Tax Formula for Individu

Income (broadly conceived)	$xx,xxx
Less: Exclusions	(x,xxx)
Gross income	$xx,xxx
Less: Deductions *for* adjusted gross income	(x,xxx)
Adjusted gross income	$xx,xxx
Less: The greater of—	
Total itemized deductions *or* standard deduction	(x,xxx)
Less: Personal and dependency exemptions	(x,xxx)
Taxable income	$xx,xxx
Tax on taxable income	$ x,xxx
Less: Tax credits (including Federal income tax withheld and other prepayments of Federal income taxes)	(xxx)
Tax due (or refund)	$ xxx

Basic Standard Deduction Amounts

	Standard Deduction Amount	
Filing Status	**2004**	**2005**
Single	$4,850	$ 5,000
Married, filing jointly	9,700	10,000
Surviving spouse	9,700	10,000
Head of household	7,150	7,300
Married, filing separately	4,850	5,000

Amount of Each Additional Standard Deduction

Filing Status	**2004**	**2005**
Single	$1,200	$1,250
Married, filing jointly	950	1,000
Surviving spouse	950	1,000
Head of household	1,200	1,250
Married, filing separately	950	1,000

Personal and Dependency Exemption

2004	**2005**
$3,100	$3,200

Comprehensive Volume

2006 EDITION

General Editors

Eugene Willis
Ph.D., CPA

William H. Hoffman, Jr.
J.D., Ph.D., CPA

David M. Maloney
Ph.D., CPA

William A. Raabe
Ph.D., CPA

Contributing Authors

James H. Boyd
Ph.D., CPA
Arizona State University

D. Larry Crumbley
Ph.D., CPA
Louisiana State University

Steven C. Dilley
J.D., Ph.D., CPA
Michigan State University

Jon S. Davis
Ph.D., CPA
University of Wisconsin, Madison

William H. Hoffman, Jr.
J.D., Ph.D., CPA
University of Houston

David M. Maloney
Ph.D., CPA
University of Virginia

Gary A. McGill
Ph.D., CPA
University of Florida

Mark B. Persellin
Ph.D., CPA, C.F.P.®
St. Mary's University

William A. Raabe
Ph.D., CPA
The Ohio State University

Boyd C. Randall
J.D., Ph.D.
Brigham Young University

Debra L. Sanders
Ph.D., CPA
Washington State University

W. Eugene Seago
J.D., Ph.D., CPA
Virginia Polytechnic Institute and State University

James E. Smith
Ph.D., CPA
College of William and Mary

Eugene Willis
Ph.D., CPA
University of Illinois, Urbana-Champaign

Australia · Canada · Mexico · Singapore · Spain · United Kingdom · United States

West Federal Taxation: Comprehensive Volume, 2006 Edition

Eugene Willis, William H. Hoffman, Jr., David M. Maloney, William A. Raabe

VP/Editorial Director
Jack W. Calhoun

Senior Acquisitions Editor
Charles E. McCormick, Jr.

Senior Developmental Editor
Craig Avery

Marketing Manager
Chris McNamee

Senior Production Editor
Tim Bailey

Manager of Technology, Editorial
Vicky True

Technology Project Editor
Christine Wittmer

Web Coordinator
Scott Cook

Manufacturing Coordinator
Doug Wilke

Art Director
Stacy Jenkins Shirley

Internal and Cover Designer
Ann Small/a small design studio

Cover Images
© William J. Hebert/Getty Images, Inc.

Production
Litten Editing and Production, Inc.

Composition
TechBooks

Printer
Thomson-West
Eagan, MN

Printed in the United States of America
1 2 3 4 5 07 06 05

Text only ISBN: 0-324-30495-1
Text with CD ISBN: 0-324-30494-3
Loose Leaf Edition ISBN: 0-324-39905-7
Instructor's Edition ISBN: 0-324-31240-7

ISSN: 0741-5184
2006 Annual Edition

For more information about our products, contact us at:

Thomson Learning Academic Resource Center

1-800-423-0563

Thomson Higher Education
5191 Natorp Boulevard
Mason, OH 45040
USA

Asia (including India)
Thomson Learning
5 Shenton Way
#01-01 UIC Building
Singapore 068808

Australia/New Zealand
Thomson Learning Australia
102 Dodds Street
Southbank, Victoria 3006
Australia

Canada
Thomson Nelson
1120 Birchmount Road
Toronto, Ontario
M1K 5G4
Canada

Latin America
Thomson Learning
Seneca, 53
Colonia Polanco
11560 Mexico
D.F.Mexico

UK/Europe/Middle East/Africa
Thomson Learning
High Holborn House
50/51 Bedford Row
London WC1R 4LR
United Kingdom

Spain (including Portugal)
Thomson Paraninfo
Calle Magallanes, 25
28015 Madrid, Spain

To the Student

YOUR SUCCESS is our key goal at *West Federal Taxation.*

♦

Comprehensive Volume, 2006 Edition comes from the most trusted and largest selling brand in college taxation—***West Federal Taxation*** (*WFT*). Twenty-eight years after we started the *WFT* series, and **almost 1.4 million users** later, we are the market leader in college taxation texts and learning materials. That's because we are focused exclusively on providing the most useful, comprehensive, and up-to-date tax texts, online study aids, tax preparation tools, and print study guides to help you succeed in your tax education.

♦

You can be sure that the 2006 Edition contains everything you'll need to succeed in your tax course—up-to-date content developed by the most respected editors and authors in taxation, free tax preparation software from TurboTax® and TaxBrain®, free access to RIA Checkpoint® (the leading tax research database), and free online quizzing for every text chapter. *WFT* also provides you with free online updates for tax legislation that affect the text.

YOUR TAX COURSE AND THIS TEXTBOOK

WFT's Comprehensive Volume, 2006 Edition is the ideal basis for your tax course focusing on both Individual and Business Entity Taxation and is perfect for both undergraduate and graduate accounting, business, and law students. In addition to Individual taxation, it provides thorough discussion of C Corporations, Flow-Through Entities, Advanced Tax Practice Considerations, and Family Tax Planning and contains material of critical interest to the serious tax practitioner. Because of its numerous straightforward examples and real-world problems, many users find it to be a valuable tool for self-study as well.

FREE RESOURCES AND STUDY TOOLS

- **Free TurboTax® Basic and TurboTax® Business CDs in every new copy.** Both the TurboTax® Basic and TurboTax® Business versions of the leading software for tax preparation come free with all new texts and provide access to tools for all your tax preparation homework. TurboTax® Basic guides users step-by-step through individual returns on IRS forms. TurboTax® Business software, designed specifically for corporations, S corporations, partnerships of up to 100 partners, and LLCs as well as estates and trusts, covers corporation, partnership, and fiduciary income taxes and gives your students practical, hands-on experience.

- **Free Online Access to TaxBrain® Tax Preparation Software—Filing Discount Included.** TaxBrain® online individual tax preparation software is used by more than 2,500 tax professionals every year. You can use TaxBrain® to work the income tax form problems in the text, developing your skills as you master course information. To access, log on to **http://www.taxbrain.com**. Take advantage of a 20 percent filing discount when filing your 2004 return with TaxBrain®—enter promotional code **SWL947.**

- **Exclusive Free Access to RIA's Checkpoint® Student Edition Online Tax Research Database.** Each *new* copy of the text contains an RIA Checkpoint® Student Edition access code, allowing you access to content from the research database most widely used by tax professionals. As you use Checkpoint® to complete problems within the text, you are building research skills and familiarity with the database—valuable preparation for your professional future.

- **Free Tutorial for RIA's Checkpoint®.** This self-paced tutorial from RIA orients you to Checkpoint® features and walks you through the application of RIA research strategies—giving you a running start on your class assignments that use Checkpoint®.

- **Free Online Self-Quizzing, Updates, and Tax Links.** *WFT: Comprehensive Volume, 2006 Edition* is supported by a text-specific Web site that offers student support and immediate access to current information. Students can take advantage of these key features:
  - **Interactive Quizzing**—25 quiz items per chapter, with automatic grading and e-mailing of results to your instructor.
  - **Tax newsletters** published twice a month written by the text authors.
  - **NewsEdge** pulls from full text articles from over 1,200 online news sources on a continuous basis and includes the following features: topic organization, personalization with the "Select My Topics/View My Topics" feature, 30-day archive, links to full online articles, and robust search functionality. NewsEdge also offers access to "Company News by Ticker," which includes stock detail, charts, financials,

management discussions, company profiles, competitor information, and company-specific news.

- **Tax Tips for the Recent Graduate** introduces the college graduate to some common tax considerations that could be beneficial in reducing the dreaded "tax-bite."
- **Tax Legislation Updates**—This resource, available to instructors and their students, provides up-to-the-minute tax information and major changes to the tax law. Tax Legislation Updates are posted as needed on the *WFT* Web site.

To start using these free study resources, go to **http://wft.swlearning.com** and select your *WFT* text.

Download a Study Guide Chapter FREE before You Buy!

Get one chapter of the print Study Guide free online. The Study Guide contains **questions and problems with solutions for self-study**, as well as **chapter highlights** that point you to the right place in the text for further study. Order it from your bookstore (ISBN 0-324-30501-X) or buy it online at **http://wft.swlearning.com.**

When you start using ***Comprehensive Volume, 2006 Edition,*** its free online study aids, its time-saving Study Guide, and other supplements your instructor may assign, you'll experience how much a new textbook from *West Federal Taxation* can add to *your* success!

The *WFT* Taxation Team

Contents in Brief

Contents

APPENDIXES

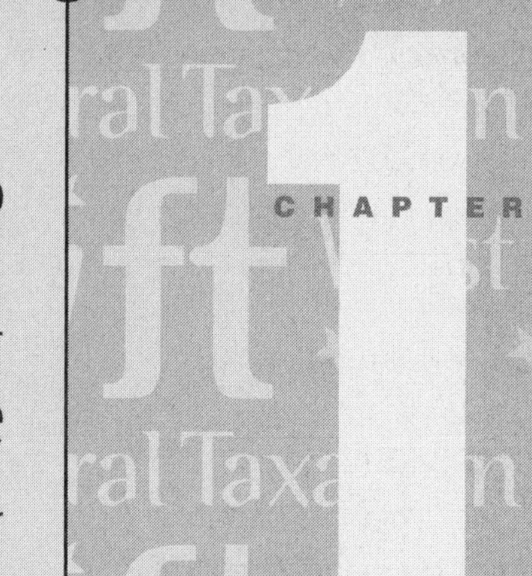

An Introduction to Taxation and Understanding the Federal Tax Law

LEARNING OBJECTIVES

After completing Chapter 1, you should be able to:

LO.1
Understand some of the history and trends of the Federal income tax.

LO.2
Know some of the criteria for selecting a tax structure; understand the components of a tax structure.

LO.3
Identify the different taxes imposed in the United States at the Federal, state, and local levels.

LO.4
Understand the administration of the tax law, including the audit process utilized by the IRS.

LO.5
Appreciate some of the ethical guidelines involved in tax practice.

LO.6
Recognize the economic, social, equity, and political considerations that justify various aspects of the tax law.

LO.7
Describe the role played by the IRS and the courts in the evolution of the Federal tax system.

OUTLINE

The primary objective of this chapter is to provide an overview of the Federal tax system. Among the topics discussed are the following:

- The history of the Federal income tax in brief.
- The types of taxes imposed at the Federal, state, and local levels.
- Some highlights of tax law administration.
- Tax concepts that help explain the reasons for various tax provisions.
- The influence that the Internal Revenue Service (IRS) and the courts have had in the evolution of current tax law.

Why does a text devoted primarily to the Federal individual income tax discuss state and local taxes? A simple illustration shows the importance of non-Federal taxes.

EXAMPLE 1

Rick is employed by Flamingo Corporation in San Antonio, Texas, at a salary of $54,000. Rick's employer offers him a chance to transfer to its New York City office at a salary of $62,000. Neither Texas nor San Antonio imposes an income tax, but New York State and New York City do. A quick computation indicates that the additional income taxes (Federal, state, and local) involve approximately $6,000. ■

Although Rick must consider many nontax factors before he decides on a job change, he should also evaluate the tax climate. How do state and local taxes compare? In this case, what appears to be a $8,000 pay increase is only $2,000 when the additional income taxes of $6,000 are taken into account.

LO.1

Understand some of the history and trends of the Federal income tax.

History of U.S. Taxation

EARLY PERIODS

The concept of an income tax can hardly be regarded as a newcomer to the Western Hemisphere. An income tax was first enacted in 1634 by the English colonists in the Massachusetts Bay Colony, but the Federal government did not adopt this form of taxation until 1861. In fact, both the Federal Union and the Confederate States of America used the income tax to raise funds to finance the Civil War. Although modest in its reach and characterized by broad exemptions and low rates, the income tax generated $376 million of revenue for the Federal government during the Civil War.

When the Civil War ended, the need for additional revenue disappeared, and the income tax was repealed. Once again the Federal government was able to finance its operations almost exclusively from customs duties (tariffs). It is interesting to note that the courts held that the Civil War income tax was not contrary to the Constitution.

When a new Federal income tax on individuals was enacted in 1894, its opponents were prepared and were able to successfully challenge its constitutionality. The U.S. Constitution provided that "No Capitation, or other direct, Tax shall be laid, unless in Proportion to the Census or Enumeration herein before directed to be taken." In *Pollock v. Farmers' Loan and Trust Co.*, the U.S. Supreme Court found that taxes on the income of real and personal property were the legal equivalent of a tax on the property involved and, therefore, required apportionment.[1]

A Federal corporate income tax, enacted by Congress in 1909, fared better in the judicial system. The U.S. Supreme Court found this tax to be constitutional because it was treated as an excise tax.[2] In essence, it was a tax on the right to do business in the corporate form. As such, it was likened to a form of the franchise tax.[3] The corporate form of doing business had been developed in the late nineteenth century and was an unfamiliar concept to the framers of the U.S. Constitution. Since a corporation is an entity created under law, jurisdictions possess the right to tax its creation and operation. Using this rationale, many states still impose franchise taxes on corporations.

The ratification of the Sixteenth Amendment to the U.S. Constitution in 1913 sanctioned both the Federal individual and corporate income taxes and, as a consequence, neutralized the continuing effect of the *Pollock* decision.

REVENUE ACTS

Following ratification of the Sixteenth Amendment, Congress enacted the Revenue Act of 1913. Under this Act, the first Form 1040 was due on March 1, 1914. The law allowed various deductions and personal exemptions of $3,000 for a single individual and $4,000 for married taxpayers. Rates ranged from a low of 2 percent to a high of 6 percent. The 6 percent rate applied only to taxable income in excess of $500,000![4]

Various revenue acts were passed between 1913 and 1939. In 1939, all of these revenue laws were codified into the Internal Revenue Code of 1939. In 1954, a similar codification of the revenue law took place. The current law is entitled the

[1] 3 AFTR 2602, 15 S.Ct. 912 (USSC, 1895). See Chapter 2 for an explanation of the citations of judicial decisions.

[2] *Flint v. Stone Tracy Co.*, 3 AFTR 2834, 31 S.Ct. 342 (USSC, 1911).

[3] See the discussion of state franchise taxes later in the chapter.

[4] This should be contrasted with the highest 2005 tax rate of 35%, which applies once taxable income exceeds $326,450.

FIGURE 1–1
Federal Budget Receipts—2005

Individual income taxes	43%
Corporation income taxes	11
Social insurance taxes and contributions	39
Excise taxes	3
Other	4
	100%

Internal Revenue Code of 1986, which largely carries over the provisions of the 1954 Code. To date, the Code has been amended several times since 1986. This matter is discussed further in Chapter 2 under Origin of the Internal Revenue Code.

HISTORICAL TRENDS

The income tax has proved to be a major source of revenue for the Federal government. Figure 1–1, which contains a breakdown of the major revenue sources,[5] demonstrates the importance of the income tax. *Estimated* income tax collections from individuals and corporations amount to 54 percent of the total receipts.

The need for revenues to finance the war effort during World War II converted the income tax into a *mass tax*. For example, in 1939, less than 6 percent of the U.S. population was subject to the Federal income tax. In 1945, over 74 percent of the population was subject to the Federal income tax.[6]

Certain changes in the income tax law are of particular significance in understanding the Federal income tax. In 1943, Congress passed the Current Tax Payment Act, which provided for the first pay-as-you-go tax system. A pay-as-you-go income tax system requires employers to withhold for taxes a specified portion of an employee's wages. Persons with income from other than wages must make quarterly payments to the IRS for estimated taxes due for the year.

One trend that has caused considerable concern is the increasing complexity of the Federal income tax laws. In the name of tax reform, Congress has added to this complexity by frequently changing the tax laws. Most recent legislation continues this trend. Increasingly, this complexity forces many taxpayers to seek the assistance of tax professionals. At this time, therefore, substantial support exists for tax law simplification.

LO.2

Know some of the criteria for selecting a tax structure; understand the components of a tax structure.

Criteria Used in the Selection of a Tax Structure

In the eighteenth century, Adam Smith identified the following *canons of taxation*, which are still considered when evaluating a particular tax structure:[7]

- *Equality*. Each taxpayer enjoys fair or equitable treatment by paying taxes in proportion to his or her income level. Ability to pay a tax is the measure of how equitably a tax is distributed among taxpayers.

[5]Budget of the United States Government for Fiscal Year 2005, Office of Management and Budget (Washington, D.C.: U.S. Government Printing Office, 2004).

[6]Richard Goode, *The Individual Income Tax* (Washington, D.C.: The Brookings Institution, 1964), pp. 2–4.

[7]*The Wealth of Nations*, Book V, Chapter II, Part II (New York: Dutton, 1910).

Adam Smith Stopped Too Soon

On July 2, 2001, the American Institute of Certified Public Accountants (AICPA) issued suggestions on Federal tax policy. Titled *Guiding Principles of Good Tax Policy: A Framework for Evaluating Tax Proposals*, the monograph sets forth 10 tax principles that are commonly used as indicators of desirable tax policy.

The first four principles are adapted from Adam Smith's *The Wealth of Nations*. The other six are summarized below:

- The tax system should be simple.
- The tax should be neutral in terms of its effect on business decisions.
- The tax system should not reduce economic growth and efficiency.
- The tax should be clear and readily understood so that taxpayers know about it and when it applies.
- The tax should be structured so as to minimize noncompliance.
- The tax system should enable the IRS to predict the amount and timing of revenue production.

SOURCE: Adapted from a Tax Policy Concept Statement issued by the Tax Division of the AICPA.

- *Convenience*. Administrative simplicity has long been valued in formulating tax policy. If a tax is easily assessed and collected and its administrative costs are low, it should be favored. An advantage of the withholding (pay-as-you-go) system is its convenience for taxpayers.
- *Certainty*. A tax structure is *good* if the taxpayer can readily predict when, where, and how a tax will be levied. Individuals and businesses need to know the likely tax consequences of a particular type of transaction.
- *Economy*. A *good* tax system involves only nominal collection costs by the government and minimal compliance costs on the part of the taxpayer. Although the government's cost of collecting Federal taxes amounts to less than one-half of 1 percent of the revenue collected, the complexity of our current tax structure imposes substantial taxpayer compliance costs.

By these canons, the Federal income tax is a contentious product. *Equality* is present as long as one accepts ability to pay as an ingredient of this component. *Convenience* exists due to a heavy reliance on pay-as-you-go procedures. *Certainty* probably generates the greatest controversy. In one sense, certainty is present since a mass of administrative and judicial guidelines exists to aid in interpreting the tax law. In another sense, however, certainty does not exist since many questions remain unanswered and frequent changes in the tax law by Congress lessen stability. *Economy* is present if only the collection procedure of the IRS is considered. Economy is not present, however, if one focuses instead on taxpayer compliance efforts and costs.

The Tax Structure

TAX BASE

A tax base is the amount to which the tax rate is applied. In the case of the Federal income tax, the tax base is *taxable income*. As noted later in the chapter (Figure

1–2), taxable income is gross income reduced by certain deductions (both business and personal).

TAX RATES

Tax rates are applied to the tax base to determine a taxpayer's liability. The tax rates may be proportional or progressive. A tax is *proportional* if the rate of tax remains constant for any given income level.

EXAMPLE 2

Bill has $10,000 of taxable income and pays a tax of $3,000, or 30%. Bob's taxable income is $50,000, and the tax on this amount is $15,000, or 30%. If this constant rate is applied throughout the rate structure, the tax is proportional. ■

A tax is *progressive* if a higher rate of tax applies as the tax base increases. The Federal income tax, Federal gift and estate taxes, and most state income tax rate structures are progressive.

EXAMPLE 3

If Cora, a married individual filing jointly, has taxable income of $10,000, her tax for 2005 is $1,000 for an average tax rate of 10%. If, however, Cora's taxable income is $50,000, her tax will be $6,770 for an average tax rate of 13.5%. The tax is progressive since higher rates are applied to greater amounts of taxable income. ■

INCIDENCE OF TAXATION

The degree to which various segments of society share the total tax burden is difficult to assess. Assumptions must be made concerning who absorbs the burden of paying the tax. For example, since dividend payments to shareholders are not deductible by a corporation and are generally taxable to shareholders, the same income is subject to a form of double taxation. Concern over double taxation is valid to the extent that corporations are *not* able to shift the corporate tax to the consumer through higher commodity prices. Many research studies have shown a high degree of shifting of the corporate income tax, converting it into a consumption tax that is borne by the ultimate purchasers of goods.

The progressiveness of the U.S. Federal income tax rate structure for individuals has varied over the years. As late as 1986, for example, there were 15 rates, ranging from 0 to 50 percent. These later were reduced to two rates of 15 and 28 percent. Currently, there are six rates ranging from 10 to 35 percent.

LO.3

Identify the different taxes imposed in the United States at the Federal, state, and local levels.

Major Types of Taxes

PROPERTY TAXES

Correctly referred to as **ad valorem taxes** because they are based on value, property taxes are a tax on wealth, or capital. In this regard, they have much in common with death taxes and gift taxes discussed later in the chapter. Although property taxes do not tax income, the income actually derived (or the potential for any income) may be relevant insofar as it affects the value of the property being taxed.

Property taxes fall into *two* categories: those imposed on realty and those imposed on personalty, or assets other than land and buildings. Both have added importance since they usually generate a deduction for Federal income tax purposes (see Chapter 10).

College Expansion May Cause Property Tax Erosion

Municipalities are very sensitive to the acquisition of additional property by nonprofit organizations. An expansion by a nonprofit can be particularly detrimental to a city's tax base if the property acquired was formerly operated as an income-producing business. As a result of the acquisition, the city permanently loses valuable ad valorem tax revenue.

Recently, Duquesne University (a nonprofit tax-exempt organization) acquired an apartment building for $22 million and converted it to a dormitory facility. The city of Pittsburgh, for obvious reasons, is challenging the tax-exempt status of the new dorm. Hopefully, a compromise can be reached whereby Duquesne will continue to pay for certain city services in return for exemption from property taxes. Such an arrangement is not uncommon in university-dominated communities—Cambridge, Massachusetts, where Harvard is located is an example. Keep in mind that Pittsburgh is also home to the University of Pittsburgh and Carnegie Mellon University, both of which are nonprofit tax-exempt organizations.

SOURCE: Adapted from "Cities Reconsidering Free Ride on Tax-Exempt College Property," *Houston Chronicle*, March 21, 2004, p. 2D.

Ad Valorem Taxes on Realty. Property taxes on realty are used exclusively by states and their local political subdivisions, such as cities, counties, and school districts. They represent a major source of revenue for *local* governments, but their importance at the *state* level has waned over the past few years. Some states, for example, have imposed freezes on upward revaluations of residential housing.

How realty is defined can have an important bearing on which assets are subject to tax. This is especially true in jurisdictions that do not impose ad valorem taxes on personalty. Primarily a question of state property law, **realty** generally includes real estate and any capital improvements that are classified as fixtures. Simply stated, a *fixture* is something so permanently attached to the real estate that its removal will cause irreparable damage. A built-in bookcase might well be a fixture, whereas a movable bookcase would not be a fixture. Certain items such as electrical wiring and plumbing cease to be personalty when installed in a building and become realty.

The following are some of the characteristics of ad valorem taxes on realty:

- Property owned by the Federal government is exempt from tax. Similar immunity usually is extended to property owned by state and local governments and by certain charitable organizations.
- Some states provide for lower valuations on property dedicated to agricultural use or other special uses (e.g., wildlife sanctuaries).
- Some states partially exempt the homestead, or personal residence, portion of property from taxation. Additionally, modern homestead laws normally protect some or all of a personal residence (including a farm or ranch) from the actions of creditors pursuing claims against the owner.
- Lower taxes may apply to a residence owned by a taxpayer age 65 or older.
- When non-income-producing property (e.g., a personal residence) is converted to income-producing property (e.g., a rental house), typically the appraised value increases.
- Some jurisdictions extend immunity from tax for a specified period of time (a *tax holiday*) to new or relocated businesses. A tax holiday can backfire, however, and cause more harm than good. If it is too generous, it can damage the local infrastructure (e.g., less funding for public works and education).

Unlike the ad valorem tax on personalty (see below), the tax on realty is difficult to avoid. Since real estate is impossible to hide, a high degree of taxpayer compliance is not surprising. The only avoidance possibility that is generally available is associated with the assessed value of the property. For this reason, the assessed value of the property—particularly, a value that is reassessed upward—may be subject to controversy and litigation.

Four methods are currently in use for assessing the value of real estate:

1. Actual purchase or construction price.
2. Contemporaneous sales prices or construction costs of comparable properties.
3. Cost of reproducing a building, less allowance for depreciation and obsolescence from the time of actual construction.
4. Capitalization of income from rental property.

Because all of these methods suffer faults and lead to inequities, a combination of two or more is not uncommon. For example, when real estate values and construction costs are rising, the use of actual purchase or construction price (method 1) places the purchaser of a new home at a definite disadvantage compared with an owner who acquired similar property years before. As another illustration, if the capitalization of income (method 4) is used for property subject to rent controls (e.g., New York City), the property may be undervalued.

The history of the ad valorem tax on realty has been marked by inconsistent application due to a lack of competent tax administration and definitive guidelines for assessment procedures. In recent years, however, some significant improvements have occurred. Some jurisdictions, for example, have computerized their reassessment procedures so that they will have an immediate effect on all property located within the jurisdiction. Nevertheless, the property tax area continues to be controversial.

Ad Valorem Taxes on Personalty. **Personalty** can be defined as all assets that are not realty. It may be helpful to distinguish between the *classification* of an asset (realty or personalty) and the *use* to which it is put. Both realty and personalty can be either business use or personal use property. Examples include a residence (realty that is personal use), an office building (realty that is business use), surgical instruments (personalty that is business use), and regular wearing apparel (personalty that is personal use).[8]

Personalty can also be classified as tangible property or intangible property. For ad valorem tax purposes, intangible personalty includes stocks, bonds, and various other securities (e.g., bank shares).

The following generalizations may be made concerning the ad valorem taxes on personalty:

- Particularly with personalty devoted to personal use (e.g., jewelry, household furnishings), taxpayer compliance ranges from poor to zero. Some jurisdictions do not even attempt to enforce the tax on these items. For automobiles devoted to personal use, many jurisdictions have converted from value as the tax base to arbitrary license fees based on the weight of the vehicle. Some jurisdictions also consider the vehicle's age (e.g., automobiles six years or older are not subject to the ad valorem tax because they are presumed to have little, if any, value).

[8]The distinction, important for ad valorem and for Federal income tax purposes, often becomes confused when personalty is referred to as "personal" property to distinguish it from "real" property. This designation does not give a complete picture of what is involved. The description "personal" residence, however, is clearer, since a residence can be identified as being realty. What is meant, in this case, is realty that is personal use property.

- For personalty devoted to business use (e.g., inventories, trucks, machinery, equipment), taxpayer compliance and enforcement procedures are measurably better.
- Which jurisdiction possesses the authority to tax movable personalty (e.g., railroad rolling stock) always has been and continues to be a troublesome issue.
- A few states levy an ad valorem tax on intangibles such as stocks and bonds. Taxpayer compliance may be negligible if the state lacks a means of verifying security transactions and ownership.

TRANSACTION TAXES

Transaction taxes, which characteristically are imposed at the manufacturer's, wholesaler's, or retailer's level, cover a wide range of transfers. Like many other types of taxes (e.g., income taxes, death taxes, and gift taxes), transaction taxes usually are not within the exclusive province of any level of taxing authority (Federal, state, local government). As the description implies, these levies place a tax on transfers of property and normally are determined by multiplying the value involved by a percentage rate.

Federal Excise Taxes. Long one of the mainstays of the Federal tax system, Federal **excise taxes** had declined in relative importance until recently. In recent years, Congress substantially increased the Federal excise taxes on such items as tobacco products, fuel and gasoline sales, telephone usage, and air travel. Other Federal excise taxes include the following:

- Manufacturers' excise taxes on trucks, trailers, tires, firearms, sporting equipment, and coal and the gas guzzler tax on automobiles.[9]
- Alcohol taxes.
- Miscellaneous taxes (e.g., the tax on wagering).

The list of transactions covered, although seemingly impressive, has diminished over the years. At one time, for example, there was a Federal excise tax on admission to amusement facilities (e.g., theaters) and on the sale of such items as leather goods, jewelry, furs, and cosmetics.

When reviewing the list of both Federal and state excise taxes, one should recognize the possibility that the tax laws may be trying to influence social behavior. For example, the gas guzzler tax is intended as an incentive for the automobile companies to build cars that are fuel efficient.

State and Local Excise Taxes. Many state and local excise taxes parallel the Federal version. Thus, all states tax the sale of gasoline, liquor, and tobacco products; however, unlike the Federal version, the rates vary significantly. For gasoline products, for example, compare the 30 cents per gallon imposed by the state of Rhode Island with the 7.5 cents per gallon levied by the state of Georgia. For tobacco sales, contrast the 3 cents per pack of 20 cigarettes in effect in Kentucky with the $2.73 per pack applicable in the state of New Jersey. Given the latter situation, is it surprising that the smuggling of cigarettes for resale elsewhere is so widespread?

Other excise taxes found at some state and local levels include those on admission to amusement facilities and on the sale of playing cards, oleomargarine products, and prepared foods. Most states impose a transaction tax on the transfer of property that requires the recording of documents (e.g., real estate sales).[10] Some extend the tax to the transfer of stocks and other securities.

---

[9]The gas guzzler tax is imposed on the manufacturers of automobiles and progresses in amount as the mileage ratings per gallon of gas decrease.

[10]This type of tax has much in common with the stamp tax levied by Great Britain on the American colonies during the pre-Revolutionary War period in U.S. history.

Over the last few years, two types of excise taxes imposed at the local level have become increasingly popular: the hotel occupancy tax and the rental car "surcharge." Since they tax the visitor who cannot vote, they are a political windfall and are often used to finance special projects that generate civic pride (e.g., convention centers, state-of-the-art sports arenas). These levies can be significant, as demonstrated by Houston's hotel tax of 17 percent and Boston's car rental tax of 28.7 percent.

General Sales Taxes. The distinction between an excise tax and a general **sales tax** is easy to make. One is restricted to a particular transaction (e.g., the 18.4 cents per gallon Federal excise tax on the sale of gasoline), while the other covers a multitude of transactions (e.g., a 5 percent tax on *all* retail sales). In actual practice, however, the distinction is not always that clear. Some state statutes exempt certain transactions from the application of the general sales taxes (e.g., sales of food to be consumed off the premises, sales of certain medicines and drugs). Also, it is not uncommon to find that rates vary depending on the commodity involved. Many states, for example, allow preferential rates for the sale of agricultural equipment or apply different rates (either higher or lower than the general rate) to the sale of automobiles. With many of these special exceptions and classifications of rates, a general sales tax can take on the appearance of a collection of individual excise taxes.

A **use tax** is an ad valorem tax, usually at the same rate as the sales tax, on the use, consumption, or storage of tangible property. The purpose of a use tax is to prevent the avoidance of a sales tax. Every state that imposes a general sales tax levied on the consumer also has a use tax. Alaska, Delaware, Montana, New Hampshire, and Oregon have neither tax.

EXAMPLE 4

Susan resides in a jurisdiction that imposes a 5% general sales tax but lives near a state that has no sales or use tax at all. Susan purchases an automobile for $10,000 from a dealer located in the neighboring state. Has she saved $500 in sales taxes? The state use tax is designed to pick up the difference between the tax paid in another jurisdiction and what would have been paid in the state in which Susan resides. ■

The use tax is difficult to enforce for many purchases and is therefore often avoided. In some cases, for example, it may be worthwhile to make purchases through an out-of-state mail-order business. In spite of shipping costs, the avoidance of the local sales tax that otherwise might be incurred can lower the cost of such products as computer components. Some states are taking steps to curtail this loss of revenue. For items such as automobiles (refer to Example 4), the use tax probably will be collected when the purchaser registers the item in his or her home state.

ETHICAL CONSIDERATIONS

Making Good Use of Out-of-State Relatives

Marcus, a resident of Maryland, has found the ideal gift for his wife in celebration of their upcoming wedding anniversary—a $22,000 diamond tennis bracelet. However, Marcus is appalled at the prospect of paying the state and local sales tax of $1,815 (combined rate of 8.25 percent). He, therefore, asks his aunt, a resident of Montana, to purchase the bracelet. The jewelry store lists the aunt as the buyer and ships the bracelet to her. Prior to the anniversary, Marcus receives the bracelet from his aunt. Is Marcus able to save $1,815 on the present for his wife? What can go wrong?

Local general sales taxes, over and above those levied by the state, are common. It is not unusual to find taxpayers living in the same state but paying different general sales taxes due to the location of their residence.

EXAMPLE 5

Pete and Sam both live in a state that has a general sales tax of 3%. Sam, however, resides in a city that imposes an additional general sales tax of 2%. Even though Pete and Sam live in the same state, one is subject to a rate of 3%, while the other pays a tax of 5%. ■

For various reasons, some jurisdictions will suspend the application of a general sales tax. New York City does so to stimulate shopping. Illinois has permanently suspended the tax on construction materials used to build power-generating plants. Texas does so annually on clothing right before the beginning of the school year. Such suspensions are similar to the tax holidays granted for ad valorem tax purposes. As state revenues have declined because of the economic slump, many states have had misgivings about the advisability of scheduling further sales tax holidays. Turning off the spigot could be political suicide, however. These holidays are extremely popular with both merchants and shoppers, and their termination could cause severe voter backlash at the polls.

Severance Taxes. **Severance taxes** are an important source of revenue for many states. These transaction taxes are based on the notion that the state has an interest in its natural resources (e.g., oil, gas, iron ore, coal). Therefore, a tax is imposed when the natural resources are extracted.

DEATH TAXES

A **death tax** is a tax on the right to transfer property or to receive property upon the death of the owner. Consequently, a death tax falls into the category of an excise tax. If the death tax is imposed on the right to pass property at death, it is classified as an **estate tax.** If it taxes the right to receive property from a decedent, it is termed an **inheritance tax.** As is typical of other types of excise taxes, the value of the property transferred provides the base for determining the amount of the death tax.

The Federal government imposes only an estate tax. State governments, however, levy inheritance taxes, estate taxes, or both.

EXAMPLE 6

At the time of her death, Wilma lived in a state that imposes an inheritance tax but not an estate tax. Mary, one of Wilma's heirs, lives in the same state. Wilma's estate is subject to the Federal estate tax, and Mary is subject to the state inheritance tax. ■

The Federal Estate Tax. The Revenue Act of 1916 incorporated the estate tax into the tax law. Never designed to generate a large amount of revenue, the tax was originally intended to prevent large concentrations of wealth from being kept within a family for many generations. Whether this objective has been accomplished is debatable. Like the income tax, estate taxes can be reduced through various planning procedures.

The gross estate includes property the decedent owned at the time of death. It also includes property interests, such as life insurance proceeds paid to the estate or to a beneficiary other than the estate if the deceased-insured had any ownership rights in the policy. Quite simply, the gross estate represents property interests subject to Federal estate taxation.[11] All property included in the gross estate is valued as of the date of death or, if the alternate valuation date is elected, six months later.[12]

Deductions from the gross estate in arriving at the taxable estate include funeral and administration expenses, certain taxes, debts of the decedent, casualty losses[13]

[11]For further information on these matters, see Chapter 27.

[12]See the discussion of the alternate valuation date in Chapter 13.

[13]For a definition of casualty losses, see the Glossary of Tax Terms in Appendix C.

incurred during the administration of the estate, transfers to charitable organizations, and, in some cases, the marital deduction. The *marital deduction* is available for amounts actually passing to a surviving spouse (a widow or widower).

Once the taxable estate has been determined and certain taxable gifts have been added to it, the estate tax can be computed. From the amount derived from the appropriate tax rate schedules, various credits should be subtracted to arrive at the tax, if any, that is due.[14] Although many other credits are also available, probably the most significant is the *unified transfer tax credit*. The main reason for this credit is to eliminate or reduce the estate tax liability for modest estates. For 2005, the amount of the credit is $555,800. Based on the estate tax rates, the credit covers a tax base of $1.5 million.

EXAMPLE 7

Ned made no taxable gifts before his death in 2005. If Ned's taxable estate amounts to $1.5 million or less, no Federal estate tax is due because of the application of the unified transfer tax credit. Under the tax law, the estate tax on a taxable estate of $1.5 million is $555,800. ■

The Federal estate tax has often been criticized for imposing a hardship on small businesses and, in particular, on family farms. Many believe that the need to pay the estate tax on the death of a major owner often forces the heirs to dissolve and liquidate the family business. In the Tax Relief Reconciliation Act of 2001, Congress responded to this criticism and scheduled a phaseout of the Federal estate tax, to be accomplished over a 10-year period by increasing the amount of the credit at periodic intervals. Consequently, the Federal estate tax is due to be eliminated in 2010. For budgetary reasons, the Act included a "sunset" provision that reinstates the Federal estate tax (as it was prior to the phaseout) as of January 1, 2011. Although the Republicans in Congress have tried to enact legislation that would repeal the sunset provision, their efforts have not been successful. As it stands now, therefore, the Federal estate tax is scheduled to end and then begin again. Obviously, this is a situation that cannot last, as it makes meaningful estate planning impossible. (Sunset provisions are discussed further later in the chapter.)

State Death Taxes. As noted earlier, states usually levy an inheritance tax, an estate tax, or both. The two forms of death taxes differ according to whether the tax is imposed on the heirs or on the estate.

Characteristically, an inheritance tax divides the heirs into classes based on their relationship to the decedent. The more closely related the heir, the lower the rates imposed and the greater the exemption allowed. Some states completely exempt from taxation amounts passing to a surviving spouse.

GIFT TAXES

Like a death tax, a **gift tax** is an excise tax levied on the right to transfer property. In this case, however, the tax is imposed on transfers made during the owner's life and not at death. Also, a gift tax applies only to transfers that are not supported by full and adequate consideration.

EXAMPLE 8

Carl sells property worth $20,000 to his daughter for $1,000. Although property worth $20,000 has been transferred, only $19,000 represents a gift, since this is the portion not supported by full and adequate consideration. ■

[14]For tax purposes, it is always crucial to appreciate the difference between a deduction and a credit. A *credit* is a dollar-for-dollar reduction of tax liability. A *deduction*, however, only benefits the taxpayer to the extent of his or her tax bracket. An estate in a 50% tax bracket, for example, would need $2 of deductions to prevent $1 of tax liability from developing. In contrast, $1 of credit neutralizes $1 of tax liability.

The Federal Gift Tax. First enacted in 1932, the Federal gift tax was intended to complement the estate tax. If lifetime transfers by gift were not taxed, it would be possible to avoid the estate tax and escape taxation entirely.

Only taxable gifts are subject to the gift tax. For this purpose, a taxable gift is measured by the fair market value of the property on the date of transfer less the *annual exclusion per donee* and, in some cases, less the *marital deduction,* which allows tax-free transfers between spouses. Each donor is allowed an annual exclusion of $11,000 in 2005 ($10,000 in 2001 and prior years) for each donee.[15]

EXAMPLE 9

On December 31, 2004, Louise (a widow) gives $11,000 to each of her four married children, their spouses, and her eight grandchildren. On January 2, 2005, she repeats the procedure. Due to the annual exclusion, Louise has not made a taxable gift, although she transferred $176,000 [$11,000 (annual exclusion) × 16 (donees)] in each year for a total of $352,000. ■

A special election applicable to married persons allows one-half of the gift made by the donor-spouse to be treated as being made by the nondonor-spouse (*gift splitting*). This election to split the gifts of property made to third persons has the effect of increasing the number of annual exclusions available. Also, it allows the use of the nondonor-spouse's unified transfer tax credit and may lower the tax brackets that will apply.

The gift tax rate schedule is the same as that applicable to the estate tax. The schedule is commonly referred to as the *unified transfer tax schedule.*

The Federal gift tax is *cumulative* in effect. What this means is that the tax base for current taxable gifts includes past taxable gifts. Although a credit is allowed for prior gift taxes, the result of adding past taxable gifts to current taxable gifts is to force the donor into a higher tax bracket.[16] Like the Federal estate tax rates, the Federal gift tax rates are progressive (see Example 3 earlier in this chapter).

The unified transfer tax credit is available for all taxable gifts; the amount of this credit for 2005 is $345,800. There is, however, only one unified transfer tax credit, and it applies both to taxable gifts and to the Federal estate tax. In a manner of speaking, therefore, once the unified transfer tax credit has been exhausted for Federal gift tax purposes, it is no longer available to insulate a decedent from the Federal estate tax, except to the extent of the excess of the credit amount for estate tax purposes over that for gift tax purposes.

As noted above, the Tax Relief Reconciliation Act of 2001 proposes to phase out the Federal estate tax. The reason for the elimination of the estate tax does not apply to the gift tax. Unlike death, which is involuntary, the making of a gift is a voluntary parting of ownership. Thus, the ownership of a business can be transferred gradually without incurring drastic and immediate tax consequences. As a result, the Federal gift tax is to be retained with the unified transfer tax credit frozen at $345,800 (which covers a taxable gift of $1 million).

State Gift Taxes. The states currently imposing a state gift tax are Connecticut, Louisiana, North Carolina, and Tennessee. Most of the laws provide for lifetime exemptions and annual exclusions. Like the Federal gift tax, the state taxes are cumulative in effect. But unlike the Federal version, the amount of tax depends on the relationship between the donor and the donee. Like state inheritance taxes, larger exemptions and lower rates apply when the donor and donee are closely related to each other.

[15]The purpose of the annual exclusion is to avoid the need to report and pay a tax on *modest* gifts. Without the exclusion, the IRS could face a real problem of taxpayer noncompliance. The annual exclusion is indexed as the level of inflation warrants.

[16]For further information on the Federal gift tax, see Chapter 27.

■ FIGURE 1–2
Formula for Federal Income Tax on Individuals

Income (broadly conceived)	$xx,xxx
Less: Exclusions (income that is not subject to tax)	(x,xxx)
Gross income (income that is subject to tax)	$xx,xxx
Less: Certain business deductions (usually referred to as deductions *for* adjusted gross income)	(x,xxx)
Adjusted gross income	$xx,xxx
Less: The greater of certain personal and employee deductions (usually referred to as *itemized deductions*) *or* The standard deduction (including any additional standard deduction)	(x,xxx)
and	
Less: Personal and dependency exemptions	(x,xxx)
Taxable income	$xx,xxx
Tax on taxable income (see the Tax Tables and Tax Rate Schedules in Appendix A)	$ x,xxx
Less: Tax credits (including Federal income tax withheld and other prepayments of Federal income taxes)	(xxx)
Tax due (or refund)	$ xxx

INCOME TAXES

Income taxes are levied by the Federal government, most states, and some local governments. The trend in recent years has been to place greater reliance on this method of taxation. This trend is not consistent with what is happening in other countries, and in this sense, our system of taxation is somewhat different.

Income taxes generally are imposed on individuals, corporations, and certain fiduciaries (estates and trusts). Most jurisdictions attempt to assure the collection of income taxes by requiring pay-as-you-go procedures, including withholding requirements for employees and estimated tax prepayments for all taxpayers.

Federal Income Taxes. Chapters 3 through 15 deal primarily with the application of the Federal income tax to individuals. The procedure for determining the Federal income tax applicable to individuals is summarized in Figure 1–2.

The application of the Federal corporate income tax does not require the computation of adjusted gross income (AGI) and does not provide for the standard deduction and personal and dependency exemptions. All allowable deductions of a corporation fall into the business-expense category. In effect, therefore, the taxable income of a corporation is the difference between gross income (net of exclusions) and deductions. Chapter 17 summarizes the rules relating to determination of taxable income of corporations.

State Income Taxes. All but the following states impose an income tax on individuals: Alaska, Florida, Nevada, South Dakota, Texas, Washington, and Wyoming.

Some of the characteristics of state income taxes are summarized as follows:

- With few exceptions, all states require some form of withholding procedures.
- Most states use as the tax base the income determination made for Federal income tax purposes.

Using the Income Tax Return As a "Use Tax" Reminder

Many consumers do not pay state and local sales tax on out-of-state purchases made online or through mail-order catalogs. In such cases, the consumer has an obligation to pay the taxing authority an equivalent use tax. Because the use tax often is not paid, either inadvertently or deliberately, some states are resorting to less subtle enforcement measures.

New York has added a separate line on its income tax return for the reporting of use taxes. The line cannot be left blank—either an amount *or* a notation of "zero" must be entered. As to the amount option, the taxpayer should list the actual amount due *or* an estimate based on a table. The table is prepared by the state and reflects the average Internet purchases for various income levels.

- A minority of states go even further and impose a flat rate upon AGI as computed for Federal income tax purposes. Several apply a rate to the Federal income tax liability. This is often referred to as the piggyback approach to state income taxation. Although the term *piggyback* does not lend itself to precise definition, in this context, it means making use, for state income tax purposes, of what was done for Federal income tax purposes.
- Some states are somewhat eroding the piggyback approach by "decoupling" from selected recent tax reductions passed by Congress. Many, for example, are not accepting for state income tax purposes the adjustments allowed by the Jobs and Growth Tax Relief Reconciliation Act (JGTRRA) of 2003. The decoupling is occurring because of the state revenue that would otherwise be lost. In other words, the state cannot afford to allow its taxpayers the same deduction for state purposes as is allowed for Federal purposes.
- Because of the tie-ins to the Federal return, a state may be notified of any changes made by the IRS upon audit of a Federal return. In recent years, the exchange of information between the IRS and state taxing authorities has increased.
- Most states allow a deduction for personal and dependency exemptions. Some states substitute a tax credit for a deduction.
- A diminishing minority of states allow a deduction for Federal income taxes.
- Most states allow their residents some form of tax credit for income taxes paid to other states.
- The objective of most states is to tax the income of residents and those who regularly conduct business within the state (e.g., nonresidents who commute to work). These states also purport to tax the income of nonresidents who earn income within the state on an itinerant basis. In practice, however, the only visitors actually taxed are highly paid athletes and entertainers. This so-called *jock tax* has been much criticized as being discriminatory due to its selective imposition.
- The due date for filing generally is the same as for the Federal income tax (the fifteenth day of the fourth month following the close of the tax year).
- Some states have occasionally instituted amnesty programs that allow taxpayers to pay back taxes (and interest) on unreported income with no (or reduced) penalty.

Nearly all states have an income tax applicable to corporations. It is difficult to determine those that do not because a state franchise tax sometimes is based in part on the income earned by the corporation.[17]

[17]See the discussion of franchise taxes later in the chapter.

Local Income Taxes. Cities imposing an income tax include, but are not limited to, Baltimore, Cincinnati, Cleveland, Detroit, Kansas City (Mo.), New York, Philadelphia, and St. Louis. The application of a city income tax is not limited to local residents.

EMPLOYMENT TAXES

Classification as an employee usually leads to the imposition of **employment taxes** and to the requirement that the employer withhold specified amounts for income taxes. The material that follows concentrates on the two major employment taxes: FICA (Federal Insurance Contributions Act—commonly referred to as the Social Security tax) and FUTA (Federal Unemployment Tax Act). Both taxes can be justified by social and public welfare considerations: FICA offers some measure of retirement security, and FUTA provides a modest source of income in the event of loss of employment.

Employment taxes come into play only if two conditions are satisfied. First, is the individual involved an *employee* (as opposed to *self-employed*)? The differences between an employee and a self-employed person are discussed in Chapter 9. Second, if the individual involved is an employee, is he or she covered under FICA or FUTA or both? Detailed coverage of both of these taxes is included in Employer's Tax Guide, an IRS Publication.[18]

FICA Taxes. The **FICA tax** rates and wage base have increased steadily over the years. It is difficult to imagine that the initial rate in 1937 was only 1 percent of the first $3,000 of covered wages. Thus, the maximum tax due was only $30!

Currently, the FICA tax has two components: Social Security tax (old age, survivors, and disability insurance) *and* Medicare tax (hospital insurance). The Social Security tax rate is 6.2 percent for 2004 and 2005, and the Medicare tax rate is 1.45 percent for these years. The base amount for Social Security is $87,900 for 2004 and $90,000 for 2005.[19] There is no limit on the base amount for the Medicare tax. The employer must match the employee's portion for both the Social Security tax and the Medicare tax.

A spouse employed by another spouse is subject to FICA. However, children under the age of 18 who are employed in a parent's trade or business are exempted.

FUTA Taxes. The purpose of the **FUTA tax** is to provide funds that the states can use to administer unemployment benefits. This leads to the somewhat unusual situation of one tax being handled by both Federal and state governments. The end result of such joint administration is to compel the employer to observe a double set of rules. Thus, state and Federal returns must be filed and payments made to both governmental units.

In 2005, FUTA applies at a rate of 6.2 percent on the first $7,000 of covered wages paid during the year to each employee. The Federal government allows a credit for FUTA paid (or allowed under a merit rating system) to the state. The credit cannot exceed 5.4 percent of the covered wages. Thus, the amount required to be paid to the IRS could be as low as 0.8 percent (6.2% – 5.4%).

States follow a policy of reducing the unemployment tax on employers who experience stable employment. Thus, an employer with little or no employee turnover might find that the state rate drops to as low as 0.1 percent or, in some states, even to zero. The reason for the merit rating credit is that the state has to pay fewer unemployment benefits when employment is steady.

---

[18]See also Circular E, Employer's Tax Guide, issued by the IRS as Publication 15.

[19]The base amount is adjusted annually.

FUTA differs from FICA in the sense that the incidence of taxation falls entirely upon the employer. A few states, however, levy a special tax on employees to provide either disability benefits or supplemental unemployment compensation, or both.

OTHER U.S. TAXES

To complete the overview of the U.S. tax system, some missing links need to be covered that do not fit into the classifications discussed elsewhere in this chapter.

Federal Customs Duties. One tax that has not yet been mentioned is the tariff on certain imported goods.[20] Generally referred to as customs duties or levies, this tax, together with selective excise taxes, provided most of the revenues needed by the Federal government during the nineteenth century. In view of present times, it is remarkable to note that tariffs and excise taxes alone paid off the national debt in 1835 and enabled the U.S. Treasury to pay a surplus of $28 million to the states.

In recent years, tariffs have served the nation more as an instrument for carrying out protectionist policies than as a means of generating revenue. Thus, a particular U.S. industry might be saved from economic disaster, so the argument goes, by placing customs duties on the importation of foreign goods that can be sold at lower prices. Protectionists contend that the tariff therefore neutralizes the competitive edge held by the producer of the foreign goods.[21]

Protectionist policies seem more appropriate for less-developed countries whose industrial capacity has not yet matured. In a world where a developed country should have everything to gain by encouraging international free trade, such policies may be of dubious value. History shows that tariffs often lead to retaliatory action on the part of the nation or nations affected.

Miscellaneous State and Local Taxes. Most states impose a franchise tax on corporations. Basically, a **franchise tax** is levied on the right to do business in the state. The base used for the determination of the tax varies from state to state. Although corporate income considerations may come into play, this tax most often is based on the capitalization of the corporation (either with or without certain long-term indebtedness).

Closely akin to the franchise tax are **occupational taxes** applicable to various trades or businesses, such as a liquor store license, a taxicab permit, or a fee to practice a profession such as law, medicine, or accounting. Most of these are not significant revenue producers and fall more into the category of licenses than taxes. The revenue derived is used to defray the cost incurred by the jurisdiction in regulating the business or profession in the interest of the public good.

PROPOSED U.S. TAXES

Considerable dissatisfaction with the U.S. Federal income tax has led to several recent proposals that, to say the least, are rather drastic in nature. One proposal would retain the income tax but with substantial change. Two other proposals would replace the Federal income tax with an entirely different system of taxation.

[20] Less-developed countries that rely principally on one or more major commodities (e.g., oil, coffee) are prone to favor *export* duties as well.

[21] The North American Free Trade Agreement (NAFTA), enacted in 1993, substantially reduced the tariffs on trade between Canada, Mexico, and the United States. The General Agreement on Tariffs and Trade (GATT) legislation enacted in 1994 also reduced tariffs on selected commodities among 124 signatory nations.

The Flat Tax. Former Representative Dick Armey (R, Texas) once proposed a **flat tax** that would replace the current graduated income tax with one rate, 17 percent. Large personal exemptions (e.g., approximately $30,000 for a family of four) would allow many low- and middle-income taxpayers to pay no tax. All other deductions would be eliminated, and no tax would be imposed on income from investments.

Various other versions of the flat tax have been suggested that would retain selected deductions (e.g., interest on home mortgages and charitable contributions) and not exclude all investment income from taxation.

The major advantage of the flat tax is its simplicity. Everyone agrees that the current Federal income tax is unbelievably complex. Consequently, compliance costs are disproportionately high. For this reason, among others, Steve Forbes, a former candidate for the Republican presidential nomination and editor of *Forbes* magazine, has been a major proponent of the flat tax approach.

Political considerations are a major obstacle to the enactment of a flat tax in its pure form (i.e., as proposed by Representative Armey). Special interest groups, such as charitable organizations and mortgage companies, are not apt to be complacent over the elimination of a tax deduction that benefits their industry. In addition, there is uncertainty as to the economic effects of the tax.

It is interesting to note that Russia's attempt at a progressive income tax was quite disastrous. Not only did high rates drive capital out of the country but also failure to report income was rampant. In early 2000, the income tax was repealed and replaced with a 13 percent flat tax. To date, the flat tax has worked quite well. Several Baltic states (Estonia, Latvia, and Slovakia) have followed Russia's example, and Poland and the Czech Republic are considering the adoption of a flat tax.

Value Added Tax. The **value added tax (VAT)** is one of two proposals that would replace the Federal income tax. Under the VAT, a business would pay the tax (approximately 17 percent) on all of the materials and services required to manufacture its product. In effect, the VAT taxes the increment in value as goods move through production and manufacturing stages to the marketplace. Moreover, the VAT paid by the producer will be reflected in the selling price of the goods. Thus, the VAT is a tax on consumption.

Many other countries (e.g., European Union countries) use the VAT either as a supplement to or a replacement for an income tax.

Sales Tax. A **national sales tax** is favored by former Representative Bill Archer (R, Texas), who was the long-time chairman of the House Ways and Means Committee. This tax differs from a VAT in that it would be collected on the final sale of goods and services. Consequently, it is collected from the consumer and not from businesses that add value to the product. Like the VAT, the national sales tax is intended to replace the Federal income tax.

The current version of the national sales tax, called the "Fair Tax," is sponsored by House Majority Leader Tom DeLay (R, Texas). It would tax all purchases, including food and medicine, at approximately 23 percent. Exempt items include business expenses, used goods, and the costs of education.

Critics contend that consumption taxes, both a VAT and a national sales tax, impose more of a burden on low-income taxpayers because they must spend larger proportions of their incomes on essential purchases. The proposal would attempt to remedy this inequity by granting some sort of credit, rebate, or exemption to low-income taxpayers.

In terms of taxpayer compliance, a value added tax is preferable to a national sales tax. Without significant collection efforts, a national sales tax could easily be circumvented by resorting to a barter system of doing business.

LO.4

Understand the administration of the tax law, including the audit process utilized by the IRS.

Tax Administration

INTERNAL REVENUE SERVICE

The responsibility for administering the Federal tax laws rests with the Treasury Department. Administratively, the IRS is part of the Department of the Treasury and is responsible for enforcing the tax laws. The Commissioner of Internal Revenue is appointed by the President and is responsible for establishing policy and supervising the activities of the entire IRS organization.

THE AUDIT PROCESS

Selection of Returns for Audit. Due to budgetary limitations, only a small minority of tax returns are audited. For the fiscal year ended September 30, 2003, the IRS audited only 0.65 percent of all individual income tax returns (about one in every 154 returns filed). The number of returns now being audited is approximately one-third of what it was five years ago.

The IRS utilizes mathematical formulas and statistical sampling techniques to select tax returns that are most likely to contain errors and to yield substantial amounts of additional tax revenues upon audit. The mathematical formula yields what is called a Discriminant Information Function (DIF) score. It is the DIF score given to a particular return that may lead to its selection for audit.

To update the DIF components, the IRS selects a cross section of returns, which are subject to various degrees of inspection (i.e., information return verification, correspondence, and face-to-face audits with filers). The results of these audits highlight areas of taxpayer noncompliance and enable the IRS to use its auditors more productively. In recent years, IRS audits have resulted in an increasing number of "no change" results (see below). This indicates that the IRS is not always choosing the right returns to audit (i.e., the ones with errors).

Though the IRS does not openly disclose all of its audit selection techniques, the following observations may be made concerning the probability of selection for audit:

- Certain groups of taxpayers are subject to audit much more frequently than others. These groups include individuals with large amounts of gross income, self-employed individuals with substantial business income and deductions, and taxpayers with prior tax deficiencies. Also vulnerable are cash businesses (e.g., cafés and small service businesses) where the potential for tax avoidance is high.

EXAMPLE 10

Jack owns and operates a liquor store on a cash-and-carry basis. Since all of Jack's sales are for cash, he might well be a prime candidate for an audit by the IRS. Cash transactions are easier to conceal than those made on credit. ■

- If information returns (e.g., Form 1099, Form W–2) are not in substantial agreement with reported income, an audit can be anticipated.
- If an individual's itemized deductions are in excess of norms established for various income levels, the probability of an audit is increased.
- Filing of a refund claim by the taxpayer may prompt an audit of the return.
- Information obtained from other sources (e.g., informants, news items) may lead to an audit. Recently, for example, the IRS advised its agents by Internet to be on the alert for newspaper accounts of large civil court judgments. The advice was based on the assumption that many successful plaintiffs were not reporting as income the punitive damages portion of awards, which is taxable.

The tax law permits the IRS to pay rewards to persons who provide information that leads to the detection and punishment of those who violate the tax laws. The rewards may not exceed 15 percent of the taxes, fines, and penalties recovered as a result of such information.

EXAMPLE 11

After 15 years of service, Rita is discharged by her employer, Dr. Smith. Shortly thereafter, the IRS receives an anonymous letter stating that Dr. Smith keeps two separate sets of books, one of which substantially understates his cash receipts. ■

EXAMPLE 12

During a divorce proceeding, it is revealed that Leo, a public official, kept large amounts of cash in a shoe box at home. This information is widely disseminated by the news media and comes to the attention of the IRS. Needless to say, the IRS would be interested in knowing whether these funds originated from a taxable source and, if so, whether they were reported on Leo's income tax returns. ■

Types of Audits. Once a return is selected for audit, the taxpayer is notified. If the issue involved is minor, the matter often can be resolved simply by correspondence (a **correspondence audit**) between the IRS and the taxpayer.

EXAMPLE 13

During 2003, Janet received dividend income from Green Corporation. In early 2004, Green Corporation reported the payment on Form 1099–DIV (an information return for reporting dividend payments), the original being sent to the IRS and a copy to Janet. When preparing her income tax return for 2003, Janet apparently overlooked this particular Form 1099–DIV and failed to include the dividend on Schedule B, Interest and Dividend Income, of Form 1040. In 2005, the IRS sends a notice to Janet calling her attention to the omission and requesting a remittance for additional tax, interest, and penalty. Janet promptly mails a check to the IRS for the requested amount, and the matter is closed. ■

Other examinations are generally classified as either office audits or field audits. An **office audit** usually is restricted in scope and is conducted in the facilities of the IRS. In contrast, a **field audit** involves an examination of numerous items reported on the return and is conducted on the premises of the taxpayer or the taxpayer's representative.

Upon the conclusion of the audit, the examining agent issues a Revenue Agent's Report (RAR) that summarizes the findings. The RAR will result in a refund (the tax was overpaid), a deficiency (the tax was underpaid), or a *no change* (the tax was correct) finding. If, during the course of an audit, a special agent accompanies (or takes over from) the regular auditor, this means the IRS suspects fraud. If the matter has progressed to an investigation for fraud, the taxpayer should retain competent counsel.

Settlement Procedures. If an audit results in an assessment of additional tax and no settlement is reached with the IRS agent, the taxpayer may attempt to negotiate a settlement with the IRS. If an appeal is desired, an appropriate request must be made to the Appeals Division of the IRS. The Appeals Division is authorized to settle all disputes based on the *hazard of litigation* (the probability of favorable resolution of the disputed issue or issues if litigated). In some cases, a taxpayer may be able to obtain a percentage settlement or a favorable settlement of one or more disputed issues.

If a satisfactory settlement is not reached within the administrative appeal process, the taxpayer may wish to litigate the case in the Tax Court, a Federal District Court, or the Court of Federal Claims. However, litigation is recommended only as a last resort because of the legal costs involved and the uncertainty of the final outcome. Tax litigation considerations are discussed more fully in Chapter 2.

THE IRS GETS TOUGH WITH TAXPAYERS WHO REFUSE TO PAY

After demanding but not obtaining payment for five years of unpaid taxes, the IRS has filed a $973,693 lien against property owned by Pete Rose. This type of publicity comes at a bad time for Rose who continues to angle for admission to baseball's Hall of Fame.

Rose was suspended from Major League Baseball after betting on games while managing the Cincinnati Reds. He also is not a stranger to tax controversy: he previously served five months in Federal prison after pleading guilty to a charge of tax evasion.

STATUTE OF LIMITATIONS

A **statute of limitations** is a provision in the law that offers a party a defense against a suit brought by another party after the expiration of a specified period of time. The purpose of a statute of limitations is to preclude parties from prosecuting stale claims. The passage of time makes the defense of such claims difficult since witnesses may no longer be available or evidence may have been lost or destroyed. Found at the state and Federal levels, such statutes cover a multitude of suits, both civil and criminal.

For our purposes, the relevant statutes deal with the Federal income tax. The two categories involved cover both the period of limitations applicable to the assessment of additional tax deficiencies by the IRS and the period that deals with claims for refunds by taxpayers.

Assessment by the IRS. Under the general rule, the IRS may assess an additional tax liability against a taxpayer within *three years* of the filing of the income tax return. If the return is filed early, the three-year period begins to run from the due date of the return (usually April 15 for a calendar year individual taxpayer). If the taxpayer files the return late (i.e., beyond the due date), the three-year period begins to run on the date filed.

If a taxpayer omits an amount of gross income in excess of 25 percent of the gross income reported on the return, the statute of limitations is increased to six years.

EXAMPLE 14

For 2000, Mark, a calendar year taxpayer, reported gross income of $400,000 on a timely filed income tax return. If Mark omitted more than $100,000 (25% × $400,000), the six-year statute of limitations would apply to the 2000 tax year. ■

The six-year provision on assessments by the IRS applies only to the omission of income and does not cover other factors that might lead to an understatement of tax liability, such as overstatement of deductions and credits.

There is *no* statute of limitations on assessments of tax if *no return* is filed or if a *fraudulent* return is filed.

Limitations on Refunds. If a taxpayer believes that an overpayment of Federal income tax was made, a claim for refund should be filed with the IRS. A *claim for refund,* therefore, is a request to the IRS that it return to the taxpayer the excessive income taxes paid.[22]

[22]Generally, an individual filing a claim for refund should use Form 1040X.

A claim for refund generally must be filed within *three years* from the date the return was filed *or* within *two years* from the date the tax was paid, whichever is later. Income tax returns that are filed early are deemed to have been filed on the date the return was due.

INTEREST AND PENALTIES

Interest rates are determined quarterly by the IRS based on the existing Federal short-term rate. Currently, the rates for tax refunds (overpayments) for individual taxpayers are the same as those applicable to assessments (underpayments). For the first quarter (January 1–March 31) of 2005, the rates are 5 percent for refunds and assessments.[23]

For assessments of additional taxes, the interest begins running on the unextended due date of the return. With refunds, however, no interest is allowed if the overpayment is refunded to the taxpayer within 45 days of the date the return is filed. For this purpose, returns filed early are deemed to have been filed on the due date.

In addition to interest, the tax law provides various penalties for lack of compliance by taxpayers. Some of these penalties are summarized as follows:

- For a *failure to file* a tax return by the due date (including extension), a penalty of 5 percent per month up to a maximum of 25 percent is imposed on the amount of tax shown as due on the return. Any fraction of a month counts as a full month.
- A penalty for a *failure to pay* the tax due as shown on the return is imposed in the amount of 0.5 percent per month up to a maximum of 25 percent. Again, any fraction of a month counts as a full month. During any month in which both the failure to file penalty and the failure to pay penalty apply, the failure to file penalty is reduced by the amount of the failure to pay penalty.

EXAMPLE 15

Adam files his tax return 18 days after the due date of the return. Along with the return, he remits a check for $1,000, which is the balance of the tax he owed. Disregarding the interest element, Adam's total penalties are as follows:

Failure to pay penalty (0.5% × $1,000)		$ 5
Plus:		
Failure to file penalty (5% × $1,000)	$50	
Less failure to pay penalty for the same period	(5)	
Failure to file penalty		45
Total penalties		$50

Note that the penalties for one full month are imposed even though Adam was delinquent by only 18 days. Unlike the method used to compute interest, any part of a month is treated as a whole month. ■

- A *negligence* penalty of 20 percent is imposed if any of the underpayment was for intentional disregard of rules and regulations without intent to defraud. The penalty applies to just that portion attributable to the negligence.

[23]The rates applicable after March 31, 2005, were not available when this text went to press.

EXAMPLE 16

Cindy underpaid her taxes for 2004 in the amount of $20,000, of which $15,000 is attributable to negligence. Cindy's negligence penalty is $3,000 (20% × $15,000). ■

- Various fraud penalties may be imposed. *Fraud* is a deliberate action on the part of the taxpayer evidenced by deceit, misrepresentation, concealment, etc. For possible fraud situations, refer to Examples 11 and 12.

TAX PRACTICE

The area of tax practice is largely unregulated. Virtually anyone can aid another in complying with the various tax laws. If a practitioner is a member of a profession, such as law or public accounting, he or she must abide by certain ethical standards. Furthermore, the Internal Revenue Code imposes penalties upon the preparers of Federal tax returns who violate proscribed acts and procedures.

LO.5

Appreciate some of the ethical guidelines involved in tax practice.

Ethical Guidelines. The American Institute of CPAs has issued numerous pronouncements dealing with CPAs engaged in tax practice. Originally called "Statements on Responsibilities in Tax Practice," these pronouncements were intended to be only *guides* to action. In 2000, however, the AICPA redesignated the pronouncements as "Statements on Standards for Tax Services" and made them *enforceable* as part of its Code of Professional Conduct. They include the provisions summarized below.

- Do not take questionable positions on a client's tax return in the hope that the return will not be selected for audit by the IRS. Any positions taken should be supported by a good-faith belief that they have a realistic possibility of being sustained if challenged. The client should be fully advised of the risks involved and of the penalties that would result if the position taken is not successful.
- A practitioner can use a client's estimates if they are reasonable under the circumstances. If the tax law requires receipts or other verification, the client should be so advised. In no event should an estimate be given the appearance of greater accuracy than is the case. For example, an estimate of $1,000 should not be deducted on a return as $999.
- Every effort should be made to answer questions appearing on tax returns. A question need not be answered if the information requested is not readily available, the answer is voluminous, or the question's meaning is uncertain. The failure to answer a question on a return cannot be justified on the grounds that the answer could prove disadvantageous to the taxpayer.
- Upon learning of an error on a past tax return, advise the client to correct it. Do not, however, inform the IRS of the error. If the error is material and the client refuses to correct it, consider withdrawing from the engagement. This will be necessary if the error has a carryover effect and prevents the current year's tax liability from being determined correctly.

ETHICAL CONSIDERATIONS

Do You Sign or Not?

In early April, a new client, Lucy Meade, comes to your office and asks you to prepare a joint return for her and her husband, Albert. They are visiting your city so that Albert can obtain medical treatment for a serious mental disorder. You suggest filing an extension so that they can have the return prepared on returning home. Lucy adamantly opposes an extension, however, as the idea of being late on her taxes frightens her. Since Lucy seems to have brought all of the information needed to prepare the return, you accept the engagement.

Several days later and after the return is prepared, you have a conference with Lucy about its content. Schedule B of Form 1040 (which reports interest and dividends), includes a question about the existence of foreign bank accounts that requires a "yes" or "no" answer. Lucy appears sincere when she says that she is unaware of any such accounts. Since she is not sure, however, she suggests that you leave the question unanswered.

If you follow Lucy's suggestion and do not answer the question, do you feel right about signing the return as the preparer?

Suppose you decide to check "no" because this response may avoid flagging the return for audit. After all, Lucy said that she was "unaware of any such accounts." Does her response support your action?

Statutory Penalties Imposed on Tax Return Preparers. In addition to ethical constraints, a tax return preparer may be subject to certain statutorily sanctioned penalties, including the following:

- Various penalties involving procedural matters. Examples include failing to furnish the taxpayer with a copy of the return; endorsing a taxpayer's refund check; failing to sign the return as a preparer; failing to furnish one's identification number; and failing to keep copies of returns or maintain a client list.
- Penalty for understatement of a tax liability based on a position that lacks any realistic possibility of being sustained. If the position is not frivolous, the penalty can be avoided by disclosing it on the return.
- Penalty for any willful attempt to understate taxes. This usually results when a preparer disregards or makes no effort to obtain pertinent information from a client.
- Penalty for failure to exercise due diligence in determining eligibility for, or the amount of, an earned income tax credit.

LO.6

Recognize the economic, social, equity, and political considerations that justify various aspects of the tax law.

Understanding the Federal Tax Law

The Federal tax law is a mosaic of statutory provisions, administrative pronouncements, and court decisions. Anyone who has attempted to work with this body of knowledge would have to admit to its complexity. For the person who has to trudge through a mass of rules to find the solution to a tax problem, it may be of some consolation to know that the law's complexity can generally be explained. Whether sound or not, there is a reason for the formulation of every rule. Knowing these reasons, therefore, is a considerable step toward understanding the Federal tax law.

The Federal tax law has as its *major objective* the raising of revenue. But although the fiscal needs of the government are important, other considerations explain certain portions of the law. Economic, social, equity, and political factors also play a significant role. Added to these factors is the marked impact the IRS and the courts have had and will continue to have on the evolution of Federal tax law. These matters are treated in the remainder of the chapter, and, wherever appropriate, the discussion is referenced to subjects covered later in the text.

REVENUE NEEDS

The foundation of any tax system has to be the raising of revenue to cover the cost of government operations. Ideally, annual outlays should not exceed anticipated revenues, thereby leading to a balanced budget with no resulting deficit.

When enacting tax legislation, a deficit-conscious Congress often has been guided by the concept of **revenue neutrality.** The concept means that the changes made will neither increase nor decrease the net result reached under the prior rules. Revenue neutrality does not mean that any one taxpayer's tax liability will

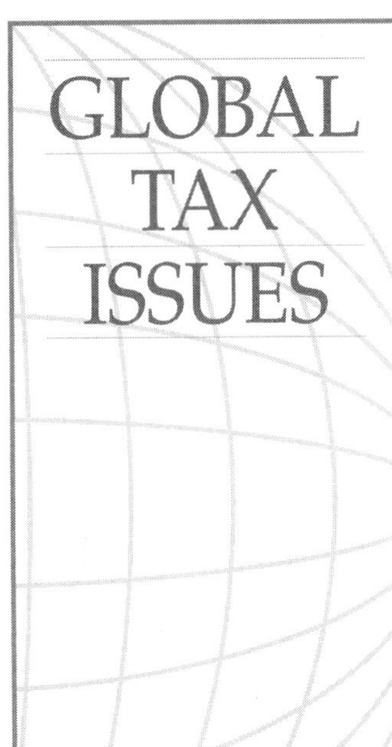

Outsourcing of Tax Return Preparation

The use of foreign nationals to carry out certain job assignments for U.S. businesses is an increasingly popular practice. Outsourcing such activities as telemarketing to India, for example, usually produces the same satisfactory result but at a much lower cost.

Outsourcing is also being applied to the preparation of tax returns. During 2003, an estimated 100,000 to 150,000 Federal and state income tax returns were outsourced to India by U.S. firms. Not only can this practice be expected to continue, but it probably will increase in volume. Outsourcing tax return preparation does not violate Federal law and is compatible with accounting ethical guidelines as long as three safeguards are followed: First, the practitioner must make sure that client confidentiality is maintained. Second, the practitioner must verify the accuracy of the work that has been outsourced. Third, the practitioner must inform clients, preferably in writing, when any third-party contractor is used to provide professional services. This last condition was promulgated by the AICPA (after much vacillation) in late 2004 and applies to services performed on or after July 1, 2005.

Practitioners justify the outsourcing practice as a means of conserving time and effort that can be applied toward more meaningful tax planning on behalf of their clients.

remain the same. Since the circumstances involved will differ, one taxpayer's increased tax liability could be another's tax savings. Although revenue-neutral tax reform does not reduce deficits, at least it does not aggravate the problem.

In addition to making changes in the tax law revenue neutral, several other procedures can be taken to mitigate any revenue loss. When tax reductions are involved, the full impact of the legislation can be phased in over a period of years.[24] Or, as an alternative, the tax reduction can be limited to a period of years. When the period expires, the prior law is reinstated through a **sunset provision.** Most of the major tax bills recently passed by Congress have contained numerous sunset provisions. They provide some semblance of revenue neutrality as some of the bills include tax cuts that were not offset by new sources of revenue. It remains to be seen, however, whether Congress will allow the sunset provisions to take effect and, thereby, kill the tax cuts that were enacted.

ECONOMIC CONSIDERATIONS

Using the tax system in an effort to accomplish economic objectives has become increasingly popular in recent years. Generally, proponents of this goal use tax legislation to amend the Internal Revenue Code in ways designed to help control the economy or encourage certain activities and businesses.

Control of the Economy. Congress has used depreciation write-offs as a means of controlling the economy. Theoretically, shorter asset lives and accelerated methods should encourage additional investment in depreciable property acquired for business use. Conversely, longer asset lives and the required use of the straight-line method of depreciation dampen the tax incentive for capital outlays.

Another approach that utilizes depreciation as a means of controlling capital investment is the amount of write-off allowed upon the acquisition of assets. This is the approach followed by the § 179 election to expense assets. It also was the

[24]An example of a gradual phase-in is the increase in the unified transfer tax credit (discussed earlier in this chapter), which does not become fully implemented at $3.5 million until year 2009.

approach used by Congress on occasions in provisions that permitted additional first-year depreciation (see Chapter 8).

A change in the tax rate structure has a more immediate impact on the economy. With lower tax rates, taxpayers are able to retain additional spendable funds. If lower tax rates are accompanied by the elimination of certain deductions, exclusions, and credits, however, the overall result may not be lower tax liabilities.

Encouragement of Certain Activities. Without passing judgment on the wisdom of any such choices, it is quite clear that the tax law does encourage certain types of economic activity or segments of the economy. For example, the favorable treatment allowed research and development expenditures can be explained by the desire to foster technological progress. Under the tax law, such expenditures can be either deducted in the year incurred or capitalized and amortized over a period of 60 months or more. In terms of the timing of the tax savings, these options usually are preferable to capitalizing the cost with a write-off over the estimated useful life of the asset created. If the asset developed has an indefinite useful life, no write-off would be available without the two options allowed by the tax law.

Is it desirable to encourage the conservation of energy resources? Considering the world energy situation and our own reliance on foreign oil, the answer to this question has to be yes. The concern over energy usage was a prime consideration in the enactment of legislation to make various tax savings for energy conservation expenditures available to taxpayers.

Is preserving the environment a desirable objective? Ecological considerations explain why the tax law permits a 60-month amortization period for costs incurred in the installation of pollution control facilities.

Is it wise to stimulate U.S. exports of services? Along this line, Congress has deemed it advisable to establish incentives for U.S. citizens who accept employment overseas. Such persons receive generous tax breaks through special treatment of their foreign-source income and certain housing costs.

Is saving desirable for the economy? Saving leads to capital formation and thereby makes funds available to finance home construction and industrial expansion. The tax law encourages saving by according preferential treatment to private retirement plans. Not only are contributions to Keogh (H.R. 10) plans and certain Individual Retirement Accounts (IRAs) deductible, but income from the contributions accumulates free of tax. As noted below, the encouragement of private-sector pension plans can also be justified under social considerations.

Encouragement of Certain Industries. No one can question the proposition that a sound agricultural base is necessary for a well-balanced national economy. Undoubtedly, this can explain why farmers are accorded special treatment under the Federal tax system. Among the benefits are the election to expense rather than capitalize certain soil and water conservation expenditures and fertilizers and the election to defer the recognition of gain on the receipt of crop insurance proceeds.

Encouragement of Small Business. At least in the United States, a consensus exists that what is good for small business is good for the economy as a whole. Whether valid or not, this assumption has led to a definite bias in the tax law favoring small business.

In the corporate tax area, several provisions can be explained by the desire to benefit small business. One provision permits the shareholders of a small business corporation to make a special election that generally will avoid the imposition of the corporate income tax.[25] Furthermore, such an election enables the corporation to pass through its operating losses to its shareholders.

[25]Known as the S election, it is discussed in Chapter 22.

SOCIAL CONSIDERATIONS

Some provisions of the Federal tax law, particularly those dealing with the income tax of individuals, can be explained by social considerations. Some notable examples and their rationales include the following:

- Certain benefits provided to employees through accident and health plans financed by employers are nontaxable to employees. Encouraging such plans is considered socially desirable since they provide medical benefits in the event of an employee's illness or injury.
- Most premiums paid by an employer for group term insurance covering the life of the employee are nontaxable to the employee. These arrangements can be justified on social grounds in that they provide funds for the family unit to help it adjust to the loss of wages caused by the employee's death.
- A contribution made by an employer to a qualified pension or profit sharing plan for an employee may receive special treatment. The contribution and any income it generates are not taxed to the employee until the funds are distributed. Such an arrangement also benefits the employer by allowing a tax deduction when the contribution is made to the qualified plan. Private retirement plans are encouraged to supplement the subsistence income level the employee otherwise would have under the Social Security system.[26]
- A deduction is allowed for contributions to qualified charitable organizations. The deduction attempts to shift some of the financial and administrative burden of socially desirable programs from the public (the government) to the private (the citizens) sector.
- A tax credit is allowed for amounts spent to furnish care for certain minor or disabled dependents to enable the taxpayer to seek or maintain gainful employment. Who could deny the social desirability of encouraging taxpayers to provide care for their children while they work?
- Various tax credits, deductions, and exclusions are designed to encourage taxpayers to obtain additional education.[27]
- A tax deduction is not allowed for certain expenditures deemed to be contrary to public policy. This disallowance extends to such items as fines, penalties, illegal kickbacks, bribes to government officials, and gambling losses in excess of gains. Social considerations dictate that the tax law should not encourage these activities by permitting a deduction.

Many other examples could be cited, but the conclusion would be unchanged. Social considerations do explain a significant part of the Federal tax law.

EQUITY CONSIDERATIONS

The concept of equity is relative. Reasonable persons can, and often do, disagree about what is fair or unfair. In the tax area, moreover, equity is most often tied to a particular taxpayer's personal situation. To illustrate, compare the tax positions of those who rent their personal residences with those who own their homes. Renters receive no Federal income tax benefit from the rent they pay. For homeowners, however, a large portion of the house payments they make may qualify for the Federal interest and property tax deductions. Although renters may have difficulty understanding this difference in tax treatment, the encouragement of home ownership can be justified on both economic and social grounds.

[26]The same rationale explains the availability of similar arrangements for self-employed persons (the H.R. 10, or Keogh, plan).

[27]These provisions can also be justified under the category of economic considerations. No one can take issue with the conclusion that a better educated workforce carries a positive economic impact.

In the same vein, compare the tax treatment of a corporation with that of a partnership. Although the two businesses may be of equal size, similarly situated, and competitors in the production of goods or services, they are not treated comparably under the tax law. The corporation is subject to a separate Federal income tax; the partnership is not. Whether the differences in tax treatment can be justified logically in terms of equity is beside the point. The point is that the tax law can and does make a distinction between these business forms.

Equity, then, is not what appears fair or unfair to any one taxpayer or group of taxpayers. Some recognition of equity does exist, however, and explains part of the law. The concept of equity appears in tax provisions that alleviate the effect of multiple taxation and postpone the recognition of gain when the taxpayer lacks the ability or wherewithal to pay the tax. Provisions that mitigate the effect of the application of the annual accounting period concept and help taxpayers cope with the eroding results of inflation also reflect equity considerations.

Alleviating the Effect of Multiple Taxation. The income earned by a taxpayer may be subject to taxes imposed by different taxing authorities. If, for example, the taxpayer is a resident of New York City, income might generate Federal, state of New York, and city of New York income taxes. To compensate for this apparent inequity, the Federal tax law allows a taxpayer to claim a deduction for state and local income taxes. The deduction does not, however, neutralize the effect of multiple taxation, since the benefit derived depends on the taxpayer's Federal income tax rate. Only a tax credit, rather than a deduction, would eliminate the effects of multiple taxation on the same income.

Equity considerations can explain the Federal tax treatment of certain income from foreign sources. Since double taxation results when the same income is subject to both foreign and U.S. income taxes, the tax law permits the taxpayer to choose between a credit and a deduction for the foreign taxes paid.

The Wherewithal to Pay Concept. The **wherewithal to pay** concept recognizes the inequity of taxing a transaction when the taxpayer lacks the means with which to pay the tax. It is particularly suited to situations in which the taxpayer's economic position has not changed significantly as a result of the transaction.

An illustration of the wherewithal to pay concept is the provision of the tax law dealing with the treatment of gain resulting from an involuntary conversion. An involuntary conversion occurs when property is destroyed by casualty or taken by a public authority through condemnation. If gain results from the conversion, it need not be recognized if the taxpayer replaces the property within a specified period of time. The replacement property must be similar or related in service or use to that involuntarily converted.

EXAMPLE 17

Some of the pasture land belonging to Ron, a rancher, is condemned by the state for use as a game preserve. The condemned pasture land cost Ron $120,000, but the state pays him $150,000 (its fair market value). Shortly thereafter, Ron buys more pasture land for $150,000. ■

In Example 17, Ron has a realized gain of $30,000 [$150,000 (condemnation award) – $120,000 (cost of land)]. It would be inequitable to force Ron to pay a tax on this gain for two reasons. First, without disposing of the property acquired (the new land), Ron would be hard-pressed to pay the tax. Second, his economic position has not changed.

A warning is in order regarding the application of the wherewithal to pay concept. If the taxpayer's economic position changes in any way, tax consequences may result.

EXAMPLE 18

Assume the same facts as in Example 17, except that Ron reinvests only $140,000 of the award in new pasture land. Now, Ron has a taxable gain of $10,000. Instead of ending up with only replacement property, Ron now has $10,000 in cash. ■

Mitigating the Effect of the Annual Accounting Period Concept. For purposes of effective administration of the tax law, all taxpayers must report to and settle with the Federal government at periodic intervals. Otherwise, taxpayers would remain uncertain as to their tax liabilities, and the government would have difficulty judging revenues and budgeting expenditures. The period selected for final settlement of most tax liabilities, in any event an arbitrary determination, is one year. At the close of each year, therefore, a taxpayer's position becomes complete for that particular year. Referred to as the annual accounting period concept, its effect is to divide each taxpayer's life, for tax purposes, into equal annual intervals.

The finality of the annual accounting period concept could lead to dissimilar tax treatment for taxpayers who are, from a long-range standpoint, in the same economic position.

EXAMPLE 19

José and Alicia, both sole proprietors, have experienced the following results during the past three years:

	Profit (or Loss)	
Year	**José**	**Alicia**
2003	$50,000	$150,000
2004	60,000	60,000
2005	60,000	(40,000)

Although José and Alicia have the same profit of $170,000 over the period from 2003 to 2005, the finality of the annual accounting period concept places Alicia at a definite disadvantage for tax purposes. The net operating loss procedure offers Alicia some relief by allowing her to apply some or all of her 2005 loss to the earlier profitable years (in this case, 2003). Thus, with a net operating loss carryback, Alicia is in a position to obtain a refund for some of the taxes she paid on the $150,000 profit reported for 2003. ■

The same reasoning used to support the deduction of net operating losses can explain the special treatment the tax law accords to excess capital losses and excess charitable contributions.[28] Carryback and carryover procedures help mitigate the effect of limiting a loss or a deduction to the accounting period in which it was realized. With such procedures, a taxpayer may be able to salvage a loss or a deduction that might otherwise be wasted.

The installment method of recognizing gain on the sale of property allows a taxpayer to spread tax consequences over the payout period.[29] The harsh effect of taxing all the gain in the year of sale is thereby avoided. The installment method can also be explained by the wherewithal to pay concept since recognition of gain is tied to the collection of the installment notes received from the sale of the property. Tax consequences, then, tend to correspond to the seller's ability to pay the tax.

Coping with Inflation. Because of the progressive nature of the income tax, a wage adjustment to compensate for inflation can increase the income tax bracket of the recipient. Known as *bracket creep*, its overall impact is an erosion of purchasing power. Congress recognized this problem and began to adjust various income tax components, such as tax brackets, standard deduction amounts, and personal and dependency exemptions, through an indexation procedure. Indexation is based upon the rise in the consumer price index over the prior year.

[28] The tax treatment of these items is discussed in Chapters 7, 10, and 14.

[29] Under the installment method, each payment received by the seller represents both a recovery of capital (the nontaxable portion) and profit from the sale (the taxable portion). The tax rules governing the installment method are discussed in Chapter 16.

POLITICAL CONSIDERATIONS

A large segment of the Federal tax law is made up of statutory provisions. Since these statutes are enacted by Congress, is it any surprise that political considerations influence tax law? For purposes of discussion, the effect of political considerations on the tax law is divided into the following topics: special interest legislation, political expediency situations, and state and local government influences.

Special Interest Legislation. There is no doubt that certain provisions of the tax law can largely be explained by the political influence some pressure groups have had on Congress. Is there any other realistic reason that, for example, prepaid subscription and dues income is not taxed until earned while prepaid rents are taxed to the landlord in the year received?

A good example of special interest legislation is contained in the Tax Relief Reconciliation Act of 2001. A provision in the bill, in effect, exempts cruise ship companies from certain antidiscrimination restrictions applicable to qualified retirement plans. This will enable corporations, such as Carnival, to establish pension plans covering only their U.S. shore-based employees without having to extend the benefits to their (almost entirely foreign) maritime employees. Carnival, along with other cruise companies, generously contributed to the campaign funds of certain key Florida and Alaska congressional representatives. Both Florida and Alaska are heavily affected by the cruise ship business.

Special interest legislation is not necessarily to be condemned if it can be justified on economic, social, or some other utilitarian grounds. At any rate, it is an inevitable product of our political system.

Political Expediency Situations. Various tax reform proposals rise and fall in favor with the shifting moods of the American public. That Congress is sensitive to popular feeling is an accepted fact. Therefore, certain provisions of the tax law can be explained by the political climate at the time they were enacted.

Measures that deter more affluent taxpayers from obtaining so-called preferential tax treatment have always had popular appeal and, consequently, the support of Congress. Provisions such as the alternative minimum tax, the imputed interest rules, and the limitation on the deductibility of interest on investment indebtedness can be explained on this basis.

Other changes explained at least partially by political expediency include the lowering of individual income tax rates, the increase in the personal and dependency exemptions, and the increase in the amount of the earned income credit.

State and Local Government Influences. Political considerations have played a major role in the nontaxability of interest received on state and local obligations. In view of the furor that has been raised by state and local political figures every time any modification of this tax provision has been proposed, one might well regard it as next to sacred.

Somewhat less apparent has been the influence state law has had in shaping our present Federal tax law. Such was the case with community property systems. The nine states with community property systems are Louisiana, Texas, New Mexico, Arizona, California, Washington, Idaho, Nevada, and Wisconsin. The rest of the states are classified as common law jurisdictions.[30] The difference between

[30]In Alaska, spouses can choose to have the community property rules apply. Otherwise, property rights are determined under common law rules.

common law and community property systems centers around the property rights possessed by married persons. In a common law system, each spouse owns whatever he or she earns. Under a community property system, one-half of the earnings of each spouse is considered owned by the other spouse.

EXAMPLE 20

Al and Fran are husband and wife, and their only income is the $60,000 annual salary Al receives. If they live in New Jersey (a common law state), the $60,000 salary belongs to Al. If, however, they live in Arizona (a community property state), the $60,000 is divided equally, in terms of ownership, between Al and Fran. ■

At one time, the tax position of the residents of community property states was so advantageous that many common law states actually adopted community property systems. Needless to say, the political pressure placed on Congress to correct the disparity in tax treatment was considerable. To a large extent this was accomplished in the Revenue Act of 1948, which extended many of the community property tax advantages to residents of common law jurisdictions.

The major advantage extended was the provision allowing married taxpayers to file joint returns and compute the tax liability as if the income had been earned one-half by each spouse. This result is automatic in a community property state, since half of the income earned by one spouse belongs to the other spouse. The income-splitting benefits of a joint return are now incorporated as part of the tax rates applicable to married taxpayers. See Chapter 3.

LO.7

Describe the role played by the IRS and the courts in the evolution of the Federal tax system.

INFLUENCE OF THE INTERNAL REVENUE SERVICE

The influence of the IRS is apparent in many areas beyond its role in issuing the administrative pronouncements that make up a considerable portion of our tax law. In its capacity as the protector of the national revenue, the IRS has been instrumental in securing the passage of much legislation designed to curtail the most flagrant tax avoidance practices (to close *tax loopholes*). In its capacity as the administrator of the tax law, the IRS has sought and obtained legislation to make its job easier (to attain administrative feasibility).

The IRS as Protector of the Revenue. Innumerable examples can be given of provisions in the tax law that stem from the direct influence of the IRS. Usually, such provisions are intended to prevent a loophole from being used to avoid the tax consequences intended by Congress. Working within the letter of existing law, ingenious taxpayers and their advisers devise techniques that accomplish indirectly what cannot be accomplished directly. As a consequence, legislation is enacted to close the loopholes that taxpayers have located and exploited. Some tax law can be explained in this fashion and is discussed in the chapters to follow.

ETHICAL CONSIDERATIONS

Deducting Uncollected Charges for Services Rendered

Dr. Taylor is a cash basis, calendar year taxpayer who maintains a dental practice as a sole proprietor. For tax year 2005, he claims $16,500 as a bad debt deduction. After performing the dental procedures and billing the patients repeatedly, he has been unable to collect the amounts due. He feels quite certain that the patients involved will never pay their bills. Comment on the propriety of Dr. Taylor's deduction.

In addition, the IRS has secured from Congress legislation of a more general nature that enables it to make adjustments based on the substance, rather than the formal construction, of what a taxpayer has done. For example, one such provision permits the IRS to make adjustments to a taxpayer's method of accounting when the method used by the taxpayer does not clearly reflect income.[31]

EXAMPLE 21

Tina, a cash basis taxpayer, owns and operates a pharmacy. All drugs and other items acquired for resale, such as cosmetics, are charged to the purchases account and written off (expensed) for tax purposes in the year of acquisition. As this procedure does not clearly reflect income, it would be appropriate for the IRS to require that Tina establish and maintain an ending inventory account. ■

Administrative Feasibility. Some tax law is justified on the grounds that it simplifies the task of the IRS in collecting the revenue and administering the law. With regard to collecting the revenue, the IRS long ago realized the importance of placing taxpayers on a pay-as-you-go basis. Elaborate withholding procedures apply to wages, while the tax on other types of income may be paid at periodic intervals throughout the year. The IRS has been instrumental in convincing the courts that accrual basis taxpayers should in most cases pay taxes on prepaid income in the year received and not when earned. The approach may be contrary to generally accepted accounting principles, but it is consistent with the wherewithal to pay concept.

Of considerable aid to the IRS in collecting revenue are the numerous provisions that impose interest and penalties on taxpayers for noncompliance with the tax law. Provisions such as the penalties for failure to pay a tax or to file a return that is due, the negligence penalty for intentional disregard of rules and regulations, and various penalties for civil and criminal fraud serve as deterrents to taxpayer noncompliance.

One of the keys to an effective administration of our tax system is the audit process conducted by the IRS. To carry out this function, the IRS is aided by provisions that reduce the chance of taxpayer error or manipulation and therefore simplify the audit effort that is necessary. An increase in the amount of the standard deduction, for example, reduces the number of individual taxpayers who will choose the alternative of itemizing their personal deductions.[32] With fewer deductions to check, the audit function is simplified.[33]

INFLUENCE OF THE COURTS

In addition to interpreting statutory provisions and the administrative pronouncements issued by the IRS, the Federal courts have influenced tax law in two other respects.[34] First, the courts have formulated certain judicial concepts that serve as guides in the application of various tax provisions. Second, certain key decisions have led to changes in the Internal Revenue Code.

Judicial Concepts Relating to Tax. A leading tax concept developed by the courts deals with the interpretation of statutory tax provisions that operate to benefit taxpayers. The courts have established the rule that these relief provisions are to be narrowly construed against taxpayers if there is any doubt about their application.

[31] See Chapter 16.

[32] For a discussion of the standard deduction, see Chapter 3.

[33] The same justification was given by the IRS when it proposed to Congress the $100 limitation on personal casualty and theft losses. Imposition of the limitation eliminated many casualty and theft loss deductions and, as a consequence, saved the IRS considerable audit time. Later legislation, in addition to retaining the $100 feature, limits deductible losses to those in excess of 10% of a taxpayer's adjusted gross income. See Chapter 7.

[34] A great deal of case law is devoted to ascertaining congressional intent. The courts, in effect, ask: What did Congress have in mind when it enacted a particular tax provision?

Important in this area is the *arm's length* concept. Particularly in dealings between related parties, transactions may be tested by looking to whether the taxpayers acted in an arm's length manner. The question to be asked is: Would unrelated parties have handled the transaction in the same way?

EXAMPLE 22

Rex, the sole shareholder of Silver Corporation, leases property to the corporation for a yearly rent of $6,000. To test whether the corporation should be allowed a rent deduction for this amount, the IRS and the courts will apply the arm's length concept. Would Silver Corporation have paid $6,000 a year in rent if it had leased the same property from an unrelated party (rather than from Rex)? Suppose it is determined that an unrelated third party would have paid an annual rent for the property of only $5,000. Under these circumstances, Silver Corporation will be allowed a deduction of only $5,000. The other $1,000 it paid for the use of the property represents a nondeductible dividend. Accordingly, Rex will be treated as having received rent income of $5,000 and dividend income of $1,000. ■

Judicial Influence on Statutory Provisions. Some court decisions have been of such consequence that Congress has incorporated them into statutory tax law. For example, many years ago the courts found that stock dividends distributed to the shareholders of a corporation were not taxable as income. This result was largely accepted by Congress, and a provision in the tax statutes now covers the issue.

On occasion, however, Congress has reacted negatively to judicial interpretations of the tax law.

EXAMPLE 23

Nora leases unimproved real estate to Wade for 40 years. At a cost of $200,000, Wade erects a building on the land. The building is worth $100,000 when the lease terminates and Nora takes possession of the property. Does Nora have any income either when the improvements are made or when the lease terminates? In a landmark decision, a court held that Nora must recognize income of $100,000 upon the termination of the lease. ■

Congress felt that the result reached in Example 23 was inequitable in that it was not consistent with the wherewithal to pay concept. Consequently, the tax law was amended to provide that a landlord does not recognize any income either when the improvements are made (unless made in lieu of rent) or when the lease terminates.

SUMMARY

In addition to its necessary revenue-raising objective, the Federal tax law has developed in response to several other factors:

- *Economic considerations.* The emphasis here is on tax provisions that help regulate the economy and encourage certain activities and types of businesses.
- *Social considerations.* Some tax provisions are designed to encourage (or discourage) certain socially desirable (or undesirable) practices.
- *Equity considerations.* Of principal concern in this area are tax provisions that alleviate the effect of multiple taxation, recognize the wherewithal to pay concept, mitigate the effect of the annual accounting period concept, and recognize the eroding effect of inflation.
- *Political considerations.* Of significance in this regard are tax provisions that represent special interest legislation, reflect political expediency, and exhibit the effect of state and local law.
- *Influence of the IRS.* Many tax provisions are intended to aid the IRS in the collection of revenue and the administration of the tax law.

- *Influence of the courts.* Court decisions have established a body of judicial concepts relating to tax law and have, on occasion, led Congress to enact statutory provisions to either clarify or negate their effect.

These factors explain various tax provisions and thereby help in understanding why the tax law developed to its present state. The next step involves learning to work with the tax law, which is the subject of Chapter 2.

KEY TERMS

Ad valorem tax, 1–6
Correspondence audit, 1–20
Death tax, 1–11
Employment taxes, 1–16
Estate tax, 1–11
Excise tax, 1–9
FICA tax, 1–16
Field audit, 1–20
Flat tax, 1–18
Franchise tax, 1–17
FUTA tax, 1–16
Gift tax, 1–12
Inheritance tax, 1–11
National sales tax, 1–18
Occupational tax, 1–17
Office audit, 1–20
Personalty, 1–8
Realty, 1–7
Revenue neutrality, 1–24
Sales tax, 1–10
Severance tax, 1–11
Statute of limitations, 1–21
Sunset provision, 1–25
Use tax, 1–10
Value added tax (VAT), 1–18
Wherewithal to pay, 1–28

PROBLEM MATERIALS

Discussion Questions

1. Irene, a middle management employee, is offered a pay increase by her employer. As a condition of the offer, Irene must move to another state. What tax considerations should Irene weigh before making a decision on whether to accept the offer?

2. Before the passage of the Sixteenth Amendment to the U.S. Constitution, there was no income tax in the United States. Please comment.

3. Did the passage of the Sixteenth Amendment to the U.S. Constitution have any effect on the income tax imposed on corporations? Explain.

4. World War II converted the Federal income tax into a *mass tax*. Explain.

5. How does the pay-as-you-go procedure apply to wage earners? To persons who have income from other than wages?

6. In terms of Adam Smith's canon of *economy*, how does the Federal income tax fare?

7. Are the following taxes *proportional* or *progressive?* Explain.
   a. Ad valorem tax on real estate.
   b. FICA tax.
   c. Federal gift tax.
   d. State income tax.

Issue ID

8. Until recently, Hunter College has relied on privately owned dormitories to provide housing for its out-of-state students. After a successful fund-raising campaign, the board of regents is considering purchasing and operating most of the privately owned dormitories. The city where Hunter College is located opposes the project. Why?

Issue ID

9. Once its new facilities are finished, the Church of the Good Samaritan moves from downtown Madison City to the suburbs. Instead of disposing of the old location, the church leases it to a former mayor of Madison City who converts the church building

and its parking lot into a high-end restaurant. Comment on any tax ramifications of this arrangement.

Issue ID

10. Before she entered a nursing home, Doris signed a deed transferring title to her personal residence to her only son, Walt. Walt has never filed the deed with the county clerk's office and continues to pay the property taxes in his mother's name. Walt and his family are the only occupants of the property. Is there an explanation for Walt's actions?

11. The commissioners for Colby County are actively negotiating with Eagle Industries regarding the location of a new manufacturing facility in the county. As Eagle is considering several other sites, a "generous tax holiday" may be needed to influence its choice. The local school district is opposed to any "generous tax holiday."
    a. In terms of a "generous tax holiday," what might the proposal entail?
    b. Why should the school district be opposed?

12. The Mayo family is selected for ABC's *Extreme Makeover: Home Edition.* The program gives the Mayos' California home the royal treatment, increasing the living area from 1,200 square feet to about 4,300—more than doubling the value of the property. Do you envision any tax problems?

13. Franklin County is in dire financial straits and is considering a number of sources for additional revenue. Evaluate the following possibilities in terms of anticipated taxpayer compliance:
    a. A property tax on business inventories.
    b. A tax on intangibles (i.e., stocks and bonds) held as investments.
    c. A property tax on boats used for recreational purposes.

14. After his first business trip to a major city, Herman is alarmed when he reviews his credit card receipts. Both the hotel bill and the car rental charge are in excess of the price he was quoted. Was Herman overcharged, or is there an explanation for the excess amounts?

Issue ID

15. Jared wants to give his wife a $30,000 diamond necklace for her birthday. To avoid the state and local general sales tax of 8.5%, he asks his aunt (who lives in New Hampshire) to make the purchase. Has Jared saved $2,550 (8.5% × $30,000)?

16. a. What is a sales tax holiday? What purpose might it serve?
    b. If a state anticipates a revenue shortfall, an easy solution is to cancel any scheduled sales tax holidays. Please assess the validity of this statement.

Issue ID

17. Velma lives in Wilson County, which is adjacent to Grimes County. Although the retail stores in both counties are comparable, Velma drives an extra 10 miles to do all of her shopping in Grimes County. Why might she do this?

Issue ID

18. During a social event, Muriel and Earl are discussing the home computer each recently purchased. Although the computers are identical makes and models, Muriel is surprised to learn that she paid a sales tax, while Earl did not. Comment as to why this could happen.

19. On a recent shopping trip to a warehouse discount store, Ruby bought goods worth $400. Although the state and local general sales tax is 7%, she was charged less than $28 (7% × $400) in tax. Why?

20. What was the original objective for the Federal estate tax? Is this objective being accomplished?

21. A decedent who leaves all of his property to his surviving spouse and to qualified charitable organizations is not subject to a Federal estate tax. Explain.

22. Petula comes to you regarding gifts to family members in the current year. When you ask her about prior gifts, she responds, "What difference does it make what I did in the past?" Please clarify matters for Petula.

23. a. What is the purpose of the unified transfer tax credit?
    b. Is the same amount available for both the Federal gift tax and the estate tax? Explain.
    c. Does the use of the credit for a gift affect the amount of credit available for the estate tax? Explain.

24. Marcus and Lottie are husband and wife and have five married daughters and 13 minor grandchildren. For year 2005, what is the maximum amount Marcus and Lottie can give their family (include the sons-in-law) without using any of their unified transfer tax credit?

25. The Tax Relief Reconciliation Act of 2001 purports to phase out the Federal estate tax but retains the Federal gift tax.
    a. What is the justification for rescinding the Federal estate tax?
    b. If the Federal estate tax is to be eliminated, why not also eliminate the Federal gift tax?

26. Errol (age 80) recently made the following remark to his new bride, Faith (age 24): "As to the tax cost, I can leave you much more property when I die than while I am alive." Is Errol telling Faith the truth? Explain.

27. Compare the Federal income tax on corporations with that applicable to individual taxpayers in terms of the following:
    a. Determination of AGI.
    b. Availability of the standard deduction.
    c. Nature of deductions allowed.

Issue ID

28. Mike Barr was an outstanding football player in college and expects to be drafted by the NFL in the first few rounds. Mike has let it be known that he would prefer to sign with a club located in Florida, Texas, or Washington. Mike sees no reason why he should have to pay state income tax on his player's salary! Is Mike under any delusions? Explain.

29. A state that uses a "piggyback" approach to its income tax has "decoupled" from a recent change in the Internal Revenue Code.
    a. What does this mean?
    b. Why might it have occurred?

Issue ID

30. A question on a state income tax return asks the taxpayer if he or she made any out-of-state Internet or mail-order catalog purchases during the year. The question requires a yes or no answer, and if the taxpayer answers yes, the amount of such purchases is to be listed.
    a. Does such an inquiry have any relevance to the state income tax? If not, why is it being asked?
    b. Your client, Harriet, wants to leave the question unanswered. As the preparer of her return, how do you respond?

31. As to those states that impose an income tax on individuals, comment on the following:
    a. Use of withholding procedures.
    b. Treatment of Federal income taxes paid.
    c. Due date for filing.
    d. Handling of personal and dependency exemptions.
    e. Credit for income taxes paid to other states.
    f. Availability of an amnesty program.

32. Contrast FICA and FUTA as to the following:
    a. Purpose of the tax.
    b. Upon whom imposed.
    c. Governmental administration of the tax.
    d. Reduction of tax based on a merit rating system.

33. Can an employee ever reach a point where salary increases are no longer subject to FICA? Explain.

34. Keith, a sole proprietor, owns and operates a grocery store. Keith's wife and his 17-year-old son work in the business and are paid wages. Will the wife and son be subject to FICA? Explain.

35. Dan, the owner and operator of a construction company that builds outdoor swimming pools, releases most of his construction personnel during the winter months. Should this hurt Dan's FUTA situation? Why or why not?

36. Regarding the proposal for a "flat tax," comment on the following:
    a. Justification for.
    b. Major obstacles to enactment.

37. In 2004, a bill was introduced in Congress that would replace the current income tax with a national sales tax, called the "Fair Tax."
    a. Describe the mechanics of the "Fair Tax" approach.
    b. What, if any, might be the shortcomings of this approach?

Issue ID

38. Serena operates a lawn maintenance service in southern California. As most of her employees are itinerant, they are paid on a day-to-day basis. Because of cash-flow problems, Serena requires her customers to pay cash for the services she provides.
    a. What are some of the tax problems Serena might have?
    b. Assess Serena's chances of audit by the IRS.

39. Assess the probability of an audit in each of the following independent situations:
    a. As a result of a jury trial, Linda was awarded $3.5 million because of job discrimination. The award included $3 million for punitive damages.
    b. Hailey, the CEO of a major corporation, is convicted by a court of wrongfully realizing $10 million in profits from insider stock trading.
    c. Gavin operates a valet parking service for several upscale restaurants and nightclubs. Gavin is paid by the customers and not by the establishments he works for.
    d. Dr. Fair just fired the accountant who maintained the records for the dental clinic he operates. The accountant received no severance pay or retirement benefits although she had been employed by the clinic for more than 15 years.
    e. Fawn works the night shift on the assembly line at a Ford Motor truck plant.

40. With regard to the IRS audit process, comment on the following:
    a. Percentage of individual returns audited.
    b. "No change" results in recent IRS audit experience.
    c. DIF score.
    d. Exchange of information with the taxing authorities of states that impose their own income tax.
    e. Type of audit (i.e., correspondence, office, field).
    f. RAR issued by the IRS agent.
    g. Special agent joins the audit team.

41. Regarding the statute of limitations on additional assessments of tax by the IRS, determine the applicable period in each of the following situations. Assume a calendar year individual with no fraud or substantial omission involved.
    a. The income tax return for 2004 was filed on February 25, 2005.
    b. The income tax return for 2004 was filed on June 28, 2005.
    c. The income tax return for 2004 was prepared on April 8, 2005, but was never filed. Through some misunderstanding between the preparer and the taxpayer, each expected the other to file the return.

42. Brianna, a calendar year taxpayer, files her income tax return for 2004 on February 7, 2005. Although she makes repeated inquiries, she does not receive her refund from the IRS until May 27, 2005. Is Brianna entitled to interest on the refund? Explain.

43. On a Federal income tax return filed five years ago, Andy inadvertently omitted a large amount of gross income.
    a. Andy seeks your advice as to whether the IRS is barred from assessing additional income tax in the event he is audited. What is your advice?
    b. Would your advice differ if you are the person who prepared the return in question? Explain.
    c. Suppose Andy asks you to prepare his current year's return. Would you do so? Explain.

44. Samantha files her income tax return 65 days after the due date of the return without obtaining an extension from the IRS. Along with the return, she remits a check for $10,000, which is the balance of the tax she owes. Disregarding the interest element, what are Samantha's penalties for failure to file and for failure to pay?

45. In March 2005, Jim asks you to prepare his Federal income tax returns for tax years 2002, 2003, and 2004. In discussing this matter with him, you discover that he also has not filed for tax year 2001. When you mention this fact, Jim tells you that the statute of limitations precludes the IRS from taking any action as to this year.
    a. Is Jim correct about the application of the statute of limitations? Why?
    b. If Jim refuses to file for 2001, should you prepare returns for 2002 through 2004?

46. Ethan owns and operates a janitorial maintenance service for commercial properties. He has instructed his new accountant that around year-end the books of the business should be kept open longer for some transactions and closed earlier for others.
    a. What does Ethan have in mind?
    b. When the accountant objects to the procedure, Ethan assures him that no distortion will occur. Because the practice has been followed in past years, the result is a "washout." Explain Ethan's reasoning and comment on the propriety of what is occurring.

47. With regard to the concept of revenue neutrality, comment on the following:
    a. A tax cut that is accompanied by a revenue offset.
    b. A tax cut that is phased in over a period of years.
    c. A tax cut that contains a sunset provision.

48. Some tax rules can be justified on multiple grounds (e.g., economic, social, etc.). In this connection, comment on the possible justification for the rules governing the following:
    a. Pension plans.
    b. Education.
    c. Home ownership.

49. Discuss the possible justifications for the following provisions of the tax law:
    a. The preferential treatment allowed U.S. citizens who work overseas.
    b. The election to expense, rather than capitalize and depreciate, certain property acquisitions.
    c. The deferral of gain recognition on the receipt of crop insurance proceeds.
    d. An election that enables certain corporations to avoid the corporate income tax and pass losses through to their shareholders.
    e. The tax treatment of premiums paid by an employer on group life insurance for employees.

50. Allowing a taxpayer a deduction for Federal income tax purposes for state income taxes paid eliminates the double taxation of the same income. Do you agree? Why or why not?

51. The state has condemned grazing land belonging to Justin, a rancher, for use as a roadside park and camping grounds. Justin paid $20,000 for the land 30 years ago. He is delighted with the condemnation award of $140,000, as he thinks the land is not worth more than $80,000. Shortly thereafter, Justin purchases additional grazing land. What are Justin's tax consequences if the replacement land costs:
    a. $15,000?
    b. $150,000?
    c. $130,000?

52. In what manner does the tax law mitigate the effect of the annual accounting period concept with the income recognition treatment allowed for installment sales?

53. How does the tax law cope with the impact of inflation?

Issue ID

54. Renee is the sole shareholder of Bronze Corporation. During the year, she leases property to Bronze for an annual rent of $24,000. Under what circumstances might this arrangement be subject to challenge by the IRS?

55. Edward leases real estate to Janet for a period of 20 years. Janet makes capital improvements to the property. When the lease expires, Edward reclaims the property, including the improvements made by Janet.
    a. Under current law, at what point does Edward recognize income as a result of Janet's improvements?
    b. Has the law in (a) always been the rule?
    c. What is the justification, if any, for the current rule?

Working with the Tax Law

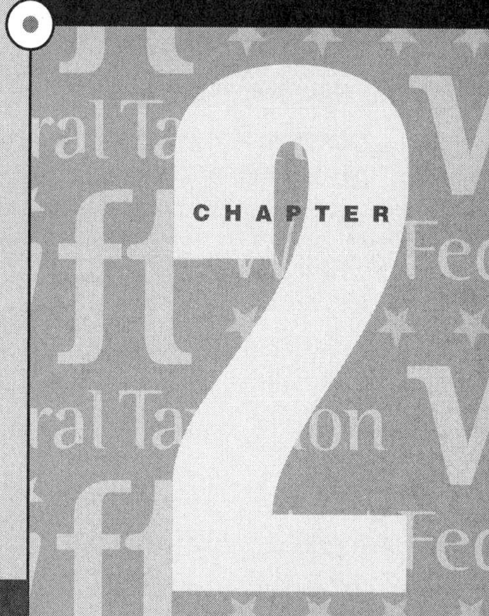

LEARNING OBJECTIVES

After completing Chapter 2, you should be able to:

LO.1

Distinguish between the statutory, administrative, and judicial sources of the tax law and understand the purpose of each source.

LO.2

Locate and work with the appropriate tax law sources.

LO.3

Understand the tax research process.

LO.4

Communicate the results of the tax research process in a client letter and a tax file memorandum.

LO.5

Apply tax research techniques and planning procedures.

LO.6

Have an awareness of electronic tax research.

http://wft.swlearning.com

OUTLINE

LO.1

Distinguish between the statutory, administrative, and judicial sources of the tax law and understand the purpose of each source.

Tax Sources

Understanding taxation requires a mastery of the sources of the *rules of tax law*. These sources include not only legislative provisions in the form of the Internal Revenue Code, but also congressional Committee Reports, Treasury Department Regulations, other Treasury Department pronouncements, and court decisions. Thus, the *primary sources* of tax information include pronouncements from all three branches of government: legislative, executive, and judicial.

In addition to being able to locate and interpret the sources of the tax law, a tax professional must understand the relative weight of authority within these sources. The tax law is of little significance, however, until it is applied to a set of facts and circumstances. This chapter, therefore, both introduces the statutory, administrative, and judicial sources of the tax law *and* explains how the law is applied to individual and business transactions. It also explains how to apply research techniques and use planning procedures effectively.

A large part of tax research focuses on determining the intent of Congress. While Congress often claims simplicity as one of its goals, a cursory examination of the tax law indicates that it has not been very successful. Faced with a 48-page tax return, James Michener, the author, said, "it is unimaginable in that I graduated from one of America's better colleges, yet I am totally incapable of understanding tax returns." David Brinkley, the former television news commentator, observed that "settling a dispute is difficult when our tax regulations are all written in a foreign tongue whose language flows like damp sludge leaking from a sanitary landfill."

Frequently, uncertainty in the tax law causes disputes between the Internal Revenue Service (IRS) and taxpayers. Due to these *gray areas* and the complexity of the tax law, a taxpayer may have more than one alternative for structuring a business transaction. In structuring business transactions and engaging in other tax planning activities, the tax adviser must be cognizant that the objective of tax planning is not necessarily to minimize the tax liability. Instead a taxpayer should maximize his or her after-tax return, which may include maximizing nontax as well as noneconomic benefits.

STATUTORY SOURCES OF THE TAX LAW

Origin of the Internal Revenue Code. Before 1939, the statutory provisions relating to taxation were contained in the individual revenue acts enacted by Congress. The inconvenience and confusion that resulted from dealing with many sepa-

TAX FREEDOM DAY?

In income tax history, 1913 was an important year. In that year, the Sixteenth Amendment to the Constitution was ratified:

> The Congress shall have power to tax and collect taxes on incomes, from whatever source derived, without apportionment among the several States, and without regard to any census or enumeration.

The first income tax legislation that definitely was constitutional was passed that same year.

According to the Tax Foundation, Tax Freedom Day fell on April 11, 2004, the earliest in 37 years. Tax Freedom Day is the date on which a taxpayer through working has paid off his or her taxes for the year. Of course, if you lived in Connecticut with the heaviest total tax burden, Tax Freedom Day fell on April 28, 2004. Alaskans paid the least and finished paying off their tax burden on March 26, 2004.

SOURCE: Tax Foundation, "Tax Freedom Day Arrives on April 11th in 2004," **http://www.taxfoundation.org/taxfreedomday.html**.

rate acts led Congress to codify all of the Federal tax laws. Known as the Internal Revenue Code of 1939, the codification arranged all Federal tax provisions in a logical sequence and placed them in a separate part of the Federal statutes. A further rearrangement took place in 1954 and resulted in the Internal Revenue Code of 1954, which continued in effect until it was replaced by the Internal Revenue Code of 1986.

The following observations help clarify the codification procedure:

- Neither the 1939, the 1954, nor the 1986 Code changed all of the tax law existing on the date of enactment. Much of the 1939 Code, for example, was incorporated into the 1954 Code. The same can be said for the transition from the 1954 to the 1986 Code. This point is important in assessing judicial and administrative decisions interpreting provisions under prior codes. For example, a decision interpreting § 121 of the Internal Revenue Code of 1954 will have continuing validity since this provision carried over unchanged to the Internal Revenue Code of 1986.
- Statutory amendments to the tax law are integrated into the existing Code. Thus, subsequent tax legislation, such as the Tax Relief Reconciliation Act of 2001, the Job Creation and Worker Assistance Act of 2002, the Jobs and Growth Tax Relief Reconciliation Act (JGTRRA) of 2003, the Working Families Tax Relief Act of 2004, and the American Jobs Creation Act of 2004, has all become part of the Internal Revenue Code of 1986. In view of the frequency with which tax legislation has been enacted in recent years, it appears that the tax law will continue to be amended frequently.

The Legislative Process. Federal tax legislation generally originates in the House of Representatives, where it is first considered by the House Ways and Means Committee. Tax bills originate in the Senate when they are attached as riders to other legislative proposals.[1] If acceptable to the committee, the proposed bill is referred to the entire

[1]The Tax Equity and Fiscal Responsibility Act of 1982 originated in the Senate, and its constitutionality was unsuccessfully challenged in the courts. The Senate version of the Deficit Reduction Act of 1984 was attached as an amendment to the Federal Boat Safety Act.

House of Representatives for approval or disapproval. Approved bills are sent to the Senate, where they initially are considered by the Senate Finance Committee.

The next step is referral from the Senate Finance Committee to the entire Senate. Assuming no disagreement between the House and Senate, passage by the Senate means referral to the President for approval or veto. The passage of JGTRRA of 2003 required the vote of Vice President Dick Cheney to break a 50–50 tie in the Senate. If the bill is approved or if the President's veto is overridden, the bill becomes law and part of the Internal Revenue Code of 1986.

House and Senate versions of major tax bills frequently differ. One reason bills are often changed in the Senate is that each individual senator has considerable latitude to make amendments when the Senate as a whole is voting on a bill referred to it by the Senate Finance Committee. In contrast, the entire House of Representatives either accepts or rejects what is proposed by the House Ways and Means Committee, and changes from the floor are rare. When the Senate version of the bill differs from that passed by the House, the Joint Conference Committee, which includes members of both the House Ways and Means Committee and the Senate Finance Committee, is called upon to resolve the differences. The deliberations of the Joint Conference Committee usually produce a compromise between the two versions, which is then voted on by both the House and the Senate. If both bodies accept the bill, it is referred to the President for approval or veto. Former Senator Daniel Patrick Moynihan observed that it is common in the last hours of Congress for the White House and lawmakers to agree on a "1,200-page monster, we vote for it; nobody knows what is in it." Figure 2–1 summarizes the typical legislative process for tax bills.

The role of the Joint Conference Committee indicates the importance of compromise in the legislative process. As an example of the practical effect of the compromise process, consider Figure 2–2, which shows what happened to a limitation on contributions by employees to their education Individual Retirement Accounts (now Coverdell Education Savings Accounts) in the Taxpayer Relief Act of 1997.

Referrals from the House Ways and Means Committee, the Senate Finance Committee, and the Joint Conference Committee are usually accompanied by Committee Reports. These Committee Reports often explain the provisions of the proposed legislation and are therefore a valuable source for ascertaining the *intent of Congress*. What Congress had in mind when it considered and enacted tax legislation is the key to interpreting the legislation. Since Regulations normally are not issued immediately after a statute is enacted, taxpayers and the courts look to Committee Reports to determine congressional intent.

Arrangement of the Code. The Internal Revenue Code of 1986 is found in Title 26 of the U.S. Code. In working with the Code, it helps to understand the format. Note the following partial table of contents:

Subtitle A. Income Taxes
- Chapter 1. Normal Taxes and Surtaxes
  - Subchapter A. Determination of Tax Liability
    - Part I. Tax on Individuals
      - Sections 1–5
    - Part II. Tax on Corporations
      - Sections 11–12

* * *

In referring to a provision of the Code, the key is usually the Section number. In citing Section 2(a) (dealing with the status of a surviving spouse), for example, it is unnecessary to include Subtitle A, Chapter 1, Subchapter A, Part I. Merely mentioning Section 2(a) will suffice, since the Section numbers run consecutively and do not begin again with each new Subtitle, Chapter, Subchapter, or Part. Not

■ **FIGURE 2–1**
Legislative Process for Tax Bills

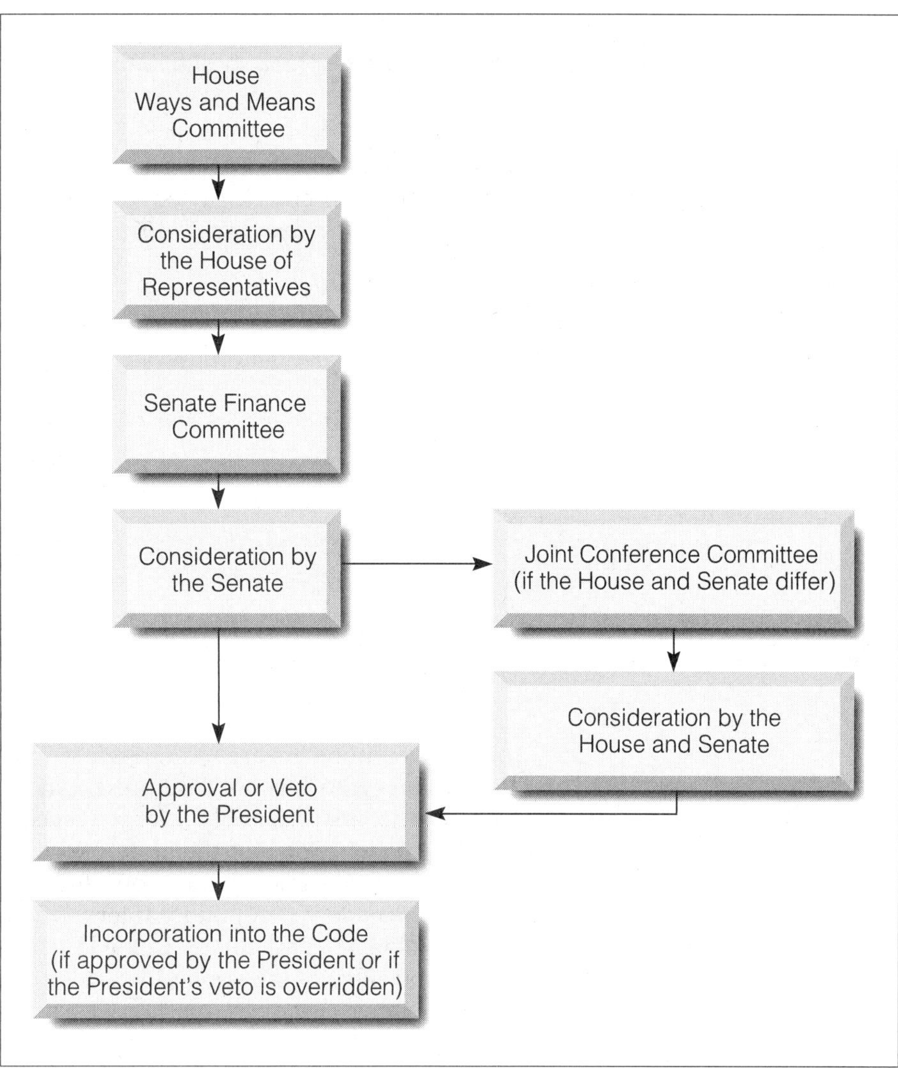

■ **FIGURE 2–2**
Example of Compromise in the Joint Conference Committee

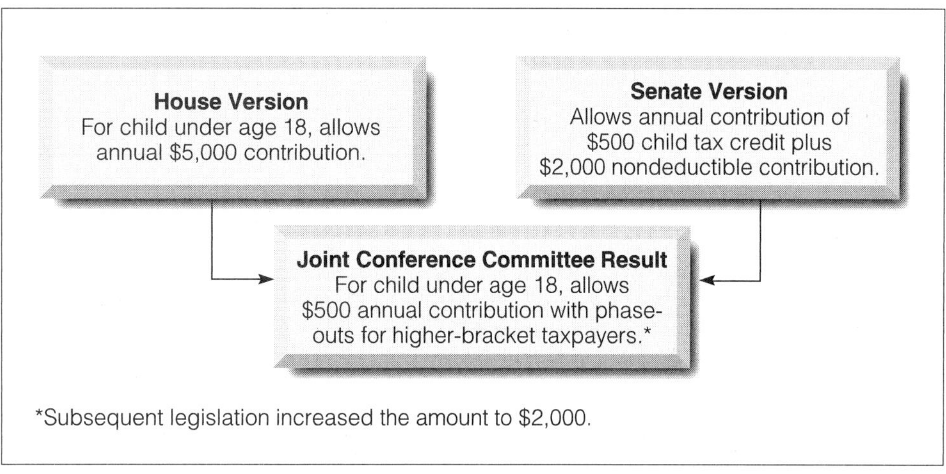

THOSE DISAPPEARING DEPENDENTS

Tax law changes can have unforeseen or peculiar impacts. In 1986, 77 million dependents were claimed on U.S. individual income tax returns, but a year later, in 1987, more than 7 million of those dependents had disappeared. More than 11,000 taxpayers who claimed seven or more dependents in 1986 claimed none in 1987. Had some disaster or plague occurred?

No, according to former IRS Commissioner Donald C. Alexander. A 1987 tax law change required taxpayers to provide a dependent's Social Security number on their tax returns. Apparently, those 7 million disappearing dependents were fakes who never existed.

Two years later 2.6 million babysitters disappeared. Kidnapped maybe? No, a change in the tax law required taxpayers to provide the babysitter's name, address, and Social Security number on the income tax return. Alexander says that tax laws must be enforced to be effective.

SOURCE: Adapted from "An Open Letter to the New Commissioner of the IRS from Donald C. Alexander," *Tax Notes* (May 17, 1993): 975.

all Code Section numbers are used, however. Note that Part I ends with Section 5 and Part II starts with Section 11 (at present there are no Sections 6, 7, 8, 9, and 10).[2]

Tax practitioners commonly refer to a specific area of income tax law by Subchapter designation. Some of the more common Subchapter designations include Subchapter C ("Corporate Distributions and Adjustments"), Subchapter K ("Partners and Partnerships"), and Subchapter S ("Tax Treatment of S Corporations and Their Shareholders"). Particularly in the last situation, it is much more convenient to describe the effect of the applicable Code provisions (Sections 1361–1379) as "S corporation status" than as the "Tax Treatment of S Corporations and Their Shareholders."

Citing the Code. Code Sections are often broken down into subparts.[3] Section 2(a)(1)(A) serves as an example.

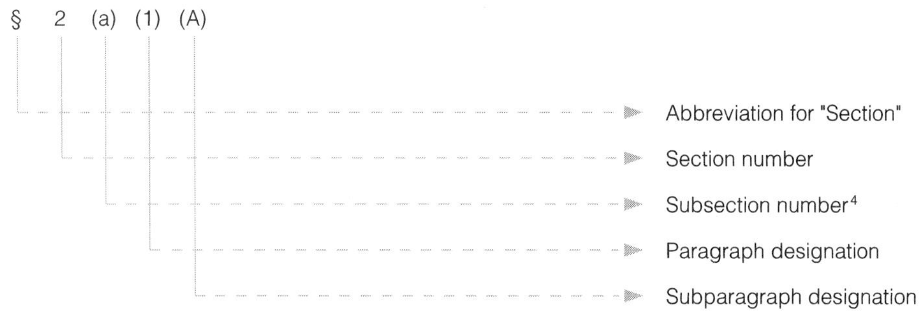

[2]When the Code was drafted, Section numbers were intentionally omitted so that later changes could be incorporated into the Code without disrupting its organization. When Congress does not leave enough space, subsequent Code Sections are given A, B, C, etc., designations. A good example is the treatment of Sections 280A through 280H.

[3]Some Code Sections do not have subparts. See, for example, §§ 211 and 241.

[4]Some Code Sections omit the subsection designation and use, instead, the paragraph designation as the first subpart. See, for example, §§ 212(1) and 1222(1).

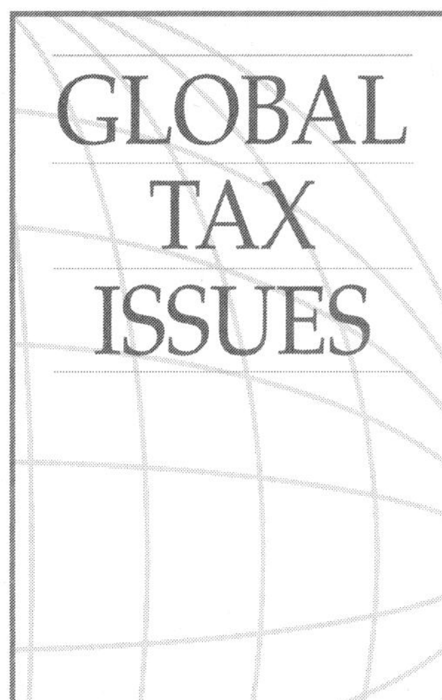

Tax Treaties

The United States has entered into treaties with most of the major countries of the world in order to eliminate possible double taxation. For example, nonresident alien students wishing to claim exemption from taxation are required to provide an information statement as set forth in several Revenue Procedures. The withholding agent must also certify the form.

Chinese students are required to prepare a four-part statement. Part 3 of the student's statement is as follows:

> I will receive compensation for personal services performed in the United States. This compensation qualifies for exemption from withholding of Federal income tax under the tax treaty between the United States and the People's Republic of China in an amount not in excess of $5,000 for any taxable year.

Broken down by content, Section 2(a)(1)(A) appears as follows:

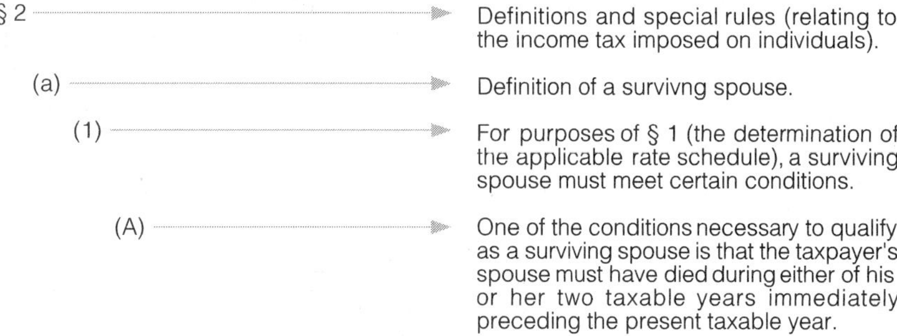

§ 2
Definitions and special rules (relating to the income tax imposed on individuals).
(a)
Definition of a survivng spouse.
(1)
For purposes of § 1 (the determination of the applicable rate schedule), a surviving spouse must meet certain conditions.
(A)
One of the conditions necessary to qualify as a surviving spouse is that the taxpayer's spouse must have died during either of his or her two taxable years immediately preceding the present taxable year.

Throughout the text, references to Code Sections are in the form given above. The symbols "§" and "§§" are used in place of "Section" and "Sections." Unless otherwise stated, all Code references are to the Internal Revenue Code of 1986. The following table summarizes the format used in the text:

Complete Reference	Text Reference
Section 2(a)(1)(A) of the Internal Revenue Code of 1986	§ 2(a)(1)(A)
Sections 1 and 2 of the Internal Revenue Code of 1986	§§ 1 and 2
Section 2 of the Internal Revenue Code of 1954	§ 2 of the Internal Revenue Code of 1954
Section 12(d) of the Internal Revenue Code of 1939[5]	§ 12(d) of the Internal Revenue Code of 1939

Effect of Treaties. The United States signs certain tax treaties (sometimes called tax conventions) with foreign countries to render mutual assistance in tax enforcement and to avoid double taxation. Neither a tax law nor a tax treaty automatically takes precedence. When there is a direct conflict, the most recent item will take

[5]Section 12(d) of the Internal Revenue Code of 1939 is the predecessor to § 2 of the Internal Revenue Code of 1954 and the Internal Revenue Code of 1986.

precedence. A taxpayer must disclose on the tax return any position where a treaty overrides a tax law.[6] There is a $1,000 per *failure to disclose* penalty for individuals and a $10,000 per failure to disclose penalty for corporations.[7]

ETHICAL CONSIDERATIONS

The President and the IRS

President Franklin Delano Roosevelt once said, "I am wholly unable to figure out the amount of tax." In a letter to the then Commissioner of the IRS, Roosevelt said, "as this is a problem in higher mathematics, may I ask the Bureau [IRS] to let me know the amount of the balance due."

When a friend of FDR was ordered to pay $420,000 in tax penalties, the President called the Commissioner within earshot of reporters and told him to cut the penalties to $3,000. One listener, David Brinkley, recalled years later: "Nobody seemed to think it was news or very interesting." Evaluate the President's actions.

ADMINISTRATIVE SOURCES OF THE TAX LAW

The administrative sources of the Federal tax law can be grouped as follows: Treasury Department Regulations, Revenue Rulings and Revenue Procedures, and various other administrative pronouncements (see Exhibit 2–1). All are issued by either the U.S. Treasury Department or the IRS.

■ EXHIBIT 2–1
Administrative Sources

Source	**Location**	**Authority****
Regulations	*Federal Register**	Force and effect of law.
Temporary Regulations	*Federal Register** *Internal Revenue Bulletin* *Cumulative Bulletin*	May be cited as a precedent.
Proposed Regulations	*Federal Register** *Internal Revenue Bulletin* *Cumulative Bulletin*	Preview of final Regulations.
Revenue Rulings Revenue Procedures Treasury Decisions Actions on Decisions	*Internal Revenue Bulletin* *Cumulative Bulletin*	Do not have the force and effect of law.
General Counsel Memoranda Technical Advice Memoranda	*Tax Analysts' Tax Notes* RIA's *Internal Memoranda of the IRS* CCH's *IRS Position Reporter*	May not be cited as a precedent.
Letter Rulings	Research Institute of America and Commerce Clearing House loose-leaf services	Applicable only to taxpayer addressed. No precedential force.

*Finalized, Temporary, and Proposed Regulations are published in soft-cover form by several publishers.
**Each of these sources may be substantial authority for purposes of the accuracy-related penalty in § 6662. Notice 90–20, 1990–1 C.B. 328.

[6]§ 7852(d).
[7]Reg. §§ 301.6114–1, 301.6712–1, and 301.7701(b)(7).

Treasury Department Regulations. Regulations are issued by the U.S. Treasury Department under authority granted by Congress.[8] Interpretive by nature, they provide taxpayers with considerable guidance on the meaning and application of the Code. Regulations carry considerable authority as the official interpretation of tax statutes. They are an important factor to consider in complying with the tax law.

Since Regulations interpret the Code, they are arranged in the same sequence as the Code. A number is added at the beginning, however, to indicate the type of tax or administrative, procedural, or definitional matter to which they relate. For example, the prefix 1 designates the Regulations under the income tax law. Thus, the Regulations under Code § 2 would be cited as Reg. § 1.2, with subparts added for further identification. The numbering patterns of these subparts often have no correlation with the Code subsections. The prefix 20 designates estate tax Regulations, 25 covers gift tax Regulations, 31 relates to employment taxes, and 301 refers to procedure and administration. This list is not all-inclusive.

New Regulations and changes in existing Regulations are usually issued in proposed form before they are finalized. The interval between the proposal of a Regulation and its finalization permits taxpayers and other interested parties to comment on the propriety of the proposal. **Proposed Regulations** under Code § 2, for example, are cited as Prop.Reg. § 1.2. The Tax Court indicates that Proposed Regulations carry little weight—no more than a position advanced in a written brief prepared by a litigating party before the Tax Court. **Finalized Regulations** have the force and effect of law.[9]

Sometimes the Treasury Department issues **Temporary Regulations** relating to matters where immediate guidance is important. These Regulations are issued without the comment period required for Proposed Regulations. Temporary Regulations have the same authoritative value as final Regulations and may be cited as precedents. Temporary Regulations must also be issued as Proposed Regulations and automatically expire within three years after the date of issuance.[10]

Proposed, Temporary, and final Regulations are published in the *Federal Register*, in the *Internal Revenue Bulletin* (I.R.B.), and by major tax services. Final Regulations are issued as Treasury Decisions (TDs).

Regulations may also be classified as *legislative, interpretive*, or *procedural*. This classification scheme is discussed under Assessing the Validity of a Treasury Regulation later in the chapter.

Revenue Rulings and Revenue Procedures. **Revenue Rulings** are official pronouncements of the National Office of the IRS.[11] They typically provide one or more examples of how the IRS would apply a law to specific fact situations. Like Regulations, Revenue Rulings are designed to provide interpretation of the tax law. However, they do not carry the same legal force and effect as Regulations and usually deal with more restricted problems. Regulations are approved by the Secretary of the Treasury, whereas Revenue Rulings generally are not.

A Revenue Ruling often results from a specific taxpayer's request for a letter ruling. If the IRS believes that a taxpayer's request for a letter ruling deserves official publication due to its widespread impact, the letter ruling will be converted into a Revenue Ruling and issued for the information and guidance of taxpayers, tax practitioners, and IRS personnel. Names, identifying descriptions, and money amounts are changed to conceal the identity of the requesting taxpayer. Revenue

[8] § 7805.

[9] *F. W. Woolworth Co.*, 54 T.C. 1233 (1970); *Harris M. Miller*, 70 T.C. 448 (1978); and *James O. Tomerlin Trust*, 87 T.C. 876 (1986).

[10] § 7805(e).

[11] § 7805(a).

Rulings also arise from technical advice to District Offices of the IRS, court decisions, suggestions from tax practitioner groups, and various tax publications.

Revenue Procedures are issued in the same manner as Revenue Rulings, but deal with the internal management practices and procedures of the IRS. Familiarity with these procedures increases taxpayer compliance and helps make the administration of the tax laws more efficient. The failure of a taxpayer to follow a Revenue Procedure can result in unnecessary delay or, in a discretionary situation, can cause the IRS to decline to act on behalf of the taxpayer.

Both Revenue Rulings and Revenue Procedures serve an important function in that they provide *guidance* to IRS personnel and taxpayers in handling routine tax matters. Revenue Rulings and Revenue Procedures generally apply retroactively and may be revoked or modified by subsequent rulings or procedures, Regulations, legislation, or court decisions.

Revenue Rulings and Revenue Procedures are published weekly by the U.S. Government in the *Internal Revenue Bulletin* (I.R.B.). Semiannually, the *Bulletins* for a six-month period are gathered together and published in a bound volume called the *Cumulative Bulletin* (C.B.).[12]

The proper form for citing Rulings and Procedures depends on whether the item has been published in the *Cumulative Bulletin* or is available only in I.R.B. form. Consider, for example, the following transition:

Temporary Citation	Rev.Rul. 2004–18, I.R.B. No. 8, 509. *Explanation:* Revenue Ruling Number 18, appearing on page 509 of the 8th weekly issue of the *Internal Revenue Bulletin* for 2004.
Permanent Citation	Rev.Rul. 2004–18, 2004–1 C.B. 509. *Explanation:* Revenue Ruling Number 18, appearing on page 509 of Volume 1 of the *Cumulative Bulletin* for 2004.

Note that the page reference of 509 is the same for both the I.R.B. (temporary) and C.B. (permanent) versions of the ruling. The IRS numbers the pages of the I.R.B.s consecutively for each six-month period so as to facilitate their conversion to C.B. form.

Revenue Procedures are cited in the same manner, except that "Rev.Proc." is substituted for "Rev.Rul." Some recent Revenue Procedures dealt with the following matters:

- Deduction limits on luxury automobile depreciation.
- Revised procedures for the issuance of letter rulings.
- Automatic consent procedure for a change in accounting method.

Letter Rulings. **Letter rulings** are issued for a fee upon a taxpayer's request and describe how the IRS will treat a *proposed* transaction for tax purposes. They apply only to the taxpayer who asks for and obtains the ruling, but post-1984 letter rulings may be substantial authority for purposes of the accuracy-related penalty.[13] Letter rulings can be useful to taxpayers who wish to be certain of how a transaction

[12]Usually, only two volumes of the *Cumulative Bulletin* are published each year. However, when Congress has enacted major tax legislation, other volumes may be published containing the Congressional Committee Reports supporting the Revenue Act. See, for example, the two extra volumes for 1984 dealing with the Deficit Reduction Act of 1984. The 1984–3 *Cumulative Bulletin*, Volume 1, contains the text of the law itself; 1984–3, Volume 2, contains the Committee Reports. There are a total of four volumes of the *Cumulative Bulletin* for 1984: 1984–1; 1984–2; 1984–3, Volume 1; and 1984–3, Volume 2.

[13]Notice 90–20, 1990–1 C.B. 328. In this regard, letter rulings differ from Revenue Rulings, which are applicable to *all* taxpayers. A letter ruling may later lead to the issuance of a Revenue Ruling if the holding affects many taxpayers. In its Agents' Manual, the IRS indicates that letter rulings may be used as a guide with other research materials in formulating a District Office position on an issue. The IRS is required to charge a taxpayer a fee for letter rulings, determination letters, etc.

will be taxed before proceeding with it. Letter rulings also allow taxpayers to avoid unexpected tax costs. Although the procedure for requesting a ruling can be quite cumbersome, sometimes requesting a ruling is the most effective way to carry out tax planning. Nevertheless, the IRS limits the issuance of individual rulings to restricted, preannounced areas of taxation. The main reason the IRS will not rule in certain areas is that they involve fact-oriented situations. Thus, a ruling may not be obtained on many of the problems that are particularly troublesome to taxpayers.[14] The IRS issues over 2,000 letter rulings each year.

Although letter rulings once were private and not available to the public, the law now requires the IRS to make such rulings available for public inspection after identifying details are deleted.[15] Published digests of private letter rulings can be found in RIA's *Private Letter Rulings*, BNA *Daily Tax Reports*, and Tax Analysts' *Tax Notes. IRS Letter Rulings Reports* (published by Commerce Clearing House) contain both digests and full texts of all letter rulings. *Letter Ruling Review* (published by Tax Analysts), a monthly publication, selects and discusses the more important letter rulings issued each month. In addition, computerized databases of letter rulings are available through several private publishers.

Letter rulings are issued multidigit file numbers, which indicate the year and week of issuance as well as the number of the ruling during that week. Consider, for example, Ltr.Rul. 200414039, which ruled that grants awarded under a tax-exempt theology school's scholarship program do not represent compensation for services.

2004	14	039
Year 2004	14th week of issuance	39th ruling issued during the 14th week

Other Administrative Pronouncements. *Treasury Decisions* (TDs) are issued by the Treasury Department to promulgate new Regulations, amend or otherwise change existing Regulations, or announce the position of the Government on selected court decisions. Like Revenue Rulings and Revenue Procedures, TDs are published initially in the *Internal Revenue Bulletin* and subsequently transferred to the *Cumulative Bulletin*.

The IRS publishes other administrative communications in the *Internal Revenue Bulletin*, such as Announcements, Notices, LRs (Proposed Regulations), and Prohibited Transaction Exemptions.

Like letter rulings, **determination letters** are issued at the request of taxpayers and provide guidance on the application of the tax law. They differ from letter rulings in that the issuing source is an Area Director rather than the National Office of the IRS. Also, determination letters usually involve *completed* (as opposed to proposed) transactions. Determination letters are not published and are made known only to the party making the request.

EXAMPLE 1

The shareholders of Red Corporation and Green Corporation want assurance that the consolidation of the corporations into Blue Corporation will be a nontaxable reorganization. The proper approach is to ask the National Office of the IRS to issue a letter ruling concerning the income tax effect of the proposed transaction. ■

[14]Rev.Proc. 2005–3, I.R.B. No. 1, 118 contains a list of areas in which the IRS will not issue advance rulings. From time to time, subsequent Revenue Procedures are issued that modify or amplify Rev.Proc. 2005–3.

[15]§ 6110.

EXAMPLE 2

Chris operates a barber shop in which he employs eight barbers. To comply with the rules governing income tax and payroll tax withholdings, Chris wants to know whether the barbers working for him are employees or independent contractors. The proper procedure is to request a determination letter on their status from the appropriate Area Director. ■

The law now requires that several internal memoranda that constitute the working law of the IRS be released. These General Counsel Memoranda (GCMs), Technical Advice Memoranda (TAMs), and Field Service Advice (FSAs) are not officially published, and the IRS indicates that they may not be cited as precedents by taxpayers.[16] However, these working documents do explain the IRS's position on various issues.

The National Office of the IRS releases **Technical Advice Memoranda (TAMs)** weekly. TAMs resemble letter rulings in that they give the IRS's determination of an issue. Letter rulings, however, are responses to requests by taxpayers, whereas TAMs are issued by the National Office of the IRS in response to questions raised by IRS field personnel during audits. TAMs deal with completed rather than proposed transactions and are often requested for questions relating to exempt organizations and employee plans. TAMs are not officially published and may not be cited or used as precedent.[17]

The Office of Chief Counsel prepares Field Service Advices (FSAs) to help IRS employees. They are issued in response to requests for advice, guidance, and analysis on difficult or significant tax issues. FSAs are not binding on either the taxpayer to whom they pertain or the IRS.

Field Service Advices are being replaced by a new form of field guidance called Technical Expedited Advice Memoranda (TEAMs). The purpose of TEAMs is to expedite legal guidance to field agents as disputes are developing. FSAs are reverting to their original purpose of case-specific development of facts.

A TEAM guidance differs from a TAM in several ways, including a mandatory presubmission conference involving the taxpayer. In the event of a tentatively adverse conclusion for the taxpayer or the field agent, a conference of right is offered to the taxpayer and to the field agent; once the conference of right is held, no further conferences are offered.

JUDICIAL SOURCES OF THE TAX LAW

The Judicial Process in General. After a taxpayer has exhausted some or all of the remedies available within the IRS (i.e., no satisfactory settlement has been reached at the agent level or at the Appeals Division level), the dispute can be taken to the Federal courts. The dispute is first considered by a **court of original jurisdiction** (known as a trial court), with any appeal (either by the taxpayer or the IRS) taken to the appropriate appellate court. In most situations, the taxpayer has a choice of any of four trial courts: a **Federal District Court,** the **U.S. Court of Federal Claims,** the **U.S. Tax Court,** or the **Small Cases Division** of the U.S. Tax Court. The trial and *appellate court* system for Federal tax litigation is illustrated in Figure 2–3.

The broken line between the U.S. Tax Court and the Small Cases Division indicates that there is no appeal from the Small Cases Division. The jurisdiction of the Small Cases Division is limited to cases involving amounts of $50,000 or

[16]These are unofficially published by the publishers listed in Exhibit 2–1. Such internal memoranda for post-1984 may be substantial authority for purposes of the accuracy-related penalty. Notice 90–20, 1990–1 C.B. 328.

[17]§ 6110(j)(3).

■ **FIGURE 2–3**
Federal Judicial System

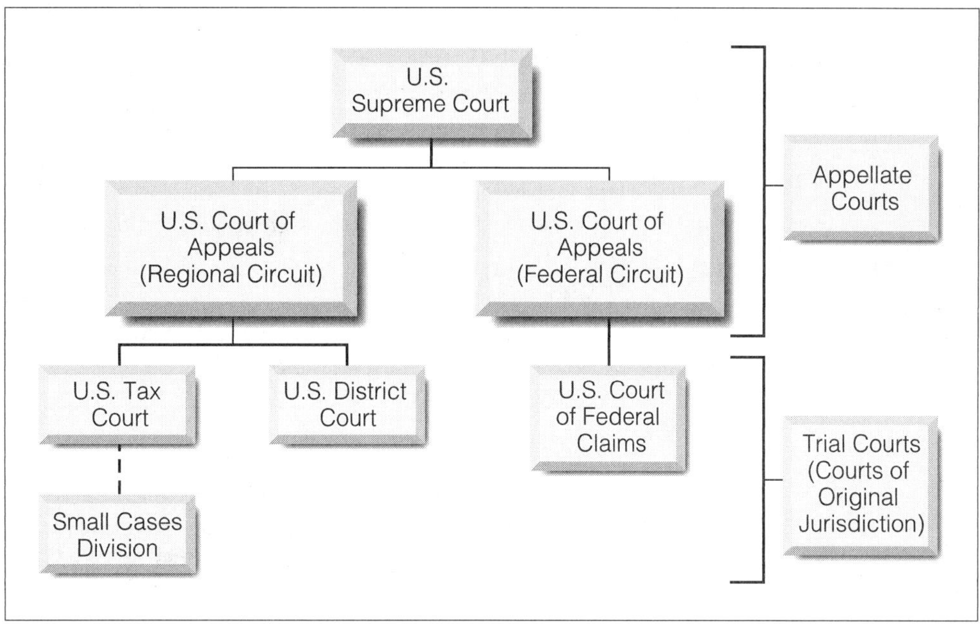

less, and some of its decisions can now be found on the U.S. Tax Court Internet Web site.

American law, following English law, is frequently "made" by judicial decisions. Under the doctrine of *stare decisis,* each case (except in the Small Cases Division) has precedential value for future cases with the same controlling set of facts. Most Federal and state appellate court decisions and some decisions of trial courts are published. More than 4 million judicial opinions have been published in the United States, and over 130,000 cases are published each year. Published court decisions are organized by jurisdiction (Federal or state) and level of court (trial or appellate).

A decision of a particular court is called its *holding*. Sometimes a decision includes dicta or incidental opinions beyond the current facts. Such passing remarks, illustrations, or analogies are not essential to the current holding. Although the holding has precedential value under *stare decisis,* dicta are not binding on a future court.

Trial Courts. The differences among the various trial courts (courts of original jurisdiction) can be summarized as follows:

- *Number of courts*. There is only one U.S. Court of Federal Claims and only one Tax Court, but there are many Federal District Courts. The taxpayer does not select the District Court that will hear the dispute but must sue in the one that has jurisdiction where the taxpayer resides.
- *Number of judges*. District Courts have various numbers of judges, but only one judge hears a case. The Court of Federal Claims has 16 judges, and the Tax Court has 19 regular judges. The entire Tax Court, however, reviews a case (the case is sent to court conference) only when important or novel tax issues are involved. Most cases are heard and decided by 1 of the 19 judges.
- *Location*. The Court of Federal Claims meets most often in Washington, D.C., while a District Court meets at a prescribed seat for the particular district. Each state has at least one District Court, and many of the populous states

Changing the Face of Russia

Peter the Great, the ruler of Russia from 1682 to 1725, imposed a tax on beards (except for clergy) because he felt that beards were "unnecessary, uncivilized, and ridiculous." If an individual did not pay the tax, a tax official would scrape off the beard. Without warning Peter himself would take a straight razor to the faces of bearded men appearing before him. When Peter attended a ceremony or banquet, anyone arriving with a beard would depart without it.

SOURCE: Adapted from Erik Jensen, "Taxation of Beards," *Tax Notes* (January 5, 2004): 153–157.

have more than one. Choosing the District Court usually minimizes the inconvenience and expense of traveling for the taxpayer and his or her counsel. The Tax Court is officially based in Washington, D.C., but the various judges travel to different parts of the country and hear cases at predetermined locations and dates. This procedure eases the distance problem for the taxpayer, but it can mean a delay before the case comes to trial and is decided.

- *Jurisdiction of the Court of Federal Claims.* The Court of Federal Claims has jurisdiction over any claim against the United States that is based upon the Constitution, any Act of Congress, or any Regulation of an executive department. Thus, the Court of Federal Claims hears nontax litigation as well as tax cases. This forum appears to be more favorable for issues having an equitable or pro-business orientation (as opposed to purely technical issues) and those requiring extensive discovery.
- *Jurisdiction of the Tax Court and District Courts.* The Tax Court hears only tax cases and is the most popular forum. The District Courts hear a wide variety of nontax cases, including drug crimes and other Federal violations, as well as tax cases. Some Tax Court justices have been appointed from IRS or Treasury Department positions. For this reason, some people suggest that the Tax Court has more expertise in tax matters.
- *Jury trial.* The only court in which a taxpayer can obtain a jury trial is a District Court. Juries can decide only questions of fact and not questions of law. Therefore, taxpayers who choose the District Court route often do not request a jury trial. If a jury trial is not elected, the judge will decide all issues. Note that a District Court decision is controlling only in the district in which the court has jurisdiction.
- *Payment of deficiency.* Before the Court of Federal Claims or a District Court can have jurisdiction, the taxpayer must pay the tax deficiency assessed by the IRS and then sue for a refund. If the taxpayer wins (assuming no successful appeal by the Government), the tax paid plus appropriate interest will be recovered. Jurisdiction in the Tax Court, however, is usually obtained without first paying the assessed tax deficiency. In the event the taxpayer loses in the Tax Court (and no appeal is taken or an appeal is unsuccessful), the deficiency must be paid with accrued interest. With the elimination of the deduction for personal (consumer) interest, the Tax Court route of delaying payment of the deficiency can become expensive. For example, to earn 7 percent after tax in 2005, a taxpayer with a 35 percent marginal tax rate will have to earn 10.77 percent. By paying the tax, a taxpayer limits underpayment interest and penalties on the underpayment.

CONCEPT SUMMARY 2–1

Federal Judicial System: Trial Courts

Issue	U.S. Tax Court	U.S. District Court	U.S. Court of Federal Claims
Number of judges per court	19*	Varies	16
Payment of deficiency before trial	No	Yes	Yes
Jury trial available	No	Yes	No
Types of disputes	Tax cases only	Mostly criminal and civil issues	Claims against the United States
Jurisdiction	Nationwide	Location of taxpayer	Nationwide
IRS acquiescence policy	Yes	Yes	Yes
Appeal route	U.S. Court of Appeals	U.S. Court of Appeals	U.S. Court of Appeals for the Federal Circuit

*There are also 14 special trial judges and 9 senior judges.

- *Termination of running of interest.* A taxpayer who selects the Tax Court may deposit a cash bond to stop the running of interest. The taxpayer must deposit both the amount of the tax and any accrued interest. If the taxpayer wins and the deposited amount is returned, the Government does not pay interest on the deposit.
- *Appeals.* Appeals from a District Court or a Tax Court decision are to the U.S. Court of Appeals for the circuit in which the taxpayer resides. Appeals from the Court of Federal Claims go to the Court of Appeals for the Federal Circuit. Few Tax Court cases are appealed, and when appeals are made, most are filed by the taxpayer rather than the IRS.
- *Bankruptcy.* When a taxpayer files a bankruptcy petition, the IRS, like other creditors, is prevented from taking action against the taxpayer. Sometimes a bankruptcy court may settle a tax claim.

For a summary of the Federal trial courts, see Concept Summary 2–1.

Appellate Courts. The losing party can appeal a trial court decision to a **Circuit Court of Appeals.** The 11 geographic circuits, the circuit for the District of Columbia, and the Federal Circuit[18] are shown in Figure 2–4. The appropriate circuit for an appeal depends on where the litigation originated. For example, an appeal from New York goes to the Second Circuit.

If the Government loses at the trial court level (District Court, Tax Court, or Court of Federal Claims), it need not (and frequently does not) appeal. The fact that an appeal is not made, however, does not indicate that the IRS agrees with the result and will not litigate similar issues in the future. The IRS may decide not to appeal for a number of reasons. First, if the current litigation load is heavy, the IRS may decide that available personnel should be assigned to other, more important cases. Second, the IRS may determine that this case is not a good one to

[18]The Court of Appeals for the Federal Circuit was created, effective October 1, 1982, by P.L. 97–164 (4/2/82) to hear decisions appealed from the Claims Court (now the Court of Federal Claims).

■ **FIGURE 2–4**
The Federal Circuit Courts of Appeals

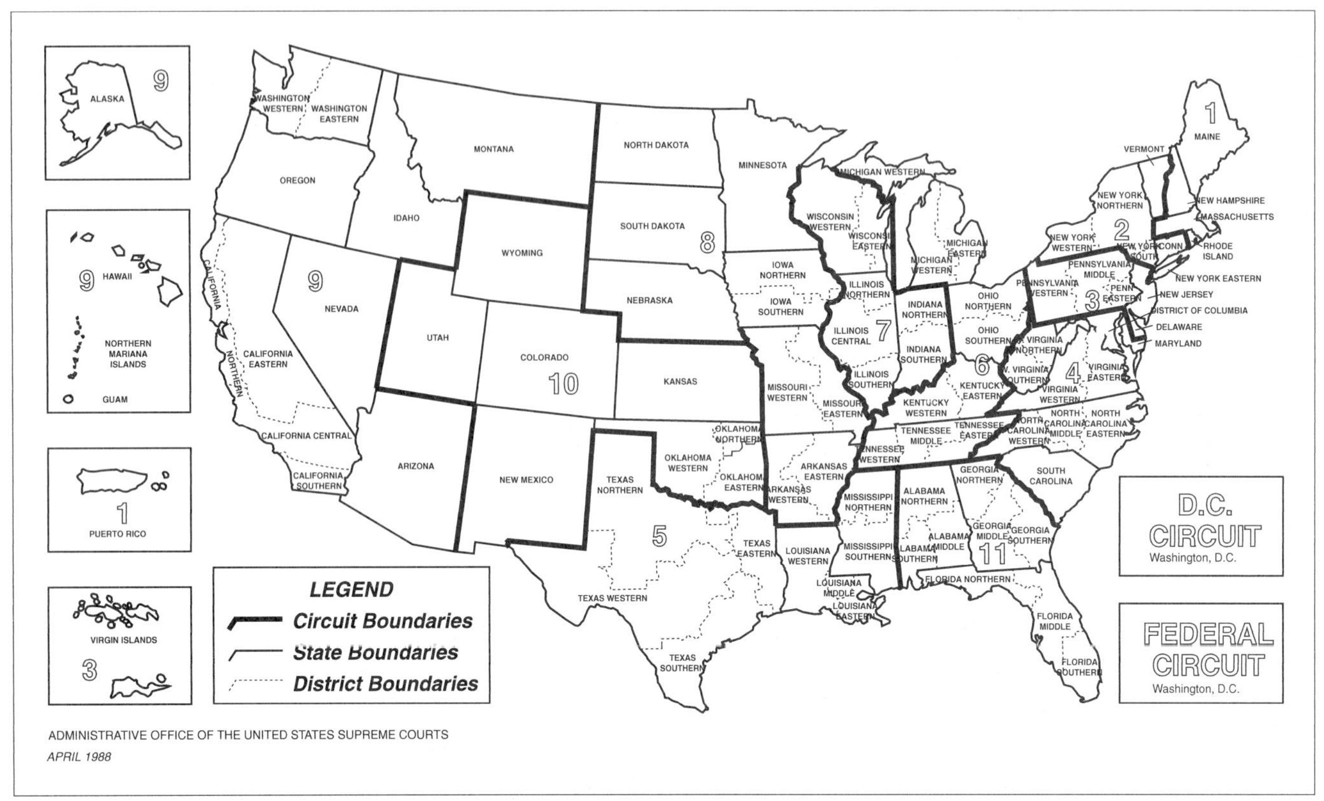

appeal. For example, the taxpayer may be in a sympathetic position, or the facts may be particularly strong in his or her favor. In that event, the IRS may wait to test the legal issues involved with a taxpayer who has a much weaker case. Third, if the appeal is from a District Court or the Tax Court, the Court of Appeals of jurisdiction could have some bearing on whether the IRS decides to pursue an appeal. Based on past experience and precedent, the IRS may conclude that the chance for success on a particular issue might be more promising in another Court of Appeals. If so, the IRS will wait for a similar case to arise in a different jurisdiction.

The Federal Circuit at the appellate level provides a taxpayer with an alternative forum to the Court of Appeals of his or her home circuit for the appeal. Appeals from both the Tax Court and the District Court go to a taxpayer's home circuit. When a particular circuit has issued an adverse decision, the taxpayer may prefer the Court of Federal Claims route since any appeal will be to the Federal Circuit.

District Courts, the Tax Court, and the Court of Federal Claims must abide by the **precedents** set by the Court of Appeals of jurisdiction. A particular Court of Appeals need not follow the decisions of another Court of Appeals. All courts, however, must follow the decisions of the **U.S. Supreme Court.**

This pattern of appellate precedents raises an issue for the Tax Court. Because the Tax Court is a national court, it decides cases from all parts of the country. For many years, the Tax Court followed a policy of deciding cases based on what it thought the result should be, even when its decision might be appealed to a Court of Appeals that had previously decided a similar case differently. A number of years ago this policy was changed in the *Golsen*[19] decision. Now the Tax Court will decide a case as it feels the law should be applied *only* if the Court of Appeals of appropriate jurisdiction has not yet passed on the issue or has previously decided a similar case in accord with the Tax Court's decision. If the Court of Appeals of appropriate jurisdiction has previously held otherwise, the Tax Court will conform even though it disagrees with the holding. This policy is known as the *Golsen* rule.

EXAMPLE 3

Emily lives in Texas and sues in the Tax Court on Issue A. The Fifth Circuit Court of Appeals is the appellate court of appropriate jurisdiction. It has already decided, in a case involving similar facts but a different taxpayer, that Issue A should be resolved against the Government. Although the Tax Court feels that the Fifth Circuit Court of Appeals is wrong, under its *Golsen* policy it will render judgment for Emily. Shortly thereafter, Rashad, a resident of New York, in a comparable case, sues in the Tax Court on Issue A. Assume that the Second Circuit Court of Appeals, the appellate court of appropriate jurisdiction, has never expressed itself on Issue A. Presuming the Tax Court has not reconsidered its position on Issue A, it will decide against Rashad. Thus, it is entirely possible for two taxpayers suing in the same court to end up with opposite results merely because they live in different parts of the country. ■

Appeal to the U.S. Supreme Court is by **Writ of Certiorari.** If the Court agrees to hear the case, it will grant the Writ (*Cert. granted*). Most often, it will deny jurisdiction (*Cert. denied*). For whatever reason or reasons, the Supreme Court rarely hears tax cases. The Court usually grants certiorari to resolve a conflict among the Courts of Appeals (e.g., two or more appellate courts have assumed opposing positions on a particular issue) or where the tax issue is extremely important. The granting of a *Writ of Certiorari* indicates that at least four members of the Supreme Court believe that the issue is of sufficient importance to be heard by the full Court.

The *role* of appellate courts is limited to a review of the record of trial compiled by the trial courts. Thus, the appellate process usually involves a determination of whether the trial court applied the proper law in arriving at its decision. Usually, an appellate court will not dispute a lower court's fact-finding determination.

An appeal can have any of a number of possible outcomes. The appellate court may approve (affirm) or disapprove (reverse) the lower court's finding, or it may send the case back for further consideration (remand). When many issues are involved, a mixed result is not unusual. Thus, the lower court may be affirmed (*aff'd.*) on Issue A and reversed (*rev'd.*) on Issue B, while Issue C is remanded (*rem'd.*) for additional fact finding.

When more than one judge is involved in the decision-making process, disagreements are not uncommon. In addition to the majority view, one or more judges may concur (agree with the result reached but not with some or all of the reasoning) or dissent (disagree with the result). In any one case, the majority view controls. But concurring and dissenting views can have influence on other courts or, at some subsequent date when the composition of the court has changed, even on the same court.

Knowledge of several terms is important in understanding court decisions. The term *plaintiff* refers to the party requesting action in a court, and the *defendant* is the party against whom the suit is brought. Sometimes a court uses the terms *petitioner* and *respondent.* In general, "petitioner" is a synonym for "plaintiff," and "respondent" is a synonym for "defendant." At the trial court level, a taxpayer is normally the plaintiff (or petitioner), and the Government is the defendant (or respondent). If the taxpayer wins and the Government appeals as the new petitioner (or appellee), the taxpayer becomes the new respondent.

[19]*Jack E. Golsen,* 54 T.C. 742 (1970).

LO.2

Locate and work with the appropriate tax law sources.

Judicial Citations—General. Having briefly described the judicial process, it is appropriate to consider the more practical problem of the relationship of case law to tax research. As previously noted, court decisions are an important source of tax law. The ability to locate a case and to cite it is therefore a must in working with the tax law. Judicial citations usually follow a standard pattern: case name, volume number, reporter series, page or paragraph number, court (where necessary), and the year of decision. Specific citation formats for each court are presented in the following sections.

Judicial Citations—The U.S. Tax Court. A good starting point is the U.S. Tax Court (formerly the Board of Tax Appeals). The Tax Court issues two types of decisions: Regular and Memorandum. The Chief Judge decides whether the opinion is issued as a Regular or Memorandum decision. The distinction between the two involves both substance and form. In terms of substance, *Memorandum* decisions deal with situations necessitating only the application of already established principles of law. *Regular* decisions involve novel issues not previously resolved by the court. In actual practice, however, this distinction is not always preserved. Not infrequently, Memorandum decisions will be encountered that appear to warrant Regular status, and vice versa. At any rate, do not conclude that Memorandum decisions possess no value as precedents. Both represent the position of the Tax Court and, as such, can be relied on.

The Regular and Memorandum decisions issued by the Tax Court also differ in form. Memorandum decisions are not officially published, while regular decisions are published by the U.S. Government in a series called *Tax Court of the United States Reports* (T.C.). Each volume of these *Reports* covers a six-month period (January 1 through June 30 and July 1 through December 31) and is given a succeeding volume number. But, as is true of the *Cumulative Bulletins,* there is usually a time lag between the date a decision is rendered and the date it appears in bound form. A temporary citation may be necessary to help the researcher locate a recent Regular decision. Consider, for example, the temporary and permanent citations for *Estate of Leona Engelman,* a decision filed on July 24, 2003:

Temporary Citation	*Estate of Leona Engelman,* 121 T.C. _____, No. 4 (2003). *Explanation:* Page number left blank because not yet known.
Permanent Citation	*Estate of Leona Engelman,* 121 T.C. 54 (2003). *Explanation:* Page number now available.

Both citations tell us that the case will ultimately appear in Volume 121 of the *Tax Court of the United States Reports.* Until this volume is bound and made available to the general public, however, the page number must be left blank. Instead, the temporary citation identifies the case as being the 4th Regular decision issued by the Tax Court since Volume 120 ended. With this information, the decision can easily be located in either of the special Tax Court services published by Commerce Clearing House and Research Institute of America (formerly by Prentice-Hall). Once Volume 121 is released, the permanent citation can be substituted and the number of the case dropped. Starting in 1999, both Regular decisions and Memorandum decisions are published on the U.S. Tax Court Web site (**http://www.ustaxcourt.gov**).

Before 1943, the Tax Court was called the Board of Tax Appeals, and its decisions were published as the *United States Board of Tax Appeals Reports* (B.T.A.). These 47 volumes cover the period from 1924 to 1942. For example, the citation *Karl Pauli,* 11 B.T.A. 784 (1928) refers to the 11th volume of the *Board of Tax Appeals Reports,* page 784, issued in 1928.

If the IRS loses in a decision, it may indicate whether it agrees or disagrees with the results reached by the court by publishing an **acquiescence** ("A" or "*Acq.*")

or **nonacquiescence** ("NA" or "*Nonacq.*"), respectively. Until 1991, acquiescences and nonacquiescences were published only for certain Regular decisions of the Tax Court, but the IRS has expanded its acquiescence program to include other civil tax cases where guidance is helpful. The acquiescence or nonacquiescence is published in the *Internal Revenue Bulletin* and the *Cumulative Bulletin* as an *Action on Decision*. The IRS can retroactively revoke an acquiescence.

Although Memorandum decisions were not published by the U.S. Government until recently (they are now published on the U.S. Tax Court Web site), they were—and continue to be—published by Commerce Clearing House (CCH) and Research Institute of America (RIA [formerly by Prentice-Hall]). Consider, for example, the three different ways that *Jack D. Carr* can be cited:

> *Jack D. Carr*, T.C.Memo. 1985–19
> The 19th Memorandum decision issued by the Tax Court in 1985.
>
> *Jack D. Carr*, 49 TCM 507
> Page 507 of Vol. 49 of the CCH *Tax Court Memorandum Decisions*.
>
> *Jack D. Carr*, RIA T.C.Mem.Dec. ¶85,019
> Paragraph 85,019 of the RIA *T.C. Memorandum Decisions*.

Note that the third citation contains the same information as the first. Thus, ¶85,019 indicates the following information about the case: year 1985, 19th T.C. Memo. decision.[20] Although the RIA citation does not include a specific volume number, the paragraph citation (85,019) indicates that the decision can be found in the 1985 volume of the RIA Memorandum Decision service.

Starting in 2001, U.S. Tax Court Summary Opinions are published on the U.S. Tax Court Web site, with the warning that they may not be treated as precedent for any other case. For example, *Edward Charles Jones*, filed on May 27, 2003, is cited as follows:

> *Edward Charles Jones*, T.C. Summary Opinion, 2003–61.

Judicial Citations—The U.S. District Court, Court of Federal Claims, and Courts of Appeals. District Court, Court of Federal Claims, Court of Appeals, and Supreme Court decisions dealing with Federal tax matters are reported in both the CCH *U.S. Tax Cases* (USTC) and the RIA *American Federal Tax Reports* (AFTR) series.

Federal District Court decisions, dealing with *both* tax and nontax issues, are also published by West Publishing Company in its *Federal Supplement Series* (F.Supp.). Volume 999, published in 1998, is the last volume of the *Federal Supplement Series*. It is followed by the *Federal Supplement Second Series* (F.Supp.2d). A District Court case can be cited in three different forms as the following examples illustrate:

> *Simons-Eastern Co. v. U.S.*, 73–1 USTC ¶9279 (D.Ct. Ga., 1972).
> *Explanation:* Reported in the first volume of the *U.S. Tax Cases* (USTC) published by Commerce Clearing House for calendar year 1973 (73–1) and located at paragraph 9279 (¶9279).
>
> *Simons-Eastern Co. v. U.S.*, 31 AFTR2d 73–640 (D.Ct. Ga., 1972).
> *Explanation:* Reported in the 31st volume of the second series of the *American Federal Tax Reports* (AFTR2d) published by RIA and beginning on page 640. The "73" preceding the page number indicates the year the case was published but is a designation used only in recent decisions.
>
> *Simons-Eastern Co. v. U.S.*, 354 F.Supp. 1003 (D.Ct. Ga., 1972).
> *Explanation:* Reported in the 354th volume of the *Federal Supplement Series* (F.Supp.) published by West Publishing Company and beginning on page 1003.

[20]In this text, this Memorandum decision of the U.S. Tax Court would be cited as *Jack D. Carr*, 49 TCM 507, T.C.Memo. 1985–19.

In all of the preceding citations, note that the name of the case is the same (Simons-Eastern Co. being the taxpayer), as are the references to the Federal District Court of Georgia (D.Ct. Ga.) and the year the decision was rendered (1972).[21]

Decisions of the Court of Federal Claims[22] and the Courts of Appeals are published in the USTCs, AFTRs, and a West Publishing Company reporter called the *Federal Second Series* (F.2d). Volume 999, published in 1993, is the last volume of the *Federal Second Series*. It is followed by the *Federal Third Series* (F.3d). Beginning with October 1982, decisions of the Court of Federal Claims are published in another West Publishing Company reporter entitled the *Claims Court Reporter* (abbreviated as Cls. Ct.). Beginning with Volume 27 on October 30, 1992, the name of the reporter changed to the *Federal Claims Reporter* (abbreviated as Fed.Cl.). The following examples illustrate the different forms:

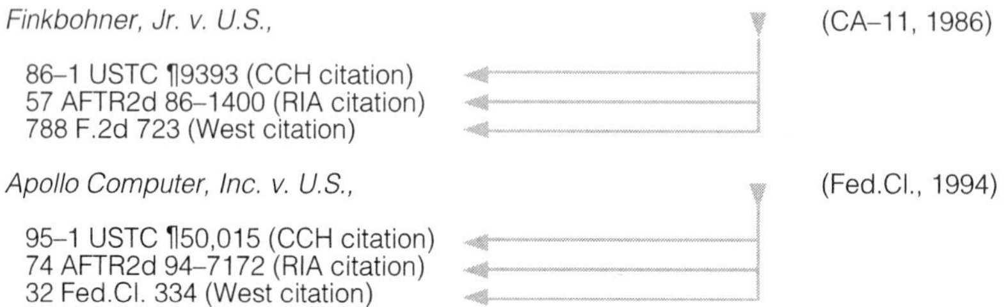

Note that *Finkbohner, Jr.* is a decision rendered by the Eleventh Circuit Court of Appeals in 1986 (CA–11, 1986), while *Apollo Computer, Inc.* was issued by the Court of Federal Claims in 1994 (Fed.Cl., 1994).

Judicial Citations—The U.S. Supreme Court. Like all other Federal tax decisions (except those rendered by the U.S. Tax Court), Supreme Court decisions are published by Commerce Clearing House in the USTCs and by RIA (formerly by Prentice-Hall) in the AFTRs. The U.S. Government Printing Office also publishes these decisions in the *United States Supreme Court Reports* (U.S.), as do West Publishing Company in its *Supreme Court Reporter* (S.Ct.) and the Lawyer's Co-operative Publishing Company in its *United States Reports, Lawyer's Edition* (L.Ed.). The following illustrates the different ways the same decision can be cited:

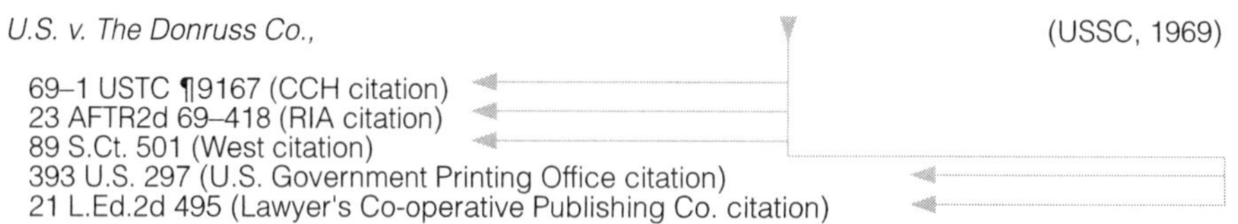

U.S. v. The Donruss Co.,
(USSC, 1969)
69–1 USTC ¶9167 (CCH citation)
23 AFTR2d 69–418 (RIA citation)
89 S.Ct. 501 (West citation)
393 U.S. 297 (U.S. Government Printing Office citation)
21 L.Ed.2d 495 (Lawyer's Co-operative Publishing Co. citation)

The parenthetical reference (USSC, 1969) identifies the decision as having been rendered by the U.S. Supreme Court in 1969. In this text, the citations of Supreme Court decisions are limited to the CCH (USTC), RIA (AFTR), and West (S.Ct.) versions. See Concept Summary 2–2.

[21] In this text, the case would be cited in the following form: *Simons-Eastern Co. v. U.S.*, 73–1 USTC ¶9279, 31 AFTR2d 73–640, 354 F.Supp. 1003 (D.Ct. Ga., 1972). Prentice-Hall Information Services is now owned by Research Institute of America. Although recent volumes contain the RIA imprint, many of the older volumes continue to have the P-H imprint.

[22] Before October 29, 1992, the Court of Federal Claims was called the Claims Court. Before October 1, 1982, the Court of Federal Claims was called the Court of Claims.

CONCEPT SUMMARY 2–2

Judicial Sources

Court	Location	Authority
U.S. Supreme Court	S.Ct. Series (West) U.S. Series (U.S. Gov't.) L.Ed. (Lawyer's Co-op.) AFTR (RIA) USTC (CCH)	Highest authority
U.S. Courts of Appeal	Federal 3d (West) AFTR (RIA) USTC (CCH)	Next highest appellate court
Tax Court (Regular decisions)	U.S. Gov't. Printing Office RIA/CCH separate services	Highest trial court*
Tax Court (Memorandum decisions)	RIA T.C.Memo. (RIA) TCM (CCH)	Less authority than Regular T.C. decision
U.S. Court of Federal Claims**	Federal Claims Reporter (West) AFTR (RIA) USTC (CCH)	Similar authority as Tax Court
U.S. District Courts	F.Supp.2d Series (West) AFTR (RIA) USTC (CCH)	Lowest trial court
Small Cases Division of Tax Court	U.S. Tax Court Web site***	No precedent value

*Theoretically, the Tax Court, Court of Federal Claims, and District Courts are on the same level of authority. But some people believe that since the Tax Court hears and decides tax cases from all parts of the country (i.e., it is a national court), its decisions may be more authoritative than a Court of Federal Claims or District Court decision.
**Before October 29, 1992, the U.S. Claims Court.
***Starting in 2001.

LO.3

Understand the tax research process.

Working with the Tax Law—Tax Research

Tax research is the method used to determine the best available solution to a situation that possesses tax consequences. In other words, it is the process of finding a competent and professional conclusion to a tax problem. The problem may originate from completed or proposed transactions. In the case of a completed transaction, the objective of the research is to determine the tax result of what has already taken place. For example, is the expenditure incurred by the taxpayer deductible or not deductible for tax purposes? When dealing with proposed transactions, the tax research process is concerned with the determination of possible alternative tax consequences. To the extent that tax research leads to a choice of alternatives or otherwise influences the future actions of the taxpayer, it becomes the key to effective tax planning.

Tax research involves the following procedures:

- Identifying and refining the problem.
- Locating the appropriate tax law sources.
- Assessing the validity of the tax law sources.
- Arriving at the solution or at alternative solutions while giving due consideration to nontax factors.
- Effectively communicating the solution to the taxpayer or the taxpayer's representative.
- Following up on the solution (where appropriate) in light of new developments.

■ **FIGURE 2–5**
Tax Research Process

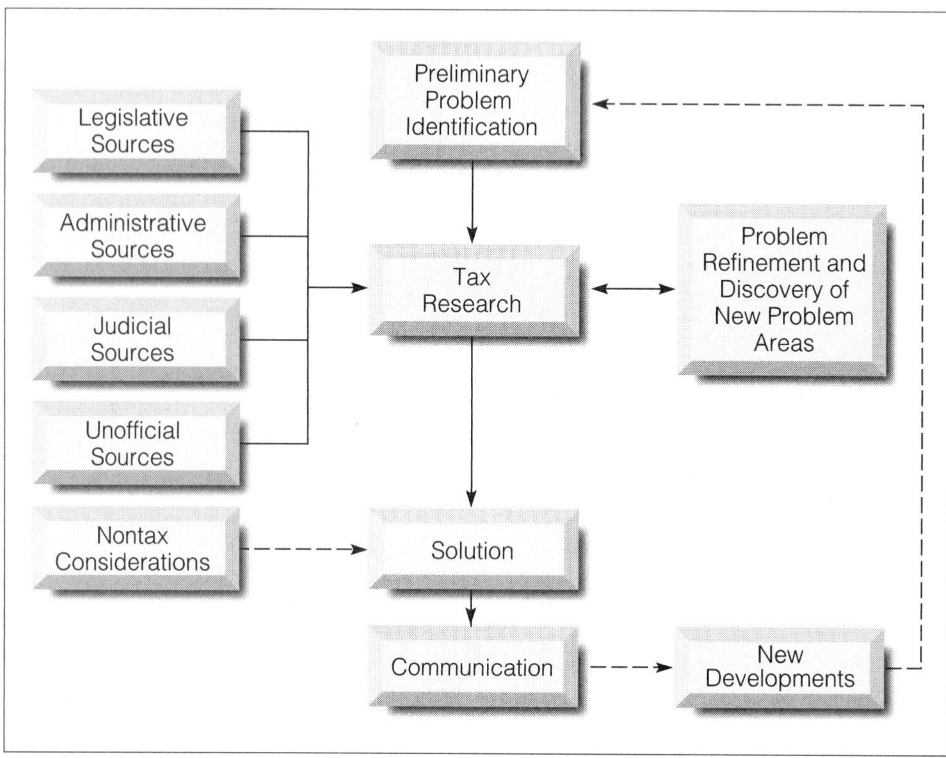

This process is depicted schematically in Figure 2–5. The broken lines indicate steps of particular interest when tax research is directed toward proposed, rather than completed, transactions.

IDENTIFYING THE PROBLEM

Problem identification starts with a compilation of the relevant facts involved. In this regard, *all* of the facts that may have a bearing on the problem must be gathered, as any omission could modify the solution reached. To illustrate, consider what appears to be a very simple problem.

EXAMPLE 4

Early in December, Fred and Megan review their financial and tax situation with their son, Sam, and daughter-in-law, Dana, who live with them. Fred and Megan are in the 28% tax bracket in 2005. Both Sam and Dana are age 21. Sam, a student at a nearby university, owns some publicly traded stock that he inherited from his grandmother. A current sale of the stock would result in approximately $8,000 of gross income. At this point, Fred and Megan provide about 55% of Sam and Dana's support. Although neither is now employed, Sam has earned $960 and Dana has earned $900. The problem: Should the stock be sold, and would the sale prohibit Fred and Megan from claiming Sam and Dana as dependents? ■

REFINING THE PROBLEM

Initial reaction is that Fred and Megan in Example 4 could not claim Sam and Dana as dependents if the stock is sold, since Sam would then have gross income of more than the exemption amount under § 151(d). However, Sam is a full-time student, and § 152(c)(3)(A)(ii) allows a son or daughter who is a full-time student and is under age 24 (a qualifying child) to generate income that is greater than the exemption amount without penalizing the parents with the loss of the dependency exemption. Thus, Sam could sell the stock without penalizing his parents under the gross income test. However, the $8,000 income from the sale of the stock might lead to the failure of the greater-than-50 percent support test, depending on how much Sam spends for his (or Dana's) support.

Assume, however, that further fact gathering reveals the following additional information:

- Sam does not really need to spend the proceeds from the sale of the stock.
- Sam receives a sizable portion of his own support from a scholarship.

With these new facts, additional research leads to § 152(f)(5) and Regulation § 1.152–1(c), which indicate that a scholarship received by a student is not included for purposes of determining whether the parents furnished more than one-half of the child's support (the child is not self-supporting). Further, if Sam does not spend the proceeds from the sale of stock, the unexpended amount is not counted for purposes of the support test. Thus, it appears that the parents would not be denied the dependency exemptions for Sam and Dana.

LOCATING THE APPROPRIATE TAX LAW SOURCES

Once the problem is clearly defined, what is the next step? Although the next step is a matter of individual judgment, most tax research begins with the index volume of the tax service, a keyword search on an online tax service, or a CD-ROM search (see the subsequent discussion of Electronic Tax Research). If the problem is not complex, the researcher may bypass the tax service or online service and turn directly to the Internal Revenue Code and the Treasury Regulations. For the beginner, the latter procedure saves time and will solve many of the more basic problems. If the researcher does not have a personal copy of the Code or Regulations, resorting to the appropriate volume(s) of a tax service or a CD-ROM is necessary.[23] The major tax services available are as follows:

Standard Federal Tax Reporter, Commerce Clearing House.

United States Tax Reporter, Research Institute of America (entitled *Federal Taxes* prior to July 1992).

Federal Tax Coordinator 2d, Research Institute of America.

Tax Management Portfolios, Bureau of National Affairs.

Federal Income, Gift and Estate Taxation, Warren, Gorham and Lamont.

CCH's Federal Tax Service, Commerce Clearing House.

Mertens Law of Federal Income Taxation, Callaghan and Co.

Working with Tax Services. In this text, it is not feasible to explain the use of any particular tax service—this ability can be obtained only by practice.[24] However, several important observations about the use of tax services cannot be overemphasized. First, always check for current developments. The main text of any paper-based service is revised too infrequently to permit reliance on that portion as the *latest* word on any subject. Where current developments can be found depends on

[23]Several of the major tax services publish paperback editions of the Code and Treasury Regulations that can be purchased at modest prices. These editions are usually revised twice each year. For an annotated and abridged version of the Code and Regulations that is published annually, see James E. Smith, *West's Internal Revenue Code of 1986 and Treasury Regulations: Annotated and Selected* (Thomson/South-Western, 2006).

[24]The representatives of the various tax services are prepared to provide the users of their services with printed booklets and individual instruction on the use of the materials.

which service is being used. Commerce Clearing House's *Standard Federal Tax Reporter* contains a special volume devoted to current matters. Both RIA's *U.S. Tax Reporter* and *Federal Tax Coordinator 2d* integrate the new developments into the body of the service throughout the year. Second, when dealing with a tax service synopsis of a Treasury Department pronouncement or a judicial decision, remember there is no substitute for the original source.

To illustrate, do not base a conclusion solely on a tax service's commentary on a potentially relevant court case. If the case is vital to the research, look it up! The facts of the case may be distinguishable from those involved in the problem being researched. This is not to say that the case synopsis contained in the tax service is wrong—it might just be misleading or incomplete.

Tax Periodicals. The various tax periodicals are another source of information. The easiest way to locate a journal article on a particular tax problem is through Commerce Clearing House's *Federal Tax Articles*. This multivolume service includes a subject index, a Code Section number index, and an author's index. In addition, the RIA tax service has a topical "Index to Tax Articles" section that is organized using the RIA paragraph index system. Also, beginning in 1992, *The Accounting & Tax Index* is available in three quarterly issues plus a cumulative year-end volume covering all four quarters. The original *Accountant's Index* started in 1921 and ended in 1991.

The following are some of the more useful tax periodicals:

The Journal of Taxation
Warren, Gorham and Lamont
395 Hudson Street
4th Floor
New York, NY 10014

Tax Law Review
Warren, Gorham and Lamont
395 Hudson Street
4th Floor
New York, NY 10014

Trusts and Estates
249 W. 17th Street
New York, NY 10011

Oil, Gas, and Energy Quarterly
Matthew Bender & Co.
1275 Broadway
Albany, NY 12204

The Practical Accountant
One State Street Plaza
New York, NY 10004

Estate Planning
Warren, Gorham and Lamont
395 Hudson Street
4th Floor
New York, NY 10014

Taxation for Accountants
Warren, Gorham and Lamont
395 Hudson Street
4th Floor
New York, NY 10014

The International Tax Journal
Aspen Publishing, Inc.
1185 Avenue of the Americas
New York, NY 10036

TAXES—The Tax Magazine
Commerce Clearing House, Inc.
2700 Lake Cook Road
Riverwood, IL 60015

National Tax Journal
725 15th Street, NW
Suite 600
Washington, D.C. 20005

The Tax Adviser
Harborside Financial Center
201 Plaza III
Jersey City, NJ 07311-3881

Journal of Taxation for Individuals
Warren, Gorham and Lamont
395 Hudson Street
4th Floor
New York, NY 10014

The Tax Lawyer
American Bar Association
750 N. Lake Shore Drive
Chicago, IL 60611

Journal of American Taxation Association
American Accounting Association
5717 Bessie Drive
Sarasota, FL 34233

The Tax Executive
1200 G Street, NW
Suite 300
Washington, D.C. 20005

Tax Notes
6830 Fairfax Drive
Arlington, VA 22213

Journal of Corporate Taxation
Warren, Gorham and Lamont
395 Hudson Street
4th Floor
New York, NY 10014

ASSESSING THE VALIDITY OF THE TAX LAW SOURCES

Once a source has been located, the next step is to assess it in light of the problem at hand. Proper assessment involves careful interpretation of the tax law and consideration of its relevance and validity.

Interpreting the Internal Revenue Code. The language of the Code often is difficult to comprehend fully. Contrary to many people's suspicions, the Code is not written deliberately to confuse. Unfortunately, though, it often has that effect. The Code is intended to apply to more than 200 million taxpayers, many of whom are willing to exploit any linguistic imprecision to their benefit—to find a "loophole" in popular parlance. Many of the Code's provisions are limitations or restrictions involving two or more variables. Expressing such concepts algebraically would be more direct; using words to accomplish this task instead is often quite cumbersome. Among the worst such attempts was former § 341(e) relating to so-called collapsible corporations. One sentence had more than 450 words (twice as many as in the Gettysburg Address). Within this same subsection was another sentence of 300 words.

Assessing the Validity of a Treasury Regulation. Treasury Regulations are the official interpretation of the Code and are entitled to great deference. Occasionally, however, a court will invalidate a Regulation or a portion thereof on the grounds that the Regulation is contrary to the intent of Congress. Usually, the courts do not question the validity of Regulations because of the belief that "the first administrative interpretation of a provision as it appears in a new act often expresses the general understanding of the times or the actual understanding of those who played an important part when the statute was drafted."[25]

Keep in mind the following observations when assessing the validity of a Regulation:

- IRS agents must give the Code and the Regulations issued thereunder equal weight when dealing with taxpayers and their representatives.
- Proposed Regulations provide a preview of future final Regulations, but they are not binding on the IRS or taxpayers.
- In a challenge, the burden of proof is on the taxpayer to show that a Regulation varies from the language of the statute and has no support in the Committee Reports.
- If the taxpayer loses the challenge, the negligence penalty may be imposed.[26] This accuracy-related penalty applies to any failure to make a reasonable attempt to comply with the tax law and to any disregard of rules and Regulations.[27]
- Final Regulations can be classified as procedural, interpretive, or legislative. **Procedural Regulations** neither establish tax laws nor attempt to explain tax laws. Procedural Regulations are *housekeeping-type* instructions, indicating

[25] *Augustus v. Comm.*, 41–1 USTC ¶9255, 26 AFTR 612, 118 F.2d 38 (CA–6, 1941).

[26] §§ 6662(a) and (b)(1).

[27] § 6662(c).

information that taxpayers should provide the IRS, as well as information about the internal management and conduct of the IRS itself.

- Some **interpretive Regulations** rephrase and elaborate what Congress stated in the Committee Reports that were issued when the tax legislation was enacted. Such Regulations are *hard and solid* and almost impossible to overturn because they clearly reflect the intent of Congress.
- In some Code Sections, Congress has given the *Secretary or his delegate* the authority to prescribe Regulations to carry out the details of administration or to otherwise complete the operating rules. Under such circumstances, Congress effectively is delegating its legislative powers to the Treasury Department. Regulations issued pursuant to this type of authority possess the force and effect of law and are often called **legislative Regulations** (e.g., consolidated return Regulations).

Assessing the Validity of Other Administrative Sources of the Tax Law. Revenue Rulings issued by the IRS carry less weight than Treasury Department Regulations. Revenue Rulings are important, however, in that they reflect the position of the IRS on tax matters. In any dispute with the IRS on the interpretation of tax law, taxpayers should expect agents to follow the results reached in any applicable Revenue Rulings.

Actions on Decisions further tell the taxpayer the IRS's reaction to certain court decisions. Recall that the IRS follows a practice of either acquiescing (agreeing) or nonacquiescing (not agreeing) with selected judicial decisions. A nonacquiescence does not mean that a particular court decision is of no value, but it does indicate that the IRS may continue to litigate the issue involved.

Assessing the Validity of Judicial Sources of the Tax Law. The judicial process as it relates to the formulation of tax law has been described. How much reliance can be placed on a particular decision depends upon the following variables:

- The higher the level of the court that issued a decision, the greater the weight accorded to that decision. A decision rendered by a trial court (e.g., a Federal District Court) carries less weight than one issued by an appellate court (e.g., the Fifth Circuit Court of Appeals). Unless Congress changes the Code, decisions by the U.S. Supreme Court represent the last word on any tax issue.
- More reliance is placed on decisions of courts that have jurisdiction in the area where the taxpayer's legal residence is located. If, for example, a taxpayer lives in Texas, a decision of the Fifth Circuit Court of Appeals means more than one rendered by the Second Circuit Court of Appeals. This is the case because any appeal from a District Court or the Tax Court would be to the Fifth Circuit Court of Appeals and not to the Second Circuit Court of Appeals.[28]
- A Tax Court Regular decision carries more weight than a Memorandum decision because the Tax Court does not consider Memorandum decisions to be binding precedents.[29] Furthermore, a Tax Court *reviewed* decision carries even more weight. All of the Tax Court judges participate in a reviewed decision.
- A Circuit Court decision where certiorari has been requested and denied by the Supreme Court carries more weight than a Circuit Court decision that was not appealed. A Circuit Court decision heard *en banc* (all the judges participate) carries more weight than a normal Circuit Court case.

[28]Before October 1, 1982, an appeal from the then-named U.S. Court of Claims (the other trial court) was directly to the U.S. Supreme Court.

[29]*Severino R. Nico, Jr.*, 67 T.C. 647 (1977).

- A decision that is supported by cases from other courts carries more weight than a decision that is not supported by other cases.
- The weight of a decision also can be affected by its status on appeal. For example, was the decision affirmed or overruled?

In connection with the last two variables, a citator is helpful to tax research.[30] A **citator** provides the history of a case and lists subsequently published opinions that refer to the case being assessed. Reviewing these references enables the tax researcher to determine whether the decision in question has been reversed, affirmed, followed by other courts, or distinguished in some way. If one intends to rely on a judicial decision to any significant degree, "running" the case through a citator is imperative.

Assessing the Validity of Other Sources. *Primary sources* of tax law include the Constitution, legislative history materials, statutes, treaties, Treasury Regulations, IRS pronouncements, and judicial decisions. In general, the IRS regards only primary sources as substantial authority. However, reference to *secondary materials* such as legal periodicals, treatises, legal opinions, General Counsel Memoranda, and written determinations may be useful. In general, secondary sources are not authority.

Although the statement that the IRS regards only primary sources as substantial authority is generally true, there is one exception. In Notice 90–20,[31] the IRS expanded the list of substantial authority *for purposes of* the accuracy-related penalty in § 6662 to include a number of secondary materials (e.g., letter rulings, General Counsel Memoranda, the Bluebook). "Authority" does not include conclusions reached in treatises, legal periodicals, and opinions rendered by tax professionals.

A letter ruling or determination letter is substantial authority *only* for the taxpayer to whom it is issued, except as noted above with respect to the accuracy-related penalty.

Upon the completion of major tax legislation, the staff of the Joint Committee on Taxation (in consultation with the staffs of the House Ways and Means and Senate Finance Committees) often will prepare a General Explanation of the Act, commonly known as the Bluebook because of the color of its cover. The IRS will not accept this detailed explanation as having legal effect. The Bluebook does, however, provide valuable guidance to tax advisers and taxpayers until Regulations are issued. Some letter rulings and General Counsel Memoranda of the IRS cite Bluebook explanations.

ARRIVING AT THE SOLUTION OR AT ALTERNATIVE SOLUTIONS

Example 4 raised the question of whether a taxpayer would be denied dependency exemptions for a son and a daughter-in-law if the son sold some stock near the end of the year. A refinement of the problem supplies the following additional information:

- Sam was a full-time student during four calendar months of the year.
- Sam and Dana anticipate filing a joint return.

Additional research leads to § 152(f)(2) and Regulation § 1.151–3(b), which indicate that to qualify as a student, Sam must be a full-time student during each of *five*

[30]The major citators are published by Commerce Clearing House, RIA, and Shepard's Citations, Inc. These citators are available in published and electronic formats. WESTLAW has a citator that is available only in electronic format.

[31]1990–1 C.B. 328; see also Reg. § 1.6661–3(b)(2).

calendar months of the year at an educational institution. Thus, proceeds from Sam's sale of the stock would cause his parents to lose at least one dependency exemption because Sam's gross income would exceed the exemption amount. The parents still might be able to claim Dana as an exemption if the support test is met.

Section 152(b)(2) indicates that a supporting taxpayer is not permitted a dependency exemption for a married dependent if the married individual files a joint return. Initial reaction is that a joint return by Sam and Dana would be disastrous to the parents. However, more research uncovers two Revenue Rulings that provide an exception if neither the dependent nor the dependent's spouse is required to file a return but does so solely to claim a refund of tax withheld. The IRS asserts that each spouse must have gross income of less than the exemption amount.[32] Therefore, if Sam sells the stock and he and Dana file a joint return, the parents would lose the dependency exemption for both Sam and Dana.

If the stock is not sold until January, both exemptions may still be available to the parents. However, under § 151(d)(2), a personal exemption is not available to a taxpayer who can be claimed as a dependent by another taxpayer (whether actually claimed or not). Thus, if the parents can claim Sam and Dana as dependents, Sam and Dana would lose their personal exemptions on their tax return.

LO.4

Communicate the results of the tax research process in a client letter and a tax file memorandum.

COMMUNICATING TAX RESEARCH

Once the problem has been researched adequately, a memo, letter, or oral presentation setting forth the result may need to be prepared. The form such a communication takes could depend on a number of considerations. For example, does the employer or instructor recommend a particular procedure or format for tax research memos? Is the memo to be given directly to the client, or will it first go to the preparer's employer? Who is the audience for the oral presentation? How long should you talk?[33] Whatever form it takes, a good tax research communication should contain the following elements.

- A clear statement of the issue.
- In more complex situations, a short review of the fact pattern that raises the issue.
- A review of the pertinent tax law sources (e.g., Code, Regulations, Revenue Rulings, judicial authority).
- Any assumptions made in arriving at the solution.
- The solution recommended and the logic or reasoning supporting it.
- The references consulted in the research process.

Illustrations of the memos for the tax file and the client letter associated with Example 4 appear in Figures 2–6, 2–7, and 2–8.

LO.5

Apply tax research techniques and planning procedures.

Working with the Tax Law—Tax Planning

Tax research and tax planning are inseparable. The *primary* purpose of effective tax planning is to maximize the taxpayer's after-tax wealth. This statement does not mean that the course of action selected must produce the lowest possible tax under the circumstances. The minimization of tax liability must be considered in the context of the legitimate business goals of the taxpayer.

[32]Rev.Rul. 54–567, 1954–2 C.B. 108; Rev.Rul. 65–34, 1965–1 C.B. 86.

[33]For more on crafting oral presentations, see W. A. Raabe and G. E. Whittenburg, "Talking Tax: How to Make a Tax Presentation," *The Tax Adviser,* March 1997, pp. 179–182.

■ FIGURE 2-6
Tax File Memorandum

August 16, 2005

TAX FILE MEMORANDUM

FROM: John J. Jones

SUBJECT: Fred and Megan Taxpayer
Engagement: Issues

Today I talked to Fred Taxpayer with respect to his August 12, 2005 letter requesting tax assistance. He wishes to know if his son, Sam, can sell stock worth $19,000 (basis = $11,000) without the parents losing the dependency exemptions for Sam and Sam's wife, Dana.

Fred Taxpayer is married to Megan, and Sam is a full-time student at a local university. Sam inherited the stock from his grandmother about five years ago. If he sells the stock, he will save the proceeds from the sale. Sam does not need to spend the proceeds if he sells the stock because he receives a $5,500 scholarship that he uses for his own support (i.e., to pay for tuition, books, and fees). Fred and Megan are in the 28% tax bracket and furnish approximately 55% of Sam and Dana's support.

ISSUE: If the stock is sold, would the sale prohibit Fred and Megan from claiming Sam and Dana as dependents? I told Fred that we would have an answer for him within two weeks.

■ FIGURE 2-7
Tax File Memorandum

August 26, 2005

TAX FILE MEMORANDUM

FROM: John J. Jones

SUBJECT: Fred and Megan Taxpayer
Engagement: Conclusions

See the Tax File Memorandum dated August 16, 2005, which contains the facts and identifies the tax issues.

Section 152(a) provides that in order for a taxpayer to take a dependency exemption, the potential dependent must satisfy either the qualifying child requirements or the qualifying relative requirements (see Chapter 3). Fred and Megan provide about 55% of the support of their son, Sam, and their daughter-in-law, Dana. If Sam should sell the stock in 2005, he would not need to spend the proceeds for support purposes (i.e., he would save the proceeds). Thus, the stock sale would not affect his qualifying as self-supporting under § 152(c)(1)(D). In calculating the percentage of support provided by Fred and Megan, a $5,500 scholarship received by Sam is not counted in determining the amount of support Sam provides for himself [see §152(f)(5) and Reg. § 1.152–1(c)].

Section 152(d)(1)(B) provides that in order to qualify for a dependency exemption as a qualifying relative, the potential dependent's gross income must be less than the exemption amount (i.e., $3,200 in 2005). Without the stock sale, the gross income of both Sam ($960) and Dana ($900) will be below the exemption amount in 2005. The $5,500 Sam receives as a scholarship is excluded from his gross income under § 117(a) because he uses the entire amount to pay for his tuition, books, and fees at a local university.

The key issue then is whether the stock, which will generate $8,000 of gain for Sam, will cause the gross income test to be violated. The gain will increase Sam's gross income to $8,960 ($8,000 + $960). However, § 152(c)(3)(A)(ii) permits a child's gross income to exceed the exemption amount if the child is a student under the age of 24 (satisfies the qualifying child test). Under §152(f)(5) and Reg. § 1.151–3(b), to qualify as a student, the person must be a full-time student during each of five calendar months. A telephone call to Megan provided the information that Sam was a student for only four months in 2005. Thus, since Sam is not eligible for the student exception, the sale of the stock by Sam in 2005 would result in Fred and Megan losing the dependency exemption for Sam.

The stock sale would also result in the loss of the dependency exemption for Dana if Sam and Dana file a joint return for 2005 [see § 152(b)(2)].

From a tax planning perspective, Sam should not sell the stock until 2006. This delay will enable Fred and Megan to claim dependency exemptions on their 2005 return for Sam and Dana. Note, however, that neither Sam nor Dana will be permitted to take a personal exemption deduction on their 2005 tax return since they are claimed as dependents on someone else's return [see § 151(d)(2)]. However, this disallowance of the personal exemption deduction will not produce any negative tax consequences since their tax liability will be zero if the stock is not sold in 2005.

■ **FIGURE 2-8**
Client Letter

Willis, Hoffman, Maloney, and Raabe, CPAs
5191 Natorp Boulevard
Mason, Ohio 45040

August 30, 2005

Mr. and Ms. Fred Taxpayer
111 Boulevard
Williamsburg, Virginia 23185

Dear Mr. and Ms. Taxpayer:

This letter is in response to your request for us to review your family's financial and tax situation. Our conclusions are based upon the facts as outlined in your August 12th letter. Any change in the facts may affect our conclusions.

You provide over 50% of the support for your son, Sam, and his wife, Dana. The scholarship Sam receives is not included in determining support. If the stock is not sold, you will qualify for a dependency exemption for both Sam and Dana.

However, if the stock is sold, a gain of approximately $8,000 will result. This amount will result in the gross income requirement being violated (i.e., potential dependent's gross income must not equal or exceed $3,200) for Sam. Therefore, you will not qualify to receive a dependency exemption for Sam. In addition, if Sam sells the stock and he and Dana file a joint return, you also will not qualify for a dependency exemption for Dana.

From a tax planning perspective, Sam should not sell the stock in 2005. Delaying the stock sale will enable you to claim dependency exemptions for both Sam and Dana. If the stock is sold, Sam and Dana should not file a joint return. If they file separate returns, you will still be able to qualify for a dependency exemption for Dana.

Should you need more information or need to clarify our conclusions, do not hesitate to contact me.

Sincerely yours,

John J. Jones, CPA
Partner

A *secondary* objective of effective tax planning is to reduce or defer the tax in the current tax year. Specifically, this objective aims to accomplish one or more results. Some possibilities are eradicating the tax entirely, eliminating the tax in the current year, deferring the receipt of income, proliferating taxpayers (i.e., forming partnerships and corporations or making lifetime gifts to family members), eluding double taxation, avoiding ordinary income, or creating, increasing, or accelerating deductions. However, this second objective should be approached with considerable reservation and moderation. For example, a tax election in one year may accomplish a current reduction in taxes, but it could saddle future years with a disadvantageous tax position.

NONTAX CONSIDERATIONS

There is a danger that tax motivations may take on a significance that does not conform to the true values involved. In other words, tax considerations can operate to impair the exercise of sound business judgment. Thus, the tax planning process can lead to ends that are socially and economically objectionable. Unfortunately, a tendency exists for planning to go toward the opposing extremes of either not enough or too much emphasis on tax considerations. The happy medium is a balance that recognizes the significance of taxes, but not beyond the point at which planning detracts from the exercise of good business judgment.

The remark is often made that a good rule is to refrain from pursuing any course of action that would not be followed were it not for certain tax considerations.

This statement is not entirely correct, but it does illustrate the desirability of preventing business logic from being *sacrificed at the altar of tax planning.*

TAX EVASION AND TAX AVOIDANCE

A fine line exists between legal tax planning and illegal tax planning—tax avoidance versus tax evasion. **Tax avoidance** is merely tax minimization through legal techniques. In this sense, tax avoidance is the proper objective of all tax planning. Though eliminating or reducing taxes is also a goal of tax evasion, the term implies the use of subterfuge and fraud as a means to this end. Perhaps because common goals are involved, popular usage has blurred the distinction between the two concepts. Consequently, the association of tax avoidance with tax evasion has kept some taxpayers from properly taking advantage of planning possibilities. The now classic words of Judge Learned Hand in *Commissioner v. Newman* reflect the true values a taxpayer should have:

> Over and over again courts have said that there is nothing sinister in so arranging one's affairs as to keep taxes as low as possible. Everybody does so, rich or poor; and all do right, for nobody owes any public duty to pay more than the law demands: taxes are enforced extractions, not voluntary contributions. To demand more in the name of morals is mere cant.[34]

As Denis Healy, a former British Chancellor, once said, "The difference between tax avoidance and tax evasion is the thickness of a prison wall."

ETHICAL CONSIDERATIONS

Tax Avoidance: Good or Bad?

In a speech class, a student who is a government major argues that tax advisers are immoral because they help people cheat the government. Each time a tax adviser shows a taxpayer a tax planning idea that reduces the client's tax liability, all other taxpayers have to pay more taxes. Therefore, society would be better off if all tax advisers would work at protecting our environment or improving living conditions in the inner cities.

An accounting student argues that the primary purpose of tax planning is to reduce a taxpayer's overall liability. This advisory process can result in avoiding, reducing, or postponing the tax burden until the future. There is nothing illegal or immoral about tax avoidance. Taxpayers have every legal right to be concerned about tax avoidance and to arrange their affairs so as to pay no more taxes than the law demands. There is no difference between reducing tax expense through the help of a tax adviser and reducing the cost of operating a business with the advice of a cost accountant.

Comment on each student's position.

FOLLOW-UP PROCEDURES

Because tax planning usually involves a proposed (as opposed to a completed) transaction, it is predicated upon the continuing validity of the advice based upon the tax research. A change in the tax law (either legislative, administrative, or judicial) could alter the original conclusion. Additional research may be necessary to test the solution in light of current developments (refer to the broken lines at the right in Figure 2–5).

[34] *Comm. v. Newman,* 47–1 USTC ¶9175, 35 AFTR 857, 159 F.2d 848 (CA–2, 1947).

The Disappearing Taxpayers

Should income taxes be increased, or not decreased, especially on the bottom 50 percent of taxpayers? Should the tax base be expanded? Recent tax data lend credence to such unpopular opinions.

For 2001, the top 50 percent of all taxpayers paid about 96 percent of all personal income taxes, leaving the bottom half to pay the remaining 4 percent. A large group of nontaxpayers paid nothing. The top 1 percent of taxpayers paid 33 percent of total individual income taxes, down from 37 percent in the prior year. The top 25 percent of taxpayers (making $55,000 or more) paid 83 percent of the total tax burden. A substantial majority of households with less than $50,000 of adjusted gross income paid an average tax rate of less than 10 percent.

The Internet is also helping taxpayers to disappear. In a recent *New Yorker* magazine cartoon, two dogs are sitting in front of a computer screen; one tells the other, "on the Internet, nobody knows that you are a dog." Similarly, in order to collect a tax, the government must know who is liable to pay the tax. Taxpayers are becoming increasingly more difficult to identify as anonymous electronic money and uncrackable encryption techniques are developed.

If too many taxpayers disappear via the Internet, will the government's deficit grow larger?

TAX PLANNING—A PRACTICAL APPLICATION

Returning to the facts of Example 4, what could be done to protect the dependency exemptions for the parents? If Sam and Dana refrain from filing a joint return, both could be claimed by the parents. This result assumes that the stock is not sold.

An obvious tax planning tool is the installment method. Could the securities be sold using the installment method under § 453 so that most of the gain is deferred into the next year? Under the installment method, certain gains may be postponed and recognized as the cash proceeds are received. The problem is that the installment method is not available for stock traded on an established securities market.[35]

A little more research, however, indicates that Sam may be able to sell the stock and postpone the recognition of gain until the following year by selling short an equal number of substantially identical shares and covering the short sale in the subsequent year with the shares originally held. Selling short means that Sam sells borrowed stock (substantially identical) and repays the lender with the stock held on the date of the short sale. This *short against the box* technique would allow Sam to protect his $8,000 profit and defer the closing of the sale until the following year.[36] However, additional research indicates that 1997 tax legislation provides that the short against the box technique will no longer produce the desired postponement of recognized gain. That is, at the time of the short sale, Sam will have a recognized gain of $8,000 from a constructive sale. Note the critical role of obtaining the correct facts in attempting to resolve the proper strategy for the taxpayers.

[35] See Chapter 16 for a discussion of installment sales.

[36] §§ 1233(a) and 1233(b)(2). See Chapter 14 for a discussion of short sales.

Throughout this text, most chapters include observations on Tax Planning Considerations. Such observations are not all-inclusive but are intended to illustrate some of the ways in which the material covered can be effectively utilized to minimize taxes.

LO.6

Have an awareness of electronic tax research.

ELECTRONIC TAX RESEARCH

Computer-based tax research tools hold a prominent position in tax practice. Electronic tax resources allow the tax library to reflect the tax law itself, including its dynamic and daily changes. Nevertheless, using electronic means to locate tax law sources cannot substitute for developing and maintaining a thorough knowledge of the tax law or for logical and analytical review in addressing open tax research issues.

Accessing tax documents through electronic means offers several important advantages over a strictly paper-based approach.

- Materials generally are available to the practitioner faster through an electronic system, as delays related to typesetting, proofreading, production, and distribution of the new materials are streamlined.
- Some tax documents, such as so-called slip opinions of trial-level court cases and interviews with policymakers, are available only through electronic means.
- Commercial subscriptions to electronic tax services are likely to provide, at little or no cost, additional tax law sources to which the researcher would not have access through stand-alone purchases of traditional material. For example, the full texts of letter rulings are quite costly to acquire in a paper-based format, but electronic publishers may bundle the rulings with other materials for a reasonable cost.

Strict cost comparisons of paper and electronic tax research materials are difficult to construct, especially when the practitioner uses hardware, including workstations and communications equipment, that is already in place and employed elsewhere in the practice. Over time, though, the convenience, cost, and reliability of electronic research tools clearly make them the dominant means of finding and analyzing the law in tax practice.

Using Electronic Services. Tax researchers often use electronic means to find sources of the tax law. Usually, the law is found using one of the following strategies:

- *Search* various databases using keywords that are likely to be found in the underlying documents, as written by Congress, the judiciary, or administrative sources.
- *Link* to tax documents for which all or part of the proper citation is known.
- *Browse* the tax databases, examining various tables of contents and indexes in a traditional manner or using cross-references in the documents to jump from one tax law source to another.

Virtually all of the major commercial tax publishers and most of the primary sources of the law itself, such as the Supreme Court and some of the Courts of Appeals, provide tax materials in electronic formats. Competitive pressures have rewarded tax practitioners who have developed computer literacy skills, and the user-friendliness of the best of the tax search software is of great benefit to both the daily and the occasional user. Exhibit 2–2 summarizes the most popular of the electronic tax services on the market today.

CD-ROM Services. The CD has been a major source of electronic tax data for about a decade. Data compression techniques continue to allow more tax materials

■ EXHIBIT 2–2
Electronic Tax Services

Electronic Tax Service	Description
CCH	Includes the CCH tax service, primary sources including treatises, and other subscription materials. Ten to 20 discs and online.
RIA	Includes the RIA topical *Coordinator* and the annotated tax service formerly provided by Prentice-Hall. The citator has elaborate document-linking features, and major tax treatises are provided. One to 10 discs and online.
WESTLAW	Code, Regulations, *Cumulative Bulletins*, cases, citators, and editorial material. About 12 discs and online.
Kleinrock's	A single disc with tax statutory, administrative, and judicial law. Another single disc provides tax forms and instructions for Federal and state jurisdictions.

to fit on a single disc every year. CCH, RIA, WESTLAW, and others offer vast tax libraries to the practitioner, often in conjunction with a subscription to traditional paper-based resources or accompanied by newsletters, training seminars, and ongoing technical support.

At its best, a CD-based tax library provides the archival data that make up a permanent, core library of tax documents. For about $300 a year, the tax CD is updated quarterly, providing more comprehensive tax resources than the researcher is ever likely to need. The CD is comparable in scope to a paper-based library of a decade ago costing perhaps $20,000 to establish and $5,000 per year in perpetuity to maintain. If the library is contained on a small number of discs, it also can offer portability through use on notebook computers.

Online Systems. An online research system allows a practitioner to obtain virtually instantaneous use of tax law sources by accessing the computer of the service provider. Online services generally employ price-per-search cost structures, which can be as much as $200 per hour, significantly higher than the cost of CD materials. Thus, unless a practitioner can pass along related costs to clients or others, online searching generally is limited to the most important issues and to the researchers with the most experience and training in search techniques.

Perhaps the best combination of electronic tax resources is to conduct day-to-day work on a CD system, so that the budget for the related work is known in advance, and augment the CD search with online access where it is judged to be critical. Exhibit 2–3 provides details on the contents of the most commonly used commercial online tax services.

The Internet. The Internet provides a wealth of tax information in several popular forms, sometimes at no direct cost to the researcher. Using so-called browser software that often is distributed with new computer systems and their communication devices, the tax professional can access information provided around the world that can aid the research process.

- *Home pages (sites) on the World Wide Web (WWW)* are provided by accounting and consulting firms, publishers, tax academics and libraries, and governmental bodies as a means of making information widely available or of soliciting subscriptions or consulting engagements. The best sites offer links to other sites and direct contact to the site providers. One of the best sites

■ **EXHIBIT 2–3**
Online Tax Services

Online Service	Description
LEXIS/NEXIS	Federal and state statutory, administrative, and judicial material. Extensive libraries of newspapers, magazines, patent records, and medical and economic databases, both U.S. and foreign-based.
RIA	Includes the RIA tax services, major tax treatises, Federal and state statutes, administrative documents, and court opinions. Extensive citator access, editorial material, and practitioner aids.
CCH	Includes the CCH tax service, primary sources including treatises, and other subscription materials. Tax and economic news sources, extensive editorial material, and practitioner support tools.
WESTLAW	Federal and state statutes, administrative documents, and court opinions. Extensive citator access, editorial material, and gateways to third-party publications. Extensive government document databases.

available to the tax practitioner is the Internal Revenue Service's *Digital Daily*, illustrated in Exhibit 2–4. This site offers downloadable forms and instructions, "plain English" versions of Regulations, and news update items. Exhibit 2–5 lists some of the Web sites that may be most useful to tax researchers and their Internet addresses as of press date.

- *Newsgroups* provide a means by which information related to the tax law can be exchanged among taxpayers, tax professionals, and others who subscribe to the group's services. Newsgroup members can read the exchanges among other members and offer replies and suggestions to inquiries as desired. Discussions address the interpretation and application of existing law, analysis of proposals and new pronouncements, and reviews of tax software.

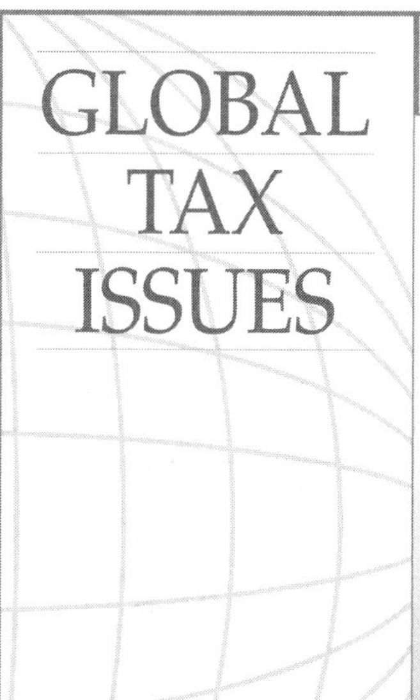

Data Warehousing Reduces Global Taxes

Many global companies are using data warehouses to collect data, which can be analyzed and used to minimize their global tax liabilities. "You take all of your tax data and dump it into a data warehouse," says Michael S. Burke of KPMG's e-tax solutions. "Next, it's applying a tool to define user requirements—compliance, real time analysis, etc." The company can then manipulate all of this information to reduce compliance costs, facilitate planning for value added taxes, and minimize time spent dealing with international tax problems.

For example, a company wishes to implement an e-procurement technique that would save it $100 million in expenses and increase taxable income. That could mean that about $40 million in additional taxes would go to the U.S. Treasury and state treasuries. By looking at the tax laws worldwide, the company may decide to base the operation in Bermuda, Ireland, or the Philippines where the tax will be only $20 million. That's a savings of $20 million, which is not taxable.

SOURCE: Adapted from Jay Weinstein, "Internet Tax Solutions Proliferate," *Global Finance*, January 2001, pp. 74–75.

■ EXHIBIT 2–4
The IRS's *Digital Daily*

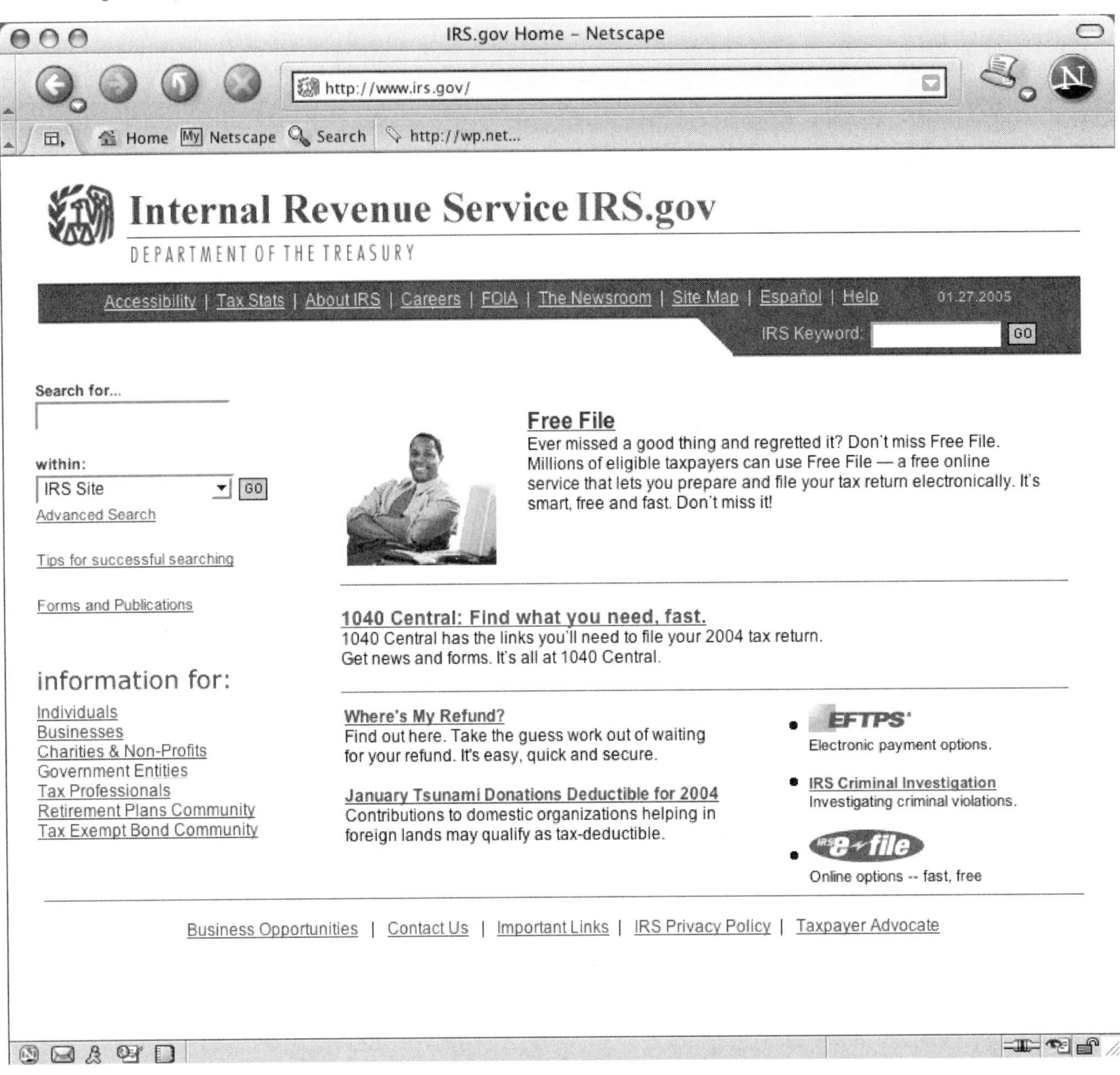

- *E-mail capabilities* are available to most tax professionals through an employer's equipment or by a subscription providing Internet access at a low and usually fixed cost for the period. E-mail allows for virtually instantaneous sending and receiving of messages, letters, tax returns and supporting data, spreadsheets, and other documents necessary to solve tax problems.

In many situations, solutions to research problems benefit from, or require, the use of various electronic tax research tools. A competent tax professional must become familiar and proficient with these tools and be able to use them to meet the expectations of clients and the necessities of work in the modern world.[37]

[37]For a more detailed discussion of the use of electronic tax research in the modern tax practice, see Raabe, Whittenburg, and Sanders, *West's Federal Tax Research*, 7th ed. (Thomson/South-Western, 2006).

EXHIBIT 2-5
Tax-Related Web Sites

Web Site	WWW Address at Press Date (Usually preceded by http://www.)	Description
Internal Revenue Service	**irs.gov/**	News releases, downloadable forms and instructions, tables, and e-mail
Court opinions	The site at **law.emory.edu/caselaw** allows the researcher to link to the site of the jurisdiction (other than the Tax Court) that is the subject of the query.	
Tax Analysts	**taxanalysts.com**	Policy-oriented readings on the tax law and proposals to change it, moderated bulletins on various tax subjects
Tax Sites Directory	**taxsites.com**	References and links to tax sites on the Internet, including state and Federal tax sites, academic and professional pages, tax forms, and software
Tax laws online	Regulations are at **cfr.law.cornell.edu/cfr/** and the Code is at **uscode.house.gov/search/criteria.php** and **www4.law.cornell.edu/uscode/**	
Commercial tax publishers	For instance, **tax.com** and **cch.com**	Information about products and services available for subscription and newsletter excerpts
Large accounting firms and professional organizations	For instance, the AICPA's page is at **aicpa.org**, Ernst and Young is at **ey.com/home.asp**, and KPMG is at **kpmg.com**	Tax planning newsletters, descriptions of services offered and career opportunities, and exchange of data with clients and subscribers
Thomson South-Western	**wft.swlearning.com**	Informational updates, newsletters, support materials for students and adopters, and continuing education
U.S. Tax Court decisions	**ustaxcourt.gov**	Recent U.S. Tax Court decisions

NOTE: Caution: addresses change frequently.

KEY TERMS

Acquiescence, 2–18
Circuit Court of Appeals, 2–15
Citator, 2–27
Court of original jurisdiction, 2–12
Determination letters, 2–11
Federal District Court, 2–12
Finalized Regulations, 2–9
Interpretive Regulations, 2–26
Legislative Regulations, 2–26
Letter rulings, 2–10
Nonacquiescence, 2–19
Precedents, 2–16
Procedural Regulations, 2–25
Proposed Regulations, 2–9
Revenue Procedures, 2–10
Revenue Rulings, 2–9
Small Cases Division, 2–12
Tax avoidance, 2–31
Tax research, 2–21
Technical Advice Memoranda (TAMs), 2–12
Temporary Regulations, 2–9
U.S. Court of Federal Claims, 2–12
U.S. Supreme Court, 2–16
U.S. Tax Court, 2–12
Writ of Certiorari, 2–17

PROBLEM MATERIALS

Discussion Questions

1. What is a primary source of tax information?
2. With proper research methods and tools, a researcher generally will arrive at one alternative for structuring a business transaction. Assess the validity of this statement.
3. Tax legislation normally originates in the Senate Finance Committee. Assess the validity of this statement.
4. What is the function of the Joint Conference Committee of the House Ways and Means Committee and the Senate Finance Committee?
5. In which title and subtitle of the U.S. Code is the income tax portion of the Internal Revenue Code of 1986 found?

Communications

6. Paul Bishop operates a small international firm named Teal, Inc. A new treaty between the United States and France conflicts with a Section of the Internal Revenue Code. Paul asks you for advice. If he follows the treaty position, does he need to disclose this on his tax return? If he is required to disclose, are there any penalties for failure to disclose? Prepare a letter in which you respond to Paul. Teal's address is 100 International Drive, Tampa, FL 33620.
7. Interpret this Regulation citation: Reg. § 301.7701–2(c)(2).
8. Explain how Regulations are arranged. How would the following Regulations be cited?
   a. Finalized Regulations under § 442.
   b. Proposed Regulations under § 318.
   c. Temporary Regulations under § 446.
   d. Legislative Regulations under § 1501.
9. Distinguish between legislative, interpretive, and procedural Regulations.
10. In the citation Rev.Rul. 99–5, 1999–1 C.B. 434, to what do the 5 and the 434 refer?
11. Rank the following items from the highest authority to the lowest in the Federal tax law system:
    a. Interpretive Regulation.
    b. Legislative Regulation.
    c. Letter ruling.
    d. Revenue Ruling.
    e. Internal Revenue Code.
    f. Proposed Regulation.
12. Interpret each of the following citations:
    a. Prop.Reg. § 1.280A–3(c)(4).
    b. Rev.Rul. 67–74, 1967–1 C.B. 194.
    c. Ltr.Rul. 200409001.

Issue ID

13. Caleb receives a 90-day letter after his discussion with an appeals officer. He is not satisfied with the $92,000 settlement offer. Identify the relevant tax research issues facing Caleb.
14. Which of the following would be considered advantages of the Small Cases Division of the Tax Court?
    a. Appeal to the U.S. Tax Court is possible.
    b. A hearing of a deficiency of $65,000 is considered on a timely basis.
    c. Taxpayer can handle the litigation without using a lawyer or certified public accountant.
    d. Taxpayer can use Small Cases Division decisions for precedential value.
    e. The actual hearing is conducted informally.
    f. Travel time will probably be reduced.

15. List an advantage and a disadvantage of using the U.S. District Court as the trial court for Federal tax litigation.

Communications

16. Dwain Toombs is considering litigating a tax deficiency of approximately $311,000 in the court system. He asks you to provide him with a short description of his alternatives indicating the advantages and disadvantages of each. Prepare your response to Dwain in the form of a letter. His address is 200 Mesa Drive, Tucson, AZ 85714.

17. List an advantage and a disadvantage of using the U.S. Court of Federal Claims as the trial court for Federal tax litigation.

18. A taxpayer lives in Michigan. In a controversy with the IRS, the taxpayer loses at the trial court level. Describe the appeal procedure for each of the following trial courts:
    a. Small Cases Division of the U.S. Tax Court.
    b. U.S. Tax Court.
    c. U.S. District Court.
    d. U.S. Court of Federal Claims.

19. Suppose the U.S. Government loses a tax case in the U.S. District Court but does not appeal the result. What does the failure to appeal signify?

20. For the U.S. Tax Court, U.S. District Court, and U.S. Court of Federal Claims, indicate the following:
    a. Number of regular judges per court.
    b. Availability of a jury trial.
    c. Whether the deficiency must be paid before the trial.

21. In which of the following states could a taxpayer appeal the decision of a U.S. District Court to the Fifth Circuit Court of Appeals?
    a. Alaska.
    b. Arkansas.
    c. Florida.
    d. New York.
    e. Texas.

22. What is the Supreme Court's policy on hearing tax cases?

23. In assessing the validity of a prior court decision, discuss the significance of the following on the taxpayer's issue:
    a. The decision was rendered by the U.S. District Court of Wyoming. Taxpayer lives in Wyoming.
    b. The decision was rendered by the U.S. Court of Federal Claims. Taxpayer lives in Wyoming.
    c. The decision was rendered by the Second Circuit Court of Appeals. Taxpayer lives in California.
    d. The decision was rendered by the U.S. Supreme Court.
    e. The decision was rendered by the U.S. Tax Court. The IRS has acquiesced in the result.
    f. Same as (e), except that the IRS has nonacquiesced in the result.

24. What is the difference between a Regular decision, a Memorandum decision, and a Summary Opinion of the U.S. Tax Court?

25. Interpret each of the following citations:
    a. 54 T.C. 1514 (1970).
    b. 408 F.2d 117 (CA–2, 1969).
    c. 69–1 USTC ¶9319 (CA–2, 1969).
    d. 23 AFTR2d 69–1090 (CA–2, 1969).
    e. 293 F.Supp. 1129 (D.Ct. Miss., 1967).
    f. 67–1 USTC ¶9253 (D.Ct. Miss., 1967).
    g. 19 AFTR2d 647 (D.Ct. Miss., 1967).
    h. 56 S.Ct. 289 (USSC, 1935).
    i. 36–1 USTC ¶9020 (USSC, 1935).
    j. 16 AFTR 1274 (USSC, 1935).
    k. 422 F.2d 1336 (Ct.Cls., 1970).

26. Explain the following abbreviations:
    a. CA–2.
    b. Fed.Cl.
    c. *aff'd.*
    d. *rev'd.*
    e. *rem'd.*
    f. *Cert. denied.*
    g. *acq.*
    h. B.T.A.
    i. USTC.
    j. AFTR.
    k. F.3d.
    l. F.Supp.
    m. USSC.
    n. S.Ct.
    o. D.Ct.

27. Give the Commerce Clearing House citation for each of the following courts:
    a. Small Cases Division of the Tax Court.
    b. Federal District Court.
    c. U.S. Supreme Court.
    d. U.S. Court of Federal Claims.
    e. Tax Court Memorandum decision.

28. Where can you locate a published decision of the U.S. Court of Federal Claims?

29. Which of the following items can probably be found in the *Cumulative Bulletin*?
    a. Action on Decision.
    b. Small Cases Division of the U.S. Tax Court decision.
    c. Letter ruling.
    d. Revenue Procedure.
    e. Finalized Regulation.
    f. U.S. Court of Federal Claims decision.
    g. Senate Finance Committee Report.
    h. Acquiescences to Tax Court decisions.
    i. U.S. Circuit Court of Appeals decision.

Issue ID

30. Ashley has to prepare a research paper discussing the differences between alimony and child care support for her tax class. Explain to Ashley how she can research these differences.

31. Define the following terms:
    a. *Golsen* rule.
    b. Small Cases Division of the U.S. Tax Court.
    c. Writ of Certiorari.
    d. Tax evasion.

Problems

32. Tom has just been audited by the IRS and, as a result, has been assessed a substantial deficiency (which he has not yet paid) in additional income taxes. In preparing his defense, Tom advances the following possibilities:
    a. Although a resident of Kentucky, Tom plans to sue in a U.S. District Court in Oregon that appears to be more favorably inclined toward taxpayers.
    b. If (a) is not possible, Tom plans to take his case to a Kentucky state court where an uncle is the presiding judge.
    c. Since Tom has found a B.T.A. decision that seems to help his case, he plans to rely on it under alternative (a) or (b).
    d. If he loses at the trial court level, Tom plans to appeal to either the U.S. Court of Federal Claims or the U.S. Second Circuit Court of Appeals because he has relatives in both Washington, D.C., and New York. Staying with these relatives could save Tom lodging expense while his appeal is being heard by the court selected.
    e. Even if he does not win at the trial court or appeals court level, Tom feels certain of success on an appeal to the U.S. Supreme Court.

    Evaluate Tom's notions concerning the judicial process as it applies to Federal income tax controversies.

33. Using the legend provided, classify each of the following statements (more than one answer per statement may be appropriate):

Legend
D = Applies to the U.S. District Court
T = Applies to the U.S. Tax Court
C = Applies to the U.S. Court of Federal Claims
A = Applies to the U.S. Circuit Court of Appeals
U = Applies to the U.S. Supreme Court
N = Applies to none of the above

a. Decides only Federal tax matters.
b. Decisions are reported in the F.3d Series.
c. Decisions are reported in the USTCs.
d. Decisions are reported in the AFTRs.
e. Appeal is by *Writ of Certiorari.*
f. Court meets most often in Washington, D.C.
g. Offers the choice of a jury trial.
h. Is a trial court.
i. Is an appellate court.
j. Allows appeal to the Court of Appeals for the Federal Circuit and bypasses the taxpayer's particular Court of Appeals.
k. Has a Small Cases Division.
l. Is the only trial court where the taxpayer does not have to first pay the tax assessed by the IRS.

34. Using the legend provided, classify each of the following citations as to the type of court:

Legend
D = Applies to the U.S. District Court
T = Applies to the U.S. Tax Court
C = Applies to the U.S. Court of Federal Claims
A = Applies to the U.S. Circuit Court of Appeals
U = Applies to the U.S. Supreme Court
N = Applies to none of the above

a. *Peter M. Schaeffer*, T.C.Memo. 1997–263.
b. Rev.Rul. 83–78, 1983–1 C.B. 245.
c. *Tufts v. Comm.*, 52 AFTR2d 83–5759 (CA–5, 1983).
d. *Farm Service Cooperative*, 70 T.C. 145 (1978).
e. *Korn Industries v. U.S.*, 532 F.2d 1352 (Ct.Cl., 1976).
f. *Zeeman v. Comm.*, 275 F.Supp. 235 (D.Ct. N.Y., 1967).
g. *Clark v. Comm.*, 489 U.S. 726 (1989).
h. Rev.Proc. 2001–43, 2001–2 C.B. 191.
i. 3 B.T.A. 1042 (1926).

35. Using the legend provided, classify each of the following citations as to publisher:

Legend	
RIA	= Research Institute of America
CCH	= Commerce Clearing House
W	= West Publishing Company
U.S.	= U.S. Government
O	= Others

a. 103 T.C. 80.
b. 69 TCM 3042.
c. 839 F.Supp. 933.
d. 56 AFTR2d 85–5926.
e. 92–1 USTC ¶50,186.
f. RIA T.C.Mem.Dec. ¶80,582.
g. Rev.Proc. 92–16, 1992–1 C.B. 673.
h. Rev.Proc. 77–37, 1977–2 C.B. 568.
i. 110 S.Ct. 589.
j. 493 U.S. 203.

36. Using the legend provided, classify each of the following statements:

Legend
A = Tax avoidance
E = Tax evasion
N = Neither

a. Terry writes a $250 check for a charitable contribution on December 28, 2005, but does not mail the check to the charitable organization until January 10, 2006. She takes a deduction in 2005.
b. Robert decides not to report interest income from a bank because the amount is only $11.75.
c. Jim pays property taxes on his home in December 2005 rather than waiting until February 2006.
d. Jane switches her investments from taxable corporate bonds to tax-exempt municipal bonds.
e. Ted encourages his mother to save most of her Social Security benefits so that he will be able to claim her as a dependent.

Research Problems

*Note: Solutions to Research Problems can be prepared by using the **RIA Checkpoint® Student Edition** online research product, which is available to accompany this text. It is also possible to prepare solutions to the Research Problems by using tax research materials found in a standard tax library.*

Research Problem 1. Complete the following citations:
a. *Figgie International, Inc.*, T.C.Memo. 1985–_____.
b. *S. Morton*, 38 B.T.A. _____ (1938).
c. *Northern Coal & Dock Co.*, 12 T.C. _____ (1949).
d. *Winn-Dixie Stores, Inc.*, 254 F.3d _____ (CA–11, 2001).
e. Rev.Rul. 59–_____, 1959–2 C.B. 87.
f. *Upjohn Co. v. U.S.*, 449 U.S. _____ (1981).
g. *In re Sealed Case*, 737 F.2d 94 (_____, 1984).

Decision Making

Research Problem 2. During 2005, Frank lived with and supported a 20-year-old woman who was not his wife. He resides in a state that has a statute that makes it a misdemeanor for a man and woman who are not married to each other to live together. May Frank claim his *friend* as a dependent assuming he satisfies the normal tax rules for the deduction? Should Frank consider moving to another state?

Partial list of research aids:
§ 152(f)(3).
John T. Untermann, 38 T.C. 93 (1962).
S.Rept. 1983, 85th Cong., 2d Sess., reprinted in the 1958 Code Cong. & Adm. News 4791, 4804.

Use the tax resources of the Internet to address the following question. Do not restrict your search to the World Wide Web, but include a review of newsgroups and general reference materials, practitioner sites and resources, primary sources of the tax law, chat rooms and discussion groups, and other opportunities.

Research Problem 3. Go to the U.S. Tax Court Internet site:

a. What different types of cases can be found on the site?
b. What is a Summary Opinion? Find one.
c. What is a Memorandum Opinion? Find one.
d. Find the "Rules and Parctices and Procedures."
e. Is the site user-friendly? E-mail suggested improvements to the webmaster.

Tax Determination; Personal and Dependency Exemptions; An Overview of Property Transactions

LEARNING OBJECTIVES

After completing Chapter 3, you should be able to:

LO.1
Understand and apply the components of the Federal income tax formula.

LO.2
Apply the rules for arriving at personal and dependency exemptions.

LO.3
Use the proper method for determining the tax liability.

LO.4
Identify and work with kiddie tax situations.

LO.5
Recognize the filing requirements and the proper filing status.

LO.6
Possess an overview of property transactions.

LO.7
Identify tax planning opportunities associated with the individual tax formula.

http://wft.swlearning.com

OUTLINE

Individuals are subject to Federal income tax based on taxable income. This chapter explains how taxable income and the income tax of an individual taxpayer are determined.

To compute taxable income, it is necessary to understand the tax formula in Figure 3–1. Although the tax formula is rather simple, determining an individual's taxable income can be quite complex. The complexity stems from the numerous provisions that govern the determination of gross income and allowable deductions.

FIGURE 3–1
Tax Formula

Income (broadly conceived)	$xx,xxx
Less: Exclusions	(x,xxx)
Gross income	$xx,xxx
Less: Deductions *for* adjusted gross income	(x,xxx)
Adjusted gross income	$xx,xxx
Less: The greater of total itemized deductions *or* the standard deduction	(x,xxx)
Personal and dependency exemptions	(x,xxx)
Taxable income	$xx,xxx
Tax on taxable income (see Tax Tables or Tax Rate Schedules)	$ x,xxx
Less: Tax credits (including income taxes withheld and prepaid)	(xxx)
Tax due (or refund)	$ xxx

After computing taxable income, the appropriate rates must be applied. This requires a determination of the individual's filing status, since different rates apply for single taxpayers, married taxpayers, and heads of household. The basic tax rate structure is progressive, with rates for 2005 ranging from 10 percent to 35 percent.[1] For comparison, the lowest rate structure, which was in effect in 1913–1915, ranged from 1 to 7 percent, and the highest, in effect during 1944–1945, ranged from 23 to 94 percent.

Once the individual's tax has been computed, prepayments and credits are subtracted to determine whether the taxpayer owes additional tax or is entitled to a refund.

When property is sold or otherwise disposed of, a gain or loss may result, which can affect the determination of taxable income. Although property transactions are covered in detail in Chapters 13 and 14, an understanding of certain basic concepts helps in working with some of the materials to follow. The concluding portion of this chapter furnishes an overview of property transactions, including the distinction between realized and recognized gain or loss, the classification of such gain or loss (ordinary or capital), and the treatment for income tax purposes.

LO.1

Understand and apply the components of the Federal income tax formula.

Tax Formula

Most individuals compute taxable income using the tax formula shown in Figure 3–1. Special provisions govern the computation of taxable income and the tax liability for certain minor children who have unearned income in excess of specified amounts. These provisions are discussed later in the chapter.

Before illustrating the application of the tax formula, a brief discussion of its components is helpful.

COMPONENTS OF THE TAX FORMULA

Income (Broadly Conceived). This includes all the taxpayer's income, both taxable and nontaxable. Although it is essentially equivalent to gross receipts, it does not include a return of capital or receipt of borrowed funds.

EXAMPLE 1

Dave needed money to purchase a house. He sold 5,000 shares of stock for $100,000. He had paid $40,000 for the stock. In addition, he borrowed $75,000 from a bank. Dave has income that is taxable of $60,000 from the sale of the stock ($100,000 selling price – $40,000 return of capital). He has no income from the $75,000 borrowed from the bank because he has an obligation to repay that amount. ■

Exclusions. For various reasons, Congress has chosen to exclude certain types of income from the income tax base. The principal income exclusions are discussed in Chapter 5. A partial list of these exclusions is shown in Exhibit 3–1.

Gross Income. The Internal Revenue Code defines gross income broadly as "except as otherwise provided . . ., all income from whatever source derived."[2] The "except as otherwise provided" refers to exclusions. Gross income includes, but is not limited to, the items in the partial list in Exhibit 3–2. It does not include unrealized gains. Gross income is discussed in Chapters 4 and 5.

---

[1]Prior to the Tax Relief Reconciliation Act of 2001, the tax rates ranged from 15% to 39.6%. The Act established 10% as the new lowest bracket. Later legislation lowered the top rate to 35%.

[2]§ 61(a).

■ EXHIBIT 3–1
Partial List of Exclusions from Gross Income

- Accident insurance proceeds
- Annuities (cost element)
- Bequests
- Child support payments
- Cost-of-living allowance (for military)
- Damages for personal injury or sickness
- Gifts received
- Group term life insurance, premium paid by employer (for coverage up to $50,000)
- Inheritances
- Interest from state and local (i.e., municipal) bonds
- Life insurance paid on death
- Meals and lodging (if furnished for employer's convenience)
- Military allowances
- Minister's dwelling rental value allowance
- Railroad retirement benefits (to a limited extent)
- Scholarship grants (to a limited extent)
- Social Security benefits (to a limited extent)
- Veterans' benefits
- Welfare payments
- Workers' compensation benefits

■ EXHIBIT 3–2
Partial List of Gross Income Items

- Alimony
- Annuities (income element)
- Awards
- Back pay
- Bargain purchase from employer
- Bonuses
- Breach of contract damages
- Business income
- Clergy fees
- Commissions
- Compensation for services
- Death benefits
- Debts forgiven
- Director's fees
- Dividends
- Embezzled funds
- Employee awards (in certain cases)
- Employee benefits (except certain fringe benefits)
- Estate and trust income
- Farm income
- Fees
- Gains from illegal activities
- Gains from sale of property
- Gambling winnings
- Group term life insurance, premium paid by employer (for coverage over $50,000)
- Hobby income
- Interest
- Jury duty fees
- Living quarters, meals (unless furnished for employer's convenience)
- Mileage allowance
- Military pay (unless combat pay)
- Notary fees
- Partnership income
- Pensions
- Prizes
- Professional fees
- Punitive damages
- Rents
- Rewards
- Royalties
- Salaries
- Severance pay
- Strike and lockout benefits
- Supplemental unemployment benefits
- Tips and gratuities
- Travel allowance (in certain cases)
- Wages

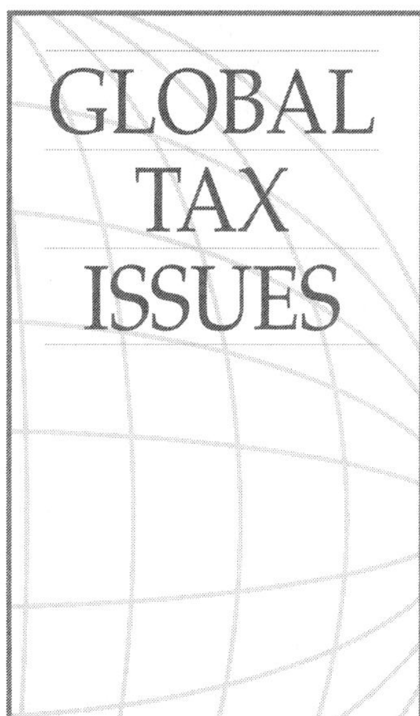

Citizenship Is Not Tax-Free

Gross income from "whatever source derived" includes income from both U.S. and foreign sources. This approach to taxation, where the government taxes its citizens and residents on their worldwide income regardless of where earned, is referred to as a *global* system. Income earned by U.S. citizens outside the United States can be subject to additional taxes, however, because all countries maintain the right to tax income earned within their borders. Consequently, the U.S. tax law includes various mechanisms to alleviate the double taxation that arises when income is subject to tax in multiple jurisdictions. These mechanisms include the foreign tax deduction, the foreign tax credit, the foreign earned income exclusion for U.S. citizens and residents working abroad, and various tax treaty provisions.

Most industrialized countries use variants of the global system. An alternative approach is the *territorial* system, where a government taxes only the income earned within its borders. Hong Kong and Guatemala, for example, use a territorial approach.

EXAMPLE 2

Beth received the following amounts during the year:

Salary	$30,000
Interest on savings account	900
Gift from her aunt	10,000
Prize won in state lottery	1,000
Alimony from ex-husband	12,000
Child support from ex-husband	6,000
Damages for injury in auto accident	25,000
Increase in the value of stock held for investment	5,000

Review Exhibits 3–1 and 3–2 to determine the amount Beth must include in the computation of taxable income and the amount she may exclude. Then check your answer in footnote 3.[3] ■

Deductions for Adjusted Gross Income. Individual taxpayers have two categories of deductions: (1) deductions *for* adjusted gross income (deductions to arrive at adjusted gross income) and (2) deductions *from* adjusted gross income.

Deductions *for* adjusted gross income (AGI) include ordinary and necessary expenses incurred in a trade or business, one-half of self-employment tax paid, alimony paid, certain payments to an Individual Retirement Account and Health Savings Accounts, moving expenses, forfeited interest penalty for premature withdrawal of time deposits, the capital loss deduction, and others.[4] Deductions *for* AGI are sometimes known as *above-the-line* deductions because on the tax return they are taken before the "line" designating AGI. The principal deductions *for* AGI are discussed in Chapters 6, 7, 8, 9, and 11.

Adjusted Gross Income (AGI). AGI is an important subtotal that serves as the basis for computing percentage limitations on certain itemized deductions, such as medical expenses, charitable contributions, and certain casualty losses.

[3]Beth must include $43,900 in computing taxable income ($30,000 salary + $900 interest + $1,000 lottery prize + $12,000 alimony). She can exclude $41,000 ($10,000 gift from aunt + $6,000 child support + $25,000 damages). The unrealized gain on the stock held for investment also is not included in gross income. Such gain will be included in gross income only when it is realized upon disposition of the stock.

[4]§ 62.

For example, medical expenses are deductible only to the extent they exceed 7.5 percent of AGI, and charitable contribution deductions may not exceed 50 percent of AGI. These limitations might be described as a 7.5 percent *floor* under the medical expense deduction and a 50 percent *ceiling* on the charitable contribution deduction.

EXAMPLE 3

Keith earned a salary of $24,000 in the current tax year. He contributed $4,000 to his traditional Individual Retirement Account (IRA) and sustained a $1,000 capital loss on the sale of Wren Corporation stock. His AGI is computed as follows:

Gross income		
Salary		$24,000
Less: Deductions *for* AGI		
IRA contribution	$4,000	
Capital loss	1,000	(5,000)
AGI		$19,000

■

EXAMPLE 4

Assume the same facts as in Example 3, and that Keith also had medical expenses of $1,800. Medical expenses may be included in itemized deductions to the extent they exceed 7.5% of AGI. In computing his itemized deductions, Keith may include medical expenses of $375 [$1,800 medical expenses – $1,425 (7.5% × $19,000 AGI)]. ■

Itemized Deductions. As a general rule, personal expenditures are disallowed as deductions in arriving at taxable income. However, Congress has chosen to allow specified personal expenses as **itemized deductions.** Such expenditures include medical expenses, certain taxes and interest, and charitable contributions.

In addition to these personal expenses, taxpayers are allowed itemized deductions for expenses related to (1) the production or collection of income and (2) the management of property held for the production of income.[5] These expenses, sometimes referred to as *nonbusiness expenses,* differ from trade or business expenses (discussed previously). Trade or business expenses, which are deductions *for* AGI, must be incurred in connection with a trade or business. Nonbusiness expenses, on the other hand, are expenses incurred in connection with an income-producing activity that does not qualify as a trade or business. Such expenses are itemized deductions.

EXAMPLE 5

Leo is the owner and operator of a video game arcade. All allowable expenses he incurs in connection with the arcade business are deductions *for* AGI. In addition, Leo has an extensive portfolio of stocks and bonds. Leo's investment activity is not treated as a trade or business. All allowable expenses that Leo incurs in connection with these investments are itemized deductions. ■

Itemized deductions include, but are not limited to, the expenses listed in Exhibit 3–3. See Chapter 10 for a detailed discussion of itemized deductions.

Standard Deduction. The **standard deduction,** which is set by Congress, is a specified amount that depends on the filing status of the taxpayer. The effect of the standard deduction is to exempt a taxpayer's income, up to the specified amount, from Federal income tax liability. In the past, Congress has attempted to

[5] § 212.

EXHIBIT 3–3
Partial List of Itemized Deductions

- Medical expenses in excess of 7.5% of AGI
- State and local income or sales taxes
- Real estate taxes
- Personal property taxes
- Interest on home mortgage
- Investment interest (to a limited extent)
- Charitable contributions (within specified percentage limitations)
- Casualty and theft losses in excess of 10% of AGI
- Miscellaneous expenses (to the extent such expenses exceed 2% of AGI)
    - Union dues
    - Professional dues and subscriptions
    - Certain educational expenses
    - Tax return preparation fee
    - Investment counsel fees
    - Unreimbursed employee business expenses (after a percentage reduction for meals and entertainment)

set the tax-free amount represented by the standard deduction approximately equal to an estimated poverty level,[6] but it has not always been consistent in doing so.

The standard deduction is the sum of two components: the *basic* standard deduction and the *additional* standard deduction.[7] Table 3–1 lists the basic standard deduction allowed for taxpayers in each filing status. All taxpayers allowed a *full* standard deduction are entitled to the applicable amount listed in Table 3–1. The standard deduction amounts are subject to adjustment for inflation each year.

Certain taxpayers are not allowed to claim *any* standard deduction, and the standard deduction is *limited* for others. These provisions are discussed later in the chapter.

A taxpayer who is age 65 or over *or* blind qualifies for an *additional standard deduction* of $1,000 or $1,250, depending on filing status (see amounts in Table 3–2). Two additional standard deductions are allowed for a taxpayer who is age 65 or

TABLE 3–1
Basic Standard Deduction Amounts

	Standard Deduction Amount	
Filing Status	**2004**	**2005**
Single	$4,850	$ 5,000
Married, filing jointly	9,700	10,000
Surviving spouse	9,700	10,000
Head of household	7,150	7,300
Married, filing separately	4,850	5,000

[6] S.Rep. No. 92–437, 92nd Cong., 1st Sess., 1971, p. 54. Another purpose of the standard deduction was discussed in Chapter 1 under Influence of the Internal Revenue Service—Administrative Feasibility. The size of the standard deduction has a direct bearing on the number of taxpayers who are in a position to itemize deductions. Reducing the number of taxpayers who itemize also reduces the audit effort required from the IRS.

[7] § 63(c)(1).

TABLE 3–2
Amount of Each Additional Standard Deduction

Filing Status	2004	2005
Single	$1,200	$1,250
Married, filing jointly	950	1,000
Surviving spouse	950	1,000
Head of household	1,200	1,250
Married, filing separately	950	1,000

over *and* blind. The additional standard deduction provisions also apply for a qualifying spouse who is age 65 or over or blind, but a taxpayer may not claim an additional standard deduction for a dependent.

To determine whether to itemize, the taxpayer compares the *total* standard deduction (the sum of the basic standard deduction and any additional standard deductions) with total itemized deductions. Taxpayers are allowed to deduct the *greater* of itemized deductions or the standard deduction. Taxpayers whose itemized deductions are less than the standard deduction compute their taxable income using the standard deduction rather than itemizing. Approximately 70 percent of individual taxpayers choose the standard deduction option.

EXAMPLE 6

Sara, who is single, is 66 years old. She had total itemized deductions of $5,900 during 2005. Her total standard deduction is $6,250 ($5,000 basic standard deduction plus $1,250 additional standard deduction). Sara should compute her taxable income for 2005 using the standard deduction ($6,250), since it exceeds her itemized deductions ($5,900). ■

Personal and Dependency Exemptions. Exemptions are allowed for the taxpayer, for the taxpayer's spouse, and for each dependent of the taxpayer. The exemption amount is $3,100 in 2004 and $3,200 in 2005.

APPLICATION OF THE TAX FORMULA

The tax formula shown in Figure 3–1 is illustrated in Example 7.

EXAMPLE 7

Grace, age 25, is single and has no dependents. She is a high school teacher and earned a $30,000 salary in 2005. Her other income consisted of a $1,000 prize won in a sweepstakes contest and $500 interest on municipal bonds received as a graduation gift in 2002. During 2005, she sustained a deductible capital loss of $1,000. Her itemized deductions are $5,400. Grace's taxable income for the year is computed as follows:

Income (broadly conceived)	
Salary	$30,000
Prize	1,000
Interest on municipal bonds	500
	$31,500
Less: Exclusion—	
Interest on municipal bonds	(500)
Gross income	$31,000
Less: Deduction *for* adjusted gross income—	
Capital loss	(1,000)
Adjusted gross income	$30,000

Less: The greater of total itemized deductions ($5,400) *or* the standard deduction ($5,000)	(5,400)
Personal and dependency exemptions (1 × $3,200)	(3,200)
Taxable income	$21,400

The structure of the individual income tax return (Form 1040, 1040A, or 1040EZ) differs somewhat from the tax formula in Figure 3–1. On the tax return, gross income generally is the starting point in computing taxable income. With few exceptions, exclusions are not reported on the tax return.

INDIVIDUALS NOT ELIGIBLE FOR THE STANDARD DEDUCTION

The following individual taxpayers are ineligible to use the standard deduction and must therefore itemize:[8]

- A married individual filing a separate return where either spouse itemizes deductions.
- A nonresident alien.
- An individual filing a return for a period of less than 12 months because of a change in the annual accounting period.

SPECIAL LIMITATIONS FOR INDIVIDUALS WHO CAN BE CLAIMED AS DEPENDENTS

Special rules apply to the standard deduction and personal exemption of an individual who can be claimed as a dependent on another person's tax return.

When filing his or her own tax return, a *dependent's* basic standard deduction in 2005 is limited to the greater of $800 or the sum of the individual's earned income for the year plus $250.[9] However, if the sum of the individual's earned income plus $250 exceeds the normal standard deduction, the standard deduction is limited to the appropriate amount shown in Table 3–1. These limitations apply only to the basic standard deduction. A dependent who is 65 or over or blind or both is also allowed the additional standard deduction amount on his or her own return (refer to Table 3–2). These provisions are illustrated in Examples 8 through 11.

EXAMPLE 8

Susan, who is 17 years old and single, is claimed as a dependent on her parents' tax return. During 2005, she received $1,200 interest (unearned income) on a savings account. She also earned $300 from a part-time job. When Susan files her own tax return, her standard deduction is $800 (the greater of $800 or the sum of earned income of $300 plus $250).

EXAMPLE 9

Assume the same facts as in Example 8, except that Susan is 67 years old and is claimed as a dependent on her son's tax return. In this case, when Susan files her own tax return, her standard deduction is $2,050 [$800 (the greater of $800 or the sum of earned income of $300 plus $250) + $1,250 (the additional standard deduction allowed because Susan is 65 or over)].

EXAMPLE 10

Peggy, who is 16 years old and single, earned $600 from a summer job and had no unearned income during 2005. She is claimed as a dependent on her parents' tax return. Her standard deduction is $850 (the greater of $800 or the sum of $600 earned income plus $250).

[8] § 63(c)(6).

[9] § 63(c)(5). Both the $800 amount and the $250 amount are subject to adjustment for inflation each year. The amounts were also $800 and $250, respectively, for 2004.

EXAMPLE 11

Jack, who is a 20-year-old, single, full-time college student, is claimed as a dependent on his parents' tax return. He worked as a musician during the summer of 2005, earning $5,300. Jack's standard deduction is $5,000 (the greater of $800 or the sum of $5,300 earned income plus $250, but limited to the $5,000 standard deduction for a single taxpayer). ■

A taxpayer who claims an individual as a dependent is allowed to claim an exemption for the dependent. The dependent cannot claim a personal exemption on his or her own return. Based on the tax formula, Jack in Example 11 would have taxable income of $300, determined as follows:

Gross income	$ 5,300
Less: Standard deduction	(5,000)
Personal exemption	(–0–)
Taxable income	$ 300

LO.2

Apply the rules for arriving at personal and dependency exemptions.

Personal and Dependency Exemptions

The use of exemptions in the tax system is based in part on the idea that a taxpayer with a small amount of income should be exempt from income taxation. An exemption frees a specified amount of income from tax ($3,100 in 2004 and $3,200 in 2005). The exemption amount is indexed (adjusted) annually for inflation. An individual who is not claimed as a dependent by another taxpayer is allowed to claim his or her own personal exemption. In addition, a taxpayer may claim an exemption for each dependent.

EXAMPLE 12

Bonnie, who is single, supports her mother and father, who have no income of their own, and claims them as dependents on her tax return. Bonnie may claim a personal exemption for herself plus an exemption for each dependent. On her 2005 tax return, Bonnie may deduct $9,600 for exemptions ($3,200 per exemption × 3 exemptions). ■

PERSONAL EXEMPTIONS

The Code provides a **personal exemption** for the taxpayer and an exemption for the spouse if a joint return is filed. However, when separate returns are filed, a married taxpayer cannot claim an exemption for his or her spouse *unless* the spouse has no gross income and is not claimed as the dependent of another taxpayer.

The determination of marital status generally is made at the end of the taxable year, except when a spouse dies during the year. Spouses who enter into a legal separation under a decree of divorce or separate maintenance before the end of the year are considered to be unmarried at the end of the taxable year. The following table illustrates the effect of death or divorce upon marital status:

	Marital Status for 2005
• Walt is the widower of Helen who died on January 3, 2005.	Walt and Helen are considered to be married for purposes of filing the 2005 return.
• Bill and Jane entered into a divorce decree that is effective on December 31, 2005.	Bill and Jane are considered to be unmarried for purposes of filing the 2005 return.

For *Federal* tax purposes, the law does not recognize same-sex marriages. By virtue of the Defense of Marriage Act (P.L. 104–199), a marriage means a legal union only between a man and a woman as husband and wife.

DEPENDENCY EXEMPTIONS—PRIOR TO 2005

The Working Families Tax Relief Act of 2004 has modified the rules applicable to dependency exemptions. Because the new rules do not become effective until 2005, preexisting law remains applicable through 2004. Consequently, preexisting law will govern tax returns filed in 2005 for calendar year 2004. As will be pointed out later, many of the old rules dealing with dependency exemptions remain unchanged under the new law. A **dependency exemption** may be claimed for each individual for whom the following five tests are met:

- Support.
- Relationship or member of the household.
- Gross income.
- Joint return.
- Citizenship or residency.

A person who dies during the year can still be claimed as a dependent if all of the tests are met. In such a case, no proration is necessary, and the full amount of the exemption is allowed.

Support Test. Over one-half of the support of the individual must be furnished by the taxpayer. Support includes food, shelter, clothing, medical and dental care, education, etc. However, a scholarship received by a student is not included for purposes of computing whether the taxpayer furnished more than half of the child's support.[10]

EXAMPLE 13

Hal contributed $3,400 (consisting of food, clothing, and medical care) toward the support of his cousin, Sam, who lives with him. Sam earned $1,500 from a part-time job and received a $2,000 scholarship to attend a local university. Assuming that the other dependency tests are met, Hal can claim Sam as a dependent since he has contributed more than half of Sam's support. The $2,000 scholarship is not included as support for purposes of this test. ■

If the individual does not spend funds that have been received from any source, the unexpended amounts are not counted for purposes of the support test.

EXAMPLE 14

Emily contributed $3,000 to her father's support during the year. In addition, her father received $2,400 in Social Security benefits, $200 of interest, and wages of $600. Her father deposited the Social Security benefits, interest, and wages in his own savings account and did not use any of the funds for his support. Thus, the Social Security benefits, interest, and wages are not considered as support provided by Emily's father. Emily may claim her father as a dependent if the other tests are met. ■

Capital expenditures for items such as furniture, appliances, and automobiles are included in total support if the item does, in fact, constitute support.[11]

EXAMPLE 15

Norm purchased a television set costing $250 and gave it to his mother who lives with him. The television set was placed in the mother's bedroom and was used exclusively by her. Norm should include the cost of the television set in determining the support of his mother. ■

---

[10]Reg. § 1.152–1(c).

[11]Rev.Rul. 57–344, 1957–2 C.B. 112; Rev.Rul. 58–419, 1958–2 C.B. 57.

An exception to the support test involves a **multiple support agreement.** A multiple support agreement permits one of a group of taxpayers who furnish support for an individual to claim a dependency exemption for that individual even if no one person provides more than 50 percent of the support.[12] The group together must provide more than 50 percent of the support. Any person who contributed *more than 10 percent* of the support is entitled to claim the exemption if each person in the group who contributed more than 10 percent files a written consent. This provision frequently enables one of the children of aged dependent parents to claim an exemption when none of the children meets the 50 percent support test. Each person who is a party to the multiple support agreement must meet all other requirements (except the support requirement) for claiming the exemption. A person who does not meet the relationship or member-of-household requirement, for instance, cannot claim the dependency exemption under a multiple support agreement. It does not matter if he or she contributes more than 10 percent of the individual's support.

EXAMPLE 16

Wanda, who resides with her son, Adam, received $12,000 from various sources during the year. This constituted her entire support for the year. She received support from the following:

	Amount	Percentage of Total
Adam, a son	$ 5,760	48
Bob, a son	1,200	10
Carol, a daughter	3,600	30
Diane, a friend	1,440	12
	$12,000	100

If Adam and Carol file a multiple support agreement, either may claim the dependency exemption for Wanda. Bob may not claim Wanda because he did not contribute more than 10% of her support. Bob's consent is not required in order for Adam and Carol to file a multiple support agreement. Diane does not meet the relationship or member-of-household test and cannot be a party to the agreement. The decision as to who claims Wanda rests with Adam and Carol. It is possible for Carol to claim Wanda, even though Adam furnished more of Wanda's support. ■

ETHICAL CONSIDERATIONS

Discovering Lost Dependency Exemptions

For the six years prior to his death in late 2005, Jesse lived with his daughter, Hannah. Because he had no source of income, Jesse was supported by equal contributions from Hannah and his two sons, Bill and Bob. At Jesse's funeral, his surviving children are amazed to discover that none of them has been claiming Jesse as a dependent. Upon the advice of the director of the funeral home, they decide to divide, among themselves, the dependency exemptions for the past six years. Multiple Forms 2120 are executed, and each of the three children files amended returns for different past years. As Jesse died before the end of the current year, no deduction is planned for 2005.

Comment on the tax expectations of the parties involved.

Each person who qualifies under the more-than-10 percent rule (except for the person claiming the exemption) must complete Form 2120 (Multiple Support

[12] § 152(d)(3).

Declaration) waiving the exemption. The person claiming the exemption must attach all Forms 2120 to his or her own return.

A special rule applies for a child of parents who are divorced or separated under a decree of separate maintenance. For decrees executed after 1984, the custodial parent is allowed to claim the exemption unless that parent agrees in writing not to claim a dependency exemption for the child.[13] Thus, claiming the exemption is dependent on whether or not a written agreement exists, *not* on meeting the support test.

EXAMPLE 17

Ira and Rita obtain a divorce decree in 1994. In 2005, their two children are in Rita's custody. Ira contributed over half of the support for each child. In the absence of a written agreement on the dependency exemptions, Rita (the custodial parent) is entitled to the exemptions in 2005. However, Ira may claim the exemptions if Rita agrees in writing. ■

For the noncustodial parent to claim the exemption, the custodial parent must complete Form 8332 (Release of Claim to Exemption for Child of Divorced or Separated Parents). The release can apply to a single year, a number of specified years, or all future years. The noncustodial parent must attach a copy of Form 8332 to his or her return.

Relationship or Member-of-the-Household Test. To be claimed as a dependent, an individual must be either a relative of the taxpayer or a member of the taxpayer's household. The Code contains a detailed listing of the various blood and marriage relationships that qualify. Note, however, that the relationship test is met if the individual is a relative of either spouse. Once established by marriage, a relationship continues regardless of subsequent changes in marital status.

The following individuals may be claimed as dependents of the taxpayer if the other tests for dependency are met:[14]

- A son or daughter of the taxpayer or a descendant of either, such as a grandchild.
- A stepson or stepdaughter of the taxpayer.
- A brother, sister, half brother, half sister, stepbrother, or stepsister of the taxpayer.
- The father or mother of the taxpayer or an ancestor of either, such as a grandparent.
- A stepfather or stepmother of the taxpayer.
- A nephew or niece of the taxpayer.
- An uncle or aunt of the taxpayer.
- A son-in-law, daughter-in-law, father-in-law, mother-in-law, brother-in-law, or sister-in-law of the taxpayer.
- An individual who, for the entire taxable year of the taxpayer, has as his or her principal place of abode the home of the taxpayer and is a member of the taxpayer's household.

The following rules are also prescribed in the Code:[15]

- A legally adopted child is treated as a natural child.
- A foster child qualifies if the child's principal place of abode is the taxpayer's household.

---

[13] § 152(e).

[14] § 152(d)(2). However, under § 152(f)(3), a taxpayer may not claim someone who is a member of his or her household as a dependent if their relationship is in violation of local law. For example, the dependency exemption was denied because the taxpayer's relationship to the person claimed as a dependent constituted *cohabitation,* a crime under applicable state law. *Cassius L. Peacock, III,* 37 TCM 177, T.C.Memo. 1978–30.

[15] § 152(f)(1).

Note that the relationship test does not include an ex-spouse of the taxpayer. Except for the year of divorce, however, an ex-spouse could qualify by being a member of the taxpayer's household.

Gross Income Test. The dependent's gross income must be less than the exemption amount ($3,100 in 2004 and $3,200 in 2005).[16] The gross income test is measured by income that is taxable. In the case of scholarships, for example, it excludes the nontaxable portion (e.g., amounts received for books and tuition) but includes the taxable portion (e.g., amounts received for room and board).

A parent may claim a dependency exemption for his or her child in 2004, even when the child's gross income is $3,100 or more, if the parent provided over half of the child's support and the child, at year-end, is under age 19 or is a full-time student under age 24. If the parent claims a dependency exemption, the dependent child may not claim a personal exemption on his or her own income tax return.

A child is defined as a son, stepson, daughter, stepdaughter, adopted son, or adopted daughter and may include a foster child.[17] For the child to qualify as a student for purposes of the dependency exemption, he or she must be a full-time student at an educational institution during some part of five calendar months of the year.[18] This exception to the gross income test for dependent children who are (1) under age 19 or (2) full-time students under age 24 (applicable to 2004 and prior years) permits a child or college student to earn money from part-time or summer jobs without penalizing the parent with the loss of the dependency exemption.

Joint Return Test. If a dependent is married, the supporting taxpayer (e.g., the parent of a married child) generally is not permitted a dependency exemption if the married individual files a joint return with his or her spouse.[19] The joint return rule does not apply, however, if the following conditions are met:

- The reason for filing is to claim a refund for tax withheld.
- No tax liability would exist for either spouse on separate returns.
- Neither spouse is required to file a return.

See Table 3–4 later in the chapter and the related discussion concerning income level requirements for filing a return.

EXAMPLE 18

Paul provides over half of the support of his son Quinn. He also provides over half of the support of Vera, who is Quinn's wife. During the year, both Quinn and Vera had part-time jobs. In order to recover the taxes withheld, they file a joint return. If Quinn and Vera are not required to file a return, Paul is allowed to claim both as dependents. ■

Citizenship or Residency Test. To be a dependent, the individual must be either a U.S. citizen, a U.S. resident, or a resident of Canada or Mexico for some part of the calendar year in which the taxpayer's tax year begins.

ETHICAL CONSIDERATIONS

A Change of Residence Can Be Rewarding

Linda is a citizen of Honduras and a resident of Chicago. For many years she has supported her parents and grandparents, who were citizens and residents of Honduras. In 2005, Linda convinces her relatives to relocate and become residents of Mexico. For tax purposes, what is Linda trying to accomplish? Is this an appropriate thing for Linda to do?

[16] § 151(c)(1).
[17] Reg. § 1.151–3(a).
[18] Reg. §§ 1.151–3(b) and (c).
[19] § 151(c)(2).

DEPENDENCY EXEMPTIONS—AFTER 2004

One of the objectives of the Working Families Tax Relief Act of 2004 was to establish a uniform definition of qualifying child for purposes of the dependency exemption, the child tax credit, the earned income credit, the dependent care credit, and head-of-household filing status. This would resolve the confusion that existed with varying definitions of "child" applying to the different Code provisions. One effect of the new uniform definition is to modify the existing rules governing dependency exemptions.

Under the new law, a dependent is one who is either a qualifying child *or* a qualifying relative.[20]

Qualifying Child. A **qualifying child** must meet the tests of relationship, domicile, and age.[21] For the relationship test, the child must be the taxpayer's son, daughter, stepson, stepdaughter, brother, sister, stepbrother, stepsister, half brother, half sister, or a descendant of such individual (e.g., grandchildren, nephews, nieces). A child who has been adopted, or whose adoption is pending, qualifies. Under certain circumstances, a foster child also can qualify.[22]

Under the domicile test, the child must have the same principal place of abode as the taxpayer for more than half of the taxable year. In satisfying this requirement, temporary absences from the household due to special circumstances (e.g., illness, education) are not considered.

The last test for qualifying child status pertains to age. The child must be under age 19 (or under age 24 in the case of a full-time student). An exception provides that individuals who are disabled[23] are not subject to any limitations as to age.

Except in one situation, the definition of qualifying child makes the support of an individual irrelevant. The one case where support becomes relevant involves self-support. A child who provides more than one-half of his or her own support cannot be claimed as a dependent.[24]

In the event that a child satisfies the requirements of a qualified child for more than one taxpayer, the following tie-breaking rules apply:[25]

- If one of the individuals eligible to claim the child is a parent, that person prevails.
- If both parents qualify (separate returns are filed), then the parent with whom the child resides the longest during the year prevails. If the residence period is the same (or is not ascertainable), then the parent with the highest AGI prevails.
- If no parents are involved, the claimant with the highest AGI prevails.

EXAMPLE 19

Tim, age 15, lives in the same household with Mike, his father, and Aaron, his uncle. Since Tim is a qualified child to both Mike and Aaron, as a parent Mike prevails. ■

EXAMPLE 20

Assume the same facts as in Example 19, except that Mike is an uncle and not a parent. If Aaron has a higher AGI than Mike, he gets to claim Tim as a dependent. ■

Resort to the tie-breaking rules is not necessary if the party who would prevail does not claim the exemption. Thus, in Example 19, Aaron can claim Tim if Mike does not. Likewise, in Example 20, Aaron can make the exemption available to Mike by not claiming Tim as a dependent on his own return.

[20] §§ 152(a)(1) and (2).
[21] § 152(c)(1).
[22] An eligible foster child is an individual who is placed with the taxpayer by an authorized placement agency or by judgment, decree, or other order of any court of competent jurisdiction.
[23] Within the meaning of § 22(a)(3). See the discussion of the credit for the elderly and disabled in Chapter 12.
[24] § 152(c)(1)(D).
[25] § 152(c)(4).

Concept Summary 3–1

Tests for Dependency Exemption after 2004

Category	
Qualifying Child	**Qualifying Relative**[1]
Relationship[2]	Support
Domicile[3]	Relationship[4] or member of household[3]
Age	Gross income
Joint return[5]	Joint return[5]
Citizenship or residency[6]	Citizenship or residency[6]

[1]These rules are largely the same as those applicable to pre-2005 years.
[2]Children, siblings, and their descendants.
[3]The rules for domicile are the same as for member of the household.
[4]Children and their descendants, siblings and their children, parents and their ascendants, uncles and aunts, stepparents and stepsiblings, and certain in-laws.
[5]The joint return rules are the same for each category.
[6]The citizenship or residency rules are the same for each category.

Although the gross income and support tests are inapplicable to the status of a qualifying child (but note the self-support exception previously discussed), other dependency tests apply. In the case of a married child, for example, the joint return test may come into play. Barring the usual refund exception, qualifying child status excludes a married child who files a joint return with his or her spouse.[26]

With one minor exception, the citizenship or residency test also applies. Under the exception, an adopted child need not be a citizen or resident of the United States (or a contiguous country) as long as his or her principal abode is with a U.S. citizen.[27]

EXAMPLE 21

Esther is a U.S. citizen who lives and works in Spain. She has adopted Benito, a four-year-old Italian national, who lives with her and is a member of her household. Although Benito does not meet the usual citizenship or residency test, he is covered by the exception. Benito is a qualifying child, and Esther can claim him as a dependent. ■

In the case of divorced or legally separated parents with children, the custodian rules continue to apply. Thus, the dependency exemption for a child (or children) belongs to whichever parent has custody. The exemption can be shifted to the noncustodial parent if the custodial parent issues the appropriate waiver.

Qualifying Relative. Under the **qualifying relative** category for the dependency exemption, individuals must also satisfy the gross income and support tests.[28] In large part, therefore, the pre-2005 rules are carried over. A comparison of the tests governing the qualifying child and the qualifying relative categories appears in Concept Summary 3–1.

The designation "qualifying relative" is somewhat misleading in that a "relative" need not be involved. An unrelated individual who is a member of the taxpayer's household can qualify if the other dependency tests are satisfied. Also, not every "relative" is eligible; only those who meet the relationship test set forth in the Code qualify.[29]

[26]§ 152(b)(2).
[27]§ 152(b)(3).
[28]§§ 152(d)(1)(B) and (C).
[29]§ 152(d)(2).

EXAMPLE 22

Andy provides all of the support of an unrelated family friend who lives with him for the entire tax year. He also supports a cousin who lives elsewhere. The family friend can qualify as Andy's dependent, but the cousin cannot. The family friend meets the member-of-the-household test, whereas the cousin satisfies neither the relationship test nor the member-of-the-household test. ■

Though the relationship test under the qualifying relative category includes those covered by the qualifying child definition, it is more expansive. Also included are lineal ascendants (e.g., parents, grandparents), collateral ascendants (e.g., uncles and aunts), and certain in-laws (son-, daughter-, father-, mother-, brother- and sister-in-law). A son or daughter who is not a qualifying child can be a dependent.

EXAMPLE 23

Greta furnished more than half of the support of her father who lives with her and of a daughter (age 26) who lives elsewhere. Presuming the other tests are met (i.e., gross income, etc.), Greta can claim both the father and the daughter as her dependents. [Note: The daughter is not a qualifying child because she does not meet the abode and age tests.] ■

PHASEOUT OF EXEMPTIONS

Several provisions of the tax law are intended to increase the tax liability of more affluent taxpayers who might otherwise enjoy some benefit from having some of their taxable income subject to the lower income tax brackets (e.g., 10 percent, 15 percent, 25 percent). One such provision phases out personal and dependency exemptions as AGI exceeds specified threshold amounts. For 2004 and 2005, the phaseout *begins* at the following threshold amounts:

	2004	2005
Joint returns/surviving spouse	$214,050	$218,950
Head of household	178,350	182,450
Single	142,700	145,950
Married, filing separately	107,025	109,475

These threshold amounts are indexed for inflation each year.

Exemptions are phased out by 2 percent for each $2,500 (or fraction thereof) by which the taxpayer's AGI exceeds the threshold amounts. For a married taxpayer filing separately, the phaseout is 2 percent for each $1,250 or fraction thereof.

The allowable exemption amount can be determined with the following steps:

1. AGI – threshold amount = excess amount
2. Excess amount ÷ $2,500 = reduction factor [rounded up to the next whole increment (e.g., 18.1 = 19)] × 2 = phaseout percentage
3. Phaseout percentage (from step 2) × exemption amount = amount of exemptions phased out
4. Exemption amounts – phaseout amount = allowable exemption deduction

EXAMPLE 24

Frederico is married but files a separate return in 2005. His AGI is $129,475. He is entitled to one personal exemption.

1. $129,475 – $109,475 = $20,000 excess amount
2. [($20,000 ÷ $1,250) × 2] = 32% (phaseout percentage)
3. 32% × $3,200 = $1,024 amount of exemption phased out
4. $3,200 – $1,024 = $2,176 allowable exemption deduction ■

How to Subtly Pluck the Chicken

No government likes to admit that it is enacting new taxes or even raising the rates on existing taxes. Needless to say, this is particularly true of the U.S. Congress. But there are more subtle ways to raise revenue (or to curtail revenue loss). The most popular way is to use a so-called *stealth tax.* A stealth tax is not really a tax at all. Instead, it is a means of depriving higher-income taxpayers of the benefits of certain tax provisions thought to be available to all.

The heart and soul of the stealth tax is the phaseout approach. Thus, as income increases, the tax benefit thought to be derived from a particular relief provision decreases. Since the phaseout is gradual and not drastic, many affected taxpayers are unaware of what has happened. Although the tax law is rampant with phaseouts, the two most flagrant limit the deductibility of personal and dependency exemptions and itemized deductions. (The itemized deduction phaseout is discussed in Chapter 10.)

As noted in the text, perhaps Congress has had some misgivings about the stealth tax imposed on personal and dependency exemptions. These misgivings cannot be too severe, however, as any scheduled relief does not even *start* until year 2006 and is not *completed* until year 2010!

Note that the exemption amount is completely phased out when the taxpayer's AGI exceeds the threshold amount by more than \$122,500 (\$61,250 for a married taxpayer filing a separate return), calculated as follows:

$122,501 ÷ $2,500 = 49.0004, rounded to 50 and multiplied by 2 = 100%
(phaseout percentage)

EXAMPLE 25

Bill and Isabella file a joint return in 2005 claiming two personal exemptions and one dependency exemption for their child. Their AGI equals \$341,800.

$341,800 – $218,950 = $122,850 excess amount

Since the excess amount exceeds \$122,500, the exemptions are completely phased out. ■

Under the Tax Relief Reconciliation Act of 2001, the exemption phaseout is repealed as to post-2009 years. The repeal takes place over a five-year period beginning in year 2006.

CHILD TAX CREDIT

In addition to providing a dependency exemption, a child of the taxpayer may also generate a tax credit. Called the **child tax credit,** the amount allowed is \$1,000 through 2009 for each dependent child (including stepchildren and eligible foster children) under the age of 17.[30] For a more complete discussion of the child tax credit, see Chapter 12.

[30] § 24(a). The credit was scheduled to be reduced to \$700 in 2005, but the reduction was canceled by the Working Families Tax Relief Act of 2004 and remains at \$1,000.

LO.3

Use the proper method for determining the tax liability.

Tax Determination

TAX TABLE METHOD

The tax liability is computed using either the Tax Table method or the Tax Rate Schedule method. Most taxpayers compute their tax using the **Tax Table.** Eligible taxpayers compute taxable income (as shown in Figure 3–1) and *must* determine their tax by reference to the Tax Table. The following taxpayers, however, may not use the Tax Table method:

- An individual who files a short period return (see Chapter 16).
- Individuals whose taxable income exceeds the maximum (ceiling) amount in the Tax Table. The 2004 Tax Table applies to taxable income below $100,000 for Form 1040.
- An estate or trust.

The IRS does not release the Tax Tables until late in the year to which they apply. The Tax Rate Schedules, however, are released at the end of the year preceding their applicability. To illustrate, the Tax Table for 2005 will be available at the end of 2005. The Tax Rate Schedules for 2005, however, were released at the end of 2004.[31] For purposes of estimating tax liability and making quarterly prepayments, the Tax Rate Schedules will usually need to be consulted. Based on its availability, the 2004 Tax Table will be used to illustrate the tax computation using the Tax Table method.

Although the Tax Table is derived by using the Tax Rate Schedules (discussed below), the tax calculated using the two methods may vary slightly. This variation occurs because the tax for a particular income range in the Tax Table is based on the midpoint amount.

EXAMPLE 26

Linda is single and has taxable income of $30,000 for calendar year 2004. To determine Linda's tax using the Tax Table (see Appendix A), find the $30,000 to $30,050 income line. The tax of $4,244 is actually the tax the Tax Rate Schedule would yield on taxable income of $30,025 (i.e., the midpoint amount between $30,000 and $30,050). ■

TAX RATE SCHEDULE METHOD

Prior to 2001 tax legislation, the **Tax Rate Schedules** contained rates of 15, 28, 31, 36, and 39.6 percent. These rates were scheduled to be reduced to 10, 15, 25, 28, 33, and 35 percent by year 2006. JGTRRA of 2003, however, accelerated the phase-in and made the new rates effective as of January 1, 2003.[32] A sunset provision reinstates the original rates (pre-2001) after 2010.

The 2005 rate schedule for single taxpayers is reproduced in Table 3–3. This schedule is used to illustrate the tax computations in Examples 27, 28, and 29.

EXAMPLE 27

Pat is single and had $5,870 of taxable income in 2005. His tax is $587 ($5,870 × 10%). ■

Several terms are used to describe tax rates. The rates in the Tax Rate Schedules are often referred to as *statutory* (or nominal) rates. The *marginal* rate is the highest rate that is applied in the tax computation for a particular taxpayer. In Example 27, the statutory rate and the marginal rate are both 10 percent.

[31] The 2005 Tax Table was not available from the IRS at the date of publication of this text. The Tax Table for 2004 and the Tax Rate Schedules for 2004 and 2005 are reproduced in Appendix A. For quick reference, the 2004 and 2005 Tax Rate Schedules are also reproduced inside the front cover of this text.

[32] § 1(i).

■ **TABLE 3–3**
2005 Tax Rate Schedule for Single Taxpayers

If Taxable Income Is			Of the
Over	**But Not Over**	**The Tax Is:**	**Amount Over**
$ -0-	$ 7,300	10%	$ -0-
7,300	29,700	$ 730.00 + 15%	7,300
29,700	71,950	4,090.00 + 25%	29,700
71,950	150,150	14,652.50 + 28%	71,950
150,150	326,450	36,548.50 + 33%	150,150
326,450		94,727.50 + 35%	326,450

EXAMPLE 28

Chris is single and had taxable income of $50,000 in 2005. Her tax is $9,165 [$4,090 + 25% ($50,000 – $29,700)]. ■

The *average* rate is equal to the tax liability divided by taxable income. In Example 28, Chris has statutory rates of 10 percent, 15 percent, and 25 percent, and a marginal rate of 25 percent. Chris's average rate is 18.33 percent ($9,165 tax liability ÷ $50,000 taxable income).

Note that $4,090, which is the starting point in the tax computation in Example 28, is 10 percent of the $7,300 taxable income in the first bracket + 15 percent of the $22,400 ($29,700 – $7,300) taxable income in the second bracket. Chris's income in excess of $29,700 is taxed at a 25 percent rate. This reflects the *progressive* (or graduated) rate structure on which the U.S. income tax system is based. A tax is progressive if a higher rate of tax applies as the tax base increases.

EXAMPLE 29

Carl is single and had taxable income of $80,000 in 2005. His tax is $16,906.50 [$14,652.50 + 28%($80,000 – $71,950)]. Note that the effect of this computation is to tax part of Carl's income at 10%, part at 15%, part at 25%, and part at 28%. An alternative computational method provides a clearer illustration of the progressive rate structure:

Tax on $7,300 at 10%	$ 730.00
Tax on $29,700 – $7,300 at 15%	3,360.00
Tax on $71,950 – $29,700 at 25%	10,562.50
Tax on $80,000 – $71,950 at 28%	2,254.00
Total	$16,906.50

■

A special computation limits the effective tax rate on qualified dividends (see Chapter 4) and net long-term capital gain (see Chapter 16).

COMPUTATION OF NET TAXES PAYABLE OR REFUND DUE

The pay-as-you-go feature of the Federal income tax system requires payment of all or part of the taxpayer's income tax liability during the year. These payments take the form of Federal income tax withheld by employers or estimated tax paid by the taxpayer or both.[33] The payments are applied against the tax from the Tax Table or Tax Rate Schedules to determine whether the taxpayer will get a refund or pay additional tax.

Employers are required to withhold income tax on compensation paid to their employees and to pay this tax over to the government. The employer notifies the employee of the amount of income tax withheld on Form W–2 (Wage and Tax Statement). The employee should receive this form by January 31 after the year in which the income tax is withheld.

[33]§ 3402 for withholding; § 6654 for estimated payments.

TAX RATE TRAUMA

One of Adam Smith's canons of taxation is the notion of certainty. A desirable tax structure must possess the degree of certainty necessary to predict what the law will be. Otherwise, meaningful tax planning becomes impossible.

That our Federal tax law often lacks certainty is illustrated by the many recent changes in the income tax brackets applicable to individual taxpayers.

In 2001, the top four tax brackets were 28, 31, 36, and 39.6 percent. Because these rates were considered to be too high, Congress arranged for reductions. Under the Tax Relief Reconciliation Act of 2001, the rates were scheduled to be reduced until the brackets reached 25, 28, 33, and 35 percent. To avoid an immediate large revenue loss, the reductions were to be phased in at periodic intervals from 2001 to 2006. After 2010, a sunset provision restored the 2001 brackets.

In 2003 at the instigation of President Bush, Congress decided to forgo any delay in the rate reductions. In JGTRRA of 2003, the phase-in period was canceled, and the rates scheduled for 2006 became effective immediately.

This lack of certainty as to what the tax law will be generates an instability that can have a demoralizing effect on taxpayers. Suppose, for example, that a promising athlete was drafted by a major league ball club in May 2001. Upon the advice of his agent, the athlete asked the ball club not to pay his $500,000 signing bonus until 2006. Thus, the athlete agreed to a five-year delay in the payment in order to benefit from the reduction in the top tax rate from 39.6 percent to 35 percent. Now, with the enactment of JGTRRA of 2003, imagine the athlete's reaction when he learns that he could have enjoyed the same tax reduction by being paid in 2003—a delay of only two years!

If taxpayers receive income that is not subject to withholding or income from which not enough tax is withheld, they must pay estimated tax. These individuals must file Form 1040–ES (Estimated Tax for Individuals) and pay in quarterly installments the income tax and self-employment tax estimated to be due.

The income tax from the Tax Table or the Tax Rate Schedules is reduced first by the individual's tax credits. There is an important distinction between tax credits and tax deductions. Tax credits reduce the tax liability dollar-for-dollar. Tax deductions reduce taxable income on which the tax liability is based.

EXAMPLE 30

Gail is a taxpayer in the 25% tax bracket. As a result of incurring $1,000 in child care expenses (see Chapter 12 for details), she is entitled to a $200 child care credit ($1,000 child care expenses × 20% credit rate). She also contributed $1,000 to the American Cancer Society and included this amount in her itemized deductions. The child care credit results in a $200 reduction of Gail's tax liability for the year. The contribution to the American Cancer Society reduces taxable income by $1,000 and results in a $250 reduction in Gail's tax liability ($1,000 reduction in taxable income × 25% tax rate). ■

Tax credits are discussed in Chapter 12. The following are several of the more common credits:

- Earned income credit.
- Credit for child and dependent care expenses.
- Credit for the elderly.
- Foreign tax credit.
- Child tax credit.

EXAMPLE 31

Kelly, age 30, is a head of household with a disabled and dependent mother living with him. During 2005, Kelly had the following: taxable income, $30,000; income tax withheld, $3,250; estimated tax payments, $600; and credit for dependent care expenses, $200. Kelly's net tax payable is computed as follows:

Income tax (from 2005 Tax Rate Schedule, Appendix A)		$ 3,978
Less: Tax credits and prepayments—		
Credit for dependent care expenses	$ 200	
Income tax withheld	3,250	
Estimated tax payments	600	(4,050)
Net taxes payable (or refund due if negative)		$ (72)

LO.4

Identify and work with kiddie tax situations.

UNEARNED INCOME OF CHILDREN UNDER AGE 14 TAXED AT PARENTS' RATE

At one time, a dependent child could claim an exemption on his or her own return even if claimed as a dependent by the parents. This enabled a parent to shift investment income (such as interest and dividends) to a child by transferring ownership of the assets producing the income. The child would pay no tax on the income to the extent that it was sheltered by the child's exemption.

Also, an additional tax motivation existed for shifting income from parents to children. Although a child's unearned income in excess of the exemption amount was subject to tax, it was taxed at the child's rate, rather than the parents' rate.

To reduce the tax savings that result from shifting income from parents to children, the net **unearned income** (commonly called investment income) of certain minor children is taxed as if it were the parents' income.[34] Unearned income includes such income as taxable interest, dividends, capital gains, rents, royalties, pension and annuity income, and income (other than earned income) received as the beneficiary of a trust. This provision, commonly referred to as the **kiddie tax,** applies to any child for any taxable year if the child has not reached age 14 by the close of the taxable year, has at least one living parent, and has unearned income of more than $1,600. The *kiddie tax* provision does not apply to a child age 14 or older. However, the limitation on the use of the standard deduction and the unavailability of the personal exemption do apply to such a child as long as he or she is eligible to be claimed as a dependent by a parent.

Net Unearned Income. Net unearned income of a dependent child is computed as follows:

Unearned income

Less: $800

Less: The greater of

- $800 of the standard deduction *or*
- The amount of allowable itemized deductions directly connected with the production of the unearned income

Equals: Net unearned income

If net unearned income is zero (or negative), the child's tax is computed without using the parents' rate. If the amount of net unearned income (regardless of source) is positive, the net unearned income is taxed at the parents' rate. The $800 amounts in the preceding formula are subject to adjustment for inflation each year (refer to footnote 9).

[34] § 1(g).

Tax Determination. If a child under age 14 has net unearned income, there are two options for computing the tax on the income. A separate return may be filed for the child, or the parents may elect to report the child's income on their own return. If a separate return is filed for the child, the tax on net unearned income (referred to as the *allocable parental tax*) is computed as though the income had been included on the parents' return. Form 8615 is used to compute the tax. The steps required in this computation are illustrated below.

EXAMPLE 32

Olaf and Olga have a child, Hans (age 10). In 2005, Hans received $2,900 of interest income and paid investment-related fees of $200. Olaf and Olga had $70,000 of taxable income, not including their child's investment income. The parents have no qualified dividends or capital gains. Olaf and Olga do not make the parental election.

1. Determine Hans's net unearned income	
Gross income (unearned)	$ 2,900
Less: $800	(800)
Less: The greater of	
• $800 or	
• Investment expense ($200)	(800)
Equals: Net unearned income	$ 1,300
2. Determine allocable parental tax	
Parents' taxable income	$ 70,000
Plus: Hans's net unearned income	1,300
Equals: Revised taxable income	$ 71,300
Tax on revised taxable income	$ 11,155
Less: Tax on parents' taxable income	(10,830)
Allocable parental tax ($1,300 × 25%)	$ 325
3. Determine Hans's nonparental source tax	
Hans's AGI	$ 2,900
Less: Standard deduction	(800)
Less: Personal exemption	(–0–)
Equals: Taxable income	$ 2,100
Less: Net unearned income	(1,300)
Nonparental source taxable income	$ 800
Equals: Tax ($800 × 10% rate) rounded	$ 80
4. Determine Hans's total tax liability	
Nonparental source tax (step 3)	$ 80
Allocable parental tax (step 2)	325
Total tax	$ 405

■

Election to Claim Certain Unearned Income on Parent's Return. If a child under age 14 is required to file a tax return and meets all of the following requirements, the parent may elect to report the child's unearned income that exceeds $1,600 on the parent's own tax return:

- Gross income is from interest and dividends only.
- Gross income is more than $800 but less than $8,000.
- No estimated tax has been paid in the name and Social Security number of the child, and the child is not subject to backup withholding.

If the parental election is made, the child is treated as having no gross income and then is not required to file a tax return.

The parent(s) must also pay an additional tax equal to the smaller of $80 or 10 percent of the child's gross income over $800. Parents who have substantial itemized deductions based on AGI (see Chapter 10) may find that making the parental election increases total taxes for the family unit. Taxes should be calculated both with the parental election and without it to determine the appropriate choice.

Other Provisions. If parents have more than one child subject to the tax on net unearned income, the tax for the children is computed as shown in Example 32 and then allocated to the children based on their relative amounts of income. For children of divorced parents, the taxable income of the custodial parent is used to determine the allocable parental tax. This parent is the one who may elect to report the child's unearned income. For married individuals filing separate returns, the individual with the greater taxable income is the applicable parent.

LO.5

Recognize the filing requirements and the proper filing status.

Filing Considerations

Under the category of filing considerations, the following questions need to be resolved:

- Is the taxpayer required to file an income tax return?
- If so, which form should be used?
- When and how should the return be filed?
- In computing the tax liability, which column of the Tax Table or which Tax Rate Schedule should be used?

The first three questions are discussed under Filing Requirements, and the last is treated under Filing Status.

FILING REQUIREMENTS

General Rules. An individual must file a tax return if certain minimum amounts of gross income have been received. The general rule is that a tax return is required for every individual who has gross income that equals or exceeds the sum of the exemption amount plus the applicable standard deduction.[35] For example, a single taxpayer under age 65 must file a tax return in 2005 if gross income equals or exceeds $8,200 ($3,200 exemption plus $5,000 standard deduction). Table 3–4 lists the income levels[36] that require tax returns under the general rule and under certain special rules.

The additional standard deduction for being age 65 or older is considered in determining the gross income filing requirements. For example, note in Table 3–4 that the 2005 filing requirement for a single taxpayer age 65 or older is $9,450 ($5,000 basic standard deduction + $1,250 additional standard deduction + $3,200 exemption). However, the additional standard deduction for blindness is not taken into account. The 2005 filing requirement for a single taxpayer under age 65 and blind is $8,200 ($5,000 basic standard deduction + $3,200 exemption).

A self-employed individual with net earnings of $400 or more from a business or profession must file a tax return regardless of the amount of gross income.

[35] The gross income amounts for determining whether a tax return must be filed are adjusted for inflation each year.

[36] § 6012(a)(1).

TABLE 3-4
Filing Levels

Filing Status	2004 Gross Income	2005 Gross Income
Single		
Under 65 and not blind	$ 7,950	$ 8,200
Under 65 and blind	7,950	8,200
65 or older	9,150	9,450
Married, filing joint return		
Both spouses under 65 and neither blind	$15,900	$16,400
Both spouses under 65 and one or both spouses blind	15,900	16,400
One spouse 65 or older	16,850	17,400
Both spouses 65 or older	17,800	18,400
Married, filing separate return		
All—whether 65 or older or blind	$ 3,100	$ 3,200
Head of household		
Under 65 and not blind	$10,250	$10,500
Under 65 and blind	10,250	10,500
65 or older	11,450	11,750
Qualifying widow(er)		
Under 65 and not blind	$12,800	$13,200
Under 65 and blind	12,800	13,200
65 or older	13,750	14,200

Even though an individual has gross income below the filing level amounts and therefore does not owe any tax, he or she must file a return to obtain a tax refund of amounts withheld. A return is also necessary to obtain the benefits of the earned income credit allowed to taxpayers with little or no tax liability. Chapter 12 discusses the earned income credit.

Filing Requirements for Dependents. Computation of the gross income filing requirement for an individual who can be claimed as a dependent on another person's tax return is subject to more complex rules. Such an individual must file a return if he or she has *any* of the following:

- Earned income only and gross income that is more than the total standard deduction (including any additional standard deduction) that the individual is allowed for the year.
- Unearned income only and gross income of more than $800 plus any additional standard deduction that the individual is allowed for the year.
- Both earned and unearned income and gross income of more than the larger of $800 or the sum of earned income plus $250 (but limited to the applicable basic standard deduction), plus any additional standard deduction that the individual is allowed for the year.

Thus, the filing requirement for a dependent who has no unearned income is the total of the *basic* standard deduction plus any *additional* standard deduction, which includes both the additional deduction for blindness and the deduction for being age 65 or older. For example, the 2005 filing requirement for a single dependent who is under age 65 and not blind is $5,000, the amount of the basic standard deduction for 2005. The filing requirement for a single dependent under age 65 and blind is $6,250 ($5,000 basic standard deduction + $1,250 additional standard deduction).

Selecting the Proper Form. The 2005 tax forms had not been released at the date of publication of this text. The following comments apply to the 2004 forms. It is possible that some provisions will change for the 2005 forms.

Although a variety of forms are available to individual taxpayers, the use of some of these forms is restricted. For example, Form 1040EZ cannot be used if:

- Taxpayer claims any dependents;
- Taxpayer (or spouse) is 65 or older or blind; or
- Taxable income is $100,000 or more.

Taxpayers who desire to itemize deductions *from* AGI cannot use Form 1040A, but must file Form 1040 (the long form).

The E-File Approach. In addition to traditional paper returns, the **e-file** program is an increasingly popular alternative. Here, the required tax information is transmitted to the IRS electronically either directly from the taxpayer (i.e., an "e-file online return") or indirectly through an electronic return originator (ERO). EROs are tax professionals who have been accepted into the electronic filing program by the IRS. Such parties hold themselves out to the general public as "authorized IRS e-file providers." Providers often are also the preparers of the return.

For direct online e-filing, a taxpayer must have a personal computer and tax preparation software with the capability of conveying the information via modem to an electronic return transmitter. Otherwise a taxpayer must use an authorized provider who makes the e-file transmission. In most cases the provider charges a fee for the services rendered.

All taxpayers and tax return preparers must attest to the returns they file. For most taxpayers, this attesting can be done through an electronic return signature using a personal identification number (a Self-Select PIN). Information on establishing a Self-Select PIN can be found in the instructions to Form 1040, Form 1040A, or Form 1040EZ, or at **http://www.irs.gov/efile**. If certain paper documents must be submitted, a one-page form must be completed and filed when the return is e-filed. Form 8453 (U.S. Individual Income Tax Declaration for an IRS *e-file* Return) is the version required when a provider is used. A direct e-file online return requires the use of Form 8453–OL, which must be signed and filed by the taxpayer after the e-file return is accepted by the IRS.

The e-file approach has two major advantages. First, compliance with the format required by the IRS eliminates many errors that would otherwise occur. Second, the time required for processing a refund usually is reduced to three weeks or less.

When and Where to File. Tax returns of individuals are due on or before the fifteenth day of the fourth month following the close of the tax year. For the calendar year taxpayer, the usual filing date is on or before April 15 of the following year.[37] When the due date falls on a Saturday, Sunday, or legal holiday, the last day for filing falls on the next business day. If the return is mailed to the proper address with sufficient postage and is postmarked on or before the due date, it is deemed timely filed. The Code enables the IRS to prescribe rules governing the filing of returns using various private parcel delivery services (e.g., DHL, FedEx, UPS).[38]

If a taxpayer is unable to file the return by the specified due date, a four-month extension of time can be obtained by filing Form 4868 (Application for Automatic Extension of Time to File U.S. Individual Income Tax Return).[39] Further extensions may be granted by the IRS upon a showing of good cause by the taxpayer. For

[37] § 6072(a).
[38] § 7502(f).
[39] Reg. § 1.6081–4.

Special Rules for Certain Military Personnel

The Military Family Tax Relief Act of 2003 allows certain members of the military more time to file their Federal income tax return. If they are outside the United States and Puerto Rico *but not* in a combat zone, the filing date is extended to June 15. If additional taxes are due, however, interest still begins to accrue after April 15. For those deployed in a designated combat zone, the filing date is postponed until 180 days after the last day of combat service. Furthermore, in such cases, interest *does not* accrue during the deferral period. These filing dates are equally applicable when the military person is married and files a joint return.

this purpose, Form 2688 (Application for Extension of Time to File U.S. Individual Income Tax Return) should be used. An extension of more than six months will not be granted if the taxpayer is in the United States.

Although obtaining an extension excuses a taxpayer from a penalty for failure to file, it does not insulate against the penalty for failure to pay. If more tax is owed, the filing of Form 4868 should be accompanied by an additional remittance to cover the balance due. The failure to file and failure to pay penalties are discussed in Chapter 1.

The return should be sent or delivered to the Regional Service Center listed in the instructions for each type of return or contained in software applications.[40] Because of an IRS reorganization that began in October 2000 and is still ongoing, some taxpayers may be required to file at a different Service Center than in the past. Eventually, 8 of the 10 Service Centers will process all individual returns, and 2 will handle all business returns.

If an individual taxpayer needs to file an amended return (e.g., because of a failure to report income or to claim a deduction or tax credit), Form 1040X is filed. The form generally must be filed within three years of the filing date of the original return or within two years from the time the tax was paid, whichever is later.

Mode of Payment. Usually, payment is made by check. In that event, the check should be made out to "United States Treasury."

The IRS has approved the use of MasterCard, American Express, Discover, and Visa to pay Federal taxes. The use of a credit card to pay taxes will result in a charge against the cardholder by the credit card company.

FILING STATUS

The amount of tax will vary considerably depending on which Tax Rate Schedule is used. This is illustrated in the following example.

EXAMPLE 33

The following amounts of tax are computed using the 2005 Tax Rate Schedules for a taxpayer (or taxpayers in the case of a joint return) with $40,000 of taxable income (see Appendix A).

[40] The Regional Service Centers and the geographic area each covers can also be found at **http://www.irs.gov/file** or in tax forms packages.

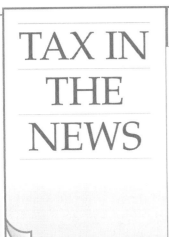

"Charge It"—Convenient But Not Cheap!

When a consumer uses a credit card to buy goods, the merchant pays a fee to the credit card company. When a credit card is used to pay income taxes, however, the law prevents the IRS from paying any such fee. Instead, the credit card company charges the user a "convenience fee" equal to 2.5 percent of the tax paid. The fee must be paid even if the user pays the credit card bill in full when it arrives. If, for example, John uses his Visa card to pay the $10,000 in taxes that he owes, he will be charged $250 (2.5% × $10,000) as a convenience fee. John will have to pay the $250 fee even if he pays Visa the $10,000 when billed. Furthermore, regular credit card interest (usually 15 percent or more) will be charged on extended time payments.

Clearly, then, using credit cards to pay income taxes, though convenient, is not without cost!

Filing Status	Amount of Tax
Single	$6,665
Married, filing joint return	5,270
Married, filing separate return	6,665
Head of household	5,498

■

Rates for Single Taxpayers. A taxpayer who is unmarried or separated from his or her spouse by a decree of divorce or separate maintenance and does not qualify for another filing status must use the rates for single taxpayers. Marital status is determined as of the last day of the tax year, except when a spouse dies during the year. In that case, marital status is determined as of the date of death. State law governs whether a taxpayer is considered married, divorced, or legally separated.

Under a special relief provision, however, married persons who live apart may be able to qualify as single. Married taxpayers who are considered single under the *abandoned spouse rules* are allowed to use the head-of-household rates. See the discussion of this filing status under Abandoned Spouse Rules later in the chapter.

Rates for Married Individuals. The joint return [Tax Rate Schedule Y, Code § 1(a)] was originally enacted in 1948 to establish equity between married taxpayers in common law states and those in community property states. Before the joint return rates were enacted, taxpayers in community property states were in an advantageous position relative to taxpayers in common law states because they could split their income. For instance, if one spouse earned $100,000 and the other spouse was not employed, each spouse could report $50,000 of income. Splitting the income in this manner caused the total income to be subject to lower marginal tax rates. Each spouse would start at the bottom of the rate structure.

Taxpayers in common law states did not have this income-splitting option, so their taxable income was subject to higher marginal rates. This inconsistency in treatment was remedied by the joint return provisions. The progressive rates in the joint return Tax Rate Schedule are constructed based on the assumption that income is earned equally by the two spouses.

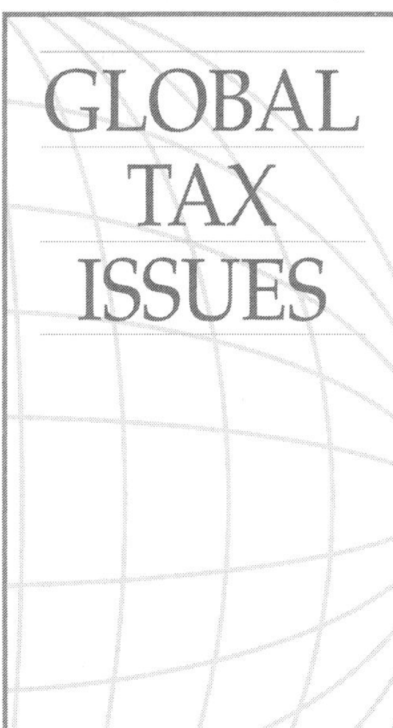

Filing a Joint Return

John Garth is a U.S. citizen and resident, but he spends a lot of time in London where his employer sends him on frequent assignments. John is married to Victoria, a citizen and resident of the United Kingdom.

Can John and Victoria file a joint return for U.S. Federal income tax purposes? Although § 6013(a)(1) specifically precludes the filing of a joint return if one spouse is a nonresident alien, another Code provision permits an exception. Under § 6013(g), the parties can elect to treat the nonqualifying spouse as a "resident" of the United States. This election would allow John and Victoria to file jointly.

But should John and Victoria make this election? If Victoria has considerable income of her own (from non-U.S. sources), the election could be ill-advised. As a nonresident alien, Victoria's non-U.S. source income *would not* be subject to the U.S. income tax. If she is treated as a U.S. resident, however, her non-U.S. source income *will be subject to U.S. tax*. Under the U.S. global approach to taxation, all income (regardless of where earned) of anyone who is a *resident* or *citizen* of the United States is subject to tax.

If married individuals elect to file separate returns, each reports only his or her own income, exemptions, deductions, and credits, and each must use the Tax Rate Schedule applicable to married taxpayers filing separately. It is generally advantageous for married individuals to file a joint return, since the combined amount of tax is lower. However, special circumstances (e.g., significant medical expenses incurred by one spouse subject to the 7.5 percent limitation) may warrant the election to file separate returns. It may be necessary to compute the tax under both assumptions to determine the most advantageous filing status.

When Congress enacted the rate structure available to those filing joint returns, it intended to favor married taxpayers. In certain situations, however, the parties would incur less tax if they were not married and filed separate returns. The additional tax that a joint return caused, commonly called the **marriage penalty,** usually developed when *both* spouses had larger taxable incomes. Long aware of the inequity of the marriage penalty, Congress reduced the effect of the problem in JGTRRA of 2003. Beginning in 2003, the standard deduction available to married filers increases to 200 percent of that applicable to single persons. Furthermore and also beginning in 2003, the 15 percent bracket for joint filers increases to 200 percent of the size of that applicable to single filers.

Although changes in the tax rates and the standard deduction have reduced the marriage penalty, the Code places some limitations on married persons who file separate returns. Some examples of these limitations are listed below.

- If either spouse itemizes deductions, the other spouse must also itemize.
- The earned income credit and the credit for child and dependent care expenses cannot be claimed (see Chapter 12).
- The special deduction for qualified tuition expenses cannot be claimed (see Chapter 9).
- Only $1,500 of excess capital losses can be claimed (see Chapter 14).

In such cases, being single would be preferable to being married and filing separately.

The joint return rates also apply for two years following the death of one spouse, if the surviving spouse maintains a household for a dependent child. This is referred to as **surviving spouse** status.[41]

EXAMPLE 34

Fred dies in 2004 leaving Ethel with a dependent child. For the year of Fred's death (2004), Ethel files a joint return with Fred (presuming the consent of Fred's executor is obtained). For the next two years (2005 and 2006), Ethel, as a surviving spouse, may use the joint return rates. In subsequent years, Ethel may use the head-of-household rates if she continues to maintain a household as her home that is the domicile of the child. ■

Keep in mind, however, that for the year of death, the surviving spouse is treated as being married. Thus, a joint return can be filed if the deceased spouse's executor agrees. If not, the surviving spouse is forced into the status of married filing separately.

Rates for Heads of Household. Unmarried individuals who maintain a household for a dependent (or dependents) are entitled to use the **head-of-household** rates.[42] The tax liability using the head-of-household rates falls between the liability using the joint return Tax Rate Schedule and the liability using the Tax Rate Schedule for single taxpayers.

To qualify for head-of-household rates, a taxpayer must pay more than half the cost of maintaining a household as his or her home. The household must also be the principal home of a dependent. Except for temporary absences (e.g., school, hospitalization), the dependent must live in the taxpayer's household for over half the year.

For tax years after 2004, a dependent must satisfy either the qualifying child or the qualifying relative category. For head-of-household purposes, a qualifying relative must also meet the relationship test.[43]

EXAMPLE 35

Dylan is single and maintains a household in which he and his cousin live. Even though the cousin may qualify as a dependent (under the member-of-the-household test), Dylan cannot claim head-of-household filing status. A cousin does not meet the relationship test. ■

EXAMPLE 36

Emma, a widow, maintains a household in which she and her aunt live. If the aunt qualifies as a dependent, Emma may file as head of household. Note that an aunt meets the relationship test. ■

For pre-2005 tax years, an exception existed to the dependent requirement for head-of-household filing status. An *unmarried child* did not have to qualify as a dependent.

EXAMPLE 37

Nancy maintains a household in which she and her daughter, Bernice, live. Bernice, age 27, is single and earns $9,000 from a part-time job. For tax years prior to 2005, Nancy qualifies for head-of-household filing status. However, she cannot claim Bernice as a dependent due to the gross income test.[44] ■

A special rule allows taxpayers to avoid having to live with their parents. Head-of-household status still may be claimed if the taxpayer maintains a *separate home* for his or her *parent or parents* if at least one parent qualifies as a dependent of the taxpayer.[45]

---

[41] § 2(a). The IRS label for surviving spouse status is "Qualifying Widow(er) with Dependent Child."

[42] § 2(b).

[43] § 2(b)(3)(B).

[44] Could Bernice be a dependent under the new qualifying child rules? Even though the gross income test is inapplicable for a qualifying child, Bernice does not meet the age test.

[45] § 2(b)(1)(B).

EXAMPLE 38

Rick, an unmarried individual, lives in New York City and maintains a household in Detroit for his dependent parents. Rick may use the head-of-household rates even though his parents do not reside in his New York home. ■

Head-of-household status is not changed during the year by the death of the dependent. As long as the taxpayer provided more than half of the cost of maintaining the household prior to the dependent's death, head-of-household status is preserved.

ETHICAL CONSIDERATIONS

The Hidden Benefits of Taking Care of a Relative

For several years, Chester, a widower, has maintained a household in which he and his aunt, Heloise, live. As the aunt has no income, Chester claims her as his dependent. In early June 2004, Heloise is admitted to a medical facility for treatment of a mental disorder. In January 2005, Heloise unexpectedly dies while still at the facility.

In completing his Federal income tax return for both 2004 and 2005, Chester intends to file as head of household and to claim Heloise as his dependent. Comment on the propriety of what Chester plans to do.

Abandoned Spouse Rules. When married persons file separate returns, several unfavorable tax consequences result. For example, the taxpayer must use the Tax Rate Schedule for married taxpayers filing separately. To mitigate such harsh treatment, Congress enacted provisions commonly referred to as the **abandoned spouse** rules. These rules allow a married taxpayer to file as a head of household if all of the following conditions are satisfied:

- The taxpayer does not file a joint return.
- The taxpayer paid more than one-half the cost of maintaining his or her home for the tax year.
- The taxpayer's spouse did not live in the home during the last six months of the tax year.
- The home was the principal residence of the taxpayer's child, stepchild, or adopted child for more than half the year.
- The taxpayer could claim the child, stepchild, or adopted child as a dependent.[46]

LO.6

Possess an overview of property transactions.

Gains and Losses from Property Transactions—In General

Gains and losses from property transactions are discussed in detail in Chapters 13 and 14. Because of their importance in the tax system, however, they are introduced briefly at this point.

When property is sold or otherwise disposed of, gain or loss may result. Such gain or loss has an effect on the income tax position of the party making the sale or other disposition when the *realized* gain or loss is *recognized* for tax purposes.

[46]The dependency requirement does not apply, however, if the taxpayer could have claimed a dependency exemption except for the fact that the exemption was claimed by the noncustodial parent under a written agreement. Refer to Example 17 and the related discussion.

Without realized gain or loss, there generally can be no recognized gain or loss. The concept of realized gain or loss is expressed as follows:

$$\text{Amount realized from the sale} - \text{Adjusted basis of the property} = \text{Realized gain (or loss)}$$

The amount realized is the selling price of the property less any costs of disposition (e.g., brokerage commissions) incurred by the seller. The adjusted basis of the property is determined as follows:

Cost (or other original basis) at date of acquisition[47]	
Add:	Capital additions
Subtract:	Depreciation (if appropriate) and other capital recoveries (see Chapter 8)
Equals:	Adjusted basis at date of sale or other disposition

All realized gains are recognized (taxable) unless some specific part of the tax law provides otherwise (see Chapter 13 dealing with certain nontaxable exchanges). Realized losses may or may not be recognized (deductible) for tax purposes, depending on the circumstances involved. Generally, losses realized from the disposition of personal use property (property neither held for investment nor used in a trade or business) are not recognized.

EXAMPLE 39

During the current year, Ted sells his sailboat (adjusted basis of $4,000) for $5,500. Ted also sells one of his personal automobiles (adjusted basis of $8,000) for $5,000. Ted's realized gain of $1,500 from the sale of the sailboat is recognized. On the other hand, the $3,000 realized loss on the sale of the automobile is not recognized and will not provide Ted with any deductible tax benefit. ■

Once it has been determined that the disposition of property results in a recognized gain or loss, the next step is to classify the gain or loss as capital or ordinary. Although ordinary gain is fully taxable and ordinary loss is fully deductible, the same may not hold true for capital gains and capital losses.

Gains and Losses from Property Transactions—Capital Gains and Losses

To obtain a good perspective on how the Federal income tax functions, some overview of property transactions is needed. This is particularly the case with capital gains and losses, which can generate unique tax consequences. For in-depth treatment of property transactions (including capital gains and losses), refer to Chapters 13 and 14. For now, the overview appearing below should suffice.

DEFINITION OF A CAPITAL ASSET

Capital assets are defined in the Code as any property held by the taxpayer *other than* property listed in § 1221. The list in § 1221 includes inventory, accounts receivable, and depreciable property or real estate used in a business. Thus, the sale or exchange of assets in these categories usually results in ordinary income or loss treatment (see Chapter 14).

[47]Cost usually means purchase price plus expenses related to the acquisition of the property and incurred by the purchaser (e.g., brokerage commissions). For the basis of property acquired by gift or inheritance and other basis rules, see Chapter 13.

EXAMPLE 40

Kelly owns a pizza parlor. During the current year, he sells two automobiles. The first automobile, which had been used as a pizza delivery car for three years, was sold at a loss of $1,000. Because this automobile is an asset used in his business, Kelly has an ordinary loss deduction of $1,000, rather than a capital loss deduction. The second automobile, which Kelly had owned for two years, was his personal use car. It was sold for a gain of $800. The personal use car is a capital asset. Therefore, Kelly has a capital gain of $800. ■

The principal capital assets held by an individual taxpayer include assets held for personal (rather than business) use, such as a personal residence or an automobile, and assets held for investment purposes (e.g., corporate securities and land). Capital assets generally include collectibles, which are subject to somewhat unique tax treatment. **Collectibles** include art, antiques, gems, metals, stamps, some coins and bullion, and alcoholic beverages that are held as investments.

TAXATION OF NET CAPITAL GAIN

In 2005, net capital gains are classified and taxed as follows:

Classification	Maximum Rate
Short-term gains (held for one year or less)	35%
Long-term gains (held for more than one year)—	
Collectibles	28%
Certain depreciable property used in a trade or business (known as unrecaptured § 1250 gain and discussed in Chapter 14)	25%
All other long-term capital gains	15% or 5%

The special tax rate applicable to long-term capital gains is called the alternative tax computation. It is to be used only if the taxpayer's regular tax rate *exceeds* the applicable alternative tax rate. In the case of the 15 percent classification (see above), the applicable alternative tax rate is 5 percent if the taxpayer's regular tax bracket is 15 percent.[48]

EXAMPLE 41

During the year, Polly is in the 15% tax bracket and has the following capital gains for the year:

Robin Corporation stock (held for 6 months)	$1,000
Crow Corporation stock (held for 13 months)	1,000

Polly's tax on these transactions is $150 ($1,000 × 15%) as to Robin and $50 ($1,000 × 5%) as to Crow. ■

EXAMPLE 42

Assume the same facts as in Example 41, except that Polly's regular tax bracket for the year is 28% (not 15%). Polly's tax on these transactions now becomes $280 ($1,000 × 28%) as to Robin and $150 ($1,000 × 15%) as to Crow. ■

DETERMINATION OF NET CAPITAL GAIN

In order to arrive at a net capital gain, capital losses must be taken into account. The capital losses are aggregated by holding period (short term and long term) and applied against the gains in that category. If excess losses result, they are then

[48] § 1(h)(1) as amended by JGTRRA of 2003. For recognized gains prior to May 6, 2003, the maximum rates were 20% and 10%.

shifted to the category carrying the *highest* tax rate. A *net capital gain* will occur if the net long-term capital gain (NLTCG) exceeds the net short-term capital loss (NSTCL).

EXAMPLE 43

In the current year, Colin is in the 35% tax bracket and has the following capital transactions:

Penguin Corporation stock (held for 8 months)	$ 1,000
Owl Corporation stock (held for 10 months)	(3,000)
Stamp collection (held for 5 years)	2,000
Land (held as an investment for 3 years)	4,000

The Penguin Corporation short-term capital gain (STCG) of $1,000 is offset by the Owl Corporation short-term capital loss (STCL) of $3,000. The net STCL of $2,000 is then applied against the collectible gain of $2,000. The end result is a net long-term capital gain of $4,000 from the land sale. Colin's net capital gain is taxed at a 15% rate. Note that the stamp collection gain would have been taxed at a higher 28% rate had it not been offset by the excess short-term capital loss. ■

TREATMENT OF NET CAPITAL LOSS

For individual taxpayers, net capital loss can be used to offset ordinary income of up to $3,000 ($1,500 for married persons filing separate returns). If a taxpayer has both short- and long-term capital losses, the short-term category is used first to arrive at the $3,000. Any remaining net capital loss is carried over indefinitely until exhausted. When carried over, the excess capital loss retains its classification as short or long term.

EXAMPLE 44

In 2005, Tina has a short-term capital loss of $2,000, a long-term capital loss of $2,500, and no capital gains. She can deduct $3,000 ($2,000 short-term + $1,000 long-term) of this amount as an ordinary loss. The remaining $1,500 is carried over to 2006 as a long-term capital loss. ■

LO.7

Identify tax planning opportunities associated with the individual tax formula.

Tax Planning Considerations

TAKING ADVANTAGE OF TAX RATE DIFFERENTIALS

It is natural for taxpayers to be concerned about the tax rates they are paying. How does a tax practitioner communicate information about rates to clients? There are several possibilities.

The marginal rate (refer to Examples 27 through 29) provides information that can help a taxpayer evaluate a particular course of action or structure a transaction in the most advantageous manner. For example, a taxpayer who is in the 15 percent bracket this year and expects to be in the 28 percent bracket next year should, if possible, defer payment of deductible expenses until next year to maximize the tax benefit of the deduction.

A note of caution is in order with respect to shifting income and expenses between years. Congress has recognized the tax planning possibilities of such shifting and has enacted many provisions to limit a taxpayer's ability to do so. Some of these limitations on the shifting of income are discussed in Chapters 4, 5, and 16. Limitations that affect a taxpayer's ability to shift deductions are discussed in Chapters 6 through 11 and in Chapter 16.

A taxpayer's *effective rate* can be an informative measure of the effectiveness of tax planning. The effective rate is computed by dividing the taxpayer's tax liability by the total amount of income. A low effective rate can be considered an indication of effective tax planning.

One way of lowering the effective rate is to exclude income from the tax base. For example, a taxpayer might consider investing in tax-free municipal bonds rather than taxable corporate bonds. Although pre-tax income from corporate bonds is usually higher, after-tax income may be higher if the taxpayer invests in tax-free municipals.

Another way of lowering the effective rate is to make sure that the taxpayer's expenses and losses are deductible. For example, losses on investments in passive activities may not be deductible (see Chapter 11). Therefore, a taxpayer who plans to invest in an activity that will produce a loss in the early years should take steps to ensure that the business is treated as active rather than passive. Active losses are deductible while passive losses are not.

INCOME OF MINOR CHILDREN

Taxpayers can use several strategies to avoid or minimize the effect of the rules that tax the unearned income of certain minor children at the parents' rate. The kiddie tax rules do not apply once a child reaches age 14. Parents should consider giving a younger child assets that defer taxable income until the child reaches age 14. For example, U.S. government Series EE savings bonds can be used to defer income until the bonds are cashed in (see Chapter 4).

Growth stocks typically pay little in the way of dividends. However, the profit on an astute investment may more than offset the lack of dividends. The child can hold the stock until he or she reaches age 14. If the stock is sold then at a profit, the profit is taxed at the child's low rates.

Taxpayers in a position to do so can employ their children in their business and pay them a reasonable wage for the work they actually perform (e.g., light office help, such as filing). The child's earned income is sheltered by the standard deduction, and the parents' business is allowed a deduction for the wages. The kiddie tax rules have no effect on earned income, even if it is earned from the parents' business.

DEPENDENCY EXEMPTIONS

The Joint Return Test. A married person can be claimed as a dependent only if that individual does not file a joint return with his or her spouse. If a joint return has been filed, the damage may be undone if separate returns are substituted on a timely basis (on or before the due date of the return).

EXAMPLE 45

While preparing a client's 2004 income tax return on April 8, 2005, the tax practitioner discovered that the client's daughter filed a joint return with her husband in late January of 2005. Presuming the daughter otherwise qualifies as the client's dependent, the exemption is not lost if she and her husband file separate returns on or before April 15, 2005. ■

An initial election to file a joint return must be considered carefully in any situation in which the taxpayers might later decide to amend their return and file separately. As indicated above, separate returns may be substituted for a joint return only if the amended returns are filed on or before the normal due date of the return. If the taxpayers in Example 45 attempt to file separate returns after April 15, 2005, the returns will not be accepted, and the joint return election is binding.[49]

Keep in mind that the filing of a joint return is not fatal to the dependency exemption if the parties are filing solely to recover all income tax withholdings, they are not required to file a return, and no tax liability would exist on separate returns.

Support Considerations. The support of a qualifying child becomes relevant only if the child is self-supporting. In cases where the child has an independent source of funds, planning could help prevent an undesirable result. When a qualifying relative is involved, meeting the support test is essential, as the dependency exemption is not otherwise available.

[49]Reg. § 1.6013–1(a)(1).

EXAMPLE 46

In 2005, Imogene maintains a household that she shares with her son and mother. The son, Barry, is 23 years of age and a full-time student in law school. The mother, Gladys, is 68 years of age and active in charitable causes. Barry works part-time for a local law firm, while Gladys has income from investments. In resolving the support issue (or self-support in the case of Barry), compare Imogene's contribution with that made by Barry and Gladys.[50] In this connection, what Barry and Gladys do with their funds becomes crucial. The funds that are used for nonsupport purposes (e.g., purchase of investments) or not used at all (e.g., deposited in a bank) should not be considered. To the extent possible, control how much Barry and Gladys contribute to their own support. Records should be maintained showing the amount of support and its source. ■

Example 46 does not mention the possible application of the gross income test. Presuming Barry is a qualifying child, the amount he earns does not matter, as the gross income test does not apply. Gladys, however, comes under the qualifying relative category, where the gross income test applies. Therefore, for her to be claimed as a dependent, her income that is taxable will have to be less than $3,200.

Community Property Ramifications. In certain cases, state law can have an effect on the availability of a dependency exemption.

EXAMPLE 47

In 2005, Mitch provides more than half of the support of his son, Ross, and daughter-in-law, Connie, who live with him. Ross, age 22, is a full-time student, while Connie earns $4,000 from a part-time job. Ross and Connie do not file a joint return. All parties live in New York, a common law state. Mitch can claim Ross as a dependent, as he is a qualifying child. Connie is not a dependent because she does not meet the gross income test under the qualifying relative category. ■

EXAMPLE 48

Assume the same facts as in Example 47, except that all parties live in Arizona, a community property state. Now, Connie also qualifies as a dependent. Since Connie's gross income is only $2,000 (one-half of the community income), she satisfies the gross income test. ■

Relationship to the Deduction for Medical Expenses. Generally, medical expenses are deductible only if they are paid on behalf of the taxpayer, his or her spouse, and their dependents. Since deductibility may rest on dependency status, planning is important in arranging multiple support agreements.

EXAMPLE 49

During the year, Zelda will be supported by her two sons (Vern and Vito) and her daughter (Maria). Each will furnish approximately one-third of the required support. If the parties decide that the dependency exemption should be claimed by the daughter under a multiple support agreement, any medical expenses incurred by Zelda should be paid by Maria. ■

In planning a multiple support agreement, take into account which of the parties is most likely to exceed the 7.5 percent limitation (see Chapter 10). In Example 49, for instance, Maria might be a poor choice if she and her family do not expect to incur many medical and drug expenses of their own.

One exception permits the deduction of medical expenses paid on behalf of someone who is not a spouse or a dependent. If the person could be claimed as a dependent *except* for the gross income or joint return test, the medical expenses are, nevertheless, deductible. For additional discussion, see Chapter 10.

---

[50] As part of her support contribution to Barry and Gladys, Imogene can count the fair market value of the meals and lodging she provides.

ETHICAL CONSIDERATIONS — Nondependents Can Provide Tax Benefits

For tax year 2005, Alexis provided more than half of the support of her parents who do not live with her. She cannot claim them as her dependents because they have too much gross income and file a joint return. Nevertheless, she pays $15,000 for her father's dental implants and $18,000 for her mother's hip replacement. From a tax standpoint, has Alexis acted wisely? Explain.

KEY TERMS

Abandoned spouse, 3–31
Child tax credit, 3–18
Collectibles, 3–33
Dependency exemption, 3–11
e-file, 3–26
Head of household, 3–30
Itemized deductions, 3–6
Kiddie tax, 3–22
Marriage penalty, 3–29
Multiple support agreement, 3–12
Personal exemption, 3–10
Qualifying child, 3–15
Qualifying relative, 3–16
Standard deduction, 3–6
Surviving spouse, 3–30
Tax Rate Schedules, 3–19
Tax Table, 3–19
Unearned income, 3–22

PROBLEM MATERIALS

Discussion Questions

1. Rearrange the following items to show the correct formula for arriving at *taxable income* of individuals under the Federal income tax:
   a. Taxable income.
   b. Income (broadly conceived).
   c. Adjusted gross income.
   d. Deductions *for* AGI.
   e. Child tax credit.
   f. The greater of the standard deduction or itemized deductions.
   g. Personal and dependency exemptions.
   h. Gross income.
   i. Exclusions.

2. During the year, a taxpayer had the following transactions: borrowed money from a bank, received repayment of a loan made to a relative several years ago, recovered a rent deposit made on an apartment recently vacated, and sold a personal automobile for a loss. Discuss the income tax ramifications of each of these transactions.

3. Which of the following are *exclusions* from gross income?
   a. Interest received from City of Seattle bonds.
   b. Workers' compensation benefits received due to job injury.
   c. Alimony received from ex-spouse.
   d. Reward received for furnishing information that led to the arrest of an arsonist.
   e. "Gift" received by justice of the peace for dismissing a traffic violation.
   f. Inheritance received upon death of uncle.

4. Which of the following items are *inclusions* in gross income?
   a. Child support received from ex-spouse.
   b. Interest received from General Electric bonds.
   c. Damages awarded due to personal injury resulting from an automobile accident.

d. Plasma TV set received for being the tenth caller in a contest sponsored by a local radio station.
e. Value of meals and lodging received by an employee while working on an oil rig in the Gulf of Mexico.
f. A cash honorarium received by a former U.S. senator for giving a college commencement address.

5. Does a U.S. citizen who works abroad run the risk of "double taxation"? Why or why not?

6. During the year, a taxpayer made a contribution to a traditional IRA and had a large personal casualty loss not covered by insurance.
   a. Does the IRA contribution have any effect on the deductibility of the casualty loss? Explain.
   b. Would it matter if the taxpayer claimed the standard deduction?

Issue ID

7. The Andersons retain you to compute their tax liability for 2005. They are expecting to pay less tax than usual for several reasons. First, both became 65 during the year. Second, they paid significant medical and dental bills that were not covered by insurance. Are the Andersons' expectations correct? Explain.

8. Christopher, a widower, is claimed as a dependent by his adult daughter. With regard to Christopher's own income tax status, comment on the possible relevance of the following:
   a. Availability of a personal exemption.
   b. $800 and $250.
   c. Earned and unearned income.
   d. Additional standard deduction.

9. In terms of meeting the requirements of a multiple support agreement, discuss the relevance of the following:
   a. Meeting the other dependency tests besides support.
   b. The percentage of support provided.
   c. Form 2120.

10. Which of the following satisfy the definition of a qualifying child? [Assume the joint return and citizenship tests are met.]
    a. Taxpayer lives alone but maintains a household that includes a 17-year-old grandson.
    b. Taxpayer's household includes a 16-year-old niece.
    c. Taxpayer's household includes a 23-year-old stepdaughter who is disabled.
    d. Taxpayer's household includes a 20-year-old nephew who is a full-time student.
    e. Taxpayer's household includes a 22-year-old son-in-law who is a full-time student.
    f. Taxpayer's household includes an 18-year-old cousin.

11. As to the dependency exemption rules applicable after 2004, contrast the following for the qualifying child and qualifying relative categories:
    a. Relationship test.
    b. Gross income test.
    c. Joint return test.
    d. Support test.
    e. Age test.
    f. Domicile test.

Issue ID

12. For years 2005 and 2006, Trevor provides more than half of the support of his ex-wife, Carrie, her mother, Adriana, and his brother-in-law, Hector. Trevor and Carrie were divorced in 2005, but for financial reasons, they continue to share the same house. Adriana lives with Hector in another city.
    a. How many dependency exemptions may Trevor claim for 2005?
    b. How many dependency exemptions may Trevor claim for 2006?
    c. If your answers in (a) and (b) are different, explain why.
    d. What circumstances might change your answer to (b)?

Issue ID

13. Roberto, who is single, is a U.S. citizen and resident. He provides almost all of the support of his parents and two aunts, who are citizens and residents of Guatemala.

Roberto's parents and aunts are seriously considering moving to and becoming residents of Mexico. Would such a move have any impact on Roberto? Why or why not?

14. What are stealth taxes?
    a. What purpose do they serve, and why are they used?
    b. Is there any hope of relief from this form of taxation?

15. Concerning income tax rates, comment on the following:
    a. Pre-2001 rates.
    b. Scheduled reductions from 2001 to 2006.
    c. Impact of JGTRRA of 2003.
    d. Sunset provision and post-2010.
    e. Adam Smith and his canon of certainty.

16. Regarding the kiddie tax, comment on the following:
    a. Minor is 14 years old.
    b. Unearned income of the minor is $1,600.
    c. Parental election as to minor's unearned income.

17. A single individual age 65 or over and blind is required to file a Federal income tax return in 2005 if he or she has gross income of $9,450 or more (refer to Table 3–4).
    a. Explain how the $9,450 filing requirement was computed.
    b. In general, explain the effect of the additional standard deduction on the determination of the gross income requirement for filing.

18. In 2005, Ginger's husband dies. Ginger plans to file as a surviving spouse for tax years 2005 through 2007. Ginger's only dependent is her mother, who lives with her. Comment on any misconceptions Ginger may have regarding the tax law.

19. Comment on the availability of head-of-household filing status for 2005 in each of the following situations:
    a. Taxpayer lives alone but maintains the household of his parents, only one of whom qualifies as his dependent.
    b. Taxpayer, a single parent, maintains a home in which she and her unmarried son live. The son, age 18, earns $4,000 from a part-time job.
    c. Assume the same facts as in (b) except that the son is age 20, not 18.
    d. Taxpayer lives alone but maintains the household where her dependent daughter lives.

20. Florence's husband died in 2002. During 2005, Florence maintains a household in which she and her son, Derrick, live. Determine Florence's filing status for 2005 based on the following independent variables:
    a. Derrick is single and does not qualify as Florence's dependent.
    b. Derrick is married and does not qualify as Florence's dependent.
    c. Derrick is married and does qualify as Florence's dependent.
    d. Would any of the previous answers change if Florence's husband died in 2003 (not 2002)? Explain.

Issue ID

21. Several years ago, after a particularly fierce argument, Fran's husband moved out and has not been heard from or seen since. Because Fran cannot locate her husband, she has been using "married, filing separate" status when filing her income tax return. Comment on Fran's status.

22. During the year, Milton sold the following items: a recreational vehicle (RV) for a $6,000 loss; unimproved land for a $10,000 gain; and a sailboat for a $1,000 gain. The RV and sailboat were personal use assets, while the land was held as an investment. How are these transactions handled for income tax purposes?

23. As soon as Kaitlyn learned about the new lower rates provided by JGTRRA of 2003, she sold her stamp collection for a $15,000 gain. Comment on Kaitlyn's tax situation if she is in the
    a. 33% tax bracket.
    b. 15% tax bracket.

24. For 2005, Arlene's only capital transactions are a short-term loss of $2,000 and a long-term loss of $2,000. How are these losses handled for tax purposes?

25. What are collectibles?
    a. How is the sale of collectibles handled for tax purposes?
    b. In connection with (a), would it matter if the collectible had been held for more than one year? For one year or less?

Issue ID

26. Marcie is divorced, and her married son, Jamie (age 25), and his wife, Audry (age 18), live with her. During 2005, Jamie earned $3,500 from a part-time job and filed a joint return with Audry to recover his withholdings. Audry has no income. Marcie can prove that she provided more than 50% of Jamie and Audry's support. Marcie does not plan to claim Jamie as a dependent because he has too much gross income. She does not plan to claim Audry as a dependent because Audry signed the joint return with Jamie. In fact, Marcie plans to use single filing status as none of the persons living in her household qualifies as her dependent. Comment on Marcie's intentions based on the following assumptions:
    a. All parties live in Indiana (a common law state).
    b. All parties live in California (a community property state).

Decision Making

27. Erica and her two brothers equally furnish all of the support of their mother. Erica is married and has four children. Her brothers are single and claim the standard deduction. Erica's mother is not in good health. What suggestions can you make regarding the tax position of the parties?

Problems

28. Compute the taxable income for 2005 in each of the following independent situations:
    a. Sidney and Cora, ages 39 and 37, are married and file a joint return. In addition to two dependent children, they have AGI of $55,000 and itemized deductions of $8,300.
    b. Kay, age 66, is unmarried and supports her two dependent parents who live in their own home. She has AGI of $70,000 and itemized deductions of $8,100.
    c. Colin, age 60, is an abandoned spouse. The household he maintains includes two unmarried stepdaughters, ages 16 and 17, who qualify as his dependents. He has AGI of $81,000 and itemized deductions of $7,900.
    d. Angel, age 33, is a surviving spouse and maintains a household for her four dependent children. She has AGI of $48,000 and itemized deductions of $8,200.
    e. Dale, age 42, is divorced but maintains the home in which he and his daughter, Jill, live. Jill is single and qualifies as Dale's dependent. Dale has AGI of $54,000 and itemized deductions of $6,900.

Note: Problems 29 and 30 can be solved by referring to Figure 3–1, Exhibits 3–1 through 3–3, Tables 3–1 and 3–2, and the discussion under Deductions for Adjusted Gross Income in this chapter.

29. Compute the taxable income for 2005 for Quincy on the basis of the following information. His filing status is head of household.

Salary	$40,000
Interest income from bonds issued by General Motors Corporation	1,200
Child support payments made	3,600
Alimony payments made	2,400
Contribution to traditional IRA	4,000
Gift from grandparents	30,000
Capital loss from stock investment	4,000
Amount won in football office pool (sports gambling is against the law where Quincy lives)	3,200
Number of dependents (parents, ages 66 and 68)	2
Age	40

30. Compute the taxable income for 2005 for Vivian on the basis of the following information. Her filing status is head of household.

Salary	$70,000
Interest on City of Chicago bonds	2,000
Insurance proceeds (Vivian was the named beneficiary of her uncle's life insurance)	50,000
Damages awarded for personal injuries Vivian suffered when she was struck by a delivery truck	90,000
Cash prize won from a radio call-in contest	5,000
Interest on home mortgage	4,800
Property taxes on personal residence	3,600
Number of dependents (children, ages 12, 14, and 16)	3
Age	42

31. Determine the amount of the standard deduction allowed for 2005 in the following independent situations. In each case, assume the taxpayer is claimed as another person's dependent.
    a. Hollis, age 17, has income as follows: $500 interest from a certificate of deposit and $4,800 from repairing cars.
    b. Sheila, age 18, has income as follows: $400 cash dividends from a stock investment and $3,300 from handling a paper route.
    c. Ernest, age 15, has income as follows: $1,200 interest on a bank savings account and $400 for painting a neighbor's fence.
    d. Viola, age 15, has income as follows: $300 cash dividends from a stock investment and $600 from grooming pets.
    e. Molly, age 66 and a widow, has income as follows: $900 from a bank savings account and $1,800 from baby-sitting.

32. For tax year 2005, determine the number of personal and dependency exemptions in each of the following independent situations:
    a. Leo and Amanda (ages 48 and 46) are husband and wife and furnish more than 50% of the support of their two children, Elton (age 18) and Trista (age 24). During the year, Elton earns $4,500 providing transportation for elderly persons with disabilities, and Trista receives a $5,000 scholarship for tuition at the law school she attends.
    b. Audry (age 65) is divorced and lives alone. She maintains a household in which her ex-husband, Clint, and his mother, Olive, live and furnishes more than 50% of their support. Olive is age 82 and blind.
    c. Jacque (age 52) furnishes more than 50% of the support of his married daughter, Carin, and her husband, Pierce, who live with him. Both Carin and Pierce are age 18. During the year, Pierce earned $4,000 from a part-time job. All parties live in New York (a common law state).
    d. Assume the same facts as in (c), except that all parties live in Nevada (a community property state).

33. Compute the number of personal and dependency exemptions in each of the following independent situations:
    a. Alberto, a U.S. citizen and resident, contributes 100% of the support of his parents who are citizens of Mexico and live there.
    b. Pablo, a U.S. citizen and resident, contributes 100% of the support of his parents who are citizens of Guatemala. Pablo's father is a resident of Guatemala, and his mother is a legal resident of the United States.
    c. Marlena, a U.S. citizen and resident, contributes 100% of the support of her parents who are also U.S. citizens but are residents of Germany.

34. Under the rules applicable after 2004, determine how many dependency exemptions would be available in each of the following independent situations. Specify whether any such exemptions would come under the qualifying child or the qualifying relative category.

a. Richard maintains a household that includes a cousin (age 12), a niece (age 18), and a son (age 20). The cousin and niece are full-time students, and the son is unemployed. Richard furnishes all of their support.
b. Minerva provides all of the support of a family friend's son (age 18) who lives with her. She also furnishes most of the support of her stepmother who does not live with her.
c. Raul, a U.S. citizen, lives in Costa Rica. Raul's household includes an adopted daughter, Helena, who is age 9 and a citizen of Costa Rica. Raul provides all of Helena's support.
d. Maxine maintains a household that includes her ex-husband, her mother-in-law, and her brother-in-law (age 23 and a full-time student). Maxine provides more than half of all of their support. Maxine is single and was divorced several years ago.

35. In 2005, Tommy, age 8, lives in a household with his mother, uncle, and grandfather. The household is maintained by the grandfather. The parties, all of whom file separate returns, have AGI as follows: $18,000 (mother), $50,000 (uncle), and $40,000 (grandfather).
    a. Who is eligible to claim Tommy as a dependent?
    b. Who has preference as to the exemption?

36. Determine the number of personal and dependency exemptions for 2005 in each of the following independent situations:
    a. Marcus (age 68) and Alice (age 65 and blind) file a joint return. They furnish more than 50% of the support of a cousin, Ann, who lives with them. Ann (age 20) is a full-time student and earns $4,000 during the year tutoring special needs children.
    b. Penny (age 45) is single and maintains a household in which she and her nephew, Kurt, live. Kurt (age 18) earns $3,900 from doing yard work, but receives more than 50% of his support from Penny.
    c. Trent (age 38) is single and lives alone. He provides more than 50% of the support of his parents (ages 69 and 70) who are in a nursing home.
    d. Zoe (age 65) and Rhett (age 60) are divorced during the year. Zoe furnished more than 50% of the support of Rhett and Belinda (Rhett's 80-year-old mother). All parties are members of Zoe's household.

37. Hector and Liza Canby file a joint return. Their three children and both sets of parents qualify as their dependents. If the Canbys have AGI of $230,000, what is their allowable deduction for personal and dependency exemptions for 2005?

38. Dudley and Keri North are married and file a joint return. Transactions for 2005 are summarized below:

Salaries (Dudley, $46,000; Keri, $51,000)		$97,000
Interest income—		
General Motors Corporation bonds	$2,100	
City of San Francisco bonds	900	3,000
Contribution to traditional IRAs (Keri, $4,000; Dudley, $4,000)		8,000
Cash gift from Keri's parents		24,000
Loss from the sale of an RV (previously used by the Norths on their vacations)		16,000

The Norths provide more than half of the support of Demi, Kevin, and Homer. Demi (age 22) is their daughter and is a full-time student at a medical school. She earns $3,400 during the year tutoring college athletes. Kevin (age 18) is their son; he does not go to school but earns $8,000 as a part-time security guard. Homer (age 70) is Dudley's father. His only income is $7,200 of Social Security benefits. If the Norths have $11,500 in itemized deductions, what is their taxable income for 2005?

39. Bob, age 13, is a full-time student supported by his parents who claim him on their tax return for 2005. Bob's parents present you with the following information and ask that you prepare Bob's Federal income tax return for the year:

Wages from summer job	$2,100
Interest on savings account at First National Bank	1,150
Interest on City of Chicago bonds Bob received as a gift from his grandfather two years ago	750

a. What is Bob's taxable income for 2005?
b. Bob's parents file a joint return for 2005 on which they report taxable income of $66,000 (no qualified dividends or capital gains). Compute Bob's 2005 tax liability.

Issue ID
Decision Making

40. Walter and Nancy provide 60% of the support of their daughter (age 18) and son-in-law (age 22). The son-in-law (John) is a full-time student at a local university, while the daughter (Irene) holds various part-time jobs from which she earns $11,000. Walter and Nancy engage you to prepare their tax return for 2005. During a meeting with them in late March of 2006, you learn that John and Irene have filed a joint return. What tax advice would you give based on the following assumptions:
a. All parties live in Louisiana (a community property state).
b. All parties live in New Jersey (a common law state).

Decision Making

41. Don is a wealthy executive who had taxable income of $200,000 in 2005. He is considering transferring title in a duplex he owns to his son Sam, age 16. Sam has no other income and is claimed as a dependent by Don. Net rent income from the duplex is $10,000 a year, which Sam will be encouraged to place in a savings account. Will the family save income taxes in 2005 if Don transfers title in the duplex to Sam? Explain.

42. Using the Tax Rate Schedules, compute the 2005 tax liability for each taxpayer:
a. Hector (age 42) is a surviving spouse and provides all of the support of his three minor children who live with him. He also maintains the household in which his parents live and furnished 60% of their support. Besides interest on City of Flint bonds in the amount of $1,200, Hector's father received $2,400 from a part-time job. Hector has a salary of $70,000, a short-term capital loss of $4,000, a cash prize of $2,000 from a church raffle, and itemized deductions of $9,500.
b. Penny (age 45) is single and provides more than 50% of the support of Rosalyn (a family friend), Flo (a niece, age 18), and Jerold (a nephew, age 18). Both Rosalyn and Flo live with Penny, but Jerold (a French citizen) lives in Canada. Penny earns a salary of $80,000, contributes $4,000 to a traditional IRA, and receives sales proceeds of $15,000 for an RV that cost $40,000 and was used for vacations. She has $8,000 in itemized deductions.

43. Ginni, age 13, is claimed as a dependent on her parents' 2005 return, on which they reported taxable income of $101,000. During the year, she earned $2,100 taking care of pets (e.g., walking and grooming dogs, pet sitting). She also earned $1,800 in interest from a bank savings account. Compute Ginni's taxable income and tax liability for 2005.

44. Nash, age 11, is claimed as a dependent on his parents' tax return. During 2005, he received $11,100 in interest and had no investment expenses. He also earned $1,200 wages from part-time jobs. Compute the amount of income that is taxed at Nash's parents' rate.

45. Which of the following individuals are required to file a tax return for 2005? Should any of these individuals file a return even if filing is not required? Why?
a. Sam is married and files a joint return with his spouse, Lana. Both Sam and Lana are 67 years old. Their combined gross income was $18,500.
b. Bobby is a dependent child under age 19 who received $4,600 in wages from a part-time job.
c. Mike is single and is 67 years old. His gross income from wages was $9,200.
d. Marge is a self-employed single individual with gross income of $4,500 from an unincorporated business. Business expenses amounted to $4,000.

46. Which of the following taxpayers must file a Federal income tax return for 2005?
a. Ben, age 19, is a full-time college student. He is claimed as a dependent by his parents. He earned $5,100 wages during the year.
b. Anita, age 12, is claimed as a dependent by her parents. She earned interest income of $1,200 during the year.

c. Earl, age 16, is claimed as a dependent by his parents. He earned wages of $2,700 and interest of $1,100 during the year.
d. Karen, age 16 and blind, is claimed as a dependent by her parents. She earned wages of $2,600 and interest of $1,200 during the year.
e. Pat, age 17, is claimed as a dependent by her parents. She earned interest of $300 during the year. In addition, she earned $550 during the summer operating her own business at the beach, where she painted caricatures of her customers.

47. In each of the following *independent* situations, determine Bianca's filing status for 2005.
   a. Bianca's husband died in December 2005, and she is the executor of his estate. Her late husband had no income for 2005.
   b. Same as (a), except the husband died in 2004 (not 2005). Bianca maintains a household that includes her sister who qualifies as a dependent.
   c. Same as (b). Bianca's household also includes Perry, her husband's 14-year-old son by a prior marriage. Perry qualifies as Bianca's dependent.
   d. Bianca was abandoned by her husband in 2003. She maintains a household that includes two daughters (ages 12 and 13) who qualify as her dependents.

48. In each of the following *independent* situations, determine Winston's filing status for 2005. Winston is not married.
   a. Winston maintains a household in which he and his unmarried son, Ward, live. Ward does not qualify as Winston's dependent.
   b. Same as (a), except that Ward is married.
   c. Winston lives alone, but he maintains a household in which his parents live. The mother qualifies as Winston's dependent, but the father does not.
   d. Winston lives alone but maintains a household in which his married daughter, Karin, lives. Both Karin and her husband (Winston's son-in-law) qualify as Winston's dependents.

49. Nadia died in 2003 and is survived by her husband, Jerold, and her 18-year-old daughter, Macy. Jerold is the executor of Nadia's estate. Jerold maintains the household in which he and Macy live and furnishes more than 50% of her support. Macy had earnings from part-time employment as follows: $4,000 in 2003; $5,000 in 2004; and $6,000 in 2005. She is a full-time student for 2005 (but not for 2003 and 2004). What is Jerold's filing status for:
   a. 2003?
   b. 2004?
   c. 2005?

50. Miles died in 2004 and is survived by his wife, Rosalyn (age 39), his married daughter, Sue (age 18), and his son-in-law, Peyton (age 22). Rosalyn is the executor of her husband's estate. She also maintains the household where she, Sue, and Peyton live and furnishes more than 50% of their support. During 2004 and 2005, Peyton is a full-time student, while Sue earns $16,000 ($8,000 each year) conducting aerobics classes. Sue and Peyton do not file joint returns. For years 2004 and 2005, what is Rosalyn's filing status, and how many exemptions can she claim based on each of the following assumptions?
   a. All parties live in Pennsylvania (a common law state).
   b. All parties live in Texas (a community property state).

51. During 2005, Reed had the following transactions involving capital assets:

Gain on the sale of customized ice-fishing cabin (held for 11 months and used for recreational purposes)	$ 8,000
Loss from garage sale (personal clothing, furniture, appliances held for more than a year)	(6,000)
Loss on the sale of GMC stock (held as an investment for 10 months)	(1,000)
Gain on the sale of a city lot (held as an investment for 3 years)	3,000

   a. If Reed is in the 28% tax bracket, how much income tax results?
   b. If Reed is in the 15% bracket?

52. During 2005, Valerie had the following gains and losses from the sale of capital assets:

Loss on the sale of GE stock (held for 5 months)	($2,000)
Gain on the sale of a coin collection (held for 3 years as an investment)	3,000
Gain on the sale of undeveloped land (held for 5 years as an investment)	2,000

a. If Valerie is in the 33% tax bracket, how much income tax results?
b. If Valerie is in the 15% tax bracket?

Decision Making

53. Amelia is a cash basis, single taxpayer with no dependents. In December 2005, she furnishes you with the following information:

	2005	2006
AGI	$60,000	$61,000
Property taxes on residence	1,300	1,300
Interest on home mortgage	1,100	1,000
Church pledges	2,400	2,400

Amelia wants to know if she can save on taxes over a two-year period by prepaying her 2006 church pledge in December 2005. In providing an answer, use the Tax Rate Schedules, standard deduction, and personal exemption amount applicable to 2005 for both years.

Cumulative Problems

Tax Return Problem

54. Gary and Tracy Wilmot live at 4682 Spring Road, Reno, NV 89557. Gary is a lab technician at the county hospital, and Tracy is the office manager for a local orthopedic clinic. During 2005, Gary and Tracy had the following transactions:

Salaries ($48,000 + $49,000)		$ 97,000
Income tax withheld ($6,000 + $6,200)		12,200
Interest income—		
City of Reno bonds	$ 300	
CD at Wells Fargo Bank	600	
Money market account at Sparks State Bank	400	1,300
Qualified dividend from SBC stock		3,200
Gift from Tracy's parents		22,000
Bequest from Gary's father		160,000
Prudential life insurance policy		50,000
Proceeds from sale of property—		
Garage sale	$ 4,800	
Houseboat	11,000	
Clark County land	31,000	46,800
Interest on home mortgage		(6,600)
Property taxes		(5,100)
Sales taxes (actual amount paid)		(1,800)
Payment on church pledge (receipts maintained)		(2,400)
Medical expenses (including insurance premiums) net of insurance reimbursements		(3,100)

Gary's father died in 2004, and the estate was settled and distributed in 2005. Gary was the designated beneficiary of a life insurance policy his father had purchased from Prudential.

The garage sale involved used clothing, toys, furniture, and other household items. Gary and Tracy estimate that the items sold originally cost $12,000. The houseboat was built by Gary in his spare time over a period of four years. Gary has receipts reflecting that the materials used in the construction cost $8,500. As one of their sons is afraid of water, the Wilmots decided to sell the boat. Tracy acquired the Clark County property in 1998 for $35,000. She had high expectations as to its investment potential, but restricted water rights proved to be a deterrent to its appreciation in value. She feels fortunate to have recovered as much as $31,000 of her cost.

The Wilmots have three children whom they support: Cole (age 18), Robyn (age 19), and Henry (age 21). Henry is a full-time student, while Cole and Robyn are taking time off prior to attending college. All of the Wilmot children are employed by the Reno Convention Bureau in various part-time capacities, and each earns in excess of $5,000 (which he or she saves). The Wilmots also furnish more than 50% of the support of Faye, Gary's 85-year-old mother, who is in a nursing home.

Compute the Wilmots' tax liability for 2005. Suggested software: TurboTax.

Tax Return Problem
Decision Making
Communications

55. Horace Fern, age 43, lives at 321 Grant Avenue, Cheyenne, WY 82002. Horace's mother, Kate (age 65), lived with him until her death in August 2004. Up to the time of her death, Kate qualified as Horace's dependent. Horace maintained the household where he and his mother lived.

Horace is a manager for Bison Lumber Company at a yearly salary of $62,000. Because his job duties will be expanded, Bison plans to increase Horace's salary by 10% starting in 2005.

During 2004, Horace paid $3,300 ($300 each month) in alimony to Janet, his ex-wife. As Janet was remarried in late November, Horace's alimony obligation has terminated.

Besides his salary, Horace received interest income of $5,700 from Western Bank and $6,300 from First Savings Bank on $400,000 in certificates of deposit (CDs) he owns. Horace received the CDs as a gift from his mother several years ago.

Except as otherwise noted, Horace's expenditures for 2004 are summarized below:

Interest on home mortgage	$3,300
Property taxes on home	1,200
Sales taxes (table amount)	1,300
Charitable contributions	600

Relevant Social Security numbers are as follows:

Horace Fern	520–31–4596
Kate Fern	520–32–3214
Janet Fern	520–33–4432

Federal income taxes withheld from Horace's salary amounted to $10,900.

Part 1—Tax Computation
Compute Horace's net tax payable or refund due for 2004. Horace does not wish to contribute to the Presidential Election Campaign Fund. If he has overpaid, he wants the amount refunded. If you use tax forms for your computations, you will need Form 1040 and Schedules A and B. Suggested software: TurboTax

Part 2—Tax Planning
In addition to preparing the return for 2004, Horace has asked you to advise him regarding his tax situation for 2005. He is particularly concerned about the tax effects of the following:

- The death of Kate.
- The cessation of alimony payments due to Janet's remarriage.
- The salary increase.
- Interest income on the CDs.

Write a letter to Horace in which you summarize (in approximate amounts) how much more (or less) he will owe in income taxes for 2005. Also include recommendations on what can be done to mitigate the tax consequences resulting from the investment in CDs. Assume that Horace's itemized deductions will remain constant in 2005.

Research Problems

Note: Solutions to Research Problems can be prepared by using the ***RIA Checkpoint® Student Edition*** *online research product, which is available to accompany this text. It is also possible to prepare solutions to the Research Problems by using tax research materials found in a standard tax library.*

Research Problem 1. Jeff and Suzy are the biological parents of Monique, born in 1992. The parents never married, and shortly after the birth, Suzy left the household and took Monique with her. In 1993, Jeff had Suzy sign a Form 8332 in which she waived the dependency exemption as to Monique for 1993 "and all years thereafter." Although Jeff contributes nothing toward the support of Monique, he has been claiming her as a dependent every year since 1993. Starting in 2002, Suzy has also been claiming Monique as a dependent.

Needless to say, the IRS is not likely to permit a dependent to be claimed twice! In the event of audit, should Jeff or Suzy be allowed the deduction for Monique? Why?

Partial list of research aids:
§§ 151(e)(1) and (2).
Jeffrey R. King, 121 T.C. 245 (2003).

Research Problem 2. Bart and Arlene Keating are husband and wife and live in Mineola, Oregon. They have been married for 18 years and have four children, all of whom are teenagers. After the birth of her last child, Arlene took a job as a city clerk and, over the years, has become city treasurer. Since graduating from high school, Bart has worked as a dispatcher for the city fire and ambulance departments. As Arlene has some college training in finance and accounting, she handles the family's financial affairs, including reconciling the bank account, paying bills, and preparing all tax returns. She also takes care of major purchases (e.g., autos, furniture) and servicing of debt (e.g., home mortgage, auto loans, charge accounts).

The Keatings themselves maintain a modest lifestyle, but Arlene is quite generous with the children. All are well-dressed, attend summer camp, and have their own cars. Bart believes Arlene obtains any additional funds for the children's support through credit card financing and bank loans.

The Keatings filed joint returns for 2001 and 2002 that reflected their salary income. Arlene prepared the returns, and Bart signed them without reviewing them first. The returns did not show the $90,000 Arlene had embezzled from her employer over this two-year period.

The City of Mineola discovers the theft, and Arlene is tried and convicted of grand larceny. Due to the adverse publicity generated by these events, the Keatings are divorced, and Arlene moves to another state.

In 2005, the IRS assesses a deficiency against Bart for the income taxes that would have resulted if the embezzled amounts had been reported as income.

What are the rights of the parties?

Partial list of research aids:
§§ 6013(d)(3) and 6015.
Kathryn Cheshire, 115 T.C. 183 (2000).
Evelyn M. Martin, 80 TCM 665, T.C.Memo. 2000–346.

Internet Activity

Use the tax resources of the Internet to address the following question. Do not restrict your search to the World Wide Web, but include a review of newsgroups and general reference materials, practitioner sites and resources, primary sources of the tax law, chat rooms and discussion groups, and other opportunities.

Research Problem 3. A nonresident alien earns money in the United States that is subject to Federal income tax. What guidance does the IRS provide on what tax form needs to be used and on when it should be filed? In terms of the proper filing date, does it matter whether the earnings were subject to income tax withholding?

Gross Income: Concepts and Inclusions

LEARNING OBJECTIVES

After completing Chapter 4, you should be able to:

LO.1

Explain the concepts of gross income and realization and distinguish between the economic, accounting, and tax concepts of gross income.

LO.2

Describe the cash and accrual methods of accounting and the related effects of the choice of taxable year.

LO.3

Identify who should pay the tax on a particular item of income in various situations.

LO.4

Apply the Internal Revenue Code provisions on alimony, loans made at below-market interest rates, annuities, prizes and awards, group term life insurance, unemployment compensation, and Social Security benefits.

LO.5

Identify tax planning strategies for minimizing gross income.

http://wft.swlearning.com

OUTLINE

Mr. Zarin lost over $2.5 million of his own money gambling. The casino then allowed him to gamble on credit. After several months, his liability to the casino totaled more than $3.4 million. Following protracted negotiations, the casino agreed to settle its claim against Mr. Zarin for a mere $500,000. Although Mr. Zarin had paid for gambling losses of $3 million, the IRS had the audacity to ask him to pay tax on $2.9 million, that is, the amount the casino marked down his account.[1] Mr. Zarin undoubtedly had difficulty understanding how he could be deemed to have income in this situation.

Given an understanding of the income tax formula, though, one can see how the "free" gambling Mr. Zarin enjoyed could constitute income. The starting point in the formula is the determination of gross income rather than "net income." Once gross income is determined, the next step is to determine the allowable deductions. In Mr. Zarin's way of thinking, these steps were collapsed.

This chapter is concerned with the first step in the computation of taxable income—the determination of gross income. Questions that are addressed include the following:

- What: What is income?
- When: In which tax period is the income recognized?
- Who: Who must include the item of income in gross income?

The Code provides an all-inclusive definition of gross income in § 61. Chapter 5 presents items of income that are specifically excluded from gross income (exclusions).

[1] *Zarin v. Comm.*, 90–2 USTC ¶50,530, 66 AFTR2d 90–5679, 916 F.2d 110 (CA–3, 1990).

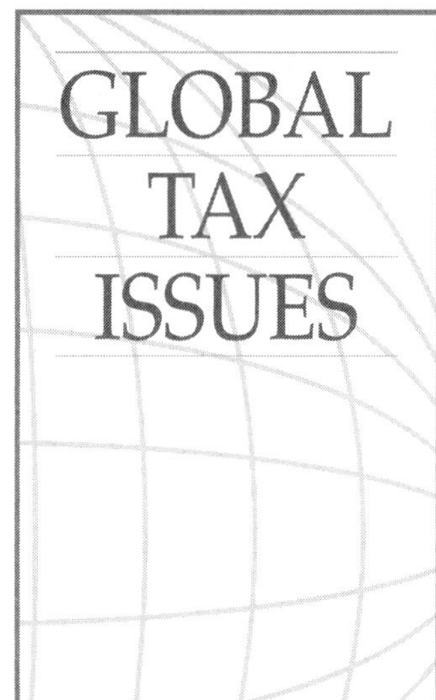

FROM "ALL SOURCES" IS A BROAD DEFINITION

When § 61 refers to "income from whatever source derived," the taxing authorities are reaching far beyond the borders of the United States. Although one interpretation of "source" in this context is type of income (wages, interest, etc.), a broader interpretation revolves around the place where the income is generated. In this context, citizens and residents of the United States are subject to taxation on income earned from sources both inside and outside the country. This "worldwide income" tax base can cause potential double taxation problems, with other countries also taxing income earned within their borders, but mechanisms such as the foreign tax credit can alleviate these tax burdens.

Recently, some U.S. corporations have relocated to other countries to avoid the higher U.S. tax rates on income earned abroad. Congress is considering ways of stopping this "flight of capital." In the American Jobs Creation Act of 2004 (AJCA), an incentive is provided to bring profits back into the United States.

LO.1

Explain the concepts of gross income and realization and distinguish between the economic, accounting, and tax concepts of gross income.

Gross Income—What Is It?

DEFINITION

Section 61(a) of the Internal Revenue Code defines the term **gross income** as follows:

> Except as otherwise provided in this subtitle, gross income means all income from whatever source derived.

This definition is derived from the language of the Sixteenth Amendment to the Constitution.

Supreme Court decisions have made it clear that all sources of income are subject to tax unless Congress specifically excludes the type of income received:

> The starting point in all cases dealing with the question of the scope of what is included in "gross income" begins with the basic premise that the purpose of Congress was to use the full measure of its taxing power.[2]

Although at this point we know that *income* is to be broadly construed, we still do not have a satisfactory definition of the term *income*. Congress left it to the judicial and administrative branches to thrash out the meaning of income. Early in the development of the income tax law, a choice was made between two competing models: economic income and accounting income.

ECONOMIC AND ACCOUNTING CONCEPTS

The term **income** is used in the Code but is not separately defined. Thus, early in the history of our tax laws, the courts were required to interpret "the commonly understood meaning of the term which must have been in the minds of the people when they adopted the Sixteenth Amendment to the Constitution."[3] In determining the definition of income, the Supreme Court rejected the economic concept of income.

Economists measure income (**economic income**) by first determining the fair market value of the individual's net assets at the beginning and end of the year

[2]*James v. U.S.*, 61–1 USTC ¶9449, 7 AFTR2d 1361, 81 S.Ct. 1052 (USSC, 1961).

[3]*Merchants Loan and Trust Co. v. Smietanka*, 1 USTC ¶42, 3 AFTR 3102, 41 S.Ct. 386 (USSC, 1921).

(change in net worth). Then, to arrive at economic income, this change in net worth is added to the goods and services that person actually consumed during the period. Economic income also includes imputed values for such items as the rental value of an owner-occupied home and the value of food a taxpayer might grow for personal consumption.[4]

EXAMPLE 1

Helen's economic income is calculated as follows:

Fair market value of Helen's assets on December 31, 2005	$220,000	
Less liabilities on December 31, 2005	(40,000)	
Net worth on December 31, 2005		$ 180,000
Fair market value of Helen's assets on January 1, 2005	$200,000	
Less liabilities on January 1, 2005	(80,000)	
Net worth on January 1, 2005		(120,000)
Increase in net worth		$ 60,000
Consumption		
Food, clothing, and other personal expenditures		25,000
Imputed rental value of the home Helen owns and occupies		12,000
Economic income		$ 97,000

The need to value assets annually would make compliance with the tax law burdensome and would cause numerous controversies between the taxpayer and the IRS over valuation. In addition, using market values to determine income for tax purposes could result in liquidity problems. That is, the taxpayer's assets may increase in value even though they are not readily convertible into the cash needed to pay the tax (e.g., commercial real estate). Thus, the IRS, Congress, and the courts have rejected the economic concept of income as impractical.

In contrast, the accounting concept of income is founded on the realization principle.[5] According to this principle, income (**accounting income**) is not recognized until it is realized. For realization to occur, (1) an exchange of goods or services must take place between the accounting entity and some independent, external group, and (2) in the exchange the accounting entity must receive assets that are capable of being objectively valued. Thus, the mere appreciation in the market value of assets before a sale or other disposition is not sufficient to warrant income recognition. In addition, the imputed savings that arise when individuals create assets for their own use (e.g., feed grown for a farmer's own livestock) are not income because no exchange has occurred. The courts and the IRS have ruled, however, that embezzlement proceeds and buried treasures found satisfy the realization requirement and, therefore, must be recognized as income.[6]

The Supreme Court expressed an inclination toward the accounting concept of income when it adopted the realization requirement in *Eisner v. Macomber*:

> Income may be defined as the gain derived from capital, from labor, or from both combined, provided it is understood to include profit gained through a sale or conversion of capital assets. . . . Here we have the essential matter: not a gain accruing to capital; not a *growth* or *increment* of value *in* investment; but a gain, a profit, something of exchangeable value, *proceeding from* the property, *severed from* the capital however invested or employed, and *coming in,* being *"derived"*—that is, *received* or *drawn by* the recipient for his separate use, benefit and disposal—*that is,* income derived from the property.[7]

[4]See Henry C. Simons, *Personal Income Taxation* (Chicago: University of Chicago Press, 1933), Chapters 2–3.

[5]See the American Accounting Association Committee Report on the "Realization Concept," *The Accounting Review* (April 1965): 312–322.

[6]*Rutkin v. U.S.*, 52–1 USTC ¶9260, 41 AFTR2d 596, 72 S.Ct. 571 (USSC, 1952); Rev.Rul. 61, 1953–1 C.B. 17.

[7]1 USTC ¶32, 3 AFTR 3020, 40 S.Ct. 189 (USSC, 1920).

Your Silent Gambling Partner: If You Win!

Gambling has become big business in the United States. But many folks fail to understand that when you win, Uncle Sam wins too, or at least he's supposed to win. Gambling payoffs, no matter how large or small, are taxable and should be reported on your Federal income tax return. This includes the fair market value of noncash prizes such as cars, trips, and dinner coupons. The provision applies to winnings from all sources, from casinos to office pools.

No one knows for sure how much in gambling winnings goes unreported. For winnings of $600 or more ($1,200 from bingo or slot machines, $1,500 from keno), however, the payer is required to notify the IRS and issue the player an IRS Form W–2G.

But what happens to all those bets you placed that didn't pay off? A person's gambling losses can be used only to offset his or her gambling gains. So, if you have a net gain, the IRS wins, and if you have a net loss, you lose.

SOURCE: Adapted from Armond Budish, "Bet On Paying Taxes When You Gamble and Win," *Cleveland Plain Dealer*, August 10, 2004, p. C5.

In summary, *income* represents an increase in wealth recognized for tax purposes only upon realization.

COMPARISON OF THE ACCOUNTING AND TAX CONCEPTS OF INCOME

Although income tax rules frequently parallel financial accounting measurement concepts, differences do exist. Of major significance, for example, is the fact that unearned (prepaid) income received by an accrual basis taxpayer often is taxed in the year of receipt. For financial accounting purposes, such prepayments are not treated as income until earned.[8] Because of this and other differences, many corporations report financial accounting income that is substantially different from the amounts reported for tax purposes (see Reconciliation of Corporate Taxable Income and Accounting Income in Chapter 17).

The Supreme Court provided an explanation for some of the variations between accounting and taxable income in a decision involving inventory and bad debt adjustments:

> The primary goal of financial accounting is to provide useful information to management, shareholders, creditors, and others properly interested; the major responsibility of the accountant is to protect these parties from being misled. The primary goal of the income tax system, in contrast, is the equitable collection of revenue. . . . Consistently with its goals and responsibilities, financial accounting has as its foundation the principle of conservatism, with its corollary that 'possible errors in measurement [should] be in the direction of understatement rather than overstatement of net income and net assets.' In view of the Treasury's markedly different goals and responsibilities, understatement of income is not destined to be its guiding light.
>
> . . . Financial accounting, in short, is hospitable to estimates, probabilities, and reasonable certainties; the tax law, with its mandate to preserve the revenue, can give no quarter to uncertainty.[9]

[8]Similar differences exist in the deduction area.

[9]*Thor Power Tool Co. v. Comm.*, 79–1 USTC ¶9139, 43 AFTR2d 79–362, 99 S.Ct. 773 (USSC, 1979).

FORM OF RECEIPT

Gross income is not limited to cash received. "It includes income realized in any form, whether in money, property, or services. Income may be realized [and recognized], therefore, in the form of services, meals, accommodations, stock or other property, as well as in cash."[10]

EXAMPLE 2

Ostrich Corporation allows Bill, an employee, to use a company car for his vacation. Bill realizes income equal to the rental value of the car for the time and mileage. ■

EXAMPLE 3

Terry owes $10,000 on a mortgage. The creditor accepts $8,000 in full satisfaction of the debt. Terry realizes income of $2,000 from retiring the debt.[11] ■

EXAMPLE 4

Martha is an attorney. She agrees to draft a will for Tom, a neighbor, who is a carpenter. In exchange, Tom repairs her back porch. Martha and Tom both have gross income equal to the fair market value of the services they provide. ■

RECOVERY OF CAPITAL DOCTRINE

The Constitution grants Congress the power to tax income but does not define the term. Because the Constitution does not define income, it would seem that Congress could simply tax gross receipts. Although Congress does allow certain deductions, none are constitutionally required. However, the Supreme Court has held that there is no income subject to tax until the taxpayer has recovered the capital invested.[12] This concept is known as the **recovery of capital doctrine.**

In its simplest application, this doctrine means that sellers can reduce their gross receipts (selling price) by the adjusted basis of the property sold.[13] This net amount, in the language of the Code, is gross income.

EXAMPLE 5

Dave sold common stock for $15,000. He had purchased the stock for $12,000. Dave's gross receipts are $15,000. This amount consists of a $12,000 recovery of capital and $3,000 of gross income. ■

Collections on annuity contracts and installment payments received from sales of property must be allocated between recovery of capital and income. Annuities are discussed in this chapter, and installment sales are discussed in Chapter 16.

LO.2

Describe the cash and accrual methods of accounting and the related effects of the choice of taxable year.

Year of Inclusion

TAXABLE YEAR

The annual accounting period or **taxable year** is a basic component of our tax system.[14] Generally, an entity must use the *calendar year* to report its income. However, a *fiscal year* (a period of 12 months ending on the last day of any month other than December) can be elected if the taxpayer maintains adequate books and

[10]Reg. § 1.61–1(a).

[11]Reg. § 1.61–12. See *U.S. v. Kirby Lumber Co.*, 2 USTC ¶814, 10 AFTR 458, 52 S.Ct. 4 (USSC, 1931). Exceptions to this general rule are discussed in Chapter 5.

[12]*Doyle v. Mitchell Bros. Co.*, 1 USTC ¶17, 3 AFTR 2979, 38 S.Ct. 467 (USSC, 1916).

[13]For a definition of "adjusted basis," see the Glossary of Tax Terms in Appendix C.

[14]See Accounting Periods in Chapter 16.

records. This fiscal year option generally is not available to partnerships, S corporations, and personal service corporations, as discussed in Chapter 16.[15]

Determining the particular year in which the income will be taxed is important for determining when the tax must be paid. But the year each item of income is subject to tax can also affect the total tax liability over the entity's lifetime. This is true for the following reasons:

- With a progressive rate system, a taxpayer's marginal tax rate can change from year to year.
- Congress may change the tax rates.
- The relevant rates may change because of a change in the entity's status (e.g., a person may marry or a business may be incorporated).
- Several provisions in the Code are dependent on the taxpayer's gross income for the year (e.g., whether the person can be claimed as a dependent, as discussed in Chapter 3).

ACCOUNTING METHODS

The year an item of income is subject to tax often depends upon which acceptable **accounting method** the taxpayer regularly employs.[16] The three primary methods of accounting are (1) the cash receipts and disbursements method, (2) the accrual method, and (3) the hybrid method. Most individuals use the cash receipts and disbursements method of accounting, whereas most corporations use the accrual method. The Regulations require the accrual method for determining purchases and sales when inventory is an income-producing factor.[17] Some businesses employ a hybrid method that is a combination of the cash and accrual methods of accounting.

In addition to these overall accounting methods, a taxpayer may choose to spread the gain from an installment sale of property over the collection periods by using the *installment method* of income recognition. Contractors may either spread profits from contracts over the periods in which the work is done (the *percentage of completion method*) or defer all profit until the year in which the project is completed (the *completed contract method*, which can be used only in limited circumstances).[18]

The IRS has the power to prescribe the accounting method to be used by the taxpayer. Section 446(b) grants the IRS broad powers to determine if the accounting method used *clearly reflects income*:

> If no method of accounting has been regularly used by the taxpayer, or *if the method used does not clearly reflect income, the computation of taxable income shall be made under such method as, in the opinion of the Secretary . . . does clearly reflect income.*

A change in the method of accounting requires the consent of the IRS.[19]

Cash Receipts Method. Under the **cash receipts method,** property or services received are included in the taxpayer's gross income in the year of actual or constructive receipt by the taxpayer or agent, regardless of whether the income was earned in that year.[20] The income received need not be reduced to cash in the same year. All that is necessary for income recognition is that property or services

[15]§§ 441(a) and (d).

[16]See Accounting Methods in Chapter 16.

[17]Reg. § 1.446–1(c)(2)(i). Other circumstances in which the accrual method must be used are presented in Chapter 16. For the small business exception to the inventory requirement, see Rev.Proc. 2002–28, 2002–1 C.B. 815.

[18]§§ 453 and 460. See Chapter 16 for limitations on the use of the installment method and the completed contract method.

[19]§ 446(e). See Chapter 16.

[20]*Julia A. Strauss,* 2 B.T.A. 598 (1925). See the Glossary of Tax Terms in Appendix C for a discussion of the terms "cash equivalent doctrine" and "constructive receipt."

received have a fair market value—a cash equivalent.[21] Thus, a cash basis taxpayer that receives a note in payment for services has income in the year of receipt equal to the fair market value of the note. However, a creditor's mere promise to pay (e.g., an account receivable), with no supporting note, usually is not considered to have a fair market value.[22] Thus, the cash basis taxpayer defers income recognition until the account receivable is collected.

EXAMPLE 6

Dana, an accountant, reports her income by the cash method. In 2005, she performed an audit for Orange Corporation and billed the client for $5,000, which was collected in 2006. In 2005, Dana also performed an audit for Blue Corporation. Because of Blue's precarious financial position, Dana required Blue to issue an $8,000 secured negotiable note in payment of the fee. The note had a fair market value of $6,000. Dana collected $8,000 on the note in 2006. Dana's gross income for the two years is as follows:

	2005	2006
Fair market value of note received from Blue	$6,000	
Cash received		
From Orange on account receivable		$ 5,000
From Blue on note receivable		8,000
Less: Recovery of capital		(6,000)
Total gross income	$6,000	$ 7,000

Generally, a check received is considered a cash equivalent. Thus, a cash basis taxpayer must recognize the income when the check is received. This is true even if the taxpayer receives the check after banking hours.[23]

Accrual Method. Under the **accrual method,** an item is generally included in the gross income for the year in which it is earned, regardless of when the income is collected. The income is earned when (1) all the events have occurred that fix the right to receive such income and (2) the amount to be received can be determined with reasonable accuracy.[24]

Generally, the taxpayer's rights to the income accrue when title to property passes to the buyer or the services are performed for the customer or client.[25] If the rights to the income have accrued but are subject to a potential refund claim (e.g., under a product warranty), the income is reported in the year of sale, and a deduction is allowed in subsequent years when actual claims accrue.[26]

Where the taxpayer's rights to the income are being contested (e.g., when a contractor fails to meet specifications), the year in which the income is subject to tax depends upon whether payment has been received. If payment has not been received, no income is recognized until the claim is settled. Only then is the right to the income established.[27] However, if the payment is received before the dispute is settled, the court-made **claim of right doctrine** requires the taxpayer to recognize the income in the year of receipt.[28]

[21] Reg. §§ 1.446–1(a)(3) and (c)(1)(i).

[22] *Bedell v. Comm.*, 1 USTC ¶359, 7 AFTR 8469, 30 F.2d 622 (CA–2, 1929).

[23] *Charles F. Kahler*, 18 T.C. 31 (1952).

[24] Reg. § 1.451–1(a).

[25] *Lucas v. North Texas Lumber Co.*, 2 USTC ¶484, 8 AFTR 10276, 50 S.Ct. 184 (USSC, 1930).

[26] *Brown v. Helvering*, 4 USTC ¶1222, 13 AFTR 851, 54 S.Ct. 356 (USSC, 1933).

[27] *Burnet v. Sanford and Brooks*, 2 USTC ¶636, 9 AFTR 603, 51 S.Ct. 150 (USSC, 1931).

[28] *North American Oil Consolidated Co. v. Burnet*, 3 USTC ¶943, 11 AFTR 16, 52 S.Ct. 613 (USSC, 1932).

EXAMPLE 7

A contractor completed a building in 2005 and presented a bill to the customer. The customer refused to pay the bill and claimed that the contractor had not met specifications. A settlement with the customer was not reached until 2006. No income accrues to the contractor until 2006. If the customer paid for the work and then filed suit for damages, the contractor cannot defer the income (the income is taxable in 2005). ■

The measure of accrual basis income is generally the amount the taxpayer has a right to receive. Unlike the cash basis, the fair market value of the customer's obligation is irrelevant in measuring accrual basis income.

EXAMPLE 8

Assume the same facts as in Example 6, except that Dana is an accrual basis taxpayer. Dana must recognize $13,000 ($8,000 + $5,000) gross income in 2005, the year her rights to the income accrued. ■

Hybrid Method. The **hybrid method** is a combination of the accrual method and the cash method. Generally, when the hybrid method is used, inventory is an income-producing factor. Therefore, the Regulations require that the accrual method be used for determining sales and cost of goods sold. In this circumstance, to simplify record keeping, the taxpayer accounts for inventory using the accrual method and uses the cash method for all other income and expense items (e.g., dividend and interest income). The hybrid method is primarily used by small businesses.

EXCEPTIONS APPLICABLE TO CASH BASIS TAXPAYERS

Constructive Receipt. Income that has not actually been received by the taxpayer is taxed as though it had been received—the income is constructively received—under the following conditions:

- The amount is made readily available to the taxpayer.
- The taxpayer's actual receipt is not subject to substantial limitations or restrictions.[29]

The rationale for the **constructive receipt** doctrine is that if the income is available, the taxpayer should not be allowed to postpone the income recognition. For instance, a taxpayer is not permitted to defer income for December services by refusing to accept payment until January. However, determining whether the income is *readily available* and whether *substantial limitations or restrictions exist* necessitates a factual inquiry that leads to a judgment call.[30] The following are some examples of the application of the constructive receipt doctrine.

EXAMPLE 9

Ted is a member of a barter club. In 2005, Ted performed services for other club members and earned 1,000 points. Each point entitles him to $1 in goods and services sold by other members of the club; the points can be used at any time. In 2006, Ted exchanged his points for a new high-definition TV. Ted must recognize $1,000 gross income in 2005 when the 1,000 points were credited to his account.[31] ■

EXAMPLE 10

On December 31, an employer issued a bonus check to an employee but asked her to hold it for a few days until the company could make deposits to cover the check. The income was not constructively received on December 31 since the issuer did not have sufficient funds in its account to pay the debt.[32] ■

[29] Reg. § 1.451–2(a).

[30] *Baxter v. Comm.*, 87–1 USTC ¶9315, 59 AFTR2d 87–1068, 816 F.2d 493 (CA–9, 1987).

[31] Rev.Rul. 80–52, 1980–1 C.B. 100.

[32] *L. M. Fischer*, 14 T.C. 792 (1950).

EXAMPLE 11

Rick owns interest coupons that mature on December 31. The coupons can be converted to cash at any bank at maturity. Thus, the income is constructively received by Rick on December 31, even though Rick failed to cash in the coupons until the following year.[33] Dove Company mails a dividend check to Rick on December 31, 2005. Rick does not receive the check until January 2006. Rick does not realize gross income until 2006.[34] ■

The constructive receipt doctrine does not reach income that the taxpayer is not yet entitled to receive even though the taxpayer could have contracted to receive the income at an earlier date.

EXAMPLE 12

Sara offers to pay Ivan $100,000 for land in December 2005. Ivan refuses but offers to sell the land to Sara on January 1, 2006, when he will be in a lower tax bracket. If Sara accepts Ivan's offer, the gain is taxed to Ivan in 2006 when the sale is completed.[35] ■

Income set apart or made available is not constructively received if its actual receipt is subject to *substantial restrictions.* The life insurance industry has used substantial restrictions as a cornerstone for designing life insurance contracts with favorable tax features. Ordinary life insurance policies provide (1) current protection—an amount payable in the event of death—and (2) a savings feature—a cash surrender value payable to the policyholder if the policy is terminated during the policyholder's life. The annual increase in cash surrender value is not taxable because the policyholder must cancel the policy to actually receive the increase in value. Because the cancellation requirement is a substantial restriction, the policyholder does not constructively receive the annual increase in cash surrender value.[36] Employees often receive from their employers property subject to substantial restrictions. Generally, no income is recognized until the restrictions lapse.[37]

EXAMPLE 13

Carlos is a key employee of Red, Inc. The corporation gives stock with a value of $10,000 to Carlos. The stock cannot be sold, however, for five years. Carlos is not required to recognize income until the restrictions lapse at the end of five years. ■

ETHICAL CONSIDERATIONS

Choosing When to File Insurance Claims

Dr. Randolph, a cash basis taxpayer, knows that he will be in a lower marginal tax bracket in 2006 than in 2005. To take advantage of the expected decrease in his tax rate, Dr. Randolph instructs his office manager to delay filing the medical insurance claims for services performed in November and December until January 2006. This will assure that the receipts will not be included in his 2005 gross income. Is Dr. Randolph abusing the cash method of accounting rules?

Original Issue Discount. Lenders frequently make loans that require a payment at maturity of more than the amount of the original loan. The difference between the amount due at maturity and the amount of the original loan is actually interest but is referred to as **original issue discount.** Under the general rules of

[33] Reg. § 1.451–2(b).
[34] Reg. § 1.451–2(b).
[35] *Cowden v. Comm.*, 61–1 USTC ¶9382, 7 AFTR2d 1160, 289 F.2d 20 (CA–5, 1961).
[36] *Theodore H. Cohen*, 39 T.C. 1055 (1963).
[37] § 83(a).

tax accounting, the cash basis lender would not report the original issue discount as interest income until the year the amount is collected, although an accrual basis borrower would deduct the interest as it is earned. However, the Code puts the lender and borrower on parity by requiring that the original issue discount be reported when it is earned, regardless of the taxpayer's accounting method.[38] The interest "earned" is calculated by the effective interest rate method.

EXAMPLE 14

On January 1, 2005, Mark, a cash basis taxpayer, pays $82,645 for a 24-month certificate. The certificate is priced to yield 10% (the effective interest rate) with interest compounded annually. No interest is paid until maturity, when Mark receives $100,000. Thus, Mark's gross income from the certificate is $17,355 ($100,000 – $82,645). Mark's income earned each year is calculated as follows:

2005 (.10 × $82,645) =	$ 8,264
2006 [.10 × ($82,645 + $8,264)] =	9,091
	$17,355

■

The original issue discount rules do not apply to U.S. savings bonds (discussed in the following paragraphs) or to obligations with a maturity date of one year or less from the date of issue.[39] See Chapter 14 for additional discussion of the tax treatment of original issue discount.

Series E and Series EE Bonds. Certain U.S. government savings bonds (Series E before 1980 and Series EE after 1979) are issued at a discount and are redeemable for fixed amounts that increase at stated intervals. No interest payments are actually made. The difference between the purchase price and the amount received on redemption is the bondholder's interest income from the investment.

The income from these savings bonds is generally deferred until the bonds are redeemed or mature. Furthermore, Series E bonds could be exchanged within one year of their maturity date for Series HH bonds, and the interest on the Series E bonds could be further deferred until maturity of the Series HH bonds.[40] Thus, U.S. savings bonds have attractive income deferral features not available with corporate bonds and certificates of deposit issued by financial institutions.

Of course, the deferral feature of government bonds issued at a discount is not an advantage if the investor has insufficient income to be subject to tax as the income accrues. In fact, the deferral may work to the investor's disadvantage if the investor has other income in the year the bonds mature or the bunching of the bond interest into one tax year creates a tax liability. Fortunately, U.S. government bonds have a provision for these investors. A cash basis taxpayer can elect to include in gross income the annual increment in redemption value.[41]

EXAMPLE 15

Kate purchases Series EE U.S. savings bonds for $500 (face value of $1,000) on January 2 of the current year. If the bonds are redeemed during the first six months, no interest is paid. At December 31, the redemption value is $519.60.

If Kate elects to report the interest income annually, she must report interest income of $19.60 for the current year. If she does not make the election, she will report no interest income for the current year. ■

[38] §§ 1272(a)(3) and 1273(a).

[39] § 1272(a)(2).

[40] Treas. Dept. Circulars No. 1–80 and No. 2–80, 1980–1 C.B. 714, 715. Note that interest is paid at semiannual intervals on the Series HH bonds and must be included in income as received. Refer to Chapter 5 for a discussion of the savings bond interest exclusion. This exchange opportunity applied through August 31, 2004.

[41] § 454(a).

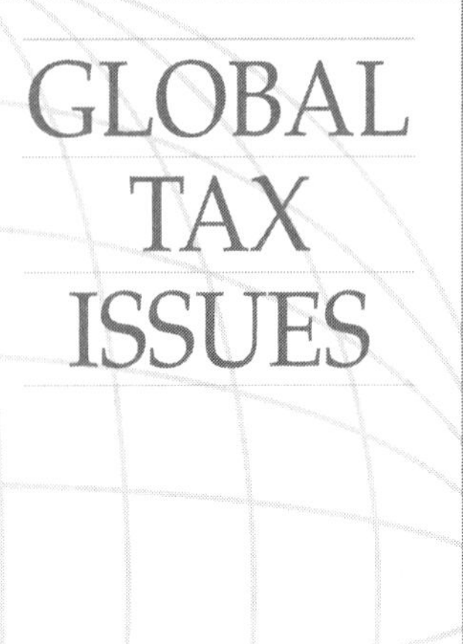

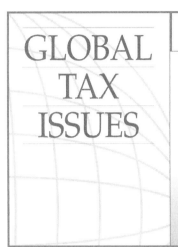

Tax Credit Neutralizes Foreign Income Taxes

When a U.S. taxpayer invests in a foreign country, that investment income is subject to tax in the United States and may also be subject to tax in the foreign country. However, the taxpayer is allowed a credit on his or her U.S. Federal income tax return for income taxes paid to the foreign country. The credit system allows the taxpayer to treat the taxes paid to the foreign country as though they were paid to the United States. If the foreign taxes paid are less than the U.S. tax on the income, the foreign taxes have cost the taxpayer nothing. On the other hand, if the foreign taxes are greater than the U.S. tax on the income, the credit is limited to the amount of the U.S. tax on the income. In this case, the taxes paid by the taxpayer will exceed what they would have been if the income had been earned in the United States.

When a taxpayer elects to report the income from the bonds on an annual basis, the election applies to all such bonds the taxpayer owns at the time of the election and to all such securities acquired subsequent to the election. A change in the method of reporting the income from the bonds requires permission from the IRS.

Amounts Received under an Obligation to Repay. The receipt of funds with an obligation to repay that amount in the future is the essence of borrowing. Because the taxpayer's assets and liabilities increase by the same amount, no income is realized when the borrowed funds are received. Because amounts paid to the taxpayer by mistake and customer deposits are often classified as borrowed funds, receipt of these funds is not a taxable event.

EXAMPLE 16

A landlord receives a damage deposit from a tenant. The landlord does not recognize income until the deposit is forfeited because the landlord has an obligation to repay the deposit if no damage occurs.[42] However, if the deposit is in fact a prepayment of rent, it is taxed in the year of receipt. ■

EXCEPTIONS APPLICABLE TO ACCRUAL BASIS TAXPAYERS

Prepaid Income. For financial reporting purposes, advance payments received from customers are reflected as prepaid income and as a liability of the seller. However, for tax purposes, the prepaid income often is taxed in the year of receipt.

EXAMPLE 17

In December 2005, a tenant pays his January 2006 rent of $1,000. The accrual basis landlord must include the $1,000 in her 2005 gross income for tax purposes, although the unearned rent income is reported as a liability on the landlord's December 31, 2005 balance sheet. ■

Taxpayers have repeatedly argued that deferral of income until it is actually earned properly matches revenues and expenses. Moreover, a proper matching of income with the expenses of earning the income is necessary to clearly reflect

[42]*John Mantell*, 17 T.C. 1143 (1952).

income, as required by the Code. The IRS responds that § 446(b) grants it broad powers to determine whether an accounting method clearly reflects income. The IRS further argues that generally accepted financial accounting principles should not dictate tax accounting for prepaid income because of the practical problems of collecting Federal revenues. Collection of the tax is simplest in the year the taxpayer receives the cash from the customer or client.

After a number of years of continual disputes between the IRS and taxpayers, in 1971 the IRS relented and modified its rules on the prepaid income issue in some situations, as explained below.

Deferral of Advance Payments for Goods. Generally, a taxpayer can elect to defer recognition of income from *advance payments for goods* if the method of accounting for the sale is the same for tax and financial reporting purposes.[43]

EXAMPLE 18

Brown Company will ship goods only after payment for the goods has been received. In December 2005, Brown received $10,000 for goods that were not shipped until January 2006. Brown can elect to report the income for tax purposes in 2006, assuming the company reports the income in 2006 for financial reporting purposes. ■

Deferral of Advance Payments for Services. Revenue Procedure 2004–34[44] permits an accrual basis taxpayer to defer recognition of income for *advance payments for services* to be performed after the end of the tax year of receipt. The portion of the advance payment that relates to services performed in the tax year of receipt is included in gross income in the tax year of receipt. The portion of the advance payment that relates to services to be performed after the tax year of receipt is included in gross income in the tax year following the tax year of receipt of the advance payment.

EXAMPLE 19

Yellow Corporation, an accrual basis calendar year taxpayer, sells its services under 12-month, 24-month, and 36-month contracts. The corporation provides services to each customer every month. On May 1, 2005, Yellow Corporation sold the following customer contracts:

Length of Contract	Total Proceeds
12 months	$3,000
24 months	4,800
36 months	7,200

Yellow may defer until 2006 all of the income that will be earned after 2005.

Length of Contract	Income Recorded in 2005	Income Recorded in 2006
12 months	$2,000 ($3,000 × 8/12)	$1,000 ($3,000 × 4/12)
24 months	1,600 ($4,800 × 8/24)	3,200 ($4,800 × 16/24)
36 months	1,600 ($7,200 × 8/36)	5,600 ($7,200 × 28/36)

■

Revenue Procedure 2004–34 does not apply to prepaid rent or prepaid interest. These items are always taxed in the year of receipt.

[43]Reg. § 1.451–5(b). See Reg. § 1.451–5(c) for exceptions to this deferral opportunity. The financial accounting conformity requirement is not applicable to contractors who use the completed contract method.

[44]I.R.B. No. 22, 991.

LO.3

Identify who should pay the tax on a particular item of income in various situations.

Income Sources

PERSONAL SERVICES

It is a well-established principle of taxation that income from personal services must be included in the gross income of the person who performs the services. This principle was first established in a Supreme Court decision, *Lucas v. Earl.*[45] Mr. Earl entered into a binding agreement with his wife under which Mrs. Earl was to receive one-half of Mr. Earl's salary. Justice Holmes used the celebrated **fruit and tree metaphor** to explain that the fruit (income) must be attributed to the tree from which it came (Mr. Earl's services). A mere **assignment of income** does not shift the liability for the tax.

Services of an Employee. Services performed by an employee for the employer's customers are considered performed by the employer. Thus, the employer is taxed on the income from the services provided to the customer, and the employee is taxed on any compensation received from the employer.[46]

EXAMPLE 20

Dr. Shontelle incorporates her medical practice and enters into a contract to work for the corporation for a salary. All patients contract to receive their services from the corporation, and those services are provided through the corporation's employee, Dr. Shontelle. The corporation must include the patients' fees in its gross income. Dr. Shontelle must include her salary in her gross income. The corporation is allowed a deduction for the reasonable salary paid to Dr. Shontelle (see the discussion of unreasonable compensation in Chapter 6). ■

Services of a Child. In the case of a child, the Code specifically provides that amounts earned from personal services must be included in the child's gross income. This result applies even though the income is paid to other persons (e.g., the parents).[47]

INCOME FROM PROPERTY

Income from property (interest, dividends, rent) must be included in the gross income of the *owner* of the property. If a father clips interest coupons from bonds shortly before the interest payment date and gives the coupons to his son, the interest will still be taxed to the father. A father who assigns rents from rental property to his daughter will be taxed on the rent since he retains ownership of the property.[48]

Often income-producing property is transferred after income from the property has accrued, but before the income is recognized under the transferor's method of accounting. The IRS and the courts have developed rules to allocate the income between the transferor and the transferee.

[45] 2 USTC ¶496, 8 AFTR 10287, 50 S.Ct. 241 (USSC, 1930).

[46] *Sargent v. Comm.*, 91–1 USTC ¶50,168, 67 AFTR2d 91–718, 929 F.2d 1252 (CA–8, 1991).

[47] § 73. For circumstances in which the child's unearned income is taxed at the parents' rate, see Unearned Income of Children under Age 14 Taxed at Parents' Rate in Chapter 3.

[48] *Galt v. Comm.*, 54–2 USTC ¶9457, 46 AFTR 633, 216 F.2d 41 (CA–7, 1954); *Helvering v. Horst*, 40–2 USTC ¶9787, 24 AFTR 1058, 61 S.Ct. 144 (USSC, 1940).

Interest. According to the IRS, interest accrues daily. Therefore, the interest for the period that includes the date of the transfer is allocated between the transferor and transferee based on the number of days during the period that each owned the property.

EXAMPLE 21

Floyd, a cash basis taxpayer, gave his son, Seth, bonds with a face amount of $10,000 and an 8% stated annual interest rate. The gift was made on January 31, 2004, and the interest was paid on December 31, 2004. Floyd must recognize $68 in interest income (8% × $10,000 × 31⁄366). Seth will recognize $732 in interest income ($800 – $68). ■

When the transferor must recognize the income from the property depends upon the method of accounting and the manner in which the property was transferred. In the case of a gift of income-producing property, the donor must recognize his or her share of the accrued income at the time it would have been recognized had the donor continued to own the property.[49] However, if the transfer is a sale, the transferor must recognize the accrued income at the time of the sale. This results because the accrued interest will be included in the sales proceeds.

EXAMPLE 22

Assume the same facts as in Example 21, except that the interest that was payable as of December 31 was not actually or constructively received by the bondholders until January 3, 2005. As a cash basis taxpayer, Floyd generally does not recognize interest income until it is received. If Floyd had continued to own the bonds, the interest would have been included in his 2005 gross income, the year it would have been received. Therefore, Floyd must include the $68 accrued income in his gross income as of January 3, 2005.

Further assume that Floyd sold identical bonds on the date of the gift. The bonds sold for $9,900, including accrued interest. On January 31, 2004, Floyd must recognize the accrued interest of $68 on the bonds sold. Thus, the selling price of the bonds is $9,832 ($9,900 – $68). ■

Dividends. A corporation is taxed on its earnings, and the shareholders are taxed on the dividends paid to them from the corporation's after-tax earnings. The dividend can take the form of an actual dividend or a constructive dividend (e.g., shareholder use of corporate assets).

Partial relief from the double taxation of dividends has been provided in the Jobs and Growth Tax Relief Reconciliation Act of 2003. Generally, dividends received in taxable years beginning after 2002 are taxed at the same marginal rate that is applicable to a net capital gain.[50] Thus, individuals otherwise subject to the 10 or 15 percent marginal tax rate pay only a 5 percent tax on qualified dividends received. Individuals subject to the 25, 28, 33, or 35 percent marginal tax rate pay a 15 percent tax on qualified dividends received. Thus, dividends receive favorable treatment as compared to interest income.

Note that qualified dividends are not treated as capital gains in the gains and losses netting process; thus, they are *not* reduced by capital losses. Qualified dividend income is merely taxed at the rates that would apply to the taxpayer if he or she had an excess of net long-term capital gain over net short-term capital loss.

Because the beneficial tax rate is intended to mitigate double taxation, only certain dividends are eligible for the beneficial treatment. Excluded are certain dividends from foreign corporations, dividends from tax-exempt entities, and dividends that do not satisfy the holding period requirement.

A dividend from a foreign corporation is eligible for qualified dividend status only if one of the following requirements is met: (1) the foreign corporation's stock

[49]Rev.Rul. 72–312, 1972–1 C.B. 22.

[50]§ 1(h)(11).

is traded on an established U.S. securities market, or (2) the foreign corporation is eligible for the benefits of a comprehensive income tax treaty between its country of incorporation and the United States.

To satisfy the holding period requirement, the stock on which the dividend is paid must have been held for more than 60 days during the 120-day period beginning 60 days before the ex-dividend date.[51] The purpose of this requirement is to prevent the taxpayer from buying the stock shortly before the dividend is paid, receiving the dividend, and then selling the stock at a loss (a capital loss) after the stock goes ex-dividend. A stock's price often declines after the stock goes ex-dividend.

EXAMPLE 23

In June 2005, Green Corporation pays a dividend of $1.50 on each share of its common stock. Madison and Daniel, two unrelated shareholders, each own 1,000 shares of the stock. Consequently, each receives $1,500 (1,000 shares × $1.50). Assume Daniel satisfies the 60/120-day holding period rule, but Madison does not. The $1,500 Daniel receives is subject to preferential 15%/5% treatment. The $1,500 Madison receives, however, is not. Because Madison did not comply with the holding period rule, her dividend is not a *qualified dividend* and is taxed at ordinary income rates. ■

EXAMPLE 24

Assume that both Madison and Daniel in Example 23 are in the 35% tax bracket. Consequently, Madison pays a tax of $525 (35% × $1,500) on her dividend, while Daniel pays a tax of $225 (15% × $1,500) on his. The $300 saving that Daniel enjoys underscores the advantages of a qualified dividend. ■

Unlike interest, dividends do not accrue on a daily basis because the declaration of a dividend is at the discretion of the corporation's board of directors. Generally, dividends are taxed to the person who is entitled to receive them—the shareholder of record as of the corporation's record date.[52] Thus, if a taxpayer sells stock after a dividend has been declared but before the record date, the dividend generally will be taxed to the purchaser.

If a donor makes a gift of stock to someone (e.g., a family member) after the declaration date but before the record date, the Tax Court has held that the donor does not shift the dividend income to the donee. The *fruit* has sufficiently ripened as of the declaration date to tax the dividend income to the donor of the stock.[53] In a similar set of facts, the Fifth Circuit Court of Appeals concluded that the dividend income should be included in the gross income of the donee (the owner at the record date). In this case, the taxpayer gave stock to a qualified charity (a charitable contribution) after the declaration date and before the record date.[54]

EXAMPLE 25

On June 20, the board of directors of Black Corporation declares a $10 per share dividend. The dividend is payable on June 30, to shareholders of record on June 25. As of June 20, Maria owned 200 shares of Black Corporation's stock. On June 21, Maria sold 100 of the shares to Norm for their fair market value and gave 100 of the shares to Sam (her son). Both Norm and Sam are shareholders of record as of June 25. Norm (the purchaser) will be taxed on $1,000 since he is entitled to receive the dividend. However, Maria (the donor) will be taxed on the $1,000 received by Sam (the donee) because the gift was made after the declaration date of the dividend. ■

[51]The ex-dividend date is the date following the record date on which the corporation finalizes the list of shareholders who will receive the dividends.

[52]Reg. § 1.61–9(c). The record date is the cutoff for determining the shareholders who are entitled to receive the dividend.

[53]*M. G. Anton*, 34 T.C. 842 (1960).

[54]*Caruth Corp. v. U.S.*, 89–1 USTC ¶9172, 63 AFTR2d 89–716, 865 F.2d 644 (CA–5, 1989).

ETHICAL CONSIDERATIONS

Enhancing Lottery Winnings

Some family members have net losses from gambling, which can be used only to reduce gambling gains. Another family member has a substantial gain from winning the lottery. Suppose that the winner gives the winning ticket to the family members with gambling losses, thereby creating what is tantamount to tax-exempt income. Evaluate this proposal.

INCOME RECEIVED BY AN AGENT

Income received by the taxpayer's agent is considered to be received by the taxpayer. A cash basis principal must recognize the income at the time it is received by the agent.[55]

EXAMPLE 26

Jack, a cash basis taxpayer, delivered cattle to the auction barn in late December. The auctioneer, acting as the farmer's agent, sold the cattle and collected the proceeds in December. The auctioneer did not pay Jack until the following January. Jack must include the sales proceeds in his gross income for the year the auctioneer received the funds. ■

INCOME FROM PARTNERSHIPS, S CORPORATIONS, TRUSTS, AND ESTATES

A **partnership** is not a separate taxable entity. Rather, the partnership merely files an information return (Form 1065), which serves to provide the data necessary for determining the character and amount of each partner's distributive share of the partnership's income and deductions. Each partner must then report his or her distributive share of the partnership's income and deductions for the partnership's tax year ending within or with the partner's tax year. The income must be reported by each partner in the year it is earned, even if such amounts are not actually distributed to the partners. Because a partner pays tax on income as the partnership earns it, a distribution by the partnership to the partner is treated under the recovery of capital rules.[56]

EXAMPLE 27

Tara owns a one-half interest in the capital and profits of T & S Company (a calendar year partnership). For tax year 2005, the partnership earned revenue of $150,000 and had operating expenses of $80,000. During the year, Tara withdrew from her capital account $2,500 per month (for a total of $30,000). For 2005, Tara must report $35,000 as her share of the partnership's profits [½ × ($150,000 − $80,000)] even though she received distributions of only $30,000. ■

Contrary to the general provision that a corporation must pay tax on its income, a *small business corporation* may elect to be taxed similarly to a partnership. Thus, the shareholders, rather than the corporation, pay the tax on the corporation's income.[57] The electing corporation is referred to as an **S corporation.** Generally, the shareholders report their proportionate shares of the corporation's income and deductions for the year, whether or not the corporation actually makes any distributions to the shareholders.

[55]Rev.Rul. 79–379, 1979–2 C.B. 204.

[56]§ 706(a) and Reg. § 1.706–1(a)(1). For further discussion, see Chapter 21.

[57]§§ 1361(a) and 1366. For further discussion, see Chapter 22.

The *beneficiaries of estates and trusts* generally are taxed on the income earned by the estates or trusts that is actually distributed or required to be distributed to them.[58] Any income not taxed to the beneficiaries is taxable to the estate or trust.

INCOME IN COMMUNITY PROPERTY STATES

General. State law in Louisiana, Texas, New Mexico, Arizona, California, Washington, Idaho, Nevada, and Wisconsin is based upon a community property system. In Alaska, spouses can choose to have the community property rules apply. All other states have a common law property system. The basic difference between common law and community property systems centers around the property rights of married persons. Questions about community property income most frequently arise when the husband and wife file separate returns.

Under a **community property** system, all property is deemed either to be separately owned by the spouse or to belong to the marital community. Property may be held separately by a spouse if it was acquired before marriage or received by gift or inheritance following marriage. Otherwise, any property is deemed to be community property. For Federal tax purposes, each spouse is taxed on one-half of the income from property belonging to the community.

The laws of Texas, Louisiana, Wisconsin, and Idaho distinguish between separate property and the income it produces. In these states, the income from separate property belongs to the community. Accordingly, for Federal income tax purposes, each spouse is taxed on one-half of the income. In the remaining community property states, separate property produces separate income that the owner-spouse must report on his or her Federal income tax return.

What appears to be income, however, may really represent a recovery of capital. A recovery of capital and gain realized on separate property retain their identity as separate property. Items such as nontaxable stock dividends, royalties from mineral interests, and gains and losses from the sale of property take on the same classification as the assets to which they relate.

EXAMPLE 28

Bob and Jane are husband and wife and reside in California. Among other transactions during the year, the following occurred:

- Nontaxable stock dividend received by Jane on stock that was given to her after her marriage by her mother.
- Gain of $10,000 on the sale of unimproved land purchased by Bob before his marriage.
- Oil royalties of $15,000 from a lease Jane acquired after marriage with her separate funds.

Since the stock dividend was distributed on stock held by Jane as separate property, it also is her separate property. The same result occurs for the oil royalties Jane receives. All of the proceeds from the sale of the unimproved land (including the gain of $10,000) are Bob's separate property. ■

In all community property states, income from personal services (e.g., salaries, wages, income from a professional partnership) is generally treated as if one-half is earned by each spouse.

EXAMPLE 29

Fred and Wilma are married but file separate returns. Fred received $25,000 salary and $300 taxable interest on a savings account he established in his name. The deposits to the savings account were made from Fred's salary that he earned since the marriage. Wilma collected

[58]§§ 652(a) and 662(a). For further discussion of the taxation of income from partnerships, S corporations, trusts, and estates, see Chapters 21, 22, and 28.

$2,000 taxable dividends on stock she inherited from her father. Wilma's gross income is computed as follows under three assumptions as to the state of residency of the couple:

	California	Texas	Common Law States
Dividends	$ 2,000	$ 1,000	$2,000
Salary	12,500	12,500	–0–
Interest	150	150	–0–
	$14,650	$13,650	$2,000

■

Community Property Spouses Living Apart. The general rules for taxing the income from services performed by residents of community property states can create complications and even inequities for spouses who are living apart.

EXAMPLE 30

Cole and Debra were married but living apart for the first nine months of 2005 and were divorced as of October 1, 2005. In December 2005, Cole married Emily, who was married but living apart from Frank before their divorce in June 2005. Cole and Frank had no income from personal services in 2005.

Cole brought into his marriage to Emily a tax liability on one-half of Debra's earnings for the first nine months of the year. However, Emily left with Frank a tax liability on one-half of her earnings for the first six months of 2005. ■

Congress has developed a simple solution to the many tax problems of community property spouses living apart. A spouse (or former spouse) is taxed only on his or her actual earnings from personal services if the following conditions are met:[59]

- The individuals live apart for the entire year.
- They do not file a joint return with each other.
- No portion of the earned income is transferred between the individuals.

EXAMPLE 31

Jim and Lori reside in a community property state, and both are gainfully employed. On July 1, 2005, they separated, and on June 30, 2006, they were divorced. Assuming their only source of income is wages, one-half of such income for each year is earned by June 30, and they did not file a joint return for 2005, each should report the following gross income:

	Jim's Separate Return	Lori's Separate Return
2005	One-half of Jim's wages	One-half of Jim's wages
	One-half of Lori's wages	One-half of Lori's wages
2006	All of Jim's wages	All of Lori's wages

The results would be the same if Jim or Lori married another person in 2006, except that the newlyweds would probably file a joint return. ■

The IRS may absolve from liability an *innocent spouse* who does not live apart for the entire year and files a separate return but omits his or her share of the community income received by the other spouse. To qualify for the innocent spouse relief, the taxpayer must not know or must have no reason to know of the omitted community income. Even if all of these requirements cannot be satisfied, the IRS has additional statutory authority to absolve the innocent spouse from tax liability. If, under the facts and circumstances, it is inequitable to hold the spouse liable for any unpaid tax, the IRS can absolve the spouse from tax liability.

[59]§ 66.

LO.4

Apply the Internal Revenue Code provisions on alimony, loans made at below-market interest rates, annuities, prizes and awards, group term life insurance, unemployment compensation, and Social Security benefits.

Items Specifically Included in Gross Income

The general principles of gross income determination (discussed in the previous sections) as applied by the IRS and the courts have on occasion yielded results Congress found unacceptable. Consequently, Congress has provided more specific rules for determining the gross income from certain sources. Some of these special rules appear in §§ 71–90 of the Code.

ALIMONY AND SEPARATE MAINTENANCE PAYMENTS

When a married couple divorce or become legally separated, state law generally requires a division of the property accumulated during the marriage. In addition, one spouse may have a legal obligation to support the other spouse. The Code distinguishes between the support payments (alimony or separate maintenance) and the property division in terms of the tax consequences.

Alimony and separate maintenance payments are *deductible* by the party making the payments and are *includible* in the gross income of the party receiving the payments.[60] Thus, income is shifted from the income earner to the income beneficiary, who is better able to pay the tax on the amount received.

EXAMPLE 32

Pete and Tina are divorced, and Pete is required to pay Tina $15,000 of alimony each year. Pete earns $31,000 a year. The tax law presumes that because Tina receives the $15,000, she is better able than Pete to pay the tax on that amount. Therefore, Tina must include the $15,000 in her gross income, and Pete is allowed to deduct $15,000 from his gross income. ■

A transfer of property *other than cash* to a former spouse under a divorce decree or agreement is not a taxable event. The transferor is not entitled to a deduction and does not recognize gain or loss on the transfer. The transferee does not recognize income and has a cost basis equal to the transferor's basis.[61]

EXAMPLE 33

Paul transfers stock to Rosa as part of a 2005 divorce settlement. The cost of the stock to Paul is $12,000, and the stock's value at the time of the transfer is $15,000. Rosa later sells the stock for $16,000. Paul is not required to recognize gain from the transfer of the stock to Rosa, and Rosa has a realized and recognized gain of $4,000 ($16,000 – $12,000) when she sells the stock. ■

In the case of *cash payments*, however, it is often difficult to distinguish payments under a support obligation (alimony) and payments for the other spouse's property (property settlement). In 1984, Congress developed objective rules to classify the payments.

Post-1984 Agreements and Decrees. Payments made under post-1984 agreements and decrees are *classified as alimony* only if the following conditions are satisfied:

1. The payments are in cash.
2. The agreement or decree does not specify that the payments are not alimony.

[60]§§ 71 and 215.

[61]§ 1041, added to the Code in 1984 to repeal the rule of *U.S. v. Davis*, 62–2 USTC ¶9509, 9 AFTR2d 1625, 82 S.Ct. 1190 (USSC, 1962). Under the *Davis* rule, which applied to pre-1985 divorces, a property transfer incident to divorce was a taxable event.

Concept Summary 4–1

Tax Treatment of Payments and Transfers Pursuant to Post-1984 Divorce Agreements and Decrees

	Payor	Recipient
Alimony	Deduction from gross income.	Included in gross income.
Alimony recapture	Included in gross income of the third year.	Deducted from gross income of the third year.
Child support	Not deductible.	Not includible in gross income.
Property settlement	No income or deduction.	No income or deduction; basis for the property is the same as the transferor's basis.

3. The payor and payee are not members of the same household at the time the payments are made.
4. There is no liability to make the payments for any period after the death of the payee.[62]

Requirement 1 simplifies the law by clearly distinguishing alimony from a property division; that is, if the payment is not in cash, it must be a property division. Requirement 2 allows the parties to determine by agreement whether or not the payments will be alimony. The prohibition on cohabitation—requirement 3—is aimed at assuring the alimony payments are associated with duplicative living expenses (maintaining two households).[63] Requirement 4 is an attempt to prevent alimony treatment from being applied to what is, in fact, a payment for property rather than a support obligation. That is, a seller's estate generally will receive payments for property due after the seller's death. Such payments after the death of the payee could not be for the payee's support.

Front-Loading. As a further safeguard against a property settlement being disguised as alimony, special rules apply to post-1986 agreements if payments in the first or second year exceed $15,000. If the change in the amount of the payments exceeds statutory limits, **alimony recapture** results to the extent of the excess alimony payments. In the *third* year, the payor must include the excess alimony payments for the first and second years in gross income, and the payee is allowed a deduction for these excess alimony payments. The recaptured amount is computed as follows:[64]

$$R = D + E$$

$$D = B - (C + \$15{,}000)$$

$$E = A - \left(\frac{B - D + C}{2} + \$15{,}000\right)$$

R = amount recaptured in Year 3 tax return

D = recapture from Year 2

E = recapture from Year 1

A, B, C = payments in the first (A), second (B), and third (C) calendar years of the agreement or decree, where $D \geq 0$, $E \geq 0$

[62] § 71(b)(1). This set of alimony rules can also apply to pre-1985 agreements and decrees if both parties agree in writing. The rules applicable to pre-1985 agreements and decrees are not discussed in this text.

[63] *Alexander Washington*, 77 T.C. 601 (1981) at 604.

[64] § 71(f).

The recapture formula provides an objective technique for determining alimony recapture. Thus, at the time of the divorce, the taxpayers can ascertain the tax consequences. The general concept is that if the alimony payments decrease by more than $15,000 between years in the first three years, there will be alimony recapture with respect to the decrease in excess of $15,000 each year. This rule is applied for the change between Year 2 and Year 3 (D in the above formula). However, rather than making the same calculation for Year 2 payments versus Year 1 payments, the Code requires that the *average* of the payments in Years 2 and 3 be compared with the Year 1 payments (E in the above formula). For this purpose, revised alimony for Year 2 (alimony deducted for Year 2 minus the alimony recapture for Year 2) is used.

EXAMPLE 34

Wes and Rita are divorced in 2005. Under the agreement, Rita is to receive $50,000 in 2005, $20,000 in 2006, and nothing thereafter. The payments are to cease upon Rita's death or remarriage. In 2007, Wes must include an additional $32,500 in gross income for alimony recapture, and Rita is allowed a deduction for the same amount.

$$D = \$20{,}000 - (\$0 + \$15{,}000) = \$5{,}000$$

$$E = \$50{,}000 - \left(\frac{\$20{,}000 - \$5{,}000 + \$0}{2} + \$15{,}000\right) = \$27{,}500$$

$$R = \$5{,}000 + \$27{,}500 = \$32{,}500$$

Note that for 2005 Wes deducts alimony of $50,000, and Rita includes $50,000 in her gross income. For 2006, the amount of the alimony deduction for Wes is $20,000, and Rita's gross income from the alimony is $20,000.

If instead Wes paid $50,000 of alimony in 2005 and nothing for the following years, $35,000 would be recaptured in 2007.

$$D = \$0 - (\$0 + \$15{,}000) = -\$15{,}000, \text{ but D must be} \geq \$0$$

$$E = \$50{,}000 - \left(\frac{\$0 - \$0 + \$0}{2} + \$15{,}000\right) = \$35{,}000$$

$$R = \$0 + \$35{,}000 = \$35{,}000$$

■

Alimony recapture does not apply if the decrease in payments is due to the death of either spouse or the remarriage of the payee.[65] Recapture is not applicable because these events typically terminate alimony under state laws. In addition, the recapture rules do not apply to payments where the amount is contingent (e.g., a percentage of income from certain property or a percentage of the pay or spouse's compensation), the payments are to be made over a period of three years or longer (unless death, remarriage, or other contingency occurs), and the contingencies are beyond the payor's control.[66]

EXAMPLE 35

Under a 2005 divorce agreement, Ed is to receive an amount equal to one-half of Nina's income from certain rental properties for 2005–2008. Payments are to cease upon the death of Ed or Nina or upon the remarriage of Ed. Ed receives $50,000 in 2005 and $50,000 in 2006; in 2007, however, the property is vacant, and Ed receives nothing. Nina, who deducted alimony in 2005 and 2006, is not required to recapture any alimony in 2007 because the payments were contingent. ■

[65] § 71(f)(5)(A).
[66] § 71(f)(5)(C).

Child Support. A taxpayer does not realize income from the receipt of child support payments made by his or her former spouse. This result occurs because the money is received subject to the duty to use the money for the child's benefit. The payor is not allowed to deduct the child support payments because the payments are made to satisfy the payor's legal obligation to support the child.

In many cases, it is difficult to determine whether an amount received is alimony or child support. If the amount of the payments would be reduced upon the happening of a contingency related to a child (e.g., the child attains age 21 or dies), the amount of the future reduction in the payment is deemed child support.[67]

EXAMPLE 36

A divorce agreement provides that Matt is required to make periodic alimony payments of $500 per month to Grace. However, when Matt and Grace's child reaches age 21, marries, or dies (whichever occurs first), the payments will be reduced to $300 per month. Grace has custody of the child. Since the required contingency is the cause for the reduction in the payments, from $500 to $300, child support payments are $200 per month, and alimony is $300 per month. ■

IMPUTED INTEREST ON BELOW-MARKET LOANS

As discussed earlier in the chapter, generally no income is recognized unless it is realized. Realization generally occurs when the taxpayer performs services or sells goods and thus becomes entitled to a payment from the other party. It follows that no income is realized if the goods or services are provided at no charge. Under this interpretation of the realization requirement, before 1984, interest-free loans were used to shift income between taxpayers.

EXAMPLE 37

Veneia (daughter) is in the 20% (combined Federal and state rates) tax bracket and has no investment income. Kareem (father) is in the 50% (combined Federal and state rates) tax bracket and has $200,000 in a money market account earning 10% interest. Kareem would like Veneia to receive and pay tax on the income earned on the $200,000. Because Kareem would also like to have access to the $200,000 should he need the money, he does not want to make an outright gift of the money, nor does he want to commit the money to a trust.

Before 1984, Kareem could achieve his goals as follows. He could transfer the money market account to Veneia in exchange for her $200,000 non-interest-bearing note, payable on Kareem's demand. As a result, Veneia would receive the income, and the family's taxes would be decreased by $6,000.

Decrease in Kareem's tax— (.10 × $200,000).50 =	($10,000)
Increase in Veneia's tax— (.10 × $200,000).20 =	4,000
Decrease in the family's taxes	($ 6,000)

■

Under the 1984 amendments to the Code, Kareem in Example 37 is required to recognize **imputed interest** income.[68] Veneia is deemed to have incurred interest expense equal to Kareem's imputed interest income. Veneia's interest may be deductible on her return as investment interest if she itemizes deductions (see Chapter 10). To complete the fictitious series of transactions, Kareem is then deemed to have given Veneia the amount of the imputed interest she did not pay. The gift received by Veneia is not subject to income tax (see Chapter 5), although Kareem

[67] § 71(c)(2).

[68] § 7872(a)(1).

may be subject to the gift tax (unified transfer tax) on the amount deemed given to Veneia (refer to Chapter 1).

Imputed interest is calculated using the rate the Federal government pays on new borrowings and is compounded semiannually. This Federal rate is adjusted monthly and is published by the IRS.[69] Actually, there are three Federal rates: short-term (not over three years and including demand loans), mid-term (over three years but not over nine years), and long-term (over nine years).[70]

EXAMPLE 38

Assume the Federal rate applicable to the loan in Example 37 is 7% through June 30 and 8% from July 1 through December 31. Kareem made the loan on January 1, and the loan is still outstanding on December 31. Kareem must recognize interest income of $15,280, and Veneia has interest expense of $15,280. Kareem is deemed to have made a gift of $15,280 to Veneia.

Interest calculations:	
January 1–June 30— .07($200,000) (½ year)	$ 7,000
July 1–December 31— .08($200,000 + $7,000) (½ year)	8,280
	$15,280

If interest is charged on the loan but is less than the Federal rate, the imputed interest is the difference between the amount that would have been charged at the Federal rate and the amount actually charged.

EXAMPLE 39

Assume the same facts as in Example 38, except that Kareem charged 6% interest, compounded annually.

Interest at the Federal rate	$ 15,280
Less interest charged (.06 × $200,000)	(12,000)
Imputed interest	$ 3,280

The imputed interest rules apply to the following *types* of below-market loans:[71]

1. Gift loans (made out of love, affection, or generosity, as in Example 37).
2. Compensation-related loans (employer loans to employees).
3. Corporation-shareholder loans (a corporation's loans to its shareholders).
4. Tax avoidance loans and other loans that significantly affect the borrower's or lender's Federal tax liability (discussed in the following paragraphs).

The effects of the first three types of loans on the borrower and lender are summarized in Concept Summary 4–2.

Tax Avoidance and Other Below-Market Loans. In addition to the three specific types of loans that are subject to the imputed interest rules, the Code includes a catchall provision for *tax avoidance loans* and other arrangements that have a significant effect on the tax liability of the borrower or lender. The Conference Report provides the following example of an arrangement that might be subject to the imputed interest rules.[72]

[69] §§ 7872(b)(2) and (f)(2).
[70] § 1274(d).
[71] § 7872(c).
[72] H. Rep. No. 98–861, 98th Cong., 2d Sess., 1984, p. 1023.

CONCEPT SUMMARY 4–2

Effect of Certain Below-Market Loans on the Lender and Borrower

Type of Loan		Lender	Borrower
Gift	Step 1	Interest income	Interest expense
	Step 2	Gift made	Gift received
Compensation-related	Step 1	Interest income	Interest expense
	Step 2	Compensation expense	Compensation income
Corporation to shareholder	Step 1	Interest income	Interest expense
	Step 2	Dividend paid	Dividend income

EXAMPLE 40

Annual dues for the Good Health Club are $400. In lieu of paying dues, a member can make a $4,000 deposit, refundable at the end of one year. The club can earn $400 interest on the deposit.

If interest were not imputed, an individual with $4,000 could, in effect, earn tax-exempt income on the deposit. That is, rather than invest the $4,000, earn $400 in interest, pay tax on the interest, and then pay $400 in dues, the individual could avoid tax on the interest by making the deposit. Thus, income and expenses are imputed as follows: interest income and nondeductible health club fees for the club member; income from fees and interest expense for the club. ■

ETHICAL CONSIDERATIONS

A Concealed Loan

You visit Ben, a client, to do some year-end tax planning for him and his wholly owned corporation. Upon reviewing the corporation's most recent balance sheet, you notice a $150,000 note receivable from Ben. No interest income appears on the income statement. You mention to Ben that some interest should be accrued on the note. He responds that it is a non-interest-bearing note. You explain how the imputed interest rules apply for income tax purposes.

After the end of the year, as you are preparing the corporate tax return, you notice that the note has been retired. Ben explains that he borrowed $150,000 from the bank on December 30 and paid off the note. Then, in early January, he borrowed $150,000 from the corporation and repaid the bank loan. The note receivable from him will not appear in the corporate balance sheet accompanying the tax return. Therefore, the IRS will never know the corporation loaned him the money.

Evaluate Ben's actions. What advice should you provide to him?

Many commercially motivated transactions could be swept into this other below-market loans category. However, the Temporary Regulations have carved out a frequently encountered exception for customer prepayments. If the prepayments are included in the recipient's income under the recipient's method of accounting, the payments are not considered loans and, thus, are not subject to the imputed interest rules.[73]

[73]Prop.Reg. § 1.7872–2(b)(1)(i).

Loans to Executives Prohibited

Interest-free loans have become a popular form of compensation for executives. Several examples of multimillion-dollar loans have come to light as a result of recent bankruptcies by large corporations. The board of directors often justifies the loans as necessary to enable the executive to purchase a residence or to buy stock in the company.

Loans by publicly held corporations to their executives are now generally prohibited by Federal law. The Sarbanes-Oxley Act of 2002 (Public Law No. 107–294) places a general prohibition on loans by corporations to their executives. However, an exception permits corporate loans to finance the acquisition of a personal residence for an executive.

Exceptions and Limitations. No interest is imputed on total outstanding *gift loans* of $10,000 or less between individuals, unless the loan proceeds are used to purchase income-producing property.[74] This exemption eliminates from these complex provisions immaterial amounts that do not result in apparent shifts of income. However, if the proceeds of such a loan are used to purchase income-producing property, the limitations discussed in the following paragraphs apply instead.

On loans of $100,000 or less between individuals, the imputed interest cannot exceed the borrower's net investment income for the year (gross income from all investments less the related expenses).[75] As discussed above, one of the purposes of the imputed interest rules is to prevent high-income taxpayers from shifting income to relatives in a lower marginal bracket. This shifting of investment income is considered to occur only to the extent the borrower has net investment income. Thus, the income imputed to the lender is limited to the borrower's net investment income. As a further limitation, or exemption, if the borrower's net investment income for the year does not exceed $1,000, no interest is imputed on loans of $100,000 or less. However, these limitations for loans of $100,000 or less do not apply if a principal purpose of a loan is tax avoidance. In such a case, interest is imputed, and the imputed interest is not limited to the borrower's net investment income.[76]

EXAMPLE 41

Vicki made interest-free gift loans as follows:

Borrower	Amount	Borrower's Net Investment Income	Purpose
Susan	$ 8,000	$ –0–	Education
Dan	9,000	500	Purchase of stock
Bonnie	25,000	–0–	Purchase of a business
Megan	90,000	15,000	Purchase of a residence
Olaf	120,000	–0–	Purchase of a residence

Assume that tax avoidance is not a principal purpose of any of the loans. The loan to Susan is not subject to the imputed interest rules because the $10,000 exception applies. The $10,000

[74] § 7872(c)(2).
[75] § 7872(d).
[76] *Deficit Reduction Tax Bill of 1984: Explanation of the Senate Finance Committee* (April 2, 1984), p. 484.

Concept Summary 4–3

Exceptions to the Imputed Interest Rules for Below-Market Loans

Exception	Eligible Loans	Ineligible Loans and Limitations
De minimis—aggregate loans of $10,000 or less	Gift loans	Proceeds used to purchase income-producing assets.
	Employer-employee	Principal purpose is tax avoidance.
	Corporation-shareholder	Principal purpose is tax avoidance.
Aggregate loans of $100,000 or less	Between individuals	Principal purpose is tax avoidance. For all other loans, interest is imputed to the extent of the borrower's net investment income if that income exceeds $1,000.

exception does not apply to the loan to Dan because the proceeds were used to purchase income-producing assets. However, under the $100,000 exception, the imputed interest is limited to Dan's investment income ($500). Since the $1,000 exception also applies to this loan, no interest is imputed.

No interest is imputed on the loan to Bonnie because the $100,000 exception applies. Interest is imputed on the loan to Megan based on the lesser of (1) the borrower's $15,000 net investment income or (2) the interest as calculated by applying the Federal rate to the outstanding loan. None of the exceptions apply to the loan to Olaf because the loan was for more than $100,000.

Assume the relevant Federal rate is 10% and the loans were outstanding for the entire year. Vicki would recognize interest income, compounded semiannually, as follows:

Loan to Megan:	
First 6 months (.10 × $90,000 × ½ year)	$ 4,500
Second 6 months (.10 × $94,500 × ½ year)	4,725
	$ 9,225
Loan to Olaf:	
First 6 months (.10 × $120,000 × ½ year)	$ 6,000
Second 6 months (.10 × $126,000 × ½ year)	6,300
	$12,300
Total imputed interest ($9,225 + $12,300)	$21,525

■

As with gift loans, there is a $10,000 exemption for *compensation-related loans* and *corporation-shareholder loans*. However, the $10,000 exception does not apply if tax avoidance is one of the principal purposes of a loan.[77] This vague tax avoidance standard makes practically all compensation-related and corporation-shareholder loans suspect. Nevertheless, the $10,000 exception should apply when an employee's borrowing was necessitated by personal needs (e.g., to meet unexpected expenses) rather than tax considerations.

These exceptions to the imputed interest rules are summarized in Concept Summary 4–3.

[77] § 7872(c)(3).

INCOME FROM ANNUITIES

Annuity contracts generally require the purchaser (the annuitant) to pay a fixed amount for the right to receive a future stream of payments. Typically, the issuer of the contract is an insurance company and will pay the annuitant a cash value if the annuitant cancels the contract. The insurance company invests the amounts received from the annuitant, and the income earned serves to increase the cash value of the policy. No income is recognized by the annuitant at the time the cash value of the annuity increases because the taxpayer has not actually received any income. The income is not constructively received because, generally, the taxpayer must cancel the policy to receive the increase in value (the increase in value is subject to substantial restrictions).

EXAMPLE 42

Jean, age 50, pays $30,000 for an annuity contract that is to pay her $500 per month beginning when she reaches age 65 and continuing until her death. If Jean should cancel the policy after one year, she would receive $30,200. The $200 increase in value is not includible in Jean's gross income as long as she does not actually receive the $200. ■

The tax accounting problem associated with receiving payments under an annuity contract is one of apportioning the amounts received between recovery of capital and income.

EXAMPLE 43

In 2005, Tom purchased for $15,000 an annuity intended as a source of retirement income. In 2007, when the cash value of the annuity is $17,000, Tom collects $1,000 on the contract. Is the $1,000 gross income, recovery of capital, or a combination of recovery of capital and income? ■

The statutory solution to this problem depends upon whether the payments began before or after the annuity starting date and upon when the policy was acquired.

Collections before the Annuity Starting Date. Generally, an annuity contract specifies a date on which monthly or annual payments will begin—the annuity starting date. Often the contract will also allow the annuitant to collect a limited amount before the starting date. The amount collected may be characterized as either an actual withdrawal of the increase in cash value or a loan on the policy. In 1982, Congress changed the rules applicable to these withdrawals and loans.

Collections (including loans) equal to or less than the post-August 13, 1982 increases in cash value must be included in gross income. Amounts received in excess of post-August 13, 1982 increases in cash value are treated as a recovery of capital until the taxpayer's cost has been entirely recovered. Additional amounts are included in gross income.[78]

The taxpayer may also be subject to a penalty on early distributions of 10 percent of the income recognized. The penalty generally applies if the amount is received before the taxpayer reaches age 59½ or is disabled.[79] The early distribution penalty is deemed necessary to prevent taxpayers from using annuities as a way of avoiding the original issue discount rules. That is, the investment in the annuity earns a return that is not taxed until it is collected under the annuity rules, whereas the interest on a certificate of deposit is taxed each year as the income accrues. Thus, the annuity offers a tax advantage (deferral of income) that Congress does not want exploited.

[78] § 72(e)(3); Reg. § 1.72–9.

[79] § 72(q).

EXAMPLE 44

Jack, age 50, purchased an annuity policy for $30,000 in 2004. In 2006, when the cash value of the policy has increased to $33,000, Jack withdraws $4,000. He must recognize $3,000 of income ($33,000 cash value – $30,000 cost) and must pay a penalty of $300 ($3,000 × 10%). The remaining $1,000 is a recovery of capital and reduces Jack's basis in the annuity policy. ■

Collections on and after the Annuity Starting Date. The annuitant can exclude from income (as a recovery of capital) the proportion of each payment that the investment in the contract bears to the expected return under the contract. The *exclusion amount* is calculated as follows:

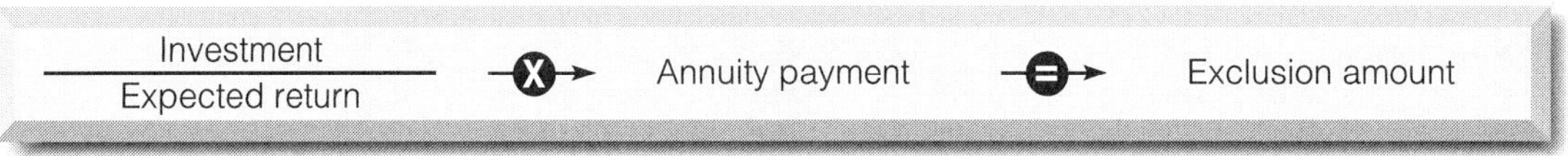

The *expected return* is the annual amount to be paid to the annuitant multiplied by the number of years the payments will be received. The payment period may be fixed (a *term certain*) or for the life of one or more individuals. When payments are for life, the taxpayer generally must use the annuity table published by the IRS to determine the expected return (see Table 4–1). This is an actuarial table that contains life expectancies.[80] The expected return is calculated by multiplying the appropriate multiple (life expectancy) by the annual payment.

EXAMPLE 45

The taxpayer, age 54, purchases an annuity from an insurance company for $90,000. She is to receive $500 per month for life. Her life expectancy (from Table 4–1) is 29.5 years from the annuity starting date. Thus, her expected return is $500 × 12 × 29.5 = $177,000, and the exclusion amount is $3,051 [($90,000 investment/$177,000 expected return) × $6,000 annual payment]. The $3,051 is a nontaxable return of capital, and $2,949 is included in gross income. ■

The *exclusion ratio* (investment ÷ expected return) applies until the annuitant has recovered his or her investment in the contract. Once the investment is recovered, the entire amount of subsequent payments is taxable. If the annuitant dies before recovering the investment, the unrecovered cost (adjusted basis) is deductible in the year the payments cease (usually the year of death).[81]

EXAMPLE 46

Assume the taxpayer in Example 45 receives annuity payments for 30.5 years (366 months). For the last 12 months [366 – (12 × 29.5) = 12], the taxpayer will include $500 each month in gross income. If instead the taxpayer dies after 36 months, she is eligible for an $80,847 deduction on her final tax return.

Cost of the contract	$90,000
Cost previously recovered $90,000/$177,000 × 36($500) =	(9,153)
Deduction	$80,847

■

Simplified Method for Annuity Distributions from Qualified Retirement Plans. A simplified method is required for allocating basis to the annuity payments received under a qualified retirement plan. The portion of each annuity payment that is excluded as a return of capital is the employee's investment in the

[80] The life expectancies in Table 4–1 apply for annuity investments made on or after July 1, 1986. See *General Rules for Pensions and Annuities*, IRS Publication 939 (Rev. April 2003), p. 25. See also *Pension and Annuity Income*, IRS Publication 575 (Rev. Feb. 2004).

[81] § 72(b).

■ TABLE 4–1
Ordinary Life Annuities: One Life—Expected Return Multiples

Age	Multiple	Age	Multiple	Age	Multiple
5	76.6	42	40.6	79	10.0
6	75.6	43	39.6	80	9.5
7	74.7	44	38.7	81	8.9
8	73.7	45	37.7	82	8.4
9	72.7	46	36.8	83	7.9
10	71.7	47	35.9	84	7.4
11	70.7	48	34.9	85	6.9
12	69.7	49	34.0	86	6.5
13	68.8	50	33.1	87	6.1
14	67.8	51	32.2	88	5.7
15	66.8	52	31.3	89	5.3
16	65.8	53	30.4	90	5.0
17	64.8	54	29.5	91	4.7
18	63.9	55	28.6	92	4.4
19	62.9	56	27.7	93	4.1
20	61.9	57	26.8	94	3.9
21	60.9	58	25.9	95	3.7
22	59.9	59	25.0	96	3.4
23	59.0	60	24.2	97	3.2
24	58.0	61	23.3	98	3.0
25	57.0	62	22.5	99	2.8
26	56.0	63	21.6	100	2.7
27	55.1	64	20.8	101	2.5
28	54.1	65	20.0	102	2.3
29	53.1	66	19.2	103	2.1
30	52.2	67	18.4	104	1.9
31	51.2	68	17.6	105	1.8
32	50.2	69	16.8	106	1.6
33	49.3	70	16.0	107	1.4
34	48.3	71	15.3	108	1.3
35	47.3	72	14.6	109	1.1
36	46.4	73	13.9	110	1.0
37	45.4	74	13.2	111	.9
38	44.4	75	12.5	112	.8
39	43.5	76	11.9	113	.7
40	42.5	77	11.2	114	.6
41	41.5	78	10.6	115	.5

contract divided by the number of anticipated monthly payments determined in accordance with Table 4–2.[82]

EXAMPLE 47

Andrea, age 62, receives an annuity distribution of $500 per month for life from her qualified retirement plan beginning in January 2005. Her investment in the contract is $100,100. The excludible amount of each payment is $385 ($100,100 investment/260 monthly payments). Thus, $115 ($500 – $385) of each annuity payment is included in Andrea's gross income. ■

[82]§ 72(d).

■ **TABLE 4–2**
Number of Anticipated Monthly Annuity Payments under the Simplified Method

Age	Number of Anticipated Monthly Payments
55 and under	360
56–60	310
61–65	260
66–70	210
71 and over	160

The rules for annuity payments received after the basis has been recovered by the annuitant and for the annuitant who dies before the basis is recovered are the same as under the exclusion ratio method discussed earlier.

PRIZES AND AWARDS

The fair market value of prizes and awards (other than scholarships exempted under § 117, to be discussed subsequently) must be included in gross income.[83] Therefore, TV giveaway prizes, magazine publisher prizes, door prizes, and awards from an employer to an employee in recognition of performance are fully taxable to the recipient.

A narrow exception permits a prize or award to be excluded from gross income if *all* of the following requirements are satisfied:

- The prize or award is received in recognition of religious, charitable, scientific, educational, artistic, literary, or civic achievement (e.g., Nobel Prize, Pulitzer Prize).
- The recipient transfers the prize or award to a qualified governmental unit or nonprofit organization.
- The recipient was selected without any action on his or her part to enter the contest or proceeding.
- The recipient is not required to render substantial future services as a condition for receiving the prize or award.[84]

Because the transfer of the property to a qualified governmental unit or nonprofit organization ordinarily would be a charitable contribution (an itemized deduction as presented in Chapter 10), the exclusion produces beneficial tax consequences in the following situations:

- The taxpayer does not itemize deductions and thus would receive no tax benefit from the charitable contribution.
- The taxpayer's charitable contributions exceed the annual statutory ceiling on the deduction.
- Including the prize or award in gross income would reduce the amount of deductions the taxpayer otherwise would qualify for because of gross income limitations (e.g., the gross income test for a dependency exemption, the adjusted gross income limitation in calculating the medical expense deduction).

Another exception is provided for certain *employee achievement awards* in the form of tangible personal property (e.g., a gold watch). The awards must be made in recognition of length of service or safety achievement. Generally, the ceiling on the excludible amount for an employee is $400 per taxable year. However, if the

[83] § 74.

[84] § 74(b).

TABLE 4–3
Uniform Premiums for $1,000 of Group Term Life Insurance Protection

Attained Age on Last Day of Employee's Tax Year	Cost per $1,000 of Protection for One-Month Period*
Under 25	$ .05
25–29	.06
30–34	.08
35–39	.09
40–44	.10
45–49	.15
50–54	.23
55–59	.43
60–64	.66
65–69	1.27
70 and above	2.06

*Reg. § 1.79–3, effective for coverage after June 30, 1999.

award is a qualified plan award, the ceiling on the exclusion is $1,600 per taxable year.[85]

GROUP TERM LIFE INSURANCE

For many years, the IRS did not attempt to tax the value of life insurance protection provided to an employee by the employer. Some companies took undue advantage of the exclusion by providing large amounts of insurance protection for executives. Therefore, Congress enacted § 79, which created a limited exclusion for **group term life insurance.** The premiums on the first $50,000 of group term life insurance protection are excludible from the employee's gross income.

The benefits of this exclusion are available only to employees. Proprietors and partners are not considered employees. The Regulations generally require broad-scale coverage of employees to satisfy the *group* requirement (e.g., shareholder-employees would not constitute a qualified group). The exclusion applies only to term insurance (protection for a period of time but with no cash surrender value) and not to ordinary life insurance (lifetime protection plus a cash surrender value that can be drawn upon before death).

As mentioned, the exclusion applies to the first $50,000 of group term life insurance protection. For each $1,000 of coverage in excess of $50,000, the employee must include the amounts indicated in Table 4–3 in gross income.[86]

EXAMPLE 48

Finch Corporation has a group term life insurance policy with coverage equal to the employee's annual salary. Keith, age 52, is president of the corporation and receives an annual salary of $75,000. Keith must include $69 in gross income from the insurance protection for the year.

$$\frac{\$75{,}000 - \$50{,}000}{\$1{,}000} \times .23 \times 12 \text{ months} = \$69$$

■

Generally, the amount that must be included in gross income, computed from Table 4–3, is much less than the price an individual would pay an insurance company for the same amount of protection. Thus, even the excess coverage pro-

[85] §§ 74(c) and 274(j).

[86] Reg. § 1.79–3(d)(2).

vides some tax-favored income for employees when group term life insurance coverage in excess of $50,000 is desirable.

If the plan discriminates in favor of certain key employees (e.g., officers), the key employees are not eligible for the exclusion. In such a case, the key employees must include in gross income the *greater* of actual premiums paid by the employer or the amount calculated from the Uniform Premiums in Table 4–3. The other employees are still eligible for the $50,000 exclusion and continue to use the Uniform Premiums table to compute the income from excess insurance protection.[87]

UNEMPLOYMENT COMPENSATION

The unemployment compensation program is sponsored and operated by the states and Federal government to provide a source of income for people who have been employed and are temporarily (hopefully) out of work. In a series of rulings over a period of 40 years, the IRS exempted unemployment benefits from tax. These payments were considered social benefit programs for the promotion of the general welfare. After experiencing dissatisfaction with the IRS's treatment of unemployment compensation, Congress amended the Code to provide that the benefits are taxable.[88]

SOCIAL SECURITY BENEFITS

If a taxpayer's income exceeds a specified base amount, as much as 85 percent of Social Security retirement benefits must be included in gross income. The taxable amount of benefits is determined through the application of one of two formulas that utilize a unique measure of income—*modified adjusted gross income* (*MAGI*).[89] MAGI is, generally, the taxpayer's adjusted gross income from all sources (other than Social Security) plus the foreign earned income exclusion and any tax-exempt interest income.

In the formulas, two sets of base amounts are established. The first set is as follows:

- $32,000 for married taxpayers who file a joint return.
- $0 for married taxpayers who do not live apart for the entire year but file separate returns.
- $25,000 for all other taxpayers.

The second set of base amounts is as follows:

- $44,000 for married taxpayers who file a joint return.
- $0 for married taxpayers who do not live apart for the entire year but file separate returns.
- $34,000 for all other taxpayers.

If MAGI plus one-half of Social Security benefits exceeds the first set of base amounts, but not the second set, the taxable amount of Social Security benefits is the *lesser* of the following:

- .50(Social Security benefits).
- .50[MAGI + .50(Social Security benefits) – first base amount].

---

[87] § 79(d).

[88] § 85.

[89] § 86. The rationale for taxing 85% of the Social Security benefits is as follows: For the average Social Security recipient, 15% of the amount received is a recovery of amounts that the individual paid into the program, and the remainder of the benefits is financed by the employer's contribution and interest earned by the Social Security fund.

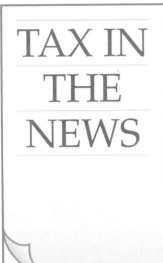

A Taxpayer Learns about the "Quirky" Social Security Benefits Taxation Formula

The "base amount" used in the formula to compute taxable Social Security benefits generally enables low-income individuals to exclude all Social Security benefits received from gross income. But in a recent Tax Court case [*Thomas W. McAdams,* 118 T.C. 373 (2002)], a taxpayer discovered that the base amount can become zero for married couples who file separate returns. If a married couple file a joint return, the base amount is $32,000 (and the adjusted base amount is $44,000). The law provides, however, that if a married couple live together at any time during the tax year and file separate returns, the base amount (and adjusted base amount) is zero. In the Tax Court case, the couple lived apart for 11 months of the year, but lived in separate portions of the same house for the remaining month. One month under the same roof with his wife caused part of the taxpayer's $12,000 in Social Security benefits to be included in his gross income.

EXAMPLE 49

A married couple with adjusted gross income of $30,000, no tax-exempt interest, and $11,000 of Social Security benefits who file jointly must include $1,750 of the benefits in gross income. This works out as the lesser of the following:

1. .50($11,000) = $5,500.
2. .50[$30,000 + .50($11,000) – $32,000] = .50($3,500) = $1,750.

If the couple's adjusted gross income were $15,000 and their Social Security benefits totaled $5,000, none of the benefits would be taxable, since .50[$15,000 + .50($5,000) – $32,000] is not a positive number. ■

If MAGI plus one-half of Social Security benefits exceeds the second set of base amounts, the taxable amount of Social Security benefits is the *lesser* of 1 or 2 below:

1. .85(Social Security benefits).
2. Sum of:
   a. .85[MAGI + .50(Social Security benefits) – second base amount], and
   b. Lesser of:
      - Amount included through application of the first formula.
      - $4,500 ($6,000 for married filing jointly).

EXAMPLE 50

A married couple who file jointly have adjusted gross income of $72,000, no tax-exempt interest, and $12,000 of Social Security benefits. Their includible Social Security benefits will be $10,200.

Include the lesser of the following:

1. .85($12,000) = $10,200.
2. Sum of:
   a. .85[$72,000 + .50($12,000) – $44,000] = $28,900, and
   b. Lesser of:
      - Amount calculated by the first formula, which is the lesser of:
        - .50($12,000) = $6,000.
        - .50[$72,000 + .50($12,000) – $32,000] = $23,000.
      - $6,000.

The sum equals $34,900 ($28,900 + $6,000). Since 85% of the Social Security benefits received is less than this amount, $10,200 is included in the couple's gross income. ■

LO.5

Identify tax planning strategies for minimizing gross income.

Tax Planning Considerations

The materials in this chapter have focused on the following questions:

- What is income?
- When is the income recognized?
- Who is the taxpayer?

Planning strategies suggested by these materials include the following:

- Maximize economic benefits that are not included in gross income.
- Defer the recognition of income.
- Shift income to taxpayers who are in a lower marginal tax bracket.

Some specific techniques for accomplishing these strategies are discussed in the following paragraphs.

NONTAXABLE ECONOMIC BENEFITS

Home ownership is the prime example of economic income from capital that is not subject to tax. If the taxpayer uses his or her capital to purchase investments, but pays rent on a personal residence, the taxpayer would pay the rent from after-tax income. However, if the taxpayer purchases a personal residence instead of the investments, he or she would give up gross income from the forgone investments in exchange for the rent savings. The savings in rent enjoyed as a result of owning the home are not subject to tax. Thus, the homeowner will have substituted nontaxable for taxable income.

TAX DEFERRAL

General. Since deferred taxes are tantamount to interest-free loans from the government, the deferral of taxes is a worthy goal of the tax planner. However, the tax planner must also consider the tax rates for the years the income is shifted from and to. For example, a one-year deferral of income from a year in which the taxpayer's tax rate was 28 percent to a year in which the tax rate will be 35 percent would not be advisable if the taxpayer expects to earn less than a 7 percent after-tax return on the deferred tax dollars.

The taxpayer can often defer the recognition of income from appreciated property by postponing the event triggering realization (the final closing on a sale or exchange of property). If the taxpayer needs cash, obtaining a loan by using the appreciated property as collateral may be the least costly alternative. When the taxpayer anticipates reinvesting the proceeds, a sale may be inadvisable.

EXAMPLE 51

Ira owns 100 shares of Pigeon Company common stock with a cost of $20,000 and a fair market value of $50,000. Although the stock's value has increased substantially in the past three years, Ira thinks the growth days are over. If he sells the Pigeon stock, Ira will invest the proceeds from the sale in other common stock. Assuming Ira's marginal tax rate on the sale is 15%, he will have only $45,500 [$50,000 – .15($50,000 – $20,000)] to reinvest. The alternative investment must substantially outperform Pigeon in the future in order for the sale to be beneficial. ■

Selection of Investments. Because no tax is due until a gain has been recognized, the law favors investments that yield appreciation rather than annual income.

EXAMPLE 52

Vera can buy a corporate bond or an acre of land for $10,000. The bond pays $1,000 of interest (10%) each year, and Vera expects the land to increase in value 10% each year for the next 10 years. She is in the 40% (combined Federal and state) tax bracket for ordinary income and 26% for qualifying capital gains. Assuming the bond would mature or the land would be sold in 10 years and Vera would reinvest the interest at a 10% before-tax return, she would accumulate the following amount at the end of 10 years.

		Bond	Land
Original investment		$10,000	$10,000
Annual income	$ 1,000		
Less tax	(400)		
	$ 600		
Compound amount reinvested for 10 years at 6% after-tax	× 13.18	7,908	
		$17,908	
Compound amount, 10 years at 10%			× 2.59
			$25,900
Less tax on sale: 26%($25,900 – $10,000)			(4,134)
			$21,766

Therefore, the value of the deferral that results from investing in the land rather than in the bond is $3,858 ($21,766 – $17,908). ■

Series E and EE bonds can also be purchased for long-term deferrals of income. In situations where the taxpayer's goal is merely to shift income one year into the future, bank certificates of deposit are useful tools. If the maturity period is one year or less, all interest is reported in the year of maturity. Time certificates are especially useful for a taxpayer who realizes an unusually large gain from the sale of property in one year (and thus is in a high tax bracket) but expects his or her gross income to be less the following year.

Cash Basis. The timing of income from services can often be controlled through the use of the cash method of accounting. Although taxpayers are somewhat constrained by the constructive receipt doctrine (they cannot turn their backs on income), seldom will customers and clients offer to pay before they are asked. The usual lag between billings and collections (e.g., December's billings collected in January) will result in a continuous deferring of some income until the last year of operations. A salaried individual approaching retirement may contract with the employer before the services are rendered to receive a portion of compensation in the lower tax bracket retirement years.

Prepaid Income. For the accrual basis taxpayer who receives advance payments from customers, the transactions should be structured to avoid payment of tax on income before the time the income is actually earned. Revenue Procedure 2004–34 provides the guidelines for deferring the tax on prepayments for services, and Regulation § 1.451–5 provides the guidelines for deferrals on sales of goods. In addition, both cash and accrual basis taxpayers can sometimes defer income by stipulating that the payments are deposits rather than prepaid income. For example, a landlord should require an equivalent damage deposit rather than prepayment of the last month's rent under the lease.

SHIFTING INCOME TO RELATIVES

The tax liability of a family can be minimized by shifting income from higher- to lower-bracket family members. This can be accomplished through gifts of income-producing property. Furthermore, in many cases, income can be shifted with no negative effect on the family's investment plans.

EXAMPLE 53

Adam, who is in the 28% tax bracket, would like to save for his children's education. All of the children are under 14 years of age. Adam could transfer income-producing properties to the children, and the children could each receive up to $800 of income each year (refer to Chapter 3) with no tax liability. The next $800 would be taxed at the child's tax rate. After a child has more than $1,600 income, there is no tax advantage to shifting more income to the child (because the income will be taxed at the parents' rate) until the child is 14 years old (when all income will be taxed according to the child's tax rate). ■

The Uniform Gifts to Minors Act, a model law adopted by all states (but with some variations among the states), facilitates income shifting. Under the Act, a gift of intangibles (e.g., bank accounts, stocks, bonds, life insurance contracts) can be made to a minor but with an adult serving as custodian. Usually, a parent who makes the gift is also named as custodian. The state laws allow the custodian to sell or redeem and reinvest the principal and to accumulate or distribute the income, practically at the custodian's discretion provided there is no commingling of the child's income with the parent's property. Thus, the parent can give appreciated securities to the child, and the donor custodian can then sell the securities and reinvest the proceeds, thereby shifting both the gain and the annual income to the child. Such planning is limited by the tax liability calculation provision for a child under the age of 14 (refer to Chapter 3).

U.S. government bonds (Series E and EE) can be purchased by parents for their children. When this is done, the children generally should file a return and elect to report the income on the accrual basis.

EXAMPLE 54

Abby pays $7,500 for Series EE bonds in 2005 and immediately gives them to Wade (her son), who will enter college the year of original maturity of the bonds. The bonds have a maturity value of $10,000. Wade elects to report the annual increment in redemption value as income for each year the bonds are held. The first year the increase is $250, and Wade includes that amount in his gross income. If Wade has no other income, no tax will be due on the $250 bond interest, since such an amount will be more than offset by his available standard deduction. The following year, the increment is $260, and Wade includes this amount in income. Thus, over the life of the bonds, Wade will include $2,500 in income ($10,000 – $7,500), none of which will result in a tax liability, assuming he has no other income. However, if the election had not been made, Wade would be required to include $2,500 in income on the bonds in the year of original maturity, if they were redeemed as planned. This amount of income might result in a tax liability. ■

In some cases, it may be advantageous for the child not to make the accrual election. For example, a child under age 14 with investment income of more than $1,600 each year and parents in the 25, 28, 33, or 35 percent tax bracket would probably benefit from deferring the tax on the savings bond interest. The child would also benefit from the use of the usually lower tax rate (rather than subjecting the income to the parents' tax rate) if the bonds mature after the child is age 14 or older.

ACCOUNTING FOR COMMUNITY PROPERTY

The classification of income as community or separate property becomes important when either of two events occurs:

- Husband and wife, married taxpayers, file separate income tax returns for the year.
- Husband and wife obtain a divorce and therefore have to file separate returns for the year (refer to Chapter 3).

For planning purposes, it behooves married persons to keep track of the source of income (community or separate). To be in a position to do this effectively when income-producing assets are involved, it may be necessary to distinguish between separate and community property.[90]

ALIMONY

The person making the alimony payments favors a divorce settlement that includes a provision for deductible alimony payments. On the other hand, the recipient prefers that the payments do not qualify as alimony. If the payor is in a higher tax bracket than the recipient, both parties may benefit by increasing the payments and structuring them so that they qualify as alimony.

EXAMPLE 55

Carl and Polly are negotiating a divorce settlement. Carl has offered to pay Polly $10,000 each year for 10 years, but payments would cease upon Polly's death. Polly is willing to accept the offer, if the agreement will specify that the cash payments are not alimony. Carl is in the 35% tax bracket, and Polly's marginal rate is 15%.

If Carl and Polly agree that Carl will pay Polly $12,000 of alimony each year, both will have improved after-tax cash flows.

	Annual Cash Flows	
	Carl	Polly
Nonalimony payments	($10,000)	$10,000
Alimony payments	($12,000)	$12,000
Tax effects		
.35($12,000)	4,200	
.15($12,000)		(1,800)
After-tax cash flows	($ 7,800)	$10,200
Benefit of alimony option	$ 2,200	$ 200

Both parties benefit at the government's expense if the $12,000 alimony option is used. ■

KEY TERMS

Accounting income, 4–4
Accounting method, 4–7
Accrual method, 4–8
Alimony and separate maintenance payments, 4–20
Alimony recapture, 4–21
Annuity, 4–28
Assignment of income, 4–14
Cash receipts method, 4–7
Claim of right doctrine, 4–8
Community property, 4–18
Constructive receipt, 4–9
Economic income, 4–3
Fruit and tree metaphor, 4–14
Gross income, 4–3
Group term life insurance, 4–32
Hybrid method, 4–9
Imputed interest, 4–23
Income, 4–3
Original issue discount, 4–10
Partnership, 4–17
Recovery of capital doctrine, 4–6
S corporation, 4–17
Taxable year, 4–6

[90] Being able to distinguish between separate and community property is crucial to the determination of a property settlement incident to a divorce. It also is vital in the estate tax area (refer to Chapter 1) since the surviving wife's or husband's share of the community property is not included in the gross estate of the deceased spouse.

PROBLEM MATERIALS

Discussion Questions

1. The conservatism principle has been found useful for financial accounting purposes. Why have the IRS and the courts chosen not to adopt this principle for tax accounting purposes?

2. In each of the following, determine the taxpayer's "income" for the current year as computed by an economist and as computed for tax purposes. Explain any differences.
   a. In the previous year, the taxpayer purchased stock for $5,000. At the beginning of the current year, the market value of the stock was $7,000. During the current year, the taxpayer sold the stock for $8,000.
   b. The individual made improvements to his personal residence. The cost of the materials was $10,000, and he provided all the labor. The improvements increased the value of the house by $18,000.
   c. The controlling shareholder in a corporation sold property to the corporation for $15,000. The value of the property was $10,000, and the shareholder's cost was $15,000.
   d. The taxpayer found a suitcase containing $25,000 in cash, and she could not determine the true owner.

Issue ID

3. Charley visits Reno, Nevada, once each year to gamble. This year his gambling loss was $15,000. He commented to you, "At least I didn't have to pay for my airfare and hotel room. The casino paid that because I am such a good customer. That was worth at least $2,500." What are the relevant tax issues for Charley?

4. Tom is in the 28% marginal tax bracket. He can work and earn $100 per day, or he can not work and paint his house. If he works, he will have to pay someone else $90 per day to paint his house. How does the tax law influence his decision?

Issue ID

5. Cecil buys wrecked cars and stores them on his property. Recently, he purchased a 1990 Ford Taurus for $250. If he can sell all of the usable parts, his total proceeds from the Taurus would be over $2,000. As of the end of the year, he has sold only the radio for $50, and he does not know how many, if any, of the remaining parts will ever be sold. What are Cecil's income recognition issues?

6. An employee receives a $3,000 payment from a customer in late 2005 and submits the payment to the employer in early 2006. When is the cash basis employer required to include the $3,000 in gross income?

7. Jared, a self-employed insect exterminator, uses the cash method of accounting to report his income. In December 2005, Jared received a check for $400 from a client. Jared deposited the check near the end of December. In early January 2006, the bank notified him that the check did not clear because of insufficient funds in the customer's account. The bank sent the check through a second time, and it cleared in January 2006. Jared computes his income using his deposit records. Therefore, he included the $400 in his 2005 gross income.
   a. In what year should Jared report the $400 of income?
   b. Why does it matter to Jared whether he reports the income in 2005 or 2006, as long as he actually reports it?

8. In 2005, Albert found dinosaur bones on a tract of land that he had owned for several years. When Albert bought the property, he was unaware that the bones were there. An appraiser told him the bones were worth $25,000. In 2006, Albert sold the bones to a museum for $26,000.
   a. What is Albert's gross income in 2005 from the discovery of the bones?
   b. What is Albert's gross income in 2006 from the sale of the bones?

9. Allyson, a cash basis taxpayer, pays $889 for a 4% certificate of deposit (CD) that is to pay her $1,000 at maturity. She purchases the certificate on July 1, 2005, and it will mature on June 30, 2008. Allyson holds the CD until maturity.
   a. Under the original issue discount (OID) rules, for which years does the CD affect Allyson's gross income?
   b. Do you think that the OID rules were enacted for equitable reasons, out of concern for the taxpayer's burden in complying with the law, or for other reasons?

10. What tax advantage does a Series EE U.S. government savings bond due in three years have over a bank CD due in three years that does not pay interest until the maturity date?

11. Coal, Inc., an accrual basis taxpayer, sells goods under terms that allow a customer who is not completely satisfied to return the goods within 30 days of receipt and receive a refund of the purchase price. On December 15, 2005, a customer purchased a product for $500. Coal's cost was $400. The customer returned the product on January 5, 2006, and received a refund of $500. How do these transactions affect Coal's gross income for:
   a. 2005?
   b. 2006?

12. Rex paid $4,000 for an automobile that needed substantial repairs. He worked nights and weekends to restore the car and spent $1,200 on parts for it. He knows he can sell the car for $9,000. His daughter's college tuition is due in a few days. Would it matter, after taxes, whether Rex sells the car and pays the tuition, or whether he gives the car to his daughter and she sells it for $9,000 and pays her tuition?

13. Sarah's major source of income is her salary of $200,000 from which she must pay $50,000 alimony to her former husband, Fred. Is the tax treatment of the $50,000 consistent with the "fruit and tree" metaphor generally applicable to income from services?

14. Who pays the tax on (a) the income of an S corporation and (b) the income of a partnership?

Issue ID

15. Mike and Debbie were residents of California. In 2005, Debbie left Mike, and he has been unable to find her even though he hired a private investigator to do so. Mike and Debbie are still married at year-end. Both Debbie and Mike were employed, and each had substantial investments. They did not have any children. How will Debbie's absence complicate Mike's 2005 income tax return?

16. Why do the alimony rules require alimony recapture when certain large cash payments are made in the first three years after a divorce?

Decision Making

17. Sam and Jean are negotiating their divorce agreement, which requires the division of their jointly owned property. Sam has proposed that he receive the couple's house (basis of $60,000 and fair market value of $100,000) while Jean would receive (a) securities (basis of $115,000 and fair market value of $100,000) or (b) five annual payments of $23,739 each, which is equivalent to a $100,000 loan at 6% interest. Jean will probably sell the securities if she receives them. Jean has too many unhappy memories about the house and does not want to live in it or own it. Which option should she accept?

Issue ID

18. William and Abigail, who live in San Francisco, have been experiencing problems with their marriage. They have a three-year-old daughter, April, who stays with William's parents during the day since both William and Abigail are employed. Abigail worked to support William while he attended medical school, and now she has been accepted by a medical school in Mexico. Abigail has decided to divorce William and attend medical school. April will stay in San Francisco because of her strong attachment to her grandparents and because they can provide her with excellent day care. Abigail knows that William will expect her to contribute to the cost of raising April. Abigail also feels that, to finance her education, she must receive cash for her share of the property they accumulated during their marriage. In addition, she feels she should receive some reimbursement for her contribution to William's support while he was in medical school. She expects the divorce proceedings will take several months. Identify the relevant tax issues for Abigail.

Decision Making

19. Bob and Mary are planning to divorce. Bob has offered to pay Mary $12,000 each year for 10 years or to transfer to her common stock he owns with a fair market value of $100,000 in satisfaction of Mary's share of the marital property. What factors should Mary consider in deciding between these two options?

20. In the case of a below-market loan between relatives, why is the lender deemed to have received interest income and made a gift?

21. What are the tax effects to a corporation of an interest-free loan to an employee?

Issue ID

22. Brad is the president of the Yellow Corporation. He and other members of his family control the corporation. Brad has a temporary need for $50,000, and the corporation has excess cash. He could borrow the money from a bank at 9%, and Yellow is earning 6% on its temporary investments. Yellow has made loans to other employees on several occasions. Therefore, Brad is considering borrowing $50,000 from the corporation. He will repay the loan principal in two years plus interest at 5%. Identify the relevant tax issues for Brad and the Yellow Corporation.

23. When Betty was 78 years old, she purchased an annuity contract for $75,600. The contract was to pay her $8,900 per year over her remaining life. How much of the annuity payment for the twelfth year would Betty be required to include in her gross income if she actually lived for 13 years after the annuity payments began?

24. Given the broad concept of gross income contained in the Internal Revenue Code, does § 79 applicable to group term life insurance assure that some premiums can be excluded from gross income, or does it assure that some of the premiums in certain circumstances will be included in gross income?

25. Evelyn, who is 66 years old and unmarried, receives a taxable pension of $22,000 annually. She also receives $10,000 a year in Social Security benefits. Evelyn claims the standard deduction. According to the tax rate schedule, her marginal tax rate is 15%. She lives in a state that bases her state taxable income on her Federal taxable income, and the state tax rate is 6%. She is considering taking on a part-time job that would pay her $3,000 a year. What would be her after-tax earnings from the part-time job?

Problems

26. Compute the taxpayer's (1) economic income and (2) gross income for tax purposes from the following events:
    a. The taxpayer sold securities for $10,000. The securities cost $6,000 in 1996. The fair market value of the securities at the beginning of the year was $9,000.
    b. The taxpayer sold his business and received $15,000 under a covenant not to compete with the new owner.
    c. The taxpayer used her controlled corporation's automobile for her vacation. The rental value of the automobile for the vacation period was $800.
    d. The taxpayer raised vegetables in her garden. The fair market value of the vegetables was $900, and the cost of raising them was $100. She ate some of the vegetables and gave the remainder to neighbors.
    e. The local government changed the zoning ordinances so that some of the taxpayer's residential property was reclassified as commercial. Because of the change, the fair market value of the taxpayer's property increased by $10,000.
    f. During the year, the taxpayer borrowed $50,000 for two years at 9% interest. By the end of the year, interest rates had increased to 12%, and the lender accepted $49,000 in full satisfaction of the debt.

Issue ID

27. Amos recently completed medical school and is beginning his medical practice. Most of his patients are covered by health insurance with a co-pay requirement (e.g., the patient pays $10, and the insurance company is billed for the remainder). It takes approximately two months to collect from the health insurance plan. What advice can you provide Amos regarding the selection of a tax accounting method?

Decision Making

Communications

28. Which of the following investments of $10,000 each will yield the greater after-tax value assuming the taxpayer is in the 35% tax bracket for ordinary income and 15% for

qualifying capital gains and dividends in all years and the investments will be liquidated at the end of five years?

a. Land that will increase in value by 6% each year.
b. A taxable bond yielding 6% before tax, and the interest can be reinvested at 6% before tax.
c. Common stock paying a 5% qualified dividend each year, which can be reinvested in common stock paying a 5% dividend each year. The value of the stock will not change.

Prepare a brief speech for your tax class in which you explain why the future value of the land will exceed the future value of the taxable bond. Also explain why the after-tax return on the stock will exceed the after-tax return earned on the bond.

Given: Compound amount of $1 and compound value of annuity payments at the end of five years:

Interest Rate	$1 Compounded for 5 Years	$1 Annuity Compounded for 5 Years
6%	$1.34	$5.64
3.90%	1.20	5.39
4.25%	1.23	5.44

29. Determine the taxpayer's gross income for tax purposes in each of the following situations:
    a. Olga, a cash basis taxpayer, sold a corporate bond with accrued interest of $200 for $10,500. Olga's cost of the bond was $10,000.
    b. Olga needed $10,000 to make a down payment on her house. She instructed her broker to sell some stock to raise the $10,000. Olga's cost of the stock was $3,000. Based on her broker's advice, instead of selling the stock, she borrowed the $10,000 using the stock as collateral for the debt.
    c. Olga owned a vacant lot that was zoned for residential housing. She spent $900 in attorney fees to get the property rezoned as commercial. The property's value increased by $10,000 as a result of the rezoning.

30. Determine Amos Seagull's gross income in each of the following cases:
    a. In the current year, Seagull Corporation purchased an automobile for $25,000. The company was to receive a $1,500 rebate from the manufacturer. However, the corporation directed that the rebate be paid to Amos, the corporation's sole shareholder.
    b. Amos sold his corporation. In addition to the selling price of the stock, he received $50,000 for a covenant not to compete—an agreement that he will not compete with his former business for five years.
    c. Amos and his neighbor got into an argument over Amos's dog. The neighbor built a fence to keep the dog out of his yard. The fence added $1,500 to the value of Amos's property.

Decision Making

31. Al is an attorney who conducts his practice as a sole proprietor. During 2005, he received cash of $150,000 for legal services. Of the amount collected, $25,000 was for services provided in 2004. At the end of 2005, Al had accounts receivable of $45,000, all for services rendered in 2005. At the end of the year, Al received $5,000 as a deposit on property a client was in the process of selling. Compute Al's gross income for 2005:
    a. Using the cash basis of accounting.
    b. Using the accrual basis of accounting.
    c. Advise Al on which method of accounting he should use.

32. Selma opened a farm implements store in 2005. The only accounting records she maintains are her cash receipts and disbursements for the business. Cash receipts for 2005 total $500,000, and cash disbursements (for inventory) total $350,000. The cash receipts include the $50,000 Selma originally invested in the business and a $5,000 customer deposit on a new tractor that is to be delivered by the factory in January 2006. You determine that there were no accounts receivable at the beginning of the year. At the end of the year, accounts receivable total $15,000. The inventory on hand at the end of the

year is $75,000, and $40,000 is owed to vendors for inventory purchases received before year-end. Determine the gross income for the store for 2005 for tax purposes.

Decision Making
Communications

33. Your client is a new partnership, Aspen Associates, which is an engineering consulting firm. Generally, Aspen bills clients for services at the end of each month. Client billings are about $50,000 each month. On average, it takes 45 days to collect the receivables. Aspen's expenses are primarily for salary and rent. Salaries are paid on the last day of each month, and rent is paid on the first day of each month. The partnership has a line of credit with a bank, which requires monthly financial statements. These must be prepared using the accrual method. Aspen's managing partner, Amanda Sims, has suggested that the firm should also use the accrual method for tax purposes and thus reduce accounting fees by $600. Assume the partners are in the 35% (combined Federal and state) marginal tax bracket. Write a letter to your client explaining why you believe it would be worthwhile for Aspen to file its tax return on the cash basis even though its financial statements are prepared on the accrual basis. Aspen's address is 100 James Tower, Denver, CO 80208.

Communications

34. Color Paint Shop, Inc. (459 Ellis Avenue, Harrisburg, PA 17111), is an accrual basis taxpayer that paints automobiles. During the year, the company painted Samuel's car and was to receive a $1,000 payment from his insurance company. Samuel was not satisfied with the work, however, and the insurance company refused to pay. In December 2005, Color and Samuel agreed that Color would receive $800 for the work, subject to final approval by the insurance company. In the past, Color had come to terms with customers only to have the insurance company negotiate an even lesser amount. In May 2006, the insurance company reviewed the claim and paid the $800 to Color. An IRS agent thinks that Color, as an accrual basis taxpayer, should report $1,000 of income in 2005, when the work was done, and then deduct a $200 loss in 2006. Prepare a memo to Susan Apple, a tax partner for whom you are working, with the recommended treatment for the disputed income.

35. Determine the effect of the following on a cash basis taxpayer's gross income for 2005:
    a. On January 2, 2005, the taxpayer negotiated his employment contract. The employer offered to pay him $10,000 on the last day of each month. The taxpayer bargained to be paid $10,000 on the first day of each month beginning February 1, 2005.
    b. In December 2004, the taxpayer received an $8,000 advance on his 2005 salary.
    c. On December 31, 2005, the employer (contrary to the taxpayer's wishes) paid the taxpayer his $10,000 salary that was due on January 1, 2006.

36. Morris is not one to take a lot of risks. All of his investments are in Series EE U.S. government savings bonds and bank CDs. Determine the tax consequences from his investments for 2005.
    a. On June 30, 2005, he cashed in Series EE bonds that he had purchased in 1995. His cost of the bonds was $6,139, and the maturity value was $10,000. This is an effective before-tax yield of 5% per year. Morris did not elect to take the annual increments in value into income each year.
    b. On September 30, 2005, Morris redeemed a two-year CD, interest rate of 4%, that he had purchased from the local bank on October 1, 2003. He paid $9,244 for the CD and received $10,000 at maturity. He immediately invested the $10,000 in a one-year CD, interest rate of 5%, with a maturity value of $10,500.

37. Swan Appliance Company, an accrual basis taxpayer, sells home appliances and service contracts. Determine the effect of each of the following transactions on the company's 2005 gross income assuming that the company uses any available options to defer its taxes.
    a. In December 2004, the company received a $1,200 advance payment from a customer for an appliance that Swan special ordered from the manufacturer. The appliance did not arrive from the manufacturer until January 2005, and Swan immediately delivered it to the customer. The sale was reported in 2005 for financial accounting purposes.
    b. In June 2005, the company sold a 12-month service contract for $240. The company also sold a 24-month service contract for $480 in December 2005.
    c. On December 31, 2005, the company sold an appliance for $1,200. The company received $500 cash and a note from the customer for $700 and $260 interest, to be

paid at the rate of $40 a month for 24 months. Because of the customer's poor credit record, the fair market value of the note was only $600. The cost of the appliance was $750.

38. Freda is a cash basis taxpayer. In 2005, she negotiated her salary for 2006. Her employer offered to pay her $20,000 each month—a total of $240,000 for the year. Freda countered that she would accept $20,000 each month for the first nine months of the year and the remaining $60,000 in January 2007. The employer accepted Freda's terms for 2006 and 2007.
    a. Did Freda actually or constructively receive $240,000 in 2006?
    b. What could explain Freda's willingness to spread her salary over a longer period of time?

Decision Making

39. The Bonhaus Apartments is a new development and is in the process of structuring its lease agreements. The company would like to set the damage deposits high enough that tenants will keep the apartments in good condition. The company is actually more concerned about damage than about tenants not paying their rent.
    a. Discuss the tax effects of the following alternatives:
        - $400 damage deposit and $400 rent for the final month of the lease.
        - $800 rent for the final two months of the lease and no damage deposit.
        - $800 damage deposit with no rent prepayment.
    b. Which option do you recommend?

40. Gus was unable to pay his bills as they came due. One of his creditors got a court order to garnish Gus's royalty receipts from a book contract. In addition, his royalties were garnished for child support. His earnings statement from the publishing company for the year reflected the following:

Royalties	$125,000
Payments to creditors	(20,000)
Child support payments	(12,000)
Received by Gus	$ 93,000

    a. Gus reasons that he received a benefit of only $93,000 and, therefore, that is what he should include in his gross income. Is Gus correct?
    b. Gus also owns all of the stock of a corporation that owns an apartment building. Gus put the apartment building in the corporation to limit his legal liability. He collects all of the rent and pays all of the expenses. Rent received is $48,000, and expenses are $30,000. Gus included $18,000 in his gross income. Is this correct?
    c. Same as (b) except the corporation made an S election.

41. Tracy, a cash basis taxpayer, is employed by Eagle Corporation, also a cash basis taxpayer. Tracy is a full-time employee of the corporation and receives a salary of $60,000 per year. He also receives a bonus equal to 10% of all collections from clients he serviced during the year. Determine the tax consequences of the following events to the corporation and to Tracy:
    a. On December 31, 2005, Tracy was visiting a customer. The customer gave Tracy a $3,000 check payable to the corporation for appraisal services Tracy performed during 2005. Tracy did not deliver the check to the corporation until January 2006.
    b. The facts are the same as in (a), except that the corporation is an accrual basis taxpayer and Tracy deposited the check on December 31, but the bank did not add the deposit to the corporation's account until January 2006.
    c. The facts are the same as in (a), except that the customer told Tracy to hold the check until January when the customer could make a bank deposit that would cover the check.

42. Eve, Fran, and Gary each have a one-third interest in the capital and profits of the EFG Partnership. At the beginning of the year, each partner had an $85,000 balance in his or her capital account. The partnership's gross income for the year was $360,000, and its total expenses were $120,000. During the year, Eve contributed an additional $23,000 to

the partnership and did not have any withdrawals from her capital account. Fran withdrew $75,000, and Gary withdrew $40,000. Compute each partner's taxable income from the partnership for the year.

43. In 2005, Alva received dividends on her stocks as follows:

Amur Corporation (a French corporation whose stock is traded on an established U.S. securities market)	$55,000
Blaze, Inc., a Delaware corporation	25,000
Grape, Inc., a Virginia corporation	12,000

a. Alva purchased the Grape stock four years ago, and she purchased the Amur stock two years ago. She purchased the Blaze stock 15 days before it went ex-dividend and sold it 20 days later at a $22,000 loss. Alva had no other capital gains and losses for the year. She is in the 35% marginal tax bracket. Compute Alva's tax on her dividend income for 2005.
b. Alva's daughter, who is not Alva's dependent, had taxable income of $10,000, which included $1,000 of dividends on Grape, Inc. stock. The daughter had purchased the stock two years ago. Compute the daughter's tax liability on the dividends.

44. Liz and Doug were divorced on July 1 of the current year after 10 years of marriage. Their current year's income received before the divorce was as follows:

Doug's salary	$41,000
Liz's salary	55,000
Rent on apartments purchased by Liz 15 years ago	6,000
Dividends on stock Doug inherited from his mother 4 years ago	1,900
Interest on a savings account in Liz's name funded with her salary	1,800

Allocate the income to Liz and Doug assuming they live in:
a. California.
b. Texas.

45. Nell and Kirby are in the process of negotiating their divorce agreement. What would be the tax consequences to Nell and Kirby if the following, considered individually, became part of the agreement?
a. Nell and Kirby will continue as joint owners of the personal residence. Nell can continue to occupy the residence as long as she so desires. If she ever sells the residence, however, Kirby will receive one-half the proceeds. The fair rental value of the residence is $2,000 per month.
b. Nell will receive $1,000 per month for 100 months, and Kirby will receive the $180,000 in securities (adjusted basis is $100,000) that were formerly owned jointly by the couple. If Nell dies before she receives all of the payments, Kirby is not required to continue the payments.
c. Nell is to have custody of their 12-year-old son and is to receive $600 per month until (1) the child dies or (2) attains age 21 (whichever occurs first).

46. Karen and Al are in the process of negotiating a divorce agreement. Al believes that Karen should pay him at least $30,000 per year, but he would like to get as much in the first two years in cash as the tax law will permit to be treated as alimony. He is willing to surrender his one-half interest in some stock in exchange for more cash. Karen and Al own stock worth $120,000 that originally cost $80,000. Al is aware that Karen is very concerned about the tax consequences of the divorce agreement. What would be the tax consequences of the following alternative agreements?
a. Al receives $30,000 per year for life and one-half of the jointly owned stock.
b. Al receives $50,000 per year in Years 1, 2, and 3 and $30,000 per year for the remainder of his life. He does not receive any of the stock.
c. Al receives $80,000 in Year 1 and $30,000 per year for the remainder of his life.

47. Under the terms of their divorce agreement, Barry is to transfer common stock (cost of $25,000, market value of $60,000) to Sandra. Barry and Sandra have a 14-year-old child.

Sandra will have custody of the child, and Barry is to pay $300 per month as child support. In addition, Sandra is to receive $1,000 per month for 10 years, or until her death if earlier. However, the payments will be reduced to $750 per month when their child reaches age 21. In the first year under the agreement, Sandra receives the common stock and the correct cash payments for six months. How will the terms of the agreement affect Sandra's gross income?

Decision Making

48. Roy decides to buy a personal residence and goes to the bank for a $150,000 loan. The bank tells him he can borrow the funds at 7% if his father will guarantee the debt. Roy's father, Hal, owns CDs currently yielding 6%. The Federal rate is 5%. Hal is willing to do either of the following:

 - Cash in the CDs and lend Roy the funds at 6% interest.
 - Guarantee the loan for Roy.

 Hal will consider lending the funds to Roy at an even lower interest rate, depending on the tax consequences. Hal is in the 35% marginal tax bracket. Roy, whose only source of income is his salary, is in the 15% marginal tax bracket. The interest Roy pays on the mortgage will be deductible by him. Considering only the tax consequences, which option will maximize the family's after-tax wealth?

49. On June 30, 2005, Ridge borrowed $62,000 from his employer. On July 1, 2005, Ridge used the money as follows:

Interest-free loan to Ridge's controlled corporation (operated by Ridge on a part-time basis)	$31,000
Interest-free loan to Tab (Ridge's son)	11,000
National Bank of Grundy 6% CD ($14,840 due at maturity, June 30, 2006)	14,000
National Bank of Grundy 6.25% CD ($6,773 due at maturity, June 30, 2007)	6,000
	$62,000

 Ridge's employer did not charge him interest. The applicable Federal rate was 7% throughout the relevant period. Tab had investment income of $800 for the year, and he used the loan proceeds to pay medical school tuition. There were no other outstanding loans between Ridge and Tab. What are the effects of the preceding transactions on Ridge's taxable income for 2005?

50. Indicate whether the imputed interest rules should apply in the following situations. Assume all the loans were made at the beginning of the tax year.
 a. Mike loaned his sister $80,000 to buy a new home. Mike did not charge interest on the loan. The Federal rate was 5.75%. Mike's sister had $900 of investment income for the year.
 b. Sam's employer maintains an emergency loan fund for its employees. During the year, Sam's wife was very ill, and he incurred unusually large medical expenses. He borrowed $9,000 from his employer's emergency loan fund for six months. The Federal rate was 5.5%. Sam and his wife had no investment income for the year.
 c. Jody borrowed $15,000 from her controlled corporation for six months. She used the funds to pay her daughter's college tuition. The corporation charged Jody 4% interest. The Federal rate was 5.5%. Jody had $3,500 of investment income for the year.

51. Vito is the sole shareholder of Vito, Inc. He is also employed by the corporation. On June 30, 2005, Vito borrowed $8,000 from Vito, Inc., and on July 1, 2006, he borrowed an additional $4,000. Both loans were due on demand. No interest was charged on the loans, and the Federal rate was 8% for all relevant dates. Vito used the money to purchase a boat, and he had $1,100 of investment income. Determine the tax consequences to Vito and Vito, Inc., in each of the following situations:
 a. The loans are considered employer-employee loans.
 b. The loans are considered corporation-shareholder loans.

52. Thelma retires after 30 years of service with her employer. She is 65 years old and has contributed $120,000 to her employer's qualified pension fund. She elects to receive her retirement benefits as an annuity of $2,000 per month for the remainder of her life.
    a. Assume that Thelma retires in June 2005 and collects six annuity payments this year. What is her gross income from the annuity payments in the first year?
    b. Assume that Thelma lives 30 years after retiring. What is her gross income from the annuity payments in the twenty-ninth year?
    c. Assume that Thelma dies after collecting 180 payments. She collected six payments in the year of her death. What are Thelma's gross income and deductions from the annuity contract in the year of her death?

53. For each of the following, determine the amount that should be included in gross income:
    a. Joe was selected as the most valuable player in the Super Bowl. In recognition of this, he was awarded a sports car worth $60,000 and $150,000 in cash.
    b. Wanda won the Mrs. America beauty contest. She received various prizes valued at $100,000. None of the $100,000 was for a scholarship or travel expenses.
    c. George was awarded the Nobel Peace Prize. He donated the $900,000 check he received to State University, his alma mater.

54. The LMN Partnership has a group term life insurance plan. Each partner has $150,000 protection, and each employee has protection equal to twice his or her annual salary. Employee Alice (age 36) has $85,000 of insurance under the plan, and partner Kay (age 54) has $150,000 of coverage. Because the plan is a "group plan," it is impossible to determine the cost of coverage for an individual employee or partner.
    a. Assuming the plan is nondiscriminatory, how much must Alice and Kay each include in gross income as a result of the partnership paying the insurance premiums?
    b. Assume that the partnership is incorporated. Kay becomes a shareholder and an employee who receives a $75,000 annual salary. The corporation provides Kay with $150,000 of group term life insurance coverage under a nondiscriminatory plan. What is Kay's gross income as a result of the corporation paying the insurance premiums?

55. Herbert was employed for the first six months of the year and earned $90,000 in salary. During the next six months, he collected $8,300 of unemployment compensation, borrowed $12,000 (using his personal residence as collateral), and withdrew $2,000 from his savings account (including $90 interest). He received dividends of $550. His luck was not all bad, for in December he won $1,500 in the lottery on a $5 ticket. Calculate Herbert's gross income.

Decision Making

56. Linda and Don are married and file a joint return. In 2005, they received $9,000 in Social Security benefits and $35,000 in taxable pension benefits and interest.
    a. Compute the couple's adjusted gross income on a joint return.
    b. Don would like to know whether they should sell for $100,000 (at no gain or loss) a corporate bond that pays 8% in interest each year and use the proceeds to buy a $100,000 nontaxable State of Virginia bond that will pay $6,000 in interest each year.
    c. If Linda in (a) works part-time and earns $30,000, how much would Linda and Don's adjusted gross income increase?

57. Melissa and Jim are married and file a joint return. Jim is 62 years old, and his employer has offered a buyout program under which Jim could retire and receive additional retirement pay. If he retires, he would receive $60,000 a year as retirement pay and approximately $12,000 a year in interest and dividends. His Social Security benefits would be $15,000 per year. Melissa is 55 years old and is not employed. Their itemized deductions and personal exemption deductions total $18,000 a year. If Jim continues to work, he will receive a salary of approximately $80,000 per year, interest and dividends of $12,000 per year, and no Social Security benefits. Assume the dividends are not qualified dividends.
    a. Melissa and Jim would like you to compute their taxable income for 2005. First assume Jim does not retire. Then assume he does retire. Assume that, based on their gross income, 85% of the Social Security benefits are included in gross income.
    b. Assume Melissa and Jim will be in the 30% bracket (combined Federal and state rates). Compute the change in their after-tax cash flow following Jim's retirement.

58. Donna does not think she has an income tax problem but would like to discuss her situation with you just to make sure she will not get hit with an unexpected tax liability. Base your suggestions on the following relevant financial information:
    a. Donna's share of the SAT Partnership income is $70,000, but none of the income can be distributed because the partnership needs the cash for operations.
    b. Donna's Social Security benefits totaled $8,400, but Donna loaned the cash received to her nephew.
    c. Donna assigned to a creditor the right to collect $1,200 interest on some bonds she owned.
    d. Donna and her husband lived together in California until September, when they separated. Donna has heard rumors that her husband had substantial gambling winnings since they separated.

Cumulative Problems

Tax Return Problem
Decision Making
Communications

59. Dan and Freida Butler, husband and wife, file a joint return. The Butlers live at 625 Oak Street, Corbin, KY 27521. Dan's Social Security number is 482–61–1231, and Freida's is 162–79–1245.

    During 2005, Dan and Freida furnished over half of the total support of each of the following individuals:
    a. Gina, their daughter, age 22, a full-time student, who was married on December 21, 2005, has no income of her own, and for 2005 did not file a joint return with her husband, who earned $10,500 during 2005.
    b. Sam, their son, age 20, who had gross income of $6,300 and who dropped out of college in October 2005. He graduated from high school in May 2005.
    c. Ben Brow, Freida's brother, age 22, who is a full-time college student with gross income of $5,200.

    Dan, a radio announcer for WJJJ, earned a salary of $86,000 in 2005. Freida was employed part-time as a real estate salesperson by Corbin Realty and was paid commissions of $31,000 in 2005. Freida sold a house on December 30, 2005, and will be paid a commission of $2,000 (not included in the $31,000) on the January 10, 2006 closing date.

    Dan and Freida collected $15,000 on a certificate of deposit that matured on September 30, 2005. The CD was purchased on October 1, 2003, for $13,868, and the yield to maturity was 4%.

    Other income received consisted of the following:

Dividends on CSX stock	$2,600
Interest on savings account at Second Bank	1,300
Interest income on City of Corbin bonds	2,900

    CSX had been instructed by Dan and Freida to pay the dividends directly to Freida's brother, Ben. CSX complied with their instructions.

    Freida is an 11% partner in the Green Partnership. Green reported taxable income of $100,000 for 2005 and made no distributions to any of the partners in 2005.

    Dan and Freida had itemized deductions as follows:

State income tax withheld	$4,500*
Personal property taxes paid	900
Real estate taxes paid	3,600
Interest on home mortgage (paid to Corbin Savings and Loan)	4,900
Cash contributions to the Boy Scouts	975

    *Sales tax from sales tax table is $1,206.

    Their employers withheld Federal income tax of $15,000 (Dan $8,400, Freida $6,600), and the Butlers paid estimated tax of $5,000.

Part 1—Tax Computation
Compute Dan and Freida's 2005 Federal income tax payable (or refund due). Suggested software: TurboTax.

Part 2—Tax Planning
Dan plans to reduce his work schedule and work only halftime for WJJJ in 2006. He has been writing songs for several years and wants to devote more time to developing a career as a songwriter. Because of the uncertainty in the music business, however, he would like you to make all computations assuming he will have no income from songwriting in 2006. To make up for the loss of income, Freida plans to increase the amount of time she spends selling real estate. She estimates she will be able to earn $60,000 in 2006. Assume all other income and expense items will be approximately the same as they were in 2005. Assume Sam will be enrolled in college as a full-time student for the summer and fall semesters. Will the Butlers have more or less disposable income (after Federal income tax) in 2006? Write a letter to the Butlers that contains your advice and prepare a memo for the tax files. Suggested software: TurboTax.

Tax Return Problem

60. Cecil C. Seymour is a 66-year-old widower. He had income for 2004 as follows:

Pension from former employer	$29,500
Interest income from Alto National Bank	5,500
Interest income on City of Alto bonds	2,700
Dividends received from AT&T	2,000
Collections on annuity contract he purchased from Great Life Insurance	4,800
Social Security benefits	12,000
Rent income on townhouse	7,600

The cost of the annuity was $52,800, and Cecil was expected to receive a total of 240 monthly payments of $400. Cecil has received 22 payments through 2004.

Cecil's 40-year-old daughter, Sarah C. Seymour, borrowed $40,000 from Cecil on January 2, 2003. She used the money to start a new business. Cecil does not charge her interest because she could not afford to pay it, but he does expect to eventually collect the principal. Sarah is living with Cecil until the business becomes profitable. Except for housing, Sarah provides her own support from her business and $1,600 in dividends on stocks that she inherited from her mother.

Other relevant information is presented below:

- Cecil's Social Security number: 259–83–4444
- Address: 3840 Springfield Blvd., Alto, GA 30754
- Sarah's Social Security number: 257–49–8862
- Expenses on rental townhouse:

Utilities	$1,500
Maintenance	1,000
Depreciation	2,000
Real estate taxes	750
Insurance	500

- State income taxes paid: $3,300
- County personal property taxes paid: $2,100
- Payments on estimated 2004 Federal income tax: $5,500
- Charitable contributions of cash to Alto Baptist Church: $6,400
- Federal interest rate: 6%
- Sales taxes paid: $912

Compute Cecil's 2004 Federal income tax payable (or refund due). If you use tax forms for your computations, you will need Form 1040 and Schedules A, B, and E. Suggested software: TurboTax.

Research Problems

*Note: Solutions to Research Problems can be prepared by using the **RIA Checkpoint® Student Edition** online research product, which is available to accompany this text. It is also possible to prepare solutions to the Research Problems by using tax research materials found in a standard tax library.*

Communications

Research Problem 1. Tranquility Funeral Home, Inc., your client, is an accrual basis taxpayer that sells pre-need funeral contracts. Under these contracts, the customer pays in advance for goods and services to be provided at the contract beneficiary's death. These payments are refundable at the contract purchaser's request, pursuant to state law, at any time until the goods and services are furnished. Tranquility, consistent with its financial accounting reporting, includes the payments in income for the year the funeral service is provided. The IRS agent insists that the payments are prepaid income subject to tax in the year of receipt. Your client believes the amounts involved are customer deposits. Write a letter to Tranquility that contains your advice about how the issue should be resolved. The client's address is 400 Rock Street, Memphis, TN 38152.

Research Problem 2. Paul is an insurance agent who receives a commission on each policy he sells. During the year, he purchased a policy on his own life, naming his wife as the beneficiary. He did not report the commission on the policy as gross income because he considered the commission a reduction in his cost for the life insurance. An IRS agent has challenged the exclusion. Who is correct?

Internet Activity

Use the tax resources of the Internet to address the following question. Do not restrict your search to the World Wide Web, but include a review of newsgroups and general reference materials, practitioner sites and resources, primary sources of the tax law, chat rooms and discussion groups, and other opportunities.

Communications

Research Problem 3. Go to the Web page of a consulting firm that offers counseling services to individuals as they negotiate the terms of a divorce. What specific tax-related services do these firms offer? Send an e-mail message to one of these firms suggesting that it add a specific service or revise its Web page to emphasize other tax-related services for its clients.

Gross Income: Exclusions

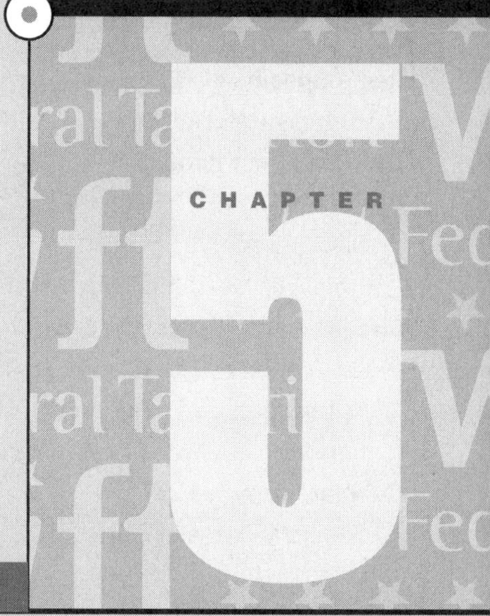

LEARNING OBJECTIVES

After completing Chapter 5, you should be able to:

LO.1

Understand that statutory authority is required to exclude an item from gross income.

LO.2

Identify the circumstances under which various items are excludible from gross income.

LO.3

Determine the extent to which receipts can be excluded under the tax benefit rule.

LO.4

Describe the circumstances under which income must be reported from the discharge of indebtedness.

LO.5

Identify tax planning strategies for obtaining the maximum benefit from allowable exclusions.

http://wft.swlearning.com

OUTLINE

Items Specifically Excluded from Gross Income

Chapter 4 discussed the concepts and judicial doctrines that affect the determination of gross income. If an income item is within the all-inclusive definition of gross income, the item can be excluded only if the taxpayer can locate specific authority for doing so. Chapter 5 focuses on the exclusions Congress has authorized. These exclusions are listed in Exhibit 5-1.

Tax advisers spend countless hours trying to develop techniques to achieve tax-exempt status for income. Employee benefits planning is greatly influenced by the availability of certain types of exclusions. Taxes play an important role in employee benefits, as well as in other situations, because attaining an exclusion is another means of enhancing after-tax income. For example, for a person whose combined Federal and state marginal tax rate is 40 percent, \$1.00 of tax-exempt income is equivalent to \$1.67 [\$1 ÷ (1 − .4)] in income subject to taxation. The tax adviser's ideal is to attach the right labels or provide the right wording to render income nontaxable without affecting the economics of the transaction.

■ EXHIBIT 5–1
Summary of Principal Exclusions from Gross Income

1. Donative items
   Gifts, bequests, and inheritances (§ 102)
   Life insurance proceeds paid by reason of death (§ 101)
   Accelerated death benefits [§ 101(g)]
   Survivor benefits for public safety officer killed in the line of duty [§ 101(h)]
   Scholarships (§ 117)
2. Personal and welfare items
   Injury or sickness payments (§ 104)
   Public assistance payments (Rev.Rul. 71–425, 1971–2 C.B. 76)
   Amounts received under insurance contracts for certain living expenses (§ 123)
   Reimbursement for the costs of caring for a foster child (§ 131)
3. Wage and salary supplements
   a. Fringe benefits
      Accident and health benefits (§§ 105 and 106)
      Health Savings Accounts [§ 106(d)]
      Lodging and meals furnished for the convenience of the employer (§ 119)
      Rental value of parsonages (§ 107)
      Employee achievement awards [§ 74(c)]
      Employer contributions to employee group term life insurance (§ 79)
      Cafeteria plans (§ 125)
      Educational assistance payments (§ 127)
      Child or dependent care (§ 129)
      Services provided to employees at no additional cost to the employer (§ 132)
      Employee discounts (§ 132)
      Working condition and *de minimis* fringes (§ 132)
      Athletic facilities provided to employees (§ 132)
      Qualified transportation fringe (§ 132)
      Qualified moving expense reimbursement (§ 132)
      Qualified retirement planning services (§ 132)
      Tuition reductions granted to employees of educational institutions (§ 117)
      Child adoption expenses (§ 137)
      Long-term care insurance (§ 7702B)
   b. Military benefits
      Combat pay (§ 112)
      Housing, uniforms, and other benefits (§ 134)
   c. Foreign earned income (§ 911)
4. Investor items
   Interest on state and local government obligations (§ 103)
   Improvements by tenant to landlord's property (§ 109)
   Fifty percent exclusion for gain from sale of certain small business stock (§ 1202)
5. Benefits for the elderly
   Social Security benefits (except in the case of certain higher-income taxpayers) (§ 86)
6. Other benefits
   Income from discharge of indebtedness (§ 108)
   Recovery of a prior year's deduction that yielded no tax benefit (§ 111)
   Gain from the sale of personal residence (§ 121)
   Educational savings bonds (§ 135)
   Qualified tuition program (§ 529)
   Coverdell Education Savings Account (§ 530)
   Lessee construction allowances for short-term leases (§ 110)

Consider the case of an employee who is in the 28 percent marginal tax bracket and is paying $3,000 a year for health insurance. If the employer provided this protection in a manner that qualified for exclusion treatment but reduced the employee's salary by $3,000, the employee's after-tax and after-insurance income would increase at no additional cost to the employer.

Salary received to use to purchase health insurance	$ 3,000
Less: Taxes ($3,000 × 28%)	(840)
Cash available to purchase health insurance	$ 2,160
Less: Cost of health insurance	(3,000)
Excess of cost of health insurance over cash available	$ 840

Thus, the employee in this case is $840 better off with a salary reduction of $3,000 and employer-provided health insurance. The employee may still decide that the $3,000 salary is preferable. For example, the employee may feel that health insurance is no longer needed. Understanding the tax influence, however, does enable the employee to make a more informed choice.

LO.1

Understand that statutory authority is required to exclude an item from gross income.

Statutory Authority

Sections 101 through 150 provide the authority for excluding specific items from gross income. In addition, other exclusions are scattered throughout the Code. Each exclusion has its own legislative history and reason for enactment. Certain exclusions are intended as a form of indirect welfare payments. Other exclusions prevent double taxation of income or provide incentives for socially desirable activities (e.g., nontaxable interest on certain U.S. government bonds where the owner uses the funds for educational expenses).

In some cases, Congress has enacted exclusions to rectify the effects of judicial decisions. For example, the Supreme Court held that the fair market value of improvements (not made in lieu of rent) made by a tenant to the landlord's property should be included in the landlord's gross income upon termination of the lease.[1] The landlord was required to include the value of the improvements in gross income even though the property had not been sold or otherwise disposed of. Congress provided relief in this situation by enacting § 109, which defers taxing the value of the improvements until the property is sold.[2]

LO.2

Identify the circumstances under which various items are excludible from gross income.

Gifts and Inheritances

GENERAL

Beginning with the Income Tax Act of 1913 and continuing to the present, Congress has allowed the recipient of a gift to exclude the value of the property from gross income. The exclusion applies to gifts made during the life of the donor (*inter vivos* gifts) and transfers that take effect upon the death of the donor (bequests and inheritances).[3] However, as discussed in Chapter 4, the recipient of a gift of income-producing property is subject to tax on the income subsequently earned from the property. Also, as discussed in Chapter 1, the donor or the decedent's estate may be subject to gift or estate taxes on the transfer.

In numerous cases, gifts are made in a business setting. For example, a salesperson gives a purchasing agent free samples; an employee receives cash from his or

[1]*Helvering v. Bruun*, 40–1 USTC ¶9337, 24 AFTR 652, 60 S.Ct. 631 (USSC, 1940).

[2]If the tenant made the improvements in lieu of rent, the value of the improvements is not eligible for exclusion.

[3]§ 102.

BEGGING AS A TAX-DISFAVORED OCCUPATION

In five recent decisions, the Tax Court ruled that amounts received from begging are nontaxable gifts. In a reversal of the normal roles, the beggars contended that the amounts received were earned income while the IRS argued that the taxpayers had merely received gifts. The beggars wanted the fruit of their efforts to be treated as earned income in order to qualify them for the earned income credit.

her employer on retirement; a corporation makes payments to employees who were victims of a natural disaster; a corporation makes a cash payment to a deceased employee's spouse. In these and similar instances, it is frequently unclear whether the payment was a gift or whether it represents compensation for past, present, or future services.

The courts have defined a **gift** as "a voluntary transfer of property by one to another without adequate [valuable] consideration or compensation therefrom."[4] If the payment is intended to be for services rendered, it is not a gift, even though the payment is made without legal or moral obligation and the payor receives no economic benefit from the transfer. To qualify as a gift, the payment must be made "out of affection, respect, admiration, charity or like impulses."[5] Thus, the cases on this issue have been decided on the basis of the donor's intent.

In a landmark case, *Comm. v. Duberstein*,[6] the taxpayer (Duberstein) received a Cadillac from a business acquaintance. Duberstein had supplied the businessman with the names of potential customers with no expectation of compensation. The Supreme Court concluded:

> . . . despite the characterization of the transfer of the Cadillac by the parties [as a gift] and the absence of any obligation, even of a moral nature, to make it, it was at the bottom a recompense for Duberstein's past service, or an inducement for him to be of further service in the future.

Duberstein was therefore required to include the fair market value of the automobile in gross income.

GIFTS TO EMPLOYEES

In the case of cash or other property *received by an employee* from his or her employer, Congress has eliminated any ambiguity. Transfers from an employer to an employee cannot be excluded as a gift.[7]

EMPLOYEE DEATH BENEFITS

Frequently, an employer makes payments (**death benefits**) to a deceased employee's surviving spouse, children, or other beneficiaries. If the decedent had a nonforfeitable right to the payments (e.g., the decedent's accrued salary), the amounts are generally taxable to the recipient just the same as if the employee had lived

[4] *Estate of D. R. Daly*, 3 B.T.A. 1042 (1926).

[5] *Robertson v. U.S.*, 52–1 USTC ¶9343, 41 AFTR 1053, 72 S.Ct. 994 (USSC, 1952).

[6] 60–2 USTC ¶9515, 5 AFTR2d 1626, 80 S.Ct. 1190 (USSC, 1960).

[7] § 102(c).

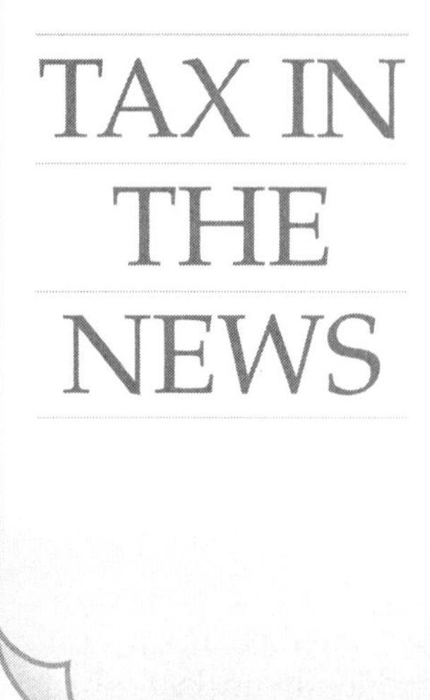

Frequent-Flier Miles Will Not Be Taxed

IRS officials believe that when a taxpayer receives frequent-flier miles in connection with business travel, the taxpayer has received income. This is clearly true if the taxpayer has deducted the cost of the airline ticket. Under the tax benefit rule, the frequent-flier miles should be included in gross income as a recovery of a prior deduction. If the employer pays for the business travel but the employee is awarded the frequent-flier miles, the employee has obviously received additional compensation.

Nevertheless, the IRS has announced (Announcement 2002–18) that it will not attempt to tax frequent-flier miles. The major consideration in creating this nonstatutory exemption was the complexity that would result from attempting to tax the miles. Distinguishing the miles awarded for personal travel (nontaxable reduction in the cost of ticket) from the business miles would be difficult. Furthermore, the valuation issues would be horrendous.

and collected the payments. But when the employer makes voluntary payments, the gift issue arises. Generally, the IRS considers such payments to be compensation for prior services rendered by the deceased employee.[8] However, some courts have held that payments to an employee's surviving spouse or other beneficiaries are gifts if the following are true:[9]

- The payments were made to the surviving spouse and children rather than to the employee's estate.
- The employer derived no benefit from the payments.
- The surviving spouse and children performed no services for the employer.
- The decedent had been fully compensated for services rendered.
- Payments were made pursuant to a board of directors' resolution that followed a general company policy of providing payments for families of deceased employees (but not exclusively for families of shareholder-employees).

When all of the above conditions are satisfied, the payment is presumed to have been made *as an act of affection or charity*. When one or more of these conditions is not satisfied, the surviving spouse and children may still be deemed the recipients of a gift if the payment is made in light of the survivors' financial needs.[10]

Life Insurance Proceeds

GENERAL RULE

Life insurance proceeds paid to the beneficiary because of the death of the insured are exempt from income tax.[11]

[8] Rev.Rul. 62–102, 1962–2 C.B. 37.

[9] *Estate of Sydney J. Carter v. Comm.*, 72–1 USTC ¶9129, 29 AFTR2d 332, 453 F.2d 61 (CA–2, 1972), and the cases cited there.

[10] *Simpson v. U.S.*, 58–2 USTC ¶9923, 2 AFTR2d 6036, 261 F.2d 497 (CA–7, 1958), *cert. denied* 79 S.Ct. 724 (USSC, 1958).

[11] § 101(a).

EXAMPLE 1

Mark purchases an insurance policy on his life and names his wife, Linda, as the beneficiary. Mark pays $45,000 in premiums. When he dies, Linda collects the insurance proceeds of $200,000. The $200,000 is exempt from Federal income tax. ■

Congress chose to exempt life insurance proceeds for the following reasons:

- For family members, life insurance proceeds serve much the same purpose as a nontaxable inheritance.
- In a business context (as well as in a family situation), life insurance proceeds replace an economic loss suffered by the beneficiary.

EXAMPLE 2

Gold Corporation purchases a life insurance policy to cover its key employee. If the proceeds were taxable, the corporation would require more insurance coverage to pay the tax as well as to cover the economic loss of the employee. ■

Thus, in general, Congress concluded that making life insurance proceeds exempt from income tax was a good policy.

ACCELERATED DEATH BENEFITS

Generally, if the owner of a life insurance policy cancels the policy and receives the cash surrender value, the taxpayer must recognize gain equal to the excess of the amount received over premiums paid on the policy (a loss is not deductible). The gain is recognized because the general exclusion provision for life insurance proceeds applies only to life insurance proceeds paid upon the death of the insured. If the taxpayer cancels the policy and receives the cash surrender value, the life insurance policy is treated as an investment by the insured.

In a limited circumstance, however, the insured is permitted to receive the benefits of the life insurance contract without having to include the gain in gross income. Under the **accelerated death benefits** provisions, exclusion treatment is available for insured taxpayers who are either terminally ill or chronically ill.[12] A terminally ill taxpayer can collect the cash surrender value of the policy from the insurance company or assign the policy proceeds to a qualified third party. The resultant gain, if any, is excluded from the insured's gross income. A *terminally ill* individual is one whom a medical doctor certifies as having an illness that is reasonably expected to cause death within 24 months.

In the case of a chronically ill patient, no gain is recognized if the proceeds of the policy are used for the long-term care of the insured. A person is *chronically ill* if he or she is certified as being unable to perform without assistance certain activities of daily living. These exclusions for the terminally ill and the chronically ill are available only to the insured. Thus, a person who purchases a life insurance policy from the insured does not qualify.

EXAMPLE 3

Tom owned a term life insurance policy at the time he was diagnosed as having a terminal illness. After paying $5,200 in premiums, he sold the policy to Amber Benefits, Inc., a company that is authorized by the State of Virginia to purchase such policies. Amber paid Tom $50,000. When Tom died six months later, Amber collected the face amount of the policy, $75,000. Tom is not required to include the $44,800 gain ($50,000 – $5,200) on the sale of the policy in his gross income. Assume Amber pays additional premiums of $4,000 during the six-month period. When Amber collects the life insurance proceeds of $75,000,

[12] § 101(g).

it must include the $21,000 gain ($75,000 proceeds – $50,000 cost – $4,000 additional premiums paid) in gross income. ■

ETHICAL CONSIDERATIONS

Should the Terminally Ill Pay Social Security Taxes?

The rationale for excluding accelerated death benefits from the gross income of the terminally ill is that they often use the funds to pay medical expenses and other costs associated with dying and do not have the ability to pay tax on the gain from the accelerated receipt of the life insurance proceeds. Yet the wages of a terminally ill person who is employed (or profits of a self-employed person) are subject to Social Security taxes. The Social Security taxes are intended to pay for retirement benefits, but a terminally ill person is unlikely to collect any Social Security benefits.

Several bills have been introduced in Congress to exempt the terminally ill from the Social Security tax. Evaluate the equity of the current tax treatment versus that in the proposed legislation.

TRANSFER FOR VALUABLE CONSIDERATION

A life insurance policy (other than one associated with accelerated death benefits) may be transferred after it is issued by the insurance company. If the policy is *transferred for valuable consideration*, the insurance proceeds are includible in the gross income of the transferee to the extent the proceeds received exceed the amount paid for the policy by the transferee plus any subsequent premiums paid.

EXAMPLE 4

Adam pays premiums of $4,000 for an insurance policy in the face amount of $10,000 upon the life of Beth and subsequently transfers the policy to Carol for $6,000. On Beth's death, Carol receives the proceeds of $10,000. The amount that Carol can exclude from gross income is limited to $6,000 plus any premiums she paid subsequent to the transfer. ■

The Code, however, provides four exceptions to the rule illustrated in the preceding example. These exceptions permit exclusion treatment for transfers to the following:

1. A partner of the insured.
2. A partnership in which the insured is a partner.
3. A corporation in which the insured is an officer or shareholder.
4. A transferee whose basis in the policy is determined by reference to the transferor's basis.

The first three exceptions facilitate the use of insurance contracts to fund buy-sell agreements.

EXAMPLE 5

Rick and Sam are equal partners who have an agreement that allows either partner to purchase the interest of a deceased partner for $50,000. Neither partner has sufficient cash to actually buy the other partner's interest, but each has a life insurance policy on his own life in the amount of $50,000. Rick and Sam could exchange their policies (usually at little or no taxable gain), and upon the death of either partner, the surviving partner could collect tax-free insurance proceeds. The proceeds could then be used to purchase the decedent's interest in the partnership. ■

The fourth exception applies to policies that were transferred pursuant to a tax-free exchange or were received by gift.[13]

Investment earnings arising from the reinvestment of life insurance proceeds are generally subject to income tax. Often the beneficiary will elect to collect the insurance proceeds in installments. The annuity rules (discussed in Chapter 4) are used to apportion the installment payment between the principal element (excludible) and the interest element (includible).[14]

Scholarships

GENERAL INFORMATION

Payments or benefits received by a student at an educational institution may be (1) compensation for services, (2) a gift, or (3) a scholarship. If the payments or benefits are received as compensation for services (past or present), the fact that the recipient is a student generally does not render the amounts received nontaxable.[15]

EXAMPLE 6

State University waives tuition for all graduate teaching assistants. The tuition waived is intended as compensation for services and is therefore included in the graduate assistant's gross income. ■

As discussed earlier, gifts are not includible in gross income.

The **scholarship** rules are intended to provide exclusion treatment for education-related benefits that cannot qualify as gifts but are not compensation for services. According to the Regulations, "a scholarship is an amount paid or allowed to, or for the benefit of, an individual to aid such individual in the pursuit of study or research."[16] The recipient must be a candidate for a degree (either undergraduate or graduate) at an educational institution.[17]

EXAMPLE 7

Terry enters a contest sponsored by a local newspaper. Each contestant is required to submit an essay on local environmental issues. The prize is one year's tuition at State University. Terry wins the contest. The newspaper has a legal obligation to Terry (as contest winner). Thus, the benefits are not a gift. However, since the tuition payment aids Terry in pursuing her studies, the payment is a scholarship. ■

A scholarship recipient may exclude from gross income the amount used for tuition and related expenses (fees, books, supplies, and equipment required for courses), provided the conditions of the grant do not require that the funds be used for other purposes.[18] Amounts received for room and board are *not* excludible and are treated as earned income for purposes of calculating the standard deduction for a taxpayer who is another taxpayer's dependent.[19]

EXAMPLE 8

Kelly receives a scholarship of $9,500 from State University to be used to pursue a bachelor's degree. She spends $4,000 on tuition, $3,000 on books and supplies, and $2,500 for room

[13]See the discussion of gifts and tax-free exchanges in Chapter 13.

[14]Reg. §§ 1.72–7(c)(1) and 1.101–7T.

[15]Reg. § 1.117–2(a). See *C. P. Bhalla*, 35 T.C. 13 (1960), for a discussion of the distinction between a scholarship and compensation. See also *Bingler v. Johnson*, 69–1 USTC ¶9348, 23 AFTR2d 1212, 89 S.Ct. 1439 (USSC, 1969). For potential exclusion treatment, see the subsequent discussion of qualified tuition reductions.

[16]Prop.Reg. § 1.117–6(c)(3)(i).

[17]§ 117(a).

[18]§ 117(b).

[19]Prop.Reg. § 1.117–6(h).

and board. Kelly may exclude $7,000 ($4,000 + $3,000) from gross income. The $2,500 spent for room and board is includible in Kelly's gross income.

The scholarship is Kelly's only source of income. Her parents provide more than 50% of Kelly's support and claim her as a dependent. Kelly's standard deduction of $2,750 ($2,500 + $250) exceeds her $2,500 gross income. Thus, she has no taxable income. ■

TIMING ISSUES

Frequently, the scholarship recipient is a cash basis taxpayer who receives the money in one tax year but pays the educational expenses in a subsequent year. The amount eligible for exclusion may not be known at the time the money is received. In that case, the transaction is held *open* until the educational expenses are paid.[20]

EXAMPLE 9

In August 2005, Sanjay received $10,000 as a scholarship for the academic year 2005–2006. Sanjay's expenditures for tuition, books, and supplies were as follows:

August–December 2005	$3,000
January–May 2006	4,500
	$7,500

Sanjay's gross income for 2006 includes $2,500 ($10,000 – $7,500) that is not excludible as a scholarship. None of the scholarship is included in his gross income in 2005. ■

DISGUISED COMPENSATION

Some employers make scholarships available solely to the children of key employees. The tax objective of these plans is to provide a nontaxable fringe benefit to the executives by making the payment to the child in the form of an excludible scholarship. However, the IRS has ruled that the payments are generally includible in the gross income of the parent-employee.[21]

QUALIFIED TUITION REDUCTION PLANS

Employees (including retired and disabled former employees) of nonprofit educational institutions are allowed to exclude a tuition waiver from gross income, if the waiver is pursuant to a **qualified tuition reduction plan.**[22] The plan may not discriminate in favor of highly compensated employees. The exclusion applies to the employee, the employee's spouse, and the employee's dependent children. The exclusion also extends to tuition reductions granted by any nonprofit educational institution to employees of any other nonprofit educational institution (reciprocal agreements).

EXAMPLE 10

ABC University allows the dependent children of XYZ University employees to attend ABC University with no tuition charge. XYZ University grants reciprocal benefits to the children of ABC University employees. The dependent children can also attend tuition-free the university where their parents are employed. Employees who take advantage of these benefits are not required to recognize gross income. ■

[20]Prop.Reg. § 1.117–6(b)(2).

[21]Rev.Rul. 75–448, 1975–2 C.B. 55. *Richard T. Armantrout*, 67 T.C. 996 (1977).

[22]§ 117(d).

Generally, the exclusion is limited to *undergraduate* tuition waivers. However, in the case of teaching or research assistants, graduate tuition waivers may also qualify for exclusion treatment. According to the Proposed Regulations, the exclusion is limited to the value of the benefit in excess of the employee's reasonable compensation.[23] Thus, a tuition reduction that is a substitute for cash compensation cannot be excluded.

EXAMPLE 11

Susan is a graduate research assistant. She receives a $5,000 salary for 500 hours of service over a nine-month period. This pay, $10 per hour, is reasonable compensation for Susan's services. In addition, Susan receives a waiver of $6,000 for tuition. Susan may exclude the tuition waiver from gross income. ■

Compensation for Injuries and Sickness

DAMAGES

A person who suffers harm caused by another is often entitled to compensatory damages. The tax consequences of the receipt of damages depend on the type of harm the taxpayer has experienced. The taxpayer may seek recovery for (1) a loss of income, (2) expenses incurred, (3) property destroyed, or (4) personal injury.

Generally, reimbursement for a loss of income is taxed the same as the income replaced (see the exception under Personal Injury below). The recovery of an expense is not income, unless the expense was deducted. Damages that are a recovery of the taxpayer's previously deducted expenses are generally taxable under the tax benefit rule, discussed later in this chapter.

A payment for damaged or destroyed property is treated as an amount received in a sale or exchange of the property. Thus, the taxpayer has a realized gain if the damage payments received exceed the property's basis. Damages for personal injuries receive special treatment under the Code.

Personal Injury. The legal theory of personal injury damages is that the amount received is intended "to make the plaintiff [the injured party] whole as before the injury."[24] It follows that if the damage payments received were subject to tax, the after-tax amount received would be less than the actual damages incurred and the injured party would not be "whole as before the injury."

In terms of personal injury damages, a distinction is made between compensatory damages and punitive damages. Under specified circumstances, compensatory damages may be excluded from gross income. Under no circumstances may punitive damages be excluded from gross income.

Compensatory damages are intended to compensate the taxpayer for the damages incurred. Only those compensatory damages received on account of *physical personal injury or physical sickness* can be excluded from gross income.[25] Such exclusion treatment includes amounts received for loss of income associated with the physical personal injury or physical sickness. Compensatory damages awarded on account of emotional distress are not received on account of physical injury or physical sickness and thus cannot be excluded (except to the extent of any amount received for medical care) from gross income. Likewise, any amounts received for age discrimination or injury to one's reputation cannot be excluded.

[23]Prop.Reg. § 1.117–6(d).

[24]*C. A. Hawkins*, 6 B.T.A. 1023 (1928).

[25]§ 104(a)(2).

CONCEPT SUMMARY 5–1

Taxation of Damages

Type of Claim	Taxation of Award or Settlement
Breach of contract (generally loss of income)	Taxable.
Property damages	Recovery of cost; gain to the extent of the excess over basis. A loss is deductible for business property and investment property to the extent of basis over the amount realized. A loss may be deductible for personal use property (see discussion of casualty losses in Chapter 7).
Personal injury	
Physical	All compensatory amounts are excluded unless previously deducted (e.g., medical expenses). Amounts received as punitive damages are included in gross income.
Nonphysical	Compensatory damages and punitive damages are included in gross income.

Punitive damages are amounts the person who caused the harm must pay to the victim as punishment for outrageous conduct. Punitive damages are not intended to compensate the victim, but rather to punish the party who caused the harm. Thus, it follows that amounts received as punitive damages may actually place the victim in a better economic position than before the harm was experienced. Logically, punitive damages are thus included in gross income.

EXAMPLE 12

Tom, a television announcer, was dissatisfied with the manner in which Ron, an attorney, was defending the television station in a libel case. Tom stated on the air that Ron was botching the case. Ron sued Tom for slander, claiming damages for loss of income from clients and potential clients who heard Tom's statement. Ron's claim is for damages to his business reputation, and the amounts received are taxable.

Ron collected on the suit against Tom and was on his way to a party to celebrate his victory when a negligent driver, Norm, drove a truck into Ron's automobile, injuring Ron. Ron filed suit for the physical personal injuries and claimed as damages the loss of income for the period he was unable to work as a result of the injuries. Ron also collected punitive damages that were awarded because of Norm's extremely negligent behavior. Ron's wife also collected damages for the emotional distress she experienced as a result of the accident. Ron may exclude the amounts he received for damages, except the punitive damages. Ron's wife must include the amounts she received for damages in gross income because the amounts were not received because of physical personal injuries or sickness. ■

WORKERS' COMPENSATION

State workers' compensation laws require the employer to pay fixed amounts for specific job-related injuries. The state laws were enacted so that the employee will not have to go through the ordeal of a lawsuit (and possibly not collect damages because of some defense available to the employer) to recover the damages. Although the payments are intended, in part, to compensate for a loss of future income, Congress has specifically exempted workers' compensation benefits from inclusion in gross income.[26]

[26]§ 104(a)(1).

Abandoning Parent Gets an "Undeserved" Benefit Tax-Free

A father who abandoned his son in infancy and refused to support him financially or emotionally was awarded half of the workers' compensation death benefit when the son was killed in the September 11, 2001 terrorist attacks. The court concluded that the Workers' Compensation Law defines *parent* in strictly biological terms and therefore the father was entitled to the benefit.

Furthermore, under IRS Regulation § 1.101–1(a)(1), the death benefit is excluded from the father's gross income because the benefit has the characteristics of life insurance proceeds payable by reason of the death of the son.

ACCIDENT AND HEALTH INSURANCE BENEFITS

The income tax treatment of accident and health insurance benefits depends on whether the policy providing the benefits was purchased by the taxpayer or the taxpayer's employer. Benefits collected under an accident and health insurance policy *purchased by the taxpayer* are excludible. In this case, benefits collected under the taxpayer's insurance policy are excluded even though the payments are a substitute for income.[27]

EXAMPLE 13

Bonnie purchases a medical and disability insurance policy. The insurance company pays Bonnie $1,000 per week to replace wages she loses while in the hospital. Although the payments serve as a substitute for income, the amounts received are tax-exempt benefits collected under Bonnie's insurance policy. ■

EXAMPLE 14

Joe's injury results in a partial paralysis of his left foot. He receives $20,000 for the injury from his accident insurance company under a policy he had purchased. The $20,000 accident insurance proceeds are tax-exempt. ■

A different set of rules applies if the accident and health insurance protection was *purchased by the individual's employer*, as discussed in the following section.

Employer-Sponsored Accident and Health Plans

Congress encourages employers to provide employees, retired former employees, and their dependents with **accident and health benefits,** disability insurance, and long-term care plans. The *premiums* are deductible by the employer and excluded from the employee's income.[28] Although § 105(a) provides the general rule that the employee has includible income when he or she collects the insurance *benefits*, two exceptions are provided.

Section 105(b) generally excludes payments received for medical care of the employee, spouse, and dependents. However, if the payments are for expenses that do not meet the Code's definition of medical care,[29] the amount received must be included in gross income. In addition, the taxpayer must include in gross income any amounts received for medical expenses that were deducted by the taxpayer on a prior return.

[27] § 104(a)(3).

[28] § 106, Reg. § 1.106–1, and Rev.Rul. 82–196, 1982–1 C.B. 106.

[29] See the discussion of medical care in Chapter 10.

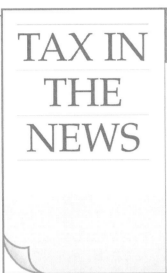

Employees Pay Tax on Disability Premiums to Attain Nontaxable Disability Pay

Generally, when an employer pays disability insurance premiums, the employee is not required to include the premiums in gross income. Any benefits collected on the policy, however, are included in gross income. On the other hand, if the employee includes the premiums in gross income, the disability payments are not taxable. An older employee with a high likelihood of disability may prefer to pay tax on the premiums so that the disability benefits will be excluded. Revenue Ruling 2004–55, I.R.B. No. 26,1081, permits the employee to elect to include disability insurance premiums in gross income. If the election is made, disability benefits received in that year and continuing into later years can be excluded from gross income, even though the employee had excluded disability insurance premiums from gross income in prior years. The election may be beneficial to older employees.

EXAMPLE 15

In 2005, Tab's employer-sponsored health insurance plan pays $4,000 for hair transplants that do not meet the Code's definition of medical care. Tab must include the $4,000 in his gross income for 2005. ■

Section 105(c) excludes payments for the permanent loss or the loss of the use of a member or function of the body or the permanent disfigurement of the employee, spouse, or a dependent. Payments that are a substitute for salary (e.g., related to the period of time absent) are includible.

EXAMPLE 16

Jill loses an eye in an automobile accident unrelated to her work. As a result of the accident, Jill incurs $2,000 of medical expenses, which she deducts on her return. She collects $10,000 from an accident insurance policy carried by her employer. The benefits are paid according to a schedule of amounts that vary with the part of the body injured (e.g., $10,000 for loss of an eye, $20,000 for loss of a hand). Because the payment is for loss of a *member or function of the body*, the $10,000 is excluded from gross income. Jill is absent from work for a week as a result of the accident. Her employer provides her with insurance for the loss of income due to illness or injury. Jill collects $500, which is includible in gross income. ■

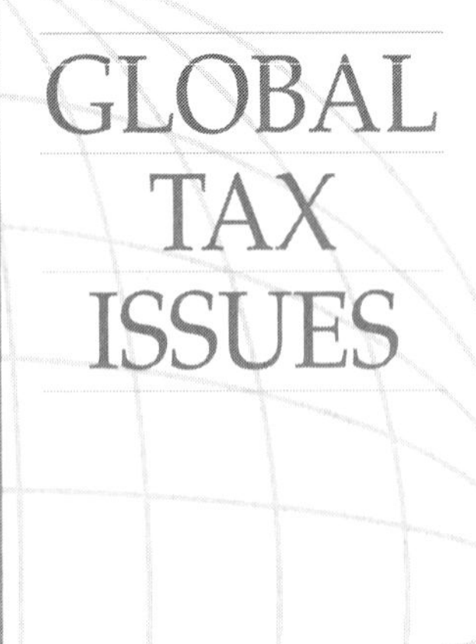

When Jobs Leave the Country, So Do the Health Insurance Benefits

Firms in the textile industry generally provided health insurance coverage for their employees. As textile mills in the United States close and production is moved to foreign countries, often the U.S. employees lose their health insurance as well as their jobs. If and when the former textile worker finds new employment, the new employer may not provide health insurance. In addition, the pay on the new job is often so low that the worker cannot afford to purchase health insurance, which may cost over $500 per month.

Among the factors contributing to increased foreign competition for the domestic textile industry are the North American Free Trade Agreement of 1993, the Caribbean Basin Initiative of 2000, and the opening up of trade with China.

The Staggering Cost of Employee Health Insurance

Some companies pay far more to provide health insurance for their retired employees than for their active employees. This is particularly true for automobile manufacturers. One giant corporation reports that it pays for health insurance for more than 1.1 million retirees. The funds to pay for these benefits must be generated by the productivity of the company's 200,000 active employees.

MEDICAL REIMBURSEMENT PLANS

In lieu of providing the employee with insurance coverage for hospital and medical expenses, the employer may agree to reimburse the employee for these expenses. The amounts received through the insurance coverage (insured plan benefits) are excluded from income under § 105 (as previously discussed). Unfortunately in terms of cost considerations, the insurance companies that issue this type of policy usually require a broad coverage of employees. An alternative is to have a plan that is not funded with insurance (a self-insured arrangement). The benefits received under a self-insured plan can be excluded from the employee's income, if the plan does not discriminate in favor of highly compensated employees.[30]

Legislation enacted in 2003 provides an alternative means of accomplishing a medical reimbursement plan. The employer can purchase a medical insurance plan with a high deductible (e.g., the employee is responsible for the first $2,000 of medical expenses) and then make contributions to the employee's **Health Savings Account (HSA).**[31] Withdrawals from the HSA must be used to reimburse the employee for the medical expenses paid by the employee that are not covered under the high-deductible plan. The employee is not taxed on the employer's contributions to the HSA, the earnings on the funds in the account, or the withdrawals made for medical expenses.[32] See additional coverage in Chapter 10.

LONG-TERM CARE INSURANCE BENEFITS

Generally, **long-term care insurance,** which covers expenses such as the cost of care in a nursing home, is treated the same as accident and health insurance benefits. Thus, the employee does not recognize income when the employer pays the premiums. When benefits are received from the policy, whether the employer or the individual purchased the policy, the exclusion from gross income is limited to the greater of the following amounts:

- $240 in 2005 (indexed amount for 2004 is $230) for each day the patient receives the long-term care.
- The actual cost of the care.

The above amount is reduced by any amounts received from other third parties (e.g., damages received).[33]

[30] § 105(h).
[31] §§ 106(d) and 223.
[32] §§ 106(d), 223(b), and 223(d).
[33] § 7702B. See § 213(d)(10) for the limitations on the amount of the employee's exclusion for premiums paid by the employer.

EXAMPLE 17

Hazel, who suffers from Alzheimer's disease, is a patient in a nursing home for the last 30 days of 2005. While in the nursing home, she incurs total costs of $7,500. Medicare pays $3,200 of the costs. Hazel receives $4,500 from her long-term care insurance policy (which pays $150 per day while she is in the facility).

The amount that Hazel may exclude is calculated as follows:

Greater of:		
Daily statutory amount of $240 ($240 × 30 days)	$7,200	
Actual cost of the care	7,500	$ 7,500
Less: Amount received from Medicare		(3,200)
Amount of exclusion		$ 4,300

Therefore, Hazel must include $200 ($4,500 – $4,300) of the long-term care benefits received in her gross income. ■

The exclusion for long-term care insurance is not available if it is provided as part of a cafeteria plan or a flexible spending plan.

Meals and Lodging

FURNISHED FOR THE CONVENIENCE OF THE EMPLOYER

As discussed in Chapter 4, income can take any form, including meals and lodging. However, § 119 excludes from income the value of meals and lodging provided to the employee and the employee's spouse and dependents under the following conditions:[34]

- The meals and/or lodging are *furnished* by the employer, on the employer's *business premises*, for the *convenience of the employer*.
- In the case of lodging, the *employee is required* to accept the lodging as a condition of employment.

The courts have construed both of these requirements strictly.

Furnished by the Employer. The following two questions have been raised with regard to the *furnished by the employer* requirement:

- Who is considered an *employee*?
- What is meant by *furnished*?

The IRS and some courts have reasoned that because a partner is not an employee, the exclusion does not apply to a partner. However, the Tax Court and the Fifth Circuit Court of Appeals have ruled in favor of the taxpayer on this issue.[35]

The Supreme Court held that a cash meal allowance was ineligible for the exclusion because the employer did not actually furnish the meals.[36] Similarly, one

[34] § 119(a). The meals and lodging are also excluded from FICA and FUTA tax. *Rowan Companies, Inc. v. U.S.*, 81–1 USTC ¶9479, 48 AFTR2d 81–5115, 101 S.Ct. 2288 (USSC, 1981).

[35] Rev.Rul. 80, 1953–1 C.B. 62; *Comm. v. Doak*, 56–2 USTC ¶9708, 49 AFTR 1491, 234 F.2d 704 (CA–4, 1956); but see *G. A. Papineau*, 16 T.C. 130 (1951); *Armstrong v. Phinney*, 68–1 USTC ¶9355, 21 AFTR2d 1260, 394 F.2d 661 (CA–5, 1968).

[36] *Comm. v. Kowalski*, 77–2 USTC ¶9748, 40 AFTR2d 6128, 98 S.Ct. 315 (USSC, 1977).

court denied the exclusion where the employer paid for the food and supplied the cooking facilities but the employee prepared the meal.[37]

On the Employer's Business Premises. The *on the employer's business premises* requirement, applicable to both meals and lodging, has resulted in much litigation. The Regulations define business premises as simply "the place of employment of the employee."[38] Thus, the Sixth Circuit Court of Appeals held that a residence, owned by the employer and occupied by an employee, two blocks from the motel that the employee managed was not part of the business premises.[39] However, the Tax Court considered an employer-owned house across the street from the hotel that was managed by the taxpayer to be on the business premises of the employer.[40] Apparently, the closer the lodging to the business operations, the more likely the convenience of the employer is served.

For the Convenience of the Employer. The *convenience of the employer* test is intended to focus on the employer's motivation for furnishing the meals and lodging rather than on the benefits received by the employee. If the employer furnishes the meals and lodging primarily to enable employees to perform their duties properly, it does not matter that the employees consider these benefits to be a part of their compensation.

The Regulations give the following examples in which the tests for excluding meals are satisfied:[41]

- A restaurant requires its service staff to eat their meals on the premises during the busy lunch and breakfast hours.
- A bank furnishes meals on the premises for its tellers to limit the time the employees are away from their booths during the busy hours.
- A worker is employed at a construction site in a remote part of Alaska. The employer must furnish meals and lodging due to the inaccessibility of other facilities.

If more than half of the employees to whom meals are furnished receive their meals for the convenience of the employer, then all such employee meals are treated as provided for the convenience of the employer.[42] Thus, in this situation, all employees are treated the same (either all of the employees are allowed exclusion treatment, or none of the employees can exclude the meals from gross income).

EXAMPLE 18

Allison's Restaurant has a restaurant area and a bar. Nine employees work in the restaurant and three work in the bar. All of the employees are provided one meal per day. In the case of the restaurant workers, the meals are provided for the convenience of the employer. The meals provided to the bar employees do not satisfy the convenience of the employer requirement. Because more than half of the employees receive their meal for the convenience of the employer, all 12 employees qualify for exclusion treatment. ■

Required as a Condition of Employment. The *employee is required to accept* test applies only to lodging. If the employee's use of the housing would serve the convenience of the employer, but the employee is not required to use the housing, the exclusion is not available.

[37] *Tougher v. Comm.*, 71–1 USTC ¶9398, 27 AFTR2d 1301, 441 F.2d 1148 (CA–9, 1971).

[38] Reg. § 1.119–1(c)(1).

[39] *Comm. v. Anderson*, 67–1 USTC ¶9136, 19 AFTR2d 318, 371 F.2d 59 (CA–6, 1966).

[40] *J. B. Lindeman*, 60 T.C. 609 (1973).

[41] Reg. § 1.119–1(f).

[42] § 119(b)(4).

EXAMPLE 19

VEP, a utilities company, has all of its service personnel on 24-hour call for emergencies. The company encourages its employees to live near the plant so that the employees can respond quickly to emergency calls. Company-owned housing is available rent-free. Only 10 of the employees live in the company housing because it is not suitable for families.

Although the company-provided housing serves the convenience of the employer, it is not required. Therefore, the employees who live in the company housing cannot exclude its value from gross income. ■

In addition, if the employee has the *option* of cash or lodging, the *required* test is not satisfied.

EXAMPLE 20

Khalid is the manager of a large apartment complex. The employer gives Khalid the option of rent-free housing (value of $6,000 per year) or an additional $5,000 per year. Khalid selects the housing option. Therefore, he must include $6,000 in gross income. ■

OTHER HOUSING EXCLUSIONS

Employees of Educational Institutions. An employee of an educational institution may be able to exclude the value of campus housing provided by the employer. Generally, the employee does not recognize income if he or she pays annual rents equal to or greater than 5 percent of the appraised value of the facility. If the rent payments are less than 5 percent of the value of the facility, the deficiency must be included in gross income.[43]

EXAMPLE 21

Swan University provides on-campus housing for its full-time faculty during the first three years of employment. The housing is not provided for the convenience of the employer. Professor Edith pays $3,000 annual rent for the use of a residence with an appraised value of $100,000 and an annual rental value of $12,000. Edith must recognize $2,000 gross income [.05($100,000) – $3,000 = $2,000] for the value of the housing provided to her. ■

Ministers of the Gospel. Ministers of the gospel can exclude (1) the rental value of a home furnished as compensation; (2) a rental allowance paid to them as compensation, to the extent the allowance is used to rent or provide a home; or (3) the rental value of a home owned by the minister.[44] The housing or housing allowance must be provided as compensation for the conduct of religious worship, the administration and maintenance of religious organizations, or the performance of teaching and administrative duties at theological seminaries.

EXAMPLE 22

Pastor Bill is allowed to live rent-free in a house owned by the congregation. The annual rental value of the house is $6,000 and is provided as part of the pastor's compensation for ministerial services. Assistant Pastor Olga is paid a $4,500 cash housing allowance. She uses the $4,500 to pay rent and utilities on a home she and her family occupy. Neither Pastor Bill nor Assistant Pastor Olga is required to recognize gross income associated with the housing or housing allowance. ■

Military Personnel. Military personnel are allowed housing exclusions under various circumstances. Authority for these exclusions generally is found in Federal laws that are not part of the Internal Revenue Code.[45]

[43]§ 119(d).
[44]§ 107 and Reg. § 1.107–1.
[45]H. Rep. No. 99–841, 99th Cong., 2d Sess., p. 548 (1986). See also § 134.

Other Employee Fringe Benefits

SPECIFIC BENEFITS

Congress has enacted exclusions to encourage employers to (1) finance and make available child care facilities, (2) provide athletic facilities for employees, (3) finance certain employees' education, and (4) pay or reimburse child adoption expenses. These provisions are summarized as follows:

- The employee does not have to include in gross income the value of child and dependent care services paid for by the employer and incurred to enable the employee to work. The exclusion cannot exceed $5,000 per year ($2,500 if married and filing separately). For a married couple, the annual exclusion cannot exceed the earned income of the spouse who has the lesser amount of earned income. For an unmarried taxpayer, the exclusion cannot exceed the taxpayer's earned income.[46]
- The value of the use of a gymnasium or other athletic facilities by employees, their spouses, and their dependent children may be excluded from an employee's gross income. The facilities must be on the employer's premises, and substantially all of the use of the facilities must be by employees and their family members.[47]
- Qualified employer-provided educational assistance (tuition, fees, books, and supplies) at the undergraduate and graduate level is excludible from gross income. The exclusion is subject to an annual employee statutory ceiling of $5,250.[48]
- The employee can exclude from gross income up to $10,630 of expenses incurred to adopt a child where the adoption expenses are paid or reimbursed by the employer under a qualified adoption assistance program.[49] The limit on the exclusion is the same even if the child has special needs (is not physically or mentally capable of caring for himself or herself). However, for a child with special needs, the $10,630 exclusion from gross income applies even if the actual adoption expenses are less than that amount. The exclusion is phased out as adjusted gross income increases from $159,450 to $199,450.

CAFETERIA PLANS

Generally, if an employee is offered a choice between cash and some other form of compensation, the employee is deemed to have constructively received the cash even when the noncash option is elected. Thus, the employee has gross income regardless of the option chosen.

An exception to this constructive receipt treatment is provided under the **cafeteria plan** rules. Under such a plan, the employee is permitted to choose between cash and nontaxable benefits (e.g., group term life insurance, health and accident protection, and child care). If the employee chooses the otherwise nontaxable benefits, the cafeteria plan rules enable the benefits to remain nontaxable.[50] Cafeteria plans provide tremendous flexibility in tailoring the employee pay package to fit individual needs. Some employees (usually the younger group) prefer cash, while others (usually the older group) will opt for the fringe benefit program. However, Congress excluded long-term

[46] § 129. The exclusion applies to the same types of expenses that, if they were paid by the employee (and not reimbursed by the employer), would be eligible for the credit for child and dependent care expense discussed in Chapter 12.

[47] § 132(j)(4).

[48] § 127.

[49] § 137.

[50] § 125.

care insurance from the excludible benefits that can be provided under a cafeteria plan.[51] Thus, the employer must provide these benefits separate from the cafeteria plan.

EXAMPLE 23

Hawk Corporation offers its employees (on a nondiscriminatory basis) a choice of any one or all of the following benefits:

Benefit	Cost
Group term life insurance	$ 200
Hospitalization insurance for family members	2,400
Child care payments	1,800
	$4,400

If a benefit is not selected, the employee receives cash equal to the cost of the benefit. Kay, an employee, has a spouse who works for another employer that provides hospitalization insurance but no child care payments. Kay elects to receive the group term life insurance, the child care payments, and $2,400 of cash. Only the $2,400 must be included in Kay's gross income. ■

FLEXIBLE SPENDING PLANS

Flexible spending plans (often referred to as flexible benefit plans) operate much like cafeteria plans. Under these plans, the employee accepts lower cash compensation in return for the employer agreeing to pay certain costs that the employer can pay without the employee recognizing gross income. For example, assume the employer's health insurance policy does not cover dental expenses. The employee could estimate his or her dental expenses for the upcoming year and agree to a salary reduction equal to the estimated dental expenses. The employer then pays or reimburses the employee for the actual dental expenses incurred, with a ceiling of the amount of the salary reduction. If the employee's actual dental expenses are less than the reduction in cash compensation, the employee cannot recover the difference. Hence, these plans are often referred to as *use or lose* plans. As is the case for cafeteria plans, flexible spending plans cannot be used to pay long-term care insurance premiums.

GENERAL CLASSES OF EXCLUDED BENEFITS

An employer can confer numerous forms and types of economic benefits on employees. Under the all-inclusive concept of income, the benefits are taxable unless one of the provisions previously discussed specifically excludes the item from gross income. The amount of the income is the fair market value of the benefit. This reasoning can lead to results that Congress considers unacceptable, as illustrated in the following example.

EXAMPLE 24

Vern is employed in New York as a ticket clerk for Trans National Airlines. He has a sick mother in Miami, Florida, but has no money for plane tickets. Trans National has daily flights from New York to Miami that often leave with empty seats. The cost of a round-trip ticket is $400, and Vern is in the 25% tax bracket. If Trans National allows Vern to fly without charge to Miami, under the general gross income rules, Vern has income equal to the value of a ticket. Therefore, Vern must pay $100 tax (.25 × $400) on a trip to Miami. Because Vern does not have $100, he cannot visit his mother, and the airplane flies with another empty seat. ■

[51] § 125(f).

If Trans National in Example 24 will allow employees to use resources that would otherwise be wasted, why should the tax laws interfere with the employee's decision to take advantage of the available benefit? Thus, to avoid the undesirable results that occur in Example 24 and in similar situations, as well as to create uniform rules for fringe benefits, Congress established seven broad classes of nontaxable employee benefits:[52]

- No-additional-cost services.
- Qualified employee discounts.
- Working condition fringes.
- *De minimis* fringes.
- Qualified transportation fringes.
- Qualified moving expense reimbursements.
- Qualified retirement planning services.

No-Additional-Cost Services. Example 24 illustrates the **no-additional-cost service** type of fringe benefit. The services will be nontaxable if all of the following conditions are satisfied:

- The employee receives services, as opposed to property.
- The employer does not incur substantial additional cost, including forgone revenue, in providing the services to the employee.
- The services are offered to customers in the ordinary course of the business in which the employee works.[53]

EXAMPLE 25

Assume that Vern in Example 24 can fly without charge only if the airline cannot fill the seats with paying customers. That is, Vern must fly on standby. Although the airplane may burn slightly more fuel because Vern is on the airplane and Vern may receive the same meal as paying customers, the additional costs would not be substantial. Thus, the trip could qualify as a no-additional-cost service.

On the other hand, assume that Vern is given a reserved seat on a flight that is frequently full. The employer would be forgoing revenue to allow Vern to fly. This forgone revenue would be a substantial additional cost, and thus the benefit would be taxable. ■

Note that if Vern were employed in a hotel owned by Trans National, the receipt of the airline ticket would be taxable because Vern did not work in that line of business. However, the Code allows the exclusion for reciprocal benefits offered by employers in the same line of business.

EXAMPLE 26

Grace is employed as a desk clerk for Plush Hotels, Inc. The company and Chain Hotels, Inc., have an agreement that allows any of their employees to stay without charge in either company's resort hotels during the off-season. If Grace takes advantage of the plan by staying in a Chain Hotel, she is not required to recognize income. ■

The no-additional-cost exclusion extends to the employee's spouse and dependent children and to retired and disabled former employees. In the Regulations, the IRS has conceded that partners who perform services for the partnership are employees for purposes of the exclusion.[54] (As discussed earlier in the chapter, the IRS's position is that partners are not employees for purposes of the § 119 meals and lodging exclusion.) However, the exclusion is not allowed to highly compensated employees unless the benefit is available on a nondiscriminatory basis.

[52]See, generally, § 132.

[53]Reg. § 1.132–2.

[54]Reg. § 1.132–1(b).

Qualified Employee Discounts. When the employer sells goods or services (other than no-additional-cost benefits just discussed) to the employee for a price that is less than the price charged regular customers, the employee realizes income equal to the discount. However, the discount, referred to as a **qualified employee discount,** can be excluded from the gross income of the employee, subject to the following conditions and limitations:

- The exclusion is not available for real property (e.g., a house) or for personal property of the type commonly held for investment (e.g., common stocks).
- The property or services must be from the same line of business in which the employee works.
- In the case of *property*, the exclusion is limited to the *gross profit component* of the price to customers.
- In the case of *services*, the exclusion is limited to 20 percent of the customer price.[55]

EXAMPLE 27

Silver Corporation, which operates a department store, sells a television set to a store employee for $300. The regular customer price is $500, and the gross profit rate is 25%. The corporation also sells the employee a service contract for $120. The regular customer price for the contract is $150. The employee must include $75 in gross income.

Customer price for property	$ 500
Less: Gross profit (25%)	(125)
	$ 375
Employee price	(300)
Income	$ 75
Customer price for service	$ 150
Less: 20 percent	(30)
	$ 120
Employee price	(120)
Income	$ -0-

EXAMPLE 28

Assume the same facts as in Example 27, except that the employee is a clerk in a hotel operated by Silver Corporation. Because the line of business requirement is not met, the employee must recognize $200 income ($500 – $300) from the purchase of the television and $30 income ($150 – $120) from the service contract.

As in the case of no-additional-cost benefits, the exclusion applies to employees (including service partners), employees' spouses and dependent children, and retired and disabled former employees. However, the exclusion does not apply to highly compensated individuals unless the discount is available on a nondiscriminatory basis.

Working Condition Fringes. Generally, an employee is not required to include in gross income the cost of property or services provided by the employer if the employee could deduct the cost of those items if he or she had actually paid for them.[56] These benefits are called **working condition fringes.**

[55] § 132(c).
[56] § 132(d).

EXAMPLE 29

Mitch is a CPA employed by an accounting firm. The employer pays Mitch's annual dues to professional organizations. Mitch is not required to include the payment of the dues in gross income because if he had paid the dues, he would have been allowed to deduct the amount as an employee business expense (as discussed in Chapter 9). ■

In many cases, this exclusion merely avoids reporting income and an offsetting deduction. However, in two specific situations, the working condition fringe benefit rules allow an exclusion where the expense would not be deductible if paid by the employee:

- Automobile salespeople are allowed to exclude the value of certain personal use of company demonstrators (e.g., commuting to and from work).[57]
- The employee business expense would be eliminated by the 2 percent floor on miscellaneous deductions under § 67 (see Chapter 10).

Unlike the other fringe benefits discussed previously, working condition fringes can be made available on a discriminatory basis and still qualify for the exclusion.

***De Minimis* Fringes.** As the term suggests, ***de minimis* fringe** benefits are so small that accounting for them is impractical.[58] The House Report contains the following examples of *de minimis* fringes:

- The typing of a personal letter by a company secretary, occasional personal use of a company copying machine, occasional company cocktail parties or picnics for employees, occasional supper money or taxi fare for employees because of overtime work, and certain holiday gifts of property with a low fair market value are excluded.
- Subsidized eating facilities (e.g., an employees' cafeteria) operated by the employer are excluded if located on or near the employer's business premises, if revenue equals or exceeds direct operating costs, and if nondiscrimination requirements are met.

When taxpayers venture beyond the specific examples contained in the House Report and the Regulations, there is obviously much room for disagreement as to what is *de minimis*. However, note that except in the case of subsidized eating facilities, the *de minimis* fringe benefits can be granted in a manner that favors highly compensated employees.

Qualified Transportation Fringes. The intent of the exclusion for **qualified transportation fringes** is to encourage the use of mass transit for commuting to and from work. Qualified transportation fringes encompass the following transportation benefits provided by the employer to the employee:[59]

1. Transportation in a commuter highway vehicle between the employee's residence and the place of employment.
2. A transit pass.
3. Qualified parking.

Statutory dollar limits are placed on the amount of the exclusion. Categories (1) and (2) above are combined for purposes of applying the limit. In this case, the limit on the exclusion for 2005 is $105 per month. Category (3) has a separate limit. For qualified parking, the limit on the exclusion for 2005 is $200 per month. Both of these dollar limits are indexed annually for inflation.

[57]§ 132(j)(3).
[58]§ 132(e).
[59]§ 132(f).

A *commuter highway vehicle* is any highway vehicle with a seating capacity of at least six adults (excluding the driver). In addition, at least 80 percent of the vehicle's use must be for transporting employees between their residences and place of employment.

Qualified parking includes the following:

- Parking provided to an employee on or near the employer's business premises.
- Parking provided to an employee on or near a location from which the employee commutes to work via mass transit, in a commuter highway vehicle, or in a carpool.

Qualified transportation fringes may be provided directly by the employer or may be in the form of cash reimbursements.

EXAMPLE 30

Gray Corporation's offices are located in the center of a large city. The company pays for parking spaces to be used by the company officers. Steve, a vice president, receives $250 of such benefits each month. The parking space rental qualifies as a qualified transportation fringe. Of the $250 benefit received each month by Steve, $200 is excludible from gross income. The balance of $50 is included in his gross income. The same result would occur if Steve paid for the parking and was reimbursed by his employer. ■

Qualified Moving Expense Reimbursements. Qualified moving expenses that are reimbursed or paid by the employer are excludible from gross income. A qualified moving expense is one that would be deductible under § 217. See the discussion of moving expenses in Chapter 9.

Qualified Retirement Planning Services. Qualified retirement planning services include any retirement planning advice or information that an employer who maintains a qualified retirement plan provides to an employee or the employee's spouse.[60] Congress decided to exclude the value of such services from gross income because they are a key part of retirement income planning. Such an exclusion should motivate more employers to provide retirement planning services to their employees.

Nondiscrimination Provisions. For no-additional-cost services, qualified employee discounts, and qualified retirement planning services, if the plan is discriminatory in favor of highly compensated employees, these key employees are denied exclusion treatment. However, the non-highly compensated employees who receive benefits from the plan can still enjoy exclusion treatment for the no-additional-cost services, qualified employee discounts, and qualified retirement planning services.[61]

EXAMPLE 31

Dove Company's officers are allowed to purchase goods from the company at a 25% discount. Other employees are allowed only a 15% discount. The company's gross profit margin on these goods is 30%.

Peggy, an officer in the company, purchased goods from the company for $750 when the price charged to customers was $1,000. Peggy must include $250 in gross income because the plan is discriminatory.

Leo, an employee of the company who is not an officer, purchased goods for $850 when the customer price was $1,000. Leo is not required to recognize income because he received a qualified employee discount. ■

[60] §§ 132(a)(7) and (m).
[61] §§ 132(j)(1) and 132(m)(2).

Concept Summary 5–2

General Classes of Excluded Benefits

Benefit	Description and Examples	Coverage Allowed	Effect of Discrimination
1. No-additional-cost services	The employee takes advantage of the employer's excess capacity (e.g., free passes for airline employees).	Current, retired, and disabled employees; their spouses and dependent children; spouses of deceased employees. Partners are treated as employees.	No exclusion for highly compensated employees.
2. Qualified discounts on goods	The employee is allowed to purchase the employer's merchandise at a price that is not less than the employer's cost.	Same as (1) above.	Same as (1) above.
3. Qualified discounts on services	The employee is allowed a discount (maximum of 20%) on services the employer offers to customers.	Same as (1) above.	Same as (1) above.
4. Working condition fringes	Expenses paid by the employer that would be deductible if paid by the employee (e.g., a mechanic's tools). Also, includes auto salesperson's use of a car held for sale.	Current employees, partners, directors, and independent contractors.	No effect.
5. *De minimis* items	Expenses so immaterial that accounting for them is not warranted (e.g., occasional supper money, personal use of the copy machine).	*Any recipient* of a fringe benefit.	No effect.
6. Qualified transportation fringes	Transportation benefits provided by the employer to employees including commuting in a commuter highway vehicle, a transit pass, and qualified parking.	Current employees.	No effect.
7. Qualified moving expense reimbursements	Qualified moving expenses that are paid or reimbursed by the employer. A qualified moving expense is one that would be deductible under § 217.	Current employees.	No effect.
8. Qualified retirement planning services	Qualified retirement planning services that are provided by the employer.	Current employees and spouses.	Same as (1) above.

De minimis (except in the case of subsidized eating facilities) and working condition fringe benefits can be provided on a discriminatory basis. The *de minimis* benefits are not subject to tax because the accounting problems that would be created are out of proportion to the amount of additional tax that would result. A nondiscrimination test would simply add to the compliance problems. In the case of working condition fringes, the types of services required vary with the job. Therefore, a nondiscrimination test probably could not be satisfied, although usually there is no deliberate plan to benefit a chosen few. Likewise, the qualified transportation fringe and the qualified moving expense reimbursement can be provided on a discriminatory basis.

TAXABLE FRINGE BENEFITS

If the fringe benefits cannot qualify for any of the specific exclusions or do not fit into any of the general classes of excluded benefits, the taxpayer must recognize gross income equal to the fair market value of the benefits. Obviously, problems are frequently encountered in determining values. The IRS has issued extensive Regulations addressing the valuation of personal use of an employer's automobiles and meals provided at an employer-operated eating facility.[62]

If a fringe benefit plan discriminates in favor of highly compensated employees, generally those employees are not allowed to exclude the benefits they receive that other employees do not enjoy. However, the highly compensated employees, as well as the other employees, are generally allowed to exclude the nondiscriminatory benefits.[63]

EXAMPLE 32

MED Company has a medical reimbursement plan that reimburses officers for 100% of their medical expenses, but reimburses all other employees for only 80% of their medical expenses. Cliff, the president of the company, was reimbursed $1,000 during the year for medical expenses. Cliff must include $200 in gross income [(1 – .80) × $1,000 = $200]. Mike, an employee who is not an officer, received $800 (80% of his actual medical expenses) under the medical reimbursement plan. None of the $800 is includible in his gross income. ■

Foreign Earned Income

A U.S. citizen is generally subject to U.S. tax on his or her income regardless of the income's geographic origin. The income may also be subject to tax in the foreign country, and thus the taxpayer must carry a double tax burden. Out of a sense of fairness and to encourage U.S. citizens to work abroad (so that exports might be increased), Congress has provided alternative forms of relief from taxes on foreign earned income. The taxpayer can elect *either* (1) to include the foreign income in his or her taxable income and then claim a credit for foreign taxes paid or (2) to exclude the foreign earnings from his or her U.S. gross income (the **foreign earned income exclusion**).[64] The foreign tax credit option is discussed in Chapter 12, but as is apparent from the following discussion, most taxpayers will choose the exclusion.

Foreign earned income consists of the earnings from the individual's personal services rendered in a foreign country (other than as an employee of the U.S. government). To qualify for the exclusion, the taxpayer must be either of the following:

- A bona fide resident of the foreign country (or countries).
- Present in a foreign country (or countries) for at least 330 days during any 12 consecutive months.[65]

[62] Reg. § 1.61–21(d). Generally, the income from the personal use of the employer's automobile is based on the lease value of the automobile (what it would have cost the employee to lease the automobile). Meals are valued at 150% of the employer's direct costs (e.g., food and labor) of preparing the meals.

[63] §§ 79(d), 105(h), 127(b)(2), and 132(j)(1).

[64] § 911(a).

[65] § 911(d). For the definition of resident, see Reg. § 1.871–2(b). Under the Regulations, a taxpayer is not a resident if he or she is there for a definite period (e.g., until completion of a construction contract).

EXAMPLE 33

Sandra's trips to and from a foreign country in connection with her work were as follows:

Arrived in Foreign Country	Arrived in United States
March 10, 2004	February 1, 2005
March 7, 2005	June 1, 2005

During the 12 consecutive months ending on March 10, 2005, Sandra was present in the foreign country for at least 330 days (365 days less 28 days in February and 7 days in March 2005). Therefore, all income earned in the foreign country through March 10, 2005, is eligible for the exclusion. The income earned from March 11, 2005, through May 31, 2005, is also eligible for the exclusion because Sandra was present in the foreign country for 330 days during the 12 consecutive months ending on May 31, 2005. ■

The exclusion is *limited* to $80,000. For married persons, both of whom have foreign earned income, the exclusion is computed separately for each spouse. Community property rules do not apply (the community property spouse is not deemed to have earned one-half of the other spouse's foreign earned income). If all the days in the tax year are not qualifying days, then the taxpayer must compute the maximum exclusion on a daily basis ($80,000 divided by the number of days in the entire year and multiplied by the number of qualifying days).

EXAMPLE 34

Keith qualifies for the foreign earned income exclusion. He was present in France for all of 2005. Keith's salary for 2005 is $90,000. Since all of the days in 2005 are qualifying days, Keith can exclude $80,000 of his $90,000 salary.

Assume instead that only 335 days were qualifying days. Then, Keith's exclusion is limited to $73,425, computed as follows:

$$\$80,000 \times \frac{335 \text{ days in foreign country}}{365 \text{ days in the year}} = \$73,425$$

■

ETHICAL CONSIDERATIONS: Who Should Benefit from the Foreign Earned Income Exclusion?

Perhaps the tax law should be changed so that when an employer transfers an employee to a foreign country for a period sufficient to qualify for the foreign earned income exclusion, the benefits of the exclusion could be allocated to the employee, the employer, or both. The purpose of the tax law in this area is to increase exports; therefore, a case can be made that all of the tax benefits should be assigned to the employer. One way of accomplishing this would be to ensure that the employer's after-tax cost for compensation paid to an employee is the same whether the employee works in the United States or in a foreign country. However, employees may not be willing to work abroad unless they receive some of the tax benefit. Evaluate the equity of a change in the tax law that would assign some or all of the tax benefit to the employer.

In addition to the exclusion for foreign earnings, the *reasonable housing costs* incurred by the taxpayer and the taxpayer's family in a foreign country in excess of a base amount may be excluded from gross income. The base amount is 16 percent of the U.S. government pay scale for a GS–14 (Step 1) employee, which varies from year to year.[66]

[66] § 911(c).

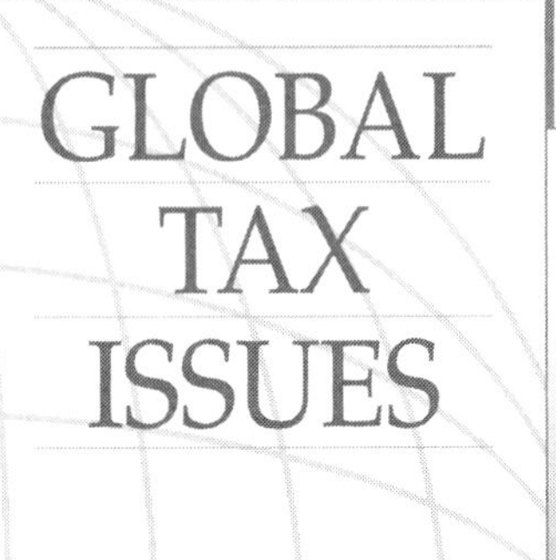

U.S. Taxpayers Abroad Are Gone but Not Forgotten

U.S. citizens and residents working and living abroad create unique compliance issues for the IRS. These individuals are potentially liable for U.S. taxes and must file U.S. tax returns, even if they earn less than the § 911 exclusion amount. However, in practical terms, many of these individuals are outside the enforcement net of the IRS. In recent years, the IRS has taken several steps to improve compliance, including taxpayer education, simplification of the filing burden, and increased enforcement efforts.

As previously mentioned, the taxpayer may elect to include the foreign earned income in gross income and claim a credit (an offset against U.S. tax) for the foreign tax paid. The credit alternative may be advantageous if the individual's foreign earned income far exceeds the excludible amount so that the foreign taxes paid exceed the U.S. tax on the amount excluded. However, once an election is made, it applies to all subsequent years unless affirmatively revoked. A revocation is effective for the year of the change and the four subsequent years.

Interest on Certain State and Local Government Obligations

At the time the Sixteenth Amendment was ratified by the states, there was some question as to whether the Federal government possessed the constitutional authority to tax interest on state and local government obligations. Taxing such interest was thought to violate the doctrine of intergovernmental immunity in that the tax would impair the state and local governments' ability to finance their operations.[67] Thus, interest on state and local government obligations was specifically exempted from Federal income taxation.[68] However, the Supreme Court has concluded that there is no constitutional prohibition against levying a nondiscriminatory Federal income tax on state and local government obligations.[69] Nevertheless, currently the statutory exclusion still exists.

Obviously, the exclusion of the interest reduces the cost of borrowing for state and local governments. A taxpayer in the 35 percent tax bracket requires only a 5.2 percent yield on a tax-exempt bond to obtain the same after-tax income as a taxable bond paying 8 percent interest [5.2% ÷ (1 – .35) = 8%].

The current exempt status applies solely to state and local government bonds. Thus, income received from the accrual of interest on a condemnation award or an overpayment of state income tax is fully taxable.[70] Nor does the exemption apply to gains on the sale of tax-exempt securities.

EXAMPLE 35

Megan purchases State of Virginia bonds for $10,000 on July 1, 2004. The bonds pay $400 interest each June 30th and December 31st. On March 31, 2005, Megan sells the bonds for $10,500 plus $200 accrued interest. Megan must recognize a $500 gain ($10,500 – $10,000), but the $200 accrued interest is exempt from taxation. ■

[67] *Pollock v. Farmer's Loan & Trust Co.*, 3 AFTR 2602, 15 S.Ct. 912 (USSC, 1895).

[68] § 103(a).

[69] *South Carolina v. Baker III*, 88–1 USTC ¶9284, 61 AFTR2d 88–995, 108 S.Ct. 1355 (USSC, 1988).

[70] *Kieselbach v. Comm.*, 43–1 USTC ¶9220, 30 AFTR 370, 63 S.Ct. 303 (USSC, 1943); *U.S. Trust Co. of New York v. Anderson*, 3 USTC ¶1125, 12 AFTR 836, 65 F.2d 575 (CA–2, 1933).

State and local governments have developed sophisticated financial schemes to attract new industry. For example, local municipalities have issued bonds to finance the construction of plants to be leased to private enterprise. By arranging the financing with low-interest municipal obligations, the plants could be leased at a lower cost than the private business could otherwise obtain. However, Congress has placed limitations on the use of tax-exempt securities to finance private business.[71]

Dividends

GENERAL INFORMATION

A *dividend* is a payment to a shareholder with respect to his or her stock (see Chapter 4). Dividends to shareholders are taxable only to the extent the payments are made from *either* the corporation's *current earnings and profits* (similar to net income per books) or its *accumulated earnings and profits* (similar to retained earnings per books).[72] Distributions that exceed earnings and profits are treated as a nontaxable recovery of capital and reduce the shareholder's basis in the stock. Once the shareholder's basis is reduced to zero, any subsequent distributions are taxed as capital gains (see Chapter 13).[73]

Some payments are frequently referred to as dividends but are not considered dividends for tax purposes:

- Dividends received on deposits with savings and loan associations, credit unions, and banks are actually interest (a contractual rate paid for the use of money).
- Patronage dividends paid by cooperatives (e.g., for farmers) are rebates made to the users and are considered reductions in the cost of items purchased from the association. The rebates are usually made after year-end (after the cooperative has determined whether it has met its expenses) and are apportioned among members on the basis of their purchases.
- Mutual insurance companies pay dividends on unmatured life insurance policies that are considered rebates of premiums.
- Shareholders in a mutual investment fund are allowed to report as capital gains their proportionate share of the fund's gains realized and distributed. The capital gain and ordinary income portions are reported on the Form 1099 that the fund supplies its shareholders each year.

STOCK DIVIDENDS

When a corporation issues a simple stock dividend (e.g., common stock issued to common shareholders), the shareholder has merely received additional shares that represent the same total investment. Thus, the shareholder does not realize income.[74] However, if the shareholder has the *option* of receiving either cash or stock in the corporation, the individual realizes gross income whether he or she receives stock or cash.[75] A taxpayer who elects to receive the stock could be deemed to be in

[71] See § 103(b).

[72] § 316(a). Refer to the discussion of the beneficial tax rates for qualified dividends in Chapter 4.

[73] § 301(c). See Chapter 19 for a detailed discussion of corporate distributions.

[74] *Eisner v. Macomber*, 1 USTC ¶32, 3 AFTR 3020, 40 S.Ct. 189 (USSC, 1920); § 305(a).

[75] § 305(b).

constructive receipt of the cash he or she has rejected.[76] However, the amount of the income in this case is the value of the stock received, rather than the cash the shareholder has rejected. See Chapter 13 for a detailed discussion of stock dividends.

Educational Savings Bonds

The cost of a college education has risen dramatically during the past 15 years. The U.S. Department of Education estimates that by the year 2007, the cost of attending a publicly supported university for four years will exceed $60,000. For a private university, the cost is expected to exceed $200,000. Consequently, Congress has attempted to assist low- to middle-income parents in saving for their children's college education.

The assistance is in the form of an interest income exclusion on **educational savings bonds.**[77] The interest on Series EE U.S. government savings bonds may be excluded from gross income if the bond proceeds are used to pay qualified higher education expenses. The exclusion applies only if both of the following requirements are satisfied:

- The savings bonds are issued after December 31, 1989.
- The savings bonds are issued to an individual who is at least 24 years old at the time of issuance.

The exclusion is not available for a married couple who file separate returns.

The redemption proceeds must be used to pay qualified higher education expenses. *Qualified higher education expenses* consist of tuition and fees paid to an eligible educational institution for the taxpayer, spouse, or dependent. In calculating qualified higher education expenses, the tuition and fees paid are reduced by excludible scholarships and veterans' benefits received. If the redemption proceeds (both principal and interest) exceed the qualified higher education expenses, only a pro rata portion of the interest will qualify for exclusion treatment.

EXAMPLE 36

Tracy's redemption proceeds from qualified savings bonds during the taxable year are $6,000 (principal of $4,000 and interest of $2,000). Tracy's qualified higher education expenses are $5,000. Since the redemption proceeds exceed the qualified higher education expenses, only $1,667 [($5,000/$6,000) × $2,000] of the interest is excludible. ■

The exclusion is limited by the application of the wherewithal to pay concept. That is, once the modified adjusted gross income exceeds a threshold amount, the phaseout of the exclusion begins. *Modified adjusted gross income* (*MAGI*) is adjusted gross income prior to the § 911 foreign earned income exclusion and the educational savings bond exclusion. The threshold amounts are adjusted for inflation each year. For 2005, the phaseout begins at $61,200 ($91,850 on a joint return).[78] The phaseout is completed when MAGI exceeds the threshold amount by more than $15,000 ($30,000 on a joint return). The otherwise excludible interest is reduced by the amount calculated as follows:

$$\frac{\text{MAGI} - \$61{,}200}{\$15{,}000} \times \begin{array}{c}\text{Excludible interest}\\ \text{before phaseout}\end{array} = \begin{array}{c}\text{Reduction in}\\ \text{excludible interest}\end{array}$$

On a joint return, $91,850 is substituted for $61,200 (in 2005), and $30,000 is substituted for $15,000.

[76] Refer to the discussion of constructive receipt in Chapter 4.
[77] § 135.
[78] The indexed amounts for 2004 are $59,850 and $89,750.

EXAMPLE 37

Assume the same facts as in Example 36, except that Tracy's MAGI for 2005 is $70,000. The phaseout results in Tracy's interest exclusion being reduced by $978 {[($70,000 – $61,200)/$15,000] × $1,667}. Therefore, Tracy's exclusion is $689 ($1,667 – $978). ■

Qualified Tuition Programs

Nearly all, if not all, states have created programs whereby parents can in effect prepay their child's college tuition. The prepayment serves as a hedge against future increases in tuition. Generally, if the child does not attend college, the parents are refunded their payments plus interest. Upon first impression, these prepaid tuition programs resemble the below-market loans discussed in Chapter 4. That is, assuming the tuition increases, the parent receives a reduction in the child's tuition in exchange for the use of the funds. However, Congress has created an exclusion provision for these programs.[79]

Under a **qualified tuition program,** the amounts contributed must be used for qualified higher education expenses. These expenses include tuition, fees, books, supplies, room and board, and equipment required for enrollment or attendance at a college, university, or certain vocational schools. Qualified higher education expenses also include the expenses for special needs services that are incurred in connection with the enrollment and attendance of special needs students.

The earnings of the contributed funds, including the discount on tuition charged to participants, are not included in gross income provided that the contributions and earnings are used for qualified higher education expenses.

EXAMPLE 38

Agnes paid $20,000 into a qualified tuition program to be used for her son's college tuition. When her son graduated from high school, the fund balance had increased to $30,000 as a result of interest credited to the account. The interest was not included in Agnes's gross income. During the current year, $7,500 of the balance in the fund was used to pay the son's tuition and fees. None of this amount is included in either Agnes's or the son's gross income. ■

If the parent receives a refund (e.g., child does not attend college), the excess of the amount refunded over the amount contributed by the parent is included in the parent's gross income.

Qualified tuition programs have been expanded to apply to private educational institutions as well as public educational institutions. Distributions made after December 31, 2003, from such a plan maintained by an entity other than the state for qualified higher education expenses are eligible for exclusion from gross income.

LO.3

Determine the extent to which receipts can be excluded under the tax benefit rule.

Tax Benefit Rule

Generally, if a taxpayer obtains a deduction for an item in one year and in a later year recovers all or a portion of the prior deduction, the recovery is included in gross income in the year received.[80]

EXAMPLE 39

A taxpayer deducted as a loss a $1,000 receivable from a customer when it appeared the amount would never be collected. The following year, the customer paid $800 on the receivable. The taxpayer must report the $800 as gross income in the year it is received. ■

[79] § 529.

[80] § 111(a).

However, the § 111 **tax benefit rule** provides that no income is recognized upon the recovery of a deduction, or the portion of a deduction, that did not yield a tax benefit in the year it was taken. If the taxpayer in Example 39 had no tax liability in the year of the deduction (e.g., itemized deductions and personal exemptions exceeded adjusted gross income), the recovery would be partially or totally excluded from gross income in the year of the recovery.[81]

EXAMPLE 40

Before deducting a $1,000 loss from an uncollectible business receivable, Ali had taxable income of $200, computed as follows:

Adjusted gross income	$ 13,300
Itemized deductions and personal exemptions	(13,100)
Taxable income	$ 200

The business bad debt deduction yields only a $200 tax benefit. That is, taxable income is reduced by only $200 (to zero) as a result of the bad debt deduction. Therefore, if the customer makes a payment on the previously deducted receivable in a subsequent year, only the first $200 is a recovery of a prior deduction and thus is taxable. Any additional amount collected is nontaxable because only $200 of the loss yielded a reduction in taxable income. ■

ETHICAL CONSIDERATIONS

Unintentional Generosity of the Tax Benefit Rule

As a result of receiving an unexpected amount of ordinary income, Albert finds himself in the 35 percent marginal tax bracket in the current tax year. In subsequent years, Albert expects his income to return to its usual level where he is subject to the 15 percent marginal rate. His tax adviser has suggested that he "overpay" his state income taxes during the current year and deduct the total state income taxes paid as an itemized deduction. The overpaid taxes will save him 35 percent of each dollar paid. In the following year, Albert will receive a state income tax refund, which will be included in his gross income under the tax benefit rule. However, this income will be taxed at only 15 percent whereas the original deduction saved 35 percent of the overpayment. When Albert asked the tax adviser how much the overpayment should be, the tax adviser answered, "The more the better." Do you concur with the tax adviser's plan?

LO.4

Describe the circumstances under which income must be reported from the discharge of indebtedness.

Income from Discharge of Indebtedness

A transfer of appreciated property (fair market value is greater than adjusted basis) in satisfaction of a debt is an event that triggers the realization of income. The transaction is treated as a sale of the appreciated property followed by payment of the debt.[82] Foreclosure by a creditor is also treated as a sale or exchange of the property.[83]

EXAMPLE 41

Juan owes State Bank $100,000 on an unsecured note. He satisfies the note by transferring to the bank common stock with a basis of $60,000 and a fair market value of $100,000. Juan must recognize a $40,000 gain on the transfer. Juan also owes the bank $50,000 on a note secured by land. When Juan's basis in the land is $20,000 and the land's fair market value is $50,000, the bank forecloses on the loan and takes title to the land. Juan must recognize a $30,000 gain on the foreclosure. ■

[81] Itemized deductions are discussed in Chapter 10.
[82] Reg. § 1.1001–2(a).
[83] *Estate of Delman v. Comm.*, 73 T.C. 15 (1979).

In some cases, a creditor will not exercise his or her right of foreclosure and will even forgive a portion of the debt to assure the vitality of the debtor. In such cases, the debtor realizes income from discharge of indebtedness.

EXAMPLE 42

Brown Corporation is unable to meet the mortgage payments on its factory building. Both the corporation and the mortgage holder are aware of the depressed market for industrial property in the area. Foreclosure would only result in the creditor's obtaining unsalable property. To improve Brown Corporation's financial position and thus improve Brown's chances of obtaining the additional credit necessary for survival from other lenders, the creditor agrees to forgive all amounts past due and to reduce the principal amount of the mortgage. ■

Generally, the income realized by the debtor from the forgiveness of a debt is taxable.[84] A similar debt discharge (produced by a different creditor motivation) associated with personal use property is illustrated in Example 43.

EXAMPLE 43

In 2000, Joyce borrowed $60,000 from National Bank to purchase her personal residence. Joyce agreed to make monthly principal and interest payments for 15 years. The interest rate on the note was 7%. In 2005, when the balance on the note has been reduced through monthly payments to $48,000, the bank offers to accept $45,000 in full settlement of the note. The bank makes the offer because interest rates have increased to 11%. Joyce accepts the bank's offer. As a result, Joyce must recognize $3,000 ($48,000 – $45,000) of gross income.[85] ■

The following discharge of indebtedness situations are subject to special treatment:[86]

1. Creditors' gifts.
2. Discharges under Federal bankruptcy law.
3. Discharges that occur when the debtor is insolvent.
4. Discharge of the farm debt of a solvent taxpayer.
5. Discharge of **qualified real property business indebtedness.**
6. A seller's cancellation of the buyer's indebtedness.
7. A shareholder's cancellation of the corporation's indebtedness.
8. Forgiveness of certain loans to students.

If the creditor reduces the debt as an act of *love, affection,* or *generosity*, the debtor has simply received a nontaxable gift (situation 1). Rarely will a gift be found to have occurred in a business context. A businessperson may settle a debt for less than the amount due, but as a matter of business expediency (e.g., high collection costs or disputes as to contract terms) rather than generosity.[87]

In situations 2, 3, 4, and 5, the Code allows the debtor to reduce his or her basis in the assets by the realized gain from the discharge.[88] Thus, the realized gain is merely deferred until the assets are sold (or depreciated). Similarly, in situation 6 (a price reduction), the debtor reduces the basis in the specific assets financed by the seller.[89]

A shareholder's cancellation of the corporation's indebtedness to him or her (situation 7) usually is considered a contribution of capital to the corporation by the shareholder. Thus, the corporation's paid-in capital is increased, and its liabilities are decreased by the same amount.[90]

[84] *U.S. v. Kirby Lumber Co.,* 2 USTC ¶814, 10 AFTR 458, 52 S.Ct. 4 (USSC, 1931), codified in § 61(a)(12).

[85] Rev.Rul. 82–202, 1982–1 C.B. 35.

[86] §§ 108 and 1017.

[87] *Comm. v. Jacobson,* 49–1 USTC ¶9133, 37 AFTR 516, 69 S.Ct. 358 (USSC, 1949).

[88] §§ 108(a), (c), (e), and (g). Note that § 108(b) provides that other tax attributes (e.g., net operating loss) will be reduced by the realized gain from the debt discharge prior to the basis adjustment unless the taxpayer elects to apply the basis adjustment first.

[89] § 108(e)(5).

[90] § 108(e)(6).

Many states make loans to students on the condition that the loan will be forgiven if the student practices a profession in the state upon completing his or her studies. The amount of the loan that is forgiven (situation 8) is excluded from gross income.[91]

LO.5

Identify tax planning strategies for obtaining the maximum benefit from allowable exclusions.

Tax Planning Considerations

The present law excludes certain types of economic gains from taxation. Therefore, taxpayers may find tax planning techniques helpful in obtaining the maximum benefits from the exclusion of such gains. Following are some of the tax planning opportunities made available by the exclusions described in this chapter.

LIFE INSURANCE

Life insurance offers several favorable tax attributes. As discussed in Chapter 4, the annual increase in the cash surrender value of the policy is not taxable (because no income has been actually or constructively received). By borrowing on the policy's cash surrender value, the owner can actually receive the policy's increase in value in cash but without recognizing income.

EMPLOYEE BENEFITS

Generally, employees view accident and health insurance, as well as life insurance, as necessities. Employees can obtain group coverage at much lower rates than individuals would have to pay for the same protection. Premiums paid by the employer can be excluded from the employees' gross income. Because of the exclusion, employees will have a greater after-tax and after-insurance income if the employer pays a lower salary but also pays the insurance premiums.

EXAMPLE 44

Pat receives a salary of $30,000. The company has group insurance benefits, but Pat is required to pay his own premiums as follows:

Hospitalization and medical insurance	$1,400
Term life insurance ($30,000 coverage)	200
Disability insurance	400
	$2,000

To simplify the analysis, assume Pat's tax rate on income is 25%. After paying taxes of $7,500 (.25 × $30,000) and $2,000 for insurance, Pat has $20,500 ($30,000 – $7,500 – $2,000) for his other living needs.

If Pat's employer reduced Pat's salary by $2,000 (to $28,000) but paid his insurance premiums, Pat's tax liability would be only $7,000 ($28,000 × .25). Thus, Pat would have $21,000 ($28,000 – $7,000) to meet his other living needs. The change in the compensation plan would save Pat $500 ($21,000 – $20,500). ■

Similarly, employees must often incur expenses for child care and parking. The employee can have more income for other uses if the employer pays these costs for the employee but reduces the employee's salary by the cost of the benefits.

The use of cafeteria plans has increased dramatically in recent years. These plans allow employees to tailor their benefits to meet their individual situations. Thus, where both spouses in a married couple are working, duplications of benefits

[91] § 108(f).

can be avoided, and other needed benefits can often be added. If less than all of the employee's allowance is spent, the employee can receive cash.

The meals and lodging exclusion enables employees to receive from their employer what they ordinarily must purchase with after-tax dollars. Although the requirements that the employee live and take his or her meals on the employer's premises limit the tax planning opportunities, the exclusion is an important factor in the employee's compensation in certain situations (e.g., hotels, motels, restaurants, farms, and ranches).

The employees' discount provision is especially important for manufacturers and wholesalers. Employees of manufacturers can avoid tax on the manufacturer's, wholesaler's, and retailer's markups. The wholesaler's employees can avoid tax on an amount equal to the wholesale and retail markups.

It should be recognized that the exclusion of benefits is generally available only to employees. Proprietors and partners must pay tax on the same benefits their employees receive tax-free. By incorporating and becoming an employee of the corporation, the former proprietor or partner can also receive these tax-exempt benefits. Thus, the availability of employee benefits is a consideration in the decision to incorporate.

INVESTMENT INCOME

Tax-exempt state and local government bonds are almost irresistible investments for many high-income taxpayers. To realize the maximum benefit from the exemption, the investor can purchase zero-coupon bonds. Like Series EE U.S. government savings bonds, these investments pay interest only at maturity. The advantage of the zero-coupon feature for a tax-exempt bond is that the investor can earn tax-exempt interest on the accumulated principal and interest. If the investor purchases a bond that pays the interest each year, the interest received may be such a small amount that an additional tax-exempt investment cannot be made. In addition, reinvesting the interest may entail transaction costs (broker's fees). The zero-coupon feature avoids these problems.

Series EE U.S. government savings bonds can earn tax-exempt interest if the bond proceeds are used for qualified higher education expenses. Many taxpayers can foresee these expenditures being made for their children's educations. In deciding whether to invest in the bonds, however, the investor must take into account the income limitations for excluding the interest from gross income.

KEY TERMS

Accelerated death benefits, 5–7
Accident and health benefits, 5–13
Cafeteria plan, 5–19
Compensatory damages, 5–11
De minimis fringes, 5–23
Death benefits, 5–5
Educational savings bonds, 5–30
Flexible spending plan, 5–20
Foreign earned income exclusion, 5–26
Gift, 5–5
Health Savings Account (HSA), 5–15
Life insurance proceeds, 5–6
Long-term care insurance, 5–15
No-additional-cost service, 5–21
Punitive damages, 5–12
Qualified employee discount, 5–22
Qualified real property business indebtedness, 5–33
Qualified transportation fringes, 5–23
Qualified tuition program, 5–31
Qualified tuition reduction plan, 5–10
Scholarship, 5–9
Tax benefit rule, 5–32
Working condition fringes, 5–22

PROBLEM MATERIALS

Discussion Questions

1. Uncle John promised Tom, "Come and take care of me and I will leave you the farm when I die." Tom took care of Uncle John for the five years preceding his death. When Uncle John died, in accordance with his will, Tom received the farm. Can Tom exclude the value of the farm from his gross income as a gift or inheritance, or has he received compensation income?

2. A few years prior to her death Hattie gave Albert, her nephew, a bond with a cost and face amount of $10,000. The bond paid $400 of interest each year. Albert collected interest on the bond for five years and then collected the face amount of the bond. The beneficiary of Hattie's life insurance policy was her niece, Samantha. Hattie had paid $6,000 in premiums, and the face amount of the policy was $10,000. When Hattie died, Samantha elected to collect the life insurance proceeds in $2,400 installments each year for five years. How much should Albert and Samantha include in their gross incomes from the bond and life insurance?

Issue ID

3. Pearl Lumber Company is located in an isolated area that is sometimes referred to as "Tornado Alley." Most of the people who live in the area are employed by Pearl. The company created a nonprofit foundation to assist tornado victims. The majority of the beneficiaries are Pearl's employees. What are the relevant issues regarding the payments made by the nonprofit foundation to tornado victims?

4. Hannah, a cash basis taxpayer, died while employed by Purple Corporation. Purple paid Hannah's husband, Wade, $6,000 in sales commissions that Hannah had earned. The company also paid Wade $4,000 for Hannah's hospital bill in excess of the amount covered by insurance. The company paid the hospital bill because of Wade's dire financial circumstances. Are any of the amounts received by Wade includible in his gross income?

5. Matt's truck was stalled on the side of the road. Abby stopped to help and called Al, who agreed to repair the truck for $75. Matt paid Al $75 and Abby $25. The payment to Al was made because of a contractual obligation and therefore is not a gift. The payment to Abby was not made because of a contractual obligation. Does this mean that the payment Abby received is a gift?

6. When Ted was age 92 and suffering from a terminal illness, he sold his life insurance policy to the Violet Capital Fund for $80,000. Ted had paid $30,000 of premiums on the policy. Later that same year Ted died, and Violet Capital collected the face amount of the policy of $100,000. Determine the effect of these transactions on Ted's gross income and on Violet Capital's gross income.

7. Amber Finance Company requires its customers to purchase a credit life insurance policy. Amber is the beneficiary of the policy to the extent of the remaining balance on the loan at the time of the customer's death. In 2003, Amber wrote off as uncollectible a $5,000 account receivable from Aly. When Aly died in 2005, the life insurance policy was still in force, and Amber received $5,000. Is the $5,000 of life insurance proceeds received by Amber included in its gross income?

8. Ed paid $39,000 of life insurance premiums before cashing in his life insurance policy for the $45,000 cash surrender value. He decided he could invest the money and earn a higher rate of return. Sarah, who has a terminal illness, cashed in her life insurance policy (cost of $39,000 and proceeds of $45,000) to go on an around-the-world cruise. Determine the amounts that Ed and Sarah should include in their gross income.

9. José is a graduate assistant at State University. He receives $7,000 a year in salary. In addition, tuition of $4,000 is waived. The tuition waiver is available to all full- and part-time employees. The fair market value of José's services is $10,000. How much is José required to include in his gross income?

Decision Making

10. Sarah's automobile was struck by a corporate truck that was driven by a drunk employee of the corporation. The company has admitted liability, and Sarah is negotiating a settlement. Sarah has asked for $100,000 for the loss of income she suffered from the injury, $50,000 in medical bills (which she has not deducted), and $80,000 in punitive damages. The company has made the following counteroffer: it will pay her $50,000 for medical expenses and $160,000 for loss wages, but no punitive damages because punitive damages create complications with its insurance company. Assuming that Sarah is in the 33% marginal tax bracket, should she accept the company's offer?

11. Sara was the victim of sexual harassment and collected the following from her employer: $45,000 for lost wages, $25,000 for emotional suffering, and $100,000 in punitive damages. How much of the damage award of $170,000 must Sara include in her gross income?

12. Wes was a major league baseball pitcher before a career-ending injury caused by a negligent driver. Wes sued the driver and collected $15 million as compensation for lost estimated future income as a pitcher and $10 million as punitive damages. Sam was also a major league baseball pitcher and earned $25 million for pitching. Do the amounts that Wes and Sam receive have the same effect on their gross income? Explain.

13. Holly worked in a factory, but was laid off. Fortunately, she is able to collect $12,000 of unemployment compensation. Jill continues to be employed at the factory and earns $12,000 which she includes in gross income. Is Holly required to include her unemployment compensation benefits in gross income even though she is unemployed and Jill is employed?

14. How are Health Savings Accounts (HSAs) used as an employee fringe benefit? How does an HSA differ from traditional health insurance?

15. Paul is in the 25% marginal tax bracket. He has received two job offers with equal salaries, but one of the potential employers will pay for his family's health insurance, which would cost approximately $9,000 a year. In terms of the work and opportunities, Paul prefers the job that does not provide health insurance. He is considering asking the company that does not offer health insurance to raise the starting salary. How much must the employer increase the salary so that the offers are equal after paying income tax and insurance?

16. What is the difference between a "cafeteria plan" and an employee "flexible spending plan"?

17. Ted works for Sage Motors, an automobile dealership. All employees can buy cars at the company's cost plus 2%. The company will sell Ted a service contract for 50% of the price it charges its regular customers. During the year, Ted purchased an automobile from Sage for $20,400. The company's cost was $20,000, and the price to regular customers was $22,000. Ted also purchased for $600 a five-year service contract that ordinarily sells for $1,200. What is Ted's gross income from the purchase of the automobile and the service contract?

18. Zack works at the Silver Life Country Club. All employees, their spouses, and children are allowed to use the club's golf and swimming facilities the same as club members. The annual membership dues are $4,000 for a family. A major consideration in Zack's accepting the job was that his son, a possible future golf professional, would be allowed to play golf each day. Is Zack required to include any of the $4,000 in gross income?

19. Eagle Life Insurance Company pays its employees $.30 per mile for driving their personal automobiles to and from work. The company reimburses each employee who rides the bus $100 a month for the cost of a pass. Tom collected $100 for his automobile mileage, and Ted received $100 as reimbursement for the cost of a bus pass.
    a. What are the effects of the above on Tom's and Ted's gross income?
    b. Assume that Tom and Ted are in the 28% marginal tax bracket and the actual before-tax cost for Tom to drive to and from work is $.30 per mile. What are Tom's and Ted's after-tax costs of commuting to and from work?

Issue ID

20. Several of Egret Company's employees have asked the company to create a hiking trail that employees could use during their lunch hours. The company owns vacant land that is being held for future expansion, but would have to spend approximately $50,000 if it were to make a trail. Nonemployees would be allowed to use the facility as part of the company's effort to build strong community support. What are the relevant tax issues for the employees?

21. Marla, a U.S. citizen, has been working on a construction project in a foreign country for the past nine months. The project will be completed in a few weeks. She has an offer to work on another three-month project in that same foreign country. Alternatively, she could return to the United States and seek employment. How does the tax law affect Marla's decision?

Decision Making

22. Tedra is in the 35% marginal tax bracket. She is very risk averse and is considering purchasing U.S. government bonds due in 10 years that yield 5.6% before tax. Triple A rated State of Virginia bonds due in 10 years yield 4%. Which is the better alternative, assuming the bonds are of equal risk?

23. Maria, a cash method farmer, owns stock in a farmers' cooperative. During 2004, she purchased from the cooperative $80,000 of feed and fertilizer, which she expensed. This was a very good year for Maria's farm, which produced a $100,000 net profit. The farm was Maria's only source of income. The cooperative also had a very good year in 2004 and declared a patronage dividend that was distributed in early 2005. Maria's dividend was $5,000. What effect does the patronage dividend have on her gross income?

24. Arthur paid $50,000 to the Virginia Qualified Tuition Program: $25,000 for his son, Robert, and $25,000 for his daughter, Peggy. Only Peggy went to college. The $25,000 in the account for her was accepted in full payment of four years of tuition, which otherwise would have been $40,000. Since Robert did not attend college, $31,100 ($25,000 plus $6,100 interest) was refunded to Arthur. What are the tax consequences to Arthur, to Peggy, and to Robert?

25. Mary is a cash basis taxpayer. In 2005, she earned only $5,400, which was less than her standard deduction and personal exemption. In January 2006, Mary's employer determined that he had miscalculated her December 2005 bonus and that she should have received an additional $1,000 of compensation in 2005. The employer paid Mary the $1,000 in 2006. If Mary had received the $1,000 in 2005, it would not have resulted in any tax liability because her gross income would still have been less than her standard deduction and personal exemption. In 2006, Mary had over $30,000 in taxable income. Does the tax benefit rule apply to Mary's situation? Explain.

26. Ida purchased a ranch. She gave the seller $50,000 cash and a 7% note for $450,000. When the principal on the note had been reduced to $420,000, the seller agreed to accept $350,000 in retirement of the debt. The creditor made the offer because interest rates had increased substantially. Ida was not undergoing bankruptcy and was not insolvent.
    a. Did Ida realize income from retiring the debt and, if so, is she required to include the amount in her gross income?
    b. What if the creditor were a bank rather than the party who sold the ranch to Ida?

Issue ID

27. Harry has experienced financial difficulties as a result of his struggling business. He has been behind on his mortgage payments for the last six months. The mortgage holder, who is a friend of Harry's, has offered to accept $80,000 in full payment of the $100,000 owed on the mortgage and payable over the next 10 years. The interest rate of the mortgage is 7%, and the market rate is now 8%. What tax issues are raised by the creditor's offer?

Problems

28. During the year, Wilbur received the following in connection with his father's estate:
    - His father's will named Wilbur as the executor of the estate. He received $7,500 for serving as executor.
    - Wilbur was also a beneficiary of his father's estate and received real estate that was included in the estate at a value of $100,000 that his father had purchased for $30,000.
    - Wilbur was the beneficiary of one of his father's life insurance policies. He elected to collect the proceeds of the $100,000 policy in four installments of $30,000 each. Each $30,000 payment consists of principal and interest. He collected $30,000 this year.

    Determine the effect on Wilbur's gross income.

29. Determine the gross income to the beneficiaries in each of the following cases:
    a. When José died, his daughter collected $2,500 in accrued vacation pay from his employer.
    b. Josh had purchased an accident insurance policy that would pay him when he was unable to work because of an accident or illness. His wife collected $4,000 on the policy for benefits accrued during the illness that preceded his death.
    c. Jay died after purchasing a $50,000 life insurance policy that was pledged to pay the $40,000 mortgage on his home, with the remaining proceeds of $10,000 paid to his wife.
    d. Lavender, Inc., was the beneficiary of a $100,000 life insurance policy it had purchased on the life of its chief executive officer who died during the year.

30. Laura was recently diagnosed with cancer and has begun chemotherapy treatments. She has incurred a lot of medical and other general living expenses and is in need of cash. Therefore, she is considering cashing in her life insurance policy. She has paid $15,000 in premiums. The policy has a face amount of $50,000, and the Viatical Benefits Company has offered to pay her $35,000 and to pay subsequent premiums.
    a. What will be the tax consequences to Laura of assigning the benefits to Viatical, assuming she has been diagnosed by a cancer specialist as having less than one year to live?
    b. Same as in (a), except that the physician has opined that Laura will live for several years, but will be unable to perform the normal functions of daily living without the assistance of a practical nurse.

31. Determine whether the taxpayer has gross income in each of the following situations:
    a. Jim is a waiter in a restaurant. The rule of thumb is that a customer should leave the waiter a tip equal to 15% of the bill. Jim has a charming personality, provides exceptionally good service, and has developed an almost personal relationship with many of his repeat customers. As a result, Jim generally receives a 20% tip. In the current year, he received $36,000 in tips. The standard 15% rate would have yielded $27,000 in tips.
    b. Tara works at a grocery store, bagging groceries and carrying them to the customers' automobiles. Her employer posts a sign saying that the employees are paid by the hour and that customers are not expected to tip them. Tara received $1,800 in tips from customers.
    c. Sheila worked at a hotel. Her home was damaged by a fire. Sheila's employer allowed her to stay at the hotel for no charge until she could return to her home. The normal charge for the room Sheila occupied during this period was $500, and the hotel had several vacant rooms.

32. Donald was killed in an accident while he was on the job. His employer provided him with group term life insurance of $150,000 (twice his annual salary), which was payable to his widow, Darlene. Premiums on this policy totaling $1,500 have been included in Donald's gross income under § 79. Darlene also received $80,000 under workers' compensation associated with the accident. In addition, Donald had purchased a $100,000 life insurance policy that paid $200,000 in the case of an accidental death. The proceeds were payable to Darlene, who elected to receive payments of $25,000 each year for a 10-year period. What is Darlene's gross income from the above in 2005?

33. Fay and Edward are partners in an accounting firm. The partners have entered into an arm's length agreement requiring Fay to purchase Edward's partnership interest from Edward's estate if he dies before Fay. The price is set at 150% of the book value of Edward's partnership interest at the time of his death. Fay purchased an insurance policy on Edward's life to fund this agreement. After Fay had paid $40,000 in premiums, Edward was killed in an automobile accident, and Fay collected $1.5 million of life insurance proceeds. Fay used the life insurance proceeds to purchase Edward's partnership interest.
    a. What amount should Fay include in her gross income from receiving the life insurance proceeds?
    b. The insurance company paid Fay $15,000 interest on the life insurance proceeds during the period Edward's estate was in administration. During this period, Fay had left the insurance proceeds with the insurance company. Is this interest taxable?
    c. When Fay paid $1.5 million for Edward's partnership interest, priced as specified in the agreement, the fair market value of Edward's interest was $2 million. How much should Fay include in her gross income from this bargain purchase?

34. Sarah was an all-state soccer player during her junior and senior years in high school. She accepted an athletic scholarship from State University. The scholarship provided the following:

Tuition and fees	$8,000
Housing and meals	7,500
Books and supplies	1,000

a. Determine the effect of the scholarship on Sarah's gross income.
b. Sarah's brother, Walt, was not a gifted athlete, but he received $8,000 from their father's employer as a scholarship during the year. The employer grants the children of all executives a scholarship equal to annual tuition and fees. Determine the effect of the scholarship on Walt's and his father's gross income.

35. Alejandro was awarded an academic scholarship to State University for the 2005–2006 academic year. He received $5,000 in August and $6,000 in December 2005. Alejandro had enough personal savings to pay all expenses as they came due. Alejandro's expenditures for the relevant period were as follows:

Tuition, August 2005	$3,300
Tuition, December 2005	3,400
Room and board	
August–December 2005	3,000
January–May 2006	2,400
Books and educational supplies	
August–December 2005	1,000
January–May 2006	1,200

Determine the effect on Alejandro's gross income for 2005 and 2006.

36. Liz sued an overzealous bill collector and received the following settlement:

Damage to her automobile the collector attempted to repossess	$ 1,000
Physical damage to her arm caused by the collector	8,000
Loss of income while her arm was healing	6,000
Punitive damages	30,000

a. What effect does the settlement have on Liz's gross income?
b. Assume Liz also collected $40,000 of damages for slander to her personal reputation caused by the bill collector misrepresenting the facts to Liz's employer and other creditors. Is this $40,000 included in Liz's gross income?

37. Determine the effect on gross income in each of the following cases:
a. Eloise received $150,000 in settlement of a sex discrimination case against her former employer.
b. Nell received $10,000 for damages to her personal reputation. She also received $40,000 punitive damages.
c. Orange Corporation, an accrual basis taxpayer, received $50,000 from a lawsuit filed against its auditor who overcharged for services rendered in a previous year.
d. Beth received $10,000 compensatory damages and $30,000 punitive damages in a lawsuit she filed against a tanning parlor for severe burns she received from using its tanning equipment.
e. Joanne received compensatory damages of $75,000 and punitive damages of $300,000 from a cosmetic surgeon who botched her nose job.

38. Rex, age 45, is an officer of Blue Company, which provides him with the following nondiscriminatory fringe benefits in 2005:

- Hospitalization insurance premiums for Rex and his dependents. The cost of the coverage for Rex is $2,700 per year, and the additional cost for his dependents is

$3,600 per year. The plan has a $2,000 deductible, but his employer contributed $1,500 to Rex's Health Savings Account. Rex withdrew only $800 from the HSA, and the account earned $50 interest during the year.

- Long-term care insurance premiums for Rex, at a cost of $3,600 per year.
- Insurance premiums of $840 for salary continuation payments. Under the plan, Rex will receive his regular salary in the event he is unable to work due to illness. Rex collected $4,500 on the policy to replace lost wages while he was ill during the year.
- Rex is a part-time student working on his bachelor's degree in engineering. His employer reimbursed his $5,200 tuition under a plan available to all full-time employees.

Determine the amount Rex must include in gross income.

Communications

39. The UVW Union and HON Corporation are negotiating contract terms. Assume the union members are in the 28% marginal tax bracket and all benefits are provided on a nondiscriminatory basis. Write a letter to the UVW Union members explaining the tax consequences of the options discussed below. The union's address is 905 Spruce Street, Washington, D.C. 20227.
    a. The company would impose a $100 deductible on medical insurance benefits. Most employees incur more than $100 each year in medical expenses.
    b. Employees would get an additional paid holiday with the same annual income (the same pay but less work).
    c. An employee who did not need health insurance (because the employee's spouse works and receives family coverage) would be allowed to receive the cash value of the coverage.

Decision Making

40. Mauve Corporation has a group hospitalization insurance plan that has a $200 deductible amount for hospital visits and a $15 deductible for doctor visits and prescriptions. The deductible portion paid by employees who have children has become substantial for some employees. The company is considering adopting a medical reimbursement plan or a flexible benefits plan to cover the deductible amounts. Either of these plans can be tailored to meet the needs of the employees. What are the cost considerations to the employer that should be considered in choosing between these plans?

41. Bertha spent the last 60 days of 2005 in a nursing home. The cost of the services provided to her was $12,000. Medicare paid $7,100 toward the cost of her stay. Bertha also received $8,000 of benefits under a long-term care insurance policy she purchased. What is the effect on Bertha's gross income?

42. Tim is the vice president of western operations for Maroon Oil Company and is stationed in San Francisco. He is required to live in an employer-owned home, which is three blocks from his company office. The company-provided home is equipped with high-speed Internet access and several telephone lines. Tim receives telephone calls and e-mails that require immediate attention any time of day or night because the company's business is spread all over the world. A full-time administrative assistant resides in the house to assist Tim with the urgent business matters. Tim often uses the home for entertaining customers, suppliers, and employees. The fair market value of comparable housing is $8,500 per month. Tim is also provided with free parking at his company's office. The value of the parking is $325 per month. Calculate the amount associated with the company-provided housing and free parking that Tim must include in his gross income.

43. Does the taxpayer recognize gross income in the following situations?
    a. Ann is a registered nurse working in a community hospital. She is not required to take her lunch on the hospital premises, but she can eat in the cafeteria at no charge. The hospital adopted this policy to encourage employees to stay on the premises and be available in case of emergencies. During the year, Ann ate most of her meals on the premises. The total value of those meals was $750.
    b. Ira is the manager of a hotel. His employer allows him to live in one of the rooms rent-free or to receive a $600 per month cash allowance for rent. Ira has elected to live in the hotel.

c. Seth is a forest ranger and lives in his employer's cabin in the forest. He is required to live there, and because there are no restaurants nearby, the employer supplies Seth with groceries that he cooks and eats on the premises.
d. Rocky is a partner in the BAR Ranch (a partnership). He is the full-time manager of the ranch. BAR has a business purpose for Rocky's living on the ranch.

Decision Making

44. Betty is considering taking an early retirement offered by her employer. She would receive $2,000 per month, indexed for inflation. However, she would no longer be able to use the company's health facilities, and she would be required to pay her hospitalization insurance of $7,800 each year. Betty and her husband will file a joint return and take the standard deduction. She currently receives a salary of $40,000 a year, and her employer pays for all of her hospitalization insurance. If she retires, Betty would not be able to use her former employer's exercise facilities because of the commuting distance. She would like to continue to exercise, however, and will therefore join a health club at a cost of $50 per month. Betty and her husband have other sources of income and are in and will remain in the 25% marginal tax bracket. She currently pays Social Security taxes of 7.65% on her salary, but her retirement pay would not be subject to this tax. She will earn about $11,000 a year from a part-time job. Betty would like to know whether she should accept the early retirement offer.

Communications

45. Finch Construction Company provides the carpenters it employs with all of the required tools. However, the company believes that this practice has led to some employees not taking care of the tools and to the mysterious disappearance of some tools. The company is considering requiring all of its employees to provide their own tools. Each employee's salary would be increased by $1,500 to compensate for the additional cost. Write a letter to Finch's management explaining the tax consequences of this plan to the carpenters. Finch's address is 300 Harbor Drive, Vermillion, SD 57069.

46. Redbird, Inc., does not provide its employees with any tax-exempt fringe benefits. The company is considering adopting a hospital and medical benefits insurance plan that will cost approximately $7,000 per employee. In order to adopt this plan, the company may have to reduce salaries and/or lower future salary increases. Redbird is in the 35% (combined Federal and state rates) bracket. Redbird is also responsible for matching the Social Security and Medicare taxes withheld on employees' salaries. The benefits insurance plan will not be subject to the Social Security and Medicare taxes. The employees generally fall into three marginal tax rate groups:

Income Tax	Social Security and Medicare Tax	Total
.15	.0765	.2265
.25	.0765	.3265
.35	.0145	.3645

The company has asked you to assist in its financial planning for the benefits insurance plan by computing the following:
a. How much taxable compensation is the equivalent of $7,000 exempt compensation for each of the three classes of employees?
b. What is the company's after-tax cost of the taxable compensation computed in (a) above?
c. What is the company's after-tax cost of the exempt compensation?
d. Briefly explain your conclusions from the above analysis.

Decision Making

47. Rosa's employer has instituted a flexible benefits program. Rosa is allowed to select from a variety of benefits, but the total cost cannot exceed $3,000. The company's medical insurance plan does not cover dental expenses. Rosa's daughter needs approximately $3,000 worth of dental work. Rosa decides to set aside the maximum amount of her salary in the flexible benefits plan for the reimbursement of dental expenses. Rosa is in the 25% marginal tax bracket.

a. Rosa uses the entire $3,000 for the reimbursement of her daughter's dental expenses. How much has Rosa decreased her tax liability? What is the after-tax cost of the dental expenses?
b. Before Rosa uses any of the available $3,000, her daughter gets married. Therefore, the daughter's dental expenses are no longer covered by the plan. Since Rosa will not need to use the $3,000, can she receive the $3,000 unused balance in the plan? If so, what are the tax consequences to Rosa?
c. Should Rosa automatically set aside the maximum amount so that she will maximize her salary deferral under the plan?

48. Canary Corporation would like you to review its employee fringe benefits program with regard to the tax consequences of the plan for the company's president (Polly), who is also the majority shareholder:
a. All executives receive free tickets to State University football games. Polly is not a football fan and usually gives her tickets to another employee. The cost to the employer for Polly's tickets for the year was $600.
b. The company owns a parking garage that is used by customers, employees, and the general public. Only the general public is required to pay for parking. The charge to the general public for Polly's parking for the year would have been $2,700 (a $225 monthly rate).
c. All employees are allowed to use the company's fixed charge long-distance telephone services, as long as the privilege is not abused. Although no one has kept track of the actual calls, Polly's use of the telephone had a value (what she would have paid on her personal telephone) of approximately $600.
d. The company owns a condominium at the beach, which it uses to entertain customers. Employees are allowed to use the facility without charge when the company has no scheduled events. Polly used the facility 10 days during the year. Her use had a rental value of $1,000.
e. The company is in the household moving business. Employees are allowed to ship goods without charge whenever there is excess space on a truck. Polly purchased a dining room suite for her daughter. Company trucks delivered the furniture to the daughter. Normal freight charges would have been $750.
f. The company has a storage facility for household goods. Officers are allowed a 20% discount on charges for storing their goods. All other employees are allowed a 10% discount. Polly's discounts for the year totaled $900.

49. George is a U.S. citizen who is employed by Hawk Enterprises, a global company. Beginning on July 1, 2005, George began working in London. He worked there until January 31, 2006, when he transferred to Paris. He worked in Paris the remainder of 2006. His salary for the first six months of 2005 was $95,000, and it was earned in the United States. His salary for the remainder of 2005 was $135,000, and it was earned in London. George's 2006 salary from Hawk was $275,000, with part being earned in London and part being earned in Paris. What is George's gross income in 2005 and 2006?

50. Determine Hazel's gross income from the following receipts for the year:

Gain on sale of Augusta County bonds	$ 600
Interest on U.S. government savings bonds	500
Interest on state income tax refund	125
Interest on Augusta County bonds	900
Patronage dividend from Potato Growers Cooperative	1,600

The patronage dividend was received in March of the current year for amounts paid and deducted in the previous year as expenses of Hazel's profitable cash basis farming business.

51. Ezra purchased 1,000 shares of Golden Gate Utility Fund for $15,000 in 2005. At the end of 2005, he received an additional 50 fund shares in lieu of receiving $700 in cash dividends. At the end of the year, the value of Ezra's Golden Gate Utility Fund shares was $14,500.

a. What is Ezra's 2005 gross income from the Golden Gate Utility Fund shares?
b. Ezra also received 100 shares of Giant, Inc. stock when the company declared a two-for-one stock dividend. At the time of the stock dividend, the shares were trading for $90 a share. Ezra did not have the option of receiving cash in lieu of the Giant stock. What are the tax consequences of Ezra's receipt of the additional shares of Giant stock?

52. Tonya purchased State of Virginia bonds in 1999 for $10,000. The bonds pay $600 interest each year. At the time she purchased the bonds, the yield on comparable taxable securities was 10%. She was in the 39.6% marginal tax bracket. Tonya's income in the current year is approximately the same as in 1999. However, Congress has lowered the tax rates, so her marginal rate is only 35%.
   a. What should be the effect of the change in the tax rates on the market value of Tonya's bonds?
   b. Assume that after she purchased the bonds, Tonya's state of residence changed its income tax law to make the Virginia bonds exempt from that state's income tax. What should be the effect of the change in the state law on the market value of Tonya's bonds?

Decision Making
Communications

53. Lynn Swartz's husband died three years ago. Her parents have an income of over $200,000 a year and want to assure that funds will be available for the education of Lynn's 8-year-old son, Eric. Lynn is currently earning $45,000 a year. Lynn's parents have suggested that they start a savings account for Eric. They have calculated that if they invest $4,000 a year for the next 8 years, at the end of 10 years sufficient funds will be available for Eric's college expenses. Lynn realizes that the tax treatment of the investments could significantly affect the amount of funds available for Eric's education. She asked you to write a letter to her advising her about options available to her parents and to her for Eric's college education. Lynn's address is 100 Myrtle Cove, Fairfield, CT 06432.

54. Starting in 1996, Chuck and Luane have been purchasing Series EE bonds in their name to use for the higher education of their daughter (Susie who currently is age 18). During the year, they cash in $12,000 of the bonds to use for freshman year tuition, fees, and room and board. Of this amount, $5,000 represents interest. Of the $12,000, $8,000 is used for tuition and fees, and $4,000 is used for room and board. Their AGI, before the educational savings bond exclusion, is $94,000.
   a. Determine the tax consequences for Chuck and Luane, who will file a joint return, and for Susie.
   b. Assume that Chuck and Luane purchased the bonds in Susie's name. Determine the tax consequences for Chuck and Luane and for Susie.
   c. How would your answer for (a) change if Chuck and Luane file separate returns?

55. Carlos is considering investing $4,000 in a qualified tuition program for the benefit of his son. He estimates that in eight years, when his son enters college, the cost of tuition will have increased by 50%. His son will go to school full-time and should be in the 15% marginal tax bracket as a result of his part-time work. Alternatively, Carlos can invest the $4,000 in a corporate bond fund, which is expected to yield 7% each year. Carlos expects to be in the 33% marginal tax bracket in all relevant years. Which alternative appears preferable? The compound amount of $1 at 4.69% in eight years is 1.44.

56. How does the tax benefit rule apply in the following cases?
   a. In December 2004, Wilma purchased a new automobile for her personal use. Early in January 2005, she received a $1,500 rebate from the manufacturer.
   b. Wilma's accountant was negligent in computing the Virginia income tax liability due on her personal return for 2000. As a result, she paid $5,000 more state income tax than she was required to pay. The error was not discovered until after the statute of limitations had run; thus, it was too late to correct the error. She had claimed the Virginia income tax paid as an itemized deduction on her Federal income tax return. The accountant paid Wilma $5,000 as compensation for his negligence.
   c. In 2005, Wilma received $400 of patronage dividends from an agricultural cooperative. The dividends were paid for $10,000 in purchases of cattle feed and $2,500 in household item purchases. She uses the cash method for her farming business.

Decision Making

57. Fran, who is in the 35% tax bracket, recently collected $100,000 on a life insurance policy she carried on her father. She currently owes $120,000 on her personal residence and $120,000 on business property. National Bank holds the mortgage on both pieces of property and has agreed to accept $100,000 in complete satisfaction of either mortgage. The interest rate on the mortgages is 8%, and both mortgages are payable over 10 years. What would be the tax consequences of each of the following alternatives, assuming Fran currently deducts the mortgage interest on her tax return?
    a. Retire the mortgage on the residence.
    b. Retire the mortgage on the business property.

    Which alternative should Fran select?

58. Robin, who was experiencing financial difficulties, was able to adjust his debts as follows:
    a. His father agreed to cancel a $10,000 debt to help him out in his time of need. Robin's father told him, "I am not going to treat you any better than I treat your brothers and sister; therefore, the $10,000 is coming out of your inheritance from me."
    b. Robin's controlled corporation canceled a $6,000 debt he owed to the company.
    c. The Trust Land Company, which had sold Robin land, reduced the mortgage on the land by $12,000 and forgave him from paying $4,000 in accrued interest. Robin had deducted the interest on the previous year's tax return.

Cumulative Problems

Tax Return Problem
Decision Making
Communications

59. Martin S. Albert (Social Security number 363–22–1141) is 39 years old and is married to Michele R. Albert (Social Security number 259–05–8242). The Alberts live at 512 Ferry Road, Newport News, VA 23100. They file a joint return and have two dependent children (Charlene, age 17, and Jordan, age 18). Charlene's Social Security number is 260–12–1234 and Jordan's Social Security number is 263–23–4321. In 2005, Martin and Michele had the following transactions:
    a. Martin received $103,000 in salary from Red Steel Corporation, where he is a construction engineer. Withholding for Federal income tax was $9,000. The proper amount of FICA tax was withheld. Martin worked in Mexico from January 1, 2004, until February 28, 2005. His $103,000 salary for 2005 includes $16,000 he earned for January and February 2005 while working in Mexico.
    b. Martin and Michele received $800 interest on U.S. savings bonds they cashed in and $400 interest on Montgomery County (Virginia) school bonds.
    c. Martin received $300 interest from a Bahamian bank account.
    d. Michele received 50 shares of Applegate Corporation common stock as a stock dividend. The shares had a fair market value of $2,000 at the time Michele received them, and she did not have the option of receiving cash.
    e. Martin and Michele received a $900 refund on their 2004 Virginia income taxes. Their itemized deductions in 2004 totaled $11,600.
    f. Martin paid $6,000 alimony to his former wife, Rose T. Morgan (Social Security number 262–55–4813).
    g. Martin and Michelle keep the receipts for their sales taxes paid of $1,100.
    h. Martin and Michele's itemized deductions were as follows:
        - State income tax paid and withheld totaled $5,100.
        - Real estate taxes on their principal residence were $3,400.
        - Mortgage interest on their principal residence was $4,500.
        - Cash contributions to the church totaled $2,800.

    Part 1—Tax Computation
    Compute the Alberts' net tax payable (or refund due) for 2005. Suggested software: TurboTax.

    Part 2—Tax Planning
    The Alberts are considering buying another house. Their house mortgage payments would increase by $500 (to $1,500) per month, which includes a $250 increase in interest and a $100 increase in property tax. The Alberts would like to know how much the

mortgage payments would increase net of any change in their income tax. Write a letter to the Alberts that contains your advice.

Tax Return Problem

60. Alfred E. Old and Beulah Crane, each age 42, married on September 7, 2004. Alfred and Beulah will file a joint return for 2004. Alfred's Social Security number is 262–60–3815. Beulah's Social Security number is 259–68–4285, and she will adopt "Old" as her married name. They live at 211 Brickstone Drive, Atlanta, GA 30304.

Alfred was divorced from Sarah Old in March 2003. Under the divorce agreement, Alfred is to pay Sarah $900 per month for the next 10 years or until Sarah's death, whichever occurs first. Alfred pays Sarah $10,800 in 2004. In addition, in January 2004, Alfred pays Sarah $50,000, which is designated as being for her share of the marital property. Also, Alfred is responsible for all prior years' income taxes. Sarah's Social Security number is 444–10–2211.

Alfred's salary for 2004 is $70,000, and his employer, Cherry, Inc., provides him with group term life insurance equal to twice his annual salary. His employer withheld $10,900 for Federal income taxes, $3,400 for state income taxes, and the appropriate amount for FICA.

Beulah recently graduated from law school and is employed by Legal Aid Society, Inc., as a public defender. She receives a salary of $38,000 in 2004. Her employer withheld $4,900 for Federal income taxes, $2,300 for state income taxes, and the appropriate amount for FICA.

Beulah has $1,500 in dividends on Yellow Corporation stock she inherited. Beulah receives a $850 refund of 2003 state income taxes. She used the standard deduction on her 2003 Federal income tax return. Alfred receives an $1,200 refund on his 2003 state income taxes. He itemized deductions on his 2003 Federal income tax return. Alfred and Beulah pay $4,300 interest and $1,450 property taxes on their personal residence in 2004. Their charitable contributions total $1,000 (all to their church). They paid sales taxes of $1,400 for which they maintain the receipts.

Compute the Olds' net tax payable (or refund due) for 2004. If you use tax forms for your solution, you will need Form 1040 and Schedules A and B. Suggested software: TurboTax.

Research Problems

THOMSON RIA™

Note: Solutions to Research Problems can be prepared by using the ***RIA Checkpoint® Student Edition*** *online research product, which is available to accompany this text. It is also possible to prepare solutions to the Research Problems by using tax research materials found in a standard tax library.*

Communications

Research Problem 1. David Hobson is the minister at the First Baptist Church. As part of his compensation, David receives an $800 per month housing allowance. David is purchasing his residence, and he uses the $800 each month to make mortgage and property tax payments. The mortgage interest and property taxes are deducted (as itemized deductions) on David's tax return. The examining IRS agent thinks David would be enjoying a double benefit if the housing allowance is excluded and the itemized deductions are allowed. In addition, the agent contends that the housing allowance exclusion should apply only where the church provides the residence or the minister uses the funds to pay rent. Therefore, the agent maintains that David should include in gross income the $800 received each month. David has asked your assistance in this matter. Write a letter to David that contains your advice and prepare a memo for the tax files. David's address is 982 Richmond Drive, Hollis, OK 73550.

Research Problem 2. Sales personnel employed by Ivory Sales, Inc., accumulate substantial frequent-flier miles traveling for the company. Since Ivory Sales reimburses its employees for travel expenses incurred, the company, rather than the employee, is entitled to the frequent-flier miles. The company is considering a change in policy that would permit the employees to retain the miles for their personal use. Ivory Sales would like to know the income tax implications to the employees of the proposed change in policy.

Research Problem 3. Herron, Inc., previously gave all of its employees a ham for Christmas. However, many of the employees do not eat ham. Therefore, Herron has decided to give each employee a coupon for $35 that can be redeemed (for food or cash) any time between

December 1 and January 31 of the following year. Herron has asked you whether the coupons can be excluded from the employees' gross income as a *de minimis* fringe benefit.

Partial list of research aids:
Ltr.Rul. 200437030.

Internet Activity

Use the tax resources of the Internet to address the following question. Do not restrict your search to the World Wide Web, but include a review of newsgroups and general reference materials, practitioner sites and resources, primary sources of the tax law, chat rooms and discussion groups, and other opportunities.

Communications

Research Problem 4. Go to the IRS site on the Internet and download instructions and regulations relative to educational savings bonds and qualified tuition programs. Summarize one of the key provisions in these materials in outline format.

Deductions and Losses: In General

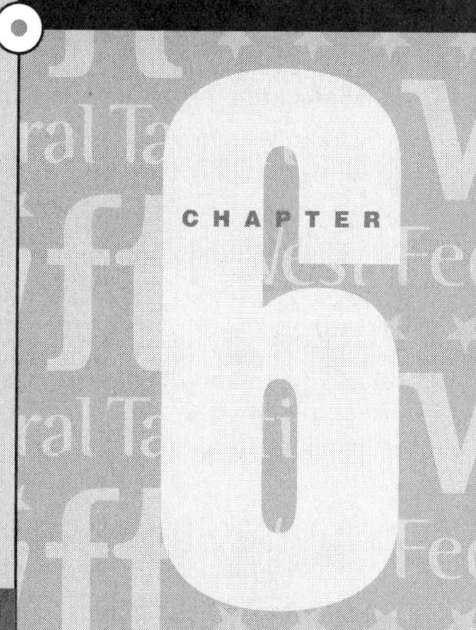

LEARNING OBJECTIVES

After completing Chapter 6, you should be able to:

LO.1

Differentiate between deductions *for* and *from* adjusted gross income and understand the relevance of the differentiation.

LO.2

Describe the cash and accrual methods of accounting.

LO.3

Apply the Internal Revenue Code deduction disallowance provisions associated with the following: public policy limitations, political activities, excessive executive compensation, investigation of business opportunities, hobby losses, vacation home rentals, payment of others' expenses, personal expenditures, capital expenditures, related-party transactions, and expenses related to tax-exempt income.

LO.4

Identify tax planning opportunities for maximizing deductions and minimizing the disallowance of deductions.

OUTLINE

LO.1

Differentiate between deductions *for* and *from* adjusted gross income and understand the relevance of the differentiation.

Classification of Deductible Expenses

The tax law has an all-inclusive definition of income; that is, income from whatever source derived is includible in gross income. Income cannot be excluded unless there is a specific statement to that effect in the Internal Revenue Code.

Similarly, deductions are disallowed unless a specific provision in the tax law permits them. The inclusive definition of income and the exclusive definition of deductions may not seem fair to taxpayers, but it is the structure of the tax law.

The courts have held that whether and to what extent deductions are allowed depends on legislative grace.[1] In other words, any exclusions from income and all deductions are gifts from Congress!

It is important to classify deductible expenses as **deductions for adjusted gross income** (AGI) or **deductions from adjusted gross income.** Deductions *for* AGI can be claimed whether or not the taxpayer itemizes. Deductions *from* AGI result in a tax benefit only if they exceed the taxpayer's standard deduction. If itemized deductions (*from* AGI) are less than the standard deduction, they provide no tax benefit.

EXAMPLE 1

Steve is a self-employed CPA. Ralph is one of Steve's employees. During the year, Steve and Ralph incur the following expenses:

[1]*New Colonial Ice Co. v. Helvering*, 4 USTC ¶1292, 13 AFTR 1180, 54 S.Ct. 788 (USSC, 1934).

	Steve	Ralph
Dues to American Institute of CPAs and State Society of CPAs	$ 400	$ 300
Subscriptions to professional journals	500	200
Registration fees for tax conferences	800	800
	$1,700	$1,300

Steve does not reimburse any of his employees for dues, subscriptions, or educational programs.

Steve's expenses are classified as a deduction *for* AGI. Therefore, he can deduct the $1,700 on his Federal income tax return. Ralph's expenses are classified as deductions *from* AGI. Ralph will be able to benefit from the $1,300 of expenses on his Federal income tax return only if he itemizes deductions. If he takes the standard deduction instead, the $1,300 of expenses will have no effect on the calculation of his taxable income. Even if Ralph does itemize deductions, he must reduce the $1,300 of expenses, which are classified as miscellaneous itemized deductions, by 2% of his AGI. As this example illustrates, whether a deduction is classified as *for* AGI or *from* AGI can affect the benefit the taxpayer receives from the deduction. ■

Deductions *for* AGI are also important in determining the *amount* of itemized deductions because many itemized deductions are limited to amounts in excess of specified percentages of AGI. Examples of itemized deductions that are limited by AGI are medical expenses and personal casualty losses. Itemized deductions that are deductible only to the extent that they exceed a specified percentage of AGI are increased when AGI is decreased. Likewise, when AGI is increased, these itemized deductions are decreased.

EXAMPLE 2

Tina earns a salary of $20,000 and has no other income. She itemizes deductions during the current year. Medical expenses for the year are $1,800. Since medical expenses are deductible only to the extent they exceed 7.5% of AGI, Tina's medical expense deduction is $300 [$1,800 – (7.5% × $20,000)]. If Tina had a $2,000 deduction *for* AGI, her medical expense deduction would be $450 [$1,800 – (7.5% × $18,000)], or $150 more. If the $2,000 deduction was *from* AGI, her medical expense deduction would remain $300 since AGI is unchanged. ■

DEDUCTIONS FOR ADJUSTED GROSS INCOME

To understand how deductions of individual taxpayers are classified, it is necessary to examine the role of § 62. The purpose of § 62 is to classify various deductions as deductions *for* AGI. It does not provide the statutory authority for taking the deduction. For example, § 212 allows individuals to deduct expenses attributable to income-producing property. Section 212 expenses that are attributable to rents or royalties are classified as deductions *for* AGI. Likewise, a deduction for trade or business expenses is allowed by § 162. These expenses are classified as deductions *for* AGI.

If a deduction is not listed in § 62, it is an itemized deduction, not a deduction *for* AGI. Following is a *partial* list of the items classified as deductions *for* AGI by § 62:

- Expenses attributable to a trade or business carried on by the taxpayer. A trade or business does not include the performance of services by the taxpayer as an employee.
- Expenses incurred by a taxpayer in connection with the performance of services as an employee if the expenses are reimbursed and other conditions are satisfied.

- Deductions that result from losses on the sale or exchange of property by the taxpayer.
- Deductions attributable to property held for the production of rents and royalties.
- The deduction for payment of alimony.
- The deduction for one-half of the self-employment tax paid by a self-employed taxpayer.
- The deduction for 100 percent of the medical insurance premiums paid by a self-employed taxpayer for coverage of the taxpayer, spouse, and any dependents.
- Certain contributions to pension, profit sharing, and annuity plans of self-employed individuals.
- The deduction for certain retirement savings allowed by § 219 (e.g., traditional IRAs).
- The penalty imposed on premature withdrawal of funds from time savings accounts or deposits.
- The deduction for moving expenses.
- The deduction for interest paid on student loans.
- The deduction for qualified tuition and related expenses under § 222 (refer to Chapter 9).
- The deduction for up to $250 for teacher supplies for elementary and secondary school teachers (refer to Chapter 9).

These items are covered in detail in various chapters in the text.

ITEMIZED DEDUCTIONS

The Code defines itemized deductions as the deductions allowed other than "the deductions allowable in arriving at adjusted gross income."[2] Thus, if a deduction is not properly classified as a deduction *for* AGI, then it is classified as an itemized deduction.

Section 212 Expenses. Section 212 allows deductions for ordinary and necessary expenses paid or incurred for the following:

- The production or collection of income.
- The management, conservation, or maintenance of property held for the production of income.
- Expenses paid in connection with the determination, collection, or refund of any tax.

Section 212 expenses related to rent and royalty income are deductions *for* AGI.[3] Expenses paid in connection with the determination, collection, or refund of taxes related to the income of sole proprietorships, rents and royalties, or farming operations are deductions *for* AGI. All other § 212 expenses are itemized deductions (deductions *from* AGI). For example, investment-related expenses (e.g., safe deposit box rentals) are deductible as itemized deductions attributable to the production of investment income.[4]

Deductible Personal Expenses. Taxpayers are allowed to deduct certain expenses that are primarily personal in nature. These expenses, which generally are not related to the production of income, are deductions *from* AGI (itemized deductions). Some of the more frequently encountered deductions in this category include the following:

[2] § 63(d).
[3] § 62(a)(4).
[4] Reg. § 1.212–1(g).

- Contributions to qualified charitable organizations (not to exceed a specified percentage of AGI).
- Medical expenses (in excess of 7.5 percent of AGI).
- Certain state and local taxes (e.g., real estate taxes and state and local income taxes).
- Personal casualty losses (in excess of an aggregate floor of 10 percent of AGI and a $100 floor per casualty).
- Certain personal interest (e.g., mortgage interest on a personal residence).

Itemized deductions are discussed in detail in Chapter 10.

TRADE OR BUSINESS EXPENSES AND PRODUCTION OF INCOME EXPENSES

Section 162(a) permits a deduction for all ordinary and necessary expenses paid or incurred in carrying on a trade or business. These include reasonable salaries paid for services, expenses for the use of business property, and one-half of self-employment taxes paid. Such expenses are deducted *for* AGI.

It is sometimes difficult to determine whether an expenditure is deductible as a trade or business expense. The term "trade or business" is not defined in the Code or Regulations, and the courts have not provided a satisfactory definition. It is usually necessary to ask one or more of the following questions to determine whether an item qualifies as a trade or business expense:

- Was the use of the particular item related to a business activity? For example, if funds are borrowed for use in a business, the interest is deductible as a business expense.
- Was the expenditure incurred with the intent to realize a profit or to produce income? For example, expenses in excess of the income from raising horses are not deductible if the activity is classified as a personal hobby rather than a trade or business.
- Were the taxpayer's operation and management activities extensive enough to indicate the carrying on of a trade or business?

Section 162 *excludes* the following items from classification as trade or business expenses:

- Charitable contributions or gifts.
- Illegal bribes and kickbacks and certain treble damage payments.
- Fines and penalties.

A bribe paid to a domestic official is not deductible if it is illegal under the laws of the United States. Foreign bribes are deductible unless they are unlawful under the Foreign Corrupt Practices Act of 1977.[5]

Ordinary and Necessary Requirement.

The terms **ordinary and necessary** are found in both §§ 162 and 212. To be deductible, any trade or business expense must be "ordinary and necessary." In addition, compensation for services must be "reasonable" in amount.

Many expenses that are necessary are *not* ordinary. Neither "ordinary" nor "necessary" is defined in the Code or Regulations. The courts have held that an expense is *necessary* if a prudent businessperson would incur the same expense and the expense is expected to be appropriate and helpful in the taxpayer's business.[6]

[5] § 162(c)(1).
[6] *Welch v. Helvering,* 3 USTC ¶1164, 12 AFTR 1456, 54 S.Ct. 8 (USSC, 1933).

Two Sides of an Issue: To Kick or to Receive?

During a televised NBA game in 1997, Dennis Rodman of the Chicago Bulls kicked Eugene Amos, Jr., a television cameraman, in the groin. The parties reached an out of court settlement under which Amos received $200,000. The agreement included a release of all claims relating to the incident, a confidentiality provision, a waiver of any criminal prosecution, and a stipulation that the parties would not disparage or defame each other.

Amos excluded the $200,000 from his gross income as damages awarded for physical personal injury. On audit, the IRS concluded that $199,999 should be included in Amos's gross income and that only $1 should be excluded. The Tax Court disagreed with both Amos and the IRS. Since no allocation was specified in the settlement, the court allocated $120,000 to physical personal injury (excluded from gross income) and $80,000 to the other settlement provisions (included in gross income).

The Tax Court decision dealt with the tax consequences for Amos but did not address Rodman's tax position. Was the $200,000 payment a deductible business expense? Since the kick occurred during the conduct of Rodman's trade or business (i.e., playing basketball), an aggressive position could be taken that the $200,000 was a legitimate business expense and deductible under § 162(a). More likely the payment is nondeductible since the game of basketball does not envision assault and battery on a nonplayer bystander. Only Rodman and the IRS know what tax position was taken and the ultimate result.

EXAMPLE 3

Pat purchased a manufacturing concern that had just been adjudged bankrupt. Because the business had a poor financial rating, Pat satisfied some of the obligations to employees and outside salespeople incurred by the former owners. Pat had no legal obligation to pay these debts, but felt this was the only way to keep salespeople and employees. The Second Circuit Court of Appeals found that the payments were necessary in that they were both appropriate and helpful.[7] However, the court held that the payments were *not* ordinary but were in the nature of capital expenditures to build a reputation. Therefore, no deduction was allowed. ■

An expense is *ordinary* if it is normal, usual, or customary in the type of business conducted by the taxpayer and is not capital in nature.[8] However, an expense need not be recurring to be deductible as ordinary.

EXAMPLE 4

Albert engaged in a mail-order business. The post office judged that his advertisements were false and misleading. Under a fraud order, the post office stamped "fraudulent" on all letters addressed to Albert's business and returned them to the senders. Albert spent $30,000 on legal fees in an unsuccessful attempt to force the post office to stop. The legal fees (though not recurring) were ordinary business expenses because they were normal, usual, or customary in the circumstances.[9] ■

For § 212 deductions, the law requires that expenses bear a reasonable and proximate relationship to (1) the production or collection of income or to (2) the management, conservation, or maintenance of property held for the production of income.[10]

[7] *Dunn and McCarthy, Inc. v. Comm.*, 43–2 USTC ¶9688, 31 AFTR 1043, 139 F.2d 242 (CA–2, 1943).

[8] *Deputy v. DuPont*, 40–1 USTC ¶9161, 23 AFTR 808, 60 S.Ct. 363 (USSC, 1940).

[9] *Comm. v. Heininger*, 44–1 USTC ¶9109, 31 AFTR 783, 64 S.Ct. 249 (USSC, 1943).

[10] Reg. § 1.212–1(d).

EXAMPLE 5

Wendy owns a small portfolio of investments, including 10 shares of Hawk, Inc. common stock worth $1,000. She incurred $350 in travel expenses to attend the annual shareholders' meeting where she voted her 10 shares against the current management group. No deduction is permitted because a 10-share investment is insignificant in value in relation to the travel expenses incurred.[11] ■

Reasonableness Requirement. The Code refers to **reasonableness** solely with respect to salaries and other compensation for services.[12] But the courts have held that for any business expense to be ordinary and necessary, it must also be reasonable in amount.[13]

What constitutes reasonableness is a question of fact. If an expense is unreasonable, the excess amount is not allowed as a deduction. The question of reasonableness generally arises with respect to closely held corporations where there is no separation of ownership and management.

Transactions between the shareholders and the closely held company may result in the disallowance of deductions for excessive salaries and rent expense paid by the corporation to the shareholders. The courts will view an unusually large salary in light of all relevant circumstances and may find that the salary is reasonable despite its size.[14] If excessive payments for salaries and rents are closely related to the percentage of stock owned by the recipients, the payments are generally treated as dividends.[15] Since dividends are not deductible by the corporation, the disallowance results in an increase in the corporate taxable income. Deductions for reasonable salaries will not be disallowed *solely* because the corporation has paid insubstantial portions of its earnings as dividends to its shareholders.

EXAMPLE 6

Sparrow Corporation, a closely held corporation, is owned equally by Lupe, Carlos, and Ramon. The company has been highly profitable for several years and has not paid dividends. Lupe, Carlos, and Ramon are key officers of the company, and each receives a salary of $200,000. Salaries for similar positions in comparable companies average only $100,000. Amounts paid the owners in excess of $100,000 may be deemed unreasonable, and, if so, a total of $300,000 in salary deductions by Sparrow is disallowed. The disallowed amounts are treated as dividends rather than salary income to Lupe, Carlos, and Ramon because the payments are proportional to stock ownership. Salaries are deductible by the corporation, but dividends are not. ■

BUSINESS AND NONBUSINESS LOSSES

Section 165 provides for a deduction for losses not compensated for by insurance. As a general rule, deductible losses of individual taxpayers are limited to those incurred in a trade or business or in a transaction entered into for profit. Individuals are also allowed to deduct losses that are the result of a casualty. Casualty losses include, but are not limited to, fire, storm, shipwreck, and theft. See Chapter 7 for a further discussion of this topic. Deductible personal casualty losses are reduced by $100 per casualty, and the aggregate of all personal casualty losses is reduced by 10 percent of AGI. A personal casualty loss is an itemized deduction. See Concept Summary 6–3 near the end of the chapter for the classification of expenses.

[11] *J. Raymond Dyer*, 36 T.C. 456 (1961).

[12] § 162(a)(1).

[13] *Comm. v. Lincoln Electric Co.*, 49–2 USTC ¶9388, 38 AFTR 411, 176 F.2d 815 (CA–6, 1949).

[14] *Kennedy, Jr. v. Comm.*, 82–1 USTC ¶9186, 49 AFTR2d 82–628, 671 F.2d 167 (CA–6, 1982), *rev'g* 72 T.C. 793 (1979).

[15] Reg. § 1.162–8.

■ **FIGURE 6–1**
Format of Form 1040

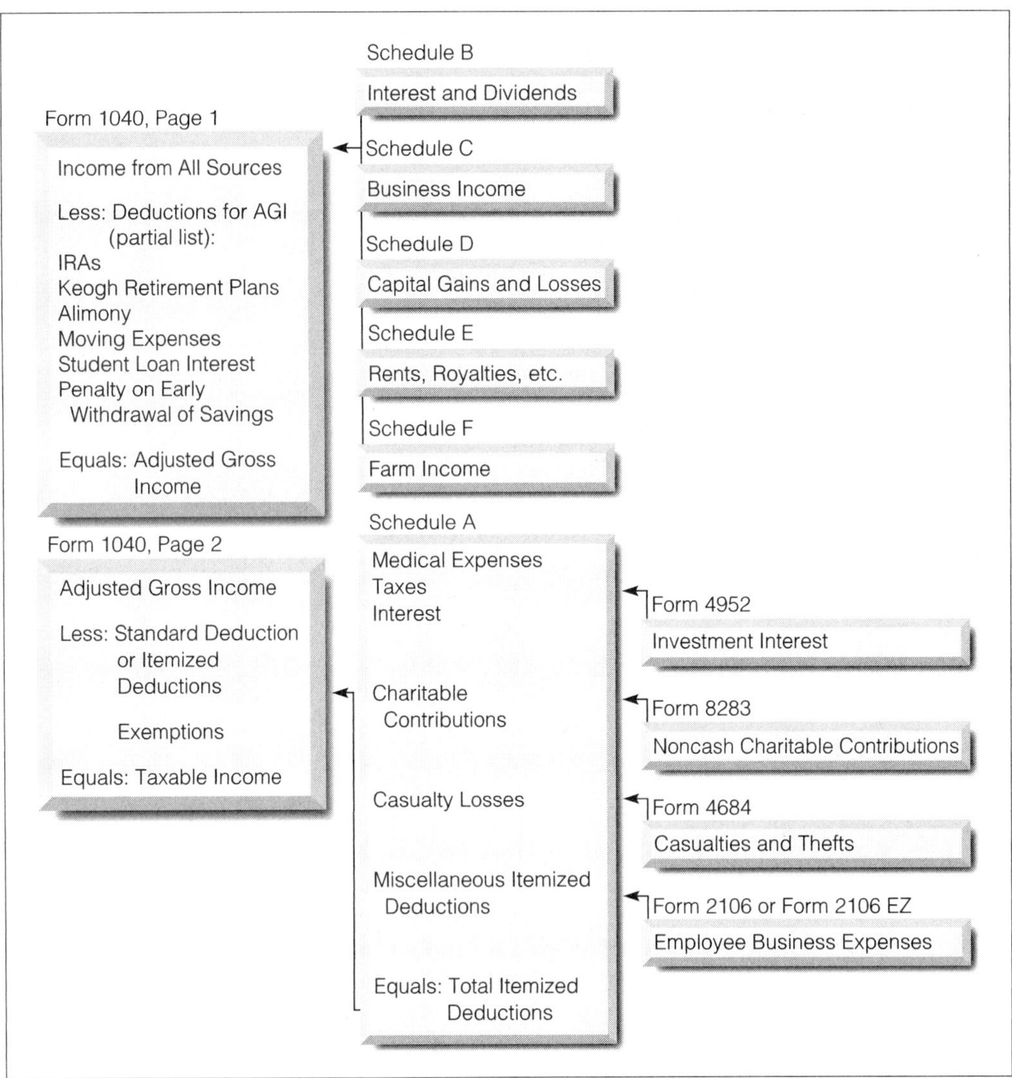

REPORTING PROCEDURES

All deductions *for* and *from* AGI wind up on pages 1 and 2 of Form 1040. All deductions *for* AGI are reported on page 1. The last line on page 1 is adjusted gross income.

The first item on page 2 is also adjusted gross income. Itemized deductions are entered next, followed by the deduction for personal and dependency exemptions. The result is taxable income.

Most of the deductions *for* AGI on page 1 originate on supporting schedules. Examples include business expenses (Schedule C) and rent, royalty, partnership, and fiduciary deductions (Schedule E). Other deductions *for* AGI, such as traditional IRAs, Keogh retirement plans, and alimony, are entered directly on page 1 of Form 1040.

All itemized deductions on page 2 are carried over from Schedule A. Some Schedule A deductions originate on other forms. Examples include investment interest, noncash charitable contributions in excess of $500, casualty losses, and unreimbursed employee expenses.

Form 1040 becomes a summary of the detailed information entered on the other schedules and forms. See Figure 6–1.

LO.2

Describe the cash and accrual methods of accounting.

Deductions and Losses—Timing of Expense Recognition

IMPORTANCE OF TAXPAYER'S METHOD OF ACCOUNTING

A taxpayer's **accounting method** is a major factor in determining taxable income. The method used determines when an item is includible in income and when an item is deductible on the tax return. Usually, the taxpayer's regular method of record keeping is used for income tax purposes.[16] The taxing authorities do not require uniformity among all taxpayers. They do require that the method used clearly reflect income and that items be handled consistently.[17] The most common methods of accounting are the cash method and the accrual method.

Throughout the portions of the Code dealing with deductions, the phrase "paid or incurred" is used. *Paid* refers to the cash basis taxpayer who gets a deduction only in the year of payment. *Incurred* concerns the accrual basis taxpayer who obtains the deduction in the year in which the liability for the expense becomes certain (refer to Chapter 4).

CASH METHOD REQUIREMENTS

The expenses of cash basis taxpayers are deductible only when they are actually paid with cash or other property. Promising to pay or issuing a note does not satisfy the actually paid requirement.[18] However, the payment can be made with borrowed funds. At the time taxpayers charge expenses on their credit cards, they are allowed to claim the deduction. They are deemed to have simultaneously borrowed money from the credit card issuer and constructively paid the expenses.[19]

Although the cash basis taxpayer must have actually or constructively paid the expense, payment does not assure a current deduction. Cash basis and accrual basis taxpayers cannot take a current deduction for capital expenditures except through amortization, depletion, or depreciation over the life (actual or statutory) of the asset. The Regulations set forth the general rule that an expenditure that creates an asset having a useful life that extends substantially beyond the end of the tax year must be capitalized.[20]

EXAMPLE 7

John, a cash basis taxpayer, rents property from Carl. On July 1, 2005, John pays $2,400 rent for the 24 months ending June 30, 2007. The prepaid rent extends 18 months after the close of the tax year—substantially beyond the year of payment. Therefore, John must capitalize the prepaid rent and amortize the expense on a monthly basis. His deduction for 2005 is $600. ■

The Tax Court and the IRS took the position that an asset that will expire or be consumed by the end of the tax year following the year of payment must be prorated. The Ninth Circuit Court of Appeals held that such expenditures are currently deductible, however, and the Supreme Court apparently concurs (the one-year rule for prepaid expenses).[21]

---

[16] § 446(a).

[17] §§ 446(b) and (e); Reg. § 1.446–1(a)(2).

[18] *Page v. Rhode Island Trust Co., Exr.*, 37–1 USTC ¶9138, 19 AFTR 105, 88 F.2d 192 (CA–1, 1937).

[19] Rev.Rul. 78–39, 1978–1 C.B. 73. See also Rev.Rul. 80–335, 1980–2 C.B. 170, which applies to pay-by-phone arrangements.

[20] Reg. § 1.461–1(a).

[21] *Zaninovich v. Comm.*, 80–1 USTC ¶9342, 45 AFTR2d 80–1442, 616 F.2d 429 (CA–9, 1980), *rev'g* 69 T.C. 605 (1978). Cited by the Supreme Court in *Hillsboro National Bank v. Comm.*, 83–1 USTC ¶9229, 51 AFTR2d 83–874, 103 S.Ct. 1134 (USSC, 1983).

EXAMPLE 8

Assume the same facts as in Example 7 except that John is required to pay only 12 months' rent in 2005. He pays $1,200 on July 1, 2005. The entire $1,200 is deductible in 2005. ■

The payment must be required, not a voluntary prepayment, to obtain the current deduction under the one-year rule.[22] The taxpayer must also demonstrate that allowing the current deduction will not result in a material distortion of income. Generally, the deduction will be allowed if the item is recurring or was made for a business purpose rather than to manipulate income.[23]

As Chapter 16 explains, not all taxpayers are allowed to use the cash method.[24] For example, in most cases the taxpayer is required to use the accrual method for sales and cost of goods sold if inventories are an income-producing factor of the business.

ACCRUAL METHOD REQUIREMENTS

The period in which an accrual basis taxpayer can deduct an expense is determined by applying the *all events test* and the *economic performance test*. A deduction cannot be claimed until (1) all the events have occurred to create the taxpayer's liability and (2) the amount of the liability can be determined with reasonable accuracy. Once these requirements are satisfied, the deduction is permitted only if economic performance has occurred. The economic performance test is met only when the service, property, or use of property giving rise to the liability is actually performed for, provided to, or used by the taxpayer.[25]

EXAMPLE 9

On December 22, 2005, Chris's entertainment business sponsored a jazz festival in a rented auditorium at a local college. His business is responsible for cleaning up the auditorium after the festival and for reinstalling seats that were removed so more people could attend the festival. Since the college is closed over the Christmas holidays, the company hired by Chris to perform the work did not begin these activities until January 2, 2006. The cost to Chris is $1,200. Chris cannot deduct the $1,200 until 2006, when the services are performed. ■

An exception to the economic performance requirements allows certain *recurring items* to be deducted if the following conditions are met:

- The item is recurring in nature and is treated consistently by the taxpayer.
- Either the accrued item is not material, or accruing it results in better matching of income and expenses.
- All the events have occurred that determine the fact of the liability, and the amount of the liability can be determined with reasonable accuracy.
- Economic performance occurs within a reasonable period (but not later than 8½ months after the close of the taxable year).[26]

EXAMPLE 10

Rick, an accrual basis, calendar year taxpayer, entered into a monthly maintenance contract during the year. He makes a monthly accrual at the end of every month for this service and pays the fee sometime between the first and fifteenth of the following month when services are performed. The amount involved is immaterial, and all the other tests are met. The December 2005 accrual is deductible in 2005 even though the service is performed on January 12, 2006. ■

---

[22] *Bonaire Development Co. v. Comm.*, 82–2 USTC ¶9428, 50 AFTR2d 82–5167, 679 F.2d 159 (CA–9, 1982).

[23] *Keller v. Comm.*, 84–1 USTC ¶9194, 53 AFTR2d 84–663, 725 F.2d 1173 (CA–8, 1984), *aff'g* 79 T.C. 7 (1982).

[24] § 448.

[25] § 461(h).

[26] § 461(h)(3)(A).

EXAMPLE 11

Rita, an accrual basis, calendar year taxpayer, shipped merchandise sold on December 30, 2005, via Greyhound Van Lines on January 2, 2006, and paid the freight charges at that time. Since Rita reported the sale of the merchandise in 2005, the shipping charge should also be deductible in 2005. This procedure results in a better matching of income and expenses. ■

Reserves for estimated expenses (frequently employed for financial accounting purposes) generally are not allowed for tax purposes because the economic performance test cannot be satisfied.

EXAMPLE 12

Blackbird Airlines is required by Federal law to test its engines after 3,000 flying hours. Aircraft cannot return to flight until the tests have been conducted. An unrelated aircraft maintenance company does all of the company's tests for $1,500 per engine. For financial reporting purposes, the company accrues an expense based upon $.50 per hour of flight and credits an allowance account. The actual amounts paid for maintenance are offset against the allowance account. For tax purposes, the economic performance test is not satisfied until the work has been done. Therefore, the reserve method cannot be used for tax purposes. ■

LO.3

Apply the Internal Revenue Code deduction disallowance provisions associated with the following: public policy limitations, political activities, excessive executive compensation, investigation of business opportunities, hobby losses, vacation home rentals, payment of others' expenses, personal expenditures, capital expenditures, related-party transactions, and expenses related to tax-exempt income.

Disallowance Possibilities

The tax law provides for the disallowance of certain types of expenses. Without specific restrictions in the tax law, taxpayers might attempt to deduct certain items that in reality are personal expenditures. For example, specific tax rules are provided to determine whether an expenditure is for trade or business purposes or related to a personal hobby.

Certain disallowance provisions are a codification or extension of prior court decisions. After the courts denied deductions for payments considered to be in violation of public policy, the tax law was changed to provide specific authority for the disallowance of these deductions. Discussions of specific disallowance provisions in the tax law follow.

PUBLIC POLICY LIMITATION

Justification for Denying Deductions. The courts developed the principle that a payment that is in violation of public policy is not a necessary expense and is not deductible.[27] Although a bribe or fine may be appropriate, helpful, and even contribute to the profitability of an activity, the courts held that to allow such expenses would frustrate clearly defined public policy. A deduction would dilute the effect of the penalty since the government would be indirectly subsidizing a taxpayer's wrongdoing.

Accordingly, the IRS was free to restrict deductions if, in its view, the expenses were contrary to public policy. But since the law did not explain which actions violated public policy, taxpayers often had to go to court to determine whether or not their expense fell into this category.

Furthermore, the public policy doctrine could be arbitrarily applied in cases where no clear definition had emerged. To solve these problems, Congress enacted legislation that attempts to limit the use of the doctrine. Under the legislation, deductions are disallowed for certain specific types of expenditures that are considered contrary to public policy:

[27]*Tank Truck Rentals, Inc. v. Comm.*, 58–1 USTC ¶9366, 1 AFTR2d 1154, 78 S.Ct. 507 (USSC, 1958).

- Bribes and kickbacks including those associated with Medicare or Medicaid (in the case of foreign bribes and kickbacks, only if the payments violate the U.S. Foreign Corrupt Practices Act of 1977).
- Fines and penalties paid to a government for violation of law.

EXAMPLE 13

Brown Corporation, a moving company, consistently loads its trucks with weights in excess of the limits allowed by state law. The additional revenue more than offsets the fines levied. The fines are for a violation of public policy and are not deductible. ■

- Two-thirds of the treble damage payments made to claimants resulting from violation of the antitrust law.[28]

To be disallowed, the bribe or kickback must be illegal under either Federal or state law and must also subject the payer to a criminal penalty or the loss of a license or privilege to engage in a trade or business. For a bribe or kickback that is illegal under state law, a deduction is denied only if the state law is generally enforced.

ETHICAL CONSIDERATIONS

Knowing the Right People

Abner, a real estate developer, has a contract with a major retailer to handle its land acquisitions in the southeastern part of the state. One of Abner's major responsibilities is to secure the requisite zoning to enable the retailer to build and operate its outlets. Typically, obtaining proper zoning is not a difficult matter.

Abner has identified a site that his client would like to acquire. It is located in a small community of historic repute and is surrounded by two counties with large populations. Unfortunately, the community has very restrictive zoning rules for commercial properties, and obtaining zoning variances will be challenging.

Abner's normal strategy in such a situation is to hire the leading law firm in the community to represent him in purchasing the property and securing the desired zoning. In this instance, however, the senior partner in the leading law firm is also the mayor. To avoid an obvious conflict of interest, Abner hires another law firm to carry out the acquisition. To avoid antagonizing the mayor, he pays a $25,000 retainer to the mayor's law firm to serve as his legal representative on any other real estate acquisitions during the coming year in the two adjoining counties. Abner is successful in securing the zoning variances and acquires the site for the retailer. During the following 12-month period, Abner does not utilize the services of the mayor's law firm. Abner deducts the $25,000 payment as an ordinary and necessary business expense.

What is Abner trying to achieve, and will he be successful?

EXAMPLE 14

During the year, Keith, an insurance salesman, paid $5,000 to Karen, a real estate broker. The payment represented 20% of the commissions Keith earned from customers referred by Karen. Under state law, the splitting of commissions by an insurance salesperson is an act of misconduct that could warrant a revocation of the salesperson's license. Keith's $5,000 payments to Karen are not deductible provided the state law is generally enforced. ■

Legal Expenses Incurred in Defense of Civil or Criminal Penalties. To deduct legal expenses, the taxpayer must be able to show that the origin and character of the claim are directly related to a trade or business, an income-producing activity, or the determination, collection, or refund of a tax. Personal legal expenses are not deductible. Thus, legal fees incurred in connection with a

[28]§§ 162(c), (f), and (g).

criminal defense are deductible only if the crime is associated with the taxpayer's trade or business or income-producing activity.[29]

EXAMPLE 15

Debra, a financial officer of Blue Corporation, incurs legal expenses in connection with her defense in a criminal indictment for evasion of Blue's income taxes. Debra may deduct her legal expenses because she is deemed to be in the trade or business of being an executive. The legal action impairs her ability to conduct this business activity.[30] ■

Deductible legal expenses associated with the following are deductible *for* AGI:

- Ordinary and necessary expenses incurred in connection with a trade or business.
- Ordinary and necessary expenses incurred in conjunction with rental or royalty property held for the production of income.

All other deductible legal expenses are deductible *from* AGI. For example, legal expenses generally are deductible *from* AGI if they are for fees for tax advice relative to the preparation of an individual's income tax return. Contrast this with the deduction *for* classification of legal fees for tax advice relative to the preparation of the portion of the tax return for a sole proprietor's trade or business (Schedule C) or an individual's rental or royalty income (Schedule E).

Expenses Relating to an Illegal Business. The usual expenses of operating an illegal business (e.g., a numbers racket) are deductible.[31] However, § 162 disallows a deduction for fines, bribes to public officials, illegal kickbacks, and other illegal payments.

EXAMPLE 16

Sam owns and operates an illegal gambling establishment. In connection with this activity, he has the following expenses during the year:

Rent	$ 60,000
Payoffs to the police	40,000
Depreciation on equipment	100,000
Wages	140,000
Interest	30,000
Criminal fines	50,000
Illegal kickbacks	10,000
Total	$430,000

All of the usual expenses (rent, depreciation, wages, and interest) are deductible; payoffs, fines, and kickbacks are not deductible. Of the $430,000 spent, $330,000 is deductible and $100,000 is not. ■

An exception applies to expenses incurred in illegal trafficking in drugs.[32] *Drug dealers* are not allowed a deduction for ordinary and necessary business expenses incurred in their business. In arriving at gross income from the business, however, dealers may reduce total sales by the cost of goods sold.[33] In this regard, no distinction is made between legal and illegal businesses in calculating gross income. Treating cost of goods sold as a negative income item rather than as a deduction

[29]*Comm. v. Tellier,* 66–1 USTC ¶9319, 17 AFTR2d 633, 86 S.Ct. 1118 (USSC, 1966).

[30]Rev.Rul. 68–662, 1968–2 C.B. 69.

[31]*Comm. v. Sullivan,* 58–1 USTC ¶9368, 1 AFTR2d 1158, 78 S.Ct. 512 (USSC, 1958).

[32]§ 280E.

[33]Reg. § 1.61–3(a). Gross income is defined as sales minus cost of goods sold. Thus, while § 280E prohibits any deductions for drug dealers, it does not modify the normal definition of gross income.

item produces the unseemly result that a drug dealer's taxable income is reduced by cost of goods sold.

POLITICAL CONTRIBUTIONS AND LOBBYING ACTIVITIES

Political Contributions. Generally, no business deduction is permitted for direct or indirect payments for political purposes.[34] Historically, the government has been reluctant to accord favorable tax treatment to business expenditures for political purposes. Allowing deductions might encourage abuses and enable businesses to have undue influence upon the political process.

Lobbying Expenditures. Lobbying expenses incurred in attempting to influence state or Federal legislation or the actions of certain high-ranking public officials (e.g., the President, Vice President, cabinet-level officials, and the two most senior officials in each agency of the executive branch) are not deductible.[35] The disallowance also applies to a pro rata portion of the membership dues of trade associations and other groups that are used for lobbying activities.

EXAMPLE 17

Egret Company pays a $10,000 annual membership fee to the Free Trade Group, a trade association for plumbing wholesalers. The trade association estimates that 70% of its dues are allocated to lobbying activities. Thus, Egret Company's deduction is limited to $3,000 ($10,000 × 30%). ■

There are three exceptions to the disallowance of lobbying expenses. An exception is provided for influencing local legislation (e.g., city and county governments). Second, the disallowance provision does not apply to activities devoted solely to monitoring legislation. Third, a *de minimis* exception is provided for annual in-house expenditures (lobbying expenses other than those paid to professional lobbyists or any portion of dues used by associations for lobbying) if such expenditures do not exceed $2,000. If the in-house expenditures exceed $2,000, none of the in-house expenditures can be deducted.

EXCESSIVE EXECUTIVE COMPENSATION

The deduction of executive compensation is subject to two limitations. As discussed earlier in this chapter, the compensation of shareholder-employees of closely held corporations is subject to the reasonableness requirement. The second limitation, the so-called millionaires' provision, applies to publicly held corporations (a corporation that has at least one class of stock registered under the Securities Act of 1934).[36]

The millionaires' provision does not limit the amount of compensation that can be paid to an employee. Instead, it limits the amount the employer can deduct for the compensation of a covered executive to $1 million annually. Covered employees include the chief executive officer and the four other most highly compensated officers.

Employee compensation *excludes* the following:

- Commissions based on individual performance.
- Certain performance-based compensation based on company performance according to a formula approved by a board of directors compensation committee (comprised solely of two or more outside directors) and by shareholder vote. The performance attainment must be certified by this compensation committee.

[34] § 276.
[35] § 162(e).
[36] § 162(m).

Executive Pay Abuse

The IRS has increased its scrutiny of executive pay practices. Its examination of 24 big companies found that several were evading the millionaires' limit on executive pay. Most of the abuses involve the exception for performance-based compensation. By paying bonuses based on performance, a corporation can exceed the general $1 million deduction cap. Some companies achieve this by changing the bonus plan formula or target throughout the year or, even worse, by paying the bonus even though the performance goals are not reached.

According to Catherine Livingston Fernandez, a speaker at a compensation conference, "some pretty large adjustments have been proposed" to correct such abuses. The Senate Finance Committee, in its report on the Enron investigation, proposed repealing the $1 million cap because it was not modifying corporate behavior as intended. Robert McIntyre, the director of Citizens for Tax Justice, believes that if the goal is to limit executive pay to $1 million, then nobody should be paid more than $1 million, and no exceptions should be allowed.

SOURCES: Adapted from Joan S. Lublin, "IRS Is Cracking Down on Abuse of Executive Bonus Tax Breaks," *Wall Street Journal*, June 18, 2004, p. B5; Jessee Drucker, "As CEOs Miss Bonus Goals, Goalposts Move," *Wall Street Journal*, July 7, 2004, p. C1.

- Payments to tax-qualified retirement plans.
- Payments that are excludible from the employee's gross income (e.g., certain fringe benefits).

INVESTIGATION OF A BUSINESS

Investigation expenses are expenses paid or incurred to determine the feasibility of entering a new business or expanding an existing business. They include such costs as travel, engineering and architectural surveys, marketing reports, and various legal and accounting services. How such expenses are treated for tax purposes depends on a number of variables, including the following:

- The current business, if any, of the taxpayer.
- The nature of the business being investigated.
- The extent to which the investigation has proceeded.
- Whether or not the acquisition actually takes place.

If the taxpayer is in a business the *same as or similar to* that being investigated, all investigation expenses are deductible in the year paid or incurred. The tax result is the same whether or not the taxpayer acquires the business being investigated.[37]

EXAMPLE 18

Terry, an accrual basis sole proprietor, owns and operates three motels in Georgia. In the current year, Terry incurs expenses of $8,500 in investigating the possibility of acquiring several additional motels located in South Carolina. The $8,500 is deductible in the current year whether or not Terry acquires the motels in South Carolina. ■

[37] § 195. *York v. Comm.*, 58–2 USTC ¶9952, 2 AFTR2d 6178, 261 F.2d 421 (CA–4, 1958).

Concept Summary 6-1

Costs of Investigating a Business

Are the investigation expenses for a business that the taxpayer either acquires or commences?

- Yes → Is the taxpayer already in the same or a similar business?
  - Yes → Deduct
  - No → Deduct up to $5,000 (portion not deducted, amortize over a 180-month period)
- No → Is the taxpayer already in the same or a similar business?
  - Yes → Deduct
  - No → Not deductible

When the taxpayer is *not* in a business that is the same as or similar to the one being investigated, the tax result depends on whether the new business is acquired. If the business is not acquired, all investigation expenses generally are nondeductible.[38]

EXAMPLE 19

Lynn, a retired merchant, incurs expenses in traveling from Rochester, New York, to California to investigate the feasibility of acquiring several auto care centers. If no acquisition takes place, none of the expenses are deductible. ■

If the taxpayer is *not* in a business that is the same as or similar to the one being investigated and actually acquires the new business, the expenses must be capitalized. At the election of the taxpayer, the first $5,000 of the expenses can be immediately deducted. Any excess expenses can be amortized over a period of not less than 180 months (15 years). In arriving at the $5,000 immediate deduction allowed, a dollar-for-dollar reduction must be made for those expenses in excess of $50,000.[39]

EXAMPLE 20

Tina owns and operates 10 restaurants located in various cities throughout the Southeast. She travels to Atlanta to discuss the acquisition of an auto dealership. In addition, she incurs legal and accounting costs associated with the potential acquisition. After incurring total investigation costs of $15,000, she acquires the auto dealership on October 1, 2005.

Tina may immediately deduct $3,000 [$5,000 – ($52,000 – $50,000)] and amortize the balance of $49,000 ($52,000 – $3,000) over a period of 180 months. For calendar year 2005, therefore, Tina can deduct $3,817 [$3,000 + ($49,000 × 3/180)]. ■

HOBBY LOSSES

Business or investment expenses are deductible only if the taxpayer can show that the activity was entered into for the purpose of making a profit. Certain activities

[38] Rev.Rul. 57–418, 1957–2 C.B. 143; *Morton Frank*, 20 T.C. 511 (1953); and *Dwight A. Ward*, 20 T.C. 332 (1953).

[39] § 195(b). Prior to October 22, 2004 (the effective date of the American Jobs Creation Act), no immediate deduction was available, but the amortization period was 60 months.

may have either profit-seeking or personal attributes, depending upon individual circumstances. Examples include raising horses and operating a farm used as a weekend residence. While personal losses are not deductible, losses attributable to profit-seeking activities may be deducted and used to offset a taxpayer's other income. For this reason, the tax law limits the deductibility of **hobby losses.**

General Rules. If an individual can show that an activity has been conducted with the intent to earn a profit, losses from the activity are fully deductible. The hobby loss rules apply only if the activity is not engaged in for profit. Hobby expenses are deductible only to the extent of hobby income.[40]

The Regulations stipulate that the following nine factors should be considered in determining whether an activity is profit seeking or a hobby:[41]

- Whether the activity is conducted in a businesslike manner.
- The expertise of the taxpayers or their advisers.
- The time and effort expended.
- The expectation that the assets of the activity will appreciate in value.
- The taxpayer's previous success in conducting similar activities.
- The history of income or losses from the activity.
- The relationship of profits earned to losses incurred.
- The financial status of the taxpayer (e.g., if the taxpayer does not have substantial amounts of other income, this may indicate that the activity is engaged in for profit).
- Elements of personal pleasure or recreation in the activity.

The presence or absence of a factor is not by itself determinative of whether the activity is profit seeking or a hobby. Rather, the decision is a subjective one that is based on an analysis of the facts and circumstances.

ETHICAL CONSIDERATIONS

When Is a Dairy Farm a Trade or Business?

Wes has been an orthopedic surgeon in New Orleans for 15 years. He would like to devote less time to his medical practice, spend more time with his family, and pay less income tax. His net income from his medical practice has been about $500,000 per year for the past five years.

Wes grew up on a dairy farm in southeastern Louisiana. He has many fond memories of his childhood and believes a farm would be an excellent environment for his three children.

Wes purchases a dairy farm across Lake Pontchartrain from New Orleans. He hires two full-time employees to handle the milking operations and other part-time employees as needed. In addition, Wes and his family participate in performing various activities on the farm.

Wes commutes to New Orleans four days a week to continue his medical practice. Because he is devoting less time to the practice, his net income decreases to $400,000. Wes has a loss of $75,000 for the dairy farm that he attributes to depressed milk prices and his inexperience at running the farm. He considers the medical practice and the dairy farm to be separate trades or businesses. Therefore, on the Federal income tax return, the $75,000 net loss is offset against the $400,000 net income. Assume that the net income and net loss from the medical practice and the dairy farm, respectively, remain approximately the same for the next four years.

Is the position adopted by Wes defensible? Discuss.

Presumptive Rule of § 183. The Code provides a rebuttable presumption that an activity is profit seeking if the activity shows a profit in at least three of any five prior consecutive years.[42] If the activity involves horses, a profit in at least two

[40]§ 183(b)(2).

[41]Reg. §§ 1.183–2(b)(1) through (9).

[42]§ 183(d).

of seven consecutive years meets the presumptive rule. If these profitability tests are met, the activity is presumed to be a trade or business rather than a personal hobby. In this situation, the IRS bears the burden of proving that the activity is personal rather than trade or business related.

EXAMPLE 21

Camille, an executive for a large corporation, is paid a salary of $200,000. Her husband is a collector of antiques. Several years ago, he opened an antique shop in a local shopping center and spends most of his time buying and selling antiques. He occasionally earns a small profit from this activity but more frequently incurs substantial losses. If the losses are business related, they are fully deductible against Camille's salary income on a joint return. In resolving this issue, consider the following:

- Initially determine whether the antique activity has met the three-out-of-five years profit test.
- If the presumption is not met, the activity may nevertheless qualify as a business if the taxpayer can show that the intent is to engage in a profit-seeking activity. It is not necessary to show actual profits.
- Attempt to fit the operation within the nine criteria prescribed in the Regulations and listed above. These criteria are the factors considered in trying to rebut the § 183 presumption. ■

Determining the Amount of the Deduction. If an activity is deemed to be a hobby, the expenses are deductible only to the extent of the gross income from the hobby. These expenses must be deducted in the following order:

- Amounts deductible under other Code sections without regard to the nature of the activity, such as property taxes and home mortgage interest.
- Amounts deductible under other Code sections if the activity had been engaged in for profit, but only if those amounts do not affect adjusted basis. Examples include maintenance, utilities, and supplies.
- Amounts that affect adjusted basis and would be deductible under other Code sections if the activity had been engaged in for profit.[43] Examples include depreciation, amortization, and depletion.

These deductions are deductible *from* AGI as itemized deductions to the extent they exceed 2 percent of AGI.[44] If the taxpayer uses the standard deduction rather than itemizing, all hobby loss deductions are wasted.

EXAMPLE 22

Jim, the vice president of an oil company, has AGI of $80,000. He decides to pursue painting in his spare time. He uses a home studio, comprising 10% of the home's square footage. During the current year, Jim incurs the following expenses:

Frames	$ 350
Art supplies	300
Fees paid to models	1,000
Home studio expenses:	
Total property taxes	900
Total home mortgage interest	10,000
Depreciation on 10% of home	500
Total home maintenance and utilities	3,600

[43] Reg. § 1.183–1(b)(1).
[44] Reg. § 1.67–1T(a)(1)(iv) and Rev.Rul. 75–14, 1975–1 C.B. 90.

During the year, Jim sold paintings for a total of $3,200. If the activity is held to be a hobby, Jim is allowed deductions as follows:

Gross income		$ 3,200
Deduct: Taxes and interest (10% of $10,900)		(1,090)
Remainder		$ 2,110
Deduct: Frames	$ 350	
Art supplies	300	
Models' fees	1,000	
Maintenance and utilities (10%)	360	(2,010)
Remainder		$ 100
Depreciation ($500, but limited to $100)		(100)
Net income		$ –0–

Jim includes the $3,200 of income in AGI, making his AGI $83,200. The taxes and interest are itemized deductions, deductible in full. The remaining $2,110 of expenses are reduced by 2% of his AGI ($1,664); so the net deduction is $446. Since the property taxes and home mortgage interest are deductible anyway, the net effect is a $2,754 ($3,200 less $446) increase in taxable income. ■

EXAMPLE 23

Assume that Jim's activity in Example 22 is held to be a business. The business is located in a small office building he owns. Expenses are property taxes of $90, mortgage interest of $1,000, frames of $350, art supplies of $300, models' fees of $1,000, maintenance and utilities of $360, and depreciation of $500. Under these circumstances, Jim could deduct expenses totaling $3,600. All these expenses would be trade or business expenses deductible *for* AGI. His reduction in AGI would be as follows:

Gross income		$ 3,200
Less: Taxes and interest	$1,090	
Other business expenses	2,010	
Depreciation	500	(3,600)
Reduction in AGI		($ 400)

■

RENTAL OF VACATION HOMES

Restrictions on the deductions allowed for part-year rentals of personal **vacation homes** were written into the law to prevent taxpayers from deducting essentially personal expenses as rental losses. Many taxpayers who owned vacation homes had formerly treated the homes as rental property and generated rental losses as deductions *for* AGI. For example, a summer cabin would be rented for 2 months per year, used for vacationing for 1 month, and left vacant the rest of the year. The taxpayer would then deduct 11 months' depreciation, utilities, maintenance, etc., as rental expenses, resulting in a rental loss. Section 280A eliminates this treatment by allowing deductions on residences used primarily for personal purposes only to the extent of the income generated. Only a break-even situation is allowed; no losses can be deducted.

There are three possible tax treatments for residences used for both personal and rental purposes. The treatment depends upon the *relative time* the residence is used for personal purposes versus rental use.

Primarily Personal Use. If the residence is *rented* for *fewer than 15 days* in a year, it is treated as a personal residence. The rent income is excluded from gross

Can an Extreme Makeover Produce Extreme Taxes?

While Trent Wolsum, a member of the National Guard, was deployed to Iraq, his house was selected for an extreme makeover by the television show *Extreme Makeover: Home Edition.* The estimated value of the makeover, which even included a backyard baseball diamond, was as much as $250,000.

The TV production company provided the Wolsums with a letter stating that its accountants believe that the $250,000 makeover is not subject to the Federal income tax. But how can this be since prizes are included in gross income under § 74? The producers of the show believe they have found a way around the "clutches of § 74."

During the seven-day period of the makeover and for three additional days, the show leases the house from the home owners. Normally, the owners would have to include the rent income (in this case the $250,000 makeover) in gross income under § 61. Under § 280A(g), however, if taxpayers lease their personal residence for fewer than 15 days, then the rent income is excluded from gross income.

Other tax experts contacted by *Newsweek* aren't nearly as convinced that the Wolsums are eligible for exclusion treatment.

SOURCE: Adapted from Daniel McGinn, "Tax Troubles for ABC's 'Extreme' Winners?" *Newsweek,* May 17, 2004, p. 12.

income, and mortgage interest and real estate taxes are allowed as itemized deductions, as with any personal residence.[45] No other expenses (e.g., depreciation, utilities, maintenance) are deductible. Although this provision exists primarily for administrative convenience, several bills have been introduced in Congress that would have repealed this exclusion from gross income.

EXAMPLE 24

Dixie owns a vacation cottage on the lake. During the current year, she rented it for $1,600 for two weeks, lived in it two months, and left it vacant the remainder of the year. The year's expenses amounted to $6,000 mortgage interest expense, $500 property taxes, $1,500 utilities and maintenance, and $2,400 depreciation. Since the property was not rented for at least 15 days, the income is excluded, the mortgage interest and property tax expenses are itemized deductions, and the remaining expenses are nondeductible personal expenses. ■

Primarily Rental Use. If the residence is *rented* for 15 days or more in a year and is *not used* for personal purposes for more than the greater of (1) 14 days or (2) 10 percent of the total days rented, the residence is treated as rental property.[46] The expenses must be allocated between personal and rental days if there are any personal use days during the year. The deduction of the expenses allocated to rental days can exceed rent income and result in a rental loss. The loss may be deductible under the passive activity loss rules (discussed in Chapter 11).

EXAMPLE 25

Assume instead that Dixie in Example 24 used the cottage for 12 days and rented it for 48 days for $4,800. Since she rented the cottage for 15 days or more but did not use it for more than 14 days, the cottage is treated as rental property. The expenses must be allocated between personal and rental days.

[45] § 280A(g).

[46] § 280A(d) and Prop.Reg. § 1.280A–3(c).

VACATION HOMES FOR THE RICH

If you feel that Nantucket, Hilton Head, and similar places have become too crowded for pleasant vacations, don't fret. With enough money, you can buy a vacation home that will enable you to avoid the crowds. By not renting it to other vacationers, however, you will forgo the cash flow that helps make the mortgage payments and pay property taxes.

New exclusive real estate developments, with an array of amenities, are springing up in previously isolated or unusual places (e.g., one development owns its own mountain and has 40 ski runs). The gated community concept keeps sightseers away, while the cost of the vacation home discourages low-budget buyers from becoming neighbors. Examples include:

Community	Proposed Number of Homes	Starting Price for Custom Home
Carnegie Abbey (Portsmouth, RI)	122	$3.5 million
Cherokee Plantation (Yemassee, SC)	28	4 million
Ford Plantation (Richmond Hill, GA)	400	1 million
Grand River Ranch (Kremmling, CO)	19	4 million
Yellowstone Club (Big Sky, MT)	864	3.8 million

Note, however, that people choose to live in these communities for various reasons. Jack Kemp, the former professional football player and politician, says that "nobody is snooty" at the Yellowstone Club. Jack is building a home on a $3 million lot. The size of his family and the in-place security features played a large part in his decision. He has 15 grandchildren and 13 of them ski.

SOURCE: Adapted from Danielle Reed and June Fletcher, "The Vacation-Home Frontier," *Wall Street Journal*, July 23, 2004, p. W1.

	Percentage of Use	
	Rental 80%	**Personal 20%**
Income	$ 4,800	$ -0-
Expenses		
Mortgage interest ($6,000)	($ 4,800)	($1,200)
Property taxes ($500)	(400)	(100)
Utilities and maintenance ($1,500)	(1,200)	(300)
Depreciation ($2,400)	(1,920)	(480)
Total expenses	($ 8,320)	($2,080)
Rental loss	($ 3,520)	$ -0-

Dixie deducts the $3,520 rental loss *for* AGI (assuming she meets the passive activity loss rules, discussed in Chapter 11). She also has an itemized deduction for property taxes of $100 associated with the personal use. The mortgage interest of $1,200 associated with the personal use is not deductible as an itemized deduction because the cottage is not a qualified residence (qualified residence interest) for this purpose (see Chapter 10). The portion of utilities and maintenance and depreciation attributable to personal use is not deductible. ■

EXAMPLE 26

Assume instead that Dixie in Example 24 rented the cottage for 200 days and lived in it for 19 days. The cottage is primarily rental use since she rented it for 15 days or more and did not use it for personal purposes for more than 20 days (10% of the rental days). The expenses must be allocated between personal and rental days as illustrated in Example 25. ■

Personal/Rental Use. If the residence is rented for 15 days or more in a year *and* is used for personal purposes for more than the greater of (1) 14 days or (2) 10 percent of the total days rented, it is treated as a personal/rental use residence. The expenses must be allocated between personal days and rental days. Expenses are allowed only to the extent of rent income.

EXAMPLE 27

Assume instead that Dixie in Example 24 rented the property for 30 days and lived in it for 30 days. The residence is classified as personal/rental use property since she used it more than 14 days and rented it for 15 days or more. The expenses must be allocated between rental use and personal use, and the rental expenses are allowed only to the extent of rent income. ■

If a residence is classified as personal/rental use property, the expenses that are deductible anyway (e.g., real estate taxes and mortgage interest) must be deducted first. If a positive net income results, otherwise nondeductible expenses that do not affect adjusted basis (e.g., maintenance, utilities, insurance) are allowed next. Finally, if any positive balance remains, depreciation is allowed. Any disallowed expenses allocable to rental use are carried forward and used in future years subject to the same limitations.

Expenses must be allocated between personal and rental days before the limits are applied. The courts have held that real estate taxes and mortgage interest, which accrue ratably over the year, are allocated on the basis of 365 days.[47] The IRS, however, disagrees and allocates real estate taxes and mortgage interest on the basis of total days of use.[48] Other expenses (utilities, maintenance, depreciation, etc.) are allocated on the basis of total days used.

EXAMPLE 28

Jason rents his vacation home for 60 days and lives in the home for 30 days. The limitations on personal/rental use residences apply. Jason's gross rent income is $10,000. For the entire year (not a leap year), the real estate taxes are $2,190; his mortgage interest expense is $10,220; utilities and maintenance expense equals $2,400; and depreciation is $9,000. Using the IRS approach, these amounts are deductible in this specific order:

Gross income	$10,000
Deduct: Taxes and interest ($^{60}/_{90}$ × $12,410)	(8,273)
Remainder to apply to rental operating expenses and depreciation	$ 1,727
Deduct: Utilities and maintenance ($^{60}/_{90}$ × $2,400)	(1,600)
Balance	$ 127
Deduct: Depreciation ($^{60}/_{90}$ × $9,000 = $6,000 but limited to above balance)	(127)
Net rent income	$ -0-

The nonrental use portion of real estate taxes and mortgage interest ($4,137 in this case) is deductible if the taxpayer elects to itemize (see Chapter 10). The personal use portion of utilities, maintenance, and depreciation is not deductible in any case. Jason has a carryover of $5,873 ($6,000 – $127) of the unused depreciation. Also note that the basis of the property is not reduced by the $5,873 depreciation not allowed because of the above limitation. (See Chapter 13 for a discussion of the reduction in basis for depreciation allowed or allowable.) ■

[47] *Bolton v. Comm.*, 82–2 USTC ¶9699, 51 AFTR2d 83–305, 694 F.2d 556 (CA–9, 1982).

[48] Prop.Reg. § 1.280A–3(d)(4).

EXAMPLE 29

Using the court's approach in allocating real estate taxes and mortgage interest, Jason, in Example 28, would have this result:

Gross income	$10,000
Deduct: Taxes and interest (60/365 × $12,410)	(2,040)
Remainder to apply to rental operating expenses and depreciation	$ 7,960
Deduct: Utilities and maintenance (60/90 × $2,400)	(1,600)
Balance	$ 6,360
Deduct: Depreciation (60/90 × $9,000, but limited to $6,360)	(6,000)
Net rent income	$ 360

Jason can deduct $10,370 ($12,410 paid – $2,040 deducted as expense in computing net rent income) of personal use mortgage interest and real estate taxes as itemized deductions. ■

Note the contrasting results in Examples 28 and 29. The IRS's approach (Example 28) results in no rental gain or loss and an itemized deduction for real estate taxes and mortgage interest of $4,137. In Example 29, Jason has net rent income of $360 and $10,370 of itemized deductions. The court's approach decreases his taxable income by $10,010 ($10,370 itemized deductions less $360 net rent income). The IRS's approach reduces his taxable income by only $4,137.

EXAMPLE 30

Assume instead that Jason in Example 28 had not lived in the home at all during the year. The house is rental property. The rental loss is calculated as follows:

Gross income	$10,000
Expenses	
Taxes and interest	($12,410)
Utilities and maintenance	(2,400)
Depreciation	(9,000)
Total expenses	($23,810)
Rental loss	($13,810)

Whether any of the rental loss would be deductible depends upon whether Jason actively participated in the rental activity and met the other requirements for passive activity losses (discussed in Chapter 11). ■

Conversion to Rental Property. A related issue is whether or not a taxpayer's *primary residence* is subject to the preceding rules if it is converted to rental property. If the vacation home rules apply, a taxpayer who converts a personal residence to rental property during the tax year, without any tax avoidance motive, could have the allowable deductions limited to the rent income. This would occur if the personal use exceeded the greater of 14 days or 10 percent of rental days test (a likely situation). The Code, however, provides that during a *qualified rental period*, any personal use days are not counted as personal use days in terms of classifying the use of the residence as *personal/rental use* rather than as *primarily rental use*.[49] In effect, the deduction for expenses of the property incurred during a qualified rental period is not subject to the personal use test of the vacation home rules. A qualified rental period is a consecutive period of 12 or more months. The period begins or ends in the taxable year in which the residence is rented or held for rental at a fair price. The residence must not be rented to a related party. If the property is sold before the 12-month period expires, the qualified rental period is the actual time rented.

[49] § 280A(d).

Concept Summary 6–2

Vacation/Rental Home

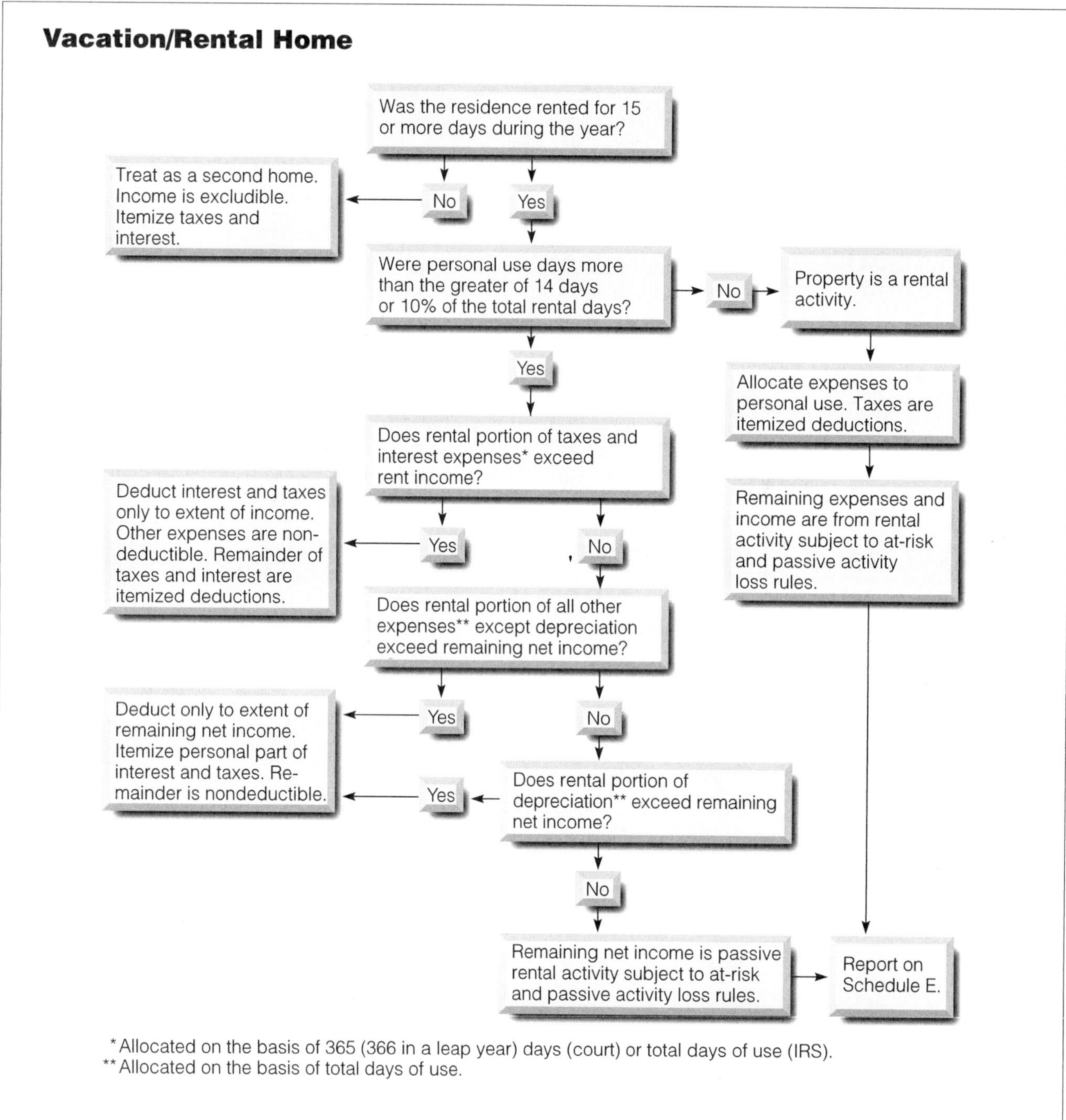
Was the residence rented for 15 or more days during the year?
No
Yes
Treat as a second home. Income is excludible. Itemize taxes and interest.
Were personal use days more than the greater of 14 days or 10% of the total rental days?
No
Property is a rental activity.
Yes
Allocate expenses to personal use. Taxes are itemized deductions.
Does rental portion of taxes and interest expenses* exceed rent income?
Remaining expenses and income are from rental activity subject to at-risk and passive activity loss rules.
Yes
Deduct interest and taxes only to extent of income. Other expenses are non-deductible. Remainder of taxes and interest are itemized deductions.
No
Does rental portion of all other expenses** except depreciation exceed remaining net income?
Yes
No
Deduct only to extent of remaining net income. Itemize personal part of interest and taxes. Remainder is nondeductible.
Yes
Does rental portion of depreciation** exceed remaining net income?
No
Remaining net income is passive rental activity subject to at-risk and passive activity loss rules.
Report on Schedule E.

*Allocated on the basis of 365 (366 in a leap year) days (court) or total days of use (IRS).
**Allocated on the basis of total days of use.

EXAMPLE 31

Rhonda converts her residence to rental property on May 1 and rents it for the remainder of 2005 for $5,600 and for all of 2006 for $8,400. The house would be classified as personal/rental use property (personal use days during 2005 are greater than both 14 days and 10% of rental days) except that this is a qualified rental period. Therefore, Rhonda's deduction for rental expenses is not limited to the gross income of $5,600 in 2005. ■

See Concept Summary 6–2 for a summary of the vacation home rules.

EXPENDITURES INCURRED FOR TAXPAYER'S BENEFIT OR TAXPAYER'S OBLIGATION

An expense must be incurred for the taxpayer's benefit or arise from the taxpayer's obligation. An individual cannot claim a tax deduction for the payment of the expenses of another individual.

EXAMPLE 32

During the current year, Fred pays the interest on his son Vern's home mortgage. Neither Fred nor Vern can take a deduction for the interest paid. Fred is not entitled to a deduction because the mortgage is not his obligation. Vern cannot claim a deduction because he did not pay the interest. The tax result would have been more favorable had Fred made a cash gift to Vern and let him pay the interest. Then Vern could have deducted the interest, and Fred might not have been liable for any gift taxes depending upon the amount involved. A deduction would have been created with no cash difference to the family. ■

One exception to this disallowance rule is the payment of medical expenses for a dependent. Such expenses are deductible by the payer subject to the normal rules that limit the deductibility of medical expenses (see Chapter 10).[50]

DISALLOWANCE OF PERSONAL EXPENDITURES

Section 262 states that "except as otherwise expressly provided in this chapter, no deduction shall be allowed for personal, living, or family expenses." To justify a deduction, an individual must be able to identify a particular section of the Code that sanctions the deduction (e.g., charitable contributions, medical expenses). Sometimes the character of a particular expenditure is not easily determined.

EXAMPLE 33

During the current year, Howard pays $1,500 in legal fees and court costs to obtain a divorce from his wife, Vera. Included in the divorce action is a property settlement concerning the disposition of income-producing property owned by Howard. In a similar situation, the Tax Court held that the taxpayer could not deduct any such costs.[51] "Although fees primarily related to property division concerning his income-producing property, they weren't ordinary and necessary expenses paid for conservation or maintenance of property held for production of income. Legal fees incurred in defending against claims that arise from a taxpayer's marital relationship aren't deductible expenses regardless of possible consequences on taxpayer's income-producing property." ■

The IRS has clarified the issue of the deduction of legal fees incurred in connection with a divorce.[52] To be deductible, an expense must relate solely to tax advice in a divorce proceeding. For example, legal fees attributable to the determination of dependency exemptions of children are deductible if the fees are distinguishable from the general legal fees incurred in obtaining a divorce. Other examples are the costs of creating a trust to make periodic alimony payments and the determination of the tax consequences of a property settlement. Therefore, it is advisable to request an itemization of attorney's fees to substantiate a deduction for the tax-related amounts.

[50]§ 213(a).

[51]*Harry H. Goldberg*, 29 TCM 74, T.C.Memo. 1970–27.

[52]Rev.Rul. 72–545, 1972–2 C.B. 179.

DISALLOWANCE OF DEDUCTIONS FOR CAPITAL EXPENDITURES

The Code specifically disallows a deduction for "any amount paid out for new buildings or for permanent improvements or betterments made to increase the value of any property or estate."[53] The Regulations further define capital expenditures to include those expenditures that add to the value or prolong the life of property or adapt the property to a new or different use.[54] Incidental repairs and maintenance of the property are not capital expenditures and can be deducted as ordinary and necessary business expenses. Repairing a roof is a deductible expense, but replacing a roof is a capital expenditure subject to depreciation deductions over its useful life. The tune-up of a delivery truck is an expense; a complete overhaul probably is a capital expenditure.

Capitalization versus Expense. When an expenditure is capitalized rather than expensed, the deduction is at best deferred and at worst lost forever. Although an immediate tax benefit for a large cash expenditure is lost, the cost may be deductible in increments over a longer period of time.

If the expenditure is for a tangible asset that has an ascertainable life, it is capitalized and may be deducted as depreciation (or cost recovery) over the life of the asset (for depreciation) or over a statutory period (for cost recovery under either ACRS or MACRS).[55] Land is not subject to depreciation (or cost recovery) since it does not have an ascertainable life.

EXAMPLE 34

Stan purchased a prime piece of land located in an apartment-zoned area. Stan paid $500,000 for the property, which had an old but usable apartment building on it. He immediately had the building demolished at a cost of $100,000. The $500,000 purchase price and the $100,000 demolition costs must be capitalized, and the basis of the land is $600,000. Since land is a nondepreciable asset, no deduction is allowed. More favorable tax treatment might result if Stan rented the apartments in the old building for a period of time to attempt to establish that there was no intent to demolish the building. If Stan's attempt is successful, it might be possible to allocate a substantial portion of the original purchase price of the property to the building (a depreciable asset). When the building is later demolished, any remaining adjusted basis can be deducted as an ordinary (§ 1231) loss. (See Chapter 14 for a discussion of the treatment of § 1231 assets.) ■

If the expenditure is for an intangible asset (e.g., copyright, patent, covenant not to compete, goodwill), the capitalized expenditure can be amortized, regardless of whether or not the intangible asset has an ascertainable life. Intangible assets, referred to as § 197 intangibles, are amortized over a 15-year statutory period using the straight-line method. See Chapter 8 for additional discussion of the amortization of intangibles.

TRANSACTIONS BETWEEN RELATED PARTIES

The Code places restrictions on the recognition of gains and losses from **related-party transactions.** Without these restrictions, relationships created by birth, marriage, and business would provide endless possibilities for engaging in financial transactions that produce tax savings with no real economic substance or change. For example, to create an artificial loss, a wife could sell investment property to her husband at a loss and deduct the loss on their joint return. Her husband could

[53] § 263(a)(1).
[54] Reg. § 1.263(a)–1(b).
[55] See Chapter 8 for the discussion of depreciation and cost recovery.

then hold the asset indefinitely, and the family would sustain no real economic loss. A complex set of laws has been designed to eliminate such possibilities.

Losses. The Code provides for the disallowance of any "losses from sales or exchanges of property . . . directly or indirectly" between related parties.[56] When the property is subsequently sold to a nonrelated party, any gain recognized is reduced by the loss previously disallowed. Any disallowed loss not used by the related-party buyer to offset the recognized gain on a subsequent sale or exchange to an unrelated party is permanently lost.

EXAMPLE 35

Freida sells common stock with a basis of $1,000 to her son, Bill, for $800. Bill sells the stock several years later for $1,100. Freida's $200 loss is disallowed upon the sale to Bill, and only $100 of gain ($1,100 selling price – $800 basis – $200 disallowed loss) is taxable to him upon the subsequent sale. ■

EXAMPLE 36

George sells common stock with a basis of $1,050 to his son, Ray, for $800. Ray sells the stock eight months later to an unrelated party for $900. Ray's gain of $100 ($900 selling price – $800 basis) is not recognized because of George's previously disallowed loss of $250. Note that the offset may result in only partial tax benefit upon the subsequent sale (as in this case). If the property had not been transferred to Ray, George could have recognized a $150 loss upon the subsequent sale to the unrelated party ($1,050 basis – $900 selling price). ■

EXAMPLE 37

Pete sells common stock with a basis of $1,000 to an unrelated third party for $800. Pete's son repurchased the same stock in the market on the same day for $800. The $200 loss is not allowed because the transaction is an indirect sale between related parties.[57] ■

Unpaid Expenses and Interest. The law prevents related taxpayers from engaging in tax avoidance schemes where one related taxpayer uses the accrual method of accounting and the other uses the cash basis. An accrual basis, closely held corporation, for example, could borrow funds from a cash basis individual shareholder. At the end of the year, the corporation would accrue and deduct the interest, but the cash basis lender would not recognize interest income since no interest had been paid. Section 267 specifically defers the deduction of the accruing taxpayer until the recipient taxpayer must include it in income; that is, when it is actually paid to the cash basis taxpayer. This *matching* provision applies to interest as well as other expenses, such as salaries and bonuses.

This deduction deferral provision does not apply if both of the related taxpayers use the accrual method or both use the cash method. Likewise, it does not apply if the related party reporting income uses the accrual method and the related party taking the deduction uses the cash method.

Relationships and Constructive Ownership. Section 267 operates to disallow losses and defer deductions only between related parties. Losses or deductions generated by similar transactions with an unrelated party are allowed. *Related parties* include the following:

- Brothers and sisters (whether whole, half, or adopted), spouse, ancestors (parents, grandparents), and lineal descendants (children, grandchildren) of the taxpayer.
- A corporation owned more than 50 percent (directly or indirectly) by the taxpayer.
- Two corporations that are members of a controlled group.

[56]§ 267(a)(1).

[57]*McWilliams v. Comm.*, 47–1 USTC ¶9289, 35 AFTR 1184, 67 S.Ct. 1477 (USSC, 1947).

- A series of other complex relationships between trusts, corporations, and individual taxpayers.

Constructive ownership provisions are applied to determine whether the taxpayers are related. Under these provisions, stock owned by certain relatives or related entities is *deemed* to be owned by the taxpayer for purposes of applying the loss and expense deduction disallowance provisions. A taxpayer is deemed to own not only his or her stock but also the stock owned by lineal descendants, ancestors, brothers and sisters or half-brothers and half-sisters, and spouse. The taxpayer is also deemed to own his or her proportionate share of stock owned by any partnership, corporation, estate, or trust of which the taxpayer is a member. An individual is deemed to own any stock owned, directly or indirectly, by his or her partner. However, constructive ownership by an individual of the partnership's and the other partner's shares does not extend to the individual's spouse or other relatives (no double attribution).

EXAMPLE 38

The stock of Sparrow Corporation is owned 20% by Ted, 30% by Ted's father, 30% by Ted's mother, and 20% by Ted's sister. On July 1 of the current year, Ted loaned $10,000 to Sparrow Corporation at 8% annual interest, principal and interest payable on demand. For tax purposes, Sparrow uses the accrual basis, and Ted uses the cash basis. Both are on a calendar year. Since Ted is deemed to own the 80% owned by his parents and sister, he constructively owns 100% of Sparrow Corporation. If the corporation accrues the interest within the taxable year, no deduction can be taken until payment is made to Ted. ■

SUBSTANTIATION REQUIREMENTS

The tax law is built on a voluntary system. Taxpayers file their tax returns, report income and take deductions to which they are entitled, and pay their taxes through withholding or estimated tax payments during the year. The taxpayer has the burden of proof for substantiating expenses deducted on the returns and must retain adequate records. Upon audit, the IRS will disallow any undocumented or unsubstantiated deductions. These requirements have resulted in numerous conflicts between taxpayers and the IRS.

Some events throughout the year should be documented as they occur. For example, it is generally advisable to receive a pledge payment statement from one's church, in addition to a canceled check (if available) for proper documentation of a charitable contribution.[58] In addition, for charitable contributions, a donor must obtain a receipt from the donee for contributions of $250 or more. Other types of deductible expenditures may require receipts or some other type of support.

Specific and *more stringent* rules for deducting travel, entertainment, and gift expenses are discussed in Chapter 9. Certain mixed-use (both personal and business use) and listed property are also subject to the adequate records requirement (discussed in Chapter 8).

EXPENSES AND INTEREST RELATING TO TAX-EXEMPT INCOME

Certain income, such as interest on municipal bonds, is tax-exempt.[59] The law also allows the taxpayer to deduct expenses incurred for the production of income.[60] Deduction disallowance provisions, however, make it impossible to make money

[58] Rev.Proc. 92–71, 1992–2 C.B. 437, addresses circumstances where checks are not returned by a financial institution or where electronic transfers are made.

[59] § 103.

[60] § 212.

at the expense of the government by excluding interest income and deducting interest expense.[61]

EXAMPLE 39

Sandy, a taxpayer in the 35% bracket, purchased $100,000 of 6% municipal bonds. At the same time, she used the bonds as collateral on a bank loan of $100,000 at 8% interest. A positive cash flow would result from the tax benefit as follows:

Cash paid out on loan	($8,000)
Cash received from bonds	6,000
Tax savings from deducting interest expense (35% of $8,000 interest expense)	2,800
Net positive cash flow	$ 800

■

To eliminate the possibility illustrated in Example 39, the Code specifically disallows as a deduction the expenses of producing tax-exempt income. Interest on any indebtedness incurred or continued to purchase or carry tax-exempt obligations also is disallowed.

Judicial Interpretations. It is often difficult to show a direct relationship between borrowings and investment in tax-exempt securities. Suppose, for example, that a taxpayer borrows money, adds it to existing funds, buys inventory and stocks, then later sells the inventory and buys municipal bonds. A series of transactions such as these can completely obscure any connection between the loan and the tax-exempt investment. One solution would be to disallow interest on any debt to the extent that the taxpayer holds any tax-exempt securities. This approach would preclude individuals from deducting part of their home mortgage interest if they owned any municipal bonds. The law was not intended to go to such extremes. As a result, judicial interpretations have tried to be reasonable in disallowing interest deductions.

In one case, a company used municipal bonds as collateral on short-term loans to meet seasonal liquidity needs.[62] The court disallowed the interest deduction on the grounds that the company could predict its seasonal liquidity needs. The company could anticipate the need to borrow the money to continue to carry the tax-exempt securities. The same company *was* allowed an interest deduction on a building mortgage, even though tax-exempt securities it owned could have been sold to pay off the mortgage. The court reasoned that short-term liquidity needs would have been impaired if the tax-exempt securities were sold. Furthermore, the court ruled that carrying the tax-exempt securities bore no relationship to the long-term financing of a construction project.

EXAMPLE 40

In January of the current year, Alan borrowed $100,000 at 8% interest. He used the loan proceeds to purchase 5,000 shares of stock in White Corporation. In July, he sold the stock for $120,000 and reinvested the proceeds in City of Denver bonds, the income from which is tax-exempt. Assuming the $100,000 loan remained outstanding throughout the entire year, Alan cannot deduct the interest attributable to the period in which he held the bonds. ■

---

[61] § 265.

[62] *The Wisconsin Cheeseman, Inc. v. U.S.*, 68–1 USTC ¶9145, 21 AFTR2d 383, 388 F.2d 420 (CA–7, 1968).

LO.4

Identify tax planning opportunities for maximizing deductions and minimizing the disallowance of deductions.

Tax Planning Considerations

TIME VALUE OF TAX DEDUCTIONS

Cash basis taxpayers often have the ability to make early payments for their expenses at the end of the tax year. This may permit the payments to be deducted currently instead of in the following tax year. In view of the time value of money, a tax deduction this year may be worth more than the same deduction next year. Before employing this strategy, the taxpayer must consider next year's expected income and tax rates and whether a cash-flow problem may develop from early payments. Thus, the time value of money as well as tax rate changes must be considered when an expense can be paid and deducted in either of two years.

EXAMPLE 41

Jena pledged $5,000 to her church's special building fund. She can make the contribution in December 2005 or January 2006. Jena is in the 35% tax bracket in 2005, and in the 28% bracket in 2006. She itemizes in both years. Assume Jena's discount rate is 8%. If she takes the deduction in 2005, she saves $454 ($1,750 – $1,296), due to the decrease in the tax rates and the time value of money.

	2005	2006
Contribution	$5,000	$5,000
Tax bracket	.35	.28
Tax savings	$1,750	$1,400
Discounted @ 8%	1.0	.926
Savings in present value	$1,750	$1,296

■

UNREASONABLE COMPENSATION

In substantiating the reasonableness of a shareholder-employee's compensation, an internal comparison test is sometimes useful. If it can be shown that nonshareholder-employees and shareholder-employees in comparable positions receive comparable compensation, it is indicative that compensation is not unreasonable.

Another possibility is to demonstrate that the shareholder-employee has been underpaid in prior years. For example, the shareholder-employee may have agreed to take a less-than-adequate salary during the unprofitable formative years of the business. The expectation is that the "postponed" compensation would be paid in later, more profitable years. The agreement should be documented, if possible, in the corporate minutes.

Keep in mind that in testing for reasonableness, the *total* pay package must be considered. Look at all fringe benefits or perquisites, such as contributions by the corporation to a qualified pension plan. Even though those amounts are not immediately available to the covered shareholder-employee, they must be taken into account.

EXCESSIVE EXECUTIVE COMPENSATION

With the $1 million limit on the deduction of compensation of covered employees, many corporations and their executives must engage in additional tax planning. Previously, concerns over the deductibility of compensation related primarily to closely held corporations. The $1 million limit applies specifically to publicly held corporations. In many instances, it is now necessary for these corporations to restructure the compensation packages of their top executives in order to deduct payments in excess of $1 million. Opportunities include compensation payable on

Concept Summary 6–3

Classification of Expenses

	Deductible			
Expense Item	**For AGI**	**From AGI**	**Not Deductible**	**Applicable Code §**
Investment expenses				
Rent and royalty	X			§ 62(a)(4)
All other investments		X[4]		§ 212
Employee expenses				
Commuting expenses			X	§ 262
Travel and transportation[1]		X[4,5]		§ 162(a)(2)
Reimbursed expenses[1]	X			§ 62(a)(2)(A)
Moving expenses	X			§ 62(a)(15)
Entertainment[1]		X[4,5]		§ 162(a)
Teacher supplies	X[11]	X[4]		§ 62(a)(2)(D)
All other employee expenses[1]		X[4,5]		§ 162(a)
Certain expenses of performing artists	X			§ 62(a)(2)(B)
Trade or business expenses	X			§§ 162 and 62(a)(1)
Casualty losses				
Business	X			§ 165(c)(1)
Personal		X[6]		§ 165(c)(3)
Tax determination				
Collection or refund expenses	X[8]	X[4]		§§ 212 and 62(a)(1) or (4)
Bad debts	X			§§ 166 and 62(a)(1) or (3)
Medical expenses		X[7]		§ 213
Charitable contributions		X		§ 170
Taxes				
Trade or business	X			§§ 162 and 62(a)(1)
Personal taxes				
Real property		X		§ 164(a)(1)
Personal property		X		§ 164(a)(2)
State and local income *or* sales		X		§§ 164(a)(3) and (b)(5)
Investigation of a business[2]	X			§§ 162 and 62(a)(1)
Interest				
Business	X			§§ 162 and 62(a)(1)
Personal	X[9]	X[3]	X[10]	§§ 163(a), (d), and (h)
Qualified tuition and related expenses	X			§§ 62(a)(18) and 222
All other personal expenses			X	§ 262

1. Deduction *for* AGI if reimbursed, an adequate accounting is made, and employee is required to repay excess reimbursements.
2. Provided certain criteria are met.
3. Subject to the excess investment interest and the qualified residence interest provisions.
4. Subject (in the aggregate) to a 2%-of-AGI floor imposed by § 67.
5. Only 50% of meals and entertainment are deductible.
6. Subject to a $100 floor per event and a 10%-of-AGI floor per tax year.
7. Subject to a 7.5%-of-AGI floor.
8. Only the portion relating to business, rental, or royalty income or losses.
9. Only the portion relating to student loans.
10. Other personal interest is disallowed.
11. Subject to a statutory limit of $250.

a commission basis, certain other performance-based compensation, payments to qualified retirement plans, and payments that are excludible fringe benefits.

SHIFTING DEDUCTIONS

Taxpayers should manage their obligations to avoid the loss of a deduction. Deductions can be shifted among family members, depending upon which member makes the payment. For example, a father buys a condo for his daughter and puts the title in both names. The taxpayer who makes the payment gets the deduction for the property taxes. If the condo is owned by the daughter only and her father makes the payment, neither is entitled to a deduction. In this case, the father should make a cash gift to the daughter who then makes the payment to the taxing authority.

HOBBY LOSSES

To demonstrate that an activity has been entered into for the purpose of making a profit, a taxpayer should treat the activity as a business. The business should engage in advertising, use business letterhead stationery, and maintain a business phone.

If a taxpayer's activity earns a profit in three out of five consecutive years, the presumption is that the activity is engaged in for profit. It may be possible for a cash basis taxpayer to meet these requirements by timing the payment of expenses or the receipt of revenues. The payment of certain expenses incurred before the end of the year might be made in the following year. The billing of year-end sales might be delayed so that collections are received in the following year.

Keep in mind that the three-out-of-five-years rule under § 183 is not absolute. All it does is shift the presumption. If a profit is not made in three out of five years, the losses may still be allowed if the taxpayer can show that they are due to the nature of the business. For example, success in artistic or literary endeavors can take a long time. Also, depending on the state of the economy, even full-time farmers and ranchers are often unable to show a profit. How can one expect a part-time farmer or rancher to do so?

Merely satisfying the three-out-of-five-years rule does not guarantee that a taxpayer is automatically home free. If the three years of profits are insignificant relative to the losses of other years, or if the profits are not from the ordinary operation of the business, the taxpayer is vulnerable. The IRS may still be able to establish that the taxpayer is not engaged in an activity for profit.

EXAMPLE 42

Ashley had the following gains and losses in an artistic endeavor:

2001	($50,000)
2002	(65,000)
2003	400
2004	200
2005	125

Under these circumstances, the IRS might try to overcome the presumption. ■

If Ashley in Example 42 could show conformity with the factors enumerated in the Regulations or could show evidence of business hardships (e.g., injury, death, or illness), the government cannot override the presumption.[63]

[63] *Faulconer, Sr. v. Comm.*, 84–2 USTC ¶9955, 55 AFTR2d 85–302, 748 F.2d 890 (CA–4, 1984), *rev'g* 45 TCM 1084, T.C. Memo. 1983–165.

CAPITAL EXPENDITURES

On the sale of a sole proprietorship where the sales price exceeds the fair market value of the tangible assets and stated intangible assets, a planning opportunity may exist for both the seller and the buyer. The seller's preference is for the excess amount to be allocated to goodwill. Goodwill is a capital asset whereas a covenant not to compete produces ordinary income treatment (see Chapter 14).

Because both a covenant and goodwill are amortized over a statutory 15-year period, the tax results of a covenant and goodwill are the same for the buyer. However, the buyer should recognize that an allocation to goodwill rather than a covenant may provide a tax benefit to the seller. Therefore, the seller and buyer, in negotiating the sales price, should factor in the tax benefit to the seller of having the excess amount labeled goodwill rather than a covenant not to compete. Of course, if the noncompetition aspects of a covenant are important to the buyer, part of the excess amount can be assigned to a covenant.

KEY TERMS

Accounting method, 6–9

Deductions *for* adjusted gross income, 6–2

Deductions *from* adjusted gross income, 6–2

Hobby losses, 6–17

Ordinary and necessary, 6–5

Reasonableness, 6–7

Related-party transactions, 6–26

Vacation home, 6–19

PROBLEM MATERIALS

Discussion Questions

1. "All income must be reported and all deductions are allowed unless specifically disallowed in the Code." Discuss.

2. Terry, who has AGI of $60,000, has deductions of $6,500. Does it matter to Terry whether they are *for* or *from* AGI? Why or why not?

3. Does an expenditure that is classified as a deduction *from* AGI produce the same tax benefit as an expenditure that is classified as a deduction *for* AGI? Explain.

4. Classify each of the following expenditures as a deduction *for* AGI, a deduction *from* AGI, or not deductible:
   a. Pete gives $1,000 to his mother for her birthday.
   b. Janet gives $1,000 to the First Baptist Church.
   c. Alex pays Dr. Dafashy $1,000 for medical services rendered.
   d. Susan pays alimony of $1,000 to Herman.
   e. Rex, who is self-employed, contributes $1,000 to his pension plan.
   f. April pays expenses of $500 associated with her rental property.

5. Classify each of the following expenditures as a deduction *for* AGI, a deduction *from* AGI, or not deductible:
   a. Amos contributes $500 to his H.R. 10 plan (i.e., a retirement plan for a self-employed individual).
   b. Keith pays $500 of child support to his former wife, Renee, for the support of their son, Chris.
   c. Judy pays $500 for professional dues that are reimbursed by her employer.
   d. Ted pays $500 as the monthly mortgage payment on his personal residence. Of this amount, $100 represents a payment on principal, and $400 represents an interest payment.

e. Lynn pays $500 to a moving company for moving her household goods to Detroit where she is starting a new job. She is not reimbursed by her employer.
f. Ralph pays property taxes of $1,500 on his personal residence.

6. Larry and Susan each invest $10,000 in separate investment activities. They each incur deductible expenses of $800 associated with their respective investments. Explain why Larry's expenses are properly classified as deductions *from* AGI (itemized deductions) and Susan's expenses are appropriately classified as deductions *for* AGI.

7. Must an expense be both ordinary and necessary in order to be deducted as a trade or business expense under § 162?

8. Wanda, a machinist employed by Silver Airlines, owns 25 shares of Silver Airlines stock. Silver has 900,000 shares of stock outstanding. Wanda spends $800 to travel to Chicago for Silver's annual meeting. Her expenses would have been $500 more, but she was permitted to fly free on Silver. She attended both days of the shareholders' meeting and actively participated. What are the tax consequences of the trip for Wanda?

9. Sid and Vienne are the owners of a corporation. To reduce the corporation's taxable income, they pay a $3,000 salary each month to their eight-year-old daughter, Paula. Why is this salary disallowed as a deduction?

10. Dave uses the second floor of a building for his residence and the first for his business. The uninsured building is destroyed by fire. Are the tax consequences the same for the residence part of the building and the business part?

11. Mary Kate owns a building that she leases to an individual who operates a grocery store. Rent income is $10,000 and rental expenses are $6,000. On what Form 1040 schedule or schedules are the income and expenses reported?

12. Distinguish between the timing for the recording of a deduction under the cash method versus the accrual method.

13. What is the "actually paid" requirement for the deduction of an expense by a cash basis taxpayer? Does actual payment ensure a deduction?

14. What is the significance of the all events and economic performance tests?

15. Why is the reserve method not allowed to be used for Federal income tax purposes?

16. Clear, Inc., is a bottled water distributor. Clear's delivery trucks frequently are required to park in "No Parking" zones in order to make their deliveries. If the trucks are occasionally ticketed, can Clear deduct the fines it pays?

Issue ID

17. Ted is an agent for an airline manufacturer and is negotiating a sale with a representative of the U.S. government and with a representative of a developing country. Ted's company has sufficient capacity to handle only one of the orders. Both orders will have the same contract price. Ted believes that if his employer will authorize a $500,000 payment to the representative of the foreign country, he can guarantee the sale. He is not sure that he can obtain the same result with the U.S. government. Identify the relevant tax issues for Ted.

18. Stuart, an insurance salesman, is arrested for allegedly robbing a convenience store. He hires an attorney who is successful in getting the charges dropped. Is the attorney's fee deductible?

19. Linda operates a drug-running operation. Which of the following expenses she incurs can reduce taxable income?
    a. Bribes paid to border guards.
    b. Salaries to employees.
    c. Price paid for drugs purchased for resale.
    d. Kickbacks to police.
    e. Rent on an office.
    f. Depreciation on office furniture and equipment.
    g. Tenant's casualty insurance.

20. Gordon anticipates that being positively perceived by the individual who is elected mayor will be beneficial for his business. Therefore, he contributes to the campaigns of both the Democratic and the Republican candidates. The Republican candidate is elected mayor. Can Gordon deduct any of the political contributions he made?

21. Melissa, the owner of a sole proprietorship, does not provide health insurance for her 20 employees. She plans to spend $1,500 lobbying in opposition to legislation that would require her to provide health insurance for her employees. Discuss the tax advantages and disadvantages of paying the $1,500 to a professional lobbyist rather than spending the $1,500 on in-house lobbying expenditures.

22. What limits exist on the deductibility of executive compensation? Do the limits apply to all types of business entities? Are there any exceptions to the limitations?

23. What is the significance of one's present occupation in the deductibility of expenses incurred in investigating another business?

24. Hector conducts a business with the following results for the year:

Revenue	$22,000
Depreciation on car	2,960
Operating expenses of car	2,100
Rent	650
Wages	8,200
Amortization of intangibles	680

Hector estimates that due to a depressed real estate market, the value of land owned by the business declined by $5,200. Calculate the effect of Hector's business on his AGI.

25. Sarah owns a vacation home in the Tennessee mountains. Without considering the vacation home, she has gross income of $65,000. During the year, she rented the cabin for two weeks to a friend for $2,500. Sarah herself used the cabin during four weeks of the year. The total expenses for the year consisted of $10,000 mortgage interest, $1,500 property tax, $2,000 utilities and maintenance, and $3,200 depreciation.
    a. What effect does the rental of the vacation cabin have on Sarah's AGI?
    b. What expenses can Sarah deduct? Which are deductible *for* AGI, and which are deductible *from* AGI?

26. Contrast the differing results obtained by using the IRS's approach and the court's approach to allocating property taxes and mortgage interest in a personal/rental situation. Which method would the taxpayer prefer?

Issue ID

27. Karen and Andy own a beach house. They have an agreement with a rental agent to rent it up to 200 days per year. For the past three years, the agent has been successful in renting it for 200 days. Karen and Andy use the beach house for one week during the summer and one week during Thanksgiving. Their daughter, Sarah, a college student, has asked if she and some friends can use the beach house for the week of spring break. Advise Karen and Andy how they should respond and identify any relevant tax issues.

28. Hank was transferred from Phoenix to North Dakota on March 1 of the current year. He immediately put his home in Phoenix up for rent. The home was rented May 1 to November 30 and was vacant during the month of December. It was rented again on January 1 for six months. What expenses, if any, can Hank deduct on his return? Which deductions are *for* AGI and which ones are *from* AGI?

Decision Making

29. Erika would like to help Hillary and James, her daughter and son-in-law, with their short-term financial problems. To help them avoid foreclosure, she proposes to make the monthly mortgage payments on their home for the past six months. Erika's preference is to make the payments directly to the mortgage company. However, she is willing to give the money to Hillary and James who would then make the payments. Advise Erika on which option, if either, offers preferential tax treatment to her.

30. Isiah repaired the roof on his apartment building at a cost of $9,200. During the same year, Rachel replaced the roof on her rental house for $9,200. Both taxpayers are on the cash basis. Are their expenditures treated the same on their tax returns? Why or why not?

Issue ID

31. Ella owns 60% of the stock of Peach, Inc. The stock has declined in value since Ella purchased it five years ago. She is going to sell 5% of her stock to a relative to pay her 12-year-old daughter's private school tuition. Ella is also going to make a gift of 10% of her stock to another relative. Identify the relevant tax issues for Ella.

32. Jake owns City of Charleston bonds with an adjusted basis of $100,000. During the year, he receives interest payments of $4,000. Jake partially financed the purchase of the bonds by borrowing $70,000 at 6% interest. Jake's interest payments on the loan this year are $4,100, and his principal payments are $1,000.
    a. Should Jake report any interest income this year?
    b. Can Jake deduct any interest expense this year?

Problems

33. Sandra is an attorney. She incurs the following expenses when she and her employee, Fred, attend the American Bar Association convention in San Francisco:

Conference registration:	
Sandra	$800
Fred	800
Airline tickets from Pittsburgh to San Francisco:	
Sandra	900
Fred	400
Lodging in San Francisco:	
Sandra	650
Fred	350
Rental car in San Francisco:	
Sandra	325
Fred	–0–

Calculate the effect of these expenses on Sandra's AGI.

Decision Making

34. Carlton received the following income and incurred and paid the following expenses during the current year:

Salary income	$72,000
Dividend income	4,000
Interest income	3,000
Contributions to First Church	2,500
Real estate taxes on personal residence	1,800
Alimony paid to former spouse	12,000
Contribution to traditional IRA	3,000
Mortgage interest on personal residence	6,000
State income taxes	3,500
Loss on the sale of stock	900

Carlton is not yet eligible to participate in his employer's retirement plan.
    a. Calculate Carlton's AGI.
    b. Should Carlton itemize deductions *from* AGI or take the standard deduction?

35. Julie is a student and earns $10,200 working part-time at the college ice cream shop. She has no other income. Her medical expenses for the year totaled $2,200. During the year, she suffered a casualty loss of $3,500 when her apartment burned. Julie contributed

$2,000 to her church. Upon the advice of her parents, Julie is trying to decide whether to contribute $3,000 to the traditional IRA her parents have set up for her. What effect would the IRA contribution have on Julie's itemized deductions?

36. Drew and his wife Cassie own all of the stock of Thrush. Cassie is the president and Drew is the vice president. Cassie and Drew are paid salaries of $400,000 and $300,000, respectively, each year. They consider the salaries to be reasonable based on a comparison with salaries paid for comparable positions in comparable companies. They project Thrush's taxable income for next year, before their salaries, to be $800,000. They decide to place their four teenage children on the payroll and to pay them total salaries of $100,000. The children will each work about five hours per week for Thrush.
    a. What are Drew and Cassie trying to achieve by hiring the children?
    b. Calculate the tax consequences of hiring the children on Thrush, and on Drew and Cassie's family.

37. Audra incurs the following losses during the current tax year from the sale of:

Brown, Inc. stock	$ 1,100
Audra's personal use car	11,000
Audra's personal residence	12,000
City of Newburyport bonds	900

She also had a theft loss on her uninsured business use car of $1,500. Calculate Audra's deductible losses.

38. Falcon, Inc., paid salaries of $500,000 to its employees during its first year of operations. At the end of the year, Falcon had unpaid salaries of $45,000.
    a. Calculate the salary deduction if Falcon is a cash basis taxpayer.
    b. Calculate the salary deduction if Falcon is an accrual basis taxpayer.

39. Doris, a calendar year taxpayer, is the owner of a sole proprietorship that uses the cash method. She leases an office building for $72,000 for an 18-month period on August 1, 2005. In order to obtain this favorable lease rate, she pays the $72,000 at the inception of the lease. How much rent expense may Doris deduct on her 2005 tax return?

40. Duck, an accrual basis corporation, sponsored a rock concert on December 29, 2005. Gross receipts were $300,000. The following expenses were incurred and paid as indicated:

Expense		Payment Date
Rental of coliseum	$ 25,000	December 21, 2005
Cost of goods sold:		
Food	30,000	December 30, 2005
Souvenirs	60,000	December 30, 2005
Performers	100,000	January 5, 2006
Cleaning of coliseum	10,000	February 1, 2006

Since the coliseum was not scheduled to be used again until January 15, the company with which Duck had contracted did not actually perform the cleanup until January 8–10, 2006.

Calculate Duck's net income from the concert for tax purposes for 2005.

41. Mercedes, an attorney with a leading Miami law firm, is convicted of failing to file Federal income tax returns for 2000–2002. Her justification for failing to do so was the pressures of her profession (80- to 90-hour workweeks). She is assessed taxes, interest, and penalties of $112,000 by the IRS. In addition, she incurs related legal fees of $75,000. Determine the amount that Mercedes can deduct, and classify it as a deduction *for* or a deduction *from* AGI.

42. Darby runs an illegal numbers racket. His gross revenues are $550,000, and he incurs the following expenses:

Illegal kickbacks	$20,000
Salaries	80,000
Rent	24,000
Utilities and telephone	9,000
Bribes to police	25,000
Interest	6,000
Medical insurance premiums for employees	4,000
Depreciation on equipment	12,000

a. What is Darby's net income from this business that is includible in taxable income?
b. If the business was an illegal drug operation and cost of goods sold was $100,000, how would your answer differ?

43. Polly made the following political contributions:

To national Republican Party	$1,000
To national Democratic Party	1,000
To local candidate for mayor	700
To candidate for state senate	200
To candidate for school board	250

How much can Polly deduct?

Decision Making

Communications

44. Amber, a publicly held corporation, currently pays its president an annual salary of $900,000. In addition, it contributes $20,000 annually to a defined contribution pension plan for him. As a means of increasing company profitability, the board of directors decides to increase the president's compensation. Two proposals are being considered. Under the first proposal, the salary and pension contribution for the president would be increased by 30%. Under the second proposal, Amber would implement a performance-based compensation program that is projected to provide about the same amount of additional compensation and pension contribution for the president.
a. Evaluate the alternatives from the perspective of Amber, Inc.
b. Prepare a letter to Amber's board of directors that contains your recommendations. Address the letter to the board chairperson, Agnes Riddle, whose address is 100 James Tower, Cleveland, OH 44106.

45. Vermillion, Inc., a publicly held corporation, pays the following salaries to its executives:

	Salary	Bonus	Retirement Plan Contribution
CEO	$2,000,000	$100,000	$80,000
Executive vice president	1,800,000	90,000	72,000
Treasurer	1,600,000	–0–	64,000
Marketing vice president	1,500,000	75,000	60,000
Operations vice president	1,400,000	70,000	56,000
Distribution vice president	1,200,000	60,000	48,000
Research vice president	1,100,000	–0–	44,000
Controller	800,000	–0–	32,000

Vermillion normally does not pay bonuses, but after reviewing the results of operations for the year, the board of directors decided to pay a 5% bonus to selected executives. What is the amount of these payments that Vermillion may deduct?

46. Jenny, the owner of a very successful restaurant chain, is exploring the possibility of expanding the chain into a city in the neighboring state. She incurs $25,000 of expenses

associated with this investigation. Based on the regulatory environment for restaurants in the city, she decides not to do so. During the year, she also investigates opening a hotel that will be part of a national hotel chain. Her expenses for this are $51,000. The hotel begins operations on November 1. Determine the amount that Jenny can deduct in the current year for investigating these two businesses.

47. Tim traveled to a neighboring state to investigate the purchase of two restaurants. His expenses included travel, legal, accounting, and miscellaneous expenses. The total was $30,000. He incurred the expenses in June and July 2005.
    a. What can Tim deduct in 2005 if he was in the restaurant business and did not acquire the two restaurants?
    b. What can Tim deduct in 2005 if he was in the restaurant business and acquired the two restaurants and began operating them on October 1, 2005?
    c. What can Tim deduct in 2005 if he did not acquire the two restaurants and was not in the restaurant business?
    d. What can he deduct in 2005 if he acquired the two restaurants, but was not in the restaurant business when he acquired them? Operations began on September 1, 2005.

48. Alex, who is single, conducts an activity that is appropriately classified as a hobby. The activity produces the following revenues and expenses:

Revenue	$18,000
Property taxes	3,000
Materials and supplies	4,500
Utilities	2,000
Advertising	5,000
Insurance	750
Depreciation	4,000

Without regard to this activity, Alex's AGI is $42,000. Determine how much income Alex must report, the amount of the expenses he is permitted to deduct, and his taxable income.

49. Samantha is an executive with an AGI of $100,000 before considering income or loss from her miniature horse business. Her income comes from prizes for winning horse shows, stud fees, and sales of yearlings. Samantha's home is on 20 acres; she uses 10 of these 20 acres for the horses and has erected stables, paddocks, fences, tack houses, and other related improvements there.

    Samantha uses an office in her home that is 10% of the square footage of the house. She uses the office exclusively for maintaining files of breeding lines, histories, and show and veterinary records. Her books show the following income and expenses for the current year:

Income from fees, prizes, and sales	$22,000
Expenses	
Entry fees	1,000
Feed and veterinary bills	4,000
Supplies	900
Publications and dues	500
Travel to horse shows (no meals)	2,300
Salaries and wages of employees	8,000
Depreciation on horse equipment	3,000
Depreciation on horse farm improvements	7,000
Depreciation on 10% of home	1,000
Total home mortgage interest	24,000
Total property taxes on home	2,200
Total property taxes on horse farm improvements	800

The mortgage interest is only on her home. The horse farm improvements are not mortgaged.

a. How must Samantha treat the income and expenses of the operation if the miniature horse activity is held to be a hobby?
b. How would your answer in part (a) differ if the horse operation is held to be a business?

50. Arlene, who lives in a winter resort area, rented her personal residence for 14 days while she was visiting Madrid. Rent income was $4,000. Related expenses for the year were as follows:

Real property taxes	$ 2,800
Mortgage interest	7,000
Utilities	3,700
Insurance	1,500
Repairs	2,100
Depreciation	12,000

Determine the effect on Arlene's AGI.

51. During the year (not a leap year), Anna rented her vacation home for 45 days, used it personally for 20 days, and left it vacant for 300 days. She had the following income and expenses:

Rent income	$ 7,000
Expenses	
Real estate taxes	2,500
Interest on mortgage	9,000
Utilities	2,400
Repairs	1,000
Roof replacement (a capital expenditure)	12,000
Depreciation	7,000

a. Compute Anna's net rent income or loss and the amounts she can itemize on her tax return, using the court's approach to allocating property taxes and interest.
b. How would your answer in part (a) differ using the IRS's method of allocating property taxes and interest?

52. How would your answer in Problem 51 differ if Anna had rented the house for 90 days and had used it personally for 12 days?

53. Chee, single, age 40, had the following income and expenses during the year (not a leap year):

Income	
Salary	$43,000
Rental of vacation home (rented 60 days, used personally 60 days, vacant 245 days)	4,000
Municipal bond interest	2,000
Dividend from General Motors	400
Expenses	
Interest	
On home mortgage	8,400
On vacation home	4,758
On loan used to buy municipal bonds	3,100
Taxes	
Property tax on home	2,200
Property tax on vacation home	1,098
State income tax	3,300

Charitable contributions	$1,100
Tax return preparation fee	300
Utilities and maintenance on vacation home	2,600
Depreciation on rental 50% of vacation home	3,500

Calculate Chee's taxable income for the year before personal exemptions.

Decision Making

54. Velma and Clyde operate a retail sports memorabilia shop. For the current year, sales revenue is $50,000 and expenses are as follows:

Cost of goods sold	$19,000
Advertising	1,000
Utilities	2,000
Rent	4,000
Insurance	1,500
Wages to Boyd	7,000

Velma and Clyde pay $7,000 in wages to Boyd, a part-time employee. Since this amount is $1,000 below the minimum wage, Boyd threatens to file a complaint with the appropriate Federal agency. Although Velma and Clyde pay no attention to Boyd's threat, Chelsie (Velma's mother) gives Boyd a check for $1,000 for the disputed wages. Both Velma and Clyde ridicule Chelsie for wasting money when they learn what she has done. The retail shop is the only source of income for Velma and Clyde.

a. Calculate Velma and Clyde's AGI.
b. Can Chelsie deduct the $1,000 payment on her tax return?
c. How could the tax position of the parties be improved?

55. Terry is purchasing a business from Anne. The amount being paid exceeds the fair market value of the identifiable assets of the business by $400,000. Advise Terry on the tax consequences of the $400,000 being allocated to goodwill versus it being allocated to a 10-year covenant not to compete.

Decision Making

56. Jay's sole proprietorship has the following assets:

	Basis	Fair Market Value
Cash	$ 10,000	$ 10,000
Accounts receivable	18,000	18,000
Inventory	25,000	30,000
Patent	22,000	40,000
Land	50,000	75,000
	$125,000	$173,000

The building in which Jay's business is located is leased. The lease expires at the end of the year.

Jay is age 70 and would like to retire. He expects to be in the 35% tax bracket. Jay is negotiating the sale of the business with Lois, a key employee. They have agreed on the fair market value of the assets, as indicated above, and agree the total purchase price should be about $200,000.

a. Advise Jay regarding how the sale should be structured.
b. Advise Lois regarding how the purchase should be structured.
c. What might they do to achieve an acceptable compromise?

Decision Making
Communications

57. Janet Saxon sold stock (basis of $82,000) to her brother, Fred, for $70,000, the fair market value.

a. What are the tax consequences to Janet?
b. What are the tax consequences to Fred if he later sells the stock for $90,000? For $50,000? For $75,000?

c. Write a letter to Janet in which you inform her of the tax consequences if she sells the stock to Fred for $70,000 and explain how a sales transaction could be structured that would produce better tax consequences for her. Janet's address is 32 Country Lane, Lawrence, KS 66045.

58. The Robin Corporation is owned as follows:

Irene	29%
Paul, Irene's husband	16%
Sylvia, Irene's mother	15%
Ron, Irene's father	25%
Quinn, an unrelated party	15%

Robin is on the accrual basis, and Irene and Paul are on the cash basis. Irene and Paul each loaned the Robin Corporation $40,000 out of their separate funds. On December 31, 2005, Robin accrued interest at 8% on both loans. The interest was paid on February 4, 2006. What is the tax treatment of this interest expense/income to Irene, Paul, and Robin?

59. For each of the following independent transactions, calculate the recognized gain or loss to the seller and the adjusted basis to the buyer:
   a. Bonnie sells Parchment, Inc. stock to Phillip, her brother, for its fair market value of $12,000. Bonnie's adjusted basis is $17,000.
   b. Amos sells land to his nephew, Boyd, for its fair market value of $70,000. Amos's adjusted basis is $85,000.
   c. Susan sells a tax-exempt bond to her wholly owned corporation for its fair market value of $19,000. Susan's adjusted basis is $20,000.
   d. Ron sells a business truck that he uses in his sole proprietorship to his cousin, Agnes, for its fair market value of $18,500. Ron's adjusted basis is $20,000.
   e. Martha sells her partnership interest in Pearl Partnership to her adult daughter, Kim, for $220,000. Martha's adjusted basis is $175,000.

60. Chris has a brokerage account and buys on the margin, which resulted in an interest expense of $15,000 during the year. Income generated through the brokerage account was as follows:

Municipal interest	$ 40,000
Taxable dividends and interest	160,000

How much investment interest can Chris deduct?

Decision Making

61. During the current year, Robert pays the following amounts associated with his own residence and that of his daughter, Anne:

Property taxes:	
On home owned by Robert	$3,000
On home owned by Anne	1,500
Mortgage interest:	
Associated with Robert's home	8,000
Associated with Anne's home	4,500
Repairs to:	
Robert's home	1,200
Anne's home	700
Utilities:	
Robert's home	2,700
Anne's home	1,600
Replacement of roof:	
Robert's home	4,000

a. Which of these expenses can Robert deduct?
b. Which of these expenses can Anne deduct?
c. Are the deductions *for* AGI or *from* AGI (itemized)?
d. How could the tax consequences be improved?

Cumulative Problems

Tax Return Problem
Decision Making
Communications

62. John and Mary Jane Sanders are married, filing jointly. Their address is 204 Shoe Lane, Blacksburg, VA 24061. They are expecting their first two children (twins) in early 2006. John's salary in 2005 was $91,000, from which $12,400 of Federal income tax and $4,500 of state income tax were withheld. Mary Jane made $47,000 and had $3,100 of Federal income tax and $2,050 of state income tax withheld. The appropriate amount of FICA tax was withheld for John and for Mary Jane.

John and Mary Jane are both covered by their employer's medical insurance policies with three-fourths of the premiums being paid by the employers. The total premiums were $4,500 for John and $3,300 for Mary Jane. Mary Jane received medical benefits of $6,200 under the plan. John was not ill during 2005.

John makes alimony payments of $30,000 per year to June, his former wife. He also makes child support payments of $12,000 for his son, Rod, who lives with June except for two months in the summer when he visits John and Mary Jane. At the time of the divorce, John worked for a Fortune 500 company and received a salary of $250,000. As a result of corporate downsizing, he lost his job.

Mary Jane's father lived with them until his death in November. His only sources of income were salary of $1,900, unemployment compensation benefits of $3,500, and Social Security benefits of $3,200. Of this amount, he deposited $5,000 in a savings account. The remainder of his support of $7,500, which included funeral expenses of $5,100, was provided by John and Mary Jane.

Other income received by the Sanderses was as follows:

Interest on certificates of deposit	$5,000
Share of S corporation taxable income (distributions from the S corporation to Mary Jane were $350)	600
Award received by Mary Jane from employer for outstanding suggestion for cutting costs	2,000

John has always wanted to operate his own business. In October 2005, he incurred expenses of $8,000 in investigating the establishment of a retail computer franchise. With the birth of the twins expected next year, however, he decides to forgo self-employment for at least a couple of years.

John and Mary Jane made charitable contributions of $3,600 during the year and paid an additional $1,200 in state income taxes in 2005 upon filing their 2004 state income tax return. Their deductible home mortgage interest was $9,000, and their property taxes came to $3,500. They paid sales taxes of $1,700 for which they have receipts.

Part 1—Tax Computation
Calculate John and Mary Jane's tax (or refund) due for 2005. Suggested software: TurboTax.

Part 2—Tax Planning
Assume that the Sanderses come to you for advice in December 2005. John has learned that he will receive a $30,000 bonus. He wants to know if he should take it in December 2005 or in January 2006. Mary Jane will quit work on December 31 to stay home with the twins. Their itemized deductions will decrease by $2,050 because Mary Jane will not have state income taxes withheld. Mary Jane will not receive the employee award in 2006. She expects the medical benefits received to be $5,000. The Sanderses expect all of their other income items to remain the same in 2006. Write a letter to John and Mary Jane that contains your advice and prepare a memo for the tax files. Suggested software: TurboTax.

Tax Return Problem

63. Helen Archer, age 38, is single and lives at 120 Sanborne Avenue, Springfield, IL 60740. Her Social Security number is 648–11–9981. Helen has been divorced from her former husband, Albert, for three years. She has a son, Jason, who is age 17. His Social Security number is 648–98–3471. Helen does not wish to contribute $3 to the Presidential Election Campaign Fund.

Helen, an advertising executive, earned a salary of $65,000 in 2004. Her employer withheld $7,700 in Federal income tax, $3,200 in state income tax, and the appropriate amount of FICA tax.

Helen has legal custody of Jason. Jason lives with his father during summer vacation. Albert indicates that his expenses for Jason are $11,000. Helen can document that she spent $5,500 for Jason's support during 2004. In prior years, Helen gave a signed Form 8332 to Albert regarding Jason. For 2004, she has decided not to do so.

Helen's mother died on January 7, 2004. Helen inherited assets worth $250,000 from her mother. As the sole beneficiary of her mother's life insurance policy, Helen received insurance proceeds of $125,000. Her mother's cost basis for the life insurance policy was $40,000. Helen's favorite aunt gave her $15,000 for her birthday in October.

On November 8, 2004, Helen sells for $19,000 Amber stock that she had purchased for $20,000 from her first cousin, Walt, on December 5, 1997. Walt's cost basis for the stock was $12,000, and the stock was worth $20,000 on December 5, 1997. On December 1, 2004, Helen sold Falcon stock for $17,000. She had acquired the stock on July 2, 2004, for $11,000.

An examination of Helen's records reveals the following information:

- Received interest income of $2,800 from First Savings Bank.
- Received groceries valued at $1,000 from a local grocery store for being the 100,000th customer.
- Received qualified dividend income of $1,400 from Amber.
- Received $1,900 of interest income on City of Springfield school bonds.
- Received alimony of $15,000 from Albert.
- Received a distribution of $2,900 from ST Partnership. Her distributive share of the partnership passive taxable income was $3,100.

From her checkbook records, she determines that she made the following payments during 2004:

- Charitable contributions of $1,600 to First Presbyterian Church and $800 to the American Red Cross.
- Mortgage interest on her residence of $6,700.
- Property taxes of $2,100 on her residence and $600 on her car.
- Estimated Federal income taxes of $7,000 and estimated state income taxes of $1,000.
- Medical expenses of $5,000 for her and $800 for Jason. In December her medical insurance policy reimbursed $1,200 of her medical expenses.
- A $400 ticket for parking in a handicapped space.
- Attorney's fees of $200 associated with unsuccessfully contesting the parking ticket.
- Contribution of $50 to the campaign of a candidate for governor.
- Since she did not maintain records of the sales tax she paid, she calculates the amount from the sales tax table to be $1,197.

Calculate Helen's net tax payable or refund due for 2004. If you use tax forms, you will need Form 1040 and Schedules A, B, D, and E. Suggested software: TurboTax.

Research Problems

Note: Solutions to Research Problems can be prepared by using the ***RIA Checkpoint® Student Edition*** *online research product, which is available to accompany this text. It is also possible to prepare solutions to the Research Problems by using tax research materials found in a standard tax library.*

Research Problem 1. Green Motor Transportation Corporation is a nationwide long-haul freight concern that owns and operates approximately 15,000 trucks. For tax purposes, Green uses a calendar year and the accrual method of accounting.

Every year, Green is required to pay for a large number of fees, licenses, insurance, and permits (designated as FLIP expenses) in order to legally operate its fleet of vehicles in the large number of states in which it does business. Although the FLIP expenses are accrued for financial accounting purposes, they are expensed for tax purposes. None of the FLIP expenses covers a period of more than one year in duration. This practice has been followed consistently by Green for many years and, until recently, has never been questioned by the IRS.

Upon audit of Green's tax return, the IRS disallowed approximately 55% of the FLIP expenses that had been claimed as a deduction. Although the disallowed expenses were paid in 2002, the IRS held that they were applicable to year 2003. Because Green used the accrual method both for accounting and for tax purposes, the IRS found that a prorating of these expenses was necessary. Green disputed the proration based on the notion that the expenses did not provide a "substantial" benefit to future years. Under an informal policy followed by the IRS, prepaid expenses of less than a year can be expensed in the year paid if certain conditions are met. Green contended that these conditions were met as the FLIP expenses were routine in nature, did not distort income, and were not designed to be manipulative.

The IRS disputed the existence of any such "one-year rule" being available to preclude deducting prepaid expenses. But regardless of whether the rule existed, it would, in any event, not apply to accrual basis taxpayers.

Who is right? Can Green Motor Transportation Corporation deduct all of the FLIP expenses paid in 2002, or must 55% of this amount be deferred to 2003?

Research Problem 2. Professor Shelia Crane is a drama professor at Municipal University with an annual salary of $75,000. In addition, Professor Crane is a playwright. She normally writes two plays each year. Her revenues and expenses from the playwright activity are as follows:

	Revenues	Expenses
2000	$ -0-	$ 9,000
2001	-0-	7,000
2002	500	10,000
2003	2,000	8,500
2004	-0-	6,000

Professor Crane works diligently to get her plays produced. One of her plays has been read at Lincoln Center, and two have been performed by local theater groups. In 2000, she was awarded a sabbatical, and in 2003, she received a $10,000 summer research grant from the university.

The IRS audited Professor Crane's 2002 return and classified her playwright activity as a hobby. Professor Crane comes to you for advice.

Internet Activity

Use the tax resources of the Internet to address the following question. Do not restrict your search to the World Wide Web, but include a review of newsgroups and general reference materials, practitioner sites and resources, primary sources of the tax law, chat rooms and discussion groups, and other opportunities.

Research Problem 3. Locate and read a recent judicial or administrative ruling regarding the deductibility of hobby losses. Look for rulings that deal with horse breeding, professional sports teams, or art collecting activities. Which criteria did the ruling emphasize in upholding or reversing the taxpayer's deduction for such losses?

Deductions and Losses: Certain Business Expenses and Losses

LEARNING OBJECTIVES

After completing Chapter 7, you should be able to:

LO.1

Determine the amount, classification, and timing of the bad debt deduction.

LO.2

Understand the tax treatment of worthless securities including § 1244 stock.

LO.3

Distinguish between deductible and nondeductible losses of individuals.

LO.4

Identify a casualty and determine the amount, classification, and timing of casualty and theft losses.

LO.5

Recognize and apply the alternative tax treatments for research and experimental expenditures.

LO.6

Calculate the manufacturers' deduction.

LO.7

Understand the tax impact of a net operating loss and recognize the effect of the carryback and carryover provisions.

LO.8

Identify tax planning opportunities in deducting certain business expenses, business losses, and personal losses.

OUTLINE

Working with the tax formula for individuals requires the proper classification of items that are deductible *for* adjusted gross income (AGI) and items that are deductions *from* AGI (itemized deductions). Business expenses and losses, discussed in this chapter, are reductions of gross income to arrive at the taxpayer's AGI. Expenses and losses incurred in connection with a transaction entered into for profit and attributable to rents and royalties are deducted *for* AGI. All other expenses and losses incurred in connection with a transaction entered into for profit are deducted *from* AGI.

The situation of Robert P. Groetzinger provides an interesting insight into the importance of the proper classification for the individual taxpayer. Groetzinger terminated his employment with a private company and devoted virtually all of his working time to pari-mutuel wagering on dog races. He had no other profession or employment, and his only sources of income, apart from his gambling winnings, were interest, dividends, and sales from investments. During the tax year in question, he went to the track six days a week and devoted 60 to 80 hours per week to preparing and making wagers on his own account.

The tax question that this case presents is whether Groetzinger's gambling activities constitute a trade or business. If the gambling is a trade or business, his gambling losses are deductions *for* AGI. If the gambling activity is not a trade or business, the losses are itemized deductions, and Groetzinger's taxes increase by $2,142.[1]

Deductible losses on personal use property are deducted as an itemized deduction. Itemized deductions are deductions *from* AGI. While the general coverage of

[1]*Groetzinger v. Comm.*, 85–2 USTC ¶9622, 56 AFTR2d 85–5683, 771 F.2d 269 (CA–7, 1985).

A Deduction for Bad Debts

When computing Federal taxable income, a business is allowed a deduction for bad debts. The city of Los Angeles, however, does not allow a deduction for bad debts when determining the city's business tax. Los Angeles city councilman Greg Smith feels this treatment of bad debts does not promote a business-friendly environment in the city. In his opinion, not allowing a deduction is " just plain bad policy."

SOURCE: Adapted from "Business Taxes," *City News Service*, May 4, 2004.

itemized deductions is in Chapter 10, casualty and theft losses on personal use property are discussed in this chapter.

In determining the amount and timing of the deduction for bad debts, proper classification is again important. A business bad debt is classified as a deduction *for* AGI, and a nonbusiness bad debt is classified as a short-term capital loss.

Other topics discussed in Chapter 7 are research and experimental expenditures and the net operating loss deduction.

LO.1

Determine the amount, classification, and timing of the bad debt deduction.

Bad Debts

If a taxpayer sells goods or provides services on credit and the account receivable subsequently becomes worthless, a **bad debt** deduction is permitted only if income arising from the creation of the account receivable was previously included in income.[2] No deduction is allowed, for example, for a bad debt arising from the sale of a product or service when the taxpayer is on the cash basis because no income is reported until the cash has been collected. Permitting a bad debt deduction for a cash basis taxpayer would amount to a double deduction because the expenses of the product or service rendered are deducted when payments are made to suppliers and to employees, or at the time of the sale.

EXAMPLE 1

Tracy, an individual engaged in the practice of accounting, performed accounting services for Pat for which she charged $8,000. Pat never paid the bill, and his whereabouts are unknown.

If Tracy is an accrual basis taxpayer, she includes the $8,000 in income when the services are performed. When she determines that Pat's account will not be collected, she deducts the $8,000 as a bad debt expense.

If Tracy is a cash basis taxpayer, she does not include the $8,000 in income until payment is received. When she determines that Pat's account will not be collected, she cannot deduct the $8,000 as a bad debt expense because it was never recognized as income. ■

A bad debt can also result from the nonrepayment of a loan made by the taxpayer or from purchased debt instruments.

SPECIFIC CHARGE-OFF METHOD

Taxpayers (other than certain financial institutions) may use only the **specific charge-off method** in accounting for bad debts. Certain financial institutions are allowed to use the **reserve method** for computing deductions for bad debts.

[2]Reg. § 1.166–1(e).

Concept Summary 7–1

Specific Charge-Off Method

Expense deduction and account write-off	The expense arises and the write-off takes place when a specific business account becomes either partially or wholly worthless or when a specific nonbusiness account becomes wholly worthless.
Recovery of accounts previously written off	If the account recovered was written off during the current taxable year, the write-off entry is reversed. If the account recovered was written off during a previous taxable year, income is created subject to the tax benefit rule.

A taxpayer using the specific charge-off method may claim a deduction when a specific business debt becomes either partially or wholly worthless or when a specific nonbusiness debt becomes wholly worthless.[3] For the business debt, the taxpayer must satisfy the IRS that the debt is partially worthless and must demonstrate the amount of worthlessness.

If a business debt previously deducted as partially worthless becomes totally worthless in a future year, only the remainder not previously deducted can be deducted in the future year.

In the case of total worthlessness, a deduction is allowed for the entire amount in the year the debt becomes worthless. The amount of the deduction depends on the taxpayer's basis in the bad debt. If the debt arose from the sale of services or products and the face amount was previously included in income, that amount is deductible. If the taxpayer purchased the debt, the deduction is equal to the amount the taxpayer paid for the debt instrument.

One of the more difficult tasks is determining if and when a bad debt is worthless. The loss is deductible only in the year of partial or total worthlessness for business debts and only in the year of total worthlessness for nonbusiness debts. Legal proceedings need not be initiated against the debtor when the surrounding facts indicate that such action will not result in collection.

EXAMPLE 2

In 2003, Ross loaned $1,000 to Kay, who agreed to repay the loan in two years. In 2005, Kay disappeared after the note became delinquent. If a reasonable investigation by Ross indicates that he cannot find Kay or that a suit against Kay would not result in collection, Ross can deduct the $1,000 in 2005. ■

Bankruptcy is generally an indication of at least partial worthlessness of a debt. Bankruptcy may create worthlessness before the settlement date. If this is the case, the deduction may be taken in the year of worthlessness.

EXAMPLE 3

In Example 2, assume that Kay filed for personal bankruptcy in 2004 and that the debt is a business debt. At that time, Ross learned that unsecured creditors (including Ross) were ultimately expected to receive 20 cents on the dollar. In 2005, settlement is made and Ross receives only $150. He should deduct $800 ($1,000 loan – $200 expected settlement) in 2004 and $50 in 2005 ($200 balance – $150 proceeds). ■

If a receivable has been written off as uncollectible during the current tax year and is subsequently collected during the current tax year, the write-off entry is reversed. If a receivable has been written off as uncollectible, the collection of the

[3] § 166(a) and Reg. § 1.166.

Writing Off Bad Debts in Australia

In Australia, a small business must identify bad debts and physically write them off by June 30, or the business will not be allowed a deduction. Even if the debts have been referred to a collection agency, they must be physically written off the books. To claim a bad debt under Australian law, the business must be on the accrual basis, there must be little possibility of the debt being paid, and the debt must be written off before June 30.

receivable in a later tax year may result in income being recognized. Income will result if the deduction yielded a tax benefit in the year it was taken. See Examples 39 and 40 in Chapter 5.

BUSINESS VERSUS NONBUSINESS BAD DEBTS

A **nonbusiness bad debt** is a debt unrelated to the taxpayer's trade or business either when it was created or when it became worthless. The nature of a debt depends on whether the lender was engaged in the business of lending money or whether there is a proximate relationship between the creation of the debt and the lender's trade or business. The use to which the borrowed funds are put by the debtor is of no consequence. Loans to relatives or friends are the most common type of nonbusiness bad debt.

EXAMPLE 4

Jamil loaned his friend, Esther, $1,500. Esther used the money to start a business, which subsequently failed. Even though the proceeds of the loan were used in a business, the loan is a nonbusiness bad debt because the business was Esther's, not Jamil's. ■

The distinction between a business bad debt and a nonbusiness bad debt is important. A **business bad debt** is deductible as an ordinary loss in the year incurred, whereas a nonbusiness bad debt is always treated as a short-term capital loss. Thus, regardless of the age of a nonbusiness bad debt, the deduction may be of limited benefit due to the capital loss limitations on deductibility in any one year. The maximum amount of a net short-term capital loss that an individual can deduct against ordinary income in any one year is $3,000 (see Chapter 14 for a detailed discussion). Although no deduction is allowed when a nonbusiness bad debt is partially worthless, the taxpayer is entitled to deduct the net amount of the loss upon final settlement.

The following example is an illustration of business bad debts adapted from the Regulations.[4]

EXAMPLE 5

In 2004, Leif sold his business but retained a claim (note or account receivable) against Bob. The claim became worthless in 2005. Leif's loss is treated as a business bad debt because the debt was created in the conduct of his former trade or business. Leif is accorded business bad debt treatment even though he was holding the note as an investor and was no longer in a trade or business when the claim became worthless. ■

The nonbusiness bad debt provisions are *not* applicable to corporations. It is assumed that any loans made by a corporation are related to its trade or business. Therefore, any bad debts of a corporation are business bad debts.

[4]Reg. § 1.166–5(d).

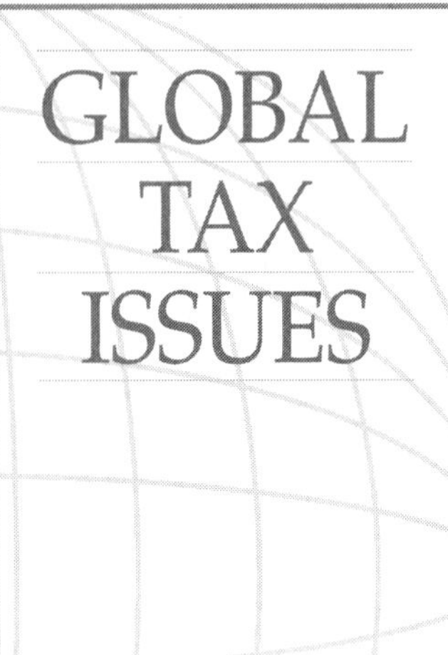

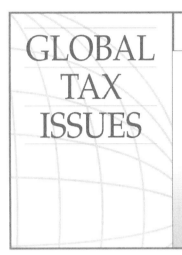

MACAU—THE NEW LAS VEGAS?

Recently, the Las Vegas Sands opened the first U.S.-operated casino in the People's Republic of China in Macau, the former Portuguese colony handed over to the People's Republic by Portugal in 1999. Because gambling is illegal in most of East Asia, including the rest of China, Macau's casino industry is expected to grow rapidly. Some believe that Macau, once best known for its seedy gambling dens, will become the Las Vegas of the East. An issue facing the gambling industry, however, is the fact that casinos cannot write off bad debts against profits. The authorities are reluctant to allow this deduction because Macau gets two-thirds of its tax revenue from gambling profits.

SOURCE: Adapted from Keith Bradsher, "Macau Famously Seedy, Now Bets on Vegas Plush," *The International Herald Tribune*, May 26, 2004, News, p. 1.

LOANS BETWEEN RELATED PARTIES

Loans between related parties (especially family members) raise the issue of whether the transaction was a *bona fide* loan or a gift. The Regulations state that a bona fide debt arises from a debtor-creditor relationship based on a valid and enforceable obligation to pay a fixed or determinable sum of money. Thus, individual circumstances must be examined to determine whether advances between related parties are gifts or loans. Some considerations are these:

- Was a note properly executed?
- Was there a reasonable rate of interest?
- Was collateral provided?
- What collection efforts were made?
- What was the intent of the parties?

EXAMPLE 6

Lana loans $2,000 to her widowed mother for an operation. Lana's mother owns no property and is not employed, and her only income consists of Social Security benefits. No note is issued for the loan, no provision for interest is made, and no repayment date is mentioned. In the current year, Lana's mother dies leaving no estate. Assuming the loan is not repaid, Lana cannot take a deduction for a nonbusiness bad debt because the facts indicate that no debtor-creditor relationship existed. ■

LO.2

Understand the tax treatment of worthless securities including § 1244 stock.

Worthless Securities

A loss is allowed for securities that become *completely* worthless during the year (**worthless securities**).[5] Such securities are shares of stock, bonds, notes, or other evidence of indebtedness issued by a corporation or government. The losses generated are treated as capital losses deemed to have occurred on the *last day* of the taxable year. By treating the loss as having occurred on the last day of the taxable year, a loss that would otherwise have been classified as short term (if the date of worthlessness was used) may be classified as a long-term capital loss. Capital losses may be of limited benefit due to the $3,000 capital loss limitation.[6]

[5] § 165(g).

[6] § 1211(b).

CONCEPT SUMMARY 7–2

Bad Debt Deductions

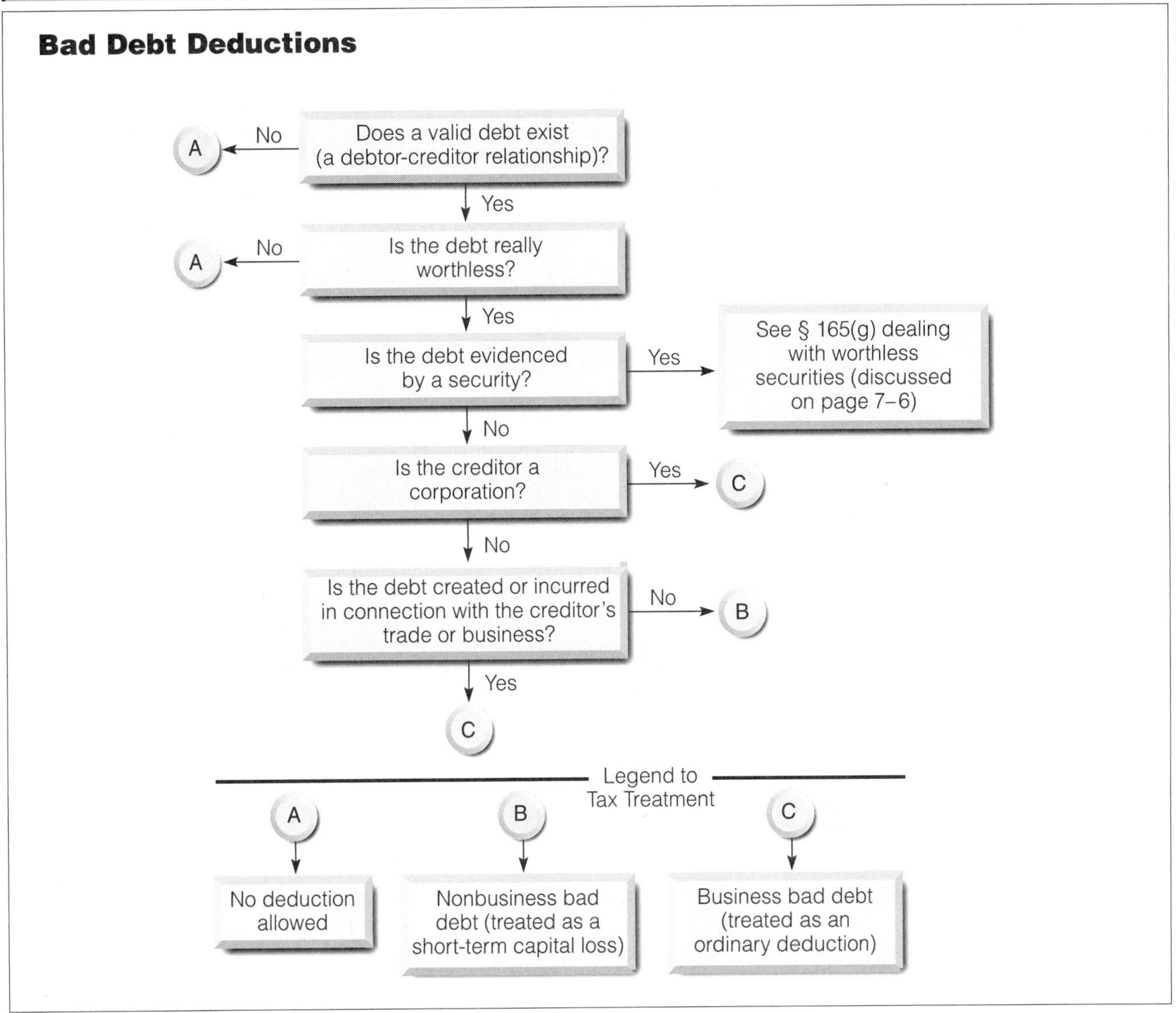

EXAMPLE 7

Ali, a calendar year taxpayer, owns stock in Owl Corporation (a publicly held company). The stock was acquired as an investment on May 31, 2004, at a cost of $5,000. On April 1, 2005, the stock became worthless. Since the stock is deemed to have become worthless as of December 31, 2005, Ali has a capital loss from an asset held for 19 months (a long-term capital loss). ■

SMALL BUSINESS STOCK

The general rule is that shareholders receive capital gain or loss treatment upon the sale or exchange of stock. However, it is possible to receive an ordinary loss deduction if the loss is sustained on **small business stock (§ 1244 stock).** This loss could arise from a sale of the stock or from the stock becoming worthless. Only *individuals*[7] who acquired the stock *from* the corporation are eligible to receive

[7]The term "individuals" for this purpose includes a partnership but not a trust or an estate.

ordinary loss treatment under § 1244. The ordinary loss treatment is limited to $50,000 ($100,000 for married individuals filing jointly) per year. Losses on § 1244 stock in excess of the statutory limits receive capital loss treatment.

The corporation must meet certain requirements for the loss on § 1244 stock to be treated as an *ordinary*—rather than a capital—loss. The major requirement is that the total amount of money and other property received by the corporation for stock as a contribution to capital (or paid-in surplus) does not exceed $1 million. The $1 million test is made at the time the stock is issued. Section 1244 stock can be common or preferred stock. Section 1244 applies only to losses. If § 1244 stock is sold at a gain, the Section is not applicable, and the gain is capital gain.

EXAMPLE 8

On July 1, 2003, Iris, a single individual, purchased 100 shares of Eagle Corporation common stock for $100,000. The Eagle stock qualifies as § 1244 stock. On June 20, 2005, Iris sells all of the Eagle stock for $20,000. Because the Eagle stock is § 1244 stock, Iris has $50,000 of ordinary loss and $30,000 of long-term capital loss. ■

LO.3

Distinguish between deductible and nondeductible losses of individuals.

Losses of Individuals

An individual may deduct the following losses under § 165(c):

- Losses incurred in a trade or business.
- Losses incurred in a transaction entered into for profit.
- Losses caused by fire, storm, shipwreck, or other casualty or by theft.

An individual taxpayer may deduct losses to property used in the taxpayer's trade or business or losses to property used in a transaction entered into for profit. Examples include a loss on property used in a proprietorship, a loss on property held for rent, or a loss on stolen bearer bonds. Note that an individual's losses on property used in a trade or business or on transactions entered into for profit are not limited to losses caused by fire, storm, shipwreck, or other casualty or by theft.

An individual taxpayer suffering losses from damage to nonbusiness property can deduct only those losses attributable to fire, storm, shipwreck, or other casualty or theft. Although the meaning of the terms *fire, storm, shipwreck,* and *theft* is relatively free from dispute, the term *other casualty* needs further clarification. It means casualties analogous to fire, storm, or shipwreck. The term also includes accidental loss of property provided the loss qualifies under the same rules as any other casualty. These rules are that the loss must result from an event that is (1) identifiable; (2) damaging to property; and (3) sudden, unexpected, and unusual in nature.

A *sudden event* is one that is swift and precipitous and not gradual or progressive. An *unexpected event* is an event that is ordinarily unanticipated and occurs without the intent of the individual who suffers the loss. An *unusual event* is one that is extraordinary and nonrecurring and does not commonly occur during the activity in which the taxpayer was engaged when the destruction occurred.[8] Examples include hurricanes, tornadoes, floods, storms, shipwrecks, fires, auto accidents, mine cave-ins, sonic booms, and vandalism. Weather that causes damages (drought, for example) must be unusual and severe for the particular region. Damage must be to the taxpayer's property to qualify as a **casualty loss.**

[8] Rev.Rul. 72–592, 1972–2 C.B. 101.

ETHICAL CONSIDERATIONS

What Is a Casualty Loss?

Casualty loss deductions are limited when the losses involve property not connected with a trade or business or a transaction entered into for profit. To be eligible for deduction, such losses must arise from fire, storm, shipwreck, or other casualty or from theft.

Joe purchased a home for $150,000. Shortly after Joe moved into his home, his neighbors began harassing him and vandalizing his property. Joe notified the police but felt that they did little to stop the harassment. Because Joe could not resolve his problems with his neighbors, he sold his house for $110,000 and moved. Joe plans to take the $40,000 loss he incurred on the sale of his house as a casualty loss on his current-year tax return.

Evaluate Joe's plan.

A taxpayer can take a deduction for a casualty loss from an automobile accident only if the damage was not caused by the taxpayer's willful act or willful negligence.

EXAMPLE 9

Ted parks his car on a hill and fails to set the brake properly and to curb the wheels. As a result of Ted's negligence, the car rolls down the hill and is damaged. The repairs to Ted's car should qualify for casualty loss treatment since Ted's act of negligence appears to be simple rather than willful. ■

LO.4

Identify a casualty and determine the amount, classification, and timing of casualty and theft losses.

EVENTS THAT ARE NOT CASUALTIES

Not all acts of God are treated as casualty losses for income tax purposes. Because a casualty must be sudden, unexpected, and unusual, progressive deterioration (such as erosion due to wind or rain) is not a casualty because it does not meet the suddenness test.

Examples of nonsudden events that generally do not qualify as casualties include disease and insect damage. When the damage was caused by termites over a period of several years, some courts have disallowed a casualty loss deduction.[9] On the other hand, some courts have held that termite damage over periods of up to 15 months after infestation constituted a sudden event and was, therefore, deductible as a casualty loss.[10] Despite the existence of some judicial support for the deductibility of termite damage as a casualty loss, the current position of the IRS is that termite damage is not deductible.[11]

Other examples of events that are not casualties are losses resulting from a decline in value rather than an actual loss of the property. No loss was allowed where the taxpayer's home declined in value as a result of a landslide that destroyed neighboring homes but did no actual damage to the taxpayer's home.[12] Similarly, a taxpayer was allowed a loss for the actual flood damage to his property but not for the decline in market value due to the property's being flood-prone.[13]

THEFT LOSSES

Theft includes, but is not necessarily limited to, larceny, embezzlement, and robbery.[14] Theft does not include misplaced items.[15]

---

[9] *Fay v. Helvering*, 41–2 USTC ¶9494, 27 AFTR 432, 120 F.2d 253 (CA–2, 1941); *U.S. v. Rogers*, 41–1 USTC ¶9442, 27 AFTR 423, 120 F.2d 244 (CA–9, 1941).

[10] *Rosenberg v. Comm.*, 52–2 USTC ¶9377, 42 AFTR 303, 198 F.2d 46 (CA–8, 1952); *Shopmaker v. U.S.*, 54–1 USTC ¶9195, 45 AFTR 758, 119 F.Supp. 705 (D.Ct. Mo., 1953).

[11] Rev.Rul. 63–232, 1963–2 C.B. 97.

[12] *H. Pulvers v. Comm.*, 69–1 USTC ¶9222, 23 AFTR2d 69–678, 407 F.2d 838 (CA–9, 1969).

[13] *S. L. Solomon*, 39 TCM 1282, T.C.Memo. 1980–87.

[14] Reg. § 1.165–8(d).

[15] *Mary Francis Allen*, 16 T.C. 163 (1951).

Theft losses are computed like other casualty losses (discussed in the following section), but the *timing* for recognition of the loss differs. A theft loss is deducted in the year of discovery, not the year of the theft (unless, of course, the discovery occurs in the same year as the theft). If, in the year of the discovery, a claim exists (e.g., against an insurance company) and there is a reasonable expectation of recovering the adjusted basis of the asset from the insurance company, no deduction is permitted.[16] If, in the year of settlement, the recovery is less than the asset's adjusted basis, a partial deduction may be available. If the recovery is greater than the asset's adjusted basis, gain may be recognized.

EXAMPLE 10

Keith's new sailboat, which he uses for personal purposes, was stolen from the storage marina in December 2003. He discovered the loss on June 3, 2004, and filed a claim with his insurance company that was settled on January 30, 2005. Assuming there is a reasonable expectation of full recovery, no deduction is allowed in 2004. A partial deduction may be available in 2005 if the actual insurance proceeds are less than the lower of the fair market value or the adjusted basis of the asset. (Loss measurement rules are discussed later in this chapter.) ■

WHEN TO DEDUCT CASUALTY LOSSES

General Rule. Generally, a casualty loss is deducted in the year the loss occurs. However, no casualty loss is permitted if a reimbursement claim with a *reasonable prospect of full recovery* exists.[17] If the taxpayer has a partial claim, only part of the loss can be claimed in the year of the casualty, and the remainder is deducted in the year the claim is settled.

EXAMPLE 11

Brian's new sailboat was completely destroyed by fire in 2005. Its cost and fair market value were $10,000. Brian's only claim against the insurance company was on a $7,000 policy that was not settled by year-end. The following year, 2006, Brian settled with the insurance company for $6,000. He is entitled to a $3,000 deduction in 2005 and a $1,000 deduction in 2006. If Brian held the sailboat for personal use, the $3,000 deduction in 2005 is reduced first by $100 and then by 10% of his 2005 AGI. The $1,000 deduction in 2006 is reduced by 10% of his 2006 AGI (see the following discussion on the $100 and 10% floors). ■

If a taxpayer receives reimbursement for a casualty loss sustained and deducted in a previous year, an amended return is not filed for that year. Instead, the taxpayer must include the reimbursement in gross income on the return for the year in which it is received to the extent that the previous deduction resulted in a tax benefit.

EXAMPLE 12

Fran had a deductible casualty loss of $5,000 on her 2004 tax return. Fran's taxable income for 2004 was $60,000. In June 2005, Fran is reimbursed $3,000 for the prior year's casualty loss. Fran includes the entire $3,000 in gross income for 2005 because the deduction in 2004 produced a tax benefit. ■

Disaster Area Losses. An exception to the general rule for the time of deduction is allowed for **disaster area losses,** which are casualties sustained in an area designated as a disaster area by the President of the United States.[18] In such cases, the taxpayer may *elect* to treat the loss as having occurred in the taxable year immediately *preceding* the taxable year in which the disaster actually occurred. The rationale for this exception is to provide immediate relief to disaster victims in the form of accelerated tax benefits.

[16] Reg. §§ 1.165–1(d)(2) and 1.165–8(a)(2).

[17] Reg. § 1.165–1(d)(2)(i).

[18] § 165(h).

If the due date, plus extensions, for the prior year's return has not passed, a taxpayer makes the election to claim the disaster area loss on the prior year's tax return. If the disaster occurs after the prior year's return has been filed, it is necessary to file either an amended return or a refund claim. In any case, the taxpayer must show clearly that such an election is being made.

Disaster loss treatment also applies in the case of a personal residence that has been rendered unsafe for use as a residence because of a disaster. This provision applies when, within 120 days after the President designates the area as a disaster area, the state or local government where the residence is located orders the taxpayer to demolish or relocate the residence.[19]

EXAMPLE 13

Janice owns a personal residence in Florida. On September 28, 2005, a hurricane severely damaged Janice's home. The amount of her uninsured loss was $50,000. Because of the extent of the damage in the area, the President of the United States designated the area a disaster area. Because Janice's loss is a disaster area loss, she may elect to file an amended return for 2004 and take the loss in that year. If Janice elects this course of action, the amount of the loss will be reduced first by $100 and then by 10% of her 2004 AGI. If Janice forgoes the election, she may take the loss on her 2005 income tax return. The amount of the loss will be reduced first by $100 and then by 10% of her 2005 AGI. ■

MEASURING THE AMOUNT OF LOSS

Amount of Loss. The rules for determining the amount of a loss depend in part on whether business use, income-producing use, or personal use property was involved. Another factor that must be considered is whether the property was partially or completely destroyed.

If business property or property held for the production of income (e.g., rental property) is *completely destroyed*, the loss is equal to the adjusted basis of the property at the time of destruction.

EXAMPLE 14

Vicki's automobile, which was used only for business purposes, was destroyed by fire. Vicki had unintentionally allowed her insurance coverage to expire. The fair market value of the automobile was $9,000 at the time of the fire, and its adjusted basis was $10,000. Vicki is allowed a loss deduction of $10,000 (the basis of the automobile). The $10,000 loss is a deduction *for* AGI. ■

A different measurement rule applies for *partial destruction* of business property and income-producing property and for *partial* or *complete destruction* of personal use property. In these situations, the loss is the *lesser* of the following:

- The adjusted basis of the property.
- The difference between the fair market value of the property before the event and the fair market value immediately after the event.

EXAMPLE 15

Kelly's uninsured automobile, which was used only for business purposes, was damaged in a wreck. At the date of the wreck, the fair market value of the automobile was $12,000, and its adjusted basis was $9,000. After the wreck, the automobile was appraised at $4,000. Kelly's loss deduction is $8,000 (the lesser of the adjusted basis or the decrease in fair market value). The $8,000 loss is a deduction *for* AGI. ■

The deduction for the loss of property that is part business and part personal must be computed separately for the business portion and the personal portion.

[19]§ 165(k).

Any insurance recovery reduces the loss for business, production of income, and personal use losses. In fact, a taxpayer may realize a gain if the insurance proceeds exceed the amount of the loss. Chapter 14 discusses the treatment of net gains and losses on business property and income-producing property.

A taxpayer is not permitted to deduct a casualty loss for damage to insured personal use property unless a *timely insurance claim* is filed with respect to the damage to the property. This rule applies to the extent that any insurance policy provides for full or partial reimbursement for the loss.[20]

Generally, an appraisal before and after the casualty is needed to measure the amount of the loss. However, the *cost of repairs* to the damaged property is acceptable as a method of establishing the loss in value provided the following criteria are met:

- The repairs are necessary to restore the property to its condition immediately before the casualty.
- The amount spent for such repairs is not excessive.
- The repairs do not extend beyond the damage suffered.
- The value of the property after the repairs does not, as a result of the repairs, exceed the value of the property immediately before the casualty.[21]

Reduction for $100 and 10 Percent-of-AGI Floors. The amount of the loss for personal use property must be further reduced by a $100 *per event* floor and a 10 percent-of-AGI *aggregate* floor.[22] The $100 floor applies separately to each casualty and applies to the entire loss from each casualty (e.g., if a storm damages both a taxpayer's residence and automobile, only $100 is subtracted from the total amount of the loss). The losses are then added together, and the total is reduced by 10 percent of the taxpayer's AGI. The resulting loss is the taxpayer's itemized deduction for casualty and theft losses.

EXAMPLE 16

Rocky, who had AGI of $30,000, was involved in a motorcycle accident. His motorcycle, which was used only for personal use and had a fair market value of $12,000 and an adjusted basis of $9,000, was completely destroyed. He received $5,000 from his insurance company. Rocky's casualty loss deduction is $900 [$9,000 basis – $5,000 insurance – $100 floor – $3,000 (.10 × $30,000 AGI)]. The $900 casualty loss is an itemized deduction (*from* AGI). ■

When a nonbusiness casualty loss is spread between two taxable years because of the *reasonable prospect of recovery* doctrine, the loss in the second year is not reduced by the $100 floor. This result occurs because this floor is imposed per event and has already reduced the amount of the loss in the first year. However, the loss in the second year is still subject to the 10 percent floor based on the taxpayer's second-year AGI (refer to Example 11).

Taxpayers who suffer qualified disaster area losses can elect to deduct the losses in the year preceding the year of occurrence. The disaster loss is treated as having occurred in the preceding taxable year. Hence, the 10 percent-of-AGI floor is determined by using the AGI of the year for which the deduction is claimed.[23]

Multiple Losses. The rules for computing loss deductions where multiple losses have occurred are explained in Examples 17 and 18.

---

[20] § 165(h)(4)(E).
[21] Reg. § 1.165–7(a)(2)(ii).
[22] § 165(c)(3).
[23] § 165(i).

EXAMPLE 17

During the year, Tim had the following casualty losses:

		Fair Market Value of Asset		
Asset	**Adjusted Basis**	**Before the Casualty**	**After the Casualty**	**Insurance Recovery**
A	$900	$600	$–0–	$400
B	300	800	250	100

Assets A and B were used in Tim's business at the time of the casualty. The following losses are allowed:

Asset A: $500. The complete destruction of a business asset results in a deduction of the adjusted basis of the property (reduced by any insurance recovery) regardless of the asset's fair market value.

Asset B: $200. The partial destruction of a business (or personal use) asset results in a deduction equal to the lesser of the adjusted basis ($300) or the decline in value ($550), reduced by any insurance recovery ($100).

Both the Asset A and Asset B losses are deductions *for* AGI. The $100 floor and the 10%-of-AGI floor do not apply because the assets are business assets. ■

EXAMPLE 18

During the year, Emily had AGI of $20,000 and the following casualty losses:

		Fair Market Value of Asset		
Asset	**Adjusted Basis**	**Before the Casualty**	**After the Casualty**	**Insurance Recovery**
A	$ 900	$ 600	$ –0–	$200
B	2,500	4,000	1,000	–0–
C	800	400	100	250

Assets A, B, and C were held for personal use, and the losses to these three assets are from three different casualties. The loss for each asset is computed as follows:

Asset A: $300. The lesser of the adjusted basis of $900 or the $600 decline in value, reduced by the insurance recovery of $200, minus the $100 floor.

Asset B: $2,400. The lesser of the adjusted basis of $2,500 or the $3,000 decline in value, minus the $100 floor.

Asset C: $0. The lesser of the adjusted basis of $800 or the $300 decline in value, reduced by the insurance recovery of $250, minus the $100 floor.

Emily's itemized casualty loss deduction for the year is $700:

Asset A loss	$ 300
Asset B loss	2,400
Asset C loss	–0–
Total loss	$ 2,700
Less: 10% of AGI (10% × $20,000)	(2,000)
Itemized casualty loss deduction	$ 700

■

STATUTORY FRAMEWORK FOR DEDUCTING LOSSES OF INDIVIDUALS

Casualty and theft losses incurred by an individual in connection with a trade or business are deductible *for* AGI.[24] These losses are not subject to the $100 per event and the 10 percent-of-AGI limitations.

Casualty and theft losses incurred by an individual in a transaction entered into for profit are not subject to the $100 per event and the 10 percent-of-AGI limitations. If these losses are attributable to rents or royalties, the deduction is *for* AGI.[25] However, if these losses are not connected with property held for the production of rents and royalties, they are deductions *from* AGI. More specifically, these losses are classified as other miscellaneous itemized deductions. An example of this type of loss would be the theft of a security. However, theft losses of investment property are not subject to the 2 percent-of-AGI floor on certain miscellaneous itemized deductions (explained in Chapter 9).

Casualty and theft losses attributable to personal use property are subject to the $100 per event and the 10 percent-of-AGI limitations. These losses are itemized deductions, but they are not subject to the 2 percent-of-AGI floor.[26]

PERSONAL CASUALTY GAINS AND LOSSES

If a taxpayer has personal casualty and theft gains as well as losses, a special set of rules applies for determining the tax consequences. A **personal casualty gain** is the recognized gain from a casualty or theft of personal use property. A **personal casualty loss** for this purpose is a casualty or theft loss of personal use property after the application of the $100 floor. A taxpayer who has both gains and losses for the taxable year must first net (offset) the personal casualty gains and personal casualty losses. If the gains exceed the losses, the gains and losses are treated as gains and losses from the sale of capital assets. The capital gains and losses are short term or long term, depending on the period the taxpayer held each of the assets. In the netting process, personal casualty and theft gains and losses are not netted with the gains and losses on business and income-producing property.

EXAMPLE 19

During the year, Cliff had the following personal casualty gains and losses (after deducting the $100 floor):

Asset	Holding Period	Gain or (Loss)
A	Three months	($ 300)
B	Three years	(2,400)
C	Two years	3,200

Cliff computes the tax consequences as follows:

Personal casualty gain	$ 3,200
Personal casualty loss ($300 + $2,400)	(2,700)
Net personal casualty gain	$ 500

[24]§ 62(a)(1).
[25]§ 62(a)(4).
[26]§ 67(b)(3).

CONCEPT SUMMARY 7–3

Casualty Gains and Losses

	Business Use or Income-Producing Property	Personal Use Property
Event creating the loss	Any event.	Casualty or theft.
Amount	The lesser of the decline in fair market value or the adjusted basis, but always the adjusted basis if the property is totally destroyed.	The lesser of the decline in fair market value or the adjusted basis.
Insurance	Insurance proceeds received reduce the amount of the loss.	Insurance proceeds received (or for which there is an unfiled claim) reduce the amount of the loss.
$100 floor	Not applicable.	Applicable per event.
Gains and losses	Gains and losses are netted (see detailed discussion in Chapter 14).	Personal casualty and theft gains and losses are netted.
Gains exceeding losses		The gains and losses are treated as gains and losses from the sale of capital assets.
Losses exceeding gains		The gains—and the losses to the extent of gains—are treated as ordinary items in computing AGI. The losses in excess of gains, to the extent they exceed 10% of AGI, are itemized deductions.

Cliff treats all of the gains and losses as capital gains and losses and has the following:

Short-term capital loss (Asset A)	$ 300
Long-term capital loss (Asset B)	2,400
Long-term capital gain (Asset C)	3,200

■

If personal casualty losses exceed personal casualty gains, all gains and losses are treated as ordinary items. The gains—and the losses to the extent of gains—are treated as ordinary income and ordinary loss in computing AGI. Losses in excess of gains are deducted as itemized deductions to the extent the losses exceed 10 percent of AGI.[27]

EXAMPLE 20

During the year, Hazel had AGI of $20,000 and the following personal casualty gain and loss (after deducting the $100 floor):

Asset	Holding Period	Gain or (Loss)
A	Three years	($2,700)
B	Four months	200

[27] § 165(h).

Hazel computes the tax consequences as follows:

Personal casualty loss	($2,700)
Personal casualty gain	200
Net personal casualty loss	($2,500)

Hazel treats the gain and the loss as ordinary items. The $200 gain and $200 of the loss are included in computing AGI. Hazel's itemized deduction for casualty losses is computed as follows:

Casualty loss in excess of gain ($2,700 – $200)	$ 2,500
Less: 10% of AGI (10% × $20,000)	(2,000)
Itemized deduction	$ 500

■

ETHICAL CONSIDERATIONS

The Amount of a Casualty Loss

In the case of a casualty loss to personal use property, the loss is allowed only to the extent that it exceeds $100 and the net casualty loss for the tax year exceeds 10 percent of AGI. The amount of the loss allowed is the lesser of (1) the decline in the fair market value of the property as a result of the casualty or (2) the adjusted basis of the property.

Milt and his family sold their home, put their belongings in storage units, and rented a smaller residence. Abnormally wet weather during the year caused the storage units to leak badly. Among the items in storage was a large personal library that Milt's wife had inherited from her father many years ago. The collection included books that were leather bound, antebellum, and signed editions. Most of the books suffered water damage and were destroyed beyond repair. Following the damage, Milt had the books appraised. The books were appraised at a replacement value of $35,000. Milt is considering claiming a loss deduction of $35,000 for the damage to the books. Evaluate Milt's plan.

LO.5

Recognize and apply the alternative tax treatments for research and experimental expenditures.

Research and Experimental Expenditures

Section 174 covers the treatment of research and experimental expenditures. The Regulations define **research and experimental expenditures** as follows:

> all such costs incident to the development of an experimental or pilot model, a plant process, a product, a formula, an invention, or similar property, and the improvement of already existing property of the type mentioned. The term does not include expenditures such as those for the ordinary testing or inspection of materials or products for quality control or those for efficiency surveys, management studies, consumer surveys, advertising, or promotions.[28]

Expenses in connection with the acquisition or improvement of land or depreciable property are not research and experimental expenditures. Rather, they increase the basis of the land or depreciable property. However, depreciation on a building used for research may be a research and experimental expense. Only the depreciation that is a research and experimental expense (not the cost of the asset) is subject to the three alternatives discussed below.

[28] Reg. § 1.174–2(a)(1).

The law permits the following *three alternatives* for the handling of research and experimental expenditures:

- Expensed in the year paid or incurred.
- Deferred and amortized.
- Capitalized.

If the costs are capitalized, a deduction is not available until the research project is abandoned or is deemed worthless. Since many products resulting from research projects do not have a definite and limited useful life, a taxpayer should ordinarily elect to write off the expenditures immediately or to defer and amortize them. It is generally preferable to elect an immediate write-off of the research expenditures because of the time value of the tax deduction.

The law also provides for a research activities credit. The credit amounts to 20 percent of certain research and experimental expenditures.[29] (The credit is discussed more fully in Chapter 12.)

EXPENSE METHOD

A taxpayer can elect to expense all of the research and experimental expenditures incurred in the current year and all subsequent years. The consent of the IRS is not required if the method is adopted for the first taxable year in which such expenditures were paid or incurred. Once the election is made, the taxpayer must continue to expense all qualifying expenditures unless a request for a change is made to, and approved by, the IRS. In certain instances, a taxpayer may incur research and experimental expenditures before actually engaging in any trade or business activity. In such instances, the Supreme Court has applied a liberal standard of deductibility and permitted a deduction in the year of incurrence.[30]

DEFERRAL AND AMORTIZATION METHOD

Alternatively, research and experimental expenditures may be deferred and amortized if the taxpayer makes an election.[31] Under the election, research and experimental expenditures are amortized ratably over a period of not less than 60 months. A deduction is allowed beginning with the month in which the taxpayer first realizes benefits from the experimental expenditure. The election is binding, and a change requires permission from the IRS.

EXAMPLE 21

Gold Corporation decides to develop a new line of adhesives. The project begins in 2005. Gold incurs the following expenses in 2005 in connection with the project:

Salaries	$25,000
Materials	8,000
Depreciation on machinery	6,500

Gold incurs the following expenses in 2006 in connection with the project:

Salaries	$18,000
Materials	2,000
Depreciation on machinery	5,700

[29]§ 41. See the information in Chapter 12 on the termination date for the research activities credit.

[30]*Snow v. Comm.*, 74–1 USTC ¶9432, 33 AFTR2d 74–1251, 94 S.Ct. 1876 (USSC, 1974).

[31]§ 174(b)(2).

The benefits from the project will be realized starting in March 2007. If Gold Corporation elects a 60-month deferral and amortization period, there is no deduction prior to March 2007, the month benefits from the project begin to be realized. The deduction for 2007 is $10,867, computed as follows:

Salaries ($25,000 + $18,000)	$43,000
Materials ($8,000 + $2,000)	10,000
Depreciation ($6,500 + $5,700)	12,200
Total	$65,200
$65,200 × (10 months/60 months) =	$10,867

■

The option to treat research and experimental expenditures as deferred expense is usually employed when a company does not have sufficient income to offset the research and experimental expenses. Rather than create net operating loss carryovers that might not be utilized because of the 20-year limitation on such carryovers, the deferral and amortization method may be used. The deferral of research and experimental expenditures should also be considered if the taxpayer expects higher tax rates in the future.

LO.6

Calculate the manufacturers' deduction.

Manufacturers' Deduction

The American Jobs Creation Act of 2004 was enacted to replace certain tax provisions that our world trading partners regarded as allowing unfair advantage to U.S. exports. Among other changes, the Act creates a new deduction based on the income from manufacturing activities (designated as *production activities*). The new **manufacturers' deduction** is contained in § 199 and is effective for taxable years beginning after December 31, 2004.

OPERATIONAL RULES

At present, the manufacturers' deduction is based on the following formula:

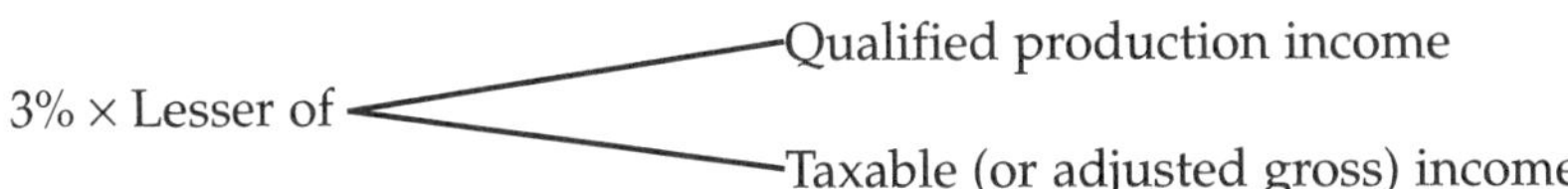

The deduction, however, cannot exceed 50 percent of an employer's W–2 wages.

A phase-in provision increases the 3 percent rate that is applicable for 2005–2006 to 6 percent for 2007 through 2009 and to 9 percent for 2010 and thereafter. Ultimately, therefore, the deduction will be determined under a 9 percent rate.

Eligible Taxpayers. The deduction is available to a variety of taxpayers including individuals, partnerships, S corporations, C corporations, cooperatives, estates, and trusts. For a pass-through entity (e.g., partnerships, S corporations), the deduction flows through to the individual owners. In the case of a sole proprietor, a deduction *for* AGI results and probably will be reflected as a Schedule C item.

EXAMPLE 22

Amanda, a calendar year taxpayer, owns and operates a shop that manufactures costume jewelry. For 2005, she has AGI of $360,000 and qualified production income of $380,000. Amanda's manufacturers' deduction is $10,800 [3% × $360,000 (the lesser of $380,000 or $360,000)]. Thus, Amanda's AGI becomes $349,200 ($360,000 – $10,800). (It has been assumed that the W–2 wage limitation is not a problem.) ■

Eligible Income. **Qualified production income** is the total of qualified production receipts reduced by:

- Cost of goods sold that are attributable to such receipts.
- Other deductions, expenses, or losses that are directly allocable to such receipts.
- A share of other deductions, expenses, and losses that are not directly allocable to such receipts or another class of income.

The term also includes receipts for certain services rendered in connection with construction projects in the United States.

Qualified production receipts do not include proceeds from the sale of food and beverages prepared at a retail establishment.

OBSERVATIONS AND OPERATIONAL PROBLEMS

Although it is called the "manufacturers' deduction," note the broad definition of production receipts. Not only is traditional manufacturing included, but so are other activities such as agriculture, extraction, and construction. Also note that the manufacturers' deduction, unlike the export subsidies it replaced, is not conditioned on the foreign sale of the goods produced. In this regard, domestic and foreign activities will be treated alike.

Because many of the concepts introduced by the manufacturers' deduction are unique, current tax law offers little assistance in resolving the problems that are bound to arise. Some of these are noted in the observations that follow.

- How much activity must take place before manufacturing occurs? For example, is the mere packaging of another's product enough? The law recognizes that production *in part* will suffice, but only if such production is *significant*.
- As to construction projects, qualifying activities are limited to structural improvements—cosmetic changes will not be enough. So, can repainting a house (cosmetic) be accompanied by some sheet rock replacement to make it structural?
- When a taxpayer has integrated businesses with some that qualify as manufacturing and others that do not, manipulation is to be expected. Income will be shifted *to* and expenses will be shifted *from* the businesses that qualify. What safeguards will be imposed to preclude this type of manipulation?

The IRS can be expected to provide answers to these questions and to issue guidelines that will aid taxpayers in utilizing the manufacturers' deduction correctly.

LO.7

Understand the tax impact of a net operating loss and recognize the effect of the carryback and carryover provisions.

Net Operating Losses

The requirement that every taxpayer file an annual income tax return (whether on a calendar year or a fiscal year) may result in certain inequities for taxpayers who experience cyclical patterns of income or expense. Inequities result from the application of a progressive rate structure to taxable income determined on an annual basis. A **net operating loss (NOL)** in a particular tax year would produce no tax benefit if the Code did not provide for the carryback and carryforward of such losses to profitable years.

EXAMPLE 23

Juanita has a business and realizes the following taxable income or loss over a five-year period: Year 1, $50,000; Year 2, ($30,000); Year 3, $100,000; Year 4, ($200,000); and Year 5, $380,000. She is married and files a joint return. Hubert also has a business and has a taxable income pattern of $60,000 every year. He, too, is married and files a joint return. Note that both Juanita and Hubert have total taxable income of $300,000 over the five-year period. Assume there is no provision for carryback or carryover of NOLs. Juanita and Hubert would have the following five-year tax bills:

Year	Juanita's Tax	Hubert's Tax
1	$ 6,770	$ 8,330
2	-0-	8,330
3	18,330	8,330
4	-0-	8,330
5	107,063	8,330
	$132,163	$41,650

The computation of tax is made without regard to any NOL benefit. Rates applicable to 2005 are used to compute the tax.

Even though Juanita and Hubert realized the same total taxable income ($300,000) over the five-year period, Juanita had to pay taxes of $132,163, while Hubert paid taxes of only $41,650. ■

To provide partial relief from this inequitable tax treatment, a deduction is allowed for NOLs.[32] This provision permits NOLs for any one year to be offset against taxable income of other years. The NOL provision is intended as a form of relief for business income and losses. Thus, only losses from the operation of a trade or business (or profession), casualty and theft losses, or losses from the confiscation of a business by a foreign government can create an NOL. In other words, a salaried individual with itemized deductions and personal exemptions in excess of gross income is not permitted to deduct the excess amounts as an NOL. On the other hand, a personal casualty loss is treated as a business loss and can therefore create (or increase) an NOL for an individual.

CARRYBACK AND CARRYOVER PERIODS

General Rules. An NOL must be applied initially to the two taxable years preceding the year of the loss (unless an election is made not to carry the loss back at all). It is carried first to the second prior year, and then to the immediately preceding tax year (or until used up). If the loss is not fully used in the carryback period, it must be carried forward to the first year after the loss year, and then forward to the second, third, etc., year after the loss year. The carryover period is 20 years. A loss sustained in 2005 is used in this order: 2003, 2004, 2006 through 2025.

A three-year carryback period is available for any portion of an individual's NOL resulting from a casualty or theft loss. The three-year carryback rule also applies to NOLs that are attributable to presidentially declared disasters that are incurred by a small business or a taxpayer engaged in farming. A small business is one whose average annual gross receipts for a three-year period are $5 million or less.

If the loss is being carried to a preceding year, an amended return is filed on Form 1040X, or a quick refund claim is filed on Form 1045. In either case, a refund of taxes previously paid is requested. Form 1045 is an application for a tentative refund. The IRS normally will process Form 1045 and pay the refund within 90 days of the date it is filed. When the loss is carried forward, the current return shows an NOL deduction for the prior year's loss.

[32] § 172.

Increased Net Operating Loss Cap

The Pennsylvania General Assembly is considering a measure that would increase the cap on the net operating loss carryover provision. The change would increase the amount from $2 million to $5 million.

SOURCE: Adapted from "Manufacturing Initiatives May Pass Before Summer Recess," *Pennsylvania Law Weekly*, May 10, 2004, News, p. 13.

Sequence of Use of NOLs. When there are NOLs in two or more years, the rule is always to use the earliest year's loss first until it is completely absorbed. The later years' losses can then be used until they also are absorbed or lost. Thus, one year's return could show NOL carryovers from two or more years. Each loss is computed and applied separately.

Election to Forgo Carryback. A taxpayer can *irrevocably elect* not to carry back an NOL to any of the prior years. In that case, the loss is available as a carryover for 20 years. The election is made if it is to the taxpayer's tax advantage. For example, a taxpayer might be in a low marginal tax bracket in the carryback years but expect to be in a high marginal tax bracket in future years. Therefore, it would be to the taxpayer's advantage to use the NOL to offset income in years when the tax rate is high rather than use it when the tax rate is relatively low.

EXAMPLE 24

For 2005, taxpayer and spouse have an NOL of $10,000. The NOL may be carried back and applied against taxable income first in 2003 and then in 2004. Any remaining NOL is carried forward to years 2006 through 2025. If, however, the taxpayer and spouse elect to forgo the carryback period, the NOL initially is carried to 2006 and then to years 2007 through 2025. ■

LO.8

Identify tax planning opportunities in deducting certain business expenses, business losses, and personal losses.

Tax Planning Considerations

TAX CONSEQUENCES OF THE *GROETZINGER* CASE

In the *Groetzinger* case discussed earlier in the chapter, the court established that the appropriate tests for determining if gambling is a trade or business are whether an individual engages in gambling full-time in good faith, with regularity, and for the production of income as a livelihood, and not as a mere hobby. The court held that Robert Groetzinger satisfied the tests because of his constant and large-scale effort. Skill was required and was applied. He did what he did for a livelihood, though with less than successful results. His gambling was not a hobby, a passing fancy, or an occasional bet for amusement. Therefore, his gambling was a trade or business, and hence, he was able to deduct his gambling losses *for* AGI. If the court had ruled that Groetzinger's gambling was not a trade or business, his gambling losses would have been limited to his gambling winnings and would have been classified as itemized deductions.

DOCUMENTATION OF RELATED-TAXPAYER LOANS, CASUALTY LOSSES, AND THEFT LOSSES

Since non-bona fide loans between related taxpayers may be treated as gifts, adequate documentation is needed to substantiate a bad debt deduction if the loan subsequently becomes worthless. Documentation should include proper execution of the note (legal form) and the establishment of a bona fide purpose for the loan. In

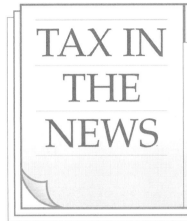

New York at a Disadvantage

The New York Senate's NextGen Task Force has issued a report expressing concern that the state is at a tax disadvantage with the state of New Jersey. In New Jersey, if a highly profitable company buys a start-up company that has net operating losses, the profitable company is allowed to apply those losses against its income and thus decrease its taxable income. According to the chairman of the task force, Dean Skelos, this offset puts emerging New York biotech and high-tech firms at a competitive disadvantage.

SOURCE: Adapted from John Kiernan, "Commentary: NY State Targets Economic Development," *Long Island Business News*, March 19, 2004.

addition, it is desirable to stipulate a reasonable rate of interest and a fixed maturity date.

Since a theft loss is not permitted for misplaced items, a loss should be documented by a police report and evidence of the value of the property (e.g., appraisals, pictures of the property, newspaper clippings). Similar documentation of the value of property should be provided to support a casualty loss deduction because the amount of loss is measured, in part, by the decline in fair market value of the property.

Casualty loss deductions must be reported on Form 4684.

SMALL BUSINESS STOCK

Because § 1244 limits the amount of loss classified as ordinary loss on a yearly basis, a taxpayer might maximize the benefits of § 1244 by selling the stock in more than one taxable year. The result could be that the losses in any one taxable year would not exceed the § 1244 limits on ordinary loss.

EXAMPLE 25

Mitch, a single individual, purchased small business stock in 2003 for $150,000 (150 shares at $1,000 per share). On December 20, 2005, the stock is worth $60,000 (150 shares at $400 per share). Mitch wants to sell the stock at this time. Mitch earns a salary of $80,000 a year, has no other capital transactions, and does not expect any in the future. If Mitch sells all of the small business stock in 2005, his recognized loss will be $90,000 ($60,000 – $150,000). The loss will be characterized as a $50,000 ordinary loss and a $40,000 long-term capital loss. In computing taxable income for 2005, Mitch could deduct the $50,000 ordinary loss but could deduct only $3,000 of the capital loss. The remainder of the capital loss could be carried over and used in future years subject to the $3,000 limitation if Mitch has no capital gains. If Mitch sells 82 shares in 2005, he will recognize an ordinary loss of $49,200 [82 × ($1,000 – $400)]. If Mitch then sells the remainder of the shares in 2006, he will recognize an ordinary loss of $40,800 [68 × ($1,000 – $400)]. Mitch could deduct the $49,200 ordinary loss in computing 2005 taxable income and the $40,800 ordinary loss in computing 2006 taxable income. ■

CASUALTY LOSSES

A special election is available for taxpayers who sustain casualty losses in an area designated by the President as a disaster area. This election affects only the timing, not the calculation, of the deduction. The deduction can be taken in the year before the year in which the loss occurred. Thus, an individual can take the deduction on the 2004 return for a loss occurring between January 1 and December 31, 2005. The benefit, of course, is a faster refund (or reduction in tax). It will also be advantageous to carry the loss back if the taxpayer's tax rate in the carryback year is higher than the tax rate in the year of the loss.

To find out if an event qualifies as a disaster area loss, one can look in any of the major tax services, the Weekly Compilation of Presidential Documents, or the *Internal Revenue Bulletin*.

NET OPERATING LOSSES

In certain instances, it may be advisable for a taxpayer to elect not to carry back an NOL. For an individual, the benefits from the loss carryback could be scaled down or lost due to the economic adjustments that must be made to taxable income for the year to which the loss is carried. For example, a taxpayer should attempt to minimize the number of taxable years to which an NOL is carried. The more years to which the NOL is applied, the more benefits are lost from adjustments for items such as personal and dependency exemptions.

The election not to carry back the loss might also be advantageous if there is a disparity in marginal tax rates applicable to different tax years.

EXAMPLE 26

Abby sustained an NOL of $10,000 in Year 3. Her marginal tax bracket in Year 1 was 15%. In Year 4, however, she expects her bracket to be 35% due to a large profit she will make on a business deal. If Abby carries her loss back, her refund will be $1,500 (15% × $10,000). If she elects not to carry it back to Year 1 but chooses, instead, to carry it forward, her savings will be $3,500 (35% × $10,000). Even considering the time value of an immediate tax refund, Abby appears to be better off using the carryover approach. ■

KEY TERMS

Bad debt, 7–3
Business bad debt, 7–5
Casualty loss, 7–8
Disaster area losses, 7–10
Manufacturers' deduction, 7–18
Net operating loss (NOL), 7–19
Nonbusiness bad debt, 7–5
Personal casualty gain, 7–14
Personal casualty loss, 7–14
Qualified production income, 7–19
Research and experimental expenditures, 7–16
Reserve method, 7–3
Section 1244 stock, 7–7
Small business stock, 7–7
Specific charge-off method, 7–3
Theft loss, 7–10
Worthless securities, 7–6

PROBLEM MATERIALS

West Federal Taxation

Discussion Questions

1. Discuss whether a cash basis taxpayer can take a bad debt deduction.
2. Ron loaned his friend Bob $10,000. Bob used the $10,000 to start a new business. In the current year, Bob notified Ron that he would be unable to repay the $10,000. Discuss whether Ron has a business bad debt, a nonbusiness bad debt, or a nondeductible loss.
3. Discuss whether legal proceedings are necessary to show that a debt is worthless.
4. Discuss the tax treatment for the recovery of an account receivable previously written off as uncollectible.

5. Discuss the application of the nonbusiness bad debt provisions to an individual taxpayer.

6. Discuss whether a bona fide loan can exist between related parties.

Issue ID

7. John was the sole shareholder of Blonde, Inc. The corporation had 26 salaried employees, which included John. Several years ago Blonde began experiencing financial difficulties. As a result, John made several loans to the corporation in an attempt to continue business operations and pay employee salaries. The corporation eventually filed for bankruptcy under Chapter 7 of the bankruptcy code. Upon the final discharge of the corporation's debts, John's loans remained unpaid and were worthless. Identify the relevant tax issues for John with respect to his loans to Blonde, Inc.

8. Mary purchased stocks two years ago for $4,000. At the end of the current year, the stocks are worth only $300. Discuss whether Mary can take a loss for the decline in value of her stocks on her current year's tax return. If so, what is the character of the loss?

9. Discuss the ordinary loss limitations on the sale of § 1244 stock and the advantages of such a characterization.

10. Jim discovers that his sea wall, which protects his home from the ocean, has been extensively damaged by the ocean. Discuss whether he may take a deduction for the damage to the wall.

11. Janice was involved in an automobile accident, and the police cited her for driving under the influence of alcohol. Discuss whether Janice may claim a casualty loss deduction for the damage to her car.

12. Discuss the tax treatment when a taxpayer has a partial claim for a personal casualty loss in 2004 and an additional loss in 2005 when the claim is settled.

13. Discuss the treatment for a reimbursement received for a casualty loss sustained and deducted in a previous tax year.

14. Discuss the measurement rule for partial or complete destruction of personal use property.

15. Discuss the tax consequences of not making an insurance claim when insured personal use property is subject to a loss.

16. Discuss the circumstances under which the cost of repairs to the damaged property can be used to measure the amount of a casualty loss.

17. Jim has a nonbusiness casualty loss that he must spread between two years because of the reasonable prospect of recovery doctrine. Discuss how the 10%-of-AGI floor applies to this casualty loss.

18. Ben sustained a loss on the theft of bearer bonds that he owned. Discuss the tax treatment of the loss on Ben's individual tax return.

19. When casualty losses exceed casualty gains, only the amount of the casualty loss in excess of casualty gains is subject to the 10%-of-AGI floor. Discuss the significance of netting losses against gains in this manner rather than having the entire casualty loss be subject to the 10%-of-AGI floor.

Issue ID

20. Monte owned property containing a pond that was built around 1980. The trees bordering the pond were primarily willows but also included red cedars, sycamores, and cottonwoods. In 2000, a wet, heavy snowfall damaged or destroyed 8 to 10 of the red cedar trees bordering the pond. The weight of the snow also broke many of the other trees. Trees and tree limbs fell into the pond from 2000 to early 2005. Late in 2004 the water became stagnant and polluted because trees had fallen into the pond and had not been removed. Sediment had accumulated in the pond, and brush had grown up around it. By the summer of 2005, the pond was shallow and smelled bad. In late summer of 2005, Monte hired a construction company to restore the pond. The company deepened the pond by removing sediment and trees from the bottom of the pond, rebuilt a road around the levee, removed two peninsulas from the pond, created an island in the pond from sediment dredged from the bottom, and removed trees surrounding the

pond, including some trees that had not been damaged. The construction company charged Monte $40,000 for the work performed. Identify the relevant tax issues for Monte.

Issue ID

21. Henry owned 1,000 acres of unimproved farmland. During the spring of the current year, shortly after Henry had tilled the ground, a storm blew away four inches of topsoil from 60% of his acreage. Identify the relevant tax issues for Henry.

22. Discuss whether depreciation can qualify as a research and experimental expenditure.

23. Discuss the alternatives for the tax treatment of research and experimental expenditures.

Issue ID

24. Power and Light, a public utility company, planned a research and development project. To obtain a construction permit to expand its facilities, the company filed an application with state regulatory agencies and conducted various studies to support its application as required by the agencies. Because the taxpayer's expansion involved both the construction of a nuclear power plant and the installation of an ultrahigh voltage electric transmission line, the agencies required that the company conduct several types of environmental impact studies for site selection. The studies measured specific site conditions and the resulting environmental impact of the construction and operation of the project. The company conducted part of the studies directly and used a research organization to conduct the remainder of the studies on its behalf. Identify the relevant tax issues for Power and Light.

25. Discuss the periods to which an individual taxpayer's 2005 NOL may be carried.

Problems

Communications

26. Several years ago John Johnson, who is not in the lending business, loaned Sara $30,000 to purchase an automobile to be used for personal purposes. In August of the current year, Sara filed for bankruptcy, and John was notified that he could not expect to receive more than $4,000. As of the end of the current year, John has received $1,000. John has contacted you about the possibility of taking a bad debt deduction for the current year.

    Write a letter to John that contains your advice as to whether he can claim a bad debt deduction for the current year. Also, prepare a memo for the tax files. John's address is 100 Tyler Lane, Erie, PA 16563.

27. Sue loaned her sister Janice $10,000 three years ago. Janice has never made any payments to Sue, and Sue has never tried to collect from Janice. This year, Janice filed for bankruptcy and told Sue that she would not be able to repay any of the $10,000 loan. Determine Sue's tax treatment for the loan for the current year.

28. Ron is in the business of purchasing accounts receivable. Last year, Ron purchased an account receivable with a face value of $100,000 for $72,000. During the current year, Ron was notified that he could not expect to collect more than 20 cents on the dollar with respect to the receivable. Determine the maximum amount of the bad debt deduction for Ron for the current year.

29. Mable and Jack file a joint return. For the current year, they had the following items:

Salaries	$180,000
Loss on sale of § 1244 stock acquired two years ago	95,000
Gain on sale of § 1244 stock acquired six months ago	12,000
Nonbusiness bad debt	16,000

Determine their AGI for the current year.

Decision Making

30. Mary, a single taxpayer, purchased 10,000 shares of § 1244 stock several years ago at a cost of $20 per share. In November of the current year, Mary received an offer to sell the stock for $12 per share. She has the option of either selling all of the stock now or selling half of the stock now and half of the stock in January of next year. Mary will receive a salary of $80,000 for the current year and $90,000 next year. Mary will have long-term capital gains of $8,000 for the current year and $10,000 next year. If Mary's

goal is to minimize her AGI for the two years, determine whether she should sell all of her stock this year or half of her stock this year and half next year.

31. During the current year, Jacob's personal residence, some of the contents, and his car were damaged or destroyed by a fire. Information with respect to the damaged and destroyed assets is as follows:

Asset	Adjusted Basis	FMV Before	FMV After	Insurance Recovery
Home	$300,000	$400,000	$350,000	$70,000
Car	60,000	55,000	–0–	20,000
Contents	80,000	60,000	10,000	10,000

If Jacob's AGI is $100,000 before considering the effects of the fire, determine the amount of his deduction for the loss.

Decision Making

32. Olaf owns a 500-acre farm in Minnesota. A tornado hit the area and destroyed a farm building and some farm equipment and damaged a barn. Fortunately for Olaf, the tornado occurred after he had harvested his corn crop. Applicable information is as follows:

Item	Adjusted Basis	FMV Before	FMV After	Insurance Proceeds
Building	$90,000	$ 70,000	$ –0–	$70,000
Equipment	40,000	50,000	–0–	25,000
Barn	90,000	120,000	70,000	25,000

Because of the extensive damage caused by the tornado, the President designated the area as a disaster area.

Olaf, who files a joint return with his wife, Anna, had $174,000 of taxable income last year. Their taxable income for the current year, excluding the loss from the tornado, is $250,000.

Determine the amount of Olaf and Anna's loss and the year in which they should take the loss.

33. Heather owns a two-story building. The first floor houses her business, and the second floor is her personal residence. During the current year, a fire caused major damage to the building and its contents. Heather purchased the building for $800,000 and has taken depreciation of $150,000 on the business portion. At the time of the fire, the building had a fair market value of $900,000. Immediately after the fire, the fair market value was $200,000. The insurance recovery on the building was $600,000. The contents of the building were insured for any loss at fair market value. The first-floor assets had an adjusted basis of $220,000 and a fair market value of $175,000. These assets were totally destroyed. The second-floor assets had an adjusted basis of $130,000 and a fair market value of $65,000. These assets were also totally destroyed. If Heather's AGI is $100,000 before considering the effects of the fire, determine her itemized deduction as a result of the fire. Also determine Heather's AGI.

Decision Making
Communications

34. On July 24 of the current year, Sam Smith was involved in an accident with his business use automobile. Sam had purchased the car for $30,000. The automobile had a fair market value of $20,000 before the accident and $8,000 immediately after the accident. Sam has taken $20,000 of depreciation on the car. The car is insured for the fair market value of any loss. Because of Sam's history, he is afraid that if he submits a claim, his policy will be canceled. Therefore, he is considering not filing a claim. Sam believes that the tax loss deduction will help mitigate the loss of the insurance reimbursement. Sam's current marginal tax rate is 35%.

Write a letter to Sam that contains your advice with respect to the tax and cash-flow consequences of filing versus not filing a claim for the insurance reimbursement for the damage to his car. Also, prepare a memo for the tax files. Sam's address is 450 Colonel's Way, Warrensburg, MO 64093.

35. Blue Corporation, a manufacturing company, decided to develop a new line of merchandise. The project began in 2005. Blue had the following expenses in connection with the project:

	2005	2006
Salaries	$300,000	$400,000
Materials	80,000	70,000
Insurance	10,000	15,000
Utilities	7,000	8,000
Cost of inspection of materials for quality control	4,000	4,000
Promotion expenses	10,000	7,000
Advertising	–0–	30,000
Equipment depreciation	10,000	12,000
Cost of market survey	8,000	–0–

The new product will be introduced for sale beginning in July 2007. Determine the amount of the deduction for research and experimental expenditures for 2005, 2006, and 2007 if:

a. Blue Corporation elects to expense the research and experimental expenditures.
b. Blue Corporation elects to amortize the research and experimental expenditures over 60 months.

36. Nell, single and age 38, had the following income and expense items in 2005:

Nonbusiness bad debt	$ 6,000
Business bad debt	2,000
Nonbusiness long-term capital gain	4,000
Nonbusiness short-term capital loss	3,000
Salary	40,000
Interest income	1,000

Determine Nell's AGI for 2005.

37. Assume that in addition to the information in Problem 36, Nell had the following items in 2005:

Personal casualty gain on an asset held for four months	$10,000
Personal casualty loss on an asset held for two years	1,000

Determine Nell's AGI for 2005.

Cumulative Problems

Tax Return Problem

38. Alan Rice, age 45, and his wife, Ruth, live at 230 Wood Lane, Salt Lake City, UT 84201. Alan's Social Security number is 885–33–3774. Ruth's Social Security number is 885–33–4985. Alan and Ruth had the following items for the year 2005:

- Salary of $100,000.
- Nonbusiness bad debt of $10,000.
- Sale of § 1244 stock resulting in a gain of $25,000. The stock was acquired nine months earlier.
- Rental income of $35,000.
- Rental expenses of $20,000.
- Casualty loss on rental property of $8,000.
- Personal casualty loss (from one event) of $23,000.

- Other itemized deductions of $21,000.
- NOL carryover from 2004 of $14,000.
- Federal income tax withheld of $12,500.

Compute Alan and Ruth's 2005 Federal income tax payable (or refund due). Suggested software: TurboTax.

Tax Return Problem
Decision Making
Communications

39. Jane Smith, age 40, is single and has no dependents. She is employed as a legal secretary by Legal Services, Inc. She owns and operates Typing Services located near the campus of Florida Atlantic University at 1986 Campus Drive. Jane is a material participant in the business. She is a cash basis taxpayer. Jane lives at 2020 Oakcrest Road, Boca Raton, FL 33431. Jane's Social Security number is 123–89–6666. Jane indicates that she wishes to designate $3 to the Presidential Election Campaign Fund. During 2004, Jane had the following income and expense items:
    a. $50,000 salary from Legal Services, Inc.
    b. $20,000 gross receipts from her typing services business.
    c. $700 interest income from Acme National Bank.
    d. $1,000 Christmas bonus from Legal Services, Inc.
    e. $60,000 life insurance proceeds on the death of her sister.
    f. $5,000 check given to her by her wealthy aunt.
    g. $100 won in a bingo game.
    h. Expenses connected with the typing service:

Office rent	$7,000
Supplies	4,400
Utilities and telephone	4,680
Wages to part-time typists	5,000
Payroll taxes	500
Equipment rentals	3,000

    i. $8,346 interest expense on a home mortgage (paid to San Jose Savings and Loan).
    j. $5,000 fair market value of silverware stolen from her home by a burglar on October 12, 2004. Jane had paid $4,000 for the silverware on July 1, 1995. She was reimbursed $1,500 by her insurance company.
    k. Jane had loaned $2,100 to a friend, Joan Jensen, on June 3, 2001. Joan declared bankruptcy on August 14, 2004, and was unable to repay the loan.
    l. Legal Services, Inc., withheld Federal income tax of $7,500 and the required amount of FICA tax.
    m. Alimony of $10,000 received from her former husband, Ted Smith.
    n. Interest income of $800 on City of Boca Raton bonds.
    o. Jane made estimated Federal tax payments of $1,000.
    p. Sales taxes from the sales tax table of $654.

Part 1—Tax Computation
Compute Jane Smith's 2004 Federal income tax payable (or refund due). If you use tax forms for your computations, you will need Forms 1040 and 4684 and Schedules A, C, and D. Suggested software: TurboTax.

Part 2—Tax Planning
In 2005, Jane plans to continue her job with Legal Services, Inc. Therefore, items a, d, and l will recur in 2005. Jane plans to continue her typing services business (refer to item b) and expects gross receipts of $26,000. She projects that all business expenses (refer to item h) will increase by 10%, except for office rent, which, under the terms of her lease, will remain the same as in 2004. Items e, f, g, j, and k will not recur in 2005. Items c, i, m, and n will be approximately the same as in 2004.

Jane would like you to compute the minimum amount of estimated tax she will have to pay for 2005 so that she will not have to pay any additional tax upon filing her 2005 Federal income tax return. Write a letter to Jane that contains your advice and prepare a memo for the tax files. Suggested software: TurboTax.

Research Problems

Note: Solutions to Research Problems can be prepared by using the ***RIA Checkpoint® Student Edition*** *online research product, which is available to accompany this text. It is also possible to prepare solutions to the Research Problems by using tax research materials found in a standard tax library.*

Research Problem 1. Jane was divorced from Bob and was granted custody of their three minor children. Pursuant to a property settlement and support agreement that was incorporated into their divorce decree, Bob was to pay Jane $2,000 per month for child support. During the current year, Bob failed to pay $18,000 of his obligation. Because of Bob's nonpayment, Jane had to spend $18,000 of her own funds in support of the children. Discuss whether Jane is entitled to a nonbusiness bad debt deduction for the amount of her own payment in support of the children caused by Bob's failure to make the court-ordered child support payments.

Partial list of research aids:
Imeson v. Comm., 32 AFTR2d 73–6073, 73–2 USTC ¶9775, 487 F.2d 319 (CA–9, 1973).
Dale A. Swenson, 43 T.C. 897 (1965).

Research Problem 2. James Morgan invested $40,000 in a company that issued him a short-term promissory note bearing an interest rate of 28%. Unbeknownst to James, the company was part of a pyramid scheme. During the current year, James was notified that he had lost his entire investment. Evaluate the possibility of James claiming a theft loss on his current year's tax return.

Internet Activity

Use the tax resources of the Internet to address the following question. Do not restrict your search to the World Wide Web, but include a review of newsgroups and general reference materials, practitioner sites and resources, primary sources of the tax law, chat rooms and discussion groups, and other opportunities.

Research Problem 3. Find a newspaper article that discusses tax planning for casualty losses when a disaster area designation is made. Does the article convey the pertinent tax rules correctly? Then list all of the locations identified by the President as Federal disaster areas in the last two years.

Depreciation, Cost Recovery, Amortization, and Depletion

LEARNING OBJECTIVES

After completing Chapter 8, you should be able to:

LO.1

Understand the rationale for the cost consumption concept and identify the relevant time periods for depreciation, ACRS, and MACRS.

LO.2

Determine the amount of cost recovery under MACRS.

LO.3

Recognize when and how to make the § 179 expensing election, calculate the amount of the deduction, and apply the effect of the election in making the MACRS calculation.

LO.4

Identify listed property and apply the deduction limitations on listed property and on luxury automobiles.

LO.5

Determine when and how to use the alternative depreciation system (ADS).

LO.6

Be aware of the major characteristics of ACRS.

LO.7

Identify intangible assets that are eligible for amortization and calculate the amount of the deduction.

LO.8

Determine the amount of depletion expense including being able to apply the alternative tax treatments for intangible drilling and development costs.

LO.9

Identify tax planning opportunities for cost recovery, amortization, and depletion.

http://wft.swlearning.com

OUTLINE

Overview

LO.1

Understand the rationale for the cost consumption concept and identify the relevant time periods for depreciation, ACRS, and MACRS.

GENERAL

The Internal Revenue Code provides for a deduction for the consumption of the cost of an asset through depreciation, cost recovery, amortization, or depletion. These deductions are applications of the recovery of capital doctrine (discussed in Chapter 4). The concept of depreciation is based on the premise that the asset acquired (or improvement made) benefits more than one accounting period. Otherwise, the expenditure is deducted in the year incurred—see Chapter 6 and the discussion of capitalization versus expense.

Congress completely overhauled the **depreciation** rules in 1981 tax legislation by creating the accelerated **cost recovery** system (ACRS). Substantial modifications were made to ACRS in 1986 tax legislation (MACRS). These changes to the depreciation rules and the time frames involved are noted in Concept Summary 8–1. A knowledge of all of the depreciation and cost recovery rules may be needed as Example 1 illustrates for cost recovery.

EXAMPLE 1

The Brown Company owns a building purchased in 1986 that has a 19-year cost recovery life. In 2005, the business purchased a computer. To compute the cost recovery for 2005, Brown will use the ACRS rules for the building and the MACRS rules for the computer. ■

The statutory changes that have taken place since 1980 have widened the gap that exists between the accounting and tax versions of depreciation. The tax rules that existed prior to 1981 were much more compatible with generally accepted accounting principles.

This chapter initially focuses on the MACRS rules.[1] Because they cover more recent property acquisitions (i.e., after 1986), their use is more widespread. The ACRS rules, however, are reviewed in Concept Summary 8–5 and briefly discussed on page 8–19. The chapter concludes with a discussion of the amortization of intangible property and the depletion of natural resources.

[1]§ 168. The terms "depreciation" and "cost recovery" are used interchangeably in the text and in § 168.

CONCEPT SUMMARY 8–1

Depreciation and Cost Recovery: Relevant Time Periods

System	Date Property Is Placed in Service
Pre-1981 depreciation	Before January 1, 1981, and *certain* property placed in service after December 31, 1980.
Original accelerated cost recovery system (ACRS)	After December 31, 1980, and before January 1, 1987.
Modified accelerated cost recovery system (MACRS)	After December 31, 1986.
Additional first-year depreciation	Acquired after September 10, 2001, and before September 11, 2004, and placed in service before January 1, 2005.
Additional first-year depreciation increased	Acquired after May 5, 2003, and placed in service before January 1, 2005.

Taxpayers may write off the cost of certain assets that are used in a trade or business or held for the production of income. A write-off may take the form of depreciation (or cost recovery), depletion, or amortization. Tangible assets, other than natural resources, are *depreciated*. Natural resources, such as oil, gas, coal, and timber, are *depleted*. Intangible assets, such as copyrights and patents, are *amortized*. Generally, no write-off is allowed for an asset that does not have a determinable useful life.

CONCEPTS RELATING TO DEPRECIATION

Nature of Property. Property includes both realty (real property) and personalty (personal property). Realty generally includes land and buildings permanently affixed to the land. Personalty is defined as any asset that is not realty.[2] Personalty includes furniture, machinery, equipment, and many other types of assets. Do not confuse personalty (or personal property) with *personal use* property. Personal use property is any property (realty or personalty) that is held for personal use rather than for use in a trade or business or an income-producing activity. Write-offs are not allowed for personal use assets.

In summary, both realty and personalty can be either business use/income-producing property or personal use property. Examples include a residence (realty that is personal use), an office building (realty that is business use), a dump truck (personalty that is business use), and regular wearing apparel (personalty that is personal use). It is imperative that this distinction between the *classification* of an asset (realty or personalty) and the *use* to which the asset is put (business or personal) be understood.

Assets used in a trade or business or for the production of income are eligible for cost recovery if they are subject to wear and tear, decay or decline from natural causes, or obsolescence. Assets that do not decline in value on a predictable basis or that do not have a determinable useful life (e.g., land, stock, antiques) are not eligible for cost recovery.

[2]Refer to Chapter 1 for a further discussion.

Placed in Service Requirement. The key date for the commencement of depreciation is the date an asset is placed in service. This date, and not the purchase date of an asset, is the relevant date. This distinction is particularly important for an asset that is purchased near the end of the tax year, but not placed in service until after the beginning of the following tax year.

Cost Recovery Allowed or Allowable. The basis of cost recovery property must be reduced by the cost recovery allowed and by not less than the allowable amount. The *allowed* cost recovery is the cost recovery actually taken, whereas the *allowable* cost recovery is the amount that could have been taken under the applicable cost recovery method. If the taxpayer does not claim any cost recovery on property during a particular year, the basis of the property must still be reduced by the amount of cost recovery that should have been deducted (the allowable cost recovery).

EXAMPLE 2

On March 15, Jack paid $10,000 for a copier to be used in his business. The copier is five-year property. Jack elected to use the straight-line method of cost recovery, but did not take cost recovery in years 3 or 4. Therefore, the allowed cost recovery (cost recovery actually deducted) and the allowable cost recovery are as follows:

	Cost Recovery Allowed	Cost Recovery Allowable
Year 1	$1,000	$1,000
Year 2	2,000	2,000
Year 3	–0–	2,000
Year 4	–0–	2,000
Year 5	2,000	2,000
Year 6	1,000	1,000

If Jack sold the copier for $800 in year 7, he would recognize an $800 gain ($800 amount realized – $0 adjusted basis) because the adjusted basis of the copier is zero. ■

Cost Recovery Basis for Personal Use Assets Converted to Business or Income-Producing Use. If personal use assets are converted to business or income-producing use, the basis for cost recovery and for loss is the *lower* of the adjusted basis or the fair market value at the time the property was converted. As a result of this lower-of-basis rule, losses that occurred while the property was personal use property will not be recognized for tax purposes through the cost recovery of the property.

EXAMPLE 3

Hans acquires a personal residence for $120,000. Four years later, when the fair market value is only $100,000, he converts the property to rental use. The basis for cost recovery is $100,000, since the fair market value is less than the adjusted basis. The $20,000 decline in value is deemed to be personal (since it occurred while the property was held for personal use) and therefore nondeductible. ■

LO.2

Determine the amount of cost recovery under MACRS.

Modified Accelerated Cost Recovery System (MACRS)

Under the **modified accelerated cost recovery system (MACRS),** the cost of an asset is recovered over a predetermined period that is generally shorter than the useful life of the asset or the period the asset is used to produce income. The MACRS rules were designed to encourage investment, improve productivity, and simplify the law and its administration.

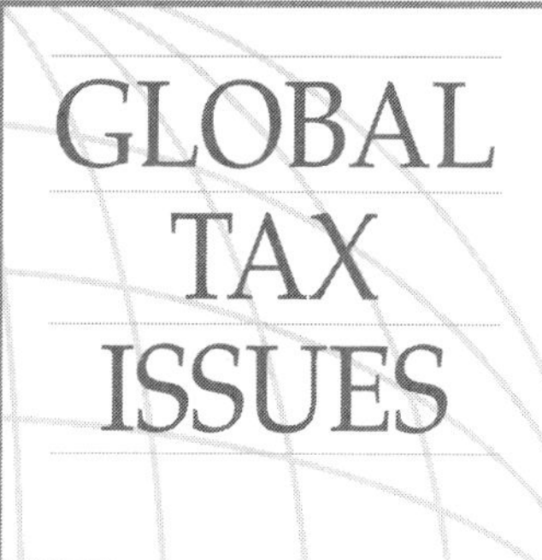

Changing the Life of a Truck

The Australian Tax Office changed the life of a truck, for depreciation computations, from five years to seven and one-half years with the effective date being January 1, 2005. Because of this change, truck operators could reduce their tax liability by buying a new truck before the end of 2004. Under the diminishing value of depreciation method, the write-off was 30 percent for 2004. Starting in 2005, the write-off is only 20 percent.

SOURCE: Adapted from MATP, "Truckload of Tax Savings," *The Daily Telegraph* (Sydney, Australia), September 25, 2004, p. G42.

MACRS provides separate cost recovery tables for realty (real property) and personalty (personal property). Write-offs are not available for land because it does not have a determinable useful life. Cost recovery allowances for real property, other than land, are based on recovery lives specified in the law. The IRS provides tables that specify cost recovery allowances for personalty and for realty.

PERSONALTY: RECOVERY PERIODS AND METHODS

Classification of Property. The general effect of TRA of 1986 was to lengthen asset lives compared to those used under ACRS. MACRS provides that the cost recovery basis of eligible personalty (and certain realty) is recovered over 3, 5, 7, 10, 15, or 20 years. Property is classified by recovery period under MACRS as follows (see Exhibit 8–1 for examples):[3]

3-year 200% class............ ADR midpoints of 4 years and less.[4] Excludes automobiles and light trucks. Includes racehorses more than 2 years old and other horses more than 12 years old.

5-year 200% class............ ADR midpoints of more than 4 years and less than 10 years, adding automobiles, light trucks, qualified technological equipment, renewable energy and biomass properties that are small power production facilities, research and experimentation property, semiconductor manufacturing equipment, and computer-based central office switching equipment.

7-year 200% class............ ADR midpoints of 10 years and more and less than 16 years, adding property with no ADR midpoint not classified elsewhere. Includes railroad track and office furniture, fixtures, and equipment.

10-year 200% class........... ADR midpoints of 16 years and more and less than 20 years, adding single-purpose agricultural or horticultural structures, any tree or vine bearing fruits or nuts.

15-year 150% class........... ADR midpoints of 20 years and more and less than 25 years, including sewage treatment plants, and telephone distribution plants and comparable equipment used for the two-way exchange of voice and data communications.

20-year 150% class........... ADR midpoints of 25 years and more, other than real property with an ADR midpoint of 27.5 years and more, and including sewer pipes.

[3]§ 168(e).

[4]Rev.Proc. 87–56, 1987–2 C.B. 674 is the source for the ADR midpoint lives.

■ EXHIBIT 8–1
Cost Recovery Periods: MACRS Personalty

Class of Property	Examples
3-year	Tractor units for use over-the-road.
	Any horse that is not a racehorse and is more than 12 years old at the time it is placed in service.
	Any racehorse that is more than 2 years old at the time it is placed in service.
	Breeding hogs.
	Special tools used in the manufacturing of motor vehicles such as dies, fixtures, molds, and patterns.
5-year	Automobiles and taxis.
	Light and heavy general-purpose trucks.
	Buses.
	Trailers and trailer-mounted containers.
	Typewriters, calculators, and copiers.
	Computers and peripheral equipment.
	Breeding and dairy cattle.
	Rental appliances, furniture, carpets, etc.
7-year	Office furniture, fixtures, and equipment.
	Breeding and work horses.
	Agricultural machinery and equipment.
	Railroad track.
10-year	Vessels, barges, tugs, and similar water transportation equipment.
	Assets used for petroleum refining or for the manufacture of grain and grain mill products, sugar and sugar products, or vegetable oils and vegetable oil products.
	Single-purpose agricultural or horticultural structures.
15-year	Land improvements.
	Assets used for industrial steam and electric generation and/or distribution systems.
	Assets used in the manufacture of cement.
	Assets used in pipeline transportation.
	Electric utility nuclear production plant.
	Municipal wastewater treatment plant.
20-year	Farm buildings except single-purpose agricultural and horticultural structures.
	Gas utility distribution facilities.
	Water utilities.
	Municipal sewer.

Accelerated depreciation is allowed for these six MACRS classes of property. Two hundred percent declining-balance is used for the 3-, 5-, 7-, and 10-year classes, with a switchover to straight-line depreciation when it yields a larger amount. One hundred and fifty percent declining-balance is allowed for the 15- and 20-year classes, with an appropriate straight-line switchover.[5] The appropriate computation methods and conventions are built into the tables, so it is not necessary to calculate the appropriate percentages. To determine the amount of the cost recovery allowances, simply identify the asset by class and go to the appropriate table for the

[5]§ 168(b).

percentage. The MACRS percentages for personalty appear in Table 8–1 *(all tables are located at the end of the chapter prior to the Problem Materials).*

Taxpayers may *elect* the straight-line method to compute cost recovery allowances for each of these classes of property. Certain property is not eligible for accelerated cost recovery and must be depreciated under an alternative depreciation system (ADS). Both the straight-line election and ADS are discussed later in the chapter.

MACRS views property as placed in service in the middle of the first year (the **half-year convention**).[6] Thus, for example, the statutory recovery period for three-year property begins in the middle of the year an asset is placed in service and ends three years later. In practical terms, this means that taxpayers must wait an extra year to recover the cost of depreciable assets. That is, the actual write-off periods are 4, 6, 8, 11, 16, and 21 years. MACRS also allows for a half-year of cost recovery in the year of disposition or retirement.

EXAMPLE 4

Kareem acquires a five-year class asset on April 10, 2005, for $30,000. Kareem's cost recovery deduction for 2005 is $6,000, computed as follows:

MACRS cost recovery [$30,000 × .20 (Table 8–1)]	$6,000

■

EXAMPLE 5

Assume the same facts as in Example 4 and that Kareem disposes of the asset on March 5, 2007. Kareem's cost recovery deduction for 2007 is $2,880 [$30,000 × ½ × .192 (Table 8–1)]. ■

Additional First-Year Depreciation. The Job Creation and Worker Assistance Act of 2002 provided for **additional first-year depreciation** on qualified property acquired after September 10, 2001, and before September 11, 2004, and placed in service before January 1, 2005. The provision allows for an additional 30 percent cost recovery in the year the asset is placed in service. The term *qualified property* includes most types of *new* property other than buildings. The term *new* means original or first use of the property. Property that is used but new to the taxpayer does not qualify. The Jobs and Growth Tax Relief Reconciliation Act of 2003 increased the additional first-year depreciation allowance percentage from 30 percent to 50 percent. To qualify for the higher percentage, the property must be acquired after May 5, 2003, and placed in service before January 1, 2005. Fifty percent additional first-year property must meet the same requirements as the 30 percent additional first-year property except for the May 5, 2003 acquisition date.[7]

The additional first-year depreciation is taken in the year in which the qualifying property is placed in service and may be claimed in addition to the otherwise available depreciation deduction. After calculating the additional first-year depreciation, the standard cost recovery allowance under MACRS is calculated by multiplying the cost recovery basis (original cost recovery basis less additional first-year depreciation) by the percentage that reflects the applicable cost recovery method and the applicable cost recovery convention.

EXAMPLE 6

Morgan acquires a five-year class asset on March 20, 2004, for $50,000. Morgan's cost recovery deduction for 2004 is $30,000, computed as follows:

50% additional first-year depreciation ($50,000 × .50)	$25,000
MACRS cost recovery [($50,000 – $25,000) × .20 (Table 8–1)]	5,000
Total cost recovery	$30,000

■

[6] § 168(d)(4)(A).

[7] § 168(k).

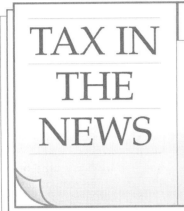

Capital Investment Write-Offs Reduce Corporate Taxes

A study by the Citizens for Tax Justice and its affiliate, the Institute on Taxation and Economic Policy, found that over the last three years the largest and most profitable U.S. companies paid less in corporate income taxes. This decline in tax liability occurred as corporate profits increased. The study attributed the decline in tax payments in part to the changes in the tax laws allowing additional first-year depreciation and increased expensing under § 179.

SOURCE: Adapted from Lynnley Browning, "Study Finds Accelerating Decline in Corporate Taxes," *New York Times*, September 23, 2004, p. C3.

EXAMPLE 7

Assume the same facts as in Example 6, except that the asset was acquired on April 24, 2005. Because additional first-year depreciation is not allowed on property placed in service after December 31, 2004, Morgan's cost recovery deduction for 2005 is $10,000 [$50,000 × .20 (Table 8–1)]. ■

EXAMPLE 8

Assume the same facts as in Example 7 and that Morgan disposes of the asset on October 17, 2007. Morgan's cost recovery deduction for 2007 is $4,800 [$50,000 × ½ × .192 (Table 8–1)]. ■

Mid-Quarter Convention. If more than 40 percent of the value of property other than eligible real estate (see Realty: Recovery Periods and Methods for a discussion of eligible real estate) is placed in service during the last quarter of the year, a **mid-quarter convention** applies.[8] Under this convention, property acquisitions are grouped by the quarter they were acquired for cost recovery purposes. Acquisitions during the first quarter are allowed 10.5 months of cost recovery; the second quarter, 7.5 months; the third quarter, 4.5 months; and the fourth quarter, 1.5 months. The percentages are shown in Table 8–2.

EXAMPLE 9

Silver Corporation acquires the following five-year class property in 2005:

Property Acquisition Dates	Cost
February 15	$ 200,000
July 10	400,000
December 5	600,000
Total	$1,200,000

If Silver Corporation uses the statutory percentage method, the cost recovery allowances for the first two years are computed as indicated below. Since more than 40% ($600,000/ $1,200,000 = 50%) of the acquisitions are in the last quarter, the mid-quarter convention applies.

[8] § 168(d)(3).

2005		
	Mid-Quarter Convention Depreciation	**Total Depreciation**
February 15	$200,000 × .35 (Table 8–2)	$ 70,000
July 10	$400,000 × .15	60,000
December 5	$600,000 × .05	30,000
		$160,000

2006		
	Mid-Quarter Convention Depreciation	**Total Depreciation**
February 15	$200,000 × .26 (Table 8–2)	$ 52,000
July 10	$400,000 × .34	136,000
December 5	$600,000 × .38	228,000
		$416,000

When property to which the mid-quarter convention applies is disposed of, the property is treated as though it were disposed of at the midpoint of the quarter. Hence, in the quarter of disposition, cost recovery is allowed for one-half of the quarter.

EXAMPLE 10

Assume the same facts as in Example 9, except that Silver Corporation sells the $400,000 asset on November 30 of 2006. The cost recovery allowance for 2006 is computed as follows:

February 15	$200,000 × .26 (Table 8–2)	$ 52,000
July 10	$400,000 × .34 × (3.5/4)	119,000
December 5	$600,000 × .38	228,000
Total		$399,000

REALTY: RECOVERY PERIODS AND METHODS

Under MACRS, the cost recovery period for residential rental real estate is 27.5 years, and the straight-line method is used for computing the cost recovery allowance. **Residential rental real estate** includes property where 80 percent or more of the gross rental revenues are from nontransient dwelling units (e.g., an apartment building). Hotels, motels, and similar establishments are not residential rental property. Low-income housing is classified as residential rental real estate. Nonresidential real estate has a recovery period of 39 years (31.5 years for such property placed in service before May 13, 1993) and is also depreciated using the straight-line method.[9]

Some items of real property are not treated as real estate for purposes of MACRS. For example, single-purpose agricultural structures are in the 10-year MACRS class. Land improvements are in the 15-year MACRS class.

All eligible real estate is depreciated using the **mid-month convention.** Regardless of when during the month the property is placed in service, it is deemed to have been placed in service at the middle of the month. This allows for one-half month's cost recovery for the month the property is placed in service. If the property is disposed of before the end of the recovery period, one-half month's cost recovery is permitted for the month of disposition regardless of the specific date of disposition.

[9]§§ 168(b), (c), and (e).

CONCEPT SUMMARY 8–2

Statutory Percentage Method under MACRS

	Personal Property	Real Property*
Convention	Half-year or mid-quarter	Mid-month
Cost recovery deduction in the year of disposition	Half-year for year of disposition or half-quarter for quarter of disposition	Half-month for month of disposition

*Straight-line method must be used.

Cost recovery is computed by multiplying the applicable rate (Table 8–8) by the cost recovery basis.

EXAMPLE 11

Alec acquired a building on April 1, 1993, for $800,000. If the building is classified as residential rental real estate, the cost recovery allowance for 2005 is $29,088 (.03636 × $800,000). If the building is classified as nonresidential real estate, the 2005 cost recovery allowance is $25,400 (.03175 × $800,000). (See Table 8–8 for percentages.) ■

EXAMPLE 12

Assume the same facts as in Example 11, except that Alec acquired the nonresidential building on November 19, 2005. The 2005 cost recovery allowance is $2,568 [$800,000 × .00321 (Table 8–8)]. ■

STRAIGHT-LINE ELECTION

Although MACRS requires straight-line depreciation for all eligible real estate as previously discussed, the taxpayer may *elect* to use the straight-line method for personal property.[10] The property is depreciated using the class life (recovery period) of the asset with a half-year convention or a mid-quarter convention, whichever is applicable. The election is available on a class-by-class and year-by-year basis. The percentages for the straight-line election with a half-year convention appear in Table 8–3.

EXAMPLE 13

Terry acquires a 10-year class asset on August 4, 2005, for $100,000. He elects the straight-line method of cost recovery. Terry's cost recovery deduction for 2005 is $5,000 ($100,000 × .050). His cost recovery deduction for 2006 is $10,000 ($100,000 × .100). (See Table 8–3 for percentages.) ■

LO.3

Recognize when and how to make the § 179 expensing election, calculate the amount of the deduction, and apply the effect of the election in making the MACRS calculation.

ELECTION TO EXPENSE ASSETS

Section 179 (Election to Expense Certain Depreciable Business Assets) permits the taxpayer to elect to write off up to $105,000 in 2005 ($102,000 in 2004) of the acquisition cost of *tangible personal property* used in a trade or business. Amounts that are expensed under § 179 may not be capitalized and depreciated. The **§ 179 expensing** election is an annual election and applies to the acquisition cost of property placed in service that year. The immediate expense election is not available for real property or for property used for the production of income.[11] In addition, any elected § 179 expense is taken *before* the 50 or 30 percent additional first-year depreciation is computed. The base for calculating the standard MACRS deduction is net of the § 179 expense and the 50 or 30 percent additional first-year depreciation.

[10] § 168(b)(5).

[11] §§ 179(b) and (d). The § 179 amount allowed is per taxpayer, per year. On a joint return, the statutory amount applies to the couple. If the taxpayers are married and file separate returns, each spouse is eligible for 50% of the statutory amount.

CHANGING BUSINESS DEDUCTIONS

The Oregon legislature is considering a bill to increase revenues so as to balance the state budget for the next three years. The new law, if enacted, would require companies using sport utility vehicles to add back, in computing Oregon taxable income, the § 179 expense deduction and the bonus depreciation deduction allowed under Federal tax law. The changes affecting business taxes would provide $146 million of the $800 million additional revenue required to balance the state budget.

SOURCE: Adapted from Boaz Herzog, "Businesses Split on Merits of Measure 30," *The Oregonian*, January 19, 2004, p. E01.

EXAMPLE 14

Kelly acquires machinery (five-year class asset) on February 1, 2004, at a cost of $152,000 and elects to expense $102,000 under § 179. Kelly also takes the 50% additional first-year depreciation and the statutory percentage cost recovery (see Table 8–1 for percentage) for 2004. As a result, the total deduction for the year is calculated as follows:

§ 179 expense	$102,000
50% additional first-year depreciation [($152,000 – $102,000) × .50]	25,000
Standard MACRS calculation [($152,000 – $102,000 – $25,000) × .20]	5,000
	$132,000

■

EXAMPLE 15

Assume the same facts as in Example 14, except that the machinery is acquired on February 15, 2005, and Kelly elects to expense $105,000 under § 179. Kelly also takes the statutory percentage cost recovery for 2005. As a result, the total deduction for the year is calculated as follows:

§ 179 expense	$105,000
Standard MACRS calculation [($152,000 – $105,000) × .20]	9,400
	$114,400

■

Annual Limitations. Two additional limitations apply to the amount deductible under § 179. First, the ceiling amount on the deduction is reduced dollar-for-dollar when property (other than eligible real estate) placed in service during the taxable year exceeds $420,000 in 2005 ($410,000 in 2004). Second, the amount expensed under § 179 cannot exceed the aggregate amount of taxable income derived from the conduct of any trade or business by the taxpayer. Taxable income of a trade or business is computed without regard to the amount expensed under § 179. Any § 179 expensed amount in excess of taxable income is carried forward to future taxable years and added to other amounts eligible for expensing. The § 179 amount eligible for expensing in a carryforward year is limited to the *lesser* of (1) the statutory dollar amount ($105,000 in 2005) reduced by the cost of § 179 property placed in service in excess of $420,000 in the carryforward year or (2) the business income limitation in the carryforward year.

CONCEPT SUMMARY 8–3

Straight-Line Election under MACRS

	Personal Property	Real Property*
Convention	Half-year or mid-quarter	Mid-month
Cost recovery deduction in the year of disposition	Half-year for year of disposition or half-quarter for quarter of disposition	Half-month for month of disposition
Elective or mandatory	Elective	Mandatory
Breadth of election	Class by class	

*Straight-line method must be used.

EXAMPLE 16

Jill owns a computer service and operates it as a sole proprietorship. In 2005, she will net $11,000 before considering any § 179 deduction. If Jill spends $491,000 on new equipment, her § 179 expense deduction is computed as follows:

§ 179 deduction before adjustment	$105,000
Less: Dollar limitation reduction ($491,000 – $420,000)	(71,000)
Remaining § 179 deduction	$ 34,000
Business income limitation	$ 11,000
§ 179 deduction allowed	$ 11,000
§ 179 deduction carryforward ($34,000 – $11,000)	$ 23,000

■

Effect on Basis. The basis of the property for cost recovery purposes is reduced by the § 179 amount after it is adjusted for property placed in service in excess of $420,000. This adjusted amount does not reflect any business income limitation.

EXAMPLE 17

Assume the same facts as in Example 16 and that the new equipment is five-year class property. After considering the § 179 deduction, Jill's cost recovery deduction for 2005 (see Table 8–1 for percentage) is calculated as follows:

Standard MACRS calculation [($491,000 – $34,000) × .20]	$91,400

■

Conversion to Personal Use. Conversion of the expensed property to personal use at any time results in recapture income (see Chapter 14). A property is converted to personal use if it is not used predominantly in a trade or business. Regulations provide for the mechanics of the recapture.[12]

LO.4

Identify listed property and apply the deduction limitations on listed property and on luxury automobiles.

BUSINESS AND PERSONAL USE OF AUTOMOBILES AND OTHER LISTED PROPERTY

Limits exist on MACRS deductions for automobiles and other listed property that are used for both personal and business purposes.[13] If the listed property is *predominantly used* for business, the taxpayer is allowed to use the *statutory percentage method* to recover the cost. In cases where the property is *not predominantly used* for business, the cost is recovered using the *straight-line method*.

[12] Reg. § 1.179–1(e).

[13] § 280F.

Spreading the Impact of the § 179 Expense Deduction

In computing Ohio taxable income, taxpayers are not allowed to claim the entire § 179 expense deduction in the year it is taken on the Federal return. The state requires a taxpayer to add back five-sixths of the excess of the § 179 deduction taken on the Federal return over $25,000. In each of the next five years, the taxpayer can deduct one-fifth of the amount that was added back on the Ohio return.

SOURCE: Adapted from Mary Vanac, "Tax Changes Benefit Small Businesses: Limit on Expense Deductions Quadruples, Depreciation Rate Nearly Doubles," *Plain Dealer* (Cleveland, Ohio), March 8, 2004, p. E14.

Listed property includes the following:

- Any passenger automobile.
- Any other property used as a means of transportation.
- Any property of a type generally used for purposes of entertainment, recreation, or amusement.
- Any computer or peripheral equipment, with the exception of equipment used exclusively at a regular business establishment, including a qualifying home office.
- Any cellular telephone or other similar telecommunications equipment.
- Any other property specified in the Regulations.

Automobiles and Other Listed Property Used Predominantly in Business. For listed property to be considered as *predominantly used in business*, its *business usage* must exceed 50 percent.[14] The use of listed property for production of income does not qualify as business use for purposes of the more-than-50 percent test. However, both production of income and business use percentages are used to compute the cost recovery deduction.

EXAMPLE 18

On September 1, 2005, Emma places in service listed five-year recovery property. The property cost $10,000. If Emma uses the property 40% for business and 25% for the production of income, the property is not considered as predominantly used for business. The cost is recovered using straight-line cost recovery. Emma's cost recovery allowance for the year is $650 ($10,000 × 10% × 65%). If, however, Emma uses the property 60% for business and 25% for the production of income, the property is considered as used predominantly for business. Therefore, she may use the statutory percentage method. Emma's cost recovery allowance for the year is $1,700 ($10,000 × .200 × 85%). ■

The method for determining the percentage of business usage for listed property is specified in the Regulations. The Regulations provide that for automobiles a mileage-based percentage is to be used. Other listed property is to use the most appropriate unit of time (e.g., hours) the property is actually used (rather than available for use).[15]

Limits on Cost Recovery for Automobiles. The law places special limitations on the cost recovery deduction for passenger automobiles. These statutory dollar limits were imposed on passenger automobiles because of the belief that the tax

[14] § 280F(b)(3).

[15] Reg. § 1.280F–6T(e).

system was being used to underwrite automobiles whose cost and luxury far exceeded what was needed for their business use.

A *passenger automobile* is any four-wheeled vehicle manufactured for use on public streets, roads, and highways with an unloaded gross vehicle weight (GVW) rating of 6,000 pounds or less.[16] This definition specifically excludes vehicles used directly in the business of transporting people or property for compensation such as taxicabs, ambulances, hearses, and trucks and vans as prescribed by the Regulations.

The following limits apply to the cost recovery deductions for passenger automobiles for 2004:[17]

Year	Recovery Limitation*
1	$2,960
2	4,800
3	2,850
Succeeding years until the cost is recovered	1,675

*The indexed amounts for 2005 were not available at the time of this writing.

There are also separate cost recovery limitations for trucks and vans and for electric automobiles. Because these limitations are applied in the same manner as those imposed on passenger automobiles, these additional limitations are not discussed further in this chapter.

The limits are imposed before any percentage reduction for personal use. In addition, the limitation in the first year includes any amount the taxpayer elects to expense under § 179.[18] If the passenger automobile is used partly for personal use, the personal use percentage is ignored for the purpose of determining the unrecovered cost available for deduction in later years.

EXAMPLE 19

On July 1, 2005, Dan places in service a new automobile that cost $40,000. He does not elect § 179 expensing. The car is always used 80% for business and 20% for personal. Dan chooses the MACRS 200% declining-balance method of cost recovery (see the 5-year column in Table 8–1). The depreciation computation for 2005–2010 is summarized below:

Year	MACRS Amount	Recovery Limitation	Depreciation Allowed
2005	$6,400 ($40,000 × 20% × 80%)	$2,368 ($2,960 × 80%)	$2,368
2006	$10,240 ($40,000 × 32% × 80%)	$3,840 ($4,800 × 80%)	$3,840
2007	$6,144 ($40,000 × 19.2% × 80%)	$2,280 ($2,850 × 80%)	$2,280
2008	$3,686 ($40,000 × 11.52% × 80%)	$1,340 ($1,675 × 80%)	$1,340
2009	$3,686 ($40,000 × 11.52% × 80%)	$1,340 ($1,675 × 80%)	$1,340
2010	$1,843 ($40,000 × 5.76% × 80%)	$1,340 ($1,675 × 80%)	$1,340

[16] § 280F(d)(5).

[17] § 280F(a)(1). Since the 2005 indexed amounts were not available at the time of this writing, the 2004 amounts are used in the Examples and in the Problem Materials.

[18] § 280F(d)(1).

The cost recovery allowed is the lesser of the MACRS amount or the recovery limitation. If Dan continues to use the car after 2010, his cost recovery is limited to the lesser of the recoverable basis or the recovery limitation (i.e., $1,675 × business use percentage). For this purpose, the recoverable basis is computed as if the full recovery limitation was allowed even if it was not. Thus, the recoverable basis as of January 1, 2011, is $24,365 ($40,000 – $2,960 – $4,800 – $2,850 – $1,675 – $1,675 – $1,675). ■

The cost recovery limitations are maximum amounts. If the regular calculation produces a lesser amount of cost recovery, the lesser amount is used.

EXAMPLE 20

On April 2, 2005, Gail places in service a used automobile that cost $10,000. The car is always used 70% for business and 30% for personal use. Therefore, the cost recovery allowance for 2005 is $1,400 ($10,000 × 20% × 70%), which is less than $2,072 ($2,960 × 70%). ■

Note that the cost recovery limitations apply *only* to passenger automobiles and not to other listed property.

Special Limitation. The American Jobs Creation Act of 2004 (AJCA) placed a limit on the § 179 deduction for certain vehicles not subject to the statutory dollar limits on cost recovery deductions that are imposed on passenger automobiles. This new limit is $25,000. The limit applies to sport utility vehicles with an unloaded GVW rating of more than 6,000 pounds and not more than 14,000 pounds.[19]

EXAMPLE 21

During 2005, Jay acquires and places in service a sport utility vehicle that cost $70,000 and has a GVW of 8,000 pounds. Jay uses the vehicle 100% of the time for business use. The total deduction for 2005 with respect to the SUV is $34,000, computed as follows:

§ 179 expense	$25,000
Standard MACRS calculation	
[($70,000 – $25,000) × .20 (Table 8–1)]	9,000
	$34,000

■

Automobiles and Other Listed Property Not Used Predominantly in Business. The cost of listed property that does not pass the more-than-50 percent business usage test in the year the property is placed in service must be recovered using the straight-line method.[20] The straight-line method to be used is that required under the alternative depreciation system (explained later in the chapter). This system requires a straight-line recovery period of five years for automobiles. However, even though the straight-line method is used, the cost recovery allowance for passenger automobiles cannot exceed the dollar limitations.

EXAMPLE 22

On July 27, 2005, Fred places in service an automobile that cost $20,000. The auto is used 40% for business and 60% for personal use. The cost recovery allowance for 2005 is $800 [$20,000 × 10% (Table 8–5) × 40%]. ■

EXAMPLE 23

Assume the same facts as in Example 22, except that the automobile cost $50,000. The cost recovery allowance for 2005 is $1,184 [$50,000 × 10% (Table 8–5) = $5,000 (limited to $2,960) × 40%]. ■

If the listed property fails the more-than-50 percent business usage test, the straight-line method must be used for the remainder of the property's life. This applies even if at some later date the business usage of the property increases to

[19] § 179(b)(6). The effective date for this provision is for vehicles placed in service after October 22, 2004, the date of enactment for the AJCA.

[20] § 280F(b)(1).

more than 50 percent. Even though the straight-line method must continue to be used, however, the amount of cost recovery will reflect the increase in business usage.

EXAMPLE 24

Assume the same facts as in Example 23, except that in 2006, Fred uses the automobile 70% for business and 30% for personal use. Fred's cost recovery allowance for 2006 is $2,800 [$20,000 × 20% (Table 8–5) × 70%], which is less than 70% of the second-year limit. ■

Change from Predominantly Business Use. If the business use percentage of listed property falls to 50 percent or lower after the year the property is placed in service, the property is subject to *cost recovery recapture*. The amount required to be recaptured and included in the taxpayer's return as ordinary income is the excess cost recovery.

Excess cost recovery is the excess of the cost recovery deduction taken in prior years using the statutory percentage method over the amount that would have been allowed if the straight-line method had been used since the property was placed in service.[21]

EXAMPLE 25

Seth purchased a car on January 22, 2005, at a cost of $20,000. Business usage was 80% in 2005, 70% in 2006, 40% in 2007, and 60% in 2008. Seth's excess cost recovery to be recaptured as ordinary income in 2007 is computed as follows:

2005	
MACRS [($20,000 × .20 × .80) (limited to $2,960) × .80]	$ 2,368
Straight-line [($20,000 × .10 × .80) (limited to $2,960) × .80]	(1,600)
Excess	$ 768
2006	
MACRS [($20,000 × .32 × .70) (limited to $4,800) × .70]	$ 3,360
Straight-line [($20,000 × .20 × .70) (limited to $4,800) × .70]	(2,800)
Excess	$ 560
2007	
2005 excess	$ 768
2006 excess	560
Ordinary income recapture	$ 1,328

■

After the business usage of the listed property drops below the more-than-50 percent level, the straight-line method must be used for the remaining life of the property.

EXAMPLE 26

Assume the same facts as in Example 25. Seth's cost recovery allowance for the years 2007 and 2008 would be $1,140 and $1,005, computed as follows:

2007—$1,140	[($20,000 × 20% × .40) limited to $2,850 × 40%]
2008—$1,005	[($20,000 × 20% × .60) limited to $1,675 × 60%]

■

[21] § 280F(b)(2).

Leased Automobiles. A taxpayer who leases a passenger automobile must report an *inclusion amount* in gross income. The inclusion amount is computed from an IRS table for each taxable year for which the taxpayer leases the automobile. The purpose of this provision is to prevent taxpayers from circumventing the cost recovery dollar limitations by leasing, instead of purchasing, an automobile.

The dollar amount of the inclusion is based on the fair market value of the automobile and is prorated for the number of days the auto is used during the taxable year. The prorated dollar amount is then multiplied by the business and income-producing usage percentage to determine the amount to be included in gross income.[22] The taxpayer deducts the lease payments, multiplied by the business and income-producing usage percentage. The net effect is that the annual deduction for the lease payment is reduced by the inclusion amount.

EXAMPLE 27

On April 1, 2005, Jim leases and places in service a passenger automobile worth $40,000. The lease is to be for a period of five years. During the taxable years 2005 and 2006, Jim uses the automobile 70% for business and 30% for personal use. Assuming the dollar amounts from the IRS table for 2005 and 2006 are $83 and $184, Jim must include $44 in gross income for 2005 and $129 for 2006, computed as follows:

2005	$83 × (275/365) × 70% = $44
2006	$184 × (365/365) × 70% = $129

In addition, Jim can deduct 70% of the lease payments each year because this is the business use percentage. ■

Substantiation Requirements. Listed property is now subject to the substantiation requirements of § 274. This means that the taxpayer must prove the business usage as to the amount of expense or use, the time and place of use, the business purpose for the use, and the business relationship to the taxpayer of persons using the property. Substantiation requires adequate records or sufficient evidence corroborating the taxpayer's statement. However, these substantiation requirements do not apply to vehicles that, by reason of their nature, are not likely to be used more than a *de minimis* amount for personal purposes.[23]

ETHICAL CONSIDERATIONS

Substantiating Business Usage of an Automobile

Joan operates a store in the city and uses her farmhouse on rural property 10 miles from the store for business meetings and storage. Joan works seven days a week and spends some nights in an apartment above the store and others at the farmhouse. She owns an Acura MDX that she uses to drive between the store and the farmhouse. Joan keeps a record of the business use of the SUV, but the record is very incomplete and lists the business usage for only about half of the weeks during the year. Joan is planning to take a statistical sampling from the records she has kept and extrapolate her results to determine her business usage for the SUV. She will use the automatic mileage method with these extrapolated results to determine her deductible expense for the year. Evaluate Joan's plan.

[22] Reg. § 1.280F–7(a).
[23] §§ 274(d) and (i).

CONCEPT SUMMARY 8–4

Listed Property Cost Recovery

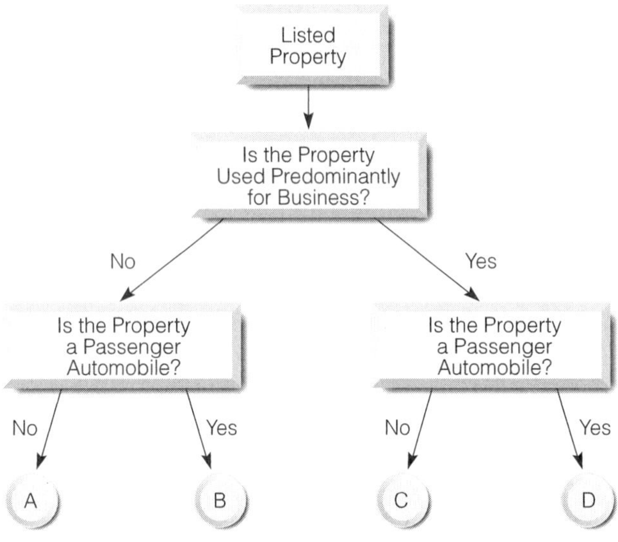

Legend to Tax Treatment

A Straight-line cost recovery reduced by the personal use percentage.

B Straight-line cost recovery subject to the recovery limitations ($2,960, $4,800, $2,850, $1,675) and reduced by the personal use percentage.

C Statutory percentage cost recovery reduced by the personal use percentage.

D Statutory percentage cost recovery subject to the recovery limitations ($2,960, $4,800, $2,850, $1,675) and reduced by the personal use percentage.

LO.5

Determine when and how to use the alternative depreciation system (ADS).

ALTERNATIVE DEPRECIATION SYSTEM (ADS)

The **alternative depreciation system (ADS)** must be used for the following:[24]

- To calculate the portion of depreciation treated as an alternative minimum tax (AMT) adjustment for purposes of the corporate and individual AMT (see Chapter 15).[25]
- To compute depreciation allowances for property for which any of the following is true:
  - Used predominantly outside the United States.
  - Leased or otherwise used by a tax-exempt entity.
  - Financed with the proceeds of tax-exempt bonds.
  - Imported from foreign countries that maintain discriminatory trade practices or otherwise engage in discriminatory acts.
- To compute depreciation allowances for earnings and profits purposes (see Chapter 19).

In general, ADS depreciation is computed using straight-line recovery without regard to salvage value. However, for purposes of the AMT, depreciation of

[24]§ 168(g).

[25]This AMT adjustment applies for real and personal property placed in service before January 1, 1999. However, it will continue to apply for personal property placed in service after December 31, 1998, if the taxpayer uses the 200% declining-balance method for regular income tax purposes. See Chapter 15.

personal property is computed using the 150 percent declining-balance method with an appropriate switch to the straight-line method.

The taxpayer must use the half-year or the mid-quarter convention, whichever is applicable, for all property other than eligible real estate. The mid-month convention is used for eligible real estate. The applicable ADS rates are found in Tables 8–4, 8–5, and 8–9.

The recovery periods under ADS are as follows:[26]

- The ADR midpoint life for property that does not fall into any of the following listed categories.
- Five years for qualified technological equipment, automobiles, and light-duty trucks.
- Twelve years for personal property with no class life.
- Forty years for all residential rental property and all nonresidential real property.

Taxpayers may *elect* to use the 150 percent declining-balance method to compute the regular income tax rather than the 200 percent declining-balance method that is available for personal property. Hence, if the election is made, there will be no difference between the cost recovery for computing the regular income tax and the AMT.[27]

EXAMPLE 28

On March 1, 2005, Abby purchases computer-based telephone central office switching equipment for $80,000. If Abby uses statutory percentage cost recovery (assuming no § 179 election), the cost recovery allowance for 2005 is $16,000 [$80,000 × 20% (Table 8–1, five-year class property)]. If Abby elects to use ADS 150% declining-balance cost recovery for the regular income tax (assuming no § 179 election), the cost recovery allowance for 2005 is $12,000 [$80,000 × 15% (Table 8–4, five-year class property)]. ■

In lieu of depreciation under the regular MACRS method, taxpayers may *elect* straight-line under ADS for property that qualifies for the regular MACRS method. The election is available on a class-by-class and year-by-year basis for property other than eligible real estate. The election for eligible real estate is on a property-by-property basis. One reason for making this election is to avoid a difference between deductible depreciation and earnings and profits depreciation.

EXAMPLE 29

Polly acquires an apartment building on March 17, 2005, for $700,000. She takes the maximum cost recovery allowance for determining taxable income. Polly's cost recovery allowance for computing 2005 taxable income is $20,153 [$700,000 × .02879 (Table 8–8)]. However, Polly's cost recovery for computing her earnings and profits is only $13,853 [$700,000 × .01979 (Table 8–9)]. ■

LO.6

Be aware of the major characteristics of ACRS.

Accelerated Cost Recovery System (ACRS)

The major characteristics of the **accelerated cost recovery system (ACRS)** are listed in Concept Summary 8–5. Note that for personalty, except for 20-year property, the recovery period has expired (all of the cost recovery basis has been recovered). For realty, the recovery period will expire in 2005.

[26]The class life for certain properties described in § 168(e)(3) is specially determined under § 168(g)(3)(B).

[27]For personal property placed in service before January 1, 1999, taxpayers making the election are required to use the ADS recovery periods in computing cost recovery for the regular income tax. The ADS recovery periods generally are longer than the regular recovery periods under MACRS.

CONCEPT SUMMARY 8–5

Characteristics of ACRS

Property	Accounting Convention	Life	Method
Personalty	Half-year or mid-quarter	3, 5, 7, 10, 15, or 20 years	Accelerated or straight-line
Realty	Mid-month	15, 18, or 19 years	Accelerated or straight-line

LO.7

Identify intangible assets that are eligible for amortization and calculate the amount of the deduction.

Amortization

Taxpayers can claim an **amortization** deduction on intangible assets called "amortizable § 197 intangibles." The amount of the deduction is determined by amortizing the adjusted basis of such intangibles ratably over a 15-year period beginning in the month in which the intangible is acquired.[28]

An *amortizable § 197 intangible* is any § 197 intangible acquired after August 10, 1993, and held in connection with the conduct of a trade or business or for the production of income. Section 197 intangibles include goodwill and going-concern value, franchises, trademarks, and trade names. Covenants not to compete, copyrights, and patents are also included if they are acquired in connection with the acquisition of a business. Generally, self-created intangibles are not § 197 intangibles. The 15-year amortization period applies regardless of the actual useful life of an amortizable § 197 intangible. No other depreciation or amortization deduction is permitted with respect to any amortizable § 197 intangible except those permitted under the 15-year amortization rules.

EXAMPLE 30

On June 1, 2005, Neil purchased and began operating the Falcon Café. Of the purchase price, $90,000 is correctly allocated to goodwill. The deduction for amortization for 2005 is $3,500 [($90,000/15) × (7/12)]. ■

ETHICAL CONSIDERATIONS

Computing § 197 Amortization

Lime Motors entered into an agreement to buy out Clarissa's interest in Lime Motors. Part of the agreement calls for Lime Motors to pay Clarissa $300,000 for a covenant not to compete for a period of three years. Under the agreement, Clarissa will be paid $5,000 per month plus interest for 60 months. Oscar, the accountant for Lime Motors, intends to expense the payments of $5,000 plus interest because they are to be made over a 60-month period (rather than over the three-year period). Evaluate the appropriateness of Oscar's plan.

LO.8

Determine the amount of depletion expense including being able to apply the alternative tax treatments for intangible drilling and development costs.

Depletion

Natural resources (e.g., oil, gas, coal, gravel, timber) are subject to **depletion,** which is simply a form of depreciation applicable to natural resources. Land generally cannot be depleted.

[28] § 197(a).

The owner of an interest in the natural resource is entitled to deduct depletion. An owner is one who has an economic interest in the property.[29] An economic interest requires the acquisition of an interest in the resource in place and the receipt of income from the extraction or severance of that resource. Like depreciation, depletion is a deduction *for* adjusted gross income.

Although all natural resources are subject to depletion, oil and gas wells are used as an example in the following paragraphs to illustrate the related costs and issues.

In developing an oil or gas well, the producer must make four types of expenditures:

- Natural resource costs.
- Intangible drilling and development costs.
- Tangible asset costs.
- Operating costs.

Natural resources are physically limited, and the costs to acquire them (e.g., oil under the ground) are, therefore, recovered through depletion. Costs incurred in making the property ready for drilling such as the cost of labor in clearing the property, erecting derricks, and drilling the hole are **intangible drilling and development costs (IDC).** These costs generally have no salvage value and are a lost cost if the well is dry. Costs for tangible assets such as tools, pipes, and engines are capital in nature. These costs must be capitalized and recovered through depreciation (cost recovery). Costs incurred after the well is producing are operating costs. These costs would include expenditures for such items as labor, fuel, and supplies. Operating costs are deductible when incurred (on the accrual basis) or when paid (on the cash basis).

The expenditures for depreciable assets and operating costs pose no unusual problems for producers of natural resources. The tax treatment of depletable costs and intangible drilling and development costs is quite a different matter.

INTANGIBLE DRILLING AND DEVELOPMENT COSTS (IDC)

Intangible drilling and development costs can be handled in one of two ways at the option of the taxpayer. They can be *either* charged off as an expense in the year in which they are incurred *or* capitalized and written off through depletion. The taxpayer makes the election in the first year such expenditures are incurred either by taking a deduction on the return or by adding them to the depletable basis. No formal statement of intent is required. Once made, the election is binding on both the taxpayer and the IRS for all such expenditures in the future. If the taxpayer fails to make the election to expense IDC on the original timely filed return the first year such expenditures are incurred, an automatic election to capitalize them has been made and is irrevocable.

As a general rule, it is more advantageous to expense IDC. The obvious benefit of an immediate write-off (as opposed to a deferred write-off through depletion) is not the only advantage. Since a taxpayer can use percentage depletion, which is calculated without reference to basis (see Example 34), the IDC may be completely lost as a deduction if they are capitalized.

DEPLETION METHODS

There are two methods of calculating depletion: cost and percentage. Cost depletion can be used on any wasting asset (and is the only method allowed for timber). Percentage depletion is subject to a number of limitations, particularly for oil and gas deposits. Depletion should be calculated both ways, and generally the method

[29] Reg. § 1.611–1(b).

that results in the *larger* deduction is used. The choice between cost and percentage depletion is an annual election.

Cost Depletion. **Cost depletion** is determined by using the adjusted basis of the asset.[30] The basis is divided by the estimated recoverable units of the asset (e.g., barrels, tons) to arrive at the depletion per unit. The depletion per unit then is multiplied by the number of units sold (*not* the units produced) during the year to arrive at the cost depletion allowed. Cost depletion, therefore, resembles the units-of-production method of calculating depreciation.

EXAMPLE 31

On January 1, 2005, Pablo purchases the rights to a mineral interest for $1 million. At that time, the remaining recoverable units in the mineral interest are estimated to be 200,000. The depletion per unit is $5 [$1,000,000 (adjusted basis) ÷ 200,000 (estimated recoverable units)]. If during the year 60,000 units are mined and 25,000 are sold, the cost depletion is $125,000 [$5 (depletion per unit) × 25,000 (units sold)]. ■

If the taxpayer later discovers that the original estimate was incorrect, the depletion per unit for future calculations must be redetermined based on the revised estimate.[31]

EXAMPLE 32

Assume the same facts as in Example 31. In 2006, Pablo realizes that an incorrect estimate was made. The remaining recoverable units now are determined to be 400,000. Based on this new information, the revised depletion per unit is $2.1875 [$875,000 (adjusted basis) ÷ 400,000 (estimated recoverable units)]. Note that the adjusted basis is the original cost ($1,000,000) reduced by the depletion claimed in 2005 ($125,000). If 30,000 units are sold in 2006, the depletion for the year is $65,625 [$2.1875 (depletion per unit) × 30,000 (units sold)]. ■

Percentage Depletion. **Percentage depletion** (also referred to as statutory depletion) is a specified percentage provided for in the Code. The percentage varies according to the type of mineral interest involved. A sample of these percentages is shown in Exhibit 8–2. The rate is applied to the gross income from the property, but in no event may percentage depletion exceed 50 percent of the taxable income from the property before the allowance for depletion.[32]

EXAMPLE 33

Assuming gross income of $100,000, a depletion rate of 22%, and other expenses relating to the property of $60,000, the depletion allowance is determined as follows:

Gross income	$100,000
Less: Other expenses	(60,000)
Taxable income before depletion	$ 40,000
Depletion allowance [the lesser of $22,000 (22% × $100,000) or $20,000 (50% × $40,000)]	(20,000)
Taxable income after depletion	$ 20,000

The adjusted basis of the property is reduced by $20,000, the depletion allowed. If the other expenses had been only $55,000, the full $22,000 could have been deducted, and the adjusted basis would have been reduced by $22,000. ■

Note that percentage depletion is based on a percentage of the gross income from the property and makes no reference to cost. Thus, when percentage depletion

[30] § 612.

[31] § 611(a).

[32] § 613(a). Special rules apply for certain oil and gas wells under § 613A (e.g., the 50% ceiling is replaced with a 100% ceiling, and the percentage depletion may not exceed 65% of the taxpayer's taxable income from all sources before the allowance for depletion).

■ **EXHIBIT 8–2**
Sample of Percentage Depletion Rates

22% Depletion	
Cobalt	Sulfur
Lead	Tin
Nickel	Uranium
Platinum	Zinc
15% Depletion	
Copper	Oil and gas
Gold	Oil shale
Iron	Silver
14% Depletion	
Borax	Magnesium carbonates
Calcium carbonates	Marble
Granite	Potash
Limestone	Slate
10% Depletion	
Coal	Perlite
Lignite	Sodium chloride
5% Depletion	
Gravel	Pumice
Peat	Sand

is used, it is possible to deduct more than the original cost of the property. If percentage depletion is used, however, the adjusted basis of the property (for computing cost depletion) must be reduced by the amount of percentage depletion taken until the adjusted basis reaches zero.

Effect of Intangible Drilling Costs on Depletion. The treatment of IDC has an effect on the depletion deduction in two ways. If the costs are capitalized, the basis for cost depletion is increased. As a consequence, the cost depletion is increased. If IDC are expensed, they reduce the taxable income from the property. This reduction may result in application of the provision that limits depletion to 50 percent (100 percent for certain oil and gas wells) of taxable income before deducting depletion.

EXAMPLE 34

Iris purchased the rights to an oil interest for $1 million. The recoverable barrels were estimated to be 200,000. During the year, 50,000 barrels were sold for $2 million. Regular expenses amounted to $800,000, and IDC were $650,000. If the IDC are capitalized, the depletion per unit is $8.25 ($1,000,000 + $650,000 ÷ 200,000 barrels), and the following taxable income results:

Gross income	$2,000,000
Less: Expenses	(800,000)
Taxable income before depletion	$1,200,000
Cost depletion ($8.25 × 50,000) = $412,500	
Percentage depletion (15% × $2,000,000) = $300,000	
Greater of cost or percentage depletion	(412,500)
Taxable income	$ 787,500

If the IDC are expensed, the taxable income is $250,000, calculated as follows:

Gross income	$ 2,000,000
Less: Expenses, including IDC	(1,450,000)
Taxable income before depletion	$ 550,000
Cost depletion [($1,000,000 ÷ 200,000 barrels) × 50,000 barrels] = $250,000	
Percentage depletion (15% of $2,000,000 = $300,000, limited to 100% of $550,000 taxable income before depletion) = $300,000	
Greater of cost or percentage depletion	(300,000)
Taxable income	$ 250,000

■

For further restrictions on the use or availability of the percentage depletion method, see § 613.

Tax Planning Considerations

COST RECOVERY

Cost recovery schedules should be reviewed annually for possible retirements, abandonments, and obsolescence.

EXAMPLE 35

An examination of the cost recovery schedule of Eagle Company reveals the following:

- Asset A was abandoned when it was discovered that the cost of repairs would be in excess of the cost of replacement. Asset A had an adjusted basis of $3,000.
- Asset J became obsolete this year, at which point, its adjusted basis was $8,000.

Assets A and J should be written off for an additional expense of $11,000 ($3,000 + $8,000). ■

LO.9 Identify tax planning opportunities for cost recovery, amortization, and depletion.

Because of the deductions for cost recovery, interest, and ad valorem property taxes, investments in real estate can be highly attractive. In figuring the economics of such investments, one should be sure to take into account any tax savings that result.

EXAMPLE 36

In early January 2004, Vern purchased residential rental property for $170,000 (of which $20,000 was allocated to the land and $150,000 to the building). Vern made a down payment of $25,000 and assumed the seller's mortgage for the balance. Under the mortgage agreement, monthly payments of $1,000 are required and are applied toward interest, taxes, insurance, and principal. Since the property was already occupied, Vern continued to receive rent of $1,200 per month from the tenant. Vern actively participates in this activity and hence comes under the special rule for a rental real estate activity with respect to the limitation on passive activity losses (refer to Chapter 11). Vern is in the 33% tax bracket.

During 2005, Vern's expenses were as follows:

Interest	$10,000
Taxes	800
Insurance	1,000
Repairs and maintenance	2,200
Depreciation ($150,000 × .03636)	5,454
Total	$19,454

The deductible loss from the rental property is computed as follows:

Rent income ($1,200 × 12 months)	$ 14,400
Less expenses (see above)	(19,454)
Net loss	($ 5,054)

But what is Vern's overall position for the year when the tax benefit of the loss is taken into account? Considering just the cash intake and outlay, it is summarized below:

Intake—		
Rent income	$14,400	
Tax savings [33% (income tax bracket) × $5,054 (loss from the property)]	1,668	$ 16,068
Outlay—		
Mortgage payments ($1,000 × 12 months)	$12,000	
Repairs and maintenance	2,200	(14,200)
Net cash benefit		$ 1,868

■

It should be noted, however, that should Vern cease being an active participant in the rental activity, the passive activity loss rules would apply, and Vern could lose the current period benefit of the loss.

AMORTIZATION

When a business is purchased, goodwill and covenants not to compete are both subject to a statutory amortization period of 15 years. Therefore, the purchaser does not derive any tax benefits when part of the purchase price is assigned to a covenant rather than to goodwill.

Thus, from the purchaser's perspective, bargaining for a covenant should be based on legal rather than tax reasons. Note, however, that from the seller's perspective, goodwill is a capital asset and the covenant is an ordinary income asset.

Since the amortization period for both goodwill and a covenant is 15 years, the purchaser may want to attempt to minimize these amounts if the purchase price can be assigned to assets with shorter lives (e.g., inventory, receivables, and personalty). Conversely, the purchaser may want to attempt to maximize these amounts if part of the purchase price will otherwise be assigned to assets with longer recovery periods (e.g., realty) or to assets not eligible for cost recovery (e.g., land).

DEPLETION

Since the election to use the cost or percentage depletion method is an annual election, a taxpayer can use cost depletion (if higher) until the basis is exhausted and then switch to percentage depletion in the following years.

EXAMPLE 37

Assume the following facts for Melissa:

Remaining depletable basis	$ 11,000
Gross income (10,000 units)	100,000
Expenses (other than depletion)	30,000

Since cost depletion is limited to the basis of $11,000 and if the percentage depletion is $22,000 (assume a 22% rate), Melissa would choose the latter. Her basis is then reduced to zero. In future years, however, she can continue to take percentage depletion since percentage depletion is taken without reference to the remaining basis. ■

The election to expense intangible drilling and development costs is a one-time election. Once the election is made to either expense or capitalize the IDC, it is binding on all future expenditures. The permanent nature of the election makes it extremely important for the taxpayer to determine which treatment will provide the greatest tax advantage. (Refer to Example 34 for an illustration of the effect of using the two different alternatives for a given set of facts.)

Tables

Summary of Tables

Table 8–1	Modified ACRS statutory percentage table for personalty. Applicable depreciation methods: 200 or 150 percent declining-balance switching to straight-line. Applicable recovery periods: 3, 5, 7, 10, 15, 20 years. Applicable convention: half-year.
Table 8–2	Modified ACRS statutory percentage table for personalty. Applicable depreciation method: 200 percent declining-balance switching to straight-line. Applicable recovery periods: 3, 5, 7 years. Applicable convention: mid-quarter.
Table 8–3	Modified ACRS optional straight-line table for personalty. Applicable depreciation method: straight-line. Applicable recovery periods: 3, 5, 7, 10, 15, 20 years. Applicable convention: half-year.
Table 8–4	Alternative minimum tax declining-balance table for personalty. Applicable depreciation method: 150 percent declining-balance switching to straight-line. Applicable recovery periods: 3, 5, 7, 9.5, 10, 12 years. Applicable convention: half-year.
Table 8–5	Alternative depreciation system straight-line table for personalty. Applicable depreciation method: straight-line. Applicable recovery periods: 5, 9.5, 12 years. Applicable convention: half-year.
Table 8–6	Original ACRS statutory percentage table for realty. Applicable depreciation method: 175 percent declining-balance switching to straight-line. Applicable recovery period: 19 years. Applicable convention: mid-month.
Table 8–7	Original ACRS optional straight-line table for realty. Applicable depreciation method: straight-line. Applicable recovery period: 19 years. Applicable convention: mid-month.
Table 8–8	Modified ACRS straight-line table for realty. Applicable depreciation method: straight-line. Applicable recovery periods: 27.5, 31.5, 39 years. Applicable convention: mid-month.
Table 8–9	Alternative depreciation system straight-line table for realty. Applicable depreciation method: straight-line. Applicable recovery period: 40 years. Applicable convention: mid-month.

■ **TABLE 8–1**
MACRS Accelerated Depreciation for Personal Property Assuming Half-Year Convention

For Property Placed in Service after December 31, 1986

Recovery Year	3-Year (200% DB)	5-Year (200% DB)	7-Year (200% DB)	10-Year (200% DB)	15-Year (150% DB)	20-Year (150% DB)
1	33.33	20.00	14.29	10.00	5.00	3.750
2	44.45	32.00	24.49	18.00	9.50	7.219
3	14.81*	19.20	17.49	14.40	8.55	6.677
4	7.41	11.52*	12.49	11.52	7.70	6.177
5		11.52	8.93*	9.22	6.93	5.713
6		5.76	8.92	7.37	6.23	5.285
7			8.93	6.55*	5.90*	4.888
8			4.46	6.55	5.90	4.522
9				6.56	5.91	4.462*
10				6.55	5.90	4.461
11				3.28	5.91	4.462
12					5.90	4.461
13					5.91	4.462
14					5.90	4.461
15					5.91	4.462
16					2.95	4.461
17						4.462
18						4.461
19						4.462
20						4.461
21						2.231

*Switchover to straight-line depreciation.

■ **TABLE 8–2**
MACRS Accelerated Depreciation for Personal Property Assuming Mid-Quarter Convention

For Property Placed in Service after December 31, 1986 (Partial Table*)

		3-Year		
Recovery Year	First Quarter	Second Quarter	Third Quarter	Fourth Quarter
1	58.33	41.67	25.00	8.33
2	27.78	38.89	50.00	61.11
		5-Year		
Recovery Year	First Quarter	Second Quarter	Third Quarter	Fourth Quarter
1	35.00	25.00	15.00	5.00
2	26.00	30.00	34.00	38.00
		7-Year		
Recovery Year	First Quarter	Second Quarter	Third Quarter	Fourth Quarter
1	25.00	17.85	10.71	3.57
2	21.43	23.47	25.51	27.55

*The figures in this table are taken from the official tables that appear in Rev.Proc. 87–57, 1987–2 C.B. 687. Because of their length, the complete tables are not presented.

■ TABLE 8–3
MACRS Straight-Line Depreciation for Personal Property Assuming Half-Year Convention*

For Property Placed in Service after December 31, 1986

MACRS Class	% First Recovery Year	Other Recovery Years		Last Recovery Year	
		Years	%	Year	%
3-year	16.67	2–3	33.33	4	16.67
5-year	10.00	2–5	20.00	6	10.00
7-year	7.14	2–7	14.29	8	7.14
10-year	5.00	2–10	10.00	11	5.00
15-year	3.33	2–15	6.67	16	3.33
20-year	2.50	2–20	5.00	21	2.50

*The official table contains a separate row for each year. For ease of presentation, certain years are grouped in this table. In some instances, this will produce a difference of .01 for the last digit when compared with the official table.

■ TABLE 8–4
Alternative Minimum Tax: 150% Declining-Balance Assuming Half-Year Convention

For Property Placed in Service after December 31, 1986 (Partial Table*)

Recovery Year	3-Year 150%	5-Year 150%	7-Year 150%	9.5-Year 150%	10-Year 150%	12-Year 150%
1	25.00	15.00	10.71	7.89	7.50	6.25
2	37.50	25.50	19.13	14.54	13.88	11.72
3	25.00**	17.85	15.03	12.25	11.79	10.25
4	12.50	16.66**	12.25**	10.31	10.02	8.97
5		16.66	12.25	9.17**	8.74**	7.85
6		8.33	12.25	9.17	8.74	7.33**
7			12.25	9.17	8.74	7.33
8			6.13	9.17	8.74	7.33
9				9.17	8.74	7.33
10				9.16	8.74	7.33
11					4.37	7.32
12						7.33
13						3.66

*The figures in this table are taken from the official table that appears in Rev.Proc. 87–57, 1987–2 C.B. 687. Because of its length, the complete table is not presented.
**Switchover to straight-line depreciation.

■ **TABLE 8–5**
ADS Straight-Line for Personal Property Assuming Half-Year Convention

For Property Placed in Service after December 31, 1986 (Partial Table)*

Recovery Year	5-Year Class	9.5-Year Class	12-Year Class
1	10.00	5.26	4.17
2	20.00	10.53	8.33
3	20.00	10.53	8.33
4	20.00	10.53	8.33
5	20.00	10.52	8.33
6	10.00	10.53	8.33
7		10.52	8.34
8		10.53	8.33
9		10.52	8.34
10		10.53	8.33
11			8.34
12			8.33
13			4.17

*The figures in this table are taken from the official table that appears in Rev.Proc. 87–57, 1987–2 C.B. 687. Because of its length, the complete table is not presented. The tables for the mid-quarter convention also appear in Rev.Proc. 87–57.

■ **TABLE 8–6**
ACRS Cost Recovery Table for 19-Year Real Property

For Property Placed in Service after May 8, 1985, and before January 1, 1987
19-Year Real Property (19-Year 175% Declining Balance)
(Assuming Mid-Month Convention)

If the Recovery Year Is:	And the Month in the First Recovery Year the Property Is Placed in Service Is: 1	2	3	4	5	6	7	8	9	10	11	12
	The Applicable Percentage Is (Use the Column for the Month in the First Year the Property Is Placed in Service):											
1	8.8	8.1	7.3	6.5	5.8	5.0	4.2	3.5	2.7	1.9	1.1	0.4
2	8.4	8.5	8.5	8.6	8.7	8.8	8.8	8.9	9.0	9.0	9.1	9.2
3	7.6	7.7	7.7	7.8	7.9	7.9	8.0	8.1	8.1	8.2	8.3	8.3
4	6.9	7.0	7.0	7.1	7.1	7.2	7.3	7.3	7.4	7.4	7.5	7.6
5	6.3	6.3	6.4	6.4	6.5	6.5	6.6	6.6	6.7	6.8	6.8	6.9
6	5.7	5.7	5.8	5.9	5.9	5.9	6.0	6.0	6.1	6.1	6.2	6.2
7	5.2	5.2	5.3	5.3	5.3	5.4	5.4	5.5	5.5	5.6	5.6	5.6
8	4.7	4.7	4.8	4.8	4.8	4.9	4.9	5.0	5.0	5.1	5.1	5.1
9	4.2	4.3	4.3	4.4	4.4	4.5	4.5	4.5	4.5	4.6	4.6	4.7
10	4.2	4.2	4.2	4.2	4.2	4.2	4.2	4.2	4.2	4.2	4.2	4.2
11	4.2	4.2	4.2	4.2	4.2	4.2	4.2	4.2	4.2	4.2	4.2	4.2
12	4.2	4.2	4.2	4.2	4.2	4.2	4.2	4.2	4.2	4.2	4.2	4.2
13	4.2	4.2	4.2	4.2	4.2	4.2	4.2	4.2	4.2	4.2	4.2	4.2
14	4.2	4.2	4.2	4.2	4.2	4.2	4.2	4.2	4.2	4.2	4.2	4.2
15	4.2	4.2	4.2	4.2	4.2	4.2	4.2	4.2	4.2	4.2	4.2	4.2
16	4.2	4.2	4.2	4.2	4.2	4.2	4.2	4.2	4.2	4.2	4.2	4.2
17	4.2	4.2	4.2	4.2	4.2	4.2	4.2	4.2	4.2	4.2	4.2	4.2
18	4.2	4.2	4.2	4.2	4.2	4.2	4.2	4.2	4.2	4.2	4.2	4.2
19	4.2	4.2	4.2	4.2	4.2	4.2	4.2	4.2	4.2	4.2	4.2	4.2
20	0.2	0.5	0.9	1.2	1.6	1.9	2.3	2.6	3.0	3.3	3.7	4.0

■ **TABLE 8–7**
ACRS Cost Recovery Table for 19-Year Real Property: Optional Straight-Line

For Property Placed in Service after May 8, 1985, and before January 1, 1987: 19-Year Real Property for Which an Optional 19-Year Straight-Line Method Is Elected (Assuming Mid-Month Convention)

If the Recovery Year Is:	And the Month in the First Recovery Year the Property Is Placed in Service Is: 1	2	3	4	5	6	7	8	9	10	11	12
	The Applicable Percentage Is (Use the Column for the Month in the First Year the Property Is Placed in Service):											
1	5.0	4.6	4.2	3.7	3.3	2.9	2.4	2.0	1.5	1.1	.7	.2
2	5.3	5.3	5.3	5.3	5.3	5.3	5.3	5.3	5.3	5.3	5.3	5.3
3	5.3	5.3	5.3	5.3	5.3	5.3	5.3	5.3	5.3	5.3	5.3	5.3
4	5.3	5.3	5.3	5.3	5.3	5.3	5.3	5.3	5.3	5.3	5.3	5.3
5	5.3	5.3	5.3	5.3	5.3	5.3	5.3	5.3	5.3	5.3	5.3	5.3
6	5.3	5.3	5.3	5.3	5.3	5.3	5.3	5.3	5.3	5.3	5.3	5.3
7	5.3	5.3	5.3	5.3	5.3	5.3	5.3	5.3	5.3	5.3	5.3	5.3
8	5.3	5.3	5.3	5.3	5.3	5.3	5.3	5.3	5.3	5.3	5.3	5.3
9	5.3	5.3	5.3	5.3	5.3	5.3	5.3	5.3	5.3	5.3	5.3	5.3
10	5.3	5.3	5.3	5.3	5.3	5.3	5.3	5.3	5.3	5.3	5.3	5.3
11	5.3	5.3	5.3	5.3	5.3	5.3	5.3	5.3	5.3	5.3	5.3	5.3
12	5.3	5.3	5.3	5.3	5.3	5.3	5.3	5.3	5.3	5.3	5.3	5.3
13	5.3	5.3	5.3	5.3	5.3	5.3	5.3	5.3	5.3	5.3	5.3	5.3
14	5.2	5.2	5.2	5.2	5.2	5.2	5.2	5.2	5.2	5.2	5.2	5.2
15	5.2	5.2	5.2	5.2	5.2	5.2	5.2	5.2	5.2	5.2	5.2	5.2
16	5.2	5.2	5.2	5.2	5.2	5.2	5.2	5.2	5.2	5.2	5.2	5.2
17	5.2	5.2	5.2	5.2	5.2	5.2	5.2	5.2	5.2	5.2	5.2	5.2
18	5.2	5.2	5.2	5.2	5.2	5.2	5.2	5.2	5.2	5.2	5.2	5.2
19	5.2	5.2	5.2	5.2	5.2	5.2	5.2	5.2	5.2	5.2	5.2	5.2
20	.2	.6	1.0	1.5	1.9	2.3	2.8	3.2	3.7	4.1	4.5	5.0

■ TABLE 8–8
MACRS Straight-Line Depreciation for Real Property Assuming Mid-Month Convention*

For Property Placed in Service after December 31, 1986: 27.5-Year Residential Real Property

Recovery Year(s)	The Applicable Percentage Is (Use the Column for the Month in the First Year the Property Is Placed in Service): 1	2	3	4	5	6	7	8	9	10	11	12
1	3.485	3.182	2.879	2.576	2.273	1.970	1.667	1.364	1.061	0.758	0.455	0.152
2–18	3.636	3.636	3.636	3.636	3.636	3.636	3.636	3.636	3.636	3.636	3.636	3.636
19–27	3.637	3.637	3.637	3.637	3.637	3.637	3.637	3.637	3.637	3.637	3.637	3.637
28	1.970	2.273	2.576	2.879	3.182	3.485	3.636	3.636	3.636	3.636	3.636	3.636
29	0.000	0.000	0.000	0.000	0.000	0.000	0.152	0.455	0.758	1.061	1.364	1.667

For Property Placed in Service after December 31, 1986, and before May 13, 1993: 31.5-Year Nonresidential Real Property

Recovery Year(s)	The Applicable Percentage Is (Use the Column for the Month in the First Year the Property Is Placed in Service): 1	2	3	4	5	6	7	8	9	10	11	12
1	3.042	2.778	2.513	2.249	1.984	1.720	1.455	1.190	0.926	0.661	0.397	0.132
2–19	3.175	3.175	3.175	3.175	3.175	3.175	3.175	3.175	3.175	3.175	3.175	3.175
20–31	3.174	3.174	3.174	3.174	3.174	3.174	3.174	3.174	3.174	3.174	3.174	3.174
32	1.720	1.984	2.249	2.513	2.778	3.042	3.175	3.175	3.175	3.175	3.175	3.175
33	0.000	0.000	0.000	0.000	0.000	0.000	0.132	0.397	0.661	0.926	1.190	1.455

For Property Placed in Service after May 12, 1993: 39-Year Nonresidential Real Property

Recovery Year(s)	The Applicable Percentage Is (Use the Column for the Month in the First Year the Property Is Placed in Service): 1	2	3	4	5	6	7	8	9	10	11	12
1	2.461	2.247	2.033	1.819	1.605	1.391	1.177	0.963	0.749	0.535	0.321	0.107
2–39	2.564	2.564	2.564	2.564	2.564	2.564	2.564	2.564	2.564	2.564	2.564	2.564
40	0.107	0.321	0.535	0.749	0.963	1.177	1.391	1.605	1.819	2.033	2.247	2.461

*The official tables contain a separate row for each year. For ease of presentation, certain years are grouped in these tables. In some instances, this will produce a difference of .001 for the last digit when compared with the official tables.

■ TABLE 8–9
ADS Straight-Line for Real Property Assuming Mid-Month Convention

For Property Placed in Service after December 31, 1986

Recovery Year	Month Placed in Service 1	2	3	4	5	6	7	8	9	10	11	12
1	2.396	2.188	1.979	1.771	1.563	1.354	1.146	0.938	0.729	0.521	0.313	0.104
2–40	2.500	2.500	2.500	2.500	2.500	2.500	2.500	2.500	2.500	2.500	2.500	2.500
41	0.104	0.312	0.521	0.729	0.937	1.146	1.354	1.562	1.771	1.979	2.187	2.396

KEY TERMS

Accelerated cost recovery system (ACRS), 8–19
Additional first-year depreciation, 8–7
Alternative depreciation system (ADS), 8–18
Amortization, 8–20
Cost depletion, 8–22
Cost recovery, 8–2
Depletion, 8–20
Depreciation, 8–2
Half-year convention, 8–7
Intangible drilling and development costs (IDC), 8–21
Listed property, 8–13
Mid-month convention, 8–9
Mid-quarter convention, 8–8
Modified accelerated cost recovery system (MACRS), 8–4
Percentage depletion, 8–22
Residential rental real estate, 8–9
Section 179 expensing, 8–10

PROBLEM MATERIALS

West Federal Taxation

Discussion Questions

1. Discuss whether property that is classified as personalty is subject to cost recovery.
2. If a taxpayer does not take any cost recovery on an asset during the year, what will be the impact on the basis of the asset?
3. Discuss whether landscaping costs are eligible for cost recovery.

Issue ID

4. At the beginning of the current year, Henry purchased a ski resort for $10 million. Henry does not own the land on which the resort is located. The Federal government owns the land, and Henry has the right to operate the resort on the land pursuant to Special Use Permits, which are terminable at will by the Federal government, and Term Special Use Permits, which allow the land to be used for a fixed number of years. In preparing the income tax return for the current year, Henry properly allocated $2 million of the purchase price to the costs of constructing mountain roads, slopes, and trails. Since the acquisition, Henry has spent an additional $1 million on maintaining the mountain roads, slopes, and trails. Identify the relevant tax issues for Henry.

Issue ID

5. During the taxable year, Pale, an electric utility company, constructed a hydroelectric dam and placed it in service. In connection with the dam, Pale was required under a Federal Power Commission license to construct and maintain various facilities for the preservation of fish and for public recreation. The fish preservation facilities constructed below the dam consisted of an entrance pool, a fish ladder, and a holding pool. The recreational facilities located above the dam included access roads, fixed wharves, landings, and other facilities. All of these facilities are tangible properties, some of which are inextricably associated with the land. Identify the relevant tax issues for Pale.
6. Discuss when the half-year convention must be used.
7. Discuss the computation of cost recovery in the year of sale of an asset when the half-year convention is being used.
8. Discuss whether the acquisition of real property affects the 40% test to determine whether the mid-quarter convention must be used.
9. Discuss the computation of cost recovery in the year of sale of an asset when the mid-quarter convention is being used.

Issue ID

10. Jed is in the business of manufacturing flat glass. He uses the "float" manufacturing process, in which limestone, sand, soda ash, and other glass components are melted to form liquefied molten glass. The molten glass then proceeds into a "tin bath" structure that holds up to 200 tons of liquefied, molten tin. The molten glass "floats" upon and is also conveyed across the surface of the molten tin, which absorbs sufficient heat from the glass to enable it to begin forming a cohesive and continuous sheet or "ribbon" of

glass. To begin operations, 168 tons of tin were melted and placed in the tin bath portion of the plant. Because tin is a highly reactive metal, it combines with oxygen, sulfur, iron, and the glass in the tin bath. As a result of these combinations and reactions, tin oxide and tin sulfide impurities continuously form on the surface of the molten tin and must be removed. Removal of these compounds causes the tin to lose volume, which is critical to the process. To maintain the needed volume of liquefied tin, additional tin is liquefied and added to the bath as needed. Identify the relevant tax issues for Jed.

11. Discuss whether an election may be made to use MACRS straight-line cost recovery on only a portion of the personalty placed in service during the tax year.

12. Discuss whether the mid-quarter convention applies if a taxpayer makes a straight-line election under MACRS.

13. Discuss whether § 179 expensing may be taken on an asset that a taxpayer acquires to help with her personal investments.

14. Explain how the § 179 limited expensing deduction affects the computation of MACRS cost recovery.

15. Discuss the treatment of a § 179 expensing carryforward.

16. Discuss the definition of *taxable income* as it is used in limiting the § 179 expensing amount.

Issue ID

17. Ana owns a motor home sales and rental business. During the current year, her rental fleet had a total of 33 motor homes, including a new Gulfstream Motor Home. The Gulfstream was purchased for $80,000 in July of the current year. The usual terms of the motor home rentals are much like those for car rentals—a daily or weekly fee, a daily mileage allowance of 100 miles, and a mileage charge of $.50 for each additional mile. Most renters use the motor homes for fewer than 30 days. Although the motor homes are rented out, they are also listed for sale. As such, any motor home can be sold at any time. Identify the relevant tax issues for Ana with respect to the new Gulfstream Motor Home.

18. Discuss the implications of an automobile used in a trade or business having a gross vehicle weight (GVW) exceeding 6,000 pounds.

19. Discuss whether an automobile is subject to the statutory dollar limits on cost recovery if the automobile fails the more-than-50% business use test for listed property.

20. Discuss the purpose of the lease inclusion amount and explain how it is determined with respect to leased passenger automobiles.

21. Explain the amortization period of a § 197 intangible if the actual useful life is less than 15 years.

22. What is the amortization period for self-created goodwill?

Issue ID

23. Harold and Bart own 75% of the stock of Orange Motors. The other 25% of the stock is owned by Jeb. Orange Motors entered into an agreement with Harold and Bart to acquire all of their stock in Orange Motors. In addition, Harold and Bart signed a noncompete agreement with Orange Motors. Under the terms of the noncompete agreement, Orange will pay Harold and Bart $15,000 each per year for four years. Identify the relevant tax issues for Orange Motors.

24. Discuss the options for handling intangible drilling and development costs.

25. Briefly discuss how cost depletion is computed for a particular tax year.

Problems

26. On November 4, 2003, Blue Company acquired an asset (27.5-year residential real property) for $100,000 for use in its business. In 2003 and 2004, respectively, Blue took $321 and $2,564 of cost recovery. These amounts were incorrect because Blue applied the wrong percentages (i.e., those for 39-year rather than 27.5-year). Blue should have

taken $455 and $3,636 cost recovery in 2003 and 2004. On January 1, 2005, the asset was sold for $98,000. Calculate the gain or loss on the sale of the asset in 2005.

27. José purchased a house for $175,000 in 2002. He used the house as his personal residence. In March 2005, when the fair market value of the house was $210,000, he converted the house to rental property. What is José's basis in the house for cost recovery?

28. Blue Corporation acquired a new tractor on August 15, 2005, for $150,000. Blue did not elect immediate expensing under § 179. Determine Blue's cost recovery for 2005.

29. Walt acquires a new 10-year class asset on June 17, 2005, for $220,000. This is the only asset acquired by Walt during the year. He does not elect immediate expensing under § 179. Compute Walt's cost recovery for 2005.

30. Juan acquires a new five-year class asset on March 14, 2005, for $200,000. This is the only asset acquired by Juan during the year. He does not elect immediate expensing under § 179. On July 15, 2006, Juan sells the asset.
   a. Determine Juan's cost recovery for 2005.
   b. Determine Juan's cost recovery for 2006.

31. Debra acquired the following new assets during the current year:

Date	Asset	Cost
April 11	Furniture	$50,000
July 28	Trucks	30,000
November 3	Computers	60,000

Determine the cost recovery for the current year. Debra does not elect immediate expensing under § 179.

32. On July 10, 1996, Wade purchased and placed in service a warehouse. The warehouse cost $850,000. On May 7, 2005, Wade sold the warehouse.
   a. Determine Wade's cost recovery for 1996.
   b. Determine Wade's cost recovery for 2005.

33. On April 3, 2005, Terry purchased and placed in service a building. The building cost $2 million. An appraisal determined that 25% of the total cost was attributed to the value of the land. The bottom three floors of the building are leased to a retail business for $72,000. The other two floors of the building are rental apartments with an annual rent of $60,000. Determine Terry's cost recovery for 2005.

34. On November 5, 2005, Chris acquires land with a warehouse on it for $3 million. The land was valued at $1 million. On January 10, 2016, Chris sells the land and warehouse for $4.5 million. Calculate Chris's cost recovery for 2005. For 2016.

35. Janice acquired an apartment building on June 4, 2005, for $1.4 million. The value of the land is $200,000. Janice sold the apartment building on November 29, 2011.
   a. Determine Janice's cost recovery for 2005.
   b. Determine Janice's cost recovery for 2011.

Decision Making

36. Lori, who is single, purchased a new copier (five-year class property) for $30,000 and new furniture (seven-year class property) for $112,000 on May 20, 2005. Lori expects the taxable income derived from her business (without regard to the amount expensed under § 179) to be about $200,000. Lori wants to elect immediate § 179 expensing, but she doesn't know which asset she should expense under § 179.
   a. Determine Lori's total deduction if the § 179 expense is first taken with respect to the copier.
   b. Determine Lori's total deduction if the § 179 expense is first taken with respect to the furniture.
   c. What is your advice to Lori?

37. Jack owns a small business that he operates as a sole proprietor. In 2005, Jack will net $80,000 of business income before consideration of any § 179 deduction. Jack spends $428,000 on new equipment in 2005. If Jack also has $4,000 of § 179 deduction carryforwards from 2004, determine his § 179 expense deduction for 2005 and the amount of any carryforward.

38. Olga is the proprietor of a small business. In 2005, the business income, before consideration of any cost recovery or § 179 deduction, is $180,000. Olga spends $132,000 for new furniture and elects to take the § 179 deduction on the furniture. Olga's cost recovery deduction for 2005, except for the cost recovery deduction with respect to the furniture, is $86,000. Determine Olga's total cost recovery for 2005 with respect to the furniture and the amount of any § 179 carryforward.

Decision Making

39. On March 10, 2005, Yoon purchased three-year class property for $20,000. On December 15, 2005, Yoon purchased five-year class property for $127,000. He has net business income of $140,000 before consideration of any § 179 deduction.
    a. Calculate Yoon's cost recovery for 2005, assuming he does not make the § 179 election or use straight-line cost recovery.
    b. Calculate Yoon's cost recovery for 2005, assuming he does elect to use § 179 and does not elect to use straight-line cost recovery.
    c. Assuming Yoon's marginal tax rate is 33%, determine his tax benefit from electing § 179.

40. Martha owns a business that she operates as a sole proprietor. In 2005, she will have net income of $22,000 before regular MACRS and the § 179 expense are deducted. Martha spent $40,000 on a new five-year class asset in June 2005. She also has $5,000 of § 179 carryforwards from prior years. Determine Martha's § 179 deduction for 2005 and any § 179 carryforward.

Communications

41. John Johnson is considering acquiring an automobile at the beginning of 2005 that he will use 100% of the time as a taxi. The purchase price of the automobile is $35,000. John has heard of cost recovery limits on automobiles and wants to know how much of the $35,000 he can deduct in the first year. Write a letter to John in which you present your calculations. Also, prepare a memo for the tax files. John's address is 100 Morningside, Clinton, MS 39058.

42. On October 15, 2005, Jon purchased and placed in service a new car. The purchase price was $30,000. This was the only business use asset Jon acquired in 2005. He used the car 80% of the time for business and 20% for personal use. Jon used the statutory percentage method of cost recovery. Calculate the total deduction Jon may take for 2005 with respect to the car.

43. On June 5, 2005, Leo purchased and placed in service a new car that cost $18,000. The business use percentage for the car is always 100%. Compute Leo's cost recovery deduction in 2005 and 2006.

44. On March 15, 2005, Helen purchased and placed in service a new Ford Excursion. The purchase price was $60,000, and the vehicle had a rating of 6,500 GVW. The vehicle was used 100% for business. Calculate the maximum total deduction Helen may take with respect to the vehicle in 2005.

45. On May 28, 2005, Mary purchased and placed in service a new $20,000 car. The car was used 60% for business, 20% for production of income, and 20% for personal use. In 2006, the usage changed to 40% for business, 30% for production of income, and 30% for personal use. Mary did not elect immediate expensing under § 179. Compute the cost recovery and any cost recovery recapture in 2006.

Decision Making

46. Sally purchased a new computer (five-year property) on June 1, 2005, for $4,000. Sally could use the computer 100% of the time in her business, or she could allow her family to also use the computer. Sally estimates that if her family uses the computer, the business use will be 45% and the personal use will be 55%. Determine the tax cost to Sally, in the year of acquisition, of allowing her family to use the computer. Assume that Sally would not elect § 179 limited expensing and that her marginal tax rate is 28%.

47. At the beginning of the current year, Abdel purchased a new computer (five-year class property) for $8,000. During the year, Abdel used the computer 80% of the time for his personal investments and 20% of the time for personal use. Calculate the maximum total deduction Abdel can take with respect to the computer for the current tax year.

48. Midway through 2005, Abdel leases and places in service a passenger automobile. The lease will run for five years, and the payments are $700 per month. During 2005, Abdel uses the car 65% for business use and 35% for personal use. Assuming the inclusion dollar amount from the IRS table is $80, determine the tax consequences to Abdel from the lease for the year 2005.

Decision Making
Communications

49. Dennis Harding is considering acquiring a new automobile that he will use 100% for business. The purchase price of the automobile would be $35,000. If Dennis leased the car for five years, the lease payments would be $375 per month. Dennis will acquire the car on January 1, 2005. The inclusion dollar amounts from the IRS table for the next five years are $52, $115, $171, $205, and $236. Dennis desires to know the effect on his adjusted gross income of purchasing versus leasing the car for the next five years. Write a letter to Dennis and present your calculations. Also, prepare a memo for the tax files. His address is 150 Avenue I, Memphis, TN 38112.

50. On March 5, 2005, Nell purchased new equipment for $90,000. The equipment has an ADS midpoint of 9.5 years. Determine Nell's cost recovery deduction for computing 2005 taxable income using the straight-line method under ADS and assuming she does not make a § 179 election.

51. In 2005, Muhammad purchased a new computer for $14,000. The computer is used 100% for business. Muhammad did not make a § 179 election with respect to the computer. If Muhammad uses the statutory percentage method, determine his cost recovery deduction for 2005 for computing taxable income and for computing his alternative minimum tax.

52. In June 2005, Cardinal, Inc., purchased and placed in service railroad track costing $800,000. Calculate Cardinal's cost recovery deduction for 2005 for computing taxable income if:
   a. Cardinal does not make the § 179 election or use straight-line cost recovery.
   b. Cardinal does not make the § 179 election but does elect to use ADS 150% declining-balance cost recovery.

Decision Making

53. Jamie purchased $100,000 of new office furniture for her business in June of the current year. Jamie understands that if she elects to use ADS to compute her regular income tax, there will be no difference between the cost recovery for computing the regular income tax and the AMT. Jamie wants to know the *regular* income tax cost, after three years, of using ADS rather than MACRS. Assume that Jamie does not elect § 179 limited expensing and that her marginal tax rate is 28%.

54. In 1997, Jake started his own dental practice. Because the practice has become very successful, Jake has been offered $800,000 for it. Of this offer price, $450,000 is estimated to be the value of the goodwill. As of December 31 of the current year, Jake has not sold his practice. Determine Jake's deduction for the amortization of the goodwill for the current year.

Decision Making
Communications

55. Mike Saxon is negotiating the purchase of a business. The final purchase price has been agreed upon, but the allocation of the purchase price to the assets is still being discussed. Appraisals on a warehouse range from $1.2 to $1.5 million. If a value of $1.2 million is used for the warehouse, the remainder of the purchase price, $800,000, will be allocated to goodwill. If $1.5 million is allocated to the warehouse, goodwill will be $500,000. Mike wants to know what effect each alternative will have on cost recovery and amortization during the first year. Under the agreement, Mike will take over the business on January 1 of next year. Write a letter to Mike in which you present your calculations and recommendation. Also, prepare a memo for the tax files. Mike's address is 200 Rolling Hills Drive, Shavertown, PA 18708.

56. Wes acquired a mineral interest during the year for $10 million. A geological survey estimated that 250,000 tons of the mineral remained in the deposit. During the year, 80,000 tons were mined, and 45,000 tons were sold for $12 million. Other expenses amounted to $5 million. Assuming the mineral depletion rate is 22%, calculate Wes's lowest taxable income.

Decision Making

57. Chris purchased an oil interest for $2 million. Recoverable barrels were estimated to be 500,000. During the year, 120,000 barrels were sold for $3.84 million, regular expenses (including cost recovery) were $1.24 million, and IDC were $1 million. Calculate Chris's taxable income under the expensing and capitalization methods of handling IDC.

Cumulative Problems

Tax Return Problem
Decision Making
Communications

58. John Smith, age 31, is single and has no dependents. At the beginning of 2005, John started his own excavation business and named it Earth Movers. John lives at 1045 Center Street, Lindon, UT, and his business is located at 381 State Street, Lindon, UT. The zip code for both addresses is 84059. John's Social Security number is 321–09–6456, and the business identification number is 98–1234567. John is a cash basis taxpayer. During 2005, John had the following items in connection with his business:

Fees for services	$500,000
Building rental expense	36,000
Office furniture and equipment rental expense	5,000
Office supplies	2,500
Utilities	4,000
Salary for secretary	35,000
Salary for equipment operators	42,000
Payroll taxes	9,000
Fuel and oil for the equipment	21,000
Purchase of three new front-end loaders on January 15, 2005, for $380,000. John made the election under § 179.	380,000
Purchase of a new dump truck on January 18, 2005	50,000

During 2005, John had the following additional items:

Interest income from First National Bank	$ 10,000
Dividends from ExxonMobil	9,500
Quarterly estimated tax payments	11,500

On October 8, 2005, John inherited IBM stock from his Aunt Mildred. John had been her favorite nephew. According to the data provided by the executor of Aunt Mildred's estate, the stock had been valued for estate tax purposes at $110,000. John is considering selling the IBM stock for $115,000 on December 29, 2005, and using $75,000 of the proceeds to purchase an Acura NSX. He would use the car 100% for business. John wants to know what effect these transactions would have on his 2005 adjusted gross income.

Write a letter to John in which you present your calculations. Also, prepare a memo for the tax files. Suggested software: TurboTax.

Tax Return Problem

59. Janice Morgan, age 32, is single and has no dependents. She is a freelance writer. In January 2004, Janice opened her own office located at 2751 Waldham Road, Pleasantville, NM 17196. She called her business Writers Anonymous. Janice is a cash basis taxpayer. She lives at 132 Stone Avenue, Pleasantville, NM 17196. Her Social Security number is 189–57–6691. Janice desires to contribute to the Presidential Election Campaign Fund.

During 2004, Janice had the following income and expense items connected with her business:

Income from sale of articles	$115,000
Rent	16,500
Utilities	7,900
Supplies	1,800
Insurance	5,000
Travel (including meals of $1,200)	3,500

Janice purchased and placed in service the following fixed assets for her business:

- Furniture and fixtures (new) costing $19,000 on January 10, 2004.
- Computer equipment (new) costing $40,000 on July 28, 2004.

Janice would like to deduct these costs as soon as possible.

Janice's itemized deductions are as follows:

State income tax	$2,000
Home mortgage interest paid to First Bank	6,000
Property taxes on home	1,500
Charitable contributions	1,200

Janice did not keep a record of the sales tax she paid. The amount from the sales tax table is $437.

Janice has interest income of $4,000 on certificates of deposit at Second Bank. Janice makes estimated tax payments of $5,000 for 2004.

Compute Janice Morgan's 2004 Federal income tax payable (or refund due). If you use tax forms for your computations, you will need Form(s) 1040 and 4562 and Schedules A, B, C, and SE. Suggested software: TurboTax.

Research Problems

Note: Solutions to Research Problems can be prepared by using the ***RIA Checkpoint® Student Edition*** *online research product, which is available to accompany this text. It is also possible to prepare solutions to the Research Problems by using tax research materials found in a standard tax library.*

Research Problem 1. Osprey Corporation operates a pipeline system to transport unprocessed "raw" or "wet" natural gas from the gas wellheads to its natural gas processing plant. The pipeline system consists of a central line leading into the processing plant. The central line is fed by lateral adjoining pipelines that link specific wellheads. At all times, Osprey has owned and operated the pipeline system while the "raw" natural gas remains the property of its producer. The producers compensate Osprey for the use of the pipeline on a contractual "fee-for-service" basis.

Determine whether Osprey should depreciate the pipeline over a 7-year period or a 15-year period. Explain.

Research Problem 2. Bud purchased farmland from Enos. Bud paid Enos $400,000 for the land. Bud also paid Enos $100,000 for the peanut base acres and payment yield assigned to the land. Bud would like to know whether he can take cost recovery or amortization on the $100,000 payment.

Internet Activity

Use the tax resources of the Internet to address the following question. Do not restrict your search to the World Wide Web, but include a review of newsgroups and general reference materials, practitioner sites and resources, primary sources of the tax law, chat rooms and discussion groups, and other opportunities.

Research Problem 3. Locate a financial calculator program that assesses the wisdom of buying versus leasing a new car. Install the program on your computer and become familiar with it. Use the program to work through Problem 49 in this chapter.

Deductions: Employee and Self-Employed-Related Expenses

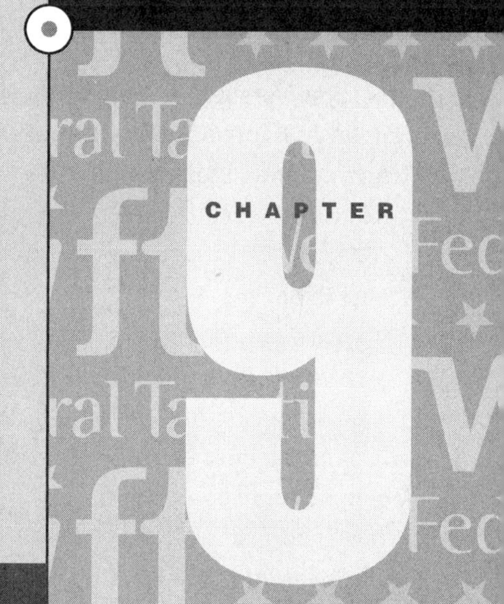

LEARNING OBJECTIVES

After completing Chapter 9, you should be able to:

LO.1

Distinguish between employee and self-employed status.

LO.2

Recognize deductible transportation expenses.

LO.3

Know how travel expenses are treated.

LO.4

Determine the moving expense deduction.

LO.5

Differentiate between deductible and nondeductible education expenses.

LO.6

Understand how entertainment expenses are treated.

LO.7

Identify other employee expenses.

LO.8

Become familiar with various deductions for contributions to retirement accounts.

LO.9

Appreciate the difference between accountable and nonaccountable employee plans.

LO.10

Work with the limitations on miscellaneous itemized deductions.

LO.11

Develop tax planning ideas related to employee business expenses.

http://wft.swlearning.com

OUTLINE

Considering the large number of taxpayers affected, the tax treatment of job-related expenses is unusually complex. To resolve this matter in a systematic fashion, a number of key questions must be asked:

- Is the taxpayer an *employee* or *self-employed?*
- If an employee, what expenses *qualify* as deductions?
- How are the expenses that qualify *classified* for tax purposes?
- To the extent the expenses are classified as deductions *from* AGI, are they subject to any *limitation?*

Once these questions have been posed and answered, the chapter considers various planning procedures available to maximize the deductibility of employee expenses.

LO.1

Distinguish between employee and self-employed status.

Employee versus Self-Employed

When one person performs services for another, the person performing the service is either an employee or self-employed (an **independent contractor**). Failure to recognize employee status can have serious consequences. Not only can interest and penalties result, but negative media coverage can impair career opportunities.

The problem is likely to intensify since businesses are increasingly relying on the services of self-employed persons for numerous reasons. Unlike employees, self-employed persons do not have to be included in various fringe benefit programs (e.g., group term life insurance) and retirement plans. Since they are not covered by FICA and FUTA (see Chapter 1), these payroll costs are avoided. The IRS is very much aware of the tendency of businesses to wrongly classify workers as self-employed rather than as employees.

In terms of tax consequences, employment status also makes a great deal of difference to the persons who perform the services. Expenses of self-employed taxpayers, to the extent allowable, are classified as deductions *for* AGI and are reported on Schedule C (Profit or Loss From Business) of Form 1040.[1] With the exception of reimbursement under an accountable plan (see later in the chapter), expenses of employees are deductions *from* AGI. They are reported on Form 2106 (Employee Business Expenses) and Schedule A (Itemized Deductions) of Form 1040.[2]

But when does an employer-employee relationship exist? Such a relationship exists when the employer has the right to specify the end result and the ways and means by which that result is to be attained.[3] An employee is subject to the will and control of the employer with respect not only to what shall be done but also to how it shall be done. If the individual is subject to the direction or control of another only to the extent of the end result but not as to the means of accomplishment, an employer-employee relationship does not exist. An example is the preparation of a taxpayer's return by an independent CPA.

Certain factors indicate an employer-employee relationship. They include (1) the right to discharge without legal liability the person performing the service, (2) the furnishing of tools or a place to work, and (3) payment based on time spent rather than the task performed. Each case is tested on its own merits, and the right to control the means and methods of accomplishment is the definitive test. Generally, physicians, lawyers, dentists, contractors, subcontractors, and others who offer services to the public are not classified as employees.

EXAMPLE 1

Arnold is a lawyer whose major client accounts for 60% of his billings. He does the routine legal work and income tax returns at the client's request. He is paid a monthly retainer in addition to amounts charged for extra work. Arnold is a self-employed individual. Even though most of his income comes from one client, he still has the right to determine how the end result of his work is attained. ■

EXAMPLE 2

Ellen is a lawyer hired by Arnold to assist him in the performance of services for the client mentioned in Example 1. Ellen is under Arnold's supervision; he reviews her work and pays her an hourly fee. Ellen is an employee of Arnold. ■

[1]§§ 62(a)(1) and 162(a). See Appendix B for a reproduction of Schedule C.

[2]See Appendix B for a reproduction of Schedule A.

[3]Reg. § 31.3401(c)–(1)(b).

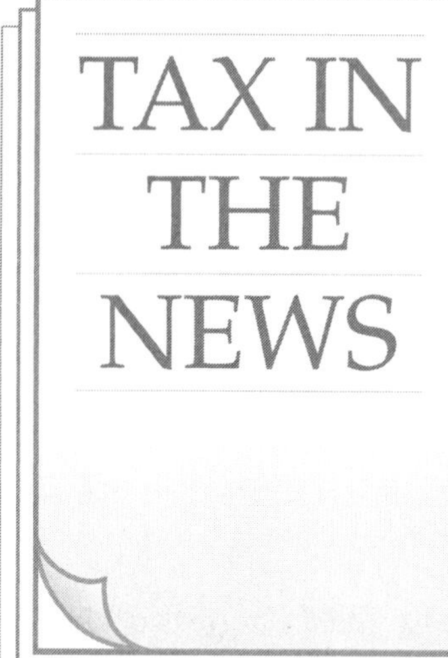

Caddies or Golf Carts?

For many years, the IRS has not questioned the tax classification of caddies as independent contractors. See, for example, Revenue Ruling 69–26 (1969–1 C.B. 251). This classification is consistent with the manner in which the services are performed. Most caddies work when they want, receive minimum training at their golf courses, and are paid "by the bag" (not by the hour). Further, they are paid by the golfer and not by the club.

Recent actions by the IRS, however, indicate that it might treat caddies as employees. If this happens, most golf courses will take steps to avoid the compliance nightmare of payroll withholding. The caddies will be replaced by golf carts!

If the IRS pursues this matter, Congress appears ready to negate any such reclassification. After all, great golfers such as Charlie Stafford, Lee Trevino, Chi Chi Rodriguez, and the late Ben Hogan were once caddies!

EXAMPLE 3

Frank is a licensed practical nurse who works as a private-duty nurse. He is under the supervision of the patient's doctor and is paid by the patient. Frank is not an employee of either the patient (who pays him) or the doctor (who supervises him). The ways and means of attaining the end result (care of the patient) are under his control. ■

Employees in a special category are also allowed to file Schedule C to report income and deduct expenses *for* AGI. These employees are called **statutory employees** because they are not common law employees under the rules explained above. The wages or commissions paid to statutory employees are not subject to Federal income tax withholding but are subject to Social Security tax.[4]

Employee Expenses—In General

Once the employment relationship is established, employee expenses fall into one of the following categories:

- Transportation.
- Travel.
- Moving.
- Education.
- Entertainment.
- Other.

These expenses are discussed below in the order presented.

Keep in mind, however, that these expenses are not necessarily limited to employees. A deduction for business transportation, for example, is equally available to taxpayers who are self-employed.

[4]See Circular E, *Employer's Tax Guide* (IRS Publication 15), for further discussion of statutory employees.

LO.2

Recognize deductible transportation expenses.

Transportation Expenses

QUALIFIED EXPENDITURES

An employee may deduct unreimbursed employment-related transportation expenses as an itemized deduction *from* AGI. **Transportation expenses** include only the cost of transporting the employee from one place to another in the course of employment when the employee is *not* away from home *in travel status*. Such costs include taxi fares, automobile expenses, tolls, and parking.

Commuting Expenses. Commuting between home and one's place of employment is a personal, nondeductible expense. The fact that one employee drives 30 miles to work and another employee walks six blocks is of no significance.[5]

EXAMPLE 4

Geraldo is employed by Sparrow Corporation. He drives 22 miles each way to work. The 44 miles he drives each workday are nondeductible commuting expenses. ■

The rule that disallows a deduction for commuting expenses has several exceptions. An employee who uses an automobile to transport heavy tools to work and who otherwise would not drive to work is allowed a deduction, but only for the additional costs incurred to transport the work implements. Additional costs are those exceeding the cost of commuting by the same mode of transportation without the tools. For example, the rental of a trailer for transporting tools is deductible, but the expenses of operating the automobile generally are not deductible.[6] The Supreme Court has held that a deduction is permitted only when the taxpayer can show that the automobile would not have been used without the necessity to transport tools or equipment.[7]

Another exception is provided for an employee who has a second job. The expenses of getting from one job to another are deductible. If the employee goes home between jobs, the deduction is based on the distance between jobs.

EXAMPLE 5

In the current year, Cynthia holds two jobs, a full-time job with Blue Corporation and a part-time job with Wren Corporation. During the 250 days that she works (adjusted for weekends, vacation, and holidays), Cynthia customarily leaves home at 7:30 A.M. and drives 30 miles to the Blue Corporation plant, where she works until 5:00 P.M. After dinner at a nearby café, Cynthia drives 20 miles to Wren Corporation and works from 7:00 to 11:00 P.M. The distance from the second job to Cynthia's home is 40 miles. Her deduction is based on 20 miles (the distance between jobs). ■

If the taxpayer is required to incur a transportation expense to travel between work stations, that expense is deductible.

EXAMPLE 6

Norman is the local manager for a national chain of fast-food outlets. Each workday he drives from his home to his office to handle administrative matters. Most of his day, however, is then spent making the rounds of the retail outlets, after which he drives home. The costs incurred in driving to his office and driving home from the last outlet are nondeductible commuting expenses. The other transportation costs are deductible. ■

---

[5] *Tauferner v. U.S.*, 69–1 USTC ¶9241, 23 AFTR2d 69–1025, 407 F.2d 243 (CA–10, 1969).

[6] Rev.Rul. 75–380, 1975–2 C.B. 59.

[7] *Fausner v. Comm.*, 73–2 USTC ¶9515, 32 AFTR2d 73–5202, 93 S.Ct. 2820 (USSC, 1973).

Likewise, the commuting costs from home to a temporary work station and from the temporary work station to home are deductible.[8]

EXAMPLE 7

Vivian works for a firm in downtown Denver and commutes to work. She occasionally works in a customer's office. On one such occasion, Vivian drove directly to the customer's office, a round-trip distance from her home of 40 miles. She did not go into her office, which is a 52-mile round-trip. Her mileage for going to and from the temporary work station is deductible. ■

Also deductible is the reasonable travel cost between the general working area and a temporary work station outside that area.[9]

EXAMPLE 8

Sam, a building inspector in Minneapolis, regularly inspects buildings for building code violations for his employer, a general contractor. During one busy season, the St. Paul inspector became ill, and Sam was required to inspect several buildings in St. Paul. The expenses for transportation for the trips to St. Paul are deductible. ■

What constitutes the general working area depends on the facts and circumstances of each situation. Furthermore, if an employee customarily works on several temporary assignments in a localized area, that localized area becomes the regular place of employment. Transportation from home to these locations becomes a personal, nondeductible commuting expense.

COMPUTATION OF AUTOMOBILE EXPENSES

A taxpayer has two choices in computing automobile expenses. The actual operating cost, which includes depreciation (cost recovery), gas, oil, repairs, licenses, and insurance, may be used. Records must be kept that detail the automobile's personal and business use. Only the percentage allocable to business transportation and travel is allowed as a deduction. Complex rules for the computation of depreciation (discussed in Chapter 8) apply if the actual expense method is used.

Use of the **automatic mileage method** (also called the standard mileage method) is the second alternative. For 2005, the deduction is based on 40.5 cents per mile for business miles.[10] Parking fees and tolls are allowed in addition to expenses computed using the automatic mileage method.

Generally, a taxpayer may elect either method for any particular year. However, the following restrictions apply:

- The vehicle must be owned or leased by the taxpayer.
- The vehicle is not used for hire (e.g., taxicab).
- If five or more vehicles are in use (for business purposes) at the *same* time (not alternately), a taxpayer may not use the automatic mileage method.
- A basis adjustment is required if the taxpayer changes from the automatic mileage method to the actual operating cost method. Depreciation is considered allowed for the business miles in accordance with the following schedule for the most recent five years:

[8]Rev.Rul. 90–23, 1990–1 C.B. 28 as amplified by Rev.Rul. 94–47, 1994–2 C.B. 18.

[9]Rev.Rul. 190, 1953–2 C.B. 303 as amplified by Rev.Rul. 94–47, 1994–2 C.B. 18.

[10]Rev.Proc. 2004–64, 2004–2 C.B. 898. For 2004, the rate was 37.5 cents per mile for business miles.

Year	Rate per Mile
2005	17 cents
2004	16 cents
2003	16 cents
2002	15 cents
2001	15 cents

EXAMPLE 9

Tim purchased his automobile in 2002 for $36,000. It is used 90% for business purposes. Tim drove the automobile for 10,000 business miles in 2004; 8,500 business miles in 2003; and 6,000 business miles in 2002. At the beginning of 2005, the basis of the business portion is $28,540.

Depreciable basis ($36,000 × 90%)	$32,400
Less depreciation:	
2004 (10,000 miles × 16 cents)	(1,600)
2003 (8,500 miles × 16 cents)	(1,360)
2002 (6,000 miles × 15 cents)	(900)
Adjusted business basis 1/1/2005	$28,540

■

- Use of the automatic mileage method in the first year the auto is placed in service is considered an election to exclude the auto from the MACRS method of depreciation (discussed in Chapter 8).
- A taxpayer may not switch to the automatic mileage method if the MACRS statutory percentage method or the election to expense under § 179 has been used.

LO.3

Know how travel expenses are treated.

Travel Expenses

DEFINITION OF TRAVEL EXPENSES

An itemized deduction is allowed for unreimbursed travel expenses related to a taxpayer's employment. **Travel expenses** are more broadly defined in the Code than are transportation expenses. Travel expenses include transportation expenses and meals and lodging while away from home in the pursuit of a trade or business. Meals cannot be lavish or extravagant under the circumstances. Transportation expenses (as previously discussed) are deductible even though the taxpayer is not away from home. A deduction for travel expenses is available only if the taxpayer is away from his or her tax home. Travel expenses also include reasonable laundry and incidental expenses.

AWAY-FROM-HOME REQUIREMENT

The crucial test for the deductibility of travel expenses is whether the employee is away from home overnight. "Overnight" need not be a 24-hour period, but it must be a period substantially longer than an ordinary day's work and must require rest, sleep, or a relief-from-work period.[11] A one-day business trip is not travel status, and meals and lodging for such a trip are not deductible.

Temporary Assignments. The employee must be away from home for a temporary period. If the taxpayer-employee is reassigned to a new post for an indefinite period of time, that new post becomes his or her tax home. *Temporary* indicates that the assignment's termination is expected within a reasonably short period of time. The position of the IRS is that the tax home is the business location, post, or station of the taxpayer. Thus, travel expenses are not deductible if a taxpayer is reassigned for an indefinite period and does not move his or her place of residence to the new location.

EXAMPLE 10

Malcolm's employer opened a branch office in San Diego. Malcolm was assigned to the new office for three months to train a new manager and to assist in setting up the new office. He tried commuting from his home in Los Angeles for a week and decided that he could not continue driving several hours a day. He rented an apartment in San Diego, where he lived during the week. He spent weekends with his wife and children at their home in Los Angeles. Malcolm's rent, meals, laundry, incidentals, and automobile expenses in San Diego are deductible. To the extent that Malcolm's transportation expense related to his weekend trips home exceeds what his cost of meals and lodging would have been, the excess is personal and nondeductible. ■

EXAMPLE 11

Assume that Malcolm in Example 10 was transferred to the new location to become the new manager permanently. His wife and children continued to live in Los Angeles until the end of the school year. Malcolm is no longer "away from home" because the assignment is not temporary. His travel expenses are not deductible. ■

To curtail controversy in this area, the Code specifies that a taxpayer "*shall not* be treated as *temporarily* away from home during any period of employment if such period exceeds 1 year."[12]

Determining the Tax Home. Under ordinary circumstances, determining the location of a taxpayer's tax home does not present a problem. The tax home is the area in which the taxpayer derives his or her principal source of income. When the taxpayer has more than one place of employment, the tax home is based on the amount of time spent in each area.

It is possible for a taxpayer never to be away from his or her tax home. In other words, the tax home follows the taxpayer. Thus, all meals and lodging remain personal and are not deductible. The reason for this result is that there is no duplication of expenses.[13]

EXAMPLE 12

Jim is single and lives with his parents. Although he is employed full-time as a long-haul truck driver, he contributes nothing toward the cost of maintaining his parents' household. The meals and lodging expenses Jim incurs while on the road are not deductible. ■

---

[11] *U.S. v. Correll*, 68–1 USTC ¶9101, 20 AFTR2d 5845, 88 S.Ct. 445 (USSC, 1967); Rev.Rul. 75–168, 1975–1 C.B. 58.

[12] § 162(a).

[13] Rev.Rul. 73–539, 1973–2 C.B. 37 and *James O. Henderson*, 70 TCM 1407, T.C.Memo. 1995–559, *aff'd* by 98–1 USTC ¶50,375, 81 AFTR2d 98–1748, 143 F.3d 497 (CA–9, 1998).

RESTRICTIONS ON TRAVEL EXPENSES

The possibility always exists that taxpayers will attempt to treat vacation or pleasure travel as deductible business travel. To prevent such practices, the law contains restrictions on certain travel expenses.

Conventions. For travel expenses to be deductible, a convention must be directly related to the taxpayer's trade or business.[14]

EXAMPLE 13

Dr. Hill, a pathologist who works for a hospital in Ohio, travels to Las Vegas to attend a two-day session on recent developments in estate planning. No deduction is allowed for Dr. Hill's travel expenses. ■

EXAMPLE 14

Assume the same facts as in Example 13, except that the convention deals entirely with recent developments in forensic medicine. Under these circumstances, a travel deduction is allowed. ■

If the proceedings of the convention are videotaped, the taxpayer must attend convention sessions to view the videotaped materials along with other participants. This requirement does not disallow deductions for costs (other than travel, meals, and entertainment) of renting or using videotaped materials related to business.

EXAMPLE 15

A CPA is unable to attend a convention at which current developments in taxation are discussed. She pays $200 for videotapes of the lectures and views them at home later. The $200 is an itemized deduction if the CPA is an employee. If she is self-employed, the $200 is a deduction *for* AGI. ■

The Code places stringent restrictions on the deductibility of travel expenses of the taxpayer's spouse or dependent.[15] Generally, the accompaniment by the spouse or dependent must serve a bona fide business purpose, and the expenses must be otherwise deductible.

EXAMPLE 16

Assume the same facts as in Example 14 with the additional fact that Dr. Hill is accompanied by Mrs. Hill. Mrs. Hill is not employed, but possesses secretarial skills and takes notes during the proceedings. No deduction is allowed for Mrs. Hill's travel expenses. ■

EXAMPLE 17

Modify the facts in Example 16 to make Mrs. Hill a nurse trained in pathology, who is employed by Dr. Hill as his assistant. Now, Mrs. Hill's travel expenses qualify as deductions. ■

Education. Travel as a form of education is not deductible.[16] If, however, the education qualifies as a deduction, the travel involved is allowed.

EXAMPLE 18

Greta, a German teacher, travels to Germany to maintain general familiarity with the language and culture. No travel expense deduction is allowed. ■

EXAMPLE 19

Jean-Claude, a scholar of French literature, travels to Paris to do specific library research that cannot be done elsewhere and to take courses that are offered only at the Sorbonne. The travel costs are deductible, assuming that the other requirements for deducting education expenses (discussed later in the chapter) are met. ■

---

[14] § 274(h)(1).
[15] § 274(m)(3).
[16] § 274(m)(2).

COMBINED BUSINESS AND PLEASURE TRAVEL

To be deductible, travel expenses need not be incurred in the performance of specific job functions. Travel expenses incurred in attending a professional convention are deductible by an employee if attendance is connected with services as an employee. For example, an employee of a law firm can deduct travel expenses incurred in attending a meeting of the American Bar Association.

Domestic Travel. Travel deductions have been used in the past by persons who claimed a tax deduction for what was essentially a personal vacation. As a result, several provisions have been enacted to govern deductions associated with combined business and pleasure trips. If the business/pleasure trip is from one point in the United States to another point in the United States, the transportation expenses are deductible only if the trip is *primarily for business*.[17] If the trip is primarily for pleasure, no transportation expenses qualify as a deduction. Meals, lodging, and other expenses are allocated between business and personal days.

EXAMPLE 20

In the current year, Hana travels from Seattle to New York primarily for business. She spends five days conducting business and three days sightseeing and attending shows. Her plane and taxi fare amounts to $560. Her meals amount to $100 per day, and lodging and incidental expenses are $150 per day. She can deduct the transportation charges of $560, since the trip is primarily for business (five days of business versus three days of sightseeing). Meals are limited to five days and are subject to the 50% cutback (discussed later in the chapter) for a total of $250 [5 days × ($100 × 50%)], and other expenses are limited to $750 (5 days × $150). If Hana is an employee, the unreimbursed travel expenses are miscellaneous itemized deductions. ■

EXAMPLE 21

Assume Hana goes to New York for a two-week vacation. While there, she spends several hours renewing acquaintances with people in her company's New York office. Her transportation expenses are not deductible. ■

Foreign Travel. When the trip is *outside the United States*, special rules apply. Transportation expenses must be allocated between business and personal unless (1) the taxpayer is away from home for seven days or less *or* (2) less than 25 percent of the time was for personal purposes. No allocation is required if the taxpayer has no substantial control over arrangements for the trip or the desire for a vacation is not a major factor in taking the trip. If the trip is primarily for pleasure, no transportation charges are deductible. Days devoted to travel are considered business days. Weekends, legal holidays, and intervening days are considered business days, provided that both the preceding and succeeding days were business days.[18]

EXAMPLE 22

In the current year, Robert takes a trip from New York to Japan primarily for business purposes. He is away from home from June 10 through June 19. He spends three days vacationing and seven days conducting business (including two travel days). His airfare is $2,500, his meals amount to $100 per day, and lodging and incidental expenses are $160 per day. Since Robert is away from home for more than seven days and more than 25% of his time is devoted to personal purposes, only 70% (7 days business/10 days total) of the transportation is deductible. His deductions are as follows:

[17]Reg. § 1.162–2(b)(1).

[18]§ 274(c) and Reg. § 1.274–4. For purposes of the seven-days-or-less exception, the departure travel day is not counted.

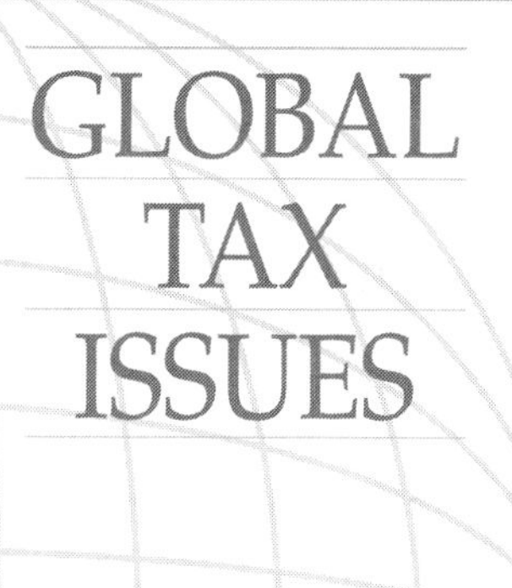

Conventions in Faraway Lands

Certain restrictions are imposed on the deductibility of expenses paid or incurred to attend conventions located outside the North American area. The expenses are disallowed unless it is established that the meeting is directly related to a trade or business of the taxpayer. Disallowance also occurs unless the taxpayer shows that it is as reasonable for the meeting to be held in a foreign location as within the North American area.

The foreign convention rules do not operate to bar a deduction to an employer if the expense is compensatory in nature. For example, a trip to Rome won by a top salesperson is included in the gross income of the employee and is fully deductible by the employer.

Transportation (70% × $2,500)		$1,750
Lodging ($160 × 7)		1,120
Meals ($100 × 7)	$ 700	
Less: 50% cutback (discussed later)	(350)	350
Total		$3,220

■

EXAMPLE 23

Assume the same facts as in Example 22. Robert is gone the same period of time, but spends only two days (rather than three) vacationing. Now no allocation of transportation is required. Since the pleasure portion of the trip is less than 25% of the total, all of the airfare qualifies for the travel deduction. ■

LO.4

Determine the moving expense deduction.

Moving Expenses

Moving expenses are deductible for moves in connection with the commencement of work at a new principal place of work.[19] Both employees and self-employed individuals can deduct these expenses. To be eligible for a moving expense deduction, a taxpayer must meet two basic tests: distance and time.

DISTANCE TEST

To meet the distance test, the taxpayer's new job location must be at least 50 miles farther from the taxpayer's old residence than the old residence was from the former place of employment. In this regard, the location of the new residence is not relevant. This eliminates a moving deduction for taxpayers who purchase a new home in the same general area without changing their place of employment. Those who accept a new job in the same general area as the old job location are also eliminated.

EXAMPLE 24

Harry is permanently transferred to a new job location. The distance from Harry's former home to his new job (80 miles) exceeds the distance from his former home to his old job (30 miles) by at least 50 miles. Harry has met the distance test for a moving expense deduction. (See the following diagram.)

[19] § 217(a).

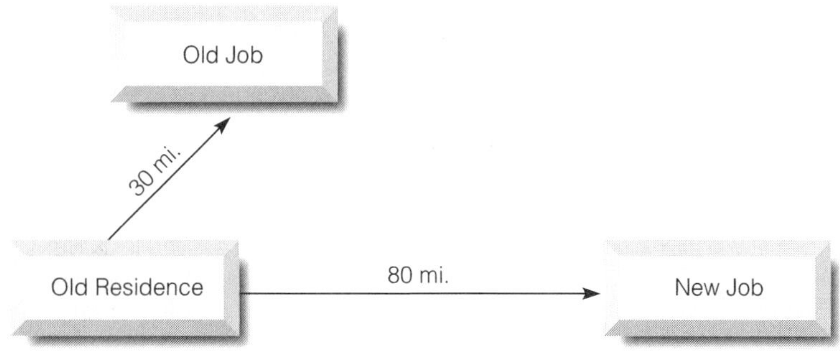

If Harry is not employed before the move, his new job must be at least 50 miles from his former residence. In this instance, Harry has met the distance test if he was not previously employed. ■

TIME TEST

To meet the time test, an employee must be employed on a full-time basis at the new location for 39 weeks in the 12-month period following the move. If the taxpayer is a self-employed individual, he or she must work in the new location for 78 weeks during the next two years. The first 39 weeks must be in the first 12 months. The time test is suspended if the taxpayer dies, becomes disabled, or is discharged or transferred by the new employer through no fault of the employee.

A taxpayer might not be able to meet the 39-week test by the due date of the tax return for the year of the move. For this reason, two alternatives are allowed. The taxpayer can take the deduction in the year the expenses are incurred, even though the 39-week test has not been met. If the taxpayer later fails to meet the test, either (1) the income of the following year is increased by an amount equal to the deduction previously claimed for moving expenses, or (2) an amended return is filed for the year of the move. The second alternative is to wait until the test is met and then file an amended tax return for the year of the move.

TREATMENT OF MOVING EXPENSES

What Is Included. "Qualified" moving expenses include *reasonable* expenses of:

- Moving household goods and personal effects.
- Traveling from the former residence to the new place of residence.

For this purpose, *traveling* includes lodging, but not meals, for the taxpayer and members of the household.[20] It does not include the cost of moving servants or others who are not members of the household. The taxpayer can elect to use actual auto expenses (no depreciation is allowed) or the automatic mileage method. In this case, moving expense mileage is limited in 2005 to 15 cents per mile (14 cents in 2004) for each car. These expenses are also limited by the reasonableness standard. For example, if one moves from Texas to Florida via Maine and takes six weeks to do so, the transportation and lodging must be allocated between personal and moving expenses.

EXAMPLE 25

Jill is transferred by her employer from the Atlanta office to the San Francisco office. In this connection, she spends the following amounts:

[20]§ 217(b).

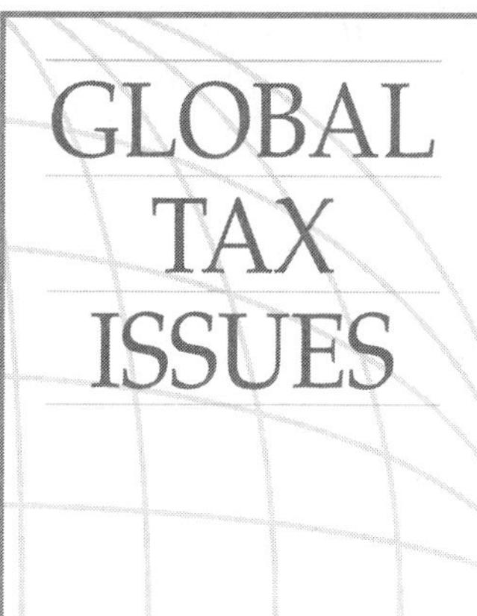

EXPATRIATES AND THE MOVING EXPENSE DEDUCTION

Expatriates, U.S. persons who accept work assignments overseas, enjoy several favorable tax advantages regarding foreign moves. First, the cost of storing household goods qualifies as a moving expense. This could lead to a major tax saving since expatriates do not ship most of their household effects to the foreign location. Furthermore, the cost of storage, particularly in a climate-controlled facility, is not insignificant.

The second advantage expatriates could enjoy is an exemption from the time test. Those who return to the United States to retire are absolved from the 39-week or 78-week work requirement. Thus, the return home expenses are treated as qualified moving expenses.

Cost of moving furniture	$2,800
Transportation	700
Meals	200
Lodging	300

Jill's total qualified moving expense is $3,800 ($2,800 + $700 + $300). ■

The moving expense deduction is allowed regardless of whether the employee is transferred by the existing employer or is employed by a new employer. It is allowed if the employee moves to a new area and obtains employment or switches from self-employed status to employee status (and vice versa). The moving expense deduction is also allowed if an individual is unemployed before obtaining employment in a new area.

How Treated. Qualified moving expenses that are paid (or reimbursed) by the employer are not reported as part of the gross income of the employee.[21] Moving expenses that are paid (or reimbursed) by the employer and are not qualified moving expenses are included in the employee's gross income and are not deductible. The employer is responsible for allocating the reimbursement between the qualified and nonqualified moving expenses. Reimbursed qualified moving expenses are separately stated on the Form W–2 given to the employee for the year involved. Qualified moving expenses that are not reimbursed and those of self-employed taxpayers are deductions *for* AGI.[22]

Form 3903 is used to report the details of the moving expense deduction if the employee is not reimbursed or a self-employed person is involved.

LO.5

Differentiate between deductible and nondeductible education expenses.

Education Expenses

GENERAL REQUIREMENTS

An employee can deduct expenses incurred for education (**education expenses**) as ordinary and necessary business expenses provided the expenses are incurred for either of two reasons:

[21]§§ 132(a)(6) and (g).

[22]§ 62(a)(15).

- To maintain or improve existing skills required in the present job.
- To meet the express requirements of the employer or the requirements imposed by law to retain his or her employment status.

Education expenses are *not* deductible if the education is for either of the following purposes (except as discussed below under A Limited Deduction Approach):

- To meet the minimum educational standards for qualification in the taxpayer's existing job.
- To qualify the taxpayer for a new trade or business.[23]

Fees incurred for professional qualification exams (the bar exam, for example) and fees for review courses (such as a CPA review course) are not deductible.[24] If the education incidentally results in a promotion or raise, the deduction still can be taken as long as the education maintained and improved existing skills and did not qualify a person for a new trade or business. A change in duties is not always fatal to the deduction if the new duties involve the same general work. For example, the IRS has ruled that a practicing dentist's education expenses incurred to become an orthodontist are deductible.[25]

REQUIREMENTS IMPOSED BY LAW OR BY THE EMPLOYER FOR RETENTION OF EMPLOYMENT

Taxpayers are permitted to deduct education expenses if additional courses are required by the employer or are imposed by law. Many states require a minimum of a bachelor's degree and a specified number of additional courses to retain a teaching job. In addition, some public school systems have imposed a master's degree requirement and require teachers to make satisfactory progress toward a master's degree in order to keep their positions. If the required education is the minimum degree required for the job, no deduction is allowed.

A taxpayer classified as a staff accountant who went back to school to obtain a bachelor's degree in accounting was not allowed to deduct the expenses. Although some courses tended to maintain and improve his existing skills in his entry-level position, the degree was the minimum requirement for his job.[26]

Expenses incurred for education required by law for various professions will also qualify for deduction.

EXAMPLE 26

In order to satisfy the State Board of Public Accountancy rules for maintaining her CPA license, Nancy takes an auditing course sponsored by a local college. The cost of the education is deductible. ■

MAINTAINING OR IMPROVING EXISTING SKILLS

The "maintaining or improving existing skills" requirement in the Code has been difficult for both taxpayers and the courts to interpret. For example, a business executive may be permitted to deduct the costs of obtaining an MBA on the grounds that the advanced management education is undertaken to maintain and improve existing management skills. The executive is eligible to deduct the costs of specialized, nondegree management courses that are taken for continuing education or to maintain or improve existing skills. Expenses incurred by the executive

[23]Reg. §§ 1.162–5(b)(2) and (3).

[24]Reg. § 1.212–1(f) and Rev.Rul. 69–292, 1969–1 C.B. 84.

[25]Rev.Rul. 74–78, 1974–1 C.B. 44.

[26]Reg. § 1.162–5(b)(2)(iii) Example (2); *Collin J. Davidson,* 43 TCM 743, T.C.Memo. 1982–119. But see the subsequent discussion of § 222 (i.e., the deduction for higher education qualified tuition and related expenses).

Is an MBA Degree Deductible?

Education that maintains or improves existing skills is deductible, but education that qualifies a taxpayer for a new field is not. But how do these basic rules apply to a conventional (i.e., nonspecialized) MBA degree? Does being a manager or a consultant require an MBA degree? Generally, the answer has always been that it does not. In this regard, therefore, the education does not create a new skill, so its cost should be deductible.

Several recent holdings, however, have found that an MBA degree can lead to qualifying for a new trade or business. But these holdings involved situations where the education resulted in a job change and satisfied different minimum requirements set by the employer. In one case, for example, the taxpayer moved from the position of investment analyst to become an investment banker, and the latter position required an MBA degree. Under these circumstances, the cost of the education was held to be nondeductible.

But barring a change to a job where the degree is required, the cost of an MBA degree should be deductible as merely improving existing managerial skills.

to obtain a law degree are not deductible, however, because the education constitutes training for a new trade or business. The Regulations deny a self-employed accountant a deduction for expenses relating to law school.[27]

CLASSIFICATION OF SPECIFIC ITEMS

Education expenses include books, tuition, typing, and transportation (e.g., from the office to night school) and travel (e.g., meals and lodging while away from home at summer school).

EXAMPLE 27

Bill, who holds a bachelor of education degree, is a secondary education teacher in the Los Angeles school system. The school board recently raised its minimum education requirement for new teachers from four years of college training to five. A grandfather clause allows teachers with only four years of college to continue to qualify if they show satisfactory progress toward a graduate degree. Bill enrolls at the University of California and takes three graduate courses. His unreimbursed expenses for this purpose are as follows:

Books and tuition	$2,600
Lodging while in travel status (June–August)	1,150
Meals while in travel status	800
Laundry while in travel status	220
Transportation	600

Bill has an itemized deduction as follows:

Books and tuition	$2,600
Lodging	1,150
Meals less 50% cutback (see below)	400
Laundry	220
Transportation	600
	$4,970

■

[27]Reg. § 1.162–5(b)(3)(ii) Example (1).

TABLE 9–1
Phase-in Rules for Qualified Tuition Deduction

Tax Years Involved	Filing Status	AGI Limit	Maximum Deduction Allowed
2002–2003	Single	$ 65,000*	$3,000
	Married	130,000*	
2004–2005	Single	65,000	4,000
	Married	130,000	
	Single	65,001 to 80,000*	2,000
	Married	130,001 to 160,000*	2,000

*No deduction at all is available if AGI exceeds this amount.

A LIMITED DEDUCTION APPROACH

One of the major shortcomings of the education deduction, previously discussed, is that it is unavailable for taxpayers obtaining a basic skill. Thus, a taxpayer working for an accounting firm cannot deduct the cost of earning a bachelor's degree in accounting. Under 2001 tax legislation, this shortcoming has been partly resolved with the **deduction for qualified tuition and related expenses**.

A deduction *for* AGI is allowed for qualified tuition and related expenses involving higher education (i.e., postsecondary). The maximum amount of the deduction varies depending on the year involved. Further, the deduction is unavailable if the taxpayer's AGI exceeds a prescribed amount.[28] The phase-ins and limitations are summarized in Table 9–1.

Various aspects of the higher education tuition deduction are summarized below:

- Qualified tuition and related expenses include whatever is required for enrollment at the institution. Usually, student activity fees, books, and room and board are not included.[29]
- The expense need not be employment related, although it can be.
- The deduction is not available for married persons who file separate returns.[30]
- To avoid a "double benefit," the deduction must be coordinated with other education provisions (i.e., HOPE and lifetime learning credits). Along this same line, no deduction is allowed for a taxpayer who qualifies as another's dependent.[31]
- The deduction *for* AGI classification avoids the 2 percent-of-AGI floor on miscellaneous itemized deductions. As noted later in the chapter, this is the fate suffered by other education-related employee expenses.

EXAMPLE 28

Tina is single and a full-time employee of a CPA firm. During 2005, she attends law school at night and incurs the following expenses: $4,200 for tuition and $340 for books and supplies. Presuming she satisfies the AGI limitation (see Table 9–1), she can claim $4,000 as a deduction *for* AGI. If she itemizes her deductions for the year, can she claim the $540 not allowed

[28]The dollar caps, AGI limitations, and phase-ins are contained in § 222(b).

[29]Section 222(d) refers to § 25A(f), which deals with the HOPE and lifetime learning credits (see Chapter 12). Student activity fees and prescribed course-related books could be allowed if they are a condition for enrollment.

[30]§ 222(d)(4).

[31]§ 222(c).

under § 222 ($200 tuition in excess of $4,000 + $340 for books and supplies) as an education expense eligible for itemized deduction treatment? No, because obtaining a law degree leads to a new trade or business.[32] ■

OTHER PROVISIONS DEALING WITH EDUCATION

The focus of this chapter is on the deduction aspects of certain items.[33] For education, however, two important provisions involve the income aspects. One deals with the exclusion of certain scholarships from gross income.[34] The other deals with the exclusion from gross income of amounts provided by the employer under certain educational assistance programs.[35] Both of these provisions are discussed in Chapter 5.

Closely tied to the income aspects is the Coverdell Education Savings Account. Although contributions to this type of savings account are not deductible, payouts of benefits can qualify as exclusions from gross income.[36]

Further favorable tax treatment of education occurs in the form of credits. Both the HOPE and the lifetime learning credits are discussed in Chapter 12.[37]

LO.6

Understand how entertainment expenses are treated.

Entertainment Expenses

Many taxpayers attempt to deduct personal entertainment expenses as business expenses. For this reason, the tax law restricts the deductibility of entertainment expenses. The Code contains strict record-keeping requirements and provides restrictive tests for the deduction of certain types of **entertainment expenses**.

CUTBACK ADJUSTMENT

During the administration of Jimmy Carter, considerable controversy arose regarding the "three martini" business lunch. By virtue of allowing a tax deduction, should the tax law be subsidizing a practice that contained a significant element of personal pleasure? One possible remedy for the situation was to disallow any deduction for business entertainment, but this option was regarded as being too harsh. Instead the *cutback* rule was instituted. Rather than disallowing *all* of the deduction, allow only a certain percentage, and the rest of the expenditure would be cut back. Currently, only 50 percent of meal and entertainment expenses are allowed as a deduction.[38] The limitation applies in the context of both employment and self-employment status. Although the 50 percent cutback can apply to either the employer or the employee, it will not apply twice. The cutback applies to the one who really pays (economically) for the meals or entertainment.

EXAMPLE 29

Jane, an employee of Pato Corporation, entertains one of her clients. If Pato Corporation does not reimburse Jane, she is subject to the cutback adjustment. If, however, Pato Corporation reimburses Jane (or pays for the entertainment directly), Pato suffers the cutback. ■

In certain situations, however, a full 50 percent cutback seems unfair. If, for example, the hours of service are regulated (by the U.S. Department of Transportation) and away-from-home meals are frequent and necessary, the "three martini" business lunch type of abuse is unlikely. Consequently, the cutback rule is mitigated for the following types of employees:

---

[32] *Steven Galligan*, 83 TCM 1859, T.C.Memo. 2002–150.

[33] Another deduction item relating to education is the deduction of interest on education loans, which is covered in § 221 and discussed in Chapter 10.

[34] § 117.

[35] § 127.

[36] § 530.

[37] § 25A.

[38] § 274(n).

- Certain air transportation employees, such as flight crews, dispatchers, mechanics, and control tower operators.
- Interstate truck and bus drivers.
- Certain railroad employees, such as train crews and dispatchers.
- Certain merchant mariners.

Starting in 1998, the cutback for these types of employees is reduced by 5 percent at two-year intervals until it reaches 20 percent in year 2008 and thereafter. Thus, 80 percent of the cost of meals will eventually be allowed as a deduction. For 2004–2005, 70 percent is allowed (for 2002–2003, 65 percent was allowed).

ETHICAL CONSIDERATIONS

Your Turn or Mine?

Martha, a CPA, John, an attorney, Alan, a realtor, and Ivana, a physician, maintain private practices in the same business community. During the year, they get together for lunch at least once a week. They take turns paying for the group's lunch. Since they all do business with each other, each claims an entertainment expense deduction for the amount he or she paid for the lunches. Evaluate this practice.

What Is Covered. Transportation expenses are not affected by the cutback rule—only meals and entertainment. The cutback also applies to taxes and tips relating to meals and entertainment. Cover charges, parking fees at an entertainment location, and room rental fees for a meal or cocktail party are also subject to the 50 percent rule.

EXAMPLE 30

Joe pays a $30 cab fare to meet his client for dinner. The meal costs $120, and Joe leaves a $20 tip. His deduction is $100 [($120 + $20) × 50% + $30 cab fare]. ■

What Is Not Covered. The cutback rule has a number of exceptions. One exception covers the case where the full value of the meals or entertainment is included in the compensation of the employee (or independent contractor).

EXAMPLE 31

Myrtle wins an all-expense-paid trip to Europe for selling the most insurance for her company during the year. Her employer treats this trip as additional compensation to Myrtle. The cutback adjustment does not apply to the employer. ■

Another exception applies to meals and entertainment in a subsidized eating facility or where the *de minimis* fringe benefit rule is met (see Chapter 5).[39]

EXAMPLE 32

General Hospital has an employee cafeteria on the premises for its doctors, nurses, and other employees. The cafeteria operates at cost. The cutback rule does not apply to General Hospital. ■

EXAMPLE 33

Canary Corporation gives a ham, a fruitcake, and a bottle of wine to each employee at year-end. Since the *de minimis* fringe benefit exclusion applies to business gifts of packaged foods and beverages, their *full* cost is deductible by Canary. ■

A similar exception applies to employer-paid recreational activities for employees (e.g., the annual Christmas party or spring picnic).[40]

[39] § 274(n)(2).

[40] § 274(e)(4).

CLASSIFICATION OF EXPENSES

Entertainment expenses are categorized as follows: those *directly related* to business and those *associated with* business.[41] Directly related expenses are related to an actual business meeting or discussion. These expenses are distinguished from entertainment expenses that are incurred to promote goodwill, such as maintaining existing customer relations. To obtain a deduction for directly related entertainment, it is not necessary to show that actual benefit resulted from the expenditure as long as there was a reasonable expectation of benefit. To qualify as directly related, the expense should be incurred in a clear business setting. If there is little possibility of engaging in the active conduct of a trade or business due to the nature of the social facility, it is difficult to qualify the expenditure as directly related to business.

Expenses associated with, rather than directly related to, business entertainment must serve a specific business purpose, such as obtaining new business or continuing existing business. These expenditures qualify only if the expenses directly precede or follow a bona fide business discussion. Entertainment occurring on the same day as the business discussion meets the test.

RESTRICTIONS UPON DEDUCTIBILITY

Business Meals. Any business meal is deductible only if the following are true:[42]

- The meal is directly related to or associated with the active conduct of a trade or business.
- The expense is not lavish or extravagant under the circumstances.
- The taxpayer (or an employee) is present at the meal.

A business meal with a business associate or customer is not deductible unless business is discussed before, during, or after the meal. This requirement is not intended to disallow the deduction for a meal consumed while away from home on business.

EXAMPLE 34

Lacy travels to San Francisco for a business convention. She pays for dinner with three colleagues and is not reimbursed by her employer. They do not discuss business. She can deduct 50% of the cost of her meal. However, she cannot deduct the cost of her colleagues' meals. ■

The *clear business purpose* test requires that meals be directly related to or associated with the active conduct of a business. A meal is not deductible if it serves no business purpose.

The taxpayer or an employee must be present at the business meal for the meal to be deductible. An independent contractor who renders significant services to the taxpayer is treated as an employee.

EXAMPLE 35

Lance, a party to a contract negotiation, buys dinner for other parties to the negotiation but does not attend the dinner. No deduction is allowed. ■

Club Dues. The Code provides: "No deduction shall be allowed . . . for amounts paid or incurred for membership in any club organized for business, pleasure, recreation, or other social purpose."[43] Although this prohibition seems quite broad, the IRS does allow a deduction for dues to clubs whose primary purpose is public service and community volunteerism (e.g., Kiwanis, Lions, Rotary).

Even though dues are not deductible, actual entertainment at a club may qualify.

[41] § 274(a)(1)(A).
[42] § 274(k).
[43] § 274(a)(3).

EXAMPLE 36

During the current year, Vincent spent $1,400 on business lunches at the Lakeside Country Club. The annual membership fee was $6,000, and Vincent used the facility 60% of the time for business. Presuming the lunches meet the business meal test, Vincent may claim $700 (50% × $1,400) as a deduction. None of the club dues are deductible. ■

Ticket Purchases for Entertainment. A deduction for the cost of a ticket for an entertainment activity is limited to the face value of the ticket.[44] This limitation is applied before the 50 percent rule. The face value of a ticket includes any tax. Under this rule, the excess payment to a scalper for a ticket is not deductible. Similarly, the fee to a ticket agency for the purchase of a ticket is not deductible.

Expenditures for the rental or use of a luxury skybox at a sports arena in excess of the face value of regular tickets are disallowed as deductions. If a luxury skybox is used for entertainment that is directly related to or associated with business, the deduction is limited to the face value of nonluxury box seats. All seats in the luxury skybox are counted, even when some seats are unoccupied.

The taxpayer may also deduct stated charges for food and beverages under the general rules for business entertainment. The deduction for skybox seats, food, and beverages is limited to 50 percent of cost.

EXAMPLE 37

In the current year, Jay Company pays $6,000 to rent a 10-seat skybox at City Stadium for three football games. Nonluxury box seats at each event range in cost from $25 to $35 a seat. In March, a Jay representative and five clients use the skybox for the first game. The entertainment follows a bona fide business discussion, and Jay spends $86 for food and beverages during the game. The deduction for the first sports event is as follows:

Food and beverages	$ 86
Deduction for seats ($35 × 10 seats)	350
Total entertainment expense	$436
50% limitation	× .50
Deduction	$218

■

Business Gifts. Business gifts are deductible to the extent of $25 per donee per year.[45] An exception is made for gifts costing $4 or less (e.g., pens with the employee's or company's name on them) or promotional materials. Such items are not treated as business gifts subject to the $25 limitation. In addition, incidental costs such as engraving of jewelry and nominal charges for gift-wrapping, mailing, and delivery are not included in the cost of the gift in applying the limitation. Gifts to superiors and employers are not deductible.

Records must be maintained to substantiate business gifts.

LO.7

Identify other employee expenses.

Other Employee Expenses

OFFICE IN THE HOME

Employees and self-employed individuals are not allowed a deduction for **office in the home expenses** unless a portion of the residence is used *exclusively* on a *regular basis* as either of the following:

- The principal place of business for any trade or business of the taxpayer.
- A place of business used by clients, patients, or customers.

[44] § 274(l).

[45] § 274(b)(1).

Employees must meet an additional test: The use must be for the *convenience of the employer* rather than merely being "appropriate and helpful."[46]

The precise meaning of "principal place of business" has been the subject of considerable controversy.[47] Congress ultimately resolved the controversy by amending the Code.[48] The term "principal place of business" now includes a place of business that satisfies the following requirements:

- The office is used by the taxpayer to conduct administrative or management activities of a trade or business.
- There is no other fixed location of the trade or business where the taxpayer conducts these activities.

EXAMPLE 38

Dr. Smith is a self-employed anesthesiologist. During the year, he spends 30 to 35 hours per week administering anesthesia and postoperative care to patients in three hospitals, none of which provides him with an office. He also spends two or three hours per day in a room in his home that he uses exclusively as an office. He does not meet patients there, but he performs a variety of tasks related to his medical practice (e.g., contacting surgeons, bookkeeping, reading medical journals). A deduction will be allowed since Dr. Smith uses the office in the home to conduct administrative or management activities of his trade or business, and there is no other fixed location where these activities can be carried out. ■

The exclusive use requirement means that a specific part of the home must be used *solely* for business purposes. A deduction, if permitted, requires an allocation of total expenses of operating the home between business and personal use based on floor space or number of rooms.

Even if the taxpayer meets the above requirements, the allowable home office expenses cannot exceed the gross income from the business less all other business expenses attributable to the activity. Furthermore, the home office expenses that are allowed as itemized deductions anyway (e.g., mortgage interest and real estate taxes) must be deducted first. All home office expenses of an employee are miscellaneous itemized deductions, except those (such as interest and taxes) that qualify as other personal itemized deductions. Home office expenses of a self-employed individual are trade or business expenses and are deductible *for* AGI.

Any disallowed home office expenses are *carried forward* and used in future years subject to the same limitations.

EXAMPLE 39

Rick is a certified public accountant employed by a regional CPA firm as a tax manager. He operates a separate business in which he refinishes furniture in his home. For this business, he uses two rooms in the basement of his home exclusively and regularly. The floor space of the two rooms constitutes 10% of the floor space of his residence. Gross income from the business totals $8,000. Expenses of the business (other than home office expenses) are $6,500. Rick incurs the following home office expenses:

Real property taxes on residence	$4,000
Interest expense on residence	7,500
Operating expenses of residence	2,000
Depreciation on residence (based on 10% business use)	250

[46]§ 280A(c)(1).

[47]See the restrictive interpretation arrived at in *Comm. v. Soliman*, 93–1 USTC ¶50,014, 71 AFTR2d 93–463, 113 S.Ct. 701 (USSC, 1993).

[48]§ 280A(c)(1) as modified by the Tax Reform Act of 1997.

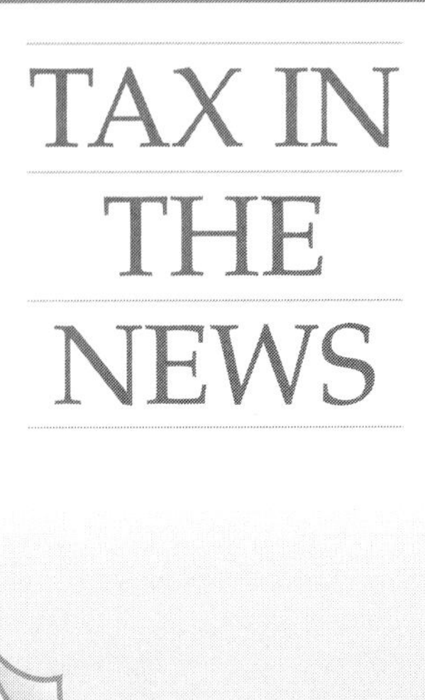

ONE SIDE EFFECT OF 9/11

Telecommuting (or working at home) has always had its advantages. For the employee, it offers flexibility as to working hours, and particularly in metropolitan areas, it avoids an often horrendous commute. For the employer, it offers the cost savings of not having to provide office space.

The tragedy of September 11 has added new variables to consider when evaluating the telecommuting approach. For the employee, there is the peace of mind that comes from the safety of home. Although no place is entirely safe, a downtown high-rise office building is clearly a more likely target of a terrorist attack. From the employer's standpoint, the "at-home workplace" guarantees employee accessibility and precludes the complete destruction of job-related business data.

As working at home becomes more popular, an obvious result will be the increased use of the office in the home deduction.

Rick's deductions are determined as follows:

Business income		$ 8,000
Less: Other business expenses		(6,500)
		$ 1,500
Less: Allocable taxes ($4,000 × 10%)	$400	
Allocable interest ($7,500 × 10%)	750	(1,150)
		$ 350
Allocable operating expenses of the residence ($2,000 × 10%)		(200)
		$ 150
Allocable depreciation ($250, limited to remaining income)		(150)
		$ -0-

Rick has a carryover of $100 (the unused excess depreciation). Because he is self-employed, the allocable taxes and interest ($1,150), the other deductible office expenses ($200 + $150), and $6,500 of other business expenses are deductible *for* AGI. ■

Form 8829 (Expenses for Business Use of Your Home) is available from the IRS for computation of the office in the home deduction.

The home office limitation cannot be circumvented by leasing part of one's home to an employer, using it as a home office, and deducting the expenses as a rental expense under § 212.

MISCELLANEOUS EMPLOYEE EXPENSES

Miscellaneous employee expenses include those costs that are job related and are not otherwise covered elsewhere. As the focus here is on their deductibility, this discussion presumes that such expenses have not been reimbursed by the employer under an accountable plan arrangement (discussed later in the chapter).

Expenses related to maintaining job status make up a significant category of miscellaneous expenses. They include such costs as union dues, membership dues to professional organizations, subscriptions to trade publications and professional journals, and various license fees paid to government agencies and other regulatory bodies.

Special Clothing. To be deductible, special clothing must be both specifically required as a condition of employment and not adaptable for regular wear. For example, a police officer's uniform must be worn when "on duty" but is not suitable for "off-duty" activities. Its cost, therefore, is deductible. When special clothing qualifies for deductibility, so does the cost of its maintenance (i.e., laundry, dry cleaning).

Whether the out-of-pocket cost of military uniforms is deductible depends on the duty status of the taxpayer. If a member of the National Guard (or reserves) is not on active duty, then the cost of the uniform qualifies for deductibility. For those on active duty, the cost of regular uniforms does not qualify because the uniforms are suitable for ordinary street wear. Even for those on active duty, some apparel, such as ceremonial attire (dress blues) or combat gear, will qualify because it is not adaptable for regular wear.

The cost of clothing possessing *safety* features to prevent workplace injuries will qualify. This includes such items as safety glasses, shoes (e.g., "steel-toed"), special gloves, lab coats, and "hard hats." The tolerance of the IRS in the area of safety clothing is partially attributable to its lack of suitability for personal use.

Job Hunting. The expenses incurred in seeking employment can be deductible under certain conditions. The search must involve the same trade or business as the taxpayer's current position. No deduction is allowed for the cost of obtaining the first job. An unemployed person, however, can qualify for the deduction if there has not been a significant time lapse since the last job. In terms of deductibility, it does not matter whether the job search is successful. Nor does a change in jobs have to result. Costs that qualify include job counseling, compilation and distribution of biographical data (such as work history), and unreimbursed travel for job interviews.

Educator Expenses. The Job Creation and Worker Assistance Act of 2002, as amended by the Working Families Tax Relief Act of 2004, provides limited relief for elementary and secondary school teachers. For taxable years beginning during 2002, 2003, 2004, or 2005, eligible educators can claim up to $250 for school supplies as a deduction *for* AGI.[49] Eligible educators must work at least 900 hours during a school year as a teacher, instructor, counselor, principal, or aide at either public or private elementary and secondary schools. Covered costs include unreimbursed expenses for books, supplies, computer and other equipment, and supplementary materials used in the classroom.

EXAMPLE 40

Hortense is a full-time teacher at Hoover Elementary. During 2005, she buys $1,200 of school supplies for her fourth grade class. Under an accountable plan (see later in the chapter), Hoover reimburses her for $400 of these supplies. As to the $800 balance, Hortense may claim $250 as a deduction *for* AGI and $550 as a miscellaneous itemized deduction (subject to the 2%-of-AGI floor). ■

Although the educator expense provision expires at the end of 2005, there is good reason to believe that Congress will extend it. When such an extension occurs, it probably will be made retroactive in application.

[49] § 62(a)(2)(D).

LO.8

Become familiar with various deductions for contributions to retirement accounts.

Contributions to Retirement Accounts

Pension considerations are an essential feature of any compensation arrangement. As noted in Chapter 1, providing retirement security for employees can be justified on both economic and social grounds. Because the public sector (i.e., Social Security) will not provide sufficient retirement security for recipients, the private sector must fill the need. Congress has given the private sector the necessary incentive by enacting various measures that provide significant tax advantages for retirement plans. These plans fall into two major classifications: those available to employees and those available to self-employed persons.

EMPLOYEE IRAs

Pension plans covering employees follow one of two income tax approaches. Most plans allow an *exclusion* for the contributions the employee makes to the plan. The employee's income tax return shows nothing regarding the contribution—no income, exclusion, or deduction. This is the case even if the contribution is funded entirely (or partially) by means of a salary reduction.[50]

The other income tax approach is followed by the **traditional IRA.** Here, the contributing employee is allowed a deduction *for* AGI. The amount, a maximum of $4,000 for 2005, is reported as a deduction on Form 1040.[51] As with the exclusion variety of pension plan, nothing is taxed to the employee-participant until distributions from the traditional IRA occur. Consequently, all of these types of retirement plans carry the advantage of deferring the taxation of income. All retirement plans are subject to various rules regarding coverage requirements, degree of vesting, excessive contributions, and premature distributions. Generally, these rules are less stringent for traditional IRAs.

The traditional IRA is to be distinguished from the **Roth IRA,** which takes a radically different tax approach. No tax benefit (i.e., exclusion or deduction) results from the initial contribution to a Roth IRA. Instead, later distributions (including postcontribution earnings) are recovered tax-free.[52]

SELF-EMPLOYED KEOGH (H.R. 10) PLANS

Self-employed taxpayers can also participate in retirement plans with tax-favored benefits. Known as Keogh (or H.R. 10) plans, these arrangements follow the deduction approach of traditional IRAs.[53] The amount contributed under a plan is a deduction *for* AGI and is reported as a deduction on Form 1040. The plan established by a self-employed taxpayer who has employees must meet stringent requirements to ensure that it provides similar retirement benefits for the group. The law is structured to ensure that employees share an owner-employer's ability to defer taxes.

LO.9

Appreciate the difference between accountable and nonaccountable employee plans.

Classification of Employee Expenses

The classification of employee expenses depends on whether they are reimbursed by the employer under an accountable plan. If so, then they are not reported by the employee at all. In effect, therefore, this result is equivalent to treating the

[50]See, for example, §§ 401(k), 403(b), and 457.

[51]§§ 219 and 408.

[52]§ 408A.

[53]§ 401(c).

expenses as deductions *for* AGI.[54] If the expenses are reimbursed under a nonaccountable plan or are not reimbursed at all, then they are classified as deductions *from* AGI and can be claimed only if the employee-taxpayer itemizes. An exception is made for moving expenses and the employment-related expenses of a qualified performing artist.[55] Here, deduction *for* AGI classification is allowed.

For classification purposes, therefore, the difference between accountable and nonaccountable plans is significant.

ACCOUNTABLE PLANS

In General. An **accountable plan** requires the employee to satisfy these two requirements:

- Adequately account for (substantiate) the expenses. An employee renders an *adequate accounting* by submitting a record, with receipts and other substantiation, to the employer.[56]
- Return any excess reimbursement or allowance. An "excess reimbursement or allowance" is any amount that the employee does not adequately account for as an ordinary and necessary business expense.

Substantiation. The law provides that no deduction is allowed for any travel, entertainment, business gift, or listed property (automobiles, computers) expenditure unless properly substantiated by adequate records. The records should contain the following information:[57]

- The amount of the expense.
- The time and place of travel or entertainment (or date of gift).
- The business purpose of the expense.
- The business relationship of the taxpayer to the person entertained (or receiving the gift).

This means the taxpayer must maintain an account book or diary in which the above information is recorded at the time of the expenditure. Documentary evidence, such as itemized receipts, is required to support any expenditure for lodging while traveling away from home and for any other expenditure of $75 or more. If a taxpayer fails to keep adequate records, each expense must be established by a written or oral statement of the exact details of the expense and by other corroborating evidence.[58]

EXAMPLE 41

Bertha has travel expenses substantiated only by canceled checks. The checks establish the date, place, and amount of the expenditure. Because neither the business relationship nor the business purpose is established, the deduction is disallowed.[59] ■

EXAMPLE 42

Dwight has travel and entertainment expenses substantiated by a diary showing the time, place, and amount of the expenditure. His oral testimony provides the business relationship and business purpose. However, since he has no receipts, any expenditures of $75 or more are disallowed.[60] ■

[54] § 62(a)(2).
[55] As defined in § 62(b).
[56] Reg. § 1.162–17(b)(4).
[57] § 274(d).
[58] Reg. § 1.274–5T(c)(3).
[59] *William T. Whitaker*, 56 TCM 47, T.C.Memo. 1988–418.
[60] *W. David Tyler*, 43 TCM 927, T.C.Memo. 1982–160.

Deemed Substantiation. In lieu of reimbursing actual expenses for travel away from home, many employers reduce their paperwork by adopting a policy of reimbursing employees with a *per diem* allowance, a flat dollar amount per day of business travel. Of the substantiation requirements listed above, the *amount* of the expense is proved, or *deemed substantiated*, by using such a per diem allowance or reimbursement procedure. The amount of expenses that is deemed substantiated is equal to the lesser of the per diem allowance or the amount of the Federal per diem rate.

The regular Federal per diem rate is the highest amount that the Federal government will pay to its employees for lodging, meals, and incidental expenses[61] while in travel status away from home in a particular area. The rates are different for different locations.[62]

The use of the standard Federal per diem rates for meals and incidental expenses constitutes an adequate accounting. Employees and self-employed persons can use these standard allowances instead of deducting the actual cost of daily meals and incidental expenses, even if not reimbursed. There is no standard lodging allowance, however.

Only the amount of the expense is considered substantiated under the deemed substantiated method. The other substantiation requirements must be provided: place, date, business purpose of the expense, and the business relationship of the parties involved.

NONACCOUNTABLE PLANS

A **nonaccountable plan** is one in which an adequate accounting or return of excess amounts, or both, is not required. All reimbursements of expenses are reported in full as wages on the employee's Form W–2. Any allowable expenses are deductible in the same manner as are unreimbursed expenses.

Unreimbursed Employee Expenses. Unreimbursed employee expenses are treated in a straightforward manner. Meals and entertainment expenses are subject to the 50 percent limit. Total unreimbursed employee business expenses are usually reported as miscellaneous itemized deductions subject to the 2 percent-of-AGI floor (see below). If the employee could have received, but did not seek, reimbursement for whatever reason, none of the employment-related expenses are deductible.

Failure to Comply with Accountable Plan Requirements. An employer may have an accountable plan and require employees to return excess reimbursements or allowances, but an employee may fail to follow the rules of the plan. In that case, the expenses and reimbursements are subject to nonaccountable plan treatment.

REPORTING PROCEDURES

The reporting requirements range from no reporting at all (accountable plans when all requirements are met) to the use of some or all of the following forms: Form W–2 (Wage and Tax Statement), Form 2106 (Employee Business Expenses) or Form 2106–EZ (Unreimbursed Employee Business Expenses), and Schedule A (Itemized Deductions) for nonaccountable plans and unreimbursed employee expenses.

[61] Incidental expenses include tips and fees to porters, bellhops, hotel maids, etc. For travel away from home after 2002, the term does *not* include expenses for laundry and dry cleaning of clothing, lodging taxes, and telephone calls.

[62] Each current edition of *Per Diem Rates* (IRS Publication 1542) contains the list and amounts for that year. Also, per diem rates, both domestic and foreign, can be found at **http://www.policyworks.gov/perdiem**.

Reimbursed employee expenses that are adequately accounted for under an accountable plan are deductible *for* AGI on Form 2106. Allowed excess expenses, expenses reimbursed under a nonaccountable plan, and unreimbursed expenses are deductible *from* AGI on Schedule A, subject to the 2 percent-of-AGI floor.

When a reimbursement under an accountable plan is paid in separate amounts relating to designated expenses such as meals or entertainment, no problem arises. The reimbursements and expenses are reported as such on the appropriate forms. If the reimbursement is made in a single amount, an allocation must be made to determine the appropriate portion of the reimbursement that applies to meals and entertainment and to other employee expenses.

EXAMPLE 43

Elizabeth, who is employed by Green Company, had AGI of $42,000. During the year, she incurred $2,000 of transportation and lodging expense and $1,000 of meals and entertainment expense, all fully substantiated. Elizabeth received $1,800 reimbursement under an accountable plan. The reimbursement rate that applies to meals and entertainment is 33.33% ($1,000 meals and entertainment expense/$3,000 total expenses). Thus, $600 ($1,800 × 33.33%) of the reimbursement applies to meals and entertainment, and $1,200 ($1,800 – $600) applies to transportation and lodging. Elizabeth's itemized deduction consists of the $800 ($2,000 total – $1,200 reimbursement) of unreimbursed transportation and lodging expenses and $400 ($1,000 – $600) of unreimbursed meal and entertainment expenses as follows:

Transportation and lodging	$ 800
Meals and entertainment ($400 × 50%)	200
Total (reported on Form 2106)	$1,000
Less: 2% of $42,000 AGI (see limitation discussed below)	(840)
Deduction (reported on Schedule A)	$ 160

In summary, Elizabeth reports $3,000 of expenses and the $1,800 reimbursement on Form 2106 and $160 as a miscellaneous itemized deduction on Schedule A. ■

ETHICAL CONSIDERATIONS

A Customized Reimbursement Agreement

In connection with his job at Yellow Corporation, Brayden incurs certain employment-related expenses. Brayden renders an adequate accounting to Yellow and is reimbursed for 50 percent of his expenditures. Under an agreement he has with Yellow, the reimbursement specifically covers the meals and entertainment portion of the employee expenses.

What tax benefit is Brayden trying to obtain as a result of the reimbursement agreement with Yellow? Will he succeed? Should employers and employees enter into such agreements?

LO.10

Work with the limitations on miscellaneous itemized deductions.

Limitations on Itemized Deductions

Many itemized deductions, such as medical expenses and charitable contributions, are subject to limitations expressed as a percentage of AGI. These limitations may be expressed as floors or ceilings and are discussed in Chapter 10.

MISCELLANEOUS ITEMIZED DEDUCTIONS SUBJECT TO THE 2 PERCENT FLOOR

Certain miscellaneous itemized deductions, including most *unreimbursed employee business expenses*, are aggregated and then reduced by 2 percent of AGI.[63] Expenses subject to the 2 percent floor include the following:

- All § 212 expenses, except expenses of producing rent and royalty income (refer to Chapter 6).
- All unreimbursed employee expenses (after the 50 percent reduction, if applicable) except moving.
- Professional dues and subscriptions.
- Union dues and work uniforms.
- Employment-related education expenses (except for § 222 qualified tuition and related expenses).
- Malpractice insurance premiums.
- Expenses of job hunting (including employment agency fees and résumé-writing expenses).
- Home office expenses of an employee or outside salesperson.
- Legal, accounting, and tax return preparation fees.
- Hobby expenses (up to hobby income).
- Investment expenses, including investment counsel fees, subscriptions, and safe deposit box rental.
- Custodial fees relating to income-producing property or a traditional IRA or a Keogh plan.
- Any fees paid to collect interest or dividends.
- Appraisal fees establishing a casualty loss or charitable contribution.

ETHICAL CONSIDERATIONS

Will Separate Returns by Married Persons Save Taxes?

Andy and Nancy are married and live in Connecticut. Both are employed and work at home. Nancy's employer pays for her employment-related expenses. Unfortunately, Andy's employee expenses, although considerable in amount, are not reimbursed. Every year Andy and Nancy file separate Federal income tax returns, and each itemizes. On his return, Andy also claims the expenses relating to the office in the home they share and deducts the fees he pays for the preparation of their tax returns.

How is the procedure Andy and Nancy are following saving them income taxes? Evaluate the appropriateness of the procedure.

MISCELLANEOUS ITEMIZED DEDUCTIONS NOT SUBJECT TO THE 2 PERCENT FLOOR

Certain miscellaneous itemized deductions, including the following, are not subject to the 2 percent floor:

- Impairment-related work expenses of handicapped individuals.
- Gambling losses to the extent of gambling winnings.
- Certain terminated annuity payments.

[63] § 67.

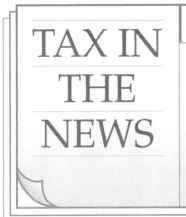

RELIEF FOR MEMBERS OF THE ARMED FORCES RESERVES

In the Military Family Tax Relief Act of 2003, Congress provided various tax benefits for reservists, one of which deals with the classification of travel expenses. Members of the Reserves or National Guard who travel to drills and other service-related activities may claim the expenses as deductions *for* AGI. Previously, the expenses were not deductible unless the taxpayer itemized. (As miscellaneous itemized deductions, they were subject to the 2 percent-of-AGI floor.) To qualify for the deduction *for* AGI classification, the trip must be more than 100 miles from home and include an overnight stay. Any deduction is limited to the Federal per diem rates applicable to the area involved.

EXAMPLE 44

Ted, who has AGI of $20,000, has the following miscellaneous itemized deductions:

Gambling losses (to extent of gains)	$1,200
Tax return preparation fees	300
Unreimbursed employee transportation	200
Professional dues and subscriptions	260
Safe deposit box rental	30

Ted's itemized deductions are as follows:

Deduction not subject to 2% floor (gambling losses)		$1,200
Deductions subject to 2% floor ($300 + $200 + $260 + $30)	$ 790	
Less 2% of AGI	(400)	390
Total miscellaneous itemized deductions		$1,590

If instead Ted's AGI is $40,000, the floor is $800 (2% of $40,000), and he cannot deduct any expenses subject to the 2% floor. ■

LO.11

Develop tax planning ideas related to employee business expenses.

Tax Planning Considerations

SELF-EMPLOYED INDIVIDUALS

Some taxpayers have the flexibility to be classified as either employees or self-employed individuals. Examples include real estate agents and direct sellers. These taxpayers should carefully consider all factors and not automatically assume that self-employed status is preferable.

It is advantageous to deduct one's business expenses *for* AGI and avoid the 2 percent floor. However, a self-employed individual may have higher expenses, such as local gross receipts taxes, license fees, franchise fees, personal property taxes, and occupation taxes. In addition, the record-keeping and filing requirements can be quite burdensome.

One of the most expensive considerations is the Social Security tax versus the self-employment tax. For an employee in 2005, for example, the Social Security tax applies at a rate of 6.2 percent on a base amount of wages of $90,000, and the Medicare tax applies at a rate of 1.45 percent with no limit on the base amount. For self-employed persons, the rate, but not the base amount, for each tax doubles. Even though a deduction *for* AGI is allowed for one-half of the self-employment tax paid, an employee and a self-employed individual are not in the same tax position on equal amounts of earnings. For the applicability of these taxes to employees, see Chapter 1.

After analyzing all these factors, a taxpayer may decide that employee status is preferable to self-employed status.

ETHICAL CONSIDERATIONS

Travel Expenses Can Be a Profit Center

A national accounting firm bills its audit clients for the market rate its auditors would have paid for airline tickets, hotel rooms, and car rentals. Not disclosed to the client, however, are the significant "upfront discounts" and "year-end rebates" the accounting firm receives from the providers of these services. Some of these savings amount to as much as 40 percent of the market rate. The pricing arrangements with the providers are negotiated in advance and are based on the accounting firm's volume of business and agreement for exclusive use.

Comment on the propriety of the accounting firm's billing practices.

SHIFTING DEDUCTIONS BETWEEN EMPLOYER AND EMPLOYEE

An employee can avoid the 2 percent floor for employee business expenses. Typically, an employee incurs travel and entertainment expenses in the course of employment. The employer gets the deduction if it reimburses the employee, and the employee gets the deduction *for* AGI. An adequate accounting must be made, and excess reimbursements cannot be kept by the employee.

TRANSPORTATION AND TRAVEL EXPENSES

Adequate detailed records of all transportation and travel expenses should be kept. Since the regular mileage allowance often is modest in amount, a new, expensive automobile used primarily for business may generate a higher expense based on actual cost. In using the operating cost method, include the business portion of depreciation, repairs and maintenance, automobile club dues, insurance, gasoline and oil, and other related costs. The cost of gasoline, when coupled with the poor mileage performance of some vehicles, can be a significant factor. If the taxpayer is located in a metropolitan area, automobile insurance is more expensive. For the self-employed taxpayer, the business portion of finance charges (i.e., interest on car loans) can be included.

Once a method is chosen, a later change may be possible. Conversion from the automatic mileage method to the operating cost method is allowed if a basis adjustment is made for depreciation deemed taken (see Example 9). Conversion from the operating cost method to the automatic mileage method is possible only if the taxpayer has not used the MACRS statutory percentage method or claimed § 179 limited expensing.

If a taxpayer wishes to sightsee or vacation on a business trip, it would be beneficial to schedule business on both a Friday and a Monday to turn the weekend into business days for allocation purposes. It is especially crucial to schedule appropriate business days when foreign travel is involved.

MOVING EXPENSES

Persons who retire and move to a new location incur personal nondeductible moving expenses. If the retired person accepts a full-time job in the new location, the moving expenses are deductible.

EXAMPLE 45

At the time of his retirement from the national office of a major accounting firm, Gordon had an annual salary of $220,000. He moves from New York City to Seattle to retire. To qualify for the moving expense deduction, Gordon accepts a full-time teaching position at a Seattle junior college at an annual salary of $15,000. If Gordon satisfies the 39-week test, his moving expenses are deductible. The disparity between the two salaries (previous and current) is of no consequence. ■

EDUCATION EXPENSES

Education expenses are treated as nondeductible personal items unless the individual is employed or is engaged in a trade or business. A temporary leave of absence for further education is one way to reasonably assure that the taxpayer is still qualified, even if a full-time student. An individual was permitted to deduct education expenses even though he resigned from his job, returned to school full-time for two years, and accepted another job in the same field upon graduation. The court held that the student had merely suspended active participation in his field.[64]

If the time out of the field is too long, educational expense deductions will be disallowed. For example, a teacher who left the field for four years to raise her child and curtailed her employment searches and writing activities was denied a deduction. She was not actively engaged in the trade or business of being an educator.[65]

To secure the deduction, an individual should arrange his or her work situation to preserve employee or business status.

The deduction for qualified tuition and related expenses provides some relief from the current restrictions on the deduction of education expenses by employees. First, the education expense does not have to be work related. Second, it is a deduction *for* (not *from*) AGI. Unfortunately, the deduction possesses severe shortcomings: not only is the annual amount allowed quite modest, but it may be unavailable to certain taxpayers. It is not available, for example, to those who exceed an AGI ceiling or to someone who can be claimed as a dependent of another.

ENTERTAINMENT EXPENSES

Proper documentation of expenditures is essential because of the strict recordkeeping requirements and the restrictive tests that must be met. For example, documentation that consists solely of credit card receipts and canceled checks may be inadequate to substantiate the business purpose and business relationship.[66] Taxpayers should maintain detailed records of amounts, time, place, business purpose, and business relationships. A credit card receipt details the place, date, and amount of the expense. A notation made on the receipt of the names of the person(s) attending, the business relationship, and the topic of discussion should constitute proper documentation.

Associated with or goodwill entertainment is not deductible unless a business discussion is conducted immediately before or after the entertainment. Furthermore, a business purpose must exist for the entertainment. Taxpayers should arrange for a business discussion before or after such entertainment. They must provide documentation of the business purpose, such as obtaining new business from a prospective customer.

[64]*Stephen G. Sherman*, 36 TCM 1191, T.C.Memo. 1977–301.

[65]*Brian C. Mulherin*, 42 TCM 834, T.C.Memo. 1981–454; *George A. Baist*, 56 TCM 778, T.C.Memo. 1988–554.

[66]*Kenneth W. Guenther*, 54 TCM 382, T.C.Memo. 1987–440.

Unreimbursed meals and entertainment are subject to the 50 percent cutback rule in addition to the 2 percent floor. Consequently, the procedure of negotiating a salary reduction, as discussed in the next section, is even more valuable to the taxpayer.

UNREIMBURSED EMPLOYEE BUSINESS EXPENSES

The 2 percent floor for unreimbursed employee business expenses offers a tax planning opportunity for married couples. If one spouse has high miscellaneous expenses subject to the floor, it may be beneficial for the couple to file separate returns. If they file jointly, the 2 percent floor is based on the incomes of both. Filing separately lowers the reduction to 2 percent of only one spouse's income.

Other provisions of the law should be considered, however. For example, filing separately could cost a couple losses of up to $25,000 from self-managed rental units under the passive activity loss rules (discussed in Chapter 11).

Another possibility is to negotiate a salary reduction with one's employer in exchange for the 100 percent reimbursement of employee expenses. The employee is better off because the 2 percent floor does not apply. The employer is better off because certain expense reimbursements are not subject to Social Security and other payroll taxes.

KEY TERMS

PROBLEM MATERIALS

Discussion Questions

1. Lyle and Joan are married and file a joint return for the year. Both incur work-related expenses that are not reimbursed. If Lyle is employed and Joan is self-employed, how should the expenses be handled for tax purposes?

Decision Making

2. Bernard operates a hair styling salon as a sole proprietor. Because his shop has several extra work stations that are not being used, he is considering renting these to other stylists, but he wants to avoid any employer-employee relationship with them. Advise Bernard on the type of working arrangement he should set up to ensure that any new stylists will be classified as independent contractors and not as employees.

3. Alexis is a CPA employed by the Tampa office of a national accounting firm. Although she usually commutes daily to the downtown office, on occasion she goes from her home directly to a client's business location. Also, on weekends she drives to a local university to attend classes leading toward a master's degree in accounting. If Alexis uses her personal automobile in these activities, what mileage can qualify as deductible?

Issue ID

4. Dan, a well-known former war correspondent and TV news commentator, authors a syndicated newspaper column, which he prepares at home. Most of his income comes from this source, but he also teaches several graduate courses in journalism at a nearby

university. Is Dan's use of his car to carry out the teaching assignments at the university deductible? Why or why not?

Issue ID

5. In 2003, Emma purchased an automobile, which she uses for both business and personal purposes. Although Emma does not keep records as to operating expenses (e.g., gas, oil, repairs), she can prove the percentage of business use and the miles driven each year. In March 2005, Emma seeks your advice as to what income tax benefit, if any, she can derive from the use of her automobile. What would you suggest?

6. Tyler, a member of a St. Louis law firm, travels to Chicago for business conferences on Friday and Monday. During the intervening weekend, he attends a Cubs baseball game and visits various museums. Discuss the deductibility of Tyler's expenses for the trip.

Issue ID

7. Dr. Werner is a full-time professor of accounting at Pelican University. During the year, he teaches continuing education programs for CPA groups in several cities. He also serves as an expert witness in numerous lawsuits involving accounting fraud. Comment on the possible tax treatment of Dr. Werner's job-related expenses.

8. What tax effect, if any, does an employee's temporary assignment to another job site have? Does the employee's tax home change?

9. a. Under what circumstances might a taxpayer never be away from home for income tax purposes?
   b. What are the tax consequences of such a status?
   c. What is the principal consideration in avoiding this result?

10. Dr. and Mrs. Hampton attend a two-day seminar in Baltimore on current developments in orthopedic surgery. Dr. Hampton owns and operates a bone and joint clinic in Charleston, West Virginia. Mrs. Hampton is the office manager and accountant for the clinic and also schedules all the surgeries performed. Comment on the deductibility of the Hamptons' expenses in attending the seminar.

11. Wyatt teaches French in high school. To stay proficient in the language and improve his accent, he spends six weeks in France during the summer break. Comment on the deductibility of the expenses he incurs for this travel.

Decision Making

12. Marge is scheduled to go to Paris on business. While there, she would like to do some sightseeing. When she mentions this to a friend, the friend suggests that she plan her weekends wisely. What does the friend's suggestion mean from a tax perspective?

13. In November 2005, Quincy moves from Minneapolis to Baltimore to accept a new job. On his 2005 timely filed income tax return, Quincy deducts the qualified moving expenses involved. In June 2006, Quincy becomes unhappy with his work situation, quits the job, and moves back to Minneapolis. Comment on Quincy's income tax problem.

14. In terms of the moving expense deduction, expatriates (persons who work overseas) enjoy several distinct tax advantages over their domestic counterparts. Explain.

Issue ID

15. During 2005, Kaitlyn incurs both deductible and nondeductible education expenses. Some of the deductible expenses are deductions *for* AGI, while the rest are deductions *from* AGI. Provide examples of Kaitlyn's expenses that could be:
    a. Nondeductible.
    b. Deductible as deductions *for* AGI.
    c. Deductible as deductions *from* AGI.

16. In connection with § 222 (deduction for qualified tuition and related expenses), comment on the relevance of the following:
    a. The education involved must be employment related.
    b. The deduction avoids the 2%-of-AGI floor.
    c. The deduction is subject to an AGI limitation.
    d. The taxpayers are married persons who file separate returns.

17. What was the original justification for the cutback adjustment?
    a. Does the cutback adjustment completely solve the problem it was intended to correct?
    b. Are any exceptions made to the cutback adjustment? Why?

18. In each of the following situations, indicate whether there is a cutback adjustment and, if so, to whom it applies (i.e., employer or employee):
    a. The employer expects certain employees to entertain their key customers. The employer does not reimburse the employees for these costs.
    b. Same as (a) except that the employees are reimbursed for these costs.
    c. Each year the employer awards its top salesperson an expense-paid trip to the Cayman Islands.
    d. The employer has a cafeteria for its employees where meals are furnished at cost.
    e. The employer sponsors an annual Fourth of July picnic for its employees.
    f. Every Christmas, the employer gives each employee a turkey.

Issue ID

19. Madison, an independent commercial real estate broker, belongs to the Spring Country Club, which she utilizes for both business and pleasure. In terms of business use, she has lunches and dinners there with prospective clients and holds an annual Christmas party at the club for existing clients and her employees. Although not a golfer, Madison also pays the green fees and caddie charges for selected prospects. Discuss Madison's available deductions regarding Spring Country Club.

Issue ID

20. At the last minute, a law firm purchases 10 tickets to the Super Bowl in order to entertain certain key clients. Comment on some possible tax ramifications of this situation.

21. In connection with the office in the home deduction, comment on the following factors:
    a. Taxpayer claims the standard deduction.
    b. The office is also used to pay personal bills.
    c. The expenses exceed the income from the business.
    d. Taxpayer rents, rather than owns, the home.

22. In 2005, Myrna, a full-time fifth grade teacher, spent $1,400 on supplies for her classes. The school district, upon the rendition of an adequate accounting, reimbursed her for $400 of these expenses. How should Myrna handle this matter for income tax purposes?

Issue ID

23. Trent, a resident of Florida, attends Vanderbilt University. After graduation, he moves to New Orleans where he begins a job search. Shortly thereafter, he accepts a position with a local radio station as an announcer. Trent's college degree is in management. Presuming no reimbursement, what employment-related expenses might Trent be eligible to deduct?

24. Distinguish between these different types of retirement plans:
    a. A traditional IRA and a Roth IRA.
    b. A traditional IRA and a Keogh (H.R. 10) plan.

25. Nicholas is a self-employed claims adjuster for several casualty insurance companies. During the year, he incurs significant transportation and travel expenses for which he is not reimbursed. His only records of such expenses are credit card receipts. Does Nicholas have a problem regarding his tax deductions? Explain.

26. What tax return reporting procedures must be followed by an employee under the following circumstances?
    a. Expenses and reimbursements are equal under an accountable plan.
    b. Reimbursements at the appropriate Federal per diem rate exceed expenses, and an adequate accounting is made to the employer.
    c. Expenses exceed reimbursements under a nonaccountable plan.

Issue ID

27. Olivia, a recent graduate from law school, is employed by a law firm as an attorney. In order to specialize, she would like to continue her education and earn a graduate degree in tax law. She is hesitant to quit her job and go back to school full-time, however, as that might jeopardize her deduction for education expenses. Furthermore, she is concerned that developing a tax specialty could be treated as acquiring skills for a new trade or business. Comment on Olivia's concerns and provide constructive planning advice.

Decision Making

28. Kim has just graduated from college and is interviewing for a position in marketing. Crane Corporation has offered her a job as a sales representative that will require extensive travel and entertainment but provide valuable experience. Under the offer,

she has two options: a salary of $48,000 and she absorbs all expenses; a salary of $35,000 and Crane reimburses for all expenses. Crane assures Kim that the $13,000 difference in the two options will be adequate to cover the expenses incurred. What issues should have an impact on Kim's choice?

29. Jeff has been practicing as a physician in Boston. Shortly, he plans to sell his practice to his partners and retire in Taos, New Mexico. Besides the sale of his practice, what should be some of Jeff's concerns?

30. Comment on the deductibility of each of the following items:
   a. Expenses incurred by taxpayer, a member of the New Mexico National Guard, to participate in a three-day training session conducted in Texas.
   b. Dues to a teamster's union paid by a truck driver.
   c. Computer supplies purchased by a college professor for use in the graduate seminars she teaches.
   d. Fee paid to take the state bar exam. Taxpayer is employed as a paralegal by a law firm.
   e. Job-hunting expenses paid by a schoolteacher seeking employment as a stockbroker.
   f. Cost of attending an investment seminar. Taxpayer is a self-employed dentist.
   g. Cost of safety work shoes. Taxpayer is a self-employed stonemason.

Problems

31. During the year, Marlon holds two jobs. After an eight-hour day at his first job, he works three hours at the second job. On Mondays and Fridays of each week, he returns home for dinner before going to the second job. On the midweek days (Tuesday through Thursday), he goes directly from the first job to the second job, stopping along the way for a meal. The mileage involved is as follows:

Home to first job	20
First job to second job	25
Home to second job	30

   a. Assuming Marlon works 50 weeks during the year, how much of his mileage is deductible?
   b. Can Marlon deduct the midweek meals he purchased? Why or why not?

32. Jenny is the regional sales manager for a bagel retail chain. She starts her working day by driving from home to the regional office, works there for several hours, and then visits the three sales outlets in her region. Relevant mileage is as follows:

Home to regional office	15
Regional office to sales outlet #1	10
Sales outlet #1 to sales outlet #2	8
Sales outlet #2 to sales outlet #3	12
Sales outlet #3 to home	18

If Jenny uses the automatic mileage method and works on 240 days in 2005, what is her deduction for the year?

33. On July 1, 2003, Nelson purchased a new automobile for $38,000. Miles driven are as follows: 15,000 in 2003; 20,000 in 2004; and 18,000 in 2005. If Nelson uses the auto 90% for business and 10% for personal use, determine its basis as of January 1, 2006, based on the following assumptions:
   a. Nelson uses the automatic mileage method.
   b. Nelson uses the actual operating cost method. (Assume that *no* § 179 expensing or additional first-year depreciation is claimed and that 200% declining-balance with the half-year convention is used—see Chapter 8.)

34. Margaret went from San Francisco to Rome (Georgia) on business. Her time was spent as follows:

Tuesday	Travel
Wednesday	Business
Thursday	Sightseeing
Friday	Business
Saturday and Sunday	Sightseeing
Monday	Business
Tuesday	Travel

Margaret's expenses are summarized below:

Airfare	$2,200
Lodging (Tuesday through Monday at $150 per day)	1,050
Meals (Wednesday through Monday at $130 per day)	780

Margaret is a self-employed real estate consultant who specializes in assisted-living housing projects.

a. How much can Margaret deduct for the trip?
b. Assume instead that the destination of Margaret's business trip is Rome, Italy (not Rome, Georgia). How much can she deduct?
c. How will any deductions in (a) and (b) be classified?

35. Graham, the regional manager for a national retail drug chain, is based in Denver, Colorado. During March and April of this year, he has to replace temporarily the district manager in Cheyenne, Wyoming. During this period, Graham flies to Cheyenne on Sunday night, spends the week at the district office, and returns home to Denver on Friday afternoon. The cost of returning home is $360, while the cost of spending the weekend in Cheyenne would have been $320.

a. Presuming no reimbursement by his employer, how much, if any, of these weekend expenses may Graham deduct?
b. Would your answer in (a) change if the amounts involved are reversed (i.e., the trip home cost $320; staying in Cheyenne would have been $360)?

36. In June of this year, Dr. and Mrs. Alvin Lord traveled to Memphis to attend a three-day conference sponsored by the American Society of Implant Dentistry. Alvin, a practicing oral surgeon, participated in scheduled technical sessions dealing with the latest developments in surgical procedures. On two days, Mrs. Lord attended group meetings where various aspects of family tax planning were discussed. On the other day, she went sightseeing. Mrs. Lord does not work for her husband, but she does their tax returns and handles the family investments. Expenses incurred in connection with the conference are summarized below:

Airfare (two tickets)	$1,040
Lodging (single and double occupancy are the same rate—$220 each day)	660
Meals ($200 × 3 days)*	600
Conference registration fee (includes $120 for Family Tax Planning sessions)	520
Car rental	240

*Split equally between Dr. and Mrs. Lord.

How much, if any, of these expenses can the Lords deduct?

37. On Thursday, Justin flies from Baltimore (his home office) to Cadiz (Spain). He conducts business on Friday and Tuesday; vacations on Saturday, Sunday, and Monday (a legal holiday in Spain); and returns to Baltimore on Thursday. Justin was scheduled to return

home on Wednesday, but all flights were canceled due to bad weather. Therefore, he spent Wednesday watching floor shows at a local casino.

a. For tax purposes, what portion of Justin's trip is regarded as being for business?
b. Suppose Monday had not been a legal holiday. Would this change your answer in (a)?
c. Under either (a) or (b), how much of Justin's airfare qualifies as a deductible business expense?

Decision Making

38. Monica travels from her office in Boston to Lisbon, Portugal, on business. Her absence of 13 days was spent as follows:

Thursday	Depart for and arrive at Lisbon
Friday	Business transacted
Saturday and Sunday	Vacationing
Monday through Friday	Business transacted
Saturday and Sunday	Vacationing
Monday	Business transacted
Tuesday	Depart Lisbon and return to office in Boston

a. For tax purposes, how many days has Monica spent on business?
b. What difference does it make?
c. Could Monica have spent more time than she did vacationing on the trip without loss of existing tax benefits? Explain.

39. Layton is an accountant and works in Boston, Massachusetts. After an extensive job search, he obtains a position as a CFO with a company located in Denver, Colorado. Expenses incurred in connection with the new job are as follows:

Job search expenses	$4,800
Loss on sale of Boston residence	8,000
Packing and moving household and personal effects	6,000
Lodging during move	620
Meals during move	740
Mileage for three personal autos	6,600 miles

a. How should Layton handle these costs for income tax purposes?
b. Suppose Layton's new job is as director of human resources (rather than CFO). Would this change your answer in (a)? Explain.

40. Marvin is employed as a full-time high school teacher. The school district where he works recently instituted a policy requiring all of its teachers to start working on a master's degree. Pursuant to this new rule, Marvin spent most of the summer of 2005 taking graduate courses at an out-of-town university. His expenses are as follows:

Tuition	$4,300
Books and course materials	650
Lodging	1,200
Meals	1,600
Laundry and dry cleaning	220
Campus parking	300

In addition, Marvin drove his personal automobile 1,500 miles in connection with the education. He uses the automatic mileage method.

a. How much, if any, of these expenses might qualify as deductions *for* AGI?
b. How much, if any, of these expenses might qualify as deductions *from* AGI?

41. In each of the following independent situations, determine how much, if any, qualifies as a deduction *for* AGI under § 222 (qualified tuition and related expenses):

a. Ruby is single and is employed as a nurse practitioner. During 2005, she spends $4,200 in tuition to attend law school at night. Her AGI is $64,000.

b. Jacque is single and is employed as a pharmacist. During 2005, he spends $2,100 ($1,900 for tuition and $200 for books) to take a course in herbal supplements at a local university. His AGI is $70,000.
c. How much, if any, of the above amounts *not allowed under* § 222 might otherwise qualify as a deduction *from* AGI?

Issue ID

42. Calvin is a long-haul truck driver who is employed by Heron Freight Corporation and based in Searcy, Arkansas. During 2005, Calvin spends approximately 44 weeks on the road and operates in 18 states. Besides a wage plus commissions, Calvin's employer furnishes him with a monthly travel allowance of $1,000. No accounting for this allowance is required. Calvin absorbs his own meals and lodging expenses while on trips, and these are supported by receipts and other substantiation. During 2005, his trip expenses are $12,480 for meals and $13,600 for lodging.
    a. What is Calvin's income tax situation?
    b. Is it possible that Calvin may find it advantageous to claim the standard deduction for 2005?

43. Grebe Associates paid $40,000 for a 20-seat skybox at Municipal Stadium for eight professional football games. Regular seats to these games range from $50 to $70 each. At one game, an employee of Grebe entertained 19 clients. Grebe furnished food and beverages for the event at a cost of $450. The game was preceded by a bona fide business discussion, and all expenses are adequately substantiated.
    a. How much may Grebe deduct for this event?
    b. Would your answer in (a) change if only 15 (not 19) clients participated—four of the seats were not occupied?

44. During the current year, Kevin, the assistant manager of a truck leasing firm, made gifts that cost the following amounts:

To Darlene (Kevin's secretary) for Christmas ($2 was for gift wrapping)	$32
To George (Kevin's boss) on his birthday	31
To Susan (a key client) for Christmas	20
To John (a key client) for Christmas	28

Kevin also took Darlene to lunch (cost of $88) on her birthday. Presuming Kevin has adequate substantiation and is not reimbursed, how much can he deduct?

45. Brittany is a broker who works full-time for a national brokerage firm. She also maintains an office in her home for her sole proprietorship, which she uses to provide financial planning services to clients. Expenses of the business (other than home office expenses) are $3,200. Brittany's home expenses are as follows:

Real property taxes	$4,000
Interest on home mortgage	5,000
Operating expenses of home	1,000
Depreciation (based on 20% business use)	1,500

Brittany's gross income from the consulting activity is $5,500.
    a. Compute Brittany's office in the home deduction.
    b. How are these items classified?

46. Victor has AGI of $94,000 during the year and the following expenses related to his employment:

Lodging while in travel status	$3,400
Meals during travel	3,200
Business transportation	5,200
Entertainment of clients	2,200
Professional dues and subscriptions	900

Victor is reimbursed $10,000 under his employer's accountable plan. What are Victor's deductions *for* and *from* AGI?

47. During the year, Cole has the following expenses related to his employment:

Airfare	$9,200
Meals during travel	4,100
Lodging while in travel status	5,300
Entertainment of clients	3,100

Cole's AGI is $98,000. He renders an adequate accounting to his employer and receives reimbursement of $15,000. How much can Cole deduct *for* and *from* AGI? Assume he has no other itemized deductions.

48. Audry, age 38 and single, earned a salary of $59,000. She had interest income of $1,600 and had a $2,000 long-term capital loss from the sale of a stock investment. Audry incurred the following employment-related expenses during the year:

Transportation	$5,500
Meals	2,800
Lodging	4,200
Entertaining clients	2,200
Professional dues and subscriptions	300

Under an accountable plan, Audry receives reimbursements of $4,500 from her employer. Calculate her AGI and itemized employee business expenses.

49. Nat and Eva Pitt are husband and wife and are full-time employees—Nat as a machinist and Eva as a sixth grade teacher. During 2005, their salaries are $51,750 and $48,000, and they have employment-related expenses (not reimbursable) as follows:

Contributions to traditional IRAs ($4,000 each)	$8,000
Union dues for Nat paid in 2005 (for years 2004–2005)	1,200
Safety clothing for Nat (glasses, shoes, gloves)	500
Professional dues and subscriptions	400
Eva's share of the cost of refreshments for the annual school picnic	200
Correspondence study course on "Coping with Pre-Teen Behavior" taken by Eva	320

In addition, the Pitts have a short-term capital gain of $3,000 from the sale of land that Nat received as a gift from his aunt. Their other itemized deductions (e.g., interest on home mortgage, property taxes on personal residence, charitable contributions) amount to $13,100.

a. Determine the Pitts' AGI for 2005.
b. Determine the total of their deductions *from* AGI.

Cumulative Problems

Tax Return Problem

50. Brenda Luce, age 39 and single, lives at 1329 Yorkchester Drive, Spring Valley, TX 77024. Her Social Security number is 444–00–1111. She is the regional sales manager for Style-Smart, a national chain of retail outlets specializing in women's clothing. As such, she oversees the sales performance of the stores in her territory, handles employee relations, and resolves customer disputes. Style-Smart pays Brenda an annual salary of $70,000 plus a bonus based on performance. She also receives a yearly travel and entertainment allowance of $24,000. Style-Smart expects its employees to use the allowance to absorb their employment-related expenses but does not require them to submit any accounting or repay any excess amounts. Federal income tax withheld was $11,000. The appropriate amount was withheld for FICA taxes.

Brenda's expenses during 2005 that relate to her work are summarized below.

Airfare (includes European trip)	$11,200
Meals	3,100
Lodging	3,900
Entertainment	3,800
Taxis, limousines, and car rentals	1,200
Valet service	420
Professional dues and subscriptions	390
Business gifts	400
Online self-study course	240

During the summer of 2005, Brenda went to France and Italy to visit various fashion houses and attend several style shows. During the trip, she spent one week on business and two weeks vacationing. Her plane ticket cost $3,300 (business class). She could have saved $1,200 by flying coach but declined to do so. The fashion houses she visited paid for the one-week business portion of her meals and lodging.

The business gifts consisted of a box of Godiva chocolates given to each of 10 store managers at Christmas. The candy cost $36 plus $4 for wrapping and shipping. The online self-study course, "Creative Fashion Displays," is part of a home study series sponsored by the National Retail Association. Brenda has a college degree in marketing and is not pursuing any further postsecondary education.

Brenda's performance bonus for 2005 turned out to be $15,000 and was paid to her in January 2006. In the past, Style-Smart always paid the bonus in the year awarded. Thus, Brenda received her $12,000 bonus for 2004 in December 2004. In 2005, however, Style-Smart changed its policy in order to improve its year-end cash flow.

In connection with her work, Brenda drives her own car. She uses the actual expense method based on 80% business/20% personal use. She purchased her present car in June 2004 at a cost of $40,000 (no trade-in was involved). She uses MACRS accelerated depreciation (200% declining-balance assuming half-year convention) and took the additional first-year allowance of 50% but no § 179 deduction. Depreciation previously claimed was $8,488 ($10,610 × 80%) for 2004. Expenses relating to the automobile are as follows:

Insurance	$1,300
Registration, inspection, license	70
Gasoline and oil	1,500
Tire replacement	300
Tolls and parking (business related)	620
Mechanical repairs	410
Traffic fines (business related)	320

During the year, Brenda had the following additional expenditures:

Contribution to a traditional IRA	$4,000
Premiums on policy covering Brenda's life (Brenda is the owner of the policy, and her parents are the designated beneficiaries.)	1,200
Premiums on medical insurance policy (sponsored by Style-Smart for its employees)	900
Contribution to the reelection campaign of the mayor of Spring Valley	200
Dental bills (not covered by insurance)	9,200
Property taxes on residence	2,800
Sales taxes (receipts available)	1,200
Interest on home mortgage	2,200
Interest on loan to purchase City of Dallas bonds	600
Charitable contributions	1,300

Besides employment-related income, Brenda had the following receipts during 2005:

Federal income tax refund (for year 2004)		$ 180
Interest income—		
City of Dallas bonds	$1,410	
Interest on CD issued by Spring Valley State Bank	800	
Interest on bonds issued by General Motors Corporation	360	2,570
Qualified dividends on stock investment in General Electric Company		940

Brenda buys all of her clothing from Style-Smart stores. Pursuant to the employer's policy, employees receive a 30% discount from the listed price (gross profit rate is 20%). In 2005, this enabled Brenda to purchase clothes listed at $3,000 for $2,100.

Based on the information given, determine Brenda's tax liability for 2005 and the related additional tax payable or refund due. Suggested software: TurboTax.

Tax Return Problem
Decision Making
Communications

51. George M. and Martha J. Jordan have no dependents and are both under age 65. George is a statutory employee of Consolidated Jobbers, a wholesaler of commercial equipment (business code is 421400), and his Social Security number is 582–99–4444. Martha is an executive with General Corporation, and her Social Security number is 241–88–6642. The Jordans live at 321 Oak Street, Lincoln, NV 89553. They both want to contribute to the Presidential Election Campaign Fund.

In 2004, George earned $49,200 in commissions. His employer withholds FICA but not Federal income taxes. George paid $4,000 in estimated taxes. Martha earned $61,900, from which $6,250 was withheld for Federal income taxes and the appropriate amount was withheld for FICA taxes. Neither George nor Martha received any expense reimbursements.

George uses his automobile in his employment, and during 2004, his business mileage is 24,800 miles. Parking and tolls in connection with business use are $340 and $280, respectively. Fines paid for traffic violations (during business use) total $420. In deducting business use of his automobile, George always uses the automatic mileage method. His other employment-related expenses for the year are as follows:

Airfare	$1,820
Meals	2,600
Lodging	1,700
Entertainment	1,400
Business gifts	1,320

The business gifts consist of 30 fruit baskets George sent to key customers during the Christmas season. Each basket cost $40 (not including $4 for wrapping and shipping).

During the year, Martha enrolled in a weekend MBA program at a local university. In this regard, she spent the following amounts: $2,800 (tuition), $360 (books and computer supplies), $190 (meals while on campus), and $120 (bus fare to and from campus). Martha took her secretary to lunch on two occasions ($68 and $74) and her boss on one occasion ($120). She spent $140 on professional dues and $220 on trade journals.

Neither George nor Martha is covered under an employer-sponsored retirement plan. However, each contributes $3,000 (for a total of $6,000) to a traditional IRA.

In addition to their salaries, the Jordans received the amounts listed below during the year:

Interest on certificate of deposit issued by Reno State Bank	$ 1,500
Gifts from Martha's parents ($25,000 apiece to Martha and George)	50,000
Distribution from Pyramid Life	100,600

The distribution from Pyramid Life represents the maturity value ($100,000) plus interest ($600) of an insurance policy on Harvey Jordan's life. Harvey was George's uncle and had designated George as the beneficiary of the policy. Because Harvey died overseas, the insurance company had delayed in making the distribution to George. The gifts from Martha's parents are belated wedding presents and are not expected to occur again.

The Jordans had other expenditures as follows:

Charitable contributions (cash)	$2,100
Medical and dental expenses	7,800
Real property taxes on residence	3,200
Sales taxes (table amount)	1,000
Home mortgage interest	7,000
Tax return preparation fee	300

Part 1—Tax Computation

Compute the Jordans' Federal income tax payable or refund due, assuming they file a joint income tax return, for 2004. If they have overpaid, they want the amount refunded. You will need Form 1040 and Schedules A, B, and C. Suggested software: TurboTax.

Part 2—Tax Planning

Martha and George request your help in deciding where to invest the extra $150,000 (life insurance and gift proceeds) they received in 2004. They are considering two alternatives:

- Municipal bonds that yield 4.5%.
- Common stock that regularly pays cash dividends of 6%.

a. Calculate the better alternative for next year. Assume that Martha and George will have the same income and deductions in 2005, except for the income from the investment they choose. In computing the tax, use the tax rate schedules for 2005.

b. What other factors should the Jordans take into account?

c. Write a memo to the Jordans, explaining their alternatives.

Suggested software: TurboTax.

Research Problems

Note: Solutions to Research Problems can be prepared by using the ***RIA Checkpoint® Student Edition*** *online research product, which is available to accompany this text. It is also possible to prepare solutions to the Research Problems by using tax research materials found in a standard tax library.*

Research Problem 1. Richard Harding is the sheriff of Howard County, Indiana. In addition to the usual law enforcement duties, the sheriff has the responsibility of maintaining the detention facility (i.e., county jail). Further, he must furnish meals for all prisoners in accordance with certain nutritional standards prescribed by the state. Although the sheriff must absorb the cost of the meals, the county provides a personal allowance.

During the year, Sheriff Harding received a salary of $35,000 (as reported on a Form W–2 issued by Howard County). He spent $90,000 on prisoner meals and received meal allowances of $110,000. On his income tax return, he reported the salary as employee income, but listed the allowances and meals on a Schedule C. Thus, he treated himself as self-employed by claiming the cost of the meals as a deduction *for* AGI.

Upon audit, the IRS determined that the Schedule C treatment was improper. Harding was not in a separate trade or business of providing meals, but was merely carrying out his employment-related duties. The costs of the meals are employee business expenses deductible only as miscellaneous itemized deductions on Schedule A. As such, they are subject to the 2%-of-AGI floor.

Is Sheriff Harding or the IRS correct? Why?

Research Problem 2. After graduating from high school, Joe attended various colleges, earning degrees in business (BBA) and law (JD). He accepted employment with Eagle Associates, a regional accounting firm. Soon thereafter, Joe took and passed the CPA exam. While at Eagle, his usual work assignment was as follows: 30% to 40% preparing tax returns, 40% to 50% researching the tax law, and the remainder consulting with clients about tax matters.

Several years later, Joe quit his job with Eagle and pursued, on a full-time basis, a master of laws degree with a specialization in taxation. Upon graduation, Joe accepted employment with Finch Trust Company. In his capacity as a trust officer with Finch, Joe manages clients' assets, acquires new clients, and prepares and files the fiduciary income tax returns that are the responsibility of the branch office where he works.

When Joe files his own income tax return, he claims a deduction for the education expenses incurred in obtaining the master of laws degree. In the event of an audit by the IRS, assess Joe's chances of sustaining the deduction.

Partial list of research aids:
Harold Haft, 40 T.C. 2 (1963).
Stephen G. Sherman, 36 TCM 1191, T.C.Memo. 1997–301.
Kenneth C. Davis, 65 T.C. 1014 (1976).
John H. Hudgens III, 73 TCM 1790, T.C.Memo. 1997–33.

Internet Activity

Use the tax resources of the Internet to address the following question. Do not restrict your search to the World Wide Web, but include a review of newsgroups and general reference materials, practitioner sites and resources, primary sources of the tax law, chat rooms and discussion groups, and other opportunities.

Research Problem 3. What are the guidelines regarding the deductibility of conventions held outside the North American area? Refer to Chapter 1 of IRS Publication No. 463.

Deductions and Losses: Certain Itemized Deductions

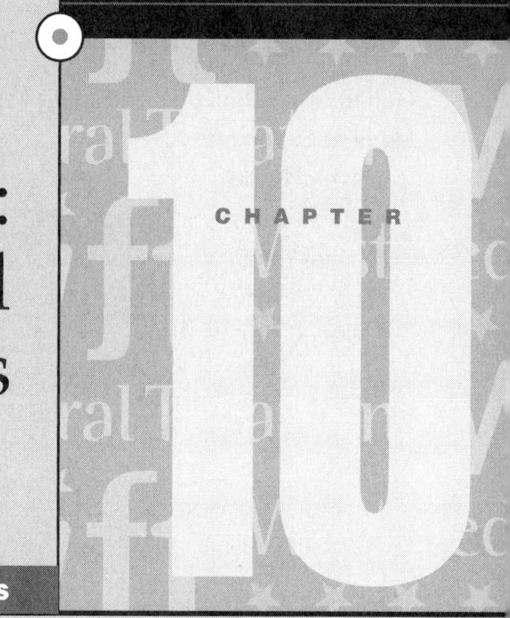

LEARNING OBJECTIVES

After completing Chapter 10, you should be able to:

LO.1
Distinguish between deductible and nondeductible personal expenses.

LO.2
Define medical expenses and compute the medical expense deduction.

LO.3
Contrast deductible taxes and nondeductible fees, licenses, etc.

LO.4
Understand the Federal income tax treatment of state and local income taxes and sales taxes.

LO.5
Distinguish between deductible and nondeductible interest and apply the appropriate limitations to deductible interest.

LO.6
Understand charitable contributions and their related measurement problems and percentage limitations.

LO.7
List the business and personal expenditures that are deductible either as miscellaneous itemized deductions or as other itemized deductions.

LO.8
Recognize the limitation on certain itemized deductions applicable to high-income taxpayers.

LO.9
Identify tax planning procedures that can maximize the benefit of itemized deductions.

OUTLINE

LO.1

Distinguish between deductible and nondeductible personal expenses.

General Classification of Expenses

As a general rule, the deduction of personal expenditures is disallowed by § 262 of the Code. However, Congress has chosen to allow certain personal expenditures to be deducted as itemized deductions. Personal expenditures that are deductible as itemized deductions include medical expenses, certain taxes, mortgage interest, investment interest, and charitable contributions. These expenditures and other personal expenditures that are allowed as itemized deductions are covered in this chapter. Any personal expenditures not specifically allowed as itemized deductions by the tax law are nondeductible.

Allowable itemized deductions are deductible *from* AGI in arriving at taxable income if the taxpayer elects to itemize. The election to itemize is appropriate when total itemized deductions exceed the standard deduction based on the taxpayer's filing status (refer to Chapter 3).[1]

[1]The total standard deduction is the sum of the basic standard deduction and the additional standard deduction (refer to Chapter 3).

The President and Vice President Itemize

Approximately two-thirds of all individual taxpayers take the standard deduction each year rather than itemize. President George W. Bush and Vice President Richard B. Cheney are among the one-third who itemize. Both the President and Vice President, who file joint returns with their wives, released their 2003 tax returns to the public. Their itemized deductions, along with certain other information from their tax returns, are shown below.

	President Bush	**Vice President Cheney**
Gross income	$822,126	$1,273,334*
Adjusted gross income	$822,126	$1,267,915
Itemized deductions:		
Medical expenses	$ –0–	$ –0–
Taxes	21,352	44,728
Interest	–0–	–0–
Charitable contributions	68,360	321,141
Job expenses and most other miscellaneous deductions	25,810	122,632
Total itemized deductions	$115,522	$ 488,501

*It is interesting to note that Vice President Cheney also reported tax-exempt interest of $627,005 on his return.

LO.2

Define medical expenses and compute the medical expense deduction.

Medical Expenses

GENERAL REQUIREMENTS

Medical expenses paid for the care of the taxpayer, spouse, and dependents are allowed as an itemized deduction to the extent the expenses are not reimbursed. The **medical expense** deduction is limited to the amount by which such expenses *exceed* 7.5 percent of the taxpayer's AGI.

EXAMPLE 1

During the year, Iris had medical expenses of $4,800, of which $1,000 was reimbursed by her insurance company. If her AGI for the year is $40,000, the itemized deduction for medical expenses is limited to $800 [$4,800 – $1,000 = $3,800 – (7.5% × $40,000)]. ■

MEDICAL EXPENSES DEFINED

The term *medical care* includes expenditures incurred for the "diagnosis, cure, mitigation, treatment, or prevention of disease, or for the purpose of affecting any structure or function of the body."[2] A *partial* list of deductible and nondeductible medical items appears in Exhibit 10–1.

[2]§ 213(d)(1)(A).

■ **EXHIBIT 10–1**
Examples of Deductible and Nondeductible Medical Expenses

Deductible	Nondeductible
Medical (including dental, mental, and hospital) care	Funeral, burial, or cremation expenses
Prescription drugs	Nonprescription drugs (except insulin)
Special equipment	Bottled water
Wheelchairs	Toiletries, cosmetics
Crutches	Diaper service, maternity clothes
Artificial limbs	Programs for the *general* improvement of health
Eyeglasses (including contact lenses)	Weight reduction
Hearing aids	Health spas
Transportation for medical care	Social activities (e.g., dancing and swimming lessons)
Medical and hospital insurance premiums	Unnecessary cosmetic surgery
Long-term care insurance premiums (subject to limitations)	
Cost of alcohol and drug rehabilitation	
Certain costs to stop smoking	
Weight reduction programs related to obesity	

A medical expense does not have to relate to a particular ailment to be deductible. Since the definition of medical care is broad enough to cover preventive measures, the cost of periodic physical and dental exams qualifies even for a taxpayer in good health.

Amounts paid for unnecessary *cosmetic surgery* are not deductible medical expenses. However, if cosmetic surgery is deemed necessary, it is deductible as a medical expense. Cosmetic surgery is necessary when it ameliorates (1) a deformity arising from a congenital abnormality, (2) a personal injury, or (3) a disfiguring disease.

EXAMPLE 2

Art, a calendar year taxpayer, paid $11,000 to a plastic surgeon for a face lift. Art, age 75, merely wanted to improve his appearance. The $11,000 does not qualify as a medical expense since the surgery was unnecessary. ■

EXAMPLE 3

As a result of a serious automobile accident, Marge's face is disfigured. The cost of restorative cosmetic surgery is deductible as a medical expense. ■

The cost of care in a *nursing home or home for the aged*, including meals and lodging, can be included in deductible medical expenses if the primary reason for being in the home is to get medical care. If the primary reason for being there is personal, any costs for medical or nursing care can be included in deductible medical expenses, but the cost of meals and lodging must be excluded.[3]

EXAMPLE 4

Norman has a chronic heart ailment. His family decides to place Norman in a nursing home equipped to provide medical and nursing care facilities. Total nursing home expenses amount to $15,000 per year. Of this amount, $4,500 is directly attributable to medical and nursing

[3] Reg. § 1.213–1(e)(1)(v).

care. Since Norman is in need of significant medical and nursing care and is placed in the facility primarily for this purpose, all $15,000 of the nursing home costs are deductible (subject to the 7.5% floor). ■

Tuition expenses of a dependent at a special school may be deductible as a medical expense. The cost of medical care can include the expenses of a special school for a mentally or physically handicapped individual. The deduction is allowed if a principal reason for sending the individual to the school is the school's special resources for alleviating the infirmities. In this case, the cost of meals and lodging, in addition to the tuition, is a proper medical expense deduction.[4]

EXAMPLE 5

Jason's daughter Marcia attended public school through the seventh grade. Because Marcia was a poor student, she was examined by a psychiatrist who diagnosed an organic problem that created a learning disability. Upon the recommendation of the psychiatrist, Marcia is enrolled in a private school so that she can receive individual attention. The school has no special program for students with learning disabilities and does not provide special medical treatment. The expense related to Marcia's attendance is not deductible as a medical expense. The cost of any psychiatric care, however, qualifies as a medical expense. ■

Example 5 shows that the recommendation of a physician does not automatically make the expenditure deductible.

CAPITAL EXPENDITURES FOR MEDICAL PURPOSES

Some examples of *capital expenditures* for medical purposes are swimming pools if the taxpayer does not have access to a neighborhood pool and air conditioners if they do not become permanent improvements (e.g., window units).[5] Other examples include dust elimination systems,[6] elevators,[7] and a room built to house an iron lung. These expenditures are medical in nature if they are incurred as a medical necessity upon the advice of a physician, the facility is used primarily by the patient alone, and the expense is reasonable.

Capital expenditures normally are adjustments to basis and are not deductible. However, both a capital expenditure for a permanent improvement and expenditures made for the operation or maintenance of the improvement may qualify as medical expenses. If a capital expenditure qualifies as a medical expense, the allowable cost is deductible in the year incurred. Although depreciation is required for most other capital expenditures, it is not required for capital expenditures for medical purposes.

A capital improvement that ordinarily would not have a medical purpose qualifies as a medical expense if it is directly related to prescribed medical care and is deductible to the extent that the expenditure *exceeds* the increase in value of the related property. Appraisal costs related to capital improvements are also deductible, but not as medical expenses. These costs are expenses incurred in the determination of the taxpayer's tax liability.[8]

EXAMPLE 6

Fred is afflicted with heart disease. His physician advises him to install an elevator in his residence so he will not be required to climb the stairs. The cost of installing the elevator is $3,000, and the increase in the value of the residence is determined to be only $1,700.

[4]*Donald R. Pfeifer*, 37 TCM 816, T.C.Memo. 1978–189. Also see Rev.Rul. 78–340, 1978–2 C.B. 124.

[5]Rev.Rul. 55–261, 1955–1 C.B. 307, modified by Rev.Rul. 68–212, 1968–1 C.B. 91.

[6]*F. S. Delp*, 30 T.C. 1230 (1958).

[7]*Riach v. Frank*, 62–1 USTC ¶9419, 9 AFTR2d 1263, 302 F.2d 374 (CA–9, 1962).

[8]§ 212(3).

Therefore, $1,300 ($3,000 – $1,700) is deductible as a medical expense. Additional utility costs to operate the elevator and maintenance costs are deductible as medical expenses as long as the medical reason for the capital expenditure continues to exist. ■

The full cost of certain home-related capital expenditures incurred to enable a *physically handicapped* individual to live independently and productively qualifies as a medical expense. Qualifying costs include expenditures for constructing entrance and exit ramps to the residence, widening hallways and doorways to accommodate wheelchairs, installing support bars and railings in bathrooms and other rooms, and adjusting electrical outlets and fixtures.[9] These expenditures are subject to the 7.5 percent floor only, and the increase in the home's value is deemed to be zero.

MEDICAL EXPENSES INCURRED FOR SPOUSE AND DEPENDENTS

In computing the medical expense deduction, a taxpayer may include medical expenses for a spouse and for a person who was a dependent at the time the expenses were paid or incurred. Of the five requirements that normally apply in determining dependency status,[10] neither the gross income nor the joint return test applies in determining dependency status for medical expense deduction purposes.

EXAMPLE 7

Ernie (age 22) is married and a full-time student at a university. During the year, Ernie incurred medical expenses that were paid by Matilda (Ernie's mother). She provided more than half of Ernie's support for the year. Even if Ernie files a joint return with his wife, Matilda may claim the medical expenses she paid for him. Matilda would combine Ernie's expenses with her own before applying the 7.5% floor. ■

For *divorced persons* with children, a special rule applies to the noncustodial parent. The noncustodial parent may claim any medical expenses he or she pays even though the custodial parent claims the children as dependents. This rule applies if the dependency exemptions could have been shifted to the noncustodial parent by the custodial parent's waiver (refer to Chapter 3).

EXAMPLE 8

Irv and Joan are divorced in 2004, and Joan is awarded custody of their child, Keith. During 2005, Irv makes the following payments to Joan: $3,600 for child support and $2,500 for Keith's medical bills. Together, Irv and Joan provide more than half of Keith's support. Even though Joan claims Keith as a dependent, Irv can combine the $2,500 of medical expenses that he pays for Keith with his own when calculating his medical expense deduction. ■

TRANSPORTATION, MEAL, AND LODGING EXPENSES FOR MEDICAL TREATMENT

Payments for transportation to and from a point of treatment for medical care are deductible as medical expenses (subject to the 7.5 percent floor). Transportation expenses for medical care include bus, taxi, train, or plane fare, charges for ambulance service, and out-of-pocket expenses for the use of an automobile. A mileage allowance of 15 cents per mile[11] may be used instead of actual out-of-pocket automobile expenses. Whether the taxpayer chooses to claim out-of-pocket automobile expenses or the 15 cents per mile automatic mileage option, related parking fees

[9]For a complete list of the items that qualify, see Rev.Rul. 87–106, 1987–2 C.B. 67.

[10]Refer to Chapter 3 for discussion of these requirements.

[11]This amount is adjusted periodically. The allowance was 14 cents in 2004.

and tolls can also be deducted. The cost of meals while en route to obtain medical care is not deductible.

A deduction is also allowed for the transportation expenses of a parent who must accompany a child who is receiving medical care or for a nurse or other person giving assistance to a person who is traveling to get medical care and cannot travel alone.

A deduction is allowed for lodging while away from home for medical expenses if the following requirements are met:[12]

- The lodging is primarily for and essential to medical care.
- Medical care is provided by a doctor in a licensed hospital or a similar medical facility (e.g., a clinic).
- The lodging is not lavish or extravagant under the circumstances.
- There is no significant element of personal pleasure, recreation, or vacation in the travel away from home.

The deduction for lodging expenses included as medical expenses cannot exceed $50 *per* night for *each* person. The deduction is allowed not only for the patient but also for a person who must travel with the patient (e.g., a parent traveling with a child who is receiving medical care).

EXAMPLE 9

Herman, a resident of Winchester, Kentucky, is advised by his family physician that Martha, Herman's dependent and disabled mother, needs specialized treatment for her heart condition. Consequently, Herman and Martha fly to Cleveland, Ohio, where Martha receives the therapy at a heart clinic on an out-patient basis. Expenses in connection with the trip are as follows:

Round trip airfare ($250 each)	$500
Lodging in Cleveland for two nights ($60 each per night)	240

Herman's medical expense deduction for transportation is $500, and his medical expense deduction for lodging is $200 ($50 per night per person). Because Martha is disabled, it is assumed that his accompanying her is justified. ■

No deduction is allowed for the cost of meals unless they are part of the medical care and are furnished at a medical facility. When allowable, such meals are not subject to the 50 percent limit applicable to business meals.

AMOUNTS PAID FOR MEDICAL INSURANCE PREMIUMS

Medical insurance premiums are included with other medical expenses subject to the 7.5 percent floor. Premiums paid by the taxpayer under a group plan or an individual plan are included as medical expenses. If an employer pays all or part of the taxpayer's medical insurance premiums, the amount paid by the employer is not included in gross income by the employee. Likewise, the premium is not included in the employee's medical expenses.

If a taxpayer is *self-employed*, insurance premiums paid for medical coverage are deductible as a *business* expense (*for* AGI).[13] The deduction *for* AGI is allowed for premiums paid on behalf of the taxpayer, the taxpayer's spouse, and dependents of the taxpayer. The deduction is not allowed to any taxpayer who is eligible to participate in a subsidized health plan maintained by any employer of the taxpayer or of the taxpayer's spouse. Premiums paid for medical insurance coverage of *employees* are deductible as business expenses.

[12]§ 213(d)(2).

[13]§ 162(l).

EXAMPLE 10

Ellen, a sole proprietor of a restaurant, has two dependent children. During the year, she paid health insurance premiums of $1,800 for her own coverage and $1,000 for coverage of her two children. Ellen can deduct $2,800 as a business deduction (for AGI) in computing net income from her business. ■

YEAR OF DEDUCTION

Regardless of a taxpayer's method of accounting, medical expenses are deductible only in the year *paid*. In effect, this places all individual taxpayers on a cash basis as far as the medical expense deduction is concerned. One exception, however, is allowed for deceased taxpayers. If the medical expenses are paid within one year from the day following the day of death, they can be treated as being paid at the time they were *incurred*. Thus, such expenses may be reported on the final income tax return of the decedent or on earlier returns if incurred before the year of death.

No current deduction is allowed for payment for medical care to be rendered in the future unless the taxpayer is under an obligation to make the payment.[14] Whether an obligation to make the payment exists depends upon the policy of the physician or the institution furnishing the medical care.

EXAMPLE 11

Upon the recommendation of his regular dentist, in late December 2005 Gary consults Dr. Smith, a prosthodontist, who specializes in crown and bridge work. Dr. Smith tells Gary that he can do the restorative work for $12,000. To cover his lab bill, however, Dr. Smith requires that 40% of this amount be prepaid. Accordingly, Gary pays $4,800 in December 2005. The balance of $7,200 is paid when the work is completed in July 2006. Under these circumstances, the qualifying medical expenses are $4,800 for 2005 and $7,200 in 2006. The result would be the same even if Gary prepaid the full $12,000 in 2005. ■

REIMBURSEMENTS

If medical expenses are reimbursed in the same year as paid, no problem arises. The reimbursement merely reduces the amount that would otherwise qualify for the medical expense deduction. But what happens if the reimbursement occurs in a later year than the expenditure? In computing casualty losses, any reasonable prospect of recovery must be considered (refer to Chapter 7). For medical expenses, however, any expected reimbursement is disregarded in measuring the amount of the deduction. Instead, the reimbursement is accounted for separately in the year in which it occurs.

Under the *tax benefit rule*, a taxpayer who receives an insurance reimbursement for medical expenses deducted in a previous year might have to include the reimbursement in gross income in the year of receipt. However, a taxpayer who did not itemize deductions in the year the expenses were paid did not receive a tax benefit and is *not* required to include a reimbursement in gross income.

The tax benefit rule applies to reimbursements if the taxpayer itemized deductions in the previous year. In this case, the taxpayer may be required to report some or all of the medical expense reimbursement in income in the year the reimbursement is received. Under the tax benefit rule, the taxpayer must include the reimbursement in income up to the amount of the deductions that decreased taxable income in the earlier year.

EXAMPLE 12

Homer had AGI of $20,000 for 2005. He was injured in a car accident and paid $1,300 for hospital expenses and $700 for doctor bills. Homer also incurred medical expenses of $600 for his dependent child. In 2006, Homer was reimbursed $650 by his insurance company

[14] *Robert S. Basset*, 26 T.C. 619 (1956).

for the medical expenses attributable to the car accident. His deduction for medical expenses in 2005 is computed as follows:

Hospitalization	$ 1,300
Bills for doctor's services	700
Medical expenses for dependent	600
Total	$ 2,600
Less: 7.5% of $20,000	(1,500)
Medical expense deduction (assuming Homer itemizes his deductions)	$ 1,100

Assume that Homer would have elected to itemize his deductions even if he had no medical expenses in 2005. If the reimbursement for medical care had occurred in 2005, the medical expense deduction would have been only $450 [$2,600 (total medical expenses) – $650 (reimbursement) – $1,500 (floor)], and Homer would have paid more income tax.

Since the reimbursement was made in a subsequent year, Homer will include $650 in gross income for 2006. If Homer had not itemized in 2005, he would not include the $650 reimbursement in 2006 gross income because he would have received no tax benefit in 2005. ■

HEALTH SAVINGS ACCOUNTS

In December 2003, President Bush signed legislation creating **Health Savings Accounts (HSAs)** as a replacement for Archer Medical Savings Accounts (MSAs).[15] A taxpayer can use an HSA in conjunction with a high-deductible medical insurance policy to help reduce the overall cost of medical coverage. Converting from a low-deductible to a high-deductible plan can generally save an individual 20 to 40 percent in premiums.

A high-deductible policy provides coverage for extraordinary medical expenses (in excess of the deductible), and expenses not covered by the policy can be paid with funds withdrawn from the HSA.

EXAMPLE 13

Sanchez, who is married and has three dependent children, carries a high-deductible medical insurance policy with a deductible of $4,400. He rolls over the balance in his Archer MSA into the HSA and contributes the maximum allowable amount to the HSA in 2005. During 2005, the Sanchez family incurs medical expenses of $12,000. The high-deductible policy covers $7,600 of the expenses ($12,000 expenses – $4,400 deductible). Sanchez may withdraw $4,400 from the HSA to pay the medical expenses not covered by the high-deductible policy. ■

High-Deductible Plans. High-deductible policies are less expensive than low-deductible policies, so taxpayers with low medical costs can benefit from the lower premiums and use funds from the HSA to pay costs not covered by the high-deductible policy. A plan must meet two requirements to qualify as a high-deductible plan.[16]

1. The annual deductible is not less than $1,000 for self-only coverage ($2,000 for family coverage).
2. The sum of the annual deductible and other out-of-pocket costs (excluding premiums) under the plan does not exceed $5,100 for self-only coverage ($10,200 for family coverage).

[15] § 223. The HSA legislation was part of the Medicare reform law. The HSA has been described as a new and improved Archer MSA.

[16] § 223(c)(2).

Tax Treatment of HSA Contributions and Distributions. To establish an HSA, a taxpayer contributes funds to a tax-exempt trust.[17] As illustrated in the preceding example, funds can be withdrawn from an HSA to pay medical expenses that are not covered by the high-deductible policy. The following general tax rules apply to HSAs:

1. Contributions made by the taxpayer to an HSA are deductible from gross income to arrive at AGI (deduction *for* AGI). Thus, the taxpayer does not need to itemize in order to take the deduction.
2. Earnings on HSAs are not subject to taxation unless distributed, in which case taxability depends on the way the funds are used.[18]
   - Distributions from HSAs are excluded from gross income if they are used to pay for medical expenses not covered by the high-deductible policy.
   - Distributions that are not used to pay for medical expenses are included in gross income and are subject to an additional 10 percent penalty if made before age 65, death, or disability. Such distributions made by reason of death or disability and distributions made after the HSA beneficiary becomes eligible for Medicare are taxed but not penalized.

HSAs have at least two other attractive features. First, an HSA is portable. Taxpayers who switch jobs can take their HSAs with them. Second, coverage is more widely available under the HSA rules than under the previous Archer MSA rules. Generally, anyone under age 65 who has a high-deductible plan and is not covered by another policy that is not a high-deductible plan can establish an HSA.

Deductible Amount. The annual deduction for contributions to an HSA is limited to the sum of the monthly limitations. The monthly limitation is calculated for each month that the individual is an eligible individual. The monthly deduction is not allowed after the individual becomes eligible for Medicare coverage.

The amount of the monthly limitation for an individual who has self-only coverage in 2005 is the *lesser* of one-twelfth of the annual deductible under the high-deductible plan or $2,650. An individual who has family coverage in 2005 is limited to the *lesser* of one-twelfth of the annual deductible under the high-deductible plan or $5,250.[19] For an eligible taxpayer who has attained age 55 by the end of the tax year, the limit on annual contributions in 2005 is increased by $600. This additional amount is referred to as a *catchup* contribution. These amounts are subject to annual cost-of-living adjustments.

EXAMPLE 14

Liu, who is married and self-employed, carries a high-deductible medical insurance policy with a deductible of $4,000. In addition, he has established an HSA. Liu's maximum annual contribution to the HSA is $4,000 (the lesser of $5,250 or the annual deductible). ■

EXAMPLE 15

During 2005, Adam, who is self-employed, made 12 monthly payments of $700 for an HSA contract that provides medical insurance coverage with a $3,600 deductible. The plan covers Adam, his wife, and two children. Of the $700 monthly fee, $400 was for the high-deductible policy and $300 was deposited into an HSA. The deductible monthly contribution to the HSA is calculated as follows:

Amount of the annual deductible under the plan	$3,600
Maximum annual deduction for family coverage	$5,250
Monthly limitation (1/12 of $3,600)	$ 300

[17] § 223(d).
[18] § 223(f).
[19] § 223(b)(2).

Because Adam is self-employed, he can deduct $4,800 of the amount paid for the high-deductible policy ($400 per month × 12 months) as a deduction *for* AGI (refer to Example 10). In addition, he can deduct the $3,600 ($300 × 12) paid to the HSA as a deduction *for* AGI. ■

LO.3

Contrast deductible taxes and nondeductible fees, licenses, etc.

Taxes

A deduction is allowed for certain state and local taxes paid or accrued by a taxpayer.[20] The deduction was created to relieve the burden of multiple taxes upon the same source of revenue.

DEDUCTIBILITY AS A TAX

A distinction must be made between a tax and a fee, since fees are not deductible unless incurred as an ordinary and necessary business expense or as an expense in the production of income. The IRS has defined a tax as follows:

> A tax is an enforced contribution exacted pursuant to legislative authority in the exercise of taxing power, and imposed and collected for the purpose of raising revenue to be used for public or governmental purposes, and not as payment for some special privilege granted or service rendered. Taxes are, therefore, distinguished from various other contributions and charges imposed for particular purposes under particular powers or functions of the government. In view of such distinctions, the question whether a particular contribution or charge is to be regarded as a tax depends upon its real nature.[21]

Accordingly, fees for dog licenses, automobile inspection, automobile titles and registration, hunting and fishing licenses, bridge and highway tolls, drivers' licenses, parking meter deposits, postage, etc., are not deductible if personal in nature. These items, however, could be deductible if incurred as a business expense or for the production of income. Deductible and nondeductible taxes are summarized in Exhibit 10–2.

■ **EXHIBIT 10–2**
Deductible and Nondeductible Taxes

Deductible	Nondeductible
State, local, and foreign real property taxes	Federal income taxes
State and local personal property taxes	FICA taxes imposed on employees
State and local income taxes *or* sales/use taxes	Employer FICA taxes paid on domestic household workers
Foreign income taxes	Estate, inheritance, and gift taxes
The environmental tax	Federal, state, and local excise taxes (e.g., gasoline, tobacco, spirits)
	Foreign income taxes if the taxpayer chooses the foreign tax credit option
	Taxes on real property to the extent such taxes are to be apportioned and treated as imposed on another taxpayer

[20] Most deductible taxes are listed in § 164, while nondeductible items are included in § 275.

[21] Rev.Rul. 57–345, 1957–2 C.B. 132, and Rev.Rul. 70–622, 1970–2 C.B. 41.

PROPERTY TAXES

State, local, and foreign taxes on real property are generally deductible only by the person upon whom the tax is imposed. Deductible personal property taxes must be *ad valorem* (assessed in relation to the value of the property). Therefore, a motor vehicle tax based on weight, model, year, and horsepower is not an ad valorem tax. However, a tax based on value and other criteria may qualify in part.

EXAMPLE 16

A state imposes a motor vehicle registration tax on 4% of the value of the vehicle plus 40 cents per hundredweight. Belle, a resident of the state, owns a car having a value of $4,000 and weighing 3,000 pounds. Belle pays an annual registration fee of $172. Of this amount, $160 (4% of $4,000) is deductible as a personal property tax. The remaining $12, based on the weight of the car, is not deductible. ■

Assessments for Local Benefits. As a general rule, real property taxes do not include taxes assessed for local benefits since such assessments tend to increase the value of the property (e.g., special assessments for streets, sidewalks, curbing, and other similar improvements). A taxpayer was denied a deduction for the cost of a new sidewalk (relative to a personal residence), even though the construction was required by the city and the sidewalk may have provided an incidental benefit to the public welfare.[22] Such assessments are added to the adjusted basis of the taxpayer's property.

Apportionment of Real Property Taxes between Seller and Purchaser. Real estate taxes for the entire year are apportioned between the buyer and seller on the basis of the number of days the property was held by each during the real property tax year. This apportionment is required whether the tax is paid by the buyer or the seller or is prorated according to the purchase agreement. It is the apportionment that determines who is entitled to deduct the real estate taxes in the year of sale. The required apportionment prevents the shifting of the deduction for real estate taxes from the buyer to the seller, or vice versa.

In making the apportionment, the assessment date and the lien date are disregarded. The date of sale counts as a day the property is owned by the buyer. In leap years, the taxes are prorated over 366 days.[23]

EXAMPLE 17

A county's real property tax year runs from April 1 to March 31. Susan, the owner on April 1, 2005, of real property located in the county, sells the real property to Bob on June 30, 2005. Bob owns the real property from June 30, 2005, through March 31, 2006. The tax for the real property tax year April 1, 2005, through March 31, 2006, is $3,650. The portion of the real property tax treated as imposed upon Susan, the seller, is $900 [(90/365) × $3,650, April 1 through June 29, 2005], and $2,750 [(275/365) × $3,650 June 30, 2005 through March 31, 2006] of the tax is treated as imposed upon Bob, the purchaser. ■

If the actual real estate taxes are not prorated between the buyer and seller as part of the purchase agreement, adjustments are required. The adjustments are necessary to determine the amount realized by the seller and the adjusted basis of the property to the buyer. If the buyer pays the entire amount of the tax, he or she has, in effect, paid the seller's portion of the real estate tax and has therefore paid more for the property than the actual purchase price. Thus, the amount of real estate tax that is apportioned to the seller (for Federal income tax purposes) and paid by the buyer is added to the buyer's adjusted basis. The seller must increase the amount realized on the sale by the same amount.

[22] *Erie H. Rose*, 31 TCM 142, T.C.Memo. 1972–39; Reg. § 1.164–4(a).

[23] A year is a leap year if its number is divisible by 4.

Deductibility of Foreign Taxes

Josef, a citizen of the United States who works primarily in New York, also works several months each year in Austria. He owns a residence in Austria and pays income taxes to Austria on the income he earns there. Both the property tax he pays on his Austrian residence and the income tax he pays on his Austrian income are deductible in computing U.S. taxable income.

EXAMPLE 18

Seth sells real estate on October 3, 2006, for $100,000. The buyer, Wilma, pays the real estate taxes of $3,650 for the 2006 calendar year, which is the real estate property tax year. Of the real estate taxes, $2,750 (for 275 days) is apportioned to and is deductible by the seller, Seth, and $900 (for 90 days) of the taxes is deductible by Wilma. The buyer has, in effect, paid Seth's real estate taxes of $2,750 and has therefore paid $102,750 for the property. Wilma's basis is increased to $102,750, and the amount realized by Seth from the sale is increased to $102,750. ■

The opposite result occurs if the seller (rather than the buyer) pays the real estate taxes. In this case, the seller reduces the amount realized from the sale by the amount that has been apportioned to the buyer. The buyer is required to reduce his or her adjusted basis by a corresponding amount.

EXAMPLE 19

Ruth sells real estate to Butch for $50,000 on October 3, 2006. While Ruth held the property, she paid the real estate taxes of $1,095 for the calendar year, which is the real estate property tax year. Although Ruth paid the entire $1,095 of real estate taxes, $270 of that amount is apportioned to Butch, based on the number of days he owned the property, and is therefore deductible by him. The effect is that the buyer, Butch, has paid only $49,730 ($50,000 – $270) for the property. The amount realized by Ruth, the seller, is reduced by $270, and Butch reduces his basis in the property to $49,730. ■

LO.4

Understand the Federal income tax treatment of state and local income taxes and sales taxes.

STATE AND LOCAL INCOME TAXES AND SALES TAXES

The position of the IRS is that state and local income taxes imposed upon an individual are deductible only as itemized deductions, even if the taxpayer's sole source of income is from a business, rents, or royalties.

Cash basis taxpayers are entitled to deduct state income taxes withheld by the employer in the year the taxes are withheld. In addition, estimated state income tax payments are deductible in the year the payment is made by cash basis taxpayers even if the payments relate to a prior or subsequent year.[24] If the taxpayer overpays state income taxes because of excessive withholdings or estimated tax payments, the refund received is included in gross income of the following year to the extent that the deduction reduced taxable income in the prior year.

EXAMPLE 20

Leona, a cash basis, unmarried taxpayer, had $800 of state income tax withheld during 2005. Additionally in 2005, Leona paid $100 that was due when she filed her 2004 state income tax return and made estimated payments of $300 on her 2005 state income tax. When Leona files her 2005 Federal income tax return in April 2006, she elects to itemize deductions, which amount to $5,500, including the $1,200 of state income tax payments and withholdings, all of which reduce her taxable income.

[24] Rev.Rul. 71–190, 1971–1 C.B. 70. See also Rev.Rul. 82–208, 1982–2 C.B. 58, where a deduction is not allowed when the taxpayer cannot, in good faith, reasonably determine that there is additional state income tax liability.

As a result of overpaying her 2005 state income tax, Leona receives a refund of $200 early in 2006. She will include this amount in her 2006 gross income in computing her Federal income tax. It does not matter whether Leona received a check from the state for $200 or applied the $200 toward her 2006 state income tax. ■

Itemized Deduction for Sales Taxes Paid. Individuals can elect to deduct either their state and local income taxes *or* their sales/use taxes paid as an itemized deduction on Schedule A of Form 1040. This American Jobs Creation Act provision is effective beginning with 2004 returns. The new, annual election can reflect actual sales/use tax payments *or* an amount from an IRS table (see Appendix A). The amount from the table may be increased by sales tax paid on the purchase of motor vehicles, boats, and other specified items. Most likely, the sales tax deduction will be elected by those living in states with no individual income tax (e.g., Texas and Washington).

LO.5

Distinguish between deductible and nondeductible interest and apply the appropriate limitations to deductible interest.

Interest

A deduction for interest has been allowed since the income tax law was enacted in 1913. Despite its long history of congressional acceptance, the interest deduction has been one of the most controversial areas in the tax law. The controversy centered around the propriety of allowing the deduction of interest charges for the purchase of consumer goods and services and interest on borrowings used to acquire investments (investment interest). Personal (consumer) interest is not deductible. This includes credit card interest, interest on car loans, and any other interest that is not interest on qualified education loans, **investment interest,** home mortgage interest, or business interest. Interest on qualified education loans, investment interest, and **qualified residence** (home mortgage) **interest** continue to be deductible, subject to limits discussed on the following pages.

ALLOWED AND DISALLOWED ITEMS

The Supreme Court has defined *interest* as compensation for the use or forbearance of money.[25] The general rule permits a deduction for interest paid or accrued within the taxable year on indebtedness.

Interest on Qualified Education Loans. Taxpayers who pay interest on a qualified education loan may deduct the interest as a deduction *for* AGI. A qualified education loan does not include indebtedness to certain related parties. The maximum deduction is $2,500. The deduction is phased out for taxpayers with modified AGI (MAGI) between $50,000 and $65,000 ($105,000 and $135,000 on joint returns). The deduction is not allowed for taxpayers who are claimed as dependents or for married taxpayers filing separately.[26]

Investment Interest. Taxpayers frequently borrow funds that they use to acquire investment assets. When the interest expense is large relative to the income from the investments, substantial tax benefits could result. Congress has therefore limited the deductibility of interest on funds borrowed for the purpose of purchasing or continuing to hold investment property. Investment interest expense is *now* limited to net investment income for the year.

[25]*Old Colony Railroad Co. v. Comm.*, 3 USTC ¶880, 10 AFTR 786, 52 S.Ct. 211 (USSC, 1932).

[26]§ 221. See § 221(b)(2)(c) for the definition of MAGI. The phaseout amounts are subject to adjustments for inflation. The $2,500 limitation and the phaseout amounts apply to tax returns for 2005. For 2004, the amounts were the same except for joint returns ($100,000 and $130,000).

Investment income is gross income from interest, dividends (see below), annuities, and royalties not derived in the ordinary course of a trade or business. Income from a passive activity and income from a real estate activity in which the taxpayer actively participates are not included in investment income (see Chapter 11).

The following types of income are not included in investment income unless the taxpayer *elects* to do so.

- Net capital gain attributable to the disposition of (a) property producing the types of income just enumerated or (b) property held for investment purposes.
- Qualified dividends that are taxed at the same marginal rate that is applicable to a net capital gain.

A taxpayer may include net capital gain and qualifying dividends as investment income by electing to do so on Form 4952. The election is available only if the taxpayer agrees to reduce amounts qualifying for the 15 percent (5 percent for low-income taxpayers) rates that otherwise apply to net capital gain (see Chapter 14) and qualifying dividends (refer to Chapter 4) by an equivalent amount.

EXAMPLE 21

Terry incurred $13,000 of interest expense related to her investments during the year. Her investment income included $4,000 of interest, $2,000 of qualifying dividends, and a $5,000 net capital gain on the sale of investment securities. If Terry does not make the election to include the net capital gain and qualified dividends in investment income, her investment income for purposes of computing the investment income limitation is $4,000 (interest income). If she does make the election, her investment income is $11,000 ($4,000 interest + $2,000 qualifying dividends + $5,000 net capital gain). ■

Net investment income is the excess of investment income over investment expenses. Investment expenses are those deductible expenses directly connected with the production of investment income. Investment expenses *do not* include interest expense. When investment expenses fall into the category of miscellaneous itemized deductions that are subject to the 2 percent-of-AGI floor, some may not enter into the calculation of net investment income because of the floor.

EXAMPLE 22

Gina has AGI of $80,000, which includes qualified dividends of $15,000 and interest income of $3,000. Besides investment interest expense, she paid $3,000 of city ad valorem property tax on stocks and bonds and had the following miscellaneous itemized expenses:

Safe deposit box rental (to hold investment securities)	$ 120
Investment counsel fee	1,200
Unreimbursed business travel	850
Uniforms	600

Before Gina can determine her investment expenses for purposes of calculating net investment income, those miscellaneous expenses that are not investment expenses are disallowed before any investment expenses are disallowed under the 2%-of-AGI floor. This is accomplished by selecting the *lesser* of the following:

1. The amount of investment expenses included in the total of miscellaneous itemized deductions subject to the 2%-of-AGI floor.
2. The amount of miscellaneous expenses deductible after the 2%-of-AGI rule is applied.

The amount under item 1 is $1,320 [$120 (safe deposit box rental) + $1,200 (investment counsel fee)]. The item 2 amount is $1,170 [$2,770 (total of miscellaneous expenses) – $1,600 (2% of $80,000 AGI)].

Then, Gina's investment expenses are calculated as follows:

Deductible miscellaneous deductions investment expense (the lesser of item 1 or item 2)	$1,170
Plus: Ad valorem tax on investment property	3,000
Total investment expenses	$4,170

Gina elects to include the qualified dividends in investment income. Gina's net investment income is $13,830 ($18,000 investment income – $4,170 investment expenses). ■

After net investment income is determined, deductible investment interest expense can be calculated.

EXAMPLE 23

Adam is a single person employed by a law firm. His investment activities for the year are as follows:

Net investment income	$30,000
Investment interest expense	44,000

Adam's investment interest deduction is $30,000. ■

The amount of investment interest disallowed is carried over to future years. In Example 23, therefore, the amount that is carried over to the following year is $14,000 ($44,000 investment interest expense – $30,000 allowed). No limit is placed on the length of the carryover period. The investment interest expense deduction is determined by completing Form 4952.

Qualified Residence Interest. *Qualified residence interest* is interest paid or accrued during the taxable year on indebtedness (subject to limitations) *secured* by any property that is a qualified residence of the taxpayer. Qualified residence interest falls into two categories: (1) interest on acquisition indebtedness and (2) interest on home equity loans. Before discussing each of these categories, however, the term qualified residence must be defined.

A *qualified residence* includes the taxpayer's principal residence and one other residence of the taxpayer or spouse. The *principal residence* is one that meets the requirement for nonrecognition of gain upon sale under § 121 (see Chapter 13). The *one other residence*, or second residence, refers to one that is used as a residence if not rented or, if rented, meets the requirements for a personal residence under the rental of vacation home rules (refer to Chapter 6). A taxpayer who has more than one second residence can make the selection each year of which one is the qualified second residence. A residence includes, in addition to a house in the ordinary sense, cooperative apartments, condominiums, and mobile homes and boats that have living quarters (sleeping accommodations and toilet and cooking facilities).

Although in most cases interest paid on a home mortgage is fully deductible, there are limitations.[27] Interest paid or accrued during the tax year on aggregate **acquisition indebtedness** of $1 million or less ($500,000 for married persons filing separate returns) is deductible as qualified residence interest. *Acquisition indebtedness* refers to amounts incurred in acquiring, constructing, or substantially improving a qualified residence of the taxpayer.

Qualified residence interest also includes interest on **home equity loans.** These loans utilize the personal residence of the taxpayer as security. Because the funds from home equity loans can be used for personal purposes (e.g., auto purchases,

[27] § 163(h)(3).

medical expenses), what would otherwise have been nondeductible consumer interest becomes deductible qualified residence interest.

However, interest is deductible only on the portion of a home equity loan that does not exceed the *lesser of*:

- The fair market value of the residence, reduced by the acquisition indebtedness, *or*
- $100,000 ($50,000 for married persons filing separate returns).

EXAMPLE 24

Larry owns a personal residence with a fair market value of $150,000 and an outstanding first mortgage of $120,000. Therefore, his equity in his home is $30,000 ($150,000 – $120,000). Larry issues a lien on the residence and in return borrows $15,000 to purchase a new family automobile. All interest on the $135,000 of debt is treated as qualified residence interest. ■

EXAMPLE 25

Leon and Pearl, married taxpayers, took out a mortgage on their home for $290,000 in 1989. In March of the current year, when the home has a fair market value of $400,000 and they owe $195,000 on the mortgage, Leon and Pearl take out a home equity loan for $120,000. They use the funds to purchase a boat to be used for recreational purposes. The boat, which does not have living quarters, does not qualify as a personal residence. On a joint return, Leon and Pearl can deduct all of the interest on the first mortgage since it is acquisition indebtedness. Of the $120,000 home equity loan, only the interest on the first $100,000 is deductible. The interest on the remaining $20,000 is not deductible because it exceeds the statutory ceiling of $100,000. ■

Interest Paid for Services. Mortgage loan companies commonly charge a fee for finding, placing, or processing a mortgage loan. Such fees are often called **points** and are expressed as a percentage of the loan amount. Borrowers often have to pay points to obtain the necessary financing. To qualify as deductible interest, the points must be considered compensation to a lender solely for the use or forbearance of money. The points cannot be a form of service charge or payment for specific services if they are to qualify as deductible interest.[28]

Points must be capitalized and are amortized and deductible ratably over the life of the loan. A special exception permits the purchaser of a personal residence to deduct qualifying points in the year of payment.[29] The exception also covers points paid to obtain funds for home improvements.

EXAMPLE 26

During 2005, Thelma purchases a new residence for $130,000 and pays points of $2,600 to obtain mortgage financing. At Thelma's election, the $2,600 can be claimed as an interest deduction for tax year 2005. ■

Points paid to *refinance* an existing home mortgage cannot be immediately expensed, but must be capitalized and amortized as interest expense over the life of the new loan.[30]

EXAMPLE 27

Sandra purchased her residence several years ago, obtaining a 30-year mortgage at an annual interest rate of 9%. In the current year, Sandra refinances the mortgage in order to reduce the interest rate to 6%. To obtain the refinancing, she has to pay points of $2,600. The $2,600 paid comes under the usual rule applicable to points. The $2,600 must be capitalized and amortized over the life of the mortgage. ■

Points paid by the seller for a buyer are, in effect, treated as an adjustment to the price of the residence, and the buyer is treated as having used cash to pay the points that were paid by the seller. A buyer may deduct seller-paid points in the

[28]Rev.Rul. 67–297, 1967–2 C.B. 87.

[29]§ 461(g)(2).

[30]Rev.Rul. 87–22, 1987–1 C.B. 146.

tax year in which they are paid if several conditions are met. Refer to Revenue Procedure 94–27 for a complete list of these conditions.[31]

Prepayment Penalty. When a mortgage or loan is paid off in full in a lump sum before its term (early), the lending institution may require an additional payment of a certain percentage applied to the unpaid amount at the time of prepayment. This is known as a prepayment penalty and is considered to be interest (e.g., personal, qualified residence, investment) in the year paid. The general rules for deductibility of interest also apply to prepayment penalties.

Interest Paid to Related Parties. Nothing prevents the deduction of interest paid to a related party as long as the payment actually took place and the interest meets the requirements for deductibility. Recall from Chapter 6 that a special rule for related taxpayers applies when the debtor uses the accrual basis and the related creditor is on the cash basis. If this rule is applicable, interest that has been accrued but not paid at the end of the debtor's tax year is not deductible until payment is made and the income is reportable by the cash basis recipient.

Tax-Exempt Securities. The tax law provides that no deduction is allowed for interest on debt incurred to purchase or carry tax-exempt securities.[32] A major problem for the courts has been to determine what is meant by the words *to purchase or carry*. Refer to Chapter 6 for a detailed discussion of these issues.

RESTRICTIONS ON DEDUCTIBILITY AND TIMING CONSIDERATIONS

Taxpayer's Obligation. Allowed interest is deductible if the related debt represents a bona fide obligation for which the taxpayer is liable.[33] Thus, a taxpayer may not deduct interest paid on behalf of another individual. For interest to be deductible, both the debtor and the creditor must intend for the loan to be repaid. Intent of the parties can be especially crucial between related parties such as a shareholder and a closely held corporation. A shareholder may not deduct interest paid by the corporation on his or her behalf.[34] Likewise, a husband may not deduct interest paid on his wife's property if he files a separate return, except in the case of qualified residence interest. If both husband and wife consent in writing, either the husband or the wife may deduct the allowed interest on the principal residence and one other residence.

Time of Deduction. Generally, interest must be paid to secure a deduction unless the taxpayer uses the accrual method of accounting. Under the accrual method, interest is deductible ratably over the life of the loan.

EXAMPLE 28

On November 1, 2005, Ramon borrows $1,000 to purchase appliances for a rental house. The loan is payable in 90 days at 12% interest. On the due date in January 2006, Ramon pays the $1,000 note and interest amounting to $30. Ramon can deduct the accrued portion ($\frac{2}{3} \times \$30 = \$20$) of the interest in 2005 only if he is an accrual basis taxpayer. Otherwise, the entire amount of interest ($30) is deductible in 2006. ■

Prepaid Interest. Accrual method reporting is imposed on cash basis taxpayers for interest prepayments that extend beyond the end of the taxable year.[35] Such payments must be allocated to the tax years to which the interest payments relate.

[31] Rev.Proc. 94–27, 1994–1 C.B. 613.

[32] § 265(a)(2).

[33] *Arcade Realty Co.*, 35 T.C. 256 (1960).

[34] *Continental Trust Co.*, 7 B.T.A. 539 (1927).

[35] § 461(g)(1).

CONCEPT SUMMARY 10–1

Deductibility of Personal, Education, Investment, and Mortgage Interest

Type	Deductible	Comments
Personal (consumer) interest	No	Includes any interest that is not home mortgage interest, qualified education loan interest, investment interest, or business interest. Examples include car loans, credit cards, etc.
Qualified education interest	Yes	Deduction *for* AGI; subject to limitations.
Investment interest (*not* related to rental or royalty property)	Yes	Itemized deduction; limited to net investment income for the year; disallowed interest can be carried over to future years.
Investment interest (related to rental or royalty property)	Yes	Deduction *for* AGI; limited to net investment income for the year; disallowed interest can be carried over to future years.
Qualified residence interest on acquisition indebtedness	Yes	Deductible as an itemized deduction; limited to indebtedness of $1 million.
Qualified residence interest on home equity indebtedness	Yes	Deductible as an itemized deduction; limited to indebtedness equal to lesser of $100,000 or FMV of residence minus acquisition indebtedness.

These provisions are intended to prevent cash basis taxpayers from *manufacturing* tax deductions before the end of the year by prepaying interest.

CLASSIFICATION OF INTEREST EXPENSE

Whether interest is deductible *for* AGI or as an itemized deduction (*from*) depends on whether the indebtedness has a business, investment, or personal purpose. If the indebtedness is incurred in relation to a business (other than performing services as an employee) or for the production of rent or royalty income, the interest is deductible *for* AGI. If the indebtedness is incurred for personal use, such as qualified residence interest, any deduction allowed is reported on Schedule A of Form 1040 if the taxpayer elects to itemize. If the taxpayer is an employee who incurs debt in relation to his or her employment, the interest is considered to be personal, or consumer, interest. Business expenses appear on Schedule C of Form 1040, and expenses related to rents or royalties are reported on Schedule E.

If a taxpayer deposits money in a certificate of deposit (CD) that has a term of one year or less and the interest cannot be withdrawn without penalty, the full amount of the interest must still be included in income, even though part of the interest is forfeited due to an early withdrawal. However, the taxpayer will be allowed a deduction *for* AGI as to the forfeited amount.

LO.6

Understand charitable contributions and their related measurement problems and percentage limitations.

Charitable Contributions

Individuals and corporations are allowed to deduct contributions made to qualified *domestic* organizations.[36] Contributions to qualified charitable organizations serve certain social welfare needs and thus relieve the government of the cost of providing these needed services to the community.

[36] § 170.

The **charitable contribution** provisions are among the most complex in the tax law. To determine the amount deductible as a charitable contribution, several important questions must be answered:

- What constitutes a charitable contribution?
- Was the contribution made to a qualified organization?
- When is the contribution deductible?
- What record-keeping and reporting requirements apply to charitable contributions?
- How is the value of donated property determined?
- What special rules apply to contributions of property that has increased in value?
- What percentage limitations apply to the charitable contribution deduction?
- What rules apply to amounts in excess of percentage limitations (carryovers)?

These questions are addressed in the sections that follow.

CRITERIA FOR A GIFT

A *charitable contribution* is defined as a gift made to a qualified organization.[37] The major elements needed to qualify a contribution as a gift are a donative intent, the absence of consideration, and acceptance by the donee. Consequently, the taxpayer has the burden of establishing that the transfer was made from motives of *disinterested generosity* as established by the courts.[38] This test is quite subjective and has led to problems of interpretation (refer to the discussion of gifts in Chapter 5).

Benefit Received Rule. When a donor derives a tangible benefit from a contribution, he or she cannot deduct the value of the benefit.

EXAMPLE 29

Ralph purchases a ticket at $100 for a special performance of the local symphony (a qualified charity). If the price of a ticket to a symphony concert is normally $35, Ralph is allowed only $65 as a charitable contribution. ■

An exception to this benefit rule provides for the deduction of an automatic percentage of the amount paid for the right to purchase athletic tickets from colleges and universities.[39] Under this exception, 80 percent of the amount paid to or for the benefit of the institution qualifies as a charitable contribution deduction.

EXAMPLE 30

Janet donates $500 to State University's athletic department. The payment guarantees that she will have preferred seating on the 50-yard line. Subsequently, Janet buys four $35 game tickets. Under the exception to the benefit rule, she is allowed a $400 (80% of $500) charitable contribution deduction for the taxable year.

If, however, Janet's $500 donation includes four $35 tickets, that portion [$140 ($35 × 4)] and the remaining portion of $360 ($500 – $140) are treated as separate amounts. Thus, Janet is allowed a charitable contribution deduction of $288 (80% of $360). ■

Contribution of Services. No deduction is allowed for a contribution of one's services to a qualified charitable organization. However, unreimbursed expenses related to the services rendered may be deductible. For example, the cost of a uniform (without general utility) that is required to be worn while performing services may be deductible, as are certain out-of-pocket transportation costs

[37] § 170(c).

[38] *Comm. v. Duberstein*, 60–2 USTC ¶9515, 5 AFTR2d 1626, 80 S.Ct. 1190 (USSC, 1960).

[39] § 170(l).

incurred for the benefit of the charity. In lieu of these out-of-pocket costs for an automobile, a standard mileage rate of 14 cents per mile is allowed.[40] Deductions are permitted for transportation, reasonable expenses for lodging, and the cost of meals while away from home incurred in performing the donated services. The travel expenses are not deductible if the travel involves a significant element of personal pleasure, recreation, or vacation.[41]

EXAMPLE 31

Grace, a delegate representing her church in Miami, Florida, travels to a two-day national meeting in Denver, Colorado, in February. After the meeting, Grace spends two weeks at a nearby ski resort. Under these circumstances, none of the transportation, meals, or lodging is deductible because the travel involved a significant element of personal pleasure, recreation, or vacation. ■

Nondeductible Items. In addition to the benefit received rule and the restrictions placed on contribution of services, the following items may *not* be deducted as charitable contributions:

- Dues, fees, or bills paid to country clubs, lodges, fraternal orders, or similar groups.
- Cost of raffle, bingo, or lottery tickets.
- Cost of tuition.
- Value of blood given to a blood bank.
- Donations to homeowners associations.
- Gifts to individuals.
- Rental value of property used by a qualified charity.

QUALIFIED ORGANIZATIONS

To be deductible, a contribution must be made to one of the following organizations:[42]

- A state or possession of the United States or any subdivisions thereof.
- A corporation, trust, community chest, fund, or foundation that is situated in the United States and is organized and operated exclusively for religious, charitable, scientific, literary, or educational purposes or for the prevention of cruelty to children or animals.
- A veterans' organization.
- A fraternal organization operating under the lodge system.
- A cemetery company.

The IRS publishes a list of organizations that have applied for and received tax-exempt status under § 501 of the Code.[43] This publication is updated frequently and may be helpful in determining if a gift has been made to a qualifying charitable organization.

Because gifts made to needy individuals are not deductible, a deduction will not be permitted if a gift is received by a donee in an individual capacity rather than as a representative of a qualifying organization.

[40] § 170(i).
[41] § 170(j).
[42] § 170(c).
[43] Although this *Cumulative List of Organizations*, IRS Publication 78 (available by purchase from the Superintendent of Documents, U.S. Government Printing Office, Washington, DC 20402), may be helpful, qualified organizations are not required to be listed. Not all organizations that qualify are listed in this publication. The list is also available on the Web at **http://www.irs.gov**.

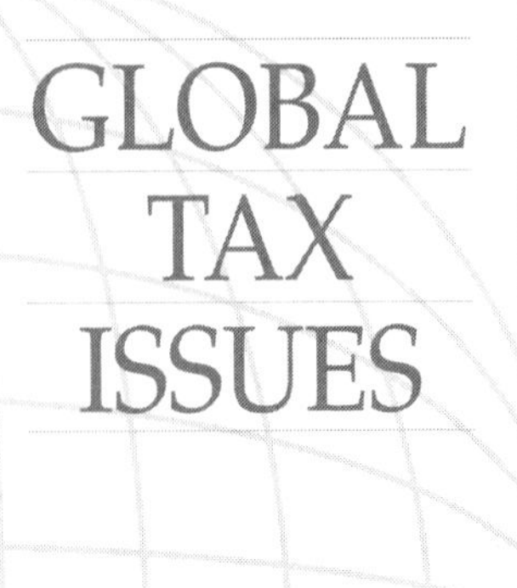

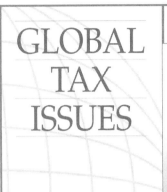

CHOOSE THE CHARITY WISELY

Ibrahim, a U.S. citizen of Turkish descent, was distressed by the damage caused by a major earthquake in Turkey. He donated $100,000 to the Earthquake Victims' Relief Fund, a Turkish charitable organization that was set up to help victims of the earthquake. Ahmed, also a U.S. citizen of Turkish descent, donated $200,000 to help with the relief effort. However, Ahmed's contribution went to his mosque, which sent the proceeds of a fund drive to the Earthquake Victims' Relief Fund in Turkey. Ibrahim's contribution is not deductible, but Ahmed's is. Why? Contributions to charitable organizations are not deductible unless the organization is a U.S. charity.

TIME OF DEDUCTION

A charitable contribution generally is deducted in the year the payment is made. This rule applies to both cash and accrual basis individuals. A contribution is ordinarily deemed to have been made on the delivery of the property to the donee. For example, if a gift of securities (properly endorsed) is made to a qualified charitable organization, the gift is considered complete on the day of delivery or mailing. However, if the donor delivers the certificate to his or her bank or broker or to the issuing corporation, the gift is considered complete on the date the stock is transferred on the books of the corporation.

A contribution made by check is considered delivered on the date of mailing. Thus, a check mailed on December 31, 2005, is deductible on the taxpayer's 2005 tax return. If the contribution is charged on a bank credit card, the date the charge is made determines the year of deduction.

RECORD-KEEPING AND VALUATION REQUIREMENTS

Record-Keeping Requirements. No deduction is allowed for contributions of $250 or more unless the taxpayer obtains *written substantiation* of the contribution from the charitable organization. The substantiation must specify the amount of cash and a description (but not value) of any property other than cash contributed. The substantiation must be obtained before the earlier of (1) the due date (including extensions) of the return for the year the contribution is claimed or (2) the date such return is filed.

Additional information is required if the value of the donated property is over $500 but not over $5,000. Also, the taxpayer must file Section A of Form 8283 (Noncash Charitable Contributions) for such contributions.

For noncash contributions with a claimed value in excess of $5,000 ($10,000 in the case of nonpublicly traded stock), the taxpayer must obtain a qualified appraisal and must file Section B of Form 8283. This schedule must show a summary of the appraisal and must be attached to the taxpayer's return. Failure to comply with these reporting rules may result in disallowance of the charitable contribution deduction. Additionally, significant overvaluation exposes the taxpayer to rather stringent penalties.[44]

Valuation Requirements. Property donated to a charity is generally valued at fair market value at the time the gift is made. The Code and Regulations give

[44]The amounts discussed in this section ($250, $500, $5,000 and $10,000) apply to 2004 tax returns. Amounts for 2005 had not been announced at the date of this writing.

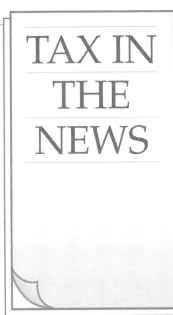

Spring Cleaning and Charitable Contributions

Two events that are usually unrelated normally occur in the spring: people clean their houses and file their tax returns. Spring housecleaning can result in a tax deduction for those who donate their unneeded items to charity. Taxpayers can load their old clothes in bags and take them to Goodwill or the Salvation Army. Instead of throwing away old furniture and appliances, these items can be donated to Empty Tomb or Habitat for Humanity. Such generosity can result in a substantial tax deduction. First, however, the taxpayer will have to determine how much to deduct. How much are old clothes worth? What value should be placed on a used sofa?

A prominent software company has created a product to help taxpayers solve the valuation problem. Based on numerous visits to thrift shops around the country, the developer of the software compiled a list of values for almost 1,000 clothing and household items. Purchasers of the software can purchase an audit protection warranty. If the IRS denies values based on the use of the product, the warranty covers any related penalties and interest.

very little guidance on the measurement of the fair market value except to say, "The fair market value is the price at which the property would change hands between a willing buyer and a willing seller, neither being under any compulsion to buy or sell and both having reasonable knowledge of relevant facts."

Generally, charitable organizations do not attest to the fair market value of the donated property. Nevertheless, the taxpayer must maintain reliable written evidence of the following information concerning the donation:

- The fair market value of the property and how that value was determined.
- The amount of the reduction in the value of the property (if required) for certain appreciated property and how that reduction was determined.
- Terms of any agreement with the charitable organization dealing with the use of the property and potential sale or other disposition of the property by the organization.
- A signed copy of the appraisal if the value of the property was determined by appraisal. Only for a contribution of art with an aggregate value of $20,000 or more must the appraisal be attached to the taxpayer's return.

LIMITATIONS ON CHARITABLE CONTRIBUTION DEDUCTION

In General. The potential charitable contribution deduction is the total of all donations, both money and property, that qualify for the deduction. After this determination is made, the actual amount of the charitable contribution deduction that is allowed for individuals for the tax year is limited as follows:

- If the qualifying contributions for the year total 20 percent or less of AGI, they are fully deductible.
- If the qualifying contributions are more than 20 percent of AGI, the deductible amount may be limited to either 20 percent, 30 percent, or 50 percent of AGI, depending on the type of property given and the type of organization to which the donation is made.
- In any case, the maximum charitable contribution deduction may not exceed 50 percent of AGI for the tax year.

To understand the complex rules for computing the amount of a charitable contribution, it is necessary to understand the distinction between capital gain property and ordinary income property. In addition, it is necessary to understand when the 50 percent, 30 percent, and 20 percent limitations apply. If a taxpayer's contributions for the year exceed the applicable percentage limitations, the excess contributions may be carried forward and deducted during a five-year carryover period. These topics are discussed in the sections that follow.

Ordinary Income Property. **Ordinary income property** is any property that, if sold, will result in the recognition of ordinary income. The term includes inventory for sale in the taxpayer's trade or business, a work of art created by the donor, and a manuscript prepared by the donor. It also includes, *for purposes of the charitable contribution calculation*, a capital asset held by the donor for less than the required holding period for long-term capital gain treatment (long term is a period longer than one year). To the extent that disposition of property results in the recognition of ordinary income due to the recapture of depreciation, it is ordinary income property.[45]

If ordinary income property is contributed, the deduction is equal to the fair market value of the property less the amount of ordinary income that would have been reported if the property were sold. In most instances, the deduction is limited to the adjusted basis of the property to the donor.

EXAMPLE 32

Tim donates stock in White Corporation to a university on May 1, 2005. Tim had purchased the stock for $2,500 on March 3, 2005, and the stock had a value of $3,600 when he made the donation. Since he had not held the property long enough to meet the long-term capital gain requirement, Tim would have recognized a short-term capital gain of $1,100 if he had sold the property. Since short-term capital gain property is treated as ordinary income property for charitable contribution purposes, Tim's charitable contribution deduction is limited to the property's adjusted basis of $2,500 ($3,600 – $1,100 = $2,500). ■

In Example 32, suppose the stock had a fair market value of $2,300 (rather than $3,600) when it was donated to charity. Because the fair market value now is less than the adjusted basis, the charitable contribution deduction is $2,300.

Capital Gain Property. **Capital gain property** is any property that would have resulted in the recognition of long-term capital gain or § 1231 gain if the property had been sold by the donor.[46] As a general rule, the deduction for a contribution of capital gain property is equal to the fair market value of the property.

Two major exceptions disallow the deductibility of the appreciation on long-term capital gain property. One exception concerns certain private foundations. Private foundations are organizations that traditionally do not receive their funding from the general public (e.g., the Ford Foundation). Generally, foundations fall into two categories: operating and nonoperating. A private *operating* foundation is one that spends substantially all of its income in the active conduct of the charitable undertaking for which it was established. Other private foundations are *nonoperating* foundations. However, if a private nonoperating foundation distributes the contributions it receives according to special rules within two and one-half months following the year of the contribution, the organization is treated the same as public charities and private operating foundations. Often, only the private foundation knows its status (operating or nonoperating) for sure, and the status can change from year to year.

[45]For a more complete discussion of the difference between ordinary income and capital gain property, see Chapter 14.

[46]See General Scheme of Taxation in Chapter 14 for a discussion of holding periods.

If capital gain property is contributed to a private nonoperating foundation, the taxpayer must reduce the contribution by the long-term capital gain that would have been recognized if the property had been sold at its fair market value. The effect of this provision is to limit the deduction to the property's adjusted basis.[47]

EXAMPLE 33

Walter purchases land for $800 on January 1, 1976, and donates it to a private nonoperating foundation on June 21, 2005, when it is worth $2,000. Walter's charitable contribution is $800 ($2,000 – $1,200), the land's basis. ■

If, in Example 33, Walter had donated the land to either a public charity or a private operating foundation, his charitable contribution would be $2,000, the fair market value of the land.

A second exception applying to capital gain property relates to *tangible personalty*. Tangible personalty is all property that is not realty (land and buildings) and does not include intangible property such as stock or securities. If tangible personalty is contributed to a public charity such as a museum, church, or university, the charitable deduction may have to be reduced. The amount of the reduction is the long-term capital gain that would have been recognized if the property had been sold for its fair market value. The reduction is required *if* the property is put to an unrelated use. The term *unrelated use* means a use that is unrelated to the exempt purpose or function of the charitable organization.

A taxpayer in this instance must establish that the property is not in fact being put to an unrelated use by the donee. The taxpayer must also establish that at the time of the contribution it was reasonable to anticipate that the property would not be put to an unrelated use. For a contribution of personalty to a museum, if the work of art is the kind of art normally retained by the museum, it is reasonable for a donor to anticipate that the work of art will not be put to an unrelated use. This is the case even if the object is later sold or exchanged by the museum.[48]

EXAMPLE 34

Myrtle contributes a Picasso painting, for which she paid $20,000, to a local museum. She had owned the painting for four years. It had a value of $30,000 at the time of the donation. The museum displays the painting for two years and subsequently sells it for $50,000. The charitable contribution is $30,000. It is not reduced by the unrealized appreciation since the painting is put to a related use even though it is later sold by the museum. ■

Fifty Percent Ceiling. Contributions made to public charities may not exceed 50 percent of an individual's AGI for the year. Excess contributions may be carried over to the next five years. The 50 percent ceiling on contributions applies to the following types of public charities:

- A church or a convention or association of churches.
- An educational organization that maintains a regular faculty and curriculum.
- A hospital or medical school.
- An organization supported by the government that holds property or investments for the benefit of a college or university.
- A Federal, state, or local governmental unit.
- An organization normally receiving a substantial part of its support from the public or a governmental unit.

In the remaining discussion of charitable contributions, public charities and private foundations (both operating and nonoperating) that qualify for the 50 percent ceiling will be referred to as *50 percent organizations*.

[47]§ 170(e)(5). Taxpayers who donate *qualified appreciated stock* to private nonoperating foundations may deduct the fair market value of the stock. Qualified appreciated stock is stock for which market quotations are readily available on an established securities market.

[48]Reg. § 1.170A–4(b)(3)(ii)(b).

The 50 percent ceiling also applies to contributions to the following organizations:

- All private operating foundations.
- Certain private nonoperating foundations that distribute the contributions they receive to public charities and private operating foundations within two and one-half months following the year they receive the contribution.
- Certain private nonoperating foundations in which the contributions are pooled in a common fund and the income and principal sum are paid to public charities.

Thirty Percent Ceiling. A 30 percent ceiling applies to contributions of cash and ordinary income property to private nonoperating foundations that are not 50 percent organizations. The 30 percent ceiling also applies to contributions of appreciated capital gain property to 50 percent organizations unless the taxpayer makes a special election (see below).

In the event the contributions for any one tax year involve both 50 percent and 30 percent property, the allowable deduction comes first from the 50 percent property.

EXAMPLE 35

During the year, Lisa makes the following donations to her church: cash of $2,000 and unimproved land worth $30,000. Lisa had purchased the land four years ago for $22,000 and held it as an investment. Therefore, it is long-term capital gain property. Lisa's AGI for the year is $60,000. Disregarding percentage limitations, Lisa's potential deduction is $32,000 [$2,000 (cash) + $30,000 (fair market value of land)].

In applying the percentage limitations, however, the *current* deduction for the land is limited to $18,000 [30% (limitation applicable to long-term capital gain property) × $60,000 (AGI)]. Thus, the total deduction is $20,000 ($2,000 cash + $18,000 land). Note that the total deduction does not exceed $30,000, which is 50% of Lisa's AGI. ■

Under a special election, a taxpayer may choose to forgo a deduction of the appreciation on capital gain property. Referred to as the *reduced deduction election*, this enables the taxpayer to move from the 30 percent limitation to the 50 percent limitation.

EXAMPLE 36

Assume the same facts as in Example 35, except that Lisa makes the reduced deduction election. Now the deduction becomes $24,000 [$2,000 (cash) + $22,000 (basis in land)] because both donations fall under the 50% limitation. Thus, by making the election, Lisa has increased her charitable contribution deduction by $4,000 [$24,000 – $20,000 (Example 35)]. ■

Although the reduced deduction election appears attractive, it should be considered carefully. The election sacrifices a deduction for the appreciation on long-term capital gain property that might eventually be allowed. Note that in Example 35, the potential deduction was $32,000, yet in Example 36 only $24,000 is allowed. The reason the potential deduction is decreased by $8,000 ($32,000 – $24,000) is that no carryover is allowed for the amount sacrificed by the election.

Twenty Percent Ceiling. A 20 percent ceiling applies to contributions of appreciated long-term capital gain property to private nonoperating foundations that are not 50 percent organizations.

Contribution Carryovers. Contributions that exceed the percentage limitations for the current year can be carried over for five years. In the carryover process, such contributions do not lose their identity for limitation purposes. Thus, if the contribution originally involved 30 percent property, the carryover will continue to be classified as 30 percent property in the carryover year.

CONCEPT SUMMARY 10–2

Determining the Deduction for Contributions of Appreciated Property by Individuals

If the Type of Property Contributed Is:	And the Property Is Contributed to:	The Contribution Is Measured by:	But the Deduction Is Limited to:
1. Capital gain property	A 50% organization	Fair market value of the property	30% of AGI
2. Ordinary income property	A 50% organization	The basis of the property*	50% of AGI
3. Capital gain property (and the property is tangible personal property put to an unrelated use by the donee)	A 50% organization	The basis of the property*	50% of AGI
4. Capital gain property (and the reduced deduction is elected)	A 50% organization	The basis of the property	50% of AGI
5. Capital gain property	A private nonoperating foundation that is not a 50% organization	The basis of the property*	The lesser of: 1. 20% of AGI 2. 50% of AGI minus other contributions to 50% organizations

*If the fair market value of the property is less than the adjusted basis (i.e., the property has declined in value instead of appreciating), the fair market value is used.

EXAMPLE 37

Assume the same facts as in Example 35. Because only $18,000 of the $30,000 value of the land is deducted in the current year, the balance of $12,000 may be carried over to the following year. But the carryover will still be treated as long-term capital gain property and is subject to the 30%-of-AGI limitation. ■

In applying the percentage limitations, current charitable contributions must be claimed first before any carryovers can be considered. If carryovers involve more than one year, they are utilized in a first-in, first-out order.

LO.7

List the business and personal expenditures that are deductible either as miscellaneous itemized deductions or as other itemized deductions.

Miscellaneous Itemized Deductions

No deduction is allowed for personal, living, or family expenses.[49] However, a taxpayer may incur a number of expenditures related to employment. If an employee or outside salesperson incurs unreimbursed business expenses or expenses that are reimbursed under a nonaccountable plan, including travel and transportation, the expenses are deductible as **miscellaneous itemized deductions.**[50] Certain other expenses also fall into the special category of miscellaneous itemized deductions. Some are deductible only if, in total, they exceed 2 percent of the taxpayer's

[49] § 262.
[50] Actors and performing artists who meet certain requirements are not subject to this rule.

AGI. These miscellaneous itemized deductions include (but are not limited to) the following:

- Professional dues to membership organizations.
- Uniforms or other clothing that cannot be used for normal wear.
- Fees incurred for the preparation of one's tax return or fees incurred for tax litigation before the IRS or the courts.
- Job-hunting costs.
- Fee paid for a safe deposit box used to store papers and documents relating to taxable income-producing investments.
- Investment expenses that are deductible under § 212 as discussed in Chapter 6.
- Appraisal fees to determine the amount of a casualty loss or the fair market value of donated property.
- Hobby losses up to the amount of hobby income (see Chapter 6).
- Unreimbursed employee expenses (see Chapter 9).

Certain employee business expenses that are reimbursed are not itemized deductions, but are deducted *for* AGI. Employee business expenses are discussed in depth in Chapter 9.

ETHICAL CONSIDERATIONS

Job Hunting in Ski Country: A Deductible Expense?

George, an avid skier, manages the ski department of a sporting goods store in St. Louis. He has been taking ski vacations in Lake Tahoe for several years and is considering finding a job in Lake Tahoe and moving there. George recently learned that he can deduct job-hunting expenses on his Federal income tax return. One of his customers, who is a CPA, told George that transportation costs can be deducted if the primary purpose of the trip is to hunt for a job. According to the CPA, other travel costs must be allocated between job-hunting days and personal days. George plans to fly to Reno on Sunday, have job interviews each morning from Monday through Thursday, and ski each afternoon after the job interviews are concluded. He plans to ski all day Friday and Saturday and fly back to St. Louis on Saturday night. Is George justified in taking a deduction for job-hunting expenses this year? Will he be justified in taking future deductions if he is unable to find a job this year and continues his job-hunting trips each year for the next several years?

Other Miscellaneous Deductions

Certain expenses and losses do not fall into any category of itemized deductions already discussed but are nonetheless deductible. The following expenses and losses are deductible on line 27 of Schedule A as Other Miscellaneous Deductions.

- Gambling losses up to the amount of gambling winnings.
- Impairment-related work expenses of a handicapped person.
- Federal estate tax on income in respect of a decedent.
- Deduction for repayment of amounts under a claim of right if more than $3,000 (discussed in Chapter 16).
- The unrecovered investment in an annuity contract when the annuity ceases by reason of death, discussed in Chapter 4.

Unlike the expenses and losses discussed previously under Miscellaneous Itemized Deductions, the above expenses and losses are not subject to the 2 percent-of-AGI floor.

Comprehensive Example of Schedule A

Harry and Jean Brown, married filing jointly, had the following transactions for the current year:

• Medicines that required a prescription	$ 430
• Doctor and dentist bills paid and not reimbursed	2,120
• Medical insurance premium payments	1,200
• Contact lenses	175
• Transportation for medical purposes (300 miles × 14 cents/mile + $1.00 parking)	43
• State income tax withheld	620
• Real estate taxes	1,580
• Interest paid on qualified residence mortgage	2,840
• Charitable contributions in cash	860
• Transportation in performing charitable services (800 miles × 14 cents/mile + $7.00 parking and tolls)	119
• Unreimbursed employee expenses (from Form 2106)	870
• Tax return preparation	150
• Safe deposit box (used for keeping investment documents and tax records)	170

The Browns' AGI is $40,000. Their completed 2004 Schedule A on the following page reports itemized deductions totaling $7,377. Schedule A for 2004 is presented because the 2005 form was not yet available.

LO.8

Recognize the limitation on certain itemized deductions applicable to high-income taxpayers.

Overall Limitation on Certain Itemized Deductions

Congress has enacted several provisions limiting tax benefits for high-income taxpayers. These limitations include the exemption phaseout (refer to Chapter 3) and a phaseout of itemized deductions. For 2005, the phaseout of itemized deductions (also referred to as a *cutback adjustment*) applies to taxpayers whose AGI exceeds $145,950 ($72,975 for married taxpayers filing separately).[51] The limitation applies to the following frequently encountered itemized deductions:[52]

- Taxes.
- Home mortgage interest, including points.
- Charitable contributions.
- Unreimbursed employee expenses subject to the 2 percent-of-AGI floor.
- All other expenses subject to the 2 percent-of-AGI floor.

The following deductions are *not* subject to the limitation on itemized deductions:

- Medical and dental expenses.
- Investment interest expense.

[51] For 2004, the limitation applied if AGI exceeded $142,700 ($71,350 for married taxpayers filing separately). The overall limitation applicable to itemized deductions will be phased out over a four-year period, beginning in 2006. The limitation will no longer exist for taxable years beginning after 2009.

[52] Other deductions subject to the limitation include Federal estate tax on income in respect of a decedent, certain amortizable bond premiums, the deduction for repayment of certain amounts, certain unrecovered investments in an annuity, and impairment-related work expenses.

SCHEDULES A&B (Form 1040)
Department of the Treasury Internal Revenue Service (99)

Schedule A—Itemized Deductions

(Schedule B is on back)

▶ **Attach to Form 1040.** ▶ **See Instructions for Schedules A and B (Form 1040).**

OMB No. 1545-0074
2004
Attachment Sequence No. **07**

Name(s) shown on Form 1040: *Harry and Jean Brown*
Your social security number: *371 30 3987*

Medical and Dental Expenses		**Caution.** Do not include expenses reimbursed or paid by others.				
	1	Medical and dental expenses (see page A-2)	1	*3,968*		
	2	Enter amount from Form 1040, line 37 [2] *40,000*				
	3	Multiply line 2 by 7.5% (.075)	3	*3,000*		
	4	Subtract line 3 from line 1. If line 3 is more than line 1, enter -0-			4	*968*
Taxes You Paid (See page A-2.)	5	State and local **(check only one box)**:				
		a ☒ Income taxes, **or**	5	*620*		
		b ☐ General sales taxes (see page A-2)				
	6	Real estate taxes (see page A-3)	6	*1,580*		
	7	Personal property taxes	7			
	8	Other taxes. List type and amount ▶	8			
	9	Add lines 5 through 8			9	*2,200*
Interest You Paid (See page A-3.)	10	Home mortgage interest and points reported to you on Form 1098	10	*2,840*		
	11	Home mortgage interest not reported to you on Form 1098. If paid to the person from whom you bought the home, see page A-4 and show that person's name, identifying no., and address ▶	11			
Note. Personal interest is not deductible.	12	Points not reported to you on Form 1098. See page A-4 for special rules	12			
	13	Investment interest. Attach Form 4952 if required. (See page A-4.)	13			
	14	Add lines 10 through 13			14	*2,840*
Gifts to Charity	15	Gifts by cash or check. If you made any gift of $250 or more, see page A-4	15	*860*		
If you made a gift and got a benefit for it, see page A-4.	16	Other than by cash or check. If any gift of $250 or more, see page A-4. You **must** attach Form 8283 if over $500	16	*119*		
	17	Carryover from prior year	17			
	18	Add lines 15 through 17			18	*979*
Casualty and Theft Losses	19	Casualty or theft loss(es). Attach Form 4684. (See page A-5.)			19	
Job Expenses and Most Other Miscellaneous Deductions	20	Unreimbursed employee expenses—job travel, union dues, job education, etc. Attach Form 2106 or 2106-EZ if required. (See page A-6.) ▶	20	*870*		
	21	Tax preparation fees	21	*150*		
(See page A-5.)	22	Other expenses—investment, safe deposit box, etc. List type and amount ▶	22	*170*		
	23	Add lines 20 through 22	23	*1,190*		
	24	Enter amount from Form 1040, line 37 [24] *40,000*				
	25	Multiply line 24 by 2% (.02)	25	*800*		
	26	Subtract line 25 from line 23. If line 25 is more than line 23, enter -0-			26	*390*
Other Miscellaneous Deductions	27	Other—from list on page A-6. List type and amount ▶			27	
Total Itemized Deductions	28	Is Form 1040, line 37, over $142,700 (over $71,350 if married filing separately)?				
		☒ **No.** Your deduction is not limited. Add the amounts in the far right column for lines 4 through 27. Also, enter this amount on Form 1040, line 39. ▶			28	*7,377*
		☐ **Yes.** Your deduction may be limited. See page A-6 for the amount to enter.				

For Paperwork Reduction Act Notice, see Form 1040 instructions. Cat. No. 11330X **Schedule A (Form 1040) 2004**

- Nonbusiness casualty and theft losses.
- Gambling losses.

Taxpayers subject to the limitation must reduce itemized deductions by the lesser of:

- 3 percent of the amount by which AGI exceeds $145,950 ($72,975 if married filing separately).
- 80 percent of itemized deductions that are affected by the limit.

The overall limitation is applied after applying all other limitations to itemized deductions that are affected by the overall limitation. Other limitations apply to charitable contributions, certain meals and entertainment expenses, and certain miscellaneous itemized deductions.

EXAMPLE 38

Herman, who is single, had AGI of $200,000 for 2005. He incurred the following expenses and losses during the year:

Medical expenses before 7.5%-of-AGI limitation	$16,000
State and local income taxes	3,200
Real estate taxes	2,800
Home mortgage interest	7,200
Charitable contributions	2,000
Casualty loss before 10% limitation (after $100 floor)	21,500
Unreimbursed employee expenses subject to 2%-of-AGI limitation	4,300
Gambling losses (Herman had $3,000 gambling income)	7,000

Herman's itemized deductions *before* the overall limitation are computed as follows:

Medical expenses [$16,000 – (7.5% × $200,000)]	$ 1,000
State and local income taxes	3,200
Real estate taxes	2,800
Home mortgage interest	7,200
Charitable contributions	2,000
Casualty loss [$21,500 – (10% × $200,000)]	1,500
Unreimbursed employee expenses [$4,300 – (2% × $200,000)]	300
Gambling losses ($7,000 loss limited to $3,000 of gambling income)	3,000
Total itemized deductions before overall limitation	$21,000

Herman's itemized deductions subject to the overall limitation are as follows:

State and local income taxes	$ 3,200
Real estate taxes	2,800
Home mortgage interest	7,200
Charitable contributions	2,000
Unreimbursed employee expenses	300
Total	$15,500

Herman must reduce this amount by the smaller of the following:

• 3% ($200,000 AGI – $145,950)	$ 1,622
• 80% of itemized deductions subject to limitation ($15,500 × .80)	12,400

The First Family and Itemized Deduction Phaseouts

President George W. and Laura Bush itemized deductions on their 2003 tax return (refer to Tax in the News, page 10–3). Because of their income level, their itemized deductions were reduced, as shown below.

Itemized Deductions	
Medical expenses	$ –0–
Taxes	21,352
Interest	–0–
Charitable contributions	68,360
Job expenses and most other miscellaneous deductions	25,810
Total itemized deductions	$115,522
Reduction due to phaseout [($822,126 AGI – $139,500) × .03]	(20,479)
Itemized deductions allowed	$ 95,043

The top marginal rate of 35 percent applied to President and Mrs. Bush's taxable income in 2003. Therefore, the phaseout of itemized deductions cost them $7,168 in additional Federal income tax ($20,479 reduction × 35% marginal tax rate).

Therefore, the amount of the reduction is $1,622, and Herman has $19,378 of deductible itemized deductions, computed as follows:

Deductible itemized deductions subject to overall limitation ($15,500 – $1,622)	$13,878
Itemized deductions not subject to overall limitation:	
Medical expenses	1,000
Casualty loss	1,500
Gambling losses	3,000
Deductible itemized deductions	$19,378

■

ETHICAL CONSIDERATIONS

Between a Rock and a Hard Place

Robert Ryan, a candidate for governor, has released his tax return to the public. As Ryan's former tax adviser, you examine the return closely and realize that a considerable amount of his income was not reported on the return. You confide in a friend in the tabloid newspaper business that you are aware that a candidate for a high public office has filed a fraudulent tax return. Your friend assures you that you will be able to sell your story for at least $25,000 to a tabloid and still remain anonymous. Another friend, a CPA, argues that you should inform Ryan and give him an opportunity to correct the problem. You tell your friend that you are concerned that Ryan will be very vindictive if you approach him about the issue. Which course of action will you choose?

LO.9

Identify tax planning procedures that can maximize the benefit of itemized deductions.

Tax Planning Considerations

EFFECTIVE UTILIZATION OF ITEMIZED DEDUCTIONS

Since an individual may use the standard deduction in one year and itemize deductions in another year, it is frequently possible to obtain maximum benefit by shifting itemized deductions from one year to another. For example, if a taxpayer's itemized deductions and the standard deduction are approximately the same for each year of a two-year period, the taxpayer should use the standard deduction in one year and shift itemized deductions (to the extent permitted by law) to the other year. The individual could, for example, prepay a church pledge for a particular year to shift the deduction to the current year or avoid paying end-of-the-year medical expenses to shift the deduction to the following year.

UTILIZATION OF MEDICAL DEDUCTIONS

When a taxpayer anticipates that medical expenses will approximate the percentage floor, much might be done to generate a deductible excess. Any of the following procedures can help build a deduction by the end of the year:

- Incur the obligation for needed dental work or have needed work carried out.[53] Orthodontic treatment, for example, may have been recommended for a member of the taxpayer's family.
- Have elective remedial surgery that may have been postponed from prior years (e.g., tonsillectomies, vasectomies, correction of hernias, hysterectomies).
- Incur the obligation for capital improvements to the taxpayer's personal residence recommended by a physician (e.g., an air filtration system to alleviate a respiratory disorder).

As an aid to taxpayers who may experience temporary cash-flow problems at the end of the year, the use of bank credit cards is deemed to be payment for purposes of timing the deductibility of charitable and medical expenses.

EXAMPLE 39

On December 13, 2005, Marge (a calendar year taxpayer) purchases two pairs of prescription contact lenses and one pair of prescribed orthopedic shoes for a total of $305. These purchases are separately charged to Marge's bank credit card. On January 6, 2006, Marge receives her statement containing these charges and makes payment shortly thereafter. The purchases are deductible as medical expenses in the year charged (2005) and not in the year the account is settled (2006). ■

Recognizing which expenditures qualify for the medical deduction also may be crucial to exceeding the percentage limitations.

EXAMPLE 40

Mortimer employs Lana (an unrelated party) to care for his incapacitated and dependent mother. Lana is not a trained nurse but spends approximately one-half of the time performing nursing duties (e.g., administering injections and providing physical therapy) and the rest of the time doing household chores. An allocable portion of Lana's wages that Mortimer pays (including the employer's portion of FICA taxes) qualifies as a medical expense. ■

TIMING THE PAYMENT OF DEDUCTIBLE TAXES

It is sometimes possible to defer or accelerate the payment of certain deductible taxes, such as state income tax, real property tax, and personal property tax. For instance, the final installment of estimated state income tax is generally due after

[53]Prepayment of medical expenses does not generate a current deduction unless the taxpayer is under an obligation to make the payment.

the end of a given tax year. Accelerating the payment of the final installment could result in larger itemized deductions for the current year.

EXAMPLE 41

Jenny, who is single, expects to have itemized deductions of $4,800 in 2005 and $2,500 in 2006. She plans to pay $900 as the final installment on her 2005 estimated state income tax, which is due on January 15, 2006. The standard deduction for 2005 is $5,000 for single taxpayers. If Jenny does not pay the final installment until 2006, she will not itemize in either 2005 or 2006. However, if she pays the final installment in December 2005, her itemized deductions will be $5,700 ($4,800 + $900) in 2005, and she will benefit from itemizing. ■

PROTECTING THE INTEREST DEDUCTION

Although the deductibility of prepaid interest by a cash basis taxpayer has been severely restricted, a notable exception allows a deduction for points paid by the buyer to obtain financing for the purchase or improvement of a principal residence in the year of payment. However, such points must actually be paid by the taxpayer obtaining the loan and must represent a charge for the use of money. It has been held that points paid from the mortgage proceeds do not satisfy the payment requirement.[54] Also, the portion of the points attributable to service charges does not represent deductible interest.[55] Taxpayers financing home purchases or improvements usually should direct their planning toward avoiding these two hurdles to immediate deductibility.

In rare instances, a taxpayer may find it desirable to forgo the immediate expensing of points in the year paid. Instead, it could prove beneficial to capitalize the points and write them off as interest expense over the life of the mortgage.

EXAMPLE 42

Gerald purchases a home on December 15, 2005, for $380,000 with $120,000 cash and a 15-year mortgage of $260,000 financed by the Greater Metropolis National Bank. Gerald pays two points in addition to interest allocated to the period from December 15 until December 31, 2005, at an annual rate of 6%. Since Gerald does not have enough itemized deductions to exceed the standard deduction for 2005, he should elect to capitalize the interest expense and amortize the points over 15 years. In this instance, Gerald would deduct $346.67 for 2006, as part of his qualified residence interest expense [$5,200 (two points) divided by 15 years], if he elects to itemize that year. ■

Because personal (consumer) interest is not deductible, taxpayers should consider making use of home equity loans. Recall that these loans utilize the personal residence of the taxpayer as security. The funds from these loans can be used for personal purposes (e.g., auto loans, vacations). By making use of home equity loans, therefore, what would have been nondeductible consumer interest becomes deductible qualified residence interest.

ASSURING THE CHARITABLE CONTRIBUTION DEDUCTION

For a charitable contribution deduction to be available, the recipient must be a qualified charitable organization. Sometimes the mechanics of how the contribution is carried out can determine whether or not a deduction results.

[54] *Alan A. Rubnitz*, 67 T.C. 621 (1977). Seller-paid points may also be deductible by the buyer under the provisions of Rev.Proc. 94–27, cited in footnote 31.

[55] *Donald L. Wilkerson*, 70 T.C. 240 (1978).

EXAMPLE 43

Fumiko wants to donate $5,000 to her church's mission in Kobe, Japan. In this regard, she considers three alternatives:

1. Send the money directly to the mission.
2. Give the money to her church with the understanding that it is to be passed on to the mission.
3. Give the money directly to the missionary in charge of the mission who is currently in the United States on a fund-raising trip.

If Fumiko wants to obtain a deduction for the contribution, she should choose alternative 2. A direct donation to the mission (alternative 1) is not deductible because the mission is a foreign charity. A direct gift to the missionary (alternative 3) does not comply since an individual cannot be a qualified charity for income tax purposes.[56] ■

When making noncash donations, the type of property chosen can have decided implications in determining the amount, if any, of the deduction.

EXAMPLE 44

Sam wants to give $60,000 in value to his church in some form other than cash. In this connection, he considers four alternatives:

1. Stock held for two years as an investment with a basis of $100,000 and a fair market value of $60,000.
2. Stock held for five years as an investment with a basis of $10,000 and a fair market value of $60,000.
3. The rent-free use for a year of a building that normally leases for $5,000 a month.
4. A valuable stamp collection held as an investment and owned for 10 years with a basis of $10,000 and a fair market value of $60,000. The church plans to sell the collection if and when it is donated.

Alternative 1 is ill-advised as the subject of the gift. Even though Sam would obtain a deduction of $60,000, he would forgo the potential loss of $40,000 that would be recognized if the property were sold.[57] Alternative 2 makes good sense since the deduction still is $60,000 and none of the $50,000 of appreciation that has occurred must be recognized as income. Alternative 3 yields no deduction at all and is not a wise choice. Alternative 4 involves tangible personalty that the recipient does not plan to use. As a result, the amount of the deduction is limited to $10,000, the stamp collection's basis.[58] ■

For property transfers (particularly real estate), the ceiling limitations on the amount of the deduction allowed in any one year (50 percent, 30 percent, or 20 percent of AGI, as the case may be) could be a factor to take into account. With proper planning, donations can be controlled to stay within the limitations and therefore avoid the need for a carryover of unused charitable contributions.

EXAMPLE 45

Andrew wants to donate a tract of unimproved land held as an investment to the University of Maryland (a qualified charitable organization). The land has been held for six years and has a current fair market value of $300,000 and a basis to Andrew of $50,000. Andrew's AGI for the current year is estimated to be $200,000, and he expects much the same for the next few years. In the current year, he deeds (transfers) an undivided one-fifth interest in the real estate to the university. ■

What has Andrew in Example 45 accomplished for income tax purposes? In the current year, he will be allowed a charitable contribution deduction of $60,000 (1/5 × $300,000), which will be within the applicable limitation of AGI (30% × $200,000).

---

[56] *Thomas E. Lesslie*, 36 TCM 495, T.C.Memo. 1977–111.

[57] *LaVar M. Withers*, 69 T.C. 900 (1978).

[58] No reduction of appreciation is necessary in alternative 2 since stock is intangible property and not tangible personalty.

Presuming no other charitable contributions for the year, Andrew has avoided the possibility of a carryover. In future years, Andrew can arrange donations of undivided interests in the real estate to stay within the bounds of the percentage limitations. The only difficulty with this approach is the need to revalue the real estate each year before the donation, since the amount of the deduction is based on the fair market value of the interest contributed at the time of the contribution.

EXAMPLE 46

Tiffany dies in October 2005. In completing her final income tax return for 2005, Tiffany's executor determines the following information: AGI of $104,000 and a donation by Tiffany to her church of stock worth $60,000. Tiffany had purchased the stock two years ago for $50,000 and held it as an investment. Tiffany's executor makes the reduced deduction election and, as a consequence, claims a charitable contribution deduction of $50,000. With the election, the potential charitable contribution deduction of $50,000 ($60,000 – $10,000) is less than the 50% ceiling of $52,000 ($104,000 × 50%). If the executor had not made the election, the potential charitable contribution deduction of $60,000 would have been reduced by the 30% ceiling to $31,200 ($104,000 × 30%). No carryover of the $28,800 ($60,000 – $31,200) would have been available. ■

KEY TERMS

Acquisition indebtedness, 10–16
Capital gain property, 10–24
Charitable contribution, 10–20
Health Savings Accounts (HSAs), 10–9
Home equity loans, 10–16
Investment income, 10–15
Investment interest, 10–14
Medical expense, 10–3
Miscellaneous itemized deductions, 10–27
Net investment income, 10–15
Ordinary income property, 10–24
Points, 10–17
Qualified residence interest, 10–14

PROBLEM MATERIALS

Discussion Questions

1. Erin, who prepared her own income tax return for the current year, failed to claim a deduction for her contribution to a traditional Individual Retirement Account (IRA). Her AGI, as reported on the incorrect return, was $100,000, and her medical expenses were $10,000.
   a. Will the correction of this omission affect the amount of medical expenses Erin can deduct? Explain.
   b. Will Erin's medical expense deduction increase or decrease when she corrects her return?

2. Roberta incurred expenses for the following items during the year:
   - Medical insurance premiums.
   - Life insurance premiums.
   - Nonprescription calcium supplements to prevent osteoporosis.
   - Fees for an alcohol rehabilitation program.
   - Contact lenses.
   - Travel expenses to obtain treatment at the Mayo Clinic in Minnesota.

   Which of these expenses can Roberta include as medical expenses for purposes of computing her medical expense deduction?

3. Joe was in an accident and required cosmetic surgery for injuries to his nose. He also had the doctor do additional surgery to reshape his chin, which had not been injured. Will the cosmetic surgery to Joe's nose qualify as a medical expense? Will the cosmetic surgery to Joe's chin qualify as a medical expense? Explain.

4. Helen pays nursing home expenses of $3,000 per month for her mother. The monthly charge covers the following items: $1,400 for medical care, $900 for lodging, and $700 for food. Under what circumstances can Helen include the $3,000 per month payment when computing her medical expense deduction for the year? If Helen is not allowed to include the entire payment, how much can she include?

5. Eduardo was injured in a diving accident and is confined to a wheelchair. In order to be able to live alone, he has entrance ramps constructed. In addition, he has the doorways and halls widened and has extensive modifications made to the kitchen and bathrooms. Do the capital expenditures incurred to modify his home constitute a valid medical expense? If so, what portion of the expense is deductible?

6. Bob and June were divorced in 2003. In July of 2005, their daughter, Harriet, broke her leg while playing soccer. Harriet lives with June, and June claims her as a dependent. Bob pays for the medical expenses related to Harriet's injury. Can Bob claim the medical expenses he pays for Harriet on his tax return?

7. In 2005, David, a sole proprietor of a bookstore, pays a $7,500 premium for medical insurance for himself and his family. Joan, an employee of a small firm that doesn't provide her with medical insurance, pays medical insurance premiums of $8,000 for herself. How does the tax treatment differ for David and Joan?

8. Arturo, a calendar year taxpayer, paid $16,000 in medical expenses and sustained a $20,000 casualty loss in 2005. He expects $12,000 of the medical expenses and $14,000 of the casualty loss to be reimbursed by insurance companies in 2006. Before considering any limitations on these deductions, how much can Arturo include in determining his itemized deductions for 2005?

9. Hubert, a self-employed taxpayer, is married and has two children. He has asked you to explain the tax and nontax advantages of creating a Health Savings Account (HSA) for himself and his family.

Issue ID

10. A local ophthalmologist's advertising campaign included a certificate for a free radial keratotomy for the lucky winner of a drawing. Ahmad held the winning ticket, which was drawn in December 2004. Ahmad had no vision problems and was uncertain what he should do with the prize. In February 2005, Ahmad's daughter, who lives with his former wife, was diagnosed with a vision problem that could be treated with either prescription glasses or a radial keratotomy. The divorce decree requires that Ahmad pay for all medical expenses incurred for his daughter. Identify the relevant tax issues for Ahmad.

11. Antonio sold his personal residence to Mina on July 1, 2005. He had paid real property taxes on March 1, 2005, the due date for property taxes for 2005. How will Antonio's payment affect his deduction for property taxes in 2005? Will Antonio's payment of the taxes have any effect on Mina's itemized deductions for 2005? What other tax or financial effects will Antonio's payment of the taxes have on either party?

Decision Making

12. Julia owns a principal residence in California, a condo in New York City, and a houseboat in Florida. All of the properties have mortgages on which Julia pays interest. What are the limitations on Julia's mortgage interest deduction? What strategy should Julia consider to maximize her mortgage interest deduction?

13. Central Bank has initiated an advertising campaign that encourages customers to take out home equity loans to pay for purchases of automobiles. Are there any tax advantages related to this type of borrowing? Explain.

14. Jerry purchased a personal residence from Kim. In order to sell the residence, Kim agreed to pay $3,000 in points related to Jerry's mortgage. Discuss the deductibility of the points.

15. Ellen borrowed $50,000 from her parents for a down payment on a condominium. She paid interest of $3,200 in 2003, $0 in 2004, and $9,000 in 2005. The IRS disallowed the deduction. Can you offer any explanation for the disallowance?

16. The city of Ogden was devastated by a tornado in April 2005, leaving many families in need of food, clothing, shelter, and other necessities. Betty contributed $500 to a family whose home was completely destroyed by the tornado. Jack contributed $700 to the family's church, which gave the money to the family. Discuss the deductibility of these contributions.

17. Andy pays tuition to a parochial school run by his church so that his daughter can attend the school. The church is a qualified charity. Can Andy deduct any portion of the tuition payments as a charitable contribution?

Issue ID

18. Nancy, who is a professor at State University, does some of her writing and class preparation at home at night. Her department provides faculty members with a $1,500 allowance for a desktop computer for use at school, but does not ordinarily provide computers for use at home. In order to have a computer for use at school and at home, Nancy has asked the department to provide her with a notebook computer that costs $2,500. The head of her department is willing to provide the standard $1,500 allowance and will permit Nancy to purchase the $2,500 notebook computer if she makes a donation of $1,000 to the department. If she acquires the notebook computer, Nancy's home use of the computer will be approximately 60% for business and 40% for personal use not related to her job. Discuss the tax issues that Nancy should consider in deciding whether to acquire the notebook computer under these conditions.

Issue ID

19. Harry, whose combined Federal and state income tax rates total 40% in 2005, expects to retire in 2006 and have a combined tax rate of 30%. He plans to donate $100,000 to his church. Because he will not have the cash available until 2006, Harry donates land (long-term capital gain property) with a basis of $20,000 and fair market value of $100,000 to the church in December 2005. He reacquires the land from the church for $100,000 in February 2006. Discuss Harry's tax objectives and all tax issues related to his actions.

Issue ID

20. Zina decided to have a garage sale to get rid of a number of items that she no longer needed, including books, old stereo equipment, clothing, bicycles, and furniture. She scheduled the sale for Friday and Saturday, but was forced to close at noon Friday because of a torrential downpour. She had collected $500 for the items she sold before closing. The heavy rains continued through the weekend, and Zina was unable to continue the sale. She had not enjoyed dealing with the people who came to the sale on Friday morning, so she donated the remaining items to several local organizations. Zina has asked your advice on how she should treat these events on her tax return. List some of the tax issues you would discuss with her.

Issue ID

21. William, a high school teacher, earns about $40,000 each year. In December 2005, he won $1 million in the state lottery. William plans to donate $100,000 to his church. He has asked you, his tax adviser, whether he should donate the $100,000 in 2005 or 2006. Identify the tax issues related to William's decision.

Issue ID

22. The Skins Game, which involves four of the top golfers on the PGA Tour, is held each year on the weekend after Thanksgiving. Total prize money amounts to $1 million, and the leading money winner also receives an automobile as a prize. Twenty percent of the money won by each player goes to charity. In addition, on the par three holes, the winner of the hole receives the keys to an automobile, which goes to the player's favorite charity. Identify the relevant tax issues for the players. Consider the following possibilities with respect to the car won by the leading money winner: (1) he might keep the car for his own use and sell his present car; (2) he might sell the new car; (3) he might give the car to a friend or relative; (4) he might donate the car to charity; or (5) he might give the car to his caddy.

Decision Making

23. Colin had AGI of $180,000 in 2005. He contributed stock in White, Inc. (a publicly traded corporation), to the United Way, a qualified charitable organization. The stock was worth $105,000 on the date it was contributed. Colin had acquired it as an investment two years ago at a cost of $84,000.

a. What is the total amount that Colin can deduct as a charitable contribution, assuming he carries over any disallowed contribution from 2005 to future years?
b. What is the maximum amount that Colin can deduct as a charitable contribution in 2005?
c. What factors should Colin consider in deciding how to treat the contribution for Federal income tax purposes?
d. Assume Colin dies in December 2005. What advice would you give the executor of his estate with regard to possible elections that can be made relative to the contribution?

Problems

24. Rita is employed as a computer consultant. For calendar year 2005, she had AGI of $200,000 and paid the following medical expenses:

Medical insurance premiums	$ 7,400
Doctor and dentist bills for Larry and Shirley (Rita's parents)	7,700
Doctor and dentist bills for Rita	10,500
Prescription medicines for Rita	1,450
Nonprescription insulin for Rita	550

Larry and Shirley would qualify as Rita's dependents except that they file a joint return. Rita's medical insurance policy does not cover them. Rita filed a claim for reimbursement of $6,000 of her own expenses with her insurance company in December 2005 and received the reimbursement in January 2006. What is Rita's maximum allowable medical expense deduction for 2005?

25. Andy had AGI of $80,000 for 2005. He was injured in a rock climbing accident and paid $5,200 for hospital expenses and $2,800 for doctor bills. Andy also incurred medical expenses of $2,400 for his child, Jodi, who lives with his former wife, Pearl, and is claimed as a dependent by her. In 2006, Andy was reimbursed $2,600 by his insurance company for the medical expenses attributable to the rock climbing accident.
a. Compute Andy's deduction for medical expenses in 2005.
b. Assume that Andy would have elected to itemize his deductions even if he had no medical expenses in 2005. How much, if any, of the $2,600 reimbursement must be included in gross income in 2006?
c. Assume that Andy's other itemized deductions in 2005 were $5,300 and that he filed as a head of household. How much of the $2,600 reimbursement must he include in gross income in 2006?

26. Jung suffers from heart problems and, upon the recommendation of a physician, has an elevator installed in his personal residence. In connection with the elevator, Jung incurs and pays the following amounts during the current year:

Elevator and cost of installation	$15,500
Increase in utility bills due to the elevator	750
Cost of certified appraisal	500

The system has an estimated useful life of 20 years. The appraisal was to determine the value of Jung's residence with and without the system. The appraisal states that the system increased the value of Jung's residence by $2,000. How much of these expenses qualifies for the medical expense deduction in the current year?

27. For calendar year 2005, Jean was a self-employed consultant with no employees. She had $80,000 net profit from consulting and paid $7,000 in medical insurance premiums on a policy covering 2005. How much of these premiums may Jean deduct as a deduction *for* AGI, and how much may she deduct as an itemized deduction (subject to the 7.5% floor)?

28. During the current year, Susan incurred and paid the following expenses for Beth (her daughter), Ed (her father), and herself:

Surgery for Beth	$4,200
Red River Academy charges for Beth:	
Tuition	5,600
Room, board, and other expenses	4,800
Psychiatric treatment	5,100
Doctor bills for Ed	2,200
Prescription drugs for Susan, Beth, and Ed	780
Insulin for Ed	540
Nonprescription drugs for Susan, Beth, and Ed	570
Charges at Heartland Nursing Home for Ed:	
Medical care	4,800
Lodging	3,700
Meals	2,650

Beth qualifies as Susan's dependent, and Ed would also qualify except that he receives $7,400 of taxable retirement benefits from his former employer. Beth's psychiatrist recommended Red River Academy because of its small classes and specialized psychiatric treatment program that is needed to treat Beth's illness. Ed is a paraplegic and diabetic, and Heartland offers the type of care that he requires.

Upon the recommendation of a physician, Susan has an air filtration system installed in her personal residence. She suffers from severe allergies. In connection with this equipment, Susan incurs and pays the following amounts during the year:

Filtration system and cost of installation	$6,500
Increase in utility bills due to the system	700
Cost of certified appraisal	360

The system has an estimated useful life of 10 years. The appraisal was to determine the value of Susan's residence with and without the system. The appraisal states that the system increased the value of Susan's residence by $2,200. Ignoring the 7.5% floor, what is the total of Susan's expenses that qualify for the medical expense deduction?

Issue ID

29. In May, Rebecca's daughter, Susan, sustained a serious injury that made it impossible for her to continue living alone. Susan, who is a novelist, moved back into Rebecca's home after the accident. Susan has begun writing a new novel based on her recent experiences. To accommodate Susan, Rebecca incurred significant remodeling expenses (widening hallways, building a separate bedroom and bathroom, making kitchen appliances accessible to Susan). In addition, Rebecca had an indoor swimming pool constructed so Susan could do rehabilitation exercises prescribed by her physician.

In September, Susan underwent major reconstructive surgery in Denver. The surgery was performed by Dr. Rama Patel, who specializes in treating injuries of the type sustained by Susan. Rebecca drove Susan from Champaign, Illinois, to Denver, a total of 1,100 miles, in Susan's specially equipped van. They left Champaign on Tuesday morning and arrived in Denver on Thursday afternoon. Rebecca incurred expenses for gasoline, highway tolls, meals, and lodging while traveling to Denver. Rebecca stayed in a motel near the clinic for eight days while Susan was hospitalized. Identify the relevant tax issues based on this information and prepare a list of questions that you would need to ask Rebecca and Susan in order to advise them as to the resolution of any issues you have identified.

30. During 2005, Felicia, who is self-employed, paid $500 per month for an HSA contract that provides medical insurance coverage with a $3,600 deductible. The plan covers Felicia, her husband, and three children. Of the $500 monthly fee, $200 was for the high-deductible policy, and $300 was deposited into an HSA. How much of the amount paid for the high-deductible policy can Felicia deduct as a deduction *for* AGI?

31. In 2005, Heather sold her personal residence to Keith for $300,000. Before the sale, Heather paid the real estate taxes of $8,030 for the calendar year. For income tax purposes, the deduction is apportioned as follows: $4,400 to Heather and $3,630 to Keith.
   a. What is Keith's basis in the residence?
   b. What is Heather's amount realized from the sale of the residence?
   c. What amount of real estate taxes can Keith deduct?
   d. What amount of real estate taxes can Heather deduct?

32. Daniel is a self-employed, calendar year taxpayer. He reports on the cash basis. Daniel made the following estimated state income tax payments:

Date	Amount
January 15, 2005	$1,200 (4th payment for 2004)
April 15, 2005	1,500 (1st payment for 2005)
June 15, 2005	1,500 (2nd payment for 2005)
September 15, 2005	1,500 (3rd payment for 2005)
January 15, 2006	1,500 (4th payment for 2005)

Daniel had a tax overpayment of $800 on his 2004 state income tax return and, rather than requesting a refund, had the overpayment applied to his 2005 state income taxes. What is the amount of Daniel's state income tax itemized deduction for his 2005 Federal income tax return?

Decision Making
Communications

33. Carol Sharp incurred $29,250 of interest expense related to her investments in 2005. Her investment income included $7,000 of interest, $5,500 of qualified dividends, and a $12,750 net capital gain on the sale of securities. Carol has asked you to compute the amount of her deduction for investment interest, taking into consideration any options she might have. In addition, she has asked for your suggestions as to any tax planning alternatives that might be available. Write a letter to her that contains your advice. Carol lives at 208 Lone Tree Circle, Napa, CA 94558.

34. Helena borrowed $300,000 to acquire a parcel of land to be held for investment purposes. During 2005, she paid interest of $30,000 on the loan. She had AGI of $75,000 for the year. Other items related to Helena's investments include the following:

Investment income	$21,150
Investment counsel fees	2,250

Helena is unmarried and elects to itemize her deductions. She has no miscellaneous itemized deductions other than the investment counsel fees.
   a. Determine Helena's investment interest deduction for 2005.
   b. Discuss the treatment of the portion of Helena's investment interest that is disallowed in 2005.
   c. Assume Helena has a long-term capital gain of $8,250 from the sale of investment land, and she elects to treat it as investment income. How would this affect her investment interest deduction and her tax computation for 2005?

35. In 1997, Huseyin, who is single, purchased a personal residence for $170,000 and took out a mortgage of $100,000 on the property. In May of the current year, when the residence had a fair market value of $220,000 and Huseyin owed $70,000 on the mortgage, he took out a home equity loan for $110,000. He used the funds to purchase a Jaguar for himself and a Cadillac SUV for his wife. For both vehicles, 100% of the use is for personal use. What is the maximum amount on which Huseyin can deduct home equity interest?

36. Ron and Tom are equal owners in Robin Corporation. On July 1, 2005, each lends the corporation $30,000 at an annual interest rate of 10%. Ron and Tom are brothers. Both shareholders are on the cash method of accounting, and Robin Corporation is on the

accrual method. All parties use the calendar year for tax purposes. On June 30, 2006, Robin repays the loans of $60,000 together with the specified interest of $6,000.

a. How much of the interest can Robin Corporation deduct in 2005? In 2006?
b. When is the interest included in Ron and Tom's gross income?

37. Nadia donates $4,000 to Eastern University's athletic department. The payment guarantees that Nadia will have preferred seating near the 50-yard line.
    a. Assume Nadia subsequently buys four $100 game tickets. How much can she deduct as a charitable contribution to the university's athletic department?
    b. Assume that Nadia's $4,000 donation includes four $100 tickets. How much can she deduct as a charitable contribution to the university's athletic department?

38. Virginia had AGI of $100,000 in 2005. She donated Amber Corporation stock with a basis of $9,000 to a qualified charitable organization on July 5, 2005.
    a. What is the amount of Virginia's deduction, assuming that she purchased the stock on December 4, 2004, and the stock had a fair market value of $16,000 when she made the donation?
    b. Assume the same facts as in (a), except that Virginia purchased the stock on July 1, 2002.
    c. Assume the same facts as in (a), except that the stock had a fair market value of $5,000 (rather than $16,000) when Virginia donated it to the charity.

Decision Making
Communications

39. Pedro contributes a painting to an art museum in 2005. He has owned the painting for 12 years, and it is worth $130,000 at the time of the donation. Pedro's adjusted basis for the painting is $90,000, and his AGI for 2005 is $250,000. Pedro has asked you whether he should make the reduced deduction election for this contribution. Write a letter to Pedro Valdez at 1289 Greenway Avenue, Foster City, CA 94404 and advise him on this matter.

40. During the year, Alvin made the following contributions to a qualified public charity:

Cash	$110,000
Stock in Goshawk, Inc. (a publicly traded corporation)	140,000

Alvin acquired the stock in Goshawk, Inc., as an investment two years ago at a cost of $60,000. Alvin's AGI is $420,000.
    a. What is Alvin's charitable contribution deduction?
    b. How are excess amounts, if any, treated?

Decision Making

41. Ramon had AGI of $180,000 in 2005. He contributed stock in Charlton, Inc. (a publicly traded corporation), to the American Heart Association, a qualified charitable organization. The stock was worth $105,000 on the date it was contributed. Ramon had acquired it as an investment two years ago at a cost of $84,000.
    a. What is the total amount that Ramon can deduct as a charitable contribution, assuming he carries over any disallowed contribution from 2005 to future years?
    b. What is the maximum amount that Ramon can deduct as a charitable contribution in 2005?
    c. What factors should Ramon consider in deciding how to treat the contribution for Federal income tax purposes?
    d. Assume Ramon dies in December 2005. What advice would you give the executor of his estate with regard to possible elections that can be made relative to the contribution?

42. On December 30, 2005, Roberta purchased four tickets to a charity ball sponsored by the city of San Diego for the benefit of underprivileged children. Each ticket cost $200 and had a fair market value of $35. On the same day as the purchase, Roberta gave the tickets to the minister of her church for personal use by his family. At the time of the gift of the tickets, Roberta pledged $4,000 to the building fund of her church. The pledge was satisfied by a check dated December 31, 2005, but not mailed until January 3, 2006.

a. Presuming Roberta is a cash basis and calendar year taxpayer, how much can she deduct as a charitable contribution for 2005?
b. Would the amount of the deduction be any different if Roberta is an accrual basis taxpayer? Explain.

Decision Making
Communications

43. In December each year, Alice Young contributes 10% of her gross income to the United Way (a 50% organization). Alice, who is in the 35% marginal tax bracket, is considering the following alternatives as charitable contributions in December 2005:

	Fair Market Value
(1) Cash donation	$21,000
(2) Unimproved land held for six years ($3,000 basis)	21,000
(3) Blue Corporation stock held for eight months ($3,000 basis)	21,000
(4) Gold Corporation stock held for two years ($26,000 basis)	21,000

Alice has asked you to help her decide which of the potential contributions listed above will be most advantageous taxwise. Evaluate the four alternatives and write a letter to Alice to communicate your advice to her. Her address is 2622 Bayshore Drive, Berkeley, CA 94709.

Decision Making
Communications

44. Manuel and Rosa Garcia, both age 45, are married and have no dependents. They have asked you to advise them whether they should file jointly or separately in 2004. They present you with the following information:

	Manuel	Rosa	Joint
Salary	$40,000		
Business net income		$100,000	
Interest income	400	1,200	$2,200
Deductions *for* AGI	2,000	13,000	
Medical expenses	9,500	600	
State income tax	800	2,000	
Real estate tax			3,400
Mortgage interest			5,200
Unreimbursed employee expenses	1,100		

If they file separately, Manuel and Rosa will split the real estate tax and mortgage interest deductions equally. Write Manuel and Rosa a letter in which you make and explain a recommendation on filing status for 2004. Manuel and Rosa reside at 5904 Stevens Avenue, Durham, NC 27707.

45. For calendar year 2005, Jon and Betty Hansen file a joint return reflecting AGI of $240,000. Their itemized deductions are as follows:

Medical expenses	$23,000
Casualty loss (not covered by insurance)	26,000
Interest on home mortgage	10,000
Property taxes on home	13,000
Charitable contributions	17,000
State income tax	15,000

After all necessary adjustments are made, what is the amount of itemized deductions the Hansens may claim?

46. Charles, who is single, had AGI of $400,000 during 2005. He incurred the following expenses and losses during the year:

Medical expenses before 7.5%-of-AGI limitation	$39,500
State and local income taxes	5,200
Real estate taxes	4,400
Home mortgage interest	5,400
Charitable contributions	4,800
Casualty loss before 10% limitation (after $100 floor)	47,000
Unreimbursed employee expenses subject to 2%-of-AGI limitation	8,900
Gambling losses (Charles had $7,400 of gambling income)	9,800

Compute Charles's itemized deductions before and after the overall limitation.

47. Gary and Carolyn Jordan are married, have two dependents, and file a joint return for 2005. Information for the year includes the following:

AGI	$252,600
State and local income taxes	5,900
Real estate taxes	8,200
Home mortgage interest	9,100
Charitable contributions	8,300
Gambling losses (gambling income of $5,300 was included in AGI)	7,400

Compute the allowable itemized deductions for 2005 for the Jordans.

48. Thomas, who is a head of household with one dependent, had AGI of $300,000 for 2005. He incurred the following expenses and losses during the year:

Medical expenses before 7.5%-of-AGI limitation	$24,000
State and local income taxes	4,500
Real estate taxes	3,100
Home mortgage interest	4,900
Charitable contribution	3,500
Casualty loss before 10% limitation (after $100 floor)	35,000
Unreimbursed employee expenses subject to 2%-of-AGI limitation	7,600
Gambling losses (Thomas had $5,800 of gambling income)	6,500

Calculate Thomas's allowable itemized deductions for the year.

Cumulative Problems

Tax Return Problem
Decision Making

49. Alice and Bruce Byrd are married taxpayers, ages 47 and 45, who file a joint return. Their Social Security numbers are 034–48–4382 and 016–50–9556, respectively. They live at 473 Revere Avenue, Ames, MA 01850. Alice is the office manager for a dental clinic and earns an annual salary of $46,200. Bruce is the manager of a fast-food outlet owned and operated by Plymouth Corporation. His annual salary is $58,300.

The Byrds have two children, Cynthia (age 24 and S.S. no. 017–44–9126) and John (age 22 and S.S. no. 017–27–4148), who live with them. Both children are full-time students at a nearby college.

During 2004, the Byrds furnished one-third of the total support of Bruce's widower father, Sam Byrd (age 70 and S.S. no. 034–82–8583). Sam lives alone and receives the rest of his support from Bruce's sister and brother (one-third each). They have signed a multiple support agreement allowing Bruce to claim Sam as a dependent for 2004. Sam died in November, and Bruce received life insurance proceeds of $600,000 on December 28.

The Byrds had the following expenses relating to their personal residence during 2004:

Property taxes	$6,840
Interest on home mortgage	8,580
Repairs to roof	2,920
Utilities	3,960
Fire and theft insurance	1,870

Medical expenses for 2004 include:

Medical insurance premiums	$7,810
Doctor bill for Sam incurred in 2003 and not paid until 2004	3,080
Operation for Sam	6,710

The operation for Sam represents the one-third Bruce contributed toward his father's support.

Other relevant information follows:

- Alice and Bruce had $4,870 ($1,980 for Alice and $2,890 for Bruce) withheld from their salaries for state income taxes. When they filed their 2003 state return in 2004, they paid additional state income tax of $880.
- During 2004, Alice and Bruce attended a dinner dance sponsored by the Ames Police Disability Association (a qualified charitable organization). The Byrds paid $220 for the tickets. Cost of comparable entertainment would normally be $90. The Byrds contributed $4,290 to their church and gave used clothing (cost of $1,100 and fair market value of $495) to the Salvation Army. All donations are supported by receipts.
- In 2004, the Byrds received interest income of $2,695 from a savings account they maintained.
- Alice's employer requires that all employees wear uniforms to work. During 2004, Alice spent $407 on new uniforms and $189 on laundry charges. Bruce paid $275 for an annual subscription to the *Journal of Franchise Management*. Neither Alice's nor Bruce's employers reimburse for employee expenses.
- The Byrds do not keep the receipts for the sales taxes they paid. The amount from the sales tax table is $974.
- Alice and Bruce had $10,570 ($4,180 for Alice and $6,390 for Bruce) of Federal income tax withheld in 2004 and paid no estimated Federal income tax. Neither Alice nor Bruce wishes to designate $3 to the Presidential Election Campaign Fund.

Part 1—Tax Computation

Compute net tax payable or refund due for Alice and Bruce Byrd for 2004. If they have overpaid, the amount is to be refunded. If you use tax forms for your computations, you will need Form 1040 and Schedules A and B. Suggested software: TurboTax.

Part 2—Tax Planning

Alice and Bruce are planning some significant changes for 2005. They have provided you with the following information and asked you to project their taxable income and tax liability for 2005.

The Byrds will use $200,000 of the life insurance proceeds they received as a result of Sam's death and pay off their mortgage in early January 2005. They will invest the remaining $400,000 in short-term certificates of deposit (CDs) and use the interest for living expenses during 2005. They expect to earn total interest of $16,000 on the CDs. Bruce has been awarded a 10% raise for 2005, and state and Federal tax withholdings on his salary will increase accordingly.

Alice, who has health problems, will take a leave of absence from work during 2005, so none of her job-related expenses or withholdings will continue. The Byrds do not expect to owe additional state income tax when they file their 2004 return, but they do expect their charitable contributions and medical insurance premiums to continue at the 2004 level. Assume all other income and deduction items will continue at the same level in 2005 unless you have information that indicates otherwise.

Tax Return Problem

50. Paul and Donna Decker are married taxpayers, ages 44 and 42, who file a joint return for 2005. The Deckers live at 1121 College Avenue, Carmel, IN 46032. Paul is an assistant manager at Carmel Motor Inn, and Donna is a teacher at Carmel Elementary School. They present you with W–2 forms that reflect the following information:

	Paul	Donna
Salary	$58,000	$56,000
Federal tax withheld	10,300	9,700
State income tax withheld	900	800
FICA (Social Security and Medicare) withheld	4,437	4,284
Social Security numbers	222–11–4567	333–11–9872

Donna is the custodial parent of two children from a previous marriage who reside with the Deckers through the school year. The children, Larry and Jane Parker, reside with their father, Bob, during the summer. Relevant information for the children follows:

	Larry	Jane
Age	17	18
Social Security numbers	305–11–4567	303–11–9872
Months spent with Deckers	9	9

Under the divorce decree, Bob pays child support of $150 per month per child during the nine months the children live with the Deckers. Bob says he spends $200 per month per child during the three summer months they reside with him. Donna and Paul can document that they provide $2,000 support per child per year. The divorce decree is silent as to which parent can claim the exemption for the children.

In August, Paul and Donna added a suite to their home to provide more comfortable accommodations for Hannah Snyder (263–33–4738), Donna's mother, who had moved in with them in February 2004 after the death of Donna's father. Not wanting to borrow money for this addition, Paul sold 300 shares of Acme Corporation stock for $50 per share on May 3, 2005, and used the proceeds of $15,000 to cover construction costs. The Deckers had purchased the stock on April 29, 2001, for $25 per share. They received dividends of $750 on the jointly owned stock a month before the sale.

Hannah, who is 66 years old, received $7,500 in Social Security benefits during the year, of which she gave the Deckers $2,000 to use toward household expenses and deposited the remainder in her personal savings account. The Deckers determine that they have spent $2,500 of their own money for food, clothing, medical expenses, and other items for Hannah. They do not know what the rental value of Hannah's suite would be, but they estimate it would be at least $300 per month.

Interest paid during the year included the following:

Home mortgage interest (paid to Carmel Federal Savings & Loan)	$7,890
Interest on an automobile loan (paid to Carmel National Bank)	1,490
Interest on Citibank Visa card	870

In July, Paul hit a submerged rock while boating. Fortunately, he was thrown from the boat, landed in deep water, and was uninjured. However, the boat, which was uninsured, was destroyed. Paul had paid $25,000 for the boat in June 2004, and its value was appraised at $18,000 on the date of the accident.

The Deckers paid doctor and hospital bills of $8,700 and were reimbursed $2,000 by their insurance company. They spent $640 for prescription drugs and medicines and $2,810 for premiums on their health insurance policy. They have filed additional claims of $1,200 with their insurance company and have been told they will receive payment for that amount in January 2006. Included in the amounts paid for doctor and hospital bills were payments of $380 for Hannah and $850 for the children.

Additional information of potential tax consequence follows:

Real estate taxes paid	$3,700
Sales taxes paid (per table)	1,379
Cash contributions to church	2,100
Appraised value of books donated to public library	740
Paul's unreimbursed employee expenses to attend hotel management convention:	
Airfare	340
Hotel	170
Meals	95
Registration fee	340
Refund of state income tax for 2004 (the Deckers itemized on their 2004 Federal tax return)	1,520

Compute net tax payable or refund due for the Deckers for 2005. Ignore the child tax credit in your computations. If they have overpaid, the amount is to be credited toward their taxes for 2006. Suggested software: TurboTax.

Research Problems

Note: Solutions to Research Problems can be prepared by using the ***RIA Checkpoint® Student Edition*** *online research product, which is available to accompany this text. It is also possible to prepare solutions to the Research Problems by using tax research materials found in a standard tax library.*

Research Problem 1. Jane suffers from a degenerative spinal disorder. Her physician said that swimming could help prevent the onset of permanent paralysis and recommended the installation of a swimming pool at her residence for her use. Jane's residence had a market value of approximately $500,000 before the swimming pool was installed. The swimming pool was built, and an appraiser estimated that the value of Jane's home increased by $98,000 because of the addition.

The pool cost $194,000, and Jane claimed a medical expense deduction of $96,000 ($194,000 – $98,000) on her tax return. Upon audit of the return, the IRS determined that an adequate pool should have cost $70,000 and would have increased the property value by only $31,000. Thus, the IRS claims that Jane is entitled to a deduction of only $39,000 ($70,000 – $31,000).

a. Is there any ceiling limitation on the amount deductible as a medical expense?
b. Can capital expenditures be deducted as medical expenses?
c. What is the significance of a "minimum adequate facility"? Should aesthetic or architectural qualities be considered in this determination?

Communications

Research Problem 2. In January, Ron, a fireman, was injured in the line of duty as a result of interference by a homeowner. He incurred medical expenses of $6,500 related to his injuries. Ron sued the homeowner and was awarded damages of $26,500 in December. The court indicated that $6,500 of the award was for payment of Ron's medical expenses and $20,000 was for punitive damages. Ron has prepared his return for the year and has asked you to review it. You notice that Ron has not reported any part of the award as income and has included the medical expense in computing his itemized deductions. Write a brief summary of the advice you should give Ron.

Internet Activity

Use the tax resources of the Internet to address the following question. Do not restrict your search to the World Wide Web, but include a review of newsgroups and general reference materials, practitioner sites and resources, primary sources of the tax law, chat rooms and discussion groups, and other opportunities.

Research Problem 3. Search the Internet for stories about major charitable contributions by individuals, including Bill Gates, Ted Turner, and at least one other individual. Briefly discuss any tax issues that are related to the contributions.

Passive Activity Losses

CHAPTER 11

LEARNING OBJECTIVES

After completing Chapter 11, you should be able to:

LO.1
Discuss tax shelters and the reasons for at-risk and passive loss limitations.

LO.2
Explain the at-risk limitation.

LO.3
Describe how the passive loss rules limit deductions for losses, and identify the taxpayers subject to these restrictions.

LO.4
Discuss the definition of passive activities and the rules for identifying an activity.

LO.5
Analyze and apply the tests for material participation.

LO.6
Understand the nature of rental activities under the passive loss rules.

LO.7
Recognize the relationship between the at-risk and passive activity limitations.

LO.8
Discuss the special treatment available to real estate activities.

LO.9
Determine the proper tax treatment upon the disposition of a passive activity.

LO.10
Suggest tax planning strategies to minimize the effect of the passive loss limitations.

OUTLINE

LO.1

Discuss tax shelters and the reasons for at-risk and passive loss limitations.

The Tax Shelter Problem

Before Congress enacted legislation to reduce or eliminate their effectiveness, **tax shelters** were popular investments for tax avoidance purposes because they could generate deductions and other benefits that could be used to offset income from other sources. Because of the tax avoidance potential of many tax shelters, they were attractive to wealthy taxpayers in high income tax brackets. Many tax shelters merely provided an opportunity for "investors" to buy deductions and credits in ventures that were not expected to generate a profit, even in the long run.

Although it may seem odd that a taxpayer would intentionally invest in an activity that was designed to produce losses, there is a logical explanation. The typical tax shelter operated as a partnership and relied heavily on nonrecourse financing.[1] Accelerated depreciation and interest expense deductions generated large losses in the early years of the activity. At the very least, the tax shelter deductions deferred the recognition of any net income from the venture until the activity was sold. In the best of situations, the investor could realize additional tax savings by offsetting other income (e.g., salary, interest, and dividends) with deductions flowing from the tax shelter. Ultimately, the sale of the investment would result in capital gain. The following examples illustrate what was possible *before* Congress enacted legislation to curb tax shelter abuses.

EXAMPLE 1

Bob, who earned a salary of $400,000 as a business executive and dividend income of $15,000, invested $20,000 for a 10% interest in a cattle-breeding tax shelter. Through the use of $800,000 of nonrecourse financing and available cash of $200,000, the partnership acquired a herd of an exotic breed of cattle costing $1 million. Depreciation, interest, and other deductions related to the activity resulted in a loss of $400,000, of which Bob's share was $40,000. Bob was allowed to deduct the $40,000 loss, even though he had invested and stood to lose only $20,000 if the investment turned sour. The net effect of the $40,000 deduction from the partnership was that a portion of Bob's salary and dividend income was "sheltered," and as a result, he was required to calculate his tax liability on only $375,000 of income [$415,000 (salary and dividends) – $40,000 (deduction)] rather than $415,000. If this deduction were available under current law and if Bob was in a combined Federal and state income tax bracket of 40%, this deduction would generate a tax savings of $16,000 ($40,000 × 40%) in the first year alone! ■

[1]Nonrecourse debt is an obligation for which the borrower is not personally liable. An example of nonrecourse debt is a liability on real estate acquired by a partnership without the partnership or any of the partners assuming any liability for the mortgage. The acquired property generally is pledged as collateral for the loan.

A review of Example 1 shows that the taxpayer took a *two-for-one* write-off ($40,000 deduction, $20,000 investment). In the heyday of tax shelters, promoters often promised *multiple* write-offs for the investor.

The first major provision aimed at tax shelters was the **at-risk limitation.** Its objective is to limit a taxpayer's deductions to the amount "at risk," which is the amount the taxpayer stands to lose if the investment turns out to be a financial disaster.

EXAMPLE 2

Returning to the facts of Example 1, under the current at-risk rules Bob would be allowed to deduct $20,000 (i.e., the amount that he could lose if the business failed). This deduction would reduce his other income, and as a result, Bob would have to report only $395,000 of income ($415,000 – $20,000). The remaining nondeductible $20,000 loss and any future losses flowing from the partnership would be suspended under the at-risk rules and would be deductible in the future only as his at-risk amount increased. ■

The second major attack on tax shelters came with the passage of the passive activity loss rules. These rules are intended to halt an investor's ability to benefit from the mismatching of an entity's expenses and income that often occurs in the early years of the business. Congress observed that despite the at-risk limitations, investors could still deduct losses flowing from an entity and thereby defer their tax liability on other income. In effect, passive activity rules have, to a great degree, made the term *tax shelter* obsolete. Now such ventures where investors are not involved in the day-to-day operations of the business are generally referred to as passive investments, or *passive activities*, rather than tax shelters.

The **passive loss** rules require the taxpayer to segregate all income and losses into three categories: active, passive, and portfolio. In general, the passive loss limits disallow the deduction of passive losses against active or portfolio income, even when the taxpayer is at risk to the extent of the loss. In general, passive losses can only offset passive income.

EXAMPLE 3

Returning to the facts of Example 1, the passive activity loss rules further restrict Bob's ability to claim the $20,000 tax deduction shown in Example 2. Because Bob is a passive investor and does not materially participate in any meaningful way in the activities of the cattle-breeding operation, the $20,000 loss allowed under the at-risk rules is disallowed under the passive loss rules. The passive loss is disallowed because Bob does not generate any passive income that could absorb his passive loss. Further, his salary (active income) and dividends (portfolio income) cannot be used to absorb any of the passive loss. Consequently, Bob's current-year taxable income must reflect his nonpassive income of $415,000, and he receives no current benefit from his share of the partnership loss. However, all is not lost because Bob's share of the entity's loss is *suspended;* it is carried forward and can be deducted in the future when he has passive income or sells his interest in the activity. ■

This chapter explores the nature of the at-risk limits and passive activity loss rules and their impact on investors. An interesting consequence of these rules is that now investors evaluating potential investments must consider mainly the economics of the venture instead of the tax benefits or tax avoidance possibilities that an investment may generate.

LO.2

Explain the at-risk limitation.

At-Risk Limits

The at-risk provisions limit the deductibility of losses from business and income-producing activities. These provisions, which apply to individuals and closely held corporations, are designed to prevent taxpayers from deducting losses in excess

With Tax Shelters in the Spotlight, Taxpayers Should Be Cautious!

Over the years, the at-risk and passive loss rules have gone a long way to curb abusive tax shelters. To the IRS's chagrin, however, some tax shelters are not restricted by these rules and continue to be a problem, as many reports in the media have shown. In response, the IRS has directed its attention toward those abusive tax shelters marketed by well-known and respected members of the financial community.

The publicity surrounding the IRS's efforts has driven a wedge between shelter marketers and their clients. As a consequence, many clients have sought damages from the accounting and law firms that developed the questionable shelters. Those corporations and executives whose shelters are under scrutiny by the IRS are at risk of losing enormous amounts of money.

But just because some taxpayers have been a bit "too creative" in using the tax law for financial advantage does not mean that all tax shelters are illegal or somehow immoral. Many "tax minimization strategies," such as pursuing well-timed property transactions that postpone taxes or sheltering assets in a § 401(k) account, are well within the bounds of appropriate tax planning. Nonetheless, in the current environment, taxpayers need to be prudent. As a safety precaution, be wary of schemes that take place only on paper and reflect no true economic gain or loss. Particularly problematic are schemes that involve so-called offshore trusts or partnerships. Remember that when something seems too good to be true, it often is!

of their actual economic investment in an activity. In the case of an S corporation or a partnership, the at-risk limits apply at the owner level. Under the at-risk rules, a taxpayer's deductible loss from an activity for any taxable year is limited to the amount the taxpayer has at risk at the end of the taxable year (the amount the taxpayer could actually lose in the activity).

While the amount at risk generally vacillates over time, the initial amount considered at risk consists of the following:[2]

- The amount of cash and the adjusted basis of property contributed to the activity by the taxpayer.
- Amounts borrowed for use in the activity for which the taxpayer is personally liable or has pledged as security property not used in the activity.

This amount generally is increased each year by the taxpayer's share of income and is decreased by the taxpayer's share of losses and withdrawals from the activity. In addition, because general partners are jointly and severally liable for recourse debts of the partnership, their at-risk amounts are increased when the partnership increases its debt and are decreased when the partnership reduces its debt. However, a taxpayer generally is not considered at risk with respect to borrowed amounts if either of the following is true:

- The taxpayer is not personally liable for repayment of the debt (e.g., nonrecourse debt).
- The lender has an interest (other than as a creditor) in the activity.

[2]§ 465(b)(1).

Concept Summary 11–1

Calculation of At-Risk Amount

Increases to a taxpayer's at-risk amount:

- Cash and the adjusted basis of property contributed to the activity.
- Amounts borrowed for use in the activity for which the taxpayer is personally liable or has pledged as security property not used in the activity.
- Taxpayer's share of amounts borrowed for use in the activity that are qualified nonrecourse financing.
- Taxpayer's share of the activity's income.

Decreases to a taxpayer's at-risk amount:

- Withdrawals from the activity.
- Taxpayer's share of the activity's loss.
- Taxpayer's share of any reductions of debt for which recourse against the taxpayer exists or reductions of qualified nonrecourse debt.

An important exception provides that in the case of an activity involving the holding of real property, a taxpayer is considered at risk for his or her share of any *qualified nonrecourse financing* that is secured by real property used in the activity.[3]

Subject to the passive activity rules discussed later in the chapter, a taxpayer may deduct a loss as long as the at-risk amount is positive. However, once the at-risk amount is exhausted, any remaining loss cannot be deducted until a later year. Any losses disallowed for any given taxable year by the at-risk rules may be deducted in the first succeeding year in which the rules do not prevent the deduction—that is, when there is, and to the extent of, a positive at-risk amount.

EXAMPLE 4

In 2005, Sue invests $40,000 in an oil partnership that, by the use of nonrecourse loans, spends $60,000 on deductible intangible drilling costs applicable to her interest. Assume Sue's interest in the partnership is subject to the at-risk limits but is not subject to the passive loss limits. Since Sue has only $40,000 of capital at risk, she cannot deduct more than $40,000 against her other income and must reduce her at-risk amount to zero ($40,000 at-risk amount – $40,000 loss deducted). The nondeductible loss of $20,000 ($60,000 loss generated – $40,000 loss allowed) can be carried over to 2006. ■

EXAMPLE 5

In 2006, Sue has taxable income of $15,000 from the oil partnership and invests an additional $10,000 in the venture. Her at-risk amount is now $25,000 ($0 beginning balance + $15,000 taxable income + $10,000 additional investment). This enables Sue to deduct the carryover loss and requires her to reduce her at-risk amount to $5,000 ($25,000 at-risk amount – $20,000 carryover loss allowed). ■

An additional complicating factor is that previously allowed losses must be recaptured to the extent the at-risk amount is reduced below zero.[4] That is, previous losses that were allowed must be offset by the recognition of enough income to bring the at-risk amount up to zero. This rule applies in such situations as when the amount at risk is reduced below zero by distributions to the taxpayer or when the status of indebtedness changes from recourse to nonrecourse.

[3]Section 465(b)(6) defines qualified nonrecourse financing.

[4]§ 465(e).

ETHICAL CONSIDERATIONS

Manipulating the At-Risk Limits

At a social function, you encounter your friend Patrick. You have long suspected that Patrick has an investment in a venture that could make him subject to the at-risk rules. Discreetly, you refer to his investment. He laughs and says, "That hasn't been a problem, I've always been able to deduct my share of losses. At the end of every year, I make a contribution to the partnership to raise my at-risk basis, and then in mid-January of the following year, I get that money back. This has worked well every year, and the IRS has never caught on. I always try to make sure that no one can link my contribution with the later withdrawal. Besides, how would they ever know what is happening?" As a respected tax accountant in the community, how do you feel about Patrick's comments?

LO.3

Describe how the passive loss rules limit deductions for losses, and identify the taxpayers subject to these restrictions.

Passive Loss Limits

CLASSIFICATION AND IMPACT OF PASSIVE INCOME AND LOSSES

Classification. The passive loss rules require income and losses to be classified into one of three categories: active, passive, or portfolio. **Active income** includes the following:

- Wages, salary, commissions, bonuses, and other payments for services rendered by the taxpayer.
- Profit from a trade or business in which the taxpayer is a material participant.
- Gain on the sale or other disposition of assets used in an active trade or business.
- Income from intangible property if the taxpayer's personal efforts significantly contributed to the creation of the property.

Portfolio income includes the following:

- Interest, dividends, annuities, and royalties not derived in the ordinary course of a trade or business.
- Gain or loss from the disposition of property that produces portfolio income or is held for investment purposes.

Section 469 provides that income or loss from the following activities is treated as *passive*:

- Any trade or business or income-producing activity in which the taxpayer does not materially participate.
- Subject to certain exceptions, all rental activities, whether the taxpayer materially participates or not.

Although the Code defines rental activities as passive activities, several exceptions allow losses from certain real estate rental activities to offset nonpassive (active or portfolio) income. The exceptions are discussed under Special Passive Activity Rules for Real Estate Activities later in the chapter.

General Impact. Losses or expenses generated by passive activities can be deducted only to the extent of income from all of the taxpayer's passive activities. Any excess may not be used to offset income from active sources or portfolio income. Instead, any unused passive losses are suspended and carried forward to future years to offset passive income generated in those years. Otherwise, suspended losses may be used only when a taxpayer disposes of his or her entire interest in an activity. In that event, all current and suspended losses related to the activity may offset active and portfolio income.

EXAMPLE 6

Kim, a physician, earns $150,000 from her full-time practice. She also receives $10,000 in dividends and interest from various portfolio investments, and her share of a passive loss from a tax shelter not limited by the at-risk rules is $60,000. Because the loss is a passive loss, it is not deductible against her other income. The loss is suspended and is carried over to the future. If Kim has passive income from this investment or from other passive investments in the future, she can offset the suspended loss against that passive income. If she does not have passive income to offset this suspended loss in the future, she will be allowed to offset the loss against other types of income when she eventually disposes of the passive activity. ■

Impact of Suspended Losses. When a taxpayer disposes of his or her entire interest in a passive activity, the actual economic gain or loss from the investment, including any suspended losses, can finally be determined. As a result, under the passive loss rules, upon a fully taxable disposition, any overall loss realized from the activity by the taxpayer is recognized and can be offset against any income.

A fully taxable disposition generally involves a sale of the property to a third party at arm's length and thus, presumably, for a price equal to the property's fair market value. Gain recognized upon a transfer of an interest in a passive activity generally is treated as passive and is first offset by the suspended losses from that activity.

EXAMPLE 7

Rex sells an apartment building, a passive activity, with an adjusted basis of $100,000 for $180,000. In addition, he has suspended losses of $60,000 associated with the building. His total gain, $80,000, and his taxable gain, $20,000, are calculated as follows:

Net sales price	$ 180,000
Less: Adjusted basis	(100,000)
Total gain	$ 80,000
Less: Suspended losses	(60,000)
Taxable gain (passive)	$ 20,000

■

If current and suspended losses of the passive activity exceed the gain realized or if the sale results in a realized loss, the amount of

- any loss from the activity for the tax year (including losses suspended in the activity disposed of)

in excess of

- net income or gain for the tax year from all passive activities (without regard to the activity disposed of)

is treated as a loss that is not from a passive activity. In computing the loss from the activity for the year of disposition, any gain or loss recognized is included.

EXAMPLE 8

Dean sells an apartment building with an adjusted basis of $100,000 for $150,000. In addition, he has current and suspended losses of $60,000 associated with the building and has no other passive activities. His total gain of $50,000 and his deductible loss of $10,000 are calculated as follows:

Net sales price	$ 150,000
Less: Adjusted basis	(100,000)
Total gain	$ 50,000
Less: Suspended losses	(60,000)
Deductible loss (not passive)	($ 10,000)

The $10,000 deductible loss is offset against Dean's active and portfolio income. ■

Carryovers of Suspended Losses. In the above examples, it was assumed that the taxpayer had an interest in only one passive activity, and as a result, the suspended loss was related exclusively to the activity that was disposed of. Taxpayers often own interests in more than one activity, however, and in that case, any suspended losses must be allocated among the activities in which the taxpayer has an interest. The allocation to an activity is made by multiplying the disallowed passive activity loss from all activities by the following fraction:

$$\frac{\text{Loss from activity}}{\text{Sum of losses for taxable year from all activities having losses}}$$

EXAMPLE 9

Diego has investments in three passive activities with the following income and losses for 2004:

Activity A	($ 30,000)
Activity B	(20,000)
Activity C	25,000
Net passive loss	($ 25,000)
Net passive loss allocated to:	
Activity A ($25,000 × $30,000/$50,000)	($ 15,000)
Activity B ($25,000 × $20,000/$50,000)	(10,000)
Total suspended losses	($ 25,000)

■

Suspended losses are carried over indefinitely and are offset in the future against any passive income from the activities to which they relate.[5]

EXAMPLE 10

Assume the same facts as in Example 9 and that Activity A produces $10,000 of income in 2005. Of the suspended loss of $15,000 from 2004 for Activity A, $10,000 is offset against the income from this activity. If Diego sells Activity A in early 2006, then the remaining $5,000 suspended loss is used in determining his taxable gain or loss. ■

Passive Credits. Credits arising from passive activities are limited in much the same way as passive losses. Passive credits can be utilized only against regular tax attributable to passive income,[6] which is calculated by comparing the tax on all income (including passive income) with the tax on income excluding passive income.

EXAMPLE 11

Sam owes $50,000 of tax, disregarding net passive income, and $80,000 of tax, considering both net passive and other taxable income (disregarding the credits in both cases). The amount of tax attributable to the passive income is $30,000.

[5] § 469(b).

[6] § 469(d)(2).

Tax due (before credits) including net passive income	$ 80,000
Less: Tax due (before credits) without including net passive income	(50,000)
Tax attributable to passive income	$ 30,000

Sam in the preceding example can claim a maximum of $30,000 of passive activity credits; the excess credits are carried over. These passive activity credits (such as the low-income housing credit and rehabilitation credit) can be used only against the *regular* tax attributable to passive income. If a taxpayer has a net loss from passive activities during a given year, no credits can be used.

Carryovers of Passive Credits. Tax credits attributable to passive activities can be carried forward indefinitely much like suspended passive losses. Unlike passive losses, however, passive credits are lost forever when the activity is disposed of in a taxable transaction where loss is recognized. Credits are allowed on dispositions only when there is sufficient tax on passive income to absorb them.

EXAMPLE 12

Alicia sells a passive activity for a gain of $10,000. The activity had suspended losses of $40,000 and suspended credits of $15,000. The $10,000 gain is offset by $10,000 of the suspended losses, and the remaining $30,000 of suspended losses is deductible against Alicia's active and portfolio income. The suspended credits are lost forever because the sale of the activity did not generate any tax. This is true even if Alicia has positive taxable income or is subject to the alternative minimum tax (discussed in Chapter 15).

EXAMPLE 13

If Alicia in Example 12 had realized a $100,000 gain on the sale of the passive activity, the suspended credits could have been used to the extent of regular tax attributable to the net passive income.

Gain on sale	$100,000
Less: Suspended losses	(40,000)
Taxable gain	$ 60,000

If the tax attributable to the taxable gain of $60,000 is $15,000 or more, the entire $15,000 of suspended credits can be used. If the tax attributable to the gain is less than $15,000, the excess of the suspended credits over the tax attributable to the gain is lost forever.

When a taxpayer has an adequate regular tax liability from passive activities to trigger the use of suspended credits, the credits lose their character as passive credits. They are reclassified as regular tax credits and made subject to the same limits as other business credits (discussed in Chapter 12).

Passive Activity Changes to Active. If a formerly passive activity becomes an active one, suspended losses are allowed to the extent of income from the now active business.[7] If any of the suspended loss remains, it continues to be treated as a loss from a passive activity. The excess suspended loss can be deducted from passive income or carried over to the next tax year and deducted to the extent of income from the now active business in the succeeding year(s). The activity must continue to be the same activity.

TAXPAYERS SUBJECT TO THE PASSIVE LOSS RULES

The passive loss rules apply to individuals, estates, trusts, personal service corporations, and closely held C corporations.[8] Passive income or loss from investments

[7] § 469(f).

[8] § 469(a).

in S corporations or partnerships (see Chapters 21 and 22) flows through to the owners, and the passive loss rules are applied at the owner level.

Personal Service Corporations. Application of the passive loss limitations to **personal service corporations** is intended to prevent taxpayers from sheltering personal service income by creating personal service corporations and acquiring passive activities at the corporate level.

EXAMPLE 14

Five tax accountants, who earn a total of $1 million a year in their individual practices, form a personal service corporation. Shortly after its formation, the corporation invests in a passive activity that produces a $200,000 loss during the year. Because the passive loss rules apply to personal service corporations, the corporation may not deduct the $200,000 loss against the $1 million of active income. ■

Determination of whether a corporation is a *personal service corporation* is based on rather broad definitions. A personal service corporation is a corporation that meets *both* of the following conditions:

- The principal activity is the performance of personal services.
- Such services are substantially performed by employee-owners.

Generally, personal service corporations include those in the fields of health, law, engineering, architecture, accounting, actuarial science, performing arts, and consulting.[9] A corporation is treated as a personal service corporation if more than 10 percent of the stock (by value) is held by employee-owners.[10] An employee is treated as an employee-owner if he or she owns stock on *any day* during the taxable year.[11] For these purposes, shareholder status and employee status do not even have to occur on the same day.

Closely Held C Corporations. Application of the passive loss rules to closely held (non-personal service) C corporations is also intended to prevent individuals from incorporating to avoid the passive loss limitations. A corporation is classified as a **closely held corporation** if at any time during the taxable year more than 50 percent of the value of its outstanding stock is owned, directly or indirectly, by or for five or fewer individuals. Closely held C corporations (other than personal service corporations) may use passive losses to offset *active* income, but not portfolio income.

EXAMPLE 15

Silver Corporation, a closely held (non-personal service) C corporation, has $500,000 of passive losses from a rental activity, $400,000 of active income, and $100,000 of portfolio income. The corporation may offset $400,000 of the $500,000 passive loss against the $400,000 of active business income, but may not offset the remainder against the $100,000 of portfolio income. Thus, $100,000 of the passive loss is suspended ($500,000 passive loss – $400,000 offset against active income). ■

Application of the passive loss limitations to closely held C corporations prevents taxpayers from transferring their portfolio investments to such corporations in order to offset passive losses against portfolio income.

[9]§ 448(d)(2)(A).
[10]§ 469(j)(2).
[11]§ 269A(b)(2).

LO.4

Discuss the definition of passive activities and the rules for identifying an activity.

PASSIVE ACTIVITIES DEFINED

Section 469 specifies that the following types of activities are to be treated as passive:

- Any trade or business or income-producing activity in which the taxpayer does not materially participate.
- Subject to certain exceptions, all rental activities.

To understand the meaning of the term *passive activity* and the impact of the rules, one must address the following issues, each of which is the subject of statutory or administrative guidance:

- What constitutes an activity?
- What is meant by material participation?
- When is an activity a rental activity?

Even though guidance is available to help the taxpayer deal with these issues, their resolution is anything but simple.

Identification of an Activity. Identifying what constitutes an activity is a necessary first step in applying the passive loss limitations. Taxpayers who are involved in complex business operations need to be able to determine whether a given segment of their overall business operations constitutes a separate activity or is to be treated as part of a single activity. Proper treatment is necessary in order to determine whether income or loss from an activity is active or passive.

EXAMPLE 16

Ben owns a business with two separate departments. Department A generates net income of $120,000, and Department B generates a net loss of $95,000. Ben participates for 700 hours in the operations of Department A and for 100 hours in Department B. If Ben is allowed to treat the departments as components of a single activity, he can offset the $95,000 loss from Department B against the $120,000 of income from Department A. ■

EXAMPLE 17

Assume the same facts as in the previous example. If Ben is required to treat each department as a separate activity, the tax result is not as favorable. Because he is a material participant in Department A (having devoted 700 hours to it), the $120,000 profit is active income. However, he is not considered a material participant in Department B (100 hours), and the $95,000 loss is a passive loss. Therefore, Ben cannot offset the $95,000 passive loss from Department B against the $120,000 of active income from Department A. (A complete discussion of the material participation rules follows.) ■

Recall that on the disposition of a passive activity, a taxpayer is allowed to offset suspended losses from the activity against other types of income. Therefore, identifying what constitutes an activity is of crucial importance for this purpose too.

EXAMPLE 18

Linda owns a business with two departments. Department A has a net loss of $125,000 in the current year, and Department B has a $70,000 net loss. She disposes of Department B at the end of the year. Assuming Linda is allowed to treat the two departments as separate passive activities, she can offset the passive loss from Department B against other types of income in the following order: gain from disposition of the passive activity, other passive income, and nonpassive income. This treatment leaves her with a suspended loss of $125,000 from Department A. If Departments A and B are treated as components of the same activity, however, on the disposal of Department B, its $70,000 net loss would be suspended along with the other $125,000 of suspended loss of the activity. ■

The current rules used to delineate what constitutes an activity for purposes of the passive loss limitations are provided in the Regulations.[12] These guidelines state that, in general, a taxpayer can treat one or more trade or business activities or rental activities as a single activity if those activities form an *appropriate economic unit* for measuring gain or loss. To determine what ventures form an appropriate economic unit, all of the relevant facts and circumstances must be considered. Taxpayers may use any reasonable method in applying the facts and circumstances. However, the following five factors are given the greatest weight in determining whether activities constitute an appropriate economic unit. It is not necessary to meet all of these conditions in order to treat multiple activities as a single activity.

- Similarities and differences in the types of business conducted in the various trade or business or rental activities.
- The extent of common control over the various activities.
- The extent of common ownership of the activities.
- The geographic location of the different units.
- Interdependencies among the activities.

The following examples, adapted from the Regulations, illustrate the application of the general rules for grouping activities.[13]

EXAMPLE 19

George owns a men's clothing store and a video game parlor in Chicago. He also owns a men's clothing store and a video game parlor in Milwaukee. Reasonable methods of applying the facts and circumstances test may result in any of the following groupings:

- All four activities may be grouped into a single activity.
- The clothing stores may be grouped into an activity, and the video game parlors may be grouped into a separate activity.
- The Chicago activities may be grouped into an activity, and the Milwaukee activities may be grouped into a separate activity.
- Each of the four activities may be treated as a separate activity. ■

EXAMPLE 20

Sharon is a partner in a business that sells snack items to drugstores. She also is a partner in a partnership that owns and operates a warehouse. Both partnerships, which are under common control, are located in the same industrial park. The predominant part of the warehouse business is warehousing items for the snack business, and it is the only warehousing business in which Sharon is involved. Sharon should treat the snack business and the warehousing business as a single activity. ■

Regrouping of Activities. Taxpayers should carefully consider all tax factors in deciding how to group their activities. Once activities have been grouped, they cannot be regrouped unless the original grouping was clearly inappropriate or there has been a material change in the facts and circumstances. If a regrouping is necessary for either of these reasons, the taxpayer is required to disclose to the IRS all information relevant to the regrouping.

The Regulations also grant the IRS the right to regroup activities when both of the following conditions exist:[14]

- The taxpayer's grouping fails to reflect one or more appropriate economic units.
- One of the primary purposes of the taxpayer's grouping is to avoid the passive loss limitations.

The following example, adapted from the Regulations, illustrates a situation where the IRS would exercise its prerogative to regroup a taxpayer's activities.

[12]Reg. § 1.469–4.
[13]Reg. § 1.469–4(c)(3).
[14]Reg. § 1.469–4(f).

EXAMPLE 21

Baker, Edwards, Andrews, Clark, and Henson are physicians who operate their own separate practices. Each of the physicians owns interests in activities that generate passive losses, so they devise a plan to set up an entity that will generate passive income. They form the BEACH Partnership to acquire and operate X-ray equipment, and each receives a limited partnership interest. They select an unrelated person to operate the X-ray business as a general partner, and none of the limited partners participates in the activity. Substantially all of the services provided by BEACH are provided to the physicians, and fees are set at a level that assures a profit for BEACH. Each physician treats his medical practice and his interest in the partnership as separate activities and offsets losses from passive investments against the passive income from the partnership. The IRS would interpret the physicians' separate groupings as attempts to avoid the passive loss limitations and would regroup each medical practice and the services performed by the partnership as an appropriate economic unit. ■

Special Grouping Rules for Rental Activities. Two rules deal specifically with the grouping of rental activities. These provisions are designed to prevent taxpayers from grouping rental activities, which are generally passive, with other businesses in a way that would result in a tax advantage.

First, a rental activity may be grouped with a trade or business activity only if one activity is insubstantial in relation to the other. That is, the rental activity must be insubstantial in relation to the trade or business activity, or the trade or business activity must be insubstantial in relation to the rental activity. The Regulations provide no clear guidelines as to the meaning of "insubstantial."[15]

EXAMPLE 22

Schemers, a firm of CPAs, owns a building in downtown Washington, D.C., in which they conduct their public accounting practice. The firm also rents space on the street level of the building to several retail establishments. Of the total revenue generated by the firm, 95% is associated with the public accounting practice, and 5% is related to the rental operation. It is likely that the rental activity would be considered insubstantial relative to the accounting practice and the two ventures could be grouped as one nonrental activity. This grouping could be advantageous to the firm, particularly if the rental operation generates a loss! Alternatively, treating the rental operation as a *separate* activity may be advantageous if this operation produces (passive) income. The passive income could then be used to absorb otherwise nondeductible passive losses. ■

Second, taxpayers generally may not treat an activity involving the rental of real property and an activity involving the rental of personal property as a single activity.

LO.5

Analyze and apply the tests for material participation.

Material Participation. If an individual taxpayer materially participates in a nonrental trade or business activity, any loss from that activity is treated as an active loss that can offset active or portfolio income. If a taxpayer does not materially participate, however, the loss is treated as a passive loss, which can only offset passive income. Therefore, controlling whether a particular activity is treated as active or passive is an important part of the tax strategy of a taxpayer who owns an interest in one or more businesses. Consider the following examples.

EXAMPLE 23

Dewayne, a corporate executive, earns a salary of $600,000 per year. In addition, he owns a separate business in which he participates. The business produces a loss of $100,000 during the year. If Dewayne materially participates in the business, the $100,000 loss is an active loss that may offset his active income from his corporate employer. If he does not materially participate, the loss is passive and is suspended. Dewayne may use the suspended loss in the future only when he has passive income or disposes of the activity. ■

[15]Reg. § 1.469–4(d).

EXAMPLE 24

Kay, an attorney, earns $350,000 a year in her law practice. She owns interests in two activities, A and B, in which she participates. Activity A, in which she does *not* materially participate, produces a loss of $50,000. Kay has not yet met the material participation standard for Activity B, which produces income of $80,000. However, she can meet the material participation standard if she spends an additional 50 hours in Activity B during the year. Should Kay attempt to meet the material participation standard for Activity B? If she continues working in Activity B and becomes a material participant, the $80,000 of income from the activity is *active*, and the $50,000 passive loss from Activity A must be suspended. A more favorable tax strategy is for Kay to *not meet* the material participation standard for Activity B, thus making the income from that activity passive. This enables her to offset the $50,000 passive loss from Activity A against the passive income from Activity B. ■

It is possible to devise numerous scenarios in which the taxpayer could control the tax outcome by increasing or decreasing his or her participation in different activities. Examples 23 and 24 demonstrate some of the possibilities. The conclusion reached in most analyses of this type is that taxpayers will benefit by having profitable activities classified as passive so that any passive losses can be used to offset that passive income. If the activity produces a loss, however, the taxpayer will benefit if it is classified as active so that the loss is not subject to the passive loss limitations.

As discussed previously, a nonrental trade or business in which a taxpayer owns an interest must be treated as a passive activity unless the taxpayer materially participates. As the Staff of the Joint Committee on Taxation explained, a material participant is one who has "a significant nontax economic profit motive" for taking on activities and selects them for their economic value. In contrast, a passive investor mainly seeks a return from a capital investment (including a possible reduction in taxes) as a supplement to an ongoing source of livelihood.[16] Even if the concept or the implication of being a material participant is clear, the precise meaning of the term **material participation** can be vague. As enacted, § 469 requires a taxpayer to participate on a *regular, continuous, and substantial* basis in order to be a material participant. In many situations, however, it is difficult or impossible to gain any assurance that this nebulous standard is met.

In response to this dilemma, Temporary Regulations[17] provide seven tests that are intended to help taxpayers cope with these issues. Material participation is achieved by meeting any *one* of the tests. These tests can be divided into three categories:

- Tests based on current participation.
- Tests based on prior participation.
- Test based on facts and circumstances.

Tests Based on Current Participation. The first four tests are quantitative tests that require measurement, in hours, of the taxpayer's participation in the activity during the year.

1. *Does the individual participate in the activity for more than 500 hours during the year?*

[16]*General Explanation of the Tax Reform Act of 1986* ("Blue Book"), prepared by The Staff of the Joint Committee on Taxation, May 4, 1987, H.R. 3838, 99th Cong., p. 212.

[17]Temp.Reg. § 1.469–5T(a). The Temporary Regulations are also Proposed Regulations. Temporary Regulations have the same effect as final Regulations. Refer to Chapter 2 for a discussion of the different categories of Regulations.

The purpose of the 500-hour requirement is to restrict deductions from the types of trade or business activities Congress intended to treat as passive activities. The 500-hour standard for material participation was adopted for the following reasons:[18]

- Few investors in traditional tax shelters devote more than 500 hours a year to such an investment.
- The IRS believes that income from an activity in which the taxpayer participates for more than 500 hours a year should not be treated as passive.

2. *Does the individual's participation in the activity for the taxable year constitute substantially all of the participation in the activity of all individuals (including nonowner employees) for the year?*

EXAMPLE 25

Ned, a physician, operates a separate business in which he participates for 80 hours during the year. He is the only participant and has no employees in the separate business. Ned meets the material participation standard of Test 2. If he had employees, it could be difficult to apply Test 2, because the Temporary Regulations do not define the term *substantially all.* ■

3. *Does the individual participate in the activity for more than 100 hours during the year, and is the individual's participation in the activity for the year not less than the participation of any other individual (including nonowner employees) for the year?*

EXAMPLE 26

Adam, a college professor, owns a separate business in which he participates 110 hours during the year. He has an employee who works 90 hours during the year. Adam meets the material participation standard under Test 3, but probably does not meet it under Test 2 because his participation is only 55% of the total participation. It is unlikely that 55% would meet the *substantially all* requirement of Test 2. ■

Tests 2 and 3 are included because the IRS recognizes that the operation of some activities does not require more than 500 hours of participation during the year.

4. *Is the activity a significant participation activity for the taxable year, and does the individual's aggregate participation in all significant participation activities during the year exceed 500 hours?*

A **significant participation activity** is a trade or business in which the individual's participation exceeds 100 hours during the year. This test treats taxpayers as material participants if their aggregate participation in several significant participation activities exceeds 500 hours. Test 4 thus accords the same treatment to an individual who devotes an aggregate of more than 500 hours to several significant participation activities as to an individual who devotes more than 500 hours to a single activity.

EXAMPLE 27

Mike owns five different businesses. He participates in each activity during the year as follows:

Activity	Hours of Participation
A	110
B	140
C	120
D	150
E	100

[18]T.D. 8175, 1988–1 C.B. 191.

Activities A, B, C, and D are significant participation activities, and Mike's aggregate participation in those activities is 520 hours. Therefore, Activities A, B, C, and D are not treated as passive activities. Activity E is not a significant participation activity (not more than 100 hours), so it is not included in applying the 500-hour test. Activity E is treated as a passive activity, unless Mike meets one of the other material participation tests for that activity. ■

EXAMPLE 28

Assume the same facts as in the previous example, except that Activity A does not exist. All of the activities are now treated as passive. Activity E is not counted in applying the more-than-500-hour test, so Mike's aggregate participation in significant participation activities is 410 hours (140 in Activity B + 120 in Activity C + 150 in Activity D). He could meet the significant participation test for Activity E by participating for one more hour in the activity. This would cause Activities B, C, D, and E to be treated as nonpassive activities. However, before deciding whether to participate for at least one more hour in Activity E, Mike should assess how the participation would affect his overall tax liability. ■

Tests Based on Prior Participation. Tests 5 and 6 are based on material participation in prior years. Under these tests, a taxpayer who is no longer a participant in an activity can continue to be *classified* as a material participant. The IRS takes the position that material participation in a trade or business for a long period of time is likely to indicate that the activity represents the individual's principal livelihood, rather than a passive investment. Consequently, withdrawal from the activity, or reduction of participation to the point where it is not material, does not change the classification of the activity from active to passive.

5. *Did the individual materially participate in the activity for any 5 taxable years (whether consecutive or not) during the 10 taxable years that immediately precede the taxable year?*

EXAMPLE 29

Dawn, who owns a 50% interest in a restaurant, was a material participant in the operations of the restaurant from 1999 through 2003. She retired at the end of 2003 and is no longer involved in the restaurant except as an investor. Dawn will be treated as a material participant in the restaurant in 2004. Even if she does not become involved in the restaurant as a material participant again, she will continue to be treated as a material participant in 2005, 2006, 2007, and 2008. In 2009 and later years, Dawn's share of income or loss from the restaurant will be classified as passive unless she materially participates in those years. ■

6. *Is the activity a personal service activity, and did the individual materially participate in the activity for any three preceding taxable years (whether consecutive or not)?*

As indicated above, the material participation standards differ for personal service activities and other businesses. An individual who was a material participant in a personal service activity for *any three years* prior to the taxable year continues to be treated as a material participant after withdrawal from the activity.

EXAMPLE 30

Evan, a CPA, retires from the EFG Partnership after working full-time in the partnership for 30 years. As a retired partner, he will continue to receive a share of the profits of the firm for the next 10 years, even though he will not participate in the firm's operations. Evan also owns an interest in a passive activity that produces a loss for the year. Because he continues to be treated as a material participant in the EFG Partnership, his income from the partnership is active income. Therefore, he is not allowed to offset the loss from his passive investment against the income from the EFG Partnership. ■

Test Based on Facts and Circumstances. Test 7 assesses the facts and circumstances to determine whether the taxpayer has materially participated.

7. *Based on all the facts and circumstances, did the individual participate in the activity on a regular, continuous, and substantial basis during the year?*

The Temporary Regulations do not define what constitutes regular, continuous, and substantial participation except to say that the taxpayer's activities will *not* be considered material participation under Test 7 in the following three circumstances:[19]

- The taxpayer satisfies the participation standards (whether or not a *material participant*) of any Code section other than § 469.
- The taxpayer manages the activity, unless
  - no other person receives compensation for management services, and
  - no individual spends more hours during the tax year managing the activity than does the taxpayer.
- The taxpayer participates in the activity for 100 hours or less during the tax year.

A part of the Temporary Regulations has been reserved for further development of this test. Presumably, additional guidelines will be issued in the future. For the time being, taxpayers should rely on Tests 1 through 6 in determining whether the material participation standards have been met.

Participation Defined. Participation generally includes any work done by an individual in an activity that he or she owns. Participation does not include work if it is of a type not customarily done by owners *and* if one of its principal purposes is to avoid the disallowance of passive losses or credits. Also, work done in an individual's capacity as an investor (e.g., reviewing financial reports in a non-managerial capacity) is not counted in applying the material participation tests. However, participation by an owner's spouse counts as participation by the owner.[20]

EXAMPLE 31

Tom, who is a partner in a CPA firm, owns a computer store that has operated at a loss during the year. In order to offset this loss against the income from his CPA practice, Tom would like to avoid having the computer business classified as a passive activity. Through December 15, he has worked 400 hours in the business in management and selling activities. During the last two weeks of December, he works 80 hours in management and selling activities and 30 hours doing janitorial chores. Also during the last two weeks in December, Tom's wife participates 40 hours as a salesperson. She has worked as a salesperson in the computer store in prior years, but has not done so during the current year. If any of Tom's work is of a type not customarily done by owners *and* if one of its principal purposes is to avoid the disallowance of passive losses or credits, it is not counted in applying the material participation tests. It is likely that Tom's 480 hours of participation in management and selling activities will count as participation, but the 30 hours spent doing janitorial chores will not. However, the 40 hours of participation by his wife will count, and as a result, Tom will qualify as a material participant under the more-than-500-hour rule (480 + 40 = 520). ■

Limited Partners. A *limited* partner is one whose liability to third-party creditors of the partnership is limited to the amount the partner has invested in the partnership. Such a partnership must have at least one *general* partner, who is fully liable in an individual capacity for the debts of the partnership to third parties. Generally, a *limited partner* is not considered a material participant unless he or she qualifies under Test 1, 5, or 6 in the above list. However, a *general partner* may qualify as a material participant by meeting any of the seven tests. If a general partner also

[19]Temp.Reg. § 1.469–5T(b)(2).

[20]Temp.Reg. § 1.469–5T(f)(3).

owns a limited interest in the same limited partnership, all interests are treated as a general interest.[21]

LO.6

Understand the nature of rental activities under the passive loss rules.

Rental Activities Defined. The Code specifies that, subject to certain exceptions, all rental activities are to be treated as passive activities.[22] A **rental activity** is defined as any activity where payments are received principally for the use of tangible (real or personal) property.[23] Importantly, an activity that is classified as a rental activity is subject to the passive activity loss rules, even if the taxpayer involved is a material participant.

EXAMPLE 32

Sarah owns an apartment building and spends an average of 60 hours a week in its operation. Assuming that the apartment building operation is classified as a rental activity, it is automatically subject to the passive activity rules, even though Sarah spends more than 500 hours a year in its operation. ■

Temporary Regulations, however, provide exceptions for certain situations where activities involving rentals of real and personal property are *not* to be *treated* as rental activities.[24]

EXAMPLE 33

Dan owns a DVD rental business. Because the average period of customer use is seven days or less, Dan's DVD business is not treated as a rental activity. ■

The fact that Dan's DVD business in the previous example is not treated as a rental activity does not necessarily mean that it is classified as a nonpassive activity. Instead, the DVD business is treated as a trade or business activity subject to the material participation standards. If Dan is a material participant, the business is treated as active. If he is not a material participant, it is treated as a passive activity.

Thus, activities covered by any of the following six exceptions provided by the Temporary Regulations are not *automatically* treated as nonpassive activities merely because they would not be classified as rental activities. Instead, the activities are subject to the material participation tests.

1. *The average period of customer use of the property is seven days or less.*

Under this exception, activities involving the short-term use of tangible property such as automobiles, DVDs, tuxedos, tools, and other such property are not treated as rental activities. The provision also applies to short-term rentals of hotel or motel rooms.

This exception is based on the presumption that a person who rents property for seven days or less is generally required to provide *significant services* to the customer. Providing such services supports a conclusion that the person is engaged in a service business rather than a rental business.

2. *The average period of customer use of the property is 30 days or less, and the owner of the property provides significant personal services.*

For longer-term rentals, the presumption that significant services are provided is not automatic, as it is in the case of the seven-day exception. Instead, the taxpayer must be able to *prove* that significant personal services are rendered in connection with the activity. Relevant facts and circumstances include the frequency with which such services are provided, the type and amount of labor required to perform the services, and the value of the services relative to the amount charged for the

[21]Temp.Reg. § 1.469–5T(e)(3)(ii).
[22]§ 469(c)(2).
[23]§ 469(j)(8).
[24]Temp.Reg. § 1.469–1T(e)(3)(ii).

use of the property. Significant personal services include only services provided by *individuals*.[25]

3. *The owner of the property provides extraordinary personal services. The average period of customer use is of no consequence in applying this test.*

Extraordinary personal services are services provided by individuals where the customers' use of the property is incidental to their receipt of the services. For example, a patient's use of a hospital bed is incidental to his or her receipt of medical services. Another example is the use of a boarding school's dormitory, which is incidental to the scholastic services received.

4. *The rental of the property is treated as incidental to a nonrental activity of the taxpayer.*

Rentals of real property incidental to a nonrental activity are not considered a passive activity. The Temporary Regulations provide that the following rentals are not passive activities:[26]

- *Property held primarily for investment.* This occurs where the principal purpose for holding the property is the expectation of gain from the appreciation of the property and the gross rent income is less than 2 percent of the lesser of (1) the unadjusted basis or (2) the fair market value of the property.

EXAMPLE 34

Ramon invests in vacant land for the purpose of realizing a profit on its appreciation. He leases the land during the period it is held. The land's unadjusted basis is $250,000, and the fair market value is $350,000. The lease payments are $4,000 per year. Because gross rent income is less than 2% of $250,000, the activity is not a rental activity. ■

- *Property used in a trade or business.* This occurs where the property is owned by a taxpayer who is an owner of the trade or business using the rental property. The property must also have been used in the trade or business during the year or during at least two of the five preceding taxable years. The 2 percent test above also applies in this situation.

EXAMPLE 35

A farmer owns land with an unadjusted basis of $250,000 and a fair market value of $350,000. He used it for farming purposes in 2003 and 2004. In 2005, he leases the land to another farmer for $4,000. The activity is not a rental activity. ■

- *Property held for sale to customers.* If property is held for sale to customers and rented during the year, the rental of the property is not a rental activity. If, for example, an automobile dealer rents automobiles held for sale to customers to persons who are having their own cars repaired, the activity is not a rental activity.
- *Lodging rented for the convenience of an employer.* If an employer provides lodging for an employee incidental to the employee's performance of services in the employer's trade or business, no rental activity exists.
- *Property rented to a partnership.* A partner who rents property to a partnership that is used in the partnership's trade or business does not have a rental activity.

These rules were written to prevent taxpayers from converting active or portfolio income into passive income for the purpose of offsetting other passive losses.

[25]Temp.Reg. § 1.469–1T(e)(3)(iv).

[26]Temp.Regs. §§ 1.469–1T(e)(3)(vi)(B) through (E).

5. *The taxpayer customarily makes the property available during defined business hours for nonexclusive use by various customers.*

EXAMPLE 36

Pat is the owner-operator of a public golf course. Some customers pay daily greens fees each time they use the course, while others purchase weekly, monthly, or annual passes. The golf course is open every day from sunrise to sunset, except on certain holidays and on days when the course is closed due to inclement weather conditions. Pat is not engaged in a rental activity, regardless of the average period customers use the course. ■

6. *The property is provided for use in an activity conducted by a partnership, S corporation, or joint venture in which the taxpayer owns an interest.*

EXAMPLE 37

Joe, a partner in the Skyview Partnership, contributes the use of a building to the partnership. The partnership has net income of $30,000 during the year, of which Joe's share is $10,000. Unless the partnership is engaged in a rental activity, none of Joe's income from the partnership is income from a rental activity. ■

LO.7

Recognize the relationship between the at-risk and passive activity limitations.

INTERACTION OF THE AT-RISK AND PASSIVE ACTIVITY LIMITS

The determination of whether a loss is suspended under the passive loss rules is made *after* application of the at-risk rules, as well as other provisions relating to the measurement of taxable income. A loss that is not allowed for the year because the taxpayer is not at risk with respect to it is suspended under the at-risk provision and not under the passive loss rules. Further, a taxpayer's basis is reduced by deductions (e.g., depreciation) even if the deductions are not currently usable because of the passive loss rules.

EXAMPLE 38

Jack's adjusted basis in a passive activity is $10,000 at the beginning of 2004. His loss from the activity in 2004 is $4,000. Since Jack has no passive activity income, the $4,000 cannot be deducted. At year-end, Jack has an adjusted basis and an at-risk amount of $6,000 in the activity and a suspended passive loss of $4,000. ■

EXAMPLE 39

Jack in Example 38 has a loss of $9,000 in the activity in 2005. Since the $9,000 exceeds his at-risk amount ($6,000) by $3,000, that $3,000 loss is disallowed by the at-risk rules. If Jack has no passive activity income, the remaining $6,000 is suspended under the passive activity rules. At year-end, he has:

- A $3,000 loss suspended under the at-risk rules.
- $10,000 of suspended passive losses.
- An adjusted basis and an at-risk amount in the activity of zero. ■

EXAMPLE 40

Jack in Example 39 realizes $1,000 of passive income from the activity in 2006. Because the $1,000 increases his at-risk amount, $1,000 of the $3,000 unused loss is reclassified as a passive loss. If he has no other passive income, the $1,000 income is offset by $1,000 of suspended passive losses. At the end of 2006, Jack has:

- No taxable passive income.
- $2,000 ($3,000 – $1,000) of unused losses under the at-risk rules.
- $10,000 of (reclassified) suspended passive losses ($10,000 + $1,000 of reclassified unused at-risk losses – $1,000 of passive losses offset against passive income).
- An adjusted basis and an at-risk amount in the activity of zero. ■

EXAMPLE 41

In 2007, Jack has no gain or loss from the activity in Example 40. He contributes $5,000 more to the passive activity. Because the $5,000 contribution increases his at-risk amount, the

NEWLY DEVELOPED TAX SHELTER STRATEGIES NOW PROTECTED BY PATENTS

A patent is generally thought of as an intangible asset that protects the intellectual property underlying a new drug, manufacturing process, or consumer item. In such cases, the U.S. Patent and Trademark Office grants a patent that legally protects the holder's exclusive right to the invention. Now, tax and financial planners are patenting their newest tax shelters and strategies to prevent competitors from using them. Some of the patented strategies involve making mixed gifts of art to charities and family or transferring appreciated assets to heirs with minimal tax consequences.

The applicant for a patent should be aware of the potential costs associated with acquiring such legal protection, however. Even if the Patent and Trademark Office grants a so-called business method patent, there is no assurance that the IRS will approve of the technique. In addition, obtaining a patent can be an expensive and involved process that can take years. Nonetheless, last year over 6,000 patent applications involving business methods were submitted for approval.

SOURCE: Adapted from Rachel Emma Silverman, "The Patented Tax Shelter," *Wall Street Journal*, June 24, 2004, pp. D1 and D2.

$2,000 of losses suspended under the at-risk rules is reclassified as passive. Jack gets no passive loss deduction in 2007. At year-end, he has:

- No suspended losses under the at-risk rules.
- $12,000 of suspended passive losses ($10,000 + $2,000 of reclassified suspended at-risk losses).
- An adjusted basis and an at-risk amount of $3,000 ($5,000 additional investment – $2,000 of reclassified losses). ■

LO.8

Discuss the special treatment available to real estate activities.

SPECIAL PASSIVE ACTIVITY RULES FOR REAL ESTATE ACTIVITIES

The passive loss rules contain two exceptions related to real estate activities. These exceptions allow all or part of real estate rental losses to offset active or portfolio income, even though the activity otherwise is defined as a passive activity.

Material Participation in a Real Property Trade or Business. Losses from real estate rental activities are *not* treated as passive losses for certain real estate professionals.[27] To qualify for nonpassive treatment, a taxpayer must satisfy both of the following requirements:

- More than half of the personal services that the taxpayer performs in trades or businesses are performed in real property trades or businesses in which the taxpayer materially participates.
- The taxpayer performs more than 750 hours of services in these real property trades or businesses as a material participant.

Taxpayers who do not satisfy the above requirements must continue to treat losses from real estate rental activities as passive losses.

[27] § 469(c)(7).

EXAMPLE 42

During the current year, Della performs personal service activities as follows: 900 hours as a personal financial planner, 550 hours in a real estate development business, and 600 hours in a real estate rental activity. Any loss Della incurs in the real estate rental activity will *not* be subject to the passive loss rules, since more than 50% of her personal services are devoted to real property trades or businesses, and her material participation in those real estate activities exceeds 750 hours. Thus, any loss from the real estate rental activity can offset active and portfolio sources of income. ■

As discussed earlier, a spouse's work is taken into consideration in satisfying the material participation requirement. However, the hours worked by a spouse are *not* taken into account when ascertaining whether a taxpayer has worked for more than 750 hours in real property trades or businesses during a year.[28] Services performed by an employee are not treated as being related to a real estate trade or business unless the employee performing the services owns more than a 5 percent interest in the employer. Additionally, a closely held C corporation may also qualify for the passive loss relief if more than 50 percent of its gross receipts for the year are derived from real property trades or businesses in which it materially participates.

Real Estate Rental Activities. The second exception is more significant in that it is not restricted to real estate professionals. This exception allows individuals to deduct up to $25,000 of losses from real estate rental activities against active and portfolio income.[29] The potential annual $25,000 deduction is reduced by 50 percent of the taxpayer's AGI in excess of $100,000. Thus, the entire deduction is phased out at $150,000 of AGI. If married individuals file separately, the $25,000 deduction is reduced to zero unless they lived apart for the entire year. If they lived apart for the entire year, the loss amount is $12,500 each, and the phaseout begins at $50,000. AGI for purposes of the phaseout is calculated without regard to IRA deductions, Social Security benefits, interest deductions on education loans, and net losses from passive activities.

To qualify for the $25,000 exception, a taxpayer must meet the following requirements:[30]

- Actively participate in the real estate rental activity.
- Own 10 percent or more (in value) of all interests in the activity during the entire taxable year (or shorter period during which the taxpayer held an interest in the activity).

The difference between *active participation* and *material participation* is that the former can be satisfied without regular, continuous, and substantial involvement in operations as long as the taxpayer participates in making management decisions in a significant and bona fide sense. In this context, relevant management decisions include such decisions as approving new tenants, deciding on rental terms, and approving capital or repair expenditures.

The $25,000 allowance is available after all active participation rental losses and gains are netted and applied to other passive income. If a taxpayer has a real estate rental loss in excess of the amount that can be deducted under the real estate rental exception, that excess is treated as a passive loss.

EXAMPLE 43

Brad, who has $90,000 of AGI before considering rental activities, has $85,000 of losses from a real estate rental activity in which he actively participates. He also actively participates

[28] § 469(c)(7)(B) and Reg. § 1.469–9.
[29] § 469(i).
[30] § 469(i)(6).

in another real estate rental activity from which he has $25,000 of income. He has other passive income of $36,000. Of the net rental loss of $60,000, $36,000 is absorbed by the $36,000 of passive income, leaving $24,000 that can be deducted against other income. ■

The $25,000 offset allowance is an aggregate of both deductions and credits in deduction equivalents. The deduction equivalent of a passive activity credit is the amount of deductions that reduces the tax liability for the taxable year by an amount equal to the credit.[31] A taxpayer with $5,000 of credits and a tax bracket of 25 percent would have a deduction equivalent of $20,000 ($5,000 ÷ 25%).

If the total deduction and deduction equivalent exceed $25,000, the taxpayer must allocate the allowance on a pro rata basis, first among the losses (including real estate rental activity losses suspended in prior years) and then to credits in the following order: (1) credits other than rehabilitation and low-income housing credits, (2) rehabilitation credits, and (3) low-income housing credits.

EXAMPLE 44

Kevin is an active participant in a real estate rental activity that produces $8,000 of income, $26,000 of deductions, and $1,500 of credits. Kevin, who is in the 25% tax bracket, may deduct the net passive loss of $18,000 ($8,000 – $26,000). After deducting the loss, he has an available deduction equivalent of $7,000 ($25,000 – $18,000 passive loss). Therefore, the maximum amount of credits that he may claim is $1,750 ($7,000 × 25%). Since the actual credits are less than this amount, Kevin may claim the entire $1,500 credit. ■

EXAMPLE 45

Kelly, who is in the 25% tax bracket, is an active participant in three separate real estate rental activities. The relevant tax results for each activity are as follows:

- Activity A: $20,000 of losses.
- Activity B: $10,000 of losses.
- Activity C: $4,200 of credits.

Kelly's deduction equivalent from the credits is $16,800 ($4,200 ÷ 25%). Therefore, the total passive deductions and deduction equivalents are $46,800 ($20,000 + $10,000 + $16,800), which exceeds the maximum allowable amount of $25,000. Consequently, Kelly must allocate pro rata first from among losses and then from among credits. Deductions from losses are limited as follows:

- Activity A {$25,000 × [$20,000 ÷ ($20,000 + $10,000)]} = $16,667.
- Activity B {$25,000 × [$10,000 ÷ ($20,000 + $10,000)]} = $8,333.

Since the amount of passive deductions exceeds the $25,000 maximum, the deduction balance of $5,000 and passive credits of $4,200 must be carried forward. Kelly's suspended losses and credits by activity are as follows:

		Activity		
	Total	**A**	**B**	**C**
Allocated losses	$ 30,000	$ 20,000	$10,000	$ –0–
Allocated credits	4,200	–0–	–0–	4,200
Utilized losses	(25,000)	(16,667)	(8,333)	–0–
Suspended losses	5,000	3,333	1,667	–0–
Suspended credits	4,200	–0–	–0–	4,200

■

[31]§ 469(j)(5).

ETHICAL CONSIDERATIONS — How Active Is Active?

Last year, George and Louise purchased several rental units near the university hoping to benefit from their expected appreciation and cash flow. Because George and Louise both have full-time jobs, they are unable to spend time managing the facilities. Consequently, they contracted with a well-regarded property manager to attract renters, collect the rents, and respond to service calls. After the close of the year, the property manager provided George and Louise with an accounting of the revenues and expenses related to the operation of the units. Though the results showed a positive cash flow, the impact of depreciation and mortgage interest expenses produced a net tax loss.

Not wanting to forgo claiming a loss on their income tax return, they chose to claim the loss under the real estate rental activity exception. Have George and Louise acted properly?

LO.9

Determine the proper tax treatment upon the disposition of a passive activity.

DISPOSITIONS OF PASSIVE INTERESTS

Recall from an earlier discussion that if a taxpayer disposes of an entire interest in a passive activity, any suspended losses (and in certain cases, suspended credits) may be utilized when calculating the final economic gain or loss on the investment. In addition, if a loss ultimately results, that loss can offset other types of income. However, the consequences may differ if the activity is disposed of in a transaction that is other than a fully taxable transaction. The following discusses the treatment of suspended passive losses in other types of dispositions.

Disposition of a Passive Activity at Death. A transfer of a taxpayer's interest in an activity by reason of the taxpayer's death results in suspended losses being allowed (to the decedent) to the extent they exceed the amount, if any, of the step-up in basis allowed.[32] Suspended losses are lost to the extent of the amount of the basis increase. The losses allowed generally are reported on the final return of the deceased taxpayer.

EXAMPLE 46

A taxpayer dies with passive activity property having an adjusted basis of $40,000, suspended losses of $10,000, and a fair market value at the date of the decedent's death of $75,000. The increase (i.e., step-up) in basis (see Chapter 13) is $35,000 (fair market value at date of death in excess of adjusted basis). None of the $10,000 suspended loss is deductible by either the decedent or the beneficiary. The suspended losses ($10,000) are lost because they do not exceed the step-up in basis ($35,000). ■

EXAMPLE 47

A taxpayer dies with passive activity property having an adjusted basis of $40,000, suspended losses of $10,000, and a fair market value at the date of the decedent's death of $47,000. Since the step-up in basis is only $7,000 ($47,000 – $40,000), the suspended losses allowed are limited to $3,000 ($10,000 suspended loss at time of death – $7,000 increase in basis). The $3,000 loss available to the decedent is reported on the decedent's final income tax return. ■

Disposition of a Passive Activity by Gift. In a disposition of a taxpayer's interest in a passive activity by gift, the suspended losses are added to the basis of the property.[33]

[32] § 469(g)(2).

[33] § 469(j)(6).

EXAMPLE 48

A taxpayer makes a gift of passive activity property having an adjusted basis of $40,000, suspended losses of $10,000, and a fair market value at the date of the gift of $100,000. The taxpayer cannot deduct the suspended losses in the year of the disposition. However, the suspended losses transfer with the property and are added to the adjusted basis of the property in the hands of the donee. ■

Installment Sale of a Passive Activity. An installment sale of a taxpayer's entire interest in a passive activity triggers the recognition of the suspended losses.[34] The losses are allowed in each year of the installment obligation in the ratio that the gain recognized in each year bears to the total gain on the sale.

EXAMPLE 49

Stan sells his entire interest in a passive activity for $100,000. His adjusted basis in the property is $60,000. If he uses the installment method, his gross profit ratio is 40% ($40,000/$100,000). If Stan receives a $20,000 down payment, he will recognize a gain of $8,000 (40% of $20,000). If the activity has a suspended loss of $25,000, Stan will deduct $5,000 [($8,000 ÷ $40,000) × $25,000] of the suspended loss in the first year. ■

Nontaxable Exchange of a Passive Activity. In a nontaxable exchange of a passive investment, the taxpayer keeps the suspended losses, which generally become deductible when the acquired property is sold. If the activity of the old and the new property is the same, suspended losses can be used before the activity's disposition.

EXAMPLE 50

A taxpayer exchanges a duplex for a limited partnership interest in a § 721 nonrecognition transaction (see Chapter 21 for details). The suspended losses from the duplex are not deductible until the limited partnership interest is sold. Two different activities exist: a real estate rental activity and a limited partnership activity. If the taxpayer had continued to own the duplex and the duplex had future taxable income, the suspended losses would have become deductible before the time of disposition. ■

EXAMPLE 51

In a § 1031 nontaxable exchange (see Chapter 13 for details), a taxpayer exchanges a duplex for an apartment building. The suspended losses from the duplex are deductible against future taxable income of the apartment building, because the same activity exists. ■

LO.10

Suggest tax planning strategies to minimize the effect of the passive loss limitations.

Tax Planning Considerations

UTILIZING PASSIVE LOSSES

Perhaps the biggest challenge individuals face with the passive loss rules is to recognize the potential impact of the rules and then to structure their affairs to minimize this impact. Taxpayers who have passive activity losses (PALs) should adopt a strategy of generating passive activity income that can be sheltered by existing passive losses. One approach is to buy an interest in a passive activity that is generating income (referred to as passive income generators, or PIGs). Then the PAL can offset income from the PIG. From a tax perspective, it would be foolish to buy a loss-generating passive activity (PAL) unless one has other passive income (PIG) to shelter or the activity is rental real estate that can qualify for the $25,000 exception or the exception available to real estate professionals.

If a taxpayer does invest in an activity that produces losses subject to the passive loss rules, the following strategies may help to minimize the loss of current deductions:

- If money is borrowed to finance the purchase of a passive activity, the associated interest expense is generally treated as part of any passive loss. Consequently, by increasing the amount of cash used to purchase the passive

[34] § 469(g)(3).

Concept Summary 11–2

Passive Activity Loss Rules: General Concepts

What is the fundamental passive activity rule?	Passive activity losses may be deducted only against passive activity income and gains. Losses not allowed are suspended and used in future years.
Who is subject to the passive activity rules?	Individuals. Estates. Trusts. Personal service corporations. Closely held C corporations.
What is a passive activity?	Trade or business or income-producing activity in which the taxpayer does not materially participate during the year, or rental activities, subject to certain exceptions, regardless of the taxpayer's level of participation.
What is an activity?	One or more trade or business or rental activities that comprise an appropriate economic unit.
How is an appropriate economic unit determined?	Based on a reasonable application of the relevant facts and circumstances.
What is material participation?	In general, the taxpayer participates in a regular, continuous, and substantial basis. More specifically, when the taxpayer meets the conditions of one of the seven tests provided in the Regulations.
What is a rental activity?	In general, an activity where payments are received for the use of tangible property. More specifically, a rental activity that does *not* meet one of the six exceptions provided in the Regulations. Special rules apply to rental real estate.

investment, the investor will need less debt and will incur less interest expense. By incurring less interest expense, a possible suspended passive loss deduction is reduced.

- If the investor does not have sufficient cash readily available for the larger down payment, it can be obtained by borrowing against the equity in his or her personal residence. The interest expense on such debt will be deductible under the qualified residence interest provisions (see Chapter 10) and will not be subject to the passive loss limitations. Thus, the taxpayer avoids the passive loss limitation and secures a currently deductible interest expense.

Often unusable passive losses accumulate and provide no current tax benefit because the taxpayer has no passive income. When the taxpayer disposes of the entire interest in a passive activity, however, any suspended losses from that activity are used to reduce the taxable gain. If any taxable gain still remains, it can be offset by losses from other passive activities. As a result, the taxpayer should carefully select the year in which a passive activity is disposed of. It is to the taxpayer's advantage to wait until sufficient passive losses have accumulated to offset any gain recognized on the asset's disposition.

EXAMPLE 52

Bill, a calendar year taxpayer, owns interests in two passive activities: Activity A, which he plans to sell in December of this year at a gain of $100,000; and Activity B, which he plans to keep indefinitely. Current and suspended losses associated with Activity B total $60,000, and Bill expects losses from the activity to be $40,000 next year. If Bill sells Activity A this year, the $100,000 gain can be offset by the current and suspended losses of $60,000 from Activity B, producing a net taxable gain of $40,000. However, if Bill delays the sale of Activity A until January of next year, the $100,000 gain will be fully offset by the $100,000 of losses generated by Activity B ($60,000 current and prior losses + $40,000 next year's loss). Consequently, by postponing the sale by one month, he could avoid recognizing $40,000 of gain that would otherwise result. ■

Taxpayers with passive losses should consider the level of their involvement in all other trades or businesses in which they have an interest. If they show that they do not materially participate in a profitable activity, the activity becomes a passive activity. Any income generated by the profitable business then could be sheltered by current and suspended passive losses. Family partnerships in which certain members do not materially participate would qualify. The silent partner in any general partnership engaged in a trade or business would also qualify.

EXAMPLE 53

Gail has an investment in a limited partnership that produces annual passive losses of approximately $25,000. She also owns a newly acquired interest in a convenience store where she works. Her share of the store's income is $35,000. If she works enough to be classified as a material participant, her $35,000 share of income is treated as active income. This results in $35,000 being subject to tax every year, while her $25,000 loss is suspended. However, if Gail reduces her involvement at the store so that she is not a material participant, the $35,000 of income receives passive treatment. Consequently, the $35,000 of income can be offset by the $25,000 passive loss, resulting in only $10,000 being subject to tax. Thus, by reducing her involvement, Gail ensures that the income from the profitable trade or business receives passive treatment and can then be used to absorb passive losses from other passive activities. ■

As this chapter has shown, the passive loss rules can have a dramatic effect on a taxpayer's ability to claim passive losses currently. As a result, it is important to keep accurate records of all sources of income and losses, particularly any suspended passive losses and credits and the activities to which they relate, so that their potential tax benefit will not be lost.

Finally, because of the restrictive nature of the passive activity loss rules, it may be advantageous for a taxpayer to use a vacation home enough to convert it to a second residence. This would enable all of the qualified interest and real estate taxes to be deducted without limitation. However, this strategy would lead to the loss of other deductions, such as repairs, maintenance, and insurance.

KEY TERMS

Active income, 11–6

At-risk limitation, 11–3

Closely held corporation, 11–10

Extraordinary personal services, 11–19

Material participation, 11–14

Passive loss, 11–3

Personal service corporation, 11–10

Portfolio income, 11–6

Rental activity, 11–18

Significant participation activity, 11–15

Tax shelters, 11–2

PROBLEM MATERIALS

West Federal Taxation

Discussion Questions

1. Congress has passed two major provisions to limit a taxpayer's ability to use tax shelters to reduce or defer Federal income tax. What are these provisions?

2. Alice invested $100,000 for a 25% interest in a partnership in which she is not a material participant. The partnership borrowed $200,000 from a bank and used the proceeds to acquire a building. What is Alice's at-risk amount if the $200,000 was borrowed on a recourse loan?

3. List some events that increase and decrease an investor's at-risk amount. What are some strategies that a taxpayer can employ to increase the at-risk amount in order to claim a higher deduction for losses?

4. James invested $10,000 in a cattle-feeding operation that used nonrecourse notes to purchase $100,000 in feed, which was fed to the cattle and expensed. His share of the expense was $18,000. How much can James deduct?

5. Explain the meaning of the terms *active income, portfolio income,* and *passive income.*

6. Manuel owns an interest in an activity that produces a $100,000 loss during the year. Would he generally prefer to have the activity classified as active or passive? Discuss.

7. Kim owns an interest in an activity that produces $100,000 of income during the year. Would Kim prefer to have the activity classified as active or passive? Discuss.

8. What is a suspended passive loss? Why is it important to allocate suspended losses in cases where a taxpayer has interests in more than one passive activity?

9. A passive activity that Lucile acquired several years ago has resulted in losses. How will these passive losses affect Lucile's taxable income when she disposes of the activity?

10. Discuss whether the passive loss rules apply to the following: individuals, closely held C corporations, S corporations, partnerships, and personal service corporations.

11. New-Tech Services, Inc., is owned by four engineers, all of whom work full-time for the corporation. The corporation has eight other full-time employees, all on the clerical staff. New-Tech provides consulting services to inventors. The corporation has invested in a passive activity that produces a $60,000 loss this year. Can New-Tech deduct the loss in the current year? Explain.

12. Gray Corporation has $100,000 of active income and a $55,000 passive loss. Under what circumstances is Gray prohibited from deducting the loss? Allowed to deduct the loss?

13. Discuss what constitutes a passive activity.

14. The Regulations prohibit grouping rental activities in certain circumstances. Discuss these rules.

15. What is the significance of the term *material participation?* Why is the extent of a taxpayer's participation in an activity important in determining whether a loss from the activity is deductible or nondeductible?

16. Why did the IRS adopt the more-than-500-hour standard for material participation?

17. Mark, a college professor, operates three separate businesses and participates less than 500 hours in each. If all three businesses incur losses during the year, are there any circumstances under which Mark may treat the losses as active?

Decision Making

18. Suzanne owns interests in a bagel shop, a lawn and garden store, and a convenience store. Several full-time employees work at each of the enterprises. As of the end of November of the current year, Suzanne has worked 150 hours in the bagel shop, 250 hours at the lawn and garden store, and 70 hours at the convenience store. In reviewing her financial records, you learn that she has no passive investments that are generating income and that she expects these three ventures collectively to produce a loss. What recommendation would you offer Suzanne as she plans her activities for the remainder of the year?

Issue ID

19. Rene retired from public accounting after a long and successful career of 45 years. As part of her retirement package, she continues to share in the profits and losses of the firm, albeit at a lower rate than when she was working full-time. Because Rene wants to stay busy during her retirement years, she has invested and works in a local hardware business, operated as a partnership. Unfortunately, the business has recently gone through a slump and has not been generating profits. Identify relevant tax issues for Rene.

20. Some types of work are counted in applying the material participation standards, and some types are not counted. Discuss and give examples of each type.

Issue ID

21. Alan is determined that during the current year, he will make better use of the tax losses that flow from various businesses that he owns. He is particularly sensitive to the limitations that the passive loss rules place on the deductibility of losses. Last year, Alan's accountant informed him that he could not claim any of the losses on his income tax return because of his lack of material participation. To circumvent the tax problem this year, Alan tells his wife that she may have to put in some time at the various businesses. Identify the tax issues that Alan faces.

22. What are *significant personal services*, and what role do they play in determining whether a rental activity is treated as a passive activity?

23. In general, the definition of a passive activity includes rental activities. However, certain activities involving rentals of real and personal property are not *treated* as rental activities. Explain.

24. How is *passive activity* defined in the Code, and what aspects of the definition have been clarified by final or Temporary Regulations?

25. Laura owns an apartment building and a videocassette and DVD rental business. She participates for more than 500 hours in the operations of each activity. Are the businesses active or passive?

26. Hilda incurs a loss of $60,000 on a real estate rental activity during the current year. Under what circumstances can Hilda treat the entire loss as nonpassive?

Issue ID

27. In the current year, George and Susie Melvin, both successful CPAs, made a cash investment in a limited partnership interest in a California orange grove. In addition to the cash generated from the investors, the venture borrowed a substantial sum to purchase assets necessary for its operation. The Melvins' investment adviser told them that their share of the tax loss in the first year alone would be in excess of their initial cash investment. This result would be followed by several more years of losses. They feel confident that their interest in the orange grove is a sound investment. Identify the tax issues facing the Melvins.

Issue ID

28. Rick, a full-time real estate professional, earns $5,000 for development services rendered to an S corporation that owns and manages apartment units held for rent. He also owns an interest in the entity. His share of the S corporation's rental losses for the year totals $5,000. Identify the issues that are relevant in determining how Rick treats the items of income and loss for tax purposes.

29. Elizabeth owns an interest in a dress shop that has three full-time employees; during the year, she works 450 hours in the shop. Elizabeth also owns an apartment building with no employees in which she works 1,200 hours. Is either activity a passive activity? Explain.

30. Matt owns a small apartment building that generates a loss during the year. Under what circumstances can Matt deduct a loss from the rental activity, and what limitations apply?

31. What are the differences between material participation and active participation under the passive loss rules?

Issue ID

32. Betty and Steve received a substantial windfall from a recent inheritance. Because they have always loved spending time at the beach, they plan to devote some of the newly available cash to a beach-related investment. Given their particular situation, their analysis identifies two possibilities that seem to be logical. First, they could purchase a beach cottage and use it for both personal and rental purposes. Second, they could pool their money with Steve's brother and purchase several cottages. One of the cottages would be held for personal use, while the others would be held for rental use. Identify the tax issues facing Betty and Steve.

Problems

33. In 2004, Fred invested $50,000 in a general partnership. Fred's interest is not considered to be a passive activity. His share of the partnership losses was $35,000 in 2004 and $25,000 in 2005. How much can Fred deduct in 2004 and 2005?

Communications

34. In the current year, Bill Parker (54 Oak Drive, St. Paul, MN 55162) is considering making an investment of $60,000 in Best Choice Partnership. The prospectus provided by Bill's broker indicates that the partnership investment is not a passive activity and that Bill's share of the entity's loss in the current year will likely be $40,000, while his share of the partnership loss next year will probably be $25,000. Write a letter to Bill in which you indicate how the losses would be treated for tax purposes in the current and next years.

Decision Making

35. Amanda wishes to invest $40,000 in a relatively safe venture and has discovered two alternatives that would produce the following reportable ordinary income and loss over the next three years:

Year	Alternative 1 Income (Loss)	Alternative 2 Income (Loss)
1	($24,000)	($48,000)
2	(24,000)	32,000
3	72,000	40,000

She is interested in the after-tax effects of these alternatives over a three-year horizon. Assume that Amanda's investment portfolio produces sufficient passive income to offset any potential passive loss that may arise from these alternatives, that her cost of capital is 8% (the present value factors are 0.92593, 0.85734, and 0.79383), that she is in the 25% tax bracket, that each investment alternative possesses equal growth potential, and that each alternative exposes her to comparable financial risk. In addition, assume that in the loss years for each alternative, there is no cash flow from or to the investment (i.e., the loss is due to depreciation), while in those years when the income is positive, cash flows to Amanda equal the amount of the income. Based on these facts, compute the present value of these two investment alternatives and determine which option Amanda should choose.

36. Dorothy acquired passive Activity A in January 2000 and Activity B in September 2001. Through 2003, Activity A was profitable, but it produced losses of $200,000 in 2004 and $100,000 in 2005. Dorothy has passive income from Activity B of $20,000 in 2004 and $40,000 in 2005. After offsetting passive income, how much of the net losses may she deduct?

37. In 2000, Russell acquired an interest in a partnership in which he is not a material participant. The partnership was profitable through 2003, and Russell's basis in his partnership interest at the beginning of 2004 was $40,000. In 2004, Russell's share of the partnership loss was $35,000, and in 2005, his share of the partnership income is $15,000. How much can Russell deduct for 2004 and 2005?

38. Bob, an attorney, earns $200,000 from his law practice in the current year. He receives $45,000 in dividends and interest during the year. In addition, he incurs a loss of $50,000 from an investment in a passive activity acquired three years ago. What is Bob's net income for the current year after considering the passive investment?

Decision Making

39. Emily has $100,000 that she wishes to invest and is considering the following two options:

- Option A: Investment in Redbird Mutual Fund, which is expected to produce interest income of $8,000 per year.

- Option B: Investment in Cardinal Limited Partnership (buys, sells, and operates wine vineyards). Emily's share of the partnership's ordinary income and loss over the next three years would be:

Year	Income (Loss)
1	($ 8,000)
2	(2,000)
3	34,000

Emily is interested in the after-tax effects of these alternatives over a three-year horizon. Assume that Emily's investment portfolio produces ample passive income to offset any passive losses that may be generated. Her cost of capital is 8% (the present value factors are 0.92593, 0.85734, and 0.79383), and she is in the 28% tax bracket. The two investment alternatives possess equal growth potential and comparable financial risk. Based on these facts, compute the present value of these two investment alternatives and determine which option Emily should choose.

40. Ray acquired an activity several years ago, and in 2005, it generated a loss of $50,000. Ray has AGI of $140,000 before considering the loss from the activity. If the activity is a bakery and Ray is not a material participant, what is his AGI?

Decision Making

41. Wade owns two passive investments, Activity A and Activity B. He plans to dispose of Activity A, either in the current year or next year. Celene has offered to buy Activity A this year for an amount that would produce a taxable passive gain to Wade of $100,000. However, if the sale, for whatever reason, is not made to Celene, Wade feels that he could find a buyer who would pay about $5,000 less than Celene. Passive losses and gains generated (and expected to be generated) by Activity B follow:

Two years ago	($35,000)
Last year	(35,000)
This year	(5,000)
Next year	(20,000)
Future years	Minimal profits

All of Activity B's losses are suspended. Should Wade close the sale of Activity A with Celene this year, or should he wait until next year and sell to another buyer? Wade is in the 35% tax bracket.

42. Rachel sells rental property with an adjusted basis of $75,000 for $125,000, its fair market value. Associated with this investment are suspended losses that have not been deducted in prior years. The anticipated tax loss from the property in the current year is expected to be $4,000. What is the current taxable gain or deductible loss on the sale of the rental property if the suspended losses from prior years total:
    a. $35,000?
    b. $60,000?

43. Saundra has investments in four passive activity partnerships purchased several years ago. Last year, the income and losses were as follows:

Activity	Income (Loss)
A	$ 10,000
B	(5,000)
C	(25,000)
D	(20,000)

In the current year, she sold her interest in Activity D for a $19,000 gain. Activity D, which had been profitable until last year, had a current loss of $1,000. How will the sale of Activity D affect Saundra's taxable income in the current year?

44. Brown Corporation, a personal service corporation, earns active income of $200,000 in the current year. The corporation receives $60,000 in dividends during the year. In addition, Brown incurs a loss of $45,000 from an investment in a passive activity acquired three years ago. What is Brown's income for the current year after considering the passive investment?

45. White, Inc., earns $400,000 from operations in the current year. White also receives $36,000 in dividends and interest on various portfolio investments. During the year, White pays $150,000 to acquire a 20% interest in a passive activity that produces a $200,000 loss. How will these facts affect White's taxable income, assuming the corporation is:
   a. A personal service corporation?
   b. A closely held (non-personal service) C corporation?

Decision Making
Communications

46. Greg Horne (431 Maple Avenue, Cincinnati, OH 45229), a syndicated radio talk show host, earns an annual salary of $400,000. He works approximately 30 hours per week in this job, which leaves him time to participate in several businesses newly acquired in 2005. He owns a movie theater and a drugstore in Cincinnati, a movie theater and a drugstore in Indianapolis, and a drugstore in Louisville. A preliminary analysis on December 1, 2005, shows the following projected income and losses and time spent for these various businesses:

	Income (Loss)
Cincinnati movie theater (95 hours participation)	$56,000
Cincinnati drugstore (140 hours participation)	(89,000)
Indianapolis movie theater (90 hours participation)	34,000
Indianapolis drugstore (170 hours participation)	(41,000)
Louisville drugstore (180 hours participation)	(15,000)

Greg has full-time employees in each of the five businesses. Write a letter to Greg suggesting a grouping method and other strategies that will provide the greatest tax advantage. As Greg is not knowledgeable about tax law, provide a nontechnical explanation.

Decision Making

47. Last year, Juan, a real estate developer, purchased 25 acres of farmland on the outskirts of town for $100,000. He expects that the land's value will appreciate rapidly as the town expands in that direction. Since the property was recently reappraised at $115,000, some of the appreciation has already taken place. To enhance his return from the investment, Juan decides he will begin renting the land to a local farmer. He has determined that a fair rent would be at least $1,500 but no more than $3,500 per year. Juan also has an interest in a passive activity that generates a $2,800 loss annually. How do the passive loss rules affect Juan's decision on how much rent to charge for the farmland?

Decision Making

48. The end of the year is approaching, and Maxine has begun to focus on ways of minimizing her income tax liability. Several years ago, she purchased an investment in Teal Limited Partnership, which is subject to both the at-risk and the passive activity loss rules. (Last year, Maxine sold a different investment that was subject to these rules but produced passive income.) She believes that her investment in Teal has good long-term

economic prospects. However, it has been generating tax losses for several years in a row. In fact, when she was discussing last year's income tax return with her tax accountant, he said that unless "things change" with respect to her investments, she would not be able to deduct losses this year.

a. What was the accountant referring to in his comment?
b. You learn that Maxine's current at-risk basis in her investment is $1,000 and her share of the current loss is expected to be $13,000. Based on these facts, how will her loss be treated?
c. After reviewing her situation, Maxine's financial adviser suggests that she invest at least an additional $12,000 in Teal in order to ensure a full loss deduction in the current year. How do you react to his suggestion?
d. What would you suggest Maxine consider as she attempts to maximize her current-year deductible loss?

49. A number of years ago, Lee acquired a 20% interest in the BlueSky Partnership for $60,000. The partnership was profitable through 2004, and Lee's amount at risk in the partnership interest was $120,000 at the beginning of 2005. BlueSky incurred a loss of $400,000 in 2005 and reported income of $200,000 in 2006. Assuming Lee is not a material participant, how much of his loss from BlueSky Partnership is deductible in 2005 and 2006?

50. Last year, Fran invested $40,000 for an interest in a partnership in which she is a material participant. Her share of the partnership's loss for the year was $50,000. In the current year, Fran's share of the partnership's income is $30,000. What is the effect on her taxable income for the current year?

51. Jonathan, a physician, earns $200,000 from his practice. He also receives $18,000 in dividends and interest on various portfolio investments. During the year, he pays $45,000 to acquire a 20% interest in a partnership that produces a $300,000 loss.
a. Compute Jonathan's AGI, assuming he does not participate in the operations of the partnership.
b. Compute Jonathan's AGI, assuming he is a material participant in the operations of the partnership.

52. Five years ago, Gerald invested $150,000 in a passive activity, his sole investment venture. On January 1, 2004, his amount at risk in the activity was $30,000. His shares of the income and losses were as follows:

Year	Income (Loss)
2004	($40,000)
2005	(30,000)
2006	50,000

How much can Gerald deduct in 2004 and 2005? What is his taxable income from the activity in 2006? Consider the at-risk rules as well as the passive loss rules.

53. Beth acquired an activity four years ago. The loss from the activity is $35,000 in the current year. She has AGI of $120,000 before considering the loss from the activity. The activity is an apartment building, and Beth is not an active participant. What is her AGI after considering the activity?

54. During the year, Roger performs personal services in three separate activities: 800 hours as a CPA in his tax practice, 400 hours in a real estate development business (i.e., not a material participant), and 600 hours in an apartment leasing operation. He expects that losses will be realized from the two real estate ventures while his tax practice will show a profit. Roger files a joint return with his wife who has salary income of $200,000. What is the character of the income and losses generated by these activities?

Decision Making

55. Ruth and Mike are married with no dependents and live in Vermont (not a community property state). Since Ruth has large medical expenses, they seek your advice about filing separately to save taxes. Their income and expenses for 2005 are as follows:

Ruth's salary	$ 30,000
Mike's salary	50,000
Interest income (joint)	1,800
Rental loss from actively managed rental property	(20,000)
Ruth's unreimbursed medical expenses	6,500
All other itemized deductions:*	
Ruth	2,000
Mike	8,000

*None subject to limitations.

Determine whether Ruth and Mike should file jointly or separately for 2005.

Decision Making

56. Mary and Charles have owned a beach cottage on the New Jersey shore for several years and have always used it as a family retreat. When they acquired the property, they had no intentions of renting it. Because family circumstances have changed, they are considering using the cottage for only two weeks a year and renting it for the remainder of the year. Their AGI approximates $80,000 per year, and they are in the 36% tax bracket (combined Federal and state). Interest and real estate taxes total $8,000 per year and are expected to continue at this level in the foreseeable future. If Mary and Charles rent the property, their *incremental* revenue and expenses are projected to be:

Rent income	$ 20,000
Rental commissions	(3,000)
Maintenance expenses	(12,000)
Depreciation expense	(10,000)

If the cottage is converted to rental property, they plan to be actively involved in key rental and maintenance decisions. Given the tax effects of converting the property to rental use, would the cash flow from renting the property be enough to meet the $12,000 annual mortgage payment?

57. During the current year, Gene performs services as follows: 1,800 hours as a CPA in his tax practice and 50 hours in an apartment leasing operation in which he has a 15% interest. Because of his oversight duties, Gene is considered to be an active participant. He expects that his share of the loss realized from the apartment leasing operation will be $30,000 while his tax practice will show a profit of approximately $80,000. Gene is single and has no other income besides that stated above. Discuss the character of the income and losses generated by these activities.

58. Ida, who has AGI of $80,000 before considering rental activities, is active in three separate real estate rental activities and is in the 28% tax bracket. She has $12,000 of losses from Activity A, $18,000 of losses from Activity B, and income of $10,000 from Activity C. She also has $2,100 of tax credits from Activity A. Calculate her deductions and credits allowed and the suspended losses and credits.

59. Ella has $105,000 of losses from a real estate rental activity in which she actively participates. She has other rental income of $25,000 and other passive income of $32,000. How much rental loss can Ella deduct against active and portfolio income (ignoring the at-risk rules)? Does she have any suspended losses to carry over?

60. Faye dies owning an interest in a passive activity property with an adjusted basis of $240,000, suspended losses of $42,000, and a fair market value of $270,000. What can be deducted on her final income tax return?

61. In the current year, Leon gives an interest in a passive activity to his daughter, Lucy. The value of the interest at the date of the gift is $25,000, and its adjusted basis to Leon is $13,000. During the time that Leon owned the investment, losses of $3,000 were not deductible because of the passive loss limitations. What is the tax treatment of the suspended passive activity losses to Leon and Lucy?

62. Tonya sells a passive activity in the current year for $150,000. Her adjusted basis in the activity is $50,000, and she uses the installment method of reporting the gain. The activity has suspended losses of $12,000. Tonya receives $60,000 in the year of sale. What is her gain? How much of the suspended losses can she deduct?

Research Problems

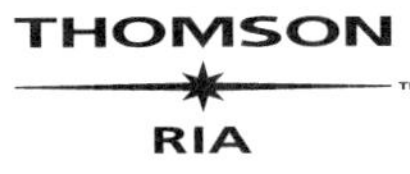

Note: Solutions to Research Problems can be prepared by using the ***RIA Checkpoint® Student Edition*** *online research product, which is available to accompany this text. It is also possible to prepare solutions to the Research Problems by using tax research materials found in a standard tax library.*

Research Problem 1. George and Judy Cash own a 30-foot yacht that is moored at Oregon Inlet on the Outer Banks of North Carolina. The yacht is offered for rent to tourists during March through November every year. George and Judy live too far away to be involved in the yacht's routine operation and maintenance. They are, however, able to perform certain periodic tasks, such as cleaning and winterizing it. Routine daily management, operating, and chartering responsibilities have been contracted to "Captain Mac." George and Judy are able to document spending 120 hours on the yacht chartering activities during the year. Determine how any losses resulting from the activity are treated under the passive activity loss rules.

Decision Making
Communications

Research Problem 2. Over the years, Julie LeDuc (117 Western Avenue, Peoria, IL 61604) has taken great pride in her ability to spot exceptional rental real estate investments, particularly in terms of their appreciation potential. As a result, she has accumulated several properties. In the past, she was able to devote only a limited amount of time to these ventures. In the current year, however, she retires from her full-time job and devotes most of her time to the management and operation of the rental activities. The relevant tax attributes of each of Julie's properties are as follows:

Property	Suspended Passive Losses	Expected Current Year's Income (Loss)
A	None	$ 25,000
B	($20,000)	15,000
C	(40,000)	(15,000)

Julie is astute enough to know that she is a qualifying real estate professional for the current year and materially participates in all three properties within the meaning of § 469(c)(7). However, she is uncertain whether she should treat the properties as three separate activities or aggregate them as one activity.

Write a letter to Julie to assist her in making the decision. Because of Julie's expertise in the tax law, feel free to use technical language in your letter.

Partial list of research aids:
Reg. § 1.469–9(e).

Internet Activity

Use the tax resources of the Internet to address the following question. Do not restrict your search to the World Wide Web, but include a review of newsgroups and general reference materials, practitioner sites and resources, primary sources of the tax law, chat rooms and discussion groups, and other opportunities.

Research Problem 3. Scan the materials offered in several newsgroups frequented by tax advisers and consultants. In what context are "tax shelters" still discussed by these professionals? Do these advisers and consultants adequately take into account the rules of §§ 465 and 469?

Tax Credits

CHAPTER 12

LEARNING OBJECTIVES

After completing Chapter 12, you should be able to:

LO.1

Explain how tax credits are used as a tool of Federal tax policy.

LO.2

Distinguish between refundable and nonrefundable credits and understand the order in which they can be used by taxpayers.

LO.3

Describe various business-related tax credits.

LO.4

Describe various tax credits that are available primarily to individual taxpayers.

LO.5

Identify tax planning opportunities related to tax credits.

http://wft.swlearning.com

OUTLINE

As explained in Chapter 1, Federal tax law often serves other purposes besides merely raising revenue for the government. Evidence of equity, social, and economic considerations, among others, is found throughout the tax law. These considerations also bear heavily in the area of **tax credits.** Consider the following examples:

EXAMPLE 1

Paul and Peggy, husband and wife, are both employed outside the home. Their combined salaries are $50,000. However, after paying for child care expenses of $2,000 on behalf of their daughter, Polly, the net economic benefit from both spouses working is $48,000. The child care expenses are, in a sense, business related since they would not have been incurred if both spouses did not work outside the home. If no tax benefits are associated with the child care expenditures, $50,000 is subject to tax.

Another couple, Alicia and Diego, also have a child, John. Diego stays at home to care for John (the value of those services is $2,000) while Alicia earns a $48,000 salary. Because the value of Diego's services rendered is not subject to tax, only Alicia's earnings of $48,000 are subject to tax. ■

The credit for child and dependent care expenses mitigates the inequity felt by working taxpayers who must pay for child care services in order to work outside the home.

EXAMPLE 2

Graham, age 66, is a retired taxpayer who receives $14,000 of Social Security benefits as his only source of income in 2005. His Social Security benefits are excluded from gross income. Therefore, Graham's income tax is $0. In 2005, Olga, a single taxpayer 66 years of age, has, as her sole source of income, $14,000 from a pension plan funded by her former employer. Assuming Olga has no itemized deductions or deductions *for* AGI, her income tax for 2005 (before credits) is $455, based on the following computation:

Pension plan benefits	$14,000
Less: Basic standard deduction	(5,000)
Additional standard deduction	(1,250)
Personal exemption	(3,200)
Taxable income	$ 4,550
Income tax (at 10%)	$ 455

The tax credit for elderly or disabled taxpayers was enacted to mitigate this inequity.

EXAMPLE 3

Jane is a single parent who depends on the government's "safety net" for survival—she receives benefits under the Temporary Assistance to Needy Families program in the amount of $15,000 per year. However, she very much wishes to work. Jane has located a job that will pay $15,500 per year and has found an individual to care for her child at no cost. But, with the $1,185.75 ($15,500 × 7.65%) withholding for Social Security and Medicare taxes, the economic benefit from working is less than remaining reliant on the government ($14,314.25 as compared to $15,000).

To help offset the effect of Social Security and Medicare taxes on wages of the working poor and to provide an incentive to work, the earned income credit is used to increase the after-tax earnings of qualified individuals. In addition, the earned income credit helps offset the regressive nature of certain taxes, such as the Social Security and Medicare taxes, which impose a relatively larger burden on low-income taxpayers than on more affluent taxpayers.

These three tax credits and many of the other important tax credits available to individuals and other types of taxpayers are a major focus of this chapter. The chapter begins by discussing important tax policy considerations relevant to tax credits. Tax credits are categorized as being either refundable or nonrefundable. The distinction between refundable and nonrefundable credits is important because it may affect the taxpayer's ability to enjoy a tax benefit from a particular credit.

Next an overview of the priority of tax credits is presented. The chapter continues with a discussion of the credits available to businesses and to individual taxpayers and the ways in which credits enter into the calculation of the tax liability.

LO.1

Explain how tax credits are used as a tool of Federal tax policy.

Tax Policy Considerations

Congress has generally used tax credits to achieve social or economic objectives or to promote equity among different types of taxpayers. For example, the disabled access credit was enacted to accomplish a social objective: to encourage taxpayers to renovate older buildings so they would be in compliance with the Americans with Disabilities Act. This Act requires businesses and institutions to make their facilities more accessible to persons with various types of disabilities. As another example, the foreign tax credit, which has been a part of the law for decades, has as its purpose the economic and equity objectives of mitigating the burden of multiple taxation on a single stream of income.

A tax credit should not be confused with an income tax deduction. Certain expenditures of individuals (e.g., business expenses) are permitted as deductions from gross income in arriving at adjusted gross income (AGI). Additionally, individuals are allowed to deduct certain nonbusiness and investment-related expenses *from* AGI. While the tax benefit received from a tax deduction depends on the tax rate, a tax credit is not affected by the tax rate of the taxpayer.

EXAMPLE 4

Assume Congress wishes to encourage a certain type of expenditure. One way to accomplish this objective is to allow a tax credit of 25% for such expenditures. Another way is to allow an itemized deduction for the expenditures. Assume that Abby's tax rate is 15%, while Bill's tax rate is 35%, and that each itemizes deductions. In addition, assume that Carmen does not incur enough qualifying expenditures to itemize deductions. The following tax benefits are available to each taxpayer for a $1,000 expenditure:

	Abby	Bill	Carmen
Tax benefit if a 25% credit is allowed	$250	$250	$250
Tax benefit if an itemized deduction is allowed	150	350	–0–

As these results indicate, tax credits provide benefits on a more equitable basis than do tax deductions. Equally apparent is that the deduction approach in this case benefits only taxpayers who itemize deductions, while the credit approach benefits all taxpayers who make the specified expenditure. ■

For many years, Congress has used the tax credit provisions of the Code liberally in implementing tax policy. Although budget constraints and economic considerations often have dictated the repeal of some credits, other credits, such as those applicable to expenses incurred for child and dependent care, have been kept to respond to important social policy considerations. Still other credits, such as the one available to low-income workers, have been retained based on economic and equity considerations. Finally, as the myriad of tax proposals so frequently pending before Congress makes clear, the use of tax credits as a tax policy tool continues to evolve as economic and political circumstances change.

LO.2

Distinguish between refundable and nonrefundable credits and understand the order in which they can be used by taxpayers.

Overview and Priority of Credits

REFUNDABLE VERSUS NONREFUNDABLE CREDITS

As illustrated in Exhibit 12–1, certain credits are refundable while others are nonrefundable. **Refundable credits** are paid to the taxpayer even if the amount of the credit (or credits) exceeds the taxpayer's tax liability.

EXAMPLE 5

Ted, who is single, had taxable income of $21,000 in 2005. His income tax from the 2005 Tax Rate Schedule is $2,785. During 2005, Ted's employer withheld income tax of $3,200. Ted is entitled to a refund of $415 because the credit for tax withheld on wages is a refundable credit. ■

Nonrefundable credits are not paid if they exceed the taxpayer's tax liability.

EXAMPLE 6

Tina is single, age 67, and retired. Her taxable income for 2005 is $1,320, and the tax on this amount is $132. Tina's tax credit for the elderly is $225. This credit can be used to reduce her net tax liability to zero, but it will not result in a refund, even though the credit ($225) exceeds Tina's tax liability ($132). This result occurs because the tax credit for the elderly is a nonrefundable credit. ■

Some nonrefundable credits, such as the foreign tax credit, are subject to carryover provisions if they exceed the amount allowable as a credit in a given year. Other nonrefundable credits, such as the tax credit for the elderly (refer to Example 6), are not subject to carryover provisions and are lost if they exceed the limitations.

EXHIBIT 12–1
Partial Listing of Refundable and Nonrefundable Credits

Refundable Credits

Taxes withheld on wages
Earned income credit

Nonrefundable Credits

Credit for child and dependent care expenses
Credit for elderly or disabled
Adoption expenses credit
Child tax credit*
Education tax credits
Credit for certain retirement plan contributions
Foreign tax credit
General business credit, which is the sum of the following:

- Tax credit for rehabilitation expenditures
- Work opportunity tax credit**
- Welfare-to-work credit**
- Research activities credit***
- Low-income housing credit
- Disabled access credit
- Credit for small employer pension plan startup costs
- Credit for employer-provided child care

*The credit is refundable to the extent of 15 percent of the taxpayer's earned income in excess of $11,000 for 2005 (indexed for inflation). Parents with three or more qualifying children may compute the refundable portion using an alternative method.
**Not available for employees hired after December 31, 2005.
***Scheduled to expire after December 31, 2005.

Because some credits are refundable and others are not and because some credits are subject to carryover provisions while others are not, the order in which credits are offset against the tax liability can be important.[1]

GENERAL BUSINESS CREDIT

As shown in Exhibit 12–1, the **general business credit** is composed of a number of other credits, each of which is computed separately under its own set of rules. The general business credit combines these credits into one amount to limit the amount of business credits that can be used to offset a taxpayer's income tax liability. The idea behind combining the credits is to prevent a taxpayer from completely avoiding an income tax liability in any one year by offsetting it with business credits that would otherwise be available.

[1]With the passage of the Tax Relief Reconciliation Act of 2001, the ordering rules and limitations applied when offsetting tax credits against both the regular income tax liability and the alternative minimum tax liability have become increasingly complex. In addition, different variations of these rules will apply over time as this legislation is fully implemented. Further discussion of the intricacies of these rules is beyond the scope of this chapter.

Two special rules apply to the general business credit. First, any unused credit must be carried back 1 year, then forward 20 years. Second, for any tax year, the general business credit is limited to the taxpayer's *net income tax* reduced by the greater of:[2]

- The *tentative minimum tax.*
- 25 percent of *net regular tax liability* that exceeds $25,000.[3]

In order to understand the general business credit limitation, several terms need defining:

- *Net income tax* is the sum of the regular tax liability and the alternative minimum tax reduced by certain nonrefundable tax credits.
- *Tentative minimum tax* for this purpose is reduced by the foreign tax credit allowed.
- *Regular tax liability* is determined from the appropriate tax table or tax rate schedule, based on taxable income. However, the regular tax liability does not include certain taxes (e.g., alternative minimum tax).
- *Net regular tax liability* is the regular tax liability reduced by certain nonrefundable credits (e.g., credit for child and dependent care expenses, foreign tax credit).

EXAMPLE 7

Floyd's general business credit for the current year is $70,000. His net income tax is $150,000, tentative minimum tax is $130,000, and net regular tax liability is $150,000. He has no other tax credits. Floyd's general business credit allowed for the tax year is computed as follows:

Net income tax	$ 150,000
Less: The greater of	
• $130,000 (tentative minimum tax)	
• $31,250 [25% × ($150,000 – $25,000)]	(130,000)
Amount of general business credit allowed for tax year	$ 20,000

Floyd then has $50,000 ($70,000 – $20,000) of unused general business credits that may be carried back or forward as discussed below. ■

TREATMENT OF UNUSED GENERAL BUSINESS CREDITS

Unused general business credits are initially carried back one year and are applied to reduce the tax liability during that year. Thus, the taxpayer may receive a tax refund as a result of the carryback. Any remaining unused credits are then carried forward 20 years.[4]

A FIFO method is applied to the carrybacks, carryovers, and utilization of credits earned during a particular year. The oldest credits are used first in determining the amount of the general business credit. The FIFO method minimizes the potential for loss of a general business credit benefit due to the expiration of credit carryovers, since the earliest years are used before the current credit for the taxable year.

[2] § 38(c).

[3] This amount is $12,500 for married taxpayers filing separately unless one of the spouses is not entitled to the general business credit.

[4] § 39(a)(1).

EXAMPLE 8

This example illustrates the use of general business credit carryovers.

General business credit carryovers		
2002	$ 4,000	
2003	6,000	
2004	2,000	
Total carryovers	$12,000	
2005 general business credit		$ 40,000
Total credit allowed in 2005 (based on tax liability)	$50,000	
Less: Utilization of carryovers		
2002	(4,000)	
2003	(6,000)	
2004	(2,000)	
Remaining credit allowed in 2005	$38,000	
Applied against		
2005 general business credit		(38,000)
2005 unused amount carried forward to 2006		$ 2,000

■

LO.3

Describe various business-related tax credits.

Specific Business-Related Tax Credit Provisions

Each component of the general business credit is determined separately under its own set of rules. The components are explained here in the order listed in Exhibit 12–1.

TAX CREDIT FOR REHABILITATION EXPENDITURES

Taxpayers are allowed a tax credit for expenditures incurred to rehabilitate industrial and commercial buildings and certified historic structures. The **rehabilitation expenditures credit** is intended to discourage businesses from moving from older, economically distressed areas (e.g., inner cities) to newer locations and to encourage the preservation of historic structures. The current operating features of this credit follow:[5]

Rate of the Credit for Rehabilitation Expenses	Nature of the Property
10%	Nonresidential buildings and residential rental property, other than certified historic structures, originally placed in service before 1936
20%	Nonresidential and residential certified historic structures

When taking the credit, the basis of a rehabilitated building must be reduced by the full rehabilitation credit allowed.[6]

EXAMPLE 9

Juan spent $60,000 to rehabilitate a building (adjusted basis of $40,000) that had originally been placed in service in 1932. He is allowed a $6,000 (10% × $60,000) credit for rehabilitation expenditures. Juan then increases the basis of the building by $54,000 [$60,000 (rehabilitation

[5] § 47.

[6] § 50(c).

TABLE 12–1
Recapture Calculation for Rehabilitation Expenditures Credit

If the Property Is Held for	The Recapture Percentage Is
Less than 1 year	100
One year or more but less than 2 years	80
Two years or more but less than 3 years	60
Three years or more but less than 4 years	40
Four years or more but less than 5 years	20
Five years or more	0

expenditures) – $6,000 (credit allowed)]. If the building were a historic structure, the credit allowed would be $12,000 (20% × $60,000), and the building's depreciable basis would increase by $48,000 [$60,000 (rehabilitation expenditures) – $12,000 (credit allowed)]. ■

To qualify for the credit, buildings must be substantially rehabilitated. A building has been *substantially rehabilitated* if qualified rehabilitation expenditures exceed the greater of:

- The adjusted basis of the property before the rehabilitation expenditures, or
- $5,000.

Qualified rehabilitation expenditures do not include the cost of acquiring a building, the cost of facilities related to a building (such as a parking lot), and the cost of enlarging an existing building.

Recapture of Tax Credit for Rehabilitation Expenditures. The rehabilitation credit taken must be recaptured if the rehabilitated property is disposed of prematurely or if it ceases to be qualifying property. The **rehabilitation expenditures credit recapture** is based on a holding period requirement of five years and is added to the taxpayer's regular tax liability in the recapture year. The recapture amount is also *added* to the adjusted basis of the rehabilitation expenditures for purposes of determining the amount of gain or loss realized on the property's disposition.

The portion of the credit recaptured is a specified percentage of the credit that was taken by the taxpayer. This percentage is based on the period the property was held by the taxpayer, as shown in Table 12–1.

EXAMPLE 10

On March 15, 2002, Rashad placed in service $30,000 of rehabilitation expenditures on a building qualifying for the 10% credit. A credit of $3,000 ($30,000 × 10%) was allowed, and the basis of the building was increased by $27,000 ($30,000 – $3,000). The building was sold on December 15, 2005. Rashad must recapture a portion of the rehabilitation credit based on the schedule in Table 12–1. Because he held the rehabilitated property for more than three years but less than four, 40% of the credit, or $1,200, is added to his 2005 tax liability. Also, the adjusted basis of the rehabilitation expenditures is increased by the $1,200 recapture amount. ■

WORK OPPORTUNITY TAX CREDIT

The **work opportunity tax credit** was enacted to encourage employers to hire individuals from one or more of a number of targeted and economically disadvantaged groups who start work by December 31, 2005.[7] Examples of such targeted persons include qualified ex-felons, high-risk youths, food stamp recipients, veterans, summer youth employees, and persons receiving certain welfare benefits.

[7] § 51.

Computation of the Work Opportunity Tax Credit: General. The credit generally is equal to 40 percent of the first $6,000 of wages (per eligible employee) for the first 12 months of employment. Thus, the credit is not available for any wages paid to an employee after the *first year* of employment. If the employee's first year overlaps two of the employer's tax years, however, the employer may take the credit over two tax years. If the credit is elected, the employer's tax deduction for wages is reduced by the amount of the credit.

For an employer to qualify for the 40 percent credit, the employee must (1) be certified by a designated local agency as being a member of one of the targeted groups and (2) have completed at least 400 hours of service to the employer. If an employee meets the first condition but not the second, the credit rate is reduced to 25 percent provided the employee has completed a minimum of 120 hours of service to the employer.

EXAMPLE 11

In January 2005, Green Company hires four individuals who are certified to be members of a qualifying targeted group. Each employee works 800 hours and is paid wages of $8,000 during the year. Green Company's work opportunity credit is $9,600 [($6,000 × 40%) × 4 employees]. If the tax credit is taken, Green must reduce its deduction for wages paid by $9,600. No credit is available for wages paid to these employees after their first year of employment. ■

EXAMPLE 12

On June 1, 2005, Maria, a calendar year taxpayer, hires Joe, a member of a targeted group, and obtains the required certification. During the last seven months of 2005, Joe is paid $3,500 for 500 hours of work. Maria is allowed a credit of $1,400 ($3,500 × 40%) for 2005. Joe continues to work for Maria in 2006 and is paid $7,000 through May 31, 2006. Because up to $6,000 of first-year wages are eligible for the credit, Maria is allowed a 40% credit on $2,500 [$6,000 – $3,500 (wages paid in 2005)] of wages paid in 2006, or $1,000 ($2,500 × 40%). None of Joe's wages paid after May 31, the end of the first year of employment, is eligible for the credit. Likewise, under current law, no credit is allowed for wages paid to persons newly hired after December 31, 2005. ■

Computation of the Work Opportunity Tax Credit: Qualified Summer Youth Employees. The credit for qualified summer youth employees is allowed on wages for services during any 90-day period between May 1 and September 15. The maximum wages eligible for the credit are $3,000 per summer youth employee. The credit rate is the same as that under the general provision for the work opportunity tax credit. If the employee continues employment after the 90-day period as a member of another targeted group, the amount of the wages eligible for the general work opportunity tax credit as a member of the new target group is reduced by the wages paid to the employee as a qualified summer youth employee.

A *qualified summer youth employee* must be age 16 or 17 on the hiring date. An additional requirement for qualifying is that the individual's principal place of abode must be within an empowerment zone or an enterprise community.

WELFARE-TO-WORK CREDIT

The **welfare-to-work credit**[8] is available to employers hiring individuals who have been long-term recipients of family assistance welfare benefits. In general, *long-term recipients* are those individuals who are certified by a designated local agency as being a member of a family receiving assistance under a public aid program for at least an 18-month period ending on the hiring date. Unlike the work opportunity credit, which applies only to first-year wages paid to qualified individuals, the

[8] § 51A.

welfare-to-work credit is available for qualified wages paid in the *first two years* of employment. If an employee's first and second work years overlap two or more of the employer's tax years, the employer may take the credit during the applicable tax years. If the welfare-to-work credit is taken, the employer's tax deduction for wages is reduced by the amount of the credit.

An employer is prohibited from taking both the work opportunity credit and the welfare-to-work credit for wages paid to a qualified employee in a given tax year. Currently, the welfare-to-work credit is not available for employees hired after December 31, 2005.

Maximum Credit. The credit is equal to 35 percent of the first $10,000 of qualified wages paid to an employee in the first year of employment, plus 50 percent of the first $10,000 of qualified wages paid in the second year of employment, resulting in a maximum credit per qualified employee of $8,500 [$3,500 (year 1) + $5,000 (year 2)]. The credit rate is higher for second-year wages to encourage employers to retain qualified individuals, thereby promoting the overall welfare-to-work goal.

EXAMPLE 13

In April 2005, Blue Company hired three individuals who are certified as long-term family assistance recipients. Each employee is paid $12,000 during 2005. Two of the three individuals continue to work for Blue Company in 2006, earning $9,000 each during the year. Blue Company's welfare-to-work credit is $10,500 [(35% × $10,000) × 3 employees] for 2005 and $9,000 [(50% × $9,000) × 2 employees] for 2006. ■

RESEARCH ACTIVITIES CREDIT

To encourage research and experimentation, usually described as research and development (R & D), a credit is allowed for certain qualifying expenditures paid or incurred not later than December 31, 2005. The **research activities credit** is the *sum* of two components: an incremental research activities credit and a basic research credit.[9]

Incremental Research Activities Credit. The incremental research activities credit is equal to 20 percent of the *excess* of qualified research expenses for the taxable year over the base amount.

In general, *research expenditures* qualify if the research relates to discovering technological information that is intended for use in the development of a new or improved business component of the taxpayer. Such expenses qualify fully if the research is performed in-house (by the taxpayer or employees). If the research is conducted by persons outside the taxpayer's business (under contract), only 65 percent of the amount paid qualifies for the credit.[10]

EXAMPLE 14

George incurs the following research expenditures during May 2005.

In-house wages, supplies, computer time	$50,000
Paid to Cutting Edge Scientific Foundation for research	30,000

George's qualified research expenditures are $69,500 [$50,000 + ($30,000 × 65%)]. ■

[9] § 41.

[10] § 41(b)(3)(A). In the case of payments to a qualified research consortium, 75% of the amount paid qualifies for the credit.

Beyond the general guidelines described above, the Code does not give specific examples of qualifying research. However, the credit is *not* allowed for research that falls into certain categories, including the following:[11]

- Research conducted after the beginning of commercial production of the business component.
- Surveys and studies such as market research, testing, and routine data collection.
- Research conducted *outside* the United States (other than research undertaken in Puerto Rico and possessions of the United States).
- Research in the social sciences, arts, or humanities.

Determining the *base amount* involves a relatively complex series of computations, meant to approximate recent historical levels of research activity by the taxpayer. Thus, the credit is allowed only for increases in research expenses. A discussion of these computations is beyond the scope of this presentation.

EXAMPLE 15

Jack, a calendar year taxpayer, incurs qualifying research expenditures of $200,000 during January 2005. Assuming the base amount is $100,000, the incremental research activities credit is $20,000 [($200,000 – $100,000) × 20%]. ■

Qualified research and experimentation expenditures are not only eligible for the 20 percent credit, but can also be *expensed* in the year incurred.[12] In this regard, a taxpayer has two choices:[13]

- Use the full credit and reduce the expense deduction for research expenses by 100 percent of the credit.
- Retain the full expense deduction and reduce the credit by the product of 100 percent of the credit times the maximum corporate tax rate (35 percent).

As an alternative to the expense deduction, the taxpayer may *capitalize* the research expenses and *amortize* them over 60 months or more. In this case, the amount capitalized and subject to amortization is reduced by the full amount of the credit *only* if the credit exceeds the amount allowable as a deduction.

EXAMPLE 16

Assume the same facts as in Example 15, which shows that the potential incremental research activities credit is $20,000. The expense that the taxpayer can deduct and the credit amount are as follows:

	Credit Amount	Deduction Amount
• Full credit and reduced deduction		
$20,000 – $0	$20,000	
$200,000 – $20,000		$180,000
• Reduced credit and full deduction		
$20,000 – [(1.00 × $20,000) × .35]	13,000	
$200,000 – $0		200,000
• Full credit and capitalize and elect to amortize costs over 60 months		
$20,000 – $0	20,000	
($200,000/60) × 12		40,000

■

[11] § 41(d). See also Reg. §§ 1.41–1 through 1.41–7.

[12] § 174. Also refer to the discussion of rules for deducting research and experimental expenditures in Chapter 7.

[13] § 280C(c).

Basic Research Credit. Corporations (other than S corporations or personal service corporations) are allowed an additional 20 percent credit for basic research payments made not later than December 31, 2005, in *excess* of a base amount. This credit is not available to individual taxpayers. *Basic research payments* are defined as amounts paid in cash to a qualified basic research organization, such as a college or university or a tax-exempt organization operated primarily to conduct scientific research.

Basic research is defined generally as any original investigation for the advancement of scientific knowledge not having a specific commercial objective. The definition excludes basic research conducted outside the United States and basic research in the social sciences, arts, or humanities. This reflects the intent of Congress to encourage high-tech research in the United States.

The calculation of this additional credit for basic research expenditures is complex and is based on expenditures in excess of a specially defined base amount.[14] The portion of the basic research expenditures not in excess of the base amount is treated as a part of the qualifying expenditures for purposes of the regular credit for incremental research activities.

EXAMPLE 17

In April 2005, Orange Corporation, a qualifying corporation, pays $75,000 to a university for basic research. Assume that Orange's base amount for the basic research credit is $50,000. The basic research activities credit allowed is $5,000 [($75,000 – $50,000) × 20%]. The $50,000 of basic research expenditures that equal the base amount are treated as research expenses for purposes of the regular incremental research activities credit. ■

LOW-INCOME HOUSING CREDIT

To encourage building owners to make affordable housing available for low-income individuals, Congress has made a credit available to owners of qualified low-income housing projects.[15]

More than any other, the **low-income housing credit** is influenced by nontax factors. For example, certification of the property by the appropriate state or local agency authorized to provide low-income housing credits is required. These credits are issued based on a nationwide allocation.

The amount of the credit is based on the qualified basis of the property. The qualified basis depends on the number of units rented to low-income tenants. Tenants are low-income tenants if their income does not exceed a specified percentage of the area median gross income. The amount of the credit is determined by multiplying the qualified basis by the applicable percentage. The credit is allowed over a 10-year period if the property continues to meet the required conditions.

EXAMPLE 18

Sarah spends $1 million to build a qualified low-income housing project completed January 1 of the current year. The entire project is rented to low-income families. Assume the credit rate for property placed in service during January is 7.96%.[16] Sarah may claim a credit of $79,600 ($1,000,000 × 7.96%) in the current year and in each of the following nine years. Generally, first-year credits are prorated based on the date the project is placed in service. A full year's credit is taken in each of the next nine years, and any remaining first-year credit is claimed in the eleventh year. ■

Recapture of a portion of the credit may be required if the number of units set aside for low-income tenants falls below a minimum threshold, if the taxpayer

[14] § 41(e).
[15] § 42.

[16] The rate is subject to adjustment every month by the IRS.

disposes of the property or the interest in it, or if the taxpayer's amount at risk decreases.

ETHICAL CONSIDERATIONS

A Win-Win Situation or an Incalculable Loss?

John and Susie rent a unit at an apartment complex owned by Mitch Brown, who has been Susie's friend since they attended business school together. One day Mitch told Susie about the thousands of tax dollars that he has saved by claiming the low-income housing credit for his investment in the apartment complex. Susie was pleased that Mitch had reduced his tax burden because she believes that the government rarely uses its resources wisely. Inadvertently, though, Mitch let the fact slip that the apartment complex "qualifies" for the credit only because he overstates the percentage of low-income tenants living in the facility. Mitch admitted that by claiming that John and Susie are low-income tenants (even though they aren't), the percentage of low-income tenants is just enough for Mitch to "qualify" for the credit. Mitch said that because John and Susie were his friends, he was passing along some of his tax savings to them in the form of lower rent.

John and Susie know that if they report Mitch to the IRS, he will not only lose the economic benefits of the credit, but will also have legal troubles. Further, if Mitch were to be sentenced to prison for the tax fraud, his children would probably become wards of the state. In addition, John and Susie would have to pay higher rent. What course of action would you recommend to John and Susie?

DISABLED ACCESS CREDIT

The **disabled access credit** is designed to encourage small businesses to make their facilities more accessible to disabled individuals. The credit is available for any eligible access expenditures paid or incurred by an eligible small business. The credit is calculated at the rate of 50 percent of the eligible expenditures that exceed $250 but do not exceed $10,250. Thus, the maximum amount for the credit is $5,000 ($10,000 × 50%).[17]

An *eligible small business* is one that during the previous year either had gross receipts of $1 million or less or had no more than 30 full-time employees. An eligible business can include a sole proprietorship, partnership, regular corporation, or S corporation.

Eligible access expenditures are generally any reasonable and necessary amounts that are paid or incurred to make certain changes to facilities. These changes must involve the removal of architectural, communication, physical, or transportation barriers that would otherwise make a business inaccessible to disabled and handicapped individuals. Examples of qualifying projects include installing ramps, widening doorways, and adding raised markings on elevator control buttons. However, eligible expenditures do *not* include amounts that are paid or incurred in connection with any facility that has been placed in service after the enactment of the credit (i.e., November 5, 1990).

To the extent a disabled access credit is available, no deduction or credit is allowed under any other provision of the tax law. The adjusted basis for depreciation is reduced by the amount of the credit.

EXAMPLE 19

This year Red, Inc., an eligible business, makes $11,000 of capital improvements to business realty that had been placed in service in June 1990. The expenditures are intended to make Red's business more accessible to the disabled and are considered eligible expenditures for

[17] § 44.

purposes of the disabled access credit. The amount of the credit is $5,000 [($10,250 – $250) × 50%]. Although $11,000 of eligible expenditures are incurred, only the excess of $10,250 over $250 qualifies for the credit. Further, the depreciable basis of the capital improvement is $6,000 because the basis must be reduced by the amount of the credit [$11,000 (cost) – $5,000 (amount of the credit)]. ■

CREDIT FOR SMALL EMPLOYER PENSION PLAN STARTUP COSTS

Small businesses are entitled to a nonrefundable credit for administrative costs associated with establishing and maintaining certain qualified retirement plans.[18] While such costs (e.g., payroll system changes, consulting fees) generally are deductible as ordinary and necessary business expenses, the credit is intended to lower the after-tax cost of establishing a qualified retirement program and thereby to encourage qualifying businesses to offer retirement plans for their employees. The **credit for small employer pension plan startup costs** is available for eligible employers at the rate of 50 percent of qualified startup costs. An eligible employer is one with fewer than 100 employees who have earned at least $5,000 of compensation. Qualified startup costs include ordinary and necessary expenses incurred in connection with establishing or maintaining an employer pension plan and retirement-related education costs.[19] The maximum credit is $500 (based on a maximum $1,000 of qualifying expenses), and the deduction for the startup costs incurred is reduced by the amount of the credit. The credit can be claimed for qualifying costs incurred in each of the three years beginning with the tax year in which the retirement plan becomes effective (maximum total credit over three years of $1,500).

EXAMPLE 20

Maple Company decides to establish a qualified retirement plan for its employees. In the process, it pays consulting fees of $1,200 to a firm that will provide educational seminars to Maple's employees and will assist the payroll department in making necessary changes to the payroll system. Maple may claim a credit for the pension plan startup costs of $500 ($1,200 of qualifying costs, limited to $1,000 × 50%), and its deduction for these expenses is reduced to $700 ($1,200 – $500). ■

CREDIT FOR EMPLOYER-PROVIDED CHILD CARE

The scope of § 162 trade or business expenses includes an employer's expenditures incurred to provide for the care of children of employees as ordinary and necessary business expenses. Another option now available permits employers to claim a credit for qualifying expenditures incurred while providing child care facilities to their employees during normal working hours.[20] The **credit for employer-provided child care,** limited annually to $150,000, is composed of the aggregate of two components: 25 percent of qualified child care expenses and 10 percent of qualified child care resource and referral services. *Qualified child care expenses* include the costs of acquiring, constructing, rehabilitating, expanding, and operating a child care facility. *Child care resource and referral services* include amounts paid or incurred under a contract to provide child care resource and referral services to an employee. To prevent an employer from obtaining a double benefit by claiming a credit and the associated deductions on the same expenditures, any qualifying expenses otherwise deductible by the taxpayer must be reduced

[18] § 45E. Currently, this credit is scheduled to expire for years after December 31, 2010.

[19] §§ 45E(c)(1) and (d)(1).

[20] § 45F. Currently, this credit is scheduled to expire for years after December 31, 2010.

by the amount of the credit. In addition, the taxpayer's basis for any property acquired or constructed and used for qualifying purposes is reduced by the amount of the credit. If within 10 years of being placed in service, a child care facility ceases to be used for a qualified use, the taxpayer will be required to recapture a portion of the credit previously claimed.[21]

EXAMPLE 21

During the year, Tan Company constructed a child care facility for $400,000 to be used by its employees who have preschool-aged children in need of child care services while their parents are at work. In addition, Tan incurred salaries for child care workers and other administrative costs associated with the facility of $100,000 during the year. As a result, Tan's credit for employer-provided child care is $125,000 [($400,000 + $100,000) × 25%]. Correspondingly, the basis of the facility is reduced to $300,000 ($400,000 – $100,000), and the deduction for salaries and administrative costs is reduced to $75,000 ($100,000 – $25,000). ■

LO.4

Describe various tax credits that are available primarily to individual taxpayers.

Other Tax Credits

EARNED INCOME CREDIT

The **earned income credit,** which has been a part of the law for many years, consistently has been justified as a means of providing tax equity to the working poor. In addition, the credit has been designed to help offset regressive taxes that are a part of our tax system, such as the gasoline and Social Security taxes. Further, the credit is intended to encourage economically disadvantaged individuals to become contributing members of the workforce.[22]

In 2005, the earned income credit is determined by multiplying a maximum amount of earned income by the appropriate credit percentage (see Table 12–2). Generally, earned income includes employee compensation and net earnings from self-employment but excludes items such as interest, dividends, pension benefits, nontaxable employee compensation, and alimony. If a taxpayer has children, the credit percentage used in the calculation depends on the number of qualifying children. Thus, in 2005, the maximum earned income credit for a taxpayer with one qualifying child is $2,662 ($7,830 × 34%) and $4,400 ($11,000 × 40%) for a taxpayer with two or more qualifying children. However, the maximum earned income credit is phased out completely if the taxpayer's earned income or AGI exceeds certain thresholds as shown in Table 12–2.[23] To the extent that the greater of earned income or AGI exceeds $16,370 in 2005 for married taxpayers filing a joint return ($14,370 for other taxpayers), the difference, multiplied by the appropriate phaseout percentage, is subtracted from the maximum earned income credit.

EXAMPLE 22

In 2005, Grace Brown, who is married, files a joint return and otherwise qualifies for the earned income credit. Grace receives wages of $25,000, and she and her husband have no other income. The Browns have one qualifying child. The current earned income credit is $2,662 ($7,830 × 34%) reduced by $1,379 [($25,000 – $16,370) × 15.98%]. Thus, the earned income credit is $1,283. If the Browns have two or more qualifying children, the calculation produces a credit of $4,400 ($11,000 × 40%) reduced by $1,817 [($25,000 – $16,370) × 21.06%]. Thus, the Brown's earned income credit is $2,583 if they have two or more children. ■

[21]§ 45F(d).

[22]§ 32. The earned income credit is not available if the taxpayer's unearned income (e.g., interest, dividends) exceeds $2,700 in 2005 ($2,650 in 2004). See § 32(i).

[23]§ 32(a)(2)(B).

■ TABLE 12–2
Earned Income Credit and Phaseout Percentages

Tax Year	Number of Qualifying Children	Maximum Earned Income	Credit Percentage	Phaseout Begins	Phaseout Percentage	Phaseout Ends
2005	*Married, Filing Joint:*					
	One child	$ 7,830	34.00	$16,370	15.98	$33,030
	Two or more children	11,000	40.00	16,370	21.06	37,263
	No qualifying children	5,220	7.65	8,530	7.65	13,750
	Other Taxpayers:					
	One child	$ 7,830	34.00	$14,370	15.98	$31,030
	Two or more children	11,000	40.00	14,370	21.06	35,263
	No qualifying children	5,220	7.65	6,530	7.65	11,750
2004	*Married, Filing Joint:*					
	One child	$ 7,660	34.00	$15,040	15.98	$31,338
	Two or more children	10,750	40.00	15,040	21.06	35,458
	No qualifying children	5,100	7.65	7,390	7.65	12,490
	Other Taxpayers:					
	One child	$ 7,660	34.00	$14,040	15.98	$30,338
	Two or more children	10,750	40.00	14,040	21.06	34,458
	No qualifying children	5,100	7.65	6,390	7.65	11,490

Earned Income Credit Table. It is not necessary to compute the credit as shown in Example 22. To simplify the compliance process, the IRS issues an Earned Income Credit Table for the determination of the appropriate amount of the credit. This table and a worksheet are included in the instructions available to individual taxpayers.

Eligibility Requirements. Eligibility for the credit may depend not only on the taxpayer meeting the earned income and AGI thresholds, but also on whether he or she has a qualifying child. The term *qualifying child* generally has the same meaning here as it does for purposes of determining who qualifies as a dependent (see Chapter 3).

ETHICAL CONSIDERATIONS

Snagging the Earned Income Credit with the Aid of a Transient Child

For many years, Loretta Johnson, a single mother of three children, has been struggling to make ends meet by working at two jobs that pay barely the minimum wage and together provide just over $15,000. Fortunately, her housing and food costs have been partially subsidized through various government programs. In addition, she has been able to take advantage of the earned income credit, which has provided around $3,000 annually to help her with living expenses. The credit has truly made a difference in the lives of Loretta and her family by helping them keep their creditors at bay. She is proud that she has worked hard and provided for her family for many years without having to accept welfare.

Now, however, Loretta faces a problem as her children have grown up and moved out of her home. With no qualified children in her household, she no longer qualifies for the earned income credit. Although she will continue working her two jobs, such a significant loss to her household budget cuts into her ability to be self-reliant. As a survival strategy and as a way of keeping the earned income credit, Loretta arranges to have one of her grandchildren live with her for just over six months every year. This enables a significant percentage of her household budget to be secure. How do you react to Loretta's strategy?

In addition to being available for taxpayers with qualifying children, the earned income credit is also available to certain *workers without children*. However, this provision is available only to taxpayers aged 25 through 64 who cannot be claimed as a dependent on another taxpayer's return. As shown in Table 12–2, the credit for 2005 is calculated on a maximum earned income of $5,220 times 7.65 percent and reduced by 7.65 percent of earned income over $8,530 for married taxpayers filing a joint return ($6,530 for other taxpayers).

EXAMPLE 23

Walt, who is single, 28 years of age, and is not claimed as a dependent on anyone else's return, earns $7,000 during 2005. Even though he does not have any qualifying children, he qualifies for the earned income credit. His credit is $399 ($5,220 × 7.65%) reduced by $36 [($7,000 – $6,530) × 7.65%]. Thus, Walt's earned income credit is $363. If, instead, Walt's earned income is $6,000, his earned income credit is $399. In this situation, there is no phaseout of the maximum credit because his earned income is not in excess of $6,530. ■

Advance Payment. The earned income credit is a form of negative income tax (a refundable credit for taxpayers who do not have a tax liability). An eligible individual may elect to receive advance payments of the earned income credit from his or her employer (rather than receiving the credit from the IRS upon filing the tax return). The amount that can be received in advance is limited to 60 percent of the credit that is available to a taxpayer with only one qualifying child. If this election is made, the taxpayer must file a certificate of eligibility (Form W–5) with his or her employer and *must* file a tax return for the year the income is earned.[24]

TAX CREDIT FOR ELDERLY OR DISABLED TAXPAYERS

The credit for the elderly was originally enacted to provide tax relief on retirement income for individuals who were not receiving substantial benefits from tax-free Social Security payments.[25] Currently, the **tax credit for the elderly or disabled** applies to the following:

- Taxpayers age 65 or older.
- Taxpayers under age 65 who are retired with a **permanent and total disability** and who have disability income from a public or private employer on account of the disability. A person generally is considered permanently and totally disabled if he or she is unable to engage in any substantial gainful activity due to a physical or mental impairment for a period of at least 12 months (or lesser period if the disability results in death).

The *maximum* allowable credit is $1,125 (15% × $7,500 of qualifying income), but the credit will be less for a taxpayer who receives Social Security benefits or has AGI exceeding specified amounts. Under these circumstances, the base used in the credit computation is reduced. Many taxpayers receive Social Security benefits or have AGI high enough to reduce the base for the credit to zero. In addition, because the credit is nonrefundable, the allowable credit cannot exceed the taxpayer's tax liability.

The eligibility requirements and the tax computation are somewhat complicated. Consequently, an individual may elect to have the IRS compute his or her tax and the amount of the tax credit.

The credit generally is based on an initial amount (referred to as the *base amount*) and the filing status of the taxpayer in accordance with Table 12–3. To qualify for the credit, married taxpayers who live together must file a joint return. For taxpayers under age 65 who are retired on permanent and total disability, the base amounts

[24] § 3507.

[25] § 22. This credit is not subject to indexation.

The Earned Income Credit: A Boost to the Working Poor and Merchants, Too!

Since 1975, the earned income credit has helped keep millions of Americans from falling below the poverty line. The tax benefits that go to over 20 million families represent one of the nation's biggest antipoverty efforts. However, these benefits don't come without problems: fraudulent claims are believed to be common (the IRS estimates that over 30 percent of the benefits are paid in error), and compliance requirements are dauntingly complex (the IRS instructions exceed 50 pages).

The benefits from the earned income credit that flow to the working poor have also led to another problem. Some merchants are targeting this group of taxpayers—and their refunds. Pawn shops, jewelers, and auto dealerships in poor neighborhoods often offer to prepare tax returns, hoping to benefit in three ways: they collect fees for preparing the returns, they offer bridge loans at exorbitant interest rates before a tax refund arrives, and they sell high-priced goods to individuals expecting a windfall from their tax refunds. Needless to say, some of these merchants provide fair and valuable assistance to many needy taxpayers; however, many other merchants are in this niche for the sole purpose of lining their own pockets. The caveat "buyer beware" could never be more appropriate.

could be less than those shown in Table 12–3 because these amounts are limited to taxable disability income.

This initial base amount is *reduced* by (1) Social Security, Railroad Retirement, and certain excluded pension benefits and (2) one-half of the taxpayer's AGI in excess of a threshold amount (see Table 12–3), which is a function of the taxpayer's filing status. The credit may be calculated using the procedure presented in the following example.

EXAMPLE 24

Paul and Peggy, husband and wife, are both over age 65 and receive Social Security benefits of $1,000 in the current year. On a joint return, they report AGI of $21,000.

Base amount (from Table 12–3)		$ 7,500
Less: Qualifying nontaxable benefits	$1,000	
One-half of excess of AGI over threshold amount from Table 12–3 [($21,000 – $10,000) × ½]	5,500	
Total reductions		(6,500)
Balance subject to credit		$ 1,000
Multiply balance subject to credit by 15%—this is the tax credit allowed, subject to tax liability limitation		$ 150

Schedule R of Form 1040 is used to calculate and report the credit.

TABLE 12–3
Base and Threshold Amounts for Tax Credit for Elderly or Disabled Taxpayers

Status	Base Amount	Threshold Amount
Single, head of household, or surviving spouse	$5,000	$ 7,500
Married, joint return, only one spouse qualifies	5,000	10,000
Married, joint return, both spouses qualify	7,500	10,000
Married, separate returns, spouses live apart the entire year (amount for each spouse)	3,750	5,000

FOREIGN TAX CREDIT

Both individual taxpayers and corporations may claim a tax credit for foreign income tax paid on income earned and subject to tax in another country or a U.S. possession.[26] As an alternative, a taxpayer may claim a deduction instead of a credit.[27] In most instances, the **foreign tax credit (FTC)** is advantageous since it provides a direct offset against the tax liability.

The purpose of the FTC is to mitigate double taxation since income earned in a foreign country is subject to both U.S. and foreign taxes. However, the ceiling limitation formula may result in some form of double taxation or taxation at rates in excess of U.S. rates when the foreign tax rates are higher than the U.S. rates. This is a distinct possibility because U.S. tax rates are often lower than those of many foreign countries.

Other special tax treatments applicable to taxpayers working outside the United States include the foreign earned income exclusion (refer to Chapter 5) and limitations on deducting expenses of employees working outside the United States (refer to Chapter 9). Recall from the earlier discussion that a taxpayer may not take advantage of *both* the FTC and the foreign earned income exclusion.

Computation. Taxpayers are required to compute the FTC based upon an overall limitation.[28] The FTC allowed is the *lesser* of the foreign taxes imposed or the *overall limitation* determined according to the following formula:

$$\frac{\text{Foreign-source taxable income}}{\text{Worldwide taxable income}} \times \text{U.S. tax before FTC}$$

For individual taxpayers, worldwide taxable income in the overall limitation formula is determined *before* personal and dependency exemptions are deducted.

EXAMPLE 25

In 2005, Carlos, a calendar year taxpayer, has $10,000 of income from Country Y, which imposes a 15% tax, and $20,000 from Country Z, which imposes a 50% tax. He has taxable income of $57,200 from within the United States, is married filing a joint return, and claims two dependency exemptions. Thus, although Carlos's taxable income for purposes of determining U.S. tax is $87,200, taxable income amounts used in the limitation formula are not reduced by personal and dependency exemptions. Thus, for this purpose, taxable income is $100,000 [$87,200 + (4 × $3,200)]. Assume that Carlos's U.S. tax before the credit is $15,130.
Overall limitation:

$$\frac{\text{Foreign-source taxable income}}{\text{Worldwide taxable income}} = \frac{\$30,000}{\$100,000} \times \$15,130 = \$4,539$$

In this case, $4,539 is allowed as the FTC because this amount is less than the $11,500 of foreign taxes imposed [$1,500 (Country Y) + $10,000 (Country Z)]. ■

Thus, the overall limitation may result in some of the foreign income being subjected to double taxation. Unused FTCs [e.g., the $6,961 ($11,500 – $4,539) from Example 25] can be carried back 1 year and forward 10 years.[29]

Only foreign income taxes, war profits taxes, and excess profits taxes (or taxes paid in lieu of such taxes) qualify for the credit.[30] In determining whether or not a tax is an income tax, U.S. criteria are applied. Thus, value added taxes (VAT), severance taxes, property taxes, and sales taxes do not qualify because they are not regarded as taxes on income. Such taxes may be deductible, however.

[26] Section 27 provides for the credit, but the qualifications and calculation procedure for the credit are contained in §§ 901–908.

[27] § 164.

[28] § 904.

[29] § 904(c) and Reg. § 1.904–2(g), Example 1. This treatment of unused FTCs applies to tax years ending after October 22, 2004. Prior law provided a two-year carryback and a five-year carryforward.

[30] Reg. § 1.901–1(a)(3)(i).

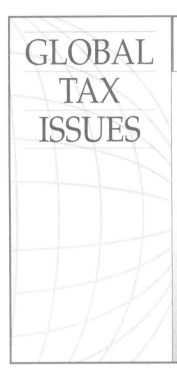

SOURCING INCOME IN CYBERSPACE—GETTING IT RIGHT WHEN CALCULATING THE FOREIGN TAX CREDIT

The overall limitation on the foreign tax credit (FTC) plays a critical role in restricting the amount of the credit available to a taxpayer. In the overall limitation formula, the taxpayer must characterize the year's taxable income as either earned (or sourced) inside the United States or earned from sources outside the United States. As a general rule, a relatively greater percentage of foreign-source income in the formula will lead to a larger FTC. Therefore, determining the source of various types of income is critical in the proper calculation of the credit. However, classifying income as either foreign or U.S. source is not always a simple matter.

For example, consumers and businesses are using the Internet to conduct more and more commerce involving both products and services. The problem is that the existing income-sourcing rules were developed long before the existence of the Internet, and taxing authorities are finding it challenging to apply these rules to Internet transactions. Where does a sale take place when the Web server is in Scotland, the seller is in India, and the customer is in Illinois? Where is a service performed when all activities take place over the Net? These questions and more will have to be answered by the United States and its trading partners as the Internet economy grows in size and importance.

ADOPTION EXPENSES CREDIT

Adoption expenses paid or incurred by a taxpayer may give rise to the **adoption expenses credit**.[31] The provision is intended to assist taxpayers who incur nonrecurring costs directly associated with the adoption process, such as adoption fees, attorney fees, court costs, social service review costs, and transportation costs.

In 2005, up to $10,630 of costs incurred to adopt an eligible child qualify for the credit.[32] An eligible child is one who is:

- under 18 years of age at the time of the adoption or
- physically or mentally incapable of taking care of himself or herself.

A taxpayer may claim the credit in the year qualifying expenses were paid or incurred if they were paid or incurred *during or after* the tax year in which the adoption was finalized. For qualifying expenses paid or incurred in a tax year *prior* to the year when the adoption was finalized, the credit must be claimed in the tax year following the tax year during which the expenses are paid or incurred. A married couple must file a joint return.

EXAMPLE 26

In late 2004, Sam and Martha pay $4,000 in legal fees, adoption fees, and other expenses directly related to the adoption of an infant daughter, Susan. In 2005, the year in which the adoption becomes final, they pay an additional $8,000. Sam and Martha are eligible for a $10,630 credit in 2005 (for expenses, limited by the $10,630 ceiling, paid in 2004 and 2005). ■

The amount of the credit that is otherwise available is phased out for taxpayers whose AGI (modified for this purpose) exceeds $159,450 in 2005, and the credit

[31] § 23.

[32] § 23(b)(1). In 2004, the maximum amount of eligible costs was $ 10,390. This ceiling is adjusted for inflation annually. Special rules are used in calculating the credit when adopting "a child with special needs." See § 23(d)(3).

is completely eliminated when the AGI reaches $199,450. The resulting credit is calculated by reducing the allowable credit (determined without this reduction) by the allowable credit multiplied by the ratio of the excess of the taxpayer's AGI over $159,450 to $40,000.[33]

EXAMPLE 27

Assume the same facts as in the previous example, except that Sam and Martha's AGI is $184,450 in 2005. As a result, their available credit in 2005 is reduced from $10,630 to $3,986 {$10,630 – [$10,630($25,000/$40,000)]}. ■

The credit is nonrefundable and is available to taxpayers only in a year in which this credit and the other nonrefundable credits do not exceed the taxpayer's tax liability. However, any unused adoption expenses credit may be carried over for up to five years, being utilized on a first-in, first-out basis.

CHILD TAX CREDIT

The **child tax credit** provisions allow individual taxpayers to take a tax credit based solely on the *number* of their qualifying children. This credit is one of several "family-friendly" provisions that currently are part of our tax law. To be eligible for the credit, the child must be under age 17, a U.S. citizen, and claimed as a dependent on the taxpayer's return.

Maximum Credit and Phaseouts. Under current law, the maximum credit available is $1,000 per child.[34] The available credit is phased out for higher-income taxpayers beginning when AGI reaches $110,000 for joint filers ($55,000 for married taxpayers filing separately) and $75,000 for single taxpayers. The credit is phased out by $50 for each $1,000 (or part thereof) of AGI above the threshold amounts.[35] Since the maximum credit amount available to taxpayers depends on the number of qualifying children, the income level at which the credit is phased out completely also depends on the number of children qualifying for the credit.

EXAMPLE 28

Juanita and Alberto are married and file a joint tax return claiming their two children, ages six and eight, as dependents. Their AGI is $122,400. Juanita and Alberto's available child tax credit is $1,350, computed as their maximum credit of $2,000 ($1,000 × 2 children) reduced by a $650 phaseout. Since Juanita and Alberto's AGI is in excess of the $110,000 threshold, the maximum credit must be reduced by $50 for every $1,000 (or part thereof) above the threshold amount {$50 × [($122,400 – $110,000)/$1,000]}. Thus, the credit reduction equals $650 [$50 × 13 (rounded from 12.4)]. Therefore, Juanita and Alberto's child tax credit is $1,350. ■

CREDIT FOR CHILD AND DEPENDENT CARE EXPENSES

A credit is allowed to taxpayers who incur employment-related expenses for child or dependent care.[36] The **credit for child and dependent care expenses** is a specified percentage of expenses incurred to enable the taxpayer to work or to seek employment. Expenses on which the credit for child and dependent care expenses is based are subject to limitations.

[33] § 23(b)(2). The AGI threshold amount is indexed for inflation. In 2004, the phaseout of the credit began when AGI exceeded $155,860.

[34] § 24. The maximum credit per child is scheduled to remain at $1,000 through 2010.

[35] AGI is modified for purposes of this calculation. The threshold amounts are *not* indexed for inflation. See §§ 24(a) and (b).

[36] § 21.

Eligibility. To be eligible for the credit, an individual must have either of the following:

- A dependent under age 13.
- A dependent or spouse who is physically or mentally incapacitated and who lives with the taxpayer for more than one-half of the year.

Generally, married taxpayers must file a joint return to obtain the credit.

Eligible Employment-Related Expenses. Eligible expenses include amounts paid for household services and care of a qualifying individual that are incurred to enable the taxpayer to be employed. Child and dependent care expenses include expenses incurred in the home, such as payments for a housekeeper. Out-of-the-home expenses incurred for the care of a dependent under the age of 13 also qualify for the credit. In addition, out-of-the-home expenses incurred for an older dependent or spouse who is physically or mentally incapacitated qualify for the credit if that person regularly spends at least eight hours each day in the taxpayer's household. This makes the credit available to taxpayers who keep handicapped older children and elderly relatives in the home instead of institutionalizing them. Out-of-the-home expenses incurred for services provided by a dependent care center will qualify only if the center complies with all applicable laws and regulations of a state or unit of local government.

Child care payments to a relative are eligible for the credit unless the relative is a child (under age 19) of the taxpayer.

EXAMPLE 29

Wilma is an employed mother of an eight-year-old child. She pays her mother, Rita, $1,500 per year to care for the child after school. Wilma pays her daughter Eleanor, age 17, $900 for the child's care during the summer. Of these amounts, only the $1,500 paid to Rita qualifies as employment-related child care expenses. ■

Earned Income Ceiling. The total for qualifying employment-related expenses is limited to an individual's earned income. For married taxpayers, this limitation applies to the spouse with the *lesser* amount of earned income. Special rules are provided for taxpayers with nonworking spouses who are disabled or are full-time students. If a nonworking spouse is physically or mentally disabled or is a full-time student, he or she is *deemed* to have earned income for purposes of this limitation. The deemed amount is $250 per month if there is one qualifying individual in the household or $500 per month if there are two or more qualifying individuals in the household. In the case of a student-spouse, the student's income is *deemed* to be earned only for the months that the student is enrolled on a full-time basis at an educational institution.[37]

Calculation of the Credit. In general, the credit is equal to a percentage of *unreimbursed* employment-related expenses up to $3,000 for one qualifying individual and $6,000 for two or more individuals. The credit rate varies between 20 percent and 35 percent, depending on the taxpayer's AGI. The following chart shows the applicable percentage for taxpayers as AGI increases:

[37] § 21(d).

Adjusted Gross Income		
Over	But Not Over	Applicable Rate of Credit
$ 0	$15,000	35%
15,000	17,000	34%
17,000	19,000	33%
19,000	21,000	32%
21,000	23,000	31%
23,000	25,000	30%
25,000	27,000	29%
27,000	29,000	28%
29,000	31,000	27%
31,000	33,000	26%
33,000	35,000	25%
35,000	37,000	24%
37,000	39,000	23%
39,000	41,000	22%
41,000	43,000	21%
43,000	No limit	20%

multiply this column by the actual cost you pay to child care

EXAMPLE 30

Nancy, who has two children under age 13, worked full-time while her spouse, Ron, was attending college for 10 months during the year. Nancy earned $22,000 and incurred $6,200 of child care expenses. Ron is *deemed* to be fully employed and to have earned $500 for each of the 10 months (or a total of $5,000). Since Nancy and Ron have AGI of $22,000, they are allowed a credit rate of 31%. Nancy and Ron are limited to $5,000 in qualified child care expenses (the lesser of $6,000 or $5,000). Therefore, they are entitled to a tax credit of $1,550 (31% × $5,000) for the year. ■

Dependent Care Assistance Program. Recall from Chapter 5 that a taxpayer is allowed an exclusion from gross income for a limited amount reimbursed for child or dependent care expenses. However, the taxpayer is not allowed both an exclusion from gross income and a child and dependent care credit on the same amount. The $3,000 and $6,000 ceilings for allowable child and dependent care expenses are reduced dollar for dollar by the amount of reimbursement.[38]

EXAMPLE 31

Assume the same facts as in Example 30, except that of the $6,200 paid for child care, Nancy was reimbursed $2,500 by her employer under a qualified dependent care assistance program. Under the employer's plan, the reimbursement reduces Nancy's taxable wages. Thus, Nancy and Ron have AGI of $19,500 ($22,000 – $2,500). The maximum amount of child care expenses for two or more dependents of $6,000 is reduced by the $2,500 reimbursement, resulting in a tax credit of $1,120 [32% × ($6,000 – $2,500)]. ■

Reporting Requirements. The credit is claimed by completing and filing Form 2441, Credit for Child and Dependent Care Expenses.

EDUCATION TAX CREDITS

Two credits, the **HOPE scholarship credit** and the **lifetime learning credit**,[39] are available to help qualifying low- and middle-income individuals defray the cost

[38] § 21(c).

[39] § 25A.

of higher education. The credits, both of which are nonrefundable, are available for qualifying tuition and related expenses incurred by students pursuing undergraduate or graduate degrees or vocational training. Room, board, and book costs are ineligible for the credits.

Maximum Credit. The HOPE scholarship credit permits a maximum credit of $1,500 per year (100 percent of the first $1,000 of tuition expenses plus 50 percent of the next $1,000 of tuition expenses) for the *first two years* of postsecondary education.[40] The lifetime learning credit permits a credit of 20 percent of qualifying expenses (up to $10,000 per year) incurred in a year in which the HOPE scholarship credit is not claimed with respect to a given student. Generally, the lifetime learning credit is used for individuals who are beyond the first two years of postsecondary education.

Eligible Individuals. Both education credits are available for qualified expenses incurred by a taxpayer, taxpayer's spouse, or taxpayer's dependent. The HOPE scholarship credit is available per eligible student, while the lifetime learning credit is calculated per taxpayer. To be eligible for the HOPE credit, a student must take at least one-half the full-time course load for at least one academic term at a qualifying educational institution. No comparable requirement exists for the lifetime learning credit. Therefore, taxpayers who are seeking new job skills or maintaining existing skills through graduate training or continuing education are eligible for the lifetime learning credit. Taxpayers who are married must file joint returns in order to claim either education credit.

Income Limitations. Both education credits are subject to income limitations and are combined for purposes of the limitation calculation. The allowable credit amount is phased out, beginning when the taxpayer's AGI (modified for this purpose) reaches $43,000 ($87,000 for married taxpayers filing jointly).[41] The reduction in 2005 is equal to the extent to which AGI exceeds $43,000 ($87,000 for married filing jointly) as a percentage of the $10,000 ($20,000 for married filing jointly) phaseout range. The credits are completely eliminated when AGI reaches $53,000 ($107,000 for married filing jointly).

EXAMPLE 32

Dean and Audry are married, file a joint tax return, have modified AGI under $87,000, and have two children, Raymond and Kelsey. During fall 2005, Raymond is beginning his freshman year at State University, and Kelsey is beginning her senior year. During the prior semester, Kelsey completed her junior year. Both Raymond and Kelsey are full-time students and may be claimed as dependents on their parents' tax return. Raymond's qualifying expenses total $4,300 for the fall semester while Kelsey's qualifying expenses total $10,200 for the prior and current semesters. For 2005, Dean and Audry may claim a $1,500 HOPE scholarship credit [(100% × $1,000) + (50% × $1,000)] relating to Raymond's expenses and a $2,000 lifetime learning credit (20% × $10,000) relating to Kelsey's expenses. Kelsey's tuition expenses are ineligible for the HOPE scholarship credit because she is beyond the first two years of postsecondary education. ■

EXAMPLE 33

Assume the same facts as in Example 32, except that Dean and Audry's modified AGI for 2005 is $99,000. Dean and Audry are eligible to claim $1,400 in total education credits for 2005. Their available credits totaling $3,500 ($1,500 HOPE scholarship credit + $2,000 lifetime learning credit) must be reduced because their AGI exceeds the $87,000 limit for married taxpayers. The percentage reduction is computed as the amount by which modified AGI

[40] The $1,000 qualifying expense base for the HOPE scholarship credit is subject to inflation adjustment. The base was $1,000 for 2004 and remains at the same level for 2005.

[41] § 25A(d). For 2004, the AGI bases were $42,000 and $85,000. § 25A(h)(2)(A).

■ **TABLE 12–4**
"Saver's" Credit Rate and AGI Thresholds

Joint Return		Head of Household		All Other Cases		Applicable Percentage
Over	**Not Over**	**Over**	**Not Over**	**Over**	**Not Over**	
$ 0	$30,000	$ 0	$22,500	$ 0	$15,000	50%
30,000	32,500	22,500	24,375	15,000	16,250	20%
32,500	50,000	24,375	37,500	16,250	25,000	10%
50,000		37,500		25,000		0%

exceeds the limit, expressed as a percentage of the phaseout range, or [($99,000 − $87,000)/$20,000)], resulting in a 60% reduction. Therefore, the maximum available credit for 2005 is $1,400 ($3,500 × 40% allowable portion). ■

Restrictions on Double Tax Benefit. Taxpayers are prohibited from receiving a double tax benefit associated with qualifying educational expenses. Therefore, taxpayers who claim an education credit may not deduct the expenses, nor may they claim the credit for amounts that are otherwise excluded from gross income (e.g., scholarships, employer-paid educational assistance). However, a taxpayer may claim an education tax credit and exclude from gross income amounts distributed from a Coverdell Education Savings Account as long as the distribution is not used for the same expenses for which the credit is claimed.

CREDIT FOR CERTAIN RETIREMENT PLAN CONTRIBUTIONS

Taxpayers may claim a nonrefundable **credit for certain retirement plan contributions** based on eligible contributions of up to $2,000 to certain qualified retirement plans established after 2001, such as traditional and Roth IRAs and § 401(k) plans.[42] This credit, sometimes referred to as the "saver's credit," was enacted to encourage lower- and middle-income taxpayers to contribute to qualified retirement plans. The benefit provided by this credit is in addition to any deduction or exclusion that otherwise is available due to the qualifying contribution. In calculating the credit, the qualifying contributions are reduced by taxable distributions from any of the qualifying plans received by the taxpayer and spouse during the tax year and the two previous tax years and during the period prior to the due date of the return.

The credit rate applied to the eligible expenses depends on the taxpayer's AGI[43] and filing status as shown in Table 12–4. However, the maximum credit allowed to an individual is $1,000 ($2,000 × 50%). As the taxpayer's AGI increases, the rate applied to contributions in calculating the credit is reduced, and once AGI exceeds the upper end of the applicable range, no credit is available. To qualify for the credit, the taxpayer must be at least 18 years of age and cannot be a dependent of another taxpayer or a full-time student.

EXAMPLE 34

Earl and Josephine, married taxpayers, each contribute $2,500 to their respective § 401(k) plans offered through their employers. The AGI reported on their joint return is $45,000. The maximum amount of contributions that may be taken into account in calculating the credit is limited to $2,000 for Earl and $2,000 for Josephine. As a result, they may claim a credit for their retirement plan contributions of $400 [($2,000 × 2) × 10%]. They would not qualify for the credit if their AGI had exceeded $50,000. ■

[42] § 25B. This credit is scheduled to expire for tax years beginning after December 31, 2006. The maximum credit allowed is not indexed for inflation.

[43] For purposes of this credit, the AGI thresholds are modified to include certain excluded income items. See § 25B(e).

Concept Summary 12–1

Tax Credits

Credit	Computation	Comments
Tax withheld on wages (§ 31)	Amount is reported to employee on Form W–2.	Refundable credit.
Earned income (§ 32)	Amount is determined by reference to Earned Income Credit Table published by IRS. Computations of underlying amounts in Earned Income Credit Table are illustrated in Example 22.	Refundable credit. A form of negative income tax to assist low-income taxpayers. Earned income and AGI must be less than certain threshold amounts. Generally, one or more qualifying children must reside with the taxpayer.
Child and dependent care (§ 21)	Rate ranges from 20% to 35% depending on AGI. Maximum base for credit is \$3,000 for one qualifying individual, \$6,000 for two or more.	Nonrefundable personal credit. No carryback or carryforward. Benefits taxpayers who incur employment-related child or dependent care expenses in order to work or seek employment. Eligible taxpayers must have a dependent under age 13 or a dependent (any age) or spouse who is physically or mentally incapacitated.
Elderly or disabled (§ 22)	15% of sum of base amount minus reductions for (a) Social Security and other nontaxable benefits and (b) excess AGI. Base amount is fixed by law (e.g., \$5,000 for a single taxpayer).	Nonrefundable personal credit. No carryback or carryforward. Provides relief for taxpayers not receiving substantial tax-free retirement benefits.
Adoption expenses (§ 23)	Up to \$10,630 of costs incurred to adopt an eligible child qualify for the credit. Taxpayer claims the credit in the year qualified expenses were paid or incurred if they were paid or incurred during or after year in which adoption was finalized. For expenses paid or incurred in a year prior to when adoption was finalized, credit must be claimed in tax year following the tax year during which the expenses are paid or incurred.	Nonrefundable credit. Unused credit may be carried forward five years. Purpose is to assist taxpayers who incur nonrecurring costs associated with the adoption process.
Child (§ 24)	Credit is based on *number* of qualifying children under age 17. Maximum credit is \$1,000 per child. Credit is phased out for higher-income taxpayers.	Generally a nonrefundable credit. Refundable in certain cases. Purpose is to provide tax relief for low- to moderate-income families with children.
Education (§ 25A)	HOPE scholarship credit is available for qualifying education expenses of students in first two years of postsecondary education. Maximum credit is \$1,500 per year per eligible student. Credit is phased out for higher-income taxpayers.	Nonrefundable credit. Credit is designed to help defray costs of first two years of higher education for low- to middle-income families.
	Lifetime learning credit permits a credit of 20% of qualifying expenses (up to \$10,000 per year) provided HOPE scholarship credit is not claimed with respect to those expenses. Credit is calculated per taxpayer, not per student, and is phased out for higher-income taxpayers.	Nonrefundable credit. Credit is designed to help defray costs of higher education beyond first two years, and for costs incurred in maintaining or improving existing job skills, for low- to middle-income taxpayers.

Tax Credits—Continued

Credit	Computation	Comments
Credit for certain retirement plan contributions (§ 25B)	Calculation is based on amount of contribution multiplied by a percentage that depends on the taxpayer's filing status and AGI.	Nonrefundable credit. Purpose is to encourage contributions to qualified retirement plans by low- and middle-income taxpayers.
Foreign tax (§ 27)	Foreign taxable income/total worldwide taxable income × U.S. tax = overall limitation. Lesser of foreign taxes imposed or overall limitation.	Nonrefundable credit. Unused credits may be carried back 1 year and forward 10 years. Purpose is to prevent double taxation of foreign income.
General business (§ 38)	May not exceed net income tax minus the greater of tentative minimum tax or 25% of net regular tax liability that exceeds $25,000.	Nonrefundable credit. Components include tax credit for rehabilitation expenditures, work opportunity tax credit, welfare-to-work credit, research activities credit, low-income housing credit, disabled access credit, credit for small employer pension plan startup costs, and credit for employer-provided child care. Unused credit may be carried back 1 year and forward 20 years. FIFO method applies to carrybacks, carryovers, and credits earned during current year.
Investment (§ 46)	Qualifying investment times rehabilitation percentage, depending on type of property. Part of general business credit and subject to its limitations.	Nonrefundable credit. Part of general business credit and therefore subject to same carryback, carryover, and FIFO rules. Regular rehabilitation rate is 10%; rate for certified historic structures is 20%.
Research activities (§ 41)	Incremental credit is 20% of excess of computation year expenditures over the base amount. Basic research credit is allowed to certain corporations for 20% of cash payments to qualified organizations that exceed a specially calculated base amount. To qualify for the credit under current law, research expenditures must be made not later than December 31, 2005.	Nonrefundable credit. Part of general business credit and therefore subject to same carryback, carryover, and FIFO rules. Purpose is to encourage high-tech research in the United States.
Low-income housing (§ 42)	Appropriate rate times eligible basis (portion of project attributable to low-income units).	Nonrefundable credit. Part of general business credit and therefore subject to same carryback, carryover, and FIFO rules. Credit is available each year for 10 years. Recapture may apply. Purpose is to encourage construction of housing for low-income individuals.
Disabled access (§ 44)	Credit is 50% of eligible access expenditures that exceed $250, but do not exceed $10,250. Maximum credit is $5,000.	Nonrefundable credit. Part of general business credit and therefore subject to same carryback, carryover, and FIFO rules. Available only to eligible small businesses. Purpose is to encourage small businesses to become more accessible to disabled individuals.

Tax Credits—Continued

Credit	Computation	Comments
Credit for small employer pension plan startup costs (§ 45E)	The credit equals 50% of qualified startup costs incurred by eligible employers. Maximum annual credit is $500. Deduction for related expenses is reduced by the amount of the credit.	Nonrefundable credit. Part of general business credit and therefore subject to same carryback, carryover, and FIFO rules. Purpose is to encourage small employers to establish qualified retirement plans for their employees.
Credit for employer-provided child care (§ 45F)	Credit is equal to 25% of qualified child care expenses plus 10% of qualified expenses for child care resource and referral services. Maximum credit is $150,000. Deduction for related expenses or basis must be reduced by the amount of the credit.	Nonrefundable credit. Part of general business credit and therefore subject to same carryback, carryover, and FIFO rules. Purpose is to encourage employers to provide child care for their employees' children during normal working hours.
Work opportunity (§ 51)	Credit is limited to 40% of the first $6,000 of wages paid to each eligible employee. Under current law, the employee must begin work by December 31, 2005.	Nonrefundable credit. Part of the general business credit and therefore subject to the same carryback, carryover, and FIFO rules. Purpose is to encourage employment of individuals in specified groups.
Welfare-to-work (§ 51A)	Credit is limited to 35% of first $10,000 of wages paid to eligible employee in first year of employment, plus 50% of first $10,000 of wages paid to eligible employee in second year of employment. Under current law, not available for employees hired after December 31, 2005.	Nonrefundable credit. Part of general business credit and therefore subject to same carryback, carryover, and FIFO rules. Purpose is to encourage employment of long-term recipients of family assistance welfare benefits.

LO.5

Identify tax planning opportunities related to tax credits.

Tax Planning Considerations

FOREIGN TAX CREDIT

A U.S. citizen or resident working abroad (commonly referred to as an *expatriate*) may elect to take either a foreign tax credit or the foreign earned income exclusion. In cases where the income tax of a foreign country is higher than the U.S. income tax, the credit choice usually is preferable. If the reverse is true, electing the foreign earned income exclusion probably reduces the overall tax burden.

Unfortunately, the choice between the credit and the earned income exclusion is not without some limitations. The election of the foreign earned income exclusion, once made, can be revoked for a later year. However, once revoked, the earned income exclusion will not be available for a period of five years unless the IRS consents to an earlier date. This will create a dilemma for expatriates whose job assignments over several years shift between low- and high-bracket countries.

EXAMPLE 35

In 2004, Ira, a calendar year taxpayer, is sent by his employer to Saudi Arabia (a low-tax country). For 2004, therefore, Ira elects the foreign earned income exclusion. In 2005, Ira's employer transfers him to France (a high-tax country). Accordingly, he revokes the foreign earned income exclusion election for 2005 and chooses instead to use the foreign tax credit. If Ira is transferred back to Saudi Arabia (or any other low-tax country) within five years, he may not utilize the foreign earned income exclusion. ■

CREDIT FOR CHILD AND DEPENDENT CARE EXPENSES

A taxpayer may incur employment-related expenses that also qualify as medical expenses (e.g., a nurse is hired to provide in-the-home care for an ill and incapacitated dependent parent). Such expenses may be either deducted as medical expenses (subject to the 7.5 percent limitation) or utilized in determining the credit for child and dependent care expenses. If the credit for child and dependent care expenses is chosen and the employment-related expenses exceed the limitation ($3,000, $6,000, or earned income, as the case may be), the excess may be considered a medical expense. If, however, the taxpayer chooses to deduct qualified employment-related expenses as medical expenses, any portion that is not deductible because of the 7.5 percent limitation may not be used in computing the credit for child and dependent care expenses.

EXAMPLE 36

Alicia has the following tax position for 2005:

Adjusted gross income		$30,000
Potential itemized deductions *from* AGI—		
Other than medical expenses	$3,500	
Medical expenses	6,600	$10,100

All of Alicia's medical expenses were incurred to provide nursing care for her disabled father while she was working. The father lives with Alicia and qualifies as her dependent. ■

What should Alicia do in this situation? One approach would be to use $3,000 of the nursing care expenses to obtain the maximum credit for child and dependent care expenses allowed of $810 (27% × $3,000). The balance of these expenses should be claimed as medical expenses. After a reduction of 7.5 percent of AGI, this would produce a medical expense deduction of $1,350 [$3,600 (remaining medical expenses) – (7.5% × $30,000)].

Another approach would be to claim the full $6,600 as a medical expense and forgo the credit for child and dependent care expenses. After the 7.5 percent adjustment of $2,250 (7.5% × $30,000), a deduction of $4,350 remains.

The choice, then, is between a credit of $810 plus a deduction of $1,350 or a credit of $0 plus a deduction of $4,350. Which is better, of course, depends on the relative tax savings involved, which in turn are dependent on the taxpayer's marginal tax bracket.

One of the traditional goals of *family tax planning* is to minimize the total tax burden within the family unit. With proper planning and implementation, the credit for child and dependent care expenses can be used to help achieve this goal. For example, payments to certain relatives for the care of qualifying dependents and children qualify for the credit if the care provider is *not* a child (under age 19) of the taxpayer. Thus, if the care provider is in a lower tax bracket than the taxpayer, the following benefits result:

- Income is shifted to a lower-bracket family member.
- The taxpayer qualifies for the credit for child and dependent care expenses.

In addition, the goal of minimizing the family income tax liability can be enhanced in some other situations, but only if the credit's limitations are recognized and avoided. For example, tax savings may still be enjoyed even if the qualifying expenditures incurred by a cash basis taxpayer have already reached the annual ceiling ($3,000 or $6,000). To the extent that any additional payments can be shifted into future tax years, the benefit from the credit may be preserved on these excess expenditures.

EXAMPLE 37

Andre, a calendar year and cash basis taxpayer, has spent $3,000 by December 1 on qualifying child care expenditures for his dependent 11-year-old son. The $250 that is due the care provider for child care services rendered in December does not generate a tax credit benefit if the amount is paid in the current year because the $3,000 ceiling has been reached. However, if the payment can be delayed until the next year, the total credit over the two-year period for which Andre is eligible may be increased. ■

A similar shifting of expenditures to a subsequent year may be wise if the potential credit otherwise generated would exceed the tax liability available to absorb the credit.

KEY TERMS

Adoption expenses credit, 12–20
Child tax credit, 12–21
Credit for certain retirement plan contributions, 12–25
Credit for child and dependent care expenses, 12–21
Credit for employer-provided child care, 12–14
Credit for small employer pension plan startup costs, 12–14
Disabled access credit, 12–13
Earned income credit, 12–15
Foreign tax credit (FTC), 12–19
General business credit, 12–5
HOPE scholarship credit, 12–23
Lifetime learning credit, 12–23
Low-income housing credit, 12–12
Nonrefundable credits, 12–4
Permanent and total disability, 12–17
Refundable credits, 12–4
Rehabilitation expenditures credit, 12–7
Rehabilitation expenditures credit recapture, 12–8
Research activities credit, 12–10
Tax credits, 12–2
Tax credit for the elderly or disabled, 12–17
Welfare-to-work credit, 12–9
Work opportunity tax credit, 12–8

PROBLEM MATERIALS

West Federal Taxation

Discussion Questions

1. Would an individual taxpayer receive greater benefit from deducting an expenditure or from taking a credit equal to 25% of the expenditure? How would your response change if the item would only be deductible *from* AGI?

2. What is a refundable credit? Give examples. What is a nonrefundable credit? Give examples.

3. In determining the maximum amount of the general business credit allowed an individual taxpayer for a tax year, *net income tax, tentative minimum tax, regular tax liability,* and *net regular tax liability* are important concepts.
   a. Define each term.
   b. Using these terms, state the general business credit limitation for an individual taxpayer for the current year.

4. Discuss the treatment of unused general business credits.

Issue ID

5. John graduated from college several years ago with high hopes and expectations of a very successful business career. Almost as soon as he completed his final exams, he borrowed over $250,000 from a local bank (the loan was guaranteed by his parents) to make several "hot" investments. The investments, as expected, spun off huge tax losses and tax credits in their early years. Recently, however, John has begun to have doubts as to the wisdom of these investments as they have not begun to generate profits as promised. As a result, he is contemplating selling the investments, at yet another loss. Because his

investments have not as yet produced any profits to support his lifestyle, he has been forced to live at home with his parents. Identify the relevant tax issues.

6. If property on which the tax credit for rehabilitation expenditures was claimed is prematurely disposed of or ceases to be qualified property, how is the tax liability affected in the year of the disposition or disqualification?

7. Discuss the purpose of the work opportunity tax credit. Who receives the tax benefits from the credit? Give examples of the types of individuals who, if hired, give rise to the credit.

8. Explain the purpose and calculation procedure of the welfare-to-work credit.

9. What credit provisions in the tax law were enacted to encourage technological development in the United States?

10. Identify several examples of the type of structural changes to a building that qualify for the disabled access credit.

11. Is the earned income credit a form of negative income tax? Why or why not?

12. Briefly discuss the requirements that must be satisfied for a taxpayer to qualify for the earned income credit.

13. Individuals who receive substantial Social Security benefits are usually not eligible for the tax credit for the elderly or disabled because these benefits effectively eliminate the base upon which the credit is computed. Explain.

14. What purpose is served by the overall limitation on the foreign tax credit?

Issue ID

15. Tara was recently called into the partner's office and offered a one-year assignment in her public accounting firm's London office. Realizing that Tara will face incremental expenses while in London, such as for foreign income taxes and rent, the firm will try to make her "whole" from a financial perspective by increasing her salary to help offset the expenses she will incur while living overseas. If Tara takes the assignment, she will likely rent her personal residence and sell several major tangible assets such as her personal automobile. Identify the relevant tax issues.

16. Discuss, in general, the calculation of the adoption expenses credit.

17. Distinguish between the child tax credit and the credit for child and dependent care expenses.

18. Gary and Gail are married and have a dependent child 8 years of age. Gary earns $15,000 during the current year. Gail, a full-time student for the entire year, is not employed. Gary and Gail believe they are not entitled to the credit for child and dependent care expenses because Gail is not employed. Is this correct? Explain your answer.

Decision Making

19. Polly and her spouse, Leo, file a joint return and expect to report AGI of $70,000 in 2005. Polly's employer offers a child and dependent care reimbursement plan that allows up to $3,500 of qualifying expenses to be reimbursed in exchange for a $3,500 reduction in the employee's salary. Because Polly and Leo have one minor child requiring child care that costs $3,500 each year, she is wondering if she should sign up for the program instead of taking advantage of the credit for child and dependent care expenses. Assuming Polly and Leo are in the 25% tax bracket, analyze the effect of the two alternatives. How would your answer differ if Polly and Leo's AGI was $14,000 instead of $70,000? Assume in this case that their marginal tax rate is 10%.

Issue ID

20. Drew and Brooke are approaching an exciting, but anxious, time in their lives as their daughter, Meg, graduates from high school and departs for college. What are some of the tax issues that Drew and Brooke should consider as they think about paying for Meg's tuition?

21. Identify two tax credits enacted by Congress that are designed to encourage the establishment of or contributions to qualified retirement plans.

22. Discuss the rationale underlying the enactment of the following tax credits:
    a. Rehabilitation expenditures credit.
    b. Low-income housing credit.
    c. Research activities credit.
    d. Earned income credit.
    e. Foreign tax credit.

Problems

23. Carol has a tentative general business credit of $110,000 for the current year. Her net regular tax liability before the general business credit is $125,000, and her tentative minimum tax is $100,000. Compute Carol's allowable general business credit for the year.

24. Tan Corporation has the following general business credit carryovers:

2001	$ 5,000
2002	15,000
2003	5,000
2004	20,000
Total carryovers	$45,000

If the general business credit generated by activities during 2005 equals $45,000 and the total credit allowed during the current year is $80,000 (based on tax liability), what amounts of the current general business credit and carryovers are utilized against the 2005 income tax liability? What is the amount of unused credit carried forward to 2006?

25. In January 2003, William purchased and placed into service a pre-1936 building that houses retail businesses. The cost was $200,000, of which $25,000 applied to the land. In modernizing the facility, William incurred $250,000 of renovation costs of the type that qualify for the tax credit for rehabilitation expenditures. These improvements were placed in service in October 2005.
    a. Compute William's tax credit for rehabilitation expenditures for 2005.
    b. Calculate the cost recovery deductions for the building and the renovation costs for 2005.

26. Red Company hires six individuals on January 15, 2005, qualifying Red for the work opportunity tax credit. Three of these individuals receive wages of $7,000 each during 2005, with each working more than 400 hours during the year. The other three receive wages of $4,000 each in 2005, with each working 300 hours during the year.
    a. Calculate the amount of Red's work opportunity tax credit for 2005.
    b. Assume Red pays total wages of $120,000 to its employees during the year. How much of this amount is deductible in 2005 if the work opportunity tax credit is taken?

27. In March 2005, Wren Corporation hired three individuals, Trent, Bernice, and Benita, all of whom are certified as long-term family assistance recipients. Each employee is paid $11,000 during 2005. Only Bernice continued to work for Wren in 2006, earning $13,500. In February 2006, Wren hired Cassie, who was also certified as a long-term family assistance recipient. During 2006, Cassie earned $14,000. Wren does not claim the work opportunity credit with respect to any of the employees hired in 2005 or 2006.
    a. Compute Wren Corporation's welfare-to-work credit for 2005 and 2006.
    b. Assume Wren Corporation pays total wages of $325,000 to its employees during 2005 and $342,000 during 2006. How much may Wren claim as a wage deduction for 2005 and 2006 if the welfare-to-work credit is claimed in both years?

Decision Making

28. Michael, a calendar year taxpayer, informs you that during June 2005, he incurs expenditures of $50,000 that qualify for the incremental research activities credit. In addition, it is determined that his base amount for the year is $35,000.
    a. Determine Michael's incremental research activities credit for the year.
    b. Michael is in the 25% tax bracket. Determine which approach to the research expenditures and the research activities credit (other than capitalization and subsequent amortization) would provide the greater tax benefit to Michael.

Communications

29. Ahmed Zinna (16 Southside Drive, Charlotte, NC 28204), one of your clients, owns two restaurants in downtown Charlotte and has come to you seeking advice concerning the tax consequences of complying with the Americans with Disabilities Act. He understands that he needs to install various features at his businesses (e.g., ramps, doorways, and restrooms that are handicapped accessible) to make them more accessible to disabled individuals. He asks whether any tax credits will be available to help offset the cost of the necessary changes. He estimates the cost of the planned changes to his facilities as follows:

Location	Projected Cost
Calvin Street	$22,000
Stowe Avenue	8,500

He reminds you that the Calvin Street restaurant was constructed in 2001 while the Stowe Avenue restaurant is in a building that was constructed in 1986. Ahmed operates his business as a sole proprietorship and has approximately eight employees at each location. Write a letter to Ahmed in which you summarize your conclusions concerning the tax consequences of his proposed capital improvements.

30. Which of the following individuals qualify for the earned income credit for 2005?
   a. Eduardo is single, 19 years of age, and has no qualifying children. His income consists of $8,000 in wages.
   b. Kate maintains a household for a dependent 12-year-old son and is eligible for head-of-household tax rates. Her income consists of $13,500 of salary and $300 of taxable interest.
   c. Keith and Susan are married and file a joint return. Keith and Susan have no dependents. Their combined income consists of $28,500 of salary and $100 of taxable interest. Adjusted gross income is $28,600.
   d. George is a 26-year-old, self-supporting, single taxpayer. He has no qualifying children and generates earnings of $9,000.

31. Vern, a widower, lives in an apartment with his three minor children (ages 3, 4, and 5) whom he fully supports. Vern earned $19,500 during 2005. He contributed $500 to a traditional IRA and uses the standard deduction. Calculate the amount, if any, of Vern's earned income credit.

Decision Making

32. Joyce, a widow, lives in an apartment with her two minor children (ages 8 and 10) whom she supports. Joyce earns $32,000 during 2005. She uses the standard deduction.
   a. Calculate the amount, if any, of Joyce's earned income credit.
   b. During the year, Joyce is offered a new job that has greater future potential than her current job. If she accepts the job offer, her earnings for the year would be $36,000; however, she will not qualify for the earned income credit. Using after-tax cash-flow calculations, determine whether Joyce should accept the new job offer.

33. Roger, age 67, and Thelma, age 66, are married retirees who receive the following income and retirement benefits during 2005:

Fully taxable pension from Roger's former employer	$ 8,000
Interest income	2,500
Social Security benefits	4,000
Total	$14,500

Assume Roger and Thelma file a joint income tax return, have no deductions *for* AGI, and do not itemize. Are they eligible for the tax credit for the elderly? If so, calculate the amount of the credit.

Decision Making

34. Kim, a U.S. citizen and resident, owns and operates a novelty goods business. During 2005, Kim has taxable income of $100,000, made up as follows: $50,000 from foreign sources and $50,000 from U.S. sources. In calculating taxable income, the standard

deduction is used. The income from foreign sources is subject to foreign income taxes of $26,000. For 2005, Kim files a joint return claiming his three children as dependents.

a. Assuming Kim chooses to claim the foreign taxes as an income tax credit, what is his income tax liability for 2005?
b. Recently, Kim has become disenchanted with the location of his business and is considering moving his foreign operation to a different country. Based on his research, if he moves his business to his country of choice, all relevant revenues and costs would remain approximately the same except that the income taxes payable to that country would be only $8,000. Given that all of the foreign income taxes paid are available to offset the U.S. tax liability (whether he operates in a high-tax or a low-tax foreign jurisdiction), what impact will this have on his decision regarding the potential move?

35. Blue Corporation, a U.S. corporation, is a manufacturing concern that sells most of its products in the United States. It also does some business in Europe through various branches. During the current year, Blue Corporation has taxable income of $500,000, of which $350,000 is U.S.-sourced and $150,000 is foreign-sourced. Foreign income taxes paid are $45,000. Blue's U.S. income tax liability before any foreign tax credit is $170,000.
    a. What is Blue Corporation's U.S. income tax liability net of the allowable foreign tax credit?
    b. What is the amount of Blue's foreign tax credit carryback and carryover?

36. Ann and Bill were on the list of a local adoption agency for several years seeking to adopt a child. Finally, in 2004, good news comes their way and an adoption seems imminent. They pay qualified adoption expenses of $4,000 in 2004 and $9,000 in 2005. Assume the adoption becomes final in 2005. Ann and Bill always file a joint income tax return.
    a. Determine the amount of the adoption expenses credit available to Ann and Bill assuming their combined annual income is $50,000. What year(s) will they benefit from the credit?
    b. Assuming Ann and Bill's modified AGI in 2004 and 2005 is $175,000, calculate the amount of the adoption expenses credit.

37. Durell and Earline are married, file a joint return, and claim dependency exemptions for their two children, ages 5 years and 6 months. They also claim Earline's son from a previous marriage, age 18, as a dependent. Durell and Earline's combined AGI is $56,000.
    a. Compute Durell and Earline's child tax credit.
    b. Assume the same facts, except that Durell and Earline's combined AGI is $119,000. Compute their child tax credit.

38. Kevin and Jane are husband and wife and have one dependent child, age 9. Kevin is a full-time student for all of the current year, while Jane earns $36,000 as a nurse's aide. To provide care for their child while Kevin attends classes and Jane works, they pay Sara (Jane's 17-year-old sister) $2,900. Sara is not a dependent of Kevin and Jane. Assuming Kevin and Jane file a joint return, what, if any, is their credit for child and dependent care expenses?

39. Ralph and Jill are husband and wife and have two dependent children under the age of 13. They both are gainfully employed and during the current year earn salaries as follows: $22,500 (Ralph) and $5,000 (Jill). To care for their children while they work, they pay Megan (Ralph's mother) $5,600. Assuming Ralph and Jill file a joint return, what, if any, is their credit for child and dependent care expenses?

Communications

40. Bernadette, a longtime client of yours, is an architect and president of the local Rotary chapter. To keep up-to-date with the latest developments in her profession, she attends continuing education seminars offered by the architecture school at State University. During 2005, Bernadette spends $2,000 on course tuition to attend such seminars. She also spends another $400 on architecture books during the year. Bernadette's son is a senior majoring in engineering at the University of the Midwest. During the 2005 calendar year, Bernadette's son incurs the following expenses: $8,200 for tuition ($4,100 per

semester) and $750 for books and supplies. Bernadette's son, whom she claims as a dependent, lives at home while attending school full-time. Bernadette is married, files a joint return, and has a combined AGI with her husband of $95,000.

a. Calculate Bernadette's education tax credit for 2005.

b. In her capacity as president of the local Rotary chapter, Bernadette has asked you to make a 30–45 minute speech outlining the different ways the tax law helps defray (1) the cost of higher education and (2) the cost of continuing education once someone is in the workforce. Prepare an outline of possible topics for presentation. A tentative title for your presentation is "How Can the Tax Law Help Pay for College and Continuing Professional Education?"

41. Kathleen and Glenn decide that this is the year to begin getting serious about saving for their retirement by participating in their employers' § 401(k) plans. As a result, they each have $3,000 of their salary set aside in their qualified plans.

a. Calculate the credit for certain retirement plan contributions available to Kathleen and Glenn if the AGI on their joint return is $32,000.

b. Kathleen and Glenn persuade their dependent 15-year-old son, Joel, to put $500 of his part-time earnings into a Roth IRA during the year. What is the credit for certain retirement plan contributions available to Joel? His AGI is $7,000.

Cumulative Problems

Tax Return Problem

42. Wade and Jane Lawrence are married and file a joint return. Wade's Social Security number is 222–33–1111, and Jane's Social Security number is 111–22–5555. They reside at 100 Olive Lane, Covington, LA 70400. They have two dependent children, Sean and Debra, ages 12 and 16, respectively. Wade is a self-employed businessman (sole proprietor of an unincorporated business), and Jane is a corporate executive. Wade has the following income and expenses from his business:

Gross income	$280,000
Business expenses	200,000

Records related to Jane's employment provide the following information:

Salary	$160,000
Unreimbursed travel expenses (including $200 of meals)	1,000
Unreimbursed entertainment expenses	600

Other pertinent information relating to 2005 follows:

Proceeds from sale of stock acquired on July 15, 2005 (cost of $10,000), and sold on August 1, 2005	$ 8,000
Proceeds from sale of stock acquired on September 18, 2004 (cost of $6,000), and sold on October 5, 2005	4,800
Wages paid to full-time domestic worker for housekeeping and child supervision	10,000
Interest income received	8,000
Total itemized deductions (not including any potential deductions above)	26,900
Federal income tax withheld	29,000
Estimated payments of Federal income tax	30,000

Compute the net tax payable or refund due for Wade and Jane Lawrence for 2005. Suggested software: TurboTax.

Tax Return Problem

43. Beth R. Jordan lives at 2322 Skyview Road, Mesa, AZ 85202. She is a tax accountant with Mesa Manufacturing Company. She also writes computer software programs for tax practitioners and has a part-time tax practice. Beth, age 35, is single and has no

dependents. Her Social Security number is 111–35–2222. She wants to contribute $3 to the Presidential Election Campaign Fund.

During 2004, Beth earned a salary of $63,000 from her employer. She received interest of $1,300 from Home Federal Savings and Loan and $400 from Home State Bank. She received qualified dividends of $500 from Gray Corporation, $400 from Blue Corporation, and $1,200 from Orange Corporation.

Beth received a $1,600 income tax refund from the state of Arizona on May 12, 2004. On her 2003 Federal income tax return, she reported total itemized deductions of $7,700, which included $2,400 of state income tax withheld by her employer.

Fees earned from her part-time tax practice in 2004 totaled $3,800. She paid $600 to have the tax returns processed by a computerized tax return service.

On February 1, 2004, Beth bought 500 shares of Gray Corporation common stock for $17.60 a share. On July 16, Beth sold the stock for $14 a share.

Beth bought a used sport utility vehicle for $3,000 on June 5, 2004. She purchased the vehicle from her brother-in-law, who was unemployed and was in need of cash. On November 2, 2004, she sold the vehicle to a friend for $3,400.

On January 2, 2004, Beth acquired 100 shares of Blue Corporation common stock for $30 a share. She sold the stock on December 19, 2004, for $55 a share.

During 2004, Beth received royalties of $16,000 on a software program she had written. Beth incurred the following expenditures in connection with her software-writing activities:

Cost of personal computer (100% business use)	$7,000
Cost of printer (100% business use)	2,000
Furniture	3,000
Supplies	650
Fee paid to computer consultant	3,500

Beth elected to expense the maximum portion of the cost of the computer, printer, and furniture allowed under the provisions of § 179. This equipment and furniture were placed in service on January 15, 2004.

Although her employer suggested that Beth attend a convention on current developments in corporate taxation, Beth was not reimbursed for the travel expenses of $1,420 she incurred in attending the convention. The $1,420 included $200 for the cost of meals.

During 2004, Beth paid $300 for prescription medicines and $2,875 in doctor bills, hospital bills, and medical insurance premiums. Her employer withheld state income tax of $1,650. Beth paid real property taxes of $1,766 on her home. Interest on her home mortgage was $3,845, and interest to credit card companies was $320. Beth contributed $30 each week to her church and $10 each week to the United Way. Professional dues and subscriptions totaled $350. Beth maintained her sales tax receipts. The total is $1,954.

Beth's employer withheld Federal income taxes of $11,000 during 2004. Beth paid estimated taxes of $1,000. What is the amount of Beth's net tax payable or refund due for 2004? If Beth has a tax refund due, she wants to have it credited toward her 2005 income tax. If you use tax forms for your solution, you will need Forms 1040, 2106–EZ, and 4562 and Schedules A, B, C, D, and SE. Suggested software: TurboTax.

Research Problems

Note: Solutions to Research Problems can be prepared by using the ***RIA Checkpoint® Student Edition*** *online research product, which is available to accompany this text. It is also possible to prepare solutions to the Research Problems by using tax research materials found in a standard tax library.*

Decision Making

Research Problem 1. During a recent Sunday afternoon excursion, Miriam, an admirer of early twentieth-century architecture, discovers a 1920s-era house in the countryside outside Mobile, Alabama. She desires not only to purchase and renovate this particular house, but also to move the structure into Mobile so her community can enjoy its architectural features. Being aware of the availability of the tax credit for rehabilitation expenditures, she wishes to maximize her use of the provision, if it is available in this case, once the renovation work begins in Mobile. Miriam also informs you that she will pursue the purchase, relocation, and renovation of the house only if the tax credit is available. Comment on Miriam's decision and whether any renovation expenditures incurred will qualify for the tax credit for rehabilitation expenditures.

Partial list of research aids:
George S. Nalle, III, 99 T.C. 187 (1992).

Decision Making

Research Problem 2. George and Louise's dependent daughter, Jamie, is a full-time university student who recently completed her first semester. The tuition expense for Jamie's first semester was $11,000. George and Louise have read about various education credits that are generally available to offset the cost of higher education, but they have concluded that they do not qualify because their AGI is too high.

Nonetheless, George asks you about a tax strategy that he recently overheard being discussed. According to his recollection of the discussion, if he and Louise would forgo claiming Jamie as a dependent on their joint income tax return, Jamie could claim the HOPE scholarship credit on her income tax return. What do you tell George about this strategy? Under what conditions should George and Louise take advantage of this approach if it is available?

Partial list of research aids:
Reg. § 1.25A–1(f).

Internet Activity

Use the tax resources of the Internet to address the following question. Do not restrict your search to the World Wide Web, but include a review of newsgroups and general reference materials, practitioner sites and resources, primary sources of the tax law, chat rooms and discussion groups, and other opportunities.

Research Problem 3. Find several news stories or government reports that document the incentive effect of the research activities credit.

Property Transactions: Determination of Gain or Loss, Basis Considerations, and Nontaxable Exchanges

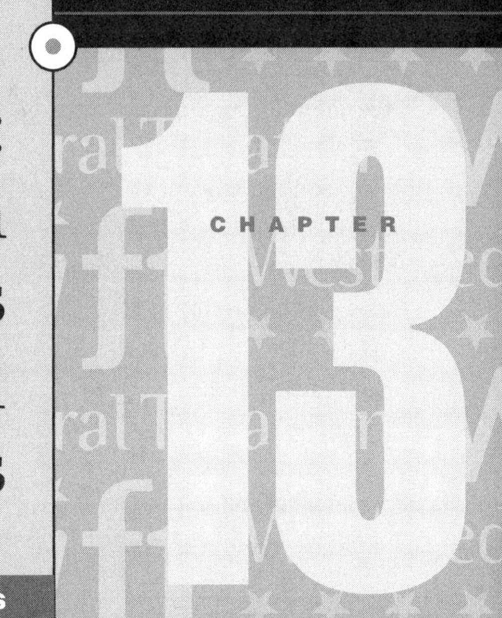

LEARNING OBJECTIVES

After completing Chapter 13, you should be able to:

LO.1
Understand the computation of realized gain or loss on property dispositions.

LO.2
Distinguish between realized and recognized gain or loss.

LO.3
Apply the recovery of capital doctrine.

LO.4
Explain how basis is determined for various methods of asset acquisition.

LO.5
Describe various loss disallowance provisions.

LO.6
Understand the rationale for nonrecognition (postponement) of gain or loss in certain property transactions.

LO.7
Apply the nonrecognition provisions and basis determination rules for like-kind exchanges.

LO.8
Explain the nonrecognition provisions available on the involuntary conversion of property.

LO.9
Describe the provision for the permanent exclusion of gain on the sale of a personal residence.

LO.10
Identify other nonrecognition provisions contained in the Code.

LO.11
Identify tax planning opportunities related to selected property transactions.

http://wft.swlearning.com

OUTLINE

This chapter and Chapter 14 are concerned with the income tax consequences of property transactions (the sale or other disposition of property). The following questions are considered with respect to the sale or other disposition of property:

- Is there a realized gain or loss?
- If so, is the gain or loss recognized?
- If the gain or loss is recognized, is it ordinary or capital?
- What is the basis of any replacement property that is acquired?

EXAMPLE 1

Alice owns a house that she received from her mother seven months ago. Her mother's cost for the house was $75,000. Alice is considering selling the house to her favorite nephew, Dan, for $75,000. Alice anticipates she will have no gain or loss on the transaction. She comes to you for advice.

As Alice's tax adviser, you need answers to the following questions:

- You are aware that Alice's mother died around the time Alice indicates she received the house from her mother. Did Alice receive the house by gift prior to her mother's death? If so, what was the mother's adjusted basis? Did Alice instead inherit the house from her mother? If so, what was the fair market value of the house on the date of her mother's death?
- Has the house been Alice's principal residence during the period she has owned it? Was it her principal residence before she received it from her mother?
- How long did Alice's mother own the house?
- What is the fair market value of the house?
- Does Alice intend for the transaction with Dan to be a sale or part sale and part gift?
- What does Alice intend to do with the sale proceeds?

Once you have the answers to these questions, you can advise Alice on the tax consequences of the proposed transaction. ■

This chapter discusses the determination of realized and recognized gain or loss and the basis of property. Chapter 14 covers the classification of the recognized gain or loss as ordinary or capital.

LO.1

Understand the computation of realized gain or loss on property dispositions.

Determination of Gain or Loss

REALIZED GAIN OR LOSS

Realized gain or loss is the difference between the amount realized from the sale or other disposition of property and the property's adjusted basis on the date of disposition. If the amount realized exceeds the property's adjusted basis, the result is a **realized gain.** Conversely, if the property's adjusted basis exceeds the amount realized, the result is a **realized loss.**[1]

EXAMPLE 2

Tab sells Swan Corporation stock with an adjusted basis of $3,000 for $5,000. Tab's realized gain is $2,000. If Tab had sold the stock for $2,000, he would have had a realized loss of $1,000. ■

Sale or Other Disposition. The term *sale or other disposition* is defined broadly in the tax law and includes virtually any disposition of property. Thus, transactions such as trade-ins, casualties, condemnations, thefts, and bond retirements are treated as dispositions of property. The most common disposition of property is through a sale or exchange. Usually, the key factor in determining whether a disposition has taken place is whether an identifiable event has occurred[2] as opposed to a mere fluctuation in the value of the property.[3]

EXAMPLE 3

Lori owns Tan Corporation stock that cost $3,000. The stock has appreciated in value by $2,000 since Lori purchased it. Lori has no realized gain since mere fluctuation in value is not a disposition or identifiable event for tax purposes. Nor would Lori have a realized loss had the stock declined in value by $2,000. ■

[1]§ 1001(a) and Reg. § 1.1001–1(a).

[2]Reg. § 1.1001–1(c)(1).

[3]*Lynch v. Turrish*, 1 USTC ¶18, 3 AFTR 2986, 38 S.Ct. 537 (USSC, 1918).

Reevaluating Your Investment Strategy

One of the many ways stocks are distinguished for investment purposes is by growth potential versus income yield. A growth stock is expected to appreciate over time and to pay few, if any, dividends. In contrast, an income stock pays regular dividends but is not expected to appreciate significantly.

Historically, growth and income stocks have also been taxed differently. The long-term capital gain on growth stocks was eligible for beneficial alternative tax treatment, whereas the dividend income on income stocks was taxed as ordinary income.

The Jobs and Growth Tax Relief Reconciliation Act of 2003 changed this historical difference. Long-term capital gains continue to be eligible for the beneficial alternative tax treatment but with rates reduced from 20%/10% to 15%/5%. Under the Act, moreover, qualified dividends are now eligible for a beneficial 15%/5% tax treatment.

These changes may well cause some taxpayers to rethink their investment strategy regarding the choice between growth and income stocks.

Amount Realized. The **amount realized** from a sale or other disposition of property is the sum of any money received plus the fair market value of other property received. The amount realized also includes any real property taxes treated as imposed on the seller that are actually paid by the buyer.[4] The reason for including these taxes in the amount realized is that by paying the taxes, the purchaser is, in effect, paying an additional amount to the seller of the property.

The amount realized also includes any liability on the property disposed of, such as a mortgage debt, if the buyer assumes the mortgage or the property is sold subject to the mortgage.[5] The amount of the liability is included in the amount realized even if the debt is nonrecourse and the amount of the debt is greater than the fair market value of the mortgaged property.[6]

EXAMPLE 4

Barry sells property on which there is a mortgage of $20,000 to Cole for $50,000 cash. Barry's amount realized from the sale is $70,000 if Cole assumes the mortgage or takes the property subject to the mortgage. ■

The **fair market value** of property received in a sale or other disposition has been defined by the courts as the price at which property will change hands between a willing seller and a willing buyer when neither is compelled to sell or buy.[7] Fair market value is determined by considering the relevant factors in each case.[8] An expert appraiser is often required to evaluate these factors in arriving at fair market value. When the fair market value of the property received cannot be determined, the value of the property given up by the taxpayer may be used.[9]

In calculating the amount realized, selling expenses such as advertising, commissions, and legal fees relating to the disposition are deducted. The amount

[4] § 1001(b) and Reg. § 1.1001–1(b). Refer to Chapter 10 for a discussion of this subject.

[5] *Crane v. Comm.*, 47–1 USTC ¶9217, 35 AFTR 776, 67 S.Ct. 1047 (USSC, 1947). Although a legal distinction exists between the direct assumption of a mortgage and taking property subject to a mortgage, the tax consequences in calculating the amount realized are the same.

[6] *Comm. v. Tufts*, 83–1 USTC ¶9328, 51 AFTR2d 83–1132, 103 S.Ct. 1826 (USSC, 1983).

[7] *Comm. v. Marshman*, 60–2 USTC ¶9484, 5 AFTR2d 1528, 279 F.2d 27 (CA–6, 1960).

[8] *O'Malley v. Ames*, 52–1 USTC ¶9361, 42 AFTR 19, 197 F.2d 256 (CA–8, 1952).

[9] *U.S. v. Davis*, 62–2 USTC ¶9509, 9 AFTR2d 1625, 82 S.Ct. 1190 (USSC, 1962).

realized is the net amount that the taxpayer received directly or indirectly, in the form of cash or anything else of value, from the disposition of the property.

Adjusted Basis. The **adjusted basis** of property disposed of is the property's original basis adjusted to the date of disposition.[10] Original basis is the cost or other basis of the property on the date the property is acquired by the taxpayer. Considerations involving original basis are discussed later in this chapter. *Capital additions* increase and *recoveries of capital* decrease the original basis so that on the date of disposition the adjusted basis reflects the unrecovered cost or other basis of the property.[11] Adjusted basis is determined as follows:

Cost (or other adjusted basis) on date of acquisition

+ Capital additions

– Capital recoveries

= Adjusted basis on date of disposition

Capital Additions. Capital additions include the cost of capital improvements and betterments made to the property by the taxpayer. These expenditures are distinguishable from expenditures for the ordinary repair and maintenance of the property, which are neither capitalized nor added to the original basis (refer to Chapter 6). The latter expenditures are deductible in the current taxable year if they are related to business or income-producing property. Amounts representing real property taxes treated as imposed on the seller but paid or assumed by the buyer are part of the cost of the property.[12] Any liability on property that is assumed by the buyer is also included in the buyer's original basis of the property. The same rule applies if property is acquired subject to a liability. Amortization of the discount on bonds increases the adjusted basis of the bonds.[13]

Capital Recoveries. Capital recoveries decrease the adjusted basis of property. The following are examples of capital recoveries:

1. *Depreciation and cost recovery allowances.* The original basis of depreciable property is reduced by the annual depreciation charges (or cost recovery allowances) while the property is held by the taxpayer. The amount of depreciation that is subtracted from the original basis is the greater of the *allowed* or *allowable* depreciation calculated on an annual basis.[14] In most circumstances, the allowed and allowable depreciation amounts are the same (refer to Chapter 8).
2. *Casualties and thefts.* A casualty or theft may result in the reduction of the adjusted basis of property.[15] The adjusted basis is reduced by the amount of the deductible loss. In addition, the adjusted basis is reduced by the amount of insurance proceeds received. However, the receipt of insurance proceeds may result in a recognized gain rather than a deductible loss. The gain increases the adjusted basis of the property.[16]

EXAMPLE 5

An insured truck used in a trade or business is destroyed in an accident. The adjusted basis is $8,000, and the fair market value is $6,500. Insurance proceeds of $6,500 are received. The amount of the casualty loss is $1,500 ($6,500 insurance proceeds – $8,000 adjusted basis).

[10]§ 1011(a) and Reg. § 1.1011–1.
[11]§ 1016(a) and Reg. § 1.1016–1.
[12]Reg. §§ 1.1001–1(b)(2) and 1.1012–1(b). Refer to Chapter 10 for a discussion of this subject.
[13]See Chapter 14 for a discussion of bond discount and the related amortization.
[14]§ 1016(a)(2) and Reg. § 1.1016–3(a)(1)(i).
[15]Refer to Chapter 7 for the discussion of casualties and thefts.
[16]Reg. § 1.1016–6(a).

The adjusted basis is reduced by the $1,500 casualty loss and the $6,500 of insurance proceeds received. ■

EXAMPLE 6

An insured truck used in a trade or business is destroyed in an accident. The adjusted basis is $6,500, and the fair market value is $8,000. Insurance proceeds of $8,000 are received. The amount of the casualty gain is $1,500 ($8,000 insurance proceeds – $6,500 adjusted basis). The adjusted basis is increased by the $1,500 casualty gain and is reduced by the $8,000 of insurance proceeds received ($6,500 basis before casualty + $1,500 casualty gain – $8,000 insurance proceeds = $0 basis). ■

3. *Certain corporate distributions.* A corporate distribution to a shareholder that is not taxable is treated as a return of capital, and it reduces the basis of the shareholder's stock in the corporation.[17] For example, if a corporation makes a cash distribution to its shareholders and has no earnings and profits, the distributions are treated as a return of capital. Once the basis of the stock is reduced to zero, the amount of any subsequent distributions is a capital gain if the stock is a capital asset. These rules are illustrated in Example 1 of Chapter 18.

ETHICAL CONSIDERATIONS

Reporting a Distribution: Dividend or Return of Capital?

Rebecca purchased 100 shares of stock in Bluebird, Inc., on December 24, 2005, for $50,000. In January 2006, Rebecca receives a Form 1099 for 2005 from the corporation indicating that she had dividend income of $2,000. Although Rebecca received a check from Bluebird on January 4, 2006 (postmarked December 31), she believes that it is a return of capital. Therefore, she reduces her basis in the stock to $48,000 and reports no dividend income for 2005. Her justification is that the corporation reported a loss in its fourth quarter financial statements. Since she did not purchase her stock until late in the fourth quarter, no corporate earnings could be identified with her shares. Evaluate Rebecca's reporting of the $2,000 distribution.

4. *Amortizable bond premium.* The basis in a bond purchased at a premium is reduced by the amortizable portion of the bond premium.[18] Investors in taxable bonds may *elect* to amortize the bond premium, but the premium on tax-exempt bonds *must be* amortized.[19] The amount of the amortized premium on taxable bonds is permitted as an interest deduction. Therefore, the election enables the taxpayer to take an annual interest deduction to offset ordinary income in exchange for a larger capital gain or smaller capital loss on the disposition of the bond. No such interest deduction is permitted for tax-exempt bonds.

   The amortization deduction is allowed for taxable bonds because the premium is viewed as a cost of earning the taxable interest from the bonds. The reason the basis of taxable bonds is reduced is that the amortization deduction is a recovery of the cost or basis of the bonds. The basis of tax-exempt bonds is reduced even though the amortization is not allowed as a deduction. No amortization deduction is permitted on tax-exempt bonds because the interest income is exempt from tax and the amortization of the bond premium merely represents an adjustment of the effective amount of such income.

[17] § 1016(a)(4) and Reg. § 1.1016–5(a).

[18] § 1016(a)(5) and Reg. § 1.1016–5(b). The accounting treatment of bond premium amortization is the same as for tax purposes. The amortization results in a decrease in the bond investment account.

[19] § 171(c).

CONCEPT SUMMARY 13–1

Recognized Gain or Loss

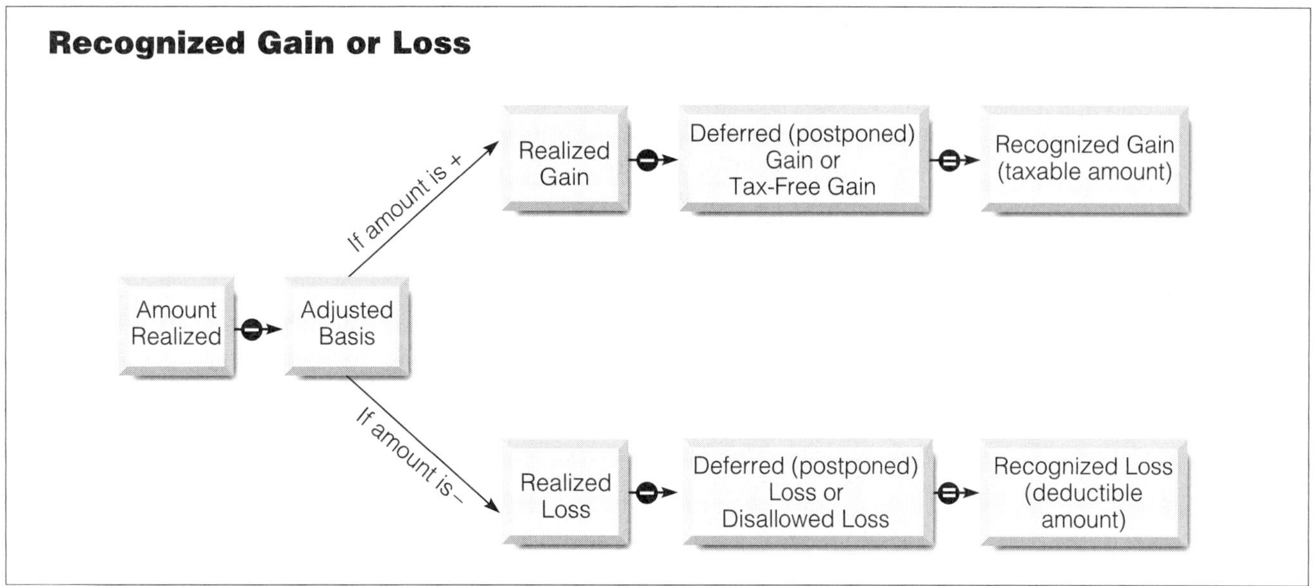

EXAMPLE 7

Antonio purchases Eagle Corporation taxable bonds with a face value of $100,000 for $110,000, thus paying a premium of $10,000. The annual interest rate is 7%, and the bonds mature 10 years from the date of purchase. The annual interest income is $7,000 (7% × $100,000). If Antonio elects to amortize the bond premium, the $10,000 premium is deducted over the 10-year period. Antonio's basis for the bonds is reduced each year by the amount of the amortization deduction. Note that if the bonds were tax-exempt, amortization of the bond premium and the basis adjustment would be mandatory. However, no deduction would be allowed for the amortization. ■

5. *Easements.* An easement is the legal right to use another's land for a special purpose. Historically, easements were commonly used to obtain rights-of-way for utility lines and roads. In recent years, grants of conservation easements have become a popular means of obtaining charitable contribution deductions and reducing the value of real estate for transfer tax (i.e., estate and gift) purposes. Likewise, scenic easements are used to reduce the value of land as assessed for ad valorem property tax purposes.

   If the taxpayer does not retain any right to the use of the land, all of the basis is assigned to the easement. However, if the use of the land is only partially restricted, an allocation of some of the basis to the easement is appropriate.

LO.2

Distinguish between realized and recognized gain or loss.

RECOGNIZED GAIN OR LOSS

Recognized gain is the amount of the realized gain that is included in the taxpayer's gross income.[20] A **recognized loss,** on the other hand, is the amount of a realized loss that is deductible for tax purposes.[21] As a general rule, the entire amount of a realized gain or loss is recognized.[22]

Concept Summary 13–1 summarizes the realized gain or loss and recognized gain or loss concepts.

[20] § 61(a)(3) and Reg. § 1.61–6(a).

[21] § 165(a) and Reg. § 1.165–1(a).

[22] § 1001(c) and Reg. § 1.1002–1(a).

NONRECOGNITION OF GAIN OR LOSS

In certain cases, a realized gain or loss is not recognized upon the sale or other disposition of property. One such case involves nontaxable exchanges, which are covered later in this chapter. Others include losses realized upon the sale, exchange, or condemnation of personal use assets (as opposed to business or income-producing property) and gains realized upon the sale of a residence. In addition, realized losses from the sale or exchange of business or income-producing property between certain related parties are not recognized.[23]

Sale, Exchange, or Condemnation of Personal Use Assets. A realized loss from the sale, exchange, or condemnation of personal use assets (e.g., a personal residence or an automobile not used at all for business or income-producing purposes) is not recognized for tax purposes. An exception exists for casualty or theft losses from personal use assets (see Chapter 7). In contrast, any gain realized from the sale or other disposition of personal use assets is, generally, fully taxable.

EXAMPLE 8

Freda sells an automobile, which she has held exclusively for personal use, for $6,000. The adjusted basis of the automobile is $5,000. Freda has a realized and recognized gain of $1,000. ■

EXAMPLE 9

Freda sells the automobile in Example 8 for $4,000. She has a realized loss of $1,000, but the loss is not recognized. ■

LO.3

Apply the recovery of capital doctrine.

RECOVERY OF CAPITAL DOCTRINE

Doctrine Defined. The **recovery of capital doctrine** pervades all the tax rules relating to property transactions. The doctrine derives its roots from the very essence of the income tax—a tax on income. Under the doctrine, as a general rule, a taxpayer is entitled to recover the cost or other original basis of property acquired and is not taxed on that amount.

The cost or other original basis of depreciable property is recovered through annual depreciation deductions. The basis is reduced as the cost is recovered over the period the property is held. Therefore, when property is sold or otherwise disposed of, it is the adjusted basis (unrecovered cost or other basis) that is compared with the amount realized from the disposition to determine realized gain or loss.

Relationship of the Recovery of Capital Doctrine to the Concepts of Realization and Recognition. If a sale or other disposition results in a realized gain, the taxpayer has recovered more than the adjusted basis of the property. Conversely, if a sale or other disposition results in a realized loss, the taxpayer has recovered less than the adjusted basis.

The general rules for the relationship between the recovery of capital doctrine and the realized and recognized gain and loss concepts are summarized as follows:

Rule 1. A realized gain that is *never recognized* results in the *permanent recovery* of more than the taxpayer's cost or other basis for tax purposes. For example, all or a portion of the realized gain on the sale of a personal residence can be excluded from gross income under § 121.

Rule 2. A realized gain on which *recognition is postponed* results in the *temporary recovery* of more than the taxpayer's cost or other basis for tax purposes. For example, an exchange of like-kind property under § 1031 and an involuntary conversion under § 1033 are both eligible for postponement treatment.

[23] § 267(a)(1).

Rule 3. A realized loss that is *never recognized* results in the *permanent recovery* of less than the taxpayer's cost or other basis for tax purposes. For example, a loss on the sale of an automobile held for personal use is not deductible.

Rule 4. A realized loss on which *recognition is postponed* results in the *temporary recovery* of less than the taxpayer's cost or other basis for tax purposes. For example, the realized loss on the exchange of like-kind property under § 1031 is postponed.

These rules are illustrated in discussions to follow in this chapter.

LO.4

Explain how basis is determined for various methods of asset acquisition.

Basis Considerations

DETERMINATION OF COST BASIS

As noted earlier, the basis of property is generally the property's cost. Cost is the amount paid for the property in cash or other property.[24] This general rule follows logically from the recovery of capital doctrine; that is, the cost or other basis of property is to be recovered tax-free by the taxpayer.

A *bargain purchase* of property is an exception to the general rule for determining basis. A bargain purchase may result when an employer transfers property to an employee at less than the property's fair market value (as compensation for services) or when a corporation transfers property to a shareholder at less than the property's fair market value (a dividend). The amount included in income either as compensation for services or dividend income is the difference between the bargain purchase price and the property's fair market value. The basis of property acquired in a bargain purchase is the property's fair market value.[25] If the basis of the property were not increased by the bargain amount, the taxpayer would be taxed on this amount again at disposition.

EXAMPLE 10

Wade buys land from his employer for $10,000 on December 30. The fair market value of the land is $15,000. Wade must include the $5,000 difference between the cost and the fair market value of the land in gross income for the taxable year. The bargain element represents additional compensation to Wade. His basis for the land is $15,000, the land's fair market value. ■

Identification Problems. Cost identification problems are frequently encountered in securities transactions. For example, the Regulations require that the taxpayer adequately identify the particular stock that has been sold.[26] A problem arises when the taxpayer has purchased separate lots of stock on different dates or at different prices and cannot adequately identify the lot from which a particular sale takes place. In this case, the stock is presumed to come from the first lot or lots purchased (a FIFO presumption).[27] When securities are left in the custody of a broker, it may be necessary to provide specific instructions and receive written confirmation as to which securities are being sold.

EXAMPLE 11

Polly purchases 100 shares of Olive Corporation stock on July 1, 2003, for $5,000 ($50 a share) and another 100 shares of Olive stock on July 1, 2004, for $6,000 ($60 a share). She sells 50 shares of the stock on January 2, 2005. The cost of the stock sold, assuming Polly

[24] § 1012 and Reg. § 1.1012–1(a).
[25] Reg. §§ 1.61–2(d)(2)(i) and 1.301–1(j).
[26] Reg. § 1.1012–1(c)(1).
[27] *Kluger Associates, Inc.*, 69 T.C. 925 (1978).

cannot adequately identify the shares, is $50 a share, or $2,500. This is the cost Polly will compare with the amount realized in determining the gain or loss from the sale. ■

Allocation Problems. When a taxpayer acquires *multiple assets in a lump-sum purchase*, the total cost must be allocated among the individual assets.[28] Allocation is necessary for several reasons:

- Some of the assets acquired may be depreciable (e.g., buildings), while others may not be (e.g., land).
- Only a portion of the assets acquired may be sold.
- Some of the assets may be capital or § 1231 assets that receive special tax treatment upon subsequent sale or other disposition.

The lump-sum cost is allocated on the basis of the fair market values of the individual assets acquired.

EXAMPLE 12

Harry purchases a building and land for $800,000. Because of the depressed nature of the industry in which the seller was operating, Harry was able to negotiate a very favorable purchase price. Appraisals of the individual assets indicate that the fair market value of the building is $600,000 and that of the land is $400,000. Harry's basis for the building is $480,000 [($600,000/$1,000,000) × $800,000], and his basis for the land is $320,000 [($400,000/$1,000,000) × $800,000]. ■

If a business is purchased and **goodwill** is involved, a special allocation rule applies. Initially, the purchase price is assigned to the assets, excluding goodwill, to the extent of their total fair market value. This assigned amount is allocated among the assets on the basis of the fair market value of the individual assets acquired. Goodwill is then assigned the residual amount of the purchase price. The resultant allocation is applicable to both the buyer and the seller.[29]

EXAMPLE 13

Rocky sells his business to Paul. They agree that the values of the individual assets are as follows:

Inventory	$ 50,000
Building	500,000
Land	200,000
Goodwill	150,000

After negotiations, Rocky and Paul agree on a sales price of $1 million. Applying the residual method with respect to goodwill results in the following allocation of the $1 million purchase price:

Inventory	$ 50,000
Building	500,000
Land	200,000
Goodwill	250,000

The residual method requires that all of the excess of the purchase price over the fair market value of the assets ($1,000,000 – $900,000 = $100,000) be allocated to goodwill. Without this requirement, the purchaser could allocate the excess pro rata to all of the assets, including goodwill, based on their respective fair market values. This would have resulted in only $166,667 [$150,000 + ($150,000 ÷ $900,000 × $100,000)] being assigned to goodwill. ■

[28] Reg. § 1.61–6(a).

[29] § 1060.

In the case of *nontaxable stock dividends*, the allocation depends on whether the dividend is a common stock dividend on common stock or a preferred stock dividend on common stock. If the dividend is common on common, the cost of the original common shares is allocated to the total shares owned after the dividend.[30]

EXAMPLE 14

Susan owns 100 shares of Sparrow Corporation common stock for which she paid $1,100. She receives a 10% common stock dividend, giving her a new total of 110 shares. Before the stock dividend, Susan's basis was $11 per share ($1,100 ÷ 100 shares). The basis of each share after the stock dividend is $10 ($1,100 ÷ 110 shares). ■

If the nontaxable stock dividend is preferred stock on common, the cost of the original common shares is allocated between the common and preferred shares on the basis of their relative fair market values on the date of distribution.[31]

EXAMPLE 15

Fran owns 100 shares of Cardinal Corporation common stock for which she paid $1,000. She receives a nontaxable stock dividend of 50 shares of preferred stock on her common stock. The fair market values on the date of distribution of the preferred stock dividend are $30 a share for common stock and $40 a share for preferred stock.

Fair market value of common ($30 × 100 shares)	$3,000
Fair market value of preferred ($40 × 50 shares)	2,000
	$5,000
Basis of common: 3/5 × $1,000	$ 600
Basis of preferred: 2/5 × $1,000	$ 400

The basis per share for the common stock is $6 ($600/100 shares). The basis per share for the preferred stock is $8 ($400/50 shares). ■

The holding period for a nontaxable stock dividend, whether received in the form of common stock or preferred stock, includes the holding period of the original shares.[32] The significance of the holding period for capital assets is discussed in Chapter 14.

In the case of *nontaxable stock rights*, the basis of the rights is zero unless the taxpayer elects or is required to allocate a portion of the cost of the stock already held to the newly received stock rights. If the fair market value of the rights is 15 percent or more of the fair market value of the stock, the taxpayer is required to allocate. If the value of the rights is less than 15 percent of the fair market value of the stock, the taxpayer may elect to allocate.[33] When allocation is required or elected, the cost of the stock on which the rights are received is allocated between the stock and the rights on the basis of their relative fair market values.

EXAMPLE 16

Donald receives nontaxable stock rights with a fair market value of $1,000. The fair market value of the stock on which the rights were received is $8,000 (cost $10,000). Donald does not elect to allocate. The basis of the rights is zero. If he exercises the rights, the basis of the new stock is the exercise (subscription) price. ■

EXAMPLE 17

Assume the same facts as in Example 16, except the fair market value of the rights is $3,000. Donald must allocate because the value of the rights ($3,000) is 15% or more of the value of the stock ($3,000/$8,000 = 37.5%).

- The basis of the stock is $7,273 [($8,000/$11,000) × $10,000].
- The basis of the rights is $2,727 [($3,000/$11,000) × $10,000].

[30]§§ 305(a) and 307(a).
[31]Reg. § 1.307–1(a).
[32]§ 1223(5) and Reg. § 1.1223–1(e).
[33]§ 307(b).

Frequent-Flier Miles and Basis

There are many ways to get frequent-flier miles. Perhaps the most logical is to fly on an airplane, but staying in a hotel, renting a car, and using your credit card can also generate frequent-flier miles. A more novel approach is to buy shares in a mutual fund.

Always watch out for the tax consequences, though. In a letter ruling, the IRS held that taxpayers who receive frequent-flier miles for buying mutual fund shares must reduce their mutual fund basis by the fair market value of the miles received. The mutual fund must notify its shareholders of the fair market value, which is based on the cost of buying frequent-flier miles from the airlines.

If Donald exercises the rights, the basis of the new stock is the exercise (subscription) price plus the basis of the rights. If he sells the rights, he recognizes gain or loss equal to the difference between the amount realized and the basis of the rights. This allocation rule applies only when the rights are exercised or sold. Therefore, if the rights are allowed to lapse (expire), they have no basis, and the basis of the original stock is the stock's cost, $10,000. ■

The holding period of nontaxable stock rights includes the holding period of the stock on which the rights were distributed. However, if the rights are exercised, the holding period of the newly acquired stock begins with the date the rights are exercised.[34]

GIFT BASIS

When a taxpayer receives property as a gift, there is no cost to the donee (recipient). Thus, under the cost basis provision, the donee's basis would be zero. However, this would violate the statutory intent that gifts not be subject to the income tax.[35] With a zero basis, if the donee sold the property, all of the amount realized would be treated as realized gain. Therefore, a basis is assigned to the property received depending on the following:

- The date of the gift.
- The basis of the property to the donor.
- The amount of the gift tax paid.
- The fair market value of the property.

Gift Basis Rules if No Gift Tax Is Paid. Property received by gift can be referred to as *dual basis* property; that is, the basis for gain and the basis for loss might not be the same amount. The present basis rules for gifts of property are as follows:

- If the donee disposes of gift property in a transaction that results in a gain, the basis to the donee is the same as the donor's adjusted basis.[36] The donee's basis in this case is referred to as the *gain basis*. Therefore, a *realized gain* results if the amount realized from the disposition exceeds the donee's gain basis.

[34] § 1223(5) and Reg. §§ 1.1223–1(e) and (f).
[35] § 102(a).
[36] § 1015(a) and Reg. § 1.1015–1(a)(1). See Reg. § 1.1015–1(a)(3) for cases in which the facts necessary to determine the donor's adjusted basis are unknown. Refer to Example 24 for the effect of depreciation deductions by the donee.

EXAMPLE 18

Melissa purchased stock in 2004 for $10,000. She gave the stock to her son, Joe, in 2005, when the fair market value was $15,000. No gift tax is paid on the transfer, and Joe subsequently sells the property for $15,000. Joe's basis is $10,000, and he has a realized gain of $5,000. ■

- If the donee disposes of gift property in a transaction that results in a loss, the basis to the donee is the *lower* of the donor's adjusted basis or the fair market value on the date of the gift. The donee's basis in this case is referred to as the *loss basis*. Therefore, a *realized loss* results if the amount realized from the disposition is less than the donee's loss basis.

EXAMPLE 19

Burt purchased stock in 2004 for $10,000. He gave the stock to his son, Cliff, in 2005, when the fair market value was $7,000. No gift tax is paid on the transfer. Cliff later sells the stock for $6,000. Cliff's basis is $7,000 (fair market value is less than donor's adjusted basis of $10,000), and the realized loss from the sale is $1,000 ($6,000 amount realized – $7,000 basis). ■

The amount of the loss basis will *differ* from the amount of the gain basis only if, at the date of the gift, the adjusted basis of the property exceeds the property's fair market value. Note that the loss basis rule prevents the donee from receiving a tax benefit from a decline in value that occurred while the donor held the property. Therefore, in Example 19, Cliff has a loss of only $1,000 rather than a loss of $4,000. The $3,000 difference represents the decline in value that occurred while Burt held the property. Ironically, however, the gain basis rule may result in the donee being subject to income tax on the appreciation that occurred while the donor held the property, as illustrated in Example 18.

If the amount realized from a sale or other disposition is *between* the basis for loss and the basis for gain, no gain or loss is realized.

EXAMPLE 20

Assume the same facts as in Example 19, except that Cliff sells the stock for $8,000. Application of the gain basis rule produces a loss of $2,000 ($8,000 – $10,000). Application of the loss basis rule produces a gain of $1,000 ($8,000 – $7,000). Because the amount realized is between the gain basis and the loss basis, Cliff recognizes neither a gain nor a loss. ■

Adjustment for Gift Tax. If gift taxes are paid by the donor, the donee's gain basis may exceed the adjusted basis of the property to the donor. This occurs only if the fair market value of the property at the date of the gift is greater than the donor's adjusted basis (the property has appreciated in value). The portion of the gift tax paid that is related to the appreciation is added to the donor's basis in calculating the donee's gain basis for the property. In this circumstance, the following formula is used for calculating the donee's gain basis:[37]

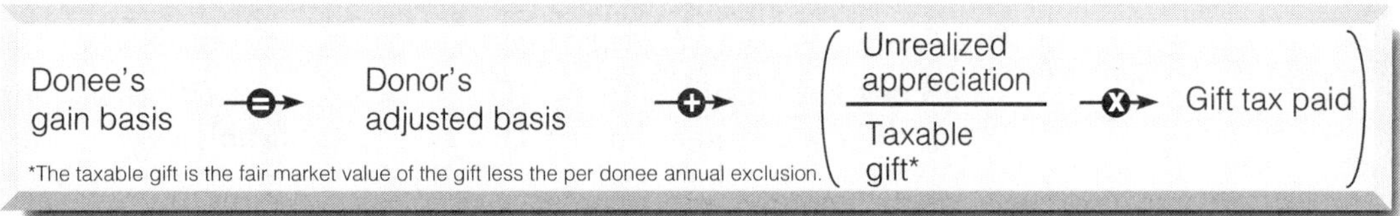

Donee's gain basis
=
Donor's adjusted basis
+
Unrealized appreciation
Taxable gift*
×
Gift tax paid
*The taxable gift is the fair market value of the gift less the per donee annual exclusion.

EXAMPLE 21

In 2005, Bonnie made a gift of stock (adjusted basis of $15,000) to Peggy. The stock had a fair market value of $50,000, and the transfer resulted in a gift tax of $4,000. The unrealized appreciation of the stock is $35,000 ($50,000 fair market value – $15,000 adjusted basis),

[37]§ 1015(d)(6) and Reg. § 1.1015–5(c)(2).

while the taxable gift is $39,000 ($50,000 fair market value of gift – $11,000 annual exclusion). Peggy's basis in the stock is $18,600, determined as follows:

Donor's adjusted basis	$15,000
Gift tax attributable to appreciation— $35,000/$39,000 = 90% (rounded) × $4,000	3,600
Donee's gain basis	$18,600

EXAMPLE 22

Don made a gift of stock to Matt in 2005, when the fair market value of the stock was $50,000. Don paid gift tax of $4,000. Don had purchased the stock in 1986 for $65,000. Because there is no unrealized appreciation at the date of the gift, none of the gift tax paid is added to Don's basis in calculating Matt's gain basis. Therefore, Matt's gain basis is $65,000.

For *gifts made before 1977*, the full amount of the gift tax paid is added to the donor's basis. However, the ceiling on this total is the fair market value of the property at the date of the gift. Thus, in Example 21, if the gift had been made before 1977, the basis of the property would be $19,000 ($15,000 + $4,000). In Example 22, the gain basis would still be $65,000 ($65,000 + $0).

Holding Period. The **holding period** for property acquired by gift begins on the date the donor acquired the property if the gain basis rule applies.[38] The holding period starts on the date of the gift if the loss basis rule applies.[39] The significance of the holding period for capital assets is discussed in Chapter 14.

The following example summarizes the basis and holding period rules for gift property:

EXAMPLE 23

Jill acquired 100 shares of Wren Corporation stock on December 30, 1987, for $40,000. On January 3, 2005, when the stock has a fair market value of $38,000, Jill gives it to Dennis and pays gift tax of $4,000. The basis is not increased by a portion of the gift tax paid because the property has not appreciated in value at the time of the gift, Therefore, Dennis's gain basis is $40,000. Dennis's basis for determining loss is $38,000 (fair market value) because the fair market value on the date of the gift is less than the donor's adjusted basis.

- If Dennis sells the stock for $45,000, he has a recognized gain of $5,000. The holding period for determining whether the capital gain is short term or long term begins on December 30, 1987, the date Jill acquired the property.
- If Dennis sells the stock for $36,000, he has a recognized loss of $2,000. The holding period for determining whether the capital loss is short term or long term begins on January 3, 2005, the date of the gift.
- If Dennis sells the property for $39,000, there is no loss because the amount realized is less than the gain basis of $40,000 and more than the loss basis of $38,000.

Basis for Depreciation. The basis for depreciation on depreciable gift property is the donee's gain basis.[40] This rule is applicable even if the donee later sells the property at a loss and uses the loss basis rule in calculating the amount of the realized loss.

EXAMPLE 24

Vito gave a machine to Tina in 2005. At that time, the adjusted basis was $32,000 (cost of $40,000 – accumulated depreciation of $8,000), and the fair market value was $26,000. No gift tax was paid. Tina's gain basis at the date of the gift is $32,000, and her loss basis is $26,000. During 2005, Tina deducts depreciation (cost recovery) of $6,400 ($32,000 × 20%).

[38] § 1223(2) and Reg. § 1.1223–1(b).
[39] Rev.Rul. 59–86, 1959–1 C.B. 209.
[40] § 1011 and Reg. §§ 1.1011–1 and 1.167(g)–1.

(Refer to Chapter 8 for the cost recovery tables.) At the end of 2005, Tina's gain basis and loss basis are calculated as follows:

	Gain Basis	Loss Basis
Donor's basis or fair market value	$32,000	$26,000
Depreciation	(6,400)	(6,400)
	$25,600	$19,600

■

PROPERTY ACQUIRED FROM A DECEDENT

General Rules. The basis of property acquired from a decedent is generally the property's fair market value at the date of death (referred to as the *primary valuation amount*).[41] The property's basis is the fair market value six months after the date of death if the executor or administrator of the estate *elects* the alternate valuation date for estate tax purposes. This amount is referred to as the *alternate valuation amount*.

EXAMPLE 25

Linda and various other family members inherited property from Linda's father, who died in 2005. At the date of death, her father's adjusted basis for the property Linda inherited was $35,000. The property's fair market value at the date of death was $50,000. The alternate valuation date was not elected. Linda's basis for income tax purposes is $50,000. This is commonly referred to as a *stepped-up basis*. ■

EXAMPLE 26

Assume the same facts as in Example 25, except the property's fair market value at the date of death was $20,000. Linda's basis for income tax purposes is $20,000. This is commonly referred to as a *stepped-down basis*. ■

No estate tax return must be filed for estates below a threshold amount. In such cases, the alternate valuation date and amount are not available. Even if an estate tax return is filed and the executor elects the alternate valuation date, the six months after death date is available only for property that the executor has not distributed before this date. For any property distributed or otherwise disposed of by the executor during the six-month period preceding the alternate valuation date, the adjusted basis to the beneficiary will equal the fair market value on the date of distribution or other disposition.[42]

The alternate valuation date can be *elected only* if, as a result of the election, both the value of the gross estate and the estate tax liability are lower than they would have been if the primary valuation date had been used. This provision prevents the alternate valuation election from being used to increase the basis of the property to the beneficiary for income tax purposes without simultaneously increasing the estate tax liability (because of estate tax deductions or credits).[43]

EXAMPLE 27

Nancy inherited all the property of her father, who died in 2005. Her father's adjusted basis for the property at the date of death was $350,000. The property's fair market value was $1,750,000 at the date of death and $1,760,000 six months after death. The alternate valuation date cannot be elected because the value of the gross estate has increased during the six-month period. Nancy's basis for income tax purposes is $1,750,000. ■

[41] § 1014(a).
[42] § 2032(a)(1) and Rev.Rul. 56–60, 1956–1 C.B. 443.
[43] § 2032(c).

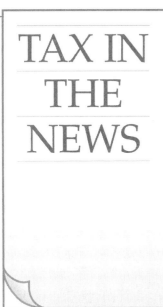

Effect of 2001 Tax Legislation on the Basis of Inherited Property: Bad News/Good News!

The *bad news* is that the Tax Relief Reconciliation Act of 2001 repeals the current step-up or step-down (i.e., fair market value) rules for the beneficiary's basis in inherited property and replaces them with a modified carryover basis. By itself, this change significantly increases the complexity of the tax law. A potential decedent will need to maintain detailed records on the cost of his or her assets and have such data readily available for the executor. Otherwise, the executor will be unable to determine the cost of many assets included in the estate.

So what is the *good news*? First, the effective date for this new carryover basis provision is deferred to deaths occurring after December 31, 2009. Second, the carryover basis approach for inherited property has been tried before. The results were so unsuccessful that the legislation was repealed retroactively by Congress. Hopefully, if the new carryover basis ever becomes effective, history will repeat itself, and another retroactive repeal by Congress will occur.

EXAMPLE 28

Assume the same facts as in Example 27, except the property's fair market value six months after death was $1,745,000. If the executor elects the alternate valuation date, Nancy's basis for income tax purposes is $1,745,000. ■

EXAMPLE 29

Assume the same facts as in the previous example, except the property is distributed four months after the date of the decedent's death. At the distribution date, the property's fair market value is $1,747,500. Since the executor elected the alternate valuation date, Nancy's basis for income tax purposes is $1,747,500. ■

For inherited property, both unrealized appreciation and decline in value are taken into consideration in determining the basis of the property for income tax purposes. Contrast this with the carryover basis rules for property received by gift.

Deathbed Gifts. The Code contains a provision designed to eliminate a tax avoidance technique referred to as *deathbed gifts*. With this technique, a donor makes a gift of appreciated property to a dying person with the understanding that the donor (or the donor's spouse) will inherit the property on the donee's death. If the time period between the date of the gift and the date of the donee's death is not longer than one year, the usual basis rule (stepped-up basis) for inherited property may not apply. The adjusted basis of such property inherited by the donor or his or her spouse from the donee is the same as the decedent's adjusted basis for the property rather than the fair market value at the date of death or the alternate valuation date.[44]

EXAMPLE 30

Ned gives stock to his uncle, Vern, in 2005. Ned's basis for the stock is $1,000, and the fair market value is $9,000. No gift tax is paid. Eight months later, Ned inherits the stock from Vern. At the date of Vern's death, the fair market value of the stock is $12,000. Ned's adjusted basis for the stock is $1,000. ■

Survivor's Share of Property. Both the decedent's share and the survivor's share of *community property* have a basis equal to the fair market value on the date of

[44]§ 1014(e).

the decedent's death.[45] This result applies to the decedent's share of the community property because the property flows to the surviving spouse from the estate (fair market value basis is assigned to inherited property). Likewise, the surviving spouse's share of the community property is deemed to be acquired by bequest, devise, or inheritance from the decedent. Therefore, it also has a basis equal to the fair market value.

EXAMPLE 31

Floyd and Vera reside in a community property state. They own as community property 200 shares of Crow stock acquired in 1981 for $100,000. Floyd dies in 2005, when the securities are valued at $300,000. One-half of the Crow stock is included in Floyd's estate. If Vera inherits Floyd's share of the community property, the basis for determining gain or loss is $300,000, determined as follows:

Vera's one-half of the community property (stepped up from $50,000 to $150,000 due to Floyd's death)	$150,000
Floyd's one-half of the community property (stepped up from $50,000 to $150,000 due to inclusion in his gross estate)	150,000
Vera's new basis	$300,000

In a *common law* state, only one-half of jointly held property of spouses (tenants by the entirety or joint tenants with rights of survivorship) is included in the estate.[46] In such a case, no adjustment of the basis is permitted for the excluded property interest (the surviving spouse's share).

EXAMPLE 32

Assume the same facts as in the previous example, except that the property is jointly held by Floyd and Vera who reside in a common law state. Floyd purchased the property and made a gift of one-half of the property to Vera when the stock was acquired. No gift tax was paid. Only one-half of the Crow stock is included in Floyd's estate. Vera's basis for determining gain or loss in the excluded half is not adjusted upward for the increase in value to date of death. Therefore, Vera's basis is $200,000, determined as follows:

Vera's one-half of the jointly held property (carryover basis of $50,000)	$ 50,000
Floyd's one-half of the jointly held property (stepped up from $50,000 to $150,000 due to inclusion in his gross estate)	150,000
Vera's new basis	$200,000

Holding Period of Property Acquired from a Decedent. The holding period of property acquired from a decedent is *deemed to be long term* (held for the required long-term holding period). This provision applies regardless of whether the property is disposed of at a gain or at a loss.[47]

LO.5

Describe various loss disallowance provisions.

DISALLOWED LOSSES

Related Taxpayers. Section 267 provides that realized losses from sales or exchanges of property, directly or indirectly, between certain related parties are not recognized. This loss disallowance provision applies to several types of related-party transactions. The most common involve (1) members of a family and (2) an individual and a corporation in which the individual owns, directly or indirectly, more than 50 percent in value of the corporation's outstanding stock. Section 707 provides a similar loss disallowance provision where the related parties are a partner and a partnership in which the partner owns, directly or indirectly, more

[45] § 1014(b)(6). See the listing of community property states in Chapter 4.

[46] § 2040(b).

[47] § 1223(11).

than 50 percent of the capital interests or profits interests in the partnership. The rules governing the relationships covered by § 267 were discussed in Chapter 6. See the discussion of the special rules under § 1041 for property transfers between spouses or incident to divorce later in this chapter.

If income-producing or business property is transferred to a related taxpayer and a loss is disallowed, the basis of the property to the recipient is the property's cost to the transferee. However, if a subsequent sale or other disposition of the property by the original transferee results in a realized gain, the amount of gain is reduced by the loss that was previously disallowed.[48] This *right of offset* is not applicable if the original sale involved the sale of a personal use asset (e.g., the sale of a personal residence between related taxpayers). Furthermore, the right of offset is available only to the original transferee (the related-party buyer).

EXAMPLE 33

Pedro sells business property with an adjusted basis of $50,000 to his daughter, Josefina, for its fair market value of $40,000. Pedro's realized loss of $10,000 is not recognized.

- How much gain does Josefina recognize if she sells the property for $52,000? Josefina recognizes a $2,000 gain. Her realized gain is $12,000 ($52,000 less her basis of $40,000), but she can offset Pedro's $10,000 loss against the gain.
- How much gain does Josefina recognize if she sells the property for $48,000? Josefina recognizes no gain or loss. Her realized gain is $8,000 ($48,000 less her basis of $40,000), but she can offset $8,000 of Pedro's $10,000 loss against the gain. Note that Pedro's loss can only offset Josefina's gain. It cannot create a loss for Josefina.
- How much loss does Josefina recognize if she sells the property for $38,000? Josefina recognizes a $2,000 loss, the same as her realized loss ($38,000 less $40,000 basis). Pedro's loss does not increase Josefina's loss. His loss can be offset only against a gain. Since Josefina has no realized gain, Pedro's loss cannot be used and is never recognized. This part of the example assumes that the property is business or income-producing property to Josefina. If not, her $2,000 loss is personal and is not recognized. ■

The loss disallowance rules are designed to achieve two objectives. First, the rules prevent a taxpayer from directly transferring an unrealized loss to a related taxpayer in a higher tax bracket who could receive a greater tax benefit from recognition of the loss. Second, the rules eliminate a substantial administrative burden on the Internal Revenue Service as to the appropriateness of the selling price (fair market value or not). The loss disallowance rules are applicable even where the selling price is equal to the fair market value and can be validated (e.g., listed stocks).

The holding period of the buyer for the property is not affected by the holding period of the seller. That is, the buyer's *holding period* includes only the period of time he or she has held the property.[49]

ETHICAL CONSIDERATIONS

Transactions between Spouses

At the time of their marriage, Ted and Lisa each had substantial assets. Consequently, they signed a premarital agreement to keep their assets separate and avoid any commingling. They do, however, own some undeveloped land jointly, with each having contributed $500,000 toward the $1 million purchase price. Though the value of the land is currently depressed, considerable profit would result if they could successfully have the land rezoned from residential to commercial use. Lisa has serious doubts that a rezoning request would be approved, but Ted thinks otherwise.

[48] § 267(d) and Reg. § 1.267(d)–1(a).

[49] §§ 267(d) and 1223(2) and Reg. § 1.267(d)–1(c)(3).

Ted has offered to buy Lisa's 50 percent interest in the land for $300,000. Lisa's CPA informs her that her realized loss of $200,000 on the sale would be disallowed under § 267 as a transaction between related parties. He also informs her that Ted, but not Lisa, could use this disallowed loss to reduce any recognized gain he might have on a subsequent sale of the land.

Horrified by these results, Lisa concludes that their marriage relationship is producing too many negative tax consequences. She proposes to Ted that they get a divorce "for tax purposes" and continue to live together as man and wife. Only Lisa, Ted, and their attorney would know that they are no longer married. Being no longer legally married, she could carry out the sale to Ted and avoid the related-party disallowance of loss rules of § 267. Comment on the propriety of Lisa's proposal.

Wash Sales. Section 1091 stipulates that in certain cases, a realized loss on the sale or exchange of stock or securities is not recognized. Specifically, if a taxpayer sells or exchanges stock or securities and within 30 days before *or* after the date of the sale or exchange acquires substantially identical stock or securities, any loss realized from the sale or exchange is not recognized because the transaction is a **wash sale.**[50] The term *acquire* means acquire by purchase or in a taxable exchange and includes an option to purchase substantially identical securities. *Substantially identical* means the same in all important particulars. Corporate bonds and preferred stock are normally not considered substantially identical to the corporation's common stock. However, if the bonds and preferred stock are convertible into common stock, they may be considered substantially identical under certain circumstances.[51] Attempts to avoid the application of the wash sales rules by having a related taxpayer repurchase the securities have been unsuccessful.[52] The wash sales provisions do *not* apply to gains.

Recognition of the loss is disallowed because the taxpayer is considered to be in substantially the same economic position after the sale and repurchase as before the sale and repurchase. This disallowance rule does not apply to taxpayers engaged in the business of buying and selling securities.[53] Investors, however, are not allowed to create losses through wash sales to offset income for tax purposes.

Realized loss that is not recognized is added to the *basis* of the substantially identical stock or securities whose acquisition resulted in the nonrecognition of loss.[54] In other words, the basis of the replacement stock or securities is increased by the amount of the unrecognized loss. If the loss were not added to the basis of the newly acquired stock or securities, the taxpayer would never recover the entire basis of the old stock or securities.

The basis of the new stock or securities includes the unrecovered portion of the basis of the formerly held stock or securities. Therefore, the *holding period* of the new stock or securities begins on the date of acquisition of the old stock or securities.[55]

EXAMPLE 34

Bhaskar owns 100 shares of Green Corporation stock (adjusted basis of $20,000). He sells 50 shares for $8,000. Ten days later, he purchases 50 shares of the same stock for $7,000. Bhaskar's realized loss of $2,000 ($8,000 amount realized – $10,000 adjusted basis of 50 shares) is not recognized because it resulted from a wash sale. Bhaskar's basis in the newly acquired stock is $9,000 ($7,000 purchase price + $2,000 unrecognized loss from the wash sale). ■

A taxpayer may acquire fewer shares than the number sold in a wash sale. In this case, the loss from the sale is prorated between recognized and unrecognized loss on the basis of the ratio of the number of shares acquired to the number of shares sold.[56]

---

[50] § 1091(a) and Reg. §§ 1.1091–1(a) and (f).
[51] Rev.Rul. 56–406, 1956–2 C.B. 523.
[52] *McWilliams v. Comm.*, 47–1 USTC ¶9289, 35 AFTR 1184, 67 S.Ct. 1477 (USSC, 1947).
[53] Reg. § 1.1091–1(a).
[54] § 1091(d) and Reg. § 1.1091–2(a).
[55] § 1223(4) and Reg. § 1.1223–1(d).
[56] § 1091(b) and Reg. § 1.1091–1(c).

CONVERSION OF PROPERTY FROM PERSONAL USE TO BUSINESS OR INCOME-PRODUCING USE

As discussed previously, losses from the sale of personal use assets are not recognized for tax purposes, but losses from the sale of business and income-producing assets are deductible. Can a taxpayer convert a personal use asset that has declined in value to business or income-producing use and then sell the asset to recognize a business or income-producing loss? The tax law prevents this practice by specifying that the *original basis for loss* on personal use assets converted to business or income-producing use is the *lower* of the property's adjusted basis or fair market value on the date of conversion.[57] The *gain basis* for converted property is the property's adjusted basis on the date of conversion. The tax law is not concerned with gains on converted property because gains are recognized regardless of whether property is business, income-producing, or personal use.

EXAMPLE 35

Diane's personal residence has an adjusted basis of $175,000 and a fair market value of $160,000. Diane converts the personal residence to rental property. Her basis for loss is $160,000 (lower of $175,000 adjusted basis and fair market value of $160,000). The $15,000 decline in value is a personal loss and can never be recognized for tax purposes. Diane's basis for gain is $175,000. ■

The basis for loss is also the *basis for depreciating* the converted property.[58] This is an exception to the general rule that the basis for depreciation is the gain basis (e.g., property received by gift). This exception prevents the taxpayer from recovering a personal loss indirectly through depreciation of the higher original basis. After the property is converted, both its basis for loss and its basis for gain are adjusted for depreciation deductions from the date of conversion to the date of disposition. These rules apply only if a conversion from personal to business or income-producing use has actually occurred.

EXAMPLE 36

At a time when his personal residence (adjusted basis of $140,000) is worth $150,000, Keith converts one-half of it to rental use. Assume the property is not MACRS recovery property. At this point, the estimated useful life of the residence is 20 years, and there is no estimated salvage value. After renting the converted portion for five years, Keith sells the property for $144,000. All amounts relate only to the building; the land has been accounted for separately. Keith has a $2,000 realized gain from the sale of the personal use portion of the residence and a $19,500 realized gain from the sale of the rental portion. These gains are computed as follows:

	Personal Use	Rental
Original basis for gain and loss—adjusted basis on date of conversion (fair market value is greater than the adjusted basis)	$70,000	$70,000
Depreciation—five years	None	17,500
Adjusted basis—date of sale	$70,000	$52,500
Amount realized	72,000	72,000
Realized gain	$ 2,000	$19,500

■

As discussed later in this chapter, Keith may be able to exclude the $2,000 realized gain from the sale of the personal use portion of the residence under § 121. If the § 121 exclusion applies, only $17,500 (equal to the depreciation deducted) of the $19,500 realized gain from the rental portion is recognized.

[57] Reg. § 1.165–9(b)(2).

[58] Reg. § 1.167(g)–1.

EXAMPLE 37

Assume the same facts as in the previous example, except that the fair market value on the date of conversion is $130,000 and the sales proceeds are $90,000. Keith has a $25,000 realized loss from the sale of the personal use portion of the residence and a $3,750 realized loss from the sale of the rental portion. These losses are computed as follows:

	Personal Use	Rental
Original basis for loss—fair market value on date of conversion (fair market value is less than the adjusted basis)	*	$65,000
Depreciation—five years	None	16,250
Adjusted basis—date of sale	$70,000	$48,750
Amount realized	45,000	45,000
Realized loss	($25,000)	($ 3,750)

*Not applicable.

The $25,000 loss from the sale of the personal use portion of the residence is not recognized. The $3,750 loss from the rental portion is recognized. ■

ADDITIONAL COMPLEXITIES IN DETERMINING REALIZED GAIN OR LOSS

Amount Realized. The calculation of the amount realized may appear to be one of the least complex areas associated with property transactions. However, because numerous positive and negative adjustments may be required, this calculation can be complex and confusing. In addition, determining the fair market value of the items received by the taxpayer can be difficult. The following example provides insight into various items that can affect the amount realized.

EXAMPLE 38

Ridge sells an office building and the associated land on October 1, 2005. Under the terms of the sales contract, Ridge is to receive $600,000 in cash. The purchaser is to assume Ridge's mortgage of $300,000 on the property. To enable the purchaser to obtain adequate financing, Ridge is to pay the $15,000 in points charged by the lender. The broker's commission on the sale is $45,000. The purchaser agrees to pay the $12,000 in property taxes for the entire year. The amount realized by Ridge is calculated as follows:

Selling price		
Cash	$600,000	
Mortgage assumed by purchaser	300,000	
Seller's property taxes paid by purchaser ($12,000 × $\frac{9}{12}$)	9,000	$909,000
Less		
Broker's commission	$ 45,000	
Points paid by seller	15,000	(60,000)
Amount realized		$849,000

■

Adjusted Basis. Three types of issues tend to complicate the determination of adjusted basis. First, the applicable tax provisions for calculating the adjusted basis depend on how the property was acquired (e.g., purchase, taxable exchange, nontaxable exchange, gift, inheritance). Second, if the asset is subject to depreciation, cost recovery, amortization, or depletion, adjustments must be made to the basis during the time period the asset is held by the taxpayer. Upon disposition of the asset, the taxpayer's records for both of these items may be deficient. For example, the donee does not know the amount of the donor's basis or the amount of gift tax paid by the donor, or the taxpayer does not know how much depreciation he or she has deducted. Third, the complex positive and negative adjustments encountered in calculating the amount realized are also involved in calculating the adjusted basis.

EXAMPLE 39

Jane purchased a personal residence in 1996. The purchase price and the related closing costs were as follows:

Purchase price	$125,000
Recording costs	140
Title fees and title insurance	815
Survey costs	115
Attorney's fees	750
Appraisal fee	60

Other relevant tax information for the house during the time Jane owned it is as follows:

- Constructed a swimming pool for medical reasons. The cost was $10,000, of which $3,000 was deducted as a medical expense.
- Added a solar heating system. The cost was $15,000.
- Deducted home office expenses of $6,000. Of this amount, $3,200 was for depreciation.

The adjusted basis for the house is calculated as follows:

Purchase price	$125,000
Recording costs	140
Title fees and title insurance	815
Survey costs	115
Attorney's fees	750
Appraisal fee	60
Swimming pool ($10,000 – $3,000)	7,000
Solar heating system	15,000
	$148,880
Less: Depreciation deducted on home office	(3,200)
Adjusted basis	$145,680

■

SUMMARY OF BASIS ADJUSTMENTS

Some of the more common items that either increase or decrease the basis of an asset appear in Concept Summary 13–2.

In discussing the topic of basis, a number of specific techniques for determining basis have been presented. Although the various techniques are responsive to and mandated by transactions occurring in the marketplace, they do possess enough common characteristics to be categorized as follows:

- The basis of the asset may be determined by reference to the asset's cost.
- The basis of the asset may be determined by reference to the basis of another asset.
- The basis of the asset may be determined by reference to the asset's fair market value.
- The basis of the asset may be determined by reference to the basis of the asset to another taxpayer.

Concept Summary 13–2

Adjustments to Basis

Item	Effect	Refer to Chapter	Explanation
Amortization of bond discount.	Increase	14	Amortization is mandatory for certain taxable bonds and elective for tax-exempt bonds.
Amortization of bond premium.	Decrease	13	Amortization is mandatory for tax-exempt bonds and elective for taxable bonds.
Amortization of covenant not to compete.	Decrease	14	Covenant must be for a definite and limited time period. The amortization period is a statutory period of 15 years.
Amortization of intangibles.	Decrease	8	Intangibles are amortized over a 15-year period.
Assessment for local benefits.	Increase	10	To the extent not deductible as taxes (e.g., assessment for streets and sidewalks that increase the value of the property versus one for maintenance or repair or for meeting interest charges).
Bad debts.	Decrease	7	Only the specific charge-off method is permitted.
Capital additions.	Increase	13	Certain items, at the taxpayer's election, can be capitalized or deducted (e.g., selected medical expenses).
Casualty.	Decrease	7	For a casualty loss, the amount of the adjustment is the summation of the deductible loss and the insurance proceeds received. For a casualty gain, the amount of the adjustment is the insurance proceeds received reduced by the recognized gain.
Condemnation.	Decrease	13	See casualty explanation.
Cost recovery.	Decrease	8	§ 168 is applicable to tangible assets placed in service after 1980 whose useful life is expressed in terms of years.
Depletion.	Decrease	8	Use the greater of cost or percentage depletion. Percentage depletion can still be deducted when the basis is zero.
Depreciation.	Decrease	8	§ 167 is applicable to tangible assets placed in service before 1981 and to tangible assets not depreciated in terms of years.
Easement.	Decrease	13	If the taxpayer does not retain any use of the land, all of the basis is allocable to the easement transaction. However, if only part of the land is affected by the easement, only part of the basis is allocable to the easement transaction.
Improvements by lessee to lessor's property.	Increase	5	Adjustment occurs only if the lessor is required to include the fair market value of the improvements in gross income under § 109.
Imputed interest.	Decrease	16	Amount deducted is not part of the cost of the asset.
Inventory: lower of cost or market.	Decrease	16	Not available if the LIFO method is used.
Limited expensing under § 179.	Decrease	8	Occurs only if the taxpayer elects § 179 treatment.

Item	Effect	Refer to Chapter	Explanation
Medical capital expenditure permitted as a medical expense.	Decrease	10	Adjustment is the amount of the deduction (the effect on basis is to increase it by the amount of the capital expenditure net of the deduction).
Real estate taxes: apportionment between the buyer and seller.	Increase or decrease	10	To the extent the buyer pays the seller's pro rata share, the buyer's basis is increased. To the extent the seller pays the buyer's pro rata share, the buyer's basis is decreased.
Rebate from manufacturer.	Decrease		Since the rebate is treated as an adjustment to the purchase price, it is not included in the buyer's gross income.
Stock dividend.	Decrease	5	Adjustment occurs only if the stock dividend is nontaxable. While the basis per share decreases, the total stock basis does not change.
Stock rights.	Decrease	13	Adjustment to stock basis occurs only for nontaxable stock rights and only if the fair market value of the rights is at least 15% of the fair market value of the stock or, if less than 15%, the taxpayer elects to allocate the basis between the stock and the rights.
Theft.	Decrease	7	See casualty explanation.

LO.6

Understand the rationale for nonrecognition (postponement) of gain or loss in certain property transactions.

General Concept of a Nontaxable Exchange

A taxpayer who is going to replace a productive asset (e.g., machinery) used in a trade or business may structure the transactions as a sale of the old asset and the purchase of a new asset. When this approach is used, any realized gain or loss on the asset sale is recognized. The basis of the new asset is its cost. Alternatively, the taxpayer may be able to trade the old asset for the new asset. This exchange of assets may produce beneficial tax consequences by qualifying for nontaxable exchange treatment.

The tax law recognizes that nontaxable exchanges result in a change in the *form* but not in the *substance* of the taxpayer's relative economic position. The replacement property received in the exchange is viewed as substantially a continuation of the old investment.[59] Additional justification for nontaxable exchange treatment is that this type of transaction does not provide the taxpayer with the wherewithal to pay the tax on any realized gain.

The nonrecognition provisions for nontaxable exchanges do not apply to realized losses from the sale or exchange of personal use assets. Such losses are not recognized (are disallowed) because they are personal in nature and not because of any nonrecognition provision.

In a **nontaxable exchange,** realized gains or losses are not recognized. However, the nonrecognition is usually temporary. The recognition of gain or loss is *postponed* (deferred) until the property received in the nontaxable exchange is subsequently

[59] Reg. § 1.1002–1(c).

disposed of in a taxable transaction. This is accomplished by assigning a carryover basis to the replacement property.

EXAMPLE 40

Debra exchanges property with an adjusted basis of $10,000 and a fair market value of $12,000 for property with a fair market value of $12,000. The transaction qualifies for nontaxable exchange treatment. Debra has a realized gain of $2,000 ($12,000 amount realized – $10,000 adjusted basis). Her recognized gain is $0. Her basis in the replacement property is a carryover basis of $10,000. Assume the replacement property is nondepreciable and Debra subsequently sells it for $12,000. Her realized and recognized gain will be the $2,000 gain that was postponed (deferred) in the nontaxable transaction. If the replacement property is depreciable, the carryover basis of $10,000 is used in calculating depreciation. ■

In some nontaxable exchanges, only part of the property involved in the transaction qualifies for nonrecognition treatment. If the taxpayer receives cash or other nonqualifying property, part or all of the realized gain from the exchange is recognized. In these instances, gain is recognized because the taxpayer has changed or improved his or her relative economic position and has the wherewithal to pay income tax to the extent of cash or other property received.

It is important to distinguish between a nontaxable disposition, as the term is used in the statute, and a tax-free transaction. First, a direct exchange is not required in all circumstances (e.g., replacement of involuntarily converted property). Second, as previously mentioned, the term *nontaxable* refers to postponement of recognition via a carryover basis. In a *tax-free* transaction, the nonrecognition is permanent (e.g., see the discussion later in the chapter of the § 121 exclusion of realized gain on the sale of a personal residence). Therefore, the basis of any property acquired in a tax-free transaction does not depend on the basis of the property disposed of by the taxpayer.

LO.7

Apply the nonrecognition provisions and basis determination rules for like-kind exchanges.

Like-Kind Exchanges—§ 1031

Section 1031 provides for nontaxable exchange treatment if the following requirements are satisfied:[60]

- The form of the transaction is an exchange.
- Both the property transferred and the property received are held either for productive use in a trade or business or for investment.
- The property is like-kind property.

Like-kind exchanges include business for business, business for investment, investment for business, or investment for investment property. Property held for personal use, inventory, and partnership interests (both limited and general) do not qualify under the like-kind exchange provisions. Securities, even though held for investment, do not qualify for like-kind exchange treatment.

The nonrecognition provision for like-kind exchanges is *mandatory* rather than elective. A taxpayer who wants to recognize a realized gain or loss will have to structure the transaction in a form that does not satisfy the statutory requirements for a like-kind exchange. This topic is discussed further under Tax Planning Considerations.

[60] § 1031(a) and Reg. § 1.1031(a)–1(a).

LIKE-KIND PROPERTY

"The words 'like-kind' refer to the nature or character of the property and not to its grade or quality. One kind or class of property may not . . . be exchanged for property of a different kind or class."[61]

The term *like-kind* is intended to be interpreted very broadly. However, three categories of exchanges are not included. First, livestock of different sexes do not qualify as like-kind property. Second, real estate can be exchanged only for other real estate, and personalty can be exchanged only for other personalty. For example, the exchange of a machine (personalty) for an office building (realty) is not a like-kind exchange. *Real estate* (or realty) includes principally rental buildings, office and store buildings, manufacturing plants, warehouses, and land. It is immaterial whether real estate is improved or unimproved. Thus, unimproved land can be exchanged for an apartment house. Personalty includes principally machines, equipment, trucks, automobiles, furniture, and fixtures. Third, real property located in the United States exchanged for foreign real property (and vice versa) does not qualify as like-kind property.

EXAMPLE 41

Wade made the following exchanges during the taxable year:

a. Inventory for a machine used in business.
b. Land held for investment for a building used in business.
c. Stock held for investment for equipment used in business.
d. A business truck for a business truck.
e. An automobile used for personal transportation for an automobile used in business.
f. Livestock for livestock of a different sex.
g. Land held for investment in New York for land held for investment in London.

Exchanges (b), investment real property for business real property, and (d), business personalty for business personalty, qualify as exchanges of like-kind property. Exchanges (a), inventory; (c), stock; (e), personal use automobile (not held for business or investment purposes); (f), livestock of different sexes; and (g), U.S. and foreign real estate do not qualify. ■

A special provision relates to the location where personal property is used. Personal property used predominantly within the United States and personal property used predominantly outside the United States are not like-kind property. The location of use for the personal property given up is its location during the two-year period ending on the date of disposition of the property. The location of use for the personal property received is its location during the two-year period beginning on the date of the acquisition.

EXAMPLE 42

In October 2004, Walter exchanges a machine used in his factory in Denver for a machine that qualifies as like-kind property. In January 2005, the factory, including the machine, is moved to Berlin, Germany. As of January 2005, the exchange is not an exchange of like-kind property. The predominant use of the original machine was in the United States, whereas the predominant use of the new machine is foreign. ■

Another special provision applies if the taxpayers involved in the exchange are *related parties* under § 267(b). To qualify for like-kind exchange treatment, the taxpayer and the related party must not dispose of the like-kind property received in the exchange within the two-year period following the date of the exchange. If such an early disposition does occur, the postponed gain is recognized as of the date of the early disposition. Dispositions due to death, involuntary conversions, and certain non-tax avoidance transactions are not treated as early dispositions.

[61]Reg. § 1.1031(a)–1(b).

ETHICAL CONSIDERATIONS

An Assumption for a Related-Party Exchange

Marcie owns a 10 percent interest in a shopping mall located in Portland, Maine. Her adjusted basis for her interest is $250,000, and its fair market value is $900,000. She exchanges it for undeveloped land in York, Pennsylvania, that is held by her sister, Sandra. Marcie is aware of the § 1031 related-party requirement that neither she nor Sandra dispose of the property received for a two-year period. Both Marcie and Sandra intend to hold the property as long-term investments. However, they agree to notify each other if a disposition does take place within two years of the exchange.

During the next six months, the land that Marcie received in the exchange continues to appreciate. Due to poor management, however, the value of Sandra's interest in the shopping mall declines to $700,000. As a result, Sandra is angry with Marcie and vows "never to speak to Marcie, her husband, or any of Marcie's children again."

As Marcie receives no communication from Sandra during the next 18 months, she assumes that her gain of $650,000 will continue to be deferred. Evaluate Marcie's assumption.

Regulations dealing with § 1031 like-kind exchange treatment provide that if the exchange transaction involves multiple assets of a business (e.g., a television station for another television station), the determination of whether the assets qualify as like-kind property will not be made at the business level.[62] Instead, the underlying assets must be evaluated.

The Regulations also provide for greater specificity in determining whether depreciable tangible personal property is of a like kind or class. Such property held for productive use in a business is of a like class only if the exchanged property is within the same *general business asset class* (as specified by the IRS in Revenue Procedure 87–57 or as subsequently modified) or the same *product class* (as specified by the Department of Commerce). Property included in a general business asset class is evaluated under this system rather than under the product class system.

The following are examples of general business asset classes:

- Office furniture, fixtures, and equipment.
- Information systems (computers and peripheral equipment).
- Airplanes.
- Automobiles and taxis.
- Buses.
- Light general-purpose trucks.
- Heavy general-purpose trucks.

These Regulations have made it more difficult for depreciable tangible personal property to qualify for § 1031 like-kind exchange treatment. For example, the exchange of office equipment for a computer does not qualify as an exchange of like-kind property. Even though both assets are depreciable tangible personal property, they are not like-kind property because they are in different general business asset classes.

EXCHANGE REQUIREMENT

The transaction must involve a direct exchange of property to qualify as a like-kind exchange. The sale of old property and the purchase of new property, even though like kind, is generally not an exchange. However, if the two transactions are mutually dependent, the IRS may treat them as a like-kind exchange. For example, if

[62] Reg. § 1.1031(j)–1.

the taxpayer sells an old business machine to a dealer and purchases a new one from the same dealer, like-kind exchange treatment could result.[63]

The taxpayer may want to avoid nontaxable exchange treatment. Recognition of gain gives the taxpayer a higher basis for depreciation (see Example 74). To the extent that such gains would, if recognized, either receive favorable capital gain treatment or be passive activity income that could offset passive activity losses, it might be preferable to avoid the nonrecognition provisions through an indirect exchange transaction. For example, a taxpayer may sell property to one individual, recognize the gain, and subsequently purchase similar property from another individual. The taxpayer may also want to avoid nontaxable exchange treatment so that a realized loss can be recognized.

If the exchange is a delayed (nonsimultaneous) exchange, there are time limits on its completion. In a delayed like-kind exchange, one party fails to take immediate title to the new property because it has not yet been identified. The Code provides that the delayed swap will qualify as a like-kind exchange if the following requirements are satisfied:

- *Identification period.* The new property must be identified within 45 days of the date when the old property was transferred.
- *Exchange period.* The new property must be received by the earlier of the following:
  - Within 180 days of the date when the old property was transferred.
  - The due date (including extensions) for the tax return covering the year of the transfer.

Are these time limits firm, or can they be extended due to unforeseen circumstances? Indications are that the IRS will allow no deviation from either the identification period or the exchange period even when events outside the taxpayer's control preclude strict compliance.

BOOT

If the taxpayer in a like-kind exchange gives or receives some property that is not like-kind property, recognition may occur. Property that is not like-kind property, including cash, is referred to as **boot.** Although the term *boot* does not appear in the Code, tax practitioners commonly use it rather than saying "property that is not like-kind property."

The *receipt* of boot will trigger recognition of gain if there is realized gain. The amount of the recognized gain is the *lesser* of the boot received or the realized gain (realized gain serves as the ceiling on recognition).

EXAMPLE 43

Emily and Fran exchange machinery, and the exchange qualifies as like kind under § 1031. Since Emily's machinery (adjusted basis of $20,000) is worth $24,000 and Fran's machine has a fair market value of $19,000, Fran also gives Emily cash of $5,000. Emily's recognized gain is $4,000, the lesser of the realized gain ($24,000 amount realized − $20,000 adjusted basis = $4,000) or the fair market value of the boot received ($5,000). ■

EXAMPLE 44

Assume the same facts as in the previous example, except that Fran's machine is worth $21,000 (not $19,000). Under these circumstances, Fran gives Emily cash of $3,000 to make up the difference. Emily's recognized gain is $3,000, the lesser of the realized gain of $4,000 ($24,000 amount realized − $20,000 adjusted basis) or the fair market value of the boot received of $3,000. ■

[63] Rev.Rul. 61–119, 1961–1 C.B. 395.

The receipt of boot does not result in recognition if there is realized loss.

EXAMPLE 45

Assume the same facts as in Example 43, except that the adjusted basis of Emily's machine is $30,000. Emily's realized loss is $6,000 ($24,000 amount realized – $30,000 adjusted basis). The receipt of the boot of $5,000 does not trigger recognition. Therefore, the recognized loss is $0. ■

The *giving* of boot usually does not trigger recognition. If the boot given is cash, no realized gain or loss is recognized.

EXAMPLE 46

Fred and Gary exchange equipment in a like-kind exchange. Fred receives equipment with a fair market value of $25,000 and transfers equipment worth $21,000 (adjusted basis of $15,000) and cash of $4,000. Fred's realized gain is $6,000 ($25,000 amount realized – $15,000 adjusted basis – $4,000 cash). However, none of the realized gain is recognized. ■

If, however, the boot given is appreciated or depreciated property, gain or loss is recognized to the extent of the difference between the adjusted basis and the fair market value of the boot. For this purpose, *appreciated or depreciated property* is defined as property whose adjusted basis is not equal to the fair market value.

EXAMPLE 47

Assume the same facts as in the previous example, except that Fred transfers equipment worth $10,000 (adjusted basis of $12,000) and boot worth $15,000 (adjusted basis of $9,000). Fred's realized gain appears to be $4,000 ($25,000 amount realized – $21,000 adjusted basis). Since realization previously has served as a ceiling on recognition, it appears that the recognized gain is $4,000 (lower of realized gain of $4,000 or amount of appreciation on boot of $6,000). However, the recognized gain actually is $6,000 (full amount of the appreciation on the boot). In effect, Fred must calculate the like-kind and boot parts of the transaction separately. That is, the realized loss of $2,000 on the like-kind property is not recognized ($10,000 fair market value – $12,000 adjusted basis), and the $6,000 realized gain on the boot is recognized ($15,000 fair market value – $9,000 adjusted basis). ■

BASIS AND HOLDING PERIOD OF PROPERTY RECEIVED

If an exchange does not qualify as nontaxable under § 1031, gain or loss is recognized, and the basis of property received in the exchange is the property's fair market value. If the exchange qualifies for nonrecognition, the basis of property received must be adjusted to reflect any postponed (deferred) gain or loss. The *basis of like-kind property* received in the exchange is the property's fair market value less postponed gain or plus postponed loss. If the exchange partially qualifies for nonrecognition (if recognition is associated with boot), the basis of like-kind property received in the exchange is the property's fair market value less postponed gain or plus postponed loss. The *basis* of any *boot* received is the boot's fair market value.

If there is a postponed loss, nonrecognition creates a situation in which the taxpayer has recovered *less* than the cost or other basis of the property exchanged in an amount equal to the unrecognized loss. If there is a postponed gain, the taxpayer has recovered *more* than the cost or other basis of the property exchanged in an amount equal to the unrecognized gain.

EXAMPLE 48

Jaime exchanges a building (used in his business) with an adjusted basis of $30,000 and a fair market value of $38,000 for land with a fair market value of $38,000. The land is to be held as an investment. The exchange qualifies as like kind (an exchange of business real property for investment real property). Thus, the basis of the land is $30,000 (the land's fair market value of $38,000 less the $8,000 postponed gain on the building). If the land is later sold for its fair market value of $38,000, the $8,000 postponed gain is recognized. ■

EXAMPLE 49

Assume the same facts as in the previous example, except that the building has an adjusted basis of $48,000 and a fair market value of only $38,000. The basis in the newly acquired land is $48,000 (fair market value of $38,000 plus the $10,000 postponed loss on the building). If the land is later sold for its fair market value of $38,000, the $10,000 postponed loss is recognized. ■

The Code provides an alternative approach for determining the basis of like-kind property received:

Adjusted basis of like-kind property surrendered
+ Adjusted basis of boot given
+ Gain recognized
– Fair market value of boot received
– Loss recognized
= *Basis of like-kind property received*

This approach is logical in terms of the recovery of capital doctrine. That is, the unrecovered cost or other basis is increased by additional cost (boot given) or decreased by cost recovered (boot received). Any gain recognized is included in the basis of the new property. The taxpayer has been taxed on this amount and is now entitled to recover it tax-free. Any loss recognized is deducted from the basis of the new property. The taxpayer has received a tax benefit on that amount.

The holding period of the property surrendered in the exchange carries over and *tacks on* to the holding period of the like-kind property received.[64] See Chapter 14 for a discussion of the relevance of the holding period.

Depreciation recapture potential carries over to the property received in a like-kind exchange.[65] See Chapter 14 for a discussion of this topic.

The following comprehensive example illustrates the like-kind exchange rules.

EXAMPLE 50

Vicki exchanged the following old machines for new machines in five independent like-kind exchanges:

Exchange	Adjusted Basis of Old Machine	Fair Market Value of New Machine	Adjusted Basis of Boot Given	Fair Market Value of Boot Received
1	$4,000	$9,000	$ -0-	$ -0-
2	4,000	9,000	3,000	-0-
3	4,000	9,000	6,000	-0-
4	4,000	9,000	-0-	3,000
5	4,000	3,500	-0-	300

Vicki's realized and recognized gains and losses and the basis of each of the like-kind properties received are as follows:

[64] § 1223(1) and Reg. § 1.1223–1(a). For this carryover holding period rule to apply to like-kind exchanges after March 1, 1954, the like-kind property surrendered must have been either a capital asset or § 1231 property. See Chapter 14 for the discussion of capital assets and § 1231 property.

[65] Reg. §§ 1.1245–2(a)(4) and 1.1250–2(d)(1).

			New Basis Calculation											
Exchange	**Realized Gain (Loss)**	**Recognized Gain (Loss)**	Old Adj. Basis	+	Boot Given	+	Gain Recognized	–	Boot Received	=	New Basis
1	$ 5,000	$ –(0)–	$4,000	+	$ –0–	+	$ –0–	–	$ –0–	=	$ 4,000*
2	2,000	–(0)–	4,000	+	3,000	+	–0–	–	–0–	=	7,000*
3	(1,000)	–(0)–	4,000	+	6,000	+	–0–	–	–0–	=	10,000**
4	8,000	3,000	4,000	+	–0–	+	3,000	–	3,000	=	4,000*
5	(200)	–(0)–	4,000	+	–0–	+	–0–	–	300	=	3,700**

*Basis may be determined in gain situations under the alternative method by subtracting the gain not recognized from the fair market value of the new property:
$9,000 – $5,000 = $4,000 for exchange 1.
$9,000 – $2,000 = $7,000 for exchange 2.
$9,000 – $5,000 = $4,000 for exchange 4.

**In loss situations, basis may be determined by adding the loss not recognized to the fair market value of the new property:
$9,000 + $1,000 = $10,000 for exchange 3.
$3,500 + $200 = $3,700 for exchange 5.
The basis of the boot received is the boot's fair market value. ■

If the taxpayer either assumes a liability or takes property subject to a liability, the amount of the liability is treated as boot given. For the taxpayer whose liability is assumed or whose property is taken subject to the liability, the amount of the liability is treated as boot received. Example 51 illustrates the effect of such a liability. In addition, the example illustrates the tax consequences for both parties involved in the like-kind exchange.

EXAMPLE 51

Jane and Leo exchange real estate investments. Jane gives up property with an adjusted basis of $250,000 (fair market value of $400,000) that is subject to a mortgage of $75,000 (assumed by Leo). In return for this property, Jane receives property with a fair market value of $300,000 (adjusted basis of $200,000) and cash of $25,000.

- Jane's realized gain is $150,000. She gave up property with an adjusted basis of $250,000. Jane received $400,000 from the exchange ($300,000 fair market value of like-kind property plus $100,000 boot received). The boot received consists of the $25,000 cash received from Leo and Jane's mortgage of $75,000, which Leo assumes.
- Jane's recognized gain is $100,000. The realized gain of $150,000 is recognized to the extent of boot received.
- Jane's basis in the real estate received from Leo is $250,000. This basis can be computed by subtracting the postponed gain ($50,000) from the fair market value of the real estate received ($300,000). It can also be computed by adding the recognized gain ($100,000) to the adjusted basis of the real estate given up ($250,000) and subtracting the boot received ($100,000).
- Leo's realized gain is $100,000. Leo gave up property with an adjusted basis of $200,000 plus boot of $100,000 ($75,000 mortgage assumed + $25,000 cash) or a total of $300,000. Leo received $400,000 from the exchange (fair market value of like-kind property received).
- Leo has no recognized gain because he did not receive any boot. The entire realized gain of $100,000 is postponed.
- Leo's basis in the real estate received from Jane is $300,000. This basis can be computed by subtracting the postponed gain ($100,000) from the fair market value of the real estate received ($400,000). It can also be computed by adding the boot given ($75,000 mortgage assumed by Leo + $25,000 cash) to the adjusted basis of the real estate given up ($200,000).[66] ■

[66]Example (2) of Reg. § 1.1031(d)–2 illustrates a special situation in which both the buyer and the seller transfer liabilities that are assumed by the other party or both parties acquire property that is subject to a liability.

LO.8

Explain the nonrecognition provisions available on the involuntary conversion of property.

Involuntary Conversions—§ 1033

Section 1033 provides that a taxpayer who suffers an involuntary conversion of property may postpone recognition of *gain* realized from the conversion. The objective of this provision is to provide relief to the taxpayer who has suffered hardship and does not have the wherewithal to pay the tax on any gain realized from the conversion. Postponement of realized gain is permitted to the extent that the taxpayer *reinvests* the amount realized from the conversion in replacement property. The rules for nonrecognition of gain are as follows:

- If the amount reinvested in replacement property *equals or exceeds* the amount realized, realized gain is *not recognized.*
- If the amount reinvested in replacement property is *less than* the amount realized, realized gain *is recognized* to the extent of the deficiency.

If a *loss* occurs on an involuntary conversion, § 1033 does not modify the normal rules for loss recognition. That is, if a realized loss would otherwise be recognized, § 1033 does not change the result.

INVOLUNTARY CONVERSION DEFINED

An **involuntary conversion** results from the destruction (complete or partial), theft, seizure, requisition or condemnation, or sale or exchange under threat or imminence of requisition or condemnation of the taxpayer's property.[67] To prove the existence of a threat or imminence of condemnation, the taxpayer must obtain confirmation that there has been a decision to acquire the property for public use. In addition, the taxpayer must have reasonable grounds to believe the property will be taken.[68] The property does not have to be sold to the authority threatening to condemn it to qualify for § 1033 postponement. If the taxpayer satisfies the confirmation and reasonable grounds requirements, he or she can sell the property to another party.[69] Likewise, the sale of property to a condemning authority by a taxpayer who acquired the property from its former owner with the knowledge that the property was under threat of condemnation also qualifies as an involuntary conversion under § 1033.[70] A voluntary act, such as a taxpayer destroying the property by arson, is not an involuntary conversion.[71]

COMPUTING THE AMOUNT REALIZED

The amount realized from the condemnation of property usually includes only the amount received as compensation for the property.[72] Any amount received that is designated as severance damages by both the government and the taxpayer is not included in the amount realized. *Severance awards* usually occur when only a portion of the property is condemned (e.g., a strip of land is taken to build a highway). Severance damages are awarded because the value of the taxpayer's remaining property has declined as a result of the condemnation. Such damages reduce the

[67] § 1033(a) and Reg. §§ 1.1033(a)–1(a) and –2(a).
[68] Rev.Rul. 63–221, 1963–2 C.B. 332, and *Joseph P. Balistrieri*, 38 TCM 526, T.C.Memo. 1979–115.
[69] Rev.Rul. 81–180, 1981–2 C.B. 161.
[70] Rev.Rul. 81–181, 1981–2 C.B. 162.
[71] Rev.Rul. 82–74, 1982–1 C.B. 110.
[72] *Pioneer Real Estate Co.*, 47 B.T.A. 886 (1942), *acq.* 1943 C.B. 18.

A Court Limits the Government's Taking of Property

Under eminent domain, governmental units have the right to take private property for public use. As fair compensation must be paid, disagreement often arises over the fair market value of condemned property.

In recent years, there has also been controversy over what constitutes "public use." Courts have expanded the definition of public use beyond the traditional public projects (such as roads, bridges, schools, hospitals, and slum clearance) to allow the taking of unblighted property for commercial development purposes. The objective in taking such property is to create jobs and increase tax revenues by means of new office parks, big box stores, racetracks, and other businesses. For example, one Mississippi case dealt with the right of a governmental agency to condemn farmland for use by Nissan as a site for a truck factory.

Recently, though, the Michigan Supreme Court in a unanimous decision refused to allow the taking of 1,300 acres near the Detroit airport for a business complex. The effect of this decision was to reverse the position the court had taken in the 1981 landmark *Poletown* case (so called for the ethnic neighborhood involved). The *Poletown* decision had permitted the city of Detroit to condemn 1,000 homes and 600 businesses to enable General Motors to acquire the land necessary for a plant. The public use was determined to be the economic benefits that resulted. In effect, the Michigan Supreme Court has now overturned the precedential value of *Poletown.*

Other courts, however, are continuing to follow the rationale set forth in *Poletown.* The time seems right for the U.S. Supreme Court to address and resolve this issue.

SOURCES: Adapted from Dean Starkman, "Michigan Upholds Property Rights in Broad Ruling," *Wall Street Journal*, August 2, 2004, p. A6; Editorial, "Poletown's Revenge," *Wall Street Journal*, August 3, 2004, p. A10.

basis of the property. However, if either of the following requirements is satisfied, the nonrecognition provision of § 1033 applies to the severance damages:

- The severance damages are used to restore the usability of the remaining property.
- The usefulness of the remaining property is destroyed by the condemnation, and the property is sold and replaced at a cost equal to or exceeding the sum of the condemnation award, severance damages, and sales proceeds.

EXAMPLE 52

The government condemns a portion of Ron's farmland to build part of an interstate highway. Because the highway denies his cattle access to a pond and some grazing land, Ron receives severance damages in addition to the condemnation proceeds for the land taken. Ron must reduce the basis of the property by the amount of the severance damages. If the amount of the severance damages received exceeds the adjusted basis, Ron recognizes gain. ■

EXAMPLE 53

Assume the same facts as in the previous example, except that Ron uses the proceeds from the condemnation and the severance damages to build another pond and to clear woodland for grazing. Therefore, all the proceeds are eligible for § 1033 treatment. There is no possibility of gain recognition as the result of the amount of the severance damages received exceeding the adjusted basis. ■

REPLACEMENT PROPERTY

The requirements for replacement property generally are more restrictive than those for like-kind property under § 1031. The basic requirement is that the replacement property be similar or related in service or use to the involuntarily converted property.[73]

Different interpretations of the phrase *similar or related in service or use* apply depending on whether the involuntarily converted property is held by an *owner-user* or by an *owner-investor* (e.g., lessor). A taxpayer who uses the property in his or her trade or business is subject to a more restrictive test in terms of acquiring replacement property. For an owner-user, the *functional use test* applies, and for an owner-investor, the *taxpayer use test* applies.

Taxpayer Use Test. The taxpayer use test for owner-investors provides the taxpayer with more flexibility in terms of what qualifies as replacement property than does the functional use test for owner-users. Essentially, the properties must be used by the taxpayer (the owner-investor) in similar endeavors. For example, rental property held by an owner-investor qualifies if replaced by other rental property, regardless of the type of rental property involved. The test is met when an investor replaces a manufacturing plant with a wholesale grocery warehouse if both properties are held for the production of rent income.[74] The replacement of a rental residence with a personal residence does not meet the test.[75]

Functional Use Test. The functional use test applies to owner-users (e.g., a manufacturer whose manufacturing plant is destroyed by fire is required to replace the plant with another facility of similar functional use). Under this test, the taxpayer's use of the replacement property and of the involuntarily converted property must be the same. Replacing a manufacturing plant with a wholesale grocery warehouse does not meet this test. Neither does replacing a rental residence with a personal residence.

Special Rules. Under one set of circumstances, the broader replacement rules for like-kind exchanges are substituted for the narrow replacement rules normally used for involuntary conversions. This beneficial provision applies if business real property or investment real property is condemned. This provision gives the taxpayer substantially more flexibility in selecting replacement property. For example, improved real property can be replaced with unimproved real property.

The rules concerning the nature of replacement property are illustrated in Concept Summary 13–3.

TIME LIMITATION ON REPLACEMENT

The taxpayer normally has a two-year period after the close of the taxable year in which gain is realized from an involuntary conversion to replace the property (*the latest date*).[76] This rule affords as much as three years from the date of realization of gain to replace the property if the realization of gain took place on the first day of the taxable year.[77] If the involuntary conversion involved the condemnation of real property used in a trade or business or held for investment, a three-year period

[73] § 1033(a) and Reg. § 1.1033(a)–1.

[74] *Loco Realty Co. v. Comm.*, 62–2 USTC ¶9657, 10 AFTR2d 5359, 306 F.2d 207 (CA–8, 1962).

[75] Rev.Rul. 70–466, 1970–2 C.B. 165.

[76] §§ 1033(a)(2)(B) and (g)(4) and Reg. § 1.1033(a)–2(c)(3).

[77] The taxpayer can apply for an extension of this time period anytime before its expiration [Reg. § 1.1033(a)–2(c)(3)]. Also, the period for filing the application for extension can be extended if the taxpayer shows reasonable cause.

CONCEPT SUMMARY 13–3

Replacement Property Tests

Type of Property and User	Like-Kind Test	Taxpayer Use Test	Functional Use Test
Land used by a manufacturing company is condemned by a local government authority.	X		
Apartment and land held by an investor are sold due to the threat or imminence of condemnation.	X		
An investor's rented shopping mall is destroyed by fire; the mall may be replaced by other rental properties (e.g., an apartment building).		X	
A manufacturing plant is destroyed by fire; replacement property must consist of another manufacturing plant that is functionally the same as the property converted.			X
Personal residence of taxpayer is condemned by a local government authority; replacement property must consist of another personal residence.			X

is substituted for the normal two-year period. In this case, the taxpayer can actually have as much as four years from the date of realization of gain to replace the property.

EXAMPLE 54

Megan's warehouse is destroyed by fire on December 16, 2004. The adjusted basis is $325,000. Megan receives $400,000 from the insurance company on January 10, 2005. She is a calendar year taxpayer. The latest date for replacement is December 31, 2007 (the end of the taxable year in which realized gain occurred plus two years). The critical date is not the date the involuntary conversion occurred, but rather the date of gain realization. ■

EXAMPLE 55

Assume the same facts as in the previous example, except that Megan's warehouse is condemned. The latest date for replacement is December 31, 2008 (the end of the taxable year in which realized gain occurred plus three years). ■

The *earliest date* for replacement typically is the date the involuntary conversion occurs. However, if the property is condemned, it is possible to replace the condemned property before this date. In this case, the earliest date is the date of the threat or imminence of requisition or condemnation of the property. The purpose of this provision is to enable the taxpayer to make an orderly replacement of the condemned property.

EXAMPLE 56

Assume the same facts as in Example 55. Megan can replace the warehouse before December 16, 2004 (the condemnation date). The earliest date for replacement is the date of the threat or imminence of requisition or condemnation of the warehouse. ■

NONRECOGNITION OF GAIN

Nonrecognition of gain can be either mandatory or elective, depending on whether the conversion is direct (into replacement property) or indirect (into money).

Direct Conversion. If the conversion is directly into replacement property rather than into money, nonrecognition of realized gain is *mandatory*. In this case, the basis of the replacement property is the same as the adjusted basis of the converted property. Direct conversion is rare in practice and usually involves condemnations.

EXAMPLE 57

Lupe's property, with an adjusted basis of $20,000, is condemned by the state. Lupe receives property with a fair market value of $50,000 as compensation for the property taken. Since the nonrecognition of realized gain is mandatory for direct conversions, Lupe's realized gain of $30,000 is not recognized, and the basis of the replacement property is $20,000 (adjusted basis of the condemned property). ■

Conversion into Money. If the conversion is into money, at the election of the taxpayer, the realized gain is recognized only to the extent the amount realized from the involuntary conversion exceeds the cost of the qualifying replacement property.[78] This is the usual case, and nonrecognition (postponement) is *elective*. If the election is not made, the realized gain is recognized.

The basis of the replacement property is the property's cost less postponed (deferred) gain.[79] If the election to postpone gain is made, the holding period of the replacement property includes the holding period of the converted property.

Section 1033 applies *only to gains* and *not to losses*. Losses from involuntary conversions are recognized if the property is held for business or income-producing purposes. Personal casualty losses are recognized, but condemnation losses related to personal use assets (e.g., a personal residence) are neither recognized nor postponed.

EXAMPLE 58

Walt's building (used in his trade or business), with an adjusted basis of $50,000, is destroyed by fire on October 5, 2005. Walt is a calendar year taxpayer. On November 17, 2005, he receives an insurance reimbursement of $100,000 for the loss. Walt invests $80,000 in a new building.

- Walt has until December 31, 2007, to make the new investment and qualify for the nonrecognition election.
- Walt's realized gain is $50,000 ($100,000 insurance proceeds received – $50,000 adjusted basis of old building).
- Assuming the replacement property qualifies as similar or related in service or use, Walt's recognized gain is $20,000. He reinvested $20,000 less than the insurance proceeds received ($100,000 proceeds – $80,000 reinvested). Therefore, his realized gain is recognized to that extent.
- Walt's basis in the new building is $50,000. This is the building's cost of $80,000 less the postponed gain of $30,000 (realized gain of $50,000 – recognized gain of $20,000).
- The computation of realization, recognition, and basis would apply even if Walt was a real estate dealer and the building destroyed by fire was part of his inventory. Unlike § 1031, § 1033 generally does not exclude inventory. ■

EXAMPLE 59

Assume the same facts as in the previous example, except that Walt receives only $45,000 of insurance proceeds. He has a realized and recognized loss of $5,000. The basis of the new building is the building's cost of $80,000. If the destroyed building had been held for personal use, the recognized loss would have been subject to the following additional limitations.[80] The loss of $5,000 would have been limited to the decline in fair market value of the property, and the amount of the loss would have been reduced first by $100 and then by 10% of adjusted gross income (refer to Chapter 7). ■

[78] § 1033(a)(2)(A) and Reg. § 1.1033(a)–2(c)(1).
[79] § 1033(b).
[80] § 165(c)(3) and Reg. § 1.165–7.

INVOLUNTARY CONVERSION OF A PERSONAL RESIDENCE

The tax consequences of the involuntary conversion of a personal residence depend on whether the conversion is a casualty or condemnation and whether a realized loss or gain results.

Loss Situations. If the conversion is a condemnation, the realized loss is not recognized. Loss from the condemnation of a personal use asset is never recognized. If the conversion is a casualty (a loss from fire, storm, etc.), the loss is recognized subject to the personal casualty loss limitations (refer to Chapter 7).

Gain Situations. If the conversion is a casualty, theft, or condemnation, the gain may be postponed under § 1033 or excluded under § 121. That is, the taxpayer may treat the involuntary conversion as a sale under the exclusion of gain rules relating to the sale of a personal residence under § 121 (presented subsequently).

Under certain circumstances, the taxpayer may use both the § 121 exclusion of gain and the § 1033 postponement of gain provisions. See the discussion under Involuntary Conversion and Using §§ 121 and 1033 later in this chapter.

REPORTING CONSIDERATIONS

Involuntary conversions from casualty and theft are reported first on Form 4684, Casualties and Thefts. Casualty and theft losses on personal use property for the individual taxpayer are carried from Form 4684 to Schedule A of Form 1040. For other casualty and theft items, the Form 4684 amounts are generally reported on Form 4797, Sales of Business Property, unless Form 4797 is not required. In the latter case, the amounts are reported directly on the tax return involved.

Except for personal use property, recognized gains and losses from involuntary conversions other than by casualty and theft are reported on Form 4797. As stated previously, if the property involved in the involuntary conversion (other than by casualty and theft) is personal use property, any realized loss is not recognized. Any realized gain is treated as gain on a voluntary sale.

LO.9

Describe the provision for the permanent exclusion of gain on the sale of a personal residence.

Sale of a Residence—§ 121

A taxpayer's **personal residence** is a personal use asset. Therefore, a realized loss from the sale of a personal residence is not recognized.[81]

A realized gain from the sale of a personal residence is subject to taxation. However, favorable relief from recognition of gain is provided in the form of the **§ 121 exclusion.** Under this provision, a taxpayer can exclude up to $250,000 of realized gain on the sale.[82]

REQUIREMENTS FOR EXCLUSION TREATMENT

To qualify for exclusion treatment, at the date of the sale, the residence must have been *owned* and *used* by the taxpayer as the principal residence for at least two years during the five-year period ending on the date of the sale.[83]

EXAMPLE 60

Alice sells her principal residence on September 18, 2005. She had purchased it on July 5, 2003, and lived in it since then. The sale of Alice's residence qualifies for the § 121 exclusion. ■

[81] § 165(c).
[82] § 121(b).
[83] § 121(a). However, § 121(d)(10) provides that exclusion treatment does not apply if the residence was acquired in a like-kind exchange within the prior five years of the sale of the residence.

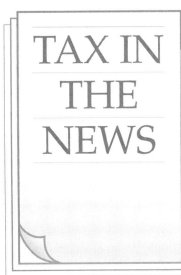

A Tax Break for Those Who Serve

To qualify for exclusion treatment on the gain from the sale of a principal residence, a two-year ownership and occupancy requirement during the five-year period preceding the sale must be satisfied. As satisfying this provision was difficult for those in the military, Congress enacted the Military Family Tax Relief Act of 2003 to provide some relief. The two-out-of-five-years requirement still must be satisfied, but at the election of the taxpayer, the running of the five-year period can be suspended during any period that the taxpayer or spouse is serving on qualified official extended duty in the military. Since this extension is limited to 10 years, the maximum period allowed is 15 years. This provision is retroactive to home sales after May 6, 1997.

SOURCE: Adapted from Sandra Block, "For Those Who Serve Their Country, Thanks Come in Form of Tax Relief," *USA Today*, April 13, 2004, p. 3B.

The five-year window enables the taxpayer to qualify for the § 121 exclusion even though the property is not his or her principal residence at the date of the sale.

EXAMPLE 61

Benjamin sells his principal residence on August 16, 2005. He had purchased it on April 1, 1997, and lived in it until July 1, 2004, when he converted it to rental property. Even though the property is rental property on August 16, 2005, rather than Benjamin's principal residence, the sale qualifies for the § 121 exclusion.[84] During the five-year period from August 16, 2000, to August 16, 2005, Benjamin owned and used the property as his principal residence for at least two years. ■

Taxpayers might be tempted to make liberal use of the § 121 exclusion as a means of speculating when the price of residential housing is rising. Without any time restriction on its use, § 121 would permit the exclusion of realized gain on multiple sales of principal residences. The Code curbs this approach by denying the application of the § 121 exclusion to sales occurring within two years of its last use.[85]

EXAMPLE 62

Seth sells his principal residence (the first residence) in June 2004 for $150,000 (realized gain of $60,000). He then buys and sells the following (all of which qualify as principal residences):

	Date of Purchase	Date of Sale	Amount Involved
Second residence	July 2004		$160,000
Second residence		April 2005	180,000
Third residence	May 2005		200,000

Because multiple sales have taken place within a period of two years, § 121 does not apply to the sale of the second residence. Thus, the realized gain of $20,000 [$180,000 (selling price) – $160,000 (purchase price)] must be recognized. ■

[84]However, any realized gain on the sale that is attributable to depreciation is not eligible for the § 121 exclusion. See Example 79.
[85]§ 121(b)(3).

EXCEPTIONS TO THE TWO-YEAR OWNERSHIP RULE

The two-year ownership and use requirement and the "only once every two years" provision could create a hardship for taxpayers in certain situations that are beyond their control. Thus, under the following special circumstances, the requirements are waived:[86]

- Change in place of employment.
- Health.
- To the extent provided in the Regulations, other unforeseen circumstances.

These three exceptions have recently been amplified by the IRS and are discussed in the sections that follow.

Change in Place of Employment. In order for this exception to apply, the distance requirements applicable to the deductibility of moving expenses must be satisfied (see Chapter 9).[87] Consequently, the location of the taxpayer's new employment must be at least 50 miles further from the old residence than the old residence was from the old job. The house must be used as the principal residence of the taxpayer at the time of the change in the place of employment. Employment includes the commencement of employment with a new employer, the continuation of employment with the same employer, and the commencement or continuation of self-employment.

EXAMPLE 63

Assume the same facts as in the previous example, except that in March 2005, Seth's employer transfers him to a job in another state that is 400 miles away. Thus, the sale of the second residence and the purchase of the third residence were due to relocation of employment. Consequently, the § 121 exclusion is partially available on the sale of the second residence. ■

Keep in mind, however, that the change in place of employment exception, or any of the other exceptions noted below, does not make the full amount of the exclusion available. See the discussion under Relief Provision later in this chapter for determining the amount of the partial exclusion allowed.

Health Considerations. For the health exception to apply, health must be the primary reason for the sale or exchange of the residence.[88] A sale or exchange that is merely beneficial to the general health or well-being of the individual will not qualify. A safe harbor applies if there is a physician's recommendation for a change of residence (1) to obtain, provide, or facilitate the diagnosis, cure, mitigation, or treatment of disease, illness, or injury or (2) to obtain or provide medical or personal care for an individual suffering from a disease, illness, or injury. If the safe harbor is not satisfied, then the determination is made using a facts and circumstances approach. Examples that qualify include the following:

- A taxpayer who is injured in an accident is unable to care for herself. She sells her residence and moves in with her daughter.
- A taxpayer's father has a chronic disease. The taxpayer sells his house in order to move into the father's house to provide the care the father requires as a result of the disease.
- A taxpayer's son suffers from a chronic disease. The taxpayer sells his house and moves his family so the son can begin a new treatment recommended by the son's physician that is available at a medical facility 100 miles away.
- A taxpayer suffers from chronic asthma. Her physician recommends that she move to a warm, dry climate. She moves from Minnesota to Arizona.

[86] § 121(c)(2)(B).
[87] Reg. § 1.121–3T(c).
[88] Reg. § 1.121–3T(d).

Unforeseen Circumstances. For the unforeseen circumstances exception to apply, the primary reason for the sale or exchange of the residence must be an event that the taxpayer did not anticipate before purchasing and occupying the residence.[89] This requirement is satisfied under a safe-harbor provision by any of the following:

- Involuntary conversion of the residence.
- Natural or human-made disasters or acts of war or terrorism resulting in a casualty to the residence.
- Death of a qualified individual.
- Cessation of employment that results in eligibility for unemployment compensation.
- Change in employment or self-employment that results in the taxpayer being unable to pay housing costs and reasonable basic living expenses for the taxpayer's household.
- Divorce or legal separation.
- Multiple births resulting from the same pregnancy.

If the safe harbor is not satisfied, then the determination is made using a facts and circumstances approach.

EXAMPLE 64

Debra and Roy are engaged and buy a house (sharing the mortgage payments) and live in it as their personal residence. Eighteen months after the purchase, they cancel their wedding plans, and Roy moves out of the house. Because Debra cannot afford to make the payments alone, they sell the house. While the sale does not fit under the safe harbor, the sale does qualify under the unforeseen circumstances exception. ■

CALCULATION OF THE AMOUNT OF THE EXCLUSION

General Provisions. The amount of the available § 121 exclusion on the sale of a principal residence is $250,000.[90] If the realized gain does not exceed $250,000, there is no recognized gain.

Realized gain is calculated in the normal manner. The *amount realized* is the selling price less the selling expenses, which include items such as the cost of advertising the property for sale, real estate broker commissions, legal fees in connection with the sale, and loan placement fees paid by the taxpayer as a condition of arranging financing for the buyer. Repairs and maintenance performed by the seller to aid in selling the property are treated neither as selling expenses nor as adjustments to the taxpayer's adjusted basis for the residence.

EXAMPLE 65

Mandy, who is single, sells her personal residence (adjusted basis of $130,000) for $290,000. She has owned and lived in the residence for three years. Her selling expenses are $18,000. Three weeks prior to the sale, Mandy paid a carpenter and a painter $1,000 to make some repairs and paint the two bathrooms. Her recognized gain is calculated as follows:

Amount realized ($290,000 – $18,000)	$ 272,000
Adjusted basis	(130,000)
Realized gain	$ 142,000
§ 121 exclusion	(142,000)
Recognized gain	$ –0–

Since the available § 121 exclusion of $250,000 exceeds Mandy's realized gain of $142,000, her recognized gain is $0. ■

[89] Reg. § 1.121–3T(e).

[90] § 121(b)(1).

EXAMPLE 66

Assume the same facts as in the previous example, except that the selling price is $490,000.

Amount realized ($490,000 – $18,000)	$ 472,000
Adjusted basis	(130,000)
Realized gain	$ 342,000
§ 121 exclusion	(250,000)
Recognized gain	$ 92,000

Since the realized gain of $342,000 exceeds the § 121 exclusion amount of $250,000, Mandy's recognized gain is $92,000 ($342,000 – $250,000). ■

Effect on Married Couples. If a married couple files a joint return, the $250,000 amount is increased to $500,000 if the following requirements are satisfied:[91]

- Either spouse meets the at-least-two-years *ownership* requirement.
- Both spouses meet the at-least-two-years *use* requirement.
- Neither spouse is ineligible for the § 121 exclusion on the sale of the current principal residence because of the sale of another principal residence within the prior two years.

EXAMPLE 67

Margaret sells her personal residence (adjusted basis of $150,000) for $650,000. She has owned and lived in the residence for six years. Her selling expenses are $40,000. Margaret is married to Ted, and they file a joint return. Ted has lived in the residence since they were married two and one-half years ago.

Amount realized ($650,000 – $40,000)	$ 610,000
Adjusted basis	(150,000)
Realized gain	$ 460,000
§ 121 exclusion	(460,000)
Recognized gain	$ -0-

Since the realized gain of $460,000 is less than the available § 121 exclusion amount of $500,000, no gain is recognized. ■

If each spouse owns a qualified principal residence, each spouse can separately qualify for the $250,000 exclusion on the sale of his or her own residence even if the couple files a joint return.[92]

EXAMPLE 68

Anne and Samuel are married on August 1, 2005. Each owns a residence that is eligible for the § 121 exclusion. Anne sells her residence on September 7, 2005, and Samuel sells his residence on October 9, 2005. Relevant data on the sales are as follows:

	Anne	Samuel
Selling price	$320,000	$425,000
Selling expenses	20,000	25,000
Adjusted basis	190,000	110,000

Anne and Samuel intend to rent a condo in Florida or Arizona and to travel. The recognized gain of each is calculated as follows:

[91] § 121(b)(2).
[92] § 121(b)(1).

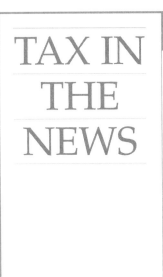

The Gains Keep Growing

When Congress created the $250,000 exclusion ($500,000 for qualified married couples filing jointly) of gain on the sale of principal residences in 1997, sympathy for those taxpayers whose realized gain exceeded those amounts was not widespread. That may no longer be the case.

Two factors are contributing to this change. First, the $250,000 and $500,000 amounts are not indexed for inflation. Second, in some areas of the country, property values are increasing dramatically.

Research by the Joint Center for Housing Studies at Harvard found that as many as 850,000 American homes may be worth at least $1 million. Most of these homes are located in areas that have experienced substantial appreciation (i.e., frequently double-digit increases each year) since the mid-1990s. In Harvard's hometown of Cambridge, one in every 11 homes is worth at least $1 million. Other high-value locations include San Francisco, the District of Columbia, Los Angeles, Pasadena, Berkeley, Boston, New York, Stamford, Fort Lauderdale, Atlanta, and Honolulu.

Congress could help relieve the problem by increasing the dollar amount of the exclusion or by indexing it to reflect inflation.

SOURCES: Adapted from Kenneth R. Harney, "Homeowners Outstrip Tax-Free Exclusion Limits," *Newport News Daily Press*, February 25, 2004, p. C9; James R. Hagerty, "Million-Dollar Home? Don't Brag," *Wall Street Journal*, February 19, 2004, p. D9.

	Anne	Samuel
Amount realized	$ 300,000	$ 400,000
Adjusted basis	(190,000)	(110,000)
Realized gain	$ 110,000	$ 290,000
§ 121 exclusion	(110,000)	(250,000)
Recognized gain	$ -0-	$ 40,000

Anne has no recognized gain because the available $250,000 exclusion amount exceeds her realized gain of $110,000. Samuel's recognized gain is $40,000 as his realized gain of $290,000 exceeds the $250,000 exclusion amount. The recognized gains calculated above result regardless of whether Anne and Samuel file a joint return or separate returns. ■

Relief Provision. As discussed earlier in Requirements for Exclusion Treatment, partial § 121 exclusion treatment may be available when not all of the statutory requirements are satisfied. Under the relief provision, the § 121 exclusion amount ($250,000 or $500,000) is multiplied by a fraction, the numerator of which is the number of qualifying months and the denominator of which is 24 months. The resulting amount is the excluded gain.[93]

EXAMPLE 69

On October 1, 2004, Rich and Audrey, who file a joint return and live in Chicago, sell their personal residence, which they have owned and lived in for eight years. The realized gain of $325,000 is excluded under § 121. They purchase another personal residence for $525,000

[93] § 121(c)(1).

on October 2, 2004. Audrey's employer transfers her to the Denver office in August 2005. Rich and Audrey sell their Chicago residence on August 2, 2005, and purchase a residence in Denver shortly thereafter. The realized gain on the sale is $300,000.

The $325,000 gain on the first Chicago residence is excluded under § 121. The sale of the second Chicago residence is within the two-year window of the prior sale, but because it resulted from a change in employment, Rich and Audrey can qualify for partial § 121 exclusion treatment as follows:

Realized gain	$ 300,000
§ 121 exclusion:	
$\frac{10 \text{ months}}{24 \text{ months}} \times \$500,000 = \$208,333$	(208,333)
Recognized gain	$ 91,667

Basis of New Residence. Because § 121 is an exclusion provision rather than a postponement of gain provision, the basis of a new residence is its cost.[94]

PRINCIPAL RESIDENCE

To be eligible for the § 121 exclusion, the residence must have been owned and used by the taxpayer as the principal residence for at least two years during the five-year window (subject to partial exclusion treatment under the relief provision). Whether property is the taxpayer's principal residence "depends upon all of the facts and circumstances in each case."[95]

EXAMPLE 70

Mitch graduates from college and moves to Boston, where he is employed. He decides to rent an apartment in Boston because of its proximity to his place of employment. He purchases a beach condo in the Cape Cod area that he occupies most weekends. Mitch does not intend to live at the beach condo except on weekends. The apartment in Boston is his principal residence.

A residence does not have to be a house. For example, a houseboat, a house trailer, or a motor home can qualify.[96] Land, under certain circumstances, can qualify for exclusion treatment. The lot on which a house is built obviously qualifies. An adjacent lot can qualify if it is regularly used by the owner as part of the residential property. To qualify, the land must be sold along with the residence or within two years before or after the sale of the residence.

INVOLUNTARY CONVERSION AND USING §§ 121 AND 1033

As mentioned earlier (see Involuntary Conversion of a Personal Residence), a taxpayer can use both the § 121 exclusion of gain provision and the § 1033 postponement of gain provision.[97] The taxpayer initially can elect to exclude realized gain under § 121 to the extent of the statutory amount. Then a qualified replacement of the residence under § 1033 can be used to postpone the remainder of the realized gain. In applying § 1033, the amount of the required reinvestment is reduced by the amount of the § 121 exclusion.

[94] § 1012.
[95] Regulation § 1.121–1(b)(2) includes factors to be considered in determining a taxpayer's principal residence.
[96] Reg. § 1.1034–1(c)(3)(i).
[97] § 121(d)(5).

EXAMPLE 71

Angel's principal residence is destroyed by a tornado. Her adjusted basis for the residence is $140,000. She receives insurance proceeds of $480,000.

If Angel does not elect to use the § 121 exclusion, her realized gain on the involuntary conversion of her principal residence is $340,000 ($480,000 amount realized – $140,000 adjusted basis). Thus, to postpone the $340,000 realized gain under § 1033, she would need to acquire qualifying property costing at least $480,000.

Using the § 121 exclusion enables Angel to reduce the amount of the required reinvestment for § 1033 purposes from $480,000 to $230,000. That is, by using § 121 in conjunction with § 1033, the amount realized, for § 1033 purposes, is reduced to $230,000 ($480,000 – $250,000 § 121 exclusion).

Note that if Angel does not acquire qualifying replacement property for § 1033 purposes, her recognized gain is $90,000 ($480,000 – $140,000 adjusted basis – $250,000 § 121 exclusion). ■

If § 1033 is used in conjunction with the § 121 exclusion on an involuntary conversion of a principal residence, the holding period of the replacement residence includes the holding period of the involuntarily converted residence. This can be beneficial in satisfying the § 121 two-out-of-five-years ownership and use requirement on a subsequent sale of the replacement residence.

LO.10

Identify other nonrecognition provisions contained in the Code.

Other Nonrecognition Provisions

The typical taxpayer experiences the sale of a personal residence or an involuntary conversion more frequently than the other types of nontaxable exchanges. Several less common nonrecognition provisions are treated briefly in the remainder of this chapter.

EXCHANGE OF STOCK FOR PROPERTY—§ 1032

Under § 1032, a corporation does not recognize gain or loss on the receipt of money or other property in exchange for its stock (including treasury stock). In other words, a corporation does not recognize gain or loss when it deals in its own stock. This provision is consistent with the accounting treatment of such transactions.

CERTAIN EXCHANGES OF INSURANCE POLICIES—§ 1035

Under § 1035, no gain or loss is recognized from the exchange of certain insurance contracts or policies. The rules relating to exchanges not solely in kind and the basis of the property acquired are the same as under § 1031. Exchanges qualifying for nonrecognition include the following:

- The exchange of life insurance contracts.
- The exchange of a life insurance contract for an endowment or annuity contract.
- The exchange of an endowment contract for another endowment contract that provides for regular payments beginning at a date not later than the date payments would have begun under the contract exchanged.
- The exchange of an endowment contract for an annuity contract.
- The exchange of annuity contracts.

EXCHANGE OF STOCK FOR STOCK OF THE SAME CORPORATION—§ 1036

Section 1036 provides that a shareholder does not recognize gain or loss on the exchange of common stock solely for common stock in the same corporation or from the exchange of preferred stock for preferred stock in the same corporation. Exchanges between individual shareholders as well as between a shareholder and the corporation are included. The rules relating to exchanges not solely in kind and the basis of the property acquired are the same as under § 1031. For example, a nonrecognition exchange occurs when common stock with different rights, such as voting for nonvoting, is exchanged. A shareholder usually recognizes gain or loss from the exchange of common for preferred or preferred for common even though the stock exchanged is in the same corporation.

CERTAIN REACQUISITIONS OF REAL PROPERTY—§ 1038

Under § 1038, no loss is recognized from the repossession of real property sold on an installment basis. Gain is recognized to a limited extent.

TRANSFERS OF PROPERTY BETWEEN SPOUSES OR INCIDENT TO DIVORCE—§ 1041

Section 1041 provides that transfers of property *between spouses or former spouses incident to divorce* are nontaxable transactions. Therefore, the basis to the recipient is a carryover basis. To be treated as incident to the divorce, the transfer must be related to the cessation of marriage or occur within one year after the date on which the marriage ceases.

Section 1041 also provides for nontaxable exchange treatment on property transfers *between spouses during marriage*. The basis to the recipient spouse is a carryover basis.

ROLLOVERS INTO SPECIALIZED SMALL BUSINESS INVESTMENT COMPANIES—§ 1044

A postponement opportunity is available for some sellers of publicly traded securities under § 1044. If the amount realized is reinvested in the common stock or partnership interest of a specialized small business investment company (SSBIC), the realized gain is not recognized. Any amount not reinvested will trigger recognition of the realized gain to the extent of the deficiency. The taxpayer must reinvest the proceeds within 60 days of the date of sale in order to qualify. In calculating the basis of the SSBIC stock, the amount of the purchase price is reduced by the amount of the postponed gain.

Statutory ceilings are imposed on the amount of realized gain that can be postponed for any taxable year as follows:

- For an individual taxpayer, the lesser of:
  - $50,000 ($25,000 for married filing separately).
  - $500,000 ($250,000 for married filing separately) reduced by the amount of such nonrecognized gain in prior taxable years.
- For a corporate taxpayer, the lesser of:
  - $250,000.
  - $1 million reduced by the amount of such nonrecognized gain in prior taxable years.

Investors *ineligible* for this postponement treatment include partnerships, S corporations, estates, and trusts.

ROLLOVER OF GAIN FROM QUALIFIED SMALL BUSINESS STOCK INTO ANOTHER QUALIFIED SMALL BUSINESS STOCK—§ 1045

Under § 1045, realized gain from the sale of qualified small business stock held for more than six months may be postponed if the taxpayer acquires other qualified small business stock within 60 days. Any amount not reinvested will trigger the recognition of the realized gain on the sale to the extent of the deficiency. In calculating the basis of the acquired qualified small business stock, the amount of the purchase price is reduced by the amount of the postponed gain.

Qualified small business stock is stock of a qualified small business that is acquired by the taxpayer at its original issue in exchange for money or other property (excluding stock) or as compensation for services. A qualified small business is a domestic corporation that satisfies the following requirements:

- The aggregate gross assets prior to the issuance of the small business stock do not exceed $50 million.
- The aggregate gross assets immediately after the issuance of the small business stock do not exceed $50 million.

LO.11

Identify tax planning opportunities related to selected property transactions.

Tax Planning Considerations

TAX CONSEQUENCES OF ALICE'S PROPOSED TRANSACTION

In Example 1 earlier in the chapter, Alice's tax adviser asked a number of questions in order to advise her on a proposed transaction. Alice provided the following answers:

- Alice inherited the house from her mother. The fair market value of the house at the date of her mother's death, based on the estate tax return, was $225,000. Based on an appraisal, the house is worth $230,000. Alice's mother lived in the house for 48 years. According to the mother's attorney, her adjusted basis for the house was $75,000.
- As a child, Alice lived in the house for 10 years. She has not lived there during the 35 years she has been married.
- The house has been vacant during the seven months that Alice has owned it. She has been trying to decide whether she should sell it for its fair market value or sell it to her nephew for $75,000. Alice has suggested a $75,000 price for the sale to Dan because she believes this is the amount at which she will have no gain or loss.
- Alice intends to invest the $75,000 in stock.

You advise Alice that her adjusted basis for the house is the $225,000 fair market value on the date of her mother's death. If Alice sells the house for $230,000 (assuming no selling expenses), she would have a recognized gain of $5,000 ($230,000 amount realized – $225,000 adjusted basis). The house is a capital asset, and Alice's holding period is long term since she inherited the house. Thus, the gain would be classified as a long-term capital gain. If, instead, Alice sells the house to her nephew for $75,000, she will have a part sale and part gift. The realized gain on the sale of $1,630 is recognized.

Amount realized	$ 75,000
Less: Adjusted basis	(73,370)*
Realized gain	$ 1,630
Recognized gain	$ 1,630

*[($75,000/$230,000) × $225,000] = $73,370.

The gain is classified as a long-term capital gain. Alice is then deemed to have made a gift to Dan of $155,000 ($230,000 – $75,000).

With this information, Alice can make an informed selection between the two options.

COST IDENTIFICATION AND DOCUMENTATION CONSIDERATIONS

When multiple assets are acquired in a single transaction, the contract price must be allocated for several reasons. First, some of the assets may be depreciable, while others are not. From the different viewpoints of the buyer and the seller, this may produce a tax conflict that needs to be resolved. That is, the seller prefers a high allocation for nondepreciable assets, whereas the purchaser prefers a high allocation for depreciable assets (see Chapter 14). Second, the seller needs to know the amount realized on the sale of the capital assets and the ordinary income assets so that the recognized gains and losses can be classified as capital or ordinary. For example, an allocation to goodwill or to a covenant not to compete (see Chapters 8 and 14) produces different tax consequences to the seller. Third, the buyer needs the adjusted basis of each asset to calculate the realized gain or loss on a subsequent sale or other disposition of each asset.

SELECTION OF PROPERTY FOR MAKING GIFTS

A donor can achieve several tax advantages by making gifts of appreciated property. The donor avoids income tax on the unrealized gain that would have occurred had the donor sold the property. A portion of this amount can be permanently avoided because the donee's adjusted basis is increased by part or all of any gift tax paid by the donor. Even without this increase in basis, the income tax liability on the sale of the property by the donee can be less than the income tax liability that would have resulted from the donor's sale of the property, if the donee is in a lower tax bracket than the donor. In addition, any subsequent appreciation during the time the property is held by the lower tax bracket donee results in a tax savings on the sale or other disposition of the property. Such gifts of appreciated property can be an effective tool in family tax planning.

Taxpayers should generally not make gifts of depreciated property (property that, if sold, would produce a realized loss) because the donor does not receive an income tax deduction for the unrealized loss element. In addition, the donee receives no benefit from this unrealized loss upon the subsequent sale of the property because of the loss basis rule. The loss basis rule provides that the donee's basis is the lower of the donor's basis or the fair market value at the date of the gift. If the donor anticipates that the donee will sell the property upon receiving it, the donor should sell the property and take the loss deduction, assuming the loss is deductible. The donor can then give the proceeds from the sale to the donee.

SELECTION OF PROPERTY FOR MAKING BEQUESTS

A taxpayer should generally make bequests of appreciated property in his or her will. Doing so enables both the decedent and the heir to avoid income tax on the unrealized gain because the recipient takes the fair market value as his or her basis.

Taxpayers generally should not make bequests of depreciated property (property that, if sold, would produce a realized loss) because the decedent does not receive an income tax deduction for the unrealized loss element. In addition, the heir will receive no benefit from this unrealized loss upon the subsequent sale of the property.

EXAMPLE 72

On the date of her death, Marta owned land held for investment purposes. The land had an adjusted basis of $130,000 and a fair market value of $100,000. If Marta had sold the property before her death, the recognized loss would have been $30,000. If Roger inherits the property and later sells it for $90,000, the recognized loss is $10,000 (the decline in value since Marta's death). In addition, regardless of the period of time Roger holds the property, the holding period is long term (see Chapter 14). ■

From an income tax perspective, it is preferable to transfer appreciated property as a bequest rather than as a gift. The reason is that inherited property receives a step-up in basis, whereas property received by gift has a carryover basis to the donee. However, in making this decision, the estate tax consequences of the bequest should also be weighed against the gift tax consequences of the gift.

DISALLOWED LOSSES

Section 267 Disallowed Losses. Taxpayers should be aware of the desirability of avoiding transactions that activate the loss disallowance provisions for related parties. This is so even in light of the provision that permits the related-party buyer to offset his or her realized gain by the related-party seller's disallowed loss. Even with this offset, several inequities exist. First, the tax benefit associated with the disallowed loss ultimately is realized by the wrong party (the related-party buyer rather than the related-party seller). Second, the tax benefit of this offset to the related-party buyer does not occur until the buyer disposes of the property. Therefore, the longer the time period between the purchase and disposition of the property by the related-party buyer, the less the economic benefit. Third, if the property does not appreciate to at least its adjusted basis to the related-party seller during the time period the related-party buyer holds it, part or all of the disallowed loss is permanently lost. Fourth, since the right of offset is available only to the original transferee (the related-party buyer), all of the disallowed loss is permanently lost if the original transferee subsequently transfers the property by gift or bequest.

EXAMPLE 73

Tim sells property with an adjusted basis of $35,000 to Wes, his brother, for $25,000, the fair market value of the property. The $10,000 realized loss to Tim is disallowed by § 267. If Wes subsequently sells the property to an unrelated party for $37,000, he has a recognized gain of $2,000 (realized gain of $12,000 reduced by disallowed loss of $10,000). Therefore, from the perspective of the family unit, the original $10,000 realized loss ultimately is recognized. However, if Wes sells the property for $29,000, he has a recognized gain of $0 (realized gain of $4,000 reduced by disallowed loss of $4,000 necessary to offset the realized gain). From the perspective of the family unit, $6,000 of the realized loss of $10,000 is permanently wasted ($10,000 realized loss – $4,000 offset permitted). ■

Wash Sales. The wash sales provisions can be avoided if the security that was sold is replaced within the statutory time period with a similar rather than a substantially identical security. For example, a sale of Dell, Inc. common stock accompanied by a purchase of Hewlett-Packard common stock is not treated as a wash sale. Such a procedure can enable the taxpayer to use an unrealized capital loss to offset a recognized capital gain. The taxpayer can sell the security before the end of the taxable year, offset the recognized capital loss against the capital gain, and invest the sales proceeds in a similar security.

Because the wash sales provisions do not apply to gains, it may be desirable to engage in a wash sale before the end of the taxable year. The recognized capital gain may be used to offset capital losses or capital loss carryovers from prior years. Since the basis of the replacement stock or securities will be the purchase price, the taxpayer in effect has exchanged a capital gain for an increased basis for the stock or securities.

LIKE-KIND EXCHANGES

Since application of the like-kind exchange provisions is mandatory rather than elective, in certain instances it may be preferable to avoid qualifying for § 1031 nonrecognition. If the like-kind exchange provisions do not apply, the end result may be the recognition of capital gain in exchange for a higher basis in the newly acquired asset. Also, the immediate recognition of gain may be preferable in certain situations. Examples where immediate recognition is beneficial include the following:

- Taxpayer has unused net operating loss carryovers.
- Taxpayer has unused general business credit carryovers.
- Taxpayer has suspended or current passive activity losses.
- Taxpayer expects his or her effective tax rate to increase in the future.

EXAMPLE 74

Alicia disposes of a machine (used in her business) with an adjusted basis of $3,000 for $4,000. She also acquires a new business machine for $9,000. If § 1031 applies, the $1,000 realized gain is not recognized, and the basis of the new machine is reduced by $1,000 (from $9,000 to $8,000). If § 1031 does not apply, a $1,000 gain is recognized and may receive favorable capital gain treatment to the extent that the gain is not recognized as ordinary income due to the depreciation recapture provisions (see Chapter 14). In addition, the basis for depreciation on the new machine is $9,000 rather than $8,000 since there is no unrecognized gain. ■

The application of § 1031 nonrecognition treatment should also be avoided when the adjusted basis of the property being disposed of exceeds the fair market value.

EXAMPLE 75

Assume the same facts as in the previous example, except that the fair market value of the machine is $2,500. If § 1031 applies, the $500 realized loss is not recognized. To recognize the loss, Alicia should sell the old machine and purchase the new one. The purchase and sale transactions should be with different taxpayers. ■

On the other hand, the like-kind exchange procedure can be utilized to control the amount of recognized gain.

EXAMPLE 76

Rex has property with an adjusted basis of $40,000 and a fair market value of $100,000. Sandra wants to buy Rex's property, but Rex wants to limit the amount of recognized gain on the proposed transaction. Sandra acquires other like-kind property (from an outside party) for $80,000. She then exchanges this property and $20,000 cash for Rex's property. Rex has a realized gain of $60,000 ($100,000 amount realized – $40,000 adjusted basis). His recognized gain is only $20,000, the lower of the $20,000 boot received or the $60,000 realized gain. Rex's basis for the like-kind property is $40,000 ($40,000 adjusted basis + $20,000 gain recognized – $20,000 boot received). If Rex had sold the property to Sandra for its fair market value of $100,000, the result would have been a $60,000 recognized gain ($100,000 amount realized – $40,000 adjusted basis) to him. It is permissible for Rex to identify the like-kind property that he wants Sandra to purchase.[98] ■

INVOLUNTARY CONVERSIONS

In certain cases, a taxpayer may prefer to recognize gain from an involuntary conversion. Keep in mind that § 1033, unlike § 1031 (dealing with like-kind exchanges), generally is an elective provision.

[98] *Franklin B. Biggs*, 69 T.C. 905 (1978); Rev.Rul. 73–476, 1973–2 C.B. 300; and *Starker v. U.S.*, 79–2 USTC ¶9541, 44 AFTR2d 79–5525, 602 F.2d 1341 (CA–9, 1979).

EXAMPLE 77

Ahmad has a $40,000 realized gain from the involuntary conversion of an office building. He reinvests the entire proceeds of $450,000 in a new office building. He does not elect to postpone gain under § 1033, however, because of an expiring net operating loss carryover that is offset against the gain. Therefore, none of the realized gain of $40,000 is postponed. Because Ahmad did not elect § 1033 postponement, his basis in the replacement property is the property's cost of $450,000 rather than $410,000 ($450,000 reduced by the $40,000 realized gain). ■

SALE OF A PRINCIPAL RESIDENCE

Election to Forgo. The § 121 exclusion automatically applies if the taxpayer is eligible. That is, the taxpayer does not have to make an election. However, if the taxpayer wishes to avoid § 121 exclusion treatment on an otherwise eligible sale, the taxpayer may elect to do so.[99]

EXAMPLE 78

George owns two personal residences that satisfy the two-year ownership and use test with respect to the five-year window. The Elm Street residence has appreciated by $25,000, and the Maple Street residence has appreciated by $230,000. He intends to sell both of them and move into rental property. He sells the Elm Street residence in December 2005 and expects to sell the Maple Street residence early next year.

Unless George elects not to apply the § 121 exclusion to the sale of the Elm Street residence, he will exclude the $25,000 realized gain on that residence in 2005. In 2006, however, he will have a recognized gain of $230,000 on the sale of the Maple Street residence.

If George makes the election to forgo, he will report a recognized gain of $25,000 on the sale of the Elm Street residence in 2005. But by using the § 121 exclusion in 2006, he will eliminate the recognized gain of $230,000 on the sale of the Maple Street residence. ■

Negative Effect of Renting or Using as a Home Office. The residence does not have to be the taxpayer's principal residence at the date of sale to qualify for the § 121 exclusion. During part of the five-year window, it could have been rental property (e.g., either a vacation home or entirely rental property). In addition, the taxpayer can have used part of the principal residence as a qualifying home office.

In either the rental or the home office setting, the taxpayer will have deducted depreciation. Any realized gain on the sale that is attributable to depreciation claimed after May 5, 1997, is not eligible for the § 121 exclusion.[100]

EXAMPLE 79

On December 5, 2005, Amanda sells her principal residence, which qualifies for the § 121 exclusion. Her realized gain is $190,000. From January through November 2004, she was temporarily out of town on a job assignment in another city and rented the residence to a college student. For this period, she deducted MACRS cost recovery of $7,000. Without the depreciation provision, Amanda could exclude the $190,000 realized gain. However, the depreciation taken requires her to recognize $7,000 of the realized gain. ■

Qualification for § 121 Exclusion. The key requirement for the § 121 exclusion is that the taxpayer must have *owned* and *used* the property as a principal residence for at least two years during the five-year window. As taxpayers advance in age, they quite frequently make decisions such as the following:

- Sell the principal residence and buy a smaller residence or rent the principal residence.
- Sell vacation homes they own.
- Sell homes they are holding as rental property.

[99] § 121(f).

[100] § 121(d)(6).

Sale of a Residence and the Home Office Deduction

If various requirements are satisfied, a taxpayer who uses his or her residence for business may claim a deduction for the expenses attributable to such use. But what effect, if any, does claiming an office in the home deduction have on a later sale of the residence? Do the sale proceeds still qualify for nonrecognition of gain treatment under § 121?

Until recently, the answers to these questions were unknown. In fact, concern that the § 121 exclusion might be denied may have deterred some taxpayers from claiming legitimate office in the home deductions. Such caution appears to have been unnecessary. The IRS has clarified its position. Only the depreciation deducted on the office portion of the residence after May 5, 1997, is not eligible for the § 121 exclusion.

These properties may have experienced substantial appreciation during the ownership period. Clearly, the sale of the principal residence is eligible for the § 121 exclusion. Less clear, however, is that proper planning can make it possible for a vacation home or rental property to qualify for the exclusion. Although this strategy may require taxpayers to be flexible about where they live, it can result in substantial tax savings.

EXAMPLE 80

Thelma and David are approaching retirement. They have substantial appreciation on their principal residence and on a house they own at the beach (about two hours away). After retirement, they plan to move to Florida. They have owned and lived in the principal residence for 28 years and have owned the beach house for 9 years. If they sell their principal residence, it qualifies for the § 121 exclusion. At retirement, they could move into their beach house for two years and make it eligible for the exclusion. If the beach house were not so far away, they could sell the principal residence now and move into the beach house to start the running of the two-year use period. Note that any realized gain on the beach house attributable to depreciation is not eligible for the § 121 exclusion. ■

ETHICAL CONSIDERATIONS

A Realtor's Recommendation for the § 121 Exclusion

Bob, age 64, and Sandra, age 50, live in Compton, California, where each owns a personal residence. The combined realized gain from sales of the residences would be about $400,000. Bob and Sandra plan to marry and move to Palm Springs, where they intend to rent a house.

Bob and Sandra both satisfy the requirements for the § 121 exclusion, but due to the soft real estate market, they have been unsuccessful in selling their personal residences. Aware that the statutory limit on the § 121 exclusion is only $250,000 for singles, the realtor suggests the following plan. Bob will sell his house to Sandra, and Sandra will sell her house to Bob for the fair market value. Each will apply § 121 exclusion treatment. As soon as possible, they will sell one of the houses, marry, and move into the other house. After they live in the remaining house for at least two years, they will sell it and move to Palm Springs.

Bob's sale of his house to Sandra and her sale to Bob will yield no tax as the realized gain in each case, being less than $250,000, is covered by § 121. When they resell one of the two houses on the market, § 121 will not apply if any gain results. But substantial gain is unlikely because the recent purchases will have stepped up the bases of both houses.

After the two-year occupancy has run, § 121 will be available again and now will shield $500,000 of realized gain (because of their marriage). In all probability, this shelter plus the higher basis will enable them to avoid any recognized gain on the sale of the remaining house.

Evaluate the realtor's proposal for Bob and Sandra.

Record Keeping. Since the amount of the available exclusion ($250,000 or $500,000) for most taxpayers will exceed the realized gain on the sale of the residence, the IRS has discontinued the form that previously was used to report the sale of a principal residence. If the sale of the residence does result in a gain that is not excluded from gross income, the gain is reported on Schedule D of Form 1040 (Capital Gains and Losses).

However, it is a good idea for all taxpayers who own residences to continue to maintain records on the adjusted basis of the residence including the original cost, any capital improvements, and any deductions that decrease basis (e.g., depreciation on a home office or on rental use) for the following reasons:

- The sale of the residence may not qualify for the § 121 exclusion.
- The realized gain may exceed the § 121 exclusion amount.
- The residence may be converted to rental or business use.
- If part of the residence has been rental or business use property (e.g., a qualifying home office) and depreciation has been deducted, the realized gain is recognized to the extent of the depreciation deducted.

KEY TERMS

Adjusted basis, 13–5
Amount realized, 13–4
Boot, 13–28
Fair market value, 13–4
Goodwill, 13–10
Holding period, 13–14
Involuntary conversion, 13–32
Like-kind exchange, 13–25
Nontaxable exchange, 13–24
Personal residence, 13–37
Realized gain, 13–3
Realized loss, 13–3
Recognized gain, 13–7
Recognized loss, 13–7
Recovery of capital doctrine, 13–8
Section 121 exclusion, 13–37
Wash sale, 13–19

PROBLEM MATERIALS

Discussion Questions

Decision Making

1. Ivan invests in land and Grace invests in taxable bonds. The land appreciates by $8,000 each year, and the bonds earn interest of $8,000 each year. After holding the land and bonds for five years, Ivan and Grace sell them. There is a $40,000 realized gain on the sale of the land and no realized gain or loss on the sale of the bonds. Are the tax consequences to Ivan and Grace the same for each of the five years? Explain.

2. Carol and Dave each purchase 100 shares of stock of Burgundy, Inc., a publicly owned corporation, in July for $10,000 each. Carol sells her stock on December 31 for $8,000. Since Burgundy's stock is listed on a national exchange, Dave is able to ascertain that his shares are worth $8,000 on December 31. Does the tax law treat the decline in value of the stock differently for Carol and Dave? Explain.

3. If a taxpayer sells property for cash, the amount realized consists of the net proceeds from the sale. For each of the following, indicate the effect on the amount realized:
   a. The property is sold on credit.
   b. A mortgage on the property is assumed by the buyer.
   c. The buyer acquires the property subject to a mortgage of the seller.
   d. The seller pays real property taxes that are treated as imposed on the purchaser.
   e. Stock that has a basis to the purchaser of $6,000 and a fair market value of $10,000 is received by the seller as part of the consideration.

Decision Making

4. Tad is negotiating to buy some land. Under the first option, Tad will give Sandra \$120,000 and assume her mortgage on the land for \$80,000. Under the second option, Tad will give Sandra \$200,000, and she will immediately pay off the mortgage. Tad wants his basis for the land to be as high as possible. Given this objective, which option should Tad select?

5. Eve purchases land from Gillen. Eve gives Gillen \$100,000 in cash and agrees to pay Gillen an additional \$400,000 one year later plus interest at 6%.
   a. What is Eve's adjusted basis for the land at the acquisition date?
   b. What is Eve's adjusted basis for the land one year later?

6. A taxpayer owns land and a building with an adjusted basis of \$75,000 and a fair market value of \$240,000. The property is subject to a mortgage of \$360,000. Since the taxpayer is in arrears on the mortgage payments, the creditor is willing to accept the property in return for canceling the amount of the mortgage.
   a. How can the adjusted basis of the property be less than the amount of the mortgage?
   b. If the creditor's offer is accepted, what are the effects on the amount realized, the adjusted basis, and the realized gain or loss?
   c. Does it matter in (b) if the mortgage is recourse or nonrecourse?

7. Distinguish between the terms *allowed depreciation* and *allowable depreciation*. What effects do allowed depreciation and allowable depreciation have on adjusted basis?

8. On August 16, 2005, Todd acquires land and a building for \$300,000 to use in his sole proprietorship. Of the purchase price, \$200,000 is allocated to the building, and \$100,000 is allocated to the land. Cost recovery of \$1,926 is deducted in 2005 for the building.
   a. What is the adjusted basis for the land and the building at the acquisition date?
   b. What is the adjusted basis for the land and the building at the end of 2005?

9. Abby owns stock in Orange Corporation and Blue Corporation. She receives a \$1,000 distribution from both corporations. The instructions from Orange state that the \$1,000 is a dividend. The instructions from Blue state that the \$1,000 is not a dividend. What could cause the instructions to differ as to the tax consequences?

Decision Making

10. Rachel owns her personal use automobile, which has an adjusted basis of \$26,000. Since she is interested in purchasing a newer model, she sells her car to Mason for \$12,000.
    a. What are Rachel's realized and recognized loss resulting from this transaction?
    b. Could Rachel achieve better tax consequences if she traded her old car in for the newer model rather than selling it to Mason?

Issue ID

11. Ron sold his sailboat for a \$5,000 loss in the current year because he was diagnosed as having skin cancer. His spouse wants him to sell his Harley Davidson motorcycle because her brother broke his leg while riding his motorcycle. Since Ron no longer has anyone to ride with, he is seriously considering accepting his wife's advice. Because the motorcycle is a classic, Ron has received two offers. Each offer would result in a \$5,000 gain. Joe would like to purchase the motorcycle before Christmas, and Jeff would like to purchase it after New Year's. Identify the relevant tax issues Ron faces in making his decision.

12. Lee owns a life insurance policy that will pay \$100,000 to Rita, his spouse, on his death. At the date of Lee's death, he had paid total premiums of \$65,000 on the policy. In accordance with § 101(a)(1), Rita excludes the \$100,000 of insurance proceeds. Discuss the relationship, if any, between the § 101 exclusion and the recovery of capital doctrine.

13. Helen purchases a one-acre lot from her employer, a real estate developer, for \$80,000. Is it possible that Helen's adjusted basis for the lot on the date of the purchase could be \$100,000? Could it be \$90,000? Explain.

14. How is cost allocated when a taxpayer acquires multiple assets in a lump-sum purchase?

15. Explain how a donee can sell investment property received by gift and recognize neither gain nor loss even though the selling price differs from the donee's adjusted basis.

Issue ID

16. Simon, who is retired, owns Teal, Inc. stock that has declined in value since he purchased it. He has decided either to give the stock to his nephew, Fred, who is a high school

teacher, or to sell the stock and give the proceeds to Fred. Because nearly all of his wealth is invested in tax-exempt bonds, Simon is in the 15% tax bracket. If Fred receives the stock, he will sell it himself. In either case, he will use the cash or the proceeds from his sale of the stock to make the down payment on the purchase of a house. Based on a recent conversation, Simon is aware that Fred is in the 25% bracket. Identify the tax issues relevant to Simon in deciding whether to give the stock or the sale proceeds to Fred.

17. Different basis rules apply for property received by gift and that received by inheritance. Under what circumstances will the basis of property received by gift and that received by inheritance be the same?

18. Immediately before his death in 2005, Karl sells securities (adjusted basis of $95,000) for their fair market value of $20,000. The sale was not to a related party. Karl is survived by his wife, Zoe, who inherits all of his property.
    a. Did Karl act wisely? Why or why not?
    b. Suppose the figures are reversed (sale for $95,000 of property with an adjusted basis of $20,000). Would the sale be wise? Why or why not?

19. Gary makes a gift of an appreciated building to Carmen. She dies three months later, and Gary inherits the building from her. During the period that Carmen held the building, she deducted depreciation and made a capital expenditure. What effect might these items have on Gary's basis for the inherited building?

20. a. In a community property state, what effect does the death of one spouse have on the adjusted basis of the surviving spouse's one-half interest in the community property?
    b. Presuming the property is jointly owned, would the result be different in a common law state?

21. Mort owns 500 shares of Pear, Inc. stock with an adjusted basis of $22,000. On July 28, 2005, he sells 100 of these shares for $3,000. On August 16, 2005, he purchases another 100 shares for $3,400. Mort's realized loss of $1,400 ($3,000 – $4,400) on the July 28 sale is not recognized, and his adjusted basis for the 100 shares purchased on August 16 is $4,800. Explain.

22. What are the three requirements that must be satisfied for a transaction to qualify for nontaxable exchange treatment under § 1031?

23. Which of the following qualify as like-kind exchanges under § 1031?
    a. Improved for unimproved real estate.
    b. Vending machine (used in business) for inventory.
    c. Rental house for personal residence.
    d. Business equipment for securities.
    e. Warehouse for office building (both used for business).
    f. Truck for computer (both used in business).
    g. Rental house for land (both held for investment).
    h. Ten shares of stock in Blue Corporation for 10 shares of stock in Red Corporation.
    i. Office furniture for office equipment (both used in business).
    j. Unimproved land in Jackson, Mississippi, for unimproved land in Toledo, Spain.

Issue ID

24. Melissa owns a residential lot in Spring Creek that has appreciated substantially in value. She holds the lot for investment. She is considering exchanging the lot with her father for a residential lot in McComb that she also will hold for investment. Identify the relevant tax issues for Melissa.

25. Waldo owns a 20% interest in the AMW Partnership. He exchanges it with Karen for her 20% interest in the JKT Partnership. Does the trade qualify for nontaxable treatment as a like-kind exchange? Explain.

26. What is boot, and how does it affect the recognition of gain or loss on a like-kind exchange when received by the taxpayer? How is the recognition of gain or loss affected when boot is given?

27. Beverly exchanges undeveloped real estate for developed real estate on March 3, 2005. The fair market value of each property is $260,000. Beverly had purchased the undeveloped real estate on February 25, 2002, for $325,000.

a. When does Beverly's holding period begin for the developed real estate?
b. Assume that Beverly's cost for the undeveloped real estate was $200,000. When does her holding period begin for the developed real estate?

28. Mortgaged real estate may be received in a like-kind exchange. If the taxpayer's mortgage is assumed, what effect does the mortgage have on the recognition of realized gain? On the basis of the real estate received?

29. A taxpayer's appreciated property is involuntarily converted. She receives insurance proceeds equal to the fair market value of the property. What is the minimum amount the taxpayer must reinvest in qualifying property to defer recognition of realized gain?

30. Ed receives severance damages from the state government for a public road built across his property. Under what circumstances can the § 1033 involuntary conversion provision apply to prevent the recognition of gain?

31. Distinguish between the taxpayer use test and the functional use test for involuntary conversions. When does each test apply?

32. On June 5, 2005, Tan, Inc., a calendar year taxpayer, receives cash of $520,000 from the county upon condemnation of its office building (adjusted basis of $250,000 and fair market value of $520,000).
   a. What must Tan do to qualify for § 1033 postponement of gain treatment?
   b. How would your advice to Tan differ if the adjusted basis were $550,000?

33. In January 2005, Stanley's warehouse (basis of $570,000) is destroyed by fire. Two months later, Stanley collects insurance proceeds of $610,000.
   a. If Stanley is a calendar year taxpayer, what is the latest date that he can reinvest the insurance proceeds and avoid recognition of gain?
   b. Suppose the warehouse was condemned by the city (instead of being destroyed by fire). What would be the latest date for reinvestment to avoid recognition of gain?

34. Bob is notified by the city public housing authority on May 3, 2005, that his apartment building is going to be condemned as part of an urban renewal project. On June 1, 2005, Carol offers to buy the building from Bob. Bob sells the building to Carol on June 30, 2005. Condemnation occurs on September 1, 2005, and Carol receives the condemnation proceeds from the city. Assume both Bob and Carol are calendar year taxpayers.
   a. What is the earliest date on which Bob can dispose of the building and qualify for § 1033 postponement treatment?
   b. Does the sale to Carol qualify as a § 1033 involuntary conversion?
   c. What is the latest date on which Carol can acquire qualifying replacement property and qualify for postponement of the realized gain?
   d. What type of property will be qualifying replacement property?

Issue ID

35. A warehouse owned by Martha and used in her business (i.e., to store inventory) is being condemned by the city to provide a right of way for a highway. The warehouse has appreciated by $100,000 based on Martha's estimate of its fair market value. In the negotiations, the city is offering $40,000 less than what Martha believes the property is worth. Alan, a real estate broker, has offered to purchase Martha's property for $25,000 more than the city's offer. Martha plans to invest the proceeds she will receive in an office building that she will lease to various tenants. Identify the relevant tax issues for Martha.

36. When does the holding period begin for replacement property acquired in an involuntary conversion? For property received in a like-kind exchange?

37. Gus, who is single, sells his principal residence (owned and occupied for seven years) in November 2005 for a realized gain of $148,000. He had purchased a more expensive new principal residence eight months prior to the sale. He anticipates that he will occupy this house as his principal residence for only about 18 additional months. He expects it to appreciate substantially while he owns it. Gus would like to recognize the realized gain on the 2005 sale because he has a large investment loss from the sale of stock. Can he recognize the realized gain of $148,000 on the sale of his principal residence?

38. Arnold, who is single, sold his principal residence on April 10, 2005, and excluded the realized gain under § 121 (exclusion on the sale of a principal residence). On April 12, 2005, he purchased another principal residence, which he sells on January 12, 2006, for a realized gain of $80,000. Can Arnold exclude the $80,000 realized gain on the January 2006 sale if his reason for selling was:
    a. His noisy neighbors?
    b. A job transfer to another city?

Issue ID

39. Sandy owns a personal residence in which she has lived since she acquired it. It has appreciated by $90,000 during this period. Now, however, the school board has redrawn the boundaries for the school districts, and her son will have to transfer to a different high school for his senior year. Sandy is considering selling her residence and buying another one that will enable her son to remain in the same high school. Without this reason, she would not sell the house. Identify the relevant tax issues for Sandy.

40. To qualify for exclusion treatment on the sale of a principal residence, the residence must have been owned and used by the taxpayer for at least two years during the five-year period ending on the date of the sale. Are there any exceptions to this provision?

41. On May 5, 2005, Nancy sells her stock (adjusted basis of $13,000) in Lime, Inc., a publicly traded company, for $17,000. On May 31, 2005, she pays $20,000 for stock in Rose, Inc., a specialized small business investment company. Nancy believes that her adjusted basis for the Rose stock is $10,000. Evaluate Nancy's calculation of the adjusted basis for her Rose stock.

Problems

42. Anne sold her home for $260,000 in 2005. Selling expenses were $15,000. She had purchased it in 1998 for $190,000. During the period of ownership, Anne had done the following:

    - Deducted $50,500 office-in-home expenses, which included $14,500 in depreciation. (Refer to Chapter 9.)
    - Deducted a casualty loss for residential trees destroyed by a hurricane. The total loss was $19,000 (after the $100 floor and the 10%-of-AGI floor), and Anne's insurance company reimbursed her for $13,500. (Refer to Chapter 7.)
    - Paid street paving assessment of $7,000 and added sidewalks for $11,000.
    - Installed an elevator for medical reasons. The total cost was $20,000, and Anne deducted $12,000 as medical expenses. (Refer to Chapter 10.)

    What is Anne's realized gain?

43. Kareem bought a rental house at the beginning of 2000 for $80,000, of which $10,000 is allocated to the land and $70,000 to the building. Early in 2002, he had a tennis court built in the backyard at a cost of $5,000. Kareem has deducted $32,200 for depreciation on the house and $1,300 for depreciation on the court. At the beginning of 2005, he sells the house and tennis court for $125,000 cash.
    a. What is Kareem's realized gain or loss?
    b. If an original mortgage of $20,000 is still outstanding and the buyer assumes the mortgage in addition to the cash payment, what is Kareem's realized gain or loss?
    c. If the buyer takes the property subject to the mortgage, what is Kareem's realized gain or loss?

44. Gayla owns a building (adjusted basis of $375,000 on January 1, 2005) that she rents to Len who operates a restaurant in the building. The municipal health department closed the restaurant for two months during 2005 because of health code violations. Under MACRS, the cost recovery deduction for 2005 would be $24,000. However, Gayla deducted cost recovery only for the 10 months the restaurant was open since she waived the rent income during the two-month period the restaurant was closed.
    a. What is the amount of the cost recovery deduction that Gayla should report on her 2005 income tax return?
    b. Calculate the adjusted basis of the building at the end of 2005.

45. Nina owns a personal use boat that has a fair market value of $12,500 and an adjusted basis of $17,000. Nina's AGI is $60,000. Calculate the realized and recognized loss if:
   a. Nina sells the boat for $12,500.
   b. Nina exchanges the boat for another boat worth $12,500.
   c. The boat is stolen and Nina receives insurance proceeds of $12,500.

46. Alton owns stock in Dove Corporation. His adjusted basis for the stock is $85,000. During the year, he receives a distribution from the corporation of $65,000 that is labeled a return of capital (i.e., Dove has no earnings and profits).
   a. Determine the tax consequences to Alton.
   b. Assume instead that the amount of the distribution is $100,000. Determine the tax consequences to Alton.
   c. Assume instead in (a) that the $65,000 distribution is labeled a taxable dividend (i.e., Dove has earnings and profits of at least $65,000).

47. Hubert's personal residence is condemned as part of an urban renewal project. His adjusted basis for the residence is $325,000. He receives condemnation proceeds of $300,000 and invests the proceeds in stock.
   a. Calculate Hubert's realized and recognized gain or loss.
   b. If the condemnation proceeds are $355,000, what are Hubert's realized and recognized gain or loss?
   c. What are Hubert's realized and recognized gain or loss if the house was rental property?

Communications

48. Walt Barnes is a real estate agent for Governor's Estates, a residential real estate development. Because of his outstanding sales performance, Walt is permitted to buy a lot that normally would sell for $350,000 for $225,000. Walt is the only real estate agent for Governor's Estates who is permitted to do so.
   a. Does Walt have gross income from the transaction?
   b. What is Walt's adjusted basis for the land?
   c. Write a letter to Walt informing him of the tax consequences of his acquisition of the lot. His address is 100 Tower Road, San Diego, CA 92182.

49. Karen makes the following purchases and sales of stock:

Transaction	Date	Number of Shares	Company	Price per Share
Purchase	1–1–2003	300	MDG	$ 75
Purchase	6–1–2003	150	GRU	300
Purchase	11–1–2003	60	MDG	70
Sale	12–3–2003	180	MDG	70
Purchase	3–1–2004	120	GRU	375
Sale	8–1–2004	90	GRU	330
Sale	1–1–2005	150	MDG	90
Sale	2–1–2005	75	GRU	500

Assuming that Karen is unable to identify the particular lots that are sold with the original purchase, what is the recognized gain or loss on each type of stock as of the following dates:
   a. 7–1–2003.
   b. 12–31–2003.
   c. 12–31–2004.
   d. 7–1–2005.

50. Frank purchases 100 shares of Bluebird Corporation stock on June 3, 2005, for $150,000. On August 25, 2005, Frank purchases an additional 50 shares of Bluebird stock for $60,000. According to market quotations, Bluebird stock is selling for $1,100 per share on December 31, 2005. Frank sells 60 shares of Bluebird stock on March 1, 2006, for $51,000.

a. What is the adjusted basis of Frank's Bluebird stock on December 31, 2005?
b. What is Frank's recognized gain or loss from the sale of Bluebird stock on March 1, 2006, assuming the shares sold are from the shares purchased on June 3, 2005?
c. What is Frank's recognized gain or loss from the sale of Bluebird stock on March 1, 2006, assuming Frank cannot adequately identify the shares sold?

Communications

51. Rod Mitchell purchases Agnes's sole proprietorship for $975,000 on August 15, 2005. The assets of the business are as follows:

Asset	Agnes's Adjusted Basis	FMV
Accounts receivable	$ 70,000	$ 70,000
Inventory	90,000	100,000
Equipment	150,000	160,000
Furniture and fixtures	95,000	130,000
Building	190,000	250,000
Land	25,000	75,000

Rod and Agnes agree that $50,000 of the purchase price is for Agnes's five-year covenant not to compete.
a. Calculate Agnes's realized and recognized gain.
b. Determine Rod's basis for each of the assets.
c. Write a letter to Rod informing him of the tax consequences of the purchase. His address is 300 Riverview Drive, Delaware, OH 43015.

52. Donna owns 800 shares of common stock in Macaw Corporation, which have an adjusted basis of $40,000. She receives a 5% stock dividend. Shareholders do not have the option to receive cash. At the date she receives the stock dividend, the common stock is selling for $60 per share.
a. Determine the amount of gross income Donna must recognize as a result of receiving the stock dividend.
b. Calculate Donna's adjusted basis for her 840 shares of Macaw common stock.

53. Sherry owns 1,000 shares of Taupe Corporation stock with a basis of $15,000 and a fair market value of $20,000. She receives nontaxable stock rights to purchase additional shares. The rights have a fair market value of $2,000.
a. What are the basis of the stock and the basis of the stock rights?
b. What is the holding period for the stock rights?
c. What is the recognized gain or loss if the stock rights are sold for $2,000?
d. What is the recognized gain or loss if the stock rights are allowed to lapse?

54. Beth receives a car from Sam as a gift. Sam paid $18,000 for the car. He had used it for business purposes and had deducted $8,000 for depreciation up to the time he gave the car to Beth. The fair market value of the car is $6,000.
a. Assuming Beth uses the car for business purposes, what is her basis for depreciation?
b. If the estimated useful life is two years (from the date of the gift), what is her depreciation deduction for each year? Assume Beth elects the straight-line method.
c. If Beth sells the car for $900 one year after receiving it, what is her gain or loss?
d. If Beth sells the car for $6,000 one year after receiving it, what is her gain or loss?

55. On September 18, 2005, Gerald received land and a building from his Uncle Frank as a gift. Uncle Frank's adjusted basis and the fair market value at the date of the gift were as follows:

Asset	Adjusted Basis	FMV
Land	$100,000	$211,000
Building	80,000	100,000

Uncle Frank paid gift tax of $45,000.

a. Determine Gerald's adjusted basis for the land and building.
b. Assume instead that the fair market value of the land was $87,000 and that of the building was $65,000. Determine Gerald's adjusted basis for the land and building.

Decision Making
Communications

56. Ira Cook is planning to make a charitable contribution of Crystal, Inc. stock worth $20,000 to the Boy Scouts. The stock has an adjusted basis of $15,000. A friend has suggested that Ira sell the stock and contribute the $20,000 in proceeds rather than contribute the stock.
    a. Should Ira follow the friend's advice? Why?
    b. Assume the fair market value is only $13,000. In this case, should Ira follow the friend's advice? Why?
    c. Rather than make a charitable contribution to the Boy Scouts, Ira is going to make a gift to Nancy, his niece. Advise Ira regarding (a) and (b).
    d. Write a letter to Ira regarding whether in (a) he should sell the stock and contribute the cash or contribute the stock. He has informed you that he purchased the stock six years ago. Ira's address is 500 Ireland Avenue, De Kalb, IL 60115.

57. Catherine died in March 2005 leaving real estate (adjusted basis of $500,000) to her niece, Amanda. The fair market value of the real estate at the date of Catherine's death is $1,825,000. The executor of the estate does not distribute the real estate to Amanda until November 2005, when its fair market value is $1,813,000. The fair market value of the real estate six months after Catherine's death is $1,815,000.
    a. What are the possibilities as to Amanda's adjusted basis in the real estate?
    b. What purpose does the alternate valuation date serve?
    c. Assume instead that the fair market value six months after Catherine's death is $1,860,000. What is Amanda's basis in the real estate?

58. Dan bought a hotel for $2,720,000 in January 2002. In January 2005, he died and left the hotel to Ed. Dan had deducted $20,930 of cost recovery on the hotel before his death. The fair market value in January 2005 was $2,780,000. The fair market value six months later was $2,850,000.
    a. What is the basis of the property to Ed?
    b. What is the basis of the property to Ed if the fair market value six months later was $2,500,000 and the objective of the executor was to minimize the estate tax liability?

59. Larry and Grace live in Arizona, a community property state. They own land (community property) that has an adjusted basis to them of $150,000. When Grace dies, Larry inherits her share of the land. At the date of Grace's death, the fair market value of the land is $200,000. Six months after Grace's death, the land is worth $220,000.
    a. What is Larry's basis for the land?
    b. What would Larry's basis for the land be if he and Grace lived in Kansas, a common law state, and Larry inherited Grace's share?

60. Sheila sells land to Elane, her sister, for the fair market value of $40,000. Six months later when the land is worth $42,000, Elane gives it to Jacob, her son. No gift taxes are paid. Shortly thereafter, Jacob sells the land for $43,000.
    a. Assuming Sheila's adjusted basis for the land is $25,000, what are Sheila's and Jacob's recognized gain or loss on their respective sales?
    b. Assuming Sheila's adjusted basis for the land is $50,000, what are Sheila's and Jacob's recognized gain or loss on their respective sales?

61. Doug owns three pieces of land in Clay County. Parcel A has an adjusted basis of $75,000; parcel B, $125,000; and parcel C, $175,000. Doug sells parcel A to his father-in-law for $50,000, parcel B to his partner for $120,000, and parcel C to his mother for $150,000.
    a. What is the recognized gain or loss from the sale of each of the parcels of land?
    b. If Doug's father-in-law eventually sells his land for $90,000, what is his recognized gain or loss?
    c. If Doug's partner eventually sells his land for $130,000, what is his recognized gain or loss?
    d. If Doug's mother eventually sells her land for $165,000, what is her recognized gain or loss?

Decision Making

62. Justin owns 1,000 shares of Oriole Corporation common stock (adjusted basis of $9,800). On April 27, 2005, he sells 300 of these shares for $2,800. On May 5, 2005, Justin purchases 200 shares of Oriole Corporation common stock for $2,500.
    a. What is Justin's recognized gain or loss resulting from these transactions?
    b. What is Justin's basis for the stock acquired on May 5?
    c. Could Justin have obtained different tax consequences in (a) and (b) if he had sold the 300 shares on December 27, 2005, and purchased the 200 shares on January 5, 2006?

63. Jeffrey leaves a public accounting firm to enter private practice. He had bought a home two years earlier for $56,000 (ignore land). When starting his business, he converts one-fourth of the home into an office. The fair market value of the home on the date of the conversion (January 1, 2000) is $75,000, while the adjusted basis remains at $56,000. Jeffery lives and works in the home for six years and sells it at the end of the sixth year. He deducted $2,124 of cost recovery (using the statutory percentage method). How much gain or loss is recognized if Jeffrey sells the home for:
    a. $44,000?
    b. $70,000?

Decision Making

64. Hun, age 93, has accumulated substantial assets during his life. Among his many assets are the following, which he is considering giving to Koji, his grandson.

Asset	Adjusted Basis	Fair Market Value
Red Corporation stock	$900,000	$700,000
Silver Corporation stock	70,000	71,000
Emerald Corporation stock	200,000	500,000

Hun has been in ill health for the past five years. His physician has informed him that he probably will not live for more than six months. Advise Hun on which of the stocks should be transferred as gifts and which as bequests.

65. Kareem owns an automobile that he uses exclusively in his business. The adjusted basis is $19,000, and the fair market value is $16,000. Kareem exchanges the car for a car that he will use exclusively in his business.
    a. What are Kareem's realized and recognized gain or loss?
    b. What is his basis in the new car?
    c. What are the tax consequences to Kareem in (a) and (b) if he used the old car and will use the new car exclusively for personal purposes?

Decision Making
Communications

66. Tex Watson owns undeveloped land (basis of $350,000) held as an investment. On October 7, 2005, he exchanges the land with his 27-year-old daughter, Porchia, for other undeveloped land also to be held as an investment. The appraised value of Porchia's land is $500,000.
    a. On February 15, 2006, Tex sells the land to Baxter, a real estate broker, for $600,000. Calculate Tex's realized and recognized gain or loss from the exchange with Porchia and on the subsequent sale of the land to Baxter.
    b. Calculate Tex's realized and recognized gain or loss on the exchange with Porchia if Tex does not sell the land. Instead, on February 15, 2006, Porchia sells the land received from Tex. Calculate Tex's basis for the land on October 7, 2005, and on February 15, 2006.
    c. Write a letter to Tex advising him on how he could avoid any recognition of gain associated with the October 7, 2005 exchange. His address is The Corral, El Paso, TX 79968.

67. Bonnie owns a personal computer (adjusted basis of $3,000) that she uses exclusively in her business. Bonnie transfers the computer and cash of $1,500 to Green Computers for a laser printer (worth $5,500) also to be used in her business.
    a. Calculate Bonnie's recognized gain or loss on the exchange.
    b. Calculate Bonnie's basis for the printer.

Decision Making

68. Clarence exchanges a light-duty truck used in his business for one to be similarly used. The adjusted basis of the old truck is $17,000 (fair market value of $11,000).
    a. Calculate Clarence's recognized gain or loss on the exchange.
    b. What is Clarence's basis in the new truck?
    c. How could the transaction have been structured to produce better tax results?
    d. How would your answers in (a), (b), and (c) change if the fair market value of the original truck was $19,000 and the fair market value of the replacement truck was $25,000 (i.e., cash payment of $6,000 was required from Clarence)?

69. Susan owns a car that she uses exclusively for personal purposes. Its original cost was $26,000, and the fair market value is $12,000. She exchanges the car and $18,000 cash for a new car.
    a. Calculate Susan's realized and recognized gain or loss.
    b. Calculate Susan's basis for the new car.
    c. Determine when Susan's holding period for the new car begins.

70. Tom owns land and a building that he uses in his business (adjusted basis of $125,000 and fair market value of $275,000). Tom exchanges the land and building for land with a fair market value of $175,000 that he will use as a parking lot. In addition, he receives stock worth $100,000.
    a. What is Tom's realized gain or loss?
    b. His recognized gain or loss?
    c. The basis of the land and the stock received?
    d. How would the answers in (a), (b), and (c) change if the stock is worth $175,000 (not $100,000) and the land Tom receives has a fair market value of $100,000 (not $175,000)?

71. What is the basis of the new property in each of the following exchanges?
    a. Apartment building held for investment (adjusted basis $145,000) for office building to be held for investment (fair market value $225,000).
    b. Land and building used as a barber shop (adjusted basis $190,000) for land and building used as a grocery store (fair market value $350,000).
    c. Office building (adjusted basis $45,000) for bulldozer (fair market value $42,000), both held for business use.
    d. IBM common stock (adjusted basis $20,000) for ExxonMobil common stock (fair market value $28,000).
    e. Rental house (adjusted basis $90,000) for mountain cabin to be held for rental use (fair market value $225,000).

Decision Making

72. Steve owns Machine A (adjusted basis of $12,000 and fair market value of $15,000), which he uses in his business. Steve sells Machine A for $15,000 to Tom (a dealer). Steve then purchases Machine B for $15,000 from Joan (also a dealer). Machine B would normally qualify as like-kind property.
    a. What are Steve's realized and recognized gain on the sale of Machine A?
    b. What is Steve's basis for Machine B?
    c. What factors would motivate Steve to sell Machine A and purchase Machine B rather than exchange one machine for the other?
    d. Assume that the adjusted basis of Machine A is $15,000 and the fair market value of both machines is $12,000. Respond to (a) through (c).

73. Gene exchanges real estate held for investment plus stock for real estate to be held for investment. The stock transferred has an adjusted basis of $30,000 and a fair market value of $20,000. The real estate transferred has an adjusted basis of $30,000 and a fair market value of $90,000. The real estate acquired has a fair market value of $110,000.
    a. What is Gene's realized gain or loss?
    b. His recognized gain or loss?
    c. The basis of the newly acquired real estate?

74. Determine the realized, recognized, and postponed gain or loss and the new basis for each of the following like-kind exchanges:

	Adjusted Basis of Old Asset	Boot Given	Fair Market Value of New Asset	Boot Received
a.	$ 7,000	$ –0–	$12,000	$4,000
b.	14,000	2,000	15,000	–0–
c.	3,000	7,000	8,000	500
d.	22,000	–0–	32,000	–0–
e.	10,000	–0–	11,000	1,000
f.	10,000	–0–	8,000	–0–

75. Carla's office building (adjusted basis of $290,000) is destroyed by a tornado. Since Carla has excess office space, she decides not to replace the building. Instead, she adds the proceeds to the working capital of her business. What is Carla's recognized gain or loss if the insurance proceeds are:
   a. $325,000?
   b. $150,000?

76. Albert owns 100 acres of land on which he grows spruce Christmas trees. His adjusted basis for the land is $100,000. He receives condemnation proceeds of $10,000 when the city's new beltway takes 5 acres along the eastern boundary of his property. He also receives a severance award of $6,000 associated with the possible harmful effects of exhaust fumes on his Christmas trees. Albert invests the $16,000 in a growth mutual fund. Determine the tax consequences to Albert of the:
   a. Condemnation proceeds.
   b. Severance award.

77. For each of the following involuntary conversions, indicate whether the property acquired qualifies as replacement property, the recognized gain, and the basis for the property acquired:
   a. Frank owns a warehouse that is destroyed by a tornado. The space in the warehouse was rented to various tenants. The adjusted basis was $470,000. Frank uses all of the insurance proceeds of $700,000 to build a shopping mall in a neighboring community where no property has been damaged by tornadoes. The shopping mall is rented to various tenants.
   b. Ivan owns a warehouse that he uses in his business. The adjusted basis is $300,000. The warehouse is destroyed by fire. Because of economic conditions in the area, Ivan decides not to rebuild the warehouse. Instead, he uses all of the insurance proceeds of $400,000 to build a warehouse to be used in his business in another state.
   c. Ridge's personal residence is condemned as part of a local government project to widen the highway from two lanes to four lanes. The adjusted basis is $170,000. Ridge uses all of the condemnation proceeds of $200,000 to purchase another personal residence.
   d. Juanita owns a building that she uses in her retail business. The adjusted basis is $250,000. The building is destroyed by a hurricane. Because of an economic downturn in the area caused by the closing of a military base, Juanita decides to rent space for her retail outlet rather than to replace the building. She uses all of the insurance proceeds of $300,000 to buy a four-unit apartment building in another city. A realtor in that city will handle the rental of the apartments for her.
   e. Susan and Rick's personal residence is destroyed by a tornado. The adjusted basis was $170,000. Since they would like to travel, they decide not to acquire a replacement residence. Instead, they invest all of the insurance proceeds of $200,000 in a duplex, which they rent to tenants.

78. Leslie's office building (adjusted basis of $325,000) is destroyed by a hurricane in November 2005. Leslie, a calendar year taxpayer, receives insurance proceeds of $450,000 in January 2006. Calculate Leslie's realized gain or loss, recognized gain or loss, and basis for the replacement property if she:

a. Acquires a new office building for $460,000 in January 2006.
b. Acquires a new office building for $430,000 in January 2006.
c. Does not acquire replacement property.

79. What are the *maximum* postponed gain or loss and the basis for the replacement property for the following involuntary conversions?

	Property	Type of Conversion	Amount Realized	Adjusted Basis	Amount Reinvested
a.	Drugstore (business)	Casualty	$160,000	$130,000	$110,000
b.	Apartments (investment)	Condemned	100,000	125,000	175,000
c.	Grocery store (business)	Casualty	400,000	300,000	450,000
d.	Residence (personal)	Casualty	16,000	18,000	17,000
e.	Vacant lot (investment)	Condemned	240,000	160,000	220,000
f.	Residence (personal)	Casualty	20,000	18,000	19,000
g.	Residence (personal)	Condemned	18,000	20,000	26,000
h.	Apartments (investment)	Condemned	150,000	100,000	200,000

Decision Making

80. Rental property owned by Faye, a calendar year taxpayer, is destroyed by a tornado on January 1, 2005. Faye had originally paid $150,000 for the property ($125,000 allocated to the building and $25,000 allocated to the land). During the time Faye owned the property, MACRS deductions of $46,250 were claimed. MACRS deductions of $57,500 would have been claimed, except that Faye chose to forgo $11,250 one year when she had a net operating loss. Faye receives insurance proceeds of $60,000 in November 2005. As a result of continuing negotiations with the insurance company, Faye receives additional proceeds of $35,000 in August 2006.
   a. What is Faye's adjusted basis for the property?
   b. What is Faye's realized gain or loss on the involuntary conversion in 2005? In 2006?
   c. What is the latest date that Faye can replace the involuntarily converted property to qualify for § 1033 postponement?
   d. What is the latest date that Faye can replace the involuntarily converted property to qualify for § 1033 postponement if the form of the involuntary conversion is a condemnation?
   e. What should Faye do regarding the omitted MACRS deductions of $11,250?

Decision Making

81. Katie purchased her residence on January 2, 2004, for $180,000 after having lived in it during 2003 as a tenant under a lease with an option to buy clause. On June 1, 2005, Katie sells the residence for $335,000. On June 13, 2005, Katie purchases a new residence for $360,000.
   a. What is Katie's recognized gain? Her basis for the new residence?
   b. Assume instead that Katie purchased her original residence on January 2, 2003 (rather than on January 2, 2004). What is Katie's recognized gain? Her basis for the new residence?
   c. In (a), what could Katie do to minimize her recognized gain?

82. Taylor has owned and occupied her personal residence (adjusted basis of $190,000) for four years. In April 2005, she sells the residence for $300,000 (selling expenses are $20,000). On the same day as the sale, Taylor purchases another house for $350,000. Because of noisy neighbors, she sells the new house after just 10 months. The selling price is $483,000 (selling expenses are $18,000).
   a. What is Taylor's recognized gain on the sale of the first residence?
   b. What is Taylor's basis for her second residence?
   c. What is Taylor's recognized gain on the sale of the second residence?
   d. Assume instead that the sale of the second residence was due to Taylor's job transfer to another state. What is her recognized gain on the sale of the second residence?

83. Milton, who is single, listed his personal residence with a realtor on March 3, 2005, at a price of $250,000. He rejected several offers in the $200,000 range during the summer. Finally, on August 16, 2005, he and the purchaser signed a contract to sell for $245,000.

The sale (i.e., closing) took place on September 7, 2005. The closing statement showed the following disbursements:

Realtor's commission	$ 14,000
Appraisal fee	500
Exterminator's certificate	300
Recording fees	400
Mortgage to First Bank	180,000
Cash to seller	49,800

Milton's adjusted basis for the house is $150,000. He owned and occupied the house for eight years. On October 1, 2005, Milton purchases another residence for $210,000.

a. Calculate Milton's recognized gain on the sale.
b. What is Milton's adjusted basis for the new residence?
c. Assume instead that the selling price is $735,000. What is Milton's recognized gain? His adjusted basis for the new residence?

84. Assuming § 121 applies, what are the realized, recognized, and excluded gain or loss and the new basis in each of the following cases?
    a. Susan sold her residence for $390,000. The adjusted basis was $55,000. The selling expenses were $15,000. Repair expenses incurred to get the house ready to sell were $3,000. She did not reinvest in a new residence.
    b. Rocky sold his residence for $270,000. The adjusted basis was $120,000. The selling expenses were $9,000. Repair expenses incurred to get the house ready to sell were $6,000. Rocky reinvested $260,000 in a new residence.
    c. Veneia sold her residence for $465,000. The adjusted basis was $35,000. The selling expenses were $17,000. Repair expenses incurred to get the house ready to sell were $2,000. She reinvested $400,000 in a new residence.
    d. Barry sold his residence for $70,000. The adjusted basis was $65,000. The selling expenses were $6,000. He reinvested $80,000 in a new residence.
    e. Carl sold his residence for $100,000 in cash, and his mortgage is assumed by the buyer. The adjusted basis was $80,000; the mortgage, $50,000. The selling expenses were $4,000. Repair expenses incurred to get the house ready to sell were $2,000. He reinvested $120,000 in a new residence.

85. Pedro, age 57, is the sole owner of his principal residence. He has owned and occupied it for 10 years. Maria, his spouse, has also lived there for 10 years. He sells the house for a realized gain of $340,000. Pedro does not intend to acquire a replacement residence.
    a. Can Pedro use the § 121 exclusion if he and Maria file a joint return? If so, what are the available amount of the exclusion and the recognized gain?
    b. Can Pedro use the § 121 exclusion if he files a separate return? If so, what are the available amounts of the exclusion and the recognized gain?
    c. Assume instead that the realized gain is $550,000 and a joint return is filed.
    d. Assume instead that the realized gain is $550,000 and separate returns are filed.
    e. Assume instead that Maria and Pedro have been married for only 18 months and that she has lived in his house only since their marriage. They file a joint return.

Decision Making

86. Meg and Walt are going to be married in three months. Meg has owned and lived in her home for 42 years, and Walt has owned and occupied his home for 35 years. They both have listed their homes for sale. They anticipate the sales results will be as follows:

	Meg	Walt
Selling price	$450,000	$190,000
Selling expenses	40,000	19,000
Adjusted basis	75,000	60,000

They intend to purchase a residence in an extended care facility for $400,000. They have come to you for advice regarding the following:

a. What is their recognized gain if they marry before they sell their residences?
b. What is their recognized gain if they marry after they sell their residences?
c. Walt would prefer to invest his sales proceeds in the stock market. Does it matter whether the new residence is jointly owned or owned only by Meg?
d. Should Meg and Walt delay their marriage if they have not yet sold their residences?

Communications

87. Nell, Nina, and Nora Sanders, who are sisters, sell their principal residence (owned as tenants in common) in which they have lived for the past 20 years. The youngest of the sisters is age 58. The selling price is $750,000, selling expenses and legal fees are $75,000, and the adjusted basis is $60,000 (the fair market value of the residence when inherited from their parents 20 years ago). Since the sisters are going to live in rental housing, they do not plan to acquire another residence. Nell has contacted you on behalf of the three sisters regarding the tax consequences of the sale.
a. Write a letter to Nell advising her of the tax consequences and how taxes can be minimized. Nell's address is 100 Oak Avenue, Billings, MT 59101.
b. Prepare a memo for the tax files.

Decision Making

88. Sam, a calendar year taxpayer who is age 63, owns a residence in which he has lived for 20 years. The residence is destroyed by fire on August 8, 2005. The adjusted basis is $170,000, and the fair market value is $350,000. Sam receives insurance proceeds of $350,000 for the residence on September 1, 2005. He is trying to decide whether to purchase a comparable house. He anticipates that he will retire in two years and will move to a warmer climate where he will rent in case he decides to live in different places.
a. Advise Sam of the tax consequences of replacing versus not replacing the residence.
b. Which do you recommend to him?
c. How would your answer in (a) change if the fair market value and insurance proceeds received were $600,000?

Decision Making

89. Roby and Sid have been married for 12 years. Roby sells Peach, Inc. stock that she has owned for four years to Sid for its fair market value of $120,000. Her adjusted basis is $150,000.
a. Calculate Roby's recognized gain or recognized loss.
b. Calculate Sid's adjusted basis for the stock.
c. How would the tax consequences in (a) and (b) differ if Roby had made a gift of the stock to Sid? Which form of the transaction would you recommend?

Cumulative Problems

Tax Return Problem

90. Albert Sims, age 67, is married and files a joint return with his wife, Carol, age 65. Albert and Carol are both retired, and during 2004, they received Social Security benefits of $11,000. Albert's Social Security number is 366–55–1111, and Carol's is 555–66–2222. They reside at 210 College Drive, Columbia, SC 29201.

Albert, who retired on January 1, 2004, receives benefits from a qualified pension plan of $600 a month for life. His total contributions to the plan (none of which were deductible) were $63,000. In January 2004, he received a bonus of $5,000 from his former employer for service performed in 2003. Although the former employer accrued the bonus in 2003, it was not paid until 2004.

Carol, who retired on December 31, 2003, started receiving benefits of $800 a month on January 1, 2004. Her contributions to the qualified pension plan (none of which were deductible) were $59,800.

Albert has been paying alimony of $12,000 each year to his former wife, Nancy. As Nancy died on September 1, the payments for 2004 were limited to $8,000. Nancy's Social Security number is 400–60–1234.

Carol had casino winnings for the year of $1,500, while Albert won $25,000 on a $1 lottery ticket.

On September 27, 2004, Albert and Carol received a 10% stock dividend on 60 shares of stock they owned. They had bought the stock on March 5, 1997, for $11 a share. On December 16, 2004, they sold the 6 dividend shares for $45 a share.

On January 10, 2004, Carol sold the car she had used in commuting to and from work for $5,000. She had paid $19,000 for the car in 1998.

On July 14, 1995, Albert and Carol received a gift of 500 shares of stock from their son, Thomas. Thomas's basis in the stock was $30 a share (fair market value at the date of gift was $22). No gift tax was paid on the transfer. Albert and Carol sold the stock on October 8, 2004, for $19 a share.

On May 1, 2004, Carol's mother died, and Carol inherited her personal residence. The residence had a fair market value of $112,000 and an adjusted basis to the mother of $130,000. Carol listed the house with a realtor, who estimated it was worth $120,000 as of December 31, 2004.

Carol received rent income of $2,000 on a beach house she inherited three years ago from her Uncle Chuck. She had rented the property for one week during the July 4th weekend and one week during the Thanksgiving holidays. Uncle Chuck's adjusted basis in the beach house was $150,000, and its fair market value on the date of his death was $225,000. Carol and Albert used the beach house for personal purposes for 42 days during the year. Expenses associated with the house were $3,400 for utilities, maintenance, and repairs and $2,000 for property taxes. There are no mortgages on the property.

Albert and Carol paid estimated Federal income tax of $3,100 and had itemized deductions of $8,800 (excluding any itemized deductions associated with the beach house). If they have overpaid their Federal income tax, they want the amount refunded. Both Albert and Carol wish to have $3 go to the Presidential Election Campaign Fund.

Compute their net tax payable or refund due for 2004. If you use tax forms for your computations, you will need Form 1040 and Schedules A and D. Suggested software: TurboTax.

Tax Return Problem
Decision Making
Communications

91. Tammy Walker, age 37, is a self-employed accountant. Tammy's Social Security number is 333–40–1111. Her address is 101 Glass Road, Richmond, VA 23236. Her income and expenses associated with her accounting practice for 2005 are as follows:

Revenues (cash receipts during 2005)	$320,000
Expenses	
Salaries	$ 85,000
Office supplies	2,100
Postage	2,900
Depreciation of equipment	30,000
Telephone	800
	$120,800

Since Tammy is a cash method taxpayer, she does not record her receivables as revenue until she receives cash payment. At the beginning of 2005, her accounts receivable were $90,000, and the balance had decreased to $35,000 by the end of the year. The balance on December 31, 2005, would have been $40,000, except that an account for $5,000 had become uncollectible in November.

Tammy used one room in her 10-room house as the office for her accounting practice (300 square feet out of a total square footage of 3,000). She paid the following expenses related to the house during 2005:

Utilities	$3,600
Insurance	1,000
Property taxes	5,000
Repairs	2,700

Tammy had purchased the house on September 1, 2004, for $275,000 (exclusive of land cost).

Tammy has one child, Thomas, age 16. Thomas lives with his father during the summer and with Tammy for the rest of the year. Tammy can document that she spent $16,000 during 2005 for the child's support. The father normally provides about $8,000 per year, but this year he gave Thomas a new car for Christmas. The cost of the car was $25,000. The divorce decree is silent regarding the dependency exemption for Thomas. Tammy does not provide her former spouse with a signed Form 8332 for 2005.

Under the terms of the divorce decree, Tammy is to receive alimony of $10,000 per month. The payments will terminate at Tammy's death or at her remarriage.

Tammy provides part of the support of her mother, age 67. The total support in 2005 for her mother was as follows:

Social Security benefits	$5,200
From Tammy	2,900
From Bob, Tammy's brother	2,000
From Susan, Tammy's sister	1,900

Bob and Susan have both indicated their willingness to sign a multiple support waiver form if it will benefit Tammy.

Tammy's deductible itemized deductions during 2005, excluding any itemized deductions related to the house, were $16,000. She made estimated tax payments of $98,000.

Part 1—Tax Computation
Compute Tammy's lowest net tax payable or refund due for 2005. Suggested software: TurboTax.

Part 2—Tax Planning
Tammy and her former husband have been discussing the $10,000 alimony he pays her each month. Because his new wife has a health problem, he does not feel that he can afford to continue to pay the $10,000 each month. He is in the 15% tax bracket. If Tammy will agree to decrease the amount by 25%, he will agree that the amount paid is not alimony for tax purposes. Assume that the other data used in calculating Tammy's taxable income for 2005 will apply for her 2006 tax return. Write a letter to Tammy that contains your advice on whether she should agree to her former husband's proposal. Also prepare a memo for the tax files. Suggested software: TurboTax.

Tax Return Problem

92. Arnold Young, age 39, is single. He lives at 1507 Iris Lane, Albuquerque, NM 87131. His Social Security number is 999–55–2000. Arnold does not wish to have $3 go to the Presidential Election Campaign Fund.

Arnold was divorced in 2000 after 15 years of marriage. He pays alimony of $32,000 a year to his former spouse, Carol. Carol's Social Security number is 999–33–3000. Arnold's son, Tom, who is age 13, resides with Carol. Arnold pays child support of $10,000 per year. Carol has provided Arnold with a signed Form 8332 in which she releases the dependency deduction to him for 2004. Tom's Social Security number is 999–09–1000.

Arnold owns a sole proprietorship for which he uses the accrual method of accounting. His revenues and expenses for 2004 are as follows:

Sales revenue	$654,000
Cost of goods sold	399,000
Salary expense	85,000
Rent expense	29,000
Utilities	5,000
Telephone	3,000
Advertising	4,000
Bad debts	8,000
Depreciation	15,000
Health insurance*	10,000
Accounting and legal fees	4,000
Supplies	1,000

*$6,000 for employees and $4,000 for Arnold.

Other income received by Arnold includes the following:

Dividend income:	
Swan, Inc.	$7,000
Wren, Inc.	5,000
Interest income:	
First Bank	6,000
Second Bank	1,500
City of Asheville bonds	9,000
Lottery winnings (tickets purchased cost $900)	8,500

During the year, Arnold and his sole proprietorship had the following property transactions:

a. Sold Blue, Inc. stock for $26,000 on March 12, 2004. He had purchased the stock on September 5, 2001, for $30,000.
b. Received an inheritance of $75,000 from his Uncle Henry. Arnold used the $75,000 to purchase Green, Inc. stock on May 15, 2004.
c. Received Orange, Inc. stock worth $8,500 as a gift from his Aunt Jane on June 17, 2004. Her adjusted basis for the stock was $4,000. No gift taxes were paid on the transfer. Aunt Jane had purchased the stock on April 1, 1998. Arnold sold the stock on July 1, 2004, for $18,000.
d. On July 15, 2004, Arnold sold one-half of the Green, Inc. stock for $22,500.
e. Arnold was notified on August 1, 2004, that Yellow, Inc. stock he purchased from a colleague on September 1, 2003, for $19,000 had become worthless. While he perceived that the investment was risky, he did not anticipate that the corporation would declare bankruptcy.
f. On August 15, 2004, Arnold received a parcel of land in Phoenix worth $185,000 in exchange for a parcel of land he owned in Tucson. Since the Tucson parcel was worth $200,000, he also received $15,000 cash. Arnold's adjusted basis for the Tucson parcel was $181,000. He originally purchased it on September 18, 2001.
g. On December 1, 2004, Arnold sold the condominium in which he had been living for the past 10 years. The sales price was $410,000, selling expenses were $15,000, and repair expenses related to the sale were $5,000. Arnold and Carol had purchased the condominium as joint owners for $140,000. Arnold had received Carol's ownership interest as part of the divorce proceedings. The fair market value at that time was $150,000.

Arnold's potential itemized deductions, exclusive of the aforementioned information, are as follows:

Medical expenses (before the 7.5% floor)	$ 7,000
Property taxes on residence	5,000
State income taxes	3,500
Charitable contributions	12,000
Mortgage interest on residence	8,500
Sales taxes paid	4,000

During the year, Arnold makes estimated Federal income tax payments of $20,000.

Compute Arnold's lowest net tax payable or refund due for 2004, assuming he makes any available elections that will reduce the tax. If you use tax forms for your computations, you will need Forms 1040, 8332, and 8824 and Schedules A, B, C, D, and SE. Suggested software: TurboTax.

Research Problems

Note: Solutions to Research Problems can be prepared by using the ***RIA Checkpoint® Student Edition*** *online research product, which is available to accompany this text. It is also possible to prepare solutions to the Research Problems by using tax research materials found in a standard tax library.*

Research Problem 1. Mitchell died on April 13, 2002. The executor of his estate made the § 2032(a) election to use the alternate valuation date in filing Mitchell's estate tax return. Using the primary valuation date and amount, the estate assets would have been valued at $1.5 million. With the election, the estate assets were valued at $1.25 million.

A major asset of the estate consisted of shares of BFI Corporation. The shares of BFI were traded on an established securities market. Since the estate owned 2% of BFI's stock, the executor secured the services of a major brokerage firm to calculate the blockage discount on the BFI stock. Shortly before the estate tax return due date of January 13, 2003, the executor filed a Form 4768 (Application for Extension of Time To File a Return and/or Pay U.S. Estate Taxes) requesting an extension for filing to July 13, 2003. At this time, the estate paid estimated estate taxes of $400,000. In early June, a representative of the brokerage firm notified the executor that it would not be able to finish the valuation on time. Another firm was engaged, and it completed the valuation as of November 29, 2003. Mitchell's executor finally filed the return on January 19, 2005, and made the § 2032(a) election.

The IRS determined that a § 2032(a) election cannot be made unless the estate tax return is timely filed. A deficiency was assessed based on an asset valuation of $1.5 million rather than $1.25 million. Evaluate the position of the IRS.

Research Problem 2. Asa operated his business in a building on Mason Drive. Due to changing residential housing patterns in the city, he decided to move the business to a new location on Leigh Lane. His adjusted basis for the Mason Drive property is $120,000, and the fair market value is $500,000. He purchased the Leigh Lane property for $500,000 on September 1, 2005. Asa quitclaimed title to the Leigh Lane property to Ivory Enterprises on September 1, 2005, in exchange for a nonrecourse and non-interest-bearing single payment note for $500,000 (to be paid at the second closing). Ivory was to have a building constructed on the Leigh Lane property in accordance with specifications provided by Asa. The construction of the building was financed by a $700,000 note that was guaranteed by Asa and was nonrecourse to Ivory.

Another agreement provided that Asa would convey the Mason Drive property to Ivory on completion of the building in exchange for the Leigh Lane property and the new building. At that time, Asa would assume the $700,000 note.

On December 1, the Leigh Lane property was conveyed to Asa, the Mason Drive property was conveyed to Ivory, and Ivory paid the $500,000 note to Asa (the second closing). Asa assumed the $700,000 note associated with the construction and reported his recognized gain as follows:

	Exchange of Mason Drive	**Sale of Leigh Lane**
Amount realized	$ 500,000	$ 1,210,000
Basis	(120,000)	(1,200,000)
Realized gain	$ 380,000	$ 10,000
Recognized gain	$ –0–*	$ 10,000

* § 1031 like-kind exchange.

An IRS agent treated the transactions as the sale of the Mason Drive property and a § 1031 exchange of the Leigh Lane property, producing a recognized gain of $380,000 rather than $10,000.

Evaluate the position of the IRS and of Asa.

Internet Activity

Use the tax resources of the Internet to address the following question. Do not restrict your search to the World Wide Web, but include a review of newsgroups and general reference materials, practitioner sites and resources, primary sources of the tax law, chat rooms and discussion groups, and other opportunities.

Research Problem 3. A number of public policy think tanks, taxpayer unions, and other private interest groups have proposed changes to the tax rules that apply to like-kind exchanges of realty. Summarize several of these proposals, including your assessment of the motivations underlying the suggested changes.

Property Transactions: Capital Gains and Losses, § 1231, and Recapture Provisions

LEARNING OBJECTIVES

After completing Chapter 14, you should be able to:

LO.1

Understand the rationale for separate reporting of capital gains and losses.

LO.2

Distinguish capital assets from ordinary assets.

LO.3

Understand the relevance of a sale or exchange to classification as a capital gain or loss and apply the special rules for the capital gain or loss treatment of the retirement of corporate obligations, options, patents, franchises, and lease cancellation payments.

LO.4

Determine whether the holding period for a capital asset is long term or short term.

LO.5

Describe the beneficial tax treatment for capital gains and the detrimental tax treatment for capital losses for noncorporate taxpayers.

LO.6

Describe the tax treatment for capital gains and the detrimental tax treatment for capital losses for corporate taxpayers.

LO.7

Understand the rationale for and the nature and treatment of gains and losses from the disposition of business assets.

LO.8

Distinguish § 1231 assets from ordinary assets and capital assets and calculate the § 1231 gain or loss.

LO.9

Determine when § 1245 recapture applies and how it is computed.

LO.10

Determine when § 1250 recapture applies and how it is computed.

http://wft.swlearning.com

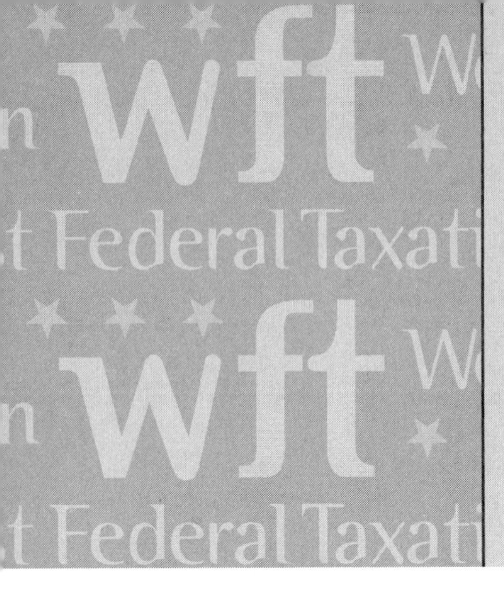

LO.11

Understand considerations common to §§ 1245 and 1250.

LO.12

Apply the special recapture provisions for related parties and IDC and be aware of the special recapture provision for corporations.

LO.13

Describe and apply the reporting procedures for §§ 1231, 1245, and 1250.

LO.14

Identify tax planning opportunities arising from the sale or exchange of capital assets and avoid pitfalls associated with the recapture provisions.

OUTLINE

LO.1

Understand the rationale for separate reporting of capital gains and losses.

General Considerations

RATIONALE FOR SEPARATE REPORTING OF CAPITAL GAINS AND LOSSES

Fourteen years ago, a taxpayer purchased 100 shares of IBM stock for $17 a share. This year the taxpayer sells the shares for $84 a share. Should the $67 per share gain receive any special tax treatment? The $67 gain has built up over 14 years, so it may not be fair to tax it the same as income that was all earned this year.

What if the stock had been purchased for $84 per share and sold for $17 a share? Should the loss be fully deductible? The tax law has an intricate approach to answering these investment activity–related questions.

As you study this chapter, keep in mind that how investment-related gains and losses are taxed can dramatically affect whether taxpayers make investments and which investments are made. Except for a brief discussion in Chapter 3, earlier chapters dwelt on how to determine the amount of gain or loss from a property disposition, but did not discuss the classification of gains and losses. This chapter will focus on that topic.

The tax law requires **capital gains** and **capital losses** to be separated from other types of gains and losses. There are two reasons for this treatment. First, long-term capital gains may be taxed at a lower rate than ordinary gains. An *alternative tax computation* is used to determine the tax when taxable income includes net long-term capital gain. Capital gains and losses must therefore be matched with one another to see if a net long-term capital gain exists. The alternative tax computation is discussed later in the chapter under Tax Treatment of Capital Gains and Losses of Noncorporate Taxpayers.

The second reason the Code requires separate reporting of gains and losses and a determination of their tax character is that a net capital loss is only deductible up to $3,000 per year. Excess loss over the annual limit carries over and may be deductible in a future tax year. Capital gains and losses must be matched with one another to see if a net capital loss exists.

For these reasons, capital gains and losses must be distinguished from other types of gains and losses. Most of this chapter describes the intricate rules for determining what type of gains and losses the taxpayer has.

GENERAL SCHEME OF TAXATION

Recognized gains and losses must be properly classified. Proper classification depends upon three characteristics:

- The tax status of the property.
- The manner of the property's disposition.
- The holding period of the property.

The three possible tax statuses are capital asset, § 1231 asset, or ordinary asset. Property disposition may be by sale, exchange, casualty, theft, or condemnation.

There are two holding periods: short term and long term. The short-term holding period is one year or less. The long-term holding period is more than one year.

The major focus of this chapter is capital gains and losses. Capital gains and losses usually result from the disposition of a capital asset. The most common disposition is a sale of the asset. Capital gains and losses can also result from the disposition of § 1231 assets, which is discussed later in this chapter.

Switching Funds Creates a Loss

Many individual taxpayers own shares in mutual funds, which invest in a wide variety of stocks and bonds. These mutual fund shares are a capital asset to the individual investor. Many mutual funds that invest in stocks have suffered losses since 2000; consequently, the value of their shares has declined. A taxpayer can usually switch between mutual funds in the same "family" of funds without any charge. For instance, a taxpayer may switch out of a stock fund and into a bond fund that is, hopefully, a "safer" investment. The switch is a sale of the shares in the stock fund and a purchase of the shares in the bond fund. The sale of the stock fund shares is taxable and, in this example, results in a capital loss. The loss may be long term or short term depending upon how long the taxpayer held the shares of the stock fund.

LO.2

Distinguish capital assets from ordinary assets.

Capital Assets

DEFINITION OF A CAPITAL ASSET

Personal use assets and investment assets are the most common capital assets owned by individual taxpayers. Personal use assets usually include items such as clothing, recreational equipment, a residence, and automobiles. Investment assets usually include investments in mutual funds, corporate stocks and bonds, government bonds, and vacant land. Remember, however, that losses from the sale or exchange of personal use assets are not recognized. Therefore, the classification of such losses as capital losses can be ignored.

Due to the historical preferential treatment of capital gains, taxpayers have preferred that gains be capital gains rather than ordinary gains. As a result, a great many statutes, cases, and rulings have accumulated in the attempt to define what is and what is not a capital asset.

Capital assets are not directly defined in the Code. Instead, § 1221(a) defines what is *not* a capital asset. A **capital asset** is property held by the taxpayer (whether or not it is connected with the taxpayer's business) that is *not* any of the following:

- Inventory or property held primarily for sale to customers in the ordinary course of a business. The Supreme Court, in *Malat v. Riddell*, defined *primarily* as meaning *of first importance* or *principally*.[1]
- Accounts and notes receivable acquired from the sale of inventory or acquired for services rendered in the ordinary course of business.
- Depreciable property or real estate used in a business.
- Certain copyrights; literary, musical, or artistic compositions; or letters, memoranda, or similar property held by (1) a taxpayer whose efforts created the property; (2) in the case of a letter, memorandum, or similar property, a taxpayer for whom it was produced; or (3) a taxpayer in whose hands the basis of the property is determined, for purposes of determining gain from a sale or exchange, in whole or in part by reference to the basis of such property in the hands of a taxpayer described in (1) or (2).

[1]66–1 USTC ¶9317, 17 AFTR2d 604, 86 S.Ct. 1030 (USSC, 1966).

- U.S. government publications that are (1) received by a taxpayer from the U.S. government other than by purchase at the price at which they are offered for sale to the public or (2) held by a taxpayer whose basis, for purposes of determining gain from a sale or exchange, is determined by reference to a taxpayer described in (1).
- Supplies of a type regularly used or consumed in the ordinary course of a business.

The Code defines what is not a capital asset. From the preceding list, it is apparent that inventory, accounts and notes receivable, supplies, and most fixed assets of a business are not capital assets. The following discussion provides further detail on each part of the capital asset definition.

Inventory. What constitutes inventory is determined by the taxpayer's business.

EXAMPLE 1

Green Company buys and sells used cars. Its cars are inventory. Its gains from the sale of the cars are ordinary income. ■

EXAMPLE 2

Soong sells her personal use automobile at a $500 gain. The automobile is a personal use asset and, therefore, a capital asset. The gain is a capital gain. ■

Accounts and Notes Receivable. Collection of an accrual basis account receivable usually does not result in a gain or loss because the amount collected equals the receivable's basis. The sale of an account or note receivable may generate a gain or loss, and the gain or loss is ordinary because the receivable is not a capital asset. The sale of an accrual basis receivable may result in a gain or loss because it will probably be sold for more or less than its basis. A cash basis account receivable has no basis. Sale of such a receivable generates a gain. Collection of a cash basis receivable generates ordinary income rather than a gain. A gain usually requires a sale of the receivable. See the discussion of Sale or Exchange later in this chapter.

EXAMPLE 3

Oriole Company has accounts receivable of $100,000. Because it needs working capital, it sells the receivables for $83,000 to a financial institution. If Oriole is an accrual basis taxpayer, it has a $17,000 ordinary loss. Revenue of $100,000 would have been recorded and a $100,000 basis would have been established when the receivable was created. If Oriole is a cash basis taxpayer, it has $83,000 of ordinary income because it would not have recorded any revenue earlier; thus, the receivable has no tax basis. ■

Business Fixed Assets. Depreciable personal property and real estate (both depreciable and nondepreciable) used by a business are not capital assets. Thus, *business fixed assets* are generally not capital assets.

The Code has a very complex set of rules pertaining to such property. One of these rules is discussed under Real Property Subdivided for Sale; the remainder of the rules are discussed later in this chapter. Although business fixed assets are not capital assets, a long-term capital gain can sometimes result from their sale. The potential capital gain treatment for business fixed assets under § 1231 is also discussed later in this chapter.

Copyrights and Creative Works. Generally, the person whose efforts led to the copyright or creative work has an ordinary asset, not a capital asset. *Creative works* include the works of authors, composers, and artists. Also, the person for whom a letter, memorandum, or other similar property was created has an ordinary asset. Finally, a person receiving a copyright, creative work, letter, memorandum, or similar property by gift from the creator or the person for whom the work was created has an ordinary asset.

EXAMPLE 4

Wanda is a part-time music composer. A music publisher purchases one of her songs for $5,000. Wanda has a $5,000 ordinary gain from the sale of an ordinary asset. ■

EXAMPLE 5

Ed received a letter from the President of the United States in 1982. In the current year, Ed sells the letter to a collector for $300. Ed has a $300 ordinary gain from the sale of an ordinary asset (because the letter was created for Ed). ■

EXAMPLE 6

Isabella gives a song she composed to her son. The son sells the song to a music publisher for $5,000. The son has a $5,000 ordinary gain from the sale of an ordinary asset. If the son inherits the song from Isabella, his basis for the song is its fair market value at Isabella's death. The song is a capital asset because the son's basis is not related to Isabella's basis for the song. ■

(Patents are subject to special statutory rules discussed later in the chapter.)

ETHICAL CONSIDERATIONS

Capital Assets for a Song

Jeremy is the composer of 10 hit songs. He wrote the songs many years ago, but they are still played regularly on the radio and in concerts. Jeremy has no tax basis for the songs. The song copyrights are worth a total of $5 million. Jeremy forms a corporation and contributes the song copyrights to it. He holds the shares in the corporation for 14 months and then sells the shares to a group of investors who want to control the song copyrights. He wants to treat the gain on the sale of the corporate shares as a long-term capital gain. Evaluate the propriety of Jeremy's plan.

U.S. Government Publications. U.S. government publications received from the U.S. government (or its agencies) for a reduced price are not capital assets. This prevents a taxpayer from later donating the publications to charity and claiming a charitable contribution equal to the fair market value of the publications. A charitable contribution of a capital asset generally yields a deduction equal to the fair market value. A charitable contribution of an ordinary asset generally yields a deduction equal to less than the fair market value. If such property is received by gift from the original purchaser, the property is not a capital asset to the donee. (For a more comprehensive explanation of charitable contributions of property, refer to Chapter 10.)

EFFECT OF JUDICIAL ACTION

Court decisions play an important role in the definition of capital assets. Because the Code only lists categories of what are *not* capital assets, judicial interpretation is sometimes required to determine whether a specific item fits into one of those categories. The Supreme Court follows a literal interpretation of the categories. For instance, corporate stock is not mentioned in § 1221. Thus, corporate stock is *usually* a capital asset. However, what if corporate stock is purchased for resale to customers? Then it is *inventory* and not a capital asset because inventory is one of the categories in § 1221. (See the discussion of Dealers in Securities below.)

A Supreme Court decision was required to distinguish between capital asset and non-capital asset status when a taxpayer who did not normally acquire stock for resale to customers acquired stock with the intention of resale.[2] The Court decided that since the stock was not acquired primarily for sale to customers (the taxpayer did not sell the stock to its regular customers), the stock was a capital asset.

[2]*Arkansas Best v. Comm.*, 88–1 USTC ¶9210, 61 AFTR2d 88–655, 108 S.Ct. 971 (USSC, 1988).

Often the crux of the capital asset determination hinges on whether the asset is held for investment purposes (capital asset) or business purposes (ordinary asset). The taxpayer's *use* of the property often provides objective evidence.

EXAMPLE 7

David's business buys an expensive painting. If the painting is used to decorate David's office and is not of investment quality, the painting is depreciable and, therefore, not a capital asset. If David's business is buying and selling paintings, the painting is inventory and, therefore, an ordinary asset. If the painting is of investment quality and the business purchased it for investment, the painting is a capital asset, even though it serves a decorative purpose in David's office. *Investment quality* generally means that the painting is expected to appreciate in value. If David depreciates the painting, that would be objective evidence that the painting is held for use in his business, is not being held for investment or as inventory, and is not a capital asset. ■

Because of the uncertainty associated with capital asset status, Congress has enacted several Code Sections to clarify the definition. These statutory expansions of the capital asset definition are discussed in the following section.

STATUTORY EXPANSIONS

Congress has often expanded the § 1221 general definition of what is *not* a capital asset.

Dealers in Securities. As a general rule, securities (stocks, bonds, and other financial instruments) held by a dealer are considered to be inventory and are, therefore, not subject to capital gain or loss treatment. A *dealer in securities* is a merchant (e.g., a brokerage firm) that regularly engages in the purchase and resale of securities to customers. The dealer must identify any securities being held for investment. Generally, if a dealer clearly identifies certain securities as held for investment purposes by the close of business on the acquisition date, gain from the securities' sale will be capital gain. However, the gain will not be capital gain if the dealer ceases to hold the securities for investment prior to the sale. Losses are capital losses if at any time the securities have been clearly identified by the dealer as held for investment.[3]

EXAMPLE 8

Tracy is a securities dealer. She purchases 100 shares of Swan stock. If Tracy takes no further action, the stock is inventory and an ordinary asset. If she designates in her records that the stock is held for investment, the stock is a capital asset. Tracy must designate the investment purpose by the close of business on the acquisition date. If Tracy maintains her investment purpose and later sells the stock, the gain or loss is capital gain or loss. If Tracy redesignates the stock as held for resale (inventory) and then sells it, any gain is ordinary, but any loss is capital loss. Stock designated as held for investment and then sold at a loss always yields a capital loss. ■

Real Property Subdivided for Sale. Substantial real property development activities may result in the owner being considered a dealer for tax purposes. Income from the sale of real estate property lots is treated as the sale of inventory (ordinary income) if the owner is considered to be a dealer. However, § 1237 allows real estate investors capital gain treatment if they engage *only* in *limited* development activities. To be eligible for § 1237 treatment, the following requirements must be met:

- The taxpayer may not be a corporation.
- The taxpayer may not be a real estate dealer.

[3]§§ 1236(a) and (b) and Reg. § 1.1236–1(a).

- No substantial improvements may be made to the lots sold. *Substantial* generally means more than a 10 percent increase in the value of a lot. Shopping centers and other commercial or residential buildings are considered substantial, while filling, draining, leveling, and clearing operations are not.
- The taxpayer must have held the lots sold for at least 5 years, except for inherited property. The substantial improvements test is less stringent if the property is held at least 10 years.

If the preceding requirements are met, all gain is capital gain until the tax year in which the *sixth* lot is sold. Sales of contiguous lots to a single buyer in the same transaction count as the sale of one lot. Beginning with the tax year the *sixth* lot is sold, some of the gain may be ordinary income. Five percent of the revenue from lot sales is potential ordinary income. That potential ordinary income is offset by any selling expenses from the lot sales. Practically, sales commissions often are at least 5 percent of the sales price, so none of the gain is treated as ordinary income.

Section 1237 does not apply to losses. A loss from the sale of subdivided real property is an ordinary loss unless the property qualifies as a capital asset under § 1221. The following example illustrates the application of § 1237.

EXAMPLE 9

Jack owns a large tract of land and subdivides it for sale. Assume Jack meets all the requirements of § 1237 and during the tax year sells the first 10 lots to 10 different buyers for $10,000 each. Jack's basis in each lot sold is $3,000, and he incurs total selling expenses of $4,000 on the sales. Jack's gain is computed as follows:

Selling price (10 × $10,000)	$100,000	
Less: Selling expenses (10 × $400)	(4,000)	
Amount realized		$ 96,000
Basis (10 × $3,000)		(30,000)
Realized and recognized gain		$ 66,000
Classification of recognized gain:		
Ordinary income		
Five percent of selling price (5% × $100,000)	$ 5,000	
Less: Selling expenses	(4,000)	
Ordinary gain		1,000
Capital gain		$ 65,000

Nonbusiness Bad Debts. A loan not made in the ordinary course of business is classified as a nonbusiness receivable. In the year the receivable becomes completely worthless, it is a *nonbusiness bad debt,* and the bad debt is treated as a short-term capital loss. Even if the receivable was outstanding for more than one year, the loss is still a short-term capital loss. Chapter 7 discusses nonbusiness bad debts more thoroughly.

LO.3

Understand the relevance of a sale or exchange to classification as a capital gain or loss and apply the special rules for the capital gain or loss treatment of the retirement of corporate obligations, options, patents, franchises, and lease cancellation payments.

Sale or Exchange

Recognition of capital gain or loss usually requires a sale or exchange of a capital asset. The Code uses the term **sale or exchange,** but does not define it. Generally, a property sale involves the receipt of money by the seller and/or the assumption by the purchaser of the seller's liabilities. An exchange involves the transfer of property for other property. Thus, an involuntary conversion (casualty, theft, or condemnation) is not a sale or exchange. In several situations, the determination of whether a sale or exchange has taken place has been clarified by the enactment of Code Sections that specifically provide for sale or exchange treatment.

All Is Not Lost—It's Just Less Valuable

A young woman inherited all the assets of her deceased financé. In going through his financial records, she found stock certificates of a large publicly traded, but now defunct, corporation where the deceased financé formerly worked. The financé had never taken a capital loss on the worthless securities even though he had paid $2 a share for them and had 50,000 shares. The young woman cannot take a capital loss for the worthless securities because the basis of the securities to her is their fair market value at the date of the financé's death—zero. The financé should have taken the loss while he was still alive, or, if the securities became worthless during the year of his death, the loss may be claimed on his income tax return for the year of his death.

Recognized gains or losses from the cancellation, lapse, expiration, or any other termination of a right or obligation with respect to personal property (other than stock) that is or would be a capital asset in the hands of the taxpayer are capital gains or losses.[4] See the discussion under Options later in the chapter for more details.

WORTHLESS SECURITIES AND § 1244 STOCK

Occasionally, securities such as stock and, especially, bonds may become worthless due to the insolvency of their issuer. If such a security is a capital asset, the loss is deemed to have occurred as the result of a sale or exchange on the *last day* of the tax year.[5] This last-day rule may have the effect of converting what otherwise would have been a short-term capital loss into a long-term capital loss. See Treatment of Capital Losses later in this chapter.

Section 1244 allows an ordinary deduction on disposition of stock at a loss. The stock must be that of a small business company, and the ordinary deduction is limited to $50,000 ($100,000 for married individuals filing jointly) per year. For a more detailed discussion, refer to Chapter 7.

SPECIAL RULE—RETIREMENT OF CORPORATE OBLIGATIONS

A debt obligation (e.g., a bond or note payable) may have a tax basis in excess of or less than its redemption value because it may have been acquired at a premium or discount. Consequently, the collection of the redemption value may result in a loss or gain. Generally, the collection of a debt obligation is *treated* as a sale or exchange.[6] Therefore, any loss or gain can be a capital loss or capital gain because a sale or exchange has taken place. However, if the debt obligation was issued by a human being prior to June 9, 1997, and/or purchased by the taxpayer prior to June 9, 1997, the collection of the debt obligation is not a sale or exchange.

EXAMPLE 10

Fran acquires $1,000 of Osprey Corporation bonds for $980 in the open market. If the bonds are held to maturity, the $20 difference between Fran's collection of the $1,000 redemption value and her cost of $980 is treated as capital gain. If the obligation had been issued to Fran by an individual prior to June 9, 1997, her $20 gain would be ordinary, since she did not sell or exchange the debt. ■

[4] § 1234A.
[5] § 165(g)(1).
[6] § 1271.

Original Issue Discount. The benefit of the sale or exchange exception that allows a capital gain from the collection of certain obligations is reduced when the obligation has original issue discount. **Original issue discount (OID)** arises when the issue price of a debt obligation is less than the maturity value of the obligation. OID must generally be amortized over the life of the debt obligation using the effective interest method. The OID amortization increases the basis of the bond. Most new publicly traded bond issues do not carry OID since the stated interest rate is set to make the market price on issue the same as the bond's face amount. In addition, even if the issue price is less than the face amount, the difference is not considered to be OID if the difference is less than one-fourth of 1 percent of the redemption price at maturity multiplied by the number of years to maturity.[7]

In the case where OID does exist, it may or may not have to be amortized, depending upon the date the obligation was issued. When OID is amortized, the amount of gain upon collection, sale, or exchange of the obligation is correspondingly reduced. The obligations covered by the OID amortization rules and the method of amortization are presented in §§ 1272–1275. Similar rules for other obligations can be found in §§ 1276–1288.

EXAMPLE 11

Jerry purchases $10,000 of newly issued White Corporation bonds for $6,000. The bonds have OID of $4,000. Jerry must amortize the discount over the life of the bonds. The OID amortization *increases* his interest income. (The bonds were selling at a discount because the market rate of interest was greater than the bonds' interest rate.) After Jerry has amortized $1,800 of OID, he sells the bonds for $8,000. Jerry has a capital gain of $200 [$8,000 – ($6,000 cost + $1,800 OID amortization)]. The OID amortization rules prevent him from converting ordinary interest income into capital gain. Without the OID amortization, Jerry would have capital gain of $2,000 ($8,000 – $6,000 cost). ■

OPTIONS

Frequently, a potential buyer of property wants some time to make the purchase decision, but wants to control the sale and/or the sale price in the meantime. **Options** are used to achieve these objectives. The potential purchaser (grantee) pays the property owner (grantor) for an option on the property. The grantee then becomes the option holder. The option usually sets a price at which the grantee can buy the property and expires after a specified period of time.

Sale of an Option. A grantee may sell or exchange the option rather than exercising it or letting it expire. Generally, the grantee's sale or exchange of the option results in capital gain or loss if the option property is (or would be) a capital asset to the grantee.[8]

EXAMPLE 12

Rosa wants to buy some vacant land for investment purposes. She cannot afford the full purchase price. Instead, she convinces the landowner (grantor) to sell her the right to purchase the land for $100,000 anytime in the next two years. Rosa (grantee) pays $3,000 to obtain this option to buy the land. The option is a capital asset for Rosa because if she actually purchased the land, the land would be a capital asset. Three months after purchasing the option, Rosa sells it for $7,000. She has a $4,000 ($7,000 – $3,000) short-term capital gain on this sale since she held the option for one year or less. ■

Failure to Exercise Options. If an option holder (grantee) fails to exercise the option, the lapse of the option is considered a sale or exchange on the option expiration date. Thus, the loss is a capital loss if the property subject to the option is (or would be) a capital asset in the hands of the grantee.

[7] § 1273(a)(3).

[8] § 1234(a) and Reg. § 1.1234–1(a)(1).

The grantor of an option on *stocks, securities, commodities, or commodity futures* receives short-term capital gain treatment upon the expiration of the option. Options on property other than stocks, securities, commodities, or commodity futures result in ordinary income to the grantor when the option expires. For example, an individual investor who owns certain stock (a capital asset) may sell a call option, entitling the buyer of the option to acquire the stock at a specified price higher than the value at the date the option is granted. The writer of the call receives a premium (e.g., 10 percent) for writing the option. If the price of the stock does not increase during the option period, the option will expire unexercised. Upon the expiration of the option, the grantor must recognize short-term capital gain. These provisions do not apply to options held for sale to customers (the inventory of a securities dealer).

Exercise of Options by Grantee. If the option is exercised, the amount paid for the option is added to the optioned property's selling price. This increases the gain (or reduces the loss) to the grantor resulting from the sale of the property. The grantor's gain or loss is capital or ordinary depending on the tax status of the property. The grantee adds the cost of the option to the basis of the property purchased.

EXAMPLE 13

On September 1, 2001, Wes purchases 100 shares of Eagle Company stock for $5,000. On April 1, 2005, he writes a call option on the stock, giving the grantee the right to buy the stock for $6,000 during the following six-month period. Wes (the grantor) receives a call premium of $500 for writing the call.

- If the call is exercised by the grantee on August 1, 2005, Wes has $1,500 ($6,000 + $500 – $5,000) of long-term capital gain from the sale of the stock. The grantee has a $6,500 ($500 option premium + $6,000 purchase price) basis for the stock.
- Assume that Wes decides to sell his stock prior to exercise for $6,000 and enters into a closing transaction by purchasing a call on 100 shares of Eagle Company stock for $5,000. Since the Eagle stock is selling for $6,000, Wes must pay a call premium of $1,000. He recognizes a $500 short-term capital loss [$1,000 (call premium paid) – $500 (call premium received)] on the closing transaction. On the actual sale of the Eagle stock, Wes has a long-term capital gain of $1,000 [$6,000 (selling price) – $5,000 (cost)]. The grantee is not affected by Wes's closing transaction. The original option is still in existence, and the grantee's tax consequences will depend on what action the grantee takes—exercising the option, letting the option expire, or selling the option.
- Assume that the original option expired unexercised. Wes has a $500 short-term capital gain equal to the call premium received for writing the option. This gain is not recognized until the option expires. The grantee has a loss from expiration of the option. The nature of the loss will depend upon whether the option was a capital asset or an ordinary asset. ■

Concept Summary 14–1 summarizes the rules for options.

PATENTS

Transfer of a **patent** is treated as the sale or exchange of a long-term capital asset when all substantial rights to the patent (or an undivided interest that includes all such rights) are transferred by a holder.[9] The transferor/holder may receive payment in virtually any form. Lump-sum or periodic payments are most common. The amount of the payments may also be contingent on the transferee/purchaser's productivity, use, or disposition of the patent. If the transfer meets these requirements, any gain or loss is *automatically a long-term* capital gain or loss. Whether the asset was a capital asset for the transferor, whether a sale or exchange occurred, and how long the transferor held the patent are not relevant.

[9] § 1235.

CONCEPT SUMMARY 14–1

Options

Event	Effect on Grantor	Effect on Grantee
Option is granted.	Receives value and has a contract obligation (a liability).	Pays value and has a contract right (an asset).
Option expires.	Has a short-term capital gain if the option property is stocks, securities, commodities, or commodity futures. Otherwise, gain is ordinary income.	Has a loss (capital loss if option property would have been a capital asset for the grantee).
Option is exercised.	Amount received for option increases proceeds from sale of the option property.	Amount paid for option becomes part of the basis of the option property purchased.
Option is sold or exchanged by grantee.	Result depends upon whether option later expires or is exercised (see above).	Could have gain or loss (capital gain or loss if option property would have been a capital asset for the grantee).

This special long-term capital gain or loss treatment for patents is intended to encourage technological progress. Ironically, authors, composers, and artists are not eligible for capital gain treatment when their creations are transferred. Books, songs, and artists' works may be copyrighted, but copyrights and the assets they represent are not capital assets. Thus, the disposition of those assets by their creators usually results in ordinary gain or loss. The following example illustrates the special treatment for patents.

EXAMPLE 14

Diana, a druggist, invents a pill-counting machine, which she patents. In consideration of a lump-sum payment of $200,000 plus $10 per machine sold, Diana assigns the patent to Drug Products, Inc. Assuming Diana has transferred all substantial rights, the question of whether the transfer is a sale or exchange of a capital asset is not relevant. Diana automatically has a long-term capital gain from both the lump-sum payment and the $10 per machine royalty to the extent these proceeds exceed her basis for the patent. ■

Substantial Rights. To receive favorable capital gain treatment, all *substantial rights* to the patent (or an undivided interest in it) must be transferred. All substantial rights to a patent means all rights (whether or not then held by the grantor) that are valuable at the time the patent rights (or an undivided interest in the patent) are transferred. All substantial rights have not been transferred when the transfer is limited geographically within the issuing country or when the transfer is for a period less than the remaining life of the patent. The circumstances of the entire transaction, rather than merely the language used in the transfer instrument, are to be considered in deciding whether all substantial rights have been transferred.[10]

EXAMPLE 15

Assume Diana, the druggist in Example 14, only licensed Drug Products, Inc., to manufacture and sell the invention in Michigan. She retained the right to license the machine elsewhere in the United States. Diana has retained a substantial right and is not eligible for automatic long-term capital gain treatment. ■

Holder Defined. The *holder* of a patent must be an *individual* and is usually the invention's creator. A holder may also be an individual who purchases the patent

[10] Reg. § 1.1235–2(b)(1).

rights from the creator before the patented invention is reduced to practice. However, the creator's employer and certain parties related to the creator do not qualify as holders. Thus, in the common situation where an employer has all rights to an employee's inventions, the employer is not eligible for long-term capital gain treatment. More than likely, the employer will have an ordinary asset because the patent was developed as part of its business.

FRANCHISES, TRADEMARKS, AND TRADE NAMES

A mode of operation, a widely recognized brand name (trade name), and a widely known business symbol (trademark) are all valuable assets. These assets may be licensed (commonly known as franchising) by their owner for use by other businesses. Many fast-food restaurants (such as McDonald's and Taco Bell) are franchises. The franchisee usually pays the owner (franchisor) an initial fee plus a contingent fee. The contingent fee is often based upon the franchisee's sales volume.

For Federal income tax purposes, a **franchise** is an agreement that gives the franchisee the right to distribute, sell, or provide goods, services, or facilities within a specified area.[11] A franchise transfer includes the grant of a franchise, a transfer by one franchisee to another person, or the renewal of a franchise.

A franchise transfer is generally not a sale or exchange of a capital asset. Section 1253 provides that a transfer of a franchise, trademark, or trade name is not a transfer of a capital asset when the transferor retains any significant power, right, or continuing interest in the property transferred.

Significant Power, Right, or Continuing Interest. *Significant powers, rights, or continuing interests* include control over assignment, quality of products and services, and sale or advertising of other products or services, and the right to require that substantially all supplies and equipment be purchased from the transferor. Also included are the right to terminate the franchise at will and the right to substantial contingent payments. Most modern franchising operations involve some or all of these powers, rights, or continuing interests.

In the unusual case where no significant power, right, or continuing interest is retained by the transferor, a sale or exchange may occur, and capital gain or loss treatment may be available. For capital gain or loss treatment to be available, the asset transferred must qualify as a capital asset.

EXAMPLE 16

Orange, Inc., a franchisee, sells the franchise to a third party. Payments to Orange are not contingent, and all significant powers, rights, and continuing interests are transferred. The gain (payments – adjusted basis) on the sale is a capital gain to Orange. ■

Noncontingent Payments. When the transferor retains a significant power, right, or continuing interest, the transferee's noncontingent payments to the transferor are ordinary income to the transferor. The franchisee capitalizes the payments and amortizes them over 15 years. The amortization is subject to recapture under § 1245.[12]

EXAMPLE 17

Grey Company signs a 10-year franchise agreement with DOH Donuts. Grey (the franchisee) makes payments of $3,000 per year for the first 8 years of the franchise agreement—a total of $24,000. Grey cannot deduct $3,000 per year as the payments are made. Instead, Grey may amortize the $24,000 total over 15 years. Thus, Grey may deduct $1,600 per year for each of the 15 years of the amortization period. The same result would occur if Grey made a $24,000 lump-sum payment at the beginning of the franchise period. Assuming DOH

[11]§ 1253(b)(1).

[12]The recapture provisions are discussed later in this chapter.

Concept Summary 14–2

Franchises

Event	Effect on Franchisor	Effect on Franchisee
Franchisor Retains Significant Powers and Rights		
Noncontingent payment	Ordinary income.	Capitalized and amortized over 15 years as an ordinary deduction; if franchise is sold, amortization is subject to recapture under § 1245.
Contingent payment	Ordinary income.	Ordinary deduction.
Franchisor Does *Not* Retain Significant Powers and Rights		
Noncontingent payment	Ordinary income if franchise rights are an ordinary asset; capital gain if franchise rights are a capital asset (unlikely).	Capitalized and amortized over 15 years as an ordinary deduction; if the franchise is sold, amortization is subject to recapture under § 1245.
Contingent payment	Ordinary income.	Ordinary deduction.

Donuts (the franchisor) retains significant powers, rights, or a continuing interest, it will have ordinary income when it receives the payments from Grey. ■

Contingent Payments. Whether or not the transferor retains a significant power, right, or continuing interest, contingent franchise payments are ordinary income for the franchisor and an ordinary deduction for the franchisee. For this purpose, a payment qualifies as a contingent payment only if the following requirements are met:

- The contingent amounts are part of a series of payments that are paid at least annually throughout the term of the transfer agreement.
- The payments are substantially equal in amount or are payable under a fixed formula.

EXAMPLE 18

TAK, a spicy chicken franchisor, transfers an eight-year franchise to Otis. TAK retains a significant power, right, or continuing interest. Otis, the franchisee, agrees to pay TAK 15% of sales. This contingent payment is ordinary income to TAK and a business deduction for Otis as the payments are made. ■

Sports Franchises. Professional sports franchises (e.g., the Detroit Tigers) are now covered by § 1253.[13] Player contracts are usually one of the major assets acquired with a sports franchise. These contracts last only for the time stated in the contract. By being classified as § 197 intangibles, the player contracts and other intangible assets acquired in the purchase of the sports franchise are amortized over a statutory 15-year period.[14]

Concept Summary 14–2 summarizes the rules for franchises.

[13]§ 1253(e).

[14]§ 197(a).

LEASE CANCELLATION PAYMENTS

The tax treatment of payments received for canceling a lease depends on whether the recipient is the **lessor** or the **lessee** and whether the lease is a capital asset or not.

Lessee Treatment. Lease cancellation payments received by a lessee are treated as an exchange.[15] Thus, these payments are capital gains if the lease is a capital asset. Generally, a lessee's lease is a capital asset if the property (either personalty or realty) is used for the lessee's personal use (e.g., his or her residence). A lessee's lease is an ordinary asset if the property is used in the lessee's trade or business and the lease has existed for one year or less when it is canceled. A lessee's lease is a § 1231 asset if the property is used in the lessee's trade or business and the lease has existed for more than a year when it is canceled.[16]

EXAMPLE 19

Mark owns an apartment building that he is going to convert into an office building. Vicki is one of the apartment tenants and receives $1,000 from Mark to cancel the lease. Vicki has a capital gain of $1,000 (which is long term or short term depending upon how long she has held the lease). Mark has an ordinary deduction of $1,000. ■

Lessor Treatment. Payments received by a lessor for a lease cancellation are always ordinary income because they are considered to be in lieu of rental payments.[17]

EXAMPLE 20

Floyd owns an apartment building near a university campus. Hui-Fen is one of the tenants. Hui-Fen is graduating early and offers Floyd $800 to cancel the apartment lease. Floyd accepts the offer. Floyd has ordinary income of $800. Hui-Fen has a nondeductible payment since the apartment was personal use property. ■

LO.4

Determine whether the holding period for a capital asset is long term or short term.

Holding Period

Property must be held more than one year to qualify for long-term capital gain or loss treatment.[18] Property not held for the required long-term period results in short-term capital gain or loss. To compute the **holding period,** start counting on the day after the property was acquired and include the day of disposition.

EXAMPLE 21

Marge purchases a capital asset on January 15, 2004, and sells it on January 16, 2005. Marge's holding period is more than one year. If Marge had sold the asset on January 15, 2005, the holding period would have been exactly one year, and the gain or loss would have been short term. ■

To be held for more than one year, a capital asset acquired on the last day of any month must not be disposed of until on or after the first day of the thirteenth succeeding month.[19]

[15] § 1241 and Reg. § 1.1241–1(a).
[16] Reg. § 1.1221–1(b) and PLR 200045019.
[17] *Hort v. Comm.,* 41–1 USTC ¶9354, 25 AFTR 1207, 61 S.Ct. 757 (USSC, 1941).
[18] § 1222.
[19] Rev.Rul. 66–7, 1966–1 C.B. 188.

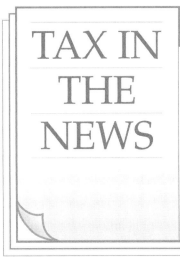

How Long Was the Holding Period for That Property?

An individual taxpayer exchanged rental real estate in Michigan that she had owned for 16 years for rental real estate in Florida. The transaction qualified as a nontaxable like-kind exchange. Within eight months of acquiring the Florida property, the taxpayer sold it when she received a very substantial unsolicited offer for the property. The local newspaper highlighted the transaction as an example of how out-of-state taxpayers were driving up real estate prices by buying and quickly reselling Florida property. Even though the taxpayer actually owned the Florida property for only eight months, her holding period for Federal income tax purposes was 16 years and eight months because the holding period of the property given up in the like-kind exchange is tacked on to the holding period of the property acquired in the exchange.

EXAMPLE 22

Leo purchases a capital asset on February 29, 2004. If Leo sells the asset on February 28, 2005, the holding period is one year, and Leo will have a short-term capital gain or loss. If Leo sells the asset on March 1, 2005, the holding period is more than one year, and he will have a long-term capital gain or loss. ■

REVIEW OF SPECIAL HOLDING PERIOD RULES

There are several special holding period rules.[20] The application of these rules depends on the type of asset and how it was acquired.

Nontaxable Exchanges. The holding period of property received in a like-kind exchange includes the holding period of the former asset if the property that has been exchanged is a capital asset or a § 1231 asset. In certain nontaxable transactions involving a substituted basis, the holding period of the former property is *tacked on* to the holding period of the newly acquired property.

EXAMPLE 23

Vern exchanges a business truck for another truck in a like-kind exchange. The holding period of the exchanged truck tacks on to the holding period of the new truck. ■

Certain Nontaxable Transactions Involving a Carryover of Another Taxpayer's Basis. A former owner's holding period is tacked on to the present owner's holding period if the transaction is nontaxable and the former owner's basis carries over to the present owner.

EXAMPLE 24

Kareem acquires 100 shares of Robin Corporation stock for $1,000 on December 31, 2001. He transfers the shares by gift to Megan on December 31, 2004, when the stock is worth $2,000. Kareem's basis of $1,000 becomes the basis for determining gain or loss on a subsequent sale by Megan. Megan's holding period begins with the date the stock was acquired by Kareem. ■

[20] § 1223.

EXAMPLE 25

Assume the same facts as in Example 24, except that the fair market value of the shares is only $800 on the date of the gift. The holding period begins on the date of the gift if Megan sells the stock for a loss. The value of the shares at the date of the gift is used in the determination of her basis for loss. If she sells the shares for $500 on April 1, 2005, Megan has a $300 recognized capital loss, and the holding period is from December 31, 2004, to April 1, 2005 (thus, the loss is short term). ■

Certain Disallowed Loss Transactions. Under several Code provisions, realized losses are disallowed. When a loss is disallowed, there is no carryover of holding period. Losses can be disallowed under § 267 (sale or exchange between related taxpayers) and § 262 (sale or exchange of personal use assets) as well as other Code Sections. Taxpayers who acquire property in a disallowed loss transaction will have a new holding period begin and will have a basis equal to the purchase price.

EXAMPLE 26

Janet sells her personal automobile at a loss. She may not deduct the loss because it arises from the sale of personal use property. Janet purchases a replacement automobile for more than the selling price of her former automobile. Janet has a basis equal to the cost of the replacement automobile, and her holding period begins when she acquires the replacement automobile. ■

Inherited Property. The holding period for inherited property is treated as long term no matter how long the property is actually held by the heir. The holding period of the decedent or the decedent's estate is not relevant for the heir's holding period.[21]

EXAMPLE 27

Shonda inherits Blue Company stock from her father. She receives the stock on April 1, 2005, and sells it on November 1, 2005. Even though Shonda did not hold the stock more than one year, she receives long-term capital gain or loss treatment on the sale. ■

SPECIAL RULES FOR SHORT SALES

General. The Code provides special rules for determining the holding period of property sold short.[22] A **short sale** occurs when a taxpayer sells borrowed property and repays the lender with substantially identical property either held on the date of the sale or purchased after the sale. Short sales usually involve corporate stock. The seller's objective is to make a profit in anticipation of a decline in the stock's price. If the price declines, the seller in a short sale recognizes a profit equal to the difference between the sales price of the borrowed stock and the price paid for the replacement stock.

A *short sale against the box* occurs when the stock is borrowed from a broker by a seller who already owns the same stock. The box is the safe deposit box where stock owners routinely used to keep stock certificates. Although today stockbrokers generally keep stock certificates for their customers, the terminology short sale against the box is still used.

EXAMPLE 28

Chris does not own any shares of Brown Corporation. However, Chris sells 30 shares of Brown. The shares are borrowed from Chris's broker and must be replaced within 45 days. Chris has a short sale because he was short the shares he sold. He will *close* the short sale by purchasing Brown shares and delivering them to his broker. If the original 30 shares

[21] In 2010, there will be no estate tax, and not all inherited assets will receive an automatic long-term holding period. Some inherited assets will have a "carryover" basis and holding period that are calculated similarly to the basis and holding period for property received by gift. See § 1022 after the effective date for this provision in the Tax Relief Reconciliation Act of 2001.

[22] § 1233.

Trading ADRs on U.S. Stock Exchanges

Many non-U.S. companies now have subsidiaries that were formerly U.S. companies. For instance, Chrysler Corporation is now a subsidiary of DaimlerChrysler (formed when the German company Daimler-Benz acquired Chrysler). Shares in such foreign companies generally cannot be traded directly on U.S. stock exchanges. Instead, the foreign companies issue instruments called American Depository Receipts (ADRs) that can be traded on U.S. stock exchanges. Purchases and sales of ADRs are treated for tax purposes as though the ADRs were shares in the corporation that issued them.

were sold for $10,000 and Chris later purchases 30 shares for $8,000, he has a gain of $2,000. Chris's hunch that the price of Brown stock would decline was correct. Chris was able to profit from selling high and buying low. If Chris had to purchase Brown shares for $13,000 to close the short sale, he would have a loss of $3,000. In this case, Chris would have sold low and bought high—not the result he wanted! Chris would be making a short sale against the box if he borrowed shares from his broker to sell and then closed the short sale by delivering other Brown shares he owned at the time he made the short sale. ■

A short sale gain or loss is a capital gain or loss to the extent that the short sale property constitutes a capital asset of the taxpayer. The gain or loss is not recognized until the short sale is closed. Generally, the holding period of the short sale property is determined by how long the property used to close the short sale was held. However, if *substantially identical property* (e.g., other shares of the same stock) is held by the taxpayer, the short-term or long-term character of the short sale gain or loss may be affected:

- If substantially identical property has *not* been held for the long-term holding period on the short sale date, the short sale *gain or loss* is short term.
- If substantially identical property has *been* held for the long-term holding period on the short sale date, the short sale *gain* is long term if the substantially identical property is used to close the short sale and short term if it is not used to close the short sale.
- If substantially identical property has *been* held for the long-term holding period on the short sale date, the short sale *loss* is long term whether or not the substantially identical property is used to close the short sale.
- If substantially identical property is acquired *after* the short sale date and on or before the closing date, the short sale *gain or loss* is short term.

Concept Summary 14–3 summarizes the short sale rules. These rules are intended to prevent the conversion of short-term capital gains into long-term capital gains and long-term capital losses into short-term capital losses.

Disposition Rules for Short Sales against the Box. In a short sale against the box, the taxpayer either owns securities that are substantially identical to the securities sold short at the short sale date or acquires such securities before the closing date. To remove the taxpayer's flexibility as to when the short sale gain must be reported, a constructive sale approach is used. If the taxpayer has not closed the short sale by delivering the short sale securities to the broker *before* January 31 of the year following the short sale, the short sale is deemed to have been closed on the *earlier* of two events:

CONCEPT SUMMARY 14–3

Short Sales of Securities

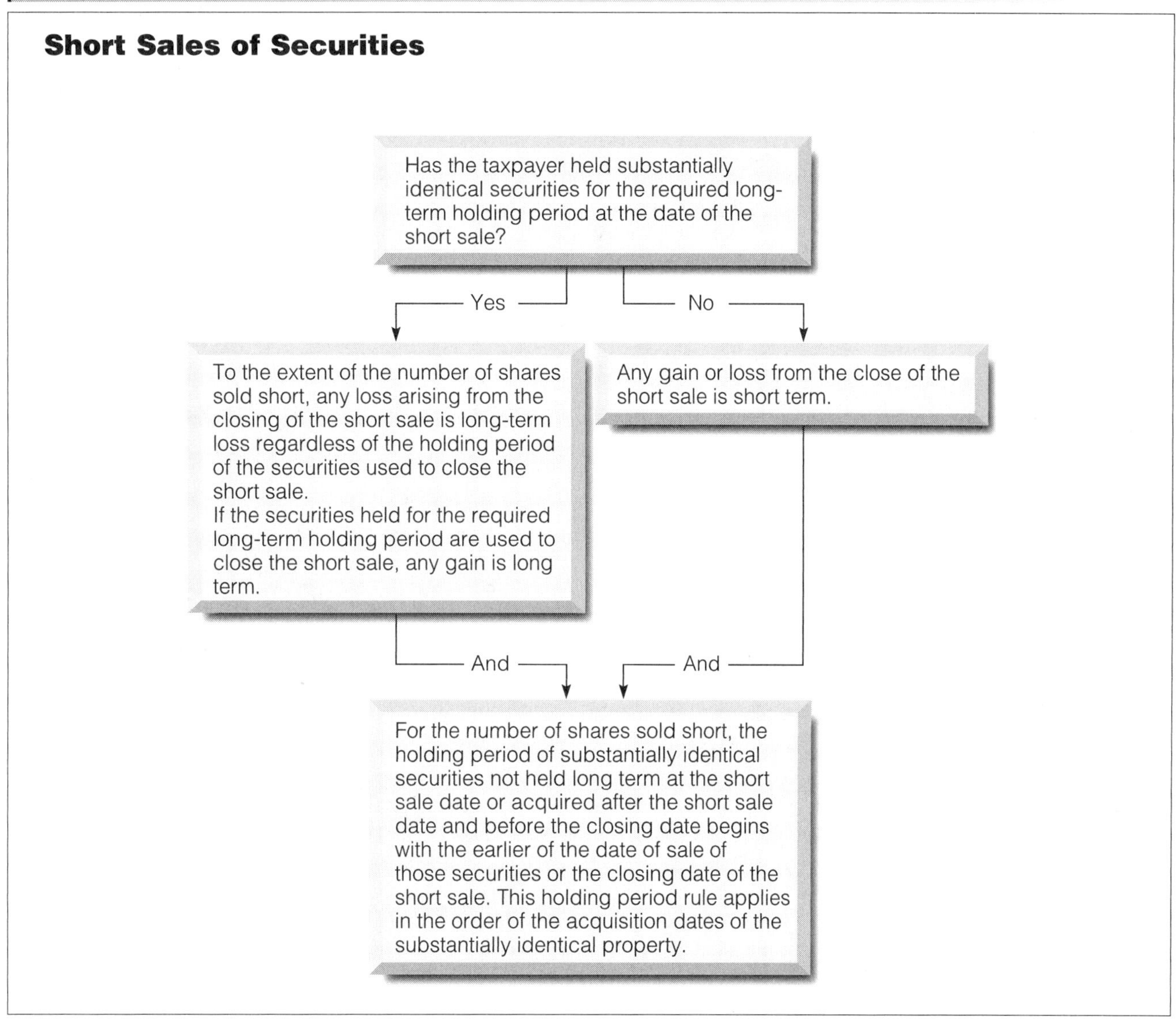

- On the short sale date if the taxpayer owned substantially identical securities at that time.
- On the date during the year of the short sale that the taxpayer acquired substantially identical securities.[23]

The basis of the shares in the deemed transfer of shares is used to compute the gain or loss on the short sale. Later, when shares are *actually* transferred to the broker to close the short sale, there may be a gain or loss because the shares transferred will have a basis equal to the short sale date price and the value at the *actual* short sale closing date may be different from the short sale date price.

Illustrations. The following examples illustrate the treatment of short sales and short sales against the box.

[23] § 1259.

EXAMPLE 29

On January 4, 2005, Donald purchases five shares of Osprey Corporation common stock for $100. On April 14, 2005, he engages in a short sale of five shares of the same stock for $150. On August 15, Donald closes the short sale by repaying the borrowed stock with the five shares purchased on January 4. Donald has a $50 short-term capital gain from the short sale because he had not held substantially identical shares for the long-term holding period on the short sale date. ■

EXAMPLE 30

Assume the same facts as in the previous example, except that Donald closes the short sale on January 28, 2006, by repaying the borrowed stock with five shares purchased on January 27, 2006, for $200. The stock used to close the short sale was not the property purchased on January 4, 2005, but since Donald held short-term property at the April 14, 2005 short sale date, the gain or loss from closing the short sale is short term. Donald has a $50 short-term capital loss ($200 cost of stock purchased on January 27, 2006, and a short sale selling price of $150). ■

EXAMPLE 31

On January 18, 2004, Rita purchases 200 shares of Owl Corporation stock for $1,000. On November 11, 2005, she sells short for $1,300 200 shares of Owl Corporation stock that she borrows from her broker. On February 10, 2006, Rita closes the short sale by delivering the 200 shares of Owl Corporation stock that she had acquired in 2004. On that date, Owl Corporation stock had a market price of $3 per share. Since Rita owned substantially identical stock on the date of the short sale and did not close the short sale before January 31, 2006, she is *deemed* to have closed the short sale on November 11, 2005 (the date of the short sale). On her 2005 tax return, she reports a $300 long-term capital gain ($1,300 short sale price – $1,000 basis). On February 10, 2006, Rita has a $700 short-term capital loss [$600 short sale closing date price (200 shares × $3 per share) – $1,300 basis] because the holding period of the shares used to close the short sale commences with the date of the short sale. ■

EXAMPLE 32

Assume the same facts as in Example 31, except that Rita did not own any Owl Corporation stock on the short sale date and acquired the 200 shares of Owl Corporation stock for $1,000 on December 12, 2005 (after the November 11, 2005 short sale date). The *deemed* closing of the short sale is December 12, 2005, because Rita held substantially identical shares at the end of 2005 and did not close the short sale before January 31, 2006. Her 2005 short sale gain is a *short-term* gain of $300 ($1,300 short sale price – $1,000 basis), and she still has a short-term capital loss of $700 on February 10, 2006. ■

LO.5

Describe the beneficial tax treatment for capital gains and the detrimental tax treatment for capital losses for noncorporate taxpayers.

Tax Treatment of Capital Gains and Losses of Noncorporate Taxpayers

All taxpayers net their capital gains and losses. Short-term gains and losses (if any) are netted against one another, and long-term gains and losses (if any) are netted against one another. The results will be net short-term gain or loss and net long-term gain or loss. If these two net positions are of opposite sign (one is a gain and one is a loss), they are netted against one another.

Six possibilities exist for the result after all possible netting has been completed. Three of these final results are gains, and three are losses. One possible result is a net long-term capital gain (NLTCG). Net long-term capital gains of noncorporate taxpayers are subject to beneficial treatment. A second possibility is a net short-term capital gain (NSTCG). Third, the netting may result in both NLTCG and NSTCG.

The NLTCG portion of these results is eligible for an alternative tax calculation. As many as four different tax rates may be used in the calculation—5, 15, 25, and 28 percent. The tax savings from the alternative tax calculation range from a low of 5 percentage points (10 percent regular tax rate – 5 percent alternative tax rate) to a high of 20 percentage points (35 percent regular tax rate – 15 percent alternative tax rate). The alternative tax computation is discussed later in the chapter under Alternative Tax on Net Capital Gain.

The last three results of the capital gain and loss netting process are losses. Thus, a fourth possibility is a net long-term capital loss (NLTCL). A fifth result is a net short-term capital loss (NSTCL). Finally, a sixth possibility includes both an NLTCL and an NSTCL. Neither NLTCLs nor NSTCLs are treated as ordinary losses. Treatment as an ordinary loss generally is preferable to capital loss treatment since ordinary losses are deductible in full while the deductibility of capital losses is subject to certain limitations. An individual taxpayer may deduct a maximum of $3,000 of net capital losses for a taxable year.[24]

CAPITAL GAIN AND LOSS NETTING PROCESS

Holding Periods for Capital Gain and Loss Netting Purposes. As mentioned earlier in this chapter, there are two holding periods for purposes of the capital gain and loss netting process:

- *Short term*—Assets held one year or less.
- *Long term*—Assets held more than one year.

Net short-term capital gain is not eligible for any special tax rate. It is taxed at the same rate as the taxpayer's other taxable income. *Net long-term capital gain* is eligible for one or more of *four* alternative tax rates: 5 percent, 15 percent, 25 percent, and 28 percent. The 25 percent and 28 percent rates are used only in somewhat unusual circumstances, so the discussion below concentrates more heavily on the other two rates.[25] The net long-term capital gain components are referred to as the *5%/15% gain*, the *25% gain*, and the *28% gain*.

The *25% gain* is technically called the **unrecaptured § 1250 gain** and is related to gain from disposition of § 1231 assets. Gains and losses from disposition of § 1231 assets are discussed later in this chapter. The following discussion will focus only on how the *25% gain* is taxed and not how it is determined. The *28% gain* relates to collectibles and § 1202 gain (see Chapter 5). Collectibles gain is discussed later in this chapter.

The *5% gain* portion of the *5%/15% gain* applies when the taxable income before taxing the *5%/15% gain* does not put the taxpayer out of the 15 percent bracket. Once the taxable income (including any portion of the *5%/15% gain* taxed at 5 percent) puts the taxpayer above the 15 percent bracket, the remaining portion of the *5%/15% gain* is taxed at 15 percent rather than at the regular tax rate.

When the long-term capital gain exceeds the short-term capital loss, a **net capital gain (NCG)** exists. Net capital gain qualifies for beneficial alternative tax treatment (see the coverage later in the chapter).[26]

Since there are both short- and long-term capital gains and losses and because the long-term capital gains may be taxed at various rates, an *ordering procedure* is required. The ordering procedure tends to preserve the lowest tax rate long-term

[24] § 1211(b).

[25] For property disposed of prior to May 6, 2003, there were alternative tax rates of 8%, 10%, and 20%.

[26] § 1222(11).

capital gain when there is a net long-term capital gain. This ordering procedure is explained in the steps below and then illustrated by several examples.

Step 1. Group all gains and losses into short term and 28%, 25%, and 5%/15% long term.
Step 2. Net the gains and losses within each group.
Step 3. Offset the net 28% and net 25% amounts if they are of opposite sign.
Step 4. Offset the results after step 3 against the 5%/15% amount if they are of opposite sign. If the 5%/15% amount is a loss, offset it against the *highest taxed gain first*. After this step, there is a net long-term capital gain or loss. If there is a net long-term capital gain, it may consist of only 28% gain, only 25% gain, only 5%/15% gain, or some combination of all of these gains. If there is a net long-term capital loss, it is simply a net long-term capital loss.
Step 5. Offset the net short-term amount against the results of step 4 if they are of opposite sign. The netting rules offset net short-term capital loss against the *highest taxed gain first*. Consequently, if there is a net short-term capital loss and a net gain from step 4, the short-term capital loss offsets first the 28% gain, then the 25% gain, and finally the 5%/15% gain.

If the result of step 5 is *only* a short-term capital gain, the taxpayer is not eligible for a reduced tax rate. If the result of step 5 is a loss, the taxpayer may be eligible for a *capital loss deduction* (discussed later in this chapter). If there was no offsetting in step 5 because the short-term and step 4 results were both gains *or* if the result of the offsetting is a long-term gain, a net capital gain exists, and the taxpayer may be eligible for a reduced tax rate. The net capital gain may consist of *28% gain*, *25% gain*, and/or *5%/15% gain*.

The five steps outlined above can have many unique final results. See Concept Summary 14–5 later in the chapter for a summary of the netting rules and how capital gains and losses are taxed. The following series of examples illustrates the capital gain and loss netting process.

EXAMPLE 33

This example shows how a net short-term capital gain may result from the netting process.

		Long-Term Gains and Losses			
Step	**Short Term**	**28%**	**25%**	**5%/15%**	**Comment**
1	$13,000	$ 12,000		$ 3,000	
	(2,000)	(20,000)			
2	$11,000	($ 8,000)		$ 3,000	
3					No 28%/25% netting because no opposite sign.
4		3,000	←	(3,000)	Netted because of opposite sign.
		($ 5,000)		$ -0-	
5	(5,000) ←	5,000			The net short-term capital gain is taxed as ordinary income.
	$ 6,000	$ -0-			
	Net short-term capital gain				

EXAMPLE 34

This example shows how a net long-term capital gain may result from the netting process.

		Long-Term Gains and Losses			
Step	**Short Term**	**28%**	**25%**	**5%/15%**	**Comment**
1	$ 3,000	$15,000	$4,000	$ 3,000	
	(5,000)	(7,000)		(8,000)	
2	($ 2,000)	$ 8,000	$4,000	($ 5,000)	
3					No 28%/25% netting because no opposite sign.
4		(5,000)	←	5,000	Netted because of opposite sign. Net 5%/15% loss is netted against 28% gain first.
		$ 3,000		$ -0-	
5	2,000 →	(2,000)			The net short-term capital loss is netted against 28% gain first. The net long-term capital gain is $5,000 ($1,000 + $4,000).
	$ -0-	$ 1,000	$4,000		
		Net 28% gain	Net 25% gain		

EXAMPLE 35

This example shows how a net long-term capital loss may result from the netting process.

		Long-Term Gains and Losses			
Step	**Short Term**	**28%**	**25%**	**5%/15%**	**Comment**
1	$ 3,000	$ 1,000		$ 3,000	
				(8,000)	
2	$ 3,000	$ 1,000		($ 5,000)	
3					No 28%/25% netting because no opposite sign.
4		(1,000)	→	1,000	Netted because of opposite sign.
		$ -0-		($ 4,000)	
5	(3,000)	→	→	3,000	The net short-term capital gain is netted against the net long-term capital loss, and the remaining loss is eligible for the capital loss deduction.
	$ -0-			($ 1,000)	
				Net long-term capital loss	

Use of Capital Loss Carryovers. A short-term capital loss carryover to the current year retains its character as short term and is combined with the short-term items of the current year. A long-term net capital loss carries over as a long-term capital loss and is combined with the current-year long-term items. The long-term loss carryover is first offset with 28% gain of the current year, then 25% gain, and then 5%/15% gain until it is absorbed.

EXAMPLE 36

In 2005, Abigail has a $4,000 short-term capital gain, a $36,000 28% long-term capital gain, and a $13,000 5%/15% long-term capital gain. She also has a $3,000 short-term capital loss carryover and a $2,000 long-term capital loss carryover from 2004. This produces a

$1,000 net short-term capital gain ($4,000 – $3,000), a $34,000 net 28% long-term capital gain ($36,000 – $2,000), and a $13,000 net 5%/15% long-term capital gain for 2005. ■

Definition of Collectibles. Capital assets that are collectibles, even though they are held long term, are not eligible for the *5%/15%* alternative tax rate. Instead, a 28 percent alternative tax rate applies.

For capital gain or loss purposes, **collectibles** include:[27]

- Any work of art.
- Any rug or antique.
- Any metal or gem.
- Any stamp.
- Any alcoholic beverage.
- Most coins.
- Any historical objects (documents, clothes, etc.).

ETHICAL CONSIDERATIONS

Is That Capital Gain Taxable?

In 2005, a U.S. taxpayer has a capital gain from the disposition of shares of a Japanese mutual fund. The mutual fund invested in securities of Japanese banks. The taxpayer's practitioner recommends that the taxpayer not report the capital gain because a special tax treaty with Japan allows such capital gains to be excluded from U.S. taxable income. None of the documents that the taxpayer has received from the mutual fund mentions this exclusion. Evaluate the practitioner's advice.

QUALIFIED DIVIDEND INCOME

Dividends paid from current or accumulated earnings and profits of domestic and certain foreign corporations are eligible to be taxed at the 5%/15% long-term capital gain rates if they are **qualified dividend income.** The question of which dividends constitute qualified dividend income is discussed more fully in Chapter 4. Here the discussion focuses on how the qualified dividend income is taxed.

After the net capital gain or loss has been determined, the qualified dividend income is added to the net long-term capital gain portion of the net capital gain and is taxed as 5%/15% gain. If there is a net capital loss, the net capital loss is still deductible *for* AGI up to $3,000 per year with the remainder of the loss (if any) carrying forward. In this case, the qualified dividend income is still eligible to be treated as *5%/15% gain* in the alternative tax calculation (it is *not* offset by the net capital loss).

EXAMPLE 37

Refer to Example 34, but assume there is qualified dividend income of $2,500 in addition to the items shown. The qualified dividend income *is not* netted against the capital gains and losses. Instead, the taxpayer has $1,000 of 28% gain, $4,000 of 25% gain, *and* $2,500 of qualified dividend income taxed at 5%/15%. ■

EXAMPLE 38

Refer to Example 35, but assume there is qualified dividend income of $2,500 in addition to the items shown. The qualified dividend income *is not* netted against the net capital loss. The taxpayer has a $1,000 capital loss deduction *and* $2,500 of qualified dividend income taxed at 5%/15%. ■

[27]§ 408(m) and Reg. § 1.408–10(b).

ALTERNATIVE TAX ON NET CAPITAL GAIN

Section 1 contains the statutory provisions that enable the *net capital gain* to be taxed at special rates (5, 15, 25, and 28 percent). This calculation is referred to as the **alternative tax** on net capital gain.[28] The alternative tax applies only if taxable income includes some long-term capital gain (there is net capital gain). Taxable income includes *all* of the net capital gain unless taxable income is less than the net capital gain. In addition, the net capital gain is taxed *last*, after other taxable income (including any short-term capital gain).

EXAMPLE 39

Joan, an unmarried taxpayer, has 2005 taxable income of $88,000, including a $12,000 net capital gain. The last $12,000 of her $88,000 taxable income is the layer related to the net capital gain. The first $76,000 ($88,000 – $12,000) of her taxable income is not subject to any special tax rate, so it is taxed using the regular tax rates. ■

Since the net capital gain may be made up of various *rate layers*, it is important to know in what order those layers will be taxed. For *each* of the layers, the taxpayer compares the regular tax rate on that layer of income and the alternative tax rate on that portion of the net capital gain. The layers are taxed in the following order: *25% gain*, *28% gain*, the 5 percent portion of the *5%/15% gain*, and then the 15 percent portion of the *5%/15% gain*. As a result of this layering, the taxpayer will benefit from the 5 percent portion of the net capital gain if the taxpayer is still in the 10 percent or 15 percent regular rate bracket after taxing other taxable income and the 25 percent and 28 percent portions of the net capital gain.

EXAMPLE 40

Assume that Joan's $12,000 net capital gain in Example 39 is made up of $10,000 *25% gain* and $2,000 *5%/15% gain*. Examination of the 2005 tax rates reveals that $76,000 of taxable income for a single individual puts Joan at a marginal tax rate of 28%. Consequently, she will use the alternative tax on both the $10,000 gain and the $2,000 gain. Her alternative tax liability for 2005 is $18,587 [$15,787 (tax on $76,000 of taxable income) + $2,500 ($10,000 × .25) + $300 ($2,000 × .15)]. Since the combination of the $76,000 taxable income and her $10,000 25% gain puts her above the 15% regular tax bracket, none of the $2,000 *5%/15% gain* is taxed at 5%. Her regular tax liability on $88,000 would be $19,147. Thus, Joan saves $560 ($19,147 – $18,587) by using the alternative tax computation. ■

EXAMPLE 41

Joan, an unmarried taxpayer, has 2005 taxable income of $25,000. Of this amount, $12,000 is net capital gain, and $13,000 is other taxable income. The net capital gain is made up of $8,300 of *25% gain* and $3,700 of *5%/15% gain* (including $1,000 of qualified dividend income). Her tax liability using the alternative tax calculation is $3,015 [$1,585 (tax on $13,000 of taxable income) + $1,245 (tax on $8,300 *25% gain* at 15%) + $185 (tax on $3,700 *5%/15% gain* at 5%)]. Since her marginal rate is still 15% after taxing the $13,000 of other taxable income, she uses the 15% regular tax rate rather than the 25% alternative tax rate on the $8,300 *25% gain.* After taxing the $13,000 and the $8,300, a total of $21,300 of the $25,000 taxable income has been taxed. Since her marginal rate is still 15%, she uses the 5% alternative rate for the $3,700 of *5%/15% gain.* The $1,000 qualified dividend income is included in the $3,700 and, thus, is also taxed at 5%. Joan's regular tax liability on $25,000 would be $3,385. Thus, she saves $370 ($3,385 – $3,015) by using the alternative tax calculation. ■

The alternative tax computation allows the taxpayer to receive the *lower of* the regular tax or the alternative tax on *each layer* of net capital gain or *portion of each layer* of net capital gain.

[28] § 1(h).

CONCEPT SUMMARY 14–4

Income Layers for Alternative Tax on Capital Gain Computation

Compute tax on:		Ordinary taxable income (including net short-term capital gain) using the regular tax rates.
Compute tax on:		Each of the layers below using the *lower* of the alternative tax rate or the regular tax rate for that layer (or portion of a layer) of taxable income.
	+	25% long-term capital gain (unrecaptured § 1250 gain) portion of taxable income
	+	28% long-term capital gain
	+	5% long-term capital gain (portion of 5%/15% capital gain that is taxed at 5%; available only if ordinary taxable income plus 25% and 28% capital gain layers do not put the taxpayer above the 15% bracket; 5% rate is no longer available once income including the portion of the gain taxed at 5% puts the taxpayer out of the 15% bracket)*
	+	15% long-term capital gain (remaining portion of 5%/15% capital gain)*
	=	Alternative tax on taxable income

*May include qualified dividend income.

EXAMPLE 42

Assume the same facts as in Example 41 except that Joan's taxable income is $31,000, consisting of $12,000 of net capital gain and $19,000 of other taxable income. Not all of the $3,700 of *5%/15% gain* is taxed at 5% because Joan's taxable income exceeds $29,700, taking her out of the 15% bracket. Consequently, the last $1,300 ($31,000 – $29,700) of the $3,700 *5%/15% gain* is taxed at 15% rather than 5%. Her tax liability using the alternative tax computation is $4,045 [$2,485 (tax on $19,000 of taxable income) + $1,245 (tax on $8,300 *25% gain* at 15%) + $120 (tax on $2,400 *5%/15% gain* at 5%) + $195 (tax on $1,300 *5%/15% gain* at 15%)]. Joan's regular tax liability on $31,000 would be $4,415. Thus, she saves $370 ($4,415 – $4,045) by using the alternative tax calculation. ■

Concept Summary 14–4 summarizes the alternative tax computation.

TREATMENT OF CAPITAL LOSSES

Computation of Net Capital Loss. A **net capital loss (NCL)** results if capital losses exceed capital gains for the year. An NCL may be all long term, all short term, or part long and part short term.[29] The characterization of an NCL as long or short term is important in determining the capital loss deduction (discussed later in this chapter).

EXAMPLE 43

Three different individual taxpayers have the following capital gains and losses during the year:

Taxpayer	LTCG	LTCL	STCG	STCL	Result of Netting	Description of Result
Robert	$1,000	($ 2,800)	$1,000	($ 500)	($ 1,300)	NLTCL
Carlos	1,000	(500)	1,000	(2,800)	(1,300)	NSTCL
Troy	400	(1,200)	500	(1,200)	(1,500)	NLTCL ($800)
						NSTCL ($700)

[29]Section 1222(10) defines a net capital loss as the net loss after the capital loss deduction. However, that definition confuses the discussion of net capital loss. Therefore, net capital loss is used here to mean the result after netting capital gains and losses and before considering the capital loss deduction. The capital loss deduction is discussed under Treatment of Net Capital Loss in this chapter.

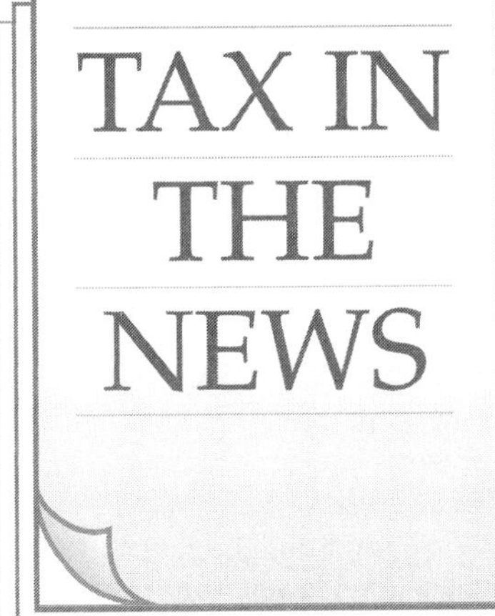

NOT ALL CORPORATE DIVIDENDS ARE "QUALIFIED DIVIDENDS"

During the 2004 presidential campaign, vice presidential candidate John Edwards's Subchapter S corporation "dividends" raised questions as to whether he had increased his dividends and reduced his corporate salary to avoid payroll taxes. Under *state corporate law*, the distributions he received from his law firm S corporation were corporate dividends from the corporation's earnings. For Federal income tax purposes, however, Edwards had already been taxed on the earnings of the S corporation as ordinary income because of the mechanics of S corporation taxation. Therefore, the S corporation distributions from earnings to him were excludible from his gross income rather than being subject to the 5%/15% alternative rates for qualified dividends.

Robert's NCL of $1,300 is all long term. Carlos's NCL of $1,300 is all short term. Troy's NCL is $1,500, $800 of which is long term and $700 of which is short term. ■

Treatment of Net Capital Loss. An NCL is deductible from gross income to the extent of $3,000 per tax year.[30] Capital losses exceeding the loss deduction limits carry forward indefinitely. Thus, although there may or may not be beneficial treatment for capital gains, there is *unfavorable* treatment for capital losses in terms of the $3,000 annual limitation on deducting NCL against ordinary income. If the NCL includes both long-term and short-term capital loss, the short-term capital loss is counted first toward the $3,000 annual limitation.

EXAMPLE 44

Burt has an NCL of $5,500, of which $2,000 is STCL and $3,500 is LTCL. Burt has a capital loss deduction of $3,000 ($2,000 of STCL and $1,000 of LTCL). He has an LTCL carryforward of $2,500 ($3,500 – $1,000). ■

Carryovers. Taxpayers are allowed to carry over unused capital losses indefinitely. The short-term capital loss (STCL) retains its character as STCL. Likewise the long-term capital loss retains its character as LTCL.

EXAMPLE 45

In 2005, Mark incurred $1,000 of STCL and $11,000 of LTCL. In 2006, Mark has a $400 LTCG.

- Mark's NCL for 2005 is $12,000. Mark deducts $3,000 ($1,000 STCL and $2,000 LTCL). He has $9,000 of LTCL carried forward to 2006.
- Mark combines the $9,000 LTCL carryforward with the $400 LTCG for 2006. He has an $8,600 NLTCL for 2006. Mark deducts $3,000 of LTCL in 2006 and carries forward $5,600 of LTCL to 2007. ■

When a taxpayer has both a capital loss deduction and negative taxable income, a special computation of the capital loss carryover is required.[31] Specifically, the capital loss carryover is the NCL minus the lesser of:

- The capital loss deduction claimed on the return.
- The negative taxable income increased by the capital loss deduction claimed on the return and the personal and dependency exemption deduction.

Without this provision, some of the tax benefit of the capital loss deduction would be wasted when the deduction drives taxable income below zero. However, the

[30] § 1211(b)(1). Married persons filing separate returns are limited to a $1,500 deduction per tax year.

[31] § 1212(b).

Concept Summary 14–5

Some Possible Final Results of the Capital Gain and Loss Netting Process and How They Are Taxed

Result	Maximum Tax Rate	Comments
Net short-term capital loss	—	Eligible for capital loss deduction ($3,000 maximum per year).
Net long-term capital loss	—	Eligible for capital loss deduction ($3,000 maximum per year).
Net short-term capital loss *and* net long-term capital loss	—	Eligible for capital loss deduction ($3,000 maximum per year). Short-term capital losses are counted first toward the deduction.
Net short-term capital gain	10–35%	Taxed as ordinary income.
Net long-term capital gain	5–28%	The net long-term capital gain may have as many as four tax rate components: 25%, 28%, and 5%/15%.
• The net long-term capital gain is the *last* portion of taxable income.		The components are taxed in the following order: 25%, 28%, 5%, 15%. They are taxed *after* the non-long-term capital gain portion of taxable income has been taxed. The 5%/15% component may include qualified dividend income.
• Each net long-term capital gain component of taxable income is taxed at the the *lower of* the regular tax on that component or the alternative tax.		The alternative tax on net long-term capital gain can never increase the tax on taxable income, but it can reduce the tax on taxable income.
Net short-term capital gain *and* net long-term capital gain	10–35% on net short-term capital gain; 5–28% on net long-term capital gain	The net short-term capital gain is taxed as ordinary income; the net long-term capital gain is taxed as discussed above for just net long-term capital gain.

capital loss deduction is not reduced if taxable income before the exemption deduction is a positive number or zero. In that situation, it is the exemption deduction, and not the capital loss deduction, that is creating the negative taxable income.

EXAMPLE 46

In 2005, Joanne has a $13,000 NCL (all long term), a $3,200 personal exemption deduction, and $4,000 negative taxable income. The negative taxable income includes a $3,000 capital loss deduction. The capital loss carryover to 2006 is $10,800 computed as follows:

- The $4,000 negative taxable income is treated as a negative number, but the capital loss deduction and personal exemption deduction are treated as positive numbers.
- The normal ceiling on the capital loss deduction is $3,000.
- However, if the $3,000 capital loss deduction and the $3,200 exemption deduction are added back to the $4,000 negative taxable income, only $2,200 of the $3,000 capital loss deduction is needed to make taxable income equal to zero.
- Therefore, this special computation results in only $2,200 of the $13,000 NCL being consumed. The LTCL carryforward is $10,800 ($13,000 – $2,200). ■

Concept Summary 14–5 summarizes the rules for noncorporate taxpayers' treatment of capital gains and losses.

LO.6

Describe the tax treatment for capital gains and the detrimental tax treatment for capital losses for corporate taxpayers.

Tax Treatment of Capital Gains and Losses of Corporate Taxpayers

The treatment of a corporation's net capital gain or loss differs from the rules for individuals. Briefly, the differences are as follows:

- There is an NCG alternative tax rate of 35 percent.[32] However, since the maximum corporate tax rate is 35 percent, the alternative tax is not beneficial.
- Capital losses offset only capital gains. No deduction of capital losses is permitted against ordinary taxable income (whereas a $3,000 deduction is allowed to individuals).[33]
- There is a three-year carryback and a five-year carryover period for net capital losses.[34] Corporate carryovers and carrybacks are always treated as short term, regardless of their original nature.

EXAMPLE 47

Sparrow Corporation has a $15,000 NLTCL for the current year and $57,000 of ordinary taxable income. Sparrow may not offset the $15,000 NLTCL against its ordinary income by taking a capital loss deduction. The $15,000 NLTCL becomes a $15,000 STCL for carryback and carryover purposes. This amount may be offset by capital gains in the three-year carryback period or, if not absorbed there, offset by capital gains in the five-year carryforward period. ■

Overview of § 1231 and the Recapture Provisions

Generic Motors Corporation sold machinery, office furniture, and unneeded production plants for $100 million last year. The corporation's disposition of these assets resulted in $60 million of gains and $13 million of losses. How are these gains and losses treated for tax purposes? Do any special tax rules apply? Could any of the gains and losses receive capital gain or loss treatment? The remainder of this chapter answers these questions by explaining how to *classify* gains and losses from the disposition of assets that are used in the business rather than held for resale. Chapter 8 discussed how to *depreciate* such assets. Chapter 13 discussed how to determine the *adjusted basis* and the *amount* of gain or loss from their disposition.

A long-term capital gain was defined earlier in this chapter as the recognized gain from the sale or exchange of a capital asset held for the required long-term holding period.[35] Long-term capital assets are capital assets held more than one year.

The remainder of this chapter is concerned with classification under § 1231, which applies to the sale or exchange of business properties and to certain involuntary conversions. The business properties are not capital assets because they are depreciable and/or real property used in business or for the production of income. Section 1221(a)(2) provides that such assets are not capital assets. Nonetheless, these business properties may be held for long periods of time and may be sold at a gain. Congress decided many years ago that such assets deserved *limited* capital gain–type treatment. Unfortunately, this limited capital gain–type treatment is very complex and difficult to understand.

[32] § 1201.
[33] § 1211(a).
[34] § 1212(a)(1).

[35] § 1222(3). To be eligible for any beneficial tax treatment, the holding period must be more than one year.

Capital Gain Confusion

A recent newspaper article discussed the special tax rates taxpayers can enjoy on long-term capital gains. In particular, the article mentioned gains from the sale of stock investments and the sale of rental real estate. The stock investment directly generates capital gain, but the gain from the rental real estate is not *directly* a capital gain because the asset would have been a § 1231 asset. The rental real estate gain may eventually be *treated as* a long-term capital gain depending on a variety of factors including depreciation recapture (partial or full).

Because the limited capital gain–type treatment sometimes gives too much tax advantage if assets are eligible for depreciation (or cost recovery), certain recapture rules may prevent the capital gain treatment when depreciation is taken. Thus, this chapter also covers the recapture provisions that tax as ordinary income certain gains that might otherwise qualify for long-term capital gain treatment.

LO.7

Understand the rationale for and the nature and treatment of gains and losses from the disposition of business assets.

Section 1231 Assets

RELATIONSHIP TO CAPITAL ASSETS

Depreciable property and real property used in business are not capital assets.[36] Thus, the recognized gains from the disposition of such property (principally machinery, equipment, buildings, and land) would appear to be ordinary income rather than capital gain. Due to § 1231, however, *net gain* from the disposition of such property is sometimes *treated* as *long-term capital gain.* A long-term holding period requirement must be met; the disposition must generally be from a sale, exchange, or involuntary conversion; and certain recapture provisions must be satisfied for this result to occur. Section 1231 may also apply to involuntary conversions of capital assets. Since an involuntary conversion is not a sale or exchange, such a disposition normally would not result in a capital gain.

If the disposition of depreciable property and real property used in business results in a *net loss,* § 1231 *treats* the *loss* as an *ordinary loss* rather than as a capital loss. Ordinary losses are fully deductible *for* adjusted gross income (AGI). Capital losses are offset by capital gains, and, if any loss remains, the loss is deductible to the extent of $3,000 per year for individuals and currently is not deductible at all by regular corporations. It seems, therefore, that § 1231 provides the *best* of both potential results: net gain may be treated as long-term capital gain, and net loss is treated as ordinary loss.

EXAMPLE 48

Roberto sells business land and a building at a $5,000 gain and business equipment at a $3,000 loss. Both properties were held for the long-term holding period. Roberto's net gain is $2,000, and that net gain may (depending on various recapture rules discussed later in this chapter) be treated as a long-term capital gain under § 1231. ■

EXAMPLE 49

Samantha sells business equipment at a $10,000 loss and business land at a $2,000 gain. Both properties were held for the long-term holding period. Samantha's net loss is $8,000, and that net loss is an ordinary loss. ■

[36] § 1221(a)(2).

The rules regarding § 1231 treatment do *not* apply to *all* business property. Important in this regard are the holding period requirements and the fact that the property must be either depreciable property or real estate used in business. Nor is § 1231 necessarily limited to business property. Transactions involving certain capital assets may fall into the § 1231 category. Thus, § 1231 singles out only some types of business property.

As discussed earlier in this chapter, long-term capital gains receive beneficial tax treatment. Section 1231 requires netting of **§ 1231 gains and losses.** If the result is a gain, it may be treated as a long-term capital gain. The net gain is added to the "real" long-term capital gains (if any) and netted with capital losses (if any). Thus, the net § 1231 gain may eventually be eligible for beneficial capital gain treatment or help avoid the unfavorable net capital loss result. The § 1231 gain and loss netting may result in a loss. In this case, the loss is an ordinary loss and is deductible *for* AGI. Finally, § 1231 assets are treated the same as capital assets for purposes of the appreciated property charitable contribution provisions (refer to Chapter 10).

JUSTIFICATION FOR FAVORABLE TAX TREATMENT

The favorable capital gain/ordinary loss treatment sanctioned by § 1231 can be explained by examining several historical developments. Before 1938, business property had been included in the definition of capital assets. Thus, if such property was sold for a loss (not an unlikely possibility during the depression years of the 1930s), a capital loss resulted. If, however, the property was depreciable and could be retained for its estimated useful life, much (if not all) of its costs could be recovered in the form of depreciation. Because the allowance for depreciation was fully deductible whereas capital losses were not, the tax law favored those who did not dispose of an asset. Congress recognized this inequity when it removed business property from the capital asset classification. During the period 1938–1942, therefore, all such gains and losses were ordinary gains and losses.

With the advent of World War II, two developments in particular forced Congress to reexamine the situation regarding business assets. First, the sale of business assets at a gain was discouraged because the gain would be ordinary income. Gains were common because the war effort had inflated prices. Second, taxpayers who did not want to sell their assets often were required to because the government acquired them through condemnation. Often, as a result of the condemnation awards, taxpayers who were forced to part with their property experienced large gains and were deprived of the benefits of future depreciation deductions. Of course, the condemnations constituted involuntary conversions, so taxpayers could defer the gain by timely reinvestment in property that was "similar or related in service or use." But where was such property to be found in view of wartime restrictions and other governmental condemnations? The end result did not seem equitable: a large ordinary gain due to government action and no possibility of deferral due to government restrictions.

In recognition of these conditions, in 1942, Congress eased the tax bite on the disposition of some business property by allowing preferential capital gain treatment. Thus, the present scheme of § 1231 and the dichotomy of capital gain/ordinary loss treatment evolved from a combination of economic considerations existing in 1938 and 1942.

LO.8

Distinguish § 1231 assets from ordinary assets and capital assets and calculate the § 1231 gain or loss.

PROPERTY INCLUDED

Section 1231 property generally includes the following assets if they are held for more than one year:

- Depreciable or real property used in business or for the production of income (principally machinery and equipment, buildings, and land).

An Environmental Fight over Timber Cutting

An investor in vacant land (owned for 20 years) wanted to sell the land to a developer. The land was "wetlands" that had a substantial growth of marketable timber on it. Without any notice to anyone, the landowner had the timber cut and sold it for $45,000 to a lumber mill. The landowner felt that the land would be more marketable without the timber obstructing its development potential. The community reacted very strongly to this "environmental degradation" and prevented the landowner from getting the zoning required for development. Now the community is left with ugly vacant land, and the landowner is left with an unmarketable property. Before the timber cutting, the landowner was holding the land for investment, not for use in a business. He was also not holding the timber for sale. Thus, § 1231 probably does not apply. However, since the timber was part of the investment land, the timber was a capital asset; so, to the extent that $45,000 exceeds the landowner's basis for the land, he has long-term capital gain.

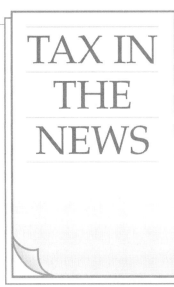

- Timber, coal, or domestic iron ore to which § 631 applies.
- Livestock held for draft, breeding, dairy, or sporting purposes.
- Unharvested crops on land used in business.
- Certain *purchased* intangible assets (such as patents and goodwill) that are eligible for amortization.

These assets are ordinary assets until they have been held for more than one year. Only then do they become § 1231 assets.

PROPERTY EXCLUDED

Section 1231 property generally does *not* include the following:

- Property not held for the long-term holding period. Since the benefit of § 1231 is long-term capital gain treatment, the holding period must correspond to the more-than-one-year holding period that applies to capital assets. Livestock must be held at least 12 months (24 months in some cases).[37] Unharvested crops do not have to be held for the required long-term holding period, but the land must be held for the long-term holding period.
- Nonpersonal use property where casualty losses exceed casualty gains for the taxable year. If a taxpayer has a net casualty loss, the individual casualty gains and losses are treated as ordinary gains and losses.
- Inventory and property held primarily for sale to customers.
- Copyrights; literary, musical, or artistic compositions, etc.; and certain U.S. government publications.
- Accounts receivable and notes receivable arising in the ordinary course of the trade or business.

SECTION 1231 ASSETS DISPOSED OF BY CASUALTY OR THEFT

When § 1231 assets are disposed of by casualty or theft, a special netting rule is applied. For simplicity, the term *casualty* is used to mean both casualty and theft dispositions. First, the casualty gains and losses from § 1231 assets *and* the casualty

[37]Note that the holding period is "12 months or more" and not "more than 12 months."

CONCEPT SUMMARY 14–6

Section 1231 Netting Procedure

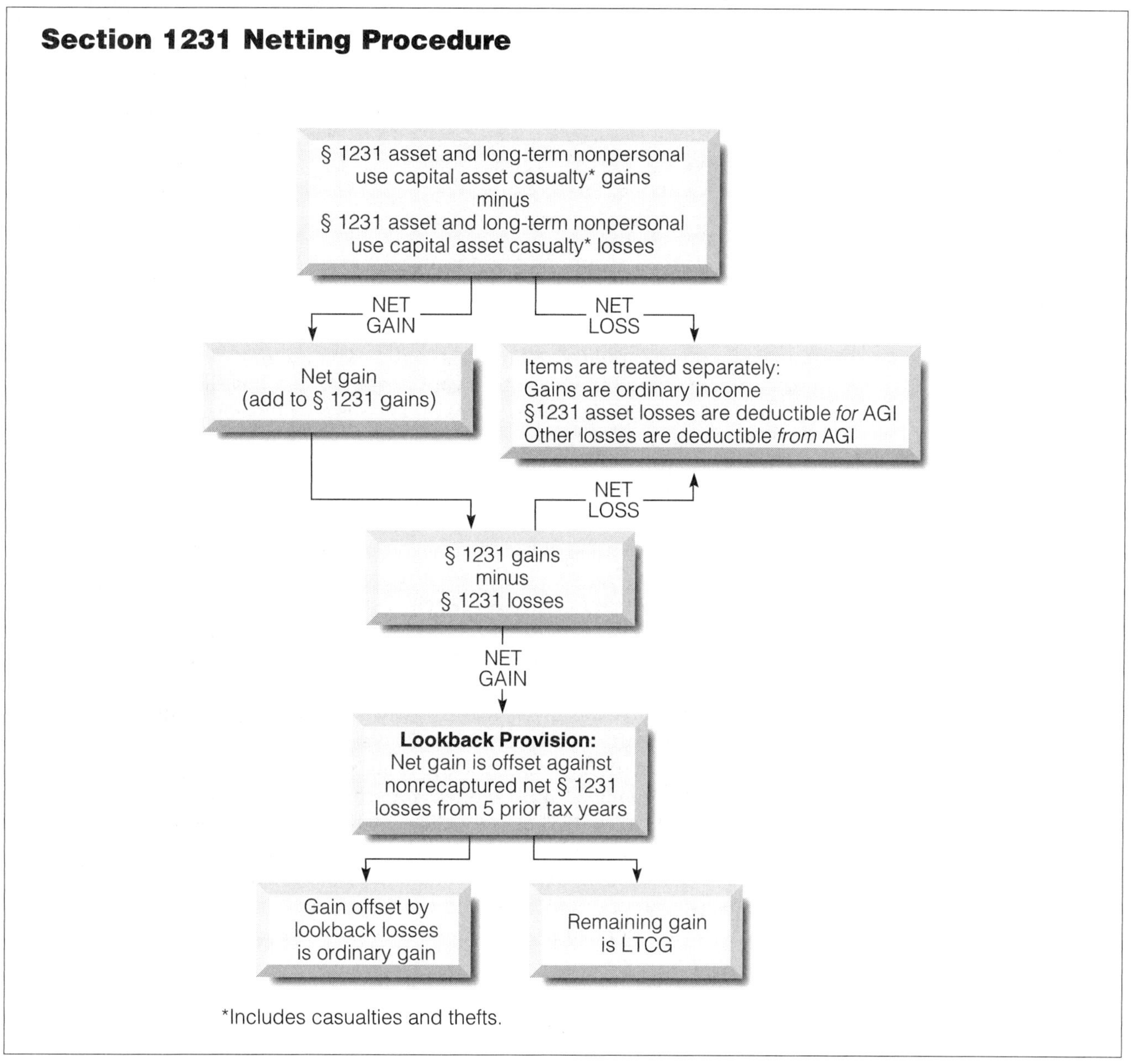

gains and losses from **long-term nonpersonal use capital assets** are determined. A nonpersonal use capital asset might be an investment painting or a baseball card collection held by a nondealer in baseball cards.

Next, the § 1231 asset casualty gains and losses and the nonpersonal use capital asset casualty gains and losses are netted together (see Concept Summary 14–6). If the result is a *net loss*, the § 1231 casualty gains and the nonpersonal use capital asset casualty gains are treated as ordinary gains, the § 1231 casualty losses are deductible *for* AGI, and the nonpersonal use capital asset casualty losses are deductible *from* AGI subject to the 2 percent-of-AGI limitation.

If the result of the netting is a *net gain*, the net gain is treated as a § 1231 gain. Thus, a § 1231 asset disposed of by casualty may or may not get § 1231 treatment, depending on whether the netting process results in a gain or a loss. Also, a

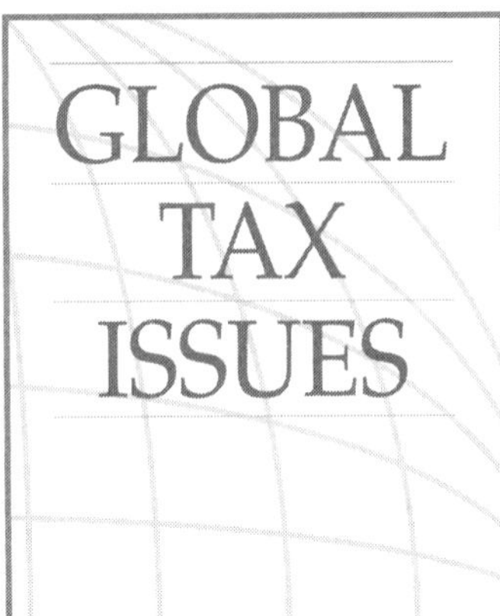

Canadian Slow Depreciation

A manufacturer has a division in Canada that manufactures auto components. The components are shipped to Detroit and become part of U.S.-manufactured automobiles. Due to slow auto sales, the manufacturer closes the Canadian plant and moves its machinery to the United States. Later, the manufacturer sells the machinery and has a tax loss because the machinery's adjusted basis is much higher than that of similar equipment that was used exclusively in the United States. The adjusted basis of the formerly Canadian equipment is higher because straight-line tax depreciation was required for the Canadian property (see Chapter 8).

nonpersonal use capital asset disposed of by casualty may get § 1231 treatment or ordinary treatment, but will not get capital gain or loss treatment!

Personal use property casualty gains and losses are not subject to the § 1231 rules. If the result of netting these gains and losses is a gain, the net gain is a capital gain. If the netting results in a loss, the net loss is a deduction *from* AGI to the extent it exceeds 10 percent of AGI.

Casualties, thefts, and condemnations are *involuntary conversions*. Involuntary conversion gains may be deferred if conversion proceeds are reinvested; involuntary conversion losses are recognized currently (refer to Chapter 13) regardless of whether the conversion proceeds are reinvested. Thus, the special netting process discussed above for casualties and thefts would not include gains that are not currently recognizable because the insurance proceeds are reinvested.

The special netting process for casualties and thefts also does not include condemnation gains and losses. Consequently, a § 1231 asset disposed of by condemnation will receive § 1231 treatment. This variation between recognized casualty and condemnation gains and losses sheds considerable light on what § 1231 is all about. Section 1231 has no effect on whether or not *realized* gain or loss is recognized. Instead, § 1231 merely dictates how such *recognized* gain or loss is *classified* (ordinary, capital, or § 1231) under certain conditions.

Personal use property condemnation gains and losses are not subject to the § 1231 rules. The gains are capital gains (because personal use property is a capital asset), and the losses are nondeductible because they arise from the disposition of personal use property.

General Procedure for § 1231 Computation

The tax treatment of § 1231 gains and losses depends on the results of a rather complex *netting* procedure. The steps in this netting procedure are as follows.

Step 1: Casualty Netting. Net all recognized long-term gains and losses from casualties of § 1231 assets and nonpersonal use capital assets. Casualty gains result when insurance proceeds exceed the adjusted basis of the property. This casualty netting is beneficial because if there is a net gain, the gain may receive long-term capital gain treatment. If there is a net loss, it receives ordinary loss treatment.

a. If the casualty gains exceed the casualty losses, add the excess to the other § 1231 gains for the taxable year.
b. If the casualty losses exceed the casualty gains, exclude all casualty losses and gains from further § 1231 computation. If this is the case, all casualty gains are ordinary income. Section 1231 asset casualty losses are deductible *for* AGI. Other casualty losses are deductible *from* AGI.

Step 2: § 1231 Netting. After adding any net casualty gain from Step 1a to the other § 1231 gains and losses (including recognized § 1231 asset condemnation gains and losses), net all § 1231 gains and losses.

a. If the gains exceed the losses, the net gain is offset by the "lookback" nonrecaptured § 1231 losses (see below) from the five prior tax years. To the extent of this offset, the net § 1231 gain is classified as ordinary gain. Any remaining gain is long-term capital gain.
b. If the losses exceed the gains, all gains are ordinary income. Section 1231 asset losses are deductible *for* AGI. Other casualty losses are deductible *from* AGI.

Step 3: § 1231 Lookback Provision. The net § 1231 gain from Step 2a is offset by the nonrecaptured net § 1231 losses for the five preceding taxable years. For 2005, the lookback years are 2000, 2001, 2002, 2003, and 2004. To the extent of the nonrecaptured net § 1231 loss, the current-year net § 1231 gain is ordinary income. The *nonrecaptured* net § 1231 losses are those that have not already been used to offset net § 1231 gains. Only the net § 1231 gain exceeding this net § 1231 loss carryforward is given long-term capital gain treatment. Concept Summary 14–6 summarizes the § 1231 computational procedure. Examples 52 and 53 illustrate the **§ 1231 lookback** provision.

Examples 50 through 53 illustrate the application of the § 1231 computation procedure.

EXAMPLE 50

During 2005, Ross had $125,000 of AGI before considering the following recognized gains and losses:

Capital Gains and Losses	
Long-term capital gain	$3,000
Long-term capital loss	(400)
Short-term capital gain	1,000
Short-term capital loss	(200)
Casualties	
Theft of diamond ring (owned four months)	($ 800)*
Fire damage to personal residence (owned 10 years)	(400)*
Gain from insurance recovery on fire loss to business building (owned two years)	200
§ 1231 Gains and Losses from Depreciable Business Assets Held Long Term	
Asset A	$ 300
Asset B	1,100
Asset C	(500)
Gains and Losses from Sale of Depreciable Business Assets Held Short Term	
Asset D	$ 200
Asset E	(300)

*As adjusted for the $100 floor on personal casualty losses.

Ross had no net § 1231 losses in tax years before 2005.

Disregarding the recapture of depreciation (discussed later in the chapter), Ross's gains and losses receive the following tax treatment:

- The diamond ring and the residence are personal use assets. Therefore, these casualties are not § 1231 transactions. The $800 (ring) plus $400 (residence) losses are potentially deductible *from* AGI. However, the total loss of $1,200 does not exceed 10% of AGI. Thus, only the business building (a § 1231 asset) casualty gain remains. The netting of the § 1231 asset and nonpersonal use capital asset casualty gains and losses contains only one item—the $200 gain from the business building. Consequently, there is a net gain and that gain is treated as a § 1231 gain (added to the § 1231 gains).
- The gains from § 1231 transactions (Assets A, B, and C and the § 1231 asset casualty gain) exceed the losses by $1,100 ($1,600 – $500). This excess is a long-term capital gain and is added to Ross's other long-term capital gains.
- Ross's net long-term capital gain is $3,700 ($3,000 + $1,100 from § 1231 transactions – $400 long-term capital loss). Ross's net short-term capital gain is $800 ($1,000 – $200). The result is capital gain net income of $4,500. The $3,700 net long-term capital gain portion is eligible for beneficial capital gain treatment [assume all the gain is 5%/15% gain (see the discussion earlier in this chapter)]. The $800 net short-term capital gain is subject to tax as ordinary income.[38]
- Ross treats the gain and loss from Assets D and E (depreciable business assets held for less than the long-term holding period) as ordinary gain and loss.

Results of the Gains and Losses on Ross's Tax Computation

NLTCG	$ 3,700
NSTCG	800
Ordinary gain from sale of Asset D	200
Ordinary loss from sale of Asset E	(300)
AGI from other sources	125,000
AGI	$129,400

- Ross will have personal use property casualty losses of $1,200 [$800 (diamond ring) + $400 (personal residence)]. A personal use property casualty loss is deductible only to the extent it exceeds 10% of AGI. Thus, none of the $1,200 is deductible ($129,400 × 10% = $12,940). ■

EXAMPLE 51

Assume the same facts as in Example 50, except the loss from Asset C was $1,700 instead of $500.

- The treatment of the casualty losses is the same as in Example 50.
- The losses from § 1231 transactions now exceed the gains by $100 ($1,700 – $1,600). As a result, the gains from Assets A and B and the § 1231 asset casualty gain are ordinary income, and the loss from Asset C is a deduction *for* AGI (a business loss). The same result can be achieved by simply treating the $100 net loss as a deduction *for* AGI.
- Capital gain net income is $3,400 ($2,600 long term + $800 short term). The $2,600 net long-term capital gain portion is eligible for beneficial capital gain treatment, and the $800 net short-term capital gain is subject to tax as ordinary income.

[38] Ross's taxable income (unless the itemized deductions and the personal exemption and dependency deductions are extremely large) will put him in at least the 28% bracket. Thus, the alternative tax computation will yield a lower tax. See Example 40.

Results of the Gains and Losses on Ross's Tax Computation	
NLTCG	$ 2,600
NSTCG	800
Net ordinary loss on Assets A, B, and C and § 1231 casualty gain	(100)
Ordinary gain from sale of Asset D	200
Ordinary loss from sale of Asset E	(300)
AGI from other sources	125,000
AGI	$128,200

- None of the personal use property casualty losses will be deductible since $1,200 does not exceed 10% of $128,200. ■

EXAMPLE 52

Assume the same facts as in Example 50, except that Ross has a $700 nonrecaptured net § 1231 loss from 2004.

- The treatment of the casualty losses is the same as in Example 50.
- The 2005 net § 1231 gain of $1,100 is treated as ordinary income to the extent of the 2004 nonrecaptured § 1231 loss of $700. The remaining $400 net § 1231 gain is a long-term capital gain and is added to Ross's other long-term capital gains.
- Ross's net long-term capital gain is $3,000 ($3,000 + $400 from § 1231 transactions – $400 long-term capital loss). Ross's net short-term capital gain is still $800 ($1,000 – $200). The result is capital gain net income of $3,800. The $3,000 net long-term capital gain portion is eligible for beneficial capital gain treatment, and the $800 net short-term capital gain is subject to tax as ordinary income.

Results of the Gains and Losses on Ross's Tax Computation	
NLTCG	$ 3,000
NSTCG	800
Ordinary gain from recapture of § 1231 losses	700
Ordinary gain from sale of Asset D	200
Ordinary loss from sale of Asset E	(300)
AGI from other sources	125,000
AGI	$129,400

- None of the personal use property casualty losses will be deductible since $1,200 does not exceed 10% of $129,400. ■

EXAMPLE 53

Assume the same facts as in Example 50, except that Ross had a net § 1231 loss of $2,700 in 2003 and a net § 1231 gain of $300 in 2004.

- The treatment of the casualty losses is the same as in Example 50.
- The 2003 net § 1231 loss of $2,700 will have carried over to 2004 and been offset against the 2004 net § 1231 gain of $300. Thus, the $300 gain will have been classified as ordinary income, and $2,400 of nonrecaptured 2003 net § 1231 loss will carry over to 2005. The 2005 net § 1231 gain of $1,100 will be offset against this loss, resulting in $1,100 of ordinary income. The nonrecaptured net § 1231 loss of $1,300 ($2,400 – $1,100) carries over to 2006.
- Capital gain net income is $3,400 ($2,600 net long-term capital gain + $800 net short-term capital gain). The $2,600 net long-term capital gain portion is eligible for beneficial capital gain treatment, and the $800 net short-term capital gain is subject to tax as ordinary income.

Results of the Gains and Losses on Ross's Tax Computation	
NLTCG	$ 2,600
NSTCG	800
Ordinary gain from recapture of § 1231 losses	1,100
Ordinary gain from sale of Asset D	200
Ordinary loss from sale of Asset E	(300)
AGI from other sources	125,000
AGI	$129,400

- None of the personal use property casualty losses will be deductible since $1,200 does not exceed 10% of $129,400. ■

LO.9

Determine when § 1245 recapture applies and how it is computed.

Section 1245 Recapture

Now that the basic rules of § 1231 have been introduced, it is time to add some complications. The Code contains two major *recapture* provisions—§§ 1245 and 1250. These provisions cause *gain* to be treated *initially* as ordinary gain. Thus, what may appear to be a § 1231 gain is ordinary gain instead. These recapture provisions may also cause a gain in a nonpersonal use casualty to be *initially* ordinary gain rather than casualty gain. Classifying gains (and losses) properly initially is important because improper initial classification may lead to incorrect mixing and matching of gains and losses. This section discusses the § 1245 recapture rules, and the next section discusses the § 1250 recapture rules.

ETHICAL CONSIDERATIONS

Preparing Tax Returns without Proper Information

Your CPA firm is preparing the tax return of a new client who says he has had numerous transactions involving the sale of depreciable business property in prior years. The client lost all his tax records in a recent hurricane. His transactions for the current year result in a net § 1231 gain. Your supervisor instructs you to complete this return without further information. Should you do so?

Section 1245 requires taxpayers to treat all gain as ordinary gain unless the property is disposed of for more than was paid for it. This result is accomplished by requiring that all gain be treated as ordinary gain to the extent of the depreciation taken on the property disposed of. Section 1231 gain results only when the property is disposed of for more than its original cost. The excess of the sales price over the original cost is § 1231 gain. Section 1245 applies *primarily* to non-real-estate property such as machinery, trucks, and office furniture. Section 1245 does not apply if property is disposed of at a loss. Generally, the loss will be a § 1231 loss unless the form of the disposition is a casualty.

EXAMPLE 54

Alice purchased a $100,000 business machine and deducted $70,000 depreciation before selling it for $80,000. If it were not for § 1245, the $50,000 gain would be § 1231 gain ($80,000 amount realized – $30,000 adjusted basis). Section 1245 prevents this potentially favorable result by treating as ordinary income (not as § 1231 gain) any gain to the extent of depreciation taken. In this example, the entire $50,000 gain would be ordinary income. If Alice had sold

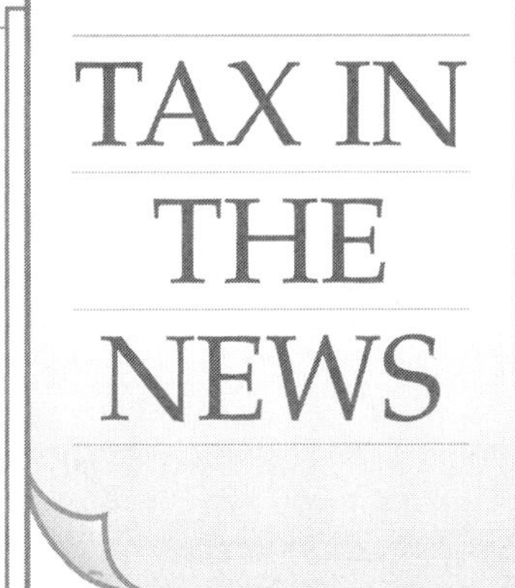

MORE DEPRECIATION AND MORE DEPRECIATION RECAPTURE

The combination of the 50 percent special depreciation allowance available under a prior law and the $102,000 (in 2004) § 179 immediate expense election permitted under the Jobs and Growth Tax Relief Reconciliation Act of 2003 dramatically increased the amount of depreciation that could be taken in the first year for certain new property (see Chapter 8). However, the increased depreciation meant that the adjusted basis of the property was reduced more quickly. Consequently, if such property is sold early in its useful life, there will very likely be a gain on its disposition, and the § 1245 depreciation recapture will be greater because the depreciation taken is greater.

the machine for $120,000, she would have a gain of $90,000 ($120,000 amount realized – $30,000 adjusted basis). The § 1245 gain would be $70,000 (equal to the depreciation taken), and the § 1231 gain would be $20,000 (equal to the excess of the sales price over the original cost). ■

Section 1245 recapture provides, in general, that the portion of recognized gain from the sale or other disposition of § 1245 property that represents depreciation (including § 167 depreciation, § 168 cost recovery, § 179 immediate expensing, § 168(k) 30 or 50 percent additional first-year depreciation, and § 197 amortization) is *recaptured* as ordinary income. Thus, in Example 54, $50,000 of the $70,000 depreciation taken is recaptured as ordinary income when the business machine is sold for $80,000. Only $50,000 is recaptured rather than $70,000 because Alice is only required to recognize § 1245 recapture ordinary gain equal to the lower of the depreciation taken or the gain recognized.

The method of depreciation (e.g., accelerated or straight-line) does not matter. All depreciation taken is potentially subject to recapture. Thus, § 1245 recapture is often referred to as *full recapture*. Any remaining gain after subtracting the amount recaptured as ordinary income will usually be § 1231 gain. If the property is disposed of in a casualty event, however, the remaining gain will be casualty gain. If the business machine in Example 54 had been disposed of by casualty and the $80,000 received had been an insurance recovery, Alice would still have a gain of $50,000, and the gain would still be recaptured by § 1245 as ordinary gain. The § 1245 recapture rules apply before there is any casualty gain. Since all the $50,000 gain is recaptured, no casualty gain arises from the casualty.

The following examples illustrate the general application of § 1245.

EXAMPLE 55

On January 1, 2005, Gary sold for $13,000 a machine acquired several years ago for $12,000. He had taken $10,000 of depreciation on the machine.

- The recognized gain from the sale is $11,000. This is the amount realized of $13,000 less the adjusted basis of $2,000 ($12,000 cost – $10,000 depreciation taken).
- Depreciation taken is $10,000. Therefore, since § 1245 recapture gain is the lower of depreciation taken or gain recognized, $10,000 of the $11,000 recognized gain is ordinary income, and the remaining $1,000 gain is § 1231 gain.
- The § 1231 gain of $1,000 is also equal to the excess of the sales price over the original cost of the property ($13,000 – $12,000 = $1,000 § 1231 gain). ■

EXAMPLE 56

Assume the same facts as in the previous example, except the asset is sold for $9,000 instead of $13,000.

- The recognized gain from the sale is $7,000. This is the amount realized of $9,000 less the adjusted basis of $2,000.
- Depreciation taken is $10,000. Therefore, since the $10,000 depreciation taken exceeds the recognized gain of $7,000, the entire $7,000 recognized gain is ordinary income.
- The § 1231 gain is zero. There is no § 1231 gain because the selling price ($9,000) does not exceed the original purchase price ($12,000). ■

EXAMPLE 57

Assume the same facts as in Example 55, except the asset is sold for $1,500 instead of $13,000.

- The recognized loss from the sale is $500. This is the amount realized of $1,500 less the adjusted basis of $2,000.
- Since there is a loss, there is no depreciation recapture. All of the loss is § 1231 loss. ■

If § 1245 property is disposed of in a transaction other than a sale, exchange, or involuntary conversion, the maximum amount recaptured is the excess of the property's fair market value over its adjusted basis. See the discussion under Considerations Common to §§ 1245 and 1250 later in the chapter.

SECTION 1245 PROPERTY

Generally, **§ 1245 property** includes all depreciable personal property (e.g., machinery and equipment), including livestock. Buildings and their structural components generally are not § 1245 property. The following property is *also* subject to § 1245 treatment:

- Amortizable personal property such as goodwill, patents, copyrights, and leaseholds of § 1245 property. Professional baseball and football player contracts are § 1245 property.
- Amortization of reforestation expenditures.
- Expensing of costs to remove architectural and transportation barriers that restrict the handicapped and/or elderly.
- Section 179 immediate expensing of depreciable tangible personal property costs.
- Property for which the § 168(k) 30 or 50 percent additional first-year depreciation was taken.
- Elevators and escalators acquired before January 1, 1987.
- Certain depreciable tangible real property (other than buildings and their structural components) employed as an integral part of certain activities such as manufacturing and production. For example, a natural gas storage tank where the gas is used in the manufacturing process is § 1245 property.
- Pollution control facilities, railroad grading and tunnel bores, on-the-job training, and child care facilities on which amortization is taken.
- Single-purpose agricultural and horticultural structures and petroleum storage facilities (e.g., a greenhouse or silo).
- Fifteen-year, 18-year, and 19-year nonresidential real estate for which accelerated cost recovery is used is subject to the § 1245 recapture rules, although it is technically not § 1245 property. Such property would have been placed in service after 1980 and before 1987.

EXAMPLE 58

James acquired nonresidential real property on January 1, 1986, for $100,000. He used the statutory percentage method to compute the ACRS cost recovery. He sells the asset on January 15, 2005, for $120,000. The amount and nature of James's gain are computed as follows:

Amount realized		$120,000
Adjusted basis		
Cost	$100,000	
Less cost recovery: 1986–2004	(99,800)	
2005	(8)	
January 15, 2005, adjusted basis		(192)
Gain realized and recognized		$119,808

The gain of $119,808 is treated as ordinary income to the extent of *all* depreciation taken because the property is 19-year nonresidential real estate for which accelerated depreciation was used. Thus, James reports ordinary income of $99,808 ($99,800 + $8) and § 1231 gain of $20,000 ($119,808 – $99,808). ■

OBSERVATIONS ON § 1245

- In most instances, the total depreciation taken will exceed the recognized gain. Therefore, the disposition of § 1245 property usually results in ordinary income rather than § 1231 gain. Thus, generally, no § 1231 gain will occur unless the § 1245 property is disposed of for more than its original cost. Refer to Examples 55 and 56.
- Recapture applies to the total amount of depreciation allowed or allowable regardless of the depreciation method used.
- Recapture applies regardless of the holding period of the property. Of course, the entire recognized gain would be ordinary income if the property were held for less than the long-term holding period because § 1231 would not apply.
- Section 1245 does not apply to losses, which receive § 1231 treatment.
- Gains from the disposition of § 1245 assets may also be treated as passive activity gains (see Chapter 11).

LO.10

Determine when § 1250 recapture applies and how it is computed.

Section 1250 Recapture

Generally, **§ 1250 property** is depreciable real property (principally buildings and their structural components) that is not subject to § 1245.[39] Intangible real property, such as leaseholds of § 1250 property, is also included.

Section 1250 recapture rarely applies since only the amount of *additional depreciation* is subject to recapture. To have additional depreciation, accelerated depreciation must have been taken on the asset. Straight-line depreciation is not recaptured (except for property held one year or less). Since depreciable real property placed in service after 1986 can only be depreciated using the straight-line method, there will be *no § 1250 depreciation recapture* on such property. Nor does § 1250 apply if the real property is sold at a loss.

If depreciable real property has been held for many years before it is sold, however, the § 1250 recapture rules may apply and are therefore discussed here. **Additional depreciation** is the excess of the accelerated depreciation actually deducted over depreciation that would have been deductible if the straight-line method had been used. Section 1250 recapture may apply when either (1) residential rental real property was acquired after 1975 and before 1987 and accelerated depreciation was taken or (2) nonresidential real property was acquired before 1981 and accelerated depreciation was taken after December 31, 1969.

[39] As noted above, in one limited circumstance, § 1245 does apply to nonresidential real estate. If the nonresidential real estate was placed in service after 1980 and before 1987 and accelerated depreciation was used, the § 1245 recapture rules rather than the § 1250 recapture rules apply.

If § 1250 property with additional depreciation is disposed of in a transaction other than a sale, exchange, or involuntary conversion, the depreciation recapture is limited to the excess of the property's fair market value over the adjusted basis. For instance, if a corporation distributes real property to its shareholders as a dividend and the fair market value of the real property is greater than its adjusted basis, the corporation will recognize a gain. If accelerated depreciation was taken on the property, § 1250 recapture will apply.

It is important to know what assets are defined as § 1250 property because even when there is no additional depreciation, the gain from such property may be subject to a special 25 percent tax rate. See the discussion of Unrecaptured § 1250 Gain later in this chapter.

The discussion below describes the computational steps when § 1250 recapture applies and indicates how that recapture is reflected on Form 4797 (Sales of Business Property).

COMPUTING RECAPTURE ON NONRESIDENTIAL REAL PROPERTY

For § 1250 property other than residential rental property, the potential recapture is equal to the amount of additional depreciation taken since December 31, 1969. This nonresidential real property includes buildings such as offices, warehouses, factories, and stores. (The definition of and rules for residential rental housing are discussed later in the chapter.) The lower of the potential § 1250 recapture amount or the recognized gain is ordinary income. The following general rules apply:

- Additional depreciation is depreciation taken in excess of straight-line after December 31, 1969, on property that was acquired before 1981.
- If the property is held for one year or less (usually not the case), all depreciation taken, even under the straight-line method, is additional depreciation.

The following procedure is used to compute recapture on nonresidential real property that was acquired before 1981 and for which accelerated depreciation was taken after December 31, 1969, under § 1250:

- Determine the recognized gain from the sale or other disposition of the property.
- Determine the additional depreciation (if any).
- The lower of the recognized gain or the additional depreciation is ordinary income.
- If any recognized gain remains (total recognized gain less recapture), it is § 1231 gain. However, it would be casualty gain if the disposition was by casualty.

The following example shows the application of the § 1250 computational procedure.

EXAMPLE 59

On January 3, 1980, Larry acquired a new building at a cost of $200,000 for use in his business. The building had an estimated useful life of 50 years and no estimated salvage value. Depreciation has been taken under the 150% declining-balance method through December 31, 2004. Pertinent information with respect to depreciation taken follows:

Year	Undepreciated Balance (Beginning of the Year)	Current Depreciation Provision	Straight-Line Depreciation	Additional Depreciation
1980–2003	$200,000	$103,810	$ 96,000	$7,810
2004	96,190	3,070	4,000	(930)
Total 1980–2004		$106,880	$100,000	$6,880

On January 2, 2005, Larry sold the building for $180,000. Compute the amount of his § 1250 ordinary income and § 1231 gain.

- Larry's recognized gain from the sale is $86,880. This is the difference between the $180,000 amount realized and the $93,120 adjusted basis ($200,000 cost – $106,880 depreciation taken).
- Additional depreciation is $6,880.
- The amount of ordinary income is $6,880. Since the additional depreciation of $6,880 is less than the recognized gain of $86,880, the entire gain is not recaptured.
- The remaining $80,000 ($86,880 – $6,880) gain is § 1231 gain. ■

COMPUTING RECAPTURE ON RESIDENTIAL RENTAL HOUSING

Section 1250 recapture sometimes applies to the sale or other disposition of residential rental housing. Property qualifies as *residential rental housing* only if at least 80 percent of gross rent income is rent income from dwelling units.[40] The rules are the same as for other § 1250 property, except that only the post-1975 additional depreciation may be recaptured on property acquired before 1987. If any of the recognized gain is not absorbed by the recapture rules pertaining to the post-1975 period, the remaining gain is § 1231 gain.

EXAMPLE 60

Assume the same facts as in the previous example, except the building is residential rental housing.

- Post-1975 ordinary income is $6,880 (post-1975 additional depreciation of $6,880).
- The remaining $80,000 ($86,880 – $6,880) gain is § 1231 gain. ■

Under § 1250, when straight-line depreciation is used, there is no § 1250 recapture potential unless the property is disposed of in the first year of use. Generally, however, the § 1250 recapture rules do not apply to depreciable real property unless the property is disposed of in the first year of use.

EXAMPLE 61

Sanjay acquires a residential rental building on January 1, 2004, for $300,000. He receives an offer of $450,000 for the building in 2005 and sells it on December 23, 2005.

- Sanjay takes $20,909 {($300,000 × .03485) + [$300,000 × .03636 × (11.5/12)] = $20,909} of total depreciation for 2004 and 2005, and the adjusted basis of the property is $279,091 ($300,000 – $20,909).
- Sanjay's recognized gain is $170,909 ($450,000 – $279,091).
- All of the gain is § 1231 gain. ■

SECTION 1250 RECAPTURE SITUATIONS

The § 1250 recapture rules apply to the following property for which accelerated depreciation was used:

- Residential rental real estate acquired before 1987.
- Nonresidential real estate acquired before 1981.
- Real property used predominantly outside the United States.
- Certain government-financed or low-income housing.[41]

[40]§ 168(e)(2)(A). Note that there may be residential, nonrental housing (e.g., a bunkhouse on a cattle ranch). Such property is commonly regarded as "nonresidential real estate." The rules for such property were discussed in the previous section.

[41]Described in § 1250(a)(1)(B).

Concept Summary 14–7

Comparison of § 1245 and § 1250 Depreciation Recapture

	§ 1245	§ 1250
Property affected	All depreciable personal property, but also nonresidential real property acquired after December 31, 1980, and before January 1, 1987, for which accelerated cost recovery was used. Also includes miscellaneous items such as § 179 expense and § 197 amortization of intangibles such as goodwill, patents, and copyrights.	Nonresidential real property acquired after December 31, 1969, and before January 1, 1981, on which accelerated depreciation was taken. Residential rental real property acquired after December 31, 1975, and before January 1, 1987, on which accelerated depreciation was taken.
Depreciation recaptured	Potentially all depreciation taken. If the selling price is greater than or equal to the original cost, all depreciation is recaptured. If the selling price is between the adjusted basis and the original cost, only some depreciation is recaptured.	Additional depreciation (the excess of accelerated cost recovery over straight-line cost recovery or the excess of accelerated depreciation over straight-line depreciation).
Limit on recapture	Lower of depreciation taken or gain recognized.	Lower of additional depreciation or gain recognized.
Treatment of gain exceeding recapture gain	Usually § 1231 gain.	Usually § 1231 gain.
Treatment of loss	No depreciation recapture; loss is usually § 1231 loss.	No depreciation recapture; loss is usually § 1231 loss.

Concept Summary 14–7 compares and contrasts the § 1245 and § 1250 depreciation recapture rules.

UNRECAPTURED § 1250 GAIN (REAL ESTATE 25% GAIN)

This section will explain what gain is eligible for the 25 percent tax rate on unrecaptured § 1250 gain. This gain is used in the alternative tax computation for net capital gain discussed earlier in this chapter. Unrecaptured § 1250 gain (25% gain) is some or all of the § 1231 gain that is treated as long-term capital gain and relates to a sale of depreciable real estate.

The maximum amount of this 25% gain is the depreciation taken on real property sold at a recognized gain. That maximum amount is reduced in one or more of the following ways:

- The recognized gain from disposition is less than the depreciation taken. The 25% gain is reduced to the recognized gain amount. Refer to Example 59. The depreciation taken was $106,880, but the recognized gain was only $86,880. Consequently, *all* of the recognized gain is potential 25% § 1231 gain.
- There is § 1250 depreciation recapture because the property is residential real estate acquired before 1987 on which accelerated depreciation was taken. The § 1250 recapture reduces the 25% gain. Refer to Example 60. Of the $86,880 recognized gain, $6,880 was recaptured by § 1250 as ordinary income, leaving $80,000 of the potential 25% § 1231 gain.

- There is § 1245 depreciation recapture because the property is nonresidential real estate acquired in 1981–1986 on which accelerated depreciation was taken. No 25% § 1231 gain will be left because § 1245 will recapture all of the depreciation or the recognized gain, whichever is less. Refer to Example 58. Depreciation of $99,808 was taken, but all of it was recaptured as ordinary income by § 1245. Thus, there is no remaining potential 25% § 1231 gain. The entire $20,000 § 1231 gain in Example 58 is potential 5%/15% gain.
- Section 1231 loss from disposition of other § 1231 assets held long term reduces the gain from real estate.
- Section 1231 lookback losses convert some or all of the potential 25% § 1231 gain to ordinary income.

Special 25% Gain Netting Rules. Where there is a § 1231 gain from real estate and that gain includes both potential *25%* gain and potential *5%/15%* gain, any § 1231 loss from disposition of other § 1231 assets *first offsets* the *5%/15%* portion of the § 1231 gain and then offsets the *25%* portion of the § 1231 gain. Also, any § 1231 lookback loss *first recharacterizes* the *25%* portion of the § 1231 gain and then recharacterizes the *5%/15%* portion of the § 1231 gain as ordinary income.

Net § 1231 Gain Limitation. The amount of unrecaptured § 1250 gain may not exceed the net § 1231 gain that is eligible to be treated as long-term capital gain. The unrecaptured § 1250 gain is the *lesser of* the unrecaptured § 1250 gain or the net § 1231 gain that is treated as capital gain. Thus, if there is a net § 1231 gain, but it is all recaptured by the five-year § 1231 lookback loss provision, there is no surviving § 1231 gain or unrecaptured § 1250 gain.

Refer to Example 52. There was $200 of § 1231 gain from the building fire that would also be potential *25%* gain if at least $200 of depreciation was taken. The net § 1231 gain was $1,100 including the $200 building gain. (The $500 loss from Asset C would offset the potential *5%/15%* § 1231 gain and not the potential *25%* gain, so all of the potential *25%* gain of $200 is in the $1,100 net § 1231 gain.) However, the $700 of § 1231 lookback losses would *first* absorb the $200 building gain, so the $400 of § 1231 gain that is treated as long-term capital gain includes no *25%* gain.

Section 1250 Property for Purposes of the Unrecaptured § 1250 Gain. Section 1250 property includes any real property (other than § 1245 property) that is or has been depreciable. Land is *not* § 1250 property because it is not depreciable.

EXAMPLE 62

Bill is a single taxpayer with 2005 taxable income of $84,000 composed of:

- $64,000 ordinary taxable income,
- $3,000 short-term capital loss,
- $15,000 long-term capital gain from sale of stock, and
- $8,000 § 1231 gain that is all unrecaptured § 1250 gain (the actual unrecaptured gain was $11,000, but net § 1231 gain is only $8,000).

Bill's net capital gain is $20,000 ($15,000 long-term capital gain + $8,000 unrecaptured § 1250 gain/net § 1231 gain – $3,000 short-term capital loss). The $3,000 short-term capital loss is offset against the $8,000 unrecaptured § 1250 gain, reducing that gain to $5,000 (see the discussion earlier in the chapter concerning netting of capital losses). Bill's adjusted net capital gain is $15,000 ($20,000 net capital gain – $5,000 unrecaptured § 1250 gain). Bill's total tax (using the alternative tax calculation discussed earlier in the chapter) is $16,165 [$12,665 (tax on ordinary taxable income) + $1,250 ($5,000 unrecaptured § 1250 gain × 25%) + $2,250 ($15,000 adjusted net capital gain × 15%)]. ■

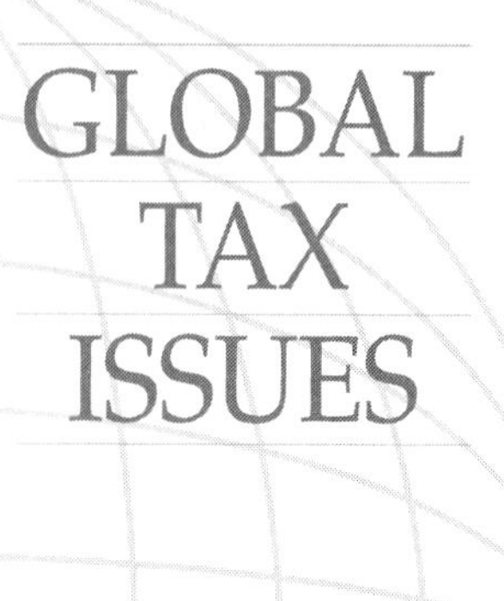

Exchange for Foreign Property Yields Recognized Recapture Gain

Tangible personal property used in a trade or business may be the subject of a § 1031 like-kind exchange, and the postponed gain is most likely postponed § 1245 gain. However, tangible personal property used predominantly within the United States cannot be exchanged for tangible personal property used predominantly outside the United States. Thus, such an exchange would cause recognized gain, and, as long as the fair market value of the property given up does not exceed its original cost, all of the gain is § 1245 depreciation recapture gain.

LO.11

Understand considerations common to §§ 1245 and 1250.

Considerations Common to §§ 1245 and 1250

EXCEPTIONS

Recapture under §§ 1245 and 1250 does not apply to the following transactions.

Gifts. The recapture potential carries over to the donee.[42]

EXAMPLE 63

Wade gives his daughter, Helen, § 1245 property with an adjusted basis of $1,000. The amount of recapture potential is $700. Helen uses the property in her business and claims further depreciation of $100 before selling it for $1,900. Helen's recognized gain is $1,000 ($1,900 amount realized – $900 adjusted basis), of which $800 is recaptured as ordinary income ($100 depreciation taken by Helen + $700 recapture potential carried over from Wade). The remaining gain of $200 is § 1231 gain. Even if Helen used the property for personal purposes, the $700 recapture potential would still be carried over. ■

Death. Although not a very attractive tax planning approach, death eliminates all recapture potential.[43] In other words, any recapture potential does not carry over from a decedent to an estate or heir.

EXAMPLE 64

Assume the same facts as in Example 63, except Helen receives the property as a result of Wade's death. The $700 recapture potential from Wade is extinguished. Helen has a basis for the property equal to the property's fair market value (assume $1,700) at Wade's death. She will have a $300 gain when the property is sold because the selling price ($1,900) exceeds the property's adjusted basis of $1,600 ($1,700 original basis to Helen – $100 depreciation) by $300. Because of § 1245, $100 is ordinary income. The remaining gain of $200 is § 1231 gain. ■

Charitable Transfers. The recapture potential reduces the amount of the charitable contribution deduction under § 170.[44]

EXAMPLE 65

Kanisha donates to her church § 1245 property with a fair market value of $10,000 and an adjusted basis of $7,000. Assume that the amount of recapture potential is $2,000 (the amount of recapture that would occur if the property were sold). Her charitable contribution deduction (subject to the limitations discussed in Chapter 10) is $8,000 ($10,000 fair market value – $2,000 recapture potential). ■

---

[42] §§ 1245(b)(1) and 1250(d)(1) and Reg. §§ 1.1245–4(a)(1) and 1.1250–3(a)(1).

[43] §§ 1245(b)(2) and 1250(d)(2).

[44] § 170(e)(1)(A) and Reg. § 1.170A–4(b)(1). In certain circumstances, § 1231 gain also reduces the amount of the charitable contribution. See § 170(e)(1)(B).

Certain Nontaxable Transactions. In certain transactions, the transferor's adjusted basis of property carries over to the transferee.[45] The recapture potential also carries over to the transferee.[46] Included in this category are transfers of property pursuant to the following:

- Nontaxable incorporations under § 351.
- Certain liquidations of subsidiary companies under § 332.
- Nontaxable contributions to a partnership under § 721.
- Nontaxable reorganizations.

Gain may be recognized in these transactions if boot is received. If gain is recognized, it is treated as ordinary income to the extent of the recapture potential or recognized gain, whichever is lower.[47]

Like-Kind Exchanges (§ 1031) and Involuntary Conversions (§ 1033). Realized gain will be recognized to the extent of boot received under § 1031. Realized gain also will be recognized to the extent the proceeds from an involuntary conversion are not reinvested in similar property under § 1033. Such recognized gain is subject to recapture as ordinary income under §§ 1245 and 1250. The remaining recapture potential, if any, carries over to the property received in the exchange. Realized losses are not recognized in like-kind exchanges, but are recognized in involuntary conversions (see Chapter 13).

EXAMPLE 66

Anita exchanges § 1245 property with an adjusted basis of $300 for § 1245 property with a fair market value of $6,000. The exchange qualifies as a like-kind exchange under § 1031. Anita also receives $1,000 cash (boot). Her realized gain is $6,700 ($7,000 amount realized – $300 adjusted basis of property). Assuming the recapture potential is $7,500, Anita recognizes § 1245 gain of $1,000 because she received boot of $1,000. The remaining recapture potential of $6,500 carries over to the like-kind property received. ■

OTHER APPLICATIONS

Sections 1245 and 1250 apply notwithstanding any other provisions in the Code.[48] That is, the recapture rules under these Sections *override* all other Sections. Special applications include installment sales and property dividends.

Installment Sales. Recapture gain is recognized in the year of the sale regardless of whether gain is otherwise recognized under the installment method.[49] All gain is ordinary income until the recapture potential is fully absorbed. Nonrecapture (§ 1231) gain is recognized under the installment method as cash is received.

EXAMPLE 67

Seth sells § 1245 property for $20,000, to be paid in 10 annual installments of $2,000 each plus interest at 10%. Seth realizes a $6,000 gain from the sale, of which $4,000 is attributable to depreciation taken. If Seth uses the installment method, he recognizes the entire $4,000 of recapture gain as ordinary income in the year of the sale. The $2,000 of nonrecapture (§ 1231) gain will be recognized at the rate of $200 per year for 10 years. ■

Gain is also recognized on installment sales in the year of the sale in an amount equal to the § 179 (immediate expensing) and § 168(k) 30 or 50 percent additional first-year depreciation deductions taken with respect to the property sold.

[45] §§ 1245(b)(3) and 1250(d)(3) and Reg. §§ 1.1245–4(c) and 1.1250–3(c).
[46] Reg. §§ 1.1245–2(a)(4) and –2(c)(2) and 1.1250–2(d)(1) and (3) and –3(c)(3).
[47] §§ 1245(b)(3) and 1250(d)(3) and Reg. §§ 1.1245–4(c) and 1.1250–3(c).
[48] §§ 1245(d) and 1250(i).
[49] § 453(i). The installment method of reporting gains on the sale of property is discussed in Chapter 16.

Concept Summary 14–8

Depreciation Recapture and § 1231 Netting Procedure

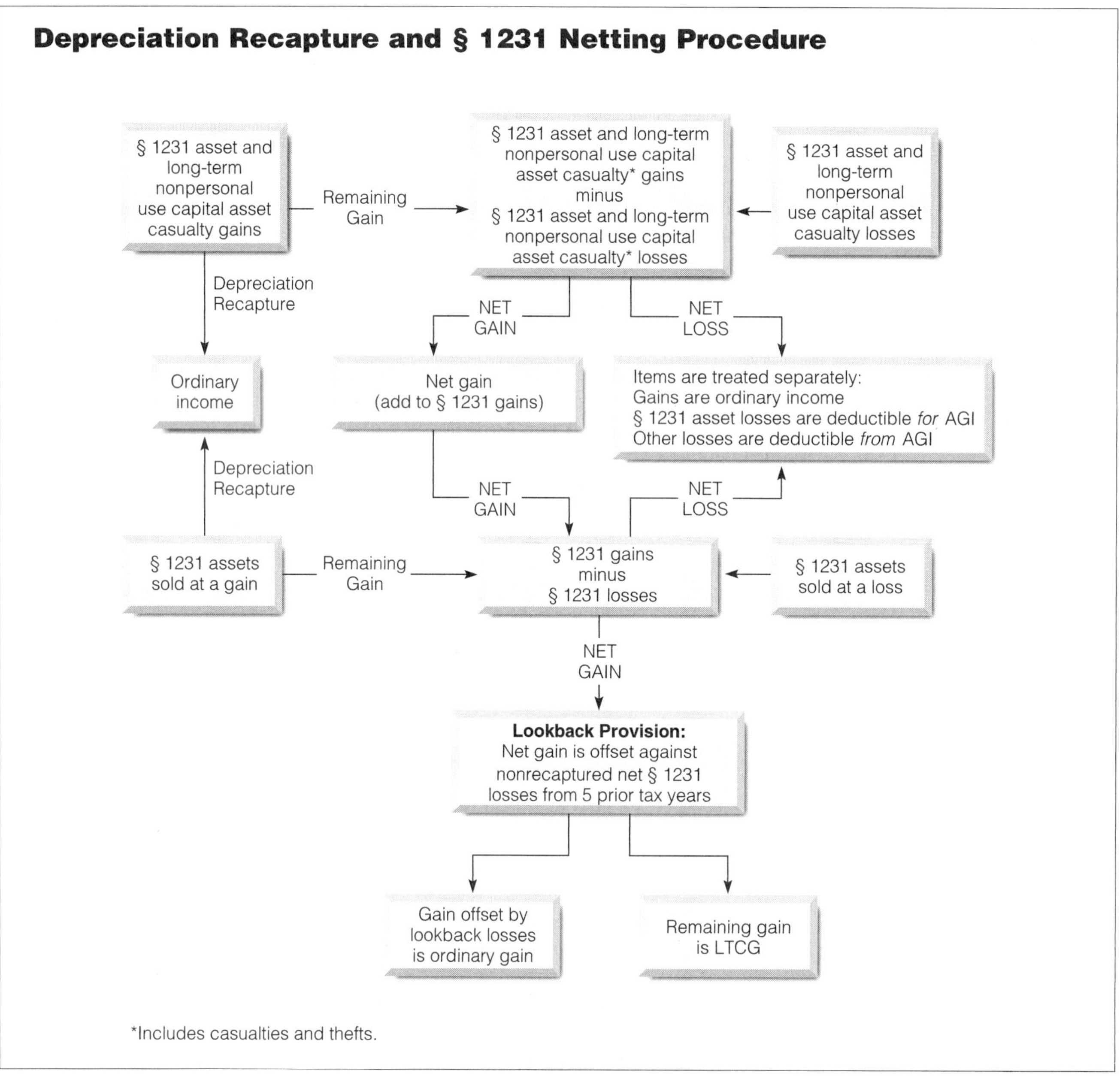

*Includes casualties and thefts.

Property Dividends. A corporation generally recognizes gain if it distributes appreciated property as a dividend. Recapture under §§ 1245 and 1250 applies to the extent of the lower of the recapture potential or the excess of the property's fair market value over the adjusted basis.[50]

EXAMPLE 68

Emerald Corporation distributes § 1245 property as a dividend to its shareholders. The amount of the recapture potential is $300, and the excess of the property's fair market value over the adjusted basis is $800. Emerald recognizes $300 of ordinary income and $500 of § 1231 gain. ■

Concept Summary 14–8 integrates the depreciation recapture rules with the § 1231 netting process. It is an expanded version of Concept Summary 14–6.

[50] § 311(b) and Reg. §§ 1.1245–1(c) and –6(b) and 1.1250–1(a)(4), –1(b)(4), and –1(c)(2).

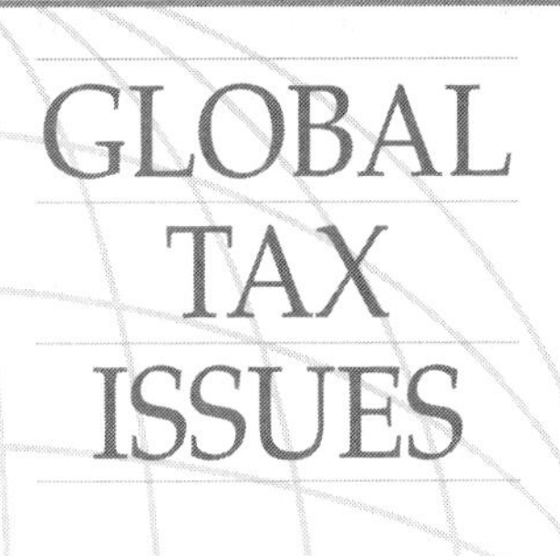

Depreciation Recapture in Other Countries

The rules for dispositions of depreciated property are more complex in the United States than in any other country. Most countries treat the gain or loss from the disposition of business depreciable assets as ordinary income or loss. Consequently, although the U.S. rules are more complex, they can be more beneficial than those of other countries because at least some gains from the disposition of depreciable business property may be taxed at the lower capital gain rates.

LO.12

Apply the special recapture provisions for related parties and IDC and be aware of the special recapture provision for corporations.

Special Recapture Provisions

SPECIAL RECAPTURE FOR CORPORATIONS

Corporations selling depreciable real estate may have ordinary income in addition to that required by § 1250.[51]

GAIN FROM SALE OF DEPRECIABLE PROPERTY BETWEEN CERTAIN RELATED PARTIES

When the sale or exchange of property, which in the hands of the *transferee* is depreciable property (principally machinery, equipment, and buildings, but not land), is between certain related parties, any gain recognized is ordinary income.[52] This provision applies to both direct and indirect sales or exchanges. A **related party** is defined as an individual and his or her controlled corporation or partnership or a taxpayer and any trust in which the taxpayer (or the taxpayer's spouse) is a beneficiary.

EXAMPLE 69

Isabella sells a personal use automobile (therefore nondepreciable) to her controlled corporation. The automobile, which was purchased two years ago, originally cost $5,000 and is sold for $7,000. The automobile is to be used in the corporation's business. If the related-party provision did not exist, Isabella would realize a $2,000 long-term capital gain. The income tax consequences would be favorable because Isabella's controlled corporation is entitled to depreciate the automobile based upon the purchase price of $7,000. Under the related-party provision, Isabella's $2,000 gain is ordinary income. ■

INTANGIBLE DRILLING COSTS

Taxpayers may elect to either *expense or capitalize* intangible drilling and development costs for oil, gas, or geothermal properties.[53] **Intangible drilling and development costs (IDC)** include operator (one who holds a working or operating interest in any tract or parcel of land) expenditures for wages, fuel, repairs, hauling, and supplies. These expenditures must be incident to and necessary for the drilling of wells and preparation of wells for production. In most instances, taxpayers elect to expense IDC to maximize tax deductions during drilling.

[51] § 291(a)(1).
[52] § 1239.
[53] § 263(c).

Intangible drilling and development costs are subject to § 1254 recapture when the property is disposed of. The gain on the disposition of the property is subject to recapture as ordinary income.

LO.13

Describe and apply the reporting procedures for §§ 1231, 1245, and 1250.

Reporting Procedures

Noncapital gains and losses are reported on Form 4797, Sales of Business Property. Before filling out Form 4797, however, Form 4684, Casualties and Thefts, Part B, must be completed to determine whether any casualties will enter into the § 1231 computation procedure. Recall that gains from § 1231 asset casualties may be recaptured by § 1245 or § 1250. These gains will not appear on Form 4684. The § 1231 gains and nonpersonal use long-term capital gains are netted against § 1231 losses and nonpersonal use long-term capital losses on Form 4684 to determine if there is a net gain to transfer to Form 4797, Part I.

ETHICAL CONSIDERATIONS

Flow-Through 25% Gain

While preparing an individual Form 1040, the tax return preparer examines a Schedule K–1 from a partnership in which the taxpayer has an ownership interest. The first page of the Schedule K–1 indicates a $23,000 § 1231 gain. On the second page of the K–1, the tax return preparer finds the following statement: "$12,300 of the $23,000 § 1231 gain reported on page 1 of this Schedule K–1 is unrecaptured § 1250 gain (25% gain)." The tax return preparer has no idea what this phrase means and does nothing with it in preparing the individual return. Could this affect the tax computation on the individual return? What is the tax return preparer's responsibility for resolving his uncertainty?

LO.14

Identify tax planning opportunities arising from the sale or exchange of capital assets and avoid pitfalls associated with the recapture provisions.

Tax Planning Considerations

IMPORTANCE OF CAPITAL ASSET STATUS

Why is capital asset status important? Capital asset status enables the taxpayer to be eligible for the alternative tax on net capital gain. For a taxpayer in the 25, 28, 33, or 35 percent regular tax bracket, a 15 percent rate is available on assets held longer than one year. For a taxpayer in the 10 or 15 percent regular tax bracket, a 5 percent rate is available on assets held longer than one year. Thus, individuals who can receive income in the form of long-term capital gains or qualified dividend income have an advantage over taxpayers who cannot receive income in these forms.

Capital asset status is also important because capital gains must be offset by capital losses. If a net capital loss results, the maximum deduction is $3,000 per year.

Consequently, capital gains and losses must be segregated from other types of gains and losses and must be reported separately on Schedule D of Form 1040.

PLANNING FOR CAPITAL ASSET STATUS

It is important to keep in mind that capital asset status often is a question of objective evidence. Thus, property that is not a capital asset to one party may qualify as a capital asset to another party.

EXAMPLE 70

Diane, a real estate dealer, transfers by gift a tract of land to Jeff, her son. The land was recorded as part of Diane's inventory (it was held for resale) and was therefore not a capital asset to her. Jeff, however, treats the land as an investment. The land is a capital asset in

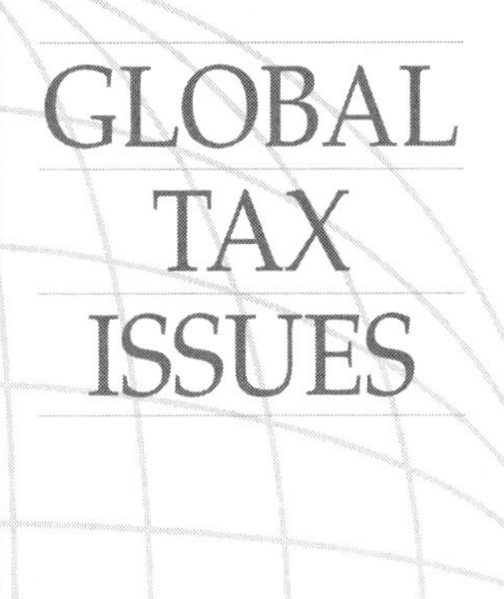

Capital Gain Treatment in the United States and Other Countries

The United States currently requires a very complex tax calculation when taxable income includes net long-term capital gain. However, the alternative tax on net long-term capital gain can generate tax savings even when the taxpayer is in the lowest regular tax bracket (10 percent) because there is an alternative tax rate of 5 percent. Many other countries do not have an alternative tax rate on long-term capital gains. Instead, those gains are taxed the same as other income. Consequently, even though the U.S. system is complex, it may be preferable because of the lower tax rates and because the lower rates are available to taxpayers in all tax brackets.

Jeff's hands, and any later taxable disposition of the property by him will yield a capital gain or loss. ■

If proper planning is carried out, even a dealer may obtain long-term capital gain treatment on the sale of the type of property normally held for resale.

EXAMPLE 71

Jim, a real estate dealer, segregates tract A from the real estate he regularly holds for resale and designates the property as being held for investment purposes. The property is not advertised for sale and is disposed of several years later. The negotiations for the subsequent sale were initiated by the purchaser and not by Jim. Under these circumstances, it would appear that any gain or loss from the sale of tract A should be a capital gain or loss.[54] ■

When a business is being sold, one of the major decisions usually concerns whether a portion of the sales price is for goodwill. For the seller, goodwill generally represents the disposition of a capital asset. Goodwill has no basis and represents a residual portion of the selling price that cannot be allocated reasonably to the known assets. The amount of goodwill thus represents capital gain.

From a legal perspective, the buyer may prefer that the residual portion of the purchase price be allocated to a covenant not to compete (a promise that the seller will not compete against the buyer by conducting a business similar to the one that the buyer has purchased). Both purchased goodwill and a covenant not to compete are § 197 intangibles. Thus, both must be capitalized and can be amortized over a 15-year statutory period.

To the seller, a covenant produces ordinary income. Thus, the seller would prefer that the residual portion of the selling price be allocated to goodwill—a capital asset. If the buyer does not need the legal protection provided by a covenant, the buyer is neutral regarding whether the residual amount be allocated to a covenant or to goodwill. Since the seller would receive a tax advantage from labeling the residual amount as goodwill, the buyer should factor this into the negotiation of the purchase price.

EXAMPLE 72

Marcia is buying Jack's dry cleaning proprietorship. An appraisal of the assets indicates that a reasonable purchase price would exceed the value of the known assets by $30,000. If the purchase contract does not specify the nature of the $30,000, the amount will be for goodwill, and Jack will have a long-term capital gain of $30,000. Marcia will have a 15-year

[54] *Toledo, Peoria & Western Railroad Co.*, 35 TCM 1663, T.C.Memo. 1976–366.

amortizable $30,000 asset. If Marcia is paying the extra $30,000 to prevent Jack from conducting another dry cleaning business in the area (a covenant not to compete), Jack will have $30,000 of ordinary income. Marcia will have a $30,000 deduction over the statutory 15-year amortization period rather than over the actual life of the covenant (e.g., 5 years). ■

EFFECT OF CAPITAL ASSET STATUS IN TRANSACTIONS OTHER THAN SALES

The nature of an asset (capital or ordinary) is important in determining the tax consequences that result when a sale or exchange occurs. It may, however, be just as significant in circumstances other than a taxable sale or exchange. When a capital asset is disposed of, the result is not always a capital gain or loss. Rather, in general, the disposition must be a sale or exchange. Collection of a debt instrument having a basis less than the face value results in a capital gain if the debt instrument is a capital asset. The collection is a sale or exchange. Sale of the debt shortly before the due date for collection will produce a capital gain.[55] If selling the debt in such circumstances could produce a capital gain but collecting could not, the consistency of what constitutes a capital gain or loss would be frustrated. Another illustration of the sale or exchange principle involves a donation of certain appreciated property to a qualified charity. Recall that in certain circumstances, the measure of the charitable contribution is fair market value when the property, if sold, would have yielded a long-term capital gain [refer to Chapter 10 and the discussion of § 170(e)].

EXAMPLE 73

Sharon wants to donate a tract of unimproved land (basis of $40,000 and fair market value of $200,000) held for the required long-term holding period to State University (a qualified charitable organization). However, Sharon currently is under audit by the IRS for capital gains she reported on certain real estate transactions during an earlier tax year. Although Sharon is not a licensed real estate broker, the IRS agent conducting the audit is contending that she has achieved dealer status by virtue of the number and frequency of the real estate transactions she has conducted. Under these circumstances, Sharon would be well-advised to postpone the donation to State University until her status is clarified. If she has achieved dealer status, the unimproved land may be inventory (refer to Example 71 for another possible result), and Sharon's charitable contribution deduction would be limited to $40,000. If not, and if the land is held as an investment, Sharon's deduction is $200,000 (the fair market value of the property). ■

STOCK SALES

The following rules apply in determining the date of a stock sale:

- The date the sale is executed is the date of the sale. The execution date is the date the broker completes the transaction on the stock exchange.
- The settlement date is the date the cash or other property is paid to the seller of the stock. This date is *not* relevant in determining the date of sale.

EXAMPLE 74

Lupe, a cash basis taxpayer, sells stock that results in a gain. The sale was executed on December 31, 2004. The settlement date is January 3, 2005. The date of sale is December 31, 2004 (the execution date). The holding period for the stock sold ends with the execution date. ■

[55] § 1271(b).

MAXIMIZING BENEFITS

Ordinary losses generally are preferable to capital losses because of the limitations imposed on the deductibility of net capital losses and the requirement that capital losses be used to offset capital gains. The taxpayer may be able to convert what would otherwise have been capital loss to ordinary loss. For example, business (but not nonbusiness) bad debts, losses from the sale or exchange of small business investment company stock, and losses from the sale or exchange of small business company stock all result in ordinary losses.[56]

Although capital losses can be carried over indefinitely, *indefinite* becomes definite when a taxpayer dies. Any loss carryovers not used by the taxpayer are permanently lost. That is, no tax benefit can be derived from the carryovers subsequent to death.[57] Therefore, the potential benefit of carrying over capital losses diminishes when dealing with older taxpayers.

It is usually beneficial to spread gains over more than one taxable year. In some cases, this can be accomplished through the installment sales method of accounting.

YEAR-END PLANNING

The following general rules can be applied for timing the recognition of capital gains and losses near the end of a taxable year:

- If the taxpayer already has recognized more than $3,000 of capital loss, sell assets to generate capital gain equal to the excess of the capital loss over $3,000.

EXAMPLE 75

Kevin has already incurred a $7,000 STCL. Kevin should generate $4,000 of capital gain. The gain will offset $4,000 of the loss. The remaining loss of $3,000 can be deducted against ordinary income. ■

- If the taxpayer already has recognized capital gain, sell assets to generate capital loss equal to the capital gain. The gain will not be taxed, and the loss will be fully *deductible* against the gain.
- Generally, if the taxpayer has a choice between recognizing short-term capital gain or long-term capital gain, long-term capital gain should be recognized because it has the lower tax rate.

TIMING OF § 1231 GAIN

Although §§ 1245 and 1250 recapture much of the gain from the disposition of business property, sometimes § 1231 gain is still substantial. For instance, land held as a business asset will generate either § 1231 gain or § 1231 loss. If the taxpayer already has a capital loss for the year, the sale of land at a gain should be postponed so that the net § 1231 gain is not netted against the capital loss. The capital loss deduction will therefore be maximized for the current tax year, and the capital loss carryforward (if any) may be offset against the gain when the land is sold. If the taxpayer already has a § 1231 loss, § 1231 gains might be postponed to maximize the ordinary loss deduction this year. However, the carryforward of unrecaptured § 1231 losses will make the § 1231 gain next year an ordinary gain.

EXAMPLE 76

Mark has a $2,000 net STCL for 2005. He could sell business land held 27 months for a $3,000 § 1231 gain. He will have no other capital gains and losses or § 1231 gains and losses in 2005 or 2006. He has no nonrecaptured § 1231 losses from prior years. Mark is in the 28% tax bracket in 2005 and will be in the 25% bracket in 2006. If he sells the land in 2005, he will

[56]§§ 166(d), 1242, and 1244. Refer to the discussion in Chapter 7.

[57]Rev.Rul. 74–175, 1974–1 C.B. 52.

have a \$1,000 net LTCG (\$3,000 § 1231 gain – \$2,000 STCL) and will pay a tax of \$150 (\$1,000 × 15%). If Mark sells the land in 2006, he will have a 2005 tax savings of \$560 (\$2,000 capital loss deduction × 28% tax rate on ordinary income). In 2006, he will pay tax of \$450 (\$3,000 × 15%). By postponing the sale for a year, Mark will have the use of \$710 (\$560 + \$150). ■

EXAMPLE 77

Beth has a \$15,000 § 1231 loss in 2005. She could sell business equipment held 30 months for a \$20,000 § 1231 gain and a \$12,000 § 1245 gain. Beth is in the 28% tax bracket in 2005 and will be in the 25% bracket in 2006. She has no nonrecaptured § 1231 losses from prior years. If she sells the equipment in 2005, she will have a \$5,000 net § 1231 gain and \$12,000 of ordinary gain. Her tax would be \$4,110 [(\$5,000 § 1231 gain × 15%) + (\$12,000 ordinary gain × 28%)].

If Beth postpones the equipment sale until 2006, she would have a 2005 ordinary loss of \$15,000 and tax savings of \$4,200 (\$15,000 × 28%). In 2006, she would have \$5,000 of § 1231 gain (the 2005 § 1231 loss carries over and recaptures \$15,000 of the 2006 § 1231 gain as ordinary income) and \$27,000 of ordinary gain. Her tax would be \$7,500 [(\$5,000 § 1231 gain × 15%) + (\$27,000 ordinary gain × 25%)]. By postponing the equipment sale, Beth has the use of \$8,310 (\$4,200 + \$4,110). ■

TIMING OF RECAPTURE

Since recapture is usually not triggered until the property is sold or disposed of, it may be possible to plan for recapture in low-bracket or loss years. If a taxpayer has net operating loss carryovers that are about to expire, the recognition of ordinary income from recapture may be advisable to absorb the loss carryovers.

EXAMPLE 78

Ahmad has a \$15,000 net operating loss carryover that will expire this year. He owns a machine that he plans to sell in the early part of next year. The expected gain of \$17,000 from the sale of the machine will be recaptured as ordinary income under § 1245. Ahmad sells the machine before the end of this year and offsets \$15,000 of the ordinary income against the net operating loss carryover. ■

POSTPONING AND SHIFTING RECAPTURE

It is also possible to postpone recapture or to shift the burden of recapture to others. For example, recapture is avoided upon the disposition of a § 1231 asset if the taxpayer replaces the property by entering into a like-kind exchange. In this instance, recapture potential is merely carried over to the newly acquired property (refer to Example 66).

Recapture can be shifted to others through the gratuitous transfer of § 1245 or § 1250 property to family members. A subsequent sale of such property by the donee will trigger recapture to the donee rather than the donor (refer to Example 63). This procedure would be advisable only if the donee is in a lower income tax bracket than the donor.

AVOIDING RECAPTURE

The immediate expensing election (§ 179) is subject to § 1245 recapture. If the election is not made, the § 1245 recapture potential will accumulate more slowly (refer to Chapter 8). Since using the immediate expense deduction complicates depreciation and book accounting for the affected asset, not taking the deduction may make sense even though the time value of money might indicate it should be taken.

KEY TERMS

Additional depreciation, 14–41
Alternative tax, 14–25
Capital asset, 14–4
Capital gains, 14–3
Capital losses, 14–3
Collectibles, 14–24
Franchise, 14–13
Holding period, 14–15
Intangible drilling and development costs (IDC), 14–49
Lessee, 14–15
Lessor, 14–15
Long-term nonpersonal use capital assets, 14–33
Net capital gain (NCG), 14–21
Net capital loss (NCL), 14–26
Options, 14–10
Original issue discount (OID), 14–10
Patent, 14–11
Qualified dividend income, 14–24
Related party, 14–49
Sale or exchange, 14–8
Section 1231 gains and losses, 14–31
Section 1231 lookback, 14–35
Section 1231 property, 14–31
Section 1245 property, 14–40
Section 1245 recapture, 14–39
Section 1250 property, 14–41
Section 1250 recapture, 14–41
Short sale, 14–17
Unrecaptured § 1250 gain, 14–21

PROBLEM MATERIALS

West Federal Taxation

Discussion Questions

Issue ID

1. Meredith, the owner of a sole proprietorship, is selling the assets of her business. The buyer is willing to pay $1,000 for various supplies (copy paper, folders, toner cartridges, etc.). Meredith deducted the $3,000 cost of these supplies as they were acquired. What issues does Meredith face from the sale of these supplies?

2. What broad class of assets is excluded from the capital asset category?

3. Martha, a real estate dealer, pays $25,000 to purchase a one-year option on 40 acres of farmland. She intends to exercise the option and purchase the farmland for $800,000 if she is able to get the property rezoned for a single-family residential development. The rezoning effort is unsuccessful, and the option expires. How should Martha treat the $25,000?

Issue ID

4. Reginald was the tenant in a rental house. The landlord sold the house and paid Reginald $4,000 to cancel the lease and move out eight months before the lease was scheduled to expire. What issues does Reginald face as a result of this transaction?

5. Stanley made a short sale of securities. Four months later he closed the short sale using substantially identical securities he had owned for two years at the date of the short sale. Stanley had a gain on the transaction. This was a "short sale against the box." Does Stanley have a short- or long-term capital gain? Explain.

Issue ID

6. Juan purchased corporate stock for $10,000 on April 10, 2003. On July 14, 2005, when the stock was worth $7,000, he gave it to his son, Miguel. What has to happen to the value of the property while Miguel holds it if Miguel is to tack Juan's holding period on to his own holding period?

Issue ID

7. Near the end of 2005, Byron realizes that he has a net short-term capital loss of $13,000 for the year. Byron has taxable income (not including the loss) of $123,000 and is single. He owns numerous stocks that could be sold for a long-term capital gain. What should he do before the end of 2005?

8. A regular corporation has a net short-term capital loss for 2005 and positive taxable income from operations. What may the corporation do with the net short-term capital loss?

9. If an asset becomes a § 1231 asset once it has been held for more than one year, what is it during that first year?

10. The taxpayer owns a Thoroughbred racehorse and is in the business of horse racing. The horse was purchased when it was one year old and has been owned by the taxpayer for over two years. What is the tax status of the racehorse?

11. Personal use property casualty gains exceed personal use property casualty losses. What is the nature of the net gain?

Issue ID

12. Examine Concept Summary 14–6. Assume that there is a net § 1231 gain of $45,000 for the year. Could some or all of the gain be treated as ordinary income?

Issue ID

13. Sally lives in an area that was hit hard by a hurricane. She has correctly determined that she has a $15,000 business property long-term casualty loss and an $11,000 business property long-term casualty gain. What tax issues must Sally deal with?

14. Does § 1231 have any effect on whether *realized* gain or loss is *recognized?*

15. Tangible personal property held more than one year and used in a trade or business is disposed of at a loss as a result of a condemnation. Is the loss subject to § 1231 treatment?

Issue ID

16. An individual taxpayer had a net § 1231 loss in 2002 and a net § 1231 gain in 2003, 2004, and 2005. What factors will influence whether any of the 2005 net § 1231 gain will be treated as long-term capital gain?

17. A depreciable business machine has been owned for four years and is no longer useful to the taxpayer. What would have to be true for the disposition of the machine to generate at least some § 1231 gain?

Issue ID

18. Sylvia owns two items of business equipment. They were both purchased in 2001 for $100,000, both have a seven-year recovery period, and both have an adjusted basis of $37,490. Sylvia is considering selling these assets in 2005. One of them is worth $40,000, and the other is worth $23,000. Since both items were used in her business, Sylvia simply assumes that the loss on one will be offset against the gain from the other and the net gain or loss will increase or reduce her business income. Is she correct?

19. If depreciable equipment used in a business is sold at a recognized gain on July 10, 2005, and it was purchased on August 21, 2004, does § 1245 depreciation recapture apply to the asset?

Issue ID

20. A professional football player's contract is sold at a gain after it has been held for two years. What issues should the team consider in determining the nature of this gain?

21. A farmer's silo is destroyed by a tornado, but is insured for its replacement cost. Consequently, the farmer has a $40,000 gain after receiving the insurance proceeds. The silo is not replaced because the farmer spends the insurance proceeds on additional cattle. What is the nature of the gain if the silo originally cost $100,000 three years ago and had an adjusted basis of $60,000 at the time of its destruction?

22. Residential real estate is sold at a gain. In what year(s) would it have to have been acquired in order for some of the gain to be recaptured as ordinary income by § 1250?

23. Residential real estate was acquired in 1992. What is the maximum amount of unrecaptured § 1250 gain from the disposition of the real estate if the real estate is sold at a gain?

24. Nonresidential real estate was acquired in 2003. What is the maximum amount of unrecaptured § 1250 gain from the disposition of the real estate if the building is sold for a loss and the land is sold for a gain?

25. An individual taxpayer has $25,000 of § 1231 gain from the disposition of nonresidential real estate. Straight-line depreciation of $43,000 was deducted on the real estate. The taxpayer also has a § 1231 loss of $56,000 from the sale of equipment. How much of the § 1231 gain is taxed as unrecaptured § 1250 gain?

26. Abigail sells one § 1231 asset during the year at a gain of $45,000. The asset was depreciable real estate she had held for seven years. She wants to know what her maximum unrecaptured § 1250 gain might be.

27. An individual taxpayer receives tangible personal property by gift. The property had been depreciated by the donor and had a fair market value greater than the donor's adjusted basis at the date of the gift. Does the § 1245 depreciation recapture potential carry over from the donor to the donee?

28. An individual taxpayer receives tangible personal property by inheritance. The property had been depreciated by the decedent and had a fair market value greater than the decedent's adjusted basis at the date of the decedent's death. Does the § 1245 depreciation recapture potential carry over from the decedent to the beneficiary?

29. A corporation distributes a truck it has owned for three years to its sole shareholder. The shareholder will use the truck for personal use activity. The truck's fair market value at the time of the distribution is greater than its adjusted basis, but less than its original cost. Does the corporation recognize a gain? If so, what is the character of the gain?

30. A corporation distributes a truck it has owned for three years to its sole shareholder. The shareholder will use the truck for business activity. The truck's fair market value at the time of the distribution is greater than its adjusted basis, but less than its original cost. Does the corporation recognize a gain? If so, what is the character of the gain?

Problems

31. During the year, Eric had the four property transactions summarized below. Eric is a collector of antique automobiles and occasionally sells one to get funds to buy another. What are the amount and nature of the gain or loss from each of these transactions?

Property	Date Acquired	Date Sold	Adjusted Basis	Sale Price
Antique truck	06/18/97	05/23/05	$47,000	$35,000
Blue Growth Fund (100 shares)	12/23/99	11/22/05	12,000	23,000
Orange bonds	02/12/00	04/11/05	34,000	42,000*
Green stock (100 shares)	02/14/05	11/23/05	13,000	11,000

*The sale price included $750 of accrued interest income.

32. All of the following assets are held by Chuck, who is not in business. Which ones are capital assets?
    a. Ten shares of Green Motors common stock.
    b. A note Chuck received when he loaned $3,000 to a friend.
    c. Chuck's personal use automobile.
    d. A letter written by Abraham Lincoln that Chuck purchased at an auction. Chuck is a collector of Lincoln memorabilia.

Communications

33. Brenda Reynolds is a dealer in securities. She has spotted a fast-rising company and would like to buy and hold its stock for investment. The stock is currently selling for $145 per share, and Brenda thinks it will climb to $200 a share within two years. Brenda's co-workers have told her that there is "no way" she can get long-term capital gain treatment when she purchases stock because she is a securities dealer. Brenda has asked you to calculate her potential gain and tell her whether her co-workers are right. Draft a letter to Brenda responding to her request. Her address is 200 Morningside Drive, Hattiesburg, MS 39406.

34. Sue Ellen meets all the requirements of § 1237 (subdivided realty). In 2005, she begins selling lots and sells four separate lots to four different purchasers. She also sells two contiguous lots to another purchaser. The sale price of each lot is $20,000. Sue Ellen's basis for each lot is $15,000. Selling expenses are $500 per lot.

a. What are the realized and recognized gain?
b. Explain the nature of the gain (i.e., ordinary income or capital gain).
c. Would your answers change if, instead, the lots sold to the fifth purchaser were not contiguous? If so, how?

Decision Making

35. Sue has had a bad year with her investments. She lent a friend $3,700; the friend did not repay the loan when it was due, and then declared bankruptcy. The loan is totally uncollectible. Sue also was notified by her broker that the Willow corporate bonds she owned became worthless on October 13, 2005. She had purchased the bonds for $12,000 on November 10, 2004. Sue also had a $30,000 loss on the disposition of § 1244 corporate stock that she purchased several years ago. Sue is single.
a. What are the nature and amount of Sue's losses?
b. What is Sue's AGI for 2005 assuming she has $65,000 of ordinary gross income from sources other than those discussed above?
c. What are the nature and amount of Sue's loss carryforwards?

36. Celia was the owner of vacant land she was holding for investment. She paid $1 million for the land in 1998. Frank is an investor in vacant land. Fourteen months ago, Frank paid Celia $10,000 for a "right of first refusal" to purchase the land. The right of first refusal was valid for four years. The land was selected as the site of a new shopping center, and Celia was offered $4 million for the land. In its title search on the land, the buyer discovered Frank's right of first refusal and involved him in the purchase negotiations. Ultimately, Celia paid Frank $120,000 to give up his right of first refusal; she then sold the land to the buyer for $4,120,000. Celia has a marginal tax rate of 35%. What are the amount and nature of Celia's gain or loss from disposition of the land?

Decision Making

37. Mateen, an inventor, obtained a patent on a chemical process to clean old aluminum siding so that it can be easily repainted. Mateen has no tax basis in the patent. Mateen does not have the capital to begin manufacturing and selling this product, so he has done nothing with the patent since obtaining it two years ago. Now a group of individuals have approached him and offered two alternatives. Under one alternative, they will pay Mateen $600,000 (payable evenly over the next 15 years) for the exclusive right to manufacture and sell the product. Under the other, they will form a business and contribute capital to it to begin manufacturing and selling the product; Mateen will receive 20% of the company's shares of stock in exchange for all of his patent rights. Discuss which alternative is better for Mateen.

38. Freys, Inc., sells a 12-year franchise to Reynaldo. The franchise contains many restrictions on how Reynaldo may operate his store. For instance, Reynaldo cannot use less than Grade 10 Idaho potatoes, must fry the potatoes at a constant 410 degrees, dress store personnel in Freys-approved uniforms, and have a Freys sign that meets detailed specifications on size, color, and construction. When the franchise contract is signed, Reynaldo makes a noncontingent $60,000 payment to Freys. During the same year, Reynaldo pays Freys $30,000—14% of Reynaldo's sales. How does Freys treat each of these payments? How does Reynaldo treat each of the payments?

Issue ID

39. Tricia owns numerous office buildings. A major tenant of one of the buildings wished to cancel its lease because it was moving to another city. After lengthy negotiations, the tenant paid Tricia $50,000 to cancel its obligations under the lease. If the tenant had fulfilled the lease terms, Tricia would have received rent of $80,000. What factors should Tricia consider to determine the amount and character of her income from these circumstances?

40. Faleh exchanges a business copying machine for another copier in a § 1031 like-kind exchange. Faleh acquired the relinquished machine on March 1, 2002, and the exchange occurred on July 3, 2005. When does the holding period of the replacement machine begin?

41. Dennis sells short 100 shares of ARC stock at $20 per share on January 15, 2005. He buys 200 shares of ARC stock on April 1, 2005, at $25 per share. On May 2, 2005, he closes the short sale by delivering 100 of the shares purchased on April 1.
a. What are the amount and nature of Dennis's loss upon closing the short sale?
b. When does the holding period for the remaining 100 shares begin?
c. If Dennis sells (at $27 per share) the remaining 100 shares on January 20, 2006, what will be the nature of his gain or loss?

Communications

42. Elaine Case (single with no dependents) has the following transactions in 2005:

Adjusted gross income (exclusive of capital gains and losses)	$240,000
Long-term capital gain	22,000
Long-term capital loss	(5,000)
Short-term capital gain	19,000
Short-term capital loss	(23,000)

What is Elaine's net capital gain or loss? Draft a letter to Elaine describing how the net capital gain or loss will be treated on her tax return. Assume Elaine's income from other sources puts her in the 35% bracket. Elaine's address is 300 Ireland Avenue, Shepherdstown, WV 25443.

Communications

43. In 2005, Betty (head of household with three dependents) had an $18,000 loss from the sale of a personal residence. She also purchased from an individual inventor for $8,000 (and resold in two months for $7,000) a patent on a rubber bonding process. The patent had not yet been reduced to practice. Betty purchased the patent as an investment. Additionally, she had the following capital gains and losses from stock transactions:

Long-term capital loss	($ 3,000)
Long-term capital loss carryover from 2004	(12,000)
Short-term capital gain	21,000
Short-term capital loss	(6,000)

What is Betty's net capital gain or loss? Draft a letter to Betty explaining the tax treatment of the sale of her personal residence. Assume Betty's income from other sources puts her in the 35% bracket. Betty's address is 1120 West Street, Ashland, OR 97520.

Issue ID

44. Bridgette is known as the "doll lady." She started collecting dolls as a child, always received one or more dolls as gifts on her birthday, never sold any dolls, and eventually owned 600 dolls. She is retiring and moving to a small apartment and has decided to sell her collection. She lists the dolls on an Internet auction site and, to her great surprise, receives an offer from another doll collector of $45,000 for the entire collection. Bridgette sells the entire collection, except for five dolls that she purchased during the last year. She had owned all the dolls sold for more than a year. What tax factors should Bridgette consider in deciding how to report the sale?

45. Asok is a head of household with two dependent children. He has $55,000 in wages, a $13,000 short-term capital loss, and $3,200 of qualified dividend income during 2005. What is his adjusted gross income?

46. For 2005, Ruth has gross income of $8,300 and a $5,000 long-term capital loss; she claims the standard deduction. Ruth is 35 years old and single with three dependent children. How much of Ruth's $5,000 capital loss carries over to 2006?

47. Roy, age 56, is a single taxpayer with no dependents. He has $65,000 of wages, $2,000 of interest income, $1,300 of qualified dividend income, and a net long-term capital gain of $4,670. What is Roy's tax on taxable income for 2005?

48. Janine and Bill are married filing jointly and have 2005 taxable income of $87,000. The taxable income includes $5,000 of gain from a capital asset held more than five years, $2,100 of gain from a capital asset held six months, and $13,000 of gain from a capital asset held four years. What is the couple's tax on taxable income?

49. Mauve, Inc., has determined that its 2005 taxable income from operations is $455,000. Mauve sold a capital asset held 10 years for a loss of $45,000. What are Mauve's 2005 taxable income and the amount, if any, of its capital loss carryback and carryover?

Decision Making

50. Hsui, who is single, is the owner of a sole proprietorship. Two years ago, Hsui developed a process for preserving fresh fruit that gives the fruit a much longer shelf life. The process is not patented or copyrighted, but only Hsui knows how it works. Hsui has been approached by a company that would like to buy the process. Hsui insists that she receive a long-term employment contract with the acquiring company as well as

be paid for the rights to the process. The acquiring company offers Hsui a choice of two options: (1) $850,000 in cash for the process and a 10-year covenant not to compete at $45,000 per year or (2) $850,000 in cash for a 10-year covenant not to compete and $45,000 per year for 10 years in payment for the process. Which option should Hsui accept? What is the tax effect on the acquiring company of each approach?

Communications

51. A painting that Kwan Lee held for investment was destroyed in a flood. The painting was insured, and Kwan had a $20,000 gain from this casualty. He also had a $7,000 loss from an uninsured antique vase that was destroyed by the flood. The vase was also held for investment. Kwan had no other property transactions during the year and has no nonrecaptured § 1231 losses from prior years. Both the painting and the vase had been held more than one year when the flood occurred. Compute Kwan's net gain or loss and identify how it would be treated. Also, write a letter to Kwan explaining the nature of the gain or loss. Kwan's address is 2367 Meridian Road, Hannibal Point, MO 34901.

52. Vicki has the following net § 1231 results for each of the years shown. What would be the nature of the net gains in 2004 and 2005?

Tax Year	Net § 1231 Loss	Net § 1231 Gain
2000	$16,000	
2001	43,000	
2002	32,000	
2003		$41,000
2004		30,000
2005		39,000

Decision Making

53. Yoshida owns two parcels of business land (§ 1231 assets). One parcel can be sold at a loss of $30,000, and the other parcel can be sold at a gain of $40,000. Yoshida has no nonrecaptured § 1231 losses from prior years. The parcels could be sold at any time because potential purchasers are abundant. Yoshida has a $25,000 short-term capital loss carryover from a prior tax year and no capital assets that could be sold to generate long-term capital gains. Both the land parcels have been held more than one year. What should Yoshida do based upon these facts? (Assume tax rates are constant and ignore the present value of future cash flow.)

54. Gray Industries (a sole proprietorship) sold three § 1231 assets during 2005. Data on these property dispositions are as follows:

Asset	Cost	Acquired	Depreciation	Sold for	Sold on
Rack	$100,000	10/10/01	$60,000	$75,000	10/10/05
Forklift	35,000	10/16/02	23,000	5,000	10/10/05
Bin	87,000	03/12/04	34,000	60,000	10/10/05

a. Determine the amount and the character of the recognized gain or loss from the disposition of each asset.
b. Assuming Gray has no nonrecaptured net § 1231 losses from prior years, how much of the 2005 recognized gains is treated as capital gains?

55. Green Industries (a sole proprietorship) sold three § 1231 assets during 2005. Data on these property dispositions are as follows:

Asset	Cost	Acquired	Depreciation	Sold for	Sold on
Rack	$100,000	10/10/01	$60,000	$135,000	10/10/05
Forklift	35,000	10/16/02	23,000	5,000	10/10/05
Bin	87,000	03/12/04	34,000	60,000	10/10/05

a. Determine the amount and the character of the recognized gain or loss from the disposition of each asset.
b. Assuming Green has $5,000 nonrecaptured net § 1231 losses from the five prior years, how much of the 2005 recognized gains is treated as capital gains?

56. Magenta Industries (a sole proprietorship) sold three § 1231 assets during 2005. Data on these property dispositions are as follows:

Asset	Cost	Acquired	Depreciation	Sold for	Sold on
Rack	$110,000	10/10/02	$60,000	$55,000	10/10/05
Forklift	45,000	10/16/01	23,000	15,000	10/10/05
Bin	97,000	03/12/04	34,000	60,000	10/10/05

a. Determine the amount and the character of the recognized gain or loss from the disposition of each asset.
b. Assuming Magenta has $2,000 nonrecaptured net § 1231 losses from prior years, how much of the 2005 recognized gains is treated as capital gains?

57. On June 1, 2001, Sparrow Enterprises (not a corporation) acquired a retail store for $500,000 (with $100,000 being allocated to the land). The store was 39-year real property, and the straight-line cost recovery method was used. The property was sold on June 21, 2005, for $470,000.
a. Compute the cost recovery and adjusted basis for the store using Table 8–8 from Chapter 8.
b. What are the amount and nature of Sparrow's gain or loss from disposition of the store? What amount, if any, of the gain is unrecaptured § 1250 gain?

58. Dave is the sole proprietor of a trampoline shop. During 2005, the following transactions occurred:

- Unimproved land adjacent to the store was condemned by the city on February 1. The condemnation proceeds were $25,000. The land, acquired in 1983, had an allocable basis of $40,000. Dave has additional parking across the street and plans to use the condemnation proceeds to build his inventory.
- A truck used to deliver trampolines was sold on January 2 for $3,500. The truck was purchased on January 2, 2001, for $6,000. On the date of sale, the adjusted basis was $2,509.
- Dave sold an antique rowing machine at an auction. Net proceeds were $3,900. The rowing machine was purchased as used equipment 17 years ago for $5,200 and is fully depreciated.
- Dave sold an apartment building for $200,000 on September 1. The rental property was purchased on September 1, 2002, for $150,000 and was being depreciated over a 27.5-year life using the straight-line method. At the date of sale, the adjusted basis was $124,783.
- Dave's personal yacht was stolen on September 5. The yacht had been purchased in August at a cost of $25,000. The fair market value immediately preceding the theft was $20,000. Dave was insured for 50% of the original cost, and he received $12,500 on December 1.
- Dave sold a Buick on May 1 for $9,600. The vehicle had been used exclusively for personal purposes. It was purchased on September 1, 2001, for $20,800.
- Dave's trampoline stretching machine (owned two years) was stolen on May 5, but the business's insurance company will not pay any of the machine's value because Dave failed to pay the insurance premium. The machine had a fair market value of $8,000 and an adjusted basis of $6,000 at the time of theft.
- Dave had AGI of $402,000 from sources other than those described above.
- Dave has no nonrecaptured § 1231 lookback losses.

a. For each transaction, what are the amount and nature of recognized gain or loss?
b. What is Dave's 2005 AGI?

Communications

59. On January 1, 1996, Cora Hassant acquired depreciable real property for $50,000. She used straight-line depreciation to compute the asset's cost recovery. The asset was sold for $89,000 on January 3, 2005, when its adjusted basis was $38,000.
    a. What are the amount and nature of the gain if the real property was residential?
    b. Cora is curious about how the recapture rules differ for residential rental real estate acquired in 1986 and for residential rental real estate acquired in 1987 and thereafter. Write a letter to Cora explaining the differences. Her address is 2345 Westridge Street #23, Homer, MT 67342.

60. In 2005, Jeremiah sold depreciable equipment used in his business for a gain of $45,000. Jeremiah had taken $33,000 of depreciation on the equipment, and his brother, Adam, had taken $27,000 of depreciation on the equipment before he gave it to Jeremiah as a gift. What is the nature of Jeremiah's gain from the disposition of the equipment?

61. In 2005, Jerry sold depreciable equipment used in his business for a gain of $45,000. He had received the equipment as a bequest from his brother, Addley. Jerry had taken $33,000 of depreciation on the equipment, and Addley had taken $27,000 of depreciation on the equipment before he died. What is the nature of Jerry's gain from the disposition of the equipment?

62. In 2005, Jerat donated to charity depreciable equipment used in his business. If Jerat had sold the equipment, he would have had a gain of $45,000. The equipment was worth $67,000 at the time of its contribution. Jerat had taken $33,000 of depreciation on the equipment. What is the amount of Jerat's charitable contribution from the donation of the equipment?

63. In 2005, Cicely sold depreciable equipment used in her business for a gain of $45,000. Cicely had taken $33,000 of depreciation on this equipment. She had also taken $27,000 of depreciation on like-kind equipment she had traded in on the equipment she sold this year. What is the nature of Cicely's gain from the disposition of the equipment?

64. Emily is the sole shareholder of Brown Corporation. Brown has a zero basis for a printing machine that Emily would like to use in a personal activity. The machine's fair market value is $4,500. Brown distributes the machine as a property dividend to Emily. Brown has accumulated earnings and profits of $3 million. What are the amount and nature of the gain recognized by Brown? What are the amount and nature of the distribution received by Emily?

65. Eli is the sole shareholder of Blue Corporation. Blue has a zero basis for a printing machine that Eli would like to use in another business he owns. The machine's fair market value is $45,000. Blue sells the machine to Eli for $45,000. What are the amount and nature of the gain recognized by Blue? What is the tax basis of the machine for Eli?

Decision Making

66. Jay sold three items of business equipment for a total of $300,000. None of the equipment was appraised to determine its value. Jay's cost and adjusted basis for the assets are as follows:

Asset	Cost	Adjusted Basis
Skidder	$230,000	$ 40,000
Driller	120,000	60,000
Platform	620,000	–0–
Total	$970,000	$100,000

Jay has been unable to establish the fair market values of the three assets. All he can determine is that combined they were worth $300,000 to the buyer in this arm's length transaction. How should Jay allocate the sales price and figure the gain or loss on the sale of the three assets?

Cumulative Problems

Tax Return Problem

67. Sue Lowe lives at 1310 Meadow Lane, Lima, OH 23412, and her Social Security number is 312–55–8000. Sue is single and has a 10-year-old son, Kania. His Social Security number is 480–01–9030. Kania lives with Sue, and she fully supports him. During 2004, Sue spent $2,700 on qualifying support for Kania at the Happy Daze Child Care Center, 18 Oak Lane, Lima, OH 23410. The center's identifying number is 38–6933367.

Sue owns the Lowe Enterprises sole proprietorship, a data processing service (38–1234567), which is located at 456 Hill Street, Lima, OH 23401. The business activity code is 514210. Her 2004 Form 1040, Schedule C for Lowe Enterprises shows revenues of $155,000, office expenses of $46,759, employee salaries of $23,000, employee payroll taxes of $1,760, meals and entertainment expenses (before the 50% reduction) of $18,000, and rent expense of $44,000. The rent expense includes payments related to renting an office ($32,000) and payments related to renting various equipment ($12,000). There is no depreciation because all depreciable equipment owned has been fully depreciated in previous years. No fringe benefits are provided to the employee. Sue personally purchases health insurance on herself and Kania. The premiums are $3,000 per year.

Sue has an extensive stock portfolio and has prepared the following analysis:

Stock	Number of Shares	Date Purchased	Date Sold	Per Share Cost	Per Share Selling Price	Total Dividends
Blue	10	10/18/03	10/11/04	$80	$72	$ 30
Green	30	10/11/95	10/11/04	33	47	70
Purple	15	3/10/04	8/11/04	62	33	45
Yellow	100	4/11/92	8/02/04	18	46	100
Gold	35	7/12/03	10/11/04	7	12	0
White	100	10/11/03		82		100

Note: The per share cost includes commissions, and the per share selling price is net of commissions. Also, the dividends are the actual dividends received in 2004.

Sue had $800 of interest income from State of Ohio bonds and $600 of interest income on her Lima Savings Bank account. She also received $5,000 of alimony payments.

Sue itemizes her deductions and had the following items, which may be relevant to her return:

Item	Amount	Comment
Unreimbursed medical expenses for Sue and Kania (all for visits to doctors)	$1,786	Does not include health insurance premiums.
State income taxes paid	1,830	
Real property taxes on personal residence	3,230	
Interest paid on home mortgage (Form 1098)	8,137	The loan is secured by the residence and was incurred when the home was purchased.
Charitable contributions	940	Cash paid to Sue's church.
Sales taxes	619	Amount per sales tax table.

Sue made a $5,000 estimated Federal income tax payment, does not wish any of her taxes to finance presidential elections, has no foreign bank accounts or trusts, and wishes any refund to be applied against her 2005 taxes.

Compute Sue's net tax payable or refund due for 2004. If you use tax forms for your computations, you will need Forms 1040, 2441, 4952, and 8812 and Schedules A, B, C, D, and SE. Suggested software: TurboTax.

Tax Return Problem

68. Justin Stone was an employee of DataCare Services, Inc. His salary was $187,000 through November 10, 2004, when he was laid off. He received $14,000 of unemployment compensation from November 11, 2004, through December 31, 2004. The appropriate amount was withheld from his salary for Social Security and Medicare. Justin lives at 112 Green Road, Sandusky, ID 45623. His Social Security number is 567–89–1234. Justin owned an apartment building until November 22, 2004, when he sold it for $400,000. For 2004, he had rent revenue of $30,000. He incurred and paid expenses as follows: $4,568 of repairs, $12,000 of mortgage interest, and $1,000 of miscellaneous expenses. He had purchased the building on January 2, 1998, for $125,000. The building generated an operating profit each year that Justin owned it.

Other information follows:

- On November 22, 2004, Justin sold for $14,000 equipment that had been used for repairing various items in the apartments. The equipment was purchased for $25,000 on July 10, 1997, and was fully depreciated prior to 2004.
- Justin has no unrecaptured § 1231 losses from prior years.
- Justin is age 38, single, divorced, and has custody of his nine-year-old son, Flint. Justin provides more than 50% of Flint's support. Flint's Social Security number is 098–77–6543.
- Justin had $5,000 interest income from Blue Corporation bonds.
- Justin had $3,000 interest income from a State Bank certificate of deposit.
- Justin had a $2,000 5%/15% long-term capital gain distribution from the Brown Stock Investment Fund.
- Justin had the following itemized deductions: $5,600 real estate taxes on his home; $8,900 mortgage interest on his home; $760 charitable contributions (all in cash, properly documented, and no single contribution exceeded $25); $2,300 state income tax withholding during 2004; $2,000 state estimated income tax payments during 2004; $2,600 sales taxes paid.
- Justin does not wish to donate to the Presidential Election Campaign Fund.
- He had $15,000 of Federal income tax withholding during 2004 and made total Federal estimated income tax payments of $95,000 during 2004.

Compute Justin's 2004 net tax payable or refund due. If you use tax forms for your computations, you will need Form 1040 and Schedules A, B, D, and E. You will also need Forms 4562 and 4797, but ignore Form 6251. Suggested software: TurboTax.

Research Problems

Note: Solutions to Research Problems can be prepared by using the ***RIA Checkpoint® Student Edition*** *online research product, which is available to accompany this text. It is also possible to prepare solutions to the Research Problems by using tax research materials found in a standard tax library.*

Communications

Research Problem 1. Clean Corporation runs a chain of dry cleaners. Borax is used heavily in Clean's dry cleaning process and has been in short supply several times in the past. Clean Corporation buys a controlling interest in Dig Corporation—a borax mining concern. Clean's sole reason for purchasing the Dig stock is to assure Clean of a continuous supply of borax if another shortage develops. Although borax must be refined before it is usable for dry cleaning purposes, a well-established commodities market exists for trading unrefined borax for refined borax. After owning the Dig stock for several years, Clean sells the stock at a loss because Dig is in difficult financial straits. Clean no longer needs to own Dig because Clean has obtained an alternative source of borax. What is the nature of Clean's loss on the disposition of the Dig Corporation stock? Write a letter to the controller, Salvio Guitterez, that contains your advice and prepare a memo for the tax files. The mailing address of Clean Corporation is 4455 Whitman Way, San Mateo, CA 44589.

Research Problem 2. Walter is both a real estate developer and the owner and manager of residential rental real estate. Walter is retiring and is going to sell both the land he is holding for future development and the rental properties he owns. Straight-line depreciation was used to depreciate the rental real estate. The rental properties will be sold at a substantial loss, and the development property will be sold at a substantial gain. What is the nature of these gains and losses?

Partial list of research aids:
§§ 1221 and 1231.
Zane R. Tollis, 65 TCM 1951, T.C.Memo. 1993–63.

Internet Activity

Use the tax resources of the Internet to address the following question. Do not restrict your search to the World Wide Web, but include a review of newsgroups and general reference materials, practitioner sites and resources, primary sources of the tax law, chat rooms and discussion groups, and other opportunities.

Research Problem 3. Summarize tax planning strategies related to each of the following topics that are presented on the Internet by tax advisers looking for clients:

a. A strategy for maximizing gains that are eligible for the 5%/15% alternative tax rate rather than the 25% rate.
b. A strategy for maximizing gains that are eligible for the 5%/15% alternative tax rate rather than the 28% rate.

Alternative Minimum Tax

LEARNING OBJECTIVES

After completing Chapter 15, you should be able to:

LO.1
Explain the rationale for the alternative minimum tax (AMT).

LO.2
Understand the formula for computing the AMT for individuals.

LO.3
Identify the adjustments made in calculating the AMT.

LO.4
Identify the tax preferences that are included in calculating the AMT.

LO.5
Apply the formula for computing the AMT and illustrate Form 6251.

LO.6
Describe the role of the AMT credit in the alternative minimum tax structure.

LO.7
Understand the basic features of the corporate AMT.

LO.8
Identify tax planning opportunities to minimize the AMT.

http://wft.swlearning.com

OUTLINE

LO.1

Explain the rationale for the alternative minimum tax (AMT).

Bob and Carol are unmarried individuals who work for the same employer and have the same amount of gross income and the same amount of deductions. Bob's tax return is prepared by Adam, and Carol's tax return is prepared by Eve. While discussing their tax liability one day at lunch, Carol is dismayed to learn that she paid $15,000 more in Federal income taxes than Bob did for the tax year. Carol meets with Eve that evening. Eve reviews Carol's tax return and assures her that her tax liability was properly calculated.

The above events raise a number of interesting questions for Bob and Carol that can be answered after completing this chapter. Why didn't Bob and Carol have the same tax liability? Were both tax returns properly prepared? Should Carol consider replacing her tax return preparer Eve with Adam? Is it possible and/or desirable for Carol to file an amended return? Should Bob do anything?

The tax law contains many incentives that are intended to influence the economic and social behavior of taxpayers (refer to Chapter 1). Some taxpayers have been able to take advantage of enough of these incentives to avoid or minimize any liability for Federal income tax. Although these taxpayers were reducing taxes legally, Congress became concerned about the inequity that results when taxpayers with substantial economic incomes can avoid paying any income tax. Such inequity undermines respect for the entire tax system.[1] To attempt to alleviate this inequity, the **alternative minimum tax (AMT)** was enacted as a backup to the regular income tax.

The individual AMT is discussed in the first part of this chapter. The corporate AMT is similar to the individual AMT, but differs in several important ways. Details of the corporate AMT are presented in the last part of the chapter.

[1]*General Explanation of the Tax Reform Act of 1986 ("Blue Book")*, prepared by The Staff of the Joint Committee on Taxation, May 4, 1987, H.R. 3838, 99th Cong., pp. 432–433.

THE AMT: FROM 155 TO 33 MILLION

Sometimes the law changes in response to the demands of society (e.g., raising the legal drinking age to 21). On other occasions, the law is changed to prevent or reduce certain perceived abuses. Such was the case when the AMT was enacted in 1969. The identifiable perceived abuse was that 155 individual taxpayers had zero Federal income tax liability despite having incomes in excess of $200,000.

The original idea behind the AMT was one of fairness, based on the premise that taxpayers with significant economic income should pay at least a minimum amount of tax. That same concept of fairness later led Nina Olsen, the IRS's Taxpayer Advocate, to identify the expanding scope of the AMT as the number one problem facing taxpayers that needs to be legislatively addressed.

What has caused this shift in what is deemed fair? The idea that taxpayers with significant economic income should pay at least a minimum amount of tax has not changed. What is new is the number of taxpayers subject to the AMT—an estimated 33 million taxpayers in 2010 if the law is not changed. Thus, a tax that was perceived as fair when it affected only a "few" now is perceived as unfair because it affects "many."

SOURCE: Adapted from Catina Downey-Stroble, "Alternative Minimum Tax: Freedom and Taxes for All," *Disclosures*, May/June 2004, pp. 7 and 8.

LO.2

Understand the formula for computing the AMT for individuals.

Individual Alternative Minimum Tax

AMT FORMULA FOR ALTERNATIVE MINIMUM TAXABLE INCOME (AMTI)

The AMT is separate from, but parallel to, the regular income tax system.[2] Most income and expense items are treated the same way for both regular income tax and AMT purposes. For example, a taxpayer's salary is included in computing taxable income and is also included in alternative minimum taxable income (AMTI). Alimony paid is allowed as a deduction *for* AGI for both regular income tax and AMT purposes. Certain itemized deductions, such as charitable contributions and gambling losses, are allowed for both regular income tax and AMT purposes.

On the other hand, some income and expense items are treated differently for regular income tax and AMT purposes. For example, interest income on bonds issued by state, county, or local governments is *excluded* in computing taxable income. However, interest on such bonds is *included* in computing AMTI if the bonds are private activity bonds. The deduction for personal and dependency exemptions is *allowed* for regular income tax purposes, but is *disallowed* for AMT purposes.

In other cases, certain items are considered in both the regular income tax and AMT computations, but the amounts are different. For example, the completed contract method can be used to report income from some long-term contracts for regular income tax purposes, but the percentage of completion method is required for AMT purposes. Thus, the amount of income included in taxable income will differ from the amount included in AMTI. Depreciation is allowed as a deduction for both regular income tax and AMT purposes, but the *amount* of the regular

[2]§ 55.

■ **FIGURE 15–1**
Alternative Minimum Taxable Income (AMTI) Formula

Taxable income
Plus: Positive AMT adjustments
Minus: Negative AMT adjustments
Equals: Taxable income after AMT adjustments
Plus: Tax preferences
Equals: Alternative minimum taxable income

income tax deduction may be different from the amount of the AMT deduction. Medical expenses are deductible in calculating both taxable income and AMTI, but the floor on the deduction is different.

The parallel but separate nature of the AMT means that AMTI will differ from taxable income. It is possible to compute AMTI by direct application of the AMT provisions, using the following formula:

Gross income computed by applying the AMT rules
Minus: Deductions computed by applying the AMT rules
Equals: AMTI before tax preferences
Plus: Tax preferences
Equals: Alternative minimum taxable income

While the direct approach for computing AMTI appears quite logical, both the tax law and the tax forms provide a very different approach. Both of these use taxable income (for Form 6251, taxable income *before* the deduction for personal exemptions and dependency deductions) as the starting point for computing AMTI, as shown in Figure 15–1. This indirect approach for computing AMTI is analogous to the indirect approach used in calculating a net operating loss.

The purpose of the AMT formula is to *reconcile* taxable income to AMTI. This reconciliation is similar to a bank reconciliation, which reconciles a checkbook balance to a bank balance by considering differences between the depositor's records and the bank's records. The reconciliation of taxable income to AMTI is accomplished by entering reconciling items to account for differences between regular income tax provisions and AMT provisions. These reconciling items are referred to as **AMT adjustments** or **tax preferences.** *Adjustments* can be either positive or negative, as shown in the formula in Figure 15–1. Tax preferences are always positive.

Adjustments. Most adjustments relate to *timing differences* that arise because of *separate* regular income tax and AMT treatments. Adjustments that are caused by timing differences will eventually *reverse;* that is, positive adjustments will be offset by negative adjustments in the future, and vice versa.[3]

For example, **circulation expenditures** can give rise to a timing difference that requires an AMT adjustment. For regular income tax purposes, circulation expenditures can be deducted in the year incurred. For AMT purposes, however, circulation expenditures must be deducted over a three-year period. This difference in treatment will be used to illustrate the role of adjustments in the formula for computing AMTI.

[3]§ 56.

EXAMPLE 1

Bob had taxable income of $100,000 in 2005. In computing taxable income, he deducted $30,000 of circulation expenditures incurred in 2005. Bob's allowable deduction for AMT purposes was only $10,000. Therefore, an AMT adjustment was required in 2005 as follows:

Taxable income		$100,000
+AMT adjustment:		
Circulation expenditures deducted for regular income tax purposes	$ 30,000	
Circulation expenditures allowed for AMT purposes	(10,000)	
Positive adjustment		20,000
=AMTI before tax preferences		$120,000
+Tax preferences		–0–
AMTI		$120,000

Analysis of this computation shows that the allowable AMT deduction is $20,000 less than the allowable regular income tax deduction. Therefore, AMTI is $20,000 greater than taxable income. This is accomplished by entering a positive AMT adjustment of $20,000. ■

EXAMPLE 2

Assume that Bob from Example 1 has taxable income of $95,000 in 2006. He is allowed to deduct $10,000 of circulation expenditures for AMT purposes, but is not allowed a deduction for regular income tax purposes because all $30,000 was deducted in 2005. Therefore, a *negative* AMT adjustment is required.

Taxable income		$ 95,000
–AMT adjustment:		
Circulation expenditures deducted for regular income tax purposes	$ –0–	
Circulation expenditures allowed for AMT purposes	(10,000)	
Negative adjustment		(10,000)
=AMTI before tax preferences		$ 85,000
+Tax preferences		–0–
AMTI		$ 85,000

Analysis of this computation shows that the allowable AMT deduction is $10,000 more than the allowable regular income tax deduction. Therefore, AMTI is $10,000 less than taxable income. This is accomplished by entering a negative AMT adjustment of $10,000. ■

As noted previously, timing differences eventually reverse. Therefore, total positive adjustments will be offset by total negative adjustments with respect to a particular item.

EXAMPLE 3

Refer to Examples 1 and 2. The difference in regular income tax and AMT treatments of circulation expenditures will result in AMT adjustments over a three-year period.

Year	Regular Income Tax Deduction	AMT Deduction	AMT Adjustment
2005	$30,000	$10,000	+$20,000
2006	–0–	10,000	–10,000
2007	–0–	10,000	–10,000
Total	$30,000	$30,000	$ –0–

As the last column illustrates, if positive and negative AMT adjustments with respect to a particular item are caused by a timing difference, they will eventually net to zero. ■

The adjustments for circulation expenditures and other items are discussed in detail under AMT Adjustments.

Although most adjustments relate to timing differences, there are exceptions. See the subsequent discussion of such items under Itemized Deductions. Adjustments that do not relate to timing differences result in a permanent difference between taxable income and AMTI.

Tax Preferences. Some deductions and exclusions allowed to taxpayers for regular income tax purposes provide extraordinary tax savings. Congress has chosen to single out these items, which are referred to as tax preferences.[4] The AMT is designed to take back all or part of the tax benefits derived through the use of preferences in the computation of taxable income for regular income tax purposes. This is why taxable income, which is the starting point in computing AMTI, is increased by tax preference items. The effect of adding these preference items is to disallow for *AMT purposes* those preferences that were allowed in the regular income tax computation. Tax preferences include the following items, which are discussed in detail under AMT Preferences:

- Percentage depletion in excess of the property's adjusted basis.
- Excess intangible drilling costs reduced by 65 percent of the net income from oil, gas, and geothermal properties.
- Interest on certain private activity bonds.
- Excess of accelerated over straight-line depreciation on real property placed in service before 1987.
- Excess of accelerated over straight-line depreciation on *leased* personal property placed in service before 1987.
- Excess of amortization allowance over depreciation on pre-1987 certified pollution control facilities.
- Seven percent of the exclusion from gross income associated with gains on the sale of certain small business stock under § 1202.

AMT FORMULA: OTHER COMPONENTS

To convert AMTI to AMT, other formula components including the exemption, rates, credit, and regular tax liability must be considered. The impact of each of these components is depicted in the AMT formula in Figure 15–2.

The relationship between the regular tax liability and the tentative AMT is key to the AMT formula. If the regular tax liability exceeds tentative AMT, then the AMT is zero. If the tentative AMT exceeds the regular tax liability, the amount of the excess is the AMT. In essence, the taxpayer will pay whichever tax liability is greater—that calculated using the regular income tax rules or that calculated using the AMT rules. However, both the tax law and Form 6251 adopt this excess approach with the taxpayer paying the regular tax liability plus any AMT.

EXAMPLE 4

Anna, an unmarried individual, has regular taxable income of $100,000. She has positive adjustments of $40,000 and tax preferences of $25,000. Calculate her AMT for 2005. Anna's regular tax liability is $22,507. Her AMT is calculated as follows:

[4] § 57.

■ FIGURE 15-2
Alternative Minimum Tax Formula

Regular taxable income
Plus or minus: Adjustments
Equals: Taxable income after AMT adjustments
Plus: Tax preferences
Equals: Alternative minimum taxable income
Minus: Exemption
Equals: Alternative minimum tax base
Times: 26% or 28% rate
Equals: Tentative minimum tax before foreign tax credit
Minus: Alternative minimum tax foreign tax credit
Equals: Tentative minimum tax
Minus: Regular tax liability*
Equals: Alternative minimum tax (if amount is positive)

*This is the regular tax liability for the year reduced by any allowable foreign tax credit.

Taxable income (TI)	$100,000
Plus: Adjustments	40,000
Equals: TI after AMT adjustments	$140,000
Plus: Tax preferences	25,000
Equals: AMTI	$165,000
Minus: AMT exemption ($40,250 – $13,125)	(27,125)*
Equals: AMT base	$137,875
Times: AMT rate	× 26%
Equals: Tentative AMT	$ 35,848
Minus: Regular tax liability	(22,507)
Equals: AMT	$ 13,341

*Discussed below under Exemption Amount.

Anna will pay the IRS a total of $35,848, consisting of her regular tax liability of $22,507 plus her AMT of $13,341. ■

Exemption Amount. The exemption amount can be thought of as a materiality provision. As such, it enables a taxpayer with a small amount of positive adjustments and tax preferences to avoid being subject to the burden of the AMT.

The *initial* exemption amount in 2005 is $58,000 for married taxpayers filing joint returns, $40,250 for single taxpayers, and $29,000 for married taxpayers filing separate returns.[5] However, the exemption is *phased out* at a rate of 25 cents on the dollar when AMTI exceeds these levels:

[5]§ 55(d). For tax years beginning in 2006 and thereafter, the exemption amount is reduced to $45,000 for married taxpayers filing jointly, $33,750 for single taxpayers, and $22,500 for married taxpayers filing separately.

- $112,500 for single taxpayers.
- $150,000 for married taxpayers filing jointly.
- $75,000 for married taxpayers filing separately.

The phaseout of the exemption amount is an application of the wherewithal to pay concept. As the income level increases, so does the taxpayer's ability to pay income taxes.

The following example explains the calculation of the phaseout of the AMT exemption.

EXAMPLE 5

Hugh, who is single, has AMTI of $192,500 for the year. His $40,250 initial exemption amount is reduced by $20,000 [($192,500 – $112,500) × 25% phaseout rate]. Hugh's AMT exemption is $20,250 ($40,250 exemption – $20,000 reduction). ■

The following table shows the beginning and end of the AMT exemption phaseout range for each filing status.

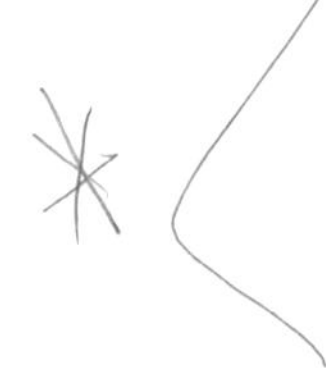

		Phaseout	
Status	**Exemption**	**Begins at**	**Ends at**
Married, joint	$58,000	$150,000	$382,000
Single or head of household	40,250	112,500	273,500
Married, separate	29,000	75,000	191,000

AMT Rate Schedule. A graduated, two-tier AMT rate schedule applies to noncorporate taxpayers. A 26 percent rate applies to the first $175,000 of the AMT base ($87,500 for married, filing separately), and a 28 percent rate applies to the AMT base in excess of $175,000 ($87,500 for married, filing separately).[6] Any net capital gain and qualified dividend income included in the AMT base are taxed at the favorable alternative tax rates for capital gains (15 percent or 5 percent) rather than at the AMT statutory rates. See the discussion of the alternative tax on capital gains in Chapter 14.

Regular Tax Liability. The AMT is equal to the tentative minimum tax minus the *regular tax liability*. In most cases, the regular tax liability is equal to the amount of tax from the Tax Table or Tax Rate Schedules decreased by any foreign tax credit allowable for regular income tax purposes. The foreign tax credit is allowed as a reduction of the tentative minimum tax.

In an AMT year, the taxpayer's total tax liability is equal to the tentative minimum tax (refer to Figure 15–2). The tentative minimum tax consists of two potential components: the regular tax liability and the AMT. The disallowance of credits does not affect a taxpayer's total liability in an AMT year. However, it does decrease the amount of the AMT and, as a consequence, reduces the minimum tax credit (discussed subsequently) available to be carried forward.

It is also possible that taxpayers who have adjustments and preferences but *do not pay* AMT will lose the benefit of some or all of their nonrefundable credits.

[6] § 55(b)(1).

ETHICAL CONSIDERATIONS

Minimizing the Tax Liability

Wilbur is single and projects his taxable income for 2005 to be about $300,000. For AMT purposes, he has positive adjustments and tax preferences of $200,000. He anticipates that his taxable income and positive adjustments and preferences will be about the same for 2006. He is evaluating several proposed transactions that could affect his 2005 tax liability.

One transaction involves an office building for which he is currently negotiating a lease. The starting date for the lease is July 1, 2005; the annual rent is $20,000, and the lease has an 18-month prepayment clause. Though Wilbur favors a five-year lease, his tax adviser has suggested an 18-month period with a 42-month renewal option. The adviser points out the tax advantages of being able to deduct the $30,000 of rent paid at the inception of the lease.

Wilbur takes his adviser's suggestion after comparing his projected tax liability for 2005 with the 18-month lease and renewal option with his liability under the five-year lease. Based on his calculations, his regular income tax liability and AMT under each option would be as follows:

	18-Month Lease	5-Year Lease
Regular income tax liability	$ 76,099	$ 82,699
AMT	52,001	51,001
Total	$128,100	$133,700

Is it appropriate for Wilbur to avoid taxes in this manner? Is it wise?

This result occurs because a taxpayer may claim many nonrefundable credits only to the extent that his or her regular tax liability exceeds the tentative minimum tax.

EXAMPLE 6

Vern has total nonrefundable *business* credits of $10,000, regular tax liability of $33,000, and tentative minimum tax of $25,000. He can claim only $8,000 of the nonrefundable credits in the current year ($33,000 – $8,000 = $25,000). The disallowed $2,000 credit is eligible for carryback and carryover. ■

For tax years 2000–2005, all nonrefundable personal credits can offset both the regular tax (less foreign tax credit) and AMT. For tax years after 2005, only *certain* nonrefundable personal tax credits (i.e., child tax credit, adoption expenses credit, and credit for elective deferrals and IRA contributions) can offset both the regular income tax (less any foreign tax credit) and the AMT in full after all other nonrefundable personal tax credits have been utilized.[7]

LO.3

Identify the adjustments made in calculating the AMT.

AMT ADJUSTMENTS

Direction of Adjustments. It is necessary to determine not only the amount of an adjustment, but also whether the adjustment is positive or negative. Careful study of Example 3 reveals the following pattern with regard to *deductions:*

- If the deduction allowed for regular income tax purposes exceeds the deduction allowed for AMT purposes, the difference is a positive adjustment.
- If the deduction allowed for AMT purposes exceeds the deduction allowed for regular income tax purposes, the difference is a negative adjustment.

[7] § 26(a)(2) as amended by the Working Families Tax Relief Act of 2004.

Conversely, the direction of an adjustment attributable to an *income* item can be determined as follows:

- If the income reported for regular income tax purposes exceeds the income reported for AMT purposes, the difference is a negative adjustment.
- If the income reported for AMT purposes exceeds the income reported for regular income tax purposes, the difference is a positive adjustment.

Circulation Expenditures. For regular income tax purposes, circulation expenditures, other than those the taxpayer elects to charge to a capital account, may be expensed in the year incurred.[8] These expenditures include expenses incurred to establish, maintain, or increase the circulation of a newspaper, magazine, or other periodical.

Circulation expenditures are not deductible in the year incurred for AMT purposes. In computing AMTI, these expenditures must be capitalized and amortized ratably over the three-year period beginning with the year in which the expenditures were made.[9]

The AMT adjustment for circulation expenditures is the amount expensed for regular income tax purposes minus the amount that can be amortized for AMT purposes. The adjustment can be either positive or negative (refer to Examples 1, 2, and 3). A taxpayer can avoid the AMT adjustments for circulation expenditures by electing to write off the expenditures over a three-year period for regular income tax purposes.[10]

Depreciation of Post-1986 Real Property. The AMT depreciation adjustment for real property applies only to real property placed in service before January 1, 1999. Real property placed in service after December 31, 1998, uses the same MACRS recovery periods (see Table 8–8) for calculating the AMT as for calculating the regular income tax. Therefore, for such property, the AMT conforms to the regular income tax.

For real property placed in service after 1986 (MACRS property) and before January 1, 1999, AMT depreciation is computed under the alternative depreciation system (ADS), which uses the straight-line method over a 40-year life. The depreciation lives for regular income tax purposes are 27.5 years for residential rental property and 39 years for all other real property.[11] The difference between AMT depreciation and regular income tax depreciation is treated as an adjustment in computing the AMT. The differences will be positive during the regular income tax life of the asset because the cost is written off over a shorter period for regular income tax purposes. For example, during the 27.5-year income tax life of residential real property, the regular income tax depreciation will exceed the AMT depreciation because AMT depreciation is computed over a 40-year period.

Table 8–8 is used to compute regular income tax depreciation on real property placed in service after 1986. For AMT purposes, depreciation on real property placed in service after 1986 and before January 1, 1999, is computed under the ADS (refer to Table 8–9).

EXAMPLE 7

In January 1998, Sara placed in service a residential building that cost $100,000. Regular income tax depreciation, AMT depreciation, and the AMT adjustment are as follows:

[8] § 173(a).
[9] § 56(b)(2)(A)(i).
[10] § 59(e)(2)(A).
[11] The 39-year life generally applies to nonresidential real property placed in service on or after May 13, 1993.

	Depreciation		
Year	**Regular Income Tax**	**AMT**	**AMT Adjustment**
1998	$3,485[a]	$2,396[b]	$1,089
1999	3,636[c]	2,500[d]	1,136
2000	3,636	2,500	1,136
2001	3,636	2,500	1,136
2002	3,636	2,500	1,136
2003	3,636	2,500	1,136
2004	3,636	2,500	1,136
2005	3,636	2,500	1,136

[a]$100,000 cost × 3.485% (Table 8–8) = $3,485.
[b]$100,000 cost × 2.396% (Table 8–9) = $2,396.
[c]$100,000 cost × 3.636% (Table 8–8) = $3,636.
[d]$100,000 cost × 2.500% (Table 8–9) = $2,500.

Note that if the building had been placed in service in 1999 or thereafter, there would have been no AMT depreciation adjustment for the tax year it was placed in service or for subsequent years. The depreciation for the tax year the building was placed in service would have been $3,485 ($100,000 × 3.485%) for both regular income tax purposes and AMT purposes. ■

After real property placed in service before January 1, 1999, has been held for the entire depreciation period for regular income tax purposes, the asset will be fully depreciated. However, the depreciation period under the ADS is 41 years due to application of the half-year convention, so depreciation will continue for AMT purposes. This causes negative adjustments after the property has been fully depreciated for regular income tax purposes.

EXAMPLE 8

Assume the same facts as in the previous example for the building placed in service in 1998, and compute the AMT adjustment for 2026 (the twenty-ninth year of the asset's life). Regular income tax depreciation is zero (refer to Table 8–8). AMT depreciation is $2,500 ($100,000 cost × 2.500% from Table 8–9). Therefore, Sara has a negative AMT adjustment of $2,500 ($0 regular income tax depreciation – $2,500 AMT depreciation). ■

After real property is fully depreciated for both regular income tax and AMT purposes, the positive and negative adjustments that have been made for AMT purposes will net to zero.

Depreciation of Post-1986 Personal Property. For most personal property placed in service after 1986 (MACRS property), the MACRS deduction for regular income tax purposes is based on the 200 percent declining-balance method with a switch to straight-line when that method produces a larger depreciation deduction for the asset. Refer to Table 8–1 for computing regular income tax depreciation.

For AMT purposes, the taxpayer must use the ADS for such property placed in service before January 1, 1999. This method is based on the 150 percent declining-balance method with a similar switch to straight-line for all personal property.[12] Refer to Table 8–4 for percentages to be used in computing AMT depreciation.

[12]§ 56(a)(1).

All personal property placed in service after 1986 may be taken into consideration in computing one net adjustment. Using this netting process, the AMT adjustment for a tax year is the difference between the total MACRS depreciation for all personal property computed for regular income tax purposes and the total ADS depreciation computed for AMT purposes. When the total of MACRS deductions exceeds the total of ADS deductions, the amount of the adjustment is positive. When the total of ADS deductions exceeds the total of MACRS deductions, the adjustment for AMTI is negative.

The MACRS deduction for personal property is larger than the ADS deduction in the early years of an asset's life. However, the ADS deduction is larger in the later years. This is so because ADS lives (based on class life) are longer than MACRS lives (based on recovery period).[13] Over the ADS life of the asset, the same amount of depreciation is deducted for both regular income tax and AMT purposes. In the same manner as other timing adjustments, the AMT adjustments for depreciation will net to zero over the ADS life of the asset.

The taxpayer may elect to use the ADS for regular income tax purposes. If this election is made, no AMT adjustment is required because the depreciation deduction is the same for regular income tax and for the AMT. The election eliminates the burden of maintaining two sets of tax depreciation records.

Tax legislation enacted in 1997 either reduced or eliminated the AMT adjustment for the depreciation of personal property. Prior to the effective date of this legislation, the difference between regular income tax depreciation and AMT depreciation was caused by longer recovery periods for the AMT (class life versus MACRS recovery periods) and more accelerated depreciation methods for the regular income tax (200 percent declining balance rather than 150 percent declining balance). The statute now provides that the MACRS recovery periods are to be used in calculating AMT depreciation. Thus, if the taxpayer elects to use the 150 percent declining-balance method for regular income tax purposes, there are no AMT adjustments. Conversely, if the taxpayer uses the 200 percent declining-balance method for regular income tax purposes, there is an AMT adjustment for depreciation. Note, however, that this AMT recovery period conformity provision applies only to property placed in service after December 31, 1998. Thus, the adjustment continues to apply for personal property placed in service before January 1, 1999.

Pollution Control Facilities. For regular income tax purposes, the cost of certified pollution control facilities may be amortized over a period of 60 months. For AMT purposes, the cost of these facilities placed in service after 1986 and before January 1, 1999, must be depreciated under the ADS over the appropriate class life, determined as explained above for depreciation of post-1986 property.[14] The required adjustment for AMTI is equal to the difference between the amortization deduction allowed for regular income tax purposes and the depreciation deduction computed under the ADS. The adjustment may be positive or negative.

Tax legislation enacted in 1997 reduced the AMT adjustment for pollution control facilities for property placed in service after December 31, 1998. This reduction is achieved by providing conformity in the recovery periods used for regular income tax purposes and AMT purposes (MACRS recovery periods).

Expenditures Requiring 10-Year Write-off for AMT Purposes. Certain expenditures that may be deducted in the year incurred for regular income tax purposes must be written off over a 10-year period for AMT purposes. These rules apply to (1) mining exploration and development costs and (2) research and experimental expenditures.

[13]Class lives and recovery periods are established for all assets in Rev.Proc. 87–56, 1987–2 C.B. 674.

[14]§ 56(a)(5).

In computing taxable income, taxpayers are allowed to deduct certain mining exploration and development expenditures. The deduction is allowed for expenditures paid or incurred during the taxable year for exploration (ascertaining the existence, location, extent, or quality of a deposit or mineral) and for development of a mine or other natural deposit, other than an oil or gas well.[15] Mining development expenditures are expenses paid or incurred after the existence of ores and minerals in commercially marketable quantities has been disclosed.

For AMT purposes, however, mining exploration and development costs must be capitalized and amortized ratably over a 10-year period.[16] The AMT adjustment for mining exploration and development costs that are expensed is equal to the amount expensed minus the allowable expense if the costs had been capitalized and amortized ratably over a 10-year period. This provision does not apply to costs relating to an oil or gas well.

EXAMPLE 9

In 2005, Audrey incurs $150,000 of mining exploration expenditures and deducts this amount for regular income tax purposes. For AMT purposes, these mining exploration expenditures must be amortized over a 10-year period. Audrey must make a positive adjustment for AMTI of $135,000 ($150,000 allowed for regular income tax – $15,000 for AMT) for 2005, the first year. In each of the next nine years for AMT purposes, Audrey is required to make a negative adjustment of $15,000 ($0 allowed for regular income tax – $15,000 for AMT). ■

To avoid the AMT adjustments for mining exploration and development costs, a taxpayer may elect to write off the expenditures over a 10-year period for regular income tax purposes.[17]

Similar rules apply to the computation of the adjustment for research and experimental expenditures.

Use of Completed Contract Method of Accounting. For a long-term contract, taxpayers are required to use the percentage of completion method for AMT purposes.[18] However, in limited circumstances, taxpayers can use the completed contract method for regular income tax purposes.[19] Thus, a taxpayer recognizes a different amount of income for regular income tax purposes than for AMT purposes. The resulting AMT adjustment is equal to the difference between income reported under the percentage of completion method and the amount reported using the completed contract method. The adjustment can be either positive or negative, depending on the amount of income recognized under the different methods.

A taxpayer can avoid an AMT adjustment on long-term contracts by using the percentage of completion method for regular income tax purposes rather than the completed contract method.

Incentive Stock Options. **Incentive stock options (ISOs)** are granted by employers to help attract new personnel and retain those already employed. At the time an ISO is granted, the employer corporation sets an option price for the corporate stock. If the value of the stock increases during the option period, the employee can obtain stock at a favorable price by exercising the option. Employees are generally restricted as to when they can dispose of stock acquired under an ISO (e.g., a certain length of employment may be required). Therefore, the stock may not be freely transferable until some specified period has passed.

[15]§§ 617(a) and 616(a).
[16]§ 56(a)(2).
[17]§§ 59(e)(2)(D) and (E).
[18]§ 56(a)(3).
[19]See Chapter 16 for a detailed discussion of the completed contract and percentage of completion methods of accounting.

The exercise of an ISO does not increase regular taxable income.[20] However, for AMT purposes, the excess of the fair market value of the stock over the exercise price (the *spread*) is treated as an adjustment in the first taxable year in which the rights in the stock are freely transferable or are not subject to a substantial risk of forfeiture.[21]

EXAMPLE 10

In 2003, Manuel exercised an ISO that had been granted by his employer, Gold Corporation. Manuel acquired 1,000 shares of Gold stock for the option price of $20 per share. The stock became freely transferable in 2005. The fair market value of the stock at the date of exercise was $50 per share. For AMT purposes, Manuel has a positive adjustment of $30,000 ($50,000 fair market value – $20,000 option price) for 2005. The transaction does not affect regular taxable income in 2003 or 2005. ■

No adjustment is required if the taxpayer exercises the option and disposes of the stock in the same tax year because the bargain element gain is reported for both regular income tax and AMT purposes in the same tax year.

The regular income tax basis of stock acquired through exercise of ISOs is different from the AMT basis. The regular income tax basis of the stock is equal to its cost, whereas the AMT basis is equal to the fair market value on the date the options are exercised. Consequently, the gain or loss upon disposition of the stock is different for regular income tax purposes and AMT purposes.

EXAMPLE 11

Assume the same facts as in the previous example and that Manuel sells the stock for $60,000 in 2007. His gain for regular income tax purposes is $40,000 ($60,000 amount realized – $20,000 regular income tax basis). For AMT purposes, the gain is $10,000 ($60,000 amount realized – $50,000 AMT basis). Therefore, Manuel has a $30,000 negative adjustment in computing AMT in 2007 ($40,000 regular income tax gain – $10,000 AMT gain). Note that the $30,000 negative adjustment upon disposition in 2007 offsets the $30,000 positive adjustment when the stock became freely transferable in 2005. ■

Adjusted Gain or Loss. When property is sold during the year or a casualty occurs to business or income-producing property, gain or loss reported for regular income tax may be different than gain or loss determined for the AMT. This difference occurs because the adjusted basis of the property for AMT purposes must reflect any current and prior AMT adjustments for the following:[22]

- Depreciation.
- Circulation expenditures.
- Research and experimental expenditures.
- Mining exploration and development costs.
- Amortization of certified pollution control facilities.

A negative gain or loss adjustment is required if:

- the gain for AMT purposes is less than the gain for regular income tax purposes;
- the loss for AMT purposes is more than the loss for regular income tax purposes; or
- a loss is computed for AMT purposes and a gain is computed for regular income tax purposes.

Otherwise, the AMT gain or loss adjustment is positive.

[20] § 421(a).
[21] § 56(b)(3).
[22] § 56(a)(6).

EXAMPLE 12

In January 1998, Kate paid $100,000 for a duplex acquired for rental purposes. Regular income tax depreciation, AMT depreciation, and the AMT adjustment are as follows:

	Depreciation		
Year	**Regular Income Tax**	**AMT**	**AMT Adjustment**
1998	$3,485[a]	$2,396[b]	$1,089
1999	3,636[c]	2,500[d]	1,136
2000	3,636	2,500	1,136
2001	3,636	2,500	1,136
2002	3,636	2,500	1,136
2003	3,636	2,500	1,136
2004	3,636	2,500	1,136

[a] $100,000 cost × 3.485% (Table 8–8) = $3,485.
[b] $100,000 cost × 2.396% (Table 8–9) = $2,396.
[c] $100,000 cost × 3.636% (Table 8–8) = $3,636.
[d] $100,000 cost × 2.500% (Table 8–9) = $2,500. ■

EXAMPLE 13

Kate sold the duplex on December 20, 2005, for $105,000. Regular income tax depreciation for 2005 is $3,485 [($100,000 cost × 3.636% from Table 8–8) × (11.5/12)]. AMT depreciation for 2005 is $2,396 [($100,000 cost × 2.500% from Table 8–9) × (11.5/12)]. Kate's positive AMT adjustment for 2005 is $1,089 ($3,485 regular income tax depreciation – $2,396 AMT depreciation). ■

Because depreciation on the duplex differs for regular income tax and AMT purposes, the adjusted basis is different for regular income tax and AMT purposes. Consequently, the gain or loss on disposition of the duplex is different for regular income tax and AMT purposes.

EXAMPLE 14

The adjusted basis of Kate's duplex is $71,214 for regular income tax purposes and $80,208 for AMT purposes.

	Regular Income Tax	**AMT**
Cost	$100,000	$100,000
Depreciation		
1998	(3,485)	(2,396)
1999	(3,636)	(2,500)
2000	(3,636)	(2,500)
2001	(3,636)	(2,500)
2002	(3,636)	(2,500)
2003	(3,636)	(2,500)
2004	(3,636)	(2,500)
2005	(3,485)	(2,396)
Adjusted basis	$ 71,214	$ 80,208

The regular income tax gain is $33,786, and the AMT gain is $24,792.

	Regular Income Tax	**AMT**
Amount realized	$105,000	$105,000
Adjusted basis	(71,214)	(80,208)
Recognized gain	$ 33,786	$ 24,792

Because the regular income tax and AMT gain on the sale of the duplex differ, Kate must make a negative AMT adjustment of $8,994 ($33,786 regular income tax gain – $24,792 AMT gain). Note that this negative adjustment offsets the $8,994 total of the eight positive adjustments for depreciation ($1,089 in 1998 + $1,136 in 1999 + $1,136 in 2000 + $1,136 in 2001 + $1,136 in 2002 + $1,136 in 2003 + $1,136 in 2004 + $1,089 in 2005). ■

Passive Activity Losses. Losses on passive activities are not deductible in computing either the regular income tax or the AMT. This does not, however, eliminate the possibility of adjustments attributable to passive activities.

The rules for computing taxable income differ from the rules for computing AMTI. It follows, then, that the rules for computing a loss for regular income tax purposes differ from the AMT rules for computing a loss. Therefore, any *passive loss* computed for regular income tax purposes may differ from the passive loss computed for AMT purposes.[23]

EXAMPLE 15

Soong acquired two passive activities in 2005. He received net passive income of $10,000 from Activity A and had no AMT adjustments or preferences in connection with the activity. Activity B had gross income of $27,000 and operating expenses (not affected by AMT adjustments or preferences) of $19,000. Soong claimed MACRS depreciation of $20,000 for Activity B; depreciation under the ADS would have been $15,000. In addition, Soong deducted $10,000 of percentage depletion in excess of basis. The following comparison illustrates the differences in the computation of the passive loss for regular income tax and AMT purposes for Activity B.

	Regular Income Tax	AMT
Gross income	$ 27,000	$ 27,000
Deductions:		
Operating expenses	($ 19,000)	($ 19,000)
Depreciation	(20,000)	(15,000)
Depletion	(10,000)	-0-
Total deductions	($ 49,000)	($ 34,000)
Passive loss	($ 22,000)	($ 7,000)

Because the adjustment for depreciation ($5,000) applies and the preference for depletion ($10,000) is not taken into account in computing AMTI, the regular income tax passive activity loss of $22,000 for Activity B is reduced by these amounts, resulting in a passive activity loss of $7,000 for AMT purposes. ■

For regular income tax purposes, Soong would offset the $10,000 of net passive income from Activity A with $10,000 of the passive loss from Activity B. For AMT purposes, he would offset the $10,000 of net passive income from Activity A with the $7,000 passive activity loss allowed from Activity B, resulting in passive activity income of $3,000. Thus, in computing AMTI, Soong makes a positive passive loss adjustment of $3,000 [$10,000 (passive activity loss allowed for regular income tax) – $7,000 (passive activity loss allowed for the AMT)]. To avoid duplication, the AMT adjustment for depreciation and the preference for depletion are *not* reported separately. They are accounted for in determining the AMT passive loss adjustment.

[23]See Chapter 11.

EXAMPLE 16

Assume the same facts as in the previous example. For regular income tax purposes, Soong has a suspended passive loss of $12,000 [$22,000 (amount of loss) – $10,000 (used in 2005)]. This suspended passive loss can offset passive income in the future or can offset active or portfolio income when Soong disposes of the loss activity (refer to Chapter 11). For AMT purposes, Soong's suspended passive loss is $0 [$7,000 (amount of loss) – $7,000 (amount used in 2005)]. ■

Alternative Tax Net Operating Loss Deduction. In computing taxable income, taxpayers are allowed to deduct net operating loss (NOL) carryovers and carrybacks (refer to Chapter 7). The regular income tax NOL must be modified, however, in computing AMTI. The starting point in computing the **alternative tax NOL deduction (ATNOLD)** is the NOL computed for regular income tax purposes. The regular income tax NOL is then modified for AMT adjustments and tax preferences with the result being the ATNOLD. Thus, preferences and adjustment items that have benefited the taxpayer in computing the regular income tax NOL are added back, thereby reducing or eliminating the ATNOLD.[24]

EXAMPLE 17

In 2005, Max incurred an NOL of $100,000. Max had no AMT adjustments, but his deductions included tax preferences of $18,000. His ATNOLD carryback to 2003 is $82,000 ($100,000 regular income tax NOL – $18,000 tax preferences deducted in computing the NOL). ■

In Example 17, if the adjustment was not made to the regular income tax NOL, the $18,000 in tax preference items deducted in 2005 would have the effect of reducing AMTI in the year (or years) the 2005 NOL is utilized. This would weaken the entire concept of the AMT.

A ceiling exists on the amount of the ATNOLD that can be deducted in the carryback or carryforward year. The deduction is limited to 90 percent of AMTI (before the ATNOLD) for the carryback or carryforward year.

EXAMPLE 18

Assume the same facts as in the previous example. Max's AMTI (before the ATNOLD) in 2003 is $90,000. Therefore, of the $82,000 ATNOLD carried back to 2003 from 2005, only $81,000 ($90,000 × 90%) can be used in recalculating the 2003 AMT. The unused $1,000 of 2005 ATNOLD is now carried to 2004 for use in recalculating the 2004 AMT. ■

A taxpayer who has an ATNOLD that is carried back or over to another year must use the ATNOLD against AMTI in the carryback or carryforward year even if the regular income tax, rather than the AMT, applies.

EXAMPLE 19

Emily's ATNOLD for 2006 (carried over from 2005) is $10,000. AMTI before considering the ATNOLD is $25,000. If Emily's regular income tax exceeds the AMT, the AMT does not apply. Nevertheless, Emily's ATNOLD of $10,000 is "used up" in 2006 and is not available for carryover to a later year. ■

For regular income tax purposes, the NOL generally can be carried back 2 years and forward 20 years. However, the taxpayer may elect to forgo the 2-year carryback. These rules generally apply to the ATNOLD as well, except that the election to forgo the 2-year carryback is available for the ATNOLD only if the taxpayer elected it for the regular income tax NOL.

Itemized Deductions. Most of the itemized deductions that are allowed for regular income tax purposes are allowed for AMT purposes. Itemized deductions that are allowed for AMT purposes include the following:

[24] § 56(a)(4).

- Casualty losses.
- Gambling losses.
- Charitable contributions.
- Medical expenses in excess of 10 percent of AGI.
- Estate tax on income in respect of a decedent.
- Qualified interest.

Taxes (state, local, foreign income, and property taxes) and miscellaneous itemized deductions that are subject to the 2 percent-of-AGI floor are not allowed in computing AMT.[25] A positive AMT adjustment in the total amount of the regular income tax deduction for each is required.

If the taxpayer's gross income includes the recovery of any tax deducted as an itemized deduction for regular income tax purposes, a negative AMT adjustment in the amount of the recovery is allowed for AMTI purposes.[26] For example, state, local, and foreign income taxes can be deducted for regular income tax purposes, but cannot be deducted in computing AMTI. Because of this, any refund of such taxes from a prior year is not included in AMTI. Therefore, in calculating AMTI, the taxpayer must make a negative adjustment for an income tax refund that has been included in computing regular taxable income. Under the tax benefit rule, a tax refund is included in regular taxable income to the extent that the taxpayer obtained a tax benefit by deducting the tax in a prior year.

Cutback Adjustment. The 3 percent cutback adjustment that applies to regular income tax itemized deductions of certain high-income taxpayers (refer to Chapter 10) does not apply in computing AMT.[27] The effect of the 3 percent cutback adjustment is to disallow a portion of the taxpayer's itemized deductions for regular income tax purposes. Because this cutback adjustment does not apply for AMT purposes, taxable income, which is the starting point for computing AMTI, must be reduced by the amount of the disallowed deductions. This reduction is a negative AMT adjustment.

Medical Expenses. The rules for determining the AMT deductions for medical expenses are sufficiently complex to require further explanation. For regular income tax purposes, medical expenses are deductible to the extent they exceed 7.5 percent of AGI. However, for AMT purposes, medical expenses are deductible only to the extent they exceed 10 percent of AGI.[28]

EXAMPLE 20

Joann incurred medical expenses of $16,000 in 2005. She had AGI of $100,000 for the year. Her AMT adjustment for medical expenses is computed as follows:

	Regular Income Tax	AMT
Medical expenses incurred	$16,000	$ 16,000
Less reduction:		
$100,000 AGI × 7.5%	(7,500)	
$100,000 AGI × 10%		(10,000)
Medical expense deduction	$ 8,500	$ 6,000

Joann's AMT adjustment for medical expenses is $2,500 ($8,500 regular income tax deduction – $6,000 AMT deduction). ■

[25] § 56(b)(1)(A).
[26] § 56(b)(1)(D).
[27] § 56(b)(1)(F).
[28] § 56(b)(1)(B).

Interest in General. The AMT itemized deduction allowed for interest expense includes only qualified housing interest and investment interest to the extent of net investment income that is included in the determination of AMTI.[29] Any interest that is deducted in calculating the regular income tax that is not permitted in calculating the AMT is treated as a positive adjustment.

In computing regular taxable income, taxpayers who itemize can deduct the following types of interest (refer to Chapter 10):

- Qualified residence interest.
- Investment interest, subject to the investment interest limitations (discussed under Investment Interest below).
- Qualified interest on student loans.

Housing Interest. Under current regular income tax rules, taxpayers who itemize can deduct *qualified residence interest* on up to two residences. The deduction is limited to interest on acquisition indebtedness up to $1 million and home equity indebtedness up to $100,000. Acquisition indebtedness is debt that is incurred in acquiring, constructing, or substantially improving a qualified residence of the taxpayer and is secured by the residence. Home equity indebtedness is indebtedness secured by a qualified residence of the taxpayer, but does not include acquisition indebtedness.

EXAMPLE 21

Gail, who used the proceeds of a mortgage to acquire a personal residence, paid mortgage interest of $112,000 in 2005. Of this amount, $14,000 is attributable to acquisition indebtedness in excess of $1 million. For regular income tax purposes, Gail may deduct mortgage interest of $98,000 ($112,000 total – $14,000 disallowed). ■

The mortgage interest deduction for AMT purposes is limited to *qualified housing interest*, rather than *qualified residence interest*. Qualified housing interest includes only interest incurred to acquire, construct, or substantially improve the taxpayer's principal residence and such interest on one other qualified dwelling used for personal purposes. A home equity loan qualifies only if it meets the definition of qualified housing interest, which frequently is not the case. When additional mortgage interest is incurred (e.g., a mortgage refinancing), interest paid is deductible as qualified housing interest for AMT purposes only if:

- The proceeds are used to acquire or substantially improve a qualified residence.
- Interest on the prior loan was qualified housing interest.
- The amount of the loan was not increased.

A positive AMT adjustment is required in the amount of the difference between qualified *residence* interest allowed as an itemized deduction for regular income tax purposes and qualified *housing* interest allowed in the determination of AMTI.

Investment Interest. Investment interest is deductible for regular income tax purposes and for AMT purposes to the extent of qualified net investment income.

EXAMPLE 22

For the year, Dan had net investment income of $16,000 before deducting investment interest. He incurred investment interest expense of $30,000 during the year. His investment interest deduction is $16,000. ■

Even though investment interest is deductible for both regular income tax and AMT purposes, an adjustment is required if the amount of investment interest

[29] § 56(b)(1)(C).

deductible for regular income tax purposes differs from the amount deductible for AMT purposes. For example, an adjustment will arise if proceeds from a home equity loan are used to purchase investments. Interest on a home equity loan is deductible as qualified residence interest for regular income tax purposes, but is not deductible for AMT purposes unless the proceeds are used to acquire or substantially improve a qualified residence. For AMT purposes, however, interest on a home equity loan is deductible as investment interest expense if proceeds from the loan are used for investment purposes.

To determine the AMT adjustment for investment interest expense, it is necessary to compute the investment interest deduction for both regular income tax and AMT purposes. This computation is illustrated in the following example.

EXAMPLE 23

Tom had $20,000 interest income from corporate bonds and $5,000 dividends from preferred stock. He reported the following amounts of investment income for regular income tax and AMT purposes:

	Regular Income Tax	AMT
Corporate bond interest	$20,000	$20,000
Preferred stock dividends	5,000	5,000
Net investment income	$25,000	$25,000

Tom incurred investment interest expense of $10,000 related to the corporate bonds. He also incurred $4,000 interest on a home equity loan and used the proceeds of the loan to purchase preferred stock. For regular income tax purposes, this $4,000 is deductible as qualified residence interest. His *investment* interest expense for regular income tax and AMT purposes is computed below:

	Regular Income Tax	AMT
To carry corporate bonds	$10,000	$10,000
On home equity loan to carry preferred stock	-0-	4,000
Total investment interest expense	$10,000	$14,000

Investment interest expense is deductible to the extent of net investment income. Because the amount deductible for regular income tax purposes ($10,000) differs from the amount deductible for AMT purposes ($14,000), an AMT adjustment is required. The adjustment is computed as follows:

AMT deduction for investment interest expense	$ 14,000
Regular income tax deduction for investment interest expense	(10,000)
Negative AMT adjustment	$ 4,000

■

As discussed subsequently under AMT Preferences, the interest on private activity bonds is a tax preference for AMT purposes. Such interest can also affect the calculation of the AMT investment interest deduction in that it is included in the calculation of net investment income.

Other Adjustments. The standard deduction and the personal and dependency exemption also give rise to AMT adjustments.[30] The standard deduction is not

[30] § 56(b)(1)(E).

allowed as a deduction in computing AMTI. Although a person who does not itemize is rarely subject to the AMT, it is possible. In such a case, the taxpayer is required to enter a positive adjustment for the standard deduction in computing the AMT.

The personal and dependency exemption amount deducted for regular income tax purposes is not allowed in computing AMT. Therefore, taxpayers must enter a positive AMT adjustment for the personal and dependency exemption amount claimed in computing the regular income tax. A separate exemption (see Exemption Amount) is allowed for AMT purposes. To allow both the regular income tax exemption amount and the AMT exemption amount would result in extra benefits for taxpayers.

EXAMPLE 24

Eli, who is single, has no dependents and does not itemize deductions. He earned a salary of $108,200 in 2005. Based on this information, Eli's taxable income for 2005 is $100,000 ($108,200 – $5,000 standard deduction – $3,200 exemption). ■

EXAMPLE 25

Assume the same facts as in Example 24. In addition, assume Eli's tax preferences for the year totaled $150,000. Eli's AMTI is $258,200 ($100,000 taxable income + $5,000 adjustment for standard deduction + $3,200 adjustment for exemption + $150,000 tax preferences). ■

LO.4

Identify the tax preferences that are included in calculating the AMT.

AMT PREFERENCES

Percentage Depletion. Congress originally enacted the percentage depletion rules to provide taxpayers with incentives to invest in the development of specified natural resources. Percentage depletion is computed by multiplying a rate specified in the Code times the gross income from the property (refer to Chapter 8).[31] The percentage rate is based on the type of mineral involved. The basis of the property is reduced by the amount of depletion taken until the basis reaches zero. However, once the basis of the property reaches zero, taxpayers are allowed to continue taking percentage depletion deductions. Thus, over the life of the property, depletion deductions may greatly exceed the cost of the property.

The percentage depletion preference is equal to the excess of the regular income tax deduction for percentage depletion over the adjusted basis of the property at the end of the taxable year.[32] Basis is determined without regard to the depletion deduction for the taxable year. This preference item is figured separately for each piece of property for which the taxpayer is claiming depletion.

EXAMPLE 26

Kim owns a mineral property that qualifies for a 22% depletion rate. The basis of the property at the beginning of the year is $10,000. Gross income from the property for the year is $100,000. For regular income tax purposes, Kim's percentage depletion deduction (assume it is not limited by taxable income from the property) is $22,000. For AMT purposes, Kim has a tax preference of $12,000 ($22,000 – $10,000). ■

Intangible Drilling Costs. In computing the regular income tax, taxpayers are allowed to deduct certain intangible drilling and development costs in the year incurred, although such costs are normally capital in nature (refer to Chapter 8). The deduction is allowed for costs incurred in connection with oil and gas wells and geothermal wells.

For AMT purposes, excess intangible drilling costs (IDC) for the year are treated as a preference.[33] The preference for excess IDC is computed as follows:

[31] § 613(a).

[32] § 57(a)(1). Note that the preference label does not apply to percentage depletion on oil and gas wells for independent producers and royalty owners as defined in § 613A(c).

[33] § 57(a)(2).

IDC expensed in the year incurred
Minus: Deduction if IDC were capitalized and amortized over 10 years
Equals: Excess of IDC expense over amortization
Minus: 65% of net oil and gas and geothermal income
Equals: Tax preference item

EXAMPLE 27

Ben, who incurred IDC of $50,000 during the year, elected to expense that amount. His net oil and gas income for the year was $60,000. Ben's tax preference for IDC is $6,000 [($50,000 IDC – $5,000 amortization) – (65% × $60,000 income)]. ■

A taxpayer can avoid the preference for IDC by electing to write off the expenditures over a 10-year period for regular income tax purposes.

Interest on Private Activity Bonds. Income from private activity bonds is not included in taxable income, and expenses related to carrying such bonds are not deductible for regular income tax purposes. However, interest on private activity bonds is included as a preference in computing AMTI. Therefore, expenses incurred in carrying the bonds are offset against the interest income in computing the tax preference.[34]

The Code contains a lengthy, complex definition of private activity bonds.[35] In general, **private activity bonds** are bonds issued by states or municipalities with more than 10 percent of the proceeds being used for private business use. For example, a bond issued by a city whose proceeds are used to construct a factory that is leased to a private business at a favorable rate is a private activity bond.

ETHICAL CONSIDERATIONS

Tax-Exempt Bonds and the AMT

Glenn, who is age 32, single, and in the 25 percent tax bracket, recently inherited $1 million of municipal bonds from his mother. Rather than change investments, Glenn decides to keep the bonds for the time being.

The information he received from the municipality shortly after the end of the year has confused Glenn about the tax treatment of the bond interest. He had thought that interest on all municipal bonds is tax-exempt, but he recently read an article that explained that interest from bonds classified as private activity bonds is excludible from income for regular income tax purposes but is a tax preference for the AMT. Glenn has asked the municipality for clarification on the status of the bonds, but he has received no answer. A review of his mother's tax returns for the past three years reveals that none included any income from the bonds.

Since he wants to file his return this week, Glenn has to decide what to do about the bond interest. He is considering not treating the bonds as private activity bonds based on what his mother did. His justification for this position is that his mother was an astute businesswoman and would have used the proper treatment. Furthermore, if Glenn does not treat the bonds as private activity bonds, the interest will not be subject to either the regular income tax or the AMT. Evaluate Glenn's proposal.

Depreciation. For real property and leased personal property placed in service before 1987, there is an AMT preference for the excess of accelerated depreciation over straight-line depreciation.[36] However, examination of the cost recovery tables for pre-1987 real property (refer to Chapter 8) reveals that from the eighth year on, accelerated depreciation will not exceed straight-line depreciation. Consequently, taxpayers no longer have preferences attributable to pre-1987 real property.

[34]§ 57(a)(5).
[35]§ 141.
[36]§ 57(a)(6).

Distinguishing between Taxable and Exempt Bonds for AMT Purposes

Interest on state and local bonds generally is exempt from the regular income tax, but it may be subject to the AMT.

If the state or local bond is a private activity bond, then the interest is a tax preference for AMT purposes. According to the Bond Market Association, interest from almost 8.7 percent of the $1.9 trillion municipal bond market is subject to the AMT. The association's Web site (**http://www.investinginbonds.com**) provides a primer on the AMT's effect on municipal bonds and explains how to determine if the related interest is subject to the AMT.

SOURCE: Adapted from Tom Herman, "A Website Can help Demystify the AMT's Impact on Municipal-Bond Investors, *Wall Street Journal*, June 17, 2004, p. D2.

Accelerated depreciation on pre-1987 leased personal property was computed using specified ACRS percentages. AMT depreciation was based on the straight-line method, which was computed using the half-year convention, no salvage value, and a longer recovery period.[37] As a result, in the early years of the life of the asset, the cost recovery allowance used in computing the regular income tax was greater than the straight-line depreciation deduction allowed in computing AMT. The excess depreciation was treated as a tax preference item. For all leased personal property placed in service before 1987 (3-year, 5-year, 10-year, and 15-year public utility property), the cost recovery period has expired. Since there is no excess depreciation, there is no tax preference for AMT purposes.

The preference item for excess depreciation on leased personal property is figured separately for each piece of property. No preference is reported in the year the taxpayer disposes of the property.

Fifty Percent Exclusion for Certain Small Business Stock. Fifty percent of the gain on the sale of certain small business stock is excludible from gross income for regular income tax purposes. Seven percent of the excluded amount is a tax preference for AMT purposes.[38]

LO.5

Apply the formula for computing the AMT and illustrate Form 6251.

ILLUSTRATION OF THE AMT COMPUTATION

The computation of the AMT is illustrated in the following example.

EXAMPLE 28

Hans Sims, who is single, had taxable income for 2005 as follows:

Salary	$ 92,000
Interest	8,000
Adjusted gross income	$100,000

[37]The specified lives for AMT purposes are 5 years for 3-year property, 8 years for 5-year property, 15 years for 10-year property, and 22 years for 15-year property.

[38]§ 57(a)(7).

Less itemized deductions:		
Medical expenses ($17,500 – 7.5% of $100,000 AGI)[a]	$10,000	
State income taxes	4,000	
Interest[b]		
Home mortgage (for qualified housing)	20,000*	
Investment interest	3,300*	
Contributions (cash)	5,000*	
Casualty losses ($14,000 – 10% of $100,000 AGI)	4,000*	(46,300)
		$ 53,700
Less personal exemption		(3,200)
Taxable income		$ 50,500

[a] Total medical expenses were $17,500, reduced by 7.5% of AGI, resulting in an itemized deduction of $10,000. However, for AMT purposes, the reduction is 10%, which leaves an AMT itemized deduction of $7,500 ($17,500 – 10% of $100,000 AGI). Therefore, an adjustment of $2,500 ($10,000 – $7,500) is required for medical expenses disallowed for AMT purposes.

[b] In this illustration, all interest is deductible in computing AMTI. Qualified housing interest is deductible. Investment interest ($3,300) is deductible to the extent of net investment income included in the minimum tax base. For this purpose, the $8,000 of interest income is treated as net investment income.

Deductions marked by an asterisk are allowed as *alternative minimum tax itemized deductions*, and AMT adjustments are required for the other itemized deductions. Thus, adjustments are required for state income taxes and for medical expenses to the extent the medical expenses deductible for regular income tax purposes are not deductible in computing AMT (see note [a] above). In addition to the items that affected taxable income, Hans had $35,000 interest on private activity bonds (an exclusion tax preference). AMTI is computed as follows:

Taxable income	$ 50,500
Plus: Adjustments	
State income taxes	4,000
Medical expenses (see note [a] above)	2,500
Personal exemption	3,200
Plus: Tax preference (interest on private activity bonds)	35,000
Equals: AMTI	$ 95,200
Minus: AMT exemption	(40,250)
Equals: Minimum tax base	$ 54,950
Times: AMT rate	× 26%
Equals: Tentative AMT	$ 14,287
Minus: Regular income tax on taxable income	(9,290)
Equals: AMT	$ 4,997

The solution to Example 28 is also presented on Form 6251. Though this example is for 2005, 2004 tax forms are used because the 2005 tax forms were not available at the time of this writing.

Note that the $3,200 personal exemption amount is a positive adjustment in the Example 28 solution, but does not appear as an adjustment in Form 6251. This difference occurs because line 1 of Form 6251 includes the amount from line 40 of Form 1040. Line 40 of Form 1040 is taxable income before the deduction for personal and dependency exemptions.

Form **6251** | **Alternative Minimum Tax—Individuals** | OMB No. 1545-0227

Department of the Treasury
Internal Revenue Service (99)

▶ See separate instructions.

▶ Attach to Form 1040 or Form 1040NR.

2004
Attachment Sequence No. **32**

Name(s) shown on Form 1040: *Hans Sims* | **Your social security number**

Part I Alternative Minimum Taxable Income (See instructions for how to complete each line.)

1	If filing Schedule A (Form 1040), enter the amount from Form 1040, line 40, and go to line 2. Otherwise, enter the amount from Form 1040, line 37, and go to line 7. (If less than zero, enter as a negative amount.)	1	*53,700*
2	Medical and dental. Enter the **smaller** of Schedule A (Form 1040), line 4, **or** 2½ % of Form 1040, line 37	2	*2,500*
3	Taxes from Schedule A (Form 1040), line 9	3	*4,000*
4	Enter the home mortgage interest adjustment, if any, from line 6 of the worksheet on page 2 of the instructions	4	
5	Miscellaneous deductions from Schedule A (Form 1040), line 26	5	
6	If Form 1040, line 37, is over $142,700 (over $71,350 if married filing separately), enter the amount from line 9 of the **Itemized Deductions Worksheet** on page B-1 of the Instructions for Schedules A & B (Form 1040)	6	( )
7	Tax refund from Form 1040, line 10 or line 21	7	( )
8	Investment interest expense (difference between regular tax and AMT)	8	
9	Depletion (difference between regular tax and AMT)	9	
10	Net operating loss deduction from Form 1040, line 21. Enter as a positive amount	10	
11	Interest from specified private activity bonds exempt from the regular tax	11	*35,000*
12	Qualified small business stock (7% of gain excluded under section 1202)	12	
13	Exercise of incentive stock options (excess of AMT income over regular tax income)	13	
14	Estates and trusts (amount from Schedule K-1 (Form 1041), line 9)	14	
15	Electing large partnerships (amount from Schedule K-1 (Form 1065-B), box 6)	15	
16	Disposition of property (difference between AMT and regular tax gain or loss)	16	
17	Depreciation on assets placed in service after 1986 (difference between regular tax and AMT)	17	
18	Passive activities (difference between AMT and regular tax income or loss)	18	
19	Loss limitations (difference between AMT and regular tax income or loss)	19	
20	Circulation costs (difference between regular tax and AMT)	20	
21	Long-term contracts (difference between AMT and regular tax income)	21	
22	Mining costs (difference between regular tax and AMT)	22	
23	Research and experimental costs (difference between regular tax and AMT)	23	
24	Income from certain installment sales before January 1, 1987	24	( )
25	Intangible drilling costs preference	25	
26	Other adjustments, including income-based related adjustments	26	
27	Alternative tax net operating loss deduction	27	( )
28	**Alternative minimum taxable income.** Combine lines 1 through 27. (If married filing separately and line 28 is more than $191,000, see page 6 of the instructions.)	28	*95,200*

Part II Alternative Minimum Tax

29 Exemption. (If this form is for a child under age 14, see page 6 of the instructions.)

IF your filing status is . . .	**AND line 28 is not over . . .**	**THEN enter on line 29 . . .**
Single or head of household	$112,500	$40,250
Married filing jointly or qualifying widow(er)	150,000	58,000
Married filing separately	75,000	29,000

If line 28 is **over** the amount shown above for your filing status, see page 6 of the instructions.

29	Exemption (from table above)	29	*40,250*
30	Subtract line 29 from line 28. If zero or less, enter -0- here and on lines 33 and 35 and stop here	30	*54,950*
31	If you reported capital gain distributions directly on Form 1040, line 13; you reported qualified dividends on Form 1040, line 9b; **or** you had a gain on both lines 15 and 16 of Schedule D (Form 1040) (as refigured for the AMT, if necessary), complete Part III on the back and enter the amount from line 55 here. **All others:** If line 30 is $175,000 or less ($87,500 or less if married filing separately), multiply line 30 by 26% (.26). Otherwise, multiply line 30 by 28% (.28) and subtract $3,500 ($1,750 if married filing separately) from the result.	31	*14,287*
32	Alternative minimum tax foreign tax credit (see page 7 of the instructions)	32	
33	Tentative minimum tax. Subtract line 32 from line 31	33	*14,287*
34	Tax from Form 1040, line 43 (minus any tax from Form 4972 and any foreign tax credit from Form 1040, line 46). If you used Schedule J to figure your tax, the amounts for lines 43 and 46 of Form 1040 must be refigured without using Schedule J (see page 8 of the instructions)	34	*9,290*
35	**Alternative minimum tax.** Subtract line 34 from line 33. If zero or less, enter -0-. Enter here and on Form 1040, line 44	35	*4,997*

For Paperwork Reduction Act Notice, see page 8 of the instructions. Cat. No. 13600G Form **6251** (2004)

CONCEPT SUMMARY 15–1

AMT Adjustments and Preferences for Individuals

Adjustments	Positive	Negative	Both*
Circulation expenditures			X
Depreciation of post-1986 real property			X
Depreciation of post-1986 personal property			X
Pollution control facilities			X
Mining exploration and development costs			X
Research and experimental expenditures			X
Completed contract method			X
Incentive stock options	X**		
Adjusted gain or loss			X
Passive activity losses			X
Alternative tax NOL deduction			X
Itemized deductions:			
Medical expenses	X		
State income tax or sales tax	X		
Property tax on realty	X		
Property tax on personalty	X		
Miscellaneous itemized deductions	X		
Tax benefit rule for state income tax refund		X	
Cutback adjustment		X	
Qualified interest on student loans	X		
Qualified residence interest that is not qualified housing interest	X		
Qualified residence interest that is AMT investment interest	X	X	
Private activity bond interest that is AMT investment interest		X	
Standard deduction	X		
Personal exemptions and dependency deductions	X		
Preferences			
Percentage depletion in excess of adjusted basis	X		
Intangible drilling costs	X		
Private activity bond interest income	X		
Depreciation on pre-1987 leased personal property	X		
§ 1202 exclusion for certain small business stock	X		

*Timing differences.
**While the adjustment is a positive adjustment, the AMT basis for the stock is increased by the amount of the positive adjustment.

LO.6

Describe the role of the AMT credit in the alternative minimum tax structure.

AMT CREDIT

As discussed previously, timing differences give rise to adjustments to the minimum tax base. In later years, the timing differences reverse, as was illustrated in several of the preceding examples. To provide equity for the taxpayer when timing differences reverse, the regular income tax liability may be reduced by a tax credit for prior years' minimum tax liability attributable to timing differences.

The **alternative minimum tax credit** may be carried over indefinitely. Therefore, there is no need to keep track of when the minimum tax credit arose.[39]

EXAMPLE 29

Assume the same facts as in Example 3. Also assume that in 2005, Bob paid AMT as a result of the $20,000 positive adjustment arising from the circulation expenditures. In 2006, $10,000 of the timing difference reverses, resulting in regular taxable income that is $10,000 greater than AMTI. Because Bob has already paid AMT as a result of the write-off of circulation expenditures, he is allowed an AMT credit in 2006. The AMT credit can offset Bob's regular income tax liability in 2006 to the extent that his regular income tax liability exceeds his tentative AMT. ■

The AMT credit is applicable only for the AMT that results from timing differences. It is not available in connection with **AMT exclusions,** which represent permanent differences rather than timing differences between the regular income tax liability and the AMT. These AMT exclusions include the following:

- The standard deduction.
- Personal exemptions.
- Medical expenses, to the extent deductible for regular income tax purposes but not deductible in computing AMT.
- Other itemized deductions not allowable for AMT purposes, including miscellaneous itemized deductions, taxes, and interest expense.
- Excess percentage depletion.
- Tax-exempt interest on specified private activity bonds.

EXAMPLE 30

Don, who is single, has zero taxable income for 2005. He also has positive timing adjustments of $300,000 and AMT exclusions of $100,000. His AMT base is $400,000 because his AMT exemption is phased out completely due to the level of AMTI. Don's tentative AMT is $108,500 [($175,000 × 26% AMT rate) + ($225,000 × 28% AMT rate)]. ■

To determine the amount of AMT credit to carry over, the AMT must be recomputed reflecting only the AMT exclusions and the AMT exemption amount.

EXAMPLE 31

Assume the same facts as in the previous example. If there had been no positive timing adjustments for the year, Don's tentative AMT would have been $15,535 [($100,000 AMT exclusions – $40,250 exemption) × 26% AMT rate]. Don may carry over an AMT credit of $92,965 ($108,500 AMT – $15,535 related to AMT exclusions) to 2006 and subsequent years. ■

LO.7

Understand the basic features of the corporate AMT.

Corporate Alternative Minimum Tax

The AMT applicable to corporations is similar to that applicable to noncorporate taxpayers. However, there are several important differences:

- The corporate AMT rate is 20 percent versus a top rate of 28 percent for noncorporate taxpayers.[40]
- The AMT exemption for corporations is $40,000 reduced by 25 percent of the amount by which AMTI exceeds $150,000.[41]
- Tax preferences applicable to noncorporate taxpayers are also applicable to corporate taxpayers, but some adjustments differ (shown later in the chapter).

Although there are computational differences, the corporate AMT and the noncorporate AMT have the identical objective: to force taxpayers who are more

[39] § 53.
[40] § 55(b)(1)(B).
[41] §§ 55(d)(2) and (3).

FIGURE 15–3
AMT Formula for Corporations

Taxable income
Plus: Income tax NOL deduction
Plus or minus: AMT adjustments
Plus: Tax preferences
Equals: AMTI before ATNOLD
Minus: ATNOLD (limited to 90% of AMTI before ATNOLD)
Equals: AMTI
Minus: Exemption
Equals: AMT base
Times: 20% rate
Equals: Tentative minimum tax before AMT foreign tax credit
Minus: AMT foreign tax credit
Equals: Tentative minimum tax
Minus: Regular tax liability before credits minus regular foreign tax credit
Equals: AMT if positive

profitable than their taxable income reflects to pay additional tax. The formula for determining the corporate AMT appears in Figure 15–3.

REPEAL OF AMT FOR SMALL CORPORATIONS

Tax legislation enacted in 1997 repealed the AMT for small corporations for tax years beginning after December 31, 1997. For this purpose, a corporation is classified as a small corporation if it had average annual gross receipts of not more than $5 million for the three-year period beginning after December 1993. A corporation will continue to be classified as a small corporation if its average annual gross receipts for the three-year period preceding the current tax year and any intervening three-year periods do not exceed $7.5 million. However, if a corporation ever fails the gross receipts test, it is ineligible for small corporation classification in future tax years.[42]

Tax legislation enacted in 1998 provided an additional opportunity for a corporation to be classified as a small corporation. A corporation will automatically be classified as a small corporation in the first tax year of existence.[43]

AMT ADJUSTMENTS

Adjustments Applicable to Individuals and Corporations. The following adjustments that were discussed in connection with the individual AMT also apply to the corporate AMT:

- Excess of MACRS over ADS depreciation on real and personal property placed in service after 1986.
- Pollution control facilities placed in service after 1986 (AMT requires ADS depreciation over the asset's ADR life if placed in service before January 1, 1999, and over the MACRS recovery period if placed in service after December 31, 1998; 60-month amortization is allowed for regular income tax purposes).

[42]§§ 55(e)(1)(A) and (B). An estimated 3 million corporations (95% of incorporated businesses) qualify for this exemption.

[43]§ 55(e)(1)(C).

- Mining and exploration expenditures (AMT requires amortization over 10 years versus immediate expensing allowed for regular income tax purposes).
- Income on long-term contracts (AMT requires percentage of completion method; completed contract method is allowed in limited circumstances for regular income tax purposes).
- Dispositions of assets (if gain or loss for AMT purposes differs from gain or loss for regular income tax purposes).
- Allowable ATNOLD (which cannot exceed 90 percent of AMTI before deduction for ATNOLD).

Adjustment Applicable Only to Corporations. An AMT adjustment applicable only to corporations is the adjusted current earnings (ACE) adjustment.[44] The **ACE adjustment** generally applies to all corporations[45] and has a significant impact on both tax and financial accounting.

Corporations are subject to an AMT adjustment equal to 75 percent of the excess of ACE over AMTI before the ACE adjustment.[46] Historically, the government has not required conformity between tax accounting and financial accounting. For many years, the only *direct* conformity requirement was that a corporation that used the LIFO method for tax accounting also had to use LIFO for financial accounting.[47] Through the ACE adjustment, Congress is *indirectly* imposing a conformity requirement on corporations. Though a corporation may still choose to use different methods for tax and financial accounting purposes, it may no longer be able to do so without incurring AMT as a result of the ACE adjustment. Thus, a corporation may incur AMT not only because of specifically targeted adjustments and preferences, but also as a result of any methods that cause ACE to exceed AMTI before the ACE adjustment.

The ACE adjustment can be either a positive or a negative amount. AMTI is increased by 75 percent of the excess of ACE over unadjusted AMTI. Or AMTI is reduced by 75 percent of the excess of unadjusted AMTI over ACE. The negative adjustment is limited to the aggregate of the positive adjustments under ACE for prior years, reduced by the previously claimed negative adjustments. See Concept Summary 15–2. Thus, the ordering of the timing differences is crucial because any lost negative adjustment is permanent. Unadjusted AMTI is AMTI without the ACE adjustment or the ATNOLD.[48]

EXAMPLE 32

A calendar year corporation has the following data:

	2004	2005	2006
Pre-adjusted AMTI	$3,000	$3,000	$3,100
Adjusted current earnings	4,000	3,000	2,000

In 2004, because ACE exceeds unadjusted AMTI by $1,000, $750 (75% × $1,000) is included as a positive adjustment to AMTI. No adjustment is necessary for 2005. As unadjusted AMTI exceeds ACE by $1,100 in 2006, there is a potential negative adjustment to AMTI of $825 ($1,100 × 75%). Since the total increases to AMTI for prior years equal $750 and there are no previously claimed negative adjustments, only $750 of the potential negative adjustment reduces AMTI for 2006. Further, $75 of the negative amount is lost forever. ■

ACE should not be confused with current earnings and profits. Although many items are treated in the same manner, certain variations exist. For example, Federal

44§ 56(c).
45The ACE adjustment does not apply to S corporations. § 56(g)(6).
46§ 56(g).
47§ 472(c).
48§§ 56(g)(1) and (2).

CONCEPT SUMMARY 15–2

Determining the ACE Adjustment*

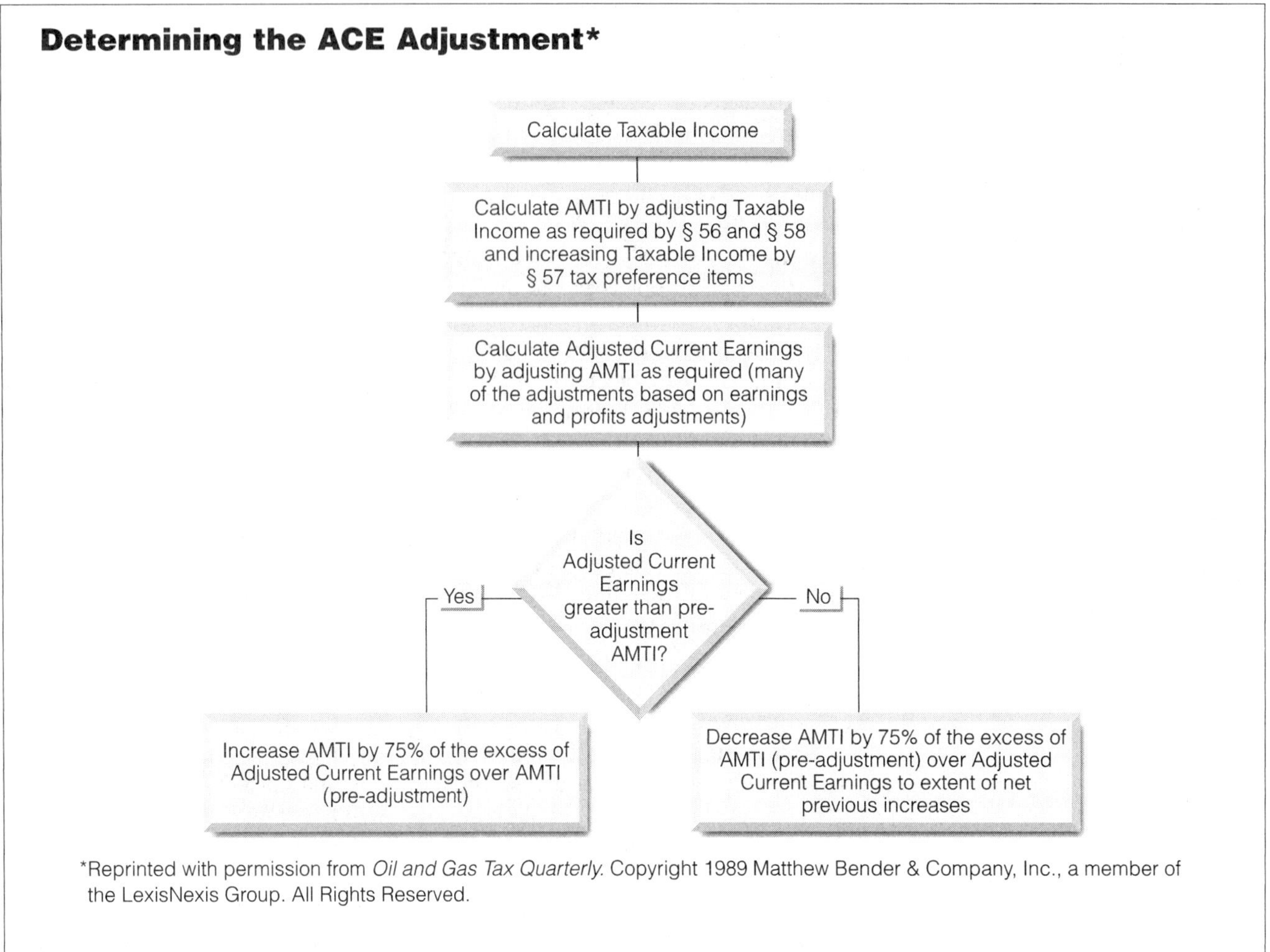
Calculate Taxable Income
Calculate AMTI by adjusting Taxable Income as required by § 56 and § 58 and increasing Taxable Income by § 57 tax preference items
Calculate Adjusted Current Earnings by adjusting AMTI as required (many of the adjustments based on earnings and profits adjustments)
Is Adjusted Current Earnings greater than pre-adjustment AMTI?
Yes
No
Increase AMTI by 75% of the excess of Adjusted Current Earnings over AMTI (pre-adjustment)
Decrease AMTI by 75% of the excess of AMTI (pre-adjustment) over Adjusted Current Earnings to extent of net previous increases

income taxes, deductible in computing earnings and profits, are not deductible in determining ACE.

The starting point for computing ACE is AMTI, which is defined as regular taxable income after AMT adjustments (other than the ATNOLD and ACE adjustments) and tax preferences. The resulting figure is adjusted for several items in order to arrive at ACE.

TAX PREFERENCES

AMTI includes designated tax preference items. In some cases, this has the effect of subjecting nontaxable income to the AMT. Tax preference items that apply to individuals also apply to corporations.

EXAMPLE 33

The following information applies to Brown Corporation (a calendar year taxpayer) for 2005:

Taxable income	$4,000,000
Mining exploration costs	500,000
Percentage depletion claimed (the property has a zero adjusted basis)	1,700,000
Interest on City of Elmira (Michigan) private activity bonds	900,000

Brown Corporation's AMTI for 2005 is determined as follows:

Taxable income		$4,000,000
Adjustments:		
Excess mining exploration costs [$500,000 (amount expensed) – $50,000 (amount allowed over a 10-year amortization period)]		450,000
Tax preferences:		
Excess depletion	$1,700,000	
Interest on private activity bonds	900,000	2,600,000
AMTI		$7,050,000

■

EXEMPTION

The tentative AMT is 20 percent of AMTI that exceeds the corporation's exemption amount. The exemption amount for a corporation is $40,000 reduced by 25 percent of the amount by which AMTI exceeds $150,000.

EXAMPLE 34

Blue Corporation has AMTI of $180,000. The exemption amount is reduced by $7,500 [25% × ($180,000 – $150,000)], and the amount remaining is $32,500 ($40,000 – $7,500). Thus, Blue Corporation's AMT base (refer to Figure 15–3) is $147,500 ($180,000 – $32,500). ■

Note that the exemption phases out entirely when AMTI reaches $310,000.

OTHER ASPECTS OF THE AMT

All of a corporation's AMT is available for carryover as a minimum tax credit. This is so regardless of whether the adjustments and preferences originate from timing differences or AMT exclusions.

EXAMPLE 35

In Example 33, the AMTI exceeds $310,000, so no exemption is allowed. The tentative minimum tax is $1,410,000 (20% of $7,050,000). Assume the regular income tax liability is $1,360,000, and the AMT liability is $50,000 ($1,410,000 – $1,360,000). The amount of the minimum tax credit carryover is $50,000, which is all of the current year's AMT. ■

LO.8

Identify tax planning opportunities to minimize the AMT.

Tax Planning Considerations

RESPONDING TO BOB AND CAROL

The chapter began with a set of circumstances involving Bob and Carol that raised a number of interesting questions. By now, the student should have arrived at a logical reason for the difference in Bob and Carol's tax liabilities and expect the following to happen to Bob.

Bob contacts Adam, his tax return preparer, and explains in an excited voice that he has received a bill from the IRS for $15,000 plus interest associated with the underpayment of his tax liability. Adam has Bob fax him a copy of the IRS deficiency notice. He checks Bob's tax file and then calls Bob to explain that Bob does owe the IRS the $15,000 plus interest. Somehow Bob's tax return was prepared without including a Form 6251 (the alternative minimum tax). Adam suggests that Bob stop by his office later that afternoon to discuss the disposition of the matter further.

AVOIDING PREFERENCES AND ADJUSTMENTS

Several strategies and elections are available to help taxpayers avoid having preferences and adjustments.

- A taxpayer who is in danger of incurring AMT liability should not invest in tax-exempt private activity bonds unless doing so makes good investment sense. Any AMT triggered by interest on private activity bonds reduces the yield on an investment in the bonds. Other tax-exempt bonds or taxable corporate bonds might yield a better after-tax return.
- A taxpayer may elect to expense certain costs in the year incurred or to capitalize and amortize the costs over some specified period. The decision should be based on the present discounted value of after-tax cash flows under the available alternatives. Costs subject to elective treatment include circulation expenditures, mining exploration and development costs, and research and experimental expenditures.

CONTROLLING THE TIMING OF PREFERENCES AND ADJUSTMENTS

The AMT exemption often keeps items of tax preference from being subject to the AMT. To use the AMT exemption effectively, taxpayers should avoid bunching preferences and positive adjustments in any one year. To avoid this bunching, taxpayers should attempt to control the timing of such items when possible.

TAKING ADVANTAGE OF THE AMT/REGULAR TAX RATE DIFFERENTIAL

A taxpayer who cannot avoid triggering the AMT in a given year can usually save taxes by taking advantage of the rate differential between the AMT and the regular income tax.

EXAMPLE 36

Peter, a real estate dealer who expects to be in the 35% regular income tax bracket in 2006, is subject to the AMT in 2005 at the 26% rate. He is considering the sale of a parcel of land (inventory) at a gain of $100,000. If he sells the land in 2006, he will have to pay tax of $35,000 ($100,000 gain × 35% regular income tax rate). However, if he sells the land in 2005, he will pay tax of $26,000 ($100,000 gain × 26% AMT rate). Thus, accelerating the sale into 2005 will save Peter $9,000 ($35,000 – $26,000) in tax. ■

EXAMPLE 37

Cora, who expects to be in the 35% tax bracket in 2006, is subject to the AMT in 2005 at the 26% rate. She is going to contribute $10,000 in cash to her alma mater, State University. If Cora makes the contribution in 2006, she will save tax of $3,500 ($10,000 contribution × 35% regular income tax rate). However, if she makes the contribution in 2005, she will save tax of $2,600 ($10,000 contribution × 26% AMT rate). Thus, deferring the contribution until 2006 will save Cora $900 ($3,500 – $2,600) in tax. ■

This deferral/acceleration strategy should be considered for any income or expenses where the taxpayer can control the timing. This strategy applies to corporations as well as to individuals.

KEY TERMS

ACE adjustment, 15–29

Alternative minimum tax (AMT), 15–2

Alternative minimum tax credit, 15–27

Alternative tax NOL deduction (ATNOLD), 15–17

AMT adjustments, 15–4

AMT exclusions, 15–27

Circulation expenditures, 15–4

Incentive stock options (ISOs), 15–13

Private activity bonds, 15–22

Tax preferences, 15–4

PROBLEM MATERIALS

Discussion Questions

1. Since there is a regular income tax, why is there a need for an AMT?
2. How can the AMT be calculated without using taxable income (as determined for purposes of the regular income tax) as a starting point?
3. What is the difference between AMT adjustments and tax preferences?
4. Identify which of the following are tax preferences:
   a. Seven percent of the exclusion associated with gains on the sale of certain small business stock.
   b. Exclusion on the receipt of property by gift or by inheritance.
   c. Exclusion associated with payment of premiums by the employer on group term life insurance for coverage not in excess of $50,000.
   d. Percentage depletion in excess of the property's adjusted basis.
   e. Tax-exempt interest on certain private activity bonds.
   f. Exclusion of life insurance proceeds received as the result of death.
5. Identify which of the following are tax preferences:
   a. Exclusion on the receipt of property by inheritance.
   b. Exclusion to employee on the employer's contribution to the employee's pension plan.
   c. Excess of deduction for circulation expenditures for regular income tax purposes over the deduction for AMT purposes.
   d. Excess of amortization allowance over depreciation on pre-1987 certified pollution control facilities.
   e. Excess of accelerated over straight-line depreciation on real property placed in service before 1987.
6. Describe the tax formula for the AMT.
7. If the regular income tax liability is greater than the tentative AMT, there is no AMT liability, and the total income tax liability is equal to the regular income tax liability. Evaluate the correctness of this statement.
8. For the exemption amount, indicate the following:
   a. Purpose for the exemption.
   b. Amount of the exemption in 2005.
   c. Reason for the phaseout of the exemption.
   d. Amount at which the phaseout of the exemption is complete.
9. What are the AMT rates for an individual taxpayer? To what levels of income do the rates apply?
10. Can any nonrefundable credits, other than the foreign tax credit, reduce the regular income tax liability below the amount of the tentative AMT?
11. Tad, who owns and operates a business, acquired machinery and placed it in service in June 1998. The machinery is 10-year property. Does Tad need to make an AMT adjustment in 1998 and in 2005 for the depreciation on the machinery? Explain.
12. How can an individual taxpayer avoid having an AMT adjustment for mining exploration and development costs?
13. **Issue ID** Rick, who is single, incurs mining exploration and development costs associated with his energy company. He would expense the costs in the current year in order to reduce his regular income tax, but is aware that this would create a positive adjustment for AMT purposes. His AGI is large enough to reduce the AMT exemption amount to zero. Therefore, he is considering electing to amortize the mining exploration and development costs over 10 years to avoid having to pay any AMT. Advise Rick.

14. Certain taxpayers have the option of using either the percentage of completion method or the completed contract method for reporting profit on long-term contracts. What impact could the AMT have on this decision?

15. Megan, a corporate executive, plans to exercise an incentive stock option (ISO) granted by her employer to purchase 200 shares of the corporation's stock for an option price of $25 per share. The stock is currently selling for $60 per share.
   a. Explain the possible consequences of this action on Megan's regular income tax and AMT.
   b. Would your response differ if Megan exercises the option and disposes of the stock in the same tax year?

16. In 1998, Desiree purchased a building for $500,000 to be used in her business. She sells the building in the current tax year. Explain why her recognized gain or loss for regular income tax purposes will be different from her recognized gain or loss for AMT purposes.

Issue ID

17. Celine is going to be subject to the AMT in 2005. She owns an investment building and is considering disposing of it and investing in other realty. Based on an appraisal of the building's value, the realized gain would be $85,000. Ed has offered to purchase the building from Celine with the closing date being December 29, 2005. Ed wants to close the transaction in 2005 because certain beneficial tax consequences will result only if the transaction is closed prior to the beginning of 2006. Abby has offered to purchase the building with the closing date being January 2, 2006. The building has a $95,000 greater AMT adjusted basis. For regular income tax purposes, Celine expects to be in the 25% tax bracket in 2005 and the 28% tax bracket in 2006. What are the relevant tax issues that Celine faces in making her decision?

18. Passive activity losses are not deductible in computing either taxable income or AMTI. Explain why an adjustment for passive activity losses may be required for AMT purposes.

19. What effect do adjustments and preferences have on the calculation of the ATNOLD?

20. The following itemized deductions are allowed for regular income tax purposes: medical expenses, state and local income taxes or sales tax, real estate taxes, personal property taxes, home mortgage interest, investment interest, charitable contributions of cash, charitable contributions of property, casualty and theft losses, unreimbursed employee business expenses, and gambling losses. Which of these itemized deductions can result in an AMT adjustment?

Issue ID

21. Matt, who is single, has always elected to itemize deductions rather than take the standard deduction. In prior years, his itemized deductions always exceeded the standard deduction by a substantial amount. As a result of paying off the mortgage on his residence, he projects that his itemized deductions for 2005 will exceed the standard deduction by only $500. Matt anticipates that the amount of his itemized deductions will remain about the same in the foreseeable future. Matt's AGI is $150,000. He is investing the amount of his former mortgage payment each month in tax-exempt bonds. A friend recommends that Matt buy a beach house in order to increase his itemized deductions with the mortgage interest deduction. What are the relevant tax issues for Matt?

22. Warren's 3% cutback adjustment for regular income tax purposes reduces his itemized deductions from $25,000 to $21,000. What effect will this have in calculating Warren's AMTI?

23. In computing the AMT itemized deduction for interest, it is possible that some interest allowed for regular income tax purposes will not be allowed. Explain.

24. Could computation of the AMT ever require an adjustment for the standard deduction or personal and dependency exemptions? Explain.

25. Alvin owns a mineral deposit that qualifies for the 15% percentage depletion rate. Under what circumstances will the depletion deduction for regular income tax purposes and AMT purposes not be the same?

Issue ID

26. Ian received a gift of $250,000 from his Aunt Nell. He is going to invest the proceeds in either taxable bonds earning interest at a 7% rate or tax-exempt bonds earning interest at a 5% rate. What are the relevant tax issues for Ian?

27. What is the purpose of the AMT credit? Briefly describe how the credit is computed.

28. What requirements must be satisfied for a corporation to be exempt from the AMT?

29. Some observers believe the ACE adjustment causes corporations to change some of the methods they use for financial accounting and tax accounting purposes. Comment.

30. Is it ever advisable for a taxpayer to defer deductions from an AMT year into a non-AMT year when the regular income tax applies? Explain and give an example of how such a deferral might be accomplished.

Problems

31. Use the following data to calculate Reba's AMT base in 2005:

Taxable income	$190,000
Positive AMT adjustments	95,000
Negative AMT adjustments	85,000
AMT preferences	28,000

Reba will file as a head of household.

Communications

32. Arthur East, an unmarried individual who is age 66, has taxable income of $130,000. He has AMT positive adjustments of $62,000 and tax preferences of $48,000.
   a. What is Arthur's AMT?
   b. What is the total amount of Arthur's tax liability?
   c. Draft a letter to Arthur explaining why he must pay more than the regular income tax liability. Arthur's address is 100 Colonel's Way, Conway, SC 29526.

33. Calculate the AMT for the following cases in 2005. The taxpayer has regular taxable income of $525,000 and does not have any credits.

	Tentative AMT	
Filing Status	**Case 1**	**Case 2**
Single	$194,000	$175,000
Married, filing jointly	194,000	175,000

34. Calculate the exemption amount for the following cases in 2005 for a single taxpayer, a married taxpayer filing jointly, and a married taxpayer filing separately.

Case	AMTI
1	$160,000
2	250,000
3	450,000

35. Leona has nonrefundable credits of $65,000 for 2005. None of these nonrefundable credits are personal credits that qualify for special treatment. Her regular income tax liability before credits is $135,000, and her tentative AMT is $78,000.
   a. What is the amount of Leona's AMT?
   b. What is the amount of Leona's regular income tax liability after credits?

Decision Making

36. Angela, who is single, incurs circulation expenditures of $123,000 during 2005. She is in the process of deciding whether to expense the $123,000 or to capitalize it and elect to deduct it over a three-year period. Angela already knows that she will be subject to the AMT for 2005 at both the 26% and the 28% rates. Angela is in the 28% bracket for regular income tax purposes this year (has regular taxable income of $123,000 before considering the circulation expenses) and expects to be in the 28% bracket in 2006 and 2007. Advise Angela on whether she should elect the three-year write-off rather than expensing the $123,000 in 2005.

37. Vito owns and operates a news agency (as a sole proprietorship). During 2005, he incurred expenses of $150,000 to increase circulation of newspapers and magazines that his agency distributes. For regular income tax purposes, he elected to expense the $150,000 in 2005. In addition, he incurred $90,000 in circulation expenditures in 2006 and again elected expense treatment. What AMT adjustments will be required in 2005 and 2006 as a result of the circulation expenditures?

38. Lonzo is a landlord who owns two apartment buildings. He acquired Forsythia Acres on February 21, 1998, for $300,000 ($90,000 allocated to the land) and Square One on November 12, 2005, for $800,000 ($100,000 allocated to the land). Neither apartment complex is low-income housing. If Lonzo elected to write off the cost of each building as fast as possible, what is the effect of depreciation (cost recovery) on his AMTI for:
   a. 1998?
   b. 2005?

Decision Making
Communications

39. In March 2005, Helen Carlon acquired used equipment for her business at a cost of $300,000. The equipment is 5-year class property for regular income tax purposes and for AMT purposes.
   a. If Helen depreciates the equipment using the method that will produce the greatest deduction for 2005 for regular income tax purposes, what is the amount of the AMT adjustment? Helen does not elect § 179 limited expensing.
   b. How can Helen reduce the AMT adjustment to $0? What circumstances would motivate her to do so?
   c. Draft a letter to Helen regarding the choice of depreciation methods. Helen's address is 500 Monticello Avenue, Glendale, AZ 85306.

Decision Making

40. In 2005, Gary incurred $600,000 of mining and exploration expenditures. He elects to deduct the expenditures as quickly as the tax law allows for regular income tax purposes.
   a. How will Gary's treatment of mining and exploration expenditures affect his regular income tax and AMT computations for 2005?
   b. How can Gary avoid having AMT adjustments related to the mining and exploration expenditures?
   c. What factors should Gary consider in deciding whether to deduct the expenditures in the year incurred?

41. Rust Company is a real estate construction business with average annual gross receipts of $3 million. Rust uses the completed contract method on a contract that requires 16 months to complete. The contract is for $500,000 with estimated costs of $300,000. At the end of 2005, $180,000 of costs had been incurred. The contract is completed in 2006 with the total cost being $295,000. Determine the amount of adjustments for AMT purposes for 2005 and 2006.

42. Burt, the CFO of Amber, Inc., is granted stock options in 2005 that qualify as incentive stock options. In 2010, the rights in the stock become freely transferable and not subject to a substantial risk of forfeiture. Burt exercises the stock options in 2009 when the option price is $70,000 and the fair market value of the stock is $100,000. He sells the stock in 2013 for $150,000. What are the regular income tax consequences and the AMT consequences for Burt in:
   a. 2005?
   b. 2009?
   c. 2010?
   d. 2013?

43. In 2005, Lori exercised an incentive stock option that had been granted by her employer, Black Corporation. Lori acquired 100 shares of Black stock for the option price of $175 per share. The rights in the stock become freely transferable and not subject to a substantial risk of forfeiture in 2005. The fair market value of the stock at the date of exercise was $210 per share. Lori sells the stock for $320 per share later in 2005.
   a. What is the amount of Lori's AMT adjustment in 2005, and what is her recognized gain on the sale for regular income tax purposes and AMT purposes?
   b. How would your answers in (a) change if Lori had sold the stock in 2006 rather than in 2005?

44. Buford sells an apartment building for $580,000. His adjusted basis is $312,000 for regular income tax purposes and $345,000 for AMT purposes. Calculate Buford's:
    a. Gain for regular income tax purposes.
    b. Gain for AMT purposes.
    c. AMT adjustment, if any.

45. Freda acquired a passive activity in 2005 for $870,000. Gross income from operations of the activity was $160,000. Operating expenses, not including depreciation, were $122,000. Regular income tax depreciation of $49,750 was computed under MACRS. AMT depreciation, computed under ADS, was $41,000. Compute Freda's passive loss deduction and passive loss suspended for regular income tax purposes and for AMT purposes.

46. Wally and Gloria incur and pay medical expenses in excess of insurance reimbursements during the year as follows:

For Wally	$11,000
For Gloria (spouse)	4,000
For Chuck (son)	1,500
For Carter (Gloria's father)	13,000

Wally and Gloria's AGI is $200,000. They file a joint return. Chuck and Carter are Wally and Gloria's dependents.
    a. What is Wally and Gloria's medical expense deduction for regular income tax purposes?
    b. What is Wally and Gloria's medical expense deduction for AMT purposes?
    c. What is the amount of the AMT adjustment for medical expenses?

47. Wolfgang's AGI is $60,000. He has the following itemized deductions for 2005:

Medical expenses [$5,500 – (7.5% × $60,000)]	$ 1,000
State income taxes	4,200
Charitable contributions	7,000
Home mortgage interest on his personal residence	6,000
Casualty loss (after $100 and 10% reductions)	1,500
Miscellaneous itemized deductions [$4,500 – 2%($60,000)]	3,300
	$23,000

    a. Calculate Wolfgang's itemized deductions for AMT purposes.
    b. What is the amount of the AMT adjustment?

48. Tom, who is single, owns a personal residence in the city. He also owns a cabin near a ski resort in the mountains. He uses the cabin as a vacation home. In February 2005, he borrowed $75,000 on a home equity loan and used the proceeds to reduce credit card obligations and other debt. During 2005, he paid the following amounts of interest:

On his personal residence	$12,000
On the cabin	6,000
On the home equity loan	4,500
On credit card obligations	1,200

What amount, if any, must Tom recognize as an AMT adjustment in 2005?

49. During the current year, Yoon earned $10,000 in dividends on corporate stock and incurred $13,000 of investment interest expense related to the stock holdings. Yoon also earned $5,000 interest on private activity bonds and incurred interest expense of $3,500 in connection with the bonds.
    a. How much investment interest expense can Yoon deduct for regular income tax and AMT purposes for the year?
    b. What is the amount of the adjustment for AMT purposes?

50. Walter and Edith, who are married with two dependents, had AGI of $110,000 in 2005. Their AGI included net investment income of $10,000 and gambling income of $2,500. They incurred the following expenses during the year (all of which resulted in itemized deductions for regular income tax purposes):

Medical expenses (before 7.5%-of-AGI floor)	$9,500
State income taxes (exceeds sales taxes)	2,800
Personal property tax	900
Real estate tax	9,100
Interest on personal residence	8,600
Interest on home equity loan (proceeds were used to buy a new fishing boat)	1,800
Investment interest expense	2,600
Charitable contribution (cash)	4,200
Unreimbursed employee expenses (before 2%-of-AGI floor)	3,800

a. What is the amount of Walter and Edith's AMT adjustment for itemized deductions in 2005? Is it positive or negative?
b. Assume the same facts as above and that Walter and Edith also earned interest of $5,000 on private activity bonds. They borrowed money to buy these bonds and paid interest of $3,900 on the loan. Determine the effect on AMTI.

51. Chuck is single, has no dependents, and does not itemize deductions. In 2005, he claims a personal exemption of $3,200 and has taxable income of $112,000. His tax preferences total $109,000. What is Chuck's AMTI for 2005?

52. Emily owns a coal mine (basis of $12,000 at the beginning of the year) that qualifies for a 15% depletion rate. Gross income from the property was $140,000, and net income before the percentage depletion deduction was $60,000. What is Emily's tax preference for excess depletion?

53. Amos incurred and expensed intangible drilling costs (IDC) of $70,000. His net oil and gas income was $60,000. What is the amount of Amos's tax preference item for IDC?

54. Jack, who is single with no dependents and does not itemize, provides you with the following information for 2005:

Short-term capital loss	$ 5,000
Long-term capital gain	25,000
Municipal bond interest received on private activity bonds acquired in 1996	9,000
Dividends from General Motors	1,500
Excess of FMV over cost of ISOs (the rights became freely transferable and not subject to a substantial risk of forfeiture in 2005)	35,000

What is the total amount of Jack's tax preference items and AMT adjustments for 2005?

55. Pat, who is single with no dependents, received a salary of $90,000 in 2005. She had interest income of $1,000, dividend income of $5,000, gambling income of $4,000, and interest income from private activity bonds of $40,000. The dividends are not qualified dividends. The following additional information is relevant:

Medical expenses (before 7.5%-of-AGI floor)	$12,000
State income taxes	4,100
Real estate taxes	2,800
Mortgage interest on residence	3,100
Investment interest expense	1,800
Gambling losses	5,100

Compute Pat's tentative minimum tax for 2005.

56. Rosa and Steve, who are married, had taxable income of $225,000 for 2005. They had positive AMT adjustments of $40,000, negative AMT adjustments of $10,000, and tax preference items of $67,500.
    a. Compute their AMTI.
    b. Compute their tentative minimum tax.

57. Farr, who is single, has no dependents and does not itemize. She has the following items relative to her tax return for 2005:

Bargain element from the exercise of an ISO (no restrictions apply to the stock)	$ 45,000
MACRS depreciation on shopping mall building acquired after 1986 and before 1999 (ADS depreciation would have yielded $26,000)	49,000
Percentage depletion in excess of property's adjusted basis	50,000
Taxable income for regular income tax purposes	121,000

    a. Determine Farr's AMT adjustments and preferences for 2005.
    b. Calculate the AMT (if any) for 2005.

58. Larry is single and has the following items for 2005:

Income—	
Salary	$141,000
Interest from bank savings account	12,000
Interest on corporate bonds	7,000
Short-term capital gain	8,000
Expenses—	
Unreimbursed employee business expenses (no meals or entertainment)	4,000
Total medical expenses	24,000
State income taxes	6,500
Real property taxes	6,800
Home mortgage (qualified housing) interest	7,200
Casualty loss on vacation home—	
Decline in value	20,000
Adjusted basis	70,000
Insurance proceeds	12,000
Tax preferences	116,000

Compute Larry's tax liability for 2005 before credits or prepayments.

59. Bonnie, who is single, has taxable income of $0 in 2005. She has positive timing adjustments of $200,000 and AMT exclusion items of $100,000 for the year. What is the amount of Bonnie's AMT credit for carryover to 2006?

60. Aqua, Inc., a calendar year corporation, has the following gross receipts and taxable income for 1993–2005:

Year	Gross Receipts	Taxable Income
1993	$11,000,000	$3,000,000
1994	4,800,000	900,000
1995	5,300,000	1,500,000
1996	4,600,000	700,000
1997	8,200,000	1,200,000
1998	8,500,000	1,900,000
1999	5,200,000	1,300,000
2000	8,000,000	1,500,000

Year	Gross Receipts	Taxable Income
2001	$ 6,000,000	$1,450,000
2002	6,200,000	1,375,000
2003	6,100,000	1,425,000
2004	10,000,000	1,400,000
2005	9,000,000	1,312,000

a. When is Aqua first exempt from the AMT as a small corporation?
b. Is Aqua subject to the AMT for 2005?

61. Gray Corporation (a calendar year corporation) reports the following information for the years listed below:

	2004	2005	2006
Unadjusted AMTI	$3,000	$2,000	$5,000
Adjusted current earnings	4,000	3,000	2,000

Compute the ACE adjustment for each year.

62. In each of the following independent situations, determine the tentative AMT:

	AMTI (Before the Exemption Amount)
Quincy Corporation	$150,000
Redland Corporation	160,000
Tanzen Corporation	320,000

63. Brown Corporation (a calendar year taxpayer) had the following transactions:

Taxable income	$2,600,000
Depreciation for regular income tax purposes on realty in excess of ADS (placed in service in 1996)	550,000
Excess amortization of certified pollution control facilities	450,000
Tax-exempt interest on private activity bonds	1,030,000
Percentage depletion in excess of the property's adjusted basis	60,000

a. Calculate Brown's regular income tax liability.
b. Calculate Brown's tentative AMT.
c. Calculate Brown's AMT.

Cumulative Problems

Tax Return Problem

64. Ron T. Freeman, age 38, is divorced and has no dependents. He pays alimony of $18,000 per year to his former wife, Kate. Kate's husband was killed in a hunting accident in 2005. At the time of the accident, their baby was only six weeks old. Ron decided to invest $10,000 each year in a mutual fund in Kate's baby's name to be used as a college fund. He made the initial $10,000 investment in 2005. Ron's Social Security number is 444–11–2222, and Kate's is 555–67–2222. Ron's address is 201 Front Street, Missoula, MT 59812. He is independently wealthy as a result of having inherited sizable holdings in real estate and corporate stocks and bonds. Ron is a minister at First Methodist Church, but he accepts no salary from the church. However, he does reside in the church's parsonage free of charge. The fair rental value of the parsonage is $2,000 a month. The church also provides him a cash grocery allowance of $200 a week. Examination of Ron's financial records provides the following information for 2005:

a. On January 16, 2005, Ron sold 2,000 shares of stock for a gain of $44,000. The stock was acquired nine months ago.
b. He received $49,000 of interest on private activity bonds.
c. He received gross rent income of $190,000 from an apartment complex he owns. He qualifies as an active participant.
d. Expenses related to the apartment complex, which he acquired in 1986, were $245,000.
e. Ron's interest income (on CDs) totaled $12,000. Since he invests only in growth stocks, he has no dividend income.
f. He won $9,000 on the lottery.
g. On October 9, 2002, Ron exercised his rights under Egret Corporation's incentive stock option plan. For an option price of $20,000, he acquired stock worth $68,000. The stock became freely transferable in 2005. At the date the stocks became freely transferable, the fair market value was $82,000.
h. Ron was the beneficiary of a $750,000 life insurance policy on his Uncle Jake. He received the proceeds in October.
i. Ron had the following potential itemized deductions *from* AGI:
   - $1,600 fair market value of stock contributed to Methodist Church (basis of stock was $1,400). He had owned the stock for two years.
   - $3,500 interest on consumer purchases.
   - $3,600 state and local income tax.
   - $4,500 medical expenses (before 7.5% floor) for himself and $8,500 of hospital expenses associated with Kate's deceased husband.
   - $200 for a safe deposit box that is used to store investments and related legal documents.
   - $8,000 paid for lottery tickets associated with playing the state lottery. Ron contributed his net winnings of $1,000 to the church.
   - $3,000 contribution to his traditional IRA.
   - Since Ron lived in Montana, he had no sales tax.

Compute Ron's tax liability, including AMT if applicable, before prepayments or credits, for 2005. Suggested software: TurboTax.

Tax Return Problem
Communications

65. Robert M. and Jane R. Armstrong live at 1802 College Avenue, Carmel, IN 46302. They are married and file a joint return for 2004. The Armstrongs have two dependent children, Ellen J. and Sean M., who are 10-year-old twins. Ellen's Social Security number is 333–42–3368, and Sean's is 333–42–3369. Robert pays child support of $16,000 for Amy, his 17-year-old daughter from his previous marriage. Amy's Social Security number is 111–22–4300. According to the divorce decree, Margaret, Robert's former wife, has legal custody of Amy. Margaret provides the balance of Amy's support (about $4,000).

Robert (224–36–9987) is a factory foreman, and Jane (443–56–3421) is a computer systems analyst. The Armstrongs' W–2 forms for 2004 reflect the following information:

	Robert	Jane
Salary (Indiana Foundry, Inc.)	$89,000	
Salary (Carmel Computer Associates)		$110,000
Federal income tax withheld	25,600	29,400
Social Security wages	87,900	87,900
Social Security withheld	5,450	5,450
Medicare wages	89,000	110,000
Medicare tax withheld	1,291	1,595
State wages	89,000	110,000
State income tax withheld	3,970	4,710

In addition to their salaries, the Armstrongs had the following income items in 2004:

Interest income (Carmel Sanitation District Bonds)	$30,200
Interest income (Carmel National Bank)	2,900
Qualified dividend income (Able Computer Corporation)	3,100
Gambling income	3,500

Jane inherited $750,000 from her grandfather in January and invested the money in the Carmel Sanitation District Bonds, which are private activity bonds. Jane was selected as the "Citizen of the Year" and received an award of $10,000. She used the $10,000 to pay credit card debt.

The Armstrongs incurred the following expenses during 2004:

Medical expenses (doctor and hospital bills)	$19,725
Real property tax on personal residence	4,900
Mortgage interest on personal residence (reported on Form 1098)	7,500
Investment interest expense	2,100
Contributions	13,000
Gambling losses	5,750
Sales taxes (from sales tax table)	1,913

On March 1, Robert and Jane contributed Ace stock to the Carmel Salvation Army, a public charity. They had acquired the stock on February 9, 1993, for $4,400. The stock was listed on the New York Stock Exchange at a value of $11,000 on the date of the contribution. In addition, Robert and Jane contributed $2,000 during the year to Second Church.

Robert sold 25 acres of land to a real estate developer on October 12, 2004, for $85,000. He had acquired it on May 15, 1998, for $67,000.

Use Forms 1040, 4952, 6251, and 8283 and Schedules A, B, and D to compute the tax liability (including AMT) for Robert and Jane Armstrong for 2004. Suggested software: TurboTax. Write a letter to the Armstrongs indicating whether they have a refund or balance due for 2004, and suggest possible tax planning strategies for 2005.

Research Problems

Note: Solutions to Research Problems can be prepared by using the ***RIA Checkpoint® Student Edition*** *online research product, which is available to accompany this text. It is also possible to prepare solutions to the Research Problems by using tax research materials found in a standard tax library.*

Research Problem 1. Gretchen is the owner of a housing unit in a cooperative housing corporation. As a tenant-stockholder, she deducts $4,800 of real estate taxes (i.e., her proportionate share of the property taxes paid by the cooperative) as an itemized deduction. She claims the $4,800 under § 216(a)(1), rather than under § 164(a)(1), because she does not have direct ownership of the housing unit.

Gretchen is aware that § 56(b)(1)(A)(ii) disallows the deduction for real estate property taxes in calculating the AMT. In calculating her AMT, Gretchen deducts the $4,800 (i.e., does not treat it as a positive adjustment) in converting regular taxable income to AMTI. Her justification for this treatment is the statutory language of § 56(b)(1)(A)(ii), which refers only to taxes deducted under § 164(a).

The IRS disagrees with Gretchen's interpretation and assesses a tax deficiency. In its opinion, the disallowance of the deduction in calculating the AMT applies to real estate taxes deducted under either § 164(a)(1) or § 216(a)(1).

Who is right?

Research Problem 2. Stuart is a journalist for a metropolitan newspaper. He has a degree in journalism from a major midwestern university.

For the past 10 years, Stuart has prepared his own income tax return. He finds doing so to be challenging and stimulating and believes that he pays lower taxes than he would if he hired a tax return preparer.

His 2003 return is audited. Although it included an AMT form (Form 6251), Stuart had not prepared it properly. Data from his Form 1040 were transferred to the wrong line in several places. In other cases, positive adjustments were not included because Stuart had failed to calculate them (e.g., did not recalculate itemized deductions for AMT purposes and did not have a positive adjustment for the personal exemption). Based on the IRS's calculation, a deficiency of $3,000 was assessed. Stuart's response to the IRS is that Form 6251 is ambiguous and misleading and, therefore, he should not be liable for the AMT. Evaluate Stuart's argument.

Partial list of research aids:
William M. Christine, 66 TCM 1025, T.C.Memo. 1993–473.

Internet Activity

Use the tax resources of the Internet to address the following question. Do not restrict your search to the World Wide Web, but include a review of newsgroups and general reference materials, practitioner sites and resources, primary sources of the tax law, chat rooms and discussion groups, and other opportunities.

Communications

Research Problem 3. Go to one of the tax newsgroups and post a short note on one of the following items relative to individuals who are subject to the AMT:

a. Interest deductions on vacation homes.
b. Charitable contributions of appreciated securities.
c. Tax preparation fees.
d. Adequacy of the exemption amount.
e. Indexing of AMT rates.

Accounting Periods and Methods

CHAPTER 16

LEARNING OBJECTIVES

After completing Chapter 16, you should be able to:

LO.1

Understand the relevance of the accounting period concept, the different types of accounting periods, and the limitations on their use.

LO.2

Apply the cash method, accrual method, and hybrid method of accounting.

LO.3

Utilize the procedure for changing accounting methods.

LO.4

Determine when the installment method of accounting can be utilized and apply the related calculation techniques.

LO.5

Understand the alternative methods of accounting for long-term contracts (the completed contract method and the percentage of completion method) including the limitations on the use of the completed contract method.

LO.6

Identify tax planning opportunities related to accounting periods and accounting methods.

OUTLINE

Tax practitioners must deal with the issue of *when* particular items of income and expense are recognized as well as the basic issue of *whether* the items are includible in taxable income. Earlier chapters discussed the types of income subject to tax (gross income and exclusions) and allowable deductions (the *whether* issue).[1] This chapter focuses on the related issue of the periods in which income and deductions are reported (the *when* issue). Generally, a taxpayer's income and deductions must be assigned to particular 12-month periods—calendar years or fiscal years.

Income and deductions are placed within particular years through the use of tax accounting methods. The basic accounting methods are the cash method, accrual method, and hybrid method. Other special purpose methods, such as the installment method and the methods used for long-term construction contracts, are available for specific circumstances or types of transactions.

Over the long run, the accounting period used by a taxpayer will not affect the aggregate amount of reported taxable income. However, taxable income for any particular year may vary significantly due to the use of a particular reporting period. Also, through the choice of accounting methods or accounting periods, it is possible to postpone the recognition of taxable income and to enjoy the benefits from deferring the related tax. This chapter discusses the taxpayer's alternatives for accounting periods and accounting methods.

LO.1

Understand the relevance of the accounting period concept, the different types of accounting periods, and the limitations on their use.

Accounting Periods

IN GENERAL

A taxpayer who keeps adequate books and records may be permitted to elect to use a **fiscal year,** a 12-month period ending on the *last day* of a month other than December, for the **accounting period.** Otherwise, a *calendar year* must be used.[2]

[1]See Chapters 4, 5, and 6.

[2]§ 441(c) and Reg. § 1.441–1(b)(1)(ii).

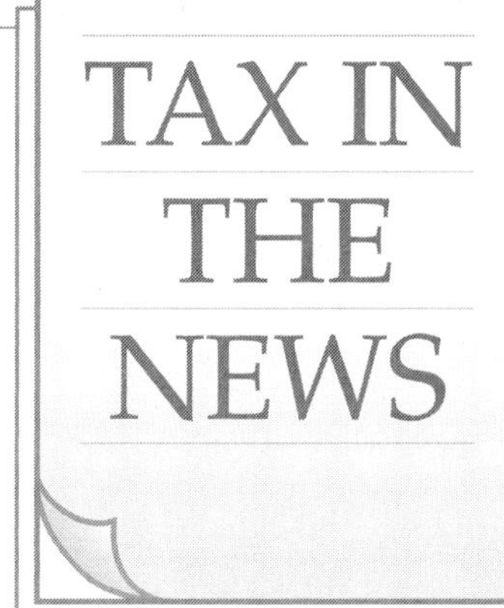

PRODUCERS' DEDUCTION CREATES TAX PLANNING OPPORTUNITIES

Under the American Jobs Creation Act of 2004, producers are allowed a deduction equal to a percentage of their income from qualified production activities: 3 percent in 2005 and 2006, 6 percent in 2007 through 2009, and 9 percent in 2010. Thus, assuming the tax rate is the same between years, a producer would prefer to take the deduction in 2007, rather than in 2006. Taking the deduction in 2006 reduces the producer's taxable income by $.03 for each dollar of production income whereas taking the deduction in 2007 reduces the producer's taxable income by $.06 on the dollar.

Frequently, corporations can satisfy the record-keeping requirements and elect to use a fiscal year.[3] Often the fiscal year conforms to a natural business year (e.g., a summer resort's fiscal year may end on September 30, after the close of the season). Individuals seldom use a fiscal year because they do not maintain the necessary books and records and because complications can arise as a result of changes in the tax law (e.g., often the transition rules and effective dates differ for fiscal year taxpayers).

Generally, a taxable year may not exceed 12 calendar months. However, if certain requirements are met, a taxpayer may elect to use an annual period that varies from 52 to 53 weeks.[4] In that case, the year-end must be on the same day of the week (e.g., the Tuesday falling closest to October 31 or the last Tuesday in October). The day of the week selected for ending the year will depend upon business considerations. For example, a retail business that is not open on Sundays may end its tax year on a Sunday so that it can take an inventory without interrupting business operations.

EXAMPLE 1

Wade is in the business of selling farm supplies. His natural business year terminates at the end of October with the completion of harvesting. At the end of the fiscal year, Wade must take an inventory, which is most easily accomplished on a Tuesday. Therefore, Wade could adopt a 52–53 week tax year ending on the Tuesday closest to October 31. If Wade selects this method, the year-end date may fall in the following month if that Tuesday is closer to October 31. The tax year ending in 2005 will contain 52 weeks beginning on Wednesday, November 3, 2004, and ending on Tuesday, November 1, 2005. The tax year ending in 2006 will have 52 weeks beginning on Wednesday, November 2, 2005, and ending on Tuesday, October 31, 2006. ■

SPECIFIC PROVISIONS FOR PARTNERSHIPS, S CORPORATIONS, AND PERSONAL SERVICE CORPORATIONS

Partnerships and S Corporations. When a partner's tax year and the partnership's tax year differ, the partner will enjoy a deferral of income. This results because the partner reports his or her share of the partnership's income and deductions for the partnership's tax year ending within or with the partner's tax year.[5] For example, if the tax year of the partnership ends on January 31, a calendar year partner will

[3]Reg. § 1.441–1(e)(2).
[4]§ 441(f).
[5]Reg. § 1.706–1(a).

not report partnership profits for the first 11 months of the partnership tax year until the following year. Therefore, partnerships are subject to special tax year requirements.

In general, the partnership tax year must be the same as the tax year of the majority interest partners. The **majority interest partners** are the partners who own a greater-than-50 percent interest in the partnership capital and profits. If there are no majority interest partners, the partnership must adopt the same tax year as its principal partners. A **principal partner** is a partner with a 5 percent or more interest in the partnership capital or profits.[6]

EXAMPLE 2

The RST Partnership is owned equally by Rose Corporation, Silver Corporation, and Tom. The partners have the following tax years.

Partner	Tax Year Ending
Rose	June 30
Silver	June 30
Tom	December 31

The partnership's tax year must end on June 30. If Silver Corporation's as well as Tom's year ended on December 31, the partnership would be required to adopt a calendar year. ■

If the principal partners do not all have the same tax year and no majority of partners have the same tax year, the partnership must use a year that results in the *least aggregate deferral* of income.[7] Under the **least aggregate deferral method,** the different tax years of the principal partners are tested to determine which produces the least aggregate deferral. This is calculated by first multiplying the combined percentages of the principal partners with the same tax year by the months of deferral for the test year. Once this is done for each set of principal partners with the same tax year, the resulting products are summed to produce the aggregate deferral. After calculating the aggregate deferral for each of the test years, the test year with the smallest summation (the least aggregate deferral) is the tax year for the partnership.

EXAMPLE 3

The DE Partnership is owned equally by Diane and Emily. Diane's fiscal year ends on March 31, and Emily's fiscal year ends on August 31. The partnership must use the partner's fiscal year that will result in the least aggregate deferral of income. Therefore, the fiscal years ending March 31 and August 31 must both be tested.

Test for Fiscal Year Ending March 31

Partner	Year Ends	Profit %	Months of Deferral	Product
Diane	3–31	50	0	0
Emily	8–31	50	5	2.5
Aggregate deferral months				2.5

Thus, with a year ending March 31, Emily would be able to defer her half of the income for five months. That is, Emily's share of the partnership income for the fiscal year ending March 31, 2006, would not be included in her income until August 31, 2006.

[6] §§ 706(b)(1)(B) and 706(b)(3).

[7] Temp.Reg. § 1.706–1T(a)(2).

Test for Fiscal Year Ending August 31

Partner	Year Ends	Profit %	Months of Deferral	Product
Diane	3–31	50	7	3.5
Emily	8–31	50	0	0
Aggregate deferral months				3.5

Thus, with a year ending August 31, Diane would be able to defer her half of the income for seven months. That is, Diane's share of the partnership income for the fiscal year ending August 31, 2006, would not be included in her income until March 31, 2007.

The year ending March 31 must be used because it results in the least aggregate deferral of income. ■

Generally, S corporations must adopt a calendar year.[8] However, partnerships and S corporations may *elect* an otherwise *impermissible year* under any of the following conditions:

- A business purpose for the year can be demonstrated.[9]
- The partnership's or S corporation's year results in a deferral of not more than three months' income, and the entity agrees to make required tax payments.[10]
- The entity retains the same year as was used for the fiscal year ending in 1987, provided the entity agrees to make required tax payments.

Business Purpose. The only business purpose for a fiscal year that the IRS has acknowledged is the need to conform the tax year to the natural business year of a business.[11] Generally, only seasonal businesses have a natural business year. For example, the natural business year for a department store may end on January 31, after Christmas returns have been processed and clearance sales have been completed.

Required Tax Payments. Under the required payments system, tax payments are due from a fiscal year partnership or S corporation by April 15 of each tax year.[12] The amount due is computed by applying the highest individual tax rate plus 1 percentage point to an estimate of the deferral period income. The deferral period runs from the close of the fiscal year to the end of the calendar year. Estimated income for this period is based on the average monthly earnings for the previous fiscal year. The amount due is reduced by the amount of required tax payments for the previous year.[13]

EXAMPLE 4

Brown, Inc., an S corporation, elected a fiscal year ending September 30. Bob is the only shareholder. For the fiscal year ending September 30, 2005, Brown earned $100,000. The required tax payment for the previous year was $5,000. The corporation must pay $4,000 by April 15, 2006, calculated as follows:

$$(\$100{,}000 \times 3/12 \times 36\%^*) - \$5{,}000 = \$4{,}000$$

*Maximum § 1 rate of 35% + 1%. ■

[8] §§ 1378(a) and (b).
[9] §§ 706(b)(1)(C) and 1378(b)(2).
[10] § 444.
[11] Rev.Rul. 87–57, 1987–2 C.B. 117.
[12] §§ 444(c) and 7519. No payment is required if the calculated amount is $500 or less.
[13] § 7519(b).

Personal Service Corporations (PSCs). A **personal service corporation (PSC)** is a corporation whose shareholder-employees provide personal services (e.g., medical, dental, legal, accounting, engineering, actuarial, consulting, or performing arts). Generally, a PSC must use a calendar year.[14] However, a PSC can *elect* a fiscal year under any of the following conditions:

- A business purpose for the year can be demonstrated.
- The PSC year results in a deferral of not more than three months' income; the corporation pays the shareholder-employee's salary during the portion of the calendar year after the close of the fiscal year; and the salary for that period is at least proportionate to the shareholder-employee's salary received for the preceding fiscal year.[15]
- The PSC retains the same year it used for the fiscal year ending in 1987, provided it satisfies the latter two requirements in the preceding option.

EXAMPLE 5

Nancy's corporation paid her a salary of $120,000 during its fiscal year ending September 30, 2005. The corporation cannot satisfy the business purpose test for a fiscal year. The corporation can continue to use its fiscal year without any negative tax effects, provided Nancy receives at least $30,000 [(3 months/12 months) × $120,000] of her salary during the period October 1 through December 31, 2005. ■

If the salary test is not satisfied, the PSC can retain the fiscal year, but the corporation's deduction for salary for the fiscal year is limited to the following:

$$A + A(F/N)$$

Where A = Amount paid after the close of the fiscal year.
F = Number of months in the fiscal year minus number of months from the end of the fiscal year to the end of the ongoing calendar year.
N = Number of months from the end of the fiscal year to the end of the ongoing calendar year.

EXAMPLE 6

Assume the corporation in the previous example paid Nancy $10,000 of salary during the period October 1 through December 31, 2005. The deduction for Nancy's salary for the corporation's fiscal year ending September 30, 2006, is thus limited to $40,000 calculated as follows:

$$\$10{,}000 + \left[\$10{,}000\left(\frac{12-3}{3}\right)\right] = \$10{,}000 + \$30{,}000 = \$40{,}000$$

■

MAKING THE ELECTION

A taxpayer elects to use a calendar or fiscal year by the timely filing of his or her initial tax return. For all subsequent years, the taxpayer must use this same period unless approval for change is obtained from the IRS.[16]

CHANGES IN THE ACCOUNTING PERIOD

A taxpayer must obtain consent from the IRS before changing the tax year.[17] This power to approve or not to approve a change is significant in that it permits the IRS to issue authoritative administrative guidelines that must be met by taxpayers

[14] § 441(i).
[15] §§ 444 and 280H.
[16] Reg. §§ 1.441–1(b)(3) and 1.441–1(b)(4).
[17] § 442. Under certain conditions, corporations are allowed to change tax years without obtaining IRS approval. See Reg. § 1.442–1(c)(1).

who wish to change their accounting period. An application for permission to change tax years must be made on Form 1128, Application for Change in Accounting Period. The application must be filed on or before the fifteenth day of the second calendar month following the close of the short period that results from the change in accounting period.[18]

EXAMPLE 7

Beginning in 2005, Gold Corporation, a calendar year taxpayer, would like to switch to a fiscal year ending March 31. The corporation must file Form 1128 by May 15, 2005. ■

IRS Requirements. The IRS will not grant permission for the change unless the taxpayer can establish a substantial business purpose for the request. One substantial business purpose is to change to a tax year that coincides with the *natural business year* (the completion of an annual business cycle). The IRS applies an objective gross receipts test to determine if the entity has a natural business year. Under this test, at least 25 percent of the entity's gross receipts for the 12-month period must be realized in the final 2 months of the 12-month period for three consecutive years.[19]

EXAMPLE 8

A Virginia Beach motel had gross receipts as follows:

	2003	2004	2005
July–August receipts	$ 300,000	$250,000	$ 325,000
September 1–August 31 receipts	1,000,000	900,000	1,250,000
Receipts for 2 months divided by receipts for 12 months	30.0%	27.8%	26.0%

Since it satisfies the natural business year test, the motel will be allowed to use a fiscal year ending August 31. ■

The IRS usually establishes certain conditions that the taxpayer must accept if the approval for change is to be granted. In particular, if the taxpayer has a net operating loss (NOL) for the short period, the IRS requires that the loss be carried forward; the loss cannot be carried back to prior years.[20] As you may recall (refer to Chapter 7), NOLs are ordinarily carried back for 2 years and forward for 20 years.

EXAMPLE 9

Parrot Corporation changed from a calendar year to a fiscal year ending September 30. The short-period return for the nine months ending September 30, 2005, reflected a $60,000 NOL. The corporation had taxable income for 2003 and 2004. As a condition for granting approval, the IRS requires Parrot to carry the loss forward rather than carrying the loss back to the two preceding years (the usual order for applying an NOL). ■

TAXABLE PERIODS OF LESS THAN ONE YEAR

A **short taxable year** (or **short period**) is a period of less than 12 calendar months. A taxpayer may have a short year for (1) the first income tax return, (2) the final income tax return, or (3) a change in the tax year. If the short period results from a change in the taxpayer's annual accounting period, the taxable income for the

[18]Reg. § 1.442–1(b)(1). In Example 7, the first period after the change in accounting period (January 1, 2005 through March 31, 2005) is less than a 12-month period and is referred to as a *short period*.

[19]Rev.Proc. 87–32, 1987–1 C.B. 131 and Rev.Rul. 87–57, 1987–2 C.B. 117.

[20]Rev.Proc. 2002–39, 2002–1 C.B. 1046.

period must be *annualized.* Due to the progressive tax rate structure, taxpayers could reap benefits from a short-period return if some adjustments were not required. Thus, the taxpayer is required to do the following:

1. Annualize the short-period income.

$$\text{Annualized income} = \text{Short-period income} \times \frac{12}{\text{Number of months in the short period}}$$

2. Compute the tax on the annualized income.
3. Convert the tax on the annualized income to a short-period tax.

$$\text{Short-period tax} = \text{Tax on annualized income} \times \frac{\text{Number of months in the short period}}{12}$$

EXAMPLE 10

Gray Corporation obtained permission to change from a calendar year to a fiscal year ending September 30, beginning in 2005. For the short period January 1 through September 30, 2005, the corporation's taxable income was $48,000. The relevant tax rates and the resultant short-period tax are as follows:

Amount of Taxable Income	Tax Rates
Not over $50,000	15% of taxable income
Over $50,000 but not over $75,000	$7,500 plus 25% of taxable income in excess of $50,000

Calculation of Short-Period Tax	
Annualized income ($48,000 × 12/9) = $64,000	
Tax on annualized income [$7,500 + .25($64,000 − $50,000)] = $7,500 + $3,500 = $11,000	
Short-period tax = ($11,000 × 9/12) = $8,250	
Annualizing the income increases the tax by $1,050:	
Tax with annualizing	$ 8,250
Tax without annualizing ($48,000 × .15)	(7,200)
Increase in tax from annualizing	$ 1,050

■

Rather than annualize the short-period income, the taxpayer can elect to (1) calculate the tax for a 12-month period beginning on the first day of the short period and (2) convert the tax in (1) to a short-period tax as follows:[21]

$$\frac{\text{Taxable income for short period}}{\text{Taxable income for the 12-month period}} \times \text{Tax on the 12 months of income}$$

EXAMPLE 11

Assume Gray Corporation's taxable income for the calendar year 2005 was $60,000. The tax on the full 12 months of income would have been $10,000 [$7,500 + .25($60,000 − $50,000)]. The short-period tax would be $8,000 [($48,000/$60,000) × $10,000]. Thus, if the corporation utilized this option, the tax for the short period would be $8,000 (rather than $8,250, as calculated in Example 10). ■

[21] §§ 443(b)(1) and (2).

For individuals, annualizing requires some special adjustments:[22]

- Deductions must be *itemized* for the short period (i.e., the standard deduction is not allowed).
- Personal and dependency exemptions must be prorated.

Fortunately, individuals rarely change tax years.

MITIGATION OF THE ANNUAL ACCOUNTING PERIOD CONCEPT

Several provisions in the Code are designed to give the taxpayer relief from the seemingly harsh results that may be produced by the combined effects of an arbitrary accounting period and a progressive rate structure. For example, under the NOL carryback and carryover rules, a loss in one year can be carried back and offset against taxable income for the preceding 2 years. Unused NOLs are then carried over for 20 years.[23] In addition, the Code provides special relief provisions for casualty losses stemming from a disaster and for the reporting of insurance proceeds from destruction of crops.[24]

Restoration of Amounts Received under a Claim of Right. The court-made **claim of right doctrine** applies when the taxpayer receives property as income and treats it as his or her own but a dispute arises over the taxpayer's rights to the income.[25] According to the doctrine, the taxpayer must include the amount as income in the year of receipt. The rationale for the doctrine is that the Federal government cannot await the resolution of all disputes before exacting a tax. As a corollary to the doctrine, if the taxpayer is later required to repay the funds, generally a deduction is allowed in the year of repayment.[26]

EXAMPLE 12

In 2005, Pedro received a $5,000 bonus computed as a percentage of profits. In 2006, Pedro's employer determined that the 2005 profits had been incorrectly computed, and Pedro had to refund the $5,000 in 2006. Pedro was required to include the $5,000 in his 2005 gross income, but he can claim a $5,000 deduction in 2006. ■

In Example 12 the transactions were a wash; that is, the income and deduction were the same ($5,000). Suppose, however, that Pedro was in the 35 percent tax bracket in 2005 but in the 15 percent bracket in 2006. Without some relief provision, the mistake would be costly to Pedro. He paid $1,750 tax in 2005 (.35 × $5,000), but the deduction reduced his tax liability in 2006 by only $750 (.15 × $5,000). The Code does provide the needed relief in such cases. Under § 1341, when income that has been taxed under the claim of right doctrine must later be repaid, in effect, the taxpayer gets to apply to the deduction the tax rate of the year that will produce the greater tax benefit. Thus, in Example 12, the repayment in 2006 would reduce Pedro's 2006 tax liability by the greater 2005 rate (.35) applied to the $5,000. However, relief is provided only in cases where the tax is significantly different; that is, when the deduction for the amount previously included in income exceeds $3,000.

[22] § 443(b)(3), § 443(c), and Reg. § 1.443–1(b).

[23] § 172. Refer to Chapter 7.

[24] §§ 165(i) and 451(d). Refer to Chapter 7.

[25] *North American Oil Consolidated v. Burnet*, 3 USTC ¶943, 11 AFTR 16, 52 S.Ct. 613 (USSC, 1932).

[26] *U.S. v. Lewis*, 51–1 USTC ¶9211, 40 AFTR 258, 71 S.Ct. 522 (USSC, 1951).

ETHICAL CONSIDERATIONS

Net Operating Loss Carryback Limits Can Put the Government Ahead of Creditors

A company may pay Federal income tax for several years, but then suffer heavy losses in excess of all of its prior income. The losses mean that assets are being consumed and are no longer available for either creditors or stockholders. Yet the government has profited from the revenue and loss stream of this company that was ultimately unsuccessful. If the loss occurs in 2003 or thereafter, the NOL provisions allow the company to recover only the taxes paid in the two years preceding the loss. Meanwhile, the company's creditors may not be able to collect their receivables from the company. One could reason that the government has collected an income tax when, in fact, there was no income, while the other creditors are unable to collect.

Tax legislation enacted in 2002 extended the two-year carryback period to five years for losses arising in taxable years ending during 2001 and 2002. This measure was largely a response to the losses suffered as a result of the 9/11 terrorist attacks. Evaluate the equity of the two-year carryback period. Should the five-year carryback period be made permanent?

LO.2

Apply the cash method, accrual method, and hybrid method of accounting.

Accounting Methods

PERMISSIBLE METHODS

Section 446 requires the taxpayer to compute taxable income using the method of accounting regularly employed in keeping his or her books, provided the method clearly reflects income. The Code recognizes the following as generally permissible **accounting methods:**

- The cash receipts and disbursements method.
- The accrual method.
- A hybrid method (a combination of cash and accrual).

The Regulations under § 446 refer to these alternatives as *overall methods* and add that the term *method of accounting* includes not only the taxpayer's overall method of accounting, but also the accounting treatment of any item.[27]

Generally, any of the three methods of accounting may be used if the method is consistently employed and clearly reflects income. However, in most cases the taxpayer is required to use the accrual method for sales and cost of goods sold if inventories are an income-producing factor to the business.[28] Other situations in which the accrual method is required are discussed later. Special methods are also permitted for installment sales, long-term construction contracts, and farmers.

A taxpayer who has more than one trade or business may use a different method of accounting for each trade or business activity. Furthermore, a taxpayer may use one method of accounting to determine income from a trade or business and use another method to compute nonbusiness items of income and deductions.[29]

EXAMPLE 13

Linda operates a grocery store and owns stocks and bonds. The sales and cost of goods sold from the grocery store must be computed by the accrual method because inventories are material. However, Linda can report her dividends and interest from the stocks and bonds under the cash method. ■

[27]Reg. § 1.446–1(a)(1).
[28]Reg. § 1.446–1(a)(4)(i).
[29]§ 446(d) and Reg. § 1.446–1(c)(1)(iv)(b).

The Code grants the IRS broad powers to determine whether the taxpayer's accounting method *clearly reflects income*. Thus, if the method employed does not clearly reflect income, the IRS has the power to prescribe the method to be used by the taxpayer.[30]

CASH RECEIPTS AND DISBURSEMENTS METHOD—CASH BASIS

Most individuals and many businesses use the cash basis to report income and deductions. The popularity of this method can largely be attributed to its simplicity and flexibility.

Under the **cash method,** income is not recognized until the taxpayer actually receives, or constructively receives, cash or its equivalent. Cash is constructively received if it is available to the taxpayer.[31] Generally, a cash equivalent is anything with a fair market value, including a note receivable from a customer.

EXAMPLE 14

Don, a dentist, does not accept credit cards. He requires that his patients either pay cash at the time the services are performed or give him a note receivable with interest at the market rate. Generally, the notes can be sold to the local banks for 95% of their face amount. At the end of 2005, Don has $60,000 in notes receivable from patients. The notes receivable are a cash equivalent and have a fair market value of $57,000 ($60,000 × 95%). Therefore, Don must include the $57,000 in his gross income for 2005. ■

Deductions are generally permitted in the year of payment. Thus, year-end accounts receivable, accounts payable, and accrued income and deductions are not included in the determination of taxable income.

In many cases, a taxpayer using the cash method can choose the year in which a deduction is claimed simply by postponing or accelerating the payment of expenses. For fixed assets, however, the cash basis taxpayer claims deductions through depreciation or amortization, the same as an accrual basis taxpayer does. In addition, prepaid expenses must be capitalized and amortized if the life of the asset extends substantially beyond the end of the tax year.[32] Most courts have applied the one-year rule (**one-year rule for prepaid expenses**) to determine whether capitalization and amortization are required. According to this rule, capitalization is required only if the asset has a life that extends beyond the tax year following the year of payment.[33]

Restrictions on Use of the Cash Method. Using the cash method to measure income from a merchandising or manufacturing operation would often yield a distorted picture of the results of operations. Income for the period would largely be a function of when payments were made for goods or materials. Thus, the Regulations prohibit the use of the cash method (and require the accrual method) to measure sales and cost of goods sold if inventories are material to the business.[34]

The prohibition on the use of the cash method if inventories are material and the rules regarding prepaid expenses (discussed above) are intended to assure that annual income is clearly reflected. However, certain taxpayers may not use the cash method of accounting for Federal income tax purposes regardless of whether inventories are material. The accrual basis must be used to report the income earned

[30]§ 446(b).

[31]Reg. § 1.451–1(a). Refer to Chapter 4 for a discussion of constructive receipt.

[32]Reg. § 1.461–1(a)(1).

[33]*Zaninovich v. Comm.*, 80–1 USTC ¶9342, 45 AFTR2d 80–1442, 616 F.2d 429 (CA–9, 1980), *rev'g* 69 T.C. 605 (1978); *U.S. Freightways Corp. v. Comm.*, 2001–2 USTC ¶50,731, 88 AFTR2d 2001–6703, 270 F.3d 1137 (CA–7, 2001), *rev'g* 113 T.C. 329 (1999). Refer to Chapter 6 for further discussion of the one-year rule. See also Reg. § 1.263(a)–4(f) for the application of the one-year rule to prepayments for intangibles.

[34]Reg. § 1.446–1(a)(4)(i).

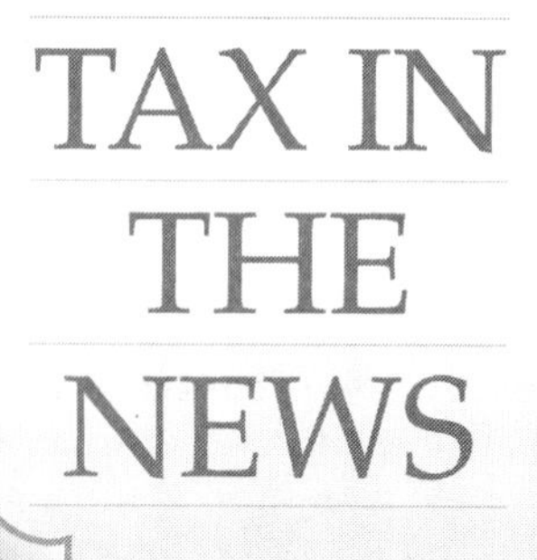

Who Wants to Be a Producer?

For many years, small businesses wanted to be considered service providers rather than producers of products. Service provider classification meant that the cash method could be used. Now, however, classification as a producer can be advantageous. As a result of the American Jobs Creation Act of 2004, producers can deduct 3 percent of their production income in calculating taxable income for 2005 and 2006 (6 percent in 2007–2009 and 9 percent in 2010). Thus, a company that develops advertising materials might argue that it is a producer rather than a provider of advertising services.

by (1) a corporation (other than an S corporation), (2) a partnership with a corporate partner, and (3) a tax shelter.[35] This accrual basis requirement has three exceptions:[36]

- A farming business.
- A qualified personal service corporation (a corporation performing services in health, law, engineering, architecture, accounting, actuarial science, performing arts, or consulting).
- An entity that is not a tax shelter whose average annual gross receipts for the most recent three-year period are $5 million or less.

As a matter of administrative convenience, the IRS will permit any entity with average annual gross receipts of not more than $1 million for the most recent three-year period to use the cash method. This applies even if the taxpayer is buying and selling inventory. Also as a matter of administrative convenience, the IRS will permit certain entities whose average annual gross receipts are greater than $1 million but are not more than $10 million for the most recent three-year period to use the cash method. However, under the $10 million exception, inventory on hand at the end of the tax year cannot be deducted until the inventory is sold (i.e., it must be capitalized). Not eligible for the cash method under the $10 million exception are entities whose principal business activity (the activity producing the largest percentage of gross receipts) is selling goods, manufacturing, mining, and certain publishing activities. Also not eligible are the C corporations, partnerships, and tax shelters discussed above that must use the accrual method. The major beneficiaries of the $10 million exception are small construction companies and small service businesses that sell some goods in conjunction with the services provided.[37]

Farming. Although inventories are material to farming operations, the IRS long ago created an exception to the general rule that allows farmers to use the cash method of accounting.[38] The purpose of the exception is to relieve the small farmer from the bookkeeping burden of accrual accounting. However, tax shelter promoters recognized, for example, that by deducting the costs of a crop in one tax year and harvesting the crop in a later year, income could be deferred from tax. Thus, §§ 447 and 464 were enacted to prevent certain farming corporations and limited partnerships (farming syndicates) from using the cash method.[39]

[35] § 448(a). For this purpose, the hybrid method of accounting is considered the same as the cash method.

[36] § 448(b).

[37] Rev.Proc. 2001–10, 2001–1 C.B. 272 and Rev.Proc. 2002–28, 2002–1 C.B. 815.

[38] Reg. § 1.471–6(a).

[39] Section 447(c) contains counterexceptions that allow certain closely held corporations to use the cash method. See also § 464(c).

Cash method farmers must nevertheless capitalize their costs of raising trees that have a preproduction period of more than two years.[40] Thus, an apple farmer generally must capitalize the costs of raising the trees until they produce apples in merchantable quantities. However, to simplify the farmer's tax accounting, the cash method farmer is given an option: the preproduction cost of the trees can be expensed if the taxpayer elects to use the alternative depreciation system (refer to Chapter 8) for all the farming assets.

Generally, the cost of purchasing an animal must be capitalized. However, the cash basis farmer's cost of raising the animal can be expensed.[41]

ACCRUAL METHOD

All Events Test for Income. Under the **accrual method,** an item is generally included in gross income for the year in which it is earned, regardless of when the income is collected. An item of income is earned when (1) all the events have occurred to fix the taxpayer's right to receive the income and (2) the amount of income (the amount the taxpayer has a right to receive) can be determined with reasonable accuracy.[42]

EXAMPLE 15

Andre, a calendar year taxpayer who uses the accrual method of accounting, was to receive a bonus equal to 6% of Blue Corporation's net income for its fiscal year ending each June 30. For the fiscal year ending June 30, 2005, Blue had net income of $240,000, and for the six months ending December 31, 2005, the corporation's net income was $150,000. Andre will report $14,400 (.06 × $240,000) for 2005 because his right to the amount became fixed when Blue's year closed. However, Andre would not accrue income based on the corporation's profits for the last six months of 2005 since his right to the income does not accrue until the close of the corporation's tax year. ■

An accrual basis taxpayer's amount of income and the tax year the income is recognized are based on his or her right to receive the income. Thus, the fair market value of a receivable is irrelevant.

EXAMPLE 16

Marcey, an accrual basis taxpayer, has provided services to clients and has the right to receive $60,000. The clients have signed notes receivable to Marcey that have a fair market value of $57,000. Marcey must include $60,000, the amount she has the right to receive, in her gross income, rather than the fair market value of the notes of $57,000. Compare this treatment to that required for the cash basis taxpayer in Example 14. ■

As discussed in Chapter 4, when an accrual basis taxpayer receives prepaid income that will not all be earned by the end of the tax year following the tax year of receipt, generally the income that is not earned by the end of the year of receipt must be allocated to the following year.

EXAMPLE 17

Troy sells computers and two-year service contracts on the computers. On November 1, 2005, Troy sold a 24-month service contract and received $240. He recognizes $20 gross income in 2005 ($240 × 2/24) and $220 ($240 – $20) in 2006. ■

However, the deferral of prepaid income is not available for prepaid rent and prepaid interest.

In a situation where the accrual basis taxpayer's right to income is being contested and the income has not yet been collected, generally no income is recog-

[40] § 263A(d).

[41] Reg. § 1.162–12(a).

[42] Reg. § 1.451–1(a). Refer to Chapter 4 for further discussion of the accrual method.

Applying the All Events Test to Cooperative Advertising

Manufacturers often offer local dealers a rebate for a portion of the cost of advertising that includes the manufacturer's brand. Automobile manufacturers make extensive use of these cooperative advertising plans. Under such a plan, the dealer runs advertisements in local newspapers and applies for a rebate from the manufacturer. The tax accounting issue is when should the manufacturer take the deduction for the rebate. Is the all events test satisfied when the dealer places the advertisement or not until the dealer applies for the rebate?

The IRS has ruled that the all events test is satisfied when the advertising occurs and that the filing of a claim for a rebate is merely a ministerial act. Therefore, the manufacturer can take the deduction in the year the advertising occurs, rather than when the dealer's claim is filed.

nized until the dispute has been settled.[43] Before the settlement, "all of the events have not occurred that fix the right to receive the income."

All Events and Economic Performance Tests for Deductions. An **all events test** applies to accrual basis deductions. A deduction cannot be claimed until (1) all the events have occurred to create the taxpayer's liability and (2) the amount of the liability can be determined with reasonable accuracy.[44] Once these requirements are satisfied, the deduction will be permitted only if economic performance has occurred.[45]

The **economic performance test** addresses situations in which the taxpayer has either of the following obligations:

1. To pay for services or property to be provided in the future.
2. To provide services or property (other than money) in the future.

When services or property are to be provided to the taxpayer in the future (situation 1), economic performance occurs when the property or services are actually provided by the other party.

EXAMPLE 18

An accrual basis, calendar year taxpayer, JAB, Inc., promoted a boxing match held in the company's arena on December 31, 2005. CLN, Inc., had contracted to clean the arena for $5,000, but did not actually perform the work until January 1, 2006. JAB, Inc., did not pay the $5,000 until 2007. Although financial accounting would require JAB, Inc., to accrue the $5,000 cleaning expense in 2005 to match the revenues from the fight, the economic performance test was not satisfied until 2006, when CLN, Inc., performed the service. Thus, JAB, Inc., must deduct the expense in 2006. ■

If the taxpayer is obligated to provide property or services (situation 2), economic performance occurs (and thus the deduction is allowed) in the year the taxpayer provides the property or services.

EXAMPLE 19

Copper Corporation, an accrual basis taxpayer, is in the strip mining business. According to the contract with the landowner, the company must reclaim the land. The estimated cost of reclaiming land mined in 2005 was $500,000, but the land was not actually reclaimed

[43] *Burnet v. Sanford & Brooks Co.*, 2 USTC ¶636, 9 AFTR 603, 51 S.Ct. 150 (USSC, 1931).

[44] § 461(h)(4).

[45] § 461(h).

until 2007. The all events test was satisfied in 2005. The obligation existed, and the amount of the liability could be determined with reasonable accuracy. However, the economic performance test was not satisfied until 2007. Therefore, the deduction is not allowed until 2007.[46] ■

The economic performance test is waived if the *recurring item exception* applies. Year-end accruals can be deducted if all the following conditions are met:

- The obligation exists and the amount of the liability can be reasonably estimated.
- Economic performance occurs within a reasonable period (but not later than 8½ months after the close of the taxable year).
- The item is recurring in nature and is treated consistently by the taxpayer.
- Either the accrued item is not material, or accruing it results in a better matching of revenues and expenses.

EXAMPLE 20

Green Corporation often sells goods that are on hand but cannot be shipped for another week. Thus, the sales account usually includes revenues for some items that have not been shipped at year-end. Green Corporation is obligated to pay shipping costs. Although the company's obligation for shipping costs can be determined with reasonable accuracy, economic performance is not satisfied until Green (or its agent) actually delivers the goods. However, accruing shipping costs on sold items will better match expenses with revenues for the period. Therefore, the company should be allowed to accrue the shipping costs on items sold but not shipped at year-end. ■

The economic performance test as set forth in the Code does not address all possible accrued expenses. That is, in some cases the taxpayer incurs costs even though no property or services were received. In these instances, according to the Regulations, economic performance generally is not satisfied until the liability is paid. The following liabilities are cases in which payment is generally the only means of satisfying economic performance:[47]

1. Workers' compensation.
2. Torts.
3. Breach of contract.
4. Violation of law.
5. Rebates and refunds.
6. Awards, prizes, and jackpots.
7. Insurance, warranty, and service contracts.[48]
8. Taxes.

EXAMPLE 21

Yellow Corporation sold defective merchandise that injured a customer. Yellow admitted liability in 2005, but did not pay the claim until January 2006. The customer's tort claim cannot be deducted until it is paid. ■

However, items (5) through (8) above are eligible for the aforementioned recurring item exception.

EXAMPLE 22

Pelican Corporation filed its 2005 state income tax return in March 2006. At the time the return was filed, Pelican was required to pay an additional $5,000. The state taxes are eligible for the recurring item exception. Thus, the $5,000 of state income taxes can be deducted on

[46]See § 468 for an elective method for reporting reclamation costs.

[47]Reg. §§ 1.461–4(g)(2)–(6) and 1.461–5(c).

[48]This item applies to contracts the taxpayer enters into for his or her own protection, rather than the taxpayer's liability as insurer, warrantor, or service provider.

the corporation's 2005 Federal tax return. The deduction is allowed because all the events had occurred to fix the liability as of the end of 2005, the payment was made within 8½ months after the end of the tax year, the item is recurring in nature, and allowing the deduction in 2005 produces a good matching of revenues and expenses. ■

Reserves. Generally, the all events and economic performance tests will prevent the use of reserves (e.g., for product warranty expense) frequently used in financial accounting to match expenses with revenues. However, small banks are allowed to use a bad debt reserve.[49] Furthermore, an accrual basis taxpayer in a service business is permitted to not accrue revenue that appears uncollectible based on experience. In effect, this approach indirectly allows a reserve.[50]

HYBRID METHOD

A **hybrid method** of accounting involves the use of more than one method. For example, a taxpayer who uses the accrual basis to report sales and cost of goods sold but uses the cash basis to report other items of income and expense is employing a hybrid method. The Code permits the use of a hybrid method provided the taxpayer's income is clearly reflected.[51] A taxpayer who uses the accrual method for business expenses must also use the accrual method for business income (the cash method may not be used for income items if the taxpayer's expenses are accounted for under the accrual method).

It may be preferable for a business that is required to report sales and cost of goods sold on the accrual method to report other items of income and expense under the cash method. The cash method permits greater flexibility in the timing of income and expense recognition.

LO.3

Utilize the procedure for changing accounting methods.

CHANGE OF METHOD

The taxpayer, in effect, makes an election to use a particular accounting method when an initial tax return is filed using that method. If a subsequent change in method is desired, the taxpayer must obtain the permission of the IRS. The request for change is made on Form 3115, Application for Change in Accounting Method. Generally, the form must be filed within the taxable year of the desired change.[52]

As previously mentioned, the term *accounting method* encompasses not only the overall accounting method used by the taxpayer (the cash or accrual method) but also the treatment of any material item of income or deduction.[53] Thus, a change in the method of deducting property taxes from a cash basis to an accrual basis that results in a deduction for taxes in a different year constitutes a change in an accounting method. Another example of an accounting method change is a change involving the method or basis used in the valuation of inventories. However, a change in treatment resulting from a change in the underlying facts does not constitute a change in the taxpayer's method of accounting.[54] For example, a change in employment contracts so that an employee accrues one day of vacation pay for each month of service rather than 12 days of vacation pay for a full year of service is a change in the underlying facts and, thus, is not an accounting method change.

Correction of an Error. A change in accounting method should be distinguished from the *correction of an error*. The taxpayer can correct an error (by filing amended returns) without permission, and the IRS can simply adjust the taxpayer's liability

[49] § 585.
[50] § 448(d)(5).
[51] § 446(c).
[52] Rev.Proc. 99–49, 1999–2 C.B. 725.
[53] Reg. § 1.446–1(a)(1).
[54] Reg. § 1.446–1(e)(2)(ii).

if an error is discovered on audit of the return. Some examples of errors are incorrect postings, errors in the calculation of tax liability or tax credits, deductions of business expense items that are actually personal, and omissions of income and deductions.[55] Unless the taxpayer or the IRS corrects the error within the statute of limitations, the taxpayer's total lifetime taxable income will be overstated or understated by the amount of the error.

Change from an Incorrect Method. An *incorrect accounting method* is the consistent (year-after-year) use of an incorrect rule to report an item of income or expense. The incorrect accounting method generally will not affect the taxpayer's total lifetime income (unlike the error). That is, an incorrect method has a self-balancing mechanism. For example, deducting freight on inventory in the year the goods are purchased, rather than when the inventory is sold, is an incorrect accounting method. The total cost of goods sold over the life of the business is not affected, but the year-to-year income is incorrect.[56]

If a taxpayer is employing an incorrect method of accounting, permission must be obtained from the IRS to change to a correct method. An incorrect method is not treated as a mechanical error that can be corrected by merely filing an amended tax return.

The tax return preparer as well as the taxpayer will be subject to penalties if the tax return is prepared using an incorrect method of accounting and permission for a change to a correct method has not been requested.[57]

Net Adjustments Due to Change in Accounting Method. In the year of a change in accounting method, some items of income and expense may have to be adjusted to prevent the change from distorting taxable income.

EXAMPLE 23

In 2005, White Corporation, with consent from the IRS, switched from the cash to the accrual basis for reporting sales and cost of goods sold. The corporation's accrual basis gross profit for the year was computed as follows:

Sales		$100,000
Beginning inventory	$ 15,000	
Plus: Purchases	60,000	
Less: Ending inventory	(10,000)	
Cost of goods sold		(65,000)
Gross profit		$ 35,000

At the end of the previous year, White Corporation had accounts receivable of $25,000 and accounts payable for merchandise of $34,000. The accounts receivable from the previous year in the amount of $25,000 were never included in gross income since White was on the cash basis and did not recognize the uncollected receivables. In the current year, the $25,000 was not included in the accrual basis sales since the sales were made in a prior year. Therefore, a $25,000 adjustment to income is required to prevent the receivables from being omitted from income.

The corollary of the failure to recognize a prior year's receivables is the failure to recognize a prior year's accounts payable. The beginning of the year's accounts payable were not included in the current or prior year's purchases. Thus, a deduction for the $34,000 was not taken in either year and is therefore included as an adjustment to income for the period of change.

[55]Reg. § 1.446–1(e)(2)(ii)(b).

[56]But see *Korn Industries v. U.S.*, 76–1 USTC ¶9354, 37 AFTR2d 76–1228, 532 F.2d 1352 (Ct.Cls., 1976).

[57]§ 446(f). See Chapter 26.

An adjustment is also required to reflect the $15,000 beginning inventory that White deducted (due to the use of a cash method of accounting) in the previous year. In this instance, the cost of goods sold during the year of change was increased by the beginning inventory and resulted in a double deduction.

The net adjustment due to the change in accounting method is computed as follows:

Beginning inventory (deducted in prior and current year)	$ 15,000
Beginning accounts receivable (omitted from income)	25,000
Beginning accounts payable (omitted from deductions)	(34,000)
Net increase in taxable income	$ 6,000

Disposition of the Net Adjustment. Required changes in accounting methods are the result of an IRS examination. The IRS usually will examine all years that are open under the statute of limitations. Generally, this means that the three preceding years are examined. The IRS will not require a change unless the net adjustment is positive. That adjustment generally must be included in gross income for the year of the change. Additional tax and interest on the tax will be due. However, if the adjustment is greater than $3,000, the taxpayer can elect to calculate the tax by spreading the adjustment over one or more previous years.[58] The election is beneficial if the taxpayer's marginal tax rate for the prior years is lower than the marginal tax rate for the year of the change.

To encourage taxpayers to *voluntarily* change from incorrect methods and to facilitate changes from one correct method to another, the IRS generally allows the taxpayer to spread a positive adjustment into future years. One-fourth of the adjustment is applied to the year of the change, and one-fourth of the adjustment is applied to each of the next three taxable years. A negative adjustment can be deducted in the year of the change.[59]

LO.4

Determine when the installment method of accounting can be utilized and apply the related calculation techniques.

Special Accounting Methods

Generally, accrual basis taxpayers recognize income when goods are sold and shipped to the customer. Cash basis taxpayers generally recognize income from a sale on the collection of cash from the customer. The tax law provides special accounting methods for certain installment sales and long-term contracts. These special methods were enacted, in part, to assure that the tax will be due when the taxpayer is best able to pay the tax.

INSTALLMENT METHOD

Under the general rule for computing the gain or loss from the sale of property, the taxpayer recognizes the entire amount of gain or loss upon the sale or other disposition of the property.

EXAMPLE 24

Mark sells property to Fran for $10,000 cash plus Fran's note (fair market value and face amount of $90,000). Mark's basis for the property was $15,000. Gain or loss is computed under either the cash or accrual basis as follows:

[58] § 481(b). See also Notice 98–31, 1998–1 C.B. 1165.

[59] Rev.Proc. 99–49, 1999–2 C.B. 725 and Rev.Proc. 2002–19, 2002–1 C.B. 696.

Selling price:	
Cash down payment	$ 10,000
Note receivable	90,000
	$100,000
Less: Basis in the property	(15,000)
Realized gain	$ 85,000

In Example 24, the general rule for recognizing gain or loss requires Mark to pay a substantial amount of tax on the gain in the year of sale even though he receives only $10,000 of cash. Congress enacted the installment sales provisions to prevent this sort of hardship by allowing the taxpayer to spread the gain from installment sales over the collection period. The *installment method* is a very important planning tool because of the tax deferral possibilities.

Eligibility and Calculations. The **installment method** applies to *gains* (but not losses) from the sale of property by a taxpayer who will receive at least one payment *after* the year of sale. For many years, practically all gains from the sale of property were eligible for the installment method. However, over the years, the Code has been amended to *deny* the use of the installment method for the following:[60]

- Gains on property held for sale in the ordinary course of business.
- Depreciation recapture under § 1245 or § 1250.
- Gains on stocks or securities traded on an established market.

As an exception to the first item, the installment method may be used to report gains from sales of the following:[61]

- Time-share units (e.g., the right to use real property for two weeks each year).
- Residential lots (if the seller is not to make any improvements).
- Any property used or produced in the trade or business of farming.

The Nonelective Aspect. As a general rule, eligible sales *must* be reported by the installment method.[62] A special election is required to report the gain by any other method of accounting (see the discussion in a subsequent section of this chapter).

Computing the Gain for the Period. The gain reported on each sale is computed by the following formula:

$$\frac{\text{Total gain}}{\text{Contract price}} \times \text{Payments received} = \text{Recognized gain}$$

The taxpayer must compute each variable as follows:

1. *Total gain* is the selling price reduced by selling expenses and the adjusted basis of the property. The selling price is the total consideration received by the seller, including notes receivable from the buyer, and the seller's liabilities assumed by the buyer.
2. *Contract price* is the selling price less the seller's liabilities that are assumed by the buyer. Generally, the contract price is the amount, other than interest, the seller will receive from the purchaser.
3. *Payments received* are the collections on the contract price received in the tax year. This generally is equal to the cash received less the interest income

[60]§§ 453(b), (i), and (l).
[61]§ 453(l)(2).
[62]§ 453(a).

collected for the period. If the buyer pays any of the seller's expenses, the seller regards the amount paid as a payment received.

EXAMPLE 25

The seller is not a dealer, and the facts are as follows:

Sales price (amount realized):		
Cash down payment	$ 1,000	
Seller's mortgage assumed	3,000	
Notes payable to the seller	13,000	$ 17,000
Less: Selling expenses		(500)
Less: Seller's basis		(10,000)
Total gain		$ 6,500

The contract price is $14,000 ($17,000 – $3,000). Assuming the $1,000 is the only payment in the year of sale, the recognized gain in that year is computed as follows:

$$\frac{\$6{,}500 \text{ (total gain)}}{\$14{,}000 \text{ (contract price)}} \times \$1{,}000 = \$464 \text{ (gain recognized in year of sale)}$$ ■

If the sum of the seller's basis and selling expenses is less than the liabilities assumed by the buyer, the difference must be added to the contract price and to the payments (treated as *deemed payments*) received in the year of sale.[63] This adjustment to the contract price is required so that the ratio of total gain to contract price will not be greater than one. The adjustment also accelerates the reporting of income from the deemed payments.

EXAMPLE 26

Assume the same facts as in Example 25, except that the seller's basis in the property is only $2,000. The total gain, therefore, is $14,500 [$17,000 – ($2,000 + $500)]. Payments in the year of sale are $1,500 and are calculated as follows:

Down payment	$1,000
Excess of mortgage assumed over seller's basis and selling expenses ($3,000 – $2,000 – $500)	500
	$1,500

The contract price is $14,500 [$17,000 (sales price) – $3,000 (seller's mortgage assumed) + $500 (excess of mortgage assumed over seller's basis and selling expenses)]. The gain recognized in the year of sale is computed as follows:

$$\frac{\$14{,}500 \text{ (total gain)}}{\$14{,}500 \text{ (contract price)}} \times \$1{,}500 = \$1{,}500$$

In subsequent years, all amounts the seller collects on the note principal ($13,000) will be recognized gain ($13,000 × 100%). ■

As previously discussed, gains attributable to ordinary income recapture under §§ 1245 and 1250 are *ineligible* for installment reporting. Therefore, the § 1245 or § 1250 gain realized must be recognized in the year of sale, and the installment sale gain is the remaining gain.

EXAMPLE 27

Olaf sold an apartment building for $50,000 cash and a $75,000 note due in two years. Olaf's basis in the property was $25,000, and he recaptured $40,000 ordinary income under § 1250.

[63] Temp.Reg. § 15a.453–1(b)(2)(iii).

Olaf's realized gain is $100,000 ($125,000 – $25,000), and the $40,000 recapture must be recognized in the year of sale. Of the $60,000 remaining § 1231 gain, $24,000 must be recognized in the year of sale:

$$\frac{\text{§ 1231 gain}}{\text{Contract price}} \times \text{Payments received} = \frac{\$125{,}000 - \$25{,}000 - \$40{,}000}{\$125{,}000} \times \$50{,}000$$

$$= \frac{\$60{,}000}{\$125{,}000} \times \$50{,}000 = \$24{,}000$$

The remaining realized gain of $36,000 ($60,000 – $24,000) will be recognized as the $75,000 note is collected. ■

Imputed Interest. If a deferred payment contract for the sale of property with a selling price greater than $3,000 does not contain a reasonable interest rate, a reasonable rate is imputed.[64] The imputing of interest effectively restates the selling price of the property to equal the sum of the payments at the date of the sale and the discounted present value of the future payments. The difference between the present value of a future payment and the payment's face amount is taxed as interest income, as discussed in the following paragraphs. Thus, the **imputed interest** rules prevent sellers of capital assets from increasing the selling price to reflect the equivalent of unstated interest on deferred payments and thereby converting ordinary (interest) income into long-term capital gains. In addition, the imputed interest rules are important because they affect the timing of income recognition.

Generally, if the contract does not charge at least the Federal rate, interest will be imputed at the Federal rate. The Federal rate is the interest rate the Federal government pays on new borrowing and is published monthly by the IRS.[65]

As a general rule, the buyer and seller must account for interest on the accrual basis with semiannual compounding.[66] Requiring the use of the accrual basis assures that the seller's interest income and the buyer's interest expense are reported in the same tax year. The following example illustrates the calculation and amortization of imputed interest.

EXAMPLE 28

Peggy, a cash basis taxpayer, sold land on January 1, 2005, for $200,000 cash and $6 million due on December 31, 2006, with 5% interest payable December 31, 2005, and December 31, 2006. Assume that at the time of the sale, the Federal rate was 8% (compounded semiannually). Because Peggy did not charge at least the Federal rate, interest will be imputed at 8% (compounded semiannually).

Date	Payment	Present Value (at 8%) on 1/1/2005	Imputed Interest
12/31/2005	$ 300,000	$ 277,500	$ 22,500
12/31/2006	6,300,000	5,386,500	913,500
	$6,600,000	$5,664,000	$936,000

Thus, the selling price will be restated to $5,864,000 ($200,000 + $5,664,000) rather than $6,200,000 ($200,000 + $6,000,000), and Peggy will recognize interest income in accordance with the following amortization schedule:

[64] §§ 483 and 1274.

[65] § 1274(d)(1). There are three Federal rates: short term (not over three years), midterm (over three years but not over nine years), and long term (over nine years).

[66] §§ 1274(a), 1273(a), and 1272(a).

Concept Summary 16–1

Interest on Installment Sales

	Imputed Interest Rate
General rule	Federal rate
Exceptions:	
• Principal amount not over $2.8 million.[1]	Lesser of Federal rate or 9%
• Sale of land (with a calendar year ceiling of $500,000) between family members (the seller's spouse, brothers, sisters, ancestors, or lineal descendants).[2]	Lesser of Federal rate or 6%

	Method of Accounting for Interest	
	Seller's Interest Income	Buyer's Interest Expense
General rule[3]	Accrual	Accrual
Exceptions:		
• Total payments under the contract are $250,000 or less.[4]	Taxpayer's overall method	Taxpayer's overall method
• Sale of a farm (sales price of $1 million or less).[5]	Taxpayer's overall method	Taxpayer's overall method
• Sale of a principal residence.[6]	Taxpayer's overall method	Taxpayer's overall method
• Sale for a note with a principal amount of not over $2 million, the seller is on the cash basis, the property sold is not inventory, and the buyer agrees to report expense by the cash method.[7]	Cash	Cash

[1]§ 1274A(b). This amount is adjusted annually for inflation. For 2005, the amount is $4,483,000.
[2]§§ 1274(c)(3)(F) and 483(e).
[3]§§ 1274(a) and 1272(a)(3).
[4]§§ 1274(c)(3)(C) and 483.
[5]§§ 1274(c)(3)(A) and 483.
[6]§§ 1274(c)(3)(B) and 483.
[7]§ 1274A(c). This amount is adjusted annually for inflation. For 2005, the amount is $3,202,100.

Year	Beginning Balance	Interest Income (at 8%)*	Received	Ending Balance
2005	$5,664,000	$462,182	$ 300,000	$5,826,182
2006	5,826,182	473,818	6,300,000	–0–

*Compounded semiannually.

Congress has created several exceptions regarding the rate at which interest is imputed and the method of accounting for the interest income and expense. The general rules and exceptions are summarized in Concept Summary 16–1.

Related-Party Sales of Nondepreciable Property. If the Code did not contain special rules, a taxpayer could make an installment sale of property to a related party (e.g., a family member) who would obtain a basis in the property equal to the purchase price (the fair market value of the property). Then, the purchasing family member could immediately sell the property to an unrelated party for cash with no recognized gain or loss (the amount realized would equal the basis). The related-party purchaser would not pay the installment note to the selling family member until a later year or years. The net result would be that the family has the cash, but no taxable gain is recognized until the intrafamily transfer of the cash (i.e., when the purchasing family member makes payments on the installment note).

Under special rules designed to combat this scheme, the proceeds from the subsequent sale (the second sale) by the purchasing family member are treated as though they were used to pay the installment note due the selling family member (the first sale). As a result, the recognition of gain from the original sale between the related parties is accelerated.[67]

However, even with these special rules, Congress did not eliminate the benefits of all related-party installment sales.

- Related parties include the first seller's brothers, sisters, ancestors, lineal descendants, controlled corporations, and partnerships, trusts, and estates in which the seller has an interest.[68]
- There is no acceleration if the second disposition occurs more than two years after the first sale.[69]

Thus, if the taxpayer can sell the property to a relative who is not a "related party" or to a patient family member, the intrafamily installment sale is still a powerful tax planning tool. Other exceptions also can be applied in some circumstances.[70]

Related-Party Sales of Depreciable Property. The installment method cannot be used to report a gain on the sale of depreciable property to a controlled entity. The purpose of this rule is to prevent the seller from deferring gain (until collections are received) while the related purchaser is enjoying a stepped-up basis for depreciation purposes.[71]

The prohibition on the use of the installment method applies to sales between the taxpayer and a partnership or corporation in which the taxpayer holds a more-than-50 percent interest. Constructive ownership rules are used in applying the ownership test (i.e., the taxpayer is considered to own stock owned by a spouse and certain other family members).[72] However, if the taxpayer can establish that tax avoidance was not a principal purpose of the transaction, the installment method can be used to report the gain.

EXAMPLE 29

Alan purchased an apartment building from his controlled corporation, Emerald Corporation. Alan was short of cash at the time of the purchase (December 2005), but was to collect a large cash payment in January 2006. The agreement required Alan to pay the entire arm's length price in January 2006. Alan had good business reasons for acquiring the building. Emerald Corporation should be able to convince the IRS that tax avoidance was not a principal purpose for the installment sale because the tax benefits are not overwhelming. The corporation will report all of the gain in the year following the year of sale, and the building must be depreciated over 27.5 years (the cost recovery period). ■

DISPOSITION OF INSTALLMENT OBLIGATIONS

Generally, a taxpayer must recognize the deferred profit from an installment sale when the obligation is transferred to another party or otherwise relinquished. The rationale for accelerating the gain is that the deferral should continue for no longer than the period during which the taxpayer owns the installment obligation.[73]

[67] § 453(e).

[68] § 453(f)(1), cross-referencing §§ 267(b) and 318(a). Although spouses are related parties, the exemption of gain between spouses (§ 1041) makes the second-disposition rules inapplicable when the first sale was between spouses.

[69] § 453(e)(2). But see § 453(e)(2)(B) for extensions of the two-year period.

[70] See §§ 453(e)(6) and (7).

[71] § 453(g).

[72] §§ 1239(b) and (c).

[73] § 453B(a).

The gift or cancellation of an installment note is treated as a taxable disposition by the donor. The amount realized from the cancellation is the face amount of the note if the parties (obligor and obligee) are related to each other.[74]

EXAMPLE 30

Liz cancels a note issued by Tina (Liz's daughter) that arose in connection with the sale of property. At the time of the cancellation, the note had a basis to Liz of $10,000, a face amount of $25,000, and a fair market value of $20,000. Presuming the initial sale by Liz qualified as an installment sale, the cancellation results in gain of $15,000 ($25,000 – $10,000) to Liz. ■

Certain exceptions to the recognition of gain provisions are provided for transfers of installment obligations pursuant to tax-free incorporations under § 351, contributions of capital to a partnership, certain corporate liquidations, transfers due to the taxpayer's death, and transfers between spouses or incident to divorce.[75] In such situations, the deferred profit is merely shifted to the transferee, who is responsible for the payment of tax on the subsequent collections of the installment obligations.

INTEREST ON DEFERRED TAXES

With the installment method, the seller earns interest on the receivable. The receivable includes the deferred gain. Thus, one could argue that the seller is earning interest on the deferred taxes. Some commentators reason that the government is, in effect, making interest-free loans to taxpayers who report gains by the installment method. Following the argument that the amount of the deferred taxes is a loan, in some situations, the taxpayer is required to pay interest on the deferred taxes.[76]

ELECTING OUT OF THE INSTALLMENT METHOD

A taxpayer can *elect not to use* the installment method. The election is made by reporting on a timely filed return the gain computed by the taxpayer's usual method of accounting.[77] However, the Regulations provide that the amount realized by a cash basis taxpayer cannot be less than the value of the property sold. This rule differs from the usual cash basis accounting rules (discussed earlier),[78] which measure the amount realized in terms of the fair market value of the property received. The net effect of the Regulations is to allow the cash basis taxpayer to report his or her gain as an accrual basis taxpayer. The election is frequently applied to year-end sales by taxpayers who expect to be in a higher tax bracket in the following year.

EXAMPLE 31

On December 31, 2005, Kurt sold land to Jodie for $20,000 (fair market value). The cash was to be paid on January 4, 2006. Kurt is a cash basis taxpayer, and his basis in the land is $8,000. Kurt has a large casualty loss and very little other income in 2005. Thus, his marginal tax rate in 2005 is 15%. He expects his rate to increase to 35% in 2006.

The transaction constitutes an installment sale because a payment will be received in a tax year after the tax year of disposition. Jodie's promise to pay Kurt is an installment obligation, and under the Regulations, the value of the installment obligation is equal to the value of the property sold ($20,000). If Kurt elects out of the installment method, he would shift $12,000 of gain ($20,000 – $8,000) from the expected higher rate in 2006 to the

[74] § 453B(f)(2).
[75] §§ 453B(c), (d), and (g).
[76] See § 453A for details.
[77] § 453(d) and Temp.Reg. § 15a.453–1(d). See also Rev.Rul. 82–227, 1982–2 C.B. 89.
[78] Refer to Chapter 4.

15% rate in 2005. The expected tax savings based on the rate differentials may exceed the benefit of the tax deferral available with the installment method. ■

Permission of the IRS is required to revoke an election not to use the installment method.[79]

ETHICAL CONSIDERATIONS

Electing Out of Electing Out of the Installment Sale Method

The general rule is that gain on a transaction eligible to use the installment sale method is to be reported by that method. However, the taxpayer can elect not to use the installment method. What if the taxpayer elects not to use the installment method but later discovers he or she has made an improvident election (e.g., the taxpayer thought he or she would have a loss to offset the gain)? Generally, the taxpayer cannot revoke the election.

If the election was "inadvertent," however, the IRS will grant permission to amend the return and to use the installment method. For example, the IRS has frequently allowed revocation when the taxpayer's accountant prepared the tax return without using the installment method (reporting the entire gain in the year of sale), and the taxpayer filed the return not realizing that the election to forgo the use of the installment method had been made.

Martha, the tax adviser for Swan Partnership, analyzed Swan's situation and incorrectly concluded that the partnership should elect out of the installment method. Martha had discussed the tax return with Swan's CFO when she presented the tax return to him. Upon discovering her error in "electing out," Martha contacts Swan's new CFO (the CFO with whom she discussed the tax return has died), informs him of the benefit of amending the election out, and tells him that when she tried to discuss the tax return with the deceased CFO, he said, "I have complete confidence in you and do not need to discuss any aspect of the tax return." Evaluate what Martha has done.

LO.5

Understand the alternative methods of accounting for long-term contracts (the completed contract method and the percentage of completion method) including the limitations on the use of the completed contract method.

LONG-TERM CONTRACTS

A **long-term contract** is a building, installation, construction, or manufacturing contract that is entered into but not completed within the same tax year. However, a *manufacturing* contract is long term *only* if the contract is to manufacture (1) a unique item not normally carried in finished goods inventory or (2) items that normally require more than 12 calendar months to complete.[80] An item is *unique* if it is designed to meet the customer's particular needs and is not suitable for use by others. A contract to perform services (e.g., auditing or legal services) is not considered a contract for this purpose and thus cannot qualify as a long-term contract.

EXAMPLE 32

Rocky, a calendar year taxpayer, entered into two contracts during the year. One contract was to construct a building foundation. Work was to begin in October 2005 and was to be completed by June 2006. The contract is long term because it will not be entered into and completed in the same tax year. The fact that the contract requires less than 12 calendar months to complete is not relevant because the contract is not for manufacturing. The second contract was for architectural services to be performed over two years. These services will not qualify for long-term contract treatment because the taxpayer will not build, install, construct, or manufacture a product. ■

Generally, the taxpayer must accumulate all of the direct and indirect costs incurred under a contract. This means the production costs must be accumulated

[79] § 453(d)(3) and Temp.Reg. § 15a.453–1(d)(4).

[80] § 460(f) and Reg. § 1.451–3(b).

and allocated to individual contracts. Furthermore, mixed services costs, costs that benefit contracts as well as the general administrative operations of the business, must be allocated to production. Exhibit 16–1 lists the types of costs that must be accumulated and allocated to contracts. The taxpayer must develop reasonable bases for cost allocations.[81]

EXAMPLE 33

Falcon, Inc., uses detailed cost accumulation records to assign labor and materials to its contracts in progress. The total cost of fringe benefits is allocated to a contract on the following basis:

$$\frac{\text{Labor on the contract}}{\text{Total salaries and labor}} \times \text{Total cost of fringe benefits}$$

Similarly, storage and handling costs for materials are allocated to contracts on the following basis:

$$\frac{\text{Contract materials}}{\text{Materials purchases}} \times \text{Storage and handling costs}$$

The cost of the personnel operations, a mixed services cost, is allocated between production and general administration based on the number of employees in each function. The personnel cost allocated to production is allocated to individual contracts on the basis of the formula used to allocate fringe benefits. ■

The accumulated costs are deducted when the revenue from the contract is recognized. Generally, two methods of accounting are used in varying circumstances to determine when the revenue from a contract is recognized:[82]

- The completed contract method.
- The percentage of completion method.

The *completed contract method may be used* for (1) home construction contracts (contracts in which at least 80 percent of the estimated costs are for dwelling units in buildings with four or fewer units) and (2) certain other real estate construction contracts. Other real estate contracts can qualify for the completed contract method if the following requirements are satisfied:

- The contract is expected to be completed within the two-year period beginning on the commencement date of the contract.
- The contract is performed by a taxpayer whose average annual gross receipts for the three taxable years preceding the taxable year in which the contract is entered into do not exceed $10 million.

All other contractors must use the percentage of completion method.

Completed Contract Method. Under the **completed contract method,** no revenue from the contract is recognized until the contract is completed and accepted. However, a taxpayer may not delay completion of a contract for the principal purpose of deferring tax.[83]

In some situations, the original contract price may be disputed, or the buyer may want additional work to be done on a long-term contract. If the disputed amount is substantial (e.g., it is not possible to determine whether a profit or loss will ultimately be realized on the contract), the Regulations provide that no amount

[81] Reg. §§ 1.263A–1T(b)(3)(iii)(A)(1) and 1.451–3(d)(9).
[82] § 460.
[83] Reg. § 1.451–3(b)(2).

■ EXHIBIT 16–1
Contract Costs, Mixed Services Costs, and Current Expense Items for Contracts

	Contracts Eligible for the Completed Contract Method	Other Contracts
Contract costs:		
Direct materials (a part of the finished product).	Capital	Capital
Indirect materials (consumed in production but not in the finished product, e.g., grease and oil for equipment).	Capital	Capital
Storage, handling, and insurance on materials.	Expense	Capital
Direct labor (worked on the product).	Capital	Capital
Indirect labor (worked in the production process but not directly on the product, e.g., a construction supervisor).	Capital	Capital
Fringe benefits for direct and indirect labor (e.g., vacation, sick pay, unemployment, and other insurance).	Capital	Capital
Pension costs for direct and indirect labor:		
• Current cost.	Expense	Capital
• Past service costs.	Expense	Capital
Depreciation on production facilities:		
• For financial statements.	Capital	Capital
• Tax depreciation in excess of financial statements.	Expense	Capital
Depreciation on idle facilities.	Expense	Expense
Property taxes, insurance, rent, and maintenance on production facilities.	Capital	Capital
Bidding expenses—successful.	Expense	Capital
Bidding expenses—unsuccessful.	Expense	Expense
Interest to finance real estate construction.	Capital	Capital
Interest to finance personal property:		
• Production period of one year or less.	Expense	Expense
• Production period exceeds one year and costs exceed $1 million.	Capital	Capital
• Production period exceeds two years.	Capital	Capital
Mixed services costs:		
Personnel operations.	Expense	Allocate
Data processing.	Expense	Allocate
Purchasing.	Expense	Allocate
Selling, general, and administrative expenses (including an allocated share of mixed services).	Expense	Expense
Losses.	Expense	Expense

of income or loss is recognized until the dispute is resolved. In all other cases, the profit or loss (reduced by the amount in dispute) is recognized in the current period on completion of the contract. However, additional work may need to be performed with respect to the disputed contract. In this case, the difference between the amount in dispute and the actual cost of the additional work is recognized in the year the work is completed rather than in the year in which the dispute is resolved.[84]

[84]Reg. §§ 1.451–3(d)(2)(ii)–(vii), Example (2).

EXAMPLE 34

Ted, a calendar year taxpayer utilizing the completed contract method of accounting, constructed a building for Brad under a long-term contract. The gross contract price was $500,000. Ted finished construction in 2005 at a cost of $475,000. When Brad examined the building, he insisted that it be repainted or the contract price be reduced. The estimated cost of repainting is $10,000. Since under the terms of the contract, Ted is assured of a profit of at least $15,000 ($500,000 – $475,000 – $10,000) even if the dispute is ultimately resolved in Brad's favor, Ted must include $490,000 ($500,000 – $10,000) in gross income and is allowed deductions of $475,000 for 2005.

In 2006, Ted and Brad resolve the dispute, and Ted repaints certain portions of the building at a cost of $6,000. Ted must include $10,000 in 2006 gross income and may deduct the $6,000 expense in that year. ■

EXAMPLE 35

Assume the same facts as in the previous example, except the estimated cost of repainting the building is $50,000. Since the resolution of the dispute completely in Brad's favor would mean a net loss on the contract for Ted ($500,000 – $475,000 – $50,000 = $25,000 loss), he does not recognize any income or loss until the year the dispute is resolved. ■

Frequently, a contractor receives payment at various stages of completion. For example, when the contract is 50 percent complete, the contractor may receive 50 percent of the contract price less a retainage. The taxation of these payments is generally governed by Regulation § 1.451–5 "advance payments for goods and long-term contracts" (discussed in Chapter 4). Generally, contractors are permitted to defer the advance payments until the payments are recognized as income under the taxpayer's method of accounting.

Percentage of Completion Method. The percentage of completion method must be used to account for long-term contracts unless the taxpayer qualifies for one of the two exceptions that permit the completed contract method to be used (home construction contracts and certain other real estate construction contracts).[85] Under the **percentage of completion method,** a portion of the gross contract price is included in income during each period as the work progresses. The revenue accrued each period (except for the final period) is computed as follows:[86]

$$\frac{C}{T} \times P$$

Where C = Contract costs incurred during the period.
T = Estimated total cost of the contract.
P = Contract price.

All of the costs allocated to the contract during the period are deductible from the accrued revenue.[87] The revenue reported in the final period is simply the unreported revenue from the contract. Because T in this formula is an estimate that frequently differs from total actual costs, which are not known until the contract has been completed, the profit on a contract for a particular period may be overstated or understated.

EXAMPLE 36

Tan, Inc., entered into a contract that was to take two years to complete, with an estimated cost of $2,250,000. The contract price was $3,000,000. Costs of the contract for 2004, the first year, totaled $1,350,000. The gross profit reported by the percentage of completion method for 2004 was $450,000 [($1,350,000/$2,250,000 × $3,000,000) – $1,350,000]. The contract was

[85] Certain residential construction contracts that do not qualify for the completed contract method may nevertheless use that method to account for 30% of the profit from the contract, with the remaining 70% reported by the percentage of completion method.

[86] § 460(b)(1)(A).

[87] Reg. § 1.451–3(c)(3).

completed at the end of 2005 at a total cost of $2,700,000. In retrospect, 2004 profit should have been $150,000 [($1,350,000/$2,700,000 × $3,000,000) – $1,350,000]. Thus, taxes were overpaid for 2004. ■

A *de minimis* rule enables the contractor to delay the recognition of income for a particular contract under the percentage of completion method. If less than 10 percent of the estimated contract costs have been incurred by the end of the taxable year, the taxpayer can elect to defer the recognition of income and the related costs until the taxable year in which cumulative contract costs are at least 10 percent of the estimated contract costs.[88]

Lookback Provisions. In the year a contract is completed, a *lookback* provision requires the recalculation of annual profits reported on the contract under the percentage of completion method. Interest is paid to the taxpayer if taxes were overpaid, and interest is payable by the taxpayer if there was an underpayment.[89] For a corporate taxpayer, the lookback interest paid by the taxpayer is deductible, but for an individual taxpayer, it is nondeductible personal interest associated with a tax liability.

EXAMPLE 37

Assume Tan, Inc., in Example 36, was in the 34% tax bracket in both years and the relevant interest rate was 10%. For 2004, the company paid excess taxes of $102,000 [($450,000 – $150,000) × .34]. When the contract is completed at the end of 2005, Tan, Inc., should receive interest of $10,200 for one year on the tax overpayment ($102,000 × .10). ■

LO.6

Identify tax planning opportunities related to accounting periods and accounting methods.

Tax Planning Considerations

TAXABLE YEAR

Under the general rules for tax years, partnerships and S corporations frequently will be required to use a calendar year. However, if the partnership or S corporation can demonstrate a business purpose for a fiscal year, the IRS will allow the entity to use the requested year. The advantage to a fiscal year is that the calendar year partners and S corporation shareholders may be able to defer from tax the income earned from the close of the fiscal year until the end of the calendar year. Tax advisers for these entities should apply the IRS's gross receipts test described in Revenue Procedure 87–32 to determine if permission for the fiscal year will be granted.

CASH METHOD OF ACCOUNTING

The cash method of accounting gives the taxpayer considerable control over the recognition of expenses and some control over the recognition of income. This method can be used by proprietorships, partnerships, and small corporations (gross receipts of $5 million or less) that provide services (inventories are not material to the service business). Farmers (except certain farming corporations) can also use the cash method.

INSTALLMENT METHOD

Unlike the cash and accrual methods, the installment method often results in an interest-free loan (of deferred taxes) from the government. The installment method is not available for the sale of inventory. Nevertheless, the installment method is

[88] § 460(b)(5).

[89] §§ 460(b)(2) and (b)(6). The taxpayer can elect to not apply the lookback method in situations where the cumulative taxable income as of the close of each prior year is within 10% of the correct income for each prior year.

an important tax planning technique and should be considered when a sale of eligible property is being planned. That is, if the taxpayer can benefit from deferring the tax, the terms of sale can be arranged so that the installment method rules apply. If, on the other hand, the taxpayer expects to be in a higher tax bracket when the payments will be received, he or she can elect not to use the installment method.

Related Parties. Intrafamily installment sales can still be a useful family tax planning tool. If the related party holds the property more than two years, a subsequent sale will not accelerate the gain from the first disposition. Patience and forethought are rewarded.

The 6 percent limitation on imputed interest on sales of land between family members (see Concept Summary 16–1) enables the seller to convert ordinary income into capital gain or make what is, in effect, a nontaxable gift. If the selling price is raised to adjust for the low interest rate charges on an installment sale, the seller has more capital gain but less ordinary income than would be realized from a sale to an unrelated party. If the selling price is not raised and the specified interest of 6 percent is charged, the seller enables the relative to have the use of the property without having to pay its full market value. As an additional benefit, the bargain sale is not a taxable gift.

Disposition of Installment Obligations. A disposition of an installment obligation is also a serious matter. Gifts of the obligations will accelerate income to the seller. The list of taxable and nontaxable dispositions of installment obligations should not be trusted to memory. In each instance where transfers of installment obligations are contemplated, the practitioner should conduct research to be sure he or she knows the consequences.

COMPLETED CONTRACT METHOD

Generally, large contractors must use the percentage of completion method of accounting for reporting the income from long-term contracts. Under the percentage of completion method, the taxpayer must recognize profit in each period costs are incurred. Profit is reported in proportion to the cost incurred for the period as a proportion of the total contract cost. However, small contractors (average annual gross receipts do not exceed $10 million) working on contracts that are completed within a two-year period can elect to use the completed contract method and defer profit until the year in which the contract is completed.

KEY TERMS

Accounting methods, 16–10
Accounting period, 16–2
Accrual method, 16–13
All events test, 16–14
Cash method, 16–11
Claim of right doctrine, 16–9
Completed contract method, 16–26
Economic performance test, 16–14
Fiscal year, 16–2
Hybrid method, 16–16
Imputed interest, 16–21
Installment method, 16–19
Least aggregate deferral method, 16–4
Long-term contract, 16–25
Majority interest partners, 16–4
One-year rule for prepaid expenses, 16–11
Percentage of completion method, 16–28
Personal service corporation (PSC), 16–6
Principal partner, 16–4
Short taxable year (short period), 16–7

PROBLEM MATERIALS

Discussion Questions

1. Why would December 31 be an inappropriate year-end for a chain of toy stores?

2. Your client, an individual whose accounting period is the calendar year, recently formed an S corporation. The business of the S corporation is to sell materials used in planting farm crops in the spring and early summer. The business will be dormant during the remainder of the year. The business is expected to generate losses for each of the first two years of operations and thereafter to produce profits. Should the corporation use a calendar year, or should the client seek permission to use a fiscal year ending in the summer?

Decision Making

3. A medical practice was incorporated on January 1, 2005, and expects to earn $25,000 per month before deducting the medical doctor's salary. The doctor owns 100% of the stock. The corporation and the doctor both use the cash method of accounting. The corporation does not need to retain any of the earnings in the business; thus, the salary of the doctor (a calendar year taxpayer) will equal the corporation's net income before salary expense. If the corporation could choose any tax year it wished and pay the doctor's salary at the time that would be the most tax efficient (but at least once every 12 months), what tax year should the corporation choose, and when should the salary be paid each year?

4. Freda is a cash basis farmer. She was in the 35% marginal tax bracket in 2004, the 15% marginal tax bracket in 2005, and the 35% marginal tax bracket in 2006. In 2004, she received $10,000 from the sale of produce. The customer complained that the produce was unfit for consumption, and in 2005 Freda refunded the $10,000. Also in 2005, Freda paid her farmers' cooperative $50,000 for seeds and fertilizer. In 2006, the cooperative paid Freda a dividend of $5,000 based on the cooperative's 2005 earnings.
   a. What are the tax consequences of the payment to the customer in 2005?
   b. What are the tax consequences of the refund from the cooperative in 2006?
   c. Were the tax accounting rules "kind" to Freda?

Decision Making

5. The Cardinal Insurance Agency is a newly formed corporation, and its gross receipts will probably never exceed $2 million in a year. Generally, it takes approximately two months to collect accounts receivable. Accounts payable generally equal expenses for one month. Cardinal does not expect accounts payable and accounts receivable to increase significantly. It prepares monthly financial statements using the accrual method of accounting. Given that the accounts receivable and accounts payable will not significantly change, would Cardinal derive any benefit from filing its tax return using the cash method of accounting?

6. A cash basis taxpayer owns rental properties. The insurance on the properties is renewed each January 1. On December 30, 2005, the taxpayer paid the premium of $12,000 for the period January 1, 2006 through December 31, 2006. Can the taxpayer deduct the premium of $12,000 in 2005?

7. Under what circumstances, if any, can a grocery store use the cash method of accounting?

8. Compare the cash basis and accrual basis of accounting as applied to the following:
   a. Fixed assets.
   b. Prepaid rent income.
   c. Prepaid interest expense.
   d. A note received for services performed if the market value and face amount of the note differ.

Decision Making

9. Edgar uses the cash method to report the income from his software consulting business. A large publicly held corporation has offered to invest in Edgar's business as a limited partner. What tax accounting complications would be created if Edgar and the corporation become partners?

10. Orange Freight Corporation is an accrual basis taxpayer with a fiscal year ending January 31. The company must pay annual license fees to several different states. The

annual payments total $500,000. Some of the license fees are for a fiscal year ending June 30, others are for a fiscal year ending September 30, and still others are for a calendar year. Allocating the fees based on time, $200,000 of the amount paid in the fiscal year ending January 31, 2005, will expire in the fiscal year ending January 31, 2006. Would the company benefit from adopting the "one-year rule" with respect to the annual license fees?

11. Ruby, Inc., manufactures consumer products and provides a 12-month warranty. The company can accurately predict the cost of services to be provided under the warranty. Therefore, the company's financial statements reflect an estimated future cost of warranty services. Discuss the tax accounting principle that prevents the company from accruing the estimated costs of services to be provided under the warranty.

Decision Making

12. Irene has made Sara an offer on the purchase of a capital asset. Irene will pay (1) $200,000 cash or (2) $50,000 cash and a 6% installment note for $150,000 guaranteed by City Bank of New York. If Sara sells for $200,000 cash, she will invest the after-tax proceeds in certificates of deposit yielding 6% interest. Sara's cost of the asset is $25,000. Why would Sara prefer the installment sale?

13. Warren owns property with a basis of $100,000 that is subject to a mortgage of $60,000. Felix is willing to pay Warren $140,000 cash and assume the mortgage. Alternatively, Felix is willing to pay Warren $200,000, and Warren will pay off the mortgage. Compare the tax consequences to Warren under the two options.

Decision Making

14. On June 1, 2003, Father sold land to Son for $200,000. Father reported the gain by the installment method, with the gain to be spread over five years. In May 2005, Son received an offer of $300,000 for the land, to be paid over three years. What would be the tax consequences of Son's sale? How could the tax consequences be improved?

Decision Making

15. In December 2005, Juan Corporation sold land it held as an investment. The corporation received $50,000 in 2005 and a note payable (with adequate interest) for $150,000 to be paid in 2007. Juan Corporation's cost of the land was $80,000. The corporation has a $90,000 net capital loss carryover that will expire in 2005. Should Juan Corporation report the sale in 2005 or use the installment method to report the income as payments are received?

16. What long-term contract method generally results in the greatest deferral of income? Explain. What are the limitations on using that method for tax purposes?

17. The Eagle Corporation builds yachts. All vessels are practically identical and sell for more than $2 million. Production does not begin until the company has a contract to sell the vessel. The company has recently changed its production techniques to reduce the time for producing a yacht from 15 months to 9 months. What are the accounting method implications of the change?

Problems

18. Red, White, and Blue are unrelated corporations engaged in real estate development. The three corporations formed a joint venture (treated as a partnership) to develop a tract of land. Assuming the venture does not have a natural business year, what tax year must the joint venture adopt under the following circumstances?

	Tax Year Ending	Interest in Joint Venture
a. Red	March 31	60%
Blue	June 30	20%
White	October 31	20%
b. Red	October 31	30%
White	June 30	40%
Blue	January 31	30%

Decision Making

19. Zack conducted his professional practice through Zack, Inc. The corporation uses a fiscal year ending September 30 even though the business purpose test for a fiscal year cannot be satisfied. For the year ending September 30, 2005, the corporation paid Zack a salary of $180,000, and during the period January through September 2005, the corporation paid him a salary of $150,000.
    a. How much salary should Zack receive during the period October 1 through December 31, 2005?
    b. Assume Zack received only $30,000 of salary during the period October 1 through December 31, 2005. What would be the consequences to Zack, Inc.?

20. Mauve Corporation began operations as a farm supplies business and used a fiscal year ending September 30. The company gradually went out of the farm supplies business and into the mail-order Christmas gifts business. The company has received permission from the IRS to change to a fiscal year ending January 31, effective for the year ending January 31, 2005. For the short period October 1, 2004 through January 31, 2005, Mauve earned $25,000. Calculate Mauve's tax liability for the short period October 1, 2004 through January 31, 2005.

Communications

21. Gold, Inc., is an accrual basis taxpayer. In 2005, an employee accidentally spilled hazardous chemicals on leased property. The chemicals destroyed trees on neighboring property, resulting in $30,000 of damages. In 2005, the owner of the property sued Gold, Inc., for the $30,000. Gold's attorney feels that it is liable and the only issue is whether the neighbor will also seek punitive damages that could be as much as three times the actual damages. In addition, as a result of the spill, Gold was in violation of its lease and was therefore required to pay the landlord $15,000. However, the amount due for the lease violation is not payable until the termination of the lease in 2008. None of these costs were covered by insurance. Jeff Stuart, the president of Gold, Inc., is generally familiar with the accrual basis tax accounting rules and is concerned about when the company will be allowed to deduct the amounts the company is required to pay as a result of this environmental disaster. Write Mr. Stuart a letter explaining these issues. Gold's address is 200 Elm Avenue, San Jose, CA 95192.

22. Compute the taxpayer's income or deductions for 2005 using (1) the cash basis and (2) the accrual basis for each of the following:
    a. In March 2005, the taxpayer purchased a copying machine for $200,000. The taxpayer paid $25,000 in cash and gave a $175,000 interest-bearing note for the balance. The copying machine has an MACRS cost recovery period of five years and the § 179 election was not made.
    b. In December 2005, the taxpayer collected $10,000 for January 2006 rents. In January 2006, the taxpayer collected $2,000 for December 2005 rents.
    c. In December 2005, the taxpayer paid office equipment insurance premiums of $30,000 for January–June 2006.
    d. In June 2005, the taxpayer purchased office furniture for $180,000. The taxpayer paid $36,000 in cash and gave a $144,000 interest-bearing note for the balance. The office furniture has an MACRS cost recovery period of seven years. The taxpayer made the § 179 election.

23. What accounting method (cash or accrual) would you recommend for the following businesses?
    a. An incorporated medical practice with annual gross receipts of $12 million.
    b. A hardware store with annual gross receipts of less than $1 million.
    c. A building contractor, who builds single-family houses, with annual gross receipts of $3 million.
    d. A grocery store with annual gross receipts of $4.5 million.

24. How do the all events and economic performance requirements apply to the following transactions by an accrual basis taxpayer?
    a. The company guarantees its products for six months. At the end of 2005, customers had made valid claims for $600,000 that were not paid until 2006. Also, the company estimates that another $400,000 in claims from 2005 sales will be filed and paid in 2006.

b. The accrual basis taxpayer reported $200,000 in corporate taxable income for 2005. The state income tax rate was 6%. The corporation paid $7,000 in estimated state income taxes in 2005 and paid $2,000 in 2004 state income taxes when it filed its 2004 state income tax return in March 2005. The company filed its 2005 state income return in March 2006 and paid the remaining $5,000 of its 2005 state income tax liability.
c. An employee was involved in an accident while making a sales call. The company paid the injured victim $15,000 in 2005 and agreed to pay the victim $15,000 a year for the next nine years.

25. Moss Company is an environmental consulting firm with average annual gross receipts of $2.5 million and taxable income of $500,000. Approximately $800,000 of the receipts are from the sale of products that are used to remedy clients' environmental problems. The company has consistently used the cash method for the consulting services and the accrual method for the product sales. The company recently learned that it qualified for the small business tax accounting rules and can use the cash method for the sale of products as well as for the consulting services. At the end of the previous tax year, Moss had $100,000 in products on hand and accounts receivable from the sale of products of $90,000. What are the immediate tax consequences if Moss changes to the cash method of accounting for the sale of products effective for the current tax year?

Decision Making

26. Floyd, a cash basis taxpayer, has received an offer to purchase his land. The buyer will either pay him $100,000 at closing or pay $50,000 at closing and $52,000 one year after the date of closing. If Floyd recognizes the entire gain in the current year, his marginal tax rate will be 35% (combined Federal and state rates). However, if he spreads the gain over the two years, his marginal tax rate on the gain will be only 25%. Floyd does not consider the buyer a credit risk, but he realizes that the deferred payment will, in effect, earn only 4% interest ($2,000/$50,000 = 4%). Floyd believes he can earn a 10% before-tax rate of return on his after-tax cash. Floyd's adjusted basis for the land is $25,000, the buyer is also a cash basis taxpayer, and the short-term Federal rate is 4%. Floyd has asked you to evaluate the two alternatives on an after-tax basis.

27. Kay, who is not a dealer, sold an apartment house to Polly during 2005. The closing statement for the sale is as follows:

Total selling price		$ 150,000
Add: Polly's share of property taxes (6 months) paid by Kay		2,500
Less: Kay's 8% mortgage assumed by Polly	$55,000	
Polly's refundable binder ("earnest money") paid in 2004	1,000	
Polly's 8% installment note given to Kay	80,000	
Kay's real estate commissions and attorney's fees	7,500	(143,500)
Cash paid to Kay at closing		$ 9,000
Cash due from Polly = $9,000 + $7,500 expenses		$ 16,500

During 2005, Kay collected $4,000 in principal on the installment note and $2,000 in interest. Her basis in the property was $70,000 [$85,000 – $15,000 (depreciation)], and there was $9,000 in potential depreciation recapture under § 1250. The Federal rate is 6%.
a. Compute the following:
   1. Total gain.
   2. Contract price.
   3. Payments received in the year of sale.
   4. Recognized gain in the year of sale and the character of such gain.
   (*Hint:* Think carefully about the manner in which the property taxes are handled before you begin your computations.)
b. Same as (a)(2) and (3), except Kay's basis in the property was $45,000.

28. On June 30, 2005, Kelly sold property for $250,000 cash on the date of sale and a $750,000 note due on September 30, 2006. No interest was stated in the contract. The present value of the note (using 6.5%, which was the Federal rate) was $692,625. Kelly's basis in the property was $400,000, and $40,000 of the gain was subject to depreciation

recapture under § 1245. Expenses of the sale totaled $10,000, and Kelly was not a dealer in the property sold.

a. Compute Kelly's gain to be reported in 2005.
b. Compute Kelly's interest income for 2006.

29. On December 30, 2005, Father sold land to Son for $10,000 cash and a 7% installment note with a face amount of $260,000. In 2006, after paying $60,000 on the principal of the note, Son sold the land. In 2007, Son paid Father $40,000 on the note principal. Father's basis in the land was $50,000. Assuming Son sold the land for $300,000, compute Father's taxable gain in 2006.

30. George sold land to an unrelated party in 2004. His basis in the land was $40,000, and the selling price was $100,000: $25,000 payable at closing and $25,000 (plus 10% interest) due January 1, 2005, 2006, and 2007. What would be the tax consequences of the following? [Treat each part independently and assume (1) George did not elect out of the installment method and (2) the installment obligations have values equal to their face amounts.]
    a. In 2005, George gave to his daughter the right to collect all future payments on the installment obligations.
    b. In 2005, after collecting the payment due on January 1, George transferred the installment obligation to his 100%-controlled corporation in exchange for additional shares of stock.
    c. On December 31, 2005, George received the payment due on January 1, 2006. On December 15, 2006, George died, and the remaining installment obligation was transferred to his estate. The estate collected the amount due on January 1, 2007.

31. The Dove Construction Company reports its income by the completed contract method. At the end of 2005, the company completed a contract to construct a building at a total cost of $750,000. The contract price was $1.2 million. However, the customer refused to accept the work and would not pay anything on the contract because he claimed the roof did not meet specifications. Dove's engineers estimated it would cost $140,000 to bring the roof up to the customer's standards. In 2006, the dispute was settled in the customer's favor; the roof was improved at a cost of $170,000, and the customer accepted the building and paid the $1.2 million.
    a. What would be the effects of the above on Dove's taxable income for 2005 and 2006?
    b. Same as (a), except Dove had $1.1 million of accumulated costs under the contract at the end of 2005.

Communications

32. Rust Company is a real estate construction company with average annual gross receipts of $4 million. Rust uses the completed contract method, and the contracts require 18 months to complete.
    a. Which of the following costs would be allocated to construction in progress by Rust?
        1. The payroll taxes on direct labor.
        2. The current services pension costs for employees whose wages are included in direct labor.
        3. Accelerated depreciation on equipment used on contracts.
        4. Freight charges on materials assigned to contracts.
        5. The past service costs for employees whose wages are included in direct labor.
        6. Bidding expenses for contracts awarded.
    b. Assume that Rust generally builds commercial buildings under contracts with the owners and reports the income by the completed contract method. The company is considering building a series of similar stores for a retail chain. The gross profit margin would be a low percentage, but the company's gross receipts would triple. Write a letter to your client, Rust Company, explaining the tax accounting implications of entering into these contracts. Rust's mailing address is P.O. Box 1000, Harrisonburg, VA 22807.

33. Explain why the taxpayer may not be required to use the percentage of completion method in each of the following situations:

a. The taxpayer agrees to build six aircraft. It takes 6 months to complete each aircraft, the price is $1.5 million per aircraft, and it will take 18 months to complete all six aircraft.
b. A contract to produce and sell hot dogs at the Superbowl for the next two years.
c. A contract to build an office building. The contractor's average annual gross receipts are approximately $3 million.

34. Ostrich Company makes gasoline storage tanks. Everything produced is under contract (that is, the company does not produce until it gets a contract for a product). Ostrich makes three basic models. However, the tanks must be adapted to each individual customer's location and needs (e.g., the location of the valves, the quality of the materials and insulation). Discuss the following issues relative to Ostrich's operations:
   a. An examining IRS agent contends that each of the company's contracts is to produce a "unique product." What difference does it make whether the product is unique or a "shelf item"?
   b. Producing one of the tanks takes over one year from start to completion, and the total price is in excess of $1 million. What costs must be capitalized for this contract that are not subject to capitalization for a contract with a shorter duration and lower cost?
   c. What must Ostrich do with the costs of bidding on contracts?
   d. Ostrich frequently makes several cost estimates for a contract, using various estimates of materials costs. These costs fluctuate almost daily. Assuming Ostrich must use the percentage of completion method to report the income from the contract, what will be the consequence if the company uses the highest estimate of a contract's costs and the actual cost is closer to the lowest estimated cost?

Communications

35. Swallow Company is a large real estate construction company that reports its income by the percentage of completion method. In 2006, the company completed a contract at a total cost of $1.9 million. The contract price was $2.4 million. At the end of 2005, the year the contract was begun, Swallow estimated the total cost of the contract would be $2.1 million, and total accumulated costs on the contract at the end of 2005 were $1.4 million. The relevant tax rate is 34%, and the relevant Federal interest rate is 7%. Assume that all returns were filed and taxes were paid on March 15 following the close of the calendar tax year.
   a. Compute the gross profit on the contract for 2005 and 2006.
   b. Compute the lookback interest due with the 2006 return.
   c. Before bidding on a contract, Swallow generally makes three estimates of total contract costs: (1) optimistic, (2) pessimistic, and (3) most likely (based on a blending of optimistic and pessimistic assumptions). The company has asked you to write a letter explaining which of these estimates should be used for percentage of completion purposes. In writing your letter, you should consider the fact that Swallow is incorporated and has made an S corporation election; therefore, the income and deductions flow through to the shareholders who are all individuals in the 35% marginal tax bracket. The relevant Federal interest rate is 8%. Swallow's mailing address is 400 Front Avenue, Ashland, OR 97520.

Research Problems

Note: Solutions to Research Problems can be prepared by using the ***RIA Checkpoint® Student Edition*** *online research product, which is available to accompany this text. It is also possible to prepare solutions to the Research Problems by using tax research materials found in a standard tax library.*

Research Problem 1. Your client is a manufacturer. For several years, the company buried empty paint cans on its property. The paint was used in the production process. Recently, a state environmental agency informed the company that it was required to dig up the paint cans and decontaminate the land. The company spent a substantial amount for this environmental cleanup in the current year. An IRS agent contends that the cost must be added to the basis in the land because the cleanup improved the land. The company's CFO has asked you to determine if any authority exists that would support a current deduction for these costs.

Research Problem 2. In 2005, your client, Clear Corporation, changed from the cash to the accrual method of accounting for its radio station. The company had a positive § 481 adjustment of $2.4 million as a result of the change and began amortizing the adjustment in 2005. In 2006, Clear received an offer to purchase the assets of the radio station business (this would be considered a sale of a trade or business under § 1060). If the offer is accepted, Clear plans to purchase a satellite television business. Clear has asked you to explain the consequences of the sale of the radio station on the amortization of the § 481 adjustment.

Internet Activity

Use the tax resources of the Internet to address the following question. Do not restrict your search to the World Wide Web, but include a review of newsgroups and general reference materials, practitioner sites and resources, primary sources of the tax law, chat rooms and discussion groups, and other opportunities.

Research Problem 3. Determine the current midterm "applicable Federal rate" that would be applied to impute interest on a note receivable due in four years.

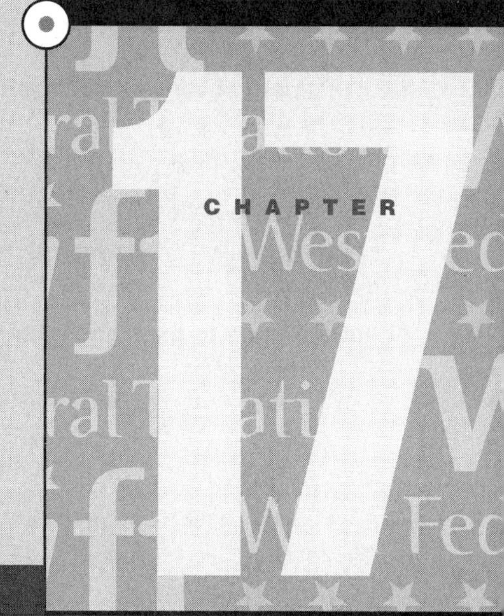

Corporations: Introduction, Operating Rules, and Related Corporations

LEARNING OBJECTIVES

After completing Chapter 17, you should be able to:

LO.1
Summarize the various forms of conducting a business.

LO.2
Compare the taxation of individuals and corporations.

LO.3
Discuss the tax rules unique to corporations.

LO.4
Compute the corporate income tax.

LO.5
Explain the tax rules unique to multiple corporations.

LO.6
Describe the reporting process for corporations.

LO.7
Evaluate corporations for conducting a business.

OUTLINE

LO.1

Summarize the various forms of conducting a business.

Tax Treatment of Various Business Forms

Business operations can be conducted in a number of different forms. Among the various possibilities are the following:

- Sole proprietorships.
- Partnerships.
- Trusts and estates.
- S corporations (also known as Subchapter S corporations).
- Regular corporations (also called Subchapter C or C corporations).

For Federal income tax purposes, the distinctions among these forms of business organization are very important. The following discussion of the tax treatment of sole proprietorships, partnerships, and regular corporations highlights these distinctions. Trusts and estates are covered in Chapter 28, and S corporations are discussed in Chapter 22.

SOLE PROPRIETORSHIPS

A sole proprietorship is not a taxable entity separate from the individual who owns the proprietorship. The owner of a sole proprietorship reports all business transactions of the proprietorship on Schedule C of Form 1040. The net profit or loss from the proprietorship is then transferred from Schedule C to Form 1040, which is used by the taxpayer to report taxable income. The proprietor reports all of the net profit from the business, regardless of the amount actually withdrawn during the year.

TAX IN THE NEWS

CORPORATE TAX BREAKS

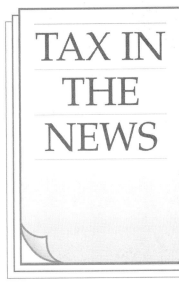

Although rates in the corporate tax schedule range from 15 percent to 39 percent, a recent Government Accountability Office study found that fewer than 40 percent of U.S. corporations paid *any* Federal income taxes from 1996 to 2000. The Commerce Department provides additional evidence of the low tax burden borne by U.S. corporations. Throughout the 1990s, the average rate paid by U.S. corporations was approximately 30 percent. Since 2001, the rate has been approximately 20 percent. A Duke University study found that the rate in 2002 was 12 percent, compared to 15 percent in 1999 and 18 percent in 1995. All of these studies show that the actual rate of Federal income tax paid by corporations is low and that it has declined steadily from the early 1990s through 2002.

SOURCE: "Corporate Tax Burden Shows Sharp Decline," *Wall Street Journal,* April 13, 2004, pp. C1–C3.

Income and expenses of the proprietorship retain their character when reported by the proprietor. For example, ordinary income of the proprietorship is treated as ordinary income when reported by the proprietor, and capital gain is treated as capital gain.

EXAMPLE 1

George is the sole proprietor of George's Record Shop. Gross income of the business for the year is $200,000, and operating expenses are $110,000. George also sells a capital asset held by the business for a $10,000 long-term capital gain. During the year, he withdraws $60,000 from the business for living expenses. George reports the income and expenses of the business on Schedule C, resulting in net profit (ordinary income) of $90,000. Even though he withdrew only $60,000, George reports all of the $90,000 net profit from the business on Form 1040, where he computes taxable income for the year. He also reports a $10,000 long-term capital gain on Schedule D. ■

PARTNERSHIPS

Partnerships are not subject to the income tax. However, a partnership is required to file Form 1065, which reports the results of the partnership's business activities. Most income and expense items are aggregated in computing the net profit of the partnership on Form 1065. Any income and expense items that are not aggregated in computing the partnership's net income are reported separately to the partners. Some examples of separately reported income items are interest income, dividend income, and long-term capital gain. Examples of separately reported expenses include charitable contributions and expenses related to interest and dividend income. Partnership reporting is discussed in detail in Chapter 21.

The partnership net profit (loss) and the separately reported items are allocated to each partner according to the partnership's profit sharing agreement, and the partners receive separate K–1 schedules from the partnership. Schedule K–1 reports each partner's share of the partnership net profit (loss) and separately reported income and expense items. Each partner reports these items on his or her own tax return.

EXAMPLE 2

Jim and Bob are equal partners in Canary Enterprises, a calendar year partnership. During the year, Canary Enterprises had $500,000 of gross income and $350,000 of operating expenses. In addition, the partnership sold land that had been held for investment purposes for a long-term capital gain of $60,000. During the year, Jim withdrew $40,000 from the partnership and Bob withdrew $45,000. The partnership's Form 1065 reports net profit of $150,000 ($500,000 income – $350,000 expenses). The partnership also reports the $60,000 long-term capital gain as a separately stated item on Form 1065. Jim and Bob both receive a Schedule K–1 reporting net profit of $75,000 and separately stated long-term capital gain of $30,000. Consequently, each partner reports net profit of $75,000 and long-term capital gain of $30,000 on his own return. ■

REGULAR CORPORATIONS

Corporations are governed by Subchapter C or Subchapter S of the Internal Revenue Code. Those governed by Subchapter C are referred to as **C corporations** or **regular corporations.** Corporations governed by Subchapter S are referred to as **S corporations.**

S corporations, which generally do not pay Federal income tax, are similar to partnerships in that net profit or loss flows through to the shareholders to be reported on their separate returns. Also like partnerships, S corporations do not aggregate all income and expense items in computing net profit or loss. Certain items flow through to the shareholders and retain their separate character when reported on the shareholders' returns. See Chapter 22 for detailed coverage of S corporations.

Unlike proprietorships, partnerships, and S corporations, C corporations are taxpaying entities. This results in what is known as a *double tax effect.* A C corporation reports its income and expenses on Form 1120 (or Form 1120–A, the corporate short form). The corporation computes tax on the net income reported on the corporate tax return using the rate schedule applicable to corporations (the rate schedule is shown on the inside front cover of this text and on page 17–6). When a corporation distributes its income, the corporation's shareholders report dividend income on their own tax returns. Thus, income that has already been taxed at the corporate level is also taxed at the shareholder level. The effects of double taxation are illustrated in Examples 3 and 4.

EXAMPLE 3

Lavender Corporation earned net profit of $100,000 in 2005. It paid corporate tax of $22,250 (refer to the corporate rate schedule on the inside front cover of this text). This left $77,750, all of which was distributed as a dividend to Mike, the corporation's sole shareholder. Mike had taxable income of $69,550 ($77,750 – $5,000 standard deduction – $3,200 personal exemption). He paid tax at the 15% rate applicable to dividends. His tax was $10,433 ($69,550 × 15%). The combined tax on the corporation's net profit was $32,683 ($22,250 paid by the corporation + $10,433 paid by the shareholder). ■

EXAMPLE 4

Assume the same facts as in Example 3, except that the business is organized as a sole proprietorship. Mike reports the $100,000 net profit from the business on his tax return. He has taxable income of $91,800 ($100,000 – $5,000 standard deduction – $3,200 personal exemption) and pays tax of $20,211. Therefore, operating the business as a sole proprietorship resulted in tax *savings* of $12,472 in 2005 ($32,683 tax from Example 3 – $20,211). ■

Examples 3 and 4 deal with a specific set of facts. The conclusions reached in this situation cannot be extended to all decisions about a form of business organization. Each specific set of facts and circumstances requires a thorough analysis of the tax factors. In many cases, the tax burden will be greater if the business is operated as a corporation (as in Example 3), but sometimes operating as a corporation can result in tax savings, as illustrated in Examples 5 and 6.

EXAMPLE 5

In 2005, Tan Corporation filed Form 1120 reporting net profit of $100,000. The corporation paid tax of $22,250 and distributed the remaining $77,750 as a dividend to Carla, the sole shareholder of the corporation. Carla had income from other sources and was in the top individual tax bracket of 35% in 2005. As a result, she paid tax of $11,663 ($77,750 × 15% rate on dividends) on the distribution. The combined tax on the corporation's net profit was $33,913 ($22,250 paid by the corporation + $11,663 paid by the shareholder). ■

EXAMPLE 6

Assume the same facts as in Example 5, except that the business is a sole proprietorship. Carla reports the $100,000 net profit from the business on her tax return and pays tax of $35,000 ($100,000 net profit × 35% marginal rate). Therefore, operating the business as a sole proprietorship resulted in a tax *cost* of $1,087 in 2005 ($35,000 – $33,913 tax from Example 5). ■

Shareholders in closely held corporations frequently attempt to avoid double taxation by paying out all the profit of the corporation as salary to themselves.

EXAMPLE 7

Orange Corporation has net income of $180,000 during the year ($300,000 revenue – $120,000 operating expenses). Emilio is the sole shareholder of Orange Corporation. In an effort to avoid tax at the corporate level, Emilio has Orange pay him a salary of $180,000, which results in zero taxable income for the corporation. ■

Will the strategy described in Example 7 effectively avoid double taxation? The answer depends on whether the compensation paid to the shareholder is *reasonable*. Section 162 provides that compensation is deductible only to the extent that it is reasonable in amount. The IRS is aware that many taxpayers use this strategy to bail out corporate profits and, in an audit, looks closely at compensation expense.

If the IRS believes that compensation is too high based on the amount and quality of services performed by the shareholder, the compensation deduction of the corporation is reduced to a reasonable amount. Compensation that is determined to be unreasonable is usually treated as a constructive dividend to the shareholder and is not deductible by the corporation.

EXAMPLE 8

Assume the same facts as in Example 7, and that the IRS determines that $80,000 of the amount paid to Emilio is unreasonable compensation. As a result, $80,000 of the corporation's compensation deduction is disallowed and treated as a constructive dividend to Emilio. Orange has taxable income of $80,000. Emilio would report salary of $100,000 and a taxable dividend of $80,000. The net effect is that $80,000 would be subject to double taxation. ■

The unreasonable compensation issue is discussed in more detail in Chapter 19.

Taxation of Dividends. The Jobs and Growth Tax Relief Reconciliation Act (JGTRRA) of 2003 reduced the impact of double taxation. Before 2003, dividends received by individuals were subject to the same rates as ordinary income. JGTRRA changed the top individual rate from 38.6 percent to 35 percent and the rate on dividend income to 15 percent (5 percent for low-income taxpayers).

The new tax-favored treatment of dividends will have a marked impact on many closely held corporations. Prior to JGTRRA, the motivation was to avoid paying dividends, as they were nondeductible to the corporation and fully taxed to the shareholders (as illustrated in Examples 3 and 5 above). To counter this problem of double taxation, corporate profits were bailed out in a manner that provided tax benefits to the corporation (refer to Example 7). Hence, liberal use was made of compensation, loan, and lease arrangements, as salaries, interest, and rent are deductible items. Now, a new variable has been interjected. Who should benefit? Shareholders will prefer dividends because salaries, interest, and rent are fully taxed, while dividends are taxed at the new 15 percent rate (5 percent for low-income taxpayers). Corporations, however, will continue to favor distributions that are deductible (e.g., salaries, interest, and rent). The ideal will be a good mix of the two approaches. Besides being attractive to shareholders, the payment of dividends

IMPACT OF THE DIVIDEND TAX CUT

The Bush administration's 2003 reduction of the tax rate on dividends to 15 percent led to much speculation as to how the cut would affect corporate dividend policy. Here is some information gleaned from the financial press on the impact to date.

- On December 2, 2004, Microsoft paid a special dividend of $32 billion to its shareholders, representing the largest dividend payout on record.
- At least 10 major corporations, including Reebok, Viacom, and Costco, paid dividends for the first time.
- Many corporations, including more than 250 of the Standard and Poor's 500, have increased the rate of dividend payouts.
- Prices of dividend-paying stocks have increased considerably relative to prices of stocks that do not pay dividends.

Although the linkage between the dividend tax cut and increased dividend payouts appears strong, additional research is needed to determine the strength of the cause-and-effect relationship.

helps the corporation ease the problems of unreasonable compensation, thin capitalization, and meeting the arm's length test as to rents. Chapter 19 presents a detailed discussion of the taxation of dividends.

Comparison of Corporations and Other Forms of Doing Business. While a detailed comparison of sole proprietorships, partnerships, S corporations, and C corporations as forms of doing business must be made, it is appropriate at this point to consider some of the tax and nontax factors that favor corporations over proprietorships.

Consideration of tax factors requires an examination of the corporate rate structure. The income tax rate schedule applicable to corporations is reproduced below.

Taxable Income		**Tax Is:**	
Over—	**But Not Over—**		**Of the Amount Over—**
$ –0–	$ 50,000	15%	$ –0–
50,000	75,000	$ 7,500 + 25%	50,000
75,000	100,000	13,750 + 34%	75,000
100,000	335,000	22,250 + 39%	100,000
335,000	10,000,000	113,900 + 34%	335,000
10,000,000	15,000,000	3,400,000 + 35%	10,000,000
15,000,000	18,333,333	5,150,000 + 38%	15,000,000
18,333,333	—	35%	–0–

As this schedule shows, corporate rates on taxable income up to $75,000 are lower than individual rates for persons in the 28 percent and higher brackets. In 2005, single individuals with taxable income over $71,950 are subject to marginal rates of 28 percent or more. Therefore, corporate tax will be lower than individual tax. Furthermore, only the corporate marginal rates of 38 and 39 percent are higher than the 35 percent top bracket for individuals. When dividends are paid, however, the double taxation problem occurs.

Another tax consideration involves the nature of dividend income. All income and expense items of a proprietorship retain their character when reported on the proprietor's tax return. In the case of a partnership, several separately reported items (e.g., charitable contributions and long-term capital gains) retain their character when passed through to the partners. However, the tax attributes of income and expense items of a corporation do not pass through the corporate entity to the shareholders.

Losses of a C corporation are treated differently than losses of a proprietorship, partnership, or S corporation. A loss incurred by a proprietorship may be deductible by the owner, because all income and expense items are reported by the proprietor. Partnership losses are passed through the partnership entity and may be deductible by the partners, and S corporation losses are passed through to the shareholders. C corporation losses, however, have no effect on the taxable income of the shareholders. Income from a C corporation is reported when the shareholders receive dividends. C corporation losses are not reported by the shareholders.

EXAMPLE 9

Franco plans to start a business this year. He expects the business will incur operating losses for the first three years and then become highly profitable. Franco decides to operate as an S corporation during the loss period, because the losses will flow through and be deductible on his personal return. When the business becomes profitable, he intends to switch to C corporation status. ■

Nontax Considerations. Nontax considerations will sometimes override tax considerations and lead to the conclusion that a business should be operated as a corporation. The following are some of the more important nontax considerations:

- Sole proprietors and *general* partners in partnerships face the danger of *unlimited liability*. That is, creditors of the business may file claims not only against the assets of the business but also against the personal assets of proprietors or general partners. Shareholders are protected from claims against their personal assets by state corporate law.
- The corporate form of business organization can provide a vehicle for raising large amounts of capital through widespread stock ownership. Most major businesses in the United States are operated as corporations.
- Shares of stock in a corporation are freely transferable, whereas a partner's sale of his or her partnership interest is subject to approval by the other partners.
- Shareholders may come and go, but a corporation can continue to exist. Death or withdrawal of a partner, on the other hand, may terminate the existing partnership and cause financial difficulties that result in dissolution of the entity. This *continuity of life* is a distinct advantage of the corporate form of doing business.
- Corporations have *centralized management*. All management responsibility is assigned to a board of directors, which appoints officers to carry out the corporation's business. Partnerships, by contrast, may have decentralized management, in which every owner has a right to participate in the organization's business decisions; **limited partnerships,** though, may have centralized management. Centralized management is essential for the smooth operation of a widely held business.

LIMITED LIABILITY COMPANIES

The **limited liability company (LLC)** has proliferated greatly in recent years, particularly since 1988 when the IRS first ruled that it would treat qualifying LLCs as partnerships for tax purposes. All 50 states and the District of Columbia have passed laws that allow LLCs, and thousands of companies have chosen LLC status.

Entity Choice: S Corporation versus C Corporation

S corporations (see Chapter 22) are subject to some restrictions that do not apply to C corporations. Among these is a requirement that the corporation be a domestic corporation, incorporated and organized in the United States. Also, an S corporation cannot have a shareholder who is a nonresident alien. Thus, the C corporation, rather than the S corporation, would be the appropriate choice for businesses that are organized outside the United States and for corporations that plan to have shareholders who are nonresident aliens.

As with a corporation, operating as an LLC allows its owners to avoid unlimited liability, which is a primary *nontax* consideration in choosing this form of business organization. The tax advantage of LLCs is that qualifying businesses may be treated as partnerships for tax purposes, thereby avoiding the problem of double taxation associated with regular corporations.

Some states allow an LLC to have centralized management, but not continuity of life or free transferability of interests. Other states allow LLCs to adopt any or all of the corporate characteristics of centralized management, continuity of life, and free transferability of interests.

ENTITY CLASSIFICATION

Can an organization not qualifying as a corporation under state law still be treated as such for Federal income tax purposes? Unfortunately, the tax law defines a corporation as including "associations, joint stock companies, and insurance companies."[1] As the Code contains no definition of what constitutes an "association," the issue became the subject of frequent litigation.

It was finally determined that an entity would be treated as a corporation if it had a majority of characteristics common to corporations. For this purpose, relevant characteristics are:

- Continuity of life.
- Centralized management.
- Limited liability.
- Free transferability of interests.

These criteria did not resolve all of the problems that continued to arise over corporate classification. When a new type of business entity—the limited liability company—was developed, the IRS was deluged with inquiries regarding its tax status. As LLCs became increasingly popular with professional groups, all states enacted statutes allowing some form of this entity. Invariably, the statutes permitted the corporate characteristic of limited liability and, often, that of centralized management. Because continuity of life and free transferability of interests are absent, partnership classification was hoped for. This treatment avoided the double tax result inherent in the corporate form.

In late 1996, the IRS eased the entity classification problem by issuing the **check-the-box Regulations.**[2] Effective beginning in 1997, the Regulations enable taxpayers to choose the tax status of a business entity without regard to its corporate (or noncorporate) characteristics. These rules have simplified tax administration

[1] § 7701(a)(3).

[2] Reg. §§ 301.7701–1 through –4, and –7.

considerably and should eliminate the type of litigation that arose with regard to the association (i.e., corporation) status.

Under the rules, entities with more than one owner can elect to be classified as either a partnership or a corporation. An entity with only one owner can elect to be classified as a sole proprietorship or as a corporation. In the event of default (i.e., no election is made), multi-owner entities are classified as partnerships and single-person businesses as sole proprietorships.

The election is not available to entities that are actually incorporated under state law or to entities that are required to be corporations under Federal law (e.g., certain publicly traded partnerships). Otherwise, LLCs are not treated as being incorporated under state law. Consequently, they can elect either corporation or partnership status. Eligible entities make the election as to tax status by filing Form 8832 (Entity Classification Election).

LO.2

Compare the taxation of individuals and corporations.

An Introduction to the Income Taxation of Corporations

AN OVERVIEW OF CORPORATE VERSUS INDIVIDUAL INCOME TAX TREATMENT

In a discussion of how corporations are treated under the Federal income tax law, a useful approach is to compare their treatment with that applicable to individual taxpayers.

Similarities. Gross income of a corporation is determined in much the same manner as it is for individuals. Thus, gross income includes compensation for services rendered, income derived from a business, gains from dealings in property, interest, rents, royalties, and dividends—to name only a few items. Both individuals and corporations are entitled to exclusions from gross income. However, corporate taxpayers are allowed fewer exclusions. Interest on municipal bonds is excluded from gross income whether the bondholder is an individual or a corporate taxpayer.

Gains and losses from property transactions are handled similarly. For example, whether a gain or loss is capital or ordinary depends upon the nature of the asset in the hands of the taxpayer making the taxable disposition. In defining what is not a capital asset, § 1221 makes no distinction between corporate and noncorporate taxpayers.

In the area of nontaxable exchanges, corporations are like individuals in that they do not recognize gain or loss on a like-kind exchange and may defer realized gain on an involuntary conversion of property. The exclusion of gain provisions dealing with the sale of a personal residence do not apply to corporations. Both corporations and individuals are vulnerable to the disallowance of losses on sales of property to related parties or on wash sales of securities. The wash sales rules do not apply to individuals who are traders or dealers in securities or to corporations that are dealers if the securities are sold in the ordinary course of the corporation's business. Upon the sale or other taxable disposition of depreciable property, the recapture rules generally make no distinction between corporate and noncorporate taxpayers.[3]

The business deductions of corporations also parallel those available to individuals. Deductions are allowed for all ordinary and necessary expenses paid or incurred in carrying on a trade or business. Specific provision is made for the

[3] §§ 1245 and 1250, but see § 291(a).

deductibility of interest, certain taxes, losses, bad debts, accelerated cost recovery, charitable contributions, net operating losses, research and experimental expenditures, and other less common deductions. A corporation does not distinguish between business and nonbusiness interest or business and nonbusiness bad debts. Thus, these amounts are deductible in full as ordinary deductions by corporations. No deduction is permitted for interest paid or incurred on amounts borrowed to purchase or carry tax-exempt securities. The same holds true for expenses contrary to public policy and certain unpaid expenses and interest between related parties.

Some of the tax credits available to individuals can also be claimed by corporations. This is the case with the foreign tax credit. Not available to corporations are certain credits that are personal in nature, such as the credit for child and dependent care expenses, the credit for elderly or disabled taxpayers, and the earned income credit.

Dissimilarities. The income taxation of corporations and individuals also differs significantly. As noted earlier, different tax rates apply to corporations and to individuals. Corporate tax rates are discussed in more detail later in the chapter (see Examples 25 and 26).

All allowable corporate deductions are treated as business deductions. Thus, the determination of adjusted gross income (AGI), so essential for individual taxpayers, has no relevance to corporations. Taxable income is computed simply by subtracting from gross income all allowable deductions and losses. Corporations thus need not be concerned with itemized deductions or the standard deduction. Likewise, the deduction for personal and dependency exemptions is not available to corporations.

Unlike individuals, corporations are not subject to the $100 floor on the deductible portion of casualty and theft losses. Also inapplicable is the provision limiting the deductibility of nonbusiness casualty losses to the amount in excess of 10 percent of AGI.

SPECIFIC PROVISIONS COMPARED

In comparing the tax treatment of individuals and corporations, the following areas warrant special discussion:

- Accounting periods and methods.
- Capital gains and losses.
- Passive losses.
- Charitable contributions.
- Manufacturers' deduction.
- Net operating losses.
- Special deductions available only to corporations.

ACCOUNTING PERIODS AND METHODS

Accounting Periods. Corporations generally have the same choices of accounting periods as do individual taxpayers. Like an individual, a corporation may choose a calendar year or a fiscal year for reporting purposes. Corporations, however, enjoy greater flexibility in the selection of a tax year. For example, corporations usually can have different tax years from those of their shareholders. Also, newly formed corporations (as new taxpayers) usually may choose any approved accounting period without having to obtain the consent of the IRS. **Personal service corporations (PSCs)** and S corporations, however, are subject to severe restrictions in the use of fiscal years. The rules applicable to S corporations are discussed in Chapter 22.

A PSC has as its principal activity the performance of personal services. Such services must be substantially performed by owner-employees and must be in the fields of health, law, engineering, architecture, accounting, actuarial science, performing arts, or consulting.[4] Barring certain exceptions, PSCs must adopt a calendar year for tax purposes.[5] The exceptions that permit the use of a fiscal year are discussed in Chapter 16.[6]

Accounting Methods. As a general rule, the cash method of accounting is unavailable to *regular* corporations.[7] Exceptions apply to the following types of corporations:

- S corporations.
- Corporations engaged in the trade or business of farming and timber.
- Qualified PSCs.
- Corporations with average annual gross receipts of $5 million or less. (In applying the $5 million-or-less test, the corporation uses the average of the three prior taxable years.)

Most individuals and corporations that maintain inventory for sale to customers are required to use the accrual method of accounting for determining sales and cost of goods sold. However, as a matter of administrative convenience, the IRS will permit any entity with average annual gross receipts of not more than $1 million for the most recent three-year period to use the cash method. This applies even if the taxpayer is buying and selling inventory. Also as a matter of administrative convenience, the IRS will permit certain entities whose average annual gross receipts are greater than $1 million but are not more than $10 million for the most recent three-year period to use the cash method.

A corporation that uses the accrual method of accounting must observe a special rule in dealing with related parties. If the corporation has an accrual outstanding at the end of any taxable year, it cannot claim a deduction until the recipient reports the amount as income.[8] This rule is most often encountered when a corporation deals with a person who owns more than 50 percent of the corporation's stock.

EXAMPLE 10

Teal, Inc., an accrual method corporation, uses the calendar year for tax purposes. Bob, a cash method taxpayer, owns more than 50% of the corporation's stock at the end of 2005. On December 31, 2005, Teal has accrued $25,000 of salary to Bob. Bob receives the salary in 2006 and reports it on his 2006 tax return. Teal cannot claim a deduction for the $25,000 until 2006. ■

CAPITAL GAINS AND LOSSES

Capital gains and losses result from the taxable sales or exchanges of capital assets.[9] Whether these gains and losses are long term or short term depends upon the holding period of the assets sold or exchanged. Each year, a taxpayer's long-term capital gains and losses are combined, and the result is either a *net* long-term capital gain or a *net* long-term capital loss. A similar aggregation is made with short-term capital gains and losses, the result being a *net* short-term capital gain or a *net* short-term capital loss. The following combinations and results are possible:

1. A net long-term capital gain and a net short-term capital loss. These are combined, and the result is either a net capital gain or a net capital loss.
2. A net long-term capital gain and a net short-term capital gain. No further combination is made.
3. A net long-term capital loss and a net short-term capital gain. These are combined, and the result is either a net capital gain or a net capital loss.
4. A net long-term capital loss and a net short-term capital loss. No further combination is made.

[4] § 448(d)(2)(A).
[5] § 441(i).
[6] §§ 444 and 280H.
[7] § 448(a).
[8] § 267(a)(2).
[9] See Chapter 14 for a detailed discussion of capital gains and losses.

Capital Gains. Individuals generally pay tax on net (long-term) capital gains at a maximum rate of 15 percent.[10] Corporations, by contrast, receive no favorable rate on capital gains and must include the net capital gain, in full, as part of taxable income.

Capital Losses. Net capital losses (refer to combination 4 and, possibly, to combinations 1 and 3) of corporate and noncorporate taxpayers receive different income tax treatment. Generally, noncorporate taxpayers can deduct up to $3,000 of such net losses against other income. Any remaining capital losses can be carried forward to future years until absorbed by capital gains or by the $3,000 deduction.[11] Carryovers do not lose their identity but remain either long term or short term.

EXAMPLE 11

Robin, an individual, incurs a net long-term capital loss of $7,500 for calendar year 2005. Assuming adequate taxable income, Robin may deduct $3,000 of this loss on his 2005 return. The remaining $4,500 ($7,500 – $3,000) of the loss is carried forward to 2006 and years thereafter until completely deducted. The $4,500 will be carried forward as a long-term capital loss. ■

Unlike individuals, corporate taxpayers are not permitted to claim any net capital losses as a deduction against ordinary income. Capital losses, therefore, can be used only as an offset against capital gains. Corporations may, however, carry back net capital losses to three preceding years, applying them first to the earliest year in point of time. Carryforwards are allowed for a period of five years from the year of the loss. When carried back or forward, a long-term capital loss is treated as a short-term capital loss.

EXAMPLE 12

Assume the same facts as in Example 11, except that Robin is a corporation. None of the $7,500 long-term capital loss incurred in 2005 can be deducted that year. Robin Corporation may, however, carry back the loss to years 2002, 2003, and 2004 (in this order) and offset it against any capital gains recognized in these years. If the carryback does not exhaust the loss, it may be carried forward to calendar years 2006, 2007, 2008, 2009, and 2010 (in this order). Either a carryback or a carryforward of the long-term capital loss converts the loss to a short-term capital loss. ■

PASSIVE LOSSES

The **passive loss** rules apply to noncorporate taxpayers and to closely held C corporations and personal service corporations (PSCs).[12] For S corporations and partnerships, passive income or loss flows through to the owners, and the passive loss rules are applied at the owner level. The passive loss rules are applied to closely held corporations and to PSCs to prevent taxpayers from incorporating to avoid the passive loss limitations (refer to Chapter 11).

A corporation is closely held if, at any time during the taxable year, more than 50 percent of the value of the corporation's outstanding stock is owned, directly or indirectly, by or for not more than five individuals. A corporation is classified as a PSC if it meets the following requirements:

- The principal activity of the corporation is the performance of personal services.
- Such services are substantially performed by owner-employees.
- More than 10 percent of the stock (in value) is held by owner-employees. *Any* stock held by an employee on *any* one day causes the employee to be an owner-employee.

[10] A maximum rate of 5% applies to taxpayers in the 10% and 15% brackets.

[11] § 1212.

[12] § 469(a).

The general passive activity loss rules apply to PSCs. Passive activity losses cannot be offset against either active income or portfolio income. The application of the passive activity rules is not as harsh for closely held corporations. They may offset passive losses against active income, but not against portfolio income.

EXAMPLE 13

Brown, a closely held C corporation that is not a PSC, has $300,000 of passive losses from a rental activity, $200,000 of active business income, and $100,000 of portfolio income. The corporation may offset $200,000 of the $300,000 passive loss against the $200,000 active business income, but may not offset the remainder against the $100,000 of portfolio income. ■

Subject to certain exceptions, individual taxpayers are not allowed to offset passive losses against *either* active or portfolio income.

CHARITABLE CONTRIBUTIONS

Both corporate and noncorporate taxpayers may deduct charitable contributions if the recipient is a qualified charitable organization. Generally, a deduction will be allowed only for the year in which the payment is made. However, an important exception is made for *accrual basis corporations*. They may claim the deduction in the year *preceding* payment if two requirements are met. First, the contribution must be authorized by the board of directors by the end of that year. Second, it must be paid on or before the fifteenth day of the third month of the next year.

EXAMPLE 14

On December 28, 2005, Blue Company, a calendar year, accrual basis partnership, authorizes a $5,000 donation to the Atlanta Symphony Association (a qualified charitable organization). The donation is made on March 14, 2006. Because Blue Company is a partnership, the contribution cannot be deducted until 2006.[13] However, if Blue Company is a corporation and the December 28, 2005 authorization was made by its board of directors, Blue may claim the $5,000 donation as a deduction for calendar year 2005. ■

Property Contributions. The amount that can be deducted for a noncash charitable contribution depends on the type of property contributed. Property must be identified as long-term capital gain property or ordinary income property. *Long-term capital gain property* is property that, if sold, would result in long-term capital gain for the taxpayer. Such property generally must be a capital asset and must be held for the long-term holding period (more than 12 months). *Ordinary income property* is property that, if sold, would result in ordinary income for the taxpayer.

The deduction for a charitable contribution of long-term capital property is generally measured by its fair market value.

EXAMPLE 15

In 2005, Mallard Corporation donates a parcel of land (a capital asset) to Oakland Community College. Mallard acquired the land in 1988 for $60,000, and the fair market value on the date of the contribution is $100,000. The corporation's charitable contribution deduction (subject to a percentage limitation discussed later) is measured by the asset's fair market value of $100,000, even though the $40,000 appreciation on the land has never been included in Mallard's income. ■

In two situations, a charitable contribution of long-term capital gain property is measured by the basis of the property, rather than fair market value. If the corporation contributes *tangible personal property* and the charitable organization

[13] Each calendar year partner will report an allocable portion of the charitable contribution deduction as of December 31, 2006 (the end of the partnership's tax year). See Chapter 21.

puts the property to an unrelated use, the appreciation on the property is not deductible. Unrelated use is defined as use that is not related to the purpose or function that qualifies the organization for exempt status.

EXAMPLE 16

White Corporation donates a painting worth $200,000 to Western States Art Museum (a qualified organization), which exhibits the painting. White had acquired the painting in 1980 for $90,000. Because the museum put the painting to a related use, White is allowed to deduct $200,000, the fair market value of the painting. ■

EXAMPLE 17

Assume the same facts as in the previous example, except that White Corporation donates the painting to the American Cancer Society, which sells the painting and deposits the $200,000 proceeds in the organization's general fund. White's deduction is limited to the $90,000 basis because it contributed tangible personal property that was put to an unrelated use by the charitable organization. ■

ETHICAL CONSIDERATIONS

Is It Better Not to Know?

Puffin Corporation, your client, donated a painting to Tri-City Art Museum. The painting, which had been displayed in the corporate offices for several years, had a basis of $20,000 and a fair market value of $100,000. Puffin deducted a charitable contribution of $100,000 on its tax return.

You have learned that Tri-City Museum, also a client of yours, did not display the painting because it did not fit well with the museum's collection. Instead, Tri-City sold the painting for $100,000 and placed the funds in its operating budget. What action, if any, should you take?

The deduction for charitable contributions of long-term capital gain property to certain *private nonoperating foundations* is also limited to the basis of the property.

Ordinary income property is property that, if sold, would result in ordinary income. Examples of ordinary income property include inventory and capital assets that have not been held long term. In addition, § 1231 property (depreciable property used in a trade or business) is treated as ordinary income property to the extent of any ordinary income recaptured under § 1245 or § 1250. As a general rule, the deduction for a contribution of ordinary income property is limited to the basis of the property. On certain contributions, however, *corporations* enjoy two special exceptions that allow a deduction for 50 percent of the appreciation (but not to exceed twice the basis) on property. The first exception concerns inventory if the property is used in a manner related to the exempt purpose of the donee. Also, the charity must use the property solely for the care of the ill, the needy, or infants.

EXAMPLE 18

Lark Corporation, a grocery chain, donates canned goods to the Salvation Army to be used to feed the needy. Lark's basis in the canned goods was $2,000, and the fair market value was $3,000. Lark's deduction is $2,500 [$2,000 basis + 50%($3,000 – $2,000)]. ■

The second exception involves gifts of scientific property to colleges and certain scientific research organizations for use in research, provided certain conditions are met.[14] As was true of the inventory exception, 50 percent of the appreciation on such property is allowed as an additional deduction.

[14]These conditions are set forth in § 170(e)(4). For the inventory exception, see § 170(e)(3).

Limitations Imposed on Charitable Contribution Deductions. Like individuals, corporations are subject to percentage limits on the charitable contribution deduction.[15] For any one year, a corporate taxpayer's contribution deduction is limited to 10 percent of taxable income. For this purpose, taxable income is computed without regard to the charitable contribution deduction, any net operating loss carryback or capital loss carryback, and the dividends received deduction. Any contributions in excess of the 10 percent limitation may be carried forward to the five succeeding tax years. Any carryforward must be added to subsequent contributions and will be subject to the 10 percent limitation. In applying this limitation, the current year's contributions must be deducted first, with excess deductions from previous years deducted in order of time.[16]

EXAMPLE 19

During 2005, Orange Corporation (a calendar year taxpayer) had the following income and expenses:

Income from operations	$140,000
Expenses from operations	110,000
Dividends received	10,000
Charitable contributions made in May 2005	5,000

For purposes of the 10% limitation *only*, Orange Corporation's taxable income is $40,000 ($140,000 – $110,000 + $10,000). Consequently, the allowable charitable contribution deduction for 2005 is $4,000 (10% × $40,000). The $1,000 unused portion of the contribution can be carried forward to 2006, 2007, 2008, 2009, and 2010 (in that order) until exhausted. ■

EXAMPLE 20

Assume the same facts as in Example 19. In 2006, Orange Corporation has taxable income (for purposes of the 10% limitation) of $50,000 and makes a charitable contribution of $4,500. The maximum deduction allowed for 2006 is $5,000 (10% × $50,000). The first $4,500 of the allowed deduction must be allocated to the contribution made in 2006, and $500 of the $1,000 unused contribution is carried over from 2005. The remaining $500 of the 2005 contribution may be carried over to 2007 (and later years, if necessary). ■

MANUFACTURERS' DEDUCTION

One important purpose of the American Jobs Creation Act of 2004 was to replace certain tax provisions that our world trading partners regarded as allowing unfair advantage to U.S. exports. Among other changes, the Act creates a new deduction based on the income from manufacturing activities (designated as *production activities*). The new **manufacturers' deduction**[17] is effective for taxable years beginning after December 31, 2004.

Operational Rules. For 2005 and 2006, the manufacturers' deduction is 3 percent of the lower of:

- qualified production income, or
- taxable income (adjusted gross income in the case of individuals).

The deduction, however, cannot exceed 50 percent of an employer's W–2 wages.

A phase-in provision increases the rate to 6 percent for 2007 through 2009 and to 9 percent for 2010 and thereafter.

[15]The percentage limitations applicable to individuals and corporations are set forth in § 170(b).

[16]The carryover rules relating to all taxpayers are in § 170(d).

[17]§ 199.

Eligible Taxpayers. The deduction is available to a variety of taxpayers including individuals, partnerships, S corporations, C corporations, cooperatives, estates, and trusts. In the case of a sole proprietor, a deduction *for* AGI results. In a pass-through entity (e.g., partnership or S corporation), the deduction flows through to the individual owners. In the case of a C corporation, the deduction is included with other expenses in computing corporate taxable income.

EXAMPLE 21

Elk Corporation, a calendar year taxpayer, manufactures golf equipment. For 2005, Elk had taxable income of $360,000 and qualified production income of $380,000. Elk's manufacturers' deduction is $10,800 [3% × $360,000 (the lesser of $380,000 or $360,000)]. Elk's W–2 wages were $30,000, so the W–2 wage limitation is not a problem. ■

Eligible Income. **Qualified production income** is the total of qualified production receipts reduced by:

- Cost of goods sold attributable to such receipts.
- Other deductions, expenses, or losses directly allocable to such receipts.
- A share of other deductions, expenses, and losses not directly allocable to such receipts or another class of income.

The term also includes receipts for certain services rendered in connection with construction projects in the United States. Qualified production receipts do not include proceeds from the sale of food and beverages prepared at a retail establishment.

Observations and Operational Problems. Although the deduction is called the manufacturers' deduction, note the broad definition of production receipts. Not only is traditional manufacturing included but so are other activities such as agriculture, extraction, and construction. Also note that the manufacturers' deduction, unlike the export subsidies it replaced, is not conditioned on the foreign sales of goods produced. In this regard, domestic and foreign activities will be treated alike.

Because the manufacturers' deduction introduces many unique concepts, current tax law offers little assistance in resolving some of the problems that are certain to arise, such as the following.

- How much activity must take place before manufacturing occurs? For example, is the mere packaging of another's product enough? The law recognizes that production *in part* will suffice but only if such production is *significant*.
- As to construction projects, qualifying activities will be limited to structural improvements—cosmetic changes will not be enough. So, can repainting a house (cosmetic) be accompanied by some sheet rock replacement to make it structural?
- When a taxpayer has integrated businesses, some that qualify as manufacturing and others that do not, manipulation is to be expected. Income will be shifted *to* and expenses will be shifted *from* the businesses that qualify. What safeguards will be imposed to preclude this type of manipulation?

The IRS is expected to provide answers to these questions and to issue guidelines that will aid taxpayers in utilizing the manufacturers' deduction correctly.

NET OPERATING LOSSES

As for individuals, the net operating loss (NOL) of a corporation may be carried back 2 years and forward 20 to offset taxable income for those years. However, a corporation does not adjust its tax loss for the year for capital losses as do individual taxpayers, because a corporation is not permitted a deduction for net capital losses. Nor does a corporation make adjustments for nonbusiness deductions as do individual taxpayers. Further, a corporation is allowed to include the dividends received deduction (discussed below) in computing its NOL.[18]

EXAMPLE 22

In 2005, Green Corporation has gross income (including dividends) of $200,000 and deductions of $300,000 excluding the dividends received deduction. Green Corporation had received taxable dividends of $100,000 from Fox, Inc. stock. Green has an NOL computed as follows:

Gross income (including dividends)		$ 200,000
Less: Business deductions	$300,000	
Dividends received deduction (70% × $100,000)*	70,000	(370,000)
Taxable income (or loss)		($ 170,000)

*See the discussion of the dividends received deduction in the next section of this chapter.

The NOL is carried back two years to 2003. (Green Corporation may *elect* to forgo the carryback option and instead carry the loss forward.) Assume Green had taxable income of $40,000 in 2003. The carryover to 2004 is computed as follows:

Taxable income for 2003	$ 40,000
Less: NOL carryback	(170,000)
Taxable income for 2003 after NOL carryback (carryover to 2004)	($ 130,000)

LO.3

Discuss the tax rules unique to corporations.

DEDUCTIONS AVAILABLE ONLY TO CORPORATIONS

Dividends Received Deduction. The purpose of the **dividends received deduction** is to mitigate triple taxation. Without the deduction, income paid to a corporation in the form of a dividend would be taxed to the recipient corporation with no corresponding deduction to the distributing corporation. Later, when the recipient corporation paid the income to its individual shareholders, the income would again be subject to taxation with no corresponding deduction to the corporation. The dividends received deduction alleviates this inequity by causing only some or none of the dividend income to be taxable to the recipient corporation.

As the following table illustrates, the amount of the dividends received deduction depends on the percentage of ownership the recipient corporate shareholder holds in a domestic corporation making the dividend distribution.[19]

Percentage of Ownership by Corporate Shareholder	Deduction Percentage
Less than 20%	70%
20% or more (but less than 80%)	80%
80% or more*	100%

*The payor corporation must be a member of an affiliated group with the recipient corporation.

The dividends received deduction is limited to a percentage of the taxable income of a corporation. For this purpose, taxable income is computed without regard to the NOL, the dividends received deduction, and any capital loss carryback

[18]The modifications required to arrive at the amount of NOL that can be carried back or forward are in § 172(d).

[19]§ 243(a).

to the current tax year. The percentage of taxable income limitation corresponds to the deduction percentage. Thus, if a corporate shareholder owns less than 20 percent of the stock in the distributing corporation, the dividends received deduction is limited to 70 percent of taxable income. However, the taxable income limitation does not apply if the corporation has an NOL for the current taxable year.[20]

In working with these myriad rules, the following steps are useful:

1. Multiply the dividends received by the deduction percentage.
2. Multiply the taxable income by the deduction percentage.
3. Limit the deduction to the lesser of step 1 or step 2, unless subtracting the amount derived in step 1 from 100 percent of taxable income *generates* an NOL. If so, use the amount derived in step 1. This is referred to as the NOL rule.

EXAMPLE 23

Red, White, and Blue Corporations are three unrelated calendar year corporations. During the year, they have the following transactions:

	Red Corporation	White Corporation	Blue Corporation
Gross income from operations	$ 400,000	$ 320,000	$ 260,000
Expenses from operations	(340,000)	(340,000)	(340,000)
Dividends received from domestic corporations (less than 20% ownership)	200,000	200,000	200,000
Taxable income before the dividends received deduction	$ 260,000	$ 180,000	$ 120,000

In determining the dividends received deduction, use the three-step procedure described above:

Step 1 (70% × $200,000)	$140,000	$140,000	$140,000
Step 2			
70% × $260,000 (taxable income)	$182,000		
70% × $180,000 (taxable income)		$126,000	
70% × $120,000 (taxable income)			$ 84,000
Step 3			
Lesser of step 1 or step 2	$140,000	$126,000	
Deduction generates an NOL			$140,000

White Corporation is subject to the 70% of taxable income limitation. It does not qualify for NOL rule treatment since subtracting $140,000 (step 1) from $180,000 (100% of taxable income before the dividends received deduction) does not yield a negative figure. Blue Corporation qualifies for NOL rule treatment because subtracting $140,000 (step 1) from $120,000 (100% of taxable income before the dividends received deduction) yields a negative figure. In summary, each corporation has a dividends received deduction for the year: $140,000 for Red Corporation, $126,000 for White Corporation, and $140,000 for Blue Corporation. ■

Deduction of Organizational Expenditures. Expenses incurred in connection with the organization of a corporation normally are chargeable to a capital account. That they benefit the corporation during its existence seems clear. But how can they be amortized when most corporations possess unlimited life? The

[20] § 246(b).

lack of a determinable and limited estimated useful life would therefore preclude any tax write-off. Section 248 was enacted to solve this problem.

Under § 248, a corporation may elect to amortize **organizational expenditures** over a period of 180 months or more. The period begins with the month in which the corporation begins business.[21] Organizational expenditures *subject to the election* include the following:

- Legal services incident to organization (e.g., drafting the corporate charter, bylaws, minutes of organizational meetings, terms of original stock certificates).
- Necessary accounting services.
- Expenses of temporary directors and of organizational meetings of directors or shareholders, and fees paid to the state of incorporation.

Expenditures that *do not qualify* include those connected with issuing or selling shares of stock or other securities (e.g., commissions, professional fees, and printing costs) or with the transfer of assets to a corporation. Such expenditures reduce the amount of capital raised and are not deductible at all.

A special exception allows the corporation to immediately expense the first $5,000 of organizational costs. The exception, however, is phased out on a dollar-for-dollar basis when these expenses exceed $50,000. A corporation, for example, with $52,000 of organizational expenditures could elect to expense $3,000 [$5,000 – ($52,000 – $50,000)] of this amount and amortize the $49,000 balance ($52,000 – $3,000) over 180 months.[22]

To qualify for the election, the expenditures must be *incurred* before the end of the tax year in which the corporation begins business. In this regard, the corporation's method of accounting is of no consequence. Thus, an expense incurred by a cash basis corporation in its first tax year qualifies even though it is not paid until a subsequent year.

The election is made in a statement attached to the corporation's return for its first tax year. The return and statement must be filed no later than the due date of the return (including any extensions).

If the election is not made on a timely basis, organizational expenditures cannot be deducted until the corporation ceases to do business and liquidates. These expenditures will be deductible if the corporate charter limits the life of the corporation.

EXAMPLE 24

Black Corporation, an accrual basis taxpayer, was formed and began operations on May 1, 2005. The following expenses were incurred during its first year of operations (May 1 through December 31, 2005):

Expenses of temporary directors and of organizational meetings	$15,000
Fee paid to the state of incorporation	2,000
Accounting services incident to organization	18,000
Legal services for drafting the corporate charter and bylaws	32,000
Expenses incident to the printing and sale of stock certificates	48,000

Because of the dollar cap (i.e., dollar-for-dollar reduction for amounts in excess of $50,000), no immediate expensing under the $5,000 rule is available. Assume, however, that Black Corporation elects to amortize the qualifying organizational expenses over a period of 180 months. The monthly amortization is $372 [($15,000 + $2,000 + $18,000 + $32,000) ÷ 180

[21]The month in which a corporation begins business may not be immediately apparent. See Reg. § 1.248–1(a)(3). For a similar problem in the Subchapter S area, see Chapter 22.

[22]Organizational expenditures incurred before October 23, 2004, could not be immediately expensed but could be amortized over a period of 60 months or more. The change to § 248 was made by the American Jobs Creation Act of 2004.

months], and $2,976 ($372 × 8 months) is deductible for tax year 2005. Note that the $48,000 of expenses incident to the printing and sale of stock certificates does not qualify for the election. These expenses cannot be deducted at all but reduce the amount of the capital realized from the sale of stock. ■

LO.4

Compute the corporate income tax.

Determining the Corporate Income Tax Liability

CORPORATE INCOME TAX RATES

Corporate income tax rates have fluctuated widely over past years. Refer to the inside front cover of the text for a schedule of the current corporate income tax rates.

EXAMPLE 25

Gold Corporation, a calendar year taxpayer, has taxable income of $90,000 for 2005. Its income tax liability is $18,850, determined as follows:

Tax on $75,000	$13,750
Tax on $15,000 × 34%	5,100
Tax liability	$18,850

■

For a corporation that has taxable income in excess of $100,000 for any tax year, the amount of the tax is increased by the lesser of (1) 5 percent of the excess or (2) $11,750. In effect, the additional tax means a 39 percent rate for every dollar of taxable income from $100,000 to $335,000.

EXAMPLE 26

Silver Corporation, a calendar year taxpayer, has taxable income of $335,000 for 2005. Its income tax liability is $113,900, determined as follows:

Tax on $100,000	$ 22,250
Tax on $235,000 × 39%	91,650
Tax liability	$113,900

Note that the tax liability of $113,900 is 34% of $335,000. Thus, due to the 39% rate (34% normal rate + 5% additional tax on taxable income between $100,000 and $335,000), the benefit of the lower rates on the first $75,000 of taxable income completely phases out at $335,000. The normal rate drops back to 34% on taxable income between $335,000 and $10 million. ■

Under § 11(b), personal service corporations are taxed at a flat 35 percent rate on all taxable income. Thus, they do not enjoy the tax savings of the 15 percent to 34 percent brackets applicable to other corporations. For this purpose, a PSC is a corporation that is substantially employee owned. Also, it must engage in one of the following activities: health, law, engineering, architecture, accounting, actuarial science, performing arts, or consulting.

ALTERNATIVE MINIMUM TAX

Corporations are subject to an alternative minimum tax (AMT) that is structured similarly to the AMT applicable to individuals.[23] The AMT for corporations, as for

[23]Small corporations are not subject to the alternative minimum tax. See Chapter 15 for details.

individuals, involves a broader tax base than does the regular tax. Like an individual, a corporation is required to apply a minimum tax rate to the expanded base and to pay the difference between the tentative AMT liability and the regular tax. Many of the adjustments and tax preference items necessary to arrive at alternative minimum taxable income (AMTI) are the same for individuals and corporations. Although the objective of the AMT is the same for individual and corporate taxpayers, the rate and exemptions are different. Refer to Chapter 15 for a detailed discussion of the corporate AMT.

LO.5

Explain the tax rules unique to multiple corporations.

TAX LIABILITY OF RELATED CORPORATIONS

Related corporations are subject to special rules for computing the income tax, the expense of certain depreciable assets under § 179, and the AMT exemption.[24] If these restrictions did not exist, the shareholders of a corporation could gain significant tax advantages by splitting a single corporation into *multiple* corporations. The next two examples illustrate the potential *income tax* advantage of multiple corporations.

EXAMPLE 27

Gray Corporation annually yields taxable income of $300,000. The corporate tax on $300,000 is $100,250, computed as follows:

Tax on $100,000	$ 22,250
Tax on $200,000 × 39%	78,000
Tax liability	$100,250

■

EXAMPLE 28

Assume that Gray Corporation in the previous example is divided equally into four corporations. Each corporation would have taxable income of $75,000, and the tax for each (absent the special provisions for related corporations) would be computed as follows:

Tax on $50,000	$ 7,500
Tax on $25,000 × 25%	6,250
Tax liability	$13,750

The total liability for the four corporations would be $55,000 ($13,750 × 4). The savings would be $45,250 ($100,250 – $55,000). ■

To preclude the advantages that could be gained by using multiple corporations, the tax law requires special treatment for *controlled groups* of corporations. A comparison of Examples 27 and 28 reveals that the income tax savings that could be achieved by using multiple corporations result from having more of the total income taxed at lower rates. To close this potential loophole, the law limits a controlled group's taxable income in the tax brackets below 35 percent to the amount the corporations in the group would have if they were one corporation. Thus, in Example 28, under the controlled corporation rules, only $12,500 (one-fourth of the first $50,000 of taxable income) for each of the four related corporations would be taxed at the 15 percent rate. The 25 percent rate would apply to the next $6,250 (one-fourth of the next $25,000) of taxable income of each corporation. This equal allocation of the $50,000 and $25,000 amounts is required unless all members of the controlled group consent to an apportionment plan providing for an unequal allocation.

Similar limitations apply to the election to expense certain depreciable assets under § 179 (see Chapter 8) and to the $40,000 exemption amount for purposes of computing the AMT (see Chapter 15).

[24] § 1561(a).

■ **FIGURE 17–1**
Controlled Groups—
Parent-Subsidiary Corporations

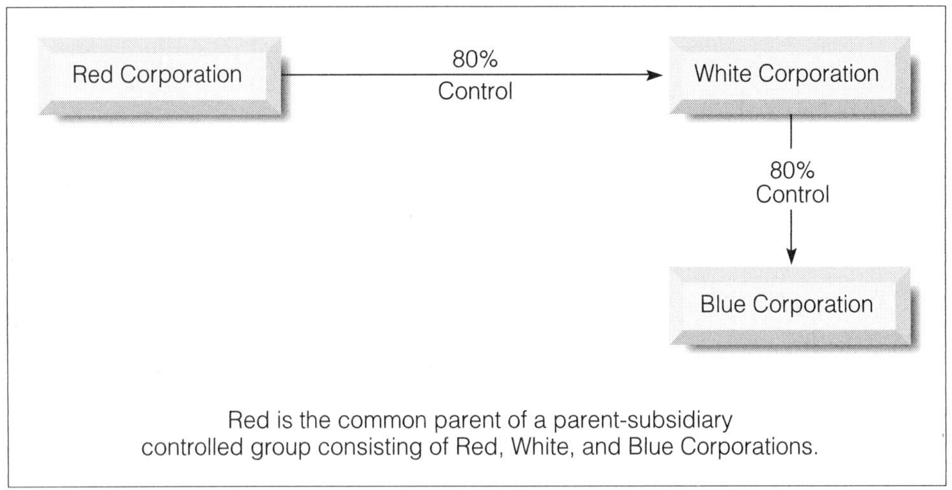

CONTROLLED GROUPS

A **controlled group** of corporations includes parent-subsidiary groups, brother-sister groups, combined groups, and certain insurance companies. Groups of the first two types are discussed in the following sections.

Parent-Subsidiary Controlled Group. A **parent-subsidiary controlled group** consists of one or more *chains* of corporations connected through stock ownership with a common parent corporation. The ownership connection can be established through either a *voting power test* or a *value test*. The voting power test requires ownership of stock possessing at least 80 percent of the total voting power of all classes of stock entitled to vote.[25]

EXAMPLE 29

Acqua Corporation owns 80% of White Corporation. Acqua and White Corporations are members of a parent-subsidiary controlled group. Acqua is the parent corporation, and White is the subsidiary. ■

The parent-subsidiary relationship described in Example 29 is easy to recognize because Acqua Corporation is the direct owner of White Corporation. Real-world business organizations are often much more complex, sometimes including numerous corporations with chains of ownership connecting them. In these complex corporate structures, determining whether the controlled group classification is appropriate becomes more difficult. The ownership requirements can be met through direct ownership (refer to Example 29) or through indirect ownership, as illustrated in the two following examples.

EXAMPLE 30

Red Corporation owns 80% of the voting stock of White Corporation, and White Corporation owns 80% of the voting stock of Blue Corporation. Red, White, and Blue Corporations constitute a controlled group in which Red is the common parent and White and Blue are subsidiaries. The same result would occur if Red Corporation, rather than White Corporation, owned the Blue Corporation stock. This parent-subsidiary relationship is diagrammed in Figure 17–1. ■

EXAMPLE 31

Brown Corporation owns 80% of the stock of Green Corporation, which owns 30% of Blue Corporation. Brown also owns 80% of White Corporation, which owns 50% of Blue Corporation. Brown, Green, Blue, and White Corporations constitute a parent-subsidiary controlled group in which Brown is the common parent and Green, Blue, and White are subsidiaries. This parent-subsidiary relationship is diagrammed in Figure 17–2. ■

---

[25]§ 1563(a)(1).

■ **FIGURE 17-2**
Controlled Groups—
Parent-Subsidiary Corporations

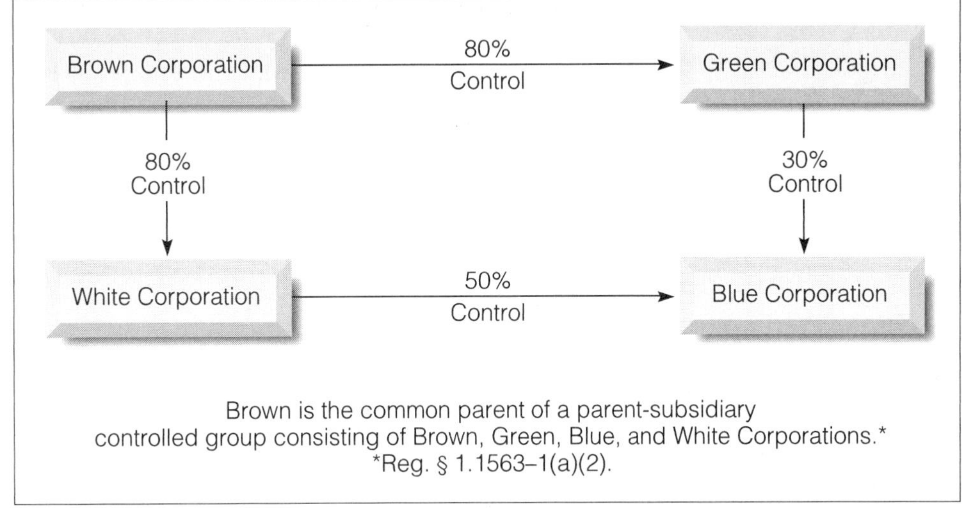

Brown is the common parent of a parent-subsidiary controlled group consisting of Brown, Green, Blue, and White Corporations.*
*Reg. § 1.1563–1(a)(2).

The value test requires ownership of at least 80 percent of the total value of all shares of all classes of stock of each of the corporations, except the parent corporation, by one or more of the other corporations.

Brother-Sister Corporations. A **brother-sister controlled group** *may* exist if two or more corporations are owned by five or fewer *persons* (individuals, estates, or trusts).[26] The ownership test is met if the shareholder group possesses stock representing more than 50 percent of the total combined voting power of all classes of stock entitled to vote, *or* more than 50 percent of the total value of shares of all classes of stock of each corporation.

In applying the more than 50 percent ownership test, the stock held by each person is considered only to the extent that the stock ownership is *identical* for each corporation. That is, if a shareholder owns 30 percent of Silver Corporation and 20 percent of Gold Corporation, that shareholder has identical ownership of 20 percent of each corporation.

EXAMPLE 32

The outstanding stock of Hawk, Eagle, Crane, and Dove Corporations, each of which has only one class of stock outstanding, is owned by the following unrelated individuals:

	Corporations				
Shareholders	**Hawk**	**Eagle**	**Crane**	**Dove**	**Identical Ownership**
Allen	10%	20%	30%	25%	20%
Barton	20%	20%	15%	20%	15%
Carter	10%	15%	10%	10%	10%
Dixon	10%	10%	15%	10%	10%
Total	50%	65%	70%	65%	55%

[26]§ 1563(a)(2). AJCA of 2004 changed the definition of brother-sister controlled groups only with respect to computing the corporate income tax, accumulated earnings credit, and AMT exemption. For other purposes, an 80% total ownership test and the 50% identical ownership test apply.

In determining whether a brother-sister controlled group exists, a corporation is considered only if the shareholder group of five or fewer persons owns more than 50% of the stock of the corporation. Therefore, Hawk Corporation is not considered as a potential member of the brother-sister group because the shareholder group does not own *more than* 50% of that corporation. It is then necessary to apply the identical ownership test to the shareholders' ownership in the remaining corporations. Under the identical ownership test, five or fewer persons (Allen, Barton, Carter, and Dixon) own 55% of all classes of stock in Eagle, Crane, and Dove Corporations. Consequently, Eagle, Crane, and Dove are regarded as members of a brother-sister controlled group. ■

ETHICAL CONSIDERATIONS

A Bookkeeper's Mistake

You recently agreed to prepare a tax return for Fox Corporation. Fox's bookkeeper, who has little tax experience, has filed a tax return for Fox each year during the corporation's existence. In your discussions with Maria Fox, president and majority shareholder of Fox Corporation, you find that she also owns substantial interests in Wolf Corporation and Coyote Corporation. You also find that two other individuals own stock in each of the three corporations, and that, along with Maria, the group owns 100 percent of all three corporations. Both Wolf and Coyote Corporations have always filed separate returns. What are the tax issues, and what action, if any, should you take?

CONSOLIDATED RETURNS

The privilege of filing a consolidated return is based on the concept that an affiliated group of corporations constitutes a single taxable entity despite the existence of technically separate businesses. By filing a consolidated return, the corporation can eliminate intercompany profits and losses on the principle that tax liability should be based on transactions with outsiders rather than on intragroup affairs.

Advantages and Disadvantages of Filing Consolidated Returns. The advantages of a consolidated return are summarized below.

- Losses of one group member can be used to shelter the income of other members. See Example 35 below.
- Taxation of intercompany dividends may be eliminated.
- Recognition of income from certain intercompany transactions can be deferred. See Example 37 below.
- Deductions may be optimized due to percentage limitations being modified as a result of the consolidation process. See Example 35 below.

Consolidation also eliminates any intercompany pricing problems among related corporations that might arise under § 482.[27]

EXAMPLE 33

Rust Corporation leases a building to Crimson Corporation for $6,000 a month. If the IRS determines that the market value is really $9,000 per month, a § 482 allocation would increase Rust Corporation's monthly rent income by $3,000. If, however, Rust and Crimson are members of an affiliated group that files a consolidated return, the § 482 adjustment would not be made. Increasing Rust Corporation's rent income by $3,000 is meaningless as it is offset by a $3,000 increase in Crimson Corporation's deduction for rent expense. ■

[27] § 482 (Allocation of Income and Deductions Among Taxpayers) is further discussed in Chapter 25 in regard to international situations.

The disadvantages of filing a consolidated return are as follows.

- An election is binding on subsequent years and can be avoided only if the makeup of the affiliated group changes or the IRS consents to the revocation of consolidated return status.
- Recognition of losses from certain intercompany transactions is deferred.
- The requirement that all group members use the parent's tax year could create short tax years for the subsidiaries. This could cause a bunching of income and use up a full year for carryover purposes.
- Additional administrative compliance costs may be incurred as the consolidated return tax provisions are extensive and complex.

A further negative consideration is that the tax rules for filing a consolidated return may not mesh with those applicable for financial accounting purposes. For example, foreign corporations cannot be included in the consolidated tax return but should be considered when preparing financial statements. This variance in treatment may require explanatory reconciliation and will further add to the administrative burden.

Eligibility and the Election. The election to file a consolidated return is available only to an **affiliated group.**[28] An affiliated group exists when one corporation owns at least 80 percent of the voting power *and* stock value of another corporation. The stock ownership test must be met on every day of the tax year. Multiple tiers and chains of corporations are allowed as long as the group has an identifiable parent corporation (i.e., at least 80 percent of one corporation must be owned by another).

An affiliated group is similar but not identical to a parent-subsidiary controlled group discussed earlier in this chapter. Two major differences are noted below.

- In meeting the 80 percent stock ownership requirement, the affiliated group must satisfy *both* the voting power test and the stock value test. As to a parent-subsidiary controlled group, the satisfaction of either test suffices.
- In the parent-subsidiary controlled group, the stock ownership test is applied only on the last day of the year—not every day as in the case of an affiliated group.

Members of an affiliated group need not file a consolidated return and, absent an election to consolidate, each corporation files its own Form 1120. If and when an election is made, all of the transactions for the group are combined and reported on one Form 1120. A Form 1122 (Authorization and Consent of Subsidiary Corporation to be Included in a Consolidated Income Tax Return) should be attached to the first consolidated Form 1120 for every subsidiary included in the group. Each subsequent consolidated Form 1120 must include a Form 851 (Affiliation Schedule) that provides pertinent information as to the members of the group.

Computing Consolidated Taxable Income. Several categories of transactions do not enter into the determination of taxable income.

- Some intercompany transactions are forever disregarded. Examples would be dividends paid by one group member to another. See also the factual situation presented in Example 33 above.
- Gains and losses from certain intercompany transactions are deferred until a restoration event occurs (e.g., disposition of the property to an outside party). See Examples 37 and 38 below.

[28]§ 1504(a). Most of the tax rules governing consolidated returns are contained in the Regulations. The delegation of this rule-making authority is contained in § 1502.

In computing the taxable income for any consolidated return year, several items are computed on a group basis. These include net capital (and § 1231) gain or loss, casualty gain or loss, charitable contributions, the dividends received deduction, and net operating loss. The importance of this grouping is illustrated below.

EXAMPLE 34

Maize Corporation owns 100% of the stock of Ecru Corporation, and both use a calendar year for tax purposes. For 2005, they had the following transactions and filed *separate* returns:

	Maize	**Ecru**
Income from operations	$300,000	$170,000
Capital gain	50,000	
Capital loss of $45,000		(–0–)*
Charitable contribution of $40,000	(35,000)**	
Taxable income	$315,000	$170,000

*No deduction is allowed to a corporation for a net capital loss.
**The charitable deduction is limited to 10% of taxable income, as computed prior to the charitable contribution deduction. Thus, 10% × $350,000 ($300,000 + $50,000) = $35,000.

EXAMPLE 35

Assume the same facts as in Example 34 except that a consolidated return is filed for 2005. The results are:

Income from operations ($300,000 + $170,000)		$470,000
Capital transactions—		
Capital gain	$50,000	
Capital loss	(45,000)*	5,000
Charitable contribution		(40,000)**
Taxable income		$435,000

*A capital loss can be used to offset a capital gain.
**The 10% of taxable income limitation now becomes 10% × $475,000 = $47,500. Thus, the full charitable deduction is allowed.

One of the advantages of filing a consolidated return can be seen by comparing the results reached in Examples 34 and 35. Note that in Example 34 the combined taxable income is $485,000 ($315,000 + $170,000), while in Example 35, taxable income is $435,000, or $50,000 less ($485,000 – $435,000).

The consolidated return rules allow the group to make use of the losses of one (or more) of its members. Because this possibility could lead to major tax avoidance (e.g., a profitable corporation acquires a loss corporation to take advantage of its loss carryovers), multiple safeguards have been enacted by Congress to preclude (or curtail) such potential abuse.

One such safeguard protects against the use of losses and deductions that arose in a separate return year.[29]

[29]Aside from the Regulations issued by the Treasury Department, the separate return limitation year (SRLY) safeguards can be invoked pursuant to § 269 (Acquisitions Made to Evade or Avoid Income Tax) and § 482 (Allocation of Income and Deductions Among Taxpayers).

EXAMPLE 36

For calendar year 2005, Kingfisher Corporation and Starling Corporation first elect to file a consolidated return. As of January 1, 2005, Starling owned land (held as an investment) with a basis of $300,000 and a fair market value of $280,000. During 2005, the land is sold for $270,000. On a consolidated return, only $10,000 of the loss can be claimed. The other $20,000 loss comes from a separate return year(s) and relates only to Starling Corporation. It cannot be used by the affiliated group. ■

A further safeguard limits the use of losses and deductions when ownership changes within the affiliated group have taken place.[30]

Deferral and Restoration Events. As noted previously, the deferral of certain intercompany sales can be advantageous (if gains are involved) or disadvantageous (if losses are involved). The realized gain or loss from the intercompany sale is not recognized but is deferred.

EXAMPLE 37

In 2005, Peach Corporation sells land (basis of $100,000) to Beige Corporation for its fair market value of $180,000. Both Peach and Beige are members of the same affiliated group that files a consolidated return for 2005. None of the $80,000 realized gain is recognized on this return. ■

The deferred gain or loss may be recognized in a later year when a restoration event occurs. Usually, the restoration event is the sale of property to outsiders.

EXAMPLE 38

Assume the same facts as in Example 37. In 2007, Beige Corporation sells the land to a Danish real estate developer for $210,000. A consolidated return for 2007 should report a recognized gain of $110,000 ($80,000 of which was previously deferred). ■

LO.6

Describe the reporting process for corporations.

Procedural Matters

FILING REQUIREMENTS FOR CORPORATIONS

A corporation must file a Federal income tax return whether it has taxable income or not.[31] A corporation that was not in existence throughout an entire annual accounting period is required to file a return for the fraction of the year during which it was in existence. In addition, a corporation must file a return even though it has ceased to do business if it has valuable claims for which it will bring suit. A corporation is relieved of filing income tax returns only when it ceases to do business and retains no assets.

The corporate return is filed on Form 1120 unless the corporation is a small corporation entitled to file the shorter Form 1120–A. A corporation may file Form 1120–A if it meets all the following requirements:

[30]The major statutory weapons available to the IRS are § 381 (Carryovers in Certain Corporate Acquisitions) and § 382 (Limitation on Net Operating Loss Carryforwards and Certain Built-in Losses Following Ownership Change).

[31]§ 6012(a)(2).

- Gross receipts or sales are under $500,000.
- Total income (gross profit plus other income including gains on sales of property) is under $500,000.
- Total assets are under $500,000.
- The corporation is not involved in a dissolution or liquidation.
- The corporation is not a member of a controlled group.
- The corporation does not file a consolidated return.
- The corporation does not have ownership in a foreign corporation.
- The corporation does not have foreign shareholders who directly or indirectly own 25 percent or more of its stock.

Corporations electing under Subchapter S (see Chapter 22) file on Form 1120S. Forms 1120, 1120–A, and 1120S are reproduced in Appendix B.

The return must be filed on or before the fifteenth day of the third month following the close of a corporation's tax year. Corporations can receive an automatic extension of six months for filing the corporate return by filing Form 7004 by the due date for the return.[32] However, the IRS may terminate the extension by mailing a 10-day notice to the corporation.

ESTIMATED TAX PAYMENTS

A corporation must make payments of estimated tax unless its tax liability can reasonably be expected to be less than $500. The required annual payment (which includes any estimated AMT liability) is the lesser of (1) 100 percent of the corporation's final tax or (2) 100 percent of the tax for the preceding year (if that was a 12-month tax year and the return filed showed a tax liability).[33] Estimated payments can be made in four installments due on or before the fifteenth day of the fourth month, the sixth month, the ninth month, and the twelfth month of the corporate taxable year. The full amount of the unpaid tax is due on the due date of the return.

Failure to make the required estimated tax prepayments results in a nondeductible penalty being imposed on the corporation. The penalty is avoided, however, if any of various exceptions apply.[34]

RECONCILIATION OF TAXABLE INCOME AND FINANCIAL NET INCOME

Conventional Reconciliations. **Schedule M–1** on the last page of Form 1120 is used to reconcile net income as computed for financial accounting purposes with taxable income reported on the corporation's income tax return. The starting point on Schedule M–1 is net income per books (financial accounting net income). Additions and subtractions are entered for items that affect net income per books and taxable income differently. The following items are entered as additions (see lines 2 through 5 of Schedule M–1):

- Federal income tax expense (deducted in computing net income per books but not deductible in computing taxable income).
- The excess of capital losses over capital gains (deducted for financial accounting purposes but not deductible by corporations for income tax purposes).
- Income that is reported in the current year for tax purposes that is not reported in computing net income per books (e.g., prepaid income).
- Various expenses that are deducted in computing net income per books but are not allowed in computing taxable income (e.g., charitable contributions in excess of the 10 percent ceiling applicable to corporations).

[32] § 6081.

[33] §§ 6655(d) and (e).

[34] See § 6655 for the penalty involved and the various exceptions to it.

The following subtractions are entered on lines 7 and 8 of Schedule M–1:

- Income reported for financial accounting purposes but not included in taxable income (e.g., tax-exempt interest).
- Expenses deducted on the tax return but not deducted in computing net income per books (e.g., a charitable contributions carryover deducted in a prior year for financial accounting purposes but deductible in the current year for tax purposes).

The result is taxable income (before the NOL deduction and the dividends received deduction).

EXAMPLE 39

During the current year, Tern Corporation had the following transactions:

Net income per books (after tax)	$92,400
Taxable income	50,000
Federal income tax expense per books	7,500
Interest income from tax-exempt bonds	5,000
Interest paid on a loan, the proceeds of which were used to purchase the tax-exempt bonds	500
Life insurance proceeds received as a result of the death of a key employee	50,000
Premiums paid on the key employee life insurance policy	2,600
Excess of capital losses over capital gains	2,000

For book and tax purposes, Tern determines depreciation under the straight-line method. Tern's Schedule M–1 for the current year follows.

Schedule M-1 **Reconciliation of Income (Loss) per Books With Income per Return**

1	Net income (loss) per books	92,400	7	Income recorded on books this year not included on this return (itemize): Tax-exempt interest $ 5,000; *Life insurance proceeds on key employee $50,000*	55,000
2	Federal income tax per books	7,500			
3	Excess of capital losses over capital gains	2,000			
4	Income subject to tax not recorded on books this year (itemize):		8	Deductions on this return not charged against book income this year (itemize):	
5	Expenses recorded on books this year not deducted on this return (itemize):			a Depreciation $	
	a Depreciation $			b Charitable contributions $	
	b Charitable contributions $				
	c Travel and entertainment $				
	Prem.–life ins. $2,600; Int.–exempt bonds $500	3,100	9	Add lines 7 and 8	55,000
6	Add lines 1 through 5	105,000	10	Income (page 1, line 28)—line 6 less line 9	50,000

Schedule M–2 reconciles unappropriated retained earnings at the beginning of the year with unappropriated retained earnings at year-end. Beginning balance plus net income per books, as entered on line 1 of Schedule M–1, less dividend distributions during the year equals ending retained earnings. Other sources of increases or decreases in retained earnings are also listed on Schedule M–2.

EXAMPLE 40

Assume the same facts as in Example 39. Tern Corporation's beginning balance in unappropriated retained earnings is $125,000. During the year, Tern distributed a cash dividend of $30,000 to its shareholders. Based on these further assumptions, Tern's Schedule M–2 for the current year is as follows:

Schedule M-2 **Analysis of Unappropriated Retained Earnings per Books (Line 25, Schedule L)**

1	Balance at beginning of year	125,000	5	Distributions: a Cash	30,000
2	Net income (loss) per books	92,400		b Stock	
3	Other increases (itemize):			c Property	
			6	Other decreases (itemize):	
			7	Add lines 5 and 6	30,000
4	Add lines 1, 2, and 3	217,400	8	Balance at end of year (line 4 less line 7)	187,400

Corporations with less than $250,000 of gross receipts and less than $250,000 in assets do not have to complete Schedule L (balance sheet) and Schedules M–1 and M–2 of Form 1120. Similar rules apply to Form 1120–A and 1120S. These rules are intended to ease the compliance burden on small business.

Expanded Reconciliation of Book and Tax Differences—Schedule M–3. Corporate taxpayers with total assets of $10 million or more are now required to report much greater detail relative to differences between income (loss) reported for financial purposes and income (loss) reported for tax purposes. This expanded reconciliation of book and tax income (loss) is reported on new **Schedule M–3,** which must be filed for years ending on or after December 31, 2004. One objective of Schedule M–3 is to create greater transparency between corporate financial statements and tax returns. Another objective is to identify corporations that engage in aggressive tax practices by requiring that transactions that create book/tax differences be disclosed on corporate tax returns. Comparison of Schedule M–3 (available at **http://www.irs.gov**) with Schedule M–1 (demonstrated in Example 39) reveals the significantly greater disclosure requirements that now apply to corporations with total assets of $10 million or more.

LO.7

Evaluate corporations for conducting a business.

Tax Planning Considerations

CORPORATE VERSUS NONCORPORATE FORMS OF BUSINESS ORGANIZATION

The decision to use the corporate form in conducting a trade or business must be weighed carefully. Besides the nontax considerations associated with the corporate form (limited liability, continuity of life, free transferability of interests, centralized management), tax ramifications will play an important role in any such decision. Close attention should be paid to the following:

1. Operating as a regular corporate entity (C corporation) results in the imposition of the corporate income tax. Corporate taxable income will be taxed twice—once as earned by the corporation and again when distributed to the shareholders. Since dividends are not deductible, a closely held corporation may have a strong incentive to structure corporate distributions in a deductible form. Before JGTRRA of 2003 lowered the rate on qualified dividends to 15 percent, shareholders had a tax incentive to bail out profits in the form of salaries, interest, or rent.[35] With the new 15 percent rate on qualified dividends, shareholders may save taxes by having the corporation pay dividends rather than salaries, rent, or interest, which could be taxed at an individual marginal rate as high as 35 percent. The decision should be made only after comparing the tax cost of the two alternatives.
2. The pre-JGTRRA of 2003 tax rates appeared to favor corporations over individuals, since corporations had a maximum tax rate of 35 percent and individuals were subject to a top marginal rate of 38.6 percent. JGTRRA of 2003 lowered the maximum individual rate to 35 percent, the same as the maximum marginal rate applicable to corporations. Even for moderate-income taxpayers, the differences in Federal tax brackets between an individual and a corporation may not be substantial. Furthermore, several state and local governments impose higher taxes on corporations than on individuals. In these jurisdictions, the combined Federal, state, and local tax rates on the two types of taxpayers are practically identical. Consequently, the tax ramifications of incorporating can be determined only on a case-by-case basis. If a corporation's taxable income does not exceed $100,000, a substantial tax savings may be achieved by accumulating income inside the corporation.

[35]Such procedures lead to a multitude of problems, one of which, the reclassification of debt as equity, is discussed in Chapter 18. The problems of unreasonable salaries and rents are covered in Chapter 19 in the discussion of constructive dividends.

3. Corporate-source income loses its identity as it passes through the corporation to the shareholders. Thus, preferential tax treatment of certain items by the corporation (e.g., interest on municipal bonds) does not carry over to the shareholders.
4. As noted in Chapter 19, it may be difficult for shareholders to recover some or all of their investment in the corporation without an ordinary income result. Most corporate distributions are treated as dividends to the extent of the corporation's earnings and profits. However, with the new 15 percent rate on qualified dividends, dividends are taxed at the same rate as net capital gains.
5. Corporate losses cannot be passed through to the shareholders.[36]
6. The liquidation of a corporation will normally generate tax consequences to both the corporation and its shareholders (see Chapter 20).
7. The corporate form provides shareholders with the opportunity to be treated as employees for tax purposes if the shareholders render services to the corporation. Such status makes a number of attractive tax-sheltered fringe benefits available. They include, but are not limited to, group term life insurance and excludible meals and lodging. One of the most attractive benefits of incorporation is the ability of the business to provide accident and health insurance to its employees, including shareholders. Such benefits are not included in the employee's gross income. Similar rules apply to other medical costs paid by the employer. These benefits are not available to partners and sole proprietors.

OPERATING THE CORPORATION

Tax planning to reduce corporate income taxes should occur before the end of the tax year. Effective planning can cause income to be shifted to the next tax year and can produce large deductions by incurring expenses before year-end. Particular attention should be focused on the following.

Charitable Contributions. Recall that accrual basis corporations may claim a deduction for charitable contributions in the year preceding payment. The contribution must be authorized by the board of directors by the end of the tax year and paid on or before the fifteenth day of the third month of the following year. Even though the contribution may not ultimately be made, it might well be authorized. A deduction cannot be thrown back to the previous year (even if paid within the two and a half months) if it has not been authorized.

Timing of Capital Gains and Losses. A corporation should consider offsetting profits on the sale of capital assets by selling some of the depreciated securities in the corporate portfolio. In addition, any already realized capital losses should be carefully monitored. Recall that corporate taxpayers are not permitted to claim any net capital losses as deductions against ordinary income. Capital losses can be used only as an offset against capital gains. Further, net capital losses can only be carried back three years and forward five. Gains from the sales of capital assets should be timed to offset any capital losses. The expiration of the carryover period for any net capital losses should be watched carefully so that sales of appreciated capital assets occur before that date.

Net Operating Losses. In some situations, electing to forgo an NOL carryback and utilizing the carryforward option may generate greater tax savings. When deciding whether to forgo the carryback option, take into account three considerations.

[36]Points 1, 2, and 5 could be resolved by making a Subchapter S election (see Chapter 22), assuming the corporation qualifies for the election. In part, the same can be said for point 3.

First, the time value of the tax refund that is lost by not using the carryback procedure should be calculated. Second, the election to forgo an NOL carryback is irrevocable. Thus, one cannot later choose to change if the predicted high profits do not materialize. Third, consider the future increases (or decreases) in corporate income tax rates that can reasonably be anticipated. This last consideration is the most difficult to work with. Although corporate tax rates have remained relatively stable in recent years, taxpayers have little assurance that future rates will remain constant.

Dividends Received Deduction. The dividends received deduction is normally limited to the lesser of 70 percent of the qualifying dividends or 70 percent of taxable income. The deduction limits are raised to 80 percent for a dividend received from a corporation in which the recipient owns 20 percent or more but less than 80 percent of the stock. An exception is made when the full deduction yields an NOL. In close situations, therefore, the proper timing of income or deductions to generate an NOL may yield a larger dividends received deduction.

Organizational Expenditures. To qualify for the 180-month amortization procedure of § 248, only organizational expenditures incurred in the first tax year of the corporation can be considered. This rule could prove to be an unfortunate trap for corporations formed late in the year.

EXAMPLE 41

Thrush Corporation is formed in December 2005. Qualified organizational expenditures are incurred as follows: $62,000 in December 2005 and $30,000 in January 2006. If Thrush uses the calendar year for tax purposes, only $62,000 of the organizational expenditures can be written off over a period of 180 months. ■

The solution to the problem posed by Example 41 is for Thrush Corporation to adopt a fiscal year that ends at or beyond January 31. All organizational expenditures will then have been incurred before the close of the first tax year.

Shareholder-Employee Payment of Corporate Expenses. In a closely held corporate setting, shareholder-employees often pay corporate expenses (e.g., travel and entertainment) for which they are not reimbursed by the corporation. The IRS often disallows the deduction of these expenses by the shareholder-employee since the payments are voluntary on his or her part. If the deduction is more beneficial at the shareholder-employee level, a corporate policy against reimbursement of such expenses should be established. Proper planning in this regard would be to decide before the beginning of each tax year where the deduction would do the most good. Corporate policy on reimbursement of such expenses could be modified on a year-to-year basis depending upon the circumstances.

In deciding whether corporate expenses should be kept at the corporate level or shifted to the shareholder-employee, the treatment of unreimbursed employee expenses must be considered. First, since employee expenses are itemized deductions, they will be of no benefit to the taxpayer who chooses the standard deduction option. Second, these expenses will be subject to the 2 percent-of-AGI floor. No such limitation will be imposed if the corporation claims the expenses.

RELATED CORPORATIONS

Recall that § 1561 was designed to prevent shareholders from operating a business as multiple corporations to obtain lower tax brackets and multiple AMT exemptions. Corporations in which substantially all the stock is held by five or fewer persons are subject to the provisions of § 1561. Dividing ownership so that control of each corporation does not lie with five or fewer persons having identical control of all corporations avoids the prohibitions of § 1561.

CONCEPT SUMMARY 17–1

Income Taxation of Individuals and Corporations Compared

	Individuals	Corporations
Computation of gross income	§ 61.	§ 61.
Computation of taxable income	§ 62 and §§ 63(b) through (h).	§ 63(a). Concept of AGI has no relevance.
Deductions	Trade or business (§ 162); nonbusiness (§ 212); some personal and employee expenses (generally deductible as itemized deductions).	Trade or business (§ 162).
Charitable contributions	Limited in any tax year to 50% of AGI; 30% for long-term capital gain property unless election is made to reduce fair market value of gift.	Limited in any tax year to 10% of taxable income computed without regard to the charitable contribution deduction, NOL carryback, capital loss carryback, and dividends received deduction.
	Excess charitable contributions carried over for five years.	Same as for individuals.
	Amount of contribution is the fair market value of the property; if lower, ordinary income property is limited to adjusted basis; capital gain property is treated as ordinary income property if certain tangible personalty is donated to a nonuse charity or a private nonoperating foundation is the donee.	Same as for individuals, but exceptions allowed for certain inventory and for scientific property where one-half of the appreciation also is allowed as a deduction.
	Time of deduction is the year in which payment is made.	Time of deduction is the year in which payment is made unless accrual basis taxpayer. Accrual basis corporation can take deduction in year preceding payment if contribution was authorized by board of directors by end of year and contribution is paid by fifteenth day of third month of following year.
Casualty losses	$100 floor on personal casualty and theft losses; personal casualty losses deductible only to extent losses exceed 10% of AGI.	Deductible in full.
Net operating loss	Adjusted for several items, including nonbusiness deductions over nonbusiness income and personal exemptions.	Generally no adjustments.
	Carryback period is 2 years and carryforward period is 20 years.	Same as for individuals.
Dividends received deduction	None.	70%, 80%, or 100% of dividends received depending on percentage of ownership by corporate shareholder.

	Individuals	Corporations
Net capital gains	Taxed in full. Tax rate generally cannot exceed 15% on net long-term capital gains.	Taxed in full.
Capital losses	Only $3,000 of capital loss per year can offset ordinary income; loss is carried forward indefinitely to offset capital gains or ordinary income up to $3,000; short-term and long-term carryovers retain their character.	Can offset only capital gains; carried back three years and forward five; carryovers and carrybacks are short-term losses.
Passive losses	In general, passive activity losses cannot offset either active income or portfolio income.	Passive loss rules apply to closely held C corporations and personal service corporations. For personal service corporations, passive losses cannot offset either active income or portfolio income. For closely held C corporations, passive losses may offset active income but not portfolio income.
Tax rates	Progressive with six rates (10%, 15%, 25%, 28%, 33%, 35%).	Progressive with four rates (15%, 25%, 34%, 35%). Two lowest brackets phased out between $100,000 and $335,000 of taxable income, and additional tax imposed between $15,000,000 and $18,333,333 of taxable income.
Alternative minimum tax	Applied at a graduated rate schedule of 26% and 28%. Exemption allowed depending on filing status (e.g., $58,000 for married filing jointly in 2005); phaseout begins when AMTI reaches a certain amount (e.g., $150,000 for married filing jointly).	Applied at a 20% rate on AMTI less exemption; $40,000 exemption allowed but phaseout begins when AMTI reaches $150,000; adjustments and tax preference items are similar to those applicable to individuals, but also include 75% adjusted current earnings adjustment. Small corporations (gross receipts of $5 million or less) are not subject to AMT.

KEY TERMS

Affiliated group, 17–25

Brother-sister controlled group, 17–23

C corporation, 17–4

Check-the-box Regulations, 17–8

Controlled group, 17–22

Dividends received deduction, 17–17

Limited liability company (LLC), 17–7

Limited partnerships, 17–7

Manufacturers' deduction, 17–15

Organizational expenditures, 17–19

Parent-subsidiary controlled group, 17–22

Passive loss, 17–12

Personal service corporation (PSC), 17–10

Qualified production income, 17–16

Regular corporation, 17–4

Related corporations, 17–21

S corporation, 17–4

Schedule M–1, 17–28

Schedule M–3, 17–30

PROBLEM MATERIALS

Discussion Questions

1. Compare the basic tax and nontax factors of doing business as a partnership, an S corporation, and a C corporation.

2. George owns a sole proprietorship, and Mike is the sole shareholder of a corporation. Both businesses make a profit of $75,000 in 2005. Neither owner withdraws any funds from his business during 2005. How much income must George and Mike report on their individual tax returns for 2005?

Decision Making

3. Art, an executive with Azure Corporation, plans to start a part-time business selling products on the Internet. He will devote about 15 hours each week to running the business. Art's salary from Azure places him in the 35% tax bracket. He projects substantial losses from the new business in each of the first three years and expects sizable profits thereafter. Art plans to leave the profits in the business for several years, sell the business, and retire. Would you advise Art to incorporate the business or operate it as a sole proprietorship?

4. Lucille owns a sole proprietorship, and Mabel is the sole shareholder of a C (regular) corporation. Each business sustained a $20,000 operating loss and a $7,000 capital loss for the year. How will these losses affect the taxable income of the two owners?

5. Harry is the sole shareholder of Purple Corporation, which is an S corporation. Purple earned net operating income of $60,000 during the year and had a long-term capital loss of $8,000. Harry withdrew $30,000 of the profit from the corporation. How much income must Harry report on his individual tax return for 2005?

Issue ID

6. Tanesha is the sole shareholder of Egret Corporation. Egret's sales have doubled in the last four years, and Tanesha has determined that the business needs a new warehouse. Tanesha has asked your advice as to whether she should (1) have the corporation acquire the warehouse or (2) acquire the warehouse herself and rent it to the corporation. What are the relevant tax issues that you will discuss with Tanesha?

7. Jay is a 25% shareholder and the president of JKL, Inc. The board of directors of JKL has decided to pay him an additional $20,000 for the year based on outstanding performance. The directors want to pay the $20,000 as salary, but Jay would prefer to have it paid as a dividend. Discuss.

8. Erica has chosen to operate her new business as an LLC. Discuss the primary tax and nontax advantages of Erica's choice.

9. Rose Corporation sells and installs heating and air conditioning units. Violet Corporation provides repair, inspection, and maintenance services for heating and air conditioning units. Which corporation is more likely to be required to use the accrual basis of accounting? Why?

10. Kathy owns all of the stock in Eagle Corporation. During 2005, Kathy incurs a $25,000 long-term capital loss, and Eagle Corporation also incurs a $25,000 long-term capital loss. Compare the treatment of these transactions on the tax returns of Kathy and Eagle.

11. Judy, a sole proprietor, sold one of her business assets for a $20,000 long-term capital gain. Judy's marginal tax rate is 35%. Link Corporation sold one of its assets for a $20,000 long-term capital gain. Link's marginal tax rate is 35%. What tax rates are applicable to these capital gains?

12. John, a sole proprietor, incurs a $7,000 capital loss from the sale of an asset held by his business. Fox Corporation incurs a $7,000 capital loss on the sale of an asset held by the corporation. How do John and Fox Corporation treat these losses in computing taxable income?

13. Falcon Corporation, a closely held corporation that is a personal service corporation, has $60,000 of active income, $36,000 of portfolio income, and a $90,000 loss from a passive activity. How much of the passive loss can Falcon deduct?

14. On December 30, 2005, Andrea, a sole proprietor, pledged to make a $20,000 charitable contribution on or before January 15, 2006. Aqua Corporation made a similar pledge on the same date, and the contribution was authorized by Aqua's board of directors. When can Andrea and Aqua Corporation, both calendar year taxpayers, deduct these contributions?

15. Discuss the manufacturers' deduction that was enacted in AJCA of 2004, including reasons for the legislation and operational details.

16. Martin Corporation was organized in 2004 and had profits in 2004 and 2005. The corporation had an NOL in 2006. Under what circumstances should the corporation elect to forgo carrying the NOL back to the two prior years?

17. Amber Corporation owns 75% of the stock of Mauve Corporation and has net operating income of $500,000 for the year. Mauve Corporation pays Amber a dividend of $100,000. What amount of dividends received deduction may Amber claim? What amount of dividends received deduction may Amber claim if it acquires an additional 10% of the stock of Mauve Corporation, receives a dividend of $110,000, and files a consolidated return with Mauve?

18. George is the sole shareholder of Palmetto Corporation, which has annual taxable income of approximately $75,000. He decides to form two new corporations and transfer one-third of the Palmetto assets to Poplar Corporation and one-third to Spruce Corporation. This will result in each of the three corporations having approximately $25,000 of taxable income each year. George believes this plan will reduce overall corporate income taxes. Will George's plan work? Discuss.

19. Ted, an individual, owns 80% of all classes of stock of Brown Corporation and Green Corporation. Brown Corporation, in turn, owns all the stock of White Corporation, and Green Corporation owns 80% of the stock of Orange Corporation. Are Brown, Green, Orange, and White Corporations members of a brother-sister controlled group? Explain.

20. Schedule M–1 of Form 1120 is used to reconcile financial net income with taxable income reported on the corporation's income tax return as follows: net income per books + additions – subtractions = taxable income. Classify the following items as additions or subtractions in the Schedule M–1 reconciliation.
    a. Charitable contributions carryover from previous year.
    b. Travel and entertainment expenses in excess of deductible limits.
    c. Book depreciation in excess of allowable tax depreciation.
    d. Federal income tax per books.
    e. Charitable contributions in excess of deductible limits.
    f. Premiums paid on life insurance policy on key employee.
    g. Proceeds of life insurance paid on death of key employee.
    h. Tax-exempt interest.
    i. Interest incurred to carry tax-exempt bonds.

21. For years ending after December 31, 2004, corporate taxpayers with total assets of $10 million or more are required to report much greater detail relative to differences between book and tax income (loss). What were the government's objectives in creating this new reporting requirement?

Problems

22. Emu Company, which was formed in 2005, had operating income of $100,000 and operating expenses of $80,000 in 2005. In addition, Emu had a long-term capital loss of $5,000. How does Andrew, the owner of Emu Company, report this information on his individual tax return under the following assumptions?
    a. Emu Company is a proprietorship, and Andrew does not withdraw any funds from Emu during the year.
    b. Emu Company is a corporation and pays no dividends during the year.

23. Lewis and Burton are equal partners in Wolverine Enterprises, a calendar year partnership. During the year, Wolverine Enterprises had $500,000 of gross income and $350,000 of operating expenses. In addition, the partnership sold land that had been held for investment purposes for a long-term capital gain of $60,000. During the year, Lewis withdrew $40,000 from the partnership, and Burton withdrew $45,000. Discuss the impact of this information on the taxable income of Wolverine, Lewis, and Burton.

24. Pink Company had $100,000 of net profit from operations in 2005 and paid Sandra Pink, its sole shareholder, a dividend of $77,750 ($100,000 net profit – $22,250 corporate tax). Sandra has a large amount of income from other sources and is in the 35% marginal tax bracket. Would Sandra's tax situation be better or worse if Pink Company were a proprietorship and Sandra withdrew $77,750 from the business during the year?

25. Dakota Enterprises, a calendar year taxpayer, suffers a casualty loss of $75,000. How much of the casualty loss will be a tax deduction to Dakota under the following circumstances?
    a. Dakota is an individual and has AGI of $110,000. The casualty loss was a personal loss, and the insurance recovered is $30,000.
    b. Dakota is a corporation, and the insurance recovered is $30,000.

Decision Making

Communications

26. Benton Company has one owner, who is in the 35% Federal income tax bracket. Benton's gross income is $200,000, and its ordinary trade or business deductions are $97,000. Compute the tax liability on Benton's income for 2005 under the following assumptions:
    a. Benton Company is operated as a proprietorship, and the owner withdraws $70,000 for personal use.
    b. Benton is operated as a corporation, pays out $70,000 as salary, and pays no dividends to its shareholder.
    c. Benton is operated as a corporation and pays out no salary or dividends to its shareholder.
    d. Benton is operated as a corporation, pays out $70,000 as salary to its shareholder, and pays out the remainder of its earnings as dividends.
    e. Assume Robert Benton of 1121 Monroe Street, Ironton, OH 45638 is the owner of Benton Company, which was operated as a proprietorship in 2005. Robert is thinking about incorporating the business in 2006 and asks your advice. He expects about the same amounts of income and expenses in 2006 and plans to take $70,000 per year out of the company whether he incorporates or not. Write a letter to Robert [based on your analysis in (a) and (b) above] containing your recommendations.

27. Mallard Corporation had $400,000 of operating income and $350,000 of operating expenses during the year. In addition, Mallard had a $30,000 long-term capital gain and a $52,000 short-term capital loss.
    a. Compute Mallard's taxable income for the year.
    b. Assume the same facts as above except that Mallard's long-term capital gain was $64,000. Compute Mallard's taxable income for the year.

28. In 2005, a business sells a capital asset, which it had held for two years, at a loss of $15,000. How much of the capital loss may be deducted in 2005, and how much is carried back or forward under the following circumstances?
    a. The business was a sole proprietorship owned by Joe. Joe had a short-term capital gain of $3,000 and a long-term capital gain of $2,000 in 2005. Joe had ordinary net income from the proprietorship of $60,000.
    b. The business is incorporated. The corporation had a short-term capital gain of $3,000 and a long-term capital gain of $2,000. Its ordinary net income from the business was $60,000.

29. Pelican Corporation has net short-term capital gains of $30,000 and net long-term capital losses of $190,000 during 2005. Pelican Corporation had taxable income from other sources of $500,000.

Prior years' transactions included the following:

2001	Net short-term capital gains	$100,000
2002	Net long-term capital gains	40,000
2003	Net short-term capital gains	30,000
2004	Net long-term capital gains	70,000

a. How are the capital gains and losses treated on Pelican's 2005 tax return?
b. Determine the amount of the 2005 capital loss that is carried back to each of the previous years.
c. Compute the amount of capital loss carryover, if any, and indicate the years to which the loss may be carried.
d. If Pelican were a proprietorship, how would Sylvia, the owner, report these transactions on her 2005 tax return?

30. Condor Corporation, a closely held corporation, has $45,000 of active business income, $35,000 of portfolio income, and an $80,000 passive loss from a rental activity. Can Condor deduct the passive loss? Would your answer differ if Condor were a PSC?

Decision Making
Communications

31. Joseph Thompson is president and sole shareholder of Jay Corporation. In December 2005, Joe asks your advice regarding a charitable contribution he plans to have the corporation make to the University of Maine, a qualified public charity. Joe is considering the following alternatives as charitable contributions in December 2005:

	Fair Market Value
(1) Cash donation	$120,000
(2) Unimproved land held for six years ($20,000 basis)	120,000
(3) Maize Corporation stock held for eight months ($20,000 basis)	120,000
(4) Brown Corporation stock held for two years ($170,000 basis)	120,000

Joe has asked you to help him decide which of these potential contributions will be most advantageous taxwise. Jay's taxable income is $3.5 million before considering the contribution. Rank the four alternatives and write a letter to Joe communicating your advice. The corporation's address is 1442 Main Street, Freeport, ME 04032.

32. Coyote, Inc. (a calendar year C corporation) had the following income and expenses in 2006:

Income from operations	$200,000
Expenses from operations	80,000
Dividends received (less than 20% ownership)	16,000
Charitable contribution	16,000

a. How much is Coyote, Inc.'s charitable contribution deduction for 2006?
b. What happens to the portion of the contribution not deductible in 2006?

Decision Making
Communications

33. Dan Simms is the president and sole shareholder of Simms Corporation, 1121 Madison Street, Seattle, WA 98121. Dan plans for the corporation to make a charitable contribution to the University of Washington, a qualified public charity. He will have the corporation donate Jaybird Corporation stock, held for five years, with a basis of $8,000 and a fair market value of $20,000. Dan projects a $200,000 net profit for Simms Corporation in 2005 and a $100,000 net profit in 2006. Dan calls you on December 3, 2005, and asks whether he should make the contribution in 2005 or 2006. Write a letter advising Dan about the timing of the contribution.

34. Zebra, Inc., a calendar year C corporation, manufactures board games. For 2005, Zebra had taxable income of $400,000, qualified production income of $500,000, and W–2 wages of $70,000. How much is Zebra's manufacturers' deduction for 2005?

35. Swallow, Inc., a calendar year C corporation, manufactures plumbing fixtures. For 2005, Swallow had taxable income of $1.2 million, qualified production income of $900,000, and W–2 wages of $25,000.
    a. How much is Swallow's manufacturers' deduction for 2005?
    b. Assume Swallow's W–2 wages were $50,000. How much is Swallow's manufacturers' deduction for 2005?

36. During the year, Crimson Corporation (a calendar year taxpayer) has the following transactions:

Income from operations	$220,000
Expenses from operations	240,000
Dividends received from Scarlet Corporation	80,000

    a. Crimson owns 15% of Scarlet Corporation's stock. How much is Crimson Corporation's taxable income or NOL for the year?
    b. Would your answer change if Crimson owned 60% of Scarlet Corporation's stock?

37. In each of the following independent situations, determine the dividends received deduction. Assume that none of the corporate shareholders owns 20% or more of the stock in the corporations paying the dividends.

	Red Corporation	**White Corporation**	**Blue Corporation**
Income from operations	$ 700,000	$ 800,000	$ 700,000
Expenses from operations	(600,000)	(900,000)	(740,000)
Qualifying dividends	100,000	200,000	200,000

38. Owl Corporation was formed on December 1, 2005. Qualifying organizational expenses were incurred and paid as follows:

Incurred and paid in December 2005	$12,000
Incurred in December 2005 but paid in January 2006	6,000
Incurred and paid in February 2006	3,600

Assuming that Owl Corporation makes a timely election under § 248 to expense and amortize organizational expenditures, what amount may be deducted in the corporation's first tax year under each of the following assumptions?
    a. Owl Corporation adopts a calendar year and the cash basis of accounting for tax purposes.
    b. Same as (a), except that Owl Corporation chooses a fiscal year of December 1 through November 30.
    c. Owl Corporation adopts a calendar year and the accrual basis of accounting for tax purposes.
    d. Same as (c), except that Owl Corporation chooses a fiscal year of December 1 through November 30.

39. Hummingbird Corporation, an accrual basis taxpayer, was formed and began operations on July 1, 2005. The following expenses were incurred during the first tax year (July 1 to December 31, 2005) of operations:

Expenses of temporary directors and of organizational meetings	$12,000
Fee paid to the state of incorporation	3,000
Accounting services incident to organization	15,000
Legal services for drafting the corporate charter and bylaws	21,000
Expenses incident to the printing and sale of stock certificates	18,000
	$69,000

Assume Hummingbird Corporation makes an appropriate and timely election under § 248 and the related Regulations. What is the maximum organizational expense Hummingbird may write off for tax year 2005?

40. In each of the following *independent* situations, determine the corporation's income tax liability. Assume that all corporations use a calendar year for tax purposes and that the tax year involved is 2005.

	Taxable Income
Violet Corporation	$ 38,000
Indigo Corporation	180,000
Orange Corporation	335,000
Blue Corporation	4,620,000
Green Corporation	18,500,000

41. The outstanding stock in Red, Blue, and Green Corporations, each of which has only one class of stock, is owned by the following unrelated individuals:

	Corporations		
Shareholders	**Red**	**Blue**	**Green**
Marrin	20%	10%	30%
Murray	10%	50%	20%
Moses	50%	30%	35%

a. Determine whether Red, Blue, and Green Corporations constitute a brother-sister controlled group.
b. Assume that Murray does not own stock in any of the corporations. Would a brother-sister controlled group exist?

42. Adams, Burke, and Chan, who are unrelated individuals, have voting stock in Pink, Purple, and Red Corporations as follows:

	Corporations		
Shareholders	**Pink**	**Purple**	**Red**
Adams	20%	20%	10%
Burke	15%	25%	35%
Chan	30%	25%	20%

Are Pink, Purple, and Red Corporations treated as a brother-sister controlled group?

43. For 2006, Cedar Corporation, an accrual basis, calendar year taxpayer, had net income per books of $172,750 and the following special transactions:

Life insurance proceeds received as a result of the death of the corporation's president	$100,000
Premiums paid on the life insurance policy on the president	10,000
Prepaid rent received and properly taxed in 2005 but credited as rent income in 2006	15,000
Rent income received in 2006 ($10,000 is prepaid and relates to 2007)	25,000
Interest income on tax-exempt bonds	5,000
Interest on loan to carry tax-exempt bonds	3,000
MACRS depreciation in excess of straight-line (straight-line was used for book purposes)	4,000
Capital loss in excess of capital gains	6,000
Federal income tax liability and accrued tax provision for 2006	22,250

Using Schedule M–1 of Form 1120 (the most recent version available), determine Cedar Corporation's taxable income for 2006.

Issue ID

44. In January, Don and Steve each invested $100,000 of cash to form a corporation to conduct business as a retail golf equipment store. On January 5, they paid Bill, an attorney, to draft the corporate charter, file the necessary forms with the state, and write the bylaws. They leased a building and began to acquire inventory, furniture, display equipment, and office equipment in February. They hired a sales staff and clerical personnel in March and conducted training sessions during the month. They had a successful opening on April 1, and sales increased steadily throughout the summer. The weather turned cold in October, and all local golf courses closed by October 15, which resulted in a drastic decline in sales. Don and Steve expect business to be very good during the Christmas season and then to taper off significantly from January 1 through February 28. The corporation accrued bonuses to Don and Steve on December 31, payable on April 15 of the following year. The corporation made timely estimated tax payments throughout the year. The corporation hired a bookkeeper in February, but he does not know much about taxation. Don and Steve have hired you as a tax consultant and have asked you to identify the tax issues that they should consider.

Research Problems

*Note: Solutions to Research Problems can be prepared by using the **RIA Checkpoint® Student Edition** online research product, which is available to accompany this text. It is also possible to prepare solutions to the Research Problems by using tax research materials found in a standard tax library.*

Communications

Research Problem 1. On August 15, Juniper Corporation declared a dividend payable on August 29 to shareholders of record on August 22. On August 20, Aspen Corporation acquired 15% of the outstanding shares of Juniper Corporation, and on August 26, it acquired another 10% of Juniper's outstanding shares. Juniper paid Aspen a dividend of $400,000 on August 29. How much is Aspen's dividends received deduction? Write a letter containing your answer to Frank Hopkins, Chief Financial Officer, Aspen Corporation, 3440 Perry Avenue, Larkspur, CO 80118.

Communications

Research Problem 2. Joe and Tom Moore are brothers and equal shareholders in Black Corporation, a calendar year taxpayer. In 2002, they incurred certain travel and entertainment expenditures, as employees, on behalf of Black Corporation. Because Black was in a precarious financial condition, Joe and Tom decided not to seek reimbursement for these expenditures. Instead, each brother deducted what he spent on his own individual return (Form 1040). Upon audit of the returns filed by Joe and Tom for 2002, the IRS disallowed these expenditures. Write a letter to Joe at 568 Inwood Avenue, Waynesburg, PA 15370, and indicate whether he should challenge the IRS action. Explain your conclusion using nontechnical language.

Internet Activity

Use the tax resources of the Internet to address the following question. Do not restrict your search to the World Wide Web, but include a review of newsgroups and general reference materials, practitioner sites and resources, primary sources of the tax law, chat rooms and discussion groups, and other opportunities.

Research Problem 3. Find the IRS Web site and print a copy of Schedule M–3. Compare it with the Schedule M–1 used in Example 39 and discuss the differences.

Corporations: Organization and Capital Structure

LEARNING OBJECTIVES

After completing Chapter 18, you should be able to:

LO.1
Identify the tax consequences of incorporating a business.

LO.2
Understand the special rules that apply when liabilities are assumed by a corporation.

LO.3
Recognize the basis issues relevant to the shareholder and the corporation.

LO.4
Appreciate the tax aspects of the capital structure of a corporation.

LO.5
Recognize the tax differences between debt and equity investments.

LO.6
Handle the tax treatment of shareholder debt and stock losses.

LO.7
Identify tax planning opportunities associated with organizing and financing a corporation.

http://wft.swlearning.com

OUTLINE

Chapter 17 dealt with three principal areas fundamental to working with corporations: (1) determination of whether an entity is a corporation for Federal income tax purposes, (2) tax rules applicable to the day-to-day operation of a corporation, and (3) filing and reporting procedures governing corporations.

Chapter 18 addresses more sophisticated issues involving corporations:

- The tax consequences to the shareholders and the corporation upon the organization of and original transfer of property to the corporation.
- The tax result that ensues when shareholders make transfers of property to a corporation after organization.
- The capital structure of a corporation, including equity and debt financing.
- The tax treatment of investor losses.

LO.1

Identify the tax consequences of incorporating a business.

Organization of and Transfers to Controlled Corporations

IN GENERAL

Property transactions normally produce tax consequences if a gain or loss is realized. As a result, unless an exception in the Code applies, a transfer of property to a corporation in exchange for stock constitutes a taxable sale or exchange of property. The amount of gain or loss is measured by the difference between the value of the stock received and the tax basis of the property transferred.

When a taxpayer's economic status has not changed and the wherewithal to pay is lacking, however, the Code does provide special exceptions to the requirement that gain or loss be recognized. One such exception is a like-kind exchange. When a taxpayer exchanges property for other property of a like kind, § 1031 provides that gain (or loss) on the exchange is postponed because there has not been a substantive change in the taxpayer's investment. Section 1031 is merely a deferral mechanism and does not authorize the permanent nonrecognition of gain or loss. The deferral mechanism is accomplished by calculating a substituted basis

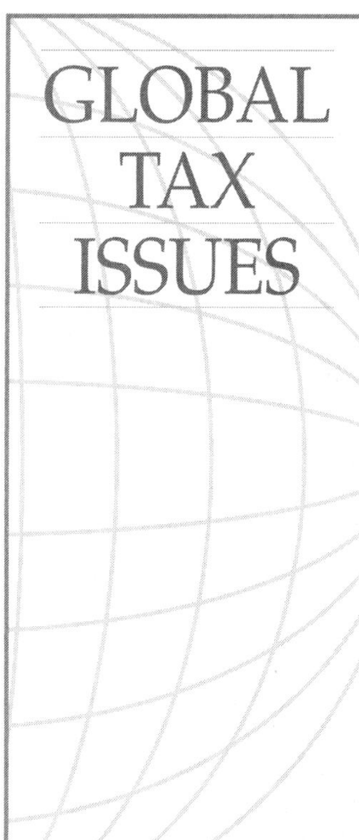

Choice of Organizational Form When Operating Overseas

When the management of a corporation decides to expand its business by establishing a presence in a foreign market, the new business venture may take one of several organizational forms. As each form comes with its respective advantages and disadvantages, making the best choice can be difficult.

One common approach is to conduct the foreign activity as a *branch* operation of the U.S. corporation. The foreign branch is not a separate legal entity, but a division of the U.S. corporation established overseas. As a result, any gains and losses produced by the foreign unit are included in the corporation's overall financial results.

Another possibility is to organize the foreign operations as a *subsidiary* of the U.S. parent corporation. If this route is chosen, the subsidiary may be either a *domestic* subsidiary (i.e., organized in the United States) or a *foreign* subsidiary (organized under the laws of a foreign country).

One fundamental tax difference between these two approaches is that the gains and losses of a *domestic* subsidiary may be consolidated with the operations of the U.S. parent, while the operations of a *foreign* subsidiary may not. Thus, the use of a domestic subsidiary to conduct foreign operations will generally yield the same final result as the use of a branch. With both approaches, the financial statements of the U.S. parent reflect the results of its worldwide operations.

for the like-kind property received. With this substituted basis, the potential gain or loss on the property given up is recognized when the property received in the exchange is sold.

Another exception to the general rule deals with transfers to controlled corporations. Section 351 provides for the nonrecognition of gain or loss upon the transfer of property to a corporation when certain conditions are met. This provision also reflects the principle that gain should not be recognized when a taxpayer's investment has not substantively changed. When a business is incorporated, the owner's economic status remains the same; only the *form* of the investment has changed. The investment in the business assets carries over to the investment in corporate stock. Further, if only stock in the corporation is received, the taxpayer is hardly in a position to pay a tax on any realized gain. Thus, this approach also is justified under the wherewithal to pay concept discussed in Chapter 1. As noted later, however, if the taxpayer receives property other than stock (i.e., boot) from the corporation, realized gain may be recognized.

Finally, § 351 exists because Congress believes that tax rules should not impede the exercise of sound business judgment (e.g., choice of corporate form of doing business). For example, a taxpayer would think twice about forming a corporation if gain recognition (and the payment of a tax) would always be a consequence.

Therefore, the same principles govern the nonrecognition of gain or loss under § 1031 and § 351. With both provisions, gain or loss is postponed until a substantive change in the taxpayer's investment occurs (e.g., a sale to outsiders).

EXAMPLE 1

Ron is considering incorporating his donut shop in order to obtain the limited liability of the corporate form. Ron realizes that if he incorporates the shop, he will be personally liable only for the debts of the business that he has guaranteed. If Ron incorporates, the following assets will be transferred to the corporation:

	Tax Basis	Fair Market Value
Cash	$10,000	$ 10,000
Furniture and fixtures	20,000	60,000
Land and building	40,000	100,000
	$70,000	$170,000

In this change of business form, Ron will receive the corporation's stock worth $170,000 in exchange for the assets he transfers. Without the nonrecognition provisions of § 351, Ron would recognize a taxable gain of $100,000 on the transfer ($170,000 value of the stock received – $70,000 basis of the assets transferred). Under § 351, however, Ron does not recognize any gain because his economic status has not really changed. Ron's investment in the assets of his unincorporated donut shop is now represented by his ownership of stock in the incorporated donut shop. Thus, § 351 provides for tax neutrality on the incorporation decision. ■

In a like-kind exchange, the recognition of gain is avoided only to the extent that the taxpayer receives like-kind property. However, the taxpayer must recognize any realized gain when receiving "boot" (i.e., property of an unlike kind, such as cash). For example, if a taxpayer exchanges a truck used in a business for another truck to be used in the business and also receives cash, the taxpayer has the wherewithal to pay an income tax on the cash involved. Further, the taxpayer's economic status has changed to the extent that cash is received. Thus, any realized gain on the exchange is recognized to the extent of the cash received. In like manner, if a taxpayer transfers property to a corporation and receives cash or property other than stock, gain (but not loss) is recognized to the extent of the lesser of the gain realized or the boot received (i.e., the amount of cash and the fair market value of other property received). Any gain recognized is classified (e.g., ordinary, capital) according to the type of assets transferred.[1] As discussed later, the nonrecognition of gain or loss is accompanied by a substituted basis in the shareholder's stock.[2]

EXAMPLE 2

Amanda and Calvin form Quail Corporation. Amanda transfers property with an adjusted basis of $30,000, fair market value of $60,000, for 50% of the stock, worth $60,000. Calvin transfers property with an adjusted basis of $70,000, fair market value of $60,000, for the remaining 50% of the stock. The transfer qualifies under § 351. Amanda has an unrecognized gain of $30,000, and Calvin has an unrecognized loss of $10,000. Both have a substituted basis in the stock in Quail Corporation. Amanda has a basis of $30,000 in her stock, and Calvin has a basis of $70,000 in his stock. Therefore, if either Amanda or Calvin later disposes of the Quail stock in a taxable transaction (e.g., a sale), this deferred gain/loss will then be fully recognized—a $30,000 gain to Amanda and a $10,000 loss to Calvin. ■

Section 351 is mandatory if a transaction satisfies the provision's requirements. The three requirements for nonrecognition of gain or loss under § 351 are that (1) *property* is transferred (2) in exchange for *stock* and (3) the property transferors are in *control* of the corporation after the exchange. Therefore, if recognition of gain or loss is *desired*, the taxpayer must plan to fail to meet at least one of these requirements.

PROPERTY DEFINED

Questions have arisen concerning what constitutes **property** for purposes of § 351. In general, the definition of property is comprehensive. For example, along with

[1] § 351(b) and Rev.Rul. 68–55, 1968–1 C.B. 140.

[2] § 358(a). See the discussion preceding Example 19.

plant and equipment, unrealized receivables of a cash basis taxpayer and installment obligations are considered property.[3] Although the disposition of an installment note receivable normally triggers deferred gain, its transfer under § 351 is not treated as a disposition. Thus, gain is not recognized to the transferor. Secret processes and formulas, as well as secret information in the general nature of a patentable invention, also qualify as property under § 351.[4]

However, the Code specifically excludes services rendered from the definition of property. Services are not considered to be property under § 351 for a critical reason. A taxpayer must report as income the fair market value of any consideration received as compensation for services rendered.[5] Consequently, when a taxpayer receives stock in a corporation as consideration for rendering services to the corporation, taxable income results. In this case, the amount of income recognized by the taxpayer is equal to the fair market value of the stock received. The taxpayer's basis in the stock received is its fair market value.

EXAMPLE 3

Ann and Bob form Olive Corporation with the transfer of the following consideration:

	Consideration Transferred		
	Basis to Transferor	**Fair Market Value**	**Number of Shares Issued**
From Ann:			
Personal services rendered to Olive Corporation	$ –0–	$20,000	200
From Bob:			
Installment obligation	5,000	40,000	
Inventory	10,000	30,000	800
Secret process	–0–	10,000	

The value of each share in Olive Corporation is $100.[6] Ann has income of $20,000 on the transfer because services do not qualify as "property." She has a basis of $20,000 in her 200 shares of Olive. Bob has no recognized gain on the receipt of stock because all of the consideration he transfers to Olive qualifies as "property" and he has "control" of Olive after the transfer; see the discussion concerning control that follows. Bob has a substituted basis of $15,000 in the Olive stock. ■

STOCK TRANSFERRED

Nonrecognition of gain occurs only when the shareholder receives stock. Stock for this purpose includes both common and preferred. However, it does not include "nonqualified preferred stock," which possesses many of the attributes of debt. In addition, the Regulations state that the term "stock" does not include stock rights and stock warrants. Otherwise, the term "stock" generally needs no clarification.[7]

Thus, any corporate debt or **securities** (e.g., long-term debt such as bonds) received are treated as boot because they are not an equity interest or stock.

[3] *Hempt Brothers, Inc. v. U.S.*, 74–1 USTC ¶9188, 33 AFTR2d 74–570, 490 F.2d 1172 (CA–3, 1974), and Reg. § 1.453–9(c)(2).

[4] Rev.Rul. 64–56, 1964–1 C.B. 133; Rev.Rul. 71–564, 1971–2 C.B. 179.

[5] §§ 61 and 83.

[6] The value of closely held stock normally is presumed to be equal to the value of the property transferred.

[7] § 351(g). Examples of nonqualified preferred stock include preferred stock that is redeemable within 20 years of issuance and whose dividend rate is based on factors other than corporate performance. Therefore, gain is recognized up to the fair market value of the nonqualified preferred stock received. Loss may be recognized when the transferor receives *only* nonqualified preferred stock (or nonqualified preferred stock and other boot) in exchange for property. See also Reg. § 1.351–1(a)(1)(ii).

Therefore, the receipt of debt in exchange for the transfer of appreciated property to a controlled corporation causes recognition of gain.

CONTROL OF THE CORPORATION

For the transaction to qualify as nontaxable under § 351, the property transferors must be in **control** of the corporation immediately after the exchange. Control means that the person or persons transferring the property must have at least an 80 percent stock ownership in the transferee corporation. More specifically, the transferor-shareholders must own stock possessing at least 80 percent of the total combined *voting power* of all classes of stock entitled to vote *and* at least 80 percent of the total *number of shares* of all other classes of stock.[8]

Control Immediately after the Transfer. Immediately after the exchange, the property transferors must control the corporation. Control can apply to a single person or to several taxpayers if they are all parties to an integrated transaction. When more than one person is involved, the exchange does not necessarily require simultaneous exchanges by those persons. However, the rights of those transferring property to the corporation must be previously set out and determined. Also, the agreement to transfer property should be executed "with an expedition consistent with orderly procedure."[9] Therefore, if two or more persons transfer property to a corporation for stock and want to defer gain, it is helpful if the transfers occur close together in time and are made in accordance with an agreement among the parties.

EXAMPLE 4

Jack exchanges property, basis of $60,000 and fair market value of $100,000, for 70% of the stock of Gray Corporation. The other 30% of the stock is owned by Jane, who acquired it several years ago. The fair market value of Jack's stock is $100,000. Jack recognizes a taxable gain of $40,000 on the transfer because he does not have control of the corporation after his transfer and his transaction cannot be integrated with Jane's for purposes of the control requirement. ■

EXAMPLE 5

Rebecca, Daryl, and Paige incorporate their businesses by forming Green Corporation. Rebecca exchanges her property for 300 shares in Green on January 6, 2005. Daryl exchanges his property for 400 shares of Green Corporation stock on January 12, 2005, and Paige exchanges her property for 300 shares in Green on March 5, 2005. Because the three exchanges are part of a prearranged plan and the control test is met, the nonrecognition provisions of § 351 apply to all of the exchanges. ■

Stock need not be issued to the property transferors in the same proportion as the relative value of the property transferred by each. However, when stock received is not proportionate to the value of the property transferred, the actual effect of the transactions must be properly characterized. For example, in such situations one transferor may actually be making a gift of valuable consideration to another transferor.

EXAMPLE 6

Ron and Shelia, father and daughter, form Oak Corporation. Ron transfers property worth $50,000 in exchange for 100 shares of stock, while Shelia transfers property worth $50,000 for 400 shares of stock. The transfers qualify under § 351 because Ron and Shelia have control of the Oak stock immediately after the transfers of property. However, the implicit

[8]§ 368(c). Nonqualified preferred stock is treated as stock, and not boot, for purposes of this control test.

[9]Reg. § 1.351–1(a)(1).

gift by Ron to Shelia must be recognized and appropriately characterized. As such, the value of the gift might be subject to the gift tax (see Chapter 27). ■

Once control has been achieved, it is not necessarily lost if stock received by shareholders is sold or given to persons who are not parties to the exchange shortly after the transaction. However, a different result might materialize if a *plan* for the ultimate disposition of the stock existed *before* the exchange.[10]

EXAMPLE 7

Naomi and Eric form Eagle Corporation. They transfer appreciated property to the corporation with each receiving 50 shares of the stock. Shortly after the formation, Naomi gives 25 shares to her son. Because Naomi was not committed to make the gift, she is considered to own her original shares of Eagle Corporation stock and, along with Eric, to control Eagle "immediately after the exchange." Therefore, the requirements of § 351 are met, and neither Naomi nor Eric is taxed on the exchange. Alternatively, had Naomi immediately given 25 shares to a business associate pursuant to a plan to satisfy an outstanding obligation, the formation of Eagle would be taxable to Naomi and Eric because of their lack of control. ■

ETHICAL CONSIDERATIONS

Proper Timing of a Gift of Shares

Naomi, in Example 7, intends to give half of her shares to her son when she incorporates. Her attorney, who is not well versed in tax law, initially prepares stock certificates evidencing 50 shares to Eric, 25 shares to Naomi, and 25 shares to Naomi's son. Prior to the transfer of property in exchange for the stock certificates, the attorney realizes that the transfer of appreciated property to the corporation might produce recognized gain to Eric and Naomi, because they would not have 80 percent control. Accordingly, the attorney shreds the original certificates and prepares new ones. Fifty of the shares are then issued to Eric and 50 to Naomi. Six months later, Naomi gives 25 shares to her son. Have the parties acted correctly?

Transfers for Property and Services. Nonrecognition treatment for the property transferors may be lost if "too much" stock is transferred to persons who did not contribute property.

EXAMPLE 8

Kate transfers property with a value of $60,000 and a basis of $5,000 for 60% of the stock in newly formed Wren Corporation. Rodney receives 40% of the stock in Wren for services worth $40,000 rendered to the corporation. Both Kate and Rodney have taxable gain on the transaction. Rodney has taxable income of $40,000 because he does not transfer property in exchange for stock. Kate has a taxable gain of $55,000 [$60,000 (fair market value of the stock in Wren Corporation) – $5,000 (basis in the transferred property)] because she, as the sole property transferor, receives only 60% of the stock in Wren Corporation. ■

A person who receives stock both in exchange for services and for property transferred may be treated as a member of the transferring group for purposes of the control test. When this is the case, the person is taxed on the value of the stock issued for services but not on the stock issued for property, assuming the property transferors control the corporation. In this case, all the stock received by the person transferring both property and services is counted in determining whether the transferors acquired control of the corporation.[11]

[10] *Wilgard Realty Co. v. Comm.*, 42–1 USTC ¶9452, 29 AFTR 325, 127 F.2d 514 (CA–2, 1942).

[11] Reg. § 1.351–1(a)(2), Ex. 3.

EXAMPLE 9

Assume the same facts as in Example 8 except that Rodney transfers property worth $30,000 (basis of $3,000) in addition to services rendered to the corporation (valued at $10,000). Now Rodney becomes a part of the control group. Kate and Rodney, as property transferors, together receive 100% of the stock in Wren Corporation. Consequently, § 351 is applicable to the exchanges. As a result, Kate has no recognized gain. Rodney does not recognize gain on the transfer of the property, but he has taxable income to the extent of the value of the shares issued for services rendered. Therefore, Rodney has current taxable income of $10,000. ■

Transfers for Services and Nominal Property. To be a member of the group and aid in qualifying all transferors under the 80 percent control test, the person contributing services must transfer property having more than a "relatively small value" compared to the services performed. The Regulations provide that stock issued for property whose value is relatively small compared to the value of the stock already owned (or to be received for services rendered) will not be treated as issued in return for property. This will be the result when the primary purpose of the transfer is to qualify the transaction under § 351 for concurrent transferors.[12]

EXAMPLE 10

Rosalyn and Mark transfer property to Redbird Corporation, each in exchange for one-third of the stock. Reed receives the other one-third of the stock for services rendered. The transaction does not qualify under § 351 because Reed is not a member of the group transferring property and Rosalyn and Mark, as the sole property transferors, together receive only 66⅔% of the stock. As a result, the post-transfer control requirement is not met.

Assume instead that Reed also transfers a substantial amount of property. Then he is a member of the group, and the transaction qualifies under § 351. Reed is taxed on the value of the stock issued for services, but the remainder of the transaction does not trigger gain or loss recognition. However, if the property transferred by Reed is of a relatively small value in comparison to the stock he receives for his services, and the primary purpose for transferring the property is to cause the transaction to be tax-free for Rosalyn and Mark, the exchange does not qualify under § 351 for any of the taxpayers. ■

Exactly when a taxpayer who renders services and transfers property is included in the control group is often subject to question. However, the IRS has stated that such a transferor can be included in the control group if the value of the property transferred is at least 10 percent of the value of the services provided.[13] If the value of the property transferred is less than this amount, the IRS will not issue an advance ruling that the exchange meets the requirements of § 351.

EXAMPLE 11

Sara and Rick form Grouse Corporation. Sara transfers land (worth $100,000, basis of $20,000) for 50% of the stock in Grouse. Rick transfers equipment (worth $50,000, adjusted basis of $10,000) and provides services worth $50,000 for 50% of the stock. Because the relative amount of property Rick transfers is not small compared to the value of the services he renders, his stock in Grouse Corporation is counted in determining control for purposes of § 351; thus, the transferors own 100% of the stock in Grouse. In addition, all of Rick's stock, not just the shares received for the equipment, is counted in determining control. As a result, Sara does not recognize gain on the transfer of the land. Rick, however, must recognize income of $50,000 on the transfer of services. Even though the transfer of the equipment qualifies under § 351, his transfer of services for stock does not.

Alternatively, had the value of Rick's property been small relative to the value of his services, the transaction would be fully taxable to both Sara and Rick. In that situation, Sara, the sole property transferor, would not have at least 80% control of Grouse Corporation following the transfer. As a result, she would fully recognize her realized gain. Further, because Rick would not be treated as having transferred property, the § 351 deferral would not be available to him either. ■

[12]Reg. § 1.351–1(a)(1)(ii).

[13]Rev.Proc. 77–37, 1977–2 C.B. 568.

Transfers to Existing Corporations. Once a corporation is in operation, § 351 also applies to any later transfers of property for stock by either new or existing shareholders.

EXAMPLE 12

Tyrone and Seth formed Blue Corporation three years ago. Both Tyrone and Seth transferred appreciated property to Blue in exchange for 50 shares each in the corporation. The original transfers qualified under § 351, and neither Tyrone nor Seth was taxed on the exchange. In the current year, Tyrone transfers property (worth $90,000, adjusted basis of $5,000) for 50 additional Blue shares. Tyrone has a taxable gain of $85,000 on the transfer. The exchange does not qualify under § 351 because Tyrone does not have 80% control of Blue Corporation immediately after the transfer—he owns 100 shares of the 150 shares outstanding, or a $66\frac{2}{3}$% interest. ■

See the Tax Planning Considerations portion of this chapter for additional discussion of this issue.

LO.2

Understand the special rules that apply when liabilities are assumed by a corporation.

ASSUMPTION OF LIABILITIES—§ 357

Without a provision to the contrary, the transfer of mortgaged property to a controlled corporation could trigger gain to the property transferor if the corporation took over the mortgage. This would be consistent with the rule dealing with like-kind exchanges under § 1031. Generally, when liabilities are assumed by another party, the party no longer responsible for the debt is treated as having received cash or boot. Section 357(a) provides, however, that when the acquiring corporation **assumes a liability** in a § 351 transaction, the transfer does *not* result in boot to the transferor-shareholder for gain recognition purposes. Nevertheless, liabilities assumed by the transferee corporation are treated as boot in determining the basis of the stock received by the shareholder. As a result, the basis of the stock received is reduced by the amount of the liabilities assumed by the corporation. See the more complete discussion of basis computations later.

EXAMPLE 13

Vera transfers property with an adjusted basis of $60,000, fair market value of $100,000, to Oriole Corporation for 100% of the stock in Oriole. The property is subject to a liability of $25,000 that Oriole Corporation assumes. The exchange is tax-free under §§ 351 and 357. However, the basis to Vera of the Oriole stock is $35,000 [$60,000 (basis of property transferred) – $25,000 (amount of the liability assumed by Oriole)]. ■

The general rule of § 357(a) has two exceptions: (1) § 357(b) provides that if the principal purpose of the assumption of the liabilities is to avoid tax *or* if there is no bona fide business purpose behind the exchange, the liabilities are treated as boot; and (2) § 357(c) provides that if the sum of the liabilities exceeds the adjusted basis of the properties transferred, the excess is taxable gain.

Exception (1): Tax Avoidance or No Bona Fide Business Purpose. Unless liabilities are incurred shortly before incorporation, § 357(b) generally poses few problems. A tax avoidance purpose for transferring liabilities to a controlled corporation normally is not a concern in view of the basis adjustment as noted above. Since the liabilities transferred reduce the basis of the stock received, any realized gain merely is deferred and not completely eliminated. Any postponed gain is recognized when and if the stock is disposed of in a taxable sale or exchange.

Satisfying the bona fide business purpose requirement is not difficult if the liabilities were incurred in connection with the transferor's normal course of conducting a trade or business. But this requirement can cause difficulty if the liability is taken out shortly before the property is transferred and the proceeds are utilized for personal purposes.[14] This type of situation is analogous to a cash distribution by the corporation to the shareholder, which is taxed as boot.

EXAMPLE 14

Dan transfers real estate (basis of $40,000 and fair market value of $90,000) to a controlled corporation in return for stock in the corporation. However, shortly before the transfer, Dan mortgages the real estate and uses the $20,000 proceeds to meet personal obligations. Thus, along with the real estate, the mortgage is transferred to the corporation. In this case, the assumption of the mortgage lacks a bona fide business purpose. Consequently, the release of the liability is treated as boot received, and Dan has a taxable gain on the transfer of $20,000.[15]

Amount realized:	
Stock	$ 70,000
Release of liability—treated as boot	20,000
Total amount realized	$ 90,000
Less: Basis of real estate	(40,000)
Realized gain	$ 50,000
Recognized gain	$ 20,000

The effect of the application of § 357(b) is to taint *all* liabilities transferred even if some are supported by a bona fide business purpose.

EXAMPLE 15

Tim, an accrual basis taxpayer, incorporates his sole proprietorship. Among the liabilities transferred to the new corporation are trade accounts payable of $100,000 and a credit card bill of $5,000. Tim had used the credit card to purchase a wedding anniversary gift for his wife. Under these circumstances, *all* of the $105,000 liabilities are treated as boot and trigger the recognition of gain to the extent gain is realized.

Exception (2): Liabilities in Excess of Basis. The second exception, § 357(c), provides that if the amount of the **liabilities** assumed **exceeds** the total of the adjusted **bases** of the properties transferred, the excess is taxable gain. Without this provision, when liabilities exceed the basis in property exchanged, a taxpayer would have a negative basis in the stock received in the controlled corporation.[16] Section 357(c) precludes the negative basis possibility by treating the excess over basis as gain to the transferor.

EXAMPLE 16

Andre transfers land and equipment with adjusted bases of $35,000 and $5,000, respectively, to a newly formed corporation in exchange for 100% of the stock. The corporation assumes the liability on the transferred land in the amount of $50,000. Without § 357(c), Andre's basis in the stock of the new corporation would be a negative $10,000 [$40,000 (bases of properties transferred) + $0 (gain recognized) – $0 (boot received) – $50,000 (liability assumed)]. Section 357(c), however, requires Andre to recognize a gain of $10,000 ($50,000 liability assumed – $40,000 bases of assets transferred). As a result, the stock has a zero basis in Andre's hands, determined as follows:

Bases in the properties transferred ($35,000 + $5,000)	$ 40,000
Plus: Gain recognized	10,000
Less: Boot received	–0–
Less: Liability assumed	(50,000)
Basis in the stock received	$ –0–

Thus, Andre recognizes $10,000 of gain, and a negative stock basis is avoided.

[14]See, for example, *Campbell, Jr. v. Wheeler*, 65–1 USTC ¶9294, 15 AFTR2d 578, 342 F.2d 837 (CA–5, 1965).

[15]§ 351(b).

[16]*Jack L. Easson*, 33 T.C. 963 (1960), *rev'd* in 61–2 USTC ¶9654, 8 AFTR2d 5448, 294 F.2d 653 (CA–9, 1961).

The definition of liabilities under § 357(c) excludes obligations that would have been deductible to the transferor had those obligations been paid before the transfer. Therefore, accounts payable of a cash basis taxpayer are not considered to be liabilities for purposes of § 357(c). In addition, they are not considered in the computation of stock basis.

EXAMPLE 17

Tina, a cash basis taxpayer, incorporates her sole proprietorship. In return for all of the stock of the new corporation, she transfers the following items:

	Adjusted Basis	Fair Market Value
Cash	$10,000	$10,000
Unrealized accounts receivable (amounts due to Tina but not yet received by her)	–0–	40,000
Trade accounts payable	–0–	30,000
Note payable	5,000	5,000

Because the unrealized accounts receivable and trade accounts payable have a zero basis under the cash method of accounting, no income is recognized until the receivables are collected, and no deduction materializes until the payables are satisfied. The note payable has a basis because it was issued for consideration received.

In this situation, the trade accounts payable are disregarded for gain recognition purposes and in determining Tina's stock basis. Thus, for purposes of § 357(c), because the balance of the note payable does not exceed the basis of the assets transferred, Tina does not have a problem of liabilities in excess of basis (i.e., the note payable of $5,000 does not exceed the aggregate basis in the cash and accounts receivable of $10,000). ■

Conceivably, a situation could arise where both §§ 357(b) and (c) apply in the same transfer. In such a situation, § 357(b) predominates.[17] This could be significant because § 357(b) does not create gain on the transfer, as does § 357(c), but merely converts the liability to boot. Thus, the realized gain limitation continues to apply to § 357(b) transactions.

EXAMPLE 18

Chris forms Robin Corporation by transferring land with a basis of $100,000, fair market value of $1 million. The land is subject to a mortgage of $300,000. One month prior to incorporating Robin, Chris borrows $200,000 for personal purposes and gives the lender a second mortgage on the land. Therefore, on the incorporation, Robin issues stock worth $500,000 to Chris and assumes the two mortgages on the land. Section 357(c) seems to apply to the transfer, given that the mortgages on the property ($500,000) exceed the basis of the property ($100,000). Thus, Chris would have a gain of $400,000 under § 357(c). Section 357(b), however, also applies to the transfer because Chris borrowed $200,000 just prior to the transfer and used the loan proceeds for personal purposes. Thus, under § 357(b), Chris has boot of $500,000 in the amount of the liabilities. Note that *all* of the liabilities are treated as boot, not just the tainted $200,000 liability. Consequently, he has realized gain of $900,000 [$1,000,000 (stock of $500,000 and assumption of liabilities of $500,000) – $100,000 (basis in the land)], and gain is recognized to the extent of the boot of $500,000. Unfortunately for Chris, the relatively more onerous rule of § 357(b) predominates over § 357(c). ■

[17]§ 357(c)(2)(A).

■ FIGURE 18–1
Shareholder's Basis in Stock Received

Adjusted basis of property transferred	$xx,xxx
Plus: Gain recognized	x,xxx
Minus: Boot received (including any liabilities transferred)	(x,xxx)
Equals: Basis of stock received	$xx,xxx

■ FIGURE 18–2
Corporation's Basis in Property Received

Adjusted basis of property transferred	$xx,xxx
Plus: Gain recognized by transferor-shareholder	xxx
Equals: Basis of property to corporation	$xx,xxx

LO.3

Recognize the basis issues relevant to the shareholder and the corporation.

BASIS DETERMINATION AND RELATED ISSUES

Recall that § 351(a) postpones gain or loss until the transferor-shareholder disposes of the stock in a taxable transaction. The postponement of shareholder gain or loss has a corollary effect on the basis of the stock received by the shareholder and the basis of the property received by the corporation. This procedure ensures that any gain or loss postponed under § 351 ultimately will be recognized when the affected asset is disposed of in a taxable transaction.

Basis of Stock to Shareholder. For a taxpayer transferring property to a corporation in a § 351 transaction, the *stock* received in the transaction is given a substituted basis. Essentially, the stock's basis is the same as the basis the taxpayer had in the property transferred, increased by any gain recognized on the exchange and decreased by boot received. Recall that for basis purposes, boot received includes any liabilities transferred by the shareholder to the corporation. Also note that if the shareholder receives any *other property* (i.e., boot) along with the stock, it takes a basis equal to its fair market value.[18]

Basis of Property to Corporation. The basis of *property* received by the corporation is determined under a carryover basis rule. This rule provides that the basis to the corporation is equal to the basis in the hands of the transferor increased by the amount of any gain recognized by the transferor-shareholder.[19]

The basis rules are summarized in Figures 18–1 and 18–2 and illustrated in Examples 19 and 20.

EXAMPLE 19

Kesha and Ned form Brown Corporation. Kesha transfers land (basis of $30,000 and fair market value of $70,000); Ned invests cash ($60,000). They each receive 50 shares in Brown Corporation, worth $60,000, but Kesha also receives $10,000 in cash from Brown. The transfers of property, the realized and recognized gain on the transfers, and the basis of the stock in Brown Corporation to Kesha and Ned are as follows:

[18] § 358(a).

[19] § 362(a).

	A	B	C	D	E	F
	Basis of Property Transferred	**FMV of Stock Received**	**Boot Received**	**Realized Gain (B + C – A)**	**Recognized Gain (Lesser of C or D)**	**Basis of Stock in Brown (A – C + E)**
From Kesha:						
Land	$30,000	$60,000	$10,000	$40,000	$10,000	$30,000
From Ned:						
Cash	60,000	60,000	–0–	–0–	–0–	60,000

Brown Corporation has a basis of $40,000 in the land: Kesha's basis of $30,000 plus her recognized gain of $10,000. ■

EXAMPLE 20

Assume the same facts as in Example 19 except that Kesha's basis in the land is $68,000 (instead of $30,000). Because recognized gain cannot exceed realized gain, the transfer generates only $2,000 of gain to Kesha. The realized and recognized gain and the basis of the stock in Brown Corporation to Kesha are as follows:

	A	B	C	D	E	F
	Basis of Property Transferred	**FMV of Stock Received**	**Boot Received**	**Realized Gain (B + C – A)**	**Recognized Gain (Lesser of C or D)**	**Basis of Stock in Brown (A – C + E)**
Land	$68,000	$60,000	$10,000	$2,000	$2,000	$60,000

Brown's basis in the land is $70,000 ($68,000 basis to Kesha + $2,000 gain recognized by Kesha). ■

Stock Issued for Services Rendered. A transfer of shares for services is not a taxable transaction to a corporation.[20] But another issue arises: Can a corporation deduct the fair market value of the stock it issues in consideration of services as a business expense? Yes, unless the services are such that the payment is characterized as a capital expenditure.[21]

EXAMPLE 21

Esther and Carl form White Corporation. Esther transfers cash of $500,000 for 100 shares of White Corporation stock. Carl transfers property worth $400,000 (basis of $90,000) and agrees to serve as manager of the corporation for one year; in return, Carl receives 100 shares of stock in White. The value of Carl's services to White Corporation is $100,000. Esther's and Carl's transfers qualify under § 351. Neither Esther nor Carl is taxed on the transfer of their property. However, Carl has income of $100,000, the value of the stock received for the services he will render to White Corporation. White has a basis of $90,000 in the property it acquired from Carl, and it may claim a compensation expense deduction under § 162 for $100,000. Carl's stock basis is $190,000 ($90,000 + $100,000). ■

EXAMPLE 22

Assume the same facts as in Example 21 except that Carl provides legal services (instead of management services) in organizing the corporation. The value of Carl's legal services is $100,000. Carl has no gain on the transfer of the property but has income of $100,000 for the value of the stock received for the services rendered. White Corporation has a basis of $90,000 in the property it acquired from Carl and must capitalize the $100,000 as an organizational expense. Carl's stock basis is $190,000 ($90,000 + $100,000). ■

[20]Reg. § 1.1032–1(a).

[21]Rev.Rul. 62–217, 1962–2 C.B. 59, modified by Rev.Rul. 74–503, 1974–2 C.B. 117.

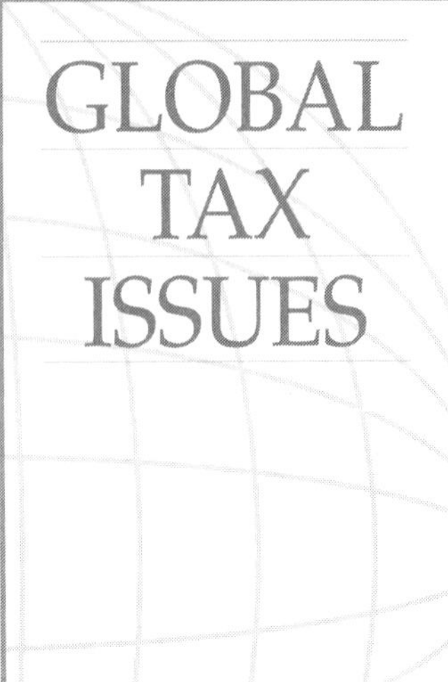

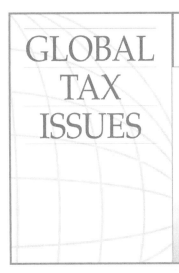

DOES § 351 COVER THE INCORPORATION OF A FOREIGN BUSINESS?

When a taxpayer wishes to incorporate a business overseas by moving assets across U.S. borders, the deferral mechanism of § 351 applies in certain situations, but not in others. In general, § 351 is available to defer gain recognition when starting up a new corporation outside the United States unless so-called tainted assets are involved. Under § 367, tainted assets, which include assets such as inventory and accounts receivable, are treated as having been sold by the taxpayer prior to the corporate formation; therefore, their transfer results in the current recognition of gain. The presence of tainted assets triggers gain because Congress does not want taxpayers to be able to shift the gain outside the U.S. jurisdiction. The gain recognized is ordinary or capital, depending on the nature of the asset involved.

Holding Period for Shareholder and Transferee Corporation. In a § 351 transfer, the shareholder's holding period for stock received in exchange for a capital asset or § 1231 property includes the holding period of the property transferred to the corporation. That is, the holding period of the property is "tacked on" to the holding period of the stock. The holding period for stock received for any other property (e.g., inventory) begins on the day after the exchange. The corporation's holding period for property acquired in a § 351 transfer is the holding period of the transferor-shareholder, regardless of the character of the property in the transferor's hands.[22]

Recapture Considerations. In a pure § 351(a) transfer where no gain is recognized, the recapture of accelerated cost recovery rules do not apply.[23] However, any recapture potential associated with the property carries over to the corporation as it steps into the shoes of the transferor-shareholder for purposes of basis determination.

EXAMPLE 23

Paul transfers equipment (adjusted basis of $30,000, original cost of $120,000, and fair market value of $100,000) to a controlled corporation in return for stock. If Paul had sold the equipment, it would have yielded a gain of $70,000, all of which would be recaptured as ordinary income under § 1245. Because the transfer comes within § 351(a), Paul has no recognized gain and no accelerated cost recovery to recapture. However, if the corporation later disposes of the equipment in a taxable transaction, it must take into account the § 1245 recapture potential originating with Paul. ■

LO.4

Appreciate the tax aspects of the capital structure of a corporation.

Capital Structure of a Corporation

CAPITAL CONTRIBUTIONS

When a corporation receives money or property in exchange for capital stock (including treasury stock), neither gain nor loss is recognized by the corporation.[24] Nor does a corporation's gross income include shareholders' contributions of money or property to the capital of the corporation. Moreover, additional money or property

[22]§§ 1223(1) and (2).
[23]§§ 1245(b)(3) and 1250(d)(3).
[24]§ 1032.

received from shareholders through voluntary pro rata transfers also is not income to the corporation. This is the case even though there is no increase in the number of outstanding shares of stock of the corporation. The contributions represent an additional price paid for the shares held by the shareholders and are treated as additions to the operating capital of the corporation.[25]

Contributions by nonshareholders, such as land contributed to a corporation by a civic group or a governmental group to induce the corporation to locate in a particular community, are also excluded from the gross income of a corporation.[26] However, if the property is transferred to a corporation by a nonshareholder in exchange for goods or services, then the corporation must recognize income.[27]

EXAMPLE 24

A cable television company charges its customers an initial fee to hook up to a new cable system installed in the area. These payments are used to finance the total cost of constructing the cable facilities. In addition, the customers will make monthly payments for the cable service. The initial payments are used for capital expenditures, but they represent payments for services to be rendered by the cable company. As such, they are taxable income to the cable company and not contributions to capital by nonshareholders. ■

The basis of property received by a corporation from a shareholder as a **capital contribution** is equal to the basis of the property in the hands of the shareholder. The basis of property transferred to a corporation by a nonshareholder as a contribution to capital is zero.

If a corporation receives *money* as a contribution to capital from a nonshareholder, a special rule applies. The basis of any property acquired with the money during a 12-month period beginning on the day the contribution was received is reduced by the amount of the contribution. The excess of money received over the cost of new property reduces the basis of other property held by the corporation and is applied in the following order:

- Depreciable property.
- Property subject to amortization.
- Property subject to depletion.
- All other remaining properties.

The basis of property within each category is reduced in proportion to the relative bases of the properties.[28]

EXAMPLE 25

A city donates land to Teal Corporation as an inducement for Teal to locate in the city. The receipt of the land produces no taxable income to Teal, and the land's basis to the corporation is zero. If, in addition, the city gives the corporation $10,000 in cash, the money is not taxable income to the corporation. However, if the corporation purchases property with the $10,000 within the next 12 months, the basis of the acquired property is reduced by $10,000. Any excess cash not used is handled according to the ordering rules noted above. ■

LO.5

Recognize the tax differences between debt and equity investments.

DEBT IN THE CAPITAL STRUCTURE

Advantages of Debt. Significant tax differences exist between debt and equity in the capital structure. The advantages of issuing long-term debt instead of stock are numerous. Interest on debt is deductible by the corporation, while dividend payments are not. Further, loan repayments are not taxable to investors unless the

[25] § 118 and Reg. § 1.118–1.

[26] See *Edwards v. Cuba Railroad Co.,* 1 USTC ¶139, 5 AFTR 5398, 45 S.Ct. 614 (USSC, 1925).

[27] Reg. § 1.118–1. See also *Teleservice Co. of Wyoming Valley,* 27 T.C. 722 (1957), *aff'd* in 58–1 USTC ¶9383, 1 AFTR2d 1249, 254 F.2d 105 (CA–3, 1958), *cert. den.* 78 S.Ct. 1360 (USSC, 1958).

[28] § 362(a) and Reg. § 1.362–2(b).

repayments exceed basis. A shareholder's receipt of property from a corporation, however, cannot be tax-free as long as the corporation has earnings and profits (see Chapter 19). Such distributions will be deemed to be taxable dividends to the extent of earnings and profits of the distributing corporation. Beginning in 2003, the advantages of debt over equity from the investor's perspective have lessened. Dividend income on equity holdings now is taxed to individual investors at the low capital gains rates, while interest income on debt continues to be taxed at the higher ordinary income rates.

EXAMPLE 26

Wade transfers cash of $100,000 to a newly formed corporation for 100% of the stock. In its initial year, the corporation has net income of $40,000. The income is credited to the earnings and profits account of the corporation. If the corporation distributes $9,500 to Wade, the distribution is a taxable dividend to Wade with no corresponding deduction to the corporation. Assume, instead, that Wade transfers to the corporation cash of $50,000 for stock and cash of $50,000 for a note of the same amount. The note is payable in equal annual installments of $5,000 and bears interest at the rate of 9%. At the end of the year, the corporation pays Wade interest of $4,500 ($50,000 × 9%) and a note repayment of $5,000. The interest payment is deductible to the corporation and taxable to Wade. The $5,000 principal repayment on the note is neither deducted by the corporation nor taxed to Wade. The after-tax impact to Wade and the corporation under each alternative is illustrated below.

	If the Distribution Is	
	$9,500 Dividend	**$5,000 Note Repayment and $4,500 Interest**
*After-tax benefit to Wade**		
[$9,500 x (1 – 15%)]	$8,075	
{$5,000 + [$4,500 x (1 – 35%)]}		$7,925
*After-tax cost to corporation***		
No deduction to corporation	9,500	
{$5,000 + [$4,500 x (1 – 35%)]}		7,925

*Assumes Wade's dividend income is taxed at the 15% capital gains rate and his interest income is taxed at the 35% ordinary income rate.

**Assumes the corporation is in the 35% marginal tax bracket.

Reclassification of Debt as Equity (Thin Capitalization Problem). In situations where the corporation is said to be thinly capitalized, the IRS contends that debt is really an equity interest and denies the corporation the tax advantages of debt financing. If the debt instrument has too many features of stock, it may be treated for tax purposes as stock. In that case, the principal and interest payments are considered dividends. In the current environment, however, the IRS may be less inclined to raise the thin capitalization issue because the conversion of interest income to dividend income would produce a tax benefit to individual investors.

Section 385 lists several factors that *may* be used to determine whether a debtor-creditor relationship or a shareholder-corporation relationship exists. The section authorizes the Treasury to prescribe Regulations that provide more definitive guidelines. To date, the Treasury has not drafted acceptable Regulations. Consequently, taxpayers must rely on judicial decisions to determine whether a true debtor-creditor relationship exists.

For the most part, the principles used to classify debt as equity developed in connection with closely held corporations. Here, the holders of the debt are also shareholders. Consequently, the rules have often proved inadequate for dealing with such problems in large, publicly traded corporations.

Together, Congress, through § 385, and the courts have identified the following factors to be considered in resolving the **thin capitalization** issue:

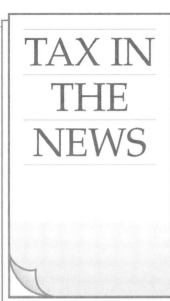

Conflict Arises between Corporations and Their Shareholders

Throughout the history of income taxation in the United States, applicable law has favored financing regular corporations with debt rather than equity. This corporate preference for debt exists because interest is deductible by the corporation, while dividends are not. Thus, if a corporation raises capital by issuing debt, the deductibility of the interest reduces the after-tax cost of obtaining financing. From the shareholders' perspective, the difference between debt and equity was not important because both interest and dividend income were taxed at ordinary income tax rates.

Now, with most dividend income being taxed at lower rates than interest income, investors will have a bias toward dividends. In contrast, corporations will still prefer debt financing because interest payments remain deductible while dividend payments are not. The chart in Example 26 illustrates this divergence between corporate and shareholder preferences. It will be interesting to see how the market will respond.

- Whether the debt instrument is in proper form. An open account advance is more easily characterized as a contribution to capital than a loan evidenced by a properly written note.[29]
- Whether the debt instrument bears a reasonable rate of interest and has a definite maturity date. When a shareholder advance does not provide for interest, the return expected may appear to be a share of the profits or an increase in the value of the shares.[30] Likewise, a lender unrelated to the corporation will usually be unwilling to commit funds to the corporation without a definite due date.
- Whether the debt is paid on a timely basis. A lender's failure to insist upon timely repayment or satisfactory renegotiation indicates that the return sought does not depend upon interest income and the repayment of principal.
- Whether payment is contingent upon earnings. A lender ordinarily will not advance funds that are likely to be repaid only if the venture is successful.
- Whether the debt is subordinated to other liabilities. Subordination tends to eliminate a significant characteristic of the creditor-debtor relationship. Creditors should have the right to share with other general creditors in the event of the corporation's dissolution or liquidation. Subordination also destroys another basic attribute of creditor status—the power to demand payment at a fixed maturity date.[31]
- Whether holdings of debt and stock are proportionate (e.g., each shareholder owns the same percentage of debt as stock). When debt and equity obligations are held in the same proportion, shareholders are, apart from tax considerations, indifferent as to whether corporate distributions are in the form of interest or dividends.
- Whether funds loaned to the corporation are used to finance initial operations or capital asset acquisitions. Funds used to finance initial operations or to acquire assets the corporation needs in the business are generally obtained through equity investments.

[29] *Estate of Mixon, Jr. v. U.S.*, 72–2 USTC ¶9537, 30 AFTR2d 72–5094, 464 F.2d 394 (CA–5, 1972).

[30] *Slappey Drive Industrial Park v. U.S.*, 77–2 USTC ¶9696, 40 AFTR2d 77–5940, 561 F.2d 572 (CA–5, 1977).

[31] *Fin Hay Realty Co. v. U.S.*, 68–2 USTC ¶9438, 22 AFTR2d 5004, 398 F.2d 694 (CA–3, 1968).

- Whether the corporation has a high ratio of shareholder debt to shareholder equity. Thin capitalization occurs when shareholder debt is high relative to shareholder equity. This indicates the corporation lacks reserves to pay interest and principal on debt when corporate income is insufficient to meet current needs.[32] In determining a corporation's debt-equity ratio, courts look at the relation of the debt both to the book value of the corporation's assets and to their actual fair market value.[33]

Under § 385, the IRS also has the authority to classify an instrument either as *wholly* debt or equity or as *part* debt and *part* equity. This flexible approach is important because some instruments cannot readily be classified either wholly as stock or wholly as debt. It may also provide an avenue for the IRS to address problems in publicly traded corporations.

LO.6

Handle the tax treatment of shareholder debt and stock losses.

Investor Losses

The difference between equity and debt financing involves a consideration of the tax treatment of worthless stock and securities versus that applicable to bad debts.

STOCK AND SECURITY LOSSES

If stocks and bonds are capital assets in their owner's hands, losses from their worthlessness are governed by § 165(g)(1). Under this provision, a capital loss materializes as of the last day of the taxable year in which the stocks or bonds become worthless. No deduction is allowed for a mere decline in value. The burden of proving complete worthlessness is on the taxpayer claiming the loss. One way to recognize partial worthlessness is to dispose of the stocks or bonds in a taxable sale or exchange.[34] But even then, the **investor loss** is disallowed if the sale or exchange is to a related party.

When the stocks or bonds are not capital assets, worthlessness yields an ordinary loss.[35] For example, if the stocks or bonds are held by a broker for resale to customers in the normal course of business, they are not capital assets. Usually, however, stocks and bonds are held as investments and, as a result, are capital assets.

Under certain circumstances involving stocks and bonds of affiliated corporations, an ordinary loss is allowed upon worthlessness.[36] A corporation is an affiliate of another corporation if the corporate shareholder owns at least 80 percent of the voting power of all classes of stock entitled to vote and 80 percent of each class of nonvoting stock. Further, to be considered affiliated, the corporation must have derived more than 90 percent of its aggregate gross receipts for all taxable years from sources other than passive income. Passive income for this purpose includes such items as rents, royalties, dividends, and interest.

BUSINESS VERSUS NONBUSINESS BAD DEBTS

In addition to worthlessness of stocks and bonds, the financial demise of a corporation can result in bad debt deductions to those who have extended credit to the corporation. These deductions can be either business bad debts or **nonbusiness**

[32] A court held that a debt-equity ratio of approximately 14.6:1 was not excessive. See *Tomlinson v. 1661 Corp.*, 67–1 USTC ¶9438, 19 AFTR2d 1413, 377 F.2d 291 (CA–5, 1967). A 26:1 ratio was found acceptable in *Delta Plastics, Inc.*, 85 TCM 940, T.C.Memo. 2003–54.

[33] In *Bauer v. Comm.*, 84–2 USTC ¶9996, 55 AFTR2d 85–433, 748 F.2d 1365 (CA–9, 1984), a debt-equity ratio of 92:1 resulted when book value was used. But the ratio ranged from 2:1 to 8:1 when equity included both paid-in capital and accumulated earnings.

[34] Reg. § 1.165–4(a).

[35] § 165(a) and Reg. § 1.165–5(b).

[36] § 165(g)(3).

bad debts. The distinction between the two types of deductions is important for tax purposes in the following respects:

- Business bad debts are deducted as ordinary losses while nonbusiness bad debts are treated as short-term capital losses.[37] A business bad debt can generate a net operating loss while a nonbusiness bad debt cannot.[38]
- A deduction is allowed for the partial worthlessness of a business debt while nonbusiness debts can be written off only when they become entirely worthless.[39]
- Nonbusiness bad debt treatment is limited to noncorporate taxpayers. However, all of the bad debts of a corporation qualify as business bad debts.[40]

When is a debt business or nonbusiness? Unfortunately, since the Code sheds little light on the matter, the distinction has been left to the courts.[41] In a leading decision, the Supreme Court somewhat clarified the picture when it held that if individual shareholders lend money to a corporation in their capacity as investors, any resulting bad debt is classified as nonbusiness.[42] Nevertheless, the Court did not preclude the possibility of a shareholder-creditor incurring a business bad debt.

If a loan is made in some capacity that qualifies as a trade or business, nonbusiness bad debt treatment is avoided. For example, if an employee, who is also a shareholder, makes a loan to preserve his or her employment, the loan qualifies for business bad debt treatment.[43] Shareholders also receive business bad debt treatment if they are in the trade or business of lending money or of buying, promoting, and selling corporations. If the shareholder has multiple motives for making the loan, according to the Supreme Court, the "dominant" or "primary" motive for making the loan controls the classification of the loss.[44]

EXAMPLE 27

Norman owns 48% of the stock of Lark Corporation, which he acquired several years ago at a cost of $200,000. Norman is also employed by the corporation at an annual salary of $80,000. At a time when Lark Corporation is experiencing financial problems, Norman lends it $100,000. Subsequently, the corporation becomes bankrupt, and both Norman's stock investment and his loan become worthless. ■

The loss from Norman's stock investment is treated as a long-term capital loss (assuming § 1244 does not apply, as discussed below). But how is the bad debt classified? If Norman can prove that his dominant or primary reason for making the loan was to protect his salary, a business bad debt deduction results. If not, it is assumed that Norman was trying to protect his stock investment, and nonbusiness bad debt treatment results. Factors to be considered in resolving this matter include the following:

- A comparison of the amount of the stock investment with the trade or business benefit derived. In Example 27, the stock investment of $200,000 is compared with the annual salary of $80,000. In this regard, the salary should be considered as a recurring item and not viewed in isolation. A salary of $80,000 each year means a great deal to a person who has no other means of support and may have difficulty obtaining similar employment elsewhere.
- A comparison of the amount of the loan with the stock investment and the trade or business benefit derived.

[37] Compare § 166(a) with § 166(d)(1)(B).

[38] Note the modification required by § 172(d)(2).

[39] Compare § 166(a)(2) with § 166(d)(1)(A).

[40] § 166(d)(1).

[41] For definitional purposes, § 166(d)(2) is almost as worthless as the debt it purports to describe.

[42] *Whipple v. Comm.*, 63–1 USTC ¶9466, 11 AFTR2d 1454, 83 S.Ct. 1168 (USSC, 1963).

[43] *Trent v. Comm.*, 61–2 USTC ¶9506, 7 AFTR2d 1599, 291 F.2d 669 (CA–2, 1961).

[44] *U.S. v. Generes*, 72–1 USTC ¶9259, 29 AFTR2d 72–609, 92 S.Ct. 827 (USSC, 1972).

- The percentage of ownership held by the shareholder. A minority shareholder, for example, is under more compulsion to lend the corporation money to protect a job than one who is in control of corporate policy.

In summary, it is impossible to conclude whether Norman in Example 27 suffered a business or nonbusiness bad debt without additional facts. Even with such facts, the guidelines are vague. Recall that a taxpayer's intent or motivation is at issue. For this reason, the problem is the subject of frequent litigation.[45]

SECTION 1244 STOCK

In an exception to the capital treatment that generally results, § 1244 permits ordinary loss treatment for losses on the sale or worthlessness of stock of so-called small business corporations. By placing shareholders on a more nearly equal basis with proprietors and partners in terms of the tax treatment of losses, the provision encourages investment of capital in small corporations. Gain on the sale of § 1244 stock remains capital. Consequently, the shareholder has nothing to lose and everything to gain by complying with § 1244.

Qualification for § 1244. Only a *small business corporation* can issue qualifying **§ 1244 stock.** To be a small business corporation, the total amount of stock that can be offered under the plan to issue § 1244 stock cannot exceed $1 million. For these purposes, property received in exchange for stock is valued at its adjusted basis, reduced by any liabilities assumed by the corporation or to which the property is subject. The fair market value of the property is not considered. The $1 million limitation is determined on the date the stock is issued. Consequently, even though a corporation fails to meet these requirements when the stock later is disposed of by the shareholder, the stock can still qualify as § 1244 stock if the requirements were met on the date the stock was issued.

Mechanics of the Loss Deduction. The amount of ordinary loss deductible in any one year from the disposition of § 1244 stock is limited to $50,000 (or $100,000 for taxpayers filing a joint return with a spouse). If the amount of the loss sustained in the taxable year exceeds these amounts, the remainder is considered a capital loss.

EXAMPLE 28

Harvey acquires § 1244 stock at a cost of $100,000. He sells the stock for $10,000 in the current year. He has an ordinary loss of $50,000 and a capital loss of $40,000. Alternatively, on a joint return, the entire $90,000 loss is ordinary. ■

Only the original holder of § 1244 stock, whether an individual or a partnership, qualifies for ordinary loss treatment. If the stock is sold or donated, it loses its § 1244 status.

Special treatment applies if § 1244 stock is issued by a corporation in exchange for property that has an adjusted basis above its fair market value immediately before the exchange. For purposes of determining ordinary loss upon a subsequent sale, the stock basis is reduced to the fair market value of the property on the date of the exchange.

EXAMPLE 29

Dana transfers property with a basis of $10,000 and a fair market value of $5,000 to a corporation in exchange for shares of § 1244 stock. Assuming the transfer qualifies under § 351, the basis of the stock is $10,000, the same as Dana's basis in the property. However, for purposes of § 1244 and measuring the amount of ordinary loss, the stock basis is only

[45]See, for example, *Kelson v. U.S.*, 74–2 USTC ¶9714, 34 AFTR2d 74–6007, 503 F.2d 1291 (CA–10, 1974) and *Kenneth W. Graves*, 87 TCM 1409, T.C.Memo. 2004–140.

$5,000. If the stock is later sold for $3,000, the total loss sustained is $7,000 ($3,000 – $10,000); however, only $2,000 of the loss is ordinary ($3,000 – $5,000). The remaining portion of the loss, $5,000, is a capital loss. ■

Recall the advantages of issuing some debt to shareholders in exchange for cash contributions to a corporation. A disadvantage of issuing debt is that it does not qualify under § 1244. Should the debt become worthless, the taxpayer generally has a short-term capital loss rather than the ordinary loss for § 1244 stock.

Gain from Qualified Small Business Stock

Shareholders are given special tax relief for gains recognized on the sale or exchange of stock acquired in a **qualified small business corporation.** The holder of **qualified small business stock** may exclude 50 percent of any gain from the sale or exchange of such stock.[46] To qualify for the exclusion, the taxpayer must have held the stock for more than five years and must have acquired the stock as part of an original issue.[47] Only noncorporate shareholders qualify for the exclusion.

A qualified small business corporation is a C corporation whose aggregate gross assets did not exceed $50 million on the date the stock was issued.[48] The corporation must be actively involved in a trade or business. This means that at least 80 percent of the corporation's assets must be used in the active conduct of one or more qualified trades or businesses.

A shareholder can apply the 50 percent exclusion to the greater of (1) $10 million or (2) 10 times the shareholder's aggregate adjusted basis in the qualified stock disposed of during a taxable year.[49]

LO.7

Identify tax planning opportunities associated with organizing and financing a corporation.

Tax Planning Considerations

WORKING WITH § 351

Effective tax planning with transfers of property to corporations requires a clear understanding of § 351 and its related Code provisions. The most important question in planning is simply: Does the desired tax result come from complying with § 351 or from avoiding it?

Utilizing § 351. If the tax-free treatment of § 351 is desired, ensure that the parties transferring property (which includes cash) receive control of the corporation. Simultaneous transfers are not necessary, but a long period of time between transfers could be disastrous if the transfers are not properly documented as part of a single plan. The parties should document and preserve evidence of their intentions. Also, it is helpful to have some reasonable explanation for any delay in the transfers.

To meet the requirements of § 351, mere momentary control on the part of the transferor may not suffice if loss of control is compelled by a prearranged agreement.[50]

EXAMPLE 30

For many years, Paula operated a business as a sole proprietor employing Brooke as manager. To dissuade Brooke from quitting and going out on her own, Paula promised her a 30% interest in the business. To fulfill this promise, Paula transfers the business to newly formed

[46] § 1202. The 5% and 15% capital gains rates do not apply. Thus, the maximum effective tax rate on the sale of qualified small business stock is 14% (28% × 50%).

[47] The stock must have been issued after August 10, 1993, which is the effective date of § 1202.

[48] § 1202(d). Its aggregate assets may not exceed this amount at any time between August 10, 1993, and the date the stock was issued.

[49] § 1202(b). The amount is $5 million for married taxpayers filing separately.

[50] Rev.Rul. 54–96, 1954–1 C.B. 111.

Green Corporation in return for all its stock. Immediately thereafter, Paula transfers 30% of the stock to Brooke. Section 351 probably does not apply to Paula's transfer to Green Corporation because it appears that Paula was under an obligation to relinquish control. However, if this is not the case and the loss of control was voluntary on Paula's part, momentary control would suffice.[51] ■

Be sure that later transfers of property to an existing corporation satisfy the control requirement if recognition of gain is to be avoided. In this connection, another transferor's interest cannot be counted if the value of stock received is relatively small compared with the value of stock already owned and the primary purpose of the transfer is to qualify other transferors for § 351 treatment.[52]

Avoiding § 351. Because § 351 provides for the nonrecognition of gain on transfers to controlled corporations, it is often regarded as a favorable relief provision. In some situations, however, avoiding § 351 may produce a more advantageous tax result. The transferors might prefer to recognize gain on the transfer of property if they cannot be particularly harmed by the gain. For example, they may be in low tax brackets, or the gain may be a capital gain from which substantial capital losses can be offset. The corporation will then have a stepped-up basis in the transferred property.

A transferor might also prefer to avoid § 351 to allow for immediate recognition of a loss. Recall that § 351 provides for the nonrecognition of both gains and losses. A transferor who wishes to recognize loss has several alternatives:

- Sell the property to the corporation for its stock. The IRS could attempt to collapse the "sale," however, by taking the approach that the transfer really falls under § 351.[53] If the sale is disregarded, the transferor ends up with a realized, but unrecognized, loss.
- Sell the property to the corporation for other property or boot. Because the transferor receives no stock, § 351 is inapplicable.
- Transfer the property to the corporation in return for securities or nonqualified preferred stock. Recall that § 351 does not apply to a transferor who receives securities or nonqualified preferred stock. In both this and the previous alternatives, watch for the possible disallowance of the loss under the related-party rules.

Suppose the loss property is to be transferred to the corporation and no loss is recognized by the transferor due to § 351. This could present an interesting problem in terms of assessing the economic realities involved.

EXAMPLE 31

Iris and Lamont form Wren Corporation with the following investments: property by Iris (basis of $40,000 and fair market value of $50,000) and property by Lamont (basis of $60,000 and fair market value of $50,000). Each receives 50% of the Wren stock. Has Lamont acted wisely in settling for only 50% of the stock? At first, it would appear so, since Iris and Lamont each invested property of the same value ($50,000). But what about tax considerations? Due to the carryover basis rules, the corporation now has a basis of $40,000 in Iris's property and $60,000 in Lamont's property. In essence, Iris has shifted a possible $10,000 gain to the corporation while Lamont has transferred a $10,000 potential loss. With this in mind, an equitable allocation of the Wren stock would call for Lamont to receive a greater percentage interest than Iris. ■

[51] Compare *Fahs v. Florida Machine and Foundry Co.*, 48–2 USTC ¶9329, 36 AFTR 1161, 168 F.2d 957 (CA–5, 1948), with *John C. O'Connor*, 16 TCM 213, T.C.Memo. 1957–50, *aff'd* in 58–2 USTC ¶9913, 2 AFTR2d 6011, 260 F.2d 358 (CA–6, 1958).

[52] Reg. § 1.351–1(a)(1)(ii).

[53] *U.S. v. Hertwig*, 68–2 USTC ¶9495, 22 AFTR2d 5249, 398 F.2d 452 (CA–5, 1968).

SELECTING ASSETS TO TRANSFER

When a business is incorporated, the organizers must determine which assets and liabilities should be transferred to the corporation. Leasing property to the corporation may be a more attractive alternative than transferring ownership. Leasing provides the taxpayer with the opportunity to withdraw money from the corporation in a deductible form without the payment being characterized as a nondeductible dividend. If the property is given to a family member in a lower tax bracket, the lease income can be shifted as well. If the depreciation and other deductions available in connection with the property are larger than the lease income, the taxpayer would retain the property until the income exceeds the deductions.

When an existing cash basis business is incorporated, an important issue to consider is whether the business's accounts receivable and accounts payable will be transferred to the new corporation or be retained by the owner of the unincorporated business. Depending on the approach taken, either the new corporation or the owner of the old unincorporated business will recognize the income associated with the cash basis receivables when they are collected. The cash basis accounts payable raise the corresponding issue of who will claim the deduction.

Another way to shift income to other taxpayers is by the use of corporate debt. Shareholder debt in a corporation can be given to family members in a lower tax bracket. This technique also causes income to be shifted without a loss of control of the corporation.

ETHICAL CONSIDERATIONS

The Control of a New Corporation: Insiders versus Outsiders

Your friend Harriet has decided to incorporate her business under the name "Out of This World.Com." She believes the corporation's prospects for growth are excellent because of its new and exciting products. To achieve this growth, however, capital from other investors will be needed.

Harriet hopes to attract funds from outsiders who will not be involved in the business. By limiting any offering to nonvoting preferred stock, capital will be raised without giving the new investors any control over the corporation's operations. Is Harriet's proposed plan ethical?

DEBT IN THE CAPITAL STRUCTURE

The advantages and disadvantages of debt as opposed to equity have previously been noted. To increase debt without incurring the thin capitalization problem, consider the following:

- Preserve the formalities of the debt. This includes providing for written instruments, realistic interest rates, and specified due dates.
- If possible, have the corporation repay the debt when it becomes due. If this is not possible, have the parties renegotiate the arrangement. Try to proceed as a nonshareholder creditor would. It is not unusual, for example, for bondholders of publicly held corporations to extend due dates when default occurs. The alternative is to foreclose and perhaps seriously impair the amount the creditors will recover.
- Avoid provisions in the debt instrument that make the debt convertible to equity in the event of default. These provisions are standard practice when nonshareholder creditors are involved. They serve no purpose if the shareholders are also the creditors and hold debt in proportion to ownership shares.

EXAMPLE 32

Gail, Gary, and Grace are equal shareholders in Magenta Corporation. Each transfers cash of $100,000 to Magenta in return for its bonds. The bond agreement provides that the holders will receive additional voting rights in the event Magenta Corporation defaults on its bonds. The voting rights provision is worthless and merely raises the issue of thin capitalization. Gail, Gary, and Grace already control Magenta Corporation, so what purpose is served by increasing their voting rights? The parties probably used a "boilerplate" bond agreement that was designed for third-party lenders (e.g., banks and other financial institutions). ■

- Pro rata holding of debt is difficult to avoid. For example, if each of the shareholders owns one-third of the stock, then each will want one-third of the debt. Nevertheless, some variation is possible.

EXAMPLE 33

Assume the same facts as Example 32 except that only Gail and Gary acquire the bonds. Grace leases property to Magenta Corporation at an annual rent that approximates the yield on the bonds. Presuming the rent passes the arm's length test (i.e., what unrelated parties would charge), all parties reach the desired result. Gail and Gary withdraw corporate profits in the form of interest income, and Grace is provided for with rent income. Magenta Corporation can deduct both the interest and the rent payments. ■

- Try to keep the debt-equity ratio within reasonable proportions. A problem frequently arises when the parties form the corporation. Often the amount invested in capital stock is the minimum required by state law. For example, if the state of incorporation permits a minimum of $1,000, limiting the investment to this amount does not provide much safety for later debt financing by the shareholders.
- Stressing the fair market value of the assets rather than their tax basis to the corporation can be helpful in preparing to defend debt-equity ratios.

EXAMPLE 34

Emily, Josh, and Miles form Black Corporation with the following capital investments: cash of $200,000 from Emily; land worth $200,000 (basis of $20,000) from Josh; and a patent worth $200,000 (basis of $0) from Miles. To state that the equity of Black Corporation is $220,000 (the tax basis to the corporation) does not reflect reality. The equity account is more properly stated at $600,000 ($200,000 + $200,000 + $200,000). ■

- The nature of the business can have an effect on what is an acceptable debt-equity ratio. Capital-intensive industries (e.g., manufacturing, transportation) characteristically rely heavily on debt financing. Consequently, larger debt should be tolerated.

What if a corporation's efforts to avoid the thin capitalization problem fail and the IRS raises the issue on audit? What steps should the shareholders take? They should hedge their position by filing a protective claim for refund claiming dividend treatment on the previously reported interest income. In such an event, ordinary income would be converted to preferential dividend income treatment. Otherwise, the IRS could ultimately invoke the statute of limitations and achieve the best of all possible worlds—the shareholders would have been taxed on the interest income at the ordinary income rates while the corporation would receive no deduction for what is now reclassified as a dividend. By filing the claim for refund, the shareholders have kept the statute of limitations from running until the thin capitalization issue is resolved at the corporate level.

INVESTOR LOSSES

Be aware of the danger of losing § 1244 attributes. Only the original holder of § 1244 stock is entitled to ordinary loss treatment. If, after a corporation is formed, the owner transfers shares of stock to family members to shift income within the family group, the benefits of § 1244 are lost.

EXAMPLE 35

Norm incorporates his business by transferring property with a basis of $100,000 for 100 shares of stock. The stock qualifies as § 1244 stock. Norm later gives 50 shares each to his children, Susan and Paul. Eventually, the business fails, and the shares of stock become worthless. If Norm had retained the stock, he would have had an ordinary loss deduction of $100,000 (assuming he filed a joint return). Susan and Paul, however, have a capital loss of $50,000 each because the § 1244 attributes are lost as a result of the gift (i.e., neither Susan nor Paul was an original holder of the stock). ■

KEY TERMS

Assumption of liabilities, 18–9
Capital contribution, 18–15
Control, 18–6
Investor losses, 18–18
Liabilities in excess of basis, 18–10
Nonbusiness bad debt, 18–18
Property, 18–4
Qualified small business corporation, 18–21
Qualified small business stock, 18–21
Section 1244 stock, 18–20
Securities, 18–5
Thin capitalization, 18–16

PROBLEM MATERIALS

Discussion Questions

1. In terms of justification and effect, § 351 (transfer to a controlled corporation) and § 1031 (like-kind exchange) are much alike. Explain.
2. Under what circumstances will gain and/or loss be recognized on a § 351 transfer?
3. Why are services not treated as property under § 351?
4. Does "stock" include stock rights and stock warrants under § 351? Does it include preferred stock?
5. Can the receipt of boot ever be taxable in a § 351 transfer in the absence of realized gain? Explain.
6. What is the control requirement of § 351? Describe the effect of the following in satisfying this requirement:
   a. A shareholder renders only services to the corporation for stock.
   b. A shareholder both renders services and transfers property to the corporation for stock.
   c. A shareholder has only momentary control after the transfer.
   d. A long period of time elapses between the transfers of property by different shareholders.

Issue ID

7. Nancy and her daughter, Margaret, have been working together in a cattery called "The Perfect Cat." Nancy formed the business in 1990 as a sole proprietorship. Because of the high quality and exotic lineage of the cats that Nancy breeds, the business has been very successful. It currently has assets with a fair market value of $250,000 and a basis of $180,000. On the advice of her tax accountant, Nancy decides to incorporate "The Perfect Cat." Because of Margaret's loyalty, Nancy would like her to have shares in the corporation. What are the relevant tax issues?

Issue ID
Decision Making

8. Several entrepreneurs plan to form a corporation for purposes of constructing a housing project. Randall will be contributing the land for the project and wants more security

than shareholder status provides. He is contemplating two possibilities: receive corporate bonds for his land, or take out a mortgage on the land before transferring it to the corporation. Comment on the choices Randall is considering. What alternatives can you suggest?

9. Paul and Mary transfer property to Falcon Corporation, each in exchange for one-third of Falcon's stock. Matt receives the other one-third of Falcon's stock for services rendered. Will the exchanges be taxable?

10. May a transferor who receives stock for both property and services be included in the control group in determining whether an exchange meets the requirements of § 351? Explain.

Issue ID

11. At a point when Robin Corporation has been in existence for six years, shareholder Ted transfers real estate (adjusted basis of $20,000 and fair market value of $100,000) to the corporation for additional stock. At the same time, Peggy, the other shareholder, acquires one share of stock for cash. After the two transfers, the percentages of stock ownership are as follows: 79% by Ted and 21% by Peggy.
    a. What were the parties trying to accomplish?
    b. Will it work? Explain.

12. How does the transfer of mortgaged property to a controlled corporation affect the transferor-shareholder's basis in stock received in the corporation? Assume no gain is recognized on the transfer.

13. Before incorporating her apartment rental business, Libbie takes out second mortgages on several of the units. She uses the mortgage proceeds to make capital improvements to the units. Along with all of the rental units, Libbie transfers the mortgages to the newly formed corporation in return for all of its stock. Discuss the tax consequences of these procedures.

14. Why does § 357(c) require a recognition of gain when liabilities assumed by a corporation exceed the adjusted basis of the assets transferred?

15. If both § 357(b) and § 357(c) apply to a transfer of property to a corporation under § 351, which provision takes precedence?

16. Identify a situation when a corporation can deduct the value of the stock it issues for the rendition of services. Identify a situation when a deduction is not available.

17. A corporation acquires property as a contribution to capital from a shareholder and from a nonshareholder. Are the rules pertaining to the property's basis the same? Explain.

18. In structuring the capitalization of a corporation, what are the advantages and disadvantages of utilizing debt rather than equity?

19. In determining a corporation's debt-equity ratio, should the book value or the fair market value of the assets be used?

20. Under what circumstances, if any, may a shareholder deduct a business bad debt on a loan made to the corporation?

Decision Making

21. Three years ago, Ralph purchased stock in White Corporation for $40,000. The stock has a current value of $5,000. Ralph needs to decide which of the following alternatives to pursue. Determine the tax effect of each.
    a. Without selling the stock, Ralph deducts $35,000 for the partial worthlessness of the White Corporation investment.
    b. Ralph sells the stock to his mother for $5,000 and deducts a $35,000 long-term capital loss.
    c. Ralph sells the stock to a third party and deducts a $35,000 long-term capital loss.
    d. Ralph sells the stock to his aunt for $5,000 and deducts a $35,000 long-term capital loss.
    e. Ralph sells the stock to a third party and deducts an ordinary loss.

Issue ID

22. Keith's sole proprietorship holds assets that, if sold, would yield a gain of $100,000. It also owns assets that would yield a loss of $30,000. Keith incorporates his business using only the gain assets. Two days later, Keith sells the loss assets to the newly formed corporation. What is Keith trying to accomplish? Will he be successful?

Issue ID

23. Emily incorporates her sole proprietorship, but does not transfer the building the business uses to the corporation. Subsequently, the building is leased to the corporation for an annual rent. What tax reasons might Emily have for not transferring the building to the corporation when the business was incorporated?

Problems

24. John, Brad, Kate, and Marta form Martin Corporation with the following consideration:

	Consideration Transferred		
	Basis to Transferor	**Fair Market Value**	**Number of Shares Issued**
From John—			
Personal services rendered to Martin Corporation	$ –0–	$ 30,000	30
From Brad—			
Equipment	345,000	300,000	270*
From Kate—			
Cash	60,000	60,000	
Unrealized accounts receivable	–0–	90,000	150
From Marta—			
Land and building	210,000	450,000	
Mortgage on land and building	300,000	300,000	150

*Brad receives $30,000 in cash in addition to the 270 shares.

Martin Corporation assumes the mortgage transferred by Marta. The value of each share of Martin Corporation stock is $1,000. As to these transactions, provide the following information:

a. John's recognized gain or loss.
b. John's basis in the Martin Corporation stock.
c. Brad's recognized gain or loss.
d. Brad's basis in the Martin Corporation stock.
e. Martin Corporation's basis in the equipment.
f. Kate's recognized gain or loss.
g. Kate's basis in the Martin Corporation stock.
h. Martin Corporation's basis in the unrealized accounts receivable.
i. Marta's recognized gain or loss.
j. Marta's basis in the Martin Corporation stock.
k. Martin Corporation's basis in the land and building.

25. Mark and Gail form Maple Corporation with the following consideration:

	Consideration Transferred		
	Basis to Transferor	**Fair Market Value**	**Number of Shares Issued**
From Mark—			
Cash	$ 50,000	$ 50,000	
Installment obligation	140,000	250,000	30
From Gail—			
Cash	150,000	150,000	
Equipment	125,000	250,000	
Patent	10,000	300,000	70

The installment obligation has a face amount of $250,000 and was acquired last year from the sale of land held for investment purposes (adjusted basis of $140,000). As to these transactions, provide the following information:

a. Mark's recognized gain or loss.
b. Mark's basis in the Maple Corporation stock.
c. Maple Corporation's basis in the installment obligation.
d. Gail's recognized gain or loss.
e. Gail's basis in the Maple Corporation stock.
f. Maple Corporation's basis in the equipment and the patent.
g. How would your answers to the preceding questions change if Mark received common stock and Gail received preferred stock?
h. How would your answers change if Gail was a partnership?

Decision Making

26. Jane, Jon, and Clyde incorporate their respective businesses and form Starling Corporation. On March 1 of the current year, Jane exchanges her property (basis of $100,000 and value of $400,000) for 200 shares in Starling Corporation. On April 15, Jon exchanges his property (basis of $140,000 and value of $600,000) for 300 shares in Starling. On May 10, Clyde transfers his property (basis of $1,180,000 and value of $1 million) for 500 shares in Starling.
    a. If the three exchanges are part of a prearranged plan, what gain will each of the parties recognize on the exchanges?
    b. Assume Jane and Jon exchanged their property for stock four years ago while Clyde transfers his property for 500 shares in the current year. Clyde's transfer is not part of a prearranged plan with Jane and Jon to incorporate their businesses. What gain or loss will Clyde recognize on the transfer?
    c. Which arrangement—part (a) or part (b)—would the parties prefer?

Communications

27. Andrew Boninti (1635 Maple Street, Syracuse, NY 13201) exchanges property, basis of $30,000 and fair market value of $600,000, for 60% of the stock of Gray Corporation. The other 40% is owned by Kendall Smith, who acquired her stock several years ago. You represent Andrew, who asks whether he must report gain on the transfer. Prepare a letter to Andrew and a memorandum for the tax files documenting your response.

Issue ID

28. Barbara exchanges property, basis of $20,000 and fair market value of $500,000, for 65% of the stock of Pelican Corporation. Alice, Barbara's daughter, who acquired her stock last year, owns the other 35% of Pelican. What are the tax issues?

29. Juan organized Red Corporation 10 years ago. He contributed property worth $1 million (basis of $200,000) for 2,000 shares of stock in Red (representing 100% ownership). Juan later gave each of his children, Julie and Rachel, 500 shares of the stock. In the current year, Juan transfers property worth $400,000 (basis of $150,000) to Red for 500 more of its shares. What gain, if any, will Juan recognize on the transfer?

30. Ann and Bob form Robin Corporation. Ann transfers property worth $420,000 (basis of $150,000) for 70 shares in Robin Corporation. Bob receives 30 shares for property worth $165,000 (basis of $30,000) and for legal services in organizing the corporation; the services are worth $15,000.
    a. What gain, if any, will the parties recognize on the transfer?
    b. What basis do Ann and Bob have in the stock in Robin Corporation?
    c. What is Robin Corporation's basis in the property and services it received from Ann and Bob?

Decision Making

31. Rhonda Johnson owns 50% of the stock of Peach Corporation. She and the other 50% shareholder, Rachel Powell, have decided that additional contributions of capital are needed if Peach is to remain successful in its competitive industry. The two shareholders have agreed that Rhonda will contribute assets having a value of $200,000 (adjusted basis of $15,000) in exchange for additional shares of stock. After the transaction, Rhonda will hold 75% of Peach Corporation and Rachel's interest will fall to 25%.
    a. What gain is realized on the transaction? How much of the gain will be recognized?
    b. Rhonda is not satisfied with the transaction as proposed. How would the consequences change if Rachel agrees to transfer $1,000 of cash in exchange for additional

stock? In this case, Rhonda will own slightly less than 75% of Peach and Rachel's interest will be slightly more than 25%.

c. If Rhonda still is not satisfied with the result, what should be done to avoid any gain recognition?

32. Paul transfers property with an adjusted basis of $50,000, fair market value of $400,000, to Swift Corporation for 90% of the stock. The property is subject to a liability of $60,000, which Swift assumes. What is the basis of the Swift stock to Paul? What is the basis of the property to Swift Corporation?

33. Allie forms Blue Corporation by transferring land with a basis of $125,000 (fair market value of $775,000). The land is subject to a mortgage of $375,000. One month prior to incorporating Blue, Allie borrows $100,000 for personal purposes and gives the lender a second mortgage on the land. Blue Corporation issues stock worth $300,000 to Allie and assumes the mortgages on the land.
    a. What are the tax consequences to Allie and to Blue Corporation?
    b. How would the tax consequences to Allie differ if she had not borrowed the $100,000?

34. Sara and Jane form Wren Corporation. Sara transfers property, basis of $25,000 and value of $200,000, for 50 shares in Wren Corporation. Jane transfers property, basis of $10,000 and value of $185,000, and agrees to serve as manager of Wren for one year; in return Jane receives 50 shares in Wren. The value of Jane's services to Wren is $15,000.
    a. What gain do Sara and Jane recognize on the exchange?
    b. What is Wren Corporation's basis in the property transferred by Sara and Jane? How does Wren treat the value of the services Jane renders?

35. Assume in Problem 34 that Jane receives the 50 shares of Wren Corporation stock in consideration for the appreciated property and for providing legal services in organizing the corporation. The value of Jane's services is $15,000.
    a. What gain does Jane recognize?
    b. What is Wren Corporation's basis in the property transferred by Jane? How does Wren treat the value of the services Jane renders?

36. Blue Corporation desires to set up a manufacturing facility in a southern state. After considerable negotiations with a small town in Arkansas, Blue accepts the following offer: land (fair market value of $3 million) and cash of $1 million.
    a. How much gain, if any, must Blue Corporation recognize?
    b. What basis will Blue Corporation have in the land?
    c. Within one year of the contribution, Blue constructs a building for $800,000 and purchases inventory for $300,000. What basis will Blue Corporation have in each of these assets?

Communications

37. Emily Patrick (36 Paradise Road, Northampton, MA 01060) formed Teal Corporation a number of years ago with an investment of $200,000 cash, for which she received $20,000 in stock and $180,000 in bonds bearing interest of 8% and maturing in nine years. Several years later, Emily lent the corporation an additional $50,000 on open account. In the current year, Teal Corporation becomes insolvent and is declared bankrupt. During the corporation's existence, Emily was paid an annual salary of $60,000. Write a letter to Emily in which you explain how she would treat her losses for tax purposes.

Communications

38. Stock in Jaybird Corporation (555 Industry Lane, Pueblo, CO 81001) is held equally by Vera, Wade, and Wes. Jaybird seeks additional capital in the amount of $900,000 to construct a building. Vera, Wade, and Wes each propose to lend Jaybird Corporation $300,000, taking from Jaybird a $300,000 four-year note with interest payable annually at two points below the prime rate. Jaybird Corporation has current taxable income of $2 million. You represent Jaybird Corporation. It asks you how the payments on the notes might be treated for tax purposes. Prepare a letter to the president of Jaybird, Steve Ferguson, and a memo to your tax files where you document your conclusions.

39. Sam, a single taxpayer, acquired stock in a corporation that qualified as a small business corporation under § 1244, at a cost of $100,000 three years ago. He sells the stock for $10,000 in the current tax year. How will the loss be treated for tax purposes?

Communications

40. Paul Sanders, a married taxpayer who files a joint return with his wife, acquired stock in a corporation that qualified as a small business corporation under § 1244. The stock cost $30,000 and was acquired three years ago. A few months after he acquired the stock he gave it to his brother, Mike Sanders. The stock was worth $30,000 on the date of the gift. Mike, who is married and files a joint return with his wife, sells the stock for $10,000 in the current tax year. You represent Mike who asks you whether he can take a loss deduction on the sale of the stock. If so, how will the loss be treated for tax purposes? Prepare a letter to your client and a memo to the file. Mike's address is 2600 Riverview Drive, Plank, MO 63701.

41. Susan transfers property with a basis of $50,000 and a fair market value of $25,000 to Thrush Corporation in exchange for shares of § 1244 stock. (Assume the transfer qualifies under § 351.)
   a. What is the basis of the stock to Susan?
   b. What is the basis of the stock to Susan for purposes of § 1244?
   c. If Susan sells the stock for $20,000 two years later, how will the loss be treated for tax purposes?

Decision Making

42. Frank, Cora, and Mitch are equal shareholders in Blue Corporation. The corporation's assets have a tax basis of $50,000 and a fair market value of $600,000. In the current year, Frank and Cora each loan Blue Corporation $150,000. The notes to Frank and Cora bear interest of 8% per annum. Mitch leases equipment to Blue Corporation for an annual rental of $12,000. Discuss whether the shareholder loans from Frank and Cora might be reclassified as equity. Consider in your discussion whether Blue Corporation has an acceptable debt-equity ratio.

Research Problems

Note: Solutions to Research Problems can be prepared by using the ***RIA Checkpoint® Student Edition*** *online research product, which is available to accompany this text. It is also possible to prepare solutions to the Research Problems by using tax research materials found in a standard tax library.*

Decision Making

Research Problem 1. Skeeter has owned and operated an accrual basis golf driving range for a number of years. The sole proprietorship has been successful and has grown to the point where it now also offers golf lessons and sponsors tournaments and other activities. Skeeter has been advised that incorporating his proprietorship would give him an opportunity to restructure the business debt and to acquire additional working capital at more favorable rates.

Based on this advice, Skeeter transfers the business assets (fair market value $1 million, adjusted basis $200,000) along with the associated debt ($325,000) to the newly formed corporation. As far as he is concerned, nothing has really changed in his relationship with the creditor bank; he still feels personally obligated to pay off the debt. In fact, before the debt is assigned to the newly formed corporation, the bank insists that Skeeter remain secondarily responsible for its payment. Even though the proprietorship's liabilities transferred exceed the basis of the assets transferred, Skeeter regards the transaction as tax-free because:

- nothing has changed with his business other than its form of operation,
- a business justification exists for changing its form to that of a corporation, and
- he has enjoyed no personal gain from the transaction.

Determine if Skeeter's belief is justified. If you believe that the transaction as currently planned would be taxable, identify strategies that could be employed to eliminate or minimize any recognition of gain.

Partial list of research aids:
§ 357(c).

Decision Making

Research Problem 2. Susan is the sole owner of Bluegill Corporation. The basis and value of her stock investment in Bluegill are approximately $100,000. In addition, she manages Bluegill's operations on a full-time basis and pays herself an annual salary of $40,000. Because of a recent downturn in business, she needs to put an additional $80,000 into her corporation to help meet short-term cash-flow needs (e.g., inventory costs, salaries, administrative expenses). Susan believes that the $80,000 transfer can be structured in one of three ways: as a capital contribution, as a loan made to protect her stock investment, or as a loan intended to protect her job. From a tax perspective, which alternative would be preferable in the event that Bluegill's economic slide worsens and bankruptcy results?

Partial list of research aids:
Kenneth W. Graves, 87 TCM 1409, T.C.Memo. 2004–140.

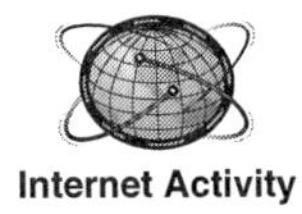

Internet Activity

Use the tax resources of the Internet to address the following question. Do not restrict your search to the World Wide Web, but include a review of newsgroups and general reference materials, practitioner sites and resources, primary sources of the tax law, chat rooms and discussion groups, and other opportunities.

Research Problem 3. Have the provisions of § 1202, which relate to qualified small business stock, been widely used since their enactment? What leads you to this conclusion?

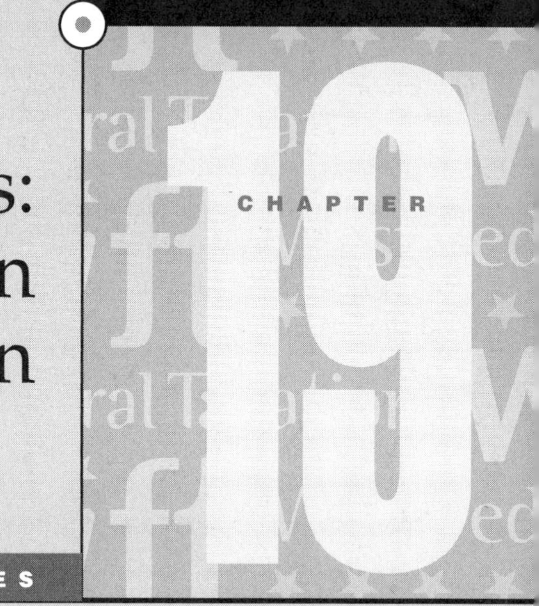

Corporations: Distributions Not in Complete Liquidation

LEARNING OBJECTIVES

After completing Chapter 19, you should be able to:

LO.1

Understand the role that earnings and profits play in determining the tax treatment of distributions.

LO.2

Compute a corporation's earnings and profits.

LO.3

Apply the rules for allocating earnings and profits to distributions.

LO.4

Understand the tax treatment of dividends for individual shareholders.

LO.5

Understand the tax impact of property dividends on the recipient shareholder and the corporation making the distribution.

LO.6

Understand the nature and treatment of constructive dividends.

LO.7

Distinguish between taxable and nontaxable stock dividends and stock rights.

LO.8

Identify various stock redemptions that qualify for sale or exchange treatment.

LO.9

Understand the tax impact of stock redemptions on the distributing corporation.

LO.10

Identify tax planning opportunities available to minimize the tax impact in corporate distributions, constructive dividends, and stock redemptions.

OUTLINE

Chapter 18 examined the tax consequences of corporate formation. In this chapter and Chapter 20, the focus shifts to the tax treatment of corporate distributions, a topic that plays a leading role in tax planning. The importance of corporate distributions derives from the variety of tax treatments that may apply. From the shareholder's perspective, distributions received from the the corporation may be treated as ordinary income, preferentially taxed dividend income, capital gain, or a nontaxable recovery of capital. From the corporation's perspective, distributions made to shareholders are generally not deductible. However, a corporation may recognize losses in liquidating distributions (see Chapter 20), and gains may be recognized at the corporate level on distributions of appreciated property. In the most common scenario, a distribution triggers dividend income to the shareholder and provides no deduction to the paying corporation, resulting in a double tax (i.e., a tax is levied at both the corporate and the shareholder levels). This double tax may be mitigated by a variety of factors including the corporate dividends received deduction and preferential tax rates on qualified dividends paid to individuals.

As will become apparent in the subsequent discussion, the tax treatment of corporate distributions can be affected by a number of considerations, including:

- The availability of earnings to be distributed.
- Whether the distribution is a "qualified dividend."
- Whether the shareholder is an individual or another kind of taxpaying entity.
- The basis of the stock in the hands of the shareholder.
- The character of the property being distributed.
- Whether the shareholder gives up ownership in return for the distribution.
- Whether the distribution is liquidating or nonliquidating.

This chapter discusses the tax rules related to nonliquidating distributions (in the form of cash and property). Distributions of stock and stock rights are also addressed along with the tax treatment of stock redemptions. Corporate liquidations are discussed in Chapter 20.

LO.1

Understand the role that earnings and profits play in determining the tax treatment of distributions.

Corporate Distributions—In General

To the extent that a distribution is made from corporate earnings and profits (E & P), the shareholder is deemed to receive a dividend, taxed as ordinary income or as preferentially taxed dividend income.[1] Generally, corporate distributions are presumed to be paid out of E & P (defined later in this chapter) and are treated as dividends, *unless* the parties to the transaction can show otherwise. Distributions that are not treated as dividends (because of insufficient E & P) are nontaxable to the extent of the shareholder's basis in the stock. The stock basis is reduced accordingly. The excess of the distribution over the shareholder's basis is treated as a gain from the sale or exchange of the stock.[2]

EXAMPLE 1

At the beginning of the year, Amber Corporation (a calendar year taxpayer) has E & P of $15,000. The corporation generates no additional E & P during the year. On July 1, the corporation distributes $20,000 to its sole shareholder, Bonnie. Assume Bonnie's stock basis is $4,000. In this situation, Bonnie recognizes dividend income of $15,000 (the amount of E & P distributed). In addition, she reduces her stock basis from $4,000 to zero, and she recognizes a taxable gain of $1,000 (the excess of the distribution over the stock basis). ■

LO.2

Compute a corporation's earnings and profits.

Earnings and Profits (E & P)

The notion of **earnings and profits** is similar in many respects to the accounting concept of retained earnings. Both are measures of the firm's accumulated capital (E & P includes both the accumulated E & P of the corporation since February 28, 1913, and the current year's E & P). However, while these two concepts are similar, they differ in a fundamental way. The computation of retained earnings is based on financial accounting rules while E & P is determined using rules specified in the tax law.

E & P fixes the upper limit on the amount of dividend income that shareholders must recognize as a result of a distribution by the corporation. In this sense, E & P represents the corporation's economic ability to pay a dividend without impairing its capital. Thus, the effect of a specific transaction on the E & P account often may be determined by considering whether the transaction increases or decreases the corporation's capacity to pay a dividend.

COMPUTATION OF E & P

The Code does not explicitly define the term *earnings and profits.* Instead, a series of adjustments to taxable income are identified to provide a measure of the corporation's economic income. Both cash basis and accrual basis corporations use the same approach when determining E & P.[3]

[1]§§ 301(c)(1), 316, and 1(h)(11).
[2]§§ 301(c)(2) and (3).
[3]Section 312 describes most of the adjustments to taxable income necessary to determine E & P. Regulations relating to E & P begin at Reg. § 1.312–6.

Additions to Taxable Income. It is necessary to add all previously excluded income items back to taxable income to determine current E & P. Included among these positive adjustments are interest on municipal bonds, excluded life insurance proceeds (in excess of cash surrender value), Federal income tax refunds from tax paid in prior years, the dividends received deduction, and the deduction for domestic manufacturing income.

EXAMPLE 2

A corporation collects $100,000 on a key employee life insurance policy (the corporation is the owner and beneficiary of the policy). At the time the policy matured on the death of the insured employee, it possessed a cash surrender value of $30,000. None of the $100,000 is included in the corporation's taxable income, but $70,000 is added to taxable income when computing current E & P (i.e., amount collected on the policy net of its cash surrender value). The collection of the $30,000 cash surrender value does not increase E & P because it does not reflect an increase in the corporation's dividend-paying capacity. Instead, it represents a shift in the corporation's assets from life insurance to cash. ■

Subtractions from Taxable Income. Some of the corporation's nondeductible expenditures are subtracted from taxable income to arrive at E & P. These negative adjustments include related-party losses, expenses incurred to produce tax-exempt income, Federal income taxes paid, nondeductible key employee life insurance premiums (net of increases in cash surrender value), and nondeductible fines and penalties.

EXAMPLE 3

A corporation sells property (basis of $10,000) to its sole shareholder for $8,000. Because of § 267 (disallowance of losses on sales between related parties), the $2,000 loss cannot be deducted in arriving at the corporation's taxable income. But since the overall economic effect of the transaction is a decrease in the corporation's assets by $2,000, the loss reduces the current E & P for the year of sale. ■

EXAMPLE 4

A corporation pays a $10,000 premium on a key employee life insurance policy covering the life of its president. As a result of the payment, the cash surrender value of the policy is increased by $7,000. Although none of the $10,000 premium is deductible for tax purposes, current E & P is reduced by $3,000 (i.e., amount of the premium payment net of the increase in the cash surrender value). The $7,000 increase in cash surrender value is not subtracted because it does not represent a decrease in the corporation's ability to pay a dividend. Instead, it is a change in the corporation's assets, from cash to life insurance. ■

Timing Adjustments. Some E & P adjustments shift the effect of a transaction from the year of its inclusion in or deduction from taxable income to the year in which it has an economic effect on the corporation. Charitable contributions, net operating losses, and capital losses all give rise to this kind of adjustment.

EXAMPLE 5

During 2005, a corporation makes charitable contributions, $12,000 of which cannot be deducted in arriving at the taxable income for the year because of the 10% taxable income limitation. Consequently, the $12,000 is carried forward to 2006 and fully deducted in that year. The excess charitable contribution reduces the corporation's current E & P for 2005 by $12,000 and increases its current E & P for 2006, when the deduction is allowed, by a like amount. The increase in E & P in 2006 is necessary because the charitable contribution carryover reduces the taxable income for that year (the starting point for computing E & P) and already has been taken into account in determining the E & P for 2005. ■

Gains and losses from property transactions generally affect the determination of E & P only to the extent that they are recognized for tax purposes. Thus, gains and losses deferred under the like-kind exchange provision and deferred involuntary conversion gains do not affect E & P until recognized. Accordingly, no adjustment is required for these items.

Accounting Method Adjustments. In addition to the above adjustments, accounting methods used for determining E & P are generally more conservative than those allowed under the income tax rules. For example, the installment method is not permitted for E & P purposes.[4] Thus, an adjustment is required for the deferred gain attributable to sales of property made during the year under the installment method. All principal payments are treated as having been received in the year of sale.

EXAMPLE 6

In 2005, Cardinal Corporation, a cash basis calendar year taxpayer, sells unimproved real estate (basis of $20,000) for $100,000. Under the terms of the sale, beginning in 2006, Cardinal will receive two annual payments of $50,000 each with interest of 9%. Cardinal Corporation does not elect out of the installment method. Since Cardinal's taxable income for 2005 will not reflect any of the gain from the sale, the corporation must make an $80,000 positive adjustment for 2005 (the deferred gain from the sale). Similarly, $40,000 negative adjustments will be required in 2006 and 2007 when the deferred gain is recognized under the installment method. ■

The alternative depreciation system (ADS) must be used for purposes of computing E & P.[5] This method requires straight-line depreciation over a recovery period equal to the Asset Depreciation Range (ADR) midpoint life.[6] Also, no 30 or 50 percent additional first-year depreciation is allowed under ADS.[7] If MACRS cost recovery is used for income tax purposes, a positive or negative adjustment equal to the difference between MACRS and ADS must be made each year. Likewise, when assets are disposed of, an additional adjustment to taxable income is required to allow for the difference in gain or loss resulting from the difference in income tax basis and the E & P basis.[8] The adjustments arising from depreciation are illustrated in the following example.

EXAMPLE 7

On January 2, 2003, White Corporation paid $30,000 to purchase equipment with an ADR midpoint life of 10 years and a MACRS class life of 7 years. The equipment was depreciated under MACRS with 30% additional first-year depreciation. The asset was sold on July 2, 2005, for $27,000. For purposes of determining taxable income and E & P, cost recovery claimed on the equipment is summarized below.

Year	Cost Recovery Computation	MACRS	ADS	Adjustment Amount
2003	$30,000 × 30% (additional first-year depreciation)	$ 9,000		
	($30,000 – $9,000) × 14.29%	3,001		
	$30,000 ÷ 10-year ADR recovery period × ½ (half-year for first year of service)		$1,500	$10,501
2004	($30,000 – $9,000) × 24.49%	5,143		
	$30,000 ÷ 10-year ADR recovery period		3,000	2,143
2005	($30,000 – $9,000) × 17.49% × ½ (half-year for year of disposal)	1,836		
	$30,000 ÷ 10-year ADR recovery period × ½ (half-year for year of disposal)		1,500	336
	Total cost recovery	$18,980	$6,000	$12,980

[4] § 312(n)(5).
[5] § 312(k)(3)(A).
[6] See § 168(g)(2). The ADR midpoint life for most assets is set out in Rev.Proc. 87–56, 1987–2 C.B. 674. The recovery period is 5 years for automobiles and light-duty trucks and 40 years for real property. For assets with no class life, the recovery period is 12 years.
[7] § 168(k)(2)(C).
[8] § 312(f)(1).

Each year White Corporation will increase taxable income by the adjustment amount indicated previously to determine E & P. In addition, when computing E & P for 2005, White will reduce taxable income by $12,980 to account for the excess gain recognized for income tax purposes, as shown below.

	Income Tax	E & P
Amount realized	$27,000	$ 27,000
Adjusted basis for income tax ($30,000 cost – $18,980 MACRS)	(11,020)	
Adjusted basis for E & P ($30,000 cost – $6,000 ADS)		(24,000)
Gain on sale	$15,980	$ 3,000
Adjustment amount ($3,000 – $15,980)	($12,980)	

In addition to more conservative depreciation methods, the E & P rules impose limitations on the deductibility of § 179 expense. In particular, this expense must be deducted over a period of five years for E & P purposes.[9] Thus, in any year that § 179 is elected, 80 percent of the resulting expense must be added back to taxable income to determine current E & P. In each of the following four years, a negative adjustment equal to 20 percent of the § 179 expense must be made.

A variety of other accounting method adjustments are also required to determine current E & P. For example, cost depletion is required for E & P purposes, so an adjustment must be made to taxable income in cases where percentage depletion is used. Similarly, the percentage of completion method is required for E & P purposes when accounting for long-term contracts, so an adjustment is required when the completed contract method is employed.[10] Intangible drilling costs and mine exploration and development costs may be deducted currently for income tax purposes, but must be capitalized for E & P. Once capitalized, these expenditures can be amortized under the E & P rules over 60 months for intangible drilling costs and over 120 months for mine exploration and development costs.[11]

SUMMARY OF E & P ADJUSTMENTS

Recall that E & P serves as a measure of the earnings of the corporation that are available for distribution as taxable dividends to the shareholders. Current E & P is determined by making a series of adjustments to the corporation's taxable income. These adjustments are reviewed in Concept Summary 19–1. Other items that affect E & P, such as property dividends and stock redemptions, are covered later in the chapter and are not included in Concept Summary 19–1.

CURRENT VERSUS ACCUMULATED E & P

Accumulated E & P is the total of all previous years' current E & P (since February 28, 1913) as computed on the first day of each tax year, reduced by distributions made from E & P. It is important to distinguish between **current E & P** and **accumulated E & P,** since the taxability of corporate distributions depends upon how these two accounts are allocated to each distribution made during the year. A complex set of rules governs the allocation process.[12] These rules are described in the following section and summarized in Concept Summary 19–2.

[9] § 312(k)(3)(B).
[10] § 312(n)(6).
[11] § 312(n)(2).

[12] Regulations relating to the source of a distribution are at Reg. § 1.316–2.

CONCEPT SUMMARY 19–1

E & P Adjustments

Nature of the Transaction	Adjustment to Taxable Income to Determine Current E & P	
	Addition	Subtraction
Tax-exempt income	X	
Dividends received deduction	X	
Deduction for domestic manufacturing income	X	
Collection of proceeds from insurance policy on life of corporate officer (in excess of cash surrender value)	X	
Deferred gain on installment sale (all gain is added to E & P in year of sale)	X	
Future recognition of installment sale gross profit		X
Excess capital loss and excess charitable contribution (over 10% limitation) in year incurred		X
Deduction of charitable contribution, NOL, or capital loss carryovers in succeeding taxable years (increases E & P because deduction reduces taxable income while E & P was reduced in a prior year)	X	
Federal income taxes paid		X
Federal income tax refund	X	
Loss on sale between related parties		X
Nondeductible fines and penalties		X
Nondeductible meal and entertainment expenses		X
Payment of premiums on insurance policy on life of corporate officer (in excess of increase in cash surrender value of policy)		X
Realized gain (not recognized) on an involuntary conversion	No effect	
Realized gain or loss (not recognized) on a like-kind exchange	No effect	
Percentage depletion (only cost depletion can reduce E & P)	X	
Accelerated depreciation (E & P is reduced only by straight-line, units-of-production, or machine hours depreciation)	X	X
Additional 30% or 50% first-year depreciation	X	
Section 179 expense in year elected (80%)	X	
Section 179 expense in four years following election (20% each year)		X
Intangible drilling costs deducted currently (reduce E & P in future years by amortizing costs over 60 months)	X	
Mine exploration and development costs (reduce E & P in future years by amortizing costs over 120 months)	X	

LO.3

Apply the rules for allocating earnings and profits to distributions.

ALLOCATING E & P TO DISTRIBUTIONS

When a positive balance exists in both the current and accumulated E & P accounts, corporate distributions are deemed to be made first from current E & P and then from accumulated E & P. When distributions exceed the amount of current E & P, it becomes necessary to allocate current and accumulated E & P to each distribution made during the year. Current E & P is allocated on a pro rata basis to each distribution. Accumulated E & P is applied in chronological order, beginning with

CONCEPT SUMMARY 19–2

Allocating E & P to Distributions

1. Current E & P is allocated first to distributions on a pro rata basis; then, accumulated E & P is applied (to the extent necessary) in chronological order beginning with the earliest distribution. See Example 8.
2. Unless and until the parties can show otherwise, it is presumed that current E & P covers all distributions. See Example 9.
3. When a deficit exists in accumulated E & P and a positive balance exists in current E & P, distributions are regarded as dividends to the extent of current E & P. See Example 10.
4. When a deficit exists in current E & P and a positive balance exists in accumulated E & P, the two accounts are netted at the date of distribution. If the resulting balance is zero or negative, the distribution is treated as a return of capital, first reducing the basis of the stock to zero, then generating taxable gain. If a positive balance results, the distribution is a dividend to the extent of the balance. Any current E & P deficit is allocated ratably during the year unless the parties can show otherwise. See Example 11.

the earliest distribution. As can be seen in the following example, this allocation is important if any shareholder sells stock during the year.

EXAMPLE 8

As of January 1 of the current year, Black Corporation has accumulated E & P of $10,000. Current E & P for the year amounts to $30,000. Megan and Matt are sole *equal* shareholders of Black from January 1 to July 31. On August 1, Megan sells all of her stock to Helen. Black makes two distributions to the shareholders during the year: $40,000 to Megan and Matt ($20,000 each) on July 1, and $40,000 to Matt and Helen ($20,000 each) on December 1. Current and accumulated E & P are allocated to the two distributions as follows:

	Source of Distribution		
	Current E & P	Accumulated E & P	Return of Capital
July 1 distribution ($40,000)	$15,000	$10,000	$15,000
December 1 distribution ($40,000)	15,000	–0–	25,000

Thus, since 50% of the total distributions are made on July 1 and December 1, respectively, one-half of current E & P is allocated to each of the two distributions. Accumulated E & P is applied in chronological order, so the entire amount is attributed to the July 1 distribution. The tax consequences to the shareholders are presented below.

	Shareholder		
	Megan	Matt	Helen
July distribution ($40,000)			
Dividend income—			
From current E & P ($15,000)	$ 7,500	$ 7,500	$ –0–
From accumulated E & P ($10,000)	5,000	5,000	–0–
Return of capital ($15,000)	7,500	7,500	–0–
December distribution ($40,000)			
Dividend income—			
From current E & P ($15,000)	–0–	7,500	7,500
From accumulated E & P ($0)	–0–	–0–	–0–
Return of capital ($25,000)	–0–	12,500	12,500

	Shareholder		
	Megan	Matt	Helen
Total dividend income	$12,500	$20,000	$ 7,500
Nontaxable return of capital (assuming sufficient basis in the stock investment)	$ 7,500	$20,000	$12,500

Because the balance in the accumulated E & P account is exhausted when it is applied to the July 1 distribution, Megan has more dividend income than Helen, even though both receive equal distributions during the year. In addition, each shareholder's basis is reduced by the nontaxable return of capital; any excess over basis results in taxable gain. ■

When the tax years of the corporation and its shareholders are not the same, it may be impossible to determine the amount of current E & P on a timely basis. For example, if shareholders use a calendar year and the corporation uses a fiscal year, then current E & P may not be ascertainable until after the shareholders' returns have been filed. To address this timing problem, the allocation rules presume that current E & P is sufficient to cover every distribution made during the year unless or until the parties can show otherwise.

EXAMPLE 9

Green Corporation uses a fiscal year of July 1 through June 30 for tax purposes. Carol, Green's only shareholder, uses a calendar year. As of July 1, 2005, Green Corporation has a zero balance in its accumulated E & P account. For fiscal year 2005–2006, the corporation suffers a $5,000 deficit in current E & P. On August 1, 2005, Green distributes $10,000 to Carol. The distribution is dividend income to Carol and is reported when she files her income tax return for the 2005 calendar year, on or before April 15, 2006. Because Carol cannot prove until June 30, 2006 that the corporation has a deficit for the 2005–2006 fiscal year, she must assume the $10,000 distribution is fully covered by current E & P. When Carol learns of the deficit, she can file an amended return for 2005 showing the $10,000 as a return of capital. ■

Additional difficulties arise when either the current or the accumulated E & P account has a deficit balance. In particular, when current E & P is positive and accumulated E & P has a deficit balance, accumulated E & P is *not* netted against current E & P. Instead, the distribution is deemed to be a taxable dividend to the extent of the positive current E & P balance.

EXAMPLE 10

At the beginning of the current year, Brown Corporation has a deficit of $30,000 in accumulated E & P. For the year, it has current E & P of $10,000 and distributes $5,000 to its shareholders. The $5,000 distribution is treated as a taxable dividend since it is deemed to have been made from current E & P. This is the case even though Brown Corporation still has a deficit in accumulated E & P at the end of the year. ■

ETHICAL CONSIDERATIONS

Shifting E & P

Ten years ago, Joe began a new business venture with his best friend and college roommate, Frankie. Joe owns 60 percent of the outstanding stock, and Frankie owns 40 percent. The business has had some difficult times, but things are starting to look up.

Yesterday, on December 1, Frankie told Joe that he wants a change of career and is planning to sell all of his stock to Joe's sister, Cindy, at the beginning of the following year. He would sell immediately, but he wants to wait until after the company pays out the current-year shareholder distribution (which is expected to be about $100,000). Cindy has been a long-time employee of the business and has often expressed an interest in becoming more involved. Joe is looking forward to working with his sister, but he now faces a terrible dilemma.

The corporation has a $350,000 deficit in accumulated E & P and only a small amount of current E & P to date (about $20,000). Within the next six weeks, however, Joe expects to sign a major deal with a very large client. If Joe signs the contract this month, the corporation will experience a $300,000 increase in current E & P for the year, causing the forthcoming distribution to be fully taxable to Frankie. As a result, most of next year's distribution would be treated as a tax-free return of capital for Cindy. Alternatively, if Joe waits until January, both he and Frankie will receive a nontaxable distribution this year, but next year's annual distribution will be taxable as a dividend to his sister. What should Joe do?

In contrast to the above rule, when a deficit exists in current E & P and a positive balance exists in accumulated E & P, the accounts are netted at the date of distribution. If the resulting balance is zero or negative, the distribution is a return of capital. If a positive balance results, the distribution is a dividend to the extent of the balance. Any current E & P deficit is allocated ratably during the year unless the parties can show otherwise.

EXAMPLE 11

At the beginning of the current year, Gray Corporation (a calendar year taxpayer) has accumulated E & P of $10,000. During the year, the corporation incurs a $15,000 deficit in current E & P that accrues ratably. On July 1, Gray distributes $6,000 in cash to Hal, its sole shareholder. To determine how much of the $6,000 cash distribution represents dividend income to Hal, the balances of both accumulated and current E & P as of July 1 are determined and netted. This is necessary because of the deficit in current E & P.

	Source of Distribution	
	Current E & P	**Accumulated E & P**
January 1		$10,000
July 1 (½ of $15,000 current E & P deficit)	($7,500)	2,500
July 1 distribution—$6,000:		
Dividend income: $2,500		
Return of capital: $3,500		

The balance in E & P on July 1 is $2,500. Thus, of the $6,000 distribution, $2,500 is taxed as a dividend, and $3,500 represents a return of capital. ■

Dividends

As noted earlier, distributions by a corporation from its E & P are treated as dividends. The tax treatment of dividends varies, depending on whether the shareholder receiving them is a corporation or another kind of taxpaying entity. All corporations treat dividends as ordinary income and are permitted a dividends received deduction (see Chapter 17). In contrast, other taxpayers may apply reduced tax rates on qualified dividends while nonqualified dividends are taxed as ordinary income.

RATIONALE FOR REDUCED TAX RATES ON DIVIDENDS

The double tax on corporate income has always been controversial. Reformers have argued that taxing corporations twice creates several distortions in the economy, including:

- An incentive to invest in noncorporate rather than corporate businesses.
- An incentive for corporations to finance operations with debt rather than equity because interest payments are deductible.
- An incentive for corporations to retain earnings and to structure distributions of profits to avoid the double tax.

Taken together, these distortions raise the cost of capital for corporate investments and increase the vulnerability of corporations in economic downturns due to excessive debt financing. Reformers argue that eliminating the double tax would remove these distortions, stimulate the economy (with estimated gains of up to $25 billion annually), and increase capital stock in the corporate sector by as much as $500 billion.[13] They also argue that elimination of the double tax would make the United States more competitive internationally, because the majority of our trading partners assess only one tax on corporate income. In contrast, supporters of the double tax argue that a double tax is appropriate because of the concentration of economic power held by publicly traded corporations, especially since the income tax is based on ability to pay and notions of fairness. They also argue that many of the distortions can already be avoided through the use of deductible payments by closely held C corporations and through partnerships, limited liability companies, and Subchapter S corporations.

In January 2003, President Bush unveiled a tax cut proposal that included a major shift in corporate tax policy toward elimination of the double tax. Most significantly, he proposed the complete elimination of any tax on dividend income received by individual taxpayers. The revenue loss from making dividends tax-free represented a significant portion of the proposal's $776 billion price tag.

Another solution to the double taxation of corporate income would have been to allow the corporation a deduction for dividend distributions. This alternative would offer the additional advantage of placing equity financing on an even playing field with debt financing. Like interest paid on debt obligations, dividends paid on stock would be deductible by the corporation. This approach was less politically feasible, however. Providing corporations with a benefit (i.e., making dividends deductible)—as opposed to providing shareholder-investors with a benefit (i.e., making dividends nontaxable)—is bound to be less acceptable to the voting public. As individuals generate more sympathy than corporations, the President opted for the solution that had a better chance of public support.

Besides being costly in terms of revenue loss, the Bush proposal was highly complex. Corporations would have been required to separate profits that had been subject to tax from those that had not. Only distributions of the former would have been nontaxable to shareholders. Otherwise what would have been intended as a single layer of taxation could have been converted to no taxation at all.

LO.4

Understand the tax treatment of dividends for individual shareholders.

QUALIFIED DIVIDENDS

Through the process of congressional compromise, the proposed zero tax rate on dividend income became a rate of 15 percent (5 percent for taxpayers in the bottom two tax brackets), and the definition of **qualified dividends** was simplified.

[13] Integration of Individual and Corporate Tax Systems, Report of the Department of the Treasury (January 1992).

Consequently, while the current tax law has moved closer to corporate tax reform, it has not yet realized the ideal of a single tax on corporate income.

Qualified Dividends—Application and Effect. Dividends that qualify under the new law are subject to a 15 percent tax rate for most individual taxpayers from 2003 to 2008. Individuals in the 10 or 15 percent rate brackets are subject to a 5 percent rate on dividends paid from 2003 to 2007. In 2008, dividends are exempt from tax for these lower-income taxpayers.[14] After 2008, unless new legislation is enacted, qualified dividends will once again be taxed as ordinary income, as they were prior to 2003. Notably, the lower rates on dividend income apply to both the regular income tax and the alternative minimum tax.

Qualified Dividends—Requirements. To be taxed at the lower rates, dividends must be paid by either domestic or certain qualified foreign corporations. Qualified foreign corporations include those traded on a U.S. stock exchange or any corporation located in a country that (1) has a comprehensive income tax treaty with the United States, (2) has an information-sharing agreement with the United States, and (3) is approved by the Treasury.[15]

Two other requirements must be met for dividends to qualify for the favorable rates. First, dividends paid to shareholders who hold both long and short positions in the stock do not qualify. Second, the stock on which the dividend is paid must be held for more than 60 days during the 121-day period beginning 60 days before the ex-dividend date.[16] To allow for settlement delays, the ex-dividend date is typically 2 days before the date of record on a dividend. This holding period rule parallels the rule applied to corporations that claim the dividends received deduction.[17]

EXAMPLE 12

In June of the current year, Green Corporation announces that a dividend of $1.50 will be paid on each share of its common stock, to shareholders of record on July 15. Amy and Corey, two unrelated shareholders, own 1,000 shares of the stock on the record date (July 15). Consequently, each receives $1,500 (1,000 shares × $1.50). Assume Amy purchased her stock on January 15 of this year, while Corey purchased her stock on July 1. Both shareholders sell their stock on July 20. To qualify for the lower dividend rate, stock must be held for more than 60 days during the 121-day period beginning 60 days prior to July 13 (the ex-dividend date). The $1,500 Amy receives is subject to preferential 15%/5% treatment. The $1,500 Corey receives, however, is not. Corey did not meet the 60-day holding requirement, so her dividend will be taxed as ordinary income. ■

LO.5

Understand the tax impact of property dividends on the recipient shareholder and the corporation making the distribution.

PROPERTY DIVIDENDS

Although most corporate distributions are cash, a corporation may distribute a **property dividend** for various reasons. The shareholders could want a particular property that is held by the corporation. Or, a corporation that is strapped for cash may want to distribute a dividend to its shareholders.

Property distributions have the same impact as distributions of cash except for effects attributable to any difference between the basis and the fair market value of the distributed property. In most situations, distributed property is appreciated, so its sale would result in a gain to the corporation. Distributions of property with a basis that differs from fair market value raise several tax questions.

[14]See §§ 1(h)(1) and (11).

[15]In Notice 2003–69, 2003–2 C.B. 851, the Treasury identified 51 qualifying countries (among those included in the list are the members of the European Union, the Russian Federation, Canada, and Mexico). Several countries were also specifically identified as nonqualifying. These include most of the former Soviet republics (except Kazakhstan), Bermuda, the Netherland Antilles, and Barbados.

[16]§ 1(h)(11)(B)(iii)(I).

[17]See § 246(c).

Companies Pay Record Dividends in 2004

In response to the 2003 tax cut on dividend income, companies in the Standard & Poor's 500 stock index are expected to pay out a record $183 billion in dividends in 2004. This continues a trend that started in late 2003, when corporations paid out a then-record $161 billion. Furthermore, a new paper published by the National Bureau of Economic Research suggests that the increase in dividend payments in the last two years extends beyond the companies in the S&P 500.

According to equity market analysts, the growth in dividend payments is being fueled both by larger dividends from companies with an established dividend-paying history (e.g., Wal-Mart, Coca-Cola, and Harley-Davidson) and by first-time dividends from growth companies that haven't paid dividends in the past (such as Staples, Cendant Corporation, and Costco Wholesale Corporation). In 2004, 374 of the S&P 500 are expected to pay dividends, up from 351 in 2002 and 370 in 2003. This is the highest rate since 1999.

The biggest dividend payers in the S&P 500 are usually Citigroup (which pays out $8.27 billion annually), General Electric (about $8.17 billion annually), and ExxonMobil (around $7 billion each year). The standout in 2004, however, was Microsoft, which paid a record one-time $32 billion dividend in December and doubled its usual quarterly dividend to boot. Some have speculated that Microsoft's large dividend reflected concerns that John Kerry might be elected president. (He was expected to eliminate the preferential tax rate on dividends.)

The sudden increase in dividend payments over the last year in response to the dividend tax cut runs counter to the expectations of many critics. They argued that corporations don't consider the taxes that their investors face when deciding whether to retain earnings or pay them out and that stock prices would not be affected by the tax cut. Consequently, they expected to see no effect on corporate behavior or the economy as a result of the cut. In their view, the rise in stock prices over the last 12 months might be attributable to economic factors that are independent of the effect of the dividend tax cut.

- For the shareholder:
  - What is the amount of the distribution?
  - What is the basis of the property in the shareholder's hands?
- For the corporation:
  - Is a gain or loss recognized as a result of the distribution?
  - What is the effect of the distribution on E & P?

Property Dividends—Effect on the Shareholder. When a corporation distributes property rather than cash to a shareholder, the amount distributed is measured by the fair market value of the property on the date of distribution.[18] As with a cash distribution, the portion of a property distribution covered by existing E & P is a dividend, and any excess is treated as a return of capital until basis is recovered. If the fair market value of the property distributed exceeds the corporation's E & P and the shareholder's basis in the stock investment, a capital gain usually results.

The amount distributed is reduced by any liabilities to which the distributed property is subject immediately before and immediately after the distribution and

[18]Section 301 describes the tax treatment of corporate distributions to shareholders.

by any liabilities of the corporation assumed by the shareholder. The basis in the distributed property to the shareholder is the fair market value of the property on the date of the distribution.

EXAMPLE 13

Robin Corporation has E & P of $60,000. It distributes land with a fair market value of $50,000 (adjusted basis of $30,000) to its sole shareholder, Charles. The land is subject to a liability of $10,000, which Charles assumes. Charles has a taxable dividend of $40,000 ($50,000 fair market value – $10,000 liability). The basis of the land to Charles is $50,000. ■

EXAMPLE 14

Red Corporation owns 10% of Tan Corporation. Tan has ample E & P to cover any distributions made during the year. One distribution made to Red Corporation consists of a vacant lot with an adjusted basis of $5,000 and a fair market value of $3,000. Red has a taxable dividend of $3,000, and its basis in the lot is $3,000. ■

Distributing property that has depreciated in value as a property dividend may reflect poor planning. Note what happens in Example 14. Basis of $2,000 disappears due to the loss (adjusted basis $5,000, fair market value $3,000). As an alternative, if Tan Corporation sells the lot, it could use the loss to reduce its taxes. Then Tan could distribute the $3,000 of proceeds to shareholders.

Property Dividends—Effect on the Corporation. All distributions of appreciated property generate gain recognition to the distributing corporation.[19] In effect, a corporation that distributes appreciated property is treated as if it had sold the property to the shareholder for its fair market value. However, the distributing corporation does *not* recognize loss on distributions of property.

EXAMPLE 15

A corporation distributes land (basis of $10,000 and fair market value of $30,000) to a shareholder. The corporation recognizes a gain of $20,000. ■

EXAMPLE 16

Assume the property in Example 15 has a basis of $30,000 and a fair market value of $10,000. The corporation does not recognize a loss on the distribution. ■

If the distributed property is subject to a liability in excess of its basis or the shareholder assumes such a liability, a special rule applies. The fair market value of the property for purposes of determining gain on the distribution is treated as not being less than the amount of the liability.[20]

EXAMPLE 17

Assume the land in Example 15 is subject to a liability of $35,000. The corporation recognizes a gain of $25,000 on the distribution ($35,000 – $10,000). ■

Corporate distributions reduce E & P by the amount of money distributed or by the *greater* of the fair market value or the adjusted basis of property distributed, less the amount of any liability on the property.[21] E & P is increased by gain recognized on appreciated property distributed as a property dividend.

EXAMPLE 18

Crimson Corporation distributes property (basis of $10,000 and fair market value of $20,000) to Brenda, its shareholder. Crimson recognizes a gain of $10,000. Crimson's E & P is increased by the $10,000 gain and decreased by the $20,000 fair market value of the distribution. Brenda has dividend income of $20,000 (presuming sufficient E & P). ■

[19]Section 311 describes how corporations are taxed on distributions.
[20]§ 311(b)(2).
[21]§§ 312(a), (b), and (c).

EXAMPLE 19

Assume the same facts as in Example 18, except that the adjusted basis of the property in the hands of Crimson Corporation is $25,000. Because the loss is not recognized and the adjusted basis is greater than fair market value, E & P is reduced by $25,000. Brenda reports dividend income of $20,000. ■

EXAMPLE 20

Assume the same facts as in Example 19, except that the property is subject to a liability of $6,000. E & P is now reduced by $19,000 ($25,000 adjusted basis – $6,000 liability). Brenda has a dividend of $14,000 ($20,000 amount of the distribution – $6,000 liability), and her basis in the property is $20,000. ■

Under no circumstances can a distribution, whether cash or property, either generate a deficit in E & P or add to a deficit in E & P. Deficits can arise only through corporate losses.

EXAMPLE 21

Teal Corporation has accumulated E & P of $10,000 at the beginning of the current tax year. During the year, it has current E & P of $15,000. At the end of the year, it distributes cash of $30,000 to its sole shareholder, Walter. Teal's E & P at the end of the year is zero. The accumulated E & P of $10,000 is increased by current E & P of $15,000 and reduced by $25,000 because of the dividend distribution. The remaining $5,000 of the distribution to Walter does not reduce E & P because a distribution cannot generate a deficit in E & P. Instead, the remaining $5,000 reduces Walter's stock basis and/or produces a capital gain to Walter. ■

LO.6

Understand the nature and treatment of constructive dividends.

CONSTRUCTIVE DIVIDENDS

Any measurable economic benefit conveyed by a corporation to its shareholders can be treated as a dividend for Federal income tax purposes even though it is not formally declared or designated as a dividend. Also, it need not be issued pro rata to all shareholders.[22] Nor must the distribution satisfy the legal requirements of a dividend as set forth by applicable state law. This benefit, often described as a **constructive dividend,** is distinguishable from actual corporate distributions of cash and property in form only.

For tax purposes, constructive distributions are treated the same as actual distributions.[23] Thus, corporate shareholders are entitled to the dividends received deduction (see Chapter 17), and other shareholders can apply the preferential tax rates (5 and 15 percent) on qualified constructive dividends. The constructive distribution is taxable as a dividend only to the extent of the corporation's current and accumulated E & P. The burden of proving that the distribution constitutes a return of capital because of inadequate E & P rests with the taxpayer.[24]

Constructive dividend situations usually arise in closely held corporations. Here, the dealings between the parties are less structured, and, frequently, formalities are not preserved. The constructive dividend serves as a substitute for actual distributions. Usually, it is intended to accomplish some tax objective not available through the use of direct dividends. The shareholders may be attempting to distribute corporate profits in a form deductible to the corporation.[25] Alternatively, the shareholders may be seeking benefits for themselves while avoiding the recognition of income. Some constructive dividends are, in reality, disguised dividends. But not all constructive dividends are deliberate attempts to avoid actual and formal

[22]See *Lengsfield v. Comm.*, 57–1 USTC ¶9437, 50 AFTR 1683, 241 F.2d 508 (CA–5, 1957).

[23]*Simon v. Comm.*, 57–2 USTC ¶9989, 52 AFTR 698, 248 F.2d 869 (CA–8, 1957).

[24]*DiZenzo v. Comm.*, 65–2 USTC ¶9518, 16 AFTR2d 5107, 348 F.2d 122 (CA–2, 1965).

[25]Recall that dividend distributions do not provide the distributing corporation with an income tax deduction, although they do reduce E & P.

dividends; many are inadvertent. Thus, an awareness of the various constructive dividend situations is essential to protect the parties from unanticipated, undesirable tax consequences. The most frequently encountered types of constructive dividends are summarized below.

Shareholder Use of Corporate-Owned Property. A constructive dividend can occur when a shareholder uses a corporation's property for personal purposes at no cost. Personal use of corporate-owned automobiles, airplanes, yachts, fishing camps, hunting lodges, and other entertainment facilities is commonplace in some closely held corporations. The shareholder has dividend income to the extent of the fair rental value of the property for the period of its personal use.

Bargain Sale of Corporate Property to a Shareholder. Shareholders often purchase property from a corporation at a cost below the fair market value of the property. These bargain sales produce dividend income to the extent that the property's fair market value on the date of sale differs from the amount the shareholder paid for the property.[26] These situations might be avoided by appraising the property on or about the date of the sale. The appraised value should become the price to be paid by the shareholder.

Bargain Rental of Corporate Property. A bargain rental of corporate property by a shareholder also produces dividend income. Here the measure of the constructive dividend is the excess of the property's fair rental value over the rent actually paid. Again, appraisal data should be used to avoid any questionable situations.

Payments for the Benefit of a Shareholder. If a corporation pays an obligation of a shareholder, the payment is treated as a constructive dividend. The obligation involved need not be legally binding on the shareholder; it may, in fact, be a moral obligation.[27] Forgiveness of shareholder indebtedness by the corporation creates an identical problem.[28] Excessive rentals paid by a corporation for the use of shareholder property also are treated as constructive dividends.

Unreasonable Compensation. A salary payment to a shareholder-employee that is deemed to be **unreasonable compensation** is frequently treated as a constructive dividend and therefore is not deductible by the corporation. In determining the reasonableness of salary payments, the following factors are considered:

- The employee's qualifications.
- A comparison of salaries with dividend distributions.
- The prevailing rates of compensation for comparable positions in comparable business concerns.
- The nature and scope of the employee's work.
- The size and complexity of the business.
- A comparison of salaries paid with both gross and net income.
- The taxpayer's salary policy toward all employees.
- For small corporations with a limited number of officers, the amount of compensation paid to the employee in question in previous years.
- Whether a reasonable shareholder would have agreed to the level of compensation paid.[29]

[26]Reg. § 1.301–1(j).

[27]*Montgomery Engineering Co. v. U.S.*, 64–2 USTC ¶9618, 13 AFTR2d 1747, 230 F.Supp. 838 (D.Ct. N.J., 1964), *aff'd* in 65–1 USTC ¶9368, 15 AFTR2d 746, 344 F.2d 996 (CA–3, 1965).

[28]Reg. § 1.301–1(m).

[29]All but the final factor in this list are identified in *Mayson Manufacturing Co. v. Comm.*, 49–2 USTC ¶9467, 38 AFTR 1028, 178 F.2d 115 (CA–6, 1949). The final factor, the "reasonable shareholder" test, is more recent. For example, see *Alpha Medical, Inc. v. Comm.*, 99–1 USTC ¶50,461, 83 AFTR2d 99–697, 172 F.3d 942 (CA–6, 1999).

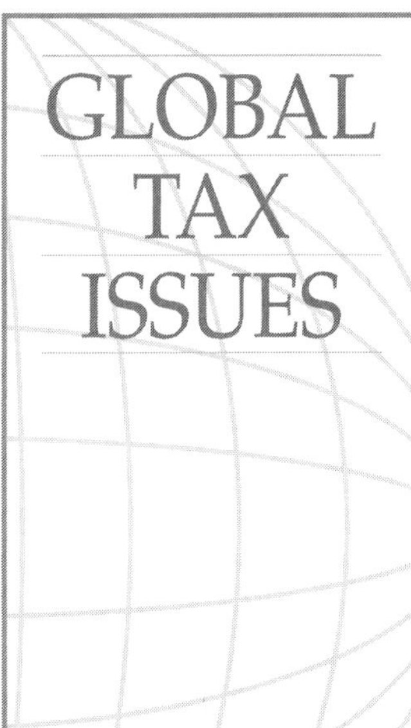

Deemed Dividends from Controlled Foreign Corporations

It is not uncommon for U.S. multinational companies to conduct business overseas through the use of foreign corporations. Most often, these foreign corporations are controlled by the U.S. parent. Called controlled foreign corporations (CFCs), such entities would be ideal for income avoidance if incorporated in a low-tax jurisdiction (i.e., a tax haven country). Further, U.S. income tax on their profits would be deferred if no dividends are distributed to the U.S. parent.

Well aware of the latter possibility, the tax law compels a U.S. shareholder to recognize as income the profits of a CFC that are not distributed. In contrast to constructive dividends, the "deemed dividend" distribution increases the basis the U.S. company has in the foreign corporation's stock. Furthermore, when the deemed dividend is ultimately distributed to the parent (i.e., repatriated), no income results. Thus, the CFC rules prevent deferral but are not intended to lead to double taxation.

Loans to Shareholders. Advances to shareholders that are not bona fide loans are constructive dividends. Whether an advance qualifies as a bona fide loan is a question of fact to be determined in light of the particular circumstances. Factors considered in determining whether the advance is a bona fide loan include the following:[30]

- Whether the advance is on open account or is evidenced by a written instrument.
- Whether the shareholder furnished collateral or other security for the advance.
- How long the advance has been outstanding.
- Whether any repayments have been made, excluding dividend sources.
- The shareholder's ability to repay the advance.
- The shareholder's use of the funds (e.g., payment of routine bills versus nonrecurring, extraordinary expenses).
- The regularity of the advances.
- The dividend-paying history of the corporation.

Even when a corporation makes a bona fide loan to a shareholder, a constructive dividend may be triggered, equal to the amount of imputed (forgone) interest on the loan.[31] Imputed interest equals the amount by which interest the Federal government pays on new borrowings, compounded semiannually, exceeds the interest charged on the loan. When the imputed interest provision applies, the shareholder is deemed to have made an interest payment to the corporation equal to the amount of imputed interest, and the corporation is deemed to have repaid the imputed interest to the shareholder through a constructive dividend. As a result, the corporation receives interest income and makes a nondeductible dividend payment, and the shareholder has taxable dividend income that may be offset with an interest deduction.

EXAMPLE 22

Mallard Corporation lends its principal shareholder, Henry, $100,000 on January 2 of the current year. The loan is interest-free and payable on demand. On December 31, the imputed interest rules are applied. Assuming the Federal rate is 6%, compounded semiannually, the

[30] *Fin Hay Realty Co. v. U.S.*, 68–2 USTC ¶9438, 22 AFTR2d 5004, 398 F.2d 694 (CA–3, 1968).

[31] See § 7872.

amount of imputed interest is $6,090. This amount is deemed paid by Henry to Mallard in the form of interest. Mallard is then deemed to return the amount to Henry as a constructive dividend. Thus, Henry has dividend income of $6,090, which may be offset with a deduction for the interest deemed paid to Mallard. Mallard has interest income of $6,090 for the interest received, with no offsetting deduction for the dividend payment. ■

Loans to a Corporation by Shareholders. Shareholder loans to a corporation may be reclassified as equity if the debt has too many features of stock. Any interest and principal payments made by the corporation to the shareholder are then treated as constructive dividends. This topic was covered more thoroughly in the discussion of "thin capitalization" in Chapter 18.

LO.7

Distinguish between taxable and nontaxable stock dividends and stock rights.

STOCK DIVIDENDS AND STOCK RIGHTS

Stock Dividends. Historically, **stock dividends** were excluded from income on the theory that the ownership interest of the shareholder was unchanged as a result of the distribution.[32] Recognizing that some distributions of stock could affect ownership interests, the 1954 Code included a provision (§ 305) taxing stock dividends where (1) the stockholder could elect to receive either stock or property or (2) the stock dividends were in discharge of preference dividends. However, because this provision applied to only a narrow range of transactions, corporations were able to develop an assortment of alternative methods that circumvented taxation and still affected shareholders' proportionate interests in the corporation.[33] In response, the scope of § 305 was expanded.

In its current state, the provisions of § 305 are based on the proportionate interest concept. As a general rule, stock dividends are excluded from income if they are pro rata distributions of stock or stock rights, paid on common stock. Five exceptions to this general rule exist. These exceptions deal with various disproportionate distribution situations. If stock dividends are not taxable, the corporation's E & P is not reduced.[34] If the stock dividends are taxable, the distributing corporation treats the distribution in the same manner as any other taxable property dividend.

If a stock dividend is taxable, the shareholder's basis in the newly received shares is fair market value, and the holding period starts on the date of receipt. If a stock dividend is not taxable, the basis of the stock on which the dividend is distributed is reallocated.[35] If the dividend shares are identical to these formerly held shares, basis in the old stock is reallocated by dividing the taxpayer's basis in the old stock by the total number of shares. If the dividend stock is not identical to the underlying shares (e.g., a stock dividend of preferred on common), basis is determined by allocating the basis of the formerly held shares between the old and new stock according to the fair market value of each. The holding period includes the holding period of the formerly held stock.[36]

EXAMPLE 23

Gail bought 1,000 shares of common stock two years ago for $10,000. In the current tax year, she receives 10 shares of common stock as a nontaxable stock dividend. Gail's basis of $10,000 is divided by 1,010. Each share of stock has a basis of $9.90 instead of the pre-dividend $10 basis. ■

[32]See *Eisner v. Macomber*, 1 USTC ¶32, 3 AFTR 3020, 40 S.Ct. 189 (USSC, 1920).
[33]See "Stock Dividends," S.Rept. 91–552, 1969–3 C.B. 519.
[34]§ 312(d)(1).
[35]§ 307(a).
[36]§ 1223(5).

THE REIT (REAL ESTATE INVESTMENT TRUST) KIND OF DIVIDENDS

REITs are tax-exempt corporations (and sometimes trusts) that receive most of their earnings from real estate activities. To qualify, the entity must pay out at least 95 percent of its taxable income as dividends each year. As a result of this requirement, REITs typically have a difficult time retaining cash to expand and acquire new properties.

Recently, in a bid to overcome the tax-based growth restriction, a REIT offered a creative dividend plan to its owners. In this plan, each shareholder could choose between two types of dividends: either a specified amount of cash per share of common stock or an equivalent value in depositary shares, representing an interest in the company's newly created class of common stock. Ordinarily, stock distributions are not considered taxable dividends and do not meet the 95 percent distribution requirement imposed on REITs. However, because shareholders were given a choice between stock and cash, the stock was considered a property distribution and, to the extent of E & P, was taxed to shareholders at its fair market value. This new technique enabled the company to meet the requirements imposed on REITs while permitting it to accumulate the cash needed to grow.

EXAMPLE 24

Assume Gail received, instead, a nontaxable preferred stock dividend of 100 shares. The preferred stock has a fair market value of $1,000, and the common stock, on which the preferred is distributed, has a fair market value of $19,000. After the receipt of the stock dividend, the basis of the common stock is $9,500, and the basis of the preferred is $500, computed as follows:

Fair market value of common	$19,000
Fair market value of preferred	1,000
	$20,000
Basis of common: $^{19}/_{20} \times \$10,000$	$ 9,500
Basis of preferred: $^{1}/_{20} \times \$10,000$	$ 500

■

Stock Rights. The rules for determining taxability of **stock rights** are identical to those for determining taxability of stock dividends. If the rights are taxable, the recipient has income to the extent of the fair market value of the rights. The fair market value then becomes the shareholder-distributee's basis in the rights.[37] If the rights are exercised, the holding period for the new stock begins on the date the rights (whether taxable or nontaxable) are exercised. The basis of the new stock is the basis of the rights plus the amount of any other consideration given.

If stock rights are not taxable and the value of the rights is less than 15 percent of the value of the old stock, the basis of the rights is zero. However, the shareholder may elect to have some of the basis in the formerly held stock allocated to the rights.[38] The election is made by attaching a statement to the shareholder's return for the year in which the rights are received.[39] If the fair market value of the rights is 15 percent or more of the value of the old stock and the rights are exercised or sold, the shareholder *must* allocate some of the basis in the formerly held stock to the rights.

[37] Reg. § 1.305–1(b).
[38] § 307(b)(1).
[39] Reg. § 1.307–2.

Corporate Cash Reserves Affect the Frequency of Stock Redemptions

The economic and financial market slumps of 2001 and 2002, along with the uneven economic recovery that followed, prompted many corporate executives to build up corporate cash reserves to record levels. However, finding productive uses for this cash in the current economic environment can be challenging. One consequence of the higher cash reserves has been an increase in stock buybacks (i.e., redemptions) over the last two years. Many corporations have also increased their dividend payouts in response to the reduction in tax rates applicable to dividends. Debt reduction also appears to have been a favorite use for the excess cash reserves.

EXAMPLE 25

A corporation with common stock outstanding declares a nontaxable dividend payable in rights to subscribe to common stock. Each right entitles the holder to purchase one share of stock for $90. One right is issued for every two shares of stock owned. Fred owns 400 shares of stock purchased two years ago for $15,000. At the time of the distribution of the rights, the market value of the common stock is $100 per share, and the market value of the rights is $8 per right. Fred receives 200 rights. He exercises 100 rights and sells the remaining 100 rights three months later for $9 per right.

Fred need not allocate the cost of the original stock to the rights because the value of the rights is less than 15% of the value of the stock ($1,600 ÷ $40,000 = 4%). If Fred does not allocate his original stock basis to the rights, the tax consequences are as follows:

- Basis in the new stock is $9,000 ($90 × 100). The holding period of the new stock begins on the date the stock was purchased.
- Sale of the rights produces long-term capital gain of $900 ($9 × 100). The holding period of the rights starts with the date the original 400 shares of stock were acquired.

If Fred elects to allocate basis to the rights, the tax consequences are as follows:

- Basis in the stock is $14,423 [$40,000 (value of stock) ÷ $41,600 (value of rights and stock) × $15,000 (cost of stock)].
- Basis in the rights is $577 [$1,600 (value of rights) ÷ $41,600 (value of rights and stock) × $15,000 (cost of stock)].
- When Fred exercises the rights, his basis in the new stock will be $9,288.50 [$9,000 (cost) + $288.50 (basis in 100 rights)].
- Sale of the rights would produce a long-term capital gain of $611.50 [$900 (selling price) – $288.50 (basis in the remaining 100 rights)]. ■

LO.8

Identify various stock redemptions that qualify for sale or exchange treatment.

Stock Redemptions

OVERVIEW

In a **stock redemption,** a corporation distributes cash or other property in exchange for a shareholder's stock in the corporation. Except for the fact that the shareholder is selling the stock back to the issuing corporation, a stock redemption resembles a sale of stock to an unrelated third party. While a sale of stock to an outsider invariably results in sale or exchange treatment, only a *qualifying* stock redemption is treated as a sale for tax purposes.

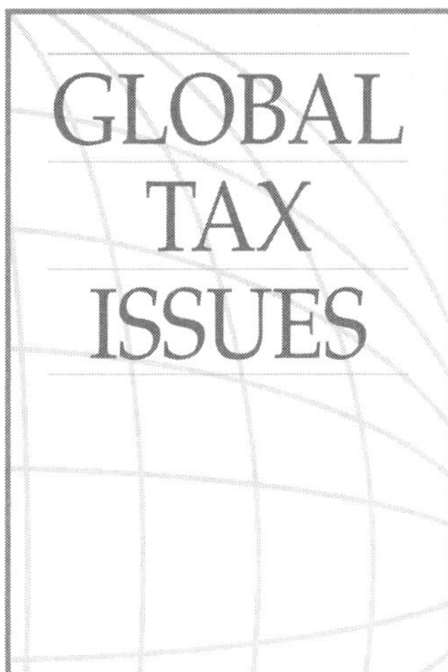

FOREIGN SHAREHOLDERS PREFER SALE OR EXCHANGE TREATMENT IN STOCK REDEMPTIONS

As a general rule, foreign shareholders of U.S. corporations are subject to U.S. tax on dividend income but not on capital gains. In some situations, a nonresident alien is taxed on a capital gain from the disposition of stock in a U.S. corporation, but only if the stock was effectively connected with the conduct of a U.S. trade or business of the individual. Foreign corporations are similarly taxed on gains from the sale of U.S. stock investments. Whether a stock redemption qualifies for sale or exchange treatment therefore takes on added significance for foreign shareholders. If one of the qualifying stock redemption rules can be satisfied, the foreign shareholder typically will avoid U.S. tax on the transaction. If, instead, dividend income is the result, a 30 percent withholding tax typically applies. For further details, see Chapter 25.

Nonqualifying stock redemptions are denied sale or exchange treatment because they are deemed to have the same effect as dividend distributions. For example, if a shareholder owns all the stock of a corporation and sells a portion of that stock to the corporation, the shareholder's ownership interest in the corporation does not change. After the redemption, the shareholder still owns all the outstanding stock of the corporation. In this situation, the stock redemption resembles a dividend distribution and is taxed as such.

Stock redemptions occur for a variety of reasons. For instance, a redemption is often used to acquire the stock of a retiring or deceased shareholder. Having the corporation provide the funds to purchase the stock relieves the remaining shareholders of the need to use their own money to aquire the stock. Further, stock redemptions also occur as a result of property settlements in divorce actions. For example, in a divorce action involving joint ownership of corporate shares, the stock interest of one spouse must be bought out. Using a redemption to buy out that spouse's shares relieves the other spouse from having to use his or her funds for the transaction.

Noncorporate shareholders generally prefer to have a stock redemption treated as a sale or exchange rather than as a dividend distribution. For such taxpayers, the maximum tax rate for long-term capital gains is currently 15 percent (5 percent for taxpayers in the 10 or 15 percent marginal tax bracket). The preference for qualifying stock redemption treatment is based on the fact that such transactions result in (1) the tax-free recovery of the redeemed stock's basis and (2) capital gains that can be offset by capital losses. In a nonqualified stock redemption, the *entire* distribution is taxed as dividend income (assuming adequate E & P), which, although taxed at the same rate as long-term capital gains, cannot be offset by capital losses.

EXAMPLE 26

Abby, an individual in the 35% tax bracket, acquired stock in Quail Corporation four years ago for $300,000. In the current year, Quail Corporation (E & P of $1 million) redeems her shares for $450,000. If the redemption qualifies for sale or exchange treatment, Abby has a long-term capital gain of $150,000 [$450,000 (redemption amount) – $300,000 (basis)]. Her tax liability on the $150,000 gain is $22,500 ($150,000 × 15%). If the stock redemption does not qualify as a sale or exchange, the entire distribution is treated as a dividend and Abby's tax liability is $67,500 ($450,000 × 15%). Thus, Abby saves $45,000 ($67,500 – $22,500) in income taxes if the transaction is a qualifying stock redemption. ■

EXAMPLE 27

Assume in Example 26 that Abby has a capital loss carryover of $100,000 in the current tax year. If the transaction is a qualifying stock redemption, Abby can offset the entire $100,000 capital loss carryover against her $150,000 long-term capital gain. As a result, only $50,000 of the gain is taxed, and her tax liability is only $7,500 ($50,000 × 15%). On the other hand, if the transaction does not qualify for sale or exchange treatment, the entire $450,000 is taxed at 15%. In addition, assuming she has no capital gains in the current year, Abby is able to deduct only $3,000 of the $100,000 capital loss carryover to offset her other (ordinary) income. ■

Corporate shareholders, however, normally receive more favorable tax treatment from a dividend distribution than would result from a qualifying stock redemption. Corporate shareholders will report only a small portion of a dividend distribution as taxable income because of the dividends received deduction (see Chapter 17). Further, the preferential tax rate applicable to dividend and long-term capital gain income is not available to corporations. Consequently, tax planning for stock redemptions must consider the varying preferences of corporate and noncorporate shareholders.

EXAMPLE 28

Assume in Example 26 that Abby is a corporation, that the stock represents a 40% ownership interest in Quail Corporation, and that Abby has corporate taxable income of $850,000 before the redemption transaction. If the transaction is a qualifying stock redemption, Abby has a long-term capital gain of $150,000 that is subject to tax at 34%, or $51,000. On the other hand, if the $450,000 distribution is treated as a dividend, Abby has a dividends received deduction of $360,000 ($450,000 × 80%), so only $90,000 of the payment is taxed. Consequently, Abby's tax liability on the transaction is only $30,600 ($90,000 × 34%). ■

When a qualifying stock redemption results in a *loss* to the shareholder rather than a gain, § 267 disallows loss recognition if the shareholder owns (directly or indirectly) more than 50 percent of the corporation's stock. A shareholder's basis in property received in a stock redemption, qualifying or nonqualified, generally will be the property's fair market value, determined as of the date of the redemption. Further, the holding period of the property begins on that date.

The Code establishes the criteria for determining whether a transaction is a qualifying stock redemption for tax purposes and thus receives sale or exchange treatment. The terminology in an agreement between the parties is not controlling, nor is state law. Under § 302(a), a redemption satisfying one of the special rules will receive sale or exchange treatment. Additionally, § 303 treats certain distributions of property to an estate in exchange for a deceased shareholder's stock as qualifying stock redemptions.

HISTORICAL BACKGROUND

Under prior law, stock redemptions that constituted ordinary dividend distributions were distinguished from those qualifying for sale or exchange treatment by the so-called *dividend equivalency rule.* When a redemption was essentially equivalent to a dividend, it did not qualify for sale or exchange treatment. The entire amount received by the shareholder was subject to taxation as dividend income to the extent of the corporation's E & P.

To eliminate the uncertainty and subjectivity surrounding the dividend equivalency rule, Congress enacted several objective tests for determining the status of a redemption. Currently, the following types of stock redemptions qualify for sale or exchange treatment:

- Distributions not essentially equivalent to a dividend (subsequently referred to as not essentially equivalent redemptions).
- Distributions substantially disproportionate in terms of shareholder effect (subsequently referred to as disproportionate redemptions).

■ **EXHIBIT 19–1**
Stock Attribution Rules

	Deemed or Constructive Ownership
• Family	An individual is deemed to own stock owned by his or her spouse, children, grandchildren, and parents (not siblings or grandparents).
• Partnership	A partner is deemed to own the stock owned by a partnership to the extent of the partner's proportionate interest in the partnership.
	Stock owned by a partner is deemed to be owned in full by a partnership.
• Estate or trust	A beneficiary or heir is deemed to own the stock owned by an estate or trust to the extent of the beneficiary's or heir's proportionate interest in the estate or trust.
	Stock owned by a beneficiary or heir is deemed to be owned in full by an estate or trust.
• Corporation	Stock owned by a corporation is deemed to be owned proportionately by any shareholder owning 50% or more of the corporation's stock.
	Stock owned by a shareholder who owns 50% or more of a corporation is deemed to be owned in full by the corporation.

- Distributions in complete termination of a shareholder's interest (subsequently referred to as complete termination redemptions).
- Distributions to pay a shareholder's death taxes (subsequently referred to as redemptions to pay death taxes).

Concept Summary 19–3 at the end of this section summarizes the requirements for each of these qualifying stock redemptions.

STOCK ATTRIBUTION RULES

To qualify for sale or exchange treatment, a stock redemption generally must result in a substantial reduction in a shareholder's ownership interest in the corporation. In the absence of this reduction in ownership interest, the redemption proceeds are taxed as dividend income. In determining whether a stock redemption has sufficiently reduced a shareholder's interest, the stock owned by certain related parties is attributed to the redeeming shareholder.[40] Thus, the stock **attribution** rules must be considered along with the stock redemption provisions. Under these rules, related parties are defined to include the following family members: spouses, children, grandchildren, and parents. Attribution also takes place *from* and *to* partnerships, estates, trusts, and corporations (50 percent or more ownership required in the case of regular corporations). Exhibit 19–1 summarizes the stock attribution rules.

EXAMPLE 29

Larry owns 30% of the stock in Blue Corporation, with the other 70% being held by his children. For purposes of the stock attribution rules, Larry is treated as owning 100% of the stock in Blue Corporation. He owns 30% directly and, because of the family attribution rules, 70% indirectly. ■

[40]§ 318.

A Novel Interpretation of Stock Attribution Rules

As part of an estate plan, a married couple made large gifts of voting stock in a family-owned corporation to several trusts set up for the benefit of their children. The stock was then transferred to a voting trust where nonfamily trustees held legal title to the stock, but the children's trusts were the beneficial owners of the stock. The taxpayers caused the corporation to twice redeem some of their stock: first, to raise funds to pay the gift tax resulting from the transfers to the children's trusts, and then again to raise funds to pay the income taxes resulting from the dividends they initially reported on the first redemption.

The taxpayers then filed amended returns for the years in question, asserting that the two stock redemptions were instead not essentially equivalent redemptions qualifying for sale or exchange treatment. This treatment was possible only if the stock held by the voting trust was not deemed to be owned by the taxpayers under the stock attribution rules, as posited by the IRS. The taxpayers offered two alternative arguments for their position: (1) the attribution rules did not apply to a not essentially equivalent redemption because such redemptions are subject to a facts and circumstance test instead, and (2) the stock held by the voting trust should be treated as nonvoting stock because the trustees were nonfamily members who would not be influenced by the taxpayers. Predictably, the IRS rejected both arguments and, having found no meaningful reduction of ownership interest, ruled that the redemptions were taxable dividends. (See Chief Counsel Advice 200409001.)

EXAMPLE 30

Chris owns 40% of the stock in Gray Corporation. The other 60% is owned by a partnership in which Chris has a 20% interest. Chris is deemed to own 52% of Gray Corporation: 40% directly and, because of the partnership interest, 12% indirectly (20% × 60%). ■

As discussed later, the *family* attribution rules (refer to Example 29) can be waived in the case of some complete termination redemptions. In addition, the stock attribution rules do not apply to stock redemptions to pay death taxes.

NOT ESSENTIALLY EQUIVALENT REDEMPTIONS

Under § 302(b)(1), a redemption qualifies for sale or exchange treatment if it is "not essentially equivalent to a dividend." This provision represents a continuation of the dividend equivalency rule applicable under prior law. The earlier redemption language was retained specifically for redemptions of preferred stock because shareholders often have no control over when corporations call in such stock.[41] Like its predecessor, the **not essentially equivalent redemption** lacks an objective test. Instead, each case must be resolved on a facts and circumstances basis.[42]

Based upon the Supreme Court's decision in *U.S. v. Davis*,[43] a redemption will qualify as a not essentially equivalent redemption only when the shareholder's interest in the redeeming corporation has been meaningfully reduced. In determining whether the **meaningful reduction test** has been met, the stock attribution rules apply. A decrease in the redeeming shareholder's voting control appears to be the most significant indicator of a meaningful reduction,[44] but reductions in

[41] See S.Rept. No. 1622, 83d Cong., 2d Sess., 44 (1954).
[42] Reg. § 1.302–2(b).
[43] 70–1 USTC ¶9289, 25 AFTR2d 70–827, 90 S.Ct. 1041 (USSC, 1970).
[44] See, for example, *Jack Paparo*, 71 T.C. 692 (1979).

the rights of redeeming shareholders to share in corporate earnings or to receive corporate assets upon liquidation are also considered.[45] The meaningful reduction test is applied whether common stock or preferred stock is being redeemed.

EXAMPLE 31

Pat owns 58% of the common stock of Falcon Corporation. After a redemption of part of Pat's stock, he owns 51% of the Falcon stock. Pat continues to have dominant voting rights in Falcon; thus, the redemption is treated as essentially equivalent to a dividend, and Pat has dividend income equal to the entire amount of the distribution, assuming adequate E & P. ■

EXAMPLE 32

Maroon Corporation redeems 2% of its stock from Maria. Before the redemption, Maria owned 10% of Maroon Corporation. In this case, the redemption may qualify as a not essentially equivalent redemption. Maria experiences a reduction in her voting rights, her right to participate in current earnings and accumulated surplus, and her right to share in net assets upon liquidation. ■

If a redemption distribution is treated as a dividend, the basis in the stock redeemed attaches to the shareholder's remaining stock (or to stock the shareholder owns constructively).[46] This is the case in any redemption that does not satisfy any of the qualifying stock redemption provisions.

EXAMPLE 33

Fran and Floyd, wife and husband, each own 50 shares in Grouse Corporation, representing 100% of the corporation's stock. All the stock was purchased for $50,000. Both Fran and Floyd serve as directors of the corporation. The corporation redeems Floyd's 50 shares, but he continues to serve as director of the corporation. The redemption is treated as a dividend distribution (assuming adequate E & P) because Floyd constructively owns Fran's stock. Floyd's basis in the 50 shares redeemed, $25,000, attaches to Fran's stock. Fran then has a basis of $50,000 in the 50 shares she owns in Grouse. ■

DISPROPORTIONATE REDEMPTIONS

A stock redemption qualifies for sale or exchange treatment under § 302(b)(2) as a **disproportionate redemption** if the following conditions are met:

- The distribution is substantially disproportionate. To be substantially disproportionate, the shareholder must own, after the distribution, *less than* 80 percent of the interest owned in the corporation before the redemption. For example, if a shareholder owns a 60 percent interest in a corporation that redeems part of the stock, the redemption is substantially disproportionate only if the shareholder's ownership interest after the redemption is less than 48 percent (80 percent of 60 percent).
- The shareholder owns, after the distribution, *less than* 50 percent of the total combined voting power of all classes of stock entitled to vote.

In determining a shareholder's ownership interest before and after a redemption, the attribution rules apply.

EXAMPLE 34

Bob, Carl, and Dan, unrelated individuals, own 30 shares, 30 shares, and 40 shares, respectively, in Wren Corporation. Wren has E & P of $200,000. The corporation redeems 20 shares of Dan's stock for $30,000. Dan paid $200 a share for the stock two years ago. Dan's ownership in Wren Corporation before and after the redemption is as follows:

[45] See, for example, *Grabowski Trust*, 58 T.C. 650 (1972).

[46] Reg. § 1.302–2(c).

	Total Shares	Dan's Ownership	Ownership Percentage	80% of Original Ownership
Before redemption	100	40	40% (40 ÷ 100)	32% (80% × 40%)
After redemption	80	20	25% (20 ÷ 80)*	

*Note that the denominator of the fraction is reduced after the redemption (from 100 to 80).

Dan's 25% ownership after the redemption meets both tests of § 302(b)(2). It is less than 80% of his original ownership and less than 50% of the total voting power. The distribution therefore qualifies as a disproportionate redemption and receives sale or exchange treatment. As a result, Dan has a long-term capital gain of $26,000 [$30,000 – $4,000 (20 shares × $200)]. ■

EXAMPLE 35

Given the situation in Example 34, assume instead that Carl and Dan are father and son. The redemption described previously would not qualify for sale or exchange treatment because of the effect of the attribution rules. Dan is deemed to own Carl's stock before and after the redemption. Dan's ownership in Wren Corporation before and after the redemption is as follows:

	Total Shares	Dan's Direct Ownership	Carl's Ownership	Dan's Direct and Indirect Ownership	Ownership Percentage	80% of Original Ownership
Before redemption	100	40	30	70	70% (70 ÷ 100)	56% (80% × 70%)
After redemption	80	20	30	50	62.5% (50 ÷ 80)	

Dan's direct and indirect ownership of 62.5% fails to meet either of the tests of § 302(b)(2). After the redemption, Dan owns more than 80% of his original ownership and more than 50% of the voting stock. Thus, the redemption does not qualify for sale or exchange treatment and results in a dividend distribution of $30,000 to Dan. The basis in the 20 shares redeemed is added to Dan's basis in his remaining 20 shares. ■

Even if a redemption does not qualify as a disproportionate redemption, it may still qualify as a not essentially equivalent redemption if it meets the meaningful reduction test (see Example 32).

COMPLETE TERMINATION REDEMPTIONS

A stock redemption that terminates a shareholder's *entire* stock ownership in a corporation will qualify for sale or exchange treatment. The attribution rules generally apply in determining whether the shareholder's stock ownership has been terminated. However, the *family* attribution rules do not apply to a **complete termination redemption** if the following conditions are met:

- The former shareholder has no interest, other than that of a creditor, in the corporation for at least 10 years after the redemption (including an interest as an officer, director, or employee).
- The former shareholder files an agreement to notify the IRS of any prohibited interest acquired within the 10-year period and to retain all necessary records pertaining to the redemption during this time period.

Acquisition of stock in the corporation by bequest or inheritance will not constitute a prohibited interest. The required agreement should be in the form of a separate statement signed by the former shareholder and attached to the return for the year in which the redemption occurs. The agreement should state that the former shareholder agrees to notify the IRS within 30 days of acquiring a prohibited interest in the corporation within the 10-year period following the redemption.[47]

EXAMPLE 36

Kevin owns 50% of the stock in Green Corporation while the remaining interest in Green is held as follows: 40% by Wilma (Kevin's wife) and 10% by Carmen (a key employee). Green redeems all of Kevin's stock for its fair market value. As a result, Wilma and Carmen are the only remaining shareholders, now owning 80% and 20%, respectively. If the requirements for the family attribution waiver are met, the transaction will qualify as a complete termination redemption and result in sale or exchange treatment. If the waiver requirements are not satisfied, Kevin will be deemed to own Wilma's (his wife's) stock, and the entire distribution will be a dividend, assuming adequate E & P. ■

EXAMPLE 37

Assume in Example 36 that Kevin qualifies for the family attribution waiver for the redemption. In the year of the redemption, Kevin treats the transaction as a sale or exchange. However, if he purchases Carmen's stock seven years after the redemption, he has acquired a prohibited interest, and the redemption distribution is reclassified as a dividend. Kevin owes additional taxes due to this revised treatment. ■

ETHICAL CONSIDERATIONS

A Friendly Dilemma

Seven years ago, Flicker Corporation redeemed all of Belinda's shares in the corporation. At that time, various members of Belinda's family owned the remaining shares of Flicker. To qualify the transaction as a complete termination redemption, Belinda resigned from all employment positions with Flicker and filed the required notification for the family attribution waiver. Belinda, a friend of yours, was also your client for the year of the redemption. As her CPA, you informed Belinda of all the requirements surrounding the family attribution waiver.

Since the redemption, Belinda has fallen upon hard times, having incurred substantial medical costs associated with her now deceased husband. Destitute and in need of some financial means, Belinda began to work for Flicker Corporation as an employee in the current year. You know that this prohibited interest results in the recharacterization of the stock redemption as a dividend distribution and that Belinda has no wherewithal to pay the additional tax burden. As Belinda's friend and former CPA, how should you proceed?

REDEMPTIONS TO PAY DEATH TAXES

Section 303 provides sale or exchange treatment to a redemption of stock included in, and representing a substantial amount of, a decedent's gross estate. The purpose of this provision is to provide an estate with liquidity to pay death-related expenses when a significant part of the estate consists of stock in a closely held corporation. Often such stock is not easily marketable, and a stock redemption represents the only viable option for its disposition. The redemption might not satisfy any of the other qualifying stock redemption rules because of the attribution rules (e.g., attribution to estate from beneficiaries). A **redemption to pay death taxes** provides sale or exchange treatment without regard to the attribution rules, but the provision limits this treatment to the sum of the death taxes and funeral and administration expenses. A redemption in excess of these expenses may qualify for sale or exchange treatment under one of the § 302 provisions.

The income tax basis of property owned by a decedent's estate is the property's fair market value on the date of death (or alternate valuation date if available and

[47]Reg. § 1.302–4(a)(1).

if elected).[48] Therefore, in a redemption to pay death taxes, the redemption price generally equals (or approximates) the basis of the stock. When the redemption price equals the estate's basis that results from the step-up to date of death value (refer to Chapter 13), the exchange is free of any income tax consequences to the estate.

Section 303 applies only to a distribution made with respect to stock of a corporation when the value of that one corporation's stock in the gross estate of a decedent *exceeds* 35 percent of the value of the adjusted gross estate. (For a definition of "gross estate," see the Glossary of Key Terms in Appendix C. The term "adjusted gross estate" refers to the gross estate reduced by certain losses and funeral and administration expenses.)

EXAMPLE 38

Juan's adjusted gross estate is $2.1 million. The death taxes and funeral and administration expenses of the estate total $320,000. Included in the gross estate is stock of Yellow Corporation, valued at $840,000. Juan had acquired the stock three years ago at a cost of $100,000. Yellow redeems $320,000 of the stock from Juan's estate. Because the value of the Yellow stock in Juan's estate exceeds the 35% threshold ($840,000 ÷ $2.1 million = 40%), the redemption qualifies under § 303 as a sale or exchange to Juan's estate. Assuming the value of the stock has remained unchanged since the date of Juan's death, there is no recognized gain (or loss) on the redemption [$320,000 (amount realized) – $320,000 (stock basis)]. ■

In determining whether the value of stock of one corporation exceeds 35 percent of the value of the adjusted gross estate of a decedent, the stock of two or more corporations may be treated as the stock of a single corporation. Stock of corporations in which the decedent held a 20 percent or more interest is treated as stock of a single corporation for this purpose.[49] When this exception is used, the stock redeemed can be that of any of the 20 percent or more shareholder interests.

EXAMPLE 39

The adjusted gross estate of a decedent is $3.3 million. The gross estate includes stock of Owl and Robin Corporations valued at $600,000 and $680,000, respectively. Unless the two corporations are treated as a single corporation, § 303 does not apply to a redemption of the stock of either corporation. Assuming the decedent owned all the stock of Owl Corporation and 80% of the stock of Robin, § 303 applies because the decedent's estate includes a 20% or more interest in stock of each corporation. The 35% test is met when the Owl and Robin stock are treated as that of a single corporation [($600,000 + $680,000) ÷ $3.3 million = 38.8%]. The stock of Owl or Robin (or both) can be redeemed under § 303. ■

LO.9

Understand the tax impact of stock redemptions on the distributing corporation.

Effect on the Corporation Redeeming Its Stock

Thus far, the discussion has focused on the effect of stock redemptions to the *shareholder*. If sale or exchange treatment is allowed for the shareholder, what is the effect on the *corporation* redeeming its stock? Does the corporation recognize gain or loss on the distribution of property to carry out the redemption? Also, what effect does the redemption have on the corporation's E & P? Furthermore, can the corporation deduct expenditures incurred in the redemption of its stock? These matters are discussed in the following paragraphs.

RECOGNITION OF GAIN OR LOSS

Section 311 provides that corporations are taxed on all nonliquidating distributions of appreciated property as if the property had been sold for its fair market value.

[48] § 1014(a).

[49] § 303(b)(2)(B).

CONCEPT SUMMARY 19–3

Summary of the Qualifying Stock Redemption Rules

Type of Redemption	Requirements to Qualify
Not essentially equivalent to a dividend [§ 302(b)(1)]	Meaningful reduction in shareholder's voting interest. If less than a majority interest, reduction in interest in assets and E & P also considered.
	Stock attribution rules apply.
Substantially disproportionate [§ 302(b)(2)]	Shareholder's interest in the corporation, after the redemption, must be less than 80% of interest before the redemption and less than 50% of total combined voting power of all classes of stock entitled to vote.
	Stock attribution rules apply.
Complete termination [§ 302(b)(3)]	Entire stock ownership terminated.
	In general, stock attribution rules apply. However, *family* stock attribution rules may be waived. Former shareholder must have no interest, other than as a creditor, in the corporation for at least 10 years and must file an agreement to notify the IRS of any prohibited interest acquired during 10-year period. Shareholder must retain all necessary records during 10-year period.
Redemption to pay death taxes [§ 303]	Value of stock of one corporation in gross estate exceeds 35% of value of adjusted gross estate.
	Stock of two or more corporations treated as stock of a single corporation in applying the 35% test if decedent held a 20% or more interest in the stock of the corporations.
	Redemption limited to amount of death taxes and funeral and administration expenses.
	Stock attribution rules do not apply.

This is the case for all stock redemptions, qualifying or not. Losses, however, are not recognized on nonliquidating distributions. When distributed property is subject to a corporate liability, the fair market value of that property is treated as not being less than the amount of the liability.

EXAMPLE 40

To carry out a redemption, Blackbird Corporation transfers land (basis of $80,000, fair market value of $300,000) to a shareholder's estate. Blackbird has a recognized gain of $220,000 ($300,000 – $80,000). If the value of the property distributed was less than its adjusted basis, the realized loss would not be recognized. ■

Because of the loss disallowance, a corporation should not use property that has declined in value as consideration in the redemption of a shareholder's stock. However, the corporation could sell the property in a taxable transaction in which it can recognize a loss and then distribute the proceeds.

EFFECT ON EARNINGS AND PROFITS

A qualifying stock redemption reduces the E & P account of a corporation in an amount not in excess of the ratable share of the distributing corporation's E & P that is attributable to the stock redeemed.[50]

[50] § 312(n)(7).

EXAMPLE 41

Navy Corporation has 100 shares of stock outstanding. It redeems 30 shares for $100,000 at a time when it has paid-in capital of $120,000 and E & P of $150,000. The charge to E & P is limited to 30% of the amount in the E & P account ($45,000), and the remainder of the redemption price ($55,000) is a reduction of the capital account. If, instead, the 30 shares were redeemed for $40,000, the charge to E & P would be limited to $40,000, the amount Navy paid for the stock. ■

REDEMPTION EXPENDITURES

In redeeming its shares, a corporation may incur certain expenditures such as accounting, brokerage, legal, and loan fees. Section 162(k) specifically denies a deduction for redemption expenditures incurred in a stock redemption.

Other Corporate Distributions

Partial liquidations of a corporation, if in compliance with the statutory requirements of § 302(e), will result in sale or exchange treatment to noncorporate shareholders. Distributions of stock and securities of a controlled corporation to the shareholders of the parent corporation will be free of any tax consequences if they fall under § 355. Both of these types of corporate distributions are similar to stock redemptions and dividend distributions in some respects but are not discussed here because of their limited applicability.

LO.10

Identify tax planning opportunities available to minimize the tax impact in corporate distributions, constructive dividends, and stock redemptions.

Tax Planning Considerations

CORPORATE DISTRIBUTIONS

In connection with the discussion of corporate distributions, the following points need reinforcement:

- Because E & P is the measure of dividend income, its periodic determination is essential to corporate planning. Thus, an E & P account should be established and maintained, particularly if the possibility exists that a corporate distribution might be a return of capital.
- Accumulated E & P is the sum of all past years' current E & P. There is no statute of limitations on the computation of E & P. The IRS can, for example, redetermine a corporation's current E & P for a tax year long since passed. Such a change affects accumulated E & P and has a direct impact on the taxability of current distributions to shareholders.
- Distributions can be planned to avoid or minimize dividend exposure.

EXAMPLE 42

After several unprofitable years, Darter Corporation has a deficit in accumulated E & P of $100,000 as of January 1, 2005. Starting in 2005, Darter expects to generate annual E & P of $50,000 for the next four years and would like to distribute this amount to its shareholders. The corporation's cash position (for dividend purposes) will correspond to the current E & P generated. Consider the following two distribution schedules:

1. On December 31 of 2005, 2006, 2007, and 2008, Darter Corporation distributes a cash dividend of $50,000.
2. On December 31 of 2006 and 2008, Darter Corporation distributes a cash dividend of $100,000.

The two alternatives are illustrated as follows.

Year	Accumulated E & P (First of Year)	Current E & P	Distribution	Amount of Dividend
		Alternative 1		
2005	($100,000)	$50,000	$ 50,000	$50,000
2006	(100,000)	50,000	50,000	50,000
2007	(100,000)	50,000	50,000	50,000
2008	(100,000)	50,000	50,000	50,000
		Alternative 2		
2005	($100,000)	$50,000	$ –0–	$ –0–
2006	(50,000)	50,000	100,000	50,000
2007	(50,000)	50,000	–0–	–0–
2008	–0–	50,000	100,000	50,000

Alternative 1 produces $200,000 of dividend income because each $50,000 distribution is fully covered by current E & P. Alternative 2, however, produces only $100,000 of dividend income to the shareholders. The remaining $100,000 is a return of capital. Why? At the time Darter Corporation made its first distribution of $100,000 on December 31, 2006, it had a deficit of $50,000 in accumulated E & P (the original deficit of $100,000 is reduced by the $50,000 of current E & P from 2005). Consequently, the $100,000 distribution yields a $50,000 dividend (the current E & P for 2006), and $50,000 is treated as a return of capital. As of January 1, 2007, Darter's accumulated E & P has a deficit balance of $50,000, since a distribution cannot increase a deficit in E & P. Adding the remaining $50,000 of current E & P from 2007, the balance as of January 1, 2008, is zero. Thus, the second distribution of $100,000 made on December 31, 2008, also yields $50,000 of dividends (the current E & P for 2008) and a $50,000 return of capital. ■

ETHICAL CONSIDERATIONS

Playing Games with the Statute of Limitations

In 1998, Beige Corporation made a cash distribution to its shareholders, one of whom was Steve Jordan. At that time, the parties involved believed that the distribution was a return of capital because Beige had no E & P. Accordingly, none of the shareholders reported dividend income. In Steve's case, he reduced the $200,000 original basis of his stock investment by $40,000, his share of the distribution. In 2005, it is discovered that E & P had been incorrectly computed. The 1998 distribution was fully covered by E & P and should not have been treated as a return of capital.

In 2006, Steve sells his stock in Beige Corporation for $350,000. He plans to report a gain of $150,000 [$350,000 (selling price) – $200,000 (original basis)] on the sale. Although Steve realizes that he should have recognized dividend income of $40,000 for 1998, the statute of limitations has made this a closed year.

Comment on Steve's situation.

PLANNING FOR QUALIFIED DIVIDENDS

Retirement Plans. The reduced tax rates available to individual taxpayers on net capital gain and qualified dividend income reinforce the inadvisability of funding retirement accounts with stock. Since § 401(k) plans and IRAs do not pay income taxes, the benefits of the lower tax rates on these forms of income are lost. Instead, distributions from the plans are taxed at ordinary income tax rates.

Closely Held Corporations. The new tax-favored treatment of dividends will have a marked impact on many closely held corporations. Prior to the Jobs and Growth Tax Relief Reconciliation Act of 2003, the motivation was to avoid paying dividends, because they were nondeductible to the corporation and fully taxed to shareholders. Instead, corporate profits were bailed out in a manner that provided tax benefits to the corporation. Hence, liberal use was made of compensation, loan, and lease arrangements—as salaries, interest, and rent are deductible items. Now, the lower tax rates on dividends must be considered. Who should benefit? Shareholders will prefer dividends because salaries, interest, and rents are fully taxed. Corporations, however, will continue to favor deductible distributions. In general, the best strategy considers the tax consequences to both parties (i.e., the corporation and the shareholder).

EXAMPLE 43

Consider a corporation paying tax at the 34% rate and an individual shareholder in the 35% tax bracket. A deductible $10,000 payment to the shareholder will *save* the corporation $3,400 in tax, resulting in an after-tax cost of $6,600. The shareholder will pay $3,500 in tax, resulting in after-tax income of $6,500. This creates a joint tax burden of $100 ($3,500 tax paid by the shareholder – $3,400 tax saved by the corporation). If, instead, the corporation paid a $10,000 qualifying dividend to the shareholder, no tax savings would be realized by the corporation, resulting in an after-tax cost of $10,000. The shareholder would owe $1,500 in taxes, leaving $8,500 of income. Considering both the corporation and the shareholder, a dividend creates $1,400 more tax liability than a deductible payment, so the deductible payment is more tax efficient. ■

In Example 43, when the deductible payment is made, the shareholder bears the burden because the tax is $2,000 higher ($3,500 tax due from the deductible payment – $1,500 tax due from the dividend), while the corporation is $3,400 better off ($3,400 tax saved because of the deductible payment – $0 tax saved because of the dividend). Both parties could be made better off by allowing the corporation to transfer part of its benefit to the shareholder through a larger deductible payment.

EXAMPLE 44

Assume the same facts as in Example 43, except that the corporation pays a $14,000 deductible payment. In this case, the corporation will save $4,760 ($14,000 × 34%) in tax, resulting in an after-tax cost of $9,240. From the corporation's perspective, this is preferable to a $10,000 dividend because it costs $760 less after tax ($10,000 dividend cost – $9,240 after-tax cost of a $14,000 deductible payment). The shareholder will pay taxes of $4,900 on the deductible payment, resulting in after-tax income of $9,100. The shareholder will also prefer this payment to a dividend because it generates $600 more after-tax income ($9,100 – $8,500 from a dividend). ■

Thus, if properly structured, deductible payments by the corporation to the shareholder still appear to be preferable to dividends in most situations (unless the corporation faces a low tax rate).

CONSTRUCTIVE DIVIDENDS

Tax planning can be particularly effective in avoiding constructive dividend situations. Shareholders should try to structure their dealings with the corporation on an arm's length basis. For example, reasonable rent should be paid for the use of corporate property, and a fair price should be paid for its purchase. The parties should make every effort to support the amount involved with appraisal data or market information obtained from reliable sources at or near the time of the transaction. Dealings between shareholders and a closely held corporation should be as formal as possible. In the case of loans to shareholders, for example, the parties should provide for an adequate rate of interest and written evidence of the debt. Shareholders should also establish and follow a realistic repayment schedule.

CONCEPT SUMMARY 19–4

Corporate Distributions

1. Without a special provision, corporate distributions are taxed as dividend income to the recipient shareholders to the extent of the distributing corporation's E & P accumulated since February 28, 1913, or to the extent of current E & P. Any excess is treated as a return of capital to the extent of the shareholder's basis in the stock and, thereafter, as capital gain.
2. Property distributions are considered dividends (taxed as noted in item 1) in the amount of their fair market value. The amount distributed is reduced by any liabilities on the property distributed. The shareholder's basis in the property is its fair market value.
3. Earnings and profits of a corporation are increased by corporate earnings for the taxable year computed in the same manner as the corporation computes its taxable income. As a general rule, the account is increased for all items of income, whether taxed or not, and reduced by all items of expense, whether deductible or not. Refer to Concept Summary 19–1 for a summary of the effect of certain transactions on taxable income in arriving at current E & P.
4. A corporation recognizes gain, but not loss, on distributions of property to its shareholders. E & P of the distributing corporation is reduced by the amount of money distributed or by the greater of the fair market value or the adjusted basis of property distributed less the amount of any liability applicable to the distributed property.
5. As a general rule, stock dividends or stock rights (representing stock in the distributing corporation) are not taxed, with certain exceptions.
6. Stock redemptions that qualify under § 302(b) are given sale or exchange treatment. This provision requires that such distributions be either substantially disproportionate, complete terminations, or not essentially equivalent to a dividend. In determining whether a transaction is a not essentially equivalent redemption or a disproportionate redemption, the attribution rules apply. However, in a complete termination redemption, the family attribution rules may be waived if certain conditions are met.
7. If stock included in a decedent's estate represents more than 35% of the adjusted gross estate, § 303 provides automatic sale or exchange treatment on its redemption.
8. A corporation is taxed on the appreciation of property distributed in redemption of its stock.
9. In a qualifying stock redemption, the E & P account of the distributing corporation is reduced by an amount not in excess of the ratable share of its E & P that is attributable to the stock redeemed.

If shareholders wish to bail out corporate profits in a form deductible to the corporation, a balanced mix of the possible alternatives lessens the risk of constructive dividend treatment. Rent for the use of shareholder property, interest on amounts borrowed from shareholders, or salaries for services rendered by shareholders are all feasible substitutes for dividend distributions. But overdoing any one approach may attract the attention of the IRS. Too much interest, for example, may mean the corporation is thinly capitalized, and some of the debt may be reclassified as equity investment.

Much can be done to protect against the disallowance of unreasonable compensation. Example 45 is an illustration, all too common in a family corporation, of what *not* to do.

EXAMPLE 45

Bob Cole wholly owns Eagle Corporation. Corporate employees and their annual salaries include Mrs. Cole ($30,000), Cole, Jr. ($20,000), Bob Cole ($160,000), and Ed ($80,000). The operation of Eagle Corporation is shared about equally between Bob Cole and Ed, who is an unrelated party. Mrs. Cole performed significant services for Eagle during its formative years but now merely attends the annual meeting of the board of directors. Cole, Jr., Bob Cole's son, is a full-time student and occasionally signs papers for the corporation in his capacity as treasurer. Eagle Corporation has not distributed a dividend for 10 years, although it has accumulated substantial E & P. Mrs. Cole, Cole, Jr., and Bob Cole run the risk of a finding of unreasonable compensation, based on the following factors:

- Mrs. Cole's salary is vulnerable unless proof is available that some or all of her $30,000 annual salary is payment for services rendered to the corporation in prior years and that she was underpaid for those years.[51]
- Cole, Jr.'s salary is also vulnerable; he does not appear to earn the $20,000 paid to him by the corporation. True, neither Cole, Jr., nor Mrs. Cole is a shareholder, but each one's relationship to Bob Cole is enough of a tie-in to raise the unreasonable compensation issue.
- Bob Cole's salary appears susceptible to challenge. Why is he receiving $80,000 more than Ed when it appears they share equally in the operation of the corporation?
- The fact that Eagle Corporation has not distributed dividends over the past 10 years, even though it is capable of doing so, increases the likelihood of a constructive dividend. ■

STOCK REDEMPTIONS

Stock redemptions offer several possibilities for tax planning:

- The alternative to a qualifying stock redemption is dividend treatment. The 15 percent (5 percent for taxpayers in the 10 or 15 percent marginal income tax brackets) preferential tax rate on dividend income reduces some of the adverse consequences of a nonqualified stock redemption. Also, a nonqualified redemption may even be preferable if the distributing corporation has little or no E & P or the distributee-shareholder is another corporation. In the latter situation, dividend treatment may be preferred because of the availability of the dividends received deduction.
- A not essentially equivalent redemption provides minimal utility and generally should be relied upon only as a last resort. Instead, the redemption should be structured to satisfy the objective tests required of one of the other qualifying redemptions. These include disproportionate redemptions, complete termination redemptions, and redemptions to pay death taxes.
- The timing and sequence of a redemption should be handled carefully, as illustrated in the following example.

EXAMPLE 46

Sparrow Corporation's stock is held as follows: Alma (60 shares), Antonio (20 shares), and Ali (20 shares). Alma, Antonio, and Ali are not related to each other. The corporation redeems 24 of Alma's shares. Shortly thereafter, it redeems 5 of Antonio's shares. Does Alma's redemption qualify as a disproportionate redemption? Taken in isolation, it would appear to meet the 80% and 50% tests. Yet, if the IRS takes into account the later redemption of Antonio's shares, Alma has not satisfied the 50% test; she still owns $^{36}/_{71}$ of the corporation after the two redemptions. A greater time lag between the redemptions places Alma in a better position to argue against collapsing the two redemptions as parts of one integrated plan. ■

- For a family corporation in which all of the shareholders are related to each other, the only hope of achieving sale or exchange treatment may lie in the use of a redemption that completely terminates a shareholder's interest or one that follows a shareholder's death. In a complete termination redemption, it is important that the family stock attribution rules be avoided. Here, strict compliance with the requirements for the family attribution waiver (e.g., the withdrawing shareholder does not acquire a prohibited interest in the corporation within 10 years) is crucial.
- In a redemption to pay death taxes, the amount to be sheltered from dividend treatment is limited to the sum of death taxes and funeral and administration expenses. However, a redemption in excess of the limitation does not destroy the applicability of § 303.

[51]See, for example, *R. J. Nicoll Co.*, 59 T.C. 37 (1972).

KEY TERMS

Accumulated earnings and profits, 19–6

Attribution, 19–23

Complete termination redemption, 19–26

Constructive dividend, 19–15

Current earnings and profits, 19–6

Disproportionate redemption, 19–25

Earnings and profits (E & P), 19–3

Meaningful reduction test, 19–24

Not essentially equivalent redemption, 19–24

Property dividend, 19–12

Qualified dividends, 19–11

Redemption to pay death taxes, 19–27

Stock dividend, 19–18

Stock redemption, 19–20

Stock rights, 19–19

Unreasonable compensation, 19–16

PROBLEM MATERIALS

Discussion Questions

1. What factors affect the tax treatment of corporate distributions?
2. What is meant by the term *earnings and profits*?
3. In determining Cassowary Corporation's current E & P for 2005, how should taxable income be adjusted by the following transactions?
   a. Interest on municipal bonds received in 2005.
   b. A net operating loss carryover from 2004, fully used in 2005.
   c. Gain deferred on an involuntary conversion that occurred in 2005.
   d. Loss on a sale between related parties in 2005.
   e. Federal income taxes paid in 2005.
   f. Section 179 expense elected and deducted in 2005.
4. Describe the effect of a distribution in a year when the distributing corporation has any of the following:
   a. A deficit in accumulated E & P and a positive amount in current E & P.
   b. A positive amount in accumulated E & P and a deficit in current E & P.
   c. A deficit in both current and accumulated E & P.
   d. A positive amount in both current and accumulated E & P.
5. A calendar year corporation has no accumulated E & P but expects to earn current E & P for the year. A cash distribution to its shareholders on January 1 should result in a return of capital. Comment on the validity of this statement.
6. Discuss the rationale for the reduced tax rates on dividends paid to individuals.
7. What requirements must be met for a dividend payment to qualify for the reduced 15%/5% tax rates?
8. Why would a corporation distribute a property dividend?

Decision Making

9. Crow Corporation owns three machines that it uses in its business. It no longer needs two of these machines and is considering distributing them to its two shareholders as a property dividend. All three machines have a fair market value of $13,000. Machine A has a basis of $7,000; machine B has a basis of $13,000; machine C has a basis of $16,000. The corporation has asked you for advice. What actions do you recommend?

Issue ID

10. A corporation is contemplating a possible property distribution to its shareholders. If appreciated property is to be used, does it matter to the distributing corporation whether the property distributed is a long-term capital asset or depreciable property subject to recapture?
11. How do liabilities affect the tax treatment of a property distribution?

Issue ID

12. Barbet Corporation distributes $112,000 to each of its three shareholders, Jim, Sharon, and Peafowl Corporation. What factors must be considered when determining how the distribution is treated for tax purposes both to the shareholders and to Barbet Corporation?

Issue ID

13. Edward is the president and sole shareholder of Kingfisher Corporation. He is paid a salary of $250,000 in the current year. His daughter, Jacqueline, is the company's chief financial officer and is paid a salary of $35,000. Jacqueline works for Kingfisher on a part-time basis while she completes her accounting degree at a local university. Kingfisher Corporation also advances $27,000 to Edward as an interest-free loan. What are the tax issues?

14. Whether compensation paid to a corporate employee is reasonable is a question of fact to be determined from the surrounding circumstances. How would the resolution of this problem be affected by each of the following factors?
    a. The employee is not a shareholder but is related to the sole owner of the corporate employer.
    b. The shareholder-employee never completed high school.
    c. The shareholder-employee is a full-time college student.
    d. The shareholder-employee was underpaid for her services during the formative period of the corporate employer.
    e. The corporate employer pays only a nominal dividend each year.
    f. Year-end bonuses are paid to all shareholder-employees, but not to nonshareholder-employees.

Decision Making

15. Condor Corporation would like to transfer excess cash to its sole shareholder, Jen, who is also an employee. Jen is in the 35% tax bracket, and Condor is in the 34% tax bracket. Because Jen's contribution to the business is substantial, Condor believes that a $50,000 bonus in the current year would be viewed as reasonable compensation and would be deductible by the corporation. However, Condor is leaning toward paying Jen a $50,000 dividend, because the tax rate on dividends is lower than the tax rate on compensation. Is Condor correct in the belief that a dividend is a better choice? Why or why not?

16. Peregrine Corporation has several employees. Their names and salaries are:

Walter	$400,000
Sam (Walter's son)	60,000
Jennifer (Walter's daughter)	60,000
Richard (an unrelated party)	50,000

Sam and Jennifer are the only shareholders of Peregrine Corporation. Walter and Richard share the company's operation equally. Sam and Jennifer are both full-time college students at a university about 600 miles away. Peregrine has substantial E & P and has distributed only one small dividend in the past 10 years. Discuss problems related to Peregrine's salary arrangement.

17. Corporate shareholders typically prefer sale or exchange treatment for a stock redemption. Assess the validity of this statement.

Issue ID

18. The stock in Brown Corporation is owned equally by Petra and Salvador, a couple in the process of divorce. Pursuant to a settlement agreement being negotiated between the two taxpayers, Salvador would be required to sell his Brown stock either to Petra or to the corporation. What issues should be considered in determining whether a redemption of Salvador's stock by Brown Corporation is the preferable alternative?

19. During the current year, Flicker, Inc., distributed $100,000 each to Kanisha and Susan in redemption of some of their Flicker stock. The two shareholders are in the 35% tax bracket, and each had a $30,000 basis in her redeemed stock. Kanisha incurred $15,000 of tax on her redemption, but Susan incurred only $10,500 on her redemption. Discuss the likely reason for the difference in their tax liabilities.

20. A shareholder realized a loss in a qualifying stock redemption. Since the redemption qualified for sale or exchange treatment, the loss will be recognized. Assess the validity of this statement.

21. For purposes of the stock attribution rules, when is stock attributed *from* and *to* a corporate shareholder?

22. The stock attribution rules generally must be considered in determining whether the requirements of a qualifying stock redemption have been satisfied. For some qualifying stock redemptions, however, some or all of the attribution rules are not relevant. Discuss those situations where the attribution rules can be ignored.

23. Under what circumstances will a stock redemption qualify as a not essentially equivalent redemption?

24. If a redemption is treated as a dividend ("nonqualifying stock redemption"), what happens to the basis of the stock redeemed?

Issue ID

25. Two years ago Jorge transferred property he had used in his sole proprietorship to Flycatcher Corporation, a newly formed corporation, for 50 shares of Flycatcher stock. The property had an adjusted basis of $300,000 and a fair market value of $800,000. Six months later Jorge's friend, Polly, transferred property she had used in her sole proprietorship to Flycatcher Corporation for 50 shares of Flycatcher stock and cash of $100,000. Her property had an adjusted basis of $150,000 and a value of $900,000. Both Jorge and Polly serve on Flycatcher's board of directors. In addition, Polly has a contract with Flycatcher to perform consulting services for the corporation. In the current year, Flycatcher Corporation redeems all of Polly's Flycatcher stock for property with a probable value of $1.4 million. What are the tax issues for Polly and Flycatcher?

26. What are the principal advantages offered by a redemption to pay death taxes?

27. At the time of her death, Yolanda owned 30% of the outstanding stock of Violet Corporation (basis of $300,000, fair market value of $900,000). Yolanda's adjusted gross estate is $2.8 million, and the death taxes and funeral and administration expenses total $550,000. Can Yolanda's estate qualify for a redemption to pay death taxes under § 303?

Issue ID

28. Angie and her daughter, Ann, who are the only shareholders of Bluebird Corporation, each paid $100,000 four years ago for their shares in Bluebird. Angie also owns 20% of the stock in Redbird Corporation. The Redbird stock is worth $500,000, and Angie's basis in the stock is $50,000. Angie died in the current year leaving all her property to her husband, Gary, but Ann wants to be the sole shareholder of Bluebird Corporation. Bluebird has assets worth $2 million (basis of $700,000) and E & P of $1 million. Angie's estate is worth approximately $4 million. Angie had made gifts during her lifetime to Ann. What are the tax issues for Angie's estate, Ann, and Bluebird?

Decision Making

29. Indigo Corporation desires to transfer cash of $30,000 or property worth $30,000 to its sole shareholder, Linda, in a redemption transaction that will be treated as a dividend to Linda. If Indigo distributes property, the corporation will choose between two assets that are each worth $30,000 and are no longer needed in its business: property A (basis of $12,000) and property B (basis of $36,000). Indigo is indifferent as to the form of the distribution, but Linda prefers a cash distribution. Considering the tax consequences to Indigo on the distribution to redeem Linda's shares, what should Indigo distribute?

Problems

30. At the start of the current year, Finch Corporation (a calendar year taxpayer) has accumulated E & P of $85,000. Finch's current E & P is $45,000, and during the year, it distributes $150,000 ($75,000 each) to its equal shareholders, George and Cindy. George has a basis of $7,000 in his stock, and Cindy has a basis of $16,000 in her stock. How is the distribution treated for tax purposes?

31. Blue Jay Corporation, a calendar year taxpayer, received dividend income of $500,000 from a corporation in which it holds a 15% interest. Blue Jay also received interest income of $75,000 from municipal bonds during the year. The municipality used the proceeds from the bond sale to construct a new jail. Blue Jay borrowed funds to purchase the municipal bonds and paid $25,000 in interest on the loan this year. Blue Jay's taxable income exclusive of the items noted above was $350,000.

a. What is Blue Jay Corporation's taxable income after considering the dividend income, the interest from the municipal bonds, and the interest paid on the indebtedness to purchase the municipals?
b. What is Blue Jay Corporation's accumulated E & P at the end of the year if its accumulated E & P account balance was $125,000 as of January 1?

32. On November 15, 2005, Red Corporation sold a parcel of land. The land had a basis of $350,000, and Red received a $900,000 note as consideration in the sale. The note is to be paid in five installments, the first of which is due on December 15, 2006. Because Red did not elect out of the installment method, none of the $550,000 gain is included in taxable income for 2005.

Red Corporation had a deficit in accumulated E & P of $280,000 on January 1, 2005. For 2005, before considering the effect of the land sale, Red had a deficit in current E & P of $120,000.

Buck, the sole shareholder in Red, has a basis of $100,000 in his stock. If Red distributes $300,000 to Buck on December 31, 2005, how much income must Buck report on the distribution for tax purposes?

33. Complete the following schedule for each case. Assume the shareholders have ample basis in the stock investment.

	Accumulated E & P Beginning of Year	Current E & P	Cash Distributions (All on Last Day of Year)	Dividend Income	Return of Capital
a.	($150,000)	$ 70,000	$130,000	$ ______	$ ______
b.	200,000	(60,000)	210,000	______	______
c.	130,000	50,000	150,000	______	______
d.	120,000	(40,000)	130,000	______	______
e.	Same as (d), except the distribution of $130,000 is made on June 30 and the corporation uses the calendar year for tax purposes.			______	______

34. Marie, the sole shareholder of Purple Corporation, had a basis of $40,000 in Purple stock that she sold to Juan on July 30 for $150,000. Purple had accumulated E & P of $100,000 on January 1 and current E & P of $90,000. During the year, Purple made the following distributions: $160,000 cash to Marie on July 1, and $160,000 cash to Juan on December 30. How will the distributions be taxed to Marie and Juan? What gain will Marie recognize on the sale of her stock to Juan?

35. Lark Corporation (a calendar year, accrual basis taxpayer) had the following transactions during 2005, its first year of operation (assume its business and existence both commenced on January 2):

Taxable income	$235,000
Federal income tax liability	74,900
Interest income from tax-exempt payors	2,300
Interest paid to carry tax-exempt bonds	800
Premiums paid on key employee life insurance	1,500
Increase in cash surrender value attributable to insurance premiums	300
Proceeds from key employee life insurance policy	54,000
Cash surrender value of life insurance policy at distribution	4,000
Excess of capital losses over capital gains	3,000
MACRS deductions	18,000
Straight-line depreciation using ADS lives	12,000
Section 179 expense elected during 2005	10,000
Organizational expenses	4,000
Dividends received from domestic corporations (less than 20% owned)	10,000

Assume Lark uses the LIFO inventory method and that its LIFO recapture amount increased $5,000 during 2005. In addition, Lark sold property on installment during 2005. The property was sold for $15,000 and had a basis of $12,000. The first payment on the installment will be received during 2006. Compute Lark Corporation's current E & P.

36. In each of the following *independent* situations, indicate the effect on taxable income and E & P, stating the amount of any increase (or decrease) as a result of the transaction. Assume E & P has already been increased by taxable income.

Transaction	**Taxable Income Increase (Decrease)**	**E & P Increase (Decrease)**
a. Sale of unimproved real estate to the sole shareholder of the corporation at a realized loss of $40,000.	_____	_____
b. Intangible drilling costs incurred on May 1 of the current year; $30,000 is deductible from current-year taxable income.	_____	_____
c. Sale of unimproved real estate to unrelated third party; basis is $200,000, fair market value is $400,000 (no election out of installment method; payments in year of sale total $100,000).	_____	_____
d. Dividends of $10,000 received from 10%-owned corporation, together with dividends received deduction (assume taxable income limit does not apply).	_____	_____
e. Realized gain of $150,000 from qualifying like-kind exchange ($30,000 of gain is recognized).	_____	_____
f. Section 179 expense deduction of $12,000 in current year.	_____	_____
g. Impact of current-year § 179 expense deduction in succeeding year.	_____	_____
h. MACRS depreciation of $80,000. ADS depreciation would have been $50,000.	_____	_____
i. A $60,000 refund of Federal income taxes paid in previous year.	_____	_____

37. Taylor, an individual, owns all of the outstanding stock in Violet Corporation. Taylor purchased his stock in Violet 11 years ago, and his basis is $15,000. At the beginning of this year, the corporation has $35,000 of accumulated E & P and no current E & P (before considering the effect of distributions). What are the tax consequences to Taylor (amount of dividend income and basis in property received) and Violet Corporation (gain or loss and effect on E & P) in each of the following situations?
    a. Violet distributes land to Taylor. The land was held as an investment and has a fair market value of $25,000 and an adjusted basis of $18,000.
    b. Assume that Violet Corporation has no current or accumulated E & P prior to the distribution. How would your answer to (a) change?
    c. Assume that the land distributed in (a) is subject to a $22,000 mortgage (which Taylor assumes). How would your answer change?
    d. Assume that the land has a fair market value of $25,000 and an adjusted basis of $28,000 on the date of distribution. How would your answer to (a) change?

   e. Instead of distributing land, assume that Violet decides to distribute furniture used in its business. The furniture has a $6,000 fair market value and $500 adjusted basis for income tax purposes and a $2,500 adjusted basis for E & P purposes. The original fair market value of the furniture when it was purchased four years ago was $8,000.

38. Raptor Corporation, with E & P of $750,000, distributes land worth $225,000, adjusted basis of $250,000, to Jaime, its sole shareholder. The land is subject to a liability of $60,000, which Jaime assumes. What are the tax consequences to Raptor and to Jaime?

39. At the beginning of the current year, Northern Fulmar Corporation (a calendar year taxpayer) has accumulated E & P of $46,000. During the year, Northern Fulmar incurs a $34,000 loss from operations that accrues ratably. On July 1, Northern Fulmar distributes $38,000 in cash to Adriana, its sole shareholder. How will the $38,000 be taxed to Adriana?

Issue ID

40. Copper Corporation has two equal shareholders, Cybil and Sally. Cybil acquired her Copper stock three years ago by transferring property worth $600,000, basis of $200,000, for 60 shares of the stock. Sally acquired 60 shares in Copper Corporation two years ago by transferring property worth $620,000, basis of $70,000. Copper Corporation's accumulated E & P as of January 1 of the current year is $300,000. On March 1 of the current year, the corporation distributed to Cybil property worth $100,000, basis to Copper of $30,000. It distributed cash of $200,000 to Sally. On July 1 of the current year, Sally sold her stock to Dana for $800,000. On December 1 of the current year, Copper distributed cash of $80,000 each to Dana and to Cybil. What are the tax issues?

41. Redwing Corporation is a closely held company with accumulated E & P of $500,000 and current E & P of $55,000. Mike and Royce are brothers, and each owns a 50% share in Redwing. On a day-to-day basis, Mike and Royce share management responsibilities equally. What are the tax consequences of the following transactions between Redwing, Mike, and Royce? How does each transaction affect Redwing's E & P? Assume each transaction is independent.
   a. Redwing sells a parking lot (adjusted basis of $33,000, fair market value of $18,000) to Mike for $5,000.
   b. Redwing lends Royce $200,000 on July 1 of this year. The loan, evidenced by a note, is due on demand. No interest is charged on the loan. The current applicable Federal interest rate is 9%.
   c. Redwing owns a yacht in Miami, Florida. It rents the yacht to vacationers throughout the year. During the current year, Mike and Royce each use the yacht for one month and pay no rent to Redwing. The rental value of the yacht is $7,500 per week. Mike has indicated that the average maintenance cost per week for the rental is $500.
   d. Mike leases equipment to Redwing for $20,000 per year. If the corporation were to lease the same equipment from another company, the cost of the lease would be $13,000.

42. Verdigris Corporation owns 25% of the stock of Rust Corporation. Rust Corporation, with E & P of $150,000 on December 20, distributes land with a fair market value of $60,000 and a basis of $90,000 to Verdigris. The land is subject to a liability of $50,000, which Verdigris assumes.
   a. How is Verdigris Corporation taxed on the distribution?
   b. What is Rust Corporation's E & P after the distribution?

43. At the beginning of its taxable year, Bunting Corporation had E & P of $175,000. Bunting sold an asset at a loss of $175,000 on June 30. It incurred a deficit in current E & P of $195,000, which includes the $175,000 loss on the sale of the asset, for the calendar year. Assume Bunting made a distribution of $40,000 to its sole individual shareholder on July 1. How will the shareholder be taxed on the $40,000?

44. Indigo Corporation and Lucy each own 50% of Tanager Corporation's common stock. On January 1, Tanager had a deficit in accumulated E & P of $250,000. Its current E & P was $180,000. During the year, Tanager made cash distributions of $70,000 each to Indigo and Lucy. How will the two shareholders be taxed on the distribution? What is the accumulated E & P of Tanager Corporation at the end of the year?

Communications

45. Julie Swanson bought 5,000 shares of Great Egret Corporation stock two years ago for $12,000. Last year, Julie received a nontaxable stock dividend of 1,000 shares in Great Egret Corporation. In the current tax year, Julie sold all of the stock received as a dividend for $9,000. Prepare a letter to Julie and a memo to the file describing the tax consequences of the stock sale. Julie's address is 3737 Canyon Drive, Minneapolis, MN 55434.

Decision Making

46. Ivana, the president and a shareholder of Robin Corporation, has earned a salary bonus of $15,000 for the current year. Because of the recent reduction in tax rates on qualified dividends, Robin is considering substituting a dividend for the bonus. Assume the tax rates are 28% for Ivana and 34% for Robin Corporation.
    a. How much better off would Ivana be if she were paid a dividend rather than salary?
    b. How much better off would Robin Corporation be if it paid Ivana salary rather than a dividend?
    c. If Robin Corporation pays Ivana a salary bonus of $20,000 instead of a $15,000 dividend, how would your answers to (a) and (b) change?
    d. What should Robin do?

47. Cardinal Corporation has 500 shares of common stock outstanding. Hubert owns 200 of the shares, Hubert's grandmother owns 100 shares, Hubert's daughter owns 50 shares, and Redbird Corporation owns 50 shares. Hubert owns 70% of the stock in Redbird Corporation.
    a. Applying the § 318 stock attribution rules, how many shares does Hubert own in Cardinal Corporation?
    b. Assume Hubert owns only 45% of Redbird Corporation. How many shares does Hubert own directly and indirectly in Cardinal Corporation?
    c. Assume the same facts as in (a) above, but in addition, Hubert owns 30% of Yellow Partnership. The partnership owns 100 shares in Cardinal Corporation. How many shares does Hubert own directly and indirectly in Cardinal Corporation?

48. Bubba owns 300 shares in Meadowlark Corporation (E & P of $1 million), which has 500 shares outstanding. The remaining 200 shares in Meadowlark are owned by several individuals unrelated to Bubba. In the current year, Meadowlark Corporation redeems 90 of Bubba's shares for $90,000. Bubba's basis in the shares redeemed is $27,000. What are the tax consequences of the redemption to Bubba and Meadowlark Corporation?

Communications

49. Stork Corporation has 1,000 shares of common stock outstanding. The shares are owned by the following unrelated shareholders: Leo Jones, 300 shares; Lori Johnson, 400 shares; and Lana Pierce, 300 shares. The corporation redeems 200 shares of the stock owned by Lana for $80,000. Lana paid $50 per share for her stock two years ago. Stork's E & P was $350,000 on the date of redemption. What is the tax effect to Lana of the redemption? Prepare a letter to Lana (1000 Main Street, Oldtown, MN 55166) and a memo for the file in which you explain your conclusions.

50. Thrush Corporation has 2,000 shares of common stock outstanding. The shares are owned as follows: Jacque Jones, 800 shares; Monique Jones (Jacque's daughter), 800 shares; and Enrique Jones (Jacque's brother), 400 shares. In the current year, Thrush redeems all of Jacque's shares. Determine whether the redemption can qualify for sale or exchange treatment under the complete termination redemption rules in the following independent circumstances.
    a. Jacque remains as a director of Thrush Corporation.
    b. Jacque resigns as director of Thrush Corporation; Monique becomes a director of Thrush to replace Jacque.
    c. Two years after the redemption, Jacque acquires 25 shares in Thrush Corporation as a gift from Enrique.

51. Roberta and Lori, sisters, own all the stock in Swan Corporation (E & P of $1.4 million). Each has a basis of $50,000 in her 200 shares. Roberta wants to sell her stock for $800,000, the fair market value, but she will continue to sit on Swan Corporation's board of directors after the sale. Lori would like to purchase Roberta's shares and, thus, become the sole shareholder in Swan, but Lori is short of funds. What are the tax consequences to Roberta, Lori, and Swan Corporation under the following circumstances?

a. Swan Corporation distributes cash of $800,000 to Lori, and she uses the cash to purchase Roberta's shares.
b. Swan Corporation redeems all of Roberta's shares for $800,000.

52. The gross estate of Bridgett, decedent, includes stock of Crane Corporation (E & P of $2 million) and Eagle Corporation (E & P of $900,000) valued at $450,000 and $220,000, respectively. At the time of her death, Bridgett owned 43% of the Crane stock outstanding and 27% of the Eagle stock outstanding. Bridgett had a basis of $97,000 in the Crane stock and $41,000 in the Eagle stock. Bridgett's adjusted gross estate is $1.8 million, and the death taxes and funeral and administration expenses total $220,000. What are the tax consequences to Bridgett's estate if Eagle Corporation redeems all of the Eagle Corporation stock for $220,000?

53. Tan Corporation (E & P of $900,000) has 1,000 shares of stock outstanding owned equally by Jacob and Julie, unrelated individuals. Both shareholders paid $100 per share for the stock six years ago. In the current year, Tan Corporation redeems 200 shares of Jacob's stock for $260,000.
a. What are the tax consequences of the stock redemption to Jacob?
b. What are the tax consequences of the stock redemption to Tan Corporation?

Communications

54. Crane Corporation has 2,000 shares of stock outstanding. It redeems 400 shares for $200,000 when it has paid-in capital of $500,000 and E & P of $1.2 million. The redemption qualifies for sale or exchange treatment for the shareholder. Crane incurred $10,000 of accounting and legal fees in connection with the redemption transaction. What is the effect of the distribution on Crane Corporation's E & P? Also, what is the proper tax treatment of the redemption expenditures? Prepare a letter to the president of Crane Corporation (506 Wall Street, Winona, MN 55987) and a memo for the file in which you explain your conclusions.

Research Problems

*Note: Solutions to Research Problems can be prepared by using the **RIA Checkpoint® Student Edition** online research product, which is available to accompany this text. It is also possible to prepare solutions to the Research Problems by using tax research materials found in a standard tax library.*

Communications

Research Problem 1. Patrick Zimbrick and his son, Dan, own all of the outstanding stock of Osprey Corporation. Both Dan and Patrick are officers in the corporation and, together with their uncle, John, comprise the entire board of directors. Osprey uses the cash method of accounting and has a calendar year-end. In late 2001, the board of directors adopted the following legally enforceable resolution (agreed to in writing by each of the officers):

> Salary payments made to an officer of the corporation that shall be disallowed in whole or in part as a deductible expense for Federal income tax purposes shall be reimbursed by such officer to the corporation to the full extent of the disallowance. It shall be the duty of the board of directors to enforce payment of each such amount.

In 2002, Osprey paid Patrick $560,000 in compensation. Dan received $400,000. On audit in late 2005, the IRS found the compensation of both officers to be excessive. It disallowed deductions for $200,000 of the payment to Patrick and $150,000 of the payment to Dan. The IRS recharacterized the disallowed payments as constructive dividends. Complying with the resolution by the board of directors, both Patrick and Dan repaid the disallowed compensation to Osprey Corporation in early 2006. Dan and Patrick have asked you to determine how their repayments should be treated for tax purposes. Dan is still working as a highly compensated executive for Osprey, while Patrick is retired and is living off his savings. Prepare a memo to your firm's client files describing the results of your research.

Communications

Research Problem 2. Twenty years ago, Galvin Alexander (6870 Broadway, San Antonio, TX 78209) formed Beige Corporation and became its sole shareholder (1,000 shares). Since that time, Galvin's son, Joseph, has been substantially involved in the management and operation of the corporation's businesses. Galvin has made several gifts of Beige stock to Joseph in an effort to increase his son's vested interest in the success of the corporation. By 2002, when Galvin owned 600 shares of Beige and Joseph owned the remaining 400 shares, the working and personal relationship between father and son had soured to the point that they refused to speak to each other. Recognizing that Beige's success was at risk, the parties agreed that the corporation (E & P of $3 million) would redeem all of Galvin's stock for $1 million (basis of $200,000). The redemption occurred in 2003, and Galvin reported the transaction as a sale or exchange, resulting in a long-term capital gain of $800,000. Under the agreement between the father and son, Galvin continued to serve as a director on the board of Beige until 2007. He was compensated $20,000 annually for serving as a director. In the current year, the IRS audited Galvin's return for 2003 and assessed additional taxes (plus penalties and interest) based on the recharacterization of the redemption as a $1 million dividend distribution. Galvin has contacted you regarding whether he should contest the proposed deficiency. Prepare a letter to Galvin and a memo for the file documenting your conclusions.

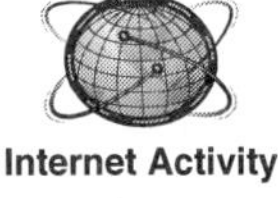
Internet Activity

Use the tax resources of the Internet to address the following question. Do not restrict your search to the World Wide Web, but include a review of newsgroups and general reference materials, practitioner sites and resources, primary sources of the tax law, chat rooms and discussion groups, and other opportunities.

Research Problem 3. Many believe that the reduced tax rate on dividends will be made permanent during President Bush's second term in office. Use the Web to search for evidence about the effects of the dividend tax cut to date. Have dividend-paying stocks experienced any increased demand relative to growth stocks? Have any other economic effects (or lack thereof) been observed by the media or by academics? On the basis of your research, would you label the dividend tax cut a success?

Corporations: Distributions in Complete Liquidation and an Overview of Reorganizations

LEARNING OBJECTIVES

After completing Chapter 20, you should be able to:

LO.1
Understand the tax consequences of complete liquidations for both the corporation and its shareholders.

LO.2
Understand the tax consequences of subsidiary liquidations for both the parent and the subsidiary corporations.

LO.3
Understand the general requirements and tax consequences of corporate reorganizations.

LO.4
Identify tax planning opportunities available to minimize the tax impact in complete liquidations and corporate reorganizations.

OUTLINE

LO.1

Understand the tax consequences of complete liquidations for both the corporation and its shareholders.

Liquidations—In General

When a corporation makes a nonliquidating distribution (e.g., stock redemption), the entity typically will continue as a going concern. With a complete liquidation, however, corporate existence terminates, as does the shareholder's ownership interest. A complete liquidation, like a qualifying stock redemption, produces sale or exchange treatment to the *shareholder*. However, the tax effects of a liquidation to the *corporation* vary somewhat from those of a redemption. Sale or exchange treatment is also the general rule for the liquidating corporation, although some losses are disallowed.

THE LIQUIDATION PROCESS

A **corporate liquidation** exists when a corporation ceases to be a going concern. The corporation continues solely to wind up affairs, pay debts, and distribute any remaining assets to its shareholders. Legal dissolution under state law is not required for a liquidation to be complete for tax purposes. A liquidation can exist even if the corporation retains a nominal amount of assets to pay remaining debts and preserve its legal status.[1]

Shareholders may decide to liquidate a corporation for one or more reasons, including the following:

- The corporate business has been unsuccessful.
- The shareholders wish to acquire the corporation's assets.

[1]Reg. § 1.332–2(c).

- Another person or corporation wants to purchase the corporation's assets. The purchaser may buy the shareholders' stock and then liquidate the corporation to acquire the assets. Alternatively, the purchaser may buy the assets directly from the corporation. After the assets are sold, the corporation distributes the sales proceeds to its shareholders and liquidates.

As one might expect, the different means used to liquidate a corporation produce varying tax results.

LIQUIDATING AND NONLIQUIDATING DISTRIBUTIONS COMPARED

As discussed in Chapter 19, a *nonliquidating* property distribution, whether in the form of a dividend or a stock redemption, produces gain (but not loss) to the distributing corporation. For the shareholder, the receipt of cash or other property produces dividend income to the extent of the corporation's E & P or, in the case of a qualifying stock redemption, results in sale or exchange treatment.

Like a qualifying stock redemption, a complete *liquidation* produces sale or exchange treatment for the shareholders. Similarly, E & P has no impact on the gain or loss to be recognized by the shareholder in either type of distribution.[2] However, a complete liquidation produces different tax consequences to the liquidating corporation. With certain exceptions, a liquidating corporation recognizes gain *and* loss upon the distribution of its assets.

EXAMPLE 1

Goose Corporation, with E & P of $40,000, makes a cash distribution of $50,000 to its sole shareholder. The shareholder's basis in the Goose stock is $20,000. If the distribution is not a qualifying stock redemption or in complete liquidation, the shareholder recognizes dividend income of $40,000 (the amount of Goose's E & P) and treats the remaining $10,000 of the distribution as a return of capital. If the distribution is a qualifying stock redemption or is pursuant to a complete liquidation, the shareholder has a capital gain of $30,000 ($50,000 distribution – $20,000 stock basis). In the latter case, Goose's E & P is of no consequence to the tax result to the shareholder. ■

In the event a corporate distribution results in a *loss* to the shareholder, an important distinction exists between qualifying stock redemptions and liquidations. Section 267 disallows recognition of losses between related parties in qualifying stock redemptions but not in complete liquidations.

EXAMPLE 2

The stock of Orange Corporation is owned equally by three brothers, Rex, Sam, and Ted. When Ted's basis in his stock is $40,000, the corporation distributes $30,000 to him in cancellation of all his shares. If the distribution is a qualifying stock redemption, the $10,000 realized loss is not recognized because Ted and Orange Corporation are related parties. Under § 267, Ted is deemed to own more than 50% in value of the corporation's outstanding stock. Ted's direct ownership is limited to 33⅓%, but through his brothers, he owns indirectly another 66⅔% for a total of 100%. On the other hand, if the distribution is pursuant to a complete liquidation, Ted's $10,000 realized loss is recognized. ■

The rules governing the basis of property received from the corporation are identical for both liquidating and nonliquidating distributions. Section 334(a) specifies that the basis of property received in a taxable complete liquidation is its fair market value on the date of distribution, while § 301(d) provides the same treatment for property received in a nonliquidating distribution.

---

[2]§ 331.

In the following pages, the tax consequences of a complete liquidation are examined, first from the view of the distributing corporation and then in terms of the shareholder. Because the tax rules differ when a subsidiary corporation is liquidated, the rules relating to the liquidation of a subsidiary corporation receive separate treatment.

Liquidations—Effect on the Distributing Corporation

THE GENERAL RULE

Section 336(a) provides that a corporation recognizes gain or loss on the distribution of property in a complete liquidation. The property is treated as if it were sold at its fair market value. This treatment is consistent with the notion of double taxation that is inherent in operating a business as a C corporation—once at the corporate level and again at the shareholder level.

As in the case of a nonliquidating distribution, when property distributed in a complete liquidation is subject to a liability of the liquidating corporation, the deemed fair market value used to calculate gain or loss may not be less than the amount of the liability.

EXAMPLE 3

Pursuant to a complete liquidation, Warbler Corporation distributes to its shareholders land held as an investment (basis of $200,000, fair market value of $300,000). If no liability is involved, Warbler has a gain of $100,000 on the distribution ($300,000 – $200,000). Likewise, if the land is subject to a liability of $250,000, Warbler Corporation has a gain of $100,000. If, instead, the liability were $350,000, Warbler's gain on the distribution would be $150,000 ($350,000 – $200,000). ■

There are four exceptions to the general rule of gain and loss recognition by a liquidating corporation:

- Losses are not recognized on certain liquidating distributions to related-party shareholders.
- Losses are not recognized on certain sales and liquidating distributions of property that was contributed to the corporation with a built-in loss shortly before the adoption of a plan of liquidation.
- A subsidiary corporation does not recognize gains or losses on liquidating distributions to its parent corporation.
- A subsidiary corporation does not recognize losses on liquidating distributions to its minority shareholders.

The first two exceptions, referred to as the "antistuffing rules," are discussed in detail in the next section and are summarized in Figure 20–1 at the end of the section. The last two exceptions, dealing with the liquidation of a subsidiary corporation, are discussed later in this chapter.

ANTISTUFFING RULES

A transfer of property to a corporation under § 351 or as a contribution of capital results in no gain or loss recognition to either the shareholder or the corporation (see Chapter 18). The shareholder's basis in the transferred property becomes the basis in the stock received (or, in the case of a capital contribution, is added to the shareholder's existing stock basis). Additionally, the corporation's basis in the transferred property is typically the shareholder's basis in such property. Concerned that these carryover basis rules would allow taxpayers to create artificial losses in liquidation transactions, Congress enacted two loss limitation provisions.

EXAMPLE 4

Nora, a shareholder in Canary Corporation, transfers property (basis of $10,000, fair market value of $3,000) to the corporation in a transaction that qualifies under § 351. Nora's basis in the additional Canary stock acquired in exchange for the property is $10,000. Canary's basis in the property also is $10,000. A few months after the transfer, Canary Corporation adopts a plan of complete liquidation. Upon liquidation, Canary distributes the property to Nora. If Canary were permitted a loss deduction of $7,000, there would be a double loss because Nora would also recognize a loss of $7,000 upon receipt of the property [$3,000 (fair market value of the property) – $10,000 (basis in Nora's stock)]. To prevent this doubling of losses, Canary Corporation's loss on the distribution is disallowed. ■

Related-Party Loss Limitation. Losses are disallowed on distributions to *related parties* in either of the following cases:

- The distribution is *not* pro rata, or
- The property distributed is *disqualified property*.[3]

A corporation and a shareholder are considered related if the shareholder owns (directly or indirectly) more than 50 percent in value of the corporation's stock.[4] A *pro rata distribution* is one where *each* shareholder receives his or her share of the corporate asset distributed. *Disqualified property* is property that is acquired by the liquidating corporation in a § 351 or contribution to capital transaction during the five-year period ending on the date of the distribution. The related-party loss limitation can apply even if the property was appreciated (fair market value greater than basis) when it was transferred to the corporation.

EXAMPLE 5

Bluebird Corporation stock is owned by Ana and Sanjay, who are unrelated. Ana owns 80% and Sanjay owns 20% of the stock in the corporation. Bluebird has the following assets (none of which was acquired in a § 351 or contribution to capital transaction) that are distributed in complete liquidation of the corporation:

	Adjusted Basis	Fair Market Value
Cash	$600,000	$600,000
Equipment	150,000	200,000
Building	400,000	200,000

Assume Bluebird Corporation distributes the equipment to Sanjay and the cash and the building to Ana. Bluebird recognizes a gain of $50,000 on the distribution of the equipment. The loss of $200,000 on the building is disallowed because the property is distributed to a related party and the distribution is not pro rata (i.e., the building is not distributed 80% to Ana and 20% to Sanjay). ■

EXAMPLE 6

Assume in Example 5 that Bluebird Corporation distributes the cash and equipment to Ana and the building to Sanjay. Again, Bluebird recognizes the $50,000 gain on the equipment. However, it now recognizes the $200,000 loss on the building because the property is not distributed to a related party (i.e., Sanjay does not own more than 50% of the stock in Bluebird Corporation). ■

[3] § 336(d)(1).

[4] Section 267 provides the definition of related party for purposes of this provision. The rules are similar to the stock attribution rules discussed in Chapter 19; one exception, however, is that stock owned by a sibling is treated as owned by the taxpayer under § 267.

EXAMPLE 7

Wren Corporation's stock is held equally by three brothers. One year before Wren's liquidation, the shareholders transfer jointly owned property (basis of $150,000, fair market value of $200,000) to the corporation in return for stock in a § 351 transaction. When the property is worth $100,000, it is transferred pro rata to the brothers in a liquidating distribution. Because each brother owns directly and indirectly more than 50% (i.e., 100% in this situation) of the stock and disqualified property is involved, Wren recognizes none of the $50,000 realized loss [$100,000 (fair market value) – $150,000 (basis)]. ■

Built-in Loss Limitation. The loss limitation provisions are extended to sales, exchanges, or distributions of built-in loss property (fair market value less than basis) that is transferred to a corporation shortly before the corporation is liquidated. The built-in loss limitation applies when both of the following conditions are met:

- The property was acquired by the corporation in a § 351 or contribution to capital transaction.
- Such acquisition was part of a plan whose principal purpose was to recognize a loss on that property by the liquidating corporation. A tax avoidance purpose is presumed in the case of transfers occurring within two years of the adoption of a plan of liquidation.

Only the built-in loss (the amount by which the property's basis exceeded its fair market value at the time it was acquired by the corporation) is disallowed under this provision.[5] Any loss attributable to a decline in value that occurs after the property's contribution to the corporation is recognized (subject to the related-party loss limitation).

The built-in loss limitation applies to a broader range of transactions than the related-party exception, which disallows losses only on certain distributions to related parties (i.e., 50 percent or more shareholders). The built-in loss limitation can apply to distributions of property to any shareholder, including an unrelated party, and to a *sale or exchange* of property by a liquidating corporation. However, the limitation is narrower than the related-party exception in that it applies only to property that had a built-in loss upon its acquisition by the corporation and only as to the amount of the built-in loss.

EXAMPLE 8

On January 2, 2005, Brown Corporation acquires property (basis of $10,000, fair market value of $3,000) in a transaction that qualifies under § 351. Brown adopts a plan of liquidation on July 1, 2005, and distributes the property to an unrelated shareholder on November 10, 2005, when the property is worth $1,000. Brown Corporation can recognize a loss of $2,000, the difference between the value of the property on the date of acquisition and the value of the property on the date of distribution. Only the built-in loss of $7,000 [$3,000 (fair market value on date of acquisition) – $10,000 (basis)] is disallowed. ■

EXAMPLE 9

Assume in Example 8 that the property had a fair market value of $12,000 on the date Brown Corporation acquired it. If the distribution is to an unrelated shareholder, Brown will recognize the entire $9,000 loss [$1,000 (fair market value on date of distribution) – $10,000 (basis)]. However, if the distribution is to a related party, Brown cannot recognize any of the loss under the related-party loss limitation because the property is disqualified property. When the distribution is to a related party, the loss is disallowed even though the entire decline in value occurred during the period the corporation held the property. ■

The built-in loss limitation will apply only in rare cases if the corporation has held the property more than two years prior to liquidation. The presumption of a tax avoidance purpose for property transferred to a corporation in the two years preceding the liquidation can be rebutted if there is a clear and substantial

[5] § 336(d)(2).

FIGURE 20–1
Distributions of Loss Property by a Liquidating Corporation

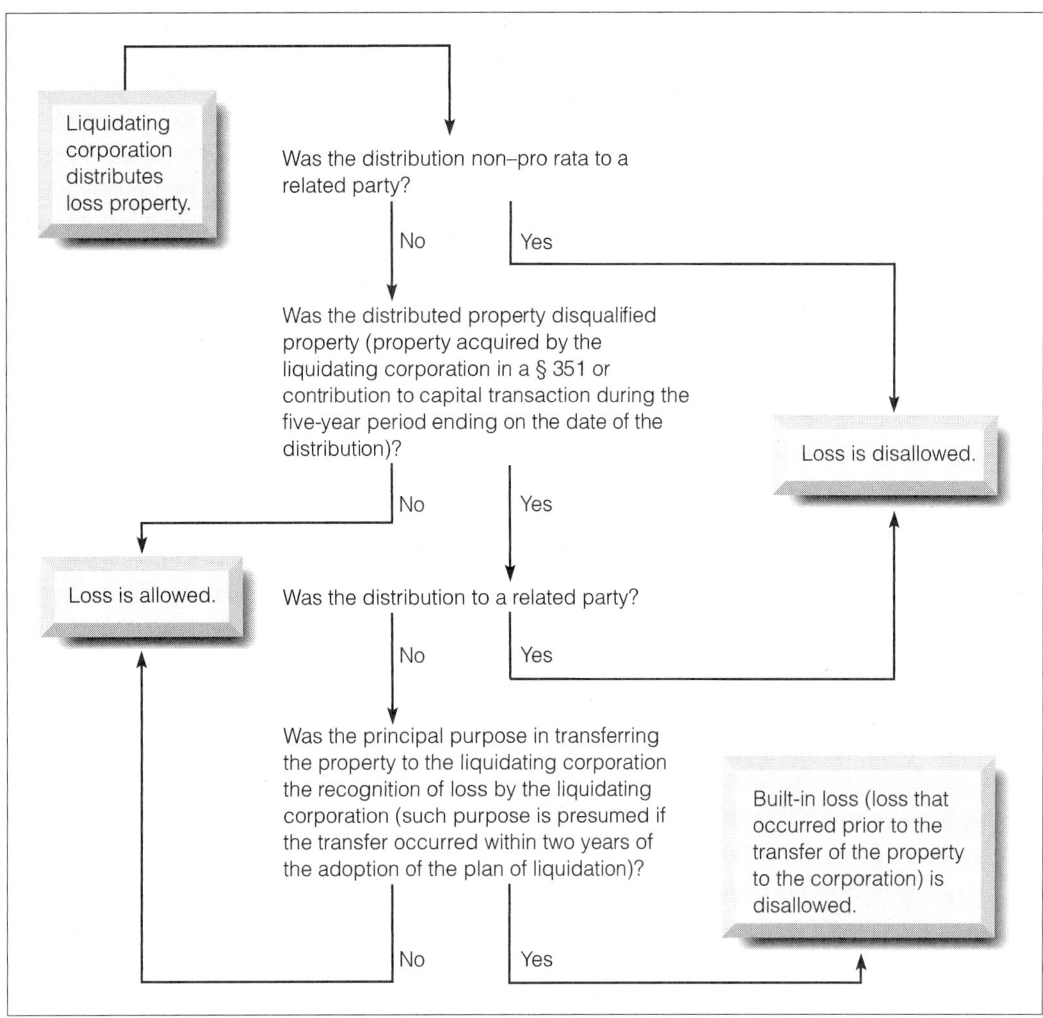

relationship between the contributed property and the (current or future) business of the corporation. When there was a business reason for the transfer, the built-in loss limitation will not apply.

EXAMPLE 10

Cardinal Corporation's stock is held by two unrelated individuals: 60% by Manuel and 40% by Jack. One year before Cardinal's liquidation, Manuel transfers property (basis of $150,000, fair market value of $100,000) to the corporation as a contribution to capital. There is no business reason for the transfer. In liquidation, Cardinal distributes the property (now with a fair market value of $90,000) to Jack. Even though the distribution is to an unrelated party, the built-in loss of $50,000 is not recognized. However, Cardinal Corporation can recognize the loss of $10,000 ($90,000 – $100,000) that occurred while it held the property. If, instead, the property is distributed to Manuel, a related party, the entire $60,000 loss is disallowed under the related-party loss limitation. ■

EXAMPLE 11

Assume in Example 10 that the property is transferred to Cardinal Corporation because a bank required the additional capital investment as a condition to making a loan to the corporation. Because there is a business purpose for the transfer, all of the $60,000 loss is recognized if the property is distributed to Jack in liquidation. If, instead, the property is distributed to Manuel, a related party, the entire loss is still disallowed under the related-party loss limitation. ■

Tax Paid on Net Gain. To the extent that a corporation pays tax on the net amount of gain recognized as a result of its liquidation, the proceeds available to be distributed to the shareholder are likewise reduced. This reduction for the payment of taxes will reduce the amount realized by the shareholder, which will then reduce the shareholder's gain (or increase the loss) recognized.

EXAMPLE 12

Purple Corporation's assets are valued at $2 million after payment of all corporate debts except for $300,000 of taxes payable on net gains it recognized on the liquidation. Therefore, the amount realized by the shareholders is $1.7 million ($2,000,000 – $300,000). As described below, in determining the gain or loss recognized by a shareholder, the amount realized is offset by the stock's adjusted basis. ■

Liquidations—Effect on the Shareholder

The tax consequences to the shareholders of a corporation in the process of liquidation are governed either by the general rule of § 331 or by the exception of § 332 relating to the liquidation of a subsidiary.

THE GENERAL RULE

In the case of a complete liquidation, § 331(a) provides for sale or exchange treatment for the shareholders. Thus, the difference between the fair market value of the assets received from the corporation and the adjusted basis of the stock surrendered is the gain or loss recognized by the shareholder. Typically, the stock is a capital asset in the hands of the shareholder, and capital gain or loss results. The burden of proof is on the taxpayer to furnish evidence as to the adjusted basis of the stock. In the absence of such evidence, the stock is deemed to have a zero basis, and the full amount of the liquidation proceeds equals the amount of the gain recognized.[6] The basis of property received in a liquidation is the property's fair market value on the date of distribution.[7]

ETHICAL CONSIDERATIONS

Shareholder Liability for Tax Deficiency of Liquidated Corporation

In 2003, Duckbill Corporation distributed all of its remaining assets to its two equal shareholders in a complete liquidation. The two shareholders, Dena Hall and Rosa Garcia, each received a distribution of $50,000 for their stock in Duckbill. In 2005, the IRS audited Duckbill Corporation and assessed additional tax of $45,000 (plus penalties and interest) against the corporation. Since Duckbill was defunct (and without assets), the IRS then assessed the entire $45,000 deficiency against Dena Hall, based on transferee liability. The IRS did not attempt to collect any of the deficiency from Rosa Garcia. Is this an equitable solution to the collection of Duckbill's tax deficiency?

SPECIAL RULE FOR CERTAIN INSTALLMENT OBLIGATIONS

Corporations often sell assets pursuant to a plan of liquidation, and sometimes these sales are made on the installment basis. If the installment notes are then distributed in liquidation, the *shareholders* can use the installment method to defer

[6]*John Calderazzo*, 34 TCM 1, T.C.Memo. 1975–1.

[7]§ 334(a).

gain to the point of collection. This treatment requires the shareholders to allocate their stock basis between the installment notes and the other assets received from the corporation.[8] The liquidating *corporation*, however, must recognize the gain on the distribution of the installment notes.[9]

EXAMPLE 13

After adopting a plan of complete liquidation, Beige Corporation sells its only asset, unimproved land held as an investment. The land has appreciated in value and is sold to Jane (an unrelated party) for $100,000. Under the terms of the sale, Beige Corporation receives cash of $25,000 and Jane's notes for the balance of $75,000. The notes are payable over 10 years ($7,500 per year) and carry an appropriate rate of interest. Immediately after the sale, Beige Corporation distributes the cash and notes to Earl, the sole shareholder. Earl has an adjusted basis of $20,000 in the Beige stock, and the installment notes have a value equal to their face amount ($75,000). These transactions have the following tax results:

- Beige Corporation recognizes gain on the distribution of the installment notes, measured by the difference between the $75,000 fair market value and the basis Beige had in the notes.
- Earl may defer the gain on the receipt of the notes to the point of collection.
- Earl must allocate the adjusted basis in his stock ($20,000) between the cash and the installment notes as follows:

$$\frac{\text{Cash}}{\text{Total receipts}} = \frac{\$25{,}000}{\$100{,}000} \times \$20{,}000 = \$5{,}000 \text{ basis allocated to the cash}$$

$$\frac{\text{Notes}}{\text{Total receipts}} = \frac{\$75{,}000}{\$100{,}000} \times \$20{,}000 = \$15{,}000 \text{ basis allocated to the notes}$$

- On the cash portion of the transaction, Earl must recognize $20,000 of gain [$25,000 (cash received) – $5,000 basis (allocated to the cash)] in the year of liquidation.
- Over the next 10 years, Earl must recognize a total gain of $60,000 on the notes, computed as follows:

$$\$75{,}000 \text{ (fair market value)} - \$15{,}000 \text{ (basis allocated to the notes)}$$
$$= \$60{,}000 \text{ (gross profit)}$$

- The gross profit percentage on the notes is 80%, computed as follows:

$$\frac{\$60{,}000 \text{ (gross profit)}}{\$75{,}000 \text{ (contract price)}} = 80\%$$

- Thus, Earl must report a gain of $6,000 [$7,500 (amount of note) × 80% (gross profit percentage)] on the collection of each note over the next 10 years.
- The interest element is accounted for separately. ■

LO.2

Understand the tax consequences of subsidiary liquidations for both the parent and the subsidiary corporations.

Liquidations—Parent-Subsidiary Situations

Section 332, an exception to the general rule of § 331, provides that a parent corporation does *not* recognize gain or loss on a liquidation of its subsidiary. In addition, the subsidiary corporation recognizes *neither gain nor loss* on distributions of property to its parent.[10]

[8] § 453(h). Installment notes attributable to the sale of inventory qualify only if the inventory was sold in a bulk sale to one person.

[9] § 453B(a). Gain is not recognized in the distribution of installment notes by a subsidiary liquidating pursuant to § 332. See the discussion below and §§ 337(a) and 453B(d).

[10] § 337(a). This is an exception to the general rule of § 336.

Include Intangible Assets When Determining a Subsidiary's Solvency

One of the requirements for the application of § 332 in a parent-subsidiary liquidation is that the subsidiary corporation must be solvent. If § 332 applies to the subsidiary's liquidation, the parent corporation will not recognize a loss for the excess of its basis in the subsidiary stock over the fair market value of the subsidiary's assets received. If, however, the subsidiary is insolvent, then the parent corporation typically can claim an ordinary loss deduction equal to its basis in the subsidiary stock. A recent ruling (Rev.Rul. 2003–125, 2003–52 I.R.B. 1243) indicates that, for purposes of determining whether a subsidiary is solvent as of the date of its liquidation, the fair market value of all the subsidiary's assets must be considered, including intangible assets such as goodwill and going-concern value. A subsidiary is insolvent if the fair market value of such assets does not exceed its liabilities.

The requirements for applying § 332 are as follows:

- The parent must own at least 80 percent of the voting stock of the subsidiary and at least 80 percent of the value of the subsidiary's stock.
- The subsidiary must distribute all of its property in complete cancellation of all of its stock within the taxable year or within three years from the close of the tax year in which the first distribution occurred.
- The subsidiary must be solvent.[11]

If these requirements are met, nonrecognition of gains and losses becomes mandatory. However, if the subsidiary is insolvent, the parent corporation will have an ordinary loss deduction under § 165(g).

When a series of distributions occurs in the liquidation of a subsidiary corporation, the parent corporation must own the required amount of stock (at least 80 percent) on the date the plan of liquidation is adopted and at all times until all property has been distributed.[12] If the parent fails the control requirement at any time, the provisions for nonrecognition of gain or loss do not apply to any distribution.[13]

MINORITY SHAREHOLDER INTERESTS

A distribution of property to a minority shareholder in a liquidation otherwise governed by § 332 is treated in the same manner as a *nonliquidating* distribution. That is, the subsidiary corporation recognizes gain (but not loss) on the property distributed to the minority shareholder.[14]

EXAMPLE 14

The stock of Tan Corporation is held as follows: 80% by Mustard Corporation and 20% by Arethia. Tan Corporation is liquidated on December 10, 2005, pursuant to a plan adopted on January 10, 2005. At the time of its liquidation, Tan has assets with a basis of $100,000 and fair market value of $500,000. Tan Corporation distributes the property pro rata to Mustard Corporation and to Arethia. Tan must recognize gain of $80,000 [($500,000 fair

[11] § 332(b) and Reg. §§ 1.332–2(a) and (b).

[12] Establishing the date of the adoption of a plan of complete liquidation could be crucial in determining whether § 332 applies. See, for example, *George L. Riggs, Inc.*, 64 T.C. 474 (1975).

[13] § 332(b)(3) and Reg. § 1.332–2(a).

[14] §§ 336(a) and (d)(3).

market value – $100,000 basis) × 20% minority interest]. Since the corporate tax due in this liquidation relates entirely to the minority shareholder distribution, that amount will most likely be deducted from the $100,000 distribution ($500,000 × 20%) going to Arethia. The remaining gain of $320,000 is not recognized because it is attributable to property being distributed to Mustard, the parent corporation. ■

A minority shareholder is subject to the general rule requiring the recognition of gain or loss in a liquidation. Accordingly, the difference between the fair market value of the assets received and the basis of the minority shareholder's stock is the amount of gain or loss recognized. Further, the basis of property received by the minority shareholder is the property's fair market value on the date of distribution.[15]

INDEBTEDNESS OF THE SUBSIDIARY TO THE PARENT

If a subsidiary transfers appreciated property to its parent to satisfy a debt, it must recognize gain on the transaction unless the subsidiary is liquidating and the conditions of § 332 (discussed above) apply. When § 332 applies, the subsidiary does not recognize gain or loss upon the transfer of properties to the parent in satisfaction of indebtedness.[16]

EXAMPLE 15

Eagle Corporation owes $20,000 to its parent, Finch Corporation. It satisfies the obligation by transferring land (basis of $8,000, fair market value of $20,000). Normally, Eagle would recognize a gain of $12,000 on the transaction. However, if the transfer is made pursuant to a liquidation under § 332, Eagle does not recognize a gain. ■

The special provision noted above does not apply to the parent corporation. The parent corporation recognizes gain or loss on the transfer of property in satisfaction of indebtedness, even if the property is received during liquidation of the subsidiary.

EXAMPLE 16

Pelican Corporation owns bonds (basis of $95,000) of its subsidiary, Crow Corporation, that were acquired at a discount. Upon liquidation of Crow pursuant to § 332, Pelican receives a distribution of $100,000, the face amount of the bonds. The transaction has no tax effect on Crow. However, Pelican Corporation recognizes gain of $5,000 [$100,000 (amount realized) – $95,000 (basis in bonds)]. ■

BASIS OF PROPERTY RECEIVED BY THE PARENT CORPORATION—THE GENERAL RULE

Property received in the complete liquidation of a subsidiary has the same basis it had in the hands of the subsidiary.[17] Unless the parent corporation makes a § 338 election (discussed below), this carryover basis in the assets generally will differ significantly from the parent's basis in the stock of the subsidiary. Since the liquidation is a nontaxable exchange, the parent's gain or loss on the difference in basis is not recognized. Further, the parent's basis in the stock of the liquidated subsidiary disappears.

EXAMPLE 17

Lark Corporation, the parent corporation, has a basis of $200,000 in the stock of Heron Corporation, a subsidiary in which it owns 85% of all classes of stock. Lark purchased the Heron stock 10 years ago. In the current year, Lark liquidates Heron Corporation and acquires assets with a fair market value of $500,000 and a tax basis to Heron of $400,000. Lark

[15] § 334(a).
[16] § 337(b)(1).
[17] § 334(b)(1) and Reg. § 1.334–1(b).

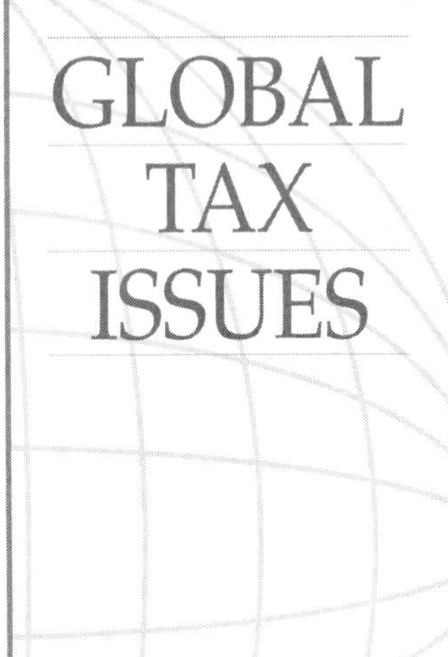

EXCEPTION TO § 332 FOR LIQUIDATIONS OF U.S. SUBSIDIARIES OF FOREIGN CORPORATIONS

When a U.S. subsidiary is liquidated into a U.S. parent, gains (or losses) are not recognized immediately, but rather are deferred as a result of the carryover basis rule. Gains inherent in the transferred assets will be recognized upon their disposition by the parent. Foreign corporations generally are not subject to U.S. taxation, so the liquidation of a U.S. subsidiary into a foreign parent could avoid gain recognition entirely if § 332 were to apply unabated. Section 367(b) overrides § 332 when a U.S. subsidiary is liquidated into a foreign parent, however. Under § 367(b), the subsidiary will recognize gain on the transfer of certain "tainted" assets. Tainted assets include inventory, installment obligations, accounts receivable, and depreciable property (to the extent of depreciation recapture). For further details, see Chapter 25.

Corporation takes a basis of $400,000 in the assets, with a potential gain upon their sale of $100,000. Lark's $200,000 basis in Heron's stock disappears. ■

EXAMPLE 18

Indigo Corporation has a basis of $600,000 in the stock of Kackie Corporation, a wholly owned subsidiary acquired 10 years ago. It liquidates Kackie Corporation and receives assets with a fair market value of $500,000 and a tax basis to Kackie of $400,000. Indigo Corporation takes a basis of $400,000 in the assets it acquires from Kackie. If it sells the assets for $500,000, it has a gain of $100,000 in spite of the fact that its basis in the Kackie stock was $600,000. Indigo's loss on its stock investment in Kackie will never be recognized. ■

In addition to the parent corporation taking the subsidiary's basis in its assets, the carryover rules of § 381 apply. Under that provision, the parent acquires other tax attributes of the subsidiary, including the subsidiary's net operating loss, business credit carryover, capital loss carryover, and E & P.

BASIS OF PROPERTY RECEIVED BY THE PARENT CORPORATION—§ 338 ELECTION

Background. As discussed above, the liquidation of a subsidiary generally is a nontaxable transaction, resulting in the nonrecognition of gain or loss for both the parent and the subsidiary corporation and the carryover of the subsidiary's asset bases (and other tax attributes). This treatment reflects the fact that such a liquidation often is merely a change in corporate structure and not a change in substance. This is particularly the case when the parent has owned the stock of the subsidiary since the subsidiary's inception. In such cases, the carried-over bases are comparable to what the parent would have in the subsidiary's assets if the parent, and not the subsidiary, had originally acquired the assets. However, inequities can develop when a subsidiary is liquidated shortly after its acquisition by the parent.

When a corporation acquires a controlling interest (80 percent) in another corporation over a short period of time, the acquisition cost of the stock will reflect the fair market value of the subsidiary's assets (including goodwill). In all but a few unusual situations, the parent's basis in the stock of the subsidiary will vary greatly from the subsidiary's basis in its assets. Under the general rule of nonrecognition, the difference between the parent's basis in the stock and the carried-over basis in the subsidiary's assets is a nonrecognized gain (if the stock basis is less than the carried-over basis) or loss (if the stock basis is greater than the carried-over basis). This is the case even if the parent acquired the subsidiary stock solely to obtain the subsidiary's assets. If the parent corporation could treat the purchase of the subsidiary stock as a purchase of its assets, the parent could take a basis in the assets equal to the acquisition cost of the stock. In most cases, this would mean a higher asset basis and, as a result, larger depreciation deductions and lower gains upon disposition for the parent corporation.

To obtain the stock-basis-for-asset-basis result, taxpayers successfully devised stock purchase/subsidiary liquidation transactions that fell outside the general rule.[18] Congress codified this treatment by enacting § 338, which permits the purchase of a controlling interest of stock to be treated as a purchase of the subsidiary's assets.

Requirements for Application. A corporation (the "parent") may *elect* the provisions of § 338 if it acquires stock representing at least 80 percent of the voting power and at least 80 percent of the value of another corporation (the "subsidiary") within a 12-month period (*"qualified stock purchase"*). The stock must be acquired in a taxable transaction (i.e., § 351 and other nonrecognition provisions do not apply). An acquisition of stock by any member of an affiliated group that includes the parent corporation is considered to be an acquisition by the parent. The **§ 338 election** must be made by the fifteenth day of the ninth month beginning after the month in which a qualified stock purchase occurs. If made, the election is irrevocable.

Tax Consequences. Upon making a qualified § 338 election, the subsidiary is treated as having sold its assets on the qualified stock purchase date for a value that is determined with reference to the parent's basis in the subsidiary stock plus any liabilities of the subsidiary.[19] The subsidiary is then treated as a new corporation that purchased those assets for a similarly computed amount on the day following the qualified stock purchase date.[20] The deemed sale results in gain (or loss) recognition to the subsidiary, and the deemed purchase results in a stepped-up (or -down) basis for the subsidiary's assets.[21] The subsidiary may, but need not, be liquidated. If the subsidiary is liquidated, the parent will obtain a carryover of the stepped-up (or -down) basis of the subsidiary's assets.

A Comparison of the General Rule and the § 338 Election. Under the general rule of nonrecognition, the liquidation of a subsidiary is tax-free to both the subsidiary (except for any minority interest) and the parent corporation. Under § 338, the subsidiary recognizes gain (or loss) on the deemed disposition of its assets. A liquidation of the subsidiary remains tax-free to the parent. While a carryover basis rule applies in both cases, the subsidiary's assets generally will have a stepped-up basis as a result of the § 338 election, and a liquidation of the subsidiary will result in a carryover of the stepped-up basis to the parent. Further, a liquidation of the subsidiary results in a carryover of its other tax attributes (e.g., E & P) to the parent whether or not a § 338 election is made. However, when the election is made, the subsidiary is treated as a new corporation as of the day following the qualified stock purchase date; as a result, any tax attributes acquired by the parent are likely to be nominal (or zero) in amount.

[18]See, e.g., *U.S. v. M.O.J. Corp.*, 60–1 USTC ¶9209, 5 AFTR2d 535, 274 F.2d 713 (CA–5, 1960). See also *Kimbell-Diamond Milling Co.*, 14 T.C. 74 (1950), *aff'd* 51–1 USTC ¶9201, 40 AFTR 328, 187 F.2d 718 (CA–5, 1951), *cert. den.* 72 S.Ct. 50 (USSC, 1951) (IRS argued stock-for-asset basis).

[19]See §§ 338(a)(1) and (b) and Reg. § 1.338–4.

[20]See §§ 338(a)(2) and (b) and Reg. § 1.338–5.

[21]For the rules governing the allocation of the purchase price to the assets, see § 338(b)(5) and Reg. § 1.338–6.

Concept Summary 20–1

Summary of Liquidation Rules

Effect on the Shareholder	Basis of Property Received	Effect on the Corporation
§ 331—The general rule provides for capital gain treatment on the difference between the FMV of property received and the basis of the stock in the corporation. Gain allocable to installment notes received can be deferred to point of collection.	§ 334(a)—Basis of assets received by the shareholder will be the FMV on the date of distribution (except for installment obligations in which gain is deferred to the point of collection).	§ 336—Gain or loss is recognized for distributions in kind and for sales by the liquidating corporation. Losses are not recognized for distributions to related parties if the distribution is not pro rata or if disqualified property is distributed. Losses may be disallowed on sales and distributions of certain other property even if made to unrelated parties.
§ 332—In liquidation of a subsidiary, no gain or loss is recognized to the parent. Subsidiary must distribute all of its property within the taxable year or within three years from the close of the taxable year in which the first distribution occurs. Minority shareholders taxed under general rule of § 331.	§ 334(b)(1)—Property has the same basis as it had in the hands of the subsidiary. Parent's basis in the stock disappears. Carryover rules of § 381 apply. Minority shareholders get FMV basis under § 334(a).	§ 337—No gain or loss is recognized to the subsidiary on distributions to the parent. Gain (but not loss) is recognized on distributions to minority shareholders.
	§ 338—Subsidiary need not be liquidated. If subsidiary is liquidated, parent's basis is now stepped-up (or -down) basis. Parent's basis in the stock disappears. Carryover rules of § 381 apply, but such amounts are likely to be nominal.	§ 338—Gain or loss is recognized to the subsidiary. Subsidiary is treated as a new corporation, and its basis in assets is stepped up (or down) to reflect parent's basis in subsidiary stock plus subsidiary's liabilities. New basis is allocated among various asset classes.

The holding period of the subsidiary's assets is determined with reference to the substance of the transaction. When the subsidiary is liquidated and there is no § 338 election, the subsidiary's historical holding period in its assets carries over to the parent. This is the typical carryover rule found in other nonrecognition provisions. A § 338 election, however, assumes a sale and repurchase of the subsidiary's assets. As a result of these deemed transactions, the holding period starts anew. If there is a § 338 election and the subsidiary is liquidated, the holding period of the property received by the parent begins on the date of the qualified stock purchase. On the other hand, if there is a § 338 election and the subsidiary is not liquidated, the holding period of the assets begins on the day after the qualified stock acquisition date. The parent-subsidiary liquidation rules are set out in Concept Summary 20–1.

LO.3

Understand the general requirements and tax consequences of corporate reorganizations.

Corporate Reorganizations

One of the tenets of U.S. tax policy is to encourage business development. To this end, the tax laws allow entities to form without taxation, assuming certain requirements are met. As an extension of this concept, corporate restructurings are also favored with tax-free treatment. Corporations may engage in a variety of acquisitions, combinations, consolidations, and divisions tax-free, as long as the "reorganization" requirements in the Code are met.

Mergers and acquisitions are a popular method of increasing the economic vitality of corporate businesses. The recent restructuring frenzy peaked in 1999–2000, when more than 20,000 major deals (values greater than $5 million) amounting to almost $2.7 trillion in value occurred. Unfortunately, the downturn in the global economy and stock market dramatically slowed merger and acquisition activity. Since the low point in 2002, however, the number and dollar value of mergers and acquisitions have been increasing. Mergers in banking and finance and in the leisure/entertainment industry have involved the highest dollar values, but the computer industry leads in the numbers of deals. The comeback seems promising, but the industry may take several years to make a full recovery. One can only guess when activity will once again reach the $1 trillion mark for a single year. Only 2 of the 10 largest mergers and acquisitions in the last seven years have occurred since 2000.

One type of restructuring has seen a dramatic increase in the past few years—mega-bankruptcies. This increase has been fueled by the economy and financial statement misstatements. In fact, seven of the largest U.S. bankruptcies in the last 18 years have occurred since 2000.

Given the magnitude of the dollar amounts involved in most reorganizations, tax planning strategies play an important role in these transactions. The taxable gain for the shareholder is likely to be treated as either a dividend or a capital gain. For individual shareholders, both of these are subject to a maximum tax rate of 15 percent. Corporate shareholders would be allowed a dividends received deduction if the gains are categorized as a dividend. However, since corporations receive no tax rate reduction for capital gains, corporate shareholders and the corporations involved in the restructuring would be taxed at their highest marginal rate on any gains classified as capital. Fortunately, careful planning can reduce or totally eliminate taxation for both the corporations and their shareholders. Consequently, tax law often dictates the form of the restructuring.

Courts originally concluded that even minor changes in a corporation's structure would produce taxable gains for the shareholders involved.[22] Congress, however, determined that businesses should be allowed to make necessary capital adjustments without being subject to taxation.[23] The theory for nonrecognition in certain corporate restructurings or "reorganizations" is similar to that underlying § 351 treatment and like-kind exchanges. As the Regulations state:

> the new property is substantially a continuation of the old investment . . . and, in the case of reorganizations, . . . the new enterprise, the new corporate structure, and the new property are substantially continuations of the old.[24]

IN GENERAL

Although the term **reorganization** is commonly associated with a corporation in financial difficulty, for tax purposes the term refers to any corporate restructuring that may be tax-free under § 368. To qualify as a tax-free reorganization, a corporate restructuring transaction must meet not only the specific requirements of § 368 but also several general requirements. These requirements include the following.

1. There must be a *plan of reorganization.*
2. The reorganization must meet the *continuity of interest* and the *continuity of business enterprise* tests set out in the Regulations.
3. The restructuring must meet the judicial doctrine of having a *sound business purpose.*
4. The court-imposed *step transaction* doctrine should not apply to the reorganization.

[22] *U.S. v. Phellis,* 1 USTC ¶54, 3 AFTR 3123, 42 S.Ct. 63 (USSC, 1921).

[23] Reg. § 1.368–1(b). See S.Rept. No. 275, 67th Cong., 1st Sess. (1921), at 1939–1 C.B. 181.

[24] Reg. § 1.1002–1(c).

When Mergers and Acquisitions Rebound, So Does Hiring

It may be that mergers and acquisitions (M&A) have turned the corner and are back on track for the first time in this century. The number of M&A transactions is finally increasing, due in part to the improving economy and the abundance of liquid financing.

Consequently, the investment banking industry is hiring rather than firing. During the past market downturn, investment bankers left Wall Street by the droves and went to specialized and regional banks. Now those same refugees are returning to their former business homes. To fulfill their growing personnel needs, the banking giants can either poach from their competitors or hire back those individuals who left and now want to come back to where the action is. The investment banks have still not jumped into the hiring game with both feet; so far, they are just looking to fill or slightly increase their strategic M&A positions. Even with this caveat, the equilibrium is shifting: these days the trend is definitely from the small banks back to Wall Street.

SOURCE: Adapted from Avital Hahn, "Back to the Big Leagues: Bankers Return to Bulge-Bracket Firms That Laid Them Off in Downturn," *Investment Dealers Digest*, June 7, 2004.

While all of these concepts are important, the initial and most important consideration is whether the reorganization qualifies for nonrecognition status under § 368, which is described below.

SUMMARY OF THE DIFFERENT TYPES OF REORGANIZATIONS

Section 368(a) specifies seven corporate restructurings or reorganizations that will qualify as nontaxable exchanges. If the transaction fails to qualify as a reorganization, it will not receive the special tax-favored treatment. Therefore, a corporation considering a business reorganization must determine in advance if the proposed transaction specifically falls within one of these seven types. In situations possibly involving substantial tax dollars, the parties should obtain a letter ruling from the IRS verifying that the proposed transaction qualifies as a tax-free reorganization under § 368.

Section 368(a)(1) states that the term reorganization applies to any of the following:

A. A statutory merger or consolidation.
B. The acquisition by a corporation of another using solely stock of each corporation (voting-stock-for-stock exchange).
C. The acquisition by a corporation of substantially all of the property of another corporation in exchange for voting stock (stock-for-asset exchange).
D. The transfer of all or part of a corporation's assets to another corporation when the original corporation's shareholders are in control of the new corporation immediately after the transfer (divisive exchange, also known as a spin-off, split-off, or split-up).
E. A recapitalization.
F. A mere change in identity, form, or place of organization.
G. A transfer by a corporation of all or a part of its assets to another corporation in a bankruptcy or receivership proceeding.

Concept Summary 20–2

Gain and Basis Rules for Nontaxable Exchanges

(1) Realized Gain/Loss	(2) Recognized Gain (Not Loss)	(3) Postponed Gain/Loss	(4) Basis of New Asset
Amount realized	Lesser of boot received or gain realized	Gain/loss realized (column 1)	FMV of asset (stock) received
– Adjusted basis of asset surrendered		– Gain recognized (column 2)	– Postponed gain (column 3) or + Postponed loss (column 3)
Gain/loss realized	Gain recognized	Gain/loss postponed	Adjusted basis in new asset (stock)

These seven types of tax-free reorganizations typically are designated by their identifying letters: "Type A," "Type B," "Type C," and so on. For the most part, excepting the recapitalization (E), the change in form (F), and the insolvent corporation (G) provisions, a tax-free reorganization is (1) a statutory merger or consolidation, (2) an exchange of stock for voting stock, (3) an exchange of assets for voting stock, or (4) a divisive reorganization (a so-called spin-off, split-off, or split-up).

SUMMARY OF THE TAX CONSEQUENCES IN A TAX-FREE REORGANIZATION

The tax treatment of the parties involved in a tax-free reorganization almost exactly parallels the treatment under the like-kind exchange provisions of § 1031. In the simplest like-kind exchange, neither gain nor loss is recognized on the exchange of "like-kind" property. When "boot" (defined as non-like-kind property) is involved, gain may be recognized. The four-column template of Concept Summary 20–2 can be used to compute the amount of gain recognized and the adjusted basis in the new asset received in the like-kind exchange.

Unfortunately, the like-kind exchange provisions do not apply to the exchange of stock or securities.[25] Therefore, the general rule is that when an investor exchanges stock in one corporation for stock in another, the exchange is a taxable transaction. If the transaction qualifies as a reorganization under § 368, however, the exchange will be nontaxable. Thus, a § 368 reorganization, in substance, is similar to a nontaxable exchange of like-kind property, and the four-column template of Concept Summary 20–2 is useful for reorganizations as well.

EXAMPLE 19

John holds 1,000 shares of Lotus stock that he purchased for $10,000 several years ago. In a merger of Lotus into Blossom, John exchanges his 1,000 shares of Lotus for 1,000 shares of Blossom. Both investments are valued at $18 per share. John's realized gain on the exchange is $8,000 [($18 per share × 1,000 shares) – $10,000 basis]. Assuming this exchange qualifies for tax-free treatment under § 368, John's recognized gain is zero. Since his postponed gain is $8,000, John's basis in his new stock is $10,000 [$18,000 (FMV of new stock) – $8,000 (postponed gain)]. The exchange of John's stock has no tax consequences for Lotus or Blossom. ■

Gain or Loss. Corporations meeting the requirements of § 368 do not recognize gain or loss on a restructuring. There are exceptions to the nonrecognition rule, however. If the acquiring corporation transfers property to the target corporation

[25] § 1031(a)(2)(B).

along with its stock and securities, gain, but not loss, may be recognized. The target may also recognize gain, but not loss, when it fails to distribute the *other property* it receives in the restructuring or distributes its own appreciated property to its shareholders. *Other property* in this case is defined as anything received other than stock or securities and, thus, is treated as boot.[26]

EXAMPLE 20

In a restructuring qualifying as a reorganization, Acquiring Corporation exchanges $80,000 of stock and land with a fair market value of $20,000 (basis of $15,000) for all of the assets of Target Corporation. Target's assets have a fair market value of $100,000 and a basis of $60,000. Due to the *other property* (land) Acquiring uses in the transfer, it recognizes a gain of $5,000 ($20,000 – $15,000) on the reorganization. If Target distributes the land to its shareholders, it does not recognize gain. If Target retains the land, however, it recognizes gain to the extent of the *other property* received, $20,000. ■

Generally, the stockholders of the corporations involved in a tax-free reorganization do not recognize gain or loss when exchanging their stock unless they receive cash or other property in addition to stock. The cash or other property is considered boot, and the gain recognized by the stockholder is the lesser of the boot received or the realized gain. This is analogous to the treatment of boot in a like-kind exchange.

EXAMPLE 21

Kalla, the sole shareholder of Target Corporation in Example 20, has a basis in her stock of $70,000. She exchanges her Target stock for the $80,000 of Acquiring stock plus the land ($20,000) transferred by Acquiring to Target. Kalla has a realized gain of $30,000 [$80,000 (value of Acquiring stock) + $20,000 (boot received) – $70,000 (basis of Target stock)]. Receiving the land (boot) causes her to recognize a $20,000 gain. ■

Once the gain is computed, its character must be determined. The following are the possibilities for gain characterization.

- Dividend to the extent of the shareholder's proportionate share of corporate earnings and profits (E & P). The remaining gain is generally capital gain.
  - For individual shareholders, the distinction between dividends and long-term capital gain may be less critical, now that the tax rate is the same for both. However, this distinction is still important when the taxpayer has capital losses to offset or when the capital gain would be classified as short term and therefore not subject to the special tax rates.
- If the requirements of § 302(b) can be met, the transaction will qualify for stock redemption treatment (see Chapter 19).
  - Gains from qualifying stock redemptions are treated as capital gains.
  - In computing the shareholder's ownership reduction, shares actually received in the acquiring corporation are compared with the number of shares the shareholder would have received if solely stock of the acquiring corporation had been distributed in the reorganization.[27]

EXAMPLE 22

Sam exchanges his 10% stock interest in Target (basis of $8,000) for $4,000 of cash and stock in Acquiring worth $11,000. At the time of the reorganization, Target's E & P is $25,000. Sam has a realized gain of $7,000 [$15,000 (value of Acquiring stock plus cash) – $8,000 (basis of Target stock)] and a $4,000 recognized gain (the cash received). The first $2,500 ($25,000 × 10%) is taxable as a dividend, and the remaining $1,500 is treated as a capital gain. Both are taxed at a maximum rate of 15%.

[26]§§ 361(a) and (b). In a Type A or Type C reorganization, gain will not be recognized due to the retention of other property because the target is liquidated under the reorganization rules (i.e, no property is retained by the target).

[27]*Comm. v. Clark*, 89–1 USTC ¶9230, 63 AFTR2d 89–860, 109 S.Ct. 1455 (USSC, 1989), and Rev.Rul. 93–61, 1993–2 C.B. 118.

CONCEPT SUMMARY 20–3

Basis Rules for a Tax-Free Reorganization

Basis to Acquiring Corporation of Property Received	
Target's basis in property transferred	$xx,xxx
Plus: Gain recognized by Target on the transaction	x,xxx
Equals: Basis of property to Acquiring Corporation	$xx,xxx
Basis to Target Shareholders of Stock and Securities Received	
Basis of stock and securities transferred	$xx,xxx
Plus: Gain and dividend income recognized	x,xxx
Less: Money and fair market value of other property received	(x,xxx)
Equals: Basis of stock and securities received	$xx,xxx

Suppose instead that Sam received 1% of Acquiring stock with a fair market value of $10,000 and $5,000 of cash. If Sam had received solely stock, he would have received 1.5% of Acquiring stock. Since Sam owns less than 80% of the stock he would have owned (1% ÷ 1.5% is less than 80%) and less than 50% of Acquiring, he meets the qualifications for sale or exchange treatment under § 302(b)(2). Therefore, all of Sam's $5,000 recognized gain is treated as a capital gain. ■

Debt security holders receive treatment similar to shareholders. They recognize gain only when the principal amount of the securities received is greater than that of the securities given up. If securities are received and none are surrendered, the gain is also recognized.[28]

The term *security* is not defined in the Code or the Regulations. Generally, however, a debt instrument with a term greater than 10 years (e.g., a bond) is treated as a security, and one with a term of five years or less (e.g., a note) is not. An exception to this general rule occurs when the debt instrument issued by the acquiring corporation is exchanged for target securities having the same term and maturity date.[29]

EXAMPLE 23

Alejandra holds a security issued by Hibiscus Corporation. The principal value of the security is $10,000, and its maturity date is December 31, 2009. In connection with the merger of Hibiscus and Tea Corporation in 2005, Alejandra exchanges her Hibiscus security for a $10,000 Tea note that matures on December 31, 2009. Even though these notes do not have a term remaining of more than five years, they qualify for tax-free reorganization treatment. ■

EXAMPLE 24

Assume the same facts as in Example 23, except that in exchange for her $10,000 security, Alejandra receives a note from Tea with a $15,000 principal value. Alejandra recognizes a $5,000 capital gain on the exchange. ■

Basis. The assets transferred from the target corporation to the acquiring corporation retain their basis. However, this carryover basis is increased by any gain recognized by the target corporation on the reorganization. Concept Summary 20–3 shows this computation.

[28] § 354(a)(2)(A).

[29] Rev.Rul. 2004–78, 2004–31 I.R.B. 108.

EXAMPLE 25

Target exchanges its assets with a fair market value of $50,000 and a basis of $30,000 for $45,000 of Acquiring stock and $5,000 of land. Target does not distribute the land to its shareholders. Target recognizes a $5,000 gain on the reorganization (due to the other property not being distributed). Acquiring's basis in the assets received from Target is $35,000 [$30,000 (Target's basis) + $5,000 (Target's gain recognized)]. ■

In general, the tax basis of the stock and securities received by a shareholder pursuant to a tax-free reorganization is the same as the basis of those surrendered. However, this basis is decreased by the fair market value of boot received and increased by the gain and/or dividend income recognized on the transaction. Concept Summary 20–3 provides a summary of these calculations. Another way to compute the basis in the stock and securities received, using the template of Concept Summary 20–2, is to subtract the gain (or add the loss) postponed from the fair market value of the stock and securities received. This basis computation ensures that the postponed gain or loss will be recognized when the new stock or securities are disposed of in a taxable transaction.

EXAMPLE 26

Quinn exchanges all of his stock in Target Corporation for stock in Acquiring plus $3,000 of cash. The exchange is pursuant to a tax-free reorganization. Quinn paid $10,000 for the stock in Target two years ago. The Acquiring stock received has a fair market value of $12,000. Quinn has a realized gain of $5,000 [$12,000 (value of Acquiring stock) + $3,000 (boot received) – $10,000 (basis of Target stock)], which is recognized to the extent of the boot received, $3,000. Quinn's basis in the Acquiring stock is $10,000. This can be computed using the template in Concept Summary 20–2 [$12,000 (value of Acquiring stock) – $2,000 (postponed gain)] or Concept Summary 20–3 [$10,000 (basis) + $3,000 (gain) – $3,000 (money received)].

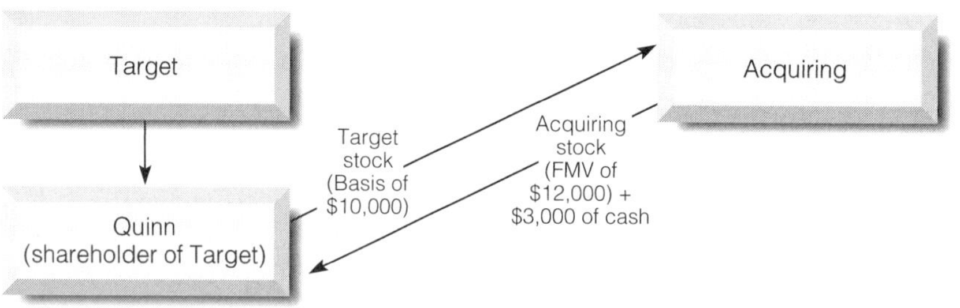

■

EXAMPLE 27

Assume the same facts as in Example 26 except that Quinn's basis in the Target stock was $16,000. Quinn realizes a loss of $1,000 on the exchange, none of which is recognized. His basis in the Acquiring stock is $13,000 [Concept Summary 20–2: $12,000 (value of stock received) + $1,000 (loss postponed) or Concept Summary 20–3: $16,000 (basis) – $3,000 (money received)]. ■

Concept Summary 20–4 furnishes a review of the tax consequences of tax-free reorganizations.

LO.4

Identify tax planning opportunities available to minimize the tax impact in complete liquidations and corporate reorganizations.

Tax Planning Considerations

EFFECT OF A LIQUIDATING DISTRIBUTION ON THE CORPORATION

With the exception of parent-subsidiary liquidations, distributions in liquidation are taxed at both the corporate level and the shareholder level. When a corporation liquidates, it generally can claim losses on assets that have declined in value. These assets should not be distributed in the form of a property dividend or stock redemption because losses are not recognized on nonliquidating distributions.

CONCEPT SUMMARY 20–4

Tax Consequences of Tax-Free Reorganizations

Treatment is similar to like-kind exchanges.

- No gain or loss is recognized by the acquiring or target corporation unless other property (i.e., boot) is transferred or received by any parties to the reorganization.
- Basis in the assets received by the acquiring corporation is generally carried over from the target corporation.
- Basis in the stock received by the target corporation's shareholders takes a substituted basis, which is derived from their basis in the target stock.
- Gain, but not loss, may be recognized when boot is transferred by the acquiring corporation.
- Gain, but not loss, may be recognized when the target corporation receives boot and does not distribute the boot to its shareholders.
- Gain, but not loss, may be recognized when target shareholders receive anything other than stock (i.e., boot) in exchange for their target stock.

EFFECT OF A LIQUIDATING DISTRIBUTION ON THE SHAREHOLDER

Shareholders faced with large prospective gains in a liquidation may consider shifting part or all of that gain to other taxpayers. One approach is to donate stock to charity. A charitable contribution of the stock produces a deduction equal to the stock's fair market value (see Chapter 17). Alternatively, the stock may be given to family members. If the family member is in the 10 or 15 percent marginal income tax bracket, some or all of the gain on liquidation could be taxed at the 5 percent preferential rate on long-term capital gains. Whether these procedures will be successful in shifting the liquidation-related gain from the taxpayer depends on the timing of the transfer. If the donee of the stock is not in a position to prevent the liquidation of the corporation, the donor may be deemed to have made an anticipatory assignment of income. In such a case, the gain is still taxed to the donor. In addition, the gift tax must be considered (see Chapter 27). Hence, advance planning of stock transfers is crucial in arriving at the desired tax result.

The installment sale provisions provide some relief from the general rule that a shareholder recognizes all gain upon receiving a liquidating distribution. If the assets of the liquidating corporation are not to be distributed in kind, a sale of the assets in exchange for installment notes should be considered. Shareholders receiving the notes in a liquidation can then report their gain on the installment method as the notes are collected.

PARENT-SUBSIDIARY LIQUIDATIONS

The nonrecognition provision applicable to the liquidation of a subsidiary, § 332, is not elective. Nevertheless, some flexibility may be available:

- Whether § 332 applies depends on the 80 percent stock ownership test. A parent corporation may be able to avoid § 332 by reducing its stock ownership in the subsidiary below this percentage to allow for recognition of a loss. On the other hand, the opposite approach may be desirable to avoid gain recognition. A corporate shareholder possessing less than the required 80 percent ownership may want to acquire additional stock to qualify for § 332 treatment.
- Once § 332 becomes effective, less latitude is allowed in determining the parent's basis in the subsidiary's assets. Generally, the subsidiary's existing

basis in its assets carries over to the parent. If a timely § 338 election is made, the subsidiary's basis in its assets is stepped up to reflect, in part, the parent's basis in the subsidiary stock. If the subsidiary also is liquidated, the parent obtains assets with the stepped-up basis.

- An election to have the § 338 rules apply should be carefully weighed as the election can be detrimental. The income tax liability on the subsidiary's recognized gain that results from the deemed sale of its assets is the cost under § 338 for obtaining the stepped-up basis. As a result, a § 338 election may be a viable option only when the subsidiary possesses loss and/or credit carryovers that can be used to offset the associated tax.

ASSET PURCHASE VERSUS STOCK PURCHASE

The acquisition of a corporation's assets generally takes one of two forms. In one form, the acquiring corporation purchases the stock of the target corporation, and then the target (subsidiary) is liquidated. In the other form, the acquiring corporation purchases the assets of the target corporation, and then the target distributes the proceeds in liquidation. Nontax considerations may affect the form of acquisition, with each form having both favorable and unfavorable aspects.

An asset purchase requires that title be transferred and that creditors be notified. Further, an asset purchase may not be feasible if valuable nontransferable trademarks, contracts, or licenses are involved. Alternatively, an asset purchase may be preferable to a stock purchase if the target's shareholders refuse to sell their stock. Additionally, an asset purchase avoids the transfer of liabilities (including unknown liabilities) generally inherent in stock acquisitions. An asset purchase also has the advantage of allowing the purchaser to avoid the acquisition of unwanted assets, whereas a stock purchase would involve all of a target's assets.

THE ROLE OF THE LETTER RULING

When feasible, the parties contemplating a corporate reorganization should apply for and obtain from the IRS a letter ruling concerning the income tax effect of the transaction(s). Assuming the parties carry out the transfers as proposed in the ruling request, a favorable ruling provides, in effect, an insurance policy. If the tax implications are significant, as they often are with corporate reorganizations, the advantage of obtaining prior IRS approval is clear.

KEY TERMS

Corporate liquidation, 20–2

Reorganization, 20–15

Section 338 election, 20–13

PROBLEM MATERIALS

Discussion Questions

1. When does a corporate liquidation exist for tax purposes?
2. Compare liquidating and nonliquidating distributions as to the recognition of gains or losses for the distributing corporation.
3. For purposes of the related-party loss limitation within the context of a complete liquidation, what is the definition of "disqualified property"?

4. For the built-in loss limitation to apply, the property must have been acquired by the corporation as part of a plan whose principal purpose was to recognize a loss on the property by the liquidating corporation. Explain this requirement.

5. Explain the tax consequences to a shareholder of a corporation in the process of liquidation under the general rule of § 331. May a shareholder use the installment method to report gain on a complete liquidation?

6. In terms of the rules applying to parent-subsidiary liquidations, describe the effect of each of the following:
   a. The date of the adoption of a plan of complete liquidation.
   b. The period of time in which the corporation must liquidate.
   c. The solvency of the subsidiary being liquidated.

7. In a liquidation subject to § 332, a subsidiary corporation distributes appreciated property (fair market value greater than basis) to a minority shareholder. Since the subsidiary is liquidated pursuant to § 332, it recognizes no gain on the distribution. Assess the validity of this statement.

8. In the context of a § 332 liquidation, does the nonrecognition rule apply to a transfer of property by a subsidiary to a parent in satisfaction of indebtedness? Explain.

9. Condor Corporation pays $1.3 million for 100% of the stock in Dove Corporation. Dove has a basis of $1.5 million in its assets. If Condor liquidates Dove and makes no special election, what are the tax consequences to Condor and to Dove?

10. What are the requirements for the application of § 338?

11. What are the tax consequences of a § 338 election to the parent and subsidiary corporations?

12. What industries currently account for the highest number and dollar value of mergers and acquisitions?

13. Taxable gains may occur in a corporate reorganization. How are the gains treated by the individual shareholders and the corporations involved in the transaction?

14. To qualify for tax-free treatment, a restructuring must meet the requirements of the Code and several general requirements. List the general requirements the restructuring must meet.

Issue ID

15. Dunn purchased 20,000 shares of stock in Pear Corporation eight years ago. This constituted 20% of Pear's outstanding shares. Last year, Pear redeemed 10,000 shares of Dunn's stock for $100 a share. In the current year, all of Pear's shareholders exchange their stock for an equal number of shares in Plum Corporation plus $5 a share. The cash payment is made because Plum stock is valued at $100 a share and Pear stock is now valued at $105 a share. Plum does not want to issue fractional shares. After the transaction, Pear becomes a subsidiary of Plum. What are the tax issues to be considered in this situation?

Problems

16. The stock of Hawk Corporation is owned equally by three sisters, Michele, Melanie, and Miranda. Hawk owns land (basis of $200,000, fair market value of $280,000) that it has held for investment for eight years. When Michele's basis in her stock is $310,000, Hawk distributes the land to her in exchange for all of her shares. What are the tax consequences for both Hawk and Michele:
    a. If the distribution is a qualifying stock redemption?
    b. If the distribution is a liquidating distribution?

17. Pursuant to a complete liquidation, Oriole Corporation distributes to its shareholders land held for three years as an investment (adjusted basis of $600,000, fair market value of $800,000). The land is subject to a liability of $500,000.
    a. What are the tax consequences to Oriole Corporation on the distribution of the land?
    b. If the land is, instead, subject to a liability of $900,000, what are the tax consequences to Oriole on the distribution?

18. Green Corporation acquired land in a § 351 exchange in 2002. The land had a basis of $625,000 and a fair market value of $700,000 on the date of the transfer. Green Corporation has two shareholders, Mark and Megan, who are brother and sister. During 2005, Green Corporation adopts a plan of liquidation, and when the fair market value of the land is $550,000, it is distributed pro rata to Mark and Megan. What amount of loss may Green Corporation recognize on the liquidating distribution of the land?

19. On April 12, 2004, Crow Corporation acquired land in a § 351 transaction. At that time, the land had a basis of $300,000 and a fair market value of $220,000. The land was transferred to Crow Corporation for use as security for a loan the corporation was in the process of obtaining from a local bank. The bank required the additional capital investment as a condition for making the loan. Crow Corporation adopted a plan of liquidation on October 3, 2005. On December 1, 2005, Crow Corporation distributes the land to Ali, a 40% shareholder. On the date of the distribution, the land had a fair market value of only $70,000. What amount of loss may Crow Corporation recognize on the distribution of the land?

20. On January 8, 2004, Grackle Corporation acquired equipment as a contribution to capital. At that time, the equipment had an adjusted basis of $200,000 and a fair market value of $110,000. On July 28, 2005, Grackle Corporation adopted a plan of liquidation. On November 15, 2005, Grackle sold the equipment to Chris, an unrelated party, for its current fair market value of $50,000. Grackle Corporation never used the equipment for any business purpose during the time it owned the equipment. What amount of loss may Grackle Corporation recognize on the sale of the equipment?

Decision Making

21. Pink Corporation acquired land in a § 351 tax-free exchange in 2004. The land had a basis of $1.7 million and a fair market value of $1.9 million on the date of the transfer. Pink Corporation has two shareholders, Maria and Paul, who are unrelated. Maria owns 70% of the stock in the corporation, and Paul owns 30%. Pink adopts a plan of liquidation in 2005. On this date, the value of the land has decreased to $700,000. What is the effect of each of the following on Pink Corporation? Which option should be selected?
    a. Distribute all the land to Maria.
    b. Distribute all the land to Paul.
    c. Distribute 70% of the land to Maria and 30% to Paul.
    d. Distribute 50% of the land to Maria and 50% to Paul.
    e. Sell the land and distribute the proceeds of $700,000 proportionately to Maria and to Paul.

Decision Making

22. Assume in Problem 21 that the land had a fair market value of $1.5 million on the date of its transfer to the corporation. On the date of the liquidation, the land's fair market value has decreased to $700,000. How would your answer to Problem 21 change if:
    a. All the land is distributed to Maria?
    b. All the land is distributed to Paul?
    c. The land is distributed 70% to Maria and 30% to Paul?
    d. The land is distributed 50% to Maria and 50% to Paul?
    e. The land is sold and the proceeds of $700,000 are distributed proportionately to Maria and to Paul?

23. After a plan of complete liquidation has been adopted, Purple Corporation sells its only asset, land, to Rex (an unrelated party) for $400,000. Under the terms of the sale, Purple receives cash of $100,000 and Rex's note in the amount of $300,000. The note is payable over five years ($60,000 per year) and carries an appropriate rate of interest. Immediately after the sale, Purple distributes the cash and note to Helen, the sole shareholder of Purple Corporation. Helen has a basis of $100,000 in the Purple stock. What are the tax results to Helen if she wishes to defer as much gain as possible on the transaction? Assume the installment note possesses a value equal to its face amount.

24. The stock of Magenta Corporation is owned by Fuchsia Corporation (95%) and Marta (5%). Magenta is liquidated on September 5, 2005, pursuant to a plan of liquidation adopted earlier in the same year. In the liquidation, Magenta distributes various assets worth $1,995,000 (basis of $950,000) to Fuchsia (basis of $1.7 million in Magenta stock) and a parcel of land worth $105,000 (basis of $125,000) to Marta (basis of $30,000 in Magenta stock). Assuming the § 338 election is not made, what are the tax consequences of the liquidation to Magenta, Fuchsia, and Marta?

25. Orange Corporation purchased bonds (basis of $680,000) of its wholly owned subsidiary, Green Corporation, at a discount. Upon liquidation of Green pursuant to § 332, Orange receives payment in the form of land worth $700,000, the face amount of the bonds. Green had a basis of $710,000 in the land. What are the tax consequences of this land transfer to Green Corporation and to Orange Corporation?

26. Three years ago, Cardinal Corporation acquired 100% of all classes of stock of Wren Corporation for $900,000. In the current year, Cardinal liquidates Wren Corporation and acquires assets worth $1.5 million with an adjusted basis to Wren of $1.2 million. At the time of its liquidation, Wren had E & P of $700,000 and a general business credit carryover of $20,000.
    a. How much gain (or loss) will Wren Corporation recognize as a result of its liquidation?
    b. How much gain (or loss) will Cardinal Corporation recognize as a result of Wren Corporation's liquidation?
    c. What basis does Cardinal Corporation take in the assets acquired in the liquidation?
    d. What happens to Wren Corporation's E & P and general business credit carryover?

Communications

27. Quail Corporation paid $5.4 million for all the stock of Sparrow Corporation 10 years ago. Sparrow Corporation's balance sheet currently reflects the following fair market values:

Assets		**Liabilities and Shareholder's Equity**	
Cash	$ 135,000	Accounts payable	$ 5,400,000
Inventory	405,000	Common stock	5,400,000
Machinery	270,000	Deficit	(7,560,000)
Equipment	1,080,000		
Land	1,350,000		
	$3,240,000		$ 3,240,000

What are the tax consequences to Quail Corporation if it liquidates Sparrow Corporation? Prepare a letter to your client, Quail Corporation (1010 Cypress Lane, Community, MN 55166), and a memo for the file in which you explain your conclusions.

28. Falcon Corporation is owned 90% by Canary Corporation. The parent is contemplating a liquidation of Falcon Corporation and the acquisition of its assets. Canary Corporation purchased the Falcon stock from Falcon's two individual shareholders a month ago on January 3, 2005, for $400,000. The financial statements of Falcon Corporation as of January 3, 2005, reflect the following:

	Assets	
	Basis to Falcon Corporation	**Fair Market Value**
Cash	$ 40,000	$ 40,000
Inventory	80,000	60,000
Accounts receivable	160,000	100,000
Equipment	400,000	320,000
Land	520,000	280,000
	$1,200,000	$800,000
	Liabilities and Shareholders' Equity	
Accounts payable	$ 120,000	$120,000
Mortgages payable	200,000	200,000
Common stock	1,000,000	480,000
Retained earnings	(120,000)	
	$1,200,000	$800,000

The management of Canary Corporation asks your advice on the feasibility of an election under § 338:

a. Can Canary Corporation make a § 338 election?
b. Assuming Canary can make a § 338 election, is such an election feasible?

29. Five years ago, Anatep paid $200,000 for 80% of Tecca Corporation's stock. In the current year, Tecca merges with Azza Corporation, and Anatep receives 25% of Azza's stock (worth $500,000) plus $100,000 cash. At the time of the transaction, Tecca's E & P was $75,000, and Azza's E & P was $800,000. How will Anatep treat this transaction for tax purposes?

30. Quinn purchased 20% of Redbird Corporation for $100,000 and a $50,000 bond five years ago. In a transaction qualifying as a reorganization under § 368, Redbird exchanges all of its assets valued at $1.6 million (basis of $900,000) for 395,000 shares of Bluebird Corporation stock plus a parcel of land. Redbird distributes 700 shares of Bluebird stock (valued at $280,000), a $60,000 Bluebird bond, and the land (valued at $20,000) to Quinn in exchange for his Redbird stock and bond. Redbird's current and accumulated E & P before the reorganization amount to $150,000.
    a. How will Quinn treat this transaction for tax purposes? What is Quinn's basis in the stock, bond, and land?
    b. How will Redbird treat this transaction for tax purposes? What is Bluebird's basis in the assets it receives from Redbird?

31. Rosa owns 60% of the stock of Pine Corporation (basis of $100,000), and the other 40% was recently purchased by Arvid (basis of $110,000). Rosa also holds a $50,000 Pine bond. Pine enters into a tax-free consolidation with Lodgepole Corporation, in which Rosa will receive a 12% interest in the new Lodgepole Pine Corporation and Arvid will receive a 6% interest plus assets worth $30,000. Pine's basis in these assets is $10,000. Rosa will also exchange her $50,000 Pine bond for a $55,000 Lodgepole Pine debenture. The interest rate on the new bond is lower than the rate on Rosa's Pine bond. At the time of the reorganization, Pine's value is $300,000, and Lodgepole's value is $1.2 million.
    a. What are Rosa's and Arvid's bases in their new Lodgepole Pine stock?
    b. What is the amount of gain (loss) recognized by Rosa, Arvid, Pine, and Lodgepole on the reorganization?

Research Problems

THOMSON RIA™

Note: Solutions to Research Problems can be prepared by using the ***RIA Checkpoint® Student Edition*** *online research product, which is available to accompany this text. It is also possible to prepare solutions to the Research Problems by using tax research materials found in a standard tax library.*

Communications

Research Problem 1. Scott Davison (255 N. Bayshore Boulevard, Clearwater, FL 34619) is the president and sole shareholder of Bluebird Corporation (stock basis of $270,000). Since 1991, Bluebird has imported fine Mexican pottery and sold it to large nurseries and hardware stores across the United States. On July 1, 2003, Bluebird transferred its entire pottery inventory to Davison in a transaction described by the parties as a sale. According to Davison and collaborated by the minutes of the corporation's board of directors, the inventory was "sold" to him for the sum of $1 million, the fair market value of the inventory (Bluebird's basis, $350,000). The terms of the sale provided that Davison would pay Bluebird the $1 million amount at some future date. This debt obligation was not evidenced by a promissory note, and, to date, Davison has made no payments (principal or interest) on the obligation. The inventory transfer was not reported on Bluebird's 2003 tax return, either as a sale or as a distribution. After the transfer of inventory to Davison, Bluebird had no remaining assets and ceased to conduct any business. Upon an audit of Bluebird's 2003 tax return, the IRS asserted that the transfer of inventory to Davison constituted a liquidation of Bluebird and, as such, that the corporation recognized a gain on the liquidating distribution in the amount of $650,000 ($1 million value – $350,000 basis). Further, the IRS has assessed a tax due from Davison for his gain recognized in the purported liquidating distribution. Davison has contacted you regarding the IRS's determination. Prepare a letter to Scott Davison and a memo for the file documenting your research.

Partial list of research aids:
Reg. § 1.332–2(c).
Kennemer v. Comm., 38–1 USTC ¶9297, 21 AFTR 103, 96 F.2d 177 (CA–5, 1938).

Research Problem 2. Four years ago, Roadrunner Corporation was completely liquidated, and all of its shareholders reported long-term capital gains as a result. One year after the liquidation, the shareholders sued a former Roadrunner Corporation CEO for large insider profits. In the current year, the shareholders' lawsuit against the former CEO was settled, and they were awarded a $3 million judgment. What is the proper tax treatment for the shareholders' judgment proceeds?

Internet Activity

Use the tax resources of the Internet to address the following question. Do not restrict your search to the World Wide Web, but include a review of newsgroups and general reference materials, practitioner sites and resources, primary sources of the tax law, chat rooms and discussion groups, and other opportunities.

Communications

Research Problem 3. The merger of Oracle and PeopleSoft received unfavorable press. Using the Internet, find two articles discussing the objections that were raised to this merger. Provide a one-page summary of your findings, and indicate whether you think the objections were valid.

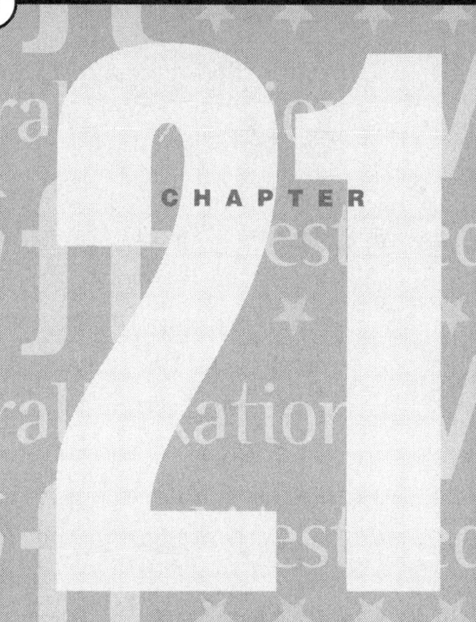

Partnerships

LEARNING OBJECTIVES

After completing Chapter 21, you should be able to:

LO.1

Discuss governing principles and theories of partnership taxation.

LO.2

Describe the tax effects of forming a partnership with cash and property contributions.

LO.3

Identify elections available to a partnership, and specify the tax treatment of expenditures of a newly formed partnership.

LO.4

Specify the accounting methods available to a partnership and the methods of determining a partnership's tax year.

LO.5

Calculate partnership taxable income and describe how partnership items affect a partner's income tax return.

LO.6

Determine a partner's basis in the partnership interest and explain how liabilities affect the basis computation.

LO.7

Describe the limitations on deducting partnership losses.

LO.8

Describe the treatment of transactions between a partner and the partnership.

LO.9

Determine the tax treatment of proportionate nonliquidating distributions from a partnership to a partner and the tax treatment of proportionate distributions that liquidate a partnership.

LO.10

Calculate the selling partner's amount and character of gain or loss on the sale or exchange of a partnership interest.

LO.11

Describe the application of partnership provisions to limited liability companies (LLCs) and limited liability partnerships (LLPs).

OUTLINE

Overview of Partnership Taxation

FORMS OF DOING BUSINESS—FEDERAL TAX CONSEQUENCES

This chapter and the next chapter analyze two types of entities that, for some taxpayers, offer certain advantages over regular corporations. These entities are partnerships and S corporations, which are called *flow-through* or *pass-through* entities because the owners of the trade or business choose to avoid treating the enterprise as a separate taxable entity. Instead, the owners are taxed on a proportionate share of the entity's taxable income at the end of each of its taxable years.

Often a partnership may provide tax advantages over a C, or regular, corporation. The income of a partnership is subject to only a single level of taxation, while C corporation income is subject to *double taxation*. Corporate income is taxed at the entity level, currently at rates up to 35 percent. Any after-tax income that is distributed to corporate owners as a dividend is taxed again at the owner level. Though partnership income may be subject to high tax rates at the partner level (currently up to 35 percent for a partner who is an individual), the resulting tax will generally

Partnerships in the Movies

As movies have become more expensive to produce, many production studios have turned to limited partnerships or limited liability companies (LLCs) as a lucrative source of investment capital. For example, Dream Works, the Walt Disney Company, and other studios have sold limited partnership (or LLC) interests in various partnerships formed to produce specific movies.

Often the sponsoring studio injects capital for a small (1–5 percent) general partnership interest, and the investors contribute the remaining capital—often many millions of dollars. The partnership agreement spells out the number and types of films the partnership intends to produce and provides a formula for allocating cash flows to the partners. The partnership agreement includes various benefits for the general partner, the studio, such as a preferred allocation of cash flows. For example, the studio may receive the first $1 million per year, distribution fees for marketing the movies, and/or reimbursement of specified amounts of corporate overhead. Any cash remaining after these expenses is allocated under a fixed formula between the general and limited partners. For example, the limited partners may receive 90 percent of remaining cash flows.

Think about bank financing in comparison, and you will see why the studio finds partnerships so appealing: How many banks would allow the general partner to receive reimbursements and allocations before debt principal and interest are paid?

This capital-raising technique has proved so advantageous to the studios that some related industries, such as movie lighting contractors and special effects companies, have also used limited partnerships (or LLCs) to raise capital. The next time you go to a movie, watch the credits at the end and think about the tremendous number of people who invested cash in the movie, hoping for a blockbuster!

be lower than a combined corporate-level tax and a second tax on a dividend distribution.

In addition, administrative and filing requirements are usually relatively simple for a partnership, and it offers certain planning opportunities not available to other entities. Both C and S corporations are subject to rigorous allocation and distribution requirements. Generally, each income or loss allocation or distribution is proportionate to the ownership interest of each shareholder. A partnership, though, may adjust its allocations of income and cash flow among the partners each year according to their needs, as long as certain standards, discussed later in this chapter, are met. Also, any previously unrealized income of an S or C corporation, such as appreciation of corporate assets, is taxed at the entity level when the corporation liquidates. However, a partnership generally may liquidate tax-free. Finally, many states impose reporting and licensing requirements on corporate entities, including S corporations. These include franchise or capital stock tax returns that may require annual assessments and costly professional preparation assistance. Partnerships, on the other hand, often have no reporting requirements beyond Federal and state informational tax returns.

For smaller business operations, a partnership enables several owners to combine their resources at low cost. It also offers simple filing requirements, the taxation of income only once, and the ability to discontinue operations relatively inexpensively.

For larger business operations, a partnership offers a unique ability to raise capital with low filing and reporting costs compared to, for example, corporate bond issuances. Special allocations of income and cash-flow items are available in all partnerships to meet the objectives of the owners.

Since partnerships and S corporations are so widespread, a study of related tax issues will prove useful to students, business owners, and consultants. This chapter addresses partnership formations, operations, and nonliquidating distributions, and, in addition, sales of partnership interests and partnership liquidating distributions. Chapter 22 discusses the taxation of S corporations.

WHAT IS A PARTNERSHIP?

A partnership is an association of two or more persons to carry on a trade or business, with each contributing money, property, labor, or skill, and with all expecting to share in profits and losses. For Federal income tax purposes, a partnership includes a syndicate, group, pool, joint venture, or other unincorporated organization through which any business, financial operation, or venture is carried on. The entity must not be otherwise classified as a corporation, trust, or estate.[1]

The four types of entities that may be taxed as partnerships are general partnerships, limited liability partnerships, limited partnerships, and limited liability companies. A partnership that conducts a service business, such as accounting, law, or medicine, is usually established as either a **general partnership** or a **limited liability partnership (LLP).** A general partnership consists of two or more general partners. Creditors of a general partnership can collect amounts owed them from both the partnership assets and the personal assets of the owner-partners. A general partner can be bankrupted by a malpractice judgment brought against the partnership, even though the partner was not personally involved in the malpractice.

An LLP is a recently created form of entity. In most states, owners of an LLP are treated much like general partners. The primary difference between an LLP and a general partnership is that an LLP partner is not personally liable for any malpractice committed by the other partners. The LLP is currently the operational form of choice for the large accounting firms.

A **limited partnership** is often used for acquiring capital in activities such as real estate development. A limited partnership has at least one general partner and often many limited partners. Typically, only the general partners are personally liable to creditors; each limited partner's risk of loss is restricted to that partner's equity investment in the entity.

An alternative entity form, the **limited liability company (LLC),** is available in all states and the District of Columbia. An LLC combines the corporate benefit of limited liability for the owners with the benefits of partnership taxation, including the single level of tax and special allocations of income, losses, and cash flows. Owners are technically considered to be "members" rather than partners, but a properly structured LLC is treated as a partnership for all tax purposes. Almost all states permit capital-intensive companies as well as nonprofessional service-oriented businesses and some professional service-providing companies to operate as LLCs. This is highly advantageous to a business entity since the LLC can protect each member's personal assets from being exposed to the entity's debts.

---

[1]A "person" can be an individual, trust, estate, corporation, association, or another partnership. §§ 7701(a)(1) and (a)(2).

The Growing Number of LLCs

In many states, including traditionally corporate-friendly states such as Delaware, Nevada, and Arizona, new limited liability companies (LLCs) are being formed at a remarkable rate. In Arizona, for example, the number of new LLCs formed in 2003 and 2004 was about double the number of corporations formed in those years. Although the state currently has more active corporations than LLCs, this is expected to change in the near future. Large Arizona businesses will probably continue to prefer the corporate form, but the LLC is clearly becoming the preferred entity for small businesses. See the additional discussion of LLCs later in this chapter.

ELECTIONS RELATED TO PARTNERSHIP STATUS

The IRS's "check-the-box" Regulations allow most unincorporated business entities—such as general partnerships, limited partnerships, LLPs, and LLCs—to select their Federal tax status.[2] If an unincorporated entity has two or more owners, it generally can choose to be taxed as either a partnership or a C corporation. This provides the entity with flexibility regarding its Federal tax classification. The Regulations, however, do not permit all unincorporated business or investment entities to choose their tax status. Newly formed publicly traded partnerships, for example, must be taxed as corporations.

A partnership generally may elect out of the partnership taxation rules if it is involved in one of the following activities:

- Investment (rather than the active conduct of a trade or business).
- Joint production, extraction, or use of property.
- Underwriting, selling, or distributing a specific security issue.[3]

If a proper election is made, the partnership is disregarded for Federal tax purposes, and its operations are reported directly on the owners' tax returns.

LO.1

Discuss governing principles and theories of partnership taxation.

PARTNERSHIP TAXATION

A partnership is not a taxable entity.[4] Rather, the taxable income or loss of the partnership flows through to the partners at the end of the entity's tax year.[5] Partners report their allocable share of the partnership's income or loss for the year on their tax returns. As a result, the partnership itself pays no Federal income tax on its income; instead, the partners' individual tax liabilities are affected by the activities of the entity.

EXAMPLE 1

Adam is a 40% partner in the ABC Partnership. Both Adam's and the partnership's tax years end on December 31. In 2005, the partnership generates $200,000 of ordinary taxable income. However, because the partnership needs capital for expansion and debt reduction, Adam makes no cash withdrawals during 2005. He meets his living expenses by reducing his investment portfolio. Adam is taxed on his $80,000 allocable share of the partnership's 2005 income, even though he receives no distributions from the entity during 2005. This allocated income is included in Adam's gross income. ■

[2] Reg. §§ 301.7701–1 to 301.7701–3.
[3] § 761(a).
[4] § 701.
[5] § 702.

EXAMPLE 2

Assume the same facts as in Example 1, except the partnership recognizes a 2005 taxable loss of $100,000. Adam's $40,000 proportionate share of the loss flows through to him from the partnership, and he can deduct the loss. (Note: Loss limitation rules discussed later in the chapter may result in some or all of this loss being deducted by Adam in a later year.) ■

Many items of partnership income, expense, gain, or loss retain their identity as they flow through to the partners. This separate flow-through of certain items is required because such **separately stated items** *might* affect any two partners' tax liabilities in different ways. When preparing a personal tax return, a partner takes each of these items into account separately.[6] For example, charitable contributions are separately stated because partners need to compute their own personal limitation on charitable contributions. Some partners are able to deduct the entire amount they are allocated. Others are limited in what they can deduct by the amount of their adjusted gross income (AGI).

EXAMPLE 3

Beth is a 25% partner in the BR Partnership. The cash basis entity collected sales income of $60,000 during 2004 and incurred $15,000 in business expenses. In addition, it sold a corporate bond in June for a $9,000 long-term capital gain. Finally, the partnership made a $1,000 contribution to the local Performing Arts Fund drive. The fund is a qualifying charity. BR and all of its partners use a calendar tax year.

For 2004, Beth is allocated ordinary taxable income of $11,250 [($60,000 – $15,000) × 25%] from the partnership. She also is allocated a flow-through of a $2,250 long-term capital gain and a $250 charitable contribution deduction. The ordinary income increases Beth's gross income. The long-term capital gain and charitable contribution are separately stated because they could be treated differently on her tax return from the way they are treated on the tax returns of the other partners. For example, Beth may have capital losses to offset the capital gain or may be subject to a percentage limitation on charitable contribution deductions for 2004. Other partners may have no capital losses or percentage limitations on charitable contribution deductions. Therefore, these items are not included in the computation of ordinary partnership income. Instead, they flow through to the partners separately. ■

The number of items that are separately reported to the partners varies and depends upon whether the partnership is an **electing large partnership.** A partnership qualifies as a large partnership if it had at least 100 partners during its immediately preceding taxable year and elects simplified reporting of its taxable items. Such partnerships separately report up to 16 different categories of items to their partners. This means that many items are netted at the partnership level. For example, items such as interest, nonqualified dividends, and royalty income are combined into one amount, and the electing large partnership reports a share of this amount to each partner. The netting of items at the partnership level makes each partner's tax return easier to complete. Unless otherwise indicated, in this chapter assume that the partnership is *not* an electing large partnership.

As most partnerships are not electing large partnerships, they may separately report more than 16 categories of items. Some partnership items are netted in these partnerships, but the netting is not as extensive as in electing large partnerships. Pass-through items that are netted in these partnerships include the ordinary income and expenses related to the partnership's trade or business activities. These ordinary income and expense items are netted to produce a single income or loss amount that is passed through to the partners. Most other partnership items are separately stated. For example, net income (loss) from rental real estate activities and net short-term capital gains (losses) are each determined at the partnership level and reported separately to the partners.

[6] § 703(a)(1).

Other items that are allocated separately to the partners include recognized gains and losses from property transactions; qualified and ordinary dividend income; tax preferences and adjustments for the alternative minimum tax; expenditures that qualify for the foreign tax credit; and expenditures the partners would treat as itemized deductions.[7]

PARTNERSHIP REPORTING

Even though it is not a taxpaying entity, a partnership must file an information tax return, Form 1065. Look at Form 1065 for 2004 in Appendix B, and refer to it during the following discussion. The ordinary income and expense items generated by the partnership's trade or business activities are netted to produce a single income or loss amount. The partnership reports this ordinary income or loss from its trade or business activities on Form 1065, page 1. Schedule K (page 3 of Form 1065) accumulates all items that must be separately reported to the partners, including net trade or business income or loss (from page 1). The amounts on Schedule K are allocated to all the partners. Each partner receives a Schedule K–1, which shows that partner's share of partnership items.

EXAMPLE 4

The BR Partnership in Example 3 reports its $60,000 sales income on Form 1065, page 1, line 1. The $15,000 of business expenses are reported in the appropriate amounts on page 1, line 2 or lines 9–20. Partnership ordinary income of $45,000 is shown on page 1, line 22, and on Schedule K, line 1. The $9,000 net long-term capital gain and the $1,000 charitable contribution are reported only on Schedule K, on lines 9a and 13a, respectively.

Beth receives a Schedule K–1 from the partnership that shows her shares of partnership ordinary income of $11,250, long-term capital gain of $2,250, and charitable contributions of $250 on lines 1, 9a, and 13, respectively. She then combines these amounts with similar items from sources other than BR on her personal tax return. For example, if she has a $5,000 long-term capital loss from a stock transaction during the year, her overall net capital loss calculated on Schedule D of her Form 1040 is $2,750 ($2,250 – $5,000). She evaluates this net amount to determine the amount she may deduct on her Form 1040. She reports the $250 of charitable contributions on her Schedule A. ■

As this example shows, one must look at both page 1 and Schedule K to get complete information regarding a partnership's operations for the year.

Certain items reported on Schedule K are netted and entered on line 1 of the Analysis of Net Income (Loss) on page 4. This total agrees with the total amount on line 9 of Schedule M–1, Reconciliation of Income (Loss) per Books with Income (Loss) per Return. Schedule L generally shows an accounting-basis balance sheet, and Schedule M–2 reconciles beginning and ending partners' capital accounts.

PARTNER'S OWNERSHIP INTEREST IN A PARTNERSHIP

Each partner typically owns both a **capital interest** and a **profits (loss) interest** in the partnership. A capital interest is measured by a partner's **capital sharing ratio,** which is the partner's percentage ownership of the capital of the partnership. A partner's capital interest can be determined in several ways. The most widely accepted method measures the capital interest as the percentage of net asset value (asset value remaining after payment of all partnership liabilities) a partner would receive on immediate liquidation of the partnership.

[7]§ 702(a).

A profits (loss) interest is simply the partner's percentage allocation of current partnership operating results. **Profit and loss sharing ratios** are usually specified in the partnership agreement and are used to determine each partner's allocation of partnership ordinary taxable income and separately stated items.[8] The partnership can change its profit and loss allocations at any time simply by amending the partnership agreement.

Each partner's profit, loss, and capital sharing ratios may appear on the partner's Schedule K–1. In many cases, the three ratios are the same. A partner's capital sharing ratio generally equals the partner's profit and loss sharing ratios if all profit and loss allocations, for each year of the partnership's existence, are in the same proportion as the partner's initial contributions to the partnership.

The partnership agreement may, in some cases, provide for a **special allocation** of certain items to specified partners, or it may allocate items in a different proportion from general profit and loss sharing ratios. These items are separately reported to the partner receiving the allocation. To be recognized for tax purposes, a special allocation must produce nontax economic consequences for the partners receiving it.[9]

EXAMPLE 5

When the George-Helen Partnership was formed, George contributed cash, and Helen contributed some City of Iuka bonds that she had held for investment purposes. The partnership agreement allocates all of the tax-exempt interest income from the bonds to Helen as an inducement for her to remain a partner. This is an acceptable special allocation for income tax purposes; it reflects the differing economic circumstances that underlie the partners' contributions to the capital of the entity. Since Helen would have received the exempt income if she had not joined the partnership, she can retain the tax-favored treatment by means of the special allocation. ■

EXAMPLE 6

Assume the same facts as in Example 5. Three years after it was formed, the George-Helen Partnership purchased some City of Butte bonds. The municipal bond interest income of $15,000 flows through to the partners as a separately stated item, so that it retains its tax-exempt status. The partnership agreement allocates all of this income to George because he is subject to a higher marginal income tax bracket than is Helen. The partnership also allocates $15,000 more of the partnership taxable income to Helen than to George. These allocations are not effective for income tax purposes because they have no purpose other than the reduction of the partners' combined income tax liability. ■

A partner has a **basis in the partnership interest.** When income flows through to a partner from the partnership, the partner's basis in the partnership interest increases. When a loss flows through to a partner, basis is reduced.

EXAMPLE 7

Paul contributes $20,000 of cash to acquire a 30% capital and profits interest in the Red Robin Partnership. In its first year of operations, the partnership earns ordinary income of $40,000 and makes no distributions to Paul. Paul's initial basis is the $20,000 he paid for the interest. He reports ordinary income of $12,000 (30% × $40,000 partnership income) on his individual return and increases his basis by the same amount, to $32,000. ■

The Code provides for the increase and decrease in a partner's basis so that the income or loss from partnership operations is taxed only once. In Example 7, if Paul sold his interest at the end of the first year for $32,000, he would have no gain or loss. If the Code did not provide for an adjustment of a partner's basis, Paul's basis would be $20,000, and he would be taxed on the gain of $12,000 in

[8] § 704(a).

[9] § 704(b).

addition to being taxed on his $12,000 share of income. In other words, without the basis adjustment, partnership income would be subject to double taxation.

As the following sections discuss in detail, a partner's basis is important for determining the treatment of distributions from the partnership to the partner, establishing the deductibility of partnership losses, and calculating gain or loss on the partner's disposition of the partnership interest.

A partner's basis is not reflected anywhere on the Schedule K–1. Instead, each partner should maintain a personal record of adjustments to basis. Schedule K–1 does reconcile a partner's **capital account,** but the ending capital account balance is rarely the same amount as the partner's basis. Just as the tax and accounting bases of a specific asset may differ, a partner's capital account and basis in the partnership interest may not be equal for a variety of reasons. For example, a partner's basis also includes the partner's share of partnership liabilities. These liabilities are not reported as part of the partner's capital account but are included in Item F at the top of the partner's Schedule K–1.

CONCEPTUAL BASIS FOR PARTNERSHIP TAXATION

The unique tax treatment of partners and partnerships can be traced to two legal concepts that evolved long ago: the **aggregate** (or conduit) **concept** and the **entity concept.** These concepts influence practically every partnership tax rule.

Aggregate (or Conduit) Concept. The aggregate (or conduit) concept treats the partnership as a channel through which income, credits, deductions, and other items flow to the partners. Under this concept, the partnership is regarded as a collection of taxpayers joined in an agency relationship with one another. The imposition of the income tax on individual partners reflects the influence of this doctrine. The aggregate concept has influenced the tax treatment of other pass-through entities, such as S corporations (Chapter 22) and trusts and estates (Chapter 28).

Entity Concept. The entity concept treats partners and partnerships as separate units and gives the partnership its own tax "personality" by (1) requiring a partnership to file an information tax return and (2) treating partners as separate and distinct from the partnership in certain transactions between a partner and the entity. A partner's recognition of capital gain or loss on the sale of the partnership interest further illustrates this doctrine.

Combined Concepts. Some rules governing the formation, operation, and liquidation of a partnership contain a blend of both the entity and aggregate concepts.

ANTI-ABUSE PROVISIONS

As this chapter reflects, partnership taxation is often flexible. For example, partnership operating income or losses can sometimes be shifted among partners, and partnership capital gains and losses can sometimes be shifted from one partner to another. The Code contains many provisions designed to thwart unwarranted allocations, but the IRS believes opportunities for tax avoidance still abound. The IRS has adopted Regulations that will allow it to recharacterize transactions that it considers to be "abusive."[10]

[10]Reg. § 1.701–2.

LO.2

Describe the tax effects of forming a partnership with cash and property contributions.

Formation of a Partnership: Tax Effects

GAIN OR LOSS ON CONTRIBUTIONS TO THE PARTNERSHIP

When a taxpayer transfers property to an entity in exchange for valuable consideration, a taxable exchange normally results. Typically, both the taxpayer and the entity realize and recognize gain or loss on the exchange.[11] The gain or loss recognized by the transferor is the difference between the fair market value of the consideration received and the adjusted basis of the property transferred.[12]

In most situations, however, neither the partner nor the partnership recognizes the realized gain or loss when a partner contributes property to a partnership in exchange for a partnership interest. Instead, the realized gain or loss is deferred.[13]

There are two reasons for this nonrecognition treatment. First, forming a partnership allows investors to combine their assets toward greater economic goals than could be achieved separately. Only the form of ownership, rather than the amount owned by each investor, has changed. Requiring that gain be recognized on such transfers would make the formation of some partnerships economically unfeasible (e.g., two existing proprietorships are combined to form one larger business). Congress does not want to hinder the creation of valid economic partnerships by requiring gain recognition when a partnership is created. Second, because the partnership interest received is typically not a liquid asset, the partner may not have sufficient cash to pay the tax. Thus, deferral of the gain recognizes the economic realities of the business world and follows the wherewithal to pay principle of taxation.

EXAMPLE 8

Alicia transfers two assets to the Wren Partnership on the day the entity is created, in exchange for a 60% profit and loss interest worth $60,000. She contributes cash of $40,000 and retail display equipment (basis to her as a sole proprietor, $8,000; fair market value, $20,000). Since an exchange has occurred between two parties, Alicia *realizes* a $12,000 gain on this transaction. The gain realized is the fair market value of the partnership interest of $60,000 less the basis of the assets that she surrendered to the partnership [$40,000 (cash) + $8,000 (equipment)].

Under § 721, Alicia *does not recognize* the $12,000 realized gain in the year of contribution. This makes sense, since all she received from the partnership was an illiquid partnership interest; she received no cash with which to pay any resulting tax liability. ■

EXAMPLE 9

Assume the same facts as in Example 8, except that the equipment Alicia contributes to the partnership has an adjusted basis of $25,000. She has a $5,000 *realized* loss [$60,000 – ($40,000 + $25,000)], but she cannot deduct the loss. Realized losses, as well as realized gains, are deferred by § 721.

Unless it is essential that the partnership receive Alicia's display equipment rather than similar equipment purchased from an outside supplier, Alicia should have considered selling the equipment to a third party. This would allow her to deduct a $5,000 loss in the year of the sale. Alicia could then contribute $60,000 of cash (including the proceeds from the sale) for her interest in the partnership, and the partnership would have funds to purchase similar equipment. ■

EXAMPLE 10

Five years after the Wren Partnership (Examples 8 and 9) was created, Alicia contributes another piece of equipment to the entity. This property has a basis of $35,000 and a fair

[11] § 1001(c).
[12] § 1001(a).
[13] § 721.

market value of $50,000. Alicia will defer the recognition of the $15,000 realized gain. Section 721 is effective whenever a partner makes a contribution to the capital of the partnership. ■

If a partner contributes only capital and § 1231 assets, the partner's holding period in the partnership interest is the same as that partner's holding period for these assets. If cash or other assets that are not capital or § 1231 assets are contributed, the holding period in the partnership interest begins on the date the partnership interest is acquired. If multiple assets are contributed, the partnership interest is apportioned, and a separate holding period applies to each portion.

EXCEPTIONS TO § 721

The nonrecognition provisions of § 721 do not apply in the following situations:

- When appreciated stocks and securities are contributed to an investment partnership.
- When the transaction is essentially a taxable exchange of properties.
- When the transaction is a disguised sale of properties.
- When the partnership interest is received in exchange for services rendered to the partnership by the partner.

Investment Partnership. If the transfer consists of appreciated stocks and securities and the partnership is an investment partnership, it is possible that the realized gain on the stocks and securities will be recognized by the contributing partner at the time of contribution.[14] This provision prevents multiple investors from using the partnership form to diversify their investment portfolios on a tax-free basis. A similar provision, § 351(e), applies to corporations (see Chapter 18).

Exchange. If a transaction is essentially a taxable exchange of properties, tax on the gain is not deferred under the nonrecognition provisions of § 721.[15]

EXAMPLE 11

Sara owns land, and Bob owns stock. Sara would like to have Bob's stock, and Bob wants Sara's land. If Sara and Bob both contribute their property to newly formed SB Partnership in exchange for interests in the partnership, the tax on the transaction appears to be deferred under § 721. If the partnership then distributes the land to Bob and the stock to Sara, the tax on this transaction also appears to be deferred under § 731 (discussed later in the chapter). According to a literal interpretation of the statutes, no taxable exchange has occurred. Sara and Bob will find, however, that this type of tax subterfuge is not permitted. The IRS will disregard the passage of the properties through the partnership and will hold, instead, that Sara and Bob exchanged the land and stock directly. Thus, the transactions will be treated as any other taxable exchange. ■

Disguised Sale. A similar result occurs in a **disguised sale** of properties. A disguised sale may occur when a partner contributes appreciated property to a partnership and soon thereafter receives a distribution from the partnership. This distribution may be viewed as a payment by the partnership for purchase of the property.[16]

EXAMPLE 12

Kim transfers property to the KLM Partnership. The property has an adjusted basis of $10,000 and a fair market value of $30,000. Two weeks later, the partnership makes a distribution of $30,000 of cash to Kim. Under the distribution rules of § 731, the distribution would not be taxable to Kim if the basis of her partnership interest prior to the distribution

[14] § 721(b).
[15] Reg. § 1.731–1(c)(3).
[16] § 707(a)(2)(B).

was greater than the $30,000 of cash distributed. However, the transaction appears to be a disguised purchase-sale transaction, rather than a contribution and distribution. Therefore, Kim must recognize gain of $20,000 on transfer of the property, and the partnership is deemed to have purchased the property for $30,000. ■

Services. A final exception to the nonrecognition provision of § 721 occurs when a partner receives an interest in the partnership as compensation for services rendered to the partnership. This is not a tax-deferred transaction because services are not treated as "property" that can be transferred to a partnership on a tax-free basis. Instead, the partner performing the services recognizes ordinary compensation income equal to the fair market value of the partnership interest received.[17]

The partnership may deduct the amount included in the service partner's income if the services are of a deductible nature. If the services are not deductible to the partnership, they must be capitalized to an asset account. For example, architectural plans created by a partner are capitalized as part of the structure built with those plans. Alternatively, day-to-day management services performed by a partner for the partnership are usually deductible by the partnership.

EXAMPLE 13

Bill, Carl, and Dave form the BCD Partnership, with each receiving a one-third interest in the entity. Dave receives his one-third interest as compensation for tax planning services he will render after the formation of the partnership. The value of a one-third interest in the partnership (for each of the parties) is $20,000. Dave recognizes $20,000 of compensation income, and he has a $20,000 basis in his partnership interest. The same result would occur if the partnership had paid Dave $20,000 for his services and he immediately contributed that amount to the entity for a one-third ownership interest. In either case the partnership deducts $20,000 in calculating its ordinary business income. ■

TAX ISSUES RELATIVE TO CONTRIBUTED PROPERTY

When a partner makes a tax-deferred contribution of an asset to the capital of a partnership, the tax law assigns a *carryover basis* to the property.[18] The partnership's basis in the asset is equal to the partner's basis in the property prior to its transfer to the partnership. The partner's basis in the new partnership interest is the same as the partner's basis in the contributed asset. The tax term for this basis concept is *substituted basis*. Thus, two assets are created out of one when a partnership is formed, namely, the property in the hands of the new entity and the new asset (the partnership interest) in the hands of the partner. Both assets are assigned a basis that is derived from the partner's existing basis in the contributed property.

These rules are logical in view of what Congress was attempting to accomplish with the deferral approach. As noted earlier, gain or loss is deferred when property is contributed to a partnership in exchange for a partnership interest. The bases are the amounts necessary to allow for recognition of the deferred gain or loss if the property or the partnership interest is subsequently disposed of in a taxable transaction. This treatment is similar to the treatment of assets transferred to a controlled corporation[19] and the treatment of like-kind exchanges.[20]

EXAMPLE 14

On June 1, 2005, Luis transfers property to the JKL Partnership in exchange for a one-third interest in the partnership. The property has an adjusted basis to Luis of $10,000 and a fair market value on June 1 of $30,000. Luis's realized gain on the exchange is $20,000 ($30,000 – $10,000), but under § 721, none of the gain is recognized. Luis's basis for his partnership interest is the amount necessary to recognize the $20,000 deferred gain if he subsequently

[17] § 83(a).
[18] § 723.
[19] § 351.
[20] § 1031.

sells the interest for its $30,000 fair market value. This amount, $10,000, is referred to as a substituted basis. The basis of the property contributed to the partnership is the amount necessary to allow for the recognition of the $20,000 deferred gain if the property is subsequently sold for its $30,000 fair market value. This amount, also $10,000, is referred to as a carryover basis. ■

The holding period for the contributed asset carries over to the partnership. Thus, the partnership's holding period for the asset includes the period during which the partner owned the asset.

Depreciation Method and Period. If depreciable property is contributed to the partnership, the partnership is usually required to use the same cost recovery method and life used by the partner. The partnership merely "steps into the shoes" of the partner and continues the same cost recovery calculations. The partnership may not elect under § 179 to immediately expense any part of the basis of depreciable property it receives from the transferor partner.

Intangible Assets. If a partner contributes an existing "§ 197" intangible asset to the partnership, the partnership generally will "step into the shoes" of the partner in determining future amortization deductions. Section 197 intangible assets include goodwill, going-concern value, information systems, customer- or supplier-related intangible assets, patents, licenses obtained from a governmental unit, franchises, trademarks, covenants not to compete, and other items.

EXAMPLE 15

On September 1, 2003, at a cost of $120,000, James obtained a license to operate a television station from the Federal Communications Commission. The license is effective for 20 years. On January 1, 2005, he contributes the license to the JS Partnership in exchange for a 60% interest. The value of the license is still $120,000 at that time.

The license is a § 197 asset since it is a license with a term greater than 15 years. The cost is amortized over 15 years. James claims amortization for 4 months in 2003 and 12 months in 2004. Thereafter, the partnership steps into James's shoes in claiming amortization deductions. ■

Intangible assets that do not fall under the § 197 rules are amortized over their useful life, if any.[21]

Receivables, Inventory, and Losses. To prevent the conversion of ordinary income into capital gain, gain or loss is treated as ordinary when the partnership disposes of either of the following:[22]

- Contributed receivables that were unrealized in the contributing partner's hands at the contribution date. Such receivables include the right to receive payment for goods or services delivered or to be delivered.
- Contributed property that was inventory in the contributor's hands on the contribution date, if the partnership disposes of the property within *five years of the contribution*. For this purpose inventory includes all tangible property except capital assets and real or depreciable business assets.

EXAMPLE 16

Tyrone operates a cash basis retail electronics and television store as a sole proprietor. Ramon is an enterprising individual who likes to invest in small businesses. On January 2

[21]Reg § 1.167(a)–3.
[22]§ 724. For this purpose, § 724(d)(2) waives the holding period requirement in defining § 1231 property.

of the current year, Tyrone and Ramon form the TR Partnership. Their partnership contributions are as follows:

	Adjusted Basis	Fair Market Value
From Tyrone:		
Receivables	$ -0-	$ 2,000
Land used as parking lot*	1,200	5,000
Inventory	2,500	5,000
From Ramon:		
Cash	12,000	12,000

*The parking lot had been held for nine months at the contribution date.

Within 30 days of formation, TR collects the receivables and sells the inventory for $5,000 of cash. It uses the land for the next 10 months as a parking lot, then sells it for $3,500 of cash. TR realizes the following income in the current year from these transactions:

- Ordinary income of $2,000 from collecting the receivables.
- Ordinary income of $2,500 from the sale of inventory.
- Section 1231 gain of $2,300 from the sale of land.

Since the land takes a carryover holding period, it is treated as having been held 19 months at the sale date. ■

A similar rule is designed to prevent a capital loss from being converted into an ordinary loss. Under the rule, if contributed property is disposed of at a loss and the property had a "built-in" capital loss on the contribution date, the loss is treated as a capital loss if the partnership disposes of the property *within five years of the contribution*. The capital loss is limited to the amount of the "built-in" loss on the date of contribution.

EXAMPLE 17

Assume the same facts as Example 16, except for the following:

- Tyrone held the land for investment purposes. It had a fair market value of $800 at the contribution date.
- TR used the land as a parking lot for 10 months and sold it for $650.

TR realizes the following income and loss from these transactions:

- Ordinary income of $2,000 from collecting the receivables.
- Ordinary income of $2,500 from the sale of inventory.
- Capital loss of $400 from the sale of land ($800 – $1,200).
- Section 1231 loss of $150 from the sale of land ($650 – $800).

Since the land was sold within five years of the contribution date, the $400 built-in loss is a capital loss. The post-contribution loss of $150 is a § 1231 loss since TR used the property in its business. ■

INSIDE AND OUTSIDE BASES

Throughout this chapter, reference is made to the partnership's inside basis and a partner's outside basis. **Inside basis** refers to the adjusted basis of each *partnership* asset, as determined from the partnership's tax accounts. **Outside basis** represents each partner's basis in the partnership interest. Each partner "owns" a share of the

CONCEPT SUMMARY 21–1

Partnership Formation and Basis Computation

1. The *entity concept* treats partners and partnerships as separate units. The nature and amount of entity gains and losses and most partnership tax elections are determined at the partnership level.
2. The *aggregate concept* is used to connect partners and partnerships. It allows income, gains, losses, credits, deductions, etc., to flow through to the partners for separate tax reporting.
3. Sometimes both the *aggregate* and the *entity* concepts apply to the same transaction, but one usually dominates.
4. Generally, partners or partnerships do not recognize gain or loss when property is contributed for capital interests.
5. Partners contributing property for partnership interests take the contributed property's adjusted basis for their *outside basis* in their partnership interest. The partners are said to take a substituted basis in their partnership interest.
6. The partnership will continue to use the contributing partner's basis for the *inside basis* in property it receives. The contributed property is said to take a carryover basis.
7. The holding period of a partner's interest includes that of contributed property when the property was a § 1231 asset or capital asset in the partner's hands. Otherwise, the holding period starts on the day the interest is acquired. The holding period of an interest acquired by a cash contribution starts at acquisition.
8. The partnership's holding period for contributed property includes the contributing partner's holding period.

partnership's inside basis for all its assets, and all partners should maintain a record of their respective outside bases.

In many cases—especially on formation of the partnership—the total of all the partners' outside bases equals the partnership's inside bases for all its assets. Differences between inside and outside basis arise when a partner's interest is sold to another person for more or less than the selling partner's share of the inside basis of partnership assets. The buying partner's outside basis equals the price paid for the interest, but the buyer's share of the partnership's inside basis is the same amount as the seller's share of the inside basis.

Concept Summary 21–1 reviews the rules that apply to partnership asset contributions and basis adjustments.

LO.3

Identify elections available to a partnership, and specify the tax treatment of expenditures of a newly formed partnership.

TAX ACCOUNTING ELECTIONS

A newly formed partnership must make numerous tax accounting elections. These elections are formal decisions on how a particular transaction or tax attribute should be handled. Most of these elections must be made by the partnership rather than by the partners individually.[23] The *partnership* makes the elections for the following items:

- Inventory method.
- Cost or percentage depletion method, excluding oil and gas wells.
- Accounting method (cash, accrual, or hybrid).
- Cost recovery methods and assumptions.
- Tax year.
- Amortization of organization costs and amortization period.
- Amortization of start-up expenditures and amortization period.
- Section 179 deductions for certain tangible personal property.
- Nonrecognition treatment for gains from involuntary conversions.

[23] § 703(b).

Each partner is bound by the decisions made by the partnership relative to the elections. If the partnership fails to make an election, a partner cannot compensate for the error by making the election individually.

Though most elections are made by the partnership, each *partner* individually is required to make a specific election on the following relatively narrow tax issues:

- Whether to reduce the basis of depreciable property when first excluding income from discharge of indebtedness.
- Whether to claim cost or percentage depletion for oil and gas wells.
- Whether to take a deduction or credit for taxes paid to foreign countries and U.S. possessions.

INITIAL COSTS OF A PARTNERSHIP

In its initial stages, a partnership incurs expenses relating to some or all of the following: forming the partnership (organization costs), admitting partners to the partnership, marketing and selling partnership units to prospective partners (syndication costs), acquiring assets, starting business operations (start-up costs), negotiating contracts, and other items. Many of these expenditures are not currently deductible. However, the Code permits a deduction for or a ratable (i.e., straight-line) amortization of "organization" and "start-up" costs; acquisition costs for depreciable assets are included in the initial basis of the acquired assets; and costs related to some intangible assets may be amortized. "Syndication costs" may be neither amortized nor deducted.

Organization Costs. These costs include expenditures that are (1) incident to the creation of the partnership; (2) chargeable to a capital account; and (3) of a character that, if incident to the creation of a partnership with an ascertainable life, would be amortized over that life. Organization costs include accounting fees and legal fees incident to the partnership's formation. The expenditures must be incurred within a period that starts a reasonable time before the partnership begins business. The period ends with the due date (without extensions) of the tax return for the initial tax year.

For organization costs incurred after October 22, 2004, the partnership may elect to deduct up to $5,000 of the costs in the year in which it begins business. This amount must be reduced, however, by the organization costs that exceed $50,000. Any organization costs that cannot be deducted under this provision are amortizable over 180 months beginning with the month in which the partnership begins business.[24] For organization costs incurred before that date, the taxpayer could elect to amortize the amount over 60 months commencing with the month the taxpayer began business.

For either set of rules, the election to deduct or amortize these amounts must be made by the due date (including extensions) of the partnership return for the year in which it begins business. Failure to make a proper election results in no deduction or amortization of the organization costs until the partnership is liquidated.

Costs incurred for the following items are not organization costs:

- Acquiring assets for the partnership.
- Transferring assets to the partnership.
- Admitting partners, other than at formation.
- Removing partners, other than at formation.
- Negotiating operating contracts.
- Syndication costs.

[24] § 709.

Start-up Costs. These costs include operating costs that are incurred after the entity is formed but before it begins business. Such costs include marketing surveys prior to conducting business, pre-operating advertising expenses, costs of establishing an accounting system, costs incurred to train employees before business begins, and salaries paid to executives and employees before the start of business.

The partnership may elect to deduct up to $5,000 of start-up costs in the year in which it begins business. This amount must be reduced, however, by the start-up costs that exceed $50,000.[25] Costs that are not deductible under this provision are amortizable over 180 months beginning with the month in which the partnership begins business. For start-up costs incurred before October 23, 2004, the taxpayer could elect to amortize those costs over 60 months commencing with the month the taxpayer began business.

For each set of rules, the election to deduct and amortize start-up costs must be made by the due date (including extensions) of the partnership return for the year it begins business. Failure to make a proper election results in no deduction or amortization of the start-up costs until the partnership is liquidated.

EXAMPLE 18

The calendar year Bluejay Partnership was formed on July 1, 2005, and immediately started business. Bluejay incurred $4,000 in legal fees for drafting the partnership agreement and $2,200 in accounting fees for tax advice of an organizational nature. In addition, the partnership incurred $20,000 of pre-opening advertising expenses and $34,000 of salaries and training costs for new employees before opening for business. The partnership selected the accrual method of accounting and made an election to deduct and amortize organization and start-up costs in 2005.

Bluejay incurred $6,200 ($4,000 + $2,200) of organization costs in 2005. The partnership may deduct $5,040 of these costs on its 2005 tax return. This deduction is the sum of the $5,000 permitted deduction and the $40 ($1,200 × 6/180) amortization deduction for the $1,200 of organization costs that exceed the $5,000 base amount.

Bluejay incurred $54,000 ($20,000 + $34,000) of start-up costs in 2005. The partnership may deduct $2,767 of these costs on its tax return for 2005. This deduction is the sum of:

- $5,000 reduced by the $4,000 ($54,000 – $50,000) amount by which the start-up costs exceed $50,000.
- $1,767 ($53,000 × 6/180) amortization of the remaining $53,000 ($54,000 – $1,000) of start-up costs for 6 months.

If Bluejay had failed to make a proper election to deduct or amortize the organization and start-up costs, none of these costs would be deductible until the partnership liquidated. ■

Acquisition Costs of Depreciable Assets. Expenditures may be incurred in changing the legal title in which certain assets are held from that of the contributing partner to the partnership name. These costs include legal fees for transferring assets and transfer taxes imposed by some states. Such costs are added to the partnership's basis for the depreciable assets and increase the amount the partnership may depreciate.

Syndication Costs. **Syndication costs** are capitalized, but no amortization election is available. Syndication costs include the following expenditures incurred for promoting and marketing partnership interests:

- Brokerage fees.
- Registration fees.

[25]§ 195.

- Legal fees paid for security advice or advice on the adequacy of tax disclosures in the prospectus or placement memo for securities law purposes.
- Accounting fees related to offering materials.
- Printing costs of prospectus, placement memos, and other selling materials.

LO.4

Specify the accounting methods available to a partnership and the methods of determining a partnership's tax year.

METHOD OF ACCOUNTING

Like a sole proprietorship, a newly formed partnership may adopt either the cash or the accrual method of accounting, or a hybrid of these two methods.

However, a few special limitations on cash basis accounting apply to partnerships.[26] The cash method of accounting may not be adopted by a partnership that:

- has one or more C corporation partners or
- is a tax shelter.

A C corporation partner does *not* preclude cash basis treatment if:

- the partnership meets the $5 million gross receipts test described below,
- the C corporation partner(s) is a qualified personal service corporation, such as an incorporated attorney, or
- the partnership is engaged in the business of farming.

A partnership meets the $5 million gross receipts test if it has not received average annual gross receipts of more than $5 million. "Average annual gross receipts" is the average of gross receipts for the three tax years ending with the tax period in question. For new partnerships, the period of existence is used. Gross receipts are annualized for short taxable periods. A partnership must change to the accrual method the first year in which its average annual gross receipts exceed $5 million and must use the accrual method thereafter.

A tax shelter is a partnership whose interests have been sold in a registered offering or a partnership in which more than 35 percent of the losses are allocated to limited partners.

TAXABLE YEAR OF THE PARTNERSHIP

Partnership taxable income (and any separately stated items) flows through to each partner at the end of the *partnership's* taxable year. A *partner's* taxable income, then, includes the distributive share of partnership income for any *partnership* taxable year that ends within the partner's tax year.

When all partners use the calendar year, it would be beneficial in present value terms for a profitable partnership to adopt a fiscal year ending with January 31. Why? As Figure 21–1 illustrates, when the adopted year ends on January 31, the reporting of income from the partnership and payment of related taxes can be deferred for up to 11 months. For instance, income earned by the partnership in September 2004 is not taxable to the partners until January 31, 2005. It is reported in the partner's tax return for the year ended December 31, 2005, which is not due until April 15, 2006. Even though each partner may be required to make quarterly estimated tax payments, some deferral is still possible.

Required Taxable Years. To prevent excessive deferral of taxation of partnership income, Congress and the IRS have adopted a series of rules that prescribe the *required* taxable year an entity must adopt if no alternative tax years (discussed on page 21–20) are available. Three rules are presented in Figure 21–2.[27] The

[26] § 448.

[27] § 706(b).

FIGURE 21–1
Deferral Benefit When Fiscal Year Is Used and All Partners Are on the Calendar Year

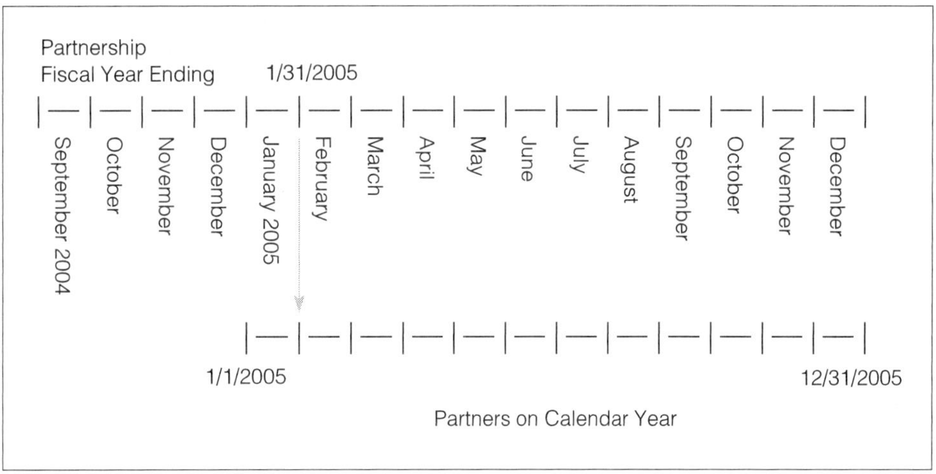

FIGURE 21–2
Required Tax Year of Partnership

In Order, Partnership Must Use	Requirements
Majority partners' tax year	• More than 50% of capital *and* profits is owned by partners who have the same taxable year.
Principal partners' tax year	• All partners who own 5% or more of capital *or* profits are principal partners. • All principal partners must have the same tax year.
Year with smallest amount of income deferred	• "Least aggregate deferral rule" (Example 19).

partnership must consider each rule in order. The partnership's required taxable year is the taxable year determined under the first rule that applies.

The first two rules in Figure 21–2 are relatively self-explanatory. Under the **least aggregate deferral method,** the partnership tests the year-ends that are used by the various partners to determine the weighted-average deferral of partnership income. The year-end that offers the least amount of deferral is the *required tax year* under this rule.

EXAMPLE 19

Anne and Bonnie are equal partners in the AB Partnership. Anne uses the calendar year, and Bonnie uses a fiscal year ending August 31. Neither Anne nor Bonnie is a majority partner since neither owns more than 50%. Although Anne and Bonnie are both principal partners, they do not have the same tax year. Therefore, the general rules indicate that the partnership's required tax year must be determined by the "least aggregate deferral rule." The following computations support August 31 as AB's tax year, since the 2.0 product using that year-end is less than the 4.0 product when December 31 is used.

Test for 12/31 Year-End

Partner	Year Ends	Profits Interest		Months of Deferral		Product
Anne	12/31	50%	×	-0-	=	0.0
Bonnie	8/31	50%	×	8	=	4.0
Aggregate number of deferral months						4.0

Test for 8/31 Year-End

Partner	Year Ends	Profits Interest		Months of Deferral		Product
Anne	12/31	50%	×	4	=	2.0
Bonnie	8/31	50%	×	–0–	=	0.0
Aggregate number of deferral months						2.0

Alternative Tax Years. If the required tax year is undesirable to the entity, three other alternative tax years may be available:

- Establish to the IRS's satisfaction that a *business purpose* exists for a different tax year, usually a natural business year at the end of a peak season or shortly thereafter.
- Elect a tax year so that taxes on partnership income are deferred for not more than *three months* from the *required* tax year.[28] Then, have the partnership maintain with the IRS a prepaid, non-interest-bearing deposit of estimated deferred taxes.[29] This alternative may not be desirable since the deposit is based on the highest individual tax rate of 35 percent plus 1 percentage point, or 36 percent.
- Elect a 52- to 53-week taxable year that ends with reference to the required taxable year or to the taxable year elected under the three-month deferral rule.

LO.5

Calculate partnership taxable income and describe how partnership items affect a partner's income tax return.

Operations of the Partnership

An individual, corporation, trust, estate, or another partnership can become a partner in a partnership. Since a partnership is a tax-reporting, rather than a taxpaying, entity for purposes of its Federal (and state) income tax computations, the partnership's income, deductions, credits, and alternative minimum tax (AMT) preferences and adjustments can ultimately be reported and taxed on any of a number of income tax forms [e.g., Forms 1040 (individuals), 1041 (fiduciaries), 1120 (C corporations), and 1120S (S corporations)].

A partnership is subject to all other taxes in the same manner as any other business. Thus, the partnership files returns and pays the outstanding amount of pertinent sales taxes, property taxes, and Social Security, unemployment, and other payroll taxes.

MEASURING AND REPORTING INCOME

The partnership's Form 1065 organizes and reports the transactions of the entity for the tax year, and each of the partnership's tax items is reported on Schedule K of that return. Each partner receives a Schedule K–1 that reports the partner's allocable share of partnership income, credits, adjustments, and preferences for the year. The IRS also receives a copy of each K–1. Form 1065 is due on the fifteenth day of the fourth month following the close of the partnership's tax year; for a calendar year partnership, this is April 15. The partnership must provide a copy of Schedule K–1 to each partner by the same date. However, partners of an electing large partnership must receive their K–1s one month earlier (March 15 for a calendar year partnership).

[28] § 444.

[29] § 7519.

Income Measurement. The measurement and reporting of partnership income require a two-step approach. Certain items must be netted at the partnership level, and other items must be segregated and reported separately on the partnership return and each partner's Schedule K–1.

Among the many items passed through separately are the following:

- Net short-term and net long-term capital gains or losses.
- Section 1231 gains and losses.
- Manufacturers' deduction (§ 199).
- Charitable contributions.
- Portfolio income items (qualified and ordinary dividends, interest, and royalties).
- Expenses related to portfolio income.
- Immediately expensed tangible personal property (§ 179).
- Items allocated among the partners in a different ratio from the general profit and loss ratio.
- Recovery of items previously deducted (tax benefit items).
- AMT preference and adjustment items.
- Self-employment income.
- Passive activity items, such as rental real estate income or loss.
- Intangible drilling and development costs.
- Taxes paid to foreign countries and U.S. possessions.[30]

The reason for separately reporting the preceding items is rooted in the aggregate or conduit concept. These items affect various exclusions, deductions, and credits at the partner level and must pass through without loss of identity so that the proper tax for each partner may be determined.[31]

A partnership is not allowed the following deductions:

- Net operating losses.
- Depletion of oil and gas interests.
- Dividends received deduction.

In addition, items that are only allowed by legislative grace to individuals, such as standard deductions or personal exemptions, are not allowed to the partnership. Also, if a partnership makes a payment on behalf of a partner, such as for alimony, medical expenses, or other items that constitute itemized deductions to individuals, the partnership treats the payment as a distribution or guaranteed payment (discussed later) to the partner, and the partner then determines whether a deduction may be claimed.

EXAMPLE 20

This year, the TUV Partnership entered into the following transactions:

Fees received	$100,000
Salaries paid	30,000
Cost recovery deductions	10,000
Supplies, repairs	3,000
Payroll taxes paid	9,000
Charitable contribution to art museum	6,000
Short-term capital gain	12,000
Passive income (rental operations)	7,500
Qualified dividends received	1,500
Tax-exempt income (bond interest)	2,100
AMT adjustment (cost recovery)	3,600
Payment of partner Vern's alimony obligations	4,000

[30] § 702(a).

[31] § 702(b).

The partnership experienced a $20,000 net loss from operations last year, its first year of business.

The partnership's current ordinary income is determined as follows:

Nonseparately Stated Items (Ordinary Income)	
Fees received	$100,000
Salaries paid	(30,000)
Cost recovery deductions	(10,000)
Supplies, repairs	(3,000)
Payroll taxes paid	(9,000)
Ordinary income	$ 48,000

The partnership is not allowed a deduction for last year's $20,000 net operating loss—this item was passed through to the partners in the previous year. Moreover, the partnership is not allowed a deduction for payment of Vern's alimony. This payment is probably handled as a distribution to Vern who may claim it as a deduction *for* AGI as if he had paid it himself.

The partnership's separately stated items are:

Separately Stated Items	
Charitable contribution to art museum	$ 6,000
Short-term capital gain	12,000
Passive income (rental operations)	7,500
Qualified dividends received	1,500
Tax-exempt income (bond interest)	2,100
AMT adjustment (cost recovery)	3,600

■

EXAMPLE 21

Assume the same facts as in Example 20. Tiwanda is a one-third partner in the TUV Partnership. The partnership will give her a Schedule K–1 on which she will be allocated a one-third share of ordinary income and one-third of each of the separately stated items. Thus, in determining her tax liability on her Form 1040, Tiwanda includes $16,000 of ordinary income, a $2,000 charitable contribution deduction, a $4,000 short-term capital gain, $2,500 of passive rent income, $500 of qualified dividend income, and a $1,200 positive adjustment in computing alternative minimum taxable income. She will disclose her $700 share of tax-exempt interest on the first page of her Form 1040. ■

Withdrawals. Capital withdrawals by partners during the year do not affect the partnership's income measuring and reporting process. These items are usually treated as distributions made on the last day of the partnership's tax year. When withdrawals exceed the partners' shares of partnership income, the excess is taxed under the distribution rules (discussed later in the chapter).[32]

Penalties. A partner's share of each partnership item should be reported on the partner's respective tax return in the same manner as presented on the Form 1065. If a partner treats an item differently, the IRS must be notified of the inconsistent treatment.[33] If a partner fails to notify the IRS, a negligence penalty may be added to the tax due.

[32] §§ 731(a)(1) and 733.

[33] § 6222.

To encourage the filing of a partnership return, a penalty is imposed on the partnership of $50, per partner, per month (or fraction thereof, but not to exceed five months) for failure to file a complete and timely information return without reasonable cause.[34] A partnership with 10 or fewer "natural persons" or corporations as partners, where each partner's share of partnership items is the same for all items, is automatically excluded from these penalties.[35]

ETHICAL CONSIDERATIONS

A Preparer's Responsibility for Partners' Tax Returns

A partnership's tax return preparer is responsible for accurately presenting information supplied by the partnership in that return. If a flow through amount is significant to a certain partner, the preparer of the *partnership* return can be treated as the preparer of a *partner's* tax return with respect to that item.

If a preparer misstates an item on a partnership return, either by taking a position that is not supportable under current law or by willfully misreporting an item on the return, "preparer penalties" can be assessed. While these penalties are relatively small, their imposition may also result in the preparer being suspended from practice before the IRS or by a state accountancy board.

As an example, assume Stan, a CPA, knowingly reported a $20,000 deduction for fines and penalties (nondeductible items) in determining the JB Partnership's $30,000 income from operations. This amount was allocated equally to partners Joe and Barb. Joe has other income of $35,000. Barb has other income of $1 million. Stan is treated as the preparer of Joe's tax return with respect to the improper $10,000 flow-through item, since the fines and penalties are significant relative to Joe's income. Stan is not considered the preparer of Barb's return, since the fines and penalties are not significant to her income.

In a recent case, the court held that the preparer of the partnership return was the preparer of several partners' returns with respect to partnership items flowing through to the partners. The court reached this decision even though the return preparer never met the individual partners, received no direct fees from the partners, and performed no other services for the partners.

Do you believe this is a reasonable approach for allocating responsibility for accurate preparation of a partner's tax return? Why or why not?

PARTNERSHIP ALLOCATIONS

So far, most examples in this chapter have assumed that the partner has the same percentage interest in capital, profits, and losses. Thus, a partner who owns a 25 percent interest in partnership capital has been assumed to own 25 percent of partnership profits and 25 percent of partnership losses.

Economic Effect. The partnership agreement can provide that any partner may share capital, profits, and losses in different ratios. For example, a partner could have a 25 percent capital sharing ratio, yet be allocated 30 percent of the profits and 20 percent of the losses of the partnership. Such special allocations have, at times, been used in an attempt to manipulate the allocation of tax benefits among partners. The Regulations[36] are designed to prevent unfair use of such manipulation. Although these rules are too complex to discuss in detail, the general outline of one of these rules—the **economic effect test**—can be easily understood.

[34]§ 6698.

[35]§§ 6231(a)(1)(B) and (I). Natural persons for this purpose include individuals who are not nonresident aliens, as well as the estate of a decedent who was not a nonresident alien.

[36]Reg. § 1.704–1(b).

In general, the economic effect test requires the following:

- An allocation of income or gain to a partner must increase the partner's capital account, and an allocation of deduction or loss must decrease the partner's capital account.
- When the partner's interest is liquidated, the partner must receive net assets that have a fair market value equal to the positive balance in the capital account.
- A partner with a negative capital account must restore that account upon liquidation of the interest. Restoration of a negative capital account can best be envisioned as a contribution of cash to the partnership equal to the negative balance.

These requirements are designed to ensure that a partner bears the economic burden of a loss or deduction allocation and receives the economic benefit of an income or gain allocation.

EXAMPLE 22

Eli and Sanjay each contribute $20,000 of cash to the newly formed ES Partnership. The partnership uses the cash to acquire a depreciable asset for $40,000. The partnership agreement provides that the depreciation is allocated 90% to Eli and 10% to Sanjay. Other items of partnership income, gain, loss, or deduction are allocated equally between the partners. Upon liquidation of the partnership, property will be distributed to the partners in accordance with their positive capital account balances. Any partner with a negative capital account must restore the capital account upon liquidation. Assume the first-year depreciation on the equipment is $4,000. Also, assume nothing else happens in the first year that affects the partners' capital accounts.

Eli's capital account is $16,400 ($20,000 – $3,600), and Sanjay's capital account has a balance of $19,600 ($20,000 – $400) after the first year of partnership operations. The Regulations require that a hypothetical sale of the asset for its $36,000 of adjusted basis on the last day of the year and an immediate liquidation of the partnership should result in Eli and Sanjay receiving distributions equal to their capital accounts. According to the partnership agreement, Eli would receive $16,400, and Sanjay would receive $19,600 of the cash in a liquidating distribution. Eli, therefore, bears the economic burden of $3,600 of depreciation since he contributed $20,000 to the partnership and would receive only $16,400 upon liquidation. Likewise, Sanjay's economic burden is $400 since he would receive only $19,600 of his original $20,000 investment. The agreement, therefore, has economic effect. ■

EXAMPLE 23

Assume the same facts as in Example 22, except that the partnership agreement provides that Eli and Sanjay will receive equal amounts of cash upon liquidation of the partnership. The hypothetical sale of the asset for its $36,000 adjusted basis and the immediate liquidation of the partnership would result in each partner receiving $18,000 cash. Since each partner contributed $20,000 to the partnership and each partner would receive $18,000 upon liquidation, each partner bears the economic burden of $2,000 of depreciation. The original 90%/10% allocation of depreciation to the two partners is defective, and the IRS will require that the depreciation be reallocated equally ($2,000 each) to the two partners to reflect the economic burden borne by each partner. ■

Precontribution Gain or Loss. Certain income, gain, loss, and deductions relative to contributed property may not be allocated under the rules described above. Instead, **precontribution gain or loss** must be allocated among the partners to take into account the variation between the basis of the property and its fair market value on the date of contribution.[37] For nondepreciable property, this means

[37]§ 704(c)(1)(A).

that *built-in* gain or loss on the date of contribution must be allocated to the contributing partner when the property is eventually disposed of by the partnership in a taxable transaction.

EXAMPLE 24

Seth and Tim form the equal profit and loss sharing ST Partnership. Seth contributes cash of $10,000, and Tim contributes land purchased two years ago that was held for investment. The land has an adjusted basis of $6,000 and fair market value of $10,000 at the contribution date. For accounting purposes, the partnership records the land at its fair market value of $10,000. For tax purposes, the partnership takes a carryover basis in the land of $6,000. After using the land as a parking lot for five months, ST sells it for $10,600. No other transactions have taken place.

The accounting and tax gain from the land sale are computed as follows:

	Accounting	Tax
Amount realized	$ 10,600	$10,600
Less: Adjusted basis	(10,000)	(6,000)
Gain realized	$ 600	$ 4,600
Built-in gain to Tim	(–0–)	(4,000)
Remaining gain (split equally)	$ 600	$ 600

Seth recognizes $300 of the gain ($600 remaining gain ÷ 2), and Tim recognizes $4,300 of gain [$4,000 built-in gain + ($600 remaining gain ÷ 2)]. ■

If the property is depreciable, Regulations describe allowable methods of allocating depreciation deductions.[38]

Concept Summary 21–2 reviews the tax reporting rules for partnership activities.

LO.6

Determine a partner's basis in the partnership interest and explain how liabilities affect the basis computation.

BASIS OF A PARTNERSHIP INTEREST

Previously, this chapter discussed how to compute a partner's basis when the partnership is formed. It was noted that the partner's basis in the newly formed partnership usually equals (1) the adjusted basis in any property contributed to the partnership plus (2) the fair market value of any services the partner performed for the partnership (i.e., the amount of ordinary income reported by the partner for services rendered to the partnership).

A partnership interest also can be acquired after the partnership has been formed. The method of acquisition controls how the partner's initial basis is computed. If the partnership interest is purchased from another partner, the purchasing partner's basis is the amount paid (cost basis) for the partnership interest. The basis of a partnership interest acquired by gift is the donor's basis for the interest plus, in certain cases, some or all of the transfer (gift) tax paid by the donor. The basis of a partnership interest acquired through inheritance generally is the fair market value of the interest on the date the partner dies.

After the partner is admitted to the partnership, the partner's basis is adjusted for numerous items. The following operating results *increase* a partner's adjusted basis:

[38]Reg. § 1.704–3.

CONCEPT SUMMARY 21–2

Tax Reporting of Partnership Activities

Event	Partnership Level	Partner Level
1. Compute partnership ordinary income.	Form 1065, line 22, page 1. Schedule K, Form 1065, line 1, page 3.	Schedule K–1 (Form 1065), line 1. Each partner's share is passed through for separate reporting. Each partner's basis is increased.
2. Compute partnership ordinary loss.	Form 1065, line 22, page 1. Schedule K, Form 1065, line 1, page 3.	Schedule K–1 (Form 1065), line 1. Each partner's share is passed through for separate reporting. Each partner's basis is decreased. The amount of a partner's loss deduction may be limited. Losses that may not be deducted are carried forward for use in future years.
3. Separately reported items such as portfolio income, capital gain and loss, and § 179 deductions.	Schedule K, Form 1065, various lines, page 3.	Schedule K–1 (Form 1065), various lines. Each partner's share of each item is passed through for separate reporting.
4. Net earnings from self-employment.	Schedule K, Form 1065, line 14, page 3.	Schedule K–1 (Form 1065), line 14.

- The partner's proportionate share of partnership income (including capital gains and tax-exempt income).
- The partner's proportionate share of any increase in partnership liabilities. (This provision is discussed in the next section.)

The following operating results *decrease* the partner's adjusted basis in the partnership:

- The partner's proportionate share of partnership deductions and losses (including capital losses).
- The partner's proportionate share of nondeductible expenses.
- The partner's proportionate share of any reduction in partnership liabilities.[39]

Under no circumstances can the partner's adjusted basis for the partnership interest be reduced below zero.

Increasing the adjusted basis for the partner's share of partnership taxable income is logical since the partner has already been taxed on the income. By increasing the partner's basis, the Code ensures that the partner is not taxed again on the income when the interest is sold or a distribution is received from the partnership.

It is also logical that the tax-exempt income should increase the partner's basis. If the income is exempt in the current period, it should not contribute to the recognition of gain when the partner either sells the interest or receives a distribution from the partnership.

[39] §§ 705 and 752.

EXAMPLE 25

Yuri is a one-third partner in the XYZ Partnership. His proportionate share of the partnership income during the current year consists of $20,000 of ordinary taxable income and $10,000 of tax-exempt income. None of the income is distributed to Yuri. The adjusted basis of Yuri's partnership interest before adjusting for his share of income is $35,000, and the fair market value of the interest before considering the income items is $50,000.

The unrealized gain inherent in Yuri's investment in the partnership is $15,000 ($50,000 – $35,000) before adjusting for his share of income. Yuri's proportionate share of the income items should increase the fair market value of the interest to $80,000 ($50,000 + $20,000 + $10,000). By increasing the adjusted basis of Yuri's partnership interest to $65,000 ($35,000 + $20,000 + $10,000), the Code ensures that the unrealized gain inherent in Yuri's partnership investment remains at $15,000. This makes sense because the $20,000 of ordinary taxable income is taxed to Yuri this year and should not be taxed again when he either sells his interest or receives a distribution. Similarly, the tax-exempt income is exempt this year and should not increase Yuri's gain when he either sells his interest or receives a distribution from the partnership. ■

Decreasing the adjusted basis for the partner's share of deductible losses, deductions, and noncapitalizable, nondeductible expenditures is logical for the same reasons. An item that is deductible currently should not contribute to creating a loss when the partnership interest is sold or a distribution is received from the partnership. Similarly, a noncapitalizable, nondeductible expenditure should never be deductible nor contribute to a loss when a subsequent sale or distribution transaction occurs.

Liability Sharing. A partner's adjusted basis is affected by the partner's share of partnership debt.[40] Partnership debt includes any partnership obligation that creates an asset, results in an expense to the partnership, or results in a nondeductible, noncapitalizable item at the partnership level. The definition of partnership debt includes most debt that is considered a liability under financial accounting rules except for accounts payable of a *cash basis* partnership and certain contingent liabilities.

Under § 752, an increase in a partner's share of partnership debt is treated as a cash contribution by the partner to the partnership. A partner's share of partnership debt increases as a result of increases in the total amount of partnership debt. A decrease in a partner's share of partnership debt is treated as a cash distribution from the partnership to the partner. A partner's share of partnership debt decreases as a result of (1) decreases in the total amount of partnership debt and (2) assumption of the partner's debt by the partnership.

EXAMPLE 26

Jim and Becky contribute property to form the JB Partnership. Jim contributes cash of $30,000. Becky contributes land with an adjusted basis and fair market value of $45,000, subject to a liability of $15,000. The partnership borrows $50,000 to finance construction of a building on the contributed land. At the end of the first year, the accrual basis partnership owes $3,500 in trade accounts payable to various vendors. Assume no other operating activities occurred.

Partnership debt sharing rules are discussed later in this section, but assuming for simplicity that Jim and Becky share equally in liabilities, the partners' bases in their partnership interests are determined as follows:

[40] § 752.

Jim's Basis		Becky's Basis	
Contributed cash	$30,000	Basis in contributed land	$ 45,000
Share of debt on land (assumed by partnership)	7,500	Less: Debt assumed by partnership	(15,000)
		Share of debt on land (assumed by partnership)	7,500
Initial basis	$37,500	Initial basis	$ 37,500
Share of construction loan	25,000	Share of construction loan	25,000
Share of trade accounts payable	1,750	Share of trade accounts payable	1,750
Basis, end of first year	$64,250	Basis, end of first year	$ 64,250

In this case, it is reasonable that the parties have an equal basis, because each is a 50% owner and they contributed property with identical *net* bases and identical *net* fair market values. ■

EXAMPLE 27

Assume the same facts as in Example 26. In the second year, the partnership generates $70,000 of taxable income from operations and repays both the $50,000 construction loan and the $3,500 trade accounts payable. The taxable income is allocated equally to each partner and increases each partner's basis by $35,000. The $26,750 ($25,000 + $1,750) reduction of each partner's share of liabilities is treated as a cash distribution to each partner and reduces each partner's adjusted basis by that amount. The $72,500 adjusted basis for each partner at the end of the second year is computed as follows:

Jim's Basis		Becky's Basis	
Basis, beginning of second year	$ 64,250	Basis, beginning of second year	$ 64,250
Share of taxable income	35,000	Share of taxable income	35,000
Share of construction loan paid	(25,000)	Share of construction loan paid	(25,000)
Share of trade accounts payable paid	(1,750)	Share of trade accounts payable paid	(1,750)
Basis, end of second year	$ 72,500	Basis, end of second year	$ 72,500

■

Two types of partnership debt exist. **Recourse debt** is partnership debt for which the partnership or at least one of the partners is personally liable. This personal liability can exist, for example, through the operation of state law or through personal guarantees that a partner makes to the creditor. Personal liability of a party related to a partner (under attribution rules) is treated as the personal liability of the partner. **Nonrecourse debt** is debt for which no partner (or party related to a partner) is personally liable. Lenders of nonrecourse debt generally require that collateral be pledged against the loan. Upon default, the lender can claim only the collateral, not the partners' personal assets.

How liabilities are shared among the partners depends upon whether the debt is recourse or nonrecourse and when the liability was incurred. For most debt *created* before January 29, 1989, the rules are relatively straightforward. Recourse debt is shared among the partners in accordance with their loss sharing ratios while nonrecourse debt is shared among the partners in accordance with the way they share partnership profits. Although questions arise about the calculation of the profit or loss sharing ratios and the treatment of personal guarantees of debt, the rules for sharing this earlier debt are easy to apply.

The rules for sharing partnership debt created after January 29, 1989, are much more complex. The basic principles of these rules are illustrated below.

Current Recourse Debt Rules. Recourse debt created after January 29, 1989, is shared in accordance with a **constructive liquidation scenario.**[41] Under this scenario, the following events are *deemed* to occur at the end of each taxable year of the partnership:

1. Most partnership assets (including cash) become worthless.
2. The worthless assets are sold at fair market value ($0), and losses on the deemed sales are determined.
3. These losses are allocated to the partners according to their loss sharing ratios. These losses reduce the partners' capital accounts.
4. Any partner with a (deemed) negative capital account balance is treated as contributing cash to the partnership to restore that negative balance to zero.
5. The cash deemed contributed by the partners with negative capital balances is used to pay the liabilities of the partnership.
6. The partnership is deemed to be liquidated immediately, and any remaining cash is distributed to partners with positive capital account balances.

The amount of a partner's cash contribution that would be used (in step 5 above) in payment of partnership recourse liabilities is that partner's share of these partnership recourse liabilities.

EXAMPLE 28

On January 1 of the current year, Nina and Otis each contribute $20,000 of cash to the newly created NO General Partnership. Each partner has a 50% interest in partnership capital, profits, and losses. The first year of partnership operations resulted in the following balance sheet as of December 31:

	Basis	FMV		Basis	FMV
Cash	$12,000	$12,000	Recourse payables	$30,000	$30,000
Receivables	7,000	7,000	Nina, capital	19,500	19,500
Land and buildings	50,000	50,000	Otis, capital	19,500	19,500
	$69,000	$69,000		$69,000	$69,000

The recourse debt is shared in accordance with the constructive liquidation scenario. All of the partnership assets (including cash) are deemed to be worthless and sold for $0. This creates a loss of $69,000 ($12,000 + $7,000 + $50,000), which is allocated equally between the two partners. The $34,500 loss allocated to each partner creates negative capital accounts of $15,000 each for Nina and Otis. If the partnership were actually liquidated, each partner would contribute $15,000 cash to the partnership; the cash would be used to pay the partnership recourse payables; and the partnership would cease to exist. Because each partner would be required to contribute $15,000 to pay the liabilities, each shares in $15,000 of the recourse payables. Accordingly, Nina and Otis will each have an adjusted basis for their partnership interests of $34,500 ($19,500 + $15,000) on December 31. ■

EXAMPLE 29

Assume the same facts as in Example 28, except that the partners allocate partnership losses 60% to Nina and 40% to Otis. The constructive liquidation scenario results in the $69,000 loss being allocated $41,400 to Nina and $27,600 to Otis. As a consequence, Nina's capital account has a negative balance of $21,900, and Otis's account has a negative balance of

[41]Transition rules (beyond the scope of this text) apply to debt created between January 29, 1989, and December 28, 1991.

$8,100. Each partner is deemed to contribute cash equal to these negative capital accounts, and the cash would be used to pay the recourse liabilities under the constructive liquidation scenario. Accordingly, Nina and Otis share $21,900 and $8,100, respectively, in the recourse debt. Note that the debt allocation percentages (73% to Nina and 27% to Otis) are different from the partners' 60%/40% loss sharing ratios. ■

Current Nonrecourse Debt Rules. Nonrecourse debt is allocated in three stages. First, an amount of debt equal to the amount of *minimum gain* is allocated to partners who share in minimum gain. The calculation of minimum gain is complex, and its details are beyond the scope of this text. In general, minimum gain approximates the amount of nonrecourse (mortgage) liability on a property in excess of the "book" basis of the property. Generally, the "book" basis for a property item is the same as the "tax" basis, although sometimes the amounts are different. For example, the "book" basis for contributed property on the date of contribution is its fair market value at that date, not its "tax" basis.

If a lender forecloses on partnership property, the result is treated as a deemed sale of the property for the mortgage balance. Gain is recognized for at least the amount of the liability in excess of the property's "book" basis—hence, minimum gain. Allocation of minimum gain among the partners should be addressed in the partnership agreement.

Second, the amount of nonrecourse debt equal to the remaining *precontribution gain* under § 704(c) is allocated to the partner who contributed the property and debt to the partnership. For this purpose, the remaining precontribution gain is the excess of the current nonrecourse debt balance on the contributed property over the current tax basis of the contributed property.[42] Note that this calculation is only relevant when the "book" and "tax" bases of the contributed property are different.

Third, any remaining nonrecourse debt is allocated to the partners in accordance with one of several different allocation methods. The partnership agreement should specify which allocation method is chosen. Most often, the profit sharing ratio is used.

EXAMPLE 30

Ted contributes a nondepreciable asset to the TK Partnership in exchange for a one-third interest in the capital, profits, and losses of the partnership. The asset has an adjusted tax basis to Ted and the partnership of $24,000 and a fair market value and "book" basis on the contribution date of $50,000. The asset is encumbered by a nonrecourse note (created January 1, 2004) of $35,000. Because the "book" basis exceeds the nonrecourse debt, there is no minimum gain. Under § 704(c) principles, the Regulations provide that the first $11,000 of the nonrecourse debt ($35,000 debt – $24,000 basis) is allocated to Ted. Assume the partnership allocates the remaining $24,000 of nonrecourse debt according to the profit sharing ratio, and Ted's share is $8,000. Therefore, Ted shares in $19,000 ($11,000 + $8,000) of the nonrecourse debt.

Ted's basis in his partnership interest is determined as follows:

Basis of contributed property	$ 24,000
Less: Liability assumed by partnership	(35,000)
Plus: Allocation of § 704(c) debt	11,000
Basis before remaining allocation	$ -0-
Plus: Allocation of remaining nonrecourse debt	8,000
Basis in partnership interest	$ 8,000

[42]Reg. § 1.704–3.

The § 704(c) allocation of nonrecourse debt prevents Ted from receiving a deemed distribution ($35,000) in excess of his basis in property he contributed ($24,000). Without this required allocation of nonrecourse debt, in some cases, a contributing partner would be required to recognize gain on a contribution of property encumbered by nonrecourse debt. ■

Other Factors Affecting Basis Calculations. The partner's basis is also affected by (1) postacquisition contributions of cash or property to the partnership; (2) postacquisition distributions of cash or property from the partnership; and (3) special calculations that are designed to allow the full deduction of percentage depletion for oil and gas wells. Postacquisition contributions of cash or property affect basis in the same manner as contributions made upon the creation of the partnership. Postacquisition distributions of cash or property reduce basis.

EXAMPLE 31

Ryan is a one-third partner in the ERM Partnership. On January 1, 2005, Ryan's basis in his partnership interest was $50,000. During 2005, the calendar year, accrual basis partnership generated ordinary taxable income of $210,000. It also received $60,000 of tax-exempt interest income from City of Buffalo bonds. It paid $3,000 in nondeductible bribes to local law enforcement officials, so that the police would not notify the Federal government about the products that the entity had imported without paying the proper tariffs. On July 1, 2005, Ryan contributed $20,000 cash and a computer (zero basis to him) to the partnership. Ryan's monthly draw from the partnership is $3,000; this is treated as a distribution and not as a guaranteed payment. The only liabilities that the partnership has incurred are trade accounts payable. On January 1, 2005, the trade accounts payable totaled $45,000; this account balance was $21,000 on December 31, 2005. Ryan shares in one-third of the partnership liabilities for basis purposes.

Ryan's basis in the partnership on December 31, 2005, is $115,000, computed as follows:

Beginning balance	$ 50,000
Share of ordinary partnership income	70,000
Share of tax-exempt income	20,000
Share of nondeductible expenditures	(1,000)
Ryan's basis in noncash capital contribution	-0-
Additional cash contribution	20,000
Capital withdrawal ($3,000 × 12)	(36,000)
Share of net decrease in partnership liabilities [⅓ × ($45,000 – $21,000)]	(8,000)
	$115,000

■

EXAMPLE 32

Assume the same facts as in Example 31. If Ryan withdraws cash of $115,000 from the partnership on January 1, 2006, the withdrawal is tax-free to him and reduces his basis to zero. The distribution is tax-free because he has recognized his share of the partnership's net income throughout his association with the entity, via the annual flow-through of his share of the partnership's income and expense items to his personal tax return. Note that the $20,000 cash withdrawal of his share of the municipal bond interest retains its nontaxable character in this distribution. Ryan receives the $20,000 tax-free because his basis was increased in 2005 when the partnership received the interest income. ■

A partner is required to compute the adjusted basis only when necessary and thus can avoid the inconvenience of making day-to-day calculations of basis. When a partnership interest is sold, exchanged, or retired, however, the partner must compute the adjusted basis as of the date the transaction occurs. Computation of gain or loss requires an accurate calculation of the partner's adjusted basis on the

■ FIGURE 21–3
Partner's Basis in Partnership Interest

Basis is generally adjusted in the following order:

Initial basis. Amount paid for partnership interest, or gift or inherited basis (including share of partnership debt). Amount paid can be amount contributed to the partnership or amount paid to another partner or former partner.

+ Partner's subsequent contributions

+ Since interest acquired, partner's share of the partnership's

- Debt increase
- Taxable income items
- Tax-exempt income items
- Excess of depletion deductions over adjusted basis of property subject to depletion

– Partner's distributions and withdrawals

– Since interest acquired, partner's share of the partnership's

- Debt decrease
- Nondeductible items not chargeable to a capital account
- Special depletion deduction for oil and gas wells
- Loss items

The basis of a partner's interest can never be negative.

transaction date. Figure 21–3 summarizes the rules for computing a partner's basis in a partnership interest.

LO.7

Describe the limitations on deducting partnership losses.

LOSS LIMITATIONS

Partnership losses flow through to the partners for use on their income tax returns. However, the amount and nature of the losses allowed in a partner's tax computations may be limited. When limitations apply, all or a portion of the losses are held in suspension until a triggering event occurs. Only then can the losses be used to determine the partner's tax liability. No time limit is imposed on such carryforwards of losses.

Three different limitations may apply to partnership losses that are passed through to a partner:

- The first is the overall limitation contained in § 704(d). This limitation allows the deduction of losses only to the extent the partner has adjusted basis for the partnership interest.
- Losses that are deductible under the overall limitation may then be subject to the at-risk limitation of § 465. Losses are deductible under this provision only to the extent the partner is at risk for the partnership interest.
- Any losses that survive this second limitation may be subject to a third limitation, the passive loss rules of § 469.

Only losses that make it through all these applicable limitations are eligible to be deducted on the partner's tax return.

EXAMPLE 33

Meg is a partner in a partnership that does not invest in real estate. On January 1, 2005, Meg's adjusted basis for her partnership interest is $50,000, and her at-risk amount is $35,000. Her share of losses from the partnership for 2005 is $60,000, all of which is passive. She has one other passive income-producing investment that produced $25,000 of passive income during 2005.

Meg will be able to deduct $25,000 of partnership losses on her Form 1040 for 2005. Her deductible loss is calculated as follows:

Applicable Provision	Deductible Loss	Suspended Loss
Overall limitation	$50,000	$10,000
At-risk limitation	35,000	15,000
Passive loss limitation	25,000	10,000

Meg can deduct only $50,000 under the overall limitation. Of this $50,000, only $35,000 is deductible under the at-risk limitation. Under the passive loss limitation, passive losses can be deducted only against passive income. Thus, Meg can deduct only $25,000 on her return in 2005. ■

Overall Limitation. A partner may only deduct losses flowing through from the partnership to the extent of the partner's adjusted basis in the partnership. A partner's adjusted basis in the partnership is determined at the end of the partnership's taxable year. It is adjusted for distributions and any partnership gains during the year, but it is determined before considering any losses for the year.

Losses that cannot be deducted because of this rule are suspended and carried forward (never back) for use against future increases in the partner's adjusted basis. Such increases might result from additional capital contributions, from sharing in additional partnership debt, or from future partnership income.

EXAMPLE 34

Carol and Dan do business as the CD Partnership, sharing profits and losses equally. All parties use the calendar year. At the start of the current year, the basis of Carol's partnership interest is $25,000. The partnership sustains an operating loss of $80,000 in the current year. For the current year, only $25,000 of Carol's $40,000 allocable share of the partnership loss can be deducted under the overall limitation. As a result, the basis of Carol's partnership interest is zero as of January 1 of the following year, and she must carry forward the remaining $15,000 of partnership losses. ■

EXAMPLE 35

Assume the same facts as in Example 34, and that the partnership earns a profit of $70,000 for the next calendar year. Carol reports net partnership income of $20,000 ($35,000 distributive share of income – the $15,000 carryforward loss). The basis of Carol's partnership interest becomes $20,000. ■

In Example 34, Carol's entire $40,000 share of the current-year partnership loss could have been deducted under the overall limitation in the current year if she had contributed an additional $15,000 or more in capital by December 31. Alternatively, if the partnership had incurred additional debt by the end of the current year, Carol's basis might have been increased to permit some or all of the loss to be deducted this year. Thus, if partnership losses are projected for a given year, careful tax planning can ensure their deductibility under the overall limitation.

At-Risk Limitation. Under the at-risk rules, the partnership losses from business and income-producing activities that individual partners and closely held C corporation partners can deduct are limited to amounts that are economically invested in the partnership. Invested amounts include cash and the adjusted basis of property contributed by the partner and the partner's share of partnership earnings that has not been withdrawn.[43] A closely held C corporation exists when five or fewer individuals own more than 50 percent of the entity's stock under appropriate attribution and ownership rules.

[43] § 465(a).

When some or all of the partners are personally liable for partnership recourse debt, that debt is included in the adjusted basis of those partners. Usually, those partners also include the debt in their amount at risk.

No partner, however, carries any financial risk on nonrecourse debt. Therefore, as a general rule, partners cannot include nonrecourse debt in their amount at risk even though that debt is included in the adjusted basis of their partnership interest. In many cases, however, an exception to this general rule applies. Real estate nonrecourse financing provided by a bank, retirement plan, or similar party, or by a Federal, state, or local government generally is deemed to be at risk.[44] Such debt is termed **qualified nonrecourse debt.** In summary, although the general rule provides that nonrecourse debt is not at risk, the overriding exception may provide that it is deemed to be at risk.

When determining a partner's loss deduction, the overall limitation rule is invoked first. That is, the deduction is limited to the partner's outside basis at the end of the partnership year. Then, the at-risk provisions are applied to see if the remaining loss is still deductible. Suspended losses are carried forward until a partner has a sufficient amount at risk in the activity to absorb them.[45]

EXAMPLE 36

Kelly invests $5,000 in the Kelly Green Limited Partnership as a 5% general partner. Shortly thereafter, the partnership acquires the master recording of a well-known vocalist for $250,000 ($50,000 from the partnership and $200,000 secured from a local bank by means of a *recourse* mortgage). Assume Kelly's share of the recourse debt is $10,000, and her basis in her partnership interest is $15,000 ($5,000 cash investment + $10,000 debt share). Since the debt is recourse, Kelly's at-risk amount is also $15,000. Kelly's share of partnership losses in the first year of operations is $11,000. She is entitled to deduct the full $11,000 of partnership losses under both the overall and the at-risk limitations because this amount is less than both her outside basis and at-risk amount. ■

EXAMPLE 37

Assume the same facts as in Example 36, except the bank loan is nonrecourse (the partners have no direct liability under the terms of the loan in the case of a default). Kelly's basis in her partnership interest still is $15,000, but she can deduct only $5,000 of the flow-through loss. The amount she has at risk in the partnership does not include the nonrecourse debt. (The debt does not relate to real estate so it is not qualified nonrecourse debt.) ■

Passive Activity Rules. A partnership loss share may be disallowed under the passive activity rules. These rules apply to partners who are individuals, estates, trusts, closely held C corporations, or personal service corporations. The rules require the partners to separate their activities into three groups:

- *Active.* Earned income, such as salary and wages; income or loss from a trade or business in which the partner materially participates; and guaranteed payments received by the partner for services.
- *Portfolio.* Annuity income, interest, dividends, guaranteed payments from a partnership for interest on capital, royalties not derived in the ordinary course of a trade or business, and gains and losses from disposal of investment assets.
- *Passive.* Income from a trade or business activity in which the partner does not materially participate on a regular, continuous, and substantial basis, or income from many rental activities.[46]

[44] § 465(b)(6).
[45] § 465(a)(2).
[46] §§ 469(c)(1) and (2).

Material participation in an activity is determined annually. The burden is on the partner to prove material participation. The IRS has provided a number of objective tests for determining material participation. These tests require the partner to have substantial involvement in daily operations of the activity. Thus, a Maine vacation resort operator investing in a California grape farm or an electrical engineer employed in Virginia investing in an Iowa corn and hog farm may have difficulty proving material participation in the activities.

Rent income from real or personal property generally is passive income, regardless of the partner's level of participation. Exceptions are made for rent income from activities where substantial services are provided (e.g., certain developers, resorts); from hotels, motels, and other transient lodging; from short-term equipment rentals; and from certain developed real estate.

Usually, passive activity losses can only offset passive activity income.[47] In determining the net passive activity loss for a year, losses and income from all passive activities are aggregated. The amount of suspended losses carried forward from a particular activity is determined by the ratio of the net loss from that activity to the aggregate net loss from all passive activities for the year. A special rule for rental real estate (discussed in the following section) allows a limited $25,000 offset against nonpassive income.[48]

A partner making a taxable disposition of an entire interest in a passive activity takes a full deduction for suspended passive activity losses from that activity in the year of disposal.[49] Suspended losses are deductible against income in the following order: income or gain from the passive activity, net income or gain from all passive activities, and other income. When a passive activity is transferred in a primarily nontaxable exchange (e.g., a like-kind exchange or contribution to a partnership), suspended losses are deductible only to the extent of gains recognized on the transfer. Remaining losses are deducted on disposal of the activity received in the exchange.

EXAMPLE 38

Debra has several investments in passive activities that generate aggregate losses of $10,000 in the current year. Debra wants to deduct all of these losses on her current-year tax return. To assure a loss deduction, she needs to invest in some passive activities that generate income. One of her long-time friends, an entrepreneur in the women's apparel business, is interested in opening a new apparel store in a nearby community. Debra is willing to finance a substantial part of the expansion but does not want to get involved with day-to-day operations. Debra also wants to limit any possible loss to her initial investment.

After substantial discussions, Debra and her friend decide to form a limited partnership, which will own the new store. Debra's friend will be the general partner, and Debra will be a limited partner. Debra invests $100,000, and her friend invests $50,000 and sweat equity (provides managerial skills and know-how). Each has a 50% interest in profits and losses. In the first year of operations, the store generates a profit of $30,000. Since Debra's share of the profit ($15,000) is passive activity income, it can be fully utilized against any of her passive activity losses from other investments. Thus, Debra's share of the apparel store profits enables her to obtain a full deduction of her $10,000 of passive activity losses. ■

Rental Real Estate Losses. In any one year, individuals can offset up to $25,000 of passive losses from rental real estate against active and portfolio income. The $25,000 maximum is reduced by 50 percent of the difference between the taxpayer's modified AGI and $100,000. Thus, when the taxpayer's modified AGI reaches $150,000, the offset is eliminated.

[47] § 469(a)(1).
[48] § 469(i).
[49] § 469(g).

The offset is available to those who actively (rather than materially) participate in rental real estate activities. Active participation is an easier test to meet. Unlike material participation, it does not require regular, continuous, and substantial involvement with the activity. However, the taxpayer must own at least 10 percent of the fair market value of all interests in the rental property and either contribute to the activity's management decisions in a significant and bona fide way or actively participate in arranging for others to make such decisions.

EXAMPLE 39

Raoul invests $10,000 cash in the Sparrow Limited Partnership in the current year for a 10% limited interest in capital and profits. Shortly thereafter, the partnership purchases rental real estate subject to a qualified nonrecourse mortgage of $120,000 obtained from a commercial bank. Raoul engages in no other passive activities during the current year.

Raoul does not participate in any of Sparrow's activities. His share of losses from Sparrow's first year of operations is $27,000. His modified AGI before considering the loss is $60,000. Before considering the loss, Raoul's basis in the partnership interest is $22,000 [$10,000 cash + (10% × $120,000 debt)], and his loss deduction is limited to this amount under the overall limitation. The debt is included in Raoul's amount at risk because it is qualified nonrecourse financing. It may seem that Raoul should be allowed to deduct the $22,000 loss share from portfolio or active income under the rental real estate exception to the passive loss rules. However, the loss may not be offset against this income because Raoul is not an active participant in the partnership. ■

LO.8

Describe the treatment of transactions between a partner and the partnership.

Transactions between Partners and Partnerships

Many types of transactions occur between a partnership and one of its partners. The partner may contribute property to the partnership, perform services for the partnership, or receive distributions from the partnership. The partner may borrow money from or lend money to the partnership. Property may be bought and sold between the partner and the partnership. Several of these transactions were discussed earlier in the chapter. The remaining types of partner-partnership transactions are the focus of this section.

GUARANTEED PAYMENTS

If a partnership makes a payment to a partner, the payment may be a draw against the partner's share of partnership income; a return of some or all of the partner's original capital contribution; or a guaranteed payment, among other treatments. A **guaranteed payment** is a payment for services performed by the partner or for the use of the partner's capital. The payment may not be determined by reference to partnership income. Guaranteed payments are usually expressed as a fixed-dollar amount or as a percentage of capital that the partner has invested in the partnership. Whether the partnership deducts or capitalizes the guaranteed payment depends on the nature of the payment.

EXAMPLE 40

David, Donald, and Dale formed the accrual basis DDD Partnership in 2005. The partnership and each of the partners are calendar year taxpayers. According to the partnership agreement, David is to manage the partnership and receive a $21,000 distribution from the entity every year, payable in 12 monthly installments. Donald is to receive an amount that is equal to 18% of his capital account, as it is computed by the firm's accountant at the beginning of the year, payable in 12 monthly installments. Dale is the partnership's advertising specialist. He withdraws approximately 3% of the partnership's net income every month for his personal use. David and Donald receive guaranteed payments from the partnership, but Dale does not. ■

Guaranteed payments resemble the salary or interest payments of other businesses and receive somewhat similar income tax treatment.[50] In contrast to the provision that usually applies to withdrawals of assets by partners from their partnerships, guaranteed payments are deductible (or capitalized) by the entity. Deductible guaranteed payments, like other deductible expenses of a partnership, can create an ordinary loss for the entity. A partner who receives guaranteed payments during a partnership year must include the payments in income as if they were received on the last day of the partnership year. Guaranteed payments are always taxable as ordinary income to the recipient partner.

EXAMPLE 41

Continue with the situation introduced in Example 40. For calendar year 2005, David receives the $21,000 as provided by the partnership agreement, Donald's guaranteed payment for 2005 is $17,000, and Dale withdraws $20,000. Before considering these amounts, the partnership's ordinary income for 2005 is $650,000.

The partnership can deduct its payments to David and Donald, so the final amount of its 2005 ordinary income is $612,000 ($650,000 – $21,000 – $17,000). Thus, each of the equal partners is allocated $204,000 of ordinary partnership income for their 2005 individual income tax returns ($612,000 ÷ 3). In addition, David reports the $21,000 of guaranteed payment income on his 2005 tax return, and Donald similarly includes the $17,000 guaranteed payment on his 2005 income. Dale's partnership draw is deemed to have come from his allocated $204,000 (or from the accumulated partnership income that was taxed in prior years) and is not taxed separately to him. Dale's basis, though, is reduced by the $20,000 distribution. ■

EXAMPLE 42

Assume the same facts as in Example 41, except that the partnership's tax year ends on March 31, 2006. The total amount of the guaranteed payments is taxable to the partners on that date. Thus, even though David receives 9 of his 12 payments for fiscal 2006 in calendar 2005, all of his guaranteed payments are taxable to him in 2006. Similarly, all of Donald's guaranteed payments are taxable to him in 2006 and not when they are received. The deduction for, and the gross income from, guaranteed payments are allowed on the same date that all of the other income and expense items relative to the partnership are allocated to the partners (on the last day of the entity's tax year). ■

OTHER TRANSACTIONS BETWEEN PARTNERS AND PARTNERSHIPS

Certain transactions between a partner and the partnership are treated as if the partner were an outsider, dealing with the partnership at arm's length.[51] Loan transactions, rental payments, and sales of property between the partner and the partnership are treated in this manner. In addition, payments for services are generally treated this way when the services are short-term technical services that the partner also provides for parties other than the partnership.

EXAMPLE 43

Emilio, a one-third partner in the CDE Partnership, owns a tract of land that the partnership wishes to purchase. The land has a fair market value of $30,000 and an adjusted basis to Emilio of $17,000. If Emilio sells the land to the partnership, he recognizes a $13,000 gain on the sale, and the partnership takes a $30,000 cost basis in the land. If the land has a fair market value of $10,000 on the sale date, Emilio recognizes a $7,000 loss. ■

[50] § 707(c).

[51] § 707(a).

The timing of the deduction for a payment by an accrual basis partnership to a cash basis service partner depends upon whether the payment is a guaranteed payment or a payment to a partner who is treated as an outsider. A guaranteed payment is includible in the partner's income on the last day of the partnership year when it is properly accrued by the partnership, even though the payment may not be made to the partner until the next taxable year. Conversely, the *partner's* method of accounting controls the timing of deduction if the payment is treated as made to an outsider. This is because a deduction cannot be claimed for such amounts until the recipient partner is required to include the amount in income under the partner's method of accounting.[52] Thus, a partnership cannot claim a deduction until it actually makes the payment to the cash basis partner, but it could accrue and deduct a payment due to an accrual basis partner even if payment was not yet made.

EXAMPLE 44

Rachel, a cash basis taxpayer, is a partner in the accrual basis RTC Partnership. On December 31, 2005, the partnership accrues but does not pay $10,000 for deductible services that Rachel performed for the partnership during the year. Both Rachel and the partnership are calendar year taxpayers.

If the $10,000 accrual is a guaranteed payment, the partnership deducts the $10,000 in its calendar year ended December 31, 2005, and Rachel includes the $10,000 in her income for the 2005 calendar year. The fact that Rachel is a cash basis taxpayer and does not actually receive the cash in 2005 is irrelevant.

If the payment is classified as a payment to an outsider, the partnership cannot deduct the payment until Rachel actually receives the cash. If, for example, Rachel performs janitorial services (i.e., not in her capacity as a partner) and receives the cash on March 25, 2006, the partnership deducts the payment and Rachel recognizes the income on that date. ■

Sales of Property. Certain sales of property fall under special rules. No loss is recognized on a sale of property between a person and a partnership when the person owns, directly or indirectly, more than 50 percent of partnership capital or profits.[53] The disallowed loss may not vanish entirely, however. If the transferee eventually sells the property at a gain, the disallowed loss reduces the gain that the transferee would otherwise recognize.

EXAMPLE 45

Barry sells land (adjusted basis $30,000; fair market value, $45,000) to a partnership in which he controls a 60% capital interest. The partnership pays him only $20,000 for the land. Barry cannot deduct his $10,000 realized loss. The sale apparently was not at arm's length, but the taxpayer's intentions are irrelevant. Barry and the partnership are related parties, and the loss is disallowed.

When the partnership sells the land to an outsider at a later date, it receives a sales price of $44,000. The partnership can offset the recognition of its $24,000 realized gain on the subsequent sale ($44,000 sales proceeds – $20,000 adjusted basis) by the amount of the $10,000 prior disallowed loss ($20,000 – $30,000). Thus, the partnership recognizes a $14,000 gain on its sale of the land. ■

Using a similar rationale, any gain that is realized on a sale or exchange between a partner and a partnership in which the partner controls a capital or profits interest of more than 50 percent must be recognized as ordinary income, unless the asset is a capital asset to both the seller and the purchaser.[54]

[52] § 267(a)(2).
[53] § 707(b).
[54] § 707(b)(2).

CONCEPT SUMMARY 21–3

Partner-Partnership Transactions

1. Partners can transact business with their partnerships in a nonpartner capacity. These transactions include the sale and exchange of property, rentals, loans of funds, etc.
2. A payment to a partner may be classified as a guaranteed payment if it is for services or use of the partner's capital and is not based on partnership income. A guaranteed payment may be deductible by the partnership and is included in the partner's income on the last day of the partnership's tax year.
3. A payment to a partner may be treated as being to an outside (though related) party. Such a payment is deductible or capitalizable by the partnership at the time the partner must include the amount in income under his or her method of accounting.
4. Guaranteed payments and payments to a partner that are treated as being to an outside party are only deductible if the underlying reason for the payment constitutes an ordinary and necessary (rather than capitalizable) business expense.
5. Losses are disallowed between a partner or related party and a partnership when the partner or related party owns more than a 50% interest in the partnership's capital or profits.
6. When there is income from a related-party sale, it is treated as ordinary income if the property is not a capital asset to both the transferor and the transferee.

EXAMPLE 46

Kristin purchases some land (adjusted basis, $30,000; fair market value, $45,000) for $45,000 from a partnership in which she controls a 90% profits interest. The land was a capital asset to the partnership. If Kristin holds the land as a capital asset, the partnership recognizes a $15,000 capital gain. However, if Kristin is a land developer and the property is not a capital asset to her, the partnership must recognize $15,000 of ordinary income from the sale, even though the property was a capital asset to the partnership. ■

PARTNERS AS EMPLOYEES

A partner usually does not qualify as an employee for tax purposes. Thus, a partner receiving guaranteed payments is not regarded as an employee of the partnership for purposes of withholding taxes. Moreover, since a partner is not an employee, the partnership cannot deduct its payments for the partner's fringe benefits. A general partner's distributive share of ordinary partnership income and guaranteed payments for services are generally subject to the Federal self-employment tax.[55]

Concept Summary 21–3 reviews partner-partnership transactions.

Distributions from the Partnership

The tax treatment of distributions from a partnership to a partner was introduced earlier in the context of routine withdrawals (or "draws") and cash distributions from a continuing partnership to a continuing partner. This section will expand that discussion by examining in greater detail the effect of nonliquidating distributions made during the normal operations of the partnership. In addition, distributions to partners in complete liquidation of their ownership interests and sales of partnership interests are discussed.

[55] § 1402(a).

A **nonliquidating distribution** is any distribution from a continuing partnership to a continuing partner—that is, any distribution that is not a liquidating distribution. There are two types of nonliquidating distributions: draws or partial liquidations. A *draw* is a distribution of a partner's share of current or accumulated partnership profits that have been taxed to the partner in current or prior taxable years of the partnership. A *partial liquidation* is a distribution that reduces the partner's interest in partnership capital but does not liquidate the partner's entire interest in the partnership. The distinction between the two types of *nonliquidating* distributions is largely semantic, since the basic tax treatment typically does not differ.

EXAMPLE 47

Kay joins the calendar year KLM Partnership on January 1, 2005, by contributing $40,000 of cash to the partnership in exchange for a one-third interest in partnership capital, profits, and losses. Her distributive share of partnership income for the year is $25,000. If the partnership distributes $65,000 ($25,000 share of partnership profits + $40,000 initial capital contribution) to Kay on December 31, 2005, the distribution is a nonliquidating distribution as long as Kay continues to be a partner in the partnership. This is true even though Kay receives her share of profits plus her entire investment in the partnership. In this case, $25,000 is considered a draw, and the remaining $40,000 is a partial liquidation of Kay's interest. ■

A payment from a partnership to a partner is not necessarily treated as a distribution. For example, as discussed earlier, a partnership may pay interest or rent to a partner for use of the partner's capital or property, make a guaranteed payment to a partner, or purchase property from a partner. If a payment *is* treated as a distribution, it is not necessarily treated under the general tax deferral rules that apply to most partnership distributions. In certain circumstances, the partner may recognize capital gain (or loss) and ordinary income (or loss) when a distribution is received from the partnership.

Finally, a distribution may be either proportionate or disproportionate. In a **proportionate distribution,** a partner receives the appropriate share of certain ordinary income-producing assets of the partnership. A **disproportionate distribution** occurs when the distribution increases or decreases the distributee partner's interest in certain ordinary income-producing assets. The tax treatment of disproportionate distributions is very complex and is beyond the scope of this discussion.

LO.9

Determine the tax treatment of proportionate nonliquidating distributions from a partnership to a partner and the tax treatment of proportionate distributions that liquidate a partnership.

PROPORTIONATE NONLIQUIDATING DISTRIBUTIONS

In general, neither the partner nor the partnership recognizes gain or loss when a nonliquidating distribution occurs.[56] The partner usually takes a carryover basis in the assets distributed.[57] The distributee partner's outside basis is reduced (but not below zero) by the amount of cash and the adjusted basis of property distributed.[58] The details of the taxation of such distributions are discussed below and are summarized at the end of this section in Concept Summary 21–4. The following examples illustrate the situation and show that a distribution does not change a partner's overall economic position.

EXAMPLE 48

Jay is a one-fourth partner in the JP Partnership. His basis in his partnership interest is $40,000 on December 31, 2005. The fair market value of the interest is $70,000. The partnership distributes $25,000 of cash to him on that date. The distribution is not taxable to Jay or the

[56] §§ 731(a) and (b).
[57] § 732(a)(1).
[58] § 733.

partnership. The distribution reduces Jay's adjusted basis in the partnership to $15,000 ($40,000 – $25,000), and the fair market value of his partnership interest is, arguably, reduced to $45,000 ($70,000 – $25,000). ■

EXAMPLE 49

Assume the same facts as in Example 48, except that the partnership distributes both the $25,000 cash and land with an adjusted basis to the partnership of $13,000 and a fair market value of $30,000 on the date of distribution. The distribution is not taxable to Jay or the partnership. Jay reduces his basis in the partnership to $2,000 [$40,000 – ($25,000 + $13,000)] and takes a carryover basis of $13,000 in the land. The fair market value of Jay's remaining interest in the partnership is, arguably, reduced to $15,000 [$70,000 – ($25,000 + $30,000)].

If Jay had sold his partnership interest for $70,000 rather than receiving the distribution, he would have realized and recognized gain of $30,000 ($70,000 selling price – $40,000 outside basis). Because he has not recognized any gain or loss on the distribution of cash and land, he should still have the $30,000 of deferred gain to recognize at some point in the future. This is exactly what will happen. If Jay sells the land and remaining partnership interest on January 1, 2006, the day after the distribution, he realizes and recognizes gains of $17,000 ($30,000 – $13,000) on the land and $13,000 ($15,000 – $2,000) on the partnership interest. These gains total $30,000, which is the amount of the original deferred gain. ■

Note the difference between the tax theory governing distributions from C corporations and partnerships. In a C corporation, a distribution from current or accumulated income (earnings and profits) is taxable as a dividend to the shareholder, and the corporation does not receive a deduction for the amount distributed. This is an example of corporate income being subject to double taxation. In a partnership, a distribution from current or accumulated profits is not taxable because Congress has decided that partnership income should be subject to only a single level of taxation. Because a partner pays taxes when the share of income is earned by the partnership, this income is not taxed again when distributed.

These results make sense under the entity and aggregate concepts. The entity concept is applicable to corporate dividends, so any amount paid as a dividend is treated as a transfer by the corporate entity to the shareholder and is taxed accordingly. Under the aggregate theory, though, a partner receiving a distribution of partnership income is treated as merely receiving something already owned. Whether the partner chooses to leave the income in the partnership or receive it in a distribution makes no difference.

Gain and Loss Recognition. A partner recognizes gain from a proportionate nonliquidating distribution to the extent that the *cash* received exceeds the outside basis of his or her interest in the partnership.[59] In a nonliquidating distribution, losses are not recognized by the partner.

EXAMPLE 50

Samantha is a one-third partner in the SMP Partnership. Her basis in this ownership interest is $50,000 on December 31, 2005, after accounting for the calendar year partnership's 2005 operations and for her 2005 capital contributions. On December 31, 2005, the partnership distributes $60,000 of cash to Samantha. She recognizes a $10,000 gain from this distribution ($60,000 cash received – $50,000 basis in her partnership interest). Most likely, this gain is taxed as a capital gain.[60] ■

[59] § 731(a)(1).

[60] § 731(a). If the partnership holds any "hot assets," however, Samantha will probably recognize some ordinary income. See § 751(b) and the related discussion of ordinary income ("hot") assets later in this chapter.

While distributions *from* current and accumulated earnings are taxed differently to shareholders and partners, cash distributions *in excess* of accumulated profits are taxed similarly for corporate shareholders and partners in partnerships. Both shareholders and partners are allowed to recover the cumulative capital invested in the entity tax-free.

Recall from earlier in the chapter that the reduction of a partner's share of partnership debt is treated as a distribution of cash from the partnership to the partner. A reduction of a partner's share of partnership debt, then, first reduces the partner's basis in the partnership. Any reduction of a share of debt in excess of a partner's basis in the partnership is taxable to the partner as a gain.

EXAMPLE 51

Returning to the facts of Example 50, assume that Samantha's $50,000 basis in her partnership interest included a $60,000 share of partnership liabilities. If the partnership repays all of its liabilities, Samantha is treated as receiving a $60,000 distribution from the partnership. The first $50,000 of this distribution reduces her basis to $0. The last $10,000 distributed creates a taxable gain to her of $10,000. ■

A distribution of marketable securities can also be treated as a distribution of cash. Determining the treatment of such distributions is complicated though, since several exceptions may apply and the basis in the distributed stock must be calculated. Discussion of such distributions is beyond the scope of this chapter.

Property Distributions. In general, a distributee partner does not recognize gain from a property distribution. If the basis of property distributed by a partnership exceeds the partner's basis in the partnership interest, the distributed asset takes a substituted basis. This ensures that the partner does not receive asset basis that is not "paid for."

EXAMPLE 52

Mary has a $50,000 basis in her partnership interest. The partnership distributes land it owns with a basis and a fair market value of $60,000. Mary does not recognize any gain on this distribution because it is a distribution of property other than cash. However, Mary should not be allowed to take a carryover basis of $60,000 in the land, when the basis in her partnership interest is only $50,000. Therefore, Mary takes a substituted basis of $50,000 in the land. Her basis in her partnership interest is reduced by the basis she takes in the asset received, or $50,000. Therefore, Mary has a $50,000 basis in the land and a $0 basis in her partnership interest, and she recognizes no gain on this distribution. ■

Ordering Rules. When the inside basis of the distributed assets exceeds the distributee partner's outside basis, the assets are deemed distributed in the following order:

- Cash is distributed first.
- Unrealized receivables and inventory are distributed second.
- All other assets are distributed last.

Unrealized receivables are receivables that have a value to the partnership, but for which the related income has not yet been realized or recognized under the partnership's method of accounting. The term *unrealized receivables* applies only to amounts that will ultimately be realized and recognized as ordinary income. If the partnership uses the cash method of accounting, trade receivables from services or sales are unrealized receivables. If the partnership uses the accrual method, they are not. Unrealized receivables include receivables from the sales of ordinary income property and rights to payments for services. For some purposes, unrealized receivables also include ordinary recapture income that would arise if the partnership sold its depreciable assets. Installment gains are unrealized receivables if the gain will be taxed as ordinary income when realized.

Inventory, for purposes of these ordering rules, includes any partnership assets except cash, capital, or § 1231 assets. For example, all accounts receivable are considered to be inventory, although only cash basis receivables are "unrealized receivables."

Since the partner typically does not recognize a gain from a *property* distribution, the Code provides that the partner's basis for property received cannot exceed the partner's basis in the partnership interest immediately before the distribution. For each level of asset distribution, the relevant adjustments are made to the partner's basis in the interest. In other words, after a cash distribution, the partner's basis in the interest is recomputed before determining the effect of a distribution of unrealized receivables or inventory. The basis is recomputed again before determining the effect of a distribution of other assets. If the remaining outside basis at the end of any step is insufficient to cover the entire inside basis of the assets in the next step, that remaining outside basis is allocated among the assets within that class.[61]

EXAMPLE 53

Sally has a $48,000 basis in her partnership interest. On September 10, 2005, the partnership distributes to her cash of $12,000, cash basis receivables with an inside basis of $0 and a fair market value of $10,000, and a parcel of land with a basis to the partnership of $60,000 and a fair market value of $100,000. Sally has realized gain on the distribution of $74,000 ($12,000 + $10,000 + $100,000 – $48,000). None of that gain is recognized, however, since the $12,000 cash distribution does not exceed her $48,000 adjusted basis for her partnership interest. In determining the basis effects of the distribution, the cash is treated as being distributed first, reducing Sally's adjusted basis to $36,000 ($48,000 – $12,000). The receivables are distributed next, taking a $0 carryover basis to Sally. Her adjusted basis remains at $36,000. The land is distributed last, taking a substituted basis of $36,000 and reducing her adjusted basis for her partnership interest to $0. ■

When more than one asset in a particular class is distributed, special rules may apply. Usually, if the partner's remaining adjusted basis for the partnership interest is less than the partnership's adjusted basis for the distributed assets in the particular class, the partner's adjusted basis for each distributed asset is computed by following three steps:

Step 1. Each distributed asset within the class initially takes a carryover basis.

Step 2. Then, this carryover basis for each of these assets is reduced in proportion to their respective amounts of unrealized depreciation (amount that carryover basis is greater than fair market value). Under no circumstances, however, can the basis of any asset be reduced below its fair market value in step 2.

Step 3. Any remaining decrease in basis is allocated among all the distributed assets in the class in proportion to their respective adjusted bases (as determined in step 2).

EXAMPLE 54

Assume the same facts as in Example 53, except that Sally receives two parcels of land, rather than a single parcel. The partnership's basis for the parcels is $15,000 for Parcel 1 and $45,000 for Parcel 2. Each parcel has a fair market value of $30,000. Sally has a realized gain on the distribution of $34,000 ($12,000 + $10,000 + $60,000 – $48,000). None of that gain

[61] § 732.

is recognized, however, because the $12,000 cash distribution does not exceed her $48,000 adjusted basis.

As in Example 53, Sally takes a $12,000 basis for the cash and a $0 carryover basis for the receivables and has a $36,000 adjusted basis for her partnership interest after these two items are distributed. Because two parcels of land are distributed, and because Sally's remaining $36,000 adjusted basis for her partnership interest is less than the partnership's $60,000 total basis for the two parcels of land, Sally's adjusted basis for each parcel of land is computed by following these steps:

Step 1. She initially takes a carryover basis of $15,000 for Parcel 1 and $45,000 for Parcel 2.

Step 2. She reduces the basis of Parcel 2 to its lower fair market value of $30,000. The basis for Parcel 1 is not adjusted in this step because Parcel 1 has a fair market value greater than its basis.

Step 3. The remaining $9,000 difference between her $36,000 basis for the partnership interest and the $45,000 ($15,000 + $30,000) basis for the land parcels after step 2 is allocated to the two parcels in proportion to their respective bases (as computed in step 2). Therefore, the amount of the step 3 basis reduction allocated to Parcel 1 is:

$$\$9,000 \times \frac{\$15,000}{\$45,000} = \$3,000$$

Sally's basis for Parcel 1 is $12,000 ($15,000 – $3,000). The amount of the step 3 basis reduction allocated to Parcel 2 is:

$$\$9,000 \times \frac{\$30,000}{\$45,000} = \$6,000$$

Sally's basis for Parcel 2 is $24,000 ($30,000 – $6,000). ■

EXAMPLE 55

Assume the same facts as in Example 54, and that Sally sells both parcels of land early in 2006 for their fair market values, receiving proceeds of $60,000 ($30,000 + $30,000). She also collects $10,000 from the cash basis receivables. Now she recognizes all of the $34,000 gain that she deferred upon receiving the property from the partnership [$60,000 amount realized – $36,000 basis for the two parcels ($12,000 + $24,000) + $10,000 collected – $0 basis for the receivables]. ■

Review the tax results of Examples 53 and 54. Although Sally does not recognize any of the gain from the distribution, she has a zero outside basis for her partnership interest. If Sally expects the partnership to generate net losses in the near future, she will *not* find this zero basis attractive. She may be unable to deduct her share of these future losses when they flow through to her on the last day of the partnership's subsequent tax year.

The low basis that Sally has assigned to the parcels of land is of no significant detriment to her if she does not intend to sell the land in the near future. Since land does not generate cost recovery deductions, the substituted basis is used only to determine Sally's gain or loss upon her disposition of the parcels in a taxable sale or exchange.

Concept Summary 21–4 reviews the general rules that apply to proportionate nonliquidating partnership distributions.

PROPORTIONATE LIQUIDATING DISTRIBUTIONS

Proportionate **liquidating distributions** consist of a single distribution or a series of distributions that result in the termination of the partner's entire interest in the partnership. This section examines situations when a partner's interest is liquidated because the partnership is liquidating.

CONCEPT SUMMARY 21–4

Proportionate Nonliquidating Distributions (General Rules)

1. In general, neither the distributee partner nor the partnership recognizes any gain or loss on a proportionate nonliquidating distribution. If cash distributed exceeds the distributee partner's outside basis, however, gain is recognized. Property distributions generally do not result in gain recognition.
2. The distributee partner usually takes the same basis in the distributed property that the property had to the partnership (carryover basis). However, where the inside basis of distributed property exceeds the partner's outside basis, the basis assigned to the distributed property cannot exceed that outside basis (substituted basis).
3. Gain recognized by the distributee partner on a proportionate nonliquidating distribution is capital in nature.
4. Loss is never recognized on a proportionate nonliquidating distribution.

Calculations

1. Partner's outside basis. __________
2. Less: Cash distributed to partner. __________
3. Gain recognized by partner (excess of Line 2 over Line 1). __________
4. Partner's remaining outside basis (Line 1 – Line 2). If less than $0, enter $0. __________
5. Partner's basis in unrealized receivables and inventory distributed (enter lesser of Line 4 or the partnership's inside basis in the unrealized receivables and inventory). __________
6. Basis available to allocate to other property distributed (Line 4 – Line 5). __________
7. Partnership's inside basis of other property distributed. __________
8. Basis to partner of other property distributed (enter lesser of Line 6 or Line 7). __________
9. Partner's remaining outside basis (Line 6 – Line 8). __________

The partnership itself typically does not recognize either gain or loss on a proportionate liquidating distribution. The following discussion outlines rules for allocation of basis and possible gain/loss recognition by partners.

Gain Recognition and Ordering Rules. When a partnership liquidates, the liquidating distributions to a partner usually consist of an interest in several or all of the partnership assets. The gain recognition and ordering rules parallel those for nonliquidating distributions, except that the partner's *entire* basis in the partnership interest is allocated to the assets received in the liquidating distribution, unless the partner is required to recognize a loss. A loss may be recognized when *only* cash, unrealized receivables, or inventory are received in the distribution. As a result of the ordering rules, the basis of some assets may be adjusted upward or downward to absorb the partner's remaining outside basis. Unrealized receivables or inventory are never "stepped up," although they may be "stepped down."

The general ordering and gain recognition rules for a proportionate liquidating distribution are summarized as follows:

- Cash is distributed first and results in a capital gain if the amount distributed exceeds the partner's basis in the partnership interest. The cash distributed reduces the liquidated partner's outside basis dollar for dollar. The partner's basis cannot be reduced below zero.
- The partner's remaining outside basis is then allocated to unrealized receivables and inventory up to the amount equal to the partnership's adjusted bases in those properties. If the partnership's bases in the unrealized receivables and inventory exceed the partner's remaining outside basis, the remaining outside basis is allocated to the unrealized receivables and inventory.

- Finally, if the liquidating partner has any outside basis left, that basis is allocated to the other assets received.[62]

EXAMPLE 56

When Tara's basis in her partnership interest is $70,000, she receives cash of $15,000, a proportionate share of inventory, and a building in a distribution that liquidates both the partnership and her entire partnership interest. The inventory has a basis to the partnership of $20,000 and a fair market value of $30,000. The building's basis is $8,000, and the fair market value is $12,000. The building is not subject to depreciation recapture. Under these circumstances, Tara recognizes no gain or loss. After reducing Tara's $70,000 basis by the $15,000 cash received, the remaining $55,000 is allocated first to the inventory and then to the building. The basis of the inventory in Tara's hands is $20,000, and the basis of the building is $35,000. ■

When more than one asset in a particular class is distributed in a proportionate liquidating distribution, special rules may apply. If the partner's remaining basis for the partnership interest is less than the partnership's basis for the distributed assets in the particular class, the partner's remaining basis for each distributed asset is computed as illustrated previously in Example 54. If, however, the partner's remaining basis for the partnership interest is greater than the partnership's basis for the distributed assets in the "other assets" class, the partner's basis for each remaining distributed asset is computed by following three steps:

Step 1. Each distributed asset within the "other asset" class initially takes a carryover basis.

Step 2. Then, this carryover basis for each of these assets is increased in proportion to their respective amounts of unrealized appreciation (amount that fair market value is greater than carryover basis). Under no circumstances, however, can the basis of any asset be increased above its fair market value in step 2.

Step 3. Any remaining increase in basis is allocated among all the distributed assets in the "other assets" class in proportion to their respective fair market values.

EXAMPLE 57

Assume the same facts as in Example 56, except that Tara receives two parcels of land, rather than a building. The partnership's basis for the parcels is $2,000 for Parcel 1 and $6,000 for Parcel 2. Each parcel has a fair market value of $6,000.

Tara takes a $15,000 basis for the cash and a $20,000 carryover basis for the inventory. She has a $35,000 basis for her partnership interest after these two items are distributed. Because two parcels of land are distributed, and because Tara's remaining $35,000 basis for her partnership interest exceeds the partnership's $8,000 basis for the two parcels of land, Tara's basis for each parcel of land is computed by following these steps:

Step 1. She initially takes a carryover basis of $2,000 for Parcel 1 and $6,000 for Parcel 2.

Step 2. She increases the basis of Parcel 1 by $4,000 to its fair market value of $6,000. The basis for Parcel 2 is not affected in this step because Parcel 2 has a fair market value equal to its basis.

Step 3. Tara's $23,000 ($35,000 – $6,000 – $6,000) remaining basis for her partnership interest is allocated to each land parcel in proportion to each parcel's respective $6,000 fair market value. Therefore, $11,500 [($6,000/$12,000) × $23,000] is allocated to each parcel. Tara's basis in Parcel 1 is $17,500 ($2,000 + $4,000 + $11,500). Her basis in Parcel 2 is $17,500 ($6,000 + $11,500). ■

[62]§§ 731 and 732.

Loss Recognition. The distributee partner may also recognize a *loss* on a liquidating distribution. The partner recognizes a loss if both of the following are true:

- The partner receives *only* cash, unrealized receivables, or inventory.
- The partner's outside basis in the partnership interest exceeds the partnership's inside basis for the assets distributed. This excess amount is the loss recognized by the distributee partner.[63]

The word "only" is important. A distribution of any other property precludes recognition of the loss.

EXAMPLE 58

When Ramon's outside basis is $40,000, he receives a liquidating distribution of $7,000 cash and a proportionate share of inventory having a partnership basis of $3,000 and a fair market value of $10,000. Ramon is not allowed to "step up" the basis in the inventory, so it is allocated a $3,000 carryover basis. Ramon's unutilized outside basis is $30,000 ($40,000 – $7,000 – $3,000). Since he receives a liquidating distribution of *only* cash and inventory, he recognizes a capital loss of $30,000 on the liquidation. ■

EXAMPLE 59

Assume the same facts as in Example 58, except that in addition to the cash and inventory, Ramon receives the desk he used in the partnership. The desk has an adjusted basis of $100 to the partnership. Applying the rules outlined above to this revised fact situation produces the following results:

Step 1. Cash of $7,000 is distributed to Ramon and reduces his outside basis to $33,000.

Step 2. Inventory is distributed to Ramon. He takes a $3,000 carryover basis in the inventory and reduces his outside basis in the partnership to $30,000.

Step 3. The desk is distributed to Ramon. Since the desk is a § 1231 asset and not cash, an unrealized receivable, or inventory, he cannot recognize a loss. Therefore, Ramon's remaining basis in his partnership interest is allocated to the desk. He takes a $30,000 basis for the desk. ■

What can Ramon do with a $30,000 desk? If he continues to use it in a trade or business, he can depreciate it. Once he has established his business use of the desk, he could sell it and recognize a large § 1231 loss. If the loss is isolated in the year of the sale, it is an ordinary loss. Thus, with proper planning, no liquidated partner should be forced to recognize a capital loss instead of an ordinary loss.

Gain recognized by the withdrawing partner on the subsequent disposition of inventory is always ordinary income, unless the disposition occurs more than five years after the distribution.[64] The withdrawing partner's holding period for all other property received in a liquidating distribution includes the partnership's related holding period.

LO.10

Calculate the selling partner's amount and character of gain or loss on the sale or exchange of a partnership interest.

Sale of a Partnership Interest

A partner can sell or exchange a partnership interest, in whole or in part. The transaction can be between the partner and a third party; in this case, it is similar in concept to a sale of corporate stock. The transfer of a partnership interest produces different results from the transfer of corporate stock because both the entity and aggregate concepts apply to the partnership situation, whereas only the entity concept applies to a sale of stock. The effect of the different rules is that gain or

[63] § 731(a)(2).

[64] § 735(a)(2).

loss resulting from a sale of a partnership interest may be divided into capital gain or loss and ordinary income or loss.

GENERAL RULES

Generally, the sale or exchange of a partnership interest results in gain or loss, measured by the difference between the amount realized and the selling partner's adjusted basis in the partnership interest.[65]

Liabilities. In computing the amount realized and the adjusted basis of the interest sold, the selling partner's share of partnership liabilities must be determined. The purchasing partner includes any assumed indebtedness as a part of the consideration paid for the partnership interest.[66]

EXAMPLE 60

Cole originally contributed $50,000 in cash for a one-third interest in the CDE Partnership. During the time Cole was a partner, his share of partnership income was $90,000, and he withdrew $60,000 cash. Cole's capital account balance is now $80,000, and partnership liabilities are $45,000, of which Cole's share is $15,000. Cole's outside basis is $95,000 ($80,000 capital account + $15,000 share of partnership debts).

Cole sells his partnership interest to Stephanie for $110,000 of cash, with Stephanie assuming Cole's share of partnership liabilities. The total amount realized by Cole is $125,000 ($110,000 cash received + $15,000 of partnership debts transferred to Stephanie). Cole's gain on the sale is $30,000 ($125,000 amount realized – adjusted basis of $95,000).

Stephanie's adjusted basis for her partnership interest is the purchase price of $125,000 ($110,000 cash paid + $15,000 assumed partnership debt). ■

Income Allocation. When a partner sells an entire interest in the partnership:

- Income for the partnership interest for the tax year is allocated between the buying partner and the selling partner, and
- The partnership's tax year "closes" with respect to the selling partner.

The closing of the tax year causes the selling partner to report the share of income on the sale date rather than at the end of the partnership's tax year. There are several acceptable methods of determining the partner's share of income.[67]

The selling partner's basis is adjusted for the allocated income or loss before the partner calculates the gain or loss on the sale of the interest.

EXAMPLE 61

On September 30, 2005, Erica sells her 20% interest in the Evergreen Partnership to Jason for $25,000. Erica is a calendar year taxpayer. Evergreen owns no hot assets (see discussion below), and its tax year ends on June 30.

Before the sale, Erica's basis in the partnership interest is $8,000. Her share of current partnership income is $10,000 for the period she owned the partnership interest. Since the partnership's tax year closes with respect to Erica, she must report $10,000 of income on her 2005 tax return. Her basis in the partnership interest is increased to $18,000, and she recognizes a $7,000 capital gain on the sale.

Note that Erica will also report income from Evergreen's tax year ending on June 30, 2005, on her 2005 tax return. ■

[65] § 741.
[66] § 742.
[67] § 706(d)(1) and related Regulations.

EFFECT OF HOT ASSETS

A major exception to capital gain or loss treatment on the sale or exchange of a partnership interest arises when a partnership has **hot assets.** In general, *hot assets* are *unrealized receivables* and *inventory*, assets that, when collected or disposed of by the partnership, would cause it to recognize ordinary income or loss. When a partner sells the interest in a partnership, it is as if the partnership had sold its hot assets and allocated to the selling partner the partner's proportionate share of the ordinary income or loss created by the sale. The primary purpose of this rule is to prevent a partner from converting ordinary income into capital gain through the sale of a partnership interest.[68]

Unrealized Receivables. As previously noted, unrealized receivables generally include the accounts receivable of a cash basis partnership and, for sale or exchange purposes, depreciation recapture potential.[69]

EXAMPLE 62

The cash basis Thrush Partnership owns only a $10,000 receivable for rendering health care advice. Its basis in the receivable is zero because no income has been recognized. This item is a hot asset because ordinary income is not generated until Thrush collects on the account.

Jacob, a 50% partner, sells his interest to Mark for $5,000. If Jacob's basis in his partnership interest is $0, his total gain is $5,000. The entire gain is attributable to Jacob's share of the unrealized receivable, so his gain is taxed as ordinary income. ■

Inventory. For a sale or exchange of a partnership interest, the term *inventory* includes all partnership property except money, capital assets, and § 1231 assets. Receivables of an accrual basis partnership are included in the definition of inventory, since they are neither capital assets nor § 1231 assets.[70] This definition also is broad enough to include all items considered to be unrealized receivables.

EXAMPLE 63

Jan sells her one-third interest in the JKL Partnership to Matt for $20,000 cash. The interest has an outside basis of $15,000. On the sale date, the partnership balance sheet reflects the following:

	Adjusted Basis	FMV		Adjusted Basis	FMV
Cash	$10,000	$10,000	Jan, capital	$15,000	$20,000
Inventory	21,000	30,000	Kelly, capital	15,000	20,000
Non-hot assets	14,000	20,000	Lynn, capital	15,000	20,000
Total	$45,000	$60,000	Total	$45,000	$60,000

The overall gain on the sale is $5,000 ($20,000 – $15,000). Jan's share of the appreciation in the inventory is $3,000 [($30,000 – $21,000) × ⅓]. Therefore, she recognizes $3,000 of ordinary income because of the inventory and $2,000 of capital gain from the rest of the sale. ■

[68] § 751(a).
[69] § 751(a)(1).
[70] § 751(d).

LO.11

Describe the application of partnership provisions to limited liability companies (LLCs) and limited liability partnerships (LLPs).

Limited Liability Entities

LIMITED LIABILITY COMPANIES

Owners of small businesses often wish to combine the limited liability of a corporation with the pass-through provisions of a partnership. S corporations, described in Chapter 22, provide some of these advantages. The limited liability company is a form of entity that goes further in combining partnership taxation with limited personal liability for all owners of the entity. All of the states and the District of Columbia have passed legislation permitting the establishment of LLCs.

Taxation of LLCs. A properly structured LLC with two or more owners is taxed as a partnership under the "check-the-box" rules. Because none of the LLC members is personally liable for any debts of the entity, the LLC is effectively treated as a limited partnership with no general partners. This may result in unusual application of partnership taxation rules. The IRS has not specifically ruled on many aspects of LLC taxation, so several of the following comments are based on speculation about how a partnership with no general partners would be taxed.

- Formation of a new LLC is treated in the same manner as formation of a partnership. Generally, no gain or loss is recognized by the LLC member or the LLC, the member takes a substituted basis in the LLC interest, and the LLC takes a carryover basis in the assets it receives.
- Contributed property with built-in gains or losses is subject to the partnership allocation rules.
- In allocating liabilities to the members for basis purposes, liabilities are generally treated as if they are nonrecourse. This occurs because under the entity's legal structure, generally none of the members individually bears the economic risk of loss for a liability.
- An LLC's income and losses are allocated proportionately. Special allocations are permitted, as long as they demonstrate economic effect.
- Losses must meet the basis, at-risk, and passive loss limitations to be currently deductible. Since the debt is generally considered nonrecourse to each of the members, it may not be included in the at-risk limitation unless it qualifies as "qualified nonrecourse financing." Also, the IRS has not issued final guidance as to whether a member is treated as a material or active participant of an LLC for passive loss purposes. Presumably, passive or active status will be based on the time the member spends in LLC activities.
- The available taxable years and initial elections discussed earlier are applicable to an LLC.
- Transactions between an LLC and its members are treated as described earlier.
- The rules described in this chapter for distributions and sales of an interest apply to an LLC. Note that a distribution of appreciated property from a C or S corporation would result in taxable gain to the entity, whereas such property takes a carryover or substituted basis when distributed from an LLC.

Converting to an LLC. A partnership can convert to an LLC with few, if any, tax ramifications: the old elections of the partnership continue, and the partners retain their bases and ownership interests in the new entity. However, a C or an S corporation that reorganizes as an LLC is treated as having liquidated prior to forming the new entity. The transaction is taxable to both the corporation and the shareholders.

Advantages of an LLC. An LLC offers certain advantages over a limited partnership, including the following:

- Generally, none of the owners of an LLC are personally liable for the entity's debts. General partners in a limited partnership have personal liability for partnership recourse debts.
- Limited partners cannot participate in the management of the partnership. All owners of an LLC have the legal right to participate in the entity's management.

Disadvantages of an LLC. The disadvantages of an LLC stem primarily from the entity's relative newness. There is no established body of case law interpreting the various state statutes, so the application of some provisions is uncertain. An additional uncertainty for LLCs that operate in more than one jurisdiction is which state's law will prevail and how it will be applied.

Among other factors, statutes differ from state to state as to the type of business an LLC can conduct—particularly as to the extent to which certain service-providing firms can operate as LLCs. A service entity may find it can operate as an LLC in one state but not in another. Despite these uncertainties, LLCs are being formed at increasing rates.

LIMITED LIABILITY PARTNERSHIPS

The difference between a general partnership and an LLP is small, but very significant. Recall that general partners are jointly and severally liable for all partnership debts. In some states, partners in a registered LLP are jointly and severally liable for contractual liability (i.e., they are treated as general partners for commercial debt). They are also always personally liable for their own malpractice or other torts. They are not, however, personally liable for the malpractice and torts of their partners. As a result, the exposure of their personal assets to lawsuits filed against other partners and the partnership is considerably reduced.

An LLP must have formal documents of organization and register with the state. Because the LLP is a general partnership in other respects, it does not have to pay any state franchise taxes on its operations—an important difference between LLPs and LLCs in states that impose franchise taxes on LLCs. LLPs are taxed as partnerships under Federal tax statutes.

See Concept Summary 22–4 in Chapter 22 for a review of the various tax implications of LLCs and LLPs.

Tax Planning Considerations

CHOOSING PARTNERSHIP TAXATION

Concept Summary 21–5 lists various factors that the owners of a business should consider in deciding whether to use a C corporation, S corporation, or partnership as a means of doing business.

FORMATION AND OPERATION OF A PARTNERSHIP

Potential partners should be cautious in transferring assets to a partnership to ensure that they are not required to recognize any gain upon the creation of the entity. The nonrecognition provisions of § 721 are relatively straightforward and resemble the provisions under § 351, which permit certain tax-free property transfers to corporations. However, any partner can make a tax-deferred contribution

Concept Summary 21–5

Advantages and Disadvantages of the Partnership Form

The partnership form may be attractive when one or more of the following factors is present:

- The entity is generating net taxable losses and/or valuable tax credits, which will be of use to the owners.
- The owners want to avoid complex corporate administrative and filing requirements.
- Other means by which to reduce the effects of the double taxation of corporate business income (e.g., compensation to owners, interest, and rental payments) have been exhausted.
- The entity does not generate material amounts of tax preference and adjustment items, which increase the alternative minimum tax liabilities of its owners.
- The entity is generating net passive income, which its owners can use to claim immediate deductions for net passive losses that they have generated from other sources.
- The owners wish to make special allocations of certain income or deduction items that are not possible under the C or S corporation forms.
- The owners anticipate liquidation of the entity within a short period of time. Liquidation of a C or S corporation would generate entity-level recognized gains on appreciated property distributed.
- The owners have adequate bases in their ownership interests to facilitate the deduction of flow-through losses and the assignment of an adequate basis to assets distributed in-kind to the owners.

The partnership form may be less attractive when one or more of the following factors is present:

- The tax paid by the individual owners on the entity's income is greater than the tax the entity would pay if it were a C corporation, and the income is not expected to be distributed soon. (If distributed by a C corporation, double taxation would likely occur.)
- The entity is generating net taxable income without distributing any cash to the owners. The owners may not have sufficient cash with which to pay the tax on the entity's earnings.
- The type of income that the entity is generating (e.g., business and portfolio income) is not as attractive to its owners as net passive income would be because the owners could use net passive income to offset the net passive losses that they have generated on their own.
- The entity is in a high-exposure business, and the owners desire protection from personal liability. An LLC or LLP structure may be available, however, to limit personal liability.
- The owners want to avoid Federal self-employment tax.

of assets to the entity either at the inception of the partnership or later. This possibility is not available to less-than-controlling shareholders in a corporation.

The partners should anticipate the tax benefits and pitfalls that are presented in the Code and should take appropriate actions to resolve any potential problems before they arise. Typically, all that is needed is an appropriate provision in the partnership agreement (e.g., with respect to differing allocation percentages for gains and losses). Recall, however, that a special allocation of income, expense, or credit items in the partnership agreement must satisfy certain requirements before it is acceptable to the IRS.

TRANSACTIONS BETWEEN PARTNERS AND PARTNERSHIPS

Partners should be careful when engaging in transactions with the partnership to ensure that no negative tax results occur. A partner who owns a majority of the partnership generally should not sell property at a loss to the partnership because the loss is disallowed. Similarly, a majority partner should not sell a capital asset to the partnership at a gain, if the asset is to be used by the partnership as other than a capital asset. The gain on this transaction is taxed as ordinary income to the selling partner rather than as capital gain.

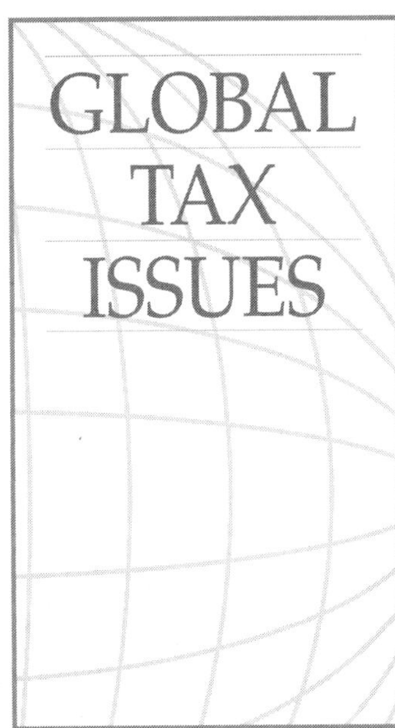

Partnerships Around the World—and Beyond

Technology continues to act as a catalyst—and incentive—for the creation of joint ventures. From Web kiosks at gas stations to global satellite networks, high-tech companies are forging alliances to bring technology to consumers.

Both Microsoft and Time Warner have teamed up with various gas stations, pizza parlors, and numerous other retail outlets to offer programming. These ventures appear to be spurred by a desire to capture larger shares of the ever-expanding advertising market.

Meanwhile, the largest U.S. telecommunications companies are continuing to align themselves with partners in foreign markets: each wants to have the widest possible service coverage area so it can offer efficient communications and computer networking to business clients with a global presence.

Other partnerships have been formed by media and cable companies to offer digital satellite television services on numerous channels to customers for a monthly rental fee. And several partnerships have been formed to establish satellite-based Web communications around the world.

As an alternative to selling property to a partnership, the partner should consider a lease arrangement. The partner recognizes rent income, and the partnership has a rent expense. If the partner needs more cash immediately, the partner can sell the property to an outside third party who leases the property to the partnership for a fair rental.

The timing of the deduction for a payment by an accrual basis partnership to a cash basis partner varies depending on whether the payment is a guaranteed payment or is treated as a payment to an outsider. If the payment is a guaranteed payment, the deduction occurs when the partnership makes the accrual. If the payment is treated as a payment to an outsider, the actual date the payment is made controls the timing of the deduction.

DRAFTING THE PARTNERSHIP AGREEMENT

Although a written partnership agreement is not required, many rules governing the tax consequences to partners and their partnership refer to such an agreement. Remember that a partner's distributive share of income, gain, loss, deduction, or credit is determined in accordance with the partnership agreement. Consequently, if taxpayers operating a business in partnership form want a measure of certainty as to the tax consequences of their activities, a carefully drafted partnership agreement is crucial. An agreement that sets forth the obligations, rights, and powers of the partners should prove invaluable in settling controversies among them and provide some degree of certainty as to the tax consequences of the partners' actions.

KEY TERMS

Inside basis, 21–14

Least aggregate deferral method, 21–19

Limited liability company (LLC), 21–4

Limited liability partnership (LLP), 21–4

Limited partnership, 21–4

Liquidating distribution, 21–44

Nonliquidating distribution, 21–40

Nonrecourse debt, 21–28

Outside basis, 21–14

Precontribution gain or loss, 21–24

Profit and loss sharing ratio, 21–8

Profits (loss) interest, 21–7

Proportionate distribution, 21–40

Qualified nonrecourse debt, 21–34

Recourse debt, 21–28

Separately stated item, 21–6

Special allocation, 21–8

Syndication costs, 21–17

Unrealized receivables, 21–42

PROBLEM MATERIALS

Discussion Questions

1. Compare the nonrecognition of gain or loss provision on contributions to a partnership with that relating to corporate formation. What are the major differences and similarities?

2. If appreciated property is contributed to a partnership in exchange for a partnership interest, what basis does the partnership take in the property?

3. In what situations can formation of a partnership result in a taxable gain to one or more of the new partners?

Issue ID
Decision Making

4. Justin and Tiffany will contribute property to form the equal TJ Partnership. Justin will contribute cash of $20,000 plus land with a fair market value of $80,000 and an adjusted basis of $65,000. Tiffany currently operates a sole proprietorship with assets valued at $100,000 and an adjusted basis of $125,000. Tiffany can either contribute these assets to the partnership or sell them to Sanford Salvage for their fair market value and then contribute the $100,000 cash to the partnership. The partnership needs assets similar to those owned by Tiffany, but it can purchase new assets for $110,000. Describe the tax consequences of the formation to Tiffany, Justin, and the partnership. Be sure to discuss how the results would differ if Tiffany sells the property rather than contributing it.

Issue ID

5. Block, Inc., a calendar year general contractor, and Strauss, Inc., a development corporation with a July 31 year-end, formed the equal SB LLC on January 1 of the current year. Both LLC members are C corporations. The limited liability company was formed to construct and lease shopping centers in Wilmington, Delaware. Block contributed equipment (basis of $650,000, fair market value of $650,000), building permits, and architectural designs created by Block's employees (basis of $0, fair market value of $100,000). Strauss contributed land (basis of $50,000, fair market value of $250,000) and cash of $500,000. The cash was used as follows:

Legal fees for drafting LLC agreement	$ 10,000
Materials and labor costs for construction in progress on shopping center	400,000
Office expense (utilities, rent, overhead, etc.)	90,000

What issues must the LLC address in preparing its initial tax return?

6. What types of expenditures might a new partnership incur? How will these costs be treated for Federal tax purposes?

Issue ID

7. Browne and Red, both C corporations, formed the BR Partnership on January 1, 2004. Neither Browne nor Red is a personal service corporation, and BR is not a tax shelter. BR's gross receipts were $4.6 million, $5 million, and $6 million, respectively, for the three tax years ending in 2004, 2005, and 2006. Describe the methods of accounting available to BR in each tax year.

8. Describe the manner in which the taxable year is determined for a newly formed partnership.
9. Discuss the adjustments that must be made to a partner's basis in the partnership interest. When are such adjustments made?
10. What is the purpose of the three rules that implement the economic effect test?

Issue ID

11. Sam has operated a microbrewery (sole proprietorship) in southern Oregon for the past 15 years. The business has been highly profitable lately, and demand for the product will soon exceed the amount Sam can produce with his present facilities. Marcie, a long-time fan of the brewery, has offered to invest $1.5 million for equipment to expand production. The assets and goodwill of the brewery are currently worth $1 million (tax basis is only $200,000). Sam will continue to manage the business. He is not willing to own less than 50% of whatever arrangement they arrive at. What issues should Sam and Marcie address and document before finalizing their venture?
12. Discuss the advantages and disadvantages of the partnership entity form compared with the C corporation form.
13. Comment on the validity of the following statements:
    a. Since a partnership is not a taxable entity, it is not required to file any type of tax return.
    b. Each partner can choose a different method of accounting and depreciation computation in determining the income from the entity.
    c. Generally, a transfer of appreciated property to a partnership results in recognized gain to the contributing partner at the time of the transfer.
    d. A partner can carry forward, for an unlimited period of time, the share of any partnership operating losses that exceed the partner's basis in the entity, provided the partner retains an ownership interest in the partnership.
    e. When a partner renders services to the entity in exchange for an unrestricted interest, that partner does not recognize any gross income.
    f. Losses on sales between a partner and the partnership always are nondeductible.
    g. A partnership may choose a year that results in the least aggregate deferral of tax to the partners, unless the IRS requires the use of an alternative tax year under the "business purpose" test.
    h. A partner's basis in a partnership interest includes that partner's share of partnership recourse and nonrecourse liabilities.
    i. Built-in loss related to nondepreciable property contributed to a partnership must be allocated to the contributing partner to the extent the loss is eventually recognized by the partnership.
    j. Property that was held as inventory by a contributing partner, but is a capital asset in the hands of the partnership, results in a capital gain if the partnership immediately sells the property.

Problems

14. Larry and Ken form an equal partnership with a cash contribution of $50,000 from Larry and a property contribution (adjusted basis of $30,000 and a fair market value of $50,000) from Ken.
    a. How much gain, if any, must Larry recognize on the transfer? Must Ken recognize any gain?
    b. What is Larry's basis in his partnership interest?
    c. What is Ken's basis in his partnership interest?
    d. What basis does the partnership take in the property transferred by Ken?

Decision Making

15. Harry and Sally form an equal partnership with a cash contribution of $100,000 from Harry and a property contribution (adjusted basis of $120,000 and a fair market value of $100,000) from Sally.
    a. How much gain or loss, if any, does Sally realize on the transfer? May Sally recognize any gain or loss?
    b. What is Harry's basis in his partnership interest?

c. What is Sally's basis in her partnership interest?
d. What basis does the partnership take in the property transferred by Sally?
e. Are there more effective ways to structure the formation?

16. Martin and Morgan formed the equal M&M Partnership on January 1 of the current year. Martin contributed $25,000 cash and land with a fair market value of $10,000 and an adjusted basis of $2,000. Morgan contributed equipment with a fair market value of $35,000 and an adjusted basis of $20,000. Morgan had previously used the equipment in his sole proprietorship.
    a. How much gain or loss will Martin, Morgan, and the partnership realize?
    b. How much gain or loss will Martin, Morgan, and the partnership recognize?
    c. What bases will Martin and Morgan take in their partnership interests?
    d. What bases will M&M take in the assets it receives?
    e. Are there any differences between inside and outside basis?
    f. How will the partnership depreciate any assets it receives from the partners?

17. Three years after the H&L Partnership is formed, Lewis, a 25% partner, contributes an additional $75,000 of cash and land he has held for investment. Lewis's basis in the land is $20,000, and its fair market value is $25,000. His basis in the partnership interest was $60,000 before this contribution. The partnership uses the land as a parking lot for four years and then sells it for $45,000.
    a. How much gain or loss does Lewis recognize on the contribution?
    b. What is Lewis's basis in his partnership interest immediately following this contribution?
    c. How much gain or loss does H&L recognize on this contribution?
    d. What is H&L's basis in the property it receives from Lewis?
    e. How much gain or loss does the partnership recognize on the later sale of the land, and what is the character of the gain or loss? How much is allocated to Lewis?

Decision Making

18. Beth and Ben are equal members of the BB Partnership, formed on June 1 of the current year. Ben contributed land that he inherited from his father three years ago. Ben's father purchased the land in 1950 for $6,000. The land was worth $50,000 when Ben's father died. The fair market value of the land was $75,000 at the date it was contributed to the partnership.

    Beth has significant experience developing real estate. After the partnership is formed, she will prepare a plan for developing the property and secure zoning approvals for the partnership. She would normally bill a third party $25,000 for these efforts. Beth will also contribute $50,000 of cash in exchange for her 50% interest in the partnership. The value of her 50% interest is $75,000.
    a. How much gain or income will Ben recognize on his contribution of the land to the partnership? What is the character of any gain or income recognized?
    b. What basis will Ben take in his partnership interest?
    c. How much gain or income will Beth recognize on the formation of the partnership? What is the character of any gain or income recognized?
    d. What basis will Beth take in her partnership interest?
    e. Construct an opening balance sheet for the partnership reflecting the partnership's basis in assets and the fair market value of these assets.
    f. Outline any planning opportunities that may minimize current taxation to any of the parties.

Decision Making

19. Continue with the facts presented in Problem 18. At the end of the first year, the partnership distributes $50,000 of cash to Ben. No distribution is made to Beth.
    a. Under general tax rules, how would the payment to Ben be treated?
    b. How much income or gain would Ben recognize as a result of the payment?
    c. Under general tax rules, what basis would the partnership take in the land Ben contributed?
    d. What alternative treatment might the IRS try to impose?
    e. Under the alternative treatment, how much income or gain would Ben recognize?
    f. Under the alternative treatment, what basis would the partnership take in the land contributed by Ben?

20. The SJ Partnership was formed to acquire land and subdivide it as residential housing lots. On July 1, 2005, Sarah contributed land valued at $200,000 to the partnership, in exchange for a 50% interest in SJ. She had purchased the land in 1998 for $160,000 and held it for investment purposes (capital asset). The partnership holds the land as inventory.

    On the same date, Joe contributed land valued at $200,000 that he had purchased in 1999 for $240,000. He also became a 50% owner. Joe is a real estate developer, but this land was held personally for investment purposes. The partnership holds this land as inventory.

    In 2006, the partnership sells the land contributed by Sarah for $220,000. In 2007, the partnership sells one-half of the subdivided real estate contributed by Joe for $88,000. The other half is finally sold in 2012 for $110,000.

    a. What is each partner's initial basis in his or her partnership interest?
    b. What is the amount of gain or loss recognized on the sale of the land contributed by Sarah? What is the character of this gain or loss?
    c. What is the amount of gain or loss recognized in 2007 and 2012 on the sale of the land contributed by Joe? What is the character of this gain or loss?

21. Continuing with Problem 20, the SJ Partnership agreement provides that all gains and losses are allocated equally between the partners, unless otherwise required under the tax law.
    a. How will the gains or losses determined in parts (b) and (c) above be allocated to each of the partners?
    b. Calculate each partner's basis in his or her partnership interest at December 31, 2012. Assume the partnership has no transactions through the end of the year 2012 other than the transactions described in Problem 20. Why are these balances the same or different?

22. On July 1 of the current year, the R & R Partnership was formed to operate a bed and breakfast inn. The partnership paid $3,000 in legal fees for drafting the partnership agreement and $5,000 for accounting fees related to organizing the entity. It also paid $10,000 in syndication costs to locate and secure investments from limited partners. In addition, before opening the inn for business, the entity paid $15,500 for advertising and $36,000 in costs related to an open house just before the grand opening of the property. The partnership opened the inn for business on October 1.
    a. How are these expenses classified?
    b. How much may the partnership deduct in its initial year of operations?
    c. How are costs treated that are not deducted currently?
    d. What elections must the partnership make in its initial tax return?

23. RonCo, PatCo, and Matt form the RPM Partnership on January 1 of the current year. Matt is a 50% partner, and RonCo and PatCo are each 25% partners. Each partner and RPM use the cash method of accounting. For reporting purposes, Matt uses a calendar year, RonCo uses a November 30 fiscal year, and PatCo uses a September 30 fiscal year. What is RPM's required tax year under the least aggregate deferral method?

24. Lisa and Lori are equal members of the Redbird Partnership. They are real estate investors who formed the partnership several years ago with equal cash contributions. Redbird then purchased a piece of land.

    On January 1 of the current year, to acquire a one-third interest in the entity, Lana contributed to the partnership some land she had held for investment. Lana purchased the land three years ago for $30,000; its fair market value at the contribution date was $40,000. No special allocation agreements were in effect before or after Lana was admitted to the partnership. The Redbird Partnership holds all land for investment.

    Immediately before Lana's property contribution, the balance sheet of the Redbird Partnership was as follows:

	Basis	FMV		Basis	FMV
Land	$5,000	$80,000	Lisa, capital	$2,500	$40,000
			Lori, capital	2,500	40,000
	$5,000	$80,000		$5,000	$80,000

a. At the contribution date, what is Lana's basis in her interest in the Redbird Partnership?
b. When does the partnership's holding period begin for the contributed land?
c. On June 30 of the current year, the partnership sold the land contributed by Lana for $40,000. How much is the recognized gain or loss, and how is it allocated among the partners?
d. Prepare a balance sheet reflecting basis and fair market value for the partnership immediately after the land sale described in (c). Assume no other transactions occurred during the year.

25. Assume the same facts as in Problem 24, with the following exceptions.

- Lana purchased the land three years ago for $50,000. Its fair market value was $40,000 when it was contributed to the partnership.
- Redbird sold the land contributed by Lana for $34,000.

a. How much is the recognized gain or loss, and how is it allocated among the partners?
b. Prepare a balance sheet reflecting basis and fair market value for the partnership immediately after the land sale. Also prepare schedules that support the amount in each partner's capital account.

26. Earl and Zelda are equal partners in the accrual basis EZ Partnership. At the beginning of 2005, Earl's capital account has a balance of $10,000, and the partnership has recourse debts of $30,000 payable to unrelated parties. All partnership recourse debt is shared equally between the partners. The following information about EZ's operations for the current year is obtained from the partnership's records.

Taxable income	$10,000
§ 1231 gain	6,000
Long-term capital gain	2,000
Short-term capital loss	600
Charitable contribution to Red Cross	200
Cash distribution to Earl	14,000
Payment of Earl's medical expenses	6,000

Assume that year-end partnership debt payable to unrelated parties is $40,000.
a. If all transactions are reflected in his beginning capital and basis in the same manner, what is Earl's basis in the partnership interest at the beginning of the year?
b. If all transactions are reflected in his beginning capital and basis in the same manner, what is Earl's basis in the partnership interest at the end of the year?

27. The RB Partnership is owned equally by Rob and Bob. Bob's basis is $14,000 at the beginning of the tax year. Rob's basis is $9,000 at the beginning of the year. RB reported the following income and expenses for the current tax year:

Sales revenue	$130,000
Cost of sales	45,000
Guaranteed payment to Rob	24,000
Depreciation expense	12,500
Utilities	15,000
Rent	16,000
Interest income	3,000
Tax-exempt interest income	4,500
Payment to Mount Vernon Hospital for Bob's medical expenses	10,000

a. Determine the ordinary partnership income and separately stated items for the partnership.
b. Calculate Bob's basis in his partnership interest at the end of the tax year. What items should Bob report on his Federal income tax return?
c. Calculate Rob's basis in his partnership interest at the end of the tax year. What items should Rob report on his Federal income tax return?

28. Assume the same facts as in Problem 27, except that partnership revenues were $90,000 instead of $130,000.
a. Redetermine the ordinary income and separately stated items for the partnership.
b. Calculate Bob's basis in his partnership interest at the end of the tax year. How much income or loss should Bob report on his Federal income tax return?
c. Calculate Rob's basis in his partnership interest at the end of the tax year. How much income or loss should Rob report on his Federal income tax return?

Decision Making

29. As of January 1 of last year, Don's outside basis and at-risk amount for his 25% interest in the DEF Partnership were $24,000. Don and the partnership use the calendar year for tax purposes. The partnership incurred an operating loss of $120,000 for last year and a profit of $40,000 for the current year. Don is a material participant in the partnership.
a. How much loss, if any, may Don recognize for last year?
b. How much net reportable income must Don recognize for the current year?
c. What is Don's basis in the partnership as of December 31 of last year?
d. What is Don's basis in the partnership as of December 31 of the current year?
e. What year-end tax planning would you suggest to ensure that Don can deduct his share of partnership losses?

30. Fred and Manuel each contribute $100,000 to the newly formed FM Partnership in exchange for a 50% interest. The partnership uses the available funds to acquire equipment costing $160,000 and to fund current operating expenses. The partnership agreement provides that depreciation will be allocated 95% to Fred and 5% to Manuel. All other items of income and loss will be allocated equally between the partners. Upon liquidation of the partnership, property will be distributed to the partners in accordance with their capital account balances. Any partner with a negative capital account must contribute cash in the amount of the negative balance to restore the capital account to $0.

In its first year, the partnership reported an ordinary loss (before depreciation) of $40,000 and depreciation expense of $32,000. In its second year, operations broke even (no gain or loss), and the partnership reported depreciation expense of $51,200. On the first day of the third year, the partnership sold the equipment for $120,000 and distributed the cash in accordance with the partnership agreement. The partnership was liquidated at this time.
a. Calculate the partners' bases in their partnership interests at the end of the first and second tax years. Are any losses suspended?
b. Calculate the partners' bases in their partnership interests after reflecting any gain or loss on disposal of the equipment.
c. How will partnership cash balances be distributed to the partners on liquidation?
d. Does the allocation provided in the partnership agreement have economic effect?
e. What observation can you make regarding the value of a deduction to each partner?

Decision Making
Communications

31. Your client, the Williams Institute of Technology (WIT), is a 60% partner in the Research Industries Partnership (RIP). WIT is located at 76 Bradford Lane, St. Paul, MN 55164. The controller, Jeanine West, has sent you the following note and a copy of WIT's 2004 Schedule K–1 from the partnership.

Excerpt from client's note:
"RIP expects its 2005 operations to include the following:

Net loss from operations	$200,000
Capital gain from sale of land	100,000

The land was contributed by DASH, the other partner, when its value was $260,000. The partnership sold the land for $300,000. The partnership used this cash to repay all the partnership debt and pay for operating expenditures, which a tax partner in your firm has said RIP can deduct this year. The net loss of $200,000 reflects that deduction.

We want to be sure we can deduct our full share of this loss, but we do not believe we will have enough basis. We are a material participant in this partnership's activities."

Items Reported on the 2004 Schedule K–1	
WIT's share of partnership recourse liabilities	$90,000
WIT's ending capital account balance	30,000

Draft a letter to the controller that describes the following:

- WIT's allocation of partnership items.
- WIT's basis in the partnership interest following the allocation.
- Any limitations on loss deductions.
- Any recommendations you have that would allow WIT to claim the full amount of losses in 2005.

Assume WIT's 2004 K–1 accurately reflects the information needed to compute the basis in the partnership interest. Also assume the operating expenditures are fully deductible this year, as the partner said.

Your client has experience researching issues in the Internal Revenue Code, so you may use some citations. However, be sure the letter is written in layperson's terms and cites are minimized.

32. Lee, Brad, and Rick form the LBR Partnership on January 1 of the current year. In return for a 25% interest, Lee transfers property (basis of $15,000, fair market value of $17,500) subject to a nonrecourse liability of $10,000. The liability is assumed by the partnership. Brad transfers property (basis of $16,000, fair market value of $7,500) for a 25% interest, and Rick transfers cash of $15,000 for the remaining 50% interest. (See Example 26 in the text.) Assume the partnership allocates all "third tier" nonrecourse liabilities in accordance with profit sharing ratios.
    a. How much gain must Lee recognize on the transfer?
    b. What is Lee's basis in his partnership interest?
    c. How much loss may Brad recognize on the transfer?
    d. What is Brad's basis in his partnership interest?
    e. What is Rick's basis in his partnership interest?
    f. What basis does the LBR Partnership take in the property transferred by Lee?
    g. What is the partnership's basis in the property transferred by Brad?

33. Assume the same facts as in Problem 32, except that the property contributed by Lee has a fair market value of $27,500 and is subject to a nonrecourse mortgage of $20,000. (See Example 30 in the text.)
    a. What is Lee's basis in his partnership interest?
    b. How much gain must Lee recognize on the transfer?
    c. What is Brad's basis in his partnership interest?
    d. What is Rick's basis in his partnership interest?
    e. What basis does the LBR Partnership take in the property transferred by Lee?

Communications

34. Kim and Craig plan to form the KC General Partnership by the end of the current year. The partners will each contribute $30,000 cash, and in addition, the partnership will borrow $140,000 from First State Bank. The partnership's land will serve as collateral, and both partners will be required to personally guarantee the debt.

    The tentative agreement provides that 75% of operating income, gains, losses, deductions, and credits will be allocated to Kim for the first five years the partnership is in existence. The remaining 25% is allocated to Craig. Thereafter, all partnership items will be allocated equally. The agreement also provides that capital accounts will be properly maintained and that each partner must restore any deficit in the capital account upon the partnership's liquidation.

    The partners would like to know, before the end of the tax year, how the $140,000 liability will be allocated for basis purposes. Using the format (1) facts, (2) issues, (3) conclusion, and (4) law and analysis, draft a memo to the tax planning file for the KC Partnership that describes how the debt will be shared between the partners for purposes of computing the adjusted basis of each partnership interest.

Communications

35. Chris Elton is a 15% partner in the Cardinal Partnership, which is a lessor of residential rental property. Her share of the partnership's losses for the current year is $70,000. Immediately before considering the deductibility of this loss, Chris's capital account (which, in this case, corresponds to her basis excluding liabilities) reflects a balance of $40,000. Her share of partnership recourse liabilities is $10,000, and her share of the nonrecourse liabilities is $6,000. The nonrecourse liability was obtained from an unrelated bank and is secured solely by the real estate.

    Chris is also a partner in the Bluebird Partnership, which has generated income from long-term (more than 30 days) equipment rental activities. Chris's share of Bluebird's income is $23,000. Chris performs substantial services for Bluebird and spends several hundred hours a year working for the Cardinal Partnership.

    Chris's modified AGI before considering partnership activities is $100,000. Your manager has asked you to determine how much of the $70,000 Cardinal loss Chris can deduct on her current calendar year return. Using the format (1) facts, (2) issues, (3) conclusion, and (4) law and analysis, draft a memo to the client's tax file describing the loss limitations. Be sure to identify the Code sections under which the losses are suspended.

36. Sonya is a 20% owner of Philadelphia Cheese Treats, Inc., a C corporation that was formed on February 1, 2005. She receives a $5,000 monthly salary from the corporation, and Cheese Treats generates $200,000 of taxable income (after the salary payment) for its tax year ending January 31, 2006.
    a. How do these activities affect Sonya's 2005 adjusted gross income?
    b. Assume, instead, that Cheese Treats is a partnership with a January 31 year-end and consider Sonya's salary to be a guaranteed payment. How do these activities affect Sonya's 2005 and 2006 adjusted gross income?

37. Ned, a 50% partner in the MN Partnership, is to receive a payment of $35,000 for services. He will also be allocated 50% of the partnership's profits or losses. After deducting the payment to Ned, the partnership has a loss of $25,000. Ned's basis in his partnership interest was $10,000 before these items.
    a. How much, if any, of the $25,000 partnership loss will be allocated to Ned?
    b. What is the net income from the partnership that Ned must report on his Federal income tax return?
    c. What is Ned's basis in his partnership interest following the guaranteed payment and loss allocation?

38. Four Lakes Partnership is owned by four sisters. Anne holds a 70% interest; each of the others owns 10%. Anne sells investment property to the partnership for its fair market value of $100,000 (Anne's basis is $150,000).
    a. How much loss, if any, may Anne recognize?
    b. If the partnership later sells the property for $160,000, how much gain must it recognize?
    c. If Anne's basis in the investment property was $20,000 instead of $150,000, how much, if any, gain would she recognize on the sale, and how would the gain be characterized?

39. When Tina's outside basis in the TNK Partnership is $80,000, the partnership distributes to her $90,000 of cash, an account receivable (fair market value of $20,000, inside basis to the partnership of $0), and a parcel of land (fair market value of $20,000, inside basis to the partnership of $30,000). Tina remains a partner in the partnership, and the distribution is proportionate to the partners.
    a. Determine the recognized gain or loss to the partnership as a result of this distribution.
    b. Determine the recognized gain or loss to Tina as a result of the distribution.
    c. Determine Tina's basis in the land, account receivable, and TNK Partnership after the distribution.

40. In each of the following independent cases in which the partnership owns no hot assets, indicate:

   - Whether the partner recognizes gain or loss.
   - Whether the partnership recognizes gain or loss.
   - The partner's adjusted basis for the property distributed.
   - The partner's outside basis in the partnership after the distribution.

   a. Mona receives $35,000 of cash in partial liquidation of her interest in the partnership. Mona's outside basis for her partnership interest immediately before the distribution is $20,000.
   b. Mark receives $15,000 of cash and land with an inside basis to the partnership of $4,000 (value $6,000) in partial liquidation of his interest. Mark's outside basis for his partnership interest immediately before the distribution is $20,000.
   c. Assume the same facts as in (b), except that Mark's outside basis for his partnership interest immediately before the distribution is $15,000.
   d. Brad receives $10,000 of cash and an account receivable with a basis of $0 and a fair market value of $12,000 in partial liquidation of his partnership interest. His basis was $6,000 before the distribution. All partners received proportionate distributions.

41. Tom's basis in his partnership interest is $41,000. In a proportionate nonliquidating distribution, Tom receives $20,000 of cash and two inventory items, each with a basis of $20,000 to the partnership. The values of the inventory items are $30,000 and $10,000.
   a. How much gain or loss, if any, must Tom recognize on the distribution?
   b. What basis will Tom take in each inventory item?

Issue ID

42. Walden is a 40% partner in the WXY Partnership. He became a partner three years ago when he contributed land with a value of $40,000 and a basis of $20,000 (current value is $90,000). Xavier and Yolanda each contributed $30,000 of cash for a 30% interest. Walden's basis in his partnership interest is currently $40,000; the other partners' bases are each $30,000. The partnership has the following assets:

	Basis	FMV
Cash	$ 60,000	$ 60,000
Accounts receivable	–0–	80,000
Marketable securities	20,000	70,000
Land	20,000	90,000
Total	$100,000	$300,000

   The partnership will make a distribution of $150,000 in value to the partners before the end of the current year, but the type of property that will be distributed has not been determined. Describe the tax effects on the partners in each of the following independent distribution alternatives:
   a. WXY distributes a $45,000 interest in the land each to Yolanda and Xavier and $60,000 of accounts receivable to Walden.
   b. WXY distributes $60,000 of cash to Walden, $45,000 of marketable securities to Yolanda, and $45,000 of accounts receivable to Xavier.
   c. WXY distributes a $36,000 interest in the land and $24,000 of accounts receivable to Walden and $27,000 of cash each and $18,000 of accounts receivable to Xavier and Yolanda.

Issue ID

43. Use the assets and partners' bases from Problem 42. Assume the partnership distributes all its assets in a liquidating distribution. In deciding the allocation of assets, what issues should the partnership consider to minimize each partner's taxable gains?

44. In 2002, Gabriella contributed land with a basis of $16,000 and a fair market value of $25,000 to the Meadowlark Partnership in exchange for a 25% interest in capital and profits. In 2005, the partnership distributes this property to Juanita, also a 25% partner,

in a nonliquidating distribution. The fair market value has increased to $30,000 at the time the property is distributed. Juanita's and Gabriella's bases in their partnership interests are each $40,000 at the time of the distribution.

a. How much gain or loss, if any, does Gabriella recognize on the distribution to Juanita? What is Gabriella's basis in her partnership interest following the distribution?
b. What is Juanita's basis in the land she received in the distribution?
c. How much gain or loss, if any, does Juanita recognize on the distribution? What is Juanita's basis in her partnership interest following the distribution?
d. How much gain or loss would Juanita recognize if she later sells the land for its $30,000 fair market value? Is this result equitable?
e. Would your answers to (a) and (b) change if Gabriella originally contributed the property to the partnership in 1995?

45. DDP Partnership has three equal partners. One of them, Donald, sells his interest to his partner, Paul, for $47,000 cash and the assumption of Donald's share of partnership liabilities. On the sale date, the partnership's cash basis balance sheet reflects the following. Assume that capital accounts reflect the partners' bases in their partnership interests, excluding liabilities.

	Basis	FMV		Basis	FMV
Cash	$51,000	$ 51,000	Note payable	$ 9,000	$ 9,000
Accounts receivable	-0-	60,000	Capital accounts		
Capital assets	9,000	39,000	Donald	17,000	47,000
			David	17,000	47,000
			Paul	17,000	47,000
Total	$60,000	$150,000	Total	$60,000	$150,000

a. What is the total amount realized by Donald on the sale?
b. How much, if any, ordinary income must Donald recognize on the sale?
c. How much capital gain must Donald report?

Research Problems

Note: Solutions to Research Problems can be prepared by using the ***RIA Checkpoint® Student Edition*** *online research product, which is available to accompany this text. It is also possible to prepare solutions to the Research Problems by using tax research materials found in a standard tax library.*

Communications

Research Problem 1. Your clients, Mark Henderson and John Burton, each contributed $10,000 of cash to form the Realty Management Partnership, a limited partnership. Mark is the general partner and John is the limited partner. The partnership used the $20,000 of cash to make a down payment on a building. The rest of the building's $200,000 purchase price was financed with an interest-only nonrecourse loan of $180,000, which was obtained from an independent third-party bank.

The partnership allocates all partnership items equally except for the MACRS deductions and building maintenance, which are allocated 70% to John and 30% to Mark. The partnership definitely wishes to satisfy the "economic effect" requirements of Reg. §§ 1.704–1 and 1.704–2 and will reallocate MACRS, if necessary, to satisfy the requirements of the Regulations.

Under the partnership agreement, liquidation distributions will be paid in proportion to the partners' positive capital account balances. Capital accounts are maintained as required in the Regulations. Mark has an unlimited obligation to restore his capital account while John is subject to a qualified income offset provision.

Assume all partnership items, except for MACRS, will net to zero throughout the first three years of the partnership operations. Also, assume that each year's MACRS deduction will be $10,000 (to simplify the calculations).

Draft a letter to the partnership evaluating the allocation of MACRS in each of the three years under Reg. §§ 1.704–1 and 1.704–2. The partnership's address is 53 East Marsh Ave., Smyrna, GA 30082. Do not address the "substantial" test.

Research Problem 2. Fred and Grady formed the FG Partnership as a retail establishment to sell antique household furnishings. Fred is the general partner, and Grady is the limited partner. Both partners contribute $15,000 to form the partnership. The partnership uses the $30,000 contributed by the partners and a recourse loan of $100,000 (obtained from an unrelated third-party lender) to acquire $130,000 of initial inventory.

The partners believe they will have extensive losses in the first year due to advertising and initial cash-flow requirements. Fred and Grady have agreed to share losses equally. To make sure the losses can be allocated to both partners, they have included a provision in the partnership agreement requiring each partner to restore any deficit balance in his partnership capital account upon liquidation of the partnership.

Fred was also willing to include a provision that requires him to make up any deficit balance within 90 days of liquidation of the partnership. As a limited partner, Grady argued that he should not be subject to such a time requirement. The partners compromised and included a provision that requires Grady to restore a deficit balance in his capital account within two years of liquidation of the partnership. No interest will be owed on the deferred restoration payment.

Determine whether FG will be able to allocate the $100,000 recourse debt equally to the two partners to ensure they will be able to deduct their respective shares of partnership losses.

Internet Activity

Use the tax resources of the Internet to address the following question. Do not restrict your search to the World Wide Web, but include a review of newsgroups and general reference materials, practitioner sites and resources, primary sources of the tax law, chat rooms and discussion groups, and other opportunities.

Research Problem 3. Download a copy of the legislation with which your state began to allow the formation of limited liability companies.

S Corporations

LEARNING OBJECTIVES

After completing Chapter 22, you should be able to:

LO.1
Explain the tax effects that S corporation status has on shareholders.

LO.2
Identify corporations that qualify for the S election.

LO.3
Understand how to make an S election.

LO.4
Explain how an S election can be terminated.

LO.5
Compute nonseparately stated income and identify separately stated items.

LO.6
Allocate income, deductions, and credits to shareholders.

LO.7
Understand how distributions to S corporation shareholders are taxed.

LO.8
Calculate a shareholder's basis in S corporation stock.

LO.9
Explain the tax effects that losses have on shareholders.

LO.10
Compute the built-in gains tax.

LO.11
Compute the passive investment income penalty tax.

http://wft.swlearning.com

OUTLINE

LO.1

Explain the tax effects that S corporation status has on shareholders.

Introduction

The major owners of a minor league baseball team have been operating as a C corporation for four years, incurring significant net operating losses (NOLs). They decide to elect S corporation status to gain immediate deductions for these NOLs. To their surprise, they learn that the NOLs incurred before the S election do not flow through. In effect, the NOLs are locked into the corporate entity until the S election is terminated. Of course, any subsequent NOLs would flow through to the owners. This scenario shows that one must be careful when selecting the form of business entity under which to operate a business.

An individual establishing a business has a number of choices as to the form of business entity under which to operate. Chapters 17 through 20 outline many of the rules, advantages, and disadvantages of operating as a regular corporation. Chapter 21 discusses both the partnership entity and the limited liability company (LLC) and limited liability partnership (LLP) forms.

Another alternative, the **S corporation**, provides many of the benefits of partnership taxation and at the same time gives the owners limited liability protection from creditors. The S corporation rules, which are contained in **Subchapter S** of the Internal Revenue Code (§§ 1361–1379), were enacted to minimize the role of tax considerations in the entity choice that businesspeople face. Thus, S status combines the legal environment of C corporations with taxation similar to that applying to partnerships. S corporation status is obtained through an election by a *qualifying* corporation with the consent of its shareholders.

S corporations are treated as corporations under state law. They are recognized as separate legal entities and generally provide shareholders with the same liability protection afforded by C corporations. For Federal income tax purposes, however, taxation of S corporations resembles that of partnerships. As with partnerships, the income, deductions, and tax credits of an S corporation flow through to shareholders annually, regardless of whether distributions are made. Thus, income is taxed at the shareholder level and not at the corporate level. Payments to S shareholders by the corporation are distributed tax-free to the extent that the distributed earnings were previously taxed. Further, certain corporate penalty taxes (e.g., accumulated earnings tax, personal holding company tax) and the alternative minimum tax do not apply to an S corporation.

Although the Federal tax treatment of S corporations and partnerships is similar, it is not identical. For example, liabilities affect an owner's basis differently, and S corporations may incur a tax liability at the corporate level. Furthermore, an S corporation may not allocate income like a partnership, and distributions of appreciated property are taxable in an S corporation situation (see Concept Summary 22–2 later in this chapter). In addition, a variety of C corporation provisions apply to S corporations. For example, the liquidation of C and S corporations is taxed in the same way. As a rule, where the S corporation provisions are silent, C corporation rules apply.

Today, the choice of a flow-through entity is often between an S corporation (a Federal tax entity) and an LLC (a state tax entity). Although an S corporation resembles an LLC, there are differences. A two-or-more-member LLC operates under partnership tax principles, whereas, as just explained, partnership taxation rules do not always apply to an S corporation.

AN OVERVIEW OF S CORPORATIONS

Since the inception of S corporations in 1958, their popularity has waxed and waned with changes in the tax law. Before the Tax Reform Act of 1986, their ranks grew slowly. In contrast, in the two years following the 1986 law changes, the population of S corporations exploded, increasing by 52 percent. By 1993, more than 1.9 million businesses were filing S corporation returns—48 percent of all corporate returns filed in that year. This rapid growth was driven by a change in the relationship of individual and corporate tax rates. Prior to 1986, maximum individual rates were higher than maximum corporate rates. Following the 1986 tax act, the relationship reversed. Now the rates are the same: 35 percent.

The growth in the number of S corporation elections continued even when the maximum individual income tax rate was above the maximum corporate rate. In 1986, only 24.1 percent of corporations were S corporations, but in 2001, almost 58.2 percent of all corporations were S corporations, up from 56.7 percent in 2000. The number of S returns filed in 2001 increased 3.4 percent to almost 3 million (up from 2.9 million in 2000). In 2001, 299,200 corporations elected S status for the first time, with 205,800 of them newly elected S corporations. Nearly two-thirds of these S corporations reported positive net income.[1] As the following examples illustrate, S corporations can be advantageous even when the individual tax rate exceeds the corporate tax rate.

EXAMPLE 1

An S corporation earns $300,000 in 2005. The marginal individual tax rate applicable to shareholders is 35% on ordinary income and 15% on dividend income. The applicable marginal corporate tax rate is 34%. All after-tax income is distributed currently. The entity's available after-tax earnings, compared with those of a similar C corporation, are as follows.

	C Corporation	S Corporation
Earnings	$ 300,000	$ 300,000
Less: Corporate tax	(102,000)	–0–
Available for distribution	$ 198,000	$ 300,000
Less: Tax at owner level	(29,700)*	(105,000)**
Available after-tax earnings	$ 168,300	$ 195,000

*$198,000 × 15% dividend income tax rate.
**$300,000 × 35% ordinary income tax rate.

[1]Kelly Bennett, "2001: S Corporations Returns," *SOI Bulletin*, Spring 2004.

The S corporation generates an extra $26,700 of after-tax earnings ($195,000 – $168,300), when compared with a similar C corporation. The C corporation might be able to reduce this disadvantage, however, by paying out its earnings as compensation, rents, or interest expense. Tax at the owner level can also be deferred or avoided by not distributing after-tax earnings. ■

EXAMPLE 2

A new corporation elects S status and incurs an NOL of $300,000. The shareholders may use their proportionate shares of the NOL to offset other taxable income in the current year, providing an immediate tax savings. In contrast, a newly formed C corporation is required to carry the NOL forward for up to 20 years and does not receive any tax benefit in the current year. Hence, an S corporation can accelerate NOL deductions and thereby provide a greater present value for tax savings generated by the loss. ■

WHEN TO ELECT S CORPORATION STATUS

Effective planning with S corporations begins with determining the appropriateness of an S election. The following factors should be considered.

- If shareholders have high marginal rates relative to C corporation rates, it may be desirable to avoid S corporation status. Although C corporation earnings can be subject to double taxation, good tax planning mitigates this result (e.g., when the owners take profits out as salary). Likewise, profits of the corporation may be taken out by the shareholders as capital gain income through stock redemptions, liquidations, or sales of stock to others. Alternatively, corporate profits may be paid out as dividends, which are subject to a maximum tax rate of 15 percent. Any distribution of profits or sale of stock can be deferred to a later year, thereby reducing the present value of potential shareholder taxes. Finally, potential shareholder-level tax on corporate profits can be eliminated by a step-up in the basis of the stock upon the shareholder's death.
- S corporation status allows shareholders to realize tax benefits from corporate losses immediately—an important consideration in new business enterprises where losses are common. Thus, if corporate NOLs are anticipated and there is unlikely to be corporate income over the near term to offset with the NOLs, S corporation status is advisable. However, the deductibility of the losses to shareholders must also be considered. The at-risk and passive loss limitations apply to losses generated by an S corporation (see Chapter 11). In addition, as discussed later in this chapter, shareholders may not deduct losses in excess of the basis in their stock. Together these limits may significantly reduce the benefits of an S corporation in a loss setting.
- If the entity electing S status is currently a C corporation, NOL carryovers from prior years cannot be used in an S corporation year. Even worse, S corporation years reduce the 20-year carryover period. Also, the corporation may be subject to some corporate-level taxes if it elects S status (see the discussion of the built-in gains tax later in this chapter).
- Distributions of earnings from C corporations are usually taxed as dividend income, subject to a maximum tax rate of 15 percent. In contrast, because S corporations are flow-through entities, all deduction and income items retain any special tax characteristics when they are reported on shareholders' returns. How this consideration affects the S status choice depends upon the character of income and deductions of the S corporation.
- The S corporation rules impose significant requirements for qualifying as an S corporation. When electing S status, one should consider whether any of these requirements are likely to be violated at some point in the future.
- State and local tax laws also should be considered when making the S election. Although an S corporation usually escapes Federal income tax, it

may not be immune from state and local taxes. State taxation of S corporations varies. Some states, including Michigan, treat them the same as C corporations, resulting in a corporate tax liability from an income or franchise tax.
- The choice of S corporation status is affected by a variety of other factors. For example, the corporate alternative minimum tax (see Chapter 15) may be avoided in an S corporation setting.

LO.2

Identify corporations that qualify for the S election.

Qualifying for S Corporation Status

DEFINITION OF A SMALL BUSINESS CORPORATION

To achieve S corporation status, a corporation *first* must qualify as a **small business corporation.** If each of the following requirements is met, then the entity can elect S corporation status.

- Is a domestic corporation (incorporated and organized in the United States).
- Is an eligible corporation (see below for ineligible types).
- Issues only one class of stock.
- Is limited to a maximum of 100 shareholders (75 before 2005).
- Has only individuals, estates, certain trusts, and certain tax-exempt organizations as shareholders.
- Has no nonresident alien shareholder.

Unlike other provisions in the tax law (e.g., § 1244), no maximum or minimum dollar sales or capitalization restrictions apply to small business corporations.

Ineligible Corporations. Small business corporation status is not permitted for non-U.S. corporations, nor for certain banks and insurance companies.

Any domestic corporation that is not an ineligible corporation can be a qualified Subchapter S corporation subsidiary (QSSS), if the S corporation holds 100 percent of its stock and elects to treat the subsidiary as a QSSS.[2] The QSSS is viewed as a division of the parent, so the parent S corporation can own a QSSS through another QSSS. QSSSs have a separate existence for legal purposes, but they exist only within the parent S corporation for tax purposes.

One Class of Stock. A small business corporation may have only one class of stock issued and outstanding.[3] This restriction permits differences in voting rights, but not differences in distribution or liquidation rights.[4] Thus, two classes of common stock that are identical except that one class is voting and the other is nonvoting would be treated as a single class of stock for small business corporation purposes. In contrast, voting common stock and voting preferred stock (with a preference on dividends) would be treated as two classes of stock. Authorized and unissued stock or treasury stock of another class does not disqualify the corporation. Likewise, unexercised stock options, phantom stock, stock appreciation rights, warrants, and convertible debentures usually do not constitute a second class of stock.

The determination of whether stock provides identical rights as to distribution and liquidation proceeds is made based on the provisions governing the operation of the corporation. These *governing provisions* include the corporate charter, articles of incorporation, bylaws, applicable state law, and binding agreements relating to distribution and liquidation proceeds. Employment contracts, loan agreements, and other commercial contracts are *not* considered governing provisions.[5]

[2] § 1361(b)(3)(B).
[3] § 1361(b)(1)(D).
[4] § 1361(c)(4).
[5] Reg. § 1.1361–1(l)(2).

Flexibility with QSSSs

An S corporation may have a wholly owned subsidiary, an opportunity that offers flexibility in tax planning. Called a qualified Subchapter S subsidiary (QSSS), the subsidiary is not treated as a separate entity for Federal income tax purposes; therefore, all of its assets, liabilities, and items of income, deductions, and credits are treated as belonging to the parent.

A number of advantages and tax planning opportunities accrue to the group. First, an S corporation may separate its lines of business. By dividing the operations among wholly owned subsidiaries, it can insulate certain businesses from the liabilities of other businesses.

Second, a profitable S corporation can make a QSSS election with respect to a nonprofitable company. Generally, when a company continually loses money, the losses may not be deductible by the shareholder because of lack of sufficient basis in the company. The QSSS election causes the nonprofitable company's stock to be a contribution of capital by the shareholder as a tax-free exchange. The deemed liquidation under § 332 creates a carryover basis, and any suspended losses of the new subsidiary are carried over. Thus, outside basis is looked at as a whole, and these suspended losses may be used against the profit of the other company.

SOURCES: Adapted from F. J. Fisher, "Qualified Subchapter S Subsidiaries: Greater Flexibility for Real Estate Practitioners," *The Real Estate Tax Digest*, March 1999, pp. 87–91; N. S. Lindholm and S. S. Karlinsky, "The Benefits and Burdens of QSubs," *The Tax Adviser*, July 1999, pp. 490–496.

EXAMPLE 3

Blue, a small business corporation, has two equal shareholders, Smith and Jones. Both shareholders are employed by Blue and have binding employment contracts with the corporation. The compensation paid by Blue to Jones under her employment contract is reasonable. The compensation paid to Smith under his employment contract, however, is excessive, resulting in a constructive dividend. Smith's employment contract was not prepared to circumvent the one-class-of-stock requirement. Because employment contracts are not considered governing provisions, Blue has only one class of stock. ■

Although the one-class-of-stock requirement seems straightforward, it is possible for debt to be reclassified as stock, resulting in unexpected loss of S corporation status.[6] To mitigate concern over possible reclassification of debt as a second class of stock, the law provides a set of *safe-harbor* provisions.

First, straight debt *issued in an S corporation year* will not be treated as a second class of stock and will not disqualify the S election.[7] The characteristics of straight debt include the following.

- The debtor is subject to a written, unconditional promise to pay on demand or on a specified date a sum certain in money.
- The interest rate and payment date are not contingent on corporate profits, management discretion, or similar factors.
- The debt is not convertible into stock.
- The debt is held by a creditor who is an individual (other than a nonresident alien), an estate, or a qualified trust.
- Straight debt can be held by creditors actively and regularly engaged in the business of lending money.

[6]Refer to the discussion of debt-versus-equity classification in Chapter 18.

[7]§ 1361(c)(5)(A).

In addition to straight debt under the safe-harbor rules, short-term unwritten advances from a shareholder that do not exceed $10,000 in the aggregate at any time during the corporation's taxable year generally are not treated as a second class of stock. Likewise, debt that is held by stockholders in the same proportion as their stock is not treated as a second class of stock, even if it would be reclassified as equity otherwise.[8]

Number of Shareholders. A small business corporation is limited to 100 shareholders (75 before 2005). If shares of stock are owned jointly by two individuals, they will generally be treated as separate shareholders.

After 2004, family members may elect to be treated as one shareholder for purposes of determining the number of shareholders. The term "members of the family" is defined as the common ancestor, the lineal descendants of the common ancestor, and the spouses (or former spouses) of the lineal descendants or common ancestor.[9] This election may be terminated.

EXAMPLE 4

Fred and Wilma (husband and wife) jointly own 10 shares in Marlins, Inc., an S corporation, with the remaining 290 shares outstanding owned by 99 other unrelated shareholders. Fred and Wilma get divorced; pursuant to the property settlement approved by the court, the 10 shares held by Fred and Wilma are divided between them—5 to each. Before the divorce settlement, Marlins had 100 shareholders under the small business corporation rules. After the settlement, it still has 100 shareholders and continues to qualify as a small business corporation. A former spouse is treated as being of the same generation as the individual to whom he or she was married. ■

Type of Shareholder Limitation. Small business corporation shareholders may be resident individuals, estates, certain trusts, and certain tax-exempt organizations.[10] This limitation prevents partnerships, corporations, LLCs, limited liability partnerships, and IRAs from owning S corporation stock. Partnerships and corporate shareholders could easily circumvent the 100-shareholder limitation as illustrated in the following example.

EXAMPLE 5

Saul and 105 of his close friends wish to form an S corporation. Saul reasons that if he and his friends form a partnership, the partnership can then form an S corporation and act as a single shareholder, thereby avoiding the 100-shareholder rule. Saul's plan will not work because partnerships cannot own stock in a small business corporation. ■

Although partnerships and corporations cannot own small business corporation stock, small business corporations can be partners in a partnership or shareholders in a corporation. This ability allows the 100-shareholder requirement to be bypassed in a limited sense. For example, if two small business corporations, each with 100 shareholders, form a partnership, then the shareholders of both corporations can enjoy the limited liability conferred by S corporation status and a single level of tax on partnership profits.

Nonresident Aliens. Nonresident aliens cannot own stock in a small business corporation.[11] That is, individuals who are not U.S. citizens *must live in the United States* to own S corporation stock. Therefore, shareholders with nonresident alien spouses in community property states[12] cannot own S corporation stock because the nonresident alien spouse would be treated as owning half of the community

[8] Reg. § 1.1361–1(l)(4).
[9] § 1361(c)(1).
[10] § 1361(b)(1)(B).
[11] § 1362(b)(1)(C).

[12] Assets acquired by a married couple are generally considered community property in these states: Louisiana, Texas, New Mexico, Arizona, California, Washington, Idaho, Nevada, Wisconsin, and (if elected by the spouses) Alaska.

property.[13] Similarly, if a resident alien shareholder moves outside the United States, the S election will be terminated.

ETHICAL CONSIDERATIONS

Extortion Payments

Burt is the custodian at Quaker Inn, an S corporation in Grand Isle, Louisiana. Over the years, he has received a total of 276 shares of stock in the corporation through bonus payments.

While listening to a debate on television about a national health care plan, Burt decides that the company's health coverage is unfair. He is concerned about this because his wife is seriously ill.

During the second week in December, Burt informs the president of Quaker that he would like a Christmas bonus of $75,000, or else he will sell 10 shares of his stock to one of his relatives who is a nonresident alien. As a C corporation, Quaker's income tax would be about $136,000.

Can you defend Burt's position?

LO.3

Understand how to make an S election.

MAKING THE ELECTION

To become an S corporation, a *small business corporation* (defined above) must file a valid election with the IRS. The election is made on Form 2553. For the election to be valid, it must be filed on a timely basis and all shareholders must consent. For S corporation status to apply in the current tax year, the election must be filed either in the previous year or on or before the fifteenth day of the third month of the current year.[14]

EXAMPLE 6

In 2005, a calendar year C corporation in Auburn, Alabama, decides to become an S corporation beginning January 1, 2006. The S corporation election can be made at any time in 2005 or by March 15, 2006. An election after March 15, 2006, will not be effective until the 2007 tax year. ■

Even if the 2½-month deadline is met, a current election is not valid unless the corporation qualifies as a small business corporation for the *entire* tax year. Otherwise, the election will be effective for the following tax year. Late current-year elections, after the 2½-month deadline, may be considered timely if there is reasonable cause for the late filing.

A corporation that does not yet exist cannot make an S corporation election.[15] Thus, for new corporations, a premature election may not be effective. A new corporation's 2½-month election period begins at the earliest occurrence of any of the following events: (1) when the corporation has shareholders, (2) when it acquires assets, or (3) when it begins doing business.[16]

EXAMPLE 7

Several individuals acquire assets on behalf of Rock Corporation on June 29, 2005, and begin doing business on July 3, 2005. They subscribe to shares of stock, file articles of incorporation for Rock, and become shareholders on July 7, 2005. The S election must be filed no later than 2½ months after June 29, 2005 (on or before September 12) to be effective for 2005. ■

[13] See *Ward v. U.S.*, 81–2 USTC ¶9674, 48 AFTR2d 81–5942, 661 F.2d 226 (Ct.Cls., 1981), where the court found that the stock was owned as community property. Since the taxpayer-shareholder (a U.S. citizen) was married to a citizen and resident of Mexico, the nonresident alien prohibition was violated. If the taxpayer-shareholder had held the stock as separate property, the S election would have been valid.

[14] § 1362(b).

[15] See, for example, *T.H. Campbell & Bros., Inc.*, 34 TCM 695, T.C.Memo. 1975–149; Ltr.Rul. 8807070.

[16] Reg. § 1.1372–2(b)(1). Also see, for example, *Nick A. Artukovich*, 61 T.C. 100 (1973).

The IRS can correct errors in electing S status where a taxpayer can show that the mistake was inadvertent, the entity otherwise was qualified to be an S corporation, and it acted as if it were an S corporation. Under certain conditions, automatic relief is granted without the need for a letter ruling request and the normal user fee.

Further, the IRS has the authority to honor S elections that were not filed by the deadline. To qualify for this relief the company must have a reasonable cause for missing the statutory deadline. Sufficient reasonable cause might occur, for example, where both the corporation's accountant and its attorney failed to file the election because each believed the other had done so or because there was miscommunication as to who was responsible for filing.

SHAREHOLDER CONSENT

A qualifying election requires the consent of all of the corporation's shareholders.[17] Consent must be in writing, and it must generally be filed by the election deadline. However, while no statutory authority exists for obtaining an extension of time for filing an S election (Form 2553), a shareholder may receive an extension of time to file consent. A consent extension is available only if Form 2553 is filed on a timely basis, reasonable cause is given, and the interests of the government are not jeopardized.[18]

EXAMPLE 8

Vern and Yvonne decide to convert their C corporation into a calendar year S corporation for 2005. At the end of February 2005 (before the election is filed), Yvonne travels to Ukraine and forgets to sign a consent to the election. Yvonne will not return to the United States until June and cannot be reached by fax or e-mail. Vern files the S election on Form 2553 and also requests an extension of time to file Yvonne's consent to the election. Vern indicates that there is a reasonable cause for the extension: a shareholder is out of the country. Since the government's interest is not jeopardized, the IRS probably will grant Yvonne an extension of time to file the consent. Vern must file the election on Form 2553 on or before March 15, 2005, for the election to be effective for the 2005 calendar year. ■

Both husband and wife must consent if they own their stock jointly (as joint tenants, tenants in common, tenants by the entirety, or community property). This requirement has led to considerable taxpayer grief—particularly in community property states where the spouses may not realize that their stock is jointly owned as a community asset.

EXAMPLE 9

Three shareholders, Amy, Monty, and Dianne, incorporate in January and file Form 2553. Amy is married and lives in California. Monty is single and Dianne is married; both live in North Carolina. Because Amy is married and lives in a community property state, her husband also must consent to the S election. Since North Carolina is not a community property state, Dianne's husband need not consent. ■

Finally, for current-year S elections, persons who were shareholders during any part of the taxable year before the election date, but were not shareholders when the election was made, must also consent to the election.[19]

EXAMPLE 10

On January 15, 2005, the stock of Columbus Corporation (a calendar year C corporation) was held equally by three individual shareholders: Jim, Sally, and LuEllen. On that date,

[17] § 1362(a)(2).

[18] Rev.Rul. 60–183, 1960–1 C.B. 625; *William Pestcoe*, 40 T.C. 195 (1963); Reg. § 1.1362–6(b)(3)(iii).

[19] § 1362(b)(2)(B)(ii).

LuEllen sells her interest to Jim and Sally. On March 14, 2005, Columbus Corporation files Form 2553. Jim and Sally indicate their consent by signing the form. Columbus cannot become an S corporation until 2006 because LuEllen did not indicate consent. Had all three shareholders consented by signing Form 2553, S status would have taken effect as of January 1, 2005. ■

LO.4

Explain how an S election can be terminated.

LOSS OF THE ELECTION

An S election remains in force until it is revoked or lost. Election or consent forms are not required for future years. However, an S election can terminate if any of the following occurs.

- Shareholders owning a majority of shares (voting and nonvoting) voluntarily revoke the election.
- A new shareholder owning more than one-half of the stock affirmatively refuses to consent to the election.
- The corporation no longer qualifies as a small business corporation.
- The corporation does not meet the passive investment income limitation.

Voluntary Revocation. A **voluntary revocation** of the S election requires the consent of shareholders owning a majority of shares on the day that the revocation is to be made.[20] A revocation filed up to and including the fifteenth day of the third month of the tax year is effective for the entire tax year, unless a later date is specified. Similarly, unless an effective date is specified, revocation made after the first 2½ months of the current tax year is effective for the following tax year.

EXAMPLE 11

The shareholders of Petunia Corporation, a calendar year S corporation, voluntarily revoke the S election on January 5, 2005. They do not specify a future effective date in the revocation. Assuming the revocation is properly executed and timely filed, Petunia will be a C corporation for the entire 2005 calendar year. If the election is not made until June 2005, Petunia will remain an S corporation in 2005 and will become a C corporation at the beginning of 2006. ■

A corporation can revoke its S status *prospectively* by specifying a future date when the revocation is to be effective. A revocation that designates a future effective date splits the corporation's tax year into a short S corporation year and a short C corporation year. The day on which the revocation occurs is treated as the first day of the C corporation year. The corporation allocates income or loss for the entire year on a pro rata basis, based on the number of days in each short year.

EXAMPLE 12

Assume the same facts as in the preceding example, except that Petunia designates July 1, 2005, as the revocation date. Accordingly, June 30, 2005, is the last day of the S corporation's tax year. The C corporation's tax year runs from July 1, 2005 to December 31, 2005. Any income or loss for the 12-month period is allocated between the two short years, based on the number of days in each short year. ■

Rather than using pro rata allocation, the corporation can elect to compute actual income or loss attributable to the two short years. This election requires the consent of everyone who was a shareholder at any time during the S corporation's short year and everyone who owns stock on the first day of the C corporation's year.[21]

[20] § 1362(d)(1).

[21] § 1362(e)(3).

Loss of Small Business Corporation Status. If an S corporation fails to qualify as a small business corporation at any time after the election has become effective, its status as an S corporation ends. The termination occurs on the day that the corporation ceases to be a small business corporation.[22] Thus, if the corporation ever has more than 100 shareholders, a second class of stock, or a nonqualifying shareholder, or otherwise fails to meet the definition of a small business corporation, the S election is immediately terminated.

EXAMPLE 13

Peony Corporation has been a calendar year S corporation for three years. On August 13, 2005, one of its 100 shareholders sells *some* of her stock to an outsider. Peony now has 101 shareholders, and it ceases to be a small business corporation. For 2005, Peony is an S corporation through August 12, 2005, and a C corporation from August 13 to December 31, 2005. ■

Passive Investment Income Limitation. The Code provides a **passive investment income (PII)** limitation for S corporations that were previously C corporations or for S corporations that have merged with C corporations. If an S corporation has C corporation E & P and passive income in excess of 25 percent of its gross receipts for three consecutive taxable years, the S election is terminated as of the beginning of the fourth year.[23]

EXAMPLE 14

For 2002, 2003, and 2004, Diapason Corporation, a calendar year S corporation, received passive income in excess of 25% of its gross receipts. If Diapason holds accumulated E & P from years in which it was a C corporation, its S election is terminated as of January 1, 2005. ■

PII includes dividends, interest, rents, gains and losses from sales of securities, and royalties net of investment deductions. Rents are not considered PII if the corporation renders significant personal services to the occupant.

EXAMPLE 15

Violet Corporation owns and operates an apartment building. The corporation provides utilities for the building, maintains the lobby, and furnishes trash collection for tenants. These activities are not considered significant personal services, so any rent income earned by the corporation will be considered PII.

Alternatively, if Violet also furnishes maid services to its tenants (personal services beyond what normally would be expected from a landlord in an apartment building), the rent income would no longer be PII. ■

Reelection after Termination. After an S election has been terminated, the corporation must wait five years before reelecting S corporation status. The five-year waiting period is waived if:

- there is a more-than-50-percent change in ownership of the corporation after the first year for which the termination is applicable, or
- the event causing the termination was not reasonably within the control of the S corporation or its majority shareholders.

Operational Rules

S corporations are treated much like partnerships for tax purposes. With a few exceptions,[24] S corporations generally make tax accounting and other elections at the corporate level. Each year, the S corporation determines nonseparately stated

[22] § 1362(d)(2)(B).
[23] § 1362(d)(3)(A)(ii).

[24] A few elections can be made at the shareholder level (e.g., the choice between a foreign tax deduction or credit).

■ **FIGURE 22–1**
Flow-Through of Separate Items of Income and Loss to S Corporation Shareholders

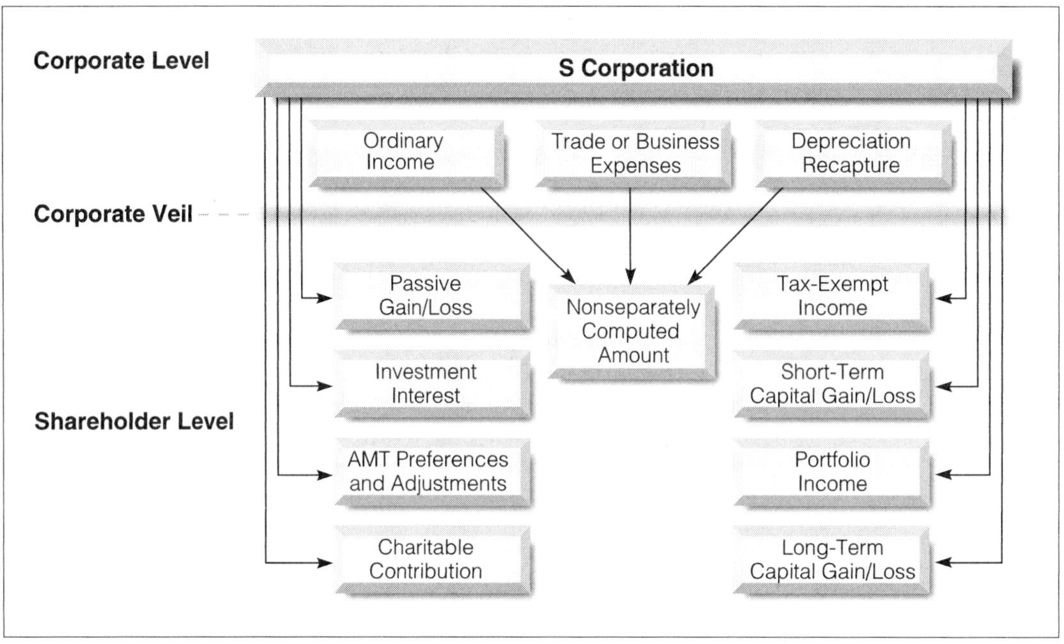

income or loss and separately stated income, deductions, and credits. These items are taxed only once, at the shareholder level. All items are allocated to each shareholder based on average ownership of stock throughout the year. The *flow-through* of each item of income, deduction, and credit from the corporation to the shareholder is illustrated in Figure 22–1.

LO.5

Compute nonseparately stated income and identify separately stated items.

COMPUTATION OF TAXABLE INCOME

Subchapter S taxable income or loss is determined in a manner similar to the tax rules that apply to partnerships, except that S corporations amortize organizational expenditures using the corporate rules[25] and must recognize gains, *but not losses*, on distributions of appreciated property to shareholders.[26] Other special provisions affecting only the computation of C corporation income, such as the dividends received deduction, do not extend to S corporations.[27] Finally, as with partnerships, certain deductions of individuals are not permitted, including alimony payments, personal moving expenses, certain dependent care expenses, the personal exemption, and the standard deduction.

In general, S corporation items are divided into (1) nonseparately stated income or loss and (2) separately stated income, losses, deductions, and credits that could affect the tax liability of any shareholder in a different manner, depending on other factors in the shareholder's tax situation. In essence, nonseparate items are aggregated into an undifferentiated amount that constitutes Subchapter S taxable income or loss. An S corporation's separately stated items are identical to those separately stated by partnerships. These items retain their tax attributes on the

[25]§§ 248 and 1363(b).
[26]§ 1363(d).
[27]§ 703(a)(2).

shareholder's return. Separately stated items are listed on Schedule K of the 1120S. They include the following.

- Tax-exempt income.
- Long-term and short-term capital gains and losses.
- Section 1231 gains and losses.
- Charitable contributions.
- Passive gains, losses, and credits.
- Certain portfolio income.
- Section 179 expense deduction.
- Tax preferences and adjustments for the alternative minimum tax.
- Depletion.
- Foreign income or loss.
- Wagering gains or losses.
- Recoveries of tax benefit items.
- Intangible drilling costs.
- Investment interest, income, and expenses.

EXAMPLE 16

The following is the income statement for Jersey, Inc., an S corporation.

Sales		$ 40,000
Less: Cost of sales		(23,000)
Gross profit on sales		$ 17,000
Less: Interest expense	$1,200	
Charitable contributions	400	
Advertising expenses	1,500	
Other operating expenses	2,000	(5,100)
		$ 11,900
Add: Tax-exempt interest	$ 300	
Dividend income	200	
Long-term capital gain	500	1,000
Less: Short-term capital loss		(150)
Net income per books		$ 12,750

Subchapter S taxable income for Jersey is calculated as follows, using net income for book purposes as the starting point.

Net income per books		$12,750
Separately stated items		
Deduct: Tax-exempt interest	$300	
Dividend income	200	
Long-term capital gain	500	(1,000)
Subtotal		$11,750
Add: Charitable contributions	$400	
Short-term capital loss	150	550
Subchapter S taxable income		$12,300

The $12,300 of Subchapter S taxable income, as well as each of the five separately stated items, are divided among the shareholders based upon their stock ownership. ■

LO.6

Allocate income, deductions, and credits to shareholders.

ALLOCATION OF INCOME AND LOSS

Each shareholder is allocated a pro rata portion of nonseparately stated income or loss and all separately stated items. The pro rata allocation method assigns an equal amount of each of the S items to each day of the year. If a shareholder's stock holding changes during the year, this allocation assigns the shareholder a pro rata share of each item for *each* day the stock is owned. On the date of transfer, the transferor (and not the transferee) is considered to own the stock.[28]

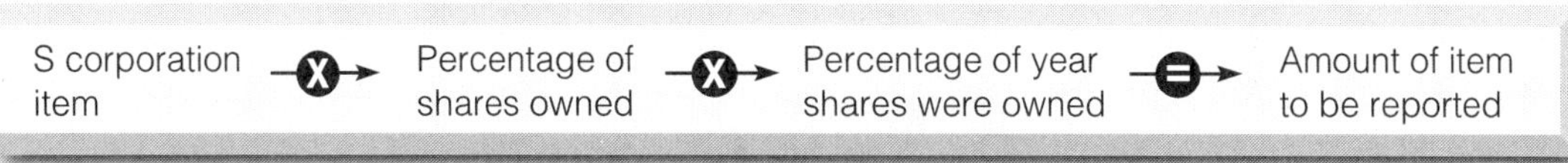

The per-day allocation must be used, unless the shareholder disposes of his or her entire interest in the entity.[29] In case of a complete termination, a short year may result, as discussed below. If a shareholder dies during the year, his or her share of the pro rata items up to the date of death is reported on the final individual income tax return.

EXAMPLE 17

Assume in the previous example that Pat, a shareholder, owned 10% of Jersey's stock for 100 days and 12% for the remaining 265 days (assume for this example that this year is not a leap year). Using the required per-day allocation method, Pat's share of the S corporation items is as follows.

	Schedule K Totals	Pat's Share		Pat's Schedule K–1 Totals
		10%	12%	
Subchapter S taxable income	$12,300	$337	$1,072	$1,409
Tax-exempt interest	300	8	26	34
Dividend income	200	5	17	22
Long-term capital gain	500	14	44	58
Charitable contributions	400	11	35	46
Short-term capital loss	150	4	13	17

Pat's share of the Subchapter S taxable income is the total of $12,300 × [0.10 × (100/365)] plus $12,300 × [0.12 × (265/365)], or $1,409. Each of the Schedule K–1 totals from the right-hand column flows through to the appropriate lines on Pat's individual income tax return (Form 1040). ■

EXAMPLE 18

If Pat in Example 17 dies after owning the stock 100 days, his share of the S corporation items is reported on his final individual income tax return (Form 1040). Thus, only the items in the column labeled 10% in Example 17 are reported on Pat's final tax return. S corporation items that occur after Pat's death most likely would flow through to the income tax return of Pat's estate (Form 1041). ■

The Short-Year Election. If a shareholder's interest is completely terminated by disposition or death during the tax year, all shareholders holding stock during the year and the corporation may elect to treat the S taxable year as two taxable years. The first year ends on the date of the termination. Under this election, an interim closing of the books is undertaken, and the shareholders report their shares of the S corporation items as they occurred during the short tax year.[30]

[28]Reg. § 1.1377–1(a)(2)(ii).
[29]§§ 1366(a)(1) and 1377(a)(1).
[30]§ 1377(a)(2).

The short-year election provides an opportunity to shift income, losses, and credits between shareholders. The election is desirable in circumstances where more loss can be allocated to taxpayers with higher marginal rates.

EXAMPLE 19

Alicia, the owner of all of the shares of an S corporation, transfers her stock to Cindy halfway through the tax year. There is a $100,000 NOL for the entire tax year, but $30,000 of the loss occurs during the first half of the year. Without a short-year election, $50,000 of the loss is allocated to Alicia, and $50,000 is allocated to Cindy. If the corporation makes the short-year election, Cindy is allocated $70,000 of the loss. Of course, the sales price of the stock would probably be increased to recognize the tax benefits being transferred from Alicia to Cindy. ■

In the case of the death of a shareholder, a short-year election prevents the income and loss allocation to a deceased shareholder from being affected by post-death events.

EXAMPLE 20

Joey and Karl equally own Rose, Inc., a calendar year S corporation. Joey dies on June 29 of a year that is not a leap year. Rose has income of $250,000 for January 1 through June 29 and $750,000 for the remainder of the year. Without a short-year election, the income is allocated by assigning an equal portion of the annual income of $1 million to each day (or $2,739.73 per day) and allocating the daily portion between the shareholders. Joey is allocated 50% of the daily income for the 180 days from January 1 to June 29, or $246,575.70 [($2,739.73/2) × 180]. Joey's *estate* is allocated 50% of the income for the 185 days from June 30 to December 31, or $253,425.02 [($2,739.73/2) × 185].

If the short-year election is made, the income of $250,000 from January 1 to June 29 is divided equally between Joey and Karl, so that each is taxed on $125,000. The income of $750,000 from June 30 to December 31 is divided equally between Joey's estate and Karl, or $375,000 to each. ■

TAX TREATMENT OF DISTRIBUTIONS TO SHAREHOLDERS

The amount of any distribution to an S corporation shareholder is equal to the cash plus the fair market value of any other property distributed. How the distribution is taxed depends upon whether the S corporation has C corporation **accumulated earnings and profits** (AEP, described in Chapter 19).

No C Corporation AEP. If the S corporation has never been a C corporation or if it has no C corporation AEP, the distribution is a tax-free recovery of capital to the extent that it does not exceed the shareholder's adjusted basis in the stock of the S corporation. When the amount of the distribution exceeds the adjusted basis of the stock, the excess is treated as a gain from the sale or exchange of property (capital gain in most cases).

EXAMPLE 21

Twirl, Inc., a calendar year S corporation, has no AEP. During the year, Juan, an individual shareholder of the corporation, receives a cash distribution of $12,200 from Twirl. Juan's basis in his stock is $9,700. Juan recognizes a capital gain of $2,500, the excess of the distribution over the stock basis ($12,200 – $9,700). The remaining $9,700 is tax-free, but it reduces Juan's basis in his stock to zero. ■

C Corporation AEP. S corporations with C corporation AEP blend the entity and conduit approaches to taxation. This blending treats distributions of pre-election (C corporation) and postelection (S corporation) earnings differently. Distributions of C corporation AEP are taxed as dividends (5/15% rate), while distributions of previously taxed S corporation earnings are tax-free to the extent of the shareholder's adjusted basis in the stock.

Concept Summary 22–1

Classification Procedures for Distributions from an S Corporation

Where Earnings and Profits Exist	Where No Earnings and Profits Exist
1. Distributions are tax-free to the extent of the AAA.*	1. Distributions are nontaxable to the extent of adjusted basis in stock.
2. Any previously taxed income (PTI) from pre-1983 tax years can be distributed tax-free.	2. Excess is treated as gain from a sale or exchange of stock (capital gain in most cases).
3. The remaining distribution constitutes dividend income from AEP.†	
4. Distributions are tax-free to the extent of the other adjustments account (OAA).	
5. Any residual amount is applied as a tax-free reduction in basis of stock.	
6. Excess is treated as gain from a sale or exchange of stock (capital gain in most cases).	

*Once stock basis reaches zero, any distribution from the AAA is treated as a gain from the sale or exchange of stock. Thus, basis is an upper limit on what a shareholder may receive tax-free.
†The AAA bypass election is available to pay out AEP before reducing the AAA [§ 1368(e)(3)].

Concept Summary 22–1 outlines the taxation of distributions. These rules are intended to prevent two problems that result when a C corporation has been converted to an S corporation.

- Tax manipulation could result in AEP from the C corporation years being withdrawn without taxation, since S corporation shareholders are taxed on income, not on distributions.
- On the other hand, double taxation could occur. Earnings from the S corporation years might both flow to the shareholders' tax returns as income and be taxed as dividends as if the corporation were a C corporation.

A special account is used to track undistributed earnings of an S corporation that have been taxed to shareholders previously. Distributions from this account, known as the **accumulated adjustments account (AAA),** are tax-free. Essentially, the AAA is the cumulative total of undistributed nonseparately and separately stated items for S corporation taxable years beginning after 1982. Thus, the account parallels the calculation of C corporation AEP. Calculation of the AAA applies to all S corporations, but the AAA is most important to those that have been C corporations. The AAA provides a mechanism to ensure that the earnings of an S corporation are taxed to shareholders only once.

The AAA is computed by making adjustments in the order specified in Exhibit 22–1. Its balance is determined at the end of each year rather than at the time distributions are made. When more than one distribution occurs in the same year, a pro rata portion of each distribution is treated as having been made out of the AAA.

In calculating the amount in the AAA for purposes of determining the tax treatment of current-year distributions, the net negative adjustments (e.g., the excess of losses and deductions over income) for that tax year are ignored.

A shareholder has a proportionate interest in the AAA, regardless of the size of his or her stock basis.[31] However, since the AAA is a corporate account, no connection exists between the prior accumulated S corporation income and any

[31] § 1368(c).

■ **EXHIBIT 22–1**
Adjustments to the Corporate AAA

Increase by:
1. Schedule K items other than tax-exempt income.
2. Nonseparately computed income.
3. Depletion in excess of basis in the property.

Decrease by:
4. Adjustments other than distributions (e.g., losses, deductions).
5. Any portion of a distribution that is considered to be tax-free from AAA (but not below zero).

NOTE: When the combination of items 1 through 4 results in a negative number, the AAA is adjusted first for the distribution and then for the adjustments in items 1 through 4.

specific shareholder.[32] Thus, the benefits of the AAA can be shifted from one shareholder to another shareholder. For example, when one S shareholder transfers stock to another shareholder, any AAA on the purchase date may be distributed tax-free to the purchaser. Similarly, issuing additional stock to a new shareholder in an S corporation having AAA dilutes the account relative to the existing shareholders.

The AAA (unlike the stock basis) can have a negative balance. All losses decrease the AAA balance, even those in excess of the shareholder's stock basis. However, *distributions* may not make the AAA negative or increase a negative balance.

Distribution Ordering Rules. A cash distribution from an S corporation with AEP comes first from the AAA (limited to stock basis). The distribution is then deemed to be made from **previously taxed income (PTI)**[33] generated under old S corporation rules (pre-1983). Distributions from the AAA and PTI are tax-free. The remaining distribution is taxed as a dividend to the extent of AEP. After AEP is fully distributed, any residual amount is applied against the shareholder's remaining stock basis. This amount is a tax-free recovery of capital.[34] Any distributions in excess of stock basis are taxed as capital gains.

EXAMPLE 22

Salvia, a calendar year S corporation, distributes $1,300 cash to its only shareholder, Otis, on December 31, 2005. Otis's basis in his stock is $1,400, his AAA is $500, and the corporation has AEP of $750 before the distribution.

According to the distribution ordering rules, the first $500 is a tax-free recovery of basis from the AAA. The next $750 is a taxable dividend distribution from AEP. Finally, the remaining $50 of cash is a tax-free recovery of basis. Immediately after the distribution, Salvia has no AAA or AEP, and Otis's stock basis equals $850.

	Corporate AAA	Corporate AEP	Otis's Stock Basis*
Beginning balance	$ 500	$ 750	$1,400
Distribution ($1,300)			
From AAA	(500)		(500)
From AEP		(750)	
From stock basis			(50)
Ending balance	$ –0–	$ –0–	$ 850

*Details of basis adjustments are discussed later in the chapter. ■

[32] § 1368(e)(1)(A).

[33] §§ 1368(c)(1) and (e)(1). Before 1983, an account similar to the AAA was in place, namely, previously taxed income (PTI). Any S corporations in existence before 1983 may have PTI, which currently may be distributed tax-free.

[34] § 1368(c).

EXAMPLE 23

Assume the same facts as in the preceding example. During the following year, Salvia has no earnings and distributes $1,000 to Otis. Of the distribution, $850 is a tax-free recovery of stock basis, and $150 is taxed to Otis as a capital gain. ■

With the consent of all of its shareholders, an S corporation can elect to have a distribution treated as if it were made first from AEP rather than from the AAA. This mechanism is known as an AAA *bypass election*. This election may be desirable as a simple means to eliminate a small AEP balance.

EXAMPLE 24

Collett, a calendar year S corporation, has AEP of $12,000 and a balance of $20,000 in the AAA. Collett Corporation may elect to distribute the AEP first, creating a $12,000 dividend for its shareholders, before using the AAA. ■

Schedule M–2. S corporations report changes in the AAA on Schedule M–2 of Form 1120S; this schedule appears below. Schedule M–2 contains a column labeled *Other adjustments account (OAA)*. This account includes items that affect basis but not the AAA, such as tax-exempt income and any related nondeductible expenses. For example, life insurance proceeds received and insurance premiums paid are traced through the OAA. Distributions are made from the OAA after AEP and the AAA are reduced to zero. Distributions from the OAA are generally tax-free.

EXAMPLE 25

During the year, Sparrow, an S corporation, records the following items.

AAA, beginning of the year	$ 8,500
Previously taxed income, beginning of the year	6,250
Ordinary income	25,000
Tax-exempt interest	4,000
Key employee life insurance proceeds received	5,000
Payroll penalty expense	2,000
Charitable contributions	3,000
Unreasonable compensation	5,000
Premiums on key employee life insurance	2,100
Distributions to shareholders	16,000

Sparrow's Schedule M–2 for the current year appears as follows.

Schedule M-2 **Analysis of Accumulated Adjustments Account, Other Adjustments Account, and Shareholders' Undistributed Taxable Income Previously Taxed**

	(a) Accumulated adjustments account	(b) Other adjustments account	(c) Shareholders' undistributed taxable income previously taxed
1 Balance at beginning of tax year . . .	*8,500*		*6,250*
2 Ordinary income from page 1, line 21 . .	*25,000*		
3 Other additions		*9,000***	
4 Loss from page 1, line 21	( )		
5 Other reductions	(*10,000**)	(*2,100*)	
6 Combine lines 1 through 5	*23,500*	*6,900*	
7 Distributions other than dividend distributions .	*16,000*		
8 Balance at end of tax year. Subtract line 7 from line 6	*7,500*	*6,900*	*6,250*

**$2,000 (payroll penalty) + $3,000 (charitable contributions) + $5,000 (unreasonable compensation).*
***$4,000 (tax-exempt interest) + $5,000 (life insurance proceeds).* ■

Effect of Terminating the S Election. Normally, distributions to shareholders from a C corporation are taxed as dividends to the extent of E & P. However, any distribution of *cash* by a corporation to shareholders during a one-year

CONCEPT SUMMARY 22–2

Distribution of Property

	Appreciated Property	Depreciated Property
S corporation	Realized gain is recognized by the corporation, which passes it through to the shareholders. Such gain increases a shareholder's stock basis, generating a basis in the property equal to FMV. On the distribution, the shareholder's stock basis is reduced by the FMV of the property (but not below zero).	Realized loss is not recognized. The shareholder assumes an FMV basis in the property.
C corporation	Realized gain is recognized under § 311(b), which increases E & P (net of tax). The shareholder has a taxable dividend to the extent of E & P.	Realized loss is not recognized. The shareholder assumes an FMV basis in the property.
Partnership	No gain to the partnership or partner. The partner takes a carryover basis in the asset, but the asset basis is limited to the partner's basis in the partnership.	Realized loss is not recognized. The partner takes a carryover basis in the asset, but the asset basis is limited to the partner's basis in the partnership.

period[35] following S election termination receives special treatment. Such a distribution is treated as a tax-free recovery of stock basis to the extent that it does not exceed the AAA.[36] Since *only* cash distributions reduce the AAA during this *postelection termination period*, a corporation should not make property distributions during this time. Instead, the entity should sell property and distribute the proceeds to shareholders. However, post-termination distributions that are charged against the OAA do not get tax-free treatment. To take advantage of post-termination benefits, an S corporation should maintain both the AAA and the OAA, although S corporations without AEP are not required to do so.

EXAMPLE 26

Quinn, the sole shareholder of Roman, Inc., a calendar year S corporation, elects during 2005 to terminate the S election, effective January 1, 2006. As of the end of 2005, Roman has an AAA of $1,300. Quinn can receive a nontaxable distribution of cash during a post-termination period of approximately one year to the extent of Roman's AAA. Although a cash distribution of $1,300 during 2006 would be nontaxable to Quinn, it would reduce the adjusted basis of his stock. ■

LO.7

Understand how distributions to S corporation shareholders are taxed.

TAX TREATMENT OF PROPERTY DISTRIBUTIONS BY THE CORPORATION

An S corporation recognizes a gain on any nonliquidating distribution of appreciated property (other than in a reorganization) in the same manner as if the asset had been sold to the shareholder at its fair market value.[37] The corporate gain is

[35]The period is *approximately* one year in length. The post-termination transition period is discussed later in the chapter.

[36]§§ 1371(e) and 1377(b).

[37]§ 311(b).

passed through to the shareholders. The character of the gain—capital gain or ordinary income—depends upon the type of asset being distributed. There is an important reason for this gain recognition rule. Without it, property might be distributed tax-free (other than for certain recapture items) and later sold without income recognition to the shareholder because the shareholder's basis equals the asset's fair market value.

The S corporation does not recognize a loss when distributing assets that are worth less than their basis. As with gain property, the shareholder's basis is equal to the asset's fair market value. Thus, the potential loss is postponed until the shareholder sells the stock of the S corporation. Since loss property receives a step-down in basis without any loss recognition by the S corporation, distributions of loss property should be avoided.

EXAMPLE 27

Turnip, Inc., an S corporation for 10 years, distributes a tract of land held as an investment to Chang, its majority shareholder. The land was purchased for $22,000 many years ago and is currently worth $82,000. Turnip recognizes a capital gain of $60,000, which increases the AAA by $60,000. The gain appears on Turnip's Schedule K, and a proportionate share of it passes through to the shareholders' tax returns. Then the property distribution reduces the AAA by $82,000 (the fair market value). The tax consequences are the same for appreciated property, whether it is distributed to the shareholders and they dispose of it, or the corporation sells the property and distributes the proceeds to the shareholders.

If the land had been purchased for $82,000 and was currently worth $22,000, Chang takes a $22,000 basis in the land. The $60,000 realized loss is not recognized at the corporate level. The loss does not reduce Turnip's AAA. Only when the S corporation sells the asset does it recognize the loss and reduce AAA. ■

EXAMPLE 28

Assume the same facts as in the previous example, except that Turnip is a C corporation ($1 million E & P balance) or a partnership. The partner's basis in the partnership interest is $100,000.

	Appreciated Property		
	S Corporation	**C Corporation**	**Partnership**
Entity gain/loss	$60,000	$60,000	$ –0–
Owner's gain/loss/dividend	60,000	82,000	–0–
Owner's basis in land	82,000	82,000	22,000
	Property That Has Declined in Value		
	S Corporation	**C Corporation**	**Partnership**
Entity gain/loss	$ –0–	$ –0–	$ –0–
Owner's gain/loss/dividend	–0–	22,000	–0–
Owner's basis in land	22,000	22,000	82,000

■

LO.8

Calculate a shareholder's basis in S corporation stock.

SHAREHOLDER'S BASIS

The calculation of the initial tax basis of stock in an S corporation is similar to that for the basis of stock in a C corporation and depends upon the manner in which the shares are acquired (e.g., gift, inheritance, purchase, exchange under § 351). Once the initial tax basis is determined, various transactions during the life of the corporation affect the shareholder's basis in the stock. Although each shareholder is required to compute his or her own basis in the S shares, neither Form 1120S nor Schedule K–1 provides a place for deriving this amount.

A shareholder's basis is increased by stock purchases and capital contributions. Operations during the year cause the following upward adjustments to basis.[38]

- Nonseparately computed income.
- Separately stated income items (e.g., nontaxable income).
- Depletion in excess of basis in the property.

Basis then is reduced by distributions not reported as income by the shareholder (e.g., an AAA or PTI distribution). Next, the following items reduce basis (*but not below zero*).

- Nondeductible expenses of the corporation (e.g., fines, penalties, illegal kickbacks).
- Nonseparately computed loss.
- Separately stated loss and deduction items.

As under the partnership rule, basis is first increased by income items; then it is decreased by distributions and finally by losses.[39] Pass-through items (other than distributions) that reduce stock basis are governed by special ordering rules. Noncapital, nondeductible expenditures reduce stock basis before losses or deductible items. A taxpayer may irrevocably elect to have deductible items pass through before any noncapital, nondeductible items. In most cases, this election is advantageous.

EXAMPLE 29

In its first year of operations, Iris, Inc., a calendar year S corporation in Clemson, South Carolina, earns income of $2,000. On February 2 in its second year of operations, Iris distributes $2,000 to Marty, its sole shareholder. During the remainder of the second year, the corporation incurs a $2,000 loss.

Under the S corporation ordering rules, the $2,000 distribution is tax-free AAA to Marty, and the $2,000 loss is *not* passed through because the stock basis cannot be reduced below zero. ■

A shareholder's basis in the stock can never be reduced below zero. Once stock basis is zero, any additional basis reductions from losses or deductions, but *not* distributions, decrease (but not below zero) the shareholder's basis in loans made to the S corporation. Any excess of losses or deductions over both bases is *suspended* until there are subsequent bases. Once the basis of any debt is reduced, it is later increased (only up to the original amount) by the subsequent *net* increase resulting from *all* positive and negative basis adjustments. The debt basis is adjusted back to the original amount before any increase is made in the stock basis.[40] A distribution in excess of stock basis does not reduce any debt basis. If a loss and a distribution occur in the same year, the loss reduces the stock basis last, *after* the distribution.

EXAMPLE 30

At the beginning of 2005, Stacey, a sole shareholder, has a $7,000 stock basis and a $2,000 basis in a loan that she made to a calendar year S corporation. The AAA and OAA balances at the beginning of the year are $0. Subchapter S ordinary income for 2005 is $8,200. During the year, the corporation received $2,000 of tax-exempt interest income. Cash of $17,300 is distributed to Stacey on November 15, 2005. Stacey recognizes only a $100 capital gain.

[38]§ 1367(a).
[39]Reg. § 1.1367–1(f).
[40]§ 1367(b)(2).

	Corporate AAA	Corporate OAA	Stacey's Stock Basis	Stacey's Loan Basis
Beginning balance	$ –0–	$ –0–	$ 7,000	$2,000
Ordinary income	8,200		8,200	
Tax-exempt income		2,000	2,000	
Subtotal	$ 8,200	$ 2,000	$17,200	$2,000
Distribution ($17,300)				
From AAA	(8,200)		(8,200)	
From OAA		(2,000)	(2,000)	
From stock basis			(7,000)	
Ending balance	$ –0–	$ –0–	$ –0–	$2,000
Distribution in excess of basis (capital gain)			$ 100	

Pass-through losses can reduce loan basis, but distributions do not. The stock basis cannot be reduced below zero, but the $100 excess distribution does not reduce Stacey's loan basis. ■

The basis rules for an S corporation are similar to the rules for determining a partner's basis in a partnership interest. However, a partner's basis in the partnership interest includes the partner's direct investment plus a *ratable share* of any partnership liabilities.[41] If a partnership borrows from a partner, the partner receives a basis increase as if the partnership had borrowed from an unrelated third party.[42] In contrast, except for loans from the shareholder to the corporation, corporate borrowing has no effect on S corporation shareholder basis. Loans from a shareholder to the S corporation have a tax basis only for the shareholder making the loan.

The fact that a shareholder has guaranteed a loan made to the corporation by a third party has no effect upon the shareholder's loan basis, unless payments actually have been made as a result of that guarantee.[43] If the corporation defaults on indebtedness and the shareholder makes good on the guarantee, the shareholder's indebtedness basis is increased to that extent.[44]

If a loan's basis has been reduced and is not restored, income is recognized when the S corporation repays the shareholder. If the corporation issued a note as evidence of the debt, repayment constitutes an amount received in exchange for a capital asset, and the amount that exceeds the shareholder's basis is entitled to capital gain treatment.[45] However, if the loan is made on open account, the repayment constitutes ordinary income to the extent that it exceeds the shareholder's basis in the loan. Each repayment is prorated between the gain portion and the repayment of the debt.[46] Thus, a note should be given to ensure capital gain treatment for the income that results from a loan's repayment.

Since the basis rule requires that corporate income be used to restore debt basis before it can be used to restore stock basis, a double tax on current income can result. Any current income distributed, after both debt and stock basis have been reduced to zero, is taxed as capital gain because it is considered a return of capital, but only to the extent of stock basis.

[41] § 752(a).

[42] Reg. § 1.752–1(e).

[43] See, for example, *Estate of Leavitt*, 90 T.C. 206 (1988), *aff'd* 89–1 USTC ¶9332, 63 AFTR2d 89–1437, 875 F.2d 420 (CA–4, 1989); *Selfe v. U.S.*, 86–1 USTC ¶9115, 57 AFTR2d 86–464, 778 F.2d 769 (CA–11, 1985); *James K. Calcutt*, 91 T.C. 14 (1988).

[44] Rev.Rul. 70–50, 1970–1 C.B. 178.

[45] *Joe M. Smith*, 48 T.C. 872 (1967), *aff'd* and *rev'd* in 70–1 USTC ¶9327, 25 AFTR2d 70–936, 424 F.2d 219 (CA–9, 1970); Rev.Rul. 64–162, 1964–1 C.B. 304.

[46] Rev.Rul. 68–537, 1968–2 C.B. 372.

EXAMPLE 31

Sammy is a 57% owner of Falcon, an S corporation in Brooklyn, New York. At the beginning of 2005, his stock basis is zero. Sammy's basis in a $12,000 loan made to Falcon and evidenced by Falcon's note has been reduced to $0 by prior losses. During the year, his share of the corporation's income is $11,000, which first is applied to increase his debt basis up to $11,000. At the end of the year, he receives a $13,000 distribution, which is treated as a capital gain because he has no stock basis. Sammy has been double taxed. ■

EXAMPLE 32

Gomez and Winn have suspended losses at the beginning of the year from their insolvent S corporation, Crocus, Inc. Crocus is a partner in a real estate partnership that realized $4 million in discharge-of-indebtedness (DOI) income. Crocus's share of the DOI income is $2 million, which is not recognized by the corporation. The DOI does not pass through to the shareholders and does not increase their stock basis. The suspended losses cannot be deducted by the shareholders.[47] ■

LO.9

Explain the tax effects that losses have on shareholders.

TREATMENT OF LOSSES

Net Operating Loss. One major advantage of an S election is the ability to pass through any net operating loss of the corporation directly to the shareholders. A shareholder can deduct an NOL for the year in which the S corporation's tax year ends. The corporation is not entitled to any deduction for the NOL. A shareholder's basis in the stock is reduced to the extent of any pass-through of the NOL, and the shareholder's AAA is reduced by the same deductible amount.[48]

EXAMPLE 33

An S corporation in Chapel Hill, North Carolina, incurs a $20,000 NOL for the current year. At all times during the tax year, the stock was owned equally by the same 10 shareholders. Each shareholder is entitled to deduct $2,000 against other income for the tax year in which the corporate tax year ends. ■

Deductions for an S corporation's NOL pass-through cannot exceed a shareholder's adjusted basis in the stock *plus* the basis of any loans made by the shareholder to the corporation. If a taxpayer is unable to prove the tax basis, the NOL pass-through can be denied.[49] As noted previously, once a shareholder's adjusted stock basis has been eliminated by an NOL, any excess NOL is used to reduce the shareholder's basis for any loans made to the corporation (*but never below zero*). The basis for loans is established by the actual advances made to the corporation, and not by indirect loans.[50] If the shareholder's basis is insufficient to allow a full flow-through and there is more than one type of loss (e.g., in the same year the S corporation incurs both a passive loss and a net capital loss), the flow-through amounts are determined on a pro rata basis.

EXAMPLE 34

Ralph is a 50% owner of an S corporation for the entire year. His stock basis is $10,000, and his shares of the various corporate losses are as follows:

Ordinary loss from operations	$8,000
Capital loss	5,000
§ 1231 loss	3,000
Passive loss	2,000

[47]Section 108(d)(7), overriding *Gitlitz v. Comm.*, 2001–1 USTC ¶50,147, 87 AFTR2d 2001–417, 121 S.Ct. 701 (USSC, 2001).

[48]§§ 1368(a)(1)(A) and (e)(1)(A).

[49]See *Donald J. Sauvigne*, 30 TCM 123, T.C.Memo. 1971–30.

[50]*Ruth M. Prashker*, 59 T.C. 172 (1972); *Frederick G. Brown v. U.S.*, 83–1 USTC ¶9364, 52 AFTR2d 82–5080, 706 F.2d 755 (CA–6, 1983).

Based upon a pro rata approach, the total $10,000 allocable flow-through would be split among the various losses as follows:

Ordinary loss	=	$\frac{\$8,000}{\$18,000}$ × $10,000	=	$ 4,444.44
Capital loss	=	$\frac{\$5,000}{\$18,000}$ × $10,000	=	$ 2,777.78
§ 1231 loss	=	$\frac{\$3,000}{\$18,000}$ × $10,000	=	$ 1,666.67
Passive loss	=	$\frac{\$2,000}{\$18,000}$ × $10,000	=	$ 1,111.11
Total allocated loss				$10,000.00

■

The distribution adjustments made by an S corporation during a tax year are taken into account *before* applying the loss limitation for the year. Thus, distributions during a year reduce the adjusted basis for determining the allowable loss for the year, but the loss for the year does *not* reduce the adjusted basis for purposes of determining the tax status of the distributions made during the year.

EXAMPLE 35

Pylon, Inc., a calendar year S corporation, is partly owned by Doris, who has a beginning stock basis of $10,000. During the year, Doris's share of a long-term capital gain (LTCG) is $2,000, and her share of an ordinary loss is $9,000. If Doris receives a $6,000 distribution, her deductible loss is calculated as follows.

Beginning stock basis	$10,000
Add: LTCG	2,000
Subtotal	$12,000
Less: Distribution	(6,000)
Basis for loss limitation purposes	$ 6,000
Deductible loss	($ 6,000)
Unused loss	($ 3,000)

Doris's stock now has a basis of zero. ■

A shareholder's share of an NOL may be greater than both stock basis and loan basis. A shareholder is entitled to carry forward a loss to the extent that the loss for the year exceeds basis. Any loss carried forward may be deducted *only* by the *same* shareholder if and when the basis in the stock of or loans to the corporation is restored.[51]

EXAMPLE 36

Dana has a stock basis of $4,000 in an S corporation. He has loaned $2,000 to the corporation and has guaranteed another $4,000 loan made to the corporation by a local bank. Although his share of the S corporation's NOL for the current year is $9,500, Dana may deduct only $6,000 of the NOL on his individual tax return. Dana may carry forward $3,500 of the NOL, to be deducted when the basis in his stock or loan to the corporation is restored. Dana has a zero basis in both the stock and the loan after the flow-through of the $6,000 NOL. ■

Any loss carryover due to insufficient basis remaining at the end of an approximately one-year post-termination transition period is *lost forever.* The post-termination period includes the 120-day period beginning on the date of any determination pursuant to an audit of a taxpayer that follows the termination of

[51] § 1366(d).

the S corporation's election and that adjusts a Subchapter S item.[52] Thus, if a shareholder has a loss carryover, he or she should increase the stock or loan basis and flow through the loss before disposing of the stock.

Net operating losses from C corporation years cannot be utilized at the corporate level (except with respect to built-in gain, discussed later in this chapter), nor can they be passed through to the shareholders. Further, the carryforward period continues to run during S status.[53] Consequently, the S election may not be appropriate for a C corporation with NOL carryforwards. When a corporation is expecting losses in the future, an S election should be made *before* the loss years.

At-Risk Rules. S corporation shareholders, like partners, are limited in the amount of losses they may deduct by their "at-risk" amounts. The rules for determining at-risk amounts are similar, but not identical, to the partner at-risk rules. These rules apply to the shareholders, but not to the corporation. An amount at risk is determined separately for each shareholder. The amount of the corporate losses that are passed through and deductible by the shareholders is not affected by the amount the corporation has at risk.

A shareholder usually is considered at risk with respect to an activity to the extent of cash and the adjusted basis of other property contributed to the S corporation, any amount borrowed for use in the activity for which the taxpayer has personal liability for payment from personal assets, and the net fair market value of personal assets that secure nonrecourse borrowing. Any losses that are suspended under the at-risk rules are carried forward and are available during the post-termination transition period. The S stock basis limitations and at-risk limitations are applied before the passive activity limitations (see below).[54]

EXAMPLE 37

Shareholder Ricketts has a basis of $35,000 in his S corporation stock. He takes a $15,000 nonrecourse loan from a local bank and lends the proceeds to the S corporation. Ricketts now has a stock basis of $35,000 and a debt basis of $15,000. However, due to the at-risk limitation, he can deduct only $35,000 of losses from the S corporation. ■

Passive Losses and Credits. Section 469 provides that net passive losses and credits are not deductible when incurred and must be carried over to a year when there is passive income. Thus, one must be aware of three major classes of income, losses, and credits—active, portfolio, and passive. S corporations are not directly subject to the limits of § 469, but corporate rental activities are inherently passive, and other activities of an S corporation may be passive unless the shareholder(s) materially participate(s) in operating the business. An S corporation may engage in more than one such activity. If the corporate activity is rental or the shareholders do not materially participate, any passive losses or credits flow through. The shareholders are able to apply the losses or credits only against their income from other passive activities.

A shareholder's stock basis is reduced by passive losses that flow through to the shareholder, even though the shareholder may not be entitled to a current deduction due to the passive loss limitations. The existence of material participation is determined at the shareholder level. There are seven tests for material participation, including a need to participate in the activity for more than 500 hours during the taxable year.[55]

EXAMPLE 38

Heather is a 50% owner of an S corporation engaged in a passive activity. A nonparticipating shareholder, she receives a salary of $6,000 for services as a result of the passive activity. Heather has $6,000 of earned income as a result of the salary. The $6,000 salary creates a $6,000 deduction/passive loss, which flows through to the shareholders. Heather's $3,000

[52] § 1377(b)(1).

[53] § 1377(b).

[54] Reg. § 1.469–2T(d)(6).

[55] Reg. § 1.469–5T(a).

share of the loss may not be deducted against the $6,000 of earned income. Under § 469(e)(3), earned income is not taken into account in computing the income or loss from a passive activity. ■

LO.10

Compute the built-in gains tax.

TAX ON PRE-ELECTION BUILT-IN GAIN

Normally, an S corporation does *not* pay an income tax, since all items flow through to the shareholders. But an S corporation that was previously a C corporation may be required to pay a built-in gains tax, a LIFO recapture tax, or a passive investment income tax.

Without the **built-in gains tax** (§ 1374), it would be possible to avoid the corporate double tax on a disposition of appreciated property by electing S corporation status.

EXAMPLE 39

Zinnia, Inc., a C corporation, owns a single asset with a basis of $100,000 and a fair market value of $500,000. If Zinnia sells this asset and distributes the cash to its shareholders, there will be two levels of tax, one at the corporate level and one at the shareholder level. Alternatively, if Zinnia distributes the asset to shareholders, a double tax will still result, since a C corporation is taxed on an implicit gain in the distribution of the appreciated property. The shareholders have a dividend equal to the property's fair market value. In an attempt to avoid the double tax, Zinnia elects S corporation status. It then sells the asset and distributes the proceeds to shareholders. Without the § 1374 tax, the gain would be taxed only once, at the shareholder level. The distribution of the sales proceeds would be a tax-free reduction of the AAA. ■

The § 1374 tax generally applies to C corporations converting to S status after 1986. It is a *corporate-level* tax on any built-in gain recognized when the S corporation disposes of an asset in a taxable disposition within 10 calendar years after the date on which the S election took effect.

General Rules. The base for the § 1374 tax includes any unrealized gain on appreciated assets (e.g., real estate, cash basis receivables, and goodwill) held by a corporation on the day it elects S status. The highest corporate tax rate (currently 35 percent) is applied to the unrealized gain when any of the assets are sold. Furthermore, the gain from the sale (net of the § 1374 tax)[56] passes through as a taxable gain to shareholders.

EXAMPLE 40

Assume the same facts as in the preceding example. Section 1374 imposes a corporate-level tax that must be paid by Zinnia if it sells the asset after electing S status. Upon sale of the asset, the corporation owes a tax of $140,000 ($400,000 × 35%). The shareholders have a $260,000 taxable gain ($400,000 – $140,000). Hence, the built-in gains tax effectively imposes a double tax on Zinnia and its shareholders. ■

ETHICAL CONSIDERATIONS

A Helpful Appraisal

Scuba Unlimited, a diving center in Miami, Florida, is in the process of converting to S corporation status. Some of the company's assets are highly appreciated. Jason, the company's accountant, is familiar with the problems the § 1374 built-in gains tax can present. His cousin, a qualified appraiser, has agreed to "lowball" the appraisal of the S corporation's assets. How would you react in Jason's situation?

[56] § 1366(f)(2).

The maximum amount of gain that is recognized over the 10-year period is limited to the *aggregate net* built-in gain of the corporation at the time it converted to S status. Thus, at the time of the S election, unrealized gains of the corporation are offset by unrealized losses. The net amount of gains and losses sets an upper limit on the tax base for the built-in gains tax. Any appreciation after the conversion to S status is subject to the regular S corporation pass-through rules.

EXAMPLE 41

Quadrant, Inc., is a former C corporation whose first S corporation year began on January 1, 2005. At that time, Quadrant had two assets: X, with a value of $1,000 and a basis of $400, and Y, with a value of $400 and a basis of $600. The net unrealized built-in gain as of January 1, 2005, is $400. If asset X is sold for $1,200 during 2005, and asset Y is retained, the recognized built-in gain is limited to $400. The additional $200 of appreciation after electing S status is not part of the built-in gain. ■

Loss assets on the date of conversion reduce the maximum built-in gain and any potential tax under § 1374.[57] In addition, built-in losses and built-in gains are netted each year to determine the annual § 1374 tax base. Thus, an incentive exists to contribute loss assets to a corporation before electing S status. However, the IRS indicates that contributions of loss property within two years before the earlier of the date of conversion or the date of filing an S election are presumed to have a tax avoidance motive and will not reduce the corporation's net unrealized built-in gain.

EXAMPLE 42

Donna owns all the stock of an S corporation, which in turn owns two assets on the S conversion date: asset 1 (basis of $5,000 and fair market value of $2,500) and asset 2 (basis of $1,000 and fair market value of $5,000). The S corporation has a potential net realized built-in gain of $1,500 (i.e., the built-in gain of $4,000 in asset 2 reduced by the built-in loss of $2,500 in asset 1). However, if Donna contributed the loss asset to the corporation within two years before the S election, the built-in gain potential becomes $4,000; the loss asset cannot be used to reduce built-in gain. ■

The amount of built-in gain recognized in any year is limited to an "as if" taxable income for the year, computed as if the corporation were a C corporation. Any built-in gain that escapes taxation due to the taxable income limitation is carried forward and recognized in future tax years. Thus, a corporation can defer § 1374 tax liability whenever it has a low or negative taxable income.

EXAMPLE 43

Assume the same facts as in Example 41, except that if Quadrant were a C corporation, its taxable income in 2005 would be $300. The amount of built-in gain subject to tax in 2005 is $300. The excess built-in gain of $100 is carried forward and taxed in 2006 (assuming adequate C corporation taxable income in that year). There is no statutory limit on the carryforward period, but the gain would effectively expire at the end of the 10-year recognition period applicable to built-in gains.[58] ■

Gains on sales or distributions of all assets by an S corporation are presumed to be built-in gains unless the taxpayer can establish that the appreciation accrued after the conversion to S status. Thus, it may be advisable to obtain an independent appraisal when converting a C corporation to an S corporation. Certainly, a memorandum should be prepared listing the fair market values of all assets, along with the methods used to arrive at the values.

Normally, tax attributes of a C corporation do *not* carry over to a converted S corporation. For purposes of the tax on built-in gains, however, certain carryovers

[57] §§ 1374(c)(2) and (d)(1).

[58] Installment sale gains can be taxed more than ten years after the S election. § 1374(d)(7); Notice 90–27, 1990–1 C.B. 336.

Concept Summary 22–3

Calculation of the Built-in Gains Tax Liability

Step 1. Select the smaller of built-in gain or taxable income (C corporation rules).*
Step 2. Deduct unexpired NOLs and capital losses from C corporation tax years.
Step 3. Multiply the tax base obtained in step 2 by the top corporate income tax rate.
Step 4. Deduct any business credit carryforwards and AMT credit carryovers arising in a C corporation tax year from the amount obtained in step 3.
Step 5. The corporation pays any tax resulting from step 4.

*Any net recognized built-in gain in excess of taxable income is carried forward to the next year, as long as the next year is within the 10-year recognition period.

are allowed. In particular, an S corporation can offset built-in gains with unexpired NOLs or capital losses from C corporation years.

EXAMPLE 44

Maple Corporation elects S status, effective for calendar year 2005. Maple has a $10,000 NOL carryover when it elects S status. As of January 1, 2005, one of Maple's capital assets has a basis of $50,000 and a fair market value of $110,000. Early in 2006, the asset is sold for $110,000. Maple recognizes a $60,000 built-in gain when the asset is sold. However, Maple's NOL reduces the built-in gain from $60,000 to $50,000. Thus, only $50,000 is subject to the built-in gains tax. ■

EXAMPLE 45

An S corporation has a built-in gain of $100,000, taxable income of $90,000, and other items as shown below. The built-in gain tax liability is calculated as follows.

Lesser of taxable income or built-in gain	$ 90,000
Less: NOL carryforward from C year	(12,000)
Capital loss carryforward from C year	(8,000)
Tax base	$ 70,000
Highest corporate tax rate	× 0.35
Tentative tax	$ 24,500
Less: Business credit carryforward from C year	(4,000)
Built-in gains tax liability	$ 20,500

The $10,000 realized (but not taxed) built-in gain in excess of taxable income must be carried forward to the next year, as long as the next year is within the 10-year recognition period. ■

Concept Summary 22–3 summarizes the calculation of the built-in gains tax.

LIFO Recapture Tax. When a corporation uses the FIFO method for its last year before making the S election, any built-in gain is recognized and taxed as the inventory is sold. A LIFO-basis corporation does not recognize this gain unless the corporation invades the LIFO layer during the 10-year recognition period. To preclude deferral of gain recognition under LIFO, any LIFO recapture amount at the time of the S election is subject to a corporate-level tax.

The taxable LIFO recapture amount equals the excess of the inventory's value under FIFO over the LIFO value. No negative adjustment is allowed if the LIFO value is higher than the FIFO value. The resulting tax is payable in four equal installments, with the first payment due on or before the due date for the corporate return for the last C corporation year (without regard to any extensions). The remaining three installments must be paid on or before the due dates of the succeeding corporate returns. No interest is due if payments are made by the due dates, and no estimated taxes are due on the four tax installments. The basis of the LIFO inventory is adjusted to account for this LIFO recapture amount, but the AAA is not decreased by payment of the tax.

EXAMPLE 46

Engelage Corporation converts from a C corporation to an S corporation at the beginning of 2005. Engelage used the LIFO inventory method in 2004 and had an ending LIFO inventory of $110,000 (FIFO value of $190,000). Engelage must add $80,000 of LIFO recapture amount to its 2004 taxable income, resulting in an increased tax liability of $28,000 ($80,000 × 35%). Thus, Engelage must pay one-fourth of the tax (or $7,000) with its 2004 corporate tax return. The three succeeding installments of $7,000 each are paid with Engelage's next three tax returns. ■

LO.11

Compute the passive investment income penalty tax.

PASSIVE INVESTMENT INCOME PENALTY TAX

A tax is imposed on the excess passive income of S corporations that possess AEP from C corporation years. The tax rate is the highest corporate rate for the year (currently, 35 percent). The rate is applied to excess net passive income (ENPI), which is determined using the following formula:

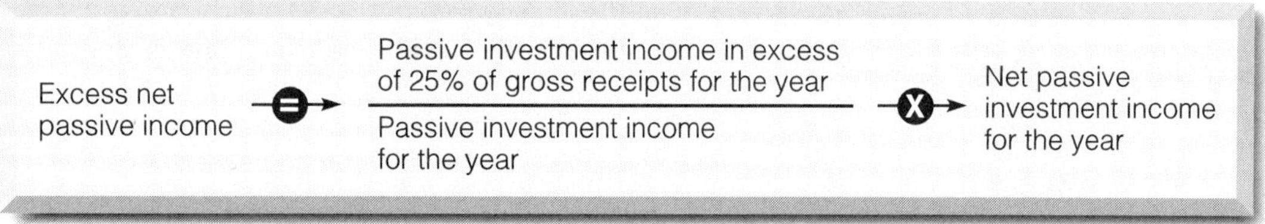

Passive investment income (PII) includes gross receipts derived from royalties, passive rents, dividends, interest, annuities, and sales and exchanges of stocks and securities.[59] Only the net gain from the disposition of capital assets (other than stocks and securities) is taken into account in computing gross receipts. Net passive income is passive income reduced by any deductions directly connected with the production of that income. Any passive income tax reduces the amount the shareholders must take into income.

The excess net passive income cannot exceed the C corporate taxable income for the year before considering any NOL deduction or the special deductions allowed by §§ 241–250 (except the organizational expense deduction of § 248).[60]

EXAMPLE 47

At the end of 2005, Barnhardt Corporation, an S corporation, has gross receipts totaling $264,000 (of which $110,000 is PII). Expenditures directly connected to the production of the PII total $30,000. Therefore, Barnhardt has net PII of $80,000 ($110,000 – $30,000), and its PII for tax year 2005 exceeds 25% of its gross receipts by $44,000 [$110,000 PII – (25% × $264,000)]. Excess net passive income (ENPI) is $32,000, calculated as follows.

$$\text{ENPI} = \frac{\$44{,}000}{\$110{,}000} \times \$80{,}000 = \$32{,}000$$

Barnhardt's PII tax for 2005 is $11,200 ($32,000 × 35%). ■

[59] § 1362(d)(3)(C)(i).
[60] §§ 1374(d)(4) and 1375(a) and (b).

OTHER OPERATIONAL RULES

Several other points may be made about the possible effects of various Code provisions on S corporations.

- An S corporation is required to make estimated tax payments with respect to tax exposure because of any recognized built-in gain and excess passive investment income.
- An S corporation may own stock in another corporation, but an S corporation may not have a C corporation shareholder. An S corporation is *not* eligible for a dividends received deduction.
- An S corporation is *not* subject to the 10 percent of taxable income limitation applicable to charitable contributions made by a C corporation.
- Any family member who renders services or furnishes capital to an S corporation must be paid reasonable compensation. Otherwise, the IRS can make adjustments to reflect the value of the services or capital.[61] This rule may make it more difficult for related parties to shift Subchapter S taxable income to children or other family members.
- Although § 1366(a)(1) provides for a flow-through of S items to a shareholder, it does not create self-employment income.[62] Compensation for services rendered to an S corporation is, however, subject to FICA taxes.

EXAMPLE 48

Cody and Dana each own one-third of a fast-food restaurant, and their 14-year-old son owns the other shares. Both parents work full-time in the restaurant operations, but the son works infrequently. Neither parent receives a salary this year, when the taxable income of the S corporation is $160,000. The IRS can require that reasonable compensation be paid to the parents to prevent the full one-third of the $160,000 from being taxed to the son. Otherwise, this would be an effective technique to shift earned income to a family member to reduce the total family tax burden. Furthermore, low or zero salaries can reduce FICA taxes due to the Federal government. ■

- An S corporation is placed on the cash method of accounting for purposes of deducting business expenses and interest owed to a cash basis related party.[63] Thus, the timing of the shareholder's income and the corporate deduction must match.
- The S election is not recognized by the District of Columbia and several states, including Michigan, New Hampshire, and Tennessee. Thus, some or all of the entity's income may be subject to a state-level income tax (e.g., a "sting tax" on large S corporations in Massachusetts).
- If § 1244 stock is issued to an S corporation, the S corporation and its shareholders may not treat losses on such stock as ordinary losses, notwithstanding § 1363, which provides that the taxable income of an S corporation must be computed in the same manner as that of an individual. However, an S corporation may issue § 1244 stock to its shareholders to obtain ordinary loss treatment.
- Losses may be disallowed due to a lack of a profit motive. If the activities at the corporate level are not profit motivated, the losses may be disallowed under the hobby loss rule of § 183.[64]

---

[61] § 1366(e). In addition, beware of an IRS search for the "real owner" of the stock under Reg. § 1.1373–1(a)(2).

[62] Rev.Rul. 59–221, 1959–1 C.B. 225.

[63] § 267(b).

[64] *Michael J. Houston*, 69 TCM 2360, T.C.Memo. 1995–159; *Mario G. De Mendoza, III*, 68 TCM 42, T.C.Memo. 1994–314.

Tax Planning Considerations

WHEN THE ELECTION IS ADVISABLE

Effective tax planning with S corporations begins with the determination of whether the election is appropriate. In this context, one should consider the following factors.

- Are losses from the business anticipated? If so, the S election may be highly attractive because these losses pass through to the shareholders.
- What are the tax brackets of the shareholders? If the shareholders are in high individual income tax brackets, it may be desirable to avoid S corporation status and have profits taxed to the corporation at lower C rates (e.g., 15 percent or 25 percent). However, the income still is not in the owner's hands.
- When the shareholders are in low individual income tax brackets, the pass-through of corporate profits is attractive, and reducing the combined income tax becomes the paramount consideration. Under these circumstances, the S election could be an effective tax planning tool. Although an S corporation usually escapes Federal taxes, it may not be immune from state and local taxes imposed on corporations or from several Federal penalty taxes.
- Does a C corporation have an NOL carryover from a prior year? Such a loss cannot be used in an S year (except for purposes of the built-in gains tax). Even worse, S years count in the 20-year carryover limitation. Thus, even if the S election is made, one might consider terminating the election before the carryover limitation expires. Such a termination would permit the loss to be utilized by what is now a C corporation.
- Both individuals and C corporations are subject to the alternative minimum tax. Many of the tax preference and adjustment items are the same, but some apply only to corporate taxpayers while others are limited to individuals. The alternative minimum tax adjustment relating to accumulated current earnings could create havoc with some C corporations (refer to Chapter 15). S corporations themselves are not subject to this tax.
- S corporations and partnerships have limited flexibility in the choice of a tax accounting period.[65]

The choice of the form of doing business often is dictated by other factors. For example, many businesses cannot qualify for the S election—due to the possibility of a public offering or a need for substantial capital inflow—or would find the partnership or limited liability company forms more practical. Therefore, freedom of action based on tax considerations may not be an attainable goal.

MAKING A PROPER ELECTION

Once the parties have decided the election is appropriate, it becomes essential to ensure that the election is made properly.

- Make sure all shareholders consent. If any doubt exists concerning the shareholder status of an individual, it would be wise to have that party issue a consent anyway.[66] Too few consents are fatal to the election; the same cannot be said for too many consents.
- Be sure that the election is timely and properly filed. Either hand carry the election to an IRS office or send it by certified or registered mail. The date used to determine timeliness is the postmark date, not the date the IRS receives the election. A copy of the election should become part of the corporation's permanent files.

[65] Entity tax-year constraints are discussed in Chapter 21.

[66] See *William B. Wilson*, 34 TCM 463, T.C.Memo. 1975–92.

- Be careful to ascertain when the timely election period begins to run for a newly formed corporation. An election made too soon (before the corporation is in existence) is worse than one made too late. If serious doubts exist as to when this period begins, filing more than one election might be considered a practical means of guaranteeing the desired result.
- It still is beneficial for an S corporation to issue § 1244 stock (refer to Chapter 18). This type of stock allows the original shareholder to obtain an ordinary deduction for a loss on the sale or worthlessness of the stock, rather than long-term capital loss treatment. Shareholders have nothing to lose by complying with § 1244.

PRESERVING THE ELECTION

Recall that an election can be lost intentionally or unintentionally in several ways and that a five-year waiting period generally is imposed before another S election is available. To preserve an S election, the following points should be kept in mind:

- As a starting point, all parties concerned should be made aware of the various transactions that lead to the loss of an election.
- Watch for possible disqualification of a small business corporation. For example, the death of a shareholder could result in a nonqualifying trust becoming a shareholder. The latter circumstance might be avoided by utilizing a buy-sell agreement or binding the deceased shareholder's estate to turn in the stock to the corporation for redemption or, as an alternative, to sell it to the surviving shareholders.[67]

PLANNING FOR THE OPERATION OF THE CORPORATION

Operating an S corporation to achieve optimum tax savings for all parties involved requires a great deal of care and, most important, an understanding of the applicable tax rules.

Accumulated Adjustments Account. Although the corporate-level accumulated adjustments account (AAA) is used primarily by an S corporation with accumulated earnings and profits (AEP) from a Subchapter C year, all S corporations should maintain an accurate record of the AAA. Because there is a grace period for distributing the AAA after termination of the S election, the parties must be in a position to determine the balance of the account.

EXAMPLE 49

Nobles, Inc., an S corporation, has no C corporation AEP. Over the years, Nobles made no attempt to maintain an accurate accounting for the AAA. In 2005, the S election is terminated, and Nobles has a grace period for distributing the AAA tax-free to its shareholders. A great deal of time and expense may be necessary to reconstruct the AAA balance in 2005. ■

When AEP is present, a negative AAA may cause double taxation of S corporation income. With a negative AAA, a distribution of current income restores the negative AAA balance to zero, but is considered to be a distribution in excess of AAA and is taxable as a dividend to the extent of AEP. Distributions during the year reduce the stock basis for determining the allowable loss for the year, but the

[67]Most such agreements do not create a second class of S stock. Rev.Rul. 85–161, 1985–2 C.B. 191; *Portage Plastics Co. v. U.S.*, 72–2 USTC ¶9567, 30 AFTR2d 72–5229, 470 F.2d 308 (CA–7, 1973).

An Abusive Tax Shelter?

During the 2004 presidential campaign, some tax practitioners pointed out that Democratic vice presidential candidate John Edwards had approximately $20 million of legal fees inside his S corporation in 1995. By paying himself a salary of only $360,000, he avoided paying almost $600,000 for the Medicare portion of FICA taxes (imposed at a rate of 2.9 percent).

There was considerable discussion of Edwards's tax situation in the media, and Vice President Dick Cheney mentioned the issue in the vice presidential debate. Reactions tended to follow the party affiliation of the commentator. In general, the $360,000 was probably less than reasonable compensation for Edwards (less than 2 percent of his legal fees), and the IRS could deem (i.e., recharacterize) any distributions as wages subject to the FICA and FUTA taxes.

Even one of Edwards's defenders said that if these funds were distributed to the senator, he "was making use of an alleged 'tax shelter' and the IRS would be quite justified in treating the distributions as salary." Another commentator said that it was somewhat hypocritical for Edwards to express concern about the solvency of Medicare and Social Security when he had engaged in what seemed to be an attempt to evade the Medicare tax.

loss does *not* reduce the stock basis for determining the tax status of distributions made during the year. In determining the tax treatment of distributions by an S corporation having AEP, any net adjustments (e.g., excess of losses and deductions over income) for the tax year are ignored.

The AAA bypass election may be used to reduce exposure to certain penalty taxes (e.g., the accumulated earnings tax or personal holding company tax) in post-S years. This bypass election allows AEP to be distributed instead.

EXAMPLE 50

Zebra, Inc., an S corporation during 2004, has a significant amount in its AEP account. The shareholders expect to terminate the election in 2005, when Zebra will be subject to the lower corporate income tax rates. Since Zebra as a C corporation may be subject to the accumulated earnings penalty tax in 2005, the shareholders may wish to use the AAA bypass election to distribute some or all of the AEP. Of course, any distributions of the AEP account in 2004 would be taxable to the shareholders. ■

A net loss allocated to a shareholder reduces the AAA. This required adjustment should encourage an S corporation to make annual distributions of net income to avoid the reduction of an AAA by a future net loss.

Salary Structure. The amount of salary paid to a shareholder-employee of an S corporation can have varying tax consequences and should be considered carefully. Larger amounts might be advantageous if the maximum contribution allowed for the shareholder-employee under the corporation's retirement plan has not been reached. Smaller amounts may be beneficial if the parties are trying to shift taxable income to lower-bracket shareholders, reduce payroll taxes, curtail a reduction of Social Security benefits, or restrict losses that do not pass through because of the basis limitation.

A strategy of decreasing compensation and correspondingly increasing distributions to shareholder-employees often results in substantial savings in employment taxes. However, a shareholder of an S corporation cannot always perform substantial services and arrange to receive distributions rather than compensation so that the corporation may avoid paying employment taxes. The IRS may deem the shareholder to be an employee, with any distributions recharacterized as wages subject to FICA and FUTA taxes.[68] In effect, the IRS requires that reasonable compensation be paid to shareholder-employees. For planning purposes, some level of compensation should be paid to all shareholder-employees to avoid any recharacterization of nonpassive distributions as deductible salaries—especially in personal service corporations.

The IRS can require that reasonable compensation be paid to family members who render services or provide capital to the S corporation. The IRS also can adjust the items taken into account by family-member shareholders to reflect the value of services or capital they provided. Refer to Example 48.

Unreasonable compensation traditionally has not been a problem for S corporations, but deductible compensation under § 162 reduces an S corporation's taxable income, which is relevant to the built-in gains tax. Compensation may be one of the larger items that an S corporation can use to reduce taxable income to minimize any built-in gains penalty tax. Thus, IRS agents may attempt to classify compensation as unreasonable to increase the § 1374 tax.

Loss Considerations. A net loss in excess of tax basis may be carried forward and deducted only by the same shareholder in succeeding years. Thus, before disposing of the stock, a shareholder should increase the basis of such stock/loan to flow through the loss. The next shareholder does not obtain the loss carryover.

Any unused loss carryover in existence upon the termination of the S election may be deducted only in the next tax year and is limited to the individual's *stock* basis (not loan basis) in the post-termination year.[69] The shareholder may wish to purchase more stock to increase the tax basis in order to absorb the loss.

The NOL provisions create a need for sound tax planning during the last election year and the post-termination transition period. If it appears that the S corporation is going to sustain an NOL or use up any loss carryover, each shareholder's basis should be analyzed to determine if it can absorb the share of the loss. If basis is insufficient to absorb the loss, further investments should be considered before the end of the post-termination transition year. Such investments can be accomplished through additional stock purchases from the corporation, or from other shareholders, to increase basis. This action ensures the full benefit from the NOL carryover.

EXAMPLE 51

A calendar year C corporation has an NOL of $20,000 in 2004. The corporation makes a valid S election in 2005 and has another $20,000 NOL in that year. At all times during 2005, the stock of the corporation was owned by the same 10 shareholders, each of whom owned 10% of the stock. Tim, one of the 10 shareholders, has an adjusted basis of $1,800 at the beginning of 2005. None of the 2004 NOL may be carried forward into the S year. Although Tim's share of the 2005 NOL is $2,000, the deduction for the loss is limited to $1,800 in 2005 with a $200 carryover. ■

Avoiding the Passive Investment Income Tax. Too much passive investment income (PII) may cause an S corporation to incur a § 1375 penalty tax

[68] Rev.Rul. 74–44, 1974–1 C.B. 287; *Spicer Accounting, Inc. v. U.S.*, 91–1 USTC ¶50,103, 66 AFTR2d 90–5806, 918 F.2d 90 (CA–9, 1990); *Radtke v. U.S.*, 90–1 USTC ¶50,113, 65 AFTR2d 90–1155, 895 F.2d 1196 (CA–7, 1990).

[69] § 1366(d)(3).

and/or terminate the S election. Several planning techniques can be used to avoid both of these unfavorable events. Where a small amount of AEP exists, an AAA bypass election may be appropriate to eliminate the AEP, thereby avoiding the passive income tax altogether. Alternatively, the corporation might reduce taxable income below the excess net passive income; similarly, PII might be accelerated into years in which there is an offsetting NOL. In addition, the tax can be avoided if the corporation manufactures needed gross receipts. By increasing gross receipts without increasing PII, the amount of PII in excess of 25 percent of gross receipts is reduced. Finally, performing significant personal services or incurring significant costs with respect to rental real estate activities can elevate the rent income to nonpassive.

EXAMPLE 52

An S corporation has paid a passive income penalty tax for two consecutive years. In the next year, the corporation has a large amount of AAA. If the AEP account is small, a bypass election may be appropriate to purge the corporation of the AEP. Without any AEP, no passive income tax applies, and the S election is not terminated. Any distribution of AEP to the shareholders constitutes taxable dividends, however.

Another alternative is to manufacture a large amount of gross receipts without increasing PII through an action such as a merger with a grocery store. If the gross receipts from the grocery store are substantial, the amount of the PII in excess of 25% of gross receipts is reduced. ■

Figure 22–2 shows four alternatives that a C corporation that intends to elect S treatment may use to reduce its tax liability.

FIGURE 22–2
Four Alternatives for Passive-Type C Corporations Electing S Treatment

Alternative 1: Eliminate AEP before the S election by paying dividends, which will be taxed at the 5/15% rate.
Alternative 2: Liquidate the C corporation and reincorporate as an S corporation. The AEP will not carryover to the S corporation after the liquidation.

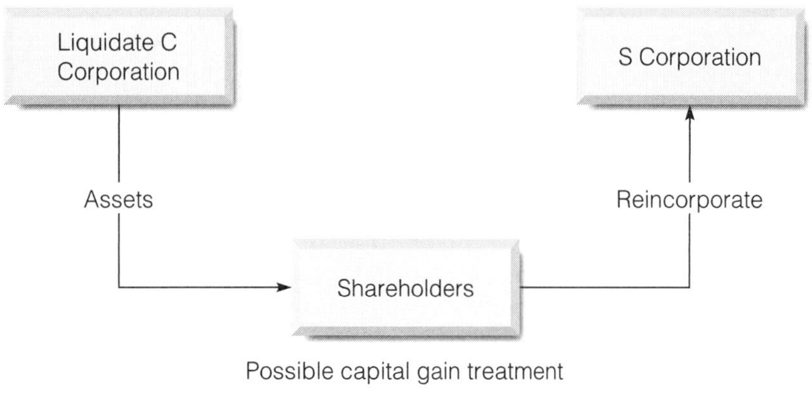

Liquidate C Corporation
S Corporation
Assets
Reincorporate
Shareholders
Possible capital gain treatment

Alternative 3: If the AEP amount is small, become an S corporation with possible built-in gains. Use a AAA bypass election to eliminate the AEP, which will be taxed at the 5/15% rate.
Alternative 4: Make an S election, but do not eliminate AEP. Use these techniques to avoid/reduce the passive investment income tax.

a. Reduce taxable income below excess passive income.
b. Accelerate PII into future years when there is an NOL.
c. Generate more gross receipts.
d. Perform significant services or incur significant costs if a rental type of business.

Managing the Built-in Gains Tax. A taxable income limitation encourages an S corporation to create deductions or accelerate deductions in the years that built-in gains are recognized. Although the postponed built-in gain is carried forward to future years, the time value of money makes the postponement beneficial. For example, payment of compensation, rather than a distribution, creates a deduction that reduces taxable income and postpones the built-in gains tax.

EXAMPLE 53

Mundy, Inc., an S corporation converted from a C corporation, has built-in gain of $110,000 and taxable income of $120,000 before payment of salaries to its two shareholders. If Mundy pays at least $120,000 in salaries to the shareholders (rather than a distribution), its taxable income drops to zero, and the built-in gains tax is postponed. Thus, Mundy needs to keep the salaries as high as possible to postpone the built-in gains tax in future years and reap a benefit from the time value of money. Of course, paying the salaries may increase the payroll tax burden if the salaries are below FICA and FUTA limits. ■

Giving built-in gain property to a charitable organization does not trigger the built-in gains tax. To reduce or eliminate the built-in gains tax, built-in *loss* property may be sold in the same year that built-in gain property is sold. Generally, the taxpayer should sell built-in loss property in a year when an equivalent amount of built-in gain property is sold. Otherwise, the built-in loss could be wasted.

EXAMPLE 54

Green Corporation elects S status effective for calendar year 2004. As of January 1, 2004, Green's only asset has a basis of $40,000 and a fair market value of $100,000. If this asset is sold for $120,000 in 2005, Green recognizes an $80,000 gain, of which $60,000 is subject to the corporate built-in gains tax. The other $20,000 of gain is subject to the S corporation pass-through rules and avoids the corporate income tax.

Unless the taxpayer can show otherwise, any appreciation existing at the time of the sale or exchange is presumed to be preconversion built-in gain. Therefore, Green incurs a built-in gain of $80,000 unless it can prove that the $20,000 gain developed after the effective date of the election. ■

Controlling Adjustments and Preference Items. The individual alternative minimum tax (AMT) affects more taxpayers than ever before, because the tax base has expanded and the difference between regular tax rates and the individual AMT rate has been narrowed. In an S corporation setting, tax preferences flow through proportionately to the shareholders, who, in computing the individual AMT, treat the preferences as if they were directly realized. Thus, the S corporation may not take advantage of the AMT exemption available to small corporations, but there is no ACE adjustment. Further, if an S corporation has a built-in gain under § 1374, the entity does not pay an AMT on the transaction (see Chapter 15).

A flow-through of tax preferences can be a tax disaster for a shareholder who is an "almost-AMT taxpayer." Certain steps can be taken to protect such a shareholder from being pushed into the AMT. For example, a large S corporation preference from tax-exempt interest on private activity bonds could adversely affect an "almost-AMT taxpayer." Certain adjustment and preference items are subject to elections that can remove them from a shareholder's AMT computation. Certain positive adjustments can be removed from a shareholder's alternative minimum taxable income base if the S corporation elects to capitalize and amortize certain expenditures over a prescribed period of time. These expenditures include excess intangible drilling and development expenditures, research and experimental costs, mining exploration and development expenditures, and circulation expenses.

Other corporate choices can protect an "almost-AMT shareholder." Using a slower method of cost recovery (rather than a more accelerated method) can be beneficial to certain shareholders. Many of these decisions and elections may generate conflicts of interest, however, with other shareholders who are not so situated and would not suffer from the flow-through of adjustments and tax preference items.

EXAMPLE 55

Tallis, Ltd., an S corporation, is owned equally by Ann, Bob, and Chris. Ann and Bob are subject to an aggregate 40% Federal and state marginal tax rate, while Chris is subject to the AMT. Tallis put the following into service this year:

- Depreciable assets: MACRS deductions per shareholder, $14,290; AMT cost recovery per shareholder, $10,714.
- Mine exploration costs: Regular tax deduction per shareholder, $30,000; AMT deduction per shareholder, $20,000.

Ann and Bob favor the larger regular tax deductions. Chris would like Tallis to elect to use the AMT deduction amounts for regular tax purposes. If the corporation does this, it eliminates the shareholders' related AMT adjustments for the lives of these assets. At the same time, the election does away with Chris's individual-level AMT on these items. Thus, Tallis's tax choice is between:

- Larger deductions at no AMT cost for Ann and Bob.
- Lower deductions and a higher tax basis for all shareholders, which would save Chris the related AMT. ■

Allocation of Tax Items. If a shareholder dies or stock is transferred during the taxable year, tax items may be allocated under the pro rata approach or the per-books method. Without the per-books election, a shareholder's pro rata share of tax items is determined by assigning an equal portion of each item to each day of the tax year and then dividing that portion pro rata among the shares outstanding on the transfer day.

With the consent of all affected shareholders and the corporation, an S corporation can elect to allocate tax items according to the permanent records using normal tax accounting rules. The allocation is made as if the taxable year consists of two taxable years. The first portion ends on the date of termination. On the day the shares are transferred, the shares are considered owned by the disposing shareholder. The selected method may be beneficial to the terminating shareholder and harmful to the acquiring shareholder. An election might result in a higher allocation of losses to a taxpayer who is better able to utilize the losses. In the case of the death of a shareholder, a per-books election prevents the income and loss allocation to a deceased shareholder from being affected by postdeath events.

Termination Aspects. It is always advisable to avoid accumulated earnings and profits (AEP) in an S corporation. There is the ever-present danger of terminating the election because of excess passive investment income in three consecutive years. Further, the § 1375 penalty tax is imposed on excess passive net income. Thus, one should try to eliminate such AEP through a dividend distribution or liquidation of the S corporation with a subsequent reincorporation. If the AEP account is small, to eliminate the problem, all of the shareholders may consent under § 1368(e)(3) to have distributions treated as made first from AEP rather than from the AAA (the AAA bypass election).

Liquidation of an S Corporation. S corporations are subject to many of the same liquidation rules applicable to C corporations (refer to Chapter 20). In general, the distribution of appreciated property to S shareholders in complete liquidation is treated as if the property were sold to the shareholders in a taxable transaction. Unlike a C corporation, however, the S corporation itself incurs no incremental tax on the liquidation gains, because such gains flow through to the shareholders subject only to the built-in gains tax of § 1374. Any corporate gain increases the shareholder's stock basis by a like amount and reduces any gain realized by the shareholder when he or she receives the liquidation proceeds. Thus, an S corporation usually avoids the double tax that is imposed on C corporations. However, when an S corporation liquidates, all of its special tax attributes disappear (e.g., AAA, AEP, PTI, C corporation NOLs, suspended losses).

OVERALL COMPARISON: FORMS OF DOING BUSINESS

See Concept Summary 22–4 for a detailed comparison of the tax consequences of the following forms of doing business: sole proprietorship, partnership, limited liability entity, S corporation, and regular corporation.

CONCEPT SUMMARY 22–4

Tax Attributes of Different Forms of Business (Assume Owners and Shareholders Are All Individuals)

	Sole Proprietorship	**Partnership/Limited Liability Entity***	**S Corporation**	**Regular (C) Corporation****
Restrictions on type or number of owners	One owner. The owner must be an individual.	Must have at least 2 owners.	Only individuals, estates, certain trusts, and certain tax-exempt entities can be owners. Maximum number of shareholders limited to 100 (spouses and family members treated as one shareholder).	None, except some states require a minimum of 2 shareholders.
Incidence of tax	Sole proprietorship's income and deductions are reported on Schedule C of the individual's Form 1040. A separate Schedule C is prepared for each business.	Entity not subject to tax. Owners in their separate capacity subject to tax on their distributive share of income. Entity files Form 1065.	Except for certain built-in gains and passive investment income when earnings and profits are present from C corporation tax years, entity not subject to Federal income tax. S corporation files Form 1120S. Shareholders are subject to tax on income attributable to their stock ownership.	Income subject to double taxation. Entity subject to tax, and shareholder subject to tax on any corporate dividends received. Corporation files Form 1120.
Highest tax rate	35% at individual level.	35% at owner level.	35% at shareholder level.	35% at corporate level plus 15%/5% on any corporate dividends at shareholder level (if qualified dividends; otherwise 35%).
Choice of tax year	Same tax year as owner.	Selection generally restricted to coincide with tax year of majority owners or principal owners, or to tax year determined under the least aggregate deferral method.	Restricted to a calendar year unless IRS approves a different year for business purposes or other exceptions apply.	Unrestricted selection allowed at time of filing first tax return.

	Sole Proprietorship	**Partnership/Limited Liability Entity***	**S Corporation**	**Regular (C) Corporation****
Timing of taxation	Based on owner's tax year.	Owners report their share of income in their tax year with or within which the entity's tax year ends. Owners in their separate capacities are subject to payment of estimated taxes.	Shareholders report their share of income in their tax year with or within which the corporation's tax year ends. Generally, the corporation uses a calendar year; but see "Choice of tax year" above. Shareholders may be subject to payment of estimated taxes. Corporation may be subject to payment of estimated taxes for any taxes imposed at the corporate level.	Corporation subject to tax at close of its tax year. May be subject to payment of estimated taxes. Dividends will be subject to tax at the shareholder level in the tax year received.
Basis for allocating income to owners	Not applicable (only one owner).	Profit and loss sharing agreement. Cash basis items of cash basis entities are allocated on a daily basis. Other entity items are allocated after considering varying interests of owners.	Pro rata share based on stock ownership. Shareholder's pro rata share is determined on a daily basis according to the number of shares of stock held on each day of the corporation's tax year.	Not applicable.
Contribution of property to the entity	Not a taxable transaction.	Generally, not a taxable transaction.	Is a taxable transaction unless the § 351 requirements are satisfied.	Is a taxable transaction unless the § 351 requirements are satisfied.
Character of income taxed to owners	Retains source characteristics.	Conduit—retains source characteristics.	Conduit—retains source characteristics.	All source characteristics are lost when income is distributed to owners.
Basis for allocating a net operating loss to owners	Not applicable (only one owner).	Profit and loss sharing agreement. Cash basis items of cash basis entities are allocated on a daily basis. Other entity items are allocated after considering varying interests of owners.	Prorated among shareholders on a daily basis.	Not applicable.
Limitation on losses deductible by owners	Investment plus liabilities.	Owner's investment plus share of liabilities.	Shareholder's investment plus loans made by shareholder to corporation.	Not applicable.
Subject to at-risk rules	Yes, at the owner level. Indefinite carryover of excess loss.	Yes, at the owner level. Indefinite carryover of excess loss.	Yes, at the shareholder level. Indefinite carryover of excess loss.	Yes, for closely held corporations. Indefinite carryover of excess loss.
Subject to passive activity loss rules	Yes, at the owner level. Indefinite carryover of excess loss.	Yes, at the owner level. Indefinite carryover of excess loss.	Yes, at the shareholder level. Indefinite carryover of excess loss.	Yes, for closely held corporations and personal service corporations. Indefinite carryover of excess loss.

	Sole Proprietorship	Partnership/Limited Liability Entity*	S Corporation	Regular (C) Corporation**
Tax consequences of earnings retained by entity	Taxed to owner when earned and increases his or her basis in the sole proprietorship.	Taxed to owners when earned and increases their respective interests in the entity.	Taxed to shareholders when earned and increases their respective bases in stock.	Taxed to corporation as earned and may be subject to penalty tax if accumulated unreasonably.
Nonliquidating distributions to owners	Not taxable.	Not taxable unless money received exceeds recipient owner's basis in entity interest. Existence of § 751 assets may cause recognition of ordinary income.	Generally not taxable unless the distribution exceeds the shareholder's AAA or stock basis. Existence of accumulated earnings and profits could cause some distributions to be dividends.	Taxable in year of receipt to extent of earnings and profits or if exceeds basis in stock.
Capital gains	Taxed at owner level with opportunity to use alternative tax rate.	Conduit—owners must account for their respective shares.	Conduit, with certain exceptions (a possible penalty tax)—shareholders must account for their respective shares.	Taxed at corporate level with a maximum 35% rate. No other benefits.
Capital losses	Only $3,000 of capital losses can be offset each tax year against ordinary income. Indefinite carryover.	Conduit—owners must account for their respective shares.	Conduit—shareholders must account for their respective shares.	Carried back three years and carried forward five years. Deductible only to the extent of capital gains.
§ 1231 gains and losses	Taxable or deductible at owner level. Five-year lookback rule for § 1231 losses.	Conduit—owners must account for their respective shares.	Conduit—shareholders must account for their respective shares.	Taxable or deductible at corporate level only. Five-year lookback rule for § 1231 losses.
Foreign tax credits	Available at owner level.	Conduit—passed through to owners.	Generally conduit—passed through to shareholders.	Available at corporate level only.
§ 1244 treatment of loss on sale of interest	Not applicable.	Not applicable.	Available.	Available.
Basis treatment of entity liabilities	Includible in interest basis.	Includible in interest basis.	Not includible in stock basis.	Not includible in stock basis.
Built-in gains	Not applicable.	Not applicable.	Possible corporate tax.	Not applicable.
Special allocations to owners	Not applicable (only one owner).	Available if supported by substantial economic effect.	Not available.	Not applicable.
Availability of fringe benefits to owners	None.	None.	None unless a 2%-or-less shareholder.	Available within antidiscrimination rules.

	Sole Proprietorship	Partnership/Limited Liability Entity*	S Corporation	Regular (C) Corporation**
Effect of liquidation/ redemption/reorganization on basis of entity assets	Not applicable.	Usually carried over from entity to owner unless a § 754 election is made, excessive cash is distributed, or more than 50% of the capital interests are transferred within 12 months.	Taxable step-up to fair market value.	Taxable step-up to fair market value.
Sale of ownership interest	Treated as the sale of individual assets. Classification of recognized gain or loss is dependent on the nature of the individual assets.	Treated as the sale of an entity interest. Recognized gain or loss is classified as capital under § 741 subject to ordinary income treatment under § 751.	Treated as the sale of corporate stock. Recognized gain is classified as capital gain. Recognized loss is classified as capital loss, subject to ordinary loss treatment under § 1244.	Treated as the sale of corporate stock. Recognized gain is classified as capital gain. Recognized loss is classified as capital loss, subject to ordinary loss treatment under § 1244.
Distribution of appreciated property	Not taxable.	No recognition at the entity level.	Recognition at the corporate level to the extent of the appreciation. Conduit—amount of recognized gain is passed through to shareholders.	Taxable at the corporate level to the extent of the appreciation.
Splitting of income among family members	Not applicable (only one owner).	Difficult—IRS will not recognize a family member as an owner unless certain requirements are met.	Rather easy—gift of stock will transfer tax on a pro rata share of income to the donee. However, IRS can make adjustments to reflect adequate compensation for services.	Same as an S corporation, except that donees will be subject to tax only on earnings actually or constructively distributed to them. Other than unreasonable compensation, IRS generally cannot make adjustments to reflect adequate compensation for services and capital.
Organization costs	Start-up expenditures are eligible for $5,000 limited expensing (subject to phaseout) and amortizing balance over 180 months.	Organization costs are eligible for $5,000 limited expensing (subject to phaseout) and amortizing balance over 180 months.	Same as partnership.	Same as partnership.
Charitable contributions	Limitations apply at owner level.	Conduit—owners are subject to deduction limitations in their own capacities.	Conduit—shareholders are subject to deduction limitations in their own capacities.	Limited to 10% of taxable income before certain deductions.
Alternative minimum tax	Applies at the owner level. AMT rates are 26% and 28%.	Applies at the owner level rather than at the entity level. AMT preferences and adjustments are passed through from the entity to the owners.	Applies at the shareholder level rather than at the corporate level. AMT preferences and adjustments are passed through from the S corporation to the shareholders.	Applies at the corporate level. AMT rate is 20%. Exception for small corporations.

	Sole Proprietorship	Partnership/Limited Liability Entity*	S Corporation	Regular (C) Corporation**
ACE adjustment	Does not apply.	Does not apply.	Does not apply.	The adjustment is made in calculating AMTI. The adjustment is 75% of the excess of adjusted current earnings over unadjusted AMTI. If the unadjusted AMTI exceeds adjusted current earnings, the adjustment is negative.
Tax preference items	Apply at owner level in determining AMT.	Conduit—passed through to owners who must account for such items in their separate capacities.	Conduit—passed through to shareholders who must account for such items in their separate capacities.	Subject to AMT at corporate level.

*Refer to Chapter 21 for additional details on partnerships and limited liability entities.
**Refer to Chapters 17 through 20 for additional details on regular corporations.

KEY TERMS

Accumulated adjustments account (AAA), 22–16

Accumulated earnings and profits, 22–15

Built-in gains tax (§ 1374), 22–26

Passive investment income (PII), 22–11

Previously taxed income (PTI), 22–17

S corporation, 22–2

Small business corporation, 22–5

Subchapter S, 22–2

Voluntary revocation, 22–10

PROBLEM MATERIALS

Discussion Questions

1. What are some tax differences between a partnership and an S corporation?
2. A current C corporation with NOL carryovers elects to be an S corporation. Can the S corporation use the NOL carryovers?
3. What are the major requirements to qualify for S corporation treatment?

Issue ID
Communications

4. Bob Roman, the major owner of an S corporation, approaches you for some tax planning help. He would like to exchange some real estate in a like-kind transaction under § 1031 for some other real estate that may have some environmental liabilities. Prepare a letter to Bob outlining your suggestion. Bob's address is 8411 Huron Boulevard, West Chester, PA 19382.

Issue ID

5. On March 2, 2005, the two 50% shareholders of a calendar year corporation decide to elect S status. One of the shareholders, Terry, purchased her stock from a previous shareholder (a nonresident alien) on January 18, 2005. Identify any potential problems for Terry or the corporation.
6. What are the characteristics of "straight debt" for purposes of avoiding second-class-of-stock treatment?

Communications

7. Elvis Samford calls you and says that his two-person S corporation was involuntarily terminated in February 2004. He asks you if they can make a new S election now, in November 2005. Draft a memo for the file outlining what you told Elvis.

8. How is a $120,000 long-term capital gain treated with respect to an S corporation and its 20% shareholder?

9. Using the categories in the following legend, classify each transaction as a plus (+) or minus (–) on Schedule M–2 of Form 1120S. An answer might look like one of these: "+AAA" or "–PTI."

Legend		
PTI	=	Shareholders' undistributed taxable income previously taxed
AAA	=	Accumulated adjustments account
OAA	=	Other adjustments account
NA	=	No direct effect on Schedule M–2

a. Receipt of tax-exempt interest income.
b. Unreasonable compensation determined.
c. Section 1245 recapture income.
d. Distribution of nontaxable income (PTI) from 1981.
e. Nontaxable life insurance proceeds.
f. Expenses related to tax-exempt securities.
g. Charitable contributions.
h. Business gifts in excess of $25.
i. Nondeductible fines and penalties.
j. Selling expenses.

Issue ID

10. Collett's S corporation has a small amount of accumulated earnings and profits (AEP), requiring the use of the more complex distribution rules. His accountant tells him that this AEP forces the maintenance of the AAA figure each year. Identify relevant tax issues facing Collett.

Communications

11. Caleb Hudson owns 10% of an S corporation. He is confused with respect to his AAA and stock basis. Write a brief memo dated November 1, 2005, to Caleb identifying the key differences between AAA and his stock basis.

12. For each of the following independent statements, indicate whether the transaction will increase (+), decrease (–), or have no effect (*NE*) on the adjusted basis of a shareholder's stock in an S corporation.
    a. Expenses related to tax-exempt income.
    b. Long-term capital gain.
    c. Nonseparately computed loss.
    d. Section 1231 gain.
    e. Depletion *not* in excess of basis.
    f. Separately computed income.
    g. Nontaxable return-of-capital distribution by the corporation.
    h. Selling expenses.
    i. Business gifts in excess of $25.
    j. Section 1245 gain.
    k. Dividends received by the S corporation.
    l. LIFO recapture tax at S election.
    m. Recovery of bad debt.
    n. Short-term capital loss.
    o. Corporate dividends out of AAA.

Issue ID

13. A C corporation that owns a subsidiary converts to an S corporation, but does not liquidate the subsidiary or convert it to a qualified Subchapter S subsidiary (QSSS). Several years later the subsidiary is liquidated. Point out any tax problems.

14. Explain how an S corporation may use unexpired NOLs or capital losses from C corporation years.

Decision Making

15. One of your clients is considering electing S status. Texas, Inc., is a six-year-old company with two equal shareholders, both of whom paid $30,000 for their stock. Going into 2005, Texas has a $110,000 NOL carryforward from prior years. Estimated income is $40,000 for 2005 and $25,000 for each of the next three years. Should Texas make an S election for 2005?

16. A corporation uses the LIFO method for its last year before making an S election. What effect will this have on any built-in gains tax?

Problems

17. An S corporation's profit and loss statement for 2005 shows net profits of $90,000 (book income). The corporation has three equal shareholders. From supplemental data, you obtain the following information about some items that are included in the $90,000.

Selling expenses	($ 21,200)
Municipal bond interest income	2,000
Dividends received on IBM stock	9,000
§ 1231 gain	6,000
§ 1245 gain	13,000
Recovery of bad debts	4,000
Long-term capital loss	(9,000)
Salary paid to owners (each)	(11,000)
Cost of goods sold	(97,000)

a. Determine nonseparately computed income or loss for 2005.
b. What would be the portion of taxable income or loss for Chang, one of the three shareholders?

18. Saul, Inc., a calendar year S corporation, incurred the following items for 2005.

Sales	$130,000
Municipal bond interest income	7,000
§ 1250 gain	12,000
Short-term capital gain	30,000
Cost of goods sold	(42,000)
Administrative expenses	(15,000)
Depreciation expense	(17,000)
Charitable contributions	(14,000)

Calculate Saul's nonseparately computed income.

19. Zebra, Inc., a calendar year S corporation, incurred the following items for 2005.

Sales income	$100,000
Cost of goods sold	(40,000)
Depreciation expense	(10,000)
Administrative expenses	(5,000)
§ 1231 gain	21,000
§ 1250 gain	20,000
Short-term capital loss from stock sale	(6,000)
Long-term capital loss from stock sale	(4,000)
Long-term capital gain from stock sale	15,000
Charitable contributions	(4,500)

Sammy is a 40% shareholder throughout the year.

a. Calculate Sammy's share of nonseparately computed income.
b. Calculate Sammy's share of the short-term capital loss.

20. Noon, Inc., a calendar year S corporation, is equally owned by Ralph and Thomas. Thomas dies on April 1 (not a leap year), and his estate selects a March 31 fiscal year. Noon has $400,000 of income for January 1 through March 31 and $600,000 for the remainder of the year.
    a. Determine how income is allocated to Ralph and Thomas under the pro rata approach.
    b. Determine how income is allocated to Ralph and Thomas under the per-books method.

21. Beginning in 2005, the AAA of Suresh, Inc., an S corporation, has a balance of $782,000. During the year, the following items occur.

Operating income	$472,000
Interest income	6,500
Dividend income	14,050
Municipal bond interest	6,000
Long-term capital loss from sale of land	(7,400)
§ 179 expense	(6,000)
Charitable contributions	(19,000)
Cash distributions	57,000

Calculate Suresh's ending AAA balance.

Decision Making

22. Goblins, Inc., a calendar year S corporation, has $90,000 of AEP. Tobias, the sole shareholder, has an adjusted basis of $80,000 in his stock with a zero balance in the AAA. Determine the tax aspects if a $90,000 salary is paid to Tobias.

Decision Making

23. Assume the same facts as in Problem 22, except that Goblins pays Tobias a $90,000 dividend.

24. Berger, Inc., a calendar year S corporation, is owned equally by three individuals: Adam, Bonnie, and Charlene. The company owns a plot of land, purchased for $110,000 three years ago. On December 3, 2005, when the land is worth $170,000, it is distributed to Charlene. Assuming Charlene's stock basis is $300,000 on the distribution date, what are the tax ramifications?

Decision Making
Communications

25. In 2005, Ourso, Inc., an S corporation with one shareholder, has a loss of $55,000 and makes a distribution of $70,000 to the shareholder, Bip Wallace. Bip's stock basis at the beginning of the year is $100,000. Write a memo dated October 21, 2005, to your manager discussing any problem that may result and the possible solution.

26. Fabrizius, Inc., an S corporation in Saint Cloud, Minnesota, had a balance in AAA of $100,000 and AEP of $55,000 on December 31, 2005. During 2006, Fabrizius distributes $70,000 to its shareholders, while sustaining a loss of $60,000. Determine any balance in the AAA and the AEP account.

27. At the beginning of the year, Malcolm, a 50% shareholder of a calendar year S corporation, has a stock basis of $22,000. During the year, the corporation has taxable income of $32,000. The following data are obtained from supplemental sources.

Dividends received from IBM	$12,000
Municipal bond interest income	18,000
Short-term capital gain	6,000
§ 1245 gain	10,000
§ 1231 gain	7,000
Charitable contributions	(5,000)
Political contributions	(8,000)

Short-term capital loss	($ 12,000)
Cash distributions to Malcolm	6,000
Selling expense	(14,000)
Beginning AAA	40,000

a. Compute Malcolm's ending stock basis.
b. Compute ending AAA.

28. Money, Inc., a calendar year S corporation in Denton, Texas, has two unrelated shareholders, each owning 50% of the stock. Both shareholders have a $400,000 stock basis as of January 1, 2005. At the beginning of 2005, Money has AAA of $300,000 and AEP of $600,000. During 2005, Money has operating income of $100,000. At the end of the year, Money distributes securities worth $1 million, with an adjusted basis of $800,000. Determine the tax effects of these transactions.

29. Assume the same facts as in Problem 28, except that the two shareholders consent to a AAA bypass election.

Issue ID

30. Red Dragon, Inc., is an S corporation with a sizable amount of AEP from a C corporation year. The S corporation has $400,000 of investment income and $400,000 of investment expenses in 2005. The company makes cash distributions to enable its sole shareholder to pay her taxes. What are the tax aspects to consider?

31. On January 1, Bobby and Alicia own equally all of the stock of an electing S corporation called Prairie Dirt Delight. The company has a $60,000 loss for the year (not a leap year). On the 219th day of the year, Bobby sells his half of the stock to his son, Bubba. How much of the $60,000 loss, if any, is allocated to Bubba?

32. Flower, Inc., an S corporation, has a $70,000 operating loss during the year (not a leap year). At the beginning of the year, Babe and Sally each own one-half of the stock. On the 219th day of the year, Babe sells her half of the stock to Sammie. How much of the ordinary loss flows through to Babe?

Communications

33. A calendar year S corporation has a taxable loss of $80,000 and a capital loss of $20,000. Ms. Muhammad owns 30% of the corporate stock and has a $24,000 basis in her stock. Determine the amounts of the taxable loss and capital loss, if any, that flow through to Ms. Muhammad. Prepare a tax memo for the files dated December 3, 2005.

34. Crew Corporation elects S status effective for tax year 2005. As of January 1, 2005, Crew's assets were appraised as follows.

	Adjusted Basis	Fair Market Value
Cash	$ 16,010	$ 16,010
Accounts receivable	-0-	55,400
Inventory (FIFO)	70,000	90,000
Investment in land	110,000	195,000
Building	220,000	275,000
Goodwill	-0-	93,000

In each of the following situations, calculate any built-in gains tax, assuming that the highest corporate tax rate is 35%. C corporation taxable income would have been $100,000.

a. During 2005, Crew collects $40,000 of the accounts receivable and sells 80% of the inventory for $99,000.
b. In 2006, Crew sells the land held for investment for $203,000.
c. In 2007, the building is sold for $270,000.

35. An S corporation in Polly Beach, South Carolina, has a recognized built-in gain of $95,000 and taxable income of $80,000. It holds a $7,000 NOL carryforward and a $9,000 business credit carryforward from a C corporation year. There are no earnings and profits from C corporation years. Calculate the built-in gains tax liability.

36. At the end of 2005, Brew, an S corporation, has gross receipts of $190,000 and gross income of $170,000. Brew has AEP of $22,000 and taxable income of $30,000. It has passive investment income of $100,000, with $40,000 of expenses directly related to the production of passive investment income. Calculate Brew's excess net passive income and any passive investment income penalty tax.

37. Savoy, Inc., in Auburn, Alabama, is an accrual basis S corporation with three equal shareholders. The three cash basis shareholders have the following stock basis at the beginning of 2005: Andre, $12,000; Crum, $22,000; and Barbara, $28,000. Savoy has the following income and expense items during 2005.

Net tax operating loss	($30,000)
Short-term capital gain	37,500
Long-term capital loss	(6,000)
Nondeductible fees and penalties	(3,000)

The electing corporation distributes $5,000 of cash to each of the shareholders during the tax year. Calculate the shareholders' stock bases at the end of 2005.

38. Yates Corporation in Cutoff, Louisiana, elects S status, effective for calendar year 2005. Yates' only asset has a basis of $50,200 and a fair market value of $110,400 as of January 1, 2005. The asset is sold at the end of 2005 for $130,800. What are the tax aspects of this transaction for Mark Farris, a 60% owner of the company?

Issue ID

39. Bonnie and Clyde each own one-third of a fast-food restaurant, and their 13-year-old daughter owns the other shares. Both parents work full-time in the restaurant, but the daughter works infrequently. Neither Bonnie nor Clyde receives a salary during the year, when the taxable income of the S corporation is $180,000. An IRS agent estimates that reasonable salaries for Bonnie, Clyde, and the daughter are $30,000, $35,000, and $10,000, respectively. What adjustments would you expect the IRS to impose upon these taxpayers?

Communications

40. Friedman, Inc., an S corporation, holds some highly appreciated land and inventory, and some marketable securities that have declined in value. It anticipates a sale of these assets and a complete liquidation of the company over the next two years. Arnold Schwartz, the CFO, calls you, asking how to treat these transactions. Prepare a tax memo dated June 18, 2005, indicating what you told Arnold over the phone.

41. Opal is the owner of all of the shares of an S corporation. In 2005, Opal is considering receiving a salary of $80,000 from the business. She will pay 7.65% FICA taxes on the salary, and the S corporation will pay the same amount of FICA tax. If Opal reduces her salary to $60,000 and takes an additional $20,000 as a distribution, how much total tax could be saved?

42. Blue Corporation elects S status effective for calendar year 2004. As of January 1, 2004, Blue holds two assets.

	Adjusted Basis	Fair Market Value
Land	$50,000	$110,000
IBM stock	55,000	40,000

Blue sells the land in 2005 for $120,000. Calculate Blue's recognized built-in gain, if any, in 2005.

Research Problems

Note: Solutions to Research Problems can be prepared by using the ***RIA Checkpoint® Student Edition*** *online research product, which is available to accompany this text. It is also possible to prepare solutions to the Research Problems by using tax research materials found in a standard tax library.*

Research Problem 1. Ewing Ballman owned a major league baseball team (the Rattlers), which was an S corporation. In 1994, Ballman sold 49% of his stock to Avon Fogel. Fogel also bought an option to purchase more of the stock. In 1998, Fogel purchased 2% more of the shares of the team, but later he encountered financial problems. In 2005, Ballman loaned $34 million to the team; then the Rattlers lent the money to Fogel, secured by his stock shares. Fogel's stock was auctioned off, but no acceptable bids were obtained. Fogel defaulted on the $34 million loan and signed a waiver allowing the Rattlers to take his stock and options. The Rattlers claimed that the collateral had no value and deducted the full amount of the loan. Ballman deducted the losses on his 2006 tax return. Do you agree with Ballman's action?

Research Problem 2. Charles, Inc., was a closely held C corporation engaged in the real estate rental business in 2003. The company had $6 million in passive activity losses. In 2004, Charles elected to be taxed as an S corporation, and the company sold a number of rental properties. May these suspended passive activity losses (PAL) be claimed as deductions under § 469(g)(1)(A)?

Recall that an S corporation cannot use carryforwards from a year in which it was a C corporation. If the PAL deductions are disallowed, may Charles readjust its cost basis in the sold property upward?

Internet Activity

Use the tax resources of the Internet to address the following question. Do not restrict your search to the World Wide Web, but include a review of newsgroups and general reference materials, practitioner sites and resources, primary sources of the tax law, chat rooms and discussion groups, and other opportunities.

Communications

Research Problem 3. Which types of trusts may be valid shareholders of an S corporation? Summarize your findings in a PowerPoint presentation for your classmates.

Exempt Entities

LEARNING OBJECTIVES

After completing Chapter 23, you should be able to:

LO.1
Identify the different types of exempt organizations.

LO.2
Enumerate the requirements for exempt status.

LO.3
Know the tax consequences of exempt status, including the different consequences for public charities and private foundations.

LO.4
Determine which exempt organizations are classified as private foundations.

LO.5
Recognize the taxes imposed on private foundations and calculate the related initial tax and additional tax amounts.

LO.6
Determine when an exempt organization is subject to the unrelated business income tax and calculate the amount of the tax.

LO.7
List the reports exempt organizations must file with the IRS and the related due dates.

LO.8
Identify tax planning opportunities for exempt organizations.

OUTLINE

General Considerations

Ideally, any entity that generates profit would prefer not to be subject to the Federal income tax. All of the types of business entities discussed thus far are subject to the Federal income tax at one level (e.g., sole proprietorships, partnerships, S corporations, and LLCs generally are subject only to single taxation) or more (e.g., C corporations are subject to double taxation). In contrast, organizations classified as **exempt organizations** may be able to escape Federal income taxation altogether.

Churches are among the types of organizations that are exempt from Federal income tax. Nevertheless, one must be careful not to conclude that everything labeled a church will qualify for exempt status.

During the 1970s and 1980s, a popular technique for attempting to avoid Federal income tax was the establishment of so-called mail-order churches. For example, in one scheme, a nurse obtained a certificate of ordination and a church charter from an organization that sold such documents.[1] The articles of incorporation stated that the church was organized exclusively for religious and charitable purposes, including a religious mission of healing the spirit, mind, emotions, and body. The nurse was the church's minister, director, and principal officer. Taking a vow of poverty, she transferred all her assets, including a house and car, to the church. The church assumed all of the nurse's liabilities, including the mortgage on her house and her credit card bills. The nurse continued to work at a hospital and deposited her salary in the church's bank account. The church provided her with a living allowance sufficient to maintain or improve her previous standard of living. She was also permitted to use the house and car for personal purposes.

The IRS declared that such organizations were shams and not bona fide churches. For a church to be tax-exempt under § 501(c)(3), none of its net earnings may be used to the benefit of any private shareholder or individual. In essence,

[1]Rev.Rul. 81–94, 1981–1 C.B. 330.

Tax-Exempts: Here Comes the IRS and Maybe Congress

Tax-exempts are facing inquiries on two fronts. First, the IRS is investigating about 2,000 tax-exempts to ascertain if they are overpaying their executives and officers. IRS audits of tax-exempts had fallen from 1,200 in 1990 to 200 in 1999.

On a related front, Senator Charles Grassley, Chairman of the Senate Finance Committee, is calling for (1) increased scrutiny of noncash donations to donor-advised funds and (2) new restrictions on insider transactions for family foundations.

A donor-advised fund enables a wealthy individual to make a lump-sum contribution, take an immediate tax deduction, and then direct which charities receive contributions and the timing of such contributions. Under the legislation Senator Grassley is considering proposing, contributions other than cash or publicly traded securities would have to be sold within one year of the gift, and grants to individuals would be prohibited.

Some 65,000 private family foundations control $500 billion in assets. Currently, a foundation may give the children and other members of the donor's family paid jobs and compensation as directors. Grassley's proposed legislation would either prohibit payments to family foundation directors or allow only minimal compensation. Travel and meal expenses for directors may also be limited. New restrictions on borrowing from family foundations may also result.

SOURCE: Adapted from Rob Wells, "IRS Inspects Family Foundations," *Wall Street Journal*, September 2, 2004, p. D2.

the organization should serve a public rather than a private interest. Though the courts have consistently upheld the IRS position, numerous avoidance schemes such as this have been attempted.

As discussed in Chapter 1, the major objective of the Federal tax law is to raise revenue. If revenue raising were the only objective, however, the Code would not contain provisions that permit certain organizations to be either partially or completely exempt from Federal income tax. Social considerations may also affect the tax law. This objective bears directly on the decision by Congress to provide for exempt organization tax status. The House Report on the Revenue Act of 1938 provides as follows:

> The exemption from taxation of money or property devoted to charitable and other purposes is based upon the theory that the Government is compensated for the loss of revenue by its relief from the financial burden which would otherwise have to be met by appropriations from public funds, and by the benefits resulting from the promotion of the general welfare.[2]

In recognition of this social consideration objective, Subchapter F (Exempt Organizations) of the Code (§§ 501–530) provides the authority under which certain organizations are exempt from Federal income tax. Exempt status is not open-ended in that two general limitations exist. First, the nature or scope of the organization may result in it being only partially exempt from tax.[3] Second, the organization may engage in activities that are subject to special taxation.[4]

[2]See 1939–1 (Part 2) C.B. 742 for a reprint of H.R. No. 1860, 75th Congress, 3rd Session.

[3]See the subsequent discussion of Unrelated Business Income Tax.

[4]See the subsequent discussions of Prohibited Transactions and Taxes Imposed on Private Foundations.

LO.1

Identify the different types of exempt organizations.

Types of Exempt Organizations

An organization qualifies for exempt status *only* if it fits into one of the categories provided in the Code. Examples of qualifying exempt organizations and the specific statutory authority for their exempt status are listed in Exhibit 23–1.[5]

LO.2

Enumerate the requirements for exempt status.

Requirements for Exempt Status

Exempt status frequently requires more than mere classification in one of the categories of exempt organizations. Many of the organizations that qualify for exempt status share the following characteristics.

- The organization serves some type of *common good*.[6]
- The organization is a *not-for-profit* entity.[7]
- *Net earnings* do not benefit the members of the organization.[8]
- The organization does not exert *political influence*.[9]

SERVING THE COMMON GOOD

The underlying rationale for all exempt organizations is that they serve some type of *common good*. However, depending on the type of the exempt organization, the term *common good* may be interpreted broadly or narrowly. If the test is interpreted broadly, the group being served is the general public or some large subgroup thereof. If it is interpreted narrowly, the group is the specific group referred to in the statutory language. One of the factors in classifying an exempt organization as a private foundation is the size of the group it serves.

NOT-FOR-PROFIT ENTITY

The organization may not be organized or operated for the purpose of making a profit. For some types of exempt organizations, the *for-profit prohibition* appears in the statutory language. For other types, the prohibition is implied.

NET EARNINGS AND MEMBERS OF THE ORGANIZATION

What uses are appropriate for the net earnings of tax-exempt organizations? The logical answer would seem to be that the earnings should be used for the exempt purpose of the organization. However, where the organization exists for the good of a specific group of members, such an open-ended interpretation could permit net earnings to benefit specific group members. Therefore, the Code specifically prohibits certain types of exempt organizations from using their earnings in this way.

> . . . no part of the net earnings . . . inures to the benefit of any private shareholder or individual.[10]

[5]Section 501(a) provides for exempt status for organizations described in §§ 401 and 501. The orientation of this chapter is toward organizations that conduct business activities. Therefore, the exempt organizations described in § 401 (qualified pension, profit sharing, and stock bonus trusts) are outside the scope of the chapter and are not discussed.

[6]See, for example, §§ 501(c)(3) and (4).

[7]See, for example, §§ 501(c)(3), (4), (6), (13), and (14).

[8]See, for example, §§ 501(c)(3), (6), (7), (9), (10), (11), and (19).

[9]See, for example, § 501(c)(3).

[10]§ 501(c)(6).

■ **EXHIBIT 23–1**
Types of Exempt Organizations

Statutory Authority	Brief Description	Examples or Comments
§ 501(c)(1)	Federal and related agencies.	Commodity Credit Corporation, Federal Deposit Insurance Corporation, Federal Land Bank.
§ 501(c)(2)	Corporations holding title to property for and paying income to exempt organizations.	Corporation holding title to college fraternity house.
§ 501(c)(3)	Religious, charitable, educational, scientific, literary, etc., organizations.	Boy Scouts of America, Red Cross, Salvation Army, Episcopal Church, United Fund, University of Richmond.
§ 501(c)(4)	Civic leagues and employee unions.	Garden club, tenants' association promoting tenants' legal rights in entire community, League of Women Voters.
§ 501(c)(5)	Labor, agricultural, and horticultural organizations.	Teachers' association, organization formed to promote effective agricultural pest control, organization formed to test soil and to educate community members in soil treatment, garden club.
§ 501(c)(6)	Business leagues, chambers of commerce, real estate boards, etc.	Chambers of Commerce, American Plywood Association, National Football League (NFL), Professional Golfers Association (PGA) Tour, medical association peer review board, organization promoting acceptance of women in business and professions.
§ 501(c)(7)	Social clubs.	Country club, rodeo and riding club, press club, bowling club, college fraternities.
§ 501(c)(8)	Fraternal beneficiary societies.	Lodges. Must provide for the payment of life, sickness, accident, or other benefits to members or their dependents.
§ 501(c)(9)	Voluntary employees' beneficiary associations.	Provide for the payment of life, sickness, accident, or other benefits to members, their dependents, or their designated beneficiaries.
§ 501(c)(10)	Domestic fraternal societies.	Lodges. Must not provide for the payment of life, sickness, accident, or other benefits; and must devote the net earnings exclusively to religious, charitable, scientific, literary, educational, and fraternal purposes.
§ 501(c)(11)	Local teachers' retirement fund associations.	Only permitted sources of income are amounts received from (1) public taxation, (2) assessments on teaching salaries of members, and (3) income from investments.
§ 501(c)(12)	Local benevolent life insurance associations, mutual or cooperative telephone companies, etc.	Local cooperative telephone company, local mutual water company, local mutual electric company.
§ 501(c)(13)	Cemetery companies.	Must be operated exclusively for the benefit of lot owners who hold the lots for burial purposes.
§ 501(c)(14)	Credit unions.	Other than credit unions exempt under § 501(c)(1).
§ 501(c)(15)	Mutual insurance companies.	Mutual fire insurance company, mutual automobile insurance company.
§ 501(c)(16)	Corporations organized by farmers' cooperatives for financing crop operations.	Related farmers' cooperative must be exempt from tax under § 521.
§ 501(c)(19)	Armed forces members' posts or organizations.	Veterans of Foreign Wars (VFW), Reserve Officers Association.
§ 501(c)(20)	Group legal service plans.	Provided by a corporation for its employees.
§ 501(d)	Religious and apostolic organizations.	Communal organization. Members must include pro rata share of the net income of the organization in their gross income as dividends.
§ 501(e)	Cooperative hospital service organizations.	Centralized purchasing organization for exempt hospitals.
§ 501(f)	Cooperative service organization of educational institutions.	Organization formed to manage universities' endowment funds.
§ 529	Qualified tuition program.	Prepaid tuition and educational savings program.
§ 530	Coverdell Education Savings Accounts.	Qualified education savings accounts.

Class-Action Lawsuits Challenge Differential Fees

If you have medical insurance, when a physician or hospital submits a claim for payment, you receive a statement from the insurance company showing the fee, the fee reduction, the amount paid by the insurance company, and the amount you owe. The fee reduction (i.e., the difference between the amount charged by the provider for the service and the amount the insurance company will pay for the service according to its fee schedule) can be a substantial amount.

If you do not have medical insurance, you are not eligible for the fee reduction and are expected to pay the full amount for the service. Some trial lawyers think this differential pricing is not appropriate for a tax-exempt entity. One such person is Richard Scruggs, the Mississippi lawyer who was one of the lead trial lawyers in the tobacco class-action settlement. Suits have been filed in eight states against about a dozen not-for-profit hospital systems challenging their exempt status under § 501(c)(3). About 85 percent of the 5,000 hospitals in the United States are not-for-profit entities.

A bright-line test for hospitals existed prior to 1969. To receive and maintain exempt status, a hospital had to provide free or discounted care to the poor. After the 1969 tax legislation, the test became more nebulous and now merely requires that the hospital "provide a community benefit."

At the state level, Illinois has revoked the exempt status of a prominent Catholic hospital located in Champaign-Urbana. The revocation decision was based on a determination by local authorities that the hospital was not a charitable institution in part because of the way it treated needy patients. The hospital has announced that it will appeal the state's revocation of its exempt status.

SOURCES: Adapted from "Lawsuits Challenge Charity Hospitals on Care for Uninsured," *Wall Street Journal*, June 17, 2004, p. B1; Lucette Lagnado, "Hospital Found 'Not Charitable' Loses Its Status as Tax Exempt," *Wall Street Journal*, February 19, 2004, p. B1.

In other instances, a statutory prohibition is unnecessary because the definition of the exempt organization in the Code effectively prevents such use.

> . . . the net earnings of which are devoted exclusively to religious, charitable, scientific, literary, educational, and fraternal purposes.[11]

ETHICAL CONSIDERATIONS

For the Good of the People

Matthew Sampson is the founder, and the man behind the throne, of the Church for Today television ministry. Ministry broadcasts originate from church services in California and New York and are transmitted via cable throughout the United States. Though the membership of the Church for Today is small (approximately 5,000 members), the typical member is quite wealthy. In addition to receiving contributions from its members, the church solicits and receives donations from viewers of the TV broadcasts. The church is tax-exempt under § 501(c)(3).

The stated mission of the church is religious in nature. However, Matthew firmly believes, as do the members of the board of deacons of the church, that certain societal goals must be accomplished for the prophecies of the church to come true (i.e., their divine being expects them to be active missionaries). Among its basic beliefs, the church advocates government control and possession of all guns, the legalization of drugs, abortion on demand once approved by the appropriate government agency, the withdrawal of all U.S. troops from foreign soil and the termination of all military

[11]§ 501(c)(10).

alliances, the abolition of capital punishment, and the availability of tuition-free university education to all U.S. citizens.

The ministers of the Church for Today are expected to include these basic beliefs, at the subliminal level, in their sermons. Some do so more effectively and more frequently than others, but all are required to do so. Matthew and the board of deacons are dismayed that American society has not adopted many of their beliefs.

Accordingly, Matthew proposes to the board of deacons that the church take a more proactive role. The employment contract of the ministers will now require them to include the basic beliefs in their sermons in an active manner. No longer can the beliefs just be incorporated subliminally. All the beliefs must be covered quarterly, and every sermon must present at least one of the basic beliefs. The ministers will encourage the church members and TV viewers to actively support these positions at both the state and Federal level.

As a new member of the board of deacons, you wholeheartedly support Matthew's position. However, you are concerned about the effects of this open advocacy of positions on the tax-exempt status of the church. Matthew responds that the "church has friends in high places" and assures you that the tax-exempt status will not be endangered. What should you do?

POLITICAL INFLUENCE

Religious, charitable, educational, etc., organizations are generally prohibited from attempting to influence legislation or participate in political campaigns. Participation in political campaigns includes participation both *on behalf of* a candidate and *in opposition to* a candidate.

Only in limited circumstances are such exempt organizations permitted to attempt to influence legislation. See the subsequent discussion under Prohibited Transactions.

LO.3

Know the tax consequences of exempt status, including the different consequences for public charities and private foundations.

Tax Consequences of Exempt Status: General

An organization that is appropriately classified as one of the types of exempt organizations is generally exempt from Federal income tax. Four exceptions to this general statement exist, however. An exempt organization that engages in a *prohibited transaction*, or is a so-called *feeder organization*, is subject to tax. If the organization is classified as a *private foundation*, it may be partially subject to tax. Finally, an exempt organization is subject to tax on its *unrelated business taxable income* (which includes unrelated debt-financed income).

In addition to being exempt from Federal income tax, an exempt organization may be eligible for other benefits, including the following.

- The organization may be exempt from state income tax, state franchise tax, sales tax, or property tax.
- The organization may receive discounts on postage rates.
- Donors of property to the exempt organization may qualify for charitable contribution deductions on their Federal and state income tax returns. However, *not* all exempt organizations are qualified charitable contribution recipients (e.g., gifts to the National Football League, PGA Tour, and Underwriters Laboratories are not deductible).

PROHIBITED TRANSACTIONS

Engaging in a prohibited transaction can produce three negative results. First, part or all of the organization's income may be subject to Federal income tax. Second and even worse, the organization may forfeit its exempt status. Finally, intermediate sanctions may be imposed on certain exempt organization insiders.

Failure to Continue to Qualify. Organizations initially qualify for exempt status only if they are organized as indicated in Exhibit 23–1. The initial qualification requirements then effectively become maintenance requirements. Failure to continue to meet the qualification requirements results in the loss of the entity's exempt status.

New Faith, Inc., is an excellent example of an exempt organization that failed to continue to qualify for tax exemption.[12] The stated purposes of the organization were to feed and shelter the poor. In its application for exempt status, New Faith indicated that it would derive its financial support from donations, bingo games, and raffles. The IRS approved the exempt status.

New Faith's only source of income was the operation of several lunch trucks, which provided food to the general public in exchange for scheduled "donations." Evidence provided by the organization to the Tax Court did not show that the food from the lunch trucks was provided free of charge or at reduced prices. In addition, no evidence was presented to show that the people who received food for free or at below-cost prices were impoverished or needy. The court concluded that the primary purpose of the activity was the conduct of a trade or business. It upheld the IRS's revocation of New Faith's exempt status.

Election Not to Forfeit Exempt Status for Lobbying. Organizations exempt under § 501(c)(3) (religious, charitable, educational, etc., organizations) are limited in their attempts to influence legislation (lobbying activities) and in participating in political campaigns.[13] Substantial lobbying or political activity can result in the forfeiture of exempt status.

Certain exempt organizations are permitted to engage in lobbying (but not political) activities that are greater than an insubstantial part of their activities, by making a § 501(h) election.[14] Eligible for the election are most § 501(c)(3) organizations (i.e., educational institutions, hospitals, and medical research organizations; organizations supporting government schools; organizations publicly supported by charitable contributions; certain organizations that are publicly supported by various sources including admissions, sales, gifts, grants, contributions, or membership fees; and certain organizations that support certain types of public charities).

An eligible § 501(c)(3) organization must make an affirmative election to participate in lobbying activities on a limited basis. The lobbying expenditures of electing organizations are subject to a ceiling. Exceeding the ceiling can lead to the forfeiture of exempt status. Even when the ceiling is not exceeded, a tax may be imposed on some of the lobbying expenditures (as discussed subsequently).

Two terms are key to the calculation of the ceiling amount: **lobbying expenditures** and **grass roots expenditures.** Lobbying expenditures are made for the purpose of influencing legislation through either of the following.

- Attempting to affect the opinions of the general public or any segment thereof.
- Communicating with any legislator or staff member or with any government official or staff member who may participate in the formulation of legislation.

Grass roots expenditures are made for the purpose of influencing legislation by attempting to affect the opinions of the general public or any segment thereof.

The statutory ceiling is imposed on both lobbying expenditures and grass roots expenditures and is computed as follows.

- 150% × lobbying nontaxable amount = lobbying expenditures ceiling.
- 150% × grass roots nontaxable amount = grass roots expenditures ceiling.

[12] *New Faith, Inc.*, 64 TCM 1050, T.C.Memo. 1992–601.

[13] § 501(c)(3). In recognition of the influence of technology, even a single Internet link to a partisan political site can taint the exempt entity.

[14] Religious organizations and private foundations cannot make this election.

■ **FIGURE 23–1**
Calculation of Lobbying Nontaxable Amount

Exempt Purpose Expenditures	Lobbying Nontaxable Amount Is
Not over $500,000	20% of exempt purpose expenditures*
Over $500,000 but not over $1 million	$100,000 + 15% of the excess of exempt purpose expenditures over $500,000
Over $1 million but not over $1.5 million	$175,000 + 10% of the excess of exempt purpose expenditures over $1 million
Over $1.5 million	$225,000 + 5% of the excess of exempt purpose expenditures over $1.5 million

*Exempt purpose expenditures generally are the amounts paid or incurred for the taxable year to accomplish the following purposes: religious, charitable, scientific, literary, educational, fostering national or international amateur sports competition, or the prevention of cruelty to children or animals.

The *lobbying nontaxable amount* is the lesser of (1) $1 million or (2) the amount determined in Figure 23–1.[15] The *grass roots nontaxable amount* is 25 percent of the lobbying nontaxable amount.[16]

A tax may be assessed on an electing exempt organization's **excess lobbying expenditures** as follows.[17]

- 25% × excess lobbying expenditures = tax liability.

Excess lobbying expenditures are the greater of the following.[18]

- Excess of the lobbying expenditures for the taxable year over the lobbying nontaxable amount.
- Excess of the grass roots expenditures for the taxable year over the grass roots nontaxable amount.

EXAMPLE 1

Tan, Inc., a qualifying § 501(c)(3) organization, incurs lobbying expenditures of $500,000 for the taxable year and grass roots expenditures of $0. Exempt purpose expenditures for the taxable year are $5 million. Tan elects to be eligible to make lobbying expenditures on a limited basis.

Applying the data in Figure 23–1, the lobbying nontaxable amount is $400,000 [$225,000 + 5%($5,000,000 – $1,500,000)]. The ceiling on lobbying expenditures is $600,000 (150% × $400,000). Therefore, the $500,000 of lobbying expenditures are under the permitted $600,000. However, the election results in the imposition of tax on the excess lobbying expenditures of $100,000 ($500,000 lobbying expenditures – $400,000 lobbying nontaxable amount). The resulting tax liability is $25,000 ($100,000 × 25%). ■

A § 501(c)(3) organization that makes disqualifying lobbying expenditures is subject to a 5 percent tax on the lobbying expenditures for the taxable year. A 5 percent tax may also be levied on the organization's management. The tax is imposed on management only if the managers knew that making the expenditures was likely to result in the organization no longer qualifying under § 501(c)(3) and if the managers' actions were willful and not due to reasonable cause. The tax does not apply to private foundations (see the subsequent discussion).[19]

Concept Summary 23–1 capsulizes the rules on influencing legislation.

Intermediate Sanctions. Prior to 1996, the IRS had only two options available for dealing with exempt organizations (other than private foundations) engaging in prohibited transactions. First, it could attempt to subject part or all of the organization's

[15]§ 4911(c)(2).
[16]§ 4911(c)(4).
[17]§ 4911(a)(1).
[18]§ 4911(b).
[19]§ 4912.

Concept Summary 23–1

Exempt Organizations and Influencing Legislation

Factor	Tax Result
Entity subject to rule	§ 501(c)(3) organization.
Effect of influencing legislation	Subject to tax on lobbying expenditures under § 4912. Forfeit exempt status under § 501(c)(3). Not eligible for exempt status under § 501(c)(4).
Effect of electing to make lobbying expenditures	Permitted to make limited lobbying expenditures. Subject to tax under § 4911.

income to Federal income tax. Second, it could revoke the exempt status of the organization. For private foundations, an additional option was available. The IRS could impose certain taxes on private foundations for engaging in so-called prohibited transactions (see Concept Summary 23–3 later in the chapter).

Tax legislation enacted in 1996 added another option to the IRS toolbox—**intermediate sanctions**—for so-called public charities.[20] The intermediate sanctions take the form of excise taxes imposed on disqualified persons (any individuals who are in a position to exercise substantial influence over the affairs of the organization) who engage in *excess benefit transactions* and on exempt organization managers who participate in such a transaction knowing that it is improper. Such excess benefit transactions include transactions in which a disqualified person engages in a non-fair-market-value transaction with the exempt organization or receives unreasonable compensation.

The excise tax on the disqualified person is imposed at a rate of 25 percent of the excess benefit. For the exempt organization manager, the excise tax is imposed at a rate of 10 percent of the excess benefit (unless such participation is not willful and is due to reasonable cause) with a statutory ceiling of $10,000 for any excess benefit transaction. These excise taxes are referred to as first-level taxes.

A second-level tax is imposed on the disqualified person if the excess benefit transaction is not corrected within the taxable period. This excise tax is imposed at a rate of 200 percent of the excess benefit.

FEEDER ORGANIZATIONS

A **feeder organization** carries on a trade or business for the benefit of an exempt organization (i.e., it remits its profits to the exempt organization). Such organizations are not exempt from Federal income tax. This provision is intended to prevent an entity whose primary purpose is to conduct a trade or business for profit from escaping taxation merely because all of its profits are payable to one or more exempt organizations.[21]

Some income and activities are *not* subject to the feeder organization rules:[22]

- Rent income that would be excluded from the definition of the term *rent* for purposes of the unrelated business income tax (discussed subsequently).
- A trade or business where substantially all the work is performed by volunteers.
- The trade or business of selling merchandise where substantially all the merchandise has been received as contributions or gifts.

Concept Summary 23–2 highlights the consequences of exempt status.

[20] § 4958.
[21] § 502(a).
[22] § 502(b).

Concept Summary 23–2

Consequences of Exempt Status

General	Exempt from Federal income tax. Exempt from most state and local income, franchise, sales, and property taxes. Qualify for reductions in postage rates. Gifts to the organization often can be deducted by donor.
Exceptions	May be subject to Federal income tax associated with the following. • Engaging in a prohibited transaction. • Being a feeder organization. • Being a private foundation. • Generating unrelated business taxable income.

Private Foundations

TAX CONSEQUENCES OF PRIVATE FOUNDATION STATUS

Certain exempt organizations are classified as **private foundations.** This classification produces two negative consequences. First, the classification may have an adverse impact on the contributions received by the donee exempt organization. Contributions may decline because the tax consequences for donors may not be as favorable as if the entity were not a private foundation.[23] Second, the classification may result in taxation at the exempt organization level. The reason for this less beneficial tax treatment is that private foundations define common good more narrowly and therefore are seen as not being supported by, and operated for the good of, the public.

ETHICAL CONSIDERATIONS

A Charity Documents the Value of Charitable Contributions

For the past three years, Helping the Poor, a private foundation, has been running radio and newspaper advertisements actively encouraging people to donate old cars and trucks to the foundation.

For the past 18 months, Helping the Poor has used the following procedure when it receives a donated automobile. If the vehicle is running, Helping the Poor gives the donor a receipt for the "blue book" value of the vehicle. If the vehicle is not running, it provides a receipt based on an appraisal. Providing such receipts has resulted in a substantial increase in the number of donated vehicles. Since Helping the Poor has no automobile facilities, it has made an arrangement with an automobile broker who sells the vehicles and receives 75 percent of the actual sales proceeds. The vehicles typically sell for about 70 percent of the "blue book" value or 90 percent of the appraisal.

You are a CPA and a new board member for Helping the Poor. Evaluate the organization's automobile donation program for 2005 and for prior years.

LO.4

Determine which exempt organizations are classified as private foundations.

Definition of a Private Foundation. The following § 501(c)(3) organizations are *not* private foundations.[24]

1. Churches; educational institutions; hospitals and medical research organizations; charitable organizations receiving a major portion of their support from the general public or the United States, a state, or a political subdivision

[23] § 170(e)(1)(B)(ii).

[24] § 509(a).

thereof that is operated for the benefit of a college or university; and governmental units (favored activities category).
2. Organizations that are broadly supported by the general public (excluding disqualified persons), by governmental units, or by organizations described in (1) above.
3. Entities organized and operated exclusively for the benefit of organizations described in (1) or (2) (a supporting organization).
4. Entities organized and operated exclusively for testing for public safety.

To meet the broadly supported requirement in (2) above, both the following tests must be satisfied.

- External support test.
- Internal support test.

Under the *external support test,* more than one-third of the organization's support each taxable year *normally* must come from the three groups listed in (2) above, in the following forms.

- Gifts, grants, contributions, and membership fees.
- Gross receipts from admissions, sales of merchandise, performance of services, or the furnishing of facilities in an activity that is not an unrelated trade or business for purposes of the unrelated business income tax (discussed subsequently). However, such gross receipts from any person or governmental agency in excess of the greater of $5,000 or 1 percent of the organization's support for the taxable year are not counted.

The *internal support test* limits the amount of support *normally* received from the following sources to one-third of the organization's support for the taxable year.[25]

- Gross investment income (gross income from interest, dividends, rents, and royalties).
- Unrelated business taxable income (discussed subsequently) minus the related tax.

EXAMPLE 2

Lion, Inc., a § 501(c)(3) organization, received the following support during the taxable year.

Governmental unit A for services rendered	$ 30,000
Governmental unit B for services rendered	20,000
General public for services rendered	20,000
Gross investment income	15,000
Contributions from individual substantial contributors (disqualified persons)	15,000
	$100,000

For purposes of the *external support test,* the support from A is counted only to the extent of $5,000 (greater of $5,000 or 1% of $100,000 support). Likewise, for B, only $5,000 is counted as support. Thus, the total countable support is $30,000 ($20,000 from the general public + $5,000 + $5,000), and Lion fails the test for the taxable year ($30,000/$100,000 = 30%; need more than 33.3%). The $15,000 received from disqualified persons is excluded from the numerator but is included in the denominator.

In calculating the *internal support test,* only the gross investment income of $15,000 is included in the numerator. Thus, the test is satisfied ($15,000/$100,000 = 15%; cannot exceed 33.3%) for the taxable year.

Since Lion did not satisfy both tests, it does not qualify as an organization that is broadly supported. ■

[25] Reg. § 1.509(a)–3(c) generally requires that the external and internal support tests be met in each of the four preceding tax years.

A Major Contribution to the Salvation Army

When the wealthy decide to make substantial charitable contributions, they normally do so by establishing private foundations. Examples of such private foundations are the Carnegie Foundation, the Ford Foundation, the Bill and Melinda Gates Foundation, the David and Lucile Packard Foundation, and the William and Flora Hewlett Foundation. By so doing, the donors can exert significant control over the timing and amounts expended for particular charitable purposes.

Joan Kroc, the widow of the founder of McDonald's, decided to follow a different approach in her charitable giving. In her pre-death estate planning, she specified that her estate make a one-time cash gift of $1.5 billion to the Salvation Army to build and operate community centers around the country. Other recipients of Mrs. Kroc's largess include National Public Radio ($200 million), Ronald McDonald Houses ($60 million), University of Notre Dame ($50 million), University of San Diego ($50 million), San Diego Hospice ($20 million), and San Diego Opera ($10 million).

SOURCE: Adapted from Shirley Leung, "Salvation Army Gets $1.5 Billion from Kroc Estate," *Wall Street Journal*, January 20, 2004, p. A1.

The intent of the two tests is to exclude from private foundation status those § 501(c)(3) organizations that are responsive to the general public rather than to the private interests of a limited number of donors or other persons.

Examples of § 501(c)(3) organizations that would be classified as private foundations, except that they receive broad public support, include the United Fund, the Boy Scouts, university alumni associations, and symphony orchestras.

LO.5

Recognize the taxes imposed on private foundations and calculate the related initial tax and additional tax amounts.

TAXES IMPOSED ON PRIVATE FOUNDATIONS

In general, a private foundation is exempt from Federal income tax. However, because a private foundation is usually not a broadly, publicly supported organization, it may be subject to the following taxes.[26]

- Tax based on investment income.
- Tax on self-dealing.
- Tax on failure to distribute income.
- Tax on excess business holdings.
- Tax on investments that jeopardize charitable purposes.
- Tax on taxable expenditures.

These taxes serve to restrict the permitted activities of private foundations. Two levels of tax may be imposed on the private foundation and the foundation manager: an initial tax and an additional tax. The initial taxes (first-level), with the exception of the tax based on investment income, are imposed because the private foundation engages in so-called *prohibited transactions*. The additional taxes (second-level) are imposed only if the prohibited transactions are not modified within a statutory time period.[27] See Concept Summary 23–3 for additional details.

The tax on a failure to distribute income will be used to illustrate how expensive these taxes can be and the related importance of avoiding their imposition. For failure to distribute a sufficient portion of a private nonoperating foundation's

[26] §§ 4940–4945.

[27] § 4961.

Concept Summary 23–3

Taxes Imposed on Private Foundations

			Private Foundation		Foundation Manager	
Type of Tax	**Code Section**	**Purpose**	**Initial Tax**	**Additional Tax**	**Initial Tax**	**Additional Tax**
On investment income	§ 4940	Audit fee to defray IRS expenses.	2%*			
On self-dealing	§ 4941	Engaging in transactions with disqualified persons.	5%**	200%**	2.5%†	50%†
On failure to distribute income	§ 4942	Failing to distribute adequate amount of income for exempt purposes.	15%	100%		
On excess business holdings	§ 4943	Investments that enable the private foundation to control unrelated businesses.	5%	200%		
On jeopardizing investments	§ 4944	Speculative investments that put the private foundation's assets at risk.	5%	25%	5%††	5%†
On taxable expenditures	§ 4945	Expenditures that should not be made by private foundations.	10%	100%	2.5%††	50%†

*May be possible to reduce the tax rate to 1%. In addition, an exempt operating foundation [see §§ 4940(d)(2) and 4942(j)(3)] is not subject to the tax.
**Imposed on the disqualified person rather than the foundation.
†Subject to a statutory ceiling of $10,000.
††Subject to a statutory ceiling of $5,000.

income, both an initial tax (first-level) and an additional tax (second-level) may be imposed. The initial tax is imposed at a rate of 15 percent on the income for the taxable year that is not distributed during the current or the following taxable year. The initial tax is imposed on the undistributed income for each year until the IRS assesses the tax.

The additional tax is imposed at a rate of 100 percent on the amount of the inadequate distribution that is not distributed by the assessment date. The additional tax is effectively waived if the undistributed income is distributed within 90 days after the mailing of the deficiency notice for the additional tax. Extensions of this period may be obtained.

Undistributed income is the excess of the distributable amount (in effect, the amount that should have been distributed) over qualifying distributions made by the entity. The distributable amount is the excess of the minimum investment return over the sum of the (1) unrelated business income tax and (2) the excise tax based on net investment income.[28] The minimum investment return is 5 percent of the excess of the fair market value of the foundation's assets over the unpaid debt associated with acquiring or improving these assets. Assets of the foundation that are employed directly in carrying on the foundation's exempt purpose are not used in making this calculation.

[28] § 4940.

■ EXHIBIT 23–2
Exempt Organizations: Classification

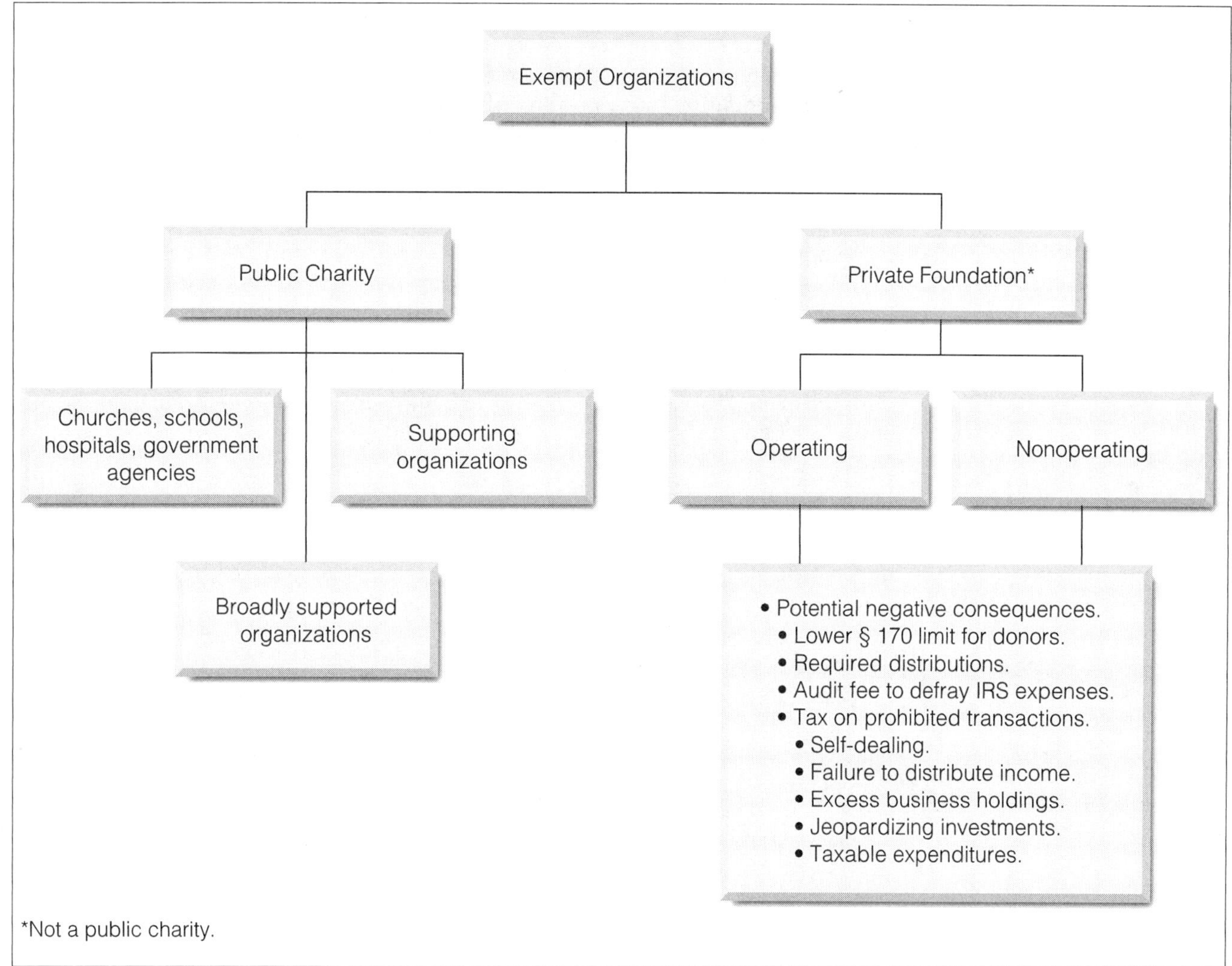

EXAMPLE 3

Gold, Inc., a private foundation, has undistributed income of $80,000 for the taxable year 2002. It distributes $15,000 of this amount during 2003 and an additional $45,000 during 2004. The IRS deficiency notice is mailed to Gold on August 5, 2005. The initial tax is $12,750 [($65,000 × 15%) + ($20,000 × 15%)].

At the date of the deficiency notice, no additional distributions have been made from the 2002 undistributed income. Therefore, since the remaining undistributed income of $20,000 has not been distributed by August 5, 2005, an additional tax of $20,000 ($20,000 × 100%) is imposed.

If Gold distributes the $20,000 of undistributed income for 2002 within 90 days of the deficiency notice, the additional tax is waived. Without this distribution, however, the foundation will owe $32,750 ($12,750 + $20,000) in taxes. ■

Exhibit 23–2 shows the classifications of exempt organizations and indicates the potential negative consequences of classification as a private foundation.

LO.6

Determine when an exempt organization is subject to the unrelated business income tax and calculate the amount of the tax.

Unrelated Business Income Tax

As explained in the previous section, private foundations are subject to excise taxes for certain actions. One of these excise taxes penalizes the private foundation for using the foundation to gain control of unrelated businesses (tax on excess business holdings). However, *unrelated business* has different meanings for purposes of that excise tax and for the unrelated business income tax.

The **unrelated business income tax (UBIT)** is designed to treat the entity as if it were subject to the corporate income tax. Thus, the rates that are used are those applicable to a corporate taxpayer.[29] In general, **unrelated business income** is derived from activities not related to the exempt purpose of the exempt organization. The tax is levied because the organization is engaging in substantial commercial activities.[30] Without such a tax, nonexempt organizations (regular taxable business entities) would be at a substantial disadvantage when trying to compete with the exempt organization. Thus, the UBIT is intended to neutralize the exempt entity's tax advantage.[31]

EXAMPLE 4

Historic, Inc., is an exempt private foundation. Its exempt activity is to maintain a restoration of eighteenth-century colonial life (houses, public buildings, taverns, businesses, and craft demonstrations) that is visited by more than a million people each year. A fee is charged for admission to the "restored area." In addition to this "museum" activity, Historic operates two hotels and three restaurants that are available to the general public. The earnings from the hotel and restaurant businesses are used to defray the costs of operating the "museum" activity.

The "museum" activity is not subject to the Federal income tax, except to the extent of any tax liability for any of the aforementioned excise taxes that are levied on private foundations. However, even though the income from the hotel and restaurant businesses is used for exempt purposes, that income is unrelated business income and is subject to the UBIT. ■

The UBIT applies to all organizations that are exempt from Federal income tax under § 501(c), except Federal agencies. In addition, the tax applies to state colleges and universities.[32]

A materiality exception generally exempts an entity from being subject to the UBIT if such income is insignificant. See the later discussion of the $1,000 statutory deduction generally available to all exempt organizations.

UNRELATED TRADE OR BUSINESS

An exempt organization may be subject to the UBIT in the following circumstances.[33]

- The organization conducts a trade or business.
- The trade or business is not substantially related to the exempt purpose of the organization.
- The trade or business is regularly carried on by the organization.

The Code specifically exempts the following activities from classification as an unrelated trade or business. Thus, even if all of the above factors are present, the activity is not classified as an unrelated trade or business.

- The individuals performing substantially all the work of the trade or business do so without compensation (e.g., an orphanage operates a retail store for sales to the general public, and all the work is done by volunteers).

[29] § 511(a)(1).
[30] § 512(a)(1).
[31] Reg. § 1.513–1(b).
[32] § 511(a)(2) and Reg. § 1.511–2(a)(2).
[33] § 513(a) and Reg. § 1.513–2(a).

- The trade or business consists of selling merchandise, and substantially all of the merchandise has been received as gifts or contributions (e.g., thrift shops).
- For § 501(c)(3) organizations and for state colleges or universities, the trade or business is conducted primarily for the convenience of the organization's members, students, patients, officers, or employees (e.g., a laundry operated by the college for laundering dormitory linens and students' clothing, a college bookstore).
- For most employee unions, the trade or business consists of selling to members, at their usual place of employment, work-related clothing and equipment and items normally sold through vending machines, snack bars, or food dispensing facilities.

Definition of Trade or Business. Trade or business, for this purpose, is broadly defined. It includes any activity conducted for the production of income through the sale of merchandise or the performance of services. An activity need not generate a profit to be treated as a trade or business. The activity may be part of a larger set of activities conducted by the organization, some of which may be related to the exempt purpose. Being included in a larger set does not cause the activity to lose its identity as an unrelated trade or business.[34]

EXAMPLE 5

Health, Inc., is an exempt hospital that operates a pharmacy. The pharmacy provides medicines and supplies to the patients in the hospital (i.e., it contributes to the conduct of the hospital's exempt purpose). In addition, the pharmacy sells medicines and supplies to the general public. The activity of selling to the general public constitutes a trade or business for purposes of the UBIT. ■

Not Substantially Related to the Exempt Purpose. Exempt organizations frequently conduct unrelated trades or businesses in order to provide income to help defray the costs of conducting the exempt purpose (like the hotel and restaurant businesses in Example 4). Providing financial support for the exempt purpose will not prevent an activity from being classified as an unrelated trade or business and thereby being subject to the UBIT.

To be related to the accomplishment of the exempt purpose, the conduct of the business activities must be causally related and contribute importantly to the exempt purpose. Whether a causal relationship exists and the degree of its importance are determined by examining the facts and circumstances. One must consider the size and extent of the activities in relation to the nature and extent of the exempt function that the activities serve.[35]

EXAMPLE 6

Art, Inc., an exempt organization, operates a school for training children in the performing arts. As an essential part of that training, the children perform for the general public. The children are paid at the minimum wage for the performances, and Art derives gross income by charging admission to the performances.

The income from admissions is not income from an unrelated trade or business, because the performances by the children contribute importantly to the accomplishment of the exempt purpose of providing training in the performing arts. ■

EXAMPLE 7

Assume the same facts as in Example 6, except that four performances are conducted each weekend of the year. Assume that this number of performances far exceeds that required for training the children. Thus, the part of the income derived from admissions for these excess performances is income from an unrelated trade or business. ■

The trade or business may sell merchandise that has been produced as part of the accomplishment of the exempt purpose. The sale of such merchandise is normally

[34] Reg. § 1.513–1(b).

[35] Reg. § 1.513–1(d).

treated as related to the exempt purpose. However, if the merchandise is not sold in substantially the same state it was in at the completion of the exempt purpose, the gross income subsequently derived from the sale of the merchandise is income from an unrelated trade or business.[36]

EXAMPLE 8

Help, Inc., an exempt organization, conducts programs for the rehabilitation of the handicapped. One of the programs includes training in radio and television repair. Help derives gross income by selling the repaired items. The income is substantially related to the accomplishment of the exempt purpose. ■

An asset or facility used in the exempt purpose may also be used in a nonexempt purpose. Income derived from the use in a nonexempt purpose is income from an unrelated trade or business.[37]

EXAMPLE 9

Civil, Inc., an exempt organization, operates a museum. As part of the exempt purpose of the museum, educational lectures are given in the museum's theater during the operating hours of the museum. In the evening, when the museum is closed, the theater is leased to an individual who operates a movie theater. The lease income received from the individual who operates the movie theater is income from an unrelated trade or business. ■

Special Rule for Corporate Sponsorship Payments. The term *unrelated trade or business* does not include the soliciting and receiving of qualified sponsorship payments.[38]

A payment qualifies as a qualified sponsorship if it meets the following requirements.

- There is no arrangement or expectation that the trade or business making the payment will receive any substantial benefit other than the use or acknowledgment of its name, logo, or product lines in connection with the activities of the exempt organization.
- Such use or acknowledgment does not include advertising the payor's products or services.
- The payment does not include any payment for which the amount is contingent upon the level of attendance at one or more events, broadcast ratings, or other factors indicating the degree of public exposure to one or more events.

EXAMPLE 10

Pets, Inc., a manufacturer of cat food, contributes $25,000 to Feline Care, Inc., an exempt organization that cares for abandoned cats. In return for the contribution, Feline agrees to put Pets' corporate logo in its monthly newsletter to donors. Under these circumstances, the $25,000 payment is a qualified sponsorship payment and is not subject to the UBIT. ■

EXAMPLE 11

Assume the same facts as in Example 10 except that Feline agrees to endorse Pets' cat food in its monthly newsletter by stating that it feeds only Pets' cat food to its cats. The $25,000 is not a qualified sponsorship payment and is subject to UBIT. ■

Special Rule for Bingo Games. A special provision applies in determining whether income from bingo games is from an unrelated trade or business. Under this provision, a *qualified bingo game* is not an unrelated trade or business if both of the following requirements are satisfied.[39]

- The bingo game is legal under both state and local law.
- Commercial bingo games (conducted for a profit motive) ordinarily are not permitted in the jurisdiction.

[36] Reg. § 1.513–1(d)(4)(ii).
[37] Reg. § 1.513–1(d)(4)(iii) addresses the allocation of expenses to exempt and nonexempt activities.
[38] § 513(i).
[39] § 513(f).

EXAMPLE 12

Play, Inc., an exempt organization, conducts weekly bingo games. The laws of the state and municipality in which Play conducts the games expressly provide that exempt organizations may conduct bingo games, but do not permit profit-oriented entities to do so. Since both of the requirements for bingo games are satisfied, the bingo games conducted by Play are not an unrelated trade or business. ■

EXAMPLE 13

Game, Inc., an exempt organization, conducts weekly bingo games in City X and City Y. State law expressly permits exempt organizations to conduct bingo games. State law also provides that profit-oriented entities may conduct bingo games in X, which is a resort community. Several businesses regularly conduct bingo games there.

The bingo games conducted by Game in Y are not an unrelated trade or business. However, the bingo games that Game conducts in X are an unrelated trade or business, because commercial bingo games are regularly permitted to be conducted there. ■

Special Rule for Distribution of Low-Cost Articles. If an exempt organization distributes low-cost items as an incidental part of its solicitation for charitable contributions, the distributions may not be considered an unrelated trade or business. A low-cost article is one that costs $8.34 (for 2005—indexed annually) or less. Examples are pens, stamps, stickers, stationery, and address labels. If more than one item is distributed to a person during the calendar year, the costs of the items are combined.[40]

Special Rule for Rental or Exchange of Membership Lists. If an exempt organization conducts a trade or business that consists of either exchanging with or renting to other exempt organizations the organization's donor or membership list (mailing lists), the activity is not an unrelated trade or business.[41]

Other Special Rules. Other special rules are used in determining whether each of the following activities is an unrelated trade or business.[42]

- Qualified public entertainment activities (e.g., a state fair).
- Qualified convention and trade show activities.
- Certain services provided at cost or less by a hospital to other small hospitals.
- Certain pole rentals by telephone or electric companies.

Discussion of these special rules is beyond the scope of this text.

UNRELATED BUSINESS INCOME

Even when an exempt organization conducts an unrelated trade or business, a tax is assessed only if the exempt organization regularly conducts the activity and the business produces unrelated business income.

Regularly Carried on by the Organization. An activity is classified as unrelated business income only if it is regularly carried on by the exempt organization. This provision assures that only activities that are actually competing with taxable organizations are subject to the UBIT. Accordingly, factors to be considered in assessing *regularly carried on* include the frequency of the activity, the continuity of the activity, and the manner in which the activity is pursued.[43]

EXAMPLE 14

Silver, Inc., an exempt organization, owns land that is located next to the state fairgrounds. During the 10 days of the state fair, Silver uses the land as a parking lot and charges individuals attending the state fair for parking there. The activity is not regularly carried on. ■

[40] § 513(h)(1)(A).
[41] § 513(h)(1)(B).
[42] §§ 513(d), (e), and (g).
[43] § 512(a)(1) and Reg. § 1.513–1(c).

■ **FIGURE 23–2**
Tax Formula for Unrelated Business Taxable Income

Gross unrelated business income
– Deductions
= Net unrelated business income
± Modifications
= Unrelated business taxable income

EXAMPLE 15

Black, Inc., an exempt organization, has its offices in the downtown area. It owns a parking lot adjacent to its offices on which its employees park during the week. On Saturdays, it rents the spaces in the parking lot to individuals shopping or working in the downtown area. Black is conducting a business activity on a year-round basis, even though it is only for one day per week. Thus, an activity is regularly being carried on. ■

Unrelated Business Income Defined. Unrelated business income is generally that derived from the unrelated trade or business. To convert it from a gross income measure to a net income measure, it must be reduced by the deductions directly connected with the conduct of the unrelated trade or business.[44]

UNRELATED BUSINESS TAXABLE INCOME

General Tax Model. The model for unrelated business taxable income (UBTI) appears in Figure 23–2.

Positive adjustments[45]

1. The charitable contribution deduction is permitted without regard to whether the charitable contributions are associated with the unrelated trade or business. However, to the extent the charitable contributions deducted in calculating net unrelated business income (see Figure 23–2) exceed 10 percent of UBTI (without regard to the charitable contribution deduction), the excess is treated as a positive adjustment.

EXAMPLE 16

Brown, Inc., an exempt organization, has UBTI of $100,000 (excluding any modifications associated with charitable contributions). Total charitable contributions (all associated with the unrelated trade or business) are $13,000. Assuming that the $13,000 is deducted in calculating net unrelated business income, the excess of $3,000 [$13,000 – 10%($100,000)] is a positive adjustment in calculating UBTI. ■

2. Unrelated debt-financed income net of the unrelated debt-financed deductions (see the subsequent discussion of Unrelated Debt-Financed Income).
3. Certain net interest, annuity, royalty, and rent income received by the exempt organization from an organization it controls (80 percent test). Note that this provision overrides the modifications for these types of income (negative adjustment 3).

Negative adjustments

1. Income from dividends, interest, and annuities net of all deductions directly related to producing such income.
2. Royalty income, regardless of whether it is measured by production, gross income, or taxable income from the property, net of all deductions directly related to producing such income.

[44] § 512(a)(1).

[45] §§ 512(a)(1) and (b) and Reg. § 1.512(b)–1.

3. Rent income from real property and from certain personal property net of all deductions directly related to producing such income. Personal property rents are included in the negative adjustment only if the personal property is leased with the real property. In addition, the personal property rent income must be incidental (does not exceed 10 percent of the gross rent income under the lease) to be used in computing the negative adjustment. In both of the following cases, however, none of the rent income is treated as a negative adjustment.
   - More than 50 percent of the rent income under the lease is from personal property.
   - Rent income is calculated using the tenant's profits.

EXAMPLE 17

Beaver, Inc., an exempt organization, leases land and a building (realty) and computers (personalty) housed in the building. Under the lease, $46,000 of the rent is for the land and building, and $4,000 is for the computers. Expenses incurred for the land and building are $10,000. The net rent income from the land and building of $36,000 ($46,000 – $10,000) and the $4,000 from the computers are negative adjustments. ■

EXAMPLE 18

Assume the same facts as in Example 17, except that the rent income is $35,000 from the land and building and $15,000 from the computers. Since the rent income from the computers exceeds $5,000 (i.e., 10% of the total rent under the lease) and is not incidental, it is not a negative adjustment. ■

EXAMPLE 19

Assume the same facts as in Example 17, except that the rent income is $20,000 from the land and building and $30,000 from the computers. Since more than 50% of the rent income under the lease is from the computers, neither the rent income from the land and building nor that from the computers is a negative adjustment. ■

If the lessor of real property provides significant services to the lessee, such income, for this purpose, is not rent income.

4. Gains and losses from the sale, exchange, or other disposition of property *except for* inventory.

EXAMPLE 20

Beaver, the owner of the land, building, and computers in Example 17, sells these assets for $450,000. Their adjusted basis is $300,000. Beaver's recognized gain of $150,000 is a negative adjustment. ■

5. Certain research income net of all deductions directly related to producing that income.
6. The charitable contribution deduction is permitted without regard to whether the charitable contributions are associated with the unrelated trade or business. Therefore, to the extent that the charitable contributions exceed those deducted in calculating net unrelated business income (see Figure 23–2), the excess is a negative adjustment in calculating UBTI. In making this calculation, be aware that the 10 percent of UBTI (without regard to the charitable contribution deduction) limit still applies (see positive adjustment 1).

EXAMPLE 21

Canine, Inc., an exempt organization, has UBTI of $100,000 (excluding any modifications associated with charitable contributions). The total charitable contributions are $9,000, of which $7,000 (those associated with the unrelated trade or business) has been deducted in calculating net unrelated business income. Therefore, the remaining $2,000 of charitable contributions is a negative adjustment in calculating UBTI. ■

7. A specific deduction of $1,000 is permitted.

EXAMPLE 22

Petit Care, Inc., an exempt organization, has net unrelated business income of $800. Since Petit will receive a specific deduction of $1,000, its UBTI is $0. Therefore, its income tax liability is $0. ■

After UBTI is determined, that amount is subject to tax using the regular corporate tax rates.

EXAMPLE 23

Patient, Inc., an exempt organization, has UBTI of $500,000. Patient's income tax liability is $170,000 ($500,000 UBTI × 34% corporate tax rate). ■

UNRELATED DEBT-FINANCED INCOME

In the formula for calculating UBTI (refer to Figure 23–2), unrelated debt-financed income is one of the positive adjustments. Examples of income from debt-financed property include rent income from real estate or tangible personal property, dividends from corporate stock, and gains from the disposition of debt-financed property. Gains from property that is unrelated business income property are also included to the extent the gains are not otherwise treated as unrelated business income. Because of the importance of this item, it is discussed separately here.

In terms of UBTI, the positive adjustment for unrelated debt-financed income is a significant one. Without this provision, a tax-exempt organization could use borrowed funds to acquire unrelated business or investment property and use the untaxed (i.e., exempt) earnings from the acquisition to pay for the property.

Definition of Debt-Financed Income. **Debt-financed income** is the gross income generated from debt-financed property. *Debt-financed property* is all property of the exempt organization that is held to produce income and on which there is acquisition indebtedness, *except* for the following.[46]

- Property where substantially all (at least 85 percent) of the use is for the achievement of the exempt purpose of the exempt organization.[47]
- Property whose gross income is otherwise treated as unrelated business income.
- Property whose gross income is from the following sources and is not otherwise treated as unrelated business income.
  - Income from research performed for the United States, a Federal governmental agency, or a state or a political subdivision thereof.
  - For a college, university, or hospital, income from research.
  - For an organization that performs fundamental (i.e., not applied) research for the benefit of the general public, income from research.
- Property used in an activity that is not an unrelated trade or business.

If the 85 percent test is not satisfied, only the portion of the property that is *not* used for the exempt purpose is debt-financed property.

EXAMPLE 24

Deer, Inc., an exempt organization, owns a five-story office building on which there is acquisition indebtedness. Three of the floors are used for Deer's exempt purpose. The two other floors are leased to Purple Corporation. In this case, the *substantially all* test is not satisfied. Therefore, 40% of the office building is debt-financed property, and 60% is not. ■

Certain land that is acquired by an exempt organization for later exempt use is excluded from debt-financed property if the following requirements are satisfied.[48]

[46] § 514(b).
[47] Reg. § 1.514(b)–1(b)(1)(ii).
[48] § 514(b)(3).

- The principal purpose of acquiring the land is for use (substantially all) in achieving the organization's exempt purpose.
- This use will begin within 10 years of the acquisition date.
- At the date when the land is acquired, it is located in the *neighborhood* of other property of the organization for which substantially all the use is for achieving the organization's exempt purpose.

Even if the third requirement is not satisfied (the property is not located in the neighborhood), the land still is excluded from debt-financed property if it is converted to use for achieving the organization's exempt purpose within the 10-year period. Qualification under this provision will result in a refund of taxes previously paid. If the exempt organization is a church, the 10-year period becomes a 15-year period, and the neighborhood requirement is waived.

Definition of Acquisition Indebtedness. Acquisition indebtedness is debt sustained by the exempt organization in association with the acquisition of property. More precisely, *acquisition indebtedness* consists of the unpaid amounts of the following for debt-financed property.[49]

- Debt incurred in acquiring or improving the property.
- Debt incurred before the property was acquired or improved, but which would not have been incurred without the acquisition or improvement.
- Debt incurred after the property was acquired or improved, but which would not have been incurred without the acquisition or improvement.

EXAMPLE 25

Red, Inc., an exempt organization, acquires land for $100,000. In order to finance the acquisition, Red mortgages the land with a bank and receives loan proceeds of $80,000. Red leases the land to Duck Corporation. The mortgage is acquisition indebtedness. ■

EXAMPLE 26

Rose, Inc., an exempt organization, makes improvements to an office building that it rents to Bird Corporation. Excess working capital funds are used to finance the improvements. Rose is later required to mortgage its laboratory building, which it uses for its exempt purpose, to replenish working capital. The mortgage is acquisition indebtedness. ■

Portion of Debt-Financed Income and Deductions Treated as Unrelated Business Taxable Income. Once the amount of the debt-financed income and deductions is determined, it is necessary to ascertain what portion is unrelated debt-financed income and deductions. Unrelated debt-financed income increases UBTI, and unrelated debt-financed deductions decrease UBTI.

The calculation is made for each debt-financed property. The gross income from the property is multiplied by the following percentage.[50]

$$\frac{\text{Average acquisition indebtedness for the property}}{\text{Average adjusted basis of the property}} = \text{Debt/basis percentage}$$

This percentage cannot exceed 100. If debt-financed property is disposed of during the taxable year at a gain, average acquisition indebtedness in the formula is replaced with highest acquisition indebtedness. *Highest acquisition indebtedness* is the largest amount of acquisition indebtedness for the property during the 12-month period preceding the date of disposition.[51]

Deductions are allowed for expenses directly related to the debt-financed property and the income from it. Cost recovery deductions must be calculated using

[49] § 514(c)(1). Educational organizations in certain limited circumstances can exclude debt incurred for real property acquisitions from classification as acquisition indebtedness.

[50] § 514(a)(1).

[51] § 514(c)(7).

the straight-line method. Once allowable deductions are determined, this amount is multiplied by the debt/basis percentage.[52]

EXAMPLE 27

White, Inc., an exempt organization, owns an office building that it leases to Squirrel Corporation for $120,000 per year. The average acquisition indebtedness is $300,000, and the average adjusted basis is $500,000. Since the office building is debt-financed property, the gross unrelated debt-financed income is:

$$\frac{\$300{,}000}{\$500{,}000} \times \$120{,}000 = \$72{,}000$$

If White's expenses associated with the office building lease (including straight-line cost recovery) equal $50,000, then allowable deductions are:

$$\frac{\$300{,}000}{\$500{,}000} \times \$50{,}000 = \$30{,}000$$

Thus, White's net unrelated debt-financed income is $42,000 ($72,000 – $30,000). ■

Average Acquisition Indebtedness. The *average acquisition indebtedness* for debt-financed property is the average amount of the outstanding debt for the taxable year (ignoring interest) during the portion of the year the property is held by the exempt organization. This amount is calculated by summing the outstanding debt on the first day of each calendar month the property is held by the exempt organization. Then this total is divided by the number of months the property is held by the organization.[53]

EXAMPLE 28

On August 12, Yellow, Inc., an exempt organization, acquires an office building that is debt-financed property for $500,000. The initial mortgage on the property is $400,000. The principal amount of the debt on August 12 and on the first of each subsequent month is as follows.

Month	Principal Amount
August 12	$ 400,000
September 1	380,000
October 1	360,000
November 1	340,000
December 1	320,000
Total	$1,800,000

Average acquisition indebtedness is $360,000 ($1,800,000 ÷ 5 months). Note that even though August is only a partial month, it is treated as a full month. ■

Average Adjusted Basis. The *average adjusted basis* of debt-financed property is calculated by summing the adjusted bases of the property on the first and last days during the taxable year the property is held by the exempt organization and then dividing by two.[54]

EXAMPLE 29

Assume the facts are the same as in Example 28. In addition, during the taxable year, depreciation of $5,900 is deducted. The average adjusted basis is $497,050 [($500,000 + $494,100) ÷ 2]. ■

Concept Summary 23–4 presents the rules concerning the UBIT.

[52]§ 514(a)(3).

[53]§ 514(c)(7) and Reg. § 1.514(a)–1(a)(3). A partial month is treated as a full month.

[54]§ 514(a)(1) and Reg. § 1.514(a)–1(a)(2).

CONCEPT SUMMARY 23–4

Unrelated Business Income Tax

Purpose	To tax the entity on unrelated business income as if it were subject to the corporate income tax.
Applicable tax rates	Corporate tax rates.
Exempt organizations to which applicable	All organizations exempt under § 501(c), except Federal agencies.
Entities subject to the tax	The organization conducts a trade or business; the trade or business is not substantially related to the exempt purpose of the organization; and the trade or business is regularly carried on by the organization.
Exceptions to the tax	• All the work is performed by volunteers. • Substantially all of the merchandise being sold has been received by gift. • For § 501(c)(3) organizations, the business is conducted primarily for the benefit of the organization's members, students, patients, officers, or employees. • For most employee unions, the trade or business consists of selling to members work-related clothing and equipment and items normally sold through vending machines, snack bars, or food-dispensing facilities.
$1,000 provision	If the gross income from an unrelated trade or business is less than $1,000, it is not necessary to file a return associated with the unrelated business income tax.

LO.7

List the reports exempt organizations must file with the IRS and the related due dates.

Reporting Requirements

OBTAINING EXEMPT ORGANIZATION STATUS

Not all exempt organizations are required to obtain IRS approval for their exempt status. Among those required by statute to do so are organizations exempt under §§ 501(c)(3), 501(c)(9), and 501(c)(20).[55] Even in these cases, exceptions are provided (e.g., churches).

Even when not required to obtain IRS approval, most exempt organizations do apply for exempt status. Typically, an organization does not want to assume that it qualifies for exempt status and describe itself in that way to the public, only to have the IRS rule later that it does not qualify.

If an organization is required to obtain IRS approval for its exempt status and does not do so, it does not qualify as an exempt organization.

ANNUAL FILING REQUIREMENTS

Most exempt organizations are required to file an annual information return.[56] The return is filed on Form 990 (Return of Organization Exempt from Income Tax). The following exempt organizations need not file Form 990.[57]

- Federal agencies.
- Churches.

[55] §§ 505(c), 508(a), and 508(c).

[56] § 6033(a)(1).

[57] § 6033(a)(2).

- Organizations whose annual gross receipts do not exceed $25,000.[58]
- Private foundations.

Private foundations are required to file Form 990–PF (Return of Private Foundation).

The due date for Form 990 or Form 990–PF is the fifteenth day of the fifth month after the end of the taxable year. These returns are filed with the appropriate IRS Service Center based on the location of the exempt organization's principal office. Requests for extensions on filing are made by filing Form 2758 (Applications for Extension of Time).

EXAMPLE 30

Green, Inc., a § 501(c)(3) organization, has a fiscal year that ends June 30, 2005. The due date for the annual return is November 15, 2005. If Green were a calendar year entity, the due date for the 2005 annual return would be May 15, 2006. ■

Exempt organizations that are subject to the UBIT may be required to file Form 990–T (Exempt Organization Business Income Tax Return). The return must be filed if the organization has gross income of at least $1,000 from an unrelated trade or business. The due date for the return is the fifteenth day of the fifth month after the end of the taxable year.

EXAMPLE 31

During the year, the First Church of Kentwood receives parishioner contributions of $450,000. Of this amount, $125,000 is designated for the church building fund. First Church is not required to file an annual return (Form 990) because churches are exempt from doing so. In addition, it is not required to file Form 990–T because it has no unrelated business income.

Colonial, Inc., is an exempt private foundation. Gross receipts for the year total $800,000, of which 40% is from admission fees paid by members of the general public who visit Colonial's museum of eighteenth-century life. The balance is endowment income and contributions from the founding donor. Because Colonial is a private foundation, it must file Form 990–PF.

Orange, Inc., is an exempt organization and is not a private foundation. Gross receipts for the year are $20,000. None of this amount is unrelated business income. Orange is not required to file Form 990 because its annual gross receipts do not exceed $25,000.

Restoration, Inc., is an exempt private foundation. Gross receipts for the year are $20,000. None of this amount is unrelated business income. Restoration must file Form 990–PF because private foundations are not eligible for the $25,000 filing exception.

During the year, the Second Church of Port Allen receives parishioner contributions of $300,000. In addition, the church has unrelated business income of $5,000. Second Church is not required to file Form 990 because churches are exempt from doing so. Form 990–T must be filed, however, because churches are not exempt from the UBIT and Second Church has exceeded the $1,000 floor. ■

DISCLOSURE REQUIREMENTS

As a result of consumer-friendly rules, exempt entities must make more information readily available to the general public.[59] Prior to the issuance of these rules, the disclosure requirements could be satisfied by making the information available for public inspection during regular business hours at the principal office of the exempt entity.

Copies of the following now must be made available to the general public.[60]

[58]The statutory amount is $5,000. However, under its discretionary authority, the IRS has expanded the exemption amount to $25,000.

[59]§ 6104(d), Reg. § 301.6104(d), and T.D. 8818 (April 1999).

[60]An Internet source of Forms 990 and 990–PF and other relevant materials on exempt entities is **http://www.guidestar.com**.

- Form 990.
- Form 1023 (or Form 1024).

Copies of the three most recent returns of the Form 990 must be made available. Private foundations must make Form 990–PF available for public inspection.

If an individual requests the entity's tax form in person, the exempt entity must provide a copy immediately. If the request is received in writing or by e-mail or fax, the copy must be provided within 30 days. The copy must be provided without charge, except for a reasonable fee for reproduction and mailing costs.

If the exempt entity has made the forms widely available to the general public, it is not required to fill individual requests. One technique for making the forms widely available is to put them on the Internet. Individual requests can also be disregarded if the exempt entity can show the request is part of a harassment campaign.

LO.8

Identify tax planning opportunities for exempt organizations.

Tax Planning Considerations

GENERAL

Exempt organization status provides at least two potential tax benefits. First, the entity may be exempt from Federal income tax. Second, contributions to the entity may be deductible by the donor.

An organization that qualifies as an exempt organization may still be subject to certain types of Federal income tax, including the following.

- Tax on prohibited transactions.
- Tax on feeder organizations.
- Tax on private foundations.
- Tax on unrelated business income.

Therefore, classification as an exempt organization should not be interpreted to mean that the organization need not be concerned with any Federal income tax. Such a belief can result in the organization engaging in transactions that produce a substantial tax liability.

An organization is exempt from taxation only if it fits into one of the categories enumerated in the Code. Thus, particular attention must be given to the qualification requirements. These requirements must continue to be satisfied to avoid termination of exempt status (in effect, they are now maintenance requirements).

MAINTAINING EXEMPT STATUS

To maintain exempt status, the organization must satisfy both an organizational test and an operational test. The organizational test requires that the entity satisfy the statutory requirements for exempt status on paper. The operational test ensures that the entity does, in fact, satisfy the statutory requirements for exempt status.

King Shipping Consum., Inc. (Zion Coptic Church, Inc.) illustrates that it is usually much easier to satisfy the organizational test than the operational test.[61] Zion's stated purpose was to engage in activities usually and normally associated with churches. Based on this, the IRS approved Zion's exempt status as a § 501(c)(3) organization.

Zion's real intent, however, was to smuggle illegal drugs into the country and to distribute them for profit. The church's justification for the drugs was that it used marijuana in its sacrament. During a four-month period, however, the police confiscated 33 tons of marijuana from church members. The IRS calculated that, even assuming the maximum alleged church membership of several thousand, each member would have had to smoke over 33 pounds of marijuana during the four-month confiscation period.

[61] 58 TCM 574, T.C.Memo. 1989–593.

Charities and Vehicle Donation Programs

Tax-exempt entities increasingly are operating vehicle donation programs. The typical donor deducts the fair market value (FMV) of the vehicle on his or her Federal income tax return. A study by the Government Accountability Office found that an estimated 4,300 charities with annual revenue of $100,000 or more are operating such programs. For 2000, the GAO estimates that 733,000 (more than one-half of 1 percent of the individual income tax returns filed) returns claimed charitable deductions for donated vehicles.

Under the tax law prior to 2005, it was the responsibility of the taxpayer, rather than the charity, to determine the FMV of the vehicle. The taxpayer was required to obtain a qualified appraisal only if the deduction claimed exceeded $5,000. A recent congressional study found that quite often the FMV (e.g., the blue book) used by the taxpayer substantially exceeded the amount the vehicle was sold for by the charity.

Because such charitable contribution deductions cost the U.S. Treasury $654 million in 2000, Congress considered various ways to limit this revenue loss. One such proposal was enacted in the American Jobs Creation Act of 2004 and is effective for contributions after 2004. For deductions of more than $500, the charitable contribution deduction cannot exceed the gross sales price received by the charity on the sale of the vehicle. The charity must provide the donor with confirmation of this dollar amount within 30 days of the sale. Charities not complying with this provision are subject to penalties.

SOURCE: Adapted from Tom Herman, "New Limits May Drive Away Used-Car Donations," *Wall Street Journal*, March 25, 2004, p. D2.

The court concluded that Zion's real purpose was to cloak a large commercial drug smuggling operation. Since this activity was inconsistent with the religious purpose for exempt status, the court upheld the IRS's revocation of Zion's exempt status and the deficiency assessment of approximately $1.6 million.

PRIVATE FOUNDATION STATUS

Exempt organizations that can qualify as public charities receive more beneficial tax treatment than those that qualify as private foundations. Thus, if possible, the organization should be structured to qualify as a public charity. The following can result when an exempt organization is classified as a private foundation.

- Taxes may be imposed on the private foundation.
  - Tax based on investment income.
  - Tax on self-dealing.
  - Tax on failure to distribute income.
  - Tax on excess business holdings.
  - Tax on investments that jeopardize charitable purposes.
  - Tax on taxable expenditures.
- Donors may receive less favorable tax deduction treatment under § 170 than they would if the exempt organization were not a private foundation.

EXAMPLE 32

David has undeveloped land ($25,000 adjusted basis, $100,000 fair market value) that he is going to contribute to one of the following exempt organizations: Blue, Inc., a public charity, or Teal, Inc., a private nonoperating foundation. David has owned the land for five years.

David asks the manager of each organization to describe the tax benefits of contributing to that organization. He tells them he is in the 35% tax bracket and his AGI exceeds $250,000.

CONCEPT SUMMARY 23–5

Private Foundation Status

	Exempt Organization Is	
	A Private Foundation	**Not a Private Foundation**
Reason for classification	Does not serve the common good because it lacks an approved exempt purpose or does not receive broad public financial support.	Serves the common good
Eligible for exempt status?	Yes	Yes
Most beneficial charitable contribution deduction treatment available to donors?	Depends. No, if the private foundation is classified as a private *nonoperating* foundation.	Yes
Subject to excise taxes levied on prohibited transactions?	Yes	No
Subject to tax on unrelated business income?	Yes	Yes

Based on the data provided by the managers, David decides to contribute the land to Blue, Inc. He calculates the benefit from the charitable contribution under each option as follows.[62]

Donee	Contribution Deduction	Tax Rate	Contribution Borne by U.S. Government
Blue	$100,000	35%	$35,000
Teal	25,000 ($100,000 – $75,000)	35%	8,750

■

One method of avoiding private foundation status is to have a tax-exempt purpose that results in the organization not being classified as a private foundation (the *organization* approach). If this is not feasible, it may be possible to operate the organization so that it receives broad public support and thereby avoids private foundation status (the *operational* approach).

If the organization is a private foundation, care must be exercised to avoid the assessment of a tax liability on prohibited transactions. This objective can best be achieved by establishing controls that prevent the private foundation from engaging in transactions that trigger the imposition of the taxes. If an initial tax is assessed, corrective actions should be implemented to avoid the assessment of an additional tax. See Concept Summary 23–5.

UNRELATED BUSINESS INCOME TAX

If the exempt organization conducts an unrelated trade or business, it may be subject to tax on the unrelated business income. Worse yet, the unrelated trade or business could result in the loss of exempt status if the IRS determines that the activity is the primary purpose of the organization. Thus, caution and planning should be used to eliminate the latter possibility and to minimize the former.

[62]See Chapter 10.

KEY TERMS

Debt-financed income, 23–22
Excess lobbying expenditure, 23–9
Exempt organization, 23–2
Feeder organization, 23–10
Grass roots expenditure, 23–8
Intermediate sanctions, 23–10
Lobbying expenditure, 23–8
Private foundation, 23–11
Unrelated business income, 23–16
Unrelated business income tax (UBIT), 23–16

PROBLEM MATERIALS

Discussion Questions

1. Are all churches exempt from Federal income tax?

2. Why are certain organizations either partially or completely exempt from Federal income tax?

3. Which of the following organizations qualify for exempt status?
   a. Tulane University.
   b. Virginia Qualified Tuition Program.
   c. Red Cross.
   d. Disneyland.
   e. Ford Foundation.
   f. Jacksonville Chamber of Commerce.
   g. Colonial Williamsburg Foundation.
   h. Professional Golfers Association (PGA) Tour.
   i. Green Bay Packers.
   j. Cleveland Indians.

4. Identify the statutory authority under which each of the following is exempt from Federal income tax.
   a. Kingsmill Country Club.
   b. Shady Lawn Cemetery.
   c. Amber Credit Union.
   d. Veterans of Foreign Wars.
   e. Boy Scouts of America.
   f. United Fund.
   g. Federal Deposit Insurance Corporation.
   h. Bruton Parish Episcopal Church.
   i. PTA.
   j. National Press Club.

5. Adrenna is the treasurer for two exempt organizations. One exempt organization pays no Federal income taxes for 2005, and the other pays Federal income taxes of $100,000 for 2005. Discuss potential reasons for this difference in tax results.

6. Robert contributes $5,000 to an exempt organization. Addie contributes $5,000 to a different exempt organization. Why is Addie permitted a $5,000 charitable contribution deduction in calculating her itemized deductions and Robert is not?

7. Can a church make an election that will enable it to engage in lobbying on a limited basis?

8. Mauve, Inc., a § 501(c)(3) organization, loses its exempt status in 2005 for attempting to influence legislation. Amber, Inc., another § 501(c)(3) organization, also attempts to influence legislation and is in no danger of losing its exempt status. Explain.

9. What are intermediate sanctions, and how are they related to forfeiture of exempt status?

10. The Living Museum is a tax-exempt organization. Dolphin Corporation, a wholly owned subsidiary of the Living Museum, sells boats. Dolphin remits all of its earnings each year to its parent. Is Dolphin exempt from Federal income tax because it is a subsidiary of a tax-exempt organization and remits all of its earnings to a tax-exempt organization?
11. What types of activities are not subject to the tax imposed on feeder organizations?
12. What is a private foundation, and what are the disadvantages of an exempt organization being classified as a private foundation?
13. Determine which of the following organizations are *not* private foundations.
    a. Crestline Baptist Church.
    b. Girl Scouts.
    c. League of Women Voters.
    d. PGA Tour.
    e. American Institute of CPAs.
    f. Homewood Middle School PTA.
    g. American Red Cross.
    h. Salvation Army.
    i. Veterans of Foreign Wars.
14. Describe the external support test and the internal support test for a private foundation.
15. Although private foundations generally are exempt from Federal income tax, they may be subject to two types of taxes. Identify these taxes, and discuss why they are imposed on private foundations.
16. A private foundation engages in a transaction with a disqualified person. What are the tax consequences to the private foundation and to the disqualified person?

Issue ID

17. Welcome, Inc., a tax-exempt organization, receives 25% of its support from disqualified persons. Another disqualified person has agreed to match this support if Welcome will appoint him to the organization's board of directors. What tax issues are relevant to Welcome as it makes this decision?
18. What is the purpose of the unrelated business income tax (UBIT)?

Issue ID

19. First Church has been selling cards and small books in the church tower. A contribution box is provided in which payments are to be deposited. To increase church revenues, a task force is evaluating setting up a gift shop in the church parish house. What tax issues are relevant to the task force as it makes its decision?
20. An exempt hospital operates a pharmacy that is staffed by a pharmacist 24 hours per day. The pharmacy serves only hospital patients. Is the pharmacy an unrelated trade or business?

Decision Making

21. An exempt hospital receives as a gift from a wealthy donor all the shares of stock of Compute, Inc., a retail computer chain. Because the chain is very profitable and its CEO has offered to continue to manage it, the hospital has decided to operate the chain rather than sell the stock. All of the chain's profits will be used in carrying out the exempt mission of the hospital. Advise the hospital on whether better tax consequences can be achieved by operating the chain as a subsidiary or as a division of the hospital corporation.
22. To which of the following tax-exempt organizations may the unrelated business income tax apply?
    a. Red Cross.
    b. Salvation Army.
    c. United Fund.
    d. College of William and Mary.
    e. Rainbow, Inc., a private foundation.
    f. Federal Land Bank.
23. Discuss the significance of the "regularly carried on" test as it relates to the unrelated business income tax.

Issue ID

24. An exempt organization is considering conducting bingo games on Thursday nights as a way of generating additional revenue to support its exempt purpose. Before doing so, however, the president of the organization has come to you for advice regarding the effect on the organization's exempt status and whether the net income from the bingo games will be taxable. Identify the relevant tax issues.

25. Define each of the following with respect to unrelated debt-financed property.
    a. Debt-financed income.
    b. Debt-financed property.
    c. Acquisition indebtedness.
    d. Average acquisition indebtedness.
    e. Average adjusted basis.

26. Tom is the treasurer of the City Garden Club, a new garden club. A friend, who is the treasurer of the garden club in a neighboring community, tells Tom that it is not necessary for the garden club to file a request for exempt status with the IRS. Has Tom received correct advice?

Issue ID

27. Abby recently became the treasurer of First Church. The church has been in existence for three years and has never filed anything with the IRS. Identify any reporting responsibilities Abby might have as church treasurer.

28. Shane and Brittany are treasurers for § 501(c)(3) exempt organizations. Neither exempt organization is a church. Each year Shane's exempt organization files a Form 990 while Brittany's exempt organization files a Form 990–PF. Discuss the public disclosure requirements for each exempt organization.

Problems

29. Wellness, Inc., a § 501(c)(3) organization, makes lobbying expenditures of $300,000 during 2005. Exempt purpose expenditures were $900,000 for the first six months of the year and $600,000 for the last six months of the year. Determine the tax consequences to Wellness if:
    a. It does not make the § 501(h) lobbying election.
    b. It does make the § 501(h) lobbying election.

Decision Making
Communications

30. Roadrunner, Inc., is an exempt medical organization. Quail, Inc., a sporting goods retailer, is a wholly owned subsidiary of Roadrunner. Roadrunner inherited the Quail stock last year from a major benefactor of the medical organization. Quail's taxable income is $550,000. Quail will remit all of its earnings, net of any taxes, to Roadrunner to support the exempt purpose of the parent.
    a. Is Quail subject to Federal income tax? If so, calculate the liability.
    b. Arthur Morgan, the treasurer of Roadrunner, has contacted you regarding minimizing or eliminating Quail's tax liability. He would like to know if the tax consequences would be better if Quail were liquidated into Roadrunner. Write a letter to Morgan that contains your advice. Roadrunner's address is 500 Rouse Tower, Rochester, NY 14627.
    c. Would your answer in (a) change if Roadrunner had acquired the Quail stock by purchase or gift rather than by inheritance? Discuss.

Communications

31. Cardinal, Inc., a § 501(c)(3) organization, received support from the following sources.

Governmental unit A for services rendered	$ 6,000
Governmental unit B for services rendered	4,000
General public for services rendered	85,000
Gross investment income	37,000
Contributions from disqualified persons	24,000
Contributions from other than disqualified persons	110,000

    a. Does Cardinal satisfy the test for receiving broad public support?
    b. Is Cardinal a private foundation?

c. Arnold Horn, Cardinal's treasurer, has asked you to advise him on whether Cardinal is a private foundation. Write a letter to him in which you address the issue. His address is 250 Bristol Road, Charlottesville, VA 22903.

32. Gray, Inc., a private foundation, has the following items of income and deductions.

Interest income	$24,000
Rent income	60,000
Dividend income	20,000
Royalty income	10,000
Unrelated business income	75,000
Rent expenses	18,000
Unrelated business expenses	10,000

Gray is not an exempt operating foundation and is not eligible for the 1% tax rate.
a. Calculate the net investment income.
b. Calculate the tax on net investment income.
c. What is the purpose of the tax on net investment income?

33. Eagle, Inc., a private foundation, has been in existence for 10 years. During this period, Eagle has been unable to satisfy the requirements for classification as a private operating foundation. At the end of 2004, it had undistributed income of $280,000. Of this amount, $120,000 was distributed in 2005, and $160,000 was distributed during the first quarter of 2006. The IRS deficiency notice was mailed on August 1, 2007.
a. Calculate the initial tax for 2004, 2005, and 2006.
b. Calculate the additional tax for 2007.

Decision Making

34. Otis is the CEO of Rectify, Inc., a private foundation. Otis invests $500,000 (80%) of the foundation's investment portfolio in derivatives. Previously, the $500,000 had been invested in corporate bonds with an AA rating that earned 7% per annum. If the derivatives investment works as Otis's investment adviser claims, the annual earnings could be as high as 20%.
a. Determine if Rectify is subject to any of the taxes imposed on private foundations.
b. If so, calculate the amount of the initial tax.
c. If so, calculate the amount of the additional tax if the act causing the imposition of the tax is not addressed within the correction period.
d. Are Otis and the foundation better off financially if the prohibited transaction, if any, is addressed within the correction period?

35. The board of directors of Pearl, Inc., a private foundation, consists of Alice, Beth, and Carlos. They vote unanimously to provide a $100,000 grant to Doug, their business associate. The grant is to be used for travel and education and does not qualify as a permitted grant to individuals (i.e., it is a taxable expenditure under § 4945). Each director knows that Doug was selected for the grant because he is a friend of the organization and that the grant is a taxable expenditure.
a. Calculate the initial tax imposed on the private foundation.
b. Calculate the initial tax imposed on the foundation manager (i.e., board of directors).

Communications

36. The Open Museum is an exempt organization that operates a gift shop. The museum's annual operations budget is $2.5 million. Gift shop sales generate a profit of $750,000. Another $500,000 of endowment income is generated. Both the income from the gift shop and the endowment income are used to support the exempt purpose of the museum. The balance of $1.25 million required for annual operations is provided through admission fees. Wayne Davis, a new board member, does not understand why the museum is subject to tax at all, particularly since the profits are used in carrying out the mission of the museum. The museum's address is 250 Oak Avenue, Peoria, IL 61625.
a. Calculate the amount of unrelated business income.
b. Assume that the endowment income is reinvested rather than being used to support annual operations. Calculate the amount of unrelated business income.
c. As the museum treasurer, write a letter to Wayne explaining the reason for the tax consequences. Mr. Davis's address is 45 Pine Avenue, Peoria, IL 61625.

Communications

37. Salmon, Inc., an exempt organization, has unrelated business taxable income of $20 million.
    a. Calculate Salmon's UBIT.
    b. Prepare an outline of a presentation you are going to give to the new members of Salmon's board on why Salmon is subject to the UBIT even though it is an exempt organization.

38. For each of the following organizations, determine the amount of the UBIT.
    a. AIDS, Inc., an exempt charitable organization that provides support for individuals with AIDS, operates a retail medical supply store open to the general public. The net income of the store, before any Federal income taxes, is $325,000.
    b. The local Episcopal Church operates a retail gift shop. The inventory consists of the typical items sold by commercial gift shops in the city. The director of the gift shop estimates that 80% of the gift shop sales are to tourists and 20% are to church members. The net income of the gift shop, before the salaries of the three gift shop employees and any Federal income taxes, is $300,000. The salaries of the employees total $80,000.
    c. Education, Inc., a private university, has vending machines in the student dormitories and academic buildings on campus. In recognition of recent tuition increases, the university has adopted a policy of merely trying to recover its costs associated with the vending machine activity. For the current year, however, the net income of the activity, before any Federal income taxes, is $75,000.
    d. Worn, Inc., an exempt organization, provides food for the homeless. It operates a thrift store that sells used clothing to the general public. The thrift shop is staffed by four salaried employees. All of the clothes it sells are received as contributions. The $100,000 profit generated for the year by the thrift shop is used in Worn's mission of providing food to the homeless.
    e. Small, Inc., an exempt organization, has unrelated business income of $900 and unrelated business expenses of $400.

39. Port Allen Sugarcane, Inc., contributes $10,000 to the Port Allen Krackers Baseball League, an exempt organization that sponsors summer baseball games for children under age 10. In return for the contribution, Port Allen Krackers includes Sugarcane's corporate logo on the cover of the program it sells at the baseball games.
    a. Determine the effect of the contribution to Port Allen Krackers.
    b. Instead of including the logo on the cover of its programs, Port Allen Krackers endorses Port Allen Sugarcane's sugar by advertising in the program that the mothers of team players use only sugar made by Port Allen Sugarcane for all their baking needs. Determine the effect of the contribution to Port Allen Krackers.

40. Fish, Inc., an exempt organization, has unrelated business taxable income of $400,000 (excluding the deduction for charitable contributions). During the year, it makes charitable contributions of $45,000, of which $38,000 are associated with the unrelated trade or business.
    a. Calculate unrelated business taxable income (UBTI).
    b. Assume that the charitable contributions are $39,000, of which $38,000 are associated with the unrelated trade or business. Calculate UBTI.

41. Tranquility, Inc., an exempt organization, leases factory equipment to Blouses, Inc. Blouses is a taxable entity that manufactures blouses for distribution through upscale department stores. Blouses owns the land and building where it conducts its manufacturing operations. The original cost of the building to Blouses was $800,000, and the cost recovery deduction for the current year is $20,512. Rent income to Tranquility for the factory equipment is $300,000, and the related expenses are $170,000. Calculate Tranquility's unrelated business taxable income.

42. Education, Inc., an exempt organization that provides educational services, has the following gains and losses from property transactions.

    - $42,000 loss on the sale of land and a building. The building had been used in carrying out Education's exempt purpose, but is no longer needed due to a contraction in the geographic area served.

- $185,000 gain on the sale of land and a building. The building had initially been acquired to lease to a national retailer. Due to a reduction in the number of its stores, the national retailer canceled the lease at the end of last year.
- $45,000 loss on the sale of investment land.
- $20,000 loss on the sale of computers. The computers had been leased to Teachers, Inc., an unrelated exempt organization. Prior to leasing the computers, Education had used them in carrying out its exempt purpose.

Determine the effect of these transactions on Education's unrelated business taxable income.

43. Fix, Inc., an exempt organization, owns a one-story building. Fix's adjusted basis for the building is $900,000. Of the building's total area of 10,000 square feet, the front portion (approximately 3,000 square feet) is used in carrying out Fix's exempt purpose. The remainder of the building is leased for $300,000 each year to Belts, Inc., a taxable entity, to use for storing its inventory. The unamortized balance of a mortgage relating to the original acquisition of the building is $600,000. Determine the portion of the adjusted basis that is treated as debt-financed property and the amount of the mortgage that is acquisition indebtedness.

44. Seagull, Inc., a § 501(c)(3) exempt organization, uses a tax year that ends on October 31, 2005. Seagull's gross receipts are $600,000, and related expenses are $580,000.
    a. Is Seagull required to file an annual Form 990?
    b. If so, what is the due date?

45. Historic Burg is an exempt organization that operates a museum depicting eighteenth-century life. Sally gives the museum an eighteenth-century chest that she has owned for 10 years. Her adjusted basis is $55,000, and the chest's appraised value is $100,000. Sally's adjusted gross income is $300,000. Calculate Sally's charitable contribution deduction if Historic Burg is:
    a. A private operating foundation.
    b. A private nonoperating foundation.

Research Problems

Note: Solutions to Research Problems can be prepared by using the ***RIA Checkpoint® Student Edition*** *online research product, which is available to accompany this text. It is also possible to prepare solutions to the Research Problems by using tax research materials found in a standard tax library.*

Research Problem 1. Allied Fund, a charitable organization exempt under § 501(c)(3), has branches located in each of the 50 states. Allied is not a private foundation. Rather than having each of the state units file an annual return with the IRS, Allied would like to file a single return that reports the activities of all of its branches. Is this permissible? What is the due date of the return?

Partial list of research aids:
§ 6033.
§ 6072.
Reg. § 1.6033–2(d).

Research Problem 2. City University has operated a television station since 1960. The station operates under a commercial license and is an affiliate of CBS. In addition to regular network programming, the television station broadcasts educational programming in the form of in-school classroom instruction, educational extension programming, and closed circuit educational programming. The station is also used in training students who are enrolled in degree programs as preparation for careers in the television industry.

City University maintains that the television station is substantially related to the purpose for which the university was granted exempt status under § 501(c)(3). The only purpose for operating the television station is to contribute to the achievement of the educational goals of the university.

Determine if the television station is subject to the tax on unrelated business income.

Internet Activity

Use the tax resources of the Internet to address the following question. Do not restrict your search to the World Wide Web, but include a review of newsgroups and general reference materials, practitioner sites and resources, primary sources of the tax law, chat rooms and discussion groups, and other opportunities.

Communications

Research Problem 3. Locate the Web site of a § 527 organization that supports the Democratic Party and a similar Web site that supports the Republican Party. If possible, determine the amount of money the organization raised and spent associated with the 2004 elections. Chart your findings in a PowerPoint presentation.

Multistate Corporate Taxation

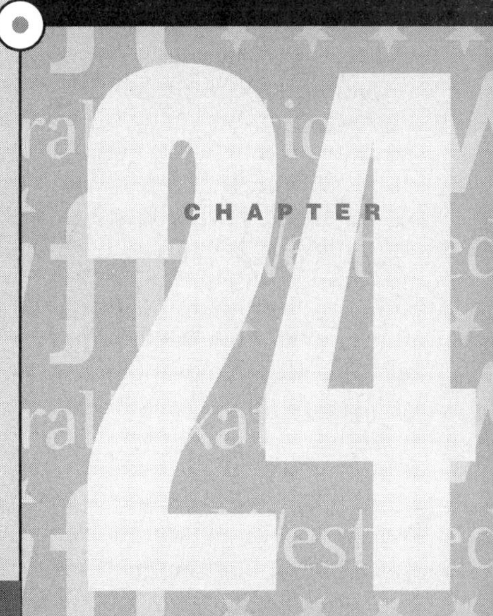

LEARNING OBJECTIVES

After completing Chapter 24, you should be able to:

LO.1
Illustrate the computation of a multistate corporation's state tax liability.

LO.2
Define nexus and explain its role in state income taxation.

LO.3
Distinguish between allocation and apportionment of a multistate corporation's taxable income.

LO.4
Describe the nature and treatment of business and nonbusiness income.

LO.5
Discuss the sales, payroll, and property apportionment factors.

LO.6
Apply the unitary method of state income taxation.

LO.7
Discuss the states' income tax treatment of S corporations, partnerships, and LLCs.

LO.8
Describe other commonly encountered state and local taxes on businesses.

LO.9
Recognize tax planning opportunities available to minimize a corporation's state and local tax liability.

http://wft.swlearning.com

OUTLINE

Although most of this text concentrates on the effects of the Federal income tax law upon the computation of a taxpayer's annual tax liability, a variety of tax bases apply to most business taxpayers. For example, a multinational corporation may be subject to tax in a number of different countries (see Chapter 25). Similarly, the taxpayer may be subject to a county-level wheel tax on its business vehicles, a state sales or use tax on many of its asset purchases, and state and local income or franchise taxes on its net income or on the privilege of doing business in the taxing jurisdiction. Indeed, estimates are that about 40 percent of the tax dollars paid by business taxpayers go to state and local authorities.

Businesses operate in a multistate environment for a variety of reasons. For the most part, nontax motivations drive such location decisions as where to build new plants or distribution centers or whether to move communications and data processing facilities and corporate headquarters. For example, a business typically wants to be close to its largest markets and to operate in a positive private- and public-sector business climate, where it has access to well-trained and reasonably priced labor, suppliers and support operations, sources of natural resources and well-educated personnel, and highway and airport facilities.

Many location decisions, though, are motivated by multistate tax considerations.

- The taxpayer's manufacturing, wholesaling, sales, retailing, and credit operations each may be centered in a different state to take advantage of various economic development incentives created by politicians.
- Mail-order and other catalog operations blur the traditional jurisdictional boundaries for buyer and seller alike. Often advertising campaigns boast "no sales tax payable."

- Similarly, the ability to transfer sales and purchase orders, pricing information, and other data via telephone lines, the Internet, and satellite transmissions may tempt the taxpayer to overlook traditional applications of the property and sales tax base. For example, is computer software tangible (and subject to property tax) or intangible property? Is canned software transferred via the Internet, rather than by disc, subject to sales tax? Which jurisdiction's property tax should apply to a communications satellite?
- In addition to flying over virtually the entire country, the major airlines depart from and land in the majority of the states. Which state's income tax should apply to the ticket income? Should sales or income tax apply to sales of movies or liquor while the plane is airborne?
- Local political concerns lead to a multiplicity of tax rules as politicians attempt to serve their constituents by introducing a variety of special tax incentives. This variety can be confusing, however. Taxpayers may have difficulty determining whether they qualify for energy or enterprise zone credits, S corporation status, exemptions from sales tax liability or income tax withholding, or passive loss relief at the local level.
- Politicians have a strong incentive to impose new tax burdens on visitors and others who have no direct say in their reelection. Thus, it is increasingly common to see tourist and hotel-bed taxes on convention delegates, city payroll taxes on commuters, and the use of obscure tax formulas that otherwise discriminate against those with limited contact in the area.
- Each jurisdiction in which the entity is subject to tax represents a geometrical increase in compliance responsibilities. For example, how many tax returns must be filed by a three-shareholder S corporation operating in 15 states?
- Various states and localities have adopted revenue-raising statutes that vary in sophistication and operate on different time schedules. For example, only a few states have adopted an alternative minimum tax, and states that impose the tax have tended to select different bases. In addition, the aggressiveness with which departments of revenue enforce their tax statutes varies greatly from state to state, even in a context of ongoing pressure to enhance revenues. Accordingly, the taxpayer must deal with a patchwork of germane taxing and enforcement provisions in an environment that is often uncertain.

This chapter reviews the basic tax concepts that are predominant among most states that impose a tax based on net income and discusses the major areas in which tax planning can reduce a corporation's overall state tax burden.

Most of this chapter is devoted to a discussion of state taxes that are based on income. Each state is free to identify its corporate tax by a different term. Not all of the states that impose a tax on corporate income call the tax an "income tax." Rather, some states refer to their tax on corporate income as a franchise tax,[1] a business tax, a license tax, or a business profits tax.

Overview of Corporate State Income Taxation

Forty-six states and the District of Columbia impose a tax based on a corporation's taxable income. Since each state is free to create its own tax provisions, the tax

[1]Although a franchise tax in some states is a business privilege tax based on a corporation's capital stock or net worth, several states use that term for the tax that they impose on a corporation's net income.

ETHICAL CONSIDERATIONS

Encouraging Economic Development through Tax Concessions

The tax professional occasionally is in a position to negotiate with a state or city taxing jurisdiction to garner tax relief for a client as an incentive to locate a plant or distribution center in that geographic area. In times when construction budgets are high and interstate competition is fierce, such tax concessions can be significant.

For instance, to encourage a business to build a large distribution center in the area, community leaders might be agreeable to (1) paying for roads, sewer, water, and other improvements through taxpayer bonds; (2) reducing property taxes by 50 percent for the first 10 years of the center's operations; and (3) permanently excluding any distribution-related vehicles and equipment from the personal property tax.

The community would grant the concessions even though the influx of new workers would place a great strain on public school facilities and likely necessitate improvements in traffic patterns and other infrastructure. Local residents, even those who obtain jobs at the new facility, and the tax adviser may wonder whether the tax concessions are supportable in light of these changes in the community's quality of life.

Take the position of a large employer that has been located in the area for more than 50 years. By how much should it be willing to absorb the tax increases that result when economic development concessions are used to attract new, perhaps temporary, businesses to the area? Should the employer challenge the constitutionality of the grant of such sizable tax breaks to some, but not all, business taxpayers in the jurisdiction?

Should higher "impact fees" be assessed on new developments? Does your analysis change if the new business competes with the long-time resident for sales? For employees? For political power?

practitioner could be faced with 47 entirely different state tax provisions.[2] Fortunately, however, to simplify the filing of tax returns and increase compliance with state tax laws, the majority of states "piggyback" onto the Federal income tax base. This means they have adopted *en masse* part or all of the Federal provisions governing the definition of income and the allowance of various exemptions, exclusions, and deductions. None of the states, however, has piggybacked its tax collections with the IRS.

LO.1

Illustrate the computation of a multistate corporation's state tax liability.

COMPUTING STATE INCOME TAX

In more than 40 of the states that impose a corporate income tax, the starting point in computing the tax base is taxable income as reflected on the Federal corporate income tax return (Form 1120). Those states whose computation of state taxable income is not coupled to the Federal tax return have their own state-specific definitions of gross and taxable income. Nonetheless, even these states typically adopt most Federal income and deduction provisions.

Although Federal tax law plays a significant role in the computation of state taxable income, there is a wide disparity in both the methods used to determine a state's taxable income and the tax rates imposed on that income. As only a few states apply more than one or two tax rates to taxable income, there is little progressivity to these tax systems. State tax credits typically are designed to encourage increased hiring and investment in local facilities. Cities and states often use targeted tax

[2]Although the District of Columbia is not a state, it operates in much the same manner as a state and imposes a tax based on income. Four states impose no corporate income tax at all: Nevada, South Dakota, Washington, and Wyoming. Corporations, however, are subject to a business and occupation tax in Washington. Several states base the tax on gross receipts, and Michigan uses a form of value added tax.

BRITNEY, YOU NEED TO PAY YOUR TAX

The state and local taxation of athletes, entertainers, and other high-income taxpayers who travel to numerous locations during the tax year has become a point of contention among the jurisdictions, the taxpayers, and policymakers. When Britney Spears comes to town for a major concert appearance, she often leaves behind thousands of dollars in state and local income taxes. California, a high-tax state with a sizable budget deficit, enforces these rules aggressively and collects over $100 million per year just from professional athletes.

The 2003 major league baseball All-Star Game was played at the home of the Chicago White Sox. Illinois is one of the few states that does not assess special taxes on visiting athletes and entertainers, as long as the athlete's home state does not tax Illinois-based professionals. This means that a player from Florida, Texas, or Washington State does not owe any Illinois income tax, but those from most other states do. Thus, as a Tax Foundation economist noted, "When Florida Marlin Dontrelle Willis replaced Los Angeles Dodger Kevin Brown in the All-Star lineup, baseball was happy, but Illinois lost over $2,200 in revenue."

Illinois does not treat its own professional athletes favorably. When income is earned in another state, say, at an away game, Illinois does not allow a tax credit for sums paid to the other state. Thus, when Chicago Cub Sammy Sosa played in the 2002 All-Star Game in Milwaukee, he was liable for both Wisconsin and Illinois income tax.

"Jock taxes" such as these have come under fire for being poorly targeted and arbitrary. There is, for instance, no special "CEO tax" or "consultant tax" for those in other businesses who must work in multiple states. Plus, the administrative burden on the tax advisers for these high-income taxpayers can be mind-boggling.

And even city-level taxes can be expensive for the professional athlete or entertainer. Philadelphia and New York City were the first to pursue such tax collections almost two decades ago, and about a half-dozen more large cities now have their hands out.

credits to entice businesses to expand within their borders. For instance, a state might offer a $1,000 credit for each new job created by the taxpayer or provide a 15 percent credit for taxpayers who purchase automobiles that were assembled in the state.

The formula used by a multistate corporation to determine its tax liability in a typical state is illustrated in Figure 24–1.

OPERATIONAL IMPLICATIONS

Generally, the accounting period and methods used by a corporation for state tax purposes must be consistent with those used on the Federal return. States often apply different rules, however, in identifying the members of a group filing a consolidated return and the income of each group member that is subject to tax.

As the starting point for computing state taxable income often is directly related to the Federal taxable income amount, most states also piggyback onto the IRS's audit process. Consequently, virtually all of the states that levy an income tax require notification of the final settlement of a Federal income tax audit. State authorities then adjust the originally calculated state tax liability appropriately.

■ **FIGURE 24–1**
Computing Corporate State Income Tax Liability

	Starting point in computing taxable income*
±	State modification items
	State tax base
±	Total net allocable income/(loss) (nonbusiness income)
	Total apportionable income/(loss) (business income)
×	State's apportionment percentage
	Income apportioned to the state
±	Income/(loss) allocated to the state
	State taxable income/(loss)
×	State tax rate
	Gross income tax liability for state
–	State's tax credits
	Net income tax liability for the state

*Most states use either line 28 or line 30 of the Federal corporate income tax return (Form 1120). In other states, the corporation is required to identify and report each element of income and deduction on the state return.

STATE MODIFICATIONS

Federal taxable income generally is used as the starting point in computing the state's income tax base, but numerous state adjustments or modifications are often made to Federal taxable income to:

- Reflect differences between state and Federal tax statutes.
- Remove income that a state is constitutionally prohibited from taxing.

The required modifications to Federal taxable income vary significantly among the states. Accordingly, this discussion is limited to the most common additions and subtractions that the states require. Exhibit 24–1 lists the most frequently encountered modifications. In computing the taxable income for a given state, only a selected number of these modifications may be applicable.

EXAMPLE 1

Blue Corporation is subject to tax only in State A. The starting point in computing State A taxable income is Federal taxable income. Modifications then are made to reflect, among other provisions, the exempt status of interest on State A obligations, all dividends received from in-state corporations, and the disallowance of a deduction for state income taxes. Blue generated the following income and deductions this year.

Sales	$1,500,000
Interest on Federal obligations	50,000
Interest on municipal obligations of State B	100,000
Dividends received from 50%-owned State A corporations	200,000
Total income	$1,850,000
Expenses related to Federal obligations	$ 1,000
Expenses related to municipal obligations	5,000
State income tax expense	50,000
Depreciation allowed for Federal tax purposes (the deduction allowed for state purposes is $300,000)	400,000
Other allowable deductions	1,000,000
Total deductions	$1,456,000

■ EXHIBIT 24–1
Common State Modifications

Addition Modifications

* Interest income received on state and municipal obligations and any other interest income that is exempt from Federal income tax. For this purpose, some states exempt interest earned on their own obligations.
* Expenses deducted in computing Federal taxable income that are directly or indirectly related to U.S. obligations.
* Income-based franchise and income taxes imposed by any state and the District of Columbia that were deducted in computing Federal taxable income.
* The amount by which the Federal deductions for depreciation, amortization, or depletion exceed those permitted by the state.
* The amount by which the state gain or loss from the disposal of assets differs from the Federal gain or loss. Due to the difference in permitted depreciation methods and other adjustments, a corporation's assets may have different Federal and state tax bases. This adjustment is not necessary if the state and Federal basis provisions are identical.

Adjustments required as a result of different elections being made for state and Federal purposes. Examples of such elections include the methods under which income from installment sales or long-term contracts is determined.

Federal net operating loss deduction. This modification is not required by states in which the starting point in the computation of taxable income is Federal income before special deductions.

Subtraction Modifications

* Interest on U.S. obligations or obligations of Federal agencies to the extent included in Federal taxable income but exempt from state income taxes under U.S. law.
* Expenses that are directly or indirectly related to the state and municipal interest that is taxable for state purposes.
* Refunds of franchise and income taxes imposed by any state and the District of Columbia, to the extent included in Federal taxable income.
* The amount by which the state deductions for depreciation, amortization, or depletion exceed the deductions permitted for Federal tax purposes.

Adjustments required as a result of different elections being made for state and Federal purposes, as above.

Dividends received from certain out-of-state corporations, to the extent included in Federal taxable income.

Net operating loss deduction as determined for state tax purposes.

Deduction for Federal income tax paid.

*Required by most states.

Blue's taxable income for Federal and state purposes is $139,000 and $295,000, respectively.

Federal Taxable Income	
Sales	$1,500,000
Interest on Federal obligations	50,000
Dividends received from domestic corporations	200,000
Total income	$1,750,000

Federal Taxable Income	
Expenses related to Federal obligations	$ 1,000
State income tax expense	50,000
Depreciation	400,000
Other allowable deductions	1,000,000
Total deductions	$1,451,000
Taxable income before special deductions	$ 299,000
Less: Dividends received deduction (80% × $200,000)	(160,000)
Federal taxable income	$ 139,000

State A Taxable Income	
Federal taxable income	$139,000
Addition Modifications	
Interest on municipal obligations of State B	100,000
State income tax expense	50,000
Excess depreciation deduction allowed for Federal purposes ($400,000 – $300,000)	100,000
Expenses related to Federal obligations	1,000
Subtraction Modifications	
Expenses related to municipal obligations	(5,000)
Dividends received from 50%-owned State A corporations included in Federal taxable income ($200,000 – $160,000)	(40,000)
Interest on Federal obligations	(50,000)
State A taxable income	$295,000

■

EXAMPLE 2

Continue with the facts of Example 1, except that the $100,000 of municipal interest was generated from State A obligations. The computation of Federal taxable income is unaffected by this change. Since State A exempts interest on its own obligations from taxation, Blue's State A taxable income is $200,000.

State A Taxable Income	
Federal taxable income	$139,000
Addition Modifications	
State income tax expense	50,000
Excess depreciation deduction allowed for Federal purposes ($400,000 – $300,000)	100,000
Expenses related to Federal obligations	1,000
Subtraction Modifications	
Dividends received from 50%-owned State A corporations included in Federal taxable income ($200,000 – $160,000)	(40,000)
Interest on Federal obligations	(50,000)
State A taxable income	$200,000

■

LO.2

Define nexus and explain its role in state income taxation.

JURISDICTION TO IMPOSE TAX: NEXUS AND PUBLIC LAW 86–272

The state in which a business is incorporated has the jurisdiction to tax the corporation, regardless of the volume of its business activity within the state. Whether a state can tax the income of a business that is incorporated in another state usually depends on the relationship between the state and the corporation.

Nexus describes the degree of business activity that must be present before a taxing jurisdiction has the right to impose a tax on an out-of-state entity's income. State law defines the measure of the relationship that is necessary to create nexus. Typically, sufficient nexus is present when a corporation derives income from sources within the state, owns or leases property in the state, employs personnel in the state, or has physical or financial capital there. **Public Law 86–272** limits the states' right to impose an income tax on interstate activities.[3] This Federal law prohibits a state from taxing a business whose only connection with the state is to solicit orders for sales of tangible personal property that is sent outside the state for approval or rejection. If approved, the orders must be filled and shipped by the business from a point outside the state.

Only the sales of tangible personal property are immune from taxation under the law, however. Leases, rentals, and other dispositions of tangible personal property are not protected activities. Moreover, dispositions of real property and intangible property, as well as sales of services, are not protected by Public Law 86–272. In this regard, each state constructs its own definition of tangible and intangible property. Thus, since property ownership is not a protected activity, providing company-owned fax, copy, or computer equipment to an out-of-state salesperson may create nexus with a state, even though the salesperson merely solicits sales orders there.

An activity that consists merely of solicitation is immune from taxation. The statute does not define the term *solicitation*, but the Supreme Court has held that *solicitation of orders* includes any explicit verbal request for orders and any speech or conduct that implicitly invites an order.[4] The Court also created a *de minimis* rule, allowing immunity from nexus where a limited amount of solicitation occurs.

Exhibit 24–2 summarizes the activities that are recognized as being directly related to solicitation (protected activities) and activities unrelated to solicitation (which establish income tax nexus for the entity).

Independent Contractors. Public Law 86–272 extends immunity to certain in-state activities conducted by an independent contractor that would not be permitted if performed directly by the taxpayer. Generally, an independent contractor may engage in the following limited activities without establishing nexus for the principal: (1) soliciting sales, (2) making sales, and (3) maintaining a sales office.

LO.3

Distinguish between allocation and apportionment of a multistate corporation's taxable income.

Allocation and Apportionment of Income

A corporation that conducts business activities in more than one state must determine the portion of its net income that is subject to tax by each state. A corporation that has established sufficient nexus with another state generally must both **allocate** and **apportion** its income.

[3]15 U.S.C. 381–385.

[4]*Wisconsin Department of Revenue v. William Wrigley, Jr., Co.*, 112 S.Ct. 2447 (1992).

■ EXHIBIT 24–2
Common Nexus Definitions under Public Law 86–272

General rule: P.L. 86–272 immunity applies where the sales representative's activities are ancillary to the order-solicitation process.

Activities That Usually Do Not Create Nexus under P.L. 86–272

- Advertising campaigns.
- Carrying free samples only for display or distribution.
- Owning or furnishing automobiles to salespersons.
- Passing inquiries or complaints on to the home office.
- Checking customers' inventories for reorder.
- Maintaining a sample or display room for two weeks or less during the year.

Activities Usually Sufficient to Establish Nexus

- Making repairs or providing maintenance.
- Collecting delinquent accounts; investigating creditworthiness.
- Installation or supervision of installation.
- Conducting training classes, seminars, or lectures for persons other than sales personnel.
- Approving or accepting orders.
- Picking up or replacing damaged or returned property.
- Hiring, training, or supervising personnel other than sales employees.
- Providing shipping information and coordinating deliveries.
- Carrying samples for sale, exchange, or distribution in any manner for consideration or other value.
- Owning, leasing, maintaining, or otherwise using any of the following facilities or property in the state: real estate; repair shop; parts department; employment office; purchasing office; warehouse; meeting place for directors, officers, or employees; stock of goods; telephone answering service; or mobile stores (i.e., trucks with driver-salespersons).
- Maintaining an office for an employee, including an office in the home.

Apportionment is a means by which a corporation's business income is divided among the states in which it conducts business. Under an apportionment procedure, a corporation determines allowable income and deductions for the company as a whole and then apportions some of its net income to a given state, according to an approved formula.

Allocation is a method under which specific components of a corporation's income, net of related expenses, are directly assigned to a certain state. Allocation differs from apportionment in that allocable income is assigned to one state, whereas apportionable income is divided among several states. Nonapportionable (nonbusiness) income generally includes:

- Income or losses derived from the sale of nonbusiness real or tangible property, or
- Income or losses derived from rentals and royalties from nonbusiness real or tangible personal property.

This income normally is allocated to the state where the property that generated the income or loss is located.

As Figure 24–1 indicated, total allocable (nonapportionable) income or loss typically is removed from corporate net income before the state's apportionment percentage is applied. The nonapportionable income or loss assigned to a state then is combined with the income apportionable to that state to arrive at total income subject to tax in the state.

EXAMPLE 3

Green Corporation conducts business in States N, O, P, and Q. Green's $900,000 taxable income is comprised of $800,000 apportionable income and $100,000 allocable income generated from transactions conducted in State Q. Green's sales, property, and payroll are evenly divided among the four states, and the states all employ an identical apportionment formula. Accordingly, $200,000 of Green's income is taxable in each of States N, O, and P. Green is subject to income tax on $300,000 of income in State Q.

Apportionable income	$800,000
Apportionment percentage (apportionable income is divided equally among the four states)	× 25%
Income apportioned to each state	$200,000

	State N	State O	State P	State Q
Income apportioned	$200,000	$200,000	$200,000	$200,000
Income allocated	-0-	-0-	-0-	100,000
Taxable income	$200,000	$200,000	$200,000	$300,000

THE APPORTIONMENT PROCEDURE

Apportionment assumes that the production of business income is linked to business activity, and the laws of each state define a number of factors believed to indicate the amount of corporate activity conducted within the state. However, apportionment often does not provide a uniform division of an organization's income based on its business activity, because each state is free to choose the type and number of factors that it believes are indicative of the business activity conducted within its borders. Therefore, a corporation may be subject to state income tax on more or less than 100 percent of its income.

An equally incongruous consequence of apportionment may occur when the operations in a state result in a loss.

EXAMPLE 4

Red Corporation's operations include two manufacturing facilities, located in States A and B, respectively. The plant located in A generated $500,000 of income, and the plant located in B generated a loss of $200,000. Therefore, Red's total taxable income is $300,000.

By applying the statutes of each state, Red determines that its apportionment factors for A and B are .65 and .35, respectively. Accordingly, Red's income is apportioned to the states as follows.

Income apportioned to State A: $300,000 × .65 = $195,000

Income apportioned to State B: $300,000 × .35 = $105,000

Red is subject to tax in B on $105,000 of income, even though the operations conducted in that state resulted in a loss.

LO.4

Describe the nature and treatment of business and nonbusiness income.

BUSINESS AND NONBUSINESS INCOME

Business income is assigned among the states by using an apportionment formula. In contrast, *nonbusiness income* is either apportioned or allocated to the state in which the income-producing asset is located. For example, income derived from the rental of nonbusiness real property generally is allocated to the state in which the property is located.

EXAMPLE 5

TNT Corporation, a manufacturer of explosive devices, is a multistate taxpayer that has nexus with States P and Q. During the taxable year, TNT's net sales of explosive devices were $900,000; $600,000 of these sales were made in P and $300,000 were made in Q. The corporation also received $90,000 from the rental of nonbusiness real property located in P.

Both states employ a three-factor apportionment formula under which sales, property, and payroll are equally weighted. However, the states do not agree on the definition of apportionable income. Under P's tax provisions, nonbusiness rent income is allocable and business income is apportionable, while Q requires a corporation to apportion all of its (business and nonbusiness) income. The sales factor (the ratio of in-state sales to total sales) for each of the states is computed as follows.

$$\text{State P: } \frac{\$600{,}000 \text{ (sales in State P)}}{\$900{,}000 \text{ (total sales)}} = 66.67\%$$

$$\text{State Q: } \frac{\$300{,}000 \text{ (sales in State Q)}}{\$990{,}000 \text{ (total sales)*}} = 30.30\%$$

*Since rent income is treated as business income, rents are included in the denominator of the sales factor. ■

EXAMPLE 6

Continue with the facts of Example 5, except that the rent income was generated from property located in Q, rather than from property located in P. Although the sales factor for P remains the same, the sales factor for Q changes.

$$\text{State P: } \frac{\$600{,}000 \text{ (sales in State P)}}{\$900{,}000 \text{ (total sales)}} = 66.67\%$$

$$\text{State Q: } \frac{\$390{,}000 \text{ (sales in State Q)}}{\$990{,}000 \text{ (total sales)}} = 39.39\%$$

Due to the composition of the sales factor in the two states, TNT's income never is perfectly apportioned: the aggregate of the sales factors is either more or less than 100%. ■

Business income arises from the taxpayer's regular course of business or constitutes an integral part of the taxpayer's regular business.[5] In determining whether an item of income is (apportionable) business income, state courts have developed a variety of approaches to determine what constitutes a taxpayer's "regular course of business."[6]

Nonbusiness income is "all income other than business income."[7] Usually, nonbusiness income comprises passive and portfolio income, such as dividends, interest, rents, royalties, and certain capital gains. However, passive or portfolio income may be classified as business income when the acquisition, management, and disposition of the underlying property constitute an integral part of the taxpayer's regular business operation.

EXAMPLE 7

Gray Corporation owns and operates two manufacturing facilities, one in State A and the other in State B. Due to a temporary decline in sales, Gray has rented 10% of its A facility to an unaffiliated corporation. Gray generated $100,000 of net rent income and $900,000 of income from manufacturing.

Both A and B classify such rent income as allocable nonbusiness income. By applying the statutes of each state, as discussed in the next section, Gray determines that its apportionment

[5]MTC Reg. IV.1.(a).

[6]*Atlantic Richfield Co. v. State of Colorado and Joseph F. Dolan*, 601 P.2d 628 (Colo.S.Ct., 1979); *Appeal of A. Epstein and Sons, Inc.* (Cal.State Bd. of Equalization, 1984).

[7]UDITPA § 1(e).

factors are 0.40 for A and 0.60 for B. Gray's income attributable to each state is determined as shown below.

Income Subject to Tax in State A	
Taxable income	$1,000,000
Less: Allocable income	(100,000)
Apportionable income	$ 900,000
Times: Apportionment factor	40%
Income apportioned to State A	$ 360,000
Plus: Income allocated to State A	100,000
Income subject to tax in State A	$ 460,000
Income Subject to Tax in State B	
Taxable income	$1,000,000
Less: Allocable income	(100,000)
Apportionable income	$ 900,000
Times: Apportionment factor	60%
Income apportioned to State B	$ 540,000
Plus: Income allocated to State B	–0–
Income subject to tax in State B	$ 540,000

■

LO.5

Discuss the sales, payroll, and property apportionment factors.

APPORTIONMENT FACTORS: ELEMENTS AND PLANNING

Business income is apportioned among the states by determining the appropriate apportionment percentage for each state that has a right to tax the entity. To determine the apportionment percentage for each state, a ratio is established for each of the factors included in the state's apportionment formula. Each ratio is calculated by comparing the level of a specific business activity within a state to the total corporate activity of that type. The ratios then are summed, averaged, and appropriately weighted (if required) to determine the corporation's apportionment percentage for a specific state.

Although apportionment formulas vary among jurisdictions, the traditional three-factor formula equally weights sales, property, and payroll.[8] This formula is derived from the Uniform Division of Income for Tax Purposes Act (**UDITPA**), a model law relating to the assignment of income among the states for corporations that maintain operations in more than one state. However, most of the states now use a modified three-factor formula, where the sales factor receives more than a one-third weight. The use of a higher-weighted sales factor tends to pull a larger percentage of an out-of-state corporation's income into the taxing jurisdiction of the state, because the corporation's major activity within the state—the sales of its products—is weighted more heavily than are its payroll and property activities. Overweighting the sales factor, however, provides tax relief for corporations that are domiciled in the state. Those corporations generally own significantly more property and incur more payroll costs (factors that are given less weight in the apportionment formula) within the state than do out-of-state corporations.

[8]Certain industries, such as financial institutions, insurance companies, air and motor carriers, pipeline companies, and public utilities, typically are required to use special apportionment formulas.

EXAMPLE 8

Musk Corporation realized $500,000 of taxable income from the sales of its products in States A and B. Musk's activities in both states establish nexus for income tax purposes. Musk's sales, payroll, and property in the states include the following.

	State A	State B	Total
Sales	$1,250,000	$750,000	$2,000,000
Property	2,500,000	–0–	2,500,000
Payroll	1,500,000	–0–	1,500,000

If State B uses an equally weighted three-factor apportionment formula, $62,500 of Musk's taxable income is apportioned to B.

Sales ($750,000/$2,000,000)	=	37.5%
Property ($0/$2,500,000)	=	–0–
Payroll ($0/$1,500,000)	=	–0–
Sum of apportionment factors		37.5%
Average	÷	3
Apportionment factor for State B		12.5%
Taxable income	×	$500,000
Taxable income apportioned to State B		$ 62,500

If State B uses a double-weighted sales factor in its three-factor apportionment formula, $93,750 of Musk's taxable income is apportioned to B.

Sales ($750,000/$2,000,000)	=	37.5% × 2	=	75%
Property ($0/$2,500,000)	=			–0–
Payroll ($0/$1,500,000)	=			–0–
Sum of apportionment factors				75%
Average			÷	4
Apportionment factor for State B				18.75%
Taxable income			×	$500,000
Taxable income apportioned to State B				$ 93,750

When a state uses a double-weighted sales factor, typically a larger percentage of an out-of-state corporation's income is subject to tax in the state. Here, an additional $31,250 ($93,750 – $62,500) of Musk's income is subject to tax in B. ■

A single-factor apportionment formula consisting solely of a sales factor is even more detrimental to an out-of-state corporation than an apportionment factor that double weights the sales factor.[9]

EXAMPLE 9

PPR Corporation, a retailer of paper products, owns retail stores in States A, B, and C. State A uses a three-factor apportionment formula under which the sales, property, and payroll factors are equally weighted. B uses a three-factor apportionment formula under which sales are double weighted. C employs a single-factor apportionment factor, based solely on sales.

[9]Currently, only Illinois, Nebraska, and Texas require the use of a single-factor apportionment formula.

PPR's operations generated $800,000 of apportionable income, and its sales, payroll activity, and average property owned in each of the three states are as follows.

	State A	State B	State C	Total
Sales	$500,000	$400,000	$300,000	$1,200,000
Payroll	100,000	125,000	75,000	300,000
Property	150,000	250,000	100,000	500,000

$280,000 of PPR's apportionable income is assigned to A.

Sales ($500,000/$1,200,000)	=	41.67%
Payroll ($100,000/$300,000)	=	33.33%
Property ($150,000/$500,000)	=	30.00%
Sum of apportionment factors		105.00%
Average	÷	3
Apportionment factor for State A		35.00%
Apportionable income	×	$800,000
Income apportioned to State A		$280,000

$316,640 of PPR's apportionable income is assigned to B.

Sales ($400,000/$1,200,000)	=	33.33% × 2	=	66.66%
Payroll ($125,000/$300,000)			=	41.67%
Property ($250,000/$500,000)			=	50.00%
Sum of apportionment factors				158.33%
Average			÷	4
Apportionment factor for State B				39.58%
Apportionable income			×	$800,000
Income apportioned to State B				$316,640

$200,000 of PPR's apportionable income is assigned to C.

Sales ($300,000/$1,200,000)	=	25.00%
Sum of apportionment factors		25.00%
Average	÷	1
Apportionment factor for State C		25.00%
Apportionable income	×	$800,000
Income apportioned to State C		$200,000

Summary	
Income apportioned to State A	$280,000
Income apportioned to State B	316,640
Income apportioned to State C	200,000
Total income apportioned	$796,640

Due to the variations in the apportionment formulas employed by the various states, only 99.58% ($796,640/$800,000) of PPR's income is apportioned to the states in which it is subject to tax. ■

THE SALES FACTOR

The **sales factor** is a fraction, whose numerator is the corporation's total sales in the state during the tax period. The denominator is the corporation's total sales everywhere during the tax period. Gross sales for this purpose generally are net of returns, allowances, and discounts. Moreover, interest income, service charges, and carrying charges are included in the sales factor. Federal and state excise taxes and state sales taxes are included in the factor, if these taxes are either passed on to the buyer or included in the selling price of the goods.

Since the sales factor is a component in the formula used to apportion a corporation's business income to a state, only sales that generate business income are includible in the fraction. The "sales" factor actually resembles a "receipts" factor since it also generally includes business income from the sale of inventory or services, interest, dividends, rentals, royalties, sales of assets, and other business income. Income on Federal obligations, however, is not included in the sales factor.

When the sale involves capital assets, some states require that the gross proceeds, rather than the net gain or loss, be included in the fraction. Most states allow incidental or occasional asset sales and sales of certain intangible assets to be excluded from gross receipts.[10]

In determining the numerator of the sales factor, most states use the UDITPA's "ultimate destination concept," under which tangible asset sales are assumed to take place at the point of delivery, not at the location at which the shipment originates.

EXAMPLE 10

Olive Corporation, whose only manufacturing plant is located in State A, sells its products to residents of A through its local retail store. Olive also ships its products to customers in States B and C. The products that are sold to residents of A are assigned to A, while the products that are delivered to B and C are assigned to B and C, respectively. ■

Throwback Rule. Out-of-state sales that are not subject to tax in the destination state are pulled back into the origination state if that state has adopted a **throwback rule.** This rule is an exception to the destination test. The rule provides that, when a corporation is not subject to tax in the destination state or the purchaser is the U.S. government, the sales are treated as in-state sales of the origination state, and the actual destination of the product is disregarded. Consequently, when the seller is immune from tax in the destination state under Public Law 86–272, the sales are considered to be in-state sales of the origination state if that state has a throwback provision.

The throwback rule seems inappropriate when the sale is made to a purchaser in a foreign country, where the transaction is subject to a gross-receipts tax (but no income tax). In these cases, the taxpayer truly is subject to double taxation, as state taxes increase but no Federal foreign tax credit is available. Nonetheless, most of the throwback states fail to distinguish between U.S. and foreign throwback sales.

EXAMPLE 11

Braun Corporation's entire operations are located in State A. Seventy percent ($700,000) of Braun's sales are made in A, and the remaining 30% ($300,000) are made in State B. Braun's solicitation of sales in B is limited to mailing a monthly catalog to its customers in that state. However, Braun employees do pick up and replace damaged merchandise in State B.

The pickup and replacement of damaged goods establish nexus with A. Braun's activities in B are sufficient (as determined by A's law) to subject Braun to a positive tax, based on its income. Therefore, Braun is permitted to apportion its income between A and B. However,

[10] MTC Reg. IV.18.(c).

B's interpretation of activities necessary to create nexus is less strict than that imposed by A; in B, the mere pickup and replacement of damaged goods do not subject a corporation's income to tax.

Braun's taxable income is $900,000. Both A and B impose a 10% corporate income tax and include only the sales factor in their apportionment formulas. If A has not adopted a throwback rule, Braun's effective state income tax rate is 7%.

	Apportionment Factors	Taxable Income	Tax Rate	Tax
State A	70%	$900,000	10%	$63,000
State B	–0–*	900,000	10%	–0–
Total tax liability				$63,000
Effective state income tax rate: $63,000/$900,000 =				7%

*As determined under B's laws, Braun's income is not apportionable to State B, because insufficient nexus is present.

If A has adopted a throwback rule, Braun does not benefit from its lack of nexus with B, because the sales in B are considered to be in-state sales of A. Thus, Braun's effective tax rate is 10%.

	Apportionment Factors	Taxable Income	Tax Rate	Tax
State A	100%	$900,000	10%	$90,000
State B	–0–	900,000	10%	–0–
Total tax liability				$90,000
Effective state income tax rate: $90,000/$900,000 =				10%
Tax increase due to throwback provision ($90,000 – $63,000)				$27,000

THE PAYROLL FACTOR

The **payroll factor** is determined by comparing the compensation paid for services rendered within a state to the total compensation paid by the corporation. Generally, the payroll factor is a fraction, whose numerator is the total amount that a corporation paid or accrued for compensation in a state during the tax period. The denominator is the total amount paid or accrued by the corporation for compensation during the tax period. For purposes of the payroll factor, compensation includes wages, salaries, commissions, and any other form of remuneration paid or accrued to employees for personal services. Compensation may also include the value of board, rent, housing, lodging, and other benefits or services furnished to employees by the taxpayer in return for personal services, if these amounts constitute Federal gross income.

Payments made to an independent contractor or any other person who is not properly classifiable as an employee generally are excluded from the numerator and denominator of the payroll factor. Some states exclude from the payroll factor the compensation paid to corporate officers.

Several states provide that earnings paid to a cash or deferred compensation plan, excluded from Federal gross income under § 401(k), are to be included in the numerator and the denominator of the payroll factor. Accordingly, the total compensation that is included in the denominator of a corporation's payroll factor may vary among the states in which the corporation's income is apportioned.

EXAMPLE 12

Mice Corporation's sales office and manufacturing plant are located in State A. Mice also maintains a manufacturing plant and sales office in State C. For purposes of apportionment, A defines payroll as all compensation paid to employees, including contributions to § 401(k) deferred compensation plans. Under the statutes of C, neither compensation paid to officers nor contributions to § 401(k) plans are included in the payroll factor. Mice incurred the following personnel costs.

	State A	State C	Total
Wages and salaries for employees other than officers	$350,000	$250,000	$600,000
Salaries for officers	150,000	100,000	250,000
Contributions to § 401(k) plans	30,000	20,000	50,000
Total	$530,000	$370,000	$900,000

The payroll factor for State A is computed as follows.

$$\frac{\$530,000}{\$900,000} = 58.89\%$$

Since C excludes from the payroll factor any compensation paid to officers and contributions to § 401(k) plans, C's factor is computed as follows.

$$\frac{\$250,000}{\$600,000} = 41.67\%$$

The aggregate of Mice's payroll factors is 100.56% (58.89% + 41.67%). In certain cases, the sum of a corporation's payroll factors may be significantly more or less than 100%. ■

Only compensation that is related to the production of apportionable income is included in the payroll factor. Accordingly, in those states that distinguish between business and nonbusiness income, compensation related to the operation, maintenance, protection, or supervision of nonbusiness income is not includible in the payroll factor.

EXAMPLE 13

Dog Corporation, a manufacturer of automobile parts, is subject to tax in States X and Y. Dog incurred the following payroll costs.

	State X	State Y	Total
Wages and salaries for officers and personnel of manufacturing facilities	$450,000	$350,000	$800,000
Wages and salaries for personnel involved in nonbusiness rental activities	50,000	-0-	50,000

If both states distinguish between business and nonbusiness income in determining apportionable income and include officers' compensation in the payroll factor, Dog's payroll factors are computed as follows.

Payroll factor for State X: $450,000/$800,000 = 56.25%

Payroll factor for State Y: $350,000/$800,000 = 43.75% ■

EXAMPLE 14

Continue with the facts of Example 13, but assume that Y defines apportionable income as the corporation's total income (business and nonbusiness income). Dog's payroll factor for X remains unchanged, but its payroll factor for Y is reduced.

Payroll factor for State X: $450,000/$800,000 = 56.25%

Payroll factor for State Y: $350,000/$850,000* = 41.18%

*$800,000 (compensation related to business income) + $50,000 (compensation related to nonbusiness income). ■

THE PROPERTY FACTOR

The **property factor** generally is a fraction, whose numerator is the average value of the corporation's real property and its tangible personal property owned and used or rented and used in the state during the taxable year. The denominator is the average value of all of the corporation's real property and its tangible personal property owned or rented and used during the taxable year, wherever it is located. In this manner, a state's property factor reflects the extent of total property usage by the taxpayer in the state.

For this purpose, property includes land, buildings, machinery, inventory, equipment, and other real and tangible personal property, other than coins or currency.[11] Other types of property that may be included in the factor are construction in progress (even though it does not yet contribute to the production of income), offshore property, outer space property (satellites), and partnership property.

In the case of property that is in transit between locations of the taxpayer or between a buyer and seller, the assets are included in the numerator of the destination state. With respect to mobile or movable property, such as construction equipment, trucks, and leased equipment, which is both in- and outside the state during the tax period, the numerator of a state's property factor generally is determined on the basis of the total time that the property was within the state.

Space satellites used in the communication industry generally are included in the numerator of the property factor based on the ratio of earth stations serviced. For example, if a satellite is being serviced by earth stations located in San Francisco, Chicago, New York, and Houston, 25 percent of the cost of the satellite is included in the numerator of the property factor for each of the four corresponding states.

Property owned by the corporation typically is valued at its average original or historical cost plus the cost of additions and improvements, but without adjusting for depreciation. Some states allow property to be included at net book value or adjusted tax basis. The value of the property usually is determined by averaging the values at the beginning and end of the tax period. Alternatively, some states allow or require the amount to be calculated on a monthly basis if annual computation results in or requires substantial distortions.

EXAMPLE 15

Blond Corporation, a calendar year taxpayer, owns property in States A and B. Both A and B require that the average value of assets be included in the property factor. A requires that the property be valued at its historical cost, and B requires that the property be included in the property factor at its net book value.

[11]MTC Reg. IV.10.(a).

Account Balances at January 1			
	State A	**State B**	**Total**
Inventories	$ 150,000	$ 100,000	$ 250,000
Building and machinery (cost)	200,000	400,000	600,000
Accumulated depreciation for building and machinery	(150,000)	(50,000)	(200,000)
Land	50,000	100,000	150,000
Total	$ 250,000	$ 550,000	$ 800,000

Account Balances at December 31			
	State A	**State B**	**Total**
Inventories	$ 250,000	$ 200,000	$ 450,000
Building and machinery (cost)	200,000	400,000	600,000
Accumulated depreciation for building and machinery	(175,000)	(100,000)	(275,000)
Land	50,000	100,000	150,000
Total	$ 325,000	$ 600,000	$ 925,000

State A Property Factor			
Historical Cost	**January 1**	**December 31**	**Average**
Property in State A	$ 400,000*	$ 500,000**	$ 450,000
Total property	1,000,000†	1,200,000††	1,100,000

* $150,000 + $200,000 + $50,000.
** $250,000 + $200,000 + $50,000.
† $250,000 + $600,000 + $150,000.
†† $450,000 + $600,000 + $150,000.

$$\text{Property factor for State A: } \frac{\$450{,}000}{\$1{,}100{,}000} = 40.91\%$$

State B Property Factor			
Net Book Value	**January 1**	**December 31**	**Average**
Property in State B	$550,000	$600,000	$575,000
Total property	800,000	925,000	862,500

$$\text{Property factor for State B: } \frac{\$575{,}000}{\$862{,}500} = 66.67\%$$

Due to the variations in the property factors, the aggregate of Blond's property factors equals 107.58%. ■

Leased property, when included in the property factor, is valued at eight times its annual rental. Annual rentals may include payments, such as real estate taxes and insurance, made by the lessee in lieu of rent.

EXAMPLE 16

Jasper Corporation is subject to tax in States D and G. Both states require that leased or rented property be included in the property factor at eight times the annual rental costs, and that the average historical cost be used for other assets. Information regarding Jasper's property and rental expenses follows.

Average Historical Cost	
Property located in State D	$ 750,000
Property located in State G	450,000
Total property	$1,200,000

Lease and Rental Expenses	
State D	$ 50,000
State G	150,000
Total	$ 200,000

$$\text{Property factor for State D: } \frac{\$750{,}000 + 8(\$50{,}000)}{\$1{,}200{,}000 + 8(\$200{,}000)} = 41.07\%$$

$$\text{Property factor for State G: } \frac{\$450{,}000 + 8(\$150{,}000)}{\$1{,}200{,}000 + 8(\$200{,}000)} = 58.93\%$$

■

Only property that is used in the production of apportionable income is includible in the numerator and denominator of the property factor. In this regard, idle property and property that is used in producing nonapportionable income generally are excluded. However, property that is temporarily idle or unused generally remains in the property factor.

LO.6

Apply the unitary method of state income taxation.

The Unitary Theory

The **unitary theory** developed in response to the early problems that states faced in attributing the income of a multistate business among the states in which the business was conducted. Originally, this theory was applied to justify apportionment of the income of multiple operating divisions within a single company. Over the years, however, the concept has been extended to require the combined reporting of certain affiliated corporations, including those outside the United States.

When two affiliated corporations are subject to tax in different states, each entity must file a return and report its income in the state in which it conducts business. Each entity reports its income separately from that of its affiliated corporations. In an effort to minimize overall state income tax, multistate entities have attempted to separate the parts of the business that are carried on in the various states.

EXAMPLE 17

Arts Corporation owns a chain of retail stores located in several states. To enable each store to file and report the income earned only in that state, each store was organized as a separate subsidiary in the state in which it did business. In this manner, each store is separately subject to tax only in the state in which it is located. ■

Since most states attempt to allocate as much income to in-state sources as possible, several states have adopted the *unitary* approach to computing state taxable income. Under this method, a corporation is required to file a "combined return" that includes the results from all of the operations of the related corporations, not just from those that transacted business in the state. In this manner, the unitary method allows a state to apply formula apportionment to a firm's nationwide or worldwide unitary income. To include the activities of the corporation's subsidiaries in the apportionment formula, the state must determine that the subsidiaries' activities are an integral part of a unitary business and, as a result, are subject to apportionment.

WHAT IS A UNITARY BUSINESS?

A unitary business operates as a unit and cannot be segregated into independently operating divisions. The operations are integrated, and each division depends on or contributes to the operation of the business as a whole. It is not necessary that each unit operating within a state contribute to the activities of all divisions outside the state. The unitary theory ignores the separate legal existence of the entities and focuses instead on practical business realities. Accordingly, the separate entities are treated as a single business for state income tax purposes, and the apportionment formula is applied to the combined income of the unitary business.

EXAMPLE 18

Continue with the facts of Example 17. Arts manufactured no goods, but conducted central management, purchasing, distributing, advertising, and administrative departments. The subsidiaries carried on a purely intrastate business, and they paid for the goods and services received at the parent company's cost, plus overhead. Arts and the subsidiaries constitute a unitary business due to their unitary operations (purchasing, distributing, advertising, and administrative functions). Accordingly, in states that have adopted the unitary method, the income and apportionment factors of the entire unitary group are combined and apportioned to the states in which at least one member of the group has nexus. ■

EXAMPLE 19

Crafts Corporation organized its departments as separate corporations on the basis of function: mining copper ore, refining the ore, and fabricating the refined copper into consumer products. Even though the various steps in the process are operated substantially independently of each other with only general supervision from Crafts's executive offices, Crafts is engaged in a single unitary business. Its various divisions are part of a large, vertically structured enterprise, in which each business segment needs the products or raw materials provided by another. The flow of products between the affiliates also provides evidence of functional integration, which generally requires some form of central decision or policy making, another characteristic of a unitary business. ■

Notice that the application of the unitary theory is based on a series of subjective observations about the organization and operation of the taxpayer's businesses, whereas the availability of Federal controlled and affiliated group status is based on objective, mechanical ownership tests. About half of the states require or allow unitary reporting, a somewhat smaller number than in the early 1980s.

TAX EFFECTS OF THE UNITARY THEORY

Use of the unitary approach by a state eliminates several of the planning techniques that could be used to shift income between corporate segments to avoid or minimize state taxes. In addition, the unitary approach usually results in a larger portion of the corporation's income being taxable in states where the compensation, property values, and sales prices are high relative to other states. This occurs because the larger in-state costs (numerators in the apportionment formula) include in the tax base a larger portion of the taxable income within the state's taxing jurisdiction.

This has an adverse effect upon the corporation's overall state tax burden if the states in which the larger portions are allocated impose a high tax rate relative to the other states in which the business is conducted.

The presence of a unitary business is favorable when losses of unprofitable affiliates may be offset against the earnings of profitable affiliates. It also is favorable when income earned in a high-tax state may be shifted to low-tax states due to the use of combined apportionment factors.

EXAMPLE 20

Rita Corporation owns two subsidiaries, Arts and Crafts. Arts, located in State K, generated taxable income of $700,000. During this same period, Crafts, located in State M, generated a loss of $400,000. If the subsidiaries are independent corporations, Arts is required to pay K tax on $700,000 of income. However, if the corporations constitute a unitary business, the incomes, as well as the apportionment factors, of the two entities are combined. As a result, the combined income of $300,000 ($700,000 – $400,000) is apportioned to unitary states K and M. ■

EXAMPLE 21

Everett Corporation, a wholly owned subsidiary of Dan Corporation, generated $1 million of taxable income. Everett's activities and sales are restricted to State P, which imposes a 10% income tax. Dan's income for the taxable period is $1.5 million. Dan's activities and sales are restricted to State Q, which imposes a 5% income tax. Both states use a three-factor apportionment formula that equally weights sales, payroll, and property. Sales, payroll, and average property for each of the corporations are as follows.

	Everett Corporation	Dan Corporation	Total
Sales	$3,000,000	$7,000,000	$10,000,000
Payroll	2,000,000	3,500,000	5,500,000
Property	2,500,000	4,500,000	7,000,000

If the corporations are independent entities, the overall state income tax liability is $175,000.

State P ($1,000,000 × 10%)	=	$100,000
State Q ($1,500,000 × 5%)	=	75,000
Total state income tax		$175,000

If the corporations are members of a unitary business, the income and apportionment factors are combined in determining the income tax liability in unitary states P and Q. As a result of the combined reporting, the overall state income tax liability is reduced.

State P Income Tax				
Total apportionable income ($1,000,000 + $1,500,000)			$2,500,000	
Apportionment formula				
Sales ($3,000,000/$10,000,000)	=	30.00%		
Payroll ($2,000,000/$5,500,000)	=	36.36%		
Property ($2,500,000/$7,000,000)	=	35.71%		
Total		102.07%		
Average (102.07% ÷ 3)			× 34.02%	
State P taxable income			$ 850,500	
Tax rate			× 10%	
State P tax liability				$85,050

Concept Summary 24–1

Principles of Multistate Corporate Taxation

1. Taxability of an organization's income in a state other than the one in which it is incorporated depends on the laws, regulations, and judicial interpretations of the other state; the nature and level of the corporation's activity in, or contacts with, that state; and, to a limited extent, the application of P.L. 86–272.
2. Each state has adopted its own multistate income tax laws, regulations, methods, and judicial interpretations; consequently, the nonuniformity of state income taxing provisions provides a multitude of planning techniques that allow a multistate corporation to reduce its overall state tax liability legally.
3. The apportionment procedure is used to assign the income of a multistate taxpayer to the various states in which business is conducted. Generally, nonbusiness income is allocated, rather than apportioned, directly to the state in which the nonbusiness income-generating assets are located.
4. The various state apportionment formulas offer planning opportunities in that more or less than 100% of the taxpayer's income may be subjected to state income tax.
5. Some states employ an equally weighted three-factor apportionment formula. In many states, the sales factor is doubled, and occasionally only the sales factor is used in apportioning multistate taxable income. Generally, the greater the relative weight assigned to the sales factor, the greater the tax burden on out-of-state taxpayers.
6. The sales factor is based upon the destination concept except where a throwback rule applies. The payroll factor generally includes compensation that is included in Federal gross income, but some states include excludible fringe benefits. An employee's compensation usually is not divided among states. The property factor is derived using the average undepreciated historical costs for the assets and eight times the rental value of the assets.
7. The unitary theory may require the taxpayer to include worldwide activities and holdings in the apportionment factors. A water's edge election can limit these amounts to U.S. transactions.

State Q Income Tax				
Total apportionable income ($1,000,000 + $1,500,000)			$2,500,000	
Apportionment formula				
Sales ($7,000,000/$10,000,000)	=	70.00%		
Payroll ($3,500,000/$5,500,000)	=	63.64%		
Property ($4,500,000/$7,000,000)	=	64.29%		
Total		197.93%		
Average (197.93% ÷ 3)			× 65.98%	
State Q taxable income			$1,649,500	
Tax rate			× 5%	
State Q tax liability				$ 82,475
Total state income tax, if unitary ($85,050 + $82,475)				$167,525
Total state income tax, if nonunitary ($100,000 + $75,000)				175,000
Tax reduction from unitary reporting				$ 7,475

The results of unitary reporting would have been detrimental if Q had imposed a higher rate of tax than P, because a larger percentage of the corporation's income is attributable to Q when the apportionment factors are combined. ■

By identifying the states that have adopted the unitary method and the criteria under which a particular state defines a unitary business, a taxpayer may reduce its overall state tax by restructuring its corporate relationships to create or guard against a unitary relationship. For instance, an independent business enterprise can be made unitary by exercising day-to-day operational control and by centralizing functions, such as marketing, financing, accounting, and legal services.

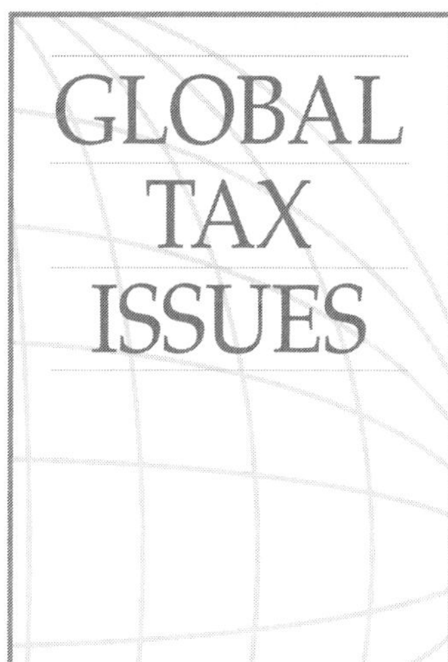

Water's Edge Is Not a Day at the Beach

As a result of pressure from the business community, the Federal government, and foreign countries, most of the states that impose an income tax on a unitary business's worldwide operations permit a multinational business to elect **water's edge** unitary reporting as an alternative to worldwide unitary filing.

The water's edge provision permits a multinational corporation to elect to limit the reach of the state's taxing jurisdiction over out-of-state affiliates to activities occurring within the boundaries of the United States. The decision to make a water's edge election may have a substantial effect on the tax liability of a multinational corporation. For instance, a water's edge election usually cannot be revoked for a number of years without permission from the appropriate tax authority. Moreover, corporations making this election may be assessed an additional tax for the privilege of excluding out-of-state entities from the combined report.

LO.7

Discuss the states' income tax treatment of S corporations, partnerships, and LLCs.

Taxation of S Corporations

The majority of the 46 states that impose a corporate income tax have special provisions, similar to the Federal law, that govern the taxation of S corporations. As of 2005, only a few states—including Michigan, New Hampshire, and Tennessee—and the District of Columbia do not provide special (i.e., no corporate-level tax) treatment for Federal S corporations. In addition, Massachusetts imposes a corporate-level tax on S corporations that have gross receipts in excess of $6 million. New Jersey and California apply a corporate-level tax, at special rates, on an S corporation.

In the non-S election states, a Federal S corporation generally is subject to tax in the same manner as a regular C corporation. Accordingly, if a multistate S corporation operates in any of these states, it is subject to state income tax and does not realize one of the primary benefits of S status—the avoidance of double taxation. Other potential tax-related benefits of the S election, including the pass-through of operating losses and the reduction in the rate of tax imposed on individual and corporate taxpayers, may be curtailed.

EXAMPLE 22

Bryan Inc., an S corporation, has established nexus in States A and B. State A recognizes S status, while B does not. Bryan generated $600,000 of ordinary business income and $100,000 of dividends that were received from corporations in which Bryan owns 50% of the stock. Bryan's State B apportionment percentage is 50%.

For B tax purposes, Bryan must first compute its income as though it were a regular corporation and then apportion the resulting income to B. Assuming that B has adopted the Federal provisions governing the dividends received deduction, Bryan's income, determined as though it were a C corporation, is $620,000 [$600,000 + (100% – 80%) × $100,000]. Accordingly, Bryan is subject to corporate income tax in B on $310,000 ($620,000 × 50% apportionment percentage) of taxable income. ■

A few states deviate from the Federal S corporation provisions and provide that an S corporation is entirely exempt from state income tax only if all of its shareholders are residents of the state. In these states, an S corporation is taxed on the portion of its income that is attributable to nonresident shareholders. Some of these states permit the S corporation to escape corporate-level tax on this income if its nonresident shareholders sign a form, agreeing to pay state tax on their share of the corporation's income. Moreover, about half of the states require the corporation to withhold taxes on the nonresident shareholders' portions of the entity's income.

EXAMPLE 23

ARGO, an S corporation, is subject to income tax only in Vermont. On the last day of its taxable year, 40% of ARGO's stock is held by nonresident shareholders. To the extent that ARGO's stock is held by resident shareholders, the corporation is not subject to income tax. Accordingly, ARGO is not subject to tax on 60% of its income.

The corporation *is* subject to tax on the remaining 40% of its income. ARGO may be able to avoid this corporate-level tax by withholding Vermont income tax for its nonresident shareholders. ■

ELIGIBILITY

All of the states that recognize S status permit a corporation to be treated as an S corporation for state purposes only if the corporation has a valid Federal S election in place. Generally, the filing of a Federal S election is sufficient to render the corporation an S corporation for state tax purposes. In most states, an entity that is an S corporation for Federal tax purposes automatically is treated as an S corporation for state tax purposes. A few states permit the entity to *elect out* of its S status for state purposes.

Taxation of Partnerships and LLCs

Most states apply income tax provisions to partnerships, limited liability companies (LLCs), and limited liability partnerships (LLPs) in a manner that parallels Federal treatment. The entity is a tax-reporting, not a taxpaying, entity. Income, loss, and credit items are allocated and apportioned among the partners according to the terms of the partnership agreement and state income tax law.

Some states require that the entity make estimated tax payments on behalf of out-of-state partners. This approach helps to assure that nonresident partners file appropriate forms and pay any resulting tax to the state. A few states, including Michigan for partnerships and Texas for LLCs, apply an entity-level tax on operating income. As is the case with S corporations, some states allow composite returns to be filed relative to out-of-state partners.

Generally, an in-state partner computes the income tax resulting from all of the flow-through income from the entity. The partner then is allowed a credit for income taxes paid to other states on this income.

Key issues facing partnerships doing business in multiple states include the following.

- Whether the partnership automatically has nexus with every state in which a partner resides.
- Whether a partner is deemed to have nexus with every state in which the partnership does business.
- How to assign the income/loss of a partner upon retirement or when a liquidating distribution is received.

Applicable law varies from state to state, and more complex transactions may not yet be addressed by existing law.

LO.8

Describe other commonly encountered state and local taxes on businesses.

Other State and Local Taxes

STATE AND LOCAL SALES AND USE TAXES

Forty-five states and the District of Columbia impose a consumers' sales tax on retail sales of tangible personal property for use or consumption. In many of these states, in-state localities, including cities, towns, school districts, or counties, also have the power to levy a sales tax. A consumers' sales tax is a tax imposed directly on the purchaser who acquires the asset at retail; the tax is measured by the price of the sale. The vendor or retailer merely acts as a collection agent for the state.

A use tax is designed to complement the sales tax. The use tax has two purposes: to prevent consumers from evading sales tax by purchasing goods outside the state for in-state use, and to provide an equitable sales environment between in-state and out-of-state retailers.

Generally, sales of tangible personal property are subject to tax. In several states, selected services are subject to tax.

A majority of the states exempt sales of certain items from the sales/use tax base. The most common exemptions and exclusions include the following.

- *Sales for resale* are exempt because the purchaser is not the ultimate user of the sold property. For instance, meat purchased by a grocer and a garment purchased by a retailer are not subject to sales/use tax under the resale rule.
- *Casual or occasional sales* that occur infrequently are exempt from the sales/use tax base chiefly for administrative convenience. Most states exclude rummage sales, the transfer of an entire business, sales of used autos, and the like under this rule.
- Most *purchases by exempt organizations* are excluded from taxable sales. Charities, governments and their agencies, and other organizations qualifying for Federal income tax exemption are relieved of sales/use tax liabilities in all of the states.
- *Sales of targeted items* can be exempt to improve the equity of the sales/use tax system. Sales of groceries, medical prescriptions and equipment, and textbooks can fall into this category and become nontaxable. Special exemptions for sales of farm, industrial, and computing equipment might also qualify under this type of exclusion.
- Certain *sales to manufacturers, producers, and processors* may also be exempt.

ETHICAL CONSIDERATIONS

Taxing Clicks and Bricks

Business has convinced Congress to enforce a politically popular "no new taxes on the Internet" pledge through 2007. But does exempting Internet sales from sales/use tax give Internet retailers an unfair advantage over "bricks and mortar" businesses that must collect sales tax on the sales that they make? These retailers have invested in physical stores and merchandise and make up most downtown and shopping mall areas. Why should we allow a full tax holiday for "clicks and mortar" Internet sellers, which have invested in just-in-time inventories and intangible assets like e-commerce Web software?

Will the next step in the saga look like this? Crate and Barrel will set up computer kiosks in all of its stores so that customers can browse the merchandise in a hands-on manner, then place a sales-tax-free order on one of the terminals.

Comment on the equity of exempting Internet sales from sales/use tax.

Collecting Those Sales/Use Tax Revenues

Today, state and local tax administrators face a major problem: How can governments get their sales/use tax revenues from mail-order, phone, and Internet sales? The problem is that the governments must rely on the seller to collect sales and use taxes, rather than collecting them directly from the purchaser. Consequently, a seller conceivably must deal with thousands of different sales/use taxing jurisdictions, each with its own forms and filing deadlines, rates of applicable tax, and definitions of what is taxable or exempt. Examples of issues on which jurisdictions may disagree include:

- Are snack foods exempt groceries or taxable candy?
- Are therapeutic stockings exempt medical supplies or taxable clothing?
- Which types of software are subject to tax?

Large retailers such as Wal-Mart, Amazon, and Radio Shack can develop software to handle these problems, but smaller businesses cannot afford to create their own software or to purchase someone else's. The result has been a very low level of compliance by sellers with respect to out-of-state sales transactions.

Governments meanwhile have limited resources to enforce tax rules that have long been on the books. Many states ask individuals and businesses to include the unpaid use taxes for Internet, phone, and mail-order purchases on their annual income tax returns, but the number of taxpayers complying is insignificant. This is not a matter of "increasing the taxes on the Internet economy," but rather of collecting revenues that already are due and are desperately needed to balance state budgets.

In an effort to solve these problems, state and local government officials and the Multistate Tax Commission have created the Streamlined Sales Tax Project (SSTP). The goal was to develop model laws that all states could adopt, thereby allowing for more uniform application of the now-disparate sales/use tax rules and more efficient exchange of information among agencies as to sellers and their transactions.

Real change, however, is likely to come only from Congress. The House Ways and Means Committee is considering a bill that would make the SSTP rules uniform law, to some extent, among all the states. In the meantime, legislatures in about two dozen states (mostly the smaller ones) have adopted the SSTP rules or are close to doing so.

So far the most popular SSTP rules are those defining what is subject to sales/use tax and what is not. For instance, the rules set out which items of clothing would be subject to tax, but each jurisdiction decides whether to include clothing in the tax base or when to allow amnesties during specific weeks of the tax year. Little interest as yet has been shown in having identical sales/use tax rates among the jurisdictions.

LOCAL PROPERTY TAXES

Property taxes, a major source of revenue at the city and county level, are referred to as *ad valorem* taxes because they are based on the value of property that is located in the state on a specific date. Generally, that date fixes taxable ownership, situs (location), and the valuation of the property. Nonetheless, to avoid tax evasion, personal property that is temporarily outside the state may be taxed at the domicile of the owner.

Property taxes can take the form of either real property taxes or personal property taxes. States apply different tax rates and means of assessment to the two classes of property. The methods of assessing the value of the real and tangible property also vary in different taxing jurisdictions.

OTHER TAXES

Jurisdictions may impose a variety of other state and local taxes on corporations, including incorporation or entrance fees or taxes; gross receipt taxes; stock transfer taxes; realty transfer and mortgage recording taxes; license taxes; and franchise taxes based on net worth or capital stock outstanding.

Tax Planning Considerations

The inconsistencies in the tax laws and rates among the states not only complicate state tax planning, but also provide the nucleus of pertinent planning opportunities. Although several tax planning devices are available to a corporation that does business in only one state, most planning techniques are directed toward corporations that do business or maintain property in more than one state. All suggested tax planning strategies should be reviewed in light of practical business considerations and the additional administrative and other costs that may be incurred, because simply minimizing state taxes may not be prudent from a business perspective.

LO.9

Recognize tax planning opportunities available to minimize a corporation's state and local tax liability.

SELECTING THE OPTIMAL STATE IN WHICH TO OPERATE

Because the states employ different definitions of the amount and type of activity necessary to establish nexus, a company has some latitude in selecting the states by which it will be taxed. When a corporation has only a limited connection with a high-tax state, it may abandon that activity by electing an alternative means of accomplishing the same result. For example, if providing a sales representative with a company-owned computer constitutes nexus in an undesired state, the company could eliminate its connection with that state by reimbursing sales personnel for equipment expenses, instead of providing a company computer. Similarly, when nexus is caused by conducting customer training sessions or seminars in the state, the corporation could bypass this connection. This can be done by sending the personnel to a nearby state in which nexus clearly has been established or in which the activity would not constitute nexus.

In addition, when sufficient activity originates from the repair and maintenance of the corporation's products or the activities performed by the sales representatives within the state, the organization could incorporate the service or sales divisions. This would invalidate a nonunitary state's right to tax the parent corporation's income; only the income of the service or sales divisions would be subject to tax. However, this technique will be successful only if the incorporated division is a *bona fide* business operation. Therefore, the pricing of any sales or services between the new subsidiary and the parent corporation must be at arm's length, and the operations of the new corporation preferably should result in a profit.

Although planning techniques often are employed to disconnect a corporation's activities from an undesirable state, they can also be utilized to create nexus in a desirable state. For example, when the presence of a company-owned computer creates nexus in a desirable state, the corporation could provide its sales representatives in that state with company-owned equipment, rather than reimbursing or providing increased compensation for equipment costs.

Establishing nexus in a state is advantageous, for instance, when that state has a lower tax rate than the state in which the income currently is taxed, or when losses or credits become available to reduce tax liabilities in the state.

EXAMPLE 24

Bird Corporation generates $500,000 of taxable income from selling goods; specifically, 40% of its product is sold in State A and 60% in State B. Both states levy a corporate income tax and include only the sales factor in their apportionment formulas. The tax rate in A is 10%; B's rate is only 3%. Bird's manufacturing operation is located in A; therefore, the corporation's income is subject to tax in that state. Currently, Bird is immune from tax under Public Law 86–272 in B. Since A has adopted a throwback provision, Bird incurs $50,000 of state income taxes.

	Apportionment Formula	Taxable Income	Tax Rate	Tax
State A	100/100	$500,000	10%	$50,000
State B	0/100	500,000	3%	–0–
Total tax liability				$50,000

Because B imposes a lower tax rate than A, Bird substantially reduces its state tax liability if sufficient nexus is created with B.

	Apportionment Formula	Taxable Income	Tax Rate	Tax
State A	40/100	$500,000	10%	$20,000
State B	60/100	500,000	3%	9,000
Total tax liability				$29,000

A corporation may benefit by storing inventory in a low- or no-tax state because the average property value in the state in which the manufacturing operation is located is reduced significantly. When the manufacturing operation is located in a high-tax state, the establishment of a distribution center in a low- or no-tax state may reduce the overall state tax liability.

EXAMPLE 25

Trill Corporation realized $200,000 of taxable income from selling its product in States A and B. Trill's manufacturing plant, product distribution center, and warehouses are located in A. The corporation's activities within the two states are as follows.

	State A	State B	Total
Sales	$500,000	$200,000	$700,000
Property	300,000	50,000	350,000
Payroll	100,000	10,000	110,000

Trill is subject to tax in A and B. Both states utilize a three-factor apportionment formula that equally weights sales, property, and payroll; however, A imposes a 10% corporate income tax, while B levies a 3% tax. Trill incurs a total income tax liability of $17,575.

	Apportionment Formulas					
	State A			State B		
Sales	$500,000/$700,000	=	71.43%	$200,000/$700,000	=	28.57%
Property	$300,000/$350,000	=	85.71%	$50,000/$350,000	=	14.29%
Payroll	$100,000/$110,000	=	90.91%	$10,000/$110,000	=	9.09%
Total			248.05%			51.95%
Apportionment factor (totals ÷ 3)			82.68%			17.32%
Taxable income apportioned to the state ($200,000 × apportionment factor)			$165,360			$34,640
Tax rate			× 10%			× 3%
Tax liability			$ 16,536			$ 1,039
Total tax liability				$17,575		

EXAMPLE 26

Continue with the facts of Example 25, and further assume that Trill's product distribution center and warehouse operations were acquired for $200,000 and the payroll of these operations is $20,000. Ignoring all nontax considerations, Trill could reduce its tax liability by $3,514 (a 20% reduction) by moving its distribution center, warehouses, and applicable personnel to B.

	State A	State B	Total
Sales	$500,000	$200,000	$700,000
Property	100,000	250,000	350,000
Payroll	80,000	30,000	110,000

Apportionment Formulas

	State A			State B		
Sales	$500,000/$700,000	=	71.43%	$200,000/$700,000	=	28.57%
Property	$100,000/$350,000	=	28.57%	$250,000/$350,000	=	71.43%
Payroll	$80,000/$110,000	=	72.73%	$30,000/$110,000	=	27.27%
Total			172.73%			127.27%
Apportionment factor (totals ÷ 3)			57.58%			42.42%
Taxable income apportioned to the state ($200,000 × apportionment factor)			$115,160			$84,840
Tax rate			× 10%			× 3%
Tax liability			$ 11,516			$ 2,545
Total tax liability				$14,061		
Tax imposed before move to State B				17,575		
Tax reduction due to move				$ 3,514		

RESTRUCTURING CORPORATE ENTITIES

One of the major objectives of state tax planning is to design the proper mix of corporate entities. An optimal mix of entities often generates the lowest combined state income tax for the corporation. Ideally, the income from all of the entities will be subject to a low tax rate or no tax at all. However, this generally is not possible. Consequently, the goal of designing a good corporate combination often is to situate the highly profitable entities in states that impose a low (or no) income tax.

Matching Tax Rates and Corporate Income. When the corporation must operate in a high-tax state, divisions that generate losses should also be located there. Alternatively, unprofitable or less profitable operations can be merged into profitable operations to reduce the overall income subject to tax in the state. An ideal candidate for this type of merger may be a research and development subsidiary that is only marginally profitable, but is vital to the parent corporation's strategic goals. By using computer simulation models, a variety of different combinations can be tested to determine the optimal corporate structure.

SUBJECTING THE CORPORATION'S INCOME TO APPORTIONMENT

When a multistate organization is domiciled in a high-tax state, some of its apportionable income is eliminated from the tax base in that state. In light of the high tax rate, this may result in significant tax savings. Apportioning income will be especially effective where the income that is attributed to the other states is not subject to income tax. The income removed from the taxing jurisdiction of the domicile state entirely escapes state income taxation when the state to which the income is attributed (1) does not levy a corporate income tax; (2) requires a higher level of activity necessary to subject an out-of-state company to taxation than that adopted by the state of domicile; or (3) is prohibited under Public Law 86–272 from taxing the income (assuming that the domicile state has not adopted a throwback provision). Thus, the right to apportion income may provide substantial benefits because the out-of-state sales are excluded from the numerator of the sales factor and may not be taxed in another state.

However, to acquire the right to apportion its income, the organization must have sufficient activities in, or contacts with, one or more other states. Whether the type and amount of activities and/or contacts are considered adequate is determined by the domicile state's nexus rules. Therefore, a corporation should analyze its current activities in, and contacts with, other states to determine which, if any, activities or contacts could be redirected so that the corporation gains the right to apportion its income.

ETHICAL CONSIDERATIONS

Can You Be a Nowhere Adviser?

The intent of much of today's multistate income tax planning is to create so-called *nowhere sales*, such that the income from the transaction is not subject to tax in any state. Suppose, for example, that a sale is made from Georgia (a state with no throwback rule) into Nevada (the place of ultimate destination, but a state with no income tax). No state-level income tax liability is generated. Is it ethical for a tax adviser to suggest such a strategy? Could you propose the establishment of a sales office in a nonthrowback state, thereby avoiding state income tax on a transaction that is fully taxable under Federal rules?

PLANNING WITH APPORTIONMENT FACTORS

Sales Factor. The sales factor often yields the greatest planning opportunities for a multistate corporation. In-state sales include those to purchasers with a destination point in that state; sales delivered to out-of-state purchasers are included in the numerator of the sales factor of the destination state. However, to be permitted to exclude out-of-state sales from the sales factor of the origination state, the seller generally must substantiate the shipment of goods to an out-of-state location. Therefore, the destinations of sales that a corporation makes and the means by which the goods are shipped must be carefully reviewed. The corporation's overall state tax can possibly be reduced by establishing a better record-keeping system or by manipulating the numerator of the sales factor by changing the delivery location or method.

For example, a corporation may substantially reduce its state tax if the delivery location of its sales is changed from a state in which the company is taxed to one in which it is not. This technique may not benefit the corporation if the state in which the sales originate has adopted the throwback rule.

Property Factor. Because most fixed assets are physically stationary in nature, the property factor is not so easily manipulated. Nonetheless, significant tax savings can be realized by establishing a leasing subsidiary in a low- or no-tax state. If the property is located in a state that does not include leased assets in the property factor, the establishment of a subsidiary from which to lease the property eliminates the assets from the property factor in the parent's state.

Permanently idle property generally is excluded from the property factor. Accordingly, a corporation should identify and remove such assets from the property factor to ensure that the factor is not distorted. It is equally important to identify and remove nonbusiness assets from the property factor in states that distinguish between business and nonbusiness income.

EXAMPLE 27

Quake Corporation's property holdings were as follows.

	State A	Total
Equipment (average historical cost)	$1,200,000	$2,000,000
Accumulated depreciation (average)	800,000	1,000,000

Twenty percent of the equipment in State A is fully depreciated and is idle. Assuming that A includes property in the factor at historical cost, Quake's property factor is 54.55% [($1,200,000 – $240,000 idle property)/($2,000,000 – $240,000)]. If the idle property is not removed from the property factor, Quake's property factor in A is incorrectly computed as 60% ($1,200,000/$2,000,000). ■

Payroll Factor. The payroll factor provides planning potential where several corporate employees spend substantial periods of time outside their state of employment, or the corporation is able to relocate highly paid employees to low- or no-tax states. Use of an independent contractor who works for more than one principal, however, can be beneficial under certain circumstances. Since the commissions paid to independent contractors are excluded from the payroll factor, the taxpayer may reduce its payroll factor in a high-tax state.

EXAMPLE 28

Yellow Corporation's total payroll costs are $1.4 million. Of this amount, $1 million was attributable to State A, a high-tax state. Yellow's payroll factor in A is 71.43% ($1,000,000/$1,400,000).

Assuming that $200,000 of the A compensation had been paid to sales representatives and that Yellow replaced its sales force with independent contractors, Yellow's payroll factor in A would be reduced to 66.67% [($1,000,000 – $200,000)/($1,400,000 – $200,000)]. ■

SALES/USE TAXES ON CAPITAL CHANGES

The tax adviser must be aware of the impact that sales and use taxes may have on a transaction that might otherwise be free from income tax. For example, although the transfer of property to a controlled corporation in exchange for its stock generally is not subject to corporate income taxes, several states provide that such transfers constitute taxable sales for sales and use tax purposes. Similarly, a corporate reorganization may be structured to avoid the imposition of income taxes, but under the statutes of several states, such transfers are considered to be taxable sales and, accordingly, will be subject to sales and use taxes.

KEY TERMS

Allocate, 24–9
Apportion, 24–9
Nexus, 24–9
Payroll factor, 24–17
Property factor, 24–19
Public Law 86–272, 24–9
Sales factor, 24–16
Throwback rule, 24–16
UDITPA, 24–13
Unitary theory, 24–21
Water's edge election, 24–25

PROBLEM MATERIALS

Discussion Questions

Issue ID

1. As a staff member of the governor of your state, you are charged with bringing new business into the jurisdiction and with keeping the industry and services that are already there. List some of the tax incentives that your Department of Revenue might provide to help meet these goals.
2. In most states, corporate taxable income is computed by reference to a series of statutes and rulings that impose a unique definition of the tax base. Evaluate the validity of this statement.
3. List the principles by which one state gains authority under its own constitution and under the U.S. Constitution to tax the in-state activities of a conglomerate doing business in a number of jurisdictions.
4. Sales representative Jones is based in Utah, where the operating plants and corporate headquarters of her employer also are located. She visits customers in Colorado for a day, soliciting orders for the seashells that she sells. The orders are approved in Utah, and the shells are shipped from Oregon within a week. Are these sales subject to the Colorado corporate income tax?
5. Continue with the facts of Question 4. In processing her orders, Jones regularly reviews the credit standing of the customer and decides whether the order should be billed on company credit or sent COD (cash on delivery). Are these sales subject to the Colorado corporate income tax?
6. Evaluate the following comment: A multistate business must allocate its income from sales among the states in which it operates. Divided in this manner, taxes are payable to states according to the income allocation.

Issue ID

7. If you were a state legislator, would you push for your state to adopt a double-weighted sales or sales-factor-only apportionment formula? Why?
8. In computing the corporate income taxes for an Arizona-based client, should a single large sale in July, in which merchandise was shipped to a customer in New Mexico, be included in the Arizona sales factor?
9. Continue with the facts of Question 8. Another large shipment was made to a customer in South Dakota, a state that does not impose any corporate income tax. Is this sale to be included in the Arizona sales factor?
10. Evaluate the following comment: The unitary concept is similar to the idea of the Federal consolidated return.
11. Name two states that do not allow single-level corporate taxation for Federal S corporations.
12. Comment on special compliance concerns for Federal S corporations in dealing with state income tax systems.
13. Describe two approaches that the states use concerning out-of-state S corporation shareholders.
14. Describe the typical state income tax system for partners and partnerships.

Issue ID

15. Evaluate this statement: The seller doesn't pay the sales tax—the customer does.

Communications

16. Create a PowerPoint outline describing the major exemptions and exclusions from the sales/use tax base of most states.

Communications

17. Your client, Ecru Limited, is considering an expansion of its sales operations, but it fears adverse resulting tax consequences. Write a memo for the tax research file identifying the planning opportunities presented by the ability of a corporation to terminate or create nexus. Be certain to discuss the *Wrigley* case in your analysis.

Decision Making

18. Mollusk Corporation generates $70 million of taxable income per year, all in State F, where its marginal state tax rate is 8%. The taxable income includes $20 million in interest income from Treasury bills. How might Mollusk reduce its state tax liability? Suggest three alternatives Mollusk should consider. Ignore any nontax considerations.

19. Parent Corporation wants to acquire Junior, Inc., in a merger transaction. Parent's advisers are consulting statutory and judicial law under § 368 to make certain that the transaction is classified as a reorganization. What advice can you offer the parties to the deal?

Problems

20. Use Figure 24–1 to compute Beta Corporation's state taxable income for the year.

Addition modifications	$ 8,000
Allocated income (total income)	15,000
Allocated income (in-state income)	3,000
Tax credits	50
Federal taxable income	50,000
Subtraction modifications	11,000
Apportionment percentage	21%
Tax rate	5%

21. Use Figure 24–1 to provide the required information for Warbler Corporation, whose Federal taxable income totals $6 million. Warbler apportions 30% of its business income to State C. Warbler generates $1 million of nonbusiness income each year, and 10% of that income is allocated to C. Warbler's business income this year is $5 million.
    a. How much of Warbler's business income does State C tax?
    b. How much of Warbler's nonbusiness income does State C tax?
    c. Explain your results.

22. For each of the following independent cases, indicate whether the circumstances call for an addition modification (*A*), a subtraction modification (*S*), or no modification (*N*) in computing state taxable income. Then indicate the amount of any modification. The starting point in computing State Q taxable income is the year's Federal taxable income.
    a. Q income taxes, deducted on the Federal return as a business expense = $10,000.
    b. State R income taxes, deducted on the Federal return as a business expense = $10,000.
    c. Federal income taxes paid = $30,000.
    d. Refund received from last year's Q income taxes = $3,000.
    e. Local property taxes, deducted on the Federal return as a business expense = $7,000.
    f. Federal cost recovery = $10,000, and Q cost recovery = $15,000.
    g. Federal cost recovery = $15,000, and Q cost recovery = $10,000.
    h. An asset was sold for $18,000; its purchase price was $20,000. Accumulated Federal cost recovery = $11,000, and accumulated Q cost recovery = $8,000.
    i. Federal investment tax credit = $0, and Q investment tax credit = $5,000.
    j. Dividend income received from State R corporation = $10,000, subject to a Federal dividends received deduction of 70%.

23. Perk Corporation is subject to tax only in State A. Perk generated the following income and deductions.

Federal taxable income	$200,000
State A income tax expense	15,000
Refund of State A income tax	13,000
Depreciation allowed for Federal tax purposes	200,000
Depreciation allowed for state tax purposes	180,000

Federal taxable income is the starting point in computing A taxable income. State income taxes are not deductible for A tax purposes. Determine Perk's A taxable income.

24. Flip Corporation is subject to tax only in State X. Flip generated the following income and deductions. State income taxes are not deductible for X income tax purposes.

Sales	$4,000,000
Cost of sales	2,250,000
State X income tax expense	110,000
Depreciation allowed for Federal tax purposes	300,000
Depreciation allowed for state tax purposes	250,000
Interest on Federal obligations	20,000
Interest on X obligations	50,000
Expenses related to X obligations	7,000

a. The starting point in computing the X income tax base is Federal taxable income. Derive this amount.
b. Determine Flip's X taxable income, assuming that interest on X obligations is exempt from X income tax.
c. Determine Flip's X taxable income, assuming that interest on X obligations is subject to X income tax.

25. Millie Corporation has nexus in States A and B. Millie's activities for the year are summarized below.

	State A	State B	Total
Sales	$1,200,000	$ 300,000	$1,500,000
Property			
Average cost	500,000	300,000	800,000
Average accumulated depreciation	(300,000)	(100,000)	(400,000)
Payroll	2,400,000	100,000	2,500,000
Rent expense	10,000	25,000	35,000

Determine the apportionment factors for A and B, assuming that A uses a three-factor apportionment formula under which sales, property (net depreciated basis), and payroll are equally weighted, and B employs a single-factor formula that consists solely of sales. State A has adopted the UDITPA with respect to the inclusion of rent payments in the property factor.

26. Assume the facts of Problem 25, except that A uses a single-factor apportionment formula that consists solely of sales, and B uses a three-factor apportionment formula that equally weights sales, property (at historical cost), and payroll. State B does not include rent payments in the property factor.

27. Assume the facts of Problem 25, except that both states employ a three-factor formula, under which sales are double weighted. The basis of the property factor in A is historical cost, while the basis of this factor in B is the net depreciated basis. Neither A nor B includes rent payments in the property factor.

28. Falcon Corporation operates in two states, as indicated below. This year's operations generated $300,000 of apportionable income.

	State A	State B	Total
Sales	$500,000	$400,000	$900,000
Property	300,000	50,000	350,000
Payroll	100,000	10,000	110,000

Compute Falcon's State A taxable income, assuming that State A apportions income based on a:

a. Three-factor formula.
b. Double-weighted sales factor.
c. Sales factor only.

29. State E applies a throwback rule to sales, while State F does not. State G has not adopted an income tax to date. Orange Corporation, headquartered in E, reported the following sales for the year. All of the goods were shipped from Orange's E manufacturing facilities. Orange's degree of operations is sufficient to establish nexus only in E and F. Determine its sales factor in those states.

Customer	Customer's Location	This Year's Sales
ShellTell, Inc.	E	$ 64,000,000
Tourists, Ltd.	F	40,000,000
PageToo Corp.	G	30,000,000
U.S. Department of Interior	All 50 states	18,000,000
Total		$152,000,000

30. Aqua Corporation is subject to tax in States G, H, and I. Aqua's compensation expense includes the following.

	State G	State H	State I	Total
Salaries and wages for nonofficers	$200,000	$400,000	$100,000	$700,000
Officers' salaries	–0–	–0–	250,000	250,000
Total				$950,000

Officers' salaries are included in the payroll factor for G and I, but not for H. Compute Aqua's payroll factors for G, H, and I.

31. Kim Corporation, a calendar year taxpayer, has manufacturing facilities in States A and B. A summary of Kim's property holdings follows.

	Beginning of Year		
	State A	State B	Total
Inventory	$ 300,000	$ 200,000	$ 500,000
Plant and equipment	2,500,000	1,500,000	4,000,000
Accumulated depreciation: plant and equipment	(1,200,000)	(500,000)	(1,700,000)
Land	600,000	600,000	1,200,000
Rental property*	900,000	300,000	1,200,000
Accumulated depreciation: rental property	(200,000)	(50,000)	(250,000)

	End of Year		
	State A	State B	Total
Inventory	$ 400,000	$ 150,000	$ 550,000
Plant and equipment	2,500,000	1,200,000	3,700,000
Accumulated depreciation: plant and equipment	(1,500,000)	(450,000)	(1,950,000)

	End of Year		
	State A	State B	Total
Land	$ 600,000	$ 400,000	$ 1,000,000
Rental property*	950,000	300,000	1,250,000
Accumulated depreciation: rental property	(300,000)	(100,000)	(400,000)

*Unrelated to Kim's regular business operations.

Determine Kim's property factors for the two states, assuming that the statutes of both A and B provide that average historical cost of business property is to be included in the property factor.

32. Assume the facts of Problem 31, except that nonbusiness income is apportionable in B.

Decision Making

33. Crate Corporation, a calendar year taxpayer, has established nexus with numerous states. On December 3, Crate sold one of its two facilities in State X. The cost of this facility was $800,000.

On January 1, Crate owned property with a cost of $3 million, $1.5 million of which was located in X. On December 31, Crate owned property with a cost of $2.2 million, $600,000 of which was located in X.

X law allows the use of average annual or monthly amounts in determining the property factor. If Crate wants to minimize the property factor in X, which method should be used to determine the property factor there?

Decision Making
Communications

34. True Corporation, a wholly owned subsidiary of Trumaine Corporation, generated a $500,000 taxable loss in its first year of operations. True's activities and sales are restricted to State A, which imposes an 8% income tax. Trumaine's income for the taxable period is $1 million. Trumaine's activities and sales are restricted to State B, which imposes an 11% income tax. Both states use a three-factor apportionment formula that equally weights sales, payroll, and property, and both require a unitary group to file on a combined basis. Sales, payroll, and average property for each corporation are as follows.

	True Corporation	Trumaine Corporation	Total
Sales	$2,500,000	$4,000,000	$6,500,000
Property	1,000,000	2,500,000	3,500,000
Payroll	800,000	1,200,000	2,000,000

True and Trumaine have been found to be members of a unitary business.

a. Determine the overall state income tax for the unitary group.
b. Determine aggregate state income tax for the entities if they were nonunitary.
c. Incorporate this analysis in a letter to Trumaine's board of directors. Corporate offices are located at 1234 Mulberry Lane, Chartown, AL 35298.

35. Gerald Corporation is part of a three-corporation unitary business. The group has a water's edge election in effect with respect to unitary State Q. State B does not apply the unitary concept with respect to its corporate income tax laws. Nor does Despina, a European country to which Geraldine paid a $4 million value added tax this year.

Geraldine was organized in Despina and conducts all of its business there. Given the summary of operations that follows, determine Gerald's and Elena's sales factors in B and Q.

Corporation	Customer's Location	Sales
Gerald	B	$10,000,000
	Q	15,000,000
Elena	Q	20,000,000
Geraldine	Despina	25,000,000

Communications

36. Hernandez, which has been an S corporation since inception, is subject to tax in States Y and Z. On Schedule K of its Federal Form 1120S, Hernandez reported ordinary income of $500,000 from its business, taxable interest income of $10,000, capital loss of $30,000, and $40,000 of dividend income from a corporation in which it owns 30%.

Both states apportion income by use of a three-factor formula that equally weights sales, payroll, and the average cost of property; both states treat interest and dividends as business income. In addition, both Y and Z follow Federal provisions with respect to the determination of taxable income for a corporation. Y recognizes S status, but Z does not. Based on the following information, write a memo to the shareholders of Hernandez, detailing the amount of taxable income on which Hernandez will pay tax in Y and Z. Hernandez corporate offices are located at 5678 Alabaster Circle, Koopville, KY 47697.

	State Y	State Z
Sales	$1,000,000	$800,000
Property (average cost)	500,000	200,000
Payroll	800,000	300,000

37. Using the following information from the books and records of Grande Corporation, determine Grande's total sales that are subject to State C's sales tax. Grande operates a retail hardware store.

Sales to C consumers, general merchandise	$700,000
Sales to C consumers, crutches and other medical supplies	111,000
Sales to consumers in State D, via mail order	84,000
Purchases from suppliers	55,000

38. Indicate for each transaction whether a sales (*S*) or use (*U*) tax applies or whether the transaction is nontaxable (*N*). Where the laws vary among states, assume that the most common rules apply. All taxpayers are individuals.
   a. A resident of State A purchases an automobile in A.
   b. A resident of State A purchases groceries in A.
   c. A resident of State B purchases an automobile in A.
   d. A charity purchases office supplies in A.
   e. An A resident purchases in B an item that will be in the inventory of her business.

Decision Making

39. Dread Corporation operates in a high-tax state. The firm asks you for advice on a plan to outsource overhead work done in its home state to independent contractors. This work now costs the company $350,000 in wages and benefits. Dread's total payroll for the year is $2 million, of which $1.5 million is for work currently done in the home state.

Issue ID

Communications

40. Prepare a PowerPoint presentation entitled "Planning Principles for Our Multistate Clients." The slides will be used to lead a 20-minute discussion with colleagues in the corporate tax department. Keep the outline general, but assume that your colleagues have clients operating in at least 15 states. Address only income tax issues.

Research Problems

Internet Activity

Use the tax resources of the Internet to address the following questions. Do not restrict your search to the World Wide Web, but include a review of newsgroups and general reference materials, practitioner sites and resources, primary sources of the tax law, chat rooms and discussion groups, and other opportunities.

Communications

Research Problem 1. Send an e-mail message to the secretary of revenue for your home state, proposing adoption of one of the following provisions that does not currently exist in your state. Justify your proposal with a numerical example.

a. Increase the apportionment weight for the sales factor.
b. Exempt computer and communications technology from the apportionment weight for the property factor.
c. Adopt a throwback rule for the sales factor.
d. Tax advertising expenditures under the sales/use tax.
e. Tax the income of an investment subsidiary set up by a domestic taxpayer.
f. Add a "nexus team" to find taxpayers operating in your state, but based in Ohio, Illinois, or Arizona.

Communications

Research Problem 2. Read the "tax footnote" of five publicly traded U.S. corporations. Find the effective state/local income tax rates of each. Create a PowerPoint presentation for your instructor, summarizing the search and reporting the findings.

Communications

Research Problem 3. Use **http://taxsites.com** or some other index to find a state/local tax organization (e.g., the Council on State Taxation). Read its current newsletter. In an e-mail to your instructor, summarize a major article at the site.

Taxation of International Transactions

LEARNING OBJECTIVES

After completing Chapter 25, you should be able to:

LO.1
Understand the framework underlying the U.S. taxation of cross-border transactions.

LO.2
Understand the interaction between Internal Revenue Code provisions and tax treaties.

LO.3
Apply the rules for sourcing income and deductions into U.S. and foreign categories.

LO.4
Explain how foreign currency exchange affects the tax consequences of international transactions.

LO.5
Work with the U.S. tax provisions affecting U.S. persons earning foreign-source income, including the rules relating to cross-border asset transfers, antideferral provisions, and the foreign tax credit.

LO.6
Apply the U.S. tax provisions concerning nonresident alien individuals and foreign corporations.

OUTLINE

LO.1

Understand the framework underlying the U.S. taxation of cross-border transactions.

Overview of International Taxation

In today's global business environment, most large businesses are truly international in scope. Consider the most recent financial results of three "all-American" companies: Coca-Cola, Ford Motor Company, and Microsoft. Coca-Cola reported that 63 percent of its total net income is from offshore operations, Ford lost money in its domestic operations but earned $1.5 billion in profits from non-U.S. operations, and Microsoft earned $3.4 billion in profits (31 percent of its book net income) from operations outside the United States. Honda, a Japanese company, reported an investment of over $5.9 billion in sales, manufacturing, and research operations in the United States; Toyota, another Japanese company, earned 24 percent of its operating income from North America; and Chrysler, one of the historical "Big 3" U.S. auto manufacturers, is now a subsidiary of a German corporation (DaimlerChrysler).

Global trade is an integral part of the U.S. economy. In 2003, U.S. exports and imports of goods and services totaled $1.02 trillion and $1.51 trillion, respectively. This international trade creates significant U.S. tax consequences for both U.S. and foreign entities. In the most recent year for which data are available, U.S. corporations reported $166 billion in foreign-source income, paid $41 billion in taxes to foreign governments, and claimed foreign tax credits in excess of $38 billion. Foreign recipients reported $140 billion in U.S.-source income subject to withholding and paid $2.3 billion in U.S. taxes. U.S. corporations controlled by foreign owners reported $102 billion in U.S. taxable income.

Cross-border transactions create the need for special tax considerations for both the United States and its trading partners. From a U.S. perspective, international tax laws should promote the global competitiveness of U.S. enterprises and at the same time protect the tax revenue base of the United States. These two objectives sometimes conflict, however. The need to deal with both contributes to the complexity of the rules governing the U.S. taxation of cross-border transactions.

■ **FIGURE 25–1**
U.S. Taxation of Cross-Border Transactions

	U.S. Person	**Foreign Person**
U.S.-source income	U.S. domestic taxation	"Inbound" taxation
Foreign-source income	"Outbound" taxation	Limited U.S. authority to tax

EXAMPLE 1

U.S. persons engage in activities outside the United States for many different reasons. Consider two U.S. corporations that have established sales subsidiaries in foreign countries. Dedalus, Inc., operates in Germany, a high-tax country, because customers demand local attention from sales agents. Mulligan, Inc., operates in the Cayman Islands, a low-tax country, simply to shift income outside the United States. U.S. tax law must fairly address both situations with the same law. ■

U.S. international tax provisions are concerned primarily with two types of potential taxpayers: U.S. persons earning foreign-source income and foreign persons earning U.S.-source income.[1] U.S. persons earning U.S.-source income are taxed under the purely domestic provisions of the Internal Revenue Code. Foreign persons earning foreign-source income are not within the taxing jurisdiction of the United States (unless this income is somehow connected to a U.S. trade or business). Figure 25–1 illustrates this categorization.

The United States taxes the worldwide income of U.S. taxpayers. Because foreign governments may also tax some of this income, these taxpayers may be subjected to double taxation. Special provisions such as the foreign tax credit can mitigate this problem. For foreign taxpayers, the United States generally taxes only income earned within its borders. The U.S. taxation of cross-border transactions can be organized in terms of "outbound" and "inbound" taxation. **Outbound taxation** refers to the U.S. taxation of foreign-source income earned by U.S. taxpayers. **Inbound taxation** refers to the U.S. taxation of U.S.-source income earned by foreign taxpayers.

EXAMPLE 2

Gator Enterprises, Inc., a U.S. corporation, operates a manufacturing branch in Italy because of customer demand in Italy, local availability of raw materials, and the high cost of shipping finished goods. This branch income is taxed in the United States as part of Gator's worldwide income, but it is also taxed in Italy. Without the availability of a foreign tax credit to mitigate this double taxation, Gator Enterprises would suffer an excessive tax burden and could not compete with local Italian companies. ■

EXAMPLE 3

Purdie, Ltd., a corporation based in the United Kingdom, operates in the United States. Although not a U.S. person, Purdie is taxed in the United States on its U.S.-source business income. If Purdie, Ltd., could operate free of U.S. tax, its U.S.-based competitors would face a serious disadvantage. ■

LO.2

Understand the interaction between Internal Revenue Code provisions and tax treaties.

Tax Treaties

The U.S. tax rules governing cross-border transactions are based on both the Internal Revenue Code and **tax treaties.** Tax treaties are bilateral agreements between countries that provide tax relief for those persons covered by the treaties. Tax treaty provisions generally override the treatment otherwise called for under the Internal Revenue Code or foreign tax statutes.

[1]The term "person" includes an individual, corporation, partnership, trust, estate, or association. § 7701(a)(1). The terms "domestic" and "foreign" are defined in §§ 7701(a)(4) and (5).

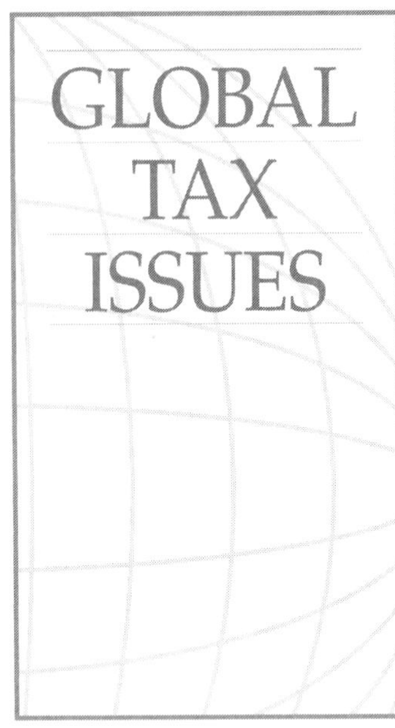

Other Countries' Taxes Are Strange, Too

People often complain about the strange provisions or workings of the U.S. Federal income tax system, but other countries can be criticized in the same way. Much of Europe, for example, is less dependent on income taxes than the United States and more dependent on transaction and wealth taxes, and these can take unusual forms. A quick survey of taxes around the globe finds the following.

Australia	68% tax on cigarette purchases
China	80–100% tax on purchase of autos built outside China
Costa Rica	170% tax on purchase of poultry raised outside the country, 96% tax on purchase of foreign dairy products
Japan	1,000% tax on purchase of rice grown outside the country
Sweden	400% tax on purchase of hard liquor
Turkmenistan	100% tax on luxury items, which include mineral water, cotton mittens, saws, blankets, pillows, mattresses

More than 50 income tax treaties between the United States and other countries are in effect (see Exhibit 25–1). These treaties generally provide *taxing rights* with regard to the taxable income of residents of one treaty country who have income sourced in the other treaty country. For the most part, neither country is prohibited from taxing the income of its residents. The treaties generally give one country primary taxing rights and require the other country to allow a credit for the taxes paid on the twice-taxed income.

EXAMPLE 4

ForCo, Ltd., a resident of a foreign country with which the United States has an income tax treaty, earns income attributable to a permanent establishment (e.g., place of business) in the United States. Under the treaty, the United States has primary taxing rights with regard

■ EXHIBIT 25–1
U.S. Income Tax Treaties in Force as of May 2004

Australia	Iceland	Pakistan
Austria	India	Philippines
Barbados	Indonesia	Poland
Belgium	Ireland	Portugal
Canada	Israel	Romania
China	Italy	Russia
Commonwealth of Independent States*	Jamaica	Slovak Republic
	Japan	Slovenia
Cyprus	Kazakhstan	South Africa
Czech Republic	Korea, Republic of	Spain
Denmark	Latvia	Sweden
Egypt	Lithuania	Switzerland
Estonia	Luxembourg	Thailand
Finland	Mexico	Trinidad and Tobago
France	Morocco	Tunisia
Germany	Netherlands	Turkey
Greece	New Zealand	United Kingdom
Hungary	Norway	Venezuela

*The income tax treaty between the United States and the former Soviet Union now applies to the countries of Armenia, Azerbaijan, Belarus, Georgia, Kyrgyzstan, Moldova, Tajikistan, Turkmenistan, Ukraine, and Uzbekistan. The Commonwealth of Independent States is an association of many of the former constituent republics of the Soviet Union.

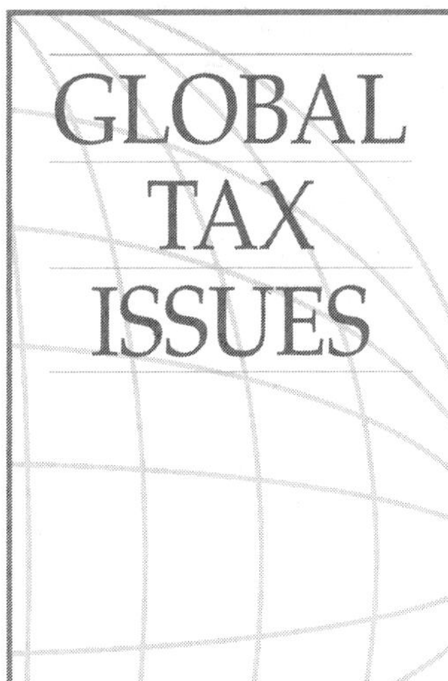

Why the Treaty Process Stalls

The United States has negotiated several income tax treaties that have never been signed or ratified (e.g., with Argentina, Bangladesh, and Brazil). The treaty process sometimes stalls for several reasons.

One is the desire on the part of some less developed countries for a tax-sparing provision in the treaty. In other words, these countries want the United States to allow a foreign tax credit against U.S. taxes even though U.S. companies operating there actually pay no foreign taxes due to local tax reduction agreements (i.e., tax holidays).

Another reason is the exchange of information provision. Some countries, for example, have anonymous bank rules that would preclude the exchange of information. Not long ago, the Parliament of Kazakhstan voted on a provision to eliminate secret bank accounts so that the United States–Kazakhstan income tax treaty could be ratified.

to this income. The other country can also require that the income be included in gross income and can subject the income to its income tax, but it must allow a credit for the taxes paid to the United States on the income. ■

Which country receives primary taxing rights usually depends on the residence of the taxpayer or the presence of a permanent establishment in a treaty country to which the income is attributable. Generally, a permanent establishment is a branch, office, factory, workshop, warehouse, or other fixed place of business.

Most U.S. income tax treaties reduce the withholding tax rate on certain items of investment income, such as interest and dividends. For example, treaties with France and Sweden reduce the withholding on portfolio dividends to 15 percent and on certain interest income to zero. Many new treaties (e.g., with the United Kingdom and Australia) provide for no withholding on dividend payments to parent corporations. The United States has developed a Model Income Tax Treaty as the starting point for negotiating income tax treaties with other countries.[2]

LO.3

Apply the rules for sourcing income and deductions into U.S. and foreign categories.

Sourcing of Income and Deductions

The sourcing of income and deductions inside or outside the United States has a direct bearing on a number of tax provisions affecting both U.S. and foreign taxpayers. For example, foreign taxpayers generally are taxed only on income sourced inside the United States, and U.S. taxpayers receive relief from double taxation under the foreign tax credit rules based on their foreign-source income. Accordingly, an examination of sourcing rules is often the starting point in addressing international tax issues.

INCOME SOURCED INSIDE THE UNITED STATES

The determination of the source of income depends on the type of income realized (e.g., income from the sale of property versus income for the use of property). This

[2]Treasury Department Model Income Tax Treaty (September 20, 1996).

makes the classification of income an important consideration. Section 861 contains source rules for most types of income. Other rules pertaining to the source of income are found in §§ 862–865.

Interest. Interest income received from the U.S. government, from the District of Columbia, and from noncorporate U.S. residents or domestic corporations is sourced inside the United States. There are a few exceptions to this rule. Certain interest received from a U.S. corporation that earned 80 percent or more of its active business income from foreign sources over the prior three-year period is treated as foreign-source income. Interest received on amounts deposited with a foreign branch of a U.S. corporation is also treated as foreign-source income if the branch is engaged in the commercial banking business.

EXAMPLE 5

John holds a bond issued by Delta, a domestic corporation. For the immediately preceding three tax years, 82% of Delta's gross income has been active foreign business income. The interest income that John receives for the current tax year from Delta is foreign-source income. ■

Dividends. Dividends received from domestic corporations (other than certain U.S. possessions corporations) are sourced inside the United States. Generally, dividends paid by a foreign corporation are foreign-source income without regard to the corporation's source of income.[3]

EXAMPLE 6

Ann receives dividend income from the following corporations for the current tax year.

Amount	Corporation	Effectively Connected U.S. Income for Past 3 Years	U.S.-Source Income
$500	Green, domestic	85%	$500
600	Brown, domestic	13%	600
300	Orange, foreign	92%	–0–

Because Green Corporation and Brown Corporation are domestic corporations, the dividends they pay are U.S.-source income. Orange Corporation is a foreign corporation that earned 92% of its business income over the prior three years from income effectively connected with a U.S. trade or business. In spite of Orange's significant U.S.-source income, the entire dividend is foreign source. ■

Personal Services Income. The source of income from personal services is determined by the location in which the services are performed (inside or outside the United States). A limited *commercial traveler* exception is available. Under this exception, personal services income must meet all the following requirements to avoid being classified as U.S.-source income.

- The services must be performed by a nonresident alien who is in the United States for 90 days or less during the taxable year.
- The compensation may not exceed $3,000 in total for the services performed in the United States.

[3]For tax years prior to 2004, a portion of a foreign corporation's dividend could be treated as U.S.-source income, if the payor earned 25% or more of its gross income from income effectively connected with a U.S. trade or business for the three tax years immediately preceding the year of the dividend payment. § 861(a)(2)(B).

- The services must be performed on behalf of:
  - a nonresident alien, foreign partnership, or foreign corporation that is not engaged in a U.S. trade or business or
  - an office or place of business maintained in a foreign country or possession of the United States by an individual who is a citizen or resident of the United States, a domestic partnership, or a domestic corporation.

EXAMPLE 7

Mark, a nonresident alien, is an engineer employed by a foreign oil company. He spent four weeks in the United States arranging the purchase of field equipment for his company. His salary for the four weeks was $3,500. Even though the oil company is not engaged in a U.S. trade or business, and Mark was in the United States for less than 90 days during the taxable year, the income is U.S.-source income because it exceeds $3,000. ■

The issue of whether income is derived from the performance of personal services is important in determining the income's source. The courts have held that a corporation can perform personal services.[4] In addition, in the absence of capital as an income-producing factor, personal services income can arise even though there is no recipient of the services.[5] If payment is received for services performed partly inside and partly outside the United States, the income must be allocated for source purposes on some reasonable basis that clearly reflects income under the facts and circumstances. The number of days worked in each country is generally acceptable.[6]

Rents and Royalties. The source of income received for the use of tangible property is the country in which the property is located. The source of income received for the use of intangible property (e.g., patents, copyrights, secret processes and formulas) is the country in which the property is used.

Sale or Exchange of Property. Generally, the location of real property determines the source of any income derived from the property. For example, income from the disposition of U.S. real property interests is U.S.-source income.

The source of income from the sale of personal property (assets other than real property) depends on several factors, including the following.

- Whether the property was produced by the seller.
- The type of property sold (e.g., inventory or a capital asset).
- The residence of the seller.

Generally, income, gain, or profit from the sale of personal property is sourced according to the residence of the seller. Income from the sale of purchased inventory, however, is sourced in the country in which the sale takes place.[7]

When the seller has produced the inventory property, the income must be apportioned between the country of production and the country of sale. Gross income is sourced under a 50/50 allocation method unless the taxpayer elects to use the independent factory price (IFP) method or the separate books and records

[4]See *British Timken Limited*, 12 T.C. 880 (1949), and Rev.Rul. 60–55, 1960–1 C.B. 270.

[5]See *Robida v. Comm.*, 72–1 USTC ¶9450, 29 AFTR2d 72–1223, 460 F.2d 1172 (CA–9, 1972). The taxpayer was employed in military PXs around the world. He had large slot machine winnings and claimed the foreign earned income exclusion. The IRS challenged the exclusion on the grounds that the winnings were not earned income because there was no recipient of Robida's services. The court, however, found that, in the absence of capital, the winnings were earned income.

[6]Reg. § 1.861–4(b). See *Stemkowski*, 76 T.C. 252 (1981).

[7]§§ 861(a)(6) and 865. The sale is deemed to take place where title passes. See Reg. § 1.861–7(c) regarding title passage. There has been considerable conflict in this area of tax law. See, for example, *Liggett Group, Inc.*, 58 TCM 1167, T.C.Memo. 1990–18.

method. The IFP method may be elected only where an IFP exists.[8] If the manufacturer or producer regularly sells to wholly independent distributors, this can establish an *independent* factory or production price.

Under § 865, income from the sale of personal property other than inventory is sourced at the residence of the seller unless one of the following exceptions applies.

- Gain on the sale of depreciable personal property is sourced according to prior depreciation deductions to the extent of the deductions. Any excess gain is sourced the same as the sale of inventory.
- Gain on the sale of intangibles is sourced according to prior amortization deductions to the extent of the deductions. Contingent payments, however, are sourced as royalty income.
- Gain attributable to an office or fixed place of business maintained outside the United States by a U.S. resident is foreign-source income.
- Income or gain attributable to an office or fixed place of business maintained in the United States by a nonresident is U.S.-source income.

The sourcing of losses is complicated and depends on the nature of the property. Different rules exist for the disposition of stock versus other personal property.[9]

Transportation and Communication Income. Income from transportation beginning *and* ending in the United States is U.S.-source income. Fifty percent of the income from transportation beginning *or* ending in the United States is U.S.-source income, unless the U.S. point is only an intermediate stop. This rule does not apply to personal services income unless the transportation is between the United States and a possession. Income from space and ocean activities conducted outside the jurisdiction of any country is sourced according to the residence of the person conducting the activity.

International communication income derived by a U.S. person is sourced 50 percent in the United States when transmission is between the United States and a foreign country. International communication income derived by foreign persons is foreign-source income unless it is attributable to an office or other fixed place of business in the United States. In that case, it is U.S.-source income.

Software Income. Income from the sale or license of software is sourced depending on how the income is classified. Under Regulation § 1.861–18, a transfer of software is classified as either the transfer of a copyright (e.g., the right to the computer program itself) or the transfer of a copyrighted article (the right to use a copy of the computer program). If the transfer is considered a transfer of a copyright, the income is sourced using the royalty income rules. If the transfer is considered a transfer of a copyrighted article, the income is treated as resulting from a sale of the article and is sourced based on the personal property sales rules.

INCOME SOURCED OUTSIDE THE UNITED STATES

The provisions for sourcing income outside the United States are not as detailed and specific as those for determining U.S.-source income. Basically, § 862 provides that if interest, dividends, compensation for personal services, income from the use or sale of property, or other income is not U.S.-source income, then it is foreign-source income.

[8] § 863(b)(2), Reg. § 1.863–3, and Notice 89–10, 1989–1 C.B. 631.

[9] See Reg. § 1.861–8(e)(7) and Temp.Reg. § 1.865–1T(a)(1). See Reg. §§ 1.865–(2)(a)(1) and (2) regarding the source of losses on the disposition of stock.

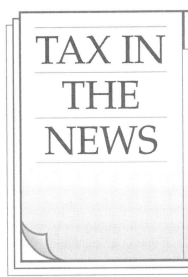

Sourcing Income in Cyberspace

The use of the Internet for more and more consumer and business transactions is posing problems for the taxing authorities. Consumers purchase books, music, clothing, and food from Internet retailers. Businesses negotiate with suppliers via online auctions of products and services. Consultants provide services to their clients over the Web. Very few transactions do not have a counterpart that takes place in cyberspace. The existing income-sourcing rules were developed long before the existence of the Internet, and taxing authorities are finding it challenging to apply these rules to Internet transactions. Where does a sale take place when the Web server is in the Cayman Islands, the seller is in Singapore, and the customer is in Texas? Where is a service performed when all activities take place over the Net? These questions and more will have to be answered by the United States and its trading partners as the Internet economy grows in size and importance.

ALLOCATION AND APPORTIONMENT OF DEDUCTIONS

The United States levies a tax on *taxable income*. Deductions and losses, therefore, must be allocated and apportioned between U.S.- and foreign-source gross income to determine U.S.- and foreign-source taxable income. Deductions directly related to an activity or property are allocated to classes of income. This is followed by apportionment between the statutory and residual groupings (e.g., foreign versus domestic) on some reasonable basis.[10] A deduction not definitely related to any class of gross income is ratably allocated to all classes of gross income and apportioned between U.S.- and foreign-source income.

EXAMPLE 8

Ace, Inc., a domestic corporation, has $2 million of gross income and a $50,000 expense, all related to real estate activities. The expense is allocated and apportioned using gross income as a basis as follows.

	Gross Income			Apportionment	
	Foreign	U.S.	Allocation	Foreign	U.S.
Sales	$1,000,000	$500,000	$37,500*	$25,000	$12,500**
Rentals	400,000	100,000	12,500	10,000	2,500***
			$50,000	$35,000	$15,000

*$50,000 × ($1,500,000/$2,000,000).
**$37,500 × ($500,000/$1,500,000).
***$12,500 × ($100,000/$500,000).

If Ace could show that $45,000 of the expense was directly related to sales income, the $45,000 would be allocated to that class of gross income, with the remainder allocated and apportioned ratably based on gross income. ■

Interest expense is allocated and apportioned based on the theory that money is fungible. With limited exceptions, interest expense is attributable to all the activities

[10]Reg. § 1.861–8.

and property of the taxpayer, regardless of the specific purpose for incurring the debt on which interest is paid.[11] Taxpayers must allocate and apportion interest expense on the basis of assets, using either the fair market value or the tax book value of the assets.[12] Once the fair market value is used, the taxpayer must continue to use this method. Special rules apply in allocating and apportioning interest expense in an affiliated group of corporations.

EXAMPLE 9

Fisher, Inc., a domestic corporation, generates U.S.-source and foreign-source gross income for the current year. Fisher's assets (tax book value) are as follows.

Assets generating U.S.-source income	$18,000,000
Assets generating foreign-source income	5,000,000
	$23,000,000

Fisher incurs interest expense of $800,000 for the current year. Using the tax book value method, interest expense is apportioned to foreign-source income as follows.

$$\frac{\$5{,}000{,}000 \text{ (foreign assets)}}{\$23{,}000{,}000 \text{ (total assets)}} \times \$800{,}000 = \$173{,}913$$

■

Specific rules also apply to research and development (R & D) expenditures, certain stewardship expenses, legal and accounting fees and expenses, income taxes, and losses. Although U.S. companies incur about 90 percent of their R & D expenditures at U.S. facilities, several billion dollars is spent on foreign R & D each year. The Regulations provide that a portion of a U.S. company's R & D expenditures must be treated as foreign-source expense if the R & D relates to foreign product sales.

SECTION 482 CONSIDERATIONS

Taxpayers may be tempted to manipulate the source of income and the allocation of deductions arbitrarily to minimize taxation. This manipulation is more easily accomplished between or among related persons. The IRS uses § 482 to counter such actions. The provision gives the IRS the power to reallocate gross income, deductions, credits, or allowances between or among organizations, trades, or businesses owned or controlled directly or indirectly by the same interests. This can be done whenever the IRS determines that reallocation is necessary to prevent the evasion of taxes or to reflect income more clearly. Section 482 is a "one-edged sword" available only to the IRS. The taxpayer generally cannot invoke it to reallocate income and expenses.[13]

The reach of § 482 is quite broad. The IRS takes the position that a corporation and its sole shareholder who works full-time for the corporation can be treated as two separate trades or businesses for purposes of § 482.[14] Two unrelated shareholders who each owned 50 percent of a corporation were held to be acting in concert for their common good and, thus, together controlled the corporation.[15]

[11]Reg. § 1.861–10T(b) describes circumstances in which interest expense can be directly allocated to specific debt. This exception to the fungibility concept is limited to cases in which specific property is purchased or improved with nonrecourse debt.

[12]Reg. § 1.861–9T.

[13]Reg. § 1.482–1(a)(3).

[14]Rev.Rul. 88–38, 1988–1 C.B. 246. But see *Foglesong v. Comm.*, 82–2 USTC ¶9650, 50 AFTR2d 82–6016, 691 F.2d 848 (CA–7, 1982), *rev'g* 77 T.C. 1102 (1981).

[15]See *B. Forman Co., Inc. v. Comm.*, 72–1 USTC ¶9182, 29 AFTR2d 72–403, 453 F.2d 1144 (CA–2, 1972).

APAs Reduce Uncertainty in Transfer Pricing Disputes

The first APA was approved in January 1991. The IRS reports that 492 APAs have been executed and 229 others are in negotiation. The taxpayers participating in the APA program come from many different industries. The five most represented industries are financial institutions, computer items and software, chemicals, transportation equipment, and electrical equipment.

Only 10 percent of the largest taxpayers involved in international intercompany transactions have participated in the APA process. However, the volume of intercompany transactions represented by these taxpayers constitutes 42 percent of the total dollar value of international intercompany transactions.

The APA process is not simple or quick. The IRS reports that the APAs approved in 2003 took an average of 34 months to complete.

SOURCE: Announcement and Report Concerning Advance Pricing Agreements, *Internal Revenue Bulletin*: 2004–15 (Announcement 2004–26).

In applying § 482, an arm's length price must be determined to assign the correct profits to related entities. Several alternative methods can be used in determining an arm's length price on the sale of tangible or intangible property. The major problem with most pricing methods is that uncontrolled comparable transactions are needed as a benchmark.

An accuracy-related penalty of 20 percent is provided by § 6662 for net § 482 transfer price adjustments (changes in profit allocations by the IRS) for a taxable year that exceed the lesser of $5 million or 10 percent of the taxpayer's gross receipts. In addition, there is a 40 percent penalty for "gross misstatements."

As an aid to reducing pricing disputes, the IRS initiated the Advance Pricing Agreement (APA) program whereby the taxpayer can propose a transfer pricing method for certain international transactions. The taxpayer provides relevant data, which are then evaluated by the IRS. If accepted, the APA provides a safe-harbor transfer pricing method for the taxpayer. Apple Computer, Inc., accomplished the first successful APA submission.

LO.4

Explain how foreign currency exchange affects the tax consequences of international transactions.

Foreign Currency Transactions

The relative value of a foreign currency and the U.S. dollar is described by the foreign exchange rate. Changes in this rate affect the dollar value of foreign property held by the taxpayer, the dollar value of foreign debts, and the dollar amount of gain or loss on a transaction denominated in a foreign currency. Almost every international tax issue requires consideration of currency exchange implications.

EXAMPLE 10

Dress, Inc., a domestic corporation, purchases merchandise for resale from Fiesta, Inc., a foreign corporation, for 50,000K (a foreign currency). On the date of purchase, 1K is equal to $1 U.S. (1K:$1). At this time, the account payable is $50,000. On the date of payment by Dress (the foreign exchange date), the exchange rate is 1.25K:$1. In other words, the foreign currency has been devalued in relation to the U.S. dollar, and Dress will pay Fiesta 50,000K, which will cost Dress only $40,000. Dress must record the purchase of the merchandise at $50,000 and recognize a foreign currency gain of $10,000 ($50,000 – $40,000). ■

In recent years, U.S. currency abroad has amounted to more than 50 percent of the U.S. currency in circulation. Taxpayers may find it necessary to translate amounts denominated in foreign currency into U.S. dollars for any of the following purposes.

- Purchase of goods, services, and property.
- Sale of goods, services, and property.
- Collection of foreign receivables.
- Payment of foreign payables.
- Foreign tax credit calculations.
- Recognition of income or loss from foreign branch activities.

The foreign currency exchange rates, however, have no effect on the transactions of a U.S. person who arranges all international transactions in U.S. dollars.

EXAMPLE 11

Sellers, Inc., a domestic corporation, purchases goods from Rose, Ltd., a foreign corporation, and pays for these goods in U.S. dollars. Rose then exchanges the U.S. dollars for the currency of the country in which it operates. Sellers has no foreign exchange considerations with which to contend. If instead Rose required Sellers to pay for the goods in a foreign currency, Sellers would have to exchange U.S. dollars to obtain the foreign currency to make payment. If the exchange rate changed from the date of purchase to the date of payment, Sellers would have a foreign currency gain or loss on the currency exchange. ■

The following concepts are important when dealing with the tax aspects of foreign exchange.

- Foreign currency is treated as property other than money.
- Gain or loss on the exchange of foreign currency is considered separately from the underlying transaction (e.g., the purchase or sale of goods).
- No gain or loss is recognized until a transaction is closed.

TAX ISSUES

The following major tax issues must be considered when dealing with foreign currency exchange.

- The date of recognition of any gain or loss (see Concept Summary 25–1).
- The source (U.S. or foreign) of the foreign currency gain or loss.
- The character of the gain or loss (ordinary or capital).

FUNCTIONAL CURRENCY

The Code generally adopted FAS 52, the Financial Accounting Standards Board standard on foreign currency translation. FAS 52 introduced the **functional currency** approach. Under this approach, the currency of the economic environment in which the foreign entity operates generally is to be used as the monetary unit to measure gains and losses.

Under § 985, all income tax determinations are to be made in the taxpayer's functional currency. A taxpayer's default functional currency is the U.S. dollar. In most cases, a **qualified business unit (QBU)** operating in a foreign country uses that country's currency as its functional currency. A QBU is a separate and clearly identified unit of a taxpayer's trade or business (e.g., a foreign branch). An individual is not a QBU; however, a trade or business conducted by an individual may be a QBU.[16]

[16]Reg. § 1.989(a)–1(b).

CONCEPT SUMMARY 25–1

Recognition of Foreign Exchange Gain or Loss

Transaction	Date of Recognition
Purchase or sale of inventory or business asset	Date of disposition of foreign currency
Branch profits	Remittance of branch profits
Subpart F income	Receipt of previously taxed income (accumulated E & P)
Dividend from untaxed current or accumulated E & P	No exchange gain or loss to recipient

BRANCH OPERATIONS

When a foreign branch (QBU) uses a foreign currency as its functional currency, profit or loss is computed in the foreign currency each year and translated into U.S. dollars for tax purposes. The entire amount of profit or loss, not taking remittances into account, is translated using the average exchange rate for the taxable year. Exchange gain or loss is recognized on remittances from the QBU. The U.S. dollar amount of the remittance at the exchange rate in effect on the date of remittance is compared with the U.S. dollar value (basis pool) of the equity pool of the branch. The equity pool comprises the branch's initial capitalization plus contributions to the branch plus undistributed profits minus remittances and losses—all measured in the QBU's functional currency.[17] This exchange gain or loss is ordinary, and it is sourced according to the income to which the remittance is attributable.

DISTRIBUTIONS FROM FOREIGN CORPORATIONS

An actual distribution of E & P from a foreign corporation is included in income by the U.S. recipient at the exchange rate in effect on the date of distribution. Thus, no exchange gain or loss is recognized. Deemed dividend distributions under Subpart F (discussed later in the chapter) are translated at the average exchange rate for the corporation's tax year to which the deemed distribution is attributable. Exchange gain or loss can result when an actual distribution of this previously taxed income is made.

FOREIGN TAXES

For purposes of the foreign tax credit, foreign taxes accrued generally are translated at the average exchange rate in effect for the tax year to which the taxes relate. Under exceptions to this rule, foreign taxes must be translated at the exchange rate in effect when the foreign taxes were paid.[18] If foreign taxes are paid within two years of accrual, and if they differ from the accrued amount merely because of currency exchange fluctuation, no redetermination is required, even though the actual dollar value paid may differ from the accrued amount. In other cases, when the taxes paid differ from the amount accrued, a redetermination is required.

EXAMPLE 12

Music, Inc., a domestic corporation, has a foreign branch. Foreign taxes attributable to branch income amount to 5,000K (a foreign currency). The taxes are paid within two years of being

[17]Prop.Reg. § 1.987–2.

[18]§§ 986(a)(1)(B) and (C).

accrued. The average foreign exchange rate for the tax year to which the foreign taxes relate is .5K:$1. On the date the taxes are paid, the rate is .6K:$1. No redetermination is required, and Music has foreign taxes of $10,000 for purposes of the foreign tax credit. ■

SECTION 988 TRANSACTIONS

The disposition of a nonfunctional currency can result in a foreign currency gain or loss under § 988. Section 988 transactions include those in which gain or loss is determined with regard to the value of a nonfunctional currency, such as the following.

- Acquiring (or becoming obligor under) a debt instrument.
- Accruing (or otherwise taking into account) any item of expense or gross income or receipts that is to be paid or received at a later date.
- Entering into or acquiring nearly any forward contract, futures contract, option, or similar investment position.
- Disposing of nonfunctional currency.

Section 988 generally treats exchange gain or loss falling within its provisions as ordinary income or loss. Capital gain or loss treatment may be elected with regard to forward contracts, futures contracts, and options that constitute capital assets in the hands of the taxpayer.

A closed or completed transaction is required. The residence of the taxpayer generally determines the source of a § 988 foreign exchange gain or loss.

LO.5

Work with the U.S. tax provisions affecting U.S. persons earning foreign-source income, including the rules relating to cross-border asset transfers, antideferral provisions, and the foreign tax credit.

U.S. Persons with Foreign Income

U.S. taxpayers often "internationalize" gradually over time. A U.S. business may operate on a strictly domestic basis for several years, then explore foreign markets by exporting its products abroad, and later license its products to a foreign manufacturer or enter into a joint venture with a foreign partner. If its forays into foreign markets are successful, the U.S. business may create a foreign subsidiary and move a portion of its operations abroad by establishing a sales or manufacturing facility. A domestically controlled foreign corporation can have significant U.S. tax consequences for the U.S. owners, and any U.S. taxpayer paying foreign taxes must consider the foreign tax credit provisions. Foreign businesses likewise enter the U.S. market in stages. In either case, each step generates increasingly significant international tax consequences.

Under § 911, qualified U.S. citizens and residents may exclude a limited amount of foreign earned income and a housing allowance from their U.S. taxable income. See Chapter 5 for more information on the § 911 exclusion.

EXPORT PROPERTY TAX INCENTIVES

The easiest way for a U.S. enterprise to engage in global commerce is simply to sell U.S.-produced goods and services abroad. These sales can be conducted with little or no foreign presence and allow the business to explore foreign markets without making costly financial commitments to foreign operations. The U.S. tax consequences of simple export sales are straightforward. All such income is taxed in the United States to the U.S. taxpayer. Whether foreign taxes must be paid on this export income depends on the particular law of the foreign jurisdiction and whether the U.S. taxpayer is deemed to have a foreign business presence there (often called a "permanent establishment"). In many cases, such export income is not taxed by any foreign jurisdiction.

To improve the U.S. balance of trade, Congress has used various export tax incentives to encourage exports of U.S.-produced property. In the late 1970s, Congress created the domestic international sales corporation (DISC) provisions that allowed a DISC to defer the tax on a portion of its export income until actual repatriation of the earnings. After the General Agreement on Tariffs and Trade (GATT) charged that the DISC provisions were a prohibited *export subsidy*, the provisions were curtailed. As an alternative, in 1984 the foreign sales corporation (FSC) provisions (§§ 921–927) were enacted to provide similar tax incentives to U.S. exporters while appeasing the GATT members. FSCs were not allowed to defer the tax on export income. Instead, a certain percentage of export income was permanently exempt from U.S. taxation.

In 2000, the United States was forced to repeal the FSC provisions after the World Trade Organization (WTO) found that the FSC benefits constituted an illegal export subsidy. Congress replaced the FSC with a benefit that excluded **extraterritorial income** from U.S. taxation. The extraterritorial income (ETI) regime preserved the basic incentives provided by the FSC rules. Consequently, it is not surprising that the WTO found that the ETI provisions also violated its rules.

The American Jobs Creation Act of 2004 repealed the ETI exclusion but provided a transition rule that allows partial ETI benefits for 2005 and 2006.[19] The Act did not replace the ETI benefit with a new tax benefit for U.S. exporters. Instead, it created a new broad-based "domestic production deduction" ("manufacturers' deduction") for U.S. manufacturers and certain other domestic producers equal to 9 percent of the taxpayer's *qualified production activities income* subject to several limitations.[20] The deduction is phased in, with a 3 percent deduction for tax years beginning in 2005 or 2006, a 6 percent deduction for tax years beginning in 2007, 2008, or 2009, and a 9 percent deduction for tax years thereafter. The domestic production deduction replacement for ETI is no longer an "international tax" issue, as the deduction does not require exporting or any other activity outside the United States. The deduction is discussed in Chapter 17.

CROSS-BORDER ASSET TRANSFERS

As part of "going international," a U.S. taxpayer may decide to transfer assets outside the United States so that any foreign business will be conducted outside the U.S. tax jurisdiction. To originate investment through, or transfer investment to, a foreign entity, the U.S. taxpayer must make some sort of transfer to the foreign entity. This may take the form of a cash investment or a transfer of assets of a U.S. entity.

In situations where potential taxable income is transferred to a corporation outside the U.S. taxing jurisdiction, the exchange may trigger a tax. The tax result of transferring property to a foreign corporation depends on the nature of the exchange, the assets involved, the income potential of the property, and the character of the property, in the hands of the transferor or transferee. Figure 25–2 summarizes the taxation of cross-border asset transfers.

Outbound Transfers. When assets are exchanged for corporate stock in a domestic transaction, realized gain or loss may be deferred rather than recognized. Similarly, deferral treatment may be available when the following "outbound" capital changes occur (i.e., moving corporate business across country borders and outside the United States).

[19]Section 101 of the American Jobs Creation Act of 2004, Public Law 108–357 (October 22, 2004).

[20]§ 199.

■ FIGURE 25–2
Taxation of Cross-Border Asset Transfers

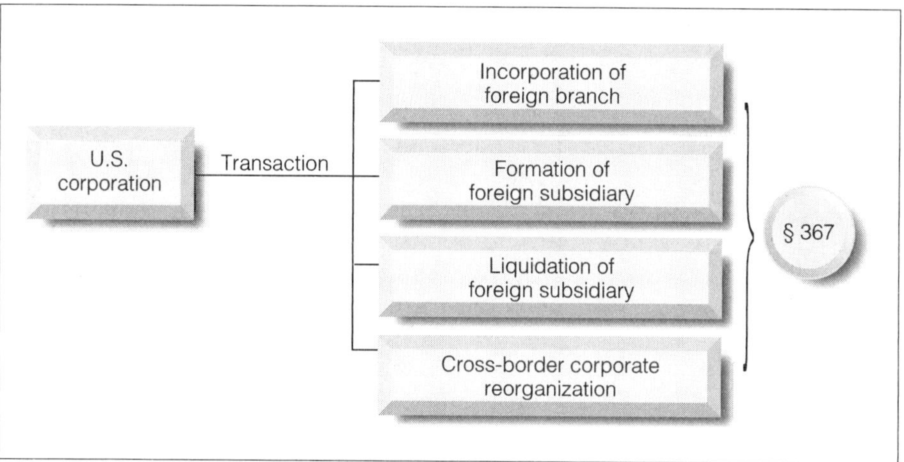

- A U.S. corporation starts up a new corporation outside the United States (§ 351).
- A U.S. corporation liquidates a U.S. subsidiary into an existing foreign subsidiary (§ 332).
- A U.S. corporation incorporates a non-U.S. branch of a U.S. corporation, forming a new foreign corporation (§ 351).
- A foreign corporation uses a stock swap to acquire a U.S. corporation (Type "B" reorganization).
- A foreign corporation acquires substantially all of a U.S. corporation's net assets (Type "C" reorganization).

These otherwise tax-deferred transactions may trigger current taxation when foreign corporations are involved. Under § 367, the general rule is that gain deferral is not allowed when assets are leaving the U.S. taxing jurisdiction. However, a major exception allows continued tax deferral for assets transferred to a foreign corporation to be used in a trade or business carried on outside the United States.

The trade or business exception does not apply to certain "tainted" assets, and the transfer of these assets outside the United States triggers immediate gain (but not loss) recognition. The following are "tainted" assets under § 367.

- Inventory (raw goods, work-in-progress, and finished goods).
- Installment obligations and unrealized accounts receivable.
- Foreign currency.
- Property leased by the transferor unless the transferee is the lessee.

These tainted assets are likely to turn over quickly once the asset transfer is completed, and any appreciation is likely to be recognized outside the U.S. taxing jurisdiction. Consequently, § 367 requires recognition of this gain upon transfer of the asset outside the United States.

EXAMPLE 13

Amelia, Inc., a domestic corporation, incorporates its profitable Irish manufacturing branch and creates a new wholly owned foreign corporation, St. George, Ltd., to engage in manufacturing activities in Ireland. The transfer qualifies as tax deferred under § 351. The branch assets have always been used in Ireland. Amelia transfers the following branch assets to St. George upon its creation.

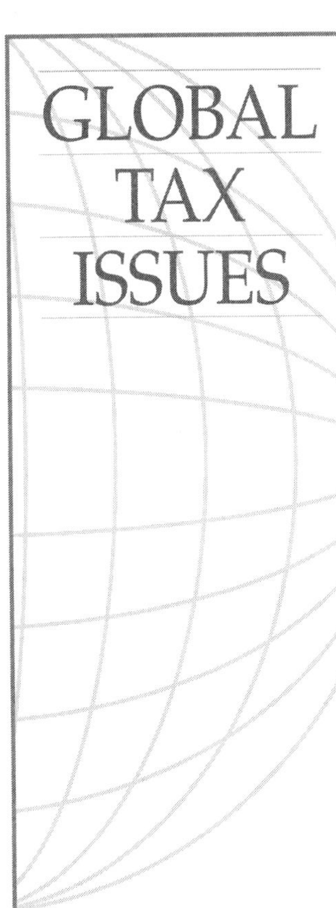

Boom in Cross-Border Mergers

Recent years have seen an increase in the number of tax-deferred mergers taking place across national borders. Helen of Troy, the publicly traded cosmetics giant, converted itself from a U.S. corporation into a tax haven corporation without triggering any tax for its shareholders. Once outside the U.S. taxing jurisdiction, the company was free from many of the restrictions imposed by U.S. tax law. U.S. taxing authorities responded to this transaction by issuing new Regulations [Reg. § 1.367(a)–3(c)] to shut down these so-called inversions unless very strict standards were met. But even after these Regulations became law, Chrysler became part of the German corporation DaimlerChrysler in a tax-deferred transaction.

The American Jobs Creation Act of 2004 created even stricter rules in an effort to deter shareholders or partners from turning domestic entities into foreign entities. A domestic corporation or partnership continues to be treated as domestic if:

- A foreign corporation acquires substantially all of its properties after March 4, 2003.
- The former shareholders (or partners) of the U.S. corporation (or partnership) hold 80 percent or more of the foreign corporation's stock after the transaction.
- The foreign corporation does not have substantial business activities in its country of incorporation.

If the former shareholders or partners own at least 60 percent but less than 80 percent of the new corporation, the foreign entity remains foreign, but any corporate-level taxes imposed because of the transfer cannot be offset with net operating losses, foreign tax credits, or certain other tax attributes. In addition, an excise tax is imposed at the maximum capital gains tax rate on the value of certain stock held by insiders at any time during the 12-month period beginning six months before the date of the inversion.

Asset	Tax Basis	Market Value	Built-in Gain/Loss
Raw materials inventory	$100	$ 400	$ 300
Accounts receivable	200	250	50
Manufacturing equipment	450	925	475
Furniture and fixtures	150	50	(100)
Total	$900	$1,625	$ 725

Although the $725 in realized gain is deferred under § 351, the gain is potentially taxable under § 367 because the assets are leaving the U.S. taxing jurisdiction. The general rule of § 367 is that all the realized gain is recognized by Amelia. However, because St. George will use the transferred assets in the active conduct of a foreign trade or business, the realized gain remains potentially deferred. But, because the inventory and accounts receivable are "tainted assets," Amelia must recognize $350 of gain upon the transfer ($300 of gain attributable to inventory and $50 related to accounts receivable). Gain is recognized on an asset-by-asset basis with no offset for losses on other assets. ■

Inbound and Offshore Transfers. One objective of Federal tax law is to prevent E & P that has accumulated in U.S.-owned foreign corporations from escaping U.S. taxation. Section 367(b) covers the tax treatment of inbound and offshore transfers with regard to stock of a **controlled foreign corporation (CFC).** (CFCs are discussed in more detail in a later section.) An example of an inbound

EXHIBIT 25–2
OECD Tax Haven Blacklist

In 2000, the OECD identified these jurisdictions as tax havens that had not cooperated with its campaign to stop harmful global tax practices. As of 2004, only the countries marked with an asterisk remained on the list.

Andorra*	Maldives
Anguilla	Marshall Islands*
Antigua and Barbuda	Monaco*
Aruba	Montserrat
Bahamas	Nauru
Bahrain	Netherlands Antilles
Barbados	Niue
Belize	Panama
British Virgin Islands	Samoa
Cook Island	Seychelles
Dominica	St. Christopher and Nevis
Gibraltar	St. Lucia
Grenada	St. Vincent and the Grenadines
Guernsey	Tonga
Isle of Man	Turks and Caicos Islands
Jersey	U.S. Virgin Islands
Liberia*	Vanuatu
Liechtenstein*	

SOURCES: Organization for Economic Cooperation and Development (OECD), *Towards Global Tax Cooperation: Progress in Identifying and Eliminating Harmful Tax Practices,* 2000; OECD News Release, April 18, 2002; and The OECD's Project on Harmful Tax Practices: The 2004 Progress Report, February 4, 2004.

transaction is the liquidation of a foreign corporation into a domestic parent under § 332.

U.S. persons that are directly or indirectly parties to an inbound or offshore transfer involving stock of a CFC generally recognize dividend income to the extent of their pro rata share of the previously untaxed E & P of the foreign corporation. In some situations, income can be deferred by entering into a gain recognition agreement with the IRS. Special rules apply to the outbound transfer of domestic or foreign shares.

TAX HAVENS

Many outbound transfers of assets to foreign corporations are to countries with tax rates higher than or equal to the U.S. rate. Thus, tax avoidance is not the motive for such transfers. Some U.S. corporations, however, make their foreign investment in (or through) a tax haven. A **tax haven** is a country where either locally sourced income or residents are subject to no or low internal taxation. Exhibit 25–2 lists countries classified as tax havens.

One method of potentially avoiding taxation is to invest through a foreign corporation incorporated in a tax haven. Because the foreign corporation is a resident of the tax haven, the income it earns is subject to no or low internal taxes. Tax haven countries may also have provisions limiting the exchange of financial and commercial information.

A tax haven can, in effect, be created by an income tax treaty. For example, under an income tax treaty between Country A and Country B, residents of Country A are subject to a withholding tax of only 5 percent on dividend and interest income sourced in Country B. The United States and Country A have a similar treaty. The United States does not have a treaty with Country B, and the withholding tax is 30 percent. A U.S. corporation can create a foreign subsidiary in Country A and use that subsidiary to make investments in Country B. This practice is referred to as **treaty shopping.** If the Country B investment income had been earned directly by the U.S. corporation, it would be subject to a 30 percent withholding tax. As a result of investing through the foreign subsidiary created in Country A, the U.S. parent corporation pays only 10 percent in foreign taxes on the income earned, that is, 5 percent to Country B and 5 percent to Country A.

In recent years, many countries have enacted "treaty shopping" provisions. Under the provisions, treaty benefits for withholding taxes are not available to a resident corporation unless a certain percentage of its beneficial interests are owned, directly or indirectly, by one or more individual residents of the country in which the corporation is resident. The most controversial article in the U.S. Model Treaty is Article 22, Limitation on Benefits, which is meant to prevent treaty shopping. Article 22 disallows treaty benefits to an entity unless more than 50 percent of the beneficial interest in the entity is owned, directly or indirectly, by one or more individual residents of the treaty country in which the entity is resident.[21]

FOREIGN CORPORATIONS CONTROLLED BY U.S. PERSONS

To minimize current tax liability, taxpayers often attempt to defer the recognition of taxable income. One way to do this is to shift the income-generating activity to a foreign entity that is not within the U.S. tax jurisdiction. A foreign corporation is the most suitable entity for such an endeavor because, unlike a partnership, it is not a conduit through which income is taxed directly to the owner. Because of the potential for abuse, Congress has enacted various provisions to limit the availability of deferral.

ETHICAL CONSIDERATIONS

A Boost to Domestic Investment or a Tax Amnesty for Outsourcers?

The American Jobs Creation Act of 2004 provided a temporary incentive to repatriate foreign profits back to the United States. Section 965 allows domestic corporations to elect to take a one-time 85 percent dividends received deduction for certain cash dividends received from controlled foreign corporations for either the taxpayer's last tax year that began before October 22, 2004, or the first tax year that began after October 22, 2004. Such dividends must be reinvested in the United States, and the eligible dividend amount is based on a calculation that considers prior-year average dividends and the amount of earnings considered "permanently reinvested" abroad under financial accounting principles. The intent was to provide a tax benefit only for earnings that would not otherwise have been repatriated to the United States. With an 85 percent dividends received deduction, the effective U.S. corporate tax rate on such dividends is 5.25 percent (35% corporate tax rate x 15% taxable amount).

Supporters of this measure argued that the inflow of cash back to the United States, along with the requirement for reinvestment here, will provide a boost to the domestic economy. The dividend income is lightly taxed but would otherwise never have been taxed in the United States. Critics argue that the tax break is simply a giveaway to U.S. multinational corporations and rewards outsourcing. They fear that with this precedent, U.S. multinationals may simply outsource more profits to low-tax countries and wait for future tax breaks before repatriating profits. Which argument do you find more convincing? How would you feel if your own company had always repatriated foreign profits back to the United States without the benefit of a special tax break?

[21]Additional limitations on the use of treaty benefits are contained in § 894(c).

A Move to the Beach for U.S. Corporations Seeking a Vacation from U.S. Tax Rules

A number of U.S.-based companies have decided to cast their lot on the golden shores of Bermuda, reincorporating as Bermuda companies and enjoying Bermuda's low-tax environment. Those with Bermuda headquarters include such well-known companies as Fruit of the Loom, Cooper Industries, Foster Wheeler, and Ingersoll Rand. Even Accenture, formerly Andersen Consulting, established itself in Bermuda.

Many of these companies argue that U.S. international tax policy compromises their ability to compete in the global marketplace. The stock market often rewarded these so-called inversion transactions (i.e., conversion from U.S. to foreign based) with increased stock prices. Although an inversion transaction often entailed a current tax cost, the long-term tax benefits were considered more important. Many other companies were preparing to invert in 2002 when Congress began developing anti-inversion legislation and the public began reacting negatively to these corporate expatriates. During mid-2002, toolmaker Stanley Works called off its previously announced, and very controversial, inversion plans. Inversions virtually ceased during 2003. Provisions in the American Jobs Creation Act of 2004 further curtailed the benefits of moving offshore.

Controlled Foreign Corporations. Subpart F, §§ 951–964 of the Code, provides that certain types of income generated by controlled foreign corporations (CFCs) are currently included in gross income by the U.S. shareholders without regard to actual distributions. For Subpart F to apply, the foreign corporation must have been a CFC for an uninterrupted period of 30 days or more during the taxable year. When this is the case, U.S. shareholders must include in gross income their pro rata share of Subpart F income and increase in earnings that the CFC has invested in U.S. property for the tax year. This rule applies to U.S. shareholders who own stock in the corporation on the last day of the tax year or on the last day the foreign corporation is a CFC. The gross income inclusion must be made for their taxable year in which the taxable year of the CFC ends.

EXAMPLE 14

Gray, Inc., a calendar year corporation, is a CFC for the entire tax year. Chance Company, a U.S. corporation, owns 60% of Gray's one class of stock for the entire year. Subpart F income is $100,000, and no distributions have been made during the year. Chance, a calendar year taxpayer, includes $60,000 in gross income as a constructive dividend for the tax year. ■

EXAMPLE 15

Gray, Inc., is a CFC until July 1 of the tax year (a calendar year) and earns $100,000 of Subpart F income. Terry, a U.S. citizen, owns 30% of its one class of stock for the entire year. She includes $14,877 [$100,000 × 30% × (181 days/365 days)] in gross income as a constructive dividend for the tax year. ■

A CFC is any foreign corporation in which more than 50 percent of the total combined voting power of all classes of stock entitled to vote or the total value of the stock of the corporation is owned by U.S. shareholders on any day during the taxable year of the foreign corporation. The foreign subsidiaries of most multinational U.S. parent corporations are CFCs. For purposes of determining if a foreign corporation is a CFC, a **U.S. shareholder** is defined as a U.S. person who owns, or is considered to own, 10 percent or more of the total combined voting power of all classes of voting stock of the foreign corporation. Stock owned directly, indirectly, and constructively is counted.

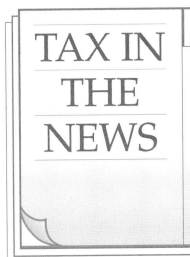

WHO ARE THESE CFCs?

The 7,500 largest CFCs accounted for $4.4 trillion of the assets and more than $2.2 trillion of the gross receipts of all CFCs for 2000, the latest year for which complete data are available. These CFCs were engaged primarily in manufacturing (29 percent), services (26 percent), or finance, insurance, or real estate (23 percent). Although these 7,500 CFCs were incorporated in over 100 different countries, CFCs in Europe, Canada, and Japan accounted for over 80 percent of the gross receipts. In 2000, CFCs distributed $94.9 billion of profits to their U.S. parents and other shareholders. This represented a 38 percent increase in distributions over 1996. A "large" CFC is one having $500 million or more in assets.

SOURCE: *Statistics of Income Bulletin*, Summer 2004, Publication 1136 (Rev. 09–2004).

Indirect ownership involves stock held through a foreign entity, such as a foreign corporation, foreign partnership, or foreign trust. This stock is considered to be actually owned proportionately by the shareholders, partners, or beneficiaries. Constructive ownership rules, with certain modifications, apply in determining if a U.S. person is a U.S. shareholder, in determining whether a foreign corporation is a CFC, and for certain related-party provisions of Subpart F.[22]

EXAMPLE 16

Shareholders of Foreign Corporation	Voting Power	Classification
Alan	30%	U.S. person
Bill	9%	U.S. person
Carla	40%	Foreign person
Dora	20%	U.S. person
Ed	1%	U.S. person

Bill is Alan's son. Alan, Bill, and Dora are U.S. shareholders. Alan owns 39%, 30% directly and 9% constructively through Bill. Bill also owns 39%, 9% directly and 30% constructively through Alan. Thus, Bill is a U.S. shareholder. Dora owns 20% directly. The corporation is a CFC because U.S. shareholders own 59% of the voting power. Ed, a U.S. person, owns 1% and is not related to any of the other shareholders. Thus, Ed is not a U.S. shareholder and would not have to include any of the Subpart F income in gross income. If Bill were not related to Alan or to any other U.S. persons who were shareholders, Bill would not be a U.S. shareholder, and the corporation would not be a CFC. ■

U.S. shareholders must include their pro rata share of the applicable income in their gross income only to the extent of their actual ownership. Stock held indirectly (but not constructively) is considered actually owned for this purpose.

EXAMPLE 17

Bill, in Example 16, would recognize only 9% of the Subpart F income as a constructive dividend. Alan would recognize 30%, and Dora would recognize 20%. If instead Bill were

[22]§§ 958 and 318(a).

a foreign corporation wholly owned by Alan, Alan would recognize 39% as a constructive dividend. ■

Subpart F Income. A U.S. shareholder of a CFC does not necessarily lose the ability to defer U.S. taxation of income earned by the CFC. Only certain income earned by the CFC triggers immediate U.S. taxation as a constructive dividend. This tainted income, referred to as Subpart F income, can be characterized as income with little or no economic connection with the CFC's country of incorporation. **Subpart F** income consists of the following.

- Insurance income (§ 953).
- Foreign base company income (§ 954).
- International boycott factor income (§ 999).
- Illegal bribes.
- Income derived from a § 901(j) foreign country.

Insurance Income. Income attributable to insuring risk of loss outside the country in which the CFC is organized is Subpart F income. This rule precludes U.S. corporations from setting up offshore insurance companies in tax havens to convert expenditures for self-insurance into a deductible insurance premium.

Foreign Base Company Income. Foreign base company income (FBCI) provisions target transactions whereby a CFC earns income that lacks any economic connection to its country of organization. There are five categories of FBCI.

- Foreign personal holding company income.
- Foreign base company sales income.
- Foreign base company services income.
- Foreign base company shipping income (for tax years beginning before 2005 only).
- Foreign base company oil-related income.

Foreign personal holding company (FPHC) income consists of the following.

- Dividends, interest, royalties, rents, and annuities.
- Excess gains over losses from the sale or exchange of property (including an interest in a trust or partnership) that gives rise to FPHC income or that does not give rise to any income.
- Excess of foreign currency gains over foreign currency losses (other than any transaction directly related to the business needs of the CFC).
- Income from notional principal contracts.
- Certain payments in lieu of dividends.
- Certain personal service contract income.

Certain FPHC income does not trigger Subpart F inclusion under exceptions for same-country payments and active rent and royalty income.

Foreign base company (FBC) sales income is income derived by a CFC where the CFC has very little connection with the process that generates the income and a related party is involved. If the CFC earns income from the sale of property to customers outside the CFC's country of incorporation, and either the supplier or the customer is related to the CFC, such income is FBC sales income.

EXAMPLE 18

Ulysses, Ltd., is a CFC organized in the United Kingdom and owned 100% by Joyce, Inc., a U.S. corporation. Ulysses purchases finished inventory from Joyce and sells the inventory to customers in Hong Kong. This sales income constitutes FBC sales income. ■

An exception applies to property that is manufactured, produced, grown, or extracted in the country in which the CFC was organized or created and also to property sold for use, consumption, or disposition within that country. In both these situations, the CFC has participated in the economic process that generates the income.

EXAMPLE 19

If Ulysses, from Example 18, purchases raw materials from Joyce and performs substantial manufacturing activity in the United Kingdom before selling the inventory to customers in Hong Kong, the income is not FBC sales income. Even without the manufacturing activity, sales to customers within the United Kingdom would not produce FBC sales income. ■

Certain income derived by a branch of the CFC in another country can be deemed FBC sales income. This is the case when the effect of using the branch is the same as if the branch were a wholly owned subsidiary.[23]

FBC services income is income derived from the performance of services for or on behalf of a related person and performed outside the country in which the CFC was created or organized. Income from services performed in connection with the sale of property by a CFC that has manufactured, produced, grown, or extracted such property is not FBC services income.

FBC oil-related income is income, other than extraction income, derived in a foreign country by large oil producers in connection with the sale of oil and gas products and sold by the CFC or a related person for use or consumption outside the country in which the oil or gas was extracted.

Subpart F Income Exceptions. A *de minimis* rule provides that if the total amount of a foreign corporation's FBCI and gross insurance income for the taxable year is less than the lesser of 5 percent of gross income or $1 million, none of its gross income is treated as FBCI for the tax year. At the other extreme, if a foreign corporation's FBCI and gross insurance income exceed 70 percent of total gross income, all the corporation's gross income for the tax year is treated as Subpart F income.

FBCI and insurance income subject to high foreign taxes are not included under Subpart F if the taxpayer establishes that the income was subject to an effective rate, imposed by a foreign country, of more than 90 percent of the maximum corporate rate under § 11. For example, the rate must be greater than 31.5 percent (90% × 35%), where 35 percent represents the highest U.S. corporate rate.

Investment in U.S. Property. In addition to Subpart F income, U.S. shareholders must include in gross income their pro rata share of the CFC's increase in investment in U.S. property for the taxable year.[24] U.S. property generally includes U.S. real property, debt obligations of U.S. persons, and stock in certain related domestic corporations. The CFC must have sufficient E & P to support a deemed dividend.

EXAMPLE 20

Fleming, Ltd., a CFC, earned no Subpart F income for the taxable year. If Fleming lends $100,000 to Lynn, its sole U.S. shareholder, this debt is considered an investment in U.S. property by Fleming because it now owns a U.S. note receivable. Holding the note triggers a constructive dividend of $100,000 to Lynn, assuming Fleming has sufficient E & P. ■

Distributions of Previously Taxed Income. Distributions from a CFC are treated as being first from E & P attributable to increases in investment in U.S. property previously taxed as a constructive dividend, second from E & P attributable to

[23]§ 954(d)(2).

[24]§ 956.

previously taxed Subpart F income, and last from other E & P.[25] Thus, distributions of previously taxed income are not taxed again as a dividend but reduce E & P. Any increase in investment in U.S. property is considered attributable first to Subpart F income and thus is not taxed twice.

EXAMPLE 21

In the current year, Jet, Inc., a U.S. shareholder, owns 100% of a CFC, from which Jet receives a $100,000 distribution. The CFC's E & P is composed of the following amounts.

- $50,000 attributable to previously taxed investment in U.S. property.
- $30,000 attributable to previously taxed Subpart F income.
- $40,000 attributable to other E & P.

Jet has a taxable dividend of only $20,000, all attributable to other E & P. The remaining $80,000 is previously taxed income. The CFC's E & P is reduced by $100,000. The remaining $20,000 E & P is all attributable to other E & P. ■

A U.S. shareholder's basis in CFC stock is increased by constructive dividends and decreased by subsequent distributions of previously taxed income. U.S. corporate shareholders who own at least 10 percent of the voting stock of a foreign corporation are allowed an indirect foreign tax credit for foreign taxes deemed paid on constructive dividends included in gross income under Subpart F. The indirect credit also is available for Subpart F income attributable to certain lower-tier foreign corporations. The various constructive dividend possibilities for CFC income appear in Concept Summary 25–2.

THE FOREIGN TAX CREDIT

The United States retains the right to tax its citizens and residents on their worldwide taxable income. This approach can result in double taxation, presenting a potential problem to U.S. persons who invest abroad.

To reduce the possibility of double taxation, Congress enacted the **foreign tax credit (FTC)** provisions. Under these provisions, a qualified taxpayer is allowed a tax credit for foreign income taxes paid. The credit is a dollar-for-dollar reduction of U.S. income tax liability.

For the most recent years data are available, corporations filing U.S. tax returns claimed $41 billion in FTCs, and individuals claimed $6.3 billion in FTCs. Income receipts on U.S. direct investment abroad were more than $100 billion. Without the benefit of the FTC, much of this income would have been subject to double taxation.

EXAMPLE 22

Ace Tools, Inc., a U.S. corporation, has a branch operation in Mexico, from which it earns taxable income of $750,000 for the current year. Ace pays income tax of $150,000 on these earnings to the Mexican tax authorities. Ace must also include the $750,000 in gross income for U.S. tax purposes. Assume that, before considering the FTC, Ace owes $255,000 in U.S. income taxes on this foreign-source income. Thus, total taxes on the $750,000 could equal $405,000 ($150,000 + $255,000), a 54% effective rate. But Ace takes an FTC of $150,000 against its U.S. tax liability on the foreign-source income. Ace's total taxes on the $750,000 now are $255,000 ($150,000 + $105,000), a 34% effective rate. ■

The FTC is elective for any particular tax year. If the taxpayer does not "choose" to take the FTC, § 164 allows a deduction for foreign taxes paid or incurred. A

[25]Prior law included another category of previously taxed income related to investment in excess passive assets under § 956A.

CONCEPT SUMMARY 25–2

Income of a CFC That Is Included in Gross Income of a U.S. Shareholder

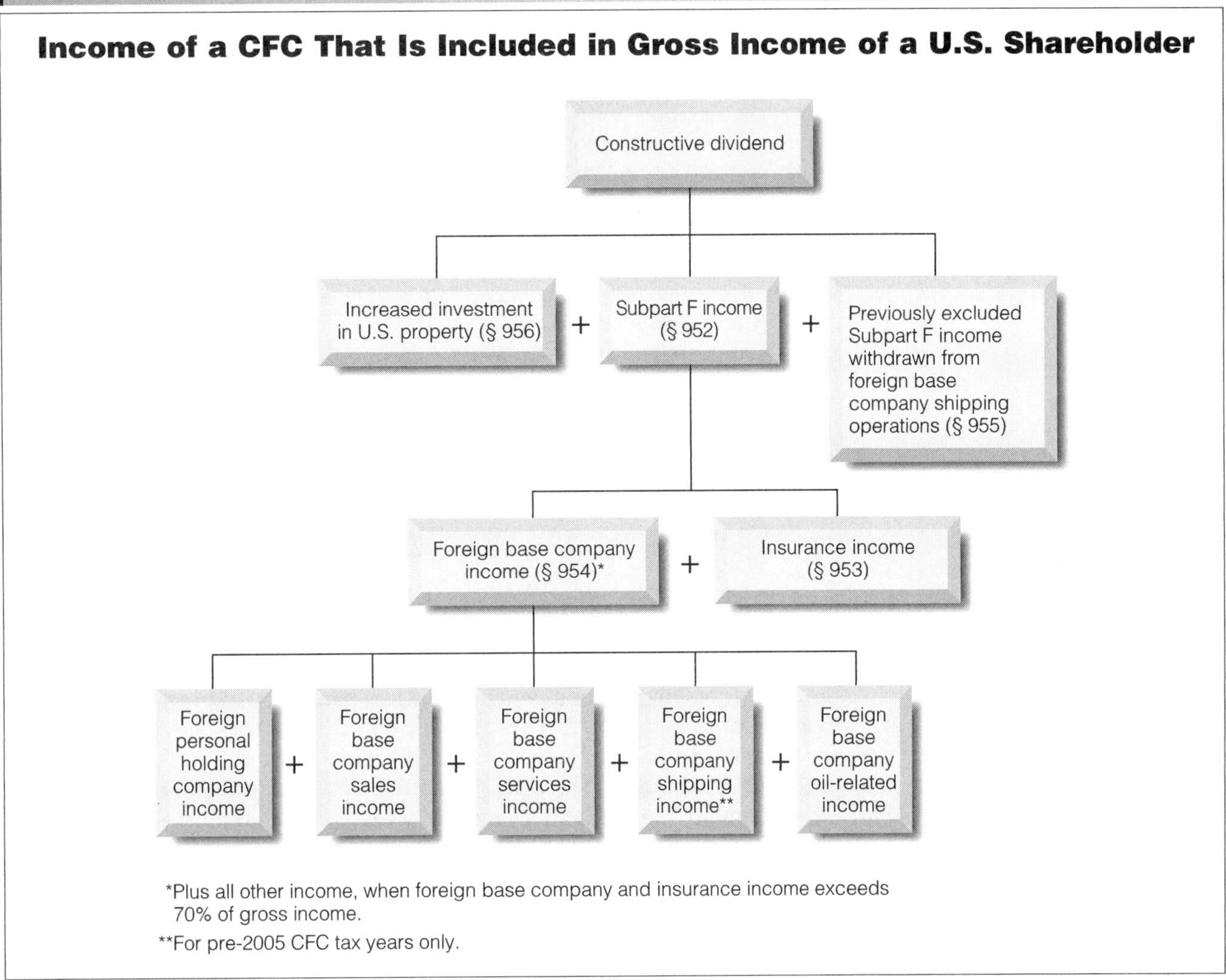

*Plus all other income, when foreign base company and insurance income exceeds 70% of gross income.

**For pre-2005 CFC tax years only.

taxpayer cannot take a credit and a deduction for the same foreign income taxes.[26] However, a taxpayer can take a deduction in the same year as an FTC for foreign taxes that are not creditable (e.g., non-income taxes).

The Direct Credit. Section 901 provides a direct FTC to U.S. taxpayers that pay or incur a foreign income tax. For purposes of the direct credit, only the taxpayer that bears the legal incidence of the foreign tax is eligible for the credit. Ace Tools in Example 22 would be eligible for the direct credit.

The Indirect Credit. If a U.S. corporation operates in a foreign country through a branch, the direct credit is available for foreign taxes paid. If, however, a U.S. corporation operates in a foreign country through a foreign subsidiary, the direct credit is not available for foreign taxes paid by the foreign corporation. An indirect credit is available to U.S. corporate taxpayers that receive actual or constructive dividends from foreign corporations that have paid foreign income taxes. These

[26]§ 275.

foreign taxes are deemed paid by the corporate shareholders in the same proportion as the dividends actually or constructively received bear to the foreign corporation's post-1986 undistributed E & P.

$$\text{Indirect FTC} = \frac{\text{Actual or constructive dividend}}{\text{Post-1986 undistributed E \& P}} \times \text{Post-1986 foreign taxes}$$

Section 78 requires a domestic corporation that chooses the FTC for deemed-paid foreign taxes to *gross up* (add to income) dividend income by the amount of deemed-paid taxes.

EXAMPLE 23

Wren, Inc., a domestic corporation, owns 50% of Finch, Inc., a foreign corporation. Wren receives a dividend of $120,000 from Finch. Finch paid foreign taxes of $500,000 on post-1986 E & P. Finch's post-1986 E & P totals $1.2 million. Wren's deemed-paid foreign taxes for FTC purposes are $50,000.

Cash dividend from Finch	$120,000
Deemed-paid foreign taxes	
$\left(\frac{\$120{,}000}{\$1{,}200{,}000} \times \$500{,}000\right)$	50,000
Gross income to Wren	$170,000

In addition to the $120,000 cash dividend, Wren must include the $50,000 in gross income for the § 78 gross-up adjustment if the FTC is elected. ■

Certain ownership requirements must be met before the indirect credit is available to a domestic corporation. The domestic corporation must own 10 percent or more of the voting stock of the foreign corporation. The credit is also available for deemed-paid foreign taxes of second- and third-tier foreign corporations if the 10 percent ownership requirement is met at the second- and third-tier level. A 5 percent indirect ownership requirement must also be met. The indirect credit is also available for foreign taxes paid by fourth- through sixth-tier foreign corporations if additional requirements are met, including the requirement that these corporations be CFCs. The § 902 ownership requirements are summarized in Figure 25–3.

FTC Limitations. To prevent taxpayers from crediting foreign taxes against U.S. taxes levied on U.S.-source taxable income, the FTC is subject to a limitation. The FTC for any taxable year cannot exceed the lesser of two amounts: (1) the actual foreign taxes paid or accrued or (2) the U.S. taxes (before the FTC) on foreign-source taxable income. The FTC limitation is derived in the following manner.

$$\text{FTC limitation} = \frac{\text{Foreign-source taxable income}}{\text{Worldwide taxable income}^{27}} \times \text{U.S. tax before FTC}$$

EXAMPLE 24

Charlotte, Inc., a domestic corporation that invests in foreign securities, has worldwide taxable income for the tax year of $120,000, consisting of $100,000 in U.S.-source business profits and $20,000 of income from foreign sources. Foreign taxes of $9,500 were withheld by foreign tax authorities. Assume that Charlotte's U.S. tax before the FTC is $42,000. The company's FTC

[27]For FTC purposes, the taxable income of an individual, estate, or trust is computed without any deduction for personal exemptions. § 904(b)(1).

■ **FIGURE 25–3**
Section 902 Ownership Requirements

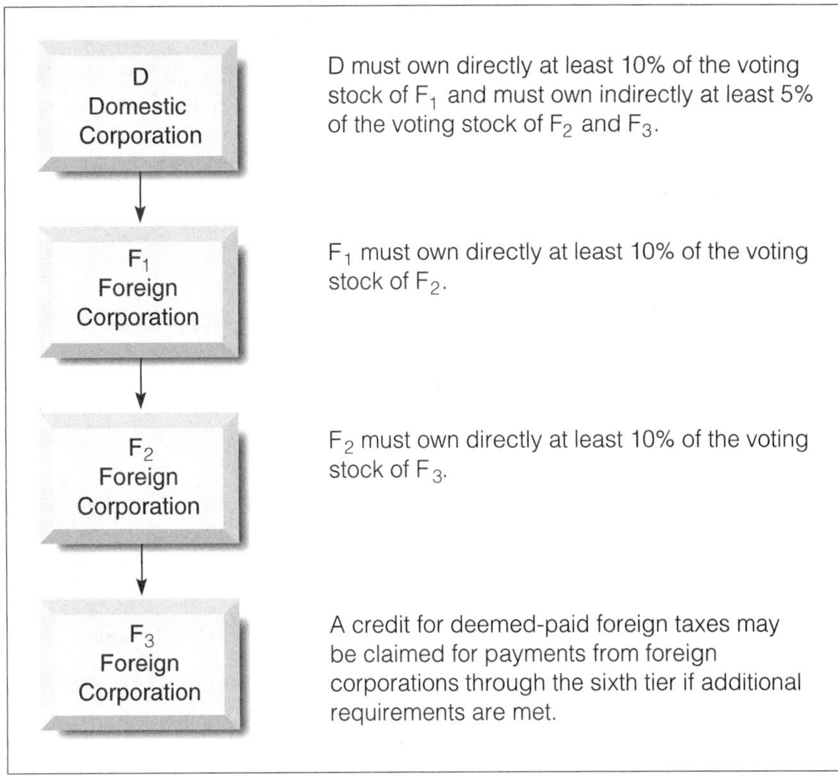

is limited to $7,000 [$42,000 × ($20,000/$120,000)]. Charlotte's net U.S. tax liability is $35,000 ($42,000 – $7,000). ■

As Example 24 illustrates, the limitation can prevent the total amount of foreign taxes paid in high-tax jurisdictions from being credited. Taxpayers could overcome this problem by generating additional foreign-source income that is subject to no, or low, foreign taxation.

EXAMPLE 25

Compare Domestic Corporation's FTC situations. In one, the corporation has only $500,000 of highly taxed foreign-source income. In the other, Domestic also has $100,000 of low-taxed foreign-source interest income.

	Only Highly Taxed Income	With Low-Taxed Interest Income
Foreign-source income	$500,000	$600,000
Foreign taxes	275,000	280,000
U.S.-source income	700,000	700,000
U.S. taxes (34%)	408,000	442,000
FTC limitation	170,000*	204,000**

*$408,000 × ($500,000/$1,200,000).
**$442,000 × ($600,000/$1,300,000).

Domestic's foreign taxes increase by only $5,000 ($280,000 – $275,000), but its FTC limitation increases by $34,000 ($204,000 – $170,000). ■

CONCEPT SUMMARY 25–3

Foreign Tax Credit: Separate Income Limitations for Tax Years Beginning before 2007

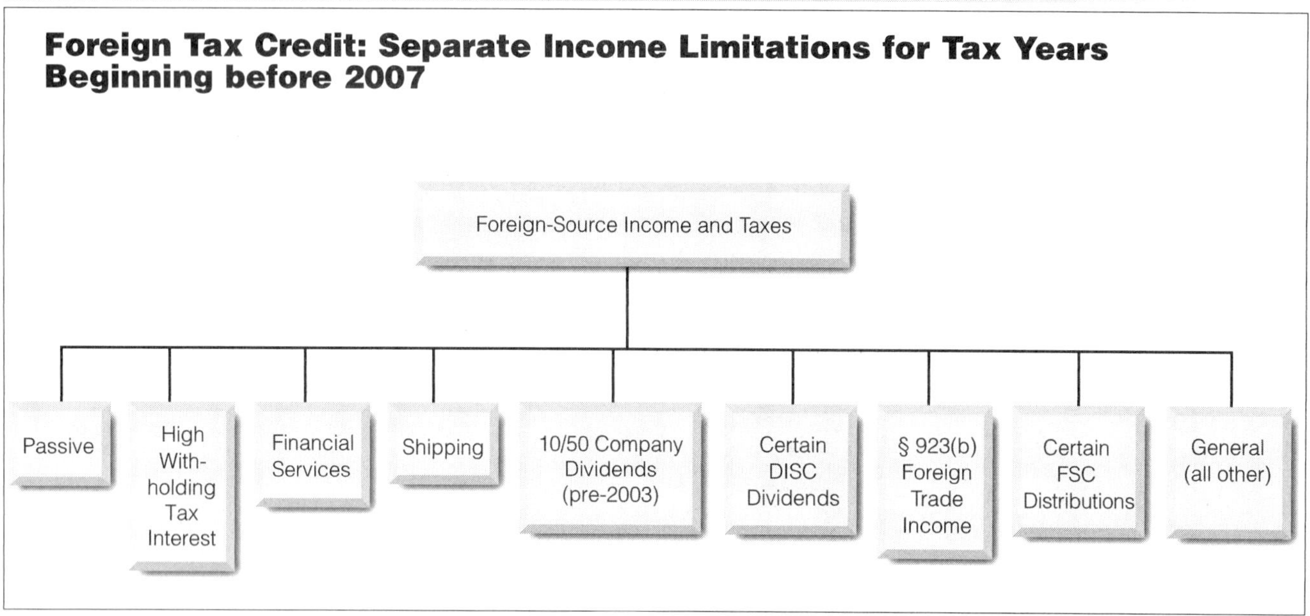

Example 25 illustrates the *cross-crediting* of foreign taxes from high- and low-taxed foreign income. To prevent this practice, the FTC rules provide for several separate limitation baskets. These provisions require that a separate limitation be calculated for each of certain categories (or baskets) of foreign-source taxable income and the foreign taxes attributable to that income. Section 904(d) provides separate limitation baskets for the following.

- Passive income.
- High withholding tax interest.
- Financial services income.
- Shipping income.
- 10/50 company dividends (dividends from a foreign corporation owned at least 10 percent but not a CFC).
- Dividends from a domestic international sales corporation (DISC) or former DISC to the extent they are treated as foreign-source income.
- Taxable income attributable to foreign trade income under § 923(b).
- Distributions from a foreign sales corporation (FSC) or former FSC out of E & P attributable to foreign trade income or qualified interest and carrying charges under § 263(c).

All other foreign-source income is included in a residual (or general) limitation basket. These separate limitations are diagrammed in Concept Summary 25–3. For tax years beginning after 2006, there are only two baskets: passive income and all other (general). Any FTC carryforwards into post-2006 years will be assigned to one of these two categories.

EXAMPLE 26

BenCo, Inc., a U.S. corporation, has a foreign branch in France that earns taxable income of $1,500,000 from manufacturing operations and $600,000 from passive activities. BenCo also earns French-source high withholding tax interest of $100,000. BenCo pays foreign taxes of $600,000 (40%), $300,000 (50%), and $15,000 (15%), respectively, on this foreign-source income. The corporation also earns $4,000,000 of U.S.-source taxable income, resulting in worldwide taxable income of $6,200,000. BenCo's U.S. taxes before the FTC are $2,108,000 (at 34%). The following tabulation illustrates the effect of the separate limitation baskets on cross-crediting in pre-2007 years.

Foreign Income Category	Net Taxable Amount	Foreign Taxes	U.S. Tax before FTC at 34%	FTC with Separate Limits
Manufacturing	$1,500,000	$600,000	$510,000	$510,000
Passive	600,000	300,000	204,000	204,000
High withholding tax interest	100,000	15,000	34,000	15,000
Total	$2,200,000	$915,000	$748,000	$729,000

Without the separate limitation provisions, the FTC would be the lesser of (1) $915,000 foreign taxes or (2) $748,000 share of U.S. tax [$2,108,000 × ($2,200,000/$6,200,000)]. The separate limitation provisions reduce the FTC by $19,000 ($748,000 – $729,000). The effect of the separate limitation rules is that the foreign-source income taxed at the foreign tax rates of 40% and 50% cannot be aggregated with foreign-source income taxed at only 15%. The reduction in the number of baskets in post-2006 years will be helpful to BenCo. ■

The limitations can result in unused (noncredited) foreign taxes for the tax year. A two-year carryback and a five-year carryforward of excess foreign taxes are allowed for tax years beginning before October 22, 2004. For later tax years, the carryback period is 1 year, and the carryforward period is 10 years. The taxes can be credited in years when the formula limitation for that year exceeds the foreign taxes attributable to the same tax year. The carryback and carryforward provisions are available only within a specific basket. In other words, excess foreign taxes in one basket cannot be carried over unless there is an excess limitation in the same basket for the carryover year.

The Alternative Minimum Tax FTC. For purposes of the alternative minimum tax (AMT), the FTC limitation is calculated by using foreign-source alternative minimum taxable income (AMTI) in the numerator and worldwide AMTI in the denominator of the formula and the tentative minimum tax rather than the regular tax.

$$\text{AMT FTC limitation} = \frac{\text{Foreign-source AMTI}}{\text{Worldwide AMTI}} \times \text{Tentative minimum tax}$$

The taxpayer may elect to use regular foreign-source taxable income in the numerator if it does not exceed total AMTI. The AMT FTC limit must also be determined on a basket-by-basket basis. Prior to 2005, only 90 percent of tentative minimum tax could be offset with an FTC.

Other Considerations. For a foreign levy to qualify for the FTC, it must be a tax, and its predominant character must be that of an income tax in the U.S. sense.[28] A levy is a tax if it is a compulsory payment, rather than a payment for a specific economic benefit such as the right to extract oil. A tax's predominant character is that of an income tax in the U.S. sense if it reaches realized net gain and is not a *soak-up* tax, that is, does not depend on being credited against the income tax of another country. A tax that is levied in lieu of an income tax is also creditable.[29]

[28] Reg. § 1.901–2.

[29] § 903 and Reg. § 1.903–1.

EXAMPLE 27

JonesCo, a domestic corporation, generates $2 million of taxable income from operations in Larissa, a foreign country. Larissan law levies a tax on income generated in Larissa by foreign residents only in cases in which the country of residence (such as the United States) allows a tax credit for foreign taxes paid. JonesCo will not be allowed an FTC for taxes paid to Larissa, because the foreign tax is a soak-up tax. ■

For purposes of the FTC, foreign taxes are attributable to the year in which they are paid or accrued. Under § 905, taxpayers using the cash method of accounting for tax purposes may elect to take the FTC in the year in which the foreign taxes accrue. The election is binding on the taxpayer for the year in which it is made and for all subsequent years. Foreign taxes generally must be translated to U.S. dollars at the average exchange rate for the tax year to which the taxes relate.[30]

LO.6

Apply the U.S. tax provisions concerning nonresident alien individuals and foreign corporations.

U.S. Taxation of Nonresident Aliens and Foreign Corporations

Generally, only the U.S.-source income of nonresident alien individuals and foreign corporations is subject to U.S. taxation. This reflects the reach of the U.S. tax jurisdiction. The constraint, however, does not prevent the United States from also taxing the foreign-source income of nonresident alien individuals and foreign corporations when that income is effectively connected with the conduct of a U.S. trade or business.[31] Concept Summary 25–4 at the end of this section summarizes these tax rules.

NONRESIDENT ALIEN INDIVIDUALS

A **nonresident alien (NRA)** individual is an individual who is not a citizen or resident of the United States. For example, Queen Elizabeth is an NRA, because she is not a citizen or resident of the United States. Citizenship is determined under the immigration and naturalization laws of the United States.[32] Basically, the citizenship statutes are broken down into two categories: nationality at birth or through naturalization.

Residency. A person is a resident of the United States for income tax purposes if he or she meets either the green card test or the substantial presence test.[33] If either of these tests is met for the calendar year, the individual is deemed a U.S. resident for the year.

A foreign person issued a green card is considered a U.S. resident on the first day he or she is physically present in the United States after issuance. The green card is Immigration Form I–551. Newly issued cards are now rose colored, but the form is still referred to as the "green card." Status as a U.S. resident remains in effect until the green card has been revoked or the individual has abandoned lawful permanent resident status.

The substantial presence test is applied to an alien without a green card. It is a mathematical test involving physical presence in the United States. An individual who is physically present in the United States for at least 183 days during the calendar year is a U.S. resident for income tax purposes. This 183-day requirement can also be met over a three-year period that includes the two immediately preceding years and the current year, as long as the individual is present in the United

[30]§ 986(a).
[31]§§ 871, 881, and 882.
[32]Title 8, Aliens and Nationality, *United States Code.*
[33]§ 7701(b).

States at least 31 days during the current year.[34] For this purpose, each day of the current calendar year is counted as a full day, each day of the first preceding year as one-third day, and each day of the second preceding year as one-sixth day.

EXAMPLE 28

Li, a foreign citizen, was present in the United States for 90 days in 2003, 180 days in 2004, and 110 days in 2005. For Federal income tax purposes, Li is a U.S. resident for 2005, because she was physically present for 185 days [(90 days × ⅙) + (180 days × ⅓) + (110 days × 1)] during the three-year period. ■

Under the substantial presence test, residence begins the first day the individual is physically present in the United States and ends the last day of physical presence for the calendar year (assuming the substantial presence test is not satisfied for the next calendar year). Nominal presence of 10 days or less can be ignored in determining whether the substantial presence test is met.

The substantial presence test allows for several exceptions. Commuters from Mexico and Canada who are employed in the United States but return home each day are excepted. Also excepted are individuals who are prevented from leaving the United States by medical conditions that arose while the individuals were in the United States. Some individuals are exempt from the substantial presence test, including foreign government-related individuals (e.g., diplomats), qualified teachers, trainees and students, and certain professional athletes.

ETHICAL CONSIDERATIONS

Should There Be Some "Heart" in Tax Law?

In determining whether an alien is a U.S. resident for U.S. income tax purposes under the substantial presence test, days on which a medical condition prevents the person from leaving the United States are not counted as days present in the United States. The medical condition (e.g., illness or injury) must have arisen after the NRA arrived in the United States. In other words, it generally must be an unexpected illness or accident. No such exception is available, however, for a family member or other NRA who is significant to the person who becomes ill or injured. Thus, under this rule, the relative or other significant person may have to either risk being classified as a U.S. resident for the tax year or leave the ill person (or accident victim) alone in the United States. Does this limited exception ignore the human element in illness and recovery?

Nonresident Aliens Not Engaged in a U.S. Trade or Business. Certain U.S.-source income that is *not* effectively connected with the conduct of a U.S. trade or business is subject to a flat 30 percent tax. This income includes dividends, interest, rents, royalties, certain compensation, premiums, annuities, and other fixed, determinable, annual or periodic (FDAP) income. This tax generally is levied by a withholding mechanism that requires the payors of the income to withhold 30 percent of gross amounts.[35] This method eliminates the problems of assuring payment by nonresidents, determining allowable deductions, and, in most instances, the filing of tax returns by nonresidents. Interest received from certain portfolio debt investments, even though U.S.-sourced, is exempt from taxation. Interest earned on deposits with banking institutions is also exempt as long as it is not effectively connected with the conduct of a U.S. trade or business.

[34] § 7701(b)(3)(A).

[35] §§ 871 and 1441.

Capital gains *not* effectively connected with the conduct of a U.S. trade or business are exempt from tax, as long as the NRA individual was not present in the United States for 183 days or more during the taxable year. If an NRA has not established a taxable year, the calendar year is used. NRAs are not permitted to carry forward capital losses.[36]

Nonresident Aliens Engaged in a U.S. Trade or Business. Two important definitions determine the U.S. tax consequences to NRAs with U.S.-source income: "the conduct of a **U.S. trade or business**" and "**effectively connected income**." Specifically, in order for an NRA's noninvestment income to be subject to U.S. taxation, the NRA must be considered engaged in a U.S. trade or business and must earn income effectively connected with that business.

General criteria for determining if a U.S. trade or business exists include the location of production activities, management, distribution activities, and other business functions. Trading in commodities and securities ordinarily does not constitute a trade or business. Dealers, however, need to avoid maintaining a U.S. trading office and trading for their own accounts. Corporations (other than certain personal holding companies) that are not dealers can trade for their own accounts. There are no restrictions on individuals who are not dealers.

The Code does not explicitly define a U.S. trade or business, but case law has defined the concept as activities carried on in the United States that are regular, substantial, and continuous.[37] Once an NRA is considered engaged in a U.S. trade or business, all U.S.-sourcc income other than FDAP and capital gain income is considered effectively connected to that trade or business and is therefore subject to U.S. taxation.

EXAMPLE 29

Vito, an NRA, produces wine for export. During the current year, Vito earns $500,000 from exporting wine to unrelated wholesalers in the United States. The title to the wine passes to the U.S. wholesalers in New York. Vito has no offices or employees in the United States. The income from wine sales is U.S.-source income, but because Vito is not engaged in a U.S. trade or business, the income is not subject to taxation in the United States.

Assume that Vito begins operating a hot dog cart in New York City. This activity constitutes a U.S. trade or business. Consequently, all U.S.-source income other than FDAP or capital gain income will be taxed in the United States as income effectively connected with a U.S. trade or business. Thus, both the hot dog cart profits and the $500,000 in wine income will be taxed in the United States. ■

FDAP and capital gain income may be considered effectively connected income if the assets that generate this income are used in, or held for use in, the trade or business (the asset-use test) or if the activities of the trade or business are a material factor in the production of the income (the business-activities test).[38] As long as FDAP and capital gain income are not effectively connected with a U.S. trade or business, the tax treatment of these income items is the same whether NRAs are engaged in a U.S. trade or business or not.

EXAMPLE 30

Ingrid, an NRA, operates a U.S. business. During the year, cash funds accumulate. Ingrid invests these funds on a short-term basis so that they remain available to meet her business needs. Any income earned from these investments is effectively connected income, under the asset-use test. ■

[36] § 871(a)(2).

[37] See, for example, *Higgins v. Comm.*, 41-1 USTC ¶9233, 25 AFTR 1160, 312 U.S. 212 (USSC, 1941) and *Continental Trading, Inc. v. Comm.*, 59-1 USTC ¶9316, 3 AFTR2d 923, 265 F.2d 40 (CA-9, 1959).

[38] § 864(c).

■ EXHIBIT 25–3
Selected Tax Treaty Withholding Rates

	Interest	Dividends in General	Dividends Paid by U.S. Subsidiary to a Foreign Parent Corporation
Australia	10%	15%	0%
Canada	10	15	5
Ireland	0	15	5
Japan	10	15	10
Mexico	15	15	0
Philippines	15	25	20

SOURCE: IRS Publication 901, *U.S. Tax Treaties.*

Effectively connected income is taxed at the same rates that apply to U.S. citizens and residents, and deductions for expenses attributable to that income are allowed. NRAs with effectively connected income are also allowed a deduction for casualty and theft losses related to property located within the United States, a deduction for qualified charitable contributions, and one personal exemption. NRAs with income effectively connected with the conduct of a U.S. trade or business may also be subject to the alternative minimum tax.

Withholding Provisions. The 30 percent U.S. tax on FDAP income is generally administered by requiring the payor of the income to withhold the tax and remit it to the U.S. tax authorities. This assures the government of timely collection and relieves it of jurisdictional problems that could arise if it had to rely on recipients residing outside the United States to pay the tax. In recent years, U.S. payors withheld taxes of $3 billion annually from payments to foreign persons. Japanese recipients received the most U.S.-source income, with recipients from the United Kingdom ranked second. As explained earlier, income tax treaties with other countries provide for reduced withholding on certain types of FDAP income (see Exhibit 25–3 for some examples of withholding rates).

FOREIGN CORPORATIONS

Definition. The classification of an entity as a foreign corporation for U.S. tax purposes is an important consideration. Section 7701(a)(5) defines a foreign corporation as one that is not domestic. A domestic corporation is a corporation that is created or organized in the United States. Thus, though McDonald's is, in reality, a global corporation, it is considered a domestic corporation for U.S. tax purposes, solely because it was organized in the United States.

Income Not Effectively Connected with a U.S. Trade or Business. U.S.-source FDAP income of foreign corporations is taxed by the United States in the same manner as that of NRA individuals—at a flat 30 percent rate. Generally, foreign corporations qualify for the same exemptions from U.S. taxation for investment income as do NRA individuals. The U.S.-source capital gains of foreign corporations are exempt from the Federal income tax if they are not effectively connected with the conduct of a U.S. trade or business.

Effectively Connected Income. Foreign corporations conducting a trade or business in the United States are subject to Federal income taxation on any U.S.-source income effectively connected with the trade or business. As with NRAs, any FDAP or capital gain income is not considered effectively connected unless the income meets the asset-use or business-activities test.[39] Foreign corporations are subject to the same tax rates on their effectively connected income as domestic corporations.

Branch Profits Tax. The objective of the **branch profits tax** is to afford equal tax treatment to income generated by a domestic corporation controlled by a foreign corporation and to income generated by other U.S. operations controlled by foreign corporations. If the foreign corporation operates through a U.S. subsidiary (a domestic corporation), the income of the subsidiary is taxable by the United States when earned and is also subject to a withholding tax when repatriated (returned as dividends to the foreign parent). Before the branch profits tax was enacted, a foreign corporation with a branch in the United States paid only the initial tax on its U.S. earnings; remittances were not taxed.

In addition to the income tax imposed under § 882 on effectively connected income of a foreign corporation, a tax equal to 30 percent of the **dividend equivalent amount (DEA)** for the taxable year is imposed on any foreign corporation with effectively connected income.[40] The DEA is the foreign corporation's effectively connected earnings for the taxable year, adjusted for increases and decreases in the corporation's U.S. net equity (investment in the U.S. operations). The DEA is limited to current E & P and post-1986 accumulated E & P that is effectively connected, or treated as effectively connected, with the conduct of a U.S. trade or business. U.S. net equity is the sum of money and the aggregate adjusted basis of assets and liabilities directly connected to U.S. operations that generate effectively connected income.

EXAMPLE 31

Robin, Inc., a foreign corporation, has a U.S. branch operation with the following tax results and other information for the year.

Pretax earnings effectively connected with a U.S. trade or business	$2,000,000
U.S. corporate tax (at 34%)	680,000
Remittance to home office	1,000,000
Increase in U.S. net equity	320,000

Robin's DEA and branch profits tax are computed as follows.

E & P effectively connected with a U.S. trade or business ($2,000,000 – $680,000)	$1,320,000
Less: Increase in U.S. net equity	(320,000)
Dividend equivalent amount	$1,000,000
Branch profits tax rate	× 30%
Branch profits tax	$ 300,000

The 30 percent rate of the branch profits tax may be reduced or eliminated by a treaty provision. If a foreign corporation is subject to the branch profits tax, no other U.S. tax is levied on the dividend actually paid by the corporation during the taxable year.

[39] § 864(c).

[40] § 884.

THE FOREIGN INVESTMENT IN REAL PROPERTY TAX ACT

Prior to 1980, NRAs and foreign corporations could avoid U.S. taxation on gains from the sale of U.S. real estate if the gains were treated as capital gains and were not effectively connected with the conduct of a U.S. trade or business. In the mid-1970s, midwestern farmers pressured Congress to eliminate what they saw as a tax advantage that would allow nonresidents to bid up the price of farmland. This and other concerns about foreign ownership of U.S. real estate led to the enactment of the Foreign Investment in Real Property Tax Act (FIRPTA) of 1980.

Under **FIRPTA,** gains and losses realized by NRAs and foreign corporations from the sale or other disposition of U.S. real property interests are treated as effectively connected with the conduct of a U.S. trade or business even when those individuals or corporations are not actually so engaged. NRA individuals must pay a tax equal to the lesser of two amounts: (1) 26 (or 28) percent of their alternative minimum taxable income or (2) regular U.S. rates on the net U.S. real property gain for the taxable year.[41] For purposes of this provision, losses are taken into account only to the extent they are deductible as business losses, losses on transactions entered into for profit, or losses from casualties and thefts.

U.S. Real Property Interest (USRPI). Any direct interest in real property situated in the United States and any interest in a domestic corporation (other than solely as a creditor) are U.S. real property interests (USRPIs). This definition applies unless the taxpayer can establish that a domestic corporation was not a U.S. real property holding corporation (USRPHC) during the shorter of two periods: (1) the period during which the taxpayer held an interest in the corporation or (2) the five-year period ending on the date on which the interest was disposed of (the base period). A domestic corporation is not a USRPHC if it holds no USRPIs on the date of disposition of its stock and if any USRPIs held by the corporation during the base period were disposed of in a transaction in which gain, if any, was fully recognized.

EXAMPLE 32

From January 1, 2000, through January 1, 2005, Francis (a foreign investor) held shares in Door, Inc., a U.S. corporation. During this period, Door held two parcels of U.S. real estate and stock of Sash, Inc., another U.S. corporation. Sash also owned U.S. real estate. The two parcels of real estate held directly by Door were disposed of on December 15, 2001, in a nontaxable transaction. Sash disposed of its U.S. real estate in a taxable transaction on January 1, 2005.

An interest in Door is treated as a USRPI because Door did not recognize gain on the December 15, 2001 disposition of the USRPIs. If Door's ownership of U.S. real estate had been limited to its indirect ownership through Sash, an interest in Door would not have constituted a USRPI as of January 2, 2005. This result would occur because Sash disposed of its USRPIs in a taxable transaction in which gain was fully recognized. ■

A USRPHC is any corporation (whether foreign or domestic) where the fair market value of the corporation's USRPIs equals or exceeds 50 percent of the aggregate of fair market value of certain specified assets. These assets are the corporation's USRPIs, its interests in real property located outside the United States, and any other of its assets that are used or held for use in a trade or business. Stock regularly traded on an established securities market is not treated as a USRPI if a person holds no more than 5 percent of the stock.

[41] § 897.

CONCEPT SUMMARY 25–4

U.S. Taxation of NRAs and Foreign Corporations (FCs)

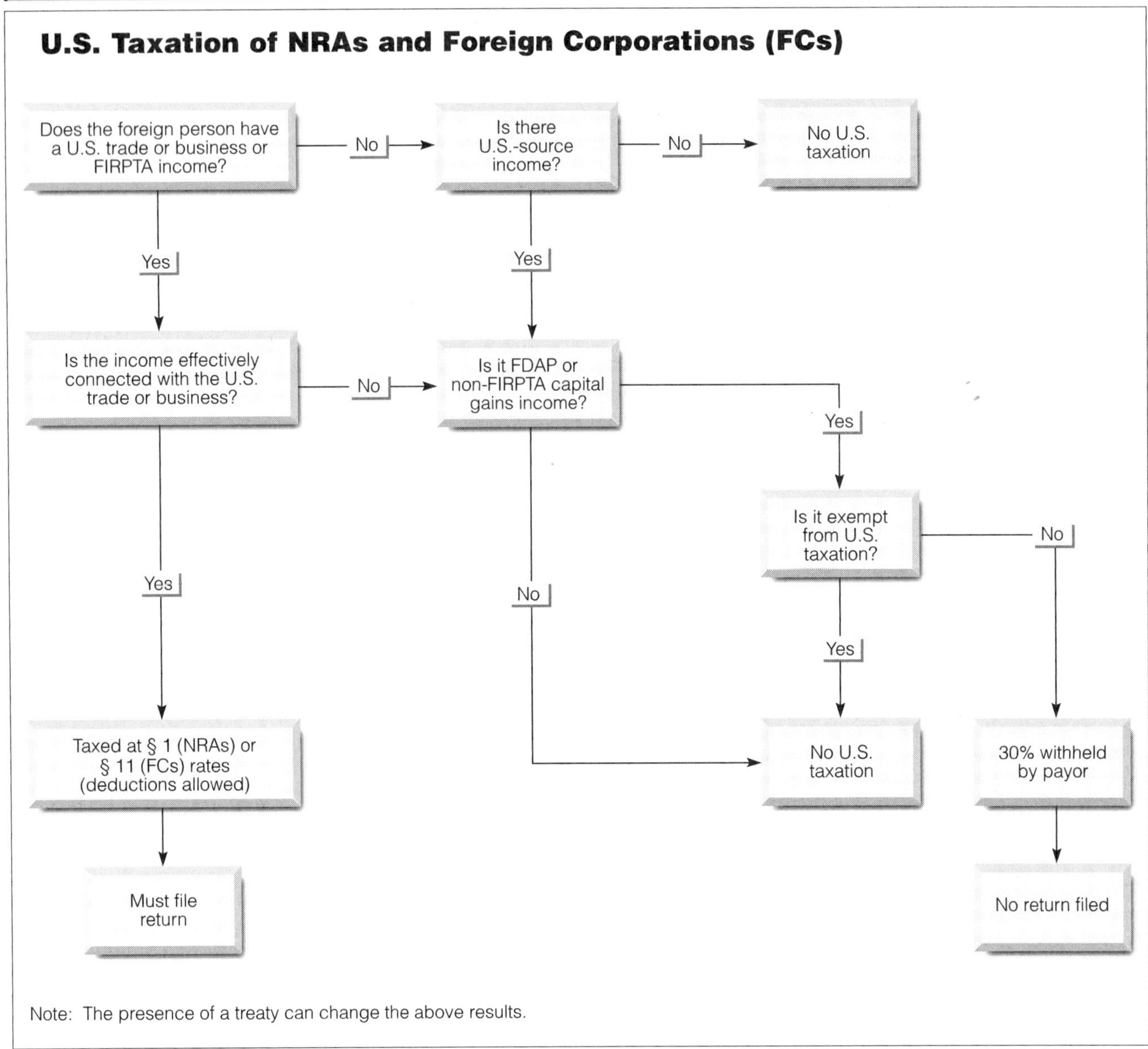

Note: The presence of a treaty can change the above results.

Withholding Provisions. The FIRPTA withholding provisions require any purchaser or agent acquiring a USRPI from a foreign person to withhold 10 percent of the amount realized on the disposition.[42] A domestic partnership, trust, or estate with a foreign partner, foreign grantor treated as owner, or foreign beneficiary generally must withhold 35 percent of the gain allocable to that person on a disposition of a USRPI. Foreign corporations are also subject to withholding provisions on certain distributions. Without this withholding, NRAs could sell USRPIs, receiving the sales proceeds outside the United States, and jurisdictional issues could

[42]§ 1445.

make it difficult for the U.S. tax authorities to collect any U.S. tax that might be due on gains. Certain exceptions to FIRPTA withholding are allowed.

Failure to withhold can subject the purchaser or the purchaser's agent to interest on any unpaid amount.[43] A civil penalty of 100 percent of the amount required to be withheld and a criminal penalty of up to $10,000 or five years in prison can be imposed for willful failure to withhold.[44]

EXPATRIATION TO AVOID U.S. TAXATION

Section 877 provides for U.S. taxation of U.S.-source income earned by individuals who relinquished their U.S. citizenship within 10 years of deriving that income if they gave up their citizenship to avoid U.S. taxation. Furthermore, NRAs who lost U.S. citizenship within a 10-year period immediately preceding the close of the tax year must pay taxes on their U.S.-source income as though they were still U.S. citizens. This provision applies only if the expatriation had as one of its principal purposes the avoidance of U.S. taxes. Individuals are presumed to have a tax avoidance purpose if they meet either of the following criteria.[45]

- Average annual net income tax for the five taxable years ending before the date of loss of U.S. citizenship is more than $124,000 (in 2005).
- Net worth as of that date is $2 million or more (in 2005).

These provisions also apply to "long-term lawful permanent residents" who cease to be taxed as U.S. residents. A long-term permanent resident is an individual (other than a citizen of the United States) who is a lawful permanent resident of the United States in at least 8 taxable years during the 15-year period ending with the taxable year in which the individual either ceases to be a lawful permanent resident of the United States or begins to be treated as a resident of another country under an income tax treaty between the United States and the other country (and does not waive the benefits of the treaty to residents of that country). An exception applies to certain individuals with dual citizenship.

The United States continues to treat individuals as U.S. citizens or residents until the taxpayers provide required information and an expatriation notice. Expatriates who are subject to the 10-year special tax regime outlined above must file a § 6039G statement annually. Additionally, if an expatriate individual is physically present in the United States for more than 30 days during a calendar year during the 10-year postexpatriation period, the individual is taxed as a U.S. citizen or resident.[46] These expatriation rules, taken as a whole, make it difficult to give up U.S. citizenship or residency simply to avoid U.S. taxation.

Tax Planning Considerations

Over time, legislation has tended to reduce the ability to plan transactions and operations in a manner that minimizes tax liability. However, taxpayers who are not limited by the constraints of a particular transaction or operation can use the following suggestions to plan for maximum tax benefits.

THE FOREIGN TAX CREDIT LIMITATION AND SOURCING PROVISIONS

The FTC limitation is partially based on the amount of foreign-source taxable income in the numerator of the limitation ratio. Consequently, the sourcing of income is extremely important. Income that is taxed by a foreign tax jurisdiction benefits from the FTC only to the extent that it is classified as foreign-source income

[43] §§ 6601, 6621, and 6651.
[44] §§ 6672 and 7202.
[45] § 877(a)(2). The dollar amounts are adjusted for inflation.
[46] § 877(g)(1).

under U.S. tax law. Thus, elements that affect the sourcing of income, such as the place of title passage, should be considered carefully before a transaction is undertaken.

It may be possible for a U.S. corporation to alleviate the problem of excess foreign taxes by using the following techniques.

- Generate "same basket" foreign-source income that is subject to a tax rate lower than the U.S. tax rate.
- Reduce highly taxed foreign-source income in favor of foreign-source income that is taxed at a lower rate by shifting operations or intangibles.
- Time the repatriation of foreign-source earnings to coincide with excess limitation years.
- Deduct foreign taxes for years when the deduction benefit would exceed the FTC benefit.

A taxpayer who can control the timing of income and loss recognition will want to avoid recognizing losses in years when the loss is apportioned among the FTC limitation baskets. Otherwise, the foreign taxes for which a credit is allowed for the tax year are reduced.

EXAMPLE 33

Della, Inc., a U.S. corporation, has U.S.-source taxable income of $200,000, worldwide taxable income of $300,000, and a U.S. tax liability (before the FTC) of $105,000. Della receives foreign-source taxable income, pays foreign income taxes, and has an FTC as shown.

Basket	Amount	Foreign Taxes	FTC Limitation	Allowed FTC
Passive	$ 20,000	$ 800	$ 7,000	$ 800
General	50,000	20,500	17,500	17,500
High withholding tax interest	15,000	3,000	5,250	3,000
Financial services	15,000	4,500	5,250	4,500
	$100,000	$28,800		$25,800

If Della also suffers a foreign-source loss of $10,000 in the oil-related limitation basket, the FTC is reduced by $1,750. The U.S. tax liability before the FTC is $101,500. Of the loss, 50% is apportioned to the general limitation basket, reducing the FTC limitation for this basket to $15,750 [$101,500 × ($45,000/$290,000)]. The remaining loss is apportioned to the other baskets, but it does not change the allowed FTC because the actual foreign taxes remain below the FTC limit. This result would be avoided if Della could defer recognition of the loss to a tax year in which it would not have a negative effect on the FTC. ■

THE FOREIGN CORPORATION AS A TAX SHELTER

An NRA who is able to hold U.S. investments through a foreign corporation can accomplish much in the way of avoiding U.S. taxation. Capital gains (other than dispositions of U.S. real property interests) are not subject to U.S. taxation. This assumes that they are not effectively connected with a U.S. trade or business. The NRA can dispose of the stock of a foreign corporation that holds U.S. real property and not be subject to taxation under § 897 (FIRPTA). Furthermore, the stock of a foreign corporation is not included in the U.S. gross estate of a deceased NRA, even if all the assets of the foreign corporation are located in the United States.

Caution is advised when the foreign corporation may generate income effectively connected with the conduct of a U.S. trade or business. The income may be taxed at a higher rate than if the NRA individually generated the income. The tradeoff between a higher U.S. tax on this income and protection from the U.S. estate tax and § 897 must be weighed.

PLANNING UNDER SUBPART F

The *de minimis* rule allows a CFC to avoid the classification of income as FBC income or insurance income and prevents the U.S. shareholder from having to include it in gross income as a constructive dividend. Thus, a CFC with total FBC income and insurance income in an amount close to the 5 percent or $1 million level should monitor income realization to assure that the *de minimis* rule applies for the tax year. At least as important is avoiding the classification of all the gross income of the CFC as FBC income or insurance income. This happens when the sum of the FBC income and gross insurance income for the taxable year exceeds 70 percent of total gross income.

Careful timing of investment in U.S. property can reduce the potential for constructive dividend income to U.S. shareholders. The gross income of U.S. shareholders attributable to investment in U.S. property is limited to the E & P of the CFC.[47] E & P that is attributable to amounts that have been included in gross income as Subpart F income in either the current year or a prior tax year is not taxed again when invested in U.S. property.

USING THE CHECK-THE-BOX REGULATIONS

The check-the-box Regulations under § 7701 provide a great deal of flexibility for U.S.-based multinational corporations. Corporations are allowed to organize their branches and subsidiaries around the world in ways that optimize both local country and U.S. taxation. For example, a U.S. corporation may choose to treat its subsidiary in the United Kingdom as a partnership or unincorporated branch for U.S. tax purposes (thus taking advantage of loss flow-throughs) and a corporation under United Kingdom law (where certain tax and liability benefits may exist). The flurry of multinational restructurings since the issuance of the check-the-box Regulations has led to some cries of foul by U.S. taxing authorities who claim that these provisions are being used in inappropriate ways. The Treasury Department and the IRS are currently exploring ways to curb some of these perceived abuses.

TRANSFERRING INTANGIBLE ASSETS OFFSHORE

In many industries, a company's intangible assets, such as licenses and patents, produce a relatively large share of total income. For example, the license to use a software program is much more valuable than the actual disk the customer purchases; thus, a large part of the profit from the sale of software accrues to the license holder.

Unlike manufacturing plants, intangible assets can be easily transferred to related entities outside the United States. Congress recognized this potential, and § 367 requires gain to be recognized if intangibles are transferred outside the United States. To avoid this § 367 "toll charge," companies should consider creating their intangibles offshore so that no subsequent transfer is required. Companies may choose to perform their R & D activities within subsidiaries located in tax haven countries in order to create and keep their valuable intangibles in low-tax jurisdictions.

[47]§§ 959(a)(1) and (2).

KEY TERMS

Branch profits tax, 25–34
Controlled foreign corporation (CFC), 25–17
Dividend equivalent amount (DEA), 25–34
Effectively connected income, 25–32
Extraterritorial income, 25–15
FIRPTA, 25–35
Foreign tax credit (FTC), 25–24
Functional currency, 25–12
Inbound taxation, 25–3
Nonresident alien (NRA), 25–30
Outbound taxation, 25–3
Qualified business unit (QBU), 25–12
Subpart F, 25–22
Tax haven, 25–18
Tax treaty, 25–3
Treaty shopping, 25–19
U.S. shareholder, 25–20
U.S. trade or business, 25–32

PROBLEM MATERIALS

Discussion Questions

1. Explain why an income tax treaty can be very favorable to a U.S. person who earns investment income from Germany.
2. Will dividends paid by a domestic corporation be treated as U.S.-source income in all cases? Explain.

Issue ID
Communications

3. Write a memo outlining the issues that arise when attempting to source income that is earned from Internet-based activities.
4. Generally, U.S. taxpayers with foreign operations desire to increase foreign-source income and reduce deductions against that foreign-source income in order to increase their FTC limitations. How does § 482 enable the IRS to prevent taxpayers from manipulating the source of income and allocation of deductions? Explain.
5. Explain how a Netherlands branch of a U.S. corporation may use the U.S. dollar as its functional currency.
6. What is a qualified business unit (QBU)? How many QBUs may a single taxpayer have?
7. What are the important concepts to be considered when U.S. assets outside the United States are transferred to foreign persons?

Communications

8. Write a memo to a U.S. client explaining why stock of a foreign corporation that it holds may be considered a tax shelter for U.S. tax purposes.

Decision Making

9. Five unrelated U.S. persons are considering forming a foreign corporation in which they will own equal interests. Will they have to be concerned with the CFC provisions?

Issue ID

10. Joanna owns 5% of Axel, a foreign corporation. Joanna's son, Fred, is considering acquiring 15% of Axel from an NRA. The remainder of Axel is owned 27% by unrelated U.S. persons and 53% by unrelated NRAs. Currently, Fred operates (as a sole proprietorship) a manufacturing business that sells goods to Axel for resale outside the United States and outside Axel's country of residence. Joanna is not concerned about the concentration of investment because she expects to sell her stock in Axel in three years at a significant capital gain. Are there tax issues that Joanna and Fred, both U.S. citizens, need to address?

Issue ID

11. Molly, Inc., a domestic corporation, owns 15% of PJ, Inc., and 12% of Emma, Inc., both foreign corporations. Molly is paid gross dividends of $35,000 and $18,000 from PJ and Emma, respectively. PJ withheld and paid more than $10,500 in foreign taxes on the $35,000 dividend. PJ's country of residence levies a 20% tax on dividends paid to nonresident corporations. However, the tax rate is increased to 30% if the recipient is a resident of a country that provides an FTC. Taxes of $3,600 are withheld on the

dividend from Emma. What tax issues must be considered in determining the availability and amount of the FTC allowed to Molly, Inc.?

12. Warren, Inc., received a $500 dividend from FrenchCo, Ltd., a foreign corporation. FrenchCo paid $300 in foreign taxes related to this $500 of distributed earnings. Explain why Warren's gross income related to this dividend is $800.

13. Carlos, a nonresident alien, is interested in acquiring U.S. real property as an investment. He knows that he will be taxed in the United States on any gains from the disposition of such property if he holds it directly. Will the result be any different if he acquires the real property within a U.S. corporation?

Issue ID

14. Old Gear, Inc., a foreign corporation, sells vacuum tubes in several countries, including the United States. In fact, currently 18% of Old Gear's sales income is sourced in the United States (through branches in New York and Miami). Old Gear is considering opening additional branches in San Francisco and Houston in order to increase U.S. sales. What tax issues must Old Gear consider before making this move?

Problems

15. Madison, a U.S. resident, received the following income items for the current tax year. Identify the source of each income item as either U.S. or foreign.
    a. $2,400 dividend from U.S. Power Company, a U.S. corporation, that operates solely in the eastern United States.
    b. $5,200 dividend from Skateworld Corporation, a U.S. corporation that had total gross income of $4 million from the active conduct of a foreign trade or business for the immediately preceding three tax years. Skateworld's worldwide gross income for the same period was $5 million.
    c. $1,500 dividend from International Consolidated, Inc., a foreign corporation that had gross income of $3.4 million effectively connected with the conduct of a U.S. trade or business for the immediately preceding three tax years. International's worldwide gross income for the same period was $6 million.
    d. $600 interest from a savings account at a Florida bank.
    e. $5,000 interest on Warren Corporation bonds. Warren is a U.S. corporation that derived $6 million of its gross income for the immediately preceding three tax years from operation of an active foreign business. Warren's worldwide gross income for this same period was $7.2 million.

Communications

16. Rita, an NRA, is a professional golfer. She played in 7 tournaments in the United States in the current year and earned $50,000 in prizes from these tournaments. She deposited the winnings in a bank account she opened in Mexico City after her first tournament win. Rita played a total of 30 tournaments for the year and earned $200,000 in total prize money. She spent 40 days in the United States, 60 days in England, 20 days in Scotland, and the rest of the time in South America. Write a letter to Rita explaining how much U.S.-source income she will generate, if any, from her participation in these tournaments and whether any of her winnings are subject to U.S. taxation. Rita's address is AV Rio Branco, 149-4#, Rio de Janeiro, RJ 22421, Brazil.

17. Determine whether the source of income for the following sales is U.S. or foreign.
    a. Kwaku, an NRA, sells stock in Home Depot, a domestic corporation, through a broker in New York.
    b. Chris sells stock in IBM, a domestic corporation, to his brother, Rich. Both Chris and Rich are NRAs, and the sale takes place outside the United States.
    c. Crows, Inc., sells inventory produced in the United States to customers in Europe. Title passes in the international waters of the Atlantic Ocean.
    d. Jordan, Inc., a domestic corporation, manufactures equipment in Taiwan and sells the equipment to customers in the United States.

Decision Making

18. Power, Inc., produces inventory in its foreign manufacturing plants for sale in the United States. Its foreign manufacturing assets have a tax book value of $6 million and a fair market value of $16 million. Its assets related to the sales activity have a tax book value of $800,000 and a fair market value of $200,000. Power's interest expense totaled $100,000 for the current year.
    a. What amount of interest expense will be allocated and apportioned to foreign-source income using the tax book value method? What amount of interest expense will be allocated and apportioned to foreign-source income using the fair market method?
    b. If Power wishes to maximize its FTC, which method should it use?

19. Weight, Inc., a domestic corporation, purchases weight-lifting equipment for resale from HiDisu, a Japanese corporation, for 75 million yen. On the date of purchase, 150 yen is equal to $1 U.S. (Y150:$1). The purchase is made on December 15, 2005, with payment due in 60 days. Weight is a calendar year taxpayer. On December 31, 2005, the foreign exchange rate is Y140:$1. What amount of foreign currency gain or loss, if any, must Weight recognize for 2005 as a result of this transaction?

20. Green, Inc., a foreign corporation, pays a dividend to its shareholders on November 30. Red, Inc., a U.S. corporation and 9% shareholder in Green, receives a dividend of 5,000K (a foreign currency). Pertinent exchange rates are as follows.

November 30	.9K:$1
Average for year	.7K:$1
December 31	2K:$1

    What is the dollar amount of the dividend received by Red, Inc., and does Red, Inc., have a foreign exchange gain or loss on receipt of the dividend?

Issue ID
Communications

21. Beach, Inc., a domestic corporation, operates a branch in Mexico. Over the last 10 years, this branch has generated $50 million in losses. For the last 3 years, however, the branch has been profitable and has earned enough income to entirely offset the prior losses. Most of the assets are fully depreciated, and a net gain would be recognized if the assets were sold. The CFO believes that Beach should incorporate the branch now so that this potential gain can be transferred to a foreign corporation, thereby avoiding U.S. tax and, as an added benefit, avoiding U.S. taxes on future income. Draft an outline of a memo to the CFO addressing the tax issues involved in the proposed transaction.

22. McDonald Enterprises, a domestic corporation, owns 100% of OK, Ltd., an Irish corporation. Determine OK's Subpart F income for the current year (before any expenses) from the following transactions.
    a. OK earned $600,000 from sales of products purchased from McDonald and sold to customers outside Ireland.
    b. OK earned $1 million from sales of products purchased from McDonald and sold to customers in Ireland.
    c. OK earned $400,000 from sales of products purchased from unrelated suppliers and sold to customers in Germany.
    d. OK purchased raw materials from McDonald, used these materials to manufacture finished goods, and sold these goods to customers in Italy. OK earned $200,000 from these sales.
    e. OK earned $120,000 for the performance of warranty services on behalf of McDonald. These services were performed in Japan for customers located in Japan.
    f. OK earned $60,000 in dividend income from investments in unrelated parties.

23. News, Inc., a U.S. corporation, owns 60% of the only class of stock of Magazine, Inc., a CFC. Magazine is a CFC until June 1 of the current tax year. News has held the stock since Magazine was organized and continues to hold it for the entire year. News and Magazine are both calendar year taxpayers. Magazine's Subpart F income for the tax year is $900,000, current E & P is $950,000, and no distributions have been made for the tax year. What amount, if any, must News include in gross income under Subpart F for the tax year?

Issue ID
Communications

24. Mary Beth Alessio, a U.S. citizen, has placed all her investments in a Cayman Island corporation owned 1% by Mary Beth and 99% by a foreign individual. She pays no income tax in the Cayman Islands on this income. The foreign corporation generates only interest and dividends. Outline a letter informing Mary Beth of the U.S. tax consequences of her foreign investments. Her address is 941 Windom Lane, Hagerstown, MD 21740.

25. Ben, Inc., a domestic corporation, operates in both Canada and the United States. This year, the business generated taxable income of $300,000 from foreign sources and $100,000 from U.S. sources. All of Ben's foreign-source income is in the general limitation basket. Ben's total worldwide taxable income is $400,000. Ben pays Canadian taxes of $130,000. Assume a 34% U.S. income tax rate. What is Ben's FTC for the tax year?

26. Elmwood, Inc., a domestic corporation, owns 15% of Correy, Ltd., a Hong Kong corporation. The remaining 85% of Correy is owned by Fortune Enterprises, a Canadian corporation. At the end of the current year, Correy has $400,000 in post-1986 undistributed E & P and $200,000 in foreign taxes related to this E & P. On the last day of the year, Correy pays a $30,000 dividend to Elmwood. Elmwood's taxable income before inclusion of the dividend is $200,000. What is Elmwood's tax liability after consideration of the dividend and any allowed FTC, assuming a 34% U.S. tax rate?

Communications

27. Your client Nashville Cats, Inc., is engaged in the music production business, with CD production plants in Tennessee and Singapore. The U.S. plant has always produced profits, but the Singapore operation has generated $200,000 in losses since inception. This year, the Singapore operation began producing net profits. Draft a brief memo to John, the CFO of Nashville Cats, explaining why a portion of the current-year foreign-source income must be recharacterized as U.S.-source for FTC limitation purposes.

28. For which of the following foreign income inclusions is a U.S. corporation potentially allowed an indirect FTC under § 902?
    a. Interest income from a 5%-owned foreign corporation.
    b. Interest income from a 60%-owned foreign corporation.
    c. Dividend income from a 5%-owned foreign corporation.
    d. Dividend income from a 60%-owned foreign corporation.

Decision Making

29. Lawn, Inc., a domestic corporation, earned $800,000 from foreign manufacturing activities on which it paid $240,000 of foreign income taxes. Lawn's foreign sales income is taxed at a 30% foreign tax rate. What amount of foreign sales income can Lawn earn without generating any excess FTCs for the current year? Assume a 34% U.S. tax rate.

30. Jones, Inc., a foreign subsidiary of Shirley, Inc., a U.S. corporation, has pretax income of 100,000 euros for 2005. Jones accrues 25,000 euros in foreign taxes on this income. The average exchange rate for the tax year to which the taxes relate is .92 euro:$1. None of the income is Subpart F income. If the net earnings of 75,000 euros are distributed when the exchange rate is 1.02 euro:$1, what are the deemed-paid taxes available to Shirley? Assume that 2005 is Jones's first year of operation.

31. Partin, Inc., a domestic corporation, operates a manufacturing branch in Ireland. During the current year, the manufacturing branch produces a loss of $50,000. Partin also operates a bank in the United Kingdom, where it earns $60,000 in financial services income. Partin paid no foreign income taxes related to the Irish branch, but it paid $15,000 in foreign income taxes related to the financial services income. Assuming that Partin pays U.S. taxes at the 34% rate, what is Partin's allowable FTC for the current year?

Decision Making
Communications

32. Money, Inc., a U.S. corporation, has $500,000 to invest overseas for 2005. For U.S. tax purposes, any additional income earned by Money will be taxed at 34%. Two possibilities for investment are:
    a. Invest the $500,000 in common stock of Exco (a foreign corporation). Exco common stock pays a dividend of $3 per share each year. The $500,000 would purchase 10,000 shares (or 10%) of Exco's only class of stock (voting common). Exco expects to earn $10 million before taxes for 2005 and to be taxed at a flat rate of 40%. Its 2005 E & P before taxes is estimated to be $9.4 million. Exco's government does not withhold on dividends paid to foreign investors.

b. Invest the $500,000 in Exco bonds that pay interest at 7% per year. Assume that the bonds will be acquired at par, or face, value. Exco's government withholds 25% on interest paid to foreign investors.

Analyze these two investment opportunities and determine which would give Money the better return after taxes. Be sure to consider the effect of the FTC. Write a memorandum to Money, Inc., advising the corporation of your findings.

33. IrishCo, a manufacturing corporation resident in Ireland, distributes products through a U.S. office. Current-year taxable income from such sales in the United States is $12 million. IrishCo's U.S. office deposits working capital funds short term in certificates of deposit with U.S. banks. Current-year income from these deposits is $100,000.
IrishCo also invests in U.S. securities traded on the New York Stock Exchange. This investing is done by the home office. For the current year, IrishCo has realized capital gains of $200,000 and dividend income of $60,000 from these stock investments. Compute IrishCo's U.S. tax liability, assuming that the U.S.-Ireland income tax treaty reduces withholding on dividends to 15% and on interest to 5%. Assume a 34% U.S. tax rate.

Communications

34. Gelati, Ltd., a foreign corporation, operates a trade or business in the United States. Gelati's U.S.-source income effectively connected with this trade or business is $400,000 for the current year. Gelati's current year E & P is $360,000. Gelati's net U.S. equity was $5.1 million at the beginning of the year and $5.3 million at year-end. Gelati is a resident in a country that has no income tax treaty with the United States. Briefly outline a memo to Gelati's Tax VP reporting Gelati's branch profits tax liability for the current year, along with a planning idea for reducing the branch profits tax.

35. Brenda, an NRA individual, owns 30% of the stock of Jeff, Inc., a U.S. corporation. Jeff's balance sheet on the last day of the taxable year is as follows.

		Adjusted Basis	Fair Market Value
Cash (used as working capital)		$ 200,000	$ 200,000
Investment in foreign land		300,000	800,000
Investment in U.S. real estate:			
Land		150,000	400,000
Buildings	$2,300,000		
Less: Depreciation	(300,000)	2,000,000	5,000,000
		$2,650,000	$6,400,000
Accounts payable		$ 300,000	$ 300,000
Notes payable		500,000	500,000
Capital stock		400,000	4,150,000
Retained earnings		1,450,000	1,450,000
		$2,650,000	$6,400,000

Brenda was in the United States only 40 days in the tax year. She sold all of her stock in Jeff on the last day of the tax year for $6.4 million. Brenda's adjusted basis in the stock sold was $500,000. She sold the stock for cash. What are the U.S. tax consequences, if any, to Brenda?

Issue ID
Communications

36. John McPherson is single, an attorney, and a U.S. citizen. He recently attended a seminar where he learned he could give up his U.S. citizenship, move to Bermuda (where he would pay no income tax), and operate his law practice long distance via the Internet with no U.S. tax consequences. Outline a letter informing John of the tax consequences of his proposed actions. His address is 1005 NE 10th Street, Gainesville, GA 32812.

Research Problems

*Note: Solutions to Research Problems can be prepared by using the **RIA Checkpoint® Student Edition** online research product, which is available to accompany this text. It is also possible to prepare solutions to the Research Problems by using tax research materials found in a standard tax library.*

Research Problem 1. A U.S. corporation had the following net taxable income (loss) for the 2005 tax year. Its U.S. taxes before the FTC are $600. Determine the FTC limitation for each basket of foreign-source income.

Source (Basket)	Income (Loss)	Foreign Taxes
U.S.-source	($68,000)	$ -0-
Foreign-source passive	70,000	21,000
Foreign-source oil and gas	30,000	6,000
Foreign-source general	(28,000)	-0-

Partial list of research aids:
§ 904(f)(5).
General Explanation of the Tax Reform Act of 1986 (the Bluebook), Joint Committee on Taxation, pp. 909–912.
Instructions accompanying *Form 1118,* Foreign Tax Credit—Corporations, Dept. of the Treasury, Internal Revenue Service.

Research Problem 2. NewCar.com, Inc., an innovative, Internet-based automobile retailer based in Ghana, is beginning to seek customers in the United States. Currently, it has no sales personnel or assets located in the United States, but it makes a few sales to U.S. customers based on orders over its Web site. NewCar.com is considering sending a few sales agents to the United States to set up sales offices in large cities. The offices will have no inventory and will merely provide a place for the sales agents to meet with interested customers. Ghana has no income tax treaty with the United States. How would you advise NewCar.com, Inc., on the tax consequences of its proposed U.S. venture?

Partial list of research aids:
§ 882(a)(1).
Higgins v. Comm., 41–1 USTC ¶9233, 25 AFTR 1160, 61 S.Ct. 475 (USSC, 1941).
Continental Trading, Inc. v. Comm., 59–1 USTC ¶9316, 3 AFTR2d 923, 265 F.2d 40 (CA–9, 1959).
Piedras Negras Broadcasting Co., 43 BTA 297 (1941), *aff'd* 42–1 USTC ¶9384, 29 AFTR 243, 127 F.2d 260 (CA–5, 1942).

Internet Activity

Use the tax resources of the Internet to address the following question. Do not restrict your search to the World Wide Web, but include a review of newsgroups and general reference materials, practitioner sites and resources, primary sources of the tax law, chat rooms and discussion groups, and other opportunities.

Research Problem 3. Locate the most recent annual report (or SEC Form 10K) for three different publicly held U.S. corporations. For each corporation, locate the income tax footnote and determine the percentage of net income before taxes from foreign operations, the current foreign income tax expense (benefit), and the deferred foreign income tax expense (benefit).

Tax Administration and Practice

LEARNING OBJECTIVES

After completing Chapter 26, you should be able to:

LO.1

Identify the various administrative pronouncements issued by the IRS and explain how they can be used in tax practice.

LO.2

Summarize the administrative powers of the IRS, including the examination of taxpayer records, the assessment and demand process, and collection procedures.

LO.3

Describe the audit process, including how returns are selected for audit and the various types of audits.

LO.4

Explain the taxpayer appeal process, including various settlement options available.

LO.5

Determine the amount of interest on a deficiency or a refund and when it is due.

LO.6

Discuss the various penalties that can be imposed on acts of noncompliance by taxpayers and return preparers.

LO.7

Understand the rules governing the statute of limitations on assessments and on refunds.

LO.8

Summarize the legal and ethical guidelines that apply to those engaged in tax practice.

http://wft.swlearning.com

OUTLINE

Few events arouse so much fear in the typical individual or corporation as the receipt of a letter from the Internal Revenue Service (IRS), notifying the taxpayer that prior years' tax returns are to be the subject of an audit. Almost immediately, calls are made to the tax adviser. Advice is sought as to what to reveal (or not reveal) in the course of the audit, how to delay or avoid the audit, and how friendly one should be with the auditor when he or she ultimately arrives.

Indeed, many tax practitioners' reputations with their clients have been made or broken by the way they are observed to behave under the pressure of an audit situation. The strategy and tactics of audits—including such seemingly unimportant issues as whether the tax adviser brings donuts or other refreshments to the audit session, the color of his or her suit and tie, and the most effective negotiation techniques—are the subject of both cocktail party banter and scholarly review.

In actuality, the practitioner can render valuable services to the taxpayer in an audit context, thereby assuring that tax payments for the disputed years are neither under- nor overreported, as part of an ongoing tax practice. In this regard, the adviser must appreciate the following.

- The elements of the Treasury's tax administration process and opportunities for appeal within the structure of the IRS.
- The extent of the negative sanctions that can be brought to bear against taxpayers whose returns are found to have been inaccurate.
- The ethical and professional constraints on the advice tax advisers can give and the actions they can take on behalf of their clients within the context of an adversarial relationship with the IRS.

Tax Administration

The Treasury has delegated the administration and enforcement of the tax laws to its subsidiary agency, the IRS. In this process, the Service is responsible for providing adequate information, in the form of publications and forms with instructions, to taxpayers so that they can comply with the laws in an appropriate manner. The IRS also identifies delinquent tax payments and carries out assessment and collection

SHOULD THE IRS BE LARGER?

What is the optimal size of the IRS? The IRS maintains in congressional testimony that it can produce three to four dollars of revenue for every dollar spent on its ongoing operations. Actually, the rate of return might be higher, especially for special projects that the Service itself devises and undertakes. As the agency becomes more proficient with computers and more aggressive in finding and treating nonfilers, the temptation to enlarge the Service increases as well.

Given concerns about the Federal deficit and an underground economy measured in the hundreds of billions of dollars, one might expect the number of IRS operatives to keep increasing, even though it already is one of the largest Federal agencies, with a staff of about 100,000 and a budget exceeding $10 billion. Yet, the last few presidents have found that pledges to cut back the size of government also apply to the IRS (i.e., the public does not apply such a rate of return test itself).

Thus, the IRS must live within its budget allocations and reallocate the resources that it now has. Can a stepped-up education campaign, further reliance on electronic filing, and an overall consumer-friendly operation produce significant revenue increases for the IRS?

procedures under the restrictions of due process and other constitutional guarantees.

In meeting these responsibilities, the Service conducts audits of selected tax returns. Fewer than 0.7 percent of all individual tax returns are subjected to audit in a given tax year. However, certain types of both taxpayers and income—including, for example, high-income individuals (about 1.5 percent), cash-oriented businesses, real estate transactions, and estate- and gift-taxable transfers (15 to 30 percent)—are subject to much higher probabilities of audit.

The audit rate for corporations with at least $250 million in assets is almost 40 percent, but the rate drops to about 0.33 percent for businesses with less than $10 million in assets. Under the present Commissioner, the IRS has pledged to increase its audit and enforcement activities and is currently hiring audit staff at a rate exceeding that of the past decade.

Recently, much of the IRS's effort has been devoted to developing statutory and administrative requirements relative to information reporting and document matching. For example, when a taxpayer engages in a like-kind exchange or sells a personal residence, various parties to the transaction are required to report the nature and magnitude of the transaction to the IRS. Later the Treasury's computers determine whether the transaction has been reported properly by comparing the information reported by the third parties with the events included on the relevant taxpayers' returns for the year.

In addition, the IRS has been placing increasing pressure on the community of tax advisers. Severe penalties may be assessed on those who have prepared a taxpayer's return when the Service's interpretation of applicable law conflicts with that of the preparer.

The IRS processes over 130 million individual income tax returns every year, almost 60 million of which are filed electronically. It collects more than $3 trillion in tax revenues and pays refunds to about 100 million taxpayers every year.

IRS Audit Initiatives

Complaints about the scope of IRS audit efforts—and the shrinking percentages of tax returns being audited—must be placed in the context of the agency's own objectives. Few taxpayers or commentators attempt to see the big picture when audit selection statistics are released.

The agency's current efforts seem to be aimed at chronic and high-risk noncompliance. In an age of shrinking real budget dollars for the Service, this "biggest bang for the buck" strategy may be appropriate. Although fewer individuals will be audited, the Service seems to be hunting for annuities of tax dollars, rather than just maximizing current collections. For example, permanently adding a noncompliant taxpayer to the tax rolls can optimize the present value of revenue collections tied to the IRS's efforts.

Announced priority areas for the IRS audit staff include the following.

- Offshore credit card users.
- High-risk, high-income taxpayers.
- Tax shelters, abusive schemes, and their promoters.
- High-income nonfilers.
- Unreported income.
- Further research as to audit initiatives.

The agency has stated that it is revising its training materials and case studies to reflect the revised priorities. "Hardball" techniques apparently will be used to deal with the priority issues. Such techniques include issuing summonses, obtaining injunctions, initiating civil audits for shelter participants, and pursuing criminal investigations of shelter promoters.

These efforts are integrated within the recent changes to the IRS's organizational plan. Audits of most individuals and businesses will be conducted through the Small Business/Self-Employed division. Reviews of tax shelters and abusive taxpayers will be centered in the Large and Mid-Size Business division.

LO.1

Identify the various administrative pronouncements issued by the IRS and explain how they can be used in tax practice.

IRS PROCEDURE—LETTER RULINGS

When a tax issue is controversial or a transaction involves considerable tax dollars, the taxpayer often wishes to obtain either assurance or direction from the IRS as to the treatment of the event. The **letter ruling** process is an effective means of dealing directly with the IRS while in the planning stages of a large or otherwise important transaction.

Rulings issued by the National Office provide a written statement of the position of the IRS concerning the tax consequences of a course of action contemplated by the taxpayer. Letter rulings do not have the force and effect of law, but they do provide guidance and support for taxpayers in similar transactions. The IRS issues rulings only on uncompleted, actual (rather than hypothetical) transactions or on transactions completed before the filing of the tax return for the year in question.

The IRS will not issue a ruling in certain circumstances. It ordinarily will not rule in cases that essentially involve a question of fact.[1] For example, no ruling will be issued to determine whether compensation paid to employees is reasonable in amount and therefore allowable as a deduction.[2]

[1] Rev.Proc. 2005–1, I.R.B. No. 1, 1.

[2] Rev.Proc. 2005–3, I.R.B. No. 1, 118.

A letter ruling represents the current opinion of the IRS on the tax consequences of a transaction with a given set of facts. IRS rulings are not unchangeable. They are frequently declared obsolete or are superseded by new rulings in response to tax law changes. However, revocation or modification of a ruling is usually not applied retroactively to the taxpayer who received the ruling, if it was relied on in good faith and if the facts in the ruling request were in agreement with the completed transaction. The IRS may revoke any ruling if, upon subsequent audit, the agent finds a misstatement or omission of facts or substantial discrepancies between the facts in the ruling request and the actual situation. A ruling may be relied upon only by the taxpayer who requested and received it.

Letter rulings benefit both the IRS and the taxpayer. Not only do they help promote a uniform application of the tax laws, but they may also reduce the potential for litigation or disputes with IRS agents. In addition, they make the IRS aware of significant transactions being consummated by taxpayers. A significant fee is charged for processing a ruling request.

IRS PROCEDURE—OTHER ISSUANCES

In addition to issuing unpublished letter rulings and published rulings and procedures, the IRS issues determination letters and technical advice memoranda.

A **determination letter** relates to a completed transaction when the issue involved is covered by judicial or statutory authority, Regulations, or rulings. Determination letters are issued for various death, gift, income, excise, and employment tax matters.

EXAMPLE 1

True Corporation recently opened a car clinic and has employed numerous mechanics. The corporation is not certain whether its educational reimbursement plan is nondiscriminatory. True may request a determination letter. ■

EXAMPLE 2

Assume the same facts as in Example 1. True would like to establish a pension plan that qualifies for the tax advantages of § 401(k). To determine whether the plan qualifies, True should request and obtain a determination letter from the IRS. ■

EXAMPLE 3

A group of physicians plans to form an association to construct and operate a hospital. The determination letter procedure is appropriate to ascertain whether the group is either subject to the Federal income tax or is tax-exempt. ■

A **technical advice memorandum (TAM)** is issued by the National Office to a Director and/or Regional Commissioner in response to a specific request by an agent, Appellate Conferee, or Director. The taxpayer may request a TAM if an issue in dispute is not treated by the law or precedent and/or published rulings or Regulations. TAMs also are appropriate when there is reason to believe that the IRS is not administering the tax law consistently. For example, a taxpayer may inquire why an agent proposes to disallow a certain expenditure when agents in other districts permit the deduction. Technical advice requests arise from the audit process, whereas ruling requests are issued before an IRS audit.

The IRS is now testing a new written determination approach, the technical expedited advice memorandum (TEAM), to be used during an office or field audit. The TEAM is designed to reflect the position of the IRS in a shorter time than the TAM now requires. This quicker response time is possible because the following occur before a TEAM request is submitted.

- The taxpayer and the IRS agree to a set of facts for the case.
- The parties conduct a presubmission conference, with attorneys for both sides in attendance.

- Technology, including e-mails and faxes, is used to gather facts as part of the process.
- The IRS holds an internal strategic planning meeting, discussing potential responses to various holdings that could be issued as part of the TEAM.

If the TEAM pilot is successful, the new procedure could see wider usage in coming years.

LO.2

Summarize the administrative powers of the IRS, including the examination of taxpayer records, the assessment and demand process, and collection procedures.

ADMINISTRATIVE POWERS OF THE IRS

Examination of Records. The Code authorizes the IRS to examine the taxpayer's books and records as part of the process of determining the correct amount of tax due. The IRS also can require the persons responsible for the return to appear and to produce any necessary books and records.[3] Taxpayers are required to maintain certain record-keeping procedures and retain the records necessary to facilitate the audit.

Burden of Proof. If the taxpayer meets the record-keeping requirement and substantiates income and deductions properly, the IRS bears the burden of proof in establishing a tax deficiency during litigation. The taxpayer must have cooperated with the IRS regarding reasonable requests for information, documents, meetings, and interviews. For individual taxpayers, the IRS's burden of proof extends to penalties and interest amounts that it assesses in a court proceeding with the taxpayer.[4]

Assessment and Demand. The Code permits the IRS to assess a deficiency and to demand payment for the tax. However, no assessment or effort to collect the tax may be made until 90 days after a statutory notice of a deficiency (the *90-day letter*) is issued. The taxpayer therefore has 90 days to file a petition to the U.S. Tax Court, effectively preventing the deficiency from being assessed or collected pending the outcome of the case.[5]

Following assessment of the tax, the IRS issues a notice and demand for payment. The taxpayer is usually given 30 days after the notice and demand for payment to pay the tax.

If the IRS believes the assessment or collection of a deficiency is in jeopardy, it may assess the deficiency and demand immediate payment.[6] The taxpayer can avoid (*stay*) the collection of the jeopardy assessment by filing a bond for the amount of the tax and interest. This action prevents the IRS from selling any property it has seized.

Collection. If the taxpayer neglects or refuses to pay the tax after receiving the demand for payment, a lien in favor of the IRS is placed on all property (realty and personalty, tangible and intangible) belonging to the taxpayer.

The levy power of the IRS is very broad. It allows the IRS to garnish (*attach*) wages and salary and to seize and sell all nonexempt property by any means. After a 30-day notice period, the IRS can also make successive seizures on any property owned by the taxpayer until the levy is satisfied.[7] A taxpayer's principal residence is exempt from the levy process, unless the disputed tax, interest, and penalty exceed $5,000 and a U.S. District Court judge approves of the seizure.[8]

[3] § 7602.
[4] §§ 7491(a)(1), (a)(2)(B), and (c).
[5] §§ 6212 and 6213.
[6] § 6861. A jeopardy assessment is appropriate, for example, where the IRS fears that the taxpayer will flee the country or destroy valuable property.
[7] The taxpayer can keep certain personal ($7,200) and business ($3,600) property and a minimal amount of his or her income as a subsistence allowance, even if a lien is outstanding. The amounts are indexed for inflation. § 6334.
[8] §§ 6334(a)(13)(A) and (e)(1).

LO.3

Describe the audit process, including how returns are selected for audit and the various types of audits.

THE AUDIT PROCESS

Selection of Returns for Audit. The IRS uses mathematical formulas to select tax returns that are most likely to contain errors and yield substantial amounts of additional tax revenues upon audit. The IRS does not openly disclose all of its audit selection techniques. However, some observations can be made regarding the probability that a return will be selected for audit.

- Certain groups of taxpayers are subject to audit more frequently than others. These groups include individuals with gross income in excess of $100,000, self-employed individuals with substantial business income and deductions, and cash businesses where the potential for tax evasion is high.

EXAMPLE 4

Tracey owns and operates a liquor store. As nearly all of her sales are for cash, Tracey might be a prime candidate for an audit by the IRS. Cash transactions are easier to conceal than those made on credit. ■

- If a taxpayer has been audited in a past year and the audit led to the assessment of a substantial deficiency, the IRS often makes a return visit.
- An audit might materialize if information returns (e.g., Form W–2, Form 1099) are not in substantial agreement with the income reported on a taxpayer's return. Obvious discrepancies do not necessitate formal audits and usually can be handled by correspondence with the taxpayer.
- If an individual's itemized deductions are in excess of norms established for various income levels, the probability of an audit increases. Certain deductions (e.g., casualty and theft losses, business use of the home, tax-sheltered investments) are sensitive areas as the IRS realizes that many taxpayers determine the amount of the deduction incorrectly or may not be entitled to the deduction at all.
- The filing of a refund claim by the taxpayer may prompt an audit of the return.
- Some returns are selected because the IRS has targeted a specific industry or type of tax return for in-depth review. This enables examiners to develop special skills and interests applicable to those returns. In the Industry Specialization Program (ISP), returns might be selected from retailers, energy developers, or health care operations for special review. In the Market Segment Specialization Program (MSSP), specialized auditors focus on returns that show passive losses, involve construction activities, or include legal or consulting income.
- Information is often obtained from other sources (e.g., other government agencies, news items, informants). The IRS then applies its own judgment and experience, and it may audit the return to address such questions as, Why did dividend income increase so much this year? Why did mortgage interest payments decrease? How did the taxpayer pay for such a large vacation home, sold this year?
- The IRS can pay rewards to persons who provide information that leads to the detection and punishment of those who violate the tax laws. The rewards are paid at the discretion of the IRS. Such a payment cannot exceed 15 percent of the taxes, fines, and penalties recovered as a result of the information.[9]

EXAMPLE 5

Phil reports to the police that burglars broke into his home while he was out of town and took a shoe box containing $25,000 in cash, among other things. A representative of the IRS reading the newspaper account of the burglary might wonder why Phil kept such a large amount of cash in a shoe box at home. ■

[9] § 7623 and Reg. § 301.7623–1T.

TABLE 26–1
IRS Audit Information by Type (Individual Returns Filed in 2002)

	Conducted (Number)	Conducted (Percent)
Correspondence audit	575,000	79%
Office audit	68,000	9%
Field audit	86,000	12%

EXAMPLE 6

After 15 years, Betty is discharged by her employer, Dr. Franklin. Shortly thereafter, the IRS receives a letter from Betty stating that Franklin keeps two sets of books, one of which substantially understates the actual cash receipts. ■

The statistical models used by the IRS to select individual tax returns for audit come from random audits of a small number of taxpayers, who are required to document every entry that they made on the Form 1040. The latest round of these National Research Program (NRP) audits took place in 2003–2004 and resulted in the construction of new Discriminant Information Function (DIF) scores that project the amount of revenue that the IRS will gain from pursuing tax returns with various statistical profiles. The higher the DIF score, the better the return to the IRS from pursuing the audit, and the higher the probability of selection for an examination.

These data-seeking audits had been delayed since the late 1980s as a result of taxpayer complaints to Congress about the stress that they create.[10] But the data from the older DIF models no longer matched the U.S. service-based, information-powered economy. Consequently, updating the underlying models was essential.

Many individual taxpayers mistakenly assume that if they do not hear from the IRS within a few weeks after filing their return or if they receive a refund check, no audit will be forthcoming. As a practical matter, most individual returns are examined about two years from the date of filing. If not, they generally remain unaudited. All large corporations, however, are subject to annual audits.

Verification and Audit Procedures. The filed tax return is immediately reviewed for mathematical accuracy. A check is also made for deductions, exclusions, etc., that are clearly erroneous. One obvious error would be the failure to comply with the 7.5 percent limitation on the deduction for medical expenses. Over 10 percent of all individual returns show a math error. In such cases, the Service Center merely sends the taxpayer revised computations and a bill or refund as appropriate. Taxpayers are usually able to settle such matters through a direct *correspondence audit* with the IRS without the necessity of a formal meeting.

Office audits are conducted by representatives of the Director's Office, either in the office of the IRS or through correspondence. Individual returns with few or no items of business income are usually handled through an office audit. In most situations, the taxpayer is required merely to substantiate a deduction, credit, or item of income that appears on the return. The taxpayer presents documentation in the form of canceled checks, invoices, etc., for the items in question.

The *field audit* is commonly used for corporate returns and for returns of individuals engaged in business or professional activities. This type of audit generally involves a more complete examination of a taxpayer's transactions.

A field audit is conducted by IRS agents at the office or home of the taxpayer or at the office of the taxpayer's representative. The agent's work may be facilitated by a review of certain tax workpapers and discussions with the taxpayer's representative about items appearing on the tax return. Table 26–1 summarizes key audit information.

[10]About 39,000 NRP audits required a meeting between the IRS and the taxpayer. The total audit sample constituted 49,000 returns. About 4,000 of these returns were analyzed without contacting the taxpayer, and another 2,000 taxpayers were contacted only by mail with queries about one or two items. The rest of the sample consisted largely of proprietors, partners, and farmers (i.e., those using Schedules C, E, and F). Only about 1,700 returns were subjected to "line-by-line" review.

Collecting Those Taxes Due

For many years, the IRS considered using third-party debt collectors as other Federal agencies (e.g., the Department of Education to collect delinquent student loans) and a few state tax departments were already doing. Now, in 2005, the IRS has negotiated a series of contracts with various collection agencies to collect unpaid Federal income and payroll taxes, estimated to exceed $120 billion.

When fully phased in by 2007, these third-party collection efforts will generate over $100 million in delinquent taxes per year. The debt collectors may focus on the more than 75,000 taxpayers who have an outstanding tax bill of more than $100,000. Best estimates are that most of the tax delinquents are not hard-core tax evaders, but individuals and businesses that are experiencing financial problems. Some have negotiated installment payment schedules that are in arrears.

This outsourcing of collection activities has led to some political opposition based on privacy and equity grounds. Can the providers of such services interpret and apply the tax laws as effectively and confidentially as the IRS? Given the level of personnel turnover that is likely to occur, can these third-party collectors be trained and controlled to stay within the boundaries of the law?

Despite these concerns, unpaid tax liabilities are now too large to ignore, especially given the record budget deficit and a more enforcement-oriented IRS. Because private collection agencies can charge a fee of up to 25 percent of the taxes collected, they have an incentive to "close the deal." The result is apt to be much tougher collection tactics than taxpayers are used to.

Prior to or at the initial interview, the IRS must provide the taxpayer with an explanation of the audit process that is the subject of the interview and describe the taxpayer's rights under that process. If the taxpayer clearly states at any time during the interview the desire to consult with an attorney, CPA, enrolled agent, or any other person permitted to represent the taxpayer before the IRS, then the IRS representative must suspend the interview.[11]

Any officer or employee of the IRS must, upon advance request, allow a taxpayer to make an audio recording of any in-person interview with the officer or employee concerning the determination and collection of any tax.[12]

Settlement with the Revenue Agent. Following an audit, the IRS agent may either accept the return as filed or recommend certain adjustments. The **Revenue Agent's Report (RAR)** is reviewed within the IRS. In most instances, the agent's proposed adjustments are approved.

Agents must adhere strictly to IRS policy as reflected in published rulings, Regulations, and other releases. The agent cannot settle an unresolved issue based upon the probability of winning the case in court. Usually, issues involving factual questions can be settled at the agent level, and it may be advantageous for both the taxpayer and the IRS to reach agreement at the earliest point in the settlement process. For example, it may be to the taxpayer's advantage to reach agreement at the agent level and avoid any further opportunity for the IRS to raise new issues.

[11] § 7521(b).

[12] § 7521(a).

If agreement is reached upon the proposed deficiency, the taxpayer signs Form 870 (Waiver of Restrictions on Assessment and Collection of Deficiency in Tax). One advantage to the taxpayer of signing Form 870 at this point is that interest stops accumulating on the deficiency 30 days after the form is filed.[13] When this form is signed, the taxpayer effectively waives the right to receive a statutory notice of deficiency (the 90-day letter) and to subsequently petition the Tax Court. In addition, it is no longer possible for the taxpayer later to go to the IRS Appeals Division. Signing Form 870 at the agent level generally closes the case. However, the IRS is not restricted by Form 870 and may assess additional deficiencies if deemed necessary.

LO.4

Explain the taxpayer appeal process, including various settlement options available.

THE TAXPAYER APPEAL PROCESS

If agreement cannot be reached at the agent level, the taxpayer receives a copy of the Revenue Agent's Report and a **30-day letter.** The taxpayer has 30 days to request an administrative appeal. If an appeal is not requested, a **90-day letter** is issued. Figure 26–1 illustrates the taxpayer's alternatives when a disagreement with the IRS persists.

A taxpayer who wishes to appeal must make an appropriate request to the Appeals Division. The request must be accompanied by a written protest except in the following cases.

- The proposed tax deficiency does not exceed $10,000 for any of the tax periods involved in the audit.
- The deficiency resulted from a correspondence or office audit (i.e., not as a result of a field audit).

The Appeals Division is authorized to settle all tax disputes based on the hazards of litigation (i.e., the chances of winning in court). Since the Appeals Division has final settlement authority until a 90-day letter has been issued, the taxpayer may be able to negotiate a settlement. In addition, an overall favorable settlement may be reached by "trading" disputed issues. The Appeals Division occasionally may raise new issues if the grounds are substantial and of significant tax impact.

Both the Appeals Division and the taxpayer have the right to request technical advice memoranda from the National Office of the IRS. A TAM that is favorable to the taxpayer is binding on the Appeals Division. Even if the TAM is favorable to the IRS, however, the Appeals Division may nevertheless settle the case based on other considerations.

A taxpayer who files a petition with the U.S. Tax Court has the option of having the case heard before the more informal Small Cases Division if the amount of tax in dispute does not exceed $50,000.[14] If the Small Cases Division is used, neither party may appeal the case.

The economic costs of a settlement offer from the Appeals Division should be weighed against the costs of litigation and the probability of winning the case. The taxpayer should also consider the impact of the settlement upon the tax liability for future periods, in addition to the years under audit.

If a settlement is reached with the Appeals Division, the taxpayer is required to sign Form 870-AD. According to the IRS, this settlement is binding upon both parties unless fraud, malfeasance, concealment, or misrepresentation of material fact has occurred.

[13] § 6601(c).

[14] § 7463(a).

■ **FIGURE 26–1**
Income Tax Appeal Procedure

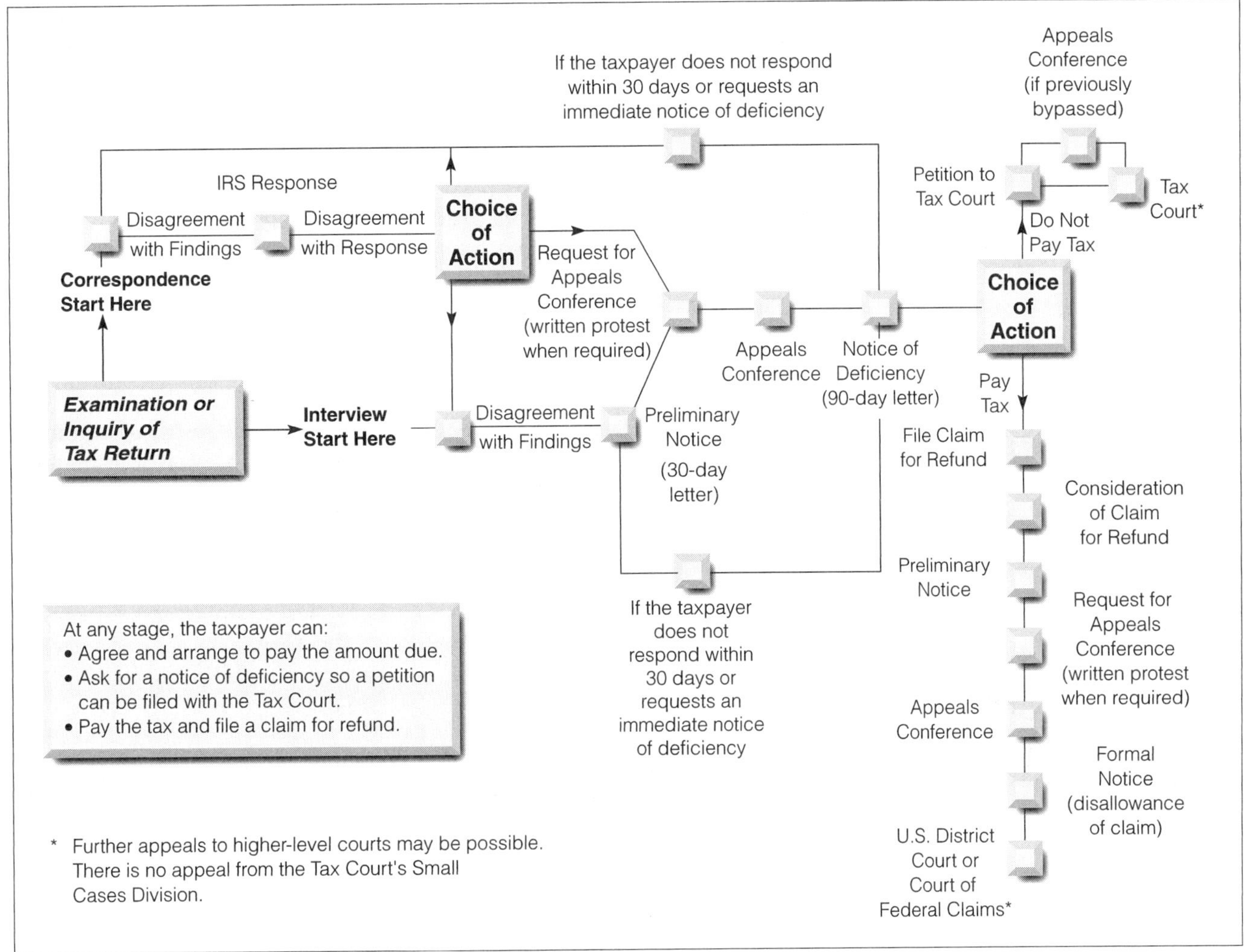

OFFERS IN COMPROMISE AND CLOSING AGREEMENTS

The IRS can negotiate a compromise if there is doubt about the taxpayer's ability to pay the tax. If the taxpayer is financially unable to pay the total amount of the tax, a Form 656 (Offer in Compromise) is filed with the Memphis Internal Revenue Service Center or the Brookhaven Internal Revenue Service Center in Holtsville, New York, depending on the location of the taxpayer. An **offer in compromise** is appropriate in the following circumstances.[15]

- There is doubt as to the taxpayer's liability for the tax (i.e., disputed issues still exist).
- There is doubt as to the collectibility of the tax (i.e., the taxpayer's net worth and earnings capacity are low).
- Payment of the disputed amount would constitute an economic hardship for the taxpayer. For example, the taxpayer is incapable of earning a living because of a long-term illness or disability, or liquidation of the taxpayer's assets to pay the amount due would leave the taxpayer unable to meet basic living expenses.

[15] § 7122 and Reg. § 301.7122–1T(b).

The IRS investigates the offer by evaluating the taxpayer's financial ability to pay the tax. In some situations, the compromise settlement includes an agreement for final settlement of the tax through payments of a specified percentage of the taxpayer's future earnings. The Director must obtain approval from the IRS Regional Counsel if the amount involved exceeds $500. This settlement procedure usually entails lengthy negotiations with the IRS, but the presumption is that the agency will find terms upon which to enter into a compromise with the taxpayer.

The IRS has statutory authority to enter into a written agreement allowing taxes to be paid on an installment basis if that arrangement facilitates the tax collection. The agency encourages its employees to use installment plans, and an individual is guaranteed the right to use an installment agreement when the amount in dispute does not exceed $10,000.

The IRS provides an annual statement accounting for the status of the agreement. The agreement may later be modified or terminated because of (1) inadequate information, (2) subsequent change in financial condition, or (3) failure to pay an installment when due or to provide requested information.[16]

A **closing agreement** is binding on both the taxpayer and the IRS except upon a subsequent showing of fraud, malfeasance, or misrepresentation of a material fact.[17] The closing agreement may be used when disputed issues carry over to future years. It may also be employed to dispose of a dispute involving a specific issue for a prior year or a proposed transaction involving future years. If, for example, the IRS is willing to make substantial concessions in the valuation of assets for estate tax purposes, it may require a closing agreement from the recipient of the property to establish the income tax basis of the assets.

LO.5

Determine the amount of interest on a deficiency or a refund and when it is due.

INTEREST

Determination of the Interest Rate. Congress sets the interest rates applicable to Federal tax underpayments (deficiencies) and overpayments (refunds) close to the rates available in financial markets. The Code provides for rates to be determined quarterly.[18] For example, the rates that are determined during March are effective for the following April through June.

IRS interest rates are based on the Federal short-term rates published periodically by the IRS in Revenue Rulings. The Federal rates are based on the average market yield on outstanding marketable obligations of the United States with remaining maturity of three years or less.

For noncorporate taxpayers, the interest rate applicable to *both* overpayments and underpayments is 5 percent for the first quarter of 2005. For most corporate taxpayers, the rate is 4 percent for overpayments and 5 percent for underpayments. Corporations with large overpayments or underpayments are subject to different rates.

Computation of the Amount of Interest. Interest is compounded daily.[19] Depending on the applicable interest rate, daily compounding doubles the payable amount over a period of five to eight years.

Tables for determining the daily compounded amount are available from the IRS and on the Internet. The tables ease the burden of those who prepare late returns where additional taxes are due.[20]

[16] § 6159.
[17] § 7121(b).
[18] § 6621.
[19] § 6622.
[20] Rev.Proc. 95–17, 1995–1 C.B. 556.

IRS Deficiency Assessments. Interest usually accrues from the unextended due date of the return until 30 days after the taxpayer agrees to the deficiency by signing Form 870. If the taxpayer does not pay the amount shown on the IRS's notice and demand (tax bill) within 30 days, interest again accrues on the deficiency.

Refund of Taxpayer's Overpayments. If an overpayment is refunded to the taxpayer within 45 days after the date the return is filed or is due, no interest is allowed. When the taxpayer files an amended return or makes a claim for refund of a prior year's tax (e.g., when net operating loss carrybacks result in refunds of a prior year's tax payments), however, interest is authorized from the original due date of the return through the date when the amended return is filed. In general, taxpayers applying for refunds receive interest as follows.

- When a return is filed after the due date, interest on any overpayment accrues from the date of filing. However, no interest is due if the IRS makes the refund within 45 days of the date of filing.

EXAMPLE 7

Naomi, a calendar year taxpayer, files her 2005 return on December 1, 2006. The return reflects an overwithholding of $2,500. On June 8, 2007, Naomi receives a refund of her 2005 overpayment. Interest on the refund began to accrue on December 1, 2006 (not April 15, 2006). ■

EXAMPLE 8

Assume the same facts as in Example 7, except that the refund is paid to Naomi on January 5, 2007 (rather than June 8, 2007). No interest is payable by the IRS, since the refund was made within 45 days of the filing of the return. ■

- In no event will interest accrue on an overpayment unless the return that is filed is in "processible form." Generally, this means that the return must contain enough information in a readable format to enable the IRS to identify the taxpayer and to determine the tax (and overpayment) involved.

LO.6

Discuss the various penalties that can be imposed on acts of noncompliance by taxpayers and return preparers.

TAXPAYER PENALTIES

To promote and enforce taxpayer compliance with the U.S. voluntary self-assessment system of taxation, Congress has enacted a comprehensive array of penalties. Tax penalties may involve both criminal and civil offenses. Criminal tax penalties are imposed only after the usual criminal process, in which the taxpayer is entitled to the same constitutional guarantees as nontax criminal defendants. Normally, a criminal penalty provides for imprisonment. Civil tax penalties are collected in the same manner as other taxes and usually provide only for monetary fines. Criminal and civil penalties are not mutually exclusive; therefore, both types of sanctions may be imposed on a taxpayer.

The Code characterizes tax penalties as additions to tax; thus, they cannot subsequently be deducted by the taxpayer. *Ad valorem penalties* are additions to tax that are based upon a percentage of the owed tax. *Assessable penalties,* on the other hand, typically include a flat dollar amount. Assessable penalties are not subject to review by the Tax Court, but *ad valorem* penalties are subject to the same deficiency procedures that apply to the underlying tax.

Failure to File and Failure to Pay. For a failure to file a tax return by the due date (including extensions), a penalty of 5 percent per month (up to a maximum of 25 percent) is imposed on the amount of tax shown as due on the return, with a minimum penalty amount of $100. If the failure to file is attributable to fraud, the penalty becomes 15 percent per month, to a maximum of 75 percent of the tax.[21]

For a failure to pay the tax due as shown on the return, a penalty of 0.5 percent per month (up to a maximum of 25 percent) is imposed on the amount of the tax. The penalty is doubled if the taxpayer fails to pay the tax after receiving a deficiency assessment.

In all of these cases, a fraction of a month counts as a full month. These penalties relate to the net amount of the tax due.

Obtaining an extension for filing a tax return does not by itself extend the date by which the taxes due must be paid. Thus, an application for an extended due date for a tax return almost always is accompanied by a payment by the taxpayer of a good faith estimate of the taxes that will be owed with the return when it is filed by the extended due date. If the taxpayer does not make such a good faith estimate and payment, the extension itself may be voided by the IRS (e.g., when the return is filed by the extended due date with a much larger amount due than had been estimated).

EXAMPLE 9

Conchita uses an automatic four-month extension for the filing of her 2004 tax return. Thus, the return is due on August 15, 2005, not on April 15. Conchita's application for the extension includes a $5,000 check, the amount that she estimates her 2004 return will show as owing for the year when she files it in August. ■

During any month in which both the failure to file penalty and the failure to pay penalty apply, the failure to file penalty is reduced by the amount of the failure to pay penalty.

EXAMPLE 10

Jason files his tax return 10 days after the due date. Along with the return, he remits a check for $3,000, which is the balance of the tax owed. Disregarding any interest liabilities, Jason's total penalties are as follows.

Failure to pay penalty (0.5% × $3,000)		$ 15
Plus: Failure to file penalty (5% × $3,000)	$150	
Less: Failure to pay penalty for the same period	(15)	
Failure to file penalty		135
Total penalties		$150

The penalties for one full month are imposed even though Jason was delinquent by only 10 days. Unlike the method used to compute interest, any part of a month is treated as a whole month. ■

These penalties can be avoided if the taxpayer shows that the failure to file and/or failure to pay was due to reasonable cause and not due to willful neglect. The Code is silent on what constitutes reasonable cause, and the Regulations do little to clarify this important concept.[22] Reasonable cause for failure to pay is presumed under the automatic four-month extension (Form 4868) when the additional tax due is not more than 10 percent of the tax liability shown on the return. In addition, the courts have ruled on some aspects of **reasonable cause.**

[21]§§ 6651(a) and (f).

[22]Reg. § 301.6651–1(c)(1) likens reasonable cause to the exercise of "ordinary business care and prudence" on the part of the taxpayer.

- Reasonable cause was found where the taxpayer relied on the advice of a competent tax adviser given in good faith, the facts were fully disclosed to the adviser, and he or she considered that the specific question represented reasonable cause.[23] No reasonable cause was found, however, where the taxpayer delegated the filing task to another, even when that person was an accountant or an attorney.[24]
- Among the reasons not qualifying as reasonable cause were lack of information on the due date of the return,[25] illness that did not incapacitate a taxpayer from completing a return,[26] refusal of the taxpayer's spouse to cooperate for a joint return,[27] and ignorance or misunderstanding of the tax law.[28]

Accuracy-Related Penalties. Major civil penalties relating to the accuracy of tax return data, including misstatements stemming from taxpayer negligence and improper valuation of income and deductions, are coordinated under the umbrella term **accuracy-related penalties.**[29] This consolidation of related penalties into a single levy eliminates the possibility that multiple penalties will apply to a single understatement of tax.

The accuracy-related penalties each amount to 20 percent of the portion of the tax underpayment that is attributable to one or more of the following infractions.

- Negligence or disregard of rules and Regulations.
- Substantial understatement of tax liability.
- Substantial valuation overstatement.
- Substantial valuation understatement.

The penalties apply only where the taxpayer fails to show a reasonable basis for the position taken on the return.[30]

Negligence. For purposes of this accuracy-related penalty, **negligence** includes any failure to make a reasonable attempt to comply with the provisions of the tax law. The penalty also applies to any disregard (whether careless, reckless, or intentional) of rules and Regulations.[31] The penalty can be avoided upon a showing of reasonable cause and that the taxpayer acted in good faith.[32] The negligence penalty applies to *all* taxes, except when fraud is involved.

A negligence penalty may be assessed when the taxpayer fails to report gross income, overstates deductions, or fails to keep adequate records. When the taxpayer takes a nonnegligent position on the return that is contrary to a published pronouncement of the IRS, the penalty is waived if the taxpayer has a reasonable basis for the interpretation and has disclosed the disputed position on Form 8275.

Substantial Understatements of Tax Liability. The understatement penalty is designed to strike at middle- and high-income taxpayers who are tempted to play the so-called *audit lottery*.[33] Some taxpayers take questionable and undisclosed positions on their tax returns in the hope that the return will not be selected for audit. Disclosing the positions would have called attention to the return and increased the probability of audit.

A *substantial understatement of a tax liability* transpires when the understatement exceeds the larger of 10 percent of the tax due or $5,000 ($10,000 for a C corporation).

[23] *Estate of Norma S. Bradley*, 33 TCM 70, T.C.Memo. 1974–17.

[24] *U.S. v. Boyle*, 85–1 USTC ¶13,602, 55 AFTR2d 85–1535, 105 S.Ct. 687 (USSC, 1985).

[25] *Beck Chemical Equipment Co.*, 27 T.C. 840 (1957).

[26] *Jacob Gassman*, 26 TCM 213, T.C.Memo. 1967–42 and *Babetta Schmidt*, 28 T.C. 367 (1957). Compare *Estate of Kirchner*, 46 B.T.A. 578 (1942).

[27] *Electric and Neon, Inc.*, 56 T.C. 1324 (1971).

[28] *Stevens Brothers Foundation, Inc.*, 39 T.C. 93 (1965).

[29] § 6662.

[30] Reg. § 1.6662–3(b)(3). Most tax professionals measure this standard as a one-fourth probability of prevailing in court.

[31] § 6662(c).

[32] § 6664(c)(1).

[33] § 6662(b)(2).

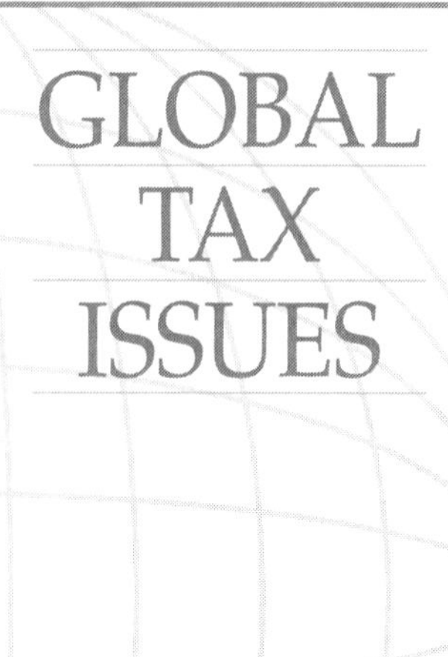

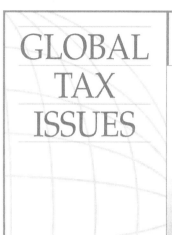

ADVANCE PRICING AGREEMENTS REDUCE INTERNATIONAL UNCERTAINTY

Two of the more severe accuracy-related penalties involve the transfer pricing issues surrounding the IRS's application of § 482. Transfer pricing issues are particularly difficult—and important—in an international context because multiple taxing authorities are involved. Consequently, taxpayers have begun to negotiate international transfer pricing agreements in advance with the IRS and other countries. Obtaining one of these *advance pricing agreements (APAs)* can require a substantial amount of work from the taxpayer, but the certainty they bring is valuable.

An estimated 400 APAs have been completed with the United States. The IRS offers a simpler APA process for small businesses.

The understatement to which the penalty applies is the difference between the amount of tax required to be shown on the return and the amount of tax actually shown on the return.

The penalty is avoided under any of the following circumstances.

- The taxpayer has **substantial authority** for the treatment.
- The relevant facts affecting the treatment are adequately disclosed in the return by attaching Form 8275.
- The IRS has not borne its burden of proof as to matters of fact in resolving a tax dispute in a court proceeding. This shift of the burden of proof does not relieve the taxpayer of documentation requirements, and it is limited to taxpayers of modest means.[34] The taxpayer retains the burden of proof in all proceedings prior to a court hearing, but the burden is on the IRS where fraud or a frivolous tax return is involved.

Penalty for Overvaluation. The objective of the overvaluation penalty is to deter taxpayers from inflating values (or basis), usually for charitable contributions of property, to reduce income taxes.[35]

- The penalty is 20 percent of the additional tax that would have been paid had the correct valuation (or basis) been used.
- The penalty applies only when the valuation (or basis) used is 200 percent or more of the correct valuation (or basis). The penalty is doubled if the valuation is overstated by 400 percent or more.
- The penalty applies only to the extent that the resulting income tax underpayment exceeds $5,000 ($10,000 for C corporations).

EXAMPLE 11

Gretchen (a calendar year taxpayer) purchased a painting for $10,000. Years later, when the painting is worth $18,000 (as later determined by the IRS), Gretchen donates the painting to an art museum. Based on the appraisal of a cousin who is an amateur artist, she deducts $40,000 for the donation. Since Gretchen was in a 33% tax bracket, overstating the deduction by $22,000 results in a tax underpayment of $7,260.

Gretchen's penalty for overvaluation is $1,452 [20% × $7,260 (the underpayment that resulted from using $40,000 instead of $18,000)]. ■

[34] The shifting of the burden is not available if the taxpayer's net worth exceeds $7 million or if the taxpayer employs more than 500 persons.

[35] §§ 6662(b)(3) and (h).

The substantial valuation overstatement penalty is avoided if the taxpayer can show reasonable cause and good faith. However, when the overvaluation involves *charitable deduction property*, the taxpayer must show *two additional* facts.

- The claimed value of the property is based on a qualified appraisal made by a qualified appraiser.
- The taxpayer made a good faith investigation of the value of the contributed property.[36]

Based on these criteria, Gretchen in Example 11 would find it difficult to avoid the penalty. A cousin who is an amateur artist does not meet the definition of a qualified appraiser. Likewise, she apparently has not made a good faith investigation of the value of the contributed property.

Penalty for Undervaluation. When attempting to minimize the income tax, it is to the benefit of taxpayers to *overvalue* deductions. When attempting to minimize transfer taxes (i.e., estate and gift taxes), however, executors and donors may be inclined to *undervalue* the assets transferred. A lower valuation reduces estate and gift taxes. An accuracy-related penalty is imposed for substantial estate or gift tax valuation understatements.[37] As with other accuracy-related penalties, reasonable cause and good faith on the part of the taxpayer are a defense.

- The penalty is 20 percent of the additional transfer tax that would have been due had the correct valuation been used on Form 706 (estate and generation-skipping transfer tax return) or Form 709 (gift and generation-skipping transfer tax return).
- The penalty applies only if the value of the property claimed on the return is 50 percent or less than the amount determined to be correct. The penalty is doubled if the reported valuation was 25 percent or less than the correct determination.
- The penalty applies only to an additional transfer tax liability in excess of $5,000.

ETHICAL CONSIDERATIONS

Good Faith Valuations

When dealing with the undervaluation penalty, the tax adviser may shift from being in adversarial alliance with the taxpayer to being a mediator for the court. Good faith estimates of value, especially for family-owned businesses, can easily vary by as much as the 50 percentage points specified for the penalty. Even a gross undervaluation can occur when someone in the business other than the donor or decedent is a particularly talented entrepreneur, an effective sales representative, and/or the founder of the company; similarly, a business may be substantially undervalued when a minority equity interest is involved, or an intangible asset conveys a sizable amount of goodwill to the valuation.

Because most taxpayers are highly averse to incurring any nondeductible penalties, the client may be tempted to compromise on the business valuation "too soon" (i.e., when the return is filed), eliminating any possibility of a more favorable valuation being presented before the Appeals Division or a court. Keeping in mind all of the potential taxpayer and preparer penalties that might apply, the tax professional should stick with a good faith appraisal of the business value, no matter what its nominal amount.

How would you react if your client, a composer, wanted to deduct $100,000 for the contribution of an obscure manuscript to the Symphony Society? What if your (first) appraiser placed the value of the manuscript at $15,000? What course of action would you propose to the client concerning the deduction? Any consequent penalties?

[36] § 6664(c)(2).

[37] § 6662(b)(5).

Civil Fraud Penalty. A 75 percent civil penalty is imposed on any underpayment resulting from **fraud** by the taxpayer who has filed a return.[38] For this penalty, the burden of proof is *on the IRS* to show by a preponderance of the evidence that the taxpayer had a specific intent to evade a tax. Once the IRS initially has established that fraud has occurred, the taxpayer then bears the burden of proof to show by a preponderance of the evidence the portion of the underpayment that is not attributable to fraud.

Although the Code and Regulations do not provide any assistance in ascertaining what constitutes civil fraud, it is clear that mere negligence on the part of the taxpayer (however great) will not suffice. Fraud has been found in cases of manipulation of the books,[39] substantial omissions from income,[40] and erroneous deductions.[41]

EXAMPLE 12

Frank underpaid his income tax by $90,000. The IRS can prove that $60,000 of the underpayment was due to fraud. Frank responds by a preponderance of the evidence that $30,000 of the underpayment was not due to fraud. The civil fraud penalty is $45,000 (75% × $60,000). ■

If the underpayment of tax is partly attributable to negligence and partly attributable to fraud, the fraud penalty is applied first.

Criminal Penalties. In addition to civil fraud penalties, the Code provides numerous criminal sanctions that carry various monetary fines and/or imprisonment. The difference between civil and criminal fraud is often one of degree. A characteristic of criminal fraud is the presence of willfulness on the part of the taxpayer. Thus, § 7201, dealing with attempts to evade or defeat a tax, contains the following language.

> Any person who *willfully* attempts in any manner to evade or defeat any tax imposed by this title or the payment thereof shall, in addition to other penalties provided by law, be guilty of a felony and, upon conviction thereof, shall be fined not more than $100,000 ($500,000 in the case of a corporation), or imprisoned not more than five years, or both, together with the costs of prosecution. (Emphasis added.)

As to the burden of proof, the IRS must show that the taxpayer was guilty of willful evasion "beyond the shadow of any reasonable doubt."

Failure to Pay Estimated Taxes. A penalty is imposed for a failure to pay estimated income taxes. The penalty applies to individuals and corporations and is based on the rate of interest in effect for deficiency assessments.[42] The penalty also applies to trusts and certain estates that are required to make estimated tax payments.

The penalty is not imposed if the tax due for the year (less amounts withheld and credits) is less than $500 for corporations, $1,000 for all others. For employees, an equal amount of withholding is deemed paid on each due date.

Quarterly payments are to be made on or before the fifteenth day of the fourth month (April 15 for a calendar year taxpayer), sixth month, and ninth month of the current year, and the first month of the following year. Corporations must make the last quarterly payment by the twelfth month of the same year.

[38] § 6663. Underpayments traceable to fraudulent acts are not subject to a statute of limitations.

[39] *Dogget v. Comm.*, 60–1 USTC ¶9342, 5 AFTR2d 1034, 275 F.2d 823 (CA–4, 1960).

[40] *Harvey Brodsky*, 21 TCM 578, T.C.Memo. 1962–105.

[41] *Lash v. Comm.*, 57–2 USTC ¶9725, 51 AFTR 492, 245 F.2d 20 (CA–1, 1957).

[42] §§ 6655 (corporations) and 6654 (other taxpayers). Other computations can avoid the penalty. See §§ 6654(d)(2) and (k), 6655(e) and (i).

An individual's underpayment of estimated tax is the difference between the estimates that were paid and the least of (1) 90 percent of the current-year tax, (2) 100 percent of the prior-year tax (the tax year must have been a full 12 months and a return must have been filed), and (3) 90 percent of the tax that would be due on an annualized income computation for the period running through the end of the quarter. When the taxpayer's prior-year adjusted gross income (AGI) exceeds $150,000, the required payment percentage for the prior-year alternative typically is 110 percent.

A corporation's underpayment of estimated tax is the difference between the estimates that were paid and the least of (1) the current-year tax, (2) the prior-year tax, and (3) the tax on an annualized income computation using one of three methods of computation sanctioned by the Code. For the prior-year alternative, (1) the prior tax year must have been a full 12 months, (2) a nonzero tax amount must have been generated for that year, and (3) large corporations (taxable income of $1 million or more in any of the three immediately preceding tax years) can use the alternative only for the first installment of a year.

In computing the penalty, Form 2210 (Underpayment of Estimated Tax by Individuals) or Form 2220 (Underpayment of Estimated Tax by Corporations) is used.

False Information with Respect to Withholding. Withholding from wages is an important element of the Federal income tax system, which is based on a pay-as-you-go approach. One way employees might hope to avoid this withholding would be to falsify the information provided to the employer on Form W–4 (Employee Withholding Allowance Certificate). For example, by overstating the number of exemptions, income tax withholdings could be reduced or completely eliminated.

To encourage compliance, a civil penalty of $500 applies when a taxpayer claims withholding allowances based on false information. The criminal penalty for willfully failing to supply information or for willfully supplying false or fraudulent information in connection with wage withholding is an additional fine of up to $1,000 and/or up to one year of imprisonment.[43]

Failure to Make Deposits of Taxes and Overstatements of Deposits. When the business is not doing well or cash-flow problems develop, employers have a great temptation to "borrow" from Uncle Sam. One way this can be done is to fail to pay to the IRS the amounts that have been withheld from the wages of employees for FICA and income tax purposes. The IRS does not appreciate being denied the use of these funds and has a number of weapons at its disposal to discourage the practice.

- A penalty of up to 15 percent of any underdeposited amount, unless the employer can show that the failure is due to reasonable cause and not to willful neglect.[44]
- Various criminal penalties.[45]
- A 100 percent penalty if the employer's actions are willful.[46] The penalty is based on the amount of the tax evaded (i.e., not collected, or not accounted for or paid over). Since the penalty is assessable against the "responsible person" of the business, more than one party may be vulnerable (e.g., the president *and* treasurer of a corporation). Although the IRS may assess the penalty against several persons, it cannot collect more than the 100 percent due.

[43]§§ 6682 and 7205.
[44]§ 6656.
[45]See, for example, § 7202 (willful failure to collect or pay over a tax).
[46]§ 6672.

Where Are All the Tax Criminals?

With Enron and other accounting scandals still destabilizing the economy, the question should be asked: What are the tax implications of these infractions? Are indictments for tax fraud and other tax-related criminal activities still to come?

Without knowing the workplan of the Treasury and Justice Departments, this question may not be answerable. But trends of the last decade or so would suggest that the Federal government is not very interested in pursuing corporate tax crimes. IRS personnel have admitted that the agency pursues only 20 to 30 percent of the known tax crime cases and that about $280 billion per year escapes collection as a result. Perhaps this is not surprising in light of the fact that the number of corporate tax returns increased by 12 percent over the last decade, while the number of revenue agents fell by 25 percent.

Today investigators of tax crimes tend to concentrate on smaller, mundane cases, not the high-profile violations of the Al Capones and Spiro Agnews of the past. And the absolute number of investigations has declined as well, according to a think tank at Syracuse University. The following table shows some examples; estimates for 2003 are for about 360 criminal tax prosecutions.

	2002	1992 or 1993
Criminal tax investigations initiated	2,500	4,000
Prosecutions for tax crimes	500	1,000
Corporate civil fraud penalties assessed	159	555
Corporate negligence penalties assessed	22	2,376

IRS data confirm a 50 percent decline in initial investigations over the last decade, but the agency maintains that actual prosecutions declined during that period by only 1.6 percent. The IRS attributes the difference in numbers to a change in its organizational structure. According to the IRS, it has a renewed commitment to pursuing tax crimes, as indicated by a new training program for younger, tech-savvy investigators.

The Service also says that some of the difficulties with the data can be traced to:

- The long lead time required to put together a criminal tax indictment.
- A de-emphasis on drug-oriented cases employing IRS investigators.
- A change in the nature of tax evasion, as new devices like credit card abuse, offshore transactions, multilayered partnerships, and abusive trusts have become more prevalent.

In addition to these penalties, the actual tax due must be remitted. An employer remains liable for the amount that should have been paid, even if the withholdings have not been taken out of the wages of its employees.[47]

LO.7

Understand the rules governing the statute of limitations on assessments and on refunds.

STATUTES OF LIMITATIONS

A **statute of limitations** defines the period of time during which one party may pursue against another party a cause of action or other suit allowed under the governing law. Failure to satisfy any requirement provides the other party with

[47] § 3403.

an absolute defense should the statute be invoked. Inequity would result if no limits were placed on such suits. Permitting an extended period of time to elapse between the initiation of a claim and its pursuit could place the defense at a serious disadvantage. Witnesses may have died or disappeared; records or other evidence may have been discarded or destroyed.

Assessment and the Statute of Limitations. In general, any tax that is imposed must be assessed within three years of the filing of the return (or, if later, the due date of the return).[48] Some exceptions to this three-year limitation exist.

- If no return is filed or a fraudulent return is filed, assessments can be made at any time. There is, in effect, no statute of limitations in these cases.
- If a taxpayer omits an amount of gross income in excess of 25 percent of the gross income stated on the return, the statute of limitations is increased to six years. The courts have interpreted this rule as including only items affecting income and not the omission of items affecting cost of sales.[49] In addition, gross income includes capital gains in the *gross* income amount (not reduced by capital losses).

EXAMPLE 13

During 2000, Jerry had the following income transactions (all of which were duly reported on his timely filed return).

Gross receipts		$ 480,000
Less: Cost of sales		(400,000)
Net business income		$ 80,000
Capital gains and losses		
Capital gain	$ 36,000	
Capital loss	(12,000)	24,000
Total income		$ 104,000

Jerry retains your services in 2005 as a tax consultant. It seems that he inadvertently omitted some income on his 2000 return and he wishes to know if he is "safe" under the statute of limitations. The six-year statute of limitations would apply, putting Jerry in a vulnerable position, only if he omitted more than $129,000 on his 2000 return [($480,000 + $36,000) × 25%]. ■

- The statute of limitations may be extended by mutual consent of the IRS and the taxpayer. This extension covers a definite period and is made by signing Form 872 (Consent to Extend the Time to Assess Tax). The extension is frequently requested by the IRS when the lapse of the statutory period is imminent and the audit has not been completed. This practice is often applied to audits of corporate taxpayers and explains why many corporations have more than three "open years."

Special rules relating to assessment are applicable in the following situations.

- Taxpayers (e.g., corporations, estates) may request a prompt assessment of the tax.
- The assessment period for capital loss and net operating loss carrybacks generally relates to the determination of tax in the year of the loss rather than in the carryback years.

[48]§§ 6501(a) and (b)(1).

[49]*The Colony, Inc. v. Comm.*, 58–2 USTC ¶9593, 1 AFTR2d 1894, 78 S.Ct. 1033 (USSC, 1958).

If the IRS issues a statutory notice of deficiency to the taxpayer, who then files a Tax Court petition, the statute is suspended on both the deficiency assessment and the period of collection until 60 days after the decision of the Tax Court becomes final. The statute is also suspended when the taxpayer is "financially disabled"; that is, the taxpayer has been rendered unable to manage his or her financial affairs by a physical or mental impairment that is likely to last for a year or more or to cause the taxpayer's death. The statute continues to run if another party is authorized to act for the taxpayer in financial matters.[50]

Refund Claims and the Statute of Limitations. To receive a tax refund, the taxpayer is required to file a valid refund claim. The official form for filing a claim is Form 1040X for individuals and Form 1120X for corporations. If the refund claim does not meet certain procedural requirements, the IRS may reject the claim with no consideration of its merit.

- A separate claim must be filed for each taxable period.
- The grounds for the claim must be stated in sufficient detail.
- The statement of facts must be sufficient to permit the IRS to evaluate the merits of the claim.

The refund claim must be filed within three years of the filing of the tax return or within two years following the payment of the tax if this period expires on a later date.[51]

EXAMPLE 14

On March 11, 2004, Louise filed her 2003 income tax return reflecting a tax of $10,500. On July 11, 2005, she filed an amended 2003 return showing an additional $3,000 of tax that was then paid. On May 19, 2007, she filed a claim for refund of $4,500.

Assuming Louise is correct in claiming a refund, how much tax can she recover? The answer is only $3,000. Because the claim was not filed within the three-year period, Louise is limited to the amount she actually paid during the last two years. ■

Special rules are available for claims relating to bad debts and worthless securities. A seven-year period of limitations applies in lieu of the normal three-year rule.[52] The extended period is provided in recognition of the inherent difficulty of identifying the exact year in which a bad debt or security becomes worthless.

LO.8

Summarize the legal and ethical guidelines that apply to those engaged in tax practice.

Tax Practice

THE TAX PRACTITIONER

Definition. Who is a tax practitioner? What service does the practitioner perform? To begin defining the term *tax practitioner*, one should consider whether the individual is qualified to practice before the IRS. Generally, practice before the IRS is limited to CPAs, attorneys, and persons who have been enrolled to practice before the IRS [called **enrolled agents (EAs)**]. In most cases, EAs are admitted to practice only if they pass an examination administered by the IRS. CPAs and

[50] "Equitable tolling" or suspension of the statute of limitations has been allowed by the courts when attributable to a taxpayer disability or IRS misconduct. See *Brockamp v. Comm.*, 97–1 USTC ¶50,216, 79 AFTR2d 97–986, 117 S.Ct. 849 (USSC, 1997). §§ 6501(c)(4) and 6511(h).

[51] §§ 6511(a) and 6513(a).

[52] § 6511(d)(1).

attorneys are not required to take this examination and are automatically admitted to practice if they are in good standing with the appropriate licensing board regulating their profession.

Persons other than CPAs, attorneys, and EAs may be allowed to practice before the IRS in limited situations. Circular 230 (entitled "Rules Governing the Practice of Attorneys and Agents Before the Internal Revenue Service") issued by the Treasury Department permits certain notable exceptions.

- A taxpayer may always represent himself or herself. A person may also represent a member of the immediate family if no compensation is received for such services.
- Regular full-time employees may represent their employers.
- Corporations may be represented by any of their bona fide officers.
- Partnerships may be represented by any of the partners.
- Trusts, receiverships, guardianships, or estates may be represented by their trustees, receivers, guardians, or administrators or executors.
- A taxpayer may be represented by whoever prepared the return for the year in question. However, such representation cannot proceed beyond the agent level.

EXAMPLE 15

Joel is currently undergoing audit by the IRS for tax years 2003 and 2004. He prepared the 2003 return but paid AddCo, a bookkeeping service, to prepare the 2004 return. AddCo may represent Joel only in matters concerning 2004. However, even for 2004, AddCo would be unable to represent Joel at an Appeals Division proceeding. Joel could represent himself, or he could retain a CPA, attorney, or EA to represent him in matters concerning both years under examination. ■

Rules Governing Tax Practice. Circular 230 further prescribes the rules governing practice before the IRS. The following are some of the most important rules imposed on CPAs, attorneys, EAs, and all others who prepare tax returns for compensation.

- A prohibition against taking a position on a tax return unless there is a *realistic possibility* of the position being sustained on its merits. Generally, the realistic possibility standard is met when a person knowledgeable in the tax law would conclude that the position has at least a one-in-three probability of prevailing in court.
- A prohibition against taking frivolous tax return positions.
- A requirement that nonfrivolous tax return positions that fail the realistic possibility standard be disclosed in the return (i.e., using Form 8275).
- A requirement to inform clients of both penalties likely to apply to return positions and ways such penalties can be avoided.
- A requirement to make known to a client any error or omission the client may have made on any return or other document submitted to the IRS.
- A duty to submit, in a timely fashion, records or information lawfully requested by the IRS.
- An obligation to exercise due diligence in preparing and filing tax returns accurately.
- A restriction against unreasonably delaying the prompt disposition of any matter before the IRS.
- A restriction against charging the client a contingent fee for preparing an original return, although such a fee can be charged when the tax professional deals with an audited or amended return.
- A restriction against charging the client "an unconscionable fee" for representation before the IRS.
- A restriction against representing clients with conflicting interests.

Anyone can prepare a tax return or render tax advice, regardless of his or her educational background or level of competence. Likewise, nothing prevents the "unlicensed" tax practitioner from advertising his or her specialty, directly soliciting clients, or otherwise violating any of the standards of conduct controlling CPAs, attorneys, and EAs. Nevertheless, some restraints do govern all parties engaged in rendering tax advice or preparing tax returns for the general public.

- A person who holds himself or herself out to the general public as possessing tax expertise could be liable to the client if services are performed in a negligent manner. At a minimum, the practitioner is liable for any interest and penalties the client incurs because of the practitioner's failure to exercise due care.
- If a practitioner agrees to perform a service (e.g., prepare a tax return) and subsequently fails to do so, the aggrieved party may be in a position to obtain damages for breach of contract.
- The IRS requires any person who prepares tax returns for a fee to sign as preparer of the return.[53] Failure to comply with this requirement could result in penalty assessment against the preparer.
- The Code prescribes various penalties for the deliberate filing of false or fraudulent returns. These penalties apply to a tax practitioner who either was aware of the situation or actually perpetrated the false filing or the fraud.[54]
- Penalties are prescribed for tax practitioners who disclose to third parties information they have received from clients in connection with the preparation of tax returns or the rendering of tax advice.[55]

EXAMPLE 16

Sarah operates a tax return preparation service. Her brother-in-law, Butch, has just taken a job as a life insurance salesman. To help Butch find contacts, Sarah furnishes him with a list of the names and addresses of all of her clients who report AGI of $50,000 or more. Sarah is subject to penalties. ■

- All nonattorney tax practitioners should avoid becoming engaged in activities that constitute the unauthorized practice of law. If they engage in this practice (e.g., by drafting legal documents for a third party), action could be instituted against them in the appropriate state court by the local or state bar association. What actions constitute the unauthorized practice of law is largely undefined, though, and such charges are filed only rarely today.

Preparer Penalties. The Code also provides for penalties to discourage improper actions by tax practitioners.

1. A $250 penalty for understatements due to taking unrealistic positions.[56] Unless the position is adequately disclosed on the tax return, the penalty is imposed if two conditions are satisfied.
   - Any part of any understatement of tax liability on any return or claim for refund is due to a position that did not have a realistic possibility of being sustained on its merits.
   - Any person who was an income tax return preparer for that return or claim knew (or should have known) of this position.

[53] Reg. § 1.6065–1(b)(1). Rev.Rul. 84–3, 1984–1 C.B. 264, contains a series of examples illustrating when a person is deemed to be a preparer of the return.

[54] § 7206.

[55] § 7216.

[56] § 6694(a).

The penalty can be avoided by showing reasonable cause and by showing that the preparer acted in good faith.

2. A $1,000 penalty for willful and reckless conduct.[57] The penalty applies if any part of the understatement of a taxpayer's liability on a return or claim for refund is due to:

   - The preparer's willful attempt to understate the taxpayer's tax liability in any manner.
   - Any reckless or intentional disregard of IRS rules or Regulations by the preparer.

   Adequate disclosure can avoid the penalty. If both this penalty and the unrealistic position penalty (see item 1 above) apply to the same return, the total penalty cannot exceed $1,000.

3. A $1,000 ($10,000 for corporations) penalty per return or document is imposed against persons who aid in the preparation of returns or other documents that they know (or have reason to believe) would result in an understatement of the tax liability of another person.[58] Clerical assistance in the preparation process does not incur the penalty.

   If this penalty applies, neither the unrealistic position penalty (item 1) nor the willful and reckless conduct penalty (item 2) is assessed.

4. A $50 penalty is assessed against the preparer for failure to sign a return or furnish the preparer's identifying number.[59]
5. A $50 penalty is assessed if the preparer fails to furnish a copy of the return or claim for refund to the taxpayer.
6. A $500 penalty may be assessed if a preparer endorses or otherwise negotiates a check for refund of tax issued to the taxpayer.

Privileged Communications. Communications between an attorney and client have long been protected from disclosure to other parties (such as the IRS and the courts). A similar privilege of confidentiality extends to tax advice between a taxpayer and tax practitioner, as that term is used above. The privilege is not available for matters involving criminal charges or questions brought by other agencies, such as the Securities and Exchange Commission.[60] Nor is it allowed in matters involving promoting or participating in tax shelters.

A taxpayer will likely want to protect documents such as the tax adviser's research memo detailing the strengths and weaknesses of a tax return position or a conversation about an appeals strategy. The confidentiality privilege should be interpreted in the following manner.

- The privilege is often available when an attorney or CPA completes a tax return for the taxpayer. But some courts have restricted the attorney's privilege in this context on the ground that the tax professional is conducting accounting work, not offering legal advice. Others assert that the confidentiality privilege is waived when the taxpayer discloses financial data on the tax return. To the contrary, if the tax professional is providing traditional legal advice to help the client decide what to disclose on a tax return, the privilege should be available.
- The privilege for CPAs applies only to tax advice. Attorneys can still exercise the privilege concerning advice rendered as a business consultant, estate/financial planner, and so on.

[57] § 6694(b).
[58] § 6701.
[59] § 6695.
[60] § 7525(a)(1).

- About a third of the states offer a similar confidentiality privilege for CPAs, but outside the Federal tax appeals process, protection is not yet the norm.
- The privilege is not available for tax accrual workpapers prepared as part of an independent financial audit.

Thus, the CPA needs to exercise care to ensure that the privilege of confidentiality will apply to his or her tax work. Taking the following steps can help.

- Segregate the time spent and documents produced in rendering services for tax compliance from the time and documents devoted to tax advice. Doing this will protect the privilege from being waived as to the tax advice.
- Explain the extent of the privilege to the client; specify what will and will not be protected from the IRS in a dispute.
- Do not inadvertently waive the privilege, say, by telling "too much" to the IRS or to a third party who is not protected by the privilege.
- Indemnify the CPA for the time spent protecting and enforcing the privilege once it is challenged.

ETHICAL CONSIDERATIONS

Where Does My Cost Saving Go?

As is the case in many other U.S. industries, tax return preparers have been outsourcing some of their operations to lower-cost locations overseas. By some estimates, almost 150,000 state and Federal tax returns are completed in India alone, and all such estimates are probably understated because of a lack of disclosure by tax practitioners.

Circular 230 does not prohibit outsourcing, and the IRS does not even require a disclosure by the tax preparer when it occurs. Tax and consulting firms defend the practice as a cost-saving measure and contend that the confidentiality of taxpayer data is not compromised.

Proposed AICPA ethics rules (applying both to tax return preparation and other work) will require:

- Notice to the taxpayer before any data are shared with a third-party service provider.
- Acceptance by the practitioner of full responsibility for the third party's work (i.e., as to quality and security).

Should any cost saving that outsourcing provides be passed on to the client in the form of lower fees? Do you expect this will occur?

AICPA STATEMENTS ON STANDARDS FOR TAX SERVICES

Tax practitioners who are CPAs, attorneys, or EAs must abide by the codes or canons of professional ethics applicable to their respective professions. The various codes and canons have much in common with and parallel the standards of conduct set forth in Circular 230.[61]

The AICPA has issued a series of Statements on Standards for Tax Services (SSTSs). The Statements are enforceable standards of professional practice for AICPA members working in state or Federal tax practice. The SSTSs comprise part of the AICPA's Code of Professional Conduct. Together with the provisions of Circular 230 and the penalty provisions of the Code, the SSTSs make up a set of guidelines for the conduct of the tax practitioner who is also a CPA. Other sources

[61] For an additional discussion of tax ethics, see Raabe, Whittenburg, and Sanders, *West's Federal Tax Research*, 7th ed. (Thomson/South-Western, 2006), Chapters 1 and 13.

of descriptions of professional ethics are issued by state bar associations and CPA societies, the American Bar Association, and the associations of enrolled agents.

Key provisions of some of the SSTSs are presented below.

Statement No. 1: Tax Return Positions. Under certain circumstances, a CPA may take a position that is contrary to that taken by the IRS. To do so, however, the CPA must have a good faith belief that the position, if challenged, has a realistic possibility of being sustained administratively or judicially on its merits.

The client should be fully advised of the risks involved and should know that certain penalties may result if the position taken by the CPA is not successful. The client should also be informed that disclosure on the return may avoid some or all of these penalties.

In no case, though, should the CPA exploit the audit lottery; that is, to take a questionable position based on the probabilities that the client's return will not be chosen by the IRS for audit. Furthermore, the CPA should not "load" the return with questionable items in the hope that they might aid the client in a later settlement negotiation with the IRS.

Statement No. 2: Questions on Returns. A CPA should make a reasonable effort to obtain from the client, and provide to the IRS, appropriate answers to all questions on a tax return before signing as preparer. Reasonable grounds may exist for omitting an answer.

- The information is not readily available, and the answer is not significant in computing the tax.
- The meaning of the question as it applies to a particular situation is genuinely uncertain.
- The answer to the question is voluminous.

The fact that an answer to a question could prove disadvantageous to the client does not justify omitting the answer.

Statement No. 3: Procedural Aspects of Preparing Returns. In preparing a return, a CPA may in good faith rely without verification on information furnished by the client or by third parties. However, the CPA should make reasonable inquiries if the information appears to be incorrect, incomplete, or inconsistent. In this regard, the CPA should refer to the client's prior returns whenever appropriate.

EXAMPLE 17

A CPA can normally take a client's word for the validity of dependency exemptions. But suppose a recently divorced client wants to claim his three children as dependents (when he does not have custody). A CPA must act in accordance with § 152(e)(2) in preparing the return. Claiming the dependency exemption will require evidence of a waiver by the custodial parent. Without this waiver, the CPA should not claim the dependency exemptions on the client's tax return. ■

EXAMPLE 18

While preparing a client's income tax return for 2005, a CPA reviews her income tax return for 2004. In comparing the dividend income reported on the 2004 Schedule B with that received in 2005, the CPA notes a significant decrease. Further investigation reveals the variation is due to a stock sale in 2005 that, until now, was unknown to the CPA. Thus, the review of the 2004 return has unearthed a transaction that should be reported on the 2005 return. ■

If the Code or Regulations require certain types of substantiation (as is the case with travel and entertainment expenditures), the CPA must advise the client of these rules. Further, inquiry must be made to ascertain whether the client has complied with the substantiation requirements.

Statement No. 4: Estimates. A CPA may prepare a tax return using estimates received from a taxpayer if it is impracticable to obtain exact data. The estimates must be reasonable under the facts and circumstances known to the CPA. When estimates are used, they should be presented in such a manner as to avoid implying that greater accuracy exists.

Statement No. 5: Recognition of Administrative Proceeding or Court Decisions. As facts may vary from year to year, so may the position taken by a CPA. In these types of situations, the CPA is not bound by an administrative or judicial proceeding involving a prior year.

EXAMPLE 19

Upon audit of Ramon Corporation's income tax return for 2003, the IRS disallowed $180,000 of the $400,000 salary paid to its president and sole shareholder on the grounds that it was unreasonable [§ 162(a)(1)]. A CPA has been engaged to prepare Ramon's income tax return for 2005. Again the corporation paid its president a salary of $400,000 and chose to deduct this amount. Because the CPA is not bound for 2005 by what the IRS deemed reasonable for 2003, the full $400,000 can be claimed as a salary deduction. ■

Other problems that require a CPA's use of judgment include reclassification of corporate debt as equity (thin capitalization) and corporate accumulations beyond the reasonable needs of the business (for the penalty tax under § 531).

Statement No. 6: Knowledge of Error. A CPA should promptly advise a client upon learning of an error on a previously filed return or upon learning of a client's failure to file a required return. The advice can be oral or written and should include a recommendation of the corrective measures, if any, to be taken. The error or other omission should not be disclosed to the IRS without the client's consent.

If the past error is material and is not corrected by the client, the CPA may be unable to prepare the current year's tax return. This situation might occur if the error has a carryover effect that prevents the CPA from determining the correct tax liability for the current year.

EXAMPLE 20

In preparing a client's 2006 income tax return, a CPA discovers that final inventory for 2005 was materially understated. First, the CPA should advise the client to file an amended return for 2005 reflecting the correct amount in final inventory. Second, if the client refuses to make this adjustment, the CPA should consider whether the error will preclude preparation of a substantially correct return for 2006. Because this will probably be the case (the final inventory for 2005 becomes the beginning inventory for 2006), the CPA should withdraw from the engagement.

If the client corrects the error, the CPA may proceed with the preparation of the tax return for 2006. However, the CPA must ensure that the error is not repeated. ■

Statement No. 8: Advice to Clients. In providing tax advice to a client, the CPA must use judgment to ensure that the advice reflects professional competence and appropriately serves the client's needs. No standard format or guidelines can be established to cover all situations and circumstances involving written or oral advice by the CPA.

The CPA may communicate with the client when subsequent developments affect previous advice on significant matters. However, the CPA cannot be expected to assume responsibility for initiating the communication, unless he or she is assisting a client in implementing procedures or plans associated with the advice. The CPA may undertake this obligation by specific agreement with the client.

CONCEPT SUMMARY 26–1

Tax Administration and Practice

1. The Internal Revenue Service (IRS) enforces the tax laws of the United States.
2. The IRS issues various pronouncements, communicating its position on certain tax issues. These pronouncements promote the uniform enforcement of the tax law among taxpayers and among the internal divisions of the IRS. Taxpayers should seek such rulings and memoranda when the nature or magnitude of a pending transaction requires a high degree of certainty in the planning process.
3. IRS audits can take several forms. Taxpayers are selected for audit based on the probable net dollar return to the Treasury from the process. Offers in compromise and closing agreements can be a useful means of completing an audit without resorting to litigation.
4. Certain IRS personnel are empowered to consider the hazards of litigation in developing a settlement with the taxpayer during the audit process.
5. The IRS pays interest to taxpayers on overpaid taxes, starting essentially 45 days after the due date of the return, in amounts tied to the Federal short-term rate. Interest paid to the IRS on underpayments is similarly based on the Federal rate, starting essentially on the due date of the return. Interest for both purposes is compounded daily.
6. The Treasury assesses penalties when the taxpayer fails to file a required tax return or pay a tax. Penalties also are assessed when an inaccurate return is filed due to negligence or other disregard of IRS rules. Tax preparers are subject to penalties for assisting a taxpayer in filing an inaccurate return, failing to follow IRS rules in an appropriate manner, or mishandling taxpayer data or funds.
7. Statutes of limitations place outer boundaries on the timing and amounts of proposed amendments to completed tax returns that can be made by the taxpayer or the IRS.
8. Tax practitioners must operate under constraints imposed on them by codes of ethics of pertinent professional societies and by Treasury Circular 230. These rules also define the parties who can represent others in an IRS proceeding.
9. A limited privilege of confidentiality exists between the taxpayer and tax preparer.

Tax Planning Considerations

STRATEGIES IN SEEKING AN ADMINISTRATIVE RULING

Determination Letters. In many instances, the request for an advance ruling or a determination letter from the IRS is a necessary or desirable planning strategy. The receipt of a favorable ruling or determination reduces the risk associated with a transaction when the tax results are in doubt. For example, the initiation or amendment of a qualified pension or profit sharing plan should be accompanied by a determination letter. Otherwise, on subsequent IRS review, the plan may not qualify, and the tax deductibility of contributions to the plan will be disallowed. In some situations, the potential tax effects of a transaction are so numerous and of such consequence that proceeding without a ruling is unwise.

Letter Rulings. In some cases, it may not be necessary or desirable to request an advance ruling. For example, it is generally not desirable to request a ruling if the tax results are doubtful and the company is committed to complete the transaction in any event. If a ruling is requested and negotiations with the IRS indicate that an adverse determination will be forthcoming, it is usually possible to have the ruling request withdrawn. However, the National Office of the IRS may forward its findings, along with a copy of the ruling request, to a Director. In determining the advisability of a ruling request, the taxpayer should consider the potential exposure of other items in the tax returns of all "open years."

A ruling request may delay the consummation of a transaction if the issues are novel or complex. Frequently, a ruling can be processed within six months, although in some instances a delay of a year or more may be encountered.

Technical Advice Memoranda. A taxpayer in the process of contesting a proposed deficiency with the Appeals Division should consider requesting a technical advice memorandum from the National Office of the IRS. If such advice is favorable to the taxpayer, it is binding on the Appeals Division. The request may be particularly appropriate when the practitioner feels that the agent or Appeals Division has been too literal in interpreting an IRS ruling.

CONSIDERATIONS IN HANDLING AN IRS AUDIT

As a general rule, a taxpayer should attempt to settle disputes at the earliest possible stage of the administrative appeal process. New issues may be raised by IRS personnel if the case goes beyond the agent level. It is usually possible to limit the scope of the examination by furnishing pertinent information requested by the agent. Extraneous information or thoughtless comments may result in the opening of new issues and should be avoided. Agents usually appreciate prompt and efficient responses to inquiries, since their performance may in part be judged by their ability to close or settle assigned cases.

To the extent possible, it is advisable to conduct the investigation of field audits in the practitioner's office, rather than the client's office. This procedure permits greater control over the audit investigation and facilitates the agent's review and prompt closure of the case.

Many practitioners feel that it is generally not advisable to have clients present at the scheduled conferences with the agent, since the client may give emotional or gratuitous comments that impair prompt settlement. If the client is not present, however, he or she should be advised of the status of negotiations. The client makes the final decision on any proposed settlement.

ETHICAL CONSIDERATIONS

Should the Client Attend an Audit?

Whether the client should be present during an audit is a matter of some debate. Certainly, the client's absence tends to slow down the negotiating process because the taxpayer must make all final decisions on settlement terms and is the best source of information for open questions of fact. Nevertheless, most practitioners discourage their clients from attending audits or conferences with the Appeals Division involving an income tax dispute. Ignorance of the law and of the conventions of the audit process can make the taxpayer a "loose cannon" that can do more harm than good if unchecked. All too often, they say, a client will "say too much" in the presence of a government official.

In reality, though, by discouraging clients from attending the audit, practitioners may be interfering with the IRS's function of gathering evidence, depending on what precisely the taxpayer is being prevented from saying. To many practitioners, a "wrong" answer is one that increases taxes, not one that misrepresents the truth. A popular saying among tax advisers is "Don't tell me more than I want to know." Although this philosophy is supportable under various professional codes of conduct, it is hardly defensible in the larger scheme of things.

In your opinion, under what circumstances should the client attend such a session? To what degree should the tax professional "coach" the client as to how to behave in that setting? Or do a taxpayer's rights include the right to increase his or her own tax liability?

Preparing for the Audit. The tax professional must prepare thoroughly for the audit or Appeals proceeding. Practitioners often cite the following steps as critical to such preparations. Carrying out a level of due diligence in preparing for the proceeding is part of the tax professional's responsibility in representing the client.

- Make certain that both sides agree on the issues to be resolved in the audit. The goal here is to limit the agent's list of open issues.
- Identify all of the facts underlying the issues in dispute, including those favorable to the IRS. Gather evidence to support the taxpayer's position, and evaluate the evidence supporting the other side.
- Research current tax law authorities that bear on the facts and open issues. Remember that the IRS agent is bound only by Supreme Court cases and IRS pronouncements. Determine the degree of discretion that the IRS is likely to have in disposing of the case.
- Prepare a list of points supporting and contradicting the taxpayer's case. Include both minor points bearing little weight and core principles. Short research memos will also be useful in the discussion with the agent. Points favoring the taxpayer should be mentioned during the discussion and "entered into the record."
- Prepare tax and interest computations showing the effects of points that are in dispute, so that the consequences of closing or compromising an issue can be readily determined.
- Determine a "litigation point" (i.e., at which the taxpayer will withdraw from further audit negotiation and pursue the case in the courts). This position should be based on the dollars of tax, interest, and penalty involved, the chances of prevailing in various trial-level courts, and other strategies discussed with the taxpayer. One must have an "end game" strategy for the audit, and thorough tax research is critical in developing that position in this context.

Offers in Compromise. By encouraging the use of offers in compromise to a greater degree than ever before, the IRS brings more nonfilers into compliance with the tax system.

Both parties to a tax dispute may find a compromise offer useful because it conclusively settles all of the issues covered by the agreement and may include a favorable payment schedule for the taxpayer. On the other hand, several attributes of an offer in compromise may work to the detriment of the taxpayer. Just as the IRS no longer can raise new issues as part of the audit proceedings against the taxpayer, he or she cannot contest or appeal any such agreement. As part of the offer process, the taxpayer must disclose all relevant finances and resources, including details he or she might not want the government to know. Furthermore, both parties are bound to the filing positions established by the compromise for five tax years, a level of inflexibility that may work against a taxpayer whose circumstances change over time.

Documentation Issues. The tax practitioner's workpapers should include all research memoranda, and a list of resolved and unresolved issues should be continually updated during the course of the IRS audit. Occasionally, agents request access to excessive amounts of accounting data in order to engage in a so-called fishing expedition. Providing blanket access to workpapers should be avoided. Workpapers should be carefully reviewed to minimize opportunities for the agent to raise new issues not otherwise apparent. It is generally advisable to provide the agent with copies of specific workpapers upon request.

In unusual situations, a Special Agent may appear to gather evidence in the investigation of possible criminal fraud. When this occurs, the taxpayer should be advised to seek legal counsel to determine the extent of his or her cooperation in providing information to the agent. Further, it is frequently desirable for the tax adviser to consult personal legal counsel in such situations. If the taxpayer receives a Revenue Agent's Report (RAR), it generally indicates that the IRS has decided not to initiate criminal proceedings. The IRS usually does not take any action upon a tax deficiency until the criminal matter has been resolved.

PENALTIES

Penalties are imposed upon a taxpayer's failure to file a return or pay a tax when due. These penalties can be avoided if the failure is due to reasonable cause and not to willful neglect. Reasonable cause, however, has not been liberally interpreted by the courts and should not be relied upon in the routine situation.[62] A safer way to avoid the failure to file penalty is to obtain an extension of time for filing the return from the IRS.

The penalty for failure to pay estimated taxes can become quite severe. Often trapped by the provision are employed taxpayers with outside income. They may forget about their outside income and assume the amount withheld from wages and salaries is adequate to cover their liability. Not only does April 15 provide a real shock (in terms of the additional tax owed) for these persons, but a penalty situation may have evolved. One way for an employee to mitigate this problem (presuming the employer is willing to cooperate) is described in the following example.

EXAMPLE 21

Patty, a calendar year taxpayer, is employed by Finn Corporation and earns (after withholding) a monthly salary of $4,000 payable at the end of each month. Patty also receives income from outside sources (interest, dividends, and consulting fees). After some quick calculations in early October, Patty determines that she has underestimated her tax liability by $7,500 and will be subject to the penalty for the first two quarters of the year and part of the third quarter. Patty, therefore, completes a new Form W–4 in which she arbitrarily raises her income tax withholding by $2,500 a month. Finn accepts the Form W–4, and as a result, an extra $7,500 is paid to the IRS on Patty's account for the payroll period from October through December.

Patty avoids penalties for the underpayment for the first three quarters because withholding of taxes is allocated pro rata over the year involved. Thus, a portion of the additional $7,500 withheld in October–December is assigned to the January 1–April 15 period, the April 16–June 15 period, etc. Had Patty merely paid the IRS an additional $7,500 in October, the penalty would still have been assessed for the earlier quarters. ■

KEY TERMS

Accuracy-related penalty, 26–15
Closing agreement, 26–12
Determination letter, 26–5
Enrolled agent (EA), 26–22
Fraud, 26–18
Letter ruling, 26–4
Negligence, 26–15
Ninety-day letter, 26–10
Offer in compromise, 26–11
Reasonable cause, 26–14
Revenue Agent's Report (RAR), 26–9
Statute of limitations, 26–20
Substantial authority, 26–16
Technical advice memorandum (TAM), 26–5
Thirty-day letter, 26–10

[62] *Dustin v. Comm.*, 72–2 USTC ¶9610, 30 AFTR2d 72–5313, 467 F.2d 47 (CA–9, 1972), *aff'g* 53 T.C. 491 (1969).

PROBLEM MATERIALS

Discussion Questions

1. Carol takes some very aggressive positions on her tax return. She maintains, "With the downsizing of the government, my chances of getting caught are virtually zero." Is Carol's approach correct?

Issue ID

2. Should the IRS audit more or fewer returns every year? What issues would you consider in this regard if you were a politician? A wealthy individual?

3. What are the most important activities that the IRS currently is carrying out in its data collection and audit efforts?

Communications

4. Your tax supervisor has informed you that the firm has received an unfavorable answer to a ruling request. In a memo to the supervisor, describe the appropriate weight that she should assign to the holding in the ruling.

5. Summarize the rules as to the burden of proof when the IRS assesses additional tax, penalties, and interest.

6. Describe the process that the IRS uses to collect the tax that is found to be due after an audit is completed. Assume that the IRS findings are not appealed but that the taxpayer does not pay the amount due as determined by the audit.

7. Sarah tells you, "I was worried about getting audited on the tax return I filed two months ago, but I received my refund check today, so the IRS must agree with my figures." Comment.

8. Describe the three types of IRS audits. Give an example of an issue that each type of audit might address, and indicate how frequently such audits are conducted by the IRS.

9. Many tax professionals encourage their clients to pursue tax disputes through the judicial system. But the courts hear only several hundred tax cases in a typical year. Identify some advantages and disadvantages of settling a tax case within IRS channels (i.e., with the auditor or the Appeals Division).

10. The taxpayer has just signed a closing agreement with the IRS. Can the amount of assessed taxes be changed later? Explain.

11. On February 10, 2005, Quon, a calendar year taxpayer, files her 2004 income tax return on which she claims a $1,200 refund. If Quon receives her refund check on May 2, 2005, will it include any interest? Explain.

12. Which of the valuation penalties is likely to arise when an aggressive taxpayer reports:
    a. A charitable contribution?
    b. A bargain purchase of property by a shareholder-employee?
    c. A gift tax?

13. Describe how the valuation penalties work. What is the rate of the penalty, and on which amount is it imposed?

14. Give two examples of a taxpayer action that would trigger a civil fraud penalty.

Issue ID

15. In early November, Brad determines that his tax for the year will total $4,000. If his employer is scheduled to withhold only $2,500 in income taxes, what can Brad do to avoid any underpayment penalty?

16. Indicate whether each of the following statements is true or false.
    a. The government never pays a taxpayer interest on an overpayment of tax.
    b. The IRS can compromise on the amount of tax liability if there is doubt as to the taxpayer's ability to pay.
    c. The statute of limitations for assessing a tax never extends beyond three years from the filing of a return.
    d. A taxpayer's claim for a refund is not subject to a statute of limitations.

17. In each of the following cases, distinguish between the terms.
    a. Offer in compromise and closing agreement.
    b. Failure to file and failure to pay.
    c. Ninety-day letter and thirty-day letter.
    d. Negligence and fraud.
    e. Criminal and civil penalties.

18. When Maggie accepted employment with Martin Corporation, she completed a Form W–4 listing 14 exemptions. Since Maggie was single and had no dependents, she misrepresented her situation on the Form W–4. What penalties, if any, might the IRS impose upon Maggie?

19. Why should the taxpayer be "let off the hook" and no longer be subject to audit exposure once the applicable statute of limitations has expired? Do statutes of limitations protect the government? Other taxpayers?

20. Lorraine, a vice president of Scott Corporation, prepared and filed the corporate Form 1120 for 2003. This return is being audited by the IRS in 2005.
    a. May Lorraine represent Scott during the audit?
    b. Can Lorraine's representation continue beyond the agent level (e.g., before the Appeals Division)?

21. Give the Circular 230 position concerning each of the following practices sometimes encountered in the tax profession.
    a. Taking an aggressive pro-taxpayer position on a tax return.
    b. Informing the client as to the risk associated with a tax return position.
    c. Delaying compliance with a document request received from the IRS.
    d. Not keeping up with changes in the tax law.
    e. Charging $1,500 to complete a Form 1040-EZ.

22. List several of the penalties that can be assessed on tax return preparers, as authorized by the Code.

23. Indicate which codes, canons, and other bodies of ethical statements apply to each of the following tax practitioners.
    a. CPAs who are members of the AICPA.
    b. CPAs who are not members of the AICPA.
    c. Attorneys.
    d. Enrolled agents.
    e. Tax preparers who are not CPAs, EAs, or attorneys.

Problems

24. On March 15, 2005, Gordon paid the $10,000 balance of his Federal income tax three months late. Ignore daily compounding of interest. Determine the interest rate that applies relative to this amount, assuming that:
    a. Gordon is an individual.
    b. Gordon is a C corporation.
    c. The $10,000 is not a tax that is due but is a refund payable by the IRS to Gordon (an individual).
    d. The $10,000 is not a tax that is due but is a refund payable by the IRS to Gordon (a C corporation).

25. Rita forgot to pay her Federal income tax on time. When she actually filed (without a valid extension), she reported a balance due. Compute Rita's failure to file penalty in each of the following cases.
    a. One month late, $1,000 additional tax due.
    b. Four months late, $1,000 additional tax due.
    c. Six months late, $1,000 additional tax due.
    d. Four months late due to fraud by Rita, $5,000 additional tax due.

26. Tom filed his Federal income tax return on time but did not remit the balance due. Compute Tom's failure to pay penalty in each of the following cases. Assume the IRS has not issued a deficiency notice.
    a. Four months late, $1,000 additional tax due.
    b. Ten months late, $1,000 additional tax due.
    c. Five years late, $1,000 additional tax due.

27. Compute the failure to pay and failure to file penalties for John, who filed his 2004 income tax return on November 10, 2005, paying the $8,000 amount due. On April 1, 2005, John had received a four-month extension of time in which to file his return. He has no reasonable cause for failing to file his return by August 15 or for failing to pay the tax that was due on April 15, 2005. John's failure to comply with the tax laws was not fraudulent.

28. Rhoda, a calendar year taxpayer, files her 2004 return on December 12, 2005. She did not obtain an extension for filing her return, and the return reflects additional income tax due of $7,000.
    a. What are Rhoda's penalties for failure to file and to pay?
    b. Would your answer change if Rhoda, before the due date of the return, had retained a CPA to prepare the return and the CPA's negligence caused the delay?

29. Dana underpaid her taxes by $250,000. A portion of the underpayment was shown to be attributable to Dana's negligence ($200,000). A court found that a portion of that deficiency constituted civil fraud ($110,000). Compute the total fraud and negligence penalties incurred.

30. Olivia, a calendar year taxpayer, does not file her 2004 return until October 4, 2005. At this point, she pays the $7,000 balance due on her 2004 tax liability of $70,000. Olivia did not apply for and obtain any extension of time for filing the 2004 return. When questioned by the IRS on her delinquency, Olivia asserts: "If I was too busy to file my regular tax return, I was too busy to request an extension."
    a. Is Olivia liable for any penalties for failure to file and for failure to pay?
    b. If so, compute the penalty amounts.

31. Compute the overvaluation penalty for each of the following independent cases involving the taxpayer's reporting of the fair market value of charitable contribution property. In each case, assume a marginal income tax rate of 35%.

Taxpayer	Corrected IRS Value	Reported Valuation
a. Individual	$ 30,000	$ 50,000
b. C corporation	30,000	50,000
c. S corporation	40,000	50,000
d. Individual	150,000	250,000
e. Individual	150,000	500,000
f. C corporation	150,000	900,000

32. Compute the undervaluation penalty for each of the following independent cases involving the executor's reporting of the value of a closely held business in the decedent's gross estate. In each case, assume a marginal estate tax rate of 47%.

	Reported Value	Corrected IRS Valuation
a.	$20,000	$ 25,000
b.	80,000	150,000
c.	80,000	250,000
d.	80,000	530,000

33. Moose, a former professional athlete, now supplements his income by signing autographs at collectors' shows. Unfortunately, Moose has not been conscientious about

reporting all of this income on his tax return. Now, the IRS has charged him with additional taxes of $80,000 due to negligence in his record-keeping and $20,000 due to an intent to defraud the U.S. government of income taxes. No criminal fraud charges are brought against Moose. The District Court finds by a preponderance of the evidence that only half of the $20,000 underpayment was due to Moose's fraudulent action; the remainder was due to mere negligence. Compute the accuracy-related and civil fraud penalties in this matter.

34. Trudy's AGI last year was $170,000. Her Federal income tax came to $60,000, which she paid through a combination of withholding and estimated payments. This year, her AGI will be $270,000, with a projected tax liability of $75,000, all to be paid through estimates. Ignore the annualized income method. Compute Trudy's quarterly estimated payment schedule for this year.

35. Kold Services Corporation estimates that its 2006 taxable income will be $500,000. Thus, it is subject to a flat 34% income tax rate and incurs a $170,000 liability. For each of the following independent cases, compute Kold's minimum quarterly estimated tax payments that will avoid an underpayment penalty.
    a. For 2005, taxable income was ($200,000). Kold carried back all of this loss to prior years and exhausted the entire net operating loss in creating a zero 2005 liability.
    b. For 2005, taxable income was $400,000, and tax liability was $136,000.
    c. For 2004, taxable income was $2 million, and tax liability was $680,000. For 2005, taxable income was $400,000, and tax liability was $136,000.

Decision Making
Communications

36. The Scooter Company, owned equally by Julie (chair of the board of directors) and Jeff (company president), is in very difficult financial straits. Last month, Jeff used the $100,000 withheld from employee paychecks for Federal payroll and income taxes to pay off a creditor who threatened to cut off all supplies. To keep the company afloat, Jeff used these government funds willfully for the operations of the business, but even that effort was not enough. The company missed the next two payrolls, and today other creditors took action to shut down Scooter altogether. How much will the IRS assess in taxes and penalties in this matter, and from whom? How can you as a tax professional best offer service to Julie, Jeff, and Scooter? Address these matters in a memo for the tax research file.

37. What is the applicable statute of limitations in each of the following independent situations?
    a. No return was filed by the taxpayer.
    b. The taxpayer incurred a bad debt loss that she failed to claim.
    c. A taxpayer inadvertently omitted a large amount of gross income.
    d. Same as (c), except that the omission was deliberate.
    e. A taxpayer innocently overstated her deductions by a large amount.

38. Suzanne, a calendar year taxpayer, had the following transactions, all of which were properly reported on a timely return.

Gross receipts		$ 960,000
Less: Cost of sales		(800,000)
Gross profit		$ 160,000
Capital gain	$ 72,000	
Less: Capital loss	(24,000)	48,000
Total income		$ 208,000

    a. Presuming the absence of fraud, how much of an omission from gross income is required before the six-year statute of limitations applies?
    b. Would it matter if cost of sales had been inadvertently overstated by $100,000?
    c. How does the situation change in the context of fraud by Suzanne?

Decision Making

39. On April 2, 2004, Mark filed his 2003 income tax return, which showed a tax due of $40,000. On June 1, 2006, he filed an amended return for 2003 that showed an additional

tax of $12,000. Mark paid the additional amount. On May 18, 2007, Mark filed a claim for a refund of $18,000.

a. If Mark's claim for a refund is correct in amount, how much tax will he recover?
b. What is the period that interest runs with respect to Mark's claim for a refund?
c. How would you have advised him differently?

Communications

40. Carol owed $4,000 in Federal income tax when she filed her Form 1040 for 2004. She attached a Post-It Note to the 1040 saying, "My inventory computations on last year's return were wrong so I paid $1,000 too much in tax." Carol then included a check for $3,000 with the Form 1040 for 2004. Write a memo to the tax research file commenting on Carol's actions.

41. Rod's Federal income tax returns (Form 1040) for the indicated three years were prepared by the following persons.

Year	Preparer
2004	Rod
2005	Ann
2006	Cheryl

Ann is Rod's next-door neighbor and owns and operates a pharmacy. Cheryl is a licensed CPA and is engaged in private practice. In the event Rod is audited and all three returns are examined, who may represent him before the IRS at the agent level? Who may represent Rod before the Appeals Division?

42. Discuss which penalties, if any, might be imposed on the tax adviser in each of the following independent circumstances. In this regard, assume that the tax adviser:
a. Suggested to the client various means by which to acquire excludible income.
b. Suggested to the client various means by which to conceal cash receipts from gross income.
c. Suggested to the client means by which to improve her cash flow by delaying for six months or more the deposit of the employees' share of Federal employment taxes.
d. Failed, because of pressing time conflicts, to conduct the usual review of the client's tax return. The IRS later discovered that the return included fraudulent data.
e. Failed, because of pressing time conflicts, to conduct the usual review of the client's tax return. The IRS later discovered a mathematical error in the computation of the personal exemption.

43. Compute the preparer penalty that the IRS could assess on Gerry in each of the following independent cases.
a. On March 21, the copy machine was not working, so Gerry gave original returns to her 30 clients that day without providing any duplicates for them. Copies for Gerry's files and for use in preparing state tax returns had been made on March 20.
b. Because Gerry extended her vacation a few days, she missed the Annual Tax Update seminar that she usually attends. As a result, she was unaware that Congress had changed a law affecting limited partnerships. The change affected the transactions of 20 of Gerry's clients, all of whom understated their tax as a result.
c. Gerry heard that the IRS was increasing its audits of corporations that hold assets in a foreign trust. As a result, Gerry instructed the intern who prepared the initial drafts of the returns for three corporate clients to leave blank the question about such trusts. Not wanting to lose his position, the intern, a senior accounting major at State University, complied with Gerry's instructions.

Decision Making

44. You are the chair of the Ethics Committee of your state's CPA Licensing Commission. Interpret controlling AICPA authority in addressing the following assertions by your membership.
a. When a CPA has reasonable grounds for not answering an applicable question on a client's return, a brief explanation of the reason for the omission should not be provided, because it would flag the return for audit by the IRS.
b. If a CPA discovers during an IRS audit that the client has a material error on the return under examination, he should immediately withdraw from the engagement.

c. If the client tells you that she had contributions of $500 for unsubstantiated cash donations to her church, you should deduct an odd amount on her return (e.g., $499), because an even amount (i.e., $500) would indicate to the IRS that her deduction was based on an estimate.
d. If a CPA knows that the client has a material error on a prior year's return, he should not, without the client's consent, disclose the error to the IRS.
e. If a CPA's client will not correct a material error on a prior year's return, the CPA should not prepare the current year's return for the client.

Research Problems

Note: Solutions to Research Problems can be prepared by using the ***RIA Checkpoint® Student Edition*** *online research product, which is available to accompany this text. It is also possible to prepare solutions to the Research Problems by using tax research materials found in a standard tax library.*

Communications

Research Problem 1. The Bird Estate committed tax fraud when it purposely understated the value of the business created and operated by the decedent, Beverly Bird. Executor Wilma Holmes (1111 East Michigan Avenue, Charleston, WV 44333) admitted to the Tax Court that she had withheld several contracts and formulas that, had they been disclosed to the valuation experts used by the government and the estate, would have added $1 million in value to the business and over half that amount in Federal estate tax liabilities. Summary data include the following.

	Reported on Form 706	Other Amounts
Gross estate	$12 million	$1 million understatement
Deductions on original return	2 million	
Interest on estate tax deficiency, professional fees incurred during administration period		400,000

Holmes asks you for advice in computing the fraud penalty. Ignore interest amounts. She wonders whether to take the 75% civil penalty against the full $1 million understatement or against the $600,000 net amount that the taxable estate would have increased had the administrative expenses been incurred prior to the filing date of the Form 706. Write Holmes, an experienced CPA with an extensive tax practice, a letter stating your opinion.

Partial list of research aids:
§ 6663.
Estate of Emanuel Trompeter, 111 T.C. 57 (1998).

Research Problem 2. Max and Annie are roommates sharing an apartment. Although they know each other well, they have respect for each other's privacy. Thus, when Max's 2003 Form 1040 was audited by the IRS, he made no mention of the audit to Annie.

When Annie was clearing the answering machine that they shared, she heard the following message: "Max, this is Richard, the IRS auditor. My figures show that you owe the government $10,000 in taxes and another $4,500 in penalties and interest."

When Annie brought up the message during dinner conversation that night, Max was furious. How could the IRS be so careless as to broadcast this news to a stranger? Didn't he have any privacy and confidentiality rights? Max calls you to determine whether he might have a case against the IRS or Richard, the agent.

Internet Activity

Use the tax resources of the Internet to address the following question. Do not restrict your search to the World Wide Web, but include a review of newsgroups and general reference materials, practitioner sites and resources, primary sources of the tax law, chat rooms and discussion groups, and other opportunities.

Communications

Research Problem 3. The Treasury has elaborate disclosure and penalty rules for "tax shelters" that are "reportable transactions." Define these two terms in an e-mail to your instructor.

The Federal Gift and Estate Taxes

LEARNING OBJECTIVES

After completing Chapter 27, you should be able to:

LO.1

Understand the nature of the Federal gift and estate taxes.

LO.2

Work with the Federal gift tax formula.

LO.3

Work with the Federal estate tax formula.

LO.4

Explain the operation of the Federal gift tax.

LO.5

Illustrate the computation of the Federal gift tax.

LO.6

Review the components of the gross estate.

LO.7

Describe the components of the taxable estate.

LO.8

Determine the Federal estate tax liability.

LO.9

Appreciate the role of the generation-skipping transfer tax.

http://wft.swlearning.com

OUTLINE

Transfer Taxes—In General

Until now, this text has dealt primarily with the various applications of the Federal income tax. Also important in the Federal tax structure are various excise taxes that cover transfers of property. Sometimes called transaction taxes, excise taxes are based on the value of the property transferred and not on the income derived from the property. Two such taxes—the Federal gift tax and the Federal estate tax—are the central focus of this chapter.

The importance of being familiar with rules governing transfer taxes can be shown with a simple illustration.

EXAMPLE 1

After 20 years of marriage to George, Helen decides to elope with Mark, a bachelor and long-time friend. Helen and Mark travel to a country in the Caribbean where Helen obtains a divorce, and she and Mark are married. Fifteen years later in 2005, Helen dies. Her will leaves all of her property (estimated value of $3 million) to Mark. Under the unlimited marital deduction (discussed later in the chapter), Helen's estate has no tax to pay. ■

But the marital deduction applies only to transfers between husband and wife. Suppose the jurisdiction where Helen and Mark live does not recognize the validity of divorces granted by the Caribbean country involved. If this is the case, Helen and Mark are not married because Helen was never legally divorced from George. If Mark is not Helen's spouse, no marital deduction is available. Disregarding any administration expenses, Helen's estate must pay an estate tax of $695,000.

LO.1
Understand the nature of the Federal gift and estate taxes.

NATURE OF THE TAXES

Before the enactment of the Tax Reform Act of 1976, Federal law imposed a tax on the gratuitous transfer of property in one of two ways. If the transfer was during the owner's life, it was subject to the Federal gift tax. If the property passed by virtue of the death of the owner, the Federal estate tax applied. The two taxes were governed by different rules including a separate set of tax rates. As Congress felt that lifetime transfers of wealth should be encouraged, the gift tax rates were lower than the estate tax rates.

An Erratic Approach to Transfer Taxes

Congressional policy toward transfer taxes has been highly erratic.

- Before the Tax Reform Act of 1976, the lower gift tax rates favored transfers by gift.
- The Tax Reform Act of 1976 took a neutral approach. It established a new unified transfer tax that applied the same tax rates to transfers by gift and transfers by death.
- The Tax Relief Reconciliation Act of 2001, once fully implemented, obviously favors transfers by death as the estate tax is to be phased out, while the gift tax is retained.

Clearly, Congress has not been consistent in its tax treatment of lifetime (i.e., gift tax) and death (i.e., estate tax) transfers.

The Tax Reform Act of 1976 significantly changed the approach taken by the Federal gift and estate taxes. Recognizing that prior rules had not significantly stimulated a preference for lifetime over death transfers, Congress decided that all transfers should be taxed the same way. Consequently, much of the distinction between life and death transfers was eliminated. Instead of subjecting these different types of transfers to two separate tax rate schedules, the Act substituted a **unified transfer tax** that covered all gratuitous transfers. Thus, gifts were subject to tax at the same rates as those applicable to transfers at death. In addition, the law eliminated the prior exemptions allowed under each tax and replaced them with a unified tax credit.

The Tax Relief Reconciliation Act of 2001 made further changes. Reacting to general public sentiment, Congress concluded that the Federal estate tax was objectionable because it leads to the breakup of family farms and other closely held businesses. This was not the case with the gift tax, since lifetime transfers are voluntary and within the control of the owner of the property. Thus, by scheduled increases in the unified tax credit applicable to estates, the estate tax will be eliminated by the year 2010, but the gift tax is retained. For budget reasons, all changes made by the 2001 Act are eliminated after December 31, 2010 (referred to as a "sunset" provision). Thus, the estate tax is reincarnated for transfers by death after 2010.

The Federal estate (or death) tax is designed to tax transfers at death. The tax differs, in several respects, from the typical **inheritance tax** imposed by several states and some local jurisdictions. First, the Federal *estate tax* is imposed on the decedent's entire taxable estate. It is a tax on the right to pass property at death. *Inheritance taxes* are taxes on the right to receive property at death and are therefore levied on the heirs. Second, the relationship of the heirs to the decedent usually has a direct bearing on the inheritance tax. In general, the more closely related the parties, the larger the exemption and the lower the applicable rates.[1] Except for transfers to a surviving spouse that may result in a marital deduction, the relationship of the heirs to the decedent has no effect on the Federal estate tax.

The Federal gift tax is imposed on the right of one person (the donor) to transfer property to another (the donee) for less than full and adequate consideration. The tax is payable by the donor.[2] If the donor fails to pay the tax when due, the donee may be held liable for the tax to the extent of the value of the property received.[3]

[1] For example, one state's inheritance tax provides an exemption of $50,000 for surviving spouses, with rates ranging from 5% to 10% on the taxable portion. This is to be contrasted with an exemption of only $1,000 for strangers (persons unrelated to the deceased), with rates ranging from 14% to 18% on the taxable portion. Other exemptions and rates fall between these extremes to cover beneficiaries variously related to the decedent.

[2] § 2502(c).

[3] § 6324(b). Known as the doctrine of transferee liability, this rule also operates to enable the IRS to enforce the collection of other taxes (e.g., income tax, estate tax).

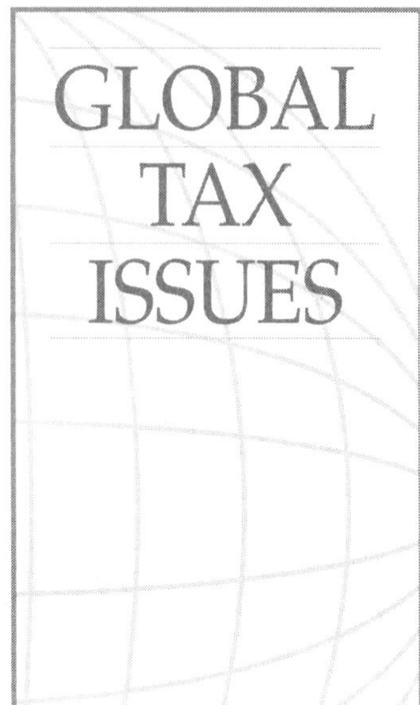

Expatriation to Avoid U.S. Taxes

Much media attention has been given to wealthy individuals who renounce their U.S. citizenship and move to another country to avoid U.S. taxes. These expatriates select a country where citizenship is easily available and low, if any, income and estate taxes are imposed.

Will this so-called expatriation to avoid taxes work? One difficulty for those who voluntarily renounce U.S. citizenship is that §§ 877 and 2107 continue to apply to their income tax and estate tax for a 10-year period. The taxpayer involved may avoid the application of these provisions by showing that the giving up of citizenship did not have as one of its principal purposes the avoidance of taxes.

Thus, the expatriation procedure will not be effective for at least 10 years. But even after this period, any income may still be subject to the Federal income tax if it is sourced in the United States. Likewise, assets located in the United States probably will be subject to the estate tax at death.

Persons Subject to the Tax. To determine whether a transfer is subject to the Federal gift tax, first ascertain if the donor is a citizen or resident of the United States. If the donor is not a citizen or a resident, it is important to determine whether the property involved in the gift was situated within the United States.

The Federal gift tax is applied to all transfers by gift of property wherever located by individuals who, at the time of the gift, were *citizens* or *residents* of the United States. The term "United States" includes only the 50 states and the District of Columbia; it does not include U.S. possessions or territories.[4] For a U.S. citizen, the place of residence at the time of the gift is irrelevant.

For individuals who are neither citizens nor residents of the United States, the Federal gift tax is applied only to gifts of property situated within the United States.[5] A gift of intangible personal property (e.g., stocks and bonds) by a nonresident alien usually is not subject to the Federal gift tax.[6]

A gift by a corporation is considered a gift by the individual shareholders. A gift to a corporation is generally considered a gift to the individual shareholders. In certain cases, however, a gift to a charitable, public, political, or similar organization may be regarded as a gift to the organization as a single entity.[7]

The Federal estate tax is applied to the entire taxable estate of a decedent who, at the time of death, was a resident or citizen of the United States. If the decedent was a U.S. citizen, the residence at death makes no difference.[8]

If the decedent was neither a resident nor a citizen of the United States at the time of death, the Federal estate tax is imposed on the value of any property located within the United States. In that case, the tax determination is controlled by a separate subchapter of the Internal Revenue Code.[9] As further coverage of this area

[4] § 7701(a)(9).

[5] § 2511(a).

[6] §§ 2501(a)(2) and (3). But see § 2511(b) and Reg. §§ 25.2511–3(b)(2), (3), and (4) for exceptions.

[7] Reg. §§ 25.0–1(b) and 25.2511–1(h)(1). But note the exemption from the Federal gift tax for certain transfers to political organizations discussed later.

[8] § 2001(a).

[9] Subchapter B (§§ 2101 through 2108) covers the estate tax treatment of decedents who are neither residents nor citizens. Subchapter A (§§ 2001 through 2058) covers the estate tax treatment of those who are either residents or citizens.

is beyond the scope of this text, the following discussion is limited to the tax treatment of decedents who were residents or citizens of the United States at the time of death.[10]

LO.2

Work with the Federal gift tax formula.

Formula for the Gift Tax. Like the income tax, which uses taxable income (and not gross income) as a tax base, the gift tax usually does not apply to the full amount of the gift. Deductions and the annual exclusion may be allowed to arrive at an amount called the **taxable gift.** However, unlike the income tax, which does not consider taxable income from prior years, *prior taxable gifts* must be added to arrive at the tax base to which the unified transfer tax rate is applied. Otherwise, the donor could start over again each year with a new set of progressive rates.

EXAMPLE 2

Don makes taxable gifts of $1 million in 1986 and $1 million in 2005. Presuming no other taxable gifts and *disregarding the effect of the unified tax credit*, Don must pay a tax of $345,800 (see Appendix A) on the 1986 transfer and a tax of $780,800 (see Appendix A) on the 2005 transfer (using a tax base of $2 million). If the 1986 taxable gift had not been included in the tax base for the 2005 gift, the tax would have been $345,800. The correct tax liability of $780,800 is more than twice $345,800! ■

Because the gift tax is cumulative in effect, a credit is allowed for the gift taxes paid (or deemed paid) on prior taxable gifts included in the tax base. The deemed paid credit is explained later in the chapter.

EXAMPLE 3

Assume the same facts as in Example 2. Don will be allowed a credit of $345,800 against the gift tax of $780,800. Thus, his gift tax liability for 2005 becomes $435,000 ($780,800 – $345,800). ■

In 1982, the annual exclusion was increased from $3,000 to $10,000 and in 2002 from $10,000 to $11,000. By allowing larger amounts to be exempt from the gift tax, taxpayer compliance may improve, as the tax will apply only to larger, planned gifts and not to day-to-day transfers. As noted in Chapter 1, the result is to ease the audit function of the IRS. Effective for years after 1998, the annual exclusion is indexed to account for *significant* inflation.[11]

The formula for the gift tax is summarized in Figure 27–1. [Note: Section (§) references are to the portion of the Internal Revenue Code involved.]

LO.3

Work with the Federal estate tax formula.

Formula for the Federal Estate Tax. The Federal unified transfer tax at death, commonly known as the Federal estate tax, is summarized in Figure 27–2. The gross estate is determined by using the fair market value of the property on the date of the decedent's death (or on the alternate valuation date if applicable).

The reason post-1976 taxable gifts are added to the taxable estate to arrive at the tax base goes back to the scheme of the unified transfer tax. Starting in 1977, all transfers, whether lifetime or by death, were to be treated the same. Consequently, taxable gifts made after 1976 must be accounted for upon the death of the donor. Note that the possible double tax effect of including these gifts is eliminated by allowing a credit against the estate tax for the gift taxes previously paid or deemed paid.

Role of the Unified Tax Credit. Before the unified transfer tax, the gift tax allowed a $30,000 specific exemption for the lifetime of the donor. A comparable

[10]Further information concerning Subchapter B (§§ 2101 through 2108) can be obtained from the relevant Code sections and the related Treasury Regulations. See also the Instructions to Form 706NA (U.S. Estate Tax Return of Nonresident Not a Citizen of the U.S.).

[11]§ 2503(b)(2).

FIGURE 27-1
Gift Tax Formula

Determine whether the transfers are considered gifts by referring to §§ 2511 through 2519; list the fair market value of only the covered transfers		$xxx,xxx
Determine the deductions allowed by §§ 2522 (charitable) and 2523 (marital)	$xx,xxx	
Claim the annual exclusion ($11,000 per donee) under § 2503(b), if available	xx,xxx	(xx,xxx)
Taxable gifts [as defined by § 2503(a)] for the current period		$ xx,xxx
Add: Taxable gifts from prior years		xx,xxx
Total of current and past taxable gifts		$ xx,xxx
Compute the gift tax on the total of current and past taxable gifts by using the rates in Appendix A		$ x,xxx
Subtract: Gift tax paid or deemed paid on past taxable gifts and the unified tax credit		(xxx)
Gift tax due on transfers during the current period		$ xxx

FIGURE 27-2
Estate Tax Formula

Gross estate (§§ 2031–2046)		$xxx,xxx
Subtract:		
Expenses, indebtedness, and taxes (§ 2053)	$xx,xxx	
Losses (§ 2054)	xx,xxx	
Charitable bequests (§ 2055)	xx,xxx	
Marital deduction (§§ 2056 and 2056A)	xx,xxx	
State death taxes (§ 2058)	xx,xxx	(xx,xxx)
Taxable estate (§ 2051)		$ xx,xxx
Add: Post-1976 taxable gifts [§ 2001(b)]		x,xxx
Tax base		$xxx,xxx
Tentative tax on total tax base [§ 2001(c)]		$ xx,xxx
Subtract:		
Unified transfer tax on post-1976 taxable gifts (gift taxes paid or deemed paid)	$ x,xxx	
Tax credits (including the unified tax credit) (§§ 2010–2016)	x,xxx	(x,xxx)
Estate tax due		$ x,xxx

$60,000 exemption was allowed for estate tax purposes. The purpose of these exemptions was to allow donors and decedents to transfer modest amounts of wealth without being subject to the gift and estate taxes. Unfortunately, inflation took its toll, and more taxpayers became subject to these transfer taxes than Congress felt was appropriate. The congressional solution, therefore, was to rescind the exemptions and replace them with the **unified tax credit.**[12]

[12]§§ 2010 and 2505.

■ **TABLE 27–1**
Phase-In of Unified Tax Credit (Applicable to *Both* Gift and Estate Taxes)

Year of Gift or Death	Amount of Credit	Exclusion Amount
1977	$ 30,000	$ 120,667
1978	34,000	134,000
1979	38,000	147,333
1980	42,500	161,563
1981	47,000	175,625
1982	62,800	225,000
1983	79,300	275,000
1984	96,300	325,000
1985	121,800	400,000
1986	155,800	500,000
1987 through 1997	192,800	600,000
1998	202,050	625,000
1999	211,300	650,000
2000 and 2001	220,550	675,000
2002	345,800	1,000,000

Note: For purposes of the *gift tax*, the unified tax credit and exclusion amount remain $345,800 and $1 million, respectively, for years after 2002.

Table 27–1 shows the unified tax credit applicable to transfers by gift and by death from 1977 through 2002. The Tax Relief Reconciliation Act of 2001 froze the credit applicable to the gift tax at $345,800 (exclusion amount of $1 million). By increasing the exclusion amount, the estate tax is scheduled to be phased out as shown in Table 27–2.

The **exclusion amount** (also termed the **exemption equivalent** and the **bypass amount**) is the amount of the transfer that will pass free of the gift or estate tax by virtue of the credit.

EXAMPLE 4

In 2005, Janet makes a taxable gift of $1 million. Presuming she has made no prior taxable gifts, Janet will not owe any gift tax. Under the applicable tax rate schedule (see Appendix A), the tax on $1 million is $345,800, which is the exact amount of the credit allowed.[13] ■

The Tax Reform Act of 1976 allowed donors one last chance to use the $30,000 specific exemption on lifetime gifts. If, however, the exemption was used on gifts made after September 8, 1976 (and before January 1, 1977), the unified tax credit must be reduced by 20 percent of the exemption utilized.[14] The credit must be readjusted whether the gift tax or the estate tax is involved. No adjustment is necessary for post-1976 gifts since the specific exemption is no longer available for such transfers.

■ **TABLE 27–2**
Scheduled Increases in Unified Tax Credit and Exclusion Amount (Applicable *Only* to Estate Taxes)

Year of Death	Amount of Credit	Exclusion Amount
2003	$ 345,800	$1,000,000
2004 and 2005	555,800	1,500,000
2006 through 2008	780,800	2,000,000
2009	1,455,800	3,500,000
2010	Estate tax repealed	Estate tax repealed

[13] The rate schedule is contained in § 2001(c). Neither the credit nor the rate schedule is subject to indexation.

[14] §§ 2010(c) and 2505(c).

What Are the Chances?

Under the Tax Relief Reconciliation Act of 2001, the estate tax is scheduled to be phased out by 2010. Even more fantastic, a "sunset" provision in the Act reincarnates this tax as of January 1, 2011. (The "sunset" provision was mandated due to budget considerations.)

What are the chances that all of these provisions will take effect as scheduled? Hopefully, not very high! The sunset reincarnation is particularly absurd and makes meaningful estate planning impossible. Tax practitioners are placed in the ridiculous posture of advising clients to live at least until 2010 but to be sure and die before 2011.

Bills that would rescind the sunset provision have been introduced in Congress. If enacted, the legislation would kill the estate tax for good (as of 2010) and keep it from coming back. Such proposals, however, are not likely to succeed. Budget deficits generated by recent tax cuts and aggravated by the conflict in Iraq do not favor any further curtailment of the revenue that transfer taxes yield. Also, there is strong conceptual support for some form of an estate tax. Perhaps an acceptable compromise would be a version that provides a generous exclusion amount and contains relief provisions to help preserve family businesses.

EXAMPLE 5

Net of the annual exclusion, Myrtle, a widow, made gifts of $10,000 in June 1976 and $20,000 in December 1976. Assume Myrtle has never used any of her specific exemption and chose to use the full $30,000 to cover the 1976 gifts. Under these circumstances, the unified tax credit will be reduced by $4,000 (20% × $20,000). The use of the specific exemption on transfers made before September 9, 1976, has no effect on the credit. ■

VALUATION FOR ESTATE AND GIFT TAX PURPOSES

The value of the property on the date of its transfer generally determines the amount that is subject to the gift tax or the estate tax. Under certain conditions, however, an executor can elect to value estate assets on the **alternate valuation date** (§ 2032).

The alternate valuation date election was designed as a relief provision to ease the economic hardship that could result when estate assets decline in value over the six months after the date of death. If the election is made, all assets of the estate are valued six months after death *or* on the date of disposition if this occurs earlier.[15] The election covers *all* assets in the gross estate and cannot be applied to only a portion of the property.

EXAMPLE 6

Robert's gross estate consists of the following property:

	Value on Date of Death	Value Six Months Later
Land	$ 800,000	$ 840,000
Stock in Brown Corporation	900,000	700,000
Stock in Green Corporation	500,000	460,000
Total	$2,200,000	$2,000,000

[15] § 2032(a). For this purpose, the term "disposition" is broadly defined. It includes the transfer of property to an heir to satisfy a bequest and the use of property to fund a testamentary trust.

If Robert's executor elects the alternate valuation date, the estate must be valued at $2 million. It is not permissible to value the land at its date of death value ($800,000) and choose the alternate valuation date for the rest of the gross estate. ■

EXAMPLE 7

Assume the same facts as in Example 6, except that the executor sells the stock in Green Corporation for $480,000 four months after Robert's death. If the alternate valuation date is elected, the estate must be valued at $2,020,000 ($840,000 + $700,000 + $480,000). As to the Green stock, the value on its date of disposition controls because that date occurred prior to the six months' alternate valuation date. ■

The election of the alternate valuation date must decrease the value of the gross estate *and* decrease the estate tax liability.[16] The reason for this last requirement is that the income tax basis of property acquired from a decedent will be the value used for estate tax purposes.[17] Without a special limitation, the alternate valuation date could be elected solely to add to income tax basis.

EXAMPLE 8

Al's gross estate is comprised of assets with a date of death value of $1 million and an alternate valuation date value of $1.1 million. Under Al's will, all of his property passes outright to Jean (Al's wife). Because of the marital deduction, no estate tax results regardless of which value is used. But if the alternate valuation date could be elected, Jean would have an income tax basis of $1.1 million in the property acquired from Al. ■

The alternate valuation date cannot be elected in Example 8 for two reasons, either of which would suffice. First, the alternate valuation date will not decrease Al's gross estate. Second, the election will not decrease Al's estate tax liability. Thus, his estate must use the date of death valuation of $1 million. As a result, Jean's income tax basis in the property received from Al is $1 million.

ETHICAL CONSIDERATIONS

An Executor's Prerogative

Denny dies in 2005 and is survived by Mary (Denny's second wife) and Rodney (a son from the first marriage). Under Denny's will his property, largely comprising marketable securities, is equally divided between Mary and Rodney with all estate expenses and taxes assigned to Rodney's portion. The will designates Mary as the executor of the estate.

Denny's gross estate has a date of death value of $4 million and an alternate valuation date value of $3.8 million. Although use of the alternate valuation date would save $45,000 in estate taxes, the election is not made. Why is the election not made? Was the failure to make the election improper?

KEY PROPERTY CONCEPTS

When property is transferred either by gift or by death, the form of ownership can have a direct bearing on any transfer tax consequences. Understanding the different forms of ownership is necessary for working with Federal gift and estate taxes.

Undivided Ownership. Assume Dan and Vicky own an undivided but equal interest in a tract of land. Such ownership can fall into any of four categories: joint tenancy, tenancy by the entirety, tenancy in common, or community property.

[16]§ 2032(c).

[17]§ 1014(a).

If Dan and Vicky hold ownership as **joint tenants** or **tenants by the entirety,** the right of survivorship exists. This means that the last tenant to survive receives full ownership of the property. Thus, if Dan predeceases Vicky, the land belongs entirely to Vicky. None of the land passes to Dan's heirs or is subject to administration by Dan's executor. A tenancy by the entirety is a joint tenancy between husband and wife.

If Dan and Vicky hold ownership as **tenants in common** or as community property, death does not defeat an owner's interest. Thus, if Dan predeceases Vicky, Dan's half interest in the land passes to his estate or heirs.

Community property interests arise from the marital relationship. Normally, all property acquired after marriage, except by gift or inheritance, by husband and wife residing in a community property state becomes part of the community. The following states have the community property system in effect: Louisiana, Texas, New Mexico, Arizona, California, Washington, Idaho, Nevada, Wisconsin, and (by election of the spouses) Alaska. All other states follow the common law system of ascertaining a spouse's rights to property acquired after marriage.

Partial Interests. Interests in assets can be divided in terms of rights to income and rights to principal. Particularly when property is placed in trust, it is not uncommon to carve out various income interests that must be accounted for separately from the ultimate disposition of the property itself.

EXAMPLE 9

Under Bill's will, a ranch is to be placed in trust, life estate to Sam, Bill's son, with remainder to Sam's children (Bill's grandchildren). Under this arrangement, Sam is the life tenant and, as such, is entitled to the use of the ranch (including any income) during his life. Upon Sam's death, the trust terminates, and its principal passes to his children. Thus, Sam's children receive outright ownership of the ranch when Sam dies. ■

The Federal Gift Tax

GENERAL CONSIDERATIONS

LO.4

Explain the operation of the Federal gift tax.

Requirements for a Gift. For a gift to be complete under state law, the following elements must be present.

- A donor competent to make the gift.
- A donee capable of receiving and possessing the property.
- Donative intent on behalf of the donor.
- Actual or constructive delivery of the property to the donee or the donee's representative.
- Acceptance of the gift by the donee.

Incomplete Transfers. The Federal gift tax does not apply to transfers that are incomplete. Thus, if the transferor retains the right to reclaim the property or has not really parted with the possession of the property, a taxable event has not taken place.

EXAMPLE 10

Lesly creates a trust with income payable to Mary for life, remainder to Paul. Under the terms of the trust instrument, Lesly can revoke the trust at any time and repossess the trust principal and the income earned. No gift takes place on the creation of the trust; Lesly has not ceased to have dominion and control over the property. ■

EXAMPLE 11

Assume the same facts as in Example 10, except that one year after the transfer, Lesly relinquishes his right to terminate the trust. At this point, the transfer becomes complete, and the Federal gift tax applies. ■

Business versus Personal Setting. In a business setting, full and adequate consideration is apt to exist. Regulation § 25.2512–8 provides that "a sale, exchange, or other transfer of property made in the ordinary course of business (a transaction that is bona fide, at arm's length, and free of any donative intent) will be considered as made for an adequate and full consideration in money or money's worth." If the parties are acting in a personal setting, a gift is usually the result. Regulation § 25.2512–8 also holds that valuable consideration (such as would preclude a gift result) does not include a payment or transfer based on "love and affection . . . promise of marriage, etc." Consequently, property settlements in consideration of marriage (i.e., pre- or antenuptial agreements) are regarded as gifts.

Do not conclude that the presence of *some* consideration is enough to preclude Federal gift tax consequences. Again, the answer may rest on whether the transfer occurred in a business setting.

EXAMPLE 12

Peter sells Bob some real estate for $40,000. Unknown to Peter, the property contains valuable mineral deposits and is really worth $200,000. Peter may have made a bad business deal, but he has not made a gift of $160,000 to Bob. ■

EXAMPLE 13

Assume the same facts as in Example 12, except that Peter and Bob are father and son. In addition, Peter is very much aware that the property is worth $200,000. Peter has made a gift of $160,000 to Bob. ■

Certain Excluded Transfers. Transfers to political organizations are exempt from the application of the Federal gift tax.[18] This provision in the Code made unnecessary the previous practice whereby candidates for public office established multiple campaign committees to maximize the number of annual exclusions available to their contributors. As noted, an annual exclusion of $11,000 for each donee passes free of the Federal gift tax.

The Federal gift tax does not apply to tuition payments made to an educational organization (e.g., a college) on another's behalf. Nor does it apply to amounts paid on another's behalf for medical care.[19] In this regard, the law is realistic since it is unlikely that most donors would recognize these items as being transfers subject to the gift tax. The payments, however, must be made directly to the provider (e.g., doctor, hospital, college). There is no requirement that the beneficiary of the service (e.g., patient, student) qualify as a dependent of the person making the payment.

Satisfying an obligation of support is not subject to the gift tax. Thus, no gift takes place when parents pay for their children's education because one of the obligations of parents is to educate their children. What constitutes an obligation of support is determined by applicable state law.

[18] § 2501(a)(5).

[19] § 2503(e).

ETHICAL CONSIDERATIONS

What Constitutes Support?

When Earl's daughter, Clara, turns 40, he gives her a Mercedes convertible as a birthday present. Clara is married and has a family of her own. She is a licensed orthopedic surgeon and maintains a successful practice in the field of sports medicine.

Earl does not regard the transfer as being subject to the gift tax. As a parent, he is merely satisfying his obligation of support. Such obligation includes providing your child with transportation. Is Earl's reasoning sound?

Lifetime versus Death Transfers. Be careful to distinguish between lifetime (*inter vivos*) and death (testamentary) transfers.

EXAMPLE 14

Dudley buys a 12-month certificate of deposit (CD) from State Bank and lists ownership as follows: "Dudley, payable on proof of death to Faye." Nine months later, Dudley dies. When the CD matures, Faye collects the proceeds from State Bank. No gift takes place when Dudley invests in the CD; Faye has received a mere expectancy (i.e., to obtain ownership of the CD upon Dudley's death). At any time before his death, Dudley may withdraw the funds or delete Faye's name from the account, thereby cutting off her expectancy. Furthermore, no gift occurs upon Dudley's death as the CD passes to Faye by testamentary disposition. As noted later, the CD will be included in Dudley's gross estate as property in which the decedent had an interest (§ 2033). ■

The arrangement used in Example 14, known as a **Totten trust,** is very similar in effect to a revocable trust (see Example 10 above). Both carry the advantage of avoiding the probate estate. A Totten trust, however, is simpler to use in the case of bank accounts and securities, and it avoids the need of having to create a formal trust.

TRANSFERS SUBJECT TO THE GIFT TAX

Whether a transfer is subject to the Federal gift tax depends upon the application of §§ 2511 through 2519 and the applicable Regulations.

Gift Loans. To understand the tax ramifications of gift loans, an illustration is helpful.

EXAMPLE 15

Before his niece Denise leaves for college, Victor lends her $300,000. Denise signs a note that provides for repayment in five years. The loan contains no interest element, and neither Victor nor Denise expects any interest to be paid. Following Victor's advice, Denise invests the loan proceeds in income-producing securities. During her five years in college, she uses the income from the investments to pay for college costs and other living expenses. On the maturity date of the note, Denise repays the $300,000 she owes Victor. ■

In a gift loan arrangement, the following consequences result:

- Victor has made a gift to Denise of the interest element. The amount of the gift is determined by the difference between the amount of interest charged (in this case, none) and the market rate (as determined by the yield on certain U.S. government securities).
- The interest element is included in Victor's gross income and is subject to the Federal income tax.

- Denise may be allowed an income tax deduction for the interest element, but *may* benefit from this result only if she is in a position to itemize her deductions *from* adjusted gross income.

The Code defines a gift loan as "any below-market loan where the forgoing of interest is in the nature of a gift."[20] Unless tax avoidance was one of the principal purposes of the loan, special limitations apply if the gift loan does not exceed $100,000. In such a case, the interest element may not exceed the borrower's net investment income.[21] Furthermore, if the net investment income does not exceed $1,000, it is treated as zero. Under a $10,000 *de minimis* rule, the interest element is disregarded.

Certain Property Settlements (§ 2516). Normally, the settlement of certain marital rights is not regarded as being for consideration and is subject to the Federal gift tax.[22] As a special exception to this general approach, Congress enacted § 2516. By this provision, transfers of property interests made under the terms of a written agreement between spouses in settlement of their marital or property rights are deemed to be for adequate consideration. The transfers are exempt from the Federal gift tax if a final decree of divorce is obtained within the three-year period beginning on the date one year before the parties entered into the agreement. Likewise excluded are transfers to provide a reasonable allowance for the support of minor children (including legally adopted children) of a marriage. The agreement need not be approved by the divorce decree.

Disclaimers (§ 2518). A **disclaimer** is a refusal by a person to accept property that is designated to pass to him or her. The effect of the disclaimer is to pass the property to someone else.

EXAMPLE 16

Earl dies without a will and is survived by a son, Andy, and a grandson, Jay. At the time of his death, Earl owned real estate that, under the applicable state law, passes to the closest lineal descendant, Andy in this case. If, however, Andy disclaims his interest in the real estate, state law provides that the property passes to Jay. At the time of Earl's death, Andy has considerable property of his own, and Jay has none. ■

Why might Andy want to consider disclaiming his inheritance and have the property pass directly from Earl to Jay? By doing so, an extra transfer tax may be avoided. If the disclaimer does not take place (Andy accepts the inheritance), and the property eventually passes to Jay (either by gift or by death), the later transfer is subject to the application of either the gift tax or the estate tax.

For many years, whether a disclaimer was effective in avoiding a Federal transfer tax depended on the application of state law. To illustrate by using the facts of Example 16, if state law determined that the real estate was deemed to have passed through Andy despite his disclaimer after Earl's death, the Federal gift tax applied. In essence, Andy was treated as if he had inherited the property from Earl and then given it to Jay. As state law was not always consistent in this regard and sometimes was not even known, the application or nonapplication of Federal transfer taxes depended on where the parties lived. To remedy this situation and provide some measure of uniformity, §§ 2046 (relating to disclaimers for estate tax purposes) and 2518 (relating to disclaimers for gift tax purposes) were added to the Code.

[20] § 7872(f)(3).

[21] Net investment income has the same meaning given to the term by § 163(d). Generally, net investment income is investment income (e.g., interest, dividends) less related expenses.

[22] Reg. § 25.2512–8.

In the case of the gift tax, when the requirements of § 2518 are met and Andy makes a timely lifetime disclaimer (refer to Example 16), the property is treated as if it goes directly from Earl to Jay. Since the property is not treated as passing through Andy (regardless of what state law holds), it is not subject to the Federal gift tax.

The tax law also permits the Federal gift tax to be avoided in cases of a partial disclaimer of an undivided interest.

EXAMPLE 17

Assume the same facts as in Example 16, except that Andy wishes to retain half of the real estate for himself. If Andy makes a timely disclaimer of an undivided one-half interest in the property, the Federal gift tax does not apply to the portion passing to Jay. ■

To be effective, the disclaimer must be timely made. Generally, this means no later than nine months after the right to the property arose. Furthermore, the person making the disclaimer must not have accepted any benefits or interest in the property.

Other Transfers Subject to Gift Tax. Other transfers that may carry gift tax consequences (e.g., the creation of joint ownership) are discussed and illustrated in connection with the Federal estate tax.

ANNUAL EXCLUSION

The first $11,000 of gifts made to any one person during any calendar year (except gifts of future interests in property) is excluded in determining the total amount of gifts for the year.[23] The **annual exclusion** applies to all gifts of a present interest made during the calendar year in the order in which they are made until the $11,000 exclusion per donee is exhausted. For a gift in trust, each beneficiary of the trust is treated as a separate person for purposes of the exclusion.

EXAMPLE 18

During the current year, Laura makes the following cash gifts: $8,000 to Rita and $12,000 to Maureen. Laura may claim an annual exclusion of $8,000 with respect to Rita and $11,000 with respect to Maureen. ■

A **future interest** is defined as one that will come into being (as to use, possession, or enjoyment) at some future date. Examples of future interests include such rights as remainder interests that are commonly encountered when property is transferred to a trust. A *present interest* is an unrestricted right to the immediate use, possession, or enjoyment of property or of the income.

EXAMPLE 19

By a lifetime gift, Ron transfers property to a trust with a life estate (with income payable annually) to June and remainder upon June's death to Albert. Ron has made two gifts: one to June of a life estate and one to Albert of a remainder interest. The life estate is a present interest and qualifies for the annual exclusion. The remainder interest granted to Albert is a future interest and does not qualify for the exclusion. Note that Albert's interest does not come into being until some future date (on the death of June). ■

Although Example 19 indicates that the gift of an income interest is a present interest, this is not always the case. If a possibility exists that the income beneficiary may not receive the immediate enjoyment of the property, the transfer is of a future interest.

[23] § 2503(b).

EXAMPLE 20

Assume the same facts as in Example 19, except that the income from the trust need not be payable annually to June. It may, at the trustee's discretion, be accumulated and added to corpus. Since June's right to receive the income from the trust is conditioned on the trustee's discretion, it is not a present interest. No annual exclusion is allowed. The mere possibility of diversion is enough. It would not matter if the trustee never exercised the discretion to accumulate and did, in fact, distribute the trust income to June annually. ■

Trust for Minors. Section 2503(c) offers an exception to the future interest rules just discussed. Under this provision, a transfer for the benefit of a person who has not attained the age of 21 years on the date of the gift may be considered a gift of a present interest. This is true even though the minor is not given the unrestricted right to the immediate use, possession, or enjoyment of the property. For the exception to apply, however, certain stringent conditions must be satisfied. One such condition is that all of the property and its income must be made available to the minor upon attaining age 21. Thus, the exception allows a trustee to accumulate income on behalf of a minor beneficiary without converting the income interest to a future interest.

From a nontax standpoint, the § 2503(c) exception makes good sense. After all, it avoids making trustees distribute income to a minor just to obtain an annual exclusion. In many situations, providing the minor with more than modest sums may be unwise.

Contributions to Qualified Tuition Programs. For income tax purposes, § 529 plans have become the best of all possible worlds. Although no up-front deduction is allowed,[24] income earned by the fund accumulates free of income tax, and distributions are not taxed if they are used for higher education purposes. A special provision allows a donor to enjoy a gift tax advantage by using five years of annual exclusions.[25]

EXAMPLE 21

Trevor and Audry would like to start building a college education fund for their 10-year-old granddaughter, Loni. In 2005, Trevor contributes $110,000 to the designated carrier of their state's § 529 plan. By electing to split the gift and using five annual exclusions [2 (number of donors) × $11,000 (annual exclusion) × 5 years = $110,000], no taxable gift results. (The gift-splitting election is discussed in detail later in this chapter.) ■

Making the five-year election precludes Trevor and Audry from using any annual exclusion on gifts to Loni for the next four years.[26]

Section 529(c)(4) provides that these college plans are not to be included in the gross estate of the transferor. This is preferential treatment because § 529 plans are incomplete transfers (the funds are returned if college is not attended). As noted later, incomplete transfers are invariably subject to the estate tax.

DEDUCTIONS

In arriving at taxable gifts, a deduction is allowed for transfers to certain qualified charitable organizations. On transfers between spouses, a marital deduction may

[24]Depending on the taxpayer's home state, some (or all) of the contributions into the plan may be deductible for *state* income tax purposes.

[25]§ 529(c)(2)(B). Subsection (A) protects against future interest treatment.

[26]Trevor and Audry could resort to § 2503(e)(2)(A) to avoid any gift at all. As mentioned earlier, a *direct* payment of tuition to certain educational institutions is exempt from the gift tax. But this rule does not help to build an education fund for future use, as § 529 does. Recall that Loni, the granddaughter, is only 10 years old.

Section 529 Plans Need Reevaluation

Contributions to § 529 plans are subject to the gift tax and are nondeductible for Federal income tax purposes. Their main advantage is that income from the plans if distributed *for education purposes* is not subject to the income tax. These plans suffer from two major drawbacks, however. First, the donor has no control over how the funds are invested. Second, there is no flexibility in the use of the funds.

Both of these disadvantages can be remedied by the use of a custodial account under a state's Uniform Gifts to Minors Act (or Uniform Transfers to Minors Act). Investments can be bought and sold and diversified (within limits prescribed by law) as the custodian chooses. Income and corpus can be used for any number of purposes (educational or otherwise) as long as they are used for the benefit of the minor. But what about the insulation from income taxation that § 529 plans provide? New rules under JGTRRA of 2003 offer a partial solution. To the extent the 25 percent bracket can be avoided, dividend income and net capital gains are subject to a maximum tax of only 5 percent. Moreover, even if the 25 percent and higher tax brackets are reached, the tax rate on this type of income increases to a relatively low 15 percent. Therefore, income tax consequences, though not completely avoided, can be substantially minimized.

In view of the lack of flexibility of § 529 plans and the reduced income tax rates now available, custodial accounts warrant serious consideration. Even if the funds are ultimately used for higher education, a custodial account may be a better choice than a § 529 plan.

be available. Since both the charitable and marital deductions apply in determining the Federal estate tax, they are discussed later in the chapter.

LO.5

Illustrate the computation of the Federal gift tax.

COMPUTING THE FEDERAL GIFT TAX

The Unified Transfer Tax Rate Schedule. The top rates of the unified transfer tax rate schedule originally reached as high as 70 percent. Over the years, these top rates were reduced to 55 percent. Under the Tax Relief Reconciliation Act of 2001, the top rate was reduced to 47 percent in 2005 (49 percent in 2003 and 48 percent in 2004), and further reductions are scheduled for future years.[27] Keep in mind that the unified transfer tax rate schedule applies to all transfers (by gift or death) after 1976 and before 2010. Different rate schedules applied for pre-1977 gifts and pre-1977 death transfers.

The Deemed-Paid Adjustment. Review the formula for the gift tax (refer to Figure 27–1) and note that the tax base for a current gift includes *all* past taxable gifts. The effect of the inclusion is to force the current taxable gift into a higher bracket due to the progressive nature of the unified transfer tax rates (refer to Example 2). To mitigate such double taxation, the donor is allowed a credit for any gift tax previously paid or deemed paid (refer to Example 3).

[27] § 2001(c)(2)(B). Scheduled reductions in the maximum tax rates are as follows: 46% (2006) and 45% (2007, 2008, 2009). As to the 2005 rates, see Appendix A.

Limiting the donor to a credit for the gift tax *actually paid* on pre-1977 taxable gifts would be unfair. Pre-1977 taxable gifts were subject to a lower set of rates than those in the unified transfer tax rate schedule. As a consequence, the donor is allowed a *deemed-paid* credit on pre-1977 taxable gifts. This is the amount that would have been due under the unified transfer tax rate schedule had it been applicable. *Post-1976* taxable gifts *also* are subject to the deemed-paid adjustment because the same rate schedule may not be involved in all gifts.

EXAMPLE 22

In 1981, Carla made a taxable gift of $3 million, which resulted in a Federal gift tax of $1,243,800*. In 2005, Carla makes another taxable gift of $3 million. The tax on the 2005 gift is determined as follows:

Taxable gift made in 2005		$3,000,000
Add: Taxable gift made in 1981		3,000,000
Total of current and past taxable gifts		$6,000,000
Unified transfer tax on $6,000,000 per Appendix A [$780,800 + 47%($6,000,000 – $2,000,000)]		$2,660,800
Subtract:		
Deemed paid tax on 1981 gift—use Appendix A [$780,800 + 47%($3,000,000 – $2,000,000)]	$1,203,800*	
Unified credit for 2005	345,800**	(1,549,600)
Gift tax due on 2005 gift		$1,111,200

*Adjusted for the $47,000 unified credit available for year 1981 (see Table 27–1).
**Recall that for *gift tax* purposes, the unified credit remains $345,800 and is not scheduled to increase (see Table 27–1).

Note that Carla's deemed paid credit allowed is $40,000 *less* than was originally paid ($1,243,800 – $1,203,800). As previously mentioned, the variance is due to the tax rate changes that have taken place since 1981. ■

The Election to Split Gifts by Married Persons. To understand the reason for the gift-splitting election of § 2513, consider the following situations:

EXAMPLE 23

Dick and Margaret are husband and wife and reside in Michigan, a common law state. Dick has been the only breadwinner in the family, and Margaret has no significant property of her own. Neither has made any prior taxable gifts or used the $30,000 specific exemption previously available for pre-1977 gifts. In 2005, Dick makes a gift to Leslie of $2,022,000. Presuming the election to split gifts did not exist, Dick's gift tax is as follows.

Amount of gift	$2,022,000
Subtract: Annual exclusion	(11,000)
Taxable gift	$2,011,000
Gift tax on $2,011,000 per Appendix A, [$780,800 + (47% × $11,000)]	$ 785,970
Subtract: Unified transfer tax credit for 2005	(345,800)
Gift tax due on the 2005 taxable gift	$ 440,170

■

EXAMPLE 24

Assume the same facts as in Example 23, except that Dick and Margaret have always resided in California, a community property state. Even though Dick is the sole breadwinner, income from personal services generally is community property. Consequently, the gift to Leslie probably involves community property. If this is the case, the gift tax is as follows.

	Dick	Margaret
Amount of gift	$1,011,000	$1,011,000
Subtract: Annual exclusion	(11,000)	(11,000)
Taxable gift	$1,000,000	$1,000,000
Gift tax on $1,000,000 per Appendix A	$ 345,800	$ 345,800
Subtract: Unified transfer tax credit for 2005	(345,800)	(345,800)
Gift tax due on the 2005 taxable gift	$ -0-	$ -0-

As the results of Examples 23 and 24 indicate, married donors residing in community property jurisdictions possessed a significant gift tax advantage over those residing in common law states. To rectify this inequity, the Revenue Act of 1948 incorporated the predecessor to § 2513 into the Code. Under this provision, a gift made by a person to someone other than his or her spouse may be considered, for Federal gift tax purposes, as having been made one-half by each spouse. Returning to Example 23, Dick and Margaret could treat the gift passing to Leslie as being made one-half by each of them, even though the property belonged to Dick. As a result, the parties are able to achieve the same tax consequence as in Example 24.

To split gifts, the spouses must be legally married to each other at the time of the gift. If they are divorced later in the calendar year, they may still split the gift if neither marries anyone else during that year. They both must indicate on their separate gift tax returns their consent to have all gifts made in that calendar year split between them. In addition, both must be citizens or residents of the United States on the date of the gift. A gift from one spouse to the other spouse cannot be split. Such a gift might, however, be eligible for the marital deduction.

The election to split gifts is not necessary when husband and wife transfer community property to a third party. It is needed if the gift consists of the separate property of one of the spouses. Generally, separate property is property acquired before marriage and property acquired after marriage by gift or inheritance. The election, then, is not limited to residents of common law states.

PROCEDURAL MATTERS

Having determined which transfers are subject to the Federal gift tax and the various deductions and exclusions available to the donor, the procedural aspects of the tax should be considered. The following section discusses the return itself, the due dates for filing and paying the tax, and other related matters.

The Federal Gift Tax Return. For transfers by gift, a Form 709 (U.S. Gift Tax Return) must be filed whenever the gifts for any one calendar year exceed the annual exclusion or involve a gift of a future interest. A Form 709 need not be filed, however, for transfers between spouses that are offset by the unlimited marital deduction, regardless of the amount of the transfer.[28]

EXAMPLE 25

In 2005, Larry makes five gifts, each in the amount of $11,000, to his five children. If the gifts do not involve future interests, a Form 709 need not be filed to report the transfers.

[28] § 6019(a)(2).

EXAMPLE 26

During 2005, Esther makes a gift of $22,000 cash of her separate property to her daughter. To double the amount of the annual exclusion allowed, Jerry (Esther's husband) is willing to split the gift. Since the § 2513 election can be made only on a gift tax return, a form must be filed even though no gift tax will be due as a result of the transfer. ■

In Example 26, no gift tax return would be necessary if the transfer consisted of community property. Since two donors are now involved, the cap for filing becomes more than $22,000, rather than more than $11,000.

Presuming a gift tax return is due, it must be filed on or before the fifteenth day of April following the year of the gift.[29] As with other Federal taxes, when the due date falls on Saturday, Sunday, or a legal holiday, the date for filing the return is the next business day. Note that the filing requirements for Form 709 have no correlation to the accounting year used by a donor for Federal income tax purposes. Thus, a fiscal year taxpayer must follow the April 15 rule for any reportable gifts. If sufficient reason is shown, the IRS is authorized to grant reasonable extensions of time for filing the return.[30]

The Federal Estate Tax

The following discussion of the estate tax coincides with the formula that appeared earlier in the chapter in Figure 27–2. The key components in the formula are the gross estate, the taxable estate, the tax base, and the credits allowed against the tentative tax. This formula can be summarized as follows:

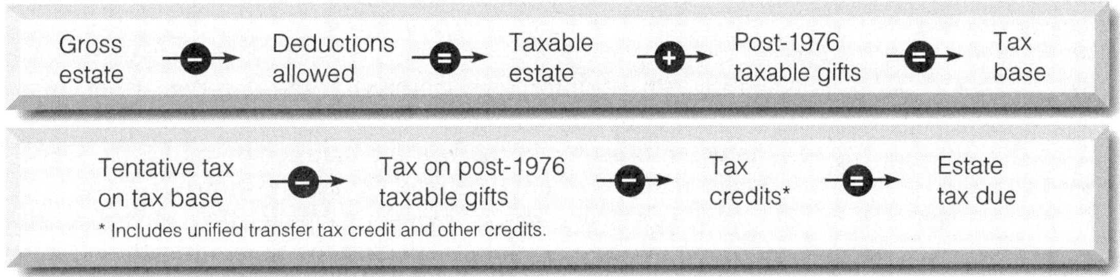

LO.6

Review the components of the gross estate.

GROSS ESTATE

Simply stated, the **gross estate** includes all property subject to the Federal estate tax. Thus, the gross estate depends on the provisions of the Internal Revenue Code as supplemented by IRS pronouncements and the judicial interpretations of Federal courts.

In contrast to the gross estate, the **probate estate** is controlled by state (rather than Federal) law. The probate estate consists of all of a decedent's property subject to administration by the executor or administrator of the estate. The administration is supervised by a local court of appropriate jurisdiction (usually called a probate

[29] § 6075(b)(1).

[30] § 6081. Under § 6075(b)(2), an extension of time granted to a calendar year taxpayer for filing an income tax return automatically extends the due date of a gift tax return.

CONCEPT SUMMARY 27–1

Federal Gift Tax Provisions

1. The Federal gift tax applies to all gratuitous transfers of property made by U.S. citizens or residents. In this regard, it does not matter where the property is located.
2. In the eyes of the IRS, a gratuitous transfer is one not supported by full and adequate consideration. If the parties are acting in a business setting, such consideration usually exists. If purported sales are between family members, a gift element may be suspected.
3. If a lender loans money to another and intends some or all of the interest element to be a gift, the arrangement is categorized as a gift loan. To the extent that the interest provided for is less than the market rate, three tax consequences result. First, a gift has taken place between the lender and the borrower as to the interest element. Second, income may result to the lender. Third, an income tax deduction may be available to the borrower.
4. Property settlements can escape the gift tax if a divorce occurs within a prescribed period of time.
5. A disclaimer is a refusal by a person to accept property designated to pass to that person. The effect of a disclaimer is to pass the property to someone else. If certain conditions are satisfied, the issuance of a disclaimer will not be subject to the Federal gift tax.
6. Except for gifts of future interests, a donor is allowed an annual exclusion of $11,000. The future interest limitation does not apply to certain trusts created for minors.
7. The election to split a gift enables a married couple to be treated as two donors. The election doubles the annual exclusion and makes the unified tax credit available to the nonowner spouse.
8. The election to split gifts is not necessary if the property is jointly owned by the spouses. That is the case when the property is part of the couple's community.
9. In determining the tax base for computing the gift tax, all prior taxable gifts must be added to current taxable gifts. Thus, the gift tax is cumulative in nature.
10. Gifts are reported on Form 709. The return is due on April 15 following the year of the gift.

court). An executor (or executrix) is the decedent's personal representative appointed under the decedent's will. When a decedent dies without a will or fails to name an executor in the will (or that person refuses to serve), the local probate court appoints an administrator (or administratrix).

The probate estate is frequently smaller than the gross estate. It contains only property owned by the decedent at the time of death and passing to heirs under a will or under the law of intestacy (the order of distribution for those dying without a will). As noted later, such items as the proceeds of many life insurance policies become part of the gross estate but are not included in the probate estate.

All states provide for an order of distribution in the event someone dies without a will. After the surviving spouse receives some or all of the estate, the preference is usually in the following order: down to lineal descendants (e.g., children, grandchildren), up to lineal ascendants (e.g., parents, grandparents), and out to collateral relations (e.g., brothers, sisters, aunts, and uncles).

Property Owned by the Decedent (§ 2033). Property owned by the decedent at the time of death is included in the gross estate. The nature of the property or the use to which it was put during the decedent-owner's lifetime has no significance as far as the estate tax is concerned. Thus, personal effects (such as clothing), stocks, bonds, furniture, jewelry, works of art, bank accounts, and interests in businesses conducted as sole proprietorships and partnerships are all included in the deceased's gross estate. No distinction is made between tangible or intangible, depreciable or nondepreciable, business or personal assets. However, a deceased spouse's gross estate does not include the surviving spouse's share of the community property.

The application of § 2033 is illustrated as follows:

EXAMPLE 27

Irma dies owning some City of Denver bonds. The fair market value of the bonds plus any interest accrued to the date of Irma's death is included in her gross estate. Although interest on municipal bonds is normally not taxable under the Federal income tax, it is property owned by Irma at the time of death. However, any interest accrued after death is not part of Irma's gross estate. ■

EXAMPLE 28

Sharon dies on April 8, 2005, at a time when she owns stock in Robin Corporation and in Wren Corporation. On March 3 of this year, both corporations had authorized a cash dividend payable on May 4. Robin's dividend is payable to shareholders of record as of April 1. Wren's date of record is April 12. Sharon's gross estate includes the following: the stock in Robin Corporation, the stock in Wren Corporation, and the dividend on the Robin stock. It does not include the dividend on the Wren stock because Sharon dies before the April 12 date of record. ■

EXAMPLE 29

Ray dies holding some promissory notes issued to him by his son. In his will, Ray forgives these notes, relieving the son of the obligation to make any payments. The fair market value of these notes is included in Ray's gross estate. ■

EXAMPLE 30

At the time of his death on a business trip, Ray was a consulting engineer for Falcon Corporation. Ray's estate receives a distribution from Falcon's qualified pension plan of $1,100,000 consisting of the following.

Falcon's contributions	$450,000
Ray's after-tax contributions	350,000
Income earned by the plan	300,000

Ray's estate also receives $150,000 from Hawk Insurance Company. The payment represents the maturity value of term life insurance from a group plan Falcon maintains for its employees. As to these amounts, Ray's gross estate includes $1,250,000 ($1,100,000 + $150,000). For income tax purposes, however, $750,000 ($450,000 + $300,000) is subject to tax, while $500,000 ($350,000 + $150,000) is not.[31] ■

Dower and Curtesy Interests (§ 2034). In its common law (nonstatutory) form, dower generally gave a surviving widow a life estate in a portion of her husband's estate (usually the real estate he owned) with the remainder passing to their children. Most states have modified and codified these common law rules, and the resulting statutes often vary among jurisdictions. In some states, for example, by statute, a widow is entitled to outright ownership of a percentage of her deceased husband's real estate and personal property. Curtesy is a similar right held by the husband in his wife's property, taking effect in the event he survives her. Most states have abolished the common law curtesy concept and have, in some cases, substituted a modified statutory version.

Dower and curtesy rights are incomplete interests and may never materialize. Thus, if a wife predeceases her husband, the dower interest in her husband's property is lost.

EXAMPLE 31

Martin dies without a will, leaving an estate of $2.1 million. Under state law, Belinda (Martin's widow) is entitled to one-third of his property. The $700,000 Belinda receives is included in Martin's gross estate. Depending on the nature of the interest Belinda receives in the $700,000, this amount could qualify Martin's estate for a marital deduction. (This

[31] Retirement plan benefits [H.R. 10 or Keogh plans, traditional IRAs, Roth IRAs, § 401(k), § 403(b)(1)] are invariably subject to estate tax. Usually, the benefits are included in the gross estate under § 2033, as was the case in Example 30. If the payout is in the form of an annuity, § 2039 applies (see later in the chapter).

possibility is discussed at greater length later in the chapter. For the time being, however, the focus is on what is or is not included as part of the decedent's gross estate.) ■

Adjustments for Gifts Made within Three Years of Death (§ 2035). At one time, all taxable gifts made within three years of death were included in the donor's gross estate unless it could be shown that the gifts were not made in contemplation of death. The prior rule was intended to preclude tax avoidance since the gift tax and estate tax rates were separate and the former was lower than the latter. When the gift and estate tax rates were combined into the unified transfer tax, the reason for the rule for gifts in contemplation of death largely disappeared. The three-year rule has, however, been retained for the following items:

- Any gift tax paid on gifts made within three years of death. Called the *gross-up* procedure, this prevents the gift tax amount from escaping the estate tax.
- Any property interests transferred by gift within three years of death that would have been included in the gross estate by virtue of the application of § 2036 (transfers with a retained life estate), § 2037 (transfers taking effect at death), § 2038 (revocable transfers), and § 2042 (proceeds of life insurance) had the gift not occurred. All except § 2037 transfers are discussed later in the chapter.

EXAMPLE 32

Before her death in 2005, Jennifer made the following taxable gifts.

Year of Gift	Nature of the Asset	Fair Market Value		Gift Tax Paid
		Date of Gift	Date of Death	
1992	Hawk Corporation stock	$100,000	$ 150,000	$ –0–
2003	Insurance policy on Jennifer's life	80,000 (cash value)	1,000,000 (face value)	–0–
2004	Land	800,000	810,000	16,000

Jennifer's *gross estate* includes $1,016,000 ($1,000,000 life insurance proceeds + $16,000 gross-up for the gift tax on the 2004 taxable gift) as to these transfers. Referring to the formula for the estate tax (Figure 27–2), the other post-1976 taxable gifts are added to the *taxable estate* (at the fair market value on the date of the gift) in arriving at the tax base. Jennifer's estate is allowed a credit for the gift tax paid (or deemed paid) on the 2004 transfer. ■

Transfers with a Retained Life Estate (§ 2036). Code §§ 2036 through 2038 were enacted on the premise that the estate tax can be avoided on lifetime transfers only if the decedent does not retain control over the property. The logic of this approach is somewhat difficult to dispute. One should not be able to escape the tax consequences of property transfers at death while remaining in a position during life to enjoy some or all of the fruits of ownership.

Under § 2036, the value of any property transferred by the deceased during lifetime for less than adequate consideration must be included if either of the following was retained:

- The possession or enjoyment of, or the right to the income from, the property.
- The right, either alone or in conjunction with any person, to designate the persons who shall possess or enjoy the property or the income.

"The possession or enjoyment of, or the right to the income from, the property," as it appears in § 2036(a)(1), is considered to have been retained by the decedent to the extent that such income, etc., is to be applied toward the discharge of a legal obligation of the decedent. The term "legal obligation" includes a legal obligation of the decedent to support a dependent during the decedent's lifetime.[32]

The following examples illustrate the practical application of § 2036.

EXAMPLE 33

Carl's will passes all of his property to a trust in which income goes to Alan for his life (Alan is given a life estate). Upon Alan's death, the principal goes to Melissa (Melissa is granted a remainder interest). On Alan's death, none of the trust property is included in his gross estate. Although Alan held a life estate, § 2036 is inapplicable because Alan was not the transferor (Carl was) of the property. Section 2033 (property owned by the decedent) causes any income distributions Alan was entitled to receive at the time of his death to be included in his gross estate. ■

EXAMPLE 34

By deed, Nora transfers the remainder interest in her ranch to Marcia, retaining for herself the right to continue occupying the property until death. Upon Nora's death, the fair market value of the ranch is included in her gross estate. Furthermore, Nora is subject to the gift tax. The amount of the gift is the fair market value of the ranch on the date of the gift less the portion applicable to Nora's retained life estate. ■

Revocable Transfers (§ 2038). Another type of lifetime transfer that is drawn into a decedent's gross estate is covered by § 2038. The gross estate includes the value of property interests transferred by the decedent (except to the extent that the transfer was made for full consideration) if the enjoyment of the property transferred was subject, at the date of the decedent's death, to any power of the decedent to *alter, amend, revoke, or terminate* the transfer. This includes the power to change beneficiaries or to accelerate or increase any beneficiary's enjoyment of the property.

The Code and the Regulations make it clear that one cannot avoid inclusion in the gross estate under § 2038 by relinquishing a power within three years of death.[33] Recall that § 2038 is one of several types of situations listed as exceptions to the usual rule excluding gifts made within three years of death from the gross estate.

In the event § 2038 applies, the amount includible in the gross estate is the portion of the property transferred that is subject, at the decedent's death, to the decedent's power to alter, amend, revoke, or terminate. The classic § 2038 situation results from the use of a revocable trust.

EXAMPLE 35

Maria creates a trust, life estate to her children, remainder to her grandchildren. Under the terms of the trust, Maria reserves the right to revoke the trust and revest the trust principal and income in herself. As noted in Example 10, the creation of the trust does not result in a gift because the transfer is not complete. However, if Maria dies still retaining the power to revoke, the trust is included in her gross estate under § 2038. ■

Annuities (§ 2039). Annuities can be divided by their origin into commercial and noncommercial contracts. Noncommercial annuities are issued by private parties and, in some cases, charitable organizations that do not regularly issue annuities. The two varieties have much in common, but noncommercial annuities present special income tax problems and are not treated further in this discussion.

Regulation § 20.2039–1(b)(1) defines an annuity as representing "one or more payments extending over any period of time." According to the Regulation, the payments may be equal or unequal, conditional or unconditional, periodic or sporadic. Annuity contracts that terminate upon the death of the person covered (i.e., annuitant) are designated as straight-life annuities. Other contracts provide for a survivorship feature (e.g., reduced payments to a surviving spouse).

[32]Reg. § 20.2036–1(b)(2).

[33]§ 2038(a)(1) and Reg. § 20.2038–1(e)(1).

In the case of a straight-life annuity, nothing is included in the gross estate of the annuitant at death. Section 2033 (property in which the decedent had an interest) does not apply because the annuitant's interest in the contract is terminated by death. Section 2036 (transfers with a retained life estate) does not cover the situation; a transfer made for full consideration is specifically excluded from § 2036 treatment. A commercial annuity is presumed to have been purchased for full consideration unless some evidence exists to indicate that the parties were not acting at arm's length.

EXAMPLE 36

Arnold purchases a straight-life annuity that will pay him $12,000 a month when he reaches age 65. Arnold dies at age 70. Except for the payments he received before his death, nothing relating to this annuity affects Arnold's gross estate. ■

In the case of a survivorship annuity, the estate tax consequences under § 2039(a) are usually triggered by the death of the first annuitant. The amount included in the gross estate is the cost from the same company of a comparable annuity covering the survivor at his or her attained age on the date of the deceased annuitant's death.

EXAMPLE 37

Assume the same facts as in Example 36, except that the annuity contract provides for Veronica to be paid $6,000 a month for life as a survivorship feature. Veronica is 62 years of age when Arnold dies. Under these circumstances, Arnold's gross estate includes the cost of a comparable contract that provides an annuity of $6,000 per month for the life of a female, age 62. ■

Full inclusion of the survivorship element in the gross estate is subject to an exception under § 2039(b). The amount includible is to be based on the proportion of the deceased annuitant's contribution to the total cost of the contract. This is expressed by the following formula:

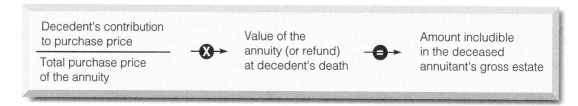

$$\frac{\text{Decedent's contribution to purchase price}}{\text{Total purchase price of the annuity}} \times \text{Value of the annuity (or refund) at decedent's death} = \text{Amount includible in the deceased annuitant's gross estate}$$

EXAMPLE 38

Assume the same facts as in Example 37, except that Arnold and Veronica are husband and wife and have always lived in a community property state. The premiums on the contract were paid with community funds. Since Veronica contributed half of the cost of the contract, only half of the amount determined under Example 37 is included in Arnold's gross estate. ■

The result reached in Example 38 is not unique to community property jurisdictions. The outcome would have been the same in a noncommunity property state if Veronica had furnished half of the consideration from her own funds.

Joint Interests (§§ 2040 and 2511). Recall that joint tenancies and tenancies by the entirety are characterized by the right of survivorship. Thus, upon the death of a joint tenant, title to the property passes to the surviving tenant. None of the property is included in the *probate* estate of the deceased tenant. In the case of tenancies in common and community property, death does not defeat an ownership interest; rather, the deceased owner's interest is part of the probate estate.

The *Federal estate tax treatment* of tenancies in common or of community property follows the logical approach of taxing only the portion of the property included in the deceased owner's probate estate. Thus, if Homer, Wilma, and Thelma are tenants in common in a tract of land, each owning an equal interest, and Homer dies, only one-third of the value of the property is included in the gross estate. This one-third interest is also the same amount that passes to Homer's heirs.

EXAMPLE 39

Homer, Wilma, and Thelma acquire a tract of land with ownership listed as tenants in common, each party furnishing $200,000 of the $600,000 purchase price. When the property is worth $900,000, Homer dies. If Homer's undivided interest in the property is 33⅓%, the gross estate *and* probate estate each include $300,000. ■

Unless the parties have provided otherwise, each tenant is deemed to own an interest equal to the portion of the original consideration he or she furnished. The parties in Example 39 could have provided that Homer would receive an undivided one-half interest in the property although he contributed only one-third of the purchase price. In that case, Wilma and Thelma have made a gift to Homer when the tenancy was created, and Homer's gross estate and probate estate each include $450,000.

For certain joint tenancies, the tax consequences are different. All of the property is included in the deceased co-owner's gross estate unless it can be proved that the surviving co-owners contributed to the cost of the property.[34] If a contribution can be shown, the amount to be *excluded* is calculated by the following formula:

$$\frac{\text{Surviving co-owner's contribution}}{\text{Total cost of the property}} \times \text{Fair market value of the property}$$

In computing a survivor's contribution, any funds received as a gift *from the deceased co-owner* and applied to the cost of the property cannot be counted. However, income or gain from gift assets can be counted.

If the co-owners receive the property as a gift *from another*, each co-owner is deemed to have contributed to the cost of his or her own interest.

The preceding rules can be illustrated as follows:

EXAMPLE 40

Keith and Steve (father and son) acquire a tract of land with ownership listed as joint tenancy with right of survivorship. Keith furnished $400,000 and Steve $200,000 of the $600,000 purchase price. Of the $200,000 provided by Steve, $100,000 had previously been received as a gift from Keith. When the property is worth $900,000, Keith dies. Because only $100,000 of Steve's contribution can be counted (the other $100,000 was received as a gift from Keith), Steve has furnished only one-sixth ($100,000/$600,000) of the cost. Thus, Keith's gross estate must include five-sixths of $900,000, or $750,000. This presumes Steve can prove that he did in fact make the $100,000 contribution. In the absence of such proof, the full value of the property is included in Keith's gross estate. Keith's death makes Steve the immediate owner of the property by virtue of the right of survivorship. None of the property is part of Keith's probate estate. ■

EXAMPLE 41

Francis transfers property to Irene and Martin as a gift, listing ownership as joint tenancy with the right of survivorship. Upon Irene's death, one-half of the value of the property is included in the gross estate. Since the property was received as a gift and the donees are equal owners, each is considered to have furnished half of the consideration. ■

[34]§ 2040(a).

To simplify the joint ownership rules for *married persons*, § 2040(b) provides for an automatic inclusion rule upon the death of the first joint-owner spouse to die. Regardless of the amount contributed by each spouse, one-half of the value of the property is included in the gross estate of the spouse who dies first. The special rule eliminates the need to trace the source of contributions and recognizes that any inclusion in the gross estate is neutralized by the marital deduction.

EXAMPLE 42

Ten years ago, Hank purchased real estate for $100,000 using his separate funds and listed title as "Hank and Louise, joint tenants with the right of survivorship." Hank predeceases Louise in the current year when the property is worth $300,000. If Hank and Louise are husband and wife, Hank's gross estate includes $150,000 (½ of $300,000) as to the property. ■

EXAMPLE 43

Assume the same facts as in Example 42, except that Louise (instead of Hank) dies first. Presuming the value at the date of death is $300,000, Louise's gross estate includes $150,000 as to the property. In this regard, it is of no consequence that Louise did not contribute to the cost of the real estate. ■

In both Examples 42 and 43, inclusion in the gross estate of the first spouse to die is neutralized by the unlimited marital deduction allowed for estate tax purposes (see the discussion of the marital deduction later in the chapter). Under the right of survivorship, the surviving joint tenant obtains full ownership of the property. The marital deduction generally is allowed for property passing from one spouse to another.

Whether or not a *gift* results when property is transferred into some form of joint ownership depends on the consideration furnished by each of the contributing parties for the ownership interest acquired.

EXAMPLE 44

Brenda and Sarah purchase real estate as tenants in common, each furnishing $400,000 of the $800,000 cost. If each is an equal owner in the property, no gift has occurred. ■

EXAMPLE 45

Assume the same facts as in Example 44, except that of the $800,000 purchase price, Brenda furnishes $600,000 and Sarah furnishes only $200,000. If they are equal owners in the property, Brenda has made a gift to Sarah of $200,000. ■

EXAMPLE 46

Martha purchases real estate for $900,000, the title to the property being listed as follows: "Martha, Sylvia, and Dan as joint tenants with the right of survivorship." If under state law the mother (Martha), the daughter (Sylvia), and the son (Dan) are deemed to be equal owners in the property, Martha is treated as having made gifts of $300,000 to Sylvia and $300,000 to Dan. ■

Several important *exceptions* exist to the general rule that the creation of a joint ownership with disproportionate interests resulting from unequal consideration triggers gift treatment. First, if the transfer involves a joint bank account, there is no gift at the time of the contribution.[35] If a gift occurs, it is when the noncontributing party withdraws the funds provided by the other joint tenant. Second, the same rule applies to the purchase of U.S. savings bonds. Again, any gift tax consequences are postponed until the noncontributing party appropriates some or all of the proceeds for his or her individual use.

Life Insurance (§ 2042). Under § 2042, the gross estate includes the proceeds of life insurance on the decedent's life if (1) they are receivable by the estate,

[35]Reg. § 25.2511–1(h)(4).

(2) they are receivable by another for the benefit of the estate, or (3) the decedent possessed an incident of ownership in the policy.

Life insurance on the life of another owned by a decedent at the time of death is included in the gross estate under § 2033 (property in which the decedent had an interest) and not under § 2042. The amount includible is the replacement value of the policy.[36] Under these circumstances, inclusion of the face amount of the policy is inappropriate as the policy has not yet matured.

EXAMPLE 47

At the time of his death, Luigi owned a life insurance policy on the life of Benito, face amount of $500,000 and replacement value of $50,000, with Sofia as the designated beneficiary. Since the policy had not matured at Luigi's death, § 2042 would be inapplicable. However, § 2033 (property in which the decedent had an interest) compels the inclusion of $50,000 (the replacement value) in Luigi's gross estate. If Luigi and Sofia owned the policy as community property, only $25,000 is included in Luigi's gross estate. ■

The term "life insurance" includes whole life policies, term insurance, group life insurance, travel and accident insurance, endowment contracts (before being paid up), and death benefits paid by fraternal societies operating under the lodge system.[37]

As just noted, proceeds of insurance on the life of the decedent receivable by the executor or administrator or payable to the decedent's estate are included in the gross estate. The estate need not be specifically named as the beneficiary. Assume, for example, the proceeds of the policy are receivable by an individual beneficiary and are subject to an obligation, legally binding upon the beneficiary, to pay taxes, debts, and other charges enforceable against the estate. The proceeds are included in the decedent's gross estate to the extent of the beneficiary's obligation. If the proceeds of an insurance policy made payable to a decedent's estate are community assets and, under state law, one-half belongs to the surviving spouse, only one-half of the proceeds will be considered as receivable by or for the benefit of the decedent's estate.

Proceeds of insurance on the life of the decedent not receivable by or for the benefit of the estate are includible if the decedent at death possessed any of the incidents of ownership in the policy. In this connection, the term "incidents of ownership" means more than the ownership of the policy in a technical legal sense. Generally speaking, the term refers to the right of the insured or his or her estate to the economic benefits of the policy. Thus, it also includes the power to change beneficiaries, revoke an assignment, pledge the policy for a loan, or surrender or cancel the policy.[38]

EXAMPLE 48

At the time of death, Broderick was the insured under a policy (face amount of $1 million) owned by Gregory with Demi as the designated beneficiary. Broderick took out the policy five years ago and immediately transferred it as a gift to Gregory. Under the assignment, Broderick transferred all rights in the policy except the right to change beneficiaries. Broderick died without having exercised this right, and the policy proceeds are paid to Demi. Under § 2042(2), Broderick's retention of an incident of ownership in the policy (i.e., the right to change beneficiaries) causes $1 million to be included in his gross estate. ■

Assuming that the deceased-insured holds the incidents of ownership in a policy, how much is included in the gross estate if the insurance policy is a

[36]Reg. § 20.2031–8(a)(1).

[37]Reg. § 20.2042–1(a)(1). As to travel and accident insurance, see *Comm. v. Estate of Noel*, 65–1 USTC ¶12,311, 15 AFTR2d 1397, 85 S.Ct. 1238 (USSC, 1965). As to employer-sponsored group term life insurance, see Example 30 earlier in this chapter.

[38]Reg. § 20.2042–1(c)(2).

community asset? Only one-half of the proceeds becomes part of the deceased spouse's gross estate.

In determining whether or not a policy is *community property* or what portion of it might be so classified, state law controls. The states appear to follow one of two general approaches. Under the inception of title approach, the classification depends on when the policy was originally purchased. If purchased before marriage, the policy is separate property regardless of how many premiums were paid after marriage with community funds. However, if the noninsured spouse is not the beneficiary of the policy, he or she may be entitled to reimbursement from the deceased-insured spouse's estate for half of the premiums paid with community funds. The inception of title approach is followed in at least three states: Louisiana, Texas, and New Mexico.

Some community property jurisdictions classify a policy using the tracing approach: The nature of the funds used to pay the premiums controls. Thus, a policy paid for 20 percent with separate funds and 80 percent with community funds is 20 percent separate property and 80 percent community property. The point in time when the policy was purchased makes no difference. Conceivably, a policy purchased after marriage with the premiums paid exclusively from separate funds is classified entirely as separate property. The tracing approach appears to be the rule in California and Washington.

Merely purchasing a life insurance contract and designating someone else as the beneficiary thereunder does not constitute a *gift*. As long as the purchaser still owns the policy, nothing has really passed to the beneficiary. Even on the death of the insured-owner, no gift takes place. The proceeds paid to the beneficiary constitute a testamentary and not a lifetime transfer. But consider the following possibility.

EXAMPLE 49

Kurt purchases an insurance policy on his own life and transfers the policy to Olga. Kurt retains no interest in the policy (such as the power to change beneficiaries). In these circumstances, Kurt has made a gift to Olga. Furthermore, if Kurt continues to pay the premiums on the transferred policy, each payment constitutes a separate gift. ■

Under certain conditions, the death of the insured may constitute a gift to the beneficiary of part or all of the proceeds. This occurs when the owner of the policy is not the insured.

EXAMPLE 50

Randolph owns an insurance policy on the life of Frank, with Tracy as the designated beneficiary. Up until the time of Frank's death, Randolph retained the right to change the beneficiary of the policy. The proceeds paid to Tracy by the insurance company by reason of Frank's death constitute a gift from Randolph to Tracy.[39] ■

LO.7

Describe the components of the taxable estate.

TAXABLE ESTATE

After the gross estate has been determined, the next step is to determine the taxable estate. By virtue of § 2051, the **taxable estate** is the gross estate less the following: expenses, indebtedness, and taxes (§ 2053); losses (§ 2054); charitable transfers (§ 2055); the marital deduction (§§ 2056 and 2056A); and the deduction for state death taxes (§ 2058). As previously noted, the charitable and marital deductions also have gift tax ramifications.

[39] *Goodman v. Comm.*, 46–1 USTC ¶10,275, 34 AFTR 1534, 156 F.2d 218 (CA–2, 1946).

Expenses, Indebtedness, and Taxes (§ 2053). A deduction is allowed for funeral expenses; expenses incurred in administering property; claims against the estate; and unpaid mortgages and other charges against property, whose value is included in the gross estate (without reduction for the mortgage or other indebtedness).

Expenses incurred in administering community property are deductible only in proportion to the deceased spouse's interest in the community.[40]

Administration expenses include commissions of the executor or administrator, attorney's fees of the estate, accountant's fees, court costs, and certain selling expenses for disposition of estate property.

Claims against the estate include property taxes accrued before the decedent's death, unpaid income taxes on income received by the decedent before he or she died, and unpaid gift taxes on gifts made by the decedent before death.

Amounts that may be deducted as claims against the estate are only for enforceable personal obligations of the decedent at the time of death. Deductions for claims founded on promises or agreements are limited to the extent that the liabilities were contracted in good faith and for adequate and full consideration. However, a pledge or subscription in favor of a public, charitable, religious, or educational organization is deductible to the extent that it would have constituted an allowable deduction had it been a bequest.[41]

Deductible funeral expenses include the cost of interment, the burial plot or vault, a gravestone, perpetual care of the grave site, and the transportation expense of the person bringing the body to the place of burial. If the decedent had, before death, acquired cemetery lots for himself or herself and family, no deduction is allowed, but the lots are not included in the decedent's gross estate under § 2033 (property in which the decedent had an interest).

ETHICAL CONSIDERATIONS

The Advantage of Being Paid Up!

While in the hospital undergoing radical treatment for a terminal condition, Faith pays her medical expenses as they are incurred and satisfies her charitable pledges for the year. Faith does not survive the medical treatment. What tax goals has Faith accomplished? Will her tax planning succeed?

Losses (§ 2054). Section 2054 permits an estate tax deduction for losses from casualty or theft incurred during the period when the estate is being settled. As is true with casualty or theft losses for income tax purposes, any anticipated insurance recovery must be taken into account in arriving at the amount of the deductible loss. Unlike the income tax, however, the deduction is not limited by a floor ($100) or a percentage amount (10 percent of adjusted gross income). If the casualty occurs to property after it has been distributed to an heir, the loss belongs to the heir and not to the estate. If the casualty occurs before the decedent's death, it should be claimed on the appropriate Form 1040. The fair market value of the property (if any) on the date of death plus any insurance recovery is included in the gross estate.

[40] *U.S. v. Stapf*, 63–2 USTC ¶12,192, 12 AFTR2d 6326, 84 S.Ct. 248 (USSC, 1963).

[41] § 2053(c)(1)(A) and Reg. § 20.2053–5.

As is true of certain administration expenses, a casualty or theft loss of estate property can be claimed as an income tax deduction on the fiduciary return of the estate (Form 1041). But a double deduction prohibition applies, and claiming the income tax deduction requires a waiver of the estate tax deduction.[42]

Transfers to Charity (§§ 2055 and 2522). A deduction is allowed for the value of property in the decedent's gross estate that is transferred by the decedent through testamentary disposition to (or for the use of) any of the following:

- The United States or any of its political subdivisions.
- Any corporation or association organized and operated exclusively for religious, charitable, scientific, literary, or educational purposes.
- Various veterans' organizations.

The organizations just described are identical to those that qualify for the Federal gift tax deduction under § 2522. With the following exceptions, they are also the same organizations that qualify a donor for an income tax deduction under § 170.

- Certain nonprofit cemetery associations qualify for income tax but not estate and gift tax purposes.
- Foreign charities may qualify under the estate and gift tax but not under the income tax.

No deduction is allowed unless the charitable bequest is specified by a provision in the decedent's will or the transfer was made before death and the property is subsequently included in the gross estate. Generally speaking, a deduction does not materialize when an individual dies intestate (without a will). The amount of the bequest to charity must be mandatory and cannot be left to someone else's discretion. It is, however, permissible to allow another person, such as the executor of the estate, to choose which charity will receive the specified donation. Likewise, a bequest may be expressed as an alternative and still be effective if the noncharitable beneficiary disclaims (refuses) the intervening interest before the due date for the filing of the estate tax return (nine months after the decedent's death plus any extensions of time granted for filing).

Marital Deduction (§§ 2056, 2056A, and 2523). The **marital deduction** originated with the Revenue Act of 1948 as part of the same legislation that permitted married persons to secure the income-splitting advantages of filing joint income tax returns. The purpose of these statutory changes was to eliminate the major tax variations that existed between taxpayers residing in community property and common law states. The marital deduction was designed to provide equity in the estate and gift tax areas.

In a community property state, for example, no marital deduction generally was allowed since the surviving spouse already owned one-half of the community and that portion was not included in the deceased spouse's gross estate. In a common law state, however, most if not all of the assets often belonged to the breadwinner of the family. When that spouse died first, all of these assets were included in the gross estate. Recall that a dower or curtesy interest (regarding a surviving spouse's right to some of the deceased spouse's property) does not reduce the gross estate. To equalize the situation, therefore, a marital deduction, usually equal to one-half of all separate assets, was allowed upon the death of the first spouse.

[42] § 642(g).

Ultimately, Congress decided to dispense with these historical justifications and recognize husband and wife as a single economic unit. Consistent with the approach taken under the income tax, spouses are considered as one for transfer tax purposes. By making the marital deduction unlimited in amount, neither the gift tax nor the estate tax is imposed on outright interspousal transfers of property. The unlimited marital deduction even includes one spouse's share of the community property transferred to the other spouse.

Under § 2056, the marital deduction is allowed only for property that is included in the deceased spouse's gross estate and that passes or has passed to the surviving spouse. In determining whether the parties are legally married, look to state law (see Example 1 earlier). Property that passes from the decedent to the surviving spouse includes any interest received as (1) the decedent's heir or donee; (2) the decedent's surviving tenant by the entirety or joint tenant; or (3) the beneficiary of insurance on the life of the decedent.

EXAMPLE 51

At the time of his death in the current year, Matthew owned an insurance policy on his own life (face amount of $500,000) with Minerva (his wife) as the designated beneficiary. Matthew and Minerva also owned real estate (worth $600,000) as tenants by the entirety (Matthew had furnished all of the purchase price). As to these transfers, $800,000 ($500,000 + $300,000) is included in Matthew's gross estate, and this amount represents the property that passes to Minerva for purposes of the marital deduction.[43] ■

ETHICAL CONSIDERATIONS

It's the Thought That Counts

Joe (age 86) and Nicole (age 22) are married. Two days later they exchange wedding gifts. Joe's gift to Nicole is stock in IBM (valued at $2 million), while Nicole's gift to Joe is a bottle of cologne (value of $32). What tax goals are they trying to accomplish? Will their plan work?

Disclaimers can affect the amount passing to the surviving spouse. If, for example, the surviving spouse is the remainderperson under the will of the deceased spouse, a disclaimer by another heir increases the amount passing to the surviving spouse. This, in turn, will increase the amount of the marital deduction allowed to the estate of the deceased spouse.

A problem arises when a property interest passing to the surviving spouse is subject to a mortgage or other encumbrance. In this case, only the net value of the interest after reduction by the amount of the mortgage or other encumbrance qualifies for the marital deduction. To allow otherwise results in a double deduction since a decedent's liabilities are separately deductible under § 2053.

EXAMPLE 52

In his will, Oscar leaves real estate (fair market value of $500,000) to his wife. If the real estate is subject to a mortgage of $100,000 (upon which Oscar was personally liable), the marital deduction is limited to $400,000 ($500,000 – $100,000). The $100,000 mortgage is deductible under § 2053 as an obligation of the decedent (Oscar). ■

[43]Inclusion in the gross estate falls under § 2042 (proceeds of life insurance) and § 2040 (joint interests). Although Matthew provided the full purchase price for the real estate, § 2040(b) requires inclusion of only half of the value of the property when one spouse predeceases the other.

However, if the executor is required under the terms of the decedent's will or under local law to discharge the mortgage out of other assets of the estate or to reimburse the surviving spouse, the payment or reimbursement is an additional interest passing to the surviving spouse.

EXAMPLE 53

Assume the same facts as in Example 52, except that Oscar's will directs that the real estate is to pass to his wife free of any liabilities. Accordingly, Oscar's executor pays off the mortgage by using other estate assets and distributes the real estate to Oscar's wife. The marital deduction now becomes $500,000. ■

Federal estate taxes or other death taxes paid out of the surviving spouse's share of the gross estate are not included in the value of property passing to the surviving spouse. Therefore, it is usually preferable for the deceased spouse's will to provide that death taxes be paid out of the portion of the estate that does not qualify for the marital deduction.

Certain interests in property passing from the deceased spouse to the surviving spouse are referred to as **terminable interests.** Such an interest will terminate or fail after the passage of time, upon the happening of some contingency, or upon the failure of some event to occur. Examples are life estates, annuities, estates for terms of years, and patents. A terminable interest will not qualify for the marital deduction if another interest in the same property passed from the deceased spouse to some other person, and by reason of the passing, that other person or his or her heirs may enjoy part of the property after the termination of the surviving spouse's interest.[44]

EXAMPLE 54

Vicky's will places her property in trust with a life estate to her husband, Brett, remainder to Andrew or his heirs. The interest passing from Vicky to Brett does not qualify for the marital deduction. Brett's interest will terminate on his death, and Andrew or his heirs will then possess or enjoy the property. ■

EXAMPLE 55

Assume the same facts as in Example 54, except that Vicky created the trust during her life. No marital deduction is available for gift tax purposes for the same reason as in Example 54.[45] ■

The justification for the terminable interest rule can be illustrated by examining the possible results of Examples 54 and 55 more closely. Without the rule, Vicky could have passed property to Brett at no cost because of the marital deduction. Yet, on Brett's death, none of the property would have been included in his gross estate. Section 2036 (transfers with a retained life estate) would not apply to Brett because he was not the original transferor of the property. The marital deduction should not be available in situations where the surviving spouse can enjoy the property and still pass it to another without tax consequences. The marital deduction is intended to merely postpone the transfer tax on the death of the first spouse and to shift any such tax to the surviving spouse.

Consistent with the objective of the terminable interest rule, an alternative means for obtaining the marital deduction is available. Under this provision, the marital deduction is allowed for transfers of **qualified terminable interest property** (commonly referred to as **QTIP**). This is defined as property that passes from one

[44]§§ 2056(b)(1) and 2523(b)(1).

[45]Both Examples 54 and 55 contain the potential for a qualified terminable interest property (QTIP) election discussed later in this section.

spouse to another by gift or at death and for which the transferee-spouse has a qualifying income interest for life.

For a donee or a surviving spouse, a qualifying income interest for life exists under the following conditions:

- The person is entitled for life to all of the income from the property (or a specific portion of it), payable at annual or more frequent intervals.
- No person (including the spouse) has a power to appoint any part of the property to any person other than the surviving spouse during his or her life.[46]

If these conditions are met, an election can be made to claim a marital deduction as to the QTIP. For estate tax purposes, the executor of the estate makes the election on Form 706 (estate tax return). For gift tax purposes, the donor spouse makes the election on Form 709 (gift tax return). The election is irrevocable.

If the election is made, a transfer tax is imposed upon the QTIP when the transferee-spouse disposes of it by gift or upon death. If the disposition occurs during life, the gift tax applies, measured by the fair market value of the property as of that time.[47] If no lifetime disposition takes place, the fair market value of the property on the date of death (or alternate valuation date if applicable) is included in the gross estate of the transferee-spouse.[48]

EXAMPLE 56

In 1980, Clyde dies and provides in his will that certain assets (fair market value of $800,000) are to be transferred to a trust under which Gertrude (Clyde's wife) is granted a life estate with the remainder passing to their children upon Gertrude's death. Presuming all of the preceding requirements are satisfied and Clyde's executor so elects, his estate receives a marital deduction of $800,000. ■

EXAMPLE 57

Assume the same facts as in Example 56, with the further stipulation that Gertrude dies in 2005 when the trust assets are worth $2.4 million. This amount is included in her gross estate. ■

Because the estate tax is imposed on assets not physically included in the probate estate, the law allows the tax liability for those assets to be shifted to the heirs. The amount shifted is determined by comparing the estate tax liability both with and without the inclusion of the QTIP. This right of recovery can be canceled by a provision in the deceased spouse's will.[49]

State Death Taxes (§ 2058). The Tax Relief Reconciliation Act of 2001 provided for a phaseout of the § 2011 credit for state death taxes. The phaseout began in 2002 and was completed in 2004. Commencing in 2005, state and local death taxes paid by the estate are allowed as deductions from the gross estate in arriving at the taxable estate.

The purpose of the new § 2058 deduction is to mitigate the effect of subjecting property to multiple death taxes (i.e., both Federal and state). In this regard, however, it provides less relief than was available with the § 2011 credit it replaces. A credit results in a dollar-for-dollar reduction in tax, whereas the benefit of a deduction is limited by the effective tax bracket of the estate.

LO.8

Determine the Federal estate tax liability.

COMPUTING THE FEDERAL ESTATE TAX

Once the taxable estate has been determined, post-1976 taxable gifts are added to arrive at the tax base. Note that pre-1977 taxable gifts do not enter into the computation of the tax base.

[46]§§ 2523(f) and 2056(b)(7).
[47]§§ 2519 and 2511.
[48]§ 2044.
[49]§ 2207A(a).

EXAMPLE 58

Joyce dies in 2005, leaving a taxable estate of $1.8 million. During her life, Joyce made taxable gifts as follows: $50,000 in 1975 and $100,000 in 1982. For estate tax purposes, the Federal estate tax base becomes $1.9 million determined as follows: $1,800,000 (taxable estate) + $100,000 taxable gift made in 1982. ■

Next the tentative tax on the tax base is computed using the unified transfer tax rate schedule contained in § 2001(c). Using the facts in Example 58, the tentative tax on $1.9 million is $735,800 [$555,800 + (45% × $400,000)]—see Appendix A.

All available estate tax credits are subtracted from the tentative estate tax to arrive at the estate tax (if any) that is due.

ESTATE TAX CREDITS

Unified Tax Credit (§ 2010). Recall from previous discussion of this credit that the amount of the credit allowed depends upon the year of the transfer. Returning to Example 58, the credit allowed on the gift in 1982 was $62,800. Since the exemption equivalent of this amount is $225,000 (refer to Table 27–1), no gift tax was due on the transfer. On Joyce's death in 2005, however, the unified tax credit is $555,800, which is less than the tentative tax of $735,800 (refer to the discussion following Example 58). Disregarding the effect of any other estate tax credits, Joyce's estate owes a tax of $180,000 [$735,800 (tentative tax on a tax base of $1,900,000) – $555,800 (unified tax credit for 2005)].

An adjustment to the unified tax credit is necessary if any portion of the specific exemption was utilized on gifts made after September 8, 1976, and before January 1, 1977. In this regard, refer to Example 5.

Credit for State Death Taxes (§ 2011). The Code allowed a limited credit for the amount of any death tax actually paid to any state (or to the District of Columbia) attributable to any property included in the gross estate. Like the credit for foreign death taxes paid, this provision mitigated the harshness of subjecting the same property to multiple death taxes.

The credit allowed was limited to the lesser of the amount of tax actually paid or the amount provided for in a table contained in § 2011(b). The table amount was based on the *adjusted taxable estate,* which for this purpose was the taxable estate less $60,000. No credit was allowed if the adjusted taxable estate was $40,000 or less.

The Tax Relief Reconciliation Act of 2001 phased out § 2011 beginning in 2002 at the rate of 25 percent per year. Thus, by 2005, the credit is completely eliminated.[50] As previously noted, the *credit* for state death taxes paid has been replaced by a *deduction* under § 2058.

The credit provision of § 2011, however, continues to be relevant. Over the years many states based their estate tax on the amount of credit allowed for Federal estate tax purposes. Called a "pick-up" ("sponge" or "soak-up") tax, its determination was convenient and added no additional cost to an estate. The application of § 2011 permitted a state to receive some of the tax that otherwise would have been paid to the IRS.

With the phaseout of the § 2011 credit, *most* states allowed the pick-up tax to phase out in a similar fashion. But some states could not afford the loss of revenue that would result, and they have retained the pick-up tax. In these cases, the table contained in § 2011 is used to compute the amount of death tax due to the state. Usually, a monetary exemption is allowed (e.g., $675,000) before an estate is subject to tax.

[50] As is the case with all estate tax changes made by the Tax Relief Reconciliation Act of 2001, a sunset provision will reinstate § 2011 as to decedents dying after 2010.

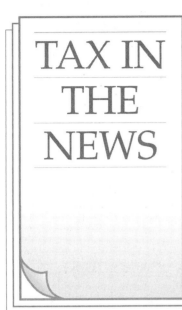

Be Careful Where You Die!

Changes in the Federal estate tax have had a significant impact on state death taxes. In 25 states, for example, there is no longer any death tax—of either the inheritance or the estate tax variety. As one might suspect, this group includes the popular retirement states, such as Arizona, Nevada, and Florida. The other 25 states and the District of Columbia continue to impose either an inheritance tax or an estate tax, or both.

To understand the different results, consider a widow who dies in 2005 with a taxable estate of $1.5 million. Further assume that all of her property is located in the state where she resides and that her sole heirs are her adult sons. If her residence is Wisconsin, her estate owes a state estate tax of $64,400. In contrast, if her residence is Arizona, no state death tax is due.

Prior to the enactment of the Tax Relief Reconciliation Act of 2001, the state of the widow's residence, at least in this case, would have made no difference. The tax due, based on the credit allowed under § 2011, would also have been $64,400 in the Arizona situation.

Credit for Tax on Prior Transfers (§ 2013). Suppose Floyd owns some property that he passes at death to Sarah. Shortly thereafter, Sarah dies and passes the property to Juan. Assuming both estates are subject to the Federal estate tax, the successive deaths result in a multiple effect. To mitigate the possible multiple taxation that might result, § 2013 provides relief in the form of a credit for a death tax on prior transfers. In the preceding hypothetical case, Sarah's estate may be able to claim as an estate tax credit some of the taxes paid by Floyd's estate.

The credit is limited to the lesser of the following:

1. The amount of the Federal estate tax attributable to the transferred property in the transferor's estate.
2. The amount of the Federal estate tax attributable to the transferred property in the decedent's estate.

To apply the limitations, certain adjustments must be made that are not covered in this text.[51] However, it is not necessary for the transferred property to be identified in the present decedent's estate or for it to be in existence at the time of the present decedent's death. It is sufficient that the transfer of property was subjected to the Federal estate tax in the estate of the transferor and that the transferor died within the prescribed period of time.

If the transferor dies within two years after or before the present decedent's death, the credit is allowed in full (subject to the preceding limitations). If the transferor died more than two years before the decedent, the credit is a certain percentage: 80 percent if the transferor died within the third or fourth year preceding the decedent's death, 60 percent if within the fifth or sixth year, 40 percent if within the seventh or eighth year, and 20 percent if within the ninth or tenth year.

EXAMPLE 59

Under Floyd's will, Sarah inherits property. One year later Sarah dies. Assume the estate tax attributable to the inclusion of the property in Floyd's gross estate was $15,000 and that attributable to the inclusion of the property in Sarah's gross estate is $12,000. Under these circumstances, Sarah's estate claims a credit against the estate tax of $12,000 (refer to limitation 2). ■

[51] See the instructions to Form 706 and Reg. §§ 20.2013–2 and –3.

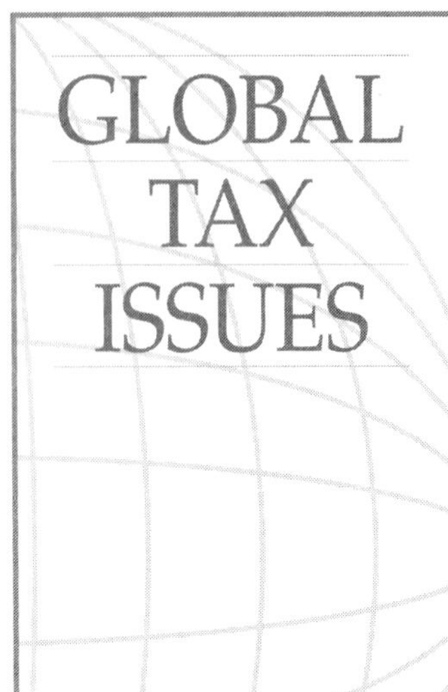

Treaty Relief Is Not Abundant!

One means of mitigating double taxation at the international level is to take advantage of treaty provisions. A treaty will determine which country has primary taxing rights, and this may depend on such factors as the domicile of the decedent or the nature of the property involved (e.g., personalty or realty). Unfortunately, the United States has death tax conventions with only 17 countries: Australia*, Austria*, Canada, Denmark*, Finland, France*, Germany*, Greece, Ireland, Italy, Japan*, the Netherlands, Norway, the Republic of South Africa, Sweden, Switzerland, and the United Kingdom*. In contrast, more than 50 countries have income tax treaties with the United States (see Exhibit 25–1 in Chapter 25). Thus, treaty relief in the estate tax area is not as widespread as with income tax situations.

*An asterisk indicates the existence of a gift tax treaty as well.

EXAMPLE 60

Assume the same facts as in Example 59, except that Sarah dies three years after Floyd. The applicable credit is now 80% of $12,000, or $9,600. ■

Credit for Foreign Death Taxes (§ 2014). A credit is allowed against the estate tax for any estate, inheritance, legacy, or succession tax actually paid to a foreign country. For purposes of this provision, the term "foreign country" means not only states in the international sense but also possessions or political subdivisions of foreign states and possessions of the United States.

PROCEDURAL MATTERS

A Federal estate tax return, if required, is due nine months after the date of the decedent's death.[52] The time limit applies to all estates regardless of the nationality or residence of the decedent. Frequently, an executor will request and obtain from the IRS an extension of time for filing Form 706 (estate tax return).[53] Also available is an *automatic* six-month extension of time to file the estate tax return. To receive the extension, the executor must file Form 4768 [Application for Extension of Time to File a Return and/or Pay U.S. Estate (and Generation-Skipping Transfer) Taxes].

The filing requirements parallel the exclusion amounts of the unified tax credit available for each year (refer to Table 27–2). The filing requirements may be lower when the decedent has made taxable gifts after 1976 or has utilized any of the $30,000 specific gift tax exemption after September 8, 1976.

EXAMPLE 61

Carlos dies in 2005, leaving a gross estate of $1.5 million. If Carlos did not make any post-1976 taxable gifts or use the specific gift tax exemption after September 8, 1976, his estate need not file Form 706. ■

EXAMPLE 62

Assume the same facts as in Example 61, except that Carlos made a taxable gift of $20,000 in 1980. Since the filing requirement now becomes $1,480,000 ($1,500,000 regular filing requirement for 2005 – $20,000 post-1976 taxable gift), Carlos's estate must file Form 706. ■

[52] § 6075(a).

[53] § 6081.

LO.9

Appreciate the role of the generation-skipping transfer tax.

The Generation-Skipping Transfer Tax

In order to prevent partial avoidance of Federal gift and estate taxes on large transfers, the tax law imposes an additional generation-skipping transfer tax.

THE PROBLEM

Previously, it was possible to bypass a generation of transfer taxes by structuring the transaction carefully.

EXAMPLE 63

Under his will, Edward creates a trust, life estate to Stephen (Edward's son) and remainder to Ava (Edward's granddaughter) upon Stephen's death. Edward is subject to the Federal estate tax, but no tax results on Stephen's death. Stephen held a life estate, but § 2036 does not apply because he was not the grantor of the trust. Nor does § 2033 (property owned by the decedent) come into play because Stephen's interest disappeared upon his death. The ultimate result is that the property in trust skips a generation of transfer taxes. ■

EXAMPLE 64

Joshua dies at age 89 and leaves all of his property to a trust. Under the terms of the trust instrument, trust income and corpus are to be distributed equally over a 10-year period to Amber and Ethan. Amber is Joshua's 22-year-old third wife, while Ethan is his 30-year-old grandson. As a result of this arrangement, the following tax consequences ensue: the estate tax applies on Joshua's death; income earned by the trust will be subject to income tax (see Chapter 28); and no transfer tax normally results when distributions of trust income and corpus occur. ■

EXAMPLE 65

Amy gives assets to Eric (her grandson). Called a direct skip, the gift would circumvent any transfer taxes that would have resulted had the assets been channeled through Eric's parents. ■

THE SOLUTION

The generation-skipping transfer tax (GSTT) is designed to preclude the avoidance of either the estate tax or the gift tax by making transfers that bypass the next lower generation. In the typical family setting, this involves transfers from grandparents to grandchildren. Such transfers, in effect, would skip any transfer tax that would result if the property were channeled through the children.

The GSTT is triggered by any of these three events: a taxable *termination* occurs; a taxable *distribution* takes place; or a *direct skip* is made.[54] Example 63 illustrates a termination event. Upon Stephen's death, the fair market value of the trust property that passes to Ava is subject to the GSTT (imposed on the trust). The GSTT will have the effect of reducing the amount Ava receives from the trust.

Example 64 illustrates a distribution event. When the trust makes a distribution to Ethan, the GSTT applies (imposed on Ethan). Any distribution to Amber is not subject to the GSTT because the spouse of the transferor (Joshua in this case) is deemed to be of the same generation.[55] The results reached in Example 64 show how ludicrous the application of the GSTT rules can be. Amber (age 22) is treated as being in the same generation as Joshua (age 89), while Ethan (age 30) is two generations removed!

[54] § 2611.

[55] § 2651(c)(1).

Example 65 illustrates a lifetime version of the direct skip event.[56] In this situation, the GSTT is imposed upon Amy when the gift is made to Eric. Not only will Amy be subject to the GSTT, but the amount of the tax represents an additional gift to Eric.[57] Thus, if a gift is a direct skip (such as Example 65), the total transfer tax (the GSTT plus the gift tax) may exceed what the donee receives.

The GSTT rate is the highest rate under the gift and estate tax schedule. Pursuant to transitional rules, these top rates are as follows: 47 percent (2005), 46 percent (2006), and 45 percent (2007). (The rates were 49 percent in 2003 and 48 percent in 2004.) To ameliorate the extra tax burden of the GSTT, an exemption is allowed equal to the exclusion amount applicable to the Federal estate tax (see Table 27–2).[58] For a donor who is married, the election to split the gift (under § 2513) will double the amount of the exemption.[59] For 2005, for example, the amount of the exemption could be $3 million ($1.5 million × 2). The exemption can be applied to whichever transfers the grantor (or personal representative of the grantor) chooses. Any appreciation attributable to the exempted portion of the transfer is not later subject to the GSTT.

EXAMPLE 66

Assume the same facts as in Example 63. Edward died in 2005, and the amount transferred to the trust was $1.5 million. Edward's executor elected to use the full $1.5 million exemption to cover the transfer. Stephen dies in 2008 when the trust is worth $2.2 million. None of this amount is subject to the GSTT. The $700,000 appreciation on the exclusion amount ($2,200,000 – $1,500,000) also escapes the GSTT. ■

Along with the estate tax, the GSTT is scheduled to be phased out by 2010.

Tax Planning Considerations

THE FEDERAL GIFT TAX

For gifts that generate a tax, consideration must be given to the time value to the donor of the gift taxes paid. Since the donor loses the use of these funds, the expected interval between a gift (the imposition of the gift tax) and death (the imposition of the death tax) may make the gift less attractive from an economic standpoint. On the plus side, however, are the estate tax savings that result from any gift tax paid. Since these funds are no longer in the gross estate of the donor (except for certain gifts within three years of death), the estate tax thereon is avoided.

Gifts possess distinct advantages. First, and often most important, income from the property is generally shifted to the donee. If the donee is in a lower bracket than the donor, the family unit will save on income taxes. Second, the proper spacing of gifts can further cut down the Federal gift tax by maximizing the number of annual exclusions available. Third, all states impose some type of death tax, but only a minority impose a gift tax. Thus, a gift may completely avoid a state transfer tax.

In minimizing gift tax liability in lifetime giving, the optimum use of the annual exclusion can have significant results. Important in this regard are the following observations:

- Because the annual exclusion is available every year, space the gifts over as many years as possible. To carry out this objective, start the program of lifetime giving as soon as is feasible. For example, assume a donor made gifts in the amount of the annual exclusion to a donee beginning in 1998.

[56] § 2612(c)(1). A direct skip can also take place in a testamentary transfer.

[57] § 2515.

[58] § 2631(c).

[59] § 2652(a)(2).

Through 2005, the donor will have transferred $84,000 [($10,000 annual exclusion for 1998–2001) × 4 (number of years at $10,000 annual exclusion) + $11,000 (annual exclusion for 2002 on) × 4 (number of years at $11,000 exclusion)] without using any of the unified tax credit and incurring any gift tax.

- To the extent consistent with the wishes of the donor, maximize the number of donees. For example, a donor could give $420,000 to five donees over the 1998–2005 period ($84,000 apiece) without using any of the unified tax credit and incurring any gift tax.
- For the married donor, make use of the election to split gifts. As an example, a married couple can give $840,000 to five donees over the 1998–2005 period [$20,000 (annual exclusion for two donors for 1998–2001) × 5 (number of donees) × 4 (number of years at $20,000 annual exclusion) + $22,000 (annual exclusion for two donors for 2002 on) × 5 (number of donees) × 4 (number of years at $22,000 annual exclusion)] without using any of their unified tax credits and incurring any gift tax.
- Watch out for gifts of future interests. As noted earlier in the chapter, the annual exclusion is available only for gifts of a present interest.

THE FEDERAL ESTATE TAX

Controlling the Amount of the Gross Estate. Presuming an estate tax problem is anticipated, the starting point for planning purposes is to reduce the size of the potential gross estate. Aside from initiating a program of lifetime giving, several other possibilities exist.

Proper Handling of Estate Tax Deductions. Estate taxes can be saved either by reducing the size of the gross estate or by increasing the total allowable deductions. Thus, the lower the taxable estate, the less the amount of estate tax generated. Planning in the deduction area generally involves the following considerations:

- Making proper use of the marital deduction.
- Working effectively with the charitable deduction.
- Taking advantage of the bypass amount.
- Properly handling other deductions and losses allowed under §§ 2053 and 2054.

Approaches to the Marital Deduction. When planning for the estate tax marital deduction, both tax and nontax factors have to be taken into account. In the tax area, planning is guided by two major goals: the *equalization* and *deferral* approaches.

- Attempt to equalize the estates of both spouses. Clearly, for example, the estate tax on $2 million is more than double the estate tax on $1 million [compare $780,800 with $691,600 ($345,800 × 2)].
- Based on the time value of taxes deferred, try to postpone estate taxation as long as possible. Also keep in mind the possible effect of the Tax Relief Reconciliation Act of 2001. If, as proposed, the estate tax is phased out, the exclusion amount (i.e., exemption equivalent) for the unified tax credit increases. The exclusion amount is $1.5 million for 2005 (and 2004) and is scheduled to increase to $2 million for 2006 to 2008 and to $3.5 million for 2009. See the earlier discussion in connection with Tables 27–1 and 27–2.

Barring certain circumstances, the deferral approach generally is preferable. By maximizing the marital deduction on the death of the first spouse to die, not only are taxes saved, but the surviving spouse is enabled to trim his or her future estate

CONCEPT SUMMARY 27–2

Federal Estate Tax Provisions

1. The Federal gift and estate taxes are both excise taxes on the transfer of wealth.
2. The starting point for applying the Federal estate tax is to determine which assets are subject to tax. Such assets constitute a decedent's gross estate.
3. The gross estate generally will not include any gifts made by the decedent within three years of death. It does include any gift tax paid on these transfers.
4. Based on the premise that one should not continue to enjoy or control property and not have it subject to the estate tax, certain incomplete transfers are included in the gross estate.
5. Upon the death of a joint tenant, the full value of the property is included in the gross estate unless the survivor(s) made a contribution toward the cost of the property. Spouses are subject to a special rule that calls for automatic inclusion of half of the value of the property in the gross estate of the first tenant to die. The creation of joint ownership is subject to the gift tax when a tenant receives a lesser interest in the property than is warranted by the consideration furnished.
6. If the decedent is the insured, life insurance proceeds are included in the gross estate if either of two conditions is satisfied. First, the proceeds are paid to the estate or for the benefit of the estate. Second, the decedent possessed incidents of ownership (e.g., the right to change beneficiaries) over the policy.
7. In moving from the gross estate to the taxable estate, certain deductions are allowed. Under § 2053, deductions are permitted for various administration expenses (e.g., executor's commissions, funeral costs), debts of the decedent, and certain unpaid taxes. Casualty and theft losses incurred during the administration of an estate can be deducted in arriving at the taxable estate under § 2054. In addition, § 2058 provides that state and local death taxes paid by the estate may be deducted from the gross estate.
8. Charitable transfers are deductible if the designated organization holds qualified status with the IRS at the time of the gift or upon death.
9. Transfers to a spouse qualify for the gift or estate tax marital deduction. Except as noted in (10), such transfers are subject to the terminable interest limitation.
10. The terminable interest limitation will not apply if the QTIP election is made. In the case of a lifetime transfer, the donor spouse makes the QTIP election. In the case of a testamentary transfer, the executor of the estate of the deceased spouse has the election responsibility.
11. The tax base for determining the estate tax is the taxable estate plus post-1976 taxable gifts. All available credits are subtracted from the tax.
12. Of prime importance in the tax credit area is the unified tax credit. The amount of the unified tax credit varies depending upon the year of death.
13. If due, a Federal estate tax return (Form 706) must be filed within nine months of the date of the decedent's death.

by entering into a program of lifetime giving. By making optimum use of the annual exclusion, considerable amounts can be shifted without incurring *any* transfer tax.

Tax planning must remain flexible and be tailored to the individual circumstances of the parties involved. Before the equalization approach is cast aside, therefore, consider the following variables:

- Both spouses are of advanced age and/or in poor health, and neither is expected to survive the other for a prolonged period of time.
- The spouse who is expected to survive has considerable assets of his or her own. Keep in mind that the transfer tax rate schedules are progressive in nature.
- Because of appreciation, property worth $250,000 when it passes to the surviving spouse today may be worth $1 million five years later when the survivor dies.

Effectively Working with the Charitable Deduction. As a general guide to obtain overall tax savings, lifetime charitable transfers are preferred over testamentary dispositions. For example, an individual who gave $20,000 to a qualified charity during his or her life would secure an income tax deduction, avoid any gift tax, and reduce the gross estate by the amount of the gift. By way of contrast, if the $20,000 had been willed to charity, no income tax deduction would be available, and the amount of the transfer would be includible in the decedent's gross estate (though later deducted for estate tax purposes). In short, the lifetime transfer provides a double tax benefit (income tax deduction plus reduced estate taxes) at no gift tax cost. The testamentary transfer merely neutralizes the effect of the inclusion of the property in the gross estate (inclusion under § 2033 and then deduction under § 2055).

On occasion, a charitable bequest depends on the issuance of a disclaimer by a noncharitable heir.[60] Such a situation frequently arises with special types of property or collections, which the decedent may feel a noncharitable heir should have a choice of receiving.

EXAMPLE 67

Megan specified in her will that her valuable art collection is to pass to her son or, if the son refuses, to a designated and qualified art museum. At the time the will was drawn, Megan knew that her son was not interested in owning the collection. If, after Megan's death, the son issues a timely disclaimer, the collection will pass to the designated museum, and Megan's estate is allowed a charitable deduction for its estate tax value. ■

EXAMPLE 68

Dick's will specifies that one-half of his disposable estate is to pass to his wife, and the remainder of his property to a designated and qualified charitable organization. If the wife issues a timely disclaimer after Dick's death, all of the property passes to the charity and qualifies for the § 2055 charitable deduction. ■

Did the son in Example 67 act wisely if he issued the disclaimer in favor of the museum? Although the disclaimer will provide Megan's estate with a deduction for the value of the art collection, consider the income tax deduction alternative. If the son accepts the bequest, he can still dispose of the collection (and fulfill his mother's philanthropic objectives) through a lifetime donation to the museum. At the same time, he obtains an income tax deduction under § 170. Whether this will save taxes for the family unit depends on a comparison of Megan's estate tax bracket with the estimated income tax bracket of the son. If the value of the collection runs afoul of the percentage limitations of § 170(b)(1), the donations can be spread over more than one year. If this is done, and to protect against the contingency of the son's dying before the entire collection is donated, the son can neutralize any potential death tax consequences by providing in his will for the undonated balance to pass to the museum.

The use of a disclaimer in Example 68 would be sheer folly. It would not reduce Dick's estate tax; it would merely substitute a charitable deduction for the marital deduction. Whether the wife issues a disclaimer or not, no estate taxes will be due. The wife should accept her bequest and, if she is so inclined, make lifetime gifts of it to a qualified charity. In so doing, she generates an income tax deduction for herself.

Taking Advantage of the Bypass Amount. The bypass amount, also known as the exclusion amount or the exemption equivalent, is the amount that can pass free of a transfer tax due to the unified credit. For a credit of $555,800, which is available for estate tax purposes for 2005, the bypass amount is $1.5 million.[61]

The availability of the bypass amount can be particularly useful in planning the marital deduction.

[60] As noted earlier in this chapter, a disclaimer is a refusal to accept the property. If the disclaimer is timely made, the property is not treated as having passed through the person issuing the disclaimer, and a gift tax is avoided.

[61] The bypass amount is reduced if the decedent has made any post-1976 taxable gifts.

EXAMPLE 69

Ethan dies in 2005 and is survived by his wife, Hope, and their children. Ethan's will passes his entire estate of $5 million to Hope. ■

EXAMPLE 70

Assume the same facts as in Example 69, except that Ethan's will passes $1.5 million to the children and the remainder of his estate to Hope. ■

Although both situations avoid any estate taxes, Example 69 represents overkill in terms of the marital deduction. Not only does it unduly concentrate wealth in the surviving spouse's estate, but it fails to take advantage of the bypass amount. Example 70 remedies this shortcoming by permitting $1.5 million to pass to another generation free of any transfer tax.

Proper Handling of Other Deductions and Losses under §§ 2053 and 2054. Many § 2053 and § 2054 deductions and losses may be claimed either as estate tax deductions or as income tax deductions of the estate on the fiduciary return (Form 1041), but a choice must be made.[62] The deduction for income tax purposes is not allowed unless the estate tax deduction is waived. It is possible for these deductions to be apportioned between the two returns.

KEY TERMS

PROBLEM MATERIALS

Discussion Questions

1. Why can the unified transfer tax be categorized as an excise tax? In this regard, how does it differ from an income tax?
2. Over the years, the tax treatment of transfers by gift and by death has not been consistent. In this regard, what was congressional justification for the rules applicable to:
   a. Pre-1977 transfers?
   b. Post-1976 and pre-2001 transfers?
   c. Current transfers?
3. What are the major differences between the Federal estate tax and the typical inheritance tax levied by some states?
4. In connection with the Federal gift tax, comment on each of the following.
   a. Upon whom it is imposed.
   b. When it is applicable to a nonresident alien.
   c. When it is applicable to property located outside the United States.

[62] § 642(g) and Reg. § 20.2053–1(d).

Issue ID

5. Evita is a citizen and resident of Costa Rica. She has investments in U.S. property consisting of unimproved land in South Carolina and stock in Ford Motor Company held by her Miami brokerage firm. If Evita makes a gift of these assets to her son (also a citizen and resident of Costa Rica), what U.S. tax consequences result?

6. To avoid Federal transfer taxes, Frank renounces his U.S. citizenship. He moves to Venice, establishes residency there, and becomes an Italian citizen. Will Frank successfully avoid the Federal gift and estate taxes? Explain.

7. Evaluate the propriety of the following statement: "The Tax Relief Reconciliation Act of 2001 eliminated the Federal estate tax."

8. What is the relationship, if any, between the *unified transfer tax credit*, the *exclusion amount*, and the *exemption equivalent*?

9. As to the alternate valuation date of § 2032, comment on the following.
   a. The justification for the election.
   b. A Form 706 need not be filed for the estate.
   c. The main heir prefers the date of death value.
   d. An estate asset is distributed to an heir three months after the decedent's death.
   e. Some estate assets have appreciated in value since the death of the decedent.

10. The alternate valuation date cannot be used unless its election decreases the value of the gross estate *and* decreases the estate tax liability. Why are these conditions imposed?

11. What are the similarities between each of the following?
    a. Joint tenancy and tenancy by the entirety.
    b. Tenancy in common and community property.
    c. Tenancy by the entirety and community property.

12. Zoe gives her son a Jaguar automobile on his fortieth birthday. The transfer is not subject to the Federal gift tax because Zoe is satisfying her obligation of support. Do you agree?

13. Can a loan between related parties ever carry gift tax ramifications? Explain.

Issue ID

14. Under Leon's will, all of his property is to pass to his son, Jody. Jody is a widower, and his only survivor is a daughter, Brenda. Jody has considerable wealth of his own and is in poor health. Do you recognize an attractive estate tax option for the parties?

15. Qualified tuition programs under § 529 enjoy significant tax advantages. Describe these advantages with regard to the Federal:
    a. Income tax.
    b. Gift tax.
    c. Estate tax.

16. In connection with the gift-splitting provision of § 2513, comment on the following.
    a. What it was designed to accomplish.
    b. How the election is made.
    c. Its utility in a community property jurisdiction.

17. In connection with the filing of a Federal gift tax return, comment on the following.
    a. No Federal gift tax is due.
    b. The § 2513 election to split gifts is to be used.
    c. A gift of a future interest is involved.
    d. The donor uses a fiscal year for Federal income tax purposes.
    e. The donor obtained from the IRS an extension of time for filing his or her Federal income tax return.

18. Distinguish between the following.
    a. The gross estate and the taxable estate.
    b. The gross estate and the probate estate.

19. Under what Code sections, if any, are the following transactions included in Mary's gross estate?
    a. A vested interest in her employer's contributory qualified pension plan with Jim, Mary's son, as the designated beneficiary.
    b. An insurance policy on her life, which Mary gave to Jim last year. Her grandson is the designated beneficiary of the policy.
    c. A CD at a local bank with ownership listed as "Mary, payable on proof of death to Jim."
    d. A revocable trust created by Mary, with a life estate to Jim, remainder to her grandson.
    e. Mary paid a gift tax last year on a gift of real estate she made to Jim.
20. At the time of Emile's death, he was a joint tenant with Colette in a parcel of real estate. With regard to the inclusion in Emile's gross estate under § 2040, comment on the following independent assumptions:
    a. Emile and Colette received the property as a gift from Douglas.
    b. Colette provided all of the purchase price of the property.
    c. Colette's contribution was received as a gift from Emile.
    d. Emile's contribution was derived from income generated by property he received as a gift from Colette.
21. With regard to "life insurance," comment on the following.
    a. What the term includes (i.e., types of policies).
    b. The meaning of "incidents of ownership."
    c. When a gift occurs upon maturity of the policy.
    d. When § 2033 (property in which the decedent had an interest) can apply as to a policy.
22. At the time of death, the decedent owned real estate that was subject to a mortgage.
    a. How does the mortgage affect the taxable estate?
    b. Can the mortgage affect the amount of any marital deduction allowed? Explain.
    c. Can the mortgage affect the amount of any charitable deduction allowed? Explain.
23. A qualified charity for estate and gift tax purposes is the same as one for Federal income tax purposes. Do you agree with this statement?
24. Sean's will creates a trust, life estate to his wife (Darcy), remainder to their children.
    a. Will Sean's estate be allowed a marital deduction? Why or why not?
    b. What course of action do you suggest to secure the deduction?
    c. What are the consequences of any such course of action?
25. In accordance with recent legislation, the credit for state death taxes (§ 2011) has been phased out. How are the states responding to this change?

Issue ID

26. Would the credit for tax on prior transfers (§ 2013) ever apply in the husband and wife–type of situation? Explain.
27. What purpose is served by the generation-skipping transfer tax?

Problems

28. An estate holds the following assets.

	Fair Market Value	
	On Date of Death	**Six Months Later**
Land	$1,200,000	$1,210,000
Stock in Pipit Corporation	1,100,000	900,000
Stock in Kinglet Corporation	800,000	850,000

Three months after the decedent's death, when the Kinglet stock is worth $820,000, the executor of the estate transfers the stock to an heir in satisfaction of a bequest. The Pipit stock is sold by the estate five months after the decedent's death for $890,000. Death occurred in 2005.

a. If the § 2032 election is made, how much is included in the gross estate?
b. Would your answer to part (a) change if the Kinglet stock was not distributed to the heir until seven months after the decedent's death, when it was worth $860,000?
c. What value should be included in the gross estate if the § 2032 election is not made?

29. In which, if any, of the following *independent* situations could the alternate valuation date *not be elected* in 2005? In all cases, assume that Bill and Nancy are husband and wife and that Nancy dies first.
   a. Nancy's will passes all of her property to Bill.
   b. Nancy's will passes all of her property to the First Baptist Church of Rome, Georgia.
   c. The election would decrease the value of Nancy's gross estate but increase her estate tax liability.
   d. The election would increase the value of Nancy's gross estate but decrease her estate tax liability.
   e. Nancy's gross estate is $1,480,000. She made a taxable gift of $40,000 in January 1976.
   f. The executor of Nancy's estate sells or otherwise disposes of all of her assets within five months of her death.

30. Using the legend provided, classify each of the following transactions.

Legend		
NT	=	No transfer tax imposed
GT	=	Subject to the Federal gift tax
ET	=	Subject to the Federal estate tax

   a. Hayden purchases a certificate of deposit listing title as "Hayden, payable on proof of death to Michele."
   b. Same as (a). Hayden dies four years later, and Michele redeems the CD.
   c. Using his funds, Marcus purchases real estate listing title as "Marcus and Kendal, joint tenancy with right of survivorship."
   d. Same as (c). Kendal predeceases Marcus four years later.
   e. Winston purchases insurance on the life of John and designates Sophia as the beneficiary.
   f. Same as (e). Two years later, John dies first, and the insurance proceeds are paid to Sophia.
   g. Pierce establishes a joint savings account listing ownership as "Pierce and Stella, joint tenants with right of survivorship."
   h. Same as (g). One year later, Stella withdraws all of the funds from the account while Pierce is hospitalized.
   i. Same as (h), except that Stella's withdrawal did not take place until after Pierce died while at the hospital.

31. In each of the following *independent* situations, indicate whether a transfer that is subject to the Federal gift tax has occurred.
   a. Jamie purchases a used car for his 20-year-old son to drive while in college.
   b. June gives her parents a new RV on their 40th wedding anniversary.
   c. As part of a prenuptial marital settlement, Blake transfers to Andrea a portfolio of municipal bonds.
   d. As part of a property settlement, Floyd transfers to Inez income-producing real estate. Six months later, Floyd and Inez are divorced.
   e. Molly reimburses her 22-year-old son for the tuition he paid to attend medical school.
   f. Logan pays State University for his niece's tuition. The niece does not qualify as Logan's dependent.
   g. Marcie pays for her aunt's heart bypass operation. The money is sent directly to the medical service providers (i.e., hospital, doctors). The aunt does not qualify as Marcie's dependent.

h. Taylor makes a substantial cash donation to the political campaign of a college classmate who is running for Congress.
i. In his will, Corrine's father leaves her a valuable gun collection. As Corrine abhors firearms, she disclaims the bequest.

Issue ID

32. In May 2004, Dudley and Eva enter into a property settlement preparatory to the dissolution of their marriage. Under the agreement, Dudley is to pay Eva $3 million in satisfaction of her marital rights. Of this amount, Dudley pays $1.5 million immediately, and the balance is due one year later. The parties are divorced in July. Dudley dies in December, and his estate pays Eva the remaining $1.5 million in May 2005. Discuss the tax ramifications of these transactions to the parties involved.

Issue ID

33. Jesse dies intestate (i.e., without a will) in May 2004. Jesse's major asset is a tract of land. Under applicable state law, Jesse's property will pass to Lorena, who is his only child. In December 2004, Lorena disclaims one-half of the property. In June 2005, Lorena disclaims the other half interest. Under state law, Lorena's disclaimer results in the property passing to Arnold (Lorena's only child). The value of the land (in its entirety) is as follows: $2 million in May 2004; $2.1 million in December 2004; and $2.2 million in June 2005. Discuss the transfer tax ramifications of these transactions.

34. In 2005, Jerold makes a gift of stock (adjusted basis of $650,000; fair market value of $1.5 million) to his daughter. Jerold has never made any prior taxable gifts. Jerold's current wife, Melanie, made a taxable gift of $750,000 in early 1976, upon which she paid a gift tax of $174,900. At the time of Melanie's gift, she was not married to Jerold. How much gift tax is due on the 2005 transfer:
   a. If the § 2513 election to split is not made?
   b. If the § 2513 election is made?

35. At the time of his death on May 12, 2005, Grover Carson held the following assets.

	Fair Market Value
Stock in Coot Corporation	$400,000
Stock in Vireo Corporation	500,000
City of Buffalo bonds	800,000
Promissory note issued by Doreen Carson	200,000

On June 1, 2005, Grover's estate received cash dividends and interest as follows: $6,000 (Coot stock), $7,500 (Vireo stock), and $12,000 (Buffalo bonds). The dividends were declared on April 8, with the record dates being May 6 for Coot and May 13 for Vireo. Of the bond interest, $1,100 had accrued since May 12. Doreen Carson is Grover's adult daughter and is a successful insurance broker. Her note was non-interest-bearing and was forgiven by Grover in his will.

As to these transactions, how much is included in Grover's gross estate?

36. Prior to his death in early 2005, Harold was involved in the following transactions.

- In late 2002, he released the power to revoke a trust he had created for his children. At the time of the release, the trust had a value of $800,000, and it was worth $900,000 when Harold died.
- In 2003, he made a gift to his wife of an insurance policy on his life (fair market value of $100,000; maturity value of $1 million). Harold's children are the designated beneficiaries.
- In 2004, he made a gift to his children of stock worth $500,000. The transfers resulted in a gift tax of $80,000. The stock is worth $600,000 on the date of Harold's death.

As to these transactions, how much is included in Harold's gross estate?

Issue ID

37. In 1976, Rita created a revocable trust with securities worth $900,000. National Trust Company was designated as the trustee. Under the terms of the trust, Rita retained a life estate with remainder to her children. Rita dies in 2005 when the trust assets have a fair market value of $2.2 million.
    a. What, if any, are Rita's gift tax consequences in 1976?
    b. What, if any, is included in Rita's gross estate in 2005?
    c. Would your answer to (b) change if Rita releases her life estate in 2001? Explain.

38. At the time of his death in 2005, Garth was involved in the following arrangements.
    - He held a life estate in the Myrtle Trust with the remainder passing to Garth's adult children. The trust was created by Myrtle (Garth's mother) in 1984 with securities worth $900,000. The Myrtle Trust had a value of $1.7 million when Garth died.
    - Under the terms of the Myrtle Trust, Garth was given the power to provide for a disproportionate distribution of the remainder interest among his children. As Garth failed to exercise this power, the remainder interest is divided equally among the children.
    - In 1998, Garth purchased a commercial single-premium annuity. Garth furnished 80% of the cost, and his wife, Ashley, provided the 20% balance. Under the terms of the policy, Garth is to receive $100,000 annually for life. If Ashley survives Garth, she is to receive $50,000 per year for life. Garth predeceases Ashley at a time when the value of her survivorship feature is worth $700,000.

    Discuss the estate tax ramifications of these arrangements as to Garth.

39. At the time of Paul's death in 2005, he was involved in the following transactions.
    - He was an equal tenant in common with Pat in real estate worth $2 million. The property had been purchased by Paul in 1980 at a cost of $400,000.
    - Paul was a participant in his employer's contributory qualified pension plan. The plan benefit of $2.1 million was paid to Pat as the designated beneficiary and was made up as follows.

Employer's contributions	$800,000
Paul's after-tax contributions	700,000
Income earned by the plan	600,000

    - Paul was covered by his employer's group term life insurance plan for employees. His policy proceeds of $50,000 were paid to Pat, the designated beneficiary.

    Discuss the tax ramifications (including gift and income) of these transactions, based on the following assumptions.
    a. Paul and Pat are father and son.
    b. Paul and Pat are husband and wife.

40. In 1990, Bertha purchased an office building for $1.2 million listing title as "Bertha and Barney, joint tenants with the right of survivorship." In the same year, as a wedding present to Barney and his new wife, Teri, Bertha gives them her former home (worth $600,000). Title to the home is recorded as "Barney and Teri, tenants by the entirety with the right of survivorship." In 2005, Barney is killed in a skiing accident and is survived by his mother (Bertha) and wife (Teri). If at the time of Barney's death the office building has a value of $1.5 million and the residence is worth $900,000, what is included in his gross estate as to these properties? Did any gift tax consequences ensue in 1990?

41. In 1990, Curt purchased realty for $1.6 million and listed title to the property as "Curt and Nell, joint tenants with right of survivorship." Curt predeceases Nell in 2005 when the realty is worth $3 million. Curt and Nell are brother and sister.
    a. What, if any, are the gift tax consequences in 1990?
    b. What, if any, are the estate tax consequences in 2005?

42. Assume the same facts as in Problem 41, except that Curt and Nell are husband and wife.
    a. What, if any, are the gift tax consequences in 1990?
    b. What, if any, are the estate tax consequences in 2005?

43. In each of the following *independent* situations, determine how much, if any, should be included in Eric's gross estate.
    a. Hope, Eric's wife, owns a policy on Eric's life (maturity value of $200,000). Upon Eric's death, the proceeds are paid to Ward, Hope's son, who is the designated beneficiary.
    b. Eric owns a policy on Hope's life (maturity value of $200,000 and current value of $40,000) with Ward, Eric's son, as the designated beneficiary.
    c. Assume the same facts as in (b) except that Eric's estate (not Ward) is the designated beneficiary.
    d. Upon Eric's death, Ward collected $200,000 on a policy he owned on Eric's life. The policy was originally taken out by Eric and was given by him to Ward two years ago.

44. In June 2005, Rudy unexpectedly died while vacationing in Maine. Discuss the tax ramifications of the following transactions involving the administration of Rudy's estate.
    a. The executor of the estate (Rudy's daughter) travels to Maine to pick up and transport the remains for burial in the family plot in Columbia, South Carolina. The expenses involved are paid by the estate.
    b. In early 2005, Rudy had promised to give his niece $10,000 if she passed the CPA exam. After Rudy's death, the niece passes the exam, and the executor of his estate pays her $10,000.
    c. In March 2005, Rudy had pledged $25,000 to the building fund of his church. The estate satisfies the pledge.
    d. Rudy had made a gift in 2004 that resulted in a gift tax. A Form 709 was completed and filed by the executor, and the gift tax was paid from estate funds.
    e. In July 2005, Rudy's hunting lodge in Colorado was destroyed by a fire started by lightning. The lodge cost Rudy $300,000 and was worth $700,000 when he died. The estate was able to recover $500,000 from the carrier that insured the property.

45. At the time of her death in the current year, Marsha owned the following real estate.

Real Property	Fair Market Value	Amount of Mortgage
Parcel A	$1,000,000	$200,000
Parcel B	1,500,000	300,000
Parcel C	900,000	200,000

    Parcels A and B pass to Felix (Marsha's surviving spouse), while Parcel C goes to the City of Bethlehem, Pennsylvania. Under the terms of Marsha's will, Parcel A is to pass free and clear of any liabilities, but no mention is made regarding the mortgages on Parcels B and C. Discuss the tax ramifications of these transactions in the context of §§ 2053, 2055, and 2056.

46. Under Nelda's will, Wanda (Nelda's sister) inherits property. Five years later Wanda dies. Determine Wanda's credit for tax on prior transfers based on the following assumptions.
    a. The estate tax attributable to the inclusion of the property in Nelda's gross estate is $800,000, and the estate tax attributable to the inclusion of the property in Wanda's gross estate is $880,000.
    b. The estate tax attributable to the inclusion of the property in Nelda's gross estate is $900,000, and the estate tax attributable to the inclusion of the property in Wanda's gross estate is $850,000.

47. In 2005, Hannah died, and her after-tax estate of $3 million passed to a trust. Under the terms of the trust, Wilma (Hannah's daughter) is granted a life estate with the remainder passing to Karl (Hannah's grandson) upon Wilma's death. The trustee elects to use $1.5 million of the generation-skipping transfer tax exemption. Wilma dies in 2008 when the trust is worth $5 million.
    a. Presuming the GSTT applies, is it caused by a termination event, a distribution event, or a direct skip?
    b. How much of the trust is subject to the GSTT?
    c. Who pays the tax?
    d. What is the GSTT rate that applies?

48. In each of the following *independent* situations, determine the decedent's final estate tax liability (net of any unified tax credit).

	Decedent			
	Brad	**Paige**	**Martina**	**Gabe**
Year of death	1998	2001	2003	2005
Taxable estate	$700,000	$900,000	$1,200,000	$ 900,000
Post-1976 taxable gifts—				
Made in 1985	600,000	—	—	—
Made in 1986	—	700,000	—	—
Made in 1999	—	—	900,000	—
Made in 2004	—	—	—	1,000,000

Research Problems

Note: Solutions to Research Problems can be prepared by using the ***RIA Checkpoint*® Student Edition** *online research product, which is available to accompany this text. It is also possible to prepare solutions to the Research Problems by using tax research materials found in a standard tax library.*

Research Problem 1. In 2003, Carol, a widow, makes substantial gifts of marketable securities (stocks and bonds) to her adult children (Peter and Susan). As a result of these transfers, Carol incurs and pays a Federal gift tax of $4 million. Carol dies in 2005 leaving an estate of inconsequential value. Carol's executor files a Form 706 for her estate reflecting a gross estate of slightly in excess of $4 million. The estate tax of $1.8 million that is attributable to the $4 million is not paid as the estate has no available funds.

Upon investigation by the IRS, the $1.8 million estate tax shortfall is assessed against Peter and Susan under the rules pertaining to transferee liability. Are Peter and Susan liable for the estate tax? Why or why not?

Partial list of research aids:
§§ 2035(b), (c)(1)(C), and 6324(a).

Research Problem 2. Grace Tipton, a widow of considerable means, dies in February 2004. One month later, her designated executor is appointed by the probate court of appropriate jurisdiction, and the administration of the Tipton estate is initiated. Among the bequests in Grace's will is one that passes $10 million to the Christian Assisted Living Foundation (CALF), but only if it is a qualified charity for purposes of § 2055. Because the status of CALF has never been evaluated by the IRS, the executor feels compelled to postpone the satisfaction of the bequest. Instead, he files the Form 706 and pays the estate tax based on the charitable deduction being allowed. Further, he requests a "closing letter" from the IRS on the Form 706 that is filed. Since the issuance of a closing letter means acceptance of the deduction, it forces the IRS to investigate the charitable nature of CALF.

After investigating the activities of CALF, the IRS finds it to be a qualified charity. Consequently, in October 2006 the IRS issues a closing letter approving the charitable deduction claimed and accepting the Form 706 as filed. Shortly thereafter, the executor transfers $11 million to CALF. The amount transferred represents $10 million for the satisfaction of the bequest and $1 million for statutory interest accrued. Under state law, interest must be paid on any bequest that is not satisfied within a one-year period after the initiation of administration. The probate court sanctions the determination and payment of the $1 million interest amount.

Subsequent to the $11 million CALF distribution, the executor files an amended Form 706. The amended return claims a refund for the estate taxes attributable to the additional $1 million paid as interest. On the amended return, the interest is classified as an administration expense under § 2053, thereby reducing the taxable estate and resulting estate tax liability. The IRS denies the claim for refund on the grounds that the interest incurred was not necessary to the administration of the estate. If the executor had satisfied the CALF bequest earlier, the accrual of interest would have been avoided. The executor counters that the delay was necessary in order to maintain fiduciary integrity in complying with the terms of the decedent's will. Who should prevail?

Partial list of research aids:
§ 2053(a)(2).
Reg. § 20.2053–3(a).
Pitner v. U.S., 68–1 USTC ¶12,499, 21 AFTR2d 1571, 388 F.2d 651 (CA–5, 1967).
Turner v. U.S., _____ USTC _____, 93 AFTR2d 2004–686, 306 F.Supp.2d 688 (D.Ct.Tex., 2004).

Internet Activity

Use the tax resources of the Internet to address the following question. Do not restrict your search to the World Wide Web, but include a review of newsgroups and general reference materials, practitioner sites and resources, primary sources of the tax law, chat rooms and discussion groups, and other opportunities.

Communications

Research Problem 3. A considerable amount of material (e.g., magazine and newspaper commentaries, journal articles, books) is available on why the Federal estate tax should not be repealed. Identify three of the more recent sources. Summarize them in an e-mail to your instructor, and include a list of citations.

Income Taxation of Trusts and Estates

LEARNING OBJECTIVES

After completing Chapter 28, you should be able to:

LO.1

Use working definitions with respect to trusts, estates, beneficiaries, and other parties.

LO.2

Identify the steps in determining the accounting and taxable income of a trust or estate, and the related taxable income of the beneficiaries.

LO.3

Illustrate the uses and implications of distributable net income.

LO.4

Understand various tax planning procedures that can be used to minimize the income tax consequences of trusts and estates and their beneficiaries.

http://wft.swlearning.com

OUTLINE

An Overview of Subchapter J

Taxpayers create trusts for a variety of reasons. Some trusts are established primarily for tax purposes, but most are designed to accomplish a specific financial goal or to provide for the orderly management of assets in case of emergency. Table 28–1 lists some of the more common reasons for creating a trust.

■ TABLE 28-1
Motivations for Creating a Trust

Type of Trust	Financial and Other Goals
Life insurance trust	Holds life insurance policies on the insured, removes the proceeds of the policies from the gross estate (if an irrevocable trust), and safeguards against a young or inexperienced beneficiary receiving the proceeds.
"Living" (revocable) trust	Manages assets, reduces probate costs, provides privacy for asset disposition, protects against medical or other emergencies, and provides relief from the necessity of day-to-day management of the underlying assets.
Trust for minors	Provides funds for a college education, shifts income to lower-bracket taxpayers, and transfers accumulated income without permanently parting with the underlying assets.
"Blind" trust	Holds and manages the assets of the grantor without his/her input or influence (e.g., while the grantor holds political office or some other sensitive position).
Retirement trust	Manages asset contributions under a qualified retirement plan.
Alimony trust	Manages the assets of an ex-spouse and assures they will be distributed in a timely fashion to specified beneficiaries.
Liquidation trust	Collects and distributes the last assets of a corporation that is undergoing a complete liquidation.

FIGURE 28–1
Structure of a Typical Trust and Estate

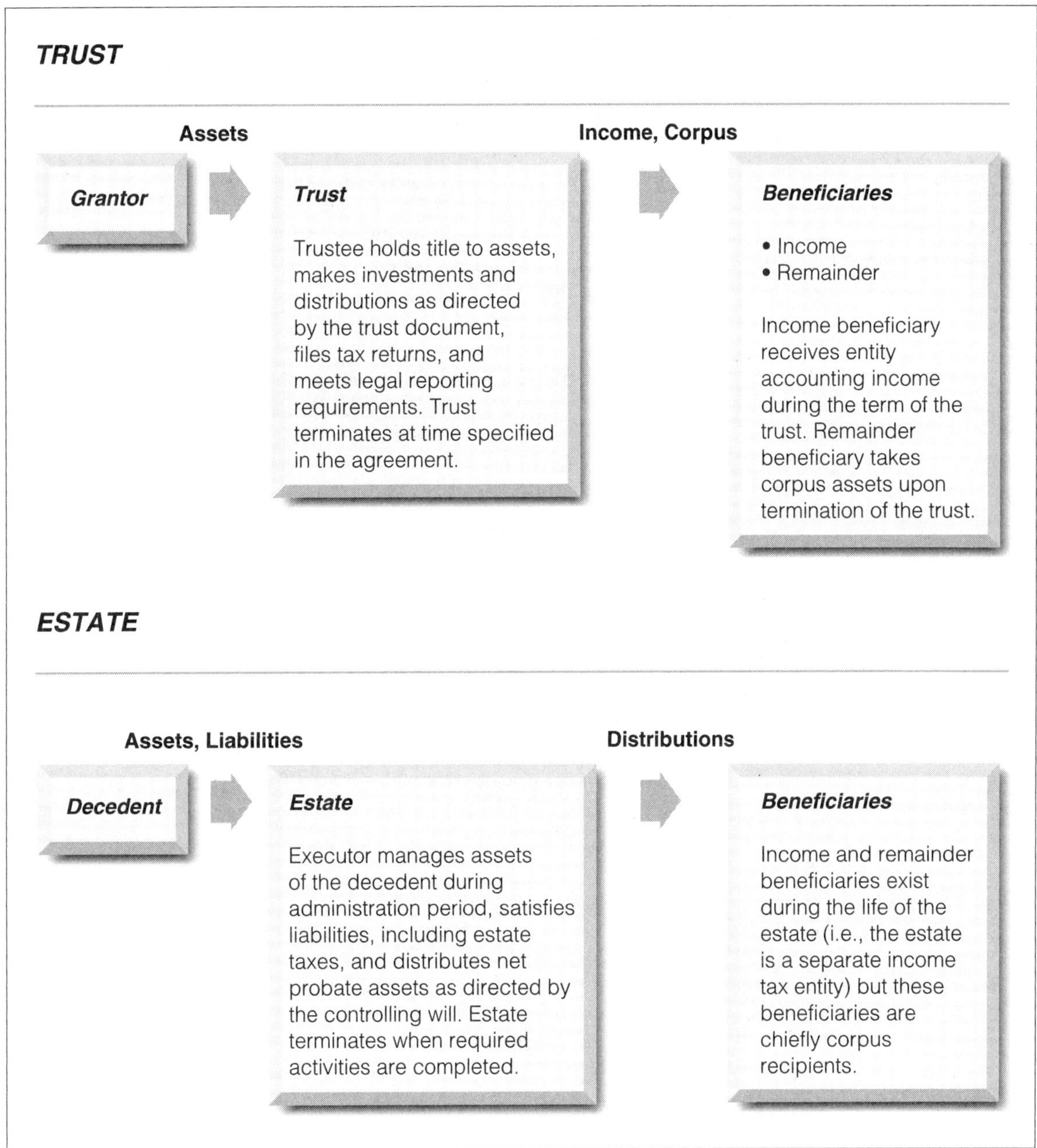

Because a trust is a separate tax entity, its gross income and deductions must be measured, and an annual tax return must be filed. Similarly, when an individual dies, a legal entity is created in the form of his or her estate. This chapter examines the rules related to the income taxation of trusts and estates. Figure 28–1 illustrates the structure of a typical trust and estate.

The income taxation of trusts and estates is governed by Subchapter J of the Internal Revenue Code, §§ 641 through 692. Certain similarities are apparent between Subchapter J and the income taxation of individuals (e.g., the definitions of gross income and deductible expenditures), partnerships and limited liability entities (e.g., the conduit principle), and S corporations (e.g., the conduit principle and the trust as a separate taxable entity). Trusts also involve several important unique concepts, however, including the determination of *distributable net income* and the *tier system* of distributions to beneficiaries.

LO.1

Use working definitions with respect to trusts, estates, beneficiaries, and other parties.

WHAT IS A TRUST?

The Code does not contain a definition of a trust. However, the term usually refers to an arrangement created by a will or by an *inter vivos* (lifetime) declaration through which trustees take title to property for the purpose of protecting or conserving it for the beneficiaries.[1]

Typically, the creation of a trust involves at least three parties: (1) The **grantor** (sometimes referred to as the settlor or donor) transfers selected assets to the trust entity. (2) The trustee, who usually is either an individual or a corporation, is charged with the fiduciary duties associated with the trust. (3) The beneficiary is designated to receive income or property from the trust; the beneficiary's rights are defined by state law and by the trust document.

In some situations, fewer than three persons may be involved, as specified by the trust agreement. For example, an elderly individual who can no longer manage his or her own property (e.g., because of ill health) may create a trust under which he or she is both the grantor and the beneficiary. In this case, a corporate trustee is charged with the management of the grantor's assets.

In another situation, the grantor might designate himself or herself as the trustee of the trust assets. For example, a parent who wants to transfer selected assets to a minor child could use a trust entity to ensure that the minor does not waste the property. By naming himself or herself as the trustee, the parent retains virtual control over the property that is transferred.

Under the general rules of Subchapter J, the **grantor trusts** just described are not recognized for income tax purposes. Similarly, when only one party is involved (when the same individual is grantor, trustee, and sole beneficiary of the trust), Subchapter J rules do not apply, and the entity is ignored for income tax purposes.

OTHER DEFINITIONS

When the grantor transfers title of selected assets to a trust, those assets become the **corpus** (body), or principal, of the trust. Trust corpus, in most situations, earns *income*, which may be distributed to the beneficiaries, or accumulated for the future by the trustee, as the trust instrument directs.

In the typical trust, the grantor creates two types of beneficiaries: one who receives the accounting income of the trust and one who receives trust corpus that remains at the termination of the trust entity. Beneficiaries in the first category hold an *income interest* in the trust, and those in the second category hold a *remainder interest* in the trust's assets. If the grantor retains the remainder interest, the interest is known as a **reversionary interest** (corpus reverts to the grantor when the trust entity terminates).

The trust document establishes the term of the trust. The term may be for a specific number of years (a *term certain*) or until the occurrence of a specified event. For example, a trust might exist (1) for the life of the income beneficiary, in which case the income beneficiary is known as a *life tenant* in trust corpus; (2) for the life

[1]Reg. § 301.7701–4(a).

of some other individual; (3) until the income or remainder beneficiary reaches the age of majority; or (4) until the beneficiary, or another individual, marries, receives a promotion, or reaches some specified age.

The trustee may be required to distribute the accounting income of the entity according to a distribution schedule specified in the agreement. Sometimes, however, the trustee is given more discretion with respect to the timing and nature of the distributions. If the trustee can determine, within guidelines that may be included in the trust document, either the timing of the income or corpus distributions or the specific beneficiaries who will receive them (from among those identified in the agreement), the trust is called a **sprinkling trust.** Here, the trustee can "sprinkle" the distributions among the various beneficiaries. Family-unit income taxes can be reduced by directing income to those who are subject to lower marginal tax rates. Thus, by giving the trustee a sprinkling power, the income tax liability of the family unit can be manipulated by applying the terms of the trust agreement.

For purposes of certain provisions of Subchapter J, a trust must be classified as either a **simple trust** or a **complex trust.** A simple trust (1) is required to distribute its entire accounting income to designated beneficiaries every year, (2) has no beneficiaries that are qualifying charitable organizations, and (3) makes no distributions of trust corpus during the year. A complex trust is any trust that is not a simple trust.[2] These criteria are applied to the trust every year. Thus, every trust is classified as a complex trust in the year in which it terminates (because it will be distributing all of its corpus during that year).

WHAT IS AN ESTATE?

An estate is created upon the death of every individual. The estate is charged with collecting and conserving all of the individual's assets, satisfying all liabilities, and distributing the remaining assets to the heirs identified by state law or the will.

Typically, the creation of an estate involves at least three parties: the decedent, all of whose probate assets are transferred to the estate for disposition; the executor, who is appointed under the decedent's valid will (or the administrator, if no valid will exists); and the beneficiaries of the estate, who are to receive assets or income from the entity, as the decedent indicated in the will. The executor or administrator holds the fiduciary responsibility to manage the estate as directed by the will, applicable state law, and the probate court.

Recall that the assets that make up the probate estate are not identical to those that constitute the gross estate for transfer tax purposes (refer to Chapter 27). Many gross estate assets are not a part of the probate estate and thus are not subject to disposition by the executor or administrator. For example, property held by the decedent as a joint tenant passes to the survivor(s) by operation of the applicable state's property law rather than through the probate estate. Proceeds of insurance policies on the life of the decedent, over which the decedent held the incidents of ownership, are not under the control of the executor or administrator. The designated beneficiaries of the policy receive the proceeds outright under the insurance contract.

An estate is a separate taxable entity. Under certain circumstances, taxpayers may find it profitable to prolong an estate's existence. This situation is likely to arise when the heirs are already in a high income tax bracket and would, therefore, prefer to have income generated by the estate so as to fully use the estate's lower marginal income tax rates. If an estate's existence is unduly prolonged, however,

[2] Reg. § 1.651(a)–1.

Should Your Trust Be All in the Family?

For decades, grantors have chosen a family member to be the trustee of the family savings, the children's education fund, or whatever other assets are placed into management by the trust. The relative chosen is often the most trusted but not always the one with the business sense. Now, however, as the financial work has become more complex, with wild stock market fluctuations, increased fiduciary standards, and potential conflicts of interest, some are questioning the wisdom of using a family member as the trustee.

Using a trust company or other financial institution as a trustee usually results in more stable investment returns, eliminating both the highs and the lows of the stock market cycle. Institutions also are more likely to be located in states that levy no income tax on trusts, preferring to attract such business with a friendly tax climate. (Delaware, South Dakota, and Alaska are known as being especially trust-friendly.) Institutions can also bring other advantages.

- They do not die, run away, develop a mental illness, or otherwise unexpectedly become unqualified for the position.
- They are not easily swayed by emotional appeals; nor do they react to family jealousies.
- They are prohibited by law from acting under a conflict of interest, such as might exist between family members when the related trustee is also a trust beneficiary.

On the negative side, human trustees often waive or discount their fiduciary fee, while institutions do not. Especially for trusts with a small corpus, institutional trustees can be prohibitively expensive. And the trust company most often is oriented toward expanding its customer base, rather than offering individual attention to existing clients.

Compromise solutions might be to:

- Appoint co-trustees. Aunt Grace or Uncle Harry can provide the personal touch and ensure that trust decisions recognize family needs, while the trust company maximizes investment returns and furnishes professional management.
- Keep the family trustee, but hire needed professionals to provide advice only when needed, at an hourly rate. This approach avoids the fees based on asset values that trust companies usually charge.
- Use the advisory services of the mutual funds in which trust assets are invested, to manage and distribute the corpus and income. These services often are discounted from market rates and can be waived for well-to-do clients.

the IRS can terminate it for Federal income tax purposes after the expiration of a reasonable period for the executor to complete the duties of administration.[3]

Nature of Trust and Estate Taxation

In general, the taxable income of a trust or estate is taxed to the entity or to its beneficiaries to the extent that each has received the accounting income of the entity. Thus, Subchapter J creates a modified conduit principle relative to the income taxation of trusts, estates, and their beneficiaries. Whoever receives the accounting income of the entity, or some portion of it, is liable for the income tax that results.

[3]Reg. § 1.641(b)–3(a).

EXAMPLE 1

Adam receives 80% of the accounting income of the Zero Trust. The trustee accumulated the other 20% of the income at her discretion under the trust agreement and added it to trust corpus. Adam is liable for income tax only on the amount of the distribution, and Zero is liable for the income tax on the accumulated portion of the income. ■

FILING REQUIREMENTS

The fiduciary is required to file a Form 1041 (U.S. Income Tax Return for Estates and Trusts) in the following situations.[4]

- For an estate that has gross income of $600 or more for the year.
- For a trust that either has any taxable income or, if there is no taxable income, has gross income of $600 or more.

The fiduciary return (and any related tax liability) is due no later than the fifteenth day of the fourth month following the close of the entity's taxable year. The IRS encourages electronic filing of the Form 1041 and schedules. A paper return is filed with the Internal Revenue Service in Philadelphia, Cincinnati, or Ogden, Utah, depending on the location of the fiduciary's principal place of business.

TAX ACCOUNTING PERIODS, METHODS, AND PAYMENTS

An estate or trust may use any of the tax accounting methods available to individuals. The method of accounting used by the grantor of a trust or the decedent of an estate need not carry over to the entity.

An estate has the same options for choosing a tax year as any new taxpayer. Thus, the estate of a calendar year decedent dying on March 3 can select any fiscal year or report on a calendar year basis. If the calendar year basis is selected, the estate's first taxable year will include the period from March 3 to December 31. If the first or last tax year of an estate is a short year (less than one calendar year), income for that year need not be annualized.

To eliminate the possibility of deferring the taxation of fiduciary-source income simply by using a fiscal tax year, virtually all trusts (other than tax-exempt trusts) are required to use a calendar tax year.[5]

Trusts and estates are required to make estimated Federal income tax payments, using the same quarterly schedule that applies to individual taxpayers. This requirement applies to estates only for tax years that end two or more years after the date of the decedent's death. Charitable trusts and private foundations are exempt from estimated payment requirements altogether.[6]

The two-year estimated tax exception for estates recognizes the liquidity problems that an executor often faces during the early months of administering the estate. The exception does not ensure, however, that an estate in existence less than 24 months will never be required to make an estimated tax payment.

EXAMPLE 2

Juanita died on March 15, 2005. Her executor elected a fiscal year ending on July 31 for the estate. Estimated tax payments will be required from the estate starting with the tax year that begins on August 1, 2006. ■

TAX RATES AND PERSONAL EXEMPTION

Congress's desire to stop trusts from being used as income-shifting devices has made the fiduciary entity the highest-taxed taxpayer in the Code.[7] The entity reaches the 35 percent marginal rate with only $9,750 of taxable income in 2005, so the

[4] § 6012(a).
[5] § 645.
[6] § 6654(l).
[7] § 1(e) (see Appendix A).

■ **TABLE 28–2**
Comparative Tax Liabilities

Filing Status/Entity	Taxable Income	Marginal Income Tax Rate (%)	2005 Tax Liability
Single	$50,000	25	$ 9,165
Married, filing jointly	50,000	15	6,770
C corporation	50,000	15	7,500
Trust or estate	50,000	35	16,607

grantor's ability to shift income in a tax-effective manner is nearly eliminated. Table 28–2, which lists the 2005 taxes paid by various entities on taxable income of $50,000, shows how expensive the accumulation of income within an estate or trust can be. Proper income shifting would move assets *out of* the estate or trust and into the hands of the grantor or beneficiary.

A fiduciary's dividend income and net long-term capital gains can be taxed at a nominal rate of no more than 15 percent. In addition to the regular income tax, an estate or trust may be subject to the alternative minimum tax, as computed on Schedule I of the Form 1041.[8]

Both trusts and estates are allowed a personal exemption in computing the fiduciary tax liability. All estates are allowed a personal exemption of $600. The exemption available to a trust depends upon the type of trust involved. A trust that is required to distribute all of its income is currently allowed an exemption of $300. All other trusts are allowed an exemption of $100 per year.[9]

The classification of trusts as to the appropriate personal exemption is similar, but not identical, to the distinction between simple and complex trusts. The classification as a simple trust is more stringent.

EXAMPLE 3

Trust Alpha is required to distribute all of its current accounting income to Susan. Trust Beta is required to distribute all of its current accounting income, one-half to Tyrone and one-half to State University, a qualifying charitable organization. The trustee of Trust Gamma can, at her discretion, distribute the current accounting income or corpus of the trust to Dr. Chapman. None of the trusts makes any corpus distributions during the year. All of the accounting income of Trust Gamma is distributed to Dr. Chapman.

Trust Alpha is a simple trust; it will receive a $300 personal exemption. Trust Beta is a complex trust; it will receive a $300 personal exemption. Trust Gamma is a complex trust; it will receive a $100 personal exemption. ■

ALTERNATIVE MINIMUM TAX

The alternative minimum tax (AMT) may apply to a trust or estate in any tax year. Given the nature and magnitude of the tax preferences, adjustments, and exemptions that determine alternative minimum taxable income (AMTI), however, most trusts and estates are unlikely to incur the tax. Nevertheless, they could be vulnerable, for example, if they are actively engaged in cashing out the stock options of a donor/decedent who was a corporate executive.

In general, derivation of AMTI for the entity follows the rules that apply to individual taxpayers. Thus, the corporate ACE adjustment does not apply to fiduciary entities, but AMTI may be created through the application of most of the other AMT preference and adjustment items discussed in Chapter 15.

[8] § 55.

[9] § 642(b).

Everyone Gets Wet When You Soak the Rich

Fiduciary taxation has fallen prey to the "soak the rich" approach to tax reform. In an environment that emphasizes taxes on millionaires, the tax rates that apply to trusts and estates have also increased, and the width of the lower brackets has become so narrow that these entities now are subject to the highest marginal rate structure in U.S. income tax law. Higher tax rates for trusts and estates affect all fiduciary arrangements, however, even those designed for reasons other than tax avoidance.

Perhaps by design, these rate changes have dampened the planning potential of fiduciary entities as a means of shifting income among generations (e.g., from parent to child) or over time (i.e., from the taxpayer's present tax return to a future one). But they have also deepened the tax burden on fixed-income retirees, handicapped individuals, children of divorced parents, and other commonly encountered fiduciary beneficiaries.

Most trust beneficiaries are passive recipients of investment income generated by a stock portfolio managed by a corporate trustee or by the distant managers of the mutual funds in which the funds are invested. In a typical year, a trust enters into very few "new" transactions. For the most part, there is little portfolio turnover, and periodic interest and dividends are collected. The beneficiaries exercise little decision-making authority over the yield or timing of the entity's distributions, which are fixed by the controlling instrument. Under such circumstances, high taxes on income other than dividends and long-term capital gains seem to punish the powerless as well as to soak the rich.

Like other taxpayers subject to the AMT, a trust or estate may claim an annual exemption. A trust or estate qualifies for a $22,500 annual exemption. The exemption phases out at a rate of one-fourth of the amount by which AMTI exceeds $75,000.

A 26 percent tax rate is applied to AMTI, increasing to 28 percent when AMTI in excess of the exemption reaches $175,000. In addition, estimated tax payments for the entity must include any applicable AMT liability.

LO.2

Identify the steps in determining the accounting and taxable income of a trust or estate, and the related taxable income of the beneficiaries.

Taxable Income of Trusts and Estates

Generally, the taxable income of a trust or estate is computed similarly to that for an individual. Subchapter J does, however, include several important exceptions and provisions that make it necessary to use a systematic approach to calculating the taxable income of these entities. Figure 28–2 illustrates the procedure implied by the Code, and Figure 28–3 presents a systematic computation method followed in this chapter.

ENTITY ACCOUNTING INCOME

The first step in determining the taxable income of a trust or estate is to compute the entity's accounting income for the period. Although this prerequisite is not apparent from a cursory reading of Subchapter J, a closer look at the Code reveals a number of references to the *income* of the entity.[10] Wherever the term *income* is used in Subchapter J without some modifier (e.g., *gross* income or *taxable* income), the statute is referring to the accounting income of the trust or estate for the tax year.

[10]For example, see §§ 651(a)(1), 652(a), and 661(a)(1).

■ **FIGURE 28-2**
Accounting Income, Distributable Net Income, and Taxable Income of the Entity and Its Beneficiaries—The Five-Step Procedure

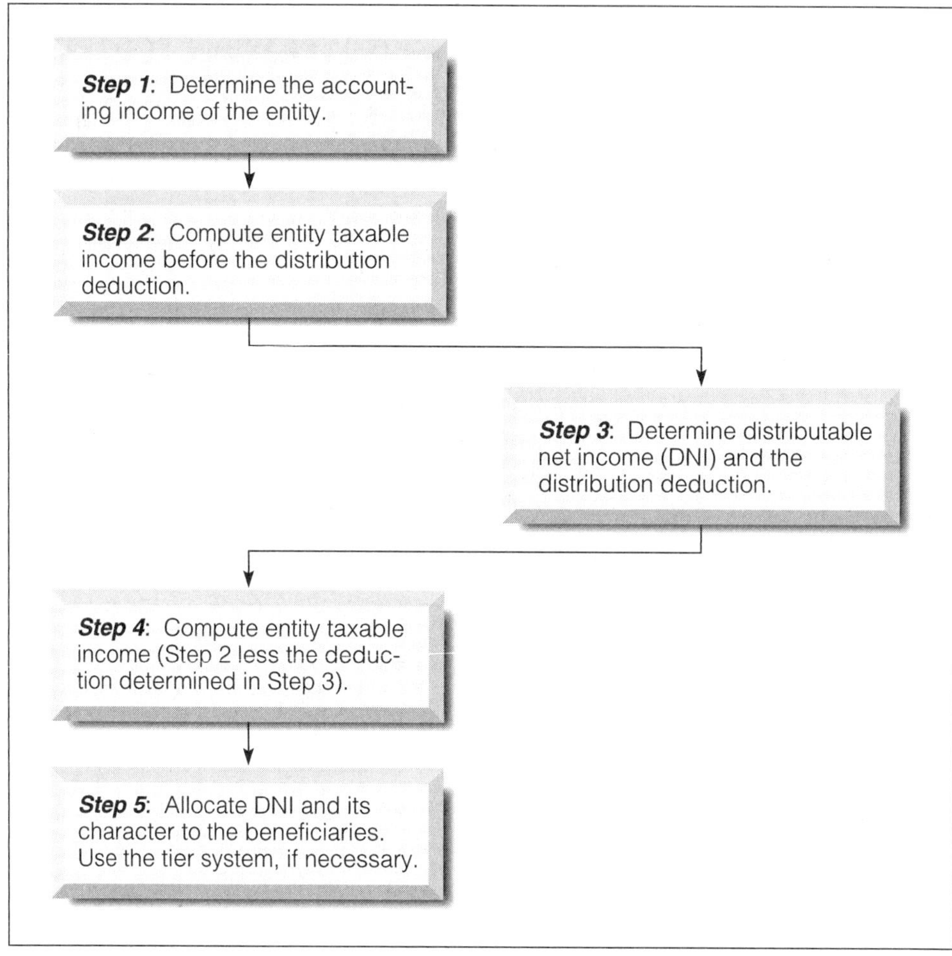

Step 1: Determine the accounting income of the entity.
Step 2: Compute entity taxable income before the distribution deduction.
Step 3: Determine distributable net income (DNI) and the distribution deduction.
Step 4: Compute entity taxable income (Step 2 less the deduction determined in Step 3).
Step 5: Allocate DNI and its character to the beneficiaries. Use the tier system, if necessary.

■ **FIGURE 28-3**
Computational Template Applying the Five-Step Procedure

Item	Totals	Accounting Income	Taxable Income	Distributable Net Income/Distribution Deduction
Income	______	______	______	
Income	______	______	______	
Expense	______	______	______	
Expense	______	______	______	
Personal exemption			______	
Accounting income/taxable income before the distribution deduction	***Step 1***	______	***Step 2*** ______	______
Personal exemption				______
Corpus capital gain/loss				______
Net tax-exempt income				______
Distributable net income				______
Distribution deduction			***Step 3*** ______	
Entity taxable income			***Step 4*** ______	

Beneficiary taxable income is addressed in ***Step 5***.

TABLE 28–3
Common Allocations of Items to Income or Corpus

Allocable to Income	Allocable to Corpus
• Ordinary and operating net income from trust assets. • Interest, dividend, rent, and royalty income. • Stock dividends. • One-half of fiduciary fees/ commissions.	• Depreciation on business assets. • Casualty gain/loss on income-producing assets. • Insurance recoveries on income-producing assets. • Capital gain/loss on investment assets. • Stock splits. • One-half of fiduciary fees/ commissions.

A definition of entity accounting income is critical to understanding the Subchapter J computation of fiduciary taxable income. Under state law, entity accounting income is the amount that the income beneficiary of the simple trust or estate is eligible to receive from the entity. More importantly, the calculation of accounting income is virtually under the control of the grantor or decedent (through a properly drafted trust agreement or will). If the document has been drafted at arm's length, a court will enforce a fiduciary's good faith efforts to carry out the specified computation of accounting income.

By allocating specific items of income and expenditure either to the income beneficiaries or to corpus, the desires of the grantor or decedent are put into effect. Table 28–3 shows typical assignments of revenue and expenditure items to fiduciary income or corpus.

Where the controlling document is silent as to whether an item should be assigned to income or corpus, state law prevails. These allocations are an important determinant of the benefits received from the entity by its beneficiaries and the timing of those benefits.

EXAMPLE 4

The Arnold Trust is a simple trust. Mrs. Bennett is its sole beneficiary. In the current year, the trust earns $20,000 in taxable interest and $15,000 in tax-exempt interest. In addition, the trust recognizes an $8,000 long-term capital gain. The trustee assesses a fee of $11,000 for the year. If the trust agreement allocates fees and capital gains to corpus, trust accounting income is $35,000, and Mrs. Bennett receives that amount. Thus, the income beneficiary receives no immediate benefit from the trust's capital gain, and she bears none of the financial burden of the fiduciary's fees.

Interest income ($20,000 + $15,000)	$35,000
Long-term capital gain—allocable to corpus	–0–
Fiduciary's fees—allocable to corpus	(–0–)
Trust accounting income	$35,000

■

EXAMPLE 5

Assume the same facts as in Example 4, except that the trust agreement allocates the fiduciary's fees to income. The trust accounting income is $24,000, and Mrs. Bennett receives that amount.

Interest income ($20,000 + $15,000)	$35,000
Long-term capital gain—allocable to corpus	–0–
Fiduciary's fees	(11,000)
Trust accounting income	$24,000

■

Pick the Home State for Your Trust Carefully

In a continuing attempt to discourage tax-motivated income shifting among family members, steep income tax rates on estates and trusts are also being seen at the state level. Although a few states (e.g., Alaska, Nevada, Texas, and Washington) do not impose any income tax on fiduciary entities, those that do are tending to increase their rates as part of their efforts to solve current budget woes.

Legal, brokerage, and accounting fees to set up and operate a trust must be accepted as necessary administrative costs inherent to the trust arrangement. But careful selection of the state in which the trust is to be created and operated could allow for an annuity of tax savings and avoid unnecessary costs. Thus, the state chosen as the situs of a trust should offer trust-friendly rules regarding disclosure and asset protection as well as a favorable tax climate.

Individuals who attempt to move their state of residence upon retirement, perhaps from New York to Florida, usually must be prepared to spend a lot of time and effort in making the transition. In contrast, changing the location of a trust is considerably simpler and may entail merely transferring assets from one trustee to another. Nevertheless, grantors are advised to make a good decision as to situs when the fiduciary entity is created. Moving a trust after it is established is more troublesome and draws unneeded attention to the parties involved.

EXAMPLE 6

Assume the same facts as in Example 4, except that the trust agreement allocates to income all capital gains and losses and one-half of the trustee's commissions. The trust accounting income is $37,500, and Mrs. Bennett receives that amount.

Interest income ($20,000 + $15,000)	$35,000
Long-term capital gain	8,000
Fiduciary's fees—one-half allocable to corpus	(5,500)
Trust accounting income	$37,500

■

GROSS INCOME

The gross income of an estate or trust is similar to that of an individual. In determining the gain or loss to be recognized by an estate or trust upon the sale or other taxable disposition of assets, the rules for basis determination are similar to those applicable to other taxpayers. Thus, an estate's basis for property received from a decedent is stepped up or stepped down to gross estate value (refer to Chapter 13 for a more detailed discussion). Property received as a gift (the usual case in most trust arrangements) usually takes the donor's basis. Property purchased by the trust from a third party is assigned a basis equal to the purchase price.

Property Distributions. In general, the entity does not recognize gain or loss upon its distribution of property to a beneficiary under the provisions of the will or trust document. The distributed property has the same basis to the beneficiary of the distribution as it did to the estate or trust. Moreover, the distribution absorbs distributable net income (DNI) and qualifies for a distribution deduction (both of which are explained later in this chapter) to the extent of the lesser of the distributed asset's basis to the beneficiary or the asset's fair market value as of the distribution date.[11]

EXAMPLE 7

The Howard Trust distributes a painting, basis of $40,000 and fair market value of $90,000, to beneficiary Kate. Kate's basis in the painting is $40,000. The distribution absorbs $40,000 of the trust's DNI, and Howard claims a $40,000 distribution deduction relative to the transaction. ■

EXAMPLE 8

Assume the same facts as in Example 7, except that Howard's basis in the painting is $100,000. Kate's basis in the painting is also $100,000. The distribution absorbs $90,000 of the trust's DNI, and Howard claims a $90,000 distribution deduction. ■

A trustee or executor can *elect* to recognize gain or loss with respect to all of the entity's in-kind property distributions for the year. If the election is made, the beneficiary's basis in the asset is equal to the asset's fair market value as of the distribution date. The distribution absorbs DNI and qualifies for a distribution deduction to the extent of the asset's fair market value. Note, however, that § 267 can restrict an estate or trust's deduction for losses.

EXAMPLE 9

The Green Estate distributes an antique piano, basis to Green of $10,000 and fair market value of $15,000, to beneficiary Kyle. The executor elects that the estate recognize the related $5,000 gain on the distribution. Accordingly, Kyle's basis in the piano is $15,000 ($10,000 basis to Green + $5,000 gain recognized). Without the election, the estate would not recognize any gain, and Kyle's basis in the piano would be $10,000. ■

EXAMPLE 10

Assume the same facts as in Example 9, except that Green's basis in the piano is $18,000. The executor elects that the estate recognize the related $3,000 loss on the distribution. Accordingly, Kyle's basis in the piano is $15,000 ($18,000 – $3,000). Without the election, the estate would not recognize any loss, and Kyle's basis in the piano would be $18,000. The estate cannot deduct this loss, however. Because an estate and its beneficiaries are related parties, realized losses cannot be recognized immediately.[12] The loss would be recognized if Kyle later sells the piano to an unrelated party. ■

Income in Respect of a Decedent. The gross income of a trust or estate includes **income in respect of a decedent (IRD)** that the entity receives.[13] For a cash basis decedent, IRD includes accrued salary, interest, rent, and other income items that were not constructively received before death. For both cash and accrual basis decedents, IRD includes, for example, death benefits from qualified retirement plans and deferred compensation contracts.

The tax consequences of IRD are as follows.

- The fair market value of the right to IRD on the appropriate valuation date is included in the decedent's gross estate. Thus, it is subject to the Federal estate tax.[14]
- The decedent's basis in the property carries over to the recipient (the estate or heirs). There is no step-up or step-down in the basis of IRD items.
- The recipient of the income recognizes gain or loss, measured by the difference between the amount realized and the adjusted basis of the IRD in the hands of the decedent. The character of the gain or loss depends upon the treatment that it would have received had it been realized by the decedent

[11] § 643(e).
[12] § 267(b)(13).
[13] § 691.
[14] To mitigate the effect of double taxation (imposition of both the estate tax and the income tax), § 691(c) allows the recipient an income tax deduction for the incremental estate tax attributable to the net IRD. For individual recipients, this is an itemized deduction, not subject to the 2%-of-AGI floor.

TAX IN THE NEWS

Coordinate Your Deductions

The deduction under § 691(c) may be one of the more obscure provisions of the tax Code, but its benefits can add up fast. The deduction is allowed on the tax return of the recipient of income in respect of a decedent (IRD). IRD often is received by the estate of the decedent or a trust that he or she created under the will or during lifetime. The deduction is for the Federal estate tax attributable to the IRD item. For an individual, it is a miscellaneous itemized deduction *not* subject to the 2 percent-of-AGI floor.

Because IRD often includes the value of the survivorship feature on pensions and other retirement plans and assets, the amount subject to the estate tax can be quite high. On top of that, recall from Chapter 27 that the marginal estate tax rate can be as high as 47 percent (in 2005). Thus, when computing the current-year income tax for the IRD recipient, the § 691(c) deduction can be extremely valuable in offsetting the IRD received.

For example, suppose that an IRA balance of $1 million generates $450,000 in attributable estate tax. If the recipient of the IRA takes the net-of-tax distribution in one year, the § 691(c) deduction shelters $450,000 in gross income and may be worth over $150,000 in Federal income taxes saved.

But taking the § 691(c) deduction is more complex than it looks. Because different tax advisers often prepare the Form 706 for the estate and the Form 1040 or 1041 for the IRD recipient, the § 691(c) deduction can get lost altogether or at least be miscomputed. When the IRD is paid out over several years, computing the § 691(c) deduction can become complex. And some tax professionals do not know the law well enough to track down the deduction, while tax software and IRS forms and publications say relatively little about it. One tax attorney believes that the omission or miscalculation of the deduction is "probably the most prevalent error today in respect to estate taxes."

As retirement assets become a larger portion of many gross estates, thanks to various rollovers from IRAs and qualified plans into the decedent's accounts, IRD and the § 691(c) deduction are likely to be encountered much more frequently in the future.

before death. Thus, if the decedent would have realized capital gain, the recipient must do likewise.

- Expenses related to the IRD (such as interest, taxes, and depletion) that properly were not reported on the final income tax return of the decedent may be claimed by the recipient. These items are known as **expenses in respect of a decedent.** Typically, such expenses also include fiduciary fees, commissions paid to dispose of estate assets, and state income taxes payable. They are deductible for both Federal estate and income tax purposes, *for* or *from* AGI as would have been the case for the decedent.
- If the IRD item would have created an AMT preference or adjustment for the decedent (e.g., with respect to the collection of certain tax-exempt interest by the entity), an identical AMT item is created for the recipient.

EXAMPLE 11

Amanda died on July 13 of the current year. On August 2, her estate received a check (before deductions) for $1,200 from Amanda's former employer; this was Amanda's compensation for the last pay period of her life. On November 23, Amanda's estate received a $45,000 distribution from her employer's qualified profit sharing plan, the full amount to which she was entitled under the plan. Both Amanda and the estate are calendar year, cash basis taxpayers.

The last salary payment and the profit sharing plan distribution constitute IRD to Amanda's estate. Amanda had earned these items during her lifetime, and the estate had an enforceable right to receive each of them after Amanda's death. Consequently, Amanda's gross estate includes $46,200 with respect to these two items. However, the income tax basis to the estate for these items is not stepped up (from zero to $1,200 and $45,000, respectively) upon distribution to the estate. Therefore, the estate must report gross income of $46,200 with respect to the IRD items upon their receipt [($1,200 + $45,000) amounts realized – ($0) adjusted bases]. ■

Including the IRD in both the taxpayer's gross estate and the gross income of the estate may seem harsh. Nonetheless, the tax consequences of IRD are similar to the treatment that applies to all of a taxpayer's earned income. The item is subject to income tax upon receipt, and to the extent that it is not consumed by the taxpayer before death, it is included in the gross estate.

EXAMPLE 12

Assume the same facts as in Example 11, except that Amanda was an accrual basis taxpayer. IRD now includes only the $45,000 distribution from the qualified retirement plan. Amanda's last paycheck is included in the gross income of her own last return (January 1 through date of death). The $1,200 salary is already recognized properly under Amanda's usual method of tax accounting. It does not constitute IRD and is not gross income when received by the executor. ■

EXAMPLE 13

Assume the same facts as in Example 11. Amanda's last paycheck was reduced by $165 for state income taxes that were withheld by her employer. The $165 tax payment is an expense in respect of a decedent and is allowed as a deduction on *both* Amanda's estate tax return *and* the estate's income tax return. ■

ORDINARY DEDUCTIONS

As a general rule, the taxable income of an estate or trust is similar to that of an individual.[15] Deductions are allowed for ordinary and necessary expenses paid or incurred in carrying on a trade or business; for the production or collection of income; for the management, conservation, or maintenance of property; and in connection with the determination, collection, or refund of any tax.[16] Reasonable administration expenses, including fiduciary fees and litigation costs in connection with the duties of administration, also can be deductible.

Expenses attributable to the production or collection of tax-exempt income are not deductible.[17] The amount of the disallowed deduction is found by using a formula based upon the composition of the income elements of entity accounting income for the year of the deduction. The § 212 deduction is apportioned without regard to the accounting income allocation of such expenses to income or to corpus. The deductibility of the fees is determined strictly by the Code (under §§ 212 and 265), and the allocation of expenditures to income and to corpus is controlled by the trust agreement or will or by state law.

Under § 642(g), amounts deductible as administration expenses or losses for estate tax purposes (under §§ 2053 and 2054) cannot be claimed by the estate for income tax purposes, unless the estate files a waiver of the estate tax deduction. Although these expenses cannot be deducted twice, they may be allocated between Forms 706 and 1041 as the fiduciary sees fit; they need not be claimed in their entirety on either return.[18] The prohibition against double deductions does not extend to expenses in respect of a decedent.

[15] § 641(b).
[16] §§ 162 and 212.
[17] § 265.
[18] Reg. § 1.642(g)–2.

Trusts and estates are allowed cost recovery deductions. However, such deductions are assigned proportionately among the recipients of entity accounting income.[19]

EXAMPLE 14

Lisa and Martin are the equal income beneficiaries of the Needle Trust. Under the terms of the trust agreement, the trustee has complete discretion as to the timing of the distributions from Needle's current accounting income. The trust agreement allocates all depreciation expense to income. In the current year, the trustee distributes 40% of the current trust accounting income to Lisa and 40% to Martin; thus, 20% of the income is accumulated. The depreciation deduction allowable to Needle is $100,000. This deduction is allocated among the trust and its beneficiaries on the basis of the distribution of current accounting income: Lisa and Martin each can claim a $40,000 deduction, and the trust can deduct $20,000. ■

EXAMPLE 15

Assume the same facts as in Example 14, except that the trust agreement allocates all depreciation expense to corpus. Lisa and Martin both still claim a $40,000 depreciation deduction, and Needle retains its $20,000 deduction. The Code assigns the depreciation deduction proportionately to the recipients of current entity accounting income. Allocation of depreciation to income or to corpus is irrelevant in determining which party can properly claim the deduction. ■

When a trust sells property received by transfer from the grantor, the amount of depreciation subject to recapture includes the depreciation claimed by the grantor before the transfer of the property to the trust. However, depreciation recapture potential disappears at death.

EXAMPLE 16

Jaime transferred an asset to the Shoulder Trust via a lifetime gift. The asset's total depreciation recapture potential was $40,000. If the trust sells the asset at a gain, it will recognize ordinary income not to exceed $40,000. Had Jaime transferred the asset after his death to his estate through a bequest, the $40,000 recapture potential would have disappeared. ■

DEDUCTIONS FOR LOSSES

An estate or trust is allowed an income tax deduction for casualty or theft losses not covered by insurance or other arrangements. Such losses may also be deductible by an estate for Federal estate tax purposes under § 2054. However, an estate is not allowed an income tax deduction unless the estate tax deduction is waived.[20]

The net operating loss (NOL) deduction is available for estates and trusts (i.e., where trade or business income is generated). The carryback of an NOL may reduce the distributable net income of the trust or estate for the carryback year and therefore affect the amount taxed to the beneficiaries for that year.

Certain losses realized by an estate or trust may also be disallowed, as they are for all taxpayers. Thus, the wash sale provisions of § 1091 disallow losses on the sale or other disposition of stock or securities when the estate or trust acquires substantially identical stock or securities within the prescribed 30-day period. Likewise, § 267 disallows certain losses, expenses, and interest with respect to transactions between related taxpayers. Generally, related parties include a trust, its trustee, grantor, and beneficiaries, as well as an estate, its executor, and beneficiaries.

Except for the possibility of unused losses in the year of termination, the net capital losses of an estate or trust are used only on the fiduciary income tax return.[21] The tax treatment of these losses is the same as for individual taxpayers.

[19] § 167(h) and §§ 611(b)(3) and (4).

[20] See Reg. § 1.642(g)–1 for the required statement waiving the estate tax deduction. In addition, see Reg. §§ 1.165–7(c) and 1.165–8(b), requiring that a statement be filed to allow an income tax deduction for such losses.

[21] § 642(h).

CHARITABLE CONTRIBUTIONS

An estate or complex trust is allowed a deduction for contributions to charitable organizations under certain conditions.

- The contribution is made pursuant to the will or trust instrument, and its amount is determinable using the language of that document.
- The recipient is a qualified organization. For this purpose, qualified organizations include the same charities for which individual and corporate donors are allowed deductions, except that estates and trusts are permitted a deduction for contributions to certain foreign charitable organizations.
- Generally, the contribution is claimed in the tax year paid, but a fiduciary can treat amounts paid in the year immediately following as a deduction for the preceding year.[22] Under this rule, estates and complex trusts receive more liberal treatment than individuals or corporations.

Unlike the charitable contribution deductions of individuals and corporations, the deductions of estates and complex trusts are not limited (e.g., to a percentage of taxable or adjusted gross income). Nonetheless, an entity's charitable contribution may not be fully deductible.[23] Specifically, the deduction is limited to amounts included in the gross income of the entity in the year of the contribution.

A contribution is deemed to have been made proportionately from each of the income elements of entity accounting income. Thus, in the event that the entity has tax-exempt income, the contribution is deductible only to the extent that the income elements of entity accounting income for the year of the deduction are included in the entity's gross income.

This rule is similar to that used to limit the § 212 deduction for fiduciary fees and other expenses incurred to generate tax-exempt income. However, if the will or trust agreement requires that the contribution be made from a specific type of income or from the current income from a specified asset, the contribution will not have to be allocated to taxable and tax-exempt income.

EXAMPLE 17

The Capper Trust has 2005 gross rent income of $80,000, expenses attributable to the rents of $60,000, and tax-exempt interest from state bonds of $20,000. Under the trust agreement, the trustee is to pay 30% of the annual trust accounting income to the United Way, a qualifying organization. Accordingly, the trustee pays $12,000 (30% × $40,000) to the charity in 2006. The charitable contribution deduction allowed for 2005 is $9,600 [($80,000/$100,000) × $12,000]. ■

EXAMPLE 18

Assume the same facts as Example 17, except that the trust instrument also requires that the contribution be paid from the net rent income. The agreement controls, and the allocation formula need not be applied. The entire $12,000 is allowed as a charitable contribution deduction. ■

LO.3

Illustrate the uses and implications of distributable net income.

DEDUCTION FOR DISTRIBUTIONS TO BENEFICIARIES

The modified conduit approach of Subchapter J is embodied in the deduction allowed to trusts and estates for the distributions made to beneficiaries during the year. Some portion of any distribution that a beneficiary receives from a trust may be subject to income tax on his or her own return. At the same time, the distributing entity is allowed a deduction for some or all of the distribution. Consequently, the modified conduit principle of Subchapter J is implemented. A good analogy is to

[22] § 642(c)(1) and Reg. § 1.642(c)–1(b).
[23] Reg. §§ 1.642(c)–3(b) and (c).

the taxability of corporate profits distributed to employees as taxable wages. The corporation is allowed a deduction for the payment, but the employee receives gross income in the form of compensation.

A critical value that is used in computing the amount of the entity's distribution deduction is **distributable net income (DNI).** As it is defined in Subchapter J, DNI serves several functions.

- DNI is the maximum amount of the distribution on which the beneficiaries can be taxed.[24]
- DNI is the maximum amount that the entity can use as a distribution deduction for the year.[25]
- The makeup of DNI carries over to the beneficiaries (the items of income and expenses retain their DNI character in the hands of the distributees).[26]

Subchapter J defines DNI in a circular manner, however. The DNI value is necessary to determine the entity's distribution deduction and therefore its taxable income for the year. Nonetheless, the Code defines DNI as a modification of the entity's taxable income itself. Using the systematic approach to determining the taxable income of the entity and of its beneficiaries, as shown earlier in Figure 28–2, one must first compute *taxable income before the distribution deduction,* modify that amount to determine DNI and the distribution deduction, return to the calculation of *taxable income,* and apply the deduction that has resulted.

Taxable income before the distribution deduction includes all of the entity's items of gross income, deductions, gains, losses, and exemptions for the year. Therefore, to compute this amount, (1) determine the appropriate personal exemption for the year and (2) account for all of the other gross income and deductions of the entity.

The next step in Figure 28–2 is the determination of *distributable net income,* computed by making the following adjustments to the entity's *taxable income before the distribution deduction.*[27]

- Add back the personal exemption.
- Add back *net* tax-exempt interest. To arrive at this amount, reduce the total tax-exempt interest by charitable contributions and by related expenses not deductible under § 265.
- Add back the entity's *net* capital losses.
- Subtract any net capital gains allocable to corpus. In other words, the only net capital gains included in DNI are those attributable to income beneficiaries or to charitable contributions.

Since taxable income before the distribution deduction is computed by deducting all of the expenses of the entity (whether they were allocated to income or to corpus), DNI is reduced by expenses that are allocated to corpus. The effect is to reduce the taxable income of the income beneficiaries. The actual distributions to the beneficiaries exceed DNI because the distributions are not reduced by expenses allocated to corpus. Aside from this shortcoming of Subchapter J, DNI offers a good approximation of the current-year economic income available for distribution to the entity's income beneficiaries.

DNI includes the net tax-exempt interest income of the entity, so that amount must be removed from DNI in computing the distribution deduction. Moreover, for estates and complex trusts, the amount actually distributed during the year may include discretionary distributions of income and distributions of corpus permissible under the will or trust instrument. Thus, the distribution deduction for estates and complex trusts is computed as the lesser of (1) the deductible portion

[24] §§ 652(a) and 662(a).
[25] §§ 651(b) and 661(c).
[26] §§ 652(b) and 662(b).
[27] These and other (less common) adjustments are detailed in § 643.

of DNI or (2) the taxable amount actually distributed to the beneficiaries during the year. For a simple trust, however, full distribution always is assumed, relative to both the entity and its beneficiaries, in a manner similar to the partnership and S corporation conduit entities.

EXAMPLE 19

The Zinc Trust is a simple trust. Because of severe liquidity problems, its 2005 accounting income is not distributed to its sole beneficiary, Mark, until early in 2006. Zinc is still allowed a full distribution deduction for, and Mark is still taxed upon, the entity's 2005 income in 2005. ■

EXAMPLE 20

The Pork Trust is required to distribute its current accounting income annually to its sole income beneficiary, Barbara. Capital gains and losses and all other expenses are allocable to corpus. For the current year, the trust records the following items.

Dividend income	$25,000
Taxable interest income	15,000
Tax-exempt interest income	20,000
Net long-term capital gain	10,000
Fiduciary fees	6,000

Item	Totals		Accounting Income		Taxable Income	Distributable Net Income/ Distribution Deduction
Dividend income	$25,000		$25,000		$ 25,000	
Taxable interest income	15,000		15,000		15,000	
Tax-exempt interest income	20,000		20,000			
Net long-term capital gain	10,000				10,000	
Fiduciary fees	6,000				(4,000)	
Personal exemption					(300)	
Accounting income/taxable income before the distribution deduction		*Step 1*	$60,000	*Step 2*	$ 45,700	$ 45,700
Personal exemption						300
Corpus capital gain/loss						(10,000)
Net tax-exempt income						18,000
Distributable net income						$ 54,000
Distribution deduction				*Step 3*	(36,000)	
Entity taxable income				*Step 4*	$ 9,700	

Step 1 Trust accounting income is $60,000; this includes the tax-exempt interest income, but not the fees or the capital gains, pursuant to the trust document. Barbara receives $60,000 from the trust for the current year.

Step 2 Taxable income before the distribution deduction is computed as directed by the Code. The tax-exempt interest is excluded under § 103. Only a portion of the fees is deductible because some of the fees are traceable to the tax-exempt income. The trust receives a $300 personal exemption as it is required to distribute its annual trust accounting income.

Step 3 DNI and the distribution deduction reflect the required adjustments. The distribution deduction is the lesser of the distributed amount ($60,000) or the deductible portion of DNI ($54,000 – $18,000 net tax-exempt income).

Step 4 Finally, return to the computation of the taxable income of the Pork Trust. A simple test should be applied at this point to ensure that the proper figure for the trust's taxable income has been determined. On what is Pork to be taxed? All of the trust's gross income has been distributed to Barbara except the $10,000 net long-term capital gain. The $300 personal exemption reduces the trust's taxable income to $9,700. ■

EXAMPLE 21

The Quick Trust is required to distribute all of its current accounting income equally to its two beneficiaries, Faith and the First Methodist Church, a qualifying charitable organization. Capital gains and losses and depreciation expenses are allocable to income. Fiduciary fees are allocable to corpus. In the current year, Quick incurs various items as indicated.

Item	Totals		Accounting Income		Taxable Income	Distributable Net Income/ Distribution Deduction
Rent income	$100,000		$100,000		$100,000	
Expenses—rent income	30,000		(30,000)		(30,000)	
Depreciation—rent income	15,000		(15,000)			
Net long-term capital gain	20,000		20,000		20,000	
Charitable contribution					(37,500)	
Fiduciary fees	18,000				(18,000)	
Personal exemption					(300)	
Accounting income/taxable income before the distribution deduction		**Step 1**	$ 75,000	**Step 2**	$ 34,200	$34,200
Personal exemption						300
Corpus capital gain/loss						
Net tax-exempt income						
Distributable net income						$34,500
Distribution deduction				**Step 3**	(34,500)	
Entity taxable income				**Step 4**	($ 300)	

Step 1 Trust accounting income of $75,000 reflects the indicated allocations of items to income and to corpus. Each income beneficiary receives $37,500.

Step 2 In the absence of tax-exempt income, a deduction is allowed for the full amount of the fiduciary's fees. Quick is a complex trust, but since it is required to distribute its full accounting income annually, a $300 exemption is allowed. The trust properly does not deduct any depreciation for the rental property. The depreciation deduction is available only to the recipients of the entity's accounting income for the period. Thus, the deduction will be split equally between Faith and the church. The deduction probably is of no direct value to the church, as the church is not subject to the income tax. The trust's charitable contribution deduction is based upon the $37,500 that the charity actually received (one-half of trust accounting income).

Step 3 As there is no tax-exempt income, the only adjustment needed to compute DNI is to add back the trust's personal exemption. Subchapter J requires no adjustment for the charitable contribution. DNI is computed only from the perspective of Faith, who also received $37,500 from the trust.

Step 4 Finally, the trust's taxable income before the distribution deduction is reduced by the distribution deduction to produce the trust's taxable income of ($300). Perform the simple test (referred to above in the previous example) to ensure that the proper taxable income for the Quick Trust has been computed. All of the trust's gross income has been distributed to Faith and the church. As is the case with most trusts that distribute all of their accounting income, the Quick Trust "wastes" the personal exemption. ■

TAX CREDITS

An estate or trust may claim the foreign tax credit to the extent that it is not passed through to the beneficiaries.[28] Similarly, other credits must be apportioned between the estate or trust and the beneficiaries on the basis of the entity accounting income allocable to each.

Taxation of Beneficiaries

The beneficiaries of an estate or trust receive taxable income from the entity under the modified conduit principle of Subchapter J. DNI determines the maximum amount that can be taxed to the beneficiaries for any tax year. The constitution of DNI also carries over to the beneficiaries (e.g., net long-term capital gains and dividends retain their character when they are distributed from the entity to the beneficiary).

The timing of any tax consequences to the beneficiary of a trust or estate presents a problem only when the parties involved use different tax years. A beneficiary must include in gross income an amount based upon the DNI of the trust for any taxable year or years of the trust or estate ending with or within his or her taxable year.[29]

EXAMPLE 22

An estate uses a fiscal year ending on March 31 for tax purposes. Its sole income beneficiary is a calendar year taxpayer. For calendar year 2007, the beneficiary reports whatever income that was assignable to her for the entity's fiscal year April 1, 2006, to March 31, 2007. If the estate is terminated by December 31, 2007, the beneficiary must also include any income assignable to her for the short year. This could result in a bunching of income in 2007. ■

DISTRIBUTIONS BY SIMPLE TRUSTS

The amount taxable to the beneficiaries of a simple trust is limited by the trust's DNI. However, since DNI includes net tax-exempt income, the amount included in the gross income of the beneficiaries could be less than DNI. When there is more than one income beneficiary, the elements of DNI must be apportioned ratably according to the amount required to be distributed currently to each.

EXAMPLE 23

A simple trust has ordinary income of $40,000, a long-term capital gain of $15,000 (allocable to corpus), and a trustee commission expense of $4,000 (payable from corpus). The two income beneficiaries, Allie and Bart, are entitled to the trust's annual accounting income, based on shares of 75% and 25%, respectively. Although Allie receives $30,000 as her share (75% × $40,000 trust accounting income), she will be allocated DNI of only $27,000 (75% × $36,000). Likewise, Bart is entitled to receive $10,000 (25% × $40,000), but he will be allocated DNI of only $9,000 (25% × $36,000). The $15,000 capital gain is taxed to the trust. ■

[28] §§ 642(a)(1) and 901.

[29] §§ 652(c) and 662(c).

DISTRIBUTIONS BY ESTATES AND COMPLEX TRUSTS

A problem arises with estates and complex trusts when more than one beneficiary receives a distribution from the entity and the controlling document does not require a distribution of the entire accounting income of the entity.

EXAMPLE 24

The trustee of the Wilson Trust has the discretion to distribute the income or corpus of the trust in any proportion between the two beneficiaries of the trust, Wong and Washington. Under the trust instrument, Wong must receive $15,000 from the trust every year. In the current year, the trust's accounting income is $50,000, and its DNI is $40,000. The trustee pays $35,000 to Wong and $25,000 to Washington for the current year. ■

How is Wilson's DNI to be divided between Wong and Washington? Several arbitrary methods of allocating DNI between the beneficiaries could be devised. Subchapter J resolves the problem by creating a two-tier system to govern the taxation of beneficiaries in such situations.[30] The tier system determines which distributions will be included in the gross income of the beneficiaries in full, which will be included in part, and which will not be included at all.

Income that is required to be distributed currently, whether or not it is distributed, is categorized as a *first-tier distribution*. All other amounts properly paid, credited, or required to be distributed are considered to be *second-tier distributions*.[31] A formula is used to allocate DNI among the appropriate beneficiaries when only first-tier distributions are made and those amounts exceed DNI.

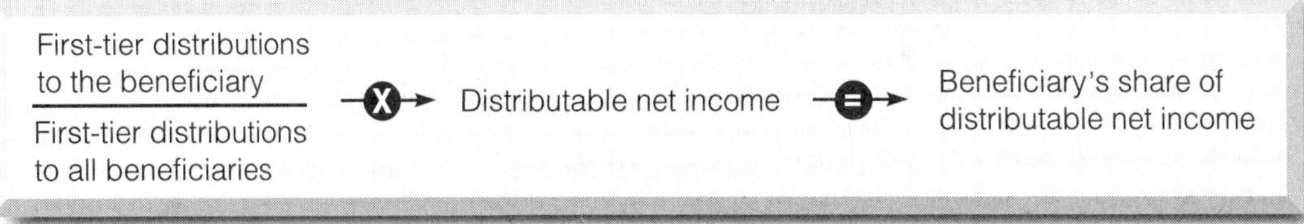

When both first-tier and second-tier distributions are made and the first-tier distributions exceed DNI, the above formula is applied to the first-tier distributions. In this case, none of the second-tier distributions are taxed because all of the DNI has been allocated to the first-tier beneficiaries.

If both first-tier and second-tier distributions are made and the first-tier distributions do not exceed DNI, but the total of both first-tier and second-tier distributions does exceed DNI, the second-tier beneficiaries must recognize income as shown below.

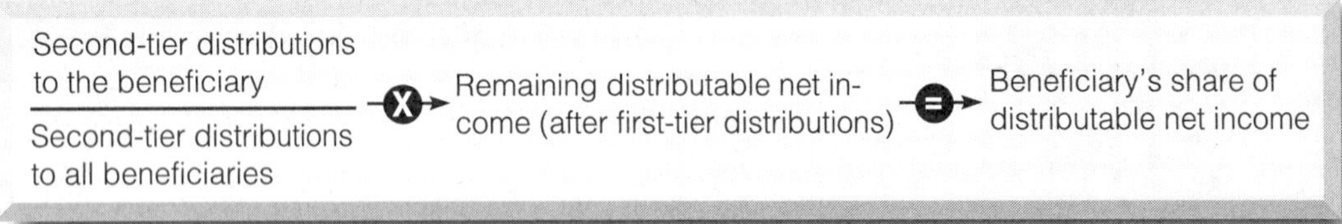

EXAMPLE 25

The trustee of the Gray Trust is required to distribute $10,000 per year to both Harriet and Wally, the two beneficiaries of the entity. In addition, the trustee is empowered to distribute other amounts of trust income or corpus at his sole discretion. In the current year, the trust has accounting income of $60,000 and DNI of $50,000. However, the trustee distributes only

[30] §§ 662(a)(1) and (2).

[31] Reg. §§ 1.662(a)–2 and –3.

the required $10,000 each to Harriet and to Wally. The balance of the income is accumulated and added to trust corpus.

In this case, only first-tier distributions have been made, but the total amount of the distributions does not exceed DNI for the year. Although DNI is the maximum amount that is included by the beneficiaries for the year, they can include no more in gross income than is distributed by the entity. Thus, both Harriet and Wally are subject to tax on $10,000 as their proportionate shares of DNI. ■

EXAMPLE 26

Assume the same facts as in Example 25, except that DNI is $12,000. Harriet and Wally each receive $10,000, but they cannot be taxed in total on more than DNI. Each is taxed on $6,000 [$12,000 DNI × ($10,000/$20,000 of the first-tier distributions)]. ■

EXAMPLE 27

Return to the facts in Example 24. Wong receives a first-tier distribution of $15,000. Second-tier distributions include $20,000 to Wong and $25,000 to Washington. Wilson Trust's DNI is $40,000. The DNI is allocated between Wong and Washington as follows.

(1) First-tier distributions	
To Wong	$15,000 DNI
To Washington	–0–
Remaining DNI = $25,000 ($40,000 DNI – $15,000 distributed)	
(2) Second-tier distributions	
To Wong [(20/45) × $25,000]	$11,111 DNI
To Washington [(25/45) × $25,000]	13,889 DNI

■

Separate Share Rule. For the sole purpose of determining the amount of DNI for a complex trust or estate with more than one beneficiary, the substantially separate and independent shares of different beneficiaries in the trust or estate are treated as *separate* trusts or estates.[32] An illustration shows the need for this special rule.

EXAMPLE 28

A trustee has the discretion to distribute or accumulate income on behalf of Greg and Hannah (in equal shares). The trustee also has the power to invade corpus for the benefit of either beneficiary to the extent of that beneficiary's one-half interest in the trust. For the current year, DNI is $10,000. Of this amount, $5,000 is distributed to Greg, and $5,000 is accumulated on behalf of Hannah. In addition, the trustee pays $20,000 from corpus to Greg. Without the separate share rule, Greg is taxed on $10,000 (the full amount of the DNI). With the separate share rule, Greg is taxed on only $5,000 (his share of the DNI) and receives the $20,000 corpus distribution tax-free. The trust will be taxed on Hannah's $5,000 share of the DNI that is accumulated. ■

The separate share rule is designed to prevent the inequity that results if the corpus payments are treated under the regular rules applicable to second-tier beneficiaries. In Example 28, the effect of the separate share rule is to produce a two-trust result: one trust for Greg and one for Hannah, each with DNI of $5,000. The rule also results in the availability of extra entity personal exemptions and in a greater use of lower entity tax brackets.

CHARACTER OF INCOME

Consistent with the modified conduit principle of Subchapter J, various classes of income (e.g., dividends, passive or portfolio gain and loss, AMT preferences and

[32] § 663(c); Reg. § 1.663(c)–1(a).

adjustments, and tax-exempt interest) retain the same character for the beneficiaries that they had when they were received by the entity. If there are multiple beneficiaries *and* if all of the DNI is distributed, a problem arises in allocating the various classes of income among the beneficiaries.

Distributions are treated as consisting of the same proportion as the items that enter into the computation of DNI. This allocation does not apply, however, if the governing instrument specifically allocates different classes of income to different beneficiaries.[33]

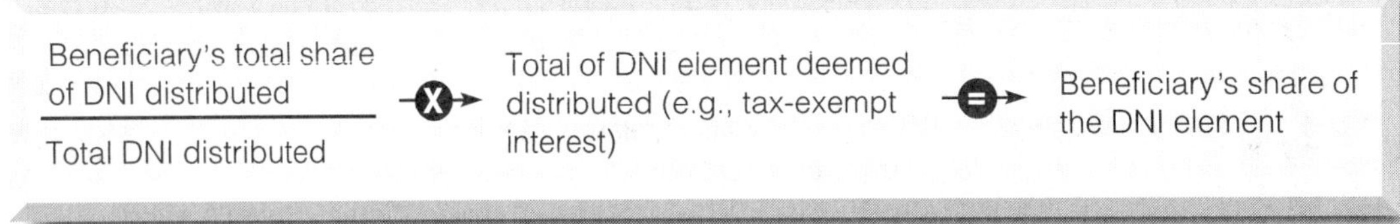

If the entity distributes only a part of its DNI, the amount of a particular class of DNI that is deemed distributed must first be determined.

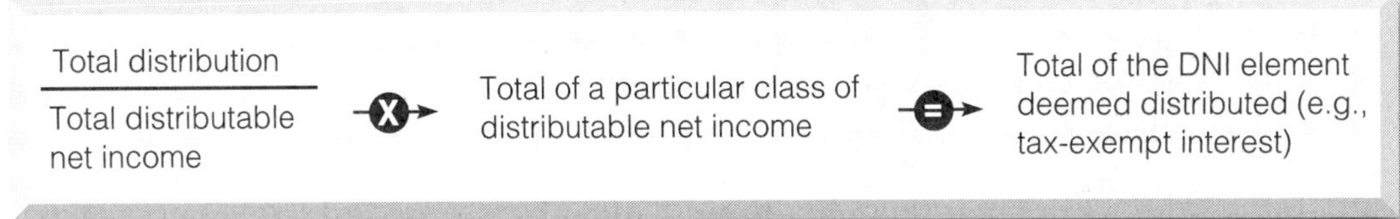

EXAMPLE 29

During the current year, a trust has DNI of $40,000, including the following: $10,000 of taxable interest, $10,000 of tax-exempt interest, and $20,000 of passive activity income. The trustee distributes, at her discretion, $8,000 to Mike and $12,000 to Nancy.

		Income Type		
Beneficiary	**Amount Received**	**Taxable Interest**	**Tax-Exempt Interest**	**Passive Income**
Mike	$ 8,000	$2,000*	$2,000	$4,000
Nancy	12,000	3,000	3,000	6,000

*$8,000 distribution/$40,000 total DNI × $10,000 taxable interest in DNI. ■

Special Allocations. Under certain circumstances, the parties may modify the character-of-income allocation method set forth above. A modification is permitted only to the extent that the allocation is required in the trust instrument and only to the extent that it has an economic effect independent of the cash-flow and income tax consequences of the allocation.[34]

EXAMPLE 30

Return to the facts in Example 29. Assume that the beneficiaries are elderly individuals who have pooled their investment portfolios to avail themselves of the trustee's professional asset management skills. Suppose the trustee has the discretion to allocate different classes

[33]Reg. § 1.662(b)–1 seems to allow special allocations, but see *Harkness v. U.S.*, 72–2 USTC ¶9740, 30 AFTR2d 72–5754, 469 F.2d 310 (Ct.Cls., 1972).

[34]Reg. § 1.652(b)–2(b). This is similar to the § 704(b) requirement for partnerships.

of income to different beneficiaries and that she designates $10,000 of Nancy's $12,000 distribution as being from the tax-exempt income. Such a designation *would not be recognized* for tax purposes, and the allocation method of Example 29 must be used.

Suppose, however, that the trust instrument stipulated that Nancy was to receive all of the income from the tax-exempt securities because she alone contributed the exempt securities to the trust corpus. Under this provision, the $10,000 of the nontaxable interest is paid to Nancy. This allocation *is recognized,* and $10,000 of Nancy's distribution is tax-exempt. ■

LOSSES IN THE TERMINATION YEAR

The ordinary net operating and capital losses of a trust or estate do not flow through to the entity's beneficiaries, as would such losses from a partnership or an S corporation. However, in the year in which an entity terminates its existence, the beneficiaries do receive a direct benefit from the loss carryovers of the trust or estate.[35]

Net operating losses and net capital losses are subject to the same carryover rules that otherwise apply to an individual. Consequently, NOLs can be carried back 2 years and then carried forward 20 years while net capital losses can be carried forward only, and for an indefinite period of time. However, if the entity incurs a negative taxable income in the last year of its existence, the excess of deductions over the entity's gross income is allowed to the beneficiaries (it will flow through to them directly). The net loss is available as a deduction *from* AGI in the beneficiary's tax year with or within which the entity's tax year ends. The amount allowed is in proportion to the relative amount of corpus assets that each beneficiary receives upon the termination of the entity, and it is subject to the 2 percent-of-AGI floor.

Any carryovers of the entity's other losses flow through to the beneficiaries in the year of termination in proportion to the relative amount of corpus assets that each beneficiary receives. The character of the loss carryforward is retained by the beneficiary, except that a carryover of a net capital loss to a corporate beneficiary is always treated as short term. Beneficiaries who are individuals use these carryforwards as deductions *for* AGI.

EXAMPLE 31

The Edgar Estate terminates on December 31, 2005. It had used a fiscal year ending July 31. For the termination year, the estate incurred a $15,000 negative taxable income. In addition, the estate had an unused NOL carryforward of $23,000 from the year ending July 31, 2001, and an unused net long-term capital loss carryforward of $10,000 from the year ending July 31, 2003. Upon termination, Dawn receives $60,000 of corpus, and Blue Corporation receives the remaining $40,000. Dawn and Blue are calendar year taxpayers.

Dawn can claim an itemized deduction of $9,000 [($60,000/$100,000) × $15,000] for the entity's negative taxable income in the year of termination. This deduction is subject to the 2%-of-AGI floor on her miscellaneous itemized deductions. In addition, she can claim a $13,800 deduction *for* AGI in 2005 (60% × $23,000) for Edgar's NOL carryforward, and she can use $6,000 (60% × $10,000) of the estate's net long-term capital loss carryforward with her other 2005 capital transactions.

Blue Corporation receives ordinary business deductions in 2005 for Edgar's NOLs: $6,000 for the loss in the year of termination and $9,200 for the carryforward from fiscal year 2001. Moreover, Blue can use the $4,000 carryforward of Edgar's net capital losses to offset against its other 2005 capital transactions, although the loss must be treated as short term. ■

[35]Reg. §§ 1.642(h)–1 and –2.

Don't Trust Your Dictionary

Today, the middle and upper classes are often including trusts in their estate plans. Usually, the purpose of the trust is to spare the survivors the time and effort required to work through a state's probate proceedings.

But planning for death can sometimes lead to confusion about terminology, especially between a living trust and a living will. A "living trust" is typically created to hold the assets of the decedent-to-be, including investments, homestead, and household goods. Assets are retitled in the name of the trustee, who periodically files a Form 1041 for the new entity. The idea underlying the living trust is to reduce the probate estate. This, in turn, lowers the fees for carrying out the probate process. Such fees often total 5 percent or so of the date of death value of the probate assets.

The living trust accomplishes virtually no Federal tax savings. The trust assets are included in the decedent's gross estate, as the living trust is an incomplete transfer under §§ 2036 and 2038. For the most part, the entity is treated as a grantor trust. Because of the retained investment and distribution powers, the donor is still liable for taxes on the taxable income of the fiduciary.

A "living will," on the other hand, is a legal document that conveys powers to relatives and third parties to make medical and financial decisions when the decedent-to-be can no longer do so. More appropriately referred to as a "medical power of attorney," the document expresses the person's wishes as to how and when to reduce specified medical treatments (including directives as to removing life support systems).

Various states and estate planners use these terms differently, and sometimes interchangeably. Consequently, it is important that the proper document is used to accomplish the desired goals. Usually, it is "too late" to amend the document once a misunderstanding is discovered!

LO.4

Understand various tax planning procedures that can be used to minimize the income tax consequences of trusts and estates and their beneficiaries.

Tax Planning Considerations

Many of the tax planning possibilities for estates and trusts were discussed in Chapter 27. However, several specific tax planning possibilities are available to help minimize the income tax effects on estates and trusts and their beneficiaries.

A TRUST OR ESTATE AS AN INCOME-SHIFTING DEVICE

The compressed tax rate schedule applicable to Subchapter J entities may have reversed the traditional techniques by which families set aside funds for long-term activities, such as business startups, college education, and home purchases. When the tax rate schedules for trusts and estates were more accommodating, high-income individuals would shift income-producing assets to trusts to take advantage of the lower tax rate that would fall on the income accumulated within the trust. The target of the plan, usually a child, would receive the accumulated income (and, perhaps, trust corpus) at a designated age, and more funds would be available because a lower tax rate had been applied over the life of the investment in the trust.

Today, such an income shift would *deplete*, rather than shelter, the family's assets, as the rates falling on individuals are much more graduated than are those applicable to fiduciaries, and the kiddie tax also penalizes attempts to shift taxable income to children. Assuming that the objectives of the plan remain unchanged, possible strategies in view of these rate changes include the following:

- Trust corpus should be invested in growth assets that are low on yield but high on appreciation, so that the trustee can determine the timing of the gain and somewhat control the effective tax rate that applies.

CONCEPT SUMMARY 28–1

Income Taxation of Trusts and Estates

1. Estates and trusts are temporary entities, created to locate, maintain, and distribute assets and to satisfy liabilities according to the wishes of the decedent or grantor as expressed in the will or trust document.
2. Generally, the estate or trust acts as a conduit of the taxable income that it receives. To the extent that the income is distributed by the entity, it is taxed to the beneficiary. Taxable income retained by the entity is taxed to the entity itself.
3. The entity's accounting income must be determined first. Accounting conventions that are stated in the controlling document or, lacking such provisions, in state law allocate specific items of receipt and expenditure either to income or to corpus. Income beneficiaries typically receive payments from the entity that are equal to the accounting income.
4. The taxable income of the entity is computed using the scheme in Figure 28–3. The entity usually recognizes income in respect of a decedent. Deductions for fiduciary's fees and for charitable contributions may be reduced if the entity received any tax-exempt income during the year. Cost recovery deductions are assigned proportionately to the recipients of accounting income. Upon election, realized gain or loss on assets that properly are distributed in kind can be recognized by the entity.
5. A distribution deduction, computationally derived from distributable net income (DNI), is allowed to the entity. DNI is the maximum amount on which entity beneficiaries can be taxed. Moreover, the constitution of DNI is assigned to the recipients of the distributions.

- Trust corpus should be invested in tax-exempt securities, such as municipal bonds and mutual funds that invest in them, to eliminate the tax costs associated with the investment. If this approach is taken, a trust might be unnecessary—the parent should simply retain full control over the assets and invest in the exempt securities in his or her own account.
- The grantor should retain high-yield assets, so that control over the assets is not surrendered when the tax cost is too high.
- Use of trust vehicles should be reserved for cases where professional management of the assets is necessary for portfolio growth and the additional tax costs can be justified.
- An income-shifting strategy may require several steps to achieve the desired result. For example, the grantor might increase contributions to his or her own qualified retirement plan, thereby sheltering the funds from all tax liabilities. Then the grantor could use the tax dollars saved from these contributions to purchase tax-deferred annuity contracts, savings bonds, exempt securities, or other assets where the tax liabilities are reduced or deferred. The grantor could then either retain these exempt securities as discussed above or transfer them to the trust at a later date.

INCOME TAX PLANNING FOR ESTATES

As a separate taxable entity, an estate can select its own tax year and accounting methods. The executor of an estate should consider selecting a fiscal year because this will determine when beneficiaries must include income distributions from the estate in their own tax returns. Beneficiaries must include the income for their tax year with or within which the estate's tax year ends. Proper selection of the estate's tax year can result in a smoothing out of income and a reduction of the income taxes for all parties involved.

Caution should be taken in determining when the estate is to be terminated. Selecting a fiscal year for the estate can result in a bunching of income to the beneficiaries in the year in which the estate is closed. Prolonging the termination of an estate can be effective income tax planning, but the IRS carefully examines the purpose of keeping the estate open. Since the unused losses of an estate pass through to the beneficiaries only in the termination year, the estate should be closed when the beneficiaries can enjoy the maximum tax benefit of the losses.

The timing and amounts of income distributions to the beneficiaries also present important tax planning opportunities. If the executor can make discretionary income distributions, he or she should evaluate the relative marginal income tax rates of the estate and its beneficiaries. By timing the distributions properly, the overall income tax liability can be minimized. Care should be taken, however, to time the distributions in light of the estate's DNI.

EXAMPLE 32

For several years before his death on March 7, Don had entered into annual deferred compensation agreements with his employer. These agreements collectively called for the payment of $200,000 six months after Don's retirement or death. To provide a maximum 12-month period within which to generate deductions to offset this large item of IRD, the executor or administrator of the estate should elect a fiscal year ending August 31. The election is made simply by filing the estate's first tax return for the short period of March 7 to August 31. ■

EXAMPLE 33

Carol, the sole beneficiary of an estate, is a calendar year, cash basis taxpayer. If the estate elects a fiscal year ending January 31, all distributions during the period of February 1 to December 31, 2005, will be reported on Carol's tax return for calendar year 2006 (due April 15, 2007). Thus, assuming estimated tax requirements have otherwise been met, any income taxes that result from a $50,000 distribution made by the estate on February 20, 2005, will be deferred until April 15, 2007. ■

EXAMPLE 34

Assume the same facts as in Example 33. If the estate is closed on December 15, 2006, the DNI for both the fiscal year ending January 31, 2006, and the final tax year ending December 15, 2006, is included in Carol's tax return for the same calendar year. To avoid the effect of this bunching of income, the estate should not be closed until calendar year 2007. ■

In general, beneficiaries who are subject to high tax rates should be made beneficiaries of second-tier (but not IRD) distributions of the estate. Most likely, these individuals will have less need for an additional steady stream of (taxable) income while their income tax savings can be relatively large. Moreover, a special allocation of tax-favored types of income and expenses should be considered. For example, tax-exempt income can be directed more easily to beneficiaries in higher income tax brackets.

ETHICAL CONSIDERATIONS

Should a Tax Adviser Also Be a Trustee?

Tax clients need to be counseled on the best use of the trust entity and the proper choice of beneficiary of the trust income. The objectives of the grantor typically will best be served by transferring more power to the trustee; sprinkling powers, in particular, enable the trustee to be sensitive to the short-term and ongoing needs of the various beneficiaries. The client, however, may not appreciate this suggestion when the trust document is drafted. Especially if the tax adviser is the trustee or a co-trustee, the client may balk at the professional's well-intended suggestion that future developments might favor one beneficiary over another in a manner that cannot be anticipated at the time.

Should the source of the estate plan—the tax adviser—also then be designated as the trustee by the grantor? When the adviser serves in that capacity, who is "the client"? Merely the grantor? How about the beneficiaries? And the trust itself? To avoid any potential for conflict with their clients, some professional firms have adopted a policy of refusing to serve as trustee of a client's trust (or executor of his or her estate). Certainly, surrendering a sprinkling power to a fiduciary who is less sensitive to the tax ramifications of Subchapter J may be costly to all of the parties, but these firms see the preservation of the client relationship as more valuable in the long term.

In creating a trust, the grantor must address critical issues: How much power and control over assets and income should be "surrendered to outsiders" through the trust? Which items lend themselves to such transfers of control?

INCOME TAX PLANNING WITH TRUSTS

The great variety of trusts provides the grantor, trustee, and beneficiaries with excellent opportunities for tax planning. Many of the same tax planning opportunities available to the executor of an estate are available to the trustee. For example, the distributions from a trust are taxable to the trust's beneficiaries to the extent of the trust's DNI. If income distributions are discretionary, the trustee can time the distributions to minimize the income tax consequences to all parties.

DISTRIBUTIONS OF IN-KIND PROPERTY

The ability of the trustee or executor to elect to recognize the realized gain or loss relative to a distributed noncash asset allows the gain or loss to be allocated to the optimal taxpayer.

EXAMPLE 35

The Yorba Linda Estate distributed some stock, basis of $40,000 and fair market value of $41,500, to beneficiary Larry. Yorba Linda is subject to a 5% capital gains tax rate, and Larry is subject to a 15% capital gains tax rate. The executor of Yorba Linda should elect that the entity recognize the related $1,500 realized gain, thereby subjecting the gain to the estate's lower tax rate and reducing Larry's future capital gain income (by increasing his basis). ■

KEY TERMS

Complex trust, 28–5
Corpus, 28–4
Distributable net income (DNI), 28–18
Expenses in respect of a decedent, 28–14
Grantor, 28–4
Grantor trusts, 28–4
Income in respect of a decedent (IRD), 28–13
Reversionary interest, 28–4
Simple trust, 28–5
Sprinkling trust, 28–5

PROBLEM MATERIALS

Discussion Questions

Issue ID

1. When should a client be counseled to create a trust? What tax motivations might lead to the use of a fiduciary? List important tax and nontax objectives that might be satisfied by the use of a trust created during the taxpayer's lifetime.

2. How many parties are needed to create an estate? A trust? Identify the titles traditionally given to each party.

3. Define the following terms.
   a. Income interest.
   b. Remainder interest.
   c. Reversionary interest.
   d. Life tenant.

4. What is a sprinkling trust? Is it a simple or a complex trust?

5. The Winter Trust must file a Form 1041 for the first time, because it has recognized about $2,000 of gross income. With respect to this trust:
   a. What tax year should be used?
   b. Are any estimated tax payments due before the return is filed? If so, when are they due?
   c. Where should the completed Form 1041 be sent?

6. Is it more or less expensive in tax terms for a married couple to shift taxable income via a trust? What if they were to use a C corporation?

7. Evaluate this comment: A fiduciary entity such as a trust or an estate is not subject to the alternative minimum tax, but its beneficiaries are.

8. Illustrate the nature and operations of each of the following trusts by creating a fact pattern to match each result. Be specific.
   a. A simple trust.
   b. A complex trust with a $300 personal exemption.
   c. A complex trust with a $100 personal exemption.

9. Using Figure 28–2 as a guide, describe the computation of a fiduciary entity's accounting income, taxable income, and distributable net income.

10. The Lopez Trust is short of cash. It is required to distribute $100,000 to Judith every year, and that payment is due in six weeks. In its asset corpus, Lopez holds a number of stocks that are valued at $100,000. One of them has a tax basis to the trust of $65,000. Assuming that the trust agreement allows, what are the tax consequences if Lopez distributes this stock to Judith?

Decision Making

11. In its first tax year, the Wittmann Estate generated $50,000 of taxable interest income and $20,000 of tax-exempt interest income. It paid fiduciary fees of $3,000. The estate is subject to a 47% marginal estate tax rate and a 33% marginal income tax rate. How should the executor assign the deductions for the payment of the fees?

12. The Red Trust generated $50,000 in cost recovery deductions this year. Can Red claim this deduction in computing its entity taxable income?

13. In 2005, the Helpful Trust agreed to make a $50,000 contribution to Local Soup Kitchen, a charitable organization. Helpful's board agreed to the gift at a November 2005 meeting, but the check was not issued until February 20, 2006. Can the trust claim a charitable contribution deduction? If so, describe how Helpful should treat its gift.

Issue ID

14. The Flan Trust is scheduled to terminate in two years, when Amy Flan reaches age 30. The trust operated a business several years ago, and it generated a sizable NOL carryforward that the trust has not been able to use. In addition, due to a bearish stock market, the value of the entity's investment portfolio declined 15% from its purchase price. What issues must you consider in giving Amy and the corporate trustee tax planning advice?

Decision Making
Communications

15. Carol wants to set up a trust that will pay her life insurance premiums. She believes that the trust will be able to deduct these premium payments, something that she cannot currently do on her Form 1040. Write a memo to the tax research file addressing Carol's ideas.

16. In planning to reduce taxes for a typical family, should income be shifted *to* a trust or *from* a trust? Why?

17. In planning to reduce taxes for a typical family, should an estate adopt a calendar or a fiscal tax year? Why?

18. In planning to reduce taxes for a typical family, should the deductions for administrative expenses be assigned to the estate tax return (i.e., Form 706) or the estate's income tax return (i.e., Form 1041)? Why?

Problems

19. Compute the Federal income tax liability for the Wren Estate. The executor reports the following transactions for the 2005 tax year.

Operating income from a business	$400,000
Dividend income, all from U.S. corporations	75,000
Interest income, City of San Antonio bonds	40,000
Fiduciary fees, deductible portion	10,000

20. The Purple Trust incurred the following items this year.

Taxable interest income	$35,000
Tax-exempt interest income, not on private activity bonds	50,000
Tax-exempt interest income, on private activity bonds	60,000

Compute Purple's tentative minimum tax for the year. Purple does not have any credits available to reduce the AMT liability.

21. Complete the following chart, indicating the comparative attributes of the typical trust and estate by answering yes/no or explaining the differences between the entities where appropriate.

Attribute	Estate	Trust
Separate income tax entity	______	______
Controlling document	______	______
Termination date is determinable from controlling document	______	______
Legal owner of assets under fiduciary's control	______	______
Document identifies both income and remainder beneficiaries	______	______
Separate share rules apply	______	______
Generally must use calendar tax year	______	______

22. Brown incurred the following items.

Business income	$75,000
Tax-exempt interest income	25,000
Payment to charity from 2006 income, paid 3/1/2007	20,000

Complete the following chart, indicating how the Code treats charitable contributions under the various assumptions.

Assumption	2006 Deduction for Contribution
Brown is a cash basis individual.	________
Brown is an accrual basis corporation.	________
Brown is a trust.	________

23. The Ricardo Trust is a simple trust that correctly uses the calendar year for tax purposes. Its three income beneficiaries (Lucy, Mark, and Ethel) are entitled to the trust's annual accounting income in shares of one-third each. For the current calendar year, the trust generates ordinary income of $75,000, a long-term capital gain of $15,000 (allocable to corpus), and a trustee commission expense of $9,000 (allocable to corpus). Use the format of Figure 28–3 to address the following items.
    a. How much income is each beneficiary entitled to receive?
    b. What is the trust's DNI?
    c. What is the trust's taxable income?
    d. How much is taxed to each of the beneficiaries?

24. Assume the same facts as in Problem 23, except that the trust instrument allocates the capital gain to income.
    a. How much income is each beneficiary entitled to receive?
    b. What is the trust's DNI?
    c. What is the trust's taxable income?
    d. How much is taxed to each of the beneficiaries?

25. Under the terms of the trust instrument, the trustee has discretion to distribute or accumulate income on behalf of Willie, Sylvia, and Doris in equal shares. The trustee also can invade corpus for the benefit of any of the beneficiaries to the extent of each person's respective one-third interest in the trust.

    In the current year, the trust has DNI of $75,000. Distributions were made as follows:

    - To Willie: $25,000 from DNI, $15,000 from corpus.
    - To Sylvia: $15,000. The remaining $10,000 DNI is accumulated.
    - To Doris: $0. The $25,000 DNI is accumulated.

    a. How much income is taxed to Willie?
    b. To Sylvia?
    c. To Doris?
    d. To the trust?

26. A trust is required to distribute $100,000 in total annually to its two equal income beneficiaries, Clare and David. If trust income is not sufficient to pay these amounts, the trustee can invade corpus to the extent necessary. During the current year, the trust generates only taxable interest income and has DNI of $120,000; the trustee distributes $75,000 to Clare and $50,000 to David.
    a. How much of the $75,000 distributed to Clare must be included in her gross income?
    b. How much of the $50,000 distributed to David must be included in his gross income?
    c. Are these distributions considered to be first-tier or second-tier distributions?

27. An estate has $75,000 of DNI, composed of $30,000 in dividends, $20,000 in taxable interest, $15,000 in passive activity income, and $10,000 in tax-exempt interest. The trust's two noncharitable income beneficiaries, Brenda and Del, receive $30,000 each. How much of each class of income is deemed to have been distributed to Brenda? To Del?

28. The trustee of the Purple Trust can distribute any amount of accounting income and corpus to the trust's beneficiaries, Lydia and Kent. This year, the trust incurred the following.

Taxable interest income	$40,000
Tax-exempt interest income	60,000
Long-term capital gains—allocable to corpus	30,000
Fiduciary's fees—allocable to corpus	10,000

    The trustee distributed $40,000 to Lydia and $30,000 to Kent.
    a. What is Purple's trust accounting income?
    b. What is Purple's DNI?
    c. What is Purple's taxable income?
    d. How much is taxed to each of the beneficiaries?

Decision Making

29. Each of the following items was incurred by José, a cash basis, calendar year decedent. Under the terms of the will, Dora took immediate ownership in all of José's assets, except the dividend-paying stocks. The estate received José's final paycheck.

    Applying the rules for income and deductions in respect of a decedent, indicate on which return each item should be reported: Dora's Form 1040 income tax (*Form 1040*); José's estate's first Form 1041 income tax (*Form 1041*); or José's estate's Form 706 estate tax (*Form 706*). More than one alternative may apply in some cases.

Item Incurred	**Form(s) Reported on**
a. Wages, last paycheck	______
b. State income tax withheld on last paycheck	______
c. Capital gain portion of installment payment received	______
d. Ordinary income portion of installment payment received	______

e. Dividend income, record date was two days prior to José's death __________
f. Unrealized appreciation on a mutual fund investment __________
g. Depreciation recapture accrued as of date of death __________
h. Medical expenses of last illness __________
i. Apartment building, rents accrued but not collected as of death __________
j. Apartment building, property tax accrued and assessed but not paid as of death __________

30. Determine the tax effects of the indicated losses for the Yellow Estate for both tax years. The estate holds a variety of investment assets, which it received from the decedent, Mrs. Yellow. The estate's sole income and remainder beneficiary is Yellow, Jr.

Tax Year	Loss Generated
2005 (first tax year)	Taxable income ($300)
	Capital loss ($8,000)
2006 (final tax year)	Taxable income ($20,000)

Research Problems

Note: Solutions to Research Problems can be prepared by using the ***RIA Checkpoint*®** ***Student Edition*** *online research product, which is available to accompany this text. It is also possible to prepare solutions to the Research Problems by using tax research materials found in a standard tax library.*

Communications

Research Problem 1. George Ruiz is an accomplished business executive and is knowledgeable about the Federal tax laws that pertain to his company's water-filtering business. George also owns several apartment complexes and has become familiar with the § 469 passive activity rules.

That is why he is worried about a new project that his family wants him to undertake. Aunt Alma died last year and left her self-service storage business in a trust for the benefit of the family's grandchildren. George was named as the sole trustee and is the only family member with the financial expertise to take over the business. Unfortunately, he has neither the time nor the inclination to assume the extensive managerial duties required. The business is barely profitable and has incurred losses for many years. To improve the profit margins and assure profits for the future, the storage units will need extensive renovation.

In the meantime, George is worried that the resulting taxable losses will be disallowed as passive. As trustee, he cannot show enough material participation in the storage facility business to meet the § 469 requirements. Virtually all of the "work" related to the business will have to be conducted by the employees and contractors that George hires. The trust produces a good deal of portfolio income, but it currently has no other sources of passive income.

How do the passive activity rules affect George's decision? Write him a letter discussing this issue. His office address is George's Clear Water, 55 Canal Street, Dunedin, FL 33761.

Research Problem 2. Happy owned and operated a hardware store that was purchased outright by The Home Depot in 2001. Under the terms of the acquisition, Happy was to receive a $100,000 payment in each of the next five years on the condition that he would not commence or acquire any hardware-store operations in Pennsylvania (Happy's state of residence) until the end of the fifth year.

Happy collected his payments under the covenant not to compete for the first four years but died in early 2006, before the last payment was made. Under the terms of his will, any postmortem payments were to be made directly to Sally, Happy's only blood relative.

How should Sally treat the final payment due under the covenant and received by her in November 2006?

Internet Activity

Use the tax resources of the Internet to address the following question. Do not restrict your search to the World Wide Web, but include a review of newsgroups and general reference materials, practitioner sites and resources, primary sources of the tax law, chat rooms and discussion groups, and other opportunities.

Communications

Research Problem 3. Find the Web site of a law firm that seems to specialize in fiduciary entities, preferably a firm located in your state. Ask the firm to quote you a fee for (1) establishing a simple trust and (2) filing the annual Form 1041. Summarize your findings, and your communications with the firm, in an e-mail to your instructor.

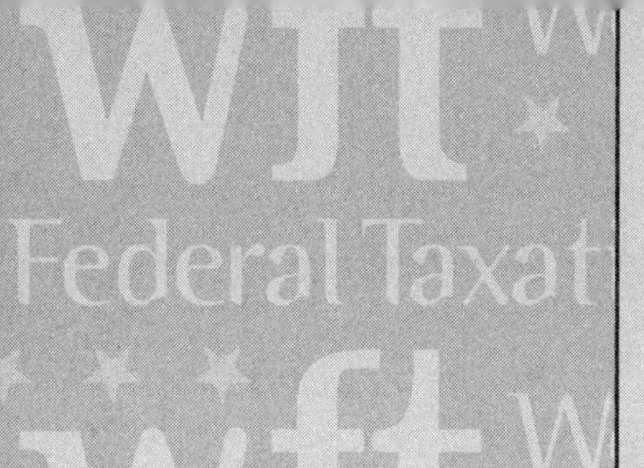

APPENDIX A

Tax Rate Schedules and Tables

(The 2005 Tax Tables and 2005 Sales Tax Tables can be accessed at the IRS web site [**http://www.irs.gov**] when released.)

2004 Tax Rate Schedules

Single—Schedule X

If taxable income is: Over—	But not over—	The tax is:	of the amount over—
$0	$ 7,150	........10%	**$0**
7,150	29,050	**$ 715.00 + 15%**	**7,150**
29,050	70,350	**4,000.00 + 25%**	**29,050**
70,350	146,750	**14,325.00 + 28%**	**70,350**
146,750	319,100	**35,717.00 + 33%**	**146,750**
319,100	....	**92,592.50 + 35%**	**319,100**

Head of household—Schedule Z

If taxable income is: Over—	But not over—	The tax is:	of the amount over—
$0	$ 10,200	........10%	**$0**
10,200	38,900	**$ 1,020.00 + 15%**	**10,200**
38,900	100,500	**5,325.00 + 25%**	**38,900**
100,500	162,700	**20,725.00 + 28%**	**100,500**
162,700	319,100	**38,141.00 + 33%**	**162,700**
319,100	....	**89,753.00 + 35%**	**319,100**

Married filing jointly or Qualifying widow(er)—Schedule Y–1

If taxable income is: Over—	But not over—	The tax is:	of the amount over—
$0	$ 14,300	........10%	**$0**
14,300	58,100	**$ 1,430.00 + 15%**	**14,300**
58,100	117,250	**8,000.00 + 25%**	**58,100**
117,250	178,650	**22,787.50 + 28%**	**117,250**
178,650	319,100	**39,979.50 + 33%**	**178,650**
319,100	....	**86,328.00 + 35%**	**319,100**

Married filing separately—Schedule Y–2

If taxable income is: Over—	But not over—	The tax is:	of the amount over—
$0	$ 7,150	........10%	**$0**
7,150	29,050	**$ 715.00 + 15%**	**7,150**
29,050	58,625	**4,000.00 + 25%**	**29,050**
58,625	89,325	**11,393.75 + 28%**	**58,625**
89,325	159,550	**19,989.75 + 33%**	**89,325**
159,550	....	**43,164.00 + 35%**	**159,550**

2005 Tax Rate Schedules

Single—Schedule X

If taxable income is: Over—	But not over—	The tax is:	of the amount over—
$0	$ 7,300	........10%	**$0**
7,300	29,700	**$ 730.00 + 15%**	**7,300**
29,700	71,950	**4,090.00 + 25%**	**29,700**
71,950	150,150	**14,652.50 + 28%**	**71,950**
150,150	326,450	**36,548.50 + 33%**	**150,150**
326,450	....	**94,727.50 + 35%**	**326,450**

Head of household—Schedule Z

If taxable income is: Over—	But not over—	The tax is:	of the amount over—
$0	$ 10,450	.......10%	**$0**
10,450	39,800	**$ 1,045.00 + 15%**	**10,450**
39,800	102,800	**5,447.50 + 25%**	**39,800**
102,800	166,450	**21,197.50 + 28%**	**102,800**
166,450	326,450	**39,019.50 + 33%**	**166,450**
326,450	....	**91,819.50 + 35%**	**326,450**

Married filing jointly or Qualifying widow(er)—Schedule Y–1

If taxable income is: Over—	But not over—	The tax is:	of the amount over—
$0	$ 14,600	........10%	**$0**
14,600	59,400	**$ 1,460.00 + 15%**	**14,600**
59,400	119,950	**8,180.00 + 25%**	**59,400**
119,950	182,800	**23,317.50 + 28%**	**119,950**
182,800	326,450	**40,915.50 + 33%**	**182,800**
326,450	....	**88,320.00 + 35%**	**326,450**

Married filing separately—Schedule Y–2

If taxable income is: Over—	But not over—	The tax is:	of the amount over—
$0	$ 7,300	........10%	**$0**
7,300	29,700	**$ 730.00 + 15%**	**7,300**
29,700	59,975	**4,090.00 + 25%**	**29,700**
59,975	91,400	**11,658.75 + 28%**	**59,975**
91,400	163,225	**20,457.75 + 33%**	**91,400**
163,225	....	**44,160.00 + 35%**	**163,225**

2004 Tax Table

See the instructions for line 43 that begin on page 33 to see if you must use the Tax Table below to figure your tax.

Example. Mr. and Mrs. Brown are filing a joint return. Their taxable income on Form 1040, line 42, is $25,300. First, they find the $25,300–25,350 taxable income line. Next, they find the column for married filing jointly and read down the column. The amount shown where the taxable income line and filing status column meet is $3,084. This is the tax amount they should enter on Form 1040, line 43.

Sample Table

At least	But less than	Single	Married filing jointly *	Married filing separately	Head of a household
		Your tax is—			
25,200	25,250	3,426	3,069	3,426	3,274
25,250	25,300	3,434	3,076	3,434	3,281
25,300	25,350	3,441	(3,084)	3,441	3,289
25,350	25,400	3,449	3,091	3,449	3,296

If line 42 (taxable income) is—		And you are—			
At least	But less than	Single	Married filing jointly *	Married filing separately	Head of a household
		Your tax is—			
0	5	0	0	0	0
5	15	1	1	1	1
15	25	2	2	2	2
25	50	4	4	4	4
50	75	6	6	6	6
75	100	9	9	9	9
100	125	11	11	11	11
125	150	14	14	14	14
150	175	16	16	16	16
175	200	19	19	19	19
200	225	21	21	21	21
225	250	24	24	24	24
250	275	26	26	26	26
275	300	29	29	29	29
300	325	31	31	31	31
325	350	34	34	34	34
350	375	36	36	36	36
375	400	39	39	39	39
400	425	41	41	41	41
425	450	44	44	44	44
450	475	46	46	46	46
475	500	49	49	49	49
500	525	51	51	51	51
525	550	54	54	54	54
550	575	56	56	56	56
575	600	59	59	59	59
600	625	61	61	61	61
625	650	64	64	64	64
650	675	66	66	66	66
675	700	69	69	69	69
700	725	71	71	71	71
725	750	74	74	74	74
750	775	76	76	76	76
775	800	79	79	79	79
800	825	81	81	81	81
825	850	84	84	84	84
850	875	86	86	86	86
875	900	89	89	89	89
900	925	91	91	91	91
925	950	94	94	94	94
950	975	96	96	96	96
975	1,000	99	99	99	99
1,000					
1,000	1,025	101	101	101	101
1,025	1,050	104	104	104	104
1,050	1,075	106	106	106	106
1,075	1,100	109	109	109	109
1,100	1,125	111	111	111	111
1,125	1,150	114	114	114	114
1,150	1,175	116	116	116	116
1,175	1,200	119	119	119	119
1,200	1,225	121	121	121	121
1,225	1,250	124	124	124	124
1,250	1,275	126	126	126	126
1,275	1,300	129	129	129	129

If line 42 (taxable income) is—		And you are—			
At least	But less than	Single	Married filing jointly *	Married filing separately	Head of a household
		Your tax is—			
1,300	1,325	131	131	131	131
1,325	1,350	134	134	134	134
1,350	1,375	136	136	136	136
1,375	1,400	139	139	139	139
1,400	1,425	141	141	141	141
1,425	1,450	144	144	144	144
1,450	1,475	146	146	146	146
1,475	1,500	149	149	149	149
1,500	1,525	151	151	151	151
1,525	1,550	154	154	154	154
1,550	1,575	156	156	156	156
1,575	1,600	159	159	159	159
1,600	1,625	161	161	161	161
1,625	1,650	164	164	164	164
1,650	1,675	166	166	166	166
1,675	1,700	169	169	169	169
1,700	1,725	171	171	171	171
1,725	1,750	174	174	174	174
1,750	1,775	176	176	176	176
1,775	1,800	179	179	179	179
1,800	1,825	181	181	181	181
1,825	1,850	184	184	184	184
1,850	1,875	186	186	186	186
1,875	1,900	189	189	189	189
1,900	1,925	191	191	191	191
1,925	1,950	194	194	194	194
1,950	1,975	196	196	196	196
1,975	2,000	199	199	199	199
2,000					
2,000	2,025	201	201	201	201
2,025	2,050	204	204	204	204
2,050	2,075	206	206	206	206
2,075	2,100	209	209	209	209
2,100	2,125	211	211	211	211
2,125	2,150	214	214	214	214
2,150	2,175	216	216	216	216
2,175	2,200	219	219	219	219
2,200	2,225	221	221	221	221
2,225	2,250	224	224	224	224
2,250	2,275	226	226	226	226
2,275	2,300	229	229	229	229
2,300	2,325	231	231	231	231
2,325	2,350	234	234	234	234
2,350	2,375	236	236	236	236
2,375	2,400	239	239	239	239
2,400	2,425	241	241	241	241
2,425	2,450	244	244	244	244
2,450	2,475	246	246	246	246
2,475	2,500	249	249	249	249
2,500	2,525	251	251	251	251
2,525	2,550	254	254	254	254
2,550	2,575	256	256	256	256
2,575	2,600	259	259	259	259
2,600	2,625	261	261	261	261
2,625	2,650	264	264	264	264
2,650	2,675	266	266	266	266
2,675	2,700	269	269	269	269

If line 42 (taxable income) is—		And you are—			
At least	But less than	Single	Married filing jointly *	Married filing separately	Head of a household
		Your tax is—			
2,700	2,725	271	271	271	271
2,725	2,750	274	274	274	274
2,750	2,775	276	276	276	276
2,775	2,800	279	279	279	279
2,800	2,825	281	281	281	281
2,825	2,850	284	284	284	284
2,850	2,875	286	286	286	286
2,875	2,900	289	289	289	289
2,900	2,925	291	291	291	291
2,925	2,950	294	294	294	294
2,950	2,975	296	296	296	296
2,975	3,000	299	299	299	299
3,000					
3,000	3,050	303	303	303	303
3,050	3,100	308	308	308	308
3,100	3,150	313	313	313	313
3,150	3,200	318	318	318	318
3,200	3,250	323	323	323	323
3,250	3,300	328	328	328	328
3,300	3,350	333	333	333	333
3,350	3,400	338	338	338	338
3,400	3,450	343	343	343	343
3,450	3,500	348	348	348	348
3,500	3,550	353	353	353	353
3,550	3,600	358	358	358	358
3,600	3,650	363	363	363	363
3,650	3,700	368	368	368	368
3,700	3,750	373	373	373	373
3,750	3,800	378	378	378	378
3,800	3,850	383	383	383	383
3,850	3,900	388	388	388	388
3,900	3,950	393	393	393	393
3,950	4,000	398	398	398	398
4,000					
4,000	4,050	403	403	403	403
4,050	4,100	408	408	408	408
4,100	4,150	413	413	413	413
4,150	4,200	418	418	418	418
4,200	4,250	423	423	423	423
4,250	4,300	428	428	428	428
4,300	4,350	433	433	433	433
4,350	4,400	438	438	438	438
4,400	4,450	443	443	443	443
4,450	4,500	448	448	448	448
4,500	4,550	453	453	453	453
4,550	4,600	458	458	458	458
4,600	4,650	463	463	463	463
4,650	4,700	468	468	468	468
4,700	4,750	473	473	473	473
4,750	4,800	478	478	478	478
4,800	4,850	483	483	483	483
4,850	4,900	488	488	488	488
4,900	4,950	493	493	493	493
4,950	5,000	498	498	498	498

(Continued on next page)

* This column must also be used by a qualifying widow(er).

2004 Tax Table—*Continued*

If line 42 (taxable income) is— At least	But less than	Single	Married filing jointly *	Married filing sepa-rately	Head of a house-hold
		Your tax is—			
5,000					
5,000	**5,050**	503	503	503	503
5,050	**5,100**	508	508	508	508
5,100	**5,150**	513	513	513	513
5,150	**5,200**	518	518	518	518
5,200	**5,250**	523	523	523	523
5,250	**5,300**	528	528	528	528
5,300	**5,350**	533	533	533	533
5,350	**5,400**	538	538	538	538
5,400	**5,450**	543	543	543	543
5,450	**5,500**	548	548	548	548
5,500	**5,550**	553	553	553	553
5,550	**5,600**	558	558	558	558
5,600	**5,650**	563	563	563	563
5,650	**5,700**	568	568	568	568
5,700	**5,750**	573	573	573	573
5,750	**5,800**	578	578	578	578
5,800	**5,850**	583	583	583	583
5,850	**5,900**	588	588	588	588
5,900	**5,950**	593	593	593	593
5,950	**6,000**	598	598	598	598
6,000					
6,000	**6,050**	603	603	603	603
6,050	**6,100**	608	608	608	608
6,100	**6,150**	613	613	613	613
6,150	**6,200**	618	618	618	618
6,200	**6,250**	623	623	623	623
6,250	**6,300**	628	628	628	628
6,300	**6,350**	633	633	633	633
6,350	**6,400**	638	638	638	638
6,400	**6,450**	643	643	643	643
6,450	**6,500**	648	648	648	648
6,500	**6,550**	653	653	653	653
6,550	**6,600**	658	658	658	658
6,600	**6,650**	663	663	663	663
6,650	**6,700**	668	668	668	668
6,700	**6,750**	673	673	673	673
6,750	**6,800**	678	678	678	678
6,800	**6,850**	683	683	683	683
6,850	**6,900**	688	688	688	688
6,900	**6,950**	693	693	693	693
6,950	**7,000**	698	698	698	698
7,000					
7,000	**7,050**	703	703	703	703
7,050	**7,100**	708	708	708	708
7,100	**7,150**	713	713	713	713
7,150	**7,200**	719	718	719	718
7,200	**7,250**	726	723	726	723
7,250	**7,300**	734	728	734	728
7,300	**7,350**	741	733	741	733
7,350	**7,400**	749	738	749	738
7,400	**7,450**	756	743	756	743
7,450	**7,500**	764	748	764	748
7,500	**7,550**	771	753	771	753
7,550	**7,600**	779	758	779	758
7,600	**7,650**	786	763	786	763
7,650	**7,700**	794	768	794	768
7,700	**7,750**	801	773	801	773
7,750	**7,800**	809	778	809	778
7,800	**7,850**	816	783	816	783
7,850	**7,900**	824	788	824	788
7,900	**7,950**	831	793	831	793
7,950	**8,000**	839	798	839	798

If line 42 (taxable income) is— At least	But less than	Single	Married filing jointly *	Married filing sepa-rately	Head of a house-hold
		Your tax is—			
8,000					
8,000	**8,050**	846	803	846	803
8,050	**8,100**	854	808	854	808
8,100	**8,150**	861	813	861	813
8,150	**8,200**	869	818	869	818
8,200	**8,250**	876	823	876	823
8,250	**8,300**	884	828	884	828
8,300	**8,350**	891	833	891	833
8,350	**8,400**	899	838	899	838
8,400	**8,450**	906	843	906	843
8,450	**8,500**	914	848	914	848
8,500	**8,550**	921	853	921	853
8,550	**8,600**	929	858	929	858
8,600	**8,650**	936	863	936	863
8,650	**8,700**	944	868	944	868
8,700	**8,750**	951	873	951	873
8,750	**8,800**	959	878	959	878
8,800	**8,850**	966	883	966	883
8,850	**8,900**	974	888	974	888
8,900	**8,950**	981	893	981	893
8,950	**9,000**	989	898	989	898
9,000					
9,000	**9,050**	996	903	996	903
9,050	**9,100**	1,004	908	1,004	908
9,100	**9,150**	1,011	913	1,011	913
9,150	**9,200**	1,019	918	1,019	918
9,200	**9,250**	1,026	923	1,026	923
9,250	**9,300**	1,034	928	1,034	928
9,300	**9,350**	1,041	933	1,041	933
9,350	**9,400**	1,049	938	1,049	938
9,400	**9,450**	1,056	943	1,056	943
9,450	**9,500**	1,064	948	1,064	948
9,500	**9,550**	1,071	953	1,071	953
9,550	**9,600**	1,079	958	1,079	958
9,600	**9,650**	1,086	963	1,086	963
9,650	**9,700**	1,094	968	1,094	968
9,700	**9,750**	1,101	973	1,101	973
9,750	**9,800**	1,109	978	1,109	978
9,800	**9,850**	1,116	983	1,116	983
9,850	**9,900**	1,124	988	1,124	988
9,900	**9,950**	1,131	993	1,131	993
9,950	**10,000**	1,139	998	1,139	998
10,000					
10,000	**10,050**	1,146	1,003	1,146	1,003
10,050	**10,100**	1,154	1,008	1,154	1,008
10,100	**10,150**	1,161	1,013	1,161	1,013
10,150	**10,200**	1,169	1,018	1,169	1,018
10,200	**10,250**	1,176	1,023	1,176	1,024
10,250	**10,300**	1,184	1,028	1,184	1,031
10,300	**10,350**	1,191	1,033	1,191	1,039
10,350	**10,400**	1,199	1,038	1,199	1,046
10,400	**10,450**	1,206	1,043	1,206	1,054
10,450	**10,500**	1,214	1,048	1,214	1,061
10,500	**10,550**	1,221	1,053	1,221	1,069
10,550	**10,600**	1,229	1,058	1,229	1,076
10,600	**10,650**	1,236	1,063	1,236	1,084
10,650	**10,700**	1,244	1,068	1,244	1,091
10,700	**10,750**	1,251	1,073	1,251	1,099
10,750	**10,800**	1,259	1,078	1,259	1,106
10,800	**10,850**	1,266	1,083	1,266	1,114
10,850	**10,900**	1,274	1,088	1,274	1,121
10,900	**10,950**	1,281	1,093	1,281	1,129
10,950	**11,000**	1,289	1,098	1,289	1,136

If line 42 (taxable income) is— At least	But less than	Single	Married filing jointly *	Married filing sepa-rately	Head of a house-hold
		Your tax is—			
11,000					
11,000	**11,050**	1,296	1,103	1,296	1,144
11,050	**11,100**	1,304	1,108	1,304	1,151
11,100	**11,150**	1,311	1,113	1,311	1,159
11,150	**11,200**	1,319	1,118	1,319	1,166
11,200	**11,250**	1,326	1,123	1,326	1,174
11,250	**11,300**	1,334	1,128	1,334	1,181
11,300	**11,350**	1,341	1,133	1,341	1,189
11,350	**11,400**	1,349	1,138	1,349	1,196
11,400	**11,450**	1,356	1,143	1,356	1,204
11,450	**11,500**	1,364	1,148	1,364	1,211
11,500	**11,550**	1,371	1,153	1,371	1,219
11,550	**11,600**	1,379	1,158	1,379	1,226
11,600	**11,650**	1,386	1,163	1,386	1,234
11,650	**11,700**	1,394	1,168	1,394	1,241
11,700	**11,750**	1,401	1,173	1,401	1,249
11,750	**11,800**	1,409	1,178	1,409	1,256
11,800	**11,850**	1,416	1,183	1,416	1,264
11,850	**11,900**	1,424	1,188	1,424	1,271
11,900	**11,950**	1,431	1,193	1,431	1,279
11,950	**12,000**	1,439	1,198	1,439	1,286
12,000					
12,000	**12,050**	1,446	1,203	1,446	1,294
12,050	**12,100**	1,454	1,208	1,454	1,301
12,100	**12,150**	1,461	1,213	1,461	1,309
12,150	**12,200**	1,469	1,218	1,469	1,316
12,200	**12,250**	1,476	1,223	1,476	1,324
12,250	**12,300**	1,484	1,228	1,484	1,331
12,300	**12,350**	1,491	1,233	1,491	1,339
12,350	**12,400**	1,499	1,238	1,499	1,346
12,400	**12,450**	1,506	1,243	1,506	1,354
12,450	**12,500**	1,514	1,248	1,514	1,361
12,500	**12,550**	1,521	1,253	1,521	1,369
12,550	**12,600**	1,529	1,258	1,529	1,376
12,600	**12,650**	1,536	1,263	1,536	1,384
12,650	**12,700**	1,544	1,268	1,544	1,391
12,700	**12,750**	1,551	1,273	1,551	1,399
12,750	**12,800**	1,559	1,278	1,559	1,406
12,800	**12,850**	1,566	1,283	1,566	1,414
12,850	**12,900**	1,574	1,288	1,574	1,421
12,900	**12,950**	1,581	1,293	1,581	1,429
12,950	**13,000**	1,589	1,298	1,589	1,436
13,000					
13,000	**13,050**	1,596	1,303	1,596	1,444
13,050	**13,100**	1,604	1,308	1,604	1,451
13,100	**13,150**	1,611	1,313	1,611	1,459
13,150	**13,200**	1,619	1,318	1,619	1,466
13,200	**13,250**	1,626	1,323	1,626	1,474
13,250	**13,300**	1,634	1,328	1,634	1,481
13,300	**13,350**	1,641	1,333	1,641	1,489
13,350	**13,400**	1,649	1,338	1,649	1,496
13,400	**13,450**	1,656	1,343	1,656	1,504
13,450	**13,500**	1,664	1,348	1,664	1,511
13,500	**13,550**	1,671	1,353	1,671	1,519
13,550	**13,600**	1,679	1,358	1,679	1,526
13,600	**13,650**	1,686	1,363	1,686	1,534
13,650	**13,700**	1,694	1,368	1,694	1,541
13,700	**13,750**	1,701	1,373	1,701	1,549
13,750	**13,800**	1,709	1,378	1,709	1,556
13,800	**13,850**	1,716	1,383	1,716	1,564
13,850	**13,900**	1,724	1,388	1,724	1,571
13,900	**13,950**	1,731	1,393	1,731	1,579
13,950	**14,000**	1,739	1,398	1,739	1,586

* This column must also be used by a qualifying widow(er).

(Continued on next page)

2004 Tax Table—*Continued*

If line 42 (taxable income) is— At least	But less than	Single	Married filing jointly *	Married filing sepa-rately	Head of a house-hold
		Your tax is—			
14,000					
14,000	14,050	1,746	1,403	1,746	1,594
14,050	14,100	1,754	1,408	1,754	1,601
14,100	14,150	1,761	1,413	1,761	1,609
14,150	14,200	1,769	1,418	1,769	1,616
14,200	14,250	1,776	1,423	1,776	1,624
14,250	14,300	1,784	1,428	1,784	1,631
14,300	14,350	1,791	1,434	1,791	1,639
14,350	14,400	1,799	1,441	1,799	1,646
14,400	14,450	1,806	1,449	1,806	1,654
14,450	14,500	1,814	1,456	1,814	1,661
14,500	14,550	1,821	1,464	1,821	1,669
14,550	14,600	1,829	1,471	1,829	1,676
14,600	14,650	1,836	1,479	1,836	1,684
14,650	14,700	1,844	1,486	1,844	1,691
14,700	14,750	1,851	1,494	1,851	1,699
14,750	14,800	1,859	1,501	1,859	1,706
14,800	14,850	1,866	1,509	1,866	1,714
14,850	14,900	1,874	1,516	1,874	1,721
14,900	14,950	1,881	1,524	1,881	1,729
14,950	15,000	1,889	1,531	1,889	1,736
15,000					
15,000	15,050	1,896	1,539	1,896	1,744
15,050	15,100	1,904	1,546	1,904	1,751
15,100	15,150	1,911	1,554	1,911	1,759
15,150	15,200	1,919	1,561	1,919	1,766
15,200	15,250	1,926	1,569	1,926	1,774
15,250	15,300	1,934	1,576	1,934	1,781
15,300	15,350	1,941	1,584	1,941	1,789
15,350	15,400	1,949	1,591	1,949	1,796
15,400	15,450	1,956	1,599	1,956	1,804
15,450	15,500	1,964	1,606	1,964	1,811
15,500	15,550	1,971	1,614	1,971	1,819
15,550	15,600	1,979	1,621	1,979	1,826
15,600	15,650	1,986	1,629	1,986	1,834
15,650	15,700	1,994	1,636	1,994	1,841
15,700	15,750	2,001	1,644	2,001	1,849
15,750	15,800	2,009	1,651	2,009	1,856
15,800	15,850	2,016	1,659	2,016	1,864
15,850	15,900	2,024	1,666	2,024	1,871
15,900	15,950	2,031	1,674	2,031	1,879
15,950	16,000	2,039	1,681	2,039	1,886
16,000					
16,000	16,050	2,046	1,689	2,046	1,894
16,050	16,100	2,054	1,696	2,054	1,901
16,100	16,150	2,061	1,704	2,061	1,909
16,150	16,200	2,069	1,711	2,069	1,916
16,200	16,250	2,076	1,719	2,076	1,924
16,250	16,300	2,084	1,726	2,084	1,931
16,300	16,350	2,091	1,734	2,091	1,939
16,350	16,400	2,099	1,741	2,099	1,946
16,400	16,450	2,106	1,749	2,106	1,954
16,450	16,500	2,114	1,756	2,114	1,961
16,500	16,550	2,121	1,764	2,121	1,969
16,550	16,600	2,129	1,771	2,129	1,976
16,600	16,650	2,136	1,779	2,136	1,984
16,650	16,700	2,144	1,786	2,144	1,991
16,700	16,750	2,151	1,794	2,151	1,999
16,750	16,800	2,159	1,801	2,159	2,006
16,800	16,850	2,166	1,809	2,166	2,014
16,850	16,900	2,174	1,816	2,174	2,021
16,900	16,950	2,181	1,824	2,181	2,029
16,950	17,000	2,189	1,831	2,189	2,036

If line 42 (taxable income) is— At least	But less than	Single	Married filing jointly *	Married filing sepa-rately	Head of a house-hold
		Your tax is—			
17,000					
17,000	17,050	2,196	1,839	2,196	2,044
17,050	17,100	2,204	1,846	2,204	2,051
17,100	17,150	2,211	1,854	2,211	2,059
17,150	17,200	2,219	1,861	2,219	2,066
17,200	17,250	2,226	1,869	2,226	2,074
17,250	17,300	2,234	1,876	2,234	2,081
17,300	17,350	2,241	1,884	2,241	2,089
17,350	17,400	2,249	1,891	2,249	2,096
17,400	17,450	2,256	1,899	2,256	2,104
17,450	17,500	2,264	1,906	2,264	2,111
17,500	17,550	2,271	1,914	2,271	2,119
17,550	17,600	2,279	1,921	2,279	2,126
17,600	17,650	2,286	1,929	2,286	2,134
17,650	17,700	2,294	1,936	2,294	2,141
17,700	17,750	2,301	1,944	2,301	2,149
17,750	17,800	2,309	1,951	2,309	2,156
17,800	17,850	2,316	1,959	2,316	2,164
17,850	17,900	2,324	1,966	2,324	2,171
17,900	17,950	2,331	1,974	2,331	2,179
17,950	18,000	2,339	1,981	2,339	2,186
18,000					
18,000	18,050	2,346	1,989	2,346	2,194
18,050	18,100	2,354	1,996	2,354	2,201
18,100	18,150	2,361	2,004	2,361	2,209
18,150	18,200	2,369	2,011	2,369	2,216
18,200	18,250	2,376	2,019	2,376	2,224
18,250	18,300	2,384	2,026	2,384	2,231
18,300	18,350	2,391	2,034	2,391	2,239
18,350	18,400	2,399	2,041	2,399	2,246
18,400	18,450	2,406	2,049	2,406	2,254
18,450	18,500	2,414	2,056	2,414	2,261
18,500	18,550	2,421	2,064	2,421	2,269
18,550	18,600	2,429	2,071	2,429	2,276
18,600	18,650	2,436	2,079	2,436	2,284
18,650	18,700	2,444	2,086	2,444	2,291
18,700	18,750	2,451	2,094	2,451	2,299
18,750	18,800	2,459	2,101	2,459	2,306
18,800	18,850	2,466	2,109	2,466	2,314
18,850	18,900	2,474	2,116	2,474	2,321
18,900	18,950	2,481	2,124	2,481	2,329
18,950	19,000	2,489	2,131	2,489	2,336
19,000					
19,000	19,050	2,496	2,139	2,496	2,344
19,050	19,100	2,504	2,146	2,504	2,351
19,100	19,150	2,511	2,154	2,511	2,359
19,150	19,200	2,519	2,161	2,519	2,366
19,200	19,250	2,526	2,169	2,526	2,374
19,250	19,300	2,534	2,176	2,534	2,381
19,300	19,350	2,541	2,184	2,541	2,389
19,350	19,400	2,549	2,191	2,549	2,396
19,400	19,450	2,556	2,199	2,556	2,404
19,450	19,500	2,564	2,206	2,564	2,411
19,500	19,550	2,571	2,214	2,571	2,419
19,550	19,600	2,579	2,221	2,579	2,426
19,600	19,650	2,586	2,229	2,586	2,434
19,650	19,700	2,594	2,236	2,594	2,441
19,700	19,750	2,601	2,244	2,601	2,449
19,750	19,800	2,609	2,251	2,609	2,456
19,800	19,850	2,616	2,259	2,616	2,464
19,850	19,900	2,624	2,266	2,624	2,471
19,900	19,950	2,631	2,274	2,631	2,479
19,950	20,000	2,639	2,281	2,639	2,486

If line 42 (taxable income) is— At least	But less than	Single	Married filing jointly *	Married filing sepa-rately	Head of a house-hold
		Your tax is—			
20,000					
20,000	20,050	2,646	2,289	2,646	2,494
20,050	20,100	2,654	2,296	2,654	2,501
20,100	20,150	2,661	2,304	2,661	2,509
20,150	20,200	2,669	2,311	2,669	2,516
20,200	20,250	2,676	2,319	2,676	2,524
20,250	20,300	2,684	2,326	2,684	2,531
20,300	20,350	2,691	2,334	2,691	2,539
20,350	20,400	2,699	2,341	2,699	2,546
20,400	20,450	2,706	2,349	2,706	2,554
20,450	20,500	2,714	2,356	2,714	2,561
20,500	20,550	2,721	2,364	2,721	2,569
20,550	20,600	2,729	2,371	2,729	2,576
20,600	20,650	2,736	2,379	2,736	2,584
20,650	20,700	2,744	2,386	2,744	2,591
20,700	20,750	2,751	2,394	2,751	2,599
20,750	20,800	2,759	2,401	2,759	2,606
20,800	20,850	2,766	2,409	2,766	2,614
20,850	20,900	2,774	2,416	2,774	2,621
20,900	20,950	2,781	2,424	2,781	2,629
20,950	21,000	2,789	2,431	2,789	2,636
21,000					
21,000	21,050	2,796	2,439	2,796	2,644
21,050	21,100	2,804	2,446	2,804	2,651
21,100	21,150	2,811	2,454	2,811	2,659
21,150	21,200	2,819	2,461	2,819	2,666
21,200	21,250	2,826	2,469	2,826	2,674
21,250	21,300	2,834	2,476	2,834	2,681
21,300	21,350	2,841	2,484	2,841	2,689
21,350	21,400	2,849	2,491	2,849	2,696
21,400	21,450	2,856	2,499	2,856	2,704
21,450	21,500	2,864	2,506	2,864	2,711
21,500	21,550	2,871	2,514	2,871	2,719
21,550	21,600	2,879	2,521	2,879	2,726
21,600	21,650	2,886	2,529	2,886	2,734
21,650	21,700	2,894	2,536	2,894	2,741
21,700	21,750	2,901	2,544	2,901	2,749
21,750	21,800	2,909	2,551	2,909	2,756
21,800	21,850	2,916	2,559	2,916	2,764
21,850	21,900	2,924	2,566	2,924	2,771
21,900	21,950	2,931	2,574	2,931	2,779
21,950	22,000	2,939	2,581	2,939	2,786
22,000					
22,000	22,050	2,946	2,589	2,946	2,794
22,050	22,100	2,954	2,596	2,954	2,801
22,100	22,150	2,961	2,604	2,961	2,809
22,150	22,200	2,969	2,611	2,969	2,816
22,200	22,250	2,976	2,619	2,976	2,824
22,250	22,300	2,984	2,626	2,984	2,831
22,300	22,350	2,991	2,634	2,991	2,839
22,350	22,400	2,999	2,641	2,999	2,846
22,400	22,450	3,006	2,649	3,006	2,854
22,450	22,500	3,014	2,656	3,014	2,861
22,500	22,550	3,021	2,664	3,021	2,869
22,550	22,600	3,029	2,671	3,029	2,876
22,600	22,650	3,036	2,679	3,036	2,884
22,650	22,700	3,044	2,686	3,044	2,891
22,700	22,750	3,051	2,694	3,051	2,899
22,750	22,800	3,059	2,701	3,059	2,906
22,800	22,850	3,066	2,709	3,066	2,914
22,850	22,900	3,074	2,716	3,074	2,921
22,900	22,950	3,081	2,724	3,081	2,929
22,950	23,000	3,089	2,731	3,089	2,936

* This column must also be used by a qualifying widow(er).

(Continued on next page)

2004 Tax Table—*Continued*

If line 42 (taxable income) is—		And you are—			
At least	But less than	Single	Married filing jointly *	Married filing separately	Head of a household
		Your tax is—			
23,000					
23,000	23,050	3,096	2,739	3,096	2,944
23,050	23,100	3,104	2,746	3,104	2,951
23,100	23,150	3,111	2,754	3,111	2,959
23,150	23,200	3,119	2,761	3,119	2,966
23,200	23,250	3,126	2,769	3,126	2,974
23,250	23,300	3,134	2,776	3,134	2,981
23,300	23,350	3,141	2,784	3,141	2,989
23,350	23,400	3,149	2,791	3,149	2,996
23,400	23,450	3,156	2,799	3,156	3,004
23,450	23,500	3,164	2,806	3,164	3,011
23,500	23,550	3,171	2,814	3,171	3,019
23,550	23,600	3,179	2,821	3,179	3,026
23,600	23,650	3,186	2,829	3,186	3,034
23,650	23,700	3,194	2,836	3,194	3,041
23,700	23,750	3,201	2,844	3,201	3,049
23,750	23,800	3,209	2,851	3,209	3,056
23,800	23,850	3,216	2,859	3,216	3,064
23,850	23,900	3,224	2,866	3,224	3,071
23,900	23,950	3,231	2,874	3,231	3,079
23,950	24,000	3,239	2,881	3,239	3,086
24,000					
24,000	24,050	3,246	2,889	3,246	3,094
24,050	24,100	3,254	2,896	3,254	3,101
24,100	24,150	3,261	2,904	3,261	3,109
24,150	24,200	3,269	2,911	3,269	3,116
24,200	24,250	3,276	2,919	3,276	3,124
24,250	24,300	3,284	2,926	3,284	3,131
24,300	24,350	3,291	2,934	3,291	3,139
24,350	24,400	3,299	2,941	3,299	3,146
24,400	24,450	3,306	2,949	3,306	3,154
24,450	24,500	3,314	2,956	3,314	3,161
24,500	24,550	3,321	2,964	3,321	3,169
24,550	24,600	3,329	2,971	3,329	3,176
24,600	24,650	3,336	2,979	3,336	3,184
24,650	24,700	3,344	2,986	3,344	3,191
24,700	24,750	3,351	2,994	3,351	3,199
24,750	24,800	3,359	3,001	3,359	3,206
24,800	24,850	3,366	3,009	3,366	3,214
24,850	24,900	3,374	3,016	3,374	3,221
24,900	24,950	3,381	3,024	3,381	3,229
24,950	25,000	3,389	3,031	3,389	3,236
25,000					
25,000	25,050	3,396	3,039	3,396	3,244
25,050	25,100	3,404	3,046	3,404	3,251
25,100	25,150	3,411	3,054	3,411	3,259
25,150	25,200	3,419	3,061	3,419	3,266
25,200	25,250	3,426	3,069	3,426	3,274
25,250	25,300	3,434	3,076	3,434	3,281
25,300	25,350	3,441	3,084	3,441	3,289
25,350	25,400	3,449	3,091	3,449	3,296
25,400	25,450	3,456	3,099	3,456	3,304
25,450	25,500	3,464	3,106	3,464	3,311
25,500	25,550	3,471	3,114	3,471	3,319
25,550	25,600	3,479	3,121	3,479	3,326
25,600	25,650	3,486	3,129	3,486	3,334
25,650	25,700	3,494	3,136	3,494	3,341
25,700	25,750	3,501	3,144	3,501	3,349
25,750	25,800	3,509	3,151	3,509	3,356
25,800	25,850	3,516	3,159	3,516	3,364
25,850	25,900	3,524	3,166	3,524	3,371
25,900	25,950	3,531	3,174	3,531	3,379
25,950	26,000	3,539	3,181	3,539	3,386

If line 42 (taxable income) is—		And you are—			
At least	But less than	Single	Married filing jointly *	Married filing separately	Head of a household
		Your tax is—			
26,000					
26,000	26,050	3,546	3,189	3,546	3,394
26,050	26,100	3,554	3,196	3,554	3,401
26,100	26,150	3,561	3,204	3,561	3,409
26,150	26,200	3,569	3,211	3,569	3,416
26,200	26,250	3,576	3,219	3,576	3,424
26,250	26,300	3,584	3,226	3,584	3,431
26,300	26,350	3,591	3,234	3,591	3,439
26,350	26,400	3,599	3,241	3,599	3,446
26,400	26,450	3,606	3,249	3,606	3,454
26,450	26,500	3,614	3,256	3,614	3,461
26,500	26,550	3,621	3,264	3,621	3,469
26,550	26,600	3,629	3,271	3,629	3,476
26,600	26,650	3,636	3,279	3,636	3,484
26,650	26,700	3,644	3,286	3,644	3,491
26,700	26,750	3,651	3,294	3,651	3,499
26,750	26,800	3,659	3,301	3,659	3,506
26,800	26,850	3,666	3,309	3,666	3,514
26,850	26,900	3,674	3,316	3,674	3,521
26,900	26,950	3,681	3,324	3,681	3,529
26,950	27,000	3,689	3,331	3,689	3,536
27,000					
27,000	27,050	3,696	3,339	3,696	3,544
27,050	27,100	3,704	3,346	3,704	3,551
27,100	27,150	3,711	3,354	3,711	3,559
27,150	27,200	3,719	3,361	3,719	3,566
27,200	27,250	3,726	3,369	3,726	3,574
27,250	27,300	3,734	3,376	3,734	3,581
27,300	27,350	3,741	3,384	3,741	3,589
27,350	27,400	3,749	3,391	3,749	3,596
27,400	27,450	3,756	3,399	3,756	3,604
27,450	27,500	3,764	3,406	3,764	3,611
27,500	27,550	3,771	3,414	3,771	3,619
27,550	27,600	3,779	3,421	3,779	3,626
27,600	27,650	3,786	3,429	3,786	3,634
27,650	27,700	3,794	3,436	3,794	3,641
27,700	27,750	3,801	3,444	3,801	3,649
27,750	27,800	3,809	3,451	3,809	3,656
27,800	27,850	3,816	3,459	3,816	3,664
27,850	27,900	3,824	3,466	3,824	3,671
27,900	27,950	3,831	3,474	3,831	3,679
27,950	28,000	3,839	3,481	3,839	3,686
28,000					
28,000	28,050	3,846	3,489	3,846	3,694
28,050	28,100	3,854	3,496	3,854	3,701
28,100	28,150	3,861	3,504	3,861	3,709
28,150	28,200	3,869	3,511	3,869	3,716
28,200	28,250	3,876	3,519	3,876	3,724
28,250	28,300	3,884	3,526	3,884	3,731
28,300	28,350	3,891	3,534	3,891	3,739
28,350	28,400	3,899	3,541	3,899	3,746
28,400	28,450	3,906	3,549	3,906	3,754
28,450	28,500	3,914	3,556	3,914	3,761
28,500	28,550	3,921	3,564	3,921	3,769
28,550	28,600	3,929	3,571	3,929	3,776
28,600	28,650	3,936	3,579	3,936	3,784
28,650	28,700	3,944	3,586	3,944	3,791
28,700	28,750	3,951	3,594	3,951	3,799
28,750	28,800	3,959	3,601	3,959	3,806
28,800	28,850	3,966	3,609	3,966	3,814
28,850	28,900	3,974	3,616	3,974	3,821
28,900	28,950	3,981	3,624	3,981	3,829
28,950	29,000	3,989	3,631	3,989	3,836

If line 42 (taxable income) is—		And you are—			
At least	But less than	Single	Married filing jointly *	Married filing separately	Head of a household
		Your tax is—			
29,000					
29,000	29,050	3,996	3,639	3,996	3,844
29,050	29,100	4,006	3,646	4,006	3,851
29,100	29,150	4,019	3,654	4,019	3,859
29,150	29,200	4,031	3,661	4,031	3,866
29,200	29,250	4,044	3,669	4,044	3,874
29,250	29,300	4,056	3,676	4,056	3,881
29,300	29,350	4,069	3,684	4,069	3,889
29,350	29,400	4,081	3,691	4,081	3,896
29,400	29,450	4,094	3,699	4,094	3,904
29,450	29,500	4,106	3,706	4,106	3,911
29,500	29,550	4,119	3,714	4,119	3,919
29,550	29,600	4,131	3,721	4,131	3,926
29,600	29,650	4,144	3,729	4,144	3,934
29,650	29,700	4,156	3,736	4,156	3,941
29,700	29,750	4,169	3,744	4,169	3,949
29,750	29,800	4,181	3,751	4,181	3,956
29,800	29,850	4,194	3,759	4,194	3,964
29,850	29,900	4,206	3,766	4,206	3,971
29,900	29,950	4,219	3,774	4,219	3,979
29,950	30,000	4,231	3,781	4,231	3,986
30,000					
30,000	30,050	4,244	3,789	4,244	3,994
30,050	30,100	4,256	3,796	4,256	4,001
30,100	30,150	4,269	3,804	4,269	4,009
30,150	30,200	4,281	3,811	4,281	4,016
30,200	30,250	4,294	3,819	4,294	4,024
30,250	30,300	4,306	3,826	4,306	4,031
30,300	30,350	4,319	3,834	4,319	4,039
30,350	30,400	4,331	3,841	4,331	4,046
30,400	30,450	4,344	3,849	4,344	4,054
30,450	30,500	4,356	3,856	4,356	4,061
30,500	30,550	4,369	3,864	4,369	4,069
30,550	30,600	4,381	3,871	4,381	4,076
30,600	30,650	4,394	3,879	4,394	4,084
30,650	30,700	4,406	3,886	4,406	4,091
30,700	30,750	4,419	3,894	4,419	4,099
30,750	30,800	4,431	3,901	4,431	4,106
30,800	30,850	4,444	3,909	4,444	4,114
30,850	30,900	4,456	3,916	4,456	4,121
30,900	30,950	4,469	3,924	4,469	4,129
30,950	31,000	4,481	3,931	4,481	4,136
31,000					
31,000	31,050	4,494	3,939	4,494	4,144
31,050	31,100	4,506	3,946	4,506	4,151
31,100	31,150	4,519	3,954	4,519	4,159
31,150	31,200	4,531	3,961	4,531	4,166
31,200	31,250	4,544	3,969	4,544	4,174
31,250	31,300	4,556	3,976	4,556	4,181
31,300	31,350	4,569	3,984	4,569	4,189
31,350	31,400	4,581	3,991	4,581	4,196
31,400	31,450	4,594	3,999	4,594	4,204
31,450	31,500	4,606	4,006	4,606	4,211
31,500	31,550	4,619	4,014	4,619	4,219
31,550	31,600	4,631	4,021	4,631	4,226
31,600	31,650	4,644	4,029	4,644	4,234
31,650	31,700	4,656	4,036	4,656	4,241
31,700	31,750	4,669	4,044	4,669	4,249
31,750	31,800	4,681	4,051	4,681	4,256
31,800	31,850	4,694	4,059	4,694	4,264
31,850	31,900	4,706	4,066	4,706	4,271
31,900	31,950	4,719	4,074	4,719	4,279
31,950	32,000	4,731	4,081	4,731	4,286

* This column must also be used by a qualifying widow(er).

(Continued on next page)

2004 Tax Table—*Continued*

If line 42 (taxable income) is— At least	But less than	And you are— Single	Married filing jointly *	Married filing sepa-rately	Head of a house-hold
		Your tax is—			
32,000					
32,000	**32,050**	4,744	4,089	4,744	4,294
32,050	**32,100**	4,756	4,096	4,756	4,301
32,100	**32,150**	4,769	4,104	4,769	4,309
32,150	**32,200**	4,781	4,111	4,781	4,316
32,200	**32,250**	4,794	4,119	4,794	4,324
32,250	**32,300**	4,806	4,126	4,806	4,331
32,300	**32,350**	4,819	4,134	4,819	4,339
32,350	**32,400**	4,831	4,141	4,831	4,346
32,400	**32,450**	4,844	4,149	4,844	4,354
32,450	**32,500**	4,856	4,156	4,856	4,361
32,500	**32,550**	4,869	4,164	4,869	4,369
32,550	**32,600**	4,881	4,171	4,881	4,376
32,600	**32,650**	4,894	4,179	4,894	4,384
32,650	**32,700**	4,906	4,186	4,906	4,391
32,700	**32,750**	4,919	4,194	4,919	4,399
32,750	**32,800**	4,931	4,201	4,931	4,406
32,800	**32,850**	4,944	4,209	4,944	4,414
32,850	**32,900**	4,956	4,216	4,956	4,421
32,900	**32,950**	4,969	4,224	4,969	4,429
32,950	**33,000**	4,981	4,231	4,981	4,436
33,000					
33,000	**33,050**	4,994	4,239	4,994	4,444
33,050	**33,100**	5,006	4,246	5,006	4,451
33,100	**33,150**	5,019	4,254	5,019	4,459
33,150	**33,200**	5,031	4,261	5,031	4,466
33,200	**33,250**	5,044	4,269	5,044	4,474
33,250	**33,300**	5,056	4,276	5,056	4,481
33,300	**33,350**	5,069	4,284	5,069	4,489
33,350	**33,400**	5,081	4,291	5,081	4,496
33,400	**33,450**	5,094	4,299	5,094	4,504
33,450	**33,500**	5,106	4,306	5,106	4,511
33,500	**33,550**	5,119	4,314	5,119	4,519
33,550	**33,600**	5,131	4,321	5,131	4,526
33,600	**33,650**	5,144	4,329	5,144	4,534
33,650	**33,700**	5,156	4,336	5,156	4,541
33,700	**33,750**	5,169	4,344	5,169	4,549
33,750	**33,800**	5,181	4,351	5,181	4,556
33,800	**33,850**	5,194	4,359	5,194	4,564
33,850	**33,900**	5,206	4,366	5,206	4,571
33,900	**33,950**	5,219	4,374	5,219	4,579
33,950	**34,000**	5,231	4,381	5,231	4,586
34,000					
34,000	**34,050**	5,244	4,389	5,244	4,594
34,050	**34,100**	5,256	4,396	5,256	4,601
34,100	**34,150**	5,269	4,404	5,269	4,609
34,150	**34,200**	5,281	4,411	5,281	4,616
34,200	**34,250**	5,294	4,419	5,294	4,624
34,250	**34,300**	5,306	4,426	5,306	4,631
34,300	**34,350**	5,319	4,434	5,319	4,639
34,350	**34,400**	5,331	4,441	5,331	4,646
34,400	**34,450**	5,344	4,449	5,344	4,654
34,450	**34,500**	5,356	4,456	5,356	4,661
34,500	**34,550**	5,369	4,464	5,369	4,669
34,550	**34,600**	5,381	4,471	5,381	4,676
34,600	**34,650**	5,394	4,479	5,394	4,684
34,650	**34,700**	5,406	4,486	5,406	4,691
34,700	**34,750**	5,419	4,494	5,419	4,699
34,750	**34,800**	5,431	4,501	5,431	4,706
34,800	**34,850**	5,444	4,509	5,444	4,714
34,850	**34,900**	5,456	4,516	5,456	4,721
34,900	**34,950**	5,469	4,524	5,469	4,729
34,950	**35,000**	5,481	4,531	5,481	4,736
35,000					
35,000	**35,050**	5,494	4,539	5,494	4,744
35,050	**35,100**	5,506	4,546	5,506	4,751
35,100	**35,150**	5,519	4,554	5,519	4,759
35,150	**35,200**	5,531	4,561	5,531	4,766
35,200	**35,250**	5,544	4,569	5,544	4,774
35,250	**35,300**	5,556	4,576	5,556	4,781
35,300	**35,350**	5,569	4,584	5,569	4,789
35,350	**35,400**	5,581	4,591	5,581	4,796
35,400	**35,450**	5,594	4,599	5,594	4,804
35,450	**35,500**	5,606	4,606	5,606	4,811
35,500	**35,550**	5,619	4,614	5,619	4,819
35,550	**35,600**	5,631	4,621	5,631	4,826
35,600	**35,650**	5,644	4,629	5,644	4,834
35,650	**35,700**	5,656	4,636	5,656	4,841
35,700	**35,750**	5,669	4,644	5,669	4,849
35,750	**35,800**	5,681	4,651	5,681	4,856
35,800	**35,850**	5,694	4,659	5,694	4,864
35,850	**35,900**	5,706	4,666	5,706	4,871
35,900	**35,950**	5,719	4,674	5,719	4,879
35,950	**36,000**	5,731	4,681	5,731	4,886
36,000					
36,000	**36,050**	5,744	4,689	5,744	4,894
36,050	**36,100**	5,756	4,696	5,756	4,901
36,100	**36,150**	5,769	4,704	5,769	4,909
36,150	**36,200**	5,781	4,711	5,781	4,916
36,200	**36,250**	5,794	4,719	5,794	4,924
36,250	**36,300**	5,806	4,726	5,806	4,931
36,300	**36,350**	5,819	4,734	5,819	4,939
36,350	**36,400**	5,831	4,741	5,831	4,946
36,400	**36,450**	5,844	4,749	5,844	4,954
36,450	**36,500**	5,856	4,756	5,856	4,961
36,500	**36,550**	5,869	4,764	5,869	4,969
36,550	**36,600**	5,881	4,771	5,881	4,976
36,600	**36,650**	5,894	4,779	5,894	4,984
36,650	**36,700**	5,906	4,786	5,906	4,991
36,700	**36,750**	5,919	4,794	5,919	4,999
36,750	**36,800**	5,931	4,801	5,931	5,006
36,800	**36,850**	5,944	4,809	5,944	5,014
36,850	**36,900**	5,956	4,816	5,956	5,021
36,900	**36,950**	5,969	4,824	5,969	5,029
36,950	**37,000**	5,981	4,831	5,981	5,036
37,000					
37,000	**37,050**	5,994	4,839	5,994	5,044
37,050	**37,100**	6,006	4,846	6,006	5,051
37,100	**37,150**	6,019	4,854	6,019	5,059
37,150	**37,200**	6,031	4,861	6,031	5,066
37,200	**37,250**	6,044	4,869	6,044	5,074
37,250	**37,300**	6,056	4,876	6,056	5,081
37,300	**37,350**	6,069	4,884	6,069	5,089
37,350	**37,400**	6,081	4,891	6,081	5,096
37,400	**37,450**	6,094	4,899	6,094	5,104
37,450	**37,500**	6,106	4,906	6,106	5,111
37,500	**37,550**	6,119	4,914	6,119	5,119
37,550	**37,600**	6,131	4,921	6,131	5,126
37,600	**37,650**	6,144	4,929	6,144	5,134
37,650	**37,700**	6,156	4,936	6,156	5,141
37,700	**37,750**	6,169	4,944	6,169	5,149
37,750	**37,800**	6,181	4,951	6,181	5,156
37,800	**37,850**	6,194	4,959	6,194	5,164
37,850	**37,900**	6,206	4,966	6,206	5,171
37,900	**37,950**	6,219	4,974	6,219	5,179
37,950	**38,000**	6,231	4,981	6,231	5,186
38,000					
38,000	**38,050**	6,244	4,989	6,244	5,194
38,050	**38,100**	6,256	4,996	6,256	5,201
38,100	**38,150**	6,269	5,004	6,269	5,209
38,150	**38,200**	6,281	5,011	6,281	5,216
38,200	**38,250**	6,294	5,019	6,294	5,224
38,250	**38,300**	6,306	5,026	6,306	5,231
38,300	**38,350**	6,319	5,034	6,319	5,239
38,350	**38,400**	6,331	5,041	6,331	5,246
38,400	**38,450**	6,344	5,049	6,344	5,254
38,450	**38,500**	6,356	5,056	6,356	5,261
38,500	**38,550**	6,369	5,064	6,369	5,269
38,550	**38,600**	6,381	5,071	6,381	5,276
38,600	**38,650**	6,394	5,079	6,394	5,284
38,650	**38,700**	6,406	5,086	6,406	5,291
38,700	**38,750**	6,419	5,094	6,419	5,299
38,750	**38,800**	6,431	5,101	6,431	5,306
38,800	**38,850**	6,444	5,109	6,444	5,314
38,850	**38,900**	6,456	5,116	6,456	5,321
38,900	**38,950**	6,469	5,124	6,469	5,331
38,950	**39,000**	6,481	5,131	6,481	5,344
39,000					
39,000	**39,050**	6,494	5,139	6,494	5,356
39,050	**39,100**	6,506	5,146	6,506	5,369
39,100	**39,150**	6,519	5,154	6,519	5,381
39,150	**39,200**	6,531	5,161	6,531	5,394
39,200	**39,250**	6,544	5,169	6,544	5,406
39,250	**39,300**	6,556	5,176	6,556	5,419
39,300	**39,350**	6,569	5,184	6,569	5,431
39,350	**39,400**	6,581	5,191	6,581	5,444
39,400	**39,450**	6,594	5,199	6,594	5,456
39,450	**39,500**	6,606	5,206	6,606	5,469
39,500	**39,550**	6,619	5,214	6,619	5,481
39,550	**39,600**	6,631	5,221	6,631	5,494
39,600	**39,650**	6,644	5,229	6,644	5,506
39,650	**39,700**	6,656	5,236	6,656	5,519
39,700	**39,750**	6,669	5,244	6,669	5,531
39,750	**39,800**	6,681	5,251	6,681	5,544
39,800	**39,850**	6,694	5,259	6,694	5,556
39,850	**39,900**	6,706	5,266	6,706	5,569
39,900	**39,950**	6,719	5,274	6,719	5,581
39,950	**40,000**	6,731	5,281	6,731	5,594
40,000					
40,000	**40,050**	6,744	5,289	6,744	5,606
40,050	**40,100**	6,756	5,296	6,756	5,619
40,100	**40,150**	6,769	5,304	6,769	5,631
40,150	**40,200**	6,781	5,311	6,781	5,644
40,200	**40,250**	6,794	5,319	6,794	5,656
40,250	**40,300**	6,806	5,326	6,806	5,669
40,300	**40,350**	6,819	5,334	6,819	5,681
40,350	**40,400**	6,831	5,341	6,831	5,694
40,400	**40,450**	6,844	5,349	6,844	5,706
40,450	**40,500**	6,856	5,356	6,856	5,719
40,500	**40,550**	6,869	5,364	6,869	5,731
40,550	**40,600**	6,881	5,371	6,881	5,744
40,600	**40,650**	6,894	5,379	6,894	5,756
40,650	**40,700**	6,906	5,386	6,906	5,769
40,700	**40,750**	6,919	5,394	6,919	5,781
40,750	**40,800**	6,931	5,401	6,931	5,794
40,800	**40,850**	6,944	5,409	6,944	5,806
40,850	**40,900**	6,956	5,416	6,956	5,819
40,900	**40,950**	6,969	5,424	6,969	5,831
40,950	**41,000**	6,981	5,431	6,981	5,844

* This column must also be used by a qualifying widow(er).

(Continued on next page)

2004 Tax Table—*Continued*

If line 42 (taxable income) is— At least	But less than	And you are— Single	Married filing jointly *	Married filing separately	Head of a household
		Your tax is—			
41,000					
41,000	**41,050**	6,994	5,439	6,994	5,856
41,050	**41,100**	7,006	5,446	7,006	5,869
41,100	**41,150**	7,019	5,454	7,019	5,881
41,150	**41,200**	7,031	5,461	7,031	5,894
41,200	**41,250**	7,044	5,469	7,044	5,906
41,250	**41,300**	7,056	5,476	7,056	5,919
41,300	**41,350**	7,069	5,484	7,069	5,931
41,350	**41,400**	7,081	5,491	7,081	5,944
41,400	**41,450**	7,094	5,499	7,094	5,956
41,450	**41,500**	7,106	5,506	7,106	5,969
41,500	**41,550**	7,119	5,514	7,119	5,981
41,550	**41,600**	7,131	5,521	7,131	5,994
41,600	**41,650**	7,144	5,529	7,144	6,006
41,650	**41,700**	7,156	5,536	7,156	6,019
41,700	**41,750**	7,169	5,544	7,169	6,031
41,750	**41,800**	7,181	5,551	7,181	6,044
41,800	**41,850**	7,194	5,559	7,194	6,056
41,850	**41,900**	7,206	5,566	7,206	6,069
41,900	**41,950**	7,219	5,574	7,219	6,081
41,950	**42,000**	7,231	5,581	7,231	6,094
42,000					
42,000	**42,050**	7,244	5,589	7,244	6,106
42,050	**42,100**	7,256	5,596	7,256	6,119
42,100	**42,150**	7,269	5,604	7,269	6,131
42,150	**42,200**	7,281	5,611	7,281	6,144
42,200	**42,250**	7,294	5,619	7,294	6,156
42,250	**42,300**	7,306	5,626	7,306	6,169
42,300	**42,350**	7,319	5,634	7,319	6,181
42,350	**42,400**	7,331	5,641	7,331	6,194
42,400	**42,450**	7,344	5,649	7,344	6,206
42,450	**42,500**	7,356	5,656	7,356	6,219
42,500	**42,550**	7,369	5,664	7,369	6,231
42,550	**42,600**	7,381	5,671	7,381	6,244
42,600	**42,650**	7,394	5,679	7,394	6,256
42,650	**42,700**	7,406	5,686	7,406	6,269
42,700	**42,750**	7,419	5,694	7,419	6,281
42,750	**42,800**	7,431	5,701	7,431	6,294
42,800	**42,850**	7,444	5,709	7,444	6,306
42,850	**42,900**	7,456	5,716	7,456	6,319
42,900	**42,950**	7,469	5,724	7,469	6,331
42,950	**43,000**	7,481	5,731	7,481	6,344
43,000					
43,000	**43,050**	7,494	5,739	7,494	6,356
43,050	**43,100**	7,506	5,746	7,506	6,369
43,100	**43,150**	7,519	5,754	7,519	6,381
43,150	**43,200**	7,531	5,761	7,531	6,394
43,200	**43,250**	7,544	5,769	7,544	6,406
43,250	**43,300**	7,556	5,776	7,556	6,419
43,300	**43,350**	7,569	5,784	7,569	6,431
43,350	**43,400**	7,581	5,791	7,581	6,444
43,400	**43,450**	7,594	5,799	7,594	6,456
43,450	**43,500**	7,606	5,806	7,606	6,469
43,500	**43,550**	7,619	5,814	7,619	6,481
43,550	**43,600**	7,631	5,821	7,631	6,494
43,600	**43,650**	7,644	5,829	7,644	6,506
43,650	**43,700**	7,656	5,836	7,656	6,519
43,700	**43,750**	7,669	5,844	7,669	6,531
43,750	**43,800**	7,681	5,851	7,681	6,544
43,800	**43,850**	7,694	5,859	7,694	6,556
43,850	**43,900**	7,706	5,866	7,706	6,569
43,900	**43,950**	7,719	5,874	7,719	6,581
43,950	**44,000**	7,731	5,881	7,731	6,594
44,000					
44,000	**44,050**	7,744	5,889	7,744	6,606
44,050	**44,100**	7,756	5,896	7,756	6,619
44,100	**44,150**	7,769	5,904	7,769	6,631
44,150	**44,200**	7,781	5,911	7,781	6,644
44,200	**44,250**	7,794	5,919	7,794	6,656
44,250	**44,300**	7,806	5,926	7,806	6,669
44,300	**44,350**	7,819	5,934	7,819	6,681
44,350	**44,400**	7,831	5,941	7,831	6,694
44,400	**44,450**	7,844	5,949	7,844	6,706
44,450	**44,500**	7,856	5,956	7,856	6,719
44,500	**44,550**	7,869	5,964	7,869	6,731
44,550	**44,600**	7,881	5,971	7,881	6,744
44,600	**44,650**	7,894	5,979	7,894	6,756
44,650	**44,700**	7,906	5,986	7,906	6,769
44,700	**44,750**	7,919	5,994	7,919	6,781
44,750	**44,800**	7,931	6,001	7,931	6,794
44,800	**44,850**	7,944	6,009	7,944	6,806
44,850	**44,900**	7,956	6,016	7,956	6,819
44,900	**44,950**	7,969	6,024	7,969	6,831
44,950	**45,000**	7,981	6,031	7,981	6,844
45,000					
45,000	**45,050**	7,994	6,039	7,994	6,856
45,050	**45,100**	8,006	6,046	8,006	6,869
45,100	**45,150**	8,019	6,054	8,019	6,881
45,150	**45,200**	8,031	6,061	8,031	6,894
45,200	**45,250**	8,044	6,069	8,044	6,906
45,250	**45,300**	8,056	6,076	8,056	6,919
45,300	**45,350**	8,069	6,084	8,069	6,931
45,350	**45,400**	8,081	6,091	8,081	6,944
45,400	**45,450**	8,094	6,099	8,094	6,956
45,450	**45,500**	8,106	6,106	8,106	6,969
45,500	**45,550**	8,119	6,114	8,119	6,981
45,550	**45,600**	8,131	6,121	8,131	6,994
45,600	**45,650**	8,144	6,129	8,144	7,006
45,650	**45,700**	8,156	6,136	8,156	7,019
45,700	**45,750**	8,169	6,144	8,169	7,031
45,750	**45,800**	8,181	6,151	8,181	7,044
45,800	**45,850**	8,194	6,159	8,194	7,056
45,850	**45,900**	8,206	6,166	8,206	7,069
45,900	**45,950**	8,219	6,174	8,219	7,081
45,950	**46,000**	8,231	6,181	8,231	7,094
46,000					
46,000	**46,050**	8,244	6,189	8,244	7,106
46,050	**46,100**	8,256	6,196	8,256	7,119
46,100	**46,150**	8,269	6,204	8,269	7,131
46,150	**46,200**	8,281	6,211	8,281	7,144
46,200	**46,250**	8,294	6,219	8,294	7,156
46,250	**46,300**	8,306	6,226	8,306	7,169
46,300	**46,350**	8,319	6,234	8,319	7,181
46,350	**46,400**	8,331	6,241	8,331	7,194
46,400	**46,450**	8,344	6,249	8,344	7,206
46,450	**46,500**	8,356	6,256	8,356	7,219
46,500	**46,550**	8,369	6,264	8,369	7,231
46,550	**46,600**	8,381	6,271	8,381	7,244
46,600	**46,650**	8,394	6,279	8,394	7,256
46,650	**46,700**	8,406	6,286	8,406	7,269
46,700	**46,750**	8,419	6,294	8,419	7,281
46,750	**46,800**	8,431	6,301	8,431	7,294
46,800	**46,850**	8,444	6,309	8,444	7,306
46,850	**46,900**	8,456	6,316	8,456	7,319
46,900	**46,950**	8,469	6,324	8,469	7,331
46,950	**47,000**	8,481	6,331	8,481	7,344
47,000					
47,000	**47,050**	8,494	6,339	8,494	7,356
47,050	**47,100**	8,506	6,346	8,506	7,369
47,100	**47,150**	8,519	6,354	8,519	7,381
47,150	**47,200**	8,531	6,361	8,531	7,394
47,200	**47,250**	8,544	6,369	8,544	7,406
47,250	**47,300**	8,556	6,376	8,556	7,419
47,300	**47,350**	8,569	6,384	8,569	7,431
47,350	**47,400**	8,581	6,391	8,581	7,444
47,400	**47,450**	8,594	6,399	8,594	7,456
47,450	**47,500**	8,606	6,406	8,606	7,469
47,500	**47,550**	8,619	6,414	8,619	7,481
47,550	**47,600**	8,631	6,421	8,631	7,494
47,600	**47,650**	8,644	6,429	8,644	7,506
47,650	**47,700**	8,656	6,436	8,656	7,519
47,700	**47,750**	8,669	6,444	8,669	7,531
47,750	**47,800**	8,681	6,451	8,681	7,544
47,800	**47,850**	8,694	6,459	8,694	7,556
47,850	**47,900**	8,706	6,466	8,706	7,569
47,900	**47,950**	8,719	6,474	8,719	7,581
47,950	**48,000**	8,731	6,481	8,731	7,594
48,000					
48,000	**48,050**	8,744	6,489	8,744	7,606
48,050	**48,100**	8,756	6,496	8,756	7,619
48,100	**48,150**	8,769	6,504	8,769	7,631
48,150	**48,200**	8,781	6,511	8,781	7,644
48,200	**48,250**	8,794	6,519	8,794	7,656
48,250	**48,300**	8,806	6,526	8,806	7,669
48,300	**48,350**	8,819	6,534	8,819	7,681
48,350	**48,400**	8,831	6,541	8,831	7,694
48,400	**48,450**	8,844	6,549	8,844	7,706
48,450	**48,500**	8,856	6,556	8,856	7,719
48,500	**48,550**	8,869	6,564	8,869	7,731
48,550	**48,600**	8,881	6,571	8,881	7,744
48,600	**48,650**	8,894	6,579	8,894	7,756
48,650	**48,700**	8,906	6,586	8,906	7,769
48,700	**48,750**	8,919	6,594	8,919	7,781
48,750	**48,800**	8,931	6,601	8,931	7,794
48,800	**48,850**	8,944	6,609	8,944	7,806
48,850	**48,900**	8,956	6,616	8,956	7,819
48,900	**48,950**	8,969	6,624	8,969	7,831
48,950	**49,000**	8,981	6,631	8,981	7,844
49,000					
49,000	**49,050**	8,994	6,639	8,994	7,856
49,050	**49,100**	9,006	6,646	9,006	7,869
49,100	**49,150**	9,019	6,654	9,019	7,881
49,150	**49,200**	9,031	6,661	9,031	7,894
49,200	**49,250**	9,044	6,669	9,044	7,906
49,250	**49,300**	9,056	6,676	9,056	7,919
49,300	**49,350**	9,069	6,684	9,069	7,931
49,350	**49,400**	9,081	6,691	9,081	7,944
49,400	**49,450**	9,094	6,699	9,094	7,956
49,450	**49,500**	9,106	6,706	9,106	7,969
49,500	**49,550**	9,119	6,714	9,119	7,981
49,550	**49,600**	9,131	6,721	9,131	7,994
49,600	**49,650**	9,144	6,729	9,144	8,006
49,650	**49,700**	9,156	6,736	9,156	8,019
49,700	**49,750**	9,169	6,744	9,169	8,031
49,750	**49,800**	9,181	6,751	9,181	8,044
49,800	**49,850**	9,194	6,759	9,194	8,056
49,850	**49,900**	9,206	6,766	9,206	8,069
49,900	**49,950**	9,219	6,774	9,219	8,081
49,950	**50,000**	9,231	6,781	9,231	8,094

* This column must also be used by a qualifying widow(er).

(Continued on next page)

2004 Tax Table—*Continued*

If line 42 (taxable income) is—		And you are—			
At least	But less than	Single	Married filing jointly *	Married filing separately	Head of a household
		Your tax is—			
50,000					
50,000	**50,050**	9,244	6,789	9,244	8,106
50,050	**50,100**	9,256	6,796	9,256	8,119
50,100	**50,150**	9,269	6,804	9,269	8,131
50,150	**50,200**	9,281	6,811	9,281	8,144
50,200	**50,250**	9,294	6,819	9,294	8,156
50,250	**50,300**	9,306	6,826	9,306	8,169
50,300	**50,350**	9,319	6,834	9,319	8,181
50,350	**50,400**	9,331	6,841	9,331	8,194
50,400	**50,450**	9,344	6,849	9,344	8,206
50,450	**50,500**	9,356	6,856	9,356	8,219
50,500	**50,550**	9,369	6,864	9,369	8,231
50,550	**50,600**	9,381	6,871	9,381	8,244
50,600	**50,650**	9,394	6,879	9,394	8,256
50,650	**50,700**	9,406	6,886	9,406	8,269
50,700	**50,750**	9,419	6,894	9,419	8,281
50,750	**50,800**	9,431	6,901	9,431	8,294
50,800	**50,850**	9,444	6,909	9,444	8,306
50,850	**50,900**	9,456	6,916	9,456	8,319
50,900	**50,950**	9,469	6,924	9,469	8,331
50,950	**51,000**	9,481	6,931	9,481	8,344
51,000					
51,000	**51,050**	9,494	6,939	9,494	8,356
51,050	**51,100**	9,506	6,946	9,506	8,369
51,100	**51,150**	9,519	6,954	9,519	8,381
51,150	**51,200**	9,531	6,961	9,531	8,394
51,200	**51,250**	9,544	6,969	9,544	8,406
51,250	**51,300**	9,556	6,976	9,556	8,419
51,300	**51,350**	9,569	6,984	9,569	8,431
51,350	**51,400**	9,581	6,991	9,581	8,444
51,400	**51,450**	9,594	6,999	9,594	8,456
51,450	**51,500**	9,606	7,006	9,606	8,469
51,500	**51,550**	9,619	7,014	9,619	8,481
51,550	**51,600**	9,631	7,021	9,631	8,494
51,600	**51,650**	9,644	7,029	9,644	8,506
51,650	**51,700**	9,656	7,036	9,656	8,519
51,700	**51,750**	9,669	7,044	9,669	8,531
51,750	**51,800**	9,681	7,051	9,681	8,544
51,800	**51,850**	9,694	7,059	9,694	8,556
51,850	**51,900**	9,706	7,066	9,706	8,569
51,900	**51,950**	9,719	7,074	9,719	8,581
51,950	**52,000**	9,731	7,081	9,731	8,594
52,000					
52,000	**52,050**	9,744	7,089	9,744	8,606
52,050	**52,100**	9,756	7,096	9,756	8,619
52,100	**52,150**	9,769	7,104	9,769	8,631
52,150	**52,200**	9,781	7,111	9,781	8,644
52,200	**52,250**	9,794	7,119	9,794	8,656
52,250	**52,300**	9,806	7,126	9,806	8,669
52,300	**52,350**	9,819	7,134	9,819	8,681
52,350	**52,400**	9,831	7,141	9,831	8,694
52,400	**52,450**	9,844	7,149	9,844	8,706
52,450	**52,500**	9,856	7,156	9,856	8,719
52,500	**52,550**	9,869	7,164	9,869	8,731
52,550	**52,600**	9,881	7,171	9,881	8,744
52,600	**52,650**	9,894	7,179	9,894	8,756
52,650	**52,700**	9,906	7,186	9,906	8,769
52,700	**52,750**	9,919	7,194	9,919	8,781
52,750	**52,800**	9,931	7,201	9,931	8,794
52,800	**52,850**	9,944	7,209	9,944	8,806
52,850	**52,900**	9,956	7,216	9,956	8,819
52,900	**52,950**	9,969	7,224	9,969	8,831
52,950	**53,000**	9,981	7,231	9,981	8,844

If line 42 (taxable income) is—		And you are—			
At least	But less than	Single	Married filing jointly *	Married filing separately	Head of a household
		Your tax is—			
53,000					
53,000	**53,050**	9,994	7,239	9,994	8,856
53,050	**53,100**	10,006	7,246	10,006	8,869
53,100	**53,150**	10,019	7,254	10,019	8,881
53,150	**53,200**	10,031	7,261	10,031	8,894
53,200	**53,250**	10,044	7,269	10,044	8,906
53,250	**53,300**	10,056	7,276	10,056	8,919
53,300	**53,350**	10,069	7,284	10,069	8,931
53,350	**53,400**	10,081	7,291	10,081	8,944
53,400	**53,450**	10,094	7,299	10,094	8,956
53,450	**53,500**	10,106	7,306	10,106	8,969
53,500	**53,550**	10,119	7,314	10,119	8,981
53,550	**53,600**	10,131	7,321	10,131	8,994
53,600	**53,650**	10,144	7,329	10,144	9,006
53,650	**53,700**	10,156	7,336	10,156	9,019
53,700	**53,750**	10,169	7,344	10,169	9,031
53,750	**53,800**	10,181	7,351	10,181	9,044
53,800	**53,850**	10,194	7,359	10,194	9,056
53,850	**53,900**	10,206	7,366	10,206	9,069
53,900	**53,950**	10,219	7,374	10,219	9,081
53,950	**54,000**	10,231	7,381	10,231	9,094
54,000					
54,000	**54,050**	10,244	7,389	10,244	9,106
54,050	**54,100**	10,256	7,396	10,256	9,119
54,100	**54,150**	10,269	7,404	10,269	9,131
54,150	**54,200**	10,281	7,411	10,281	9,144
54,200	**54,250**	10,294	7,419	10,294	9,156
54,250	**54,300**	10,306	7,426	10,306	9,169
54,300	**54,350**	10,319	7,434	10,319	9,181
54,350	**54,400**	10,331	7,441	10,331	9,194
54,400	**54,450**	10,344	7,449	10,344	9,206
54,450	**54,500**	10,356	7,456	10,356	9,219
54,500	**54,550**	10,369	7,464	10,369	9,231
54,550	**54,600**	10,381	7,471	10,381	9,244
54,600	**54,650**	10,394	7,479	10,394	9,256
54,650	**54,700**	10,406	7,486	10,406	9,269
54,700	**54,750**	10,419	7,494	10,419	9,281
54,750	**54,800**	10,431	7,501	10,431	9,294
54,800	**54,850**	10,444	7,509	10,444	9,306
54,850	**54,900**	10,456	7,516	10,456	9,319
54,900	**54,950**	10,469	7,524	10,469	9,331
54,950	**55,000**	10,481	7,531	10,481	9,344
55,000					
55,000	**55,050**	10,494	7,539	10,494	9,356
55,050	**55,100**	10,506	7,546	10,506	9,369
55,100	**55,150**	10,519	7,554	10,519	9,381
55,150	**55,200**	10,531	7,561	10,531	9,394
55,200	**55,250**	10,544	7,569	10,544	9,406
55,250	**55,300**	10,556	7,576	10,556	9,419
55,300	**55,350**	10,569	7,584	10,569	9,431
55,350	**55,400**	10,581	7,591	10,581	9,444
55,400	**55,450**	10,594	7,599	10,594	9,456
55,450	**55,500**	10,606	7,606	10,606	9,469
55,500	**55,550**	10,619	7,614	10,619	9,481
55,550	**55,600**	10,631	7,621	10,631	9,494
55,600	**55,650**	10,644	7,629	10,644	9,506
55,650	**55,700**	10,656	7,636	10,656	9,519
55,700	**55,750**	10,669	7,644	10,669	9,531
55,750	**55,800**	10,681	7,651	10,681	9,544
55,800	**55,850**	10,694	7,659	10,694	9,556
55,850	**55,900**	10,706	7,666	10,706	9,569
55,900	**55,950**	10,719	7,674	10,719	9,581
55,950	**56,000**	10,731	7,681	10,731	9,594

If line 42 (taxable income) is—		And you are—			
At least	But less than	Single	Married filing jointly *	Married filing separately	Head of a household
		Your tax is—			
56,000					
56,000	**56,050**	10,744	7,689	10,744	9,606
56,050	**56,100**	10,756	7,696	10,756	9,619
56,100	**56,150**	10,769	7,704	10,769	9,631
56,150	**56,200**	10,781	7,711	10,781	9,644
56,200	**56,250**	10,794	7,719	10,794	9,656
56,250	**56,300**	10,806	7,726	10,806	9,669
56,300	**56,350**	10,819	7,734	10,819	9,681
56,350	**56,400**	10,831	7,741	10,831	9,694
56,400	**56,450**	10,844	7,749	10,844	9,706
56,450	**56,500**	10,856	7,756	10,856	9,719
56,500	**56,550**	10,869	7,764	10,869	9,731
56,550	**56,600**	10,881	7,771	10,881	9,744
56,600	**56,650**	10,894	7,779	10,894	9,756
56,650	**56,700**	10,906	7,786	10,906	9,769
56,700	**56,750**	10,919	7,794	10,919	9,781
56,750	**56,800**	10,931	7,801	10,931	9,794
56,800	**56,850**	10,944	7,809	10,944	9,806
56,850	**56,900**	10,956	7,816	10,956	9,819
56,900	**56,950**	10,969	7,824	10,969	9,831
56,950	**57,000**	10,981	7,831	10,981	9,844
57,000					
57,000	**57,050**	10,994	7,839	10,994	9,856
57,050	**57,100**	11,006	7,846	11,006	9,869
57,100	**57,150**	11,019	7,854	11,019	9,881
57,150	**57,200**	11,031	7,861	11,031	9,894
57,200	**57,250**	11,044	7,869	11,044	9,906
57,250	**57,300**	11,056	7,876	11,056	9,919
57,300	**57,350**	11,069	7,884	11,069	9,931
57,350	**57,400**	11,081	7,891	11,081	9,944
57,400	**57,450**	11,094	7,899	11,094	9,956
57,450	**57,500**	11,106	7,906	11,106	9,969
57,500	**57,550**	11,119	7,914	11,119	9,981
57,550	**57,600**	11,131	7,921	11,131	9,994
57,600	**57,650**	11,144	7,929	11,144	10,006
57,650	**57,700**	11,156	7,936	11,156	10,019
57,700	**57,750**	11,169	7,944	11,169	10,031
57,750	**57,800**	11,181	7,951	11,181	10,044
57,800	**57,850**	11,194	7,959	11,194	10,056
57,850	**57,900**	11,206	7,966	11,206	10,069
57,900	**57,950**	11,219	7,974	11,219	10,081
57,950	**58,000**	11,231	7,981	11,231	10,094
58,000					
58,000	**58,050**	11,244	7,989	11,244	10,106
58,050	**58,100**	11,256	7,996	11,256	10,119
58,100	**58,150**	11,269	8,006	11,269	10,131
58,150	**58,200**	11,281	8,019	11,281	10,144
58,200	**58,250**	11,294	8,031	11,294	10,156
58,250	**58,300**	11,306	8,044	11,306	10,169
58,300	**58,350**	11,319	8,056	11,319	10,181
58,350	**58,400**	11,331	8,069	11,331	10,194
58,400	**58,450**	11,344	8,081	11,344	10,206
58,450	**58,500**	11,356	8,094	11,356	10,219
58,500	**58,550**	11,369	8,106	11,369	10,231
58,550	**58,600**	11,381	8,119	11,381	10,244
58,600	**58,650**	11,394	8,131	11,394	10,256
58,650	**58,700**	11,406	8,144	11,408	10,269
58,700	**58,750**	11,419	8,156	11,422	10,281
58,750	**58,800**	11,431	8,169	11,436	10,294
58,800	**58,850**	11,444	8,181	11,450	10,306
58,850	**58,900**	11,456	8,194	11,464	10,319
58,900	**58,950**	11,469	8,206	11,478	10,331
58,950	**59,000**	11,481	8,219	11,492	10,344

* This column must also be used by a qualifying widow(er).

(Continued on next page)

2004 Tax Table—*Continued*

If line 42 (taxable income) is—		And you are—			
At least	But less than	Single	Married filing jointly *	Married filing sepa-rately	Head of a house-hold
		Your tax is—			
59,000					
59,000	**59,050**	11,494	8,231	11,506	10,356
59,050	**59,100**	11,506	8,244	11,520	10,369
59,100	**59,150**	11,519	8,256	11,534	10,381
59,150	**59,200**	11,531	8,269	11,548	10,394
59,200	**59,250**	11,544	8,281	11,562	10,406
59,250	**59,300**	11,556	8,294	11,576	10,419
59,300	**59,350**	11,569	8,306	11,590	10,431
59,350	**59,400**	11,581	8,319	11,604	10,444
59,400	**59,450**	11,594	8,331	11,618	10,456
59,450	**59,500**	11,606	8,344	11,632	10,469
59,500	**59,550**	11,619	8,356	11,646	10,481
59,550	**59,600**	11,631	8,369	11,660	10,494
59,600	**59,650**	11,644	8,381	11,674	10,506
59,650	**59,700**	11,656	8,394	11,688	10,519
59,700	**59,750**	11,669	8,406	11,702	10,531
59,750	**59,800**	11,681	8,419	11,716	10,544
59,800	**59,850**	11,694	8,431	11,730	10,556
59,850	**59,900**	11,706	8,444	11,744	10,569
59,900	**59,950**	11,719	8,456	11,758	10,581
59,950	**60,000**	11,731	8,469	11,772	10,594
60,000					
60,000	**60,050**	11,744	8,481	11,786	10,606
60,050	**60,100**	11,756	8,494	11,800	10,619
60,100	**60,150**	11,769	8,506	11,814	10,631
60,150	**60,200**	11,781	8,519	11,828	10,644
60,200	**60,250**	11,794	8,531	11,842	10,656
60,250	**60,300**	11,806	8,544	11,856	10,669
60,300	**60,350**	11,819	8,556	11,870	10,681
60,350	**60,400**	11,831	8,569	11,884	10,694
60,400	**60,450**	11,844	8,581	11,898	10,706
60,450	**60,500**	11,856	8,594	11,912	10,719
60,500	**60,550**	11,869	8,606	11,926	10,731
60,550	**60,600**	11,881	8,619	11,940	10,744
60,600	**60,650**	11,894	8,631	11,954	10,756
60,650	**60,700**	11,906	8,644	11,968	10,769
60,700	**60,750**	11,919	8,656	11,982	10,781
60,750	**60,800**	11,931	8,669	11,996	10,794
60,800	**60,850**	11,944	8,681	12,010	10,806
60,850	**60,900**	11,956	8,694	12,024	10,819
60,900	**60,950**	11,969	8,706	12,038	10,831
60,950	**61,000**	11,981	8,719	12,052	10,844
61,000					
61,000	**61,050**	11,994	8,731	12,066	10,856
61,050	**61,100**	12,006	8,744	12,080	10,869
61,100	**61,150**	12,019	8,756	12,094	10,881
61,150	**61,200**	12,031	8,769	12,108	10,894
61,200	**61,250**	12,044	8,781	12,122	10,906
61,250	**61,300**	12,056	8,794	12,136	10,919
61,300	**61,350**	12,069	8,806	12,150	10,931
61,350	**61,400**	12,081	8,819	12,164	10,944
61,400	**61,450**	12,094	8,831	12,178	10,956
61,450	**61,500**	12,106	8,844	12,192	10,969
61,500	**61,550**	12,119	8,856	12,206	10,981
61,550	**61,600**	12,131	8,869	12,220	10,994
61,600	**61,650**	12,144	8,881	12,234	11,006
61,650	**61,700**	12,156	8,894	12,248	11,019
61,700	**61,750**	12,169	8,906	12,262	11,031
61,750	**61,800**	12,181	8,919	12,276	11,044
61,800	**61,850**	12,194	8,931	12,290	11,056
61,850	**61,900**	12,206	8,944	12,304	11,069
61,900	**61,950**	12,219	8,956	12,318	11,081
61,950	**62,000**	12,231	8,969	12,332	11,094
62,000					
62,000	**62,050**	12,244	8,981	12,346	11,106
62,050	**62,100**	12,256	8,994	12,360	11,119
62,100	**62,150**	12,269	9,006	12,374	11,131
62,150	**62,200**	12,281	9,019	12,388	11,144
62,200	**62,250**	12,294	9,031	12,402	11,156
62,250	**62,300**	12,306	9,044	12,416	11,169
62,300	**62,350**	12,319	9,056	12,430	11,181
62,350	**62,400**	12,331	9,069	12,444	11,194
62,400	**62,450**	12,344	9,081	12,458	11,206
62,450	**62,500**	12,356	9,094	12,472	11,219
62,500	**62,550**	12,369	9,106	12,486	11,231
62,550	**62,600**	12,381	9,119	12,500	11,244
62,600	**62,650**	12,394	9,131	12,514	11,256
62,650	**62,700**	12,406	9,144	12,528	11,269
62,700	**62,750**	12,419	9,156	12,542	11,281
62,750	**62,800**	12,431	9,169	12,556	11,294
62,800	**62,850**	12,444	9,181	12,570	11,306
62,850	**62,900**	12,456	9,194	12,584	11,319
62,900	**62,950**	12,469	9,206	12,598	11,331
62,950	**63,000**	12,481	9,219	12,612	11,344
63,000					
63,000	**63,050**	12,494	9,231	12,626	11,356
63,050	**63,100**	12,506	9,244	12,640	11,369
63,100	**63,150**	12,519	9,256	12,654	11,381
63,150	**63,200**	12,531	9,269	12,668	11,394
63,200	**63,250**	12,544	9,281	12,682	11,406
63,250	**63,300**	12,556	9,294	12,696	11,419
63,300	**63,350**	12,569	9,306	12,710	11,431
63,350	**63,400**	12,581	9,319	12,724	11,444
63,400	**63,450**	12,594	9,331	12,738	11,456
63,450	**63,500**	12,606	9,344	12,752	11,469
63,500	**63,550**	12,619	9,356	12,766	11,481
63,550	**63,600**	12,631	9,369	12,780	11,494
63,600	**63,650**	12,644	9,381	12,794	11,506
63,650	**63,700**	12,656	9,394	12,808	11,519
63,700	**63,750**	12,669	9,406	12,822	11,531
63,750	**63,800**	12,681	9,419	12,836	11,544
63,800	**63,850**	12,694	9,431	12,850	11,556
63,850	**63,900**	12,706	9,444	12,864	11,569
63,900	**63,950**	12,719	9,456	12,878	11,581
63,950	**64,000**	12,731	9,469	12,892	11,594
64,000					
64,000	**64,050**	12,744	9,481	12,906	11,606
64,050	**64,100**	12,756	9,494	12,920	11,619
64,100	**64,150**	12,769	9,506	12,934	11,631
64,150	**64,200**	12,781	9,519	12,948	11,644
64,200	**64,250**	12,794	9,531	12,962	11,656
64,250	**64,300**	12,806	9,544	12,976	11,669
64,300	**64,350**	12,819	9,556	12,990	11,681
64,350	**64,400**	12,831	9,569	13,004	11,694
64,400	**64,450**	12,844	9,581	13,018	11,706
64,450	**64,500**	12,856	9,594	13,032	11,719
64,500	**64,550**	12,869	9,606	13,046	11,731
64,550	**64,600**	12,881	9,619	13,060	11,744
64,600	**64,650**	12,894	9,631	13,074	11,756
64,650	**64,700**	12,906	9,644	13,088	11,769
64,700	**64,750**	12,919	9,656	13,102	11,781
64,750	**64,800**	12,931	9,669	13,116	11,794
64,800	**64,850**	12,944	9,681	13,130	11,806
64,850	**64,900**	12,956	9,694	13,144	11,819
64,900	**64,950**	12,969	9,706	13,158	11,831
64,950	**65,000**	12,981	9,719	13,172	11,844
65,000					
65,000	**65,050**	12,994	9,731	13,186	11,856
65,050	**65,100**	13,006	9,744	13,200	11,869
65,100	**65,150**	13,019	9,756	13,214	11,881
65,150	**65,200**	13,031	9,769	13,228	11,894
65,200	**65,250**	13,044	9,781	13,242	11,906
65,250	**65,300**	13,056	9,794	13,256	11,919
65,300	**65,350**	13,069	9,806	13,270	11,931
65,350	**65,400**	13,081	9,819	13,284	11,944
65,400	**65,450**	13,094	9,831	13,298	11,956
65,450	**65,500**	13,106	9,844	13,312	11,969
65,500	**65,550**	13,119	9,856	13,326	11,981
65,550	**65,600**	13,131	9,869	13,340	11,994
65,600	**65,650**	13,144	9,881	13,354	12,006
65,650	**65,700**	13,156	9,894	13,368	12,019
65,700	**65,750**	13,169	9,906	13,382	12,031
65,750	**65,800**	13,181	9,919	13,396	12,044
65,800	**65,850**	13,194	9,931	13,410	12,056
65,850	**65,900**	13,206	9,944	13,424	12,069
65,900	**65,950**	13,219	9,956	13,438	12,081
65,950	**66,000**	13,231	9,969	13,452	12,094
66,000					
66,000	**66,050**	13,244	9,981	13,466	12,106
66,050	**66,100**	13,256	9,994	13,480	12,119
66,100	**66,150**	13,269	10,006	13,494	12,131
66,150	**66,200**	13,281	10,019	13,508	12,144
66,200	**66,250**	13,294	10,031	13,522	12,156
66,250	**66,300**	13,306	10,044	13,536	12,169
66,300	**66,350**	13,319	10,056	13,550	12,181
66,350	**66,400**	13,331	10,069	13,564	12,194
66,400	**66,450**	13,344	10,081	13,578	12,206
66,450	**66,500**	13,356	10,094	13,592	12,219
66,500	**66,550**	13,369	10,106	13,606	12,231
66,550	**66,600**	13,381	10,119	13,620	12,244
66,600	**66,650**	13,394	10,131	13,634	12,256
66,650	**66,700**	13,406	10,144	13,648	12,269
66,700	**66,750**	13,419	10,156	13,662	12,281
66,750	**66,800**	13,431	10,169	13,676	12,294
66,800	**66,850**	13,444	10,181	13,690	12,306
66,850	**66,900**	13,456	10,194	13,704	12,319
66,900	**66,950**	13,469	10,206	13,718	12,331
66,950	**67,000**	13,481	10,219	13,732	12,344
67,000					
67,000	**67,050**	13,494	10,231	13,746	12,356
67,050	**67,100**	13,506	10,244	13,760	12,369
67,100	**67,150**	13,519	10,256	13,774	12,381
67,150	**67,200**	13,531	10,269	13,788	12,394
67,200	**67,250**	13,544	10,281	13,802	12,406
67,250	**67,300**	13,556	10,294	13,816	12,419
67,300	**67,350**	13,569	10,306	13,830	12,431
67,350	**67,400**	13,581	10,319	13,844	12,444
67,400	**67,450**	13,594	10,331	13,858	12,456
67,450	**67,500**	13,606	10,344	13,872	12,469
67,500	**67,550**	13,619	10,356	13,886	12,481
67,550	**67,600**	13,631	10,369	13,900	12,494
67,600	**67,650**	13,644	10,381	13,914	12,506
67,650	**67,700**	13,656	10,394	13,928	12,519
67,700	**67,750**	13,669	10,406	13,942	12,531
67,750	**67,800**	13,681	10,419	13,956	12,544
67,800	**67,850**	13,694	10,431	13,970	12,556
67,850	**67,900**	13,706	10,444	13,984	12,569
67,900	**67,950**	13,719	10,456	13,998	12,581
67,950	**68,000**	13,731	10,469	14,012	12,594

* This column must also be used by a qualifying widow(er).

(Continued on next page)

2004 Tax Table—*Continued*

If line 42 (taxable income) is— At least	But less than	And you are— Single	Married filing jointly *	Married filing sepa-rately	Head of a house-hold
		Your tax is—			
68,000					
68,000	68,050	13,744	10,481	14,026	12,606
68,050	68,100	13,756	10,494	14,040	12,619
68,100	68,150	13,769	10,506	14,054	12,631
68,150	68,200	13,781	10,519	14,068	12,644
68,200	68,250	13,794	10,531	14,082	12,656
68,250	68,300	13,806	10,544	14,096	12,669
68,300	68,350	13,819	10,556	14,110	12,681
68,350	68,400	13,831	10,569	14,124	12,694
68,400	68,450	13,844	10,581	14,138	12,706
68,450	68,500	13,856	10,594	14,152	12,719
68,500	68,550	13,869	10,606	14,166	12,731
68,550	68,600	13,881	10,619	14,180	12,744
68,600	68,650	13,894	10,631	14,194	12,756
68,650	68,700	13,906	10,644	14,208	12,769
68,700	68,750	13,919	10,656	14,222	12,781
68,750	68,800	13,931	10,669	14,236	12,794
68,800	68,850	13,944	10,681	14,250	12,806
68,850	68,900	13,956	10,694	14,264	12,819
68,900	68,950	13,969	10,706	14,278	12,831
68,950	69,000	13,981	10,719	14,292	12,844
69,000					
69,000	69,050	13,994	10,731	14,306	12,856
69,050	69,100	14,006	10,744	14,320	12,869
69,100	69,150	14,019	10,756	14,334	12,881
69,150	69,200	14,031	10,769	14,348	12,894
69,200	69,250	14,044	10,781	14,362	12,906
69,250	69,300	14,056	10,794	14,376	12,919
69,300	69,350	14,069	10,806	14,390	12,931
69,350	69,400	14,081	10,819	14,404	12,944
69,400	69,450	14,094	10,831	14,418	12,956
69,450	69,500	14,106	10,844	14,432	12,969
69,500	69,550	14,119	10,856	14,446	12,981
69,550	69,600	14,131	10,869	14,460	12,994
69,600	69,650	14,144	10,881	14,474	13,006
69,650	69,700	14,156	10,894	14,488	13,019
69,700	69,750	14,169	10,906	14,502	13,031
69,750	69,800	14,181	10,919	14,516	13,044
69,800	69,850	14,194	10,931	14,530	13,056
69,850	69,900	14,206	10,944	14,544	13,069
69,900	69,950	14,219	10,956	14,558	13,081
69,950	70,000	14,231	10,969	14,572	13,094
70,000					
70,000	70,050	14,244	10,981	14,586	13,106
70,050	70,100	14,256	10,994	14,600	13,119
70,100	70,150	14,269	11,006	14,614	13,131
70,150	70,200	14,281	11,019	14,628	13,144
70,200	70,250	14,294	11,031	14,642	13,156
70,250	70,300	14,306	11,044	14,656	13,169
70,300	70,350	14,319	11,056	14,670	13,181
70,350	70,400	14,332	11,069	14,684	13,194
70,400	70,450	14,346	11,081	14,698	13,206
70,450	70,500	14,360	11,094	14,712	13,219
70,500	70,550	14,374	11,106	14,726	13,231
70,550	70,600	14,388	11,119	14,740	13,244
70,600	70,650	14,402	11,131	14,754	13,256
70,650	70,700	14,416	11,144	14,768	13,269
70,700	70,750	14,430	11,156	14,782	13,281
70,750	70,800	14,444	11,169	14,796	13,294
70,800	70,850	14,458	11,181	14,810	13,306
70,850	70,900	14,472	11,194	14,824	13,319
70,900	70,950	14,486	11,206	14,838	13,331
70,950	71,000	14,500	11,219	14,852	13,344

If line 42 (taxable income) is— At least	But less than	And you are— Single	Married filing jointly *	Married filing sepa-rately	Head of a house-hold
		Your tax is—			
71,000					
71,000	71,050	14,514	11,231	14,866	13,356
71,050	71,100	14,528	11,244	14,880	13,369
71,100	71,150	14,542	11,256	14,894	13,381
71,150	71,200	14,556	11,269	14,908	13,394
71,200	71,250	14,570	11,281	14,922	13,406
71,250	71,300	14,584	11,294	14,936	13,419
71,300	71,350	14,598	11,306	14,950	13,431
71,350	71,400	14,612	11,319	14,964	13,444
71,400	71,450	14,626	11,331	14,978	13,456
71,450	71,500	14,640	11,344	14,992	13,469
71,500	71,550	14,654	11,356	15,006	13,481
71,550	71,600	14,668	11,369	15,020	13,494
71,600	71,650	14,682	11,381	15,034	13,506
71,650	71,700	14,696	11,394	15,048	13,519
71,700	71,750	14,710	11,406	15,062	13,531
71,750	71,800	14,724	11,419	15,076	13,544
71,800	71,850	14,738	11,431	15,090	13,556
71,850	71,900	14,752	11,444	15,104	13,569
71,900	71,950	14,766	11,456	15,118	13,581
71,950	72,000	14,780	11,469	15,132	13,594
72,000					
72,000	72,050	14,794	11,481	15,146	13,606
72,050	72,100	14,808	11,494	15,160	13,619
72,100	72,150	14,822	11,506	15,174	13,631
72,150	72,200	14,836	11,519	15,188	13,644
72,200	72,250	14,850	11,531	15,202	13,656
72,250	72,300	14,864	11,544	15,216	13,669
72,300	72,350	14,878	11,556	15,230	13,681
72,350	72,400	14,892	11,569	15,244	13,694
72,400	72,450	14,906	11,581	15,258	13,706
72,450	72,500	14,920	11,594	15,272	13,719
72,500	72,550	14,934	11,606	15,286	13,731
72,550	72,600	14,948	11,619	15,300	13,744
72,600	72,650	14,962	11,631	15,314	13,756
72,650	72,700	14,976	11,644	15,328	13,769
72,700	72,750	14,990	11,656	15,342	13,781
72,750	72,800	15,004	11,669	15,356	13,794
72,800	72,850	15,018	11,681	15,370	13,806
72,850	72,900	15,032	11,694	15,384	13,819
72,900	72,950	15,046	11,706	15,398	13,831
72,950	73,000	15,060	11,719	15,412	13,844
73,000					
73,000	73,050	15,074	11,731	15,426	13,856
73,050	73,100	15,088	11,744	15,440	13,869
73,100	73,150	15,102	11,756	15,454	13,881
73,150	73,200	15,116	11,769	15,468	13,894
73,200	73,250	15,130	11,781	15,482	13,906
73,250	73,300	15,144	11,794	15,496	13,919
73,300	73,350	15,158	11,806	15,510	13,931
73,350	73,400	15,172	11,819	15,524	13,944
73,400	73,450	15,186	11,831	15,538	13,956
73,450	73,500	15,200	11,844	15,552	13,969
73,500	73,550	15,214	11,856	15,566	13,981
73,550	73,600	15,228	11,869	15,580	13,994
73,600	73,650	15,242	11,881	15,594	14,006
73,650	73,700	15,256	11,894	15,608	14,019
73,700	73,750	15,270	11,906	15,622	14,031
73,750	73,800	15,284	11,919	15,636	14,044
73,800	73,850	15,298	11,931	15,650	14,056
73,850	73,900	15,312	11,944	15,664	14,069
73,900	73,950	15,326	11,956	15,678	14,081
73,950	74,000	15,340	11,969	15,692	14,094

If line 42 (taxable income) is— At least	But less than	And you are— Single	Married filing jointly *	Married filing sepa-rately	Head of a house-hold
		Your tax is—			
74,000					
74,000	74,050	15,354	11,981	15,706	14,106
74,050	74,100	15,368	11,994	15,720	14,119
74,100	74,150	15,382	12,006	15,734	14,131
74,150	74,200	15,396	12,019	15,748	14,144
74,200	74,250	15,410	12,031	15,762	14,156
74,250	74,300	15,424	12,044	15,776	14,169
74,300	74,350	15,438	12,056	15,790	14,181
74,350	74,400	15,452	12,069	15,804	14,194
74,400	74,450	15,466	12,081	15,818	14,206
74,450	74,500	15,480	12,094	15,832	14,219
74,500	74,550	15,494	12,106	15,846	14,231
74,550	74,600	15,508	12,119	15,860	14,244
74,600	74,650	15,522	12,131	15,874	14,256
74,650	74,700	15,536	12,144	15,888	14,269
74,700	74,750	15,550	12,156	15,902	14,281
74,750	74,800	15,564	12,169	15,916	14,294
74,800	74,850	15,578	12,181	15,930	14,306
74,850	74,900	15,592	12,194	15,944	14,319
74,900	74,950	15,606	12,206	15,958	14,331
74,950	75,000	15,620	12,219	15,972	14,344
75,000					
75,000	75,050	15,634	12,231	15,986	14,356
75,050	75,100	15,648	12,244	16,000	14,369
75,100	75,150	15,662	12,256	16,014	14,381
75,150	75,200	15,676	12,269	16,028	14,394
75,200	75,250	15,690	12,281	16,042	14,406
75,250	75,300	15,704	12,294	16,056	14,419
75,300	75,350	15,718	12,306	16,070	14,431
75,350	75,400	15,732	12,319	16,084	14,444
75,400	75,450	15,746	12,331	16,098	14,456
75,450	75,500	15,760	12,344	16,112	14,469
75,500	75,550	15,774	12,356	16,126	14,481
75,550	75,600	15,788	12,369	16,140	14,494
75,600	75,650	15,802	12,381	16,154	14,506
75,650	75,700	15,816	12,394	16,168	14,519
75,700	75,750	15,830	12,406	16,182	14,531
75,750	75,800	15,844	12,419	16,196	14,544
75,800	75,850	15,858	12,431	16,210	14,556
75,850	75,900	15,872	12,444	16,224	14,569
75,900	75,950	15,886	12,456	16,238	14,581
75,950	76,000	15,900	12,469	16,252	14,594
76,000					
76,000	76,050	15,914	12,481	16,266	14,606
76,050	76,100	15,928	12,494	16,280	14,619
76,100	76,150	15,942	12,506	16,294	14,631
76,150	76,200	15,956	12,519	16,308	14,644
76,200	76,250	15,970	12,531	16,322	14,656
76,250	76,300	15,984	12,544	16,336	14,669
76,300	76,350	15,998	12,556	16,350	14,681
76,350	76,400	16,012	12,569	16,364	14,694
76,400	76,450	16,026	12,581	16,378	14,706
76,450	76,500	16,040	12,594	16,392	14,719
76,500	76,550	16,054	12,606	16,406	14,731
76,550	76,600	16,068	12,619	16,420	14,744
76,600	76,650	16,082	12,631	16,434	14,756
76,650	76,700	16,096	12,644	16,448	14,769
76,700	76,750	16,110	12,656	16,462	14,781
76,750	76,800	16,124	12,669	16,476	14,794
76,800	76,850	16,138	12,681	16,490	14,806
76,850	76,900	16,152	12,694	16,504	14,819
76,900	76,950	16,166	12,706	16,518	14,831
76,950	77,000	16,180	12,719	16,532	14,844

* This column must also be used by a qualifying widow(er).

(Continued on next page)

2004 Tax Table—*Continued*

If line 42 (taxable income) is— At least	But less than	Single	Married filing jointly *	Married filing separately	Head of a household
		Your tax is—			
77,000					
77,000	**77,050**	16,194	12,731	16,546	14,856
77,050	**77,100**	16,208	12,744	16,560	14,869
77,100	**77,150**	16,222	12,756	16,574	14,881
77,150	**77,200**	16,236	12,769	16,588	14,894
77,200	**77,250**	16,250	12,781	16,602	14,906
77,250	**77,300**	16,264	12,794	16,616	14,919
77,300	**77,350**	16,278	12,806	16,630	14,931
77,350	**77,400**	16,292	12,819	16,644	14,944
77,400	**77,450**	16,306	12,831	16,658	14,956
77,450	**77,500**	16,320	12,844	16,672	14,969
77,500	**77,550**	16,334	12,856	16,686	14,981
77,550	**77,600**	16,348	12,869	16,700	14,994
77,600	**77,650**	16,362	12,881	16,714	15,006
77,650	**77,700**	16,376	12,894	16,728	15,019
77,700	**77,750**	16,390	12,906	16,742	15,031
77,750	**77,800**	16,404	12,919	16,756	15,044
77,800	**77,850**	16,418	12,931	16,770	15,056
77,850	**77,900**	16,432	12,944	16,784	15,069
77,900	**77,950**	16,446	12,956	16,798	15,081
77,950	**78,000**	16,460	12,969	16,812	15,094
78,000					
78,000	**78,050**	16,474	12,981	16,826	15,106
78,050	**78,100**	16,488	12,994	16,840	15,119
78,100	**78,150**	16,502	13,006	16,854	15,131
78,150	**78,200**	16,516	13,019	16,868	15,144
78,200	**78,250**	16,530	13,031	16,882	15,156
78,250	**78,300**	16,544	13,044	16,896	15,169
78,300	**78,350**	16,558	13,056	16,910	15,181
78,350	**78,400**	16,572	13,069	16,924	15,194
78,400	**78,450**	16,586	13,081	16,938	15,206
78,450	**78,500**	16,600	13,094	16,952	15,219
78,500	**78,550**	16,614	13,106	16,966	15,231
78,550	**78,600**	16,628	13,119	16,980	15,244
78,600	**78,650**	16,642	13,131	16,994	15,256
78,650	**78,700**	16,656	13,144	17,008	15,269
78,700	**78,750**	16,670	13,156	17,022	15,281
78,750	**78,800**	16,684	13,169	17,036	15,294
78,800	**78,850**	16,698	13,181	17,050	15,306
78,850	**78,900**	16,712	13,194	17,064	15,319
78,900	**78,950**	16,726	13,206	17,078	15,331
78,950	**79,000**	16,740	13,219	17,092	15,344
79,000					
79,000	**79,050**	16,754	13,231	17,106	15,356
79,050	**79,100**	16,768	13,244	17,120	15,369
79,100	**79,150**	16,782	13,256	17,134	15,381
79,150	**79,200**	16,796	13,269	17,148	15,394
79,200	**79,250**	16,810	13,281	17,162	15,406
79,250	**79,300**	16,824	13,294	17,176	15,419
79,300	**79,350**	16,838	13,306	17,190	15,431
79,350	**79,400**	16,852	13,319	17,204	15,444
79,400	**79,450**	16,866	13,331	17,218	15,456
79,450	**79,500**	16,880	13,344	17,232	15,469
79,500	**79,550**	16,894	13,356	17,246	15,481
79,550	**79,600**	16,908	13,369	17,260	15,494
79,600	**79,650**	16,922	13,381	17,274	15,506
79,650	**79,700**	16,936	13,394	17,288	15,519
79,700	**79,750**	16,950	13,406	17,302	15,531
79,750	**79,800**	16,964	13,419	17,316	15,544
79,800	**79,850**	16,978	13,431	17,330	15,556
79,850	**79,900**	16,992	13,444	17,344	15,569
79,900	**79,950**	17,006	13,456	17,358	15,581
79,950	**80,000**	17,020	13,469	17,372	15,594

If line 42 (taxable income) is— At least	But less than	Single	Married filing jointly *	Married filing separately	Head of a household
		Your tax is—			
80,000					
80,000	**80,050**	17,034	13,481	17,386	15,606
80,050	**80,100**	17,048	13,494	17,400	15,619
80,100	**80,150**	17,062	13,506	17,414	15,631
80,150	**80,200**	17,076	13,519	17,428	15,644
80,200	**80,250**	17,090	13,531	17,442	15,656
80,250	**80,300**	17,104	13,544	17,456	15,669
80,300	**80,350**	17,118	13,556	17,470	15,681
80,350	**80,400**	17,132	13,569	17,484	15,694
80,400	**80,450**	17,146	13,581	17,498	15,706
80,450	**80,500**	17,160	13,594	17,512	15,719
80,500	**80,550**	17,174	13,606	17,526	15,731
80,550	**80,600**	17,188	13,619	17,540	15,744
80,600	**80,650**	17,202	13,631	17,554	15,756
80,650	**80,700**	17,216	13,644	17,568	15,769
80,700	**80,750**	17,230	13,656	17,582	15,781
80,750	**80,800**	17,244	13,669	17,596	15,794
80,800	**80,850**	17,258	13,681	17,610	15,806
80,850	**80,900**	17,272	13,694	17,624	15,819
80,900	**80,950**	17,286	13,706	17,638	15,831
80,950	**81,000**	17,300	13,719	17,652	15,844
81,000					
81,000	**81,050**	17,314	13,731	17,666	15,856
81,050	**81,100**	17,328	13,744	17,680	15,869
81,100	**81,150**	17,342	13,756	17,694	15,881
81,150	**81,200**	17,356	13,769	17,708	15,894
81,200	**81,250**	17,370	13,781	17,722	15,906
81,250	**81,300**	17,384	13,794	17,736	15,919
81,300	**81,350**	17,398	13,806	17,750	15,931
81,350	**81,400**	17,412	13,819	17,764	15,944
81,400	**81,450**	17,426	13,831	17,778	15,956
81,450	**81,500**	17,440	13,844	17,792	15,969
81,500	**81,550**	17,454	13,856	17,806	15,981
81,550	**81,600**	17,468	13,869	17,820	15,994
81,600	**81,650**	17,482	13,881	17,834	16,006
81,650	**81,700**	17,496	13,894	17,848	16,019
81,700	**81,750**	17,510	13,906	17,862	16,031
81,750	**81,800**	17,524	13,919	17,876	16,044
81,800	**81,850**	17,538	13,931	17,890	16,056
81,850	**81,900**	17,552	13,944	17,904	16,069
81,900	**81,950**	17,566	13,956	17,918	16,081
81,950	**82,000**	17,580	13,969	17,932	16,094
82,000					
82,000	**82,050**	17,594	13,981	17,946	16,106
82,050	**82,100**	17,608	13,994	17,960	16,119
82,100	**82,150**	17,622	14,006	17,974	16,131
82,150	**82,200**	17,636	14,019	17,988	16,144
82,200	**82,250**	17,650	14,031	18,002	16,156
82,250	**82,300**	17,664	14,044	18,016	16,169
82,300	**82,350**	17,678	14,056	18,030	16,181
82,350	**82,400**	17,692	14,069	18,044	16,194
82,400	**82,450**	17,706	14,081	18,058	16,206
82,450	**82,500**	17,720	14,094	18,072	16,219
82,500	**82,550**	17,734	14,106	18,086	16,231
82,550	**82,600**	17,748	14,119	18,100	16,244
82,600	**82,650**	17,762	14,131	18,114	16,256
82,650	**82,700**	17,776	14,144	18,128	16,269
82,700	**82,750**	17,790	14,156	18,142	16,281
82,750	**82,800**	17,804	14,169	18,156	16,294
82,800	**82,850**	17,818	14,181	18,170	16,306
82,850	**82,900**	17,832	14,194	18,184	16,319
82,900	**82,950**	17,846	14,206	18,198	16,331
82,950	**83,000**	17,860	14,219	18,212	16,344

If line 42 (taxable income) is— At least	But less than	Single	Married filing jointly *	Married filing separately	Head of a household
		Your tax is—			
83,000					
83,000	**83,050**	17,874	14,231	18,226	16,356
83,050	**83,100**	17,888	14,244	18,240	16,369
83,100	**83,150**	17,902	14,256	18,254	16,381
83,150	**83,200**	17,916	14,269	18,268	16,394
83,200	**83,250**	17,930	14,281	18,282	16,406
83,250	**83,300**	17,944	14,294	18,296	16,419
83,300	**83,350**	17,958	14,306	18,310	16,431
83,350	**83,400**	17,972	14,319	18,324	16,444
83,400	**83,450**	17,986	14,331	18,338	16,456
83,450	**83,500**	18,000	14,344	18,352	16,469
83,500	**83,550**	18,014	14,356	18,366	16,481
83,550	**83,600**	18,028	14,369	18,380	16,494
83,600	**83,650**	18,042	14,381	18,394	16,506
83,650	**83,700**	18,056	14,394	18,408	16,519
83,700	**83,750**	18,070	14,406	18,422	16,531
83,750	**83,800**	18,084	14,419	18,436	16,544
83,800	**83,850**	18,098	14,431	18,450	16,556
83,850	**83,900**	18,112	14,444	18,464	16,569
83,900	**83,950**	18,126	14,456	18,478	16,581
83,950	**84,000**	18,140	14,469	18,492	16,594
84,000					
84,000	**84,050**	18,154	14,481	18,506	16,606
84,050	**84,100**	18,168	14,494	18,520	16,619
84,100	**84,150**	18,182	14,506	18,534	16,631
84,150	**84,200**	18,196	14,519	18,548	16,644
84,200	**84,250**	18,210	14,531	18,562	16,656
84,250	**84,300**	18,224	14,544	18,576	16,669
84,300	**84,350**	18,238	14,556	18,590	16,681
84,350	**84,400**	18,252	14,569	18,604	16,694
84,400	**84,450**	18,266	14,581	18,618	16,706
84,450	**84,500**	18,280	14,594	18,632	16,719
84,500	**84,550**	18,294	14,606	18,646	16,731
84,550	**84,600**	18,308	14,619	18,660	16,744
84,600	**84,650**	18,322	14,631	18,674	16,756
84,650	**84,700**	18,336	14,644	18,688	16,769
84,700	**84,750**	18,350	14,656	18,702	16,781
84,750	**84,800**	18,364	14,669	18,716	16,794
84,800	**84,850**	18,378	14,681	18,730	16,806
84,850	**84,900**	18,392	14,694	18,744	16,819
84,900	**84,950**	18,406	14,706	18,758	16,831
84,950	**85,000**	18,420	14,719	18,772	16,844
85,000					
85,000	**85,050**	18,434	14,731	18,786	16,856
85,050	**85,100**	18,448	14,744	18,800	16,869
85,100	**85,150**	18,462	14,756	18,814	16,881
85,150	**85,200**	18,476	14,769	18,828	16,894
85,200	**85,250**	18,490	14,781	18,842	16,906
85,250	**85,300**	18,504	14,794	18,856	16,919
85,300	**85,350**	18,518	14,806	18,870	16,931
85,350	**85,400**	18,532	14,819	18,884	16,944
85,400	**85,450**	18,546	14,831	18,898	16,956
85,450	**85,500**	18,560	14,844	18,912	16,969
85,500	**85,550**	18,574	14,856	18,926	16,981
85,550	**85,600**	18,588	14,869	18,940	16,994
85,600	**85,650**	18,602	14,881	18,954	17,006
85,650	**85,700**	18,616	14,894	18,968	17,019
85,700	**85,750**	18,630	14,906	18,982	17,031
85,750	**85,800**	18,644	14,919	18,996	17,044
85,800	**85,850**	18,658	14,931	19,010	17,056
85,850	**85,900**	18,672	14,944	19,024	17,069
85,900	**85,950**	18,686	14,956	19,038	17,081
85,950	**86,000**	18,700	14,969	19,052	17,094

* This column must also be used by a qualifying widow(er).

(Continued on next page)

2004 Tax Table—*Continued*

If line 42 (taxable income) is— At least	But less than	And you are— Single	Married filing jointly *	Married filing separately	Head of a household
		Your tax is—			
86,000					
86,000	86,050	18,714	14,981	19,066	17,106
86,050	86,100	18,728	14,994	19,080	17,119
86,100	86,150	18,742	15,006	19,094	17,131
86,150	86,200	18,756	15,019	19,108	17,144
86,200	86,250	18,770	15,031	19,122	17,156
86,250	86,300	18,784	15,044	19,136	17,169
86,300	86,350	18,798	15,056	19,150	17,181
86,350	86,400	18,812	15,069	19,164	17,194
86,400	86,450	18,826	15,081	19,178	17,206
86,450	86,500	18,840	15,094	19,192	17,219
86,500	86,550	18,854	15,106	19,206	17,231
86,550	86,600	18,868	15,119	19,220	17,244
86,600	86,650	18,882	15,131	19,234	17,256
86,650	86,700	18,896	15,144	19,248	17,269
86,700	86,750	18,910	15,156	19,262	17,281
86,750	86,800	18,924	15,169	19,276	17,294
86,800	86,850	18,938	15,181	19,290	17,306
86,850	86,900	18,952	15,194	19,304	17,319
86,900	86,950	18,966	15,206	19,318	17,331
86,950	87,000	18,980	15,219	19,332	17,344
87,000					
87,000	87,050	18,994	15,231	19,346	17,356
87,050	87,100	19,008	15,244	19,360	17,369
87,100	87,150	19,022	15,256	19,374	17,381
87,150	87,200	19,036	15,269	19,388	17,394
87,200	87,250	19,050	15,281	19,402	17,406
87,250	87,300	19,064	15,294	19,416	17,419
87,300	87,350	19,078	15,306	19,430	17,431
87,350	87,400	19,092	15,319	19,444	17,444
87,400	87,450	19,106	15,331	19,458	17,456
87,450	87,500	19,120	15,344	19,472	17,469
87,500	87,550	19,134	15,356	19,486	17,481
87,550	87,600	19,148	15,369	19,500	17,494
87,600	87,650	19,162	15,381	19,514	17,506
87,650	87,700	19,176	15,394	19,528	17,519
87,700	87,750	19,190	15,406	19,542	17,531
87,750	87,800	19,204	15,419	19,556	17,544
87,800	87,850	19,218	15,431	19,570	17,556
87,850	87,900	19,232	15,444	19,584	17,569
87,900	87,950	19,246	15,456	19,598	17,581
87,950	88,000	19,260	15,469	19,612	17,594
88,000					
88,000	88,050	19,274	15,481	19,626	17,606
88,050	88,100	19,288	15,494	19,640	17,619
88,100	88,150	19,302	15,506	19,654	17,631
88,150	88,200	19,316	15,519	19,668	17,644
88,200	88,250	19,330	15,531	19,682	17,656
88,250	88,300	19,344	15,544	19,696	17,669
88,300	88,350	19,358	15,556	19,710	17,681
88,350	88,400	19,372	15,569	19,724	17,694
88,400	88,450	19,386	15,581	19,738	17,706
88,450	88,500	19,400	15,594	19,752	17,719
88,500	88,550	19,414	15,606	19,766	17,731
88,550	88,600	19,428	15,619	19,780	17,744
88,600	88,650	19,442	15,631	19,794	17,756
88,650	88,700	19,456	15,644	19,808	17,769
88,700	88,750	19,470	15,656	19,822	17,781
88,750	88,800	19,484	15,669	19,836	17,794
88,800	88,850	19,498	15,681	19,850	17,806
88,850	88,900	19,512	15,694	19,864	17,819
88,900	88,950	19,526	15,706	19,878	17,831
88,950	89,000	19,540	15,719	19,892	17,844

If line 42 (taxable income) is— At least	But less than	And you are— Single	Married filing jointly *	Married filing separately	Head of a household
		Your tax is—			
89,000					
89,000	89,050	19,554	15,731	19,906	17,856
89,050	89,100	19,568	15,744	19,920	17,869
89,100	89,150	19,582	15,756	19,934	17,881
89,150	89,200	19,596	15,769	19,948	17,894
89,200	89,250	19,610	15,781	19,962	17,906
89,250	89,300	19,624	15,794	19,976	17,919
89,300	89,350	19,638	15,806	19,990	17,931
89,350	89,400	19,652	15,819	20,006	17,944
89,400	89,450	19,666	15,831	20,023	17,956
89,450	89,500	19,680	15,844	20,039	17,969
89,500	89,550	19,694	15,856	20,056	17,981
89,550	89,600	19,708	15,869	20,072	17,994
89,600	89,650	19,722	15,881	20,089	18,006
89,650	89,700	19,736	15,894	20,105	18,019
89,700	89,750	19,750	15,906	20,122	18,031
89,750	89,800	19,764	15,919	20,138	18,044
89,800	89,850	19,778	15,931	20,155	18,056
89,850	89,900	19,792	15,944	20,171	18,069
89,900	89,950	19,806	15,956	20,188	18,081
89,950	90,000	19,820	15,969	20,204	18,094
90,000					
90,000	90,050	19,834	15,981	20,221	18,106
90,050	90,100	19,848	15,994	20,237	18,119
90,100	90,150	19,862	16,006	20,254	18,131
90,150	90,200	19,876	16,019	20,270	18,144
90,200	90,250	19,890	16,031	20,287	18,156
90,250	90,300	19,904	16,044	20,303	18,169
90,300	90,350	19,918	16,056	20,320	18,181
90,350	90,400	19,932	16,069	20,336	18,194
90,400	90,450	19,946	16,081	20,353	18,206
90,450	90,500	19,960	16,094	20,369	18,219
90,500	90,550	19,974	16,106	20,386	18,231
90,550	90,600	19,988	16,119	20,402	18,244
90,600	90,650	20,002	16,131	20,419	18,256
90,650	90,700	20,016	16,144	20,435	18,269
90,700	90,750	20,030	16,156	20,452	18,281
90,750	90,800	20,044	16,169	20,468	18,294
90,800	90,850	20,058	16,181	20,485	18,306
90,850	90,900	20,072	16,194	20,501	18,319
90,900	90,950	20,086	16,206	20,518	18,331
90,950	91,000	20,100	16,219	20,534	18,344
91,000					
91,000	91,050	20,114	16,231	20,551	18,356
91,050	91,100	20,128	16,244	20,567	18,369
91,100	91,150	20,142	16,256	20,584	18,381
91,150	91,200	20,156	16,269	20,600	18,394
91,200	91,250	20,170	16,281	20,617	18,406
91,250	91,300	20,184	16,294	20,633	18,419
91,300	91,350	20,198	16,306	20,650	18,431
91,350	91,400	20,212	16,319	20,666	18,444
91,400	91,450	20,226	16,331	20,683	18,456
91,450	91,500	20,240	16,344	20,699	18,469
91,500	91,550	20,254	16,356	20,716	18,481
91,550	91,600	20,268	16,369	20,732	18,494
91,600	91,650	20,282	16,381	20,749	18,506
91,650	91,700	20,296	16,394	20,765	18,519
91,700	91,750	20,310	16,406	20,782	18,531
91,750	91,800	20,324	16,419	20,798	18,544
91,800	91,850	20,338	16,431	20,815	18,556
91,850	91,900	20,352	16,444	20,831	18,569
91,900	91,950	20,366	16,456	20,848	18,581
91,950	92,000	20,380	16,469	20,864	18,594

If line 42 (taxable income) is— At least	But less than	And you are— Single	Married filing jointly *	Married filing separately	Head of a household
		Your tax is—			
92,000					
92,000	92,050	20,394	16,481	20,881	18,606
92,050	92,100	20,408	16,494	20,897	18,619
92,100	92,150	20,422	16,506	20,914	18,631
92,150	92,200	20,436	16,519	20,930	18,644
92,200	92,250	20,450	16,531	20,947	18,656
92,250	92,300	20,464	16,544	20,963	18,669
92,300	92,350	20,478	16,556	20,980	18,681
92,350	92,400	20,492	16,569	20,996	18,694
92,400	92,450	20,506	16,581	21,013	18,706
92,450	92,500	20,520	16,594	21,029	18,719
92,500	92,550	20,534	16,606	21,046	18,731
92,550	92,600	20,548	16,619	21,062	18,744
92,600	92,650	20,562	16,631	21,079	18,756
92,650	92,700	20,576	16,644	21,095	18,769
92,700	92,750	20,590	16,656	21,112	18,781
92,750	92,800	20,604	16,669	21,128	18,794
92,800	92,850	20,618	16,681	21,145	18,806
92,850	92,900	20,632	16,694	21,161	18,819
92,900	92,950	20,646	16,706	21,178	18,831
92,950	93,000	20,660	16,719	21,194	18,844
93,000					
93,000	93,050	20,674	16,731	21,211	18,856
93,050	93,100	20,688	16,744	21,227	18,869
93,100	93,150	20,702	16,756	21,244	18,881
93,150	93,200	20,716	16,769	21,260	18,894
93,200	93,250	20,730	16,781	21,277	18,906
93,250	93,300	20,744	16,794	21,293	18,919
93,300	93,350	20,758	16,806	21,310	18,931
93,350	93,400	20,772	16,819	21,326	18,944
93,400	93,450	20,786	16,831	21,343	18,956
93,450	93,500	20,800	16,844	21,359	18,969
93,500	93,550	20,814	16,856	21,376	18,981
93,550	93,600	20,828	16,869	21,392	18,994
93,600	93,650	20,842	16,881	21,409	19,006
93,650	93,700	20,856	16,894	21,425	19,019
93,700	93,750	20,870	16,906	21,442	19,031
93,750	93,800	20,884	16,919	21,458	19,044
93,800	93,850	20,898	16,931	21,475	19,056
93,850	93,900	20,912	16,944	21,491	19,069
93,900	93,950	20,926	16,956	21,508	19,081
93,950	94,000	20,940	16,969	21,524	19,094
94,000					
94,000	94,050	20,954	16,981	21,541	19,106
94,050	94,100	20,968	16,994	21,557	19,119
94,100	94,150	20,982	17,006	21,574	19,131
94,150	94,200	20,996	17,019	21,590	19,144
94,200	94,250	21,010	17,031	21,607	19,156
94,250	94,300	21,024	17,044	21,623	19,169
94,300	94,350	21,038	17,056	21,640	19,181
94,350	94,400	21,052	17,069	21,656	19,194
94,400	94,450	21,066	17,081	21,673	19,206
94,450	94,500	21,080	17,094	21,689	19,219
94,500	94,550	21,094	17,106	21,706	19,231
94,550	94,600	21,108	17,119	21,722	19,244
94,600	94,650	21,122	17,131	21,739	19,256
94,650	94,700	21,136	17,144	21,755	19,269
94,700	94,750	21,150	17,156	21,772	19,281
94,750	94,800	21,164	17,169	21,788	19,294
94,800	94,850	21,178	17,181	21,805	19,306
94,850	94,900	21,192	17,194	21,821	19,319
94,900	94,950	21,206	17,206	21,838	19,331
94,950	95,000	21,220	17,219	21,854	19,344

* This column must also be used by a qualifying widow(er).

(Continued on next page)

2004 Tax Table—*Continued*

If line 42 (taxable income) is—		And you are—			
At least	But less than	Single	Married filing jointly *	Married filing separately	Head of a household
		Your tax is—			
95,000					
95,000	**95,050**	21,234	17,231	21,871	19,356
95,050	**95,100**	21,248	17,244	21,887	19,369
95,100	**95,150**	21,262	17,256	21,904	19,381
95,150	**95,200**	21,276	17,269	21,920	19,394
95,200	**95,250**	21,290	17,281	21,937	19,406
95,250	**95,300**	21,304	17,294	21,953	19,419
95,300	**95,350**	21,318	17,306	21,970	19,431
95,350	**95,400**	21,332	17,319	21,986	19,444
95,400	**95,450**	21,346	17,331	22,003	19,456
95,450	**95,500**	21,360	17,344	22,019	19,469
95,500	**95,550**	21,374	17,356	22,036	19,481
95,550	**95,600**	21,388	17,369	22,052	19,494
95,600	**95,650**	21,402	17,381	22,069	19,506
95,650	**95,700**	21,416	17,394	22,085	19,519
95,700	**95,750**	21,430	17,406	22,102	19,531
95,750	**95,800**	21,444	17,419	22,118	19,544
95,800	**95,850**	21,458	17,431	22,135	19,556
95,850	**95,900**	21,472	17,444	22,151	19,569
95,900	**95,950**	21,486	17,456	22,168	19,581
95,950	**96,000**	21,500	17,469	22,184	19,594
96,000					
96,000	**96,050**	21,514	17,481	22,201	19,606
96,050	**96,100**	21,528	17,494	22,217	19,619
96,100	**96,150**	21,542	17,506	22,234	19,631
96,150	**96,200**	21,556	17,519	22,250	19,644
96,200	**96,250**	21,570	17,531	22,267	19,656
96,250	**96,300**	21,584	17,544	22,283	19,669
96,300	**96,350**	21,598	17,556	22,300	19,681
96,350	**96,400**	21,612	17,569	22,316	19,694
96,400	**96,450**	21,626	17,581	22,333	19,706
96,450	**96,500**	21,640	17,594	22,349	19,719
96,500	**96,550**	21,654	17,606	22,366	19,731
96,550	**96,600**	21,668	17,619	22,382	19,744
96,600	**96,650**	21,682	17,631	22,399	19,756
96,650	**96,700**	21,696	17,644	22,415	19,769
96,700	**96,750**	21,710	17,656	22,432	19,781
96,750	**96,800**	21,724	17,669	22,448	19,794
96,800	**96,850**	21,738	17,681	22,465	19,806
96,850	**96,900**	21,752	17,694	22,481	19,819
96,900	**96,950**	21,766	17,706	22,498	19,831
96,950	**97,000**	21,780	17,719	22,514	19,844
97,000					
97,000	**97,050**	21,794	17,731	22,531	19,856
97,050	**97,100**	21,808	17,744	22,547	19,869
97,100	**97,150**	21,822	17,756	22,564	19,881
97,150	**97,200**	21,836	17,769	22,580	19,894
97,200	**97,250**	21,850	17,781	22,597	19,906
97,250	**97,300**	21,864	17,794	22,613	19,919
97,300	**97,350**	21,878	17,806	22,630	19,931
97,350	**97,400**	21,892	17,819	22,646	19,944
97,400	**97,450**	21,906	17,831	22,663	19,956
97,450	**97,500**	21,920	17,844	22,679	19,969
97,500	**97,550**	21,934	17,856	22,696	19,981
97,550	**97,600**	21,948	17,869	22,712	19,994
97,600	**97,650**	21,962	17,881	22,729	20,006
97,650	**97,700**	21,976	17,894	22,745	20,019
97,700	**97,750**	21,990	17,906	22,762	20,031
97,750	**97,800**	22,004	17,919	22,778	20,044
97,800	**97,850**	22,018	17,931	22,795	20,056
97,850	**97,900**	22,032	17,944	22,811	20,069
97,900	**97,950**	22,046	17,956	22,828	20,081
97,950	**98,000**	22,060	17,969	22,844	20,094
98,000					
98,000	**98,050**	22,074	17,981	22,861	20,106
98,050	**98,100**	22,088	17,994	22,877	20,119
98,100	**98,150**	22,102	18,006	22,894	20,131
98,150	**98,200**	22,116	18,019	22,910	20,144
98,200	**98,250**	22,130	18,031	22,927	20,156
98,250	**98,300**	22,144	18,044	22,943	20,169
98,300	**98,350**	22,158	18,056	22,960	20,181
98,350	**98,400**	22,172	18,069	22,976	20,194
98,400	**98,450**	22,186	18,081	22,993	20,206
98,450	**98,500**	22,200	18,094	23,009	20,219
98,500	**98,550**	22,214	18,106	23,026	20,231
98,550	**98,600**	22,228	18,119	23,042	20,244
98,600	**98,650**	22,242	18,131	23,059	20,256
98,650	**98,700**	22,256	18,144	23,075	20,269
98,700	**98,750**	22,270	18,156	23,092	20,281
98,750	**98,800**	22,284	18,169	23,108	20,294
98,800	**98,850**	22,298	18,181	23,125	20,306
98,850	**98,900**	22,312	18,194	23,141	20,319
98,900	**98,950**	22,326	18,206	23,158	20,331
98,950	**99,000**	22,340	18,219	23,174	20,344
99,000					
99,000	**99,050**	22,354	18,231	23,191	20,356
99,050	**99,100**	22,368	18,244	23,207	20,369
99,100	**99,150**	22,382	18,256	23,224	20,381
99,150	**99,200**	22,396	18,269	23,240	20,394
99,200	**99,250**	22,410	18,281	23,257	20,406
99,250	**99,300**	22,424	18,294	23,273	20,419
99,300	**99,350**	22,438	18,306	23,290	20,431
99,350	**99,400**	22,452	18,319	23,306	20,444
99,400	**99,450**	22,466	18,331	23,323	20,456
99,450	**99,500**	22,480	18,344	23,339	20,469
99,500	**99,550**	22,494	18,356	23,356	20,481
99,550	**99,600**	22,508	18,369	23,372	20,494
99,600	**99,650**	22,522	18,381	23,389	20,506
99,650	**99,700**	22,536	18,394	23,405	20,519
99,700	**99,750**	22,550	18,406	23,422	20,531
99,750	**99,800**	22,564	18,419	23,438	20,544
99,800	**99,850**	22,578	18,431	23,455	20,556
99,850	**99,900**	22,592	18,444	23,471	20,569
99,900	**99,950**	22,606	18,456	23,488	20,581
99,950	**100,000**	22,620	18,469	23,504	20,594

$100,000 or over — use the Tax Rate Schedules on page A–2

* This column must also be used by a qualifying widow(er).

2004 Optional Sales Tax Tables

When Used. The election to deduct state and local general sales taxes requires that the taxpayer forgo any deduction for state and local income taxes. Further, the use of the optional sales tax tables means that the actual expense method is not chosen. The actual expense method cannot be used when the amount claimed is not supported by actual receipts.

Adjustments Necessary. The optional sales tax tables are based on a number of assumptions that require adjustments to be made. As the starting point for the use of the tables is AGI, nontaxable receipts have not been included. Examples of receipts that should be added include: tax-exempt interest, veterans' benefits, workers' compensation, nontaxable social security and other retirement benefits. But do not include any large nontaxable items that are not likely to be spent. For example, a $100,000 inheritance should not be added if it was invested in a certificate of deposit.

Because the tables are based on the state general sales tax rate, an adjustment has to be made for any local (city, county, transit authority, etc.) tax imposed.

The tables represent the sales tax on the average (and recurring) expenditures based on level of income by family size and do not include exceptional purchases. Therefore, add to the table amount any sales taxes on major purchases (such as motor vehicles, aircraft, boats, and home building materials, etc.).

Use Illustrated.

EXAMPLE. The Archers file a joint return for 2004 reflecting AGI of $88,000 and claiming three exemptions. They have tax-exempt interest of $3,000, and during the year, they incurred sales tax of $1,650 on the purchase of an automobile for their dependent teenage son. They live in Bellaire, Texas, where the general sales tax rates are 6.25% (0.0625) for state and 2% (0.02) for local.

Using the Worksheet appearing below, the general sales tax deduction is $3,062. As Texas imposes no state or local income tax, no choice is necessary, and the $3,062 can be claimed by the Archers as an itemized deduction on Schedule A.

Sales Tax Deduction Worksheet

Adjusted Gross Income (AGI) as listed on line 37 of Form 1040		88,000
Add nontaxable items		3,000
Table income to be used for purposes of line 1 below		91,000
1. Use table income to determine table amount—go to state of residence and find applicable range of table income and exemption column* for *state* sales tax		1,070
2a. Enter local general sales tax rate	0.02	
2b. Enter state general sales tax rate**	0.0625	
2c. Divide 2a by 2b	0.32	
2d. Multiply line 1 by line 2c for the local sales tax		342
3. Enter general sales tax on large purchases		1,650
4. Deduction for general sales tax (add lines 1 + 2d + 3) and report on line 5 of Schedule A of Form 1040		3,062

*Use total of personal and dependency exemptions as reported in item 6d of Form 1040.
**Due to change in rates during 2004 use: .059 for Arkansas, .061 for California, and .037 for Virginia.

2004 Optional State Sales Tax Tables

Alaska residents only. If you paid any local sales taxes, you must use your actual expenses to figure your deduction.

Alabama

Income At least	But less than	Exemptions 1	2	3	4	5	Over 5
$0	$20,000	288	344	381	410	434	468
20,000	30,000	366	434	481	517	547	590
30,000	40,000	416	494	547	587	621	669
40,000	50,000	460	545	602	647	684	736
50,000	60,000	498	590	652	700	740	796
60,000	70,000	532	630	695	747	789	849
70,000	80,000	565	667	737	791	835	898
80,000	90,000	593	701	773	830	877	942
90,000	100,000	621	733	809	868	916	985
100,000	120,000	657	775	855	917	968	1040
120,000	140,000	706	832	916	982	1037	1114
140,000	160,000	749	881	971	1040	1098	1179
160,000	180,000	789	928	1022	1095	1155	1240
180,000	200,000	827	972	1070	1146	1209	1298
200,000 or more		995	1166	1281	1371	1445	1549

Arizona

Income At least	But less than	Exemptions 1	2	3	4	5	Over 5
$0	$20,000	332	374	402	422	439	463
20,000	30,000	430	485	520	547	568	598
30,000	40,000	496	558	599	629	654	688
40,000	50,000	552	621	666	699	727	765
50,000	60,000	603	678	726	763	792	833
60,000	70,000	648	728	780	819	851	895
70,000	80,000	690	776	831	872	906	952
80,000	90,000	728	818	876	920	955	1004
90,000	100,000	765	859	920	965	1003	1054
100,000	120,000	814	913	977	1026	1065	1119
120,000	140,000	878	985	1054	1106	1148	1206
140,000	160,000	935	1048	1122	1177	1222	1283
160,000	180,000	990	1109	1186	1244	1292	1357
180,000	200,000	1041	1166	1247	1308	1357	1425
200,000 or more		1267	1417	1514	1587	1647	1728

Arkansas

Income At least	But less than	Exemptions 1	2	3	4	5	Over 5
$0	$20,000	430	510	564	605	640	688
20,000	30,000	542	641	708	760	803	863
30,000	40,000	616	727	802	860	908	976
40,000	50,000	678	800	882	945	998	1072
50,000	60,000	734	864	952	1021	1077	1157
60,000	70,000	783	922	1015	1088	1148	1232
70,000	80,000	829	976	1074	1150	1214	1302
80,000	90,000	871	1023	1126	1206	1272	1365
90,000	100,000	910	1070	1177	1260	1328	1425
100,000	120,000	962	1130	1242	1330	1402	1503
120,000	140,000	1031	1210	1330	1422	1499	1607
140,000	160,000	1093	1280	1407	1504	1585	1699
160,000	180,000	1151	1347	1479	1582	1667	1785
180,000	200,000	1205	1410	1548	1654	1743	1866
200,000 or more		1443	1684	1846	1971	2074	2220

California

Income At least	But less than	Exemptions 1	2	3	4	5	Over 5
$0	$20,000	363	416	451	477	499	529
20,000	30,000	469	537	581	615	643	681
30,000	40,000	540	617	668	706	738	782
40,000	50,000	600	685	741	784	819	867
50,000	60,000	654	747	807	854	892	944
60,000	70,000	702	801	866	916	956	1012
70,000	80,000	748	853	922	974	1017	1077
80,000	90,000	789	899	971	1027	1072	1134
90,000	100,000	828	944	1019	1077	1124	1189
100,000	120,000	880	1002	1082	1143	1193	1262
120,000	140,000	949	1080	1166	1232	1285	1359
140,000	160,000	1010	1149	1240	1310	1366	1445
160,000	180,000	1069	1215	1311	1384	1444	1526
180,000	200,000	1123	1277	1377	1454	1516	1602
200,000 or more		1365	1549	1669	1761	1835	1939

Colorado

Income At least	But less than	Exemptions 1	2	3	4	5	Over 5
$0	$20,000	160	183	197	208	217	230
20,000	30,000	209	238	257	271	283	299
30,000	40,000	242	275	297	313	327	345
40,000	50,000	271	307	331	349	364	384
50,000	60,000	296	336	362	382	398	420
60,000	70,000	319	362	390	411	428	452
70,000	80,000	341	386	416	438	457	482
80,000	90,000	360	408	439	463	482	509
90,000	100,000	379	429	462	487	507	535
100,000	120,000	404	457	492	518	539	569
120,000	140,000	437	494	531	560	583	614
140,000	160,000	466	527	567	597	621	655
160,000	180,000	494	559	600	632	658	694
180,000	200,000	521	588	632	665	693	730
200,000 or more		638	720	773	813	846	891

Connecticut

Income At least	But less than	Exemptions 1	2	3	4	5	Over 5
$0	$20,000	338	387	419	444	464	492
20,000	30,000	440	503	545	577	603	639
30,000	40,000	509	581	629	665	695	736
40,000	50,000	567	647	700	740	773	819
50,000	60,000	620	707	764	808	844	894
60,000	70,000	667	760	822	869	907	960
70,000	80,000	712	811	876	926	966	1023
80,000	90,000	751	856	924	976	1019	1079
90,000	100,000	790	899	971	1026	1071	1133
100,000	120,000	840	956	1032	1090	1138	1204
120,000	140,000	908	1032	1114	1177	1228	1298
140,000	160,000	968	1100	1187	1253	1307	1382
160,000	180,000	1025	1164	1256	1325	1383	1462
180,000	200,000	1079	1225	1320	1394	1454	1536
200,000 or more		1315	1491	1606	1694	1766	1866

District of Columbia

Income At least	But less than	Exemptions 1	2	3	4	5	Over 5
$0	$20,000	327	375	407	431	451	478
20,000	30,000	428	490	531	563	588	624
30,000	40,000	496	568	615	651	680	721
40,000	50,000	555	635	687	727	759	805
50,000	60,000	608	695	752	795	831	880
60,000	70,000	655	748	810	856	894	947
70,000	80,000	700	799	864	914	954	1011
80,000	90,000	740	845	913	966	1008	1067
90,000	100,000	779	889	961	1016	1060	1122
100,000	120,000	831	947	1023	1082	1129	1195
120,000	140,000	900	1025	1107	1170	1221	1292
140,000	160,000	961	1094	1181	1248	1302	1377
160,000	180,000	1019	1160	1252	1322	1380	1459
180,000	200,000	1074	1222	1319	1393	1453	1536
200,000 or more		1319	1498	1615	1704	1777	1877

Florida

Income At least	But less than	Exemptions 1	2	3	4	5	Over 5
$0	$20,000	394	450	487	515	537	569
20,000	30,000	509	580	627	662	691	731
30,000	40,000	585	666	720	760	793	838
40,000	50,000	650	740	799	843	880	930
50,000	60,000	709	806	870	918	957	1012
60,000	70,000	761	865	933	984	1027	1085
70,000	80,000	810	920	992	1047	1092	1153
80,000	90,000	854	970	1045	1103	1150	1215
90,000	100,000	896	1018	1097	1157	1206	1274
100,000	120,000	952	1080	1164	1228	1280	1351
120,000	140,000	1026	1164	1254	1322	1378	1455
140,000	160,000	1092	1238	1333	1406	1465	1546
160,000	180,000	1155	1309	1409	1485	1547	1633
180,000	200,000	1214	1375	1480	1560	1625	1714
200,000 or more		1474	1667	1792	1888	1965	2073

Georgia

Income At least	But less than	Exemptions 1	2	3	4	5	Over 5
$0	$20,000	247	285	310	330	345	367
20,000	30,000	328	377	410	435	455	484
30,000	40,000	382	439	477	506	529	562
40,000	50,000	429	493	535	567	593	630
50,000	60,000	471	541	587	622	651	691
60,000	70,000	509	584	634	672	703	746
70,000	80,000	545	625	678	719	752	798
80,000	90,000	578	662	718	761	796	844
90,000	100,000	609	698	757	802	838	889
100,000	120,000	651	746	808	855	894	949
120,000	140,000	707	809	876	927	969	1028
140,000	160,000	757	865	937	991	1036	1099
160,000	180,000	804	919	995	1053	1100	1166
180,000	200,000	849	970	1050	1110	1160	1230
200,000 or more		1049	1196	1293	1367	1428	1512

Hawaii

Income At least	But less than	Exemptions 1	2	3	4	5	Over 5
$0	$20,000	325	386	428	460	487	525
20,000	30,000	416	493	545	586	620	667
30,000	40,000	476	564	623	669	707	761
40,000	50,000	527	624	689	739	781	840
50,000	60,000	573	677	747	802	847	911
60,000	70,000	614	725	800	858	906	974
70,000	80,000	652	770	849	910	961	1033
80,000	90,000	687	809	892	957	1010	1085
90,000	100,000	720	848	935	1002	1058	1136
100,000	120,000	763	899	990	1061	1120	1202
120,000	140,000	821	966	1063	1139	1202	1290
140,000	160,000	873	1025	1129	1209	1275	1368
160,000	180,000	921	1082	1190	1274	1344	1442
180,000	200,000	967	1135	1248	1336	1409	1511
200,000 or more		1169	1368	1502	1607	1693	1814

Idaho

Income At least	But less than	Exemptions 1	2	3	4	5	Over 5
$0	$20,000	405	482	535	575	609	657
20,000	30,000	519	615	681	732	775	835
30,000	40,000	594	703	777	835	883	951
40,000	50,000	658	778	859	923	976	1050
50,000	60,000	715	845	933	1001	1058	1138
60,000	70,000	767	904	998	1071	1131	1216
70,000	80,000	815	960	1059	1136	1200	1290
80,000	90,000	858	1010	1114	1194	1261	1355
90,000	100,000	900	1059	1166	1250	1320	1418
100,000	120,000	954	1122	1236	1324	1398	1501
120,000	140,000	1027	1206	1327	1422	1500	1611
140,000	160,000	1092	1281	1409	1508	1591	1708
160,000	180,000	1153	1352	1486	1591	1677	1800
180,000	200,000	1211	1418	1558	1668	1758	1886
200,000 or more		1467	1711	1877	2006	2113	2264

Illinois

Income At least	But less than	Exemptions 1	2	3	4	5	Over 5
$0	$20,000	480	578	644	696	740	801
20,000	30,000	603	723	806	870	924	999
30,000	40,000	683	819	911	983	1043	1128
40,000	50,000	751	899	999	1078	1144	1236
50,000	60,000	812	970	1078	1163	1233	1332
60,000	70,000	866	1034	1148	1237	1312	1417
70,000	80,000	916	1093	1213	1308	1386	1496
80,000	90,000	961	1146	1272	1370	1452	1567
90,000	100,000	1005	1197	1327	1430	1515	1635
100,000	120,000	1061	1263	1401	1508	1597	1723
120,000	140,000	1137	1351	1497	1611	1706	1840
140,000	160,000	1203	1429	1583	1703	1803	1943
160,000	180,000	1266	1503	1664	1789	1893	2041
180,000	200,000	1326	1572	1739	1870	1979	2132
200,000 or more		1585	1874	2069	2222	2349	2529

(Continued)

2004 Optional State Sales Tax Tables *(Continued)*

Indiana

Income: At least	Income: But less than	Exemptions: 1	2	3	4	5	Over 5
$0	$20,000	375	431	467	495	518	550
20,000	30,000	489	561	608	644	673	714
30,000	40,000	566	648	702	743	776	823
40,000	50,000	631	722	782	828	865	917
50,000	60,000	691	789	854	904	944	1001
60,000	70,000	744	849	919	972	1015	1076
70,000	80,000	794	906	980	1036	1082	1146
80,000	90,000	839	957	1035	1094	1142	1210
90,000	100,000	882	1006	1088	1150	1200	1271
100,000	120,000	940	1071	1157	1223	1277	1351
120,000	140,000	1016	1157	1250	1321	1379	1459
140,000	160,000	1085	1234	1333	1408	1469	1554
160,000	180,000	1150	1308	1411	1490	1555	1645
180,000	200,000	1211	1377	1485	1568	1636	1730
200,000 or more		1483	1682	1813	1913	1994	2107

Iowa

Income: At least	Income: But less than	Exemptions: 1	2	3	4	5	Over 5
$0	$20,000	304	348	377	399	417	442
20,000	30,000	400	457	494	523	546	578
30,000	40,000	465	530	573	606	632	669
40,000	50,000	520	593	641	677	707	748
50,000	60,000	570	650	702	741	774	819
60,000	70,000	616	701	757	799	834	882
70,000	80,000	658	749	808	854	891	942
80,000	90,000	696	792	855	902	941	995
90,000	100,000	734	834	900	950	991	1047
100,000	120,000	783	889	959	1012	1056	1116
120,000	140,000	848	963	1038	1095	1142	1207
140,000	160,000	906	1029	1109	1169	1219	1288
160,000	180,000	962	1091	1176	1240	1293	1365
180,000	200,000	1015	1150	1239	1307	1362	1438
200,000 or more		1249	1413	1520	1602	1669	1761

Kansas

Income: At least	Income: But less than	Exemptions: 1	2	3	4	5	Over 5
$0	$20,000	390	464	514	553	585	631
20,000	30,000	496	589	652	700	741	798
30,000	40,000	566	671	742	797	843	907
40,000	50,000	626	741	819	879	929	999
50,000	60,000	679	803	887	952	1006	1082
60,000	70,000	727	858	948	1017	1074	1155
70,000	80,000	771	910	1004	1078	1138	1223
80,000	90,000	811	957	1055	1132	1195	1284
90,000	100,000	849	1001	1104	1184	1250	1343
100,000	120,000	900	1060	1168	1252	1322	1420
120,000	140,000	966	1138	1253	1343	1417	1521
140,000	160,000	1026	1206	1328	1423	1501	1611
160,000	180,000	1082	1272	1399	1499	1581	1696
180,000	200,000	1135	1333	1466	1570	1656	1776
200,000 or more		1367	1601	1759	1881	1983	2125

Kentucky

Income: At least	Income: But less than	Exemptions: 1	2	3	4	5	Over 5
$0	$20,000	337	388	421	446	467	496
20,000	30,000	441	507	549	582	609	646
30,000	40,000	511	586	635	673	704	747
40,000	50,000	572	655	709	751	785	833
50,000	60,000	626	716	776	821	858	910
60,000	70,000	675	772	835	884	924	979
70,000	80,000	721	824	892	943	986	1045
80,000	90,000	762	871	942	997	1041	1103
90,000	100,000	802	916	991	1048	1095	1160
100,000	120,000	855	976	1055	1116	1166	1234
120,000	140,000	925	1056	1141	1206	1260	1334
140,000	160,000	988	1127	1217	1287	1343	1422
160,000	180,000	1048	1194	1290	1363	1423	1506
180,000	200,000	1104	1258	1359	1436	1498	1585
200,000 or more		1355	1541	1662	1755	1831	1936

Louisiana

Income: At least	Income: But less than	Exemptions: 1	2	3	4	5	Over 5
$0	$20,000	216	247	268	283	296	313
20,000	30,000	282	322	349	369	385	408
30,000	40,000	327	373	403	426	445	470
40,000	50,000	365	416	449	475	496	524
50,000	60,000	399	455	491	519	541	573
60,000	70,000	430	489	528	558	582	616
70,000	80,000	459	522	564	595	621	657
80,000	90,000	485	551	595	628	656	693
90,000	100,000	510	580	626	661	689	728
100,000	120,000	543	617	666	703	733	775
120,000	140,000	587	667	719	759	792	837
140,000	160,000	626	711	767	809	844	892
160,000	180,000	664	754	812	857	893	944
180,000	200,000	699	793	855	902	940	993
200,000 or more		855	969	1043	1100	1146	1209

Maine

Income: At least	Income: But less than	Exemptions: 1	2	3	4	5	Over 5
$0	$20,000	264	301	325	344	359	379
20,000	30,000	352	400	432	456	475	502
30,000	40,000	411	467	504	532	554	586
40,000	50,000	463	525	566	597	623	658
50,000	60,000	509	578	622	656	684	723
60,000	70,000	551	625	673	710	740	781
70,000	80,000	591	670	721	760	792	836
80,000	90,000	627	710	765	806	840	886
90,000	100,000	662	749	806	850	885	934
100,000	120,000	708	801	862	908	946	998
120,000	140,000	770	870	936	986	1027	1083
140,000	160,000	825	932	1002	1056	1099	1159
160,000	180,000	878	992	1066	1122	1168	1232
180,000	200,000	928	1047	1126	1185	1233	1300
200,000 or more		1151	1297	1392	1465	1524	1605

Maryland

Income: At least	Income: But less than	Exemptions: 1	2	3	4	5	Over 5
$0	$20,000	241	280	306	326	343	366
20,000	30,000	326	378	413	440	462	493
30,000	40,000	384	445	486	517	543	579
40,000	50,000	435	504	549	585	614	654
50,000	60,000	481	557	607	646	678	722
60,000	70,000	523	605	659	701	736	784
70,000	80,000	563	650	709	754	791	842
80,000	90,000	599	692	753	801	840	895
90,000	100,000	634	732	797	847	888	946
100,000	120,000	680	785	854	908	952	1014
120,000	140,000	743	856	932	990	1038	1105
140,000	160,000	799	920	1001	1063	1114	1186
160,000	180,000	852	981	1067	1133	1188	1264
180,000	200,000	903	1039	1130	1200	1257	1337
200,000 or more		1131	1299	1411	1497	1568	1667

Massachusetts

Income: At least	Income: But less than	Exemptions: 1	2	3	4	5	Over 5
$0	$20,000	279	315	339	357	372	392
20,000	30,000	370	418	449	473	492	519
30,000	40,000	432	487	524	551	573	604
40,000	50,000	485	547	588	618	643	677
50,000	60,000	534	602	646	679	706	744
60,000	70,000	578	651	698	734	763	804
70,000	80,000	619	697	748	786	817	860
80,000	90,000	656	739	792	832	865	911
90,000	100,000	692	779	835	878	912	960
100,000	120,000	740	832	892	937	974	1025
120,000	140,000	804	904	968	1017	1057	1112
140,000	160,000	861	967	1036	1088	1131	1189
160,000	180,000	916	1028	1101	1156	1201	1263
180,000	200,000	967	1086	1162	1221	1268	1333
200,000 or more		1198	1342	1436	1506	1564	1643

Michigan

Income: At least	Income: But less than	Exemptions: 1	2	3	4	5	Over 5
$0	$20,000	349	396	426	450	469	495
20,000	30,000	448	507	545	575	599	632
30,000	40,000	514	580	624	657	684	722
40,000	50,000	570	643	691	727	757	798
50,000	60,000	621	699	751	790	822	867
60,000	70,000	666	749	804	846	880	927
70,000	80,000	708	796	854	898	934	984
80,000	90,000	746	838	899	945	983	1035
90,000	100,000	783	879	942	990	1030	1084
100,000	120,000	831	933	999	1050	1091	1148
120,000	140,000	896	1004	1074	1128	1173	1234
140,000	160,000	953	1067	1141	1198	1245	1309
160,000	180,000	1007	1127	1205	1265	1313	1381
180,000	200,000	1059	1183	1264	1327	1378	1448
200,000 or more		1285	1431	1527	1600	1660	1744

Minnesota

Income: At least	Income: But less than	Exemptions: 1	2	3	4	5	Over 5
$0	$20,000	379	429	462	487	508	536
20,000	30,000	495	561	603	636	662	698
30,000	40,000	573	649	698	735	765	806
40,000	50,000	640	724	778	820	853	899
50,000	60,000	701	792	851	896	933	983
60,000	70,000	755	853	916	964	1003	1057
70,000	80,000	806	910	978	1029	1071	1128
80,000	90,000	852	962	1033	1087	1130	1191
90,000	100,000	896	1011	1086	1142	1188	1252
100,000	120,000	955	1077	1156	1216	1265	1332
120,000	140,000	1033	1164	1250	1314	1367	1439
140,000	160,000	1102	1242	1333	1401	1457	1534
160,000	180,000	1168	1316	1412	1484	1543	1624
180,000	200,000	1231	1386	1486	1562	1624	1710
200,000 or more		1507	1695	1816	1908	1983	2085

Mississippi

Income: At least	Income: But less than	Exemptions: 1	2	3	4	5	Over 5
$0	$20,000	510	607	673	724	766	826
20,000	30,000	643	762	844	907	959	1033
30,000	40,000	729	864	955	1026	1085	1167
40,000	50,000	802	949	1049	1126	1191	1281
50,000	60,000	868	1026	1133	1216	1285	1381
60,000	70,000	926	1093	1207	1295	1368	1470
70,000	80,000	980	1157	1276	1369	1446	1554
80,000	90,000	1029	1213	1338	1434	1515	1628
90,000	100,000	1075	1267	1397	1498	1581	1699
100,000	120,000	1137	1338	1475	1580	1668	1792
120,000	140,000	1218	1432	1577	1690	1783	1914
140,000	160,000	1290	1515	1668	1786	1885	2023
160,000	180,000	1358	1594	1754	1878	1981	2125
180,000	200,000	1421	1668	1834	1963	2070	2221
200,000 or more		1701	1990	2185	2336	2461	2637

Missouri

Income: At least	Income: But less than	Exemptions: 1	2	3	4	5	Over 5
$0	$20,000	323	385	427	460	488	527
20,000	30,000	409	487	539	580	614	662
30,000	40,000	466	553	612	658	697	751
40,000	50,000	514	609	674	724	766	825
50,000	60,000	557	660	729	783	828	892
60,000	70,000	595	704	778	836	883	951
70,000	80,000	631	746	824	885	935	1006
80,000	90,000	663	783	865	928	981	1055
90,000	100,000	694	819	904	970	1025	1102
100,000	120,000	735	866	955	1025	1083	1164
120,000	140,000	789	929	1024	1098	1159	1246
140,000	160,000	837	984	1084	1162	1227	1318
160,000	180,000	882	1037	1141	1223	1290	1386
180,000	200,000	925	1086	1195	1280	1350	1450
200,000 or more		1112	1301	1429	1529	1612	1728

Nebraska

Income: At least	Income: But less than	Exemptions: 1	2	3	4	5	Over 5
$0	$20,000	318	363	392	414	432	457
20,000	30,000	417	475	513	541	565	597
30,000	40,000	484	550	594	627	654	691
40,000	50,000	541	615	663	700	730	771
50,000	60,000	593	674	726	766	799	844
60,000	70,000	639	726	782	825	860	908
70,000	80,000	683	775	835	881	918	970
80,000	90,000	723	820	883	931	970	1024
90,000	100,000	761	863	929	980	1021	1078
100,000	120,000	811	920	990	1044	1087	1147
120,000	140,000	879	995	1071	1129	1176	1241
140,000	160,000	939	1063	1143	1205	1255	1324
160,000	180,000	996	1127	1212	1277	1330	1403
180,000	200,000	1050	1187	1277	1345	1400	1477
200,000 or more		1289	1456	1564	1647	1714	1806

Nevada

Income: At least	Income: But less than	Exemptions: 1	2	3	4	5	Over 5
$0	$20,000	304	355	389	415	437	467
20,000	30,000	406	472	517	551	579	619
30,000	40,000	474	551	603	643	675	721
40,000	50,000	534	620	677	722	758	810
50,000	60,000	588	682	745	794	834	890
60,000	70,000	636	738	806	858	901	961
70,000	80,000	682	791	863	919	965	1029
80,000	90,000	724	838	915	974	1022	1090
90,000	100,000	764	884	965	1027	1078	1149
100,000	120,000	817	945	1031	1097	1151	1228
120,000	140,000	888	1027	1120	1191	1250	1332
140,000	160,000	952	1100	1198	1275	1337	1425
160,000	180,000	1012	1169	1274	1355	1421	1514
180,000	200,000	1070	1235	1345	1430	1500	1597
200,000 or more		1326	1528	1662	1765	1851	1970

New Jersey

Income: At least	Income: But less than	Exemptions: 1	2	3	4	5	Over 5
$0	$20,000	317	367	400	425	446	475
20,000	30,000	418	482	525	558	585	623
30,000	40,000	485	560	610	647	679	722
40,000	50,000	544	627	682	724	759	807
50,000	60,000	597	688	748	794	831	884
60,000	70,000	644	742	806	856	896	953
70,000	80,000	689	793	862	914	957	1017
80,000	90,000	730	839	911	967	1012	1076
90,000	100,000	769	884	960	1018	1066	1132
100,000	120,000	821	943	1023	1085	1136	1206
120,000	140,000	890	1021	1108	1175	1229	1305
140,000	160,000	951	1091	1184	1255	1313	1394
160,000	180,000	1010	1158	1256	1331	1392	1478
180,000	200,000	1066	1222	1324	1403	1467	1557
200,000 or more		1313	1502	1626	1722	1800	1908

New Mexico

Income: At least	Income: But less than	Exemptions: 1	2	3	4	5	Over 5
$0	$20,000	371	439	484	519	548	589
20,000	30,000	471	555	611	655	691	742
30,000	40,000	536	631	695	744	785	842
40,000	50,000	592	696	766	820	864	927
50,000	60,000	641	753	829	887	935	1003
60,000	70,000	686	805	885	947	998	1069
70,000	80,000	727	853	937	1002	1056	1132
80,000	90,000	764	896	984	1052	1109	1188
90,000	100,000	800	937	1029	1100	1159	1241
100,000	120,000	847	991	1088	1163	1225	1312
120,000	140,000	909	1063	1166	1246	1312	1405
140,000	160,000	964	1126	1235	1320	1389	1487
160,000	180,000	1016	1187	1301	1389	1462	1564
180,000	200,000	1065	1243	1362	1454	1531	1637
200,000 or more		1281	1491	1631	1740	1830	1955

New York

Income: At least	Income: But less than	Exemptions: 1	2	3	4	5	Over 5
$0	$20,000	224	262	287	306	322	344
20,000	30,000	296	345	378	403	424	453
30,000	40,000	345	401	439	468	492	526
40,000	50,000	387	450	492	524	551	588
50,000	60,000	425	494	540	575	604	645
60,000	70,000	459	533	582	620	652	696
70,000	80,000	491	570	623	663	697	743
80,000	90,000	520	604	659	702	737	786
90,000	100,000	549	636	694	739	776	828
100,000	120,000	586	679	741	788	828	883
120,000	140,000	635	736	802	854	896	956
140,000	160,000	680	786	858	912	958	1021
160,000	180,000	722	835	910	968	1016	1083
180,000	200,000	762	881	960	1021	1071	1141
200,000 or more		940	1084	1180	1254	1315	1399

North Carolina

Income: At least	Income: But less than	Exemptions: 1	2	3	4	5	Over 5
$0	$20,000	269	304	327	344	358	377
20,000	30,000	350	395	424	445	463	488
30,000	40,000	403	455	488	513	533	561
40,000	50,000	449	506	543	571	593	624
50,000	60,000	491	552	592	622	647	681
60,000	70,000	528	594	636	669	695	731
70,000	80,000	563	633	678	712	740	778
80,000	90,000	594	668	715	751	781	821
90,000	100,000	624	701	751	789	820	862
100,000	120,000	664	746	799	839	871	916
120,000	140,000	717	805	862	905	940	988
140,000	160,000	764	857	918	963	1000	1051
160,000	180,000	809	907	971	1019	1058	1112
180,000	200,000	851	954	1021	1072	1112	1169
200,000 or more		1038	1162	1242	1303	1352	1420

North Dakota

Income: At least	Income: But less than	Exemptions: 1	2	3	4	5	Over 5
$0	$20,000	291	331	357	377	393	415
20,000	30,000	383	434	468	494	514	543
30,000	40,000	444	503	542	572	596	629
40,000	50,000	497	563	606	639	665	702
50,000	60,000	544	617	664	699	728	768
60,000	70,000	587	665	715	753	784	828
70,000	80,000	627	710	764	804	838	883
80,000	90,000	664	751	807	850	885	934
90,000	100,000	699	790	850	895	931	982
100,000	120,000	745	842	905	953	992	1046
120,000	140,000	807	912	980	1031	1073	1131
140,000	160,000	862	973	1046	1101	1145	1207
160,000	180,000	915	1032	1109	1167	1214	1279
180,000	200,000	964	1088	1168	1229	1279	1347
200,000 or more		1185	1335	1432	1505	1566	1648

Ohio

Income: At least	Income: But less than	Exemptions: 1	2	3	4	5	Over 5
$0	$20,000	364	412	443	467	486	512
20,000	30,000	475	536	576	606	631	665
30,000	40,000	549	619	665	699	727	766
40,000	50,000	612	690	741	779	810	853
50,000	60,000	670	754	809	851	885	932
60,000	70,000	721	812	871	915	951	1001
70,000	80,000	769	866	928	976	1014	1067
80,000	90,000	813	914	980	1030	1071	1126
90,000	100,000	855	961	1030	1083	1125	1184
100,000	120,000	911	1023	1096	1152	1197	1259
120,000	140,000	985	1106	1185	1244	1292	1359
140,000	160,000	1051	1180	1263	1326	1377	1448
160,000	180,000	1114	1250	1338	1404	1458	1533
180,000	200,000	1173	1316	1408	1478	1534	1612
200,000 or more		1437	1608	1719	1803	1871	1965

(Continued)

2004 Optional State Sales Tax Tables *(Continued)*

Oklahoma

Income At least	But less than	1	2	3	4	5	Over 5
$0	$20,000	327	388	430	462	489	527
20,000	30,000	412	487	539	578	612	658
30,000	40,000	468	552	609	654	691	744
40,000	50,000	515	607	669	718	759	816
50,000	60,000	557	656	723	775	818	879
60,000	70,000	595	699	770	825	871	936
70,000	80,000	630	739	814	872	920	988
80,000	90,000	661	775	853	913	964	1035
90,000	100,000	691	810	891	954	1006	1080
100,000	120,000	731	855	940	1006	1061	1139
120,000	140,000	784	915	1005	1075	1134	1216
140,000	160,000	830	968	1063	1136	1198	1284
160,000	180,000	874	1019	1117	1194	1258	1348
180,000	200,000	916	1066	1168	1248	1315	1409
200,000 or more		1098	1272	1391	1484	1561	1670

Pennsylvania

Income At least	But less than	1	2	3	4	5	Over 5
$0	$20,000	284	328	357	380	398	424
20,000	30,000	382	440	478	508	532	566
30,000	40,000	448	516	561	595	623	663
40,000	50,000	506	582	632	671	702	746
50,000	60,000	558	642	697	739	774	822
60,000	70,000	605	696	755	801	838	890
70,000	80,000	650	747	811	859	899	955
80,000	90,000	691	793	860	912	954	1013
90,000	100,000	730	838	909	963	1008	1070
100,000	120,000	782	897	973	1031	1079	1145
120,000	140,000	852	977	1059	1122	1173	1245
140,000	160,000	915	1048	1135	1203	1258	1335
160,000	180,000	975	1116	1209	1280	1339	1420
180,000	200,000	1031	1180	1278	1354	1415	1501
200,000 or more		1285	1468	1588	1681	1756	1862

Rhode Island

Income At least	But less than	1	2	3	4	5	Over 5
$0	$20,000	302	342	368	387	403	425
20,000	30,000	403	455	489	515	536	565
30,000	40,000	472	532	571	601	625	659
40,000	50,000	531	598	642	676	703	740
50,000	60,000	585	658	706	743	773	814
60,000	70,000	633	712	764	803	835	880
70,000	80,000	678	763	819	861	895	942
80,000	90,000	719	809	868	912	948	998
90,000	100,000	759	854	915	962	1000	1053
100,000	120,000	812	913	978	1028	1068	1124
120,000	140,000	882	991	1062	1116	1160	1220
140,000	160,000	945	1061	1137	1194	1241	1306
160,000	180,000	1005	1128	1208	1269	1319	1387
180,000	200,000	1062	1191	1276	1340	1392	1464
200,000 or more		1314	1472	1575	1653	1717	1805

South Carolina

Income At least	But less than	1	2	3	4	5	Over 5
$0	$20,000	379	449	496	533	563	606
20,000	30,000	481	568	627	672	710	763
30,000	40,000	547	646	712	764	806	866
40,000	50,000	604	712	785	841	888	953
50,000	60,000	655	771	849	910	960	1031
60,000	70,000	700	823	906	971	1024	1099
70,000	80,000	742	872	960	1028	1085	1164
80,000	90,000	780	916	1008	1079	1138	1221
90,000	100,000	816	958	1054	1128	1190	1276
100,000	120,000	864	1014	1114	1193	1257	1348
120,000	140,000	927	1087	1194	1278	1347	1443
140,000	160,000	983	1152	1265	1353	1426	1527
160,000	180,000	1036	1213	1332	1424	1500	1607
180,000	200,000	1086	1271	1395	1491	1570	1682
200,000 or more		1306	1523	1670	1783	1876	2008

South Dakota

Income At least	But less than	1	2	3	4	5	Over 5
$0	$20,000	263	319	358	388	414	450
20,000	30,000	344	417	466	505	538	585
30,000	40,000	399	482	539	584	621	674
40,000	50,000	446	537	601	650	692	751
50,000	60,000	488	588	656	711	756	820
60,000	70,000	526	633	706	764	813	882
70,000	80,000	562	675	753	815	867	940
80,000	90,000	594	713	796	860	915	991
90,000	100,000	625	750	836	904	961	1042
100,000	120,000	666	799	890	962	1022	1108
120,000	140,000	721	864	962	1039	1104	1195
140,000	160,000	770	921	1025	1107	1176	1273
160,000	180,000	816	976	1086	1172	1245	1347
180,000	200,000	860	1028	1143	1234	1310	1417
200,000 or more		1055	1257	1395	1504	1596	1725

Tennessee

Income At least	But less than	1	2	3	4	5	Over 5
$0	$20,000	506	601	666	717	758	817
20,000	30,000	628	745	824	886	937	1008
30,000	40,000	708	838	926	995	1052	1132
40,000	50,000	775	916	1012	1086	1148	1235
50,000	60,000	835	986	1088	1168	1233	1326
60,000	70,000	887	1047	1155	1239	1309	1407
70,000	80,000	937	1105	1218	1306	1379	1482
80,000	90,000	981	1155	1273	1365	1441	1548
90,000	100,000	1023	1204	1327	1422	1501	1612
100,000	120,000	1078	1268	1397	1496	1579	1695
120,000	140,000	1151	1353	1489	1594	1682	1805
140,000	160,000	1216	1427	1570	1681	1773	1902
160,000	180,000	1277	1498	1647	1762	1858	1993
180,000	200,000	1334	1563	1718	1838	1938	2078
200,000 or more		1583	1850	2030	2169	2284	2446

Texas

Income At least	But less than	1	2	3	4	5	Over 5
$0	$20,000	375	427	461	487	509	538
20,000	30,000	488	555	599	633	660	697
30,000	40,000	564	641	691	730	761	804
40,000	50,000	629	714	770	812	847	895
50,000	60,000	687	780	841	887	925	976
60,000	70,000	740	840	904	954	994	1049
70,000	80,000	789	895	964	1017	1059	1118
80,000	90,000	834	945	1018	1073	1118	1180
90,000	100,000	877	994	1070	1127	1174	1239
100,000	120,000	933	1057	1138	1199	1249	1318
120,000	140,000	1009	1142	1229	1294	1348	1422
140,000	160,000	1076	1217	1309	1379	1436	1515
160,000	180,000	1140	1289	1386	1460	1520	1603
180,000	200,000	1200	1357	1459	1536	1599	1686
200,000 or more		1467	1656	1779	1872	1948	2052

Utah

Income At least	But less than	1	2	3	4	5	Over 5
$0	$20,000	345	411	456	491	521	562
20,000	30,000	437	520	576	620	657	708
30,000	40,000	498	592	655	705	746	804
40,000	50,000	550	652	722	776	821	884
50,000	60,000	596	707	781	840	888	956
60,000	70,000	637	755	834	896	947	1020
70,000	80,000	676	800	884	949	1003	1079
80,000	90,000	711	840	928	996	1053	1132
90,000	100,000	744	879	970	1041	1100	1183
100,000	120,000	787	929	1026	1100	1163	1250
120,000	140,000	845	997	1099	1179	1245	1339
140,000	160,000	897	1056	1164	1248	1318	1416
160,000	180,000	945	1113	1226	1314	1387	1490
180,000	200,000	991	1166	1284	1376	1452	1559
200,000 or more		1192	1398	1537	1645	1735	1861

Vermont

Income At least	But less than	1	2	3	4	5	Over 5
$0	$20,000	259	300	327	348	365	389
20,000	30,000	352	406	442	470	493	525
30,000	40,000	416	479	521	554	581	618
40,000	50,000	471	543	590	627	657	699
50,000	60,000	522	601	653	693	726	772
60,000	70,000	568	653	710	753	789	839
70,000	80,000	612	703	764	810	849	902
80,000	90,000	651	748	812	862	902	959
90,000	100,000	690	792	859	912	955	1014
100,000	120,000	741	850	922	978	1024	1088
120,000	140,000	809	928	1006	1067	1117	1186
140,000	160,000	871	998	1082	1147	1200	1274
160,000	180,000	930	1065	1154	1223	1280	1359
180,000	200,000	986	1128	1223	1296	1355	1439
200,000 or more		1238	1414	1531	1620	1694	1797

Virginia

Income At least	But less than	1	2	3	4	5	Over 5
$0	$20,000	270	322	357	385	408	440
20,000	30,000	345	411	455	490	519	559
30,000	40,000	395	470	520	559	592	638
40,000	50,000	438	520	575	618	654	704
50,000	60,000	476	564	624	670	709	763
60,000	70,000	510	604	667	717	758	816
70,000	80,000	542	641	708	761	804	865
80,000	90,000	571	675	745	800	845	909
90,000	100,000	598	707	780	837	885	952
100,000	120,000	635	749	827	887	937	1007
120,000	140,000	683	805	888	952	1006	1081
140,000	160,000	726	855	942	1010	1067	1146
160,000	180,000	767	902	994	1065	1125	1208
180,000	200,000	805	947	1043	1117	1179	1266
200,000 or more		974	1142	1256	1344	1417	1520

Washington

Income At least	But less than	1	2	3	4	5	Over 5
$0	$20,000	389	439	471	496	516	543
20,000	30,000	500	564	605	636	662	696
30,000	40,000	574	647	694	729	758	797
40,000	50,000	637	717	769	808	840	883
50,000	60,000	694	780	836	879	913	960
60,000	70,000	744	837	896	942	978	1029
70,000	80,000	791	890	953	1001	1040	1093
80,000	90,000	834	937	1004	1054	1095	1151
90,000	100,000	875	983	1052	1105	1148	1206
100,000	120,000	929	1043	1116	1172	1217	1279
120,000	140,000	1000	1123	1201	1261	1309	1376
140,000	160,000	1064	1193	1277	1340	1391	1462
160,000	180,000	1124	1261	1349	1415	1469	1543
180,000	200,000	1181	1324	1416	1485	1542	1619
200,000 or more		1431	1602	1712	1795	1862	1955

West Virginia

Income At least	But less than	1	2	3	4	5	Over 5
$0	$20,000	493	585	646	694	734	789
20,000	30,000	622	736	812	872	921	990
30,000	40,000	706	835	921	988	1043	1121
40,000	50,000	778	918	1013	1086	1146	1231
50,000	60,000	842	993	1094	1173	1238	1329
60,000	70,000	899	1059	1166	1250	1319	1416
70,000	80,000	952	1121	1234	1322	1395	1497
80,000	90,000	999	1176	1294	1386	1462	1569
90,000	100,000	1045	1229	1352	1448	1527	1639
100,000	120,000	1105	1298	1428	1529	1612	1729
120,000	140,000	1184	1390	1528	1636	1725	1849
140,000	160,000	1254	1471	1617	1730	1824	1955
160,000	180,000	1320	1548	1701	1819	1917	2055
180,000	200,000	1383	1620	1779	1903	2005	2148
200,000 or more		1656	1935	2123	2268	2388	2556

Wisconsin

Income At least	But less than	1	2	3	4	5	Over 5
$0	$20,000	293	334	360	380	396	419
20,000	30,000	388	440	475	501	522	551
30,000	40,000	452	513	552	582	607	641
40,000	50,000	507	575	619	652	680	718
50,000	60,000	557	631	679	716	746	787
60,000	70,000	602	681	733	773	805	849
70,000	80,000	644	729	785	827	861	908
80,000	90,000	683	772	831	875	911	961
90,000	100,000	720	814	875	922	960	1012
100,000	120,000	769	869	934	983	1024	1080
120,000	140,000	834	942	1013	1066	1110	1170
140,000	160,000	893	1008	1083	1140	1186	1250
160,000	180,000	949	1071	1150	1210	1259	1327
180,000	200,000	1001	1130	1213	1276	1328	1399
200,000 or more		1237	1392	1494	1571	1633	1720

Wyoming

Income At least	But less than	1	2	3	4	5	Over 5
$0	$20,000	337	401	445	479	507	547
20,000	30,000	428	508	563	605	640	689
30,000	40,000	487	578	640	687	727	783
40,000	50,000	538	637	705	757	800	861
50,000	60,000	583	690	763	819	866	932
60,000	70,000	623	737	814	874	924	994
70,000	80,000	661	781	863	926	978	1052
80,000	90,000	695	821	906	972	1026	1104
90,000	100,000	727	858	947	1016	1073	1153
100,000	120,000	770	908	1001	1074	1134	1219
120,000	140,000	826	974	1073	1150	1215	1305
140,000	160,000	876	1032	1137	1218	1286	1381
160,000	180,000	924	1087	1197	1282	1353	1453
180,000	200,000	969	1138	1253	1342	1416	1520
200,000 or more		1164	1365	1500	1605	1692	1814

Income Tax Rates—Estates and Trusts

TAX YEAR 2004

Taxable Income		The Tax Is:	
Over—	But not Over—		Of the Amount Over—
$ 0	$1,950	15%	$ 0
1,950	4,600	$ 292.50 + 25%	1,950
4,600	7,000	955.00 + 28%	4,600
7,000	9,550	1,627.00 + 33%	7,000
9,550	....	2,468.50 + 35%	9,550

TAX YEAR 2005

Taxable Income		The Tax Is:	
Over—	But not Over—		Of the Amount Over—
$ 0	$2,000	15%	$ 0
2,000	4,700	$ 300 + 25%	2,000
4,700	7,150	975 + 28%	4,700
7,150	9,750	1,661 + 33%	7,150
9,750	....	2,519 + 35%	9,750

Income Tax Rates—Corporations

Taxable Income		Tax Is:	
Over—	But not Over—		Of the Amount Over—
$ 0	$ 50,000	15%	$ 0
50,000	75,000	$ 7,500 + 25%	50,000
75,000	100,000	13,750 + 34%	75,000
100,000	335,000	22,250 + 39%	100,000
335,000	10,000,000	113,900 + 34%	335,000
10,000,000	15,000,000	3,400,000 + 35%	10,000,000
15,000,000	18,333,333	5,150,000 + 38%	15,000,000
18,333,333	....	35%	0

Unified Transfer Tax Rates

FOR GIFTS MADE AND FOR DEATHS AFTER 1983 AND BEFORE 2002

If the Amount with Respect to Which the Tentative Tax to Be Computed Is:	The Tentative Tax Is:
Not over $10,000	18 percent of such amount.
Over $10,000 but not over $20,000	$1,800, plus 20 percent of the excess of such amount over $10,000.
Over $20,000 but not over $40,000	$3,800, plus 22 percent of the excess of such amount over $20,000.
Over $40,000 but not over $60,000	$8,200, plus 24 percent of the excess of such amount over $40,000.
Over $60,000 but not over $80,000	$13,000, plus 26 percent of the excess of such amount over $60,000.
Over $80,000 but not over $100,000	$18,200, plus 28 percent of the excess of such amount over $80,000.
Over $100,000 but not over $150,000	$23,800, plus 30 percent of the excess of such amount over $100,000.
Over $150,000 but not over $250,000	$38,800, plus 32 percent of the excess of such amount over $150,000.
Over $250,000 but not over $500,000	$70,800, plus 34 percent of the excess of such amount over $250,000.
Over $500,000 but not over $750,000	$155,800, plus 37 percent of the excess of such amount over $500,000.
Over $750,000 but not over $1,000,000	$248,300, plus 39 percent of the excess of such amount over $750,000.
Over $1,000,000 but not over $1,250,000	$345,800, plus 41 percent of the excess of such amount over $1,000,000.
Over $1,250,000 but not over $1,500,000	$448,300, plus 43 percent of the excess of such amount over $1,250,000.
Over $1,500,000 but not over $2,000,000	$555,800, plus 45 percent of the excess of such amount over $1,500,000.
Over $2,000,000 but not over $2,500,000	$780,800, plus 49 percent of the excess of such amount over $2,000,000.
Over $2,500,000 but not over $3,000,000	$1,025,800, plus 53 percent of the excess of such amount over $2,500,000.
Over $3,000,000*	$1,290,800, plus 55 percent of the excess of such amount over $3,000,000.

*For large taxable transfers (generally in excess of $10 million) there is a phaseout of the graduated rates and the unified tax credit.

Unified Transfer Tax Rates

FOR GIFTS MADE AND FOR DEATHS IN 2002

If the Amount with Respect to Which the Tentative Tax to Be Computed Is:	The Tentative Tax Is:
Not over $10,000	18 percent of such amount.
Over $10,000 but not over $20,000	$1,800, plus 20 percent of the excess of such amount over $10,000.
Over $20,000 but not over $40,000	$3,800, plus 22 percent of the excess of such amount over $20,000.
Over $40,000 but not over $60,000	$8,200, plus 24 percent of the excess of such amount over $40,000.
Over $60,000 but not over $80,000	$13,000, plus 26 percent of the excess of such amount over $60,000.
Over $80,000 but not over $100,000	$18,200, plus 28 percent of the excess of such amount over $80,000.
Over $100,000 but not over $150,000	$23,800, plus 30 percent of the excess of such amount over $100,000.
Over $150,000 but not over $250,000	$38,800, plus 32 percent of the excess of such amount over $150,000.
Over $250,000 but not over $500,000	$70,800, plus 34 percent of the excess of such amount over $250,000.
Over $500,000 but not over $750,000	$155,800, plus 37 percent of the excess of such amount over $500,000.
Over $750,000 but not over $1,000,000	$248,300, plus 39 percent of the excess of such amount over $750,000.
Over $1,000,000 but not over $1,250,000	$345,800, plus 41 percent of the excess of such amount over $1,000,000.
Over $1,250,000 but not over $1,500,000	$448,300, plus 43 percent of the excess of such amount over $1,250,000.
Over $1,500,000 but not over $2,000,000	$555,800, plus 45 percent of the excess of such amount over $1,500,000.
Over $2,000,000 but not over $2,500,000	$780,800, plus 49 percent of the excess of such amount over $2,000,000.
Over $2,500,000	$1,025,800, plus 50 percent of the excess of such amount over $2,500,000.

Unified Transfer Tax Rates

FOR GIFTS MADE AND FOR DEATHS IN 2003

If the Amount with Respect to Which the Tentative Tax to Be Computed Is:	The Tentative Tax Is:
Not over $10,000	18 percent of such amount.
Over $10,000 but not over $20,000	$1,800, plus 20 percent of the excess of such amount over $10,000.
Over $20,000 but not over $40,000	$3,800, plus 22 percent of the excess of such amount over $20,000.
Over $40,000 but not over $60,000	$8,200, plus 24 percent of the excess of such amount over $40,000.
Over $60,000 but not over $80,000	$13,000, plus 26 percent of the excess of such amount over $60,000.
Over $80,000 but not over $100,000	$18,200, plus 28 percent of the excess of such amount over $80,000.
Over $100,000 but not over $150,000	$23,800, plus 30 percent of the excess of such amount over $100,000.
Over $150,000 but not over $250,000	$38,800, plus 32 percent of the excess of such amount over $150,000.
Over $250,000 but not over $500,000	$70,800, plus 34 percent of the excess of such amount over $250,000.
Over $500,000 but not over $750,000	$155,800, plus 37 percent of the excess of such amount over $500,000.
Over $750,000 but not over $1,000,000	$248,300, plus 39 percent of the excess of such amount over $750,000.
Over $1,000,000 but not over $1,250,000	$345,800, plus 41 percent of the excess of such amount over $1,000,000.
Over $1,250,000 but not over $1,500,000	$448,300, plus 43 percent of the excess of such amount over $1,250,000.
Over $1,500,000 but not over $2,000,000	$555,800, plus 45 percent of the excess of such amount over $1,500,000.
Over $2,000,000	$780,800, plus 49 percent of the excess of such amount over $2,000,000.

Unified Transfer Tax Rates

FOR GIFTS MADE AND FOR DEATHS IN 2004

If the Amount with Respect to Which the Tentative Tax to Be Computed Is:	The Tentative Tax Is:
Not over $10,000	18 percent of such amount.
Over $10,000 but not over $20,000	$1,800, plus 20 percent of the excess of such amount over $10,000.
Over $20,000 but not over $40,000	$3,800, plus 22 percent of the excess of such amount over $20,000.
Over $40,000 but not over $60,000	$8,200, plus 24 percent of the excess of such amount over $40,000.
Over $60,000 but not over $80,000	$13,000, plus 26 percent of the excess of such amount over $60,000.
Over $80,000 but not over $100,000	$18,200, plus 28 percent of the excess of such amount over $80,000.
Over $100,000 but not over $150,000	$23,800, plus 30 percent of the excess of such amount over $100,000.
Over $150,000 but not over $250,000	$38,800, plus 32 percent of the excess of such amount over $150,000.
Over $250,000 but not over $500,000	$70,800, plus 34 percent of the excess of such amount over $250,000.
Over $500,000 but not over $750,000	$155,800, plus 37 percent of the excess of such amount over $500,000.
Over $750,000 but not over $1,000,000	$248,300, plus 39 percent of the excess of such amount over $750,000.
Over $1,000,000 but not over $1,250,000	$345,800, plus 41 percent of the excess of such amount over $1,000,000.
Over $1,250,000 but not over $1,500,000	$448,300, plus 43 percent of the excess of such amount over $1,250,000.
Over $1,500,000 but not over $2,000,000	$555,800, plus 45 percent of the excess of such amount over $1,500,000.
Over $2,000,000	$780,800, plus 48 percent of the excess of such amount over $2,000,000.

Unified Transfer Tax Rates

FOR GIFTS MADE AND FOR DEATHS IN 2005

If the Amount with Respect to Which the Tentative Tax to Be Computed Is:	The Tentative Tax Is:
Not over $10,000	18 percent of such amount.
Over $10,000 but not over $20,000	$1,800, plus 20 percent of the excess of such amount over $10,000.
Over $20,000 but not over $40,000	$3,800, plus 22 percent of the excess of such amount over $20,000.
Over $40,000 but not over $60,000	$8,200, plus 24 percent of the excess of such amount over $40,000.
Over $60,000 but not over $80,000	$13,000, plus 26 percent of the excess of such amount over $60,000.
Over $80,000 but not over $100,000	$18,200, plus 28 percent of the excess of such amount over $80,000.
Over $100,000 but not over $150,000	$23,800, plus 30 percent of the excess of such amount over $100,000.
Over $150,000 but not over $250,000	$38,800, plus 32 percent of the excess of such amount over $150,000.
Over $250,000 but not over $500,000	$70,800, plus 34 percent of the excess of such amount over $250,000.
Over $500,000 but not over $750,000	$155,800, plus 37 percent of the excess of such amount over $500,000.
Over $750,000 but not over $1,000,000	$248,300, plus 39 percent of the excess of such amount over $750,000.
Over $1,000,000 but not over $1,250,000	$345,800, plus 41 percent of the excess of such amount over $1,000,000.
Over $1,250,000 but not over $1,500,000	$448,300, plus 43 percent of the excess of such amount over $1,250,000.
Over $1,500,000 but not over $2,000,000	$555,800, plus 45 percent of the excess of such amount over $1,500,000.
Over $2,000,000	$780,800, plus 47 percent of the excess of such amount over $2,000,000.

Table for Computation of Maximum Credit for State Death Taxes**

(A) Adjusted Taxable Estate* Equal to or More Than	(B) Adjusted Taxable Estate* Less Than	(C) Credit on Amount in Column (A)	(D) Rate of Credit on Excess Over Amount in Column (A) (Percentage)
0	$ 40,000	0	None
$ 40,000	90,000	0	0.8
90,000	140,000	$ 400	1.6
140,000	240,000	1,200	2.4
240,000	440,000	3,600	3.2
440,000	640,000	10,000	4.0
640,000	840,000	18,000	4.8
840,000	1,040,000	27,600	5.6
1,040,000	1,540,000	38,800	6.4
1,540,000	2,040,000	70,800	7.2
2,040,000	2,540,000	106,800	8.0
2,540,000	3,040,000	146,800	8.8
3,040,000	3,540,000	190,800	9.6
3,540,000	4,040,000	238,800	10.4
4,040,000	5,040,000	290,800	11.2
5,040,000	6,040,000	402,800	12.0
6,040,000	7,040,000	522,800	12.8
7,040,000	8,040,000	650,800	13.6
8,040,000	9,040,000	786,800	14.4
9,040,000	10,040,000	930,800	15.2
10,040,000		1,082,800	16.0

*Adjusted Taxable Estate = Taxable Estate – $60,000.

**Although the § 2011 credit has been completely phased out for Federal estate tax purposes, the schedule continues to be used by some states as the measure of state death tax imposed.

Scheduled phaseout:

Year	Percentage Allowed
2002	75
2003	50
2004	25
2005	0

APPENDIX B
Tax Forms

(Tax forms can be obtained from the IRS Web site: **http://www.irs.gov**)

Form **709**

Department of the Treasury
Internal Revenue Service

United States Gift (and Generation-Skipping Transfer) Tax Return

(For gifts made during calendar year 2004)

▶ **See separate instructions.**

OMB No. 1545-0020

2004

Part 1—General Information

1 Donor's first name and middle initial	2 Donor's last name	3 **Donor's social security number**
4 Address (number, street, and apartment number)		5 Legal residence (domicile) (county and state)
6 City, state, and ZIP code		7 Citizenship

		Yes	No
8	If the donor died during the year, check here ▶ ☐ and enter date of death ____________ , ______		
9	If you received an extension of time to file this Form 709, check here ▶ ☐ and attach the Form 4868, 2688, 2350, or 8892		
10	Enter the total number of donees listed on Schedule A—count each person only once. ▶		
11a	Have you (the donor) previously filed a Form 709 (or 709-A) for any other year? If "No," skip line 11b		
11b	If the answer to line 11a is "Yes," has your address changed since you last filed Form 709 (or 709-A)?		
12	Gifts by husband or wife to third parties.—Do you consent to have the gifts (including generation-skipping transfers) made by you and by your spouse to third parties during the calendar year considered as made one-half by each of you? (See instructions.) (If the answer is "Yes," the following information must be furnished and your spouse must sign the consent shown below. **If the answer is "No," skip lines 13–18 and go to Schedule A.**)		
13	Name of consenting spouse 14 SSN		
15	Were you married to one another during the entire calendar year? (see instructions)		
16	If 15 is "No," check whether ☐ married ☐ divorced or ☐ widowed/deceased, and give date (see instructions) ▶		
17	Will a gift tax return for this year be filed by your spouse? (If "Yes," mail both returns in the same envelope.)		

18 **Consent of Spouse**—I consent to have the gifts (and generation-skipping transfers) made by me and by my spouse to third parties during the calendar year considered as made one-half by each of us. We are both aware of the joint and several liability for tax created by the execution of this consent.

Consenting spouse's signature ▶   **Date** ▶

Part 2—Tax Computation

1	Enter the amount from Schedule A, Part 4, line 11	1		
2	Enter the amount from Schedule B, line 3	2		
3	Total taxable gifts (add lines 1 and 2)	3		
4	Tax computed on amount on line 3 (see Table for Computing Tax in separate instructions)	4		
5	Tax computed on amount on line 2 (see Table for Computing Tax in separate instructions)	5		
6	Balance (subtract line 5 from line 4)	6		
7	Maximum unified credit (nonresident aliens, see instructions)	7	345,800	00
8	Enter the unified credit against tax allowable for all prior periods (from Sch. B, line 1, col. C)	8		
9	Balance (subtract line 8 from line 7)	9		
10	Enter 20% (.20) of the amount allowed as a specific exemption for gifts made after September 8, 1976, and before January 1, 1977 (see instructions)	10		
11	Balance (subtract line 10 from line 9)	11		
12	Unified credit (enter the smaller of line 6 or line 11)	12		
13	Credit for foreign gift taxes (see instructions)	13		
14	Total credits (add lines 12 and 13)	14		
15	Balance (subtract line 14 from line 6) (do not enter less than zero)	15		
16	Generation-skipping transfer taxes (from Schedule C, Part 3, col. H, Total)	16		
17	Total tax (add lines 15 and 16)	17		
18	Gift and generation-skipping transfer taxes prepaid with extension of time to file	18		
19	If line 18 is less than line 17, enter **balance due** (see instructions)	19		
20	If line 18 is greater than line 17, enter **amount to be refunded**	20		

Attach check or money order here.

Sign Here

Under penalties of perjury, I declare that I have examined this return, including any accompanying schedules and statements, and to the best of my knowledge and belief, it is true, correct, and complete. Declaration of preparer (other than donor) is based on all information of which preparer has any knowledge.

▶ Signature of donor   Date

Paid Preparer's Use Only

Preparer's signature ▶	Date	Check if self-employed ▶ ☐
Firm's name (or yours if self-employed), address, and ZIP code ▶	Phone no. ▶ ( )	

Form 709 (2004) Page 2

SCHEDULE A **Computation of Taxable Gifts** (Including transfers in trust) (see instructions)

A Does the value of any item listed on Schedule A reflect any valuation discount? If "Yes," see instructions. . . . . Yes ☐ No ☐

B ☐ ◄ Check here if you elect under section 529(c)(2)(B) to treat any transfers made this year to a qualified tuition program as made ratably over a 5-year period beginning this year. See instructions. Attach explanation.

Part 1—Gifts Subject Only to Gift Tax. *Gifts less political organization, medical, and educational exclusions—see instructions*

A Item number	B • Donee's name and address • Relationship to donor (if any) • Description of gift • If the gift was of securities, give CUSIP no. • If closely held entity, give EIN	C	D Donor's adjusted basis of gift	E Date of gift	F Value at date of gift	G For split gifts, enter ½ of column F	H Net transfer (subtract col. G from col. F)
1							
Gifts made by spouse—*complete **only** if you are splitting gifts with your spouse and he/she also made gifts.*							
Total of Part 1 (add amounts from Part 1, column H) . . . . ▶							

Part 2—Direct skips— gifts that are direct skips and are subject to both gift tax and generation-skipping transfer tax. You must list the gifts in chronological order.

A Item number	B • Donee's name and address • Relationship to donor (if any) • Description of gift • If the gift was of securities, give CUSIP no. • If closely held entity, give EIN	C 2632(b) election out	D Donor's adjusted basis of gift	E Date of gift	F Value at date of gift	G For split gifts, enter ½ of column F	H Net transfer (subtract col. G from col. F)
1							
Gifts made by spouse—*complete **only** if you are splitting gifts with your spouse and he/she also made gifts.*							
Total of Part 2 (add amounts from Part 2, column H) . . . . ▶							

Part 3—Indirect skips— gifts to trusts that are currently subject to gift tax and may later be subject to generation-skipping transfer tax. You must list these gifts in chronological order.

A Item number	B • Donee's name and address • Relationship to donor (if any) • Description of gift • If the gift was of securities, give CUSIP no. • If closely held entity, give EIN	C 2632(c) election	D Donor's adjusted basis of gift	E Date of gift	F Value at date of gift	G For split gifts, enter ½ of column F	H Net transfer (subtract col. G from col. F)
1							
Gifts made by spouse—*complete **only** if you are splitting gifts with your spouse and he/she also made gifts.*							
Total of Part 3 (add amounts from Part 3, column H) . . . . ▶							

(If more space is needed, attach additional sheets of same size.) Form **709** (2004)

Form 709 (2004) Page **3**

Part 4—Taxable Gift Reconciliation

1	Total value of gifts of donor (add totals from column H of Parts 1, 2, and 3)		1	
2	Total annual exclusions for gifts listed on line 1 (see instructions)		2	
3	Total included amount of gifts (subtract line 2 from line 1)		3	
	Deductions (see instructions)			
4	Gifts of interests to spouse for which a marital deduction will be claimed, based on items .... of Schedule A	4		
5	Exclusions attributable to gifts on line 4	5		
6	Marital deduction—subtract line 5 from line 4	6		
7	Charitable deduction, based on items .... less exclusions	7		
8	Total deductions—add lines 6 and 7		8	
9	Subtract line 8 from line 3		9	
10	Generation-skipping transfer taxes payable with this Form 709 (from Schedule C, Part 3, col. H, Total)		10	
11	Taxable gifts (add lines 9 and 10). Enter here and on line 1 of the Tax Computation on page 1		11	

12 **Terminable Interest (QTIP) Marital Deduction.** (See instructions for line 4 of Schedule A.)

If a trust (or other property) meets the requirements of qualified terminable interest property under section 2523(f), and

a. The trust (or other property) is listed on Schedule A, and

b. The value of the trust (or other property) is entered in whole or in part as a deduction on line 4, Part 4 of Schedule A,

then the donor shall be deemed to have made an election to have such trust (or other property) treated as qualified terminable interest property under section 2523(f).

If less than the entire value of the trust (or other property) that the donor has included in Parts 1 and 3 of Schedule A is entered as a deduction on line 4, the donor shall be considered to have made an election only as to a fraction of the trust (or other property). The numerator of this fraction is equal to the amount of the trust (or other property) deducted on line 6 of Part 4, Schedule A. The denominator is equal to the total value of the trust (or other property) listed in Parts 1 and 3 of Schedule A.

If you make the QTIP election (see instructions for line 4 of Schedule A), the terminable interest property involved will be included in your spouse's gross estate upon his or her death (section 2044). If your spouse disposes (by gift or otherwise) of all or part of the qualifying life income interest, he or she will be considered to have made a transfer of the entire property that is subject to the gift tax (see Transfer of Certain Life Estates on page 4 of the instructions).

13 **Election Out of QTIP Treatment of Annuities**

☐◄ Check here if you elect under section 2523(f)(6) **NOT** to treat as qualified terminable interest property any joint and survivor annuities that re reported on Schedule A and would otherwise be treated as qualified terminable interest property under section 2523(f). (See instructions.) Enter the item numbers (from Schedule A) for the annuities for which you are making this election ▶

SCHEDULE B Gifts From Prior Periods

If you answered "Yes" on line 11a of page 1, Part 1, see the instructions for completing Schedule B. If you answered "No," skip to the Tax Computation on page 1 (or Schedule C, if applicable).

A Calendar year or calendar quarter (see instructions)	B Internal Revenue office where prior return was filed	C Amount of unified credit against gift tax for periods after December 31, 1976	D Amount of specific exemption for prior periods ending before January 1, 1977	E Amount of taxable gifts
1 Totals for prior periods	1			

2	Amount, if any, by which total specific exemption, line 1, column D, is more than $30,000	2	
3	Total amount of taxable gifts for prior periods (add amount, column E, line 1, and amount, if any, on line 2). (Enter here and on line 2 of the Tax Computation on page 1.)	3	

(If more space is needed, attach additional sheets of same size.) Form **709** (2004)

Form 709 (2004) Page 4

SCHEDULE C Computation of Generation-Skipping Transfer Tax

Note: *Inter vivos direct skips that are completely excluded by the GST exemption must still be fully reported (including value and exemptions claimed) on Schedule C.*

Part 1—Generation-Skipping Transfers

A Item No. (from Schedule A, Part 2, col. A)	B Value (from Schedule A, Part 2, col. H)	C Nontaxable portion of transfer	D Net Transfer (subtract col. C from col. B)
1			
Gifts made by spouse (for gift splitting only)			

Part 2—GST Exemption Reconciliation (Section 2631) and Section 2652(a)(3) Election

Check box ▶ ☐ if you are making a section 2652(a)(3) (special QTIP) election (see instructions)

Enter the item numbers (from Schedule A) of the gifts for which you are making this election ▶ ....

1	Maximum allowable exemption (see instructions)	1	
2	Total exemption used for periods before filing this return	2	
3	Exemption available for this return (subtract line 2 from line 1)	3	
4	Exemption claimed on this return (from Part 3, col. C total, below)	4	
5	Automatic allocation of exemption to transfers reported on Schedule A, Part 3	5	
6	Exemption allocated to transfers not shown on line 4 or 5, above. **You must attach a Notice of Allocation.** (See instructions.)	6	
7	Add lines 4, 5, and 6	7	
8	Exemption available for future transfers (subtract line 7 from line 3)	8	

Part 3—Tax Computation

A Item No. (from Schedule C, Part 1)	B Net transfer (from Schedule C, Part 1, col. D)	C GST Exemption Allocated	D Divide col. C by col. B	E Inclusion Ratio (subtract col. D from 1.000)	F Maximum Estate Tax Rate	G Applicable Rate (multiply col. E by col. F)	H Generation-Skipping Transfer Tax (multiply col. B by col. G)
1					48% (.48)		
2					48% (.48)		
3					48% (.48)		
4					48% (.48)		
5					48% (.48)		
6					48% (.48)		
					48% (.48)		
					48% (.48)		
					48% (.48)		
					48% (.48)		
					48% (.48)		
					48% (.48)		
Total exemption claimed. Enter here and on line 4, Part 2, above. May not exceed line 3, Part 2, above		**Total generation-skipping transfer tax.** Enter here, on line 10 of Schedule A, Part 4, and on line 16 of the Tax Computation on page 1					

(If more space is needed, attach additional sheets of same size.)

Form **709** (2004)

Form 1040 — Department of the Treasury—Internal Revenue Service — U.S. Individual Income Tax Return 2004

(99) IRS Use Only—Do not write or staple in this space.

For the year Jan. 1–Dec. 31, 2004, or other tax year beginning , 2004, ending , 20 — OMB No. 1545-0074

Label

(See instructions on page 16.)

Use the IRS label. Otherwise, please print or type.

LABEL HERE

Your first name and initial	Last name	Your social security number
If a joint return, spouse's first name and initial	Last name	Spouse's social security number
Home address (number and street). If you have a P.O. box, see page 16.	Apt. no.	**Important!** You **must** enter your SSN(s) above.
City, town or post office, state, and ZIP code. If you have a foreign address, see page 16.		

Presidential Election Campaign (See page 16.)

Note. Checking "Yes" will not change your tax or reduce your refund.
Do you, or your spouse if filing a joint return, want $3 to go to this fund? ▶ You ☐ Yes ☐ No Spouse ☐ Yes ☐ No

Filing Status

Check only one box.

1 ☐ Single
2 ☐ Married filing jointly (even if only one had income)
3 ☐ Married filing separately. Enter spouse's SSN above and full name here. ▶
4 ☐ Head of household (with qualifying person). (See page 17.) If the qualifying person is a child but not your dependent, enter this child's name here. ▶
5 ☐ Qualifying widow(er) with dependent child (see page 17)

Exemptions

6a ☐ **Yourself.** If someone can claim you as a dependent, **do not** check box 6a
b ☐ **Spouse**

Boxes checked on 6a and 6b ____

c **Dependents:**

(1) First name Last name	(2) Dependent's social security number	(3) Dependent's relationship to you	(4) ✓ if qualifying child for child tax credit (see page 18)
			☐
			☐
			☐
			☐

If more than four dependents, see page 18.

No. of children on 6c who:
• lived with you ____
• did not live with you due to divorce or separation (see page 18) ____
Dependents on 6c not entered above ____

d Total number of exemptions claimed — Add numbers on lines above ▶

Income

Attach Form(s) W-2 here. Also attach Forms W-2G and 1099-R if tax was withheld.

If you did not get a W-2, see page 19.

Enclose, but do not attach, any payment. Also, please use Form 1040-V.

7	Wages, salaries, tips, etc. Attach Form(s) W-2		7
8a	**Taxable** interest. Attach Schedule B if required		8a
b	**Tax-exempt** interest. **Do not** include on line 8a	8b	
9a	Ordinary dividends. Attach Schedule B if required		9a
b	Qualified dividends (see page 20)	9b	
10	Taxable refunds, credits, or offsets of state and local income taxes (see page 20)		10
11	Alimony received		11
12	Business income or (loss). Attach Schedule C or C-EZ		12
13	Capital gain or (loss). Attach Schedule D if required. If not required, check here ▶ ☐		13
14	Other gains or (losses). Attach Form 4797		14
15a	IRA distributions 15a	b Taxable amount (see page 22)	15b
16a	Pensions and annuities 16a	b Taxable amount (see page 22)	16b
17	Rental real estate, royalties, partnerships, S corporations, trusts, etc. Attach Schedule E		17
18	Farm income or (loss). Attach Schedule F		18
19	Unemployment compensation		19
20a	Social security benefits 20a	b Taxable amount (see page 24)	20b
21	Other income. List type and amount (see page 24)		21
22	Add the amounts in the far right column for lines 7 through 21. This is your **total income** ▶		22

Adjusted Gross Income

23	Educator expenses (see page 26)	23	
24	Certain business expenses of reservists, performing artists, and fee-basis government officials. Attach Form 2106 or 2106-EZ	24	
25	IRA deduction (see page 26)	25	
26	Student loan interest deduction (see page 28)	26	
27	Tuition and fees deduction (see page 29)	27	
28	Health savings account deduction. Attach Form 8889	28	
29	Moving expenses. Attach Form 3903	29	
30	One-half of self-employment tax. Attach Schedule SE	30	
31	Self-employed health insurance deduction (see page 30)	31	
32	Self-employed SEP, SIMPLE, and qualified plans	32	
33	Penalty on early withdrawal of savings	33	
34a	Alimony paid b Recipient's SSN ▶	34a	
35	Add lines 23 through 34a		35
36	Subtract line 35 from line 22. This is your **adjusted gross income** ▶		36

For Disclosure, Privacy Act, and Paperwork Reduction Act Notice, see page 75. Cat. No. 11320B Form **1040** (2004)

Form 1040 (2004) Page 2

Tax and Credits

37 Amount from line 36 (adjusted gross income) . . . 37

38a Check if: ☐ **You** were born before January 2, 1940, ☐ Blind. ☐ **Spouse** was born before January 2, 1940, ☐ Blind. } **Total boxes checked** ▶ 38a ☐

b If your spouse itemizes on a separate return or you were a dual-status alien, see page 31 and check here ▶ 38b ☐

Standard Deduction for—
- People who checked any box on line 38a or 38b **or** who can be claimed as a dependent, see page 31.
- All others:

Single or Married filing separately, $4,850

Married filing jointly or Qualifying widow(er), $9,700

Head of household, $7,150

39 **Itemized deductions** (from Schedule A) **or** your **standard deduction** (see left margin) . . 39

40 Subtract line 39 from line 37 . . . 40

41 If line 37 is $107,025 or less, multiply $3,100 by the total number of exemptions claimed on line 6d. If line 37 is over $107,025, see the worksheet on page 33 . . . 41

42 **Taxable income.** Subtract line 41 from line 40. If line 41 is more than line 40, enter -0- . 42

43 **Tax** (see page 33). Check if any tax is from: **a** ☐ Form(s) 8814 **b** ☐ Form 4972 . . . 43

44 **Alternative minimum tax** (see page 35). Attach Form 6251 . . . 44

45 Add lines 43 and 44 . . . ▶ 45

46 Foreign tax credit. Attach Form 1116 if required . . . 46

47 Credit for child and dependent care expenses. Attach Form 2441 47

48 Credit for the elderly or the disabled. Attach Schedule R . . 48

49 Education credits. Attach Form 8863 . . . 49

50 Retirement savings contributions credit. Attach Form 8880. . 50

51 Child tax credit (see page 37) . . . 51

52 Adoption credit. Attach Form 8839 . . . 52

53 Credits from: **a** ☐ Form 8396 **b** ☐ Form 8859 . . . 53

54 Other credits. Check applicable box(es): **a** ☐ Form 3800 **b** ☐ Form 8801 **c** ☐ Specify ______ . . 54

55 Add lines 46 through 54. These are your **total credits** . . . 55

56 Subtract line 55 from line 45. If line 55 is more than line 45, enter -0- . . . ▶ 56

Other Taxes

57 Self-employment tax. Attach Schedule SE . . . 57

58 Social security and Medicare tax on tip income not reported to employer. Attach Form 4137 . . 58

59 Additional tax on IRAs, other qualified retirement plans, etc. Attach Form 5329 if required . 59

60 Advance earned income credit payments from Form(s) W-2 . . . 60

61 Household employment taxes. Attach Schedule H . . . 61

62 Add lines 56 through 61. This is your **total tax** . . . ▶ 62

Payments

If you have a qualifying child, attach Schedule EIC.

63 Federal income tax withheld from Forms W-2 and 1099 . . 63

64 2004 estimated tax payments and amount applied from 2003 return 64

65a **Earned income credit (EIC)** . . . 65a

b Nontaxable combat pay election ▶ 65b

66 Excess social security and tier 1 RRTA tax withheld (see page 54) 66

67 Additional child tax credit. Attach Form 8812 . . . 67

68 Amount paid with request for extension to file (see page 54) 68

69 Other payments from: **a** ☐ Form 2439 **b** ☐ Form 4136 **c** ☐ Form 8885 . 69

70 Add lines 63, 64, 65a, and 66 through 69. These are your **total payments** . . . ▶ 70

Refund

Direct deposit? See page 54 and fill in 72b, 72c, and 72d.

71 If line 70 is more than line 62, subtract line 62 from line 70. This is the amount you **overpaid** 71

72a Amount of line 71 you want **refunded to you** . . . ▶ 72a

▶ b Routing number ☐☐☐☐☐☐☐☐☐ ▶ **c** Type: ☐ Checking ☐ Savings

▶ d Account number ☐☐☐☐☐☐☐☐☐☐☐☐☐☐☐☐☐

73 Amount of line 71 you want **applied to your 2005 estimated tax** ▶ 73

Amount You Owe

74 **Amount you owe.** Subtract line 70 from line 62. For details on how to pay, see page 55 ▶ 74

75 Estimated tax penalty (see page 55) . . . 75

Third Party Designee

Do you want to allow another person to discuss this return with the IRS (see page 56)? ☐ **Yes.** Complete the following. ☐ **No**

Designee's name ▶ Phone no. ▶ ( ) Personal identification number (PIN) ▶ ☐☐☐☐☐

Sign Here

Joint return? See page 17.

Keep a copy for your records.

Under penalties of perjury, I declare that I have examined this return and accompanying schedules and statements, and to the best of my knowledge and belief, they are true, correct, and complete. Declaration of preparer (other than taxpayer) is based on all information of which preparer has any knowledge.

Your signature	Date	Your occupation	Daytime phone number ( )
Spouse's signature. If a joint return, **both** must sign.	Date	Spouse's occupation	

Paid Preparer's Use Only

Preparer's signature ▶	Date	Check if self-employed ☐	Preparer's SSN or PTIN
Firm's name (or yours if self-employed), address, and ZIP code ▶		EIN	
		Phone no.	( )

SCHEDULES A&B (Form 1040) Department of the Treasury Internal Revenue Service (99)	**Schedule A—Itemized Deductions** (Schedule B is on back) ▶ Attach to Form 1040. ▶ See Instructions for Schedules A and B (Form 1040).	OMB No. 1545-0074 2004 Attachment Sequence No. 07

Name(s) shown on Form 1040 | Your social security number

Medical and Dental Expenses		**Caution.** Do not include expenses reimbursed or paid by others.			
	1	Medical and dental expenses (see page A-2)	1		
	2	Enter amount from Form 1040, line 37 [2]			
	3	Multiply line 2 by 7.5% (.075).	3		
	4	Subtract line 3 from line 1. If line 3 is more than line 1, enter -0-		4	
Taxes You Paid (See page A-2.)	5	State and local **(check only one box)**: a ☐ Income taxes, **or** b ☐ General sales taxes (see page A-2)	5		
	6	Real estate taxes (see page A-3).	6		
	7	Personal property taxes	7		
	8	Other taxes. List type and amount ▶	8		
	9	Add lines 5 through 8		9	
Interest You Paid (See page A-3.)	10	Home mortgage interest and points reported to you on Form 1098	10		
	11	Home mortgage interest not reported to you on Form 1098. If paid to the person from whom you bought the home, see page A-4 and show that person's name, identifying no., and address ▶	11		
Note. Personal interest is not deductible.	12	Points not reported to you on Form 1098. See page A-4 for special rules	12		
	13	Investment interest. Attach Form 4952 if required. (See page A-4.)	13		
	14	Add lines 10 through 13		14	
Gifts to Charity If you made a gift and got a benefit for it, see page A-4.	15	Gifts by cash or check. If you made any gift of $250 or more, see page A-4	15		
	16	Other than by cash or check. If any gift of $250 or more, see page A-4. You **must** attach Form 8283 if over $500	16		
	17	Carryover from prior year	17		
	18	Add lines 15 through 17		18	
Casualty and Theft Losses	19	Casualty or theft loss(es). Attach Form 4684. (See page A-5.)		19	
Job Expenses and Most Other Miscellaneous Deductions (See page A-5.)	20	Unreimbursed employee expenses—job travel, union dues, job education, etc. Attach Form 2106 or 2106-EZ if required. (See page A-6.) ▶	20		
	21	Tax preparation fees.	21		
	22	Other expenses—investment, safe deposit box, etc. List type and amount ▶	22		
	23	Add lines 20 through 22	23		
	24	Enter amount from Form 1040, line 37 [24]			
	25	Multiply line 24 by 2% (.02)	25		
	26	Subtract line 25 from line 23. If line 25 is more than line 23, enter -0-		26	
Other Miscellaneous Deductions	27	Other—from list on page A-6. List type and amount ▶		27	
Total Itemized Deductions	28	Is Form 1040, line 37, over $142,700 (over $71,350 if married filing separately)? ☐ **No.** Your deduction is not limited. Add the amounts in the far right column for lines 4 through 27. Also, enter this amount on Form 1040, line 39. ▶ ☐ **Yes.** Your deduction may be limited. See page A-6 for the amount to enter.		28	

Schedules A&B (Form 1040) 2004 OMB No. 1545-0074 Page **2**

Name(s) shown on Form 1040. Do not enter name and social security number if shown on other side. | **Your social security number**

Schedule B—Interest and Ordinary Dividends

Attachment Sequence No. **08**

Part I Interest

(See page B-1 and the instructions for Form 1040, line 8a.)

Note. If you received a Form 1099-INT, Form 1099-OID, or substitute statement from a brokerage firm, list the firm's name as the payer and enter the total interest shown on that form.

			Amount
1	List name of payer. If any interest is from a seller-financed mortgage and the buyer used the property as a personal residence, see page B-1 and list this interest first. Also, show that buyer's social security number and address ▶	1	
2	Add the amounts on line 1	2	
3	Excludable interest on series EE and I U.S. savings bonds issued after 1989. Attach Form 8815	3	
4	Subtract line 3 from line 2. Enter the result here and on Form 1040, line 8a ▶	4	

Note. If line 4 is over $1,500, you must complete Part III.

Part II Ordinary Dividends

(See page B-2 and the instructions for Form 1040, line 9a.)

Note. If you received a Form 1099-DIV or substitute statement from a brokerage firm, list the firm's name as the payer and enter the ordinary dividends shown on that form.

			Amount
5	List name of payer ▶	5	
6	Add the amounts on line 5. Enter the total here and on Form 1040, line 9a . ▶	6	

Note. If line 6 is over $1,500, you must complete Part III.

Part III Foreign Accounts and Trusts

(See page B-2.)

	You must complete this part if you **(a)** had over $1,500 of taxable interest or ordinary dividends; or **(b)** had a foreign account; or **(c)** received a distribution from, or were a grantor of, or a transferor to, a foreign trust.	**Yes**	**No**
7a	At any time during 2004, did you have an interest in or a signature or other authority over a financial account in a foreign country, such as a bank account, securities account, or other financial account? See page B-2 for exceptions and filing requirements for Form TD F 90-22.1.		
b	If "Yes," enter the name of the foreign country ▶		
8	During 2004, did you receive a distribution from, or were you the grantor of, or transferor to, a foreign trust? If "Yes," you may have to file Form 3520. See page B-2		

For Paperwork Reduction Act Notice, see Form 1040 instructions. **Schedule B (Form 1040) 2004**

SCHEDULE C (Form 1040)

Department of the Treasury
Internal Revenue Service

Profit or Loss From Business

(Sole Proprietorship)

▶ Partnerships, joint ventures, etc., must file Form 1065 or 1065-B.

▶ Attach to Form 1040 or 1041. ▶ See Instructions for Schedule C (Form 1040).

OMB No. 1545-0074

2004

Attachment Sequence No. **09**

Name of proprietor | **Social security number (SSN)**

A Principal business or profession, including product or service (see page C-2 of the instructions) | **B** Enter code from pages C-7, 8, & 9 ▶

C Business name. If no separate business name, leave blank. | **D** Employer ID number (EIN), if any

E Business address (including suite or room no.) ▶
City, town or post office, state, and ZIP code

F Accounting method: (1) ☐ Cash (2) ☐ Accrual (3) ☐ Other (specify) ▶

G Did you "materially participate" in the operation of this business during 2004? If "No," see page C-3 for limit on losses ☐ **Yes** ☐ **No**

H If you started or acquired this business during 2004, check here . . . ▶ ☐

Part I Income

1	Gross receipts or sales. **Caution.** If this income was reported to you on Form W-2 and the "Statutory employee" box on that form was checked, see page C-3 and check here . . . ▶ ☐	1	
2	Returns and allowances	2	
3	Subtract line 2 from line 1	3	
4	Cost of goods sold (from line 42 on page 2)	4	
5	**Gross profit.** Subtract line 4 from line 3	5	
6	Other income, including Federal and state gasoline or fuel tax credit or refund (see page C-3)	6	
7	**Gross income.** Add lines 5 and 6 . . . ▶	7	

Part II Expenses. Enter expenses for business use of your home **only** on line 30.

8	Advertising	8		19	Pension and profit-sharing plans	19	
9	Car and truck expenses (see page C-3)	9		20	Rent or lease (see page C-5):		
				a	Vehicles, machinery, and equipment	20a	
10	Commissions and fees	10		b	Other business property	20b	
11	Contract labor (see page C-4)	11		21	Repairs and maintenance	21	
12	Depletion	12		22	Supplies (not included in Part III)	22	
13	Depreciation and section 179 expense deduction (not included in Part III) (see page C-4)	13		23	Taxes and licenses	23	
				24	Travel, meals, and entertainment:		
				a	Travel	24a	
14	Employee benefit programs (other than on line 19)	14		b	Meals and entertainment		
15	Insurance (other than health)	15		c	Enter nondeductible amount included on line 24b (see page C-5)		
16	Interest:						
a	Mortgage (paid to banks, etc.)	16a		d	Subtract line 24c from line 24b	24d	
b	Other	16b		25	Utilities	25	
17	Legal and professional services	17		26	Wages (less employment credits)	26	
18	Office expense	18		27	Other expenses (from line 48 on page 2)	27	

28	**Total expenses** before expenses for business use of home. Add lines 8 through 27 in columns . . ▶	28	
29	Tentative profit (loss). Subtract line 28 from line 7	29	
30	Expenses for business use of your home. Attach **Form 8829**	30	
31	**Net profit or (loss).** Subtract line 30 from line 29. • If a profit, enter on **Form 1040, line 12,** and **also** on **Schedule SE, line 2** (statutory employees, see page C-6). Estates and trusts, enter on Form 1041, line 3. • If a loss, you **must** go to line 32.	31	
32	If you have a loss, check the box that describes your investment in this activity (see page C-6). • If you checked 32a, enter the loss on **Form 1040, line 12,** and **also** on **Schedule SE, line 2** (statutory employees, see page C-6). Estates and trusts, enter on Form 1041, line 3. • If you checked 32b, you **must** attach **Form 6198.**	32a ☐ All investment is at risk. 32b ☐ Some investment is not at risk.	

For Paperwork Reduction Act Notice, see Form 1040 instructions. Cat. No. 11334P **Schedule C (Form 1040) 2004**

Schedule C (Form 1040) 2004 Page 2

Part III Cost of Goods Sold (see page C-6)

33 Method(s) used to value closing inventory: a ☐ Cost b ☐ Lower of cost or market c ☐ Other (attach explanation)

34 Was there any change in determining quantities, costs, or valuations between opening and closing inventory? If "Yes," attach explanation . . . ☐ Yes ☐ No

35 Inventory at beginning of year. If different from last year's closing inventory, attach explanation . .	35		
36 Purchases less cost of items withdrawn for personal use . . .	36		
37 Cost of labor. Do not include any amounts paid to yourself . . .	37		
38 Materials and supplies . . .	38		
39 Other costs . . .	39		
40 Add lines 35 through 39 . . .	40		
41 Inventory at end of year . . .	41		
42 **Cost of goods sold.** Subtract line 41 from line 40. Enter the result here and on page 1, line 4 . .	42		

Part IV Information on Your Vehicle.

Complete this part **only** if you are claiming car or truck expenses on line 9 and are not required to file Form 4562 for this business. See the instructions for line 13 on page C-4 to find out if you must file Form 4562.

43 When did you place your vehicle in service for business purposes? (month, day, year) ▶ ______/______/______

44 Of the total number of miles you drove your vehicle during 2004, enter the number of miles you used your vehicle for:

a Business ____________ b Commuting ____________ c Other ____________

45 Do you (or your spouse) have another vehicle available for personal use? . . . ☐ Yes ☐ No

46 Was your vehicle available for personal use during off-duty hours? . . . ☐ Yes ☐ No

47a Do you have evidence to support your deduction? . . . ☐ Yes ☐ No

b If "Yes," is the evidence written? . . . ☐ Yes ☐ No

Part V Other Expenses.

List below business expenses not included on lines 8–26 or line 30.

48 **Total other expenses.** Enter here and on page 1, line 27 . . .	48	

Schedule C (Form 1040) 2004

SCHEDULE D (Form 1040)

Department of the Treasury Internal Revenue Service (99)

Capital Gains and Losses

▶ Attach to Form 1040. ▶ See Instructions for Schedule D (Form 1040).
▶ Use Schedule D-1 to list additional transactions for lines 1 and 8.

OMB No. 1545-0074

2004

Attachment Sequence No. **12**

Name(s) shown on Form 1040 | **Your social security number**

Part I Short-Term Capital Gains and Losses—Assets Held One Year or Less

	(a) Description of property (Example: 100 sh. XYZ Co.)	(b) Date acquired (Mo., day, yr.)	(c) Date sold (Mo., day, yr.)	(d) Sales price (see page D-6 of the instructions)	(e) Cost or other basis (see page D-6 of the instructions)	(f) Gain or (loss) Subtract (e) from (d)
1						

2	Enter your short-term totals, if any, from Schedule D-1, line 2	2		
3	**Total short-term sales price amounts.** Add lines 1 and 2 in column (d)	3		
4	Short-term gain from Form 6252 and short-term gain or (loss) from Forms 4684, 6781, and 8824		4	
5	Net short-term gain or (loss) from partnerships, S corporations, estates, and trusts from Schedule(s) K-1		5	
6	Short-term capital loss carryover. Enter the amount, if any, from line 8 of your **Capital Loss Carryover Worksheet** on page D-6 of the instructions		6	( )
7	**Net short-term capital gain or (loss).** Combine lines 1 through 6 in column (f)		7	

Part II Long-Term Capital Gains and Losses—Assets Held More Than One Year

	(a) Description of property (Example: 100 sh. XYZ Co.)	(b) Date acquired (Mo., day, yr.)	(c) Date sold (Mo., day, yr.)	(d) Sales price (see page D-6 of the instructions)	(e) Cost or other basis (see page D-6 of the instructions)	(f) Gain or (loss) Subtract (e) from (d)
8						

9	Enter your long-term totals, if any, from Schedule D-1, line 9	9		
10	**Total long-term sales price amounts.** Add lines 8 and 9 in column (d)	10		
11	Gain from Form 4797, Part I; long-term gain from Forms 2439 and 6252; and long-term gain or (loss) from Forms 4684, 6781, and 8824		11	
12	Net long-term gain or (loss) from partnerships, S corporations, estates, and trusts from Schedule(s) K-1		12	
13	Capital gain distributions. See page D-1 of the instructions		13	
14	Long-term capital loss carryover. Enter the amount, if any, from line 13 of your **Capital Loss Carryover Worksheet** on page D-6 of the instructions		14	( )
15	**Net long-term capital gain or (loss).** Combine lines 8 through 14 in column (f). Then go to Part III on the back		15	

Part III **Summary**

16 Combine lines 7 and 15 and enter the result. If line 16 is a loss, skip lines 17 through 20, and go to line 21. If a gain, enter the gain on Form 1040, line 13, and then go to line 17 below . . | 16 |

17 Are lines 15 and 16 **both** gains?
☐ **Yes.** Go to line 18.
☐ **No.** Skip lines 18 through 21, and go to line 22.

18 Enter the amount, if any, from line 7 of the **28% Rate Gain Worksheet** on page D-7 of the instructions . . . . ▶ | 18 |

19 Enter the amount, if any, from line 18 of the **Unrecaptured Section 1250 Gain Worksheet** on page D-8 of the instructions . . . . ▶ | 19 |

20 Are lines 18 and 19 **both** zero or blank?
☐ **Yes.** Complete Form 1040 through line 42, and then complete the **Qualified Dividends and Capital Gain Tax Worksheet** on page 34 of the Instructions for Form 1040. **Do not** complete lines 21 and 22 below.
☐ **No.** Complete Form 1040 through line 42, and then complete the **Schedule D Tax Worksheet** on page D-9 of the instructions. **Do not** complete lines 21 and 22 below.

21 If line 16 is a loss, enter here and on Form 1040, line 13, the **smaller** of:

- The loss on line 16 or
- ($3,000), or if married filing separately, ($1,500)

} . . . . | 21 | ( ) |

Note. When figuring which amount is smaller, treat both amounts as positive numbers.

22 Do you have qualified dividends on Form 1040, line 9b?
☐ **Yes.** Complete Form 1040 through line 42, and then complete the **Qualified Dividends and Capital Gain Tax Worksheet** on page 34 of the Instructions for Form 1040.
☐ **No.** Complete the rest of Form 1040.

SCHEDULE E (Form 1040)

Department of the Treasury Internal Revenue Service (99)

Supplemental Income and Loss

(From rental real estate, royalties, partnerships, S corporations, estates, trusts, REMICs, etc.)

▶ Attach to Form 1040 or Form 1041. ▶ See Instructions for Schedule E (Form 1040).

OMB No. 1545-0074

2004

Attachment Sequence No. 13

Name(s) shown on return | **Your social security number**

Part I **Income or Loss From Rental Real Estate and Royalties** **Note.** If you are in the business of renting personal property, use **Schedule C** or **C-EZ** (see page E-3). Report farm rental income or loss from **Form 4835** on page 2, line 40.

1 List the type and location of each **rental real estate property:**	2 For each rental real estate property listed on line 1, did you or your family use it during the tax year for personal purposes for more than the greater of: • 14 days **or** • 10% of the total days rented at fair rental value? (See page E-3.)		**Yes**	**No**
A		A		
B		B		
C		C		

Income:		Properties A	Properties B	Properties C		Totals (Add columns A, B, and C.)
3 Rents received	3				3	
4 Royalties received	4				4	
Expenses:						
5 Advertising	5					
6 Auto and travel (see page E-4).	6					
7 Cleaning and maintenance	7					
8 Commissions	8					
9 Insurance	9					
10 Legal and other professional fees	10					
11 Management fees	11					
12 Mortgage interest paid to banks, etc. (see page E-4)	12				12	
13 Other interest	13					
14 Repairs	14					
15 Supplies	15					
16 Taxes	16					
17 Utilities	17					
18 Other (list) ▶	18					
19 Add lines 5 through 18	19				19	
20 Depreciation expense or depletion (see page E-4)	20				20	
21 Total expenses. Add lines 19 and 20	21					
22 Income or (loss) from rental real estate or royalty properties. Subtract line 21 from line 3 (rents) or line 4 (royalties). If the result is a (loss), see page E-4 to find out if you must file **Form 6198**	22					
23 Deductible rental real estate loss. **Caution.** Your rental real estate loss on line 22 may be limited. See page E-4 to find out if you must file **Form 8582.** Real estate professionals must complete line 43 on page 2	23	( )	( )	( )		
24 **Income.** Add positive amounts shown on line 22. **Do not** include any losses					24	
25 **Losses.** Add royalty losses from line 22 and rental real estate losses from line 23. Enter total losses here					25	( )
26 **Total rental real estate and royalty income or (loss).** Combine lines 24 and 25. Enter the result here. If Parts II, III, IV, and line 40 on page 2 do not apply to you, also enter this amount on Form 1040, line 17. Otherwise, include this amount in the total on line 41 on page 2					26	

Schedule E (Form 1040) 2004 Attachment Sequence No. 13 Page 2

Name(s) shown on return. Do not enter name and social security number if shown on other side. | **Your social security number**

Caution. The IRS compares amounts reported on your tax return with amounts shown on Schedule(s) K-1.

Part II Income or Loss From Partnerships and S Corporations

Note. If you report a loss from an at-risk activity for which **any** amount is **not** at risk, you **must** check column **(e)** on line 28 and attach **Form 6198.** See page E-1.

27 Are you reporting any loss not allowed in a prior year due to the at-risk or basis limitations, a prior year unallowed loss from a passive activity (if that loss was not reported on Form 8582), or unreimbursed partnership expenses? ☐ **Yes** ☐ **No**
If you answered "Yes," see page E-6 before completing this section.

28	**(a)** Name	**(b)** Enter **P** for partnership; **S** for S corporation	**(c)** Check if foreign partnership	**(d)** Employer identification number	**(e)** Check if any amount is not at risk
A					
B					
C					
D					

	Passive Income and Loss		Nonpassive Income and Loss		
	(f) Passive loss allowed (attach **Form 8582** if required)	**(g)** Passive income from **Schedule K–1**	**(h)** Nonpassive loss from **Schedule K–1**	**(i)** Section 179 expense deduction from **Form 4562**	**(j)** Nonpassive income from **Schedule K–1**
A					
B					
C					
D					
29a Totals					
b Totals					

30 Add columns (g) and (j) of line 29a 30

31 Add columns (f), (h), and (i) of line 29b . . . . . . 31 ( )

32 **Total partnership and S corporation income or (loss).** Combine lines 30 and 31. Enter the result here and include in the total on line 41 below 32

Part III Income or Loss From Estates and Trusts

33	**(a)** Name	**(b)** Employer identification number
A		
B		

	Passive Income and Loss		Nonpassive Income and Loss	
	(c) Passive deduction or loss allowed (attach **Form 8582** if required)	**(d)** Passive income from **Schedule K–1**	**(e)** Deduction or loss from **Schedule K–1**	**(f)** Other income from **Schedule K–1**
A				
B				
34a Totals				
b Totals				

35 Add columns (d) and (f) of line 34a 35

36 Add columns (c) and (e) of line 34b . . . . . . 36 ( )

37 **Total estate and trust income or (loss).** Combine lines 35 and 36. Enter the result here and include in the total on line 41 below 37

Part IV Income or Loss From Real Estate Mortgage Investment Conduits (REMICs)—Residual Holder

38	**(a)** Name	**(b)** Employer identification number	**(c)** Excess inclusion from **Schedules Q,** line 2c (see page E-6)	**(d)** Taxable income (net loss) from **Schedules Q,** line 1b	**(e)** Income from **Schedules Q,** line 3b

39 Combine columns (d) and (e) only. Enter the result here and include in the total on line 41 below 39

Part V Summary

40 Net farm rental income or (loss) from **Form 4835**. Also, complete line 42 below 40

41 **Total income or (loss).** Combine lines 26, 32, 37, 39, and 40. Enter the result here and on Form 1040, line 17 ▶ 41

42 **Reconciliation of farming and fishing income.** Enter your **gross** farming and fishing income reported on Form 4835, line 7; Schedule K-1 (Form 1065), box 14, code B; Schedule K-1 (Form 1120S), box 17, code N; and Schedule K-1 (Form 1041), line 14 (see page E-6) 42

43 **Reconciliation for real estate professionals.** If you were a real estate professional (see page E-1), enter the net income or (loss) you reported anywhere on Form 1040 from all rental real estate activities in which you materially participated under the passive activity loss rules . . . 43

SCHEDULE SE (Form 1040)

Department of the Treasury Internal Revenue Service

Self-Employment Tax

▶ Attach to Form 1040. ▶ See Instructions for Schedule SE (Form 1040).

OMB No. 1545-0074

2004

Attachment Sequence No. 17

Name of person with **self-employment** income (as shown on Form 1040)	Social security number of person with **self-employment** income ▶	

Who Must File Schedule SE

You must file Schedule SE if:

- You had net earnings from self-employment from **other than** church employee income (line 4 of Short Schedule SE or line 4c of Long Schedule SE) of $400 or more **or**
- You had church employee income of $108.28 or more. Income from services you performed as a minister or a member of a religious order **is not** church employee income (see page SE-1).

Note. Even if you had a loss or a small amount of income from self-employment, it may be to your benefit to file Schedule SE and use either "optional method" in Part II of Long Schedule SE (see page SE-3).

Exception. If your only self-employment income was from earnings as a minister, member of a religious order, or Christian Science practitioner **and** you filed Form 4361 and received IRS approval not to be taxed on those earnings, **do not** file Schedule SE. Instead, write "Exempt–Form 4361" on Form 1040, line 57.

May I Use Short Schedule SE or Must I Use Long Schedule SE?

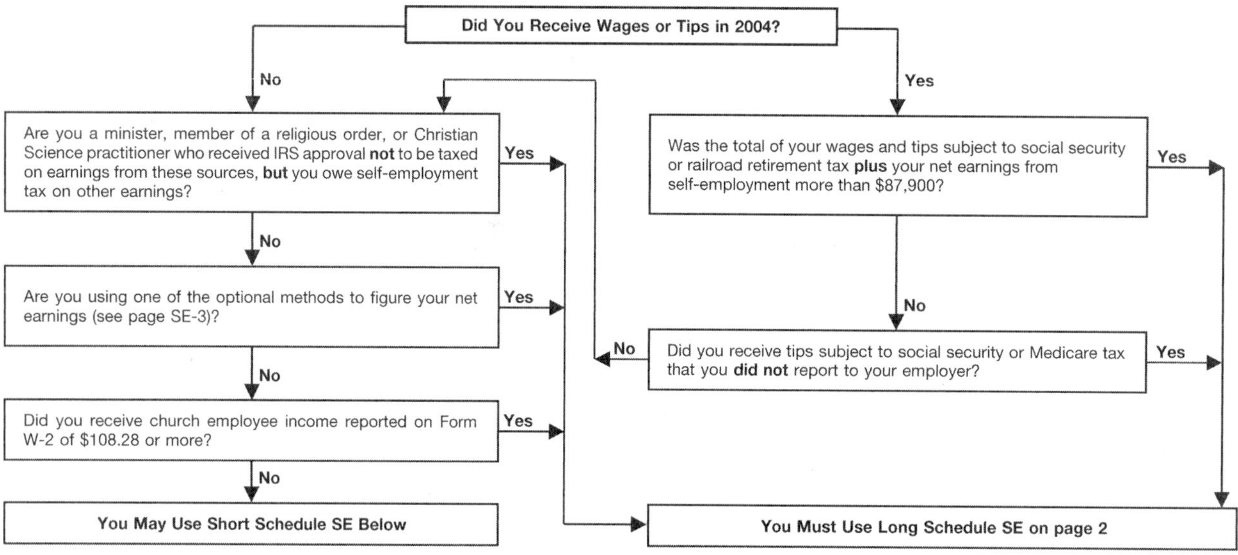

Section A—Short Schedule SE. Caution. Read above to see if you can use Short Schedule SE.

1	Net farm profit or (loss) from Schedule F, line 36, and farm partnerships, Schedule K-1 (Form 1065), box 14, code A	1	
2	Net profit or (loss) from Schedule C, line 31; Schedule C-EZ, line 3; Schedule K-1 (Form 1065), box 14, code A (other than farming); and Schedule K-1 (Form 1065-B), box 9. Ministers and members of religious orders, see page SE-1 for amounts to report on this line. See page SE-2 for other income to report	2	
3	Combine lines 1 and 2	3	
4	**Net earnings from self-employment.** Multiply line 3 by 92.35% (.9235). If less than $400, **do not** file this schedule; you do not owe self-employment tax ▶	4	
5	**Self-employment tax.** If the amount on line 4 is: • $87,900 or less, multiply line 4 by 15.3% (.153). Enter the result here and on **Form 1040, line 57.** • More than $87,900, multiply line 4 by 2.9% (.029). Then, add $10,899.60 to the result. Enter the total here and on **Form 1040, line 57.**	5	
6	**Deduction for one-half of self-employment tax.** Multiply line 5 by 50% (.5). Enter the result here and on **Form 1040, line 30** 6		

For Paperwork Reduction Act Notice, see Form 1040 instructions. Cat. No. 11358Z **Schedule SE (Form 1040) 2004**

Schedule SE (Form 1040) 2004 Attachment Sequence No. 17 Page 2

Name of person with **self-employment** income (as shown on Form 1040)	Social security number of person with **self-employment** income ▶

Section B—Long Schedule SE

Part I Self-Employment Tax

Note. If your only income subject to self-employment tax is **church employee income,** skip lines 1 through 4b. Enter -0- on line 4c and go to line 5a. Income from services you performed as a minister or a member of a religious order **is not** church employee income. See page SE-1.

A	If you are a minister, member of a religious order, or Christian Science practitioner **and** you filed Form 4361, but you had $400 or more of **other** net earnings from self-employment, check here and continue with Part I . . . . ▶ ☐			
1	Net farm profit or (loss) from Schedule F, line 36, and farm partnerships, Schedule K-1 (Form 1065), box 14, code A. **Note.** Skip this line if you use the farm optional method (see page SE-4)	1		
2	Net profit or (loss) from Schedule C, line 31; Schedule C-EZ, line 3; Schedule K-1 (Form 1065), box 14, code A (other than farming); and Schedule K-1 (Form 1065-B), box 9. Ministers and members of religious orders, see page SE-1 for amounts to report on this line. See page SE-2 for other income to report. **Note.** Skip this line if you use the nonfarm optional method (see page SE-4)	2		
3	Combine lines 1 and 2	3		
4a	If line 3 is more than zero, multiply line 3 by 92.35% (.9235). Otherwise, enter amount from line 3	4a		
b	If you elect one or both of the optional methods, enter the total of lines 15 and 17 here . . .	4b		
c	Combine lines 4a and 4b. If less than $400, **stop**; you do not owe self-employment tax. **Exception.** If less than $400 and you had **church employee income,** enter -0- and continue. . . . . . ▶	4c		
5a	Enter your **church employee income** from Form W-2. See page SE-1 for definition of church employee income **5a**			
b	Multiply line 5a by 92.35% (.9235). If less than $100, enter -0-	5b		
6	**Net earnings from self-employment.** Add lines 4c and 5b	6		
7	Maximum amount of combined wages and self-employment earnings subject to social security tax or the 6.2% portion of the 7.65% railroad retirement (tier 1) tax for 2004	7	87,900	00
8a	Total social security wages and tips (total of boxes 3 and 7 on Form(s) W-2) and railroad retirement (tier 1) compensation. If $87,900 or more, skip lines 8b through 10, and go to line 11 . . . . **8a**			
b	Unreported tips subject to social security tax (from Form 4137, line 9) **8b**			
c	Add lines 8a and 8b	8c		
9	Subtract line 8c from line 7. If zero or less, enter -0- here and on line 10 and go to line 11 . ▶	9		
10	Multiply the **smaller** of line 6 or line 9 by 12.4% (.124)	10		
11	Multiply line 6 by 2.9% (.029)	11		
12	**Self-employment tax.** Add lines 10 and 11. Enter here and on **Form 1040, line 57**	12		
13	**Deduction for one-half of self-employment tax.** Multiply line 12 by 50% (.5). Enter the result here and on **Form 1040, line 30** **13**			

Part II Optional Methods To Figure Net Earnings (see page SE-3)

Farm Optional Method. You may use this method **only** if **(a)** your gross farm income[1] was not more than $2,400 **or (b)** your net farm profits[2] were less than $1,733.

14	Maximum income for optional methods	14	1,600	00
15	Enter the **smaller** of: two-thirds (⅔) of gross farm income[1] (not less than zero) **or** $1,600. Also include this amount on line 4b above	15		

Nonfarm Optional Method. You may use this method **only** if **(a)** your net nonfarm profits[3] were less than $1,733 and also less than 72.189% of your gross nonfarm income[4] **and (b)** you had net earnings from self-employment of at least $400 in 2 of the prior 3 years.

Caution. You may use this method no more than five times.

16	Subtract line 15 from line 14	16		
17	Enter the **smaller** of: two-thirds (⅔) of gross nonfarm income[4] (not less than zero) **or** the amount on line 16. Also include this amount on line 4b above	17		

[1] From Sch. F, line 11, and Sch. K-1 (Form 1065), box 14, code B.

[2] From Sch. F, line 36, and Sch. K-1 (Form 1065), box 14, code A.

[3] From Sch. C, line 31; Sch. C-EZ, line 3; Sch. K-1 (Form 1065), box 14, code A; and Sch. K-1 (Form 1065-B), box 9.

[4] From Sch. C, line 7; Sch. C-EZ, line 1; Sch. K-1 (Form 1065), box 14, code C; and Sch. K-1 (Form 1065-B), box 9.

Form **1041** Department of the Treasury—Internal Revenue Service

U.S. Income Tax Return for Estates and Trusts 2004

OMB No. 1545-0092

For calendar year 2004 or fiscal year beginning , 2004, and ending , 20

A Type of entity (see instr.):
- ☐ Decedent's estate
- ☐ Simple trust
- ☐ Complex trust
- ☐ Qualified disability trust
- ☐ ESBT (S portion only)
- ☐ Grantor type trust
- ☐ Bankruptcy estate–Ch. 7
- ☐ Bankruptcy estate–Ch. 11
- ☐ Pooled income fund

Name of estate or trust (If a grantor type trust, see page 12 of the instructions.)

Name and title of fiduciary

Number, street, and room or suite no. (If a P.O. box, see page 12 of the instructions.)

City or town, state, and ZIP code

C Employer identification number

D Date entity created

E Nonexempt charitable and split-interest trusts, check applicable boxes (see page 13 of the instr.):
- ☐ Described in section 4947(a)(1)
- ☐ Not a private foundation
- ☐ Described in section 4947(a)(2)

B Number of Schedules K-1 attached (see instructions) ▶

F Check applicable boxes: ☐ Initial return ☐ Final return ☐ Amended return ☐ Change in trust's name ☐ Change in fiduciary ☐ Change in fiduciary's name ☐ Change in fiduciary's address

G Pooled mortgage account (see page 14 of the instructions): ☐ Bought ☐ Sold Date:

Income

1	Interest income	1	
2a	Total ordinary dividends	2a	
b	Qualified dividends allocable to: **(1)** Beneficiaries ______ **(2)** Estate or trust ______		
3	Business income or (loss) (attach Schedule C or C-EZ (Form 1040))	3	
4	Capital gain or (loss) (attach Schedule D (Form 1041))	4	
5	Rents, royalties, partnerships, other estates and trusts, etc. (attach Schedule E (Form 1040))	5	
6	Farm income or (loss) (attach Schedule F (Form 1040))	6	
7	Ordinary gain or (loss) (attach Form 4797)	7	
8	Other income. List type and amount ______	8	
9	**Total income.** Combine lines 1, 2a, and 3 through 8 ▶	9	

Deductions

10	Interest. Check if Form 4952 is attached ▶ ☐	10	
11	Taxes	11	
12	Fiduciary fees	12	
13	Charitable deduction (from Schedule A, line 7)	13	
14	Attorney, accountant, and return preparer fees	14	
15a	Other deductions **not** subject to the 2% floor (attach schedule)	15a	
b	Allowable miscellaneous itemized deductions subject to the 2% floor	15b	
16	**Total.** Add lines 10 through 15b	16	
17	Adjusted total income or (loss). Subtract line 16 from line 9. Enter here and on Schedule B, line 1 ▶	17	
18	Income distribution deduction (from Schedule B, line 15) (attach Schedules K-1 (Form 1041))	18	
19	Estate tax deduction (including certain generation-skipping taxes) (attach computation)	19	
20	Exemption	20	
21	**Total deductions.** Add lines 18 through 20 ▶	21	

Tax and Payments

22	Taxable income. Subtract line 21 from line 17. If a loss, see page 19 of the instructions	22	
23	**Total tax** (from Schedule G, line 7)	23	
24	**Payments: a** 2004 estimated tax payments and amount applied from 2003 return	24a	
b	Estimated tax payments allocated to beneficiaries (from Form 1041-T)	24b	
c	Subtract line 24b from line 24a	24c	
d	Tax paid with extension of time to file: ☐ Form 2758 ☐ Form 8736 ☐ Form 8800	24d	
e	Federal income tax withheld. If any is from Form(s) 1099, check ▶ ☐	24e	
	Other payments: **f** Form 2439 ______ ; **g** Form 4136 ______ ; Total ▶	24h	
25	**Total payments.** Add lines 24c through 24e, and 24h ▶	25	
26	Estimated tax penalty (see page 20 of the instructions)	26	
27	**Tax due.** If line 25 is smaller than the total of lines 23 and 26, enter amount owed	27	
28	**Overpayment.** If line 25 is larger than the total of lines 23 and 26, enter amount overpaid	28	
29	Amount of line 28 to be: **a Credited to 2005 estimated tax** ▶ ; **b Refunded** ▶	29	

Sign Here

Under penalties of perjury, I declare that I have examined this return, including accompanying schedules and statements, and to the best of my knowledge and belief, it is true, correct, and complete. Declaration of preparer (other than taxpayer) is based on all information of which preparer has any knowledge.

Signature of fiduciary or officer representing fiduciary | Date | ▶ EIN of fiduciary if a financial institution

May the IRS discuss this return with the preparer shown below (see instr.)? ☐ **Yes** ☐ **No**

Paid Preparer's Use Only

Preparer's signature ▶ | Date | Check if self-employed ☐ | Preparer's SSN or PTIN

Firm's name (or yours if self-employed), address, and ZIP code ▶ | EIN | Phone no. ( )

For Privacy Act and Paperwork Reduction Act Notice, see the separate instructions. Cat. No. 11370H Form **1041** (2004)

Form 1041 (2004) Page 2

Schedule A **Charitable Deduction.** Do not complete for a simple trust or a pooled income fund.

1	Amounts paid or permanently set aside for charitable purposes from gross income (see page 20)	1	
2	Tax-exempt income allocable to charitable contributions (see page 20 of the instructions)	2	
3	Subtract line 2 from line 1	3	
4	Capital gains for the tax year allocated to corpus and paid or permanently set aside for charitable purposes	4	
5	Add lines 3 and 4	5	
6	Section 1202 exclusion allocable to capital gains paid or permanently set aside for charitable purposes (see page 20 of the instructions)	6	
7	**Charitable deduction.** Subtract line 6 from line 5. Enter here and on page 1, line 13	7	

Schedule B **Income Distribution Deduction**

1	Adjusted total income (see page 21 of the instructions)	1	
2	Adjusted tax-exempt interest	2	
3	Total net gain from Schedule D (Form 1041), line 15, column (1) (see page 21 of the instructions)	3	
4	Enter amount from Schedule A, line 4 (reduced by any allocable section 1202 exclusion)	4	
5	Capital gains for the tax year included on Schedule A, line 1 (see page 21 of the instructions)	5	
6	Enter any gain from page 1, line 4, as a negative number. If page 1, line 4, is a loss, enter the loss as a positive number	6	
7	**Distributable net income (DNI).** Combine lines 1 through 6. If zero or less, enter -0-	7	
8	If a complex trust, enter accounting income for the tax year as determined under the governing instrument and applicable local law — 8		
9	Income required to be distributed currently	9	
10	Other amounts paid, credited, or otherwise required to be distributed	10	
11	Total distributions. Add lines 9 and 10. If greater than line 8, see page 22 of the instructions	11	
12	Enter the amount of tax-exempt income included on line 11	12	
13	Tentative income distribution deduction. Subtract line 12 from line 11	13	
14	Tentative income distribution deduction. Subtract line 2 from line 7. If zero or less, enter -0-	14	
15	**Income distribution deduction.** Enter the smaller of line 13 or line 14 here and on page 1, line 18	15	

Schedule G **Tax Computation** (see page 22 of the instructions)

1	**Tax:** a Tax on taxable income (see page 22 of the instructions)	1a			
	b Tax on lump-sum distributions (attach Form 4972)	1b			
	c Alternative minimum tax (from Schedule I, line 56)	1c			
	d **Total.** Add lines 1a through 1c ▶			1d	
2a	Foreign tax credit (attach Form 1116)	2a			
b	Other nonbusiness credits (attach schedule)	2b			
c	General business credit. Enter here and check which forms are attached: ☐ Form 3800 ☐ Forms (specify) ▶ ________	2c			
d	Credit for prior year minimum tax (attach Form 8801)	2d			
3	**Total credits.** Add lines 2a through 2d ▶			3	
4	Subtract line 3 from line 1d. If zero or less, enter -0-			4	
5	Recapture taxes. Check if from: ☐ Form 4255 ☐ Form 8611			5	
6	Household employment taxes. Attach Schedule H (Form 1040)			6	
7	**Total tax.** Add lines 4 through 6. Enter here and on page 1, line 23 ▶			7	

	Other Information	**Yes**	**No**
1	Did the estate or trust receive tax-exempt income? If "Yes," attach a computation of the allocation of expenses. Enter the amount of tax-exempt interest income and exempt-interest dividends ▶ $ ________		
2	Did the estate or trust receive all or any part of the earnings (salary, wages, and other compensation) of any individual by reason of a contract assignment or similar arrangement?		
3	At any time during calendar year 2004, did the estate or trust have an interest in or a signature or other authority over a bank, securities, or other financial account in a foreign country?		
	See page 24 of the instructions for exceptions and filing requirements for Form TD F 90-22.1. If "Yes," enter the name of the foreign country ▶ ________		
4	During the tax year, did the estate or trust receive a distribution from, or was it the grantor of, or transferor to, a foreign trust? If "Yes," the estate or trust may have to file Form 3520. See page 24 of the instructions		
5	Did the estate or trust receive, or pay, any qualified residence interest on seller-provided financing? If "Yes," see page 24 for required attachment		
6	If this is an estate or a complex trust making the section 663(b) election, check here (see page 24) ▶ ☐		
7	To make a section 643(e)(3) election, attach Schedule D (Form 1041), and check here (see page 24) ▶ ☐		
8	If the decedent's estate has been open for more than 2 years, attach an explanation for the delay in closing the estate, and check here ▶ ☐		
9	Are any present or future trust beneficiaries skip persons? See page 24 of the instructions		

Form 1041 (2004) Page **3**

Schedule I **Alternative Minimum Tax** (see pages 25 through 31 of the instructions)

Part I—Estate's or Trust's Share of Alternative Minimum Taxable Income

1	Adjusted total income or (loss) (from page 1, line 17)	1	
2	Interest	2	
3	Taxes	3	
4	Miscellaneous itemized deductions (from page 1, line 15b)	4	
5	Refund of taxes	5	( )
6	Depletion (difference between regular tax and AMT)	6	
7	Net operating loss deduction. Enter as a positive amount	7	
8	Interest from specified private activity bonds exempt from the regular tax	8	
9	Qualified small business stock (see page 26 of the instructions)	9	
10	Exercise of incentive stock options (excess of AMT income over regular tax income)	10	
11	Other estates and trusts (amount from Schedule K-1 (Form 1041), line 9)	11	
12	Electing large partnerships (amount from Schedule K-1 (Form 1065-B), box 6)	12	
13	Disposition of property (difference between AMT and regular tax gain or loss)	13	
14	Depreciation on assets placed in service after 1986 (difference between regular tax and AMT)	14	
15	Passive activities (difference between AMT and regular tax income or loss)	15	
16	Loss limitations (difference between AMT and regular tax income or loss)	16	
17	Circulation costs (difference between regular tax and AMT)	17	
18	Long-term contracts (difference between AMT and regular tax income)	18	
19	Mining costs (difference between regular tax and AMT)	19	
20	Research and experimental costs (difference between regular tax and AMT)	20	
21	Income from certain installment sales before January 1, 1987	21	( )
22	Intangible drilling costs preference	22	
23	Other adjustments, including income-based related adjustments	23	
24	Alternative tax net operating loss deduction (See the instructions for the limitation that applies.)	24	( )
25	Adjusted alternative minimum taxable income. Combine lines 1 through 24	25	
	Note: *Complete Part II below before going to line 26.*		
26	Income distribution deduction from Part II, line 44 ... 26		
27	Estate tax deduction (from page 1, line 19) ... 27		
28	Add lines 26 and 27	28	
29	Estate's or trust's share of alternative minimum taxable income. Subtract line 28 from line 25	29	

If line 29 is:

- $22,500 or less, stop here and enter -0- on Schedule G, line 1c. The estate or trust is not liable for the alternative minimum tax.
- Over $22,500, but less than $165,000, go to line 45.
- $165,000 or more, enter the amount from line 29 on line 51 and go to line 52.

Part II—Income Distribution Deduction on a Minimum Tax Basis

30	Adjusted alternative minimum taxable income (see page 29 of the instructions)	30	
31	Adjusted tax-exempt interest (other than amounts included on line 8)	31	
32	Total net gain from Schedule D (Form 1041), line 15, column (1). If a loss, enter -0-	32	
33	Capital gains for the tax year allocated to corpus and paid or permanently set aside for charitable purposes (from Schedule A, line 4)	33	
34	Capital gains paid or permanently set aside for charitable purposes from gross income (see page 29 of the instructions)	34	
35	Capital gains computed on a minimum tax basis included on line 25	35	( )
36	Capital losses computed on a minimum tax basis included on line 25. Enter as a positive amount	36	
37	Distributable net alternative minimum taxable income (DNAMTI). Combine lines 30 through 36. If zero or less, enter -0-	37	
38	Income required to be distributed currently (from Schedule B, line 9)	38	
39	Other amounts paid, credited, or otherwise required to be distributed (from Schedule B, line 10)	39	
40	Total distributions. Add lines 38 and 39	40	
41	Tax-exempt income included on line 40 (other than amounts included on line 8)	41	
42	Tentative income distribution deduction on a minimum tax basis. Subtract line 41 from line 40	42	
43	Tentative income distribution deduction on a minimum tax basis. Subtract line 31 from line 37. If zero or less, enter -0-	43	
44	**Income distribution deduction on a minimum tax basis.** Enter the smaller of line 42 or line 43. Enter here and on line 26	44	

Form **1041** (2004)

Form 1041 (2004) Page **4**

Part III—Alternative Minimum Tax

45	Exemption amount				45	$22,500	00
46	Enter the amount from line 29	46					
47	Phase-out of exemption amount	47	$75,000	00			
48	Subtract line 47 from line 46. If zero or less, enter -0-	48					
49	Multiply line 48 by 25% (.25)				49		
50	Subtract line 49 from line 45. If zero or less, enter -0-				50		
51	Subtract line 50 from line 46				51		
52	Go to Part IV of Schedule I to figure line 52 if the estate or trust has qualified dividends or has a gain on lines 14a and 15 of column (2) of Schedule D (Form 1041) (as refigured for the AMT, if necessary). Otherwise, if line 51 is— • $175,000 or less, multiply line 51 by 26% (.26). • Over $175,000, multiply line 51 by 28% (.28) and subtract $3,500 from the result				52		
53	Alternative minimum foreign tax credit (see page 29 of the instructions)				53		
54	Tentative minimum tax. Subtract line 53 from line 52				54		
55	Enter the tax from Schedule G, line 1a (minus any foreign tax credit from Schedule G, line 2a)				55		
56	**Alternative minimum tax.** Subtract line 55 from line 54. If zero or less, enter -0-. Enter here and on Schedule G, line 1c				56		

Part IV—Line 52 Computation Using Maximum Capital Gains Rates

Caution: *If you did not complete Part V of Schedule D (Form 1041), the Schedule D Tax Worksheet, or the Qualified Dividends Tax Worksheet, see page 31 of the instructions before completing this part.*

57	Enter the amount from line 51				57		
58	Enter the amount from Schedule D (Form 1041), line 22, line 13 of the Schedule D Tax Worksheet, or line 4 of the Qualified Dividends Tax Worksheet, whichever applies (as refigured for the AMT, if necessary)	58					
59	Enter the amount from Schedule D (Form 1041), line 14b, column (2) (as refigured for the AMT, if necessary). If you did not complete Schedule D for the regular tax or the AMT, enter -0-	59					
60	If you did not complete a Schedule D Tax Worksheet for the regular tax or the AMT, enter the amount from line 58. Otherwise, add lines 58 and 59 and enter the **smaller** of that result or the amount from line 10 of the Schedule D Tax Worksheet (as refigured for the AMT, if necessary)	60					
61	Enter the **smaller** of line 57 or line 60				61		
62	Subtract line 61 from line 57				62		
63	If line 62 is $175,000 or less, multiply line 62 by 26% (.26). Otherwise, multiply line 62 by 28% (.28) and subtract $3,500 from the result ▶				63		
64	Maximum amount subject to the 5% rate	64	$1,950	00			
65	Enter the amount from line 23 of Schedule D (Form 1041), line 14 of the Schedule D Tax Worksheet, or line 5 of the Qualified Dividends Tax Worksheet, whichever applies (as figured for the regular tax). If you did not complete Schedule D or either worksheet for the regular tax, enter -0-	65					
66	Subtract line 65 from line 64. If zero or less, enter -0-	66					
67	Enter the **smaller** of line 57 or line 58	67					
68	Enter the **smaller** of line 66 or line 67	68					
69	Multiply line 68 by 5% (.05) ▶				69		
70	Subtract line 68 from line 67	70					
71	Multiply line 70 by 15% (.15) ▶				71		
	If line 59 is zero or blank, skip lines 72 and 73 and go to line 74. Otherwise, go to line 72.						
72	Subtract line 67 from line 61	72					
73	Multiply line 72 by 25% (.25) ▶				73		
74	Add lines 63, 69, 71, and 73				74		
75	If line 57 is $175,000 or less, multiply line 57 by 26% (.26). Otherwise, multiply line 57 by 28% (.28) and subtract $3,500 from the result				75		
76	Enter the **smaller** of line 74 or line 75 here and on line 52				76		

Form **1041** (2004)

Printed on recycled paper

6611

SCHEDULE K-1 (Form 1041)

Department of the Treasury
Internal Revenue Service

Beneficiary's Share of Income, Deductions, Credits, etc.

for the calendar year 2004, or fiscal year

beginning ...., 2004, ending ...., 20 ....

► Complete a separate Schedule K-1 for each beneficiary.

OMB No. 1545-0092

2004

Name of trust or decedent's estate

☐ Amended K-1
☐ Final K-1

Beneficiary's identifying number ►

Estate's or trust's EIN ►

Beneficiary's name, address, and ZIP code

Fiduciary's name, address, and ZIP code

(a) Allocable share item		(b) Amount	(c) Calendar year 2004 Form 1040 filers enter the amounts in column (b) on:
1 Interest	1		Form 1040, line 8a
2a Qualified dividends	2a		Form 1040, line 9b
b Total ordinary dividends	2b		Form 1040, line 9a
3 Net short-term capital gain	3		Schedule D, line 5, column (f)
4a Net long-term capital gain	4a		Schedule D, line 12, column (f)
b Unrecaptured section 1250 gain	4b		Line 11 of the worksheet for Schedule D, line 19
c 28% rate gain	4c		Line 4 of the worksheet for Schedule D, line 18
5a Annuities, royalties, and other nonpassive income before directly apportioned deductions	5a		Schedule E, Part III, column (f)
b Depreciation	5b		Include on the applicable line of the appropriate tax form
c Depletion	5c		
d Amortization	5d		
6a Trade or business, rental real estate, and other rental income before directly apportioned deductions (see instructions)	6a		Schedule E, Part III
b Depreciation	6b		Include on the applicable line of the appropriate tax form
c Depletion	6c		
d Amortization	6d		
7 Income for minimum tax purposes	7		
8 Income for regular tax purposes (add lines 1, 2b, 3, 4a, 5a, and 6a)	8		
9 Adjustment for minimum tax purposes (subtract line 8 from line 7)	9		Form 6251, line 14
10 Estate tax deduction (including certain generation-skipping transfer taxes)	10		Schedule A, line 27
11 Foreign taxes	11		Form 1040, line 46 or Schedule A, line 8
12 Adjustments and tax preference items (itemize):			
a Accelerated depreciation	12a		Include on the applicable line of Form 6251
b Depletion	12b		
c Amortization	12c		
d Exclusion items	12d		2005 Form 8801
13 Deductions in the final year of trust or decedent's estate:			
a Excess deductions on termination (see instructions)	13a		Schedule A, line 22
b Short-term capital loss carryover	13b	( )	Schedule D, line 5, column (f)
c Long-term capital loss carryover	13c	( )	Sch. D, line 12, col. (f); line 5 of the wksht. for Sch. D, line 18; and line 16 of the wksht. for Sch. D, line 19
d Net operating loss (NOL) carryover for regular tax purposes	13d	( )	Form 1040, line 21
e NOL carryover for minimum tax purposes	13e		See the instructions for Form 6251, line 27
f	13f		Include on the applicable line of the appropriate tax form
g	13g		
14 Other (itemize):			
a Payments of estimated taxes credited to you	14a		Form 1040, line 64
b Tax-exempt interest	14b		Form 1040, line 8b
c	14c		Include on the applicable line of the appropriate tax form
d	14d		
e	14e		
f	14f		
g	14g		
h	14h		

For Paperwork Reduction Act Notice, see the Instructions for Form 1041. Cat. No. 11380D **Schedule K-1 (Form 1041) 2004**

Form **1065**
Department of the Treasury
Internal Revenue Service

U.S. Return of Partnership Income

For calendar year 2004, or tax year beginning .... , 2004, and ending .... , 20.... .
▶ See separate instructions.

OMB No. 1545-0099

2004

A Principal business activity	**Use the IRS label. Otherwise, print or type.**	Name of partnership	**D Employer identification number**
B Principal product or service		Number, street, and room or suite no. If a P.O. box, see page 14 of the instructions.	E Date business started
C Business code number		City or town, state, and ZIP code	F Total assets (see page 14 of the instructions) $

G Check applicable boxes: **(1)** ☐ Initial return **(2)** ☐ Final return **(3)** ☐ Name change **(4)** ☐ Address change **(5)** ☐ Amended return

H Check accounting method: **(1)** ☐ Cash **(2)** ☐ Accrual **(3)** ☐ Other (specify) ▶ ....

I Number of Schedules K-1. Attach one for each person who was a partner at any time during the tax year ▶ ....

Caution: *Include **only** trade or business income and expenses on lines 1a through 22 below. See the instructions for more information.*

Income

1a Gross receipts or sales	1a			
b Less returns and allowances	1b		1c	
2 Cost of goods sold (Schedule A, line 8)			2	
3 Gross profit. Subtract line 2 from line 1c			3	
4 Ordinary income (loss) from other partnerships, estates, and trusts *(attach schedule)*			4	
5 Net farm profit (loss) *(attach Schedule F (Form 1040))*			5	
6 Net gain (loss) from Form 4797, Part II, line 17			6	
7 Other income (loss) *(attach statement)*			7	
8 **Total income (loss).** Combine lines 3 through 7			8	

Deductions (see page 16 of the instructions for limitations)

9 Salaries and wages (other than to partners) (less employment credits)			9	
10 Guaranteed payments to partners			10	
11 Repairs and maintenance			11	
12 Bad debts			12	
13 Rent			13	
14 Taxes and licenses			14	
15 Interest			15	
16a Depreciation *(if required, attach Form 4562)*	16a			
b Less depreciation reported on Schedule A and elsewhere on return	16b		16c	
17 Depletion **(Do not deduct oil and gas depletion.)**			17	
18 Retirement plans, etc.			18	
19 Employee benefit programs			19	
20 Other deductions *(attach statement)*			20	
21 **Total deductions.** Add the amounts shown in the far right column for lines 9 through 20			21	
22 **Ordinary business income (loss).** Subtract line 21 from line 8			22	

Sign Here

Under penalties of perjury, I declare that I have examined this return, including accompanying schedules and statements, and to the best of my knowledge and belief, it is true, correct, and complete. Declaration of preparer (other than general partner or limited liability company member) is based on all information of which preparer has any knowledge.

▶ Signature of general partner or limited liability company member manager ▶ Date

May the IRS discuss this return with the preparer shown below (see instructions)? ☐ **Yes** ☐ **No**

Paid Preparer's Use Only

Preparer's signature	Date	Check if self-employed ▶ ☐	Preparer's SSN or PTIN
Firm's name (or yours if self-employed), address, and ZIP code ▶		EIN ▶	
		Phone no. ( )	

For Privacy Act and Paperwork Reduction Act Notice, see separate instructions. Cat. No. 11390Z Form **1065** (2004)

Form 1065 (2004) Page **2**

Schedule A Cost of Goods Sold (see page 19 of the instructions)

1	Inventory at beginning of year	1	
2	Purchases less cost of items withdrawn for personal use	2	
3	Cost of labor	3	
4	Additional section 263A costs *(attach statement)*	4	
5	Other costs *(attach statement)*	5	
6	**Total.** Add lines 1 through 5	6	
7	Inventory at end of year	7	
8	**Cost of goods sold.** Subtract line 7 from line 6. Enter here and on page 1, line 2	8	

9a Check all methods used for valuing closing inventory:

(i) ☐ Cost as described in Regulations section 1.471-3

(ii) ☐ Lower of cost or market as described in Regulations section 1.471-4

(iii) ☐ Other (specify method used and attach explanation) ▶

b Check this box if there was a writedown of "subnormal" goods as described in Regulations section 1.471-2(c) ▶ ☐

c Check this box if the LIFO inventory method was adopted this tax year for any goods *(if checked, attach Form 970)*. ▶ ☐

d Do the rules of section 263A (for property produced or acquired for resale) apply to the partnership? ☐ **Yes** ☐ **No**

e Was there any change in determining quantities, cost, or valuations between opening and closing inventory? ☐ **Yes** ☐ **No**
If "Yes," attach explanation.

Schedule B Other Information

		Yes	No
1	What type of entity is filing this return? Check the applicable box: **a** ☐ Domestic general partnership **b** ☐ Domestic limited partnership **c** ☐ Domestic limited liability company **d** ☐ Domestic limited liability partnership **e** ☐ Foreign partnership **f** ☐ Other ▶		
2	Are any partners in this partnership also partnerships?		
3	During the partnership's tax year, did the partnership own any interest in another partnership or in any foreign entity that was disregarded as an entity separate from its owner under Regulations sections 301.7701-2 and 301.7701-3? If yes, see instructions for required attachment		
4	Did the partnership file Form 8893, Election of Partnership Level Tax Treatment, or an election statement under section 6231(a)(1)(B)(ii) for partnership-level tax treatment, that is in effect for this tax year? See Form 8893 for more details		
5	Does this partnership meet all three of the following requirements? **a** The partnership's total receipts for the tax year were less than $250,000; **b** The partnership's total assets at the end of the tax year were less than $600,000; and **c** Schedules K-1 are filed with the return and furnished to the partners on or before the due date (including extensions) for the partnership return. If "Yes," the partnership is not required to complete Schedules L, M-1, and M-2; Item F on page 1 of Form 1065; or Item N on Schedule K-1.		
6	Does this partnership have any foreign partners? If "Yes," the partnership may have to file Forms 8804, 8805 and 8813. See page 20 of the instructions		
7	Is this partnership a publicly traded partnership as defined in section 469(k)(2)?		
8	Has this partnership filed, or is it required to file, Form 8264, Application for Registration of a Tax Shelter?		
9	At any time during calendar year 2004, did the partnership have an interest in or a signature or other authority over a financial account in a foreign country (such as a bank account, securities account, or other financial account)? See page 20 of the instructions for exceptions and filing requirements for Form TD F 90-22.1. If "Yes," enter the name of the foreign country. ▶		
10	During the tax year, did the partnership receive a distribution from, or was it the grantor of, or transferor to, a foreign trust? If "Yes," the partnership may have to file Form 3520. See page 21 of the instructions		
11	Was there a distribution of property or a transfer (e.g., by sale or death) of a partnership interest during the tax year? If "Yes," you may elect to adjust the basis of the partnership's assets under section 754 by attaching the statement described under *Elections Made By the Partnership* on page 9 of the instructions		
12	Enter the number of Forms 8865, Return of U.S. Persons With Respect to Certain Foreign Partnerships, attached to this return ▶		

Designation of Tax Matters Partner (see page 21 of the instructions)

Enter below the general partner designated as the tax matters partner (TMP) for the tax year of this return:

Name of designated TMP ▶ Identifying number of TMP ▶

Address of designated TMP ▶

Form **1065** (2004)

Form 1065 (2004) Page 3

Schedule K Partners' Distributive Share Items

				Total amount
Income (Loss)	1 Ordinary business income (loss) (page 1, line 22)		1	
	2 Net rental real estate income (loss) *(attach Form 8825)*		2	
	3a Other gross rental income (loss)	3a		
	b Expenses from other rental activities *(attach statement)*	3b		
	c Other net rental income (loss). Subtract line 3b from line 3a		3c	
	4 Guaranteed payments		4	
	5 Interest income		5	
	6 Dividends: a Ordinary dividends		6a	
	b Qualified dividends	6b		
	7 Royalties		7	
	8 Net short-term capital gain (loss) *(attach Schedule D (Form 1065))*		8	
	9a Net long-term capital gain (loss) *(attach Schedule D (Form 1065))*		9a	
	b Collectibles (28%) gain (loss)	9b		
	c Unrecaptured section 1250 gain *(attach statement)*	9c		
	10 Net section 1231 gain (loss) *(attach Form 4797)*		10	
	11 Other income (loss) *(attach statement)*		11	
Deductions	12 Section 179 deduction *(attach Form 4562)*		12	
	13a Contributions		13a	
	b Deductions related to portfolio income *(attach statement)*		13b	
	c Investment interest expense		13c	
	d Section 59(e)(2) expenditures: **(1)** Type ▶ ________ **(2)** Amount ▶		13d(2)	
	e Other deductions *(attach statement)*		13e	
Self-Employment	14a Net earnings (loss) from self-employment		14a	
	b Gross farming or fishing income		14b	
	c Gross nonfarm income		14c	
Credits & Credit Recapture	15a Low-income housing credit (section 42(j)(5))		15a	
	b Low-income housing credit (other)		15b	
	c Qualified rehabilitation expenditures (rental real estate) *(attach Form 3468)*		15c	
	d Other rental real estate credits		15d	
	e Other rental credits		15e	
	f Other credits and credit recapture *(attach statement)*		15f	
Foreign Transactions	16a Name of country or U.S. possession ▶ ________			
	b Gross income from all sources		16b	
	c Gross income sourced at partner level		16c	
	Foreign gross income sourced at partnership level			
	d Passive ▶ ________ e Listed categories *(attach statement)* ▶ ________ f General limitation ▶		16f	
	Deductions allocated and apportioned at partner level			
	g Interest expense ▶ ________ h Other ▶		16h	
	Deductions allocated and apportioned at partnership level to foreign source income			
	i Passive ▶ ________ j Listed categories *(attach statement)* ▶ ________ k General limitation ▶		16k	
	l Foreign taxes: **(1)** Paid ▶ ________ **(2)** Accrued ▶		16l(2)	
	m Reduction in taxes available for credit *(attach statement)*		16m	
Alternative Minimum Tax (AMT) Items	17a Post-1986 depreciation adjustment		17a	
	b Adjusted gain or loss		17b	
	c Depletion (other than oil and gas)		17c	
	d Oil, gas, and geothermal properties—gross income		17d	
	e Oil, gas, and geothermal properties—deductions		17e	
	f Other AMT items *(attach statement)*		17f	
Other Information	18a Tax-exempt interest income		18a	
	b Other tax-exempt income		18b	
	c Nondeductible expenses		18c	
	19a Distributions of cash and marketable securities		19a	
	b Distributions of other property		19b	
	20a Investment income		20a	
	b Investment expenses		20b	
	c Other items and amounts *(attach statement)*			

Form **1065** (2004)

Form 1065 (2004) Page **4**

Analysis of Net Income (Loss)

1 Net income (loss). Combine Schedule K, lines 1 through 11. From the result, subtract the sum of Schedule K, lines 12 through 13e, 16l(1), and 16l(2)	**1**	

2 Analysis by partner type:	**(i)** Corporate	**(ii)** Individual (active)	**(iii)** Individual (passive)	**(iv)** Partnership	**(v)** Exempt organization	**(vi)** Nominee/Other
a General partners						
b Limited partners						

Note: Schedules L, M-1, and M-2 are not required if Question 5 of Schedule B is answered "Yes."

Schedule L Balance Sheets per Books

Assets	Beginning of tax year (a)	(b)	End of tax year (c)	(d)
1 Cash				
2a Trade notes and accounts receivable				
b Less allowance for bad debts				
3 Inventories				
4 U.S. government obligations				
5 Tax-exempt securities				
6 Other current assets *(attach statement)*				
7 Mortgage and real estate loans				
8 Other investments *(attach statement)*				
9a Buildings and other depreciable assets				
b Less accumulated depreciation				
10a Depletable assets				
b Less accumulated depletion				
11 Land (net of any amortization)				
12a Intangible assets (amortizable only)				
b Less accumulated amortization				
13 Other assets *(attach statement)*				
14 Total assets				
Liabilities and Capital				
15 Accounts payable				
16 Mortgages, notes, bonds payable in less than 1 year				
17 Other current liabilities *(attach statement)*				
18 All nonrecourse loans				
19 Mortgages, notes, bonds payable in 1 year or more				
20 Other liabilities *(attach statement)*				
21 Partners' capital accounts				
22 Total liabilities and capital				

Schedule M-1 Reconciliation of Income (Loss) per Books With Income (Loss) per Return

1 Net income (loss) per books		**6** Income recorded on books this year not included on Schedule K, lines 1 through 11 (itemize):	
2 Income included on Schedule K, lines 1, 2, 3c, 5, 6a, 7, 8, 9a, 10, and 11, not recorded on books this year (itemize):		**a** Tax-exempt interest $	
3 Guaranteed payments (other than health insurance)		**7** Deductions included on Schedule K, lines 1 through 13e, 16l(1), and 16l(2), not charged against book income this year (itemize):	
4 Expenses recorded on books this year not included on Schedule K, lines 1 through 13e, 16l(1), and 16l(2) (itemize):		**a** Depreciation $	
a Depreciation $			
b Travel and entertainment $		**8** Add lines 6 and 7	
5 Add lines 1 through 4		**9** Income (loss) (Analysis of Net Income (Loss), line 1). Subtract line 8 from line 5	

Schedule M-2 Analysis of Partners' Capital Accounts

1 Balance at beginning of year		**6** Distributions: **a** Cash	
2 Capital contributed: **a** Cash		**b** Property	
b Property		**7** Other decreases (itemize):	
3 Net income (loss) per books			
4 Other increases (itemize):			
		8 Add lines 6 and 7	
5 Add lines 1 through 4		**9** Balance at end of year. Subtract line 8 from line 5	

6511

☐ Final K-1 ☐ Amended K-1 OMB No. 1545-0099

Schedule K-1 (Form 1065) **2004**

Department of the Treasury
Internal Revenue Service

Tax year beginning ________, 2004
and ending ________, 20__

Partner's Share of Income, Deductions, Credits, etc.

▶ See back of form and separate instructions.

Part I Information About the Partnership

A Partnership's employer identification number

B Partnership's name, address, city, state, and ZIP code

C IRS Center where partnership filed return

D ☐ Check if this is a publicly traded partnership (PTP)

E ☐ Tax shelter registration number, if any ________

F ☐ Check if Form 8271 is attached

Part II Information About the Partner

G Partner's identifying number

H Partner's name, address, city, state, and ZIP code

I ☐ General partner or LLC member-manager ☐ Limited partner or other LLC member

J ☐ Domestic partner ☐ Foreign partner

K What type of entity is this partner? ________

L Partner's share of profit, loss, and capital:

	Beginning	Ending
Profit	%	%
Loss	%	%
Capital	%	%

M Partner's share of liabilities at year end:

Nonrecourse . . . . $________

Qualified nonrecourse financing . . $________

Recourse . . . . $________

N Partner's capital account analysis:

Beginning capital account . . . . $________

Capital contributed during the year . $________

Current year increase (decrease) . . $________

Withdrawals & distributions . . . $(________)

Ending capital account . . . . $________

☐ Tax basis ☐ GAAP ☐ Section 704(b) book

☐ Other (explain)

Part III Partner's Share of Current Year Income, Deductions, Credits, and Other Items

1 Ordinary business income (loss)

2 Net rental real estate income (loss)

3 Other net rental income (loss)

4 Guaranteed payments

5 Interest income

6a Ordinary dividends

6b Qualified dividends

7 Royalties

8 Net short-term capital gain (loss)

9a Net long-term capital gain (loss)

9b Collectibles (28%) gain (loss)

9c Unrecaptured section 1250 gain

10 Net section 1231 gain (loss)

11 Other income (loss)

12 Section 179 deduction

13 Other deductions

14 Self-employment earnings (loss)

15 Credits & credit recapture

16 Foreign transactions

17 Alternative minimum tax (AMT) items

18 Tax-exempt income and nondeductible expenses

19 Distributions

20 Other information

*See attached statement for additional information.

For IRS Use Only

Form **1120-A**
Department of the Treasury
Internal Revenue Service

U.S. Corporation Short-Form Income Tax Return

For calendar year 2004 or tax year beginning................, 2004, ending................, 20....
▶ See separate instructions to make sure the corporation qualifies to file Form 1120-A.

OMB No. 1545-0890
2004

A Check this box if the corporation is a personal service corporation (see instructions). . ☐

Use IRS label. Otherwise, print or type.
Name
Number, street, and room or suite no. If a P.O. box, see page 9 of instructions.
City or town, state, and ZIP code

B Employer identification number
C Date incorporated
D Total assets (see page 10 of instructions)
$

E Check if: (1) ☐ Initial return (2) ☐ Final return (3) ☐ Name change (4) ☐ Address change
F Check accounting method: (1) ☐ Cash (2) ☐ Accrual (3) ☐ Other (specify) ▶

Income	1a	Gross receipts or sales ______ b Less returns and allowances ______ c Balance ▶	1c	
	2	Cost of goods sold (see page 17 of instructions)	2	
	3	Gross profit. Subtract line 2 from line 1c	3	
	4	Domestic corporation dividends subject to the 70% deduction	4	
	5	Interest	5	
	6	Gross rents	6	
	7	Gross royalties	7	
	8	Capital gain net income (attach Schedule D (Form 1120))	8	
	9	Net gain or (loss) from Form 4797, Part II, line 17 (attach Form 4797)	9	
	10	Other income (see page 11 of instructions—attach schedule)	10	
	11	**Total income.** Add lines 3 through 10 ▶	11	
Deductions (See instructions for limitations on deductions.)	12	Compensation of officers (see page 13 of instructions)	12	
	13	Salaries and wages (less employment credits)	13	
	14	Repairs and maintenance	14	
	15	Bad debts	15	
	16	Rents	16	
	17	Taxes and licenses	17	
	18	Interest	18	
	19	Charitable contributions (see page 14 of instructions for 10% limitation)	19	
	20	Depreciation (attach Form 4562) — 20		
	21	Less depreciation claimed elsewhere on return — 21a	21b	
	22	Other deductions (attach schedule)	22	
	23	**Total deductions.** Add lines 12 through 22 ▶	23	
	24	Taxable income before net operating loss deduction and special deductions. Subtract line 23 from line 11	24	
	25	**Less:** a Net operating loss deduction (see page 16 of instructions) — 25a		
		b Special deductions (see page 16 of instructions) — 25b	25c	
Tax and Payments	26	**Taxable income.** Subtract line 25c from line 24	26	
	27	**Total tax** (page 2, Part I, line 5)	27	
	28	**Payments:**		
		a 2003 overpayment credited to 2004 — 28a		
		b 2004 estimated tax payments — 28b		
		c Less 2004 refund applied for on Form 4466 — 28c ( ) Bal ▶ 28d		
		e Tax deposited with Form 7004 — 28e		
		f Credit for tax paid on undistributed capital gains (attach Form 2439) — 28f		
		g Credit for Federal tax on fuels (attach Form 4136). See instructions — 28g		
		h **Total payments.** Add lines 28d through 28g	28h	
	29	Estimated tax penalty (see page 17 of instructions). Check if Form 2220 is attached ▶ ☐	29	
	30	**Tax due.** If line 28h is smaller than the total of lines 27 and 29, enter amount owed	30	
	31	**Overpayment.** If line 28h is larger than the total of lines 27 and 29, enter amount overpaid	31	
	32	Enter amount of line 31 you want: **Credited to 2005 estimated tax ▶** ______ **Refunded ▶**	32	

Sign Here

Under penalties of perjury, I declare that I have examined this return, including accompanying schedules and statements, and to the best of my knowledge and belief, it is true, correct, and complete. Declaration of preparer (other than taxpayer) is based on all information of which preparer has any knowledge.

▶ Signature of officer — Date ▶ Title

May the IRS discuss this return with the preparer shown below (see instructions)? ☐ Yes ☐ No

Paid Preparer's Use Only

Preparer's signature ▶ — Date — Check if self-employed ☐ — Preparer's SSN or PTIN

Firm's name (or yours if self-employed), address, and ZIP code ▶ — EIN — Phone no. ( )

For Privacy Act and Paperwork Reduction Act Notice, see separate instructions. Cat. No. 11456E Form **1120-A** (2004)

Form 1120-A (2004) Page 2

Part I Tax Computation (see page 20 of instructions)

1	Income tax. If the corporation is a qualified personal service corporation (see page 21), check here ▶ ☐	1	
2	General business credit. Check box(es) and indicate which forms are attached: ☐ Form 3800 ☐ Form(s) (specify) ▶	2	
3	Subtract line 2 from line 1	3	
4	Other taxes. Check if from: ☐ Form 4255 ☐ Form 8611 ☐ Form 8697 ☐ Form 8866 ☐ Other (attach schedule)	4	
5	**Total tax.** Add lines 3 and 4. Enter here and on page 1, line 27	5	

Part II Other Information (see page 23 of instructions)

1 See page 25 of the instructions and enter the:
- a Business activity code no. ▶
- b Business activity ▶
- c Product or service ▶

2 At the end of the tax year, did any individual, partnership, estate, or trust own, directly or indirectly, 50% or more of the corporation's voting stock? (For rules of attribution, see section 267(c).) ☐ Yes ☐ No

If "Yes," attach a schedule showing name and identifying number.

3 Enter the amount of tax-exempt interest received or accrued during the tax year. ▶ $

4 Enter total amount of cash distributions and the book value of property distributions (other than cash) made during the tax year ▶ $

5a If an amount is entered on page 1, line 2, enter from worksheet on page 17 instr.:
- (1) Purchases
- (2) Additional 263A costs (attach schedule)
- (3) Other costs (attach schedule).

b If property is produced or acquired for resale, do the rules of section 263A apply to the corporation?. ☐ Yes ☐ No

6 At any time during the 2004 calendar year, did the corporation have an interest in or a signature or other authority over a financial account (such as a bank account, securities account, or other financial account) in a foreign country? ☐ Yes ☐ No

If "Yes," the corporation may have to file Form TD F 90-22.1.

If "Yes," enter the name of the foreign country ▶

7 Are the corporation's total receipts (line 1a plus lines 4 through 10 on page 1) for the tax year **and** its total assets at the end of the tax year less than $250,000? ☐ Yes ☐ No

If "Yes," the corporation is **not** required to complete Parts III and IV below.

Part III Balance Sheets per Books

			(a) Beginning of tax year	(b) End of tax year
Assets	1	Cash		
	2a	Trade notes and accounts receivable		
	b	Less allowance for bad debts	( )	( )
	3	Inventories		
	4	U.S. government obligations		
	5	Tax-exempt securities (see instructions)		
	6	Other current assets (attach schedule)		
	7	Loans to shareholders		
	8	Mortgage and real estate loans		
	9a	Depreciable, depletable, and intangible assets		
	b	Less accumulated depreciation, depletion, and amortization	( )	( )
	10	Land (net of any amortization)		
	11	Other assets (attach schedule)		
	12	Total assets		
Liabilities and Shareholders' Equity	13	Accounts payable		
	14	Other current liabilities (attach schedule)		
	15	Loans from shareholders		
	16	Mortgages, notes, bonds payable		
	17	Other liabilities (attach schedule)		
	18	Capital stock (preferred and common stock)		
	19	Additional paid-in capital		
	20	Retained earnings		
	21	Adjustments to shareholders' equity (attach schedule)		
	22	Less cost of treasury stock	( )	( )
	23	Total liabilities and shareholders' equity		

Part IV Reconciliation of Income (Loss) per Books With Income per Return

1 Net income (loss) per books		6 Income recorded on books this year not included on this return (itemize):	
2 Federal income tax per books		7 Deductions on this return not charged against book income this year (itemize):	
3 Excess of capital losses over capital gains			
4 Income subject to tax not recorded on books this year (itemize):			
5 Expenses recorded on books this year not deducted on this return (itemize):		8 Income (page 1, line 24). Enter the sum of lines 1 through 5 less the sum of lines 6 and 7	

Form **1120-A** (2004)

Form **1120**

Department of the Treasury
Internal Revenue Service

U.S. Corporation Income Tax Return

For calendar year 2004 or tax year beginning ...., 2004, ending ...., 20 ....

▶ See separate instructions.

OMB No. 1545-0123

2004

A Check if:
1 Consolidated return (attach Form 851) ☐
2 Personal holding co. (attach Sch. PH) ☐
3 Personal service corp. (see instructions) ☐
4 Schedule M-3 required (attach Sch. M-3) ☐

Use IRS label. Otherwise, print or type.

Name

Number, street, and room or suite no. If a P.O. box, see page 9 of instructions.

City or town, state, and ZIP code

B Employer identification number

C Date incorporated

D Total assets (see page 8 of instructions)
$

E Check if: (1) ☐ Initial return (2) ☐ Final return (3) ☐ Name change (4) ☐ Address change

Income

1a	Gross receipts or sales ____ b Less returns and allowances ____ c Bal ▶	1c	
2	Cost of goods sold (Schedule A, line 8)	2	
3	Gross profit. Subtract line 2 from line 1c	3	
4	Dividends (Schedule C, line 19)	4	
5	Interest	5	
6	Gross rents	6	
7	Gross royalties	7	
8	Capital gain net income (attach Schedule D (Form 1120))	8	
9	Net gain or (loss) from Form 4797, Part II, line 17 (attach Form 4797)	9	
10	Other income (see page 11 of instructions—attach schedule)	10	
11	**Total income.** Add lines 3 through 10 ▶	11	

Deductions (See instructions for limitations on deductions.)

12	Compensation of officers (Schedule E, line 4)	12	
13	Salaries and wages (less employment credits)	13	
14	Repairs and maintenance	14	
15	Bad debts	15	
16	Rents	16	
17	Taxes and licenses	17	
18	Interest	18	
19	Charitable contributions (see page 14 of instructions for 10% limitation)	19	
20	Depreciation (attach Form 4562) ... 20		
21	Less depreciation claimed on Schedule A and elsewhere on return ... 21a	21b	
22	Depletion	22	
23	Advertising	23	
24	Pension, profit-sharing, etc., plans	24	
25	Employee benefit programs	25	
26	Other deductions (attach schedule)	26	
27	**Total deductions.** Add lines 12 through 26 ▶	27	
28	Taxable income before net operating loss deduction and special deductions. Subtract line 27 from line 11	28	
29	**Less:** a Net operating loss deduction (see page 16 of instructions) ... 29a		
	b Special deductions (Schedule C, line 20) ... 29b	29c	

Tax and Payments

30	**Taxable income.** Subtract line 29c from line 28 (see instructions if Schedule C, line 12, was completed)	30	
31	**Total tax** (Schedule J, line 11)	31	
32	**Payments: a** 2003 overpayment credited to 2004 ... 32a		
b	2004 estimated tax payments ... 32b		
c	Less 2004 refund applied for on Form 4466 ... 32c ( ) d Bal ▶ 32d		
e	Tax deposited with Form 7004 ... 32e		
f	Credit for tax paid on undistributed capital gains (attach Form 2439) ... 32f		
g	Credit for Federal tax on fuels (attach Form 4136). See instructions ... 32g	32h	
33	Estimated tax penalty (see page 17 of instructions). Check if Form 2220 is attached ▶ ☐	33	
34	**Tax due.** If line 32h is smaller than the total of lines 31 and 33, enter amount owed	34	
35	**Overpayment.** If line 32h is larger than the total of lines 31 and 33, enter amount overpaid	35	
36	Enter amount of line 35 you want: **Credited to 2005 estimated tax** ▶ **Refunded** ▶	36	

Sign Here

Under penalties of perjury, I declare that I have examined this return, including accompanying schedules and statements, and to the best of my knowledge and belief, it is true, correct, and complete. Declaration of preparer (other than taxpayer) is based on all information of which preparer has any knowledge.

Signature of officer | Date | Title

May the IRS discuss this return with the preparer shown below (see instructions)? ☐ **Yes** ☐ **No**

Paid Preparer's Use Only

Preparer's signature | Date | Check if self-employed ☐ | Preparer's SSN or PTIN

Firm's name (or yours if self-employed), address, and ZIP code | EIN | Phone no. ( )

Form 1120 (2004) Page **2**

Schedule A Cost of Goods Sold (see page 17 of instructions)

1	Inventory at beginning of year	1	
2	Purchases	2	
3	Cost of labor	3	
4	Additional section 263A costs (attach schedule)	4	
5	Other costs (attach schedule)	5	
6	**Total.** Add lines 1 through 5	6	
7	Inventory at end of year	7	
8	**Cost of goods sold.** Subtract line 7 from line 6. Enter here and on page 1, line 2	8	

9a Check all methods used for valuing closing inventory:

(i) ☐ Cost as described in Regulations section 1.471-3

(ii) ☐ Lower of cost or market as described in Regulations section 1.471-4

(iii) ☐ Other (Specify method used and attach explanation.) ▶

b Check if there was a writedown of subnormal goods as described in Regulations section 1.471-2(c) ▶ ☐

c Check if the LIFO inventory method was adopted this tax year for any goods (if checked, attach Form 970) ▶ ☐

d If the LIFO inventory method was used for this tax year, enter percentage (or amounts) of closing inventory computed under LIFO **9d**

e If property is produced or acquired for resale, do the rules of section 263A apply to the corporation? ☐ Yes ☐ No

f Was there any change in determining quantities, cost, or valuations between opening and closing inventory? If "Yes," attach explanation ☐ Yes ☐ No

Schedule C Dividends and Special Deductions (see page 18 of instructions)

		(a) Dividends received	(b) %	(c) Special deductions (a) × (b)
1	Dividends from less-than-20%-owned domestic corporations that are subject to the 70% deduction (other than debt-financed stock)		70	
2	Dividends from 20%-or-more-owned domestic corporations that are subject to the 80% deduction (other than debt-financed stock)		80	
3	Dividends on debt-financed stock of domestic and foreign corporations (section 246A)		see instructions	
4	Dividends on certain preferred stock of less-than-20%-owned public utilities		42	
5	Dividends on certain preferred stock of 20%-or-more-owned public utilities		48	
6	Dividends from less-than-20%-owned foreign corporations and certain FSCs that are subject to the 70% deduction		70	
7	Dividends from 20%-or-more-owned foreign corporations and certain FSCs that are subject to the 80% deduction		80	
8	Dividends from wholly owned foreign subsidiaries subject to the 100% deduction (section 245(b))		100	
9	**Total.** Add lines 1 through 8. See page 19 of instructions for limitation			
10	Dividends from domestic corporations received by a small business investment company operating under the Small Business Investment Act of 1958		100	
11	Dividends from affiliated group members and certain FSCs that are subject to the 100% deduction		100	
12	Dividends from controlled foreign corporations subject to the 85% deduction (attach Form 8895)		85	
13	Other dividends from foreign corporations not included on lines 3, 6, 7, 8, 11, or 12			
14	Income from controlled foreign corporations under subpart F (attach Form(s) 5471)			
15	Foreign dividend gross-up (section 78)			
16	IC-DISC and former DISC dividends not included on lines 1, 2, or 3 (section 246(d))			
17	Other dividends			
18	Deduction for dividends paid on certain preferred stock of public utilities			
19	**Total dividends.** Add lines 1 through 17. Enter here and on page 1, line 4 ▶			
20	**Total special deductions.** Add lines 9, 10, 11, 12, and 18. Enter here and on page 1, line 29b ▶			

Schedule E Compensation of Officers (see instructions for page 1, line 12, on page 13 of instructions)

Note: *Complete Schedule E only if total receipts (line 1a plus lines 4 through 10 on page 1) are $500,000 or more.*

	(a) Name of officer	(b) Social security number	(c) Percent of time devoted to business	Percent of corporation stock owned: (d) Common	(e) Preferred	(f) Amount of compensation
1			%	%	%	
			%	%	%	
			%	%	%	
			%	%	%	
			%	%	%	

2	Total compensation of officers	
3	Compensation of officers claimed on Schedule A and elsewhere on return	
4	Subtract line 3 from line 2. Enter the result here and on page 1, line 12	

Form **1120** (2004)

Form 1120 (2004) Page **3**

Schedule J Tax Computation (see page 20 of instructions)

1	Check if the corporation is a member of a controlled group (see sections 1561 and 1563) . . . . . ▶ ☐ **Important:** Members of a controlled group, see page 20 of instructions.		
2a	If the box on line 1 is checked, enter the corporation's share of the $50,000, $25,000, and $9,925,000 taxable income brackets (in that order): **(1)** $ **(2)** $ **(3)** $		
b	Enter the corporation's share of: **(1)** Additional 5% tax (not more than $11,750) $ **(2)** Additional 3% tax (not more than $100,000) $		
3	Income tax. Check if a qualified personal service corporation under section 448(d)(2) (see page 21) . . ▶ ☐	3	
4	Alternative minimum tax (attach Form 4626)	4	
5	Add lines 3 and 4	5	
6a	Foreign tax credit (attach Form 1118) 6a		
b	Possessions tax credit (attach Form 5735) 6b		
c	Check: ☐ Nonconventional source fuel credit ☐ QEV credit (attach Form 8834) 6c		
d	General business credit. Check box(es) and indicate which forms are attached: ☐ Form 3800 ☐ Form(s) (specify) ▶ 6d		
e	Credit for prior year minimum tax (attach Form 8827) 6e		
f	Qualified zone academy bond credit (attach Form 8860) 6f		
7	**Total credits.** Add lines 6a through 6f	7	
8	Subtract line 7 from line 5	8	
9	Personal holding company tax (attach Schedule PH (Form 1120))	9	
10	Other taxes. Check if from: ☐ Form 4255 ☐ Form 8611 ☐ Form 8697 ☐ Form 8866 ☐ Other (attach schedule)	10	
11	**Total tax.** Add lines 8 through 10. Enter here and on page 1, line 31	11	

Schedule K Other Information (see page 23 of instructions)

		Yes	No
1	Check accounting method: a ☐ Cash b ☐ Accrual c ☐ Other (specify) ▶		
2	See page 25 of the instructions and enter the: a Business activity code no. ▶ b Business activity ▶ c Product or service ▶		
3	At the end of the tax year, did the corporation own, directly or indirectly, 50% or more of the voting stock of a domestic corporation? (For rules of attribution, see section 267(c).) . . . . If "Yes," attach a schedule showing: **(a)** name and employer identification number (EIN), **(b)** percentage owned, and **(c)** taxable income or (loss) before NOL and special deductions of such corporation for the tax year ending with or within your tax year.		
4	Is the corporation a subsidiary in an affiliated group or a parent-subsidiary controlled group? . . . . . . If "Yes," enter name and EIN of the parent corporation ▶		
5	At the end of the tax year, did any individual, partnership, corporation, estate, or trust own, directly or indirectly, 50% or more of the corporation's voting stock? (For rules of attribution, see section 267(c).) . . . . . . If "Yes," attach a schedule showing name and identifying number. (Do not include any information already entered in **4** above.) Enter percentage owned ▶		
6	During this tax year, did the corporation pay dividends (other than stock dividends and distributions in exchange for stock) in excess of the corporation's current and accumulated earnings and profits? (See sections 301 and 316.) . . If "Yes," file **Form 5452,** Corporate Report of Nondividend Distributions. If this is a consolidated return, answer here for the parent corporation and on **Form 851,** Affiliations Schedule, for each subsidiary.		
7	At any time during the tax year, did one foreign person own, directly or indirectly, at least 25% of **(a)** the total voting power of all classes of stock of the corporation entitled to vote or **(b)** the total value of all classes of stock of the corporation? . . . . If "Yes," enter: **(a)** Percentage owned ▶ and **(b)** Owner's country ▶		
c	The corporation may have to file **Form 5472,** Information Return of a 25% Foreign-Owned U.S. Corporation or a Foreign Corporation Engaged in a U.S. Trade or Business. Enter number of Forms 5472 attached ▶		
8	Check this box if the corporation issued publicly offered debt instruments with original issue discount . ▶ ☐ If checked, the corporation may have to file **Form 8281,** Information Return for Publicly Offered Original Issue Discount Instruments.		
9	Enter the amount of tax-exempt interest received or accrued during the tax year ▶ $		
10	Enter the number of shareholders at the end of the tax year (if 75 or fewer) ▶		
11	If the corporation has an NOL for the tax year and is electing to forego the carryback period, check here ▶ ☐ If the corporation is filing a consolidated return, the statement required by Temporary Regulations section 1.1502-21T(b)(3)(i) or (ii) must be attached or the election will not be valid.		
12	Enter the available NOL carryover from prior tax years (Do not reduce it by any deduction on line 29a.) ▶ $		
13	Are the corporation's total receipts (line 1a plus lines 4 through 10 on page 1) for the tax year **and** its total assets at the end of the tax year less than $250,000? . . . If "Yes," the corporation is not required to complete Schedules L, M-1, and M-2 on page 4. Instead, enter the total amount of cash distributions and the book value of property distributions (other than cash) made during the tax year. ▶ $		

Note: *If the corporation, at any time during the tax year, had assets or operated a business in a foreign country or U.S. possession, it may be required to attach* **Schedule N (Form 1120),** *Foreign Operations of U.S. Corporations, to this return. See Schedule N for details.*

Note: *The corporation is not required to complete Schedules L, M-1, and M-2 if Question 13 on Schedule K is answered "Yes."*

Schedule L Balance Sheets per Books

Assets	Beginning of tax year (a)	(b)	End of tax year (c)	(d)
1 Cash				
2a Trade notes and accounts receivable				
b Less allowance for bad debts	( )		( )	
3 Inventories				
4 U.S. government obligations				
5 Tax-exempt securities (see instructions)				
6 Other current assets (attach schedule)				
7 Loans to shareholders				
8 Mortgage and real estate loans				
9 Other investments (attach schedule)				
10a Buildings and other depreciable assets				
b Less accumulated depreciation	( )		( )	
11a Depletable assets				
b Less accumulated depletion	( )		( )	
12 Land (net of any amortization)				
13a Intangible assets (amortizable only)				
b Less accumulated amortization	( )		( )	
14 Other assets (attach schedule)				
15 Total assets				
Liabilities and Shareholders' Equity				
16 Accounts payable				
17 Mortgages, notes, bonds payable in less than 1 year				
18 Other current liabilities (attach schedule)				
19 Loans from shareholders				
20 Mortgages, notes, bonds payable in 1 year or more				
21 Other liabilities (attach schedule)				
22 Capital stock: a Preferred stock				
b Common stock				
23 Additional paid-in capital				
24 Retained earnings—Appropriated (attach schedule)				
25 Retained earnings—Unappropriated				
26 Adjustments to shareholders' equity (attach schedule)				
27 Less cost of treasury stock		( )		( )
28 Total liabilities and shareholders' equity				

Schedule M-1 Reconciliation of Income (Loss) per Books With Income per Return (see page 24 of instructions)

1 Net income (loss) per books		7 Income recorded on books this year not included on this return (itemize): Tax-exempt interest $	
2 Federal income tax per books			
3 Excess of capital losses over capital gains			
4 Income subject to tax not recorded on books this year (itemize):		8 Deductions on this return not charged against book income this year (itemize):	
5 Expenses recorded on books this year not deducted on this return (itemize):		a Depreciation . . . . $	
a Depreciation . . . . $		b Charitable contributions $	
b Charitable contributions $			
c Travel and entertainment $			
		9 Add lines 7 and 8	
6 Add lines 1 through 5		10 Income (page 1, line 28)—line 6 less line 9	

Schedule M-2 Analysis of Unappropriated Retained Earnings per Books (Line 25, Schedule L)

1 Balance at beginning of year		5 Distributions: a Cash	
2 Net income (loss) per books		b Stock	
3 Other increases (itemize):		c Property	
		6 Other decreases (itemize):	
		7 Add lines 5 and 6	
4 Add lines 1, 2, and 3		8 Balance at end of year (line 4 less line 7)	

Form **1120S** | Department of the Treasury Internal Revenue Service

U.S. Income Tax Return for an S Corporation

▶ **Do not file this form unless the corporation has timely filed Form 2553 to elect to be an S corporation.**
▶ **See separate instructions.**

OMB No. 1545-0130

2004

For calendar year 2004, or tax year beginning , 2004, and ending , 20

	Use the IRS label. Otherwise, print or type.		
A Effective date of S election		Name	**C Employer identification number**
		Number, street, and room or suite no. (If a P.O. box, see page 12 of the instructions.)	D Date incorporated
B Business code number (see pages 36–38 of the Insts.)		City or town, state, and ZIP code	E Total assets (see page 12 of instructions) $

F Check applicable boxes: (1) ☐ Initial return (2) ☐ Final return (3) ☐ Name change (4) ☐ Address change (5) ☐ Amended return

G Enter number of shareholders in the corporation at end of the tax year ▶

Caution: *Include **only** trade or business income and expenses on lines 1a through 21. See page 13 of the instructions for more information.*

Income	1a	Gross receipts or sales ____ **b** Less returns and allowances ____ **c** Bal ▶		1c	
	2	Cost of goods sold (Schedule A, line 8)		2	
	3	Gross profit. Subtract line 2 from line 1c		3	
	4	Net gain (loss) from Form 4797, Part II, line 17 *(attach Form 4797)*		4	
	5	Other income (loss) *(attach schedule)*		5	
	6	**Total income (loss).** Add lines 3 through 5 ▶		6	
Deductions (see page 14 of the instructions for limitations)	7	Compensation of officers		7	
	8	Salaries and wages (less employment credits)		8	
	9	Repairs and maintenance		9	
	10	Bad debts		10	
	11	Rents		11	
	12	Taxes and licenses		12	
	13	Interest		13	
	14a	Depreciation *(attach Form 4562)*	14a		
	b	Depreciation claimed on Schedule A and elsewhere on return	14b		
	c	Subtract line 14b from line 14a		14c	
	15	Depletion **(Do not deduct oil and gas depletion.)**		15	
	16	Advertising		16	
	17	Pension, profit-sharing, etc., plans		17	
	18	Employee benefit programs		18	
	19	Other deductions *(attach schedule)*		19	
	20	**Total deductions.** Add the amounts shown in the far right column for lines 7 through 19 ▶		20	
	21	Ordinary business income (loss). Subtract line 20 from line 6		21	
Tax and Payments	22	**Tax: a** Excess net passive income tax *(attach schedule)*	22a		
	b	Tax from Schedule D (Form 1120S)	22b		
	c	Add lines 22a and 22b (see page 18 of the instructions for additional taxes)		22c	
	23	**Payments: a** 2004 estimated tax payments and amount applied from 2003 return	23a		
	b	Tax deposited with Form 7004	23b		
	c	Credit for Federal tax paid on fuels *(attach Form 4136)*	23c		
	d	Add lines 23a through 23c		23d	
	24	Estimated tax penalty (see page 18 of instructions). Check if Form 2220 is attached ▶ ☐		24	
	25	**Tax due.** If line 23d is smaller than the total of lines 22c and 24, enter amount owed		25	
	26	**Overpayment.** If line 23d is larger than the total of lines 22c and 24, enter amount overpaid		26	
	27	Enter amount of line 26 you want: **Credited to 2005 estimated tax** ▶ | **Refunded** ▶		27	

Sign Here

Under penalties of perjury, I declare that I have examined this return, including accompanying schedules and statements, and to the best of my knowledge and belief, it is true, correct, and complete. Declaration of preparer (other than taxpayer) is based on all information of which preparer has any knowledge.

▶ Signature of officer | Date | ▶ Title

May the IRS discuss this return with the preparer shown below (see instructions)? ☐ **Yes** ☐ **No**

Paid Preparer's Use Only			
Preparer's signature ▶	Date	Check if self-employed ☐	Preparer's SSN or PTIN
Firm's name (or yours if self-employed), address, and ZIP code ▶		EIN	
		Phone no. ( )	

Form 1120S (2004) Page **2**

Schedule A Cost of Goods Sold (see page 18 of the instructions)

1	Inventory at beginning of year	1	
2	Purchases	2	
3	Cost of labor	3	
4	Additional section 263A costs *(attach schedule)*	4	
5	Other costs *(attach schedule)*	5	
6	**Total.** Add lines 1 through 5	6	
7	Inventory at end of year	7	
8	**Cost of goods sold.** Subtract line 7 from line 6. Enter here and on page 1, line 2	8	

9a Check all methods used for valuing closing inventory: *(i)* ☐ Cost as described in Regulations section 1.471-3

(ii) ☐ Lower of cost or market as described in Regulations section 1.471-4

(iii) ☐ Other (specify method used and attach explanation) ▶ ____________

b Check if there was a writedown of subnormal goods as described in Regulations section 1.471-2(c) ▶ ☐

c Check if the LIFO inventory method was adopted this tax year for any goods (if checked, attach Form 970) ▶ ☐

d If the LIFO inventory method was used for this tax year, enter percentage (or amounts) of closing inventory computed under LIFO **9d** ____

e If property is produced or acquired for resale, do the rules of Section 263A apply to the corporation? ☐ Yes ☐ No

f Was there any change in determining quantities, cost, or valuations between opening and closing inventory? ☐ Yes ☐ No
If "Yes," attach explanation.

Schedule B Other Information (see page 19 of instructions)

		Yes	No
1	Check method of accounting: **(a)** ☐ Cash **(b)** ☐ Accrual **(c)** ☐ Other (specify) ▶ ____		
2	See pages 36 through 38 of the instructions and enter the: **(a)** Business activity ▶ ____ **(b)** Product or service ▶ ____		
3	At the end of the tax year, did the corporation own, directly or indirectly, 50% or more of the voting stock of a domestic corporation? (For rules of attribution, see section 267(c).) If "Yes," attach a schedule showing: **(a)** name, address, and employer identification number and **(b)** percentage owned		
4	Was the corporation a member of a controlled group subject to the provisions of section 1561?		
5	Check this box if the corporation has filed or is required to file **Form 8264,** Application for Registration of a Tax Shelter ▶ ☐		
6	Check this box if the corporation issued publicly offered debt instruments with original issue discount ▶ ☐ If checked, the corporation may have to file **Form 8281,** Information Return for Publicly Offered Original Issue Discount Instruments.		
7	If the corporation: **(a)** was a C corporation before it elected to be an S corporation **or** the corporation acquired an asset with a basis determined by reference to its basis (or the basis of any other property) in the hands of a C corporation **and (b)** has net unrealized built-in gain (defined in section 1374(d)(1)) in excess of the net recognized built-in gain from prior years, enter the net unrealized built-in gain reduced by net recognized built-in gain from prior years ▶ $ ____		
8	Check this box if the corporation had accumulated earnings and profits at the close of the tax year ▶ ☐		
9	Are the corporation's total receipts (see page 19 of the instructions) for the tax year **and** its total assets at the end of the tax year less than $250,000? If "Yes," the corporation is not required to complete Schedules L and M-1.		

Note: *If the corporation had assets or operated a business in a foreign country or U.S. possession, it may be required to attach* ***Schedule N (Form 1120),*** *Foreign Operations of U.S. Corporations, to this return. See Schedule N for details.*

Schedule K Shareholders' Shares of Income, Deductions, Credits, etc.

Income (Loss)

Shareholders' Pro Rata Share Items				Total amount
1	Ordinary business income (loss) (page 1, line 21)		1	
2	Net rental real estate income (loss) *(attach Form 8825)*		2	
3a	Other gross rental income (loss)	3a		
b	Expenses from other rental activities *(attach schedule)*	3b		
c	Other net rental income (loss). Subtract line 3b from line 3a		3c	
4	Interest income		4	
5	Dividends: **a** Ordinary dividends		5a	
	b Qualified dividends	5b		
6	Royalties		6	
7	Net short-term capital gain (loss)		7	
8a	Net long-term capital gain (loss)		8a	
b	Collectibles (28%) gain (loss)	8b		
c	Unrecaptured section 1250 gain *(attach schedule)*	8c		
9	Net section 1231 gain (loss) (attach Form 4797)		9	
10	Other income (loss) *(attach schedule)*		10	

Form **1120S** (2004)

Form 1120S (2004) Page **3**

	Shareholders' Pro Rata Share Items (continued)		Total amount
Deductions	**11** Section 179 deduction *(attach Form 4562)*	11	
	12a Contributions	12a	
	b Deductions related to portfolio income *(attach schedule)*	12b	
	c Investment interest expense	12c	
	d Section 59(e)(2) expenditures **(1)** Type ▶ **(2)** Amount ▶	12d(2)	
	e Other deductions *(attach schedule)*	12e	
Credits & Credit Recapture	**13a** Low-income housing credit (section 42(j)(5))	13a	
	b Low-income housing credit (other)	13b	
	c Qualified rehabilitation expenditures (rental real estate) *(attach Form 3468)*	13c	
	d Other rental real estate credits	13d	
	e Other rental credits	13e	
	f Credit for alcohol used as fuel *(attach Form 6478)*	13f	
	g Other credits and credit recapture *(attach schedule)*	13g	
Foreign Transactions	**14a** Name of country or U.S. possession ▶		
	b Gross income from all sources	14b	
	c Gross income sourced at shareholder level	14c	
	Foreign gross income sourced at corporate level:		
	d Passive	14d	
	e Listed categories *(attach schedule)*	14e	
	f General limitation	14f	
	Deductions allocated and apportioned at shareholder level:		
	g Interest expense	14g	
	h Other	14h	
	Deductions allocated and apportioned at corporate level to foreign source income:		
	i Passive	14i	
	j Listed categories *(attach schedule)*	14j	
	k General limitation	14k	
	Other information:		
	l Foreign taxes paid	14l	
	m Foreign taxes accrued	14m	
	n Reduction in taxes available for credit *(attach schedule)*	14n	
Alternative Minimum Tax (AMT) Items	**15a** Post-1986 depreciation adjustment	15a	
	b Adjusted gain or loss	15b	
	c Depletion (other than oil and gas)	15c	
	d Oil, gas, and geothermal properties—gross income	15d	
	e Oil, gas, and geothermal properties—deductions	15e	
	f Other AMT items *(attach schedule)*	15f	
Items Affecting Shareholder Basis	**16a** Tax-exempt interest income	16a	
	b Other tax-exempt income	16b	
	c Nondeductible expenses	16c	
	d Property distributions	16d	
	e Repayment of loans from shareholders	16e	
Other Information	**17a** Investment income	17a	
	b Investment expenses	17b	
	c Dividend distributions paid from accumulated earnings and profits	17c	
	d Other items and amounts *(attach schedule)*		
	e Income/loss reconciliation. (Required only if Schedule M-1 must be completed.) Combine the amounts on lines 1 through 10 in the far right column. From the result, subtract the sum of the amounts on lines 11 through 12e and lines 14l or 14m, whichever applies	17e	

Form **1120S** (2004)

Note: The corporation is not required to complete Schedules L and M-1 if question 9 of Schedule B is answered "Yes."

Schedule L Balance Sheets per Books

Assets	Beginning of tax year (a)	(b)	End of tax year (c)	(d)
1 Cash				
2a Trade notes and accounts receivable				
b Less allowance for bad debts				
3 Inventories				
4 U.S. government obligations				
5 Tax-exempt securities				
6 Other current assets *(attach schedule)*				
7 Loans to shareholders				
8 Mortgage and real estate loans				
9 Other investments *(attach schedule)*				
10a Buildings and other depreciable assets				
b Less accumulated depreciation				
11a Depletable assets				
b Less accumulated depletion				
12 Land (net of any amortization)				
13a Intangible assets (amortizable only)				
b Less accumulated amortization				
14 Other assets *(attach schedule)*				
15 Total assets				
Liabilities and Shareholders' Equity				
16 Accounts payable				
17 Mortgages, notes, bonds payable in less than 1 year				
18 Other current liabilities *(attach schedule)*				
19 Loans from shareholders				
20 Mortgages, notes, bonds payable in 1 year or more				
21 Other liabilities *(attach schedule)*				
22 Capital stock				
23 Additional paid-in capital				
24 Retained earnings				
25 Adjustments to shareholders' equity *(attach schedule)*				
26 Less cost of treasury stock		( )		( )
27 Total liabilities and shareholders' equity				

Schedule M-1 Reconciliation of Income (Loss) per Books With Income (Loss) per Return

1 Net income (loss) per books		5 Income recorded on books this year not included on Schedule K, lines 1 through 10 (itemize): a Tax-exempt interest $	
2 Income included on Schedule K, lines 1, 2, 3c, 4, 5a, 6, 7, 8a, 9, and 10, not recorded on books this year (itemize):			
3 Expenses recorded on books this year not included on Schedule K, lines 1 through 12, and 14l or (14m) (itemize): a Depreciation $ b Travel and entertainment $		6 Deductions included on Schedule K, lines 1 through 12, and 14l or (14m), not charged against book income this year (itemize): a Depreciation $	
		7 Add lines 5 and 6	
4 Add lines 1 through 3		8 Income (loss) (Schedule K, line 17e). Line 4 less line 7	

Schedule M-2 Analysis of Accumulated Adjustments Account, Other Adjustments Account, and Shareholders' Undistributed Taxable Income Previously Taxed (see page 32 of the instructions)

	(a) Accumulated adjustments account	(b) Other adjustments account	(c) Shareholders' undistributed taxable income previously taxed
1 Balance at beginning of tax year			
2 Ordinary income from page 1, line 21			
3 Other additions			
4 Loss from page 1, line 21	( )		
5 Other reductions	( )	( )	
6 Combine lines 1 through 5			
7 Distributions other than dividend distributions			
8 Balance at end of tax year. Subtract line 7 from line 6			

6711

☐ Final K-1 ☐ Amended K-1 OMB No. 1545-0130

Schedule K-1 (Form 1120S) **2004**

Department of the Treasury
Internal Revenue Service

Tax year beginning ____________, 2004
and ending ____________, 20__

Shareholder's Share of Income, Deductions, Credits, etc.

► See back of form and separate instructions.

Part I Information About the Corporation

A Corporation's employer identification number

B Corporation's name, address, city, state, and ZIP code

C IRS Center where corporation filed return

D ☐ Tax shelter registration number, if any ____________

E ☐ Check if Form 8271 is attached

Part II Information About the Shareholder

F Shareholder's identifying number

G Shareholder's name, address, city, state and ZIP code

H Shareholder's percentage of stock ownership for tax year . . . . ____________ %

For IRS Use Only

Part III Shareholder's Share of Current Year Income, Deductions, Credits, and Other Items

1	Ordinary business income (loss)	13	Credits & credit recapture
2	Net rental real estate income (loss)		
3	Other net rental income (loss)		
4	Interest income		
5a	Ordinary dividends		
5b	Qualified dividends	14	Foreign transactions
6	Royalties		
7	Net short-term capital gain (loss)		
8a	Net long-term capital gain (loss)		
8b	Collectibles (28%) gain (loss)		
8c	Unrecaptured section 1250 gain		
9	Net section 1231 gain (loss)		
10	Other income (loss)	15	Alternative minimum tax (AMT) items
11	Section 179 deduction	16	Items affecting shareholder basis
12	Other deductions		
		17	Other information

* See attached statement for additional information.

For Privacy Act and Paperwork Reduction Act Notice, see Instructions for Form 1120S. Cat. No. 11520D **Schedule K-1 (Form 1120S) 2004**

APPENDIX C

Glossary of Key Terms

The key terms in this glossary have been defined to reflect their conventional use in the field of taxation. The definitions may therefore be incomplete for other purposes.

A

Abandoned spouse. The abandoned spouse provision enables a married taxpayer with a dependent child whose spouse did not live in the taxpayer's home during the last six months of the tax year to file as a head of household rather than as married filing separately.

Accelerated cost recovery system (ACRS). A method in which the cost of tangible property is recovered over a prescribed period of time. The approach disregards salvage value, imposes a period of cost recovery that depends upon the classification of the asset into one of various recovery periods, and prescribes the applicable percentage of cost that can be deducted each year. § 168.

Accelerated death benefits. The amount received from a life insurance policy by the insured who is terminally ill or chronically ill. Any realized gain may be excluded from the gross income of the insured if the policy is surrendered to the insurer or is sold to a licensed viatical settlement provider. § 101(g).

Accident and health benefits. Employee fringe benefits provided by employers through the payment of health and accident insurance premiums or the establishment of employer-funded medical reimbursement plans. Employers generally are entitled to a deduction for such payments, whereas employees generally exclude such fringe benefits from gross income. §§ 105 and 106.

Accountable plan. An accountable plan is a type of expense reimbursement plan that requires an employee to render an adequate accounting to the employer and return any excess reimbursement or allowance. If the expense qualifies, it will be treated as a deduction *for* AGI.

Accounting income. The accountant's concept of income is generally based upon the realization principle. Financial accounting income may differ from taxable income (e.g., accelerated depreciation might be used for Federal income tax and straight-line depreciation for financial accounting purposes). Differences are included in a reconciliation of taxable and accounting income on Schedule M–1 or Schedule M–3 of Form 1120 for corporations.

Accounting method. The method under which income and expenses are determined for tax purposes. Important accounting methods include the cash basis and the accrual basis. Special methods are available for the reporting of gain on installment sales, recognition of income on construction projects (the completed contract and percentage of completion methods), and the valuation of inventories (last-in, first-out and first-in, first-out). §§ 446–474.

Accounting period. The period of time, usually a year, used by a taxpayer for the determination of tax liability. Unless a fiscal year is chosen, taxpayers must determine and pay their income tax liability by using the calendar year (January 1 through December 31) as the period of measurement. An example of a fiscal year is July 1 through June 30. A change in accounting period (e.g., from a calendar year to a fiscal year) generally requires the consent of the IRS. Some new taxpayers, such as a newly formed corporation, are free to select either an initial calendar or a fiscal year without the consent of the IRS. §§ 441–444.

Accrual method. A method of accounting that reflects expenses incurred and income earned for any one tax year. In contrast to the cash basis of accounting, expenses need not be paid to be deductible, nor need income be received to be taxable. Unearned income (e.g., prepaid interest and rent) generally is taxed in the year of receipt regardless of the method of accounting used by the taxpayer. § 446(c)(2).

Accumulated adjustments account (AAA). An account that aggregates an S corporation's post-1982 income, loss, and deductions for the tax year (including nontaxable income and nondeductible losses and expenses). After the year-end income and expense adjustments are made, the account is reduced by distributions made during the tax year.

Accumulated earnings and profits. Net undistributed tax-basis earnings of a corporation aggregated from March 1, 1913, to the end of the prior tax year. Used to determine the amount of dividend income associated with a distribution to shareholders. § 316 and Reg. § 1.316–2.

Accuracy-related penalty. Major civil taxpayer penalties relating to the accuracy of tax return data, including misstatements stemming from taxpayer negligence and improper valuation of income and deductions, are coordinated under this umbrella term. The penalty usually equals 20 percent of the understated tax liability.

ACE adjustment. An adjustment in computing corporate alternative minimum taxable income (AMTI), computed at 75 percent of the excess of adjusted current earnings (ACE) over unadjusted AMTI. ACE computations reflect longer and slower cost recovery deductions and other restrictions on the timing of certain recognition events. Exempt interest, life insurance proceeds, and other receipts that are included in earnings and profits but not in taxable income also increase the ACE adjustment. If unadjusted AMTI exceeds ACE, the ACE adjustment is negative. The negative adjustment is limited to the aggregate of the positive adjustments under ACE for prior years, reduced by any previously claimed negative adjustments.

Acquiescence. Agreement by the IRS on the results reached in certain judicial decisions; sometimes abbreviated *Acq.* or *A.*

Acquisition indebtedness. Debt incurred in acquiring, constructing, or substantially improving a qualified residence of the taxpayer. The interest on such loans is deductible as qualified residence interest. However, interest on such debt is deductible only on the portion of the indebtedness that does not exceed $1,000,000 ($500,000 for married persons filing separate returns). § 163(h)(3).

Active income. Active income includes wages, salary, commissions, bonuses, profits from a trade or business in which the taxpayer is a material participant, gain on the sale or other disposition of assets used in an active trade or business, and income from intangible property if the taxpayer's personal efforts significantly contributed to the creation of the property. The passive activity loss rules require classification of income and losses into three categories with active income being one of them.

Ad valorem tax. A tax imposed on the value of property. The most common ad valorem tax is that imposed by states, counties, and cities on real estate. Ad valorem taxes can be imposed on personal property as well.

Additional depreciation. The excess of the amount of depreciation actually deducted over the amount that would have been deducted had the straight-line method been used. § 1250(b).

Additional first-year depreciation. One such beneficial provision, which is effective for property acquired after September 10, 2001 and before September 11, 2004, provides for an additional cost recovery deduction of 30 percent in the tax year that qualified property is placed in service. A more recently enacted provision, which is effective for property acquired after May 5, 2003 and placed in service before January 1, 2005, provides for an additional cost recovery deduction of 50 percent in the tax year the qualified property is placed in service. Qualified property includes most types of new property other than buildings. The taxpayer can elect to forgo the bonus depreciation provisions. The taxpayer also can elect to use 30 percent bonus depreciation rather than the 50 percent bonus depreciation. § 168(k).

Adjusted basis. The cost or other basis of property reduced by depreciation allowed or allowable and increased by capital improvements. Other special adjustments are provided in § 1016 and the related Regulations.

Adoption expenses credit. A provision intended to assist taxpayers who incur nonrecurring costs directly associated with the adoption process such as legal costs, social service review costs, and transportation costs. Up to $10,630 ($10,630 for a child with special needs regardless of the actual adoption expenses) of costs incurred to adopt an eligible child qualify for the credit. A taxpayer may claim the credit in the year qualifying expenses are paid or incurred if the expenses are paid during or after the year in which the adoption is finalized. For qualifying expenses paid or incurred in a tax year prior to the year the adoption is finalized, the credit must be claimed in the tax year following the tax year during which the expenses are paid or incurred. § 23.

Affiliated group. A parent-subsidiary group of corporations that is eligible to elect to file on a consolidated basis. Eighty percent ownership of the voting power and value of all of the corporations must be achieved on every day of the tax year, and an identifiable parent corporation must exist (i.e., it must own at least 80 percent of another group member without applying attribution rules).

Aggregate concept. The theory of partnership taxation under which, in certain cases, a partnership is treated as a mere extension of each partner.

Alimony and separate maintenance payments. Alimony deductions result from the payment of a legal obligation arising from the termination of a marital relationship. Payments designated as alimony generally are included in the gross income of the recipient and are deductible *for* AGI by the payer.

Alimony recapture. The amount of alimony that previously has been included in the gross income of the recipient and deducted by the payor that now is deducted by the recipient and included in the gross income of the payor as the result of front-loading. § 71(f).

All events test. For accrual method taxpayers, income is earned when (1) all the events have occurred that fix the right to receive the income and (2) the amount can be determined with reasonable accuracy. Accrual of income cannot be postponed simply because a portion of the income may have to be returned in a subsequent period. The all events test also is utilized to determine when expenses can be deducted by an accrual basis taxpayer. The application of the test could cause a variation between the treatment of an item for accounting and for tax purposes. For example, a reserve for warranty expense may be properly accruable under generally accepted accounting principles but not be deductible under the Federal income tax law. Because of the application of the all events test, the deduction becomes available in the year the warranty obligation becomes fixed and the amount is determinable with reasonable certainty. Reg §§ 1.446–1(c)(1)(ii) and 1.461–1(a)(2).

Allocate. The assignment of income for various tax purposes. A multistate corporation's nonbusiness income usually is allocated to the state where the nonbusiness assets are located; it is not apportioned with the rest of the entity's income. The income and expense items of an estate or trust are allocated between income and corpus components. Specific items of income, expense, gain, loss, and credit can be allocated to specific partners, if a substantial economic nontax purpose for the allocation is established.

Alternate valuation date. Property passing from a decedent by death may be valued for estate tax purposes as of the date of death or the alternate valuation date. The alternate valuation date is six months from the date of death or the date the property is disposed of by the estate, whichever comes first. To use the alternate valuation date, the executor or administrator of the estate must make an affirmative election. Election of the alternate valuation date is not available unless it decreases the amount of the gross estate *and* reduces the estate tax liability.

Alternative depreciation system (ADS). A cost recovery system that produces a smaller deduction than would be calculated under ACRS or MACRS. The alternative system must be used in certain instances and can be elected in other instances. § 168(g).

Alternative minimum tax (AMT). The AMT is a fixed percentage of alternative minimum taxable income (AMTI). AMTI generally starts with the taxpayer's adjusted gross income (for individuals) or taxable income (for other taxpayers). To this amount, the taxpayer (1) adds designated preference items (e.g., tax-exempt interest income on private activity bonds), (2) makes other specified adjustments (e.g., to reflect a longer, straight-line cost recovery deduction), (3) subtracts certain AMT itemized deductions for individuals (e.g., interest incurred on housing but not taxes paid), and (4) subtracts an exemption amount. The taxpayer must pay the greater of the resulting AMT (reduced by only the foreign tax credit) or the regular income tax (reduced by all allowable tax credits). The AMT does not apply to certain small C corporations. AMT preferences and adjustments are assigned to partners and S corporation shareholders.

Alternative minimum tax credit. The AMT can result from timing differences that give rise to positive adjustments in calculating the AMT base. To provide equity for the taxpayer when these timing differences reverse, the regular tax liability may be reduced by a tax credit for a prior year's minimum tax liability attributable to timing differences. § 53.

Alternative tax. An option that is allowed in computing the tax on net capital gain. For the corporate taxpayer, the rate is 35 percent (the same as the highest regular corporate tax rate). Thus, for corporate taxpayers, the alternative tax does not produce a beneficial result. For noncorporate taxpayers, the rate is usually 15 percent (but is 25 percent for unrecaptured § 1250 gain and 28 percent for collectibles and § 1202 gain). However, if the noncorporate taxpayer is in either the 10 percent or the 15 percent tax bracket, the alternative tax rate is 5 percent (rather than 15 percent). §§ 1(h) and 1201.

Alternative tax NOL deduction (ATNOLD). In calculating the AMT, the taxpayer is allowed to deduct NOL carryovers and carrybacks. However, for this purpose, a special calculation is required that is referred to as the ATNOLD. The regular income tax is modified for AMT adjustments and preferences to produce the ATNOLD. § 56(d).

Amortization. The tax deduction for the cost or other basis of an intangible asset over the asset's estimated useful life. Examples of amortizable intangibles include patents, copyrights, and leasehold interests. The intangible goodwill can be amortized for income tax purposes over a 15-year period.

Amount realized. The amount received by a taxpayer upon the sale or exchange of property. Amount realized is the sum of the cash and the fair market value of any property or services received by the taxpayer, plus any related debt assumed by the buyer. Determining the amount realized is the starting point for arriving at realized gain or loss. § 1001(b).

AMT adjustments. In calculating AMTI, certain adjustments are added to or deducted from taxable income. These adjustments generally reflect timing differences. § 56.

AMT exclusions. A credit that can be used to reduce the regular tax liability in future tax years is available in connection with the AMT (AMT credit). The credit is applicable only with respect to the AMT that results from timing differences. It is not available in connection with AMT exclusions, which include the standard deduction, personal exemptions, medical expenses deductible in calculating the regular income tax that are not deductible in computing the AMT, other itemized deductions that are not allowable for AMT purposes, excess percentage depletion, and tax-exempt interest on specified private activity bonds.

Annual exclusion. In computing the taxable gifts for the year, each donor excludes the first $11,000 of a gift to each donee. Usually, the annual exclusion is not available for gifts of future interests. § 2503(b).

Annuity. A fixed sum of money payable to a person at specified times for a specified period of time or for life. If the party making the payment (i.e., the obligor) is regularly engaged in this type of business (e.g., an insurance company), the arrangement is classified as a commercial annuity. A so-called private annuity involves an obligor that is not regularly engaged in selling annuities (e.g., a charity or family member).

Apportion. The assignment of the business income of a multistate corporation to specific states for income taxation. Usually, the apportionment procedure accounts for the property, payroll, and sales activity levels of the various states, and a proportionate assignment of the entity's total income is made, using a three-factor apportionment formula. These activities indicate the commercial domicile of the corporation, relative to that income. Some states exclude nonbusiness income from the apportionment procedure; they allocate nonbusiness income to the states where the nonbusiness assets are located.

Assignment of income. A procedure whereby a taxpayer attempts to avoid the recognition of income by assigning to another the property that generates the income. Such a procedure will not avoid the recognition of income by the taxpayer making the assignment if it can be said that the income was earned at the point of the transfer. In this case, usually referred to as an anticipatory assignment of income, the income will be taxed to the person who earns it.

Assumption of liabilities. In a corporate formation, corporate takeover, or asset purchase, the new owner often takes assets and agrees to assume preexisting debt. Such actions do not create boot received on the transaction for the new shareholder, unless there is no *bona fide* business purpose for the exchange, or the principal purpose of the debt assumption is the avoidance of tax liabilities. Gain is recognized to the extent that liabilities assumed exceed the aggregated bases of the transferred assets. § 357.

At-risk limitation. Generally, a taxpayer can deduct losses related to a trade or business, S corporation, partnership, or investment asset only to the extent of the at-risk amount.

Attribution. Under certain circumstances, the tax law applies attribution (constructive ownership) rules to assign to one taxpayer the ownership interest of another taxpayer. If, for example, the stock of Gold Corporation is held 60 percent by Marsha and 40 percent by Sidney, Marsha may be deemed to own 100 percent of Gold Corporation if Marsha and Sidney are mother and son. In that case, the stock owned by Sidney is attributed to Marsha. Stated differently, Marsha has a 60 percent direct and a 40 percent indirect interest in Gold Corporation. It can also be said that Marsha is the constructive owner of Sidney's interest.

Automatic mileage method. Automobile expenses are generally deductible only to the extent the automobile is used in business or for the production of income. Personal commuting expenses are not deductible. The taxpayer may deduct actual expenses (including depreciation and insurance), or the standard (automatic) mileage rate may be used (36 cents per mile for 2003, 37.5 cents per mile for 2004, and 40.5 cents per mile for 2005) during any one year. Automobile expenses incurred for medical purposes or in connection with job-related moving expenses are deductible to the extent of actual out-of-pocket expenses or at the rate of 15 cents per mile in 2005 (14 cents per mile in 2004). For charitable activities, the rate is 14 cents per mile.

B

Bad debts. A deduction is permitted if a business account receivable subsequently becomes partially or completely worthless, providing the income arising from the debt previously was included in income. Available methods are the specific charge-off method and the reserve method. However, except for certain financial institutions, TRA of 1986 repealed the use of the reserve method for 1987 and thereafter. If the reserve method is used, partially or totally worthless accounts are charged to the reserve. A nonbusiness bad debt deduction is allowed as a short-term capital loss if the loan did not arise in connection with the creditor's trade or business activities. Loans between related parties (family members) generally are classified as nonbusiness. § 166.

Basis in partnership interest. The acquisition cost of the partner's ownership interest in the partnership. Includes purchase price and associated debt acquired from other partners and in the course of the entity's trade or business.

Boot. Cash or property of a type not included in the definition of a nontaxable exchange. The receipt of boot causes an otherwise nontaxable transfer to become taxable to the extent of the lesser of the fair market value of the boot or the realized gain on the transfer. For example, see transfers to controlled corporations under § 351(b) and like-kind exchanges under § 1031(b).

Branch profits tax. A tax on the effectively connected earnings and profits of the U.S. branch of a foreign corporation. The tax is levied in addition to the usual § 11 tax, in an amount equal to 30 percent of the dividend equivalent amount. Treaties can override the tax or reduce the withholding percentage. Earnings reinvested in the U.S. operations of the entity are not subject to the tax until repatriation.

Brother-sister controlled group. More than one corporation owned by the same shareholders. If, for example, Chris and Pat each own one-half of the stock in Wren Corporation and Redbird Corporation, Wren and Redbird form a brother-sister controlled group.

Built-in gains tax. A penalty tax designed to discourage a shift of the incidence of taxation on unrealized gains from a C corporation to its shareholders, via an S election. Under this provision, any recognized gain during the first 10 years of S status generates a corporate-level tax on a base not to exceed the aggregate untaxed built-in gains brought into the S corporation upon its election from C corporation taxable years.

Business bad debt. A tax deduction allowed for obligations obtained in connection with a trade or business that have become either partially or completely worthless. In contrast to nonbusiness bad debts, business bad debts are deductible as business expenses. § 166.

Bypass amount. The amount that can be transferred by gift or at death free of any unified transfer tax. Currently, the by-pass amount is $1,500,000 for estate tax and $1 million for gift tax.

C

C corporation. A separate taxable entity, subject to the rules of Subchapter C of the Code. This business form may create a double taxation effect relative to its shareholders. The entity is subject to the regular corporate tax and a number of penalty taxes at the Federal level.

Cafeteria plan. An employee benefit plan under which an employee is allowed to select from among a variety of employer-provided fringe benefits. Some of the benefits may be taxable, and some may be statutory nontaxable benefits (e.g., health and accident insurance and group term life insurance). The employee is taxed only on the taxable benefits selected. A cafeteria benefit plan is also referred to as a flexible benefit plan. § 125.

Capital account. The financial accounting analog of a partner's tax basis in the entity.

Capital asset. Broadly speaking, all assets are capital except those specifically excluded by the Code. Major categories of noncapital assets include property held for resale in the normal course of business (inventory), trade accounts and notes receivable, and depreciable property and real estate used in a trade or business (§ 1231 assets). § 1221.

Capital contribution. Various means by which a shareholder makes additional funds available to the corporation (placed at the risk of the business), sometimes without the receipt of additional stock. If no stock is received, the contributions are added to the basis of the shareholder's existing stock investment and do not generate gross income to the corporation. § 118.

Capital gain. The gain from the sale or exchange of a capital asset.

Capital gain property. Property contributed to a charitable organization that, if sold rather than contributed, would have resulted in long-term capital gain to the donor.

Capital interest. Usually, the percentage of the entity's net assets that a partner would receive on liquidation. Typically determined by the partner's capital sharing ratio.

Capital loss. The loss from the sale or exchange of a capital asset.

Capital sharing ratio. A partner's percentage ownership of the entity's capital.

Cash method. See *cash receipts method.*

Cash receipts method. A method of accounting that reflects deductions as paid and income as received in any one tax year. However, deductions for prepaid expenses that benefit more than one tax year (e.g., prepaid rent and prepaid interest) usually must be spread over the period benefited rather than deducted in the year paid. § 446(c)(1).

Casualty loss. A casualty is defined as "the complete or partial destruction of property resulting from an identifiable event of a sudden, unexpected or unusual nature" (e.g., floods, storms, fires, auto accidents). Individuals may deduct a casualty loss only if the loss is incurred in a trade or business or in a transaction entered into for profit or arises from fire, storm, shipwreck, or other casualty or from theft. Individuals usually deduct personal casualty losses as itemized deductions subject to a $100 nondeductible amount and to an annual floor equal to 10 percent of adjusted gross income that applies after the $100 per casualty floor has been applied. Special rules are provided for the netting of certain casualty gains and losses.

Charitable contributions. Contributions are deductible (subject to various restrictions and ceiling limitations) if made to qualified nonprofit charitable organizations. A cash basis taxpayer is entitled to a deduction solely in the year of payment. Accrual basis corporations may accrue contributions at year-end if payment is properly authorized before the end of the year and payment is made within two and one-half months after the end of the year. § 170.

Check-the-box regulation. A business entity can elect to be taxed as a partnership, S corporation, or C corporation by indicating its preference on the tax return. Legal structure and operations are irrelevant in this regard. Thus, by using the check-the-box rules prudently, an entity can select the most attractive tax results offered by the Code, without being bound by legal forms. Not available if the entity is incorporated under state law.

Child tax credit. A tax credit based solely on the number of qualifying children under age 17. The maximum credit available is $1,000 per child through 2010. A qualifying child must be claimed as a dependent on a parent's tax return in order to qualify for the credit. Taxpayers who qualify for the child tax credit may also qualify for a supplemental credit. The supplemental credit is treated as a component of the earned income credit and is therefore refundable. The credit is phased out for higher-income taxpayers. § 24.

Circuit Court of Appeals. Any of 13 Federal courts that consider tax matters appealed from the U.S. Tax Court, a U.S. District Court, or the U.S. Court of Federal Claims. Appeal from a U.S. Court of Appeals is to the U.S. Supreme Court by *Certiorari.*

Circulation expenditures. Expenditures of establishing or increasing the circulation of a periodical that may be either expensed or capitalized. If such expenses are expensed, an adjustment will occur for AMT purposes, since the expenses are deducted over a three-year period for AMT purposes. Over the three-year period, both positive and negative AMT adjustments will be produced. § 173.

Citator. A tax research resource that presents the judicial history of a court case and traces the subsequent references to the case. When these references include the citating cases' evaluations of the cited case's precedents, the research can obtain some measure of the efficacy and reliability of the original holding.

Claim of right doctrine. A judicially imposed doctrine applicable to both cash and accrual basis taxpayers that holds that an amount is includible in income upon actual or constructive receipt if the taxpayer has an unrestricted claim to the payment. For the tax treatment of amounts repaid when previously included in income under the claim of right doctrine, see § 1341.

Closely held corporation. A corporation where stock ownership is not widely dispersed. Rather, a few shareholders are in control of corporate policy and are in a position to benefit personally from that policy.

Closing agreement. In a tax dispute, the parties sign a closing agreement to spell out the terms under which the matters are settled. The agreement is binding on both the Service and the taxpayer, for the disputed year and for all future years.

Collectibles. A special type of capital asset, the gain from which is taxed at a maximum rate of 28 percent if the holding period is more than one year. Examples include art, rugs, antiques, gems, metals, stamps, some coins and bullion, and alcoholic beverages held for investment.

Community property. Louisiana, Texas, New Mexico, Arizona, California, Washington, Idaho, Nevada, and Wisconsin have community property systems. Alaska residents can elect community property status for assets. The rest of the states are common law property jurisdictions. The difference between common law and community property systems centers around the property rights possessed by married persons. In a common law system, each spouse owns whatever he or she earns. Under a community property system, one-half of the earnings of each spouse is considered owned by the other spouse. Assume, for example, Jeff and Alice are husband and wife and their only income is the $50,000 annual salary Jeff receives. If they live in New York (a common law state), the $50,000 salary belongs to Jeff. If, however, they live in Texas (a community property state), the $50,000 salary is owned one-half each by Jeff and Alice.

Compensatory damages. Damages received or paid by the taxpayer can be classified as compensatory damages or as punitive damages. Compensatory damages are those paid to compensate one for harm caused by another. Compensatory damages are excludible from the recipient's gross income.

Complete termination redemption. Sale or exchange treatment is available relative to this type of redemption. The shareholder must retire all of his or her outstanding shares in the corporation (ignoring family attribution rules), and cannot hold an interest, other than that of a creditor, for the 10 years following the redemption. § 302(b)(3).

Completed contract method. A method of reporting gain or loss on certain long-term contracts. Under this method of accounting, gross income and expenses are recognized in the tax year in which the contract is completed. Reg. § 1.451–3.

Complex trust. Not a simple trust. Such trusts may have charitable beneficiaries, accumulate income, and distribute corpus. §§ 661–663.

Constructive dividend. A taxable benefit derived by a shareholder from his or her corporation that is not actually called a dividend. Examples include unreasonable compensation, excessive rent payments, bargain purchases of corporate property, and shareholder use of corporate property. Constructive dividends generally are found in closely held corporations.

Constructive liquidation scenario. The means by which recourse debt is shared among partners in basis determination.

Constructive receipt. If income is unqualifiedly available although not physically in the taxpayer's possession, it is subject to the income tax. An example is accrued interest on a savings account. Under the constructive receipt of income concept, the interest is taxed to a depositor in the year available, rather than the year actually withdrawn. The fact that the depositor uses the cash basis of accounting for tax purposes is irrelevant. See Reg. § 1.451–2.

Control. Holding a specified level of stock ownership in a corporation. For § 351, the new shareholder(s) must hold at least 80 percent of the total combined voting power of all voting classes of stock and at least 80 percent of the shares of all nonvoting classes. Other tax provisions require different levels of control to bring about desired effects, such as 50 or 100 percent.

Controlled foreign corporation (CFC). A non-U.S. corporation in which more than 50 percent of the total combined voting power of all classes of stock entitled to vote or the total value of the stock of the corporation is owned by "U.S. shareholders" on any day during the taxable year of the foreign corporation. For purposes of this definition, a U.S. shareholder is any U.S. person who owns, or is considered to own, 10 percent or more of the total combined voting power of all classes of voting stock of the foreign corporation. Stock owned directly, indirectly, and constructively is used in this measure.

Controlled group. A controlled group of corporations is required to share the lower-level corporate tax rates and various other tax benefits among the members of the group. A controlled group may be either a brother-sister or a parent-subsidiary group.

Corporate liquidation. Occurs when a corporation distributes its net assets to its shareholders and ceases to be a going concern. Generally, a shareholder recognizes capital gain or loss upon the liquidation of the entity, regardless of the corporation's balance in its earnings and profits account. However, the distributing corporation recognizes gain and loss on assets that it distributes to shareholders in kind.

Corpus. The body or principal of a trust. Suppose, for example, Grant transfers an apartment building into a trust, income payable to Ruth for life, remainder to Shawn upon Ruth's death. Corpus of the trust is the apartment building.

Correspondence audit. An audit conducted by the IRS by mail. Typically, the IRS writes to the taxpayer requesting the verification of a particular deduction or exemption. The completion of a special form or the remittance of copies of records or other support is all that is requested of the taxpayer.

Cost depletion. Depletion that is calculated based on the adjusted basis of the asset. The adjusted basis is divided by the expected recoverable units to determine the depletion per unit. The depletion per unit is multiplied by the units sold during the tax year to calculate cost depletion.

Cost recovery. The portion of the cost of an asset written off under ACRS (or MACRS), which replaced the depreciation system as a method for writing off the cost of an asset for most assets placed in service after 1980 (after 1986 for MACRS). § 168.

Court of original jurisdiction. The Federal courts are divided into courts of original jurisdiction and appellate courts. A dispute between a taxpayer and the IRS is first considered by a court of original jurisdiction (i.e., a trial court). The four Federal courts of original jurisdiction are the U.S. Tax Court, U.S. District Court, the Court of Federal Claims, and the Small Cases Division of the U.S. Tax Court.

Credit for certain retirement plan contributions. A nonrefundable credit is available based on eligible contributions of up to $2,000 to certain qualified retirement plans, such as traditional and Roth IRAs and § 401(k) plans, for taxable years beginning after 2001 and before 2007. The benefit provided by this credit is in addition to any deduction or exclusion that otherwise is available resulting from the qualifying contribution. The amount of the credit depends on the taxpayer's AGI and filing status. § 25B.

Credit for child and dependent care expenses. A tax credit ranging from 20 percent to 35 percent of employment-related expenses (child and dependent care expenses) for amounts of up to $6,000 is available to individuals who are employed (or deemed to be employed) and maintain a household for a dependent child under age 13, disabled spouse, or disabled dependent. § 21.

Credit for employer-provided child care. A nonrefundable credit is available to employers who provide child care facilities to their employees during normal working hours. The credit, limited to $150,000, is comprised of two components. The portion of the credit for qualified child care expenses is equal to 25 percent of these expenses while the portion of the credit for qualified child care resource and referral services is equal to 10 percent of these expenses. Any qualifying expenses otherwise deductible by the taxpayer must be reduced by the amount of the credit. In addition, the taxpayer's basis for any property used for qualifying purposes is reduced by the amount of the credit. § 45F.

Credit for small employer pension plan startup costs. A nonrefundable credit available to small businesses based on administrative costs associated with establishing and maintaining certain qualified plans. While such qualifying costs generally are deductible as ordinary and necessary business expenses, the availability of the credit is intended to lower the costs of starting a qualified retirement program, and therefore encourage qualifying businesses to establish retirement plans for their employees. The credit is available for eligible employers at the rate of 50 percent of qualified startup costs. The maximum credit is $500 (based on a maximum $1,000 of qualifying expenses). § 45E.

Current earnings and profits. Net tax-basis earnings of a corporation aggregated during the current tax year. A corporate distribution is deemed to be first from the entity's current earnings and profits and then from accumulated earnings and profits. Shareholders recognize dividend income to the extent of the earnings and profits of the corporation. A dividend results to the extent of current earnings and profits, even if there is a larger negative balance in accumulated earnings and profits.

D

***De minimis* fringe.** Benefits provided to employees that are too insignificant to warrant the time and effort required to account for the benefits received by each employee and the value of those benefits. Such amounts are excludible from the employee's gross income. § 132.

Death benefit. A payment made by an employer to the beneficiary or beneficiaries of a deceased employee on account of the death of the employee.

Death tax. A tax imposed on property transferred by the death of the owner.

Debt-financed income. Included in computations of the unrelated business income of an exempt organization, the gross income generated from debt-financed property.

Deduction for qualified tuition and related expenses. Taxpayers are allowed a deduction of up to $4,000 for higher education expenses. Certain taxpayers are not eligible for the deduction: those whose gross AGI exceeds a specified amount and those who can be claimed as a dependent by another taxpayer. These expenses are classified as a deduction *for* AGI, and they need not be employment related. § 222.

Deductions for adjusted gross income. The Federal income tax is not imposed upon gross income. Rather, it is imposed upon taxable income. Congressionally identified deductions for individual taxpayers are subtracted either from gross income to arrive at adjusted gross income or from adjusted gross income to arrive at the tax base, taxable income.

Deductions from adjusted gross income. See *deductions for adjusted gross income.*

Dependency exemption. The tax law provides an exemption for each individual taxpayer and an additional exemption for the taxpayer's spouse if a joint return is filed. An individual may also claim a dependency exemption for each dependent, provided certain tests are met. The amount of the personal and dependency exemptions is $3,200 in 2005 ($3,100 in 2004). The exemption is subject to phaseout once adjusted gross income exceeds certain statutory threshold amounts.

Depletion. The process by which the cost or other basis of a natural resource (e.g., an oil or gas interest) is recovered upon extraction and sale of the resource. The two ways to determine the depletion allowance are the cost and percentage (or statutory) methods. Under cost depletion, each unit of production sold is assigned a portion of the cost or other basis of the interest. This is determined by dividing the cost or other basis by the total units expected to be recovered. Under percentage (or statutory) depletion, the tax law provides a special percentage factor for different types of minerals and other natural resources. This percentage is multiplied by the gross income from the interest to arrive at the depletion allowance. §§ 613 and 613A.

Depreciation. The deduction for the cost or other basis of a tangible asset over the asset's estimated useful life.

Determination letter. Upon the request of a taxpayer, the IRS will comment on the tax status of a completed transaction. Determination letters frequently are used to clarify employee status, determine whether a retirement or profit sharing plan qualifies under the Code, and determine the tax-exempt status of certain nonprofit organizations.

Disabled access credit. A tax credit designed to encourage small businesses to make their facilities more accessible to disabled individuals. The credit is equal to 50 percent of the eligible expenditures that exceed $250 but do not exceed $10,250. Thus, the maximum amount for the credit is $5,000. The adjusted basis for depreciation is reduced by the amount of the credit. To qualify, the facility must have been placed in service before November 6, 1990. § 44.

Disaster area loss. A casualty sustained in an area designated as a disaster area by the President of the United States. In such an event, the disaster loss may be treated as having occurred in the taxable year immediately preceding the year in which the disaster actually occurred. Thus, immediate tax benefits are provided to victims of a disaster. § 165(i).

Disclaimers. Rejections, refusals, or renunciations of claims, powers, or property. Section 2518 sets forth the conditions required to avoid gift tax consequences as the result of a disclaimer.

Disguised sale. When a partner contributes property to the entity and soon thereafter receives a distribution from the partnership, the transactions are collapsed, and the distribution is seen as a purchase of the asset by the partnership. § 707(a)(2)(B).

Disproportionate distribution. A distribution from a partnership to one or more of its partners in which at least one partner's interest in partnership hot assets is increased or decreased. For example, a distribution of cash to one partner and hot assets to another changes both partners' interest in hot assets and is disproportionate. The intent of rules for taxation of disproportionate distributions is to ensure each partner eventually recognizes his or her proportionate share of partnership ordinary income.

Disproportionate redemption. Sale or exchange treatment is available relative to this type of redemption. After the exchange, the shareholder owns less than 80 percent of his or her pre-redemption interest in the corporation, and only a minority interest in the entity. § 302(b)(2).

Distributable net income (DNI). The measure that determines the nature and amount of the distributions from estates and trusts that the beneficiaries must include in income. DNI also limits the amount that estates and trusts can claim as a deduction for such distributions. § 643(a).

Dividend equivalent amount (DEA). The amount subject to the branch profits tax, it is equal to the effectively connected E & P of the U.S. branch of a foreign corporation, reduced/(increased) by an increase/(reduction) in U.S. net equity.

Dividends received deduction. A deduction allowed a shareholder that is a corporation for dividends received from a domestic corporation. The deduction usually is 70 percent of the dividends received, but it could be 80 or 100 percent depending upon the ownership percentage held by the recipient corporation. §§ 243–246.

E

Earned income credit. A tax credit designed to provide assistance to certain low-income individuals who generally have a qualifying child. This is a refundable credit. To receive the most beneficial treatment, the taxpayer must have qualifying children. However, it is possible to qualify for the credit without having a child. To calculate the credit for a taxpayer with one or more children for 2005, a statutory rate of 34 percent for one child (40 percent for two or more children) is multiplied by the earned income (subject to a statutory maximum of $7,830 with one qualifying child or $11,000 with two or more qualifying children). Once the earned income exceeds certain thresholds, the credit is phased out using a 15.98 percent rate for one qualifying child and a 21.06 percent rate for two qualifying children. For the qualifying taxpayer without children, the credit is calculated on a maximum earned income of $5,220 applying a 7.65 percent rate with the phaseout beginning later applying the same rate.

Earnings and profits (E & P). Measures the economic capacity of a corporation to make a distribution to shareholders that is not a return of capital. Such a distribution results in dividend income to the shareholders to the extent of the corporation's current and accumulated earnings and profits.

Economic effect test. Requirements that must be met before a special allocation may be used by a partnership. The premise behind the test is that each partner who receives an allocation of income or loss from a partnership bears the economic benefit or burden of the allocation.

Economic income. The change in the taxpayer's net worth, as measured in terms of market values, plus the value of the assets the taxpayer consumed during the year. Because of the impracticality of this income model, it is not used for tax purposes.

Economic performance test. One of the requirements that must be satisfied in order for an accrual basis taxpayer to deduct an expense. The accrual basis taxpayer first must satisfy the all events test. That test is not deemed satisfied until economic performance occurs. This occurs when property or services are provided to the taxpayer, or in the case in which the taxpayer is required to provide property or services, whenever the property or services are actually provided by the taxpayer.

Education expenses. Employees may deduct education expenses that are incurred either (1) to maintain or improve existing job-related skills or (2) to meet the express requirements of the employer or the requirements imposed by law to retain employment status. The expenses are not deductible if the education is required to meet the minimum educational standards for the taxpayer's job or if the education qualifies the individual for a new trade or business. Reg. § 1.162–5.

Educational savings bonds. U.S. Series EE bonds whose proceeds are used for qualified higher educational expenses for the taxpayer, the taxpayer's spouse, or a dependent. The interest may be excluded from gross income, provided the taxpayer's adjusted gross income does not exceed certain amounts. § 135.

Effectively connected income. Income of a nonresident alien or foreign corporation that is attributable to the operation of a U.S. trade or business under either the asset-use or business-activities test.

e-file. The electronic filing of a tax return. The filing is either direct or indirect. As to direct, the taxpayer goes online using a computer and tax return preparation software. Indirect filing occurs when a taxpayer utilizes an authorized IRS e-file provider. The provider often is the tax return preparer.

Electing large partnership. A partnership with 100 or more partners may elect to be subject to simplified tax reporting and audit procedures. The election allows the partnership to combine certain income and expense amounts and report net amounts to the partners. The result is fewer "pass-through" items to the partners, which makes the partners' tax returns easier to prepare. As an example, an electing large partnership with a long-term capital gain and a short-term capital loss would offset the two amounts and allocate the net amount among the partners.

Employment taxes. Employment taxes are those taxes that an employer must pay on account of its employees. Employment taxes include FICA (Federal Insurance Contributions Act) and FUTA (Federal Unemployment Tax Act) taxes. Employment taxes are paid to the IRS in addition to income tax withholdings at specified intervals. Such taxes can be levied on the employees, the employer, or both.

Enrolled agent (EA). A tax practitioner who has gained admission to practice before the IRS by passing an IRS examination.

Entertainment expenses. These expenses are deductible only if they are directly related to or associated with a trade or business. Various restrictions and documentation requirements have been imposed upon the deductibility of entertainment expenses to prevent abuses by taxpayers. See, for example, the provision contained in § 274(n) that disallows 50 percent (20 percent prior to 1994) of entertainment expenses. § 274.

Entity concept. The theory of partnership taxation under which a partnership is treated as a separate and distinct entity from the partners and has its own tax attributes.

Estate tax. A tax imposed on the right to transfer property by death. Thus, an estate tax is levied on the decedent's estate and not on the heir receiving the property.

Excess lobbying expenditure. An excise tax is applied on otherwise tax-exempt organizations with respect to the excess of total lobbying expenditures over grass roots lobbying expenditures for the year.

Excise tax. A tax on the manufacture, sale, or use of goods; on the carrying on of an occupation or activity; or on the transfer of property. Thus, the Federal estate and gift taxes are, theoretically, excise taxes.

Exclusion amount. The value of assets that is equal to the credit allowed for gifts or transfers by death. Thus, if the estate tax unified transfer tax credit is $555,800, the exclusion amount is $1,500,000. The gift tax exclusion amount is $1 million, based on its $345,800 unified credit. Often called the *exemption equivalent amount.*

Exemption equivalent. The amount of value (currently $1,500,000 for estate tax and $1 million for gift tax) that is the equivalent of the unified transfer tax credit allowed.

Exempt organization. An organization that is either partially or completely exempt from Federal income taxation. § 501.

Expenses in respect of a decedent. Deductions accrued at the moment of death but not recognizable on the final income tax return of a decedent because of the method of accounting used. Such items are allowed as deductions on the estate tax return and on the income tax return of the estate (Form 1041) or the heir (Form 1040). An example of a deduction in respect of a decedent is interest expense accrued to the date of death by a cash basis debtor.

Extraordinary personal services. These are services provided by individuals where the customers' use of the property is incidental to their receipt of the services. For example, a patient's use of a hospital bed is incidental to his or her receipt of medical services. This is one of the six exceptions to determine whether an activity is a passive rental activity. § 469.

Extraterritorial income. A device by which the United States encouraged outbound (export) sales, services, and leases. An exclusion from gross income computed under § 114 for certain transactions of U.S. taxpayers.

F

Fair market value. The amount at which property would change hands between a willing buyer and a willing seller, neither being under any compulsion to buy or to sell, and both having reasonable knowledge of the relevant facts. Reg. §§ 1.1001–1(a) and 20.2031–1(b).

Federal District Court. A Federal District Court is a trial court for purposes of litigating Federal tax matters. It is the only trial court in which a jury trial can be obtained.

Feeder organization. An entity that carries on a trade or business for the benefit of an exempt organization. However, such a relationship does not result in the feeder organization itself being tax-exempt. § 502.

FICA tax. An abbreviation that stands for Federal Insurance Contributions Act, commonly referred to as the Social Security tax. The FICA tax is comprised of the Social Security tax (old age, survivors, and disability insurance) and the Medicare tax (hospital insurance) and is imposed on both employers and employees. The employer is responsible for withholding from the employee's wages the Social Security tax at a rate of 6.2 percent on a maximum wage base of $90,000 (for 2005) and the Medicare tax at a rate of 1.45 percent (no maximum wage base). The employer is required to match the employee's contribution.

Field audit. An audit conducted by the IRS on the business premises of the taxpayer or in the office of the tax practitioner representing the taxpayer.

Finalized Regulation. The U.S. Treasury Department Regulations (abbreviated Reg.) represent the position of the IRS as to how the Internal Revenue Code is to be interpreted. Their purpose is to provide taxpayers and IRS personnel with rules of general and specific application to the various provisions of the tax law. Regulations are published in the *Federal Register* and in all tax services.

FIRPTA. Under the Foreign Investment in Real Property Tax Act, gains or losses realized by nonresident aliens and non-U.S. corporations on the disposition of U.S. real estate create U.S.-source income and are subject to U.S. income tax.

Fiscal year. A fiscal year is a 12-month period ending on the last day of a month other than December. In certain circumstances, a taxpayer is permitted to elect a fiscal year instead of being required to use a calendar year.

Flat tax. In its pure form, a flat tax would eliminate all exclusions, deductions, and credits and impose a one-rate tax on gross income.

Flexible spending plan. An employee benefit plan that allows the employee to take a reduction in salary in exchange for the employer paying benefits that can be provided by the employer without the employee being required to recognize income (e.g., medical and child care benefits).

Foreign earned income exclusion. The Code allows exclusions for earned income generated outside the United States to alleviate any tax base and rate disparities among countries. In addition, the exclusion is allowed for housing expenditures incurred by the taxpayer's employer with respect to the non-U.S. assignment, and self-employed individuals can deduct foreign housing expenses incurred in a trade or business. The exclusion is limited to $80,000 per year. § 911.

Foreign tax credit. A U.S. citizen or resident who incurs or pays income taxes to a foreign country on income subject to U.S. tax may be able to claim some of these taxes as a credit against the U.S. income tax. §§ 27 and 901–905.

Franchise. An agreement that gives the transferee the right to distribute, sell, or provide goods, services, or facilities within a specified area. The cost of obtaining a franchise may be amortized over a statutory period of 15 years. In general, the franchisor's gain on the sale of franchise rights is an ordinary gain because the franchisor retains a significant power, right, or continuing interest in the subject of the franchise. §§ 197 and 1253.

Franchise tax. A tax levied on the right to do business in a state as a corporation. Although income considerations may come into play, the tax usually is based on the capitalization of the corporation.

Fraud. Tax fraud falls into two categories: civil and criminal. Under civil fraud, the IRS may impose as a penalty an amount equal to as much as 75 percent of the underpayment [§ 6651(f)]. Fines and/or imprisonment are prescribed for conviction of various types of criminal tax fraud (§§ 7201– 7207). Both civil and criminal fraud involve a specific intent on the part of the taxpayer to evade the tax; mere negligence is not enough. Criminal fraud requires the additional element of willfulness (i.e., done deliberately and with evil purpose). In practice, it becomes difficult to distinguish between the degree of intent necessary to support criminal, rather than civil, fraud. In either situation, the IRS has the burden of proving fraud.

Fruit and tree metaphor. The courts have held that an individual who earns income from property or services cannot assign that income to another. For example, a father cannot assign his earnings from commissions to his child and escape income tax on those amounts.

Functional currency. The currency of the economic environment in which the taxpayer carries on most of its activities, and in which the taxpayer transacts most of its business.

FUTA tax. An employment tax levied on employers. Jointly administered by the Federal and state governments, the tax provides funding for unemployment benefits. FUTA applies at a rate of 6.2 percent on the first $7,000 of covered wages paid during the year for each employee. The Federal government allows a credit for FUTA paid (or allowed under a merit rating system) to the state. The credit cannot exceed 5.4 percent of the covered wages.

Future interest. An interest that will come into being at some future time. It is distinguished from a present interest, which already exists. Assume that Dan transfers securities to a newly created trust. Under the terms of the trust instrument, income from the securities is to be paid each year to Wilma for her life, with the securities passing to Sam upon Wilma's death. Wilma has a present interest in the trust since she is currently entitled to receive the income from the securities. Sam has a future interest since he must wait for Wilma's death to benefit from the trust. The annual exclusion of $11,000 is not allowed for a gift of a future interest. § 2503(b).

G

General business credit. The summation of various nonrefundable business credits, including the tax credit for rehabilitation expenditures, business energy credit, welfare-to-work credit, work opportunity credit, research activities credit, low-income housing credit, and disabled access credit. The amount of general business credit that can be used to reduce the tax liability is limited to the taxpayer's net income tax reduced by the greater of (1) the tentative minimum tax or (2) 25 percent of the net regular tax liability that exceeds

$25,000. Unused general business credits can be carried back 1 year and forward 20 years. § 38.

General partnership. A partnership that is owned by one or more general partners. Creditors of a general partnership can collect amounts owed them from both the partnership assets and the assets of the partners individually.

Gift. A transfer of property for less than adequate consideration. Gifts usually occur in a personal setting (such as between members of the same family). They are excluded from the income tax base but may be subject to a transfer tax.

Gift tax. A tax imposed on the transfer of property by gift. The tax is imposed upon the donor of a gift and is based on the fair market value of the property on the date of the gift.

Goodwill. The reputation and built-up business of a company. For accounting purposes, goodwill has no basis unless it is purchased. In the purchase of a business, goodwill generally is the difference between the purchase price and the fair market value of the assets acquired. The intangible asset goodwill can be amortized for tax purposes over a 15-year period. Reg. § 1.167(a)–3.

Grantor. A transferor of property. The creator of a trust is usually referred to as the grantor of the trust.

Grantor trust. A trust under which the grantor retains control over the income or corpus (or both) to such an extent that he or she is treated as the owner of the property and its income for income tax purposes. Income from a grantor trust is taxable to the grantor and not to the beneficiary who receives it. §§ 671–679.

Grass roots expenditures. Exempt organizations are prohibited from engaging in political activities, but spending incurred to influence the opinions of the general public relative to specific legislation is permitted by the law.

Gross estate. The property owned or previously transferred by a decedent that is subject to the Federal estate tax. The gross estate can be distinguished from the probate estate, which is property actually subject to administration by the administrator or executor of an estate. §§ 2031–2046.

Gross income. Income subject to the Federal income tax. Gross income does not include all economic income. That is, certain exclusions are allowed (e.g., interest on municipal bonds). For a manufacturing or merchandising business, gross income usually means gross profit (gross sales or gross receipts less cost of goods sold). § 61 and Reg. § 1.61–3(a).

Group term life insurance. Life insurance coverage provided by an employer for a group of employees. Such insurance is renewable on a year-to-year basis, and typically no cash surrender value is built up. The premiums paid by the employer on the insurance are not taxed to the employees on coverage of up to $50,000 per person. § 79 and Reg. § 1.79–1(b).

Guaranteed payments. Payments made by a partnership to a partner for services rendered or for the use of capital to the extent that the payments are determined without regard to the income of the partnership. The payments are treated as though they were made to a nonpartner and thus are usually deductible by the entity.

H

Half-year convention. The half-year convention is a cost recovery convention that assumes all property is placed in service at mid-year and thus provides for a half-year's cost recovery for that year.

Head of household. An unmarried individual who maintains a household for another and satisfies certain conditions set forth in § 2(b). This status enables the taxpayer to use a set of income tax rates that are lower than those applicable to other unmarried individuals but higher than those applicable to surviving spouses and married persons filing a joint return.

Health savings account (HSA). A medical savings account created in legislation enacted in December 2003 that is designed to replace and expand Archer Medical Savings Accounts. See also *medical savings account.*

Hobby losses. Losses from an activity not engaged in for profit. The Code restricts the amount of losses that an individual can deduct for hobby activities so that these transactions cannot be used to offset income from other sources. § 183.

Holding period. The period of time during which property has been held for income tax purposes. The holding period is significant in determining whether gain or loss from the sale or exchange of a capital asset is long term or short term. § 1223.

Home equity loans. Loans that utilize the personal residence of the taxpayer as security. The interest on such loans is deductible as qualified residence interest. However, interest is deductible only on the portion of the loan that does not exceed the lesser of (1) the fair market value of the residence, reduced by the acquisition indebtedness, or (2) $100,000 ($50,000 for married persons filing separate returns). A major benefit of a home equity loan is that there are no tracing rules regarding the use of the loan proceeds. § 163(h)(3).

HOPE scholarship credit. A tax credit for qualifying expenses paid for the first two years of postsecondary education. Room, board, and book costs are ineligible for the credit. The maximum credit available is $1,500 per year per student, computed as 100 percent of the first $1,000 of qualifying expenses, plus 50 percent of the second $1,000 of qualifying expenses. Eligible students include the taxpayer, taxpayer's spouse, and taxpayer's dependents. To qualify for the credit, a student must take at least one-half the full-time course load for at least one academic term at a qualifying educational institution. The credit is phased out for higher-income taxpayers. § 25A.

Hot assets. Unrealized receivables and substantially appreciated inventory under § 751. When hot assets are present, the sale of a partnership interest or the disproportionate distribution of the assets can cause ordinary income to be recognized.

Hybrid method. A combination of the accrual and cash methods of accounting. That is, the taxpayer may account for some items of income on the accrual method (e.g., sales and cost of goods sold) and other items (e.g., interest income) on the cash method.

I

Imputed interest. For certain long-term sales of property, the IRS can convert some of the gain from the sale into interest income if the contract does not provide for a minimum rate of interest to be paid by the purchaser. The application of this procedure has the effect of forcing the seller to recognize less long-term capital gain and more ordinary income (interest income). § 483 and the related Regulations.

Inbound taxation. U.S. tax effects when a non-U.S. person begins an investment or business activity in the United States.

Incentive stock option (ISO). A type of stock option that receives favorable tax treatment. If various qualification requirements can be satisfied, there are no recognition tax consequences when the stock option is granted. However, the spread (the excess of the fair market value at the date of exercise over the option price) is a tax preference item for purposes of the alternative minimum tax. The gain on disposition of the stock resulting from the exercise of the stock option will be classified as long-term capital gain if certain holding period requirements are met (the employee must not dispose of the stock within two years after the option is granted or within one year after acquiring the stock). § 422.

Income. For tax purposes, an increase in wealth that has been realized.

Income in respect of a decedent (IRD). Income earned by a decedent at the time of death but not reportable on the final income tax return because of the method of accounting that appropriately is utilized. Such income is included in the gross estate and is taxed to the eventual recipient (either the estate or heirs). The recipient is, however, allowed an income tax deduction for the estate tax attributable to the income. § 691.

Independent contractor. A self-employed person as distinguished from one who is employed as an employee.

Individual retirement account (IRA). A type of retirement plan to which an individual with earned income can contribute a maximum of $3,000 ($3,000 each in the case of a married couple with a spousal IRA) per tax year for 2002–2004. The maximum amount increases to $4,000 in 2005 and to $5,000 in 2008. IRAs can be classified as traditional IRAs or Roth IRAs. With a traditional IRA, an individual can contribute and deduct a maximum of $4,000 per tax year in 2005. The deduction is a deduction *for* AGI. However, if the individual is an active participant in another qualified retirement plan, the deduction is phased out proportionally between certain AGI ranges (note that the phaseout limits the amount of the deduction and not the amount of the contribution). With a Roth IRA, an individual can contribute a maximum of $4,000 per tax year in 2005. No deduction is permitted. However, if a five-year holding period requirement is satisfied and if the distribution is a qualified distribution, the taxpayer can make tax-free withdrawals from a Roth IRA. The maximum annual contribution is phased out proportionally between certain AGI ranges. §§ 219 and 408A.

Inheritance tax. A tax imposed on the right to receive property from a decedent. Thus, theoretically, an inheritance tax is imposed on the heir. The Federal estate tax is imposed on the estate.

Inside basis. A partnership's basis in the assets it owns.

Installment method. A method of accounting enabling certain taxpayers to spread the recognition of gain on the sale of property over the collection period. Under this procedure, the seller arrives at the gain to be recognized by computing the gross profit percentage from the sale (the gain divided by the contract price) and applying it to each payment received. § 453.

Intangible drilling and development costs (IDC). Taxpayers may elect to expense or capitalize (subject to amortization) intangible drilling and development costs. However, ordinary income recapture provisions apply to oil and gas properties on a sale or other disposition if the expense method is elected. §§ 263(c) and 1254(a).

Intermediate sanctions. The IRS can assess excise taxes on disqualified persons and organization managers associated with so-called public charities engaging in excess benefit transactions. An excess benefit transaction is one in which a disqualified person engages in a non-fair market value transaction with the exempt organization or receives unreasonable compensation. Prior to the idea of intermediate sanctions, the only option available to the IRS was to revoke the organization's exempt status.

Interpretive Regulation. A Regulation issued by the Treasury Department that purports to explain the meaning of a particular Code Section. An interpretive Regulation is given less deference than a legislative Regulation.

Investment income. Consisting of virtually the same elements as portfolio income, a measure by which to justify a deduction for interest on investment indebtedness.

Investment interest. Payment for the use of funds used to acquire assets that produce investment income. The deduction for investment interest is limited to net investment income for the tax year.

Investor losses. Losses on stock and securities. If stocks and bonds are capital assets in the hands of the holder, a capital loss materializes as of the last day of the taxable year in which the stocks or bonds become worthless. Under certain circumstances involving stocks and bonds of affiliated corporations, an ordinary loss is permitted upon worthlessness.

Involuntary conversion. The loss or destruction of property through theft, casualty, or condemnation. Any gain realized on an involuntary conversion can, at the taxpayer's election, be deferred for Federal income tax purposes if the owner reinvests the proceeds within a prescribed period of time in property that is similar or related in service or use. § 1033.

IRAs (traditional). See *Individual retirement account (IRA).*

Itemized deductions. Personal and employee expenditures allowed by the Code as deductions from adjusted gross income. Examples include certain medical expenses, interest on home mortgages, state income taxes, and charitable contributions. Itemized deductions are reported on Schedule A of Form 1040. Certain miscellaneous itemized deductions are reduced by 2 percent of the taxpayer's adjusted gross income. In addition, a taxpayer whose adjusted gross income exceeds a certain level (indexed annually) must reduce the itemized deductions by 3 percent of the excess of adjusted gross income over that level. Medical, casualty and theft, and investment interest deductions are not subject to the 3 percent reduction. The 3 percent reduction may not reduce itemized deductions that are subject to the reduction to below 20 percent of their initial amount.

J

Joint tenants. Two or more persons having undivided ownership of property with the right of survivorship. Right of survivorship gives the surviving owner full ownership of the property. Suppose Bob and Tami are joint tenants of a tract of land. Upon Bob's death, Tami becomes the sole owner of the property. For the estate tax consequences upon the death of a joint tenant, see § 2040.

K

Kiddie tax. Passive income, such as interest and dividends, that is recognized by a child under age 14 is taxed to him or her at the rates that would have applied had the income been incurred by the child's parents, generally to the extent that the income exceeds $1,600. The additional tax is assessed regardless of the source of the income or the income's underlying property. If the child's parents are divorced, the custodial parent's rates are used. The parents' rates reflect any applicable alternative minimum tax and the phaseouts of lower tax brackets and other deductions. § 1(g).

L

Least aggregate deferral method. An algorithm set forth in the Regulations to determine the tax year for a partnership or S corporation with owners whose tax years differ. The tax year selected is the one that produces the least aggregate deferral of income for the owners.

Legislative Regulation. Some Code Sections give the Secretary of the Treasury or his delegate the authority to prescribe Regulations to carry out the details of administration or to otherwise complete the operating rules. Regulations issued pursuant to this type of authority truly possess the force and effect of law. In effect, Congress is almost delegating its legislative powers to the Treasury Department.

Lessee. One who rents property from another. In the case of real estate, the lessee is also known as the tenant.

Lessor. One who rents property to another. In the case of real estate, the lessor is also known as the landlord.

Letter ruling. The written response of the IRS to a taxpayer's request for interpretation of the revenue laws, with respect to a proposed transaction (e.g., concerning the tax-free status of a reorganization). Not to be relied on as precedent by other than the party who requested the ruling.

Liabilities in excess of basis. On the contribution of capital to a corporation, an investor recognizes gain on the exchange to the extent that contributed assets carry liabilities with a face amount in excess of the tax basis of the contributed assets. This rule keeps the investor from holding the investment asset received with a negative basis. § 357(c).

Life insurance proceeds. A specified sum (the face value or maturity value of the policy) paid to the designated beneficiary of the policy by the life insurance company upon the death of the insured.

Lifetime learning credit. A tax credit for qualifying expenses for taxpayers pursuing education beyond the first two years of postsecondary education. Individuals who are completing their last two years of undergraduate studies, pursuing graduate or professional degrees, or otherwise seeking new job skills or maintaining existing job skills are all eligible for the credit. Eligible individuals include the taxpayer, taxpayer's spouse, and taxpayer's dependents. The maximum credit is 20 percent of the first $10,000 of qualifying expenses and is computed per taxpayer. The credit is phased out for higher-income taxpayers. § 25A.

Like-kind exchange. An exchange of property held for productive use in a trade or business or for investment (except inventory and stocks and bonds) for other investment or trade or business property. Unless non-like-kind property (boot) is received, the exchange is fully nontaxable. § 1031.

Limited liability company (LLC). A form of entity allowed by all of the states. The entity is taxed as a partnership in which all members or owners of the LLC are treated much like limited partners. There are no restrictions on ownership, all members may participate in management, and none has personal liability for the entity's debts.

Limited liability partnership (LLP). A form of entity allowed by many of the states, where a general partnership registers with the state as an LLP. Owners are general partners, but a partner is not liable for any malpractice committed by other partners. The personal assets of the partners are at risk for the entity's contractual liabilities, such as accounts payable. The personal assets of a specific partner are at risk for his or her own professional malpractice and tort liability, and for malpractice and torts committed by those whom he or she supervises.

Limited partnership. A partnership in which some of the partners are limited partners. At least one of the partners in a limited partnership must be a general partner.

Liquidating distribution. A distribution by a partnership or corporation that is in complete liquidation of the entity's trade or business activities. Typically, such distributions generate capital gain or loss to the investors without regard, for instance, to the earnings and profits of the corporation or to the partnership's basis in the distributed property. They can, however, lead to recognized gain or loss at the corporate level.

Listed property. The term listed property includes (1) any passenger automobile, (2) any other property used as a means of transportation, (3) any property of a type generally used for purposes of entertainment, recreation, or amusement, (4) any computer or peripheral equipment (with an exception for exclusive business use), (5) any cellular telephone (or other similar telecommunications equipment), and (6) any other property of a type specified in the Regulations. If listed property is predominantly used for business, the taxpayer is allowed to use the statutory percentage method of cost recovery. Otherwise, the straight-line cost recovery method must be used. § 280F.

Lobbying expenditure. An expenditure made for the purpose of influencing legislation. Such payments can result in the loss of the exempt status of, and the imposition of Federal income tax on, an exempt organization.

Long-term care insurance. Insurance that helps pay the cost of care when the insured is unable to care for himself or herself. Such insurance is generally thought of as insurance against the cost of an aged person entering a nursing home. The employer can provide the insurance, and the premiums may be excluded from the employee's gross income. § 7702B.

Long-term contract. A building, installation, construction, or manufacturing contract that is entered into but not completed within the same tax year. A manufacturing contract is a long-term contract only if the contract is to manufacture (1) a unique item not normally carried in finished goods inventory or (2) items that normally require more than 12 calendar months to complete. The two available methods to account for long-term contracts are the percentage of completion method and the completed contract method. The completed contract method can be used only in limited circumstances. § 460.

Long-term nonpersonal use capital assets. Includes investment property with a long-term holding period. Such property disposed of by casualty or theft may receive § 1231 treatment.

Low-income housing credit. Beneficial treatment to owners of low-income housing is provided in the form of a tax credit. The calculated credit is claimed in the year the building is placed in service and in the following nine years. § 42.

M

Majority interest partners. Partners who have more than a 50 percent interest in partnership profits and capital, counting only those partners who have the same taxable year, are referred to as majority interest partners. The term is of significance in determining the appropriate taxable year of a partnership. § 706(b).

Manufacturers' deduction. A deduction allowed to sole proprietors, C corporations, partnerships, S corporations, cooperatives, estates, and trusts for certain production activities. The deduction rate is 3% of qualified production income for 2005–2006 and is scheduled to increase to 6% for 2007 through 2009 and to 9% for 2010 and thereafter. § 199.

Marital deduction. A deduction allowed against the taxable estate or taxable gifts upon the transfer of property from one spouse to another.

Marriage penalty. The additional tax liability that results for a married couple when compared with what their tax liability would be if they were not married and filed separate returns.

Material participation. If an individual taxpayer materially participates in a nonrental trade or business activity, any loss from that activity is treated as an active loss that can be offset against active income. Material participation is achieved by meeting any one of seven tests provided in the Regulations. § 469(h).

Meaningful reduction test. A decrease in the shareholder's voting control. Used to determine whether a redemption qualifies for sale or exchange treatment.

Medical expenses. Medical expenses of an individual, spouse, and dependents are allowed as an itemized deduction to the extent that such amounts (less insurance reimbursements) exceed 7.5 percent of adjusted gross income. § 213.

Mid-month convention. A cost recovery convention that assumes property is placed in service in the middle of the month that it is actually placed in service.

Mid-quarter convention. A cost recovery convention that assumes property placed in service during the year is placed in service at the middle of the quarter in which it is actually placed in service. The mid-quarter convention applies if more than 40 percent of the value of property (other than eligible real estate) is placed in service during the last quarter of the year.

Miscellaneous itemized deductions. A special category of itemized deductions that includes such expenses as professional dues, tax return preparation fees, job-hunting costs, unreimbursed employee business expenses, and certain investment expenses. Such expenses are deductible only to the extent they exceed 2 percent of adjusted gross income. § 67.

Modified accelerated cost recovery system (MACRS). A method in which the cost of tangible property is recovered over a prescribed period of time. Enacted by the Economic Recovery Tax Act (ERTA) of 1981 and substantially modified by the Tax Reform Act (TRA) of 1986 (the modified system is referred to as MACRS), the approach disregards salvage value, imposes a period of cost recovery that depends upon the classification of the asset into one of various recovery periods, and prescribes the applicable percentage of cost that can be deducted each year. § 168.

Moving expenses. A deduction *for* AGI is permitted to employees and self-employed individuals provided certain tests are met. The taxpayer's new job must be at least 50 miles farther from the old residence than the old residence was from the former place of work. In addition, an employee must be employed on a full-time basis at the new location for 39 weeks in the 12-month period following the move. Deductible moving expenses include the cost of moving the household and personal effects, transportation, and lodging expenses during the move. The cost of meals during the move is not deductible. Qualified moving expenses that are paid (or reimbursed) by the employer can be excluded from the employee's gross income. In this case, the related deduction by the employee is not permitted. §§ 62(a)(15), 132(a)(6), and 217.

Multiple support agreement. To qualify for a dependency exemption, the support test must be satisfied. This requires that over 50 percent of the support of the potential dependent be provided by the taxpayer. Where no one person provides more than 50 percent of the support, a multiple support agreement enables a taxpayer to still qualify for the dependency exemption. Any person who contributed more than 10 percent of the support is entitled to claim the exemption if each person in the group who contributed more than 10 percent files a written consent (Form 2120). Each person who is a party to the multiple support agreement must meet all the other requirements for claiming the dependency exemption. § 152(c).

N

National sales tax. Intended as a replacement for the current Federal income tax. Unlike a value added tax (VAT), which is levied on the manufacturer, it would be imposed on the consumer upon the final sale of goods and services. To keep the tax from being regressive, low-income taxpayers would be granted some kind of credit or exemption.

Negligence. Failure to exercise the reasonable or ordinary degree of care of a prudent person in a situation that results in harm or damage to another. Code § 6651 imposes a penalty on taxpayers who exhibit negligence or intentional disregard of rules and Regulations with respect to the underpayment of certain taxes.

Net capital gain. The excess of the net long-term capital gain for the tax year over the net short-term capital loss. The net capital gain of an individual taxpayer is eligible for the alternative tax. § 1222(11).

Net capital loss. The excess of the losses from sales or exchanges of capital assets over the gains from sales or exchanges of such assets. Up to $3,000 per year of the net capital loss may be deductible by noncorporate taxpayers against ordinary income. The excess net capital loss carries over to future tax years. For corporate taxpayers, the net capital loss cannot be offset against ordinary income, but it can be carried back three years and forward five years to offset net capital gains. §§ 1211, 1212, and 1221(10).

Net investment income. The excess of investment income over investment expenses. Investment expenses are those deductible expenses directly connected with the production of investment income. Investment expenses do not include investment interest. The deduction for investment interest for the tax year is limited to net investment income. § 163(d).

Net operating loss. To mitigate the effect of the annual accounting period concept, § 172 allows taxpayers to use an excess loss of one year as a deduction for certain past or future years. In this regard, a carryback period of 2 years and a carryforward period of 20 years currently are allowed.

Nexus. A multistate corporation's taxable income can be apportioned to a specific state only if the entity has established a sufficient presence, or nexus, with that state. State law, which often follows the Uniform Division of Income for Tax Purposes Act (UDITPA), specifies various activities that lead to nexus in various states.

Ninety-day letter. Commonly referred to as the 90-day letter, this notice is sent to a taxpayer upon request, upon the expiration of the 30-day letter, or upon exhaustion by the taxpayer of his or her administrative remedies before the IRS. The notice gives the taxpayer 90 days in which to file a petition with the U.S. Tax Court. If a petition is not filed, the IRS will demand payment of the assessed deficiency. §§ 6211–6216.

No-additional-cost services. Services that the employer may provide the employee at no additional cost to the employer. Generally, the benefit is the ability to utilize the employer's excess capacity (e.g., vacant seats on an airliner). Such amounts are excludible from the recipient's gross income.

Nonaccountable plan. An expense reimbursement plan that does not have an accountability feature. The result is that employee expenses must be claimed as deductions *from* AGI. An exception is moving expenses that are deductions *for* AGI.

Nonacquiescence. Disagreement by the IRS on the result reached in certain judicial decisions. *Nonacq.* or *NA*.

Nonbusiness bad debt. A bad debt loss that is not incurred in connection with a creditor's trade or business. The loss is classified as a short-term capital loss and is allowed only in the year the debt becomes entirely worthless. In addition to family loans, many investor losses are nonbusiness bad debts. § 166(d).

Nonliquidating distribution. A payment made by a partnership or corporation to the entity's owner is a nonliquidating distribution when the entity's legal existence does not cease thereafter. If the payor is a corporation, such a distribution can result in dividend income to the shareholders. If the payor is a partnership, the partner usually assigns a basis in the distributed property that is equal to the lesser of the partner's basis in the partnership interest or the basis of the distributed asset to the partnership. In this regard, the partner first assigns basis to any cash that he or she receives in the distribution. The partner's remaining basis, if any, is assigned to the noncash assets according to their relative bases to the partnership.

Nonrecourse debt. Debt secured by the property that it is used to purchase. The purchaser of the property is not personally liable for the debt upon default. Rather, the creditor's recourse is to repossess the related property. Nonrecourse debt generally does not increase the purchaser's at-risk amount.

Nonrefundable credit. A nonrefundable credit is a credit that is not paid if it exceeds the taxpayer's tax liability. Some nonrefundable credits qualify for carryback and carryover treatment.

Nonresident alien. An individual who is neither a citizen nor a resident of the United States. Citizenship is determined under the immigration and naturalization laws of the United States. Residency is determined under § 7701(b) of the Internal Revenue Code.

Nontaxable exchange. A transaction in which realized gains or losses are not recognized. The recognition of gain or loss is postponed (deferred) until the property received in the nontaxable exchange is subsequently disposed of in a taxable transaction. Examples are § 1031 like-kind exchanges and § 1033 involuntary conversions.

Not essentially equivalent redemption. Sale or exchange treatment is given to this type of redemption. Although various safe-harbor tests are failed, the nature of the redemption is such that dividend treatment is avoided, because it represents a meaningful reduction in the shareholder's interest in the corporation. § 302(b)(1).

O

Occupational tax. A tax imposed on various trades or businesses. A license fee that enables a taxpayer to engage in a particular occupation.

Offer in compromise. A settlement agreement offered by the IRS in a tax dispute, especially where there is doubt as to the collectibility of the full deficiency. Offers in compromise can include installment payment schedules, as well as reductions in the tax and penalties owed by the taxpayer.

Office audit. An audit conducted by the IRS in the agent's office.

Office in the home expenses. Employment and business-related expenses attributable to the use of a residence (e.g., den or office) are allowed only if the portion of the residence is exclusively used on a regular basis as a principal place of business of the taxpayer or as a place of business that is used by patients, clients, or customers. If the expenses are incurred by an employee, the use must be for the convenience of the employer as opposed to being merely appropriate and helpful. § 280A.

One-year rule for prepaid expenses. Taxpayers who use the cash method are required to use the accrual method for deducting certain prepaid expenses (i.e., must capitalize the item and can deduct only when used). If a prepayment will not be consumed or expire by the end of the tax year following the year of payment, the prepayment must be capitalized and prorated over the benefit period. Conversely, if the prepayment will be consumed by the end of the tax year following the year of payment, it can be expensed when paid. To obtain the current deduction under the one-year rule, the payment must be a required payment rather than a voluntary payment.

Options. The sale or exchange of an option to buy or sell property results in capital gain or loss if the property is a capital asset. Generally, the closing of an option transaction results in short-term capital gain or loss to the writer of the call and the purchaser of the call option. § 1234.

Ordinary and necessary. An ordinary expense is one that is common and accepted in the general industry or type of activity in which the taxpayer is engaged. It comprises one of the tests for the deductibility of expenses incurred or paid in connection with a trade or business; for the production or collection of income; for the management, conservation, or maintenance of property held for the production of income; or in connection with the determination, collection, or refund of any tax. §§ 162(a) and 212. A necessary expense is one that is appropriate and helpful in furthering the taxpayer's business or income-producing activity. §§ 162(a) and 212.

Ordinary income property. Property contributed to a charitable organization that, if sold rather than contributed, would have resulted in other than long-term capital gain to the donor (i.e., ordinary income property and short-term capital gain property). Examples are inventory and capital assets held for less than the long-term holding period.

Organizational expenditures. Items incurred early in the life of a corporate entity that are eligible for a $5,000 limited expensing (subject to phaseout) and an amortization of the balance over 180 months or more. Organizational expenditures exclude those incurred to obtain capital (underwriting fees) or assets (subject to cost recovery). Typically, eligible expenditures include legal and accounting fees and state incorporation payments. Such items must be incurred by the end of the entity's first tax year. § 248.

Original issue discount. The difference between the issue price of a debt obligation (e.g., a corporate bond) and the maturity value of the obligation when the issue price is *less than* the maturity value. OID represents interest and must be amortized over the life of the debt obligation using the effective interest method. The difference is not considered to be original issue discount for tax purposes when it is less than one-fourth of 1 percent of the redemption price at maturity multiplied by the number of years to maturity. §§ 1272 and 1273(a)(3).

Outbound taxation. U.S. tax effects when a U.S. person begins an investment or business activity outside the United States.

Outside basis. A partner's basis in his or her partnership interest.

P

Parent-subsidiary controlled group. A controlled or affiliated group of corporations, where at least one corporation is at least 80 percent owned by one or more of the others. The affiliated group definition is more difficult to meet.

Partnership. For income tax purposes, a partnership includes a syndicate, group, pool, or joint venture, as well as ordinary partnerships. In an ordinary partnership, two or more parties combine capital and/or services to carry on a business for profit as co-owners. § 7701(a)(2).

Passive investment income (PII). Gross receipts from royalties, certain rents, dividends, interest, annuities, and gains from the sale or exchange of stock and securities. With certain exceptions, if the passive investment income of an S corporation exceeds 25 percent of the corporation's gross receipts for three consecutive years, S status is lost.

Passive loss. Any loss from (1) activities in which the taxpayer does not materially participate or (2) rental activities (subject to certain exceptions). Net passive losses cannot be used to offset income from nonpassive sources. Rather, they are suspended until the taxpayer either generates net passive income (and a deduction of such losses is allowed) or disposes of the underlying property (at which time the loss deductions are allowed in full). One relief provision allows landlords who actively participate in the rental activities to deduct up to $25,000 of passive losses annually. However, a phaseout of the $25,000 amount commences when the landlord's AGI exceeds $100,000. Another relief provision applies for material participation in a real estate trade or business.

Patent. A patent is an intangible asset that may be amortized over a statutory 15-year period as a § 197 intangible. The sale of a patent usually results in favorable long-term capital gain treatment. §§ 197 and 1235.

Payroll factor. The proportion of a multistate corporation's total payroll that is traceable to a specific state. Used in determining the taxable income that is to be apportioned to that state.

Percentage depletion. Percentage depletion is depletion based on a statutory percentage applied to the gross income from the property. The taxpayer deducts the greater of cost depletion or percentage depletion. § 613.

Percentage of completion method. A method of reporting gain or loss on certain long-term contracts. Under this method of accounting, the gross contract price is included in income as the contract is completed. Reg. § 1.451–3.

Permanent and total disability. A person is considered permanently and totally disabled if he or she is unable to engage in any substantial gainful activity due to a physical or mental impairment. In addition, this impairment must be one that can be expected to result in death or that has lasted or can be expected to last for a continuous period of not less than 12 months. The taxpayer generally must provide the IRS a physician's statement documenting this condition.

Personal casualty gain. The recognized gain from any involuntary conversion of personal use property arising from fire, storm, shipwreck, or other casualty, or from theft.

Personal casualty loss. The recognized loss from any involuntary conversion of personal use property arising from fire, storm, shipwreck, or other casualty, or from theft.

Personal exemption. The tax law provides an exemption for each individual taxpayer and an additional exemption for the taxpayer's spouse if a joint return is filed. An individual may also claim a dependency exemption for each dependent, provided certain tests are met. The amount of the personal and dependency exemptions is $3,200 in 2005 ($3,100 in 2004). The exemption is subject to phaseout once adjusted gross income exceeds certain statutory threshold amounts.

Personal residence. If a residence has been owned and used by the taxpayer as the principal residence for at least two years during the five-year period ending on the date of sale, up to $250,000 of realized gain is excluded from gross income. For a married couple filing a joint return, the $250,000 is increased to $500,000 if either spouse satisfies the ownership requirement and both spouses satisfy the use requirement. § 121.

Personal service corporation (PSC). A corporation whose principal activity is the performance of personal services (e.g., health, law, engineering, architecture, accounting, actuarial science, performing arts, or consulting) and where such services are substantially performed by the employee-owners. The 35 percent statutory income tax rate applies to PSCs.

Personalty. All property that is not attached to real estate (realty) and is movable. Examples of personalty are machinery, automobiles, clothing, household furnishings, inventory, and personal effects.

Points. Loan origination fees that may be deductible as interest by a buyer of property. A seller of property who pays points reduces the selling price by the amount of the points paid for the buyer. While the seller is not permitted to deduct this amount as interest, the buyer may do so.

Portfolio income. Income from interest, dividends, rentals, royalties, capital gains, or other investment sources. Net passive losses cannot be used to offset net portfolio income.

Precedent. A previously decided court decision that is recognized as authority for the disposition of future decisions.

Precontribution gain or loss. Partnerships allow for a variety of special allocations of gain or loss among the partners, but gain or loss that is "built in" on an asset contributed to the partnership is assigned specifically to the contributing partner. § 704(c)(1)(A).

Previously taxed income (PTI). Under prior law, the undistributed taxable income of an S corporation was taxed to the shareholders as of the last day of the corporation's tax year and usually could be withdrawn by the shareholders without tax consequences at some later point in time. The role of PTI has been taken over by the accumulated adjustments account. See also *acculated adjustments account*.

Principal partner. A partner with a 5 percent or greater interest in partnership capital or profits. § 706(b)(3).

Private activity bond. Interest on state and local bonds is excludible from gross income. § 103. Certain such bonds are labeled private activity bonds. Although the interest on such bonds is excludible for regular income tax purposes, it is treated as a tax preference in calculating the AMT.

Private foundation. An exempt organization that is subject to additional statutory restrictions on its activities and on contributions made to it. Excise taxes may be levied on certain prohibited transactions, and the Code places more stringent restrictions on the deductibility of contributions to private foundations. § 509.

Probate estate. The property of a decedent that is subject to administration by the executor or administrator of an estate.

Procedural Regulation. A Regulation issued by the Treasury Department that is a housekeeping-type instruction indicating information that taxpayers should provide the IRS as well as information about the internal management and conduct of the IRS itself.

Profit and loss sharing ratios. Specified in the partnership agreement and used to determine each partner's allocation of ordinary taxable income and separately stated items. Profits and losses can be shared in different ratios. The ratios can be changed by amending the partnership agreement. § 704(a).

Profits (loss) interest. A partner's percentage allocation of partnership operating results, determined by the profit and loss sharing ratios.

Property. Assets defined in the broadest legal sense. Property includes the unrealized receivables of a cash basis taxpayer, but not services rendered. § 351.

Property dividend. Generally treated in the same manner as a cash distribution, measured by the fair market value of the property on the date of distribution. The portion of the distribution representing E & P is a dividend; any excess is treated as a return of capital. Distribution of appreciated property causes the distributing corporation to recognize gain. The distributing corporation does not recognize loss on property that has depreciated in value.

Property factor. The proportion of a multistate corporation's total property that is traceable to a specific state. Used in determining the taxable income that is to be apportioned to that state.

Proportionate distribution. A distribution in which each partner in a partnership receives a pro rata share of hot assets being distributed. For example, a distribution of $10,000 of hot assets equally to two 50 percent partners is a proportionate distribution.

Proposed Regulation. A Regulation issued by the Treasury Department in proposed, rather than final, form. The interval between the proposal of a Regulation and its finalization permits taxpayers and other interested parties to comment on the propriety of the proposal.

Public Law 86–272. A congressional limit on the ability of the state to force a multistate corporation to assign income to that state. Under P.L. 86–272, where orders for tangible personal property are both filled and delivered outside the state, the entity must establish more than the mere solicitation of such orders before any income can be apportioned to the state.

Punitive damages. Damages received or paid by the taxpayer can be classified as compensatory damages or as punitive damages. Punitive damages are those awarded to punish the defendant for gross negligence or the intentional infliction of harm. Such damages are includible in gross income. § 104.

Q

Qualified business unit (QBU). A subsidiary, branch, or other business entity that conducts business using a currency other than the U.S. dollar.

Qualified dividend income. See *Qualified dividends.*

Qualified dividends. Distributions made by domestic (and certain non-U.S.) corporations to noncorporate shareholders that are subject to tax at the same rates as those applicable to net long-term capital gains (15 percent and 5 percent). The dividends must be paid out of earnings and profits, and the shareholders must meet certain holding period requirements as to the stock. Qualified dividend treatment applies to distributions made after 2002 and before 2009. Beginning in 2009, dividends are scheduled to be taxed at ordinary income rates. §§ 1(h)(1) and (11).

Qualified employee discounts. Discounts offered employees on merchandise or services that the employer ordinarily sells or provides to customers. The discounts must be generally available to all employees. In the case of property, the discount cannot exceed the employer's gross profit (the sales price cannot be less than the employer's cost). In the case of services, the discounts cannot exceed 20 percent of the normal sales price. § 132.

Qualified nonrecourse debt. Debt issued on realty by a bank, retirement plan, or governmental agency. Included in the at-risk amount by the investor. § 465(b)(6).

Qualified production income. The base for computing the manufacturers' deduction. It comprises qualified production receipts less allocable cost of goods sold and other deductions. § 199.

Qualified real property business indebtedness. Indebtedness that was incurred or assumed by the taxpayer in connection with real property used in a trade or business and is secured by such real property. The taxpayer must not be a C corporation. For qualified real property business indebtedness, the taxpayer may elect to exclude some or all of the income realized from cancellation of debt on qualified real property. If the election is made, the basis of the property must be reduced by the amount excluded. The amount excluded cannot be greater than the excess of the principal amount of the outstanding debt over the fair market value (net of any other debt outstanding on the property) of the property securing the debt. § 108(c).

Qualified residence interest. A term relevant in determining the amount of interest expense the individual taxpayer may deduct as an itemized deduction for what otherwise would be disallowed as a component of personal interest (consumer interest). Qualified residence interest consists of interest paid on qualified residences (principal residence and one other residence) of the taxpayer. Debt that qualifies as qualified residence interest is limited to $1 million of debt to acquire, construct, or substantially improve qualified residences (acquisition indebtedness) plus $100,000 of other debt secured by qualified residences (home equity indebtedness). The home equity indebtedness may not exceed the fair market value of a qualified residence reduced by the acquisition indebtedness for that residence. § 163(h)(3).

Qualified small business corporation. A C corporation that has aggregate gross assets not exceeding $50 million and that is conducting an active trade or business. § 1202.

Qualified small business stock. Stock in a qualified small business corporation, purchased as part of an original issue after August 10, 1993. The shareholder may exclude from gross income 50 percent of the realized gain on the sale of the stock, if he or she held the stock for more than five years. § 1202.

Qualified terminable interest property (QTIP). Generally, the marital deduction (for gift and estate tax purposes) is not available if the interest transferred will terminate upon the death of the transferee spouse and pass to someone else. Thus, if Jim (the husband) places property in trust, life estate to Mary (the wife), and remainder to their children upon Mary's death, this is a terminable interest that will not provide Jim (or Jim's estate) with a marital deduction. If, however, the transfer in trust is treated as qualified terminable interest property (the QTIP election is made), the terminable interest restriction is waived and the marital deduction becomes available. In exchange for this deduction, the surviving spouse's gross estate must include the value of the QTIP election assets, even though he or she has no control over the ultimate disposition of the asset. Terminable interest property qualifies for this election if the donee (or heir) is the only beneficiary of the asset during his or her lifetime and receives income distributions relative to the property at least annually. For gifts, the donor spouse is the one who makes the QTIP election. For property transferred by death, the executor of the estate of the deceased spouse has the right to make the election. §§ 2056(b)(7) and 2523(f).

Qualified transportation fringes. Transportation benefits provided by the employer to the employee. Such benefits include (1) transportation in a commuter highway vehicle between the employee's residence and the place of employment, (2) a transit pass, and (3) qualified parking. Qualified transportation fringes are excludible from the employee's gross income to the extent categories (1) and (2) above do not exceed $105 per month in 2005 and category (3) does not exceed $200 per month in 2005. These amounts are indexed annually for inflation. § 132.

Qualified tuition program. A program that allows college tuition to be prepaid for a beneficiary. When amounts in the plan are used, nothing is included in gross income provided they are used for qualified higher education expenses. § 529.

Qualified tuition reduction plan. A type of fringe benefit plan that is available to employees of nonprofit educational institutions. Such employees (and the spouse and dependent children) are allowed to exclude from gross income a tuition waiver pursuant to a qualified tuition reduction plan. The exclusion applies to undergraduate tuition. In limited circumstances, the exclusion also applies to the graduate tuition of teaching and research assistants. § 117(d).

Qualifying child. An individual who, as to the taxpayer, satisfies the relationship, abode, and age tests. To be claimed as a dependent, such individual must also meet the citizenship and joint return tests and not be self-supporting. §§ 152(a)(1) and (c).

Qualifying relative. An individual who, as to the taxpayer, satisfies the relationship, gross income, support, citizenship, and joint return tests. Such an individual can be claimed as a dependent of the taxpayer. §§ 152(a)(2) and (d).

R

Realized gain or loss. The difference between the amount realized upon the sale or other disposition of property and the adjusted basis of the property. § 1001.

Realty. Real estate.

Reasonable cause. Relief from taxpayer and preparer penalties often is allowed where reasonable cause is found for the taxpayer's actions. For example, reasonable cause for the late filing of a tax return might be a flood that damaged the taxpayer's record-keeping systems and made a timely completion of the return difficult.

Reasonableness. The Code includes a reasonableness requirement with respect to the deduction of salaries and other compensation for services. What constitutes reasonableness is a question of fact. If an expense is unreasonable, the amount that is classified as unreasonable is not allowed as a deduction. The question of reasonableness generally arises with respect to closely held corporations where there is no separation of ownership and management. § 162(a)(1).

Recognized gain or loss. The portion of realized gain or loss subject to income taxation.

Recourse debt. Debt for which the lender may both foreclose on the property and assess a guarantor for any payments due under the loan. A lender may also make a claim against the assets of any general partner in a partnership to which debt is issued, without regard to whether the partner has guaranteed the debt.

Recovery of capital doctrine. When a taxable sale or exchange occurs, the seller may be permitted to recover his or her investment (or other adjusted basis) in the property before gain or loss is recognized.

Redemption to pay death taxes. Sale or exchange treatment is available relative to this type of redemption, to the extent of the proceeds up to the total amount paid by the estate or heir for death taxes and administration expenses. The stock value must exceed 35 percent of the value of the decedent's adjusted gross estate. In meeting this test, one can combine shareholdings in corporations where the decedent held at least 20 percent of the outstanding shares.

Refundable credit. A refundable credit is a credit that is paid to the taxpayer even if the amount of the credit (or credits) exceeds the taxpayer's tax liability.

Regular corporation. See *C corporation.*

Rehabilitation expenditures credit. A credit that is based on expenditures incurred to rehabilitate industrial and commercial buildings and certified historic structures. The credit is intended to discourage businesses from moving from older, economically distressed areas to newer locations and to encourage the preservation of historic structures. § 47.

Rehabilitation expenditures credit recapture. When property that qualifies for the rehabilitation expenditures credit is disposed of or ceases to be used in the trade or business of the taxpayer, some or all of the tax credit claimed on the property may be recaptured as additional tax liability. The amount of the recapture is the difference between the amount of the credit claimed originally and what should have been claimed in light of the length of time the property was actually held or used for qualifying purposes. § 50.

Related corporation. See *controlled group.*

Related parties. Various Code Sections define related parties and often include a variety of persons within this (usually detrimental) category. Generally, related parties are accorded different tax treatment from that applicable to other taxpayers who enter into similar transactions. For instance, realized losses that are generated between related parties are not recognized in the year of the loss. However, these deferred losses can be used to offset recognized gains that occur upon the subsequent sale of the asset to a nonrelated party. Other uses of a related-party definition include the conversion of gain upon the sale of a depreciable asset into all ordinary income (§ 1239) and the identification of constructive ownership of stock relative to corporate distributions, redemptions, liquidations, reorganizations, and compensation.

Related-party transactions. The tax law places restrictions upon the recognition of gains and losses between related parties because of the potential for abuse. For example, restrictions are placed on the deduction of losses from the sale or exchange of property between related parties. In addition, under certain circumstances, related-party gains that would otherwise be classified as capital gain are classified as ordinary income. §§ 267, 707(b), and 1239.

Rental activity. Any activity where payments are received principally for the use of tangible property is a rental activity. Temporary Regulations provide that in certain circumstances activities involving rentals of real and personal property are not to be *treated* as rental activities. The Temporary Regulations list six exceptions.

Reorganization. Occurs, among other instances, when one corporation acquires another in a merger or acquisition, a single corporation divides into two or more entities, a corporation makes a substantial change in its capital structure, or a corporation undertakes a change in its legal name or domicile. The exchange of stock and other securities in a corporate reorganization can be effected favorably for tax purposes if certain statutory requirements are followed strictly. Tax consequences include the nonrecognition of any gain that is realized by the shareholders except to the extent of boot received.

Research activities credit. A tax credit whose purpose is to encourage research and development. It consists of two components: the incremental research activities credit and the basic research credit. The incremental research activities credit is equal to 20 percent of the excess qualified research expenditures over the base amount. The basic research credit is equal to 20 percent of the excess of basic research payments over the base amount. § 41.

Research and experimental expenditures. The Code provides three alternatives for the tax treatment of research and experimentation expenditures. They may be expensed in the year paid or incurred, deferred subject to amortization, or capitalized. If the taxpayer does not elect to expense such costs or to defer them subject to amortization (over 60 months), the expenditures must be capitalized. § 174. Two types of research activities credits are available: the basic research credit and the incremental research activities credit. The rate for each type is 20 percent. § 41.

Reserve method. A method of accounting whereby an allowance is permitted for estimated uncollectible accounts. Actual write-offs are charged to the reserve, and recoveries of amounts previously written off are credited to the reserve. The Code permits only certain financial institutions to use the reserve method. § 166.

Residential rental real estate. Buildings for which at least 80 percent of the gross rents are from dwelling units (e.g., an apartment building). This type of building is distinguished from nonresidential (commercial or industrial) buildings in applying the recapture of depreciation provisions. The term also is relevant in distinguishing between buildings that are eligible for a 27.5-year life versus a 39-year life for MACRS purposes. Generally, residential buildings receive preferential treatment.

Revenue Agent's Report. A Revenue Agent's Report (RAR) reflects any adjustments made by the agent as a result of an audit of the taxpayer. The RAR is mailed to the taxpayer along with the 30-day letter, which outlines the appellate procedures available to the taxpayer.

Revenue neutrality. A description that characterizes tax legislation when it neither increases nor decreases the revenue result. Thus, any tax revenue losses are offset by tax revenue gains.

Revenue Procedure. A matter of procedural importance to both taxpayers and the IRS concerning the administration of the tax laws is issued as a Revenue Procedure (abbreviated Rev.Proc.). A Revenue Procedure is first published in an *Internal Revenue Bulletin* (I.R.B.) and later transferred to the appropriate *Cumulative Bulletin* (C.B.). Both the *Internal Revenue Bulletins* and the *Cumulative Bulletins* are published by the U.S. Government Printing Office.

Revenue Ruling. A Revenue Ruling (abbreviated Rev.Rul.) is issued by the National Office of the IRS to express an official interpretation of the tax law as applied to specific transactions. It is more limited in application than a Regulation. A Revenue Ruling is first published in an *Internal Revenue Bulletin* (I.R.B.) and later transferred to the appropriate *Cumulative Bulletin* (C.B.). Both the *Internal Revenue Bulletins* and the *Cumulative Bulletins* are published by the U.S. Government Printing Office.

Reversionary interest. The property that reverts to the grantor after the expiration of an intervening income interest. Assume Phil places real estate in trust with income to Junior for 11 years, and upon the expiration of this term, the property returns to Phil. Under these circumstances, Phil holds a reversionary interest in the property. A reversionary interest is the same as a remainder interest, except that, in the latter case, the property passes to someone other than the original owner (e.g., the grantor of a trust) upon the expiration of the intervening interest.

Roth IRAs. See *Individual retirement account (IRA).*

S

S corporation. The designation for a small business corporation. See also *Subchapter S.*

Sale or exchange. A requirement for the recognition of capital gain or loss. Generally, the seller of property must receive money or relief from debt in order to have sold the property. An exchange involves the transfer of property for other property. Thus, collection of a debt is neither a sale nor an exchange. The term *sale or exchange* is not defined by the Code.

Sales factor. The proportion of a multistate corporation's total sales that is traceable to a specific state. Used in determining the taxable income that is to be apportioned to that state.

Sales tax. A state- or local-level tax on the retail sale of specified property. Generally, the purchaser pays the tax, but the seller collects it, as an agent for the government. Various taxing jurisdictions allow exemptions for purchases of specific items, including certain food, services, and manufacturing equipment. If the purchaser and seller are in different states, a use tax usually applies.

Schedule M–1. On the Form 1120, a reconciliation of book net income with Federal taxable income. Accounts for timing and permanent differences in the two computations, such as depreciation differences, exempt income, and nondeductible items. On Forms 1120S and 1065, the Schedule M–1 reconciles book income with the owners' aggregate ordinary taxable income.

Schedule M–3. An *expanded* reconciliation of book net income with Federal taxable income (see *Schedule M–1*). Applies to corporations with total assets of $10 million or more.

Scholarships. Scholarships are generally excluded from the gross income of the recipient unless the payments are a disguised form of compensation for services rendered. However, the Code imposes restrictions on the exclusion. The recipient must be a degree candidate. The excluded amount is limited to amounts used for tuition, fees, books, supplies, and equipment required for courses of instruction. Amounts received for room and board are not eligible for the exclusion. § 117.

Section 121 exclusion. If a residence has been owned and used by the taxpayer as the principal residence for at least two years during the five-year period ending on the date of sale, up to $250,000 of realized gain is excluded from gross income. For a married couple filing a joint return, the $250,000 is increased to $500,000 if either spouse satisfies the ownership requirement and both spouses satisfy the use requirement.

Section 179 expensing. The ability to deduct a capital expenditure in the year an asset is placed in service rather than over the asset's useful life or cost recovery period. The annual ceiling on the deduction is $105,000 for 2005. However, the deduction is reduced dollar for dollar when § 179 property placed in service during the taxable year exceeds $420,000 in 2005. In addition, the amount expensed under § 179 cannot exceed the aggregate amount of taxable income derived from the conduct of any trade or business by the taxpayer.

Section 338 election. When a corporation acquires at least 80 percent of a subsidiary in a 12-month period, it can elect to treat the acquisition of such stock as an asset purchase. The acquiring corporation's basis in the subsidiary's assets then is the cost of the stock. The subsidiary is deemed to have sold its assets for an amount equal to the grossed-up basis in its stock.

Section 1231 gains and losses. If the combined gains and losses from the taxable dispositions of § 1231 assets plus the net gain from business involuntary conversions (of both § 1231 assets and long-term capital assets) is a gain, the gains and losses are treated as long-term capital gains and losses. In arriving at § 1231 gains, however, the depreciation recapture provisions (e.g., §§ 1245 and 1250) are first applied to produce ordinary income. If the net result of the combination is a loss, the gains and losses from § 1231 assets are treated as ordinary gains and losses. § 1231(a).

Section 1231 lookback. In order for gain to be classified as § 1231 gain, the gain must survive the § 1231 lookback. To the extent of nonrecaptured § 1231 losses for the five prior tax years, the gain is classified as ordinary income. § 1231(c).

Section 1231 property. Depreciable assets and real estate used in trade or business and held for the required long-term holding period. Under certain circumstances, the classification also includes timber, coal, domestic iron ore, livestock (held for draft, breeding, dairy, or sporting purposes), and unharvested crops. § 1231(b).

Section 1244 stock. Stock issued under § 1244 by qualifying small business corporations. If § 1244 stock becomes worthless, the shareholders may claim an ordinary loss rather than the usual capital loss, within statutory limitations.

Section 1245 property. Property that is subject to the recapture of depreciation under § 1245. For a definition of § 1245 property, see § 1245(a)(3).

Section 1245 recapture. Upon a taxable disposition of § 1245 property, all depreciation claimed on the property is recaptured as ordinary income (but not to exceed recognized gain from the disposition).

Section 1250 property. Real estate that is subject to the recapture of depreciation under § 1250. For a definition of § 1250 property, see § 1250(c).

Section 1250 recapture. Upon a taxable disposition of § 1250 property, some of the depreciation or cost recovery claimed on the property may be recaptured as ordinary income.

Securities. Generally, stock, debt, and other financial assets. To the extent securities other than the stock of the transferee corporation are received in a § 351 exchange, the new shareholder realizes a gain.

Separately stated item. Any item of a partnership or S corporation that might be taxed differently to any two owners of the entity. These amounts are not included in ordinary income of the entity, but are instead reported separately to the owners; tax consequences are determined at the owner level.

Severance tax. A tax imposed upon the extraction of natural resources.

Short sale. A short sale occurs when a taxpayer sells borrowed property (usually stock) and repays the lender with substantially identical property either held on the date of the short sale or purchased after the sale. No gain or loss is recognized until the short sale is closed, and such gain or loss is generally short term. § 1233.

Short taxable year (short period). A tax year that is less than 12 months. A short taxable year may occur in the initial reporting period, in the final tax year, or when the taxpayer changes tax years.

Significant participation activity. There are seven tests to determine whether an individual has achieved material participation in an activity, one of which is based on more than 500 hours of participation in significant participation activities. A significant participation activity is one in which the individual's participation exceeds 100 hours during the year. Reg. § 1.469–5T.

Simple trust. Simple trusts are those that are not complex trusts. Such trusts may not have a charitable beneficiary, accumulate income, or distribute corpus.

Small business corporation. A corporation that satisfies the definition of § 1361(b), § 1244(c), or both. Satisfaction of § 1361(b) permits an S election, and satisfaction of § 1244 enables the shareholders of the corporation to claim an ordinary loss on the worthlessness of stock.

Small business stock. See *small business corporation*.

Small Cases Division. A division within the U.S. Tax Court where jurisdiction is limited to claims of $50,000 or less. There is no appeal from this court.

Special allocation. Any amount for which an agreement exists among the partners of a partnership outlining the method used for spreading the item among the partners.

Specific charge-off method. A method of accounting for bad debts in which a deduction is permitted only when an account becomes partially or completely worthless.

Sprinkling trust. When a trustee has the discretion to either distribute or accumulate the entity accounting income of the trust and to distribute it among the trust's income beneficiaries in varying magnitudes, a sprinkling trust exists. The trustee can "sprinkle" the income of the trust.

Standard deduction. The individual taxpayer can either itemize deductions or take the standard deduction. The amount of the standard deduction depends on the taxpayer's filing status (single, head of household, married filing jointly, surviving spouse, or married filing separately). For 2005, the amount of the standard deduction ranges from $5,000 (for married, filing separately) to $10,000 (for married, filing jointly). Additional standard deductions of either $1,000 (for married taxpayers) or $1,250 (for single taxpayers) are available if the taxpayer is either blind or age 65 or over. Limitations exist on the amount of the standard deduction of a taxpayer who is another taxpayer's dependent. The standard deduction amounts are adjusted for inflation each year. § 63(c).

Statute of limitations. Provisions of the law that specify the maximum period of time in which action may be taken on a past event. Code §§ 6501–6504 contain the limitation periods applicable to the IRS for additional assessments, and §§ 6511–6515 relate to refund claims by taxpayers.

Statutory employee. Statutory employees are considered self-employed independent contractors for purposes of reporting income and expenses on their tax returns. Generally, a statutory employee must meet three tests:

- It is understood from a service contract that the services will be performed by the person.
- The person does not have a substantial investment in facilities (other than transportation used to perform the services).
- The services involve a continuing relationship with the person for whom they are performed.

For further information on statutory employees, see Circular E *Employer's Tax Guide* IRS Publication 15.

Stock dividend. Not taxable if pro rata distributions of stock or stock rights on common stock. Section 305 governs the taxability of stock dividends and sets out five exceptions to the general rule that stock dividends are nontaxable.

Stock redemption. A corporation buys back its own stock from a specified shareholder. Typically, the corporation recognizes any realized gain on the noncash assets that it uses to effect a redemption, and the shareholder obtains a capital gain or loss upon receipt of the purchase price.

Stock rights. Assets that convey to the holder the power to purchase corporate stock at a specified price, often for a limited period of time. Stock rights received may be taxed as a distribution of earnings and profits. After the right is exercised, the basis of the acquired share includes the investor's purchase price or gross income, if any, to obtain the right. Disposition of the right also is a taxable event, with basis often assigned from the shares held prior to the issuance of the right.

Subchapter S. Sections 1361–1379 of the Internal Revenue Code. An elective provision permitting certain small business corporations (§ 1361) and their shareholders (§ 1362) to elect to be treated for income tax purposes in accordance with the operating rules of §§ 1363–1379. However, some S corporations usually avoid the corporate income tax, and corporate losses can be claimed by the shareholders.

Subpart F. That subpart of the Code that identifies the current tax treatment of income earned by a controlled foreign corporation. Certain types of income are included in U.S. gross income by U.S. shareholders of such an entity as they are generated, not when they are repatriated.

Substantial authority. Taxpayer understatement penalties are waived where substantial authority existed for the disputed position taken on the return.

Sunset provision. A provision attached to new tax legislation that will cause such legislation to expire at a specified date. Sunset provisions are attached to tax cut bills for long-term budgetary reasons in order to make their effect temporary. Once the sunset provision comes into play, the tax cut is rescinded and former law is reinstated. An example of a sunset provision is the one contained in the Tax Relief Reconciliation Act of 2001 that relates to the estate tax. After the estate tax is phased out in 2010, a sunset provision reinstates the estate tax as of January 1, 2011.

Surviving spouse. When a husband or wife predeceases the other spouse, the survivor is known as a surviving spouse. Under certain conditions, a surviving spouse may be entitled to use the income tax rates in § 1(a) (those applicable to married persons filing a joint return) for the two years after the year of death of his or her spouse. § 2.

Syndication costs. Incurred in promoting and marketing partnership interests for sale to investors. Examples include legal and accounting fees, printing costs for prospectus and placement documents, and state registration fees. These items are capitalized by the partnership as incurred, with no amortization thereof allowed.

T

Tax avoidance. The minimization of one's tax liability by taking advantage of legally available tax planning opportunities. Tax avoidance can be contrasted with tax evasion, which entails the reduction of tax liability by illegal means.

Tax benefit rule. A provision that limits the recognition of income from the recovery of an expense or loss properly deducted in a prior tax year to the amount of the deduction that generated a tax saving. Assume that last year Gary had medical expenses of $3,000 and adjusted gross income of $30,000. Because of the 7.5 percent limitation, Gary could deduct only $750 of these expenses [$3,000 – (7.5% × $30,000)]. If, this year, Gary is reimbursed by his insurance company for $900 of these expenses, the tax benefit rule limits the amount of income from the reimbursement to $750 (the amount previously deducted with a tax saving).

Tax credit for the elderly or disabled. An elderly (age 65 and over) or disabled taxpayer may receive a tax credit amounting to 15 percent of $5,000 ($7,500 for qualified married individuals filing jointly). This amount is reduced by Social Security benefits, excluded pension benefits, and one-half of the taxpayer's adjusted gross income in excess of $7,500 ($10,000 for married taxpayers filing jointly). § 22.

Tax credits. Tax credits are amounts that directly reduce a taxpayer's tax liability. The tax benefit received from a tax credit is not dependent on the taxpayer's marginal tax rate, whereas the benefit of a tax deduction or exclusion is dependent on the taxpayer's tax bracket.

Tax haven. A country in which either locally sourced income or residents of the country are subject to a low rate of taxation.

Tax preferences. Various items that may result in the imposition of the alternative minimum tax. §§ 55–58.

Tax rate schedules. Rate schedules that are used by upper-income taxpayers and those not permitted to use the tax table. Separate rate schedules are provided for married individuals filing jointly, heads of households, single taxpayers, estates and trusts, and married individuals filing separate returns. § 1.

Tax research. The method used to determine the best available solution to a situation that possesses tax consequences. Both tax and nontax factors are considered.

Tax shelters. The typical tax shelter generated large losses in the early years of the activity. Investors would offset these losses against other types of income and, therefore, avoid paying income taxes on this income. These tax shelter investments could then be sold after a few years and produce capital gain income, which is taxed at a lower rate than ordinary income. The passive activity loss rules and the at-risk rules now limit tax shelter deductions.

Tax table. A tax table that is provided for taxpayers with less than $100,000 of taxable income. Separate columns are provided for single taxpayers, married taxpayers filing jointly, heads of households, and married taxpayers filing separately. § 3.

Tax treaty. An agreement between the U.S. Department of State and another country, designed to alleviate double taxation of income and asset transfers, and to share administrative information useful to tax agencies in both countries. The United States has income tax treaties with over 40 countries, and transfer tax treaties with about 20.

Taxable estate. The taxable estate is the gross estate of a decedent reduced by the deductions allowed by §§ 2053–2057 (e.g., administration expenses, marital and charitable deductions). The taxable estate is subject to the unified transfer tax at death. § 2051.

Taxable gift. The amount of a gift that is subject to the unified transfer tax. Thus, a taxable gift has been adjusted by the annual exclusion and other appropriate deductions (e.g., marital and charitable). § 2053.

Taxable year. The annual period over which income is measured for income tax purposes. Most individuals use a calendar year, but many businesses use a fiscal year based on the natural business year.

Technical advice memoranda (TAMs). TAMs are issued by the IRS in response to questions raised by IRS field personnel during audits. They deal with completed rather than proposed transactions and are often requested for questions related to exempt organizations and employee plans.

Temporary Regulation. A Regulation issued by the Treasury Department in temporary form. When speed is critical, the Treasury Department issues Temporary Regulations that take effect immediately. These Regulations have the same authoritative value as Final Regulations and may be cited as precedent for three years. Temporary Regulations are also issued as proposed Regulations.

Tenants by the entirety. Essentially, a joint tenancy between husband and wife.

Tenants in common. A form of ownership where each tenant (owner) holds an undivided interest in property. Unlike a joint tenancy or a tenancy by the entirety, the interest of a tenant in common does not terminate upon that individual's death (there is no right of survivorship). Assume Tim and Cindy acquire real estate as equal tenants in common, each having furnished one-half of the purchase price. Upon Tim's death, his one-half interest in the property passes to his estate or heirs, not to Cindy.

Terminable interest. An interest in property that terminates upon the death of the holder or upon the occurrence of some other specified event. The transfer of a terminable interest by one spouse to the other may not qualify for the marital deduction. §§ 2056(b) and 2523(b).

Theft loss. A loss from larceny, embezzlement, or robbery. It does not include misplacement of items.

Thin capitalization. When debt owed by a corporation to the shareholders becomes too large in relation to the corporation's capital structure (i.e., stock and shareholder equity), the IRS may contend that the corporation is thinly capitalized. In effect, this means that some or all of the debt is reclassified as equity. The immediate result is to disallow any interest deduction to the corporation on the reclassified debt. To the extent of the corporation's earnings and profits, interest payments and loan repayments on the reclassified debt are treated as dividends to the shareholders.

Thirty-day letter. A letter that accompanies an *RAR* (Revenue Agent's Report) issued as a result of an IRS audit of a taxpayer (or the rejection of a taxpayer's claim for refund). The letter outlines the taxpayer's appeal procedure before the IRS. If the taxpayer does not request any such procedures within the 30-day period, the IRS will issue a statutory notice of deficiency (the 90-day letter).

Throwback rule. If there is no income tax in the state to which a sale otherwise would be apportioned, the sale essentially is exempt from state income tax, even though the seller is domiciled in a state that levies an income tax. Nonetheless, if the seller's state has adopted a throwback rule, the sale is attributed to the *seller's* state, and the transaction is subjected to a state-level tax.

Totten trust. A bank account (checking, savings, money market, CD) that designates a survivor in the event the owner predeceases. As an example, Dan purchases a $50,000 CD and lists ownership as follows: "Dan, payable on proof of Dan's death to Nancy." The transfer is incomplete and can be revoked or changed by Dan as he sees fit. Once Dan dies, however, the CD belongs to Nancy. In effect, the Totten trust arrangement carries the same tax consequences as a revocable trust. It is a simpler and cheaper way to avoid probate as no formal trust need be created. The Totten trust arrangement also can be used with most securities (i.e., stocks and bonds).

Transportation expenses. Transportation expenses for an employee include only the cost of transportation (taxi fares, automobile expenses, etc.) in the course of employment when the employee is not away from home in travel status. Commuting expenses are not deductible.

Travel expenses. Travel expenses include meals (generally subject to a 50 percent disallowance) and lodging and transportation expenses while away from home in the pursuit of a trade or business (including that of an employee).

Treaty shopping. An international investor attempts to use the favorable aspects of a tax treaty to his or her advantage, often elevating the form of the transaction over its substance (e.g., by establishing only a nominal presence in the country offering the favorable treaty terms).

U

UDITPA. The Uniform Division of Income for Tax Purposes Act has been adopted in some form by many of the states. The Act develops criteria by which the total taxable income of a multistate corporation can be assigned to specific states.

Unearned income. Income received but not yet earned. Normally, such income is taxed when received, even for accrual basis taxpayers.

Unified tax credit. A credit allowed against any unified transfer tax. §§ 2010 and 2505.

Unified transfer tax. Rates applicable to transfers by gift and death made after 1976. § 2001(c).

Unitary theory. Sales, property, and payroll of related corporations are combined for nexus and apportionment purposes, and the worldwide income of the unitary entity is apportioned to the state. Subsidiaries and other affiliated corporations found to be part of the corporation's unitary business (because they are subject to overlapping ownership, operation, or management) are included in the apportionment procedure. This approach can be limited if a water's edge election is in effect.

Unrealized receivables. Amounts earned by a cash basis taxpayer but not yet received. Because of the method of accounting used by the taxpayer, these amounts have no income tax basis. When unrealized receivables are distributed to a partner, they generally convert a transaction from nontaxable to taxable or convert otherwise capital gain to ordinary income.

Unreasonable compensation. A deduction is allowed for "reasonable" salaries or other compensation for personal services actually rendered. To the extent compensation is "excessive" ("unreasonable"), no deduction is allowed. The problem of unreasonable compensation usually is limited to closely held corporations, where the motivation is to pay out profits in some form that is deductible to the corporation. Deductible compensation therefore becomes an attractive substitute for nondeductible dividends when the shareholders also are employed by the corporation.

Unrecaptured § 1250 gain (25 percent gain). Gain from the sale of depreciable real estate held more than one year. The gain is equal to or less than the depreciation taken on such property and is reduced by § 1245 and § 1250 gain.

Unrelated business income. Income recognized by an exempt organization that is generated from activities not related to the exempt purpose of the entity. For instance, the pharmacy located in a hospital often generates unrelated business income. § 511.

Unrelated business income tax. Levied on the unrelated business income of an exempt organization.

U.S. Court of Federal Claims. A trial court (court of original jurisdiction) that decides litigation involving Federal tax matters. Appeal from this court is to the Court of Appeals for the Federal Circuit.

U.S. shareholder. For purposes of classification of an entity as a controlled foreign corporation, a U.S. person who owns, or is considered to own, 10 percent or more of the total combined voting power of all classes of voting stock of a foreign corporation. Stock owned directly, indirectly, and constructively is counted for this purpose.

U.S. Supreme Court. The highest appellate court or the court of last resort in the Federal court system and in most states. Only a small number of tax decisions of the U.S. Courts of Appeal are reviewed by the U.S. Supreme Court under its certiorari procedure. The Supreme Court usually grants certiorari to resolve a conflict among the Courts of Appeal (e.g., two or more appellate courts have assumed opposing positions on a particular issue) or when the tax issue is extremely important (e.g., size of the revenue loss to the Federal government).

U.S. Tax Court. The U.S. Tax Court is one of four trial courts of original jurisdiction that decides litigation involving Federal income, death, or gift taxes. It is the only trial court where the taxpayer must not first pay the deficiency assessed by the IRS. The Tax Court will not have jurisdiction over a case unless a statutory notice of deficiency (90-day letter) has been issued by the IRS and the taxpayer files the petition for hearing within the time prescribed.

U.S. trade or business. A set of activities that is carried on in a regular, continuous, and substantial manner. A non-U.S. taxpayer is subject to U.S. tax on the taxable income that is effectively connected with a U.S. trade or business.

Use tax. A sales tax that is collectible by the seller where the purchaser is domiciled in a different state.

V

Vacation home. The Code places restrictions upon taxpayers who rent their residences or vacation homes for part of the tax year. The restrictions may result in a scaling down of expense deductions for the taxpayers. § 280A.

Value added tax (VAT). A national sales tax that taxes the increment in value as goods move through the production process. A VAT is much used in other countries but has not yet been incorporated as part of the U.S. Federal tax structure.

Voluntary revocation. The owners of a majority of shares in an S corporation elect to terminate the S status of the entity, as of a specified date. The day on which the revocation is effective is the first day of the corporation's C tax year.

W

Wash sale. A loss from the sale of stock or securities that is disallowed because the taxpayer, within 30 days before or after the sale, has acquired stock or securities substantially identical to those sold. § 1091.

Water's edge election. A limitation on the worldwide scope of the unitary theory. If a corporate water's edge election is in effect, the state can consider only the activities that occur within the boundaries of the United States in the apportionment procedure.

Welfare-to-work credit. A tax credit available to employers hiring individuals who have been long-term recipients of family assistance welfare benefits. In general, long-term recipients are those individuals who are certified by a designated local agency as being members of a family receiving assistance under a public aid program for at least an 18-month period ending on the hiring date. The welfare-to-work credit is available for qualified wages paid in the first two years of employment. The maximum credit is equal to $8,500 per qualified employee, computed as 35 percent of the first $10,000 of qualified wages paid in the first year of employment, plus 50 percent of the first $10,000 of qualified wages paid in the second year of employment. § 51A.

Wherewithal to pay. This concept recognizes the inequity of taxing a transaction when the taxpayer lacks the means with which to pay the tax. Under it, there is a correlation between the imposition of the tax and the ability to pay the tax. It is particularly suited to situations in which the taxpayer's economic position has not changed significantly as a result of the transaction.

Working condition fringe. A type of fringe benefit received by the employee that is excludible from the employee's gross income. It consists of property or services provided (paid or reimbursed) by the employer for which the employee could take a tax deduction if the employee had paid for them. § 132.

Work opportunity tax credit. Employers are allowed a tax credit equal to 40 percent of the first $6,000 of wages (per eligible employee) for the first year of employment. Eligible employees include certain hard-to-employ individuals (e.g., qualified ex-felons, high-risk youth, food stamp recipients, and veterans). The employer's deduction for wages is reduced by the amount of the credit taken. For qualified summer youth employees, the 40 percent rate is applied to the first $3,000 of qualified wages. §§ 51 and 52.

Worthless securities. A loss (usually capital) is allowed for a security that becomes worthless during the year. The loss is deemed to have occurred on the last day of the year. Special rules apply to securities of affiliated companies and small business stock. § 165.

Writ of Certiorari. Appeal from a U.S. Court of Appeals to the U.S. Supreme Court is by Writ of Certiorari. The Supreme Court need not accept the appeal, and it usually does not (*cert. den.*) unless a conflict exists among the lower courts that must be resolved or a constitutional issue is involved.

APPENDIX D-1

Table of Code Sections Cited

[See Title 26 U.S.C.A.]

I.R.C. Sec.	This Work Page

APPENDIX D-2

Table of Regulations Cited

Temporary Treasury Regulations

Temp.Reg. Sec.	This Work Page
1.2	2–9
1.67–1T(a)(1)(iv)	6–18
1.101–7T	5–9
1.117–6(b)(2)	5–10
1.117–6(c)(3)(i)	5–9
1.117–6(d)	5–11
1.117–6(h)	5–9
1.263A–1T(b)(3)(iii)(A)(1)	16–26
1.280A–3(c)	6–20
1.280A–3(c)(4)	2–38
1.280A–3(d)(4)	6–22
1.987–2	25–13
1.469–1T(e)(3)(ii)	11–18
1.469–1T(e)(3)(iv)	11–19
1.469–1T(e)(3)(vi)(B)	11–19
1.469–1T(e)(3)(vi)(C)	11–19
1.469–1T(e)(3)(vi)(D)	11–19
1.469–1T(e)(3)(vi)(E)	11–19
1.469–5T(a)	11–14
1.469–5T(b)(2)	11–17
1.469–5T(e)(3)(ii)	11–18
1.469–5T(f)(3)	11–17
1.706–1T(a)(2)	16–4
1.865–1T(a)(1)	25–8
1.7872–2(b)(1)(i)	4–25
15a.453–1(b)(2)(iii)	16–20
15a.453–1(d)	16–24
15a.453–1(d)(4)	16–25

Treasury Regulations

Reg. Sec.	This Work Page
1.25A–1(f)	12–37
1.41–1 through 1.41–7	12–11
1.61–1(a)	4–6
1.61–2(d)(2)(i)	13–9
1.61–3(a)	6–13
1.61–6(a)	13–7, 13–10
1.61–9(c)	4–16
1.61–12	4–6
1.61–21(d)	5–26
1.72–7(c)(1)	5–9
1.72–9	4–28
1.79–3	4–32
1.79–3(d)(2)	4–32
1.101–1(a)(1)	5–13
1.106–1	5–13
1.107–1	5–18
1.117–2(a)	5–9
1.118–1	18–15
1.119–1(c)(1)	5–17
1.119–1(f)	5–17
1.121–1(b)(2)	13–43
1.121–3T(c)	13–39
1.121–3T(d)	13–39
1.121–3T(e)	13–40
1.132–1(b)	5–21
1.132–2	5–21
1.151–3(a)	3–14
1.151–3(b)	2–27, 2–29, 3–14
1.151–3(c)	3–14
1.152–1(c)	2–23, 2–29, 3–11
1.162–2(b)(1)	9–10
1.162–5(b)(2)	9–14
1.162–5(b)(2)(iii)	9–14
1.162–5(b)(3)	9–14
1.162–5(b)(3)(ii)	9–15
1.162–8	6–7
1.162–12(a)	16–13
1.162–17(b)(4)	9–25
1.164–4(a)	10–12
1.165–1(a)	13–7
1.165–1(d)(2)	7–10
1.165–1(d)(2)(i)	7–10
1.165–4(a)	18–18
1.165–5(b)	18–18
1.165–7	13–36, 28–16
1.165–7(c)	28–16
1.165–7(a)(2)(ii)	7–12
1.165–8(a)(2)	7–10
1.165–8(b)	28–16
1.165–8(d)	7–9
1.165–9(b)(2)	13–20

Treasury Regulations

Treasury Regulations

Treasury Regulations

Treasury Regulations

APPENDIX D-3

Table of Revenue Procedures and Revenue Rulings Cited

Revenue Procedure

Rev.Proc.	This Work Page
77–37	2–42, 18–8
87–32	16–7
87–56	8–5, 15–12, 19–5
87–57	8–27, 8–28, 8–29, 13–27
92–16	2–42
92–71	6–28
94–27	10–18, 10–34
95–17	26–12
99–49	16–16, 16–18
2001–10	16–12
2001–43	2–41
2002–19	16–18
2002–28	4–7, 16–12
2002–39	16–7
2004–34	4–13, 4–36
2004–64	9–6
2005–1	26–4
2005–3	2–11, 26–4

Revenue Rulings

Rev.Rul.	This Work Page
53–61	4–4
53–80	5–16
53–190	9–6
54–96	18–21
54–567	2–28
55–261	10–5
56–60	13–15
56–406	13–19
57–344	3–11
57–345	10–11
57–418	6–16
58–419	3–11
59–86	13–14
59–221	22–30
60–55	25–7
60–183	22–9
61–119	13–28

Revenue Rulings

Rev.Rul.	This Work Page
62–102	5–6
62–217	18–13
63–221	13–32
63–232	7–9
64–56	18–5
64–162	22–22
65–34	2–28
66–7	14–15
67–74	2–38
67–297	10–17
68–55	18–4
68–212	10–5
68–537	22–22
68–662	6–13
69–26	9–4
69–292	9–14
70–50	22–22
70–466	13–34
70–622	10–11
71–190	10–13
71–425	5–3
71–564	18–5
72–312	4–15
72–545	6–25
72–592	7–8
73–476	13–49
73–539	9–8
74–44	22–34
74–78	9–14
74–175	14–53
74–503	18–13
75–14	6–18
75–168	9–8
75–380	9–5
75–448	5–10
78–39	6–9
78–340	10–5
79–379	4–17
80–52	4–9
80–335	6–9
81–94	23–2

Revenue Rulings

APPENDIX E

Comprehensive Tax Return Problems

PROBLEM 1—INDIVIDUALS

Timothy (Tim) R. and Polly M. Landry are ages 40 and 39, married, and live at 1318 Camden Road, Garfield, NJ 07026.

1. Tim is a self-employed claims adjuster for several major casualty insurance companies (professional activity code is 524290). He maintains an office at 418 Clark Street, Suite 320, Garfield, NJ 07026. His only employee is a receptionist, whom he shares with several other professionals. Workforce Associates provides the receptionist on an annual contract basis and handles her salary and payroll taxes. Except as noted below, Tim's office equipment (e.g., desk, chairs, file cabinets) has been expensed under § 179 in the year acquired.
2. Polly is the manager of the local Fashion-All, a national chain of clothing stores specializing in business wear. Further, she is an adviser to the chain's buyers. She is paid a flat annual salary of $60,000, receives no commissions, and is expected to absorb her business-related expenses. She also is eligible for a bonus based on her input to the buyers of Fashion-All. Furthermore and as noted below, Polly can take advantage of the employee discount policy on her in-store clothing purchases.
3. For 2004, Tim's work-related expenses are as follows:

Office rent	$7,200
Utilities (includes telephone, fax)	2,100
Receptionist (paid to Workforce Associates)	5,000
Advertising	1,200
Accounting services	1,400
Legal services (see item 10 below)	2,000
Office expenses (supplies, postage)	600
Renters' insurance (covers personal liability, casualty, theft)	1,300
State and local license fees	650
Professional dues and subscriptions to trade publications	450
Repairs to copy machine	110
Business lunches	1,820
Replacement of reception room furnishings, 5/10/04	2,100
Purchase of notebook computer, 2/9/04	1,600
Contribution to H.R. 10 (Keogh) plan	7,000
Medical insurance premiums	4,000

Although Tim does not advertise his services to the general public, he does produce and distribute a public relations brochure. The brochure emphasizes his qualifications as a claims adjuster and is sent to present and potential customers (e.g., insurance companies, repair facilities). The business meals Tim paid for were to entertain various visiting executives from the insurance companies he does business with. As is the case with all of Tim's business transactions, the lunches are properly documented and supported by receipts.

Because the reception room furnishings were looking shabby, Tim and his officemates had them replaced. The $2,100 Tim spent was his share (i.e., three chairs and a lamp) of the refurnishing cost. Except as to his automobile (see item 4 below), Tim follows a policy of avoiding depreciation by utilizing the § 179 election to expense assets.

4. On July 7, 2003, Tim paid $34,530 to purchase a BMW 325i sedan, which he uses 90% for business. He did not choose to use any § 179 expenses but elected 50% additional first-year depreciation. Under the actual operating cost method, he uses 200% declining-balance with a half-year convention. His expenses relating to the BMW for 2004 are as follows:

Gasoline	$2,650
Oil and lubrication	150
Auto insurance	1,200
Auto club dues	180
Interest on car loan	600

In addition and in connection with the business use, Tim paid $380 for parking, $420 for tolls, and $290 in fines for parking violations. During 2004, he drove the BMW 20,000 miles (18,000 business, 1,000 personal, and 1,000 commuting).

5. Polly's employment-related expenses for 2004 are listed below:

Business lunches	$ 980
Christmas gifts ($32 × 18)	576
Business trips (see item 6)	7,020

Regarding the business lunches, she entertains visiting company officials and employees on special occasions (e.g., birthdays, anniversaries). The Christmas gifts consist of fruit baskets (cost of $30, gift wrapping of $2) sent to key employees and major customers.

6. To stay abreast of fashion trends and consumer tastes, Polly attends at least five fashion shows per year. Her unreimbursed expenses for this activity during 2004 are as follows:

Transportation (air, bus, rail)	$3,200
Lodging	1,500
Meals	1,300
Entertainment of show sponsors	420
Incidentals (taxis, limos, valet service)	600
	$7,020

At the conclusion of these trips, Polly forwards her opinions to the buyers of Fashion-All. Depending on the value of the contribution, Fashion-All awards an annual bonus to its advisers. Polly was awarded a bonus of $6,000 for 2003 and a bonus of $8,000 for 2004. The bonus is paid in January of the year following the award. Thus, Polly did not receive her 2004 bonus until January 2005.

7. Fashion-All has a discount plan that allows its employees to purchase its merchandise at 30% of the customer price. (The gross profit component is 50%.) During 2004, Polly purchased $8,000 (customer price) of clothing for $2,400. Although most of the clothing was for herself, some of the items were gifts for family members.

8. Polly attends evening classes at a local university to earn credits toward a master's degree in marketing. Her expenses for 2004 are summarized below:

Tuition	$4,150
Books and computer supplies	930
Bus fare	62
Meals while on campus	110

9. In addition to the items already mentioned, the Landrys received the following amounts:

Payments to Tim for services rendered (as reported on Forms 1099 issued by several payor insurance companies) pursuant to contractual arrangement		$76,000
Cash payments received by Tim from numerous repair facilities and building contractors that he deals with frequently (see item 10 below)		24,000
Annual installment from Cardinal Life Insurance Company (see item 11 below)		12,000
Return of deductible by Hawk Casualty (see item 12 below)		1,000
Income tax refunds for tax year 2003—		
Federal tax	$2,100	
State tax	300	2,400
Proceeds from the sale of Stockton Road lot (see item 13 below)		32,500
Interest income—		
Billy Landry loan (see item 14 below)	$1,200	
City of Newark bonds	1,800	
CD at Chase Bank	800	3,800
Qualified dividends (American Electric Power)		600
Proceeds from church bazaar (see item 15 below)		3,900
Cash gifts from Polly's parents		22,000

10. The cash payments are delivered to Tim during the Christmas season by special courier. They are enclosed in an envelope marked "GIFT" with a note expressing thanks for the business referrals. No arrangement exists, contractual or otherwise, that requires Tim to be compensated for any referrals he makes. Although Tim realizes that kickbacks are not uncommon in the repair business, he is concerned about the legality of the procedure. During 2004, therefore, he retains an attorney to research the matter. Without passing judgment on the status of the payors, the attorney finds that Tim's acceptance of the payments does not violate any state or local law. The attorney charges Tim $2,000 for his advice (see item 3).

11. On May 9, 2001, Polly's widowed aunt, Marie, died. Among her assets was a life insurance policy naming Polly as the sole beneficiary. Although Polly was entitled to an immediate distribution of the $100,000 maturity value, Cardinal Life convinced Polly that it was financially advantageous to accept a settlement option of $12,000 a year for 10 years.

12. In 2003, the Landrys were rear-ended while in the family Volvo by a hit-and-run driver. Their insurance carrier, Hawk Casualty, paid for the damage but charged them for the $1,000 deductible on the policy. In 2004 and after the police located the other driver, Hawk was able to recover the repair cost. Consequently, it refunded the deductible previously withheld. The Landrys were unable to claim any tax deduction for the casualty even though they itemized their deductions for 2003.

13. The Stockton Road lot was inherited by Polly from Marie (see item 11). It was acquired by Marie on August 4, 2000, for $30,000 and had a value of $35,000 when she died. Marie bought the property because it was adjacent to a school that was expected to expand. By 2004, it had become clear that the expansion was not going to take place and that no condemnation would occur. Polly could see no reason to keep the property, so she sold it on August 17, 2004, through a classified ad in the suburban newspaper.

14. In December 2002, Tim loaned his nephew, Billy, $10,000 to help finance a new catering business. No note was signed and no due date specified, but Billy agreed to pay annual interest of 6%. The $1,200 represents interest accrued for both 2003 and 2004.

15. The Landrys participated in the annual fund-raising bazaar sponsored by their church. Under the bazaar rules, parishioners contribute household items (e.g., clothing, furniture) for resale to the general public. The church retains half of the sale proceeds, and the other half belongs to the owner; any unsold property is returned to the owners. The Landrys contributed property with a basis of $11,000 (estimated in part) that sold for $7,800. Much of the property they contributed had been received from Aunt Marie's estate (see item 11 above).

16. Besides items previously noted, the Landrys had the following expenditures for 2004:

Medical—		
Expenses not covered by insurance (deductible and copay features and those relating to Claire)	$2,300	
Modifications to personal residence (see item 17 below)	9,200	$11,500
Taxes—		
Ad valorem taxes on personal residence	$4,800	
Special property tax assessment (see item 18 below)	1,300	
State income taxes (see items 22 and 23 below)	x,xxx	x,xxx
Interest—		
Interest on home mortgage	$3,600	
Interest on home equity loan (see item 19 below)	1,200	4,800
Church pledge		2,400
Contribution to traditional IRA (see item 20 below)		3,000
Fee for preparation of income tax returns (50% of fee relates to Tim's business)		800

17. The medical expenses listed do not include the 880 miles the family Volvo was driven for medical reasons (e.g., dentist appointments). Tim's mother, Claire, lives with them and qualifies as a dependent. Claire suffers from severe osteoarthritis and has limited mobility. To ease the problem, Tim had certain portions of their personal residence modified (e.g., ramps added, counters lowered, hallways widened) to facilitate wheelchair and walker access. A neighbor of the Landrys who is a realtor estimates that the $9,200 of improvements increased the value of the residence by $5,000.

18. The City of Garfield made a special assessment to repave Camden Road. The Landrys' share of the assessment, $1,300, is based on the frontage of their residential property on Camden Road. To expedite the process, the city chose to bypass any escrow accounts the property owners might have with their mortgage carriers and made the assessment directly on the owners.

19. The home equity loan was for $20,000. The funds were used to help finance the purchase of the family Volvo.

20. Because Fashion-All has no retirement plan for its employees, Polly has established an IRA. She chooses not to be covered under the optional Fashion-All health plan as Tim's policy provides better benefits for the cost.

21. In addition to Claire, the Landrys provide all of the support of their three children who live with them. The children, Celeste (age 17), Daniel (age 15), and Bridget (age 14), are all full-time students. Celeste, an accomplished musician, earns $4,200 during the year performing at various events and giving lessons.

22. For Federal income tax purposes, the Landrys choose to deduct state income taxes rather than state and local sales taxes.

23. Polly's Form W–2 from Fashion-All shows $4,750 and $1,390 withheld for Federal and state income taxes, respectively. Tim made quarterly payments of $3,500 (Federal) and $350 (state) for a total of $14,000 (Federal) and $1,400 (state).

24. Relevant Social Security numbers are:

Name	Social Security Number
Timothy Landry	136–94–4596
Polly Landry	137–47–7892
Claire Landry	135–29–5102
Celeste Landry	138–61–8245
Daniel Landry	139–37–2918
Bridget Landry	138–52–6821

Prepare a joint return (with appropriate schedules) for the Landrys for year 2004. Assume that any refund is to be sent to the Landrys and that they do not wish to contribute to the Presidential Election Campaign Fund.

PROBLEM 2—INDIVIDUALS

Joseph (Joe) L. and Robyn N. Sadler, ages 66 and 61, are married and live at 1320 Photinia Avenue, Dallas, TX 75280.

1. Joe holds degrees in geology and petroleum engineering and prior to his retirement was a manager in the exploration and production division of Pajaro International. Pajaro has extensive offshore oil and gas interests in the Gulf of Mexico. Joe is very familiar with its operations and helped situate several of the platforms and conduct the drilling of wells. Because of Joe's expertise, Pajaro still utilizes his services on a consulting basis (see item 4 below).
2. Robyn, an accomplished artist, is well known regionally for her oil portraits. Because her work is meticulous and she refuses to accept deadlines, her output averages around one portrait a month. Her fee, which was set several years ago, is $3,000 per portrait. As this is quite reasonable for a good quality oil portrait, Robyn has a long waiting list of clients who have not yet been scheduled for sittings.
3. Joe retired from Pajaro at age 65. Under the company's contributory qualified pension plan, he selected an annuity option providing annual payments of $60,000 for life. During his employment, Joe contributed $300,000 (nondeductible) to the plan. Pajaro provides its retirees with continued coverage under the company health plan, but they are subject to higher deductible and copay amounts.
4. During 2004, Joe made six trips on behalf of Pajaro. On a typical trip, Joe flies by commercial airline to New Orleans, Houston, or Corpus Christi and then takes a company helicopter to the offshore platform. If necessary, he rents a room at a local motel. Sometimes offsite consultations can resolve the problem, and trips to the rigs are not necessary. His expenses for these trips are summarized below:

Airfare	$3,300
Meals	1,800
Lodging	2,200
Ground transportation (limos, taxis)	400

   After each trip, Joe recovers his expenses when he is paid by Pajaro for the services rendered. Pajaro does not require an accounting for the expenses and reimburses Joe based on the amount he says he spent.
5. For convenience and security reasons, Robyn prefers to work at home. The Sadlers had this in mind when they built their present home. One-third of the 3,600-square-foot living area is devoted to Robyn's studio. The house was built in 2000 at a cost of $300,000 on a lot that the Sadlers had previously acquired for $120,000. Besides home mortgage

interest and property taxes (see item 20 below), residential expenses for 2004 are as follows:

Homeowner's insurance	$ 980
Security system service fee	1,800
Utilities	4,100
Molly Maid cleaning service	2,400
Repairs to studio skylight	380
Repainting of studio	1,200

6. During 2004, Robyn completed 15 portraits, 12 of which were delivered and paid for. Two portraits were delivered but were not paid for until January 2005. One portrait was commissioned by the CEO of a company that has since entered bankruptcy. As the CEO has been indicted for securities fraud, Robyn feels certain that she will not be paid for the work. Although she did not like the arrangement, in December she accepted $6,000 as a prepayment for two portraits to be done in 2005. Apparently, the corporation making the prepayment was motivated by income tax considerations. Lastly, in January 2004, Robyn was paid for a portrait she painted and delivered in 2003.
7. Although Robyn keeps receipts, she does not classify her expenses by category. At the end of each year, she adds the receipts and arrives at a total. The total for 2004 (which includes canvases, brushes, oils, smocks, palettes) is $2,312. As frames are a matter of personal taste and depend on the setting where the painting is exhibited, the framing of a finished portrait is left up to the customer.
8. On March 10, 1998, Robyn's father, John Newton, gave her his antique gun collection as a birthday present. A reasonable approximation of the cost basis of the collection to John is $6,500. At the time of the gift, however, it was appraised at $12,000. On April 21, 2004 (San Jacinto Day), Robyn donated the collection to the Texas Battleground Museum. The museum is a qualified charity and gave Robyn a receipt that shows the value of the collection as $15,000.
9. On John's death on December 3, 2003, Robyn inherited his stamp collection. Again, a reasonable approximation of the cost basis is $2,750. A date of death appraisal reflects a value of $20,000. Robyn sold the collection on November 26, 2004, for $21,500. Robyn regretted disposing of her father's collections (see item 8 above), but keeping them would have created maintenance and security problems she prefers to avoid. Also, none of the immediate family has any interest in either antique guns or stamps.
10. While on a business trip to south Texas to acquire some oil leases, Joe attended a mortgage foreclosure auction. At the auction (held on May 30, 1997), he acquired an abandoned rice farm near Pearland, known as the Hebert Place. Joe financed most of the $20,000 purchase price with help from Pajaro's credit union. In view of the expanding Houston area, he considered the purchase to be a good investment. On March 4, 2004, he was contacted by a Houston real estate developer who offered $200,000 for the Hebert Place. Appalled by the prospect of a taxable gain of $180,000, Joe eventually agreed to an exchange transaction. Under the exchange, Joe transferred the Hebert Place in return for four undeveloped lots in Sugar Land (TX) worth $180,000 and cash of $20,000. The exchange took place on July 14, 2004, at an attorney's office in Pearland.
11. On another business trip in Texas, Joe purchased unimproved land at an estate sale. Described as Block 31, the property is located in Huntsville (TX) and is adjacent to the Texas Department of Corrections (TDC) prison farm. Block 31 was purchased on June 12, 1984, for $16,200. As Joe hoped, he was ultimately contacted by the State of Texas, which offered him $100,000 for Block 31 in late 2003 and advised him that condemnation proceedings would be instituted in the event of refusal. After several counteroffers, Joe accepted $126,000 on January 22, 2004. On March 17, 2005, Joe reinvested $120,000 of the proceeds in a trailer park facility near Raton (NM). He does not plan any further reinvestment of the condemnation award.
12. On February 12, 2002, Robyn was contacted by one of her former college roommates, Esther. At lunch, Esther asked Robyn for a loan of $5,000 to help finance a new venture.

Because the venture, a summertime art camp in Santa Fe (NM), sounded interesting, Robyn made the loan. Esther signed a note payable due in two years at 10% interest. In late 2004, Robyn learned that Esther had disappeared after being charged by New Mexico authorities with grand theft. Even worse, Esther is wanted for a parole violation from a prior felony conviction.

13. On November 4, 2003, and upon the advice of a former business friend, Joe purchased 10,000 shares of Pelican Energy preferred stock at $1 per share. Although Pelican had recently entered bankruptcy, the friend believed that the liquidation value of the company would far exceed the current price of the stock. On May 4, 2004, the trustees in bankruptcy announced that Pelican's energy reserves had been significantly overvalued and, as a result, the shareholders would receive nothing for their stock. On that same day, Pelican stock ceased to trade on any organized exchange.

14. In 2003 and to celebrate Joe's retirement, the Sadlers decided to take a one-month road trip through the West. For this purpose and to use on future vacations, they purchased an RV (Republic Coach, model 800i) on July 31 for $110,000. They did not enjoy this means of travel, however, and sold the RV on January 8, 2004, for $95,000. The purchaser, a family friend, made a down payment of $15,000 and issued four notes of $20,000 each, payable at annual intervals over four years.

15. In addition to the items already noted, the Sadlers had the following stock transactions during 2004:

Description	Date Acquired	Date Sold	Sale Price	Cost
100 shares Wren Co.	3/10/97	5/5/04	$13,000	$?
300 shares Owl Co.	12/3/03	8/5/04	38,000	?
500 shares Lark Co.	11/5/03	12/22/04	25,000	28,000
1,000 shares Teal Energy Co.	6/5/03	5/4/04	36,500	32,000

Robyn received the Wren stock as a gift from her father, John. The stock cost John $9,000 and was worth $12,000 on the date of the gift. No gift tax was incurred on the transfer. Robyn inherited the Owl stock from John. The stock cost John $18,000 and was worth $40,000 when he died. The Sadlers sold the Lark stock to generate a loss to offset part of the gain generated from the sale of the Teal Energy stock. However, the Sadlers felt that Lark had good growth potential, so they repurchased 500 shares on January 26, 2005, for $25,100. Teal Energy was purchased purely for quick profit, but after the stock peaked at $38 a share and started to decline, the Sadlers decided to sell.

16. The Sadlers have a $9,000 long-term capital loss carryover from 2003. Due to their unhappy experience with an investment in Enron, they have not had any taxable capital gains for a number of years.

17. In November 2003 and while on his morning walk, Joe was injured when he was sideswiped by a delivery truck. Joe was hospitalized for several days, and the driver of the truck was ticketed and charged with DUI. The owner of the truck, a national parcel delivery service, was very disturbed by the adverse publicity that resulted. To keep Joe from taking the matter to court, the company offered him a settlement if he would sign a release. Under the settlement, Joe's medical expenses were paid, and he was to receive a cash award of $110,000. The award was designated as being $100,000 for personal injury and $10,000 for loss of consulting income (Joe had already retired). Joe agreed to the settlement, signed the release, and received $110,000 in January 2004.

18. Joe furnishes more than 50% of the support of his parents, Ernest and Imogene Sadler. Unfortunately, he cannot claim them as dependents due to the gross income and joint return tests. Imogene suffers from Alzheimer's disease and until December 2003 was cared for at home. When her condition worsened, the family was forced to admit her to a nursing home. The home, Azalea Manor, provides full-time medical care at a cost of $3,500 per month. Imogene died on January 29, 2004. Joe reimbursed Ernest for $4,000 of the funeral expenses and paid Azalea Manor $7,000 (the charge for Imogene for December 2003 and January 2004). Joe made both payments on April 1, 2004.

19. Besides the items already mentioned, the Sadlers had the following receipts for 2004:

Social Security benefits		$18,200
Consulting income (does not include expense reimbursement—see item 4)		24,100
Qualified dividends from investment in ChevronTexaco stock		2,000
Interest income—		
City of San Antonio bonds	$1,300	
General Electric bonds	800	
Wells Fargo CD	900	
Bank of America money market fund	200	3,200

20. Expenditures for 2004 not already described include the following:

Medical—		
Deductible and copay amounts of medical insurance	$ 2,900	
Dental bills (not covered by insurance)	11,700	$14,600
Property taxes on personal residence		3,900
Interest on home mortgage		3,600
Charitable contribution—church pledge		3,000
Professional journals—		
Oil and gas related (Joe)	$380	
Art related (Robyn)	240	620
Dues to professional organization (Joe)		240
Special clothing (used at drilling and production sites)		210
Tax return preparation fee		800

21. Joe paid $1,000 of the $3,000 church pledge on December 30, 2004, using a Visa credit card. Joe did not pay the Visa charges for the month of December until January 20, 2005. Of the tax return preparation fee, 50% is for transactions pertaining to the two Schedule C forms (allocate equally to each).

22. Besides personal use, the Sadlers drove their cars as follows: 3,000 miles business (Joe); 2,500 miles business (Robyn); 1,200 miles medical; and 900 miles charitable. They have always utilized the automatic (standard) mileage method of determining automobile expenses.

23. The Sadlers do not keep track of the state and local sales taxes they pay. They use the optional state sales tax tables issued by the IRS (Publication 600)—the state rate is 6¼%; the local rate is 2%.

24. The trustee of Pajaro's retirement plan withheld $5,664 from the $60,000 in pension payments it distributed to Joe in 2004. In addition Joe and Robyn made quarterly payments to the IRS of $4,500 (for a total of $18,000). They had last year's tax refund of $620 applied toward their 2004 income tax liability.

25. Relevant Social Security numbers are 450–26–4596 for Robyn and 466–59–6844 for Joe. Professional activity codes are 711510 for Robyn and 541330 for Joe.

Prepare a joint return (with appropriate schedules) for the Sadlers for 2004. In claiming business use of their home, complete Form 8829 and base depreciation on MACRS straight-line (using the mid-month convention) applicable to 39-year nonresidential realty. Assume that any refund is to be applied toward the prepayment of the Sadlers' income tax liability for 2005. They do not wish to contribute to the Presidential Election Campaign fund.

PROBLEM 3—C CORPORATION (Form 1120)

On September 9, 1992, Jennifer Jones and Jeff Shurts formed SnowPro Corporation to sell ski equipment. Pertinent information regarding SnowPro is summarized as follows:

- The business address is 2120 Adobe Drive, Las Cruces, NM 88011.
- The employer identification number is 75–3392543; the principal business activity code is 451110.
- Jennifer and Jeff each own one-half of the outstanding common stock; no other class of stock is authorized. Jennifer is president of the company, and Jeff is secretary-treasurer. Both are full-time employees of the corporation, and each receives a salary of $189,500. Jennifer's Social Security number is 399–50–2953; Jeff's Social Security number is 400–30–4495.
- The corporation uses the accrual method of accounting and reports on a calendar year basis. Inventories are determined using the lower of cost or market method. For book and tax purposes, the straight-line method of depreciation is used.
- During 2004, the corporation distributed a cash dividend of $72,000.

Selected portions of SnowPro's profit and loss statement for 2004 reflect the following debits and credits:

Account		Debit	Credit
Gross sales			$2,556,000
Sales returns and allowances		$ 72,000	
Cost of goods sold		925,000	
Dividends received from stock investments in less-than-20%-owned U.S corporations			108,000
Interest income			
State bonds	$12,600		
Certificates of deposit	23,000		35,600
Premiums on term life insurance policies on the lives of Jennifer and Jeff; SnowPro Corporation is the designated beneficiary		14,000	
Salaries—officers		379,000	
Salaries—clerical and sales		370,000	
Taxes (state, local, and payroll)		92,000	
Repairs		72,500	
Interest expense			
Loan to purchase state bonds	$ 7,200		
Other business loans	16,800	24,000	
Advertising		83,400	
Rental expense		177,700	
Depreciation		36,000	

A comparative balance sheet for SnowPro Corporation reveals the following information:

Assets	January 1, 2004	December 31, 2004
Cash	$ 369,000	$ 251,194
Trade notes and accounts receivable	790,560	956,140
Inventories	540,000	640,800
Federal bonds	127,000	154,000
State bonds	143,000	186,000
Prepaid Federal tax	—	1,620

Assets	January 1, 2004	December 31, 2004
Buildings and other depreciable assets	$ 216,000	$ 216,000
Accumulated depreciation	(79,920)	(115,920)
Land	18,500	18,500
Other assets	2,740	1,300
Total assets	$2,126,880	$2,309,634

Liabilities and Equity		
Accounts payable	$ 208,000	$ 214,004
Other current liabilities	134,270	69,600
Mortgages	214,000	205,000
Capital stock	425,000	425,000
Retained earnings	1,145,610	1,396,030
Total liabilities and equity	$2,126,880	$2,309,634

Net income per books (before any income tax accrual) is $454,000. During 2004, SnowPro Corporation made estimated tax payments of $133,200 to the IRS. Prepare a Form 1120 for SnowPro Corporation for tax year 2004.

Business entity but not taxable to entity but to partners

PROBLEM 4—PARTNERSHIP (Form 1065)

Craig Howard (623–98–0123), Josh Edwards (410–63–4297), and Dana Prosky (896–49–1235) are equal partners in TDP—the "Tile Doctors Partnership"—a general partnership engaged in residential tile installation in Baton Rouge, Louisiana. TDP's Federal ID number is 42–1234598. The partnership uses the accrual method of accounting and the calendar year for reporting purposes. It began business operations on October 15, 2002. Its current address is 5917 La Rue, Baton Rouge, LA 70825. The 2004 income statement for the partnership reflected net income of $161,520. The following information was taken from the partnership's financial statements for the current year:

Receipts:	
Sales revenues	$740,925
Qualified dividend income	2,700
Long-term capital gain	1,275
Long-term capital loss	(300)
Total revenues	$744,600
Cash payments related to cost of goods sold:	
Materials purchases	$162,250
Direct job costs	26,450
Additional § 263A costs	2,950
Contract labor	278,300
Total cash payments—work-in-progress:	$469,950
Other cash disbursements (net of additional § 263A costs):	
Rent	$ 8,400
Utilities	6,580
Office employee salaries	25,400
Contribution to Red Cross	1,500
Meals and entertainment, subject to 50% disallowance	1,200

Guaranteed payment, Dana Prosky, managing partner	$ 30,000
Office expense	2,820
Accounting fees	3,500
Payroll taxes	2,680
Business interest on operating line of credit	9,500
Repairs	1,420
Payment of beginning accounts payable	8,200
Tile cutting equipment	9,000
Total other cash disbursements	$110,200
Noncash expenses:	
Amortization	$ 600
Accrual of ending accounts payable	–0–
Depreciation on equipment owned previously (reported on Schedule A)	16,620

The beginning and ending balance sheets for the partnership were as follows for 2004:

	Beginning	Ending
Cash	$ 28,730	$ 38,180
Inventory (jobs in progress)	36,850	42,940
Long-term investments	46,000	42,000
Equipment	95,000	104,000
Accumulated depreciation	(26,660)	(52,280)
Organization fees	3,000	3,000
Accumulated amortization	(750)	(1,350)
Total assets	$182,170	$176,490
Accounts payable	$ 8,200	$ –0–
Recourse operating line of credit (note payable in less than one year)	75,000	60,000
Capital, Howard	32,990	38,830
Capital, Edwards	32,990	38,830
Capital, Prosky	32,990	38,830
Total liabilities and capital	$182,170	$176,490

The partnership uses the lower of cost or market method for valuing inventory. TDP is subject to § 263A; for simplicity, assume § 263A costs are reflected in the same manner for book and tax purposes. TDP did not change its inventory accounting method during the year. There were no writedowns of inventory items, and TDP does not use the LIFO method.

The partnership claimed $16,620 of depreciation expense for both tax and financial accounting purposes; all $16,620 should be reported on Schedule A. Assume that none of the depreciation creates a tax preference. The partnership will claim a § 179 deduction for the tile cutting equipment purchased during the year.

None of the long-term capital gain or loss is taxable at a 28% rate. All line-of-credit borrowings were used exclusively for business operations; consequently, none of the interest expense is considered investment interest expense.

No guaranteed payments were paid to partners other than Dana Prosky. Instead, each partner (including Prosky) withdrew $4,000 per month as a distribution (draw) of operating profits. There were no distributions of noncash property.

All debts are recourse debt. The partners share equally in all partnership liabilities, since all initial contributions and all ongoing allocations and distributions are pro rata. All partners are considered "active" for purposes of the passive loss rules.

None of the partners sold any portion of their interests in the partnership during 2004. The partnership's operations are entirely restricted to southern Louisiana. All partners are U.S. citizens. The partnership had no foreign operations, no foreign bank accounts, and no interest in any foreign trusts or other partnerships. The partnership is not publicly traded and is not a statutory tax shelter. No Forms 8865 are required to be attached to the return.

The IRS's business code for "tile contractors" is 238340. The partnership is not subject to the consolidated audit procedures and does not have a tax matters partner. The partnership files its tax return in Ogden, Utah. Partner Dana Prosky lives at 1423 N. Louisiana Boulevard, Baton Rouge, LA 70823. The capital account reconciliation on Schedules K–1 is prepared on a GAAP basis, which, in this case, corresponds to the tax basis.

a. Prepare pages 1–4 of Form 1065 for TDP. Do not prepare Form 4562. Leave any items blank where insufficient information has been provided. Prepare supporting schedules as necessary if adequate information is provided. (You will not be able to prepare a schedule for additional § 263A costs.) *Hint:* Prepare Schedule A first to determine cost of goods sold.
b. Prepare Schedule K–1 for partner Dana Prosky.

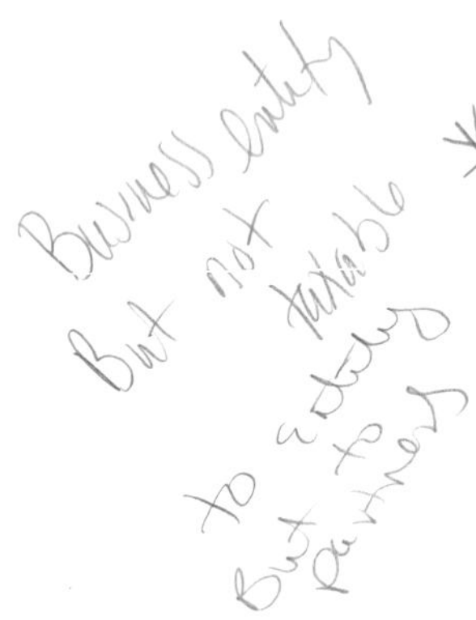

PROBLEM 5—S CORPORATION (Form 1120S)

John Martin (Social Security number 234–10–5214) and Stan Mitchell (Social Security number 244–58–8695) are 55% and 45% owners of Ram, Inc. (74–8265910), a small textile manufacturing company located at 1011 Wright Avenue, Kannapolis, NC 28083. The company's first S election was made on January 1, 1984. The following information was taken from the income statement for 2004.

Other income (active)	$ 380
Interest income	267
Gross sales	1,376,214
Beginning inventory	7,607
Direct labor	303,102
Direct materials purchased	278,143
Direct other costs	149,356
Ending inventory	13,467
Taxes	39,235
Contributions to United Fund	445
Contributions to Senator Brown's campaign	5,000
Fines on illegal activities	34
Life insurance premiums (the corporation is the beneficiary)	98
Compensation to shareholder/officers (proportionate to ownership)	34,934
Salaries and wages	62,103
Interest	17,222
Repairs	16,106
Depreciation	16,154
Advertising	3,246
Pension plan contributions	6,000
Employee benefit programs	2,875
Other deductions	63,784
Net income	384,884

A comparative balance sheet appears below.

	January 1, 2004	December 31, 2004
Cash	$ 47,840	$ 61,242
Accounts receivable	93,100	153,136
Inventories	7,607	13,467
Prepaid expenses	10,333	7,582
Loans to shareholders	313	727
Building and trucks	138,203	244,348
Accumulated depreciation	(84,235)	(100,389)
Land	1,809	16,513
Life insurance	11,566	18,344
Total Assets	$226,536	$ 414,970
Accounts payable	$ 52,404	$ 82,963
Notes payable (less than one year)	5,122	8,989
Loans from shareholders	155,751	191,967
Notes payable (more than one year)	21,821	33,835
Loan on life insurance	5,312	16,206
Capital stock	1,003	1,003
Paid-in capital	9,559	9,559
Retained earnings (unappropriated)	(8,314)	?
Accumulated adjustments account	–0–	?
Other adjustments account	–0–	?
Treasury stock	(16,122)	(16,122)
Total liabilities and capital	$226,536	$ 414,970

Ram's accounting firm provides the following additional information.

Dividends paid to shareholders	$290,000
AMT depreciation adjustment	(1,075)
AMT interest on private activity bonds preference	11,070

Using the above information, prepare a complete Form 1120S and a Schedule K–1 for John Martin (596 Lane Street, Kannapolis, NC 28083). If any information is missing, make realistic assumptions and list them.

PROBLEM 6—GIFT TAX (Form 709)

Melvin (Mel) C. and Jane W. Bird (Social Security numbers 521–68–4596 and 522–49–5482) reside at 420 Spruce Trace, Lark, CO 80523. They have three children: Kirk (age 22), Ruth (age 21), and Edward (age 20). During their 23 years of marriage, the Birds have always lived in a common law state. Both Mel and Jane are successful professionals—Mel is an oral surgeon in private practice, and Jane is a trial attorney in a local law firm.

In 2004, the Birds made the following transfers [without regard to any annual exclusion or deductions (marital, charitable) otherwise available].

Transfer	Mel	Jane
Melvin and Jane purchase a tract of undeveloped land in Morgan County and list title as follows: "Melvin, Kirk, Ruth, and Edward Bird equal tenants in common."	$100,000	$20,000
Room and board and college tuition (paid to provider) for Kirk, Ruth, and Edward (Mel paid for the room and board; Jane paid for the tuition).	14,200	75,000

Transfer	Mel	Jane
Jane obtains a divorce for Donald (Mel's brother) who has been abandoned by his wife. Court costs were $4,200 and Jane's usual charge for legal services would have been $8,000.		$12,200
Mel establishes a joint checking account with Donald at Washington County State Bank—Donald withdrew $19,100 during 2004.	$ 30,000	
Mel reimbursed his aunt, Maureen, for part of the $42,000 she spent on a heart bypass operation.	24,000	
Deluxe houseboat purchased for Ida and Roger Webb (Jane's parents) on their 50th wedding anniversary.	35,000	35,000
Contribution to the reelection campaign of their state representative.	2,000	2,000
Mel and Jane exchanged Rolex watches as birthday presents.	13,000	18,000

In the past, the Birds have made the following *taxable gifts;* for each year involved, the § 2513 election to split the gifts was made.

Year of Gift	Amount of Taxable Gift
1999	$1,400,000
2003	1,200,000

a. Determine the gift tax liability for the transfers made by the Birds prior to 2004.
b. Determine the gift tax liability for the transfers made in 2004. Complete Form 709 (U.S. Federal Gift Tax Return). The Birds continue to make the § 2513 election to split gifts.

PROBLEM 7—ESTATE TAX (Form 706)

Albert (Al) F. Harper died on May 9, 2004, at Buncombe County Hospital as a result of injuries from an automobile accident occurring four days earlier. At the time of his death, Al was 62 years of age and resided at 1482 Dogwood Lane, Asheville, NC 28804. He is survived by his wife, Mona Spain Harper (age 60); two married sons, Baker and Donald; several grandchildren; and four brothers and sisters.

1. When he died, Al was CEO and one-third owner of Old North State Entertainment (ONSE), a family-owned corporation founded by his parents. ONSE operates a chain of theaters located throughout a nine-county area. The business has been quite successful, and over the years it has adopted a number of fringe benefits for long-term, full-time employees. One such benefit, a $5,000 death gratuity, is paid to the estate of any employee who dies prior to retirement. ONSE pays the $5,000 death gratuity to Al's estate on June 7, 2004.
2. Al was covered under a group-term life insurance policy sponsored by ONSE for its employees. Although Al's coverage was for $50,000, the policy had a double indemnity clause in case of accidental death. The carrier of the insurance, Crane Life, paid Al's estate $100,000 on July 6, 2004. [Note: Al had designated his mother as the beneficiary under the policy, but since she was deceased and no secondary beneficiary was listed, the proceeds were paid to his estate.]
3. ONSE maintains a contributory qualified pension plan for its full-time employees. As of May 9, 2004, Al's vested interest in the plan is as follows.

ONSE's contribution	$300,000
Al's contribution	300,000
Plan earnings	400,000

Al has designated Mona as his beneficiary. Shortly after Al's death, the trustee of the plan, Eagle Trust Company, notifies Mona regarding the availability of Al's vested interest.

4. Several years ago, Al and his brothers and sisters became concerned about the continued existence of ONSE in the event that one of them, voluntarily or otherwise, withdrew from the business. To provide a smooth transition and keep the ownership of the corporation within the family, they entered into a buy-sell agreement. Under the agreement, each shareholder agreed to have his or her stock interest redeemed by ONSE. The value of the stock was to be determined periodically by a specified appraisal procedure. To assist in funding the redemption obligation, ONSE purchased insurance policies on several key shareholders. In the case of Al, it acquired a policy from Cardinal Life with a maturity value of $600,000. In late 2003, the total value of ONSE's stock was appraised at $3 million. [Note: A national theater chain had offered $2.5 million, but the offer was declined.] On August 4, 2004, ONSE redeems Al's one-third interest (5,000 shares of common stock) for $1 million. It pays cash of $800,000 and issues four notes of $50,000 payable at six-month intervals and carrying 5% interest.
5. When Al's mother died in 1985, her will provided that the family vacation lodge pass to her three children (Albert, Jill, and Evan) as equal joint tenants with the right of survivorship. The property is located in Greene County (TN) and was worth $240,000 on May 9, 2004. Al is survived by Jill and Evan.
6. The house where the Harpers currently reside (the Dogwood property) was built by them in 2000 at a cost of $380,000. Mona paid for the construction using funds she had inherited from her father. Title to the property is listed as "Albert and Mona Harper, tenants by the entirety with right of survivorship." The house is valued at $410,000 on May 9, 2004.
7. In 2001, Al and his two sons purchased some timberland in Clay County (NC) for $300,000 and listed title to the property as equal tenants in common. As his sons could only finance $100,000 ($50,000 each) of the purchase price, Al paid the $200,000 balance due. Each son issued a note to Al, face amount of $50,000 payable in four years at 6% annual interest. The sons paid Al the interest accrued at the end of 2001, 2002, and 2003. The Clay County property had a value of $330,000 on May 9, 2004.
8. In late 2003, Al acquired a tract of undeveloped land in Polk County (NC) for $140,000. He paid $40,000 in cash and financed the balance with a mortgage obtained from Jackson State Bank. Since he wanted the purchase to be Mona's Christmas present, he had title to the property listed as "Albert and Mona Harper, equal tenants in common." The property is still worth $140,000 on May 9, 2004.
9. For several years, Al and Mona have maintained insurance coverage on each other. Each policy, issued by Osprey Group, has a maturity value of $200,000 and names the other spouse as the beneficiary. On June 23, Mona receives $200,000 from Osprey on the policy she held on Al's life. Al's policy on Mona's life is worth $90,000 on May 9, 2004. Ultimately, it is sold by Al's estate for this amount to his sons, Baker and Donald.
10. Besides the items previously noted, Al has interests in the following.

• Joint checking account with Mona at Asheville National Bank	$ 4,396
• Money market account at Asheville State Bank*	26,400
• Certificate of deposit at Durham State Bank*	113,100
• City of Asheville bonds*	106,000
• Crimson Corporation common stock (400 shares)	62,000
• Maize Corporation common stock (500 shares)	83,000
• Personal and household effects (e.g., clothing, furniture, camper, hunting and fishing equipment)	63,000
• Four cemetery lots ($2,500 apiece) purchased by Al and intended for family use	10,000

*Includes interest accrued to May 9, 2004.

11. On May 24, 2004, Mona files Al's will with the probate division of the Buncombe County Court of Law. Pursuant to Al's will, she is appointed independent executor of his estate and is allowed to serve without posting bond. After establishing a bank account for the estate, she pays $15,200 in funeral expenses. This includes the cost of the service, hearse, casket, and marble family marker—but not the cemetery lot.

12. In accordance with a provision in Al's will, the estate transfers $50,000 to the University of North Carolina at Asheville to help fund the Charles Spain Professorship in Drama. The chair was established when Mona's father died.

13. In late June, Al's bass boat and trailer were stolen from his garage. A police report was filed, but the property was never recovered. The rig had just recently been acquired by Al at a cost of $18,000 and is included in his household effects (see item 10 above) at a value of $15,000. Mona had not insured the property as she had hoped to sell it to either Baker or Donald soon after the funeral.

14. Shortly after the accident, Al's family files a claim with his automobile insurance company. The carrier, Falcon Casualty, decides that the car Al was driving is a total loss and determines its value as being $39,000 at the time of the accident. In July, Al's estate receives a check from Falcon for $38,000 [$39,000 (value) – $1,000 (policy deductible)].

15. During the administration of Al's estate and in addition to the events already noted, all of the following take place.

• Received cash dividend on Crimson Corporation common stock (date of record was May 7, 2004)	$ 300
• Received cash dividend on Maize Corporation common stock (date of record was May 10, 2004)	415
• Paid dental bills incurred by Al and not covered by employer's (ONSE) group medical insurance policy for employees	11,100
• Paid Al's outstanding credit card debt and other predeath bills	9,400

• Professional fees incurred in connection with the administration of the estate.

Accounting	$18,000	
Legal	31,000	
Appraisal	4,600	$53,600

• Although Al and Mona will file a joint return for 2004, she determines that Al's allocable portion of income taxes is $4,244 (Federal) and $1,889 (state) determined in accordance with the procedure prescribed by Reg. § 20.2053–6(f).

• Under state law, Mona is entitled to a fee for serving as executor of Al's estate. Because Mona does not want to pay income tax on the fee she receives and since she is already financially secure, she decides against claiming any such fee.

• In addition to the charitable provision (see item 12 above), the estate satisfies the other cash bequests specified in Al's will. In making the transfers to Baker and Donald (see item 16 below), the estate first offsets the $50,000 note each son owes Al (see item 7 above).

• After paying all required taxes and disposing of the remainder of the estate, Mona files a final accounting with the probate court. On January 10, 2005, the court approves Mona's administration, discharges her from the duties of executor, and closes the Estate of Albert F Harper.

16. In addition to the charitable donation, Al's will provides monetary bequests of $100,000 each to Baker and Donald. The remainder of the estate (net of taxes and administration expenses) is to pass to a newly created trust, to be called the "Albert Harper Trust" for the benefit of Al and Mona's grandchildren. Jill Harper, Al's younger sister, is designated as the trustee of the new trust.

Other relevant information includes:

• Taxpayer identification numbers—

Albert F. Harper	240–64–2245
Mona Spain Harper	241–35–8123
Baker Harper	244–51–3496
Donald Harper	244–69–8438
Jill Harper	246–81–9654
Albert Harper Trust	34–8765123

- North Carolina imposes a death tax. The death tax is a sponge tax based on the full amount that *would have been* allowed as a credit under § 2011.

Assumptions to be made are as follows:

- No § 2032 election is made, and Code §§ 2032A and 6166 are inappropriate.
- Disregard requests for information that is not available.
- Some deductions require a choice (e.g., Form 706 or Form 1041, Form 706 or Form 1040) and cannot be claimed twice. Resolve all such choices in favor of the Form 706 deduction.
- The Harpers have never made any prior taxable gifts nor have they ever filed a Form 709.

Complete a Form 706 for the estate of Albert F. Harper.

PROBLEM 8—TRUST (Form 1041)

Prepare the 2004 fiduciary income tax return (Form 1041) for the Green Trust. In addition, determine the amount and character of the income and expense items that each beneficiary must report for 2004 and prepare a Schedule K–1 for Marcus White. Omit all alternative minimum tax computations.

The 2004 activities of the trust include the following.

Dividend income, all U.S. stocks	$25,000
Taxable interest income	20,000
Tax-exempt interest income	30,000
Net long-term capital gain, incurred 11/1/04	27,000
Fiduciary's fees	6,000

Under the terms of the trust instrument, depreciation, net capital gains and losses, and any fiduciary's fees are allocable to corpus. The trustee is required to distribute $15,000 to Marcus every year. For 2004, the trustee distributed $25,000 to Marcus and $50,000 to Marcus's sister, Ellen Hayes. No other distributions were made.

In computing DNI, the trustee properly assigned all of the deductible fiduciary fees to the interest income.

The trustee paid $4,000 in estimated taxes for the year on behalf of the trust. Any 2004 refund is to be credited to 2005 estimates. The exempt income was not derived from private activity bonds.

The trust was created on December 14, 1953. It is not subject to any recapture taxes, nor does it have any tax credits. None of its income was derived under a personal services contract. Ignore the AMT for all parties. The trust has no economic interest in any foreign trust. Its Federal identification number is 79–2635151.

The trustee, Wisconsin State National Bank, is located at 3100 East Wisconsin Avenue, Milwaukee, WI 53201. Its employer identification number is 66–7602487.

Marcus lives at 9880 East North Avenue, Shorewood, WI 53211. His identification number is 498–98–8058.

Ellen lives at 6772 East Oklahoma Avenue, St. Cecilia, WI 53204. Her identification number is 499–97–6531.

Index

B

C

D

E

F

G

M

S

T

U

V

W

Y